# TEXAS CRIMINAL LAW AND MOTOR VEHICLE HANDBOOK

–Including–

**Penal Code, Code of Criminal Procedure, Rules of Evidence, Transportation Code, Vehicle Laws,**

***and Related Statutes from***

**Civil Statutes; Agriculture, Alcoholic Beverage, Business and Commerce, Civil Practice and Remedies, Education, Election, Family, Finance, Government, Health and Safety, Human Resources, Insurance, Local Government, Natural Resources, Occupations Code, Parks and Wildlife, Property, Tax, Utilities and Water Codes; U.S. Code; U.S. Constitution; Texas Constitution**

***(Includes the enactments of the 1999 Regular Session through Chapter 1590)***

**2000**

**GOULD PUBLICATIONS of Texas, Inc.**

Published by
**GOULD PUBLICATIONS of Texas Inc.**
1333 North US Highway 17-92
Longwood, FL 32750-3724
(407) 695-9500
**World Wide Web**—http://www.gouldlaw.com
**E-mail**—info@gouldlaw.com

**ISBN** 0-9629210-0-9



**Every attempt has been made to ensure the accuracy and the completeness of the law contained herein. No express or implied guarantees or warranties are made.**

**Since laws change very often and vary from jurisdiction to jurisdiction, it is very important to check the timeliness and applicability of the laws contained herein.**

# FOREWORD

The material presented herewith in convenient form is Gould's **Texas Criminal Law and Motor Vehicle Handbook**, as currently amended to include the enactments of the 1999 Regular Session of the 76th Legislature through Chapter 1590, for use in 2000. All changes to these laws have been incorporated in text, and effective dates have been added where applicable.

The new ***Rules of Evidence*** are included in this edition, effective March 1, 1998. Pertinent portions of the ***Transportation Code***, effective September 1, 1995, are also included in this edition following the Rules of Evidence. The ***Vehicle Laws*** portion, following the Transportation Code, contains the ***Civil Statutes*** relating to vehicles which are still in force and effect.

A complete, up-to-date, integrated index is also included.

At the end of this volume is Gould's handy ***Quick Find Locator***™ which helps you find the law you need.

Annual editions will incorporate changes as enacted. Please return the "IMPORTANT" subscription card at the front of this volume to ensure that you receive the latest changes to the laws contained herein.

Comments from users of this book and ways to improve it to facilitate its use would be appreciated by the publisher.

In this edition of Gould's **Texas Criminal Law and Motor Vehicle Handbook**, section headings/catchlines which have become so associated with the law that they cannot be separated therefrom, are designated by the symbol †.

More descriptive section headings/catchlines have been added by the editors of this publication. They appear in brackets [ ] in bold italics immediately following the symbol †.

Where only one section heading/catchline appears, with neither brackets ([ ]) nor symbol (†), it has been enacted officially by the Texas State Legislature.

*This product is also available on **CD-ROM** as **Texas Penal Code, Transportation Code, Vehicle Laws & Related Statutes DiskLaw**™. For details on how to obtain the laws you need and enforce for use on a single computer or on a network, please contact the publisher.*

This page intentionally left blank.

# 1999 Legislative Changes to the TEXAS CRIMINAL LAW and MOTOR VEHICLE HANDBOOK (for use in 2000)

## Penal Code

| *Section(s)* | *Change* | *Chap.* | *Eff. Date* |
|---|---|---|---|
| 12.42(g) | Amend | 62(15.01) | 9/1/99 |
| 12.43 | Amend | 564(1) | 9/1/99 |
| 12.48 | New | 417(2(a)) | 9/1/99 |
| 12.48 | New | 439(4) | 9/1/99 |
| 15.031 | Amend | 1415(22(a)) | 9/1/99 |
| Chap. 16, heading | Amend | 728(2) | 9/1/99 |
| 16.06 | New | 728(1) | 9/1/99 |
| 20.01(1) | Amend | 790(1) | 9/1/99 |
| 20.02(c) | Amend | 790(2) | 9/1/99 |
| 20.02(e) | New | 790(2) | 9/1/99 |
| 20.05 | New | 1014(1) | 9/1/99 |
| 21.11(b) | Amend | 1415(23) | 9/1/99 |
| 22.01(b) | Amend | 1158(1) | 9/1/99 |
| 22.01(e) | Amend | 62(15.02(a)) | 9/1/99 |
| 22.01(e) | Amend | 1158(1) | 9/1/99 |
| 22.01(f) | New | 1158(1) | 9/1/99 |
| 22.011(c)(4) | New | 1102(3) | 9/1/99 |
| 22.011(e) | Amend | 1415(24) | 9/1/99 |
| 22.015 | New | 708(1) | 9/1/99 |
| 22.021(a) | Amend | 417(1) | 9/1/99 |
| 22.04(k)(2) | Amend | 62(15.02(b)) | 9/1/99 |
| 22.041(h) | New | 1087(3) | 9/1/99 |
| 22.11 | New | 335(1) | 9/1/99 |
| 25.04(b) | Amend | 685(7) | 9/1/99 |
| 25.07(b) | Amend | 62(15.02(c)) | 9/1/99 |
| 25.07(f) | Amend | 62(15.02(c)) | 9/1/99 |
| 28.03(b) | Amend | 686(1) | 9/1/99 |
| 28.08(a) | Amend | 695(1) | 9/1/99 |
| 28.08(d) | Amend | 166(1) | 9/1/99 |
| 28.08(e) | Amend | 695(1) | 9/1/99 |
| 28.08(e)(3) | New | 166(2) | 9/1/99 |
| 28.08(e)(4) | New | 166(2) | 9/1/99 |
| 30.02(a) | Amend | 727(1) | 9/1/99 |
| 30.04 | Amend | 916(1) | 9/1/99 |
| 30.05(a) | Amend | 161(1) | 9/1/99 |
| 30.05(b)(5) | New | 169(1) | 9/1/99 |
| 30.05(b)(5) | New | 765(1) | 9/1/99 |
| 30.05(d) | Amend | 169(2) | 9/1/99 |
| 30.05(d) | Amend | 765(2) | 9/1/99 |
| 30.05(e) | New | 169(2) | 9/1/99 |
| 30.06(a) | Amend | 62(9.24) | 9/1/99 |
| 30.06(c) | Amend | 62(9.24) | 9/1/99 |
| 31.04(b) | Amend | 843(1) | 9/1/99 |
| 31.12 | Amend | 858(1) | 9/1/99 |
| 31.13 | Amend | 858(2) | 9/1/99 |

*(continued)*

# 1999 Legislative Changes to the TEXAS CRIMINAL LAW and MOTOR VEHICLE HANDBOOK
*(Continued)*

## Penal Code
*(Continued)*

| *Section(s)* | *Change* | *Chap.* | *Eff. Date* |
|---|---|---|---|
| 31.14 | New | 858(3) | 9/1/99 |
| 32.24 | New | 1413(1) | 9/1/99 |
| 32.35(a)(5) | Amend | 62(7.83) | 9/1/99 |
| 32.50 | Renumber | 62(19.01(88)) | 9/1/99 |
| 32.51 | New | 1159(1) | 9/1/99 |
| 33.01(13) | Amend | 62(18.44) | 9/1/99 |
| 37.01(2) | Amend | 659(1) | 9/1/99 |
| 37.081 | New | 200(3) | 9/1/99 |
| 37.10(c) | Amend | 659(2) | 9/1/99 |
| 37.10(d) | Amend | 659(2) | 9/1/99 |
| 37.10(d) | Amend | 718(1) | 9/1/99 |
| 38.06(c) | Amend | 526(1) | 9/1/99 |
| 38.11(d) | Amend | 649(1) | 9/1/99 |
| 38.11(i) | New | 362(1) | 9/1/99 |
| 38.111 | Repeal | 1196(3) | 9/1/99 |
| 38.14 | Amend | 714(1) | 9/1/99 |
| 38.17 | New | 1344(1) | 9/1/99 |
| 39.04(a) | Amend | 158(1) | 9/1/99 |
| 39.04(e) | Amend | 158(2) | 9/1/99 |
| 39.04(f) | New | 158(3) | 9/1/99 |
| 39.04(g) | New | 158(3) | 9/1/99 |
| 42.07(b) | Amend | 62(15.02(d)) | 9/1/99 |
| 42.072(c) | Amend | 62(15.02(e)) | 9/1/99 |
| 43.25(a)(2) | Amend | 1415(22(b)) | 9/1/99 |
| 43.26(g) | Amend | 1415(22(c)) | 9/1/99 |
| 46.01(3) | Amend | 1445(1) | 9/1/99 |
| 46.06(b) | Amend | 62(15.02(f)) | 9/1/99 |
| 46.13(f) | Amend | 62(15.02(g)) | 9/1/99 |
| 46.15(a) | Amend | 62(9.25) | 9/1/99 |
| 46.15(e) | New | 1445(2) | 9/1/99 |
| 47.09(b) | Amend | 844(1) | 9/1/99 |
| 49.01(2) | Amend | 234(1) | 9/1/99 |
| 49.01(5) | New | 1364(8) | 1/1/2000 |
| 49.01(6) | New | 1364(8) | 1/1/2000 |
| 49.065 | New | 1364(9) | 1/1/2000 |
| 49.07(a) | Amend | 1364(10) | 1/1/2000 |
| 49.08(a) | Amend | 1364(11) | 1/1/2000 |
| 49.09(a) | Amend | 1364(12) | 1/1/2000 |
| 49.09(b) | Amend | 1364(12) | 1/1/2000 |
| 49.09(c)(4) | New | 1364(13) | 1/1/2000 |
| 49.09(d) | Amend | 1364(12) | 1/1/2000 |
| 49.09(e) | Amend | 1364(12) | 1/1/2000 |

*(continued)*

# 1999 Legislative Changes to the TEXAS CRIMINAL LAW and MOTOR VEHICLE HANDBOOK
*(Continued)*

## Penal Code
*(Continued)*

| *Section(s)* | *Change* | *Chap.* | *Eff. Date* |
|---|---|---|---|
| 49.10 | Amend | 1364(14) | 1/1/2000 |
| 71.02(a) | Amend | 685(8) | 9/1/99 |
| 71.022 | New | 1555(1) | 9/1/99 |



## Code of Criminal Procedure

| *Article(s)* | *Change* | *Chap.* | *Eff. Date* |
|---|---|---|---|
| 2.025 | New | 40(1) | 9/1/99 |
| 2.07(g) | New | 1545(1) | 9/1/99 |
| 2.09 | Amend | 586(2) | 6/18/99 |
| 2.09 | Amend | 1503(2) | 9/1/99 |
| 2.12 | Amend | 90(1) | 9/1/99 |
| 2.12 | Amend | 322(2) | 5/29/99 |
| 2.12 | Amend | 882(2) | 6/18/99 |
| 2.12 | Amend | 974(37) | 9/1/99 |
| 2.121(c) | Amend | 62(3.01) | 9/1/99 |
| 2.122(a) | Amend | 197(1) | 5/24/99 |
| 2.122(c) | Amend | 863(1) | 6/18/99 |
| 2.122(d) | New | 197(1) | 5/24/99 |
| 2.122(d) | New | 628(1) | 6/18/99 |
| 2.124 | Amend | 107(1) | 9/1/99 |
| 2.13 | Amend | 685(1) | 9/1/99 |
| 2.21(a) | Amend | 580(1) | 9/1/99 |
| 2.21(b) | Amend | 580(1) | 9/1/99 |
| 2.26 | New | 701(1) | 6/18/99 |
| 4.12 | Amend | 1545(2) | 9/1/99 |
| 4.18, heading | Amend | 1477(27) | 9/1/99 |
| 4.18(g) | New | 1477(28) | 9/1/99 |
| 5.08 | New | 389(1) | 5/31/99 |
| 11.051 | New | 392(1) | 5/31/99 |
| 11.07, Sec. 3(b) | Amend | 580(2) | 9/1/99 |
| 11.071, Sec. 2 | Amend | 803(1) | 9/1/99 |
| 11.071, Sec. 2A | New | 803(2) | 9/1/99 |
| 11.071, Sec. 3(b) | Amend | 803(3) | 9/1/99 |
| 11.071, Sec. 3(d) | Amend | 803(3) | 9/1/99 |
| 11.071, Sec. 4 | Amend | 803(4) | 9/1/99 |
| 11.071, Sec. 4A | New | 803(5) | 9/1/99 |
| 11.071, Sec. 5 heading | Amend | 803(7) | 9/1/99 |
| 11.071, Sec. 5(a) | Amend | 803(6) | 9/1/99 |
| 11.071, Sec. 5(b) | Amend | 803(6) | 9/1/99 |
| 11.071, Sec. 5(f) | New | 803(6) | 9/1/99 |

*(continued)*

## 1999 Legislative Changes to the TEXAS CRIMINAL LAW and MOTOR VEHICLE HANDBOOK
*(Continued)*

### Code of Criminal Procedure
*(Continued)*

| *Article(s)* | *Change* | *Chap.* | *Eff. Date* |
|---|---|---|---|
| 11.071, Sec. 6(b) | Amend | 803(8) | 9/1/99 |
| 11.071, Sec. 7(a) | Amend | 803(9) | 9/1/99 |
| 11.071, Sec. 9(b) | Amend | 803(10) | 9/1/99 |
| 12.01 | Amend | 39(1) | 9/1/99 |
| 12.01 | Amend | 1285(33) | 9/1/2000 |
| 13.27 | Renumber | 62(19.01(6)) | 9/1/99 |
| 14.03(g) | Amend | 62(3.02) | 9/1/99 |
| 14.03(g) | Amend | 210(2) | 5/24/99 |
| 17.08 | Amend | 1506(1) | 9/1/99 |
| 17.11, Sec. 2 | Amend | 1506(2) | 9/1/99 |
| 17.19(a) | Amend | 1506(3) | 9/1/99 |
| 17.291(b) | Amend | 1341(1) | 9/1/99 |
| 17.292 | Amend | 1412(1) | 9/1/99 |
| 17.292(i) | Amend | 514(1) | 9/1/99 |
| 17.293 | New | 1412(2) | 9/1/99 |
| 17.40 | New | 768(1) | 9/1/99 |
| 17.441(d) | Amend | 537(1) | 9/1/99 |
| 18.01(b) | Amend | 167(1) | 5/21/99 |
| 18.01(d) | Amend | 1469(1) | 6/19/99 |
| 18.21, Sec. 1(7) | Amend | 62(18.20) | 9/1/99 |
| 19.08 | Amend | 1177(1) | 9/1/99 |
| 19.18 | Amend | 1065(1) | 9/1/99 |
| 19.21 | Amend | 1065(2) | 9/1/99 |
| 19.25 | Amend | 1177(2) | 9/1/99 |
| 19.26 | Amend | 1065(3) | 9/1/99 |
| 19.41 | Amend | 1065(4) | 9/1/99 |
| 19.42 | New | 1177(3) | 9/1/99 |
| 20.22 | Amend | 580(3) | 9/1/99 |
| 22.10 | Amend | 1506(4) | 9/1/99 |
| 22.125 | Amend | 1506(5) | 9/1/99 |
| 22.18 | New | 1506(6) | 9/1/99 |
| 23.05 | Amend | 1506(7) | 9/1/99 |
| 24.03(a) | Amend | 580(4) | 9/1/99 |
| 24.03(a) | Amend | 614(2) | 6/18/99 |
| 24.04 | Amend | 580(5) | 9/1/99 |
| 26.05(f) | New | 837(1) | 9/1/99 |
| 26.052(*l*) | Amend | 837(2) | 9/1/99 |
| 26.13(a) | Amend | 1415(1) | 9/1/99 |
| 26.13(h) | New | 425(1) | 6/18/99 |
| 26.13(h) | New | 1415(1) | 9/1/99 |
| 30.03 | Repeal | 1388(14) | 9/1/99 |
| 30.04 | Repeal | 1388(14) | 9/1/99 |

*(continued)*

# 1999 Legislative Changes to the TEXAS CRIMINAL LAW and MOTOR VEHICLE HANDBOOK
*(Continued)*

## Code of Criminal Procedure
*(Continued)*

| *Article(s)* | *Change* | *Chap.* | *Eff. Date* |
|---|---|---|---|
| 30.05 | Repeal | 1388(14) | 9/1/99 |
| 30.06 | Repeal | 1388(14) | 9/1/99 |
| 37.07, Sec. 3(i) | Reletter | 62(19.01(7)) | 9/1/99 |
| 37.071, Sec. 2(e) | Amend | 140(1) | 9/1/99 |
| 39.14 | Amend | 578(1) | 9/1/99 |
| 42.01, Sec. 2 | Amend | 580(6) | 9/1/99 |
| 42.01, Sec. 7 | New | 1193(1) | 9/1/99 |
| 42.01, Sec. 7 | New | 1415(2) | 9/1/99 |
| 42.015 | New | 417(2(b)) | 9/1/99 |
| 42.015 | New | 1193(2) | 9/1/99 |
| 42.015 | New | 1415(3) | 9/1/99 |
| 42.016 | New | 1401(1) | 9/1/2000 |
| 42.032, Sec. 5 | Amend | 655(2(a)) | 6/18/99 |
| 42.037(g)(4) | Amend | 40(2) | 9/1/99 |
| 42.037(n) | New | 40(3) | 9/1/99 |
| 42.0371 | New | 657(1) | 9/1/99 |
| 42.038 | New | 295(1) | 9/1/99 |
| 42.09, Sec. 8(a) | Amend | 1188(1.42) | 9/1/99 |
| 42.09, Sec. 8(c) | Amend | 1477(29) | 9/1/99 |
| 42.09, Sec. 9 | New | 655(1) | 6/18/99 |
| 42.111 | Amend | 62(3.03) | 9/1/99 |
| 42.111 | Amend | 1545(62) | 9/1/99 |
| 42.12, Sec. 3g(a) | Amend | 806(1) | 9/1/99 |
| 42.12, Sec. 5(c) | Amend | 1415(5(a)) | 9/1/99 |
| 42.12, Sec. 5(e) | New | 580(7) | 9/1/99 |
| 42.12, Sec. 5(e) | New | 1193(3) | 9/1/99 |
| 42.12, Sec. 5(e) | New | 1415(4) | 9/1/99 |
| 42.12, Sec. 9(j) | Amend | 1263(1) | 9/1/99 |
| 42.12, Sec. 9(k) | Amend | 1188(1.43) | 9/1/99 |
| 42.12, Sec. 11(a) | Amend | 323(1) | 9/1/99 |
| 42.12, Sec. 11(g) | New | 27(1) | 9/1/99 |
| 42.12, Sec. 11(g) | New | 1415(6(a)) | 9/1/99 |
| 42.12, Sec. 13(g) | Amend | 62(3.04) | 9/1/99 |
| 42.12, Sec. 13(h) | Amend | 62(3.04) | 9/1/99 |
| 42.12, Sec. 13(h) | Amend | 580(8) | 9/1/99 |
| 42.12, Sec. 13(i) | Amend | 62(3.04) | 9/1/99 |
| 42.12, Sec. 13(i) | Amend | 1105(3) | 9/1/99 |
| 42.12, Sec. 13(j) | Amend | 62(3.04) | 9/1/99 |
| 42.12, Sec. 13(j) | Amend | 580(8) | 9/1/99 |
| 42.12, Sec. 13(k) | Amend | 62(3.04) | 9/1/99 |
| 42.12, Sec. 13(m) | Amend | 62(3.04) | 9/1/99 |
| 42.12, Sec. 13D | New | 56(1) | 9/1/99 |

*(continued)*

## 1999 Legislative Changes to the TEXAS CRIMINAL LAW and MOTOR VEHICLE HANDBOOK

*(Continued)*

### Code of Criminal Procedure

*(Continued)*

| *Article(s)* | *Change* | *Chap.* | *Eff. Date* |
|---|---|---|---|
| 42.12, Sec. 14(c) | Amend | 910(1) | 9/1/99 |
| 42.12, Sec. 14(c) | Amend | 1188(1.44) | 9/1/99 |
| 42.12, Sec. 14(e) | New | 1188(1.44) | 9/1/99 |
| 42.12, Sec. 15A | New | 564(2) | 9/1/99 |
| 42.12, Sec. 20(b) | Amend | 1415(5(b)) | 9/1/99 |
| 42.18, Sec. 2(10) | Repeal | 62(10.39(3)) | 9/1/99 |
| 42.18, Sec. 4 | Repeal | 62(10.39(3)) | 9/1/99 |
| 42.18, Sec. 5 | Repeal | 62(10.39(3)) | 9/1/99 |
| 42.18, Sec. 6 | Repeal | 62(10.39(3)) | 9/1/99 |
| 42.18, Sec. 6A | Repeal | 62(10.39(3)) | 9/1/99 |
| 42.18, Sec. 6C | Repeal | 62(10.39(3)) | 9/1/99 |
| 42.18, Sec. 6D | Repeal | 62(10.39(3)) | 9/1/99 |
| 42.18, Sec. 7(c) | Repeal | 62(10.39(3)) | 9/1/99 |
| 42.18, Sec. 7(d) | Repeal | 62(10.39(3)) | 9/1/99 |
| 42.18, Sec. 7(f) | Repeal | 62(10.39(3)) | 9/1/99 |
| 42.18, Sec. 7(h) | Repeal | 62(10.39(3)) | 9/1/99 |
| 42.18, Sec. 7(*i*) | Repeal | 62(10.39(3)) | 9/1/99 |
| 42.18, Sec. 7(j) | Repeal | 62(10.39(3)) | 9/1/99 |
| 42.18, Sec. 7(k) | Repeal | 62(10.39(3)) | 9/1/99 |
| 42.18, Sec. 8(b)(2) | Repeal | 62(10.39(9)) | 9/1/99 |
| 42.18, Sec. 8(c) | Repeal | 62(10.39(5)) | 9/1/99 |
| 42.18, Sec. 8(g) | Repeal | 62(10.39(3)) | 9/1/99 |
| 42.18, Sec. 8(h) | Repeal | 62(10.39(8)) | 9/1/99 |
| 42.18, Sec. 8(*o*)(1) | Repeal | 62(10.39(1)) | 9/1/99 |
| 42.18, Sec. 8(*o*)(1) | Repeal | 62(10.39(4)) | 9/1/99 |
| 42.18, Sec. 8(*o*)(1) | Repeal | 62(10.39(11)) | 9/1/99 |
| 42.18, Sec. 8(r) | Repeal | 62(10.39(10)) | 9/1/99 |
| 42.18, Sec. 8(s) | Repeal | 62(10.39(2)) | 9/1/99 |
| 42.18, Sec. 8A(e) | Repeal | 62(10.39(8)) | 9/1/99 |
| 42.18, Sec. 8A(g) | Repeal | 62(10.39(12)) | 9/1/99 |
| 42.18, Sec. 8C | Repeal | 62(10.39(11)) | 9/1/99 |
| 42.18, Sec. 11(a) | Repeal | 62(10.39(3)) | 9/1/99 |
| 42.18, Sec. 13(a) | Repeal | 62(10.39(6)) | 9/1/99 |
| 42.18, Sec. 13A | Repeal | 62(10.39(6)) | 9/1/99 |
| 42.18, Sec. 14 | Repeal | 62(10.39(3)) | 9/1/99 |
| 42.18, Sec. 14 | Repeal | 62(10.39(6)) | 9/1/99 |
| 42.18, Sec. 14A | Repeal | 62(10.39(3)) | 9/1/99 |
| 42.18, Sec. 18(b) | Repeal | 62(10.39(10)) | 9/1/99 |
| 42.18, Sec. 24 | Repeal | 62(10.39(13)) | 9/1/99 |
| 42.18, Sec. 25(c) | Repeal | 62(10.39(7)) | 9/1/99 |
| 42.18, Sec. 30 | Repeal | 62(10.39(11)) | 9/1/99 |
| 42.22, Sec. 2(b) | Amend | 295(2) | 9/1/99 |

*(continued)*

# 1999 Legislative Changes to the TEXAS CRIMINAL LAW and MOTOR VEHICLE HANDBOOK
*(Continued)*

## Code of Criminal Procedure
*(Continued)*

| *Article(s)* | *Change* | *Chap.* | *Eff. Date* |
|---|---|---|---|
| 43.09(k) | Amend | 1545(3) | 9/1/99 |
| 44.04(b) | Amend | 546(1) | 9/1/99 |
| 44.04(c) | Amend | 546(1) | 9/1/99 |
| 44.13 | Repeal | 1545(75) | 9/1/99 |
| 44.14 | Redesignate | 1545(42) | 9/1/99 |
| 44.181(a) | Amend | 1545(4) | 9/1/99 |
| 44.281 | Redesignate & Amend | 1545(65) | 9/1/99 |
| Chap. 45, heading | Amend | 1545(5) | 9/1/99 |
| Chap. 45, Subchap. A | New | 1545(6) | 9/1/99 |
| 45.001 | New | 1545(6) | 9/1/99 |
| 45.002 | New | 1545(6) | 9/1/99 |
| 45.003 | New | 1545(6) | 9/1/99 |
| 45.01 | Repeal | 1545(75) | 9/1/99 |
| 45.02 | Repeal | 1545(75) | 9/1/99 |
| 45.021(a) [now 45.012] | Amend | 701(2) | 6/18/99 |
| 45.021(f) [now 45.012] | New | 701(2) | 6/18/99 |
| 45.05 | Repeal | 1545(75) | 9/1/99 |
| 45.06 [now 45.203] | Amend | 62(3.05) | 9/1/99 |
| 45.07 | Repeal | 1545(75(a)) | 9/1/99 |
| 45.08 | Repeal | 1545(75(a)) | 9/1/99 |
| 45.09 | Repeal | 1545(75(a)) | 9/1/99 |
| Chap. 45 Subchap. B, heading | New | 1545(7) | 9/1/99 |
| 45.011 | Redesignate & Amend | 1545(8) | 9/1/99 |
| 45.012 | Redesignate & Amend | 1545(9) | 9/1/99 |
| 45.013 | New | 1545(10) | 9/1/99 |
| 45.014 | Redesignate & Amend | 1545(11) | 9/1/99 |
| 45.015 | Redesignate & Amend | 1545(12) | 9/1/99 |
| 45.016 | Redesignate & Amend | 1545(13) | 9/1/99 |
| 45.017 | Redesignate & Amend | 1545(14) | 9/1/99 |
| 45.018 | New | 1545(15) | 9/1/99 |
| 45.019 | Redesignate & Amend | 1545(16) | 9/1/99 |
| 45.020 | Redesignate & Amend | 1545(17) | 9/1/99 |
| 45.021 | Redesignate & Amend | 1545(18) | 9/1/99 |
| 45.0215 | Redesignate & Amend | 1545(19) | 9/1/99 |
| 45.022 | Redesignate & Amend | 1545(20) | 9/1/99 |
| 45.023 | Redesignate & Amend | 1545(21) | 9/1/99 |
| 45.024 | Redesignate & Amend | 1545(22) | 9/1/99 |
| 45.025 | Redesignate & Amend | 1545(23) | 9/1/99 |
| 45.026 | Redesignate & Amend | 1545(24) | 9/1/99 |
| 45.027 | Redesignate & Amend | 1545(25) | 9/1/99 |

*(continued)*

# 1999 Legislative Changes to the TEXAS CRIMINAL LAW and MOTOR VEHICLE HANDBOOK
*(Continued)*

## Code of Criminal Procedure
*(Continued)*

| *Article(s)* | *Change* | *Chap.* | *Eff. Date* |
|---|---|---|---|
| 45.028 | Redesignate & Amend | 1545(26) | 9/1/99 |
| 45.029 | Redesignate & Amend | 1545(27) | 9/1/99 |
| 45.030 | Redesignate & Amend | 1545(28) | 9/1/99 |
| 45.031 | Redesignate & Amend | 1545(29) | 9/1/99 |
| 45.032 | Redesignate & Amend | 1545(30) | 9/1/99 |
| 45.033 | New | 1545(31) | 9/1/99 |
| 45.034 | Redesignate & Amend | 1545(32) | 9/1/99 |
| 45.035 | Redesignate & Amend | 1545(33) | 9/1/99 |
| 45.036 | Redesignate & Amend | 1545(34) | 9/1/99 |
| 45.037 | Redesignate & Amend | 1545(35) | 9/1/99 |
| 45.038 | Redesignate & Amend | 1545(36) | 9/1/99 |
| 45.039 | Redesignate & Amend | 1545(37) | 9/1/99 |
| 45.040 | Redesignate & Amend | 1545(38) | 9/1/99 |
| 45.041 | Redesignate & Amend | 1545(39) | 9/1/99 |
| 45.042 | Redesignate & Amend | 1545(40) | 9/1/99 |
| 45.0425 | New | 1545(41) | 9/1/99 |
| 45.0426 | Redesignate & Amend | 1545(42) | 9/1/99 |
| 45.043 | Redesignate & Amend | 1545(43) | 9/1/99 |
| 45.044 | Redesignate & Amend | 1545(44) | 9/1/99 |
| 45.045 | Redesignate & Amend | 1545(45) | 9/1/99 |
| 45.046 | Redesignate & Amend | 1545(46) | 9/1/99 |
| 45.047 | New | 1545(47) | 9/1/99 |
| 45.048 | Redesignate & Amend | 1545(48) | 9/1/99 |
| 45.049 | Redesignate & Amend | 1545(49) | 9/1/99 |
| 45.050 | Redesignate & Amend | 1545(49) | 9/1/99 |
| 45.051 | Redesignate & Amend | 1545(50) | 9/1/99 |
| 45.0511 | New | 1545(51) | 9/1/99 |
| 45.052 | Redesignate & Amend | 1545(52) | 9/1/99 |
| 45.053 | Redesignate | 1545(53) | 9/1/99 |
| Chap. 45, Subchap. C | New | 1545(54) | 9/1/99 |
| 45.101 | New | 1545(55) | 9/1/99 |
| 45.102 | Redesignate & Amend | 1545(56) | 9/1/99 |
| 45.103 | Redesignate & Amend | 1545(57) | 9/1/99 |
| 45.12 | Repeal | 1545(75(a)) | 9/1/99 |
| 45.16 | Repeal | 1545(75(a)) | 9/1/99 |
| 45.19 | Repeal | 1545(75(a)) | 9/1/99 |
| Chap. 45, Subchap. D | New | 1545(58) | 9/1/99 |
| 45.201 | Redesignate & Amend | 1545(59) | 9/1/99 |
| 45.202 | Redesignate & Amend | 1545(60) | 9/1/99 |
| 45.203 | Redesignate & Amend | 1545(61) | 9/1/99 |



*(continued)*

# 1999 Legislative Changes to the TEXAS CRIMINAL LAW and MOTOR VEHICLE HANDBOOK
*(Continued)*

## Code of Criminal Procedure
*(Continued)*

| *Article(s)* | *Change* | *Chap.* | *Eff. Date* |
|---|---|---|---|
| 45.22 | Repeal | 1545(75(a)) | 9/1/99 |
| 45.23 | Repeal | 1545(75(a)) | 9/1/99 |
| 45.26 | Repeal | 1545(75(a)) | 9/1/99 |
| 45.27 | Repeal | 1545(75(a)) | 9/1/99 |
| 45.32 | Repeal | 1545(75(a)) | 9/1/99 |
| 45.49 | Repeal | 1545(75(a)) | 9/1/99 |
| 45.522(b) [now 45.050] | Amend | 76(7) | 9/1/99 |
| 45.54 [now 45.051] | Amend | 1387(1) | 9/1/99 |
| 45.54(1) [now 45.051] | Amend | 62(3.06) | 9/1/99 |
| 45.54(2) [now 45.051] | Amend | 62(3.06) | 9/1/99 |
| 45.54(3) [now 45.051] | Amend | 62(3.06) | 9/1/99 |
| 45.54(3) [now 45.051] | Amend | 532(1) | 9/1/99 |
| 45.541 [now 45.0511] | New | 1387(2) | 9/1/99 |
| 45.55(a) [now 45.052] | Amend | 76(6) | 9/1/99 |
| 45.55(f) [now 45.052] | Amend | 76(6) | 9/1/99 |
| 46.01 | Repeal | 561(8) | 9/1/99 |
| 46.02, Sec. 1 | New | 561(1) | 9/1/99 |
| 46.02, Sec. 1A | Redesignate | 561(1) | 9/1/99 |
| 46.02, Sec. 3(d) | Amend | 561(2) | 9/1/99 |
| 46.02, Sec. 3(e) | Amend | 561(2) | 9/1/99 |
| 46.02, Sec. 4(a) | Amend | 561(3) | 9/1/99 |
| 46.02, Sec. 4(h) | Amend | 561(3) | 9/1/99 |
| 46.02, Sec. 4(i) | Amend | 561(3) | 9/1/99 |
| 46.02, Sec. 5(a) | Amend | 561(4) | 9/1/99 |
| 46.02, Sec. 5(b) | Amend | 561(4) | 9/1/99 |
| 46.02, Sec. 5(i) | Amend | 561(4) | 9/1/99 |
| 46.02, Sec. 6 | Amend | 561(5) | 9/1/99 |
| 46.02, Sec. 7 | Amend | 561(6) | 9/1/99 |
| 46.02, Sec. 8 | Amend | 561(7) | 9/1/99 |
| 46.04 | New | 654(1) | 9/1/99 |
| 46.04 | New | 1512(6) | 9/1/99 |
| 47.01 | Amend | 62(3.07) | 9/1/99 |
| 49.04(a) | Amend | 785(2) | 9/1/99 |
| 49.10(c) | Amend | 1071(1) | 6/18/99 |
| 49.10(j) | Amend | 1132(1) | 9/1/99 |
| 49.25, Sec. 11 | Amend | 607(2) | 9/1/99 |
| 55.01 | Amend | 1236(1) | 6/18/99 |
| 55.02 | Amend | 1236(2) | 6/18/99 |
| 55.03 | Amend | 1236(3) | 6/18/99 |
| 55.06 | Amend | 62(3.08) | 9/1/99 |
| 55.06 | Amend | 1236(4) | 6/18/99 |
| 56.32(9) | Amend | 1470(1) | 6/19/99 |

*(continued)*

## 1999 Legislative Changes to the TEXAS CRIMINAL LAW and MOTOR VEHICLE HANDBOOK
*(Continued)*

### Code of Criminal Procedure
*(Continued)*

| *Article(s)* | *Change* | *Chap.* | *Eff. Date* |
|---|---|---|---|
| 56.42(d) | New | 1470(2) | 6/19/99 |
| 56.54(j) | New | 1302(13) | 9/1/99 |
| 56.541(e) | Amend | 1077(1) | 6/18/99 |
| 59.01(2) | Amend | 62(7.48) | 9/1/99 |
| 59.01(3) | Amend | 62(3.09) | 9/1/99 |
| 59.05(f) | New | 582(1) | 9/1/99 |
| 59.06 | Amend | 707(1) | 9/1/99 |
| 59.06(a) | Amend | 582(2) | 9/1/99 |
| 59.06(c) | Amend | 582(2) | 9/1/99 |
| 59.06(g) | Amend | 481(1) | 9/1/99 |
| 59.06(j) | Amend | 481(2) | 9/1/99 |
| 60.061(a) | Amend | 1189(43) | 9/1/99 |
| 60.061(b) | Amend | 1189(43) | 9/1/99 |
| 60.19 | New | 1334(2) | 9/1/99 |
| Chap. 61, heading | Amend | 1154(1) | 9/1/99 |
| 61.01(1) | Amend | 1154(2) | 9/1/99 |
| 61.01(7) | New | 1154(2) | 9/1/99 |
| 61.01(8) | New | 1154(2) | 9/1/99 |
| 61.01(9) | New | 1154(2) | 9/1/99 |
| 61.02 | Amend | 1154(3) | 9/1/99 |
| 61.03(c) | Amend | 1154(4) | 9/1/99 |
| 61.03(d) | Amend | 1154(4) | 9/1/99 |
| 61.03(e) | New | 1154(4) | 9/1/99 |
| 61.04(a) | Amend | 1154(5) | 9/1/99 |
| 61.04(d) | New | 1154(5) | 9/1/99 |
| 61.06 | Amend | 1154(6) | 9/1/99 |
| 61.07 | New | 492(1) | 6/18/99 |
| 61.07 | New | 1154(7) | 9/1/99 |
| 61.08 | New | 491(1) | 6/18/99 |
| 61.08 | New | 1154(7) | 9/1/99 |
| 61.09 | New | 1154(7) | 9/1/99 |
| 62.001(3) | Redesignate & Amend | 62(3.10) | 9/1/99 |
| 62.0015 | New | 685(2) | 9/1/99 |
| 62.006(b) | Amend | 685(3) | 9/1/99 |
| 62.009 | Redesignate | 62(3.12) | 9/1/99 |
| 62.009(a) | Amend | 200(1) | 9/1/99 |
| 62.009(a) | Amend & Reenact | 685(4) | 9/1/99 |
| 62.009(a) | Redesignate & Amend | 62(3.11) | 9/1/99 |
| 62.009(g) | New | 200(2) | 9/1/99 |
| 62.009(g) | New | 685(5) | 9/1/99 |
| 62.01(3) | Amend | 1415(7) | 9/1/99 |
| 62.01(5) | Amend | 1193(4) | 9/1/99 |

*(continued)*

# 1999 Legislative Changes to the TEXAS CRIMINAL LAW and MOTOR VEHICLE HANDBOOK
*(Continued)*

## Code of Criminal Procedure
*(Continued)*



| *Article(s)* | *Change* | *Chap.* | *Eff. Date* |
|---|---|---|---|
| 62.01(5) | Amend | 1415(8) | 9/1/99 |
| 62.01(6) | Amend | 1193(4) | 9/1/99 |
| 62.01(6) | Amend | 1415(8) | 9/1/99 |
| 62.01(7) | New | 1193(4) | 9/1/99 |
| 62.01(7) | New | 1415(8) | 9/1/99 |
| 62.011 | New | 1193(8) | 9/1/99 |
| 62.011 | New | 1415(9) | 9/1/99 |
| 62.02(a) | Amend | 444(1) | 9/1/99 |
| 62.02(a) | Amend | 1415(10) | 9/1/99 |
| 62.02(g) | New | 1193(5) | 9/1/99 |
| 62.02(g) | New | 1415(10) | 9/1/99 |
| 62.021 | New | 444(2) | 9/1/99 |
| 62.021 | New | 1415(11) | 9/1/99 |
| 62.03(a) | Amend | 1401(2) | 9/1/2000 |
| 62.03(a) | Amend | 1557(1) | 6/19/99 |
| 62.03(b) | Amend | 1557(1) | 6/19/99 |
| 62.03(c) | Amend | 1557(1) | 6/19/99 |
| 62.03(d) | Amend | 1193(6) | 9/1/99 |
| 62.03(d) | Amend | 1415(12) | 9/1/99 |
| 62.03(e) | Amend | 444(3) | 9/1/99 |
| 62.03(e) | Amend | 1415(12) | 9/1/99 |
| 62.03(e) | Amend | 1557(1) | 6/19/99 |
| 62.03(f) | Amend | 1415(12) | 9/1/99 |
| 62.03(f) | Amend | 1557(1) | 6/19/99 |
| 62.03(h) | New | 1193(7) | 9/1/99 |
| 62.03(h) | New | 1415(12) | 9/1/99 |
| 62.035 | New | 1557(2) | 6/19/99 |
| 62.04(a) | Amend | 444(4) | 9/1/99 |
| 62.04(a) | Amend | 1415(13) | 9/1/99 |
| 62.04(d) | Amend | 1557(3) | 6/19/99 |
| 62.04(f) | Amend | 444(4) | 9/1/99 |
| 62.04(f) | Amend | 1415(13) | 9/1/99 |
| 62.04(f) | Amend | 1557(3) | 6/19/99 |
| 62.04(g) | Amend | 1415(13) | 9/1/99 |
| 62.04(g) | Amend | 1557(3) | 6/19/99 |
| 62.045 | New | 1557(4) | 6/19/99 |
| 62.0451 | New | 444(5(a)) | 1/1/2000 |
| 62.05 | Amend | 444(6) | 9/1/99 |
| 62.05 | Amend | 1415(14) | 9/1/99 |
| 62.06(a) | Amend | 444(7) | 9/1/99 |
| 62.06(a) | Amend | 1415(15) | 9/1/99 |
| 62.06(b) | Amend | 444(7) | 9/1/99 |

*(continued)*

# 1999 Legislative Changes to the TEXAS CRIMINAL LAW and MOTOR VEHICLE HANDBOOK
*(Continued)*

## Code of Criminal Procedure
*(Continued)*

| *Article(s)* | *Change* | *Chap.* | *Eff. Date* |
|---|---|---|---|
| 62.06(b) | Amend | 1415(15) | 9/1/99 |
| 62.061 | New | 444(5(b)) | 1/1/2000 |
| 62.061 | New | 1193(8) | 9/1/99 |
| 62.061 | New | 1415(16) | 9/1/99 |
| 62.062 | New | 444(8) | 9/1/99 |
| 62.062 | New | 1415(16) | 9/1/99 |
| 62.065 | New | 1401(3) | 9/1/2000 |
| 62.08(b) | Amend | 1415(17) | 9/1/99 |
| 62.085 | New | 1401(3) | 9/1/2000 |
| 62.10(b) | Amend | 444(9) | 9/1/99 |
| 62.10(b) | Amend | 1415(18) | 9/1/99 |
| 62.10(c) | Amend | 444(9) | 9/1/99 |
| 62.10(c) | Amend | 1415(18) | 9/1/99 |
| 62.101 | New | 444(5(c)) | 1/1/2000 |
| 62.12(c) | Repeal | 1415(25) | 9/1/99 |
| Chap. 63, 63.001-63.018 | Renumber | 62(19.01(8(A))) | 9/1/99 |
| 63.001(3) | Redesignate & Amend | 62(3.10) | 9/1/99 |
| 63.009 | Redesignate | 62(3.12) | 9/1/99 |
| 63.009(3) | Redesignate & Amend | 62(3.11) | 9/1/99 |
| 63.009(g) | New | 62(3.12) | 9/1/99 |
| 63.012 | Renumber & Amend | 62(19.02(1)) | 9/1/99 |
| 63.019 | Transferred | 62(19.01)(8(B)) | 9/1/99 |
| 63.020 | Transferred | 62(19.01)(8(B)) | 9/1/99 |
| 63.021 | Transferred | 62(19.01)(8(B)) | 9/1/99 |
| 63.022 | Transferred | 62(19.01)(8(B)) | 9/1/99 |
| 63.023 | Transferred | 62(19.01(8(C))) | 9/1/99 |
| 63.023 | Repeal | 1081(8) | 9/1/99 |
| 63.023(c) | Amend | 62(19.02(2)) | 9/1/99 |
| 63.024 | Transferred | 62(19.01(8(C))) | 9/1/99 |
| 63.024 | Repeal | 1081(8) | 9/1/99 |
| 63.024(a) | Amend | 62(19.02(3)) | 9/1/99 |
| 102.002(a) | Repeal | 580(11(a)) | 9/1/99 |
| 102.002(b) | Repeal | 580(11(a)) | 9/1/99 |
| 102.002(b) | Amend | 1545(63) | 9/1/99 |
| 102.002(c) | Repeal | 580(11(a)) | 9/1/99 |
| 102.002(c) | Amend | 1545(63) | 9/1/99 |
| 102.004 | Amend | 1545(64) | 9/1/99 |
| 102.005(e) | Repeal | 580(11(b)) | 9/1/99 |
| 102.005(f) | Amend | 1031(1) | 9/1/99 |
| 102.007(c) | Amend | 49(1) | 9/1/99 |
| 102.011(a) | Amend | 44(1) | 9/1/99 |

*(continued)*

# 1999 Legislative Changes to the TEXAS CRIMINAL LAW and MOTOR VEHICLE HANDBOOK
*(Continued)*

## Code of Criminal Procedure
*(Continued)*

| *Article(s)* | *Change* | *Chap.* | *Eff. Date* |
|---|---|---|---|
| 102.017(d) | Amend | 110(1) | 5/17/99 |
| 102.0172 | New | 285(1) | 9/1/99 |
| 102.072 | Amend | 1345(1) | 9/1/99 |
| 102.075(g) | Amend | 1467(2.01) | 10/1/99 |
| 103.004 | Amend | 1462(1) | 9/1/99 |
| 103.010(c) | New | 412(1) | 6/18/99 |
| 103.011 | Amend | 412(2) | 6/18/99 |
| 104.004 | New | 664(1) | 9/1/99 |

## Transportation Code

| *Section(s)* | *Change* | *Chap.* | *Eff. Date* |
|---|---|---|---|
| 251.016 | New | 62(13.11(b)) | 9/1/99 |
| 251.159(a) | Amend | 885(1) | 6/18/99 |
| 391.035 | Amend | 442(1) | 6/18/99 |
| 391.063 | Amend | 62(17.03) | 9/1/99 |
| 391.093(f) | New | 841(1) | 6/18/99 |
| 391.125 | New | 442(2) | 6/18/99 |
| 391.126 | New | 442(2) | 6/18/99 |
| 391.127 | New | 442(2) | 6/18/99 |
| 392.0325 | New | 442(3) | 6/18/99 |
| 471.007(a) | Repeal & New | 1023(1) | 9/1/99 |
| 471.007(b) | Amend | 1023(1) | 9/1/99 |
| 471.007(c) | Amend | 1023(1) | 9/1/99 |
| 471.007(d) | Repeal & New | 1023(1) | 9/1/99 |
| 472.022(d) | Amend | 789(1) | 9/1/99 |
| 472.022(e)(2) | Amend | 789(2) | 9/1/99 |
| 472.022(e)(2) | Amend | 965(1) | 9/1/99 |
| 472.022(f) | New | 1088(1) | 9/1/99 |
| 501.002(9) | Amend | 414(2.42) | 7/1/2001 |
| 501.021(a) | Amend | 1423(1) | 9/1/99 |
| 501.023(c) | New | 1423(2) | 9/1/99 |
| 501.0234(a) | Amend | 1423(3) | 9/1/99 |
| 501.0275 | New | 1423(4) | 9/1/99 |
| 501.031 | Amend | 241(1) | 9/1/99 |
| 501.031(a) | Amend | 62(17.05) | 9/1/99 |
| 501.115(a) | Amend | 268(1) | 5/28/99 |
| 502.0021 | Renumber | 62(19.01(100)) | 9/1/99 |
| 502.0025 | New | 836(1) | 9/1/99 |
| 502.006(e) | New | 311(1) | 5/29/99 |
| 502.153(a) | Amend | 260(1) | 5/28/99 |

*(continued)*

## 1999 Legislative Changes to the TEXAS CRIMINAL LAW and MOTOR VEHICLE HANDBOOK
*(Continued)*

### Transportation Code
*(Continued)*

| *Section(s)* | *Change* | *Chap.* | *Eff. Date* |
|---|---|---|---|
| 502.153(j) | New | 260(1) | 5/28/99 |
| 502.158(f) | Repeal | 641(2) | 9/1/99 |
| 502.1585 | New | 732(1) | 9/1/99 |
| 502.1585 | New | 1197(1) | 9/1/99 |
| 502.1705 | New | 1455(1) | 9/1/99 |
| 502.174(b) | Amend | 1459(15) | 6/19/99 |
| 502.176 | Amend | 641(1) | 9/1/99 |
| 502.180(e) | Amend | 1455(2) | 9/1/99 |
| 502.184(a) | Amend | 1455(3) | 9/1/99 |
| 502.184(*i*) | Amend | 1455(3) | 9/1/99 |
| 502.185(h) | New | 97(1) | 5/17/99 |
| 502.202(a) | Amend | 62(17.06) | 9/1/99 |
| 502.2035 | New | 1194(1) | 9/1/99 |
| 502.2525 | New | 951(1) | 8/30/99 |
| 502.2526 | New | 951(1) | 8/30/99 |
| 502.253(e) | Amend | 1172(1) | 6/18/99 |
| 502.2531 | New | 513(1) | 9/1/99 |
| 502.254(a) | Amend | 993(1) | 9/1/99 |
| 502.254(b) | Amend | 993(1) | 9/1/99 |
| 502.254(c) | Amend | 993(1) | 9/1/99 |
| 502.254(d) | Amend | 993(1) | 9/1/99 |
| 502.254(g) | New | 993(1) | 9/1/99 |
| 502.254(h) | Reletter & Amend | 993(1) | 9/1/99 |
| 502.254(*i*) | Reletter | 993(1) | 9/1/99 |
| 502.2585 | New | 991(1) | 9/1/99 |
| 502.262 | Amend | 1249(1) | 9/1/99 |
| 502.263, sec. heading | Amend | 590(1) | 6/18/99 |
| 502.263 | Amend | 1249(1) | 9/1/99 |
| 502.264 | Amend | 1249(1) | 9/1/99 |
| 502.265 | Amend | 1249(1) | 9/1/99 |
| 502.266 | Amend | 530(1) | 9/1/99 |
| 502.2661 | Renumber | 62(19.01(103)) | 9/1/99 |
| 502.2663 | New | 763(1) | 9/1/99 |
| 502.268(a) | Amend | 818(1) | 9/1/99 |
| 502.2704 | Renumber | 62(19.01(101)) | 9/1/99 |
| 502.2721 | Renumber | 62(19.01(105)) | 9/1/99 |
| 502.2731(c) | Amend | 951(2) | 8/30/99 |
| 502.2731(e) | Amend | 951(2) | 8/30/99 |
| 502.2732 | Renumber | 62(19.01(106)) | 9/1/99 |
| 502.2733 | New | 1220(1) | 9/1/99 |
| 502.276(c) | Amend | 572(1) | 9/1/99 |
| 502.2761 | New | 186(3) | 9/1/99 |

*(continued)*

# 1999 Legislative Changes to the TEXAS CRIMINAL LAW and MOTOR VEHICLE HANDBOOK
*(Continued)*

## Transportation Code
*(Continued)*

| *Section(s)* | *Change* | *Chap.* | *Eff. Date* |
|---|---|---|---|
| 502.284(a) | Amend | 780(1) | 9/1/99 |
| 502.291 | Repeal | 951(5) | 8/30/99 |
| 502.292(e) | Amend | 1108(1) | 9/1/99 |
| 502.2921 | Renumber | 62(19.01(102)) | 9/1/99 |
| 502.2931 | New | 550(1) | 9/1/99 |
| 502.2951 | Renumber | 62(19.01(104)) | 9/1/99 |
| 502.298 | New | 862(1) | 9/1/99 |
| 502.298 | New | 951(4) | 8/30/99 |
| 502.299 | New | 433(1) | 9/1/99 |
| 502.299 | New | 634(1) | 9/1/99 |
| 502.299 | New | 1230(1) | 9/1/99 |
| 502.303 | New | 951(3) | 8/30/99 |
| 502.407(a) | Amend | 207(1) | 9/1/99 |
| 502.409(a) | Amend | 1189(17) | 9/1/99 |
| 503.0618 | New | 964(1) | 9/1/99 |
| 503.0625 | New | 964(2) | 9/1/99 |
| 520.002 | New | 876(1) | 6/18/99 |
| 520.022(a) | Amend | 1423(5) | 9/1/99 |
| 520.0225 | New | 836(2) | 9/1/99 |
| 520.031(a) | Amend | 836(3) | 9/1/99 |
| 520.031(a) | Amend | 1423(6) | 9/1/99 |
| 520.031(b) | Amend | 1423(6) | 9/1/99 |
| Chap. 520, Subchap. E | New | 1478(2) | 9/1/99 |
| 520.051 | New | 1478(2) | 9/1/99 |
| 520.052 | New | 1478(2) | 9/1/99 |
| 520.053 | New | 1478(2) | 9/1/99 |
| 520.054 | New | 1478(2) | 9/1/99 |
| 520.055 | New | 1478(2) | 9/1/99 |
| 520.056 | New | 1478(2) | 9/1/99 |
| 520.057 | New | 1478(2) | 9/1/99 |
| 520.058 | New | 1478(2) | 9/1/99 |
| 520.059 | New | 1478(2) | 9/1/99 |
| 520.060 | New | 1478(2) | 9/1/99 |
| 520.061 | New | 1478(2) | 9/1/99 |
| 520.062 | New | 1478(2) | 9/1/99 |
| 520.063 | New | 1478(2) | 9/1/99 |
| 521.006 | New | 1258(1) | 8/30/99 |
| 521.022(c) | Amend | 786(1) | 6/18/99 |
| 521.022(i) | New | 663(3) | 6/18/99 |
| 521.044(f) | New | 556(77(a)) | 9/1/99 |
| 521.044(f) | New | 1189(18) | 9/1/99 |

*(continued)*

# 1999 Legislative Changes to the TEXAS CRIMINAL LAW and MOTOR VEHICLE HANDBOOK
*(Continued)*

## Transportation Code
*(Continued)*

| *Section(s)* | *Change* | *Chap.* | *Eff. Date* |
|---|---|---|---|
| 521.057 | New | 1401(4) | 9/1/2000 |
| 521.101(h) | New | 1401(5) | 9/1/2000 |
| 521.101(*i*) | New | 1401(5) | 9/1/2000 |
| 521.103 | New | 1189(19) | 9/1/99 |
| 521.103 | New | 1401(6) | 9/1/2000 |
| 521.125 | Amend | 1189(20) | 9/1/99 |
| 521.126 | New | 1340(1) | 9/1/99 |
| 521.141(a) | Amend | 1189(21) | 9/1/99 |
| 521.142(c) | Amend | 640(3) | 9/1/99 |
| 521.142(g) | New | 556(78(a)) | 9/1/99 |
| 521.142(g) | New | 1189(22) | 9/1/99 |
| 521.1425 | Amend | 640(4) | 9/1/99 |
| 521.143(a) | Amend | 1189(23) | 9/1/99 |
| 521.201 | Amend | 1080(1) | 9/1/99 |
| 521.205(a) | Amend | 721(1) | 9/1/99 |
| 521.224(b) | Amend | 797(1) | 9/1/99 |
| 521.224(e) | Amend | 797(1) | 9/1/99 |
| 521.225(d) | New | 797(2) | 9/1/99 |
| 521.226 | Repeal | 797(4) | 9/1/99 |
| 521.246(f) | New | 1105(1) | 9/1/99 |
| 521.2476 | New | 1105(2) | 9/1/99 |
| Chap. 521, Subchap. M heading | Amend | 709(1) | 9/1/99 |
| Chap. 521, Subchap. M heading | Amend | 1189(25) | 9/1/99 |
| 521.272 | New | 1401(7) | 9/1/2000 |
| 521.274 | Amend | 1189(24) | 9/1/99 |
| 521.274(b) | Amend | 1401(8) | 9/1/2000 |
| 521.275 | New | 709(2) | 9/1/99 |
| 521.275 | New | 1189(26) | 9/1/99 |
| 521.291 | Repeal & New | 1117(1) | 9/1/2000 |
| 521.291(b) | Amend | 1409(1) | 9/1/99 |
| 521.292 | Repeal & New | 1117(1) | 9/1/2000 |
| 521.293 | Repeal & New | 1117(1) | 9/1/2000 |
| 521.294 | Repeal & New | 1117(1) | 9/1/2000 |
| 521.295 | Repeal & New | 1117(1) | 9/1/2000 |
| 521.295 | Repeal | 1409(9) | 9/1/99 |
| 521.296 | New | 1117(1) | 9/1/2000 |
| 521.297 | New | 1117(1) | 9/1/2000 |
| 521.298 | New | 1117(1) | 9/1/2000 |
| 521.299 | New | 1117(1) | 9/1/2000 |
| 521.300 | New | 1117(1) | 9/1/2000 |

*(continued)*

# 1999 Legislative Changes to the TEXAS CRIMINAL LAW and MOTOR VEHICLE HANDBOOK
*(Continued)*

## Transportation Code
*(Continued)*

| *Section(s)* | *Change* | *Chap.* | *Eff. Date* |
|---|---|---|---|
| 521.301 | Repeal & New | 1117(1) | 9/1/2000 |
| 521.302 | New | 1117(1) | 9/1/2000 |
| 521.303 | New | 1117(1) | 9/1/2000 |
| 521.304 | Renumber | 1117(1) | 9/1/2000 |
| 521.305 | Renumber | 1117(1) | 9/1/2000 |
| 521.306 | Renumber | 1117(1) | 9/1/2000 |
| 521.306(d) | Amend | 1189(27) | 9/1/99 |
| 521.307 | Renumber | 1117(1) | 9/1/2000 |
| 521.308 | Amend | 884(1) | 9/1/99 |
| 521.308 | Renumber & Amend | 1117(1) | 9/1/2000 |
| 521.309 | Renumber & Amend | 1117(1) | 9/1/2000 |
| 521.310 | Renumber & Amend | 1117(1) | 9/1/2000 |
| 521.311 | Renumber & Amend | 1117(1) | 9/1/2000 |
| 521.312 | Renumber & Amend | 1117(1) | 9/1/2000 |
| 521.313 | New | 1117(1) | 9/1/2000 |
| 521.314 | Renumber | 1117(1) | 9/1/2000 |
| 521.315 | Renumber & Amend | 1117(1) | 9/1/2000 |
| 521.316 | Renumber | 1117(1) | 9/1/2000 |
| 521.317 | Renumber | 1117(1) | 9/1/2000 |
| 521.318 | Renumber | 1117(1) | 9/1/2000 |
| 521.319 | Renumber & Amend | 1117(1) | 9/1/2000 |
| 521.320 | Renumber | 1117(1) | 9/1/2000 |
| 521.342(b) | Amend | 580(9) | 9/1/99 |
| 521.344(g) | Amend | 1409(2) | 9/1/99 |
| 521.344(h) | Amend | 1117(2) | 9/1/2000 |
| 521.344(*i*) | Amend | 580(10) | 9/1/99 |
| 521.347(a) | Amend | 884(2) | 9/1/99 |
| 521.347(c) | Amend | 581(1) | 6/18/99 |
| 521.348 | New | 1401(9) | 9/1/2000 |
| 521.421(g) | New | 1516(2) | 9/1/99 |
| 521.422(c) | New | 1516(3) | 9/1/99 |
| 521.427 | New | 1189(28) | 9/1/99 |
| 521.451 | Amend | 659(3) | 9/1/99 |
| 521.454(c) | Amend | 658(1) | 9/1/99 |
| 521.457(a) | Amend | 1207(6) | 9/1/99 |
| 522.071(c) | Amend | 1409(3) | 9/1/99 |
| 522.087(b) | Amend | 1117(3) | 9/1/2000 |
| 523.004 | Amend | 1257(1) | 9/1/99 |
| 524.013(a) | Amend | 1409(4) | 9/1/99 |
| 541.201(10) | Amend | 797(3) | 9/1/99 |
| 541.201(15) | New | 663(1) | 6/18/99 |
| 541.201(16) | Renumber & Amend | 663(1) | 6/18/99 |

*(continued)*

# 1999 Legislative Changes to the TEXAS CRIMINAL LAW and MOTOR VEHICLE HANDBOOK
*(Continued)*

## Transportation Code
*(Continued)*

| *Section(s)* | *Change* | *Chap.* | *Eff. Date* |
|---|---|---|---|
| 541.201(17) to (23) | Renumber | 663(1) | 6/18/99 |
| 542.006(a) | Amend | 308(1) | 5/29/99 |
| 542.007 | New | 1393(1) | 9/1/99 |
| 542.402 | Amend | 1336(1) | 9/1/99 |
| 542.402(b) | Amend | 1545(72) | 9/1/99 |
| 542.404(a) | Amend | 789(3) | 9/1/99 |
| 542.501 | Amend | 724(1) | 6/18/99 |
| 543.003 | Amend | 701(3) | 6/18/99 |
| 543.004(c) | New | 62(17.07) | 9/1/99 |
| 543.005 | Amend | 701(4) | 6/18/99 |
| 543.007 | Amend | 701(5) | 6/18/99 |
| 543.102 | Repeal | 1387(3) | 9/1/99 |
| 543.102 | Repeal | 1545(75(b)) | 9/1/99 |
| 543.103 | Repeal | 1387(3) | 9/1/99 |
| 543.103 | Repeal | 1545(75(b)) | 9/1/99 |
| 543.104 | Repeal | 1387(3) | 9/1/99 |
| 543.104 | Repeal | 1545(75(b)) | 9/1/99 |
| 543.105 | Repeal | 1387(3) | 9/1/99 |
| 543.105 | Repeal | 1545(75(b)) | 9/1/99 |
| 543.106 | Repeal | 1387(3) | 9/1/99 |
| 543.106 | Repeal | 1545(75(b)) | 9/1/99 |
| 543.107 | Repeal | 1387(3) | 9/1/99 |
| 543.107 | Repeal | 1545(75(b)) | 9/1/99 |
| 543.108 | Repeal | 1387(3) | 9/1/99 |
| 543.108 | Repeal | 1545(75(b)) | 9/1/99 |
| 543.109 | Repeal | 1387(3) | 9/1/99 |
| 543.109 | Repeal | 1545(75(b)) | 9/1/99 |
| 543.110 | Repeal | 1387(3) | 9/1/99 |
| 543.110 | Repeal | 1545(75(b)) | 9/1/99 |
| 543.117 | New | 1088(2) | 9/1/99 |
| 543.204(a) | Amend | 1545(73) | 9/1/99 |
| 544.011 | Amend | 62(17.08) | 9/1/99 |
| 545.302(g) | New | 814(1) | 6/18/99 |
| 545.303(e) | New | 814(2) | 6/18/99 |
| 545.307(a)(1) | Amend | 731(1) | 9/1/99 |
| 545.307(a)(2) | Amend | 1419(1) | 6/19/99 |
| 545.352(b) | Amend | 663(2) | 6/18/99 |
| 545.352(b) | Amend | 739(1) | 9/1/99 |
| 545.352(b) | Amend | 1346(1) | 9/1/99 |
| 545.352(c) | Amend | 663(2) | 6/18/99 |
| 545.3535 | Amend | 1346(2) | 9/1/99 |
| 545.354, heading | Amend | 576(3) | 9/1/99 |

*(continued)*

 Zt

# 1999 Legislative Changes to the TEXAS CRIMINAL LAW and MOTOR VEHICLE HANDBOOK
*(Continued)*

## Transportation Code
*(Continued)*

| *Section(s)* | *Change* | *Chap.* | *Eff. Date* |
|---|---|---|---|
| 545.354(a) | Amend | 576(3) | 9/1/99 |
| 545.364 | Repeal | 1346(3) | 9/1/99 |
| 545.410(a) | Amend | 1357(1) | 9/1/99 |
| 545.410(b) | Amend | 1357(1) | 9/1/99 |
| 545.410(d) | Amend | 1357(1) | 9/1/99 |
| 545.413(b) | Amend | 515(1) | 9/1/99 |
| 545.413(e) | Amend | 316(1) | 9/1/99 |
| 545.413(h) | Amend | 515(1) | 9/1/99 |
| 547.305(d) | Amend | 380(1) | 7/1/99 |
| 547.701(b) | Amend | 183(1) | 9/1/99 |
| 547.801(d) | Amend | 1022(1) | 9/1/99 |
| 548.001 | Amend | 663(4) | 6/18/99 |
| 548.051(a) | Amend | 1189(29) | 9/1/99 |
| 548.052 | Amend | 963(1) | 6/18/99 |
| 548.052 | Amend | 1423(7) | 9/1/99 |
| 548.201(b) | Amend | 663(5) | 6/18/99 |
| 548.256, heading | Amend | 1423(9) | 9/1/99 |
| 548.256(a) | Amend | 1423(8) | 9/1/99 |
| 548.306(k) | New | 1189(30) | 9/1/99 |
| 548.306(*l*) | New | 1189(30) | 9/1/99 |
| 548.306(m) | New | 1189(30) | 9/1/99 |
| 548.306(n) | New | 1189(30) | 9/1/99 |
| 548.405(a) | Amend | 1189(31) | 9/1/99 |
| 548.405(c) | Amend | 1189(31) | 9/1/99 |
| 548.407(*l*) | Amend | 1189(32) | 9/1/99 |
| 548.408(a) | Amend | 1189(33) | 9/1/99 |
| 548.408(b) | Amend | 1189(33) | 9/1/99 |
| 548.408(f) | New | 1189(33) | 9/1/99 |
| 548.501(a) | Amend | 1189(34) | 9/1/99 |
| 548.503(a) | Amend | 1189(35) | 9/1/99 |
| 548.601(a) | Amend | 1189(36) | 9/1/99 |
| 548.602(a) | Amend | 1189(37) | 9/1/99 |
| 548.605 | Amend | 688(1) | 9/1/99 |
| 600.004 | New | 724(2) | 6/18/99 |
| 601.087 | Repeal | 659(4) | 9/1/99 |
| 601.156(a) | Amend | 1117(4) | 9/1/2000 |
| 601.156(c) | Amend | 1409(6) | 9/1/99 |
| 601.158(b) | Amend | 1117(5) | 9/1/2000 |
| 601.158(c) | New | 1117(5) | 9/1/2000 |
| 601.158(d) | New | 1117(5) | 9/1/2000 |
| 601.158(e) | New | 1117(5) | 9/1/2000 |
| 601.158(f) | New | 1117(5) | 9/1/2000 |

*(continued)*

## 1999 Legislative Changes to the TEXAS CRIMINAL LAW and MOTOR VEHICLE HANDBOOK
*(Continued)*

### Transportation Code
*(Continued)*

| *Section(s)* | *Change* | *Chap.* | *Eff. Date* |
|---|---|---|---|
| 601.193 | Amend | 961(1) | 9/1/99 |
| 601.196 | Repeal | 659(4) | 9/1/99 |
| 601.372(c) | Amend | 884(3) | 9/1/99 |
| 601.373(b) | Amend | 884(4) | 9/1/99 |
| 601.376(a) | Amend | 1189(38) | 9/1/99 |
| 601.401 | Amend | 1117(6) | 9/1/2000 |
| 601.402 | Repeal | 1117(9) | 9/1/2000 |
| 601.403 | Repeal | 1117(9) | 9/1/2000 |
| 601.404 | Repeal | 1117(9) | 9/1/2000 |
| 601.405 | Repeal | 1117(9) | 9/1/2000 |
| 601.406 | Repeal | 1117(9) | 9/1/2000 |
| 601.407 | Repeal | 1117(9) | 9/1/2000 |
| 601.408 | Repeal | 1117(9) | 9/1/2000 |
| 601.409 | Repeal | 1117(9) | 9/1/2000 |
| 601.410 | Repeal | 1117(9) | 9/1/2000 |
| 621.101(a) | Amend | 601(1) | 9/1/99 |
| 621.401 | Amend | 62(17.09) | 9/1/99 |
| 621.401 | Amend | 1523(1) | 9/1/99 |
| 621.408 | Amend | 601(2) | 9/1/99 |
| 621.408 | Amend | 1523(2) | 9/1/99 |
| 621.506(g) | Amend | 1101(1) | 9/1/99 |
| 622.042 | Amend | 749(1) | 9/1/99 |
| 622.052, heading | Amend | 749(2) | 9/1/99 |
| 622.052(b) | Amend | 749(3) | 9/1/99 |
| 622.062, heading | Amend | 749(4) | 9/1/99 |
| 622.062(b) | Amend | 749(5) | 9/1/99 |
| 623.071(d) | New | 807(1) | 9/1/99 |
| 623.071(e) | Reletter | 807(1) | 9/1/99 |
| 623.071(f) | Reletter | 807(1) | 9/1/99 |
| 623.071(g) | Repeal | 807(1) | 9/1/99 |
| 623.071(g) | Reletter | 807(1) | 9/1/99 |
| 623.076(c) | Amend | 807(2) | 9/1/99 |
| 623.093(f) | Reletter | 62(19.01(107)) | 9/1/99 |
| 623.214(b) | Amend | 624(1) | 6/18/99 |
| 623.215(a) | Amend | 624(2) | 6/18/99 |
| 623.219 | Amend | 624(3) | 6/18/99 |
| 642.002 | Amend | 566(1) | 6/18/99 |
| 643.002 | Amend | 62(17.10(a)) | 9/1/99 |
| 643.002 | Amend | 603(1) | 6/18/99 |
| 643.004 | Amend | 62(17.11(a)) | 9/1/99 |
| 643.054(c) | New | 62(17.12(a)) | 9/1/99 |
| 643.058(a) | Amend | 603(2) | 6/18/99 |

*(continued)*

# 1999 Legislative Changes to the TEXAS CRIMINAL LAW and MOTOR VEHICLE HANDBOOK
*(Continued)*

## Transportation Code
*(Continued)*

| *Section(s)* | *Change* | *Chap.* | *Eff. Date* |
|---|---|---|---|
| 643.058(b) | New | 62(17.13(a)) | 9/1/99 |
| 643.058(c) | Reletter | 62(17.13(a)) | 9/1/99 |
| 643.059(b) | Amend | 603(3) | 6/18/99 |
| 643.059(e) | Amend | 603(3) | 6/18/99 |
| 643.059(f) | New | 603(3) | 6/18/99 |
| 643.061 | New | 62(17.14(a)) | 9/1/99 |
| 643.061 | New | 603(4) | 6/18/99 |
| 643.062 | New | 62(17.14(a)) | 9/1/99 |
| 643.062 | New | 603(4) | 6/18/99 |
| 643.063 | New | 62(17.15(a)) | 9/1/99 |
| 643.106(a) | Amend | 62(17.17(a)) | 9/1/99 |
| 643.106(a) | Amend | 886(1) | 6/18/99 |
| 643.153(a) | Amend | 62(17.19(a)) | 9/1/99 |
| 643.153(b) | Repeal | 62(17.19(a)) | 9/1/99 |
| 643.153(b) | Reletter | 62(17.19(a)) | 9/1/99 |
| 643.153(c) | New | 62(17.19(a)) | 9/1/99 |
| 643.153(f) | Amend | 62(17.19(a)) | 9/1/99 |
| 643.153(f) | Amend | 603(5) | 6/18/99 |
| 643.155 | Repeal & New | 62(17.19(b)) | 9/1/99 |
| 643.156 | New | 62(17.20(a)) | 9/1/99 |
| 643.252 | Amend | 62(17.21(a)) | 9/1/99 |
| 643.253 | Amend | 62(17.22(a)) | 9/1/99 |
| 643.254(a) | Amend | 603(6) | 6/18/99 |
| 643.254(c) | New | 603(6) | 6/18/99 |
| 643.254(d) | New | 603(6) | 6/18/99 |
| 644.001(1) | Amend | 62(17.24(a)) | 9/1/99 |
| 644.001(5) | Amend | 62(17.25(a)) | 9/1/99 |
| 644.004 | New | 62(17.26(a)) | 9/1/99 |
| 644.053(a) | Amend | 62(17.27(a)) | 9/1/99 |
| 644.053(c) | New | 62(17.27(a)) | 9/1/99 |
| 644.053(d) | New | 62(17.27(b)) | 9/1/99 |
| 644.054 | New | 62(17.28(a)) | 9/1/99 |
| 644.101 | Amend | 62(17.29(a)) | 9/1/99 |
| 644.101(b) | Amend | 1189(39) | 9/1/99 |
| 644.102(a) | Amend | 292(1) | 9/1/99 |
| 644.102(b) | Amend | 292(1) | 9/1/99 |
| 644.102(f) | New | 292(1) | 9/1/99 |
| 644.103 | Amend | 62(17.31(a)) | 9/1/99 |
| 644.103(d) | New | 1189(40) | 9/1/99 |
| 644.103(e) | New | 1189(40) | 9/1/99 |
| 644.104(c) | New | 1189(41) | 9/1/99 |
| 644.104(d) | New | 1189(41) | 9/1/99 |

*(continued)*

# 1999 Legislative Changes to the TEXAS CRIMINAL LAW and MOTOR VEHICLE HANDBOOK
*(Continued)*

## Transportation Code
*(Continued)*

| *Section(s)* | *Change* | *Chap.* | *Eff. Date* |
|---|---|---|---|
| 644.153(d) | New | 292(2) | 9/1/99 |
| 644.153(e) | New | 292(2) | 9/1/99 |
| 644.153(f) | New | 292(2) | 9/1/99 |
| 644.153(g) | New | 292(2) | 9/1/99 |
| 644.153(h) | New | 292(2) | 9/1/99 |
| 644.155 | Amend | 292(3) | 9/1/99 |
| Chap. 644, Subchap. E | New | 62(17.32(a)) | 9/1/99 |
| 644.201 | New | 62(17.32(a)) | 9/1/99 |
| 644.202 | New | 62(17.32(a)) | 9/1/99 |
| 644.203 | New | 62(17.32(a)) | 9/1/99 |
| 645.002(b) | Amend | 62(17.33(a)) | 9/1/99 |
| 645.002(c) | New | 62(17.33(a)) | 9/1/99 |
| Chap. 647 | New | 62(17.34(a)) | 9/1/99 |
| 647.001 | New | 62(17.34(a)) | 9/1/99 |
| 647.002 | New | 62(17.34(a)) | 9/1/99 |
| 647.003 | New | 62(17.34(a)) | 9/1/99 |
| 647.004 | New | 62(17.34(a)) | 9/1/99 |
| 647.005 | New | 62(17.34(a)) | 9/1/99 |
| 647.006 | New | 62(17.34(a)) | 9/1/99 |
| 647.007 | New | 62(17.34(a)) | 9/1/99 |
| 647.008 | New | 62(17.34(a)) | 9/1/99 |
| 647.009 | New | 62(17.34(a)) | 9/1/99 |
| 647.010 | New | 62(17.34(a)) | 9/1/99 |
| 647.011 | New | 62(17.34(a)) | 9/1/99 |
| 647.012 | New | 62(17.34(a)) | 9/1/99 |
| 647.013 | New | 62(17.34(a)) | 9/1/99 |
| 647.014 | New | 62(17.34(a)) | 9/1/99 |
| 647.015 | New | 62(17.34(a)) | 9/1/99 |
| 647.016 | New | 62(17.34(a)) | 9/1/99 |
| 647.017 | New | 62(17.34(a)) | 9/1/99 |
| 647.018 | New | 62(17.34(a)) | 9/1/99 |
| 647.019 | New | 62(17.34(a)) | 9/1/99 |
| Chap. 648 | New | 62(17.35(a)) | 9/1/99 |
| 648.001 | New | 62(17.35(a)) | 9/1/99 |
| 648.002 | New | 62(17.35(a)) | 9/1/99 |
| 648.003 | New | 62(17.35(a)) | 9/1/99 |
| 648.051 | New | 62(17.35(a)) | 9/1/99 |
| 648.052 | New | 62(17.35(a)) | 9/1/99 |
| 648.101 | New | 62(17.35(a)) | 9/1/99 |
| 648.102 | New | 62(17.35(a)) | 9/1/99 |
| 648.103 | New | 62(17.35(a)) | 9/1/99 |

*(continued)*

# 1999 Legislative Changes to the TEXAS CRIMINAL LAW and MOTOR VEHICLE HANDBOOK
*(Continued)*

## Transportation Code
*(Continued)*

| *Section(s)* | *Change* | *Chap.* | *Eff. Date* |
|---|---|---|---|
| 661.003(d) | Amend | 62(17.36) | 9/1/99 |
| 661.003(e) | Amend | 62(17.36) | 9/1/99 |
| 661.003(f) | Amend | 62(17.36) | 9/1/99 |
| 661.003(g) | Amend | 62(17.36) | 9/1/99 |
| 681.001(5) | Amend | 1172(2) | 6/18/99 |
| 681.002(b) | Amend | 1362(1) | 9/1/99 |
| 681.002(e) | New | 1362(1) | 9/1/99 |
| 681.003(c) | Amend | 1172(3) | 6/18/99 |
| 681.003(c) | Amend | 1362(2) | 9/1/99 |
| 681.0032 | New | 513(2) | 9/1/99 |
| 681.006 | Amend | 1362(3) | 9/1/99 |
| 681.008 | Amend | 738(1) | 9/1/99 |
| 681.008 | Amend | 1195(1) | 6/18/99 |
| 681.008 | Amend | 1362(4) | 9/1/99 |
| 681.009(b) | Amend | 1246(9) | 9/1/99 |
| 681.009(e) | New | 1362(5) | 9/1/99 |
| 681.011(a) | Amend | 738(2) | 9/1/99 |
| 681.011(b) | Amend | 738(2) | 9/1/99 |
| 681.011(b) | Amend | 1362(6) | 9/1/99 |
| 681.011(g) | Amend | 1362(6) | 9/1/99 |
| 681.011(h) | Amend | 1362(6) | 9/1/99 |
| 681.011(*i*) | Amend | 1362(6) | 9/1/99 |
| 681.011(j) | Amend | 1362(6) | 9/1/99 |
| 681.011(k) | Amend | 1362(6) | 9/1/99 |
| 681.011(*l*) | Repeal | 1362(7) | 9/1/99 |
| 681.011(m) | New | 1362(6) | 9/1/99 |
| Chap. 682, heading | Amend | 156(1) | 5/21/99 |
| 682.001 | Amend | 156(2) | 5/21/99 |
| 682.001 | Amend | 310(1) | 5/29/99 |
| 682.002 | Amend | 156(2) | 5/21/99 |
| 682.003 | Amend | 156(2) | 5/21/99 |
| 682.004 | Amend | 156(2) | 5/21/99 |
| 682.009(b) | Amend | 156(3) | 5/21/99 |
| 682.010 | Amend | 156(4) | 5/21/99 |
| 682.011(c) | Amend | 156(5) | 5/21/99 |
| 683.051 | Amend | 612(1) | 9/1/99 |
| 683.054(b) | Amend | 612(2) | 9/1/99 |
| 683.071 | Amend | 746(1) | 9/1/99 |
| 683.074(g) | New | 1226(1) | 6/18/99 |
| 702.002 | Amend | 744(1) | 6/18/99 |
| 706.001 | Amend | 62(17.37(a)) | 9/1/99 |
| 706.001(1) | Amend | 1545(74) | 9/1/99 |

*(continued)*

# 1999 Legislative Changes to the TEXAS CRIMINAL LAW and MOTOR VEHICLE HANDBOOK
*(Continued)*

## Transportation Code
*(Continued)*

| *Section(s)* | *Change* | *Chap.* | *Eff. Date* |
|---|---|---|---|
| 706.002(a) | Amend | 62(17.37(b)) | 9/1/99 |
| 706.002(a) | Amend | 999(1) | 9/1/99 |
| 706.004 | Amend | 62(17.37(c)) | 9/1/99 |
| 706.004 | Amend | 999(2) | 9/1/99 |
| 706.005 | Amend | 62(17.37(c)) | 9/1/99 |
| 706.005 | Amend | 999(2) | 9/1/99 |
| 706.006(a) | Amend | 62(17.37(d)) | 9/1/99 |
| 706.006(a) | Amend | 999(3) | 9/1/99 |
| 721.005(b) | Amend | 62(17.38) | 9/1/99 |
| 722.013 | Repeal | 1530(5.02) | 9/1/99 |
| 724.033(a) | Amend | 1409(5) | 9/1/99 |
| 729.001(c) | Amend | 1477(36) | 9/1/99 |
| 729.002(b) | Amend | 1477(37) | 9/1/99 |
| 729.004(b) | Amend | 789(4) | 9/1/99 |

## Vehicle Laws

| *Article(s)* | *Change* | *Chap.* | *Eff. Date* |
|---|---|---|---|
| 4413(29c), Sec. 3(23) | New | 1489(1) | 9/1/99 |
| 4413(29c), Sec. 4(c) | New | 762(1) | 6/18/99 |
| 4413(29c), Sec. 4A | New | 1489(2) | 9/1/99 |
| 4413(29c), Sec. 6 | Amend | 604(1) | 6/18/99 |
| 4413(29c), Sec. 15A(c) | Amend | 1166(1) | 6/18/99 |
| 4413(29c), Sec. 15A(f) | New | 1166(1) | 6/18/99 |
| 6675c, Sec. 2 | Repeal | 62(17.10(b)) | 9/1/99 |
| 6675c, Sec. 2 | Repeal | 603(7(a)) | 6/18/99 |
| 6675c, Sec. 3(a), (e) | Repeal | 62(17.12(b)) | 9/1/99 |
| 6675c, Sec. 3(i) | Repeal | 62(17.13(b)) | 9/1/99 |
| 6675c, Sec. 3(*l*), (m) | Repeal | 62(17.14(b)) | 9/1/99 |
| 6675c, Sec. 3(*l*) | Repeal | 603(7(a)) | 6/18/99 |
| 6675c, Sec. 3(m) | Repeal | 603(7(a)) | 6/18/99 |
| 6675c, Sec. 3A | Repeal | 62(17.15(b)) | 9/1/99 |
| 6675c, Sec. 4(a), (b), (d) | Repeal | 62(17.16) | 9/1/99 |
| 6675c, Sec. 4(j) | Repeal | 62(17.17(b)) | 9/1/99 |
| 6675c, Sec. 6(a) | Repeal | 62(17.18) | 9/1/99 |
| 6675c, Sec. 7 | Repeal | 62(17.21(b)) | 9/1/99 |
| 6675c, Sec. 7(a) | Repeal | 62(17.21(b)) | 9/1/99 |
| 6675c, Sec. 8(c), (f), (g) | Repeal | 62(17.19(c)) | 9/1/99 |
| 6675c, Sec. 8(h) | Repeal | 62(17.20(b)) | 9/1/99 |
| 6675c, Sec. 10 | Repeal | 62(17.22(b)) | 9/1/99 |
| 6675c, Sec. 13(a) | Repeal | 62(17.23) | 9/1/99 |

*(continued)*

# 1999 Legislative Changes to the TEXAS CRIMINAL LAW and MOTOR VEHICLE HANDBOOK
*(Continued)*

## Vehicle Laws
*(Continued)*

| *Article(s)* | *Change* | *Chap.* | *Eff. Date* |
|---|---|---|---|
| 6675c, Sec. 15 | Repeal | 62(17.11(b)) | 9/1/99 |
| 6675c-1(e), (f) | Repeal | 62(17.33(b)) | 9/1/99 |
| 6675-c2 | Repeal | 62(17.35(b)) | 9/1/99 |
| 6675d, Sec. 1(1) | Repeal | 62(17.24(b)) | 9/1/99 |
| 6675d, Sec. 1(1) | Repeal | 62(17.24(b)) | 9/1/99 |
| 6675d, Sec. 1(5) | Repeal | 62(17.25(b)) | 9/1/99 |
| 6675d, Sec. 3A | Repeal | 62(17.28(b)) | 9/1/99 |
| 6675d, Sec. 3A | Repeal | 62(17.32(b)) | 9/1/99 |
| 6675d, Sec. 5(a), (c) | Repeal | 62(17.27(c)) | 9/1/99 |
| 6675d, Sec. 5(c) | Repeal | 62(17.27(c)) | 9/1/99 |
| 6675d, Sec. 5(c) | Repeal | 62(17.27(c)) | 9/1/99 |
| 6675d, Sec. 6 | Repeal | 62(17.29(b)) | 9/1/99 |
| 6675d, Sec. 7(e) | Repeal | 62(17.30) | 9/1/99 |
| 6675d, Sec. 7(f) | Repeal | 62(17.32(b)) | 9/1/99 |
| 6675d, Sec. 8 | Repeal | 62(17.31(b)) | 9/1/99 |
| 6675d, Sec. 16 | Repeal | 62(17.26(b)) | 9/1/99 |
| 6687d, Sec. 1(5-9) | Repeal | 62(17.37(e)) | 9/1/99 |
| 6687d, Sec. 2(a) | Repeal | 62(17.37(e)) | 9/1/99 |
| 6687d, Sec. 4(a), (b), (c) | Repeal | 62(17.37(e)) | 9/1/99 |
| 6687-9a, Sec. 13 | Amend | 1376(1) | 9/1/99 |
| 6687-9a, Sec. 14(d) | Amend | 1376(3) | 9/1/99 |
| 6687-9a, Sec. 14B(a) | Amend | 1376(2) | 9/1/99 |



## Agriculture Code

| *Section(s)* | *Change* | *Chap.* | *Eff. Date* |
|---|---|---|---|
| 102.0195 | Repeal | 358(27) | 9/1/99 |

## Alcoholic Beverage Code

| *Section(s)* | *Change* | *Chap.* | *Eff. Date* |
|---|---|---|---|
| 11.09 | Amend | 517(1) | 9/1/99 |
| 11.61(e) | Amend | 62(9.19) | 9/1/99 |
| 61.03 | Amend | 517(3) | 9/1/99 |
| 61.11(a) | Amend | 62(9.20) | 9/1/99 |
| 61.71(f) | Amend | 62(9.21) | 9/1/99 |
| 106.04(d) | Amend | 1207(1) | 9/1/99 |
| 106.041(f) | Amend | 1207(2) | 9/1/99 |
| 106.041(h) | Amend | 1207(2) | 9/1/99 |
| 106.071(d) | Amend | 1207(3) | 9/1/99 |

*(continued)*

# 1999 Legislative Changes to the TEXAS CRIMINAL LAW and MOTOR VEHICLE HANDBOOK
*(Continued)*

## Alcoholic Beverage Code
*(Continued)*

| *Section(s)* | *Change* | *Chap.* | *Eff. Date* |
|---|---|---|---|
| 106.071(e) | Amend | 76(4) | 9/1/99 |
| 106.071(f) | Amend | 1207(3) | 9/1/99 |
| 106.071(h) | New | 1207(3) | 9/1/99 |
| 106.071(i) | New | 1207(3) | 9/1/99 |
| 106.115 | Amend | 62(2.01) | 9/1/99 |
| 106.115(a) | Amend | 1207(4) | 9/1/99 |
| 106.115(d) | Amend | 76(5) | 9/1/99 |
| 106.115(e) | Amend | 1409(7) | 9/1/99 |
| 106.117(a) | Amend | 1207(5) | 9/1/99 |
| 106.15 | New | 80(2) | 9/1/99 |

## Civil Practice and Remedies Code

| *Section(s)* | *Change* | *Chap.* | *Eff. Date* |
|---|---|---|---|
| 74.001(a) | Amend | 679(2) | 9/1/99 |
| 125.001(c) | Amend | 1161(1) | 9/1/99 |

## Civil Statutes

| *Article(s)* | *Change* | *Chap.* | *Eff. Date* |
|---|---|---|---|
| 4413(29ee), Sec. 1(4) | Repeal | 62(9.01(b)) | 9/1/99 |
| 4413(29ee), Sec. 1(4) | Repeal | 62(9.02(b)) | 9/1/99 |
| 4413(29ee), Sec. 2(a) | Repeal | 62(9.03(b)) | 9/1/99 |
| 4413(29ee), Sec. 2(d) | Repeal | 62(9.04(b)) | 9/1/99 |
| 4413(29ee), Sec. 3(a) | Repeal | 62(9.06(b)) | 9/1/99 |
| 4413(29ee), Sec. 5(b) | Repeal | 62(9.07(b)) | 9/1/99 |
| 4413(29ee), Sec. 6(b) | Repeal | 62(9.08(b)) | 9/1/99 |
| 4413(29ee), Sec. 6(g) | Repeal | 62(9.17(b)) | 9/1/99 |
| 4413(29ee), Sec. 6(h) | Repeal | 62(9.17(b)) | 9/1/99 |
| 4413(29ee), Sec. 12(a) | Repeal | 62(9.09(b)) | 9/1/99 |
| 4413(29ee), Sec. 13(a) | Repeal | 62(9.10(b)) | 9/1/99 |
| 4413(29ee), Sec. 13(c) | Repeal | 62(9.10(b)) | 9/1/99 |
| 4413(29ee), Sec. 16(a) | Repeal | 62(9.11(b)) | 9/1/99 |
| 4413(29ee), Sec. 17(c) | Repeal | 62(9.12(b)) | 9/1/99 |
| 4413(29ee), Sec. 18(c) | Repeal | 62(9.13(b)) | 9/1/99 |
| 4413(29ee), Sec. 18(f) | Repeal | 62(9.13(b)) | 9/1/99 |
| 4413(29ee), Sec. 28 | Repeal | 62(9.15(b)) | 9/1/99 |
| 4413(29ee), Sec. 28A | Repeal | 62(9.15(b)) | 9/1/99 |
| 4413(29ee), Sec. 31(a) | Repeal | 62(9.16(b)) | 9/1/99 |
| 4413(29ee), Sec. 31(c) | Repeal | 62(9.16(b)) | 9/1/99 |

*(continued)*

# 1999 Legislative Changes to the TEXAS CRIMINAL LAW and MOTOR VEHICLE HANDBOOK
*(Continued)*

## Civil Statutes
*(Continued)*

| *Article(s)* | *Change* | *Chap.* | *Eff. Date* |
|---|---|---|---|
| 4413(29ee), Sec. 31(d) | Repeal | 62(9.16(b)) | 9/1/99 |
| 4413(29ee), Sec. 31(e) | Repeal | 62(9.16(b)) | 9/1/99 |
| 4413(29ee), Sec. 35 | Repeal | 62(9.05(b)) | 9/1/99 |
| 4495b | Repeal | 388(6(a)) | 9/1/99 |
| 4542a-1 | Repeal | 388(6(a)) | 9/1/99 |
| 4542a-1, Sec. 33(f) | New | 428(3) | 9/1/99 |
| 9003 | Repeal | 388(6(a)) | 9/1/99 |
| 9023 | Repeal | 388(6(a)) | 9/1/99 |
| 9023c | Repeal | 388(6(a)) | 9/1/99 |

## Education Code

| *Section(s)* | *Change* | *Chap.* | *Eff. Date* |
|---|---|---|---|
| 25.085(d) | Amend | 396(2.10) | 9/1/99 |
| 25.085(e) | New | 711(1) | 6/18/99 |
| 25.086(a) | Amend | 1282(2) | 6/18/99 |
| 25.093(f) | Amend | 1403(1) | 9/1/99 |
| 37.006(f) | Amend | 396(2.15) | 9/1/99 |
| 37.006(*l*) | New | 396(2.15) | 9/1/99 |
| 37.007(b) | Amend | 542(1) | 6/18/99 |
| 37.007(d) | Amend | 542(1) | 6/18/99 |

## Family Code

| *Sections* | *Change* | *Chap.* | *Eff. Date* |
|---|---|---|---|
| 6.405 | Amend | 62(6.04) | 9/1/99 |
| 6.501(b) | Amend | 1081(6) | 9/1/99 |
| 51.04(f) | Amend | 232(2) | 9/1/99 |
| 51.04(g) | Amend | 232(2) | 9/1/99 |
| 51.06(a) | Amend | 488(1) | 9/1/99 |
| 51.095(a) | Amend | 982(1) | 9/1/99 |
| 51.095(b) | Amend | 982(1) | 9/1/99 |
| 51.095(d) | New | 982(1) | 9/1/99 |
| 51.095(d) | New | 1477(1) | 9/1/99 |
| 51.12 | Amend | 62(6.07) | 9/1/99 |
| 51.12 | Amend | 232(3) | 9/1/99 |
| 51.12(h) | Amend | 1477(2) | 9/1/99 |
| 51.13(a) | Amend | 1188(4.02) | 9/1/99 |
| 51.13(b) | Amend | 1188(4.02) | 9/1/99 |
| 51.17(c) | Amend | 1477(3) | 9/1/99 |

*(continued)*

# 1999 Legislative Changes to the TEXAS CRIMINAL LAW and MOTOR VEHICLE HANDBOOK
*(Continued)*

## Family Code
*(Continued)*

| *Section(s)* | *Change* | *Chap.* | *Eff. Date* |
|---|---|---|---|
| 51.20 | New | 1477(4) | 9/1/99 |
| 52.02(a) | Amend | 62(6.08) | 9/1/99 |
| 52.02(c) | Amend | 1477(5) | 9/1/99 |
| 52.026(b) | Amend | 62(6.09) | 9/1/99 |
| 52.026(b) | Amend | 1082(1) | 6/18/99 |
| 52.027(a) | Amend | 76(1) | 9/1/99 |
| 52.027(f) | Amend | 76(1) | 9/1/99 |
| 52.027(h) | Amend | 76(1) | 9/1/99 |
| 52.027(h) | Amend | 1545(66) | 9/1/99 |
| 52.027(*i*) | Amend | 76(1) | 9/1/99 |
| 52.027(j) | New | 76(1) | 9/1/99 |
| 52.027(j) | New | 1545(66) | 9/1/99 |
| 52.03(a) | Amend | 48(1) | 9/1/99 |
| 52.031(c) | Amend | 48(2) | 9/1/99 |
| 52.032 | New | 48(3) | 9/1/99 |
| 53.02(b) | Amend | 232(1) | 9/1/99 |
| 53.02(f) | New | 232(1) | 9/1/99 |
| 53.03(h) | Reletter | 62(19.01(17)) | 9/1/99 |
| 53.035 | New | 1477(6) | 9/1/99 |
| 54.01(a) | Amend | 232(4) | 9/1/99 |
| 54.01(p) | Amend | 232(4) | 9/1/99 |
| 54.01(p) | New | 1477(7) | 9/1/99 |
| 54.02(h) | Amend | 1477(8) | 9/1/99 |
| 54.02(j) | Amend | 1477(8) | 9/1/99 |
| 54.02(*o*) | New | 1477(8) | 9/1/99 |
| 54.02(p) | New | 1477(8) | 9/1/99 |
| 54.02(q) | New | 1477(8) | 9/1/99 |
| 54.02(r) | New | 1477(8) | 9/1/99 |
| 54.021(d) | Amend | 76(2) | 9/1/99 |
| 54.022 | Amend | 76(3) | 9/1/99 |
| 54.03(d) | Amend | 1477(9) | 9/1/99 |
| 54.03(f) | Amend | 1477(9) | 9/1/99 |
| 54.034 | New | 74(1) | 9/1/99 |
| 54.04(d) | Amend | 1448(1) | 9/1/99 |
| 54.04(*l*) | Amend | 1477(10) | 9/1/99 |
| 54.04(q) | New | 1193(9) | 9/1/99 |
| 54.04(q) | New | 1415(19) | 9/1/99 |
| 54.04(q) | New | 1448(1) | 9/1/99 |
| 54.04(q) | New | 1477(10) | 9/1/99 |
| 54.0406 | New | 1446(1) | 9/1/99 |
| 54.042(h) | Reletter | 62(19.01(18)) | 9/1/99 |
| 54.0461 | New | 174(1) | 9/1/99 |

*(continued)*

Printed in the U.S.A. Zt

# 1999 Legislative Changes to the TEXAS CRIMINAL LAW and MOTOR VEHICLE HANDBOOK
*(Continued)*

## Family Code
*(Continued)*

| *Section(s)* | *Change* | *Chap.* | *Eff. Date* |
|---|---|---|---|
| 54.047 | Renumber | 62(19.01(19)) | 9/1/99 |
| 54.05(f) | Amend | 1448(2) | 9/1/99 |
| 54.05(f) | Amend | 1477(11) | 9/1/99 |
| 54.05(g) | Amend | 1448(2) | 9/1/99 |
| 54.05(g) | Amend | 1477(11) | 9/1/99 |
| 54.05(h) | Amend | 1477(11) | 9/1/99 |
| 54.05(j) | New | 1448(2) | 9/1/99 |
| 54.05(j) | New | 1477(11) | 9/1/99 |
| 54.051 | New | 1477(12) | 9/1/99 |
| 54.10 | Amend | 232(5) | 9/1/99 |
| 54.10(a) | Amend | 1477(13) | 9/1/99 |
| Chap. 55, Subchap. A, heading | New | 1477(14) | 9/1/99 |
| 55.01 | Repeal & New | 1477(14) | 9/1/99 |
| 55.02 | New | 1477(14) | 9/1/99 |
| 55.03 | Repeal & New | 1477(14) | 9/1/99 |
| Chap. 55, Subchap. B, heading | New | 1477(14) | 9/1/99 |
| 55.11 | New | 1477(14) | 9/1/99 |
| 55.12 | New | 1477(14) | 9/1/99 |
| 55.13 | New | 1477(14) | 9/1/99 |
| 55.14 | New | 1477(14) | 9/1/99 |
| 55.15 | New | 1477(14) | 9/1/99 |
| 55.16 | New | 1477(14) | 9/1/99 |
| 55.17 | New | 1477(14) | 9/1/99 |
| 55.18 | New | 1477(14) | 9/1/99 |
| 55.19 | New | 1477(14) | 9/1/99 |
| Chap. 55, Subchap. C, heading | New | 1477(14) | 9/1/99 |
| 55.31 | New | 1477(14) | 9/1/99 |
| 55.32 | New | 1477(14) | 9/1/99 |
| 55.33 | New | 1477(14) | 9/1/99 |
| 55.34 | New | 1477(14) | 9/1/99 |
| 55.35 | New | 1477(14) | 9/1/99 |
| 55.36 | New | 1477(14) | 9/1/99 |
| 55.37 | New | 1477(14) | 9/1/99 |
| 55.38 | New | 1477(14) | 9/1/99 |
| 55.39 | New | 1477(14) | 9/1/99 |
| 55.40 | New | 1477(14) | 9/1/99 |
| 55.41 | New | 1477(14) | 9/1/99 |
| 55.42 | New | 1477(14) | 9/1/99 |
| 55.43 | New | 1477(14) | 9/1/99 |

*(continued)*

# 1999 Legislative Changes to the TEXAS CRIMINAL LAW and MOTOR VEHICLE HANDBOOK

*(Continued)*

## Family Code

*(Continued)*

| *Section(s)* | *Change* | *Chap.* | *Eff. Date* |
|---|---|---|---|
| 55.44 | New | 1477(14) | 9/1/99 |
| Chap. 55, Subchap. D, heading | New | 1477(14) | 9/1/99 |
| 55.51 | New | 1477(14) | 9/1/99 |
| 55.52 | New | 1477(14) | 9/1/99 |
| 55.53 | New | 1477(14) | 9/1/99 |
| 55.54 | New | 1477(14) | 9/1/99 |
| 55.55 | New | 1477(14) | 9/1/99 |
| 55.56 | New | 1477(14) | 9/1/99 |
| 55.57 | New | 1477(14) | 9/1/99 |
| 55.58 | New | 1477(14) | 9/1/99 |
| 55.59 | New | 1477(14) | 9/1/99 |
| 55.60 | New | 1477(14) | 9/1/99 |
| 55.61 | New | 1477(14) | 9/1/99 |
| 56.01(c) | Amend | 74(2) | 9/1/99 |
| 56.01(c) | Amend | 1477(15) | 9/1/99 |
| 56.01(d) | Amend | 74(2) | 9/1/99 |
| 56.01(n) | New | 74(2) | 9/1/99 |
| 58.001(c) | Amend | 1477(16) | 9/1/99 |
| 58.002(a) | Amend | 1477(17) | 9/1/99 |
| 58.003(g) | Amend | 147(1) | 9/1/99 |
| 58.003(n) | Reletter | 62(19.01(20)) | 9/1/99 |
| 58.003(*o*) | New | 147(1) | 9/1/99 |
| 58.0051 | New | 217(1) | 5/24/99 |
| 58.007(a) | Amend | 815(1) | 6/18/99 |
| 58.007(a) | Amend | 1415(20)) | 9/1/99 |
| 58.007(c) | Amend | 815(1) | 6/18/99 |
| 58.007(h) | New | 1477(18) | 9/1/99 |
| 58.106(c) | Amend | 1477(19) | 9/1/99 |
| 58.106(d) | New | 407(1) | 9/1/99 |
| 59.003(a) | Amend | 1477(20) | 9/1/99 |
| 59.005(a) | Amend | 1477(21) | 9/1/99 |
| 59.014 | Amend | 1011(1) | 9/1/99 |
| 59.014 | Amend | 1477(22) | 9/1/99 |
| 71.09(a) | Repeal | 62(6.10(b)) | 9/1/99 |
| 82.008(a) | Amend | 1160(1) | 9/1/99 |
| 82.0085 | New | 1160(2) | 9/1/99 |
| 84.005 | New | 62(6.10(a)) | 9/1/99 |
| 85.022(d) | New | 1412(3) | 9/1/99 |
| 85.025 | Amend | 1160(3) | 9/1/99 |
| 85.026 | Amend | 178(3) | 5/21/99 |
| 85.026 | Amend | 1160(4) | 9/1/99 |

*(continued)*

# 1999 Legislative Changes to the TEXAS CRIMINAL LAW and MOTOR VEHICLE HANDBOOK
*(Continued)*

## Family Code
*(Continued)*

| *Section(s)* | *Change* | *Chap.* | *Eff. Date* |
|---|---|---|---|
| 85.042(e) | New | 1412(4) | 9/1/99 |
| 87.002 | Amend | 1160(5) | 9/1/99 |
| 105.001(b) | Amend | 1390(3) | 9/1/99 |
| 105.001(d) | Amend | 1390(3) | 9/1/99 |
| 156.006(b) | Amend | 1390(15) | 9/1/99 |
| 157.102 | Amend | 556(16) | 9/1/99 |
| 232.002 | Amend | 1254(4) | 9/1/99 |
| 232.002 | Amend | 1477(23) | 9/1/99 |
| 232.003(a) | Amend | 556(59) | 9/1/99 |
| 232.004(b) | Amend | 556(60) | 9/1/99 |
| 232.006(c) | Amend | 178(11) | 5/21/99 |
| 232.008(a) | Amend | 556(61) | 9/1/99 |
| 261.001(8) | Renumber | 62(19.01(26)) | 9/1/99 |
| 261.101(b) | Amend | 62(6.29) | 9/1/99 |
| 261.101(d) | Amend | 1150(2) | 9/1/99 |
| 261.101(d) | Amend | 1390(21) | 9/1/99 |
| 261.103 | Amend | 1477(24) | 9/1/99 |
| 261.105(e) | New | 1477(25) | 9/1/99 |
| 261.107 | Reenact | 62(6.30) | 9/1/99 |
| 261.201(b) | Amend | 1150(3) | 9/1/99 |
| 261.201(b) | Amend | 1390(22) | 9/1/99 |
| 261.201(c) | Amend | 1150(3) | 9/1/99 |
| 261.201(c) | Amend | 1390(22) | 9/1/99 |
| 261.201(h) | New | 1150(3) | 9/1/99 |
| 261.201(h) | New | 1390(22) | 9/1/99 |
| 261.301(b) | Amend | 1150(4) | 9/1/99 |
| 261.301(b) | Amend | 1390(23) | 9/1/99 |
| 261.3019(g) | Amend | 907(38) | 9/1/99 |
| 261.303(c) | Amend | 1150(5) | 9/1/99 |
| 261.303(c) | Amend | 1390(24) | 9/1/99 |
| 261.303(d) | New | 1150(5) | 9/1/99 |
| 261.303(d) | New | 1390(24) | 9/1/99 |
| 261.305(a) | Amend | 1150(6) | 9/1/99 |
| 261.305(a) | Amend | 1390(25) | 9/1/99 |
| 261.305(b) | Amend | 1150(6) | 9/1/99 |
| 261.305(b) | Amend | 1390(25) | 9/1/99 |
| 261.305(c) | Amend | 1150(6) | 9/1/99 |
| 261.305(c) | Amend | 1390(25) | 9/1/99 |
| 261.3125 | New | 1490(1) | 9/1/99 |
| 261.316 | Renumber | 62(19.01(27)) | 9/1/99 |
| 261.404 | Amend | 907(39) | 9/1/99 |
| 261.405 | Reenact | 1150(7) | 9/1/99 |

*(continued)*

## 1999 Legislative Changes to the TEXAS CRIMINAL LAW and MOTOR VEHICLE HANDBOOK
*(Continued)*

### Family Code
*(Continued)*

| *Section(s)* | *Change* | *Chap.* | *Eff. Date* |
|---|---|---|---|
| 261.405 | Reenact | 1390(26) | 9/1/99 |
| 261.405 | Reenact & Amend | 1477(26) | 9/1/99 |
| 261.406(b) | Amend | 1150(8) | 9/1/99 |
| 261.406(b) | Amend | 1390(27) | 9/1/99 |
| Chap. 262, heading | Amend | 1150(9) | 9/1/99 |
| Chap. 262, heading | Amend | 1390(28) | 9/1/99 |
| 262.001 | Amend | 1150(10) | 9/1/99 |
| 262.001 | Amend | 1390(29) | 9/1/99 |
| 262.002 | Amend | 1150(11) | 9/1/99 |
| 262.002 | Amend | 1390(30) | 9/1/99 |
| 262.007(a) | Amend | 685(6) | 9/1/99 |
| 262.007(c) | Amend | 1150(12) | 9/1/99 |
| 262.007(c) | Amend | 1390(31) | 9/1/99 |
| Chap. 262, Subchap. B, heading | Amend | 1150(13) | 9/1/99 |
| Chap. 262 Subchap. B, heading | Amend | 1390(32) | 9/1/99 |
| 262.101 | Amend | 1150(14) | 9/1/99 |
| 262.101 | Amend | 1390(33) | 9/1/99 |
| 262.102(a) | Amend | 1150(15) | 9/1/99 |
| 262.102(a) | Amend | 1390(34) | 9/1/99 |
| 262.106(d) | New | 1150(16) | 9/1/99 |
| 262.106(d) | New | 1390(35) | 9/1/99 |
| 262.109(d) | Amend | 1150(17) | 9/1/99 |
| 262.109(d) | Amend | 1390(36) | 9/1/99 |
| 262.110 | Amend | 1150(18) | 9/1/99 |
| 262.110 | Amend | 1390(37) | 9/1/99 |
| 262.113 | New | 1150(19) | 9/1/99 |
| 262.113 | New | 1390(38) | 9/1/99 |

### Government Code

| *Section(s)* | *Change* | *Chap.* | *Eff. Date* |
|---|---|---|---|
| 29.003(a) | Amend | 611(1) | 9/1/99 |
| 29.003(a) | Amend | 660(1) | 6/18/99 |
| 29.003(b) | Amend | 660(1) | 6/18/99 |
| 29.003(f) | New | 611(1) | 9/1/99 |
| 29.012 | New | 912(1) | 9/1/99 |
| 62.001(f) | Amend | 640(1) | 9/1/99 |
| 62.001(i) | Amend | 640(1) | 9/1/99 |
| 62.001(j) | New | 640(1) | 9/1/99 |

*(continued)*

# 1999 Legislative Changes to the TEXAS CRIMINAL LAW and MOTOR VEHICLE HANDBOOK

*(Continued)*

## Government Code

*(Continued)*

| *Section(s)* | *Change* | *Chap.* | *Eff. Date* |
|---|---|---|---|
| 76.006(a) | Amend | 875(1) | 6/18/99 |
| 76.006(g) | Reletter | 62(19.01(29)) | 9/1/99 |
| 76.006(h) | New | 875(1) | 6/18/99 |
| 76.018 | New | 399(3) | 6/10/99 |
| 411.047(a) | Amend | 1189(12) | 9/1/99 |
| 411.0098 | New | 150(1) | 9/1/99 |
| 411.0098 | New | 1189(7) | 9/1/99 |
| 411.135(a) | Amend | 1415(21) | 9/1/99 |
| 411.171(4) | Amend | 62(9.01(a)) | 9/1/99 |
| 411.171(8) | Repeal | 62(9.02(a)) | 9/1/99 |
| 411.172(a) | Amend | 62(9.03(a)) | 9/1/99 |
| 411.172(d) to (f) | New | 62(9.04(a)) | 9/1/99 |
| 411.173 | Amend | 62(9.05(a)) | 9/1/99 |
| 411.174(a) | Amend | 62(9.06(a)) | 9/1/99 |
| 411.176(b) | Amend | 62(9.07(a)) | 9/1/99 |
| 411.177(b) | Amend | 62(9.08(a)) | 9/1/99 |
| 411.178 | Amend | 1189(14) | 9/1/99 |
| 411.180(i) | New | 1412(5) | 9/1/99 |
| 411.181(f) | Amend | 1189(15) | 9/1/99 |
| 411.186(a) | Amend | 62(9.09(a)) | 9/1/99 |
| 411.187(a) | Amend | 62(9.10(a)) | 9/1/99 |
| 411.187(a) | Amend | 1412(6) | 9/1/99 |
| 411.187(c) | Amend | 62(9.10(a)) | 9/1/99 |
| 411.187(c) | Amend | 1412(6) | 9/1/99 |
| 411.188(a) | Amend | 62(9.11(a)) | 9/1/99 |
| 411.189(c) | Amend | 62(9.12(a)) | 9/1/99 |
| 411.190(c) | Amend | 62(9.13(a)) | 9/1/99 |
| 411.190(c) | Amend | 199(1) | 9/1/99 |
| 411.190(f) | Amend | 62(9.13(a)) | 9/1/99 |
| 411.199(b) | Amend | 62(9.14) | 9/1/99 |
| 411.199(g) | Amend | 62(9.14) | 9/1/99 |
| 411.1991 | New | 62(9.15(a)) | 9/1/99 |
| 411.204(a) | Amend | 62(9.16(a)) | 9/1/99 |
| 411.204(b) | Amend | 523(1) | 6/18/99 |
| 411.204(c) | Amend | 62(9.16(a)) | 9/1/99 |
| 411.204(d) | New | 62(9.16(a)) | 9/1/99 |
| 411.204(e) | New | 62(9.16(a)) | 9/1/99 |
| 411.205 | Amend | 62(9.17(a)) | 9/1/99 |
| 414.009 | Amend | 1560(1) | 6/19/99 |
| Chap. 415 | Repeal | 388(6(b(1))) | 9/1/99 |
| 466.254 | Amend | 678(2) | 9/1/99 |

*(continued)*

## 1999 Legislative Changes to the TEXAS CRIMINAL LAW and MOTOR VEHICLE HANDBOOK
*(Continued)*

### Government Code
*(Continued)*

| *Section(s)* | *Change* | *Chap.* | *Eff. Date* |
|---|---|---|---|
| 466.3052 | Amend | 687(1) | 9/1/99 |
| 508.001(8) | New | 62(10.01) | 9/1/99 |
| 508.001(9) | Renumber | 62(10.01) | 9/1/99 |
| 508.031(b) | Amend | 554(1) | 9/1/99 |
| 508.033 | Amend | 554(2) | 9/1/99 |
| 508.033(c) | Amend | 62(10.02) | 9/1/99 |
| 508.033(d) | Amend | 62(10.03) | 9/1/99 |
| 508.033(e) | Amend | 62(10.04) | 9/1/99 |
| 508.034 | Amend | 62(10.05) | 9/1/99 |
| 508.034(a) | Amend | 554(3) | 9/1/99 |
| 508.036 | Repeal & New | 62(10.06) | 9/1/99 |
| 508.0361 | New | 62(10.07) | 9/1/99 |
| 508.0362 | New | 62(10.08) | 9/1/99 |
| 508.0362(a) | Amend | 554(4) | 9/1/99 |
| 508.0362(c) | Amend | 554(4) | 9/1/99 |
| 508.040 | Amend | 62(10.09) | 9/1/99 |
| 508.040 | Amend | 554(5) | 9/1/99 |
| 508.041 | Repeal & New | 62(10.10) | 9/1/99 |
| 508.042(a) | Amend | 62(10.11) | 9/1/99 |
| 508.042(b) | Amend | 554(6) | 9/1/99 |
| 508.044(c) | Amend | 62(10.12) | 9/1/99 |
| 508.044(d) | Amend | 62(10.13) | 9/1/99 |
| 508.044(e) | Amend | 62(10.14) | 9/1/99 |
| 508.047(a) | Amend | 62(10.15) | 9/1/99 |
| 508.049 | Amend | 62(10.16) | 9/1/99 |
| 508.051 | Amend | 62(10.17) | 9/1/99 |
| 508.082 | Amend | 62(10.18) | 9/1/99 |
| 508.1141 | New | 490(1) | 9/1/99 |
| 508.115(a) | Amend | 62(10.19) | 9/1/99 |
| 508.115(c) | Amend | 62(10.19) | 9/1/99 |
| 508.119(*i*) | New | 62(10.20) | 9/1/99 |
| 508.145(c) | Amend | 62(10.21) | 9/1/99 |
| 508.149(a) | Amend | 62(10.22) | 9/1/99 |
| 508.181(g) | New | 62(10.23) | 9/1/99 |
| 508.181(h) | New | 62(10.24) | 9/1/99 |
| 508.186(a) | Amend | 62(10.25) | 9/1/99 |
| 508.190 | New | 62(10.26) | 9/1/99 |
| 508.191 | New | 62(10.27) | 9/1/99 |
| 508.223 | Amend | 62(10.28) | 9/1/99 |
| 508.225 | New | 56(2) | 9/1/99 |
| 508.225 | New | 62(10.29) | 9/1/99 |
| 508.252 | Amend | 62(10.30) | 9/1/99 |

*(continued)*

# 1999 Legislative Changes to the TEXAS CRIMINAL LAW and MOTOR VEHICLE HANDBOOK
*(Continued)*

## Government Code
*(Continued)*

| *Section(s)* | *Change* | *Chap.* | *Eff. Date* |
|---|---|---|---|
| 508.281(a) | Amend | 62(10.31) | 9/1/99 |
| 508.2811 | New | 62(10.32) | 9/1/99 |
| 508.282 | Repeal & New | 62(10.33) | 9/1/99 |
| 508.283 | Amend | 62(10.34) | 9/1/99 |
| 508.284 | New | 62(10.35) | 9/1/99 |
| 508.313(e) | Amend | 62(10.36) | 9/1/99 |
| 508.313(f) | New | 783(3) | 6/18/99 |
| 508.317 | Amend | 62(10.37) | 9/1/99 |
| 508.324 | New | 62(10.38) | 9/1/99 |



## Health and Safety Code

| *Section(s)* | *Change* | *Chap.* | *Eff. Date* |
|---|---|---|---|
| 12.092(b) | Amend | 62(9.23) | 9/1/99 |
| 161.086(b) | Amend | 567(1) | 9/1/99 |
| 161.088(a) | Amend | 1156(1) | 9/1/99 |
| 161.088(b) | Amend | 1156(1) | 9/1/99 |
| 161.088(d) | Amend | 1156(1) | 9/1/99 |
| 161.254(b) | Amend | 1409(8) | 9/1/99 |
| Title 2, Subtitle H, Chap. 166, heading | New | 450(1.01) | 9/1/99 |
| Title 2, Subtitle H, Chap. 166 | New | 642(1) | 6/18/99 |
| Chap. 166, Subchap. B, heading | Redesignate & Amend | 450(1.03) | 9/1/99 |
| 166.001 | New | 642(1) | 6/18/99 |
| 166.048 | Renumber | 450(1.03) | 9/1/99 |
| 382.0374(c) | New | 1189(42) | 9/1/99 |
| 382.0374(d) | New | 1189(42) | 9/1/99 |
| 431.006 | New | 132(1) | 5/20/99 |
| 431.006 | New | 1298(1) | 6/18/99 |
| 431.022 | New | 151(1) | 9/1/99 |
| 466.001(a) | Amend | 1411(1.12) | 9/1/99 |
| 466.002 | Amend | 1411(1.13) | 9/1/99 |
| 466.004(a) | Amend | 1411(1.14) | 9/1/99 |
| 466.005 | Repeal | 1411(1.18) | 9/1/99 |
| 466.022 | Amend | 1411(1.15) | 9/1/99 |
| 481.002(47) | Amend | 145(1) | 9/1/99 |
| 481.002(51) | Repeal | 145(5)(1) | 9/1/99 |
| 481.002(53) | Repeal | 145(5)(1) | 9/1/99 |
| 481.002(54) | Repeal | 145(5)(1) | 9/1/99 |

*(continued)*

# 1999 Legislative Changes to the TEXAS CRIMINAL LAW and MOTOR VEHICLE HANDBOOK
*(Continued)*

## Health and Safety Code
*(Continued)*

| *Section(s)* | *Change* | *Chap.* | *Eff. Date* |
|---|---|---|---|
| 481.002(55) | Repeal | 145(5)(1) | 9/1/99 |
| 481.003 | Amend | 1266(1) | 9/1/99 |
| 481.074(n) | Amend | 145(2) | 9/1/99 |
| 481.075(a) | Amend | 145(3) | 9/1/99 |
| 481.075(b) | Amend | 145(3) | 9/1/99 |
| 481.075(c) | Amend | 145(3) | 9/1/99 |
| 481.075(d) | Amend | 145(3) | 9/1/99 |
| 481.075(e) | Amend | 145(3) | 9/1/99 |
| 481.075(i) | Amend | 145(3) | 9/1/99 |
| 481.075(k) | Amend | 145(3) | 9/1/99 |
| 481.075(*l*) | Amend | 145(3) | 9/1/99 |
| 481.075(m) | Amend | 145(3) | 9/1/99 |
| 481.075(n) | Repeal | 145(5)(2) | 9/1/99 |
| 481.076(g) | Amend | 145(4) | 9/1/99 |
| 481.076(h) | Amend | 145(4) | 9/1/99 |
| 481.076(j) | Repeal | 145(5)(3) | 9/1/99 |
| 481.0761(g) | Repeal | 145(5)(4) | 9/1/99 |
| 483.022(f) | New | 428(4) | 9/1/99 |
| 483.042(f) | New | 1404(1) | 9/1/99 |
| 484.005(e) | Amend | 684(1) | 9/1/99 |
| 484.005(f) | New | 684(1) | 9/1/99 |
| 484.005(g) | New | 684(1) | 9/1/99 |
| 484.005(h) | New | 684(1) | 9/1/99 |
| Chap. 485, Subchap. D | New | 1411(6.01) | 9/1/99 |
| 485.101 | New | 1411(6.01) | 9/1/99 |
| 485.102 | New | 1411(6.01) | 9/1/99 |
| 485.103 | New | 1411(6.01) | 9/1/99 |
| 485.104 | New | 1411(6.01) | 9/1/99 |
| 485.105 | New | 1411(6.01) | 9/1/99 |
| 485.106 | New | 1411(6.01) | 9/1/99 |
| 485.107 | New | 1411(6.01) | 9/1/99 |
| 485.108 | New | 1411(6.01) | 9/1/99 |
| 485.109 | New | 1411(6.01) | 9/1/99 |
| 485.110 | New | 1411(6.01) | 9/1/99 |
| 485.111 | New | 1411(6.01) | 9/1/99 |
| 485.112 | New | 1411(6.01) | 9/1/99 |
| 485.113 | New | 1411(6.01) | 9/1/99 |
| 751.002(1) | Amend | 553(1) | 6/18/99 |
| 751.005 | Amend | 553(2) | 6/18/99 |
| 751.012 | New | 553(3) | 6/18/99 |
| 751.013 | New | 553(3) | 6/18/99 |

*(continued)*

# 1999 Legislative Changes to the TEXAS CRIMINAL LAW and MOTOR VEHICLE HANDBOOK
*(Continued)*

## Health and Safety Code
*(Continued)*

| *Section(s)* | *Change* | *Chap.* | *Eff. Date* |
|---|---|---|---|
| Title 11, Chap. 841 | New | 1188(4.01) | 9/1/99 |
| 841.001 | New | 1188(4.01) | 9/1/99 |
| 841.002 | New | 1188(4.01) | 9/1/99 |
| 841.003 | New | 1188(4.01) | 9/1/99 |
| 841.004 | New | 1188(4.01) | 9/1/99 |
| 841.005 | New | 1188(4.01) | 9/1/99 |
| 841.006 | New | 1188(4.01) | 9/1/99 |
| 841.007 | New | 1188(4.01) | 9/1/99 |
| 841.021 | New | 1188(4.01) | 9/1/99 |
| 841.022 | New | 1188(4.01) | 9/1/99 |
| 841.023 | New | 1188(4.01) | 9/1/99 |
| 841.041 | New | 1188(4.01) | 9/1/99 |
| 841.061 | New | 1188(4.01) | 9/1/99 |
| 841.062 | New | 1188(4.01) | 9/1/99 |
| 841.063 | New | 1188(4.01) | 9/1/99 |
| 841.064 | New | 1188(4.01) | 9/1/99 |
| 841.081 | New | 1188(4.01) | 9/1/99 |
| 841.082 | New | 1188(4.01) | 9/1/99 |
| 841.083 | New | 1188(4.01) | 9/1/99 |
| 841.084 | New | 1188(4.01) | 9/1/99 |
| 841.085 | New | 1188(4.01) | 9/1/99 |
| 841.101 | New | 1188(4.01) | 9/1/99 |
| 841.102 | New | 1188(4.01) | 9/1/99 |
| 841.103 | New | 1188(4.01) | 9/1/99 |
| 841.121 | New | 1188(4.01) | 9/1/99 |
| 841.122 | New | 1188(4.01) | 9/1/99 |
| 841.123 | New | 1188(4.01) | 9/1/99 |
| 841.124 | New | 1188(4.01) | 9/1/99 |
| 841.141 | New | 1188(4.01) | 9/1/99 |
| 841.142 | New | 1188(4.01) | 9/1/99 |
| 841.143 | New | 1188(4.01) | 9/1/99 |
| 841.144 | New | 1188(4.01) | 9/1/99 |
| 841.145 | New | 1188(4.01) | 9/1/99 |
| 841.146 | New | 1188(4.01) | 9/1/99 |
| 841.147 | New | 1188(4.01) | 9/1/99 |

## Insurance Code

| *Section(s)* | *Change* | *Chap.* | *Eff. Date* |
|---|---|---|---|
| Title 1, heading | New | 101(2) | 9/1/99 |

*(continued)*

## 1999 Legislative Changes to the TEXAS CRIMINAL LAW and MOTOR VEHICLE HANDBOOK
*(Continued)*

### Occupations Code

| *Section(s)* | *Change* | *Chap.* | *Eff. Date* |
|---|---|---|---|
| Chap. 158, heading | New | 388(1) | 9/1/99 |
| 158.001 | New | 388(1) | 9/1/99 |
| 158.002 | New | 388(1) | 9/1/99 |
| 158.003 | New | 388(1) | 9/1/99 |
| Chap. 563, heading | New | 388(1) | 9/1/99 |
| 563.001 | New | 388(1) | 9/1/99 |
| 563.002 | New | 388(1) | 9/1/99 |
| Chap. 563, Subchap. B, heading | New | 388(1) | 9/1/99 |
| 563.051 | New | 388(1) | 9/1/99 |
| 563.052 | New | 388(1) | 9/1/99 |
| 563.053 | New | 388(1) | 9/1/99 |
| 563.054 | New | 388(1) | 9/1/99 |
| Title 10, heading | New | 388(1) | 9/1/99 |
| Chap.1701, heading | New | 388(1) | 9/1/99 |
| Chap. 1701, Subchap. F, heading | New | 388(1) | 9/1/99 |
| 1701.253 | New | 388(1) | 9/1/99 |
| Chap. 1701, Subchap. H, heading | New | 388(1) | 9/1/99 |
| 1701.351 | New | 388(1) | 9/1/99 |
| 1701.352 | New | 388(1) | 9/1/99 |
| 1701.353 | New | 388(1) | 9/1/99 |
| 1701.355 | New | 388(1) | 9/1/99 |
| Title 11, heading | New | 388(1) | 9/1/99 |
| Chap. 1803, heading | New | 388(1) | 9/1/99 |
| Chap. 1803, Subchap. A, heading | New | 388(1) | 9/1/99 |
| 1803.001 | New | 388(1) | 9/1/99 |
| 1803.002 | New | 388(1) | 9/1/99 |
| Chap. 1803, Subchap. B, heading | New | 388(1) | 9/1/99 |
| 1803.051 | New | 388(1) | 9/1/99 |
| 1803.052 | New | 388(1) | 9/1/99 |
| 1803.053 | New | 388(1) | 9/1/99 |
| 1803.054 | New | 388(1) | 9/1/99 |
| 1803.055 | New | 388(1) | 9/1/99 |
| 1803.056 | New | 388(1) | 9/1/99 |
| 1803.101 | New | 388(1) | 9/1/99 |
| Chap. 1803, Subchap. C, heading | New | 388(1) | 9/1/99 |
| 1803.102 | New | 388(1) | 9/1/99 |
| 1803.103 | New | 388(1) | 9/1/99 |

*(continued)*

# 1999 Legislative Changes to the TEXAS CRIMINAL LAW and MOTOR VEHICLE HANDBOOK

*(Continued)*

## Occupations Code

*(Continued)*

| *Section(s)* | *Change* | *Chap.* | *Eff. Date* |
|---|---|---|---|
| 1803.104 | New | 388(1) | 9/1/99 |
| Chap. 1803, Subchap. D, heading | New | 388(1) | 9/1/99 |
| 1803.151 | New | 388(1) | 9/1/99 |
| 1803.152 | New | 388(1) | 9/1/99 |
| 1803.153 | New | 388(1) | 9/1/99 |
| 1803.154 | New | 388(1) | 9/1/99 |
| 1803.155 | New | 388(1) | 9/1/99 |
| Title 13, heading | New | 388(1) | 9/1/99 |
| Title 13, Subtitle A, heading | New | 388(1) | 9/1/99 |
| Chap. 2003, heading | New | 388(1) | 9/1/99 |
| Chap. 2003, Subchap. A, heading | New | 388(1) | 9/1/99 |
| 2003.001 | New | 388(1) | 9/1/99 |
| 2003.002 | New | 388(1) | 9/1/99 |
| Chap. 2003, Subchap. B, heading | New | 388(1) | 9/1/99 |
| 2003.051 | New | 388(1) | 9/1/99 |
| 2003.052 | New | 388(1) | 9/1/99 |
| Chap. 2003, Subchap. C, heading | New | 388(1) | 9/1/99 |
| 2003.101 | New | 388(1) | 9/1/99 |
| 2003.102 | New | 388(1) | 9/1/99 |
| Title 13, Subtitle B, heading | New | 388(1) | 9/1/99 |
| Chap. 2053, heading | New | 388(1) | 9/1/99 |
| Chap. 2053, Subchap. C, heading | New | 388(1) | 9/1/99 |
| 2053.021 | New | 388(1) | 9/1/99 |
| 2053.038 | New | 388(1) | 9/1/99 |
| Chap. 2104, heading | New | 388(1) | 9/1/99 |
| Chap. 2104, Subchap. A, heading | New | 388(1) | 9/1/99 |
| 2104.001 | New | 388(1) | 9/1/99 |
| Chap. 2104, Subchap. B, heading | New | 388(1) | 9/1/99 |
| 2104.051 | New | 388(1) | 9/1/99 |
| Chap. 2104, Subchap. C, heading | New | 388(1) | 9/1/99 |
| 2104.101 | New | 388(1) | 9/1/99 |
| 2104.102 | New | 388(1) | 9/1/99 |

*(continued)*

# 1999 Legislative Changes to the TEXAS CRIMINAL LAW and MOTOR VEHICLE HANDBOOK
*(Continued)*

## Occupations Code
*(Continued)*

| *Section(s)* | *Change* | *Chap.* | *Eff. Date* |
|---|---|---|---|
| 2104.103 | New | 388(1) | 9/1/99 |
| 2104.104 | New | 388(1) | 9/1/99 |
| 2104.105 | New | 388(1) | 9/1/99 |
| 2104.106 | New | 388(1) | 9/1/99 |
| 2104.107 | New | 388(1) | 9/1/99 |
| Chap. 2104, Subchap. D, heading | New | 388(1) | 9/1/99 |
| 2104.151 | New | 388(1) | 9/1/99 |
| Chap. 2152, Subchap. C, heading | New | 388(1) | 9/1/99 |
| 2152.101 | New | 388(1) | 9/1/99 |
| Chap. 2152, Subchap. E, heading | New | 388(1) | 9/1/99 |
| 2152.202 | New | 388(1) | 9/1/99 |

## Parks and Wildlife Code

| *Section(s)* | *Change* | *Chap.* | *Eff. Date* |
|---|---|---|---|
| 12.101(2) | Amend | 959(1) | 9/1/99 |
| 12.1105(c) | Amend | 851(1) | 9/1/99 |
| 12.1106(b) | Amend | 851(2) | 9/1/99 |
| 12.1106(b) | Amend | 959(2) | 9/1/99 |
| 12.1106(d) | Amend | 959(2) | 9/1/99 |

## Property

| *Section(s)* | *Change* | *Chap.* | *Eff. Date* |
|---|---|---|---|
| 70.001(b) | Amend | 414(2.38) | 7/1/2001 |
| 70.001(b) | Amend | 978(1) | 9/1/99 |
| 70.001(e) | Amend | 978(1) | 9/1/99 |
| 70.001(f) | Amend | 978(1) | 9/1/99 |
| 70.003(d)(1) | Amend | 414(2.39) | 7/1/2001 |
| 70.004 | Amend | 70(2) | 9/1/99 |
| 70.006 | Amend | 70(3) | 9/1/99 |
| 70.302(b) | Amend | 414(2.41) | 7/1/2001 |

## Texas Constitution

| *Article(s)* | *Change* | *H.J.R.* | *Eff. Date* |
|---|---|---|---|
| III, Sec. 14 | Amend | 62(7) | 11/2/99 |
| XVII, Sec. 1 | Amend | 62(54) | 11/2/99 |

# TABLE OF CONTENTS
# TEXAS CRIMINAL LAW AND MOTOR VEHICLE HANDBOOK

*Page*

# PENAL CODE



## TITLE 1. INTRODUCTORY PROVISIONS



## CHAPTER 1. GENERAL PROVISIONS



### §1.01. Short title.

This code shall be known and may be cited as the Penal Code. *(Chgd. by L.1993, chap. 900(1.01), eff. 9/1/94.)*

### §1.02. Objectives of code.

The general purposes of this code are to establish a system of prohibitions, penalties, and correctional measures to deal with conduct that unjustifiably and inexcusably causes or threatens harm to those individual or public interests for which state protection is appropriate. To this end, the provisions of this code are intended, and shall be construed, to achieve the following objectives:

(1) to insure the public safety through:

(A) the deterrent influence to the penalties hereinafter provided;

(B) the rehabilitation of those convicted of violations of this code; and

(C) such punishment as may be necessary to prevent likely recurrence of criminal behavior;

(2) by definition and grading of offenses to give fair warning of what is prohibited and of the consequences of violation;

(3) to prescribe penalties that are proportionate to the seriousness of offenses and that permit recognition of differences in rehabilitation possibilities among individual offenders;

(4) to safeguard conduct that is without guilt from condemnation as criminal;

(5) to guide and limit the exercise of official discretion in law enforcement to prevent arbitrary or oppressive treatment of persons suspected, accused, or convicted of offenses; and

(6) to define the scope of state interest in law enforcement against specific offenses and to systematize the exercise of state criminal jurisdiction.

*(Chgd. by L.1993, chap. 900(1.01), eff. 9/1/94.)*

### §1.03. Effect of code.

(a) Conduct does not constitute an offense unless it is defined as an offense by statute, municipal ordinance, order of a county commissioners court, or rule authorized by and lawfully adopted under a statute.

(b) The provisions of Titles 1, 2, and 3 apply to offenses defined by other laws, unless the statute defining the offense provides otherwise; however, the punishment affixed to an offense defined outside this code shall be applicable unless the punishment is classified in accordance with this code.

(c) This code does not bar, suspend, or otherwise affect a right or liability to damages, penalty, forfeiture, or other remedy authorized by law to be recovered or enforced in a civil suit for conduct this code defines as an offense, and the civil injury is not merged in the offense.

*(Chgd. by L.1993, chap. 900(1.01), eff. 9/1/94.)*

### §1.04. Territorial jurisdiction.

(a) This state has jurisdiction over an offense that a person commits by his own conduct or the conduct of another for which he is criminally responsible if:

(1) either the conduct or a result that is an element of the offense occurs inside this state;

(2) the conduct outside this state constitutes an attempt to commit an offense inside this state;

(3) the conduct outside this state constitutes a conspiracy to commit an offense inside this state, and an act in furtherance of the conspiracy occurs inside this state; or

(4) the conduct inside this state constitutes an attempt, solicitation, or conspiracy to commit, or establishes criminal responsibility for the commission of, an offense in another jurisdiction that is also an offense under the laws of this state.

(b) If the offense is criminal homicide, a "result" is either the physical impact causing death or the death itself. If the body of a criminal homicide victim is found in this state, it is presumed that the death occurred in this state. If death alone is the basis for jurisdiction, it is a defense to the exercise of jurisdiction by this state that the conduct that constitutes the offense is not made criminal in the jurisdiction where the conduct occurred.

(c) An offense based on an omission to perform a duty imposed on an actor by a statute of this state is committed inside this state regardless of the location of the actor at the time of the offense.

(d) This state includes the land and water and the air space above the land and water over which this state has power to define offenses.

*(Chgd. by L.1993, chap. 900(1.01), eff. 9/1/94.)*

### §1.05. Construction of code.

(a) The rule that a penal statute is to be strictly construed does not apply to this code. The provisions of this code shall be construed according to the fair import of their terms, to promote justice and effect the objectives of the code.

(b) Unless a different construction is required by the context, Sections 311.011, 311.012, 311.014, 311.015, and 311.021 through 311.032 of Chapter 311, Government Code (Code Construction Act), apply to the construction of this code.

(c) In this code:

(1) a reference to a title, chapter, or section without further identification is a reference to a title, chapter, or section of this code; and

(2) a reference to a subchapter, subsection, subdivision, paragraph, or other numbered or lettered unit without further identification is a reference to a unit of the next-larger unit of this code in which the reference appears.

*(Chgd. by L.1993, chap. 900(1.01), eff. 9/1/94.)*

### §1.06. Computation of age.

A person attains a specified age on the day of the anniversary of his birthdate. *(Chgd. by L.1993, chap. 900(1.01), eff. 9/1/94.)*

### §1.07. Definitions.

(a) In this code:

(1) "Act" means a bodily movement, whether voluntary or involuntary, and includes speech.

(2) "Actor" means a person whose criminal responsibility is in issue in a criminal action. Whenever the term "suspect" is used in this code, it means "actor."

(3) "Agency" includes authority, board, bureau, commission, committee, council, department, district, division, and office.

(4) "Alcoholic beverage" has the meaning assigned by Section 1.04, Alcoholic Beverage Code.

(5) "Another" means a person other than the actor.

(6) "Association" means a government or governmental subdivision or agency, trust, partnership, or two or more persons having a joint or common economic interest.

(7) "Benefit" means anything reasonably regarded as economic gain or advantage, including benefit to any other person in whose welfare the beneficiary is interested.

(8) "Bodily injury" means physical pain, illness, or any impairment of physical condition.

(9) "Coercion" means a threat, however communicated:

(A) to commit an offense;

(B) to inflict bodily injury in the future on the person threatened or another;

(C) to accuse a person of any offense;

(D) to expose a person to hatred, contempt, or ridicule;

(E) to harm the credit or business repute of any person; or

(F) to take or withhold action as a public servant, or to cause a public servant to take or withhold action.

(10) "Conduct" means an act or omission and its accompanying mental state.

(11) "Consent" means assent in fact, whether express or apparent.

(12) "Controlled substance" has the meaning assigned by Section 481.002, Health and Safety Code.

(13) "Corporation" includes nonprofit corporations, professional associations created pursuant to statute, and joint stock companies.

(14) "Correctional facility" means a place designated by law for the confinement of a person arrested for, charged with, or convicted of a criminal offense. The term includes:

(A) a municipal or county jail;

(B) a confinement facility operated by the Texas Department of Criminal Justice;

(C) a confinement facility operated under contract with any division of the Texas Department of Criminal Justice;

(D) a community corrections facility operated by a community supervision and corrections department.

(15) "Criminal negligence" is defined in Section 6.03 (Culpable Mental States).

(16) "Dangerous drug" has the meaning assigned by Section 483.001, Health and Safety Code.

(17) "Deadly weapon" means:

(A) a firearm or anything manifestly designed, made, or adapted for the purpose of inflicting death or serious bodily injury; or

(B) anything that in the manner of its use or intended use is capable of causing death or serious bodily injury.

(18) "Drug" has the meaning assigned by Section 481.002, Health and Safety Code.

(19) "Effective consent" includes consent by a person legally authorized to act for the owner. Consent is not effective if:

(A) induced by force, threat, or fraud;

(B) given by a person the actor knows is not legally authorized to act for the owner;

(C) given by a person who by reason of youth, mental disease or defect, or intoxication is known by the actor to be unable to make reasonable decisions; or

(D) given solely to detect the commission of an offense.

(20) "Electric generating plant" means a facility that generates electric energy for distribution to the public.

(21) "Electric utility substation" means a facility used to switch or change voltage in connection with the transmission of electric energy for distribution to the public.

(22) "Element of offense" means:

(A) the forbidden conduct;

(B) the required culpability;

(C) any required result; and

(D) the negation of any exception to the offense.

(23) "Felony" means an offense so designated by law or punishable by death or confinement in a penitentiary.

(24) "Government" means:

(A) the state;

(B) a county, municipality, or political subdivision of the state; or

(C) any branch or agency of the state, a county, municipality, or political subdivision.

(25) "Harm" means anything reasonably regarded as loss, disadvantage, or injury, including harm to another person in whose welfare the person affected is interested.

(26) "Individual" means a human being who has been born and is alive.

(27) "Institutional division" means the institutional division of the Texas Department of Criminal Justice.

(28) "Intentional" is defined in Section 6.03 (Culpable Mental States).

(29) "Knowing" is defined in Section 6.03 (Culpable Mental States).

(30) "Law" means the constitution or a statute of this state or of the United States, a written opinion of a court of record, a municipal ordinance, an order of a county commissioners court, or a rule authorized by and lawfully adopted under a statute.

(31) "Misdemeanor" means an offense so designated by law or punishable by fine, by confinement in jail, or by both fine and confinement in jail.

(32) "Oath" includes affirmation.

(33) "Official proceeding" means any type of administrative, executive, legislative, or judicial proceeding that may be conducted before a public servant.

(34) "Omission" means failure to act.

(35) "Owner" means a person who:

(A) has title to the property, possession of the property, whether lawful or not, or a greater right to possession of the property than the actor; or

(B) is a holder in due course of a negotiable instrument.

(36) "Peace officer" means a person elected, employed, or appointed as a peace officer under Article 2.12, Code of Criminal Procedure, Section 51.212 or 51.214, Education Code, or other law.

(37) "Penal institution" means a place designated by law for confinement of persons arrested for, charged with, or convicted of an offense.

(38) "Person" means an individual, corporation, or association.

(39) "Possession" means actual care, custody, control, or management.

(40) "Public place" means any place to which the public or a substantial group of the public has access and includes, but is not limited to streets, highways, and the common areas of schools, hospitals, apartment houses, office buildings, transport facilities, and shops.

(41) "Public servant" means a person elected, selected, appointed, employed, or otherwise designated as one of the following, even if he has not yet qualified for office or assumed his duties:

(A) an officer, employee, or agent of government;

(B) a juror or grand juror; or

(C) an arbitrator, referee, or other person who is authorized by law or private written agreement to hear or determine a cause or controversy; or

(D) an attorney at law or notary public when participating in the performance of a governmental function; or

(E) a candidate for nomination or election to public office; or

(F) a person who is performing a governmental function under a claim of right although he is not legally qualified to do so.

(42) "Reasonable belief" means a belief that would be held by an ordinary and prudent man in the same circumstances as the actor.

(43) "Reckless" is defined in Section 6.03 (Culpable Mental States).

(44) "Rule" includes regulation.

(45) "Secure correctional facility" means:

(A) a municipal or county jail; or

(B) a confinement facility operated by or under a contract with any division of the Texas Department of Criminal Justice.

(46) "Serious bodily injury" means bodily injury that creates a substantial risk of death or that causes death, serious permanent disfigurement, or protracted loss or impairment of the function of any bodily member or organ.

(47) "Swear" includes affirm.

(48) "Unlawful" means criminal or tortious or both and includes what would be criminal or tortious but for a defense not amounting to justification or privilege.

(b) The definition of a term in this code applies to each grammatical variation of the term. *(Chgd. by L.1989, chap. 997(1); L.1991, chap. 543(1); L.1993, chap. 900(1.01), eff. 9/1/94.)*

### §1.08. Preemption.

No governmental subdivision or agency may enact or enforce a law that makes any conduct covered by this code an offense subject to a criminal penalty. This section shall apply only as long as the law governing the conduct proscribed by this code is legally enforceable. *(Chgd. by L.1993, chap. 900(1.01), eff. 9/1/94.)*

# CHAPTER 2. BURDEN OF PROOF



### §2.01. Proof beyond a reasonable doubt.

All persons are presumed to be innocent and no person may be convicted of an offense unless each element of the offense is proved beyond a reasonable doubt. The fact that he has been arrested, confined, or indicted for, or otherwise charged with, the offense gives rise to no inference of guilt at his trial. *(Chgd. by L.1993, chap. 900(1.01), eff. 9/1/94.)*

### §2.02. Exception.

(a) An exception to an offense in this code is so labeled by the phrase: "It is an exception to the application of . . . ."

(b) The prosecuting attorney must negate the existence of an exception in the accusation charging commission of the offense and prove beyond a reasonable doubt that the defendant or defendant's conduct does not fall within the exception.

(c) This section does not affect exceptions applicable to offenses enacted prior to the effective date of this code.

*(Chgd. by L.1993, chap. 900(1.01), eff. 9/1/94.)*

### §2.03. Defense.

(a) A defense to prosecution for an offense in this code is so labeled by the phrase: "It is a defense to prosecution . . . ."

(b) The prosecuting attorney is not required to negate the existence of a defense in the accusation charging commission of the offense.

(c) The issue of the existence of a defense is not submitted to the jury unless evidence is admitted supporting the defense.

(d) If the issue of the existence of a defense is submitted to the jury, the court shall charge that a reasonable doubt on the issue requires that the defendant be acquitted.

(e) A ground of defense in a penal law that is not plainly labeled in accordance with this chapter has the procedural and evidentiary consequences of a defense.

*(Chgd. by L.1993, chap. 900(1.01), eff. 9/1/94.)*

### §2.04. Affirmative defense.

(a) An affirmative defense in this code is so labeled by the phrase: "It is an affirmative defense to prosecution . . . ."

(b) The prosecuting attorney is not required to negate the existence of an affirmative defense in the accusation charging commission of the offense.

(c) The issue of the existence of an affirmative defense is not submitted to the jury unless evidence is admitted supporting the defense.

(d) If the issue of the existence of an affirmative defense is submitted to the jury, the court shall charge that the defendant must prove the affirmative defense by a preponderance of evidence.

*(Chgd. by L.1993, chap. 900(1.01), eff. 9/1/94.)*

### §2.05. Presumption.

When this code or another penal law establishes a presumption with respect to any fact, it has the following consequences:

(1) if there is sufficient evidence of the facts that give rise to the presumption, the issue of the existence of the presumed fact must be submitted to the jury, unless the court is satisfied that the evidence as a whole clearly precludes a finding beyond a reasonable doubt of the presumed fact; and

(2) if the existence of the presumed fact is submitted to the jury, the court shall charge the jury, in terms of the presumption and the specific element to which it applies, as follows:

(A) that the facts giving rise to the presumption must be proven beyond a reasonable doubt;

(B) that if such facts are proven beyond a reasonable doubt the jury may find that the element of the offense sought to be presumed exists, but is not bound to so find;

(C) that even though the jury may find the existence of such element, the state must prove beyond a reasonable doubt each of the other elements of the offense charged; and

(D) if the jury has a reasonable doubt as to the existence of a fact or facts giving rise to the presumption, the presumption fails and the jury shall not consider the presumption for any purpose.
*(Chgd. by L.1993, chap. 900(1.01), eff. 9/1/94.)*

## CHAPTER 3. MULTIPLE PROSECUTIONS

Section



### §3.01. Definition.

In this chapter, "criminal episode" means the commission of two or more offenses, regardless of whether the harm is directed toward or inflicted upon more than one person or item of property, under the following circumstances:

(1) the offenses are committed pursuant to the same transaction or pursuant to two or more transactions that are connected or constitute a common scheme or plan; or

(2) the offenses are the repeated commission of the same or similar offenses.
*(Chgd. by L.1993, chap. 900(1.01), eff. 9/1/94.)*

### §3.02. Consolidation and joinder of prosecutions.

(a) A defendant may be prosecuted in a single criminal action for all offenses arising out of the same criminal episode.

(b) When a single criminal action is based on more than one charging instrument within the jurisdiction of the trial court, the state shall file written notice of the action not less than 30 days prior to the trial.

(c) If a judgment of guilt is reversed, set aside, or vacated, and a new trial ordered, the state may not prosecute in a single criminal action in the new trial any offense not joined in the former prosecution unless evidence to establish probable guilt for that offense was not known to the appropriate prosecuting official at the time the first prosecution commenced.
*(Chgd. by L.1993, chap. 900(1.01), eff. 9/1/94.)*

### §3.03. Sentences for offenses arising out of same criminal episode.

(a) When the accused is found guilty of more than one offense arising out of the same criminal episode prosecuted in a single criminal action, a sentence for each offense for which he has been found guilty shall be pronounced. Except as provided by Subsection (b), the sentences shall run concurrently.

(b) If the accused is found guilty of more than one offense arising out of the same criminal episode, the sentences may run concurrently or consecutively if each sentence is for a conviction of:

(1) an offense:

(A) under Section 49.08; or

(B) for which a plea agreement was reached in a case in which the accused was charged with more than one offense under Section 49.08; or

(2) an offense:

(A) under Section 21.11, 22.011, 22.021, 25.02, or 43.25 committed against a victim younger than 17 years of age at the time of the commission of the offense regardless of whether the accused is convicted of violations of the same section more than once or is convicted of violations of more than one section; or

(B) for which a plea agreement was reached in a case in which the accused was charged with more than one offense listed in Paragraph (A) committed against a victim younger than 17 years of age at the time of the commission of the offense regardless of whether the accused is charged with violations of the same section more than once or is charged with violations of more than one section.
*(Chgd. by L.1993, chap. 900(1.01); L.1995, chap. 596(1); L.1997, chap. 667(2), eff. 9/1/97.)*

### §3.04. Severance.

(a) Whenever two or more offenses have been consolidated or joined for trial under Section 3.02, the defendant shall have a right to a severance of the offenses.

(b) In the event of severance under this section, the provisions of Section 3.03 do not apply, and the court in its discretion may order the sentences to run either concurrently or consecutively.

(c) The right to severance under this section does not apply to a prosecution for offenses described by Section 3.03(b)(2) unless the court determines that the defendant or the state would be unfairly prejudiced by a joinder of offenses, in which event the judge may order the offenses to be tried separately or may order other relief as justice requires.

*(Chgd. by L.1993, chap. 900(1.01); L.1997, chap. 667(3), eff. 9/1/97.)*

# TITLE 2. GENERAL PRINCIPLES OF CRIMINAL RESPONSIBILITY



## CHAPTER 6. CULPABILITY GENERALLY



### §6.01. Requirement of voluntary act or omission.

(a) A person commits an offense only if he voluntarily engages in conduct, including an act, an omission, or possession.

(b) Possession is a voluntary act if the possessor knowingly obtains or receives the thing possessed or is aware of his control of the thing for a sufficient time to permit him to terminate his control.

(c) A person who omits to perform an act does not commit an offense unless a law as defined by Section 1.07 provides that the omission is an offense or otherwise provides that he has a duty to perform the act.

*(Chgd. by L.1993, chap. 900(1.01), eff. 9/1/94.)*

### §6.02. Requirement of culpability.

(a) Except as provided in Subsection (b), a person does not commit an offense unless he intentionally, knowingly, recklessly, or with criminal negligence engages in conduct as the definition of the offense requires.

(b) If the definition of an offense does not prescribe a culpable mental state, a culpable mental state is nevertheless required unless the definition plainly dispenses with any mental element.

(c) If the definition of an offense does not prescribe a culpable mental state, but one is nevertheless required under Subsection (b), intent, knowledge, or recklessness suffices to establish criminal responsibility.

(d) Culpable mental states are classified according to relative degrees, from highest to lowest, as follows:

(1) intentional;
(2) knowing;
(3) reckless;
(4) criminal negligence.

(e) Proof of a higher degree of culpability than that charged constitutes proof of the culpability charged.

*(Chgd. by L.1993, chap. 900(1.01), eff. 9/1/94.)*

### §6.03. Definitions of culpable mental states.

(a) A person acts intentionally, or with intent, with respect to the nature of his conduct or to a result of his conduct when it is his conscious objective or desire to engage in the conduct or cause the result.

(b) A person acts knowingly, or with knowledge, with respect to the nature of his conduct or to circumstances surrounding his conduct when he is aware of the nature of his conduct or that the circumstances exist. A person acts knowingly, or with knowledge, with respect to a result of his conduct when he is aware that his conduct is reasonably certain to cause the result.

(c) A person acts recklessly, or is reckless, with respect to circumstances surrounding his conduct or the result of his conduct when he is aware of but consciously disregards a substantial and unjustifiable risk that the circumstances exist or the result will occur. The risk must be of such a nature and degree that its disregard constitutes a gross deviation from the standard of care that an ordinary person would exercise under all the circumstances as viewed from the actor's standpoint.

(d) A person acts with criminal negligence, or is criminally negligent with respect to circumstances surrounding his conduct or the result of his conduct when he ought to be aware of a substantial and unjustifiable risk that the circumstances exist or the result will occur. The risk must be of such a nature and degree that the failure to perceive it constitutes a gross deviation from the standard of care that an ordinary person would exercise under all the circumstances as viewed from the actor's standpoint.

*(Chgd. by L.1993, chap. 900(1.01), eff. 9/1/94.)*

### §6.04. Causation: conduct and results.

(a) A person is criminally responsible if the result would not have occurred but for his conduct, operating either alone or concurrently with another cause, unless the concurrent cause was clearly sufficient to produce the result and the conduct of the actor clearly insufficient.

(b) A person is nevertheless criminally responsible for causing a result if the only difference between what actually occurred and what he desired, contemplated, or risked is that:

(1) a different offense was committed; or

(2) a different person or property was injured, harmed, or otherwise affected.

*(Chgd. by L.1993, chap. 900(1.01), eff. 9/1/94.)*

## CHAPTER 7. CRIMINAL RESPONSIBILITY FOR CONDUCT OF ANOTHER

### SUBCHAPTER A. COMPLICITY

Section



### SUBCHAPTER B. CORPORATIONS AND ASSOCIATIONS



### SUBCHAPTER A. COMPLICITY

### §7.01. Parties to offenses.

(a) A person is criminally responsible as a party to an offense if the offense is committed by his own conduct, by the conduct of another for which he is criminally responsible, or by both.

(b) Each party to an offense may be charged with commission of the offense.

(c) All traditional distinctions between accomplices and principals are abolished by this section, and each party to an offense may be charged and convicted without alleging that he acted as a principal or accomplice.

*(Chgd. by L.1993, chap. 900(1.01), eff. 9/1/94.)*

### §7.02. Criminal responsibility for conduct of another.

(a) A person is criminally responsible for an offense committed by the conduct of another if:

(1) acting with the kind of culpability required for the offense, he causes or aids an innocent or nonresponsible person to engage in conduct prohibited by the definition of the offense;

(2) acting with intent to promote or assist the commission of the offense, he solicits, encourages, directs, aids, or attempts to aid the other person to commit the offense; or

(3) having a legal duty to prevent commission of the offense and acting with intent to promote or assist its commission, he fails to make a reasonable effort to prevent commission of the offense.

(b) If, in the attempt to carry out a conspiracy to commit one felony, another felony is committed by one of the conspirators, all conspirators are guilty of the felony actually committed, though having no intent to commit it, if the offense was committed in furtherance of the unlawful purpose and was one that should have been anticipated as a result of the carrying out of the conspiracy.
*(Chgd. by L.1993, chap. 900(1.01), eff. 9/1/94.)*

### §7.03. Defenses excluded.

In a prosecution in which an actor's criminal responsibility is based on the conduct of another, the actor may be convicted on proof of commission of the offense and that he was a party to its commission, and it is no defense:

(1) that the actor belongs to a class of persons that by definition of the offense is legally incapable of committing the offense in an individual capacity; or

(2) that the person for whose conduct the actor is criminally responsible has been acquitted, has not been prosecuted or convicted, has been convicted of a different offense or of a different type or class of offense, or is immune from prosecution.
*(Chgd. by L.1993, chap. 900(1.01), eff. 9/1/94.)*

## SUBCHAPTER B. CORPORATIONS AND ASSOCIATIONS

### §7.21. Definitions.

In this subchapter:

(1) "Agent" means a director, officer, employee, or other person authorized to act in behalf of a corporation or association.

(2) "High managerial agent" means:

(A) a partner in a partnership;

(B) an officer of a corporation or association;

(C) an agent of a corporation or association who has duties of such responsibility that his conduct reasonably may be assumed to represent the policy of the corporation or association.
*(Chgd. by L.1993, chap. 900(1.01), eff. 9/1/94.)*

### §7.22. Criminal responsibility of corporation or association.

(a) If conduct constituting an offense is performed by an agent acting in behalf of a corporation or association and within the scope of his office or employment, the corporation or association is criminally responsible for an offense defined:

(1) in this code where corporations and associations are made subject thereto;

(2) by law other than this code in which a legislative purpose to impose criminal responsibility on corporations or associations plainly appears; or

(3) by law other than this code for which strict liability is imposed, unless a legislative purpose not to impose criminal responsibility on corporations or associations plainly appears.

(b) A corporation or association is criminally responsible for a felony offense only if its commission was authorized, requested, commanded, performed, or recklessly tolerated by:

(1) a majority of the governing board acting in behalf of the corporation or association; or

(2) a high managerial agent acting in behalf of the corporation or association and within the scope of this office or employment.
*(Chgd. by L.1993, chap. 900(1.01), eff. 9/1/94.)*

### §7.23. Criminal responsibility of person for conduct in behalf of corporation or association.

(a) An individual is criminally responsible for conduct that he performs in the name of or in behalf of a corporation or association to the same extent as if the conduct were performed in his own name or behalf.

(b) An agent having primary responsibility for the discharge of a duty to act imposed by law on a corporation or association is criminally responsible for omission to discharge the duty to the same extent as if the duty were imposed by law directly on him.

(c) If an individual is convicted of conduct constituting an offense performed in the name of or on behalf of a corporation or association, he is subject to the sentence authorized by law for an individual convicted of the offense.
*(Chgd. by L.1993, chap. 900(1.01), eff. 9/1/94.)*

### §7.24. Defense to criminal responsibility of corporation or association.

It is an affirmative defense to prosecution of a corporation or association under Section 7.22(a)(1) or (a)(2) that the high managerial agent having supervisory responsibility over the subject matter of the offense employed due diligence to prevent its commission. *(Chgd. by L.1993, chap. 900(1.01), eff. 9/1/94.)*

## CHAPTER 8. GENERAL DEFENSES TO CRIMINAL RESPONSIBILITY

Section


### §8.01. Insanity.

(a) It is an affirmative defense to prosecution that, at the time of the conduct charged, the actor, as a result of severe mental disease or defect, did not know that his conduct was wrong.

(b) The term "mental disease or defect" does not include an abnormality manifested only by repeated criminal or otherwise antisocial conduct.

*(Chgd. by L.1993, chap. 900(1.01), eff. 9/1/94.)*

### §8.02. Mistake of fact.

(a) It is a defense to prosecution that the actor through mistake formed a reasonable belief about a matter of fact if his mistaken belief negated the kind of culpability required for commission of the offense.

(b) Although an actor's mistake of fact may constitute a defense to the offense charged, he may nevertheless be convicted of any lesser included offense of which he would be guilty if the fact were as he believed.

*(Chgd. by L.1993, chap. 900(1.01), eff. 9/1/94.)*

### §8.03. Mistake of law.

(a) It is no defense to prosecution that the actor was ignorant of the provisions of any law after the law has taken effect.

(b) It is an affirmative defense to prosecution that the actor reasonably believed the conduct charged did not constitute a crime and that he acted in reasonable reliance upon:

(1) an official statement of the law contained in a written order or grant of permission by an administrative agency charged by law with responsibility for interpreting the law in question; or

(2) a written interpretation of the law contained in an opinion of a court of record or made by a public official charged by law with responsibility for interpreting the law in question.

(c) Although an actor's mistake of law may constitute a defense to the offense charged, he may nevertheless be convicted of a lesser included offense of which he would be guilty if the law were as he believed.

*(Chgd. by L.1993, chap. 900(1.01), eff. 9/1/94.)*

### §8.04. Intoxication.

(a) Voluntary intoxication does not constitute a defense to the commission of crime.

(b) Evidence of temporary insanity caused by intoxication may be introduced by the actor in mitigation of the penalty attached to the offense for which he is being tried.

(c) When temporary insanity is relied upon as a defense and the evidence tends to show that such insanity was caused by intoxication, the court shall charge the jury in accordance with the provisions of this section.

(d) For purposes of this section "intoxication" means disturbance of mental or physical capacity resulting from the introduction of any substance into the body.

*(Chgd. by L.1993, chap. 900(1.01), eff. 9/1/94.)*

### §8.05. Duress.

(a) It is an affirmative defense to prosecution that the actor engaged in the proscribed conduct because he was compelled to do so by threat of imminent death or serious bodily injury to himself or another.

(b) In a prosecution for an offense that does not constitute a felony, it is an affirmative defense to prosecution that the actor engaged in the proscribed conduct because he was compelled to do so by force or threat of force.

(c) Compulsion within the meaning of this section exists only if the force or threat of force would render a person of reasonable firmness incapable of resisting the pressure.

(d) The defense provided by this section is unavailable if the actor intentionally, knowingly, or recklessly placed himself in a situation in which it was probable that he would be subjected to compulsion.

(e) It is no defense that a person acted at the command or persuasion of his spouse, unless he acted under compulsion that would establish a defense under this section.

*(Chgd. by L.1993, chap. 900(1.01), eff. 9/1/94.)*



### §8.06. Entrapment.

(a) It is a defense to prosecution that the actor engaged in the conduct charged because he was induced to do so by a law enforcement agent using persuasion or other means likely to cause persons to commit the offense. Conduct merely affording a person an opportunity to commit an offense does not constitute entrapment.

(b) In this section "law enforcement agent" includes personnel of the state and local law enforcement agencies as well as of the United States and any person acting in accordance with instructions from such agents.

*(Chgd. by L.1993, chap. 900(1.01), eff. 9/1/94.)*

### §8.07. Age affecting criminal responsibility.

(a) A person may not be prosecuted for or convicted of any offense that he committed when younger than 15 years of age except:

(1) perjury and aggravated perjury when it appears by proof that he had sufficient discretion to understand the nature and obligation of an oath;

(2) a violation of a penal statute cognizable under Chapter 729, Transportation Code, except for:

(A) an offense under Section 550.021, Transportation Code;

(B) an offense punishable as a Class B misdemeanor under Section 550.022, Transportation Code; or

(C) an offense punishable as a Class B misdemeanor under Section 550.024, Transportation Code;

(3) a violation of a motor vehicle traffic ordinance of an incorporated city or town in this state;

(4) a misdemeanor punishable by fine only other than public intoxication;

(5) a violation of a penal ordinance of a political subdivision; or

(6) a violation of a penal statute that is, or is a lesser included offense of, a capital felony, an aggravated controlled substance felony, or a felony of the first degree for which the person is transferred to the court under Section 54.02, Family Code, for prosecution if the person committed the offense when 14 years of age or older.

(b) Unless the juvenile court waives jurisdiction under Section 54.02, Family Code, and certifies the individual for criminal prosecution or the juvenile court has previously waived jurisdiction under that section and certified the individual for criminal prosecution, a person may not be prosecuted for or convicted of any offense committed before reaching 17 years of age except an offense described by Subsections (a)(1)-(5).

(c) No person may, in any case, be punished by death for an offense committed while he was younger than 17 years.

*(Chgd. by L.1989, chap. 1245(3); L.1991, chap. 169(3); L.1993, chap. 900(1.01); L.1995, chap. 262(77); L.1997, chaps. 165(30.236), 822(4), 1086(42), eff. 9/1/97, 6/18/97, 9/1/97, respectively.)*

# CHAPTER 9. JUSTIFICATION EXCLUDING CRIMINAL RESPONSIBILITY

## SUBCHAPTER A. GENERAL PROVISIONS



## SUBCHAPTER B. JUSTIFICATION GENERALLY



## SUBCHAPTER C. PROTECTION OF PERSONS



## SUBCHAPTER D. PROTECTION OF PROPERTY



## SUBCHAPTER E. LAW ENFORCEMENT



## SUBCHAPTER F. SPECIAL RELATIONSHIPS



## SUBCHAPTER A. GENERAL PROVISIONS

### §9.01. Definitions.

In this chapter:

(1) "Custody" has the meaning assigned by Section 38.01.

(2) "Escape" has the meaning assigned by Section 38.01.

(3) "Deadly force" means force that is intended or known by the actor to cause, or in the manner of its use or intended use is capable of causing, death or serious bodily injury.
*(Chgd. by L.1993, chap. 900(1.01); L.1997, chap. 293(1), eff. 9/1/97.)*

### §9.02. Justification as a defense.

It is a defense to prosecution that the conduct in question is justified under this chapter. *(Chgd. by L.1993, chap. 900(1.01), eff. 9/1/94.)*

### §9.03. Confinement as justifiable force.

Confinement is justified when force is justified by this chapter if the actor takes reasonable measures to terminate the confinement as soon as he knows he safely can unless the person confined has been arrested for an offense. *(Chgd. by L.1993, chap. 900(1.01), eff. 9/1/94.)*

### §9.04. Threats as justifiable force.

The threat of force is justified when the use of force is justified by this chapter. For purposes of this section, a threat to cause death or serious bodily injury by the production of a weapon or otherwise, as long as the actor's purpose is limited to creating an apprehension that he will use deadly force if necessary, does not constitute the use of deadly force. *(Chgd. by L.1993, chap. 900(1.01), eff. 9/1/94.)*

### §9.05. Reckless injury of innocent third person.

Even though an actor is justified under this chapter in threatening or using force or deadly force against another, if in doing so he also recklessly injures or kills an innocent third person, the justification afforded by this chapter is unavailable in a prosecution for the reckless injury or killing of the innocent third person. *(Chgd. by L.1993, chap. 900(1.01), eff. 9/1/94.)*

### §9.06. Civil remedies unaffected.

The fact that conduct is justified under this chapter does not abolish or impair any remedy for the conduct that is available in a civil suit. *(Chgd. by L.1993, chap. 900(1.01), eff. 9/1/94.)*

## SUBCHAPTER B. JUSTIFICATION GENERALLY



### §9.21. Public duty.

(a) Except as qualified by Subsections (b) and (c), conduct is justified if the actor reasonably believes the conduct is required or authorized by law, by the judgment or order of a competent court or other governmental tribunal, or in the execution of legal process.

(b) The other sections of this chapter control when force is used against a person to protect persons (Subchapter C), to protect property (Subchapter D), for law enforcement (Subchapter E) or by virtue of a special relationship (Subchapter F).

(c) The use of deadly force is not justified under this section unless the actor reasonably believes the deadly force is specifically required by statute or unless it occurs in the lawful conduct of war. If deadly force is so justified, there is no duty to retreat before using it.

(d) The justification afforded by this section is available if the actor reasonably believes:

(1) the court or governmental tribunal has jurisdiction or the process is lawful, even though the court or governmental tribunal lacks jurisdiction or the process is unlawful; or

(2) his conduct is required or authorized to assist a public servant in the performance of his official duty, even though the servant exceeds his lawful authority.

*(Chgd. by L.1993, chap. 900(1.01), eff. 9/1/94.)*

### §9.22. Necessity.

Conduct is justified if:

(1) the actor reasonably believes the conduct is immediately necessary to avoid imminent harm;

(2) the desirability and urgency of avoiding the harm clearly outweigh, according to ordinary standards of reasonableness, the harm sought to be prevented by the law proscribing the conduct; and

(3) a legislative purpose to exclude the justification claimed for the conduct does not otherwise plainly appear.

*(Chgd. by L.1993, chap. 900(1.01), eff. 9/1/94.)*

## SUBCHAPTER C. PROTECTION OF PERSONS

### §9.31. Self-defense.

(a) Except as provided in Subsection (b), a person is justified in using force against another when and to the degree he reasonably believes the force is immediately necessary to protect himself against the other's use or attempted use of unlawful force.

(b) The use of force against another is not justified:

(1) in the response to verbal provocation alone;

(2) to resist an arrest or search that the actor knows is being made by a peace officer, or by a person acting in a peace officer's presence and at his direction, even though the arrest or search is unlawful, unless the resistance is justified under Subsection (c);

(3) if the actor consented to the exact force used or attempted by the other;

(4) if the actor provoked the other's use or attempted use of unlawful force, unless:

(A) the actor abandons the encounter, or clearly communicates to the other his intent to do so reasonably believing he cannot safely abandon the encounter; and

(B) the other nevertheless continues or attempts to use unlawful force against the actor; or

(5) if the actor sought an explanation from or discussion with the other person concerning the actor's differences with the other person while the actor was:

(A) carrying a weapon in violation of Section 46.02; or

(B) possessing or transporting a weapon in violation of Section 46.05.

(c) The use of force to resist an arrest or search is justified:

(1) if, before the actor offers any resistance, the peace officer (or person acting at his direction) uses or attempts to use greater force than necessary to make the arrest or search; and

(2) when and to the degree the actor reasonably believes the force is immediately necessary to protect himself against the peace officer's (or other person's) use or attempted use of greater force than necessary.

(d) The use of deadly force is not justified under this subchapter except as provided in Sections 9.32, 9.33, and 9.34.

*(Chgd. by L.1993, chap. 900(1.01); L.1995, chap. 190(1), eff. 9/1/95.)*

### §9.32. Deadly force in defense of person.

(a) A person is justified in using deadly force against another:

(1) if he would be justified in using force against the other under Section 9.31;

(2) if a reasonable person in the actor's situation would not have retreated; and

(3) when and to the degree he reasonably believes the deadly force is immediately necessary:

(A) to protect himself against the other's use or attempted use of unlawful deadly force; or

(B) to prevent the other's imminent commission of aggravated kidnapping, murder, sexual assault, aggravated sexual assault, robbery, or aggravated robbery.

(b) The requirement imposed by Subsection (a)(2) does not apply to an actor who uses force against a person who is at the time of the use of force committing an offense of unlawful entry in the habitation of the actor.

*(Chgd. by L.1993, chap. 900(1.01); L.1995, chap. 235(1), eff. 9/1/95.)*

### §9.33. Defense of third person.

A person is justified in using force or deadly force against another to protect a third person if:

(1) under the circumstances as the actor reasonably believes them to be, the actor would be justified under Section 9.31 or 9.32 in using force or deadly force to protect himself against the unlawful force or unlawful deadly force he reasonably believes to be threatening the third person he seeks to protect; and

(2) the actor reasonably believes that his intervention is immediately necessary to protect the third person.

*(Chgd. by L.1993, chap. 900(1.01), eff. 9/1/94.)*

### §9.34. Protection of life or health.

(a) A person is justified in using force, but not deadly force, against another when and to the degree he reasonably believes the force is immediately necessary to prevent the other from committing suicide or inflicting serious bodily injury to himself.

(b) A person is justified in using both force and deadly force against another when and to the degree he reasonably believes the force or deadly force is immediately necessary to preserve the other's life in an emergency.

*(Chgd. by L.1993, chap. 900(1.01), eff. 9/1/94.)*

## SUBCHAPTER D. PROTECTION OF PROPERTY

### §9.41. Protection of one's own property.

(a) A person in lawful possession of land or tangible, movable property is justified in using force against another when and to the degree the actor reasonably believes the force is immediately necessary to prevent or terminate the other's trespass on the land or unlawful interference with the property.

(b) A person unlawfully dispossessed of land or tangible, movable property by another is justified in using force against the other when and to the degree the actor reasonably believes the force is immediately necessary to reenter the land or recover the property if the actor uses the force immediately or in fresh pursuit after the dispossession and:

(1) the actor reasonably believes the other had no claim of right when he dispossessed the actor; or

(2) the other accomplished the dispossession by using force, threat, or fraud against the actor.

*(Chgd. by L.1993, chap. 900(1.01), eff. 9/1/94.)*

### §9.42. Deadly force to protect property.

A person is justified in using deadly force against another to protect land or tangible, movable property:

(1) if he would be justified in using force against the other under Section 9.41; and

(2) when and to the degree he reasonably believes the deadly force is immediately necessary:

(A) to prevent the other's imminent commission of arson, burglary, robbery, aggravated robbery, theft during the nighttime, or criminal mischief during the nighttime; or

(B) to prevent the other who is fleeing immediately after committing burglary, robbery, aggravated robbery, or theft during the nighttime from escaping with the property; and

(3) he reasonably believes that:

(A) the land or property cannot be protected or recovered by any other means; or

(B) the use of force other than deadly force to protect or recover the land or property would expose the actor or another to a substantial risk of death or serious bodily injury.

*(Chgd. by L.1993, chap. 900(1.01), eff. 9/1/94.)*

### §9.43. Protection of third person's property.

A person is justified in using force or deadly force against another to protect land or tangible, movable property of a third person if, under the circumstances as he reasonably believes them to be, the actor would be justified under Section 9.41 or 9.42 in using force or deadly force to protect his own land or property and:

(1) the actor reasonably believes the unlawful interference constitutes attempted or consummated theft of or criminal mischief to the tangible, movable property; or

(2) the actor reasonably believes that:

(A) the third person has requested his protection of the land or property;

(B) he has a legal duty to protect the third person's land or property; or

(C) the third person whose land or property he uses force or deadly force to protect is the actor's spouse, parent, or child, resides with the actor, or is under the actor's care.

*(Chgd. by L.1993, chap. 900(1.01), eff. 9/1/94.)*



### §9.44. Use of device to protect property.

The justification afforded by Sections 9.41 and 9.43 applies to the use of a device to protect land or tangible, movable property if:

(1) the device is not designed to cause, or known by the actor to create a substantial risk of causing, death or serious bodily injury; and

(2) use of the device is reasonable under all the circumstances as the actor reasonably believes them to be when he installs the device.

*(Chgd. by L.1993, chap. 900(1.01), eff. 9/1/94.)*

## SUBCHAPTER E. LAW ENFORCEMENT

### §9.51. Arrest and search.

(a) A peace officer, or a person acting in a peace officer's presence and at his direction, is justified in using force against another when and to the degree the actor reasonably believes the force is immediately necessary to make or assist in making an arrest or search, or to prevent or assist in preventing escape after arrest if:

(1) the actor reasonably believes the arrest or search is lawful or, if the arrest or search is made under a warrant, he reasonably believes the warrant is valid; and

(2) before using force, the actor manifests his purpose to arrest or search and identifies himself as a peace officer or as one acting at a peace officer's direction, unless he reasonably believes his purpose and identity are already known by or cannot reasonably be made known to the person to be arrested.

(b) A person other than a peace officer (or one acting at his direction) is justified in using force against another when and to the degree the actor reasonably believes the force is immediately necessary to make or assist in making a lawful arrest, or to prevent or assist in preventing escape after lawful arrest if, before using force, the actor manifests his purpose to and the reason for the arrest or reasonably believes his purpose and the reason are already known by or cannot reasonably be made known to the person to be arrested.

(c) A peace officer is justified in using deadly force against another when and to the degree the peace officer reasonably believes the deadly force is immediately necessary to make an arrest, or to prevent escape after arrest, if the use of force would have been justified under Subsection (a) and:

(1) the actor reasonably believes the conduct for which arrest is authorized included the use or attempted use of deadly force; or

(2) the actor reasonably believes there is a substantial risk that the person to be arrested will cause death or serious bodily injury to the actor or another if the arrest is delayed.

(d) A person other than a peace officer acting in a peace officer's presence and at his direction is justified in using deadly force against another when and to the degree the person reasonably believes the deadly force is immediately necessary to make a lawful arrest, or to prevent escape after a lawful arrest, if the use of force would have been justified under Subsection (b) and:

(1) the actor reasonably believes the felony or offense against the public peace for which arrest is authorized included the use or attempted use of deadly force; or

(2) the actor reasonably believes there is a substantial risk that the person to be arrested will cause death or serious bodily injury to another if the arrest is delayed.

(e) There is no duty to retreat before using deadly force justified by Subsection (c) or (d).

(f) Nothing in this section relating to the actor's manifestation of purpose or identity shall be construed as conflicting with any other law relating to the issuance, service, and execution of an arrest or search warrant either under the laws of this state or the United States.

(g) Deadly force may only be used under the circumstances enumerated in Subsections (c) and (d).

*(Chgd. by L.1993, chap. 900(1.01), eff. 9/1/94.)*

### §9.52. Prevention of escape from custody.

The use of force to prevent the escape of an arrested person from custody is justifiable when the force could have been employed to effect the arrest under which the person is in custody, except that a guard employed by a correctional facility or a peace officer is justified in using any force, including deadly force, that he reasonably believes to be immediately necessary to prevent the escape of a person from the correctional facility. *(Chgd. by L.1993, chap. 900(1.01), eff. 9/1/94.)*

### §9.53. Maintaining security in correctional facility.

An officer or employee of a correctional facility is justified in using force against a person in custody when and to the degree the officer or employee reasonably believes the force is necessary to maintain the security of the correctional facility, the safety or security of other persons in custody or employed by the correctional facility, or his own safety or security. *(Chgd. by L.1993, chap. 900(1.01), eff. 9/1/94.)*

## SUBCHAPTER F. SPECIAL RELATIONSHIPS

### §9.61. Parent—child.

(a) The use of force, but not deadly force, against a child younger than 18 years is justified:

(1) if the actor is the child's parent or stepparent or is acting in loco parentis to the child; and

(2) when and to the degree the actor reasonably believes the force is necessary to discipline the child or to safeguard or promote his welfare.

(b) For purposes of this section, "in loco parentis" includes grandparent and guardian, any person acting by, through, or under the direction of a court with jurisdiction over the child, and anyone who has express or implied consent of the parent or parents.

*(Chgd. by L.1993, chap. 900(1.01), eff. 9/1/94.)*

### §9.62. Educator—student.

The use of force, but not deadly force, against a person is justified:

(1) if the actor is entrusted with the care, supervision, or administration of the person for a special purpose; and

(2) when and to the degree the actor reasonably believes the force is necessary to further the special purpose or to maintain discipline in a group.

*(Chgd. by L.1993, chap. 900(1.01), eff. 9/1/94.)*

### §9.63. Guardian—incompetent.

The use of force, but not deadly force, against a mental incompetent is justified:

(1) if the actor is the incompetent's guardian or someone similarly responsible for the general care and supervision of the incompetent; and

(2) when and to the degree the actor reasonably believes the force is necessary:

(A) to safeguard and promote the incompetent's welfare; or

(B) if the incompetent is in an institution for his care and custody, to maintain discipline in the institution.

*(Chgd. by L.1993, chap. 900(1.01), eff. 9/1/94.)*

# TITLE 3. PUNISHMENTS



## CHAPTER 12. PUNISHMENTS

### SUBCHAPTER A. GENERAL PROVISIONS



### SUBCHAPTER B. ORDINARY MISDEMEANOR PUNISHMENTS



### SUBCHAPTER C. ORDINARY FELONY PUNISHMENTS



### SUBCHAPTER D. EXCEPTIONAL SENTENCES



### SUBCHAPTER E. CORPORATIONS AND ASSOCIATIONS



### SUBCHAPTER A. GENERAL PROVISIONS

#### §12.01. Punishment in accordance with code.

(a) A person adjudged guilty of an offense under this code shall be punished in accordance with this chapter and the Code of Criminal Procedure.

(b) Penal laws enacted after the effective date of this code shall be classified for punishment purposes in accordance with this chapter.

(c) This chapter does not deprive a court of authority conferred by law to forfeit property, dissolve a corporation, suspend or cancel a license or permit, remove a person from office, cite for contempt, or impose any other civil penalty. The civil penalty may be included in the sentence. *(Chgd. by L.1993, chap. 900(1.01), eff. 9/1/94.)*

#### §12.02. Classification of offenses.

Offenses are designated as felonies or misdemeanors. *(Chgd. by L.1993, chap. 900(1.01), eff. 9/1/94.)*

#### §12.03. Classification of misdemeanors.

(a) Misdemeanors are classified according to the relative seriousness of the offense into three categories:

(1) Class A misdemeanors;
(2) Class B misdemeanors;
(3) Class C misdemeanors.

(b) An offense designated a misdemeanor in this code without specification as to punishment or category is a Class C misdemeanor.

(c) Conviction of a Class C misdemeanor does not impose any legal disability or disadvantage.

*(Chgd. by L.1993, chap. 900(1.01), eff. 9/1/94.)*

### §12.04. Classification of felonies.

(a) Felonies are classified according to the relative seriousness of the offense into five categories:

(1) capital felonies;
(2) felonies of the first degree;
(3) felonies of the second degree;
(4) felonies of the third degree; and
(5) state jail felonies.

(b) An offense designated a felony in this code without specification as to category is a state jail felony.

*(Chgd. by L.1993, chap. 900(1.01), eff. 9/1/94.)*



## SUBCHAPTER B. ORDINARY MISDEMEANOR PUNISHMENTS

### §12.21. Class A misdemeanor.

An individual adjudged guilty of a Class A misdemeanor shall be punished by:

(1) a fine not to exceed $4,000;
(2) confinement in jail for a term not to exceed one year; or
(3) both such fine and confinement.

*(Chgd. by L.1991, chap. 108(1); L.1993, chap. 900(1.01), eff. 9/1/94.)*

### §12.22. Class B misdemeanor.

An individual adjudged guilty of a Class B misdemeanor shall be punished by:

(1) a fine not to exceed $2,000;
(2) confinement in jail for a term not to exceed 180 days; or
(3) both such fine and confinement.

*(Chgd. by L.1991, chap. 108(1); L.1993, chap. 900(1.01), eff. 9/1/94.)*

### §12.23. Class C misdemeanor.

An individual adjudged guilty of a Class C misdemeanor shall be punished by a fine not to exceed $500. *(Chgd. by L.1991, chap. 108(1); L.1993, chap. 900(1.01), eff. 9/1/94.)*

## SUBCHAPTER C. ORDINARY FELONY PUNISHMENTS

### §12.31. Capital felony.

(a) An individual adjudged guilty of a capital felony in a case in which the state seeks the death penalty shall be punished by imprisonment in the institutional division for life or by death. An individual adjudged guilty of a capital felony in a case in which the state does not seek the death penalty shall be punished by imprisonment in the institutional division for life.

(b) In a capital felony trial in which the state seeks the death penalty, prospective jurors shall be informed that a sentence of life imprisonment or death is mandatory on conviction of a capital felony. In a capital felony trial in which the state does not seek the death penalty, prospective jurors shall be informed that the state is not seeking the death penalty and that a sentence of life imprisonment is mandatory on conviction of the capital felony.

*(Chgd. by L.1991, chaps. 652(12), 838(4); L.1993, chap. 900(1.01), eff. 9/1/94. This Section is exempt from the repeal of the Penal Code, L.1991, 2nd C.S., chap. 10(11.17), eff. 9/1/94.)*

### §12.32. First degree felony punishment.

(a) An individual adjudged guilty of a felony of the first degree shall be punished by imprisonment in the institutional division for life or for any term of not more than 99 years or less than 5 years.

(b) In addition to imprisonment, an individual adjudged guilty of a felony of the first degree may be punished by a fine not to exceed $10,000.
*(Chgd. by L.1993, chap. 900(1.01), eff. 9/1/94.)*

### §12.33. Second degree felony punishment.

(a) An individual adjudged guilty of a felony of the second degree shall be punished by imprisonment in the institutional division for any term of not more than 20 years or less than 2 years.

(b) In addition to imprisonment, an individual adjudged guilty of a felony of the second degree may be punished by a fine not to exceed $10,000.
*(Chgd. by L.1993, chap. 900(1.01), eff. 9/1/94.)*

### §12.34. Third degree felony punishment.

(a) An individual adjudged guilty of a felony of the third degree shall be punished by imprisonment in the institutional division for any term of not more than 10 years or less than 2 years.

(b) In addition to imprisonment an individual adjudged guilty of a felony of the third degree may be punished by a fine not to exceed $10,000.
*(Chgd. by L.1989, chap. 785(4.01); L.1990, 6th C. S., chap. 25(7); L.1993, chap. 900(1.01), eff. 9/1/94.)*



### §12.35. State jail felony punishment.

(a) Except as provided by Subsection (c), an individual adjudged guilty of a state jail felony shall be punished by confinement in a state jail for any term of not more than two years or less than 180 days.

(b) In addition to confinement, an individual adjudged guilty of a state jail felony may be punished by a fine not to exceed $10,000.

(c) An individual adjudged guilty of a state jail felony shall be punished for a third degree felony if it is shown on the trial of the offense that:

(1) a deadly weapon as defined by Section 1.07 was used or exhibited during the commission of the offense or during immediate flight following the commission of the offense, and that the individual used or exhibited the deadly weapon or was a party to the offense and knew that a deadly weapon would be used or exhibited; or

(2) the individual has previously been finally convicted of any felony:

(A) listed in Section 3g(a)(1), Article 42.12, Code of Criminal Procedure; or

(B) for which the judgment contains an affirmative finding under Section 3g(a)(2), Article 42.12, Code of Criminal Procedure.
*(Added by L.1993, chap. 900(1.01), eff. 9/1/94.)*

## SUBCHAPTER D. EXCEPTIONAL SENTENCES

### §12.41. Classification of offenses outside this code.

For purposes of this subchapter, any conviction not obtained from a prosecution under this code shall be classified as follows:

(1) "felony of the third degree" if imprisonment in a penitentiary is affixed to the offense as a possible punishment;

(2) "Class B misdemeanor" if the offense is not a felony and confinement in a jail is affixed to the offense as a possible punishment;

(3) "Class C misdemeanor" if the offense is punishable by fine only.
*(Chgd. by L.1993, chap. 900(1.01), eff. 9/1/94.)*

### §12.42. Penalties for repeat and habitual felony offenders.

(a)(1) If it is shown on the trial of a state jail felony punishable under Section 12.35(a) that the defendant has previously been finally convicted of two state jail felonies, on conviction the defendant shall be punished for a third-degree felony.

(2) If it is shown on the trial of a state jail felony punishable under Section 12.35(a) that the defendant has previously been finally convicted of two felonies, and the second previous felony conviction is for an offense that occurred subsequent to the first previous conviction having become final, on conviction the defendant shall be punished for a second-degree felony.

(3) If it is shown on the trial of a state jail felony punishable under Section 12.35(c) or on the trial of a third-degree felony that the defendant has been once before convicted of a felony, on conviction he shall be punished for a second-degree felony.

(b) If it is shown on the trial of a second-degree felony that the defendant has been once before convicted of a felony, on conviction he shall be punished for a first-degree felony.

(c)(1) Except as provided by Subdivision (2), if it is shown on the trial of a first-degree felony that the defendant has been once before convicted of a felony, on conviction he shall be punished by imprisonment in the institutional division of the Texas Department of Criminal Justice for life, or for any term of not more than 99 years or less than 15 years. In addition to imprisonment, an individual may be punished by a fine not to exceed $10,000.

(2) A defendant shall be punished by imprisonment in the institutional division for life if:

(A) the defendant is convicted of an offense:

(i) under Section 22.021 or 22.011, Penal Code;

(ii) under Section 20.04(a)(4), Penal Code, if the defendant committed the offense with the intent to violate or abuse the victim sexually; or

(iii) under Section 30.02, Penal Code, punishable under Subsection (d) of that section, if the defendant committed the offense with the intent to commit a felony described by Subparagraph (i) or (ii) or a felony under Section 21.11 or 22.011, Penal Code; and

(B) the defendant has been previously convicted of an offense:

(i) under Section 43.25 or 43.26, Penal Code;

(ii) under Section 21.11, 22.011, 22.021, or 25.02, Penal Code;

(iii) under Section 20.04(a)(4), Penal Code, if the defendant committed the offense with the intent to violate or abuse the victim sexually;

(iv) under Section 30.02, Penal Code, punishable under Subsection (d) of that section, if the defendant committed the offense with the intent to commit a felony described by Subparagraph (ii) or (iii); or

(v) under the laws of another state containing elements that are substantially similar to the elements of an offense listed in Subparagraph (i), (ii), (iii), or (iv).

(d) If it is shown on the trial of a felony offense other than a state jail felony punishable under Section 12.35(a) that the defendant has previously been finally convicted of two felony offenses, and the second previous felony conviction is for an offense that occurred subsequent to the first previous conviction having become final, on conviction he shall be punished by imprisonment in the institutional division of the Texas Department of Criminal Justice for life, or for any term of not more than 99 years or less than 25 years.

(e) A previous conviction for a state jail felony punished under Section 12.35(a) may not be used for enhancement purposes under Subsection (b), (c), or (d).

(f) For the purposes of Subsections (a)-(c) and (e), an adjudication by a juvenile court under Section 54.03, Family Code, that a child engaged in delinquent conduct constituting a felony offense for which the child is committed to the Texas Youth Commission under Section 54.04(d)(2), (d)(3), or (m), Family Code, or Section 54.05(f), Family Code, is a final felony conviction.

(g) For the purposes of Subsection (c)(2):

(1) a defendant has been previously convicted of an offense listed under Subsection (c)(2)(B) if the defendant was adjudged guilty of the offense or entered a plea of guilty or nolo contendere in return for a grant of deferred adjudication, regardless of whether the sentence for the offense was ever imposed or whether the sentence was probated and the defendant was subsequently discharged from community supervision; and

(2) a conviction under the laws of another state for an offense containing elements that are substantially similar to the elements of an offense listed under Subsection (c)(2)(B) is a conviction of an offense listed under Subsection (c)(2)(B).

*(Chgd. by L.1993, chap. 900(1.01); L.1995, chaps. 250(1), 262(78), 318(1); L.1997, chaps. 665(1), (2); 667(4); L.1999, chap. 62(15.01), eff. 9/1/99.)*

**§12.422.** *(Deleted by amendment by L.1993, chap. 900(1.01), eff. 9/1/93.)*

### §12.43. Penalties for repeat and habitual misdemeanor offenders.

(a) If it is shown on the trial of a Class A misdemeanor that the defendant has been before convicted of a Class A misdemeanor or any degree of felony, on conviction he shall be punished by:

(1) a fine not to exceed $4,000;

(2) confinement in jail for any term of not more than one year or less than 90 days; or

(3) both such fine and confinement.

(b) If it is shown on the trial of a Class B misdemeanor that the defendant has been before convicted of a Class A or Class B misdemeanor or any degree of felony, on conviction he shall be punished by:

(1) a fine not to exceed $2,000;

(2) confinement in jail for any term of not more than 180 days or less than 30 days; or

(3) both such fine and confinement.

(c) If it is shown on the trial of an offense punishable as a Class C misdemeanor under Section 42.01 or 49.02 that the defendant has been before convicted under either of those sections three times or three times for any combination of those offenses and each prior offense was committed in the 24 months preceding the date of commission of the instant offense, the defendant shall be punished by:

(1) a fine not to exceed $2,000;

(2) confinement in jail for a term not to exceed 180 days; or

(3) both such fine and confinement.

(d) If the punishment scheme for an offense contains a specific enhancement provision increasing punishment for a defendant who has previously been convicted of the offense, the specific enhancement provision controls over this section.

*(Chgd. by L.1993, chap. 900(1.01); L.1995, chap. 318(2); L.1999, chap. 564(1), eff. 9/1/99.)*

### §12.44. Reduction of state jail felony punishment to misdemeanor punishment.

(a) A court may punish a defendant who is convicted of a state jail felony by imposing the confinement permissible as punishment for a Class A misdemeanor if, after considering the gravity and circumstances of the felony committed and the history, character, and rehabilitative needs of the defendant, the court finds that such punishment would best serve the ends of justice.

(b) When a court is authorized to impose punishment for a lesser category of offense as provided in Subsection (a), the court may authorize the prosecuting attorney to prosecute initially for the lesser category of offense.

*(Chgd. by L.1989, chap. 785(4.02); L.1993, chap. 900(1.01); L.1995, chap. 318(3), eff. 9/1/95.)*



### §12.45. Admission of unadjudicated offense.

(a) A person may, with the consent of the attorney for the state, admit during the sentencing hearing his guilt of one or more unadjudicated offenses and request the court to take each into account in determining sentence for the offense or offenses of which he stands adjudged guilty.

(b) Before a court may take into account an admitted offense over which exclusive venue lies in another county or district, the court must obtain permission from the prosecuting attorney with jurisdiction over the offense.

(c) If a court lawfully takes into account an admitted offense, prosecution is barred for that offense.

*(Chgd. by L.1993, chap. 900(1.01), eff. 9/1/94.)*

### §12.46. Use of prior convictions.

The use of a conviction for enhancement purposes shall not preclude the subsequent use of such conviction for enhancement purposes. *(Chgd. by L.1993, chap. 900(1.01), eff. 9/1/94.)*

### §12.47. Penalty if offense committed because of bias or prejudice.

If the judge or jury, whichever assesses punishment in the case, makes an affirmative finding under Article 42.014, Code of Criminal Procedure, in the punishment phase of the trial of an offense other than a first degree felony or a Class A misdemeanor, the punishment for the offense is increased to the punishment prescribed for the next highest category of offense. If the offense is a Class A misdemeanor, the minimum term of confinement for the offense is increased to 180 days. *(Added by L.1993, chap. 987(1); chgd. by L.1997, chap. 751(1), eff. 9/1/97. Former 12.47 deleted by amendment by L.1993, chap. 900(1.01), eff. 9/1/94.)*

### §12.48. Penalty if controlled substance used to commit offense.

If the court makes an affirmative finding under Article 42.015, Code of Criminal Procedure, in the punishment phase of the trial of an offense under Chapter 29, Chapter 31, or Title 5, other than a first degree felony or a Class A misdemeanor, the punishment for the offense is increased to the punishment prescribed for the next highest category of offense. If the offense is a Class A misdemeanor, the minimum term of confinement for the offense is increased to 180 days. *(Added by L.1999, chap. 417(2(a)), eff. 9/1/99. See other section 12.48 below.)*

### §12.48. Certain offenses resulting in loss to nursing and convalescent homes.

If it is shown on the trial of an offense under Chapter 31 or 32 that, as a result of a loss incurred because of the conduct charged, a trustee was appointed and emergency assistance funds, other than funds used to pay the expenses of the trustee, were used for a nursing or convalescent home under Subchapter D, Chapter 242, Health and Safety Code, the punishment for the offense is increased to the punishment prescribed for the next higher category of offense except that a felony of the first degree is punished as a felony of the first degree. *(Added by L.1999, chap. 439(4), eff. 9/1/99. See other section 12.48 above.)*

## SUBCHAPTER E. CORPORATIONS AND ASSOCIATIONS

### §12.51. Authorized punishments for corporations and associations.

(a) If a corporation or association is adjudged guilty of an offense that provides a penalty consisting of a fine only, a court may sentence the corporation or association to pay a fine in an amount fixed by the court, not to exceed the fine provided by the offense.

(b) If a corporation or association is adjudged guilty of an offense that provides a penalty including imprisonment, or that provides no specific penalty, a court may sentence the corporation or association to pay a fine in an amount fixed by the court, not to exceed:

(1) $20,000 if the offense is a felony of any category;

(2) $10,000 if the offense is a Class A or Class B misdemeanor;

(3) $2,000 if the offense is a Class C misdemeanor; or

(4) $50,000 if, as a result of an offense classified as a felony or Class A misdemeanor, an individual suffers serious bodily injury or death.

(c) In lieu of the fines authorized by Subsections (a), (b)(1), (b)(2), and (b)(4), if a court finds that the corporation or association gained money or property or caused personal injury or death, property damage, or other loss through the commission of a felony or Class A or Class B misdemeanor, the court may sentence the corporation or association to pay a fine in an amount fixed by the court, not to exceed double the amount gained or caused by the corporation or association to be lost or damaged, whichever is greater.

(d) In addition to any sentence that may be imposed by this section, a corporation or association that has been adjudged guilty of an offense may be ordered by the court to give notice of the conviction to any person the court deems appropriate.

(e) On conviction of a corporation or association, the court shall notify the attorney general of that fact.

*(Chgd. by L.1993, chap. 900(1.01), eff. 9/1/94.)*

# TITLE 4. INCHOATE OFFENSES



## CHAPTER 15. PREPARATORY OFFENSES



### §15.01. Criminal attempt.

(a) A person commits an offense if, with specific intent to commit an offense, he does an act amounting to more than mere preparation that tends but fails to effect the commission of the offense intended.

(b) If a person attempts an offense that may be aggravated, his conduct constitutes an attempt to commit the aggravated offense if an element that aggravates the offense accompanies the attempt.

(c) It is no defense to prosecution for criminal attempt that the offense attempted was actually committed.

(d) An offense under this section is one category lower than the offense attempted, and if the offense attempted is a state jail felony, the offense is a Class A misdemeanor.

*(Chgd. by L.1993, chap. 900(1.01), eff. 9/1/94.)*

### §15.02. Criminal conspiracy.

(a) A person commits criminal conspiracy if, with intent that a felony be committed:

(1) he agrees with one or more persons that they or one or more of them engage in conduct that would constitute the offense; and

(2) he or one or more of them performs an overt act in pursuance of the agreement.

(b) An agreement constituting a conspiracy may be inferred from acts of the parties.

(c) It is no defense to prosecution for criminal conspiracy that:

(1) one or more of the coconspirators is not criminally responsible for the object offense;

(2) one or more of the coconspirators has been acquitted, so long as two or more coconspirators have not been acquitted;

(3) one or more of the coconspirators has not been prosecuted or convicted, has been convicted of a different offense, or is immune from prosecution;

(4) the actor belongs to a class of persons that by definition of the object offense is legally incapable of committing the object offense in an individual capacity; or

(5) the object offense was actually committed.

(d) An offense under this section is one category lower than the most serious felony that is the object of the conspiracy, and if the most serious felony that is the object of the conspiracy is a state jail felony, the offense is a Class A misdemeanor.

*(Chgd. by L.1993, chap. 900(1.01), eff. 9/1/94.)*



### §15.03. Criminal solicitation.

(a) A person commits an offense if, with intent that a capital felony or felony of the first degree be committed, he requests, commands, or attempts to induce another to engage in specific conduct that, under the circumstances surrounding his conduct as the actor believes them to be, would constitute the felony or make the other a party to its commission.

(b) A person may not be convicted under this section on the uncorroborated testimony of the person allegedly solicited and unless the solicitation is made under circumstances strongly corroborative of both the solicitation itself and the actor's intent that the other person act on the solicitation.

(c) It is no defense to prosecution under this section that:

(1) the person solicited is not criminally responsible for the felony solicited;

(2) the person solicited has been acquitted, has not been prosecuted or convicted, has been convicted of a different offense or of a different type or class of offense, or is immune from prosecution;

(3) the actor belongs to a class of persons that by definition of the felony solicited is legally incapable of committing the offense in an individual capacity; or

(4) the felony solicited was actually committed.

(d) An offense under this section is:

(1) a felony of the first degree if the offense solicited is a capital offense; or

(2) a felony of the second degree if the offense solicited is a felony of the first degree.

*(Chgd. by L.1993, chap. 900(1.01), eff. 9/1/94.)*

### §15.031. Criminal solicitation of a minor.

(a) A person commits an offense if, with intent that an offense listed by Section 3g(a)(1), Article 42.12, Code of Criminal Procedure, be committed, the person requests, commands, or attempts to induce a minor to engage in specific conduct that, under the circumstances surrounding the actor's conduct as the actor believes them to be, would constitute an offense listed by Section 3g(a)(1), Article 42.12, or make the minor a party to the commission of an offense listed by Section 3g(a)(1), Article 42.12.

(b) A person commits an offense if, with intent that an offense under Section 21.11, 22.011, 22.021, or 43.25 be committed, the person by any means requests, commands, or attempts to induce a minor or another whom the person believes to be a minor to engage in specific conduct that, under circumstances surrounding the actor's conduct as the actor believes them to be, would constitute an offense under one of those sections or would make the minor or other believed by the person to be a minor a party to the commission of an offense under one of those sections.

(c) A person may not be convicted under this section on the uncorroborated testimony of the minor allegedly solicited unless the solicitation is made under circumstances strongly corroborative of both the solicitation itself and the actor's intent that the minor act on the solicitation.

(d) It is no defense to prosecution under this section that:

(1) the minor solicited is not criminally responsible for the offense solicited;

(2) the minor solicited has been acquitted, has not been prosecuted or convicted, has been convicted of a different offense or of a different type or class of offense, or is immune from prosecution;

(3) the actor belongs to a class of persons that by definition of the offense solicited is legally incapable of committing the offense in an individual capacity; or

(4) the offense solicited was actually committed.

(e) An offense under this section is one category lower than the solicited offense.

(f) In this section, "minor" means an individual younger than 17 years of age.

*(Added by L.1995, chap. 262(79); chgd. by L.1999, chap. 1415(22(a)), eff. 9/1/99.)*

### §15.04. Renunciation defense.

(a) It is an affirmative defense to prosecution under Section 15.01 that under circumstances manifesting a voluntary and complete renunciation of his criminal objective the actor avoided commission of the offense attempted by abandoning his criminal conduct or, if abandonment was insufficient to avoid commission of the offense, by taking further affirmative action that prevented the commission.

(b) It is an affirmative defense to prosecution under Section 15.02 or 15.03 that under circumstances manifesting a voluntary and complete renunciation of his criminal objective the actor countermanded his solicitation or withdrew from the conspiracy before commission of the object offense and took further affirmative action that prevented the commission of the object offense.

(c) Renunciation is not voluntary if it is motivated in whole or in part:

(1) by circumstances not present or apparent at the inception of the actor's course of conduct that increase the probability of detection or apprehension or that make more difficult the accomplishment of the objective; or

(2) by a decision to postpone the criminal conduct until another time or to transfer the criminal act to another but similar objective or victim.

(d) Evidence that the defendant renounced his criminal objective by abandoning his criminal conduct, countermanding his solicitation, or withdrawing from the conspiracy before the criminal offense was committed and made substantial effort to prevent the commission of the object offense shall be admissible as mitigation at the hearing on punishment if he has been found guilty of criminal attempt, criminal solicitation, or criminal conspiracy; and in the event of a finding of renunciation under this subsection, the punishment shall be one grade lower than that provided for the offense committed.

*(Chgd. by L.1993, chap. 900(1.01), eff. 9/1/94.)*

### §15.05. No offense.

Attempt or conspiracy to commit, or solicitation of, a preparatory offense defined in this chapter is not an offense. *(Chgd. by L.1993, chap. 900(1.01), eff. 9/1/94.)*

## CHAPTER 16. CRIMINAL INSTRUMENTS, INTERCEPTION OF WIRE OR ORAL COMMUNICATION, AND INSTALLATION OF TRACKING DEVICE

*(Heading chgd. by L.1999, chap. 728(2), eff. 9/1/99.)*

Section



### §16.01. Unlawful use of criminal instrument.

(a) A person commits an offense if:

(1) he possesses a criminal instrument with intent to use it in the commission of an offense; or

(2) with knowledge of its character and with intent to use or aid or permit another to use in the commission of an offense, he manufactures, adapts, sells, installs, or sets up a criminal instrument.

(b) For the purpose of this section, "criminal instrument" means anything, the possession, manufacture, or sale of which is not otherwise an offense, that is specially designed, made, or adapted for use in the commission of an offense.

(c) An offense under Subsection (a)(1) is one category lower than the offense intended. An offense under Subsection (a)(2) is a state jail felony.

*(Chgd. by L.1993, chap. 900(1.01), eff. 9/1/94.)*

**§16.02. Unlawful interception, use, or disclosure of wire, oral, or electronic communications.**

(a) In this section, "covert entry," "communication common carrier," "contents," "electronic, mechanical, or other device," "intercept," "investigative or law enforcement officer," "oral communication," " electronic communication," "readily accessible to the general public," and "wire communication" have the meanings given those terms in Article 18.20, Code of Criminal Procedure.

(b) A person commits an offense if he:

(1) intentionally intercepts, endeavors to intercept, or procures another person to intercept or endeavor to intercept a wire, oral, or electronic communication;

(2) intentionally discloses or endeavors to disclose to another person the contents of a wire, oral, or electronic communication if he knows or has reason to know the information was obtained through the interception of a wire, oral, or electronic communication in violation of this subsection;

(3) intentionally uses or endeavors to use the contents of a wire, oral, or electronic communication if he knows or is reckless about whether the information was obtained through the interception of a wire, oral, or electronic communication in violation of this subsection;

(4) knowingly or intentionally effects a covert entry for the purpose of intercepting wire, oral, or electronic communications without court order or authorization; or

(5) intentionally uses, endeavors to use, or procures any other person to use or endeavor to use any electronic, mechanical, or other device to intercept any oral communication when the device:

(A) is affixed to, or otherwise transmits a signal through a wire, cable, or other connection used in wire communications; or

(B) transmits communications by radio or interferes with the transmission of communications by radio.

(c) It is an affirmative defense to prosecution under Subsection (b) that:

(1) an operator of a switchboard or an officer, employee, or agent of a communication common carrier whose facilities are used in the transmission of a wire or electronic communication intercepts a communication or discloses or uses an intercepted communication in the normal course of employment while engaged in an activity that is a necessary incident to the rendition of service or to the protection of the rights or property of the carrier of the communication, unless the interception results from the communication common carrier's use of service observing or random monitoring for purposes other than mechanical or service quality control checks;

(2) an officer, employee, or agent of a communication common carrier provides information, facilities, or technical assistance to an investigative or law enforcement officer who is authorized as provided by this article to intercept a wire, oral, or electronic communication;

(3) a person acting under color of law intercepts a wire, oral, or electronic communication if the person is a party to the communication or if one of the parties to the communication has given prior consent to the interception;

(4) a person not acting under color of law intercepts a wire, oral, or electronic communication if the person is a party to the communication or if one of the parties to the communication has given prior consent to the interception unless the communication is intercepted for the purpose of committing any criminal or tortious act in violation of the constitution or laws of the United States or of this state or for the purpose of committing any other injurious act;

(5) a person acting under color of law intercepts a wire, oral, or electronic communication if:

(A) oral or written consent for the interception is given by a magistrate before the interception;

(B) an immediate life-threatening situation exists;

(C) the person is a member of a law enforcement unit specially trained to:

(i) respond to and deal with life-threatening situations; or

(ii) install electronic, mechanical, or other devices; and

(D) the interception ceases immediately on termination of the life-threatening situation;

(6) an officer, employee, or agent of the Federal Communications Commission intercepts a communication transmitted by radio or discloses or uses an intercepted communication in the normal course of employment and in the discharge of the monitoring responsibilities exercised by the Federal Communications Commission in the enforcement of Chapter 5, Title 47, United States Code;

(7) a person intercepts or obtains access to an electronic communication that was made through an electronic communication system that is configured to permit the communication to be readily accessible to the general public;

(8) a person intercepts radio communication, other than a cordless telephone communication that is transmitted between a cordless telephone handset and a base unit, that is transmitted:


Zt

(A) by a station for the use of the general public;

(B) to ships, aircraft, vehicles, or persons in distress;

(C) by a governmental, law enforcement, civil defense, private land mobile, or public safety communications system that is readily accessible to the general public, unless the radio communication is transmitted by a law enforcement representative to or from a mobile data terminal;

(D) by a station operating on an authorized frequency within the bands allocated to the amateur, citizens band, or general mobile radio services; or

(E) by a marine or aeronautical communications system;

(9) a person intercepts a wire or electronic communication the transmission of which causes harmful interference to a lawfully operating station or consumer electronic equipment, to the extent necessary to identify the source of the interference;

(10) a user of the same frequency intercepts a radio communication made through a system that uses frequencies monitored by individuals engaged in the provision or the use of the system, if the communication is not scrambled or encrypted; or

(11) a provider of electronic communications service records the fact that a wire or electronic communication was initiated or completed in order to protect the provider, another provider furnishing service towards the completion of the communication, or a user of that service from fraudulent, unlawful, or abusive use of the service.

(d)(1) A person commits an offense if he:

(A) intentionally manufactures, assembles, possesses, or sells an electronic, mechanical, or other device knowing or having reason to know that the device is designed primarily for nonconsensual interception of wire, electronic, or oral communications and that the device or a component of the device has been or will be used for an unlawful purpose; or

(B) places in a newspaper, magazine, handbill, or other publication an advertisement of an electronic, mechanical, or other device:

(i) knowing or having reason to know that the device is designed primarily for nonconsensual interception of wire, electronic, or oral communications;

(ii) promoting the use of the device for the purpose of nonconsensual interception of wire, electronic, or oral communications; or

(iii) knowing or having reason to know that the advertisement will promote the use of the device for the purpose of nonconsensual interception of wire, electronic, or oral communications.

(2) An offense under Subdivision (1) is a state jail felony.

(e) It is an affirmative defense to prosecution under Subsection (d) that the manufacture, assembly, possession, or sale of an electronic, mechanical, or other device that is designed primarily for the purpose of nonconsensual interception of wire, electronic, or oral communication is by:

(1) a communication common carrier or a provider of wire or electronic communications service or an officer, agent, or employee of or a person under contract with a communication common carrier or provider acting in the normal course of the provider's or communication carrier's business;

(2) an officer, agent, or employee of a person under contract with, bidding on contracts with, or doing business with the United States or this state acting in the normal course of the activities of the United States or this state; or

(3) a law enforcement agency that has an established unit specifically designated to respond to and deal with life-threatening situations or specifically trained to install wire, oral, or electronic communications intercept equipment.

(f) Except as provided by Subsections (d) and (h), an offense under this section is a felony of the second degree.

(g) For purposes of this section:

(1) An immediate life-threatening situation exists when human life is directly threatened in either a hostage or barricade situation.

(2) "Member of a law enforcement unit specially trained to respond to and deal with life-threatening situations" means a peace officer who has received a minimum of 40 hours a year of training in hostage and barricade suspect situations. This training must be evidenced by the submission of appropriate documentation to the Commission on Law Enforcement Officer Standards and Education.

(h)(1) A person commits an offense if, knowing that a government attorney or an investigative or law enforcement officer has been authorized or has applied for authorization to intercept wire, electronic, or oral communications, the person obstructs, impedes, prevents, gives notice to another of, or attempts to give notice to another of the interception.

(2) An offense under this subsection is a state jail felony.

(i) This section expires September 1, 2005, and shall not be in force on and after that date. *(Chgd. by L.1989, chap. 1166(16); L.1993, chap. 900(1.01); L.1997, chap. 1051(9), eff. 9/1/97. Expires 9/1/2005.)*

**§16.021.** *(Deleted by amendment by L.1993, chap. 900(1.01), eff. 9/1/94.)*

**§16.03. Unlawful use of pen register or trap and trace device.**

(a) A person commits an offense if the person knowingly installs or uses a pen register or trap and trace device to record or decode electronic or other impulses for the purpose of identifying telephone numbers dialed or otherwise transmitted on a telephone line.

(b) In this section, "authorized peace officer," "communications common carrier," "pen register," and "trap and trace device" have the meanings assigned by Article 18.21, Code of Criminal Procedure.

(c) It is an affirmative defense to prosecution under Subsection (a) that the actor is:

(1) an officer, employee, or agent of a communications common carrier and the actor installs or uses a device or equipment to record a number dialed from or to a telephone instrument in the normal course of business of the carrier for purposes of:

(A) protecting property or services provided by the carrier; or

(B) assisting another who the actor reasonably believes to be a peace officer authorized to install or use a pen register or trap and trace device under Article 18.21, Code of Criminal Procedure;

(2) an officer, employee, or agent of a lawful enterprise and the actor installs or uses a device or equipment while engaged in an activity that:

(A) is a necessary incident to the rendition of service or to the protection of property of or services provided by the enterprise; and

(B) is not made for the purpose of gathering information for a law enforcement agency or private investigative agency, other than information related to the theft of communication or information services provided by the enterprise; or

(3) a person authorized to install or use a pen register or trap and trace device under Article 18.21, Code of Criminal Procedure.

(d) An offense under this section is a state jail felony.

(e) *(Relettered by L.1997, chap. 1051(10), eff. 9/1/97.)*

(f) *(Deleted by amendment by L.1993, chap. 900(1.01), eff. 9/1/94.)*

*(Chgd. by L.1989, chap. 958(2); L.1993, chap. 900(1.01); L.1997, chap. 1051(10), eff. 9/1/97.)*

**§16.04. Unlawful access to stored communications.**

(a) In this section, "electronic communication," "electronic storage," "user," and "wire communication" have the meanings assigned to those terms in Article 18.21, Code of Criminal Procedure.

(b) A person commits an offense if the person obtains, alters, or prevents authorized access to a wire or electronic communication while the communication is in electronic storage by:

(1) intentionally obtaining access without authorization to a facility through which a wire or electronic communications service is provided; or

(2) intentionally exceeding an authorization for access to a facility through which a wire or electronic communications service is provided.

(c) Except as provided by Subsection (d), an offense under Subsection (b) is a Class A misdemeanor.

(d) If committed to obtain a benefit or to harm another, an offense is a state jail felony.

(e) It is an affirmative defense to prosecution under Subsection (b) that the conduct was authorized by:

(1) the provider of the wire or electronic communications service;

(2) the user of the wire or electronic communications service;

(3) the addressee or intended recipient of the wire or electronic communication; or

(4) Article 18.21, Code of Criminal Procedure.

*(Added by L.1989, chap. 958(3); chgd. by L.1993, chap. 900(1.01); L.1997, chap. 1051(11), eff. 9/1/97.)*

**§16.05. Illegal divulgence of public communications.**

(a) In this section, "electronic communication," "electronic communications service," and "electronic communications system" have the meanings given those terms in Article 18.20, Code of Criminal Procedure.

(b) A person who provides electronic communications service to the public commits an offense if the person knowingly divulges the contents of a communication to another who is not the intended recipient of the communication.

(c) It is an affirmative defense to prosecution under Subsection (b) that the actor divulged the contents of the communication:

(1) as authorized by federal or state law;

(2) to a person employed, authorized, or whose facilities are used to forward the communication to the communication's destination; or

(3) to a law enforcement agency if the contents reasonably appear to pertain to the commission of a crime.

(d) Except as provided by Subsection (e), an offense under Subsection (b) that involves a scrambled or encrypted radio communication is a state jail felony.

(e) If committed for a tortious or illegal purpose or to gain a benefit, an offense under Subsection (b) that involves a radio communication that is not scrambled or encrypted:

(1) is a Class A misdemeanor if the communication is not a public land mobile radio service communication or a paging service communication; or

(2) is a Class C misdemeanor if the communication is a public land mobile radio service communication or a paging service communication.

(f) *(Repealed by L.1997, chap. 1051(13), eff. 9/1/97.)*

*(Added by L.1989, chap. 1166(17); redes. by L.1990, 6th C.S., chap. 12(2(24)); chgd. by L.1993, chap. 900(1.01); L.1997, chap. 1051(12), eff. 9/1/97.)*



### §16.06. Unlawful installation of tracking device.

(a) In this section:

(1) "Electronic or mechanical tracking device" means a device capable of emitting an electronic frequency or other signal that may be used by a person to identify, monitor, or record the location of another person or object.

(2) "Motor vehicle" has the meaning assigned by Section 501.002, Transportation Code.

(b) A person commits an offense if the person knowingly installs an electronic or mechanical tracking device on a motor vehicle owned or leased by another person.

(c) An offense under this section is a Class A misdemeanor.

(d) It is an affirmative defense to prosecution under this section that the person:

(1) obtained the effective consent of the owner or lessee of the motor vehicle before the electronic or mechanical tracking device was installed;

(2) was a peace officer who installed the device in the course of a criminal investigation or pursuant to an order of a court to gather information for a law enforcement agency;

(3) assisted another whom the person reasonably believed to be a peace officer authorized to install the device in the course of a criminal investigation or pursuant to an order of a court to gather information for a law enforcement agency; or

(4) was a private investigator licensed under the Private Investigators and Private Security Agencies Act (Article 4413(29bb), Vernon's Texas Civil Statutes) who installed the device:

(A) with written consent:

(i) to install the device given by the owner or lessee of the motor vehicle; and

(ii) to enter private residential property, if that entry was necessary to install the device, given by the owner or lessee of the property; or

(B) pursuant to an order of or other authorization from a court to gather information.

*(Added by L.1999, chap. 728(1), eff. 9/1/99.)*

# TITLE 5. OFFENSES AGAINST THE PERSON



## CHAPTER 19. CRIMINAL HOMICIDE

### §19.01. Types of criminal homicide.

(a) A person commits criminal homicide if he intentionally, knowingly, recklessly, or with criminal negligence causes the death of an individual.

(b) Criminal homicide is murder, capital murder, manslaughter, or criminally negligent homicide.

*(Chgd. by L.1993, chap. 900(1.01), eff. 9/1/94.)*

### §19.02. Murder.

(a) In this section:

(1) "Adequate cause" means cause that would commonly produce a degree of anger, rage, resentment, or terror in a person of ordinary temper, sufficient to render the mind incapable of cool reflection.

(2) "Sudden passion" means passion directly caused by and arising out of provocation by the individual killed or another acting with the person killed which passion arises at the time of the offense and is not solely the result of former provocation.

(b) A person commits an offense if he:

(1) intentionally or knowingly causes the death of an individual;

(2) intends to cause serious bodily injury and commits an act clearly dangerous to human life that causes the death of an individual; or

(3) commits or attempts to commit a felony, other than manslaughter, and in the course of and in furtherance of the commission or attempt, or in immediate flight from the commission or attempt, he commits or attempts to commit an act clearly dangerous to human life that causes the death of an individual.

(c) Except as provided by Subsection (d), an offense under this section is a felony of the first degree.

(d) At the punishment stage of a trial, the defendant may raise the issue as to whether he caused the death under the immediate influence of sudden passion arising from an adequate cause. If the defendant proves the issue in the affirmative by a preponderance of the evidence, the offense is a felony of the second degree.

*(This Section is exempt from the repeal of the Penal Code, L.1991, 2nd C.S., chap. 10(11.17), eff. 9/1/94; chgd. by L.1993, chap. 900(1.01), eff. 9/1/94.)*

### §19.03. Capital murder.

(a) A person commits an offense if he commits murder as defined under Section 19.02(b)(1) and:

(1) the person murders a peace officer or fireman who is acting in the lawful discharge of an official duty and who the person knows is a peace officer or fireman;

(2) the person intentionally commits the murder in the course of committing or attempting to commit kidnapping, burglary, robbery, aggravated sexual assault, arson, or obstruction or retaliation;

(3) the person commits the murder for remuneration or the promise of remuneration or employs another to commit the murder for remuneration or the promise of remuneration;

(4) the person commits the murder while escaping or attempting to escape from the penal institution;

(5) the person, while incarcerated in a penal institution, murders another:

(A) who is employed in the operation of the penal institution; or

(B) with the intent to establish, maintain, or participate in a combination or in the profits of a combination;

(6) the person:

(A) while incarcerated for an offense under this section or Section 19.02, murders another; or

(B) while serving a sentence of life imprisonment or a term of 99 years for an offense under Section 20.04, 22.021, or 29.03, murders another;

(7) the person murders more than one person:

(A) during the same criminal transaction; or

(B) during different criminal transactions but the murders are committed pursuant to the same scheme or course of conduct; or

(8) the person murders an individual under six years of age.

(b) An offense under this section is a capital felony.

(c) If the jury or, when authorized by law, the judge does not find beyond a reasonable doubt that the defendant is guilty of an offense under this section, he may be convicted of murder or of any other lesser included offense.

*(This Section is exempt from the repeal of the Penal Code, L.1991, 2nd C.S., chap. 10(11.17), eff. 9/1/94; chgd. by L.1991, chap. 652(13); L.1993, chap. 900(1.01), eff. 9/1/94.)*

### §19.04. Manslaughter.

(a) A person commits an offense if he recklessly causes the death of an individual.

(b) An offense under this section is a felony of the second degree.

*(Deleted by amendment and renum. from §19.05 and chgd. by L.1993, chap. 900(1.01), eff. 9/1/94.)*

### §19.05. Criminally negligent homicide.

(a) A person commits an offense if he causes the death of an individual by criminal negligence.

(b) An offense under this section is a state jail felony.

*(Renumbered from §19.07 and chgd. by L.1993, chap. 900(1.01), eff. 9/1/94.)*

**§19.06.** *(Deleted by amendment by L.1993, chap. 900(1.01), eff. 9/1/94.)*

**§19.07.** *(Renumbered to §19.05 by L.1993, chap. 900(1.01), eff. 9/1/94.)*

## CHAPTER 20. KIDNAPPING AND UNLAWFUL RESTRAINT

*(Heading chgd. by L.1997, chap. 707(1(a)), eff. 9/1/97.)*

Section



### §20.01. Definitions.

In this chapter:

(1) "Restrain" means to restrict a person's movements without consent, so as to interfere substantially with the person's liberty, by moving the person from one place to another or by confining the person. Restraint is "without consent" if it is accomplished by:

(A) force, intimidation, or deception; or

(B) any means, including acquiescence of the victim, if:

(i) the victim is a child who is less than 14 years of age or an incompetent person and the parent, guardian, or person or institution acting in loco parentis has not acquiesced in the movement or confinement; or

(ii) the victim is a child who is 14 years of age or older and younger than 17 years of age, the victim is taken outside of the state and outside a 120-mile radius from the victim's residence, and the parent, guardian, or person or institution acting in loco parentis has not acquiesced in the movement.

(2) "Abduct" means to restrain a person with intent to prevent his liberation by:

(A) secreting or holding him in a place where he is not likely to be found; or

(B) using or threatening to use deadly force.

(3) "Relative" means a parent or stepparent, ancestor, sibling, or uncle or aunt, including an adoptive relative of the same degree through marriage or adoption.

*(Chgd. by L.1993, chap. 900(1.01); L.1999, chap. 790(1), eff. 9/1/99.)*

### §20.02. Unlawful restraint.

(a) A person commits an offense if he intentionally or knowingly restrains another person.

(b) It is an affirmative defense to prosecution under this section that:

(1) the person restrained was a child younger than 14 years of age;

(2) the actor was a relative of the child; and

(3) the actor's sole intent was to assume lawful control of the child.

Printed in the U.S.A.

(c) An offense under this section is a Class A misdemeanor unless:

(1) the person restrained was a child younger than 17 years of age, in which event the offense is a state jail felony; or

(2) the actor recklessly exposes the victim to a substantial risk of serious bodily injury, in which event it is a felony of the third degree.

(d) It is no offense to detain or move another under this section when it is for the purpose of effecting a lawful arrest or detaining an individual lawfully arrested.

(e) It is an affirmative defense to prosecution under this section that:

(1) the person restrained was a child who is 14 years of age or older and younger than 17 years of age;

(2) the actor does not restrain the child by force, intimidation, or deception; and

(3) the actor is not more than three years older than the child.

*(Chgd. by L.1993, chap. 900(1.01); L.1997, chap. 707(1(b)), (2); L.1999, chap. 790(2), eff. 9/1/99.)*



### §20.03. Kidnapping.

(a) A person commits an offense if he intentionally or knowingly abducts another person.

(b) It is an affirmative defense to prosecution under this section that:

(1) the abduction was not coupled with intent to use or to threaten to use deadly force;

(2) the actor was a relative of the person abducted; and

(3) the actor's sole intent was to assume lawful control of the victim.

(c) An offense under this section is a felony of the third degree.

*(Chgd. by L.1993, chap. 900(1.01), eff. 9/1/94.)*

### §20.04. Aggravated kidnapping.

(a) A person commits an offense if he intentionally or knowingly abducts another person with the intent to:

(1) hold him for ransom or reward;

(2) use him as a shield or hostage;

(3) facilitate the commission of a felony or the flight after the attempt or commission of a felony;

(4) inflict bodily injury on him or violate or abuse him sexually;

(5) terrorize him or a third person; or

(6) interfere with the performance of any governmental or political function.

(b) A person commits an offense if the person intentionally or knowingly abducts another person and uses or exhibits a deadly weapon during the commission of the offense.

(c) Except as provided by Subsection (d), an offense under this section is a felony of the first degree.

(d) At the punishment stage of a trial, the defendant may raise the issue as to whether he voluntarily released the victim in a safe place. If the defendant proves the issue in the affirmative by a preponderance of the evidence, the offense is a felony of the second degree.

*(Chgd. by L.1993, chap. 900(1.01); L.1995, chap. 318(4), eff. 9/1/95.)*

### §20.05. Unlawful transport.

(a) A person commits an offense if the person for pecuniary benefit transports an individual in a manner that:

(1) is designed to conceal the individual from local, state, or federal law enforcement authorities; and

(2) creates a substantial likelihood that the individual will suffer serious bodily injury or death.

(b) An offense under this section is a state jail felony.

*(Added by L.1999, chap. 1014(1), eff. 9/1/99.)*

## CHAPTER 21. SEXUAL OFFENSES

Section

### §21.01. Definitions.

In this chapter:

(1) "Deviate sexual intercourse" means:

(A) any contact between any part of the genitals of one person and the mouth or anus of another person; or

(B) the penetration of the genitals or the anus of another person with an object.

(2) "Sexual contact" means any touching of the anus, breast, or any part of the genitals of another person with intent to arouse or gratify the sexual desire of any person.

(3) "Sexual intercourse" means any penetration of the female sex organ by the male sex organ.

*(Chgd. by L.1993, chap. 900(1.01), eff. 9/1/94.)*

### §21.06. Homosexual conduct.

(a) A person commits an offense if he engages in deviate sexual intercourse with another individual of the same sex.

(b) An offense under this section is a Class C misdemeanor.

*(Chgd. by L.1993, chap. 900(1.01), eff. 9/1/94.)*

### §21.07. Public lewdness.

(a) A person commits an offense if he knowingly engages in any of the following acts in a public place or, if not in a public place, he is reckless about whether another is present who will be offended or alarmed by his:

(1) act of sexual intercourse;

(2) act of deviate sexual intercourse;

(3) act of sexual contact;

(4) act involving contact between the person's mouth or genitals and the anus or genitals of an animal or fowl.

(b) An offense under this section is a Class A misdemeanor.

*(Chgd. by L.1993, chap. 900(1.01), eff. 9/1/94.)*

### §21.08. Indecent exposure.

(a) A person commits an offense if he exposes his anus or any part of his genitals with intent to arouse or gratify the sexual desire of any person, and he is reckless about whether another is present who will be offended or alarmed by his act.

(b) An offense under this section is a Class B misdemeanor.

*(Chgd. by L.1993, chap. 900(1.01), eff. 9/1/94.)*

### §21.11. Indecency with a child.

(a) A person commits an offense if, with a child younger than 17 years and not his spouse, whether the child is of the same or opposite sex, he:

(1) engages in sexual contact with the child; or

(2) exposes his anus or any part of his genitals, knowing the child is present, with intent to arouse or gratify the sexual desire of any person.

(b) It is an affirmative defense to prosecution under this section that the actor:

(1) was not more than three years older than the victim and of the opposite sex;

(2) did not use duress, force, or a threat against the victim at the time of the offense; and

(3) at the time of the offense:

(A) was not required under Chapter 62, Code of Criminal Procedure, as added by Chapter 668, Acts of the 75th Legislature, Regular Session, 1997, to register for life as a sex offender; or

(B) was not a person who under Chapter 62 had a reportable conviction or adjudication for an offense under this section.

(c) An offense under Subsection (a)(1) is a felony of the second degree and an offense under Subsection (a)(2) is a felony of the third degree.

*(Chgd. by L.1993, chap. 900(1.01); L.1999, chap. 1415(23), eff. 9/1/99.)*

## CHAPTER 22. ASSAULTIVE OFFENSES

Section

### §22.01. Assault.

(a) A person commits an offense if the person:

(1) intentionally, knowingly, or recklessly causes bodily injury to another, including the person's spouse;

(2) intentionally or knowingly threatens another with imminent bodily injury, including the person's spouse; or

(3) intentionally or knowingly causes physical contact with another when the person knows or should reasonably believe that the other will regard the contact as offensive or provocative.

(b) An offense under Subsection (a)(1) is a Class A misdemeanor, except that the offense is a felony of the third degree if the offense is committed against:

(1) a person the actor knows is a public servant while the public servant is lawfully discharging an official duty, or in retaliation or on account of an exercise of official power or performance of an official duty as a public servant; or

(2) a member of the defendant's family or household, if it is shown on the trial of the offense that the defendant has been previously convicted of an offense against a member of the defendant's family or household under this section.

(c) An offense under Subsection (a)(2) or (3) is a Class C misdemeanor, except that an offense under Subsection (a)(3) is a Class A misdemeanor if the offense was committed against an elderly individual or disabled individual, as those terms are defined by Section 22.04.

(d) For purposes of Subsection (b), the actor is presumed to have known the person assaulted was a public servant if the person was wearing a distinctive uniform or badge indicating the person's employment as a public servant.

(e) In this section:

(1) "Family" has the meaning assigned by Section 71.003, Family Code.

(2) "Household" has the meaning assigned by Section 71.005, Family Code.

(f) For the purposes of this section, a defendant has been previously convicted of an offense against a member of the defendant's family or a member of the defendant's household under this section if the defendant was adjudged guilty of the offense or entered a plea of guilty or nolo contendere in return for a grant of deferred adjudication, regardless of whether the sentence for the offense was ever imposed or whether the sentence was probated and the defendant was subsequently discharged from community supervision.

*(Chgd. by L.1989, chap. 739(1-3); L.1991, chaps. 14(284(23-26)), 334(1), 366(1); L.1993, chap. 900(1.01); L.1995, chaps. 318(5), 659(1); L.1997, chap. 165(27.01), (31.01(68)); L.1999, chaps. 62(15.02(a)), 1158(1), eff. 9/1/99.)*

### §22.011. Sexual assault.

(a) A person commits an offense if the person:

(1) intentionally or knowingly:

(A) causes the penetration of the anus or female sexual organ of another person by any means, without that person's consent;

(B) causes the penetration of the mouth of another person by the sexual organ of the actor, without that person's consent; or

(C) causes the sexual organ of another person, without that person's consent, to contact or penetrate the mouth, anus, or sexual organ of another person, including the actor; or

(2) intentionally or knowingly:

(A) causes the penetration of the anus or female sexual organ of a child by any means;

(B) causes the penetration of the mouth of a child by the sexual organ of the actor;

(C) causes the sexual organ of a child to contact or penetrate the mouth, anus, or sexual organ of another person, including the actor;

(D) causes the anus of a child to contact the mouth, anus, or sexual organ of another person, including the actor; or

(E) causes the mouth of a child to contact the anus or sexual organ of another person, including the actor.

(b) A sexual assault under Subsection (a)(1) is without the consent of the other person if:

(1) the actor compels the other person to submit or participate by the use of physical force or violence;

(2) the actor compels the other person to submit or participate by threatening to use force or violence against the other person, and the other person believes that the actor has the present ability to execute the threat;

(3) the other person has not consented and the actor knows the other person is unconscious or physically unable to resist;

(4) the actor knows that as a result of mental disease or defect the other person is at the time of the sexual assault incapable either of appraising the nature of the act or of resisting it;

(5) the other person has not consented and the actor knows the other person is unaware that the sexual assault is occurring;

(6) the actor has intentionally impaired the other person's power to appraise or control the other person's conduct by administering any substance without the other person's knowledge;

(7) the actor compels the other person to submit or participate by threatening to use force or violence against any person, and the other person believes that the actor has the ability to execute the threat;

(8) the actor is a public servant who coerces the other person to submit or participate;

(9) the actor is a mental health services provider or a health care services provider who causes the other person, who is a patient or former patient of the actor, to submit or participate by exploiting the other person's emotional dependency on the actor; or

(10) the actor is a clergyman who causes the other person to submit or participate by exploiting the other person's emotional dependency on the clergyman in the clergyman's professional character as spiritual adviser.

(c) In this section:

(1) "Child" means a person younger than 17 years of age who is not the spouse of the actor.

(2) "Spouse" means a person who is legally married to another.

(3) "Health care services provider" means:

(A) a physician licensed under the Medical Practice Act (Article 4495b, Texas Civil Statutes);

(B) a chiropractor licensed under Chapter 94, Acts of the 51st Legislature, Regular Session, 1949 (Article 4512b, Texas Civil Statutes);

(C) a licensed vocational nurse licensed under Chapter 118, Acts of the 52nd Legislature, 1951 (Article 4528c, Texas Civil Statutes);

(D) a physical therapist licensed under Chapter 836, Acts of the 62nd Legislature, Regular Session, 1971 (Article 4512e, Texas Civil Statutes);

(E) a physician assistant licensed under the Physician Assistant Licensing Act (Article 4495b-1, Texas Civil Statutes); or

(F) a registered nurse or an advanced practice nurse licensed under Chapter 7, Title 71, Revised Statutes.

(4) "Mental health services provider" means an individual, licensed or unlicensed, who performs or purports to perform mental health services, including a:

(A) licensed social worker as defined by Section 50.001, Human Resources Code;

(B) chemical dependency counselor as defined by Section 1, Chapter 635, Acts of the 72nd Legislature, Regular Session, 1991 (Article 4512*o*, Vernon's Texas Civil Statutes);

(C) licensed professional counselor as defined by Section 2, Licensed Professional Counselor Act (Article 4512g, Vernon's Texas Civil Statutes);

(D) licensed marriage and family therapist as defined by Section 2, Licensed Marriage and Family Therapist Act (Article 4512c-1, Vernon's Texas Civil Statutes);

(E) member of the clergy;

(F) psychologist offering psychological services as defined by Section 2, Psychologists' Licensing Act (Article 4512c, Vernon's Texas Civil Statutes); or

(G) special officer for mental health assignment certified under Section 415.037, Government Code.

(d) It is a defense to prosecution under Subsection (a)(2) that the conduct consisted of medical care for the child and did not include any contact between the anus or sexual organ of the child and the mouth, anus, or sexual organ of the actor or a third party.

(e) It is an affirmative defense to prosecution under Subsection (a)(2) that:

(1) the actor was not more than three years older than the victim and at the time of the offense:

(A) was not required under Chapter 62, Code of Criminal Procedure, as added by Chapter 668, Acts of the 75th Legislature, Regular Session, 1997, to register for life as a sex offender; or

(B) was not a person who under Chapter 62 had a reportable conviction or adjudication for an offense under this section; and

(2) the victim was a child of 14 years of age or older.

(f) An offense under this section is a felony of the second degree.

(g) *(Deleted by amendment by L.1993, chap. 900(1.01), eff. 9/1/94.)*

*(Chgd. by L.1991, chap. 662(1); L.1993, chap. 900(1.01); L.1995, chaps. 273(1), 318(6); L.1997, chaps. 1031(1), (2); 1286(1); L.1999, chaps. 1102(3), 1415(24), eff. 9/1/99.)*

**§22.012.** *(Deleted by amendment by L.1993, chap. 900(1.01), eff. 9/1/94.)*



### §22.015. Coercing, soliciting, or inducing gang membership.

(a) In this section:

(1) "Child" means an individual younger than 17 years of age.

(2) "Criminal street gang" has the meaning assigned by Section 71.01.

(b) A person commits an offense if, with intent to coerce, induce, or solicit a child to actively participate in the activities of a criminal street gang, the person:

(1) threatens the child with imminent bodily injury; or

(2) causes bodily injury to the child.

(c) An offense under Subsection (b)(1) is a state jail felony. An offense under Subsection (b)(2) is a felony of the third degree.

*(Added by L.1999, chap. 708(1), eff. 9/1/99.)*

### §22.02. Aggravated assault.

(a) A person commits an offense if the person commits assault as defined in Section 22.01 and the person:

(1) causes serious bodily injury to another, including the person's spouse; or

(2) uses or exhibits a deadly weapon during the commission of the assault.

(b) An offense under this section is a felony of the second degree, except that the offense is a felony of the first degree if the offense is committed:

(1) by a public servant acting under color of the servant's office or employment;

(2) against a person the actor knows is a public servant while the public servant is lawfully discharging an official duty, or in retaliation or on account of an exercise of official power or performance of an official duty as a public servant; or

(3) in retaliation against or on account of the service of another as a witness, prospective witness, informant, or person who has reported the occurrence of a crime.

(c) The actor is presumed to have known the person assaulted was a public servant if the person was wearing a distinctive uniform or badge indicating the person's employment as a public servant.

*(Chgd. by L.1989, chap. 939(1-3); L.1991, chaps. 334(2), 903(1); L.1993, chap. 900(1.01), eff. 9/1/94.)*

### §22.021. Aggravated sexual assault.

(a) A person commits an offense:

(1) if the person:

(A) intentionally or knowingly:

(i) causes the penetration of the anus or female sexual organ of another person by any means, without that person's consent;

(ii) causes the penetration of the mouth of another person by the sexual organ of the actor, without that person's consent; or

(iii) causes the sexual organ of another person, without that person's consent, to contact or penetrate the mouth, anus, or sexual organ of another person, including the actor; or

(B) intentionally or knowingly:

(i) causes the penetration of the anus or female sexual organ of a child by any means;

(ii) causes the penetration of the mouth of a child by the sexual organ of the actor;

(iii) causes the sexual organ of a child to contact or penetrate the mouth, anus, or sexual organ of another person, including the actor;

(iv) causes the anus of a child to contact the mouth, anus, or sexual organ of another person, including the actor; or

(v) causes the mouth of a child to contact the anus or sexual organ of another person, including the actor; and

(2) if:

(A) the person:

(i) causes serious bodily injury or attempts to cause the death of the victim or another person in the course of the same criminal episode;

(ii) by acts or words places the victim in fear that death, serious bodily injury, or kidnapping will be imminently inflicted on any person;

(iii) by acts or words occurring in the presence of the victim threatens to cause the death, serious bodily injury, or kidnapping of any person;

(iv) uses or exhibits a deadly weapon in the course of the same criminal episode;

(v) acts in concert with another who engages in conduct described by Subdivision (1) directed toward the same victim and occurring during the course of the same criminal episode; or

(vi) administers or provides flunitrazepam, otherwise known as rohypnol, or gamma hydroxybutyrate to the victim of the offense with the intent of facilitating the commission of the offense;

(B) the victim is younger than 14 years of age; or

(C) the victim is 65 years of age or older.

(b) In this section, "child" has the meaning assigned that term by Section 22.011(c).

(c) An aggravated sexual assault under this section is without the consent of the other person if the aggravated sexual assault occurs under the same circumstances listed in Section 22.011(b).

(d) The defense provided by Section 22.011(d) applies to this section.

(e) An offense under this section is a felony of the first degree.

*(Chgd. by L.1993, chap. 900(1.01); L.1995, chap. 318(7); L.1997, chap. 1286(2); L.1999, chap. 417(1), eff. 9/1/99.)*

**§22.03.** *(Deleted by amendment by L.1993, chap. 900(1.01), eff. 9/1/94.)*

## §22.04. Injury to a child, elderly individual, or disabled individual.

(a) A person commits an offense if he intentionally, knowingly, recklessly, or with criminal negligence, by act or intentionally, knowingly, or recklessly by omission, causes to a child, elderly individual, or disabled individual:

(1) serious bodily injury;

(2) serious mental deficiency, impairment, or injury; or

(3) bodily injury.

(b) An omission that causes a condition described by Subsections (a)(1) through (a)(3) is conduct constituting an offense under this section if:

(1) the actor has a legal or statutory duty to act; or

(2) the actor has assumed care, custody, or control of a child, elderly individual, or disabled individual.

(c) In this section:

(1) "Child" means a person 14 years of age or younger.

(2) "Elderly individual" means a person 65 years of age or older.

(3) "Disabled individual" means a person older than 14 years of age who by reason of age or physical or mental disease, defect, or injury is substantially unable to protect himself from harm or to provide food, shelter, or medical care for himself.

(d) The actor has assumed care, custody, or control if he has by act, words, or course of conduct acted so as to cause a reasonable person to conclude that he has accepted responsibility for protection, food, shelter, and medical care for a child, elderly individual, or disabled individual.

(e) An offense under Subsection (a)(1) or (2) is a felony of the first degree when the conduct is committed intentionally or knowingly. When the conduct is engaged in recklessly it shall be a felony of the second degree.

(f) An offense under Subsection (a)(3) is a felony of the third degree when the conduct is committed intentionally or knowingly. When the conduct is engaged in recklessly it shall be a state jail felony.

(g) An offense under Subsection (a) when the person acts with criminal negligence shall be a state jail felony.

(h) A person who is subject to prosecution under both this section and another section of this code may be prosecuted under either or both sections. Section 3.04 does not apply to criminal episodes prosecuted under both this section and another section of this code. If a criminal episode is prosecuted under both this section and another section of this code and sentences are assessed for convictions under both sections, the sentences shall run concurrently.

(i) It is an affirmative defense to prosecution under Subsection (b)(2) that before the offense the actor:

(1) notified in person the child, elderly individual, or disabled individual that he would no longer provide any of the care described by Subsection (d); and

(2) notified in writing the parents or person other than himself acting in loco parentis to the child, elderly individual, or disabled individual that he would no longer provide any of the care described by Subsection (d); or

(3) notified in writing the Department of Protective and Regulatory Services that he would no longer provide any of the care set forth in Subsection (d).

(j) Written notification under Subsection (i)(2) or (i)(3) is not effective unless it contains the name and address of the actor, the name and address of the child, elderly individual, or disabled individual, the type of care provided by the actor, and the date the care was discontinued.

(k)(1) It is a defense to prosecution under this section that the act or omission consisted of:

(A) reasonable medical care occurring under the direction of or by a licensed physician; or

(B) emergency medical care administered in good faith and with reasonable care by a person not licensed in the healing arts.

(2) It is an affirmative defense to prosecution under this section that the act or omission was based on treatment in accordance with the tenets and practices of a recognized religious method of healing with a generally accepted record of efficacy. It is an affirmative defense to prosecution for a person charged with an act of omission under this section causing to a child, elderly individual, or disabled individual a condition described by Subsection (a)(1), (2), or (3) that:

(A) there is no evidence that, on the date prior to the offense charged, the defendant was aware of an incident of injury to the child, elderly individual, or disabled individual and failed to report the incident; and

(B) the person:

(i) was a victim of family violence, as that term is defined by Section 71.004, Family Code, committed by a person who is also charged with an offense against the child, elderly individual, or disabled individual under this section or any other section of this title;

(ii) did not cause a condition described by Subsection (a)(1), (2), or (3); and

(iii) did not reasonably believe at the time of the omission that an effort to prevent the person also charged with an offense against the child, elderly individual, or disabled individual from committing the offense would have an effect.

*(Chgd. by L.1989, chap. 357(1); L.1991, chap. 497(1); L.1993, chap. 900(1.01); L.1995, chap. 76(8.139); L.1999, chap. 62(15.02(b)), eff. 9/1/99.)*

### §22.041. Abandoning or endangering child.

(a) In this section, "abandon" means to leave a child in any place without providing reasonable and necessary care for the child, under circumstances under which no reasonable, similarly situated adult would leave a child of that age and ability.

(b) A person commits an offense if, having custody, care, or control of a child younger than 15 years, he intentionally abandons the child in any place under circumstances that expose the child to an unreasonable risk of harm.

(c) A person commits an offense if he intentionally, knowingly, recklessly, or with criminal negligence, by act or omission, engages in conduct that places a child younger than 15 years in imminent danger of death, bodily injury, or physical or mental impairment.

(d) Except as provided by Subsection (e), an offense under Subsection (b) is:

(1) a state jail felony if the actor abandoned the child with intent to return for the child; or

(2) a felony of the third degree if the actor abandoned the child without intent to return for the child.

(e) An offense under Subsection (b) is a felony of the second degree if the actor abandons the child under circumstances that a reasonable person would believe would place the child in imminent danger of death, bodily injury, or physical or mental impairment.

(f) An offense under Subsection (c) is a state jail felony.

(g) It is a defense to prosecution under Subsection (c) that the act or omission enables the child to practice for or participate in an organized athletic event and that appropriate safety equipment and procedures are employed in the event.

(h) It is an affirmative defense to prosecution under Subsection (b) that the actor voluntarily delivered the child to an emergency medical services provider under Section 262.301, Family Code.

*(Chgd. by L.1989, chap. 904(1); L.1993, chap. 900(1.01); L.1997, chap. 687(1); L.1999, chap. 1087(3), eff. 9/1/99.)*

## §22.05. Deadly conduct.

(a) A person commits an offense if he recklessly engages in conduct that places another in imminent danger of serious bodily injury.

(b) A person commits an offense if he knowingly discharges a firearm at or in the direction of:

(1) one or more individuals; or

(2) a habitation, building, or vehicle and is reckless as to whether the habitation, building, or vehicle is occupied.

(c) Recklessness and danger are presumed if the actor knowingly pointed a firearm at or in the direction of another whether or not the actor believed the firearm to be loaded.

(d) For purposes of this section, "building," "habitation," and "vehicle" have the meanings assigned those terms by Section 30.01.

(e) An offense under Subsection (a) is a Class A misdemeanor. An offense under Subsection (b) is a felony of the third degree.

*(Chgd. by L.1993, chap. 900(1.01), eff. 9/1/94.)*

## §22.06. Consent as defense to assaultive conduct.

The victim's effective consent or the actor's reasonable belief that the victim consented to the actor's conduct is a defense to prosecution under Section 22.01 (Assault), 22.02 (Aggravated Assault), or 22.05 (Deadly Conduct) if:

(1) the conduct did not threaten or inflict serious bodily injury; or

(2) the victim knew the conduct was a risk of:

(A) his occupation;

(B) recognized medical treatment; or

(C) a scientific experiment conducted by recognized methods.

*(Chgd. by L.1993, chap. 900(1.01), eff. 9/1/94.)*

## §22.07. Terroristic threat.

(a) A person commits an offense if he threatens to commit any offense involving violence to any person or property with intent to:

(1) cause a reaction of any type to his threat by an official or volunteer agency organized to deal with emergencies;

(2) place any person in fear of imminent serious bodily injury; or

(3) prevent or interrupt the occupation or use of a building; room; place of assembly; place to which the public has access; place of employment or occupation; aircraft, automobile, or other form of conveyance; or other public place; or

(4) cause impairment or interruption of public communications, public transportation, public water, gas, or power supply or other public service.

(b) An offense under Subdivision (1) or (2) of Subsection (a) is a Class B misdemeanor. An offense under Subdivision (3) of Subsection (a) is a Class A misdemeanor. An offense under Subdivision (4) of Subsection (a) is a felony of the third degree.

*(Chgd. by L.1993, chap. 900(1.01), eff. 9/1/94.)*

## §22.08. Aiding suicide.

(a) A person commits an offense if, with intent to promote or assist the commission of suicide by another, he aids or attempts to aid the other to commit or attempt to commit suicide.

(b) An offense under this section is a Class C misdemeanor unless the actor's conduct causes suicide or attempted suicide that results in serious bodily injury, in which event the offense is a state jail felony.

*(Chgd. by L.1993, chap. 900(1.01), eff. 9/1/94.)*

## §22.09. Tampering with consumer product.

(a) In this section:

(1) "Consumer Product" means any product offered for sale to or for consumption by the public and includes "food" and "drugs" as those terms are defined in Section 431.002, Health and Safety Code.

(2) "Tamper" means to alter or add a foreign substance to a consumer product to make it probable that the consumer product will cause serious bodily injury.

(b) A person commits an offense if he knowingly or intentionally tampers with a consumer product knowing that the consumer product will be offered for sale to the public or as a gift to another.

(c) A person commits an offense if he knowingly or intentionally threatens to tamper with a consumer product with the intent to cause fear, to affect the sale of the consumer product, or to cause bodily injury to any person.

(d) An offense under Subsection (b) is a felony of the second degree unless a person suffers serious bodily injury, in which event it is a felony of the first degree. An offense under Subsection (c) is a felony of the third degree.

*(Chgd. by L.1989, chap. 1008(1); L.1991, chap. 14(284(32)); L.1993, chap. 900(1.01), eff. 9/1/94.)*

### §22.10. Leaving a child in a vehicle.

(a) A person commits an offense if he intentionally or knowingly leaves a child in a motor vehicle for longer than five minutes, knowing that the child is:

(1) younger than seven years of age; and

(2) not attended by an individual in the vehicle who is 14 years of age or older.

(b) An offense under this section is a Class C misdemeanor.

*(Chgd. by L.1993, chap. 900(1.01), eff. 9/1/94.)*

### §22.11. Harassment by persons in certain correctional facilities.

(a) A person commits an offense if the person, while imprisoned or confined in a secure correctional facility or a facility operated by or under contract with the Texas Youth Commission and with intent to harass, alarm, or annoy another person, causes the other person to contact the blood, seminal fluid, urine, or feces of the actor or any other person.

(b) An offense under this section is a felony of the third degree.

(c) If conduct constituting an offense under this section also constitutes an offense under another section of this code, the actor may be prosecuted under either section.

*(Added by L.1999, chap. 335(1), eff. 9/1/99.)*



# TITLE 6. OFFENSES AGAINST THE FAMILY



## CHAPTER 25. OFFENSES AGAINST THE FAMILY



### §25.01. Bigamy.

(a) An individual commits an offense if:

(1) he is legally married and he:

(A) purports to marry or does marry a person other than his spouse in this state, or any other state or foreign country, under circumstances that would, but for the actor's prior marriage, constitute a marriage; or

(B) lives with a person other than his spouse in this state under the appearance of being married; or

(2) he knows that a married person other than his spouse is married and he:

(A) purports to marry or does marry that person in this state, or any other state or foreign country, under circumstances that would, but for the person's prior marriage, constitute a marriage; or

(B) lives with that person in this state under the appearance of being married.

(b) For purposes of this section, "under the appearance of being married" means holding out that the parties are married with cohabitation, and an intent to be married by either party.

(c) It is a defense to prosecution under Subsection (a)(1) that the actor reasonably believed that his marriage was void or had been dissolved by death, divorce, or annulment.

(d) For the purposes of this section, the lawful wife or husband of the actor may testify both for or against the actor concerning proof of the original marriage.

(e) An offense under this section is a Class A misdemeanor.

*(Chgd. by L.1993, chap. 900(1.01), eff. 9/1/94.)*

### §25.02. Prohibited sexual conduct.

(a) An individual commits an offense if he engages in sexual intercourse or deviate sexual intercourse with a person he knows to be, without regard to legitimacy:

(1) his ancestor or descendant by blood or adoption;

(2) his stepchild or stepparent, while the marriage creating that relationship exists;

(3) his parent's brother or sister of the whole or half blood;

(4) his brother or sister of the whole or half blood or by adoption; or

(5) the children of his brother or sister of the whole or half blood or by adoption.

(b) For purposes of this section:

(1) "Deviate sexual intercourse" means any contact between the genitals of one person and the mouth or anus of another person with intent to arouse or gratify the sexual desire of any person.

(2) "Sexual intercourse" means any penetration of the female sex organ by the male sex organ.

(c) An offense under this section is a felony of the third degree.

*(Chgd. by L.1993, chap. 900(1.01), eff. 9/1/94.)*

### §25.03. Interference with child custody.

(a) A person commits an offense if he takes or retains a child younger than 18 years when he:

(1) knows that his taking or retention violates the express terms of a judgment or order of a court disposing of the child's custody; or

(2) has not been awarded custody of the child by a court of competent jurisdiction, knows that a suit for divorce or a civil suit or application for habeas corpus to dispose of the child's custody has been filed, and takes the child out of the geographic area of the counties composing the judicial district if the court is a district court or the county if the court is a statutory county court, without the permission of the court and with the intent to deprive the court of authority over the child.

(b) A noncustodial parent commits an offense if, with the intent to interfere with the lawful custody of a child younger than 18 years, he knowingly entices or persuades the child to leave the custody of the custodial parent, guardian, or person standing in the stead of the custodial parent or guardian of the child.

(c) It is a defense to prosecution under Subsection (a)(2) that the actor returned the child to the geographic area of the counties composing the judicial district if the court is a district court or the county if the court is a statutory county court, within three days after the date of the commission of the offense.

(d) An offense under this section is a state jail felony.

*(Chgd. by L.1989, chap. 830(1); L.1993, chap. 900(1.01), eff. 9/1/94.)*

### §25.031. Agreement to abduct from custody.

(a) A person commits an offense if the person agrees, for remuneration or the promise of remuneration, to abduct a child younger than 18 years of age by force, threat of force, misrepresentation, stealth, or unlawful entry, knowing that the child is under the care and control of a person having custody or physical possession of the child under a court order or under the care and control of another person who is exercising care and control with the consent of a person having custody or physical possession under a court order.

(b) An offense under this section is a state jail felony.

*(Chgd. by L.1993, chap. 900(1.01), eff. 9/1/94.)*

### §25.04. Enticing a child.

(a) A person commits an offense if, with the intent to interfere with the lawful custody of a child younger than 18 years, he knowingly entices, persuades, or takes the child from the custody of the parent or guardian or person standing in the stead of the parent or guardian of such child.

(b) An offense under this section is a Class B misdemeanor, unless it is shown on the trial of the offense that the actor intended to commit a felony against the child, in which event an offense under this section is a felony of the third degree.

*(Chgd. by L.1993, chap. 900(1.01); L.1999, chap. 685(7), eff. 9/1/99.)*

## §25.05. Criminal nonsupport.

(a) An individual commits an offense if he intentionally or knowingly fails to provide support for his child younger than 18 years of age, or for his child who is the subject of a court order requiring the individual to support the child.

(b) For purposes of this section, "child" includes a child born out of wedlock whose paternity has either been acknowledged by the actor or has been established in a civil suit under the Family Code or the law of another state.

(c) Under this section, a conviction may be had on the uncorroborated testimony of a party to the offense.

(d) It is an affirmative defense to prosecution under this section that the actor could not provide support for his child.

(e) The pendency of a prosecution under this section does not affect the power of a court to enter an order for child support under the Family Code.

(f) An offense under this section is a state jail felony.

*(Chgd. by L.1993, chap. 900(1.01), eff. 9/1/94.)*



## §25.06. Harboring runaway child.

(a) A person commits an offense if he knowingly harbors a child and he is criminally negligent about whether the child:

(1) is younger than 18 years; and

(2) has escaped from the custody of a peace officer, a probation officer, the Texas Youth Council, or a detention facility for children, or is voluntarily absent from the child's home without the consent of the child's parent or guardian for a substantial length of time or without the intent to return.

(b) It is a defense to prosecution under this section that the actor was related to the child within the second degree by consanguinity or affinity, as determined under Chapter 573, Government Code.

(c) It is a defense to prosecution under this section that the actor notified:

(1) the person or agency from which the child escaped or a law enforcement agency of the presence of the child within 24 hours after discovering that the child had escaped from custody; or

(2) a law enforcement agency or a person at the child's home of the presence of the child within 24 hours after discovering that the child was voluntarily absent from home without the consent of the child's parent or guardian.

(d) An offense under this section is a Class A misdemeanor.

(e) On the receipt of a report from a peace officer, probation officer, the Texas Youth Council, a foster home, or a detention facility for children that a child has escaped its custody or upon receipt of a report from a parent, guardian, conservator, or legal custodian that a child is missing, a law enforcement agency shall immediately enter a record of the child into the National Crime Information Center.

*(Chgd. by L.1991, chap. 561(40); deleted by amendment and renum. from §25.07 and chgd. by L.1993, chap. 900(1.01); chgd. by L.1995, chap. 76(5.95(27)), eff. 9/1/95.)*

## §25.07. Violation of protective order or magistrate's order.

(a) A person commits an offense if, in violation of an order issued under Section 6.504 or Chapter 85, Family Code, under Article 17.292, Code of Criminal Procedure, or by another jurisdiction as provided by Chapter 88, Family Code, the person knowingly or intentionally:

(1) commits family violence or an act in furtherance of an offense under Section 42.072;

(2) communicates:

(A) directly with a protected individual or a member of the family or household in a threatening or harassing manner;

(B) a threat through any person to a protected individual or a member of the family or household; and

(C) in any manner with the protected individual or a member of the family or household except through the person's attorney or a person appointed by the court, if the order prohibits any communication with a protected individual or a member of the family or household; or

(3) goes to or near any of the following places as specifically described in the order:

(A) the residence or place of employment or business of a protected individual or a member of the family or household; or

(B) any child care facility, residence, or school where a child protected by the order normally resides or attends.

(b) For the purposes of this section, "family violence," "family," "household," and "member of a household" have the meanings assigned by Chapter 71, Family Code.

(c) If conduct constituting an offense under this section also constitutes an offense under another section of this code, the actor may be prosecuted under either section or under both sections.

(d) Reconciliatory actions or agreements made by persons affected by an order do not affect the validity of the order or the duty of a peace officer to enforce this section.

(e) A peace officer investigating conduct that may constitute an offense under this section for a violation of an order may not arrest a person protected by that order for a violation of that order.

(f) It is not a defense to prosecution under this section that certain information has been excluded, as provided by Section 85.007, Family Code, or Article 17.292, Code of Criminal Procedure, from an order to which this section applies.

(g) An offense under this section is a Class A misdemeanor unless it is shown on the trial of the offense that the defendant has previously been convicted under this section two or more times or has violated the protective order by committing an assault or the offense of stalking, in which event the offense is a third degree felony.
*(Chgd. by L.1989, chaps. 614(23-26), 739(4-7); L.1991, chap. 366(2); renum. from §25.08 and chgd. by L.1993, chap. 900(1.01); chgd. by L.1995, chaps. 658(2),(3), 660(1), 1024(23); L.1997, chaps. 1(2), 1193(21); L.1999, chap. 62(15.02(c)), eff. 9/1/99.)*

### §25.08. Sale or purchase of child.

(a) A person commits an offense if he:

(1) possesses a child younger than 18 years of age or has the custody, conservatorship, or guardianship of a child younger than 18 years of age, whether or not he has actual possession of the child, and he offers to accept, agrees to accept, or accepts a thing of value for the delivery of the child to another or for the possession of the child by another for purposes of adoption; or

(2) offers to give, agrees to give, or gives a thing of value to another for acquiring or maintaining the possession of a child for the purpose of adoption.

(b) It is an exception to the application of this section that the thing of value is:

(1) a fee paid to a child-placing agency as authorized by law;

(2) a fee paid to an attorney or physician for services rendered in the usual course of legal or medical practice; or

(3) a reimbursement of legal or medical expenses incurred by a person for the benefit of the child.

(c) An offense under this section is a felony of the third degree.
*(Renumbered from §25.11 and chgd. by L.1993, chap. 900(1.01), eff. 9/1/94.)*

### §25.09. Advertising for placement of child.

(a) A person commits an offense if the person advertises in the public media that the person will place a child for adoption or will provide or obtain a child for adoption.

(b) This section does not apply to a licensed child-placing agency that is identified in the advertisement as a licensed child-placing agency.

(c) An offense under this section is a Class A misdemeanor unless the person has been convicted previously under this section, in which event the offense is a felony of the third degree.

(d) In this section:

(1) "Child" has the meaning assigned by Section 101.003, Family Code.

(2) "Public media" has the meaning assigned by Section 38.01. The term also includes communications through the use of the Internet or another public computer network.
*(Added by L.1997, chap. 561(31), eff. 9/1/97.)*

**§25.11.** *(Renumbered to §25.08 by L.1993, chap. 900(1.01), eff. 9/1/94.)*

## TITLE 7. OFFENSES AGAINST PROPERTY

## CHAPTER 28. ARSON, CRIMINAL MISCHIEF, AND OTHER PROPERTY DAMAGE OR DESTRUCTION

Section


### §28.01. Definitions.

In this chapter:

(1) "Habitation" means a structure or vehicle that is adapted for the overnight accommodation of persons and includes:

(A) each separately secured or occupied portion of the structure or vehicle; and

(B) each structure appurtenant to or connected with the structure or vehicle.

(2) "Building" means any structure or enclosure intended for use or occupation as a habitation or for some purpose of trade, manufacture, ornament, or use.

(3) "Property" means:

(A) real property;

(B) tangible or intangible personal property, including anything severed from land; or

(C) a document, including money, that represents or embodies anything of value.

(4) "Vehicle" includes any device in, on, or by which any person or property is or may be propelled, moved, or drawn in the normal course of commerce or transportation.

(5) "Open-space land" means real property that is undeveloped for the purpose of human habitation.

(6) "Controlled burning" means the burning of unwanted vegetation with the consent of the owner of the property on which the vegetation is located and in such a manner that the fire is controlled and limited to a designated area.

*(Chgd. by L.1989, chap. 31(1); L.1993, chap. 900(1.01), eff. 9/1/94.)*

### §28.02. Arson.

(a) A person commits an offense if he starts a fire or causes an explosion with intent to destroy or damage:

(1) any vegetation, fence, or structure on open-space land; or

(2) any building, habitation, or vehicle:

(A) knowing that it is within the limits of an incorporated city or town;

(B) knowing that it is insured against damage or destruction;

(C) knowing that it is subject to a mortgage or other security interest;

(D) knowing that it is located on property belonging to another;

(E) knowing that it has located within it property belonging to another; or

(F) when he is reckless about whether the burning or explosion will endanger the life of some individual or the safety of the property of another.

(b) It is an exception to the application of Subsection (a)(1) that the fire or explosion was a part of the controlled burning of open-space land.

(c) It is a defense to prosecution under Subsection (a)(2)(A) that prior to starting the fire or causing the explosion, the actor obtained a permit or other written authorization granted in accordance with a city ordinance, if any, regulating fires and explosions.

(d) An offense under this section is a felony of the second degree, except that the offense is a felony of the first degree if it is shown on the trial of the offense that:

(1) bodily injury or death was suffered by any person by reason of the commission of the offense; or

(2) the actor committed the offense knowing that the property intended to be damaged or destroyed was a place of worship.

*(Chgd. by L.1989, chap. 31(2); L.1993, chap. 900(1.01); L.1997, chap. 1006(1), eff. 9/1/97.)*

## §28.03. Criminal mischief.

(a) A person commits an offense if, without the effective consent of the owner:

(1) he intentionally or knowingly damages or destroys the tangible property of the owner;

(2) he intentionally or knowingly tampers with the tangible property of the owner and causes pecuniary loss or substantial inconvenience to the owner or a third person; or

(3) he intentionally or knowingly makes markings, including inscriptions, slogans, drawings, or paintings, on the tangible property of the owner.

(b) Except as provided by Subsection (f), an offense under this section is:

(1) a Class C misdemeanor if:

(A) the amount of pecuniary loss is less than $50; or

(B) except as provided in Subdivision (3)(B), it causes substantial inconvenience to others;

(2) a Class B misdemeanor if the amount of pecuniary loss is $50 or more but less than $500;

(3) a Class A misdemeanor if the amount of pecuniary loss is:

(A) $500 or more but less than $1,500; or

(B) less than $1,500 and the actor causes in whole or in part impairment or interruption of public communications, public transportation, public water, gas, or power supply, or other public service, or causes to be diverted in whole, in part, or in any manner, including installation or removal of any device for any such purpose, any public communications, public water, gas, or power supply;

(4) a state jail felony if the amount of pecuniary loss is:

(A) $1,500 or more but less than $20,000;

(B) less than $1,500, if the property damaged or destroyed is a habitation and if the damage or destruction is caused by a firearm or explosive weapon; or

(C) less than $1,500, if the property was a fence used for the production or containment of:

(i) cattle, bison, horses, sheep, swine, goats, exotic livestock, or exotic poultry; or

(ii) game animals as that term is defined by Section 63.001, Parks and Wildlife Code;

(5) a felony of the third degree if the amount of the pecuniary loss is $20,000 or more but less than $100,000;

(6) a felony of the second degree if the amount of pecuniary loss is $100,000 or more but less than $200,000; or

(7) a felony of the first degree if the amount of pecuniary loss is $200,000 or more.

(c) For the purposes of this section, it shall be presumed that a person who is receiving the economic benefit of public communications, public water, gas, or power supply, has knowingly tampered with the tangible property of the owner if the communication or supply has been:

(1) diverted from passing through a metering device; or

(2) prevented from being correctly registered by a metering device; or

(3) activated by any device installed to obtain public communications, public water, gas, or power supply without a metering device.

(d) The term "public communication, public transportation, public water, gas, or power supply, or other public service" shall mean, refer to, and include any such services subject to regulation by the Public Utility Commission of Texas, the Railroad Commission of Texas, or the Texas Natural Resource Conservation Commission or any such services enfranchised by the State of Texas or any political subdivision thereof.

(e) When more than one item of tangible property, belonging to one or more owners, is damaged, destroyed, or tampered with in violation of this section pursuant to one scheme or continuing course of conduct, the conduct may be considered as one offense, and the amounts of pecuniary loss to property resulting from the damage to, destruction of, or tampering with the property may be aggregated in determining the grade of the offense.

(f) An offense under this section is a state jail felony if the damage or destruction is inflicted on a place of worship or human burial, a public monument, or a community center that provides medical, social, or educational programs and the amount of the pecuniary loss to real property or to tangible personal property is less than $20,000.

(g) For the purposes of this section, "firearm" and "explosive weapon" have the meanings assigned those terms by Section 46.01.

*(Chgd. by L.1989, chaps. 559(1), 1253(1); 1st C.S., chap. 42(1); L.1993, chap. 900(1.01); L.1995, chap. 76(11.280); L.1997, chap. 1083(1); L.1999, chap. 686(1), eff. 9/1/99.)*

## §28.04. Reckless damage or destruction.

(a) A person commits an offense if, without the effective consent of the owner, he recklessly damages or destroys property of the owner.

(b) An offense under this section is a Class C misdemeanor.

*(Chgd. by L.1993, chap. 900(1.01), eff. 9/1/94.)*

### §28.05. Actor's interest in property.

It is no defense to prosecution under this chapter that the actor has an interest in the property damaged or destroyed if another person also has an interest that the actor is not entitled to infringe.
*(Chgd. by L.1993, chap. 900(1.01), eff. 9/1/94.)*

### §28.06. Amount of pecuniary loss.

(a) The amount of pecuniary loss under this chapter, if the property is destroyed, is:

(1) the fair market value of the property at the time and place of the destruction; or

(2) if the fair market value of the property cannot be ascertained, the cost of replacing the property within a reasonable time after the destruction.

(b) The amount of pecuniary loss under this chapter, if the property is damaged, is the cost of repairing or restoring the damaged property within a reasonable time after the damage occurred.

(c) The amount of pecuniary loss under this chapter for documents, other than those having a readily ascertainable market value, is:

(1) the amount due and collectible at maturity less any part that has been satisfied, if the document constitutes evidence of a debt; or

(2) the greatest amount of economic loss that the owner might reasonably suffer by virtue of the destruction or damage if the document is other than evidence of a debt.

(d) If the amount of pecuniary loss cannot be ascertained by the criteria set forth in Subsections (a) through (c), the amount of loss is deemed to be greater than $500 but less than $1,500.

(e) If the actor proves by a preponderance of the evidence that he gave consideration for or had a legal interest in the property involved, the value of the interest so proven shall be deducted from:

(1) the amount of pecuniary loss if the property is destroyed; or

(2) the amount of pecuniary loss to the extent of an amount equal to the ratio the value of the interest bears to the total value of the property, if the property is damaged.
*(Chgd. by L.1993, chap. 900(1.01), eff. 9/1/94.)*

### §28.07. Interference with railroad property.

(a) In this section:

(1) "Railroad property" means:

(A) a train, locomotive, railroad car, caboose, work equipment, rolling stock, safety device, switch, or connection that is owned, leased, operated, or possessed by a railroad; or

(B) a railroad track, rail, bridge, trestle, or right-of-way owned or used by a railroad.

(2) "Tamper" means to move, alter, or interfere with railroad property.

(b) A person commits an offense if the person:

(1) throws an object or discharges a firearm or weapon at a train or rail-mounted work equipment; or

(2) without the effective consent of the owner:

(A) enters or remains on railroad property, knowing that it is railroad property;

(B) tampers with railroad property;

(C) places an obstruction on a railroad track or right-of-way; or

(D) causes in any manner the derailment of a train, railroad car, or other railroad property that moves on tracks.

(c) An offense under Subsection (b)(1) is a Class B misdemeanor unless the person causes bodily injury to another, in which event the offense is a felony of the third degree.

(d) An offense under Subsection (b)(2)(A) is a Class C misdemeanor.

(e) An offense under Subsection (b)(2)(B), (b)(2)(C), or (b)(2)(D) is a Class C misdemeanor unless the person causes pecuniary loss, in which event the offense is:

(1) a Class B misdemeanor if the amount of pecuniary loss is $20 or more but less than $500;

(2) a Class A misdemeanor if the amount of pecuniary loss is $500 or more but less than $1,500;

(3) a state jail felony if the amount of pecuniary loss is $1,500 or more but less than $20,000;

(4) a felony of the third degree if the amount of the pecuniary loss is $20,000 or more but less than $100,000;

(5) a felony of the second degree if the amount of pecuniary loss is $100,000 or more but less than $200,000; or

(6) a felony of the first degree if the amount of the pecuniary loss is $200,000 or more.

(f) The conduct described in Subsection (b)(2)(A) is not an offense under this section if it is undertaken by an employee of the railroad or by a representative of a labor organization which represents or is seeking to represent the employees of the railroad as long as the employee or representative has a right to engage in such conduct under the Railway Labor Act (45 U.S.C. Section 151 et seq.).
*(Added by L.1989, chap. 908(1); chgd. by L.1993, chap. 900(1.01), eff. 9/1/94.)*

### §28.08. Graffiti.

(a) A person commits an offense if, without the effective consent of the owner, the person intentionally or knowingly makes markings, including inscriptions, slogans, drawings, or paintings, on the tangible property of the owner with:

(1) aerosol paint;

(2) an indelible marker; or

(3) an etching or engraving device.

(b) Except as provided by Subsection (d), an offense under this section is:

(1) a Class B misdemeanor if the amount of pecuniary loss is less than $500;

(2) a Class A misdemeanor if the amount of pecuniary loss is $500 or more but less than $1,500;

(3) a state jail felony if the amount of pecuniary loss is $1,500 or more but less than $20,000;

(4) a felony of the third degree if the amount of pecuniary loss is $20,000 or more but less than $100,000;

(5) a felony of the second degree if the amount of pecuniary loss is $100,000 or more but less than $200,000; or

(6) a felony of the first degree if the amount of pecuniary loss is $200,000 or more.

(c) When more than one item of tangible property, belonging to one or more owners, is marked in violation of this section pursuant to one scheme or continuing course of conduct, the conduct may be considered as one offense, and the amounts of pecuniary loss to property resulting from the marking of the property may be aggregated in determining the grade of the offense.

(d) An offense under this section is a state jail felony if:

(1) the marking is made on a school, an institution of higher education, a place of worship or human burial, a public monument, or a community center that provides medical, social, or educational programs; and

(2) the amount of the pecuniary loss to real property or to tangible personal property is less than $20,000.

(e) In this section:

(1) "Aerosol paint" means an aerosolized paint product.

(2) "Etching or engraving device" means a device that makes a delineation or impression on tangible property, regardless of the manufacturer's intended use for that device.

(3) "Indelible marker" means a device that makes a mark with a paint or ink product that is specifically formulated to be more difficult to erase, wash out, or remove than ordinary paint or ink products. *(Renumbered by L.1999, chap. 695(1), eff. 9/1/99. See other subdivision (3) below.)*

(3) "Institution of higher education" has the meaning assigned by Section 481.134, Health and Safety Code. *(Added by L.1999, chap. 166(2), eff. 9/1/99. See other subdivision (3) above.)*

(4) "School" means a private or public elementary or secondary school.

*(Added by L.1997, chap. 593(1); chgd. by L.1999, chaps. 166(1), (2), 695(1), eff. 9/1/99.)*

## CHAPTER 29. ROBBERY

Section



### §29.01. Definitions.

In this chapter:

(1) "In the course of committing theft" means conduct that occurs in an attempt to commit, during the commission, or in immediate flight after the attempt or commission of theft.

(2) "Property" means:

(A) tangible or intangible personal property including anything severed from land; or

(B) a document, including money, that represents or embodies anything of value.

*(Chgd. by L.1993, chap. 900(1.01), eff. 9/1/94.)*

### §29.02. Robbery.

(a) A person commits an offense if, in the course of committing theft as defined in Chapter 31 and with intent to obtain or maintain control of the property, he:

(1) intentionally, knowingly, or recklessly causes bodily injury to another; or

(2) intentionally or knowingly threatens or places another in fear of imminent bodily injury or death.

(b) An offense under this section is a felony of the second degree.
*(Chgd. by L.1993, chap. 900(1.01), eff. 9/1/94.)*

### §29.03. Aggravated robbery.

(a) A person commits an offense if he commits robbery as defined in Section 29.02, and he:
(1) causes serious bodily injury to another;
(2) uses or exhibits a deadly weapon; or
(3) causes bodily injury to another person or threatens or places another person in fear of imminent bodily injury or death, if the other person is:
(A) 65 years of age or older; or
(B) a disabled person.
(b) An offense under this section is a felony of the first degree.
(c) In this section, "disabled person" mean an individual with a mental, physical, or developmental disability who is substantially unable to protect himself from harm.
*(Chgd. by L.1989, chap. 357(2); L.1993, chap. 900(1.01), eff. 9/1/94.)*

## CHAPTER 30. BURGLARY AND CRIMINAL TRESPASS

Section


### §30.01. Definitions.

In this chapter:
(1) "Habitation" means a structure or vehicle that is adapted for the overnight accommodation of persons, and includes:
(A) each separately secured or occupied portion of the structure or vehicle; and
(B) each structure appurtenant to or connected with the structure or vehicle.
(2) "Building" means any enclosed structure intended for use or occupation as a habitation or for some purpose of trade, manufacture, ornament, or use.
(3) "Vehicle" includes any device in, on, or by which any person or property is or may be propelled, moved, or drawn in the normal course of commerce or transportation, except such devices as are classified as "habitation."
*(Chgd. by L.1993, chap. 900(1.01), eff. 9/1/94.)*

### §30.02. Burglary.

(a) A person commits an offense if, without the effective consent of the owner, the person:
(1) enters a habitation, or a building (or any portion of a building) not then open to the public, with intent to commit a felony, theft, or an assault; or
(2) remains concealed, with intent to commit a felony, theft, or an assault, in a building or habitation; or
(3) enters a building or habitation and commits or attempts to commit a felony, theft, or an assault.
(b) For purposes of this section, "enter" means to intrude:
(1) any part of the body; or
(2) any physical object connected with the body.
(c) Except as provided in Subsection (d), an offense under this section is a:
(1) state jail felony if committed in a building other than a habitation; or
(2) felony of the second degree if committed in a habitation.
(d) An offense under this section is a felony of the first degree if:
(1) the premises are a habitation; and
(2) any party to the offense entered the habitation with intent to commit a felony other than felony theft or committed or attempted to commit a felony other than felony theft.
*(Chgd. by L.1993, chap. 900(1.01); L.1995, chap. 318(8); L.1999, chap. 727(1), eff. 9/1/99.)*

### §30.03. Burglary of coin-operated or coin collection machines.

(a) A person commits an offense if, without the effective consent of the owner, he breaks or enters into any coin-operated machine, coin collection machine, or other coin-operated or coin collection receptacle, contrivance, apparatus, or equipment used for the purpose of providing lawful amusement, sales of goods, services, or other valuable things, or telecommunications with intent to obtain property, or services.

(b) For purposes of this section, "entry" includes every kind of entry except one made with the effective consent of the owner.

(c) An offense under this section is a Class A misdemeanor.

*(Chgd. by L.1993, chap. 900(1.01), eff. 9/1/94.)*

## §30.04. Burglary of vehicles.

(a) A person commits an offense if, without the effective consent of the owner, he breaks into or enters a vehicle or any part of a vehicle with intent to commit any felony or theft.

(b) For purposes of this section, "enter" means to intrude:

(1) any part of the body; or

(2) any physical object connected with the body.

(c) For purposes of this section, a container or trailer carried on a rail car is a part of the rail car.

(d) An offense under this section is a Class A misdemeanor unless the vehicle or part of the vehicle broken into or entered is a rail car, in which event the offense is a state jail felony.

(e) It is a defense to prosecution under this section that the actor entered a rail car or any part of a rail car and was at that time an employee or a representative of employees exercising a right under the Railway Labor Act (45 U.S.C. Section 151 et seq.).

*(Chgd. by L.1993, chap. 900(1.01); chgd. by L.1999, chap. 916(1), eff. 9/1/99.)*

## §30.05. Criminal trespass.

(a) A person commits an offense if he enters or remains on property, including an aircraft, of another without effective consent or he enters or remains in a building of another without effective consent and he:

(1) had notice that the entry was forbidden; or

(2) received notice to depart but failed to do so.

(b) For purposes of this section:

(1) "Entry" means the intrusion of the entire body.

(2) "Notice" means:

(A) oral or written communication by the owner or someone with apparent authority to act for the owner;

(B) fencing or other enclosure obviously designed to exclude intruders or to contain livestock;

(C) a sign or signs posted on the property or at the entrance to the building, reasonably likely to come to the attention of intruders, indicating that entry is forbidden;

(D) the placement of identifying purple paint marks on trees or posts on the property, provided that the marks are:

(i) vertical lines of not less than eight inches in length and not less than one inch in width;

(ii) placed so that the bottom of the mark is not less than three feet from the ground or more than five feet from the ground; and

(iii) placed at locations that are readily visible to any person approaching the property and no more than:

(a) 100 feet apart on forest land; or

(b) 1,000 feet apart on land other than forest land; or

(E) the visible presence on the property of a crop grown for human consumption that is under cultivation, in the process of being harvested, or marketable if harvested at the time of entry.

(3) "Shelter center" has the meaning assigned by Section 51.002(1), Human Resources Code.

(4) "Forest land" means land on which the trees are potentially valuable for timber products.

(5) "Agricultural land" has the meaning assigned by Section 75.001, Civil Practice and Remedies Code. *(Added by L.1999, chap. 169(1), eff. 9/1/99. See other subdivision (b)(5) below.)*

(5) "Superfund site" means a facility that:

(A) is on the National Priorities List established under Section 105 of the federal Comprehensive Environmental Response, Compensation, and Liability Act of 1980 (42 U.S.C. Section 9605); or

(B) is listed on the state registry established under Section 361.181, Health and Safety Code. *(Added by L.1999, chap. 765(1), eff. 9/1/99. See other subdivision (b)(5) above.)*

(c) It is a defense to prosecution under this section that the actor at the time of the offense was a fire fighter or emergency medical services personnel, as that term is defined by Section 773.003,

Health and Safety Code, acting in the lawful discharge of an official duty under exigent circumstances.

(d) An offense under Subsection (a) is a Class B misdemeanor, except that the offense is a Class A misdemeanor if:

(1) the offense is committed:

(A) in a habitation or a shelter center; or

(B) on a Superfund site; or

(2) the actor carries a deadly weapon on or about the actor's person during the commission of the offense. An offense under Subsection (e) is a Class C misdemeanor unless it is committed in a habitation or unless the actor carries a deadly weapon on or about the actor's person during the commission of the offense, in which event it is a Class A misdemeanor.

(e) A person commits an offense if without express consent or if without authorization provided by any law, whether in writing or other form, the person:

(1) enters or remains on agricultural land of another;

(2) is on the agricultural land and within 100 feet of the boundary of the land when apprehended; and

(3) had notice that the entry was forbidden or received notice to depart but failed to do so.

*(Chgd. by L.1989, chap. 139(1); L.1991, chap. 308(1); L.1993, chap. 900(1.01); L.1997, chap. 1229(1), (2); L.1999, chaps. 161(1), 169(1), (2), 765(1), (2), eff. 9/1/99.)*

### §30.06. Trespass by holder of license to carry concealed handgun.

(a) A license holder commits an offense if the license holder:

(1) carries a handgun under the authority of Subchapter H, Chapter 411, Government Code, on property of another without effective consent; and

(2) received notice that:

(A) entry on the property by a license holder with a concealed handgun was forbidden; or

(B) remaining on the property with a concealed handgun was forbidden and failed to depart.

(b) For purposes of this section, a person receives notice if the owner of the property or someone with apparent authority to act for the owner provides notice to the person by oral or written communication.

(c) In this section:

(1) "Entry" has the meaning assigned by Section 30.05(b).

(2) "License holder" has the meaning assigned by Section 46.035(f).

(3) "Written communication" means:

(A) a card or other document on which is written language identical to the following: "Pursuant to Section 30.06, Penal Code (trespass by holder of license to carry a concealed handgun), a person licensed under Subchapter H, Chapter 411, Government Code (concealed handgun law), may not enter this property with a concealed handgun"; or

(B) a sign posted on the property that:

(i) includes the language described by Paragraph (A) in both English and Spanish;

(ii) appears in contrasting colors with block letters at least one inch in height; and

(iii) is displayed in a conspicuous manner clearly visible to the public.

(d) An offense under this section is a Class A misdemeanor.

*(Added by L.1997, chap. 1261(23); L.1999, chap. 62(9.24), eff. 9/1/99.)*

## CHAPTER 31. THEFT

Section

## §31.01. Definitions.

In this chapter:

(1) "Deception" means:

(A) creating or confirming by words or conduct a false impression of law or fact that is likely to affect the judgment of another in the transaction, and that the actor does not believe to be true;

(B) failing to correct a false impression of law or fact that is likely to affect the judgment of another in the transaction, that the actor previously created or confirmed by words or conduct, and that the actor does not now believe to be true;

(C) preventing another from acquiring information likely to affect his judgment in the transaction;

(D) selling or otherwise transferring or encumbering property without disclosing a lien, security interest, adverse claim, or other legal impediment to the enjoyment of the property, whether the lien, security interest, claim, or impediment is or is not valid, or is or is not a matter of official record; or

(E) promising performance that is likely to affect the judgment of another in the transaction and that the actor does not intend to perform or knows will not be performed, except that failure to perform the promise in issue without other evidence of intent or knowledge is not sufficient proof that the actor did not intend to perform or knew the promise would not be performed.

(2) "Deprive" means:

(A) to withhold property from the owner permanently or for so extended a period of time that a major portion of the value or enjoyment of the property is lost to the owner;

(B) to restore property only upon payment of reward or other compensation; or

(C) to dispose of property in a manner that makes recovery of the property by the owner unlikely.

(3) "Effective consent" includes consent by a person legally authorized to act for the owner. Consent is not effective if:

(A) induced by deception or coercion;

(B) given by a person the actor knows is not legally authorized to act for the owner;

(C) given by a person who by reason of youth, mental disease or defect, or intoxication is known by the actor to be unable to make reasonable property dispositions;

(D) given solely to detect the commission of an offense; or

(E) given by a person who by reason of advanced age is known by the actor to have a diminished capacity to make informed and rational decisions about the reasonable disposition of property.

(4) "Appropriate" means:

(A) to bring about a transfer or purported transfer of title to or other nonpossessory interest in property, whether to the actor or another; or

(B) to acquire or otherwise exercise control over property other than real property.

(5) "Property" means:

(A) real property;

(B) tangible or intangible personal property including anything severed from land; or

(C) a document, including money, that represents or embodies anything of value.

(6) "Service" includes:

(A) labor and professional service;

(B) telecommunication, public utility, or transportation service;

(C) lodging, restaurant service, and entertainment; and

(D) the supply of a motor vehicle or other property for use.

(7) "Steal" means to acquire property or service by theft.

(8) "Certificate of title" has the meaning assigned by Section 501.002, Transportation Code.

(9) "Used or secondhand motor vehicle" means a used motor vehicle, as that term is defined by Section 501.002, Transportation Code.

*(Chgd. by L.1993, chap. 900(1.01); L.1997, chap. 165(30.237), eff. 9/1/97.)*

## §31.02. Consolidation of theft offenses.

Theft as defined in Section 31.03 constitutes a single offense superseding the separate offenses previously known as theft, theft by false pretext, conversion by a bailee, theft from the person, shoplifting, acquisition of property by threat, swindling, swindling by worthless check, embezzlement, extortion, receiving or concealing embezzled property, and receiving or concealing stolen property. *(Chgd. by L.1993, chap. 900(1.01), eff. 9/1/94.)*

**§31.03. Theft.**

(a) A person commits an offense if he unlawfully appropriates property with intent to deprive the owner of property.

(b) Appropriation of property is unlawful if:

(1) it is without the owner's effective consent;

(2) the property is stolen and the actor appropriates the property knowing it was stolen by another; or

(3) property in the custody of any law enforcement agency was explicitly represented by any law enforcement agent to the actor as being stolen and the actor appropriates the property believing it was stolen by another.

(c) For purposes of Subsection (b):

(1) evidence that the actor has previously participated in recent transactions other than, but similar to, that which the prosecution is based is admissible for the purpose of showing knowledge or intent and the issues of knowledge or intent are raised by the actor's plea of not guilty;

(2) the testimony of an accomplice shall be corroborated by proof that tends to connect the actor to the crime, but the actor's knowledge or intent may be established by the uncorroborated testimony of the accomplice;

(3) an actor engaged in the business of buying and selling used or secondhand personal property, or lending money on the security of personal property deposited with him, is presumed to know upon receipt by the actor of stolen property (other than a motor vehicle subject to Chapter 501, Transportation Code) that the property has been previously stolen from another if the actor pays for or loans against the property $25 or more (or consideration of equivalent value) and the actor knowingly or recklessly:

(A) fails to record the name, address, and physical description or identification number of the seller or pledgor;

(B) fails to record a complete description of the property, including the serial number, if reasonably available, or other identifying characteristics; or

(C) fails to obtain a signed warranty from the seller or pledgor that the seller or pledgor has the right to possess the property. It is the express intent of this provision that the presumption arises unless the actor complies with each of the numbered requirements;

(4) for the purposes of Subdivision (3)(A), "identification number" means driver's license number, military identification number, identification certificate, or other official number capable of identifying an individual;

(5) stolen property does not lose its character as stolen when recovered by any law enforcement agency;

(6) an actor engaged in the business of obtaining abandoned or wrecked motor vehicles or parts of an abandoned or wrecked motor vehicle for resale, disposal, scrap, repair, rebuilding, demolition, or other form of salvage is presumed to know on receipt by the actor of stolen property that the property has been previously stolen from another if the actor knowingly or recklessly:

(A) fails to maintain an accurate and legible inventory of each motor vehicle component part purchased by or delivered to the actor, including the date of purchase or delivery, the name, age, address, sex, and driver's license number of the seller or person making the delivery, the license plate number of the motor vehicle in which the part was delivered, a complete description of the part, and the vehicle identification number of the motor vehicle from which the part was removed, or in lieu of maintaining an inventory, fails to record the name and certificate of inventory number of the person who dismantled the motor vehicle from which the part was obtained;

(B) fails on receipt of a motor vehicle to obtain a certificate of authority, sales receipt, or transfer document as required by Chapter 683, Transportation Code, or a certificate of title showing that the motor vehicle is not subject to a lien or that all recorded liens on the motor vehicle have been released; or

(C) fails on receipt of a motor vehicle to immediately remove an unexpired license plate from the motor vehicle, to keep the plate in a secure and locked place, or to maintain an inventory, on forms provided by the Texas Department of Transportation, of license plates kept under this paragraph, including for each plate or set of plates the license plate number and the make, motor number, and vehicle identification number of the motor vehicle from which the plate was removed;

(7) an actor who purchases or receives a used or secondhand motor vehicle is presumed to know on receipt by the actor of the motor vehicle that the motor vehicle has been previously stolen from another if the actor knowingly or recklessly:

(A) fails to report to the Texas Department of Transportation the failure of the person who sold or delivered the motor vehicle to the actor to deliver to the actor a properly executed certificate of title to the motor vehicle at the time the motor vehicle was delivered; or

(B) fails to file with the county tax assessor-collector of the county in which the actor received the motor vehicle, not later than the 20th day after the date the actor received the motor vehicle, the registration license receipt and certificate of title or evidence of title delivered to the actor in accordance with Subchapter D, Chapter 520, Transportation Code, at the time the motor vehicle was delivered; and

(8) an actor who purchases or receives from any source other than a licensed retailer or distributor of pesticides a restricted-use pesticide or a state-limited-use pesticide or a compound, mixture, or preparation containing a restricted-use or state-limited-use pesticide is presumed to know on receipt by the actor of the pesticide or compound, mixture, or preparation that the pesticide or compound, mixture, or preparation has been previously stolen from another if the actor:

(A) fails to record the name, address, and physical description of the seller or pledgor;

(B) fails to record a complete description of the amount and type of pesticide or compound, mixture, or preparation purchased or received; and

(C) fails to obtain a signed warranty from the seller or pledgor that the seller or pledgor has the right to possess the property.

(d) It is not a defense to prosecution under this section that:

(1) the offense occurred as a result of a deception or strategy on the part of a law enforcement agency, including the use of an undercover operative or peace officer;

(2) the actor was provided by a law enforcement agency with a facility in which to commit the offense or an opportunity to engage in conduct constituting the offense; or

(3) the actor was solicited to commit the offense by a peace officer, and the solicitation was of a type that would encourage a person predisposed to commit the offense to actually commit the offense, but would not encourage a person not predisposed to commit the offense to actually commit the offense.

(e) Except as provided by Subsection (f), an offense under this section is:

(1) a Class C misdemeanor if the value of the property stolen is less than:

(A) $50; or

(B) $20 and the defendant obtained the property by issuing or passing a check or similar sight order in a manner described by Section 31.06;

(2) a Class B misdemeanor if:

(A) the value of the property stolen is:

(i) $50 or more but less than $500; or

(ii) $20 or more but less than $500 and the defendant obtained the property by issuing or passing a check or similar sight order in a manner described by Section 31.06; or

(B) the value of the property stolen is less than:

(i) $50 and the defendant has previously been convicted of any grade of theft; or

(ii) $20, the defendant has previously been convicted of any grade of theft, and the defendant obtained the property by issuing or passing a check or similar sight order in a manner described by Section 31.06;

(3) a Class A misdemeanor if the value of the property stolen is $500 or more but less than $1,500;

(4) a state jail felony if:

(A) the value of the property stolen is $1,500 or more but less than $20,000, or the property is less than 10 head of cattle, horses, or exotic livestock or exotic fowl as defined by Section 142.001, Agriculture Code, or any part thereof under the value of $20,000, or less than 100 head of sheep, swine, or goats or any part thereof under the value of $20,000;

(B) regardless of value, the property is stolen from the person of another or from a human corpse or grave;

(C) the property stolen is a firearm, as defined by Section 46.01; or

(D) the value of the property stolen is less than $1,500 and the defendant has been previously convicted two or more times of any grade of theft;

(5) a felony of the third degree if the value of the property stolen is $20,000 or more but less than $100,000, or the property is:

(A) 10 or more head of cattle, horses, or exotic livestock or exotic fowl as defined by Section 142.001, Agriculture Code, stolen during a single transaction and having an aggregate value of less than $100,000; or

(B) 100 or more head of sheep, swine, or goats stolen during a single transaction and having an aggregate value of less than $100,000;

(6) a felony of the second degree if the value of the property stolen is $100,000 or more but less than $200,000; or

(7) a felony of the first degree if the value of the property stolen is $200,000 or more.

(f) An offense described for purposes of punishment by Subsections (e)(1)-(6) is increased to the next higher category of offense if it is shown on the trial of the offense that:

(1) the actor was a public servant at the time of the offense and the property appropriated came into the actor's custody, possession, or control by virtue of his status as a public servant; or

(2) the actor was in a contractual relationship with government at the time of the offense and the property appropriated came into the actor's custody, possession, or control by virtue of the contractual relationship.

(g) For the purposes of Subsection (a), a person is the owner of exotic livestock or exotic fowl as defined by Section 142.001, Agriculture Code, only if the person qualifies to claim the animal under Section 142.0021, Agriculture Code, if the animal is an estray.

(h) In this section:

(1) "Restricted-use pesticide" means a pesticide classified as a restricted-use pesticide by the administrator of the Environmental Protection Agency under 7 U.S.C. Section 136a, as that law existed on January 1, 1995, and containing an active ingredient listed in the federal regulations adopted under that law (40 C.F.R. Section 152.175) and in effect on that date.

(2) "State-limited-use pesticide" means a pesticide classified as a state-limited-use pesticide by the Department of Agriculture under Section 76.003, Agriculture Code, as that section existed on January 1, 1995, and containing an active ingredient listed in the rules adopted under that section (4 TAC Section 7.24) as that section existed on that date.

*(Chgd. by L.1989, chaps. 245(1), 724(2); L.1991, chaps. 14(284(80)), 565(1); L.1993, chap. 900(1.01); L.1995, chaps. 318(9), 734(1), 843(1); L.1997, chaps. 165(30.238), (31.01(69)), 1153(7.01(a)), eff. 9/1/97.)*

### §31.04. Theft of service.

(a) A person commits theft of service if, with intent to avoid payment for service that he knows is provided only for compensation:

(1) he intentionally or knowingly secures performance of the service by deception, threat, or false token;

(2) having control over the disposition of services of another to which he is not entitled, he intentionally or knowingly diverts the other's services to his own benefit or to the benefit of another not entitled to them; or

(3) having control of personal property under a written rental agreement, he holds the property beyond the expiration of the rental period without the effective consent of the owner of the property, thereby depriving the owner of the property of its use in further rentals.

(b) For purposes of this section, intent to avoid payment is presumed if:

(1) the actor absconded without paying for the service or expressly refused to pay for the service in circumstances where payment is ordinarily made immediately upon rendering of the service, as in hotels, campgrounds, recreational vehicle parks, restaurants, and comparable establishments;

(2) the actor failed to return the property held under a rental agreement within 10 days after receiving notice demanding return; or

(3) the actor returns property held under a rental agreement after the expiration of the rental agreement and fails to pay the applicable rental charge for the property within 10 days after the date on which the actor received notice demanding payment.

(c) For purposes of Subsection (b)(2), notice shall be notice in writing, sent by registered or certified mail with return receipt requested or by telegram with report of delivery requested, and addressed to the actor at his address shown on the rental agreement.

(d) If written notice is given in accordance with Subsection (c), it is presumed that the notice was received not later than five days after it was sent.

(e) An offense under this section is:

(1) a Class C misdemeanor if the value of the service stolen is less than $20;

(2) a Class B misdemeanor if the value of the service stolen is $20 or more but less than $500;

(3) a Class A misdemeanor if the value of the service stolen is $500 or more but less than $1,500;

(4) a state jail felony if the value of the service stolen is $1,500 or more but less than $20,000;

(5) a felony of the third degree if the value of the service stolen is $20,000 or more but less than $100,000;

(6) a felony of the second degree if the value of the service stolen is $100,000 or more but less than $200,000; or

(7) a felony of the first degree if the value of the service stolen is $200,000 or more.

(f) Notwithstanding any other provision of this code, any police or other report of stolen vehicles by a political subdivision of this state shall include on the report any rental vehicles whose

renters have been shown to such reporting agency to be in violation of Subsection (b)(2) and shall indicate that the renting agency has complied with the notice requirements demanding return as provided in this section.
*(Chgd. by L.1991, chap. 565(15); L.1993, chap. 900(1.01); L.1995, chap. 479(1); L.1999, chap. 843(1), eff. 9/1/99.)*

## §31.05. Theft of trade secrets.

(a) For purposes of this section:

(1) "Article" means any object, material, device, or substance or any copy thereof, including a writing, recording, drawing, sample, specimen, prototype, model, photograph, microorganism, blueprint, or map.

(2) "Copy" means a facsimile, replica, photograph, or other reproduction of an article or a note, drawing, or sketch made of or from the article.

(3) "Representing" means describing, depicting, containing, constituting, reflecting or recording.

(4) "Trade secret" means the whole or any part of any scientific or technical information, design, process, procedure, formula, or improvement that has value and that the owner has taken measures to prevent from becoming available to persons other than those selected by the owner to have access for limited purposes.

(b) A person commits an offense if, without the owner's effective consent, he knowingly:

(1) steals a trade secret;

(2) makes a copy of an article representing a trade secret; or

(3) communicates or transmits a trade secret.

(c) An offense under this section is a felony of the third degree.
*(Chgd. by L.1993, chap. 900(1.01), eff. 9/1/94.)*

## §31.06. Presumption for theft by check.

(a) If the actor obtained property or secured performance of service by issuing or passing a check or similar sight order for the payment of money, when the issuer did not have sufficient funds in or on deposit with the bank or other drawee for the payment in full of the check or order as well as all other checks or orders then outstanding, it is prima facie evidence of his intent to deprive the owner of property under Section 31.03 (Theft) including a drawee or third-party holder in due course who negotiated the check or to avoid payment for service under Section 31.04 (Theft of Service) (except in the case of a postdated check or order) if:

(1) he had no account with the bank or other drawee at the time he issued the check or order; or

(2) payment was refused by the bank or other drawee for lack of funds or insufficient funds, on presentation within 30 days after issue, and the issuer failed to pay the holder in full within 10 days after receiving notice of that refusal.

(b) For purposes of Subsection (a)(2) or (f)(3), notice may be actual notice or notice in writing that:

(1) is sent by registered or certified mail with return receipt requested or by telegram with report of delivery requested;

(2) is addressed to the issuer at his address shown on:

(A) the check or order;

(B) the records of the bank or other drawee; or

(C) the records of the person to whom the check or order has been issued or passed; and

(3) contains the following statement:

"This is a demand for payment in full for a check or order not paid because of a lack of funds or insufficient funds. If you fail to make payment in full within 10 days after the date of receipt of this notice, the failure to pay creates a presumption for committing an offense, and this matter may be referred for criminal prosecution."

(c) If written notice is given in accordance with Subsection (b), it is presumed that the notice was received not later than five days after it was sent.

(d) Nothing in this section prevents the prosecution from establishing the requisite intent by direct evidence.

(e) Partial restitution does not preclude the presumption of the requisite intent under this section.

(f) If the actor obtained property by issuing or passing a check or similar sight order for the payment of money, the actor's intent to deprive the owner of the property under Section 31.03 (Theft) is presumed, except in the case of a postdated check or order, if:

(1) the actor ordered the bank or other drawee to stop payment on the check or order;

(2) the bank or drawee refused payment to the holder on presentation of the check or order within 30 days after issue;

(3) the owner gave the actor notice of the refusal of payment and made a demand to the actor for payment or return of the property; and

(4) the actor failed to:

(A) pay the holder within 10 days after receiving the demand for payment; or

(B) return the property to the owner within 10 days after receiving the demand for return of the property.

*(Chgd. by L.1991, chap. 543(2); L.1993, chap. 900(1.01); L.1995, chap. 753(1), eff. 9/1/95.)*

### §31.07. Unauthorized use of a vehicle.

(a) A person commits an offense if he intentionally or knowingly operates another's boat, airplane, or motor-propelled vehicle without the effective consent of the owner.

(b) An offense under this section is a state jail felony.

*(Chgd. by L.1993, chap. 900(1.01), eff. 9/1/94.)*

### §31.08. Value.

(a) Subject to the additional criteria of Subsections (b) and (c), value under this chapter is:

(1) the fair market value of the property or service at the time and place of the offense; or

(2) if the fair market value of the property cannot be ascertained, the cost of replacing the property within a reasonable time after the theft.

(b) The value of documents, other than those having a readily ascertainable market value, is:

(1) the amount due and collectible at maturity less that part which has been satisfied, if the document constitutes evidence of a debt; or

(2) the greatest amount of economic loss that the owner might reasonably suffer by virtue of loss of the document, if the document is other than evidence of a debt.

(c) If property or service has value that cannot be reasonably ascertained by the criteria set forth in Subsections (a) and (b), the property or service is deemed to have a value of $500 or more but less than $1,500.

(d) If the actor proves by a preponderance of the evidence that he gave consideration for or had a legal interest in the property or service stolen, the amount of the consideration or the value of the interest so proven shall be deducted from the value of the property or service ascertained under Subsection (a), (b), or (c) to determine value for purposes of this chapter.

*(Chgd. by L.1993, chap. 900(1.01), eff. 9/1/94.)*

### §31.09. Aggregation of amounts involved in theft.

When amounts are obtained in violation of this chapter pursuant to one scheme or continuing course of conduct, whether from the same or several sources, the conduct may be considered as one offense and the amounts aggregated in determining the grade of the offense. *(Chgd. by L.1993, chap. 900(1.01), eff. 9/1/94.)*

### §31.10. Actor's interest in property.

It is no defense to prosecution under this chapter that the actor has an interest in the property or service stolen if another person has the right of exclusive possession of the property. *(Chgd. by L.1993, chap. 900(1.01), eff. 9/1/94.)*

### §31.11. Tampering with identification numbers.

(a) A person commits an offense if the person:

(1) knowingly or intentionally removes, alters, or obliterates the serial number or other permanent identification marking on tangible personal property; or

(2) possesses, sells, or offers for sale tangible personal property and:

(A) the actor knows that the serial number or other permanent identification marking has been removed, altered, or obliterated; or

(B) a reasonable person in the position of the actor would have known that the serial number or other permanent identification marking has been removed, altered, or obliterated.

(b) It is an affirmative defense to prosecution under this section that the person was:

(1) the owner or acting with the effective consent of the owner of the property involved;

(2) a peace officer acting in the actual discharge of official dutes; or

(3) acting with respect to a number assigned to a vehicle by the Texas Department of Transportation and the person was:

(A) in the actual discharge of official duties as an employee or agent of the department; or

(B) in full compliance with the rules of the department as an applicant for an assigned number approved by the department.

(c) Property involved in a violation of this section may be treated as stolen for purposes of custody and disposition of the property.

(d) An offense under this section is a Class A misdemeanor.

(e) In this section, "vehicle" has the meaning given by Section 541.201, Transportation Code.

(f) *(Relettered.)*

*(Chgd. by L.1991, chap. 113(1); L.1993, chap. 900(1.01); L.1997, chap. 165(30.239), eff. 9/1/97.)*

### §31.12. Theft of or tampering with multichannel video or information services.

(a) A person commits an offense if, without the authorization of the multichannel video or information services provider, the person intentionally or knowingly:

(1) makes or maintains a connection, whether physically, electrically, electronically, or inductively, to:

(A) a cable, wire, or other component of or media attached to a multichannel video or information services system; or

(B) a television set, videotape recorder, or other receiver attached to a multichannel video or information system;

(2) attaches, causes to be attached, or maintains the attachment of a device to:

(A) a cable, wire, or other component of or media attached to a multichannel video or information services system; or

(B) a television set, videotape recorder, or other receiver attached to a multichannel video or information services system;

(3) tampers with, modifies, or maintains a modification to a device installed by a multichannel video or information services provider; or

(4) tampers with, modifies, or maintains a modification to an access device or uses that access device or any unauthorized access device to obtain services from a multichannel video or information services provider.

(b) In this section:

(1) "Access device," "connection," and "device" mean an access device, connection, or device wholly or partly designed to make intelligible an encrypted, encoded, scrambled, or other nonstandard signal carried by a multichannel video or information services provider.

(2) "Encrypted, encoded, scrambled, or other nonstandard signal" means any type of signal or transmission not intended to produce an intelligible program or service without the use of a device, signal, or information provided by a multichannel video or information services provider.

(3) "Multichannel video or information services provider" means a licensed cable television system, video dialtone system, multichannel multipoint distribution services system, direct broadcast satellite system, or other system providing video or information services that are distributed by cable, wire, radio frequency, or other media.

(c) This section does not prohibit the manufacture, distribution, sale, or use of satellite receiving antennas that are otherwise permitted by state or federal law.

(d) An offense under this section is a Class C misdemeanor unless it is shown on the trial of the offense that the actor:

(1) has been previously convicted one time of an offense under this section, in which event the offense is a Class B misdemeanor, or convicted two or more times of an offense under this section, in which event the offense is a Class A misdemeanor; or

(2) committed the offense for remuneration, in which event the offense is a Class A misdemeanor, unless it is also shown on the trial of the offense that the actor has been previously convicted two or more times of an offense under this section, in which event the offense is a Class A misdemeanor with a minimum fine of $2,000 and a minimum term of confinement of 180 days.

(e) For the purposes of this section, each connection, attachment, modification, or act of tampering is a separate offense.

*(Added by L.1995, chap. 318(10); chgd. by L.1999, chap. 858(1), eff. 9/1/99.)*

### §31.13. Manufacture, distribution, or advertisement of multichannel video or information services device.

(a) A person commits an offense if the person for remuneration intentionally or knowingly manufactures, assembles, modifies, imports into the state, exports out of the state, distributes, advertises, or offers for sale, with an intent to aid in the commission of an offense under Section 31.12, a device, a kit or part for a device, or a plan for a system of components wholly or partly designed to make intelligible an encrypted, encoded, scrambled, or other nonstandard signal carried or caused by a multichannel video or information services provider.

(b) In this section, "device," "encrypted, encoded, scrambled, or other nonstandard signal," and "multichannel video or information services provider" have the meanings assigned by Section 31.12.

(c) This section does not prohibit the manufacture, distribution, advertisement, offer for sale, or use of satellite receiving antennas that are otherwise permitted by state or federal law.

(d) An offense under this section is a Class A misdemeanor.

*(Added by L.1995, chap. 318(10); chgd. by L.1999, chap. 858(2), eff. 9/1/99.)*

### §31.14. Sale or lease of multichannel video or information services device.

(a) A person commits an offense if the person intentionally or knowingly sells or leases, with an intent to aid in the commission of an offense under Section 31.12, a device, a kit or part for a device, or a plan for a system of components wholly or partly designed to make intelligible an encrypted, encoded, scrambled, or other nonstandard signal carried or caused by a multichannel video or information services provider.

(b) In this section, "device," "encrypted, encoded, scrambled, or other nonstandard signal," and "multichannel video or information services provider" have the meanings assigned by Section 31.12.

(c) This section does not prohibit the sale or lease of satellite receiving antennas that are otherwise permitted by state or federal law without providing notice to the comptroller.

(d) An offense under this section is a Class A misdemeanor.

*(Added by L.1999, chap. 858(3), eff. 9/1/99.)*

## CHAPTER 32. FRAUD

### SUBCHAPTER A. GENERAL PROVISIONS

Section

32.01. Definitions.

32.02. Value.

32.03. Aggregation of amounts involved in fraud.

### SUBCHAPTER B. FORGERY

32.21. Forgery.

32.22. Criminal simulation.

32.23. Trademark counterfeiting.

32.24. Stealing or receiving stolen check or similar sight order.

### SUBCHAPTER C. CREDIT

32.31. Credit card or debit card abuse.

32.32. False statement to obtain property or credit.

32.33. Hindering secured creditors.

32.34. Fraudulent transfer of a motor vehicle.

32.35. Credit card transaction record laundering.

32.36. *(Renumbered.)*

32.37. *(Renumbered.)*

### SUBCHAPTER D. OTHER DECEPTIVE PRACTICES

32.41. Issuance of bad check.

32.42. Deceptive business practices.

32.43. Commercial bribery.

32.44. Rigging publicly exhibited contest.

32.441. Illegal recruitment of an athlete.

32.45. Misapplication of fiduciary property or property of financial institution.

32.46. Securing execution of document by deception.

32.47. Fraudulent destruction, removal, or concealment of writing.

32.48. Simulating legal process.

32.49. Refusal to execute release of fraudulent lien or claim.

32.50. Deceptive preparation and marketing of academic product.

32.51. Fraudulent use or possession of identifying information.

32.52 to 32.54. *(Deleted.)*

### SUBCHAPTER E. SAVINGS AND LOAN ASSOCIATIONS

32.71,
32.72. *(Deleted.)*

### SUBCHAPTER A. GENERAL PROVISIONS

## §32.01. Definitions.

In this chapter:

(1) "Financial institution" means a bank, trust company, insurance company, credit union, building and loan association, savings and loan association, investment trust, investment company, or any other organization held out to the public as a place for deposit of funds or medium of savings or collective investment.

(2) "Property" means:

(A) real property;

(B) tangible or intangible personal property including anything severed from land; or

(C) a document, including money, that represents or embodies anything of value.

(3) "Service" includes:

(A) labor and professional service;

(B) telecommunication, public utility, and transportation service;

(C) lodging, restaurant service, and entertainment; and

(D) the supply of a motor vehicle or other property for use.

(4) "Steal" means to acquire property or service by theft.

*(Chgd. by L.1993, chap. 900(1.01), eff. 9/1/94.)*

## §32.02. Value.

(a) Subject to the additional criteria of Subsections (b) and (c), value under this chapter is:

(1) the fair market value of the property or service at the time and place of the offense; or

(2) if the fair market value of the property cannot be ascertained, the cost of replacing the property within a reasonable time after the offense.

(b) The value of documents, other than those having a readily ascertainable market value, is:

(1) the amount due and collectible at maturity less any part that has been satisfied, if the document constitutes evidence of a debt; or

(2) the greatest amount of economic loss that the owner might reasonably suffer by virtue of loss of the document, if the document is other than evidence of a debt.

(c) If property or service has value that cannot be reasonably ascertained by the criteria set forth in Subsections (a) and (b), the property or service is deemed to have a value of $500 or more but less than $1,500.

(d) If the actor proves by a preponderance of the evidence that he gave consideration for or had a legal interest in the property or service stolen, the amount of the consideration or the value of the interest so proven shall be deducted from the value of the property or service ascertained under Subsection (a), (b), or (c) to determine value for purposes of this chapter.

*(Chgd. by L.1993, chap. 900(1.01), eff. 9/1/94.)*

## §32.03. Aggregation of amounts involved in fraud.

When amounts are obtained in violation of this chapter pursuant to one scheme or continuing course of conduct, whether from the same or several sources, the conduct may be considered as one offense and the amounts aggregated in determining the grade of offense. *(Chgd. by L.1993, chap. 900(1.01), eff. 9/1/94.)*

### SUBCHAPTER B. FORGERY

## §32.21. Forgery.

(a) For purposes of this section:

(1) "Forge" means:

(A) to alter, make, complete, execute, or authenticate any writing so that it purports:

(i) to be the act of another who did not authorize that act;

(ii) to have been executed at a time or place or in a numbered sequence other than was in fact the case; or

(iii) to be a copy of an original when no such original existed;

(B) to issue, transfer, register the transfer of, pass, publish, or otherwise utter a writing that is forged within the meaning of Paragraph (A); or

(C) to possess a writing that is forged within the meaning of Paragraph (A) with intent to utter it in a manner specified in Paragraph (B).

(2) "Writing" includes:

(A) printing or any other method of recording information;

(B) money, coins, tokens, stamps, seals, credit cards, badges, and trademarks; and

(C) symbols of value, right, privilege, or identification.

(b) A person commits an offense if he forges a writing with intent to defraud or harm another.

(c) Except as provided in Subsections (d) and (e) an offense under this section is a Class A misdemeanor.

(d) An offense under this section is a state jail felony if the writing is or purports to be a will, codicil, deed, deed of trust, mortgage, security instrument, security agreement, credit card, check or similar sight order for payment of money, contract, release, or other commercial instrument.

(e) An offense under this section is a felony of the third degree if the writing is or purports to be:

(1) part of an issue of money, securities, postage or revenue stamps;

(2) a government record listed in Section 37.01(2)(C); or

(3) other instruments issued by a state or national government or by a subdivision of either, or part of an issue of stock, bonds, or other instruments representing interests in or claims against another person.

(f) A person is presumed to intend to defraud or harm another if the person acts with respect to two or more writings of the same type and if each writing is a government record listed in Section 37.01(2)(C).

*(Chgd. by L.1991, chap. 113(2); L.1993, chap. 900(1.01); L.1997, chap. 189(1), eff. 5/21/97.)*

### §32.22. Criminal simulation.

(a) A person commits an offense if, with intent to defraud or harm another:

(1) he makes or alters an object, in whole or in part, so that it appears to have value because of age, antiquity, rarity, source, or authorship that it does not have;

(2) he possesses an object so made or altered, with intent to sell, pass, or otherwise utter it; or

(3) he authenticates or certifies an object so made or altered as genuine or as different from what it is.

(b) An offense under this section is a Class A misdemeanor.

*(Chgd. by L.1993, chap. 900(1.01), eff. 9/1/94.)*

### §32.23. Trademark counterfeiting.

(a) In this section:

(1) "Counterfeit mark" means a mark that is identical to or substantially indistinguishable from a protected mark the use or production of which is not authorized by the owner of the protected mark.

(2) "Identification mark" means a data plate, serial number, or part identification number.

(3) "Protected mark" means a trademark or service mark or an identification mark that is:

(A) registered with the secretary of state;

(B) registered on the principal register of the United States Patent and Trademark Office;

(C) registered under the laws of another state; or

(D) protected by Section 16.30, Business & Commerce Code, or by 36 U.S.C. Section 371 et seq.

(4) "Retail value" means the actor's regular selling price for a counterfeit mark or an item or service that bears or is identified by a counterfeit mark, except that if an item bearing a counterfeit mark is a component of a finished product, the retail value means the actor's regular selling price of the finished product on or in which the component is used, distributed, or sold.

(5) "Service mark" has the meaning assigned by Section 16.01, Business & Commerce Code.

(6) "Trademark" has the meaning assigned by Section 16.01, Business & Commerce Code.

(b) A person commits an offense if the person intentionally manufactures, displays, advertises, distributes, offers for sale, sells, or possesses with intent to sell or distribute a counterfeit mark or an item or service that:

(1) bears or is identified by a counterfeit mark; or

(2) the person knows or should have known bears or is identified by a counterfeit mark.

(c) A state or federal certificate of registration of intellectual property is prima facie evidence of the facts stated in the certificate.

(d) For the purposes of Subsection (e), when items or services are the subject of counterfeiting in violation of this section pursuant to one scheme or continuing course of conduct, the conduct may be considered as one offense and the retail value of the items or services aggregated in determining the grade of offense.

(e) An offense under this section is a:

(1) Class C misdemeanor if the retail value of the item or service is less than $20;

(2) Class B misdemeanor if the retail value of the item or service is $20 or more but less than $500;

(3) Class A misdemeanor if the retail value of the item or service is $500 or more but less than $1,500;

(4) state jail felony if the retail value of the item or service is $1,500 or more but less than $20,000;

(5) felony of the third degree if the retail value of the item or service is $20,000 or more but less than $100,000;

(6) felony of the second degree if the retail value of the item or service is $100,000 or more but less than $200,000; or

(7) felony of the first degree if the retail value of the item or service is $200,000 or more.

*(Added by L.1997, chap. 1161(2), eff. 9/1/97.)*

### §32.24. Stealing or receiving stolen check or similar sight order.

(a) A person commits an offense if the person steals an unsigned check or similar sight order or, with knowledge that an unsigned check or similar sight order has been stolen, receives the check or sight order with intent to use it, to sell it, or to transfer it to a person other than the person from whom the check or sight order was stolen.

(b) An offense under this section is a Class A misdemeanor.

*(Added by L.1999, chap. 1413(1), eff. 9/1/99.)*

## SUBCHAPTER C. CREDIT

### §32.31. Credit card or debit card abuse.

(a) For purposes of this section:

(1) "Cardholder" means the person named on the face of a credit card or debit card to whom or for whose benefit the card is issued.

(2) "Credit card" means an identification card, plate, coupon, book, number, or any other device authorizing a designated person or bearer to obtain property or services on credit. The term includes the number or description of the device if the device itself is not produced at the time of ordering or obtaining the property or service.

(3) "Expired credit card" means a credit card bearing an expiration date after that date has passed.

(4) "Debit card" means an identification card, plate, coupon, book, number, or any other device authorizing a designated person or bearer to communicate a request to an unmanned teller machine or a customer convenience terminal. The term includes the number or description of the device if the device itself is not produced at the time of ordering or obtaining the benefit.

(5) "Expired debit card" means a debit card bearing as its expiration date a date that has passed.

(6) "Unmanned teller machine" means a machine, other than a telephone, capable of being operated by a customer, by which a customer may communicate to a financial institution a request to withdraw a benefit for himself or for another directly from the customer's account or from the customer's account under a line of credit previously authorized by the institution for the customer.

(7) "Customer convenience terminal" means an unmanned teller machine the use of which does not involve personnel of a financial institution.

(b) A person commits an offense if:

(1) with intent to obtain a benefit fraudulently, he presents or uses a credit card or debit card with knowledge that:

(A) the card, whether or not expired, has not been issued to him and is not used with the effective consent of the cardholder; or

(B) the card has expired or has been revoked or cancelled;

(2) with intent to obtain a benefit, he uses a fictitious credit card or debit card or the pretended number or description of a fictitious card;

(3) he receives a benefit that he knows has been obtained in violation of this section;

(4) he steals a credit card or debit card or, with knowledge that it has been stolen, receives a credit card or debit card with intent to use it, to sell it, or to transfer it to a person other than the issuer or the cardholder;

(5) he buys a credit card or debit card from a person who he knows is not the issuer;

(6) not being the issuer, he sells a credit card or debit card;

(7) he uses or induces the cardholder to use the cardholder's credit card to obtain property or service for the actor's benefit for which the cardholder is financially unable to pay;

(8) not being the cardholder, and without the effective consent of the cardholder, he signs or writes his name or the name of another on a credit card or debit card with intent to use it;

(9) he possesses two or more incomplete credit cards or debit cards that have not been issued to him with intent to complete them without the effective consent of the issuer. For purposes of this subdivision, a card is incomplete if part of the matter that an issuer requires to appear on the card before it can be used, other than the signature of the cardholder, has not yet been stamped, embossed, imprinted, or written on it;

(10) being authorized by an issuer to furnish goods or services on presentation of a credit card, he, with intent to defraud the issuer or the cardholder, furnishes goods or services on presentation of a credit card obtained or retained in violation of this section or a credit card that is forged, expired, or revoked; or

(11) being authorized by an issuer to furnish goods or services on presentation of a credit card, he, with intent to defraud the issuer or a cardholder fails to furnish goods or services that he represents in writing to the issuer that he has furnished.

(c) It is presumed that a person who used a revoked, cancelled, or expired credit card or debit card had knowledge that the card had been revoked, cancelled, or expired if he had received notice of revocation, cancellation, or expiration from the issuer. For purposes of this section, notice may be either notice given orally in person or by telephone, or in writing by mail or by telegram. If written notice was sent by registered or certified mail with return receipt requested, or by telegram with report of delivery requested, addressed to the cardholder at the last address shown by the records of the issuer, it is presumed that the notice was received by the cardholder no later than five days after sent.

(d) An offense under this section is a state jail felony.

*(Chgd. by L.1993, chap. 900(1.01), eff. 9/1/94.)*

### §32.32. False statement to obtain property or credit.

(a) For purposes of this section, "credit" includes:

(1) a loan of money;

(2) furnishing property or service on credit;

(3) extending the due date of an obligation;

(4) comaking, endorsing, or guaranteeing a note or other instrument for obtaining credit;

(5) a line or letter of credit; and

(6) a credit card, as defined in Section 32.31 (Credit Card or Debit Card Abuse).

(b) A person commits an offense if he intentionally or knowingly makes a materially false or misleading written statement to obtain property or credit for himself or another.

(c) An offense under this section is a Class A misdemeanor.

*(Chgd. by L.1993, chap. 900(1.01); L.1995, chap. 76(14.50), eff. 9/1/95.)*

### §32.33. Hindering secured creditors.

(a) For purposes of this section:

(1) "Remove" means transport, without the effective consent of the secured party, from the state in which the property was located when the security interest or lien attached.

(2) "Security interest" means an interest in personal property or fixtures that secures payment or performance of an obligation.

(b) A person who has signed a security agreement creating a security interest in property or a mortgage or deed of trust creating a lien on property commits an offense if, with intent to hinder enforcement of that interest or lien, he destroys, removes, conceals, encumbers, or otherwise harms or reduces the value of the property.

(c) For purposes of this section, a person is presumed to have intended to hinder enforcement of the security interest or lien if, when any part of the debt secured by the security interest or lien was due, he failed:

(1) to pay the part then due; and

(2) if the secured party had made demand, to deliver possession of the secured property to the secured party.

(d) An offense under Subsection (b) is a:

(1) Class C misdemeanor if the value of the property destroyed, removed, concealed, encumbered, or otherwise harmed or reduced in value is less than $20;

(2) Class B misdemeanor if the value of the property destroyed, removed, concealed, encumbered, or otherwise harmed or reduced in value is $20 or more but less than $500;

(3) Class A misdemeanor if the value of the property destroyed, removed, concealed, encumbered, or otherwise harmed or reduced in value is $500 or more but less than $1,500;

(4) state jail felony if the value of the property destroyed, removed, concealed, encumbered, or otherwise harmed or reduced in value is $1,500 or more but less than $20,000;

(5) felony of the third degree if the value of the property destroyed, removed, concealed, encumbered, or otherwise harmed or reduced in value is $20,000 or more but less than $100,000;

(6) felony of the second degree if the value of the property destroyed, removed, concealed, encumbered, or otherwise harmed or reduced in value is $100,000 or more but less than $200,000; or

(7) felony of the first degree if the value of the property destroyed, removed, concealed, encumbered, or otherwise harmed or reduced in value is $200,000 or more.

(e) A person who is a debtor under a security agreement, and who does not have a right to sell or dispose of the secured property or is required to account to the secured party for the proceeds of a permitted sale or disposition, commits an offense if the person sells or otherwise disposes of the secured property, or does not account to the secured party for the proceeds of a sale or other disposition as required, with intent to appropriate (as defined in Chapter 31) the proceeds or value of the secured property. A person is presumed to have intended to appropriate proceeds if the person does not deliver the proceeds to the secured party or account to the secured party for the proceeds before the 11th day after the day that the secured party makes a lawful demand for the proceeds or account. An offense under this subsection is:

(1) a Class C misdemeanor if the proceeds obtained from the sale or other disposition are money or goods having a value of less than $20;

(2) a Class B misdemeanor if the proceeds obtained from the sale or other disposition are money or goods having a value of $20 or more but less than $500;

(3) a Class A misdemeanor if the proceeds obtained from the sale or other disposition are money or goods having a value of $500 or more but less than $1,500;

(4) a state jail felony if the proceeds obtained from the sale or other disposition are money or goods having a value of $1,500 or more but less than $20,000;

(5) a felony of the third degree if the proceeds obtained from the sale or other disposition are money or goods having a value of $20,000 or more but less than $100,000;

(6) a felony of the second degree if the proceeds obtained from the sale or other disposition are money or goods having a value of $100,000 or more but less than $200,000;

(7) a felony of the first degree if the proceeds obtained from the sale or other disposition are money or goods having a value of $200,000 or more.

(f) *(Relettered.)*

*(Chgd. by L.1993, chap. 900(1.01), eff. 9/1/94.)*

### §32.34. Fraudulent transfer of a motor vehicle.

(a) In this section:

(1) "Lease" means the grant of use and possession of a motor vehicle for consideration, whether or not the grant includes an option to buy the vehicle.

(2) "Motor vehicle" means a device in, on, or by which a person or property is or may be transported or drawn on a highway, except a device used exclusively on stationary rails or tracks.

(3) "Security interest" means an interest in personal property or fixtures that secures payment or performance of an obligation.

(4) "Third party" means a person other than the actor or the owner of the vehicle.

(5) "Transfer" means to transfer possession, whether or not another right is also transferred, by means of a sale, lease, sublease, lease assignment, or other property transfer.

(b) A person commits an offense if the person acquires, accepts possession of, or exercises control over the motor vehicle of another under a written or oral agreement to arrange for the transfer of the vehicle to a third party and:

(1) knowing the vehicle is subject to a security interest, lease, or lien, the person transfers the vehicle to a third party without first obtaining written authorization from the vehicle's secured creditor, lessor, or lienholder;

(2) intending to defraud or harm the vehicle's owner, the person transfers the vehicle to a third party;

(3) intending to defraud or harm the vehicle's owner, the person disposes of the vehicle in a manner other than by transfer to a third party; or

(4) the person does not disclose the location of the vehicle on the request of the vehicle's owner, secured creditor, lessor, or lienholder.

(c) For the purposes of Subsection (b)(2), the actor is presumed to have intended to defraud or harm the motor vehicle's owner if the actor does not take reasonable steps to determine whether or not the third party is financially able to pay for the vehicle.

(d) It is a defense to prosecution under Subsection (b)(1) that the entire indebtedness secured by or owed under the security interest, lease, or lien is paid or satisfied in full not later than the 30th day after the date that the transfer was made.

(e) It is not a defense to prosecution under Subsection (b)(1) that the motor vehicle's owner has violated a contract creating a security interest, lease, or lien in the motor vehicle.

(f) An offense under Subsection (b)(1), (b)(2), or (b)(3) is:

(1) a state jail felony if the value of the motor vehicle is less than $20,000; or

(2) a felony of the third degree if the value of the motor vehicle is $20,000 or more.

(g) An offense under Subsection (b)(4) is a Class A misdemeanor.

*(Added by L.1989, chap. 954(1); deleted by amendment and renum. from §32.36 and chgd. by L.1993, chap. 900(1.01), eff. 9/1/94.)*

### §32.35. Credit card transaction record laundering.

(a) In this section:

(1) "Agent" means a person authorized to act on behalf of another and includes an employee.

(2) "Authorized vendor" means a person authorized by a creditor to furnish property, service, or anything else of value upon presentation of a credit card by a cardholder.

(3) "Cardholder" means the person named on the face of a credit card to whom or for whose benefit the credit card is issued, and includes the named person's agents.

(4) "Credit card" means an identification card, plate, coupon, book, number, or any other device authorizing a designated person or bearer to obtain property or services on credit. It includes the number or description on the device if the device itself is not produced at the time of ordering or obtaining the property or service.

(5) "Creditor" means a person licensed under Chapter 342, Finance Code, a bank, savings and loan association, credit union, or other regulated financial institution that lends money or otherwise extends credit to a cardholder through a credit card and that authorizes other persons to honor the credit card.

(b) A person commits an offense if the person is an authorized vendor who, with intent to defraud the creditor or cardholder, presents to a creditor, for payment, a credit card transaction record of a sale that was not made by the authorized vendor or the vendor's agent.

(c) A person commits an offense if, without the creditor's authorization, the person employs, solicits, or otherwise causes an authorized vendor or the vendor's agent to present to a creditor, for payment, a credit card transaction record of a sale that was not made by the authorized vendor or the vendor's agent.

(d) It is presumed that a person is not the agent of an authorized vendor if a fee is paid or offered to be paid by the person to the authorized vendor in connection with the vendor's presentment to a creditor of a credit card transaction record.

(e) An offense under this section is a:

(1) Class C misdemeanor if the amount of the record of a sale is less than $20;

(2) Class B misdemeanor if the amount of the record of a sale is $20 or more but less than $500;

(3) Class A misdemeanor if the amount of the record of a sale is $500 or more but less than $1,500;

(4) state jail felony if the amount of the record of a sale is $1,500 or more but less than $20,000;

(5) felony of the third degree if the amount of the record of a sale is $20,000 or more but less than $100,000;

(6) felony of the second degree if the amount of the record of a sale is $100,000 or more but less than $200,000; or

(7) felony of the first degree if the amount of the record of a sale is $200,000 or more.

*(Added by L.1991, chap. 792(1); deleted by amendment and renum. from §32.37 and chgd. by L.1993, chap. 900(1.01); chgd. by L.1997, chap. 1396(38); L.1999, chap. 62(7.83), eff. 9/1/99.)*

**§32.36.** *(Renumbered to §32.34 by L.1993, chap. 900(1.01), eff. 9/1/94.)*

**§32.37.** *(Renumbered to §32.35 by L.1993, chap. 900(1.01), eff. 9/1/94.)*

## SUBCHAPTER D. OTHER DECEPTIVE PRACTICES

### §32.41. Issuance of bad check.

(a) A person commits an offense if he issues or passes a check or similar sight order for the payment of money knowing that the issuer does not have sufficient funds in or on deposit with the bank or other drawee for the payment in full of the check or order as well as all other checks or orders outstanding at the time of issuance.

(b) This section does not prevent the prosecution from establishing the required knowledge by direct evidence; however, for purposes of this section, the issuer's knowledge of insufficient funds is presumed (except in the case of a postdated check or order) if:

(1) he had no account with the bank or other drawee at the time he issued the check or order; or

(2) payment was refused by the bank or other drawee for lack of funds or insufficient funds on presentation within 30 days after issue and the issuer failed to pay the holder in full within 10 days after receiving notice of that refusal.

(c) Notice for purposes of Subsection (b)(2) may be actual notice or notice in writing that:

(1) is sent by registered or certified mail with return receipt requested, by telegram with report of delivery requested, or by first class mail if the letter was returned unopened with markings indicating that the address is incorrect and that there is no current forwarding order;

(2) is addressed to the issuer at his address shown on:

(A) the check or order;

(B) the records of the bank or other drawee; or

(C) the records of the person to whom the check or order has been issued or passed; and

(3) contains the following statement:

"This is a demand for payment in full for a check or order not paid because of a lack of funds or insufficient funds. If you fail to make payment in full within 10 days after the date of receipt of this notice, the failure to pay creates a presumption for committing an offense, and this matter may be referred for criminal prosecution."

(d) If notice is given in accordance with Subsection (c), it is presumed that the notice was received no later than five days after it was sent.

(e) A person charged with an offense under this section may make restitution for the bad checks. Restitution shall be made through the prosecutor's office if collection and processing were initiated through that office. In other cases restitution may, with the approval of the court in which the offense is filed, be made through the court.

(f) Except as otherwise provided by this subsection, an offense under this section is a Class C misdemeanor. If the check or similar sight order that was issued or passed was for a child support payment the obligation for which is established under a court order, the offense is a Class B misdemeanor.

(g) An offense under this section is not a lesser included offense of an offense under Section 31.03 or 31.04.

*(Chgd. by L.1989, chap. 1038(1); L.1993, chap. 900(1.01); L.1995, chap. 753(2); L.1997, chap. 702(14), eff. 9/1/97.)*

### §32.42. Deceptive business practices.

(a) For purposes of this section:

(1) "Adulterated" means varying from the standard of composition or quality prescribed by law or set by established commercial usage.

(2) "Business" includes trade and commerce and advertising, selling, and buying service or property.

(3) "Commodity" means any tangible or intangible personal property.

(4) "Contest" includes sweepstake, puzzle, and game of chance.

(5) "Deceptive sales contest" means a sales contest:

(A) that misrepresents the participant's chance of winning a prize;

(B) that fails to disclose to participants on a conspicuously displayed permanent poster (if the contest is conducted by or through a retail outlet) or on each card game piece, entry blank, or other paraphernalia required for participation in the contest (if the contest is not conducted by or through a retail outlet):

(i) the geographical area or number of outlets in which the contest is to be conducted;

(ii) an accurate description of each type of prize;

(iii) the minimum number and minimum amount of cash prizes; and

(iv) the minimum number of each other type of prize; or

(C) that is manipulated or rigged so that prizes are given to predetermined persons or retail establishments. A sales contest is not deceptive if the total value of prizes to each retail outlet is in a uniform ratio to the number of game pieces distributed to that outlet.

(6) "Mislabeled" means varying from the standard of truth or disclosure in labeling prescribed by law or set by established commercial usage.

(7) "Prize" includes gift, discount, coupon, certificate, gratuity, and any other thing of value awarded in a sales contest.

(8) "Sales contest" means a contest in connection with the sale of a commodity or service by which a person may, as determined by drawing, guessing, matching, or chance, receive a prize and which is not regulated by the rules of a federal regulatory agency.

(9) "Sell" and "sale" include offer for sale, advertise for sale, expose for sale, keep for the purpose of sale, deliver for or after sale, solicit and offer to buy, and every disposition for value.

(b) A person commits an offense if in the course of business he intentionally, knowingly, recklessly, or with criminal negligence commits one or more of the following deceptive business practices:

(1) using, selling, or possessing for use or sale a false weight or measure, or any other device for falsely determining or recording any quality or quantity;

(2) selling less than the represented quantity of a property or service;

(3) taking more than the represented quantity of property or service when as a buyer the actor furnishes the weight or measure;

(4) selling an adulterated or mislabeled commodity;

(5) passing off property or service as that of another;

(6) representing that a commodity is original or new if it is deteriorated, altered, rebuilt, reconditioned, reclaimed, used, or secondhand;

(7) representing that a commodity or service is of a particular style, grade, or model if it is of another;

(8) advertising property or service with intent:

(A) not to sell it as advertised, or

(B) not to supply reasonably expectable public demand, unless the advertising adequately discloses a time or quantity limit;

(9) representing the price of property or service falsely or in a way tending to mislead;

(10) making a materially false or misleading statement of fact concerning the reason for, existence of, or amount of a price or price reduction;

(11) conducting a deceptive sales contest; or

(12) making a materially false or misleading statement:

(A) in an advertisement for the purchase or sale of property or service; or

(B) otherwise in connection with the purchase or sale of property or service.

(c) An offense under Subsections (b)(1), (b)(2), (b)(3), (b)(4), (b)(5), and (b)(6) is:

(1) a Class C misdemeanor if the actor commits an offense with criminal negligence and if he has not previously been convicted of a deceptive business practice; or

(2) a Class A misdemeanor if the actor commits an offense intentionally, knowingly, recklessly or if he has been previously convicted of a Class B or C misdemeanor under this section.

(d) An offense under Subsections (b)(7), (b)(8), (b)(9), (b)(10), (b)(11), and (b)(12) is a Class A misdemeanor.

*(Chgd. by L.1993, chap. 900(1.01), eff. 9/1/94.)*

### §32.43. Commercial bribery.

(a) For purposes of this section:

(1) "Beneficiary" means a person for whom a fiduciary is acting.

(2) "Fiduciary" means:

(A) an agent or employee;

(B) a trustee, guardian, custodian, administrator, executor, conservator, receiver, or similar fiduciary;

(C) a lawyer, physician, accountant, appraiser, or other professional advisor; or

(D) an officer, director, partner, manager, or other participant in the direction of the affairs of a corporation or association.

(b) A person who is a fiduciary commits an offense if, without the consent of his beneficiary, he intentionally or knowingly solicits, accepts, or agrees to accept any benefit from another person on agreement or understanding that the benefit will influence the conduct of the fiduciary in relation to the affairs of his beneficiary.

(c) A person commits an offense if he offers, confers, or agrees to confer any benefit the acceptance of which is an offense under Subsection (b).

(d) An offense under this section is a state jail felony.

(e) In lieu of a fine that is authorized by Subsection (d), and in addition to the imprisonment that is authorized by that subsection, if the court finds that an individual who is a fiduciary gained a benefit through the commission of an offense under Subsection (b), the court may sentence the individual to pay a fine in an amount fixed by the court, not to exceed double the value of the benefit gained. This subsection does not affect the application of Section 12.51(c) to an offense under this section committed by a corporation or association.

*(Chgd. by L.1993, chap. 900(1.01), eff. 9/1/94.)*

### §32.44. Rigging publicly exhibited contest.

(a) A person commits an offense if, with intent to affect the outcome (including the score) of a publicly exhibited contest:

(1) he offers, confers, or agrees to confer any benefit on, or threatens harm to:

(A) a participant in the contest to induce him not to use his best efforts; or

(B) an official or other person associated with the contest; or

(2) he tampers with a person, animal, or thing in a manner contrary to the rules of the contest.

(b) A person commits an offense if he intentionally or knowingly solicits, accepts, or agrees to accept any benefit the conferring of which is an offense under Subsection (a).

(c) An offense under this section is a Class A misdemeanor.

(d) *(Deleted by amendment by L.1993, chap. 900(1.01), eff. 9/1/94.)*

*(Chgd. by L.1993, chap. 900(1.01), eff. 9/1/94.)*

### §32.441. Illegal recruitment of an athlete.

(a) A person commits an offense if, without the consent of the governing body or a designee of the governing body of an institution of higher education, the person intentionally or knowingly solicits, accepts, or agrees to accept any benefit from another on an agreement or understanding that the benefit will influence the conduct of the person in enrolling in the institution and participating in intercollegiate athletics.

(b) A person commits an offense if he offers, confers, or agrees to confer any benefit the acceptance of which is an offense under Subsection (a).

(c) It is an exception to prosecution under this section that the person offering, conferring, or agreeing to confer a benefit and the person soliciting, accepting, or agreeing to accept a benefit are related within the second degree of consanguinity or affinity, as determined under Chapter 573, Government Code.

(d) It is an exception to prosecution under Subsection (a) that, not later than the 60th day after the date the person accepted or agreed to accept a benefit, the person contacted a law enforcement agency and furnished testimony or evidence about the offense.

(e) An offense under this section is a:

(1) Class C misdemeanor if the value of the benefit is less than $20;

(2) Class B misdemeanor if the value of the benefit is $20 or more but less than $500;

(3) Class A misdemeanor if the value of the benefit is $500 or more but less than $1,500;

(4) state jail felony if the value of the benefit is $1,500 or more but less than $20,000;

(5) felony of the third degree if the value of the benefit is $20,000 or more but less than $100,000;

(6) felony of the second degree if the value of the benefit is $100,000 or more but less than $200,000; or

(7) felony of the first degree if the value of the benefit is $200,000 or more.

*(Added by L.1989, chap. 125(1); L.1991, chap. 561(41); L.1993, chap. 900(1.01); L.1995, chap. 76(5.95(27)), eff. 9/1/95.)*

### §32.45. Misapplication of fiduciary property or property of financial institution.

(a) For purposes of this section:

(1) "Fiduciary" includes:

(A) trustee, guardian, administrator, executor, conservator, and receiver;

(B) any other person acting in a fiduciary capacity, but not a commercial bailee unless the commercial bailee is a party in a motor fuel sales agreement with a distributor or supplier, as those terms are defined by Section 153.001, Tax Code; and

(C) an officer, manager, employee, or agent carrying on fiduciary functions on behalf of a fiduciary.

(2) "Misapply" means deal with property contrary to:

(A) an agreement under which the fiduciary holds the property; or

(B) a [illegible] ...ribing the custody or disposition of the property.

(b) A person commits an offense if he intentionally, knowingly, or recklessly misapplies property he holds as a fiduciary or property of a financial institution in a manner that involves substantial risk of loss to the owner of the property or to a person for whose benefit the property is held.

(c) An offense under this section is:

(1) a Class C misdemeanor if the value of the property misapplied is less than $20;

(2) a Class B misdemeanor if the value of the property misapplied is $20 or more but less than $500;

(3) a Class A misdemeanor if the value of the property misapplied is $500 or more but less than $1,500;

(4) a state jail felony if the value of the property misapplied is $1,500 or more but less than $20,000;

(5) a felony of the third degree if the value of the property misapplied is $20,000 or more but less than $100,000;

(6) a felony of the second degree if the value of the property misapplied is $100,000 or more but less than $200,000; or

(7) a felony of the first degree if the value of the property misapplied is $200,000 or more.

*(Chgd. by L.1991, chap. 565(2); L.1993, chap. 900(1.01); L.1997, chap. 1036(14), eff. 9/1/97.)*

### §32.46. Securing execution of document by deception.

(a) A person commits an offense if, with intent to defraud or harm any person, he, by deception:

(1) causes another to sign or execute any document affecting property or service or the pecuniary interest of any person; or

(2) causes or induces a public servant to file or record any purported judgment or other document purporting to memorialize or evidence an act, an order, a directive, or process of:

(A) a purported court that is not expressly created or established under the constitution or the laws of this state or of the United States;

(B) a purported judicial entity that is not expressly created or established under the constitution or laws of this state or of the United States; or

(C) a purported judicial officer of a purported court or purported judicial entity described by Paragraph (A) or (B).

(b) An offense under Subsection (a)(1) is a:

(1) Class C misdemeanor if the value of the property, service, or pecuniary interest is less than $20;

(2) Class B misdemeanor if the value of the property, service, or pecuniary interest is $20 or more but less than $500;

(3) Class A misdemeanor if the value of the property, service, or pecuniary interest is $500 or more but less than $1,500;

(4) state jail felony if the value of the property, service, or pecuniary interest is $1,500 or more but less than $20,000;

(5) felony of the third degree if the value of the property, service, or pecuniary interest is $20,000 or more but less than $100,000;

(6) felony of the second degree if the value of the property, service, or pecuniary interest is $100,000 or more but less than $200,000; or

(7) felony of the first degree if the value of the property, service, or pecuniary interest is $200,000 or more.

(c) An offense under Subsection (a)(2) is a state jail felony.

(d) In this section, "deception" has the meaning assigned by Section 31.01.

*(Chgd. by L.1993, chap. 900(1.01); L.1997, chap. 189(2), eff. 5/21/97.)*

### §32.47. Fraudulent destruction, removal, or concealment of writing.

(a) A person commits an offense if, with intent to defraud or harm another, he destroys, removes, conceals, alters, substitutes, or otherwise impairs the verity, legibility, or availability of a writing, other than a governmental record.

(b) For purposes of this section,"writing" includes:

(1) printing or any other method of recording information;

(2) money, coins, tokens, stamps, seals, credit cards, badges, trademarks;

(3) symbols of value, right, privilege, or identification; and

(4) labels, price tags, or markings on goods.

(c) Except as provided in Subsection (d), an offense under this section is a Class A misdemeanor.

(d) An offense under this section is a state jail felony if the writing:

(1) is a will or codicil of another, whether or not the maker is alive or dead and whether or not it has been admitted to probate; or

(2) is a deed, mortgage, deed of trust, security instrument, security agreement, or other writing for which the law provides public recording or filing, whether or not the writing has been acknowledged.

*(Chgd. by L.1993, chap. 900(1.01), eff. 9/1/94.)*

## §32.48. Simulating legal process.

(a) A person commits an offense if the person recklessly causes to be delivered to another any document that simulates a summons, complaint, judgment, or other court process with the intent to:

(1) induce payment of a claim from another person; or

(2) cause another to:

(A) submit to the putative authority of the document; or

(B) take any action or refrain from taking any action in response to the document, in compliance with the document, or on the basis of the document.

(b) Proof that the document was mailed to any person with the intent that it be forwarded to the intended recipient is a sufficient showing that the document was delivered.

(c) It is not a defense to prosecution under this section that the simulating document:

(1) states that it is not legal process; or

(2) purports to have been issued or authorized by a person or entity who did not have lawful authority to issue or authorize the document.

(d) If it is shown on the trial of an offense under this section that the simulating document was filed with, presented to, or delivered to a clerk of a court or an employee of a clerk of a court created or established under the constitution or laws of this state, there is a rebuttable presumption that the document was delivered with the intent described by Subsection (a).

(e) Except as provided by Subsection (f), an offense under this section is a Class A misdemeanor.

(f) If it is shown on the trial of an offense under this section that the defendant has previously been convicted of a violation of this section, the offense is a state jail felony.

*(Added by L.1997, chap. 189(3), eff. 5/21/97.)*

## §32.49. Refusal to execute release of fraudulent lien or claim.

(a) A person commits an offense if, with intent to defraud or harm another, the person:

(1) owns, holds, or is the beneficiary of a purported lien or claim asserted against real or personal property or an interest in real or personal property that is fraudulent, as described by Section 51.901(c), Government Code; and

(2) not later than the 21st day after the date of receipt of actual or written notice sent by either certified or registered mail, return receipt requested, to the person's last known address, or by telephonic document transfer to the recipient's current telecopier number, requesting the execution of a release of the fraudulent lien or claim, refuses to execute the release on the request of:

(A) the obligor or debtor; or

(B) any person who owns any interest in the real or personal property described in the document or instrument that is the basis for the lien or claim.

(b) A person who fails to execute a release of the purported lien or claim within the period prescribed by Subsection (a)(2) is presumed to have had the intent to harm or defraud another.

(c) An offense under this section is a Class A misdemeanor.

*(Added by L.1997, chap. 189(4), eff. 5/21/97.)*

## §32.50. Deceptive preparation and marketing of academic product.

(a) For purposes of this section:

(1) "Academic product" means a term paper, thesis, dissertation, essay, report, recording, work of art, or other written, recorded, pictorial, or artistic product or material submitted or intended to be submitted by a person to satisfy an academic requirement of the person.

(2) "Academic requirement" means a requirement or prerequisite to receive course credit or to complete a course of study or degree, diploma, or certificate program at an institution of higher education.

(3) "Institution of higher education" means an institution of higher education or private or independent institution of higher education as those terms are defined by Section 61.003, Education Code, or a private postsecondary educational institution as that term is defined by Section 61.302, Education Code.

(b) A person commits an offense if, with intent to make a profit, the person prepares, sells, offers or advertises for sale, or delivers to another person an academic product when the person knows, or should reasonably have known, that a person intends to submit or use the academic product to satisfy an academic requirement of a person other than the person who prepared the product.

(c) A person commits an offense if, with intent to induce another person to enter into an agreement or obligation to obtain or have prepared an academic product, the person knowingly makes or disseminates a written or oral statement that the person will prepare or cause to be prepared an academic product to be sold for use in satisfying an academic requirement of a person other than the person who prepared the product.

(d) It is a defense to prosecution under this section that the actor's conduct consisted solely of action taken as an employee of an institution of higher education in providing instruction, counseling, or tutoring in research or writing to students of the institution.

(e) It is a defense to prosecution under this section that the actor's conduct consisted solely of offering or providing tutorial or editing assistance to another person in connection with the other person's preparation of an academic product to satisfy the other person's academic requirement, and the actor does not offer or provide substantial preparation, writing, or research in the production of the academic product.

(f) It is a defense to prosecution under this section that the actor's conduct consisted solely of typing, transcribing, or reproducing a manuscript for a fee, or of offering to do so.

(g) An offense under this section is a Class C misdemeanor.

*(Added by L.1997, chap. 730(1), eff; renumbered from section 32.49 by L.1999, chap. 62(19.01(88)), eff. 9/1/99.)*

**§32.51. Fraudulent use or possession of identifying information.**

(a) In this section:

(1) "Identifying information" means information that alone or in conjunction with other information identifies an individual, including an individual's:

(A) name, social security number, date of birth, and government-issued identification number;

(B) unique biometric data, including the individual's fingerprint, voice print, and retina or iris image;

(C) unique electronic identification number, address, and routing code; and

(D) telecommunication identifying information or access device.

(2) "Telecommunication access device" means a card, plate, code, account number, personal identification number, electronic serial number, mobile identification number, or other telecommunications service, equipment, or instrument identifier or means of account access that alone or in conjunction with another telecommunication access device may be used to:

(A) obtain money, goods, services, or other thing of value; or

(B) initiate a transfer of funds other than a transfer originated solely by paper instrument.

(b) A person commits an offense if the person obtains, possesses, transfers, or uses identifying information of another person without the other person's consent and with intent to harm or defraud another.

(c) An offense under this section is a state jail felony.

(d) If a court orders a defendant convicted of an offense under this section to make restitution to the victim of the offense, the court may order the defendant to reimburse the victim for lost income or other expenses, other than attorney's fees, incurred as a result of the offense.

(e) If conduct that constitutes an offense under this section also constitutes an offense under any other law, the actor may be prosecuted under this section or the other law.

*(Added by L.1999, chap. 1159(1), eff. 9/1/99.)*

**§§32.52 to 32.54.** *(Deleted by amendment by L.1993, chap. 900(1.01), eff. 9/1/94.)*

### SUBCHAPTER E. SAVINGS AND LOAN ASSOCIATIONS

**§§32.71, 32.72.** *(Deleted by amendment by L.1993, chap. 900(1.01), eff. 9/1/94.)*

## CHAPTER 33. COMPUTER CRIMES

Section

## §33.01. Definitions.

In this chapter:

(1) "Access" means to approach, instruct, communicate with, store data in, retrieve or intercept data from, alter data or computer software in, or otherwise make use of any resource of a computer, computer network, computer program, or computer system.

(2) "Aggregate amount" means the amount of:

(A) any direct or indirect loss incurred by a victim, including the value of money, property, or service stolen or rendered unrecoverable by the offense; or

(B) any expenditure required by the victim to verify that a computer, computer network, computer program, or computer system was not altered, acquired, damaged, deleted, or disrupted by the offense.

(3) "Communications common carrier" means a person who owns or operates a telephone system in this state that includes equipment or facilities for the conveyance, transmission, or reception of communications and who receives compensation from persons who use that system.

(4) "Computer" means an electronic, magnetic, optical, electrochemical, or other high-speed data processing device that performs logical, arithmetic, or memory functions by the manipulations of electronic or magnetic impulses and includes all input, output, processing, storage, or communication facilities that are connected or related to the device.

(5) "Computer network" means the interconnection of two or more computers or computer systems by satellite, microwave, line, or other communication medium with the capability to transmit information among the computers.

(6) "Computer program" means an ordered set of data representing coded instructions or statements that when executed by a computer cause the computer to process data or perform specific functions.

(7) "Computer services" means the product of the use of a computer, the information stored in the computer, or the personnel supporting the computer, including computer time, data processing, and storage functions.

(8) "Computer system" means any combination of a computer or computer network with the documentation, computer software, or physical facilities supporting the computer or computer network.

(9) "Computer software" means a set of computer programs, procedures, and associated documentation related to the operation of a computer, computer system, or computer network.

(10) "Computer virus" means an unwanted computer program or other set of instructions inserted into a computer's memory, operating system, or program that is specifically constructed with the ability to replicate itself or to affect the other programs or files in the computer by attaching a copy of the unwanted program or other set of instructions to one or more computer programs or files.

(11) "Data" means a representation of information, knowledge, facts, concepts, or instructions that is being prepared or has been prepared in a formalized manner and is intended to be stored or processed, is being stored or processed, or has been stored or processed in a computer. Data may be embodied in any form, including but not limited to computer printouts, magnetic storage media, laser storage media, and punchcards, or may be stored internally in the memory of the computer.

(12) "Effective consent" includes consent by a person legally authorized to act for the owner. Consent is not effective if:

(A) induced by deception, as defined by Section 31.01, or induced by coercion;

(B) given by a person the actor knows is not legally authorized to act for the owner;

(C) given by a person who by reason of youth, mental disease or defect, or intoxication is known by the actor to be unable to make reasonable property dispositions;

(D) given solely to detect the commission of an offense; or

(E) used for a purpose other than that for which the consent was given.

(13) "Electric utility" has the meaning assigned by Section 31.002, Utilities Code.

(14) "Harm" includes partial or total alteration, damage, or erasure of stored data, interruption of computer services, introduction of a computer virus, or any other loss, disadvantage, or injury that might reasonably be suffered as a result of the actor's conduct.

(15) "Owner" means a person who:

(A) has title to the property, possession of the property, whether lawful or not, or a greater right to possession of the property than the actor;

(B) has the right to restrict access to the property; or

(C) is the licensee of data or computer software.

(16) "Property" means:

(A) tangible or intangible personal property including a computer, computer system, computer network, computer software, or data; or

(B) the use of a computer, computer system, computer network, computer software, or data. *(Chgd. by L.1989, chap. 306(1); L.1993, chap. 900(1.01); L.1997, chap. 306(1); L.1999, chap. 62(18.44), eff. 9/1/99.)*

### §33.02. Breach of computer security.

(a) A person commits an offense if the person knowingly accesses a computer, computer network, or computer system without the effective consent of the owner.

(b) An offense under this section is a Class B misdemeanor unless in committing the offense the actor knowingly obtains a benefit, defrauds or harms another, or alters, damages, or deletes property, in which event the offense is:

(1) a Class A misdemeanor if the aggregate amount involved is less than $1,500;

(2) a state jail felony if:

(A) the aggregate amount involved is $1,500 or more but less than $20,000; or

(B) the aggregate amount involved is less than $1,500 and the defendant has been previously convicted two or more times of an offense under this chapter;

(3) a felony of the third degree if the aggregate amount involved is $20,000 or more but less than $100,000;

(4) a felony of the second degree if the aggregate amount involved is $100,000 or more but less than $200,000; or

(5) a felony of the first degree if the aggregate amount involved is $200,000 or more.

(d) A person who his* subject to prosecution under this section and any other section of this code may be prosecuted under either or both sections.

**So in original. Probably should be "is".*

*(Chgd. by L.1989, chap. 306(2); L.1993, chap. 900(1.01); L.1997, chap. 306(2), eff. 9/1/97.)*

### §33.03. Defenses.

It is an affirmative defense to prosecution under Section 33.02 that the actor was an officer, employee, or agent of a communications common carrier or electric utility and committed the proscribed act or acts in the course of employment while engaged in an activity that is a necessary incident to the rendition of service or to the protection of the rights or property of the communications common carrier or electric utility. *(Deleted by amendment and renum. from §33.04 and chgd. by L.1993, chap. 900(1.01), eff. 9/1/94.)*

### §33.04. Assistance by attorney general.

The attorney general, if requested to do so by a prosecuting attorney, may assist the prosecuting attorney in the investigation or prosecution of an offense under this chapter or of any other offense involving the use of a computer. *(Renumbered from §33.05 by L.1993, chap. 900(1.01), eff. 9/1/94.)*

### §33.05. *(Renumbered to §33.04 by L.1993, chap. 900(1.01), eff. 9/1/94.)*

## CHAPTER 33A. TELECOMMUNICATIONS CRIMES

*(Added by L.1997, chap. 306(3), eff. 9/1/97.)*



### §33A.01. Definitions.

In this chapter:

(1) "Counterfeit telecommunications access device" means a telecommunications access device that is false, fraudulent, not issued to a legitimate telecommunications access device subscriber account, or otherwise unlawful or invalid.

(2) "Counterfeit telecommunications device" means a telecommunications device that has been altered or programmed alone or with another telecommunications device to acquire, intercept, receive, or otherwise facilitate the use of a telecommunications service without the authority or consent of the telecommunications service provider and includes a clone telephone, clone microchip, tumbler telephone, tumbler microchip, or wireless scanning device capable of acquiring, intercepting, receiving, or otherwise facilitating the use of a telecommunications service without immediate detection.

(3) "Deliver" means to actually or constructively sell, give, loan, or otherwise transfer a telecommunications device, or a counterfeit telecommunications device or any telecommunications plans, instructions, or materials, to another person.

(4) "Publish" means to communicate information or make information available to another person orally, in writing, or by means of telecommunications and includes communicating information on a computer bulletin board or similar system.

(5) "Telecommunications" means the origination, emission, transmission, or reception of data, images, signals, sounds, or other intelligence or equivalence of intelligence over a communications system by any method, including an electronic, magnetic, optical, digital, or analog method.

(6) "Telecommunications access device" means an instrument, device, card, plate, code, account number, personal identification number, electronic serial number, mobile identification number, counterfeit number, or financial transaction device that alone or with another telecommunications access device can acquire, intercept, provide, receive, use, or otherwise facilitate the use of a telecommunications device, counterfeit telecommunications device, or telecommunications service.

(7) "Telecommunications device" means any instrument, equipment, machine, or device that facilitates telecommunications and includes a computer, computer chip or circuit, telephone, pager, personal communications device, transponder, receiver, radio, modem, or device that enables use of a modem.

(8) "Telecommunications service" means the provision, facilitation, or generation of telecommunications through the use of a telecommunications device or telecommunications access device over a telecommunications system.

(9) "Value of the telecommunications service obtained or attempted to be obtained" includes the value of:

(A) a lawful charge for telecommunications service avoided or attempted to be avoided;

(B) money, property, or telecommunications service lost, stolen, or rendered unrecoverable by an offense; and

(C) an expenditure incurred by a victim to verify that a telecommunications device or telecommunications access device or telecommunications service was not altered, acquired, damaged, or disrupted as a result of an offense.

*(Added by L.1997, chap. 306(3), eff. 9/1/97.)*

## §33A.02. Unauthorized use of telecommunications service.

(a) A person commits an offense if the person is an officer, shareholder, partner, employee, agent, or independent contractor of a telecommunications service provider and the person knowingly and without authority uses or diverts telecommunications service for the person's own benefit or to the benefit of another.

(b) An offense under this section is:

(1) a Class B misdemeanor if the value of the telecommunications service used or diverted is less than $500;

(2) a Class A misdemeanor if:

(A) the value of the telecommunications service used or diverted is $500 or more but less than $1,500; or

(B) the value of the telecommunications service used or diverted is less than $500 and the defendant has been previously convicted of an offense under this chapter;

(3) a state jail felony if:

(A) the value of the telecommunications service used or diverted is $1,500 or more but less than $20,000; or

(B) the value of the telecommunications service used or diverted is less than $1,500 and the defendant has been previously convicted two or more times of an offense under this chapter;

(4) a felony of the third degree if the value of the telecommunications service used or diverted is $20,000 or more but less than $100,000;

(5) a felony of the second degree if the value of the telecommunications service used or diverted is $100,000 or more but less than $200,000; or

(6) a felony of the first degree if the value of the telecommunications service used or diverted is $200,000 or more.

(c) When telecommunications service is used or diverted in violation of this section pursuant to one scheme or continuing course of conduct, whether or not in a single incident, the conduct may be considered as one offense and the values of the service used or diverted may be aggregated in determining the grade of the offense.
*(Added by L.1997, chap. 306(3), eff. 9/1/97.)*

### §33A.03. Manufacture, possession, or delivery of unlawful telecommunications device.

(a) A person commits an offense if the person manufactures, possesses, delivers, offers to deliver, or advertises:

(1) a counterfeit telecommunications device; or

(2) a telecommunications device that is intended to be used to:

(A) commit an offense under Section 33A.04; or

(B) conceal the existence or place of origin or destination of a telecommunications service.

(b) A person commits an offense if the person delivers, offers to deliver, or advertises plans, instructions, or materials for manufacture of:

(1) a counterfeit telecommunications device; or

(2) a telecommunications device that is intended to be used to commit an offense under Subsection (a).

(c) An offense under this section is a felony of the third degree.

(d) It is a defense to prosecution under this section that the person was an officer, agent, or employee of a telecommunications service provider who engaged in the conduct for the purpose of gathering information for a law enforcement investigation related to an offense under this chapter.
*(Added by L.1997, chap. 306(3), eff. 9/1/97.)*

### §33A.04. Theft of telecommunications service.

(a) A person commits an offense if the person knowingly obtains or attempts to obtain telecommunications service to avoid or cause another person to avoid a lawful charge for that service by using:

(1) a telecommunications access device without the authority or consent of the subscriber or lawful holder of the device or pursuant to an agreement for an exchange of value with the subscriber or lawful holder of the device to allow another person to use the device;

(2) a counterfeit telecommunications access device;

(3) a telecommunications device or counterfeit telecommunications device; or

(4) a fraudulent or deceptive scheme, pretense, method, or conspiracy, or other device or means, including a false, altered, or stolen identification.

(b) An offense under this section is:

(1) a Class B misdemeanor if the value of the telecommunications service obtained or attempted to be obtained is less than $500;

(2) a Class A misdemeanor if:

(A) the value of the telecommunications service obtained or attempted to be obtained is $500 or more but less than $1,500; or

(B) the value of the telecommunications service obtained or attempted to be obtained is less than $500 and the defendant has been previously convicted of an offense under this chapter;

(3) a state jail felony if:

(A) the value of the telecommunications service obtained or attempted to be obtained is $1,500 or more but less than $20,000; or

(B) the value of the telecommunications service obtained or attempted to be obtained is less than $1,500 and the defendant has been previously convicted two or more times of an offense under this chapter;

(4) a felony of the third degree if the value of the telecommunications service obtained or attempted to be obtained is $20,000 or more but less than $100,000;

(5) a felony of the second degree if the value of the telecommunications service obtained or attempted to be obtained is $100,000 or more but less than $200,000; or

(6) a felony of the first degree if the value of the telecommunications service obtained or attempted to be obtained is $200,000 or more.

(c) When telecommunications service is obtained or attempted to be obtained in violation of this section pursuant to one scheme or continuing course of conduct, whether or not in a single incident, the conduct may be considered as one offense and the values of the service obtained or attempted to be obtained may be aggregated in determining the grade of the offense.
*(Added by L.1997, chap. 306(3), eff. 9/1/97.)*

### §33A.05. Publication of telecommunications access device.

(a) A person commits an offense if the person with criminal negligence publishes a telecommunications access device or counterfeit telecommunications access device that is designed to be used to commit an offense under Section 33A.04.

(b) Except as otherwise provided by this subsection, an offense under this section is a Class A misdemeanor. An offense under this section is a felony of the third degree if the person has been previously convicted of an offense under this chapter.
*(Added by L.1997, chap. 306(3), eff. 9/1/97.)*

### §33A.06. Assistance by attorney general.

The attorney general, if requested to do so by a prosecuting attorney, may assist the prosecuting attorney in the investigation or prosecution of an offense under this chapter or of any other offense involving the use of telecommunications equipment, services, or devices. *(Added by L.1997, chap. 306(3), eff. 9/1/97.)*

## CHAPTER 34. MONEY LAUNDERING
*(Added by L.1993, chap. 761(2), eff. 9/1/93.)*

Section


### §34.01. Definitions.

In this chapter:

(1) "Criminal activity" means any offense, including any preparatory offense, that is:

(A) classified as a felony under the laws of this state or the United States; or

(B) punishable by confinement for more than one year under the laws of another state.

(2) "Funds" includes:

(A) coin or paper money of the United States or any other country that is designated as legal tender and that circulates and is customarily used and accepted as a medium of exchange in the country of issue;

(B) United States silver certificates, United States Treasury notes, and Federal Reserve System notes; and

(C) official foreign bank notes that are customarily used and accepted as a medium of exchange in a foreign country and foreign bank drafts.

(3) "Peace officer" means a person who is elected, appointed, or employed by a governmental entity and who is a peace officer under Article 2.12, Code of Criminal Procedure, or other law.

(4) "Proceeds" means funds acquired or derived directly or indirectly from, produced through, or realized through an act.
*(Added by L.1993, chap. 761(2), eff. 9/1/93.)*

### §34.02. Money laundering.

(a) A person commits an offense if the person knowingly:

(1) acquires or maintains an interest in, receives, conceals, possesses, transfers, or transports the proceeds of criminal activity;

(2) conducts, supervises, or facilitates a transaction involving the proceeds of criminal activity; or

(3) invests, expends, or receives, or offers to invest, expend, or receive, the proceeds of criminal activity or funds that the person believes are the proceeds of criminal activity.

(b) For purposes of Subsection (a)(3) of this section, a person is presumed to believe that funds are the proceeds of criminal activity if a peace officer or a person acting at the direction of a peace officer represents to the person that the funds are proceeds of criminal activity, regardless of whether the peace officer or person acting at the peace officer's direction discloses the person's status as a peace officer or that the person is acting at the direction of a peace officer.

(c) It is a defense to prosecution under this section that the person acted with intent to facilitate the lawful seizure, forfeiture, or disposition of funds or other legitimate law enforcement purpose pursuant to the laws of this state or the United States.

(d) It is a defense to prosecution under this section that the transaction was necessary to preserve a person's right to representation as guaranteed by the Sixth Amendment of the United States Constitution and by Article 1, Section 10, of the Texas Constitution or that the funds were received as bona fide legal fees by a licensed attorney and at the time of their receipt, the attorney did not have actual knowledge that the funds were derived from criminal activity.

(e) An offense under this section is:

(1) a felony of the third degree if the value of the funds is $3,000 or more but less than $20,000;

(2) a felony of the second degree if the value of the funds is $20,000 or more but less than $100,000; or

(3) a felony of the first degree if the value of the funds is $100,000 or more.

*(Added by L.1993, chap. 761(2), eff. 9/1/93.)*

### §34.03. Assistance by attorney general.

The attorney general, if requested to do so by a prosecuting attorney, may assist in the prosecution of an offense under this chapter. *(Added by L.1993, chap. 761(2), eff. 9/1/93.)*



## CHAPTER 35. INSURANCE FRAUD

*(Added by L.1995, chap. 621(1), eff. 9/1/95.)*

Section



### §35.01. Definitions.

In this chapter:

(1) "Health care goods" means a tangible product, device, medicine, or other object provided in conjunction with a health care service.

(2) "Health care provider" means a person who renders health care services or an agent or employee of an organization that renders or provides a facility and means to render health care services. The term includes a physician, surgeon, person who may be selected by an insured or a beneficiary under Article 21.52, Insurance Code, and person defined as a provider of health care under Section 2.05(d)(1), Medical Practice Act (Article 4495b, Texas Civil Statutes).

(3) "Health care service" means a service that is intended to improve or maintain the physical or mental condition of an individual and that is rendered, directed, or supervised by a health care provider.

(4) "Insurer" means a person who engages in the business of insurance in this state, including:

(A) an insurer that is not authorized to do business in this state;

(B) a health maintenance organization;

(C) a group hospital service corporation regulated under Chapter 20, Insurance Code; and

(D) any person who self-insures and provides health care benefits to the person's employees.

(5) "Statement" means an oral or written communication or a record or documented representation of fact evidencing a loss, injury, or expense. The term includes computer-generated information.

*(Added by L.1995, chap. 621(1), eff. 9/1/95.)*

### §35.02. Insurance fraud.

(a) A person commits an offense if, with intent to defraud or deceive an insurer, the person causes to be prepared or presents to an insurer in support of a claim for payment under a health or property and casualty insurance policy a statement that the person knows contains false or misleading information concerning a matter that is material to the claim, and the matter affects a person's right to a payment or the amount of payment to which a person is entitled.

(b) A person commits an offense if, with intent to defraud or deceive an insurer, the person solicits, offers, pays, or receives a benefit in connection with the furnishing of health care goods or services for which a claim for payment is submitted under a health or property and casualty insurance policy.

(c) For purposes of Subsection (a), information concerning a matter that is material to a claim for payment under an insurance policy includes information concerning:

(1) whether health care goods or services were provided;

(2) whether health care goods or services were medically necessary under professionally accepted standards;

(3) the nature of the health care goods or services provided;

(4) the date on which health care goods or services were provided;

(5) the medical record of goods or services provided;
(6) the condition treated or diagnosis made;
(7) the identity and applicable license of the provider or the recipient of health care goods or services;
(8) whether property was damaged or lost in the manner and under the circumstances described in a statement related to a claim for insurance payment; or
(9) whether any other claim for insurance payment has been communicated to any other insurer concerning property damage or loss to the same property.
(d) An offense under this section is:
(1) a Class C misdemeanor if the value of the claim is less than $20;
(2) a class B misdemeanor if the value of the claim is $20 or more but less than $500;
(3) a Class A misdemeanor if the value of the claim is $500 or more but less than $1,500;
(4) a state jail felony if the value of the claim is $1,500 or more but less than $20,000;
(5) a felony of the third degree if the value of the claim is $20,000 or more but less than $100,000;
(6) a felony of the second degree if the value of the claim is $100,000 or more but less than $200,000; or
(7) a felony of the first degree if:
(A) the value of the claim is $200,000 or more; or
(B) the value of the claim is less than $200,000 and the commission of the offense placed a person at risk of death or serious bodily injury.
*(Added by L.1995, chap. 621(1), eff. 9/1/95.)*



### §35.03. Aggregation and multiple offenses.

(a) When separate claims in violation of this chapter are communicated to an insurer or group of insurers pursuant to one scheme or continuing course of conduct, the conduct may be considered as one offense and the value of the claims aggregated in determining the classification of the offense. If claims are aggregated under this subsection, Subsection (b) shall not apply.

(b) When three or more separate claims in violation of this chapter are communicated to an insurer or group of insurers pursuant to one scheme or continuing course of conduct, the conduct may be considered as one offense, and the classification of the offense shall be one category higher than the most serious single offense proven from the separate claims, except that if the most serious offense is a felony of the first degree, the offense is a felony of the first degree. This subsection shall not be applied if claims are aggregated under Subsection (a).
*(Added by L.1995, chap. 621(1), eff. 9/1/95.)*

### §35.04. Jurisdiction of attorney general.

(a) The attorney general may offer to an attorney representing the state in the prosecution of an offense under Section 35.02 the investigative, technical, and litigation assistance of the attorney general's office.

(b) The attorney general may prosecute or assist in the prosecution of an offense under Section 35.02 on the request of the attorney representing the state described by Subsection (a).
*(Added by L.1995, chap. 621(1), eff. 9/1/95.)*

# TITLE 8. OFFENSES AGAINST PUBLIC ADMINISTRATION



## CHAPTER 36. BRIBERY AND CORRUPT INFLUENCE

## §36.01. Definitions.

In this chapter:

(1) "Custody" means:

(A) detained or under arrest by a peace officer; or

(B) under restraint by a public servant pursuant to an order of a court.

(2) "Party official" means a person who holds any position or office in a political party, whether by election, appointment, or employment.

(3) "Benefit" means anything reasonably regarded as pecuniary gain or pecuniary advantage, including benefit to any other person in whose welfare the beneficiary has a direct and substantial interest.

(4) "Vote" means to cast a ballot in an election regulated by law.

*(Chgd. by L.1991, chap. 304(4.01); L.1993, chap. 900(1.01), eff. 9/1/94.)*



## §36.02. Bribery.

(a) A person commits an offense if he intentionally or knowingly offers, confers, or agrees to confer on another, or solicits, accepts, or agrees to accept from another:

(1) any benefit as consideration for the recipient's decision, opinion, recommendation, vote, or other exercise of discretion as a public servant, party official, or voter;

(2) any benefit as consideration for the recipient's decision, vote, recommendation, or other exercise of official discretion in a judicial or administrative proceeding;

(3) any benefit as consideration for a violation of a duty imposed by law on a public servant or party official; or

(4) any benefit that is a political contribution as defined by Title 15, Election Code, or that is an expenditure made and reported in accordance with Chapter 305, Government Code, if the benefit was offered, conferred, solicited, accepted, or agreed to pursuant to an express agreement to take or withhold a specific exercise of official discretion if such exercise of official discretion would not have been taken or withheld but for the benefit; notwithstanding any rule of evidence or jury instruction allowing factual inferences in the absence of certain evidence, direct evidence of the express agreement shall be required in any prosecution under this subdivision.

(b) It is no defense to prosecution under this section that a person whom the actor sought to influence was not qualified to act in the desired way whether because he had not yet assumed office or he lacked jurisdiction or for any other reason.

(c) It is no defense to prosecution under this section that the benefit is not offered or conferred or that the benefit is not solicited or accepted until after:

(1) the decision, opinion, recommendation, vote, or other exercise of discretion has occurred; or

(2) the public servant ceases to be a public servant.

(d) It is an exception to the application of Subdivisions (1), (2), and (3) of Subsection (a) that the benefit is a political contribution as defined by Title 15, Election Code, or an expenditure made and reported in accordance with Chapter 305, Government Code.

(e) An offense under this section is a felony of the second degree.

*(Chgd. by L.1991, chap. 304(4.02); L.1993, chap. 900(1.01), eff. 9/1/94.)*

## §36.03. Coercion of public servant or voter.

(a) A person commits an offense if by means of coercion he:

(1) influences or attempts to influence a public servant in a specific exercise of his official power or a specific performance of his official duty or influences or attempts to influence a public servant to violate the public servant's known legal duty; or

(2) influences or attempts to influence a voter not to vote or to vote in a particular manner.

(b) An offense under this section is a Class A misdemeanor unless the coercion is a threat to commit a felony, in which event it is a felony of the third degree.

(c) It is an exception to the application of Subsection (a)(1) of this section that the person who influences or attempts to influence the public servant is a member of the governing body of a governmental entity, and that the action that influences or attempts to influence the public servant is an official action taken by the member of the governing body. For the purposes of this subsection, the term "official action" includes deliberations by the governing body of a governmental entity.

*(Chgd. by L.1989, chap. 67(1), (3); L.1993, chap. 900(1.01), eff. 9/1/94.)*

## §36.04. Improper influence.

(a) A person commits an offense if he privately addresses a representation, entreaty, argument, or other communication to any public servant who exercises or will exercise official discretion in an adjudicatory proceeding with an intent to influence the outcome of the proceeding on the basis of considerations other than those authorized by law.

(b) For purposes of this section, "adjudicatory proceeding" means any proceeding before a court or any other agency of government in which the legal rights, powers, duties, or privileges of specified parties are determined.

(c) An offense under this section is a Class A misdemeanor.

*(Chgd. by L.1993, chap. 900(1.01), eff. 9/1/94.)*

## §36.05. Tampering with witness.

(a) A person commits an offense if, with intent to influence the witness, he offers, confers, or agrees to confer any benefit on a witness or prospective witness in an official proceeding or coerces a witness or prospective witness in an official proceeding:

(1) to testify falsely;

(2) to withhold any testimony, information, document, or thing;

(3) to elude legal process summoning him to testify or supply evidence;

(4) to absent himself from an official proceeding to which he has been legally summoned; or

(5) to abstain from, discontinue, or delay the prosecution of another.

(b) A witness or prospective witness in an official proceeding commits an offense if he knowingly solicits, accepts, or agrees to accept any benefit on the representation or understanding that he will do any of the things specified in Subsection (a).

(c) It is a defense to prosecution under Subsection (a)(5) that the benefit received was:

(1) reasonable restitution for damages suffered by the complaining witness as a result of the offense; and

(2) a result of an agreement negotiated with the assistance or acquiescence of an attorney for the state who represented the state in the case.

(d) An offense under this section is a state jail felony.

*(Chgd. by L.1993, chap. 900(1.01); L.1997, chap. 721(1), eff. 9/1/97.)*

## §36.06. Obstruction or retaliation.

(a) A person commits an offense if he intentionally or knowingly harms or threatens to harm another by an unlawful act:

(1) in retaliation for or on account of the service or status of another as a:

(A) public servant, witness, prospective witness, or informant; or

(B) person who has reported or who the actor knows intends to report the occurrence of a crime; or

(2) to prevent or delay the service of another as a:

(A) public servant, witness, prospective witness, or informant; or

(B) person who has reported or who the actor knows intends to report the occurrence of a crime.

(b) For purposes of this section, "informant" means a person who has communicated information to the government in connection with any governmental function.

(c) An offense under this section is a felony of the third degree.

*(Chgd. by L.1989, chap. 557(1); L.1993, chap. 900(1.01); L.1997, chap. 239(1), eff. 9/1/97.)*

## §36.07. Acceptance of honorarium.

(a) A public servant commits an offense if the public servant solicits, accepts, or agrees to accept an honorarium in consideration for services that the public servant would not have been requested to provide but for the public servant's official position or duties.

(b) This section does not prohibit a public servant from accepting transportation and lodging expenses in connection with a conference or similar event in which the public servant renders services, such as addressing an audience or engaging in a seminar, to the extent that those services are more than merely perfunctory, or from accepting meals in connection with such an event.

(c) An offense under this section is a Class A misdemeanor.

*(Added by L.1991, chap. 304(4.03); chgd. by L.1993, chap. 900(1.01), eff. 9/1/94.)*

## §36.08. Gift to public servant by person subject to his jurisdiction.

(a) A public servant in an agency performing regulatory functions or conducting inspections or investigations commits an offense if he solicits, accepts, or agrees to accept any benefit from a person the public servant knows to be subject to regulation, inspection, or investigation by the public servant or his agency.

(b) A public servant in an agency having custody of prisoners commits an offense if he solicits, accepts, or agrees to accept any benefit from a person the public servant knows to be in his custody or the custody of his agency.

(c) A public servant in an agency carrying on civil or criminal litigation on behalf of government commits an offense if he solicits, accepts, or agrees to accept any benefit from a person against whom the public servant knows litigation is pending or contemplated by the public servant or his agency.

(d) A public servant who exercises discretion in connection with contracts, purchases, payments, claims, or other pecuniary transactions of government commits an offense if he solicits, accepts, or agrees to accept any benefit from a person the public servant knows is interested in or likely to become interested in any contract, purchase, payment, claim, or transaction involving the exercise of his discretion.

(e) A public servant who has judicial or administrative authority, who is employed by or in a tribunal having judicial or administrative authority, or who participates in the enforcement of a tribunal's decision, commits an offense if he solicits, accepts, or agrees to accept any benefit from a person the public servant knows is interested in or likely to become interested in any matter before the public servant or tribunal.

(f) A member of the legislature, the governor, the lieutenant governor, or a person employed by a member of the legislature, the governor, the lieutenant governor, or an agency of the legislature commits an offense if he solicits, accepts, or agrees to accept any benefit from any person.

(g) A public servant who is a hearing examiner employed by an agency performing regulatory functions and who conducts hearings in contested cases commits an offense if the public servant solicits, accepts, or agrees to accept any benefit from any person who is appearing before the agency in a contested case, who is doing business with the agency, or who the public servant knows is interested in any matter before the public servant. The exception provided by Section 36.10(b) does not apply to a benefit under this subsection.

(h) An offense under this section is a Class A misdemeanor.

(i) A public servant who receives an unsolicited benefit that the public servant is prohibited from accepting under this section may donate the benefit to a governmental entity that has the authority to accept the gift or may donate the benefit to a recognized tax-exempt charitable organization formed for educational, religious, or scientific purposes.

*(Chgd. by L.1991, chap. 304(4.04); L.1993, chap. 900(1.01), eff. 9/1/94.)*

## §36.09. Offering gift to public servant.

(a) A person commits an offense if he offers, confers, or agrees to confer any benefit on a public servant that he knows the public servant is prohibited by law from accepting.

(b) An offense under this section is a Class A misdemeanor.

*(Chgd. by L.1993, chap. 900(1.01), eff. 9/1/94.)*

## §36.10. Non-applicable.

(a) Sections 36.08 (Gift to Public Servant) and 36.09 (Offering Gift to Public Servant) do not apply to:

(1) a fee prescribed by law to be received by a public servant or any other benefit to which the public servant is lawfully entitled or for which he gives legitimate consideration in a capacity other than as a public servant;

(2) a gift or other benefit conferred on account of kinship or a personal, professional, or business relationship independent of the official status of the recipient; or

(3) a benefit to a public servant required to file a statement under Chapter 572, Government Code, or a report under Title 15, Election Code, that is derived from a function in honor or appreciation of the recipient if:

(A) the benefit and the source of any benefit in excess of $50 is reported in the statement; and

(B) the benefit is used solely to defray the expenses that accrue in the performance of duties or activities in connection with the office which are nonreimbursable by the state or political subdivision;

(4) a political contribution as defined by Title 15, Election Code;

(5) a gift, award, or memento to a member of the legislative or executive branch that is required to be reported under Chapter 305, Government Code;

(6) an item with a value of less than $50, excluding cash or a negotiable instrument as described by Section 3.104, Business & Commerce Code; or

(7) an item issued by a governmental entity that allows the use of property or facilities owned, leased, or operated by the governmental entity.

(b) Section 36.08 (Gift to Public Servant) does not apply to food, lodging, transportation, or entertainment accepted as a guest and, if the donee is required by law to report those items, reorted by the donee in accordance with that law.

(c) Section 36.09 (Offering Gift to Public Servant) does not apply to food, lodging, transportation, or entertainment accepted as a guest and, if the donor is required by law to report those items, reported by the donor in accordance with that law.

*(Chgd. by L.1991, chap. 304(4.05); L.1993, chap. 900(1.01); L.1995, chap. 76(5.95)(38), eff. 9/1/95.)*

## CHAPTER 37. PERJURY AND OTHER FALSIFICATION

Section



### §37.01. Definitions.

In this chapter:

(1) "Court record" means a decree, judgment, order, subpoena, warrant, minutes, or other document issued by a court of:

(A) this state;

(B) another state;

(C) the United States;

(D) a foreign country recognized by an act of congress or a treaty or other international convention to which the United States is a party;

(E) an Indian tribe recognized by the United States; or

(F) any other jurisdiction, territory, or protectorate entitled to full faith and credit in this state under the United States Constitution.

(2) "Governmental record" means:

(A) anything belonging to, received by, or kept by government for information, including a court record;

(B) anything required by law to be kept by others for information of government;

(C) a license, certificate, permit, seal, title, letter of patent, or similar document issued by government, by another state, or by the United States; or

(D) a standard proof of motor vehicle liability insurance form described by Section 601.081, Transportation Code, a certificate of an insurance company described by Section 601.083 of that code, a document purporting to be such a form or certificate that is not issued by an insurer authorized to write motor vehicle liability insurance in this state, an electronic submission in a form described by Section 502.153(i), Transportation Code, or an evidence of financial responsibility described by Section 601.053 of that code.

(3) "Statement" means any representation of fact.

*(Chgd. by L.1991, chap. 113(3); L.1993, chap. 900(1.01); L.1997, chaps. 189(5), 823(3); L.1999, chap. 659(1), eff. 9/1/99.)*

### §37.02. Perjury.

(a) A person commits an offense if, with intent to deceive and with knowledge of the statement's meaning:

(1) he makes a false statement under oath or swears to the truth of a false statement previously made and the statement is required or authorized by law to be made under oath; or

(2) he makes a false unsworn declaration under Chapter 132, Civil Practice and Remedies Code.

• (b) An offense under this section is a Class A misdemeanor.
*(Chgd. by L.1993, chap. 900(1.01), eff. 9/1/94.)*

### §37.03. Aggravated perjury.

(a) A person commits an offense if he commits perjury as defined in Section 37.02, and the false statement:

(1) is made during or in connection with an official proceeding; and

(2) is material.

(b) An offense under this section is a felony of the third degree.
*(Chgd. by L.1993, chap. 900(1.01), eff. 9/1/94.)*

### §37.04. Materiality.

(a) A statement is material, regardless of the admissibility of the statement under the rules of evidence, if it could have affected the course or outcome of the official proceeding.

(b) It is no defense to prosecution under Section 37.03 (Aggravated Perjury) that the declarant mistakenly believed the statement to be immaterial.

(c) Whether a statement is material in a given factual situation is a question of law.
*(Chgd. by L.1993, chap. 900(1.01), eff. 9/1/94.)*

### §37.05. Retraction.

It is a defense to prosecution under Section 37.03 (Aggravated Perjury) that the actor retracted his false statement:

(1) before completion of the testimony at the official proceeding; and

(2) before it became manifest that the falsity of the statement would be exposed.
*(Chgd. by L.1993, chap. 900(1.01), eff. 9/1/94.)*

### §37.06. Inconsistent statements.

An information or indictment for perjury under Section 37.02 or aggravated perjury under Section 37.03 that alleges that the declarant has made statements under oath, both of which cannot be true, need not allege which statement is false. At the trial the prosecution need not prove which statement is false. *(Chgd. by L.1993, chap. 900(1.01), eff. 9/1/94.)*

### §37.07. Irregularities no defense.

(a) It is no defense to prosecution under Section 37.02 (Perjury) or 37.03 (Aggravated Perjury) that the oath was administered or taken in an irregular manner, or that there was some irregularity in the appointment or qualification of the person who administered the oath.

(b) It is no defense to prosecution under Section 37.02 (Perjury) or 37.03 (Aggravated Perjury) that a document was not sworn to if the document contains a recital that it was made under oath, the declarant was aware of the recital when he signed the document, and the document contains the signed jurat of a public servant authorized to administer oaths.
*(Chgd. by L.1993, chap. 900(1.01), eff. 9/1/94.)*

### §37.08. False report to peace officer or law enforcement employee.

(a) A person commits an offense if, with intent to deceive, he knowingly makes a false statement that is material to a criminal investigation and makes the statement to:

(1) a peace officer conducting the investigation; or

(2) any employee of a law enforcement agency that is authorized by the agency to conduct the investigation and that the actor knows is conducting the investigation.

(b) In this section, "law enforcement agency" has the meaning assigned by Article 59.01, Code of Criminal Procedure.

(c) An offense under this section is a Class B misdemeanor.
*(Chgd. by L.1993, chap. 900(1.01); L.1997, chap. 925(1), eff. 9/1/97.)*

### §37.081. False report regarding missing child or missing person.

(a) A person commits an offense if, with intent to deceive, the person knowingly:

(1) files a false report of a missing child or missing person with a law enforcement officer or agency; or

(2) makes a false statement to a law enforcement officer or other employee of a law enforcement agency relating to a missing child or missing person.

(b) An offense under this section is a Class C misdemeanor.

*(Added by L.1999, chap. 200(3), eff. 9/1/99.)*

### §37.09. Tampering with or fabricating physical evidence.

(a) A person commits an offense if, knowing that an investigation or official proceeding is pending or in progress, he:

(1) alters, destroys, or conceals any record, document, or thing with intent to impair its verity, legibility, or availability as evidence in the investigation or official proceeding; or

(2) makes, presents, or uses any record, document, or thing with knowledge of its falsity and with intent to affect the course or outcome of the investigation or official proceeding.

(b) This section shall not apply if the record, document, or thing concealed is privileged or is the work product of the parties to the investigation or official proceeding.

(c) An offense under Subsection (a) or Subsection (d)(1) is a felony of the third degree. An offense under Subsection (d)(2) is a Class A misdemeanor.

(d) A person commits an offense if the person:

(1) knowing that an offense has been committed, alters, destroys, or conceals any record, document, or thing with intent to impair its verity, legibility, or availability as evidence in any subsequent investigation of or official proceeding related to the offense; or

(2) observes human remains under circumstances in which a reasonable person would believe that an offense had been committed, knows or reasonably should know that a law enforcement agency is not aware of the existence of or location of the remains, and fails to report the existence of and location of the remains to a law enforcement agency.

*(Chgd. by L.1991, chap. 565(4); L.1993, chap. 900(1.01); L.1997, chap. 1284(1), eff. 9/1/97.)*

### §37.10. Tampering with governmental record.

(a) A person commits an offense if he:

(1) knowingly makes a false entry in, or false alteration of, a governmental record;

(2) makes, presents, or uses any record, document, or thing with knowledge of its falsity and with intent that it be taken as a genuine governmental record;

(3) intentionally destroys, conceals, removes, or otherwise impairs the verity, legibility, or availability of a governmental record;

(4) possesses, sells, or offers to sell a governmental record or a blank governmental record form with intent that it be used unlawfully;

(5) makes, presents, or uses a governmental record with knowledge of its falsity; or

(6) possesses, sells, or offers to sell a governmental record or a blank governmental record form with knowledge that is was obtained unlawfully.

(b) It is an exception to the application of Subsection (a)(3) that the governmental record is destroyed pursuant to legal authorization. With regard to the destruction of a local government record, legal authorization includes compliance with the provisions of Subtitle C, Title 6, Local Government Code.

(c)(1) Except as provided by Subdivision (2) and by Subsection (d), an offense under this section is a Class A misdemeanor unless the actor's intent is to defraud or harm another, in which event the offense is a state jail felony.

(2) An offense under this section is a felony of the third degree if it is shown on the trial of the offense that the governmental record was a public school record, report, or assessment instrument required under Chapter 39, Education Code, or was a license, certificate, permit, seal, title, letter of patent, or similar document issued by government, by another state, or by the United States, unless the actor's intent is to defraud or harm another, in which event the offense is a felony of the second degree.

(d) An offense under this section, if it is shown on the trial of the offense that the governmental record is described by Section 37.01(2)(D), is:

(1) a Class B misdemeanor if the offense is committed under Subsection (a)(2) or Subsection (a)(5) and the defendant is convicted of presenting or using the record;

(2) a felony of the third degree if the offense is committed under:

(A) Subsection (a)(1), (3), (4), or (6); or

(B) Subsection (a)(2) or (5) and the defendant is convicted of making the record; and

(3) a felony of the second degree, notwithstanding Subdivisions (1) and (2), if the actor's intent in committing the offense was to defraud or harm another.

(e) It is an affirmative defense to prosecution for possession under Subsection (a)(6) that the possession occurred in the actual discharge of official duties as a public servant.

Printed in the U.S.A. Zt

(f) It is a defense to prosecution under Subsection (a)(1), (a)(2), or (a)(5) that the false entry or false information could have no effect on the government's purpose for requiring the governmental record.

(g) A person is presumed to intend to defraud or harm another if the person acts with respect to two or more of the same type of governmental records or blank governmental record forms and if each governmental record or blank governmental record form is a license, certificate, permit, seal, title, or similar document issued by government.

(h) If conduct that constitutes an offense under this section also constitutes an offense under Section 32.48 or 37.13, the actor may be prosecuted under any of those sections.
*(Chgd. by L.1989, chap. 1248(66); L.1991, chaps. 113(4), 565(5); L.1993, chap. 900(1.01); L.1997, chaps. 189(6), 823(4); L.1999, chaps. 659(2), 718(1), eff. 9/1/99.)*

### §37.101. Fraudulent filing of financing statement.

(a) A person commits an offense if the person knowingly presents for filing or causes to be presented for filing a financing statement that the person knows:

(1) is forged;

(2) contains a material false statement; or

(3) is groundless.

(b) An offense under Subsection (a)(1) is a felony of the third degree, unless it is shown on the trial of the offense that the person had previously been convicted under this section on two or more occasions, in which event the offense is a felony of the second degree. An offense under Subsection (a)(2) or (a)(3) is a Class A misdemeanor, unless the person commits the offense with the intent to defraud or harm another, in which event the offense is a state jail felony.
*(Added by L.1997, chap. 189(10), eff. 5/21/97.)*



### §37.11. Impersonating public servant.

(a) A person commits an offense if he:

(1) impersonates a public servant with intent to induce another to submit to his pretended official authority or to rely on his pretended official acts; or

(2) knowingly purports to exercise any function of a public servant or of a public office, including that of a judge and court, and the position or office through which he purports to exercise a function of a public servant or public office has no lawful existence under the constitution or laws of this state or of the United States.

(b) An offense under this section is a felony of the third degree.
*(Chgd. by L.1993, chap. 900(1.01); L.1997, chap. 189(7), eff. 5/21/97.)*

### §37.12. False identification as peace officer; misrepresentation of property.

(a) A person commits an offense if:

(1) the person makes, provides to another person, or possesses a card, document, badge, insignia, shoulder emblem, or other item bearing an insignia of a law enforcement agency that identifies a person as a peace officer or a reserve law enforcement officer; and

(2) the person who makes, provides, or possesses the item bearing the insignia knows that the person so identified by the item is not commissioned as a peace officer or reserve law enforcement officer as indicated on the item.

(b) It is a defense to prosecution under this section that:

(1) the card, document, badge, insignia, shoulder emblem, or other item bearing an insignia of a law enforcement agency clearly identifies the person as an honorary or junior peace officer or reserve law enforcement officer, or as a member of a junior posse;

(2) the person identified as a peace officer or reserve law enforcement officer by the item bearing the insignia was commissioned in that capacity when the item was made; or

(3) the item was used or intended for use exclusively for decorative purposes or in an artistic or dramatic presentation.

(c) In this section, "reserve law enforcement officer" has the same meaning as is given that term in Section 415.001, Government Code.

(d) A person commits an offense if the person intentionally or knowingly misrepresents an object as property belonging to a law enforcement agency.

(e) An offense under this section is a Class B misdemeanor.
*(Chgd. by L.1993, chap. 900(1.01), eff. 9/1/94.)*

### §37.13. Record of a fraudulent court.

(a) A person commits an offense if the person makes, presents, or uses any document or other record with:

(1) knowledge that the document or other record is not a record of a court created under or established by the constitution or laws of this state or of the United States; and

(2) the intent that the document or other record be given the same legal effect as a record of a court created under or established by the constitution or laws of this state or of the United States.

(b) An offense under this section is a Class A misdemeanor, except that the offense is a felony of the third degree if it is shown on the trial of the offense that the defendant has previously been convicted under this section on two or more occasions.

(c) If conduct that constitutes an offense under this section also constitutes an offense under Section 32.48 or 37.10, the actor may be prosecuted under any of those sections.
*(Added by L.1997, chap. 189(8), eff. 5/21/97.)*

## CHAPTER 38. OBSTRUCTING GOVERNMENTAL OPERATION

Section



### §38.01. Definitions.

In this chapter:

(1) "Custody" means:

(A) under arrest by a peace officer or under restraint by a public servant pursuant to an order of a court of this state or another state of the United States; or

(B) under restraint by an agent or employee of a facility that is operated by or under contract with the United States and that confines persons arrested for, charged with, or convicted of criminal offenses.

(2) "Escape" means unauthorized departure from custody or failure to return to custody following temporary leave for a specific purpose or limited period or leave that is part of an intermittent sentence, but does not include a violation of conditions of community supervision or parole other than conditions that impose a period of confinement in a secure correctional facility.

(3) "Economic benefit" means anything reasonably regarded as an economic gain or advantage, including accepting or offering to accept employment for a fee, accepting or offering to accept a fee, entering into a fee contract, or accepting or agreeing to accept money or anything of value.

(4) "Finance" means to provide funds or capital or to furnish with necessary funds.

(5) "Fugitive from justice" means a person for whom a valid arrest warrant has been issued.

(6) "Governmental function" includes any activity that a public servant is lawfully authorized to undertake on behalf of government.

(7) "Invest funds" means to commit money to earn a financial return.

(8) "Member of the family" means anyone related within the third degree of consanguinity or affinity, as determined under Chapter 573, Government Code.

Printed in the U.S.A.

(9) "Qualified nonprofit organization" means a nonprofit organization that meets the following conditions:

(A) the primary purposes of the organization do not include the rendition of legal services or education regarding legal services;

(B) the recommending, furnishing, paying for, or educating persons regarding legal services is incidental and reasonably related to the primary purposes of the organization;

(C) the organization does not derive a financial benefit from the rendition of legal services by a lawyer; and

(D) the person for whom the legal services are rendered, and not the organization, is recognized as the client of a lawyer.

(10) "Public media" means a telephone directory or legal directory, newspaper or other periodical, billboard or other sign, radio or television broadcast, recorded message the public may access by dialing a telephone number, or a written communication not prohibited by Section 38.12(d).

(11) "Solicit employment" means to communicate in person or by telephone with a prospective client or a member of the prospective client's family concerning professional employment within the scope of a professional's license, registration, or certification arising out of a particular occurrence or event, or series of occurrences or events, or concerning an existing problem of the prospective client within the scope of the professional's license, registration, or certification, for the purpose of providing professional services to the prospective client, when neither the person receiving the communication nor anyone acting on that person's behalf has requested the communication. The term does not include a communication initiated by a family member of the person receiving a communication, a communication by a professional who has a prior or existing professional-client relationship with the person receiving the communication, or communication by an attorney for a qualified nonprofit organization with the organization's members for the purpose of educating the organization's members to understand the law, to recognize legal problems, to make intelligent selection of legal counsel, or to use available legal services. The term does not include an advertisement by a professional through public media.

(12) "Professional" means an attorney, chiropractor, physician, surgeon, private investigator, or any other person licensed, certified, or registered by a state agency that regulates a health care profession.

*(Chgd. by L.1989, chap. 866(1); L.1991, chaps. 14(284)(14), 561(42); L.1993, chap. 900(1.01); L.1995, chaps. 76(5.95)(27), 321(1.103); L.1997, chaps. 293(2), 750(1), eff. 9/1/97.)*

## §38.02. Failure to identify.

(a) A person commits an offense if he intentionally refuses to give his name, residence address, or date of birth to a peace officer who has lawfully arrested the person and requested the information.

(b) A person commits an offense if he intentionally gives a false or fictitious name, residence address, or date of birth to a peace officer who has:

(1) lawfully arrested the person;

(2) lawfully detained the person; or

(3) requested the information from a person that the peace officer has good cause to believe is a witness to a criminal offense.

(c) Except as provided by Subsection (d), an offense under this section is a Class C misdemeanor.

(d) If it is shown on the trial of an offense under this section that the defendant was a fugitive from justice at the time of the offense, the offense is a Class B misdemeanor.

*(Chgd. by L.1991, chap. 821(1); L.1993, chap. 900(1.01), eff. 9/1/94.)*

## §38.03. Resisting arrest, search, or transportation.

(a) A person commits an offense if he intentionally prevents or obstructs a person he knows is a peace officer or a person acting in a peace officer's presence and at his direction from effecting an arrest, search, or transportation of the actor or another by using force against the peace officer or another.

(b) It is no defense to prosecution under this section that the arrest or search was unlawful.

(c) Except as provided in Subsection (d), an offense under this section is a Class A misdemeanor.

(d) An offense under this section is a felony of the third degree if the actor uses a deadly weapon to resist the arrest or search.

*(Chgd. by L.1991, chap. 277(1, 2); L.1993, chap. 900(1.01), eff. 9/1/94.)*

Printed in the U.S.A. 12

### §38.04. Evading arrest or detention.

(a) A person commits an offense if he intentionally flees from a person he knows is a peace officer attempting lawfully to arrest or detain him.

(b) An offense under this section is a Class B misdemeanor, except that the offense is:

(1) a Class A misdemeanor if the actor uses a vehicle while the actor is in flight and the actor has not been previously convicted under this section;

(2) a state jail felony if the actor uses a vehicle while the actor is in flight and the actor has been previously convicted under this section;

(3) a felony of the third degree if another suffers serious bodily injury as a direct result of an attempt by the officer from whom the actor is fleeing to apprehend the actor while the actor is in flight; or

(4) a felony of the second degree if another suffers death as a direct result of an attempt by the officer from whom the actor is fleeing to apprehend the actor while the actor is in flight.

(c) In this section, "vehicle" has the meaning assigned by Section 541.201, Transportation Code.

(d) A person who is subject to prosecution under both this section and another law may be prosecuted under either or both this section and the other law.

*(Chgd. by L.1989, chap. 126(1); L.1993, chap. 900(1.01); L.1995, chap. 708(1); L.1997, chap. 165(30.240), eff. 9/1/97.)*

### §38.05. Hindering apprehension or prosecution.

(a) A person commits an offense if, with intent to hinder the arrest, prosecution, conviction, or punishment of another for an offense or, with intent to hinder the arrest, detention, adjudication, or disposition of a child for engaging in delinquent conduct that violates a penal law of the grade of felony, he:

(1) harbors or conceals the other;

(2) provides or aids in providing the other with any means of avoiding arrest or effecting escape; or

(3) warns the other of impending discovery or apprehension.

(b) It is a defense to prosecution under Subsection (a)(3) that the warning was given in connection with an effort to bring another into compliance with the law.

(c) An offense under this section is a Class A misdemeanor, except that the offense is a felony of the third degree if the person who is harbored, concealed, provided with a means of avoiding arrest or effecting escape, or warned of discovery or apprehension is under arrest for, charged with, or convicted of a felony, or is in custody or detention for, is alleged in a petition to have engaged in, or has been adjudicated as having engaged in delinquent conduct that violates a penal law of the grade of felony, and the person charged under this section knew that the person they harbored, concealed, provided with a means of avoiding arrest or effecting escape, or warned of discovery or apprehension is under arrest for, charged with, or convicted of a felony, or is in custody or detention for, is alleged in a petition to have engaged in, or has been adjudicated as having engaged in delinquent conduct that violates a penal law of the grade of felony.

*(Chgd. by L.1991, chap. 748(1); L.1993, chap. 900(1.01); L.1995, chap. 318(11), eff. 9/1/95.)*

### §38.06. Escape.

(a) A person commits an offense if he escapes from custody when he is:

(1) under arrest for, charged with, or convicted of an offense; or

(2) in custody pursuant to a lawful order of a court.

(b) Except as provided in Subsections (c), (d), and (e), an offense under this section is a Class A misdemeanor.

(c) An offense under this section is a felony of the third degree if the actor:

(1) is under arrest for, charged with, or convicted of a felony;

(2) is confined in a secure correctional facility; or

(3) is committed to a secure correctional facility, as defined by Section 51.02, Family Code, other than a halfway house, operated by or under contract with the Texas Youth Commission.

(d) An offense under this section is a felony of the second degree if the actor to effect his escape causes bodily injury.

(e) An offense under this section is a felony of the first degree if to effect his escape the actor:

(1) causes serious bodily injury; or

(2) uses or threatens to use a deadly weapon.

*(Deleted by amendment and renum. from §38.07 and chgd. by L.1993, chap. 900(1.01); L.1999, chap. 526(1), eff. 9/1/99.)*

**§38.07. Permitting or facilitating escape.**

(a) An official or employee of a correctional facility commits an offense if he knowingly permits or facilitates the escape of a person in custody.

(b) A person commits an offense if he knowingly causes or facilitates the escape of one who is in custody pursuant to:

(1) an allegation or adjudication of delinquency; or

(2) involuntary commitment for mental illness under Subtitle C, Title 7, Health and Safety Code, or for chemical dependency under Chapter 462, Health and Safety Code.

(c) Except as provided in Subsections (d) and (e), an offense under this section is a Class A misdemeanor.

(d) An offense under this section is a felony of the third degree if the person in custody:

(1) was under arrest for, charged with, or convicted of a felony; or

(2) was confined in a correctional facility other than a secure correctional facility after conviction of a felony.

(e) An offense under this section is a felony of the second degree if:

(1) the actor or the person in custody used or threatened to use a deadly weapon to effect the escape; or

(2) the person in custody was confined in a secure correctional facility after conviction of a felony.

*(Renumbered from §38.08 and chgd. by L.1993, chap. 900(1.01), eff. 9/1/94.)*

**§38.08. Effect of unlawful custody.**

It is no defense to prosecution under Section 38.06 or 38.07 that the custody was unlawful.

*(Renumbered from §38.09 and chgd. by L.1993, chap. 900(1.01), eff. 9/1/94.)*

**§38.09. Implements for escape.**

(a) A person commits an offense if, with intent to facilitate escape, he introduces into a correctional facility, or provides a person in custody or an inmate with, a deadly weapon or anything that may be useful for escape.

(b) An offense under this section is a felony of the third degree unless the actor introduced or provided a deadly weapon, in which event the offense is a felony of the second degree.

*(Renumbered from §38.10 and chgd. by L.1993, chap. 900(1.01), eff. 9/1/94.)*

**§38.10. Bail jumping and failure to appear.**

(a) A person lawfully released from custody, with or without bail, on condition that he subsequently appear commits an offense if he intentionally or knowingly fails to appear in accordance with the terms of his release.

(b) It is a defense to prosecution under this section that the appearance was incident to community supervision, parole, or an intermittent sentence.

(c) It is a defense to prosecution under this section that the actor had a reasonable excuse for his failure to appear in accordance with the terms of his release.

(d) Except as provided in Subsections (e) and (f), an offense under this section is a Class A misdemeanor.

(e) An offense under this section is a Class C misdemeanor if the offense for which the actor's appearance was required is punishable by fine only.

(f) An offense under this section is a felony of the third degree if the offense for which the actor's appearance was required is classified as a felony.

*(Renumbered from §38.11 and chgd. by L.1993, chap. 900(1.01), eff. 9/1/94.)*

**§38.11. Prohibited substances in correctional facility or on property of Texas Department of Criminal Justice.**

(a) A person commits an offense if the person provides an alcoholic beverage, controlled substance, or dangerous drug to an inmate of a correctional facility, except on the prescription of a physician.

(b) A person commits an offense if the person takes an alcoholic beverage, controlled substance, or dangerous drug into a correctional facility, except for delivery to a correctional facility warehouse, pharmacy, or physician.

(c) A person commits an offense if the person takes a controlled substance or dangerous drug on property owned, used, or controlled by the Texas Department of Criminal Justice, except for delivery to a warehouse, pharmacy, or physician on property owned, used, or controlled by the department.

(d) A person commits an offense if the person possesses a controlled substance or dangerous drug while:

(1) on property owned, used, or controlled by the Texas Department of Criminal Justice; or

(2) in a correctional facility.

(e) It is an affirmative defense to prosecution under Subsection (d) of this section that the person possessed the controlled substance or dangerous drug pursuant to a prescription issued by a practitioner or while delivering the substance or drug to a warehouse, pharmacy, or physician on property owned, used, or controlled by the department.

(f) In this section:

(1) "Practitioner" has the meaning assigned by Section 481.002, Health and Safety Code.

(2) "Prescription" has the meaning assigned by Section 481.002, Health and Safety Code.

(g) An offense under this section is a felony of the third degree.

(h) Notwithstanding Section 15.01(d), if a person commits the offense of criminal attempt to commit an offense under Subsection (a) or (b), the offense committed under Section 15.01 is a felony of the third degree.

(i) It is an affirmative defense to prosecution under Subsection (b) that the actor:

(1) is a duly authorized member of the clergy with rights and privileges granted by an ordaining authority that includes administration of a religious ritual or ceremony requiring the presence or consumption of an alcoholic beverage; and

(2) takes four ounces or less of an alcoholic beverage into the correctional facility and personally consumes all of the alcoholic beverage or departs from the facility with any portion of the beverage not consumed.

*(Added by L.1991, 2nd C.S., chap. 10(5.01); renum. from §38.112 and chgd. by L.1993, chap. 900(1.01); chgd. by L.1999, chaps. 362(1), 649(1), eff. 9/1/99.)*

**§38.111.** *(Repealed by L.1999, chap. 1196(3), eff. 9/1/99.)*

**§38.112.** *(Renumbered to §38.11 by L.1993, chap. 900(1.01), eff. 9/1/94.)*

**§38.113. Unauthorized absence from community corrections facility, county correctional center, or assignment site.**

(a) A person commits an offense if the person:

(1) is sentenced to or is required as a condition of community supervision or correctional programming to submit to a period of detention or treatment in a community corrections facility or county correctional center;

(2) fails to report to or leaves the facility, the center, or a community service assignment site as directed by the court, community supervision and corrections department supervising the person, or director of the facility or center in which the person is detained or treated, as appropriate; and

(3) in failing to report or leaving acts without the approval of the court, the community supervision and corrections department supervising the person, or the director of the facility or center in which the person is detained or treated.

(b) An offense under this section is a state jail felony.

*(Added by L.1993, chap. 900(1.01); chgd. by L.1995, chap. 318(12), eff. 9/1/95.)*

**§38.12. Barratry and solicitation of professional employment.**

(a) A person commits an offense if, with intent to obtain an economic benefit the person:

(1) knowingly institutes a suit or claim that the person has not been authorized to pursue;

(2) solicits employment, either in person or by telephone, for himself or for another;

(3) pays, gives, or advances or offers to pay, give, or advance to a prospective client money or anything of value to obtain employment as a professional from the prospective client;

(4) pays or gives or offers to pay or give a person money or anything of value to solicit employment;

(5) pays or gives or offers to pay or give a family member of a prospective client money or anything of value to solicit employment; or

(6) accepts or agrees to accept money or anything of value to solicit employment.

(b) A person commits an offense if the person:

(1) knowingly finances the commission of an offense under Subsection (a);

(2) invests funds the person knows or believes are intended to further the commission of an offense under Subsection (a); or

(3) is a professional who knowingly accepts employment within the scope of the person's license, registration, or certification that results from the solicitation of employment in violation of Subsection (a).

(c) It is an exception to prosecution under Subsection (a) or (b) that the person's conduct is authorized by the Texas Disciplinary Rules of Professional Conduct or any rule of court.

(d) A person commits an offense if the person:

(1) is an attorney, chiropractor, physician, surgeon, or private investigator licensed to practice in this state or any person licensed, certified, or registered by a health care regulatory agency of this state;

(2) with the intent to obtain professional employment for himself or for another, sends or knowingly permits to be sent to an individual who has not sought the person's employment, legal representation, advice, or care a written communication that:

(A) concerns an action for personal injury or wrongful death or otherwise relates to an accident or disaster involving the person to whom the communication is addressed or a relative of that person and that was mailed before the 31st day after the date on which the accident or disaster occurred;

(B) concerns a specific matter and relates to legal representation and the person knows or reasonably should know that the person to whom the communication is directed is represented by a lawyer in the matter;

(C) concerns an arrest of or issuance of a summons to the person to whom the communication is addressed or a relative of that person and that was mailed before the 31st day after the date on which the arrest or issuance of the summons occurred;

(D) concerns a lawsuit of any kind, including an action for divorce, in which the person to whom the communication is addressed is a defendant or a relative of that person, unless the lawsuit in which the person is named as a defendant has been on file for more than 31 days before the date on which the communication was mailed;

(E) is sent or permitted to be sent by a person who knows or reasonably should know that the injured person or relative of the injured person has indicated a desire not to be contacted by or receive communications concerning employment;

(F) involves coercion, duress, fraud, overreaching, harassment, intimidation, or undue influence; or

(G) contains a false, fraudulent, misleading, deceptive, or unfair statement or claim.

(e) For purposes of Subsection (d)(2)(E), a desire not to be contacted is presumed if an accident report reflects that such an indication has been made by an injured person or that person's relative.

(f) An offense under Subsection (a) or (b) is a felony of the third degree.

(g) Except as provided by Subsection (h), an offense under Subsection (d) is a Class A misdemeanor.

(h) An offense under Subsection (d) is a felony of the third degree if it is shown on the trial of the offense that the defendant has previously been convicted under Subsection (d).

(i) Final conviction of felony barratry is a serious crime for all purposes and acts, specifically including the State Bar Rules and the Texas Rules of Disciplinary Procedure.

*(Chgd. by L.1989, chap. 866(2); L.1993, chap. 900(1.01); L.1997, chap. 750(2), eff. 9/1/97.)*

## §38.122. Falsely holding oneself out as a lawyer.

(a) A person commits an offense if, with intent to obtain an economic benefit for himself or herself, the person holds himself or herself out as a lawyer, unless he or she is currently licensed to practice law in this state, another state, or a foreign country and is in good standing with the State Bar of Texas and the state bar or licensing authority of any and all other states and foreign countries where licensed.

(b) An offense under Subsection (a) of this section is a felony of the third degree.

(c) Final conviction of falsely holding oneself out to be a lawyer is a serious crime for all purposes and acts, specifically, including the State Bar Rules.

*(Added by L.1993, chap. 723(5), eff. 9/1/93. See note following §38.123.)*

## §38.123. Unauthorized practice of law.

(a) A person commits an offense if, with intent to obtain an economic benefit for himself or herself, the person:

(1) contracts with any person to represent that person with regard to personal causes of action for property damages or personal injury;

(2) advises any person as to the person's rights and the advisability of making claims for personal injuries or property damages;

(3) advises any person as to whether or not to accept an offered sum of money in settlement of claims for personal injuries or property damages;

(4) enters into any contract with another person to represent that person in personal injury or property damage matters on a contingent fee basis with an attempted assignment of a portion of the person's cause of action; or

(5) enters into any contract with a third person which purports to grant the exclusive right to select and retain legal counsel to represent the individual in any legal proceeding.

(b) This section does not apply to a person currently licensed to practice law in this state, another state, or a foreign country and in good standing with the State Bar of Texas and the state bar or licensing authority of any and all other states and foreign countries where licensed.

(c) Except as provided by Subsection (d) of this section, an offense under Subsection (a) of this section is a Class A misdemeanor.

(d) An offense under Subsection (a) of this section is a felony of the third degree if it is shown on the trial of the offense that the defendant has previously been convicted under Subsection (a) of this section.

*(Added by L.1993, chap. 723(5), eff. 9/1/93.)*

**Note:** Section 8 of L.1993, chap. 723 states:

"If enacted, S.B. No. 1067, Acts of the 73rd Legislature, Regular Session, 1993 [chap. 900] does not affect Sections 38.122 and 38.123, Penal Code, as added by Section 5 of this Act, and those sections continue in effect on and after the enactment and effective date of S.B. No. 1067, Acts of the 73rd Legislature, Regular Session, 1993, as a part, and subject to the general provisions, of the Penal Code, as amended."

### §38.13. Hindering proceedings by disorderly conduct.

(a) A person commits an offense if he intentionally hinders an official proceeding by noise or violent or tumultuous behavior or disturbance.

(b) A person commits an offense if he recklessly hinders an official proceeding by noise or violent or tumultuous behavior or disturbance and continues after explicit official request to desist.

(c) An offense under this section is a Class A misdemeanor.

*(Chgd. by L.1993, chap. 900(1.01), eff. 9/1/94.)*

### §38.14. Taking or attempting to take weapon from peace officer, parole officer, or community supervision and corrections department officer.

(a) In this section, "firearm" has the meanings assigned by Section 46.01.

(b) A person commits an offense if the person intentionally or knowingly and with force takes or attempts to take from a peace officer, parole officer, or community supervision and corrections department officer the officer's firearm, nightstick, or personal protection chemical dispensing device with the intention of harming the officer or a third person.

(c) The actor is presumed to have known that the peace officer, parole officer, or community supervision and corrections department officer was a peace officer, parole officer, or community supervision and corrections department officer if the officer was wearing a distinctive uniform or badge indicating his employment, or if the officer identified himself as a peace officer, parole officer, or community supervision and corrections department officer.

(d) It is a defense to prosecution under this section that the defendant took or attempted to take the weapon from a peace officer, parole officer, or community supervision and corrections department officer who was using force against the defendant or another in excess of the amount of force permitted by law.

(e) An offense under this section is a state jail felony.

*(Added by L.1989, chap. 986(1); redes. by L.1990, 6th C.S., chap. 12(2)(25); deleted by amendment and renum. from §38.17 and chgd. by L.1993, chap. 900(1.01); chgd. by L.1999, chap. 714(1), eff. 9/1/99.)*

### §38.15. Interference with public duties.

(a) A person commits an offense if the person with criminal negligence interrupts, disrupts, impedes, or otherwise interferes with:

(1) a peace officer while the peace officer is performing a duty or exercising authority imposed or granted by law;

(2) a person who is employed to provide emergency medical services including the transportation of ill or injured persons while the person is performing that duty;

(3) a fire fighter, while the fire fighter is fighting a fire or investigating the cause of a fire;

Printed in the U.S.A. 17

(4) an animal under the supervision of a peace officer, corrections officer, or jailer, if the person knows the animal is being used for law enforcement, corrections, prison or jail security, or investigative purposes; or

(5) the transmission of a communication over a citizen's band radio channel, the purpose of which communication is to inform or inquire about an emergency.

(b) An offense under this section is a Class B misdemeanor.

(c) It is a defense to prosecution under Subsection (a)(1) that the conduct engaged in by the defendant was intended to warn a person operating a motor vehicle of the presence of a peace officer who was enforcing Subtitle C, Title 7, Transportation Code.

(d) It is a defense to prosecution under this section that the interruption, disruption, impediment, or interference alleged consisted of speech only.

(e) In this section, "emergency" means a condition or circumstance in which an individual is or is reasonably believed by the person transmitting the communication to be in imminent danger of serious bodily injury or in which property is or is reasonably believed by the person transmitting the communication to be in imminent danger of damage or destruction.

*(Added by L.1989, chap. 1162(1); redes. by L.1990, 6th C.S., chap. 12(2)(26); deleted by amendment and renum. from §38.18 and chgd. by L.1993, chap. 900(1.01); L.1997, chap. 165(30.241), eff. 9/1/97.)*



### §38.16. Preventing execution of civil process.

(a) A person commits an offense if he intentionally or knowingly by words or physical action prevents the execution of any process in a civil cause.

(b) It is an exception to the application of this section that the actor evaded service of process by avoiding detection.

(c) An offense under this section is a Class C misdemeanor.

*(Added by L.1995, chap. 318(13), eff. 9/1/95.)*

### §38.17. Failure to stop or report aggravated sexual assault of child.

(a) A person, other than a person who has a relationship with a child described by Section 22.04(b), commits an offense if:

(1) the actor observes the commission or attempted commission of an offense prohibited by Section 22.021(a)(2)(B) under circumstances in which a reasonable person would believe that an offense of a sexual or assaultive nature was being committed or was about to be committed against the child;

(2) the actor fails to assist the child or immediately report the commission of the offense to a peace officer or law enforcement agency; and

(3) the actor could assist the child or immediately report the commission of the offense without placing the actor in danger of suffering serious bodily injury or death.

(b) An offense under this section is a Class A misdemeanor.

*(Added by L.1999, chap. 1344(1), eff. 9/1/99.)*

### §38.18. *(Renumbered to §38.15 by L.1993, chap. 900(1.01), eff. 9/1/94.)*

## CHAPTER 39. ABUSE OF OFFICE

Section



### §39.01. Definitions.

In this chapter:

(1) "Law relating to a public servant's office or employment" means a law that specifically applies to a person acting in the capacity of a public servant and that directly or indirectly:

(A) imposes a duty on the public servant; or

(B) governs the conduct of the public servant.

(2) "Misuse" means to deal with property contrary to:

(A) an agreement under which the public servant holds the property;

(B) a contract of employment or oath of office of a public servant;

(C) a law, including provisions of the General Appropriations Act specifically relating to government property, that prescribes the manner of custody or disposition of the property; or

(D) a limited purpose for which the property is delivered or received.

*(Added by L.1993, chap. 900(1.01), eff. 9/1/94.)*

## §39.02. Abuse of official capacity.

(a) A public servant commits an offense if, with intent to obtain a benefit or with intent to harm or defraud another, he intentionally or knowingly:

(1) violates a law relating to the public servant's office or employment; or

(2) misuses government property, services, personnel, or any other thing of value belonging to the government that has come into the public servant's custody or possession by virtue of the public servant's office or employment.

(b) An offense under Subsection (a)(1) is a Class A misdemeanor.

(c) An offense under Subsection (a)(2) is:

(1) a Class C misdemeanor if the value of the use of the thing misused is less than $20;

(2) a Class B misdemeanor if the value of the use of the thing misused is $20 or more but less than $500;

(3) a Class A misdemeanor if the value of the use of the thing misused is $500 or more but less than $1,500;

(4) a state jail felony if the value of the use of the thing misused is $1,500 or more but less than $20,000;

(5) a felony of the third degree if the value of the use of the thing misused if $20,000 or more but less than $100,000;

(6) a felony of the second degree if the value of the use of the thing misused is $100,000 or more but less than $200,000; or

(7) a felony of the first degree if the value of the use of the thing misused is $200,000 or more.

(d) A discount or award given for travel, such as frequent flyer miles, rental car or hotel discounts, or food coupons, are not things of value belonging to the government for purposes of this section due to the administrative difficulty and cost involved in recapturing the discount or award for a governmental entity.

*(Renumbered from §39.01 and chgd. by L.1993, chap. 900(1.01), eff. 9/1/94.)*

## §39.021. *(Renumbered to §39.04 by L.1993, chap. 900(1.01), eff. 9/1/94.)*

## §39.022. *(Renumbered to §39.05 by L.1993, chap. 900(1.01), eff. 9/1/94.)*

## §39.03. Official oppression.

(a) A public servant acting under color of his office or employment commits an offense if he:

(1) intentionally subjects another to mistreatment or to arrest, detention, search, seizure, dispossession, assessment, or lien that he knows is unlawful;

(2) intentionally denies or impedes another in the exercise or enjoyment of any right, privilege, power, or immunity, knowing his conduct is unlawful; or

(3) intentionally subjects another to sexual harassment.

(b) For purposes of this section, a public servant acts under color of his office or employment if he acts or purports to act in an official capacity or takes advantage of such actual or purported capacity.

(c) In this section, "sexual harassment" means unwelcome sexual advances, requests for sexual favors, or other verbal or physical conduct of a sexual nature, submission to which is made a term or condition of a person's exercise or enjoyment of any right, privilege, power, or immunity, either explicitly or implicitly.

(d) An offense under this section is a Class A misdemeanor.

*(Chgd. by L.1989, chap. 1217(1); L.1991, chap. 16(19.01)(34); renum. from §39.02 by L.1993, chap. 900(1.01), eff. 9/1/94.)*

## §39.04. Violations of the civil rights of person in custody; improper sexual activity with person in custody.

(a) An official or employee of a correctional facility or a peace officer commits an offense if he intentionally:

(1) denies or impedes a person in custody in the exercise or enjoyment of any right, privilege, or immunity knowing his conduct is unlawful; or

(2) engages in sexual contact, sexual intercourse, or deviate sexual intercourse with an individual in custody.

(b) An offense under Subsection (a)(1) is a Class A misdemeanor. An offense under Subsection (a)(2) is a state jail felony.

(c) This section shall not preclude prosecution for any other offense set out in this code.

(d) The Attorney General of Texas shall have concurrent jurisdiction with law enforcement agencies to investigate violations of this statute involving serious bodily injury or death.

(e) In this section:

(1) "Correctional facility" means:

(A) any place described by Section 1.07(a)(14); or

(B) a "secure correctional facility" or "secure detention facility" as defined by Section 51.02, Family Code.

(2) "Custody" means the detention, arrest, or confinement of an adult offender or the detention or the commitment to a facility operated by or under a contract with the Texas Youth Commission of a juvenile offender.

(3) "Sexual contact," "sexual intercourse," and "deviate sexual intercourse" have the meanings assigned by Section 21.01.

(f) An employee of the Texas Department of Criminal Justice commits an offense if the employee engages in sexual contact, sexual intercourse, or deviate sexual intercourse with an individual who is not the employee's spouse and who the employee knows is under the supervision of the department but not in the custody of the department.

(g) An offense under Subsection (f) is a state jail felony.

*(Renumbered from §39.021 and chgd. by L.1993, chap. 900(1.01); chgd. by L.1997, chap. 1406(1); L.1999, chap. 158(1) to (3), eff. 9/1/99.)*

### §39.05. Failure to report death of prisoner.

(a) A person commits an offense if the person is required to conduct an investigation and file a report by Article 49.18, Code of Criminal Procedure, and the person fails to investigate the death, fails to file the report as required, or fails to include in a filed report facts known or discovered in the investigation.

(b) A person commits an offense if the person is required by Section 501.055, Government Code, to:

(1) give notice of the death of an inmate and the person fails to give the notice; or

(2) conduct an investigation and file a report and the person:

(A) fails to conduct the investigation or file the report; or

(B) fails to include in the report facts known to the person or discovered by the person in the investigation.

(c) An offense under this section is a Class B misdemeanor.

*(Renumbered from §39.022 and chgd. by L.1993, chap. 900(1.01); chgd. by L.1995, chap. 321(1.104), eff. 9/1/95.)*

### §39.06. Misuse of official information.

(a) A public servant commits an offense if, in reliance on information to which he has access by virtue of his office or employment and that has not been made public, he:

(1) acquires or aids another to acquire a pecuniary interest in any property, transaction, or enterprise that may be affected by the information;

(2) speculates or aids another to speculate on the basis of the information; or

(3) as a public servant, including as a principal of a school, coerces another into suppressing or failing to report that information to a law enforcement agency.

(b) A public servant commits an offense if with intent to obtain a benefit or with intent to harm or defraud another, he discloses or uses information for a nongovernmental purpose that:

(1) he has access to by means of his office or employment; and

(2) has not been made public.

(c) A person commits an offense if, with intent to obtain a benefit or with intent to harm or defraud another, he solicits or receives from a public servant information that:

(1) the public servant has access to by means of his office or employment; and

(2) has not been made public.

(d) In this section, "information that has not been made public" means any information to which the public does not generally have access, and that is prohibited from disclosure under Chapter 552, Government Code.

(e) Except as provided by Subsection (f), an offense under this section is a felony of the third degree.

(f) An offense under Subsection (a)(3) is a Class C misdemeanor.

*(Chgd. by L.1989, chap. 927(1); renum. from §39.03 and chgd. by L.1993, chap. 900(1.01); chgd. by L.1995, chap. 76(5.95)(90), (14.52), eff. 9/1/95.)*

# TITLE 9. OFFENSES AGAINST PUBLIC ORDER AND DECENCY



## CHAPTER 42. DISORDERLY CONDUCT AND RELATED OFFENSES



### §42.01. Disorderly conduct.

(a) A person commits an offense if he intentionally or knowingly:

(1) uses abusive, indecent, profane, or vulgar language in a public place, and the language by its very utterance tends to incite an immediate breach of the peace;

(2) makes an offensive gesture or display in a public place, and the gesture or display tends to incite an immediate breach of the peace;

(3) creates, by chemical means, a noxious and unreasonable odor in a public place;

(4) abuses or threatens a person in a public place in an obviously offensive manner;

(5) makes unreasonable noise in a public place other than a sport shooting range, as defined by Section 250.001, Local Government Code, or in or near a private residence that he has no right to occupy;

(6) fights with another in a public place;

(7) enters on the property of another and for a lewd or unlawful purpose looks into a dwelling on the property through any window or other opening in the dwelling;

(8) while on the premises of a hotel or comparable establishment, for a lewd or unlawful purpose looks into a guest room not his own through a window or other opening in the room;

(9) discharges a firearm in a public place other than a public road or a sport shooting range, as defined by Section 250.001, Local Government Code;

(10) displays a firearm or other deadly weapon in a public place in a manner calculated to alarm;

(11) discharges a firearm on or across a public road; or

(12) exposes his anus or genitals in a public place and is reckless about whether another may be present who will be offended or alarmed by his act.

(b) It is a defense to prosecution under Subsection (a)(4) that the actor had significant provocation for his abusive or threatening conduct.

(c) For purposes of this section:

(1) an act is deemed to occur in a public place or near a private residence if it produces its offensive or proscribed consequences in the public place or near a private residence; and

(2) a noise is presumed to be unreasonable if the noise exceeds a decibel level of 85 after the person making the noise receives notice from a magistrate or peace officer that the noise is a public nuisance.

(d) An offense under this section is a Class C misdemeanor unless committed under Subsection (a)(9) or (a)(10), in which event it is a Class B misdemeanor.
*(Chgd. by L.1991, chap. 145(2); L.1993, chap. 900(1.01); L.1995, chap. 318(14), eff. 9/1/95.)*

### §42.02. Riot.

(a) For the purpose of this section, "riot" means the assemblage of seven or more persons resulting in conduct which:

(1) creates an immediate danger of damage to property or injury to persons;

(2) substantially obstructs law enforcement or other governmental functions or services; or

(3) by force, threat of force, or physical action deprives any person of a legal right or disturbs any person in the enjoyment of a legal right.

(b) A person commits an offense if he knowingly participates in a riot.

(c) It is a defense to prosecution under this section that the assembly was at first lawful and when one of those assembled manifested an intent to engage in conduct enumerated in Subsection (a), the actor retired from the assembly.

(d) It is no defense to prosecution under this section that another who was a party to the riot has been acquitted, has not been arrested, prosecuted, or convicted, has been convicted of a different offense or of a different type or class of offense, or is immune from prosecution.

(e) Except as provided in Subsection (f), an offense under this section is a Class B misdemeanor.

(f) An offense under this section is an offense of the same classification as any offense of a higher grade committed by anyone engaged in the riot if the offense was:

(1) in the furtherance of the purpose of the assembly; or

(2) an offense which should have been anticipated as a result of the assembly.
*(Chgd. by L.1993, chap. 900(1.01), eff. 9/1/94.)*

### §42.03. Obstructing highway or other passageway.

(a) A person commits an offense if, without legal privilege or authority, he intentionally, knowingly, or recklessly:

(1) obstructs a highway, street, sidewalk, railway, waterway, elevator, aisle, hallway, entrance, or exit to which the public or a substantial group of the public has access, or any other place used for the passage of persons, vehicles, or conveyances, regardless of the means of creating the obstruction and whether the obstruction arises from his acts alone or from his acts and the acts of others; or

(2) disobeys a reasonable request or order to move issued by a person the actor knows to be or is informed is a peace officer, a fireman, or a person with authority to control the use of the premises:

(A) to prevent obstruction of a highway or any of those areas mentioned in Subdivision (1); or

(B) to maintain public safety by dispersing those gathered in dangerous proximity to a fire, riot, or other hazard.

(b) For purposes of this section, "obstruct" means to render impassable or to render passage unreasonably inconvenient or hazardous.

(c) An offense under this section is a Class B misdemeanor.
*(Chgd. by L.1993, chap. 900(1.01), eff. 9/1/94.)*

### §42.04. Defense when conduct consists of speech or other expression.

(a) If conduct that would otherwise violate Section 42.01(a)(5) (Unreasonable Noise) or 42.03 (Obstructing Passageway) consists of speech or other communication, of gathering with others to hear or observe such speech or communication, or of gathering with others to picket or otherwise express in a nonviolent manner a position on social, economic, political, or religious questions, the actor must be ordered to move, disperse, or otherwise remedy the violation prior to his arrest if he has not yet intentionally harmed the interests of others which those sections seek to protect.

(b) The order required by this section may be given by a peace officer, a fireman, a person with authority to control the use of the premises, or any person directly affected by the violation.

(c) It is a defense to prosecution under Section 42.01(a)(5) or 42.03:

(1) that in circumstances in which this section requires an order no order was given;

(2) that an order, if given, was manifestly unreasonable in scope; or

(3) that an order, if given, was promptly obeyed.

*(Chgd. by L.1993, chap. 900(1.01), eff. 9/1/94.)*

## §42.05. Disrupting meeting or procession.

(a) A person commits an offense if, with intent to prevent or disrupt a lawful meeting, procession, or gathering, he obstructs or interferes with the meeting, procession, or gathering by physical action or verbal utterance.

(b) An offense under this section is a Class B misdemeanor.

*(Chgd. by L.1993, chap. 900(1.01), eff. 9/1/94.)*

## §42.06. False alarm or report.

(a) A person commits an offense if he knowingly initiates, communicates or circulates a report of a present, past, or future bombing, fire, offense, or other emergency that he knows is false or baseless and that would ordinarily:

(1) cause action by an official or volunteer agency organized to deal with emergencies;

(2) place a person in fear of imminent serious bodily injury; or

(3) prevent or interrupt the occupation of a building, room, place of assembly, place to which the public has access, or aircraft, automobile, or other mode of conveyance.

(b) An offense under this section is a Class A misdemeanor unless the false report is of an emergency involving a public primary or secondary school, public communications, public transportation, public water, gas, or power supply or other public service, in which event the offense is a state jail felony.

*(Chgd. by L.1993, chap. 900(1.01), eff. 9/1/94.)*

## §42.061. Silent or abusive calls to 9-1-1 service.

(a) In this section "9-1-1 service" and "public safety answering point" or "PSAP" have the meanings assigned by Section 772.001, Health and Safety Code.

(b) A person commits an offense if the person makes a telephone call to 9-1-1 when there is not an emergency and knowingly or intentionally:

(1) remains silent; or

(2) makes abusive or harassing statements to a PSAP employee.

(c) A person commits an offense if the person knowingly permits a telephone under the person's control to be used by another person in a manner described in Subsection (b).

(d) An offense under this section is a Class B misdemeanor.

*(Added by L.1989, chap. 582(1); chgd. by L.1991, chap. 14(284)(2); L.1993, chap. 900(1.01), eff. 9/1/94.)*

## §42.07. Harassment.

(a) A person commits an offense if, with intent to harass, annoy, alarm, abuse, torment, or embarrass another, he:

(1) initiates communication by telephone or in writing and in the course of the communication makes a comment, request, suggestion, or proposal that is obscene;

(2) threatens, by telephone or in writing, in a manner reasonably likely to alarm the person receiving the threat, to inflict bodily injury on the person or to commit a felony against the person, a member of his family, or his property;

(3) conveys, in a manner reasonably likely to alarm the person receiving the report, a false report, which is known by the conveyor to be false, that another person has suffered death or serious bodily injury;

(4) causes the telephone of another to ring repeatedly or makes repeated telephone communications anonymously or in a manner reasonably likely to harass, annoy, alarm, abuse, torment, embarrass, or offend another;

(5) makes a telephone call and intentionally fails to hang up or disengage the connection; or

(6) knowingly permits a telephone under his control to be used by a person to commit an offense under this section.

(b) For purposes of Subsection (a)(1), "obscene" means containing a patently offensive description of or a solicitation to commit an ultimate sex act, including sexual intercourse, masturbation, cunnilingus, fellatio, or anilingus, or a description of an excretory function. In this section, "family" has the meaning assigned by Section 71.003, Family Code.

(c) An offense under this section is a Class B misdemeanor.

*(Chgd. by L.1993, chap. 900(1.01); L.1995, chap. 657(1); L.1999, chap. 62(15.02(d)), eff. 9/1/99.)*

**§42.071.** *(Repealed by L.1997, chap. 1(10), eff. 1/28/97.)*

## §42.072. Stalking.

(a) A person commits an offense if the person, on more than one occasion and pursuant to the same scheme or course of conduct that is directed specifically at another person, knowingly engages in conduct, including following the other person, that:

(1) the actor knows or reasonably believes the other person will regard as threatening:

(A) bodily injury or death for the other person;

(B) bodily injury or death for a member of the other person's family or household; or

(C) that an offense will be committed against the other person's property;

(2) causes the other person or a member of the other person's family or household to be placed in fear of bodily injury or death or fear that an offense will be committed against the other person's property; and

(3) would cause a reasonable person to fear:

(A) bodily injury or death for himself or herself;

(B) bodily injury or death for a member of the person's family or household; or

(C) that an offense will be committed against the person's property.

(b) An offense under this section is a Class A misdemeanor, except that the offense is a felony of the third degree if the actor has previously been convicted under this section.

(c) In this section, "family," "household," and "member of a household" have the meanings assigned by Chapter 71, Family Code.

*(Added by L.1997, chap. 1(1); chgd. by L.1999, chap. 62(15.02(e)), eff. 9/1/99.)*



## §42.08. Abuse of corpse.

(a) A person commits an offense if, not authorized by law, he intentionally or knowingly:

(1) disinters, disturbs, removes, dissects, in whole or in part, carries away, or treats in a seriously offensive manner a human corpse;

(2) conceals a human corpse knowing it to be illegally disinterred;

(3) sells or buys a human corpse or in any way traffics in a human corpse; or

(4) transmits or conveys, or procures to be transmitted or conveyed, a human corpse to a place outside the state.

(b) An offense under this section is a Class A misdemeanor.

*(Deleted by amendment and renum. from §42.10 by L.1993, chap. 900(1.01), eff. 9/1/94.)*

## §42.09. Cruelty to animals.

(a) A person commits an offense if he intentionally or knowingly:

(1) tortures or seriously overworks an animal;

(2) fails unreasonably to provide necessary food, care, or shelter for an animal in his custody;

(3) abandons unreasonably an animal in his custody;

(4) transports or confines an animal in a cruel manner;

(5) kills, injures, or administers poison to an animal, other than cattle, horses, sheep, swine, or goats, belonging to another without legal authority or the owner's effective consent;

(6) causes one animal to fight with another;

(7) uses a live animal as a lure in dog race training or in dog coursing on a racetrack; or

(8) trips a horse.

(b) It is a defense to prosecution under this section that the actor was engaged in bona fide experimentation for scientific research.

(c) For purposes of this section:

(1) "Animal" means a domesticated living creature and wild living creature previously captured. "Animal" does not include an uncaptured wild creature or a wild creature whose capture was accomplished by conduct at issue under this section.

(2) "Trip" means to use an object to cause a horse to fall or lose its balance.

(d) An offense under this section is a Class A misdemeanor, except that the offense is a state jail felony if the person has previously been convicted two times under this section.

(e) It is a defense to prosecution under Subsection (a)(5) that the animal was discovered on the person's property in the act of or immediately after injuring or killing the person's goats, sheep, cattle, horses, swine, or poultry and that person killed or injured the animal at the time of this discovery.

(f) It is a defense to prosecution under Subsection (a)(8) that the actor tripped the horse for the purpose of identifying the ownership of the horse or giving veterinary care to the horse.

*(Chgd. by L.1991, chap. 78(1); deleted by amendment and renum. from §42.11 and chgd. by L.1993, chap. 900(1.01); chgd. by L.1995, chap. 318(15); L.1997, chap. 1283(1), eff. 9/1/97.)*

### §42.10. Dog fighting.

(a) A person commits an offense if he intentionally or knowingly:

(1) causes a dog to fight with another dog;

(2) for a pecuniary benefit causes a dog to fight with another dog;

(3) participates in the earnings of or operates a facility used for dog fighting;

(4) uses or permits another to use any real estate, building, room, tent, arena, or other property for dog fighting;

(5) owns or trains a dog with the intent that the dog be used in an exhibition of dog fighting; or

(6) attends as a spectator an exhibition of dog fighting.

(b) In this section, "dog fighting" means any situation in which one dog attacks or fights with another dog.

(c) A conviction under Subdivision (2), (3), or (4) of Subsection (a) may be had upon the uncorroborated testimony of a party to the offense.

(d) It is a defense to prosecution under Subdivision (1) or (2) of Subsection (a) that the actor caused a dog to fight with another dog to protect livestock, other property, or a person from the other dog, and for no other purpose.

(e) An offense under Subdivision (1) or (5) of Subsection (a) is a Class A misdemeanor. An offense under Subdivision (2), (3), or (4) of Subsection (a) is a state jail felony. An offense under Subdivision (6) of Subsection (a) is a Class C misdemeanor.

*(Renumbered from §42.111 and chgd. by L.1993, chap. 900(1.01), eff. 9/1/94.)*



### §42.11. Destruction of flag.

(a) A person commits an offense if the person intentionally or knowingly damages, defaces, mutilates, or burns the flag of the United States or the State of Texas.

(b) In this section, "flag" means an emblem, banner, or other standard or a copy of an emblem, standard, or banner that is an official or commonly recognized depiction of the flag of the United States or of this state and is capable of being flown from a staff of any character or size. The term does not include a representation of a flag on a written or printed document, a periodical, stationery, a painting or photograph, or an article of clothing or jewelry.

(c) It is an exception to the application of this section that the act that would otherwise constitute an offense is done in conformity with statutes of the United States or of this state relating to the proper disposal of damaged flags.

(d) An offense under this section is a Class A misdemeanor.

*(Added by L.1989, 1st C.S., chap. 27(1); renum. from §42.14 by L.1993, chap. 900(1.01), eff. 9/1/94.)*

### §42.111. *(Renumbered to §42.10 by L.1993, chap. 900(1.01), eff. 9/1/94.)*

### §42.12. Discharge of firearm in certain municipalities.

(a) A person commits an offense if the person recklessly discharges a firearm inside the corporate limits of a municipality having a population of 100,000 or more.

(b) An offense under this section is a Class A misdemeanor.

(c) If conduct constituting an offense under this section also constitutes an offense under another section of this code, the person may be prosecuted under either section.

(d) Subsection (a) does not affect the authority of a municipality to enact an ordinance which prohibits the discharge of a firearm.

*(Added by L.1995, chap. 663(1), eff. 9/1/95.)*

### §42.13. *(Deleted by amendment by L.1993, chap. 900(1.01), eff. 9/1/94.)*

### §42.14. *(Renumbered to §42.11 by L.1993, chap. 900(1.01), eff. 9/1/94.)*

## CHAPTER 43. PUBLIC INDECENCY

### SUBCHAPTER A. PROSTITUTION

Section

## SUBCHAPTER B. OBSCENITY



## SUBCHAPTER A. PROSTITUTION

### §43.01 Definitions.

In this subchapter:

(1) "Deviate sexual intercourse" means any contact between the genitals of one person and the mouth or anus of another person.

(2) "Prostitution" means the offense defined in Section 43.02.

(3) "Sexual contact" means any touching of the anus, breast, or any part of the genitals of another person with intent to arouse or gratify the sexual desire of any person.

(4) "Sexual conduct" includes deviate sexual intercourse, sexual contact, and sexual intercourse.

(5) "Sexual intercourse" means any penetration of the female sex organ by the male sex organ.

*(Chgd. by L.1993, chap. 900(1.01), eff. 9/1/94.)*



### §43.02. Prostitution.

(a) A person commits an offense if he knowingly:

(1) offers to engage, agrees to engage, or engages in sexual conduct for a fee; or

(2) solicits another in a public place to engage with him in sexual conduct for hire.

(b) An offense is established under Subsection (a)(1) whether the actor is to receive or pay a fee. An offense is established under Subsection (a)(2) whether the actor solicits a person to hire him or offers to hire the person solicited.

(c) An offense under this section is a Class B misdemeanor, unless the actor has been convicted previously under this section, in which event it is a Class A misdemeanor.

*(Chgd. by L.1993, chap. 900(1.01), eff. 9/1/94.)*

### §43.03. Promotion of prostitution.

(a) A person commits an offense if, acting other than as a prostitute receiving compensation for personally rendered prostitution services, he or she knowingly:

(1) receives money or other property pursuant to an agreement to participate in the proceeds of prostitution; or

(2) solicits another to engage in sexual conduct with another person for compensation.

(b) An offense under this section is a Class A misdemeanor.

*(Chgd. by L.1993, chap. 900(1.01), eff. 9/1/94.)*

### §43.04. Aggravated promotion of prostitution.

(a) A person commits an offense if he knowingly owns, invests in, finances, controls, supervises, or manages a prostitution enterprise that uses two or more prostitutes.

(b) An offense under this section is a felony of the third degree.

*(Chgd. by L.1993, chap. 900(1.01), eff. 9/1/94.)*

### §43.05. Compelling prostitution.

(a) A person commits an offense if he knowingly:

(1) causes another by force, threat, or fraud to commit prostitution; or

(2) causes by any means a person younger than 17 years to commit prostitution.

(b) An offense under this section is a felony of the second degree.

*(Chgd. by L.1993, chap. 900(1.01), eff. 9/1/94.)*

### §43.06. Accomplice witness: testimony and immunity.

(a) A party to an offense under this subchapter may be required to furnish evidence or testify about the offense.

(b) A party to an offense under this subchapter may not be prosecuted for any offense about which he is required to furnish evidence or testify, and the evidence and testimony may not be used against the party in any adjudicatory proceeding except a prosecution for aggravated perjury.

(c) For purposes of this section, "adjudicatory proceeding" means a proceeding before a court or any other agency of government in which the legal rights, powers, duties, or privileges of specified parties are determined.

(d) A conviction under this subchapter may be had upon the uncorroborated testimony of a party to the offense.

*(Chgd. by L.1993, chap. 900(1.01), eff. 9/1/94.)*

## SUBCHAPTER B. OBSCENITY

### §43.21. Definitions.

(a) In this subchapter:

(1) "obscene" means material or a performance that:

(A) the average person, applying contemporary community standards, would find that taken as a whole appeals to the prurient interest in sex;

(B) depicts or describes:

(i) patently offensive representations or descriptions of ultimate sexual acts, normal or perverted, actual or simulated, including sexual intercourse, sodomy, and sexual bestiality; or

(ii) patently offensive representations or descriptions of masturbation, excretory functions, sadism, masochism, lewd exhibition of the genitals, the male or female genitals is a state of sexual stimulation or arousal, covered male genitals in a discernibly turgid state or a device designed and marketed as useful primarily for stimulation of the human genital organs; and

(C) taken as a whole, lacks serious literary, artistic, political, and scientific value.

(2) "Material" means anything tangible that is capable of being used or adapted to arouse interest, whether through the medium of reading, observation, sound, or in any other manner, but does not include an actual three dimensional obscene device.

(3) "Performance" means a play, motion picture, dance, or other exhibition performed before an audience.

(4) "Patently offensive" means so offensive on its face as to affront current community standards of decency.

(5) "Promote" means to manufacture, issue, sell, give, provide, lend, mail, deliver, transfer, transmit, publish, distribute, circulate, disseminate, present, exhibit, or advertise, or to offer or agree to do the same.

(6) "Wholesale promote" means to manufacture, issue, sell, provide, mail, deliver, transfer, transmit, publish, distribute, circulate, disseminate, or to offer or agree to do the same for purpose of resale.

(7) "Obscene device" means a device including a dildo or artificial vagina, designed or marketed as useful primarily for the stimulation of human genital organs.

(b) If any of the depictions or descriptions of sexual conduct described in this section are declared by a court of competent jurisdiction to be unlawfully included herein, this declaration shall not invalidate this section as to other patently offensive sexual conduct included herein.

*(Chgd. by L.1993, chap. 900(1.01), eff. 9/1/94.)*

### §43.22. Obscene display or distribution.

(a) A person commits an offense if he intentionally or knowingly displays or distributes an obscene photograph, drawing, or similar visual representation or other obscene material and is reckless about whether a person is present who will be offended or alarmed by the display or distribution.

(b) An offense under this section is a Class C misdemeanor.

*(Chgd. by L.1993, chap. 900(1.01), eff. 9/1/94.)*

### §43.23. Obscenity.

(a) A person commits an offense if, knowing its content and character, he wholesale promotes or possesses with intent to wholesale promote any obscene material or obscene device.

(b) An offense under Subsection (a) is a state jail felony.

(c) A person commits an offense if, knowing its content and character, he:

(1) promotes or possesses with intent to promote any obscene material or obscene device; or

(2) produces, presents, or directs an obscene performance or participates in a portion thereof that is obscene or that contributes to its obscenity.

(d) An offense under Subsection (c) is a Class A misdemeanor.

(e) A person who promotes or wholesale promotes obscene material or an obscene device or possesses the same with intent to promote or wholesale promote it in the course of his business is presumed to do so with knowledge of its content and character.

(f) A person who possesses six or more obscene devices or identical or similar obscene articles is presumed to possess them with intent to promote the same.

(g) It is an affirmative defense to prosecution under this section that the person who possesses or promotes material or a device proscribed by this section does so for a bona fide medical, psychiatric, judicial, legislative, or law enforcement purpose.

*(Chgd. by L.1993, chap. 900(1.01), eff. 9/1/94.)*

## §43.24. Sale, distribution, or display of harmful material to minor.

(a) For purposes of this section:

(1) "Minor" means an individual younger than 18 years.

(2) "Harmful material" means material whose dominant theme taken as a whole:

(A) appeals to the prurient interest of a minor, in sex, nudity, or excretion;

(B) is patently offensive to prevailing standards in the adult community as a whole with respect to what is suitable for minors; and

(C) is utterly without redeeming social value for minors.

(b) A person commits an offense if, knowing that the material is harmful:

(1) and knowing the person is a minor, he sells, distributes, exhibits, or possesses for sale, distribution, or exhibition to a minor harmful material;

(2) he displays harmful material and is reckless about whether a minor is present who will be offended or alarmed by the display; or

(3) he hires, employs, or uses a minor to do or accomplish or assist in doing or accomplishing any of the acts prohibited in Subsection (b)(1) or (b)(2).

(c) It is a defense to prosecution under this section that:

(1) the sale, distribution, or exhibition was by a person having scientific, educational, governmental, or other similar justification; or

(2) the sale, distribution, or exhibition was to a minor who was accompanied by a consenting parent, guardian, or spouse.

(d) An offense under this section is a Class A misdemeanor unless it is committed under Subsection (b)(3) in which event it is a felony of the third degree.

*(Chgd. by L.1993, chap. 900(1.01), eff. 9/1/94.)*

## §43.25. Sexual performance by a child.

(a) In this section:

(1) "Sexual performance" means any performance or part thereof that includes sexual conduct by a child younger than 18 years of age.

(2) "Sexual conduct" means actual or simulated sexual intercourse, deviate sexual intercourse, sexual bestiality, masturbation, sado-masochistic abuse, or lewd exhibition of the genitals, the anus, or any portion of the female breast below the top of the areola.

(3) "Performance" means any play, motion picture, photograph, dance, or other visual representation that can be exhibited before an audience of one or more persons.

(4) "Produce" with respect to a sexual performance includes any conduct that directly contributes to the creation or manufacture of the sexual performance.

(5) "Promote" means to procure, manufacture, issue, sell, give, provide, lend, mail, deliver, transfer, transmit, publish, distribute, circulate, disseminate, present, exhibit, or advertise or to offer or agree to do any of the above.

(6) "Simulated" means the explicit depiction of sexual conduct that creates the appearance of actual sexual conduct during which a person engaging in the conduct exhibits any uncovered portion of the breasts, genitals, or buttocks.

(7) "Deviate sexual intercourse" has the meaning defined by Section 43.01.

(b) A person commits an offense if, knowing the character and content thereof, he employs, authorizes, or induces a child younger than 18 years of age to engage in sexual conduct or a sexual performance. A parent or legal guardian or custodian of a child younger than 18 years of age commits an offense if he consents to the participation by the child in a sexual performance.

(c) An offense under Subsection (b) is a felony of the second degree.

(d) A person commits an offense if, knowing the character and content of the material, he produces, directs, or promotes a performance that includes sexual conduct by a child younger than 18 years of age.

(e) An offense under Subsection (d) is a felony of the third degree.

(f) It is an affirmative defense to a prosecution under this section that:

(1) the defendant, in good faith, reasonably believed that the child who engaged in the sexual conduct was 18 years of age or older;

(2) the defendant was the spouse of the child at the time of the offense;

(3) the conduct was for a bona fide educational, medical, psychological, psychiatric, judicial, law enforcement, or legislative purpose; or

(4) the defendant is not more than two years older than the child.

(g) When it becomes necessary for the purposes of this section or Section 43.26 to determine whether a child who participated in sexual conduct was younger than 18 years of age, the court or jury may make this determination by any of the following methods:

(1) personal inspection of the child;

(2) inspection of the photograph or motion picture that shows the child engaging in the sexual performance;

(3) oral testimony by a witness to the sexual performance as to the age of the child based on the child's appearance at the time;

(4) expert medical testimony based on the appearance of the child engaging in the sexual performance; or

(5) any other method authorized by law or by the rules of evidence at common law.

*(Chgd. by L.1993, chap. 900(1.01); L.1999, chap. 1415(22(b)), eff. 9/1/99.)*

**§43.251. Employment harmful to children.**

(a) In this section:

(1) "Child" means a person younger than 18 years of age.

(2) "Massage" has the meaning assigned to the term "massage therapy" by Section 1, Chapter 752, Acts of the 69th Legislature, Regular Session, 1985 (Article 4512k, Texas Civil Statutes).

(3) "Massage establishment" has the meaning assigned by Section 1, Chapter 752, Acts of the 69th Legislature, Regular Session, 1985 (Article 4512k, Texas Civil Statutes).

(4) "Nude" means a child who is:

(A) entirely unclothed; or

(B) clothed in a manner that leaves uncovered or visible through less than fully opaque clothing any portion of the breasts below the top of the areola of the breasts, if the child is female, or any portion of the genitals or buttocks.

(5) "Sexually oriented commercial activity" means a massage establishment, nude studio, modeling studio, love parlor, or other similar commercial enterprise the primary business of which is the offering of a service that is intended to provide sexual stimulation or sexual gratification to the customer.

(6) "Topless" means a female child clothed in a manner that leaves uncovered or visible through less then fully opaque clothing any portion of her breasts below the top of the areola.

(b) A person commits an offense if the person employs, authorizes, or induces a child to work:

(1) in a sexually oriented commercial activity; or

(2) in any place of business permitting, requesting, or requiring a child to work nude or topless.

(c) An offense under this section is a Class A misdemeanor.

*(Chgd. by L.1993, chap. 900(1.01), eff. 9/1/94.)*

**§43.26. Possession or promotion of child pornography.**

(a) A person commits an offense if:

(1) the person knowingly or intentionally possesses visual material that visually depicts a child younger than 18 years of age at the time the image of the child was made who is engaging in sexual conduct; and

(2) the person knows that the material depicts the child as described by Subdivision (1).

(b) In this section:

(1) "Promote" has the meaning assigned by Section 43.25.

(2) "Sexual conduct" has the meaning assigned by Section 43.25.

(3) "Visual material" means:

(A) any film, photograph, videotape, negative, or slide or any photographic reproduction that contains or incorporates in any manner any film, photograph, videotape, negative, or slide; or

(B) any disk, diskette, or other physical medium that allows an image to be displayed on a computer or other video screen and any image transmitted to a computer or other video screen by telephone line, cable, satellite transmission, or other method.

(c) The affirmative defenses provided by Section 43.25(f) also apply to a prosecution under.

(d) An offense under Subsection (a) is a felony of the third degree.

(e) A person commits an offense if:

 Zt

(1) the person knowingly or intentionally promotes or p[illegible]ses with intent to promote material described by Subsection (a)(1); and

(2) the person knows that the material depicts the child as described by Subsection (a)(1).

(f) A person who possesses visual material that contains six or more identical visual depictions of a child as described by Subsection (a)(1) is presumed to possess the material with the intent to promote the material.

(g) An offense under Subsection (e) is a felony of the second degree.

*(Chgd. by L.1989, chap. 968(1); L.1993, chap. 900(1.01); L.1995, chap. 76(14.51); L.1997, chap. 933(1); L.1999, chap. 1415(22(c)), eff. 9/1/99.)*

# TITLE 10. OFFENSES AGAINST PUBLIC HEALTH, SAFETY, AND MORALS





## CHAPTER 46. WEAPONS



### §46.01. Definitions.

In this chapter:

(1) "Club" means an instrument that is specially designed, made, or adapted for the purpose of inflicting serious bodily injury or death by striking a person with the instrument, and includes but is not limited to the following:

(A) blackjack;

(B) nightstick;

(C) mace;

(D) tomahawk.

(2) "Explosive weapon" means any explosive or incendiary bomb, grenade, rocket, or mine, that is designed, made, or adapted for the purpose of inflicting serious bodily injury, death, or substantial property damage, or for the principal purpose of causing such a loud report as to cause undue public alarm or terror, and includes a device designed, made, or adapted for delivery or shooting an explosive weapon.

(3) "Firearm" means any device designed, made, or adapted to expel a projectile through a barrel by using the energy generated by an explosion or burning substance or any device readily convertible to that use. Firearm does not include a firearm that may have, as an integral part, a folding knife blade or other characteristics of weapons made illegal by this chapter and that is:

(A) an antique or curio firearm manufactured before 1899; or

(B) a replica of an antique or curio firearm manufactured before 1899, but only if the replica does not use rim fire or center fire ammunition.

(4) "Firearm silencer" means any device designed, made, or adapted to muffle the report of a firearm.

(5) "Handgun" means any firearm that is designed, made, or adapted to be fired with one hand.

(6) "Illegal knife" means a:

(A) knife with a blade over five and one-half inches;

(B) hand instrument designed to cut or stab another by being thrown;

(C) dagger, including but not limited to a dirk, stilletto*, and poniard;

**So in original. Probably should be "stiletto".*

(D) bowie knife;

(E) sword; or

(F) spear.

(7) "Knife" means any bladed hand instrument that is capable of inflicting serious bodily injury or death by cutting or stabbing a person with the instrument.

(8) "Knuckles" means any instrument that consists of finger rings, or guards made of a hard substance and that is designed, made, or adapted for the purpose of inflicting serious bodily injury or death by striking a person with a fist enclosed in the knuckles.

(9) "Machine gun" means any firearm that is capable of shooting more than two shots automatically, without manual reloading, by a single function of the trigger.

(10) "Short-barrel firearm" means a rifle with a barrel length of less than 16 inches or a shotgun with a barrel length of less than 18 inches, or any weapon made from a shotgun or rifle if, as altered, it has an overall length of less than 26 inches.

(11) "Switchblade knife" means any knife that has a blade that folds, closes, or retracts into the handle or sheath, and that:

(A) opens automatically by pressure applied to a button or other device located on the handle; or

(B) opens or releases a blade from the handle or sheath by the force of gravity or by the application of centrifugal force.

(12) "Armor-piercing ammunition" means handgun ammunition that is designed primarily for the purpose of penetrating metal or body armor and to be used principally in pistols and revolvers.

(13) "Hoax bomb" means a device that:

(A) reasonably appears to be an explosive or incendiary device; or

(B) by its design causes alarm or reaction of any type by an official of a public safety agency or a volunteer agency organized to deal with emergencies.

(14) "Chemical dispensing device" means a device, other than a small chemical dispenser sold commercially for personal protection, that is designed, made, or adapted for the purpose of dispensing a substance capable of causing an adverse psychological or physiological effect on a human being.

(15) "Racetrack" has the meaning assigned that term by the Texas Racing Act (Article 179e, Texas Civil Statutes).

(16) "Zip gun" means a device or combination of devices that was not originally a firearm and is adapted to expel a projectile through a smooth-bore or rifled-bore barrel by using the energy generated by an explosion or burning substance.

*(Chgd. by L.1989, chap. 749(1); L.1991, chap. 229(1); L.1993, chap. 900(1.01); L.1999, chap. 1445(1), eff. 9/1/99.)*

### §46.02. Unlawful carrying weapons.

(a) A person commits an offense if he intentionally, knowingly, or recklessly carries on or about his person a handgun, illegal knife, or club.

(b) Except as provided by Subsection (c), an offense under this section is a Class A misdemeanor.

(c) An offense under this section is a felony of the third degree if the offense is committed on any premises licensed or issued a permit by this state for the sale of alcoholic beverages.

*(Chgd. by L.1991, chap. 168(1); renum. from §46.03 and chgd. by L.1993, chap. 900(1.01); chgd. by L.1995, chaps. 229(2), 318(16), 754(15), 790(16), 998(3); L.1997, chaps. 165(10.02), 1221(1), 1261(24), eff. 9/1/97, 6/20/97, 9/1/97, respectively.)*

### §46.03. Places weapons prohibited.

(a) A person commits an offense if the person intentionally, knowingly, or recklessly possesses or goes with a firearm, illegal knife, club, or prohibited weapon listed in Section 46.05(a):

(1) on the physical premises of a school or educational institution, any grounds or building on which an activity sponsored by a school or educational institution is being conducted, or a passenger transportation vehicle of a school or educational

institution is public or private, unless pursuant to written regulations or written authorization of the institution;

(2) on the premises of a polling place on the day of an election or while early voting is in progress;

(3) in any government court or offices utilized by the court, unless pursuant to written regulations or written authorization of the court;

(4) on the premises of a racetrack; or

(5) in a secured area of an airport.

(b) It is a defense to prosecution under Subsections (a)(1)-(4) that the actor possessed a firearm while in the actual discharge of his official duties as a member of the armed forces or national guard or a guard employed by a penal institution, or an officer of the court.

(c) In this section:

(1) "Premises" has the meaning assigned by Section 46.035.

(2) "Secured area" means an area of an airport terminal building to which access is controlled by the inspection of persons and property under federal law.

(d) It is a defense to prosecution under Subsection (a)(5) that the actor possessed a firearm or club while traveling to or from the actor's place of assignment or in the actual discharge of duties as:

(1) a member of the armed forces or national guard;

(2) a guard employed by a penal institution;

(3) a security officer commissioned by the Texas Board of Private Investigators and Private Security Agencies if:

(A) the actor is wearing a distinctive uniform; and

(B) the firearm or club is in plain view; or

(4) *(Renumbered.)*

(5) a security officer who holds a personal protection authorization under the Private Investigators and Private Security Agencies Act (Article 4413(29bb), Texas Civil Statutes).

(e) It is a defense to prosecution under Subsection (a)(5) that the actor checked all firearms as baggage in accordance with federal or state law or regulations before entering a secured area.

(f) It is not a defense to prosecution under this section that the actor possessed a handgun and was licensed to carry a concealed handgun under Subchapter H, Chapter 411, Government Code.

(g) An offense under this section is a third degree felony.

(h) It is a defense to prosecution under Subsection (a)(4) that the actor possessed a firearm or club while traveling to or from the actor's place of assignment or in the actual discharge of duties as a security officer commissioned by the Texas Board of Private Investigators and Private Security Agencies, if:

(1) the actor is wearing a distinctive uniform; and

(2) the firearm or club is in plain view.

*(Chgd. by L.1989, chap. 749(2); L.1991, chaps. 203(2.79), 386(71), 433(1), 554(50); renum. from §46.04 and chgd. by L.1993, chap. 900(1.01); chgd. by L.1995, chaps. 229(3), 260(42), 318(17), 790(17); L.1997, chaps. 165(10.03), (31.01(70)); 1043(1); 1221(2), (3); 1261(25), eff. 9/1/97, 9/1/97, 6/20/97, 9/1/97, respectively.)*

## §46.035. Unlawful carrying of handgun by license holder.

(a) A license holder commits an offense if the license holder carries a handgun on or about the license holder's person under the authority of Subchapter H, Chapter 411, Government Code, and intentionally fails to conceal the handgun.

(b) A license holder commits an offense if the license holder intentionally, knowingly, or recklessly carries a handgun under the authority of Subchapter H, Chapter 411, Government Code, regardless of whether the handgun is concealed, on or about the license holder's person:

(1) on the premises of a business that has a permit or license issued under Chapter 25, 28, 32, 69, or 74, Alcoholic Beverage Code, if the business derives 51 percent or more of its income from the sale or service of alcoholic beverages for on-premises consumption, as determined by the Texas Alcoholic Beverage Commission under Section 104.06, Alcoholic Beverage Code;

(2) on the premises where a high school, collegiate, or professional sporting event or interscholastic event is taking place, unless the license holder is a participant in the event and a handgun is used in the event;

(3) on the premises of a correctional facility;

(4) on the premises of a hospital licensed under Chapter 241, Health and Safety Code, or on the premises of a nursing home licensed under Chapter 242, Health and Safety Code, unless the license holder has written authorization of the hospital or nursing home administration, as appropriate;

(5) in an amusement park; or

(6) on the premises of a church, synagogue, or other established place of religious worship.

(c) A license holder commits an offense if the license holder intentionally, knowingly, or recklessly carries a handgun under the authority of Subchapter H, Chapter 411, Government Code, regardless of whether the handgun is concealed, at any meeting of a governmental entity.

(d) A license holder commits an offense if, while intoxicated, the license holder carries a handgun under the authority of Subchapter H, Chapter 411, Government Code, regardless of whether the handgun is concealed.

(e) A license holder who is licensed as a security officer under the Private Investigators and Private Security Agencies Act (Article 4413(29bb), Texas Civil Statutes) and employed as a security officer commits an offense if, while in the course and scope of the security officer's employment, the security officer violates a provision of Subchapter H, Chapter 411, Government Code.

(f) In this section:

(1) "Amusement park" means a permanent indoor or outdoor facility or park where amusement rides are available for use by the public that is located in a county with a population of more than one million, encompasses at least 75 acres in surface area, is enclosed with access only through controlled entries, is open for operation more than 120 days in each calendar year, and has security guards on the premises at all times. The term does not include any public or private driveway, street, sidewalk or walkway, parking lot, parking garage, or other parking area.

(2) "License holder" means a person licensed to carry a handgun under Subchapter H, Chapter 411, Government Code.

(3) "Premises" means a building or a portion of a building. The term does not include any public or private driveway, street, sidewalk or walkway, parking lot, parking garage, or other parking area.

(g) An offense under Subsection (a), (b), (c), (d), or (e) is a Class A misdemeanor, unless the offense is committed under Subsection (b)(1) or (b)(3), in which event the offense is a felony of the third degree.

(h) It is a defense to prosecution under Subsection (a) that the actor, at the time of the commission of the offense, displayed the handgun under circumstances in which the actor would have been justified in the use of deadly force under Chapter 9.

(i) Subsections (b)(4), (b)(5), (b)(6), and (c) do not apply if the actor was not given effective notice under Section 30.06.

*(Added by L.1995, chap. 229(4); chgd. by L.1997, chaps. 165(10.04); 1261(26), (27), eff. 9/1/97.)*

## §46.04. Unlawful possession of firearm by felon.

(a) A person who has been convicted of a felony commits an offense if he possesses a firearm:

(1) after conviction and before the fifth anniversary of the person's release from confinement following conviction of the felony or the person's release from supervision under community supervision, parole, or mandatory supervision, whichever date is later; or

(2) after the period described by Subdivision (1), at any location other than the premises at which the person lives.

(b) An offense under this section is a felony of the third degree.

*(Renumbered from §46.05 and chgd. by L.1993, chap. 900(1.01), eff. 9/1/94.)*

## §46.05. Prohibited weapons.

(a) A person commits an offense if he intentionally or knowingly possesses, manufactures, transports, repairs, or sells:

(1) an explosive weapon;

(2) a machine gun;

(3) a short-barrel firearm;

(4) a firearm silencer;

(5) a switchblade knife;

(6) knuckles;

(7) armor-piercing ammunition;

(8) a chemical dispensing device; or

(9) a zip gun.

(b) It is a defense to prosecution under this section that the actor's conduct was incidental to the performance of official duty by the armed forces or national guard, a governmental law enforcement agency, or a correctional facility.

(c) It is a defense to prosecution under this section that the actor's possession was pursuant to registration pursuant to the National Firearms Act, as amended.

(d) It is an affirmative defense to prosecution under this section that the actor's conduct:

(1) was incidental to dealing with a switchblade knife, springblade knife, or short-barrel firearm solely as an antique or curio; or

(2) was incidental to dealing with armor-piercing ammunition solely for the purpose of making the ammunition available to an organization, agency, or institution listed in Subsection (b).

(e) An offense under this section is a felony of the third degree unless it is committed under Subsection (a)(5) or (a)(6), in which event, it is a Class A misdemeanor.
*(Chgd. by L.1991, chap. 229(2); renum. from §46.06 and chgd. by L.1993, chap. 900(1.01), eff. 9/1/94.)*

### §46.06. Unlawful transfer of certain weapons.

(a) A person commits an offense if the person:

(1) sells, rents, leases, loans, or gives a handgun to any person knowing that the person to whom the handgun is to be delivered intends to use it unlawfully or in the commission of an unlawful act;

(2) intentionally or knowingly sells, rents, leases, or gives or offers to sell, rent, lease, or give to any child younger than 18 years any firearm, club, or illegal knife;

(3) intentionally, knowingly, or recklessly sells a firearm or ammunition for a firearm to any person who is intoxicated;

(4) knowingly sells a firearm or ammunition for a firearm to any person who has been convicted of a felony before the fifth anniversary of the later of the following dates:

(A) the person's release from confinement following conviction of the felony; or

(B) the person's release from supervision under community supervision, parole, or mandatory supervision following conviction of the felony;

(5) sells, rents, leases, loans, or gives a handgun to any person knowing that an active protective order is directed to the person to whom the handgun is to be delivered; or

(6) knowingly purchases, rents, leases, or receives as a loan or gift from another a handgun while an active protective order is directed to the actor.

(b) In this section:

(1) "Intoxicated" means substantial impairment of mental or physical capacity resulting from introduction of any substance into the body.

(2) "Active protective order" means a protective order issued under Title 4, Family Code, that is in effect. The term does not include a temporary protective order issued before the court holds a hearing on the matter.

(c) It is an affirmative defense to prosecution under Subsection (a)(2) that the transfer was to a minor whose parent or the person having legal custody of the minor had given written permission for the sale or, if the transfer was other than a sale, the parent or person having legal custody had given effective consent.

(d) An offense under this section is a Class A misdemeanor, except that an offense under Subsection (a)(2) is a state jail felony if the weapon that is the subject of the offense is a handgun.
*(Renumbered from §46.07 and chgd. by L.1993, chap. 900(1.01); chgd. by L.1995, chap. 324(1); L.1997, chaps. 1193(22), 1304(1); L.1999, chap.62(15.02(f)), eff. 9/1/99.)*

### §46.07. Interstate purchase.

A resident of this state may, if not otherwise precluded by law, purchase firearms, ammunition, reloading components, or firearm accessories in contiguous states. This authorization is enacted in conformance with Section 922(b)(3)(A), Public Law 90-618, 90th Congress.
*(Renumbered from §46.08 by L.1993, chap. 900(1.01), eff. 9/1/94.)*

### §46.08. Hoax bombs.

(a) A person commits an offense if the person knowingly manufactures, sells, purchases, transports, or possesses a hoax bomb with intent to use the hoax bomb to:

(1) make another believe that the hoax bomb is an explosive or incendiary device; or

(2) cause alarm or reaction of any type by an official of a public safety agency or volunteer agency organized to deal with emergencies.

(b) An offense under this section is a Class A misdemeanor.
*(Renumbered from §46.09 by L.1993, chap. 900(1.01), eff. 9/1/94.)*

### §46.09. Components of explosives.

(a) A person commits an offense if the person knowingly possesses components of an explosive weapon with the intent to combine the components into an explosive weapon for use in a criminal endeavor.

(b) An offense under this section is a felony of the third degree.
*(Renumbered from §46.10 by L.1993, chap. 900(1.01), eff. 9/1/94.)*

### §46.10. Deadly weapon in a penal institution.

(a) A person commits an offense if, while confined in a penal institution, he intentionally, knowingly, or recklessly:

(1) carries on or about his person a deadly weapon; or

(2) possesses or conceals a deadly weapon in the penal institution.

(b) It is an affirmative defense to prosecution under this section that at the time of the offense the actor was engaged in conduct authorized by an employee of the penal institution.

(c) A person who is subject to prosecution under both this section and another section under this chapter may be prosecuted under either section.

(d) An offense under this section is a felony of the third degree.
*(Renumbered from §46.11 by L.1993, chap. 900(1.01), eff. 9/1/94.)*

### §46.11. Penalty if offense committed within weapon-free school zone.

(a) Except as provided by Subsection (b), the punishment prescribed for an offense under this chapter is increased to the punishment prescribed for the next highest category of offense if it is shown beyond a reasonable doubt on the trial of the offense that the actor committed the offense in a place that the actor knew was:

(1) within 300 feet of the premises of a school; or

(2) on premises where:

(A) an official school function is taking place; or

(B) an event sponsored or sanctioned by the University Interscholastic League is taking place.

(b) This section does not apply to an offense under Section 46.03(a)(1).

(c) In this section:

(1) "Institution of higher education" and "premises" have the meanings assigned by Section 481.134, Health and Safety Code.

(2) "School" means a private or public elementary or secondary school.
*(Added by L.1995, chap. 320(1); chgd. by L.1997, chap. 1063(10), eff. 9/1/97.)*

### §46.12. Maps as evidence of location or area.

(a) In a prosecution of an offense for which punishment is increased under Section 46.11, a map produced or reproduced by a municipal or county engineer for the purpose of showing the location and boundaries of weapon-free zones is admissible in evidence and is prima facie evidence of the location or boundaries of those areas if the governing body of the municipality or county adopts a resolution or ordinance approving the map as an official finding and record of the location or boundaries of those areas.

(b) A municipal or county engineer may, on request of the governing body of the municipality or county, revise a map that has been approved by the governing body of the municipality or county as provided by Subsection (a).

(c) A municipal or county engineer shall file the original or a copy of every approved or revised map approved as provided by Subsection (a) with the county clerk of each county in which the area is located.

(d) This section does not prevent the prosecution from:

(1) introducing or relying on any other evidence or testimony to establish any element of an offense for which punishment is increased under Section 46.11; or

(2) using or introducing any other map or diagram otherwise admissible under the Texas Rules of Criminal Evidence.
*(Added by L.1995, chap. 320(2), eff. 9/1/95.)*

### §46.13. Making a firearm accessible to a child.

(a) In this section:

(1) "Child" means a person younger than 17 years of age.

(2) "Readily dischargeable firearm" means a firearm that is loaded with ammunition, whether or not a round is in the chamber.

(3) "Secure" means to take steps that a reasonable person would take to prevent the access to a readily dischargeable firearm by a child, including but not limited to placing a firearm in a locked container or temporarily rendering the firearm inoperable by a trigger lock or other means.

(b) A person commits an offense if a child gains access to a readily dischargeable firearm and the person with criminal negligence:

(1) failed to secure the firearm; or

(2) left the firearm in a place to which the person knew or should have known the child would gain access.

(c) It is an affirmative defense to prosecution under this section that the child's access to the firearm:

(1) was supervised by a person older than 18 years of age and was for hunting, sporting, or other lawful purposes;

(2) consisted of lawful defense by the child of people or property;

(3) was gained by entering property in violation of this code; or

(4) occurred during a time when the actor was engaged in an agricultural enterprise.

(d) Except as provided by Subsection (e), an offense under this section is a Class C misdemeanor.

(e) An offense under this section is a Class A misdemeanor if the child discharges the firearm and causes death or serious bodily injury to himself or another person.

(f) A peace officer or other person may not arrest the actor before the seventh day after the date on which the offense is committed if:

(1) the actor is a member of the family, as defined by Section 71.003, Family Code, of the child who discharged the firearm; and

(2) the child in discharging the firearm caused the death of or serious injury to the child.

(g) A dealer of firearms shall post in a conspicuous position on the premises where the dealer conducts business a sign that contains the following warning in block letters not less than one inch in height:

> "IT IS UNLAWFUL TO STORE, TRANSPORT, OR ABANDON AN UNSECURED FIREARM IN A PLACE WHERE CHILDREN ARE LIKELY TO BE AND CAN OBTAIN ACCESS TO THE FIREARM."

*(Added by L.1995, chap. 83(1); chgd. by L.1999, chap. 62(15.02(g)), eff. 9/1/99.)*

### §46.15. Nonapplicability.

(a) Sections 46.02 and 46.03 do not apply to:

(1) peace officers and neither section prohibits a peace officer from carrying a weapon in this state, regardless of whether the officer is engaged in the actual discharge of the officer's duties while carrying the weapon;

(2) parole officers and neither section prohibits an officer from carrying a weapon in this state if the officer is:

(A) engaged in the actual discharge of the officer's duties while carrying the weapon; and

(B) in compliance with policies and procedures adopted by the Texas Department of Criminal Justice regarding the possession of a weapon by an officer while on duty;

(3) community supervision and corrections department officers appointed or employed under Section 76.004, Government Code, and neither section prohibits an officer from carrying a weapon in this state if the officer is:

(A) engaged in the actual discharge of the officer's duties while carrying the weapon; and

(B) authorized to carry a weapon under Section 76.0051, Government Code; or

(4) a judge or justice of the supreme court, the court of criminal appeals, a court of appeals, a district court, a criminal district court, a constitutional county court, a statutory county court, a justice court, or a municipal court who is licensed to carry a concealed handgun under Subchapter H, Chapter 411, Government Code.

(b) Section 46.02 does not apply to a person who:

(1) is in the actual discharge of official duties as a member of the armed forces or state military forces as defined by Section 431.001, Government Code, or as a guard employed by a penal institution; *(Chgd. by L.1997, chap. 1261(28), eff. 9/1/97. See other paragraph (1) below.)*

(1) is in the actual discharge of official duties as a member of the armed forces or state military forces as defined by Section 431.001, Government Code, or as an employee of a penal institution who is performing a security function; *(Chgd. by L.1997, chap. 1221(4), eff. 6/20/97. See other paragraph (1) above.)*

(2) is on the person's own premises or premises under the person's control unless the person is an employee or agent of the owner of the premises and the person's primary responsibility is to act in the capacity of a security guard to protect persons or property, in which event the person must comply with Subdivision (5);

(3) is traveling;

(4) is engaging in lawful hunting, fishing, or other sporting activity on the immediate premises where the activity is conducted, or is directly en route between the premises and the actor's residence, if the weapon is a type commonly used in the activity;

(5) holds a security officer commission issued by the Texas Board of Private Investigators and Private Security Agencies, if:

(A) the person is engaged in the performance of the person's duties as a security officer or traveling to and from the person's place of assignment;

(B) the person is wearing a distinctive uniform; and

(C) the weapon is in plain view;

(6) is carrying a concealed handgun and a valid license issued under Article 4413(29ee), Revised Statutes, to carry a concealed handgun of the same category as the handgun the person is carrying;

(7) holds a security officer commission and a personal protection authorization issued by the Texas Board of Private Investigators and Private Security Agencies and who is providing personal protection under the Private Investigators and Private Security Agencies Act (Article 4413(29bb), Texas Civil Statutes); or

(8) holds an alcoholic beverage permit or license or is an employee of a holder of an alcoholic beverage permit or license if the person is supervising the operation of the permitted or licensed premises.

(c) The provision of Section 46.02 prohibiting the carrying of a club does not apply to a noncommissioned security guard at an institution of higher education who carries a nightstick or similar club, and who has undergone 15 hours of training in the proper use of the club, including at least seven hours of training in the use of the club for nonviolent restraint. For the purposes of this subsection, "nonviolent restraint" means the use of reasonable force, not intended and not likely to inflict bodily injury.

(d) The provisions of Section 46.02 prohibiting the carrying of a firearm or carrying of a club do not apply to a public security officer employed by the adjutant general under Section 431.029, Government Code, in performance of official duties or while traveling to or from a place of duty.

(e) The provisions of Section 46.02 prohibiting the carrying of an illegal knife do not apply to an individual carrying a bowie knife or a sword used in a historical demonstration or in a ceremony in which the knife or sword is significant to the performance of the ceremony.

*(Added by L.1995, chap. 318(18); chgd. by L.1997, chaps. 1221(4),1261(28); L.1999, chaps. 62(9.25), 1445(2), eff. 9/1/99.)*

# CHAPTER 47. GAMBLING

Section



## §47.01. Definitions.

In this chapter:

(1) "Bet" means an agreement to win or lose something of value solely or partially by chance. A bet does not include:

(A) contracts of indemnity or guaranty, or life, health, property, or accident insurance;

(B) an offer of a prize, award, or compensation to the actual contestants in a bona fide contest for the determination of skill, speed, strength, or endurance or to the owners of animals, vehicles, watercraft, or aircraft entered in a contest; or

(C) an offer of merchandise, with a value not greater than $25, made by the proprietor of a bona fide carnival contest conducted at a carnival sponsored by a nonprofit religious, fraternal, school, law enforcement, youth, agricultural, or civic group, including any nonprofit agricultural or civic group incorporated by the state before 1955, if the person to receive the merchandise from the proprietor is the person who performs the carnival contest.

(2) "Bookmaking" means:

(A) to receive and record or to forward more than five bets or offers to bet in a period of 24 hours;

(B) to receive and record or to forward bets or offers to bet totaling more than $1,000 in a period of 24 hours; or

(C) a scheme by three or more persons to receive, record, or forward a bet or an offer to bet.

(3) "Gambling place" means any real estate, building, room, tent, vehicle, boat, or other property whatsoever, one of the uses of which is the making or settling of bets, bookmaking, or the conducting of a lottery or the playing of gambling devices.

(4) "Gambling device" means any electronic, electromechanical, or mechanical contrivance not excluded under Paragraph (B) that for a consideration affords the player an opportunity to obtain anything of value, the award of which is determined solely or partially by chance, even though accompanied by some skill, whether or not the prize is automatically paid by the contrivance. The term:

(A) includes, but is not limited to, gambling device versions of bingo, keno, blackjack, lottery, roulette, video poker, or similar electronic, electromechanical, or mechanical games, or facsimiles thereof, that operate by chance or partially so, that as a result of the play or operation of the game award credits or free games, and that record the number of free games or credits so awarded and the cancellation or removal of the free games or credits; and

(B) does not include any electronic, electromechanical, or mechanical contrivance designed, made, and adapted solely for bona fide amusement purposes if the contrivance rewards the player exclusively with noncash merchandise prizes, toys, or novelties, or a representation of value redeemable for those items, that have a wholesale value available from a single play of the game or device of not more than 10 times the amount charged to play the game or device once or $5, whichever is less.

(5) "Altered gambling equipment" means any contrivance that has been altered in some manner, including, but not limited to, shaved dice, loaded dice, magnetic dice, mirror rings, electronic sensors, shaved cards, marked cards, and any other equipment altered or designed to enhance the actor's chances of winning.

(6) "Gambling paraphernalia" means any book, instrument, or apparatus by means of which bets have been or may be recorded or registered; any record, ticket, certificate, bill, slip, token, writing, scratch sheet, or other means of carrying on bookmaking, wagering pools, lotteries, numbers, policy, or similar games.

(7) "Lottery" means any scheme or procedure whereby one or more prizes are distributed by chance among persons who have paid or promised consideration for a chance to win anything of value, whether such scheme or procedure is called a pool, lottery, raffle, gift, gift enterprise, sale, policy game, or some other name.

(8) "Private place" means a place to which the public does not have access, and excludes, among other places, streets, highways, restaurants, taverns, nightclubs, schools, hospitals, and the common areas of apartment houses, hotels, motels, office buildings, transportation facilities, and shops.

(9) "Thing of value" means any benefit, but does not include an unrecorded and immediate right of replay not exchangeable for value.

*(Chgd. by L.1989, chap. 396(1); L.1993, chap. 900(1.01); L.1995, chap. 318(19), eff. 9/1/95.)*

### §47.02. Gambling.

(a) A person commits an offense if he:

(1) makes a bet on the partial or final result of a game or contest or on the performance of a participant in a game or contest;

(2) makes a bet on the result of any political nomination, appointment, or election or on the degree of success of any nominee, appointee, or candidate; or

(3) plays and bets for money or other thing of value at any game played with cards, dice, balls, or any other gambling device.

(b) It is a defense to prosecution under this section that:

(1) the actor engaged in gambling in a private place;

(2) no person received any economic benefit other than personal winnings; and

(3) except for the advantage of skill or luck, the risks of losing and the chances of winning were the same for all participants.

(c) It is a defense to prosecution under this section that the actor reasonably believed that the conduct:

(1) was permitted under the Bingo Enabling Act (Article 179d, Texas Civil Statutes);

(2) was permitted under the Charitable Raffle Enabling Act (Article 179f, Revised Statutes);

(3) consisted entirely of participation in the state lottery authorized by the State Lottery Act (Chapter 466, Government Code);

(4) was permitted under the Texas Racing Act (Article 179e, Texas Civil Statutes); or

(5) consisted entirely of participation in a drawing for the opportunity to participate in a hunting, fishing, or other recreational event conducted by the Parks and Wildlife Department.

(d) An offense under this section is a Class C misdemeanor.

(e) It is a defense to prosecution under this section that a person played for something of value other than money using an electronic, electromechanical, or mechanical contrivance excluded from the definition of "gambling device" under Section 47.01(4)(B).

*(Chgd. by L.1989, chap. 957(2); L.1991, 1st C.S., chap. 6(3); L.1993, chap. 900(1.01); L.1995, chaps. 76(14.53), 318(20), 931(79); L.1997, chap. 1256(124), eff. 9/1/97.)*

### §47.03. Gambling promotion.

(a) A person commits an offense if he intentionally or knowingly does any of the following acts:

(1) operates or participates in the earnings of a gambling place;

(2) engages in bookmaking;

(3) for gain, becomes a custodian of anything of value bet or offered to be bet;

(4) sells chances on the partial or final result of or on the margin of victory in any game or contest or on the performance of any participant in any game or contest or on the result of any political nomination, appointment, or election or on the degree of success of any nominee, appointee, or candidate; or

(5) for gain, sets up or promotes any lottery or sells or offers to sell or knowingly possesses for transfer, or transfers any card, stub, ticket, check, or other device designed to serve as evidence of participation in any lottery.

(b) An offense under this section is a Class A misdemeanor.

*(Chgd. by L.1993, chap. 900(1.01), eff. 9/1/94.)*

### §47.04. Keeping a gambling place.

(a) A person commits an offense if he knowingly uses or permits another to use as a gambling place any real estate, building, room, tent, vehicle, boat, or other property whatsoever owned by him or under his control, or rents or lets any such property with a view or expectation that it be so used.

(b) It is an affirmative defense to prosecution under this section that:

(1) the gambling occurred in a private place;

(2) no person received any economic benefit other than personal winnings; and

(3) except for the advantage of skill or luck, the risks of losing and the chances of winning were the same for all participants.

(c) An offense under this section is a Class A misdemeanor.

*(Chgd. by L.1993, chap. 900(1.01), eff. 9/1/94.)*

### §47.05. Communicating gambling information.

(a) A person commits an offense if, with the intent to further gambling, he knowingly communicates information as to bets, betting odds, or changes in betting odds or he knowingly provides, installs, or maintains equipment for the transmission or receipt of such information.

(b) It is an exception to the application of Subsection (a) that the information communicated is intended for use in placing a lawful wager under Article 11, Texas Racing Act (Article 179e, Texas Civil Statutes), and is not communicated in violation of Section 14.01 of that Act.

(c) An offense under this section is a Class A misdemeanor.

*(Chgd. by L.1993, chap. 900(1.01), eff. 9/1/94.)*

### §47.06. Possession of gambling device, equipment, or paraphernalia.

(a) A person commits an offense if, with the intent to further gambling, he knowingly owns, manufactures, transfers, or possesses any gambling device that he knows is designed for gambling purposes or any equipment that he knows is designed as a subassembly or essential part of a gambling device.

(b) A person commits an offense if, with the intent to further gambling, he knowingly owns, manufactures, transfers commercially, or possesses any altered gambling equipment that he knows is designed for gambling purposes or any equipment that he knows is designed as a subassembly or essential part of such device.

(c) A person commits an offense if, with the intent to further gambling, the person knowingly owns, manufactures, transfers commercially, or possesses gambling paraphernalia.

(d) It is a defense to prosecution under Subsections (a) and (c) that:

(1) the device, equipment, or paraphernalia is used for or is intended for use in gambling that is to occur entirely in a private place;

(2) a person involved in the gambling does not receive any economic benefit other than personal winnings; and

(3) except for the advantage of skill or luck, the chance of winning is the same for all participants.

(e) An offense under this section is a Class A misdemeanor.

(f) It is a defense to prosecution under Subsection (a) or (c) that the person owned, manufactured, transferred, or possessed the gambling device, equipment, or paraphernalia for the sole purpose of shipping it to another jurisdiction where the possession or use of the device, equipment, or paraphernalia was legal.

(g) A district or county attorney is not required to have a search warrant or subpoena to inspect a gambling device or gambling equipment or paraphernalia on an ocean-going vessel that enters the territorial waters of this state to call at a port in this state.

*(Chgd. by L.1991, chap. 44(1); 1st C.S., chap. 6(4); L.1993, chap. 900(1.01), eff. 9/1/94.)*

## §47.07. Evidence.

In any prosecution under this chapter in which it is relevant to prove the occurrence of a sporting event, a published report of its occurrence in a daily newspaper, magazine, or other periodically printed publication of general circulation shall be admissible in evidence and is prima facie evidence that the event occurred. *(Deleted by amendment and renum. from §47.08 and chgd. by L.1993, chap. 900(1.01), eff. 9/1/94.)*

## §47.08. Testimonial immunity.

(a) A party to an offense under this chapter may be required to furnish evidence or testify about the offense.

(b) A party to an offense under this chapter may not be prosecuted for any offense about which he is required to furnish evidence or testify, and the evidence and testimony may not be used against the party in any adjudicatory proceeding except a prosecution for aggravated perjury.

(c) For purposes of this section, "adjudicatory proceeding" means a proceeding before a court or any other agency of government in which the legal rights, powers, duties, or privileges of specified parties are determined.

(d) A conviction under this chapter may be had upon the uncorroborated testimony of a party to the offense.

*(Renumbered from §47.09 by L.1993, chap. 900(1.01), eff. 9/1/94.)*

## §47.09. Other defenses.

(a) It is a defense to prosecution under this chapter that the conduct:

(1) was authorized under:

(A) the Bingo Enabling Act (Article 179d, Texas Civil Statutes);

(B) the Texas Racing Act (Article 179e, Texas Civil Statutes); or

(C) the Charitable Raffle Enabling Act (Article 179f, Revised Statutes);

(2) consisted entirely of participation in the state lottery authorized by Chapter 466, Government Code; or

(3) was a necessary incident to the operation of the state lottery and was directly or indirectly authorized by:

(A) Chapter 466, Government Code;

(B) the lottery division of the Texas Lottery Commission;

(C) the Texas Lottery Commission; or

(D) the director of the lottery division of the Texas Lottery Commission.

(b) It is an affirmative defense to prosecution under Sections 47.04, 47.06(a), and 47.06(c) that the gambling device, equipment, or paraphernalia is aboard an ocean-going vessel that enters the territorial waters of this state to call at a port in this state if:

(1) before the vessel enters the territorial waters of this state, the district attorney or, if there is no district attorney, the county attorney for the county in which the port is located receives notice of the existence of the device, equipment, or paraphernalia on board the vessel and of the anticipated dates on which the vessel will enter and leave the territorial waters of this state;

(2) at all times while the vessel is in the territorial waters of this state all devices, equipment, or paraphernalia are disabled, electronically or by another method, from a remote and secured area of the vessel in a manner that allows only the master or crew of the vessel to remove any disabling device;

(3) at all times while the vessel is in the territorial waters of this state any disabling device is not removed except for the purposes of inspecting or repairing the device, equipment, or paraphernalia; and

(4) the device, equipment, or paraphernalia is not used for gambling or other gaming purposes while the vessel is in the territorial waters of this state.
*(Added by L.1993, chap. 900(1.01); chgd. by L.1995, chap. 76(14.54); L.1997, chaps. 111(1), 1035(55); L.1999, chap. 844(1), eff. 9/1/99.)*

### §47.10. American documentation of vessel required.

If 18 U.S.C. Section 1082 is repealed, the affirmative defenses provided by Section 47.09(b) apply only if the vessel is documented under the laws of the United States. *(Added by L.1989, chap. 1030(4); redes. by L.1990, 6th C.S., chap. 12(2)(27); deleted by amendment and renum. from §47.13 and chgd. by L.1993, chap. 900(1.01), eff. 9/1/94.)*

### §§47.11, 47.12. *(Deleted by amendment by L.1993, chap. 900(1.01), eff. 9/1/94.)*

### §47.13. *(Renumbered to §47.10 by L.1993, chap. 900(1.01), eff. 9/1/94.)*

### §47.14. *(Deleted by amendment by L.1993, chap. 900(1.01), eff. 9/1/94.)*

## CHAPTER 48. CONDUCT AFFECTING PUBLIC HEALTH

Section


### §48.01. Smoking tobacco.

(a) A person commits an offense if he is in possession of a burning tobacco product or smokes tobacco in a facility of a public primary or secondary school or an elevator, enclosed theater or movie house, library, museum, hospital, transit system bus, or intrastate bus, as defined by Section 541.201, Transportation Code, plane, or train which is a public place.

(b) It is a defense to prosecution under this section that the conveyance or public place in which the offense takes place does not have prominently displayed a reasonably sized notice that smoking is prohibited by state law in such conveyance or public place and that an offense is punishable by a fine not to exceed $500.

(c) All conveyances and public places set out in Subsection (a) of Section 48.01 shall be equipped with facilities for extinguishment of smoking materials and it shall be a defense to prosecution under this section if the conveyance or public place within which the offense takes place is not so equipped.

(d) It is an exception to the application of Subsection (a) if the person is in possession of the burning tobacco product or smokes tobacco exclusively with in an area designated for smoking tobacco or as a participant in an authorized theatrical performance.

(e) An area designated for smoking tobacco on a transit system bus or intrastate plane or train must also include the area occupied by the operator of the transit system bus, plane, or train.

(f) An offense under this section is punishable as a Class C misdemeanor.
*(Chgd. by L.1991, chap. 108(2); L.1993, chap. 900(1.01); L.1997, chap. 165(30.242), eff. 9/1/97.)*

### §48.02. Prohibition of the purchase and sale of human organs.

(a) "Human organ" means the human kidney, liver, heart, lung, pancreas, eye, bone, skin, fetal tissue, or any other human organ or tissue, but does not include hair or blood, blood components (including plasma), blood derivatives, or blood reagents.

(b) A person commits an offense if he or she knowingly or intentionally offers to buy, offers to sell, acquires, receives, sells, or otherwise transfers any human organ for valuable consideration.

(c) It is an exception to the application of this section that the valuable consideration is: (1) a fee paid to a physician or to other medical personnel for services rendered in the usual course of medical practice or a fee paid for hospital or other clinical services; (2) reimbursement of legal or medical expenses incurred for the benefit of the ultimate receiver of the organ; or (3) reimbursement of expenses of travel, housing, and lost wages incurred by the donor of a human organ in connection with the donation of the organ.

(d) A violation of this section is a Class A misdemeanor.
*(Chgd. by L.1993, chap. 900(1.01), eff. 9/1/94.)*

Printed in the U.S.A. 27

# CHAPTER 49. INTOXICATION AND ALCOHOLIC BEVERAGE OFFENSES

*(Added by L.1993, chap. 900(1.01), eff. 9/1/94.)*

Section





## §49.01. Definitions.

In this chapter:

(1) "Alcohol concentration" means the number of grams of alcohol per:

(A) 210 liters of breath;

(B) 100 milliliters of blood; or

(C) 67 milliliters of urine.

(2) "Intoxicated" means:

(A) not having the normal use of mental or physical faculties by reason of the introduction of alcohol, a controlled substance, a drug, a dangerous drug, a combination of two or more of those substances, or any other substance into the body; or

(B) having an alcohol concentration of 0.08 or more.

(3) "Motor vehicle" has the meaning assigned by Section 32.24(a).

(4) "Watercraft" means a vessel, one or more water skis, an aquaplane, or another device used for transporting or carrying a person on water, other than a device propelled only by the current of water.

*(5) "Amusement ride" has the meaning assigned by Section 2, Article 21.60, Insurance Code.*

*(6) "Mobile amusement ride" has the meaning assigned by Section 2, Article 21.60, Insurance Code.*

*(Added by L.1993, chap. 900(1.01); chgd. by L.1999, chaps. 234(1), 1364(8), eff. 9/1/99, 1/1/2000, respectively. Matter in italics eff. 1/1/2000.)*

## §49.02. Public intoxication.

(a) A person commits an offense if the person appears in a public place while intoxicated to the degree that the person may endanger the person or another.

(b) It is a defense to prosecution under this section that the alcohol or other substance was administered for therapeutic purposes and as a part of the person's professional medical treatment by a licensed physician.

(c) Except as provided by Subsection (e), an offense under this section is a Class C misdemeanor.

(d) An offense under this section is not a lesser included offense under Section 49.04.

(e) An offense under this section committed by a person younger than 21 years of age is punishable in the same manner as if the minor committed an offense to which Section 106.071, Alcoholic Beverage Code, applies.

*(Added by L.1993, chap. 900(1.01); chgd. by L.1997, chap. 1013(12), eff. 9/1/97.)*

## §49.03. Consumption or possession of alcoholic beverage in motor vehicle.

(a) A person commits an offense if the person consumes an alcoholic beverage while operating a motor vehicle in a public place and is observed doing so by a peace officer.

(b) An offense under this section is a Class C misdemeanor.

*(Added by L.1993, chap. 900(1.01), eff. 9/1/94.)*

## §49.04. Driving while intoxicated.

(a) A person commits an offense if the person is intoxicated while operating a motor vehicle in a public place.

(b) Except as provided by Subsection (c) and Section 49.09, an offense under this section is a Class B misdemeanor, with a minimum term of confinement of 72 hours.

(c) If it is shown on the trial of an offense under this section that at the time of the offense the person operating the motor vehicle had an open container of alcohol in the person's immediate possession, the offense is a Class B misdemeanor, with a minimum term of confinement of six days.

*(Added by L.1993, chap. 900(1.01); chgd. by L.1995, chap. 76(14.55), eff. 9/1/95.)*

### §49.05. Flying while intoxicated.

(a) A person commits an offense if the person is intoxicated while operating an aircraft.

(b) Except as provided by Section 49.09, an offense under this section is a Class B misdemeanor, with a minimum term of confinement of 72 hours.

*(Added by L.1993, chap. 900(1.01), eff. 9/1/94.)*

### §49.06. Boating while intoxicated.

(a) A person commits an offense if the person is intoxicated while operating a watercraft.

(b) Except as provided by Section 49.09, an offense under this section is a Class B misdemeanor, with a minimum term of confinement of 72 hours.

*(Added by L.1993, chap. 900(1.01), eff. 9/1/94.)*

### §49.065. Assembling or operating an amusement ride while intoxicated.

(a) A person commits an offense if the person is intoxicated while operating an amusement ride or while assembling a mobile amusement ride.

(b) Except as provided by Subsection (c) and Section 49.09, an offense under this section is a Class B misdemeanor with a minimum term of confinement of 72 hours.

(c) If it is shown on the trial of an offense under this section that at the time of the offense the person operating the amusement ride or assembling the mobile amusement ride had an open container of alcohol in the person's immediate possession, the offense is a Class B misdemeanor with a minimum term of confinement of six days.

*(Added by L.1999, chap. 1364(9), eff. 1/1/2000.)*

### §49.07. Intoxication assault.

(a) A person commits an offense if the person, by accident or mistake[,]*:*

*(1)* while operating an aircraft, watercraft, or *amusement ride while intoxicated,* or *while operating a* motor vehicle in a public place while intoxicated, by reason of that intoxication causes serious bodily injury to another*; or*

*(2) as a result of assembling a mobile amusement ride while intoxicated causes serious bodily injury to another.*

(b) In this section, "serious bodily injury" means injury that creates a substantial risk of death or that causes serious permanent disfigurement or protracted loss or impairment of the function of any bodily member or organ.

(c) An offense under this section is a felony of the third degree.

*(Added by L.1993, chap. 900(1.01); chgd. by L.1999, chap. 1364(10), eff. 1/1/2000. Matter in brackets eff. only until 1/1/2000. Matter in italics eff. 1/1/2000.)*

### §49.08. Intoxication manslaughter.

(a) A person commits an offense if the person:

(1) operates a motor vehicle in a public place, *operates* an aircraft, [or] a watercraft, *or an amusement ride, or assembles a mobile amusement ride*; and

(2) is intoxicated and by reason of that intoxication causes the death of another by accident or mistake.

(b) An offense under this section is a felony of the second degree.

*(Added by L.1993, chap. 900(1.01); chgd. by L.1999, chap. 1364(11), eff. 1/1/2000. Matter in brackets eff. only until 1/1/2000. Matter in italics eff. 1/1/2000.)*

### §49.09. Enhanced offenses and penalties.

(a) If it is shown on the trial of an offense under Section 49.04, 49.05, [or] 49.06, *or 49.065* that the person has previously been convicted one time of an offense relating to the operating of a motor vehicle while intoxicated, an offense of operating an aircraft while intoxicated, [or] an offense of operating a watercraft while intoxicated, *or an offense of operating or assembling an amusement ride while intoxicated,* the offense is a Class A misdemeanor, with a minimum term of confinement of 30 days.

(b) If it is shown on the trial of an offense under Section 49.04, 49.05, [or] 49.06, *or 49.065* that the person has previously been convicted two times of an offense relating to the operating of a motor vehicle while intoxicated, an offense of operating an aircraft while intoxicated, [or] an offense of operating a watercraft while intoxicated, *or an offense of operating or assembling an amusement ride while intoxicated,* the offense is a felony of the third degree.

(c) For the purposes of this section:

(1) "Offense relating to the operating of a motor vehicle while intoxicated" means:

(A) an offense under Section 49.04;

(B) an offense under Section 49.07 or 49.08, if the vehicle operated was a motor vehicle;

(C) an offense under Article 6701*l*-1, Revised Statutes, as that law existed before September 1, 1994;

(D) an offense under Article 6701*l*-2, Revised Statutes, as that law existed before January 1, 1984;

(E) an offense under Section 19.05(a)(2), as that law existed before September 1, 1994, if the vehicle operated was a motor vehicle; or

(F) an offense under the laws of another state that prohibit the operation of a motor vehicle while intoxicated.

(2) "Offense of operating an aircraft while intoxicated" means:

(A) an offense under Section 49.05;

(B) an offense under Section 49.07 or 49.08, if the vehicle operated was an aircraft;

(C) an offense under Section 1, Chapter 46, Acts of the 58th Legislature, Regular Session, 1963 (Article 46f-3, Texas Civil Statutes), as that law existed before September 1, 1994;

(D) an offense under Section 19.05(a)(2), as that law existed before September 1, 1994, if the vehicle operated was an aircraft; or

(E) an offense under the laws of another state that prohibit the operation of an aircraft while intoxicated.

(3) "Offense of operating a watercraft while intoxicated" means:

(A) an offense under Section 49.06;

(B) an offense under Section 49.07 or 49.08, if the vehicle operated was a watercraft;

(C) an offense under Section 31.097, Parks and Wildlife Code, as that law existed before September 1, 1994;

(D) an offense under Section 19.05(a)(2), as that law existed before September 1, 1994, if the vehicle operated was a watercraft; or

(E) an offense under the laws of another state that prohibit the operation of a watercraft while intoxicated.

*(4) "Offense of operating or assembling an amusement ride while intoxicated" means:*

*(A) an offense under Section 49.065;*

*(B) an offense under Section 49.07 or 49.08, if the offense involved the operation or assembly of an amusement ride; or*

*(C) an offense under the law of another state that prohibits the operation of an amusement ride while intoxicated or the assembly of a mobile amusement ride while intoxicated.*

(d) For the purposes of this section, a conviction for an offense under Section 49.04, 49.05, 49.06, *49.065,* 49.07, or 49.08 that occurs on or after September 1, 1994, is a final conviction, whether the sentence for the conviction is imposed or probated.

(e) A conviction may not be used for purposes of enhancement under this section if:

(1) the conviction was a final conviction under Subsection (d) and was for an offense committed more than 10 years before the offense for which the person is being tried was committed; and

(2) the person has not been convicted of an offense under Section 49.04, 49.05, 49.06, *49.065,* 49.07, or 49.08 or any offense related to operating a motor vehicle while intoxicated committed within 10 years before the date on which the offense for which the person is being tried was committed.

(f) A conviction may be used for purposes of enhancement under this section or enhancement under Subchapter D, Chapter 12, but not under both this section and Subchapter D.
*(Added by L.1993, chap. 900(1.01); chgd. by L.1995, chaps. 76(14.56), 318(21); L.1999, chap. 1364(12), (13), eff. 1/1/2000. Matter in brackets eff. only until 1/1/2000. Matter in italics eff. 1/1/2000.)*

## §49.10. No defense.

In a prosecution under Section 49.03, 49.04, 49.05, 49.06, *49.065,* 49.07, or 49.08, the fact that the defendant is or has been entitled to use the alcohol, controlled substance, drug, dangerous drug, or other substance is not a defense. *(Added by L.1993, chap. 900(1.01); chgd. by L.1999, chap. 1364(14), eff. 1/1/2000. Matter in italics eff. 1/1/2000.)*

### §49.11. Proof of mental state unnecessary.

Notwithstanding Section 6.02(b), proof of a culpable mental state is not required for conviction of an offense under this chapter. *(Added by L.1995, chap. 318(22), eff. 9/1/95.)*

# TITLE 11. ORGANIZED CRIME

*(Title heading chgd. by L.1991, chap. 555(2)(a); L.1993, chap. 900(1.01), eff. 9/1/94.)*



## CHAPTER 71. ORGANIZED CRIME

*(Chapter heading chgd. by L.1991, chap. 555(2)(b); L.1993, chap. 900(1.01), eff. 9/1/94.)*



### §71.01. Definitions.

In this chapter,

(a) "Combination" means three or more persons who collaborate in carrying on criminal activities, although:

(1) participants may not know each other's identity;

(2) membership in the combination may change from time to time; and

(3) participants may stand in a wholesaler-retailer or other arm's-length relationship in illicit distribution operations.

(b) "Conspires to commit" means that a person agrees with one or more persons that they or one or more of them engage in conduct that would constitute the offense and that person and one or more of them perform an overt act in pursuance of the agreement. An agreement constituting conspiring to commit may be inferred from the acts of the parties.

(c) "Profits" means property constituting or derived from any proceeds obtained, directly or indirectly, from an offense listed in Section 71.02.

(d) "Criminal street gang" means three or more persons having a common identifying sign or symbol or an identifiable leadership who continuously or regularly associate in the commission of criminal activities.

*(Chgd. by L.1989, chap. 782(1); L.1993, chap. 900(1.01); L.1995, chap. 318(23), eff. 9/1/95.)*

### §71.02. Engaging in organized criminal activity.

(a) A person commits an offense if, with the intent to establish, maintain, or participate in a combination or in the profits of a combination or as a member of a criminal street gang, he commits or conspires to commit one or more of the following:

(1) murder, capital murder, arson, aggravated robbery, robbery, burglary, theft, aggravated kidnapping, kidnapping, aggravated assault, aggravated sexual assault, sexual assault, forgery, deadly conduct, assault punishable as a Class A misdemeanor, burglary of a motor vehicle, or unauthorized use of a motor vehicle;

(2) any gambling offense punishable as a Class A misdemeanor;

(3) promotion of prostitution, aggravated promotion of prostitution, or compelling prostitution;

(4) unlawful manufacture, transportation, repair, or sale of firearms or prohibited weapons;

(5) unlawful manufacture, delivery, dispensation, or distribution of a controlled substance or dangerous drug, or unlawful possession of a controlled substance or dangerous drug through forgery, fraud, misrepresentation, or deception;

(6) any unlawful wholesale promotion or possession of any obscene material or obscene device with the intent to wholesale promote the same;

(7) any offense under Subchapter B, Chapter 43, depicting or involving conduct by or directed toward a child younger than 18 years of age;

(8) any felony offense under Chapter 32, Penal Code;

(9) any offense under Chapter 36, Penal Code;

(10) any offense under Chapter 34, Penal Code; or

(11) any offense under Section 37.11(a), Penal Code.

(b) Except as provided in Subsection (c) of this section, an offense under this section is one category higher than the most serious offense listed in Subdivisions (1) through (10) of Subsection (a) of this section that was committed, and if the most serious offense is a Class A misdemeanor, the offense is a felony of the third degree, except that if the most serious offense is a felony of the first degree, the offense is a felony of the first degree. *(See other subsec. (b) below.)*

(b) Except as provided in Subsections (c) and (d), an offense under this section is one category higher than the most serious offense listed in Subsection (a) that was committed, and if the most serious offense is a Class A misdemeanor, the offense is a state jail felony, except that if the most serious offense is a felony of the first degree, the offense is a felony of the first degree. *(See other subsec. (b) above.)*

(c) Conspiring to commit an offense under this section is of the same degree as the most serious offense listed in Subdivisions (1) through (10) of Subsection (a) of this section that the person conspired to commit. *(See other subsec. (c) below.)*

(c) Conspiring to commit an offense under this section is of the same degree as the most serious offense listed in Subsection (a) that the person conspired to commit. *(See other subsec. (c) above.)*

(d) At the punishment stage of a trial, the defendant may raise the issue as to whether in voluntary and complete renunciation of the offense he withdrew from the combination before commission of an offense listed in Subsection (a) and made substantial effort to prevent the commission of the offense. If the defendant proves the issue in the affirmative by a preponderance of the evidence the offense is the same category of offense as the most serious offense listed in Subsection (a) that is committed, unless the defendant is convicted of conspiring to commit the offense, in which event the offense is one category lower than the most serious offense that the defendant conspired to commit.

*(Chgd. by L.1989, chap. 782(2); L.1991, chap. 555(1); L.1993, chaps. 761(3), 900(1.01); L.1995, chap. 318(24); L.1997, chap. 189(9); L.1999, chap. 685(8), eff. 9/1/99.)*

### §71.021. Violation of court order enjoining organized criminal activity.

(a) A person commits an offense if the person knowingly violates a temporary or permanent order issued under Section 125.065(a) or (b), Civil Practice and Remedies Code.

(b) If conduct constituting an offense under this section also constitutes an offense under another section of this code, the actor may be prosecuted under either section or under both sections.

(c) An offense under this section is a Class A misdemeanor.

*(Added by L.1995, chap. 584(1), eff. 9/1/95.)*

### §71.022. Soliciting membership in a criminal street gang.

(a) A person commits an offense if the person knowingly causes, enables, encourages, recruits, or solicits another person to become a member of a criminal street gang which, as a condition of initiation, admission, membership, or continued membership, requires the commission of any conduct which constitutes an offense punishable as a Class A misdemeanor or a felony.

(b) Except as provided by Subsection (c), an offense under this section is a felony of the third degree.

(c) A second or subsequent offense under this section is a felony of the second degree.

*(Added by L.1999, chap. 1555(1), eff. 9/1/99.)*

### §71.03. Defenses excluded.

It is no defense to prosecution under Section 71.02 that:

(1) one or more members of the combination are not criminally responsible for the object offense;

(2) one or more members of the combination have been acquitted, have not been prosecuted or convicted, have been convicted of a different offense, or are immune from prosecution;

(3) a person has been charged with, acquitted, or convicted of any offense listed in Subsection (a) of Section 71.02; or

(4) once the initial combination of three or more persons is formed there is a change in the number or identity of persons in the combination as long as two or more persons remain in the

combination and are involved in a continuing course of conduct constituting an offense under this chapter.
*(Chgd. by L.1993. chap. 900(1.01), eff. 9/1/94.)*

**§71.04. Testimonial immunity.**

(a) A party to an offense under this chapter may be required to furnish evidence or testify about the offense.

(b) No evidence or testimony required to be furnished under the provisions of this section nor any information directly or indirectly derived from such evidence or testimony may be used against the witness in any criminal case, except a prosecution for aggravated perjury or contempt.
*(Chgd. by L.1993, chap. 900(1.01), eff. 9/1/94.)*

**§71.05. Renunciation defense.**

(a) It is an affirmative defense to prosecution under Section 71.02 of this code that under circumstances manifesting a voluntary and complete renunciation of his criminal objective the actor withdrew from the combination before commission of an offense listed in Subdivisions (1) through (7) or Subdivision (10) of Subsection (a) of Section 71.02 of this code and took further affirmative action that prevented the commission of the offense. *(See other subsec. (a) below.)*

(a) It is an affirmative defense to prosecution under Section 71.02 that under circumstances manifesting a voluntary and complete renunciation of his criminal objective the actor withdrew from the combination before commission of an offense listed in Subsection (a) of Section 71.02 and took further affirmative action that prevented the commission of the offense. *(See other subsec. (a) above.)*

(b) For the purposes of this section and Subsection (d) of Section 71.02, renunciation is not voluntary if it is motivated in whole or in part:

(1) by circumstances not present or apparent at the inception of the actor's course of conduct that increase the probability of detection or apprehension or that make more difficult the accomplishment of the objective; or

(2) by a decision to postpone the criminal conduct until another time or to transfer the criminal act to another but similar objective or victim.

(c) Evidence that the defendant withdrew from the combination before commission of an offense listed in Subdivisions (1) through (7) or Subdivision (10) of Subsection (a) of Section 71.02 of this code and made substantial effort to prevent the commission of an offense listed in Subdivisions (1) through (7) or Subdivision (10) of Subsection (a) of Section 71.02 of this code shall be admissible as mitigation at the hearing on punishment if he has been found guilty under Section 71.02 of this code, and in the event of a finding of renunciation under this subsection, the punishment shall be one grade lower than that provided under Section 71.02 of this code.
*(Chgd. by L.1993, chaps. 761(4), 900(1.01), eff. 9/1/93, 9/1/94, respectively.)*

# CODE OF CRIMINAL PROCEDURE



## PART I

### INTRODUCTORY



### COURTS AND CRIMINAL JURISDICTION



### PREVENTION AND SUPPRESSION OF OFFENSES



### HABEAS CORPUS



### LIMITATION AND VENUE



### ARREST, COMMITMENT AND BAIL



### SEARCH WARRANTS



### AFTER COMMITMENT OR BAIL AND BEFORE THE TRIAL

TRIAL AND ITS INCIDENTS



PROCEEDINGS AFTER VERDICT



APPEAL AND WRIT OF ERROR



JUSTICE AND MUNICIPAL COURTS



MISCELLANEOUS PROCEEDINGS



# INTRODUCTORY

## CHAPTER 1. GENERAL PROVISIONS

Article

### Art. 1.01. Short title.

This Act shall be known, and may be cited, as the "Code of Criminal Procedure."

### Art. 1.02. Effective date.

This Code shall take effect and be in force on and after January 1, 1966. The procedure herein prescribed shall govern all criminal proceedings instituted after the effective date of this Act and all proceedings pending upon the effective date hereof insofar as are applicable.

### Art. 1.03. Object of this code.† [*Objective of Code.*]

This Code is intended to embrace rules applicable to the prevention and prosecution of offenses against the laws of this State, and to make the rules of procedure in respect to the prevention and punishment of offenses intelligible to the officers who are to act under them, and to all persons whose rights are to be affected by them. It seeks:

(1) To adopt measures for preventing the commission of crime;

(2) To exclude the offender from all hope of escape;

(3) To insure a trial with as little delay as is consistent with the ends of justice;

(4) To bring to the investigation of each offense on the trial all the evidence tending to produce conviction or acquittal;

(5) To insure a fair and impartial trial; and

(6) The certain execution of the sentence of the law when declared.

### Art. 1.04. Due course of law.† [*Due process of law.*]

No citizen of this State shall be deprived of life, liberty, property, privileges or immunities, or in any manner disfranchised, except by the due course of the law of the land.

### Art. 1.05. Rights of accused.

In all criminal prosecutions the accused shall have a speedy public trial by an impartial jury. He shall have the right to demand the nature and cause of the accusation against him, and to have a copy thereof. He shall not be compelled to give evidence against himself. He shall have the right of being heard by himself, or counsel, or both; shall be confronted with the witnesses against him, and shall have compulsory process for obtaining witnesses in his favor. No person shall be held to answer for a felony unless on indictment of a grand jury.

### Art. 1.051. Right to representation by counsel.† [*Right to be represented by counsel.*]

(a) A defendant in a criminal matter is entitled to be represented by counsel in an adversarial judicial proceeding. The right to be represented by counsel includes the right to consult in private with counsel sufficiently in advance of a proceeding to allow adequate preparation for the proceeding.

(b) For the purposes of this article and Articles 26.04 and 26.05 of this code, "indigent" means a person who is not financially able to employ counsel.

(c) An indigent defendant is entitled to have an attorney appointed to represent him in any adversary judicial proceeding that may result in punishment by confinement and in any other criminal proceeding if the court concludes that the interests of justice require representation. If an indigent defendant is entitled to and requests appointed counsel, the court shall appoint counsel to represent the defendant as soon as possible.

(d) An eligible indigent defendant is entitled to have the trial court appoint an attorney to represent him in the following appellate and postconviction habeas corpus matters:

(1) an appeal to a court of appeals;

(2) an appeal to the Court of Criminal Appeals if the appeal is made directly from the trial court or if a petition for discretionary review has been granted;

(3) a habeas corpus proceeding if the court concludes that the interests of justice require representation; and

(4) any other appellate proceeding if the court concludes that the interests of justice require representation.

(e) An appointed counsel is entitled to 10 days to prepare for a proceeding but may waive the preparation time with the consent of the defendant in writing or on the record in open court. If a nonindigent defendant or an indigent defendant who has refused appointed counsel in order to retain private counsel appears without counsel at a proceeding after having been given a reasonable opportunity to retain counsel, the court, on 10 days' notice to the defendant of a dispositive setting, may proceed with the matter without securing a written waiver or appointing counsel.

(f) A defendant may voluntarily and intelligently waive in writing the right to counsel.

(g) If a defendant wishes to waive his right to counsel, the court shall advise him of the dangers and disadvantages of self-representation. If the court determines that the waiver is voluntarily and intelligently made, the court shall provide the defendant with a statement substantially in the following form, which, if signed by the defendant, shall be filed with and become part of the record of the proceedings:

"I have been advised this ____ day of __________, 19__, by the (name of court) Court of my right to representation by counsel in the trial of the charge pending against me. I have been further advised that if I am unable to afford counsel, one will be appointed for me free of charge. Understanding my right to have counsel appointed for me free of charge if I am not financially able to employ counsel, I wish to waive that right and request the court to proceed with my case without an attorney being appointed for me. I hereby waive my right to counsel. (signature of the defendant)"

(h) A defendant may withdraw a waiver of the right to counsel at any time but is not entitled to repeat a proceeding previously held or waived solely on the grounds of the subsequent appointment or retention of counsel. If the defendant withdraws a waiver, the trial court, in its discretion, may provide the appointed counsel 10 days to prepare.

### Art. 1.052. Signed pleadings of defendant.

(a) A pleading, motion, and other paper filed for or on behalf of a defendant represented by an attorney must be signed by at least one attorney of record in the attorney's name and state the attorney's address. A defendant who is not represented by an attorney must sign any pleading, motion, or other paper filed for or on the defendant's behalf and state the defendant's address.

(b) The signature of an attorney or a defendant constitutes a certificate by the attorney or defendant that the person has read the pleading, motion, or other paper and that to the best of the person's knowledge, information, and belief formed after reasonable inquiry that the instrument is not groundless and brought in bad faith or groundless and brought for harassment, unnecessary delay, or other improper purpose.

(c) If a pleading, motion, or other paper is not signed, the court shall strike it unless it is signed promptly after the omission is called to the attention of the attorney or defendant.

(d) An attorney or defendant who files a fictitious pleading in a cause for an improper purpose described by Subsection (b) or who makes a statement in a pleading that the attorney or defendant knows to be groundless and false to obtain a delay of the trial of the cause or for the purpose of harassment shall be held guilty of contempt.

(e) If a pleading, motion, or other paper is signed in violation of this article, the court, on motion or on its own initiative, after notice and hearing, shall impose an appropriate sanction, which may include an order to pay to the other party or parties to the prosecution or to the general fund of the county in which the pleading, motion, or other paper was filed the amount of reasonable expenses incurred because of the filing of the pleading, motion, or other paper, including reasonable attorney's fees.

(f) A court shall presume that a pleading, motion, or other paper is filed in good faith. Sanctions under this article may not be imposed except for good cause stated in the sanction order.

(g) A plea of "not guilty" or "no contest" or "nolo contendere" does not constitute a violation of this article. An allegation that an event took place or occurred on or about a particular date does not constitute a violation of this article.

(h) In this article, "groundless" means without basis in law or fact and not warranted by a good faith argument for the extension, modification, or reversal of existing law.

*(Added by L.1997, chap. 189(11), eff. 5/21/97.)*

**Art. 1.06. Searches and seizures.† [*Unreasonable searches and seizures.*]**

The people shall be secure in their persons, houses, papers and possessions from all unreasonable seizures or searches. No warrant to search any place or to seize any person or thing shall issue without describing them as near as may be, nor without probable cause supported by oath or affirmation.

**Art. 1.07. Right to bail.† [*Prisoner has right to bail.*]**

All prisoners shall be bailable unless for capital offenses when the proof is evident. This provision shall not be so construed as to prevent bail after indictment found upon examination of the evidence, in such manner as may be prescribed by law.

**Art. 1.08. Habeas corpus.**

The writ of habeas corpus is a writ of right and shall never be suspended.

**Art. 1.09. Cruelty forbidden.† [*Cruel and unusual punishment.*]**

Excessive bail shall not be required, nor excessive fines imposed, nor cruel or unusual punishment inflicted.

**Art. 1.10. Jeopardy.† [*Double jeopardy.*]**

No person for the same offense shall be twice put in jeopardy of life or liberty; nor shall a person be again put upon trial for the same offense, after a verdict of not guilty in a court of competent jurisdiction.

**Art. 1.11. Acquittal a bar.**

An acquittal of the defendant exempts him from a second trial or a second prosecution for the same offense, however irregular the proceedings may have been; but if the defendant shall have been acquitted upon trial in a court having no jurisdiction of the offense, he may be prosecuted again in a court having jurisdiction.

**Art. 1.12. Right to jury.† [*Right to jury trial.*]**

The right of trial by jury shall remain inviolate.

**Art. 1.13. Waiver of trial by jury.**

(a) The defendant in a criminal prosecution for any offense other than a capital felony case in which the State notifies the court and the defendant that it will seek the death penalty shall have the right, upon entering a plea, to waive the right of trial by jury, conditioned, however, that such waiver must be made in person by the defendant in writing in open court with the consent and approval of the court, and the attorney representing the State. The consent and approval by the court shall be entered of record on the minutes of the court, and the consent and approval of the attorney representing the State shall be in writing, signed by him, and filed in the papers of the cause before the defendant enters his plea.

(b) In a capital felony case in which the attorney representing the State notifies the court and the defendant that it will not seek the death penalty, the defendant may waive the right to trial by jury but only if the attorney representing the State, in writing and in open court, consents to the waiver.

(c) A defendant may agree to waive a jury trial regardless of whether the defendant is represented by an attorney at the time of making the waiver, but before a defendant charged with a felony who has no attorney can agree to waive the jury, the court must appoint an attorney to represent him.

*(Chgd. by L.1991, chap. 652(1); L.1997, chap. 285(1), eff. 9/1/97.)*

**Art. 1.14. Waiver of rights.**

(a) The defendant in a criminal prosecution for any offense may waive any rights secured him by law except that a defendant in a capital felony case may waive the right of trial by jury only in the manner permitted by Article 1.13(b) of this code.

(b) If the defendant does not object to a defect, error, or irregularity of form or substance in an indictment or information before the date on which the trial on the merits commences, he waives and forfeits the right to object to the defect, error, or irregularity and he may not raise the objection on appeal or in any other postconviction proceeding. Nothing in this article prohibits a trial court from requiring that an objection to an indictment or information be made at an earlier time in compliance with Article 28.01 of this code.
*(Chgd. by L.1991, chap. 652(2), eff. 9/1/91.)*

**Art. 1.141. Waiver of indictment for noncapital felony.† [*Noncapital felony waiver of indictment.*]**

A person represented by legal counsel may in open court or by written instrument voluntarily waive the right to be accused by indictment of any offense other than a capital felony. On waiver as provided in this article, the accused shall be charged by information.

**Art. 1.15. Jury in felony.† [*Jury required for felony trial.*]**

No person can be convicted of a felony except upon the verdict of a jury duly rendered and recorded, unless the defendant, upon entering a plea, has in open court in person waived his right of trial by jury in writing in accordance with Articles 1.13 and 1.14; provided, however, that it shall be necessary for the state to introduce evidence into the record showing the guilt of the defendant and said evidence shall be accepted by the court as the basis for its judgment and in no event shall a person charged be convicted upon his plea without sufficient evidence to support the same. The evidence may be stipulated if the defendant in such case consents in writing, in open court, to waive the appearance, confrontation, and cross-examination of witnesses, and further consents either to an oral stipulation of the evidence and testimony or to the introduction of testimony by affidavits, written statements of witnesses, and any other documentary evidence in support of the judgment of the court. Such waiver and consent must be approved by the court in writing, and be filed in the file of the papers of the cause. *(Chgd. by L.1991, chap. 652(3), eff. 9/1/91.)*

**Art. 1.16. Liberty of speech and press.† [*Freedom of speech and press.*]**

Every person shall be at liberty to speak, write or publish his opinion on any subject, being liable for the abuse of that privilege; and no law shall ever be passed curtailing the liberty of speech or of the press. In prosecutions for the publication of papers investigating the conduct of officers or men in public capacity, or when the matter published is proper for public information, the truth thereof may be given in evidence. In all indictments for libels, the jury shall have the right to determine the law and the facts, under the direction of the court, as in other cases.

**Art. 1.17. Religious belief.† [*Religious belief not a bar in giving evidence.*]**

No person shall be disqualified to give evidence in any court of this State on account of his religious opinions, or for the want of any religious belief; but all oaths or affirmations shall be administered in the mode most binding upon the conscience, and shall be taken subject to the pains and penalties of perjury.

**Art. 1.18. Outlawry and transportation.† [*Prohibition of outlawry and transportation.*]**

No citizen shall be outlawed, nor shall any person be transported out of the State for any offense committed within the same.

**Art. 1.19. Corruption of blood, etc.**

No conviction shall work corruption of blood or forfeiture of estate.

**Art. 1.20. Conviction of treason.† [*Treason.*]**

No person shall be convicted of treason except on the testimony of two witnesses to the same overt act, or on confession in open court.

**Art. 1.21. Privilege of legislators.**

Senators and Representatives shall, except in cases of treason, felony or breach of the peace, be privileged from arrest during the session of the Legislature, and in going to and returning from the same, allowing one day for every twenty miles such member may reside from the place at which the Legislature is convened.

### Art. 1.23. Dignity of State.

All justices of the Supreme Court, judges of the Court of Criminal Appeals, justices of the Courts of Appeals and judges of the District Courts, shall, by virtue of their offices, be conservators of the peace throughout the State. The style of all writs and process shall be "The State of Texas". All prosecutions shall be carried on "in the name and by authority of The State of Texas," and conclude,"against the peace and dignity of the State".

### Art. 1.24. Public trial.† [*Trials must be public.*]

The proceedings and trials in all courts shall be public.

### Art. 1.25. Confronted by witnesses.† [*Defendant must be confronted by witnesses.*]

The defendant, upon a trial, shall be confronted with the witnesses, except in certain cases provided for in this Code where depositions have been taken.

### Art. 1.26. Construction of this Code.

The provisions of this Code shall be liberally construed, so as to attain the objects intended by the Legislature: The prevention, suppression and punishment of crime.

### Art. 1.27. Common law governs.† [*Application and governing of common law.*]

If this code fails to provide a rule of procedure in any particular state of case which may arise, the rules of the common law shall be applied and govern.

## CHAPTER 2. GENERAL DUTIES OF OFFICERS

Article



### Art. 2.01. Duties of district attorneys.† [*District attorneys: duties.*]

Each district attorney shall represent the State in all criminal cases in the district courts of his district and in appeals therefrom, except in cases where he has been, before his election, employed adversely. When any criminal proceeding is had before an examining court in his district or before a judge upon habeas corpus, and he is notified of the same, and is at the time within his district, he shall represent the State therein, unless prevented by other official duties. It shall be the primary duty of all prosecuting attorneys, including any special prosecutors, not to convict, but to see that justice is done. They shall not suppress facts or secrete witnesses capable of establishing the innocence of the accused.

**Art. 2.02. Duties of county attorneys.† [*County attorneys: duties.*]**

The county attorney shall attend the terms of court in his county below the grade of district court, and shall represent the State in all criminal cases under examination or prosecution in said county; and in the absence of the district attorney he shall represent the State alone and, when requested, shall aid the district attorney in the prosecution of any case in behalf of the State in the district court. He shall represent the State in cases he has prosecuted which are appealed.

**Art. 2.025. Special duty of district or county attorney relating to child support.**

If a district or county attorney receives money from a person who is required by a court order to pay child support through a local registry or the Title IV-D agency and the money is presented to the attorney as payment for the court-ordered child support, the attorney shall transfer the money to the local registry or Title IV-D agency designated as the place of payment in the child support order. *(Added by L.1999, chap. 40(1), eff. 9/1/99.)*

**Art. 2.03. Neglect of duty.† [*Neglecting duties.*]**

(a) It shall be the duty of the attorney representing the State to present by information to the court having jurisdiction, any officer for neglect or failure of any duty enjoined upon such officer, when such neglect or failure can be presented by information, whenever it shall come to the knowledge of said attorney that there has been a neglect or failure of duty upon the part of said officer; and he shall bring to the notice of the grand jury any act of violation of law or neglect or failure of duty upon the part of any officer, when such violation, neglect or failure is not presented by information, and whenever the same may come to his knowledge.

(b) It is the duty of the trial court, the attorney representing the accused, the attorney representing the state and all peace officers to so conduct themselves as to insure a fair trial for both the state and the defendant, not impair the presumption of innocence, and at the same time afford the public the benefits of a free press.

**Art. 2.04. Shall draw complaints.† [*Attorney shall act upon complaints.*]**

Upon complaint being made before a district or county attorney that an offense has been committed in his district or county, he shall reduce the complaint to writing and cause the same to be signed and sworn to by the complainant, and it shall be duly attested by said attorney.

**Art. 2.05. When complaint is made.† [*Processing of complaint.*]**

If the offense be a misdemeanor, the attorney shall forthwith prepare an information based upon such complaint and file the same in the court having jurisdiction; provided, that in counties having no county attorney, misdemeanor cases may be tried upon complaint alone, without an information, provided, however, in counties having one or more criminal district courts an information must be filed in each misdemeanor case. If the offense be a felony, he shall forthwith file the complaint with a magistrate of the county.

**Art. 2.06. May administer oaths.† [*Administration of oaths.*]**

For the purpose mentioned in the two preceding Articles, district and county attorneys are authorized to administer oaths.

**Art. 2.07. Attorney pro tem.**

(a) Whenever an attorney for the state is disqualified to act in any case or proceeding, is absent from the county or district, or is otherwise unable to perform the duties of his office, or in any instance where there is no attorney for the state, the judge of the court in which he represents the state may appoint any competent attorney to perform the duties of the office during the absence or disqualification of the attorney for the state.

(b) Except as otherwise provided by this subsection, if the appointed attorney is also an attorney for the state, the duties of the appointed office are additional duties of his present office, and he is not entitled to additional compensation. Nothing herein shall prevent a commissioners court of a county from contracting with another commissioners court to pay expenses and reimburse compensation paid by a county to an attorney for the state who is appointed to perform additional duties.

(b-1) An attorney for the state who is not disqualified to act may request the court to permit him to recuse himself in a case for good cause and upon approval by the court is disqualified.

(c) If the appointed attorney is not an attorney for the state, he is qualified to perform the duties of the office for the period of absence or disqualification of the attorney for the state on filing an oath with the clerk of the court. He shall receive compensation in the same amount and manner as an attorney appointed to represent an indigent person.

(d) In this article, "attorney for the state" means a county attorney, a district attorney, or a criminal district attorney.

(e) In Subsections (b) and (c) of this article, "attorney for the state" includes an assistant attorney general.

(f) In Subsection (a) of this article, "competent attorney" includes an assistant attorney general.

(g) An attorney appointed under Subsection (a) of this article to perform the duties of the office of an attorney for the state in a justice or municipal court may be paid a reasonable fee for performing those duties.

*(Chgd. by L.1995, chap. 785(1); L.1999, chap. 1545(1), eff. 9/1/99.)*

### Art. 2.08. Disqualified.† [*Disqualification of district or county attorneys.*]

District and county attorneys shall not be of counsel adversely to the State in any case, in any court, nor shall they, after they cease to be such officers, be of counsel adversely to the State in any case in which they have been of counsel for the State.

### Art. 2.09. Who are magistrates.

Each of the following officers is a magistrate within the meaning of this Code: The justices of the Supreme Court, the judges of the Court of Criminal Appeals, the justices of the Courts of Appeals, the judges of the District Court, the magistrates appointed by the judges of the district courts of Bexar County, Dallas County, Tarrant County, or Travis County that give preference to criminal cases, the criminal law hearing officers for Harris County appointed under Subchapter L, Chapter 54, Government Code, the magistrates appointed by the judges of the district courts of Lubbock County or Webb County, the magistrates appointed by the judges of the criminal district courts of Dallas County or Tarrant County, the masters appointed by the judges of the district courts and the county courts at law that give preference to criminal cases in Jefferson County, the magistrates appointed by the judges of the district courts and the statutory county courts of Williamson County, the county judges, the judges of the county courts at law, judges of the county criminal courts, the judges of statutory probate courts, the masters appointed by the judges of the statutory probate courts under Subchapter G, Chapter 54, Government Code, the justices of the peace, the mayors and recorders and the judges of the municipal courts of incorporated cities or towns. *(Chgd. by L.1989, chaps. 25(2), 79(1), 916(1), 1068(2); reenacted by L.1991, chap. 16(4.01); chgd. by L.1993, chaps. 224(2), 413(1), 468(1), 577(2); L.1999, chaps. 586(2), 1503(2), eff. 6/18/99, 9/1/99, respectively.)*

### Art. 2.10. Duty of magistrates.† [*Magistrates: duties.*]

It is the duty of every magistrate to preserve the peace within his jurisdiction by the use of all lawful means; to issue all process intended to aid in preventing and suppressing crime; to cause the arrest of offenders by the use of lawful means in order that they may be brought to punishment.

### Art. 2.11. Examining court.

When the magistrate sits for the purpose of inquiring into a criminal accusation against any person, this is called an examining court.

### Art. 2.12. Who are peace officers.

The following are peace officers:

(1) sheriffs, their deputies, and those reserve deputies who hold a permanent peace officer license issued under Chapter 415, Government Code;

(2) constables, deputy constables, and those reserve deputy constables who hold a permanent peace officer license issued under Chapter 415, Government Code;

(3) marshals or police officers of an incorporated city, town, or village, and those reserve municipal police officers who hold a permanent peace officer license issued under Chapter 415, Government Code;

(4) rangers and officers commissioned by the Public Safety Commission and the Director of the Department of Public Safety;

(5) investigators of the district attorneys', criminal district attorneys', and county attorneys' offices;

(6) law enforcement agents of the Texas Alcoholic Beverage Commission;

(7) each member of an arson investigating unit commissioned by a city, a county, or the state;

(8) officers commissioned under Section 37.081, Education Code, or Subchapter E, Chapter 51, Education Code;

(9) officers commissioned by the General Services Commission;

(10) law enforcement officers commissioned by the Parks and Wildlife Commission;

(11) airport police officers commissioned by a city with a population of more than one million, according to the most recent federal census, that operates an airport that serves commercial air carriers;

(12) airport security personnel commissioned as peace officers by the governing body of any political subdivision of this state, other than a city described by Subdivision (11), that operates an airport that serves commercial air carriers;

(13) municipal park and recreational patrolmen and security officers;

(14) security officers commissioned as peace officers by the comptroller;

(15) officers commissioned by a water control and improvement district under Section 49.216, Water Code;

(16) officers commissioned by a board of trustees under Chapter 341, Acts of the 57th Legislature, Regular Session, 1961 (Article 1187f, Vernon's Texas Civil Statutes);

(17) investigators commissioned by the Texas State Board of Medical Examiners;

(18) officers commissioned by the board of managers of the Dallas County Hospital District, the Tarrant County Hospital District, or the Bexar County Hospital District under Section 281.057, Health and Safety Code;

(19) county park rangers commissioned under Subchapter E, Chapter 351, Local Government Code;

(20) investigators employed by the Texas Racing Commission;

(21) officers commissioned by the State Board of Pharmacy;

(22) officers commissioned by the governing body of a metropolitan rapid transit authority under Section 451.108, Transportation Code, or by a regional transportation authority under Section 452.110, Transportation Code;

(23) investigators commissioned by the attorney general under Section 402.009, Government Code;

(24) security officers and investigators commissioned as peace officers under Chapter 466, Government Code;

(25) an officer employed by the Texas Department of Health under Section 431.2471, Health and Safety Code;

(26) officers appointed by an appellate court under Subchapter F, Chapter 53, Government Code;

(27) officers commissioned by the state fire marshal under Chapter 417, Government Code;

(28) an investigator commissioned by the commissioner of insurance under Article 1.10D, Insurance Code;

(29) apprehension specialists commissioned by the Texas Youth Commission as officers under Section 61.0931, Human Resources Code; and

(30) officers appointed by the executive director of the Texas Department of Criminal Justice under Section 493.019, Government Code. *(Added by L.1999, chap. 322, eff. 5/29/99. See other subdivisions 30 below.)*

(30) investigators commissioned by the Commission on Law Enforcement Officer Standards and Education under Section 415.016, Government Code. *(Added by L.1999, chap. 882, eff. 6/18/99. See other subdivisions 30 above and below.)*

(30) board investigators commissioned by the Texas Commission on Private Security under Section 10(f), Private Investigators and Private Security Agencies Act (Article 4413(29bb), Vernon's Texas Civil Statutes). *(Added by L.1999, chap. 974, eff. 9/1/99. See other subdivisions 30 above.)*

*(Chgd. by L.1989, chaps. 277(4), 794(1), 1104(4); L.1991, chaps. 16(4.02), 228(1), 287(24), 386(70, 75), 446(1), 544(1), 545(2), 597(57), 853(2); L.1991, 1st C.S., chaps. 6(6), 14(3.01); L.1993, chaps. 107(4.07), 116(1), 339(2), 695(2), 912(25); L.1995, chaps. 260(10), 621(2), 729(1); L.1997, chap. 1423(4.01); L.1999, chaps. 90(1), 322(2), 882(2), 974(37), eff. 9/1/99, 5/29/99, 6/18/99, 9/1/99, respectively.)*

### Art. 2.121. Railroad peace officers.

(a) The director of the Department of Public Safety may appoint up to 250 railroad peace officers who are employed by a railroad company to aid law enforcement agencies in the protection of railroad property and the protection of the persons and property of railroad passengers and employees.

(b) Except as provided by Subsection (c) of this article, a railroad peace officer may make arrests and exercise all authority given peace officers under this code when necessary to prevent or abate the commission of an offense involving injury to passengers and employees of the railroad or damage to railroad property or to protect railroad property or property in the custody or control of the railroad.

(c) A railroad peace officer may not issue a traffic citation for a violation of Chapter 521, Transportation Code, or Subtitle C, Title 7, Transportation Code.

(d) A railroad peace officer is not entitled to state benefits normally provided by the state to a peace officer.

(e) A person may not serve as a railroad peace officer for a railroad company unless:

(1) the Texas Railroad Association submits the person's application for appointment and certification as a railroad peace officer to the director of the Department of Public Safety and to the executive director of the Commission on Law Enforcement Officer Standards and Education;

(2) the director of the department issues the person a certificate of authority to act as a railroad peace officer; and

(3) the executive director of the commission determines that the person meets minimum standards required of peace officers by the commission relating to competence, reliability, education, training, morality, and physical and mental health and issues the person a license as a railroad peace officer; and

(4) the person has met all standards for certification as a peace officer by the Commission on Law Enforcement Officer Standards and Education.

(f) For good cause, the director of the department may revoke a certificate of authority issued under this article and the executive director of the commission may revoke a license issued under this article. Termination of employment with a railroad company, or the revocation of a railroad peace officer license, shall constitute an automatic revocation of a certificate of authority to act as a railroad peace officer.

(g) A railroad company is liable for any act or omission by a person serving as a railroad peace officer for the company that is within the person's scope of employment. Neither the state nor any political subdivision or agency of the state shall be liable for any act or omission by a person appointed as a railroad peace officer. All expenses incurred by the granting or revocation of a certificate of authority to act as a railroad peace officer shall be paid by the employing railroad company.

(h) A railroad peace officer who is a member of a railroad craft may not perform the duties of a member of any other railroad craft during a strike or labor dispute.

(i) The director of the department and the executive director of the commission shall have the authority to promulgate rules necessary for the effective administration and performance of the duties and responsibilities delegated to them by this article.

*(Chgd. by L.1999, chap. 62(3.01), eff. 9/1/99.)*

## Art. 2.122. Special investigators.

(a) The following named criminal investigators of the United States shall not be deemed peace officers, but shall have the powers of arrest, search and seizure as to felony offenses only under the laws of the State of Texas:

(1) Special Agents of the Federal Bureau of Investigation;

(2) Special Agents of the Secret Service;

(3) Special Agents of the United States Customs Service;

(4) Special Agents of Alcohol, Tobacco and Firearms;

(5) Special Agents of Federal Drug Enforcement Agency;

(6) Inspectors of the United States Postal Service;

(7) Special Agents of the Criminal Investigation Division and Inspectors of the Internal Security Division of the Internal Revenue Service;

(8) Civilian Special Agents of the United States Naval Investigative Service;

(9) Marshals and Deputy Marshals of the United States Marshals Service;

(10) Special Agents of the United States Immigration and Naturalization Service; and

(11) Special Agents of the United States Department of State, Bureau of Diplomatic Security.

(b) A person designated as a special policeman by the Federal Protective Services division of the General Services Administration under 40 U.S.C. Section 318 or 318d is not a peace officer but has the powers of arrest and search and seizure as to any offense under the laws of this state.

(c) A customs inspector of the United States Customs Service or a border patrolman or immigration officer of the United States Department of Justice is not a peace officer under the laws of this state but, on the premises of a port facility designated by the commissioner of the United States Immigration and Naturalization Service as a port of entry for arrival in the United States by land transportation from the United Mexican States into the State of Texas or at a permanent established border patrol traffic check point, has the authority to detain a person pending transfer without unnecessary delay to a peace officer if the inspector, patrolman, or officer has probable cause to believe that the person has engaged in conduct that is a violation of Section 49.02, 49.04, 49.07, or 49.08, Penal Code, regardless of whether the violation may be disposed of in a criminal proceeding or a juvenile justice proceeding.

(d) A Special Agent or Law Enforcement Officer of the United States Forest Service is not a peace officer under the laws of this state, except that the agent or officer has the powers of arrest, search, and seizure as to any offense under the laws of this state committed within the National Forest System. In this subsection, "National Forest System" has the meaning assigned by 16 U.S.C. Section 1609. *(Added by L.1999, chap. 197(1), eff. 5/24/99. See other paragraph (d) below.)*

(d) A commissioned law enforcement officer of the National Park Service is not a peace officer under the laws of this state, except that the officer has the powers of arrest, search, and seizure as to any offense under the laws of this state committed within the boundaries of a national park or national recreation area. In this subsection, "national park or national recreation area" means a national park or national recreation area included in the National Park System as defined by 16 U.S.C. Section 1c(a). *(Added by L.1999, chap. 628(1), eff. 6/18/99. See other paragraph (d) above.)*

*(Chgd. by L.1989, chap. 841(1); L.1993, chap. 927(1); L.1997, chaps. 290(1), 717(1); L.1999, chaps. 197(1), 628(1), 863(1), eff. 5/24/99, 6/18/99, 6/18/99, respectively.)*

## Art. 2.123. Adjunct police officers.

(a) Within counties under 200,000 population, the chief of police of a municipality or the sheriff of the county, if the institution is outside the corporate limits of a municipality, that has jurisdiction over the geographical area of a private institution of higher education, provided the governing board of such institution consents, may appoint up to 50 peace officers who are commissioned under Section 51.212, Education Code, and who are employed by a private institution of higher education located in the municipality or county, to serve as adjunct police officers of the municipality or county. Officers appointed under this article shall aid law enforcement agencies in the protection of the municipality or county in a geographical area that is designated by agreement on an annual basis between the appointing chief of police or sheriff and the private institution.

(b) The geographical area that is subject to designation under Subsection (a) of this article may include only the private institution's campus area and an area that:

(1) is adjacent to the campus of the private institution;

(2) does not extend further than a distance of one mile from the perimeter of the campus of the private institution; and

(3) is inhabited primarily by students or employees of the private institution.

(c) A peace officer serving as an adjunct police officer may make arrests and exercise all authority given peace officers under this code only within the geographical area designated by agreement between the appointing chief of police or sheriff and the private institution.

(d) A peace officer serving as an adjunct police officer has all the rights, privileges, and immunities of a peace officer but is not entitled to state compensation and retirement benefits normally provided by the state to a peace officer.

(e) A person may not serve as an adjunct police officer for a municipality or county unless:

(1) the institution of higher education submits the person's application for appointment and certification as an adjunct police officer to the chief of police of the municipality or, if outside a municipality, the sheriff of the county that has jurisdiction over the geographical area of the institution;

(2) the chief of police of the municipality or sheriff of the county to whom the application was made issues the person a certificate of authority to act as an adjunct police officer; and

(3) the person undergoes any additional training required for that person to meet the training standards of the municipality or county for peace officers employed by the municipality or county.

(f) For good cause, the chief of police or sheriff may revoke a certificate of authority issued under this article.

(g) A private institution of higher education is liable for any act or omission by a person while serving as an adjunct police officer outside of the campus of the institution in the same manner as the municipality or county governing that geographical area is liable for any act or omission of a peace officer employed by the municipality or county. This subsection shall not be construed to act as a limitation on the liability of a municipality or county for the acts or omissions of a person serving as an adjunct police officer.

(h) The employing institution shall pay all expenses incurred by the municipality or county in granting or revoking a certificate of authority to act as an adjunct police officer under this article.

(i) This article does not affect any duty of the municipality or county to provide law enforcement services to a geographical area designated under Subsection (a) of this article.

### Art. 2.124. Peace officers from adjoining states.

(a) A commissioned peace officer of a state of the United States of America adjoining this state, while the officer is in this state, has under this subsection the same powers, duties, and immunities as a peace officer of this state who is acting in the discharge of an official duty, but only:

(1) during a time in which:

(A) the peace officer from the adjoining state has physical custody of an inmate or criminal defendant and is transporting the inmate or defendant from a county in the adjoining state that is on the border between the two states to a hospital or other medical facility in a county in this state that is on the border between the two states; or

(B) the peace officer has physical custody of the inmate or defendant and is returning the inmate or defendant from the hospital or facility to the county in the adjoining state; and

(2) to the extent necessary to:

(A) maintain physical custody of the inmate or defendant while transporting the inmate or defendant; or

(B) regain physical custody of the inmate or defendant if the inmate or defendant escapes while being transported.

(b) A commissioned peace officer of a state of the United States of America adjoining this state, while the officer is in this state, has under this subsection the same powers, duties, and immunities as a peace officer of this state who is acting in the discharge of an official duty, but only in a municipality some part of the municipal limits of which are within one mile of the boundary between this state and the adjoining state and only at a time the peace officer is regularly assigned to duty in a county, parish, or municipality that adjoins this state. A peace officer described by this subsection may also as part of the officer's powers in this state enforce the ordinances of a Texas municipality described by this subsection but only after the governing body of the municipality authorizes that enforcement by majority vote at an open meeting.

*(Added by L.1995, chap. 156(1); chgd. by L.1999, chap. 107(1), eff. 9/1/99.)*

### Art. 2.13. Duties and powers.

(a) It is the duty of every peace officer to preserve the peace within the officer's jurisdiction. To effect this purpose, the officer shall use all lawful means.

(b) The officer shall:

(1) in every case authorized by the provisions of this Code, interfere without warrant to prevent or suppress crime;

(2) execute all lawful process issued to the officer by any magistrate or court;

(3) give notice to some magistrate of all offenses committed within the officer's jurisdiction, where the officer has good reason to believe there has been a violation of the penal law; and

(4) arrest offenders without warrant in every case where the officer is authorized by law, in order that they may be taken before the proper magistrate or court and be tried.

(c) It is the duty of every officer to take possession of a child under Article 62.009(g).

*(Chgd. by L.1999, chap. 685(1), eff. 9/1/99.)*

### Art. 2.14. May summon aid.† [*Peace officer may request assistance.*]

Whenever a peace officer meets with resistance in discharging any duty imposed upon him by law, he shall summon a sufficient number of citizens of his county to overcome the resistance; and all persons summoned are bound to obey.

### Art. 2.15. Person refusing to aid.

The peace officer who has summoned any person to assist him in performing any duty shall report such person, if he refuse to obey, to the proper district or county attorney, in order that he may be prosecuted for the offense.

### Art. 2.16. Neglecting to execute process.† [*Peace officer: neglecting to execute process.*]

If any sheriff or other officer shall wilfully refuse or fail from neglect to execute any summons, subpoena or attachment for a witness, or any other legal process which it is made his duty by law to execute, he shall be liable to a fine for contempt not less than ten nor more than two hundred dollars, at the discretion of the court. The payment of such fine shall be enforced in the same manner as fines for contempt in civil cases.

### Art. 2.17. Conservator of the peace.† [*Sheriff: conservator of the peace.*]

Each sheriff shall be a conservator of the peace in his county, and shall arrest all offenders against the laws of the State, in his view or hearing, and take them before the proper court for examination or trial. He shall quell and suppress all assaults and batteries, affrays, insurrections and unlawful assemblies. He shall apprehend and commit to jail all offenders, until an examination or trial can be had.

### Art. 2.18. Custody of prisoners.

When a prisoner is committed to jail by warrant from a magistrate or court, he shall be placed in jail by the sheriff. It is a violation of duty on the part of any sheriff to permit a defendant so committed to remain out of jail, except that he may, when a defendant is committed for want of bail, or when he arrests in a bailable case, give the person arrested a reasonable time to procure bail; but he shall so guard the accused as to prevent escape.

### Art. 2.19. Report as to prisoners.† [*Monthly report on prisoners.*]

On the first day of each month, the sheriff shall give notice, in writing, to the district or county attorney, where there be one, as to all prisoners in his custody, naming them, and of the authority under which he detains them.

### Art. 2.20. Deputy.

Wherever a duty is imposed by this Code upon the sheriff, the same duty may lawfully be performed by his deputy. When there is no sheriff in a county, the duties of that office, as to all proceedings under the criminal law, devolve upon the officer who, under the law, is empowered to discharge the duties of sheriff, in case of vacancy in the office.

### Art. 2.21. Duty of clerks.

(a) In a criminal proceeding, a clerk of the district or county court shall:
(1) receive and file all papers;
(2) receive all exhibits at the conclusion of the proceeding;
(3) issue all process; and
(4) perform all other duties imposed on the clerk by law.

(b) At any time during or after a criminal proceeding, the court reporter shall release to the sheriff for safekeeping any firearm or contraband received by the court as an exhibit in that proceeding.

(c) The sheriff shall receive and hold exhibits consisting of firearms or contraband and release them only to the person or persons authorized by the court in which such exhibits have been received or dispose of them as provided by Chapter 18 of this code.

(d) In this article, "eligible exhibit" means an exhibit filed with the clerk that:
(1) is not a firearm or contraband;
(2) has not been ordered by the court to be returned to its owner; and
(3) is not an exhibit in another pending criminal action.

(e) An eligible exhibit may be disposed of as provided by this article:

(1) on or after the first anniversary of the date on which a conviction becomes final in the case, if the case is a misdemeanor or a felony for which the sentence imposed by the court is five years or less; or

(2) on or after the second anniversary of the date on which a conviction becomes final in the case, if the case is a non-capital felony for which the sentence imposed by the court is greater than five years.

(f) A clerk in a county with a population of 1.7 million or more may dispose of an eligible exhibit on the date provided by Subsection (e) of this article if on that date the clerk has not received a request for the exhibit from either the attorney representing the state in the case or the attorney representing the defendant.

(g) A clerk in a county with a population of less than 1.7 million must provide written notice by mail to the attorney representing the state in the case and the attorney representing the defendant before disposing of an eligible exhibit.

(h) The notice under Subsection (g) of this article must:
(1) describe the eligible exhibit;
(2) give the name and address of the court holding the exhibit; and
(3) state that the eligible exhibit will be disposed of unless a written request is received by the clerk before the 31st day after the date of notice.

(i) If a request is not received by a clerk covered by Subsection (g) of this article before the 31st day after the date of notice, the clerk may dispose of the eligible exhibit.

(j) If a request is timely received, the clerk shall deliver the eligible exhibit to the person making the request if the court determines the requestor is the owner of the eligible exhibit.
*(Chgd. by L.1993, chap. 967(1); L.1999, chap. 580(1), eff. 9/1/99.)*

### Art. 2.22. Power of deputy clerks.† [*Deputy clerks: duties.*]

Whenever a duty is imposed upon the clerk of the district or county court, the same may be lawfully performed by his deputy.

### Art. 2.23. Report to Attorney General.† [*Court clerks: report to Attorney General.*]

The clerks of the district and county courts shall, when required by the Attorney General, report to him at such times, and in accordance with such forms as he may direct, such information in relation to criminal matters as may be shown by their records.

When any district clerk has failed, neglected or refused to make any such report after being requested in writing by the Attorney General to make such report, the Attorney General shall notify in writing the Comptroller of Public Accounts of such failure, neglect or refusal, and said Comptroller shall not thereafter draw any warrant in favor of said clerk until said report has been filed with the Attorney General.

### Art. 2.24. Authenticating officer.

(a) The governor may appoint an authenticating officer, in accordance with Subsection (b) of this article, and delegate to that officer the power to sign for the governor or to use the governor's facsimile signature for signing any document that does not have legal effect under this code unless it is signed by the governor.

(b) To appoint an authenticating officer under this article, the governor shall file with the secretary of state a document that contains:

(1) the name of the person to be appointed as authenticating officer and a copy of the person's signature;

(2) the types of documents the authenticating officer is authorized to sign for the governor; and

(3) the types of documents on which the authenticating officer is authorized to use the governor's facsimile signature.

(c) The governor may revoke an appointment made under this article by filing with the secretary of state a document that expressly revokes the appointment of the authenticating agent.

(d) If an authenticating officer signs a document described in Subsection (a) of this article, the officer shall sign in the following manner: "__________, Authenticating Officer for Governor __________."

(e) If a provision of this code requires the governor's signature on a document before that document has legal effect, the authorized signature of the authenticating officer or an authorized facsimile signature of the governor gives the document the same legal effect as if it had been signed manually by the governor.

### Art. 2.25. Reporting certain aliens to federal government.

A judge shall report to the United States Immigration and Naturalization Service a person who has been convicted in the judge's court of a crime or has been placed on deferred adjudication for a felony and is an illegal criminal alien as defined by Section 493.015(a), Government Code.
*(Added by L.1995, chap. 85(2), eff. 5/16/95.)*

### Art. 2.26. Digital signature.

(a) In this section, "digital signature" means an electronic identifier intended by the person using it to have the same force and effect as the use of a manual signature.

(b) An electronically transmitted document issued or received by a court in a criminal matter is considered signed if a digital signature is transmitted with the document.

(c) This section does not preclude any symbol from being valid as a signature under other applicable law, including Section 1.201(39), Business & Commerce Code.

(d) The use of a digital signature under this section is subject to criminal laws pertaining to fraud and computer crimes, including Chapters 32 and 33, Penal Code.
*(Added by L.1999, chap. 701(1), eff. 6/18/99.)*

## CHAPTER 3. DEFINITIONS

Article


### Art. 3.01. Words and phrases.

All words, phrases and terms used in this Code are to be taken and understood in their usual acceptation in common language, except where specially defined.

### Art. 3.02. Criminal action.

A criminal action is prosecuted in the name of the State of Texas against the accused, and is conducted by some person acting under the authority of the State, in accordance with its laws.

### Art. 3.03. Officers.

The general term "officers" includes both magistrates and peace officers.

### Art. 3.04. Official misconduct.

In this code:

(1) "Official misconduct" means an offense that is an intentional or knowing violation of a law committed by a public servant while acting in an official capacity as a public servant.

(2) "Public servant" has the meaning assigned by Section 1.07, Penal Code.

*(Added by L.1993, chap. 900(1.03), eff. 9/1/94.)*

# COURTS AND CRIMINAL JURISDICTION

## CHAPTER 4. COURTS AND CRIMINAL JURISDICTION

Article


### Art. 4.01. What courts have criminal jurisdiction.

The following courts have jurisdiction in criminal actions:

1. The Court of Criminal Appeals;
2. Courts of appeals;
3. The district courts;
4. The criminal district courts;
5. The magistrates appointed by the judges of the district courts of Bexar County, Dallas County, Tarrant County, or Travis County that give preference to criminal cases and the magistrates appointed by the judges of the criminal district courts of Dallas County or Tarrant County;
6. The county courts;
7. All county courts at law with criminal jurisdiction;
8. County criminal courts;

9. Justice courts;
10. Municipal courts; and
11. The magistrates appointed by the judges of the district courts of Lubbock County.

*(Chgd. by L.1989, chaps. 25(3), 79(2), 1068(3); reenacted by L.1991, chap. 16(4.03); chgd. by L.1993, chap. 413(2), eff. 9/1/93.)*

### Art. 4.02. Existing courts continued.† [*Continuation of existing courts.*]

No existing courts shall be abolished by this Code and shall continue with the jurisdiction, organization, terms and powers currently existing unless otherwise provided by law.

### Art. 4.03. Courts of Appeals.

The Courts of Appeals shall have appellate jurisdiction coextensive with the limits of their respective districts in all criminal cases except those in which the death penalty has been assessed. This Article shall not be so construed as to embrace any case which has been appealed from any inferior court to the county court, the county criminal court, or county court at law, in which the fine imposed by the county court, the county criminal court or county court at law does not exceed one hundred dollars, unless the sole issue is the constitutionality of the statute or ordinance on which the conviction is based.

### Art. 4.04. Court of Criminal Appeals.

**Sec. 1.** The Court of Criminal Appeals and each judge thereof shall have, and is hereby given, the power and authority to grant and issue and cause the issuance of writs of habeas corpus, and, in criminal law matters, the writs of mandamus, procedendo, prohibition, and certiorari. The court and each judge thereof shall have, and is hereby given, the power and authority to grant and issue and cause the issuance of such other writs as may be necessary to protect its jurisdiction or enforce its judgments.

**Sec. 2.** The Court of Criminal Appeals shall have, and is hereby given, final appellate and review jurisdiction in criminal cases coextensive with the limits of the state, and its determinations shall be final. The appeal of all cases in which the death penalty has been assessed shall be to the Court of Criminal Appeals. In addition, the Court of Criminal Appeals may, on its own motion, with or without a petition for such discretionary review being filed by one of the parties, review any decision of a court of appeals in a criminal case. Discretionary review by the Court of Criminal Appeals is not a matter of right, but of sound judicial discretion.

### Art. 4.05. Jurisdiction of district courts.

District courts and criminal district courts shall have original jurisdiction in criminal cases of the grade of felony, of all misdemeanors involving official misconduct, and of misdemeanor cases transferred to the district court under Article 4.17 of this code.

### Art. 4.06. When felony includes misdemeanor.† [*Misdemeanor included in felony.*]

Upon the trial of a felony case, the court shall hear and determine the case as to any grade of offense included in the indictment, whether the proof shows a felony or a misdemeanor.

### Art. 4.07. Jurisdiction of county courts.

The county courts shall have original jurisdiction of all misdemeanors of which exclusive original jurisdiction is not given to the justice court, and when the fine to be imposed shall exceed five hundred dollars. *(Chgd. by L.1991, chap. 108(3), eff. 9/1/91.)*

### Art. 4.08. Appellate jurisdiction of county courts.

The county courts shall have appellate jurisdiction in criminal cases of which justice courts and other inferior courts have original jurisdiction.

### Art. 4.09. Appeals from inferior court.

If the jurisdiction of any county court has been transferred to the district court or to a county court at law, then an appeal from a justice or other inferior court will lie to the court to which such appellate jurisdiction has been transferred.

### Art. 4.10. To forfeit bail bonds.† [*Bail bonds: forfeiture.*]

County courts and county courts at law shall have jurisdiction in the forfeiture and final judgment of all bail bonds and personal bonds taken in criminal cases of which said courts have jurisdiction.

### Art. 4.11. Jurisdiction of justice courts.

(a) Justices of the peace shall have original jurisdiction in criminal cases:

(1) punishable by fine only or punishable by:

(A) a fine; and

(B) as authorized by statute, a sanction not consisting of confinement or imprisonment; or

(2) arising under Chapter 106, Alcoholic Beverage Code, that do not include confinement as an authorized sanction.

(b) The fact that a conviction in a justice court has as a consequence the imposition of a penalty or sanction by an agency or entity other than the court, such as a denial, suspension, or revocation of a privilege, does not affect the original jurisdiction of the justice court.

*(Chgd. by L.1991, chap. 108(4); L.1995, chap. 449(1); L.1997, chaps. 533(1), 1013(38), eff. 9/1/97.)*

### Art. 4.12. Misdemeanor cases; precinct in which defendant to be tried in justice court.

(a) Except as otherwise provided by this article, a misdemeanor case to be tried in justice court shall be tried:

(1) in the precinct in which the offense was committed;

(2) in the precinct in which the defendant or any of the defendants reside; or

(3) with the written consent of the state and each defendant or the defendant's attorney, in any other precinct within the county.

(b) In any misdemeanor case in which the offense was committed in a precinct where there is no qualified justice court, then trial shall be held:

(1) in the next adjacent precinct in the same county which has a duly qualified justice court; or

(2) in the precinct in which the defendant may reside.

(c) In any misdemeanor case in which each justice of the peace in the precinct where the offense was committed is disqualified for any reason, such case may be tried in the next adjoining precinct in the same county having a duly qualified justice of the peace.

*(Chgd. by L.1999, chap. 1545(2), eff. 9/1/99.)*

### Art. 4.13. Justice may forfeit bond.† [*Bond forfeiture by justice of the peace.*]

A justice of the peace shall have the power to take forfeitures of all bonds given for the appearance of any party at his court, regardless of the amount.

### Art. 4.14. Jurisdiction of municipal court.

(a) A municipal court, including a municipal court of record, shall have exclusive original jurisdiction within the territorial limits of the municipality in all criminal cases that:

(1) arise under the ordinances of the municipality; and

(2) are punishable by a fine not to exceed:

(A) $2,000 in all cases arising under municipal ordinances that govern fire safety, zoning, or public health and sanitation, including dumping of refuse; or

(B) $500 in all other cases arising under a municipal ordinance.

(b) The municipal court shall have concurrent jurisdiction with the justice court of a precinct in which the municipality is located in all criminal cases arising under state law that:

(1) arise within the territorial limits of the municipality and are punishable only by a fine, as defined in Subsection (c) of this section; or

(2) arise under Chapter 106, Alcoholic Beverage Code, and do not include confinement as an authorized sanction.

(c) In this article, an offense which is punishable by "fine only" is defined as an offense that is punishable by fine and such sanctions, if any, as authorized by statute not consisting of confinement in jail or imprisonment.

(d) The fact that a conviction in a municipal court has as a consequence the imposition of a penalty or sanction by an agency or entity other than the court, such as a denial, suspension, or revocation of a privilege, does not affect the original jurisdiction of the municipal court.

(e) The municipal court has jurisdiction in the forfeiture and final judgment of all bail bonds and personal bonds taken in criminal cases of which the court has jurisdiction.

*(Chgd. by L.1995, chap. 449(3); L.1997, chaps. 533(2), 1013(39), eff. 9/1/97.)*

### Art. 4.15. May sit at any time.† [*Court sessions.*]

Justice courts and corporation courts may sit at any time to try criminal cases over which they have jurisdiction. Any case in which a fine may be assessed shall be tried in accordance with the rules of evidence and this Code.

### Art. 4.16. Concurrent jurisdiction.

When two or more courts have concurrent jurisdiction of any criminal offense, the court in which an indictment or a complaint shall first be filed shall retain jurisdiction except as provided in Article 4.12.

### Art. 4.17. Transfer of certain misdemeanors.

On a plea of not guilty to a misdemeanor offense punishable by confinement in jail, entered in a county court of a judge who is not a licensed attorney, on the motion of the state or the defendant, the judge may transfer the case to a district court having jurisdiction in the county or to a county court at law in the county presided over by a judge who is a licensed attorney. The judge may make the transfer on his own motion. The attorney representing the state in the case in county court shall continue the prosecution in the court to which the case is transferred. Provided, in no case may any such case be transferred to a district court except with the written consent of the judge of the district court to which the transfer is sought. *(Chgd. by L.1989, chap. 295(1), eff. 9/1/89.)*



### Art. 4.18. Claim of underage.

(a) A claim that a district court or criminal district court does not have jurisdiction over a person because jurisdiction is exclusively in the juvenile court and that the juvenile court could not waive jurisdiction under Section 8.07(a), Penal Code, or did not waive jurisdiction under Section 8.07(b), Penal Code, must be made by written motion in bar of prosecution filed with the court in which criminal charges against the person are filed.

(b) The motion must be filed and presented to the presiding judge of the court:

(1) if the defendant enters a plea of guilty or no contest, before the plea;

(2) if the defendant's guilt or punishment is tried or determined by a jury, before selection of the jury begins; or

(3) if the defendant's guilt is tried by the court, before the first witness is sworn.

(c) Unless the motion is not contested, the presiding judge shall promptly conduct a hearing without a jury and rule on the motion. The party making the motion has the burden of establishing by a preponderance of the evidence those facts necessary for the motion to prevail.

(d) A person may not contest the jurisdiction of the court on the ground that the juvenile court has exclusive jurisdiction if:

(1) the person does not file a motion within the time requirements of this article; or

(2) the presiding judge finds under Subsection (c) that a motion made under this article does not prevail.

(e) An appellate court may review a trial court's determination under this article, if otherwise authorized by law, only after conviction in the trial court.

(f) A court that finds that it lacks jurisdiction over a case because exclusive jurisdiction is in the juvenile court shall transfer the case to the juvenile court as provided by Section 51.08, Family Code.

(g) This article does not apply to a claim of a defect or error in a discretionary transfer proceeding in juvenile court. A defendant may appeal a defect or error only as provided by Article 44.47. *(Added by L.1995, chap. 262(80); chgd. by L.1999, chap. 1477(27),(28), eff. 9/1/99.)*

# PREVENTION AND SUPPRESSION OF OFFENSES

## CHAPTER 5. FAMILYVIOLENCE PREVENTION

Article

5.01. Legislative statement.

5.02. Definitions.

5.03. Family or household relationship does not create an exception to official duties.† [*Domestic violence: family or household relationship no exception.*]

5.04. Duties of peace officers.† [*Peace officers: duties.*]

5.045. Standby assistance; liability.

5.05. Reports and records.

5.06. Duties of prosecuting attorneys and courts.

5.07. Venue for protective order offenses.

5.08. Mediation in family violence cases

## Art. 5.01. Legislative statement.

(a) Family violence is a serious danger and threat to society and its members. Victims of family violence are entitled to the maximum protection from harm or abuse or the threat of harm or abuse as is permitted by law.

(b) In any law enforcement, prosecutorial, or judicial response to allegations of family violence, the responding law enforcement or judicial officers shall protect the victim, without regard to the relationship between the alleged offender and victim.

## Art. 5.02. Definitions.

In this chapter, "family violence," "family," "household," and "member of a household" have the meanings assigned by Section 71.01, Family Code.

## Art. 5.03. Family or household relationship does not create an exception to official duties.† [*Domestic violence: family or household relationship no exception.*]

A general duty prescribed for an officer by Chapter 2 of this code is not waived or excepted in any family violence case or investigation because of a family or household relationship between an alleged violator and the victim of family violence. A peace officer's or a magistrate's duty to prevent the commission of criminal offenses, including acts of family violence, is not waived or excepted because of a family or household relationship between the potential violator and victim.



## Art. 5.04. Duties of peace officers.† [*Peace officers: duties.*]

(a) The primary duties of a peace officer who investigates a family violence allegation or who responds to a disturbance call that may involve family violence are to protect any potential victim of family violence, enforce the law of this state, enforce a protective order from another jurisdiction as provided by Chapter 88, Family Code, and make lawful arrests of violators.

(b) A peace officer who investigates a family violence allegation or who responds to a disturbance call that may involve family violence shall advise any possible adult victim of all reasonable means to prevent further family violence, including giving written notice of a victim's legal rights and remedies and of the availability of shelter or other community services for family violence victims.

(c) A written notice required by Subsection (b) of this article is sufficient if it is in substantially the following form with the required information in English and in Spanish inserted in the notice:

**"NOTICE TO ADULT VICTIMS OF FAMILY VIOLENCE**

"It is a crime for any person to cause you any physical injury or harm EVEN IF THAT PERSON IS A MEMBER OR FORMER MEMBER OF YOUR FAMILY OR HOUSEHOLD.

"Please tell the investigating peace officer:

"IF you, your child, or any other household resident has been injured; or

"IF you feel you are going to be in danger when the officer leaves or later.

"You have the right to:

"ASK the local prosecutor to file a criminal complaint against the person committing family violence; and

"APPLY to a court for an order to protect you (you should consult a legal aid office, a prosecuting attorney, or a private attorney). If a family or household member assaults you and is arrested, you may request that a magistrate's order for emergency protection be issued. Please inform the investigating officer if you want an order for emergency protection. You need not be present when the order is issued. You cannot be charged a fee by a court in connection with filing, serving, or entering a protective order. For example, the court can enter an order that:

"(1) the abuser not commit further acts of violence;

"(2) the abuser not threaten, harass, or contact you at home;

"(3) directs the abuser to leave your household; and

"(4) establishes temporary custody of the children and directs the abuser not to interfere with the children or any property.

"A VIOLATION OF CERTAIN PROVISIONS OF COURT-ORDERED PROTECTION (such as (1) and (2) above) MAY BE A FELONY.

"CALL THE FOLLOWING VIOLENCE SHELTERS OR SOCIAL ORGANIZATIONS IF YOU NEED PROTECTION:

"______________________________________________

______________________________________________."

*(Chgd. by L.1991, chap. 366(4); L.1995, chap. 1024(24); L.1997, chaps. 610(2), 1193(23), eff. 9/1/97.)*

### Art. 5.045. Standby assistance; liability.

(a) In the discretion of a peace officer, the officer may stay with a victim of family violence to protect the victim and allow the victim to take the personal property of the victim or of a child in the care of the victim to a place of safety in an orderly manner.

(b) A peace officer who provides assistance under Subsection (a) of this article is not:

(1) civilly liable for an act or omission of the officer that arises in connection with providing the assistance or determining whether to provide the assistance; or

(2) civilly or criminally liable for the wrongful appropriation of any personal property by the victim.

*(Added by L.1995, chap. 565(1), eff. 6/14/95.)*

### Art. 5.05. Reports and records.

(a) A peace officer who investigates a family violence incident or who responds to a disturbance call that may involve family violence shall make a written report, including but not limited to:

(1) the names of the suspect and complainant;

(2) the date, time, and location of the incident;

(3) any visible or reported injuries; and

(4) a description of the incident and a statement of its disposition.

(b) Each local law enforcement agency shall establish a departmental code for identifying and retrieving family violence reports as outlined in Subsection (a) of this section. A district or county attorney or an assistant district or county attorney exercising authority in the county where the law enforcement agency maintains records under this section is entitled to access to the records.

(c) In order to ensure that officers responding to calls are aware of the existence and terms of protective orders, each municipal police department and sheriff shall establish procedures within the department or office to provide adequate information or access to information for law enforcement officers of the names of persons protected by a protective order and of persons to whom protective orders are directed.

(d) Each law enforcement officer shall accept a certified copy of an original or modified protective order as proof of the validity of the order and it is presumed the order remains valid unless:

(1) the order contains a termination date that has passed;

(2) it is more than one year after the date the order was issued; or

(3) the law enforcement officer has been notified by the clerk of the court vacating the order that the order has been vacated.

(e) A peace officer who makes a report under Subsection (a) of this article shall provide information concerning the incident or disturbance to the bureau of identification and records of the Department of Public Safety for its recordkeeping function under Section 411.042, Government Code. The bureau shall prescribe the form and nature of the information required to be reported to the bureau by this article.

*(Chgd. by L.1989, chaps. 614(27), 739(8); L.1993, chap. 900(8.01), eff. 9/1/93.)*

### Art. 5.06. Duties of prosecuting attorneys and courts.

(a) Neither a prosecuting attorney nor a court may:

(1) dismiss or delay any criminal proceeding that involves a prosecution for an offense that constitutes family violence because a civil proceeding is pending or not pending; or

(2) require proof that a complaining witness, victim, or defendant is a party to a suit for the dissolution of a marriage or a suit affecting the parent-child relationship before presenting a criminal allegation to a grand jury, filing an information, or otherwise proceeding with the prosecution of a criminal case.

(b) A prosecuting attorney's decision to file an application for a protective order under Chapter 71, Family Code, should be made without regard to whether a criminal complaint has been filed by the applicant. A prosecuting attorney may require the applicant to provide information for an offense report, relating to the facts alleged in the application, with a local law enforcement agency.

(c) The prosecuting attorney having responsibility under Section 71.04(c), Family Code, for filing applications for protective orders under Chapter 71, Family Code, shall provide notice of that responsibility to all law enforcement agencies within the jurisdiction of the prosecuting attorney for the prosecuting attorney.

*(Chgd. by L.1989, chaps. 614(28), 739(9); L.1995, chaps. 564(2), 1024(25), eff. 9/1/95.)*

### Art. 5.07. Venue for protective order offenses.

The venue for an offense under Section 25.07, Penal Code, is in the county in which the order was issued or, without regard to the identity or location of the court that issued the protective order, in the county in which the offense was committed. *(Added by L.1989, chaps. 614(29), 739(10); chgd. by L.1995, chap. 76(14.16), eff. 9/1/95.)*

### Art. 5.08. Mediation in family violence cases.

Notwithstanding Article 26.13(g) or Section 11(a)(16), Article 42, of this code, in a criminal prosecution arising from family violence, as that term is defined by Section 71.004, Family Code, a court shall not refer or order the victim or the defendant involved to mediation, dispute resolution, or other similar procedures. *(Added by L.1999, chap. 389(1), eff. 5/31/99.)*

## CHAPTER 6. PREVENTING OFFENSES BY THE ACT OF MAGISTRATES AND OTHER OFFICERS

Article



### Art. 6.01. When magistrate hears threat.† [*Threatened injury.*]

It is the duty of every magistrate, when he may have heard, in any manner, that a threat has been made by one person to do some injury to himself or the person or property of another, including the person or property of his spouse, immediately to give notice to some peace officer, in order that such peace officer may use lawful means to prevent the injury.

### Art. 6.02. Threat to take life.† [*Threatened fatal injury.*]

If, within the hearing of a magistrate, one person shall threaten to take the life of another, including that of his spouse, or himself, the magistrate shall issue a warrant for the arrest of the person making the threat, or in case of emergency, he may himself immediately arrest such person.

### Art. 6.03. On attempt to injure.† [*Attempted injury.*]

Whenever, in the presence or within the observation of a magistrate, an attempt is made by one person to inflict an injury upon himself or to the person or property of another, including the person or property of his spouse, it is his duty to use all lawful means to prevent the injury. This may be done, either by verbal order to a peace officer to interfere and prevent the injury, or by the issuance of an order of arrest against the offender, or by arresting the offender; for which purpose he may call upon all persons present to assist in making the arrest.

### Art. 6.04. May compel offender to give security.† [*Placing offender into custody.*]

When the person making such threat is brought before a magistrate, he may compel him to give security to keep the peace, or commit him to custody.

### Art. 6.05. Duty of peace officer as to threats.† [*Threats: duty of peace officer.*]

It is the duty of every peace officer, when he may have been informed in any manner that a threat has been made by one person to do some injury to himself or to the person or property of another, including the person or property of his spouse, to prevent the threatened injury, if within his power; and, in order to do this, he may call in aid any number of citizens in his county. He may take such measures as the person about to be injured might for the prevention of the offense.

### Art. 6.06. Peace officer to prevent injury.† [*Prevention of injury.*]

Whenever, in the presence of a peace officer, or within his view, one person is about to commit an offense against the person or property of another, including the person or property of his spouse, or injure himself, it is his duty to prevent it; and, for this purpose the peace officer may summon any number of the citizens of his county to his aid. The peace officer must use the amount of force necessary to prevent the commission of the offense, and no greater.

### Art. 6.07. Conduct of peace officer.

The conduct of peace officers, in preventing offenses about to be committed in their presence, or within their view, is to be regulated by the same rules as are prescribed to the action of the person about to be injured. They may use all force necessary to repel the aggression.

## CHAPTER 7. PROCEEDINGS BEFORE MAGISTRATES TO PREVENT OFFENSES





### Art. 7.01. Shall issue warrant.† [*Warrant issuance.*]

Whenever a magistrate is informed upon oath that an offense is about to be committed against the person or property of the informant, or of another, or that any person has threatened to commit an offense, the magistrate shall immediately issue a warrant for the arrest of the accused; that he may be brought before such magistrate or before some other named in the warrant.

### Art. 7.02. Appearance bond pending peace bond hearing.† [*Appearance bond.*]

In proceedings under this Chapter, the accused shall have the right to make an appearance bond; such bond shall be conditioned as appearance bonds in other cases, and shall be further conditioned that the accused, pending the hearing, will not commit such offense and that he will keep the peace toward the person threatened or about to be injured, and toward all others, pending the hearing. Should the accused enter into such appearance bond, such fact shall not constitute any evidence of the accusation brought against him at the hearing on the merits before the magistrate.

### Art. 7.03. Accused brought before magistrate.

When the accused has been brought before the magistrate, he shall hear proof as to the accusation, and if he be satisfied that there is just reason to apprehend that the offense was intended to be committed, or that the threat was seriously made, he shall make an order that the accused enter into bond in such sum as he may in his discretion require, conditioned that he will not commit such offense, and that he will keep the peace toward the person threatened or about to be injured, and toward all others named in the bond for any period of time, not to exceed one year from the date of the bond. The magistrate shall admonish the accused that if the accused violates a condition of the bond, the court, in addition to ordering forfeiture of the bond, may punish the accused for contempt under Section 21.002(c), Government Code. *(Chgd. by L.1997, chap. 773(1), eff. 9/1/97.)*

### Art. 7.04. Form of peace bond.† [*Peace bond: form.*]

Such bond shall be sufficient if it be payable to the State of Texas, conditioned as required in said order of the magistrate, be for some certain sum, and be signed by the defendant and his surety or sureties and dated, and the provisions of Article 17.02 permitting the deposit of current United States money in lieu of sureties is applicable to this bond. No error of form shall vitiate such bond, and no error in the proceedings prior to the execution of the bond shall be a defense in a suit thereon.

### Art. 7.05. Oath of surety; bond filed.

The officer taking such bond shall require the sureties of the accused to make oath as to the value of their property as pointed out with regard to bail bonds. Such officer shall forthwith deposit such bond and oaths in the office of the clerk of the county where such bond is taken.

### Art. 7.06. Amount of bail.† [*Fixing bail amounts.*]

The magistrate, in fixing the amount of such bonds, shall be governed by the pecuniary circumstances of the accused and the nature of the offense threatened or about to be committed.

### Art. 7.07. Surety may exonerate himself.

A surety upon any such bond may, at any time before a breach thereof, exonerate himself from the obligations of the same by delivering to any magistrate of the county where such bond was taken, the person of the defendant; and such magistrate shall in that case again require of the defendant bond, with other security in the same amount as the first bond; and the same proceeding shall be had as in the first instance, but the one year's time shall commence to run from the date of the first order.

### Art. 7.08. Failure to give bond.† [*Failing to give bond.*]

If the defendant fail to give bond, he shall be committed to jail for one year from the date of the first order requiring such bond.

### Art. 7.09. Discharge of defendant.† [*Discharging defendant.*]

A defendant committed for failing to give bond shall be discharged by the officer having him in custody, upon giving the required bond, or at the expiration of the time for which he has been committed.

### Art. 7.10. May discharge defendant.† [*Discharge of defendant.*]

If the magistrate believes from the evidence that there is no good reason to apprehend that the offense was intended or will be committed, or that no serious threat was made by the defendant, he shall discharge the accused, and may, in his discretion, tax the cost of the proceeding against the party making the complaint.

### Art. 7.13. When defendant has committed a crime.† [*Commission of a crime.*]

If it appears from the evidence before the magistrate that the defendant has committed a criminal offense, the same proceedings shall be had as in other cases where parties are charged with crime.

### Art. 7.14. Costs.

If the accused is found subject to the charge and required to give bond, the costs of the proceedings shall be adjudged against him.

### Art. 7.15. May order protection.† [*Ordering protection.*]

When, from the nature of the case and the proof offered to the magistrate, it may appear necessary and proper, he shall have a right to order any peace officer to protect the person or property of any individual threatened; and such peace officer shall have the right to summon aid by requiring any number of citizens of his county to assist in giving the protection.

### Art. 7.16. Suit on bond.

A suit to forfeit any bond taken under the provisions of this Chapter shall be brought in the name of the State by the district or county attorney in the county where the bond was taken.

### Art. 7.17. Limitation and procedure.

Suits upon such bonds shall be commenced within two years from the breach of the same, and not thereafter, and shall be governed by the same rules as civil actions, except that the sureties may be sued without joining the principal. To entitle the State to recover, it shall only be necessary to prove that the accused violated any condition of said bond. The full amount of such bond may be recovered of the accused and the sureties.

### Art. 7.18. Contempt.

Violation of a condition of bond imposed under this chapter is punishable by:

(1) forfeiture of the bond;

(2) imposition of the fine and confinement for contempt under Section 21.002(c), Government Code; or

(3) both forfeiture of the bond and imposition of the fine and confinement.

*(Added by L.1997, chap. 773(2), eff. 9/1/97.)*

 

# CHAPTER 8. SUPPRESSION OF RIOTS AND OTHER DISTURBANCES

Article





### Art. 8.01. Officer may require aid.† [*Officer may request assistance.*]

When any officer authorized to execute process is resisted, or when he has sufficient reason to believe that he will meet with resistance in executing the same, he may command as many of the citizens of his county as he may think proper; and the sheriff may call any military company in the county to aid him in overcoming the resistance, and if necessary, in seizing and arresting the persons engaged in such resistance.

### Art. 8.02. Military aid in executing process.† [*Military aid to overcome resistance.*]

If it be represented to the Governor in such manner as to satisfy him that the power of the county is not sufficient to enable the sheriff to execute process, he may, on application, order any military company of volunteers or militia company from another county to aid in overcoming such resistance.

### Art. 8.03. Military aid in suppressing riots.† [*Suppression of riots: military assistance.*]

Whenever, for the purpose of suppressing riots or unlawful assemblies, the aid of military or militia companies is called, they shall obey the orders of the civil officer who is engaged in suppressing the same.

### Art. 8.04. Dispersing riot.

Whenever a number of persons are assembled together in such a manner as to constitute a riot, according to the penal law of the State, it is the duty of every magistrate or peace officer to cause such persons to disperse. This may either be done by commanding them to disperse or by arresting the persons engaged, if necessary, either with or without warrant.

### Art. 8.05. Officer may call aid.† [*Officer may call for aid.*]

In order to enable the officer to disperse a riot, he may call to his aid the power of the county in the same manner as is provided where it is necessary for the execution of process.

### Art. 8.06. Means adopted to suppress.† [*Force to suppress riot.*]

The officer engaged in suppressing a riot, and those who aid him are authorized and justified in adopting such measures as are necessary to suppress the riot, but are not authorized to use any greater degree of force than is requisite to accomplish that object.

### Art. 8.07. Unlawful assembly.

The Articles of this Chapter relating to the suppression of riots apply equally to an unlawful assembly and other unlawful disturbances, as defined by the Penal Code.

### Art. 8.08. Suppression at election.† [*Suppression of riots: elections.*]

To suppress riots, unlawful assemblies and other disturbances at elections, any magistrate may appoint a sufficient number of special constables. Such appointments shall be made to each special constable, shall be in writing, dated and signed by the magistrate, and shall recite the purposes for which such appointment is made, and the length of time it is to continue. Before the same is delivered to such special constable, he shall take an oath before the magistrate to suppress, by lawful means, all riots, unlawful assemblies and breaches of the peace of which he may receive information, and to act impartially between all parties and persons interested in the result of the election.

**Art. 8.09. Power of special constable.† [*Special constable: powers.*]**
Special constables so appointed shall, during the time for which they are appointed, exercise the powers and perform the duties properly belonging to peace officers.

## CHAPTER 9. OFFENSES INJURIOUS TO PUBLIC HEALTH

Article


**Art. 9.01. Trade injurious to health.† [*Pursuing trade that is hazardous to health.*]**
After an indictment or information has been presented against any person for carrying on a trade, business or occupation injurious to the health of those in the neighborhood, the court shall have power, on the application of anyone interested, and after hearing proof both for and against the accused, to restrain the defendant, in such penalty as may be deemed proper, from carrying on such trade, business or occupation, or may make such order respecting the manner and place of carrying on the same as may be deemed advisable; and if upon trial, the defendant be convicted, the restraint shall be made perpetual, and the party shall be required to enter into bond, with security, not to continue such trade, business or occupation to the detriment of the health of such neighborhood, or of any other neighborhood within the county.



**Art. 9.02. Refusal to give bond.† [*Refusing to give bond.*]**
If the party refuses to give bond when required under the provisions of the preceding Article, the court may either commit him to jail, or make an order requiring the sheriff to seize upon the implements of such trade, business or occupation, or the goods and property used in conducting such trade, business or occupation, and destroy the same.

**Art. 9.03. Requisites of bond.† [*Requirements of bond.*]**
Such bond shall be payable to the State of Texas, in a reasonable amount to be fixed by the court, conditioned that the defendant will not carry on such trade, business or occupation, naming the same, at such place, naming the place, or at any other place in the county, to the detriment of the health of the neighborhood. The bond shall be signed by the defendant and his sureties and dated, and shall be approved by the court taking the same, and filed in such court.

**Art. 9.04. Suit upon bond.**
Any such bond, upon the breach thereof, may be sued upon by the district or county attorney, in the name of the State of Texas, within two years after such breach, and not afterwards; and such suits shall be governed by the same rules as civil actions.

**Art. 9.05. Proof.**
It shall be sufficient proof of the breach of any such bond to show that the party continued after executing the same, to carry on the trade, business or occupation which he bound himself to discontinue; and the full amount of such bond may be recovered of the defendant and his sureties.

**Art. 9.06. Unwholesome food.† [*Selling unwholesome food.*]**
After conviction for selling unwholesome food or adulterated medicine, the court shall enter and issue an order to the sheriff or other proper officer to seize and destroy such as remains in the hands of the defendant.

## CHAPTER 10. OBSTRUCTIONS OF PUBLIC HIGHWAYS

Article

### Art. 10.01. Order to remove.

After prosecution begun against any person for obstructing any highway, any one, in behalf of the public, may apply to the county judge of the county in which such highway is situated; and upon hearing proof, such judge, either in term time or in vacation, may issue his written order to the sheriff or other proper officer of the county, directing him to remove the obstruction. Before the issuance of such order, the applicant therefor shall give bond with security in an amount to be fixed by the judge, to indemnify the accused, in case of his acquittal, for the loss he sustains. Such bond shall be approved by the county judge and filed with the papers in the cause.

### Art. 10.02. Bond of applicant.† [*Bond.*]

If the defendant be acquitted after a trial upon the merits of the case, he may maintain a civil action against the applicant and his sureties upon such bond, and may recover the full amount of the bond, or such damages, less than the full amount thereof, as may be assessed by a court or jury; provided, he shows on the trial that the place was not in fact, at the time he placed the obstruction or impediment thereupon, a public highway established by proper authority, but was in fact his own property or in his lawful possession.



### Art. 10.03. Removal.

Upon the conviction of a defendant for obstructing a public highway, if such obstruction still exists, the court shall order the sheriff or other proper officer to forthwith remove the same at the cost of the defendant, to be taxed and collected as other costs in the case.

# HABEAS CORPUS

## CHAPTER 11. HABEAS CORPUS

Article

### Art. 11.01. What writ is.† [*Description of writ.*]

The writ of habeas corpus is the remedy to be used when any person is restrained in his liberty. It is an order issued by a court or judge of competent jurisdiction, directed to any one having a person in his custody, or under his restraint, commanding him to produce such person, at a time and place named in the writ, and show why he is held in custody or under restraint.

### Art. 11.02. To whom directed.† [*Direction of writ.*]

The writ runs in the name of "The State of Texas". It is addressed to a person having another under restraint, or in his custody, describing, as near as may be, the name of the office, if any, of the person to whom it is directed, and the name of the person said to be detained. It shall fix the time and place of return and be signed by the judge, or by the clerk with his seal, where issued by a court.

### Art. 11.03. Want of form.

The writ of habeas corpus is not invalid, nor shall it be disobeyed for any want of form, if it substantially appear that it is issued by competent authority, and the writ sufficiently shows the object of its issuance.

### Art. 11.04. Construction.

Every provision relating to the writ of habeas corpus shall be most favorably construed in order to give effect to the remedy, and protect the rights of the person seeking relief under it.

### Art. 11.05. By whom writ may be granted.† [*Power of issuance.*]

The Court of Criminal Appeals, the District Courts, the County Courts, or any Judge of said Courts, have power to issue the writ of habeas corpus; and it is their duty, upon proper motion, to grant the writ under the rules prescribed by law.

### Art. 11.051. Filing fee prohibited.

Notwithstanding any other law, a clerk of a court may not require a filing fee from an individual who files an application or petition for a writ of habeas corpus. *(Added by L.1999, chap. 392(1), eff. 5/31/99.)*

**Art. 11.06. Returnable to any county.† [*Writ returnable to any county.*]**
Before indictment found, the writ may be made returnable to any county in the State.

**Art. 11.07. Procedure after conviction without death penalty.**
**Sec. 1.** This article establishes the procedures for an application for writ of habeas corpus in which the applicant seeks relief from a felony judgment imposing a penalty other than death.

**Sec. 2.** After indictment found in any felony case, other than a case in which the death penalty is imposed, and before conviction, the writ must be made returnable in the county where the offense has been committed.

**Sec. 3.** (a) After final conviction in any felony case, the writ must be made returnable to the Court of Criminal Appeals of Texas at Austin, Texas.

(b) An application for writ of habeas corpus filed after final conviction in a felony case, other than a case in which the death penalty is imposed, must be filed with the clerk of the court in which the conviction being challenged was obtained, and the clerk shall assign the application to that court. When the application is received by that court, a writ of habeas corpus, returnable to the Court of Criminal Appeals, shall issue by operation of law. The clerk of that court shall make appropriate notation thereof, assign to the case a file number (ancillary to that of the conviction being challenged), and forward a copy of the application by certified mail, return receipt requested, or by personal service to the attorney representing the state in that court, who shall answer the application not later than the 15th day after the date the copy of the application is received. Matters alleged in the application not admitted by the state are deemed denied.

(c) Within 20 days of the expiration of the time in which the state is allowed to answer, it shall be the duty of the convicting court to decide whether there are controverted, previously unresolved facts material to the legality of the applicant's confinement. Confinement means confinement for any offense or any collateral consequence resulting from the conviction that is the basis of the instant habeas corpus. If the convicting court decides that there are no such issues, the clerk shall immediately transmit to the Court of Criminal Appeals a copy of the application, any answers filed, and a certificate reciting the date upon which that finding was made. Failure of the court to act within the allowed 20 days shall constitute such a finding.

(d) If the convicting court decides that there are controverted, previously unresolved facts which are material to the legality of the applicant's confinement, it shall enter an order within 20 days of the expiration of the time allowed for the state to reply, designating the issues of fact to be resolved. To resolve those issues the court may order affidavits, depositions, interrogatories, and hearings, as well as using personal recollection. Also, the convicting court may appoint an attorney or a magistrate to hold a hearing and make findings of fact. An attorney so appointed shall be compensated as provided in Article 26.05 of this code. It shall be the duty of the reporter who is designated to transcribe a hearing held pursuant to this article to prepare a transcript within 15 days of its conclusion. After the convicting court makes findings of fact or approves the findings of the person designated to make them, the clerk of the convicting court shall immediately transmit to the Court of Criminal Appeals, under one cover, the application, any answers filed, any motions filed, transcripts of all depositions and hearings, any affidavits, and any other matters such as official records used by the court in resolving issues of fact.
*(Chgd. by L.1999, chap. 580(2), eff. 9/1/99.)*

**Sec. 4.** (a) If a subsequent application for writ of habeas corpus is filed after final disposition of an initial application challenging the same conviction, a court may not consider the merits of or grant relief based on the subsequent application unless the application contains sufficient specific facts establishing that:

(1) the current claims and issues have not been and could not have been presented previously in an original application or in a previously considered application filed under this article because the factual or legal basis for the claim was unavailable on the date the applicant filed the previous application; or

(2) by a preponderance of the evidence, but for a violation of the United States Constitution no rational juror could have found the applicant guilty beyond a reasonable doubt.

(b) For purposes of Subsection (a)(1), a legal basis of a claim is unavailable on or before a date described by Subsection (a)(1) if the legal basis was not recognized by and could not have been reasonably formulated from a final decision of the United States Supreme Court, a court of appeals of the United States, or a court of appellate jurisdiction of this state on or before that date.

(c) For purposes of Subsection (a)(1), a factual basis of a claim is unavailable on or before a date described by Subsection (a)(1) if the factual basis was not ascertainable through the exercise of reasonable diligence on or before that date.

**Sec. 5.** The Court of Criminal Appeals may deny relief upon the findings and conclusions of the hearing judge without docketing the cause, or may direct that the cause be docketed and heard as though originally presented to said court or as an appeal. Upon reviewing the record the court shall enter its judgment remanding the applicant to custody or ordering his release, as the law and facts may justify. The mandate of the court shall issue to the court issuing the writ, as in other criminal cases. After conviction the procedure outlined in this Act shall be exclusive and any other proceeding shall be void and of no force and effect in discharging the prisoner.

**Sec. 6.** Upon any hearing by a district judge by virtue of this Act, the attorney for applicant, and the state, shall be given at least seven full days' notice before such hearing is held.

**Sec. 7.** When the attorney for the state files an answer, motion, or other pleading relating to an application for a writ of habeas corpus or the court issues an order relating to an application for a writ of habeas corpus, the clerk of the court shall mail or deliver to the applicant a copy of the answer, motion, pleading, or order.
*(Chgd. by L.1995, chap. 319(5), eff. 9/1/95.)*

**Art. 11.071. Procedure in death penalty case.**

**Sec. 1. Application to death penalty case.** Notwithstanding any other provision of this chapter, this article establishes the procedures for an application for a writ of habeas corpus in which the applicant seeks relief from a judgment imposing a penalty of death.

**Sec. 2. Representation by counsel.** (a) An applicant shall be represented by competent counsel unless the applicant has elected to proceed pro se and the convicting trial court finds, after a hearing on the record, that the applicant's election is intelligent and voluntary.

(b) If a defendant is sentenced to death the convicting court, immediately after judgment is entered under Article 42.01, shall determine if the defendant is indigent and, if so, whether the defendant desires appointment of counsel for the purpose of a writ of habeas corpus.

(c) At the earliest practical time, but in no event later than 30 days, after the convicting court makes the findings required under Subsections (a) and (b), the convicting court shall appoint competent counsel, unless the applicant elects to proceed pro se or is represented by retained counsel. On appointing counsel under this section, the convicting court shall immediately notify the court of criminal appeals of the appointment, including in the notice a copy of the judgment and the name, address, and telephone number of the appointed counsel.

(d) The court of criminal appeals shall adopt rules for the appointment of attorneys as counsel under this section and the convicting court may appoint an attorney as counsel under this section only if the appointment is approved by the court of criminal appeals in any manner provided by those rules.

(e) If the court of criminal appeals denies an applicant relief under this article, an attorney appointed under this section to represent the applicant shall, not later than the 15th day after the date the court of criminal appeals denies relief or, if the case is filed and set for submission, the 15th day after the date the court of criminal appeals issues a mandate on the initial application for a writ of habeas corpus under this article, move to be appointed as counsel in federal habeas review under 21 U.S.C. Section 848(q) or equivalent provision or, if necessary, move for the appointment of other counsel under 21 U.S.C. Section 848(q) or equivalent provision. The attorney shall immediately file a copy of the motion with the court of criminal appeals, and if the attorney fails to do so, the court may take any action to ensure that the applicant's right to federal habeas review is protected, including initiating contempt proceedings against the attorney.

(f) The convicting court shall reasonably compensate an attorney appointed under this section as provided by Section 2A.
*(Chgd. by L.1999, chap. 803(1), eff. 9/1/99.)*

**Sec. 2A. State reimbursement; county obligation.** (a) The state shall reimburse a county for compensation of counsel under Section 2 and payment of expenses under Section 3. The total amount of reimbursement to which a county is entitled under this section for an application under this article may not exceed $25,000. Compensation and expenses in excess of the $25,000 reimbursement provided by the state are the obligation of the county.

(b) A convicting court seeking reimbursement for a county shall certify to the comptroller of public accounts the amount of compensation that the county is entitled to receive under this section. The comptroller of public accounts shall issue a warrant to the county in the amount certified by the convicting court, not to exceed $25,000.

(c) The limitation imposed by this section on the reimbursement by the state to a county for compensation of counsel and payment of reasonable expenses does not prohibit a county from compensating counsel and reimbursing expenses in an amount that is in excess of the amount the county receives from the state as reimbursement, and a county is specifically granted discretion by this subsection to make payments in excess of the state reimbursement.

*(Added by L.1999, chap. 803(2), eff. 9/1/99.)*



**Sec. 3. Investigation of grounds for application.** (a) On appointment, counsel shall investigate expeditiously, before and after the appellate record is filed in the court of criminal appeals, the factual and legal grounds for the filing of an application for a writ of habeas corpus.

(b) Not later than the 30th day before the date the application for a writ of habeas corpus is filed with the convicting court, counsel may file with the convicting court an ex parte, verified, and confidential request for prepayment of expenses, including expert fees, to investigate and present potential habeas corpus claims. The request for expenses must state:

(1) the claims of the application to be investigated;

(2) specific facts that suggest that a claim of possible merit may exist; and

(3) an itemized list of anticipated expenses for each claim.

(c) The court shall grant a request for expenses in whole or in part if the request for expenses is timely and reasonable. If the court denies in whole or in part the request for expenses, the court shall briefly state the reasons for the denial in a written order provided to the applicant.

(d) Counsel may incur expenses for habeas corpus investigation, including expenses for experts, without prior approval by the convicting court. On presentation of a claim for reimbursement, which may be presented ex parte, the court shall order reimbursement of counsel for expenses, if the expenses are reasonably necessary and reasonably incurred. If the court denies in whole or in part the request for expenses, the court shall briefly state the reasons for the denial in a written order provided to the applicant. The applicant may request reconsideration of the denial for reimbursement.

(e) Materials submitted to the court under this section are a part of the court's record.

*(Chgd. by L.1999, chap. 803(3), eff. 9/1/99.)*

**Sec. 4. Filing of application.** (a) An application for a writ of habeas corpus, returnable to the court of criminal appeals, must be filed in the convicting court not later than the 180th day after the date the convicting court appoints counsel under Section 2 or not later than the 45th day after the date the state's original brief is filed on direct appeal with the court of criminal appeals, whichever date is later.

(b) The convicting court, before the filing date that is applicable to the applicant under Subsection (a), may for good cause shown and after notice and an opportunity to be heard by the attorney representing the state grant one 90-day extension that begins on the filing date applicable to the defendant under Subsection (a). Either party may request that the court hold a hearing on the request. If the convicting court finds that the applicant cannot establish good cause justifying the requested extension, the court shall make a finding stating that fact and deny the request for the extension.

(c) An application filed after the filing date that is applicable to the applicant under Subsection (a) or (b) is untimely.

(d) If the convicting court receives an untimely application or determines that after the filing date that is applicable to the applicant under Subsection (a) or (b) no application has been filed, the convicting court immediately, but in any event within 10 days, shall send to the court of criminal appeals and to the attorney representing the state:

(1) a copy of the untimely application, with a statement of the convicting court that the application is untimely, or a statement of the convicting court that no application has been filed within the time periods required by Subsections (a) and (b); and

(2) any order the judge of the convicting court determines should be attached to an untimely application or statement under Subdivision (1).

(e) A failure to file an application before the filing date applicable to the applicant under Subsection (a) or (b) constitutes a waiver of all grounds for relief that were available to the applicant before the last date on which an application could be timely filed, except as provided by Section 4A.

*(Chgd. by L.1997, chap. 1336(1); L.1999, chap. 803(4), eff. 9/1/99.)*

**Sec. 4A. Untimely application; application not filed.** (a) On command of the court of criminal appeals, a counsel who files an untimely application or fails to file an application before the filing date applicable under Section 4(a) or (b) shall show cause as to why the application was untimely filed or not filed before the filing date.

(b) At the conclusion of the counsel's presentation to the court of criminal appeals, the court may:

(1) find that good cause has not been shown and dismiss the application;

(2) permit the counsel to continue representation of the applicant and establish a new filing date for the application, which may be not more than 180 days from the date the court permits the counsel to continue representation; or

(3) appoint new counsel to represent the applicant and establish a new filing date for the application, which may be not more than 270 days after the date the court appoints new counsel.

(c) The court of criminal appeals may hold in contempt counsel who files an untimely application or fails to file an application before the date required by Section 4(a) or (b). The court of criminal appeals may punish as a separate instance of contempt each day after the first day on which the counsel fails to timely file the application. In addition to or in lieu of holding counsel in contempt, the court of criminal appeals may enter an order denying counsel compensation under Section 2A.

(d) If the court of criminal appeals establishes a new filing date for the application, the court of criminal appeals shall notify the convicting court of that fact and the convicting court shall proceed under this article.

(e) Sections 2A and 3 apply to compensation and reimbursement of counsel appointed under Subsection (b)(3) in the same manner as if counsel had been appointed by the convicting court.

(f) Notwithstanding any other provision of this article, the court of criminal appeals shall appoint counsel and establish a new filing date for application, which may be no later than the 270th day after the date on which counsel is appointed, for each applicant who before September 1, 1999, filed an untimely application or failed to file an application before the date required by Section 4(a) or (b). Section 2A applies to the compensation and payment of expenses of counsel appointed by the court of criminal appeals under this subsection.
*(Added by L.1999, chap. 803(5), eff. 9/1/99.)*

**Sec. 5. Subsequent application.** (a) If a subsequent application for a writ of habeas corpus is filed after filing an initial application, a court may not consider the merits of or grant relief based on the subsequent application unless the application contains sufficient specific facts establishing that:

(1) the current claims and issues have not been and could not have been presented previously in a timely initial application or in a previously considered application filed under this article or Article 11.07 because the factual or legal basis for the claim was unavailable on the date the applicant filed the previous application;

(2) by a preponderance of the evidence, but for a violation of the United States Constitution no rational juror could have found the applicant guilty beyond a reasonable doubt; or

(3) by clear and convincing evidence, but for a violation of the United States Constitution no rational juror would have answered in the state's favor one or more of the special issues that were submitted to the jury in the applicant's trial under Article 37.071 or 37.0711.

(b) If the convicting court receives a subsequent application, the clerk of the court shall:

(1) attach a notation that the application is a subsequent application;

(2) assign to the case a file number that is ancillary to that of the conviction being challenged; and

(3) immediately send to the court of criminal appeals a copy of:

(A) the application;

(B) the notation;

(C) the order scheduling the applicant's execution, if scheduled; and

(D) any order the judge of the convicting court directs to be attached to the application.

(c) On receipt of the copies of the documents from the clerk, the court of criminal appeals shall determine whether the requirements of Subsection (a) have been satisfied. The convicting court may not take further action on the application before the court of criminal appeals issues an order finding that the requirements have been satisfied. If the court of criminal appeals determines that the requirements have not been satisfied, the court shall issue an order dismissing the application as an abuse of the writ under this section.

(d) For purposes of Subsection (a)(1), a legal basis of a claim is unavailable on or before a date described by Subsection (a)(1) if the legal basis was not recognized by or could not have been reasonably formulated from a final decision of the United States Supreme Court, a court of appeals of the United States, or a court of appellate jurisdiction of this state on or before that date.

(e) For purposes of Subsection (a)(1), a factual basis of a claim is unavailable on or before a date described by Subsection (a)(1) if the factual basis was not ascertainable through the exercise of reasonable diligence on or before that date.

(f) If an amended or supplemental application is not filed within the time specified under Section 4(a) or (b), the court shall treat the application as a subsequent application under this section.
*(Chgd. by L.1997, chap. 1336(2); L.1999, chap. 803(6), (7), eff. 9/1/99.)*

**Sec. 6. Issuance of writ.** (a) If a timely application for a writ of habeas corpus is filed in the convicting court, a writ of habeas corpus, returnable to the court of criminal appeals, shall issue by operation of law.

(b) If the convicting court receives notice that the requirements of Section 5 for consideration of a subsequent application have been met, a writ of habeas corpus, returnable to the court of criminal appeals, shall issue by operation of law.

(c) The clerk of the convicting court shall:

(1) make an appropriate notation that a writ of habeas corpus was issued;

(2) assign to the case a file number that is ancillary to that of the conviction being challenged; and

(3) send a copy of the application by certified mail, return receipt requested, to the attorney representing the state in that court.

(d) The clerk of the convicting court shall promptly deliver copies of documents submitted to the clerk under this article to the applicant and the attorney representing the state.
*(Chgd. by L.1999, chap. 803(8), eff. 9/1/99.)*



**Sec. 7. Answer to application.** (a) The state shall file an answer to the application for a writ of habeas corpus not later than the 120th day after the date the state receives notice of issuance of the writ. The state shall serve the answer on counsel for the applicant or, if the applicant is proceeding pro se, on the applicant. The state may request from the convicting court an extension of time in which to answer the application by showing particularized justifying circumstances for the extension, but in no event may the court permit the state to file an answer later than the 180th day after the date the state receives notice of issuance of the writ.

(b) Matters alleged in the application not admitted by the state are deemed denied.
*(Chgd. by L.1997, chap. 1336(3); L.1999, chap. 803(9), eff. 9/1/99.)*

**Sec. 8. Findings of fact without evidentiary hearing.** (a) Not later than the 20th day after the last date the state answers the application, the convicting court shall determine whether controverted, previously unresolved factual issues material to the legality of the applicant's confinement exist and shall issue a written order of the determination.

(b) If the convicting court determines the issues do not exist, the parties shall file proposed findings of fact and conclusions of law for the court to consider on or before a date set by the court that is not later than the 30th day after the date the order is issued.

(c) After argument of counsel, if requested by the court, the convicting court shall make appropriate written findings of fact and conclusions of law not later than the 15th day after the date the parties filed proposed findings or not later than the 45th day after the date the court's determination is made under Subsection (a), whichever occurs first.

(d) The clerk of the court shall immediately send to:

(1) the court of criminal appeals a copy of the:

(A) application;

(B) answer;

(C) orders entered by the convicting court;

(D) proposed findings of fact and conclusions of law; and

(E) findings of fact and conclusions of law entered by the court; and

(2) counsel for the applicant or, if the applicant is proceeding pro se, to the applicant, a copy of:

(A) orders entered by the convicting court;

(B) proposed findings of fact and conclusions of law; and

(C) findings of fact and conclusions of law entered by the court.
*(Chgd. by L.1997, chap. 1336(4), eff. 9/1/97.)*

**Sec. 9. Hearing.** (a) If the convicting court determines that controverted, previously unresolved factual issues material to the legality of the applicant's confinement exist, the court shall enter an order, not later than the 20th day after the last date the state answers the application, designating the issues of fact to be resolved and the manner in which the issues shall be resolved. To resolve the issues, the court may require affidavits, depositions, interrogatories, and evidentiary hearings and may use personal recollection.

(b) The convicting court shall hold the evidentiary hearing not later than the 30th day after the date on which the court enters the order designating issues under Subsection (a). The convicting court may grant a motion to postpone the hearing, but not for more than 30 days, and only if the court states, on the record, good cause for delay.

(c) The presiding judge of the convicting court shall conduct a hearing held under this section unless another judge presided over the original capital felony trial, in which event that judge, if qualified for assignment under Section 74.054 or 74.055, Government Code, may preside over the hearing.

(d) The court reporter shall prepare a transcript of the hearing not later than the 30th day after the date the hearing ends and file the transcript with the clerk of the convicting court.

(e) The parties shall file proposed findings of fact and conclusions of law for the convicting court to consider on or before a date set by the court that is not later than the 30th day after the date the transcript is filed. If the court requests argument of counsel, after argument the court shall make written findings of fact that are necessary to resolve the previously unresolved facts and make conclusions of law not later than the 15th day after the date the parties file proposed findings or not later than the 45th day after the date the court reporter files the transcript, whichever occurs first.

(f) The clerk of the convicting court shall immediately transmit to:

(1) the court of criminal appeals a copy of:

(A) the application;

(B) the answers and motions filed;

(C) the court reporter's transcript;

(D) the documentary exhibits introduced into evidence;

(E) the proposed findings of fact and conclusions of law;

(F) the findings of fact and conclusions of law entered by the court;

(G) the sealed materials such as a confidential request for investigative expenses; and

(H) any other matters used by the convicting court in resolving issues of fact; and

(2) counsel for the applicant or, if the applicant is proceeding pro se, to the applicant, a copy of:

(A) orders entered by the convicting court;

(B) proposed findings of fact and conclusions of law; and

(C) findings of fact and conclusions of law entered by the court.

(g) The clerk of the convicting court shall forward an exhibit that is not documentary to the court of criminal appeals on request of the court.

*(Chgd. by L.1997, chap. 1336(5); L.1999, chap. 803(10), eff. 9/1/99.)*

**Sec. 10. Rules of evidence.** The Texas Rules of Criminal Evidence apply to a hearing held under this article.

**Sec. 11. Review by court of criminal appeals.** The court of criminal appeals shall expeditiously review all applications for a writ of habeas corpus submitted under this article. The court may set the cause for oral argument and may request further briefing of the issues by the applicant or the state. After reviewing the record, the court shall enter its judgment remanding the applicant to custody or ordering the applicant's release, as the law and facts may justify.

*(Added by L.1995, chap. 319(1), eff. 9/1/95.)*

### Art. 11.08. Applicant charged with felony.† [*Charge of felony.*]

If a person is confined after indictment on a charge of felony, he may apply to the judge of the court in which he is indicted; or if there be no judge within the district, then to the judge of any district whose residence is nearest to the court house of the county in which the applicant is held in custody.

### Art. 11.09. Applicant charged with misdemeanor.† [*Charge of misdemeanor.*]

If a person is confined on a charge of misdemeanor, he may apply to the county judge of the county in which the misdemeanor is charged to have been committed, or if there be no county judge in said county, then to the county judge whose residence is nearest to the courthouse of the county in which the applicant is held in custody.

**Art. 11.10. Proceedings under the writ.† [*Proceedings.*]**

When motion has been made to a judge under the circumstances set forth in the two preceding Articles, he shall appoint a time when he will examine the cause of the applicant, and issue the writ returnable at that time, in the county where the offense is charged in the indictment or information to have been committed. He shall also specify some place in the county where he will hear the motion.

**Art. 11.11. Early hearing.**

The time so appointed shall be the earliest day which the judge can devote to hearing the cause of the applicant.

**Art. 11.12. Who may present petition.† [*Presenting petition.*]**

Either the party for whose relief the writ is intended, or any person for him, may present a petition to the proper authority for the purpose of obtaining relief.

**Art. 11.13. Applicant.**

The word applicant, as used in this Chapter, refers to the person for whose relief the writ is asked, though the petition may be signed and presented by any other person.

**Art. 11.14. Requisites of petition.† [*Requirements of petition.*]**

The petition must state substantially:

1. That the person for whose benefit the application is made is illegally restrained in his liberty, and by whom, naming both parties, if their names are known, or if unknown, designating and describing them;
2. When the party is confined or restrained by virtue of any writ, order or process, or under color of either, a copy shall be annexed to the petition, or it shall be stated that a copy cannot be obtained;
3. When the confinement or restraint is not by virtue of any writ, order or process, the petition may state only that the party is illegally confined or restrained in his liberty;
4. There must be a prayer in the petition for the writ of habeas corpus; and
5. Oath must be made that the allegations of the petition are true, according to the belief of the petitioner.

**Art. 11.15. Writ granted without delay.† [*Granting writ without delay.*]**

The writ of habeas corpus shall be granted without delay by the judge or court receiving the petition, unless it be manifest from the petition itself, or some documents annexed to it, that the party is entitled to no relief whatever.

**Art. 11.16. Writ may issue without motion.† [*Issuing writ without motion.*]**

A judge of the district or county court who has knowledge that any person is illegally confined or restrained in his liberty within his district or county may, if the case be one within his jurisdiction, issue the writ of habeas corpus, without any motion being made for the same.

**Art. 11.17. Judge may issue warrant of arrest.† [*Issuance of arrest warrant.*]**

Whenever it appears by satisfactory evidence to any judge authorized to issue such writ that any one is held in illegal confinement or custody, and there is good reason to believe that he will be carried out of the State, or suffer some irreparable injury before he can obtain relief in the usual course of law, or whenever the writ of habeas corpus has been issued and disregarded, the said judge may issue a warrant to any peace officer, or to any person specially named by said judge, directing him to take and bring such person before such judge, to be dealt with according to law.

**Art. 11.18. May arrest detainer.† [*Arrest of detainer.*]**

Where it appears by the proof offered, under circumstances mentioned in the preceding Article, that the person charged with having illegal custody of the prisoner is, by such act, guilty of an offense against the law, the judge may, in the warrant, order that he be arrested and brought before him; and upon examination, he may be committed, discharged, or held to bail, as the law and the nature of the case may require.

**Art. 11.19. Proceedings under the warrant.**

The officer charged with the execution of the warrant shall bring the persons therein mentioned before the judge or court issuing the same, who shall inquire into the cause of the imprisonment or restraint, and make an order thereon, as in cases of habeas corpus, either remanding into custody, discharging or admitting to bail the party so imprisoned or restrained.

**Art. 11.20. Officer executing warrant.† [*Execution of warrant.*]**

The same power may be exercised by the officer executing the warrant in cases arising under the foregoing Articles as is exercised in the execution of warrants of arrest.

**Art. 11.21. Constructive custody.**

The words "confined", "imprisoned", "in custody", "confinement", "imprisonment", refer not only to the actual, corporeal and forcible detention of a person, but likewise to any coercive measures by threats, menaces or the fear of injury, whereby one person exercises a control over the person of another, and detains him within certain limits.

**Art. 11.22. Restraint.**

By "restraint" is meant the kind of control which one person exercises over another, not to confine him within certain limits, but to subject him to the general authority and power of the person claiming such right.

**Art. 11.23. Scope of writ.**

The writ of habeas corpus is intended to be applicable to all such cases of confinement and restraint, where there is no lawful right in the person exercising the power, or where, though the power in fact exists, it is exercised in a manner or degree not sanctioned by law.

**Art. 11.24. One committed in default of bail.† [*Commitment in default of bail.*]**

Where a person has been committed to custody for failing to enter into bond, he is entitled to the writ of habeas corpus, if it be stated in the petition that there was no sufficient cause for requiring bail, or that the bail required is excessive. If the proof sustains the petition, it will entitle the party to be discharged, or have the bail reduced.

**Art. 11.25. Person afflicted with disease.† [*Person in ill health.*]**

When a judge or court authorized to grant writs of habeas corpus shall be satisfied, upon investigation, that a person in legal custody is afflicted with a disease which will render a removal necessary for the preservation of life, an order may be made for the removal of the prisoner to some other place where his health will not be likely to suffer; or he may be admitted to bail when it appears that any species of confinement will endanger his life.

**Art. 11.26. Who may serve writ.† [*Service of writ.*]**

The service of the writ may be made by any person competent to testify.

**Art. 11.27. How writ may be served and returned.† [*Service and return of writ.*]**

The writ may be served by delivering a copy of the original to the person who is charged with having the party under restraint or in custody, and exhibiting the original, if demanded; if he refuse to receive it, he shall be informed verbally of the purport of the writ. If he refuses admittance to the person wishing to make the service, or conceals himself, a copy of the writ may be fixed upon some conspicuous part of the house where such person resides or conceals himself, or of the place where the prisoner is confined; and the person serving the writ of habeas corpus shall, in all cases, state fully, in his return, the manner and the time of the service of the writ.

**Art. 11.28. Return under oath.† [*Return of writ.*]**

The return of a writ of habeas corpus, under the provisions of the preceding Article, if made by any person other than an officer, shall be under oath.

**Art. 11.29. Must make return.† [*Return of writ required.*]**

The person on whom the writ of habeas corpus is served shall immediately obey the same, and make the return required by law upon the copy of the original writ served on him, and this, whether the writ be directed to him or not.

**Art. 11.30. How return is made.**

The return is made by stating in plain language upon the copy of the writ or some paper connected with it:

1. Whether it is true or not, according to the statement of the petition, that he has in his custody, or under his restraint, the person named or described in such petition;

2. By virtue of what authority, or for what cause, he took and detains such person;

3. If he had such person in his custody or under restraint at any time before the service of the writ, and has transferred him to the custody of another, he shall state particularly to whom, at what time, for what reason or by what authority he made such transfer;

4. He shall annex to his return the writ or warrant, if any, by virtue of which he holds the person in custody; and

5. The return must be signed and sworn to by the person making it.

### Art. 11.31. Applicant brought before judge.† [*Producing applicant.*]

The person on whom the writ is served shall bring before the judge the person in his custody, or under his restraint, unless it be made to appear that by reason of sickness he cannot be removed; in which case, another day may be appointed by the judge or court for hearing the cause, and for the production of the person confined; or the application may be heard and decided without the production of the person detained, by the consent of his counsel.



### Art. 11.32. Custody pending examination.

When the return of the writ has been made, and the applicant brought before the court, he is no longer detained on the original warrant or process, but under the authority of the habeas corpus. The safekeeping of the prisoner, pending the examination or hearing, is entirely under the direction and authority of the judge or court issuing the writ, or to which the return is made. He may be bailed from day to day, or be remanded to the same jail whence he came, or to any other place of safekeeping under the control of the judge or court, till the case is finally determined.

### Art. 11.33. Court shall allow time.

The court or judge granting the writ of habeas corpus shall allow reasonable time for the production of the person detained in custody.

### Art. 11.34. Disobeying writ.

When service has been made upon a person charged with the illegal custody of another, if he refuses to obey the writ and make the return required by law, or, if he refuses to receive the writ, or conceals himself, the court or judge issuing the writ shall issue a warrant directed to any officer or other suitable person willing to execute the same, commanding him to arrest the person charged with the illegal custody or detention of another, and bring him before such court or judge. When such person has been arrested and brought before the court or judge, if he still refuses to return the writ, or does not produce the person in his custody, he shall be committed to jail and remain there until he is willing to obey the writ of habeas corpus, and until he pays all the costs of the proceeding.

### Art. 11.35. Further penalty for disobeying writ.† [*Disobeying writ: penalty.*]

Any person disobeying the writ of habeas corpus shall also be liable to a civil action at the suit of the party detained, and shall pay in such suit fifty dollars for each day of illegal detention and restraint, after service of the writ. It shall be deemed that a person has disobeyed the writ who detains a prisoner no longer time than three days after service thereof, unless where further time is allowed in the writ for making the return thereto.

### Art. 11.36. Applicant may be brought before court.

In case of disobedience of the writ of habeas corpus, the person for whose relief it is intended may also be brought before the court or judge having competent authority, by an order for that purpose, issued to any peace officer or other proper person specially named.

### Art. 11.37. Death, etc., sufficient return of writ.

It is a sufficient return of the writ of habeas corpus that the person, once detained, has died or escaped, or that by some superior force he has been taken from the custody of the person making the return; but where any such cause shall be assigned, the court or judge shall proceed to hear testimony; and the facts stated in the return shall be proved by satisfactory evidence.

### Art. 11.38. When a prisoner dies.† [*Death of a prisoner.*]

When a prisoner confined in jail, or who is in legal custody, shall die, the officer having charge of him shall forthwith report the same to a justice of the peace of the county, who shall hold an inquest to ascertain the cause of his death. All the proceedings had in such cases shall be reduced to writing, certified and returned as in other cases of inquest; a certified copy of which shall be sufficient proof of the death of the prisoner at the hearing of a motion under habeas corpus.

**Art. 11.39. Who shall represent the state.† [*Representation of the State.*]**

If neither the county nor the district attorney be present, the judge may appoint some qualified practicing attorney to represent the State, who shall be paid the same fee allowed district attorneys for like services.

**Art. 11.40. Prisoner discharged.† [*Discharge of prisoner.*]**

The judge or court before whom a person is brought by writ of habeas corpus shall examine the writ and the papers attached to it; and if no legal cause be shown for the imprisonment or restraint, or if it appear that the imprisonment or restraint, though at first legal, cannot for any cause be lawfully prolonged, the applicant shall be discharged.

**Art. 11.41. Where party is indicted for capital offense.† [*Indictment for capital offense.*]**

If it appears by the return and papers attached that the party stands indicted for a capital offense, the judge or court having jurisdiction of the case shall, nevertheless, proceed to hear such testimony as may be offered on the part of the State and the applicant, and may either remand or admit him to bail, as the law and the facts may justify.

**Art. 11.42. If court has no jurisdiction.**

If it appear by the return and papers attached that the judge or court has no jurisdiction, such court or judge shall at once remand the applicant to the person from whose custody he has been taken.

**Art. 11.43. Presumption of innocence.**

No presumption of guilt arises from the mere fact that a criminal accusation has been made before a competent authority.

**Art. 11.44. Action of court upon examination.**

The judge or court, after having examined the return and all documents attached, and heard the testimony offered on both sides, shall, according to the facts and circumstances of the case, proceed either to remand the party into custody, admit him to bail or discharge him; provided, that no defendant shall be discharged after indictment without bail.

**Art. 11.45. Void or informal.† [*Warrant of commitment void or informal.*]**

If it appears that the applicant is detained or held under a warrant of commitment which is informal, or void; yet, if from the document on which the warrant was based, or from the proof on the hearing of the habeas corpus, it appears that there is probable cause to believe that an offense has been committed by the prisoner, he shall not be discharged, but shall be committed or held to bail.

**Art. 11.46. If proof shows offense.**

Where, upon an examination under habeas corpus, it appears to the court or judge that there is probable cause to believe that an offense has been committed by the prisoner, he shall not be discharged, but shall be committed or admitted to bail.

**Art. 11.47. May summon magistrate.† [*Summoning magistrate who issued warrant.*]**

To ascertain the grounds on which an informal or void warrant has been issued, the judge or court may cause to be summoned the magistrate who issued the warrant, and may, by an order, require him to bring with him all the papers and proceedings touching the matter. The attendance of such magistrate and the production of such papers may be enforced by warrant of arrest.

**Art. 11.48. Written issue not necessary.**

It shall not be necessary, on the trial of any cause arising under habeas corpus, to make up a written issue, though it may be done by the applicant for the writ. He may except to the sufficiency of, or controvert the return or any part thereof, or allege any new matter in avoidance. If written denial on his part be not made, it shall be considered, for the purpose of investigation, that the statements of said return are contested by a denial of the same; and the proof shall be heard accordingly, both for and against the applicant for relief.

**Art. 11.49. Order of argument.**

The applicant shall have the right by himself or counsel to open and conclude the argument upon the trial under habeas corpus.

**Art. 11.50. Costs.**

The judge trying the cause under habeas corpus may make such order as is deemed right concerning the cost of bringing the defendant before him, and all other costs of the proceeding, awarding the same either against the person to whom the writ was directed, the person seeking relief, or may award no costs at all.

**Art. 11.51. Record of proceedings.† [*Proceedings: record.*]**

If a writ of habeas corpus be made returnable before a court in session, all the proceedings had shall be entered of record by the clerk thereof, as in any other case in such court. When the motion is heard out of the county where the offense was committed, or in the Court of Criminal Appeals, the clerk shall transmit a certified copy of all the proceedings upon the motion to the clerk of the court which has jurisdiction of the offense.

**Art. 11.52. Proceedings had in vacation.† [*Court in vacation: proceedings.*]**

If the return is made and the proceedings had before a judge of a court in vacation, he shall cause all of the proceedings to be written, shall certify to the same, and cause them to be filed with the clerk of the court which has jurisdiction of the offense, who shall keep them safely.

**Art. 11.53. Construing the two preceding Articles.**

The two preceding Articles refer only to cases where an applicant is held under accusation for some offense; in all other cases the proceedings had before the judge shall be filed and kept by the clerk of the court hearing the case.

**Art. 11.54. Court may grant necessary orders.† [*Granting necessary orders.*]**

The court or judge granting a writ of habeas corpus may grant all necessary orders to bring before him the testimony taken before the examining court, and may issue process to enforce the attendance of witnesses.

**Art. 11.55. Meaning of "return".**

The word "return", as used in this Chapter, means the report made by the officer or person charged with serving the writ of habeas corpus, and also the answer made by the person served with such writ.

**Art. 11.56. Effect of discharge before indictment.† [*Discharge before indictment: effect.*]**

Where a person, before indictment found against him, has been discharged or held to bail on habeas corpus by order of a court or judge of competent jurisdiction, he shall not be again imprisoned or detained in custody on an accusation for the same offense, until after he shall have been indicted, unless surrendered by his bail.

**Art. 11.57. Writ after indictment.**

Where a person once discharged or admitted to bail is afterward indicted for the same offense for which he has been once arrested, he may be committed on the indictment, but shall be again entitled to the writ of habeas corpus, and may be admitted to bail, if the facts of the case render it proper; but in cases where, after indictment is found, the cause of the defendant has been investigated on habeas corpus, and an order made, either remanding him to custody, or admitting him to bail, he shall neither be subject to be again placed in custody, unless when surrendered by his bail, nor shall he be again entitled to the writ of habeas corpus, except in the special cases mentioned in this Chapter.

**Art. 11.58. Person committed for a capital offense.† [*Person committed for capital offense.*]**

If the accusation against the defendant for a capital offense has been heard on habeas corpus before indictment found, and he shall have been committed after such examination, he shall not be entitled to the writ, unless in the special cases mentioned in Articles 11.25 and 11.59.

### Art. 11.59. Obtaining writ a second time.

A party may obtain the writ of habeas corpus a second time by stating in a motion therefor that since the hearing of his first motion important testimony has been obtained which it was not in his power to produce at the former hearing. He shall also set forth the testimony so newly discovered; and if it be that of a witness, the affidavit of the witness shall also accompany such motion.

### Art. 11.60. Refusing to execute writ.† [*Execution of writ: refusal.*]

Any officer to whom a writ of habeas corpus, or other writ, warrant or process authorized by this Chapter shall be directed, delivered or tendered, who refuses to execute the same according to his directions, or who wantonly delays the service or execution of the same, shall be liable to fine as for contempt of court.

### Art. 11.61. Refusal to obey writ.

Any one having another in his custody, or under his power, control or restraint who refuses to obey a writ of habeas corpus, or who evades the service of the same, or places the person illegally detained under the control of another, removes him, or in any other manner attempts to evade the operation of the writ, shall be dealt with as provided in Article 11.34 of this Code.

### Art. 11.62. Refusal to give copy of process.

Any jailer, sheriff or other officer who has a prisoner in his custody and refuses, upon demand, to furnish a copy of the process under which he holds the person, is guilty of an offense, and shall be dealt with as provided in Article 11.34 of this Code for refusal to return the writ therein required.

### Art. 11.63. Held under federal authority.† [*Discharge of person held under Federal authority.*]

No person shall be discharged under the writ of habeas corpus who is in custody by virtue of a commitment for any offense exclusively cognizable by the courts of the United States, or by order or process issuing out of such courts in cases where they have jurisdiction, or who is held by virtue of any legal engagement or enlistment in the army, or who, being rightfully subject to the rules and articles of war, is confined by any one legally acting under the authority thereof, or who is held as a prisoner of war under the authority of the United States.

### Art. 11.64. Application of Chapter.

This chapter applies to all cases of habeas corpus for the enlargement of persons illegally held in custody or in any manner restrained in their personal liberty, for the admission of prisoners to bail, and for the discharge of prisoners before indictment upon a hearing of the testimony. Instead of a writ of habeas corpus in other cases heretofore used, a simple order shall be substituted.

## LIMITATION AND VENUE

## CHAPTER 12. LIMITATION



### Art. 12.01. Felonies.

Except as provided in Article 12.03, felony indictments may be presented within these limits, and not afterward:

(1) no limitation: murder and manslaughter;

(2) ten years from the date of the commission of the offense:

(A) theft of any estate, real, personal or mixed, by an executor, administrator, guardian or trustee, with intent to defraud any creditor, heir, legatee, ward, distributee, beneficiary or settlor of a trust interested in such estate;

(B) theft by a public servant of government property over which he exercises control in his official capacity;

(C) forgery or the uttering, using or passing of forged instruments; or

(D) indecency with a child under Section 21.11(a)(2), Penal Code;

(3) seven years from the date of the commission of the offense:

(A) misapplication of fiduciary property or property of a financial institution;

(B) securing execution of document by deception; or

(C) a violation under Sections 153.403(20)-(33), Tax Code; *(Chgd. by L.1999, chap. 39(1), eff. 9/1/99 only until 9/1/2000. See other paragraph (C) below, eff. 9/1/2000.)*

(C) a violation under Sections 153.403(22)-(39), Tax Code; *(Chgd. by L.1999, chap. 1285(33), eff. 9/1/2000. See other paragraph (C) above, eff. only until 9/1/2000.)*

(4) five years from the date of the commission of the offense:

(A) theft, burglary, robbery;

(B) arson; or

(C) sexual assault, except as provided in Subsection (5) of this article;

(5) ten years from the 18th birthday of the victim of the offense:

(A) indecency with a child under Section 21.11(a)(1), Penal Code;

(B) sexual assault under Section 22.011(a)(2), Penal Code; or

(C) aggravated sexual assault under Section 22.021(a)(1)(B), Penal Code; or

(6) three years from the date of the commission of the offense: all other felonies.

*(Chgd. by L.1991, chap. 565(6); L.1995, chap. 476(1); L.1997, chap. 740(1); L.1999, chaps. 39(1), 1285(33), eff. 9/1/99, 9/1/2000, respectively.)*



### Art. 12.02. Misdemeanors.

An indictment or information for any misdemeanor may be presented within two years from the date of the commission of the offense, and not afterward.

### Art. 12.03. Aggravated offenses, attempt, conspiracy, solicitation, organized criminal activity.† [*Limitation on offenses and aggravated offenses.*]

(a) The limitation period for criminal attempt is the same as that of the offense attempted.

(b) The limitation period for criminal conspiracy or organized criminal activity is the same as that of the most serious offense that is the object of the conspiracy or the organized criminal activity.

(c) The limitation period for criminal solicitation is the same as that of the felony solicited.

(d) Except as otherwise provided by this chapter, any offense that bears the title "aggravated" shall carry the same limitation period as the primary crime.

*(Chgd. by L.1997, chap. 740(2), eff. 9/1/97.)*

### Art. 12.04. Computation.

The day on which the offense was committed and the day on which the indictment or information is presented shall be excluded from the computation of time.

### Art. 12.05. Absence from State and time of pendency of indictment, etc., not computed.† [*Absence from State: effect on limitation.*]

(a) The time during which the accused is absent from the state shall not be computed in the period of limitation.

(b) The time during the pendency of an indictment, information, or complaint shall not be computed in the period of limitation.

(c) The term "during the pendency," as used herein, means that period of time beginning with the day the indictment, information, or complaint is filed in a court of competent jurisdiction, and ending with the day such accusation is, by an order of a trial court having jurisdiction thereof, determined to be invalid for any reason.

### Art. 12.06. An indictment is "presented," when.† [*Time for "presenting" an indictment.*]

An indictment is considered as "presented" when it has been duly acted upon by the grand jury and received by the court.

**Art. 12.07. An information is "presented," when.† [*Time for "presenting" an information.*]**

An information is considered as "presented," when it has been filed by the proper officer in the proper court.

## CHAPTER 13. VENUE

Article



**Art. 13.01. Offenses committed outside this State.† [*Commission of crimes outside this State.*]**

Offenses committed wholly or in part outside this State, under circumstances that give this State jurisdiction to prosecute the offender, may be prosecuted in any county in which the offender is found or in any county in which an element of the offense occurs.

**Art. 13.02. Forgery.**

Forgery may be prosecuted in any county where the writing was forged, or where the same was used or passed, or attempted to be used or passed, or deposited or placed with another person, firm, association, or corporation either for collection or credit for the account of any person, firm, association or corporation. In addition, a forging and uttering, using or passing of forged instruments in writing which concern or affect the title to land in this State may be prosecuted in the county in which such land, or any part thereof, is situated.

**Art. 13.03. Perjury.**

Perjury and aggravated perjury may be prosecuted in the county where committed, or in the county where the false statement is used or attempted to be used.

**Art. 13.04. On the boundaries of counties.† [*Crime committed on a county boundary.*]**

An offense committed on the boundaries of two or more counties, or within four hundred yards thereof, may be prosecuted and punished in any one of such counties and any offense committed on the premises of any airport operated jointly by two municipalities and situated in two counties may be prosecuted and punished in either county.

**Art. 13.05. Criminal homicide committed outside this State.**

The offense of criminal homicide committed wholly or in part outside this State, under circumstances that give this State jurisdiction to prosecute the offender, may be prosecuted in the county where the injury was inflicted, or in the county where the offender was located when he inflicted the injury, or in the county where the victim died or the body was found.

**Art. 13.06. Committed on a boundary stream.† [*Commission of a crime on a boundary stream.*]**

If an offense be committed upon any river or stream, the boundary of this State, it may be prosecuted in the county the boundary of which is upon such stream or river, and the county seat of which is nearest the place where the offense was committed.

**Art. 13.07. Injured in one county and dying in another.† [*Injury and death occurring in different counties.*]**

If a person receives an injury in one county and dies in another by reason of such injury, the offender may be prosecuted in the county where the injury was received or where the death occurred, or in the county where the dead body is found.

**Art. 13.08. Theft.**

Where property is stolen in one county and removed by the offender to another county, the offender may be prosecuted either in the county where he took the property or in any other county through or into which he may have removed the same.

**Art. 13.09. Hindering secured creditors.**

If secured property is taken from one county and unlawfully disposed of in another county or state, the offender may be prosecuted either in the county in which such property was disposed of, or in the county from which it was removed, or in the county in which the security agreement is filed.

**Art. 13.10. Persons acting under authority of this State.**

An offense committed outside this State by any officer acting under the authority of this State, under circumstances that give this state jurisdiction to prosecute the offender, may be prosecuted in the county of his residence or, if a nonresident of this State, in Travis County.

**Art. 13.11. On vessels.† [*Crimes committed on vessels.*]**

An offense committed on board a vessel which is at the time upon any navigable water within the boundaries of this State, may be prosecuted in any county through which the vessel is navigated in the course of her voyage, or in the county where the voyage commences or terminates.

**Art. 13.12. False imprisonment and kidnapping.**

Venue for false imprisonment and kidnapping is in either the county in which the offense was committed, or in any county through, into or out of which the person falsely imprisoned or kidnapped may have been taken.

**Art. 13.13. Conspiracy.**

Criminal conspiracy may be prosecuted in the county where the conspiracy was entered into, in the county where the conspiracy was agreed to be executed, or in any county in which one or more of the conspirators does any act to effect an object of the conspiracy. If a conspiracy was entered into outside this State under circumstances that give this State jurisdiction to prosecute the offender, the offender may be prosecuted in the county where the conspiracy was agreed to be executed, or in the county where any one of the conspirators was found, or in Travis County.

**Art. 13.14. Bigamy.**

Bigamy may be prosecuted:

(1) in the county where the bigamous marriage occurred;

(2) in any county in this State in which the parties to such bigamous marriage may live or cohabit together as man and wife; or

(3) in any county in this State in which a party to the bigamous marriage not charged with the offense resides.

*(Chgd. by L.1989, chap. 1112(1), eff. 8/28/89.)*

**Art. 13.15. Sexual assault.**

Sexual assault may be prosecuted in the county in which it is committed, in the county in which the victim is abducted, or in any county through or into which the victim is transported in the course of the abduction and sexual assault. When it shall come to the knowledge of any district judge whose court has jurisdiction under this Article that sexual assault has probably been committed, he shall immediately, if his court be in session, and if not in session, then, at the first term thereafter in any county of the district, call the attention of the grand jury thereto; and if the court be in session, but the grand jury has been discharged, he shall immediately recall the grand jury to investigate the accusation. The district courts are authorized and directed to change the venue in such cases whenever it shall be necessary to secure a speedy trial.

**Art. 13.16. Criminal nonsupport.**

Criminal nonsupport may be prosecuted in the county where the offended spouse or child is residing at the time the information or indictment is presented.

**Art. 13.17. Proof of venue.† [*Venue: proof.*]**

In all cases mentioned in this Chapter, the indictment or information, or any pleading in the case, may allege that the offense was committed in the county where the prosecution is carried on. To sustain the allegation of venue, it shall only be necessary to prove by the preponderance of the evidence that by reason of the facts in the case, the county where such prosecution is carried on has venue.

**Art. 13.18. Other offenses.**

If venue is not specifically stated, the proper county for the prosecution of offenses is that in which the offense was committed.

**Art. 13.19. Where venue cannot be determined.† [*Determination of venue.*]**

If an offense has been committed within the state and it cannot readily be determined within which county or counties the commission took place, trial may be held in the county in which the defendant resides, in the county in which he is apprehended, or in the county to which he is extradited.

**Art. 13.20. Venue by consent.† [*Venue by consent of defendant.*]**

The trial of all felony cases, without a jury, may, with the consent of the defendant in writing, his attorney, and the attorney for the state, be held in any county within the judicial district or districts for the county where venue is otherwise authorized by law.

**Art. 13.21. Organized criminal activity.**

The offense of engaging in organized criminal activity may be prosecuted in any county in which any act is committed to effect an objective of the combination.

**Art. 13.22. Possession and delivery of marihuana.**

An offense of possession or delivery of marihuana may be prosecuted in the county where the offense was committed or with the consent of the defendant in a county that is adjacent to and in the same judicial district as the county where the offense was committed.

**Art. 13.23. Unauthorized use of a vehicle.**

An offense of unauthorized use of a vehicle may be prosecuted in any county where the unauthorized use of the vehicle occurred or in the county in which the vehicle was originally reported stolen.

**Art. 13.24. Illegal recruitment of athletes.**

An offense of illegal recruitment of an athlete may be prosecuted in any county in which the offense was committed or in the county in which is located the institution of higher education in which the athlete agreed to enroll or was influenced to enroll. *(Added by L.1989, chap. 125(2), eff. 9/1/89.)*

**Art. 13.25. Computer crimes.**

(a) In this section "access," "computer," "computer network," "computer program," "computer system," and "owner" have the meanings assigned to those terms by Section 33.01, Penal Code.

(b) An offense under Chapter 33, Penal Code, may be prosecuted in:

(1) the county of the principal place of business of the owner or lessee of a computer, computer network, or computer system involved in the offense;

(2) any county in which a defendant had control or possession of:

(A) any proceeds of the offense; or

(B) any books, records, documents, property, negotiable instruments, computer programs, or other material used in furtherance of the offense; or

(3) any county from which, to which, or through which access to a computer, computer network, computer program, or computer system was made in violation of Chapter 33, whether by wires, electromagnetic waves, microwaves, or any other means of communication.
*(Added by L.1989, chap. 306(4); redes. by L.1991, chap. 16(19.01(1)); chgd. by L.1993, chap. 900(3.01); L.1997, chap. 306(4), eff. 9/1/97.)*

### Art. 13.26. Telecommunications crimes.

An offense under Chapter 33A, Penal Code, may be prosecuted in the county in which the telecommunications service originated or terminated or in the county to which the bill for the telecommunications service was or would have been delivered. *(Added by L.1997, chap. 306(5), eff. 9/1/97.)*



### Art. 13.27. Simulating legal process.

An offense under Section 32.46, 32.48, 32.49, or 37.13, Penal Code, may be prosecuted either in the county from which any material document was sent or in the county in which it was delivered. *(Added by L.1997, chap. 189(12); renumbered from Art. 13.26 by L.1999, chap. 62(19.01(6)), eff. 9/1/99.)*

# ARREST, COMMITMENT AND BAIL

## CHAPTER 14. ARREST WITHOUT WARRANT

Article



### Art. 14.01. Offense within view.† [*Crime committed within view of peace officer.*]

(a) A peace officer or any other person, may, without a warrant, arrest an offender when the offense is committed in his presence or within his view, if the offense is one classed as a felony or as an offense against the public peace.

(b) A peace officer may arrest an offender without a warrant for any offense committed in his presence or within his view.

### Art. 14.02. Within view of magistrate.† [*Offense committed within view of magistrate.*]

A peace officer may arrest, without warrant, when a felony or breach of the peace has been committed in the presence or within the view of a magistrate, and such magistrate verbally orders the arrest of the offender.

### Art. 14.03. Authority of peace officers.

(a) Any peace officer may arrest, without warrant:

(1) persons found in suspicious places and under circumstances which reasonably show that such persons have been guilty of some felony, violation of Title 9, Chapter 42, Penal Code, breach of the peace, or offense under Section 49.02, Penal Code, or threaten, or are about to commit some offense against the laws;

(2) persons who the peace officer has probable cause to believe have committed an assault resulting in bodily injury to another person and the peace officer has probable cause to believe that there is danger of further bodily injury to that person;

(3) persons who the peace officer has probable cause to believe have committed the offense defined by Section 25.07, Penal Code (violation of Protective Order), if the offense is not committed in the presence of the peace officer; or

(4) persons who the peace officer has probable cause to believe have committed an assault resulting in bodily injury to a member of the person's family or household.

(b) A peace officer shall arrest, without a warrant, a person the peace officer has probable cause to believe has committed an offense under Section 25.07, Penal Code (violation of Protective Order), if the offense is committed in the presence of the peace officer.

(c) If reasonably necessary to verify an allegation of a violation of a protective order or of the commission of an assault against a member of the family or household, a peace officer shall remain at the scene of the investigation to verify the allegation and to prevent the further commission of family violence.

(d) A peace officer who is outside his jurisdiction may arrest, without warrant, a person who commits an offense within the officer's presence or view, if the offense is a felony, a violation of Title 9, Chapter 42, Penal Code, a breach of the peace, or an offense under Section 49.02, Penal Code. A peace officer making an arrest under this subsection shall, as soon as practicable after making the arrest, notify a law enforcement agency having jurisdiction where the arrest was made. The law enforcement agency shall then take custody of the person committing the offense and take the person before a magistrate in compliance with Article 14.06 of this code.

(e) The justification for conduct provided under Section 9.21, Penal Code, applies to a peace officer when the peace officer is performing a duty required by this article.

(f) In this article, "family," "household," and "member of a household" have the meanings assigned to those terms by Section 71.01, Family Code.

(g) A peace officer listed in Subdivision (1), (2), (3), (4), or (5), Article 2.12, who is licensed under Chapter 415, Government Code, and is outside of the officer's jurisdiction may arrest without a warrant a person who commits any offense within the officer's presence or view, except that an officer who is outside the officer's jurisdiction may arrest a person for a violation of Subtitle C, Title 7, Transportation Code, only if the officer is listed in Subdivision (4), Article 2.12. A peace officer making an arrest under this subsection shall as soon as practicable after making the arrest notify a law enforcement agency having jurisdiction where the arrest was made. The law enforcement agency shall then take custody of the person committing the offense and take the person before a magistrate in compliance with Article 14.06.

*(Chgd. by L.1989, chap. 740(1); L.1991, chap. 542(9); L.1993, chap. 900(3.02); L.1995, chaps. 76(14.17), 829(1); L.1999, chaps. 62(3.02), 210(2), eff. 9/1/99, 5/24/99, respectively.)*

### Art. 14.031. Public intoxication.

(a) In lieu of arresting an individual who commits an offense under Section 49.02, Penal Code, a peace officer may release an individual if:

(1) the officer believes detention in a penal facility is unnecessary for the protection of the individual or others; and

(2) the individual:

(A) is released to the care of an adult who agrees to assume responsibility for the individual; or

(B) verbally consents to voluntary treatment for chemical dependency in a program in a treatment facility licensed and approved by the Texas Commission on Alcohol and Drug Abuse, and the program admits the individual for treatment.

(b) A magistrate may release from custody an individual arrested under Section 49.02, Penal Code, if the magistrate determines the individual meets the conditions required for release in lieu of arrest under Subsection (a) of this article.

(c) The release of an individual under Subsection (a) or (b) of this article to an alcohol or drug treatment program may not be considered by a peace officer or magistrate in determining whether the individual should be released to such a program for a subsequent incident or arrest under Section 49.02, Penal Code.

(d) A peace officer and the agency or political subdivision that employs the peace officer may not be held liable for damage to persons or property that results from the actions of an individual released under Subsection (a) or (b) of this article.

*(Added by L.1993, chap. 900(1.04), eff. 9/1/94.)*

### Art. 14.04. When felony has been committed.† [*Proof of commission of a felony.*]

Where it is shown by satisfactory proof to a peace officer, upon the representation of a credible person, that a felony has been committed, and that the offender is about to escape, so that there is no time to procure a warrant, such peace officer may, without warrant, pursue and arrest the accused.

### Art. 14.05. Rights of officer.

In each case enumerated where arrests may be lawfully made without warrant, the officer or person making the arrest is justified in adopting all the measures which he might adopt in cases of arrest under warrant, except that an officer making an arrest without a warrant may not enter a residence to make the arrest unless:

(1) a person who resides in the residence consents to the entry; or

(2) exigent circumstances require that the officer making the arrest enter the residence without the consent of a resident or without a warrant.

### Art. 14.051. Arrest by peace officer from other jurisdiction.

(a) A peace officer commissioned and authorized by another state to make arrests for felonies who is in fresh pursuit of a person for the purpose of arresting that person for a felony may continue the pursuit into this state and arrest the person.

(b) In this article, "fresh pursuit" means a pursuit without unreasonable delay by a peace officer of a person the officer reasonably suspects has committed a felony.

*(Added by L.1989, chap. 997(2), eff. 8/28/89.)*



### Art. 14.06. Must take offender before magistrate.

(a) Except as provided by Subsection (b), in each case enumerated in this Code, the person making the arrest shall take the person arrested or have him taken without unnecessary delay before the magistrate who may have ordered the arrest, before some magistrate of the county where the arrest was made without an order, or, if necessary to provide more expeditiously to the person arrested the warnings described by Article 15.17 of this Code, before a magistrate in a county bordering the county in which the arrest was made. The magistrate shall immediately perform the duties described in Article 15.17 of this Code.

(b) A peace officer who is charging a person, including a child, with committing an offense that is a Class C misdemeanor, other than an offense under Section 49.02, Penal Code, may, instead of taking the person before a magistrate, issue a citation to the person that contains written notice of the time and place the person must appear before a magistrate, the name and address of the person charged, and the offense charged.

*(Chgd. by L.1991, chap. 84(1); L.1993, chap. 900(1.05); L.1995, chap. 262(81), eff. 1/1/96.)*

## CHAPTER 15. ARREST UNDER WARRANT

Article

### Art. 15.01. Warrant of arrest.

A "warrant of arrest" is a written order from a magistrate, directed to a peace officer or some other person specially named, commanding him to take the body of the person accused of an offense, to be dealt with according to law.

### Art. 15.02. Requisites of warrant.† [*Requirements of warrant.*]

It issues in the name of "The State of Texas" and shall be sufficient, without regard to form, if it have these substantial requisites:

1. It must specify the name of the person whose arrest is ordered, if it be known, if unknown, then some reasonably definite description must be given of him.

2. It must state that the person is accused of some offense against the laws of the State, naming the offense.

3. It must be signed by the magistrate, and his office be named in the body of the warrant, or in connection with his signature.

### Art. 15.03. Magistrate may issue warrant or summons.† [*Issuance of warrant or summons; magistrate.*]

(a) A magistrate may issue a warrant of arrest or a summons:

1. In any case in which he is by law authorized to order verbally the arrest of an offender;

2. When any person shall make oath before the magistrate that another has committed some offense against the laws of the State; and

3. In any case named in this Code where he is specially authorized to issue warrants of arrest.

(b) A summons may be issued in any case where a warrant may be issued, and shall be in the same form as the warrant except that it shall summon the defendant to appear before a magistrate at a stated time and place. The summons shall be served upon a defendant by delivering a copy to him personally, or by leaving it at his dwelling house or usual place of abode with some person of suitable age and discretion then residing therein or by mailing it to the defendant's last known address. If a defendant fails to appear in response to the summons a warrant shall be issued.

### Art. 15.04. Complaint.

The affidavit made before the magistrate or district or county attorney is called a "complaint" if it charges the commission of an offense.

### Art. 15.05. Requisites of complaint.† [*Requirements of complaint.*]

The complaint shall be sufficient, without regard to form, if it have these substantial requisites:

1. It must state the name of the accused, if known, and if not known, must give some reasonably definite description of him.

2. It must show that the accused has committed some offense against the laws of the State, either directly or that the affiant has good reason to believe, and does believe, that the accused has committed such offense.

3. It must state the time and place of the commission of the offense as definitely as can be done by the affiant.

4. It must be signed by the affiant by writing his name or affixing his mark.

### Art. 15.051. Requiring polygraph examination of complainant prohibited.

(a) A peace officer or an attorney representing the state may not require a polygraph examination of a person who charges or seeks to charge in a complaint the commission of an offense under Section 21.11, 22.011, 22.021, or 25.02, Penal Code.

(b) If a peace officer or an attorney representing the state requests a polygraph examination of a person who charges or seeks to charge in a complaint the commission of an offense listed in Subsection (a), the officer or attorney must inform the complainant that the examination is not required and that a complaint may not be dismissed solely:

(1) because a complainant did not take a polygraph examination; or

(2) on the basis of the results of a polygraph examination taken by the complainant.

(c) A peace officer or an attorney representing the state may not take a polygraph examination of a person who charges or seeks to charge the commission of an offense listed in Subsection (a) unless the officer or attorney provides the information in Subsection (b) to the person and the person signs a statement indicating the person understands the information.

(d) A complaint may not be dismissed solely:

(1) because a complainant did not take a polygraph examination; or

(2) on the basis of the results of a polygraph examination taken by the complainant.

*(Added by L.1995, chap. 24(1); chgd. by L.1997, chap. 608(1), eff. 6/11/97.)*

**Art. 15.06. Warrant extends to every part of the state.† [*Warrant valid throughout state.*]**

A warrant of arrest, issued by any county or district clerk, or by any magistrate (except mayors of an incorporated city or town), shall extend to any part of the State; and any peace officer to whom said warrant is directed, or into whose hands the same has been transferred, shall be authorized to execute the same in any county in this State.



**Art. 15.07. Warrant issued by other magistrate.† [*Warrant issued by mayor.*]**

When a warrant of arrest is issued by any mayor of an incorporated city or town, it cannot be executed in another county than the one in which it issues, except:

1. It be endorsed by a judge of a court of record, in which case it may be executed anywhere in the State; or

2. If it be endorsed by any magistrate in the county in which the accused is found, it may be executed in such county. The endorsement may be: "Let this warrant be executed in the county of _____________". Or, if the endorsement is made by a judge of a court of record, then the endorsement may be: "Let this warrant be executed in any county of the State of Texas". Any other words of the same meaning will be sufficient. The endorsement shall be dated, and signed officially by the magistrate making it.

**Art. 15.08. Warrant may be telegraphed.† [*Warrant issued by telegraph.*]**

A warrant of arrest may be forwarded by telegraph from any telegraph office to another in this State. If issued by any magistrate named in Article 15.06, the peace officer receiving the same shall execute it without delay. If it be issued by any other magistrate than is named in Article 15.06, the peace officer receiving the same shall proceed with it to the nearest magistrate of his county, who shall endorse thereon, in substance, these words:

"Let this warrant be executed in the county of ______________", which endorsement shall be dated and signed officially by the magistrate making the same.

**Art. 15.09. Complaint by telegraph.† [*Telegraphing complaint.*]**

A complaint in accordance with Article 15.05, may be telegraphed, as provided in the preceding Article, to any magistrate in the State; and the magistrate who receives the same shall forthwith issue a warrant for the arrest of the accused; and the accused, when arrested, shall be dealt with as provided in this Chapter in similar cases.

**Art. 15.10. Copy to be deposited.† [*Depositing of certified copy.*]**

A certified copy of the original warrant or complaint, certified to by the magistrate issuing or taking the same, shall be deposited with the manager of the telegraph office from which the same is to be forwarded, taking precedence over other business, to the place of its destination or to the telegraph office nearest thereto, precisely as it is written, including the certificate of the seal attached.

**Art. 15.11. Duty of telegraph manager.† [*Delivery of warrant or complaint: duty of telegraph manager.*]**

When a warrant or complaint is received at a telegraph office for delivery, it shall be delivered to the party to whom it is addressed as soon as practicable, written on the proper blanks of the telegraph company and certified to by the manager of the telegraph office as being a true and correct copy of the warrant or complaint received at his office.

**Art. 15.12. Warrant or complaint must be under seal.† [*Telegraphing of warrant or complaint: seal must be affixed.*]**

No manager of a telegraph office shall receive and forward a warrant or complaint unless the same shall be certified to under the seal of a court of record or by a justice of the peace, with the certificate under seal of the district or county clerk of his county that he is a legally qualified justice of the peace of such county; nor shall it be lawful for any magistrate to endorse a warrant received by telegraph, or issue a warrant upon a complaint received by telegraph, unless all the requirements of the law in relation thereto have been fully complied with.

**Art. 15.13. Telegram prepaid.† [*Telegram must be prepaid.*]**

Whoever presents a warrant or complaint to the manager of a telegraph office to be forwarded by telegraph, shall pay for the same in advance, unless, by the rules of the company, it may be sent collect.

**Art. 15.14. Arrest after dismissal because of delay.**

If a prosecution of a defendant is dismissed under Article 32.01, the defendant may be rearrested for the same criminal conduct alleged in the dismissed prosecution only upon presentation of indictment or information for the offense and the issuance of a capias subsequent to the indictment or information. *(Added by L.1997, chap. 289(3), eff. 5/26/97.)*

**Art. 15.15.** *(Repealed by L.1991, chap. 446(2), eff. 6/11/91.)*

**Art. 15.16. How warrant is executed.† [*Execution of warrant.*]**

The officer or person executing a warrant of arrest shall without unnecessary delay take the person or have him taken before the magistrate who issued the warrant or before the magistrate named in the warrant, if the magistrate is in the same county where the person is arrested. If the issuing or named magistrate is in another county, the person arrested shall without unnecessary delay be taken before some magistrate in the county in which he was arrested.

**Art. 15.17. Duties of arresting officer and magistrate.**

(a) In each case enumerated in this Code, the person making the arrest shall without unnecessary delay take the person arrested or have him taken before some magistrate of the county where the accused was arrested or, if necessary to provide more expeditiously to the person arrested the warnings described by this article, before a magistrate in a county bordering the county in which the arrest was made. The arrested person may be taken before the magistrate in person or the image of the arrested person may be broadcast by closed circuit television to the magistrate. The magistrate shall inform in clear language the person arrested, either in person or by closed circuit television, of the accusation against him and of any affidavit filed therewith, of his right to retain counsel, of his right to remain silent, of his right to have an attorney present during any interview with peace officers or attorneys representing the state, of his right to terminate the interview at any time, of his right to request the appointment of counsel if he is indigent and cannot afford counsel, and of his right to have an examining trial. He shall also inform the person arrested that he is not required to make a statement and that any statement made by him may be used against him. The magistrate shall allow the person arrested reasonable time and opportunity to consult counsel and shall admit the person arrested to bail if allowed by law. A closed circuit television system may not be used under this subsection unless the system provides for a two-way communication of image and sound between the arrested person and the magistrate. A recording of the communication between the arrested person and the magistrate shall be made. The recording shall be preserved until the earlier of the following dates: (1) the date on which the pretrial hearing ends; or (2) the 91st day after the date on which the recording is made if the person is charged with a misdemeanor or the 120th day after the date on which the recording is made if the person is charged with a felony. The counsel for the defendant may obtain a copy of the recording on payment of a reasonable amount to cover costs of reproduction.

(b) After an accused charged with a misdemeanor punishable by fine only is taken before a magistrate under Subsection (a) of this article and the magistrate has identified the accused with certainty, the magistrate may release the accused without bond and order the accused to appear at a later date for arraignment in the county court or statutory county court. The order must state in writing the time, date, and place of the arraignment, and the magistrate must sign the order. The accused shall receive a copy of the order on release. If an accused fails to appear as required by the order, the judge of the court in which the accused is required to appear shall issue a warrant for the arrest of the accused. If the accused is arrested and brought before the judge, the judge may admit the accused to bail, and in admitting the accused to bail, the judge should set as the amount of bail an amount double that generally set for the offense for which the accused was arrested. This subsection does not apply to an accused who has previously been convicted of a felony or a misdemeanor other than a misdemeanor punishable by fine only.

(c) When a deaf accused is taken before a magistrate under this article or Article 14.06 of this Code, an interpreter appointed by the magistrate qualified and sworn as provided in Article 38.31

of this Code shall interpret the warning required by those articles in a language that the accused can understand, including but not limited to sign language.

(d) If a magistrate determines that a person brought before the magistrate after an arrest authorized by Article 14.051 of this code was arrested unlawfully, the magistrate shall release the person from custody. If the magistrate determines that the arrest was lawful, the person arrested is considered a fugitive from justice for the purposes of Article 51.13 of this code, and the disposition of the person is controlled by that article.

*(Chgd. by L.1989, chaps. 467(1), 977(1), 997(3); L.1991, chap. 16(19.01(2)), eff. 8/26/91.)*

### Art. 15.18. Arrest for out-of-county offense.† [*Offense committed in other county: arrest.*]

One arrested under a warrant issued in a county other than the one in which the person is arrested shall be taken before a magistrate of the county where the arrest takes place who shall take bail, if allowed by law, and immediately transmit the bond taken to the court having jurisdiction of the offense.

### Art. 15.19. Notice of arrest.

(a) If the accused fails or refuses to give bail, as provided in the preceding Article, he shall be committed to the jail of the county where he was arrested; and the magistrate committing him shall immediately notify the sheriff of the county in which the offense is alleged to have been committed of the arrest and commitment, which notice may be given by telegraph, by mail or by other written notice.

(b) If a person is arrested and taken before a magistrate in a county bordering the county in which the arrest is made under the provisions of Article 15.17(a) of this code and if the person is remanded to custody, the person may be confined in a jail in the county in which the magistrate serves for a period of not more than 72 hours after the arrest before being transferred to the county jail of the county in which the arrest occurred.

### Art. 15.20. Duty of sheriff receiving notice.

The sheriff receiving the notice shall forthwith go or send for the prisoner and have him brought before the proper court or magistrate.

### Art. 15.21. Prisoner discharged if not timely demanded.† [*Discharge of prisoner.*]

If the proper office of the county where the offense is alleged to have been committed does not demand the prisoner and take charge of him within ten days from the day he is committed, such prisoner shall be discharged from custody.

### Art. 15.22. When a person is arrested.† [*Arrest: definition.*]

A person is arrested when he has been actually placed under restraint or taken into custody by an officer or person executing a warrant of arrest, or by an officer or person arresting without a warrant.

### Art. 15.23. Time of arrest.

An arrest may be made on any day or at any time of the day or night.

### Art. 15.24. What force may be used.† [*Use of reasonable force in arrest.*]

In making an arrest, all reasonable means are permitted to be used to effect it. No greater force, however, shall be resorted to than is necessary to secure the arrest and detention of the accused.

### Art. 15.25. May break door.† [*Arresting officer may break door.*]

In case of felony, the officer may break down the door of any house for the purpose of making an arrest, if he be refused admittance after giving notice of his authority and purpose.

### Art. 15.26. Authority to arrest must be made known.† [*Officer's authority to arrest must be stated.*]

In executing a warrant of arrest, it shall always be made known to the accused under what authority the arrest is made. The warrant shall be executed by the arrest of the defendant. The officer need not have the warrant in his possession at the time of the arrest, provided the warrant was issued under the provisions of this Code, but upon request he shall show the warrant to the defendant as soon as possible. If the officer does not have the warrant in his possession at the time of arrest he shall then inform the defendant of the offense charged and of the fact that a warrant has been issued.

### Art. 15.27. Notification to schools required.

(a) A law enforcement agency that arrests any person or refers a child to the office or official designated by the juvenile court who the agency believes is enrolled as a student in a public primary or secondary school, for an offense listed in Subsection (h), shall attempt to ascertain whether the person is so enrolled. If the law enforcement agency ascertains that the individual is enrolled as a student in a public primary or secondary school, the agency shall orally notify the superintendent or a person designated by the superintendent in the school district in which the student is enrolled of that arrest or referral within 24 hours after the arrest or referral is made, or on the next school day. If the law enforcement agency cannot ascertain whether the individual is enrolled as a student, the agency shall orally notify the superintendent or a person designated by the superintendent in the school district in which the student is believed to be enrolled of that arrest or detention within 24 hours after the arrest or detention, or on the next school day. If the individual is a student, the superintendent shall promptly notify all instructional and support personnel who have responsibility for supervision of the student. All personnel shall keep the information received in this subsection confidential. The State Board for Educator Certification may revoke or suspend the certification of personnel who intentionally violate this subsection. Within seven days after the date the oral notice is given, the law enforcement agency shall mail written notification, marked "PERSONAL and CONFIDENTIAL" on the mailing envelope, to the superintendent or the person designated by the superintendent. Both the oral and written notice shall contain sufficient details of the arrest or referral and the acts allegedly committed by the student to enable the superintendent or the superintendent's designee to determine whether there is a reasonable belief that the student has engaged in conduct defined as a felony offense by the Penal Code. The information contained in the notice may be considered by the superintendent or the superintendent's designee in making such a determination.

(b) On conviction or on an adjudication of delinquent conduct of an individual enrolled as a student in a public primary or secondary school, for an offense or for any conduct listed in Subsection (h) of this article, the office of the prosecuting attorney acting in the case shall orally notify the superintendent or a person designated by the superintendent in the school district in which the student is enrolled of the conviction or adjudication. Oral notification must be given within 24 hours of the time of the determination of guilt, or on the next school day. The superintendent shall promptly notify all instructional and support personnel who have regular contact with the student. Within seven days after the date the oral notice is given, the office of the prosecuting attorney shall mail written notice, which must contain a statement of the offense of which the individual is convicted or on which the adjudication is grounded.

(c) A parole or probation office having jurisdiction over a student described by Subsection (a), (b), or (e) who transfers from a school or is subsequently removed from a school and later returned to a school or school district other than the one the student was enrolled in when the arrest, referral to a juvenile court, conviction, or adjudication occurred shall notify the new school officials of the arrest or referral in a manner similar to that provided for by Subsection (a) or (e)(1), or of the conviction or delinquent adjudication in a manner similar to that provided for by Subsection (b) or (e)(2). The new school officials shall promptly notify all instructional and support personnel who have regular contact with the student.

(d) The superintendent or a person designated by the superintendent in the school district may send to a school district employee having direct supervisory responsibility over the student the information contained in the confidential notice if the superintendent or the person designated by the superintendent determines that the school district employee needs the information for educational purposes or for the protection of the person informed or others.

(e)(1) A law enforcement agency that arrests, or refers to a juvenile court under Chapter 52, Family Code, an individual who the law enforcement agency knows or believes is enrolled as a student in a private primary or secondary school shall make the oral and written notifications described by Subsection (a) to the principal or a school employee designated by the principal of the school in which the student is enrolled.

(2) On conviction or an adjudication of delinquent conduct of an individual enrolled as a student in a private primary or secondary school, the office of prosecuting attorney shall make the oral and written notifications described by Subsection (b) of this article to the principal or a school employee designated by the principal of the school in which the student is enrolled.

(3) The principal of a private school in which the student is enrolled or a school employee designated by the principal may send to a school employee having direct supervisory responsibility over the student the information contained in the confidential notice, for the same purposes as described by Subsection (d) of this article.

(f) A person who receives information under this article may not disclose the information except as specifically authorized by this article. A person who intentionally violates this article commits an offense. An offense under this subsection is a Class C misdemeanor.

(g) The office of the prosecuting attorney or the office or official designated by the juvenile court shall, within two working days, notify the school district that removed a student to an alternative education program under Section 37.006, Education Code, if:

(1) prosecution of the student's case was refused for lack of prosecutorial merit or insufficient evidence and no formal proceedings, deferred adjudication, or deferred prosecution will be initiated; or

(2) the court or jury found the student not guilty or made a finding the child did not engage in delinquent conduct or conduct indicating a need for supervision and the case was dismissed with prejudice.

(h) This article applies to:

(1) an offense under Section 19.02, 19.03, 19.04, 19.05, 20.02, 20.03, 20.04, 21.08, 21.11, 22.01, 22.011, 22.02, 22.021, 22.04, 22.05, 22.07, 28.02, 29.02, 29.03, 30.02, or 71.02, Penal Code; *(Chgd. by L.1997, chap. 1233(1), eff. 6/20/97. See other paragraph (1) below.)*

(1) an offense listed in Section 508.149, Government Code; deadly conduct, as described by Section 22.05, Penal Code; or a terroristic threat, as described by Section 22.07, Penal Code; *(Chgd. by L.1997, chap. 165(12.02), eff. 9/1/97. See other paragraph (1) above.)*

(2) the unlawful use, sale, or possession of a controlled substance, drug paraphernalia, or marihuana, as defined by Chapter 481, Health and Safety Code;

(3) the unlawful possession of any of the weapons or devices listed in Sections 46.01(1)-(14) or (16), Penal Code; or a weapon listed as a prohibited weapon under Section 46.05, Penal Code; or

(4) a felony offense in which a deadly weapon, as defined by Section 1.07, Penal Code, was used or exhibited.

*(Chgd. by L.1997, chap. 1233(1), eff. 6/20/97. See other subsection (h) below.)*

(h) This article applies to any felony offense. *(Chgd. by L.1997, chap. 1015(12), eff. 6/19/97. See other subsection (h) above.)*

*(Added by L.1993, chap. 461(1); chgd. by L.1995, chaps. 76(14.18), 626(1); L.1997, chaps. 165(12.02); 1015(12), (13), (14); 1233(1), eff. 9/1/97, 6/19/97, 6/20/97, respectively.)*

## CHAPTER 16. THE COMMITMENT OR DISCHARGE OF THE ACCUSED

Article

16.01. Examining trial.
16.02. Examination postponed.† [*Postponement of examination.*]
16.03. Warning to accused.
16.04. Voluntary statement.
16.06. Counsel may examine witness.† [*Examination of witnesses.*]
16.07. Same rules of evidence as on final trial.† [*Examining trial: rules of evidence.*]
16.08. Presence of the accused.† [*Accused shall be present.*]
16.09. Testimony reduced to writing.† [*Testimony shall be written.*]
16.10. Attachment for witness.† [*Magistrate may issue attachment.*]
16.11. Attachment to another county.† [*Magistrate may issue attachment for another county.*]
16.12. Witness need not be tendered his witness fees or expenses.† [*Witness fees or expenses.*]
16.13. Attachment executed forthwith.† [*Prompt execution of attachment.*]
16.14. Postponing examination.† [*Postponement of examination: additional testimony.*]
16.15. Who may discharge capital offense.† [*Capital offense: examination of accused.*]
16.16. If insufficient bail has been taken.† [*Insufficient bail; warrant of arrest.*]
16.17. Decision of judge.
16.18. When no safe jail.† [*Safe jail required.*]
16.19. Warrant in such case.† [*Commitment in jail of another county: warrant.*]
16.20. "Commitment".
16.21. Duty of sheriff as to prisoners.† [*Commitment of prisoners: duty of sheriff.*]
16.22. Examination and transfer of defendant suspected of having mental illness or mental retardation.

## Art. 16.01. Examining trial.

When the accused has been brought before a magistrate for an examining trial that officer shall proceed to examine into the truth of the accusation made, allowing the accused, however, sufficient time to procure counsel. In a proper case, the magistrate may appoint counsel to represent an accused in such examining trial only, to be compensated as otherwise provided in this Code. The accused in any felony case shall have the right to an examining trial before indictment in the county having jurisdiction of the offense, whether he be in custody or on bail, at which time the magistrate at the hearing shall determine the amount or sufficiency of bail, if a bailable case. If the accused has been transferred for criminal prosecution after a hearing under Section 54.02, Family Code, the accused may be granted an examining trial at the discretion of the court.

## Art. 16.02. Examination postponed.† [*Postponement of examination.*]

The magistrate may at the request of either party postpone the examination to procure testimony; but the accused shall in the meanwhile be detained in custody unless he give bail to be present from day to day before the magistrate until the examination is concluded, which he may do in all cases except murder and treason.

## Art. 16.03. Warning to accused.

Before the examination of the witnesses, the magistrate shall inform the accused that it is his right to make a statement relative to the accusation brought against him, but at the same time shall also inform him that he cannot be compelled to make any statement whatever, and that if he does make such statement, it may be used in evidence against him.

## Art. 16.04. Voluntary statement.

If the accused desires to make a voluntary statement, he may do so before the examination of any witness, but not afterward. His statement shall be reduced to writing by or under the direction of the magistrate, or by the accused or his counsel, and shall be signed by the accused by affixing his name or mark, but shall not be sworn to by him. The magistrate shall attest by his own certificate and signature to the execution and signing of the statement.

## Art. 16.06. Counsel may examine witness.† [*Examination of witnesses.*]

The counsel for the State, and the accused or his counsel may question the witnesses on direct or cross examination. If no counsel appears for the State the magistrate may examine the witnesses.

## Art. 16.07. Same rules of evidence as on final trial.† [*Examining trial: rules of evidence.*]

The same rules of evidence shall apply to and govern a trial before an examining court that apply to and govern a final trial.

## Art. 16.08. Presence of the accused.† [*Accused shall be present.*]

The examination of each witness shall be in the presence of the accused.

## Art. 16.09. Testimony reduced to writing.† [*Testimony shall be written.*]

The testimony of each witness shall be reduced to writing by or under the direction of the magistrate, and shall then be read over to the witness, or he may read it over himself. Such corrections shall be made in the same as the witness may direct; and he shall then sign the same by affixing thereto his name or mark. All the testimony thus taken shall be certified to by the magistrate. In lieu of the above provision, a statement of facts authenticated by State and defense counsel and approved by the presiding magistrate may be used to preserve the testimony of witnesses.

## Art. 16.10. Attachment for witness.† [*Magistrate may issue attachment.*]

The magistrate has the power in all cases, where a witness resides or is in the county where the prosecution is pending, to issue an attachment for the purpose of enforcing the attendance of such witness; this he may do without having previously issued a subpoena for that purpose.

## Art. 16.11. Attachment to another county.† [*Magistrate may issue attachment for another county.*]

The magistrate may issue an attachment for a witness to any county in the State, when affidavit is made by the party applying therefor that the testimony of the witness is material to the prosecution, or the defense, as the case may be; and the affidavit shall further state the facts which it is expected will be proved by the witness; and if the facts set forth are not considered material by the magistrate, or if they be admitted to be true by the adverse party, the attachment shall not issue.

### Art. 16.12. Witness need not be tendered his witness fees or expenses.† [*Witness fees or expenses.*]

A witness attached need not be tendered his witness fees or expenses.

### Art. 16.13. Attachment executed forthwith.† [*Prompt execution of attachment.*]

The officer receiving the attachment shall execute it forthwith by bringing before the magistrate the witness named therein, unless such witness shall give bail for his appearance before the magistrate at the time and place required by the writ.

### Art. 16.14. Postponing examination.† [*Postponement of examination: additional testimony.*]

After examining the witness in attendance, if it appears to the magistrate that there is other important testimony which may be had by a postponement, he shall, at the request of the prosecutor or of the defendant, postpone the hearing for a reasonable time to enable such testimony to be procured; but in such case the accused shall remain in the custody of the proper officer until the day fixed for such further examination. No postponement shall take place, unless a sworn statement be made by the defendant, or the prosecutor, setting forth the name and residence of the witness, and the facts which it is expected will be proved. If it be testimony other than that of a witness, the statement made shall set forth the nature of the evidence. If the magistrate is satisfied that the testimony is not material, or if the same be admitted to be true by the adverse party, the postponement shall be refused.

### Art. 16.15. Who may discharge capital offense.† [*Capital offense: examination of accused.*]

The examination of one accused of a capital offense shall be conducted by a justice of the peace, county judge, county court at law, or county criminal court. The judge may admit to bail, except in capital cases where the proof is evident.

### Art. 16.16. If insufficient bail has been taken.† [*Insufficient bail; warrant of arrest.*]

Where it is made to appear by affidavit to a judge of the Court of Criminal Appeals, a justice of a court of appeals, or to a judge of the district or county court, that the bail taken in any case is insufficient in amount, or that the sureties are not good for the amount, or that the bond is for any reason defective or insufficient, such judge shall issue a warrant of arrest, and require of the defendant sufficient bond and security, according to the nature of the case.

### Art. 16.17. Decision of judge.

After the examining trial has been had, the judge shall make an order committing the defendant to the jail of the proper county, discharging him or admitting him to bail, as the law and facts of the case may require. Failure of the judge to make or enter an order within 48 hours after the examining trial has been completed operates as a finding of no probable cause and the accused shall be discharged.

### Art. 16.18. When no safe jail.† [*Safe jail required.*]

If there is no safe jail in the county in which the prosecution is carried on, the magistrate may commit defendant to the nearest safe jail in any other county.

### Art. 16.19. Warrant in such case.† [*Commitment in jail of another county: warrant.*]

The commitment in the case mentioned in the preceding Article shall be directed to the sheriff of the county to which the defendant is sent, but the sheriff of the county from which the defendant is taken shall be required to deliver the prisoner into the hands of the sheriff to whom he is sent.

### Art. 16.20. "Commitment".

A "commitment" is an order signed by the proper magistrate directing a sheriff to receive and place in jail the person so committed. It will be sufficient if it has the following requisites:

1. That it run in the name of "The State of Texas";

2. That it be addressed to the sheriff of the county to the jail of which the defendant is committed;

3. That it state in plain language the offense for which the defendant is committed, and give his name, if it be known, or if unknown, contain an accurate description of the defendant;

4. That it state to what court and at what time the defendant is to be held to answer;

5. When the prisoner is sent out of the county where the prosecution arose, the warrant of commitment shall state that there is no safe jail in the proper county; and

6. If bail has been granted, the amount of bail shall be stated in the warrant of commitment.

### Art. 16.21. Duty of sheriff as to prisoners.† [*Commitment of prisoners: duty of sheriff.*]

Every sheriff shall keep safely a person committed to his custody. He shall use no cruel or unusual means to secure this end, but shall adopt all necessary measures to prevent the escape of a prisoner. He may summon a guard of sufficient number, in case it becomes necessary to prevent an escape from jail, or the rescue of a prisoner.

### Art. 16.22. Examination and transfer of defendant suspected of having mental illness or mental retardation.

(a) Not later than 72 hours after receiving evidence or a statement that may establish reasonable cause to believe that a defendant committed to the sheriff's custody has a mental illness or is a person with mental retardation, the sheriff shall notify a magistrate of that fact. A defendant's behavior or the result of a prior evaluation indicating a need for referral for further mental health or mental retardation assessment must be considered in determining whether reasonable cause exists to believe the defendant has a mental illness or is a person with mental retardation. On a determination that there is reasonable cause to believe that the defendant has a mental illness or is a person with mental retardation, the magistrate shall order an examination of the defendant by a disinterested expert experienced and qualified in mental health or mental retardation to determine whether the defendant has a mental illness as defined by Section 571.003, Health and Safety Code, or is a person with mental retardation as defined by Section 591.003, Health and Safety Code. If the defendant fails or refuses to submit to examination, the magistrate may order the defendant to custody for examination for a reasonable period not to exceed 21 days. The magistrate may not order a defendant to a facility operated by the Texas Department of Mental Health and Mental Retardation for examination without the consent of the head of that facility. If a defendant who has been ordered to a facility operated by the Texas Department of Mental Health and Mental Retardation for examination remains in the facility for a period exceeding 21 days, the head of that facility shall cause the defendant to be immediately transported to the committing court and placed in the custody of the sheriff of the county in which the committing court is located. That county shall reimburse the Texas Department of Mental Health and Mental Retardation facility for the mileage and per diem expenses of the personnel required to transport the defendant calculated in accordance with the state travel regulations in effect at the time.

(b) A written report of the examination shall be submitted to the magistrate within 30 days of the order of examination, and the magistrate shall furnish copies of the report to the defense counsel and the prosecuting attorney. The report shall include a description of the procedures used in the examination, the examiner's observations and findings pertaining to whether the defendant is a person who has a mental illness or is a person with mental retardation, and recommended treatment.

(c) After the court receives the examining expert's report relating to the defendant under Subsection (b), the court may resume the criminal proceedings against the defendant or competency proceedings, if required, as provided by Article 46.02 of this code.

*(Added by L.1993, chap. 900(3.05); chgd. by L.1997, chap. 312(1), eff. 9/1/97.)*

## CHAPTER 17. BAIL

Article

## Art. 17.01. Definition of "bail".† [*"Bail": definition.*]

"Bail" is the security given by the accused that he will appear and answer before the proper court the accusation brought against him, and includes a bail bond or a personal bond.

## Art. 17.02. Definition of "bail bond".† [*"Bail bond": definition.*]

A "bail bond" is a written undertaking entered into by the defendant and his sureties for the appearance of the principal therein before some court or magistrate to answer a criminal accusation; provided, however, that the defendant upon execution of such bail bond may deposit with the custodian of funds of the court in which the prosecution is pending current money of the United States in the amount of the bond in lieu of having sureties signing the same. Any cash funds deposited under this Article shall be receipted for by the officer receiving the same and shall be refunded to the defendant if and when the defendant complies with the conditions of this bond, and upon order of the court.

### Art. 17.03. Personal bond.

(a) Except as provided by Subsection (b) of this article, a magistrate may, in the magistrate's discretion, release the defendant on his personal bond without sureties or other security.

(b) Only the court before whom the case is pending may release on personal bond a defendant who:

(1) is charged with an offense under the following sections of the Penal Code:

(A) Section 19.03 (Capital Murder);

(B) Section 20.04 (Aggravated Kidnapping);

(C) Section 22.021 (Aggravated Sexual Assault);

(D) Section 22.03 (Deadly Assault on Law Enforcement or Corrections Officer, Member or Employee of Board of Pardons and Paroles, or Court Participant);

(E) Section 22.04 (Injury to a Child, Elderly Individual, or Disabled Individual);

(F) Section 29.03 (Aggravated Robbery);

(G) Section 30.02 (Burglary); or

(H) Section 71.02 (Engaging in Organized Criminal Activity);

(2) is charged with a felony under Chapter 481, Health and Safety Code, or Section 485.033, Health and Safety Code, punishable by imprisonment for a minimum term or by a maximum fine that is more than a minimum term or maximum fine for a first degree felony; or

(3) does not submit to testing for the presence of a controlled substance in the defendant's body as requested by the court or magistrate under Subsection (c) of this article or submits to testing and the test shows evidence of the presence of a controlled substance in the defendant's body.

(c) When setting a personal bond under this chapter, on reasonable belief by the investigating or arresting law enforcement agent or magistrate of the presence of a controlled substance in the defendant's body or on the finding of drug or alcohol abuse related to the offense for which the defendant is charged, the court or a magistrate shall require as a condition of personal bond that the defendant submit to testing for alcohol or a controlled substance in the defendant's body and participate in an alcohol or drug abuse treatment or education program if such a condition will serve to reasonably assure the appearance of the defendant for trial.

(d) The state may not use the results of any test conducted under this chapter in any criminal proceeding arising out of the offense for which the defendant is charged.

(e) Costs of testing may be assessed as court costs or ordered paid directly by the defendant as a condition of bond.

(f) In this article, "controlled substance" has the meaning assigned by Section 481.002, Health and Safety Code.

(g) The court may order that a personal bond fee assessed under Section 17.42 be:

(1) paid before the defendant is released;

(2) paid as a condition of bond;

(3) paid as court costs;

(4) reduced as otherwise provided for by statute; or

(5) waived.

*(Chgd. by L.1989, chap. 374(1); L.1991, chap. 14(284(45), (57)); L.1995, chap. 76(14.19), eff. 9/1/95.)*

### Art. 17.031. Release on personal bond.

(a) Any magistrate in this state may release a defendant eligible for release on personal bond under Article 17.03 of this code on his personal bond where the complaint and warrant for arrest does not originate in the county wherein the accused is arrested if the magistrate would have had jurisdiction over the matter had the complaint arisen within the county wherein the magistrate presides. The personal bond may not be revoked by the judge of the court issuing the warrant for arrest except for good cause shown.

(b) If there is a personal bond office in the county from which the warrant for arrest was issued, the court releasing a defendant on his personal bond will forward a copy of the personal bond to the personal bond office in that county.

*(Chgd. by L.1989, chap. 374(2), eff. 9/1/89.)*

### Art. 17.032. Release on personal bond of certain mentally ill defendants.

(a) In this article, "violent offense" means an offense under the following sections of the Penal Code:

(1) Section 19.02 (murder);

(2) Section 19.03 (capital murder);
(3) Section 20.03 (kidnapping);
(4) Section 20.04 (aggravated kidnapping);
(5) Section 21.11 (indecency with a child);
(6) Section 22.01(a)(1) (assault);
(7) Section 22.011 (sexual assault);
(8) Section 22.02 (aggravated assault);
(9) Section 22.021 (aggravated sexual assault);
(10) Section 22.04 (injury to a child, elderly individual, or disabled individual); or
(11) Section 29.03 (aggravated robbery).

(b) A magistrate shall release a defendant on personal bond unless good cause is shown otherwise or if the:

(1) defendant is not charged with and has not been previously convicted of a violent offense;
(2) defendant is examined by a mental health expert under Article 16.22 of this code;
(3) examining expert, in a report submitted to the magistrate under Article 16.22 of this code:
(A) concludes that the defendant has a mental illness or is a person with mental retardation and is nonetheless competent to stand trial; and
(B) recommends mental health treatment for the defendant; and
(4) magistrate determines, in consultation with a local mental health or mental retardation services provider, that appropriate mental health or mental retardation services for the defendant are available through the Texas Department of Mental Health and Mental Retardation under Section 534.053, Health and Safety Code, or through another mental health or mental retardation services provider.

(c) The magistrate, unless good cause is shown for not requiring treatment, shall require as a condition of release on personal bond under this article that the defendant submit to outpatient or inpatient mental health or mental retardation treatment if the defendant's:

(1) mental illness or mental retardation is chronic in nature; or
(2) ability to function independently will continue to deteriorate if the defendant is not treated.

(d) In addition to a condition of release imposed under Subsection (c) of this article, the magistrate may require the defendant to comply with other conditions that are reasonably necessary to protect the community.

(e) In this article, a person is considered to have been convicted of an offense if:

(1) a sentence is imposed;
(2) the person is placed on community supervision or receives deferred adjudication; or
(3) the court defers final disposition of the case.

*(Added by L.1993, chap. 900(3.06); chgd. by L.1995, chap. 76(14.20); L.1997, chap. 312(2), eff. 9/1/97.)*

## Art. 17.04. Requisites of a personal bond.† [*Personal bond: requirements.*]

A personal bond is sufficient if it includes the requisites of a bail bond as set out in Article 17.08, except that no sureties are required. In addition, a personal bond shall contain:

(1) the defendant's name, address, and place of employment;
(2) identification information, including the defendant's:
(A) date and place of birth;
(B) height, weight, and color of hair and eyes;
(C) driver's license number and state of issuance, if any; and
(D) nearest relative's name and address, if any; and
(3) the following oath sworn and signed by the defendant:

"I swear that I will appear before (the court or magistrate) at (address, city, county) Texas, on the (date), at the hour of (time, a.m. or p.m.) or upon notice by the court, or pay to the court the principal sum of (amount) plus all necessary and reasonable expenses incurred in any arrest for failure to appear."

## Art. 17.045. Bail bond certificates.

A bail bond certificate with respect to which a fidelity and surety company has become surety as provided in the Automobile Club Services Act, or for any truck and bus association incorporated in this state, when posted by the person whose signature appears thereon, shall be accepted as bail bond in an amount not to exceed $200 to guarantee the appearance of such person in any court in this state when the person is arrested for violation of any motor vehicle law of this state or ordinance of any municipality in this state, except for the offense of driving while intoxicated or for any felony, and the alleged violation was committed prior to the date of expiration shown on such bail bond certificate.

### Art. 17.05. When a bail bond is given.† [*Entering into a bail bond.*]

A bail bond is entered into either before a magistrate, upon an examination of a criminal accusation, or before a judge upon an application under habeas corpus; or it is taken from the defendant by a peace officer if authorized by Article 17.20, 17.21, or 17.22.

### Art. 17.06. Corporation surety.† [*Surety for a bail bond.*]

Wherever in this Chapter, any person is required or authorized to give or execute any bail bond, such bail bond may be given or executed by such principal and any corporation authorized by law to act as surety, subject to all the provisions of this Chapter regulating and governing the giving of bail bonds by personal surety insofar as the same is applicable.

### Art. 17.07. Corporation to file with county clerk power of attorney designating agent.† [*Agent of surety corporation: power of attorney.*]

Any corporation authorized by the law of this State to act as a surety, shall before executing any bail bond as authorized in the preceding Article, first file in the office of the county clerk of the county where such bail bond is given, a power of attorney designating and authorizing the named agent, agents or attorney of such corporation to execute such bail bonds and thereafter the execution of such bail bonds by such agent, agents or attorney, shall be a valid and binding obligation of such corporation.

### Art. 17.08. Requisites of a bail bond.

A bail bond must contain the following requisites:

1. That it be made payable to "The State of Texas";

2. That the defendant and his sureties, if any, bind themselves that the defendant will appear before the proper court or magistrate to answer the accusation against him;

3. If the defendant is charged with a felony, that it state that he is charged with a felony. If the defendant is charged with a misdemeanor, that it state that he is charged with a misdemeanor;

4. That the bond be signed by name or mark by the principal and sureties, if any, each of whom shall write thereon his mailing address;

5. That the bond state the time and place, when and where the accused binds himself to appear, and the court or magistrate before whom he is to appear. The bond shall also bind the defendant to appear before any court or magistrate before whom the cause may thereafter be pending at any time when, and place where, his presence may be required under this Code or by any court or magistrate, but in no event shall the sureties be bound after such time as the defendant receives an order of deferred adjudication or is acquitted, sentenced, placed on community supervision, or dismissed from the charge;

6. The bond shall also be conditioned that the principal and sureties, if any, will pay all necessary and reasonable expenses incurred by any and all sheriffs or other peace officers in rearresting the principal in the event he fails to appear before the court or magistrate named in the bond at the time stated therein. The amount of such expense shall be in addition to the principal amount specified in the bond. The failure of any bail bond to contain the conditions specified in this paragraph shall in no manner affect the legality of any such bond, but it is intended that the sheriff or other peace officer shall look to the defendant and his sureties, if any, for expenses incurred by him, and not to the State for any fees earned by him in connection with the rearresting of an accused who has violated the conditions of his bond.

*(Chgd. by L.1999, chap. 1506(1), eff. 9/1/99.)*

### Art. 17.09. Duration; original and subsequent proceedings; new bail.† [*Bail given valid for proceedings; exceptions; new bail set.*]

**Sec. 1.** Where a defendant, in the course of a criminal action, gives bail before any court or person authorized by law to take same, for his personal appearance before a court or magistrate, to answer a charge against him, the said bond shall be valid and binding upon the defendant and his sureties, if any, thereon, for the defendant's personal appearance before the court or magistrate designated therein, as well as before any other court to which same may be transferred, and for any and all subsequent proceedings had relative to the charge, and each such bond shall be so conditioned except as hereinafter provided.

**Sec. 2.** When a defendant has once given bail for his appearance in answer to a criminal charge, he shall not be required to give another bond in the course of the same criminal action except as herein provided.

**Sec. 3.** Provided that whenever, during the course of the action, the judge or magistrate in whose court such action is pending finds that the bond is defective, excessive or insufficient in amount, or that the sureties, if any, are not acceptable, or for any other good and sufficient cause, such judge or magistrate may, either in term-time or in vacation, order the accused to be rearrested, and require the accused to give another bond in such amount as the judge or magistrate may deem proper. When such bond is so given and approved, the defendant shall be released from custody.

### Art. 17.10. Disqualified sureties.† [*Minor cannot be surety.*]

A minor cannot be surety on a bail bond, but the accused party may sign as principal.

### Art. 17.11. How bail bond is taken.† [*Taking of a bail bond.*]

**Sec. 1.** Every court, judge, magistrate or other officer taking a bail bond shall require evidence of the sufficiency of the security offered; but in every case, one surety shall be sufficient, if it be made to appear that such surety is worth at least double the amount of the sum for which he is bound, exclusive of all property exempted by law from execution, and of debts or other encumbrances; and that he is a resident of this state, and has property therein liable to execution worth the sum for which he is bound.

**Sec. 2.** Provided, however, any person who has signed as a surety on a bail bond and is in default thereon shall thereafter be disqualified to sign as a surety so long as he is in default on said bond. It shall be the duty of the clerk of the court wherein such surety is in default on a bail bond, to notify in writing the sheriff, chief of police, or other peace officer, of such default. A surety shall be deemed in default from the time execution may be issued on a final judgment in a bond forfeiture proceeding under the Texas Rules of Civil Procedure, unless the final judgment is superseded by the posting of a supersedeas bond. *(Chgd. by L.1999, chap. 1506(2), eff. 9/1/99.)*

### Art. 17.12. Exempt property.

The property secured by the Constitution and laws from forced sale shall not, in any case, be held liable for the satisfaction of bail, either as to principal or sureties, if any.

### Art. 17.13. Sufficiency of sureties ascertained.† [*Determining sufficiency of surety.*]

To test the sufficiency of the security offered to any bail bond, unless the court or officer taking the same is fully satisfied as to its sufficiency, the following oath shall be made in writing and subscribed by the sureties:

"I, do swear that I am worth, in my own right, at least the sum of (here insert the amount in which the surety is bound), after deducting all that which is exempt by the Constitution and Laws of the State from forced sale, and after the payment of all my debts of every description, whether individual or security debts, and after satisfying all encumbrances upon my property which are known to me; that I reside in __________ County, and have property in this State liable to execution worth said amount or more.

(Dated __________, and attested by the judge of the court, clerk, magistrate or sheriff.)"

Such affidavit shall be filed with the papers of the proceedings.

### Art. 17.14. Affidavit not conclusive.† [*Sufficiency of surety: affidavit.*]

Such affidavit shall not be conclusive as to the sufficiency of the security; and if the court or officer taking the bail bond is not fully satisfied as to the sufficiency of the security offered, further evidence shall be required before approving the same.

### Art. 17.15. Rules for fixing amount of bail.

The amount of bail to be required in any case is to be regulated by the court, judge, magistrate or officer taking the bail; they are to be governed in the exercise of this discretion by the Constitution and by the following rules:

1. The bail shall be sufficiently high to give reasonable assurance that the undertaking will be complied with.
2. The power to require bail is not to be so used as to make it an instrument of oppression.

3. The nature of the offense and the circumstances under which it was committed are to be considered.

4. The ability to make bail is to be regarded, and proof may be taken upon this point.

5. The future safety of a victim of the alleged offense and the community shall be considered. *(Chgd. by L.1993, chap. 396(1), eff. 9/1/93.)*

## Art. 17.151. Release because of delay.† [*Release of defendant: delay in trial.*]

**Sec. 1.** A defendant who is detained in jail pending trial of an accusation against him must be released either on personal bond or by reducing the amount of bail required, if the state is not ready for trial of the criminal action for which he is being detained within:

(1) 90 days from the commencement of his detention if he is accused of a felony;

(2) 30 days from the commencement of his detention if he is accused of a misdemeanor punishable by a sentence of imprisonment in jail for more than 180 days;

(3) 15 days from the commencement of his detention if he is accused of a misdemeanor punishable by a sentence of imprisonment for 180 days or less; or

(4) five days from the commencement of his detention if he is accused of a misdemeanor punishable by a fine only.

**Sec. 2.** The provisions of this article do not apply to a defendant who is:

(1) serving a sentence of imprisonment for another offense while he is serving that sentence;

(2) being detained pending trial of another accusation against him as to which the applicable period has not yet elapsed; or

(3) incompetent to stand trial, during the period of his incompetence.

**Sec. 3.** If a person released under this article is arrested and detained for a violation of the conditions of his release, the time for release under Section 1 of this article begins to run on the date of the arrest for violation of conditions of the release.

## Art. 17.16. Discharge of liability; surrender or incarceration of principal before forfeiture.† [*Surety may surrender accused.*]

(a) A surety may before forfeiture relieve himself of his undertaking by:

(1) surrendering the accused into the custody of the sheriff of the county where the prosecution is pending; or

(2) delivering to the sheriff of the county where the prosecution is pending an affidavit stating that the accused is incarcerated in federal custody, in the custody of any state, or in any county of this state.

(b) For the purposes of Subsection (a)(2) of this article, the bond is discharged and the surety is absolved of liability on the bond on the sheriff's verification of the incarceration of the accused.

## Art. 17.17. When surrender is made during term.† [*Accused surrendered during term of court.*]

If a surrender of the accused be made during a term of the court to which he has bound himself to appear, the sheriff shall take him before the court, and if he is willing to give other bail, the court shall forthwith require him to do so. If he fails or refuses to give bail, the court shall make an order that he be committed to jail until the bail is given, and this shall be a sufficient commitment without any written order to the sheriff.

## Art. 17.18. Surrender in vacation.† [*Accused surrendered during vacation of court.*]

When the surrender is made at any other time than during the session of the court, the sheriff may take the necessary bail bond, but if the defendant fails or refuses to give other bail, the sheriff shall take him before the nearest magistrate; and such magistrate shall issue a warrant of commitment, reciting the fact that the accused has been once admitted to bail, has been surrendered, and now fails or refuses to give other bail.

## Art. 17.19. Surety may obtain a warrant.† [*Surety may file for warrant.*]

(a) Any surety, desiring to surrender his principal and after notifying the principal's attorney, if the principal is represented by an attorney, in a manner provided by Rule 21a, Texas Rules of Civil Procedure, of the surety's intention to surrender the principal, may file an affidavit of such intention before the court or magistrate before which the prosecution is pending. The affidavit must state:

(1) the court and cause number of the case;

(2) the name of the defendant;
(3) the offense with which the defendant is charged;
(4) the date of the bond;
(5) the cause for the surrender; and
(6) that notice of the surety's intention to surrender the principal has been given as required by this subsection.

(b) If the court or magistrate finds that there is cause for the surety to surrender his principal, the court shall issue a warrant of arrest for the principal. It is an affirmative defense to any liability on the bond that:

(1) the court or magistrate refused to issue a warrant of arrest for the principal; and
(2) after the refusal to issue the warrant the principal failed to appear.

(c) If the court or magistrate before whom the prosecution is pending is not available, the surety may deliver the affidavit to any other magistrate in the county and that magistrate, on a finding of cause for the surety to surrender his principal, shall issue a warrant of arrest for the principal.

(d) An arrest warrant issued under this article shall be issued to the sheriff of the county in which the case is pending, and a copy of the warrant shall be issued to the surety or his agent.

(e) An arrest warrant issued under this article may be executed by a peace officer, a security officer, or a private investigator licensed in this state.

*(Chgd. by L.1989, chap. 374(3); L.1999, chap. 1506(3), eff. 9/1/99.)*

**Art. 17.20. Bail in misdemeanor.† [*Misdemeanor: bail.*]**

The sheriff, or other peace officer, in cases of misdemeanor, may, whether during the term of the court or in vacation, where he has a defendant in custody, take of the defendant a bail bond.

**Art. 17.21. Bail in felony.† [*Felony: bail.*]**

In cases of felony, when the accused is in custody of the sheriff or other peace officer, and the court before which the prosecution is pending is in session in the county where the accused is in custody, the court shall fix the amount of bail, if it is a bailable case and determine if the accused is eligible for a personal bond; and the sheriff, or other peace officer, unless it be the police of a city, is authorized to take a bail bond of the accused in the amount as fixed by the court, to be approved by such officer taking the same, and will thereupon discharge the accused from custody. It shall not be necessary for the defendant or his sureties to appear in court.

**Art. 17.22. May take bail in felony.† [*Felony: payment of bail.*]**

In a felony case, if the court before which the same is pending is not in session in the county where the defendant is in custody, the sheriff, or other peace officer having him in custody, may take his bail bond in such amount as may have been fixed by the court or magistrate, or if no amount has been fixed, then in such amount as such officer may consider reasonable.

**Art. 17.23. Sureties severally bound.**

In all bail bonds taken under any provision of this Code, the sureties shall be severally bound. Where a surrender of the principal is made by one or more of them, all the sureties shall be considered discharged.

**Art. 17.24. General rules applicable.**

All general rules in the Chapter are applicable to bail defendant before an examining court.

**Art. 17.25. Proceedings when bail is granted.† [*Granting of bail: proceedings.*]**

After a full examination of the testimony, the magistrate shall, if the case be one where bail may properly be granted and ought to be required, proceed to make an order that the accused execute a bail bond with sufficient security, conditioned for his appearance before the proper court.

**Art. 17.26. Time given to procure bail.† [*Procurement of bail.*]**

Reasonable time shall be given the accused to procure security.

**Art. 17.27. When bail is not given.† [*Bail not given: accused incarcerated.*]**

If, after the allowance of a reasonable time, the security be not given, the magistrate shall make an order committing the accused to jail to be kept safely until legally discharged; and he shall issue a commitment accordingly.

### Art. 17.28. When ready to give bail.† [*Accused ready to give bail: bond prepared.*]

If the party be ready to give bail, the magistrate shall cause to be prepared a bond, which shall be signed by the accused and his surety or sureties, if any.

### Art. 17.29. Accused liberated.

(a) When the accused has given the required bond, either to the magistrate or the officer having him in custody, he shall at once be set at liberty.

(b) Before releasing on bail a person arrested for an offense under Section 42.072, Penal Code, or a person arrested or held without warrant in the prevention of family violence, the law enforcement agency holding the person shall make a reasonable attempt to give personal notice of the imminent release to the victim of the alleged offense or to another person designated by the victim to receive the notice. An attempt by an agency to give notice to the victim or the person designated by the victim at the victim's or person's last known telephone number or address, as shown on the records of the agency, constitutes a reasonable attempt to give notice under this subsection. If possible, the arresting officer shall collect the address and telephone number of the victim at the time the arrest is made and shall communicate that information to the agency holding the person.

(c) A law enforcement agency or an employee of a law enforcement agency is not liable for damages arising from complying or failing to comply with Subsection (b) of this article.

(d) In this article, "family violence" has the meaning assigned by Section 71.01, Family Code.

*(Chgd. by L.1995, chaps. 656(1), 661(1); L.1997, chap. 1(3), eff. 1/28/97.)*

### Art. 17.291. Further detention of certain persons.

(a) In this article:

(1) "family violence" has the meaning assigned to that phrase by Section 71.01(b)(2), Family Code; and

(2) "magistrate" has the meaning assigned to it by Article 2.09 of this code, as amended by Chapters 25, 79, 916, and 1068 of the 71st Legislature, Regular Session, 1989.

(b) Article 17.29 does not apply when a person has been arrested or held without a warrant in the prevention of family violence if there is probable cause to believe the violence will continue if the person is immediately released. The head of the agency arresting or holding such a person may hold the person for a period of not more than four hours after bond has been posted. This detention period may be extended for an additional period not to exceed 48 hours, but only if authorized in a writing directed to the person having custody of the detained person by a magistrate who concludes that:

(1) the violence would continue if the person is released; and

(2) if the additional period exceeds 24 hours, probable cause exists to believe that the person committed the instant offense and that, during the 10-year period preceding the date of the instant offense, the person has been arrested:

(A) on more than one occasion for an offense involving family violence; or

(B) for any other offense, if a deadly weapon, as defined by Section 1.07, Penal Code, was used or exhibited during commission of the offense or during immediate flight after commission of the offense.

*(Added by L.1991, chap. 552(2); chgd. by L.1999, chap. 1341(1), eff. 9/1/99.)*

### Art. 17.292. Magistrate's order for emergency protection.

(a) At a defendant's appearance before a magistrate after arrest for an offense involving family violence or an offense under Section 42.072, Penal Code, the magistrate may issue an order for emergency protection on the magistrate's own motion or on the request of:

(1) the victim of the offense;

(2) the guardian of the victim;

(3) a peace officer; or

(4) the attorney representing the state.

(b) At a defendant's appearance before a magistrate after arrest for an offense involving family violence, the magistrate shall issue an order for emergency protection if the arrest is for an offense that also involves:

(1) serious bodily injury to the victim; or

(2) the use or exhibition of a deadly weapon during the commission of an assault.

(c) The magistrate in the order for emergency protection may prohibit the arrested party from:

(1) committing:

(A) family violence or an assault on the person protected under the order; or

(B) an act in furtherance of an offense under Section 42.072, Penal Code;

(2) communicating:

(A) directly with a member of the family or household or with the person protected under the order in a threatening or harassing manner; or

(B) a threat through any person to a member of the family or household or to the person protected under the order; or

(3) going to or near:

(A) the residence, place of employment, or business of a member of the family or household or of the person protected under the order; or

(B) the residence, child care facility, or school where a child protected under the order resides or attends.

(d) The victim of the offense need not be present in court when the order for emergency protection is issued.

(e) In the order for emergency protection the magistrate shall specifically describe the prohibited locations and the minimum distances, if any, that the party must maintain, unless the magistrate determines for the safety of the person or persons protected by the order that specific descriptions of the locations should be omitted.

(f) To the extent that a condition imposed by an order for emergency protection issued under this article conflicts with an existing court order granting possession of or access to a child, the condition imposed under this article prevails for the duration of the order for emergency protection.

(g) An order for emergency protection issued under this article must contain the following statements printed in bold-face type or in capital letters:

"A VIOLATION OF THIS ORDER BY COMMISSION OF AN ACT PROHIBITED BY THE ORDER MAY BE PUNISHABLE BY A FINE OF AS MUCH AS $4,000 OR BY CONFINEMENT IN JAIL FOR AS LONG AS ONE YEAR OR BY BOTH. AN ACT THAT RESULTS IN FAMILY VIOLENCE OR A STALKING OFFENSE MAY BE PROSECUTED AS A SEPARATE MISDEMEANOR OR FELONY OFFENSE. IF THE ACT IS PROSECUTED AS A SEPARATE FELONY OFFENSE, IT IS PUNISHABLE BY CONFINEMENT IN PRISON FOR AT LEAST TWO YEARS.

"NO PERSON, INCLUDING A PERSON WHO IS PROTECTED BY THIS ORDER, MAY GIVE PERMISSION TO ANYONE TO IGNORE OR VIOLATE ANY PROVISION OF THIS ORDER. DURING THE TIME IN WHICH THIS ORDER IS VALID, EVERY PROVISION OF THIS ORDER IS IN FULL FORCE AND EFFECT UNLESS A COURT CHANGES THE ORDER."

(h) The magistrate issuing an order for emergency protection under this article shall send a copy of the order to the chief of police in the municipality where the member of the family or household or individual protected by the order resides, if the person resides in a municipality, or to the sheriff of the county where the person resides, if the person does not reside in a municipality. If the victim of the offense is not present when the order is issued, the magistrate issuing the order shall order an appropriate peace officer to make a good faith effort to notify, within 24 hours, the victim that the order has been issued by calling the victim's residence and place of employment. The clerk of the court shall send a copy of the order to the victim.

(i) If an order for emergency protection issued under this article prohibits a person from going to or near a child care facility or school, the magistrate shall send a copy of the order to the child care facility or school.

(j) An order for emergency protection issued under this article is effective on issuance, and the defendant shall be served a copy of the order in open court. An order for emergency protection issued under this article remains in effect up to the 61st day but not less than 31 days after the date of issuance.

(k) To ensure that an officer responding to a call is aware of the existence and terms of an order for emergency protection issued under this article, each municipal police department and sheriff shall establish a procedure within the department or office to provide adequate information or access to information for peace officers of the names of persons protected by an order for emergency protection issued under this article and of persons to whom the order is directed. The police department or sheriff may enter an order for emergency protection issued under this article in the department's or office's record of outstanding warrants as notice that the order has been issued and is in effect.

(*l*) In the order for emergency protection, the magistrate may suspend a license to carry a concealed handgun issued under Section 411.177, Government Code, that is held by the defendant.

(m) In this article, "family," "family violence," and "household" have the meanings assigned by Chapter 71, Family Code.
*(Added by L.1995, chap. 658(1); chgd. by L.1997, chaps. 1(4), 610(1); L.1999, chaps. 514(1), 1412(1), eff. 9/1/99.)*

**Art. 17.293. Delivery of order for emergency protection to other persons.**
The magistrate or the clerk of the magistrate's court issuing an order for emergency protection under Article 17.292 that suspends a license to carry a concealed handgun shall immediately send a copy of the order to the appropriate division of the Department of Public Safety at its Austin headquarters. On receipt of the order suspending the license, the department shall:
(1) record the suspension of the license in the records of the department;
(2) report the suspension to local law enforcement agencies, as appropriate; and
(3) demand surrender of the suspended license from the license holder.
*(Added by L.1999, chap. 1412(2), eff. 9/1/99.)*

**Art. 17.30. Shall certify proceedings.† [*Certification of proceedings.*]**
The magistrate, before whom an examination has taken place upon a criminal accusation, shall certify to all the proceedings had before him, as well as where he discharges, holds to bail or commits, and transmit them, sealed up, to the court before which the defendant may be tried, writing his name across the seals of the envelope. The voluntary statement of the defendant, the testimony, bail bonds, and every other proceeding in the case, shall be thus delivered to the clerk of the proper court, without delay.

**Art. 17.31. Duty of clerks who receive such proceedings.† [*Report of proceedings: duty of clerks.*]**
If the proceedings be delivered to a district clerk, he shall keep them safely and deliver the same to the next grand jury. If the proceedings are delivered to a county clerk, he shall without delay deliver them to the district or county attorney of his county.

**Art. 17.32. In case of no arrest.† [*Accused not arrested.*]**
Upon failure from any cause to arrest the accused the magistrate shall file with the proper clerk the complaint, warrant of arrest, and a list of the witnesses.

**Art. 17.33. Request setting of bail.† [*Accused may request bail.*]**
The accused may at any time after being confined request a magistrate to review the written statements of the witnesses for the State as well as all other evidence available at that time in determining the amount of bail. This setting of the amount of bail does not waive the defendant's right to an examining trial as provided in Article 16.01.

**Art. 17.34. Witnesses to give bond.† [*Bond may be required of witness.*]**
Witnesses for the State or defendant may be required by the magistrate, upon the examination of any criminal accusation before him, to give bail for their appearance to testify before the proper court. A personal bond may be taken of a witness by the court before whom the case is pending.

**Art. 17.35. Security of witness.† [*Security may be required of witness.*]**
The amount of security to be required of a witness is to be regulated by his pecuniary condition, character and the nature of the offense with respect to which he is a witness.

**Art. 17.36. Effect of witness bond.† [*Bond given by witness: effect.*]**
The bond given by a witness for his appearance has the same effect as a bond of the accused and may be forfeited and recovered upon in the same manner.

**Art. 17.37. Witness may be committed.† [*Commitment of witness.*]**
A witness required to give bail who fails or refuses to do so shall be committed to jail as in other cases of a failure to give bail when required, but shall be released from custody upon giving such bail.

**Art. 17.38. Rules applicable to all cases of bail.† [*Applicability of rules.*]**
The rules in this Chapter respecting bail are applicable to all such undertakings when entered into in the course of a criminal action, whether before or after an indictment, in every case where authority is given to any court, judge, magistrate, or other officer, to require bail of a person accused of an offense, or a witness in a criminal action.

**Art. 17.39. Records of bail.† [*Bail: records.*]**

A magistrate or other officer who sets the amount of bail or who takes bail shall record in a well-bound book the name of the person whose appearance the bail secures, the amount of bail, the date bail is set, the magistrate or officer who sets bail, the offense or other cause for which the appearance is secured, the magistrate or other officer who takes bail, the date the person is released, and the name of the bondsman, if any.

**Art. 17.40. Conditions related to victim or community safety.**

(a) To secure a defendant's attendance at trial, a magistrate may impose any reasonable condition of bond related to the safety of a victim of the alleged offense or to the safety of the community.

(b) At a hearing limited to determining whether the defendant violated a condition of bond imposed under Subsection (a), the magistrate may revoke the defendant's bond only if the magistrate finds by a preponderance of the evidence that the violation occurred.

*(Added by L.1999, chap. 768(1), eff. 9/1/99.)*

**Art. 17.41. Condition where child alleged victim.† [*Child is victim of offense.*]**

(a) This article applies to a defendant charged with an offense under any of the following provisions of the Penal Code, if committed against a child 12 years of age or younger:

(1) Chapter 21 (Sexual Offenses) or 22 (Assaultive Offenses);

(2) Section 25.02 (Prohibited Sexual Conduct); or

(3) Section 43.25 (Sexual Performance by a Child).

(b) A magistrate may require as a condition of bond for a defendant charged with an offense described by Subsection (a) of this article that the defendant not directly communicate with the alleged victim of the offense or go near a residence, school, or other location, as specifically described in the bond, frequented by the alleged victim.

(c) A magistrate who imposes a condition of bond under this article may grant the defendant supervised access to the alleged victim.

(d) To the extent that a condition imposed under this article conflicts with an existing court order granting possession of or access to a child, the condition imposed under this article prevails for a period specified by the magistrate, not to exceed 90 days.

*(Chgd. by L.1995, chap. 76(14.21), eff. 9/1/95.)*

**Art. 17.42. Personal bond office.**

**Sec. 1.** Any county, or any judicial district with jurisdiction in more than one county, with the approval of the commissioners court of each county in the district, may establish a personal bond office to gather and review information about an accused that may have a bearing on whether he will comply with the conditions of a personal bond and report its findings to the court before which the case is pending.

**Sec. 2.** (a) The commissioners court of a county that establishes the office or the district and county judges of a judicial district that establishes the office may employ a director of the office.

(b) The director may employ the staff authorized by the commissioners court of the county or the commissioners court of each county in the judicial district.

**Sec. 3.** If a judicial district establishes the office, each county in the district shall pay its pro rata share of the costs of administering the office according to its population.

**Sec. 4.** (a) If a court releases an accused on personal bond on a recommendation of a personal bond office, the court shall assess a personal bond fee of $20 or of three percent of the amount of the bail fixed for the accused, whichever is greater. The court may waive the fee or assess a lesser fee if good cause is shown.

(b) Fees collected under this article may be used solely to defray expenses of the personal bond office, including defraying the expenses of extradition.

(c) Fees collected under this article shall be deposited in the county treasury, or if the office serves more than one county, the fees shall be apportioned to each county in the district according to each county's pro rata share of the costs of the office.

**Sec. 5.** (a) A personal bond pretrial release office established under this article shall:

(1) prepare a record containing information about any accused person identified by case number only who, after review by the office, is released by a court on personal bond;

(2) update the record on a monthly basis; and

(3) post a copy of the record in the office of the clerk of the county court in any county served by the office.

(b) In preparing a record under Subsection (a), the office shall include in the record a statement of:

(1) the offense with which the person is charged;

(2) the dates of any court appearances scheduled in the matter that were previously unattended by the person;

(3) whether a warrant has been issued for the person's arrest for failure to appear in accordance with the terms of the person's release;

(4) whether the person has failed to comply with conditions of release on personal bond; and

(5) the presiding judge or magistrate who authorized the personal bond.

(c) This section does not apply to a personal bond pretrial release office that on January 1, 1995, was operated by a community corrections and supervision department.

**Sec. 6.** (a) Not later than April 1 of each year, a personal bond office established under this article shall submit to the commissioners court or district and county judges that established the office an annual report containing information about the operations of the office during the preceding year.

(b) In preparing an annual report under Subsection (a), the office shall include in the report a statement of:

(1) the office's operating budget;

(2) the number of positions maintained for office staff;

(3) the number of accused persons who, after review by the office, were released by a court on personal bond; and

(4) the number of persons described in Subdivision (3):

(A) who were convicted of the same offense or of any felony within the six years preceding the date on which charges were filed in the matter pending during the person's release;

(B) who failed to attend a scheduled court appearance;

(C) for whom a warrant was issued for the person's arrest for failure to appear in accordance with the terms of the person's release; or

(D) who were arrested for any other offense while on the personal bond.

(c) This section does not apply to a personal bond pretrial release office that on January 1, 1995, was operated by a community corrections and supervision department.

*(Added by L.1989, chaps. 2(5.01(a)), 1080(1); chgd. by L.1995, chap. 318(44), eff. 9/1/95; former Art. 17.42, added by L.1989, chap. 698(1), repealed by L.1990, 6th C.S., chap. 28(2), eff. 9/6/90.)*

### Art. 17.43. Home curfew and electronic monitoring as condition.

(a) A magistrate may require as a condition of release on personal bond that the defendant submit to home curfew and electronic monitoring under the supervision of an agency designated by the magistrate.

(b) Cost of monitoring may be assessed as court costs or ordered paid directly by the defendant as a condition of bond.

*(Added by L.1989, chap. 374(4), eff. 9/1/89.)*

### Art. 17.44. Home confinement, electronic monitoring, and drug testing as condition.

(a) A magistrate may require as a condition of release on bond that the defendant submit to:

(1) home confinement and electronic monitoring under the supervision of an agency designated by the magistrate; or

(2) testing on a weekly basis for the presence of a controlled substance in the defendant's body.

(b) In this article, "controlled substance" has the meaning assigned by Section 481.002, Health and Safety Code.

(c) If a defendant violates a condition of home confinement and electronic monitoring, refuses to submit to a test for controlled substances, or submits to a test for controlled substances and the test indicates the presence of a controlled substance in the defendant's body, the magistrate may revoke the bond and order the defendant arrested.

(d) The community justice assistance division of the Texas Department of Criminal Justice may provide grants to counties to implement electronic monitoring programs authorized by this article.

*(Added by L.1989, chap. 785(4.03); chgd. by L.1991, chap. 14(284(46)); redes. by L.1991, chap. 16(19.01(3)), eff. 8/26/91.)*

### Art. 17.441. Conditions requiring motor vehicle ignition interlock.

(a) Except as provided by Subsection (b), a magistrate shall require on release that a defendant charged with a subsequent offense under Sections 49.04-49.06, Penal Code, or an offense under Section 49.07 or 49.08 of that code:

(1) have installed on the motor vehicle owned by the defendant or on the vehicle most regularly driven by the defendant, a device that uses a deep-lung breath analysis mechanism to make impractical the operation of a motor vehicle if ethyl alcohol is detected in the breath of the operator; and

(2) not operate any motor vehicle unless the vehicle is equipped with that device.

(b) The magistrate may not require the installation of the device if the magistrate finds that to require the device would not be in the best interest of justice.

(c) If the defendant is required to have the device installed, the magistrate shall require that the defendant have the device installed on the appropriate motor vehicle, at the defendant's expense, before the 30th day after the date the defendant is released on bond.

(d) The magistrate may designate an appropriate agency to verify the installation of the device and to monitor the device. If the magistrate designates an agency under this subsection, in each month during which the agency verifies the installation of the device or provides a monitoring service the defendant shall pay a fee to the designated agency in the amount set by the magistrate. The defendant shall pay the initial fee at the time the agency verifies the installation of the device. In each subsequent month during which the defendant is required to pay a fee the defendant shall pay the fee on the first occasion in that month that the agency provides a monitoring service. The magistrate shall set the fee in an amount not to exceed $10 as determined by the county auditor, or by the commissioners court of the county if the county does not have a county auditor, to be sufficient to cover the cost incurred by the designated agency in conducting the verification or providing the monitoring service, as applicable in that county.
*(Added by L.1995, chap. 318(45); chgd. by L.1999, chap. 537(1), eff. 9/1/99.)*

### Art. 17.45. Conditions requiring AIDS and HIV instruction.

A magistrate may require as a condition of bond that a defendant charged with an offense under Section 43.02, Penal Code, receive counseling or education, or both, relating to acquired immune deficiency syndrome or human immunodeficiency virus. *(Added by L.1989, chap. 1195(8); redes. by L.1991, chap. 16(19.01(4)), eff. 8/26/91.)*

### Art. 17.46. Conditions for a defendant charged with stalking.

(a) A magistrate may require as a condition of release on bond that a defendant charged with an offense under Section 42.072, Penal Code, may not:

(1) communicate directly or indirectly with the victim; or

(2) go to or near the residence, place of employment, or business of the victim or to or near a school, day-care facility, or similar facility where a dependent child of the victim is in attendance.

(b) If the magistrate requires the prohibition contained in Subsection (a)(2) of this article as a condition of release on bond, the magistrate shall specifically describe the prohibited locations and the minimum distances, if any, that the defendant must maintain from the locations.
*(Added by L.1993, chap. 10(2); chgd. by L.1995, chap. 657(3); L.1997, chap. 1(5), eff. 1/28/97.)*

## CHAPTER 17A. CORPORATIONS AND ASSOCIATIONS

Article


### Art. 17A.01. Application and definitions.† [*Application of chapter; definitions.*]

(a) This chapter sets out some of the procedural rules applicable to the criminal responsibility of corporations and associations. Where not in conflict with this chapter, the other chapters of this code apply to corporations and associations.

(b) In this code, unless the context requires a different definition:

(1) "Agent" means a director, officer, employee, or other person authorized to act in behalf of a corporation or association.

(2) "Association" means a government or governmental subdivision or agency, trust, partnership, or two or more persons having a joint or common economic interest.

(3) "High managerial agent" means:

(A) an officer of a corporation or association;

(B) a partner in a partnership; or

(C) an agent of a corporation or association who has duties of such responsibility that his conduct may reasonably be assumed to represent the policy of the corporation or association.

(4) "Person," "he," and "him" include corporation and association.

### Art. 17A.02. Allegation of name.

(a) In alleging the name of a defendant corporation, it is sufficient to state in the complaint, indictment, or information the corporate name, or to state any name or designation by which the corporation is known or may be identified. It is not necessary to allege that the defendant was lawfully incorporated.

(b) In alleging the name of a defendant association it is sufficient to state in the complaint, indictment, or information the association's name, or to state any name or designation by which the association is known or may be identified, or to state the name or names of one or more members of the association, referring to the unnamed members as "others." It is not necessary to allege the legal form of the association.

### Art. 17A.03. Summoning corporation or association.

(a) When a complaint is filed or an indictment or information presented against a corporation or association, the court or clerk shall issue a summons to the corporation or association. The summons shall be in the same form as a capias except that:

(1) it shall summon the corporation or association to appear before the court named at the place stated in the summons; and

(2) it shall be accompanied by a certified copy of the complaint, indictment, or information; and

(3) it shall provide that the corporation or association appear before the court named at or before 10 a.m. of the Monday next after the expiration of 20 days after it is served with summons, except when service is made upon the secretary of state or the Commissioner of Insurance, in which instance the summons shall provide that the corporation or association appear before the court named at or before 10 a.m. of the Monday next after the expiration of 30 days after the secretary of state or the Commissioner of Insurance is served with summons.

(b) No individual may be arrested upon a complaint, indictment, information, judgment, or sentence against a corporation or association.

### Art. 17A.04. Service on corporation.† [*Serving a summons on a corporation.*]

(a) Except as provided in Paragraph (d) of this article, a peace officer shall serve a summons on a corporation by personally delivering a copy of it to the corporation's registered agent. However, if a registered agent has not been designated, or cannot with reasonable diligence be found at the registered office, then the peace officer shall serve the summons by personally delivering a copy of it to the president or a vice-president of the corporation.

(b) If the peace officer certifies on the return that he diligently but unsuccessfully attempted to effect service under Paragraph (a) of this article, or if the corporation is a foreign corporation that has no certificate of authority, then he shall serve the summons on the secretary of state by personally delivering a copy of it to him, or to the assistant secretary of state, or to any clerk in charge of the corporation department of his office. On receipt of the summons copy, the secretary of state shall immediately forward it by certified or registered mail, return receipt requested, addressed to the defendant corporation at its registered or principal office in the state or country under whose law it was incorporated.

(c) The secretary of state shall keep a permanent record of the date and time of receipt and his disposition of each summons served under Paragraph (b) of this article together with the return receipt.

(d) The method of service on a corporation regulated under the Insurance Code is governed by that code.

### Art. 17A.05. Service on association.† [*Serving a summons on an association.*]

(a) Except as provided in Paragraph (b) of this article, a peace officer shall serve a summons on an association by personally delivering a copy of it:

(1) to a high managerial agent at any place where business of the association is regularly conducted; or

(2) if the peace officer certifies on the return that he diligently but unsuccessfully attempted to serve a high managerial agent, to any employee of suitable age and discretion at any place where business of the association is regularly conducted; or

(3) if the peace officer certifies on the return that he diligently but unsuccessfully attempted to serve a high managerial agent, or employee of suitable age and discretion, to any member of the association.

(b) The method of service on an association regulated under the Insurance Code is governed by that code.

### Art. 17A.06. Appearance.

(a) In all criminal actions instituted against a corporation or association, in which original jurisdiction is in a district or county-level court:

(1) appearance is for the purpose of arraignment;

(2) the corporation or association has 10 full days after the day the arraignment takes place and before the day the trial begins to file written pleadings.

(b) in all criminal actions instituted against a corporation or association, in which original jurisdiction is in a justice court or corporation court:

(1) appearance is for the purpose of entering a plea; and

(2) ten full days must elapse after the day of appearance before the corporation or association may be tried.

### Art. 17A.07. Presence of corporation or association.

(a) A defendant corporation or association appears through counsel.

(b) If a corporation or association does not appear in response to summons, or appears but fails or refuses to plead:

(1) it is deemed to be present in person for all purposes; and

(2) the court shall enter a plea of not guilty in its behalf; and

(3) the court may proceed with trial, judgment, and sentencing.

(c) If, having appeared and entered a plea in response to summons, a corporation or association is absent without good cause at any time during later proceedings:

(1) it is deemed to be present in person for all purposes; and

(2) the court may proceed with trial, judgment, or sentencing.

### Art. 17A.08. Probation.

The benefits of the adult probation laws shall not be available to corporations and associations.

### Art. 17A.09. Notifying attorney general of corporation's conviction.† [*Conviction of corporation: notification of attorney general.*]

If a corporation is convicted of an offense, or if a high managerial agent is convicted of an offense committed in the conduct of the affairs of the corporation, the court shall notify the attorney general in writing of the conviction when it becomes final and unappealable. The notice shall include:

(1) the corporation's name, and the name of the corporation's registered agent and the address of the registered office, or the high managerial agent's name and address, or both; and

(2) certified copies of the judgment and sentence and of the complaint, information, or indictment on which the judgment and sentence were based.

# SEARCH WARRANTS

## CHAPTER 18. SEARCH WARRANTS

Article

## Art. 18.01. Search warrant.

(a) A "search warrant" is a written order, issued by a magistrate and directed to a peace officer, commanding him to search for any property or thing and to seize the same and bring it before such magistrate or commanding him to search for and photograph a child and to deliver to the magistrate any of the film exposed pursuant to the order.

(b) No search warrant shall issue for any purpose in this state unless sufficient facts are first presented to satisfy the issuing magistrate that probable cause does in fact exist for its issuance. A sworn affidavit setting forth substantial facts establishing probable cause shall be filed in every instance in which a search warrant is requested. The affidavit is public information if executed, and the magistrate's clerk shall make a copy of the affidavit available for public inspection in the clerk's office during normal business hours.

(c) A search warrant may not be issued pursuant to Subdivision (10) of Article 18.02 of this code unless the sworn affidavit required by Subsection (b) of this article sets forth sufficient facts to establish probable cause: (1) that a specific offense has been committed, (2) that the specifically described property or items that are to be searched for or seized constitute evidence of that offense or evidence that a particular person committed that offense, and (3) that the property or items constituting evidence to be searched for or seized are located at or on the particular person, place, or thing to be searched. Except as provided by Subsections (d) and (i) of this article, only a judge of a municipal court of record or county court who is an attorney licensed by the State of Texas, statutory county court, district court, the Court of Criminal Appeals, or the Supreme Court may issue warrants pursuant to Subdivision (10), Article 18.02 of this code.

(d) Only the specifically described property or items set forth in a search warrant issued under Subdivision (10) of Article 18.02 of this code or property, items or contraband enumerated in Subdivisions (1) through (9) or in Subdivision (12) of Article 18.02 of this code may be seized. A subsequent search warrant may be issued pursuant to Subdivision (10) of Article 18.02 of this code to search the same person, place, or thing subjected to a prior search under Subdivision (10) of Article 18.02 of this code only if the subsequent search warrant is issued by a judge of a district court, a court of appeals, the court of criminal appeals, or the supreme court.

(e) A search warrant may not be issued under Subdivision (10) of Article 18.02 of this code to search for and seize property or items that are not described in Subdivisions (1) through (9) of that article and that are located in an office of a newspaper, news magazine, television station, or radio station, and in no event may property or items not described in Subdivisions (1) through (9) of that article be legally seized in any search pursuant to a search warrant of an office of a newspaper, news magazine, television station, or radio station.

(f) A search warrant may not be issued pursuant to Article 18.021 of this code unless the sworn affidavit required by Subsection (b) of this article sets forth sufficient facts to establish probable cause:

(1) that a specific offense has been committed;

(2) that a specifically described person has been a victim of the offense;

(3) that evidence of the offense or evidence that a particular person committed the offense can be detected by photographic means; and

(4) that the person to be searched for and photographed is located at the particular place to be searched.

(g) A search warrant may not be issued under Subdivision (12), Article 18.02, of this code unless the sworn affidavit required by Subsection (b) of this article sets forth sufficient facts to establish probable cause that a specific felony offense has been committed and that the specifically described property or items that are to be searched for or seized constitute contraband as defined in Article 59.01 of this code and are located at or on the particular person, place, or thing to be searched.

(h) Except as provided by Subsection (i) of this article, a warrant under Subdivision (12), Article 18.02 of this code may only be issued by:

(1) a judge of a municipal court of record who is an attorney licensed by the state;

(2) a judge of a county court who is an attorney licensed by the state; or

(3) a judge of a statutory county court, district court, the court of criminal appeals, or the supreme court.

(i) In a county in which the only judge serving the county who is a licensed attorney is a district judge whose district includes more than one county, any magistrate may issue a search warrant under Subdivision (10) or Subdivision (12) of Article 18.02 of this code. This section is not applicable to a subsequent search warrant under Subdivision (10) of Article 18.02 of this code. *(Chgd. by L.1989, 1st C.S., chap. 12(2); L.1991, chap. 73(1); L.1995, chap. 670(1); L.1997, chap. 604(1); L.1999, chaps. 167(1), 1469(1), eff. 5/21/99, 6/19/99, respectively.)*

## Art. 18.02. Grounds for issuance.

A search warrant may be issued to search for and seize:

(1) property acquired by theft or in any other manner which makes its acquisition a penal offense;

(2) property specially designed, made, or adapted for or commonly used in the commission of an offense;

(3) arms and munitions kept or prepared for the purposes of insurrection or riot;

(4) weapons prohibited by the Penal Code;

(5) gambling devices or equipment, altered gambling equipment, or gambling paraphernalia;

(6) obscene materials kept or prepared for commercial distribution or exhibition, subject to the additional rules set forth by law;

(7) drugs kept, prepared, or manufactured in violation of the laws of this state;

(8) any property the possession of which is prohibited by law;

(9) implements or instruments used in the commission of a crime;

(10) property or items, except the personal writings by the accused, constituting evidence of an offense or constituting evidence tending to show that a particular person committed an offense;

(11) persons; or

(12) contraband subject to forfeiture under Chapter 59 of this code.

*(Chgd. by L.1989, 1st C.S., chap. 12(3), eff. 9/1/89.)*

## Art. 18.021. Issuance of search warrant to photograph injured child.

(a) A search warrant may be issued to search for and photograph a child who is alleged to be the victim of the offenses of injury to a child as defined by Section 22.04, Penal Code, as amended; sexual assault of a child as defined by Section 22.011(a), Penal Code, as amended; or aggravated sexual assault of a child as defined by Section 22.021, Penal Code.

(b) The officer executing the warrant may be accompanied by a photographer who is employed by a law enforcement agency and who acts under the direction of the officer executing the warrant. The photographer is entitled to access to the child in the same manner as the officer executing the warrant.

(c) In addition to the requirements of Subdivisions (1) and (4) of Article 18.04 of this code, a warrant issued under this article shall identify, as near as may be, the child to be located and photographed, shall name or describe, as near as may be, the place or thing to be searched, and shall command any peace officer of the proper county to search for and cause the child to be photographed.

(d) After having located and photographed the child, the peace officer executing the warrant shall take possession of the exposed film and deliver it forthwith to the magistrate. The child may not be removed from the premises on which he or she is located except under Subchapters A and B, Chapter 262, Family Code.

(e) A search warrant under this section shall be executed by a peace officer of the same sex as the alleged victim or, if the officer is not of the same sex as the alleged victim, the peace officer must be assisted by a person of the same sex as the alleged victim. The person assisting an officer under this subsection must be acting under the direction of the officer and must be with the alleged victim during the taking of the photographs.
*(Chgd. by L.1997, chap. 165(7.01), eff. 9/1/97.)*

## Art. 18.03. Search warrant may authorize arrest.

If the facts presented to the magistrate under Article 18.02 of this chapter also establish the existence of probable cause that a person has committed some offense under the laws of this state, the search warrant may, in addition, order the arrest of such person.

## Art. 18.04. Contents of warrant.† [*Components of warrant.*]

A search warrant issued under this chapter shall be sufficient if it contains the following requisites:

(1) that it run in the name of "The State of Texas";

(2) that it identify, as near as may be, that which is to be seized and name or describe, as near as may be, the person, place, or thing to be searched;

(3) that it command any peace officer of the proper county to search forthwith the person, place, or thing named; and

(4) that it be dated and signed by the magistrate.

## Art. 18.05. Warrants for fire, health, and code inspections.

(a) Except as provided by Subsection (e) of this article, a search warrant may be issued to the fire marshal, health officer, or code enforcement official of the state or of any county, city or other political subdivision for the purpose of allowing the inspection of any specified premises to determine the presence of a fire or health hazard or unsafe building condition or a violation of any fire, health, or building regulation, statute, or ordinance.

(b) A search warrant may not be issued under this article except upon the presentation of evidence of probable cause to believe that a fire or health hazard or violation or unsafe building condition is present in the premises sought to be inspected.

(c) In determining probable cause, the magistrate is not limited to evidence of specific knowledge, but may consider any of the following:

(1) the age and general condition of the premises;

(2) previous violations or hazards found present in the premises;

(3) the type of premises;

(4) the purposes for which the premises are used; and

(5) the presence of hazards or violations in and the general condition of premises near the premises sought to be inspected.

(d) Each city or county may designate one code enforcement official for the purpose of being issued a search warrant as authorized by Subsection (a) of this article. A political subdivision other than a city or county may designate one code enforcement official for the purpose of being issued a search warrant as authorized by Subsection (a) of this article only if the political subdivision routinely inspects premises to determine whether there is a fire or health hazard or unsafe building condition or a violation of fire, health, or building regulation, statute, or ordinance.

(e) A search warrant may not be issued under this article to a code enforcement official of a county with a population of 2.4 million or more for the purpose of allowing the inspection of specified premises to determine the presence of an unsafe building condition or a violation of a building regulation, statute, or ordinance.
*(Chgd. by L.1989, chap. 382(1), eff. 6/14/89.)*

## Art. 18.06. Execution of warrants.

(a) A peace officer to whom a search warrant is delivered shall execute it without delay and forthwith return it to the proper magistrate. It must be executed within three days from the time of its issuance, and shall be executed within a shorter period if so directed in the warrant by the magistrate.

(b) On searching the place ordered to be searched, the officer executing the warrant shall present a copy of the warrant to the owner of the place, if he is present. If the owner of the place is not present but a person who is present is in possession of the place, the officer shall present a copy of the warrant to the person. Before the officer takes property from the place, he shall prepare a written inventory of the property to be taken. He shall legibly endorse his name on the inventory and present a copy of the inventory to the owner or other person in possession of the property. If neither the owner nor a person in possession of the property is present when the officer executes the warrant, the officer shall leave a copy of the warrant and the inventory at the place.

**Art. 18.07. Days allowed for warrant to run.† [*Time allowed for execution of warrant.*]**

The time allowed for the execution of a search warrant shall be three whole days, exclusive of the day of its issuance and of the day of its execution. The magistrate issuing a search warrant under the provisions of this chapter shall endorse on such search warrant the date and hour of the issuance of the same.

**Art. 18.08. Power of officer executing warrant.† [*Authority of officer executing warrant.*]**

In the execution of a search warrant, the officer may call to his aid any number of citizens in this county, who shall be bound to aid in the execution of the same.

**Art. 18.09. Shall seize accused and property.† [*Shall seize suspect and property.*]**

When the property which the officer is directed to search for and seize is found he shall take possession of the same and carry it before the magistrate. He shall also arrest any person whom he is directed to arrest by the warrant and immediately take such person before the magistrate.

**Art. 18.10. How return made.**

Upon returning the search warrant, the officer shall state on the back of the same, or on some paper attached to it, the manner in which it has been executed and shall likewise deliver to the magistrate a copy of the inventory of the property taken into his possession under the warrant. The officer who seized the property shall retain custody of it until the magistrate issues an order directing the manner of safekeeping the property. The property may not be removed from the county in which it was seized without an order approving the removal, issued by a magistrate in the county in which the warrant was issued; provided, however, nothing herein shall prevent the officer, or his department, from forwarding any item or items seized to a laboratory for scientific analysis.

**Art. 18.11. Custody of property found.† [*Custody of property located.*]**

Property seized pursuant to a search warrant shall be kept as provided by the order of a magistrate issued in accordance with Article 18.10 of this code.

**Art. 18.12. Magistrate shall investigate.**

The magistrate, upon the return of a search warrant, shall proceed to try the questions arising upon the same, and shall take testimony as in other examinations before him.

**Art. 18.13. Shall discharge defendant.† [*Shall discharge accused.*]**

If the magistrate be not satisfied, upon investigation, that there was good ground for the issuance of the warrant, he shall discharge the defendant and order restitution of the property taken from him, except for criminal instruments. In such case, the criminal instruments shall be kept by the sheriff subject to the order of the proper court.

**Art. 18.14. Examining trial.**

The magistrate shall proceed to deal with the accused as in other cases before an examining court if he is satisfied there was good ground for issuing the warrant.

**Art. 18.15. Certify record to proper court.**

The magistrate shall keep a record of all the proceedings had before him in cases of search warrants, and shall certify the same and deliver them to the clerk of the court having jurisdiction of the case, before the next term of said court, and accompany the same with all the original papers relating thereto, including the certified schedule of the property seized.

**Art. 18.16. Preventing consequences of theft.† [*Deterring results of theft.*]**

All persons have a right to prevent the consequences of theft by seizing any personal property which has been stolen and bringing it, with the supposed offender, if he can be taken, before a magistrate for examination, or delivering the same to a peace officer for that purpose. To justify such seizure, there must, however, be reasonable ground to suppose the property to be stolen, and the seizure must be openly made and the proceedings had without delay.

**Art. 18.17. Disposition of abandoned or unclaimed property.**

(a) All unclaimed or abandoned personal property of every kind, other than contraband subject to forfeiture under Chapter 59 of this code and whiskey, wine and beer, seized by any peace officer in the State of Texas which is not held as evidence to be used in any pending case and has not been ordered destroyed or returned to the person entitled to possession of the same by a magistrate, which shall remain unclaimed for a period of 30 days shall be delivered for disposition to a person designated by the municipality or the purchasing agent of the county in which the property was seized. If a peace officer of a municipality seizes the property, the peace officer shall deliver the property to a person designated by the municipality. If any other peace officer seizes the property, the peace officer shall deliver the property to the purchasing agent of the county. If the county has no purchasing agent, then such property shall be disposed of by the sheriff of the county.

(b) The county purchasing agent, the person designated by the municipality, or the sheriff of the county, as the case may be, shall mail a notice to the last known address of the owner of such property by certified mail. Such notice shall describe the property being held, give the name and address of the officer holding such property, and shall state that if the owner does not claim such property within 90 days from the date of the notice such property will be disposed of and the proceeds, after deducting the reasonable expense of keeping such property and the costs of the disposition, placed in the treasury of the municipality or county giving the notice.

(c) If the property has a fair market value of $500 or more and the owner or the address of the owner is unknown, the person designated by the municipality, the county purchasing agent, or the sheriff, as the case may be, shall cause to be published once in a paper of general circulation in the municipality or county a notice containing a general description of the property held, the name of the owner if known, the name and address of the officer holding such property, and a statement that if the owner does not claim such property within 90 days from the date of the publication such property will be disposed of and the proceeds, after deducting the reasonable expense of keeping such property and the costs of the disposition, placed in the treasury of the municipality or county disposing of the property. If the property has a fair market value of less than $500 and the owner or the address of the owner is unknown, the person designated by the municipality, the county purchasing agent, or the sheriff may sell or donate the property. The person designated by the municipality, the purchasing agent, or the sheriff shall deposit the sale proceeds, after deducting the reasonable expense of keeping the property and costs of the sale, in the treasury of the municipality or county selling or donating the property.

(d) The sale under this article of any property that has a fair market value of $500 or more shall be preceded by a notice published once at least 14 days prior to the date of such sale in a newspaper of general circulation in the municipality or county where the sale is to take place, stating the general description of the property, the names of the owner if known, and the date and place that such sale will occur. This article does not require disposition by sale.

(e) The real owner of any property disposed of shall have the right to file a claim to the proceeds with the commissioners court of the county or with the governing body of the municipality in which the disposition took place. A claim by the real owner must be filed not later than the 30th day after the date of disposition. If the claim is allowed by the commissioners court or the governing body of the municipality, the municipal or county treasurer shall pay the owner such funds as were paid into the treasury of the municipality or county as proceeds of the disposition. If the claim is denied by the commissioners court or the governing body or if said court or body fails to act upon such claim within 90 days, the claimant may sue the municipal or county treasurer in a court of competent jurisdiction in the county, and upon sufficient proof of ownership, recover judgment against such municipality or county for the recovery of the proceeds of the disposition.

(f) For the purposes of this article:

(1) "Person designated by a municipality" means an officer or employee of a municipality who is designated by the municipality to be primarily responsible for the disposition of property under this article.

(2) "Property held as evidence" means property related to a charge that has been filed or to a matter that is being investigated for the filing of a charge.

(g) If the provisions of this section have been met and the property is scheduled for disposition, the municipal or county law enforcement agency that originally seized the property may request and have the property converted to agency use. The agency at any time may transfer the property to another municipal or county law enforcement agency for the use of that agency. The agency last using the property shall return the property to the person designated by the municipality, county purchasing agent, or sheriff, as the case may be, for disposition when the agency has completed the intended use of the property.

(h) If the abandoned or unclaimed personal property is money, the person designated by the municipality, the county purchasing agent, or the sheriff of the county, as appropriate, may, after giving notice under Subsection (b) or (c) of this article, deposit the money in the treasury of the municipality or county giving notice without conducting the sale as required by Subsection (d) of this article.

(i) While offering the property for sale under this article, if a person designated by a municipality, county purchasing agent, or sheriff considers any bid as insufficient, the person, agent, or sheriff may decline the bid and reoffer the property for sale.
*(Chgd. by L.1989, 1st C.S., chap. 12(4); L.1991, chap. 254(1); L.1993, chaps. 157(1), 321(1)-(4); L.1995, chap. 76(3.01)-(3.05), eff. 9/1/95.)*

## Art. 18.18. Disposition of gambling paraphernalia, prohibited weapon, criminal instrument, and other contraband.† [*Treatment of gambling paraphernalia, prohibited weapon, criminal instrument, and other contraband.*]

(a) Following the final conviction of a person for possession of a gambling device or equipment, altered gambling equipment, or gambling paraphernalia, for an offense involving a criminal instrument, for an offense involving an obscene device or material, the court entering the judgment of conviction shall order that the machine, device, gambling equipment or gambling paraphernalia, instrument, obscene device or material be destroyed or forfeited to the state. Not later than the 30th day after the final conviction of a person for an offense involving a prohibited weapon, the court entering the judgment of conviction on its own motion, on the motion of the prosecuting attorney in the case, or on the motion of the law enforcement agency initiating the complaint on notice to the prosecuting attorney in the case if the prosecutor fails to move for the order shall order that the prohibited weapon be destroyed or forfeited to the law enforcement agency that initiated the complaint. If the court fails to enter the order within the time required by this subsection, any magistrate in the county in which the offense occurred may enter the order. Following the final conviction of a person for an offense involving dog fighting, the court entering the judgment of conviction shall order that any dog-fighting equipment be destroyed or forfeited to the state. Destruction of dogs, if necessary, must be carried out by a veterinarian licensed in this state or, if one is not available, by trained personnel of a humane society or an animal shelter. If forfeited, the court shall order the contraband delivered to the state, any political subdivision of the state, or to any state institution or agency. If gambling proceeds were seized, the court shall order them forfeited to the state and shall transmit them to the grand jury of the county in which they were seized for use in investigating alleged violations of the Penal Code, or to the state, any political subdivision of the state, or to any state institution or agency.

(b) If there is no prosecution or conviction following seizure, the magistrate to whom the return was made shall notify in writing the person found in possession of the alleged gambling device or equipment, altered gambling equipment or gambling paraphernalia, gambling proceeds, prohibited weapon, obscene device or material, criminal instrument, or dog-fighting equipment to show cause why the property seized should not be destroyed or the proceeds forfeited. The magistrate, on the motion of the law enforcement agency seizing a prohibited weapon, shall order the weapon destroyed or forfeited to the law enforcement agency seizing the weapon, unless a person shows cause as to why the prohibited weapon should not be destroyed or forfeited. A law enforcement agency shall make a motion under this section in a timely manner after the time at which the agency is informed in writing by the attorney representing the state that no prosecution will arise from the seizure.

(c) The magistrate shall include in the notice a detailed description of the property seized and the total amount of alleged gambling proceeds; the name of the person found in possession; the address where the property or proceeds were seized; and the date and time of the seizure.

(d) The magistrate shall send the notice by registered or certified mail, return receipt requested, to the person found in possession at the address where the property or proceeds were seized. If no one was found in possession, or the possessor's address is unknown, the magistrate shall post the notice on the courthouse door.

(e) Any person interested in the alleged gambling device or equipment, altered gambling equipment or gambling paraphernalia, gambling proceeds, prohibited weapon, obscene device or material, criminal instrument, or dog-fighting equipment seized must appear before the magistrate on the 20th day following the date the notice was mailed or posted. Failure to timely appear forfeits any interest the person may have in the property or proceeds seized, and no person after failing to timely appear may contest destruction or forfeiture.

(f) If a person timely appears to show cause why the property or proceeds should not be destroyed or forfeited, the magistrate shall conduct a hearing on the issue and determine the nature of property or proceeds and the person's interest therein. Unless the person proves by a preponderance of the evidence that the property or proceeds is not gambling equipment, altered gambling equipment, gambling paraphernalia, gambling device, gambling proceeds, prohibited weapon, criminal instrument, or dog-fighting equipment and that he is entitled to possession, the magistrate shall dispose of the property or proceeds in accordance with Paragraph (a) of this article.

(g) For purposes of this article:

(1) "criminal instrument" has the meaning defined in the Penal Code;

(2) "gambling device or equipment, altered gambling equipment or gambling paraphernalia" has the meaning defined in the Penal Code;

(3) "prohibited weapon" has the meaning defined in the Penal Code; and

(4) "dog-fighting equipment" means:

(A) equipment used for training or handling a fighting dog, including a harness, treadmill, cage, decoy, pen, house for keeping a fighting dog, feeding apparatus, or training pen;

(B) equipment used for transporting a fighting dog, including any automobile, or other vehicle, and its appurtenances which are intended to be used as a vehicle for transporting a fighting dog;

(C) equipment used to promote or advertise an exhibition of dog fighting, including a printing press or similar equipment, paper, ink, or photography equipment; or

(D) a dog trained, being trained, or intended to be used to fight with another dog.

(5) *(Blank.)*

(6) "obscene device or material" means a device or material introduced into evidence and thereafter found obscene by virtue of a final judgment after all appellate remedies have been exhausted.

*(Chgd. by L.1993, chap. 157(2), eff. 9/1/93.)*

**Art. 18.181. Disposition of explosive weapons and chemical dispensing devices.†**
**[*Treatment of explosive weapons and chemical dispensing devices.*]**

(a) After seizure of an explosive weapon or chemical dispensing device, as these terms are defined in Section 46.01, Penal Code, a peace officer or a person acting at the direction of a peace officer shall:

(1) photograph the weapon in the position where it is recovered before touching or moving it;

(2) record the identification designations printed on a weapon if the markings are intact;

(3) if the weapon can be moved, move it to an isolated area in order to lessen the danger to the public;

(4) if possible, retain a portion of a wrapper or other packaging materials connected to the weapon;

(5) retain a small portion of the explosive material and submit the material to a laboratory for chemical analysis;

(6) separate and retain components associated with the weapon such as fusing and triggering mechanisms if those mechanisms are not hazardous in themselves;

(7) destroy the remainder of the weapon in a safe manner;

(8) at the time of destruction, photograph the destruction process and make careful observations of the characteristics of the destruction;

(9) after destruction, inspect the disposal site and photograph the site to record the destructive characteristics of the weapon; and

(10) retain components of the weapon and records of the destruction for use as evidence in court proceedings.

(b) Representative samples, photographs, and records made pursuant to this article are admissible in civil or criminal proceedings in the same manner and to the same extent as if the explosive weapon were offered in evidence, regardless of whether or not the remainder of the weapon has been destroyed. No inference or presumption of spoliation applies to weapons destroyed pursuant to this article.

**Art. 18.182.** *(Repealed by L.1991, chap. 916(3), eff. 9/1/91.)*

**Art. 18.183. Deposit of money pending disposition.**

(a) If money is seized by a law enforcement agency in connection with a violation of Chapter 47, Penal Code, the state or the political subdivision of the state that employs the law enforcement agency may deposit the money in an interest-bearing bank account in the jurisdiction of the agency that made seizure or in the county in which the money was seized until a final judgment is rendered concerning the violation.

(b) If a final judgment is rendered concerning a violation of Chapter 47, Penal Code, money seized in connection with the violation that has been placed in an interest-bearing bank account

shall be distributed according to this chapter, with any interest being distributed in the same manner and used for the same purpose as the principal.
*(Renumbered by L.1989, chap. 2(16.01(6)), eff. 9/1/89.)*

**Art. 18.19. Disposition of seized weapons.† [*Treatment of seized weapons.*]**

(a) Weapons seized in connection with an offense involving the use of a weapon or an offense under Penal Code Chapter 46 shall be held by the law enforcement agency making the seizure, subject to the following provisions, unless:

(1) the weapon is a prohibited weapon identified in Penal Code Chapter 46, in which event Article 18.18 of this code applies; or

(2) the weapon is alleged to be stolen property, in which event Chapter 47 of this code applies.

(b) When a weapon described in Paragraph (a) of this article is seized, and the seizure is not made pursuant to a search or arrest warrant, the person seizing the same shall prepare and deliver to a magistrate a written inventory of each weapon seized.

(c) If there is no prosecution or conviction for an offense involving the weapon seized, the magistrate to whom the seizure was reported shall notify in writing the person found in possession that he is entitled to the weapon upon request to the court in which he was convicted. If the weapon is not requested within 60 days after notification, the magistrate shall order the weapon destroyed or forfeited to the state for use by the law enforcement agency holding the weapon.

(d) A person either convicted or receiving deferred adjudication under Penal Code Chapter 46 is entitled to the weapon seized upon request to the law enforcement agency holding the weapon. However, the court entering the judgment shall order the weapon destroyed or forfeited to the state for use by the law enforcement agency holding the weapon if:

(1) the person does not request the weapon within 60 days after the date of the judgment of conviction;

(2) the person has been previously convicted under Penal Code Chapter 46;

(3) the weapon is one defined as a prohibited weapon under Penal Code Chapter 46;

(4) the offense for which the person is convicted or receives deferred adjudication was committed in or on the premises of a playground, school, video arcade facility, or youth center, as those terms are defined by Section 481.134, Health and Safety Code; or

(5) the court determines based on the prior criminal history of the defendant or based on the circumstances surrounding the commission of the offense that possession of the seized weapon would pose a threat to the community or one or more individuals.

(e) If the person found in possession of a weapon is convicted of an offense involving the use of the weapon, the court entering judgment of conviction shall order destruction of the weapon or forfeiture to the state for use by the law enforcement agency holding the weapon.
*(Chgd. by L.1993, chap. 157(3); L.1995, chap. 318(46)(a), eff. 9/1/95.)*

**Art. 18.20. Interception and use of wire, oral, or electronic communications.**

**Sec. 1. Definitions.** In this article:

(1) "Wire communication" means an aural transfer made in whole or in part through the use of facilities for the transmission of communications by the aid of wire, cable, or other like connection between the point of origin and the point of reception, including the use of such a connection in a switching station, furnished or operated by a person authorized to engage in providing or operating the facilities for the transmission of communications as a communications common carrier. The term includes the electronic storage of a wire communication.

(2) "Oral communication" means an oral communication uttered by a person exhibiting an expectation that the communication is not subject to interception under circumstances justifying that expectation. The term does not include an electronic communication.

(3) "Intercept" means the aural acquisition of the contents of a wire, oral, or electronic communication through the use of an electronic, mechanical, or other device.

(4) "Electronic, mechanical, or other device" means a device that may be used for the nonconsensual interception of wire, oral, or electronic communications. The term does not include a telephone or telegraph instrument, the equipment or a facility used for the transmission of electronic communications, or a component of the equipment or a facility used for the transmission of electronic communications if the instrument, equipment, facility, or component is:

(A) furnished to the subscriber or user by a provider of wire or electronic communications service in the ordinary course of the provider's business and being used by the subscriber or user in the ordinary course of its business;

(B) furnished by a subscriber or user for connection to the facilities of a wire or electronic communications service for use in the ordinary course of the subscriber's or user's business;

(C) being used by a communications common carrier in the ordinary course of its business; or

(D) being used by an investigative or law enforcement officer in the ordinary course of the officer's duties.

(5) "Investigative or law enforcement officer" means an officer of this state or of a political subdivision of this state who is empowered by law to conduct investigations of or to make arrests for offenses enumerated in Section 4 of this article or an attorney authorized by law to prosecute or participate in the prosecution of the enumerated offenses.

(6) "Contents," when used with respect to a wire, oral, or electronic communication, includes any information concerning the substance, purport, or meaning of that communication.

(7) "Judge of competent jurisdiction" means a judge from the panel of nine active district judges with criminal jurisdiction appointed by the presiding judge of the court of criminal appeals as provided by Section 3 of this article.

(8) "Prosecutor" means a district attorney, criminal district attorney, or county attorney performing the duties of a district attorney, with jurisdiction in the county within an administrative judicial district described by Section 3(b).

(9) "Director" means the director of the Department of Public Safety or, if the director is absent or unable to serve, the assistant director of the Department of Public Safety.

(10) "Communication common carrier" means a person engaged as a common carrier for hire in the transmission of wire or electronic communications.

(11) "Aggrieved person" means a person who was a party to an intercepted wire, oral, or electronic communication or a person against whom the interception was directed.

(12) "Covert entry" means any entry into or onto premises which if made without a court order allowing such an entry under this Act, would be a violation of the Penal Code.

(13) "Residence" means a structure or the portion of a structure used as a person's home or fixed place of habitation to which the person indicates an intent to return after any temporary absence.

(14) "Pen register" means a device that attaches to a telephone line and records or decodes electronic or other impulses to identify numbers dialed or otherwise transmitted on the telephone line. The term does not include a device used by a provider or customer of:

(A) a wire or electronic communication service for purposes of charging a fee for the service; or

(B) a wire communication service during the ordinary course of the provider's or customer's business, including cost accounting and security control.

(15) "Electronic communication" means a transfer of signs, signals, writing, images, sounds, data, or intelligence of any nature transmitted in whole or in part by a wire, radio, electromagnetic, photoelectronic, or photo-optical system. The term does not include:

(A) a wire or oral communication;

(B) a communication made through a tone-only paging device; or

(C) a communication from a tracking device.

(16) "User" means a person who uses an electronic communications service and is authorized by the provider of the service to use the service.

(17) "Electronic communications system" means a wire, radio, electromagnetic, photo-optical or photoelectronic facility for the transmission of wire or electronic communications, and any computer facility or related electronic equipment for the electronic storage of those communications.

(18) "Electronic communications service" means a service that provides to users of the service the ability to send or receive wire or electronic communications.

(19) "Readily accessible to the general public" means, with respect to a radio communication, a communication that is not:

(A) scrambled or encrypted;

(B) transmitted using modulation techniques whose essential parameters have been withheld from the public with the intention of preserving the privacy of the communication;

(C) carried on a subcarrier or other signal subsidiary to a radio transmission;

(D) transmitted over a communication system provided by a common carrier, unless the communication is a tone-only paging system communication;

(E) transmitted on frequencies allocated under Part 25, Subpart D, E, or F of Part 74, or Part 94 of the rules of the Federal Communications Commission, unless, in the case of a communication transmitted on a frequency allocated under Part 74 that is not exclusively allocated to broadcast auxiliary services, the communication is a two-way voice communication by radio; or

(F) an electronic communication.

(20) "Electronic storage" means:

(A) a temporary, intermediate storage of a wire or electronic communication that is incidental to the electronic transmission of the communication; or

(B) storage of a wire or electronic communication by an electronic communications service for purposes of backup protection of the communication.

(21) "Aural transfer" means a transfer containing the human voice at any point between and including the point of origin and the point of reception.

*(Chgd. by L.1997, chap. 1051(1), eff. 9/1/97.)*

**Sec. 2. Prohibition of use as evidence of intercepted communications.** The contents of an intercepted communication and evidence derived from an intercepted communication may not be received in evidence in any trial, hearing, or other proceeding in or before any court, grand jury, department, officer, agency, regulatory body, legislative committee, or other authority of the United States or of this state or a political subdivision of this state if the disclosure of that information would be in violation of this article. The contents of an intercepted communication and evidence derived from an intercepted communication may be received in a civil trial, hearing, or other proceeding only if the civil trial, hearing, or other proceeding arises out of a violation of the Penal Code, Code of Criminal Procedure, Controlled Substances Act, or Dangerous Drug Act.

**Sec. 3. Judges authorized to consider interception applications.** (a) The presiding judge of the court of criminal appeals, by order filed with the clerk of that court, shall appoint one district judge from each of the administrative judicial districts of this state to serve at his pleasure as the judge of competent jurisdiction within that administrative judicial district. The presiding judge shall fill vacancies, as they occur, in the same manner.

(b) Except as provided by Subsection (c), a judge appointed under Subsection (a) may act on an application for authorization to intercept wire, oral, or electronic communications if the judge is appointed as the judge of competent jurisdiction within the administrative judicial district in which the following is located:

(1) the site of:

(A) the proposed interception; or

(B) the interception device to be installed or monitored;

(2) the communication device to be intercepted;

(3) the billing, residential, or business address of the subscriber to the electronic communications service to be intercepted;

(4) the headquarters of the law enforcement agency that makes a request for or executes an order authorizing an interception; or

(5) the headquarters of the service provider.

(c) If the judge of competent jurisdiction for an administrative judicial district is absent or unable to serve or if exigent circumstances exist, the application may be made to the judge of competent jurisdiction in an adjacent administrative judicial district. Exigent circumstances does not include a denial of a previous application on the same facts and circumstances. To be valid, the application must fully explain the circumstances justifying application under this subsection.

*(Chgd. by L.1997, chap. 1051(2), eff. 9/1/97.)*

**Sec. 4. Offenses for which interceptions may be authorized.** A judge may issue an order authorizing interception of wire, oral, or electronic communications only if the prosecutor applying for the order shows probable cause to believe that the interception will provide evidence of the commission of a felony (other than felony possession of marihuana) under Chapter 481, Health and Safety Code, or Section 485.033, Health and Safety Code or of a felony under Chapter 483, Health and Safety Code.

**Sec. 5. Control of intercepting devices.** (a) Only the Department of Public Safety is authorized by this article to own, possess, install, operate, or monitor an electronic, mechanical, or other device. The Department of Public Safety may be assisted by an investigative or law enforcement officer in the operation and monitoring of an interception of wire, oral, or electronic communications, provided that a commissioned officer of the Department of Public Safety is present at all times.

(b) The director shall designate in writing the commissioned officers of the Department of Public Safety who are responsible for the possession, installation, operation, and monitoring of electronic, mechanical, or other devices for the department.

**Sec. 6. Request for application for interception.** (a) The director may, based on written affidavits, request in writing that a prosecutor apply for an order authorizing interception of wire, oral, or electronic communications.

(b) The head of a local law enforcement agency or, if the head of the local law enforcement agency is absent or unable to serve, the acting head of the local law enforcement agency may, based on written affidavits, request in writing that a prosecutor apply for an order authorizing interception of wire, oral, or electronic communications. Prior to the requesting of an application under this subsection, the head of a local law enforcement agency must submit the request and supporting affidavits to the director, who shall make a finding in writing whether the request and supporting affidavits establish that other investigative procedures have been tried and failed or they reasonably appear unlikely to succeed or to be too dangerous if tried, is feasible, is justifiable, and whether the Department of Public Safety has the necessary resources available. The prosecutor may file the application only after a written positive finding on all the above requirements by the director.

**Sec. 7. Authorization for disclosure and use of intercepted communications.** (a) An investigative or law enforcement officer who, by any means authorized by this article, obtains knowledge of the contents of a wire, oral, or electronic communication or evidence derived from the communication may disclose the contents or evidence to another investigative or law enforcement officer to the extent that the disclosure is appropriate to the proper performance of the official duties of the officer making or receiving the disclosure.

(b) An investigative or law enforcement officer who, by any means authorized by this article, obtains knowledge of the contents of a wire, oral, or electronic communication or evidence derived from the communication may use the contents or evidence to the extent the use is appropriate to the proper performance of his official duties.

(c) A person who receives, by any means authorized by this article, information concerning a wire, oral, or electronic communication or evidence derived from a communication intercepted in accordance with the provisions of this article may disclose the contents of that communication or the derivative evidence while giving testimony under oath in any proceeding held under the authority of the United States, of this state, or of a political subdivision of this state.

(d) An otherwise privileged wire, oral, or electronic communication intercepted in accordance with, or in violation of, the provisions of this article does not lose its privileged character and any evidence derived from such privileged communication against the party to the privileged communication shall be considered privileged also.

(e) When an investigative or law enforcement officer, while engaged in intercepting wire, oral, or electronic communications in a manner authorized by this article, intercepts wire, oral, or electronic communications relating to offenses other than those specified in the order of authorization, the contents of and evidence derived from the communication may be disclosed or used as provided by Subsections (a) and (b) of this section. Such contents and any evidence derived therefrom may be used under Subsection (c) of this section when authorized by a judge of competent jurisdiction where the judge finds, on subsequent application, that the contents were otherwise intercepted in accordance with the provisions of this article. The application shall be made as soon as practicable.

**Sec. 8. Application for interception authorization.** (a) To be valid, an application for an order authorizing the interception of a wire, oral, or electronic communication must be made in writing under oath to a judge of competent jurisdiction and must state the applicant's authority to make the application. An applicant must include the following information in the application:

(1) the identity of the prosecutor making the application and of the officer requesting the application;

(2) a full and complete statement of the facts and circumstances relied on by the applicant to justify his belief that an order should be issued, including:

(A) details about the particular offense that has been, is being, or is about to be committed;

(B) a particular description of the nature and location of the facilities from which or the place where the communication is to be intercepted;

(C) a particular description of the type of communication sought to be intercepted; and

(D) the identity of the person, if known, committing the offense and whose communications are to be intercepted;

(3) a full and complete statement as to whether or not other investigative procedures have been tried and failed or why they reasonably appear to be unlikely to succeed or to be too dangerous if tried;

(4) a statement of the period of time for which the interception is required to be maintained and, if the nature of the investigation is such that the authorization for interception should not automatically terminate when the described type of communication is first obtained, a particular de-

scription of facts establishing probable cause to believe that additional communications of the same type will occur after the described type of communication is obtained;

(5) a statement whether a covert entry will be necessary to properly and safely install the wiretapping or electronic surveillance or eavesdropping equipment and, if a covert entry is requested, a statement as to why such an entry is necessary and proper under the facts of the particular investigation, including a full and complete statement as to whether other investigative techniques have been tried and have failed or why they reasonably appear to be unlikely to succeed or to be too dangerous if tried or are not feasible under the circumstances or exigencies of time;

(6) a full and complete statement of the facts concerning all applications known to the prosecutor making the application that have been previously made to a judge for authorization to intercept wire, oral, or electronic communications involving any of the persons, facilities, or places specified in the application and of the action taken by the judge on each application; and

(7) if the application is for the extension of an order, a statement setting forth the results already obtained from the interception or a reasonable explanation of the failure to obtain results.

(b) The judge may, in an ex parte hearing in chambers, require additional testimony or documentary evidence in support of the application, and such testimony or documentary evidence shall be preserved as part of the application.



**Sec. 9. Action on application for interception order.** (a) On receipt of an application, the judge may enter an ex parte order, as requested or as modified, authorizing interception of wire, oral, or electronic communications if the judge determines from the evidence submitted by the applicant that:

(1) there is probable cause to believe that a person is committing, has committed, or is about to commit a particular offense enumerated in Section 4 of this article;

(2) there is probable cause to believe that particular communications concerning that offense will be obtained through the interception;

(3) normal investigative procedures have been tried and have failed or reasonably appear to be unlikely to succeed or to be too dangerous if tried;

(4) there is probable cause to believe that the facilities from which or the place where the wire, oral, or electronic communications are to be intercepted are being used or are about to be used in connection with the commission of an offense or are leased to, listed in the name of, or commonly used by the person; and

(5) a covert entry is or is not necessary to properly and safely install the wiretapping or electronic surveillance or eavesdropping equipment.

(b) An order authorizing the interception of a wire, oral, or electronic communication must specify:

(1) the identity of the person, if known, whose communications are to be intercepted;

(2) the nature and location of the communications facilities as to which or the place where authority to intercept is granted;

(3) a particular description of the type of communication sought to be intercepted and a statement of the particular offense to which it relates;

(4) the identity of the officer making the request and the identity of the prosecutor;

(5) the time during which the interception is authorized, including a statement of whether or not the interception will automatically terminate when the described communication is first obtained; and

(6) whether or not a covert entry or surreptitious entry is necessary to properly and safely install wiretapping, electronic surveillance, or eavesdropping equipment.

(c) In an order authorizing the interception of a wire, oral, or electronic communication, the judge issuing it, on request of the applicant, shall direct that a provider of wire or electronic communications service, communication common carrier, landlord, custodian, or other person furnish the applicant all information, facilities, and technical assistance necessary to accomplish the interception unobtrusively and with a minimum of interference with the services that the provider, carrier, landlord, custodian, or other person is providing the person whose communications are to be intercepted. Any provider of wire or electronic communications service, communication common carrier, landlord, custodian, or other person furnishing facilities or technical assistance is entitled to compensation by the applicant for the facilities or assistance at the prevailing rates.

(d) An order entered pursuant to this section may not authorize the interception of a wire, oral, or electronic communication for longer than is necessary to achieve the objective of the authorization and in no event may it authorize interception for more than 30 days. The issuing judge may grant extensions of an order, but only on application for an extension made in accordance with Section 8 of this article and the court making the findings required by Subsection (a) of this section. The period of extension may not be longer than the authorizing judge deems necessary to achieve the purposes for which it is granted and in no event may the extension be for more than 30 days. To be valid, each order and extension of an order must provide that the authorization to intercept be executed as soon as practicable, be conducted in a way that minimizes the interception of communications not otherwise subject to interception under this article, and terminate on obtaining the authorized objective or within 30 days, whichever occurs sooner.

(e) An order entered pursuant to this section may not authorize a covert entry into a residence solely for the purpose of intercepting a wire or electronic communication.

(f) An order entered pursuant to this section may not authorize a covert entry into or onto a premises for the purpose of intercepting an oral communication unless:

(1) the judge, in addition to making the determinations required under Subsection (a) of this section, determines that:

(A)(i) the premises into or onto which the covert entry is authorized or the person whose communications are to be obtained has been the subject of a pen register previously authorized in connection with the same investigation;

(ii) the premises into or onto which the covert entry is authorized or the person whose communications are to be obtained has been the subject of an interception of wire or electronic communications previously authorized in connection with the same investigation; and

(iii) that such procedures have failed; or

(B) that the procedures enumerated in Paragraph (A) reasonably appear to be unlikely to succeed or to be too dangerous if tried or are not feasible under the circumstances or exigencies of time; and

(2) the order, in addition to the matters required to be specified under Subsection (b) of this section, specifies that the covert entry is for the purpose of intercepting oral communications of two or more persons and that there is probable cause to believe they are committing, have committed, or are about to commit a particular offense enumerated in Section 4 of this article.

(g) Whenever an order authorizing interception is entered pursuant to this article, the order may require reports to the judge who issued the order showing what progress has been made toward achievement of the authorized objective and the need for continued interception. Reports shall be made at any interval the judge requires.

(h) A judge who issues an order authorizing the interception of a wire, oral, or electronic communication may not hear a criminal prosecution in which evidence derived from the interception may be used or in which the order may be an issue.

**Sec. 10. Procedure for preserving intercepted communications.** (a) The contents of a wire, oral, or electronic communication intercepted by means authorized by this article shall be recorded on tape, wire, or other comparable device. The recording of the contents of a wire, oral, or electronic communication under this subsection shall be done in a way that protects the recording from editing or other alterations.

(b) Immediately on the expiration of the period of the order and all extensions, if any, the recordings shall be made available to the judge issuing the order and sealed under his directions. Custody of the recordings shall be wherever the judge orders. The recordings may not be destroyed until at least 10 years after the date of expiration of the order and the last extension, if any. A recording may be destroyed only by order of the judge of competent jurisdiction for the administrative judicial district in which the interception was authorized.

(c) Duplicate recordings may be made for use or disclosure pursuant to Subsections (a) and (b), Section 7, of this article for investigations.

(d) The presence of the seal required by Subsection (b) of this section or a satisfactory explanation of its absence is a prerequisite for the use or disclosure of the contents of a wire, oral, or electronic communication or evidence derived from the communication under Subsection (c), Section 7, of this article.

**Sec. 11. Sealing of orders and applications.** The judge shall seal each application made and order granted under this article. Custody of the applications and orders shall be wherever the judge directs. An application or order may be disclosed only on a showing of good cause before a judge of competent jurisdiction and may not be destroyed until at least 10 years after the date it is sealed. An application or order may be destroyed only by order of the judge of competent jurisdiction for the administrative judicial district in which it was made or granted.

**Sec. 12. Contempt.** A violation of Section 10 or 11 of this article may be punished as contempt of court.

**Sec. 13. Notice and disclosure of interception to a party.** (a) Within a reasonable time but not later than 90 days after the date an application for an order is denied or after the date an order or the last extension, if any, expires, the judge who granted or denied the application shall cause to be served on the persons named in the order or the application and any other parties to intercepted communications, if any, an inventory, which must include notice:

(1) of the entry of the order or the application;

(2) of the date of the entry and the period of authorized interception or the date of denial of the application; and

(3) that during the authorized period wire, oral, or electronic communications were or were not intercepted.

(b) The judge, on motion, may in his discretion make available to a person or his counsel for inspection any portion of an intercepted communication, application, or order that the judge determines, in the interest of justice, to disclose to that person.

(c) On an ex parte showing of good cause to the judge, the serving of the inventory required by this section may be postponed, but in no event may any evidence derived from an order under this article be disclosed in any trial, until after such inventory has been served.



**Sec. 14. Preconditions to use as evidence.** (a) The contents of an intercepted wire, oral, or electronic communication or evidence derived from the communication may not be received in evidence or otherwise disclosed in a trial, hearing, or other proceeding in a federal or state court unless each party, not later than the 10th day before the date of the trial, hearing, or other proceed ing, has been furnished with a copy of the court order and application under which the interception was authorized or approved. This 10-day period may be waived by the judge if he finds that it is not possible to furnish the party with the information 10 days before the trial, hearing, or proceeding and that the party will not be prejudiced by the delay in receiving the information.

(b) An aggrieved person charged with an offense in a trial, hearing, or proceeding in or before a court, department, officer, agency, regulatory body, or other authority of the United States or of this state or a political subdivision of this state may move to suppress the contents of an intercepted wire, oral, or electronic communication or evidence derived from the communication on the ground that:

(1) the communication was unlawfully intercepted;

(2) the order authorizing the interception is insufficient on its face; or

(3) the interception was not made in conformity with the order.

(c) A person identified by a party to an intercepted wire, oral, or electronic communication during the course of that communication may move to suppress the contents of the communication on the grounds provided in Subsection (b) of this section or on the ground that the harm to the person resulting from his identification in court exceeds the value to the prosecution of the disclosure of the contents.

(d) The motion to suppress must be made before the trial, hearing, or proceeding unless there was no opportunity to make the motion or the person was not aware of the grounds of the motion. The hearing on the motion shall be held in camera upon the written request of the aggrieved person. If the motion is granted, the contents of the intercepted wire, oral, or electronic communication and evidence derived from the communication shall be treated as having been obtained in violation of this article. The judge, on the filing of the motion by the aggrieved person, shall make available to the aggrieved person or his counsel for inspection any portion of the intercepted communication or evidence derived from the communication that the judge determines, in the interest of justice, to make available.

(e) Any judge of this state, upon hearing a pretrial motion regarding conversations intercepted by wire pursuant to this article, or who otherwise becomes informed that there exists on such intercepted wire, oral, or electronic communication identification of a specific individual who is not a party or suspect to the subject of interception:

(1) shall give notice and an opportunity to be heard on the matter of suppression of references to that person if identification is sufficient so as to give notice; or

(2) shall suppress references to that person if identification is sufficient to potentially cause embarrassment or harm which outweighs the probative value, if any, of the mention of such person, but insufficient to require the notice provided for in Subdivision (1), above.

**Sec. 15. Reports concerning intercepted wire, oral, or electronic communications.** (a) Within 30 days after the date an order or the last extension, if any, expires or after the denial of an order, the issuing or denying judge shall report to the Administrative Office of the United States Courts:

(1) the fact that an order or extension was applied for;

(2) the kind of order or extension applied for;

(3) the fact that the order or extension was granted as applied for, was modified, or was denied;

(4) the period of interceptions authorized by the order and the number and duration of any extensions of the order;

(5) the offense specified in the order or application or extension;

(6) the identity of the officer making the request and the prosecutor; and

(7) the nature of the facilities from which or the place where communications were to be intercepted.

(b) In January of each year each prosecutor shall report to the Administrative Office of the United States Courts the following information for the preceding calendar year:

(1) the information required by Subsection (a) of this section with respect to each application for an order or extension made;

(2) a general description of the interceptions made under each order or extension, including the approximate nature and frequency of incriminating communications intercepted, the approximate nature and frequency of other communications intercepted, the approximate number of persons whose communications were intercepted, and the approximate nature, amount, and cost of the manpower and other resources used in the interceptions;

(3) the number of arrests resulting from interceptions made under each order or extension and the offenses for which arrests were made;

(4) the number of trials resulting from interceptions;

(5) the number of motions to suppress made with respect to interceptions and the number granted or denied;

(6) the number of convictions resulting from interceptions, the offenses for which the convictions were obtained, and a general assessment of the importance of the interceptions; and

(7) the information required by Subdivisions (2) through (6) of this subsection with respect to orders or extensions obtained.

(c) Any judge or prosecutor required to file a report with the Administrative Office of the United States Courts shall forward a copy of such report to the director of the Department of Public Safety. On or before March 1 of each year, the director shall submit to the governor; lieutenant governor; speaker of the house of representatives; chairman, senate jurisprudence committee; and chairman, house of representatives criminal jurisprudence committee a report of all intercepts as defined herein conducted pursuant to this article and terminated during the preceding calendar year. Such report shall include:

(1) the reports of judges and prosecuting attorneys forwarded to the director as required in this section;

(2) the number of Department of Public Safety personnel authorized to possess, install, or operate electronic, mechanical, or other devices;

(3) the number of Department of Public Safety and other law enforcement personnel who participated or engaged in the seizure of intercepts pursuant to this article during the preceding calendar year; and

(4) the total cost to the Department of Public Safety of all activities and procedures relating to the seizure of intercepts during the preceding calendar year, including costs of equipment, manpower, and expenses incurred as compensation for use of facilities or technical assistance provided to the department.

**Sec. 16. Recovery of civil damages authorized.** (a) A person whose wire, oral, or electronic communication is intercepted, disclosed, or used in violation of this article, or in violation of Chapter 16, Penal Code, has a civil cause of action against any person who intercepts, discloses, or uses or solicits another person to intercept, disclose, or use the communication and is entitled to recover from the person:

(1) actual damages but not less than liquidated damages computed at a rate of $100 a day for each day of violation or $1,000, whichever is higher;

(2) punitive damages; and

(3) a reasonable attorney's fee and other litigation costs reasonably incurred.

(b) A good faith reliance on a court order or legislative authorization constitutes a complete defense to an action brought under this section.

(c) A person is subject to suit by the federal or state government in a court of competent jurisdiction for appropriate injunctive relief if the person engages in conduct that:

(1) constitutes an offense under Section 16.05, Penal Code, but is not for a tortious or illegal purpose or for the purpose of direct or indirect commercial advantage or private commercial gain; and

(2) involves a radio communication that is:

(A) transmitted on frequencies allocated under Subpart D of Part 74 of the rules of the Federal Communications Commission; and

(B) not scrambled or encrypted.

(d) A defendant is liable for a civil penalty of $500 if it is shown at the trial of the civil suit brought under Subsection (c) that the defendant:

(1) has been convicted of an offense under Section 16.05, Penal Code; or

(2) is found liable in a civil action brought under Subsection (a).

(e) Each violation of an injunction ordered under Subsection (c) is punishable by a fine of $500.

(f) The attorney general, or the county or district attorney of the county in which the conduct, as described by Subsection (c), is occurring, may file suit under Subsection (c) on behalf of the state.

*(Chgd. by L.1997, chap. 1051(3), eff. 9/1/97.)*



**Sec. 17. Nonapplicability.** This article does not apply to conduct described as an affirmative defense under Section 16.02(c), Penal Code. *(Chgd. by L.1997, chap. 1051(4), eff. 9/1/97.)*

**Sec. 18.** This article expires September 1, 2005, and shall not be in force on and after that date. *(Article 18.20 chgd. by L.1989, chap. 1166(1-15); L.1991, chap. 14(284(38), (57)); L.1993, chaps. 790(15), 900(1.06), eff. 9/1/93. Expires 9/1/2005.)*

## Art. 18.21. Pen registers and trap and trace devices; access to stored communications; mobile tracking devices.

**Sec. 1. Definitions.** In this article:

(1) "Aural transfer," "communication common carrier," "electronic communication," "electronic communications service," "electronic communications system," "electronic storage," "pen register," "readily accessible to the general public," "user," and "wire communication" have the meanings assigned by Article 18.20.

(2) "Authorized peace officer" means:

(A) a sheriff or a sheriff's deputy;

(B) a constable or deputy constable;

(C) a marshal or police officer of an incorporated city, town, or village;

(D) a ranger or officer commissioned by the Public Safety Commission or the director of the Department of Public Safety;

(E) an investigator of the district attorney's, criminal district attorney's, or county attorney's office;

(F) a law enforcement agent of the Alcoholic Beverage Commission;

(G) a law enforcement officer commissioned by the Parks and Wildlife Commission; or

(H) an enforcement officer employed by the Texas Department of Criminal Justice pursuant to Section 493.015, Government Code, as added by Chapter 321, Acts of the 74th Legislature, 1995.

(3) "Department" means the Department of Public Safety.

(4) "Remote computing service" means the provision to the public of computer storage or processing services by means of an electronic communications system.

(5) "Supervisory official" means:

(A) an investigative agent or an assistant investigative agent who is in charge of an investigation;

(B) an equivalent person at an investigating agency's headquarters or regional office; and

(C) the principal prosecuting attorney of the state or of a political subdivision of the state or the first assistant or chief assistant prosecuting attorney in the office of either.

(6) "Tracking device" means an electronic or mechanical device that permits only tracking the movement of a person or object.

(7) "Trap and trace device" means a device that records an incoming electronic or other impulse that identifies the originating number of an instrument or device from which a wire or electronic communication was transmitted. The term does not include a device or telecommunications network used in providing:

(A) a caller identification service authorized by the Public Utility Commission of Texas under Subchapter E, Chapter 55, Utilities Code;

(B) the services referenced in Section 55.102(b), Utilities Code; or

(C) a caller identification service provided by a commercial mobile radio service provider licensed by the Federal Communications Commission.

*(Chgd. by L.1997, chap. 1051(5); L.1999, chap. 62(18.20), eff. 9/1/99.)*

**Sec. 2. Application and order of pen registers or trap and trace devices.** (a) An authorized peace officer commissioned by the department may request an attorney for the state to file an application with a judge of the judicial district in which the proposed installation will be made for the installation and use of a pen register to obtain information material to the investigation of a criminal offense. A district or criminal district attorney may on his own motion file an application under this section. The district or criminal district attorney who is acting on his own motion must make the application personally and may not do so through an assistant or some other person acting on his behalf.

(b) An authorized peace officer may request an attorney for the state to file an application with a judge of the judicial district in which the proposed installation will be made for the installation and use of a trap and trace device to obtain information material to the investigation of a criminal offense. A district or criminal district attorney may on his own motion file an application under this section. The district or criminal district attorney who is acting on his own motion must make the application personally and may not do so through an assistant or some other person acting on his behalf.

(c) The application must be made in writing under oath and must include the name of the subscriber, the telephone number or numbers, and the location of the telephone instrument or instruments on which the pen register or trap and trace device will be utilized. The application must also state that the installation and utilization of the pen register or trap and trace device will be material to the investigation of a criminal offense.

(d) On presentation of the application, the judge may order the installation and utilization of the pen register by an authorized peace officer commissioned by the department, and, on request of the applicant, the judge shall direct in the order that a communications common carrier or a provider of electronic communications service furnish all information, facilities, and technical assistance necessary to facilitate the installation and utilization of the pen register by the department unobtrusively and with a minimum of interference to the services provided by the carrier. The carrier is entitled to compensation at the prevailing rates for the facilities and assistance provided to the department.

(e) On presentation of the application, the judge may order the installation and operation of the trap and trace device by the communications common carrier or other person on the appropriate line, and in that order the judge shall direct the communications common carrier or other person and any landlord or other custodian of equipment to furnish all information, facilities, and technical assistance necessary to install and operate the device unobtrusively and with a minimum of interference to the services provided by the communications common carrier, landlord, custodian, or other person. Unless otherwise ordered by the court, the results of the trap and trace device shall be furnished to the applicant, designated by the court, at reasonable intervals during regular business hours, for the duration of the order. The carrier is entitled to compensation at the prevailing rates for the facilities and assistance provided to the law enforcement agency.

(f) An order for the installation and utilization of a pen register or trap and trace device is valid for not more than 60 days after the date the device is installed or after 10 days after the date the order is entered, whichever occurs first, unless prior to the expiration of the order the attorney for the state applies for and obtains from the court an extension of the order. The period of extension may not exceed 60 days for each extension granted, except that with the consent of the subscriber or customer of the service on which the pen register or trap and trace device is utilized, the court may extend an order for a period not to exceed one year.

(g) The district court shall seal an application and order for the installation and utilization of a pen register or trap and trace device granted under this article. The contents of an application or order may not be disclosed except in the course of a judicial proceeding and an unauthorized disclosure is punishable as contempt of court.

*(Chgd. by L.1997, chap. 1051(6), eff. 9/1/97.)*

**Sec. 3. Emergency pen register and trap and trace device installation.** (a) An authorized peace officer, designated by the district or criminal district attorney of the county where the installation will be used, may install and use a pen register or trap and trace device if the peace officer reasonably believes that:

(1) an emergency requiring the installation of a pen register or trap and trace device before an order authorizing the installation and use can, with due diligence, be obtained, exists involving immediate danger of death or serious injury to any person; and

(2) there are grounds under this article on which an order could be entered to authorize the installation and use of a pen register or trap and trace device.

(b) If an authorized peace officer installs a pen register or trap and trace device under Subsection (a), the peace officer must obtain an order approving installation and use within 48 hours after the installation begins. If authorization is not obtained within 48 hours, the officer shall terminate use of the pen register or the trap and trace device on the expiration of the 48 hours or at the time the order is denied, whichever is earlier.

(c) The state may not use as evidence in a criminal proceeding any information gained through the use of a pen register or trap and trace device installed under this section if authorization for the pen register or trap and trace device is denied.
*(Chgd. by L.1997, chap. 1051(7), eff. 9/1/97.)*

**Sec. 4. Requirements for government access to stored communications.** (a) An authorized peace officer may require a provider of electronic communications service to disclose the contents of an electronic communication that has been in electronic storage for not longer than 180 days by obtaining a warrant.

(b) An authorized peace officer may require a provider of electronic communications service to disclose the contents of an electronic communication that has been in electronic storage for longer than 180 days:

(1) if notice is not being given to the subscriber or customer, by obtaining a warrant;

(2) if notice is being given to the subscriber or customer, by obtaining:

(A) an administrative subpoena authorized by statute;

(B) a grand jury subpoena; or

(C) a court order issued under Section 5 of this article; or

(3) as otherwise permitted by applicable federal law.

(c)(1) An authorized peace officer may require a provider of a remote computing service to disclose the contents of an electronic communication as described in Subdivision (2) of this subsection:

(A) if notice is not being given to the subscriber or customer, by obtaining a warrant issued under this code;

(B) if notice is being given to the subscriber or customer, by:

(i) an administrative subpoena authorized by statute;

(ii) a grand jury subpoena; or

(iii) a court order issued under Section 5 of this article; or

(C) as otherwise permitted by applicable federal law.

(2) Subdivision (1) of this subsection applies only to an electronic communication that is in electronic storage:

(A) on behalf of a subscriber or customer of the service and is received by means of electronic transmission from or created by means of computer processing of communications received by means of electronic transmission from the subscriber or customer; and

(B) solely for the purpose of providing storage or computer processing services to the subscriber or customer if the provider of the service is not authorized to obtain access to the contents of those communications for purposes of providing any service other than storage or computer processing.

(d) An authorized peace officer may require a provider of remote computing service to disclose records or other information pertaining to a subscriber or customer of the service, other than communications described in Subsection (c) of this section, without giving the subscriber or customer notice:

(1) by obtaining an administrative subpoena authorized by statute;

(2) by obtaining a grand jury subpoena;

(3) by obtaining a warrant;

(4) by obtaining the consent of the subscriber or customer to the disclosure of the records or information;

(5) by obtaining a court order under Section 5 of this article; or

(6) as otherwise permitted by applicable federal law.

(e) A provider of telephonic communications service shall disclose to an authorized peace officer, without any form of legal process, subscriber listing information, including name, address, and telephone number or similar access code that:

(1) the service provides to others in the course of providing publicly available directory or similar assistance; or

(2) is solely for use in the dispatch of emergency vehicles and personnel responding to a distress call directed to an emergency dispatch system or when the information is reasonably necessary to aid in the dispatching of emergency vehicles and personnel for the immediate prevention of death, personal injury, or destruction of property.

(f) A provider of telephonic communications service shall provide an authorized peace officer with the name of the subscriber of record whose published telephone number is provided to the service by an authorized peace officer.

**Sec. 5. Court order to obtain access to stored communications.** (a) A court shall issue an order authorizing disclosure of contents, records, or other information of a wire or electronic communication held in electronic storage if the court determines that there is reasonable belief that the information sought is relevant to a legitimate law enforcement inquiry.

(b) A court may grant a motion by the service provider to quash or modify the order issued under Subsection (a) of this section if the court determines that the information or records requested are unusually voluminous in nature or that compliance with the order would cause an undue burden on the provider.

**Sec. 6. Backup preservation.** (a) A subpoena or court order for disclosure of the contents of an electronic communication in a remote computing service under Section 4(c) of this article may require that the service provider to whom the request is directed create a copy of the contents of the electronic communications sought by the subpoena or court order for the purpose of preserving those contents. The service provider may not inform the subscriber or customer whose communications are being sought that the subpoena or court order has been issued. The service provider shall create the copy not later than two business days after the date of the receipt by the service provider of the subpoena or court order.

(b) The service provider shall immediately notify the authorized peace officer who presented the subpoena or court order requesting the copy when the copy has been created.

(c) Except as provided by Section 7 of this article, the authorized peace officer shall notify the subscriber or customer whose communications are the subject of the subpoena or court order of the creation of the copy not later than three days after the date of the receipt of the notification from the service provider that the copy was created.

(d) The service provider shall release the copy to the requesting authorized peace officer not earlier than the 14th day after the date of the peace officer's notice to the subscriber or customer if the service provider has not:

(1) initiated proceedings to challenge the request of the peace officer for the copy; or

(2) received notice from the subscriber or customer that the subscriber or customer has initiated proceedings to challenge the request.

(e) The service provider may not destroy or permit the destruction of the copy until the information has been delivered to the law enforcement agency or until the resolution of any court proceedings, including appeals of any proceedings, relating to the subpoena or court order requesting the creation of the copy, whichever occurs last.

(f) An authorized peace officer who reasonably believes that notification to the subscriber or customer of the subpoena or court order would result in the destruction of or tampering with information sought may request the creation of a copy of the information. The peace officer's belief is not subject to challenge by the subscriber or customer or service provider.

(g)(1) A subscriber or customer who receives notification as described in Subsection (c) of this section may file a written motion to quash the subpoena or vacate the court order in the court that issued the subpoena or court order not later than the 14th day after the date of the receipt of the notice. The motion must contain an affidavit or sworn statement stating that:

(A) the applicant is a subscriber or customer of the service from which the contents of electronic communications stored for the subscriber or customer have been sought; and

(B) the applicant's reasons for believing that the information sought is not relevant to a legitimate law enforcement inquiry or that there has not been substantial compliance with the provisions of this article in some other respect.

(2) The subscriber or customer shall give written notice to the service provider of the challenge to the subpoena or court order. The authorized peace officer or law enforcement agency requesting the subpoena or court order shall be served a copy of the papers filed by personal delivery or by registered or certified mail.

(h)(1) The court shall order the authorized peace officer to file a sworn response to the motion filed by the subscriber or customer if the court determines that the subscriber or customer has complied with the requirements of Subsection (g) of this section. On request of the peace officer, the court may permit the response to be filed in camera. The court may conduct any additional proceedings the court considers appropriate if the court is unable to make a determination on the motion on the basis of the parties' initial allegations and response.

(2) The court shall rule on the motion as soon after the filing of the officer's response as practicable. The court shall deny the motion if the court finds that the applicant is not the subscriber or

customer whose stored communications are the subject of the subpoena or court order or that there is reason to believe that the peace officer's inquiry is legitimate and that the communications sought are relevant to that inquiry. The court shall quash the subpoena or vacate the order if the court finds that the applicant is the subscriber or customer whose stored communications are the subject of the subpoena or court order and that there is not a reason to believe that the communications sought are relevant to a legitimate law enforcement inquiry or that there has not been substantial compliance with the provisions of this article.

(3) A court order denying a motion or application under this section is not a final order and no interlocutory appeal may be taken from the denial.

**Sec. 7. Delay of notification.** (a) An authorized peace officer seeking a court order to obtain information under Section 4(c) of this article may include a request for an order delaying the notification required under Section 4(c) of this article for a period not to exceed 90 days. The court shall grant the request if the court determines that there is reason to believe that notification of the existence of the court order may have an adverse result, as described in Subsection (c) of this section.

(b) An authorized peace officer who has obtained a subpoena authorized by statute or a grand jury subpoena to seek information under Section 4(c) of this article may delay the notification required under that section for a period not to exceed 90 days on the execution of a written certification of a supervisory official that there is reason to believe that notification of the existence of the subpoena may have an adverse result as described in Subsection (c) of this section. The peace officer shall maintain a true copy of the certification.

(c) In this section an "adverse result" means:

(1) endangering the life or physical safety of an individual;

(2) flight from prosecution;

(3) destruction of or tampering with evidence;

(4) intimidation of a potential witness; or

(5) otherwise seriously jeopardizing an investigation or unduly delaying a trial.

(d) A court may grant one or more extensions of the delay of notification provided by this section of up to 90 days on request or by certification by a supervisory official if the original requirements under Subsection (a) or (b) of this section are met for each extension.

(e) When the delay of notification under this section expires, the authorized peace officer shall serve, by personal delivery or registered or certified mail, the subscriber or customer a copy of the process or request together with notice that:

(1) states with reasonable specificity the nature of the law enforcement inquiry; and

(2) informs the subscriber or customer:

(A) that information stored for the subscriber or customer by the service provider named in the process or request was supplied to or requested by the peace officer and the date on which the information was supplied or requested;

(B) that notification to the subscriber or customer was delayed;

(C) of the name of the supervisory official who made the certification or the court that granted the request for the delay of notification; and

(D) of which provision of this article permitted the delay of notification.

**Sec. 8. Preclusion of notification.** When an authorized peace officer seeking information under Section 4 of this article is not required to give notice to the subscriber or customer or is delaying notification under Section 7 of this article, the peace officer may apply to the court for an order commanding the service provider to whom a warrant, subpoena, or court order is directed not to disclose to any other person the existence of the warrant, subpoena, or court order. The order is effective for the period the court considers appropriate. The court shall enter the order if the court determines that there is reason to believe that notification of the existence of the warrant, subpoena, or court order will have an adverse result as described in Section 7(c) of this article.

**Sec. 9. Reimbursement of costs.** (a) Except as provided by Subsection (c) of this section, an authorized peace officer who obtains information under this article shall reimburse the person assembling or providing the information for all costs that are reasonably necessary and that have been directly incurred in searching for, assembling, reproducing, or otherwise providing the information. These costs include costs arising from necessary disruption of normal operations of an electronic communications service or remote computing service in which the information may be stored.

(b) The authorized peace officer and the person providing the information may agree on the amount of reimbursement. If there is no agreement, the court that issued the order for production

Printed in the U.S.A. Zt

of the information shall determine the amount. If no court order was issued for production of the information, the court before which the criminal prosecution relating to the information would be brought shall determine the amount.

(c) Subsection (a) of this section does not apply to records or other information maintained by a communications common carrier that relate to telephone toll records or telephone listings obtained under Section 4(e) of this article unless the court determines that the amount of information required was unusually voluminous or that an undue burden was imposed on the provider.

**Sec. 10. No cause of action.** A subscriber or customer of a wire or electronic communications or remote computing service does not have a cause of action against a wire or electronic communications or remote computing service, its officers, employees, agents, or other specified persons for providing information, facilities, or assistance as required by a court order, warrant, subpoena, or certification under this article.

**Sec. 11. Disclosure of stored communications.** (a) Except as provided by Subsection (c) of this section, a provider of an electronic communications service may not knowingly divulge the contents of a communication that is in electronic storage.

(b) Except as provided by Subsection (c) of this section, a provider of remote computing service may not knowingly divulge the contents of any communication that is:

(1) in electronic storage;

(2) stored on behalf of a subscriber or customer of the service and is received by means of electronic transmission from or created by means of computer processing of communications received by means of electronic transmission from the subscriber or customer; and

(3) solely for the purpose of providing storage or computer processing services to the subscriber or customer if the provider of the service is not authorized to obtain access to the contents of those communications for purposes of providing any service other than storage or computer processing.

(c) A provider of an electronic communications or remote computing service may divulge the contents of an electronically stored communication:

(1) to an intended recipient of the communication or that person's agent;

(2) to the addressee or that person's agent;

(3) with the consent of the originator, to the addressee or the intended recipient of the communication, or the subscriber of a remote computing service;

(4) to a person whose facilities are used to transmit the communication to its destination or the person's employee or authorized representative;

(5) as may be necessary to provide the service or to protect the property or rights of the provider of the service;

(6) to a law enforcement agency if the contents were obtained inadvertently by the service provider and the contents appear to pertain to the commission of a crime; or

(7) as authorized under federal or other state law.

**Sec. 12. Cause of action.** (a) Except as provided by Section 10 of this article, a provider of electronic communications service or subscriber or customer of an electronic communications service aggrieved by a violation of this article has a civil cause of action if the conduct constituting the violation was committed knowingly or intentionally and is entitled to:

(1) injunctive relief;

(2) a reasonable attorney's fee and other litigation costs reasonably incurred; and

(3) the sum of the actual damages suffered and any profits made by the violator as a result of the violation or $1,000, whichever is more.

(b) The reliance in good faith on a court order, warrant, subpoena, or legislative authorization is a complete defense to any civil action brought under this article.

(c) A civil action under this section may be presented within two years after the date the claimant first discovered or had reasonable opportunity to discover the violation, and not afterward.

**Sec. 13. Exclusivity of remedies.** The remedies and sanctions described in this article are the exclusive judicial remedies and sanctions for a violation of this article other than a violation that infringes on a right of a party guaranteed by a state or federal constitution.

**Sec. 14. Mobile tracking devices.** (a) A district judge may issue an order for the installation within the judge's judicial district of one or more mobile tracking devices and for their use.

(b) The order may authorize the use of mobile tracking devices outside the judicial district but within the state if the device is installed within the district.

(c) A district judge may issue the order only on the application of an authorized peace officer. An application must be written and signed and sworn to or affirmed before the judge. The affidavit must:

(1) state the name, department, agency, and address of the applicant;

(2) identify the vehicle, container, or item to which, in which, or on which the mobile tracking device is to be attached or placed and state the name of the owner or possessor of that vehicle, container, or item;

(3) state the jurisdictional area in which the vehicle, container, or item is expected to be found; and

(4) state the facts and circumstances that provide the applicant with a reasonable suspicion that criminal activity has been, is, or will be in progress and that the use of a mobile tracking device is reasonably likely to yield information relevant to the investigation of that criminal activity.

(d) The judge that issued an order shall be notified in writing within 72 hours after the time the mobile tracking device has been activated in place on or within the vehicle, container, or item.

(e) An order authorizing the use of a mobile tracking device expires not later than the 90th day after the date that the device has been activated in place on or within the vehicle, container, or item. For good cause shown, the judge may grant an extension for an additional 90-day period.

(f) A mobile tracking device shall be removed as soon as is practicable after the authorization period expires. If removal is not practicable, monitoring of the device shall cease on expiration of the authorization order.

**Sec. 15. Subpoena authority.** The director of the department or the director's designee may issue an administrative subpoena to a communications common carrier or an electronic communications service to compel the production of the carrier's or service's business records that:

(1) disclose information about:

(A) the carrier's or service's customers; or

(B) users of the services offered by the carrier or service; and

(2) are material to a criminal investigation.

**Sec. 16. Limitation.** A governmental agency authorized to install and use a pen register under this article or other law must use reasonably available technology to only record and decode electronic or other impulses used to identify the numbers dialed or otherwise transmitted. *(Added by L.1997, chap. 1051(8), eff. 9/1/97.)*

*(Chgd. by L.1989, chap. 958(1); L.1993, chap. 659(2); L.1995, chaps. 170(1), 318(47), eff. 8/28/95, 9/1/95, respectively.)*

## AFTER COMMITMENT OR BAIL AND BEFORE THE TRIAL

## CHAPTER 19. ORGANIZATION OF THE GRAND JURY

Article

### Art. 19.01. Appointment of jury commissioners; selection without jury commission.† [*Appointment of jury commissioners; selection in lieu of commission.*]

(a) The district judge, at or during any term of court, shall appoint not less than three, nor more than five persons to perform the duties of jury commissioners, and shall cause the sheriff to notify them of their appointment, and when and where they are to appear. The district judge shall, in the order appointing such commissioners, designate whether such commissioners shall serve during the term at which selected or for the next succeeding term. Such commissioners shall receive as compensation for each day or part thereof they may serve the sum of Ten Dollars and they shall possess the following qualifications:

1. Be intelligent citizens of the county and able to read and write the English language;
2. Be qualified jurors in the county;
3. Have no suit in said court which requires intervention of a jury;
4. Be residents of different portions of the county; and
5. The same person shall not act as jury commissioner more than once in any 12-month period.

(b) In lieu of the selection of prospective jurors by means of a jury commission, the district judge may direct that 20 to 75 prospective grand jurors be selected and summoned, with return on summons, in the same manner as for the selection and summons of panels for the trial of civil cases in the district courts. The judge shall try the qualifications for and excuses from service as a grand juror and impanel the completed grand jury in the same manner as provided for grand jurors selected by a jury commission.
*(Chgd. by L.1991, chap. 67(1), eff. 9/1/91.)*

### Art. 19.02. Notified of appointment.

The judge shall cause the proper officer to notify such appointees of such appointment, and when and where they are to appear.

### Art. 19.03. Oath of commissioners.

When the appointees appear before the judge, he shall administer to them the following oath: "You do swear faithfully to discharge the duties required of you as jury commissioners; that you will not knowingly elect any man as juryman whom you believe to be unfit and not qualified; that you will not make known to any one the name of any juryman selected by you and reported to the court; that you will not, directly or indirectly, converse with anyone selected by you as a juryman concerning the merits of any case to be tried at the next term of this court, until after said cause may be tried or continued, or the jury discharged."

### Art. 19.04. Instructed.

The jury commissioners, after they have been organized and sworn, shall be instructed by the judge in their duties and shall then retire in charge of the sheriff to a suitable room to be secured by the sheriff for that purpose. The clerk shall furnish them the necessary stationery, the names of those appearing from the records of the court to be exempt or disqualified from serving on the jury at each term, and the last assessment roll of the county.

### Art. 19.05. Kept free from intrusion.† [*Freed from intrusion.*]

The jury commissioners shall be kept free from the intrusion of any person during their session, and shall not separate without leave of the court until they complete their duties.

### Art. 19.06. Shall select grand jurors.† [*Grand juror selection.*]

The jury commissioners shall select not less than 15 nor more than 20 persons from the citizens of the county to be summoned as grand jurors for the next term of court, or the term of court for which said commissioners were selected to serve, as directed in the order of the court selecting the commissioners. The commissioners shall, to the extent possible, select grand jurors who the commissioners determine represent a broad cross-section of the population of the county, considering the factors of race, sex, and age.



### Art. 19.07. Extension beyond term of period for which grand jurors shall sit.† [*Extension of grand jurors' service.*]

If prior to the expiration of the term for which the grand jury was impaneled, it is made to appear by a declaration of the foreman or of a majority of the grand jurors in open court, that the investigation by the grand jury of the matters before it cannot be concluded before the expiration of the term, the judge of the district court in which said grand jury was impaneled may, by the entry of an order on the minutes of said court, extend, from time to time, for the purpose of concluding the investigation of matters then before it, the period during which said grand jury shall sit, for not to exceed a total of ninety days after the expiration of the term for which it was impaneled, and all indictments pertaining thereto returned by the grand jury within said extended period shall be as valid as if returned before the expiration of the term. The extension of the term of a grand jury under this article does not affect the provisions of Article 19.06 relating to the selection and summoning of grand jurors for each regularly scheduled term.

### Art. 19.08. Qualifications.

No person shall be selected or serve as a grand juror who does not possess the following qualifications:

1. He must be a citizen of the state, and of the county in which he is to serve, and be qualified under the Constitution and laws to vote in said county, provided that his failure to register to vote shall not be held to disqualify him in this instance;
2. He must be of sound mind and good moral character;
3. He must be able to read and write;
4. He must not have been convicted of theft or of any felony;
5. He must not be under indictment or other legal accusation for theft or of any felony;
6. He must not be related within the third degree of consanguinity or second degree of affinity, as determined under Chapter 573, Government Code, to any person selected to serve or serving on the same grand jury;
7. He must not have served as grand juror or jury commissioner in the year before the date on which the term of court for which he has been selected as grand juror begins;
8. He must not be a complainant in any matter to be heard by the grand jury during the term of court for which he has been selected as a grand juror.

*(Chgd. by L.1989, chap. 1065(1); L.1991, chap. 561(8); L.1995, chap. 76(5.95)(27); L.1999, chap. 1177(1), eff. 9/1/99.)*

### Art. 19.09. Names returned.

The names of those selected as grand jurors by the commissioners shall be written upon a paper; and the fact that they were so selected shall be certified and signed by the jury commissioners, who shall place said paper, so certified and signed, in an envelope, and seal the same, and endorse thereon the words, "The list of grand jurors selected at ____________ term of the district court", the blank being for the month and year in which the term of the court began its session. The commissioners shall write their names across the seal of said envelope, direct the same to the district judge and deliver it to him in open court.

**Art. 19.10. List to clerk.**

The judge shall deliver the envelope containing the list of grand jurors to the clerk or one of his deputies in open court without opening the same.

**Art. 19.11. Oath to clerk.**

Before the list of grand jurors is delivered to the clerk, the judge shall administer to the clerk and each of his deputies in open court the following oath: "You do swear that you will not open the jury lists now delivered you, nor permit them to be opened until the time prescribed by law; that you will not, directly or indirectly, converse with any one selected as a juror concerning any case or proceeding which may come before such juror for trial in this court at its next term".

**Art. 19.12. Deputy clerk sworn.**

Should the clerk subsequently appoint a deputy, such clerk shall administer to him the same oath, at the time of such appointment.

**Art. 19.13. Clerk shall open lists.† [*Clerk opens lists.*]**

The grand jury may be convened on the first or any subsequent day of the term. The judge shall designate the date on which the grand jury is to be impaneled and notify the clerk of such date; and within thirty days of such date, and not before, the clerk shall open the envelope containing the list of grand jurors, make out a copy of the names of those selected as grand jurors, certify to it under his official seal, note thereon the day for which they are to be summoned, and deliver it to the sheriff.



**Art. 19.14. Summoning.**

The sheriff shall summon the persons named in the list at least three days, exclusive of the day of service, prior to the day on which the grand jury is to be impaneled, by giving personal notice to each juror of the time and place when and where he is to attend as a grand juror, or by leaving at his place of residence with a member of his family over sixteen years old, a written notice to such juror that he has been selected as a grand juror, and the time and place when and where he is to attend; or the judge, at his election, may direct the sheriff to summon the grand jurors by registered or certified mail. *(Chgd. by L.1993, chap. 268(5), eff. 9/1/93.)*

**Art. 19.15. Return of officer.**

The officer executing such summons shall return the list on the day on which the grand jury is to be impaneled, with a certificate thereon of the date and manner of service upon each juror. If any of said jurors have not been summoned, he shall also state in his certificate the reason why they have not been summoned.

**Art. 19.16. Absent juror fined.† [*Nonpresent juror fined.*]**

A juror legally summoned, failing to attend without a reasonable excuse, may, by order of the court entered on the record, be fined not less than ten dollars nor more than one hundred dollars.

**Art. 19.17. Failure to select.**

If for any reason a grand jury shall not be selected or summoned prior to the commencement of any term of court, or when none of those summoned shall attend, the district judge may at any time after the commencement of the term, in his discretion, direct a writ to be issued to the sheriff commanding him to summon a jury commission, selected by the court, which commission shall select twenty persons, as provided by law, who shall serve as grand jurors.

**Art. 19.18. If less than fourteen attend.**

When less than fourteen of those summoned to serve as grand jurors are found to be in attendance and qualified to so serve, the court shall order the sheriff to summon such additional number of persons as may be deemed necessary to constitute a grand jury of twelve persons and two alternates. *(Chgd. by L.1999, chap. 1065(1), eff. 9/1/99.)*

**Art. 19.19. Jurors to attend forthwith.† [*Jurors shall attend.*]**

The jurors provided for in the two preceding Articles shall be summoned in person to attend before the court forthwith.

**Art. 19.20. To summon qualified persons.† [*Summoning qualified candidates.*]**

Upon directing the sheriff to summon grand jurors not selected by the jury commissioners, the court shall instruct him that he must summon no person to serve as a grand juror who does not possess the qualifications prescribed by law.

**Art. 19.21. To test qualifications.**

When as many as fourteen persons summoned to serve as grand jurors are in attendance upon the court, it shall proceed to test their qualifications as such. *(Chgd. by L.1999, chap. 1065(2), eff. 9/1/99.)*

**Art. 19.22. Interrogated.**

Each person who is presented to serve as a grand juror shall, before being impaneled, be interrogated on oath by the court or under his direction, touching his qualifications.



**Art. 19.23. Mode of test.**

In trying the qualifications of any person to serve as a grand juror, he shall be asked:

1. Are you a citizen of this state and county, and qualified to vote in this county, under the Constitution and laws of this state?
2. Are you able to read and write?
3. Have you ever been convicted of a felony?
4. Are you under indictment or other legal accusation for theft or for any felony?

**Art. 19.24. Qualified juror accepted.**

When, by the answer of the person, it appears to the court that he is a qualified juror, he shall be accepted as such, unless it be shown that he is not of sound mind or of good moral character, or unless it be shown that he is in fact not qualified to serve as a grand juror.

**Art. 19.25. Excuses from service.**

Any person summoned who does not possess the requisite qualifications shall be excused by the court from serving. The following qualified persons may be excused from grand jury service:

(1) a person older than 70 years;

(2) a person responsible for the care of a child younger than 18 years;

(3) a student of a public or private secondary school;

(4) a person enrolled and in actual attendance at an institution of higher education; and

(5) any other person that the court determines has a reasonable excuse from service.

*(Chgd. by L.1999, chap. 1177(2), eff. 9/1/99.)*

**Art. 19.26. Jury impaneled.**

(a) When fourteen qualified jurors are found to be present, the court shall proceed to impanel the grand jury, unless a challenge is made, which may be to the array or to any particular person presented to serve as a grand juror or an alternate.

(b) The grand jury is composed of not more than twelve qualified jurors. In addition, the court shall qualify and impanel not more than two alternates to serve on disqualification of a juror during the term of the grand jury. On learning that a grand juror has become disqualified during the term of the grand jury, the attorney representing the state shall prepare an order for the court identifying the disqualified juror, stating the basis for the disqualification, dismissing the disqualified juror from the grand jury, and naming one of the alternates as a member of the grand jury. The procedure established by this subsection may be used on disqualification of a second grand juror during the term of the grand jury.

*(Chgd. by L.1999, chap. 1065(3), eff. 9/1/99.)*

**Art. 19.27. Any person may challenge.† [*Anyone may challenge.*]**

Before the grand jury has been impaneled, any person may challenge the array of jurors or any person presented as a grand juror. In no other way shall objections to the qualifications and legality of the grand jury be heard. Any person confined in jail in the county shall upon his request be brought into court to make such challenge.

**Art. 19.28. "Array".**

By the "array" of grand jurors is meant the whole body of persons summoned to serve as such before they have been impaneled.

**Art. 19.29. "Impaneled" and "panel".**

A grand juror is said to be "impaneled" after his qualifications have been tried and he has been sworn. By "panel" is meant the whole body of grand jurors.

**Art. 19.30. Challenge to "array".**

A challenge to the "array" shall be made in writing for these causes only:

(1) That those summoned as grand jurors are not in fact those selected by the method provided by Article 19.01(b) of this chapter or by the jury commissioners; and

(2) In case the grand jurors summoned by order of the court, that the officer who summoned them had acted corruptly in summoning any one or more of them.

**Art. 19.31. Challenge to juror.**

A challenge to a particular grand juror may be made orally for the following causes only:

1. That he is not a qualified juror; and
2. That he is the prosecutor upon an accusation against the person making the challenge.

**Art. 19.32. Summarily decided.† [*Summary decision.*]**

When a challenge to the array or to any individual has been made, the court shall hear proof and decide in a summary manner whether the challenge be well-founded or not.

**Art. 19.33. Other jurors summoned.† [*Other jurors called.*]**

The court shall order another grand jury to be summoned if the challenge to the array be sustained, or order the panel to be completed if by challenge to any particular grand juror their number be reduced below twelve.

**Art. 19.34. Oath of grand jurors.**

When the grand jury is completed, the court shall appoint one of the number foreman; and the following oath shall be administered by the court, or under its direction, to the jurors: "You solemnly swear that you will diligently inquire into, and true presentment make, of all such matters and things as shall be given you in charge; the State's counsel, your fellows and your own, you shall keep secret, unless required to disclose the same in the course of a judicial proceeding in which the truth or falsity of evidence given in the grand jury room, in a criminal case, shall be under investigation. You shall present no person from envy, hatred or malice; neither shall you leave any person unpresented for love, fear, favor, affection or hope of reward; but you shall present things truly as they come to your knowledge, according to the best of your understanding, so help you God".

**Art. 19.35. To instruct jury.**

The court shall instruct the grand jury as to their duty.

**Art. 19.36. Bailiffs appointed.**

The court and the district attorney may each appoint one or more bailiffs to attend upon the grand jury, and at the time of appointment, the following oath shall be administered to each of them by the court, or under its direction: "You solemnly swear that you will faithfully and impartially perform all the duties of bailiff of the grand jury, and that you will keep secret the proceedings of the grand jury, so help you God". Such bailiffs shall be compensated in a sum to be set by the commissioner's court of said county.

**Art. 19.37. Bailiff's duties.**

A bailiff is to obey the instructions of the foreman, to summon all witnesses, and generally, to perform all such duties as the foreman may require of him. One bailiff shall be always with the grand jury, if two or more are appointed.

**Art. 19.38. Bailiff violating duty.† [*Bailiff in violation of duty.*]**

No bailiff shall take part in the discussions or deliberations of the grand jury nor be present when they are discussing or voting upon a question. The grand jury shall report to the court any violation of duty by a bailiff and the court may punish him for such violation as for contempt.

**Art. 19.39. Another foreman appointed.† [*Appointing another foreman.*]**

If the foreman of the grand jury is from any cause absent or unable or disqualified to act, the court shall appoint in his place some other member of the body.

Printed in the U.S.A. Zt

### Art. 19.40. Quorum.

Nine members shall be a quorum for the purpose of discharging any duty or exercising any right properly belonging to the grand jury.

### Art. 19.41. Reassembled.

A grand jury discharged by the court for the term may be reassembled by the court at any time during the term. *(Chgd. by L.1999, chap. 1065(4), eff. 9/1/99.)*

### Art. 19.42. Personal information about grand jurors.

(a) Except as provided by Subsection (b), information collected by the court, court personnel, or prosecuting attorney during the grand jury selection process about a person who serves as a grand juror, including the person's home address, home telephone number, social security number, driver's license number, and other personal information, is confidential and may not be disclosed by the court, court personnel, or prosecuting attorney.

(b) On a showing of good cause, the court shall permit disclosure of the information sought to a party to the proceeding.
*(Added by L.1999, chap. 1177(3), eff. 9/1/99.)*



## CHAPTER 20. DUTIES AND POWERS OF THE GRAND JURY

Article


### Art. 20.01. Grand jury room.

After the grand jury is organized they shall proceed to the discharge of their duties in a suitable place which the sheriff shall prepare for their sessions.

### Art. 20.011. Who may be present in grand jury room.

(a) Only the following persons may be present in a grand jury room while the grand jury is conducting proceedings;

(1) grand jurors;

(2) bailiffs;

(3) the attorney representing the state;

(4) witnesses while being examined or when necessary to assist the attorney representing the state in examining other witnesses or presenting evidence to the grand jury;

(5) interpreters, if necessary; and

(6) a stenographer or person operating an electronic recording device, as provided by Article 20.012.

(b) Only a grand juror may be in a grand jury room while the grand jury is deliberating.
*(Added by L.1995, chap. 1011(1), eff. 9/1/95.)*

## Art. 20.012. Recording of certain testimony.

(a) Questions propounded by the grand jury or the attorney representing the state to a person accused or suspected and the testimony of that person to the grand jury shall be recorded either by a stenographer or by use of an electronic device capable of recording sound.

(b) The validity of a grand jury proceeding is not affected by an unintentional failure to record all or part of questions propounded or testimony made under Subsection (a).

(c) The attorney representing the state shall maintain possession of all records other than stenographer's notes made under this article and any typewritten transcription of those records, except as provided by Article 20.02.

*(Added by L.1995, chap. 1011(1), eff. 9/1/95.)*

## Art. 20.02. Proceedings secret.

(a) The proceedings of the grand jury shall be secret.

(b) A grand juror, bailiff, interpreter, stenographer or person operating an electronic recording device, or person preparing a typewritten transcription of a stenographic or electronic recording who discloses anything transpiring before the grand jury, regardless of whether the thing transpiring is recorded, in the course of the official duties of the grand jury shall be liable to a fine as for contempt of the court, not exceeding five hundred dollars, imprisonment not exceeding thirty days, or both such fine and imprisonment.

(c) A disclosure of a record made under Article 20.012, a disclosure of a typewritten transcription of that record, or a disclosure otherwise prohibited by Subsection (b) or Article 20.16 may be made by the attorney representing the state in performing the attorney's duties to a grand juror serving on the grand jury before whom the record was made, another grand jury, a law enforcement agency, or a prosecuting attorney, as permitted by the attorney representing the state and determined by the attorney as necessary to assist the attorney in the performance of the attorney's duties. The attorney representing the state shall warn any person the attorney authorizes to receive information under this subsection of the person's duty to maintain the secrecy of the information. Any person who receives information under this subsection and discloses the information for purposes other than those permitted by this subsection is subject to punishment for contempt in the same manner as persons who violate Subsection (b).

(d) The defendant may petition a court to order the disclosure of information otherwise made secret by this article or the disclosure of a recording or typewritten transcription under Article 20.012 as a matter preliminary to or in connection with a judicial proceeding. The court may order disclosure of the information, recording, or transcription on a showing by the defendant of a particularized need.

(e) A petition for disclosure under Subsection (d) must be filed in the district court in which the case is pending. The defendant must also file a copy of the petition with the attorney representing the state, the parties to the judicial proceeding, and any other persons required by the court to receive a copy of the petition. All persons receiving a petition under this subsection are entitled to appear before the court. The court shall provide interested parties with an opportunity to appear and present arguments for the continuation of or end to the requirement of secrecy.

(f) A person who receives information under Subsection (d) or (e) and discloses that information is subject to punishment for contempt in the same manner as a person who violates Subsection (b).

(g) The attorney representing the state may not disclose anything transpiring before the grand jury except as permitted by Subsections (c), (d), and (e).

*(Chgd. by L.1995, chap. 1011(2), eff. 9/1/95.)*

## Art. 20.03. Attorney representing State entitled to appear.

"The attorney representing the State" means the Attorney General, district attorney, criminal district attorney, or county attorney. The attorney representing the State, is entitled to go before the grand jury and inform them of offenses liable to indictment at any time except when they are discussing the propriety of finding an indictment or voting upon the same.

## Art. 20.04. Attorney may examine witnesses.

The attorney representing the State may examine the witnesses before the grand jury and shall advise as to proper mode of interrogating them. No person other than the attorney representing the State or a grand juror may question a witness before the grand jury. No person may address the grand jury about a matter before the grand jury other than the attorney representing the State, a witness, or the accused or suspected person or the attorney for the accused or suspected person if approved by the State's attorney. *(Chgd. by L.1989, chap. 1065(2), eff. 9/1/89.)*

### Art. 20.05. May send for attorney.

The grand jury may send for the attorney representing the state and ask his advice upon any matter of law or upon any question arising respecting the proper discharge of their duties. *(Chgd. by L.1989, chap. 1065(3), eff. 9/1/89.)*

### Art. 20.06. Advice from court.

The grand jury may also seek and receive advice from the court touching any matter before them, and for this purpose, shall go into the court in a body; but they shall so guard the manner of propounding their questions as not to divulge the particular accusation that is pending before them; or they may propound their questions in writing, upon which the court may give them the desired information in writing.

### Art. 20.07. Foreman shall preside.† [*Foreman presides.*]

The foreman shall preside over the sessions of the grand jury, and conduct its business and proceedings in an orderly manner. He may appoint one or more members of the body to act as clerks for the grand jury.

### Art. 20.08. Adjournments.

The grand jury shall meet and adjourn at times agreed upon by a majority of the body; but they shall not adjourn, at any one time, for more than three days, unless by consent of the court. With the consent of the court, they may adjourn for a longer time, and shall as near as may be, conform their adjournments to those of the court.

### Art. 20.09. Duties of grand jury.

The grand jury shall inquire into all offenses liable to indictment of which any member may have knowledge, or of which they shall be informed by the attorney representing the State, or any other credible person.

### Art. 20.10. Attorney or foreman may issue process.

The attorney representing the state, or the foreman, in term time or vacation, may issue a summons or attachment for any witness in the county where they are sitting; which summons or attachment may require the witness to appear before them at a time fixed, or forthwith, without stating the matter under investigation.

### Art. 20.11. Out-of-county witnesses.

**Sec. 1.** The foreman or the attorney representing the State may, upon written application to the district court stating the name and residence of the witness and that his testimony is believed to be material, cause a subpoena or an attachment to be issued to any county in the State for such witness, returnable to the grand jury then in session, or to the next grand jury for the county from whence the same issued, as such foreman or attorney may desire. The subpoena may require the witness to appear and produce records and documents. An attachment shall command the sheriff or any constable of the county where the witness resides to serve the witness, and have him before the grand jury at the time and place specified in the writ.

**Sec. 2.** A subpoena or attachment issued pursuant to this article shall be served and returned in the manner prescribed in Chapter 24 of this code.

A witness subpoenaed pursuant to this article shall be compensated as provided in this code.

### Art. 20.12. Attachment in vacation.

The attorney representing the state may cause an attachment for a witness to be issued, as provided in the preceding Article, either in term time or in vacation.

### Art. 20.13. Execution of process.† [*Process execution.*]

The bailiff or other officer who receives process to be served from a grand jury shall forthwith execute the same and return it to the foreman, if the grand jury be in session; and if the grand jury be not in session, the process shall be returned to the district clerk. If the process is returned not executed, the return shall state why it was not executed.

### Art. 20.14. Evasion of process.† [*Process evasion.*]

If it be made to appear satisfactorily to the court that a witness for whom an attachment has been issued to go before the grand jury is in any manner wilfully evading the service of such summons or attachment, the court may fine such witness, as for contempt, not exceeding five hundred dollars.

**Art. 20.15. When witness refuses to testify.† [*When witness won't testify.*]**

When a witness, brought in any manner before a grand jury, refuses to testify, such fact shall be made known to the attorney representing the State or to the court; and the court may compel the witness to answer the question, if it appears to be a proper one, by imposing a fine not exceeding five hundred dollars, and by committing the party to jail until he is willing to testify.

**Art. 20.16. Oaths to witnesses.**

The following oath shall be administered by the foreman, or under his direction, to each witness before being interrogated: "You solemnly swear that you will not divulge, either by words or signs, any matter about which you may be interrogated, and that you will keep secret all proceedings of the grand jury which may be had in your presence, and that you will true answers make to such questions as may be propounded to you by the grand jury, or under its direction, so help you God." Any witness who divulges any matter about which he is interrogated, or any proceedings of the grand jury had in his presence, other than when required to give evidence thereof in due course, shall be liable to a fine as for contempt of court, not exceeding $500, and to imprisonment not exceeding six months.

**Art. 20.17. How suspect or accused questioned.**

(a) The grand jury, in propounding questions to the person accused or suspected, shall first state the offense with which he is suspected or accused, the county where the offense is said to have been committed and as nearly as may be, the time of commission of the offense, and shall direct the examination to the offense under investigation.

(b) Prior to any questioning of an accused or suspected person who is subpoenaed to appear before the grand jury, the accused or suspected person shall be furnished a written copy of the warnings contained in Subsection (c) of this section and shall be given a reasonable opportunity to retain counsel or apply to the court for an appointed attorney and to consult with counsel prior to appearing before the grand jury.

(c) If an accused or suspected person is subpoenaed to appear before a grand jury prior to any questions before the grand jury, the person accused or suspected shall be orally warned as follows:

(1) "Your testimony before this grand jury is under oath";

(2) "Any material question that is answered falsely before this grand jury subjects you to being prosecuted for aggravated perjury";

(3) "You have the right to refuse to make answers to any question, the answer to which would incriminate you in any manner";

(4) "You have the right to have a lawyer present outside this chamber to advise you before making answers to questions you feel might incriminate you";

(5) "Any testimony you give may be used against you at any subsequent proceeding";

(6) "If you are unable to employ a lawyer, you have the right to have a lawyer appointed to advise you before making an answer to a question, the answer to which you feel might incriminate you."

*(Chgd. by L.1989, chap. 1065(4), eff. 9/1/89.)*

**Art. 20.18. How witness questioned.**

When a felony has been committed in any county within the jurisdiction of the grand jury, and the name of the offender is known or unknown or where it is uncertain when or how the felony was committed, the grand jury shall first state to the witness called the subject matter under investigation, then may ask pertinent questions relative to the transaction in general terms and in such a manner as to determine whether he has knowledge of the violation of any particular law by any person, and if so, by what person.

**Art. 20.19. Grand jury shall vote.† [*Grand jury votes.*]**

After all the testimony which is accessible to the grand jury shall have been given in respect to any criminal accusation, the vote shall be taken as to the presentment of an indictment, and if nine members concur in finding the bill, the foreman shall make a memorandum of the same with such data as will enable the attorney who represents the State to write the indictment.

**Art. 20.20. Indictment prepared.**

The attorney representing the State shall prepare all indictments which have been found, with as little delay as possible, and deliver them to the foreman, who shall sign the same officially, and

Printed in the U.S.A. Zt

said attorney shall endorse thereon the names of the witnesses upon whose testimony the same was found.

### Art. 20.21. Indictment presented.

When the indictment is ready to be presented, the grand jury shall through their foreman, deliver the indictment to the judge or clerk of the court. At least nine members of the grand jury must be present on such occasion.

### Art. 20.22. Presentment entered of record.

The fact of a presentment of indictment by a grand jury shall be entered upon the minutes of the court, if the defendant is in custody or under bond, noting briefly the style of the criminal action and the file number of the indictment and the defendant's name. If the defendant is not in custody or under bond at the time of the presentment of indictment, the entry in the minutes of the court relating to said indictment shall be delayed until such time as the capias is served and the defendant is placed in custody or under bond. *(Chgd. by L.1999, chap. 580(3), eff. 9/1/99.)*



## CHAPTER 21. INDICTMENT AND INFORMATION

Article



### Art. 21.01. "Indictment".

An "indictment" is the written statement of a grand jury accusing a person therein named of some act or omission which, by law, is declared to be an offense.

### Art. 21.02. Requisites of an indictment.

An indictment shall be deemed sufficient if it has the following requisites:

1. It shall commence, "In the name and by authority of The State of Texas".

2. It must appear that the same was presented in the district court of the county where the grand jury is in session.

3. It must appear to be the act of a grand jury of the proper county.

4. It must contain the name of the accused, or state that his name is unknown and give a reasonably accurate description of him.

5. It must show that the place where the offense was committed is within the jurisdiction of the court in which the indictment is presented.

6. The time mentioned must be some date anterior to the presentment of the indictment, and not so remote that the prosecution of the offense is barred by limitation.

7. The offense must be set forth in plain and intelligible words.

8. The indictment must conclude, "against the peace and dignity of the State".

9. It shall be signed officially by the foreman of the grand jury.

### Art. 21.03. What should be stated.

Everything should be stated in an indictment which is necessary to be proved.

### Art. 21.04. The certainty required.

The certainty required in an indictment is such as will enable the accused to plead the judgment that may be given upon it in bar of any prosecution for the same offense.

### Art. 21.05. Particular intent; intent to defraud.

Where a particular intent is a material fact in the description of the offense, it must be stated in the indictment; but in any case where an intent to defraud is required to constitute an offense, it shall be sufficient to allege an intent to defraud, without naming therein the particular person intended to be defrauded.

### Art. 21.06. Allegation of venue.

When the offense may be prosecuted in either of two or more counties, the indictment may allege the offense to have been committed in the county where the same is prosecuted, or in any county or place where the offense was actually committed.

### Art. 21.07. Allegation of name.

In alleging the name of the defendant, or of any other person necessary to be stated in the indictment, it shall be sufficient to state one or more of the initials of the given name and the surname. When a person is known by two or more names, it shall be sufficient to state either name. When the name of the person is unknown to the grand jury, that fact shall be stated, and if it be the accused, a reasonably accurate description of him shall be given in the indictment. *(Chgd. by L.1995, chap. 830(1), eff. 9/1/95.)*

### Art. 21.08. Allegation of ownership.

Where one person owns the property, and another person has the possession of the same, the ownership thereof may be alleged to be in either. Where property is owned in common, or jointly, by two or more persons, the ownership may be alleged to be in all or either of them. When the property belongs to the estate of a deceased person, the ownership may be alleged to be in the executor, administrator or heirs of such deceased person, or in any one of such heirs. Where the ownership of the property is unknown to the grand jury, it shall be sufficient to allege that fact.

### Art. 21.09. Description of property.

If known, personal property alleged in an indictment shall be identified by name, kind, number, and ownership. When such is unknown, that fact shall be stated, and a general classification, describing and identifying the property as near as may be, shall suffice. If the property be real estate, its general locality in the county, and the name of the owner, occupant or claimant thereof, shall be a sufficient description of the same.

### Art. 21.10. "Felonious" and "feloniously".

It is not necessary to use the words "felonious" or "feloniously" in any indictment.

### Art. 21.11. Certainty; what sufficient.

An indictment shall be deemed sufficient which charges the commission of the offense in ordinary and concise language in such a manner as to enable a person of common understanding to know what is meant, and with that degree of certainty that will give the defendant notice of the particular offense with which he is charged, and enable the court, on conviction, to pronounce the proper judgment; and in no case are the words "force and arms" or "contrary to the form of the statute" necessary.

### Art. 21.12. Special and general terms.

When a statute defining any offense uses special or particular terms, indictment on it may use the general term which, in common language, embraces the special term. To charge an unlawful sale, it is necessary to name the purchaser.

### Art. 21.13. Act with intent to commit an offense.

An indictment for an act done with intent to commit some other offense may charge in general terms the commission of such act with intent to commit such other offense.

### Art. 21.14. Perjury and aggravated perjury.

(a) An indictment for perjury or aggravated perjury need not charge the precise language of the false statement, but may state the substance of the same, and no such indictment shall be held insufficient on account of any variance which does not affect the subject matter or general import of such false statement; and it is not necessary in such indictment to set forth the pleadings, records or proceeding with which the false statement is connected, nor the commission or authority of the court or person before whom the false statement was made; but it is sufficient to state the name of the court or public servant by whom the oath was administered with the allegation of the falsity of the matter on which the perjury or aggravated perjury is assigned.

(b) If an individual is charged with aggravated perjury before a grand jury, the indictment may not be entered by the grand jury before which the false statement was alleged to have been made.

*(Chgd. by L.1989, chap. 1065(5), eff. 9/1/89.)*



### Art. 21.15. Must allege acts of recklessness or criminal negligence.† [*Must allege recklessness or criminal negligence.*]

Whenever recklessness or criminal negligence enters into or is a part or element of any offense, or it is charged that the accused acted recklessly or with criminal negligence in the commission of an offense, the complaint, information, or indictment in order to be sufficient in any such case must allege, with reasonable certainty, the act or acts relied upon to constitute recklessness or criminal negligence, and in no event shall it be sufficient to allege merely that the accused, in committing the offense, acted recklessly or with criminal negligence.

### Art. 21.16. Certain forms of indictments.

The following form of indictments is sufficient: "In the name and by authority of the State of Texas: The grand jury of ______________ County, State of Texas, duly organized at the ______________ term, A.D. ______________, of the district court of said county, in said court at said term, do present that ______________ (defendant) on the ______________ day of ______________ A.D. ______________, in said county and State, did ______________ (description of offense) against the peace and dignity of the State.

______________, Foreman of the grand jury."

### Art. 21.17. Following statutory words.

Words used in a statute to define an offense need not be strictly pursued in the indictment; it is sufficient to use other words conveying the same meaning, or which include the sense of the statutory words.

### Art. 21.18. Matters of judicial notice.

Presumptions of law and matters of which judicial notice is taken (among which are included the authority and duties of all officers elected or appointed under the General Laws of this State) need not be stated in an indictment.

### Art. 21.19. Defects of form.

An indictment shall not be held insufficient, nor shall the trial, judgment or other proceedings thereon be affected, by reason of any defect of form which does not prejudice the substantial rights of the defendant.

### Art. 21.20. "Information".

An "information" is a written statement filed and presented in behalf of the State by the district or county attorney, charging the defendant with an offense which may by law be so prosecuted.

### Art. 21.21. Requisites for an information.† [*Requirements of an information.*]

An information is sufficient if it has the following requisites:

1. It shall commence, "In the name and by authority of the State of Texas";
2. That it appear to have been presented in a court having jurisdiction of the offense set forth;
3. That it appear to have been presented by the proper officer;
4. That it contain the name of the accused, or state that his name is unknown and give a reasonably accurate description of him;
5. It must appear that the place where the offense is charged to have been committed is within the jurisdiction of the court where the information is filed;
6. That the time mentioned be some date anterior to the filing of the information, and that the offense does not appear to be barred by limitation;
7. That the offense be set forth in plain and intelligible words;
8. That it conclude, "Against the peace and dignity of the State"; and
9. It must be signed by the district or county attorney, officially.

### Art. 21.22. Information based upon complaint.

No information shall be presented until affidavit has been made by some credible person charging the defendant with an offense. The affidavit shall be filed with the information. It may be sworn to before the district or county attorney who, for that purpose, shall have power to administer the oath, or it may be made before any officer authorized by law to administer oaths.



### Art. 21.23. Rules as to indictment apply to information.

The rules with respect to allegations in an indictment and the certainty required apply also to an information.

### Art. 21.24. Joinder of certain offenses.

(a) Two or more offenses may be joined in a single indictment, information, or complaint, with each offense stated in a separate count, if the offenses arise out of the same criminal episode, as defined in Chapter 3 of the Penal Code.

(b) A count may contain as many separate paragraphs charging the same offense as necessary, but no paragraph may charge more than one offense.

(c) A count is sufficient if any one of its paragraphs is sufficient. An indictment, information, or complaint is sufficient if any one of its counts is sufficient.

### Art. 21.25. When indictment has been lost, etc.

When an indictment or information has been lost, mislaid, mutilated or obliterated, the district or county attorney may suggest the fact to the court; and the same shall be entered upon the minutes of the court. In such case, another indictment or information may be substituted, upon the written statement of such attorney that it is substantially the same as that which has been lost, mislaid, mutilated, or obliterated. Or another indictment may be presented, as in the first instance; and in such case, the period for the commencement of the prosecution shall be dated from the time of making such entry.

### Art. 21.26. Order transferring cases.

Upon the filing of an indictment in the district court which charges an offense over which such court has no jurisdiction, the judge of such court shall make an order transferring the same to such inferior court as may have jurisdiction, stating in such order the cause transferred and to what court transferred.

### Art. 21.27. Causes transferred to justice court.† [*Causes sent to justice court.*]

Causes over which justices of the peace have jurisdiction may be transferred to a justice of the peace at the county seat, or in the discretion of the judge, to a justice of the precinct in which the same can be most conveniently tried, as may appear by memorandum endorsed by the grand jury on the indictment or otherwise. If it appears to the judge that the offense has been committed in any incorporated town or city, the cause shall be transferred to a justice in said town or city, if there be one therein; and any justice to whom such cause may be transferred shall have jurisdiction to try the same.

### Art. 21.28. Duty on transfer.

The clerk of the court, without delay, shall deliver the indictments in all cases transferred, together with all the papers relating to each case, to the proper court or justice, as directed in the order of transfer; and shall accompany each case with a certified copy of all the proceedings taken therein in the district court, and with a bill of the costs that have accrued therein in the district court. The said costs shall be taxed in the court in which said cause is tried, in the event of a conviction.

### Art. 21.29. Proceedings of inferior court.

Any case so transferred shall be entered on the docket of the court to which it is transferred. All process thereon shall be issued and the defendant tried as if the case had originated in the court to which it was transferred.

### Art. 21.30. Cause improvidently transferred.

When a cause has been improvidently transferred to a court which has no jurisdiction of the same, the court to which it has been transferred shall order it to be re-transferred to the proper court; and the same proceedings shall be had as in the case of the original transfer. In such case, the defendant and the witnesses shall be held bound to appear before the court to which the case has been re-transferred, the same as they were bound to appear before the court so transferring the same.

Printed in the U.S.A. Zt

### Art. 21.31. AIDS testing.

(a) A person who is indicted for or who waives indictment for an offense under Section 21.11(a)(1), 22.011, or 22.021, Penal Code, shall, at the direction of the court, undergo a medical procedure or test designed to show or help show whether the person has a sexually transmitted disease or has acquired immune deficiency syndrome (AIDS) or human immunodeficiency virus (HIV) infection, antibodies to HIV, or infection with any other probable causative agent of AIDS. The court may direct the person to undergo the procedure or test on its own motion or on the request of the victim of the alleged offense. If the person refuses to submit voluntarily to the procedure or test, the court shall require the person to submit to the procedure or test. The court may require a defendant previously required under this article to undergo a medical procedure or test on indictment for an offense to undergo a subsequent medical procedure or test following conviction of the offense. The person performing the procedure or test shall make the test results available to the local health authority, and the local health authority shall be required to make the notification of the test result to the victim of the alleged offense and to the defendant. The state may not use the fact that a medical procedure or test was performed on a person under this subsection or use the results of the procedure or test in any criminal proceeding arising out of the alleged offense.

(b) Testing under this section shall be conducted in accordance with written infectious disease control protocols adopted by the Texas Board of Health that clearly establish procedural guidelines that provide criteria for testing and that respect the rights of the person accused and the victims of the alleged offense.

(c) Nothing in this section would allow a court to release a test result to anyone other than those specifically authorized by this law and the provisions of Section 81.103(d), Health and Safety Code, shall not be construed to allow such disclosure.

*(Chgd. by L.1991, chap. 14(284)(7); L.1993, chap. 811(1), eff. 9/1/93.)*

## CHAPTER 22. FORFEITURE OF BAIL

Article

22.15. Judgment final by default.
22.16. Remittitur after forfeiture.
22.17. Special bill of review.
22.18. Limitation.

**Art. 22.01. Bail forfeited, when.† [*Forfeit of bail, when.*]**

When a defendant is bound by bail to appear and fails to appear in any court in which such case may be pending and at any time when his personal appearance is required under this Code, or by any court or magistrate, a forfeiture of his bail and a judicial declaration of such forfeiture shall be taken in the manner provided in Article 22.02 of this Code and entered by such court.

**Art. 22.02. Manner of taking a forfeiture.† [*Method of taking a forfeiture.*]**

Bail bonds and personal bonds are forfeited in the following manner: The name of the defendant shall be called distinctly at the courthouse door, and if the defendant does not appear within a reasonable time after such call is made judgment shall be entered that the State of Texas recover of the defendant the amount of money in which he is bound, and of his sureties, if any, the amount of money in which they are respectively bound, which judgment shall state that the same will be made final, unless good cause be shown why the defendant did not appear.

**Art. 22.021. Forfeiture after violating treatment condition.† [*Forfeiture after violation of condition of treatment.*]**

On its own motion or the motion of the attorney for the state, the magistrate who set a defendant's bond or before whom a prosecution is pending may issue a warrant for the arrest of the defendant for a violation of a condition of the defendant's bond under Article 17.40 of this code. If, at a hearing, the magistrate determines that the defendant violated the condition without sufficient cause, the magistrate shall forfeit the defendant's bond and enter a final judgment of forfeiture. Citation shall be issued as provided by this chapter, except that the citation is sufficient if it is in the form provided for citations in civil cases.

**Art. 22.03. Citation to sureties.**

Upon entry of judgment, a citation shall issue forthwith notifying the sureties of the defendant, if any, that the bond has been forfeited, and requiring them to appear and show cause why the judgment of forfeiture should not be made final.

**Art. 22.04. Requisites of citation.**

A citation shall be sufficient if it be in the form provided for citations in civil cases in such court; provided, however, that a copy of the judgment of forfeiture entered by the court shall be attached to the citation and the citation shall notify the parties cited to appear and show cause why the judgment of forfeiture should not be made final.

**Art. 22.05. Citation as in civil actions.† [*Citation like civil actions.*]**

Sureties shall be entitled to notice by service of citation, the length of time and in the manner required in civil actions; and the officer executing the citation shall return the same as in civil actions. It shall not be necessary to give notice to the defendant unless he has furnished his address on the bond, in which event notice to the defendant shall be deposited in the United States mail directed to the defendant at the address shown on the bond.

**Art. 22.06. Citation by publication.**

Where the surety is a nonresident of the State, or where he is a transient person, or where his residence is unknown, the district or county attorney may, upon application in writing to the county clerk, stating the facts, obtain a citation to be served by publication; and the same shall be served by a publication and returned as in civil actions.

**Art. 22.07. Cost of publication.† [*Expense of publication.*]**

When service of citation is made by publication, the county in which the forfeiture has been taken shall pay the costs thereof, to be taxed as costs in the case.

**Art. 22.08. Service out of the State.† [*Service outside the State.*]**

Service of a certified copy of the citation upon any absent or non-resident surety may be made outside of the limits of this State by any person competent to make oath of the fact; and the affidavit of such person, stating the facts of such service, shall be a sufficient return.

### Art. 22.09. When surety is dead.

If the surety is dead at the time the forfeiture is taken, the forfeiture shall nevertheless be valid. The final judgment shall not be rendered where a surety has died, either before or after the forfeiture has been taken, unless his executor, administrator or heirs, as the case may be, have been cited to appear and show cause why the judgment should not be made final, in the same manner as provided in the case of the surety.

### Art. 22.10. Scire facias docket.

When a forfeiture has been declared upon a bond, the court or clerk shall docket the case upon the scire facias or upon the civil docket, in the name of the State of Texas, as plaintiff, and the principal and his sureties, if any, as defendants; and, except as otherwise provided by this chapter, the proceedings had therein shall be governed by the same rules governing other civil suits. *(Chgd. by L.1999, chap. 1506(4), eff. 9/1/99.)*

### Art. 22.11. Sureties may answer.

After the forfeiture of the bond, if the sureties, if any, have been duly notified, the sureties, if any, may answer in writing and show cause why the defendant did not appear, which answer may be filed within the time limited for answering in other civil actions.

### Art. 22.12. Proceedings not set aside for defect of form.† [*Proceedings not abandoned for defect of form.*]

The bond, the judgment declaring the forfeiture, the citation and the return thereupon, shall not be set aside because of any defect of form; but such defect of form may, at any time, be amended under the direction of the court.

### Art. 22.125. Powers of the court.

After a judicial declaration of forfeiture is entered, the court may proceed with the trial required by Article 22.14 of this code. The court may exonerate the defendant and his sureties, if any, from liability on the forfeiture, remit the amount of the forfeiture, or set aside the forfeiture only as expressly provided by this chapter. The court may approve any proposed settlement of the liability on the forfeiture that is agreed to by the state and by the defendant or the defendant's sureties, if any. *(Chgd. by L.1999, chap. 1506(5), eff. 9/1/99.)*

### Art. 22.13. Causes which will exonerate.† [*Exonerating causes.*]

The following causes, and no other will exonerate the defendant and his sureties, if any, from liability upon the forfeiture taken:

1. That the bond is, for any cause, not a valid and binding undertaking in law. If it be valid and binding as to the principal, and one or more of his sureties, if any, they shall not be exonerated from liability because of its being invalid and not binding as to another surety or sureties, if any. If it be invalid and not binding as to the principal, each of the sureties, if any, shall be exonerated from liability. If it be valid and binding as to the principal, but not so as to the sureties, if any, the principal shall not be exonerated, but the sureties, if any, shall be.
2. The death of the principal before the forfeiture was taken.
3. The sickness of the principal or some uncontrollable circumstance which prevented his appearance at court, and it must, in every such case, be shown that his failure to appear arose from no fault on his part. The causes mentioned in this subdivision shall not be deemed sufficient to exonerate the principal and his sureties, if any, unless such principal appear before final judgment on the bond to answer the accusation against him, or show sufficient cause for not so appearing.
4. Failure to present an indictment or information at the first term of the court which may be held after the principal has been admitted to bail, in case where the party was bound over before indictment or information, and the prosecution has not been continued by order of the court.

### Art. 22.14. Judgment final.

When, upon a trial of the issues presented, no sufficient cause is shown for the failure of the principal to appear, the judgment shall be made final against him and his sureties, if any, for the amount in which they are respectively bound; and the same shall be collected by execution as in civil actions. Separate executions shall issue against each party for the amount adjudged against him. The costs shall be equally divided between the sureties, if there be more than one.

### Art. 22.15. Judgment final by default.

When the sureties have been duly cited and fail to answer, and the principal also fails to answer within the time limited for answering in other civil actions, the court shall enter judgment final by default.

### Art. 22.16. Remittitur after forfeiture.

(a) After forfeiture of a bond and before the expiration of the time limits set by Subsection (c) of this article, the court shall, on written motion, remit to the surety the amount of the bond after deducting the costs of court, any reasonable costs to the county for the return of the principal, and the interest accrued on the bond amount as provided by Subsection (e) of this article if:

(1) the principal is incarcerated in the county in which the prosecution is pending;

(2) the principal is incarcerated in another jurisdiction and the incarceration is verified as provided by Subsection (b) of this article;

(3) the principal is released on new bail in the case;

(4) the principal is deceased; or

(5) the case for which bond was given is dismissed.

(b) For the purposes of Subsection (a)(2) of this article, a surety may request confirmation of the incarceration of his principal by written request to the law enforcement agency of the county where prosecution is pending. A law enforcement agency in this state that receives a request for verification shall notify the court in which prosecution is pending and the surety whether or not the principal is or has been incarcerated in another jurisdiction and the date of the incarceration.

(c) A final judgment may be entered against a bond not earlier than:

(1) nine months after the date the forfeiture was entered, if the offense for which the bond was given is a misdemeanor; or

(2) 18 months after the date the forfeiture was entered, if the offense for which the bond was given is a felony.

(d) After the expiration of the time limits set by Subsection (c) of this article and before the entry of a final judgment against the bond, the court in its discretion may remit to the surety all or part of the amount of the bond after deducting the costs of court, any reasonable costs to the county for the return of the principal, and the interest accrued on the bond amount as provided by Subsection (e) of this article.

(e) For the purposes of this article, interest accrues on the bond amount from the date of forfeiture in the same manner and at the same rate as provided for the accrual of prejudgment interest in civil cases.

### Art. 22.17. Special bill of review.

(a) Not later than two years after the date a final judgment is entered in a bond forfeiture proceeding, the surety on the bond may file with the court a special bill of review. A special bill of review may include a request, on equitable grounds, that the final judgment be reformed and that all or part of the bond amount be remitted to the surety, after deducting the costs of court, any reasonable costs to the county for the return of the principal, and the interest accrued on the bond amount from the date of forfeiture. The court in its discretion may grant or deny the bill in whole or in part.

(b) For the purposes of this article, interest accrues on the bond amount from the date of:

(1) forfeiture to the date of final judgment in the same manner and at the same rate as provided for the accrual of prejudgment interest in civil cases; and

(2) final judgment to the date of the order for remittitur at the same rate as provided for the accrual of postjudgment interest in civil cases.

### Art. 22.18. Limitation.

An action by the state to forfeit a bail bond under this chapter must be brought not later than the fourth anniversary of the date the principal fails to appear in court. *(Added by L.1999, chap. 1506(6), eff. 9/1/99.)*

## CHAPTER 23. THE CAPIAS

Article

### Art. 23.01. Definition of a "capias".

A "capias" is a writ issued by the court or clerk, and directed "To any peace officer of the State of Texas", commanding him to arrest a person accused of an offense and bring him before that court immediately, or on a day or at a term stated in the writ.

### Art. 23.02. Its requisites.† [*Requisites thereof.*]

A capias shall be held sufficient if it have the following requisites:

1. That it run in the name of "The State of Texas";
2. That it name the person whose arrest is ordered, or if unknown, describe him;
3. That it specify the offense of which the defendant is accused, and it appear thereby that he is accused of some offense against the penal laws of the State;
4. That it name the court to which and the time when it is returnable; and
5. That it be dated and attested officially by the authority issuing the same.

### Art. 23.03. Capias or summons in felony.

(a) A capias shall be issued by the district clerk upon each indictment for felony presented, after bail has been set or denied by the judge of the court. Upon the request of the attorney representing the State, a summons shall be issued by the district clerk. The capias or summons shall be delivered by the clerk or mailed to the sheriff of the county where the defendant resides or is to be found. A capias or summons need not issue for a defendant in custody or under bond.

(b) Upon the request of the attorney representing the State a summons instead of a capias shall issue. If a defendant fails to appear in response to the summons a capias shall issue.

(c) Summons. The summons shall be in the same form as the capias except that it shall summon the defendant to appear before the proper court at a stated time and place. The summons shall be served upon a defendant by delivering a copy to him personally, or by leaving it at his dwelling house or usual place of abode with some person of suitable age and discretion then residing therein or by mailing it to the defendant's last known address.

(d) A summons issued to any person must clearly and prominently state in English and in Spanish the following:

> "It is an offense for a person to intentionally influence or coerce a witness to testify falsely or to elude legal process. It is also a felony offense to harm or threaten to harm a witness or prospective witness in retaliation for or on account of the service of the person as a witness or to prevent or delay the person's service as a witness to a crime."

*(Chgd. by L.1995, chap. 67(1), eff. 9/1/95.)*

### Art. 23.04. In misdemeanor case.

In misdemeanor cases the capias or summons shall issue from a court having jurisdiction of the case. The summons shall be issued only upon request of the attorney representing the State and shall follow the same form and procedure as in a felony case.

### Art. 23.05. Capias after forfeiture.

(a) Where a forfeiture of bail is declared, a capias shall be immediately issued for the arrest of the defendant, and when arrested, in its discretion, the court may require the defendant, in order to be released from custody, to deposit with the custodian of funds of the court in which the prosecution is pending current money of the United States in the amount of the new bond as set by the court, in lieu of a surety bond, unless the forfeiture taken has been set aside under the third subdivision of Article 22.13 of this code, in which case the defendant and his sureties shall remain bound under the same bail.

(b) A capias issued under this article may be executed by a peace officer or by a private investigator licensed under the Private Investigators and Private Security Agencies Act (Article 4413 (29bb), Vernon's Texas Civil Statutes).
*(Chgd. by L.1999, chap. 1506(7), eff. 9/1/99.)*

**Art. 23.06. New bail in felony case.**
When a defendant who has been arrested for a felony under a capias has previously given bail to answer said charge, his sureties, if any, shall be released by such arrest, and he shall be required to give new bail.

**Art. 23.07. Capias does not lose its force.† [*Capias remains in force.*]**
A capias shall not lose its force if not executed and returned at the time fixed in the writ, but may be executed at any time afterward, and return made. All proceedings under such capias shall be as valid as if the same had been executed and returned within the time specified in the writ.

**Art. 23.08. Reasons for retaining capias.† [*Reasons to retain capias.*]**
When the capias is not returned at the time fixed in the writ, the officer holding it shall notify the court from whence it was issued, in writing, of his reasons for retaining it.

**Art. 23.09. Capias to several counties.**
Capiases for a defendant may be issued to as many counties as the district or county attorney may direct.

**Art. 23.10. Bail in felony.**
In cases of arrest for felony in the county where the prosecution is pending, during a term of court, the officer making the arrest may take bail as provided in Article 17.21.

**Art. 23.11. Sheriff may take bail in felony.**
In cases of arrest for felony less than capital, made during vacation or made in another county than the one in which the prosecution is pending, the sheriff may take bail; in such cases the amount of the bail bond shall be the same as is endorsed upon the capias; and if no amount be endorsed on the capias, the sheriff shall require a reasonable amount of bail. If it be made to appear by affidavit, made by any district attorney, county attorney, or the sheriff approving the bail bond, to a judge of the Court of Criminal Appeals, a justice of a court of appeals, or to a judge of the district or county court, that the bail taken in any case after indictment is insufficient in amount, or that the sureties are not good for the amount, or that the bond is for any reason defective or insufficient, such judge shall issue a warrant of arrest and require of the defendant sufficient bond; according to the nature of the case.

**Art. 23.12. Court shall fix bail in felony.† [*Court sets bail in felony.*]**
In felony cases which are bailable, the court shall, before adjourning, fix and enter upon the minutes the amount of the bail to be required in each case. The clerk shall endorse upon the capias the amount of bail required. In case of neglect to so comply with this Article, the arrest of the defendant, and the bail taken by the sheriff, shall be as legal as if there had been no such omission.

**Art. 23.13. Who may arrest under capias.**
A capias may be executed by any peace officer. In felony cases, the defendant must be delivered immediately to the sheriff of the county where the arrest is made together, with the writ under which he was taken.

**Art. 23.14. Bail in misdemeanor.**
Any officer making an arrest under a capias in a misdemeanor may in term time or vacation take a bail bond of the defendant.

**Art. 23.15. Arrest in capital cases.**
Where an arrest is made under a capias in a capital case, the sheriff shall confine the defendant in jail, and the capias shall, for that purpose, be a sufficient commitment. This Article is applicable when the arrest is made in the county where the prosecution is pending.

**Art. 23.16. Arrest in capital case in another county.† [*Arrest in capital case outside the county.*]**

In each capital case where a defendant is arrested under a capias in a county other than that in which the case is pending, the sheriff who arrests or to whom the defendant is delivered, shall convey him immediately to the county from which the capias issued and deliver him to the sheriff of such county.

**Art. 23.17. Return of bail and capias.**

When an arrest has been made and a bail taken, such bond, together with the capias, shall be returned forthwith to the proper court.

**Art. 23.18. Return of capias.**

The return of the capias shall be made to the court from which it is issued. If it has been executed, the return shall state what disposition has been made of the defendant. If it has not been executed, the cause of the failure to execute it shall be fully stated. If the defendant has not been found, the return shall further show what efforts have been made by the officer to find him, and what information he has as to the defendant's whereabouts.



## CHAPTER 24. SUBPOENA AND ATTACHMENT

Article



**Art. 24.01. Issuance of subpoenas.† [*Effect of subpoenas.*]**

(a) A subpoena may summon one or more persons to appear:

(1) before a court to testify in a criminal action at a specified term of the court or on a specified day; or

(2) on a specified day:

(A) before an examining court;

(B) at a coroner's inquest;

(C) before a grand jury;

(D) at a habeas corpus hearing; or

(E) in any other proceeding in which the person's testimony may be required in accordance with this code.

(b) The person named in the subpoena to summon the person whose appearance is sought must be:

(1) a peace officer; or

(2) at least 18 years old and, at the time the subpoena is issued, not a participant in the proceeding for which the appearance is sought.

(c) A person who is not a peace officer may not be compelled to accept the duty to execute a subpoena, but if he agrees in writing to accept that duty and neglects or refuses to serve or return the subpoena, he may be punished in accordance with Article 2.16 of this code.

(d) A court or clerk issuing a subpoena shall sign the subpoena and indicate on it the date it was issued, but the subpoena need not be under seal.

### Art. 24.011. Subpoenas; child witnesses.

(a) If a witness is younger than 18 years, the court may issue a subpoena directing a person having custody, care, or control of the child to produce the child in court.

(b) If a person, without legal cause, fails to produce the child in court as directed by a subpoena issued under this article, the court may impose on the person penalties for contempt provided by this chapter. The court may also issue a writ of attachment for the person and the child, in the same manner as other writs of attachment are issued under this chapter.

### Art. 24.02. Subpoena duces tecum.

If a witness have in his possession any instrument of writing or other thing desired as evidence, the subpoena may specify such evidence and direct that the witness bring the same with him and produce it in court.

### Art. 24.03. Subpoena and application therefor.

(a) Before the clerk or his deputy shall be required or permitted to issue a subpoena in any felony case pending in any district or criminal district court of this State of which he is clerk or deputy, the defendant or his attorney or the State's attorney shall make an application in writing or by electronic means to such clerk for each witness desired. Such application shall state the name of each witness desired, the location and vocation, if known, and that the testimony of said witness is material to the State or to the defense. The application must be filed with the clerk and placed with the papers in the cause or, if the application is filed electronically, placed with any other electronic information linked to the number of the cause. The application must also be made available to both the State and the defendant. Except as provided by Subsection (b), as far as is practical such clerk shall include in one subpoena the names of all witnesses for the State and for defendant, and such process shall show that the witnesses are summoned for the State or for the defendant. When a witness has been served with a subpoena, attached or placed under bail at the instance of either party in a particular case, such execution of process shall inure to the benefit of the opposite party in such case in the event such opposite party desires to use such witness on the trial of the case, provided that when a witness has once been served with a subpoena, no further subpoena shall be issued for said witness.

(b) If the defendant is a member of a combination as defined by Section 71.01, Penal Code, the clerk shall issue for each witness a subpoena that does not include a list of the names of all other witnesses for the State or the defendant.

*(Chgd. by L.1993, chap. 900(10.01); L.1999, chaps. 580(4), 614(2), eff. 9/1/99, 6/18/99, respectively.)*

### Art. 24.04. Service and return of subpoena.

(a) A subpoena is served by:

(1) reading the subpoena in the hearing of the witness;

(2) delivering a copy of the subpoena to the witness;

(3) electronically transmitting a copy of the subpoena, acknowledgment of receipt requested, to the last known electronic address of the witness; or

(4) mailing a copy of the subpoena by certified mail, return receipt requested, to the last known address of the witness unless:

(A) the applicant for the subpoena requests in writing that the subpoena not be served by certified mail; or

(B) the proceeding for which the witness is being subpoenaed is set to begin within seven business days after the date the subpoena would be mailed.

(b) The officer having the subpoena shall make due return thereof, showing the time and manner of service, if served under Subsection (a)(1) or (2) of this article, the acknowledgment of receipt, if served under Subsection (a)(3) of this article, or the return receipt, if served under Subsection (a)(4) of this article. If the subpoena is not served, the officer shall show in his return the cause of his failure to serve it. If receipt of an electronically transmitted subpoena is not acknowledged within a reasonable time or a mailed subpoena is returned undelivered, the officer shall use due diligence to locate and serve the witness. If the witness could not be found, the officer shall state the diligence he has used to find him, and what information he has as to the whereabouts of the witness.

(c) A subpoena served under Subsection (a)(3) of this article must be accompanied by notice that an acknowledgment of receipt of the subpoena must be made in a manner enabling verification of the person acknowledging receipt.

*(Chgd. by L.1995, chap. 374(1); L.1999, chap. 580(5), eff. 9/1/99.)*

**Art. 24.05. Refusing to obey.† [*Refusal to obey subpoena.*]**

If a witness refuses to obey a subpoena, he may be fined at the discretion of the court, as follows: In a felony case, not exceeding five hundred dollars; in a misdemeanor case, not exceeding one hundred dollars.

**Art. 24.06. What is disobedience of a subpoena.† [*Determination of disobedience.*]**

It shall be held that a witness refuses to obey a subpoena:

(1) If he is not in attendance on the court on the day set apart for taking up the criminal docket or on any day subsequent thereto and before the final disposition or continuance of the particular case in which he is a witness;

(2) If he is not in attendance at any other time named in a writ; and

(3) If he refuses without legal cause to produce evidence in his possession which he has been summoned to bring with him and produce.

**Art. 24.07. Fine against witness conditional.† [*Failure to appear: fine against witness.*]**

When a fine is entered against a witness for failure to appear and testify, the judgment shall be conditional; and a citation shall issue to him to show cause, at the term of the court at which said fine is entered, or at the first term thereafter, at the discretion of the judge of said court, why the same should not be final; provided, citation shall be served upon said witness in the manner and for the length of time prescribed for citations in civil cases.

**Art. 24.08. Witness may show cause.† [*Failure to appear: witness may show cause.*]**

A witness cited to show cause, as provided in the preceding Article, may do so under oath, in writing or verbally, at any time before judgment final is entered against him; but if he fails to show cause within the time limited for answering in civil actions, a judgment final by default shall be entered against him.

**Art. 24.09. Court may remit fine.† [*Remission of fine.*]**

It shall be within the discretion of the court to judge of the sufficiency of an excuse rendered by a witness, and upon the hearing the court shall render judgment against the witness for the whole or any part of the fine, or shall remit the fine altogether, as to the court may appear proper and right. Said fine shall be collected as fines in misdemeanor cases.

**Art. 24.10. When witness appears and testifies.† [*Subsequent appearance of witness.*]**

When a fine has been entered against a witness, but no trial of the cause takes place, and such witness afterward appears and testifies upon the trial thereof, it shall be discretionary with the judge, though no good excuse be rendered, to reduce the fine or remit it altogether; but the witness, in such case, shall, nevertheless, be adjudged to pay all the costs accruing in the proceeding against him by reason of his failure to attend.

**Art. 24.11. Requisites of an "attachment".† [*"Attachment": definition.*]**

An "attachment" is a writ issued by a clerk of a court under seal, or by any magistrate, or by the foreman of a grand jury, in any criminal action or proceeding authorized by law, commanding some peace officer to take the body of a witness and bring him before such court, magistrate or grand jury on a day named, or forthwith, to testify in behalf of the State or of the defendant, as the case may be. It shall be dated and signed officially by the officer issuing it.

**Art. 24.12. When attachment may issue.† [*Issuance of attachment.*]**
When a witness who resides in the county of the prosecution has been duly served with a subpoena to appear and testify in any criminal action or proceeding fails to so appear, the State or the defendant shall be entitled to have an attachment issued forthwith for such witness.

**Art. 24.13. Attachment for convict witness.† [*Convict witness: attachment.*]**
All persons who have been or may be convicted in this State, and who are confined in an institution operated by the Department of Corrections or any jail in this State, shall be permitted to testify in person in any court for the State and the defendant when the presiding judge finds, after hearing, that the ends of justice require their attendance, and directs that an attachment issue to accomplish the purpose, notwithstanding any other provision of this Code. Nothing in this Article shall be construed as limiting the power of the courts of this State to issue bench warrants.

**Art. 24.14. Attachment for resident witness.† [*Resident witness: attachment.*]**
When a witness resides in the county of the prosecution, whether he has disobeyed a subpoena or not, either in term-time or vacation, upon the filing of an affidavit with the clerk by the defendant or State's counsel, that he has good reason to believe, and does believe, that such witness is a material witness, and is about to move out of the county, the clerk shall forthwith issue an attachment for such witness; provided, that in misdemeanor cases, when the witness makes oath that he cannot give surety, the officer executing the attachment shall take his personal bond.

**Art. 24.15. To secure attendance before grand jury.† [*Grand jury proceedings: use of subpoena or attachment.*]**
At any time before the first day of any term of the district court, the clerk, upon application of the State's attorney, shall issue a subpoena for any witness who resides in the county. If at the time such application is made, such attorney files a sworn application that he has good reason to believe and does believe that such witness is about to move out of the county, then said clerk shall issue an attachment for such witness to be and appear before said district court on the first day thereof to testify as a witness before the grand jury. Any witness so summoned, or attached, who shall fail or refuse to obey a subpoena or attachment, shall be punished by the court by a fine not exceeding five hundred dollars, to be collected as fines and costs in other criminal cases.

**Art. 24.16. Application for out-county witness.† [*Subpoena for out of county witness.*]**
Where, in misdemeanor cases in which confinement in jail is a permissible punishment, or in felony cases, a witness resides out of the county in which the prosecution is pending, the State or the defendant shall be entitled, either in term-time or in vacation, to a subpoena to compel the attendance of such witness on application to the proper clerk or magistrate. Such application shall be in the manner and form as provided in Article 24.03. Witnesses in such misdemeanor cases shall be compensated in the same manner as in felony cases. This Article shall not apply to more than one character witness in a misdemeanor case.

**Art. 24.17. Duty of officer receiving said subpoena.† [*Execution of subpoena: duty of officer.*]**
The officer receiving said subpoena shall execute the same by delivering a copy thereof to each witness therein named. He shall make due return of said subpoena, showing therein the time and manner of executing the same, and if not executed, such return shall show why not executed, the diligence used to find said witness, and such information as the officer has as to the whereabouts of said witness.

**Art. 24.18. Subpoena returnable forthwith.† [*Immediate return of subpoena.*]**
When a subpoena is returnable forthwith, the officer shall immediately serve the witness with a copy of the same; and it shall be the duty of said witness to immediately make his appearance before the court, magistrate or other authority issuing the same. If said witness makes affidavit of his inability from lack of funds to appear in obedience to said subpoena, the officer executing the same shall provide said witness, if said subpoena be issued as provided in Article 24.16, with the necessary funds or means to appear in obedience to said subpoena, taking his receipt therefor, and showing in his return on said subpoena, under oath, the amount furnished to said witness, together with the amount of his fees for executing said subpoena.

**Art. 24.19. Certificate to officer.**

The clerk, magistrate, or foreman of the grand jury issuing said process, immediately upon the return of said subpoena, if issued as provided in Article 24.16, shall issue to such officer a certificate for the amount furnished such witness, together with the amount of his fees for executing the same, showing the amount of each item; which certificate shall be approved by the district judge and recorded by the district clerk in a book kept for that purpose; and said certificate transmitted to the officer executing such subpoena, which amount shall be paid by the State, as costs are paid in other criminal matters.

**Art. 24.20. Subpoena returnable at future date.† [*Future return of subpoena.*]**

If the subpoena be returnable at some future date, the officer shall have authority to take bail of such witness for his appearance under said subpoena, which bond shall be returned with such subpoena, and shall be made payable to the State of Texas, in the amount in which the witness and his surety, if any, shall be bound and conditioned for the appearance of the witness at the time and before the court, magistrate or grand jury named in said subpoena, and shall be signed by the witness and his sureties. If the witness refuses to give bond, he shall be kept in custody until such time as he starts in obedience to said subpoena, when he shall be, upon affidavit being made, provided with funds necessary to appear in obedience to said subpoena.

**Art. 24.21. Stating bail in subpoena.† [*Statement of bail included in subpoena.*]**

The court or magistrate issuing said subpoena may direct therein the amount of the bail to be required. The officer may fix the amount if not specified, and in either case, shall require sufficient security, to be approved by himself.

**Art. 24.22. Witness fined and attached.† [*Fine or attachment for out of county witness.*]**

If a witness summoned from without the county refuses to obey a subpoena, he shall be fined by the court or magistrate not exceeding five hundred dollars, which fine and judgment shall be final, unless set aside after due notice to show cause why it should not be final, which notice may immediately issue, requiring the defaulting witness to appear at once or at the next term of said court, in the discretion of the judge, to answer for such default. The court may cause to be issued at the same time an attachment for said witness, directed to the proper county, commanding the officer to whom said writ is directed to take said witness into custody and have him before said court at the time named in said writ; in which case such witness shall receive no fees, unless it appears to the court that such disobedience is excusable, when the witness may receive the same pay as if he had not been attached. Said fine when made final and all costs thereon shall be collected as in other criminal cases. Said fine and judgment may be set aside in vacation or at the time or any subsequent term of the court for good cause shown, after the witness testifies or has been discharged. The following words shall be written or printed on the face of such subpoena for out-county witnesses: "A disobedience of this subpoena is punishable by fine not exceeding five hundred dollars, to be collected as fines and costs in other criminal cases."

**Art. 24.23. Witness released.† [*Release of witness.*]**

A witness who is in custody for failing to give bail shall be at once released upon giving bail required.

**Art. 24.24. Bail for witness.† [*Bail.*]**

Witnesses on behalf of the State or defendant may, at the request of either party, be required to enter into bail in an amount to be fixed by the court to appear and testify in a criminal action; but if it shall appear to the court that any witness is unable to give security upon such bail, he shall be released without security.

**Art. 24.25. Personal bond of witness.† [*Personal bond.*]**

When it appears to the satisfaction of the court that personal bond of the witness will insure his attendance, no security need be required of him; but no bond without security shall be taken by any officer.

**Art. 24.26. Enforcing forfeiture.† [*Forfeiture of sureties.*]**

The bond of a witness may be enforced against him and his sureties, if any, in the manner pointed out in this Code for enforcing the bond of a defendant in a criminal case.

**Art. 24.27. No surrender after forfeiture.† [*Forfeiture of surety final.*]**
The sureties of a witness have no right to discharge themselves by the surrender of the witness after the forfeiture of their bond.

**Art. 24.28. Uniform Act to secure attendance of witnesses from without State.**
**Sec. 1. Short title.** This Act may be cited as the "Uniform Act to Secure the Attendance of Witnesses from Without the State in Criminal Proceedings".

**Sec. 2. Definitions.** "Witness" as used in this Act shall include a person whose testimony is desired in any proceeding or investigation by a grand jury or in a criminal action, prosecution or proceeding.

The word "State" shall include any territory of the United States and the District of Columbia.

The word "summons" shall include a subpoena, order or other notice requiring the appearance of a witness.

**Sec. 3. Summoning witnesses in this state to testify in another State.† [*Directing a witness from this State to testify in another.*]** (a) If a judge of a court of record in any State which by its laws has made provision for commanding persons within that State to attend and testify in this State certifies under the seal of such court that there is a criminal prosecution pending in such court, or that a grand jury investigation has commenced or is about to commence, that a person being within this State is a material witness in such prosecution, or grand jury investigation, and that his presence will be required for a specified number of days, upon presentation of such certificate to any judge of a court of record in the county in which such person is, such judge shall fix a time and place for a hearing, and shall make an order directing the witness to appear at a time and place certain for the hearing.

(b) If at a hearing the judge determines that the witness is material and necessary, that it will not cause undue hardship to the witness to be compelled to attend and testify in the prosecution or a grand jury investigation in the other State, and that the laws of the State in which the prosecution is pending, or grand jury investigation has commenced or is about to commence, (and of any other State through which the witness may be required to pass by ordinary course of travel), will give to him protection from arrest and the service of civil and criminal process, he shall issue a summons, with a copy of the certificate attached, directing the witness to attend and testify in the court where the prosecution is pending, or where a grand jury investigation has commenced or is about to commence at a time and place specified in the summons. In any such hearing the certificate shall be prima facie evidence of all the facts stated therein.

(c) If said certificate recommends that the witness be taken into immediate custody and delivered to an officer of the requesting State to assure his attendance in the requesting State, such judge may, in lieu of notification of the hearing, direct that such witness be forthwith brought before him for said hearing; and the judge at the hearing being satisfied of the desirability of such custody and delivery, for which determination the certificate shall be prima facie proof of such desirability may, in lieu of issuing subpoena or summons, order that said witness be forthwith taken into custody and delivered to an officer of the requesting State.

(d) If the witness, who is summoned as above provided, after being paid or tendered by some properly authorized person the compensation for nonresident witnesses authorized and provided for by Article 35.27 of this Code, fails without good cause to attend and testify as directed in the summons, he shall be punished in the manner provided for the punishment of any witness who disobeys a summons issued from a court of record in this State.

**Sec. 4. Witnesses from another state summoned to testify in this State.† [*Out of state witnesses directed to testify in this state.*]** (a) If a person in any State, which by its laws has made provision for commanding persons within its borders to attend and testify in criminal prosecutions, or grand jury investigations commenced or about to commence, in this State, is a material witness in a prosecution pending in a court of record in this State, or in a grand jury investigation which has commenced or is about to commence, a judge of such court may issue a certificate under the seal of the court stating these facts and specifying the number of days the witness will be required. Said certificate may include a recommendation that the witness be taken into immediate custody and delivered to an officer of this State to assure his attendance in this State. This certificate shall be presented to a judge of a court of record in the county in which the witness is found.

(b) If the witness is summoned to attend and testify in this State he shall be tendered the compensation for nonresident witnesses authorized by Article 35.27 of this Code, together with such additional compensation, if any, required by the other State for compliance. A witness who has appeared in accordance with the provisions of the summons shall not be required to remain within this State a longer period of time than the period mentioned in the certificate, unless otherwise ordered by the court. If such witness, after coming into this State, fails without good cause to attend and testify as directed in the summons, he shall be punished in the manner provided for the punishment of any witness who disobeys a summons issued from a court of record in this State.

**Sec. 5. Exemption from arrest and service of process.**† [***Out of state witness: exempt from other legal process.***] If a person comes into this State in obedience to the summons directing him to attend and testify in this State he shall not while in this State pursuant to such summons be subject to arrest or the service of process, civil or criminal, in connection with matters which arose before his entrance into this State under the summons.

If a person passes through this State while going to another State in obedience to a summons to attend and testify in that State or while returning therefrom, he shall not while so passing through this State be subject to arrest or the service of process, civil or criminal, in connection with matters which arose before his entrance into this State under the summons.

## Art. 24.29. Uniform Act to secure rendition of prisoners in criminal proceedings.

**Sec. 1. Short title.** This article may be cited as the "Uniform Act to Secure Rendition of Prisoners in Criminal Proceedings."

**Sec. 2. Definitions.** In this Act:

(1) "Penal institution" means a jail, prison, penitentiary, house of correction, or other place of penal detention.

(2) "State" means a state of the United States, the District of Columbia, the Commonwealth of Puerto Rico, and any territory of the United States.

(3) "Witness" means a person who is confined in a penal institution in a state and whose testimony is desired in another state in a criminal proceeding or investigation by a grand jury or in any criminal action before a court.

**Sec. 3. Summoning witness in this state to testify in another state.**† [***Directing witness in this state to testify in another state.***] (a) A judge of a state court of record in another state, which by its laws has made provision for commanding persons confined in penal institutions within that state to attend and testify in this state, may certify that:

(1) there is a criminal proceeding or investigation by a grand jury or a criminal action pending in the court;

(2) a person who is confined in a penal institution in this state may be a material witness in the proceeding, investigation, or action; and

(3) his presence will be required during a specified time.

(b) On presentation of the certificate to any judge having jurisdiction over the person confined and on notice to the attorney general, the judge in this state shall fix a time and place for a hearing and shall make an order directed to the person having custody of the prisoner requiring that the prisoner be produced before him at the hearing.

**Sec. 4. Court order.** (a) A judge may issue a transfer order if at the hearing the judge determines that:

(1) the witness may be material and necessary;

(2) his attending and testifying are not adverse to the interest of this state or to the health or legal rights of the witness;

(3) the laws of the state in which he is requested to testify will give him protection from arrest and the service of civil and criminal process because of any act committed prior to his arrival in the state under the order; and

(4) as a practical matter the possibility is negligible that the witness may be subject to arrest or to the service of civil or criminal process in any state through which he will be required to pass.

(b) If a judge issues an order under Subsection (a) of this section, the judge shall attach to the order a copy of a certificate presented under Section 3 of this Act. The order shall:

(1) direct the witness to attend and testify;

(2) except as provided by Subsection (c) of this section, direct the person having custody of the witness to produce him in the court where the criminal action is pending or where the grand jury investigation is pending at a time and place specified in the order; and

(3) prescribe such conditions as the judge shall determine.

(c) The judge, in lieu of directing the person having custody of the witness to produce him in the requesting jurisdiction's court, may direct and require in his order that:

(1) an officer of the requesting jurisdiction come to the Texas penal institution in which the witness is confined to accept custody of the witness for physical transfer to the requesting jurisdiction;

(2) the requesting jurisdiction provide proper safeguards on his custody while in transit;

(3) the requesting jurisdiction be liable for and pay all expenses incurred in producing and returning the witness, including but not limited to food, lodging, clothing, and medical care; and

(4) the requesting jurisdiction promptly deliver the witness back to the same or another Texas penal institution as specified by the Texas Department of Corrections at the conclusion of his testimony.

**Sec. 5. Terms and conditions.** An order to a witness and to a person having custody of the witness shall provide for the return of the witness at the conclusion of his testimony, proper safeguards on his custody, and proper financial reimbursement or prepayment by the requesting jurisdiction for all expenses incurred in the production and return of the witness. The order may prescribe any other condition the judge thinks proper or necessary. The judge shall not require prepayment of expenses if the judge directs and requires the requesting jurisdiction to accept custody of the witness at the Texas penal institution in which the witness is confined and to deliver the witness back to the same or another Texas penal institution at the conclusion of his testimony. An order does not become effective until the judge of the state requesting the witness enters an order directing compliance with the conditions prescribed.

**Sec. 6. Exceptions.** This Act does not apply to a person in this state who is confined as mentally ill or who is under sentence of death.

**Sec. 7. Prisoner from another state summoned to testify in this State.† [*Out of state prisoner requested to testify in this state.*]** (a) If a person confined in a penal institution in any other state may be a material witness in a criminal action pending in a court of record or in a grand jury investigation in this state, a judge of the court may certify that:

(1) there is a criminal proceeding or investigation by a grand jury or a criminal action pending in the court;

(2) a person who is confined in a penal institution in the other state may be a material witness in the proceeding, investigation, or action; and

(3) his presence will be required during a specified time.

(b) The judge of the court in this state shall:

(1) present the certificate to a judge of a court of record in the other state having jurisdiction over the prisoner confined; and

(2) give notice that the prisoner's presence will be required to the attorney general of the state in which the prisoner is confined.

**Sec. 8. Compliance.** A judge of the court in this state may enter an order directing compliance with the terms and conditions of an order specified in a certificate under Section 3 of this Act and entered by the judge of the state in which the witness is confined.

**Sec. 9. Exemption from arrest and service of process.† [*Out of state witness: exempted from other legal process.*]** If a witness from another state comes into or passes through this state under an order directing him to attend and testify in this or another state, while in this state pursuant to the order he is not subject to arrest or the service of civil or criminal process because of any act committed prior to his arrival in this state under the order.

**Sec. 10. Uniformity of interpretation.** This Act shall be so construed as to effect its general purpose to make uniform the laws of those states which enact it.

## CHAPTER 25. SERVICE OF A COPY OF THE INDICTMENT

Article

### Art. 25.01. In felony.† [*Indictment of felony.*]

In every case of felony, when the accused is in custody, or as soon as he may be arrested, the clerk of the court where an indictment has been presented shall immediately make a certified copy of the same, and deliver such copy to the sheriff, together with a writ directed to such sheriff, commanding him forthwith to deliver such certified copy to the accused.

### Art. 25.02. Service and return.† [*Service and return of indictment.*]

Upon receipt of such writ and copy, the sheriff shall immediately deliver such certified copy of the indictment to the accused and return the writ to the clerk issuing the same, with his return thereon, showing when and how the same was executed.

### Art. 25.03. If on bail in felony.† [*Felony: accused on bail.*]

When the accused, in case of felony, is on bail at the time the indictment is presented, it is not necessary to serve him with a copy, but the clerk shall on request deliver a copy of the same to the accused or his counsel, at the earliest possible time.

### Art. 25.04. In misdemeanor.† [*Service of indictment of misdemeanor.*]

In misdemeanors, it shall not be necessary before trial to furnish the accused with a copy of the indictment or information; but he or his counsel may demand a copy, which shall be given as early as possible.

## CHAPTER 26. ARRAIGNMENT

Article

### Art. 26.01. Arraignment.

In all felony cases, after indictment, and all misdemeanor cases punishable by imprisonment, there shall be an arraignment.

### Art. 26.02. Purpose of arraignment.† [*Purpose.*]

An arraignment takes place for the purpose of fixing his identity and hearing his plea.

### Art. 26.03. Time of arraignment.† [*Time.*]

No arraignment shall take place until the expiration of at least two entire days after the day on which a copy of the indictment was served on the defendant, unless the right to such copy or to such delay be waived, or unless the defendant is on bail.

### Art. 26.04. Court shall appoint counsel.† [*Appointing counsel for indigent defendant.*]

(a) Whenever the court determines that a defendant charged with a felony or a misdemeanor punishable by imprisonment is indigent or that the interests of justice require representation of a defendant in a criminal proceeding, the court shall appoint one or more practicing attorneys to defend him. An attorney appointed under this subsection shall represent the defendant until charges are dismissed, the defendant is acquitted, appeals are exhausted, or the attorney is relieved of his duties by the court or replaced by other counsel.

(b) In determining whether a defendant is indigent, the court shall consider such factors as the defendant's income, source of income, property owned, outstanding obligations, necessary expenses, the number and ages of dependents, spousal income, and whether the defendant has posted or is capable of posting bail. The court may not deny appointed counsel to a defendant solely because the defendant has posted or is capable of posting bail.

(c) A defendant who requests a determination of indigency and appointment of counsel shall:

(1) complete under oath a questionnaire concerning his financial resources;

(2) respond under oath to an examination regarding his financial resources by the judge or magistrate responsible for determining whether the defendant is indigent; or

(3) complete the questionnaire and respond to examination by the judge or magistrate.

(d) Before making a determination of whether a defendant is indigent, the court shall request the defendant to sign under oath a statement substantially in the following form:

"On this __________ day of __________, 19 ___, I have been advised by the (name of the court) Court of my right to representation by counsel in the trial of the charge pending against me. I certify that I am without means to employ counsel of my own choosing and I hereby request the court to appoint counsel for me. (signature of the defendant)"

(e) If there is a material change in circumstances after a determination of indigency or nonindigency is made, the defendant, the defendant's counsel, or the attorney representing the state may move for reconsideration of the determination.

(f) A written or oral statement elicited under this article or evidence derived from the statement may not be used for any purpose, except to determine the defendant's indigency or to impeach the direct testimony of the defendant. This subsection does not prohibit prosecution of the defendant under Chapter 37, Penal Code.

### Art. 26.041. Assistance for court-appointed counsel in Harris County.† [*Assistance for assigned counsel: Harris County.*]

(a) To assist the courts in providing timely and effective assistance of counsel to indigents in criminal cases, the Commissioners Court of Harris County may contract with:

(1) an established bar association;

(2) a nonprofit corporation;

(3) a nonprofit trust association; or

(4) any other nonprofit entity whose primary purpose is to provide timely and effective assistance of counsel for an indigent accused of a crime.

(b) The contract may provide that the contracting entity provide additional legal counseling and advice to the court-appointed attorney and provide necessary investigative services authorized by Article 26.05 of this code.

(c) To provide a judge with the necessary information to determine if a defendant should be released on personal bond, as authorized by Article 17.03 of this code, the commissioners court may contract with an entity listed in Subsection (a) of this article to:

(1) interview the defendant;

(2) verify the information given by the defendant;

(3) recommend to the judge having jurisdiction of the case if the defendant should be released on a personal bond; and

(4) assist the court in securing the presence in court of a defendant who was released on personal bond.

(d) The commissioners court may not contract for services under this article for more than one year, but the commissioners court may renew a contract. Either party to a contract may terminate the contract by giving six months' advance notice of intent to terminate.

(e) The commissioners court shall pay for contracted services from county general funds. The commissioners court may accept grants, federal funds, and other financial assistance to assist the program.

### Art. 26.042. Tarrant County public defender.† [*Public defender in Tarrant County.*]

(a) Each judge of a criminal district court having jurisdiction in Tarrant County shall appoint an attorney to serve as a public defender. The appointing judge shall define the powers and duties of the public defender appointed to serve that court.

(b) A public defender serves at the pleasure of the appointing judge. A public defender is entitled to receive an annual salary in an amount set by the commissioners court.

(c) To be eligible for appointment as a public defender, a person must:

(1) be a member of the State Bar of Texas;

(2) have practiced law for at least three years; and

(3) have experience in the practice of criminal law.

(d) Except as authorized by this article, a public defender may not engage in the private practice of criminal law or accept anything of value for services rendered in a criminal case.

(e) A public defender or a practicing attorney appointed by a court of competent jurisdiction shall represent each indigent person who is charged with a criminal offense in a Tarrant County court or who is a party in a juvenile delinquency proceeding in Tarrant County.

(f) A public defender may investigate the financial condition of any person the public defender is appointed to represent. The public defender shall report the results of any investigation to the appointing judge. The court may hold a hearing to determine if the defendant is indigent and entitled to representation by a public defender.

(g) At any stage of a criminal proceeding including appeal or other postconviction proceedings, the court may assign a substitute attorney to represent an indigent defendant.

(h) Except for the provisions relating to daily appearance fees, Article 26.05 of this code applies to public defenders.

(i) An attorney other than a public defender who is appointed to represent an indigent defendant is entitled to the compensation provided by Article 26.05 of this code.

### Art. 26.043. Public defender in Wichita County.† [*Appointment of public defender: Wichita County.*]

(a) The Commissioners Court of Wichita County may appoint an attorney to serve as a public defender. The public defender serves at the pleasure of the commissioners court.

(b) To be eligible for appointment as a public defender, a person must:

(1) be a member of the State Bar of Texas;

(2) have practiced law for at least three years; and

(3) have experience in the practice of criminal law.

(c) With the approval of the commissioners court, the public defender may employ assistant public defenders, investigators, secretaries, and other necessary personnel. An assistant public defender must be a licensed attorney and may perform the duties of a public defender under this article.

(d) Chapter 622, Acts of the 62nd Legislature, Regular Session, 1971 (Article 3912k, Texas Civil Statutes),* applies to the compensation of personnel and the payment of office expenses, except that the public defender may not receive a salary that is greater than the salary paid to the district attorney serving Wichita County.

**(Repealed, See Local Government Code, §152.011.)*

(e) Except as authorized by this article, a public defender or assistant public defender may not:

(1) engage in the private practice of criminal law;

(2) engage in the private practice of civil law in a county court, county court at law, or district court in Wichita County; or

(3) accept anything of value not authorized by this article for services rendered under this article.

(f) The commissioners court may remove a public defender or assistant public defender who violates a provision of Subsection (e) of this article.

(g) The public defender or an assistant public defender:

(1) shall represent each indigent person in Wichita County who is:

(A) charged with a criminal offense in the county; or

(B) a minor who is a party to a juvenile delinquency proceeding in the county; and

(2) may represent each indigent person in Wichita County who is entitled to representation under:

(A) Chapter 462, Health and Safety Code;

(B) Subtitle C, Title 7, Health and Safety Code; or

(C) Subtitle D, Title 7, Health and Safety Code.

(h) A public defender or an assistant public defender shall investigate the financial condition of any person the public defender is appointed to represent. The defender shall report the results of the investigation to the appointing judge. The judge may hold a hearing to determine if the defendant or minor is indigent and entitled to representation under this article.

(i) If at any stage of the proceeding the judge determines that a conflict of interest exists between the public defender and the defendant or minor, the judge may appoint another attorney to represent the person. The attorney must be licensed to practice law in this state and is entitled to the compensation provided by Article 26.05 of this code.

(j) Except for the provisions relating to daily appearance fees, Article 26.05 of this code applies to the public defender and assistant public defenders.

(k) The commissioners court may accept gifts and grants from any source to finance an adequate and effective public defender program.

*(Chgd. by L.1995, chap. 637(1), eff. 9/1/95.)*

### Art. 26.044. Public defender in county with four county courts and four district courts.† [*Appointment of public defender: county with four county courts and four district courts.*]

(a) The commissioners court of any county having four county courts and four district courts may appoint one or more attorneys to serve as a public defender. A public defender serves at the pleasure of the commissioners court.

(b) To be eligible for appointment as a public defender, a person must:

(1) be a member of the State Bar of Texas;

(2) have practiced law for at least one year; and

(3) have experience in the practice of criminal law.

(c) The public defender is entitled to receive an annual salary in an amount fixed by the commissioners court and paid out of the appropriate county fund.

(d) Except as authorized by this article, a public defender may not:

(1) engage in the private practice of criminal law; or

(2) accept anything of value not authorized by this article for services rendered under this article.

(e) The judge may remove a public defender who violates a provision of Subsection (d) of this article.

(f) A public defender or an attorney appointed by a court of competent jurisdiction shall represent each indigent person who is charged with a criminal offense in a county having at least four county courts and at least four district courts and each indigent minor who is a party to a juvenile delinquency proceeding in the county.

(g) A public defender may investigate the financial condition of any person the public defender is appointed to represent. The defender shall report the results of the investigation to the appointing judge. The judge may hold a hearing to determine if the person is indigent and entitled to representation under this article.

(h) If an attorney other than a public defender is appointed, the attorney is entitled to the compensation provided by Article 26.05 of this code.

(i) At any stage of the proceeding, including appeal or other postconviction proceedings, the judge may appoint another attorney to represent the person. The substitute attorney is entitled to the compensation provided by Article 26.05 of this code.

(j) Except for the provisions relating to daily appearance fees, Article 26.05 of this code applies to a public defender appointed under this article.

### Art. 26.045. Public defender in 33rd Judicial District.† [*Appointment of public defender: 33rd Judicial District.*]

(a) The 33rd District Court may appoint an attorney to serve as a public defender in the district court for indigents charged with a criminal offense in counties within the district, subject to the approval of the commissioners court of each participating county. If the commissioners court of a county within the district does not approve the appointment, that county is not a participating county and the public defender shall not represent indigent defendants in the district court in that county. The public defender serves at the pleasure of the district court.

(b) To be eligible to be appointed public defender, a person must:

(1) be a licensed member of the State Bar of Texas;

(2) have practiced law for at least three years; and

(3) have experience in the practice of criminal law.

(c) Except as provided by Subsection (f) of this article, a public defender shall represent each indigent person who is charged in the district court with a criminal offense.

(d) The public defender is entitled to receive an annual salary set by the district court in an amount that does not exceed the salary paid by the state to the district attorney serving the district.

(e) The district court may authorize the public defender to employ assistant public defenders, investigators, secretaries, and other necessary personnel. An assistant public defender must be an attorney licensed in this state and may perform the duties of the public defender under this article. Chapter 622, Acts of the 62nd Legislature, Regular Session, 1971 (Article 3912k, Texas Civil Statutes),* applies to the compensation of these personnel and the payment of office expenses.
**(Repealed; see Local Government Code, §152.011.)*

(f) The salary of the public defender, salaries of all employees of the public defender's office, and office expenses of the public defender's office shall be paid by participating counties on a pro rata basis in proportion to the population of each participating county. If a participating county does not pay its apportioned amount, the public defender is not required to represent indigent defendants in that county.

(g) The public defender may investigate the financial condition of a person the public defender is appointed to represent. The public defender shall report the results of the investigation to the appointing judge.

(h) If a judge who has appointed a public defender to represent a defendant determines, at any stage of a proceeding, that there is good cause to remove the public defender from the case, the judge may appoint another attorney to represent the defendant in the place of the public defender. An attorney who is appointed to represent an indigent defendant under this subsection is entitled to compensation as provided by Article 26.05 of this code.

(i) Except for the provisions relating to daily appearance fees, Article 26.05 of this code applies to a public defender appointed under this article.

(j) The commissioners court of a participating county may accept gifts and grants from any source to finance that county's apportioned share of the salaries and expenses of the office of public defender.

### Art. 26.046. Public defender in Webb County.† [*Appointment of public defender: Webb County.*]

(a) The commissioners court of Webb County may appoint an attorney to serve as a public defender. The public defender serves at the pleasure of the commissioners court.

(b) To be eligible for appointment as a public defender, a person must:

(1) be a member of the State Bar of Texas;

(2) have practiced law for at least three years; and

(3) have experience in the practice of criminal law.

(c) With the approval of the commissioners court, the public defender may employ assistant public defenders, investigators, secretaries, and other necessary personnel. An assistant public defender must be a licensed attorney and may perform the duties of a public defender under this article.

(d) Chapter 622, Acts of the 62nd Legislature, Regular Session, 1971 (Article 3912k, Texas Civil Statutes),* applies to the compensation of personnel and the payment of office expenses.
**(Repealed, See Local Government Code, §152.011.)*

(e) Except as authorized by this article, a public defender or an assistant public defender may not:

(1) engage in the private practice of criminal law;

(2) engage in the private practice of civil law in a county court, county court at law, district court, or federal court in Webb County; or

(3) accept anything of value not authorized by this article for services rendered under this article.

(f) The commissioners court may remove a public defender or assistant public defender who violates a provision of Subsection (e) of this article.

(g) The public defender or an assistant public defender shall represent each indigent person who is charged with a criminal offense in Webb County and each indigent minor who is a party to a juvenile delinquency proceeding in the county.

(h) A public defender or an assistant public defender shall investigate the financial condition of any person the public defender is appointed to represent. The defender shall report the results of the investigation to the appointing judge. The judge may hold a hearing to determine if the defendant or minor is indigent and entitled to representation under this article.

(i) If at any stage of the proceeding the judge determines that a conflict of interest exists between the public defender and the defendant or minor, the judge may appoint another attorney to represent the person. The attorney must be licensed to practice law in this state and is entitled to the compensation provided by Article 26.05 of this code.

(j) Except for the provisions relating to daily appearance fees, Article 26.05 of this code applies to the public defender and an assistant public defender.

(k) The commissioners court may accept gifts and grants from any source to finance an adequate and effective public defender program.

**Art. 26.047. Public defender in Colorado County.† [*Appointment of public defender: Colorado County.*]**

(a) The Commissioners Court of Colorado County may appoint an attorney to serve as a public defender. The public defender serves at the pleasure of the commissioners court.

(b) To be eligible for appointment as a public defender, a person must:

(1) be a member of the State Bar of Texas;

(2) have practiced law for at least two years; and

(3) have experience in the practice of criminal law.

(c) With the approval of the commissioners court, the public defender may employ assistant public defenders, investigators, secretaries, and other necessary personnel. An assistant public defender must be a licensed attorney and may perform the duties of a public defender under this article.

(d) Chapter 622, Acts of the 62nd Legislature, Regular Session, 1971 (Article 3912k, Texas Civil Statutes),* applies to the compensation of personnel and the payment of office expenses, except that the public defender may not receive a salary that is greater than the salary paid to the district attorney serving Colorado County.

**(Repealed. See Local Government Code, §152.011.)*

(e) Except as authorized by this article, a public defender or assistant public defender may not:

(1) engage in the private practice of criminal law in any court in Colorado County; or

(2) accept anything of value not authorized by this article for services rendered under this article.

(f) The commissioners court may remove a public defender or assistant public defender who violates a provision of Subsection (e) of this article.

(g) The public defender or an assistant public defender shall represent each indigent person who is charged with a criminal offense in Colorado County and each indigent minor who is a party to a juvenile delinquency proceeding in the county.

(h) A public defender or an assistant public defender shall investigate the financial condition of any person the public defender is appointed to represent. The defender shall report the results of the investigation to the appointing judge. The judge may hold a hearing to determine if the defendant or minor is indigent and entitled to representation under this article.

(i) If at any stage of the proceeding the judge determines that a conflict of interest exists between the public defender and the defendant or minor, the judge may appoint another attorney to represent the person. The attorney must be licensed to practice law in this state and is entitled to the compensation provided by Article 26.05 of this code.

(j) Except for the provisions relating to daily appearance fees, Article 26.05 of this code applies to the public defender and assistant public defenders.

(k) The commissioners court may accept gifts and grants from any source to finance an adequate and effective public defender program.

*(Renumbered from Art. 26.045 by L.1989, chap. 2(16.01)(7), eff. 9/1/89.)*

**Art. 26.048. Public defender in Cherokee County.**

(a) The Commissioners Court of Cherokee County may appoint an attorney to serve as a public defender. The public defender serves at the pleasure of the commissioners court.

(b) To be eligible for appointment as a public defender, a person must:

(1) be a member of the State Bar of Texas;

(2) have practiced law for at least two years; and

(3) have experience in the practice of criminal law.

(c) With the approval of the commissioners court, the public defender may employ assistant public defenders, investigators, secretaries, and other necessary personnel. An assistant public defender must be a licensed attorney and may perform the duties of a public defender under this article.

(d) Subchapter B, Chapter 152, Local Government Code, applies to the compensation of personnel and the payment of office expenses, except that the public defender may not receive a salary that is greater than the salary paid to the district attorney serving Cherokee County.

(e) Except as authorized by this article, a public defender or assistant public defender may not:

(1) engage in the private practice of criminal law in any court in Cherokee County; or

(2) accept anything of value not authorized by this article for services rendered under this article.

(f) The commissioners court may remove a public defender or assistant public defender who violates a provision of Subsection (e) of this article.

(g) The public defender or an assistant public defender may represent each indigent person who is charged with a criminal offense in Cherokee County and each indigent minor who is a party to a juvenile delinquency proceeding in the county. The county commissioners court may specify other types of cases in which the public defender or assistant public defender may represent persons or minors.

(h) A public defender or an assistant public defender shall investigate the financial condition of any person the public defender is appointed to represent. The defender shall report the results of the investigation to the appointing judge. The judge may hold a hearing to determine if the defendant or minor is indigent and entitled to representation under this article.

(i) If at any stage of the proceeding the judge determines that a conflict of interest exists between the public defender and the defendant or minor, the judge may appoint another attorney to represent the person. The attorney must be licensed to practice law in this state and is entitled to the compensation provided by Article 26.05 of this code.

(j) Except for the provisions relating to daily appearance fees, Article 26.05 of this code applies to the public defender and assistant public defenders.

(k) The commissioners court may accept gifts and grants from any source to finance an adequate and effective public defender program.

*(Added by L.1991, chap. 731(1), eff. 6/16/91.)*

**Art. 26.049. Public defender in Tom Green County.**

(a) The Commissioners Court of Tom Green County may appoint an attorney to serve as a public defender. The public defender serves at the pleasure of the commissioners court.

(b) To be eligible for appointment as a public defender, a person must:

(1) be a member of the State Bar of Texas;

(2) have practiced law for at least four years; and

(3) have experience in the practice of criminal law.

(c) With the approval of the commissioners court, the public defender may employ assistant public defenders, investigators, secretaries, and other necessary personnel. An assistant public defender must be a licensed attorney and may perform the duties of a public defender under this article.

(d) Subchapter B, Chapter 152, Local Government Code, applies to the compensation of personnel and the payment of office expenses in the public defender's office.

(e) Except as authorized by this article, a public defender or an assistant public defender may not:

(1) engage in the private practice of law; or

(2) accept anything of value not authorized by this article for services rendered under this article.

(f) The commissioners court may remove a public defender or an assistant public defender who violates Subsection (e).

(g) The public defender or an assistant public defender shall represent each indigent person who is charged with a criminal offense in Tom Green County or who is both a minor and a party to a juvenile delinquency proceeding in the county. The commissioners court may specify other types of cases in which the public defender or an assistant public defender may represent indigent persons.

(h) The public defender or an assistant public defender may investigate the financial condition of any person the defender is appointed to represent. The defender shall report the results of the investigation to the appointing judge. The judge may hold a hearing to determine whether the person is indigent and entitled to representation under this article.

(i) If at any stage of a proceeding the judge determines that a conflict of interest exists between the indigent person and the public defender or an assistant public defender, the judge may appoint another attorney to represent the person. The attorney must be licensed to practice law in this state and is entitled to the compensation provided by Article 26.05.

(j) Except for the provisions relating to daily appearance fees, Article 26.05 applies to the public defender and assistant public defenders.

(k) The commissioners court may accept gifts and grants from any source to finance an adequate and effective public defender program.

*(Added by L.1997, chap. 854(1), eff. 6/18/97.)*

**Art. 26.05. Compensation of counsel appointed to defend.† [*Compensation of court appointed counsel.*]**

(a) A counsel, other than an attorney with a public defender's office, appointed to represent a defendant in a criminal proceeding, including a habeas corpus hearing, shall be reimbursed for reasonable expenses incurred with prior court approval for purposes of investigation and expert testimony and shall be paid a reasonable attorney's fee for performing the following services, based on the time and labor required, the complexity of the case, and the experience and ability of the appointed counsel:

(1) time spent in court making an appearance on behalf of the defendant as evidenced by a docket entry, time spent in trial, or time spent in a proceeding in which sworn oral testimony is elicited;

(2) reasonable and necessary time spent out of court on the case, supported by any documentation that the court requires; and

(3) preparation of an appellate brief to a court of appeals or the Court of Criminal Appeals.

(b) All payments made under this article shall be paid in accordance with a schedule of fees adopted by formal action of the county and district criminal court judges within each county, except that in a county with only one judge with criminal jurisdiction the schedule will be adopted by the administrative judge for that judicial district.

(c) Each fee schedule adopted will include a fixed rate, minimum and maximum hourly rates, and daily rates and will provide a form for reporting the types of services performed in each one. No payment shall be made under this section until the form for reporting the services performed is submitted and approved by the court and is in accordance with the fee schedule for that county.

(d) All payments made under this article shall be paid from the general fund of the county in which the prosecution was instituted or habeas corpus hearing held and may be included as costs of court.

(e) If the court determines that a defendant has financial resources that enable him to offset in part or in whole the costs of the legal services provided, including any expenses and costs, the court shall order the defendant to pay the amount that it finds the defendant is able to pay.

(f) Reimbursement of expenses incurred for purposes of investigation or expert testimony may be paid directly to a private investigator licensed under the Private Investigators and Private Security Agencies Act (Article 4413(29bb), Vernon's Texas Civil Statutes) or to an expert witness in the manner designated by appointed counsel and approved by the court.

*(Chgd. by L.1999, chap. 837(1), eff. 9/1/99.)*

**Art. 26.050. Public defender in 293rd and 365th judicial districts.**

(a) The 293rd and 365th district courts may jointly appoint an attorney to serve as a public defender in the district courts for indigents charged with a criminal offense in counties within the districts, subject to the approval of the commissioners court of each participating county. If the commissioners court of a county within the districts does not approve the appointment, that county is not a participating county and the public defender may not represent indigent defendants in the district courts in that county. The public defender serves at the pleasure of the district courts.

(b) To be eligible to be appointed public defender, a person must:

(1) be a licensed member of the State Bar of Texas;

(2) have practiced law for at least two years; and

(3) have experience in the practice of criminal law.

(c) Except as provided by Subsections (g) and (j) of this article, a public defender shall represent each indigent person who is charged in the district courts with a criminal offense.

(d) The public defender is entitled to receive an annual salary set by the district courts in an amount that does not exceed either of the salaries paid to the district attorney serving the 293rd District Court or the county attorney serving the 365th District Court.

(e) The district courts may authorized the public defender to employ assistant public defenders, investigators, secretaries, and other necessary personnel. An assistant public defender must be an attorney licensed in this state and may perform the duties of the public defender under this article. Subchapter B, Chapter 152, Local Government Code, applies to the compensation of these personnel and the payment of office expenses.

(f) A public defender or assistant public defender may not engage in the private practice of criminal law and, except as authorized by this article, may not accept anything of value for services rendered in a criminal case.

(g) The salary of the public defender, salaries of all employees of the public defender's office, and office expenses of the public defender's office shall be paid by participating counties on a pro rata basis in proportion to the population of each participating county. If a participating county does not pay its apportioned amount, the public defender is not required to represent indigent defendants in that county.

(h) The public defender may investigate the financial condition of a person the public defender is appointed to represent. The public defender shall report the results of the investigation to the appointing judge.

(i) If a judge who has appointed a public defender to represent a defendant determines, at any stage of a proceeding, that there is good cause to remove the public defender from the case, the judge may appoint another attorney to represent the defendant in the place of the public defender. An attorney who is appointed to represent an indigent defendant under this subsection is entitled to compensation as provided by Article 26.05 of this code.

(j) The judge of a district court in which a capital felony is being tried may appoint any attorney as lead counsel for an indigent person. If the attorney appointed is not an employee of the public defender's office, the public defender shall assist the appointed attorney.

(k) The public defender for the 293rd and 365th judicial districts and the Webb County public defender, with the approval of all participating counties, may agree to represent indigents in each other's jurisdictions if either public defender has a conflict of interest in the representation of a particular indigent.

(*l*) Except for the provisions relating to daily appearance fees, Article 26.05 of this code applies to a public defender appointed under this article.

(m) The commissioners court of a participating county may accept gifts and grants from any source to finance that county's apportioned share of the salaries and expenses of the office of public defender.

*(Added by L.1991, chap. 922(1); renumbered from Art. 26.048 by L.1991, 1st C.S., chap. 14(8.01)(1), eff. 11/12/91.)*

## Art. 26.051. Indigent inmate defense.

(a) In this article:

(1) "Board" means the Texas Board of Criminal Justice.

(2) "Institutional division" means the institutional division of the Texas Department of Criminal Justice.

(b) This article applies only to the appointment of attorneys for indigent inmate defendants made on or after August 1, 1990.

(c) A county in which a facility of the institutional division or a correctional facility authorized by Section 495.001, Government Code, is located shall, except as provided by Subsection (f) of this article, pay from its general fund the total costs of the aggregate sum allowed and awarded by the court for attorney's fees under Article 26.05 of this code for an attorney appointed by the court, other than an attorney provided by the board in Subsection (e) of this article, to defend an indigent inmate.

(d) A court may notify the board if it determines that a defendant before the court is indigent and is an inmate charged with an offense committed while in the custody of the institutional division and request that the board provide legal representation for the inmate.

(e) The board shall provide legal representation for inmates described by Subsection (d) of this section. The board may employ attorneys, support staff, and any other personnel required to provide legal representation for those inmates. All personnel employed under this article are directly responsible to the board in the performance of their duties. The board shall pay all fees and costs associated with providing legal representation for those inmates.

(f) *(Repealed.)*

(g) The court shall appoint an attorney other than an attorney provided by the board if the court determines for any of the following reasons that a conflict of interest could arise from the use of an attorney provided by the board under Subsection (e) of this article:

(1) the case involves more than one inmate and the representation of more than one inmate could impair the attorney's effectiveness;

(2) the case is appealed and the court is satisfied that conflict of interest would prevent the presentation of a good faith allegation of ineffective assistance of counsel by a trial attorney provided by the board; or

(3) any conflict of interest exists under the Texas Disciplinary Rules of Professional Conduct of the State Bar of Texas that precludes representation by an attorney appointed by the board.

(h) When the court appoints an attorney other than an attorney provided by the board, the county shall pay from its general fund the first $250.00 of the aggregate sum allowed and awarded by the court for the attorney fees under Article 26.05 of this code. If the fees awarded for a court-appointed attorney in a case described by this subsection exceed $250.00, the court shall certify the amount in excess of $250.00 to the board. On request of the board, the comptroller shall issue a warrant to the court-appointed attorney in the amount certified to the board by the court. *(Added by L.1990, 6th C.S., chap. 15(2); chgd. by L.1991, chap. 719(1); L.1993, chap. 988(7.01), (7.02), eff. 9/1/93.)*

**Art. 26.052. Appointment of counsel in death penalty case; reimbursement of investigative expenses.**

(a) Notwithstanding any other provision of this chapter, this article establishes procedures in death penalty cases for appointment and payment of counsel to represent indigent defendants at trial and on direct appeal and to apply for writ of certiorari in the United States Supreme Court.

(b) If a county is served by a public defender's office, trial counsel and counsel for direct appeal or to apply for a writ of certiorari may be appointed as provided by the guidelines established by the public defender's office. In all other cases in which the death penalty is sought, counsel shall be appointed as provided by this article.

(c) A local selection committee is created in each administrative judicial region created under Section 74.042, Government Code. The administrative judge of the judicial region shall appoint the members of the committee. A committee shall have not less than four members, including:

(1) the administrative judge of the judicial region;

(2) at least one district judge;

(3) a representative from the local bar association; and

(4) at least one practitioner who is board certified by the State Bar of Texas in criminal law.

(d) The committee shall adopt standards for the qualification of attorneys for appointment to death penalty cases. The committee shall prominently post the standards in each district clerk's office in the region with a list of attorneys qualified for appointment.

(e) The presiding judge of the district court in which a capital felony case is filed shall appoint counsel to represent an indigent defendant as soon as practicable after charges are filed, if the death penalty is sought in the case. The judge shall appoint lead trial counsel from the list of attorneys qualified for appointment. The judge shall appoint a second counsel to assist in the defense of the defendant, unless reasons against the appointment of two counsel are stated in the record.

(f) Appointed counsel may file with the trial court a pretrial ex parte confidential request for advance payment of expenses to investigate potential defenses. The request for expenses must state:

(1) the type of investigation to be conducted;

(2) specific facts that suggest the investigation will result in admissible evidence; and

(3) an itemized list of anticipated expenses for each investigation.

(g) The court shall grant the request for advance payment of expenses in whole or in part if the request is reasonable. If the court denies in whole or in part the request for expenses, the court shall:

(1) state the reasons for the denial in writing;

(2) attach the denial to the confidential request; and

(3) submit the request and denial as a sealed exhibit to the record.

(h) Counsel may incur expenses without prior approval of the court. On presentation of a claim for reimbursement, the court shall order reimbursement of counsel for the expenses, if the expenses are reasonably necessary and reasonably incurred.

(i) If the indigent defendant is convicted of a capital felony and sentenced to death, the defendant is entitled to be represented by competent counsel on appeal and to apply for a writ of certiorari to the United States Supreme Court.

(j) As soon as practicable after a death sentence is imposed in a capital felony case, the presiding judge of the convicting court shall appoint counsel to represent an indigent defendant on appeal and to apply for a writ of certiorari, if appropriate.

(k) The court may not appoint an attorney as counsel on appeal if the attorney represented the defendant at trial, unless:

(1) the defendant and the attorney request the appointment on the record; and

(2) the court finds good cause to make the appointment.

(*l*) An attorney appointed under this article to represent a defendant at trial or on direct appeal is compensated as provided by Article 26.05 from county funds. Advance payment of expenses anticipated or reimbursement of expenses incurred for purposes of investigation or expert testimony may be paid directly to a private investigator licensed under the Private Investigators and Private Security Agencies Act (Article 4413(29bb), Vernon's Texas Civil Statutes) or to an expert witness in the manner designated by appointed counsel and approved by the court.
*(Added by L.1995, chap. 319(2); chgd. by L.1999, chap. 837(2), eff. 9/1/99.)*

## Art. 26.055. Contribution from state for defense of certain prisoners.† [*Contribution from state for defense of indigent inmates.*]

**Sec. 1.** (a) This article applies only to an attorney appointed under Article 26.05 of this code to defend an indigent inmate before August 1, 1990.

(b) A county in which a facility of the institutional division of the Texas Department of Criminal Justice, or a correctional facility authorized by Section 494.001, Government Code, is located shall pay from its general fund only the first $250 of the aggregate sum allowed and awarded by the court for attorneys' fees under Art. 26.05 toward defending an inmate committed to that facility who is being prosecuted for an offense committed in that county while in the custody of the department if the inmate was originally committed for an offense committed in another county.

**Sec. 2.** If the fees awarded for court-appointed counsel in a case covered by Sec. 1 of this article exceed $250, the court shall certify the amount in excess of $250 to the Texas Board of Criminal Justice. On request of the board, the comptroller shall issue a warrant to the court-appointed counsel in the amount certified to the board by the court.

**Sec. 3.** (a) In the defense of a prosecution of an offense committed while the actor was an inmate in the custody of the institutional division of the Texas Department of Criminal Justice, the state shall reimburse a counsel appointed to defend the actor for expenses incurred by the counsel, in an amount that the court determines to be reasonable, for payment of:

(1) salaries and expenses of foreign language interpreters and interpreters for deaf persons whose services are necessary to the defense;

(2) consultation fees of experts whose assistance is directly related to the defense;

(3) travel expenses for witnesses;

(4) compensation of witnesses;

(5) the cost of preparation of a statement of facts and a transcript of the trial for purposes of appeal; and

(6) food, lodging, and travel expenses incurred by the defense counsel and staff during travel essential to the defense, calculated on the same basis as expenses incurred by the prosecutor's staff related to essential travel are calculated.

(b) The trial court shall certify the amount of reimbursement for expenses under this section to the Texas Board of Criminal Justice. On request of the board, the comptroller shall issue a warrant in that amount to the defense counsel or, if the board determines that the amount certified by the trial court is unreasonable, in an amount that the board determines to be reasonable.

(c) Notwithstanding anything to the contrary contained in this Act, the reimbursement for expenses submitted by the defense counsel shall not exceed the amount the county would pay for the same activity or service, if that activity or service was not reimbursed by the state. The trial judge shall certify compliance with this paragraph on request by the Texas Board of Criminal Justice.
*(Chgd. by L.1990, 6th C.S., chap. 15(1), eff. 6/14/90.)*

## Art. 26.056. Contribution from State in certain counties.† [*State support for defense of minors.*]

**Sec. 1.** A county in which a state training school for delinquent children is located shall pay from its general fund the first $250 of fees awarded for court-appointed counsel under Article 26.05 toward defending a child committed to the school from another county who is being prosecuted for a felony or misdemeanor in the county where the training school is located.

**Sec. 2.** If the fees awarded for counsel compensation are in excess of $250, the court shall certify the amount in excess of $250 to the Comptroller of Public Accounts of the State of Texas. The Comptroller shall issue a warrant to the court-appointed counsel in the amount certified to the comptroller by the court.

### Art. 26.057. Cost of employment of counsel for certain minors.† [*Employing counsel for minor in criminal cases.*]

If a juvenile has been transferred to a criminal court under Section 54.02, Family Code, and if a court appoints counsel for the juvenile under Article 26.04 of this code, the county that pays for the counsel has a cause of action against a parent or other person who is responsible for the support of the juvenile and is financially able to employ counsel for the juvenile but refuses to do so. The county may recover its cost of payment to the appointed counsel and may recover attorney's fees necessary to prosecute the cause of action against the parent or other person. *(Renumbered from Art. 26.056 by L.1989, chap. 2(16.01(8)), eff. 9/1/89.)*

### Art. 26.058. Public defender in Aransas County.

(a) The Commissioners Court of Aransas County may appoint an attorney to serve as a public defender. The public defender serves at the pleasure of the commissioners court.

(b) To be eligible for appointment as a public defender, a person must:

(1) be a member of the State Bar of Texas;

(2) have practiced law for at least three years; and

(3) have experience in the practice of criminal law.

(c) With the approval of the commissioners court, the public defender may employ assistant public defenders, investigators, secretaries, and other necessary personnel. An assistant public defender must be a licensed attorney and may perform the duties of a public defender under this article.

(d) Subchapter B, Chapter 152, Local Government Code, applies to the compensation of personnel and the payment of office expenses in the public defender's office.

(e) Except as authorized by this article, a public defender or assistant public defender may not:

(1) engage in the private practice of criminal law;

(2) engage in the practice of civil law in a county court, county court at law, district court, or federal court in Aransas County; or

(3) accept anything of value not authorized by this article for services rendered under this article.

(f) The commissioners court may remove a public defender or assistant public defender who violates a provision of Subsection (e) of this article or for good cause shown.

(g) The public defender or an assistant public defender shall represent each indigent person in Aransas County who is:

(1) charged with a criminal offense in the county;

(2) a minor who is a party to a juvenile delinquency proceeding in the county; or

(3) entitled to representation under:

(A) Chapter 574, Health and Safety Code;

(B) Chapter 462, Health and Safety Code; or

(C) Subchapter B, Chapter 107, or Section 262.105, Family Code.

(D) *(Repealed.)*

(h) A public defender or an assistant public defender shall investigate the financial condition of any person the public defender is appointed to represent. The defender shall report the results of the investigation to the appointing judge. The judge may hold a hearing to determine if the person is indigent and entitled to representation under this article.

(i) If at any stage of the proceeding the judge determines that a conflict of interest exists between the public defender and the indigent person, the judge may appoint another attorney to represent the person. The attorney must be licensed to practice law in this state and is entitled to the compensation provided by Article 26.05 of this code.

(j) Subsections (d) and (e), Article 26.05, of this code apply to a person represented under this article.

(k) The commissioners court may accept gifts and grants from any source to finance an adequate and effective public defender program.

*(Added by L.1989, chap. 590(1); chgd. by L.1991, chap. 14(284)(97); L.1997, chap. 165(7.02), eff. 9/1/97.)*

**Art. 26.06. Elected officials not to be appointed.† [*Appointment of elected official.*]**

No court may appoint an elected county, district or state official to represent a person accused of crime, unless the official has notified the court of his availability for appointment. If an official has notified the court of his availability and is appointed as counsel, he may decline the appointment if he determines that it is in the best interest of his office to do so. Nothing in this Code shall modify any statutory provision for legislative continuance.

**Art. 26.07. Name as stated in indictment.**

When the defendant is arraigned, his name, as stated in the indictment, shall be distinctly called; and unless he suggest by himself or counsel that he is not indicted by his true name, it shall be taken that his name is truly set forth, and he shall not thereafter be allowed to deny the same by way of defense.

**Art. 26.08. If defendant suggest different name.† [*Name of defendant incorrect: indictment corrected.*]**

If the defendant, or his counsel for him, suggests that he bears some name different from that stated in the indictment, the same shall be noted upon the minutes of the court, the indictment corrected by inserting therein the name of the defendant as suggested by himself or his counsel for him, the style of the case changed so as to give his true name, and the cause proceed as if the true name had been first recited in the indictment.

**Art. 26.09. If accused refuses to give his real name.† [*Name in indictment incorrect: defendant refuses to give true name.*]**

If the defendant alleges that he is not indicted by his true name, and refuses to say what his real name is, the cause shall proceed as if the name stated in the indictment were true; and the defendant shall not be allowed to contradict the same by way of defense.

**Art. 26.10. Where name is unknown.† [*Name of defendant unknown.*]**

A defendant described as a person whose name is unknown may have the indictment so corrected as to give therein his true name.

**Art. 26.11. Indictment read.† [*Reading of indictment.*]**

The name of the accused having been called, if no suggestion, such as is spoken of in the four preceding Articles, be made, or being made is disposed of as before directed, the indictment shall be read, and the defendant asked whether he is guilty or not, as therein charged.

**Art. 26.12. Plea of not guilty entered.† [*Entering plea of not guilty.*]**

If the defendant answers that he is not guilty, such plea shall be entered upon the minutes of the court; if he refuses to answer, the plea of not guilty shall in like manner be entered.

**Art. 26.13. Plea of guilty.† [*Entering plea of guilty.*]**

(a) Prior to accepting a plea of guilty or a plea of nolo contendere, the court shall admonish the defendant of:

(1) the range of the punishment attached to the offense;

(2) the fact that the recommendation of the prosecuting attorney as to punishment is not binding on the court. Provided that the court shall inquire as to the existence of any plea bargaining agreements between the state and the defendant and, in the event that such an agreement exists, the court shall inform the defendant whether it will follow or reject such agreement in open court and before any finding on the plea. Should the court reject any such agreement, the defendant shall be permitted to withdraw his plea of guilty or nolo contendere;

(3) the fact that if the punishment assessed does not exceed the punishment recommended by the prosecutor and agreed to by the defendant and his attorney, the trial court must give its permission to the defendant before he may prosecute an appeal on any matter in the case except for those matters raised by written motions filed prior to trial;

(4) the fact that if the defendant is not a citizen of the United States of America, a plea of guilty or nolo contendere for the offense charged may result in deportation, the exclusion from admission to this country, or the denial of naturalization under federal law; and

(5) the fact that the defendant will be required to meet the registration requirements of Chapter 62, if the defendant is convicted of or placed on deferred adjudication for an offense for which a person is subject to registration under that chapter.

(b) No plea of guilty or plea of nolo contendere shall be accepted by the court unless it appears that the defendant is mentally competent and the plea is free and voluntary.

(c) In admonishing the defendant as herein provided, substantial compliance by the court is sufficient, unless the defendant affirmatively shows that he was not aware of the consequences of his plea and that he was misled or harmed by the admonishment of the court.

(d) The court may make the admonitions required by this article either orally or in writing. If the court makes the admonitions in writing, it must receive a statement signed by the defendant and the defendant's attorney that he understands the admonitions and is aware of the consequences of his plea. If the defendant is unable or refuses to sign the statement, the court shall make the admonitions orally.

(e) Before accepting a plea of guilty or a plea of nolo contendere, the court shall inquire as to whether a victim impact statement has been returned to the attorney representing the state and ask for a copy of the statement if one has been returned.

(f) The court must substantially comply with Subsection (e) of this article. The failure of the court to comply with Subsection (e) of this article is not grounds for the defendant to set aside the conviction, sentence, or plea.

(g) Before accepting a plea of guilty or a plea of nolo contendere and on the request of a victim of the offense, the court may assist the victim and the defendant in participating in a victim-offender mediation program.

(h) Notwithstanding this article, a court shall not order the state or any of its prosecuting attorneys to participate in mediation, dispute resolution, arbitration, or other similar procedures in relation to a criminal prosecution unless upon written consent of the state. *(Added by L.1999, chap. 425(1), eff. 6/18/99. See other subsection (h) below.)*

(h) Before accepting a plea of guilty or nolo contendere from a defendant described by Subsection (a)(5), the court shall ascertain whether the attorney representing the defendant has advised the defendant regarding registration requirements under Chapter 62. *(Added by L.1999, chap. 1415(1), eff. 9/1/99. See other subsection (h) above.)*

*(Chgd. by L.1991, chap. 202(1); L.1997, chap. 670(4); L.1999, chaps. 425(1), 1415(1), eff. 6/18/99, 9/1/99, respectively.)*

**Art. 26.14. Jury on plea of guilty.† [*Plea of guilty: jury trial.*]**

Where a defendant in a case of felony persists in pleading guilty or in entering a plea of nolo contendere, if the punishment is not absolutely fixed by law, a jury shall be impaneled to assess the punishment and evidence may be heard to enable them to decide thereupon, unless the defendant in accordance with Articles 1.13 or 37.07 shall have waived his right to trial by jury.

**Art. 26.15. Correcting name.† [*Correcting name on indictment.*]**

In any case, the same proceedings shall be had with respect to the name of the defendant and the correction of the indictment or information as provided with respect to the same in capital cases.

## CHAPTER 27. THE PLEADING IN CRIMINAL ACTIONS

Article

**Art. 27.01. Indictment or information.**

The primary pleading in a criminal action on the part of the State is the indictment or information.

**Art. 27.02. Defendant's pleadings.† [*Pleadings and motions: defendant.*]**

The pleadings and motions of the defendant shall be:

(1) A motion to set aside or an exception to an indictment or information for some matter of form or substance;

(2) A special plea as provided in Article 27.05 of this code;

(3) A plea of guilty;

(4) A plea of not guilty;

(5) A plea of nolo contendere, the legal effect of which shall be the same as that of a plea of guilty, except that such plea may not be used against the defendant as an admission in any civil suit based upon or growing out of the act upon which the criminal prosecution is based;

(6) An application for probation, if any;

(7) An election, if any, to have the jury assess the punishment if he is found guilty; and

(8) Any other motions or pleadings that are by law permitted to be filed.

**Art. 27.03. Motion to set aside indictment.† [*Indictment: motion to set aside.*]**

In addition to any other grounds authorized by law, a motion to set aside an indictment or information may be based on the following:

1. That it appears by the records of the court that the indictment was not found by at least nine grand jurors, or that the information was not based upon a valid complaint;

2. That some person not authorized by law was present when the grand jury was deliberating upon the accusation against the defendant, or was voting upon the same; and

3. That the grand jury was illegally impaneled; provided, however, in order to raise such question on motion to set aside the indictment, the defendant must show that he did not have an opportunity to challenge the array at the time the grand jury was impaneled.

**Art. 27.04. Motion tried by judge.† [*Motion to set aside tried by judge.*]**

An issue of fact arising upon a motion to set aside an indictment or information shall be tried by the judge without a jury.

**Art. 27.05. Defendant's special plea.† [*Special plea: defendant.*]**

A defendant's only special plea is that he has already been prosecuted for the same or a different offense arising out of the same criminal episode that was or should have been consolidated into one trial, and that the former prosecution:

(1) resulted in acquittal;

(2) resulted in conviction;

(3) was improperly terminated; or

(4) was terminated by a final order or judgment for the defendant that has not been reversed, set aside, or vacated and that necessarily required a determination inconsistent with a fact that must be established to secure conviction in the subsequent prosecution.

**Art. 27.06. Special plea verified.† [*Verification of special plea.*]**

Every special plea shall be verified by the affidavit of the defendant.

**Art. 27.07. Special plea tried.**

All issues of fact presented by a special plea shall be tried by the trier of the facts on the trial on the merits.

**Art. 27.08. Exception to substance of indictment.† [*Indictment: exceptions to substance.*]**

There is no exception to the substance of an indictment or information except:

1. That it does not appear therefrom that an offense against the law was committed by the defendant;

2. That it appears from the face thereof that a prosecution for the offense is barred by a lapse of time, or that the offense was committed after the finding of the indictment;

3. That it contains matter which is a legal defense or bar to the prosecution; and

4. That it shows upon its face that the court trying the case has no jurisdiction thereof.

**Art. 27.09. Exception to form of indictment.†** [*Indictment: exceptions to form.*]

Exceptions to the form of an indictment or information may be taken for the following causes only:

1. That it does not appear to have been presented in the proper court as required by law;
2. The want of any requisite prescribed by Articles 21.02 and 21.21.
3. That it was not returned by a lawfully chosen or empaneled grand jury.

**Art. 27.10. Written pleadings.†** [*Pleadings must be written.*]

All motions to set aside an indictment or information and all special pleas and exceptions shall be in writing.

**Art. 27.11. Ten days allowed for filing pleadings.†** [*Filing pleadings: ten day limit.*]

In all cases the defendant shall be allowed ten entire days, exclusive of all fractions of a day after his arrest, and during the term of the court, to file written pleadings.

**Art. 27.12. Time after service.†** [*Filing pleadings after service of indictment.*]

In cases where the defendant is entitled to be served with a copy of the indictment, he shall be allowed the ten days time mentioned in the preceding Article to file written pleadings after such service.

**Art. 27.13. Plea of guilty or nolo contendere in felony.†** [*Felony: pleas of "guilty" or "nolo contendere".*]

A plea of "guilty" or a plea of "nolo contendere" in a felony case must be made in open court by the defendant in person; and the proceedings shall be as provided in Article 26.13, 26.14 and 27.02. If the plea is before the judge alone, same may be made in the same manner as is provided for by Articles 1.13 and 1.15.

**Art. 27.14. Plea of guilty or nolo contendere in misdemeanor.†** [*Misdemeanor: pleas of "guilty" or "nolo contendere".*]

(a) A plea of "guilty" or a plea of "nolo contendere" in a misdemeanor case may be made either by the defendant or his counsel in open court; in such case, the defendant or his counsel may waive a jury, and the punishment may be assessed by the court either upon or without evidence, at the discretion of the court.

(b) A defendant charged with a misdemeanor for which the maximum possible punishment is by fine only may, in lieu of the method provided in Subsection (a) of this article, mail or deliver in person to the court a plea of "guilty" or a plea of "nolo contendere" and a waiver of jury trial. The defendant may also request in writing that the court notify the defendant, at the address stated in the request, of the amount of an appeal bond that the court will approve. If the court receives a plea and waiver before the time the defendant is scheduled to appear in court, the court shall dispose of the case without requiring a court appearance by the defendant. The court shall notify the defendant either in person or by certified mail, return receipt requested, of the amount of any fine assessed in the case and, if requested by the defendant, the amount of an appeal bond that the court will approve. The defendant shall pay any fine assessed or give an appeal bond in the amount stated in the notice before the 31st day after receiving the notice.

(c) In a misdemeanor case for which the maximum possible punishment is by fine only, payment of a fine, or an amount accepted by the court constitutes a finding of guilty in open court, as though a plea of nolo contendere had been entered by the defendant.

(d) If written notice of an offense for which maximum possible punishment is by fine only or of a violation relating to the manner, time, and place of parking has been prepared, delivered, and filed with the court and a legible duplicate copy has been given to the defendant, the written notice serves as a complaint to which the defendant may plead "guilty," "not guilty," or "nolo contendere." If the defendant pleads "not guilty" to the offense, a complaint shall be filed that conforms to the requirements of Chapter 45 of this code, and that complaint serves as an original complaint. A defendant may waive the filing of a sworn complaint and elect that the prosecution proceed on the written notice of the charged offense if the defendant agrees in writing with the prosecution, signs the agreement, and files it with the court.
*(Chgd. by L.1993, chap. 76(1), eff. 9/1/93.)*

**Art. 27.15. Change of venue to plead guilty.†** [*Change of venue to enter plea.*]

When in any county which is located in a judicial district composed of more than one county, a party is charged with a felony and the maximum punishment therefor shall not exceed fifteen years, and the district court of said county is not in session, such party may, if he desires to plead guilty, or enter a plea of nolo contendere, make application to the district judge of such district for a change of venue to the county in which said court is in session, and said district judge may enter an order changing the venue of said cause to the county in which the court is then in session, and the defendant may plead guilty or enter a plea of nolo contendere to said charge in said court to which the venue has been changed.

**Art. 27.16. Plea of not guilty, how made.† [*Entering a plea of not guilty.*]**

(a) The plea of not guilty may be made orally by the defendant or by his counsel in open court. If the defendant refuses to plead, the plea of not guilty shall be entered for him by the court.

(b) A defendant charged with a misdemeanor for which the maximum possible punishment is by fine only may, in lieu of the method provided in Subsection (a) of this article, mail to the court a plea of not guilty.

**Art. 27.17. Plea of not guilty construed.**

The plea of not guilty shall be construed to be a denial of every material allegation in the indictment or information. Under this plea, evidence to establish the insanity of defendant, and every fact whatever tending to acquit him of the accusation may be introduced, except such facts as are proper for a special plea under Article 27.05.

**Art. 27.18. Plea or waiver of rights by closed circuit video teleconferencing.**

(a) Notwithstanding any provision of this code requiring that a plea or a waiver of a defendant's right be made in open court, a court may accept the plea or waiver by broadcast by closed circuit video teleconferencing to the court if:

(1) the defendant and the attorney representing the state file with the court written consent to the use of closed circuit video teleconferencing;

(2) the closed circuit video teleconferencing system provides for a simultaneous, compressed full motion video, and interactive communication of image and sound between the judge, the attorney representing the state, the defendant, and the defendant's attorney; and

(3) on request of the defendant, the defendant and the defendant's attorney are able to communicate privately without being recorded or heard by the judge or the attorney representing the state.

(b) On motion of the defendant or the attorney representing the state or in the court's discretion, the court may terminate an appearance by closed circuit video teleconferencing at any time during the appearance and require an appearance by the defendant in open court.

(c) A recording of the communication shall be made and preserved until all appellate proceedings have been disposed of. The defendant may obtain a copy of the recording on payment of a reasonable amount to cover the costs of reproduction or, if the defendant is indigent, the court shall provide a copy to the defendant without charging a cost for the copy.

*(Added by L.1997, chap. 1014(1), eff. 6/19/97.)*

## CHAPTER 28. MOTIONS, PLEADINGS AND EXCEPTIONS

Article

## Art. 28.01. Pre-trial.

**Sec. 1.** The court may set any criminal case for a pre-trial hearing before it is set for trial upon its merits, and direct the defendant and his attorney, if any of record, and the State's attorney, to appear before the court at the time and place stated in the court's order for a conference and hearing. The defendant must be present at the arraignment, and his presence is required during any pre-trial proceeding. The pre-trial hearing shall be to determine any of the following matters:

(1) Arraignment of the defendant, if such be necessary; and appointment of counsel to represent the defendant, if such be necessary;

(2) Pleadings of the defendant;

(3) Special pleas, if any;

(4) Exceptions to the form or substance of the indictment or information;

(5) Motions for continuance either by the State or defendant; provided that grounds for continuance not existing or not known at the time may be presented and considered at any time before the defendant announces ready for trial;

(6) Motions to suppress evidence—When a hearing on the motion to suppress evidence is granted, the court may determine the merits of said motion on the motions themselves, or upon opposing affidavits, or upon oral testimony, subject to the discretion of the court;

(7) Motions for change of venue by the State or the defendant; provided, however, that such motions for change of venue, if overruled at the pre-trial hearing, may be renewed by the State or the defendant during the voir dire examination of the jury;

(8) Discovery;

(9) Entrapment; and

(10) Motion for appointment of interpreter.

**Sec. 2.** When a criminal case is set for such pre-trial hearing, any such preliminary matters not raised or filed seven days before the hearing will not thereafter be allowed to be raised or filed, except by permission of the court for good cause shown; provided that the defendant shall have sufficient notice of such hearing to allow him not less than 10 days in which to raise or file such preliminary matters. The record made at such pre-trial hearing, the rulings of the court and the exceptions and objections thereto shall become a part of the trial record of the case upon its merits.

**Sec. 3.** The notice mentioned in Section 2 above shall be sufficient if given in any one of the following ways:

(1) By announcement made by the court in open court in the presence of the defendant or his attorney of record;

(2) By personal service upon the defendant or his attorney of record;

(3) By mail to either the defendant or his attorney of record deposited by the clerk in the mail at least six days prior to the date set for hearing. If the defendant has no attorney of record such notice shall be addressed to defendant at the address shown on his bond, if the bond shows such an address, and if not, it may be addressed to one of the sureties on his bond. If the envelope containing the notice is properly addressed, stamped and mailed, the state will not be required to show that it was received.

## Art. 28.02. Order of argument.

The counsel of the defendant has the right to open and conclude the argument upon all pleadings of the defendant presented for the decision of the judge.

## Art. 28.03. Process for testimony on pleadings.† [*Pleadings process for testimony.*]

When the matters involved in any written pleading depend in whole or in part upon testimony, and not altogether upon the record of the court, every process known to the law may be obtained on behalf of either party to procure such testimony; but there shall be no delay on account of the want of the testimony, unless it be shown to the satisfaction of the court that all the means given by the law have been used to procure the same.

## Art. 28.04. Quashing charge in misdemeanor.† [*Misdemeanor: setting aside charge.*]

If the motion to set aside or the exception to an indictment or information is sustained, the defendant in a misdemeanor case shall be discharged, but may be again prosecuted within the time allowed by law.

**Art. 28.05. Quashing indictment in felony.†** [*Felony: setting aside indictment.*]

If the motion to set aside or the exception to the indictment in cases of felony be sustained, the defendant shall not therefor be discharged, but may immediately be recommitted by order of the court, upon motion of the State's attorney or without motion; and proceedings may afterward be had against him as if no prosecution had ever been commenced.

**Art. 28.06. Shall be fully discharged, when.†** [*Discharge of defendant.*]

Where, after the motion or exception is sustained, it is made known to the court by sufficient testimony that the offense of which the defendant is accused will be barred by limitation before another indictment can be presented, he shall be fully discharged.

**Art. 28.061. Discharge for delay.**

If a motion to set aside an indictment, information, or complaint for failure to provide a speedy trial is sustained, the court shall discharge the defendant. A discharge under this article is a bar to any further prosecution for the offense discharged and for any other offense arising out of the same transaction, other than an offense of a higher grade that the attorney representing the state and prosecuting the offense that was discharged does not have the primary duty to prosecute. *(Chgd. by L.1997, chap. 289(1), eff. 5/26/97.)*

**Art. 28.07. If exception is that no offense is charged.†** [*Discharge of defendant: no offense charged.*]

If an exception to an indictment or information is taken and sustained upon the ground that there is no offense against the law charged therein, the defendant shall be discharged, unless an affidavit be filed accusing him of the commission of a penal offense.

**Art. 28.08. When defendant is held by order of court.†** [*Refusal of court to discharge defendant.*]

If the motion to set aside the indictment or any exception thereto is sustained, but the court refuses to discharge the defendant, then at the expiration of ten days from the order sustaining such motions or exceptions, the defendant shall be discharged, unless in the meanwhile complaint has been made before a magistrate charging him with an offense, or unless another indictment has been presented against him for such offense.

**Art. 28.09. Exception on account of form or substance.†** [*Amending indictment or information.*]

If the exception to an indictment or information is sustained, the information or indictment may be amended if permitted by Article 28.10 of this code, and the cause may proceed upon the amended indictment or information.

**Art. 28.10. Amendment of indictment or information.†** [*Amending indictment or information: defendant's objections.*]

(a) After notice to the defendant, a matter of form or substance in an indictment or information may be amended at any time before the date the trial on the merits commences. On the request of the defendant, the court shall allow the defendant not less than 10 days, or a shorter period if requested by the defendant, to respond to the amended indictment or information.

(b) A matter of form or substance in an indictment or information may also be amended after the trial on the merits commences if the defendant does not object.

(c) An indictment or information may not be amended over the defendant's objection as to form or substance if the amended indictment or information charges the defendant with an additional or different offense or if the substantial rights of the defendant are prejudiced.

**Art. 28.11. How amended.**

All amendments of an indictment or information shall be made with the leave of the court and under its direction.

**Art. 28.12. Exception and trial of special pleas.†** [*Special pleas: exception and trial.*]

When a special plea is filed by the defendant, the State may except to it for substantial defects. If the exception be sustained, the plea may be amended. If the plea be not excepted to, it shall be considered that issue has been taken upon the same. Such special pleas as set forth matter of fact proper to be tried by a jury shall be submitted and tried with a plea of not guilty.

**Art. 28.13. Former acquittal or conviction.† [*Former acquittal or conviction bar to further prosecution.*]**

A former judgment of acquittal or conviction in a court of competent jurisdiction shall be a bar to any further prosecution for the same offense, but shall not bar a prosecution for any higher grade of offense over which said court had not jurisdiction, unless such judgment was had upon indictment or information, in which case the prosecution shall be barred for all grades of the offense.

**Art. 28.14. Plea allowed.† [*Plea permitted.*]**

Judgment shall, in no case, be given against the defendant where his motion, exception or plea is overruled; but in all cases the plea of not guilty may be made by or for him.

## CHAPTER 29. CONTINUANCE

Article



**Art. 29.01. By operation of law.**

Criminal actions are continued by operation of law if:

(1) The individual defendant has not been arrested;

(2) A defendant corporation or association has not been served with summons; or

(3) There is not sufficient time for trial at that term of court.

**Art. 29.011. Religious holy day.† [*Continuance for religious holy day: party to case.*]**

(a) In this article:

(1) "Religious organization" means an organization that meets the standards for qualifying as a religious organization under Section 11.20, Tax Code.

(2) "Religious holy day" means a day on which the tenets of a religious organization prohibit its members from participating in secular activities, such as court proceedings.

(b) If a defendant, an attorney representing the defendant, or an attorney representing the state in a criminal action is required to appear at a court proceeding on a religious holy day observed by the person, the court shall continue the action.

(c) A defendant or attorney seeking a continuance must file with the court an affidavit stating:

(1) the grounds for the continuance; and

(2) that the person holds religious beliefs that prohibit him from taking part in a court proceeding on the day for which the continuance is sought.

(d) An affidavit filed under Subsection (c) of this article is proof of the facts stated and need not be corroborated.

*(Chgd. by L.1991, chap. 815(1), eff. 9/1/91. See also §29.012 below regarding provisions for jurors on holy days.)*

**Art. 29.012. Religious holy day.† [*Continuance for religious holy day: juror.*]**

(a) In this article:

(1) "Religious organization" means an organization that meets the standards for qualification as a religious organization under Section 11.20, Tax Code.

(2) "Religious holy day" means a day on which the tenets of a religious organization prohibit its members from participating in secular activities, such as court proceedings.

(b) If a juror in a criminal action is required to appear at a court proceeding on a religious holy day observed by the juror, the court or the court's designee shall recess the criminal action until the next day the court is in session after the conclusion of the holy day.

(c) A juror seeking a recess must file with the court before the final selection of the jury an affidavit stating:

(1) the grounds for the recess; and

(2) that the juror hold religious beliefs that prohibit him from taking part in a court proceeding on the day for which the recess is sought.

(d) An affidavit filed under Subsection (c) of this section is proof of the facts stated and need not be corroborated.

*(See also §29.011 above regarding provisions for parties on holy days.)*

### Art. 29.02. By agreement.† [*Agreement of parties.*]

A criminal action may be continued by consent of the parties thereto, in open court, at any time on a showing of good cause, but a continuance may be only for as long as is necessary.

### Art. 29.03. For sufficient cause shown.† [*Continuance: cause shown.*]

A criminal action may be continued on the written motion of the State or of the defendant, upon sufficient cause shown; which cause shall be fully set forth in the motion. A continuance may be only for as long as is necessary.

### Art. 29.04. First motion by State.

It shall be sufficient, upon the first motion by the State for a continuance, if the same be for the want of a witness, to state:

1. The name of the witness and his residence, if known, or that his residence is unknown;

2. The diligence which has been used to procure his attendance; and it shall not be considered sufficient diligence to have caused to be issued, or to have applied for, a subpoena, in cases where the law authorized an attachment to issue; and

3. That the testimony of the witness is believed by the applicant to be material for the State.

### Art. 29.05. Subsequent motion by State.† [*Additional motion by State.*]

On any subsequent motion for a continuance by the State, for the want of a witness, the motion, in addition to the requisites in the preceding Article, must show:

1. The facts which the applicant expects to establish by the witness, and it must appear to the court that they are material;

2. That the applicant expects to be able to procure the attendance of the witness at the next term of the court; and

3. That the testimony cannot be procured from any other source during the present term of the court.

### Art. 29.06. First motion by defendant.

In the first motion by the defendant for a continuance, it shall be necessary, if the same be on account of the absence of a witness, to state:

1. The name of the witness and his residence, if known, or that his residence is not known.

2. The diligence which has been used to procure his attendance; and it shall not be considered sufficient diligence to have caused to be issued, or to have applied for, a subpoena, in cases where the law authorized an attachment to issue.

3. The facts which are expected to be proved by the witness, and it must appear to the court that they are material.

4. That the witness is not absent by the procurement or consent of the defendant.

5. That the motion is not made for delay.

6. That there is no reasonable expectation that attendance of the witness can be secured during the present term of the court by a postponement of the trial to some future day of said term. The truth of the first, or any subsequent motion, as well as the merit of the ground set forth therein and its sufficiency shall be addressed to the sound discretion of the court called to pass upon the same, and shall not be granted as a matter of right. If a motion for continuance be overruled, and the defendant convicted, if it appear upon the trial that the evidence of the witness or witnesses named in the motion was a material character, and that the facts set forth in said motion were probably true, a new trial should be granted, and the cause continued or postponed to a future day of the same term.

**Art. 29.07. Subsequent motion by defendant.† [*Additional motion by defendant.*]**

Subsequent motions for continuance on the part of the defendant shall, in addition to the requisites in the preceding Article, state also:

1. That the testimony cannot be procured from any other source known to the defendant; and
2. That the defendant has reasonable expectation of procuring the same at the next term of the court.

**Art. 29.08. Motion sworn to.† [*Swearing to motion.*]**

All motions for continuance must be sworn to by a person having personal knowledge of the facts relied on for the continuance.

**Art. 29.09. Controverting motion.† [*Denial of motion.*]**

Any material fact stated, affecting diligence, in a motion for a continuance, may be denied in writing by the adverse party. The denial shall be supported by the oath of some credible person, and filed as soon as practicable after the filing of such motion.

**Art. 29.10. When denial is filed.† [*Filing of denial.*]**

When such denial is filed, the issue shall be tried by the judge; and he shall hear testimony by affidavits, and grant or refuse continuance, according to the law and facts of the case.

**Art. 29.11. Argument.**

No argument shall be heard on a motion for a continuance, unless requested by the judge; and when argument is heard, the applicant shall have the right to open and conclude it.

**Art. 29.12. Bail resulting from continuance.† [*Continuance: bail.*]**

If a defendant in a capital case demand a trial, and it appears that more than one continuance has been granted to the State, and that the defendant has not before applied for a continuance, he shall be entitled to be admitted to bail, unless it be made to appear to the satisfaction of the court that a material witness of the State had been prevented from attendance by the procurement of the defendant or some person acting in his behalf.

**Art. 29.13. Continuance after trial has begun.† [*Continuance after commencement of trial.*]**

A continuance or postponement may be granted on the motion of the State or defendant after the trial has begun, when it is made to appear to the satisfaction of the court that by some unexpected occurrence since the trial began, which no reasonable diligence could have anticipated, the applicant is so taken by surprise that a fair trial cannot be had.

## CHAPTER 30. DISQUALIFICATION OF THE JUDGE

Article



**Art. 30.01. Causes which disqualify.**

No judge or justice of the peace shall sit in any case where he may be the party injured, or where he has been of counsel for the State or the accused, or where the accused or the party injured may be connected with him by consanguinity or affinity within the third degree, as determined under Chapter 573, Government Code. *(Chgd. by L.1991, chap. 561(9); L.1995, chap. 76(5.95(27)), eff. 9/1/95.)*

**Art. 30.02. District judge disqualified.† [*Disqualification of district judge.*]**

Whenever any case is pending in which the district judge or criminal district judge is disqualified from trying the case, no change of venue shall be made necessary thereby; but the judge presiding shall certify that fact to the presiding judge of the administrative judicial district in which the case is pending and the presiding judge of such administrative judicial district shall assign a judge to try such case in accordance with the provisions of Article 200a, C.S.

**Arts. 30.03 to 30.06.** *(Repealed by L.1999, chap. 1388(14), eff. 9/1/99.)*

**Art. 30.07. Justice disqualified.† [*Disqualification of justice of the peace.*]**

If a justice of the peace be disqualified from sitting in any criminal action pending before him, he shall transfer the same to any justice of the peace in the county who is not disqualified to try the case.

**Art. 30.08. Order of transfer.**

In cases provided for in the preceding Article, the order of transfer shall state the cause of the transfer, and name the court to which the transfer is made, and the time and place, when and where, the parties and witnesses shall appear before such court. The rules governing the transfer of cases from the district to inferior courts shall govern in the transfer of cases under the preceding Article.

## CHAPTER 31. CHANGE OF VENUE

Article



**Art. 31.01. On court's own motion.† [*Change of venue by motion of court.*]**

Whenever in any case of felony or misdemeanor punishable by confinement, the judge presiding shall be satisfied that a trial, alike fair and impartial to the accused and to the State, cannot, from any cause, be had in the county in which the case is pending, he may, upon his own motion, after due notice to accused and the State, and after hearing evidence thereon, order a change of venue to any county in the judicial district in which such county is located or in an adjoining district, stating in his order the grounds for such change of venue. The judge, upon his own motion, after ten days notice to the parties or their counsel, may order a change of venue to any county beyond an adjoining district; provided, however, an order changing venue to a county beyond an adjoining district shall be grounds for reversal if, upon timely contest by the defendant, the record of the contest affirmatively shows that any county in his own and the adjoining district is not subject to the same conditions which required the transfer.

**Art. 31.02. State may have.† [*Change of venue by motion of State.*]**

Whenever the district or county attorney shall represent in writing to the court before which any felony or misdemeanor case punishable by confinement, is pending, that, by reason of existing combinations or influences in favor of the accused, or on account of the lawless condition of affairs in the county, a fair and impartial trial as between the accused and the State cannot be safely and speedily had; or whenever he shall represent that the life of the prisoner, or of any witness, would be jeopardized by a trial in the county in which the case is pending, the judge shall hear proof in relation thereto, and if satisfied that such representation is well-founded and that the ends of public justice will be subserved thereby, he shall order a change of venue to any county in the judicial district in which such county is located or in an adjoining district.

**Art. 31.03. Granted on motion of defendant.† [*Change of venue by motion of defendant.*]**

(a) A change of venue may be granted in any felony or misdemeanor case punishable by confinement on the written motion of the defendant, supported by his own affidavit and the affidavit of at least two credible persons, residents of the county where the prosecution is instituted, for either of the following causes, the truth and sufficiency of which the court shall determine:

1. That there exists in the county where the prosecution is commenced so great a prejudice against him that he cannot obtain a fair and impartial trial; and

2. That there is a dangerous combination against him instigated by influential persons, by reason of which he cannot expect a fair trial.

An order changing venue to a county beyond an adjoining district shall be grounds for reversal, if upon timely contest by defendant, the record of the contest affirmatively shows that any county in his own and the adjoining district is not subject to the same conditions which required the transfer.

(b) For the convenience of parties and witnesses, and in the interest of justice, the court upon motion of the defendant and with the consent of the attorney for the state may transfer the proceeding as to him to another district.

(c) The court upon motion of the defendant and with the consent of the attorney for the state may transfer the proceedings to another district in those cases wherein the defendant stipulates that a plea of guilty will be entered.

### Art. 31.04. Motion may be controverted.† [*Denial of motion.*]

The credibility of the persons making affidavit for change of venue, or their means of knowledge, may be attacked by the affidavit of a credible person. The issue thus formed shall be tried by the judge, and the motion granted or refused, as the law and facts shall warrant.

### Art. 31.05. Clerk's duties on change of venue.† [*Change of venue: duties of court clerk.*]

Where an order for a change of venue of any court in any criminal cause in this State has been made the clerk of the court where the prosecution is pending shall make out a certified copy of the court's order directing such change of venue, together with a certified copy of the defendant's bail bond or personal bond, together with all the original papers in said cause and also a certificate of the said clerk under his official seal that such papers are the papers and all the papers on file in said court in said cause; and he shall transmit the same to the clerk of the court to which the venue has been changed.

### Art. 31.06. If defendant be in custody.† [*Transfer of defendant in custody.*]

When the venue is changed in any criminal action if the defendant be in custody, an order shall be made for his removal to the proper county, and his delivery to the sheriff thereof before the next succeeding term of the court of the county to which the case is to be taken, and he shall be delivered by the sheriff as directed in the order.

### Art. 31.07. Witness need not again be summoned.† [*Responsibilities of witnesses.*]

When the venue in a criminal action has been changed, it shall not be necessary to have the witnesses therein again subpoenaed, attached or bailed, but all the witnesses who have been subpoenaed, attached or bailed to appear and testify in the cause shall be held bound to appear before the court to which the cause has been transferred, as if there had been no such transfer.

### Art. 31.08. Return to county of original venue.

**Sec. 1.** (a) On the completion of a trial in which a change of venue has been ordered and after the jury has been discharged, the court, with the consent of counsel for the state and the defendant, may return the cause to the original county in which the indictment or information was filed. Except as provided by Subsection (b) of this section, all subsequent and ancillary proceedings, including the pronouncement of sentence after appeals have been exhausted, must be heard in the county in which the indictment or information was filed.

(b) A motion for new trial alleging jury misconduct must be heard in the county in which the cause was tried. The county in which the indictment or information was filed must pay the costs of the prosecution of the motion for new trial.

**Sec. 2.** (a) Except as provided by Subsection (b), on an order returning venue to the original county in which the indictment or information was filed, the clerk of the county in which the cause was tried shall:

(1) make a certified copy of the court's order directing the return to the original county;

(2) make a certified copy of the defendant's bail bond, personal bond, or appeal bond;

(3) gather all the original papers in the cause and certify under official seal that the papers are all the original papers on file in the court; and

(4) transmit the items listed in this section to the clerk of the court of original venue.

(b) This article does not apply to a proceeding in which the clerk of the court of original venue was present and performed the duties as clerk for the court under Article 31.09.

**Sec. 3.** Except for the review of a death sentence under Article 37.071(h) of this code, an appeal taken in a cause returned to the original county under this article must be docketed in the appellate district in which the county of original venue is located.
*(Added by L.1989, chap. 824(1); chgd. by L.1995, chap. 651(1), eff. 9/1/95.)*

### Art. 31.09. Change of venue; use of existing services.

(a) If a change of venue in a criminal case is ordered under this chapter, the judge ordering the change of venue may, with the written consent of the prosecuting attorney, the defense attorney, and the defendant, maintain the original case number on its own docket, preside over the case, and use the services of the court reporter, the court coordinator, and the clerk of the court of original venue. The court shall use the courtroom facilities and any other services or facilities of the district or county to which venue is changed. A jury, if required, must consist of residents of the district or county to which the venue is changed.

(b) Notwithstanding Article 31.05, the clerk of the court of original venue shall:

(1) maintain the original papers of the case, including the defendant's bail bond or personal bond;

(2) make the papers available for trial; and

(3) act as the clerk in the case.

*(Added by L.1995, chap. 651(2), eff. 9/1/95.)*

# TRIAL AND ITS INCIDENTS

## CHAPTER 32. DISMISSING PROSECUTIONS



### Art. 32.01. Defendant in custody and no indictment presented.

When a defendant has been detained in custody or held to bail for his appearance to answer any criminal accusation before the district court, the prosecution, unless otherwise ordered by the court, for good cause shown, supported by affidavit, shall be dismissed and the bail discharged, if indictment or information be not presented against such defendant on or before the last day of the next term of the court which is held after his commitment or admission to bail or on or before the 180th day after the date of commitment or admission to bail, whichever date is later. *(Chgd. by L.1997, chap. 289(2), eff. 5/26/97.)*

### Art. 32.02. Dismissal by State's attorney.† [*Prosecution dismissed by State's attorney.*]

The attorney representing the State may, by permission of the court, dismiss a criminal action at any time upon filing a written statement with the papers in the case setting out his reasons for such dismissal, which shall be incorporated in the judgment of dismissal. No case shall be dismissed without the consent of the presiding judge.

## CHAPTER 32A. SPEEDY TRIAL



### Art. 32A.01. Trial priorities.

Insofar as is practicable, the trial of a criminal action shall be given preference over trials of civil cases, and the trial of a criminal action against a defendant who is detained in jail pending trial of the action shall be given preference over trials of other criminal actions.

### Art. 32A.02. Time limitations.† [*Time limitations on preparations for trial.*]

**Sec. 1.** A court shall grant a motion to set aside an indictment, information, or complaint if the state is not ready for trial within:

(1) 180 days of the commencement of a criminal action if the defendant is accused of a felony;

(2) 90 days of the commencement of a criminal action if the defendant is accused of a misdemeanor punishable by a sentence of imprisonment for more than 180 days; or

(3) 60 days of the commencement of a criminal action if the defendant is accused of a misdemeanor punishable by a sentence of imprisonment for 180 days or less or punishable by a fine only.

**Sec. 2.** (a) Except as provided in Subsections (b) and (c) of this section, a criminal action commences for purposes of this article when an indictment, information, or complaint against the defendant is filed in court, unless prior to the filing the defendant is either detained in custody or released on bail or personal bond to answer for the same offense or any other offense arising out of the same transaction, in which event the criminal action commences when he is arrested.

(b) If a defendant is to be retried following a mistrial, an order granting a new trial, or an appeal or collateral attack, a criminal action commences for purposes of this article on the date of the mistrial, the order granting a new trial, or the remand.

(c) If an indictment, information, or complaint is dismissed on motion of the defendant, a criminal action commences for the purposes of the article when a new indictment, information, or complaint against the defendant is filed in court, unless the defendant is either detained in custody or released on bail or personal bond to answer for the same offense or any other offense arising out of the same transaction, in which event the criminal action commences when he is detained or released.

**Sec. 3.** The failure of a defendant to move for discharge under the provisions of this article prior to trial or the entry of a plea of guilty constitutes a waiver of the rights accorded by this article.

**Sec. 4.** In computing the time by which the state must be ready for trial, the following periods shall be excluded:

(1) a reasonable period of delay resulting from other proceedings involving the defendant, including but not limited to proceedings for the determination of competence to stand trial, hearing on pretrial motions, appeals, and trials of other charges;

(2) any period during which the defendant is incompetent to stand trial;

(3) a period of delay resulting from a continuance granted at the request or with the consent of the defendant or his counsel, except that a defendant without counsel is deemed not to have consented to a continuance unless the court advised him of his right to a speedy trial and of the effect of his consent;

(4) a period of delay resulting from the absence of the defendant because his location is unknown and:

(A) he is attempting to avoid apprehension or prosecution; or

(B) the state has been unable to determine his location by due diligence;

(5) any period of delay during which the defendant is absent because he is a fugitive or his bail is forfeited or because he resists being returned to the state for trial;

(6) a reasonable period of delay resulting from a continuance granted at the request of the state if the continuance is granted:

(A) because of the unavailability of evidence that is material to the state's case, if the state has exercised due diligence to obtain the evidence and there are reasonable grounds to believe the evidence will be available within a reasonable time; or

(B) to allow the state additional time to prepare its case and the additional time is justified because of the exceptional circumstances of the case;

(7) if the charge is dismissed upon motion of the state or the charge is disposed of by a final judgment and the defendant is later charged with the same offense or another offense arising out of the same transaction, the period of delay from the date of dismissal or the date of the final judgment to the date the time limitation would commence running on the subsequent charge had there been no previous charge;

(8) a reasonable period of delay when the defendant is joined for trial with a codefendant as to whom the time for trial has not run, if there is good cause for not granting a severance;

(9) a period of delay resulting from detention of the defendant in another jurisdiction, if the state is aware of the detention and exercises due diligence to obtain his presence for trial;

(10) any period the defendant is released from custody without bail;

(11) any reasonable period of delay caused by exceptional circumstances not under the direct control of the state's attorney, including the completion, by another agency, of scientific analysis necessary to determine the offense to be charged; and

(12) any other reasonable period of delay that is justified by exceptional circumstances.

## CHAPTER 33. THE MODE OF TRIAL

Article

### Art. 33.01. Jury; when of twelve, when of six.† [*Numbers of jurors.*]

In the district court, the jury shall consist of twelve qualified jurors; in the county court and inferior courts, the jury shall consist of six qualified jurors.

### Art. 33.011. Alternate jurors.† [*Number of alternate jurors.*]

(a) In district courts, the judge may direct that not more than four jurors in addition to the regular jury be called and impaneled to sit as alternate jurors. In county courts, the judge may direct that not more than two jurors in addition to the regular jury be called and impaneled to sit as alternate jurors.

(b) Alternate jurors in the order in which they are called shall replace jurors who, prior to the time the jury retires to consider its verdict, become or are found to be unable or disqualified to perform their duties. Alternate jurors shall be drawn and selected in the same manner, shall have the same qualifications, shall be subject to the same examination and challenges, shall take the same oath, and shall have the same functions, powers, facilities, security, and privileges as regular jurors. An alternate juror who does not replace a regular juror shall be discharged after the jury retires to consider its verdict.

### Art. 33.02. Failure to register.† [*Nonregistered voters.*]

Failure to register to vote shall not disqualify any person from jury service.

### Art. 33.03. Presence of defendant.† [*Defendant must be present.*]

In all prosecutions for felonies, the defendant must be personally present at the trial, and he must likewise be present in all cases of misdemeanor when the punishment or any part thereof is imprisonment in jail; provided, however, that in all cases, when the defendant voluntarily absents himself after pleading to the indictment or information, or after the jury has been selected when trial is before a jury, the trial may proceed to its conclusion. When the record in the appellate court shows that the defendant was present at the commencement, or any portion of the trial, it shall be presumed in the absence of all evidence in the record to the contrary that he was present during the whole trial. Provided, however, that the presence of the defendant shall not be required at the hearing on the motion for new trial in any misdemeanor case.

### Art. 33.04. May appear by counsel.† [*Counsel may appear for defendant.*]

In other misdemeanor cases, the defendant may, by consent of the State's attorney, appear by counsel, and the trial may proceed without his personal presence.

### Art. 33.05. On bail during trial.† [*Bail of defendant during trial.*]

If the defendant is on bail when the trial commences, such bail shall be considered as discharged if he is acquitted. If a verdict of guilty is returned against him, the discharge of his bail shall be governed by other provisions of this Code.

### Art. 33.06. Sureties bound in case of mistrial.† [*Sureties held in felony case.*]

If there be a mistrial in a felony case, the original sureties, if any, of the defendant shall be still held bound for his appearance until they surrender him in accordance with the provisions of this Code.

### Art. 33.07. Criminal docket.

Each clerk of a court of record having criminal jurisdiction shall keep a docket in which shall be set down the style and file number of each criminal action, the nature of the offense, the names of counsel, the proceedings had therein, and the date of each proceeding.

### Art. 33.08. To fix day for criminal docket.† [*Setting times for criminal docket.*]

The district courts and county courts shall have control of their respective dockets as to the settings of criminal cases.

Printed in the U.S.A. Zt

### Art. 33.09. Jury drawn.† [*Selection of jury.*]

Jury panels, including special venires, for the trial of criminal cases shall be selected and summoned (with return on summons) in the same manner as the selection of panels for the trial of civil cases except as otherwise provided in this Code.

## CHAPTER 34. SPECIAL VENIRE IN CAPITAL CASES

Article


### Art. 34.01. Special venire.† [*Definition.*]

A "special venire" is a writ issued in a capital case by order of the district court, commanding the sheriff to summon either verbally or by mail such a number of persons, not less than 50, as the court may order, to appear before the court on a day named in the writ from whom the jury for the trial of such case is to be selected. Where as many as one hundred jurors have been summoned in such county for regular service for the week in which such capital case is set for trial, the judge of the court having jurisdiction of a capital case in which a motion for a special venire has been made, shall grant or refuse such motion for a special venire, and upon such refusal require the case to be tried by regular jurors summoned for service in such county for the week in which such capital case is set for trial and such additional talesmen as may be summoned by the sheriff upon order of the court as provided in Article 34.02 of this Code, but the clerk of such court shall furnish the defendant or his counsel a list of the persons summoned as provided in Article 34.04.

### Art. 34.02. Additional names drawn.† [*Selection of additional names.*]

In any criminal case in which the court deems that the veniremen theretofore drawn will be insufficient for the trial of the case, or in any criminal case in which the venire has been exhausted by challenge or otherwise, the court shall order additional veniremen in such numbers as the court may deem advisable, to be summoned as follows:

(a) In a jury wheel county, the names of those to be summoned shall be drawn from the jury wheel.

(b) In counties not using the jury wheel, the veniremen shall be summoned by the sheriff.

### Art. 34.03. Instructions to sheriff.

When the sheriff is ordered by the court to summon persons upon a special venire whose names have not been selected under the Jury Wheel Law, the court shall, in every case, caution and direct the sheriff to summon such persons as have legal qualifications to serve on juries, informing him of what those qualifications are, and shall direct him, as far as he may be able to summon persons of good character who can read and write, and such as are not prejudiced against the defendant or biased in his favor, if he knows of such bias or prejudice.

### Art. 34.04. Notice of list.

No defendant in a capital case in which the state seeks the death penalty shall be brought to trial until he shall have had at least two days (including holidays) a copy of the names of the persons summoned as veniremen, for the week for which his case is set for trial except where he waives the right or is on bail. When such defendant is on bail, the clerk of the court in which the case is pending shall furnish such a list to the defendant or his counsel at least two days prior to the trial (including holidays) upon timely motion by the defendant or his counsel therefor at the office of such clerk, and the defendant shall not be brought to trial until such list has been furnished defendant or his counsel for at least two days (including holidays). When the venire is exhausted, by challenges or otherwise, and additional names are drawn, the defendant shall not be entitled to two days service of the names additionally drawn, but the clerk shall compile a list of such names promptly after they are drawn and if the defendant is not on bail, the sheriff shall serve a copy of such list promptly upon the defendant, and if on bail, the clerk shall furnish a copy of such list to the defendant or his counsel upon request, but the proceedings shall not be delayed thereby. *(Chgd. by L.1991, chap. 652(4), eff. 9/1/91.)*

### Art. 34.05. Mechanical or electronic selection method.

A mechanical or electronic method of jury selection as provided by Chapter 62, Government Code, may be used under this chapter. *(Added by L.1995, chap. 694(1), eff. 9/1/95.)*

## CHAPTER 35. FORMATION OF THE JURY

Article





### Art. 35.01. Jurors called.† [*Summoning of jurors.*]

When a case is called for trial and the parties have announced ready for trial, the names of those summoned as jurors in the case shall be called. Those not present may be fined not exceeding fifty dollars. An attachment may issue on request of either party for any absent summoned juror, to have him brought forthwith before the court. A person who is summoned but not present, may upon an appearance, before the jury is qualified, be tried as to his qualifications and impaneled as a juror unless challenged, but no cause shall be unreasonably delayed on account of his absence.

### Art. 35.02. Sworn to answer questions.† [*Oath taken by jurors.*]

To those present the court shall cause to be administered this oath: "You, and each of you, solemnly swear that you will make true answers to such questions as may be propounded to you by the court, or under its directions, touching your service and qualifications as a juror, so help you God."

### Art. 35.03. Excuses.

**Sec. 1.** Except as provided by Sections 2 and 3 of this article, the court shall then hear and determine excuses offered for not serving as a juror, and if the court deems the excuse sufficient, the court shall discharge the juror or postpone the juror's service to a date specified by the court.

**Sec. 2.** Under a plan approved by the commissioners court of the county in the same manner as a plan is approved for jury selection under Section 62.011, Government Code, in a case other than a capital felony case, the court's designee may hear and determine an excuse offered for not serving as a juror, and if the court's designee deems the excuse sufficient, he may postpone the juror's service to a date specified by the court's designee.

**Sec. 3.** A court or a court's designee may discharge a juror or postpone the juror's service on the basis of the juror's observation of a religious holy day or religious beliefs only if the juror provides an affidavit as required by Article 29.012(c) of this code.

### Art. 35.04. Claiming exemption.† [*Exemption claimed.*]

Any person summoned as a juror who is exempt by law from jury service may establish his exemption without appearing in person by filing a signed statement of the ground of his exemption with the clerk of the court at any time before the date upon which he is summoned to appear.

### Art. 35.05. Excused by consent.† [*Juror excused by consent of both parties.*]

One summoned upon a special venire may by consent of both parties be excused from attendance by the court at any time before he is impaneled.

### Art. 35.06. Challenge to array first heard.† [*Preliminary challenge to array.*]

The court shall hear and determine a challenge to the array before interrogating those summoned as to their qualifications.



### Art. 35.07. Challenge to the array.

Each party may challenge the array only on the ground that the officer summoning the jury has wilfully summoned jurors with a view to securing a conviction or an acquittal. All such challenges must be in writing setting forth distinctly the grounds of such challenge. When made by the defendant, it must be supported by his affidavit or the affidavit of any credible person. When such challenge is made, the judge shall hear evidence and decide without delay whether or not the challenge shall be sustained.

### Art. 35.08. When challenge is sustained.† [*Challenge to array sustained.*]

The array of jurors summoned shall be discharged if the challenge be sustained, and the court shall order other jurors to be summoned in their stead, and direct that the officer who summoned those so discharged, and on account of whose misconduct the challenge has been sustained shall not summon any other jurors in the case.

### Art. 35.09. List of new venire.

When a challenge to the array has been sustained, the defendant shall be entitled, as in the first instance, to service of a copy of the list of names of those summoned by order of the court.

### Art. 35.10. Court to try qualifications.

When no challenge to the array has been made, or if made, has been overruled, the court shall proceed to try the qualifications of those present who have been summoned to serve as jurors.

### Art. 35.11. Preparation of list.

The trial judge, on the demand of the defendant or his attorney, or of the State's counsel, shall cause a sufficient number of jurors from which a jury may be selected to try to case to be randomly selected from the members of the general panel drawn or assigned as jurors in the case. The clerk shall randomly select the jurors by a computer or other process of random selection and shall write or print the names, in the order selected, on the jury list from which the jury is to be selected to try the case. The clerk shall deliver a copy of the list to the State's counsel and to the defendant or his attorney. *(Chgd. by L.1991, chap. 337(1), eff. 9/1/91.)*

### Art. 35.12. Mode of testing.† [*Method of testing jurors.*]

In testing the qualification of a prospective juror after he has been sworn, he shall be asked by the court, or under its direction:

1. Except for failure to register, are you a qualified voter in this county and state under the Constitution and laws of this state?
2. Have you ever been convicted of theft or any felony?
3. Are you under indictment or legal accusation for theft or any felony?

### Art. 35.13. Passing juror for challenge.

A juror in a capital case in which the state has made it known it will seek the death penalty, held to be qualified, shall be passed for acceptance or challenge first to the state and then to the defendant. Challenges to jurors are either peremptory or for cause.

**Art. 35.14. A peremptory challenge.**

A peremptory challenge is made to a juror without assigning any reason therefor.

**Art. 35.15. Number of challenges.† [*Felony cases: number of challenges allowed.*]**

(a) In capital cases in which the State seeks the death penalty both the State and defendant shall be entitled to fifteen peremptory challenges. Where two or more defendants are tried together, the State shall be entitled to eight peremptory challenges for each defendant; and each defendant shall be entitled to eight peremptory challenges.

(b) In non-capital felony cases and in capital cases in which the State does not seek the death penalty, the State and defendant shall each be entitled to ten peremptory challenges. If two or more defendants are tried together each defendant shall be entitled to six peremptory challenges and the State to six for each defendant.

(c) The State and the defendant shall each be entitled to five peremptory challenges in a misdemeanor tried in the district court and to three in the county court, or county court at law. If two or more defendants are tried together, each defendant shall be entitled to three such challenges and the State to three for each defendant in either court.

(d) The State and the defendant shall each be entitled to one peremptory challenge in addition to those otherwise allowed by law if one or two alternate jurors are to be impaneled and two peremptory challenges if three or four alternate jurors are to be impaneled. The additional peremptory challenges provided by this subsection may be used against an alternate juror only, and the other peremptory challenges allowed by law may not be used against an alternate juror.
*(Chgd. by L.1991, chap. 652(5), eff. 9/1/91.)*



**Art. 35.16. Reasons for challenge for cause.† [*Reasons for objection to juror.*]**

(a) A challenge for cause is an objection made to a particular juror, alleging some fact which renders him incapable or unfit to serve on the jury. A challenge for cause may be made by either the state or the defense for any one of the following reasons:

1. That he is not a qualified voter in the state and county under the Constitution and laws of the state; provided, however, the failure to register to vote shall not be a disqualification;
2. That he has been convicted of theft or any felony;
3. That he is under indictment or other legal accusation for theft or any felony;
4. That he is insane;
5. That he has such defect in the organs of feeling or hearing, or such bodily or mental defect or disease as to render him unfit for jury service, or that he is legally blind and the court in its discretion is not satisfied that he is fit for jury service in that particular case;
6. That he is a witness in the case;
7. That he served on the grand jury which found the indictment;
8. That he served on a petit jury in a former trial of the same case;
9. That he has a bias or prejudice in favor of or against the defendant;
10. That from hearsay, or otherwise, there is established in the mind of the juror such a conclusion as to the guilt or innocence of the defendant as would influence him in his action in finding a verdict. To ascertain whether this cause of challenge exists, the juror shall first be asked whether, in his opinion, the conclusion so established will influence his verdict. If he answers in the affirmative, he shall be discharged without further interrogation by either party or the court. If he answers in the negative, he shall be further examined as to how his conclusion was formed, and the extent to which it will affect his action; and, if it appears to have been formed from reading newspaper accounts, communications, statements or reports or mere rumor or hearsay, and if the juror states that he feels able, notwithstanding such opinion, to render an impartial verdict upon the law and the evidence, the court, if satisfied that he is impartial and will render such verdict, may, in its discretion, admit him as competent to serve in such case. If the court, in its discretion, is not satisfied that he is impartial, the juror shall be discharged;
11. That he cannot read or write.

No juror shall be impaneled when it appears that he is subject to the second, third or fourth grounds of challenge for cause set forth above, although both parties may consent. All other grounds for challenge may be waived by the party or parties in whose favor such grounds of challenge exist.

In this subsection "legally blind" shall mean having not more than 20/200 of visual acuity in the better eye with correcting lenses, or visual acuity greater than 20/200 but with a limitation in the field of vision such that the widest diameter of the visual field subtends an angle no greater than 20 degrees.

(b) A challenge for cause may be made by the State or any of the following reasons:

1. That the juror has conscientious scruples in regard to the infliction of the punishment of death for crime, in a capital case, where the State is seeking the death penalty;

2. That he is related within the third degree of consanguinity or affinity, as determined under Chapter 573, Government Code, to the defendant; and

3. That he has a bias or prejudice against any phase of the law upon which the State is entitled to rely for conviction or punishment.

(c) A challenge for cause may be made by the defense for any of the following reasons:

1. That he is related within the third degree of consanguinity or affinity, as determined under Chapter 573, Government Code, to the person injured by the commission of the offense, or to any prosecutor in the case; and

2. That he has a bias or prejudice against any of the law applicable to the case upon which the defense is entitled to rely, either as a defense to some phase of the offense for which the defendant is being prosecuted or as a mitigation thereof or of the punishment therefor.

*(Chgd. by L.1991, chap. 561(10); L.1995, chap. 76(5.95(27)), eff. 9/1/95.)*

### Art. 35.17. Voir dire examination.

1. When the court in its discretion so directs, except as provided in Section 2, the state and defendant shall conduct the voir dire examination of prospective jurors in the presence of the entire panel.

2. In a capital felony case in which the State seeks the death penalty, the court shall propound to the entire panel of prospective jurors questions concerning the principles, as applicable to the case on trial, of reasonable doubt, burden of proof, return of indictment by grand jury, presumption of innocence, and opinion. Then, on demand of the State or defendant, either is entitled to examine each juror on voir dire individually and apart from the entire panel, and may further question the juror on the principles propounded by the court.

*(Chgd. by L.1991, chap. 652(6), eff. 9/1/91.)*

### Art. 35.18. Other evidence on challenge.

Upon a challenge for cause, the examination is not confined to the answers of the juror, but other evidence may be heard for or against the challenge.

### Art. 35.19. Absolute disqualification.† [*Juror disqualified absolutely.*]

No juror shall be impaneled when it appears that he is subject to the second, third or fourth cause of challenge in Article 35.16, though both parties may consent.

### Art. 35.20. Names called in order.† [*Jurors' names called in order.*]

In selecting the jury from the persons summoned, the names of such persons shall be called in the order in which they appear upon the list furnished the defendant. Each juror shall be tried and passed upon separately. A person who has been summoned, but who is not present, may, upon his appearance before the jury is completed, be tried as to his qualifications and impaneled as a juror, unless challenged, but no cause shall be unreasonably delayed on account of such absence.

### Art. 35.21. Judge to decide qualifications.† [*Court's decision on qualifications.*]

The court is the judge, after proper examination, of the qualifications of a juror, and shall decide all challenges without delay and without argument thereupon.

### Art. 35.22. Oath to jury.

When the jury has been selected, the following oath shall be administered them by the court or under its direction: "You and each of you do solemnly swear that in the case of the State of Texas against the defendant, you will a true verdict render according to the law and the evidence, so help you God".

### Art. 35.23. Jurors may separate.

The court may adjourn veniremen to any day of the term. When jurors have been sworn in a felony case, the court may, at its discretion, permit the jurors to separate until the court has given its charge to the jury. The court on its own motion may and on the motion of either party shall, after having given its charge to the jury, order that the jury not be allowed to separate, after which the jury shall be kept together, and not permitted to separate except to the extent of housing female jurors separate and apart from male jurors, until a verdict has been rendered or the jury finally discharged. Any person who makes known to the jury which party made the motion not to allow separation of the jury shall be punished for contempt of court. If such jurors are kept overnight, facilities shall be provided for female jurors separate and apart from the facilities provided for male jurors. In misdemeanor cases the court may, at its discretion permit the jurors to separate at any time before the verdict. In any case in which the jury is permitted to separate, the court shall first give the jurors proper instructions with regard to their conduct as jurors when so separated. *(Chgd. by L.1989, chap. 825(1), eff. 9/1/89.)*

### Art. 35.25. Making peremptory challenges.† [*Peremptory challenges.*]

In non-capital cases and in capital cases in which the State's attorney has announced that he will not qualify the jury for, or seek the death penalty, the party desiring to challenge any juror peremptorily shall strike the name of such juror from the list furnished him by the clerk.

### Art. 35.26. Lists returned to clerk.

(a) When the parties have made or declined to make their peremptory challenges, they shall deliver their lists to the clerk. Except as provided in Subsection (b) of this section, the clerk shall, if the case be in the district court, call off the first twelve names on the lists that have not been stricken. If the case be in the county court, he shall call off the first six names on the lists that have not been stricken. Those whose names are called shall be the jury.

(b) In a capital case in which the state seeks the death penalty, the court may direct that two alternate jurors be selected and that the first fourteen names not stricken be called off by the clerk. The last two names to be called are the alternate jurors.
*(Chgd. by L.1991, chap. 652(7), eff. 9/1/91.)*

### Art. 35.261. Peremptory challenges based on race prohibited.† [*Challenges based on race forbidden.*]

(a) After the parties have delivered their lists to the clerk under Article 35.26 of this code and before the court has impaneled the jury, the defendant may request the court to dismiss the array and call a new array in the case. The court shall grant the motion of a defendant for dismissal of the array if the court determines that the defendant is a member of an identifiable racial group, that the attorney representing the state exercised peremptory challenges for the purpose of excluding persons from the jury on the basis of their race, and that the defendant has offered evidence of relevant facts that tend to show that challenges made by the attorney representing the state were made for reasons based on race. If the defendant establishes a prima facie case, the burden then shifts to the attorney representing the state to give a racially neutral explanation for the challenges. The burden of persuasion remains with the defendant to establish purposeful discrimination.

(b) If the court determines that the attorney representing the state challenged prospective jurors on the basis of race, the court shall call a new array in the case.

### Art. 35.27. Compensation of nonresident witnesses.

**Sec. 1. Expenses for nonresident witnesses.** (a) Every person subpoenaed by either party or otherwise required or requested in writing by the prosecuting attorney or the court to appear for the purpose of giving testimony in a criminal proceeding who resides outside the state or the county in which the prosecution is pending shall be reimbursed by the state for the reasonable and necessary transportation, meal, and lodging expenses he incurs by reason of his attendance as a witness at such proceeding.

(b) The state may reimburse a witness for transportation only if the transportation is provided by a commercial transportation company or the witness uses the witness's personally owned or leased motor vehicle. In this article, "commercial transportation company" means an entity that offers transportation of people or goods to the public in exchange for compensation.

(c) The state may reimburse a witness for lodging only if the lodging is provided by a commercial lodging establishment. In this article, "commercial lodging establishment" means a motel, hotel, inn, apartment, or similar entity that offers lodging to the public in exchange for compensation.

**Sec. 2. Amount of reimbursement for expenses.** Any person seeking reimbursement as a witness shall make an affidavit setting out the transportation, meal, and lodging expenses necessitated by his travel to and from and attendance at the place he appeared to give testimony, together with the number of days that such travel and attendance made him absent from his place of residence. A reimbursement paid by the state to a witness for transportation, meal, or lodging expenses may not be paid at a rate that exceeds the maximum rates provided by law for state employees.

**Sec. 2A. Direct payment of transportation or lodging expenses.** If this article requires the state to reimburse a witness for transportation or lodging expenses, the state may instead directly pay a commercial transportation company or commercial lodging establishment for those expenses.

**Sec. 3. Other expenses.** In addition to reimbursement or payment for transportation, meal, and lodging expenses, the comptroller, upon proper application by the attorney for the state, shall reimburse or pay the other expenses required by the laws of this state or the state from which the attendance of the witness is sought.

**Sec. 4. Application and approval by judge.** A reimbursement to a witness as provided by this article shall be paid by the state to the witness or his assignee. Claim shall be made by sworn application to the comptroller, a copy of which shall be filed with the clerk of the court, setting out the facts showing entitlement as provided in this article to the reimbursement, which application shall be presented for approval by the judge who presided over the court or empaneled the grand jury before whom the criminal proceeding was pending. No fee shall be required of any witness for the processing of his claim for reimbursement.

**Sec. 5. Payment by state.** The Comptroller of Public Accounts, upon receipt of a claim approved by the judge, shall examine it and, if he deems the claim in compliance with and authorized by this Article, draw his warrant on the State Treasury for the amount due the witness, or to any person to which the certificate has been assigned by the witness, but no warrant may issue to any assignee of a witness claim unless the assignment is made under oath and acknowledged before some person authorized to administer oaths, certified to by the officer, and under seal. If the appropriation for paying the account is exhausted, the Comptroller of Public Accounts shall file it away and issue a certificate in the name of the witness entitled to it, stating therein the amount of the claim. Each claim not filed in the office of the Comptroller of Public Accounts within twelve months from the date it became due and payable shall be forever barred.

**Sec. 6. Advance by state.** Funds required to be tendered to an out-of-state witness pursuant to Article 24.28 of this Code shall be paid by the Comptroller of Public Accounts into the registry of the Court in which the case is to be tried upon certification by the Court such funds are necessary to obtain attendance of said witness. The court shall then cause to be issued checks drawn upon the registry of the Court to secure the attendance of such witness. In the event that such funds are not used pursuant to this Act, the Court shall return the funds to the Comptroller of Public Accounts.

**Sec. 7. Advance by county.** The county in which a criminal proceeding is pending, upon request of the district attorney or other prosecutor charged with the duty of prosecution in the proceeding, may advance funds from its treasury to any witness who will be entitled to reimbursement under this article. The amount advanced may not exceed the amount that is reasonably necessary to enable the witness to attend as required or requested. However, the amount advanced may include sums in excess of the reimbursement provided for by this article if the excess is required for compliance with Section 4 of Article 24.28 in securing the attendance of a witness from another state under the Uniform Act. A county that advances funds to a witness under this section is entitled to reimbursement by the state as an assignee of the witness.

**Sec. 8. Advance for expenses for witnesses of indigent defendant.** Upon application by a defendant shown to be indigent and a showing to the court of reasonable necessity and materiality for the testimony of a witness residing outside the State, the court shall act pursuant to Section 6 hereof to secure advance of funds necessary for the attendance of such witness.

**Sec. 9. Limitations.** A witness, when attached and conveyed by a sheriff or other officer, is not eligible to receive reimbursement of transportation, meal, or lodging expenses incurred while in the custody of the officer. A court, in its discretion, may limit the number of character witnesses allowed reimbursement under this article to not fewer than two for each defendant and two per defendant for the state.
*(Chgd. by L.1993, chap. 449(18), eff. 9/1/93.)*

### Art. 35.28. When no clerk.† [*When clerk absent.*]

In each instance in Article 35.27 in which the clerk of the court is authorized or directed to perform any act, the judge of such court shall perform the same if there is no clerk of the court.

### Art. 35.29. Personal information about jurors.

Information collected by the court or by a prosecuting attorney during the jury selection process about a person who serves as a juror, including the juror's home address, home telephone number, social security number, driver's license number, and other personal information, is confidential and may not be disclosed by the court, the prosecuting attorney, the defense counsel, or any court personnel except on application by a party in the trial or on application by a bona fide member of the news media acting in such capacity to the court in which the person is serving or did serve as a juror. On a showing of good cause, the court shall permit disclosure of the information sought. *(Added by L.1993, chap. 371(1), eff. 9/1/93.)*

## CHAPTER 36. THE TRIAL BEFORE THE JURY



Article



### Art. 36.01. Order of proceeding in trial.† [*Order of proceedings.*]

(a) A jury being impaneled in any criminal action, except as provided by Subsection (b) of this article, the cause shall proceed in the following order:

1. The indictment or information shall be read to the jury by the attorney prosecuting. When prior convictions are alleged for purposes of enhancement only and are not jurisdictional, that portion of the indictment or information reciting such convictions shall not be read until the hearing on punishment is held as provided in Article 37.07.
2. The special pleas, if any, shall be read by the defendant's counsel, and if the plea of not guilty is also relied upon, it shall also be stated.
3. The State's attorney shall state to the jury the nature of the accusation and the facts which are expected to be proved by the State in support thereof.
4. The testimony on the part of the State shall be offered.
5. The nature of the defenses relied upon and the facts expected to be proved in their support shall be stated by defendant's counsel.
6. The testimony on the part of the defendant shall be offered.
7. Rebutting testimony may be offered on the part of each party.
8. In the event of a finding of guilty, the trial shall then proceed as set forth in Article 37.07.

(b) The defendant's counsel may make the opening statement for the defendant immediately after the attorney representing the State makes the opening statement for the State. After the defendant's attorney concludes the defendant's opening statement, the State's testimony shall be offered. At the conclusion of the presentation of the State's testimony, the defendant's testimony shall be offered, and the order of proceedings shall continue in the manner described by Subsection (a) of this article.

### Art. 36.02. Testimony at any time.† [*Introduction of testimony.*]

The court shall allow testimony to be introduced at any time before the argument of a cause is concluded, if it appears that it is necessary to a due administration of justice.

### Art. 36.05. Not to hear testimony.† [*Witness excluded from other testimony.*]

Witnesses under rule shall be attended by an officer, and all their reasonable wants provided for, unless the court, in its discretion, directs that they be allowed to go at large; but in no case where the witnesses are under rule shall they be allowed to hear any testimony in the case.

### Art. 36.06. Instructed by the court.† [*Witness: instructions of court.*]

Witnesses, when placed under rule, shall be instructed by the court that they are not to converse with each other or with any other person about the case, except by permission of the court, and that they are not to read any report of or comment upon the testimony in the case while under rule. The officer who attends the witnesses shall report to the court at once any violation of its instructions, and the party violating the same shall be punished for contempt of court.



### Art. 36.07. Order of argument.

The order of argument may be regulated by the presiding judge; but the State's counsel shall have the right to make the concluding address to the jury.

### Art. 36.08. Number of arguments.

The court shall never restrict the argument in felony cases to a number of addresses less than two on each side.

### Art. 36.09. Severance on separate indictments.

Two or more defendants who are jointly or separately indicted or complained against for the same offense or any offense growing out of the same transaction may be, in the discretion of the court, tried jointly or separately as to one or more defendants; provided that in any event either defendant may testify for the other or on behalf of the state; and provided further, that in cases in which, upon timely motion to sever, and evidence introduced thereon, it is made known to the court that there is a previous admissible conviction against one defendant or that a joint trial would be prejudicial to any defendant, the court shall order a severance as to the defendant whose joint trial would prejudice the other defendant or defendants.

### Art. 36.10. Order of trial.

If a severance is granted, the defendants may agree upon the order in which they are to be tried, but if they fail to agree, the court shall direct the order of the trial.

### Art. 36.11. Discharge before verdict.† [*Discharge of jury before verdict reached.*]

If it appears during a trial that the court has no jurisdiction of the offense, or that the facts charged in the indictment do not constitute an offense, the jury shall be discharged. The accused shall also be discharged, but such discharge shall be no bar in any case to a prosecution before the proper court for any offense unless termination of the former prosecution was improper.

### Art. 36.12. Court may commit.† [*Court may place defendant in custody.*]

If the want of jurisdiction arises from the fact that the defendant is not liable to prosecution in the county where the indictment was presented, the court may in felony cases order the accused into custody for a reasonable length of time to await a warrant for his arrest from the proper county; or if the offense be bailable, may require him to enter into recognizance to answer before the proper court; in which case a certified copy of the recognizance shall be sent forthwith to the clerk of the proper court, to be enforced by that court in case of forfeiture.

### Art. 36.13. Jury is judge of facts.

Unless otherwise provided in this Code, the jury is the exclusive judge of the facts, but it is bound to receive the law from the court and be governed thereby.

**Art. 36.14. Charge of court.† [*Charge to jurors.*]**

Subject to the provisions of Article 36.07 in each felony case and in each misdemeanor case tried in a court of record, the judge shall, before the argument begins, deliver to the jury, except in pleas of guilty, where a jury has been waived, a written charge distinctly setting forth the law applicable to the case; not expressing any opinion as to the weight of the evidence, not summing up the testimony, discussing the facts or using any argument in his charge calculated to arouse the sympathy or excite the passions of the jury. Before said charge is read to the jury, the defendant or his counsel shall have a reasonable time to examine the same and he shall present his objections thereto in writing, distinctly specifying each ground of objection. Said objections may embody errors claimed to have been committed in the charge, as well as errors claimed to have been committed by omissions therefrom or in failing to charge upon issues arising from the facts, and in no event shall it be necessary for the defendant or his counsel to present special requested charges to preserve or maintain any error assigned to the charge, as herein provided. The requirement that the objections to the court's charge be in writing will be complied with if the objections are dictated to the court reporter in the presence of the court and the state's counsel, before the reading of the court's charge to the jury. Compliance with the provisions of this Article is all that is necessary to preserve, for review, the exceptions and objections presented to the charge and any amendment or modification thereof. In no event shall it be necessary for the defendant to except to the action of the court in over-ruling defendant's exceptions or objections to the charge.



**Art. 36.15. Requested special charges.† [*Counsel may present special charge to jury.*]**

Before the court reads his charge to the jury, counsel on both sides shall have a reasonable time to present written instructions and ask that they be given to the jury. The requirement that the instructions be in writing is complied with if the instructions are dictated to the court reporter in the presence of the court and the state's counsel, before the reading of the court's charge to the jury. The court shall give or refuse these charges. The defendant may, by a special requested instruction, call the trial court's attention to error in the charge, as well as omissions therefrom, the* no other exception or objection to the court's charge shall be necessary to preserve any error reflected by any special requested instruction which the trial court refuses.

**So in original.*

Any special requested charge which is granted shall be incorporated in the main charge and shall be treated as a part thereof, and the jury shall not be advised that it is a special requested charge of either party. The judge shall read to the jury only such special charges as he gives.

When the defendant has leveled objections to the charge or has requested instructions or both, and the court thereafter modifies his charge and rewrites the same and in so doing does not respond to objections or requested charges, or any of them, then the objections or requested charges shall not be deemed to have been waived by the party making or requesting the same, but shall be deemed to continue to have been urged by the party making or requesting the same unless the contrary is shown by the record; no exception by the defendant to the action of the court shall be necessary or required in order to preserve for review the error claimed in the charge.

**Art. 36.16. Final charge.**

After the judge shall have received the objections to his main charge, together with any special charges offered, he may make such changes in his main charge as he may deem proper, and the defendant or his counsel shall have the opportunity to present their objections thereto and in the same manner as is provided in Article 36.15, and thereupon the judge shall read his charge to the jury as finally written, together with any special charges given, and no further exception or objection shall be required of the defendant in order to preserve any objections or exceptions theretofore made. After the argument begins no further charge shall be given to the jury unless required by the improper argument of counsel or the request of the jury, or unless the judge shall, in his discretion, permit the introduction of other testimony, and in the event of such further charge, the defendant or his counsel shall have the right to present objections in the same manner as is prescribed in Article 36.15. The failure of the court to give the defendant or his counsel a reasonable time to examine the charge and specify the ground of objection shall be subject to review either in the trial court or in the appellate court.

**Art. 36.17. Charge certified by judge.**

The general charge given by the court and all special charges given or refused shall be certified by the judge and filed among the papers in the cause.

**Art. 36.18. Jury may take charge.**

The jury may take to their jury room the charges given by the court after the same have been filed. They shall not be permitted to take with them any charge or part thereof which the court has refused to give.

**Art. 36.19. Review of charge on appeal.**

Whenever it appears by the record in any criminal action upon appeal that any requirement of Articles 36.14, 36.15, 36.16, 36.17 and 36.18 has been disregarded, the judgment shall not be reversed unless the error appearing from the record was calculated to injure the rights of defendant, or unless it appears from the record that the defendant has not had a fair and impartial trial. All objections to the charge and to the refusal of special charges shall be made at the time of the trial.

**Art. 36.21. To provide jury room.† [*Jury room provided.*]**

The sheriff shall provide a suitable room for the deliberation of the jury and supply them with such necessary food and lodging as he can obtain. No intoxicating liquor shall be furnished them. In all cases wherein a jury consists partly of male jurors and partly of female jurors, the sheriff shall provide facilities for the female jurors separate and apart from the facilities provided for the male jurors.

**Art. 36.22. Conversing with jury.† [*Conversing with jury forbidden.*]**

No person shall be permitted to be with a jury while it is deliberating. No person shall be permitted to converse with a juror about the case on trial except in the presence and by the permission of the court.

**Art. 36.23. Violation of preceding article.† [*Violation of Article 36.22.*]**

Any juror or other person violating the preceding Article shall be punished for contempt of court by confinement in jail not to exceed three days or by fine not to exceed one hundred dollars, or by both such fine and imprisonment.

**Art. 36.24. Officer shall attend jury.† [*Sheriff shall furnish bailiff.*]**

The sheriff of the county shall furnish the court with a bailiff during the trial of any case to attend the wants of the jury and to act under the direction of the court. If the person furnished by the sheriff is to be called as a witness in the case he may not serve as bailiff.

**Art. 36.25. Written evidence.† [*Evidence.*]**

There shall be furnished to the jury upon its request any exhibits admitted as evidence in the case.

**Art. 36.26. Foreman of jury.† [*Jury foreman.*]**

Each jury shall appoint one of its members foreman.

**Art. 36.27. Jury may communicate with court.† [*Communication of jury with court.*]**

When the jury wishes to communicate with the court, it shall so notify the sheriff, who shall inform the court thereof. Any communication relative to the cause must be written, prepared by the foreman and shall be submitted to the court through the bailiff. The court shall answer any such communication in writing, and before giving such answer to the jury shall use reasonable diligence to secure the presence of the defendant and his counsel, and shall first submit the question and also submit his answer to the same to the defendant or his counsel or objections and exceptions, in the same manner as any other written instructions are submitted to such counsel, before the court gives such answer to the jury, but if he is unable to secure the presence of the defendant and his counsel, then he shall proceed to answer the same as he deems proper. The written instruction or answer to the communication shall be read in open court unless expressly waived by the defendant.

All such proceedings in felony cases shall be a part of the record and recorded by the court reporter.

**Art. 36.28. Jury may have witness re-examined or testimony read.† [*Jury may have testimony repeated.*]**

In the trial of a criminal case in a court of record, if the jury disagree as to the statement of any witness they may, upon applying to the court, have read to them from the court reporter's notes that part of such witness testimony or the particular point in dispute, and no other; but if there be no such reporter, or if his notes cannot be read to the jury, the court may cause such witness to be again brought upon the stand and the judge shall direct him to repeat his testimony as to the point in dispute, and no other, as nearly as he can in the language used on the trial.

**Art. 36.29. If a juror becomes ill.† [*Illness of juror.*]**

(a) Not less than twelve jurors can render and return a verdict in a felony case. It must be concurred in by each juror and signed by the foreman. Except as provided in Subsection (b) of this section, however, when pending the trial of any felony case, one juror may die or be disabled from sitting at any time before the charge of the court is read to the jury, the remainder of the jury shall have the power to render the verdict; but when the verdict shall be rendered by less than the whole number, it shall be signed by every member of the jury concurring in it.

(b) If alternate jurors have been selected in a capital case in which the state seeks the death penalty and a juror dies or becomes disabled from sitting at any time before the charge of the court is read to the jury, the alternate juror whose name was called first under Article 35.26 of this code shall replace the dead or disabled juror. Likewise, if another juror dies or becomes disabled from sitting before the charge of the court is read to the jury, the other alternate juror shall replace the second juror to die or become disabled.

(c) After the charge of the court is read to the jury, if any one of them becomes so sick as to prevent the continuance of his duty, or any accident of circumstance occurs to prevent their being kept together under circumstances under which the law or the instructions of the court requires that they be kept together, the jury shall be discharged, except that on agreement on the record by the defendant, the defendant's counsel, and the attorney representing the state 11 members of a jury may render a verdict and, if punishment is to be assessed by the jury, assess punishment. If a verdict is rendered by less than the whole number of the jury, each member of the jury shall sign the verdict.

(d) After the charge of the court is read to the jury, the court shall discharge an alternate juror who has not replaced a juror.

*(Chgd. by L.1991, chap. 652(8); L.1997, chap. 866(1), eff. 9/1/97.)*



**Art. 36.30. Discharging jury in misdemeanor.**

If nine of the jury can be kept together in a misdemeanor case in the district court, they shall not be discharged. If more than three of the twelve are discharged, the entire jury shall be discharged.

**Art. 36.31. Disagreement of jury.**

After the cause is submitted to the jury, it may be discharged when it cannot agree and both parties consent to its discharge; or the court may in its discretion discharge it where it has been kept together for such time as to render it altogether improbable that it can agree.

**Art. 36.32. Receipt of verdict and final adjournment.† [*Term of jury: receipt of verdict and final adjournment.*]**

During the trial of any case, the term shall be deemed to have been extended until such time as the jury has rendered its verdict or been discharged according to law.

**Art. 36.33. Discharge without verdict.† [*Trial of case after discharge without verdict.*]**

When a jury has been discharged, as provided in the four preceding Articles, without having rendered a verdict, the cause may be again tried at the same or another term.

## CHAPTER 37. THE VERDICT

Article

### Art. 37.01. Verdict.† [*Verdict defined.*]

A "verdict" is a written declaration by a jury of its decision of the issue submitted to it in the case.

### Art. 37.02. Verdict by nine jurors.† [*Verdict of nine jurors.*]

In misdemeanor cases in the district court, where one or more jurors have been discharged from serving after the cause has been submitted to them, if all the alternate jurors selected under Article 33.011 of this code have either been seated or discharged, and there be as many as nine of the jurors remaining, those remaining may render and return a verdict; but in such case, the verdict must be signed by each juror rendering it.

### Art. 37.03. In county court.† [*Verdict in county court.*]

In the county court the verdict must be concurred in by each juror.

### Art. 37.04. When jury has agreed.† [*When jury in agreement.*]

When the jury agrees upon a verdict, it shall be brought into court by the proper officer; and if it states that it has agreed, the verdict shall be read aloud by the judge, the foreman, or the clerk. If in proper form and no juror dissents therefrom, and neither party requests a poll of the jury, the verdict shall be entered upon the minutes of the court.

### Art. 37.05. Polling the jury.† [*Polling the jurors.*]

The State or the defendant shall have the right to have the jury polled, which is done by calling separately the name of each juror and asking him if the verdict is his. If all, when asked, answer in the affirmative, the verdict shall be entered upon the minutes; but if any juror answer in the negative, the jury shall retire again to consider its verdict.

### Art. 37.06. Presence of defendant.† [*Presence of the accused.*]

In felony cases the defendant must be present when the verdict is read unless his absence is wilful or voluntary. A verdict in a misdemeanor case may be received and read in the absence of the defendant.

### Art. 37.07. Verdict must be general; separate hearing on proper punishment.† [*Verdict not specific; separate hearing on proper punishment.*]

**Sec. 1.** (a) The verdict in every criminal action must be general. When there are special pleas on which a jury is to find they must say in their verdict that the allegations in such pleas are true or untrue.

(b) If the plea is not guilty, they must find that the defendant is either guilty or not guilty, and, except as provided in Section 2, they shall assess the punishment in all cases where the same is not absolutely fixed by law to some particular penalty.

(c) If the charging instrument contains more than one count or if two or more offenses are consolidated for trial pursuant to Chapter 3 of the Penal Code, the jury shall be instructed to return a finding of guilty or not guilty in a separate verdict as to each count and offense submitted to them.

**Sec. 2. Criminal cases.**

(a) In all criminal cases, other than misdemeanor cases of which the justice court or municipal court has jurisdiction, which are tried before a jury on a plea of not guilty, the judge shall, before argument begins, first submit to the jury the issue of guilt or innocence of the defendant of the offense or offenses charged, without authorizing the jury to pass upon the punishment to be imposed.

(b) Except as provided in Article 37.071, if a finding of guilty is returned, it shall then be the responsibility of the judge to assess the punishment applicable to the offense; provided, however, that (1) in any criminal action where the jury may recommend probation and the defendant filed

Printed in the U.S.A. Zt

his sworn motion for probation before the trial began, and (2) in other cases where the defendant so elects in writing before the commencement of the voir dire examination of the jury panel, the punishment shall be assessed by the same jury, except as provided in Article 44.29. If a finding of guilty is returned, the defendant may, with the consent of the attorney for the state, change his election of one who assesses the punishment.

(c) Punishment shall be assessed on each count on which a finding of guilty has been returned.

**Sec. 3. Evidence of prior criminal record in all criminal cases after a finding of guilty.**

(a) Regardless of the plea and whether the punishment be assessed by the judge or the jury, evidence may be offered by the state and the defendant as to any matter the court deems relevant to sentencing, including but not limited to the prior criminal record of the defendant, his general reputation, his character, an opinion regarding his character, the circumstances of the offense for which he is being tried, and, notwithstanding Rules 404 and 405, Texas Rules of Criminal Evidence, any other evidence of an extraneous crime or bad act that is shown beyond a reasonable doubt by evidence to have been committed by the defendant or for which he could be held criminally responsible, regardless of whether he has previously been charged with or finally convicted of the crime or act. A court may consider as a factor in mitigating punishment the conduct of a defendant while participating in a program under Chapter 17 as a condition of release on bail. Additionally, notwithstanding Rule 609(d), Texas Rules of Criminal Evidence, and subject to Subsection (h), evidence may be offered by the state and the defendant of an adjudication of delinquency based on a violation by the defendant of a penal law of the grade of:

(1) a felony; or

(2) a misdemeanor punishable by confinement in jail.

(b) After the introduction of such evidence has been concluded, and if the jury has the responsibility of assessing the punishment, the court shall give such additional written instructions as may be necessary and the order of procedure and the rules governing the conduct of the trial shall be the same as are applicable on the issue of guilt or innocence.

(c) In cases where the matter of punishment is referred to the jury, the verdict shall not be complete until the jury has rendered a verdict both on the guilt or innocence of the defendant and the amount of punishment, where the jury finds the defendant guilty. In the event the jury shall fail to agree, a mistrial shall be declared, the jury shall be discharged, and no jeopardy shall attach.

(d) When the judge assesses the punishment, he may order an investigative report as contemplated in Section 9 of Article 42.12 of this code and after considering the report, and after the hearing of the evidence hereinabove provided for, he shall forthwith announce his decision in open court as to the punishment to be assessed.

(e) Nothing herein contained shall be construed as affecting the admissibility of extraneous offenses on the question of guilt or innocence.

(f) In cases in which the matter of punishment is referred to a jury, either party may offer into evidence the availability of community corrections facilities serving the jurisdiction in which the offense was committed.

(g) On timely request of the defendant, notice of intent to introduce evidence under this article shall be given in the same manner required by Rule 404(b), Texas Rules of Criminal Evidence. If the attorney representing the state intends to introduce an extraneous crime or bad act that has not resulted in a final conviction in a court of record or a probated or suspended sentence, notice of that intent is reasonable only if the notice includes the date on which and the county in which the alleged crime or bad act occurred and the name of the alleged victim of the crime or bad act. The requirement under this subsection that the attorney representing the state give notice applies only if the defendant makes a timely request to the attorney representing the state for the notice.

(h) Regardless of whether the punishment will be assessed by the judge or the jury, neither the state nor the defendant may offer before sentencing evidence that the defendant plans to undergo an orchiectomy.

(i) Evidence of an adjudication for conduct that is a violation of a penal law of the grade of misdemeanor punishable by confinement in jail is admissible only if the conduct upon which the adjudication is based occurred on or after January 1, 1996.

*(Chgd. by L.1997, chaps. 144(2), 1086(31); L.1999, chap. 62(19.01(7)), eff. 9/1/99.)*

**Sec. 4. Felony cases; penalty phase.**

(a) In the penalty phase of the trial of a felony case in which the punishment is to be assessed by the jury rather than the court, if the offense of which the jury has found the defendant guilty is listed in Section 3g(a)(1), Article 42.12, of this code or if the judgment contains an affirmative finding under Section 3g(a)(2), Article 42.12, of this code, unless the defendant has been convicted of a capital felony the court shall charge the jury in writing as follows:

"Under the law applicable in this case, the defendant, if sentenced to a term of imprisonment, may earn time off the period of incarceration imposed through the award of good conduct time. Prison authorities may award good conduct time to a prisoner who exhibits good behavior, diligence in carrying out prison work assignments, and attempts at rehabilitation. If a prisoner engages in misconduct, prison authorities may also take away all or part of any good conduct time earned by the prisoner.

"It is also possible that the length of time for which the defendant will be imprisoned might be reduced by the award of parole.

"Under the law applicable in this case, if the defendant is sentenced to a term of imprisonment, he will not become eligible for parole until the actual time served equals one-half of the sentence imposed or 30 years, whichever is less, without consideration of any good conduct time he may earn. If the defendant is sentenced to a term of less than four years, he must serve at least two years before he is eligible for parole. Eligibility for parole does not guarantee that parole will be granted.

"It cannot accurately be predicted how the parole law and good conduct time might be applied to this defendant if he is sentenced to a term of imprisonment, because the application of these laws will depend on decisions made by prison and parole authorities.

"You may consider the existence of the parole law and good conduct time. However, you are not to consider the extent to which good conduct time may be awarded to or forfeited by this particular defendant. You are not to consider the manner in which the parole law may be applied to this particular defendant."

(b) In the penalty phase of the trial of a felony case in which the punishment is to be assessed by the jury rather than the court, if the offense is punishable as a felony of the first degree, if a prior conviction has been alleged for enhancement of punishment as provided by Section 12.42(b), (c), or (d), Penal Code, or if the offense is a felony not designated as a capital felony or a felony of the first, second, or third degree and the maximum term of imprisonment that may be imposed for the offense is longer than 60 years, unless the offense of which the jury has found the defendant guilty is listed in Section 3g(a)(1), Article 42.12, of this code or the judgment contains an affirmative finding under Section 3g(a)(2), Article 42.12, of this code, the court shall charge the jury in writing as follows:

"Under the law applicable in this case, the defendant, if sentenced to a term of imprisonment, may earn time off the period of incarceration imposed through the award of good conduct time. Prison authorities may award good conduct time to a prisoner who exhibits good behavior, diligence in carrying out prison work assignments, and attempts at rehabilitation. If a prisoner engages in misconduct, prison authorities may also take away all or part of any good conduct time earned by the prisoner.

"It is also possible that the length of time for which the defendant will be imprisoned might be reduced by the award of parole.

"Under the law applicable in this case, if the defendant is sentenced to a term of imprisonment, he will not become eligible for parole until the actual time served plus any good conduct time earned equals one-fourth of the sentence imposed or 15 years, whichever is less. Eligibility for parole does not guarantee that parole will be granted.

"It cannot accurately be predicted how the parole law and good conduct time might be applied to this defendant if he is sentenced to a term of imprisonment, because the application of these laws will depend on decisions made by prison and parole authorities.

"You may consider the existence of the parole law and good conduct time. However, you are not to consider the extent to which good conduct time may be awarded to or forfeited by this particular defendant. You are not to consider the manner in which the parole law may be applied to this particular defendant."

(c) In the penalty phase of the trial of a felony case in which the punishment is to be assessed by the jury rather than the court, if the offense is punishable as a felony of the second or third degree, if a prior conviction has been alleged for enhancement as provided by Section 12.42(a), Penal Code, or if the offense is a felony not designated as a capital felony or a felony of the first, second, or third degree and the maximum term of imprisonment that may be imposed for the offense is 60 years or less, unless the offense of which the jury has found the defendant guilty is listed in Section 3g(a)(1), Article 42.12, of this code or the judgment contains an affirmative finding under Section 3g(a)(2), Article 42.12, of this code, the court shall charge the jury in writing as follows:

"Under the law applicable in this case, the defendant, if sentenced to a term of imprisonment, may earn time off the period of incarceration imposed through the award of good conduct time. Prison authorities may award good conduct time to a prisoner who exhibits good behavior, diligence in carrying out prison work assignments, and attempts at rehabilitation. If a prisoner engages in misconduct, prison authorities may also take away all or part of any good conduct time earned by the prisoner.

"It is also possible that the length of time for which the defendant will be imprisoned might be reduced by the award of parole.

"Under the law applicable in this case, if the defendant is sentenced to a term of imprisonment, he will not become eligible for parole until the actual time served plus any good conduct time earned equals one-fourth of the sentence imposed. Eligibility for parole does not guarantee that parole will be granted.

"It cannot accurately be predicted how the parole law and good conduct time might be applied to this defendant if he is sentenced to a term of imprisonment, because the application of these laws will depend on decisions made by prison and parole authorities.

"You may consider the existence of the parole law and good conduct time. However, you are not to consider the extent to which good conduct time may be awarded to or forfeited by this particular defendant. You are not to consider the manner in which the parole law may be applied to this particular defendant."

(d) This section does not permit the introduction of evidence on the operation of parole and good conduct time laws.

*(Chgd. by L.1989, chaps. 103(1), 785(4.04); L.1990, 6th C.S., chap. 25(30); L.1993, chap. 900(5.01), (5.02), (5.05), (5.06); L.1995, chap. 262(82), eff. 1/1/96.)*



## Art. 37.071. Procedure in capital case.

**Sec. 1.** If a defendant is found guilty in a capital felony case in which the state does not seek the death penalty, the judge shall sentence the defendant to life imprisonment.

**Sec. 2.** (a) If a defendant is tried for a capital offense in which the state seeks the death penalty, on a finding that the defendant is guilty of a capital offense, the court shall conduct a separate sentencing proceeding to determine whether the defendant shall be sentenced to death or life imprisonment. The proceeding shall be conducted in the trial court and, except as provided by Article 44.29(c) of this code, before the trial jury as soon as practicable. In the proceeding, evidence may be presented by the state and the defendant or the defendant's counsel as to any matter that the court deems relevant to sentence, including evidence of the defendant's background or character or the circumstances of the offense that mitigate against the imposition of the death penalty. This subsection shall not be construed to authorize the introduction of any evidence secured in violation of the Constitution of the United States or of the State of Texas. The state and the defendant or the defendant's counsel shall be permitted to present argument for or against sentence of death. The court, the attorney representing the state, the defendant, or the defendant's counsel may not inform a juror or a prospective juror of the effect of a failure of a jury to agree on issues submitted under Subsection (c) or (e) of this article.

(b) On conclusion of the presentation of the evidence, the court shall submit the following issues to the jury:

(1) whether there is a probability that the defendant would commit criminal acts of violence that would constitute a continuing threat to society; and

(2) in cases in which the jury charge at the guilt or innocence stage permitted the jury to find the defendant guilty as a party under Sections 7.01 and 7.02, Penal Code, whether the defendant actually caused the death of the deceased or did not actually cause the death of the deceased but intended to kill the deceased or another or anticipated that a human life would be taken.

(3) *(Repealed.)*

(c) The state must prove each issue submitted under Subsection (b) of this article beyond a reasonable doubt, and the jury shall return a special verdict of "yes" or "no" on each issue submitted under Subsection (b) of this Article.

(d) The court shall charge the jury that:

(1) in deliberating on the issues submitted under Subsection (b) of this article, it shall consider all evidence admitted at the guilt or innocence stage and the punishment stage, including evidence of the defendant's background or character or the circumstances of the offense that militates for or mitigates against the imposition of the death penalty;

(2) it may not answer any issue submitted under Subsection (b) of this article "yes" unless it agrees unanimously and it may not answer any issue "no" unless 10 or more jurors agree; and

(3) members of the jury need not agree on what particular evidence supports a negative answer to any issue submitted under Subsection (b) of this article.

(e)(1) The court shall instruct the jury that if the jury returns an affirmative finding to each issue submitted under Subsection (b) of this article, it shall answer the following issue:

Whether, taking into consideration all of the evidence, including the circumstances of the offense, the defendant's character and background, and the personal moral culpability of the defendant, there is a sufficient mitigating circumstance or circumstances to warrant that a sentence of life imprisonment rather than a death sentence be imposed.

(2) The court, on the written request of the attorney representing the defendant, shall:

(A) instruct the jury that if the jury answers that a circumstance or circumstances warrant that a sentence of life imprisonment rather than a death sentence be imposed, the court will sentence the defendant to imprisonment in the institutional division of the Texas Department of Criminal Justice for life; and

(B) charge the jury in writing as follows:

"Under the law applicable in this case, if the defendant is sentenced to imprisonment in the institutional division of the Texas Department of Criminal Justice for life, the defendant will become eligible for release on parole, but not until the actual time served by the defendant equals 40 years, without consideration of any good conduct time. It cannot accurately be predicted how the parole laws might be applied to this defendant if the defendant is sentenced to a term of imprisonment for life because the application of those laws will depend on decisions made by prison and parole authorities, but eligibility for parole does not guarantee that parole will be granted."

(f) The court shall charge the jury that in answering the issue submitted under Subsection (e) of this article, the jury:

(1) shall answer the issue "yes" or "no";

(2) may not answer the issue "no" unless it agrees unanimously and may not answer the issue "yes" unless 10 or more jurors agree;

(3) need not agree on what particular evidence supports an affirmative finding on the issue; and

(4) shall consider mitigating evidence to be evidence that a juror might regard as reducing the defendant's moral blameworthiness.

(g) If the jury returns an affirmative finding on each issue submitted under Subsection (b) of this article and a negative finding on an issue submitted under Subsection (e) of this article, the court shall sentence the defendant to death. If the jury returns a negative finding on any issue submitted under Subsection (b) of this article or an affirmative finding on an issue submitted under Subsection (e) of this article or is unable to answer any issue submitted under Subsection (b) or (e) of this article, the court shall sentence the defendant to confinement in the institutional division of the Texas Department of Criminal Justice for life.

(h) The judgment of conviction and sentence of death shall be subject to automatic review by the Court of Criminal Appeals.

(i) This article applies to the sentencing procedure in a capital case for an offense that is committed on or after September 1, 1991. For the purposes of this section, an offense is committed on or after September 1, 1991, if any element of that offense occurs on or after that date.
*(Chgd. by L.1991, chaps. 652(9), 838(1); L.1993, chap. 781(1); L.1999, chap. 140(1), eff. 9/1/99.)*

### Art. 37.0711. Procedure in capital case for offense committed before September 1, 1991.

**Sec. 1.** This article applies to the sentencing procedure in a capital case for an offense that is committed before September 1, 1991, whether the sentencing procedure is part of the original trial of the offense, an award of a new trial for both the guilt or innocence stage and the punishment stage of the trial, or an award of a new trial only for the punishment stage of the trial. For the purposes of this section, an offense is committed before September 1, 1991, if every element of the offense occurs before that date.

**Sec. 2.** If a defendant is found guilty in a case in which the state does not seek the death penalty, the judge shall sentence the defendant to life imprisonment.

**Sec. 3.** (a) If a defendant is tried for a capital offense in which the state seeks the death penalty, on a finding that the defendant is guilty of a capital offense, the court shall conduct a separate sentencing proceeding to determine whether the defendant shall be sentenced to death or life imprisonment. The proceeding shall be conducted in the trial court and, except as provided by Article 44.29(c) of this code, before the trial jury as soon as practicable. In the proceeding, evidence may be presented as to any matter that the court deems relevant to sentence. This subsection shall not be construed to authorize the introduction of any evidence secured in violation of the Constitution of the United States or of this state. The state and the defendant or the defendant's counsel shall be permitted to present argument for or against sentence of death.

(b) On conclusion of the presentation of the evidence, the court shall submit the following three issues to the jury:

(1) whether the conduct of the defendant that caused the death of the deceased was committed deliberately and with the reasonable expectation that the death of the deceased or another would result;

(2) whether there is a probability that the defendant would commit criminal acts of violence that would constitute a continuing threat to society; and

(3) if raised by the evidence, whether the conduct of the defendant in killing the deceased was unreasonable in response to the provocation, if any, by the deceased.

(c) The state must prove each issue submitted under Subsection (b) of this section beyond a reasonable doubt, and the jury shall return a special verdict of "yes" or "no" on each issue submitted.

(d) The court shall charge the jury that:

(1) it may not answer any issue submitted under Subsection (b) of this section "yes" unless it agrees unanimously; and

(2) it may not answer any issue submitted under Subsection (b) of this section "no" unless 10 or more jurors agree.

(e) The court shall instruct the jury that if the jury returns an affirmative finding on each issue submitted under Subsection (b) of this section, it shall answer the following issue:

Whether, taking into consideration all of the evidence, including the circumstances of the offense, the defendant's character and background, and the personal moral culpability of the defendant, there is a sufficient mitigating circumstance or circumstances to warrant that a sentence of life imprisonment rather than a death sentence be imposed.

(f) The court shall charge the jury that, in answering the issue submitted under Subsection (e) of this section, the jury:

(1) shall answer the issue "yes" or "no";

(2) may not answer the issue "no" unless it agrees unanimously and may not answer the issue "yes" unless 10 or more jurors agree; and

(3) shall consider mitigating evidence that a juror might regard as reducing the defendant's moral blameworthiness.

(g) If the jury returns an affirmative finding on each issue submitted under Subsection (b) of this section and a negative finding on the issue submitted under Subsection (e) of this section, the court shall sentence the defendant to death. If the jury returns a negative finding on any issue submitted under Subsection (b) of this section or an affirmative finding on the issue submitted under Subsection (e) of this section or is unable to answer any issue submitted under Subsection (b) or (e) of this section, the court shall sentence the defendant to confinement in the institutional division of the Texas Department of Criminal Justice for life.

(h) If a defendant is convicted of an offense under Section 19.03(a)(7), Penal Code, the court shall submit the issues under Subsections (b) and (e) of this section only with regard to the conduct of the defendant in murdering the deceased individual first named in the indictment.

(i) The court, the attorney for the state, or the attorney for the defendant may not inform a juror or prospective juror of the effect of failure of the jury to agree on an issue submitted under this article.

(j) The Court of Criminal Appeals shall automatically review a judgment of conviction and sentence of death not later than the 60th day after the date of certification by the sentencing court of the entire record, unless the Court of Criminal Appeals extends the time for an additional period not to exceed 30 days for good cause shown. Automatic review under this subsection has priority over all other cases before the Court of Criminal Appeals, and the court shall hear automatic reviews under rules adopted by the court for that purpose.

*(Added by L.1993, chap. 781(2); chgd. by L.1995, chap. 76(14.22), eff. 9/1/95.)*

**Art. 37.072.** *(Added by L.1989, chap. 360(1); chgd. by L.1991, chap. 727(1); L.1995, chaps. 76(14.23), 260(11), (12), (13); repealed by L.1997, chap. 1100(6(1)), eff. 9/1/97.)*

### Art. 37.073. Repayment of rewards.

(a) After a defendant has been convicted of a felony offense, the judge may order a defendant to repay all or part of a reward paid by a crime stoppers organization.

(b) In determining whether the defendant must repay the reward or part of the reward, the court shall consider:

(1) the ability of the defendant to make the payment and the financial hardship on the defendant to make the required payment; and

(2) the importance of the information to the prosecution of the defendant as provided by the arresting officer or the attorney for the state with due regard for the confidentiality of the crime stoppers organization records.

(c) In this article, "crime stoppers organization" means a crime stoppers organization, as defined by Subdivision (2), Section 414.001, Government Code, that is approved by the Crime Stoppers Advisory Council to receive payments of rewards under this article and Article 42.152 of this code.

*(Added by L.1989, chap. 611(1); redes. by L.1991, chap. 16(19.01(5)); chgd. by L.1997, chap. 700(10), eff. 9/1/97.)*

### Art. 37.08. Conviction of lesser included offenses.† [*Conviction of lesser included offense.*]

In a prosecution for an offense with lesser included offenses, the jury may find the defendant not guilty of the greater offense, but guilty of any lesser included offense.

### Art. 37.09. Lesser included offenses.† [*Lesser included offense.*]

An offense is a lesser included offense if:

(1) it is established by proof of the same or less than all the facts required to establish the commission of the offense charged;

(2) it differs from the offense charged only in the respect that a less serious injury or risk of injury to the same person, property, or public interest suffices to establish its commission;

(3) it differs from the offense charged only in the respect that a less culpable mental state suffices to establish its commission; or

(4) it consists of an attempt to commit the offense charged or an otherwise included offense.

### Art. 37.10. Informal verdict.

(a) If the verdict of the jury is informal, its attention shall be called to it, and with its consent the verdict may, under the direction of the court, be reduced to the proper form. If the jury refuses to have the verdict altered, it shall again retire to its room to deliberate, unless it manifestly appear that the verdict is intended as an acquittal; and in that case, the judgment shall be rendered accordingly, discharging the defendant.

(b) If the jury assesses punishment in a case and in the verdict assesses both punishment that is authorized by law for the offense and punishment that is not authorized by law for the offense, the court shall reform the verdict to show the punishment authorized by law and to omit the punishment not authorized by law. If the trial court is required to reform a verdict under this subsection and fails to do so, the appellate court shall reform the verdict as provided by this subsection.

### Art. 37.11. Defendants tried jointly.† [*Defendants tried together.*]

Where several defendants are tried together, the jury may convict each defendant it finds guilty and acquit others. If it agrees to a verdict as to one or more, it may find a verdict in accordance with such agreement, and if it cannot agree as to others, a mistrial may be entered as to them.

### Art. 37.12. Judgment on verdict.

On each verdict of acquittal or conviction, the proper judgment shall be entered immediately. If acquitted, the defendant shall be at once discharged from all further liability upon the charge for which he was tried; provided that, in misdemeanor cases where there is returned a verdict, or a plea of guilty is entered and the punishment assessed is by fine only, the court may, on written request of the defendant and for good cause shown, defer judgment until some other day fixed by order of the court; but in no event shall the judgment be deferred for a longer period of time than six months. On expiration of the time fixed by the order of the court, the court or judge thereof, shall enter judgment on the verdict or plea and the same shall be executed as provided by Chapter 43 of this Code. Provided further, that the court or judge thereof, in the exercise of sound discretion may permit the defendant where judgment is deferred, to remain at large on his personal bond, or may require him to enter into bail bond in a sum at least double the amount of the assessed fine and costs, conditioned that the defendant and sureties, jointly and severally, will pay such fine and costs unless the defendant personally appears on the day, set in the order and discharges the judgment in the manner provided by Chapter 43 of this Code; and for the enforcement of any judgment entered, all writs, processes and remedies of this Code are made applicable so far as necessary to carry out the provisions of this Article.

**Art. 37.13. If jury believes accused insane.† [*If jury believes defendant insane.*]**
When a jury has been impaneled to assess the punishment upon a plea of guilty, it shall say in its verdict what the punishment is which it assesses; but if it is of the opinion that a person pleading guilty is insane, it shall so report to the court, and an issue as to that fact shall be tried before another jury; and if, upon such trial, it be found that the defendant is insane, such proceedings shall be had as directed in cases where a defendant becomes insane after conviction.

**Art. 37.14. Acquittal of higher offense as jeopardy.**
If a defendant, prosecuted for an offense which includes within it lesser offenses, be convicted of an offense lower than that for which he is indicted, and a new trial be granted him, or the judgment be arrested for any cause other than the want of jurisdiction, the verdict upon the first trial shall be considered an acquittal of the higher offense; but he may, upon a second trial, be convicted of the same offense of which he was before convicted, or any other inferior thereto.

**Art. 37.15.** *(Expired 9/1/94.)*



## CHAPTER 38. EVIDENCE IN CRIMINAL ACTIONS

Article
38.03. Presumption of innocence.† [*Supposition of innocence.*]
38.04. Jury are judges of facts.† [*Jury to weigh facts.*]
38.05. Judge shall not discuss evidence.† [*Judge not to discuss evidence.*]
38.07. Testimony in corroboration of victim of sexual offense.
38.071. Testimony of child who is victim of offense.
38.072. Hearsay statement of child abuse victim.† [*Hearsay statement by victim of child abuse.*]
38.08. Defendant may testify.† [*Testimony by defendant.*]
38.10. Exceptions to the spousal adverse testimony privilege.
38.101. Communications by drug abusers.† [*Drug rehab communications confidential.*]
38.12. Religious opinion.
38.14. Testimony of accomplice.† [*Accomplice's testimony.*]
38.15. Two witnesses in treason.
38.16. Evidence in treason.
38.17. Two witnesses required.† [*Two witnesses necessary.*]
38.18. Perjury and aggravated perjury.† [*Perjury; simple and aggravated.*]
38.19. Intent to defraud in forgery.† [*Forgery with intent to defraud.*]
38.21. Statement.
38.22. When statements may be used.† [*When statements usable.*]
38.23. Evidence not to be used.† [*Inadmissible evidence.*]
38.25. Written part of instrument controls.† [*Written portion of instrument authoritative.*]
38.27. Evidence of handwriting.† [*Handwriting as evidence.*]
38.30. Interpreter.
38.31. Interpreters for deaf persons.† [*Interpreters for the deaf.*]
38.32. Presumption of death.
38.33. Preservation and use of evidence of certain misdemeanor convictions.† [*Fingerprinting, etc., in certain misdemeanor convictions.*]
38.34. Photographic evidence in theft cases.† [*Photos as evidence in theft cases.*]
38.35. Forensic analysis of evidence.
38.36. Evidence in prosecutions for murder.
38.37. Evidence of extraneous offenses or acts.
38.38. Evidence relating to retaining attorney.

**Art. 38.03. Presumption of innocence.† [*Supposition of innocence.*]**
All persons are presumed to be innocent and no person may be convicted of an offense unless each element of the offense is proved beyond a reasonable doubt. The fact that he has been arrested, confined, or indicted for, or otherwise charged with, the offense gives rise to no inference of guilt at his trial.

**Art. 38.04. Jury are judges of facts.† [*Jury to weigh facts.*]**
The jury, in all cases, is the exclusive judge of the facts proved, and of the weight to be given to the testimony, except where it is provided by law that proof of any particular fact is to be taken as either conclusive or presumptive proof of the existence of another fact, or where the law directs that a certain degree of weight is to be attached to a certain species of evidence.

**Art. 38.05. Judge shall not discuss evidence.† [*Judge not to discuss evidence.*]**

In ruling upon the admissibility of evidence, the judge shall not discuss or comment upon the weight of the same or its bearing in the case, but shall simply decide whether or not it is admissible; nor shall he, at any stage of the proceeding previous to the return of the verdict, make any remark calculated to convey to the jury his opinion of the case.

**Art. 38.07. Testimony in corroboration of victim of sexual offense.**

A conviction under Chapter 21, Section 22.011, or Section 22.021, Penal Code, is supportable on the uncorroborated testimony of the victim of the sexual offense if the victim informed any person, other than the defendant, of the alleged offense within one year after the date on which the offense is alleged to have occurred. The requirement that the victim inform another person of an alleged offense does not apply if the victim was younger than 18 years of age at the time of the alleged offense. *(Chgd. by L.1993, chaps. 200(1), 900(12.01), eff. 5/19/93, 9/1/93, respectively.)*

**Art. 38.071. Testimony of child who is victim of offense.**

**Sec. 1.** This article applies only to a proceeding in the prosecution of an offense defined by any of the following sections of the Penal Code if the offense is alleged to have been committed against a child 12 years of age or younger and if the trial court finds that the child is unavailable to testify at the trial of the offense, and applies only to the statements or testimony of that child:

(1) Section 21.11 (Indecency with a Child);
(2) Section 22.011 (Sexual Assault);
(3) Section 22.02 (Aggravated Assault);
(4) Section 22.021 (Aggravated Sexual Assault);
(5) Section 22.04(e) (Injury to a Child, Elderly Individual, or Disabled Individual);
(6) Section 22.04(f) (Injury to a Child, Elderly Individual, or Disabled Individual), if the conduct is committed intentionally or knowingly;
(7) Section 25.02 (Prohibited Sexual Conduct); or
(8) Section 43.25 (Sexual Performance by a Child).

**Sec. 2. Oral statement of child.** (a) The recording of an oral statement of the child made before the indictment is returned or the complaint has been filed is admissible into evidence if the court makes a determination that the factual issues of identity or actual occurrence were fully and fairly inquired into in a detached manner by a neutral individual experienced in child abuse cases that seeks to find the truth of the matter.

(b) If a recording is made under Subsection (a) of this section and after an indictment is returned or a complaint has been filed, by motion of the attorney representing the state or the attorney representing the defendant and on the approval of the court, both attorneys may propound written interrogatories that shall be presented by the same neutral individual who made the initial inquiries, if possible, and recorded under the same or similar circumstances of the original recording with the time and date of the inquiry clearly indicated in the recording.

(c) A recording made under Subsection (a) of this section is not admissible into evidence unless a recording made under Subsection (b) is admitted at the same time if a recording under Subsection (b) was requested prior to time of trial.

**Sec. 3. Televised testimony of child.** (a) On its own motion or on the motion of the attorney representing the state or the attorney representing the defendant, the court may order that the testimony of the child be taken during the trial in a room other than the courtroom and be televised by closed circuit equipment in the courtroom to be viewed by the court and the finder of fact. To the extent practicable, only the judge, the court reporter, the attorneys for the defendant and for the state, persons necessary to operate the equipment, and any person whose presence would contribute to the welfare and well-being of the child may be present in the room with the child during his testimony. Only the attorneys and the judge may question the child. To the extent practicable, the persons necessary to operate the equipment shall be confined to an adjacent room or behind a screen or mirror that permits them to see and hear the child during his testimony, but does not permit the child to see or hear them. The court shall permit the defendant to observe and hear the testimony of the child and to communicate contemporaneously with his attorney during periods of recess or by audio contact, but the court shall attempt to ensure that the child cannot hear or see the defendant. The court shall permit the attorney for the defendant adequate opportunity to confer with the defendant during cross-examination of the child. On application of the attorney for the defendant, the court may recess the proceeding before or during cross-examination of the child for a reasonable time to allow the attorney for the defendant to confer with defendant.

Printed in the U.S.A. Zt

(b) The court may set any other conditions and limitations on the taking of the testimony that it finds just and appropriate, taking into consideration the interests of the child, the rights of the defendant, and any other relevant factors.

**Sec. 4. Indictment; persons present at child's testimony.** (a) After an indictment has been returned or a complaint filed charging the defendant with an offense to which this article applies, on its own motion or on the motion of the attorney representing the state or the attorney representing the defendant, the court may order that the testimony of the child be taken outside the courtroom and be recorded for showing in the courtroom before the court and the finder of fact. To the extent practicable, only those persons permitted to be present at the taking of testimony under Section 3 of this article may be present during the taking of the child's testimony, and the persons operating the equipment shall be confined from the child's sight and hearing as provided by Section 3. The court shall permit the defendant to observe and hear the testimony of the child and to communicate contemporaneously with his attorney during periods of recess or by audio contact but shall attempt to ensure that the child cannot hear or see the defendant.

(b) The court may set any other conditions and limitations on the taking of the testimony that it finds just and appropriate, taking into consideration the interests of the child, the rights of the defendant, and any other relevant factors. The court shall also ensure that:

(1) the recording is both visual and aural and is recorded on film or videotape or by other electronic means;

(2) the recording equipment was capable of making an accurate recording, the operator was competent, the quality of the recording is sufficient to allow the court and the finder of fact to assess the demeanor of the child and the interviewer, and the recording is accurate and is not altered;

(3) each voice on the recording is identified;

(4) the defendant, the attorneys for each party, and the expert witnesses for each party are afforded an opportunity to view the recording before it is shown in the courtroom;

(5) before giving his testimony, the child was placed under oath or was otherwise admonished in a manner appropriate to the child's age and maturity to testify truthfully;

(6) the court finds from the recording or through an in camera examination of the child that the child was competent to testify at the time the recording was made; and

(7) only one continuous recording of the child was made or the necessity for pauses in the recordings or for multiple recordings is established at trial.

(c) After a complaint has been filed or an indictment returned charging the defendant, on the motion of the attorney representing the state, the court may order that the deposition of the child be taken outside of the courtroom in the same manner as a deposition may be taken in a civil matter. A deposition taken under this subsection is admissible into evidence.

**Sec. 5. Recordings of child's statements as admissible evidence; requirements.** (a) On the motion of the attorney representing the state or the attorney representing the defendant and on a finding by the trial court that the following requirements have been substantially satisfied, the recording of an oral statement of the child made before a complaint has been filed or an indictment returned charging any person with an offense to which this article applies is admissible into evidence if:

(1) no attorney or peace officer was present when the statement was made;

(2) the recording is both visual and aural and is recorded on film or videotape or by other electronic means;

(3) the recording equipment was capable of making an accurate recording, the operator of the equipment was competent, the quality of the recording is sufficient to allow the court and the finder of fact to assess the demeanor of the child and the interviewer, and the recording is accurate and has not been altered;

(4) the statement was not made in response to questioning calculated to lead the child to make a particular statement;

(5) every voice on the recording is identified;

(6) the person conducting the interview of the child in the recording is expert in the handling, treatment, and investigation of child abuse cases, present at the proceeding, called by the state as part of the state's case in chief to testify at trial, and subject to cross-examination;

(7) immediately after a complaint was filed or an indictment returned charging the defendant with an offense to which this article applies, the attorney representing the state notified the court, the defendant, and the attorney representing the defendant of the existence of the recording and that the recording may be used at the trial of the offense;

(8) the defendant, the attorney for the defendant, and the expert witnesses for the defendant were afforded an opportunity to view the recording before it is offered into evidence and, if a pro-

ceeding was requested as provided by Subsection (b) of this section, in a proceeding conducted before a district court judge but outside the presence of the jury were afforded an opportunity to cross-examine the child as provided by Subsection (b) of this section from any time immediately following the filing of the complaint or the returning of an indictment charging the defendant with an offense to which this article applies until the date the trial begins;

(9) the recording of the cross-examination, if there is one, is admissible under Subsection (b) of this section;

(10) before giving his testimony, the child was placed under oath or was otherwise admonished in a manner appropriate to the child's age and maturity to testify truthfully;

(11) the court finds from the recording or through an in camera examination of the child that the child was competent to testify at the time that the recording was made; and

(12) only one continuous recording of the child was made or the necessity for pauses in the recordings or for multiple recordings has been established at trial.

(b) On the motion of the attorney representing the defendant, a district court may order that the cross-examination of the child be taken and be recorded before the judge of that court at any time until a recording made in accordance with Subsection (a) of this section has been introduced into evidence at the trial. On a finding by the trial court that the following requirements were satisfied, the recording of the cross-examination of the child is admissible into evidence and shall be viewed by the finder of fact only after the finder of fact has viewed the recording authorized by Subsection (a) of this section if:

(1) the recording is both visual and aural and is recorded on film or videotape or by other electronic means;

(2) the recording equipment was capable of making an accurate recording, the operator of the equipment was competent, the quality of the recording is sufficient to allow the court and the finder of fact to assess the demeanor of the child and the attorney representing the defendant, and the recording is accurate and has not been altered;

(3) every voice on the recording is identified;

(4) the defendant, the attorney representing the defendant, the attorney representing the state, and the expert witnesses for the defendant and the state were afforded an opportunity to view the recording before the trial began;

(5) the child was placed under oath before the cross-examination began or was otherwise admonished in a manner appropriate to the child's age and maturity to testify truthfully; and

(6) only one continuous recording of the child was made or the necessity for pauses in the recordings or for multiple recordings was established at trial.

(c) During cross-examination under Subsection (b) of this section, to the extent practicable, only a district court judge, the attorney representing the defendant, the attorney representing the state, persons necessary to operate the equipment, and any other person whose presence would contribute to the welfare and well-being of the child may be present in the room with the child during his testimony. Only the attorneys and the judge may question the child. To the extent practicable, the persons operating the equipment shall be confined to an adjacent room or behind a screen or mirror that permits them to see and hear the child during his testimony but does not permit the child to see or hear them. The court shall permit the defendant to observe and hear the testimony of the child and to communicate contemporaneously with his attorney during periods of recess or by audio contact, but shall attempt to ensure that the child cannot hear or see the defendant.

(d) Under Subsection (b) of this section the district court may set any other conditions and limitations on the taking of the cross-examination of a child that it finds just and appropriate, taking into consideration the interests of the child, the rights of the defendant, and any other relevant factors.

**Sec. 6. Waiver of court testimony.** If the court orders the testimony of a child to be taken under Section 3 or 4 of this article or if the court finds the testimony of the child taken under Section 2 or 5 of this article is admissible into evidence, the child may not be required to testify in court at the proceeding for which the testimony was taken, unless the court finds there is good cause.

**Sec. 7. Determination of good cause.** In making any determination of good cause under this article, the court shall consider the rights of the defendant, the interests of the child, the relationship of the defendant to the child, the character and duration of the alleged offense, any court finding related to the availability of the child to testify, the age, maturity, and emotional stability of the child, the time elapsed since the alleged offense, and any other relevant factors.

**Sec. 8. Determination of unavailability.** (a) In making a determination of unavailability under this article, the court shall consider relevant factors including the relationship of the defendant to the child, the character and duration of the alleged offense, the age, maturity, and emotional stability of the child, and the time elapsed since the alleged offense, and whether the child is more likely than not to be unavailable to testify because:

(1) of emotional or physical causes, including the confrontation with the defendant or the ordinary involvement as complainant in the courtroom trial; or

(2) the child would suffer undue psychological or physical harm through his involvement at trial.

(b) A determination of unavailability under this article can be made after an earlier determination of availability. A determination of availability under this article can be made after an earlier determination of unavailability.

**Sec. 9. Proof of identification.** If the court finds the testimony taken under Section 2 or 5 of this article is admissible into evidence or if the court orders the testimony to be taken under Section 3 or 4 of this article and if the identity of the perpetrator is a contested issue, the child additionally must make an in-person identification of the defendant either at or before trial.

**Sec. 10. Court's duty to minimize trauma to child.** In ordering a child to testify under this article, the court shall take all reasonable steps necessary and available to minimize undue psychological trauma to the child and to minimize the emotional and physical stress to the child caused by relevant factors, including the confrontation with the defendant and the ordinary participation of the complainant in the courtroom.

**Sec. 11. Court-approved counsel.** In a proceeding under Section 2, 3, or 4 or Subsection (b) of Section 5 of this article, if the defendant is not represented by counsel and the court finds that the defendant is not able to obtain counsel for the purposes of the proceeding, the court shall appoint counsel to represent the defendant at the proceeding.

**Sec. 12. Cross-examination.** In this article, "cross-examination" has the same meaning as in other legal proceedings in the state.

**Sec. 13. Attorney of States.** The attorney representing the state shall determine whether to use the procedure provided in Section 2 of this article or the procedure provided in Section 5 of this article.

*(Chgd. by L.1991, chap. 266(1); L.1995, chap. 76(14.24), eff. 9/1/95.)*

### Art. 38.072. Hearsay statement of child abuse victim.† [*Hearsay statement by victim of child abuse.*]

**Sec. 1.** This article applies to a proceeding in the prosecution of an offense under any of the following provisions of the Penal Code, if committed against a child 12 years of age or younger:

(1) Chapter 21 (Sexual Offenses) or 22 (Assaultive Offenses);

(2) Section 25.02 (Prohibited Sexual Conduct); or

(3) Section 43.25 (Sexual Performance by a Child).

**Sec. 2.** (a) This article applies only to statements that describe the alleged offense that:

(1) were made by the child against whom the offense was allegedly committed; and

(2) were made to the first person, 18 years of age or older, other than the defendant, to whom the child made a statement about the offense.

(b) A statement that meets the requirements of Subsection (a) of this article is not inadmissible because of the hearsay rule if:

(1) on or before the 14th day before the date the proceeding begins, the party intending to offer the statement:

(A) notifies the adverse party of its intention to do so;

(B) provides the adverse party with the name of the witness through whom it intends to offer the statement; and

(C) provides the adverse party with a written summary of the statement;

(2) the trial court finds, in a hearing conducted outside the presence of the jury, that the statement is reliable based on the time, content, and circumstances of the statement; and

(3) the child testifies or is available to testify at the proceeding in court or in any other manner provided by law.

*(Chgd. by L.1995, chap. 76(14.25), eff. 9/1/95.)*

**Art. 38.08. Defendant may testify.† [*Testimony by defendant.*]**

Any defendant in a criminal action shall be permitted to testify in his own behalf therein, but the failure of any defendant to so testify shall not be taken as a circumstance against him, nor shall the same be alluded to or commented on by counsel in the cause.

**Art. 38.10. Exceptions to the spousal adverse testimony privilege.**

The privilege of a person's spouse not to be called as a witness for the state does not apply in any proceeding in which the person is charged with a crime committed against the person's spouse, a minor child, or a member of the household of either spouse. *(Added by L.1995, chap. 67(2), eff. 9/1/95.)*

**Art. 38.101. Communications by drug abusers.† [*Drug rehab communications confidential.*]**

A communication to any person involved in the treatment or examination of drug abusers by a person being treated voluntarily or being examined for admission to voluntary treatment for drug abuse is not admissible. However, information derived from the treatment or examination of drug abusers may be used for statistical and research purposes if the names of the patients are not revealed.

**Art. 38.12. Religious opinion.**

No person is incompetent to testify on account of his religious opinion or for the want of any religious belief.

**Art. 38.14. Testimony of accomplice.† [*Accomplice's testimony.*]**

A conviction cannot be had upon the testimony of an accomplice unless corroborated by other evidence tending to connect the defendant with the offense committed; and the corroboration is not sufficient if it merely shows the commission of the offense.

**Art. 38.15. Two witnesses in treason.**

No person can be convicted of treason except upon the testimony of at least two witnesses to the same overt act, or upon his own confession in open court.

**Art. 38.16. Evidence in treason.**

Evidence shall not be admitted in a prosecution for treason as to an overt act not expressly charged in the indictment; nor shall any person be convicted under an indictment for treason unless one or more overt acts are expressly charged therein.

**Art. 38.17. Two witnesses required.† [*Two witnesses necessary.*]**

In all cases where, by law, two witnesses, or one with corroborating circumstances, are required to authorize a conviction, if the requirement be not fulfilled, the court shall instruct the jury to render a verdict of acquittal, and they are bound by the instruction.

**Art. 38.18. Perjury and aggravated perjury.† [*Perjury; simple and aggravated.*]**

(a) No person may be convicted of perjury or aggravated perjury if proof that his statement is false rests solely upon the testimony of one witness other than the defendant.

(b) Paragraph (a) of this article does not apply to prosecutions for perjury or aggravated perjury involving inconsistent statements.

**Art. 38.19. Intent to defraud in forgery.† [*Forgery with intent to defraud.*]**

In trials of forgery, it need not be proved that the defendant committed the act with intent to defraud any particular person. It shall be sufficient to prove that the forgery was, in its nature, calculated to injure or defraud any of the sovereignties, bodies corporate or politic, officers or persons, named in the definition of forgery in the Penal Code.

**Art. 38.21. Statement.**

A statement of an accused may be used in evidence against him if it appears that the same was freely and voluntarily made without compulsion or persuasion, under the rules hereafter prescribed.

**Art. 38.22. When statements may be used.† [*When statements usable.*]**

**Sec. 1.** In this article, a written statement of an accused means a statement signed by the accused or a statement made by the accused in his own handwriting or, if the accused is unable to write, a statement bearing his mark, when the mark has been witnessed by a person other than a peace officer.

**Sec. 2.** No written statement made by an accused as a result of custodial interrogation is admissible as evidence against him in any criminal proceeding unless it is shown on the face of the statement that:

(a) The accused, prior to making the statement, either received from a magistrate the warning provided in Article 15.17 of this code or received from the person to whom the statement is made a warning that:

(1) he has the right to remain silent and not make any statement at all and that any statement he makes may be used against him at his trial;

(2) any statement he makes may be used as evidence against him in court;

(3) he has the right to have a lawyer present to advise him prior to and during any questioning;

(4) if he is unable to employ a lawyer, he has the right to have a lawyer appointed to advise him prior to and during any questioning; and

(5) he has the right to terminate the interview at any time; and

(b) the accused, prior to and during the making of the statement, knowingly, intelligently, and voluntarily waived the rights set out in the warning prescribed by Subsection (a) of this section.



**Sec. 3.** (a) No oral or sign language statement of an accused made as a result of custodial interrogation shall be admissible against the accused in a criminal proceeding unless:

(1) an electronic recording, which may include motion picture, video tape, or other visual recording, is made of the statement;

(2) prior to the statement but during the recording the accused is given the warning in Subsection (a) of Section 2 above and the accused knowingly, intelligently, and voluntarily waives any rights set out in the warning;

(3) the recording device was capable of making an accurate recording, the operator was competent, and the recording is accurate, and has not been altered;

(4) all voices on the recording are identified; and

(5) not later than the 20th day before the date of the proceeding, the attorney representing the defendant is provided with a true, complete, and accurate copy of all recordings of the defendant made under this article.

(b) Every electronic recording of any statement made by an accused during a custodial interrogation must be preserved until such time as the defendant's conviction for any offense relating thereto is final, all direct appeals therefrom are exhausted, or the prosecution of such offenses is barred by law.

(c) Subsection (a) of this section shall not apply to any statement which contains assertions of facts or circumstances that are found to be true and which conduce to establish the guilt of the accused, such as the finding of secreted or stolen property or the instrument with which he states the offense was committed.

(d) If the accused is a deaf person, the accused's statement under Section 2 or Section 3(a) of this article is not admissible against the accused unless the warning in Section 2 of this article is interpreted to the deaf person by an interpreter who is qualified and sworn as provided in Article 38.31 of this code.

(e) The courts of this state shall strictly construe Subsection (a) of this section and may not interpret Subsection (a) as making admissible a statement unless all requirements of the subsection have been satisfied by the state, except that:

(1) only voices that are material are identified; and

(2) the accused was given the warning in Subsection (a) of Section 2 above or its fully effective equivalent.

**Sec. 4.** When any statement, the admissibility of which is covered by this article, is sought to be used in connection with an official proceeding, any person who swears falsely to facts and circumstances which, if true, would render the statement admissible under this article is presumed to have acted with intent to deceive and with knowledge of the statement's meaning for the purpose of prosecution for aggravated perjury under Section 37.03 of the Penal Code. No person prosecuted under this subsection shall be eligible for probation.

**Sec. 5.** Nothing in this article precludes the admission of a statement made by the accused in open court at his trial, before a grand jury, or at any examining trial in compliance with Articles 16.03 and 16.04 of this code, or of a statement that is the res gestae of the arrest or of the offense, or of a statement that does not stem from custodial interrogation, or of a voluntary statement, whether or not the result of custodial interrogation, that has a bearing upon the credibility of the accused as a witness, or of any other statement that may be admissible under law.

**Sec. 6.** In all cases where a question is raised as to the voluntariness of a statement of an accused, the court must make an independent finding in the absence of the jury as to whether the statement was made under voluntary conditions. If the statement has been found to have been voluntarily made and held admissible as a matter of law and fact by the court in a hearing in the absence of the jury, the court must enter an order stating its conclusion as to whether or not the statement was voluntarily made, along with the specific finding of facts upon which the conclusion was based, which order shall be filed among the papers of the cause. Such order shall not be exhibited to the jury nor the finding thereof made known to the jury in any manner. Upon the finding by the judge as a matter of law and fact that the statement was voluntarily made, evidence pertaining to such matter may be submitted to the jury and it shall be instructed that unless the jury believes beyond a reasonable doubt that the statement was voluntarily made, the jury shall not consider such statement for any purpose nor any evidence obtained as a result thereof. In any case where a motion to suppress the statement has been filed and evidence has been submitted to the court on this issue, the court within its discretion may reconsider such evidence in his finding that the statement was voluntarily made and the same evidence submitted to the court at the hearing on the motion to suppress shall be made a part of the record the same as if it were being presented at the time of trial. However, the state or the defendant shall be entitled to present any new evidence on the issue of the voluntariness of the statement prior to the court's final ruling and order stating its findings.

**Sec. 7.** When the issue is raised by the evidence, the trial judge shall appropriately instruct the jury, generally, on the law pertaining to such statement.
*(Chgd. by L.1989, chap. 777(1), (2), eff. 9/1/89.)*

### Art. 38.23. Evidence not to be used.† [*Inadmissible evidence.*]

(a) No evidence obtained by an officer or other person in violation of any provisions of the Constitution or laws of the State of Texas, or of the Constitution or laws of the United States of America, shall be admitted in evidence against the accused on the trial of any criminal case.

In any case where the legal evidence raises an issue hereunder, the jury shall be instructed that if it believes, or has a reasonable doubt, that the evidence was obtained in violation of the provisions of this article, then and in such event, the jury shall disregard any such evidence so obtained.

(b) It is an exception to the provisions of Subsection (a) of this Article that the evidence was obtained by a law enforcement officer acting in objective good faith reliance upon a warrant issued by a neutral magistrate based on probable cause.

### Art. 38.25. Written part of instrument controls.† [*Written portion of instrument authoritative.*]

When an instrument is partly written and partly printed, the written shall control the printed portion when the two are inconsistent.

### Art. 38.27. Evidence of handwriting.† [*Handwriting as evidence.*]

It is competent to give evidence of handwriting by comparison, made by experts or by the jury. Proof by comparison only shall not be sufficient to establish the handwriting of a witness who denies his signature under oath.

### Art. 38.30. Interpreter.

(a) When a motion for appointment of an interpreter is filed by any party or on motion of the court, in any criminal proceeding, it is determined that a person charged or a witness does not understand and speak the English language, an interpreter must be sworn to interpret for him. Any person may be subpoenaed, attached or recognized in any criminal action or proceeding, to appear before the proper judge or court to act as interpreter therein, under the same rules and penalties as are provided for witnesses. In the event that the only available interpreter is not considered to possess adequate interpreting skills for the particular situation or the interpreter is not familiar with use of slang, the person charged or witness may be permitted by the court to nominate another person to act as intermediary between himself and the appointed interpreter during the proceedings.

(b) Except as provided by Subsection (c) of this article, interpreters appointed under the terms of this article will receive from the general fund of the county for their services a sum not to exceed $100 a day as follows: interpreters shall be paid not less than $15 nor more than $100 a day at the discretion of the judge presiding, and when travel of the interpreter is involved all the actual expenses of travel, lodging, and meals incurred by the interpreter pertaining to the case he is appointed to serve shall be paid at the same rate applicable to state employees.

(c) A county commissioners court may set a payment schedule and expend funds for the services of interpreters in excess of the daily amount of not less than $15 or more than $100 established by Subsection (b) of this article.

*(Chgd. by L.1991, chap. 700(1), eff. 6/16/91.)*

## Art. 38.31. Interpreters for deaf persons.† [*Interpreters for the deaf.*]

(a) If the court is notified by a party that the defendant is deaf and will be present at an arraignment, hearing, examining trial, or trial, or that a witness is deaf and will be called at a hearing, examining trial, or trial, the court shall appoint a qualified interpreter to interpret the proceedings in any language that the deaf person can understand, including but not limited to sign language. On the court's motion or the motion of a party, the court may order testimony of a deaf witness and the interpretation of that testimony by the interpreter visually, electronically recorded for use in verification of the transcription of the reporter's notes. The clerk of the court shall include that recording in the appellate record if requested by a party under Article 40.09 of this Code.

(b) Following the filing of an indictment, information, or complaint against a deaf defendant, the court on the motion of the defendant shall appoint a qualified interpreter to interpret in a language that the defendant can understand, including but not limited to sign language, communications concerning the case between the defendant and defense counsel. The interpreter may not disclose a communication between the defendant and defense counsel or a fact that came to the attention of the interpreter while interpreting those communications if defense counsel may not disclose that communication or fact.

(c) In all cases where the mental condition of a person is being considered and where such person may be committed to a mental institution, and where such person is deaf, all of the court proceedings pertaining to him shall be interpreted by a qualified interpreter appointed by the court.

(d) A proceeding for which an interpreter is required to be appointed under this Article may not commence until the appointed interpreter is in a position not exceeding ten feet from and in full view of the deaf person.

(e) The interpreter appointed under the terms of this Article shall be required to take an oath that he will make a true interpretation to the person accused or being examined, which person is deaf, of all the proceedings of his case in a language that he understands; and that he will repeat said deaf person's answer to questions to counsel, court, or jury, in the English language, in his best skill and judgment.

(f) Interpreters appointed under this Article are entitled to a reasonable fee determined by the court after considering the recommendations of the Texas Commission for the Deaf and Hard of Hearing. When travel of the interpreter is involved all the actual expenses of travel, lodging, and meals incurred by the interpreter pertaining to the case he is appointed to serve shall be paid at the same rate applicable to state employees.

(g) In this Code:

(1) "Deaf person" means a person who has a hearing impairment, regardless of whether the person also has a speech impairment, that inhibits the person's comprehension of the proceedings or communication with others.

(2) "Qualified interpreter" means an interpreter for the deaf who holds a current Reverse Skills Certificate, Comprehensive Skills Certificate, Master's Comprehensive Skills Certificate, or Legal Skills Certificate issued by the National Registry of Interpreters for the Deaf or a current Level III, IV, or V Certificate issued by the Board for Evaluation of Interpreters.

*(Chgd. by L.1995, chap. 835(14), eff. 9/1/95.)*

## Art. 38.32. Presumption of death.

(a) Upon introduction and admission into evidence of a valid certificate of death wherein the time of death of the decedent has been entered by a licensed physician, a presumption exists that death occurred at the time stated in the certificate of death.

(b) A presumption existing pursuant to Section (a) of this Article is sufficient to support a finding as to time of death but may be rebutted through a showing by a preponderance of the evidence that death occurred at some other time.

**Art. 38.33. Preservation and use of evidence of certain misdemeanor convictions.† [*Fingerprinting, etc., in certain misdemeanor convictions.*]**

**Sec. 1.** The court shall order that a defendant who is convicted of a felony or a misdemeanor offense that is punishable by confinement in jail have a thumbprint of the defendant's right thumb rolled legibly on the judgment or the docket sheet in the case. The court shall order a defendant who is placed on probation under Section 5 of Article 42.12, Code of Criminal Procedure, for an offense described by this section to have a thumbprint of the defendant's right thumb rolled legibly on the order placing the defendant on probation. If the defendant does not have a right thumb, the defendant must have a thumbprint of the defendant's left thumb rolled legibly on the judgment, order, or docket sheet. The defendant must have a fingerprint of the defendant's index finger rolled legibly on the judgment, order, or docket sheet if the defendant does not have a right thumb or a left thumb. The judgment, order, or docket sheet must contain a statement that describes from which thumb or finger the print was taken, unless a rolled 10-finger print set was taken. A clerk or bailiff of the court or other person qualified to take fingerprints shall take the thumbprint or fingerprint, either by use of the ink-rolled print method or by use of a live-scanning device that prints the thumbprint or fingerprint image on the judgment, order, or docket sheet.

**Sec. 2.** This article does not prohibit a court from including in the records of the case additional information to identify the defendant.
*(Chgd. by L.1989, chap. 603(1); L.1991, 2nd C.S., chap. 10(7.01), eff. 12/1/91.)*



Zt

**Art. 38.34. Photographic evidence in theft cases.† [*Photos as evidence in theft cases.*]**

(a) As used herein, the term "property" means tangible personal property offered for sale or lease by a person engaged in the business of selling goods or services to buyers.

(b) A photograph of property which a person is alleged to have unlawfully appropriated with the intent to deprive the owner of such property is admissible into evidence under rules of law governing the admissibility of photographs and such photograph is as admissible in evidence as the property itself.

(c) The provisions of Article 18.16 of this code concerning the bringing of stolen property before a magistrate for examination are complied with if a photograph of the stolen property is brought before the magistrate.

(d) The defendant's rights of discovery and inspection of tangible physical evidence are satisfied if a photograph of the tangible property is made available to the defendant by the state upon order of any court having jurisdiction over the cause.

**Art. 38.35. Forensic analysis of evidence.**

(a) In this article:

(1) "Forensic analysis" means a medical, chemical, toxicologic, ballistic, or other expert examination and test performed on physical evidence for the purpose of determining its connection to a criminal action.

(2) "Physical evidence" means any tangible object, thing, or substance relating to a criminal offense.

(b) A law enforcement agency may procure a forensic analysis of physical evidence obtained in connection with the agency's investigation of a criminal offense.

(c) A law enforcement agency, other governmental agency, or private entity performing a forensic analysis of physical evidence may require the requesting law enforcement agency to pay a fee for such analysis.
*(Added by L.1991, chap. 298(1), eff. 9/1/91.)*

**Art. 38.36. Evidence in prosecutions for murder.**

(a) In all prosecutions for murder, the state or the defendant shall be permitted to offer testimony as to all relevant facts and circumstances surrounding the killing and the previous relationship existing between the accused and the deceased, together with all relevant facts and circumstances going to show the condition of the mind of the accused at the time of the offense.

(b) In a prosecution for murder, if a defendant raises as a defense a justification provided by Section 9.31, 9.32, or 9.33, Penal Code, the defendant, in order to establish the defendant's reasonable belief that use of force or deadly force was immediately necessary, shall be permitted to offer:

(1) relevant evidence that the defendant had been the victim of acts of family violence committed by the deceased, as family violence is defined by Section 71.01, Family Code; and

(2) relevant expert testimony regarding the condition of the mind of the defendant at the time of the offense, including those relevant facts and circumstances relating to family violence that are the basis of the expert's opinion.
*(Added by L.1993, chap. 900(7.03), eff. 9/1/94.)*

### Art. 38.37. Evidence of extraneous offenses or acts.

**Sec. 1.** This article applies to a proceeding in the prosecution of a defendant for an offense under the following provisions of the Penal Code, if committed against a child under 17 years of age:
(1) Chapter 21 (Sexual Offenses);
(2) Chapter 22 (Assaultive Offenses);
(3) Section 25.02 (Prohibited Sexual Conduct);
(4) Section 43.25 (Sexual Performance by a Child); or
(5) an attempt or conspiracy to commit an offense listed in this section.



**Sec. 2.** Notwithstanding Rules 404 and 405, Texas Rules of Criminal Evidence, evidence of other crimes, wrongs, or acts committed by the defendant against the child who is the victim of the alleged offense shall be admitted for its bearing on relevant matters, including:
(1) the state of mind of the defendant and the child; and
(2) the previous and subsequent relationship between the defendant and the child.

**Sec. 3.** On timely request by the defendant, the state shall give the defendant notice of the state's intent to introduce in the case in chief evidence described by Section 2 in the same manner as the state is required to give notice under Rule 404(b), Texas Rules of Criminal Evidence.

**Sec. 4.** This article does not limit the admissibility of evidence of extraneous crimes, wrongs, or acts under any other applicable law.
*(Added by L.1995, chap. 318(48(a)), eff. 9/1/95.)*

### Art. 38.38. Evidence relating to retaining attorney.

Evidence that a person has contacted or retained an attorney is not admissible on the issue of whether the person committed a criminal offense. In a criminal case, neither the judge nor the attorney representing the state may comment on the fact that the defendant has contacted or retained an attorney in the case. *(Added by L.1995, chap. 318(49), eff. 9/1/95.)*

## CHAPTER 39. DEPOSITIONS AND DISCOVERY

Article


### Art. 39.01. In examining trial.

When an examination takes place in a criminal action before a magistrate, the defendant may have the deposition of any witness taken by any officer or officers named in this Chapter. The defendant shall not use the deposition for any purpose unless he first consent that the entire evidence or statement of the witness may be used against him by the State on the trial of the case, subject to all legal objections. The deposition of a witness duly taken before an examining trial or a jury of inquest and reduced to writing and certified according to law where the defendant was present when such testimony was taken, and had the privilege afforded of cross-examining the witness, or taken at any prior trial of the defendant for the same offense, may be used by either the State or the defendant in the trial of such defendant's criminal case under the following circumstances:

When oath made by the party using the same that the witness resides outside the State; or that since his testimony was taken, the witness has died, or that he has removed beyond the limits of the State, or that he has been prevented from attending the court through the act or agency of the other party, or by the act or agency of any person whose object was to deprive the defendant of the benefit of the testimony; or that by reason of age or bodily infirmity, such witness cannot attend. When the testimony is sought to be used by the State, the oath may be made by any credible person. When sought to be used by the defendant, the oath shall be made by him in person.

### Art. 39.02. Depositions for defendant.

Depositions of witnesses may be taken by the defendant. When the defendant desires to take the deposition of a witness, he shall, by himself or counsel, file with the clerk of the court in which the case is pending an affidavit stating the facts necessary to constitute a good reason for taking the same, and an application to take the same. Provided that upon the filing of such application, and after notice to the attorney for the state, the courts shall hear the application and determine if good reason exists for taking the deposition. Such determination shall be based on the facts made known at the hearing and the court, in its judgment, shall grant or deny the application on such facts.

### Art. 39.03. Officers who may take the deposition.

Upon the filing of such an affidavit and application, the court shall appoint, order or designate one of the following persons before whom such deposition shall be taken:

1. A district judge.
2. A county judge.
3. A notary public.
4. A district clerk.
5. A county clerk.

Such order shall specifically name such person and the time when and place where such deposition shall be taken. Failure of a witness to respond thereto, shall be punishable by contempt by the court. Such deposition shall be oral or written, as the court shall direct.

### Art. 39.04. Applicability of civil rules.

The rules prescribed in civil cases for issuance of commissions, subpoenaing witnesses, taking the depositions of witnesses and all other formalities governing depositions shall, as to the manner and form of taking and returning the same and other formalities to the taking of the same, govern the criminal actions, when not in conflict with this Code.

### Art. 39.05. Objections.

The rules of procedure as to objections in depositions in civil actions shall govern in criminal actions when not in conflict with this Code.

### Art. 39.06. Written interrogatories.

When any such deposition is to be taken by written interrogatories, such written interrogatories shall be filed with the clerk of the court, and a copy of the same served on all other parties or their counsel for the length of time and in the manner required for service of interrogatories in civil action, and the same procedure shall also be followed with reference to cross-interrogatories as that prescribed in civil actions.

### Art. 39.07. Certificate.

Where depositions are taken under commission in criminal actions, the officer or officers taking the same shall certify that the person deposing is the identical person named in the commission; or, if they cannot certify to the identity of the witness, there shall be an affidavit of some person attached to the deposition proving the identity of such witness, and the officer or officers shall certify that the person making the affidavit is known to them.

### Art. 39.08. Authenticating the deposition.

The official seal and signature of the officer taking the deposition shall be attached to the certificate authenticating the deposition.

### Art. 39.09. Non-resident witnesses.

Depositions of a witness residing out of the State may be taken before a judge or before a commissioner of deeds and depositions for this State, who resides within the State where the deposition is to be taken, or before a notary public of the place where such deposition is to be taken, or before any commissioned officer of the armed services or before any diplomatic or consular officer. The deposition of a non-resident witness who may be temporarily within the State, may be taken under the same rules which apply to the taking of depositions of other witnesses in the State.

### Art. 39.10. Return.

In all cases the return of depositions may be made as provided in civil actions.

### Art. 39.11. Waiver.

The State and defense may agree upon a waiver of any formalities in the taking of a deposition other than that the taking of such deposition must be under oath.

### Art. 39.12. Predicate to read.

Depositions taken in criminal actions shall not be read unless oath be made that the witness resides out of the State; or that since his deposition was taken, the witness has died; or that he has removed beyond the limits of the State; or that he has been prevented from attending the court through the act or agency of the defendant; or by the act or agency of any person whose object was to deprive the defendant of the benefit of the testimony; or that by reason of age or bodily infirmity, such witness cannot attend. When the deposition is sought to be used by the State, the oath may be made by any credible person. When sought to be used by the defendant, the oath shall be made by him in person.



### Art. 39.13. Impeachment.

Nothing contained in the preceding Articles shall be construed as prohibiting the use of any such evidence for impeachment purposes under the rules of evidence heretofore existing at common law.

### Art. 39.14. Discovery.

(a) Upon motion of the defendant showing good cause therefor and upon notice to the other parties, the court in which an action is pending may order the State before or during trial of a criminal action therein pending or on trial to produce and permit the inspection and copying or photographing by or on behalf of the defendant of any designated documents, papers, written statement of the defendant, (except written statements of witnesses and except the work product of counsel in the case and their investigators and their notes or report), books, accounts, letters, photographs, objects or tangible things not privileged, which constitute or contain evidence material to any matter involved in the action and which are in the possession, custody or control of the State or any of its agencies. The order shall specify the time, place and manner of making the inspection and taking the copies and photographs of any of the aforementioned documents or tangible evidence; provided, however, that the rights herein granted shall not extend to written communications between the State or any of its agents or representatives or employees. Nothing in this Act shall authorize the removal of such evidence from the possession of the State, and any inspection shall be in the presence of a representative of the State.

(b) On motion of a party and on notice to the other parties, the court in which an action is pending may order one or more of the other parties to disclose to the party making the motion the name and address of each person the other party may use at trial to present evidence under Rules 702, 703, and 705, Texas Rules of Evidence. The court shall specify in the order the time and manner in which the other party must make the disclosure to the moving party, but in specifying the time in which the other party shall make disclosure the court shall require the other party to make the disclosure not later than the 20th day before the date the trial begins.
*(Chgd. by L.1999, chap. 578(1), eff. 9/1/99.)*

## PROCEEDINGS AFTER VERDICT

## CHAPTER 40. NEW TRIALS

Article


### Art. 40.001. New trial on material evidence.

A new trial shall be granted an accused where material evidence favorable to the accused has been discovered since trial. *(Added by L.1993, chap. 900(11.01), eff. 9/1/93.)*

# CHAPTER 42. JUDGMENT AND SENTENCE



## Art. 42.01. Judgment.

**Sec. 1.** A judgment is the written declaration of the court signed by the trial judge and entered of record showing the conviction or acquittal of the defendant. The sentence served shall be based on the information contained in the judgment. The judgment should reflect:

1. The title and number of the case;
2. That the case was called and the parties appeared, naming the attorney for the state, the defendant, and the attorney for the defendant, or, where a defendant is not represented by counsel, that the defendant knowingly, intelligently, and voluntarily waived the right to representation by counsel;
3. The plea or pleas of the defendant to the offense charged;
4. Whether the case was tried before a jury or a jury was waived;

5. The submission of the evidence, if any;
6. In cases tried before a jury that the jury was charged by the court;
7. The verdict or verdicts of the jury or the finding or findings of the court;
8. In the event of a conviction that the defendant is adjudged guilty of the offense as found by the verdict of the jury or the finding of the court, and that the defendant be punished in accordance with the jury's verdict or the court's finding as to the proper punishment;
9. In the event of conviction where death or any punishment is assessed that the defendant be sentenced to death, a term of confinement or community supervision, or to pay a fine, as the case may be;
10. In the event of conviction where the imposition of sentence is suspended and the defendant is placed on community supervision, setting forth the punishment assessed, the length of community supervision, and the conditions of community supervision;
11. In the event of acquittal that the defendant be discharged;
12. The county and court in which the case was tried and, if there was a change of venue in the case, the name of the county in which the prosecution was originated;
13. The offense or offenses for which the defendant was convicted;
14. The date of the offense or offenses and degree of offense for which the defendant was convicted;
15. The term of sentence;
16. The date judgment is entered;
17. The date sentence is imposed;
18. The date sentence is to commence and any credit for time served;
19. The terms of any order entered pursuant to Article 42.08 of this code that the defendant's sentence is to run cumulatively or concurrently with another sentence or sentences;
20. The terms of any plea bargain;
21. Affirmative findings entered pursuant to Subdivision (2) of Subsection (a) of Section 3g of Article 42.12 of this code;
22. The terms of any fee payment ordered under Articles 37.072 and 42.151 of this code;
23. The defendant's thumbprint taken in accordance with Article 38.33 of this code;
24. In the event that the judge orders the defendant to repay a reward or part of a reward under Articles 37.073 and 42.152 of this code, a statement of the amount of the payment or payments required to be made;
25. In the event that the court orders restitution to be paid to the victim, a statement of the amount of restitution ordered and:

(A) the name of the victim and the permanent mailing address of the victim at the time of the judgment; or

(B) if the court determines that the inclusion of the victim's name and address in the judgment is not in the best interest of the victim, the name and address of a person or agency that will accept and forward restitution payments to the victim;

26. In the event that a presentence investigation is required by Section 9(a), (b), (h), or (i), Article 42.12 of this code, a statement that the presentence investigation was done according to the applicable provision; and
27. In the event of conviction of an offense for which registration as a sex offender is required under Chapter 62, a statement that the registration requirement of that chapter applies to the defendant and a statement of the age of the victim of the offense.

*(Chgd. by L.1997, chap. 668(2), eff. 9/1/97.)*

**Sec. 2.** The judge may order the prosecuting attorney, or the attorney or attorneys representing any defendant, or the court clerk under the supervision of an attorney, to prepare the judgment, or the court may prepare the same. *(Chgd. by L.1999, chap. 580(6), eff. 9/1/99.)*

**Sec. 3.** The provisions of this article shall apply to both felony and misdemeanor cases.

**Sec. 4.** The Office of Court Administration of the Texas Judicial System shall promulgate a standardized felony judgment form that conforms to the requirements of Section 1 of this article.

**Sec. 5.** In addition to the information described by Section 1 of this article, the judgment should reflect affirmative findings entered pursuant to Article 42.013 of this code.

**Sec. 6.** In addition to the information described by Section 1 of this article, the judgment should reflect affirmative findings entered pursuant to Article 42.014 of this code.

**Sec. 7.** In addition to the information described by Section 1, the judgment should reflect affirmative findings entered pursuant to Article 42.015. *(Added by L.1999, chaps. 1193(1), 1415(2), eff. 9/1/99.)*
*(Chgd. by L.1989, chaps. 360(2), 603(2), 611(2), 806(1); L.1991, 16(4.04), 2nd C.S., chaps. 10(7.02); L.1993, chaps. 900(5.03), (9.02); 987(4); L.1995, chap. 258(9), eff. 9/1/95.)*

## Art. 42.011. Judgment affecting an officer or jailer.

If a person licensed under Chapter 415, Government Code, is charged with the commission of a felony and a court that knows the person is licensed under that chapter convicts the person or places the person on community supervision, the clerk of the court shall send the Commission on Law Enforcement Officer Standards and Education, by mail or electronically, the license number of the person and a certified copy of the court's judgment reflecting that the person has been convicted or placed on community supervision. *(Added by L.1995, chap. 538(10), eff. 9/1/95.)*

## Art. 42.013. Finding of family violence.

In the trial of an offense under Title 5, Penal Code, if the court determines that the offense involved family violence, as defined by Section 71.01, Family Code, the court shall make an affirmative finding of that fact and enter the affirmative finding in the judgment of the case. *(Added by L.1993, chap. 900(9.01), eff. 9/1/93.)*

## Art. 42.014. Finding that offense was committed because of bias or prejudice.

In the punishment phase of the trial of an offense under the Penal Code, if the court determines that the defendant intentionally selected the victim primarily because of the defendant's bias or prejudice against a group, the court shall make an affirmative finding of that fact and enter the affirmative finding in the judgment of that case. *(Added by L.1993, chap. 987(5); chgd. by L.1995, chap. 318(50), eff. 9/1/95.)*

## Art. 42.015. Finding that controlled substance used to commit offense.

In the punishment phase of the trial of an offense under Chapter 29, Chapter 31, or Title 5, Penal Code, if the court determines beyond a reasonable doubt that the defendant administered or provided a controlled substance to the victim of the offense with the intent of facilitating the commission of the offense, the court shall make an affirmative finding of that fact and enter the affirmative finding in the judgment of that case. *(Added by L.1999, chap. 417(2(b)), eff. 9/1/99. See other Art. 42.015 below.)*

## Art. 42.015. Finding of age of victim.

In the trial of an offense under Section 20.02, 20.03, or 20.04, Penal Code, or an attempt, conspiracy, or solicitation to commit one of those offenses, the judge shall make an affirmative finding of fact and enter the affirmative finding in the judgment in the case if the judge determines that the victim or intended victim was younger than 17 years of age at the time of the offense. *(Added by L.1999, chaps. 1193(2), 1415(3), eff. 9/1/99. See other Art. 42.015 above.)*

## Art. 42.016. Special driver's license or identification requirements for certain sex offenders.

If a person is convicted of, receives a grant of deferred adjudication for, or is adjudicated as having engaged in delinquent conduct based on a violation of an offense for which a conviction or adjudication requires registration as a sex offender under Chapter 62, as added by Chapter 668, Acts of the 75th Legislature, Regular Session, 1997, the court shall:

(1) issue an order requiring the Texas Department of Public Safety to include in any driver's license record or personal identification certificate record maintained by the department for the person an indication that the person is subject to the registration requirements of Chapter 62, as added by Chapter 668, Acts of the 75th Legislature, Regular Session, 1997;

(2) require the person to apply to the Texas Department of Public Safety in person for an original or renewal driver's license or personal identification certificate not later than the 30th day after the date the person is released or the date the department sends written notice to the person of the requirements of Article 62.065, as applicable, and to annually renew the license or certificate;

(3) notify the person of the consequence of the conviction or order of deferred adjudication as it relates to the order issued under this article; and

(4) send to the Texas Department of Public Safety a copy of the record of conviction, a copy of the order granting deferred adjudication, or a copy of the juvenile adjudication, as applicable, and a copy of the order issued under this article.

*(Added by L.1999, chap. 1401(1), eff. 9/1/2000.)*

**Art. 42.02. Sentence.**

The sentence is that part of the judgment, or order revoking a suspension of the imposition of a sentence, that orders that the punishment be carried into execution in the manner prescribed by law. *(Chgd. by L.1993, chap. 900(5.03), eff. 9/1/93.)*

**Art. 42.023. Judge may consider alternative sentencing.**

Before pronouncing sentence on a defendant convicted of a criminal offense, the judge may consider whether the defendant should be committed for care and treatment under Section 462.081, Health and Safety Code. *(Added by L.1993, chap. 900(5.03), eff. 9/1/93.)*

**Art. 42.03. Pronouncing sentence; time; credit for time spent in jail between arrest and sentence or pending appeal.**

**Sec. 1.** (a) Except as provided in Article 42.14, sentence shall be pronounced in the defendant's presence.

(b) The court shall permit a victim, close relative of a deceased victim, or guardian of a victim, as defined by Article 56.01 of this code, to appear in person to present to the court and to the defendant a statement of the person's views about the offense, the defendant, and the effect of the offense on the victim. The victim, relative, or guardian may not direct questions to the defendant while making the statement. The court reporter may not transcribe the statement. The statement must be made:

(1) after punishment has been assessed and the court has determined whether or not to grant community supervision in the case;

(2) after the court has announced the terms and conditions of the sentence; and

(3) after sentence is pronounced.

**Sec. 2.** (a) In all criminal cases the judge of the court in which the defendant was convicted shall give the defendant credit on his sentence for the time that the defendant has spent in jail in said cause, other than confinement served as a condition of community supervision, from the time of his arrest and confinement until his sentence by the trial court.

(b) In all revocations of a suspension of the imposition of a sentence the judge shall enter the restitution or reparation due and owing on the date of the revocation.

**Sec. 3.** If a defendant appeals his conviction, is not released on bail, and is retained in a jail as provided in Section 7, Article 42.09, pending his appeal, the judge of the court in which the defendant was convicted shall give the defendant credit on his sentence for the time that the defendant has spent in jail pending disposition of his appeal. The court shall endorse on both the commitment and the mandate from the appellate court all credit given the defendant under this section, and the institutional division of the Texas Department of Criminal Justice shall grant the credit in computing the defendant's eligibility for parole and discharge.

**Sec. 4.** When a defendant who has been sentenced to imprisonment in the institutional division of the Texas Department of Criminal Justice has spent time in jail pending trial and sentence or pending appeal, the judge of the sentencing court shall direct the sheriff to attach to the commitment papers a statement assessing the defendant's conduct while in jail.

**Sec. 5. to Sec. 7A.** *(Repealed.)*

**Sec. 8.** (a) - (f) *(Repealed.)*

(g) An employee of the Texas Department of Criminal Justice, sheriff, employee of a sheriff's department, county commissioner, county employee, county judge, employee of a community corrections and supervision department, restitution center, or officer or employee of a political subdivision other than a county is not liable for damages arising from an act or failure to act in connection with community service performed by an inmate pursuant to court order under this article or in connection with an inmate or offender programmatic or nonprogrammatic activity, including work, educational, and treatment activities, if the act or failure to act was not intentional, wilfully or wantonly negligent, or performed with conscious indifference or reckless disregard for the safety of others.

*(Chgd. by L.1989, chap. 785(4.06), (4.24); L.1991, chap. 278(1); 2nd C.S., chap. 10(14.01); L.1993, chaps. 201(1), 900(5.03); L.1995, chap. 556(1), eff. 9/1/95.)*

## Art. 42.031. Work release program.

**Sec. 1.** (a) The sheriff of each county may attempt to secure employment for each defendant sentenced to the county jail work release program under Article 42.034 of this code and each defendant confined in the county jail awaiting transfer to the institutional division of the Texas Department of Criminal Justice.

(b) The employer of a defendant participating in a program under this article shall pay the defendant's salary to the sheriff. The sheriff shall deposit the salary into a special fund to be given to the defendant on his release after deducting:

(1) the cost to the county for the defendant's confinement during the pay period based on the average daily cost of confining defendants in the county jail, as determined by the commissioners court of the county;

(2) support of the defendant's dependents; and

(3) restitution to the victims of an offense committed by the defendant.

(c) At the time of sentencing or at a later date, the court sentencing a defendant may direct the sheriff not to deduct the cost described under Subdivision (1) of Subsection (b) of this section or to deduct only a specified portion of the cost if the court determines that the full deduction would cause a significant financial hardship to the defendant's dependents.

(d) If the sheriff does not find employment for a defendant who would otherwise be sentenced to imprisonment in the institutional division, the sheriff shall:

(1) transfer the defendant to the sheriff of a county who agrees to accept the defendant as a participant in the county jail work release program; or

(2) retain the defendant in the county jail for employment as soon as possible in a jail work release program.

(e) *(Repealed.)*

**Sec. 2.** A defendant participating in a program under this article shall be confined in the county jail or in another facility designated by the sheriff at all times except for:

(1) time spent at work and traveling to or from work; and

(2) time spent attending or traveling to or from an education or rehabilitation program approved by the sheriff.

**Sec. 3.** (a) The sheriff of each county shall classify each felon serving a sentence in the county jail work release program for the purpose of awarding good conduct time credit in the same manner as inmates of the institutional division of the Texas Department of Criminal Justice are classified under Chapter 498, Government Code, and shall award good conduct time in the same manner as the director of the department does in that chapter.

(b) If the sheriff determines that the defendant is conducting himself in a manner that is dangerous to inmates in the county jail or to society as a whole, the sheriff may remove the defendant from participation in the program pending a hearing before the sentencing court. At the hearing, if the court determines that the sheriff's assessment of the defendant's conduct is correct, the court may terminate the defendant's participation in the program and order the defendant to the term of imprisonment that the defendant would have received has he not entered the program. If the court determines that the sheriff's assessment is incorrect, the court shall order the sheriff to readmit the defendant to the program. A defendant shall receive as credit toward his sentence any time served as a participant in the program.

*(Added by L.1989, chap. 2(5.03(a)); chgd. by L.1989, chap. 785; L.1991, 2nd C.S., chap. 10(14.10), (14.11); chgd. by L.1993, chap. 900(5.03), eff. 9/1/93.)*

## Art. 42.032. Good conduct.

**Sec. 1.** To encourage county jail discipline, a distinction may be made to give orderly, industrious, and obedient defendants the comforts and privileges they deserve. The reward for good conduct may consist of a relaxation of strict county jail rules and extension of social privileges consistent with proper discipline.

**Sec. 2.** The sheriff in charge of each county jail may grant commutation of time for good conduct, industry, and obedience. A deduction not to exceed one day for each day of the original sentence actually served may be made for the term or terms of sentences if a charge of misconduct has not been sustained against the defendant.

**Sec. 3.** This article applies whether or not the judgment of conviction is a fine or jail sentence or both, but the deduction in time may not exceed one-third of the original sentence as to fines and court costs assessed in the judgment of conviction.

**Sec. 4.** A defendant serving two or more cumulative sentences shall be allowed commutation as if the sentences were one sentence.

**Sec. 5.** Any part or all of the commutation accrued under this article may be forfeited and taken away by the sheriff:

(1) for a sustained charge of misconduct in violation of any rule known to the defendant, including escape or attempt to escape, if the sheriff has complied with discipline proceedings as approved by the Commission on Jail Standards; or

(2) on receipt by the sheriff of a certified copy of a final order of a state or federal court that dismisses as frivolous or malicious a lawsuit brought by a defendant while the defendant was in the custody of the sheriff.

*(Chgd. by L.1999, chap. 655(2(a)), eff. 6/18/99.)*

**Sec. 6.** Except for credit earned by a defendant under Article 43.10, no other time allowance or credits in addition to the commutation of time under this article may be deducted from the term or terms of sentences.

**Sec. 7.** The sheriff shall keep a conduct record in card or ledger form and a calendar card on each defendant showing all forfeitures of commutation time and the reasons for the forfeitures.

*(Added by L.1989, chap. 2(5.04(a)); chgd. by L.1991, 2nd C.S., chap. 10(14.05); L.1993, chap. 900(5.03), eff. 9/1/93.)*

### Art. 42.033. Sentence to serve time during off-work hours.

(a) Where jail time has been awarded to a person sentenced for a misdemeanor or sentenced to confinement in the county jail for a felony or when a defendant is serving a period of confinement as a condition of community supervision, the trial judge, at the time of the pronouncement of sentence or at any time while the defendant is serving the sentence or period of confinement, when in the judge's discretion the ends of justice would best be served, may permit the defendant to serve the defendant's sentence or period of confinement intermittently during his off-work hours or on weekends. The judge may require bail of the defendant to ensure the faithful performance of the sentence or period of confinement. The judge may attach conditions regarding the employment, travel, and other conduct of the defendant during the performance of such a sentence or period of confinement.

(b) The court may impose as a condition to permitting a defendant to serve the jail time assessed or period of confinement intermittently an additional requirement that the defendant make any of the following payments to the court, agencies, or persons, or that the defendant execute a letter and direct it to the defendant's employer directing the employer to deduct from the defendant's salary an amount directed by the court, which is to be sent by the employer to the clerk of the court. The money received by the court under this section may be used to pay the following expenses as directed by the court:

(1) the support of the defendant's dependents, if necessary;

(2) the defendant's documented personal, business, and travel expenses;

(3) reimbursement of the general fund of the county for the maintenance of the defendant in jail; and

(4) installment payments on restitution, fines, and court costs ordered by the court.

(c) The condition imposed under Subsection (b) of this article is not binding on an employer, except that income withheld for child support is governed by Chapter 158, Family Code.

(d) The court may permit the defendant to serve the defendant's sentence or period of confinement intermittently in order for the defendant to continue employment if the court imposes confinement for failure to pay a fine or court costs, as punishment for criminal nonsupport under Section 25.05, Penal Code, or for contempt of a court order for periodic payments for the support of a child.

(e) The court may permit the defendant to seek employment or obtain medical, psychological, or substance abuse treatment or counseling or obtain training or needed education under the same terms and conditions that apply to employment under this article.

*(Added by L.1989, chap. 785(4.07); chgd. by L.1991, 2nd C.S., chap. 10(14.06); L.1993, chap. 900(5.03); L.1997, chap. 165(7.03), eff. 9/1/97.)*

### Art. 42.034. County jail work release program.

(a) If jail time has been awarded to a person sentenced for a misdemeanor or sentenced to confinement in the county jail for a felony, the trial judge at the time of pronouncement of sentence or at any time while the defendant is serving the sentence, when in the judge's discretion the ends of justice would best be served, may require the defendant to serve an alternate term for the same period of time in the county jail work release program of the county in which the offense occurred, if the person is classified by the sheriff as a low-risk offender under the classification system developed by the Commission on Jail Standards under Section 511.009, Government Code.

(b) The sheriff shall provide a classification report for a defendant to a judge as necessary so that the judge can determine whether to require the defendant to participate in the work release program under this article.

(c) A defendant sentenced under this article who would otherwise be sentenced to confinement in jail may earn good conduct credit in the same manner as provided by Article 42.032 of this code, but only while actually confined.

*(Added by L.1989, chap. 785(4.08); chgd. by L.1991, 2nd C.S., chap. 10(14.07); L.1993, chap. 900(5.03); L.1995, chap. 722(1), eff. 9/1/95.)*

### Art. 42.035. Electronic monitoring; house arrest.

(a) A court in a county served by a community supervision and corrections department that has an electronic monitoring program approved by the community justice assistance division of the Texas Department of Criminal Justice may require a defendant to serve all or part of a sentence of confinement in county jail by submitting to electronic monitoring rather than being confined in the county jail.

(b) A judge, at the time of the pronouncement of a sentence of confinement or at any time while the defendant is serving the sentence, on the judge's own motion or on the written motion of the defendant, may permit the defendant to serve the sentence under house arrest, including electronic monitoring and any other conditions the court chooses to impose, during the person's off-work hours. The judge may require bail of the defendant to ensure the faithful performance of the sentence.

(c) The court may require the defendant to pay to the community supervision and corrections department or the county any reasonable cost incurred because of the defendant's participation in the house arrest program, including the cost of electronic monitoring.

(d) A defendant who submits to electronic monitoring or participates in the house arrest program under this section discharges a sentence of confinement without deductions, good conduct time credits, or commutations.

*(Added by L.1989, chap. 785(4.09); chgd. by L.1993, chap. 900(5.03), eff. 9/1/93.)*

### Art. 42.036. Community service.

(a) A court may require a defendant, other than a defendant convicted of an offense under Sections 49.04-49.08, Penal Code, to serve all or part of a sentence of confinement or period of confinement required as a condition of community supervision in county jail by performing community service rather than by being confined in county jail unless the sentence of confinement was imposed by the jury in the case.

(b) In its order requiring a defendant to participate in community service work, the court must specify:

(1) the number of hours the defendant is required to work; and

(2) the entity or organization for which the defendant is required to work.

(c) The court may order the defendant to perform community service work under this article only for a governmental entity or a nonprofit organization that provides services to the general public that enhance social welfare and the general well-being of the community. A governmental entity or nonprofit organization that accepts a defendant under this section to perform community service must agree to supervise the defendant in the performance of the defendant's work and report on the defendant's work to the community supervision and corrections department or court-related services office.

(d) The court may require bail of a defendant to ensure the defendant's faithful performance of community service and may attach conditions to the bail as it determines are proper.

(e) A court may not order a defendant who is employed to perform more than 16 hours per week of community service under this article unless the court determines that requiring the defendant to work additional hours does not work a hardship on the defendant or the defendant's dependents. A court may not order a defendant who is unemployed to perform more than 32 hours per week of community service under this article, but may direct the defendant to use the remaining hours of the week to seek employment.

(f) A defendant is considered to have served one day in jail for each eight hours of community service performed under this article.

(g) *(Repealed.)*

(h) *(Repealed by L.1995, chap. 76(3.14), eff. 9/1/95.)*
*(Added by L.1989, chap. 785(4.10); chgd. by L.1990, 6th C.S., chap. 25(27); L.1991, 2nd C.S., chap. 10(14.08); L.1993, chaps. 201(2), 900(5.03); L.1995, chap. 76(3.14), eff. 9/1/95.)*

**Art. 42.037. Restitution.**

(a) In addition to any fine authorized by law, the court that sentences a defendant convicted of an offense may order the defendant to make restitution to any victim of the offense. If the court does not order restitution or orders partial restitution under this subsection, the court shall state on the record the reasons for not making the order or for the limited order.

(b)(1) If the offense results in damage to or loss or destruction of property of a victim of the offense, the court may order the defendant:

(A) to return the property to the owner of the property or someone designated by the owner; or

(B) if return of the property is impossible or impractical or is an inadequate remedy, to pay an amount equal to the greater of:

(i) the value of the property on the date of the damage, loss, or destruction; or

(ii) the value of the property on the date of sentencing, less the value of any part of the property that is returned on the date the property is returned.

(2) If the offense results in bodily injury to a victim, the court may order the defendant to do any one or more of the following:

(A) pay an amount equal to the cost of necessary medical and related professional services and devices relating to physical, psychiatric, and psychological care, including nonmedical care and treatment rendered in accordance with a method of healing recognized by the law of the place of treatment;

(B) pay an amount equal to the cost of necessary physical and occupational therapy and rehabilitation; or

(C) reimburse the victim for income lost by the victim as a result of the offense.

(3) If the offense results in the death of a victim, the court may, in addition to an order under Subdivision (2) of this subsection, order the defendant to pay an amount equal to the cost of necessary funeral and related services.

(4) If the victim or the victim's estate consents, the court may, in addition to an order under Subdivision (2) of this subsection, order the defendant to make restitution by performing services instead of by paying money or make restitution to a person or organization designated by the victim or the estate.

(c) The court, in determining whether to order restitution and the amount of restitution, shall consider:

(1) the amount of the loss sustained by any victim as a result of the offense;

(2) the financial resources of the defendant;

(3) the financial needs and earning ability of the defendant and the defendant's dependents; and

(4) other factors the court deems appropriate.

(d) If the court orders restitution under this article and the victim is deceased the court shall order the defendant to make restitution to the victim's estate.

(e) The court shall impose an order of restitution that is as fair as possible to the victim. The imposition of the order may not unduly complicate or prolong the sentencing process.

(f)(1) The court may not order restitution for a loss for which the victim has received or will receive compensation. The court may, in the interest of justice, order restitution to any person who has compensated the victim for the loss to the extent the person paid compensation. An order of restitution shall require that all restitution to a victim be made before any restitution to any other person is made under the order.

(2) Any amount recovered by a victim from a person ordered to pay restitution in a federal or state civil proceeding is reduced by any amount previously paid to the victim by the person under an order of restitution.

(g)(1) The court may require a defendant to make restitution under this article within a specified period or in specified installments.

(2) The end of the period or the last installment may not be later than:

(A) the end of the period of probation, if probation is ordered;

(B) five years after the end of the term of imprisonment imposed, if the court does not order probation; or

(C) five years after the date of sentencing in any other case.

(3) If the court does not provide otherwise, the defendant shall make restitution immediately.

(4) Except as provided by Subsection (n), the order of restitution must require the defendant to make restitution directly to the victim or other person eligible for restitution under this article or

to deliver the amount or property due as restitution to a community supervision and corrections department for transfer to the victim or person.

(h) If a defendant is placed on probation or is paroled or released on mandatory supervision under this chapter, the court or the Board of Pardons and Paroles shall order the payment of restitution ordered under this article as a condition of probation, parole, or mandatory supervision. The court may revoke probation and the Board of Pardons and Paroles may revoke parole or mandatory supervision if the defendant fails to comply with the order. In determining whether to revoke probation, parole, or mandatory supervision, the court or board shall consider:

(1) the defendant's employment status;

(2) the defendant's earning ability;

(3) the defendant's financial resources;

(4) the willfulness of the defendant's failure to pay; and

(5) any other special circumstances that may affect the defendant's ability to pay.

(i) In addition to any other terms and conditions of probation imposed under Article 42.12 of this code, the court may require a probationer to reimburse the crime victims compensation fund created under Subchapter B, Chapter 56 for any amounts paid from that fund to a victim of the probationer's offense. In this subsection, "victim" has the meaning assigned by Article 56.01 of this code.

(j) The court may order a community supervision and corrections department to obtain information pertaining to the factors listed in Subsection (c) of this article. The probation officer shall include the information in the report required under Section 9(a), Article 42.12, of this code or a separate report, as the court directs. The court shall permit the defendant and the prosecuting attorney to read the report.

(k) The court shall resolve any dispute relating to the proper amount or type of restitution. The standard of proof is a preponderance of the evidence. The burden of demonstrating the amount of the loss sustained by a victim as a result of the offense is on the prosecuting attorney. The burden of demonstrating the financial resources of the defendant and the financial needs of the defendant and the defendant's dependents is on the defendant. The burden of demonstrating other matters as the court deems appropriate is on the party designated by the court as justice requires.

(*l*) Conviction of a defendant for an offense involving the act giving rise to restitution under this article estops the defendant from denying the essential allegations of that offense in any subsequent federal civil proceeding or state civil proceeding brought by the victim, to the extent consistent with state law.

(m) An order of restitution may be enforced by the state or a victim named in the order to receive the restitution in the same manner as a judgment in a civil action.

(n) If a defendant is convicted of or receives deferred adjudication for an offense under Section 25.05, Penal Code, if the child support order on which prosecution of the offense was based required the defendant to pay the support to a local registry or the Title IV-D agency, and if the court orders restitution under this article, the order of restitution must require the defendant to pay the child support in the following manner:

(1) during any period in which the defendant is under the supervision of a community supervision and corrections department, to the department for transfer to the local registry or Title IV-D agency designated as the place of payment in the child support order; and

(2) during any period in which the defendant is not under the supervision of a department, directly to the registry or agency described by Subdivision (1).

*(Added by L.1993, chap. 806(1); chgd. by L.1995, chaps. 76(5.95(111)), 318(51); L.1999, chap. 40(2), (3), eff. 9/1/99.)*

### Art. 42.0371. Mandatory restitution for kidnapped or abducted children.

(a) The court shall order a defendant convicted of an offense under Chapter 20, Penal Code, or Section 25.03, 25.031, or 25.04, Penal Code, to pay restitution in an amount equal to the cost of necessary rehabilitation, including medical, psychiatric, and psychological care and treatment, for the victim of the offense if the victim is younger than 17 years of age.

(b) The court shall, after considering the financial circumstances of the defendant, specify in a restitution order issued under Subsection (a) the manner in which the defendant must pay the restitution.

(c) A restitution order issued under Subsection (a) may be enforced by the state or a victim named in the order to receive the restitution in the same manner as a judgment in a civil action.

(d) The court may hold a hearing, make findings of fact, and amend a restitution order issued under Subsection (a) if the defendant fails to pay the victim named in the order in the manner specified by the court.
*(Added by L.1999, chap. 657(1), eff. 9/1/99.)*

## Art. 42.038. Reimbursement for confinement expenses.

(a) In addition to any fine, cost, or fee authorized by law, a court that sentences a defendant convicted of a misdemeanor to serve a term of confinement in county jail and orders execution of the sentence may require the defendant to reimburse the county for the defendant's confinement at a rate of $25 a day.

(b) A court that requires a defendant convicted of a misdemeanor or placed on deferred adjudication for a misdemeanor to submit to a period of confinement in county jail as a condition of community supervision may also require as a condition of community supervision that the defendant reimburse the county for the defendant's confinement, with the amount of reimbursement determined as if the defendant were serving an executed sentence.

(c) A judge may not require reimbursement under this article if the judge determines the defendant is indigent based on the defendant's sworn statement or affidavit filed with the court. A court that requires reimbursement under this article may require the defendant to reimburse the county only for those days the defendant is confined after the date of conviction or on which a plea of guilty or nolo contendere was entered. The court may not require a defendant to reimburse the county for those days the defendant was confined after arrest and before the date of conviction or on which the plea of guilty or nolo contendere was entered.

(d) The court, in determining whether to order reimbursement under this article, shall consider:

(1) the defendant's employment status, earning ability, and financial resources; and

(2) any other special circumstances that may affect the defendant's ability to pay, including child support obligations and including any financial responsibilities owed by the defendant to dependents or restitution payments owed by the defendant to a victim.

(e) On the day on which a defendant who is required to reimburse the county under this article discharges an executed sentence of confinement or completes the period of confinement required as a condition of community supervision, the sheriff shall present to the defendant a bill computed by multiplying the daily rate of $25 times the number of days the defendant was confined in the county jail, not counting the day on which the execution of the sentence or the period of confinement began. For purposes of this subsection, a defendant who is confined in county jail for only a portion of a day is nonetheless considered to have been confined for the whole day.

(f) The court may require a defendant to reimburse the county under this article by paying to the sheriff the bill presented by the sheriff within a specified period or in specified installments. The end of the period or the last installment may not be later than:

(1) the end of the period of community supervision, if community supervision is ordered; or

(2) the fifth anniversary of the last day of the term of confinement, if the court does not order community supervision.
*(Added by L.1999, chap. 295(1), eff. 9/1/99.)*

## Art. 42.04. Sentence when appeal is taken.

When a defendant is sentenced to death, no date shall be set for the execution of sentence until after the receipt by the clerk of the trial court of the mandate of affirmance of the court of criminal appeals.

## Art. 42.045. Issuance of mandate; judgments final.† [*Delivery of mandate; judgments final.*]

(a) When a decision of a court of appeals or the Court of Criminal Appeals becomes final, the clerk of such court shall issue a mandate in the case to the trial court.

(b) A decision of a court of appeals shall be final:

(1) at the expiration of 45 days after the final ruling of the court, unless:

(A) a petition for review has been filed within 30 days after the final ruling of the court of appeals; or

(B) the Court of Criminal Appeals has filed an order for review of the decision on its own motion; or

(2) at the expiration of 15 days from the date of refusal of the Court of Criminal Appeals to grant a petition for review.

(c) A decision of the Court of Criminal Appeals shall be final at the expiration of 15 days from the ruling on the final motion for rehearing or from the rendition of the decision if no motion for rehearing is filed.

### Art. 42.05. If court is about to adjourn.† [*Expiration of court term.*]

The time limit within which any act is to be done within the meaning of this Code shall not be affected by the expiration of the term of the court.

### Art. 42.07. Reasons to prevent sentence.† [*Sentence not pronounced.*]

Before pronouncing sentence, the defendant shall be asked whether he has anything to say why the sentence should not be pronounced against him. The only reasons which can be shown, on account of which sentence cannot be pronounced, are:

1. That the defendant has received a pardon from the proper authority, on the presentation of which, legally authenticated, he shall be discharged;
2. That the defendant is incompetent to stand trial; and if evidence be shown to support a finding of incompetency to stand trial, no sentence shall be pronounced, and the court shall proceed under Article 46.02 of this code; and
3. When a person who has been convicted escapes after conviction and before sentence and an individual supposed to be the same has been arrested he may before sentence is pronounced, deny that he is the person convicted, and an issue be accordingly tried before a jury, or before the court if a jury is waived, as to his identity.

### Art. 42.08. Cumulative or concurrent sentence.

(a) When the same defendant has been convicted in two or more cases, judgment and sentence shall be pronounced in each case in the same manner as if there had been but one conviction. Except as provided by Sections (b) and (c) of this article, in the discretion of the court, the judgment in the second and subsequent convictions may either be that the sentence imposed or suspended shall begin when the judgment and the sentence imposed or suspended in the preceding conviction has ceased to operate, or that the sentence imposed or suspended shall run concurrently with the other case or cases, and sentence and execution shall be accordingly; provided, however, that the cumulative total of suspended sentences in felony cases shall not exceed 10 years, and the cumulative total of suspended sentences in misdemeanor cases shall not exceed the maximum period of confinement in jail applicable to the misdemeanor offenses, though in no event more than three years, including extensions of periods of community supervision under Section 22, Article 42.12, of this code, if none of the offenses are offenses under Chapter 49, Penal Code, or four years, including extensions, if any of the offenses are offenses under Chapter 49, Penal Code.

(b) If a defendant is sentenced for an offense committed while the defendant was an inmate in the institutional division of the Texas Department of Criminal Justice and the defendant has not completed the sentence he was serving at the time of the offense, the judge shall order the sentence for the subsequent offense to commence immediately on completion of the sentence for the original offense.

(c) If a defendant has been convicted in two or more cases and the court suspends the imposition of the sentence in one of the cases, the court may not order a sentence of confinement to commence on the completion of a suspended sentence for an offense.
*(Chgd. by L.1989, chap. 785(4.11); L.1993, chap. 900(5.03), eff. 9/1/93.)*

### Art. 42.09. Commencement of sentence; status during appeal; pen packet.

**Sec. 1.** Except as provided in Sections 2 and 3, a defendant shall be delivered to a jail or to the institutional division of the Texas Department of Criminal Justice when his sentence is pronounced, or his sentence to death is announced, by the court. The defendant's sentence begins to run on the day it is pronounced, but with all credits, if any, allowed by Article 42.03.

**Sec. 2.** If a defendant appeals his conviction and is released on bail pending disposition of his appeal, when his conviction is affirmed, the clerk of the trial court, on receipt of the mandate from the appellate court, shall issue a commitment against the defendant. The officer executing the commitment shall endorse thereon the date he takes the defendant into custody and the defendant's sentence begins to run from the date endorsed on the commitment. The institutional division of the Texas Department of Criminal Justice shall admit the defendant named in the commitment on the basis of the commitment.

**Sec. 3.** If a defendant is convicted of a felony and sentenced to death, life, or a term of more than ten years in the institutional division of the Texas Department of Criminal Justice and he gives notice of appeal, he shall be transferred to the institutional division on a commitment pending a mandate from the court of appeals or the Court of Criminal Appeals.

**Sec. 4.** If a defendant is convicted of a felony and his sentence is a term of ten years or less and he gives notice of appeal, he shall be transferred to the institutional division of the Texas Department of Criminal Justice on a commitment pending a mandate from the court of appeals or the Court of Criminal Appeals upon request in open court or upon written request to the sentencing court. Upon a valid transfer to the institutional division under this section, the defendant may not thereafter be released on bail pending his appeal.

**Sec. 5.** If a defendant is transferred to the institutional division of the Texas Department of Criminal Justice pending appeal under Section 3 or 4, his sentence shall be computed as if no appeal had been taken if the appeal is affirmed.

**Sec. 6.** All defendants who have been transferred to the institutional division of the Texas Department of Criminal Justice pending the appeal of their convictions under this article shall be under the control and authority of the institutional division for all purposes as if no appeal were pending.

**Sec. 7.** If a defendant is sentenced to a term of imprisonment in the institutional division of the Texas Department of Criminal Justice but is not transferred to the institutional division under Section 3 or 4 of this article, the court, before the date on which it would lose jurisdiction under Section 6(a), Article 42.12, of this code, shall send to the department a document containing a statement of the date on which the defendant's sentence was pronounced and credits earned by the defendant under Article 42.03 of this code as of the date of the statement.

**Sec. 8.** (a) A county that transfers a defendant to the Texas Department of Criminal Justice under this article shall deliver to an officer designated by the department:

(1) a copy of the judgment entered pursuant to Article 42.01 of this code, completed on a standardized felony judgment form described by Section 4 of that article;

(2) a copy of any order revoking community supervision and imposing sentence pursuant to Section 23, Article 42.12, of this code, including:

(A) any amounts owed for restitution, fines, and court costs, completed on a standardized felony judgment form described by Section 4, Article 42.01, of this code; and

(B) a copy of the client supervision plan prepared for the defendant by the community supervision and corrections department supervising the defendant, if such a plan was prepared;

(3) a written report that states the nature and the seriousness of each offense and that states the citation to the provision or provisions of the Penal Code or other law under which the defendant was convicted;

(4) a copy of the victim impact statement, if one has been prepared in the case under Article 56.03 of this code;

(5) a statement as to whether there was a change in venue in the case and, if so, the names of the county prosecuting the offense and the county in which the case was tried;

(6) a copy of the record of arrest for each offense;

(7) if requested, information regarding the criminal history of the defendant, including the defendant's state identification number if the number has been issued;

(8) a copy of the indictment or information for each offense;

(9) a checklist sent by the department to the county and completed by the county in a manner indicating that the documents required by this subsection and Subsection (c) of this section accompany the defendant; and

(10) if prepared, a copy of a presentence or postsentence investigation report prepared under Section 9, Article 42.12 of this code.

(b) The Texas Department of Criminal Justice shall not take a defendant into custody under this article until the designated officer receives the documents required by Subsections (a) and (c) of this section. The designated officer shall certify under the seal of the department the documents received under Subsections (a) and (c) of this section. A document certified under this subsection is self-authenticated for the purposes of Rules 901 and 902, Texas Rules of Criminal Evidence.

(c) A county that transfers a defendant to the Texas Department of Criminal Justice under this article shall also deliver to the designated officer any presentence or postsentence investigation report, revocation report, psychological or psychiatric evaluation of the defendant, including an evaluation prepared for the juvenile court before transferring the defendant to criminal court and contained in the criminal prosecutor's file, and available social or psychological background information relating to the defendant and may deliver to the designated officer any additional information upon which the judge or jury bases the punishment decision.

(d) The institutional division of the Texas Department of Criminal Justice shall make documents received under Subsections (a) and (c) available to the pardons and paroles division on the request of the pardons and paroles division and shall, on release of a defendant on parole or to mandatory supervision, immediately provide the pardons and paroles division with copies of documents received under Subsection (a). The pardons and paroles division shall provide to the parole officer appointed to supervise the defendant a comprehensive summary of the information contained in the documents referenced in this section not later than the 14th day after the date of the defendant's release. The summary shall include a current photograph of the defendant and a complete set of the defendant's fingerprints. Upon written request from the county sheriff, the photograph and fingerprints shall be filed with the sheriff of the county to which the parolee is assigned if that county is not the county from which the parolee was sentenced.

(e) A county is not required to deliver separate documents containing information relating to citations to provisions of the Penal Code or other law and to changes of venue, as otherwise required by Subsections (a)(3) and (a)(5) of this article, if the standardized felony judgment form described by Section 4, Article 42.01, of this code is modified to require that information.

(f) Except as provided by Subsection (g) of this section, the county sheriff is responsible for ensuring that documents and information required by this section accompany defendants sentenced by district courts in the county to the Texas Department of Criminal Justice.

(g) If the presiding judge of the administrative judicial region in which the county is located determines that the county sheriff is unable to perform the duties required by Subsection (f) of this section, the presiding judge may impose those duties on:

(1) the district clerk; or

(2) the prosecutor of each district court in the county.

(h) If a parole panel releases on parole a person who is confined in a jail in this state, a federal correctional institution, or a correctional institution in another state, the Texas Department of Criminal Justice shall request the sheriff who would otherwise be required to transfer the person to the department to forward to the department the information described by Subsections (a) and (c) of this section. The sheriff shall comply with the request of the department. The department shall determine whether the information forwarded by the sheriff under this subsection contains a thumbprint taken from the person in the manner provided by Article 38.33 of this code and, if not, the department shall obtain a thumbprint taken in the manner provided by that article and shall forward the thumbprint to the department for inclusion with the information sent by the sheriff.

(i) A county may deliver the documents required under Subsections (a) and (c) of this section to the Texas Department of Criminal Justice by electronic means. For purposes of this subsection, "electronic means" means the transmission of data between word processors, data processors, or similar automated information equipment over dedicated cables, commercial lines, or other similar methods of transmission.

*(Chgd. by L.1999, chaps. 1188(1.42), 1477(29), eff. 9/1/99.)*

**Sec. 9.** A county that transfers a defendant to the Texas Department of Criminal Justice under this article may deliver to an officer designated by the department a certified copy of a final order of a state or federal court that dismisses as frivolous or malicious a lawsuit brought by the inmate while the inmate was confined in the county jail awaiting transfer to the department following conviction of a felony or revocation of community supervision, parole, or mandatory supervision. The county may deliver the copy to the department at the time of the transfer of the inmate or at any time after the transfer of the inmate. *(Added by L.1999, chap. 655(1), eff. 6/18/99.)*

*(Chgd. by L.1989, chaps. 33(2), 785(4.12); L.1991, 2nd C.S., chap. 10(11.05); L.1993, chap. 900(5.03); L.1995, chaps. 321(3.001), 723(1), eff. 9/1/95.)*

### Art. 42.10. Satisfaction of judgment as in misdemeanor convictions.† [*Judgment satisfaction same as in misdemeanor convictions.*]

When a person is convicted of a felony, and the punishment assessed is only a fine or a term in jail, or both, the judgment may be satisfied in the same manner as a conviction for a misdemeanor is by law satisfied.

### Art. 42.11. Uniform Act for out-of-state probationer and parolee supervision.

**Sec. 1.** This Act may be cited as the Uniform Act for out-of-State probationer and parolee supervision.

**Sec. 2.** The Governor of this State is hereby authorized and directed to execute a compact on behalf of the State of Texas with any of the United States legally joining therein in the form substantially as follows:

A COMPACT

Entering into by and among the contracting state, signatories hereto, with the consent of the Congress of the United States of America, granted by an Act entitled "An Act granting the consent of Congress to any two or more States to enter into agreements or compacts for cooperative effort and mutual assistance in the prevention of crime and for other purposes"

The contracting states solemnly agree:

(1) That it shall be competent for the duly constituted judicial and administrative authorities of a State party to this compact (herein called "sending State"), to permit any person convicted of an offense within such State and placed on probation or released on parole to reside in any other State party to this compact (herein called "receiving State"), while on probation or parole, if

(a) Such person is in fact a resident of or has his family residing within the receiving State and can obtain employment there; and

(b) Though not a resident of the receiving State and not having his family residing there, the receiving State consents to such person being sent there.

Before granting such permission, opportunity shall be granted to the receiving State to investigate the home and prospective employment of such person.

A resident of the receiving State, within the meaning of this section is one who has been an actual inhabitant of such State continuously for more than one year prior his coming to the sending State and has not resided within the sending State more than six continuous months immediately preceding the commission of the offense for which he has been convicted.

(2) That each receiving State will assume the duties of visitation of and supervision over probationers or parolees of any sending State and in the exercise of those duties will be governed by the same standards that prevail for its own probationers and parolees.

(3) That duly accredited officers of a sending State may at all times enter a receiving State and there apprehend and retake any person on probation or parole. For that purpose no formalities will be required other than establishing the authority of the officer and the identity of the person to be retaken. All legal requirements to obtain extradition of fugitives from justice are hereby expressly waived on the part of States party hereto, as to such persons. The decision of the sending State to retake a person on probation or parole shall be conclusive upon and not reviewable within the receiving State; provided, however, that if at the time when a State seeks to retake a probationer or parolee there should be pending against him within the receiving State any criminal charge, or he should be suspected of having committed within such State a criminal offense, he shall not be retaken without the consent of the receiving State until discharged from prosecution or from any imprisonment for such offense.

(4) That the duly accredited officers of the sending State will be permitted to transport prisoners being retaken through any and all States party to this compact, without interference.

(5) That the Governor of each State may designate an officer who, acting jointly with like officers of other contracting States, if and when appointed, shall promulgate such rules and regulations as may be deemed necessary to more effectively carry out the terms of this compact.

(6) That this compact shall become operative immediately upon its execution by any State as between it and other State or States so executing. When executed it shall have the full force and effect of law within such State, the form of execution to be in accordance with the law of the executing State.

(7) That this compact shall continue in force and remain binding upon each executing State until renounced by it. The duties and obligations hereunder of a renouncing State shall continue as to parolees or probationers residing therein at the time of withdrawal until retaken or finally discharged by the sending State. Renunciation of this compact shall be by the same authority which executed it, by sending six months notice in writing of its intention to withdraw from the compact to the other States party hereto.

**Sec. 3.** The title of the officer designated by the Governor under Subdivision (5) of the compact is the Interstate Compact Administrator for Probation and Parole. The Interstate Compact Administrator is authorized to appoint two Deputy Interstate Compact Administrators, with one deputy primarily responsible for issues dealing with probationers and the other primarily responsible for issues dealing with parolees. The executive director of the Texas Department of Criminal Justice or the executive director's designee is authorized and directed to do all things necessary or incidental to the carrying out of the compact in every particular. *(Chgd. by L.1997, chap. 514(1), eff. 5/31/97.)*

**Sec. 3a.** *(Repealed.)*
*(Chgd. by L.1991, 1st C.S., chap. 17(7.01(27)); L.1995, chap. 321(3.002), eff. 9/1/95.)*

## Art. 42.111. Deferral of proceedings in cases appealed to county court.

If a defendant convicted of a misdemeanor punishable by fine only appeals the conviction to a county court, on the trial in county court the defendant may enter a plea of guilty or nolo contendere to the offense. If the defendant enters a plea of guilty or nolo contendere, the court may defer further proceedings without entering an adjudication of guilt in the same manner as provided for the deferral of proceedings in justice court or municipal court under Article 45.051 of this code. This article does not apply to a misdemeanor case disposed of under Subchapter B, Chapter 543, Transportation Code, or a serious traffic violation as defined by Section 522.003, Transportation Code. *(Added by L.1989, chap. 399(2); chgd. by L.1991, chap. 775(18); L.1999, chaps. 62(3.03), 1545(62), eff. 9/1/99.)*

## Art. 42.12. Community supervision.

**Sec. 1. Purpose.** It is the purpose of this article to place wholly within the state courts the responsibility for determining when the imposition of sentence in certain cases shall be suspended, the conditions of community supervision, and the supervision of defendants placed on community supervision, in consonance with the powers assigned to the judicial branch of this government by the Constitution of Texas. It is the purpose of this article to remove from existing statutes the limitations, other than questions of constitutionality, that have acted as barriers to effective systems of community supervision in the public interest.

**Sec. 2. Definitions.** In this article:

(1) "Court" means a court of record having original criminal jurisdiction.

(2) "Community supervision" means the placement of a defendant by a court under a continuum of programs and sanctions, with conditions imposed by the court for a specified period during which:

(A) criminal proceedings are deferred without an adjudication of guilt; or

(B) a sentence of imprisonment or confinement, imprisonment and fine, or confinement and fine, is probated and the imposition of sentence is suspended in whole or in part.

(3) "Supervision officer" means a person appointed or employed under Section 76.004, Government Code, to supervise defendants placed on community supervision.

(4) "Electronic monitoring" includes voice tracking systems, position tracking systems, position location systems, biometric tracking systems, and any other electronic or telecommunications system that may be used to assist in the supervision of individuals under this article.
*(Chgd. by L.1997, chap. 1430(1), eff. 9/1/97.)*

**Sec. 3. Judge ordered community supervision.**

(a) A judge, in the best interest of justice, the public, and the defendant, after conviction or a plea of guilty or nolo contendere, may suspend the imposition of the sentence and place the defendant on community supervision or impose a fine applicable to the offense and place the defendant on community supervision.

(b) Except as provided by Subsection (f), in a felony case the minimum period of community supervision is the same as the minimum term of imprisonment applicable to the offense and the maximum period of community supervision is 10 years.

(c) The maximum period of community supervision in a misdemeanor case is two years.

(d) A judge may increase the maximum period of community supervision in the manner provided by Section 22(c) or 22A of this article.

(e) A defendant is not eligible for community supervision under this section if the defendant:

(1) is sentenced to a term of imprisonment that exceeds 10 years; or

(2) is sentenced to serve a term of confinement under Section 12.35, Penal Code.

(f) The minimum period of community supervision for a felony described by Section 13B(b) is five years and the maximum period of supervision is 10 years.

(g) A judge shall not deny community supervision to a defendant based solely on the defendant's inability to speak, read, write, hear, or understand English.
*(Chgd. by L.1997, chaps. 706(1), 1430(2), eff. 9/1/97.)*

**Secs. 3a to 3f.** *(Blank.)*

**Sec. 3g. Limitation on judge ordered community supervision.** (a) The provisions of Section 3 of this article do not apply:

(1) to a defendant adjudged guilty of an offense under:

(A) Section 19.02, Penal Code (Murder);

(B) Section 19.03, Penal Code (Capital murder);

(C) Section 21.11(a)(1), Penal Code (Indecency with a child);

(D) Section 20.04, Penal Code (Aggravated kidnapping);

(E) Section 22.021, Penal Code (Aggravated sexual assault);

(F) Section 29.03, Penal Code (Aggravated robbery);

(G) Chapter 481, Health and Safety Code, for which punishment is increased under Section 481.134(c), (d), (e), or (f), Health and Safety Code, if it is shown that the defendant has been previously convicted of an offense for which punishment was increased under any of those subsections; or

(H) Section 22.011, Penal Code (Sexual assault); or

(2) to a defendant when it is shown that a deadly weapon as defined in Section 1.07, Penal Code, was used or exhibited during the commission of a felony offense or during immediate flight therefrom, and that the defendant used or exhibited the deadly weapon or was a party to the offense and knew that a deadly weapon would be used or exhibited. On an affirmative finding under this subdivision, the trial court shall enter the finding in the judgment of the court. On an affirmative finding that the deadly weapon was a firearm, the court shall enter that finding in its judgment.

(b) If there is an affirmative finding under Subsection (a)(2) in the trial of a felony of the second degree or higher that the deadly weapon used or exhibited was a firearm and the defendant is granted community supervision, the court may order the defendant confined in the institutional division of the Texas Department of Criminal Justice for not less than 60 and not more than 120 days. At any time after the defendant has served 60 days in the custody of the institutional division, the sentencing judge, on his own motion or on motion of the defendant, may order the defendant released to community supervision. The institutional division shall release the defendant to community supervision after he has served 120 days.

*(Chgd. by L.1997, chap. 165(12.03); L.1999, chap. 806(1), eff. 9/1/99.)*

**Sec. 4. Jury recommended community supervision.** (a) A jury that imposes confinement as punishment for an offense may recommend to the judge that the judge suspend the imposition of the sentence and place the defendant on community supervision. A judge shall suspend the imposition of the sentence and place the defendant on community supervision if the jury makes that recommendation in the verdict.

(b) If the jury recommends to the judge that the judge place the defendant on community supervision, the judge shall place the defendant on community supervision for any period permitted under Section 3(b) or 3(c) of this article, as appropriate.

(c) A judge may increase the maximum period of community supervision in the manner provided by Section 22(c) or Section 22A of this article.

(d) A defendant is not eligible for community supervision under this section if the defendant:

(1) is sentenced to a term of imprisonment that exceeds 10 years;

(2) is sentenced to serve a term of confinement under Section 12.35, Penal Code;

(3) does not file a sworn motion under Subsection (e) of this section or for whom the jury does not enter in the verdict a finding that the information contained in the motion is true; or

(4) is adjudged guilty of an offense for which punishment is increased under Section 481.134(c), (d), (e), or (f), Health and Safety Code, if it is shown that the defendant has been previously convicted of an offense for which punishment was increased under any one of those subsections.

(e) A defendant is eligible for community supervision under this section only if before the trial begins the defendant files a written sworn motion with the judge that the defendant has not previously been convicted of a felony in this or any other state, and the jury enters in the verdict a finding that the information in the defendant's motion is true.

*(Chgd. by L.1997, chap. 1430(3), eff. 9/1/97.)*

**Sec. 5. Deferred adjudication; community supervision.** (a) Except as provided by Subsection (d) of this section, when in the judge's opinion the best interest of society and the defendant will be served, the judge may, after receiving a plea of guilty or plea of nolo contendere, hearing the evidence, and finding that it substantiates the defendant's guilt, defer further proceedings without entering an adjudication of guilt, and place the defendant on community supervision. A judge may place on community supervision under this section a defendant charged with an offense under Section 21.11, 22.011, or 22.021, Penal Code, regardless of the age of the victim, or a defendant charged with a felony described by Section 13B(b) of this article, only if the judge makes a finding in open court that placing the defendant on community supervision is in the best interest of the victim. The failure of the judge to find that deferred adjudication is in the best interest of the victim is not grounds for the defendant to set aside the plea, deferred adjudication, or any subsequent conviction or sentence. After placing the defendant on community supervision under this section, the judge shall inform the defendant orally or in writing of the possible consequences under Subsection (b) of this section of a violation of community supervision. If the information is provided orally, the judge must record and maintain the judge's statement to the defendant. The failure of a judge to inform a defendant of possible consequences under Subsection (b) of this section is not a ground for reversal unless the defendant shows that he was harmed by the failure of the judge to provide the information. In a felony case, the period of community supervision may not exceed 10 years. For a defendant charged with a felony under Section 21.11, 22.011, or 22.021, Penal Code, regardless of the age of the victim, and for a defendant charged with a felony described by Section 13B(b) of this article, the period of community supervision may not be less than five years. In a misdemeanor case, the period of community supervision may not exceed two years. A judge may increase the maximum period of community supervision in the manner provided by Section 22(c) or 22A of this article. The judge may impose a fine applicable to the offense and require any reasonable conditions of community supervision, including mental health treatment under Section 11(d) of this article, that a judge could impose on a defendant placed on community supervision for a conviction that was probated and suspended, including confinement. The provisions of Section 15 of this article specifying whether a defendant convicted of a state jail felony is to be confined in a county jail or state jail felony facility and establishing the minimum and maximum terms of confinement as a condition of community supervision apply in the same manner to a defendant placed on community supervision after pleading guilty or nolo contendere to a state jail felony. However, upon written motion of the defendant requesting final adjudication filed within 30 days after entering such plea and the deferment of adjudication, the judge shall proceed to final adjudication as in all other cases.

(b) On violation of a condition of community supervision imposed under Subsection (a) of this section, the defendant may be arrested and detained as provided in Section 21 of this article. The defendant is entitled to a hearing limited to the determination by the court of whether it proceeds with an adjudication of guilt on the original charge. No appeal may be taken from this determination. After an adjudication of guilt, all proceedings, including assessment of punishment, pronouncement of sentence, granting of community supervision, and defendant's appeal continue as if the adjudication of guilt had not been deferred. A court assessing punishment after an adjudication of guilt of a defendant charged with a state jail felony may suspend the imposition of the sentence and place the defendant on community supervision or may order the sentence to be executed, regardless of whether the defendant has previously been convicted of a felony.

(c) On expiration of a community supervision period imposed under Subsection (a) of this section, if the judge has not proceeded to adjudication of guilt, the judge shall dismiss the proceedings against the defendant and discharge him. The judge may dismiss the proceedings and discharge a defendant, other than a defendant charged with an offense requiring the defendant to register as a sex offender under Chapter 62, as added by Chapter 668, Acts of the 75th Legislature, Regular Session, 1997, prior to the expiration of the term of community supervision if in the judge's opinion the best interest of society and the defendant will be served. The judge may not dismiss the proceedings and discharge a defendant charged with an offense requiring the defendant to register under Chapter 62, as added by Chapter 668, Acts of the 75th Legislature, Regular Session, 1997. Except as provided by Section 12.42(g), Penal Code, a dismissal and discharge under this section may not be deemed a conviction for the purposes of disqualifications or disabilities imposed by law for conviction of an offense. For any defendant who receives a dismissal and discharge under this section:

(1) upon conviction of a subsequent offense, the fact that the defendant had previously received community supervision with a deferred adjudication of guilt shall be admissible before the court or jury to be considered on the issue of penalty;

(2) if the defendant is an applicant for a license or is a licensee under Chapter 42, Human Resources Code, the Texas Department of Human Services may consider the fact that the defendant previously has received community supervision with a deferred adjudication of guilt under this section in issuing, renewing, denying, or revoking a license under that chapter; and

(3) if the defendant is a person who has applied for registration to provide mental health or medical services for the rehabilitation of sex offenders, the Interagency Council on Sex Offender Treatment may consider the fact that the defendant has received community supervision under this section in issuing, renewing, denying, or revoking a license or registration issued by that council.

(d) In all other cases the judge may grant deferred adjudication unless:

(1) the defendant is charged with an offense:

(A) under Section 49.04, 49.05, 49.06, 49.07, or 49.08, Penal Code; or

(B) for which punishment may be increased under Section 481.134(c), (d), (e), or (f), Health and Safety Code, if it is shown that the defendant has been previously convicted of an offense for which punishment was increased under any one of those subsections; or

(2) the defendant:

(A) is charged with an offense under Section 21.11, 22.011, or 22.021, Penal Code, regardless of the age of the victim, or a felony described by Section 13B(b) of this article; and

(B) has previously been placed on community supervision for any offense under Paragraph (A) of this subdivision.

(e) A record in the custody of the court clerk regarding a case in which a person is granted deferred adjudication is not confidential. *(Added by L.1999, chap. 580(7), eff. 9/1/99. See other subsection (e) below.)*

(e) If a judge places on community supervision under this section a defendant charged with an offense under Section 20.02, 20.03, or 20.04, Penal Code, or an attempt, conspiracy, or solicitation to commit one of those offenses, the judge shall make an affirmative finding of fact and file a statement of that affirmative finding with the papers in the case if the judge determines that the victim or intended victim was younger than 17 years of age at the time of the offense. *(Added by L.1999, chaps. 1193(3), 1415(4), eff. 9/1/99. See other subsection (e) above.)*

*(Chgd. by L.1997, chaps. 667(1), 1430(4); L.1999, chaps. 580(7), 1193(3), 1415(4), (5(a)), eff. 9/1/99.)*

**Sec. 6. Continuing court jurisdiction in felony cases.** (a) For the purposes of this section, the jurisdiction of a court in which a sentence requiring imprisonment in the institutional division of the Texas Department of Criminal Justice is imposed by the judge of the court shall continue for 180 days from the date the execution of the sentence actually begins. Before the expiration of 180 days from the date the execution of the sentence actually begins, the judge of the court that imposed such sentence may on his own motion, on the motion of the attorney representing the state, or on the written motion of the defendant, suspend further execution of the sentence and place the defendant on community supervision under the terms and conditions of this article, if in the opinion of the judge the defendant would not benefit from further imprisonment and:

(1) the defendant is otherwise eligible for community supervision under this article; and

(2) the defendant had never before been incarcerated in a penitentiary serving a sentence for a felony.

(b) When the defendant or the attorney representing the state files a written motion requesting suspension by the judge of further execution of the sentence and placement of the defendant on community supervision, and when requested to do so by the judge, the clerk of the court shall request a copy of the defendant's record while imprisoned from the institutional division of the Texas Department of Criminal Justice or, if the defendant is confined in county jail, from the sheriff. Upon receipt of such request, the institutional division of the Texas Department of Criminal Justice or the sheriff shall forward to the judge, as soon as possible, a full and complete copy of the defendant's record while imprisoned or confined. When the defendant files a written motion requesting suspension of further execution of the sentence and placement on community supervision, he shall immediately deliver or cause to be delivered a true and correct copy of the motion to the office of the attorney representing the state.

(c) The judge may deny the motion without a hearing but may not grant the motion without holding a hearing and providing the attorney representing the state and the defendant the opportunity to present evidence on the motion.

**Sec. 7. Continuing court jurisdiction in misdemeanor cases.** (a) For the purposes of this section, the jurisdiction of the courts in this state in which a sentence requiring confinement in a jail is imposed for conviction of a misdemeanor shall continue for 180 days from the date the execution of the sentence actually begins. The judge of the court that imposed such sentence may on his own motion, on the motion of the attorney representing the state, or on the written motion of the defendant suspend further execution of the sentence and place the defendant on community supervision under the terms and conditions of this article, if in the opinion of the judge the defendant would not benefit from further confinement.

(b) When the defendant files a written motion with the court requesting suspension of further execution of the sentence and placement on community supervision or when requested to do so by the judge, the clerk of the court shall request a copy of the defendant's record while confined from the agency operating the jail where the defendant is confined. Upon receipt of such request, the agency operating the jail where the defendant is confined shall forward to the court as soon as possible a full and complete copy of the defendant's record while confined.

(c) The judge may deny the motion without a hearing but may not grant a motion without holding a hearing and allowing the attorney representing the state and the defendant to present evidence in the case.

**Sec. 8. State boot camp program.** (a) For the purposes of this section, the jurisdiction of a court in which a sentence requiring imprisonment in the institutional division of the Texas Department of Criminal Justice is imposed for conviction of a felony shall continue for 90 days from the date on which the convicted person is received into custody by the institutional division. After the expiration of 75 days but prior to the expiration of 90 days from the date on which the convicted person is received into custody by the institutional division, the judge of the court that imposed the sentence may suspend further execution of the sentence imposed and place the person on community supervision under the terms and conditions of this article, if in the opinion of the judge the person would not benefit from further imprisonment. The court shall clearly indicate in its order recommending the placement of the person in the state boot camp program that the court is not retaining jurisdiction over the person for the purposes of Section 6 of this article. A court may recommend a person for placement in the state boot camp program only if:

(1) the person is otherwise eligible for community supervision under this article;

(2) the person is 17 years of age or older but younger than 26 years and is physically and mentally capable of participating in a program that requires strenuous physical activity; and

(3) the person is not convicted of an offense punishable as a state jail felony.

(b) On the 76th day after the day on which the convicted person is received into custody by the institutional division, the institutional division shall send the convicting court the record of the person's progress, conduct, and conformity to institutional division rules.

(c) The judge's recommendation that a person be placed in an state boot camp program created under Section 499.052, Government Code, does not give the court the power to hold the Texas Department of Criminal Justice or any officer or employee of the department in contempt of court for failure to adhere to that recommendation.

**Sec. 9. Presentence investigations.** (a) Except as provided by Subsection (g) of this section, before the imposition of sentence by a judge in a felony case, and except as provided by Subsection (b) of this section, before the imposition of sentence by a judge in a misdemeanor case the judge shall direct a supervision officer to report to the judge in writing on the circumstances of the offense with which the defendant is charged, the amount of restitution necessary to adequately compensate a victim of the offense, the criminal and social history of the defendant, and any other information relating to the defendant or the offense requested by the judge. It is not necessary that the report contain a sentencing recommendation, but the report must contain a proposed client supervision plan describing programs and sanctions that the community supervision and corrections department would provide the defendant if the judge suspended the imposition of the sentence or granted deferred adjudication.

(b) The judge is not required to direct a supervision officer to prepare a report in a misdemeanor case if:

(1) the defendant requests that a report not be made and the judge agrees to the request; or

(2) the judge finds that there is sufficient information in the record to permit the meaningful exercise of sentencing discretion and the judge explains this finding on the record.

(c) The judge may not inspect a report and the contents of the report may not be disclosed to any person unless:

(1) the defendant pleads guilty or nolo contendere or is convicted of the offense; or

(2) the defendant, in writing, authorizes the judge to inspect the report.

(d) Before sentencing a defendant, the judge shall permit the defendant or his counsel to read the presentence report.

(e) The judge shall allow the defendant or his attorney to comment on a presentence investigation or a postsentence report and, with the approval of the judge, introduce testimony or other information alleging a factual inaccuracy in the investigation or report.

(f) The judge shall allow the attorney representing the state access to any information made available to the defendant under this section.

(g) Unless requested by the defendant, a judge is not required to direct an officer to prepare a presentence report in a felony case under this section if:

(1) punishment is to be assessed by a jury;

(2) the defendant is convicted of or enters a plea of guilty or nolo contendere to capital murder;

(3) the only available punishment is imprisonment; or

(4) the judge is informed that a plea bargain agreement exists, under which the defendant agrees to a punishment of imprisonment, and the judge intends to follow the agreement.

(h) On a determination by the judge that alcohol or drug abuse may have contributed to the commission of the offense, the judge shall direct a supervision officer approved by the community supervision and corrections department or the judge or a person, program, or other agency approved by the Texas Commission on Alcohol and Drug Abuse, to conduct an evaluation to determine the appropriateness of, and a course of conduct necessary for, alcohol or drug rehabilitation for a defendant and to report that evaluation to the judge. The evaluation shall be made:

(1) after arrest and before conviction, if requested by the defendant;

(2) after conviction and before sentencing, if the judge assesses punishment in the case;

(3) after sentencing and before the entry of a final judgment, if the jury assesses punishment in the case; or

(4) after community supervision is granted, if the evaluation is required as a condition of community supervision under Section 13 of this article.

(i) A presentence investigation conducted on any defendant convicted of a felony offense who appears to the judge through its* own observation or on suggestion of a party to have a mental impairment shall include a psychological evaluation which determines, at a minimum, the defendant's IQ and adaptive behavior score. The results of the evaluation shall be included in the report to the judge as required by Subsection (a) of this section.

**So in original. Probably should be "his".*

(j) The judge by order may direct that any information and records that are not privileged and that are relevant to a report required by Subsection (a) or Subsection (k) of this section be released to an officer conducting a presentence investigation under Subsection (i) of this section or a postsentence report under Subsection (k) of this section. The judge may also issue a subpoena to obtain that information. A report and all information obtained in connection with a presentence investigation or postsentence report are confidential and may be released only:

(1) to those persons and under those circumstances authorized under Subsections (d), (e), (f), (h), (k), and (*l*) of this section;

(2) pursuant to Section 614.017, Health and Safety Code; or

(3) as directed by the judge for the effective supervision of the defendant.

(k) If a presentence report in a felony case is not required under this section, the judge may direct the officer to prepare a postsentence report containing the same information that would have been required for the presentence report, other than a proposed client supervision plan and any information that is reflected in the judgment. If the postsentence report is ordered, the officer shall send the report to the clerk of the court not later than the 30th day after the date on which sentence is pronounced or deferred adjudication is granted, and the clerk shall deliver the postsentence report with the papers in the case to a designated officer of the Texas Department of Criminal Justice, as described by Section 8(a), Article 42.09.

(*l*) If a person is a sex offender, a supervision officer may release information in a presentence or postsentence report concerning the social and criminal history of the person to a person who:

(1) is licensed or certified in this state to provide mental health or medical services, including a:

(A) physician;

(B) psychiatrist;

(C) psychologist;

(D) licensed professional counselor;

(E) licensed marriage and family therapist; or

(F) certified social worker; and

(2) provides mental health or medical services for the rehabilitation of the person.

(m) In this section, "sex offender" means a person who has been convicted or has entered a plea of guilty or nolo contendere for an offense under any one of the following provisions of the Penal Code:

(1) Section 20.04(a)(4) (Aggravated Kidnapping), if the person committed the offense with the intent to violate or abuse the victim sexually;

(2) Section 21.08 (Indecent Exposure);

(3) Section 21.11 (Indecency with a Child);

(4) Section 22.011 (Sexual Assault);

(5) Section 22.021 (Aggravated Sexual Assault);

(6) Section 25.02 (Prohibited Sexual Conduct);

(7) Section 30.02 (Burglary), if:

(A) the offense is punishable under Subsection (d) of that section; and

(B) the person committed the offense with the intent to commit a felony listed in this subsection;

(8) Section 43.25 (Sexual Performance by a Child); or

(9) Section 43.26 (Possession or Promotion of Child Pornography).

*(Chgd. by L.1999, chaps. 1188(1.43), 1263(1), eff. 9/1/99.)*

**Sec. 10. Authority to impose, modify, or revoke community supervision.** (a) Only the court in which the defendant was tried may grant community supervision, impose conditions, revoke the community supervision, or discharge the defendant, unless the judge has transferred jurisdiction of the case to another court with the latter's consent. Except as provided by Subsection (d) of this section, only the judge may alter conditions of community supervision. In a felony case, only the judge who originally sentenced the defendant may suspend execution thereof and place the defendant under community supervision pursuant to Section 6 of this article. If the judge who originally sentenced the defendant is deceased or disabled or if the office is vacant and the judge who originally sentenced the defendant is deceased or disabled or if the office is vacant and a motion is filed in accordance with Section 6 of this article, the clerk of the court shall promptly forward a copy of the motion to the presiding judge of the administrative judicial district for that court, who may deny the motion without a hearing or appoint a judge to hold a hearing on the motion.

(b) After a defendant has been placed on community supervision, jurisdiction of the case may be transferred to a court of the same rank in this state having geographical jurisdiction where the defendant is residing or where a violation of the conditions of community supervision occurs. Upon transfer, the clerk of the court of original jurisdiction shall forward a transcript of such portions of the record as the transferring judge shall direct to the court accepting jurisdiction, which latter court shall thereafter proceed as if the trial and conviction had occurred in that court.

(c) Any judge of a court having geographical jurisdiction where the defendant is residing or where a violation of the conditions of community supervision occurs may issue a warrant for his arrest, but the determination of action to be taken after arrest shall be only by the judge of the court having jurisdiction of the case at the time the action is taken.

(d) A judge that places a defendant on community supervision may authorize the supervision officer supervising the defendant or a magistrate appointed by the district courts in the county that give preference to criminal cases to modify the conditions of community supervision for the limited purpose of transferring the defendant to different programs within the community supervision continuum of programs and sanctions.

(e) If a supervision officer or magistrate modifies the conditions of community supervision, the officer or magistrate shall deliver a copy of the modified conditions to the defendant, shall file a copy of the modified conditions with the sentencing court, and shall note the date of delivery of the copy in the defendant's file. If the defendant agrees to the modification in writing, the officer or magistrate shall file a copy of the modified conditions with the district clerk and the conditions shall be enforced as modified. If the defendant does not agree to the modification in writing, the supervision officer or magistrate shall refer the case to the judge of the court for modification in the manner provided by Section 22 of this article.

**Sec. 10.** (j-3) The judges of the county courts at law in Hidalgo County shall participate in the management of the probation department serving the county, and for that purpose have the same duties and powers imposed by this section as do the district judges trying criminal cases in the county.

**Secs. 10A, 10B.** *(Repealed.)*

**Sec. 11. Basic conditions of community supervision.** (a) The judge of the court having jurisdiction of the case shall determine the conditions of community supervision and may, at any time, during the period of community supervision alter or modify the conditions. The judge may impose any reasonable condition that is designed to protect or restore the community, protect or restore the victim, or punish, rehabilitate, or reform the defendant. Conditions of community supervision may include, but shall not be limited to, the conditions that the defendant shall:

(1) Commit no offense against the laws of this State or of any other State or of the United States;

(2) Avoid injurious or vicious habits;

(3) Avoid persons or places of disreputable or harmful character;

(4) Report to the supervision officer as directed by the judge or supervision officer and obey all rules and regulations of the community supervision and corrections department;

(5) Permit the supervision officer to visit him at his home or elsewhere;
(6) Work faithfully at suitable employment as far as possible;
(7) Remain within a specified place;
(8) Pay his fine, if one be assessed, and all court costs whether a fine be assessed or not, in one or several sums;
(9) Support his dependents;
(10) Participate, for a time specified by the judge in any community-based program, including a community-service work program under Section 16 of this article;
(11) Reimburse the county in which the prosecution was instituted for compensation paid to appointed counsel for defending him in the case, if counsel was appointed, or if he was represented by a county-paid public defender, in an amount that would have been paid to an appointed attorney had the county not had a public defender;
(12) Remain under custodial supervision in a community corrections facility, obey all rules and regulations of such facility, and pay a percentage of his income to the facility for room and board;
(13) Pay a percentage of his income to his dependents for their support while under custodial supervision in a community corrections facility;
(14) Submit to testing for alcohol or controlled substances;
(15) Attend counseling sessions for substance abusers or participate in substance abuse treatment services in a program or facility approved or licensed by the Texas Commission on Alcohol and Drug Abuse;
(16) With the consent of the victim of a misdemeanor offense or of any offense under Title 7, Penal Code, participate in victim-defendant mediation;
(17) Submit to electronic monitoring;
(18) Reimburse the general revenue fund for any amounts paid from that fund to a victim, as defined by Article 56.01 of this code, of the defendant's offense or if no reimbursement is required, make one payment to the fund in an amount not to exceed $50 if the offense is a misdemeanor or not to exceed $100 if the offense is a felony;
(19) Reimburse a law enforcement agency for the analysis, storage, or disposal of raw materials, controlled substances, chemical precursors, drug paraphernalia, or other materials seized in connection with the offense;
(20) Pay all or part of the reasonable and necessary costs incurred by the victim for psychological counseling made necessary by the offense or for counseling and education relating to acquired immune deficiency syndrome or human immunodeficiency virus made necessary by the offense;
(21) Make one payment in an amount not to exceed $50 to a crime stoppers organization as defined by Section 414.001, Government Code, and as certified by the Crime Stoppers Advisory Council;
(22) Submit a blood sample or other specimen to the Department of Public Safety under Subchapter G, Chapter 411, Government Code, for the purpose of creating a DNA record of the defendant; and
(23) In any manner required by the judge, provide public notice of the offense for which the defendant was placed on community supervision in the county in which the offense was committed.

(b) A judge may not order a defendant to make any payments as a term or condition of community supervision, except for fines, court costs, restitution to the victim, and other conditions related personally to the rehabilitation of the defendant or otherwise expressly authorized by law. The court shall consider the ability of the defendant to make payments in ordering the defendant to make payments under this article.

(c) If the judge or jury places a defendant on community supervision, the judge shall require the defendant to demonstrate to the court whether the defendant has an educational skill level that is equal to or greater than the average skill level of students who have completed the sixth grade in public schools in this state. If the judge determines that the defendant has not attained that skill level, the judge shall require as a condition of community supervision that the defendant attain that level of educational skill, unless the judge determines that the defendant lacks the intellectual capacity or the learning ability to ever achieve that level of skill.

(d) If the judge places a defendant on community supervision and the defendant is determined to have a mental illness or be a person with mental retardation by an examining expert under Article 16.22 or Section 3, Article 46.02, of this code or in a psychological evaluation conducted under Section 9(i) of this article, the judge may require the defendant as a condition of community supervision to submit to outpatient or inpatient mental health or mental retardation treatment if the:
(1) defendant's:

(A) mental impairment is chronic in nature; or

(B) ability to function independently will continue to deteriorate if the defendant does not receive mental health or mental retardation services; and

(2) judge determines, in consultation with a local mental health or mental retardation services provider, that appropriate mental health or mental retardation services for the defendant are available through the Texas Department of Mental Health and Mental Retardation under Section 534.053, Health and Safety Code, or through another mental health or mental retardation services provider.

(e) A judge granting community supervision to a defendant required to register as a sex offender under Chapter 62 shall require the registration as a condition of community supervision.

(f) A judge may not require a defendant to undergo an orchiectomy as a condition of community supervision.

(g) If a judge grants community supervision to a person convicted of an offense under Title 5, Penal Code, that the court determines involves family violence, the judge may require the person to make one payment in an amount not to exceed $100 to a family violence shelter center that receives state or federal funds and that serves the county in which the court is located. In this subsection, "family violence" has the meaning assigned by Section 71.004, Family Code, and "family violence shelter center" has the meaning assigned by Section 51.002, Human Resources Code. *(Added by L.1999, chap. 27(1), eff. 9/1/99. See other subsection (g) below.)*

(g) A judge who grants community supervision to a person may require the person to make one payment in an amount not to exceed $50 to a children's advocacy center established under Subchapter E, Chapter 264, Family Code, if the person is charged with or convicted of an offense under Section 21.11 or 22.011(a)(2), Penal Code. *(Added by L.1999, chap. 1415(6(a)), eff. 9/1/99. See other subsection (g) above.)*

(h) *(Repealed.)*

(i)-(k) *(None enacted.)*

(*l*)(1) If the court grants community supervision to a person convicted of an offense under Section 42.072, Penal Code, the court may require as a condition of community supervision that the person may not:

(A) communicate directly or indirectly with the victim; or

(B) go to or near the residence, place of employment, or business of the victim or to or near a school, day-care facility, or similar facility where a dependent child of the victim is in attendance.

(2) If the court requires the prohibition contained in Subdivision (1)(B) of this subsection as a condition of community supervision, the court shall specifically describe the prohibited locations and the minimum distances, if any, that the person must maintain from the locations.

*(Chgd. by L.1997, chaps. 1(6), 144(3), 312(3), 668(3), 700(11); L.1999, chaps. 27(1), 323(1), 1415(6(a)), eff. 9/1/99.)*

**Sec. 12. Confinement as a condition of community supervision.** (a) If a judge having jurisdiction of a misdemeanor case requires as a condition of community supervision that the defendant submit to a period of confinement in a county jail, the period of confinement may not exceed 30 days. If a judge having jurisdiction of a felony case requires as a condition of community supervision that the defendant submit to a period of confinement in a county jail, the period of confinement may not exceed 180 days.

(b) A judge that requires as a condition of community supervision that the defendant serve a term in a community corrections facility under Section 18 of this article may not impose a term of confinement under this section that, when added to the term imposed under Section 18, exceeds 24 months.

(c) A judge may impose confinement as a condition of community supervision under Subsection (a) of this section on placing the defendant on supervision or at any time during the supervision period. The judge may impose periods of confinement as a condition of community supervision in increments smaller than the maximum periods provided by Subsection (a) of this section but may not impose periods of confinement that if added together exceed the maximum periods provided by Subsection (a).

**Sec. 13. DWI community supervision.** (a) A judge granting community supervision to a defendant convicted of an offense under Chapter 49, Penal Code, shall require as a condition of community supervision that the defendant submit to:

(1) not less than three days of confinement in county jail if the defendant was punished under Section 49.09(a); not less than 10 days of confinement in county jail if the defendant was punished under Section 49.09(b) or (c); or not less than 30 days of confinement in county jail if the defendant was convicted under Section 49.07; and

(2) an evaluation by a supervision officer or by a person, program, or facility approved by the Texas Commission on Alcohol and Drug Abuse for the purpose of having the facility prescribe and carry out a course of conduct necessary for the rehabilitation of the defendant's drug or alcohol dependence condition.

(b) A judge granting community supervision to a defendant convicted of an offense under Section 49.08, Penal Code, shall require as a condition of community supervision that the defendant submit to a period of confinement of not less than 120 days.

(c) If the director of a facility to which a defendant is referred under Subdivision (2) of Subsection (a) of this section determines that the defendant is not making a good faith effort to participate in a program of rehabilitation, the director shall notify the judge that referred the defendant of that fact.

(d) If a judge requires as a condition of community supervision that the defendant participate in a prescribed course of conduct necessary for the rehabilitation of the defendant's drug or alcohol dependence condition, the judge shall require that the defendant pay for all or part of the cost of such rehabilitation based on the defendant's ability to pay. The judge may, in its discretion, credit such cost paid by the defendant against the fine assessed. In making a determination of a defendant's ability to pay the cost of rehabilitation under this subsection, the judge shall consider whether the defendant has insurance coverage that will pay for rehabilitation.

(e) The confinement imposed shall be treated as a condition of community supervision, and in the event of a sentence of confinement upon the revocation of community supervision, the term of confinement served may not be credited toward service of such subsequent confinement.

(f) If a judge grants community supervision to a defendant convicted of an offense under Sections 49.04-49.08, Penal Code, and if before receiving community supervision the defendant has not submitted to an evaluation under Section 9 of this article, the judge shall require the defendant to submit to the evaluation as a condition of community supervision. If the evaluation indicates to the judge that the defendant is in need of treatment for drug or alcohol dependency, the judge shall require the defendant to submit to that treatment as a condition of community supervision in a program or facility approved or licensed by the Texas Commission on Alcohol and Drug Abuse or in a program or facility that complies with standards established by the community justice assistance division of the Texas Department of Criminal Justice, after consultation by the division with the commission.

(g) A jury that recommends community supervision for a person convicted of an offense under Sections 49.04-49.08, Penal Code, may recommend that any driver's license issued to the defendant under Chapter 521, Transportation Code, not be suspended.

(h) If a person convicted of an offense under Sections 49.04-49.08, Penal Code, is placed on community supervision, the judge shall require, as a condition of the community supervision, that the defendant attend and successfully complete before the 181st day after the day community supervision is granted an educational program jointly approved by the Texas Commission on Alcohol and Drug Abuse, the Department of Public Safety, the Traffic Safety Section of the Texas Department of Transportation, and the community justice assistance division of the Texas Department of Criminal Justice designed to rehabilitate persons who have driven while intoxicated. The Texas Commission on Alcohol and Drug Abuse shall publish the jointly approved rules and shall monitor, coordinate, and provide training to persons providing the educational programs. The Texas Commission on Alcohol and Drug Abuse is responsible for the administration of the certification of approved educational programs and may charge a nonrefundable application fee for the initial certification of approval and for renewal of a certificate. The judge may waive the educational program requirement or may grant an extension of time to successfully complete the program that expires not later than one year after the beginning date of the person's community supervision, however, if the defendant by a motion in writing shows good cause. In determining good cause, the judge may consider but is not limited to: the defendant's school and work schedule, the defendant's health, the distance that the defendant must travel to attend an educational program, and the fact that the defendant resides out of state, has no valid driver's license, or does not have access to transportation. The judge shall set out the finding of good cause for waiver in the judgment. If a defendant is required, as a condition of community supervision, to attend an educational program or if the court waives the educational program requirement, the court clerk shall immediately report that fact to the Department of Public Safety, on a form prescribed by the department, for inclusion in the person's driving record. If the court grants an extension of time in which the person may complete the program, the court clerk shall immediately report that fact to the Department of Public Safety on a form prescribed by the department. The report must include the beginning date of the person's community supervision. Upon the person's successful completion of the educational program, the person's instructor shall give notice to the Department of Public Safety for inclusion in the person's driving record and to the community supervision and corrections department. The community supervision and corrections department shall then forward the notice to the court clerk for filing. If the Department of Public Safety does not receive notice that a defendant required to complete an educational program has successfully completed the program within the period required by this section, as shown on department records, the department shall revoke the defendant's driver's license, permit, or privilege or prohibit the person from obtaining a license or permit, as provided by Sections 521.344(e) and (f), Transportation Code. The Department of Public Safety may not reinstate a license suspended under this subsection unless the person whose license was suspended makes application to the department for reinstatement of the person's license and pays to the department a reinstatement fee of $50. The Department of Public Safety shall remit all fees collected under this subsection to the comptroller for deposit in the general revenue fund. This subsection does not apply to a defendant if a jury recommends community supervision for the defendant and also recommends that the defendant's driver's license not be suspended.

(i) If a person convicted of an offense under Sections 49.04-49.08, Penal Code, is placed on community supervision, the court may require as a condition of community supervision that the defendant have a device installed, on the motor vehicle owned by the defendant or on the vehicle most regularly driven by the defendant, that uses a deep-lung breath analysis mechanism to make impractical the operation of the motor vehicle if ethyl alcohol is detected in the breath of the operator and that the defendant not operate any motor vehicle that is not equipped with that device. If the person is convicted of an offense under Sections 49.04-49.06, Penal Code, and punished under Section 49.09(a) or (b), Penal Code, or of a second or subsequent offense under Section 49.07 or 49.08, Penal Code, and the person after conviction of either offense is placed on community supervision, the court shall require as a condition of community supervision that the defendant have the device installed on the appropriate vehicle and that the defendant not operate any motor vehicle unless the vehicle is equipped with that device. Before placing on community supervision a person convicted of an offense under Sections 49.04-49.08, Penal Code, the court shall determine from criminal history record information maintained by the Department of Public Safety whether the person has one or more previous convictions under Sections 49.04-49.08, Penal Code, or has one previous conviction under Sections 49.04-49.07, Penal Code, or one previous conviction under Section 49.08, Penal Code. If the court determines that the person has one or more such previous convictions, the court shall require as a condition of community supervision that the defendant have that device installed on the motor vehicle owned by the defendant or on the vehicle most regularly driven by the defendant and that the defendant not operate any motor vehicle unless the vehicle is equipped with the device described in this subsection. The court shall require the defendant to obtain the device at the defendant's own cost before the 30th day after the date of conviction unless the court finds that to do so would not be in the best interest of justice and enters its findings on record. The court shall require the defendant to provide evidence to the court within the 30-day period that the device has been installed on the appropriate vehicle and order the device to remain installed on that vehicle for a period not less than 50 percent of the supervision period. If the court determines the offender is unable to pay for the device, the court may impose a reasonable payment schedule not to exceed twice the period of the court's order. The Department of Public Safety shall approve devices for use under this subsection. Section 521.247, Transportation Code, applies to the approval of a device under this subsection and the consequences of that approval. Notwithstanding the provisions of this section, if a person is required to operate a motor vehicle in the course and scope of the person's employment and if the vehicle is owned by the employer, the person may operate that vehicle without installation of an approved ignition interlock device if the employer has been notified of that driving privilege restriction and if proof of that notification is with the vehicle. This employment exemption does not apply, however, if the business entity that owns the vehicle is owned or controlled by the person whose driving privilege has been restricted. A previous conviction may not be used for purposes of restricting a person to the operation of a motor vehicle equipped with an interlock ignition device under this subsection if:

(1) the previous conviction was a final conviction under Section 49.04, 49.05, 49.06, 49.07, or 49.08, Penal Code, and was for an offense committed more than 10 years before the instant offense for which the person was convicted and placed on community supervision; and

(2) the person has not been convicted of an offense under Section 49.04, 49.05, 49.06, 49.07, or 49.08 of that code, committed within 10 years before the date on which the instant offense for which the person was convicted and placed on community supervision.

(j) The judge shall require a defendant who is punished under Section 49.09, Penal Code, as a condition of community supervision, to attend and successfully complete an educational program for repeat offenders approved by the Texas Commission on Alcohol and Drug Abuse. The Texas Commission on Alcohol and Drug Abuse shall adopt rules and shall monitor, coordinate, and provide training to persons providing the educational programs. The Texas Commission on Alcohol and Drug Abuse is responsible for the administration of the certification of approved educational programs and may charge a nonrefundable application fee for initial certification of approval or for renewal of the certification. The judge may waive the educational program requirement only if the defendant by a motion in writing shows good cause. In determining good cause, the judge may consider the defendant's school and work schedule, the defendant's health, the distance that the defendant must travel to attend an educational program, and whether the defendant resides out of state or does not have access to transportation. The judge shall set out the finding of good cause in the judgment. If a defendant is required, as a condition of community supervision, to attend an educational program, the court clerk shall immediately report that fact to the Department of Public Safety, on a form prescribed by the department, for inclusion in the defendant's driving record. The report must include the beginning date of the defendant's community supervision. On the defendant's successful completion of the educational program for repeat offenders, the defendant's instructor shall give notice to the Department of Public Safety for inclusion in the defendant's driving record and to the community supervision and corrections department. The community supervision and corrections department shall then forward the notice to the court clerk for filing. If the Department of Public Safety does not receive notice that a defendant required to complete an educational program has successfully completed the program for repeat offenders within the period required by the judge, as shown on department records, the department shall revoke the defendant's driver's license, permit, or privilege or prohibit the defendant from obtaining a license or permit, as provided by Sections 521.344(e) and (f), Transportation Code.

(k) Notwithstanding Sections 521.344(d)-(i), Transportation Code, if the judge, under Subsection (h) or (j) of this section, permits or requires a defendant punished under Section 49.09, Penal Code, to attend an educational program as a condition of community supervision, or waives the required attendance for such a program, and the defendant has previously been required to attend such a program, or the required attendance at the program had been waived, the judge nonetheless shall order the suspension of the driver's license, permit, or operating privilege of that person for a period determined by the judge according to the following schedule:

(1) not less than 90 days or more than 365 days, if the defendant is convicted under Sections 49.04-49.08, Penal Code; or

(2) not less than 180 days or more than two years, if the defendant is punished under Section 49.09, Penal Code.

(*l*) If the Department of Public Safety receives notice that a defendant has been required or permitted to attend a subsequent educational program under Subsection (h), (j), or (k) of this section, although the previously required attendance had been waived, but the judge has not ordered a period of suspension, the department shall suspend the defendant's driver's license, permit, or operating privilege, or shall issue an order prohibiting the defendant from obtaining a license or permit for a period of 365 days.

(m) If a judge revokes the community supervision of a defendant for an offense under Section 49.04, Penal Code, or an offense involving the operation of a motor vehicle under Section 49.07, Penal Code, and the driver's license or privilege to operate a motor vehicle has not previously been ordered by the judge to be suspended, or if the suspension was previously probated, the judge shall suspend the license or privilege for a period provided under Subchapter O, Chapter 521, Transportation Code. The suspension shall be reported to the Department of Public Safety as provided under Section 521.347, Transportation Code.

(n) Notwithstanding any other provision of this section or other law, the judge who places on community supervision a defendant who is younger than 21 years of age and convicted for an offense under Sections 49.04-49.08, Penal Code, shall:

(1) order that the defendant's driver's license be suspended for 90 days beginning on the date that the person is placed on community supervision; and

(2) require as a condition of community supervision that the defendant not operate a motor vehicle unless the vehicle is equipped with the device described by Subsection (i) of this section.
*(Chgd. by L.1997, chaps. 165(31.01(10)), 577(18); L.1999, chaps. 62(3.04), 580(8), 1105(3), eff. 9/1/99.)*

**Sec. 13A. Community supervision for offense committed because of bias or prejudice.** (a) A court granting community supervision to a defendant convicted of an offense for which the court has made an affirmative finding under Article 42.014 of this code shall require as a term of community supervision that the defendant:

(1) serve a term of not more than one year imprisonment in the institutional division of the Texas Department of Criminal Justice if the offense is a felony other than an offense under Section 19.02, Penal Code; or

(2) serve a term of not more than 90 days confinement in jail if the offense is a misdemeanor.

(b) The court may not grant community supervision on its own motion or on the recommendation of the jury to a defendant convicted of an offense for which the court has made an affirmative finding under Article 42.014 of this code if:

(1) the offense is murder under Section 19.02, Penal Code; or

(2) the defendant has been previously convicted of an offense for which the court made an affirmative finding under Article 42.014 of this code.

**Sec. 13B. Defendants placed on community supervision for sexual offenses against children.** (a) If a judge grants community supervision to a defendant described by Subsection (b) and the judge determines that a child as defined by Section 22.011(c), Penal Code, was the victim of the offense, the judge shall establish a child safety zone applicable to the defendant by requiring as a condition of community supervision that the defendant:

(1) not:

(A) supervise or participate in any program that includes as participants or recipients persons who are 17 years of age or younger and that regularly provides athletic, civic, or cultural activities; or

(B) go in, on, or within a distance specified by the judge of a premises where children commonly gather, including a school, day-care facility, playground, public or private youth center, public swimming pool, or video arcade facility; and

(2) attend psychological counseling sessions for sex offenders with an individual or organization which provides sex offender treatment or counseling as specified by or approved by the judge or the community supervision and corrections department officer supervising the defendant.

(b) This section applies to a defendant placed on community supervision for an offense:

(1) under Section 43.25 or 43.26, Penal Code;

(2) under Section 21.08, 21.11, 22.011, 22.021, or 25.02, Penal Code;

(3) under Section 20.04(a)(4), Penal Code, if the defendant committed the offense with the intent to violate or abuse the victim sexually; or

(4) under Section 30.02, Penal Code, punishable under Subsection (d) of that section, if the defendant committed the offense with the intent to commit a felony listed in Subdivision (2) or (3) of this subsection.

(c) A community supervision and corrections department officer who under Subsection (a)(2) specifies a sex offender treatment provider to provide counseling to a defendant shall contact the provider before the defendant is released, establish the date, time, and place of the first session between the defendant and the provider, and request the provider to immediately notify the officer if the defendant fails to attend the first session or any subsequent scheduled session.

(d) Notwithstanding Subsection (a)(1), a judge is not required to impose the conditions described by Subsection (a)(1) if the defendant is a student at a primary or secondary school.

(e) At any time after the imposition of a condition under Subsection (a)(1), the defendant may request the court to modify the child safety zone applicable to the defendant because the zone as created by the court:

(1) interferes with the ability of the defendant to attend school or hold a job and consequently constitutes an undue hardship for the defendant; or

(2) is broader than is necessary to protect the public, given the nature and circumstances of the offense.

(f) A community supervision and corrections department officer supervising a defendant described by Subsection (b) may permit the defendant to enter on an event-by-event basis into the child safety zone from which the defendant is otherwise prohibited from entering if:

(1) the defendant has served at least two years of the period of community supervision;

(2) the defendant enters the zone as part of a program to reunite with the defendant's family;

(3) the defendant presents to the officer a written proposal specifying where the defendant intends to go within the zone, why and with whom the defendant is going, and how the defendant intends to cope with any stressful situations that occur;

(4) the sex offender treatment provider treating the defendant agrees with the officer that the defendant should be allowed to attend the event; and

(5) the officer and the treatment provider agree on a chaperon to accompany the defendant and the chaperon agrees to perform that duty.

(g) Section 10(a) does not prohibit a community supervision and corrections department officer from altering a condition of community supervision by permitting a defendant to enter a child safety zone under Subsection (f).

(h) In this section, "playground," "premises," "school," "video arcade facility," and "youth center" have the meanings assigned by Section 481.134, Health and Safety Code.

**Sec. 13C. Community supervision for making a firearm accessible to a child.** (a) A court granting community supervision to a defendant convicted of an offense under Section 46.13, Penal Code, may require as a condition of community supervision that the defendant:

(1) provide an appropriate public service activity designated by the court; or

(2) attend a firearms safety course which meets or exceeds the requirements set by the National Rifle Association as of January 1, 1995, for a firearms safety course that requires not more than 17 hours of instruction.

(b) The court shall require the defendant to pay the cost of attending the firearms safety course under Subsection (a)(2).

*(Renumbered from Sec. 13B by L.1997, chap. 165(31.01(11)), eff. 9/1/97.)*

**Sec. 13D. Defendants placed on community supervision for violent offenses; protecting children.** (a) If a judge grants community supervision to a defendant convicted of an offense listed in Section 3g(a)(1) or for which the judgment contains an affirmative finding under Section 3g(a)(2), the judge, if the nature of the offense for which the defendant is convicted warrants the establishment of a child safety zone, may establish a child safety zone applicable to the defendant by requiring as a condition of community supervision that the defendant not:

(1) supervise or participate in any program that includes as participants or recipients persons who are 17 years of age or younger and that regularly provides athletic, civic, or cultural activities; or

(2) go in or on, or within a distance specified by the judge of, a premises where children commonly gather, including a school, day-care facility, playground, public or private youth center, public swimming pool, or video arcade facility.

(b) At any time after the imposition of a condition under Subsection (a), the defendant may request the judge to modify the child safety zone applicable to the defendant because the zone as created by the judge:

(1) interferes with the ability of the defendant to attend school or hold a job and consequently constitutes an undue hardship for the defendant; or

(2) is broader than is necessary to protect the public, given the nature and circumstances of the offense.

(c) This section does not apply to a defendant described by Section 13B.

(d) In this section, "playground," "premises," "school," "video arcade facility," and "youth center" have the meanings assigned by Section 481.134, Health and Safety Code.

*(Added by L.1999, chap. 56(1), eff. 9/1/99.)*

**Sec. 14. Child abusers, sex offenders, and family violence offenders; special conditions.** (a) If the court grants probation to a person convicted of an offense described by Article 17.41(a) of this code, the court may require as a condition of probation that the defendant not directly communicate with the victim of the offense or go near a residence, school, or other location, as specifically described in the copy of terms and conditions, frequented by the victim. In imposing the condition, the court may grant the defendant supervised access to the victim. To the extent that a condition imposed under this subsection conflicts with an existing court order granting possession of or access to a child, the condition imposed under this subsection prevails for a period specified by the court granting probation, not to exceed 90 days.

(b) If the court grants probation to a person convicted of an offense under Section 21.11, 22.011, 22.021, or 22.04, Penal Code, the court may require the probationer to attend psychological counseling sessions at the direction of the probation officer and may require the probationer to pay all or a part of the reasonable and necessary costs incurred by the victim for psychological counseling made necessary by the offense, upon a finding that the probationer is financially able to make payment. Any payments ordered under this subsection may not extend past one year from the date of the order.

(c) If the court grants community supervision to a person convicted of an offense involving family violence, as defined by Section 71.004, Family Code, the court may require the defendant to attend, at the direction of the community supervision and corrections department officer, counseling sessions for the elimination of violent behavior with a licensed counselor, social worker, or other professional who has been trained in family violence intervention or to attend a battering intervention and prevention program if available that meets guidelines adopted by the community justice assistance division of the Texas Department of Criminal Justice. If the court requires the defendant to attend counseling or a program, the court shall require the defendant to begin attendance not later than the 60th day after the date the court grants community supervision, notify the community supervision and corrections department officer of the name, address, and phone number of the counselor or program, and report the defendant's attendance to the officer. The court

shall require the defendant to pay all the reasonable costs of the counseling sessions or attendance in the program on a finding that the defendant is financially able to make payment. If the court finds the defendant is unable to make payment, the court shall make the counseling sessions or enrollment in the program available without cost to the defendant. The court may also require the defendant to pay all or a part of the reasonable costs incurred by the victim for counseling made necessary by the offense, on a finding that the defendant is financially able to make payment. The court may order the defendant to make payments under this subsection for a period not to exceed one year after the date on which the order is entered.
*(Chgd. by L.1999, chap. 910(1), eff. 9/1/99. See other Section 14 below.)*

**Sec. 14. Substance abuse felony program.** (a) If a court places a defendant on community supervision under any provision of this article as an alternative to imprisonment, the judge may require as a condition of community supervision that the defendant serve a term of confinement and treatment in a substance abuse treatment facility operated by the Texas Department of Criminal Justice under Section 493.009, Government Code. A term of confinement and treatment imposed under this section must be an indeterminate term of not more than one year or less than 90 days.

(b) A judge may impose the condition of community supervision created under this section if:

(1) the judge places the defendant on community supervision under this article;

(2) the defendant is charged with or convicted of a felony other than:

(A) a felony under Section 21.11, 22.011, or 22.021, Penal Code; or

(B) criminal attempt of a felony under Section 21.11, 22.011, or 22.021, Penal Code; and

(3) the judge makes an affirmative finding that:

(A) drug or alcohol abuse significantly contributed to the commission of the crime or violation of community supervision; and

(B) the defendant is a suitable candidate for treatment, as determined by the suitability criteria established by the Texas Board of Criminal Justice under Section 493.009(b), Government Code.

(c) If a judge requires as a condition of community supervision that the defendant serve a term of confinement and treatment in a substance abuse treatment facility under this section, the judge shall also require as a condition of community supervision that on release from the facility the defendant:

(1) participate in a drug or alcohol abuse continuum of care treatment plan; and

(2) pay a fee in an amount established by the judge for residential aftercare required as part of the treatment plan.

(d) The Texas Commission on Alcohol and Drug Abuse shall develop the continuum of care treatment plan.

(e) The clerk of a court that collects a fee imposed under Subsection (c)(2) shall remit the fee to the comptroller, and the comptroller shall deposit the fee into the general revenue fund. In requiring the payment of a fee under Subsection (c)(2), the judge shall consider fines, fees, and other necessary expenses for which the defendant is obligated in establishing the amount of the fee. The judge may not:

(1) establish the fee in an amount that is greater than 25 percent of the defendant's gross income while the defendant is a participant in residential aftercare; or

(2) require the defendant to pay the fee at any time other than a time at which the defendant is both employed and a participant in residential aftercare.
*(Chgd. by L.1999, chap. 1188(1.44), eff. 9/1/99. See other Section 14 above.)*

**Sec. 15. Procedures relating to state jail felony community supervision.** (a) On conviction of a state jail felony punished under Section 12.35(a), Penal Code, the judge may suspend the imposition of the sentence and place the defendant on community supervision or may order the sentence to be executed. The judge may suspend in whole or in part the imposition of any fine imposed on conviction.

(b) The minimum period of community supervision a judge may impose under this section is two years. The maximum period of community supervision a judge may impose under this section is five years, except that the judge may extend the maximum period of community supervision under this section to not more than 10 years. A judge may extend a period of community supervision under this section at any time during the period of community supervision, or if a motion for revocation of community supervision is filed before the period of community supervision ends, before the first anniversary of the expiration of the period of community supervision.

(c) A judge may impose any condition of community supervision on a defendant that the judge could impose on a defendant placed on supervision for an offense other than a state jail felony, except that the judge may impose on the defendant a condition that the defendant submit to a period of confinement in a county jail under Section 5 or 12 of this article only if the term does not exceed 90 days.

(d) A judge may impose as a condition of community supervision that a defendant submit at the beginning of the period of community supervision to a term of confinement in a state jail felony facility for a term of not less than 90 days or more than 180 days, or a term of not less than 90 days or more than one year if the defendant is convicted of an offense punishable as a state jail felony under Section 481.112, 481.1121, 481.113, or 481.120, Health and Safety Code. A judge may not require a defendant to submit to both the term of confinement authorized by this subsection and a term of confinement under Section 5 or 12 of this article. For the purposes of this subsection, a defendant previously has been convicted of a felony regardless of whether the sentence for the previous conviction was actually imposed or was probated and suspended.

(e) If a defendant violates a condition of community supervision imposed on the defendant under this article and after a hearing under Section 21 of this article the judge modifies the defendant's community supervision, the judge may impose any sanction permitted by Section 22 of this article, except that if the judge requires a defendant to serve a period of confinement in a state jail felony facility as a modification of the defendant's community supervision, the minimum term of confinement is 90 days and the maximum term of confinement is 180 days.

(f)(1) If a defendant violates a condition of community supervision imposed on the defendant under this article and after a hearing under Section 21 of this article the judge revokes the defendant's community supervision, the judge shall dispose of the case in the manner provided by Section 23 of this article.

(2) The court retains jurisdiction over the defendant for the period during which the defendant is confined in a state jail. At any time after the 75th day after the date the defendant is received into the custody of a state jail, the judge on the judge's own motion, on the motion of the attorney representing the state, or on the motion of the defendant may suspend further execution of the sentence and place the defendant on community supervision under the conditions of this section.

(3) When the defendant or the attorney representing the state files a written motion requesting suspension by the judge of further execution of the sentence and placement of the defendant on community supervision, the clerk of the court, if requested to do so by the judge, shall request a copy of the defendant's record while confined from the facility director of the state jail felony facility in which the defendant is confined or, if the defendant is confined in a county jail, from the sheriff. On receipt of the request, the facility director or the sheriff shall forward to the judge, as soon as possible, a full and complete copy of the defendant's record while confined. When the defendant files a written motion requesting suspension of further execution of the sentence and placement on community supervision, he shall immediately deliver or cause to be delivered a true and correct copy of the motion to the office of the attorney representing the state. The judge may deny the motion without a hearing but may not grant the motion without holding a hearing and providing the attorney representing the state and the defendant the opportunity to present evidence on the motion.

(g) The facility director of a state jail felony facility shall report to a judge who orders a defendant confined in the facility as a condition of community supervision or as sanction imposed as a modification of community supervision under Subsection (e) not less than every 90 days on the defendant's programmatic progress, conduct, and conformity to the rules of the facility.

(h)(1) A defendant confined in a state jail felony facility does not earn good conduct time for time served in the facility.

(2) A judge may credit against any time a defendant is required to serve in a state jail felony facility time served by the defendant in county jail from the time of the defendant's arrest and confinement until sentencing by the trial court.

(3) A judge shall credit against any time a defendant is subsequently required to serve in a state jail felony facility after revocation of community supervision any time served by the defendant in a state jail felony facility after sentencing.

*(Chgd. by L.1997, chaps. 488(1)-(4), 745(34), eff. 9/1/97, 1/1/98, respectively.)*

**Sec. 15A. Enhanced disorderly conduct and public intoxication offenses.** (a) Except as provided by Subsection (b), on conviction of an offense for which punishment is enhanced under Section 12.43(c), Penal Code, the court shall suspend the imposition of the sentence and place the defendant on community supervision. The judge may suspend in whole or in part the imposition of any fine imposed on conviction. All provisions of this article applying to a defendant placed on community supervision for a misdemeanor apply to a defendant placed on community supervision under this section, except that the court shall require the defendant as a condition of community supervision to:

(1) submit to diagnostic testing for addiction to alcohol or a controlled substance or drug;

(2) submit to a psychological assessment;

(3) if indicated as necessary by testing and assessment, participate in an alcohol or drug abuse treatment or education program; and

(4) pay the costs of testing, assessment, and treatment or education, either directly or as a court cost.

(b) Subsection (a) does not apply if it is shown at the punishment phase of a trial in which punishment is enhanced under Section 12.43(c), Penal Code, that the defendant had previously been convicted of an offense for which punishment was enhanced under Section 12.43(c), Penal Code. *(Added by L.1999, chap. 564(2), eff. 9/1/99.)*

**Sec. 16. Community service.** (a) A judge shall require as a condition of community supervision, that the defendant work a specified number of hours at a community service project or projects for an organization or organizations approved by the judge and designated by the department, unless the judge determines and notes on the order placing the defendant on community supervision that:

(1) the defendant is physically or mentally incapable of participating in the project;

(2) participating in the project will work a hardship on the defendant or the defendant's dependents;

(3) the defendant is to be confined in a substance abuse punishment facility as a condition of community supervision; or

(4) there is other good cause shown..

(b) The amount of community service work ordered by the judge:

(1) may not exceed 1,000 hours and may not be less than 320 hours for an offense classified as a first degree felony;

(2) may not exceed 800 hours and may not be less then 240 hours for an offense classified as a second degree felony;

(3) may not exceed 600 hours and may not be less than 160 hours for an offense classified as a third degree felony;

(4) may not exceed 400 hours and may not be less than 120 hours for an offense classified as a state jail felony;

(5) may not exceed 200 hours and may not be less than 80 hours for an offense classified as a Class A misdemeanor or for any other misdemeanor for which the maximum permissible confinement, if any, exceeds six months or the maximum permissible fine, if any, exceeds $4,000; and

(6) may not exceed 100 hours and may not be less than 24 hours for an offense classified as a Class B misdemeanor or for any other misdemeanor for which the maximum permissible confinement, if any, does not exceed six months and the maximum permissible fine, if any, does not exceed $4,000.

(c) A defendant required to perform community service under this section is not a state employee for the purposes of Article 8309g or 8309h, Revised Statutes.

(d) If the court makes an affirmative finding under Article 42.014 of this code, the judge may order the defendant to perform community service under this section at a project designated by the judge that primarily serves the person or group who was the target of the defendant. If the judge orders community service under this subsection the judge shall order the defendant to perform not less than:

(1) 100 hours of service if the offense is a misdemeanor; or

(2) 300 hours of service if the offense is a felony.

**Sec. 17. Change of residence; leaving the state.** (a) If, for good and sufficient reasons, a defendant desires to change his residence within the state, the change may be effected by application to the supervising supervision officer, which change shall be subject to the judge's consent and subject to such regulations as the judge may require in the absence of an officer in the locality to which the defendant is transferred.

(b) Any defendant who removes himself from the state without permission of the judge having jurisdiction of the case shall be considered a fugitive from justice and shall be subject to extradition as provided by law.

**Sec. 18. Community corrections facilities.** (a) In this section, "community corrections facility" has the meaning assigned by Section 509.001, Government Code.

(b) If a judge requires as a condition of community supervision that the defendant serve a term in a community corrections facility, the term may not be more than 24 months.

(c) A defendant granted community supervision under this section may not earn good conduct credit for time spent in a community corrections facility or apply time spent in the facility toward completion of a prison sentence if the community supervision is revoked.

(d) As directed by the judge, the corrections facility director shall file with the community supervision and corrections department director a copy of an evaluation made by the director of the defendant's behavior and attitude at the facility. The director shall examine the evaluation, make written comments on the evaluation that he considers relevant, and file the evaluation and comments with the judge who granted community supervision to the defendant. If the evaluation indicates that the defendant has made significant progress toward compliance with court-ordered conditions of community supervision, the court may release the defendant from the community corrections facility. The defendant shall serve the remainder of his community supervision under any terms and conditions the court imposes under this article.

(e) No later than 18 months after the date on which a defendant is granted community supervision under this section, the community corrections facility director shall file with the community supervision and corrections department director a copy of an evaluation made by the director of the defendant's behavior and attitude at the center. The director shall examine the evaluation, make written comments on the evaluation that he considers relevant, and file the evaluation and comments with the judge who granted community supervision to the defendant. If the report indicates that the defendant has made significant progress toward court-ordered conditions of community supervision, the judge shall modify the judge's sentence and release the defendant in the same manner as provided by Subsection (d) of this section. If the report indicates that the defendant would benefit from continued participation in the community corrections facility program, the judge may order the defendant to remain at the community corrections facility for a period determined by the judge. If the report indicates that the defendant has not made significant progress toward rehabilitation, the judge may revoke community supervision and order the defendant to the term of confinement specified in the defendant's sentence.



(f) If ordered by the judge who placed the defendant on community supervision, a community corrections facility director shall attempt to place a defendant as a worker in a community-service project of a type described by Section 16 of this article.

(g) A defendant participating in a program under this article shall be confined in the community corrections facility at all times except for:

(1) time spent attending and traveling to and from an education or rehabilitation program as ordered by the court;

(2) time spent attending and traveling to and from a community-service project;

(3) time spent away from the facility for purposes described by this section; and

(4) time spent traveling to and from work, if applicable.

(h) A judge that requires as a condition of community supervision that the defendant serve a term in a community corrections facility may not impose a subsequent term in a community corrections facility or jail during the same supervision period that, when added to the terms previously imposed, exceeds 36 months.

(i) If a defendant participating in a program under this section is not required by the judge to deliver the defendant's salary to the restitution center director, the employer of the defendant shall deliver the salary to the director. The director shall deposit the salary into a fund to be given to the defendant on release after deducting:

(1) the cost to the center for the defendant's food, housing, and supervision;

(2) necessary travel expense to and from work and community-service projects and other incidental expenses of the defendant;

(3) support of the defendant's dependents; and

(4) restitution to the victims of an offense committed by the defendant.

**Sec. 19. Fees.** (a) Except as otherwise provided by this subsection, a judge granting community supervision shall fix a fee of not less than $25 and not more than $40 per month to be paid to the court by the defendant during the community supervision period. The judge may make payment of the fee a condition of granting or continuing the community supervision. The judge may waive or reduce the fee or suspend a monthly payment of the fee if the judge determines that payment of the fee would cause the defendant a significant financial hardship.

(b) The judge shall deposit the fees received under Subsection (a) of this section in the special fund of the county treasury, to be used for the same purposes for which state aid may be used under Chapter 76, Government Code.

(c) A judge receiving a defendant for supervision as authorized by Article 42.11 of this code may impose on the defendant any term of community supervision authorized by this article and may require the defendant to pay the fee authorized by Subsection (a) of this section. Fees received under this section shall be deposited in the same manner as required by Subsection (b) of this section.

(d) For the purpose of determining when fees due on conviction are to be paid to any officer or officers, the placing of the defendant on community supervision shall be considered a final disposition of the case, without the necessity of waiting for the termination of the period of community supervision.

(e) If the judge grants community supervision to a defendant convicted of an offense under Section 21.08, 21.11, 22.011, 22.021, 25.02, 43.25, or 43.26, Penal Code, the judge shall require as a condition of community supervision that the defendant pay to the community corrections and supervision department officer supervising the defendant a community supervision fee of $5 each month during the period of community supervision. The fee is in addition to court costs or any other fee imposed on the defendant.

(f) A community corrections and supervision department shall remit fees collected under Subsection (e) of this section to the comptroller. The comptroller shall deposit the fee in the special revenue fund to the credit of the sexual assault program established under Section 44.0061, Health and Safety Code.

(g) If the judge places on community supervision a person required to register as a sex offender under Chapter 62, the judge shall require as a condition of community supervision that the person pay to the person's supervising officer a fee that equals the actual cost to the applicable local law enforcement authority for providing notice for publication to a newspaper as required by Chapter 62. A community supervision and corrections department shall remit fees collected under this subsection to the applicable local law enforcement authority to reimburse the authority for the actual cost incurred by the authority, as evidenced by written receipt, for providing notice for publication to a newspaper as required by Chapter 62. In a community supervision revocation hearing at which it is alleged only that the person violated the terms of community supervision by failing to make a payment under this subsection, the inability of the person to pay as ordered by the judge is an affirmative defense to revocation, which the person must prove by a preponderance of the evidence.

*(Chgd. by L.1997, chap. 668(4), eff. 9/1/97.)*

**Sec. 20. Reduction or termination of community supervision.** (a) At any time, after the defendant has satisfactorily completed one-third of the original community supervision period or two years of community supervision, whichever is less, the period of community supervision may be reduced or terminated by the judge. Upon the satisfactory fulfillment of the conditions of community supervision, and the expiration of the period of community supervision, the judge, by order duly entered, shall amend or modify the original sentence imposed, if necessary, to conform to the community supervision period and shall discharge the defendant. If the judge discharges the defendant under this section, the judge may set aside the verdict or permit the defendant to withdraw his plea, and shall dismiss the accusation, complaint, information or indictment against the defendant, who shall thereafter be released from all penalties and disabilities resulting from the offense or crime of which he has been convicted or to which he has pleaded guilty, except that:

(1) proof of the conviction or plea of guilty shall be made known to the judge should the defendant again be convicted of any criminal offense; and

(2) if the defendant is an applicant for a license or is a licensee under Chapter 42, Human Resources Code, the Texas Department of Human Services may consider the fact that the defendant previously has received community supervision under this article in issuing, renewing, denying, or revoking a license under that chapter.

(b) This section does not apply to a defendant convicted of an offense under Sections 49.04-49.08, Penal Code, a defendant convicted of an offense for which on conviction registration as a sex offender is required under Chapter 62, as added by Chapter 668, Acts of the 75th Legislature, Regular Session, 1997, or a defendant convicted of an offense punishable as a state jail felony.

*(Chgd. by L.1999, chap. 1415(5(b)), eff. 9/1/99.)*

**Sec. 21. Violation of community supervision: detention and hearing.** (a) At any time during the period of community supervision the judge may issue a warrant for violation of any of the conditions of the community supervision and cause a defendant convicted under Section 43.02, Penal Code, or under Chapter 481, Health and Safety Code, or Sections 485.031 through 485.035, Health and Safety Code, or placed on deferred adjudication after being charged with one of those offenses, to be subject to the control measures of Section 81.083, Health and Safety Code, and to the court-ordered-management provisions of Subchapter G, Chapter 81, Health and Safety Code.

(b) At any time during the period of community supervision the judge may issue a warrant for violation of any of the conditions of the community supervision and cause the defendant to be arrested. Any supervision officer, police officer or other officer with power of arrest may arrest such defendant with or without a warrant upon the order of the judge to be noted on the docket of the court. A defendant so arrested may be detained in the county jail or other appropriate place of confinement until he can be taken before the judge. Such officer shall forthwith report such arrest and detention to such judge. If the defendant has not been released on bail, on motion by the defendant the judge shall cause the defendant to be brought before the judge for a hearing within 20 days of filing of said motion, and after a hearing without a jury, may either continue, modify, or revoke the community supervision. A judge may revoke the community supervision of a defendant who is imprisoned in a penal institution without a hearing if the defendant in writing before a court of record in the jurisdiction where imprisoned waives his right to a hearing and to counsel, affirms that he has nothing to say as to why sentence should not be pronounced against him, and requests the judge to revoke community supervision and to pronounce sentence. In a felony case, the state may amend the motion to revoke community supervision any time up to seven days before the date of the revocation hearing, after which time the motion may not be amended except for good cause shown, and in no event may the state amend the motion after the commencement of taking evidence at the hearing. The judge may continue the hearing for good cause shown by either the defendant or the state.

(c) In a community supervision revocation hearing at which it is alleged only that the defendant violated the conditions of community supervision by failing to pay compensation paid to appointed counsel, community supervision fees, court costs, restitution, or reparations, the inability of the defendant to pay as ordered by the judge is an affirmative defense to revocation, which the defendant must prove by a preponderance of evidence.

(d) A defendant has a right to counsel at a hearing under this section.

**Sec. 22. Continuation or modification.** (a) If after a hearing under Section 21 of this article a judge continues or modifies community supervision after determining that the defendant violated a condition of community supervision, the judge may impose any other conditions the judge determines are appropriate, including:

(1) a requirement that the defendant perform community service for a number of hours specified by the court under Section 16 of this article, or an increase in the number of hours that the defendant has previously been required to perform under those sections in an amount not to exceed double the number of hours permitted by Section 16;

(2) an increase in the period of community supervision, in the manner described by Subsection (b) of this section;

(3) an increase in the defendant's fine, in the manner described by Subsection (d) of this section; or

(4) the placement of the defendant in a substance abuse felony punishment program operated under Section 493.009, Government Code, if:

(A) the defendant is convicted of a felony other than:

(i) a felony under Section 21.11, 22.011, or 22.021, Penal Code; or

(ii) criminal attempt of a felony under Section 21.11, 22.011, or 22.021, Penal Code; and

(B) the judge makes an affirmative finding that:

(i) drug or alcohol abuse significantly contributed to the commission of the crime or violation of community supervision; and

(ii) the defendant is a suitable candidate for treatment, as determined by the suitability criteria established by the Texas Board of Criminal Justice under Section 493.009(b), Government Code.

(b) If the judge imposes a sanction under Subsection (a)(4) of this section, the judge shall also impose a condition requiring the defendant on successful completion of the program to participate in a drug or alcohol abuse continuum of care program.

(c) The judge may extend a period of community supervision under this section as often as the judge determines is necessary, but the period of community supervision in a first, second, or third degree felony case may not exceed 10 years and, except as otherwise provided by this subsection, the period of community supervision in a misdemeanor case may not exceed three years. The judge may extend the period of community supervision in a misdemeanor case for any period the judge determines is necessary, not to exceed an additional two years beyond the three-year limit, if the defendant fails to pay a previously assessed fine, costs, or restitution and the judge determines that extending the period of supervision increases the likelihood that the defendant will fully pay the fine, costs, or restitution. A court may extend a period of community supervision under this section at any time during the period of supervision or, if a motion for revocation of community supervision is filed before the period of supervision ends, before the first anniversary of the date on which the period of supervision expires.

(d) A judge may impose a sanction on a defendant described by Subsection (a)(3) of this section by increasing the fine imposed on the defendant. The original fine imposed on the defendant and an increase in the fine imposed under this subsection may not exceed the maximum fine for the offense for which the defendant was sentenced. The judge shall deposit money received from an increase in the defendant's fine under this subsection in the special fund of the county treasury to be used for the same purposes for which state aid may be used under Chapter 76, Government Code.

*(Chgd. by L.1997, chap. 754(1), eff. 9/1/97.)*

**Sec. 22A. Extending supervision period for sex offenders.** (a) If a defendant is placed on community supervision after receiving a grant of deferred adjudication for or being convicted of an offense under Section 21.11, 22.011, or 22.021, Penal Code, at any time during the period of community supervision, the judge may extend the period of community supervision as provided by this section.

(b) If at a hearing at which the defendant is provided the same rights as are provided a defendant at a hearing under Section 21 the judge determines that the defendant has not sufficiently demonstrated a commitment to avoid future criminal behavior and that the release of the defendant from supervision would endanger the public, the judge may extend the period of supervision for a period not to exceed 10 additional years.

(c) A judge may extend a period of community supervision under this section only once; however, the judge may extend a period of community supervision for a defendant under both Section 22(c) and this section, and the prohibition in Section 22(c) against a period of community supervision in a felony case exceeding 10 years does not apply to a defendant for whom community supervision is increased under this section or under both Section 22(c) and this section.

*(Added by L.1997, chap. 1430(5), eff. 9/1/97.)*

**Sec. 23. Revocation.** (a) If community supervision is revoked after a hearing under Section 21 of this article, the judge may proceed to dispose of the case as if there had been no community supervision, or if the judge determines that the best interests of society and the defendant would be served by a shorter term of confinement, reduce the term of confinement originally assessed to any term of confinement not less than the minimum prescribed for the offense of which the defendant was convicted. The judge shall enter the amount of restitution or reparation owed by the defendant on the date of revocation in the judgment in the case.

(b) No part of the time that the defendant is on community supervision shall be considered as any part of the time that he shall be sentenced to serve. The right of the defendant to appeal for a review of the conviction and punishment, as provided by law, shall be accorded the defendant at the time he is placed on community supervision. When he is notified that his community supervision is revoked for violation of the conditions of community supervision and he is called on to serve a sentence in a jail or in the institutional division of the Texas Department of Criminal Justice, he may appeal the revocation.

**Sec. 24.** *(Expired 9/1/95.)*

**Sec. 25.** *(Renumbered to Sec. 22.)*

**Sec. 26.** *(Renumbered to Sec. 23.)*

**Secs. 27, 28.** *(Repealed.)*

**Sec. 29.** *(Repealed by L.1995, chap. 76(3.15), eff. 9/1/95.)*
*(Chgd. by L.1989, 1st C.S., chaps. 6(1), 8(1); chaps. 86(1); 111(1); 191(1); 236(11); 260(1); 679(1)-(3); 785(4.17); 1135(5); 1195(9), (10); L.1990, 6th C.S., chap. 25(8), (9), (12); L.1991, 2nd C.S., chap. 10(15.02), (16.01), (19.02); chaps. 14(284(8, 9, 52, 60)); 202(2); 285(1); 343(1); 344(1); 541(1); 555(3); 572(2); 784(9); L.1993, chaps. 10(3); 107(10.01(1)); 165(1); 201(3), (4); 470(2); 662(1), (8); 790(30), (36): 796(1), (2); 805(7); 806(2)-(4); 886(15); 889(1); 900(4.01); 987(2), (3); L.1995, chaps. 76(3.06)-(3.12), (3.15)-(3.18), (7.02), (7.13)-(7.15), eff. 9/1/95; 83(2), eff. 9/1/95; 256(1)-(3), eff. 9/1/95; 257(1), eff. 9/1/95; 258(10), (11), eff. 9/1/95; 260(14)-(16), eff. 5/30/95; 318(52), eff. 9/1/95; 318(53), eff. 1/1/96; 318(54)-(59), eff. 9/1/95, 318(60), (61), eff. 1/1/96; 321(3.003)-(3.008), eff. 9/1/95; 321(3.020)(a), eff. 9/1/95; 595(2), eff. 9/1/95; 657(4), eff. 6/14/95.)*

**Art. 42.121.** *(Secs. 1.01 to 2.09(b) and 3.12 to 5.07 repealed by L.1989, chap. 785(3.10); secs. 2.09(c) and 3.111 repealed by L.1995, chap. 321(3.020(b, c)), eff. 9/1/95.)*



**Art. 42.122. Adult Probation Officer of 222nd Judicial District; salary and expenses; payment by county.**

The adult probation officer of the 222nd Judicial District receives a salary of not less than $15,000 per annum. Also, the probation officer receives allowances, not to exceed the amount allowed by the federal government for traveling the most practical route to and from the place where the duties are discharged, for his necessary travel and hotel expenses. Upon the sworn statement of the officer, approved by the judge, the respective counties of the judicial district pay the expenses incurred for their regular or special term of court out of the general county fund. In lieu of travel allowances the commissioners court of each county, by agreement, may provide transportation under the same terms and conditions as provided for sheriffs.

**Art. 42.13.** *(Repealed by L.1995, chap. 76(7.10), eff. 9/1/95; chgd. by L.1995, chaps. 318(62), 321(3.009)-(3.013), eff. 9/1/95.)*

**Sec. 1.** *(Repealed by L.1997, chap. 165(12.23(b)), eff. 9/1/97.)*

**Sec. 2.** *(Repealed by L.1997, chap. 165(12.24(b)), eff. 9/1/97.)*

**Sec. 3.** *(Repealed by L.1997, chap. 165(12.25(b)), eff. 9/1/97.)*

**Sec. 4.** *(Repealed by L.1997, chap. 165(12.26(b)), eff. 9/1/97.)*

**Sec. 7.** *(Repealed by L.1997, chap. 165(12.27(b)), eff. 9/1/97.)*

**Sec. 10.** *(Repealed by L.1997, chap. 165(12.28(b)), eff. 9/1/97.)*

**Sec. 11.** *(Repealed by L.1997, chap. 165(12.29(b)), eff. 9/1/97.)*

**Art. 42.131.** *(Repealed and the substance transferred to Chapter 76, Government Code by L.1995, chap. 76(7.11),(7.12), eff. 9/1/95; chgd. by L.1995, chaps. 76(17.01(3)), eff. 9/1/95; 185(1), eff. 5/23/95; 252(1), eff. 9/1/95; 266(1), eff. 6/5/95; 321(3.014),(3.0151, eff. 9/1/95; 611(5), eff. 8/28/95.)*

**Sec. 3.** *(Repealed by L.1997, chap. 165(9.02(b), 9.03(b)), eff. 9/1/97.)*

**Sec. 12.** *(Repealed by L.1997, chaps. 165(9.04(b)), 796(1)(c), eff. 9/1/97.)*

**Sec. 13.** *(Repealed by L.1997, chap. 165(9.05(b)), eff. 9/1/97.)*

**Sec. 14.** *(Repealed by L.1997, chap. 165(9.06), eff. 9/1/97.)*

**Sec. 14.** *(Repealed by L.1997, chap. 165(9.08(b)), eff. 9/1/97.)*

**Sec. 14.** *(Repealed by L.1997, chaps. 165(9.09(b)), 1269(6(b)), eff. 9/1/97, 6/20/97, respectively.)*

**Sec. 15.** *(Repealed by L.1997, chaps. 165(9.07(b)), 983(1)(c), eff. 9/1/97.)*

## Art. 42.14. In absence of defendant.† [*Defendant not present.*]

The judgment and sentence in a misdemeanor case may be rendered in the absence of the defendant.

## Art. 42.141. Battering intervention and prevention program.

**Sec. 1. Definitions.** In this article:

(1) "Batterer" means a person who commits repeated acts of violence or who repeatedly threatens violence against another who is:

(A) related to the actor by affinity or consanguinity, as determined under Chapter 573, Government Code;

(B) is a former spouse of the actor; or

(C) resides or has resided in the same household with the actor.

(2) "Division" means the community justice assistance division of the Texas Department of Criminal Justice.

(3) "Family" has the meaning assigned by Section 71.01, Family Code.

(4) "Family violence" has the meaning assigned by Section 71.01, Family Code.

(5) "Shelter center" has the meaning assigned by Section 51.002, Human Resources Code.

(6) "Household" has the meaning assigned by Section 71.01, Family Code.

(7) "Program" means a battering intervention and prevention program operated by a nonprofit organization that provides, on a local basis to batterers referred by the courts for treatment, treatment and educational services designed to help the batterers stop their abusive behavior.

(8) "Project" means the statewide activities for the funding of battering intervention and prevention programs, the related community educational campaign, and education and research regarding such programs.

(9) "Responsive law enforcement climate" means an area where, in cases of family violence:

(A) the local law enforcement agency has a policy or record of arresting batterers; and

(B) the local criminal justice system:

(i) cooperates with the victim in filing protective orders; and

(ii) takes appropriate action against a person who violates protective orders.

**Sec. 2. Establishment.** The battering intervention and prevention program is established in the division.

**Sec. 3. Duties of the division.** The division shall:

(1) contract with a nonprofit organization that for the five-year period before the date on which a contract is to be signed has been involved in providing to shelter centers, law enforcement agencies, and the legal community statewide advocacy and technical assistance relating to family violence, with the contract requiring the nonprofit organization to perform the duties described in Section (4) of this article;

(2) seek the input of the statewide nonprofit organization described in Subdivision (1) of this section in the development of standards for selection of programs and the review of proposals submitted by programs;

(3) issue requests for proposals for the programs and an educational campaign not later than January 1, 1990;

(4) award contracts for programs that take into consideration:

(A) a balanced geographical distribution of urban, rural, and suburban models; and

(B) the presence of a responsive law enforcement climate in the community;

(5) develop and monitor the project in cooperation with the nonprofit organization;

(6) monitor the development of a community educational campaign in cooperation with the nonprofit organization;

(7) assist the nonprofit organization in designing program evaluations and research activities; and

(8) facilitate training of probation officers and other criminal justice professionals by the nonprofit organization and by programs.

**Sec. 4. Duties of the nonprofit organization.** The nonprofit organization with which the division contracts shall:

(1) assist the division in developing and issuing requests for proposals for the programs and the educational campaign;

(2) assist the division in reviewing the submitted proposals and making recommendations for proposals to be selected for funding;

(3) develop and monitor the project in cooperation with the division;

(4) provide technical assistance to programs to:

(A) develop appropriate services for batterers;

(B) train staff;

(C) improve coordination with shelter centers, the criminal justice system, the judiciary, law enforcement agencies, prosecutors, and other appropriate officials and support services;

(D) implement the community educational campaign; and

(E) participate in project administered program evaluation and research activities;

(5) provide technical assistance to the division to:

(A) develop and implement standards for selection of programs for inclusion in the project; and

(B) develop standards for selection of the community educational campaign described in Section 6 of this article;

(6) submit an annual written report to the division and to the legislature with recommendations for continuation, elimination, or changes in the project; and

(7) evaluate the programs and the community educational campaign, including an analysis of the effectiveness of the project and the level of public awareness relating to family violence.

**Sec. 5. Programs.** (a) A program proposal must:

(1) describe the counseling or treatment the program will offer;

(2) include letters from a local law enforcement agency or agencies, courts, probation officers, and other community resources describing the community's commitment to improve the criminal justice system's response to victims and batterers and to cooperate with and interact in the programs' activities;

(3) include a letter from the local shelter center describing the support services available to victims of family violence in the community and the shelter's commitment to cooperate and work with the program; and

(4) describe the public education and local community outreach activities relating to family violence currently available in the community and a statement of commitment to participate on the local level in the public educational campaign described in Section 6 of this article.

(b) A program must:

(1) be situated in a county in which a shelter center is located;

(2) offer counseling or treatment in which the primary approach is direct intervention with the batterer, on an individual or group basis, but that does not require the victim of the family violence to participate in the counseling or treatment;

(3) offer training to law enforcement prosecutors, judges, probation officers, and others on the dynamics of family violence, treatment options, and program activities; and

(4) have a system for receiving referrals from the courts and for reporting to the court regarding batterers' compliance with the treatment program.

(c) This section does not preclude a program from serving a batterer other than one who was ordered by a court to participate in the program established under this subchapter.

**Sec. 6. Community educational campaign.** (a) The division, with assistance from the nonprofit organization, shall select the community educational campaign relating to family violence after the commission has selected the programs. The campaign is to be implemented in the areas covered by the programs.

(b) The campaign shall use a variety of media, including newspapers, radio, television, and billboards, and shall focus on:

(1) the criminality of acts of violence toward family members;

(2) the consequences of family violence crimes to the batterer; and

(3) eradicating public misconceptions of family violence.

**Sec. 7. Use of legislative appropriation.** Of a legislative appropriation for the project established under this article:

(1) not more than six percent may be used by the division for management and administration of the project;

(2) not more than 14 percent may be applied to the contract between the division and the nonprofit organization; and

(3) not more than three percent may be applied to the contract for the community educational campaign.

**Sec. 8. Contract date.** The contract required under Section 3(a) of this article shall be signed not later than November 1, 1989.
*(Added by L.1989, chap. 785(3.05); chgd. by L.1991, chap. 561(11); L.1995, chap. 76(5.95)(27)), eff. 9/1/95.)*

## Art. 42.15. Fines.

(a) When the defendant is fined, the judgment shall be that the defendant pay the amount of the fine and all costs to the state.
(b) When imposing a fine and costs a court may direct a defendant:
(1) to pay the entire fine and costs when sentence is pronounced; or
(2) to pay the entire fine and costs at some later date; or
(3) to pay a specified portion of the fine and costs at designated intervals.

## Art. 42.151. Fees for abused children's counseling.

If a court orders a defendant to pay a fee under Article 37.072 of this code, the court shall assess the fee against the defendant in the same manner as other costs of prosecution are assessed against a defendant. The court may direct a defendant:
(1) to pay the entire fee when sentence is pronounced;
(2) to pay the entire fee at some later date; or
(3) to pay a specified portion of the fee at designated intervals.
*(Added by L.1989, chap. 360(3), eff. 9/1/89.)*

## Art. 42.152. Repayment of reward.

(a) If a judge orders a defendant to repay a reward or part of a reward under Article 37.073 of this code, the court shall assess this cost against the defendant in the same manner as other costs of prosecution are assessed against a defendant. The court may order the defendant to:
(1) pay the entire amount required when sentence is pronounced;
(2) pay the entire amount required at a later date specified by the court; or
(3) pay specified portions of the required amount at designated intervals.
(b) After receiving a payment from a person ordered to make the payment under this article, the clerk of the court or fee officer shall:
(1) make a record of the payment;
(2) deduct a one-time $7 processing fee from the reward repayment;
(3) forward the payment to the designated crime stoppers organization; and
(4) make a record of the forwarding of the payment.
*(Added by L.1989, chap. 611(3); redes. by L.1991, chap. 16(19.01(6)); chgd. by L.1997, chap. 700(12), eff. 9/1/97.)*

## Art. 42.16. On other judgment.

If the punishment is any other than a fine, the judgment shall specify it, and order it enforced by the proper process. It shall also adjudge the costs against the defendant, and order the collection thereof as in other cases.

## Art. 42.17. Transfer under treaty.† [*Transfer per treaty.*]

When a treaty is in effect between the United States and a foreign country providing for the transfer of convicted offenders who are citizens or nationals of foreign countries to the foreign countries of which they are citizens or nationals, the governor is authorized, subject to the terms of such treaty, to act on behalf of the State of Texas and to consent to the transfer of such convicted offenders under the provisions of Article IV, Section 11 of the Constitution of the State of Texas.

**Art. 42.18.** *(Repealed by L.1997, chap. 165(12.22), eff. 9/1/97. Former sections transferred to Government Code, Chapter 508 by L.1997, chap. 165(12.01), eff. 9/1/97, except for Section 29(a) and (h), which was transferred to Human Resources Code section 61.084 by L.1997, chap. 165(12.20), eff. 9/1/97.)*

**Sec. 2.** *(Repealed by L.1999, chap. 62(10.39)(3), eff. 9/1/99.)*

**Sec. 4.** *(Repealed by L.1999, chap. 62(10.39)(3), eff. 9/1/99.)*

Printed in the U.S.A. Zt

**Sec. 5.** *(Repealed by L.1999, chap. 62(10.39)(3), eff. 9/1/99.)*

**Sec. 6.** *(Repealed by L.1999, chap. 62(10.39)(3), eff. 9/1/99.)*

**Sec. 6A.** *(Repealed by L.1999, chap. 62(10.39)(3), eff. 9/1/99.)*

**Sec. 6C.** *(Repealed by L.1999, chap. 62(10.39)(3), eff. 9/1/99.)*

**Sec. 6D.** *(Repealed by L.1999, chap. 62(10.39)(3), eff. 9/1/99.)*

**Sec. 7.** *(Repealed by L.1999, chap. 62(10.39)(3), eff. 9/1/99.)*

**Sec. 8.** *(Repealed by L.1999, chap. 62(10.39)(1) to (5), (8) to (11), eff. 9/1/99.)*

**Sec. 8A.** *(Repealed by L.1999, chap. 62(10.39)(8), (12), eff. 9/1/99.)*

**Sec. 8B. Parolee restitution fund.**

(b) The comptroller shall be the trustee of the parolee restitution fund as provided by Section 404.073, Government Code. *(Chgd. by L.1997, chap. 1423(4.02), eff. 9/1/97.)*

**Sec. 8C.** *(Repealed by L.1999, chap. 62(10.39)(11), eff. 9/1/99.)*

**Sec. 11.** *(Repealed by L.1999, chap. 62(10.39)(3), eff. 9/1/99.)*

**Sec. 13.** *(Repealed by L.1999, chap. 62(10.39)(6), eff. 9/1/99.)*

**Sec. 13A.** *(Repealed by L.1999, chap. 62(10.39)(6), eff. 9/1/99.)*

**Sec. 14.** *(Repealed by L.1999, chap. 62(10.39)(3), (6), eff. 9/1/99.)*

**Sec. 14A.** *(Repealed by L.1999, chap. 62(10.39)(3), eff. 9/1/99.)*

**Sec. 18.** *(Repealed by L.1999, chap. 62(10.39)(10), eff. 9/1/99.)*

**Sec. 24.** *(Repealed by L.1999, chap. 62(10.39)(13), eff. 9/1/99.)*

**Sec. 25.** *(Repealed by L.1999, chap. 62(10.39)(7), eff. 9/1/99.)*

**Sec. 30.** *(Repealed by L.1999, chap. 62(10.39)(11), eff. 9/1/99.)*

**Sec. 30.** *(Expired 1/1/99.)*

## Art. 42.19. Interstate Corrections Compact.

### Article I. Purpose and Policy

The party states, desiring by common action to fully utilize and improve their institutional facilities and provide adequate programs for the confinement, treatment, and rehabilitation of various types of offenders, declare that it is the policy of each of the party states to provide such facilities and programs on a basis of cooperation with one another, thereby serving the best interests of such offenders and of society and effecting economies in capital expenditures and operational costs. The purpose of this compact is to provide for the mutual development and execution of such programs of cooperation for the confinement, treatment, and rehabilitation of offenders with the most economical use of human and material resources.

### Article II. Definitions

As used in this compact, unless the context clearly requires otherwise:

(a) "State" means a state of the United States; the United States of America; a territory or possession of the United States; the District of Columbia; the commonwealth of Puerto Rico.

(b) "Sending state" means a state party to this compact in which conviction or court commitment was had.

(c) "Receiving state" means a state party to this compact to which an inmate is sent for confinement other than a state in which conviction or court commitment was had.

(d) "Inmate" means a male or female offender who is committed, under sentence to or confined in a penal or correctional institution.

(e) "Institution" means any penal or correctional facility, including but not limited to a facility for the mentally ill or mentally defective, in which inmates as defined in (d) above may lawfully be confined.

Article III. Contracts

(a) Each party state may make one or more contracts with any one or more of the other party states for the confinement of inmates on behalf of a sending state in institutions situated within receiving states. Any such contract shall provide for:

1. Its duration.

2. Payments to be made to the receiving state by the sending state for inmate maintenance, extraordinary medical and dental expenses, and any participation in or receipt by inmates of rehabilitative or correctional services, facilities, programs, or treatment not reasonably included as part of normal maintenance.

3. Participation in programs of inmate employment, if any; the disposition or crediting of any payments received by inmates on account thereof, and the crediting of proceeds from or disposal of any products resulting therefrom.

4. Delivery and retaking of inmates.

5. Such other matters as may be necessary and appropriate to fix the obligations, responsibilities, and rights of the sending and receiving states.

(b) The terms and provisions of this compact shall be a part of any contract entered into by the authority of or pursuant thereto, and nothing in any such contract shall be inconsistent therewith.

Article IV. Procedures and Rights

(a) Whenever the duly constituted authorities in a state party to this compact, and which has entered into a contract pursuant to Article III, shall decide that confinement in, or transfer of an inmate to, an institution within the territory of another party state is necessary or desirable in order to provide adequate quarters and care or an appropriate program of rehabilitation or treatment, such official may direct that the confinement be within an institution within the territory of such other party state, the receiving state to act in that regard solely as agent for the sending state.

(b) The appropriate officials of any state party to this compact shall have access, at all reasonable times, to any institution in which it has a contractual right to confine inmates for the purpose of inspecting the facilities thereof and visiting such of its inmates as may be confined in the institution.

(c) Inmates confined in an institution pursuant to this compact shall at all times be subject to the jurisdiction of the sending state and may at any time be removed therefrom for transfer to a prison or other institution within the sending state, for transfer to another institution in which the sending state may have a contractual or other right to confine inmates, for release on probation or parole, for discharge, or for any other purpose permitted by the laws of the sending state. However, the sending state shall continue to be obligated to such payments as may be required pursuant to the terms of any contract entered into under the terms of Article III.

(d) Each receiving state shall provide regular reports to each sending state on the inmates of that sending state who are in institutions pursuant to this compact including a conduct record of each inmate and shall certify such record to the official designated by the sending state, in order that each inmate may have official review of his or her record in determining and altering the disposition of the inmate in accordance with the law which may obtain in the sending state and in order that the same may be a source of information for the sending state.

(e) All inmates who may be confined in an institution pursuant to this compact shall be treated in a reasonable and humane manner and shall be treated equally with such similar inmates of the receiving state as may be confined in the same institution. The fact of confinement in a receiving state shall not deprive any inmate so confined of any legal rights which the inmate would have had if confined in an appropriate institution of the sending state.

(f) Any hearing or hearings to which an inmate confined pursuant to this compact may be entitled by the laws of the sending state may be had before the appropriate authorities of the sending state, or of the receiving state if authorized by the sending state. The receiving state shall provide adequate facilities for such hearing as may be conducted by the appropriate officials of a sending state. In the event such hearing or hearings are had before officials of the receiving state, the governing law shall be that of the sending state and a record of the hearing or hearings as prescribed by the sending state shall be made. The record together with any recommendations of the hearing officials shall be transmitted forthwith to the official or officials before whom the hearing would have been had if it had taken place in the sending state. In any and all proceedings had pursuant to the provisions of this paragraph (f), the officials of the receiving state shall act solely as agents of the sending state and no final determination shall be made in any matter except by the appropriate officials of the sending state.

(g) Any inmate confined pursuant to this compact shall be released within the territory of the sending state unless the inmate and the sending and receiving state shall agree upon release in some other place. The sending state shall bear the cost of such return to its territory.

(h) Any inmate confined pursuant to this compact shall have any rights and all rights to participate in and derive any benefits or incur or be relieved of any obligations or have such obligations modified or his status changed on account of any action or proceeding in which he could have participated if confined in any appropriate institution of the sending state located within such state.

(i) The parent, guardian, trustee, or other person or persons entitled under the laws of the sending state to act for, advise, or otherwise function with respect to any inmate shall not be deprived of or restricted in his exercise of any power in respect of any inmate confined pursuant to the terms of this compact.

### Article V. Act Not Reviewable in Receiving State: Extradition

(a) Any decision of the sending state in respect of any matter over which it retains jurisdiction pursuant to this compact shall be conclusive upon and not reviewable within the receiving state, but if at the time the sending state seeks to remove an inmate from an institution in the receiving state there is pending against the inmate within such state any criminal charge or if the inmate is formally accused of having committed within such state a criminal offense, the inmate shall not be returned without the consent of the receiving state until discharged from prosecution or other form of proceeding, imprisonment, or detention for such offense. The duly accredited officer of the sending state shall be permitted to transport inmates pursuant to this compact through any and all states party to this compact without interference.

(b) An inmate who escapes from an institution in which he is confined pursuant to this compact shall be deemed a fugitive from the sending state and from the state in which the institution escaped from is situated. In the case of an escape to a jurisdiction other than the sending or receiving state, the responsibility for institution of extradition or rendition proceedings shall be that of the sending state, but nothing contained herein shall be construed to prevent or affect the activities of officers and agencies of any jurisdiction directed toward the apprehension and return of an escapee.

### Article VI. Federal Aid

Any state party to this compact may accept federal aid for use in connection with any institution or program, the use of which is or may be affected by this compact or any contract pursuant thereto. Any inmate in a receiving state pursuant to this compact may participate in any such federally aided program or activity for which the sending and receiving states have made contractual provision. However, if such program or activity is not part of the customary correctional regimen, the express consent of the appropriate official of the sending state shall be required therefor.

### Article VII. Entry Into Force

This compact shall enter into force and become effective and binding upon the states so acting when it has been enacted into law by any two states. Thereafter, this compact shall enter into force and become effective and binding as to any other of such states upon similar action by such state.

### Article VIII. Withdrawal and Termination

This compact shall continue in force and remain binding upon a party state until it shall have enacted a statute repealing the compact and providing for the sending of formal written notice of withdrawal from the compact to the appropriate officials of all other party states. An actual withdrawal shall not take effect until one year after the notices provided in the statute have been sent. Such withdrawal shall not relieve the withdrawing state from its obligations assumed hereunder prior to the effective date of withdrawal. Before the effective date of withdrawal, a withdrawal state shall remove to its territory, at its own expense, such inmates as it may have confined pursuant to the provisions of this compact.

### Article IX. Other Arrangements Unaffected

Nothing contained in this compact shall be construed to abrogate or impair an agreement or other arrangement which a party state may have with a nonparty state for the confinement, rehabilitation, or treatment of inmates, nor to repeal any other laws of a party state authorizing the making of cooperative institutional arrangements.

Article X. Construction and Severability

(a) The provisions of this compact shall be liberally construed and shall be severable. If any phrase, clause, sentence, or provision of this compact is declared to be contrary to the constitution of any participating state or of the United States or the applicability thereof to any government, agency, person, or circumstance is held invalid, the validity of the remainder of this compact and the applicability thereof to any government, agency, person, or circumstance shall not be affected thereby. If this compact shall be held contrary to the constitution of any state participating therein, the compact shall remain in full force and effect as to the remaining states and in full force and effect as to the state affected as to all severable matters.

(b) Powers. The director of the Texas Department of Corrections is authorized and directed to do all things necessary or incidental to the carrying out of the compact in every particular.

## Art. 42.20. Immunities.

(a) An individual listed in Subsection (c) of this article and the governmental entity that the individual serves as an officer or employee are not liable for damages arising from an act or failure to act by the individual or governmental entity in connection with a community service program or work program established under this chapter or in connection with an inmate, offender, or releasee programmatic or nonprogrammatic activity, including work, educational, and treatment activities, if the act or failure to act:

(1) was performed pursuant to a court order or was otherwise performed in an official capacity; and

(2) was not performed with conscious indifference for the safety of others.

(b) Chapter 101, Civil Practice and Remedies Code, does not apply to a claim based on an act or a failure to act of an individual listed in Subsection (c) of this article or a governmental entity the officer serves as an officer or employee if the act or failure to act is in connection with a program described by Subsection (a) of this article.

(c) This article applies to:

(1) a director or employee of a community supervision and corrections department or a community corrections facility;

(2) a sheriff or employee of a sheriff's department;

(3) a county judge, county commissioner, or county employee;

(4) an officer or employee of a state agency; or

(5) an officer or employee of a political subdivision other than a county.

*(Added by L.1993, chap. 900(5.03); chgd. by L.1995, chap. 76(3.13), eff. 9/1/95.)*

## Art. 42.21. Notice of release of family violence offenders.

(a) Before releasing a person convicted of a family violence offense, the entity holding the person shall make a reasonable attempt to give personal notice of the imminent release to the victim of the offense or to another person designated by the victim to receive the notice. An attempt by an entity to give notice to the victim or person designated by the victim at the victim's or person's last known telephone number or address, as shown on the records of the entity, constitutes a reasonable attempt to give notice under this subsection.

(b) An entity or an employee of an entity is not liable for damages arising from complying or failing to comply with Subsection (a) of this article.

(c) In this article, "family violence" has the meaning assigned by Section 71.01, Family Code.

*(Added by L.1995, chap. 661(2), eff. 8/28/95.)*

## Art. 42.22. Restitution liens.

**Sec. 1. Definitions.** In this article:

(1) "Department" means the Texas Department of Transportation.

(2) "Motor vehicle" has the meaning assigned by Chapter 501, Transportation Code.

(3) "State" means the State of Texas and all political subdivisions thereof.

(4) "Victim" means a "close relative of a deceased victim," "guardian of a victim," or "victim," as those terms are defined by Article 56.01 of this code.

(5) "Personal property" means any property other than real property including all tangible and intangible types of property and including but not limited to copyrights, book rights, movie rights, patents, and trademarks acquired by the defendant prior to, during, and after conviction.

**Sec. 2. Lien established.** (a) The victim of a criminal offense has a restitution lien to secure the amount of restitution to which the victim is entitled under the order of a court in a criminal case.

Printed in the U.S.A.

(b) The state also has a restitution lien to secure the:

(1) amount of fines or costs entered against a defendant in the judgment in a felony criminal case; and

(2) amount of reimbursement for costs of confinement ordered under Article 42.038. *(Chgd. by L.1999, chap. 295(2), eff. 9/1/99.)*

**Sec. 3. Perfection.** (a) Except as provided by this section, a restitution lien attaches and is perfected when an affidavit to perfect the lien is filed in accordance with this article.

(b) If a lien established under this article is attached to a motor vehicle, the lien must be perfected in the manner provided by Chapter 501, Transportation Code, and the court that entered the order of restitution giving rise to the lien shall include in the order a requirement that the defendant surrender to the court evidence of current legal ownership of the motor vehicle and the title, if applicable, against which the lien attaches. A lien against a motor vehicle as provided by this article is not perfected until the defendant's title to the vehicle has been surrendered to the court and the department has issued a subsequent title that discloses on its face the fact that the vehicle is subject to a restitution lien established as provided by this article.





**Sec. 4. Judgment required.** An affidavit to perfect a restitution lien may not be filed under this article until a court has ordered restitution or entered a judgment requiring the defendant to pay a fine or costs.

**Sec. 5. Persons who may file.** The following persons may file an affidavit to perfect a restitution lien:

(1) the attorney representing the state in a criminal case in which a victim is determined by the court to be entitled to restitution or in which a defendant is ordered to pay fines or costs; or

(2) a victim in a criminal case determined by the court to be entitled to restitution.

**Sec. 6. Affidavit.** An affidavit to perfect a restitution lien must be signed by the attorney representing the state or a magistrate and must contain:

(1) the name and date of birth of the defendant whose property or other interests are subject to the lien;

(2) the residence or principal place of business of the person named in the lien, if known;

(3) the criminal proceeding giving rise to the lien, including the name of the court, the name of the case, and the court's file number for the case;

(4) the name and address of the attorney representing the state and the name of the person entitled to restitution;

(5) a statement that the notice is being filed under this article;

(6) the amount of restitution and the amount of fines and costs the defendant has been ordered to pay by the court;

(7) a statement that the amount of restitution owed at any one time may be less than the original balance and that the outstanding balance is reflected in the records of the clerk of the court hearing the criminal proceeding giving rise to the lien; and

(8) the vehicle description and vehicle identification number.

**Sec. 7. Filing.** (a) An affidavit to perfect a restitution lien may be filed with:

(1) the secretary of state;

(2) the department in the manner provided by Chapter 501, Transportation Code; or

(3) the county clerk of the county in which:

(A) the crime was committed;

(B) the defendant resides; or

(C) the property is located.

(b) The uniform fee for filing and indexing and for stamping a copy furnished by the state or victim to show the date and place of filing is $5.

(c) The secretary of state shall deposit the filing fee in the state treasury to the credit of the statutory filing fund solely to defray the costs of administration of this section. The department shall deposit the filing fee in the state treasury to the credit of the state highway fund to be used solely to defray the costs of administering this section.

(d) The county clerk shall immediately record the restitution lien in the judgment records of the county. The clerk shall note in the records the date and hour the lien is received.

(e) The secretary of state shall immediately file the restitution lien in the security interest and financing statement records of the secretary of state. The secretary of state shall note in the records the date and hour the lien is received.

(f) The department shall immediately file the restitution lien in the motor vehicle records of the department. The department shall note in the records the date and hour the lien is received.

(g) When a restitution lien is filed, the county clerk or secretary of state shall enter the restitution lien in an alphabetical index to the records in which the lien is filed showing:

(1) the name of the person entitled to restitution;

(2) the name of the defendant obligated to pay restitution, fines, or costs;

(3) the amount of the lien; and

(4) the name of the court that ordered restitution.

(h) A person who files an affidavit to perfect a restitution lien under this article shall notify in writing the clerk of the court entering the judgment creating the lien of all officers or entities with which the affidavit was filed.

**Sec. 8. Subject property.** A restitution lien extends to:

(1) any interest of the defendant in real property whether then owned or after-acquired located in a county in which the lien is perfected by the filing of an affidavit with the county clerk;

(2) any interest of the defendant in tangible or intangible personal property whether then owned or after-acquired other than a motor vehicle if the lien is perfected by the filing of the affidavit with the secretary of state; or

(3) any interest of the defendant in a motor vehicle whether then owned or after-acquired if the lien is perfected by the filing of the affidavit with the department.





**Sec. 9. Priority.** The perfection of a restitution lien under this article is notice of the claim to all persons dealing with the defendant or the property identified in the affidavit perfecting the lien. Without regard to whether perfected before or after the perfection of a restitution lien filed and perfected under this article, a perfected real estate mortgage lien, a vendor's lien, a purchase money security interest, a chattel paper security interest, a lien on a motor vehicle perfected as provided by Chapter 501, Transportation Code, or a worker's lien perfected in the manner provided by law is superior and prior to a restitution lien filed and perfected under this article. Except as provided by this article, a perfected lien in favor of a victim is superior and prior to a lien perfected by the state under this article, and the perfected lien in favor of the state is superior and prior to the claim or interest of any other person, other than:

(1) a person who acquires a valid lien or security interest perfected before the perfection of the restitution lien;

(2) a bona fide purchaser who acquires an interest in the property, if personal property, before the filing of the restitution lien, to the extent that the purchaser gives value; or

(3) a bona fide purchaser for value who acquires and files for record an interest in the property, if real property, before the perfection of the restitution lien.

**Sec. 10. Payment.** The clerk receiving a payment from a defendant ordered to pay restitution shall make payments to the person having an interest in the restitution lien on a schedule of not less than quarterly payments as determined by the clerk or agency.

**Sec. 11. Foreclosure.** If a defendant fails to timely make a payment required by the order of the court entering the judgment creating the restitution lien, the person having an interest in the lien may file suit in a court of competent jurisdiction to foreclose the lien. If the defendant cures the default on or before the 20th day after the date the suit is filed and pays the person who files the suit costs of court and reasonable attorney's fees, the court may dismiss the suit without prejudice to the person. The person may refile the suit against the defendant if the defendant subsequently defaults.

**Sec. 12. Expiration; records.** (a) A restitution lien expires on the 10th anniversary of the date the lien was filed or on the date the defendant satisfies the judgment creating the lien, whichever occurs first. The person having an interest in the lien may refile the lien before the date the lien expires. A lien that is refiled expires on the 10th anniversary of the date the lien was refiled or the date the defendant satisfies the judgment creating the lien, whichever occurs first.

(b) Failure to execute or foreclose the restitution lien does not cause dormancy of the lien.

(c) The clerk of the court entering the judgment creating the restitution lien shall maintain a record of the outstanding balance of restitution, fines, or costs owed. If the defendant satisfies the judgment, the clerk shall immediately execute and file for record a release of the restitution lien with all officers or entities with which the affidavit perfecting the lien was filed, as indicated by the notice received by the clerk under Section 7(h) of this article, unless a release was executed and filed by the person who filed the affidavit to perfect the lien.

(d) A partial release of a lien as to specific property may be executed by the attorney representing the state or a magistrate who signs an affidavit described by Section 6 of this article on payment of a sum determined to represent the defendant's interest in any property to which the lien may attach.
*(Added by L.1995, chap. 997(1); renumbered from Art. 42.21 by L.1997, chap. 165(31.01(12)), eff. 9/1/97; chgd. by L.1997, chap. 1118(1), eff. 6/19/97.)*

## CHAPTER 43. EXECUTION OF JUDGMENT

Article





### Art. 43.01. Discharging judgment for fine.

(a) When the sentence against an individual defendant is for fine and costs, he shall be discharged from the same:

(1) when the amount thereof has been fully paid;

(2) when remitted by the proper authority;

(3) when he has remained in custody for the time required by law to satisfy the amount thereof; or

(4) when the defendant has discharged the amount of fines and costs in any other manner permitted by this code.

(b) When the sentence against a defendant corporation or association is for fine and costs, it shall be discharged from same:

(1) when the amount thereof has been fully paid;

(2) when the execution against the corporation or association has been fully satisfied; or

(3) when the judgment has been fully satisfied in any other manner.

*(Chgd. by L.1993, chap. 900(5.04), eff. 9/1/93.)*

### Art. 43.02. Payable in money.† [*Fines payable in U.S. money only.*]

All recognizances, bail bonds, and undertakings of any kind, whereby a party becomes bound to pay money to the State, and all fines and forfeitures of a pecuniary character, shall be collected in the lawful money of the United States only.

## Art. 43.03. Payment of fine.

(a) If a defendant is sentenced to pay a fine or costs or both and he defaults in payment, the court after a hearing under Subsection (d) of this article may order him confined in jail until discharged as provided by law or may order him to discharge the fines and costs in any other manner provided by Article 43.09 of this code. A certified copy of the judgment, sentence, and order is sufficient to authorize confinement under this subsection.

(b) A term of confinement for default in payment of fine or costs or both may not exceed the maximum term of confinement authorized for the offense for which the defendant was sentenced to pay the fine or costs or both. If a court orders a term of confinement for default in payment of fines or costs under this article at a time during which a defendant is serving another term of confinement for default or is serving a term of confinement for conviction of an offense, the term of confinement for default runs concurrently with the other term of confinement, unless the court orders the terms to run consecutively under Article 42.08 of this code.

(c) If a defendant is sentenced both to confinement and to pay a fine or costs or both, and he defaults in payment of either, a term of confinement for the default, when combined with the term of confinement already assessed, may not exceed the maximum term of confinement authorized for the offense for which the defendant was sentenced.

(d) A court may not order a defendant confined under Subsection (a) of this article unless the court at a hearing:

(1) determines that the defendant is not indigent or determines that the defendant wilfully refused to pay or failed to make sufficient bona fide efforts legally to acquire the resources to pay and enters that determination in writing in the court docket; and

(2) determines that no alternative method of discharging fines and costs provided by Article 43.09 of this code is appropriate for the defendant.

*(Chgd. by L.1993, chap. 900(5.04), eff. 9/1/93.)*

## Art. 43.04. If defendant is absent.† [*Absence of defendant.*]

When a judgment and sentence have been rendered against a defendant for a fine in his absence, the court may order a capias issued for his arrest. The sheriff shall execute the capias by bringing the defendant before the court or by placing the defendant in jail until he can be brought before the court.

## Art. 43.05. Capias shall recite what.† [*Content of capias.*]

Where such capias issues, it shall state the rendition and amount of the judgment and sentence, and command the sheriff to bring the defendant before the court or place him in jail until he can be brought before the court.

## Art. 43.06. Capias may issue to any county.† [*Execution of capias in any county.*]

The capias provided for in this Chapter may be issued to any county in the State, and shall be executed and returned as in other cases, but no bail shall be taken in such cases.

## Art. 43.07. Execution for fine and costs.† [*Execution of capias for fine and costs.*]

In each case of pecuniary fine, an execution may issue for the fine and costs, though a capias was issued for the defendant; and a capias may issue for the defendant though an execution was issued against his property. The execution shall be collected and returned as in civil actions. When the execution has been collected, the defendant shall be at once discharged; and whenever the fine and costs have been legally discharged in any way, the execution shall be returned satisfied.

## Art. 43.08. Further enforcement of judgment.

When a defendant has been committed to jail in default of the fine and costs adjudged against him, the further enforcement of such judgment and sentence shall be in accordance with the provisions of this Code.

## Art. 43.09. Fine discharged.

(a) When a defendant is convicted of a misdemeanor and his punishment is assessed at a pecuniary fine or is confined in a jail after conviction of a felony for which a fine is imposed, if he is unable to pay the fine and costs adjudged against him, he may for such time as will satisfy the judgment be put to work in the county jail industries program, in the workhouse, or on the county farm, or public improvements and maintenance projects of the county or a political subdivision located in whole or in part in the county, as provided in the succeeding article; or if there be no such county jail industries program, workhouse, farm, or improvements and maintenance projects, he shall be confined in jail for a sufficient length of time to discharge the full amount of fine and costs adjudged against him; rating such confinement at $50 for each day and rating such labor at $50 for each day; provided, however, that the defendant may pay the pecuniary fine assessed against him at any time while he is serving at work in the county jail industries program, in the workhouse, or on the county farm, or on the public improvements and maintenance projects of the county or a political subdivision located in whole or in part in the county, or while he is serving his jail sentence, and in such instances he shall be entitled to the credit he has earned under this subsection during the time that he has served and he shall only be required to pay his balance of the pecuniary fine assessed against him. A defendant who performs labor under this article during a day in which he is confined is entitled to both the credit for confinement and the credit for labor provided by this article.

(b) In its discretion, the court may order that for each day's confinement served by a defendant under this article, the defendant receive credit toward payment of the pecuniary fine and credit toward payment of costs adjudged against the defendant. Additionally, the court may order that the defendant receive credit under this article for each day's confinement served by the defendant as punishment for the offense.

(c) In its discretion, the court may order that a defendant serving concurrent, but not consecutive, sentences for two or more misdemeanors may, for each day served, receive credit toward the satisfaction of costs and fines imposed for each separate offense.

(d) Notwithstanding any other provision of this article, in its discretion, the court or the sheriff of the county may grant an additional two days credit for each day served to any inmate participating in an approved work program under this article or a rehabilitation, restitution, or education program.

(e) A court in a county served by a community supervision and corrections department that has an electronic monitoring program approved by the community justice assistance division of the Texas Department of Criminal Justice may require a defendant who is unable to pay a fine or costs to discharge all or part of the fine or costs by submitting to electronic monitoring. A defendant that submits to electronic monitoring under this subsection discharges fines and costs in the same manner as if the defendant were confined in county jail.

(f) A court may require a defendant who is unable to pay a fine or costs to discharge all or part of the fine or costs by performing community service.

(g) In its order requiring a defendant to participate in community service work under Subsection (f) of this article, the court must specify:

(1) the number of hours the defendant is required to work; and

(2) whether the community supervision and corrections department or a court-related services office will perform the administrative duties required by the placement of the defendant in the community service program.

(h) The court may order the defendant to perform community service work under Subsection (f) of this article only for a governmental entity or a nonprofit organization that provides services to the general public that enhance social welfare and the general well-being of the community. A governmental entity or nonprofit organization that accepts a defendant under Subsection (f) of this article to perform community service must agree to supervise the defendant in the performance of the defendant's work and report on the defendant's work to the district probation department or court-related services office.

(i) The court may require bail of a defendant to ensure the defendant's faithful performance of community service under Subsection (f) of this article and may attach conditions to the bail as it determines are proper.

(j) A court may not order a defendant to perform more than 16 hours per week of community service under Subsection (f) of this article unless the court determines that requiring the defendant to work additional hours does not work a hardship on the defendant or the defendant's dependents.

(k) A defendant is considered to have discharged $100 of fines or costs for each eight hours of community service performed under Subsection (f) of this article.

(*l*) A sheriff, employee of a sheriff's department, county commissioner, county employee, county judge, an employee of a community corrections and supervision department, restitution center, or officer or employee of a political subdivision other than a county is not liable for damages arising from an act or failure to act in connection with manual labor performed by an inmate pursuant to this article if the act or failure to act:

(1) was performed pursuant to confinement or other court order; and

(2) was not intentional, wilfully or wantonly negligent, or performed with conscious indifference or reckless disregard for the safety of others.

(m) Fines and costs imposed by a municipal court, regardless of whether the court is a court of record, may be discharged in the manner provided by Subsection (f) of this article. A community supervision and corrections department or a court-related services office may provide the admin-

istrative duties and other services necessary for the placement in programs under this article of a defendant convicted in a municipal court, regardless of whether the municipal court is a court of record.
*(Chgd. by L.1989, chaps. 753(1), 785(4.13), 1040(3), (4); L.1991, chap. 16(4.06); L.1993, chaps. 414(1), 578(2), 900(5.04); L.1999, chap. 1545(3), eff. 9/1/99.)*

### Art. 43.10. Manual labor.

Where the punishment assessed in a conviction for misdemeanor is confinement in jail for more than one day, or where in such conviction the punishment is assessed only at a pecuniary fine and the party so convicted is unable to pay the fine and costs adjudged against him, or where the party is sentenced to jail for a felony or is confined in jail after conviction of a felony, the party convicted shall be required to work in the county jail industries program or shall be required to do manual labor in accordance with the provisions of this article under the following rules and regulations:

1. Each commissioners court may provide for the erection of a workhouse and the establishment of a county farm in connection therewith for the purpose of utilizing the labor of said parties so convicted;
2. Such farms and workhouses shall be under the control and management of the sheriff, and the sheriff may adopt such rules and regulations not inconsistent with the rules and regulations of the Commission on Jail Standards and with the laws as the sheriff deems necessary;
3. Such overseers and guards may be employed by the sheriff under the authority of the commissioners court as may be necessary to prevent escapes and to enforce such labor, and they shall be paid out of the county treasury such compensation as the commissioners court may prescribe;
4. They shall be put to labor upon public works and maintenance projects, including public works and maintenance projects for a political subdivision located in whole or in part in the county;
5. One who from age, disease, or other physical or mental disability is unable to do manual labor shall not be required to work. His inability to do manual labor may be determined by a physician appointed for that purpose by the county judge or the commissioners court, who shall be paid for such service such compensation as said court may allow; and
6. For each day of manual labor, in addition to any other credits allowed by law, a defendant is entitled to have one day deducted from each sentence he is serving. The deduction authorized by this article, when combined with the deduction required by Article 42.10 of this code, may not exceed two-thirds (⅔) of the sentence.

*(Chgd. by L.1989, chaps. 753(2), 785(4.14); L.1991, chap. 900(2), 2nd C.S., chap. 10(14.09); L.1993, chap. 578(3), 900(5.04); L.1995, chaps. 76(3.19), 321(3.015), eff. 9/1/95.)*

### Art. 43.101. Voluntary work.

(a) A defendant confined in county jail awaiting trial or a defendant confined in county jail after conviction of a felony or revocation of community supervision, parole, or mandatory supervision and awaiting transfer to the institutional division of the Texas Department of Criminal Justice may volunteer to participate in any work program operated by the sheriff that uses the labor of convicted defendants.

(b) The sheriff may accept a defendant as a volunteer under Subsection (a) of this section if the defendant is not awaiting trial for an offense involving violence or is not awaiting transfer to the institutional division of the Texas Department of Criminal Justice after conviction of a felony involving violence, and if the sheriff determines that the inmate has not engaged previously in violent conduct and does not pose a security risk to the general public if allowed to participate in the work program.

(c) A defendant participating in a work program under this section is not an employee for the purposes of Chapter 501 or 504, Labor Code.

*(Added by L.1989, chap. 753(3); chgd. by L.1993, chaps. 86(1), 900(5.04); L.1995, chap. 76(3.20), eff. 9/1/95.)*

### Art. 43.11. Authority for confinement.

When, by the judgment and sentence of the court, a defendant is to be confined in jail, a certified copy of such judgment and sentence shall be sufficient authority for the sheriff to place such defendant in jail. *(Chgd. by L.1993, chap. 900(5.04), eff. 9/1/93.)*

### Art. 43.12. Capias for confinement.

A capias issued for the arrest and commitment of one convicted of a misdemeanor, the penalty of which or any part thereof is a fine, shall recite the judgment and sentence and command the sheriff to immediately bring the defendant before the court; and this writ shall be sufficient to authorize the sheriff to place the defendant in jail until the defendant appears before the court. *(Chgd. by L.1993, chap. 900(5.04), eff. 9/1/93.)*

### Art. 43.13. Discharge of defendant.

(a) A defendant who has remained in jail the length of time required by the judgment and sentence shall be discharged. The sheriff shall return the copy of the judgment and sentence, or the capias under which the defendant was imprisoned, to the proper court, stating how it was executed.

(b) A defendant convicted of a misdemeanor and sentenced to a term of confinement of more than 30 days discharges the defendant's sentence at any time between the hours of 6 a.m. and 7 p.m. on the day of discharge.

*(Chgd. by L.1997, chap. 714(1), eff. 9/1/97.)*



### Art. 43.131. Immunities.

(a) An individual listed in Subsection (c) of this article and the governmental entity that the individual serves as an officer or employee are not liable for damages arising from an act or failure to act by the individual or governmental entity in connection with a community service program or work program established under this chapter if the act or failure to act:

(1) was performed pursuant to a court order or was otherwise performed in an official capacity; and

(2) was not performed with conscious indifference for the safety of others.

(b) Chapter 101, Civil Practice and Remedies Code, does not apply to a claim based on an act or a failure to act of an individual listed in Subsection (c) of this article or a governmental entity the officer serves as an officer or employee if the act or failure to act is in connection with a program described by Subsection (a) of this article.

(c) This article applies to:

(1) a director or employee of a community supervision and corrections department or a community corrections facility;

(2) a sheriff or employee of a sheriff's department;

(3) a county judge, county commissioner, or county employee;

(4) an officer or employee of a state agency; or

(5) an officer or employee of a political subdivision other than a county.

*(Added by L.1993, chap. 900(5.04), eff. 9/1/93.)*

### Art. 43.14. Execution of convict.

Whenever the sentence of death is pronounced against a convict, the sentence shall be executed at any time after the hour of 6 p.m. on the day set for the execution, by intravenous injection of a substance or substances in a lethal quantity sufficient to cause death and until such convict is dead, such execution procedure to be determined and supervised by the Director of the institutional division of the Texas Department of Criminal Justice. *(Chgd. by L.1991, chap. 652(11); L.1995, chap. 319(3), eff. 9/1/95.)*

### Art. 43.141. Scheduling of execution date; withdrawal; modification.

(a) If an initial application under Article 11.071 is timely filed, the convicting court may not set an execution date before:

(1) the court of criminal appeals denies relief; or

(2) if the case is filed and set for submission, the court of criminal appeals issues a mandate.

(b) If an original application is not timely filed under Article 11.071 or good cause is not shown for an untimely application under Article 11.071, the convicting court may set an execution date.

(c) The first execution date may not be earlier than the 91st day after the date the convicting court enters the order setting the execution date. A subsequent execution date may not be earlier than the 31st day after the date the convicting court enters the order setting the execution date.

(d) The convicting court may modify or withdraw the order of the court setting a date for execution in a death penalty case if the court determines that additional proceedings are necessary on a subsequent or untimely application for a writ of habeas corpus filed under Article 11.071.

(e) If the convicting court withdraws the order of the court setting the execution date, the court shall recall the warrant of execution. If the court modifies the order of the court setting the execution date, the court shall recall the previous warrant of execution, and the clerk of the court shall issue a new warrant.

*(Added by L.1995, chap. 319(4), eff. 9/1/95.)*

### Art. 43.15. Warrant of execution.

Whenever any person is sentenced to death, the clerk of the court in which the sentence is pronounced, shall within ten days after the court enters its order setting the date for execution, issue a warrant under the seal of the court for the execution of the sentence of death, which shall recite the fact of conviction, setting forth specifically the offense, the judgment of the court, the time fixed for his execution, and directed to the Director of the Department of Corrections at Huntsville, Texas, commanding him to proceed, at the time and place named in the order of execution, to carry the same into execution, as provided in the preceding Article, and shall deliver such warrant to the sheriff of the county in which such judgment of conviction was had, to be by him delivered to the said Director of the Department of Corrections, together with the condemned person if he has not previously been so delivered.

### Art. 43.16. Taken to Department of Corrections.† [*Prisoner conveyed to Department of Corrections.*]

Immediately upon the receipt of such warrant, the sheriff shall transport such condemned person to the Director of the Department of Corrections, if he has not already been so delivered, and shall deliver him and the warrant aforesaid into the hands of the Director of the Department of Corrections and shall take from the Director of the Department of Corrections his receipt for such person and such warrant, which receipt the sheriff shall return to the office of the clerk of the court where the judgment of death was rendered. For his services, the sheriff shall be entitled to the same compensation as is now allowed by law to sheriffs for removing or conveying prisoners under the provisions of Section 4 of Article 1029 or 1030 of the Code of Criminal Procedure of 1925, as amended.

### Art. 43.17. Visitors.

Upon the receipt of such condemned person by the Director of the Department of Corrections, the condemned person shall be confined therein until the time for his or her execution arrives, and while so confined, all persons outside of said prison shall be denied access to him or her, except his or her physician, lawyer, and clergyperson, who shall be admitted to see him or her when necessary for his or her health or for the transaction of business, and the relatives and friends of the condemned person, who shall be admitted to see and converse with him or her at all proper times, under such reasonable rules and regulations as may be made by the Board of Directors of the Department of Corrections.

### Art. 43.18. Executioner.

The Director of the Texas Department of Corrections, shall designate an executioner to carry out the death penalty provided by law.

### Art. 43.19. Place of execution.† [*Location of execution.*]

The execution shall take place at a location designated by the Texas Department of Corrections in a room arranged for that purpose.

### Art. 43.20. Present at execution.† [*Persons permitted to attend execution.*]

The following persons may be present at the execution: the executioner, and such persons as may be necessary to assist him in conducting the execution; after the Board of Directors of the Department of Corrections, two physicians, including the prison physician, the spiritual advisor of the condemned, the chaplains of the Department of Corrections, the county judge and sheriff of the county in which the Department of Corrections is situated, and any of the relatives or friends of the condemned person that he may request, not exceeding five in number, shall be admitted. No convict shall be permitted by the prison authorities to witness the execution.

### Art. 43.21. Escape after sentence.† [*Escape of condemned after sentence.*]

If the condemned escape after sentence and before his delivery to the Director of the Department of Corrections, and be not rearrested until after the time fixed for execution, any person may arrest and commit him to the jail of the county in which he was sentenced; and thereupon the court by whom the condemned was sentenced; either in term-time or vacation, on notice of such arrest being given by the sheriff, shall again appoint a time for the execution, not less than thirty days from such appointment, which appointment shall be by the clerk of said court immediately certified to the Director of the Department of Corrections and such clerk shall place such certificate in the hands of the sheriff, who shall deliver the same, together with the warrant aforesaid and the condemned person to the Director of the Department of Corrections, who shall receipt to the sheriff for the same and proceed at the appointed time to carry the sentence of death into execution as hereinabove provided.

**Art. 43.22. Escape from Department of Corrections.† [*Escape of condemned from Department of Corrections.*]**

If the condemned person escapes after his delivery to the Director of the Department of Corrections, and is not retaken before the time appointed for his execution, any person may arrest and commit him to the Director of the Department of Corrections whereupon the Director of the Department of Corrections shall certify the fact of his escape and recapture to the court in which sentence was passed; and the court, either in term-time or vacation, shall again appoint a time for the execution which shall not be less than thirty days from the date of such appointment; and thereupon the clerk of such court shall certify such appointment to the Director of the Department of Corrections, who shall proceed at the time so appointed to execute the condemned, as hereinabove provided. The sheriff or other officer or other person performing any service under this and the preceding Article shall receive the same compensation as is provided for similar services under the provisions of Articles 1029 or 1030 of the Code of Criminal Procedure of 1925, as amended. If for any reason execution is delayed beyond the date set, then the court which originally sentenced the defendant may set a later date for execution.



**Art. 43.23. Return of director.† [*Return of warrant by Director.*]**

When the execution of sentence is suspended or respited to another date, same shall be noted on the warrant and on the arrival of such date, the Director of the Department of Corrections shall proceed with such execution; and in case of death of any condemned person before the time for his execution arrives, or if he should be pardoned or his sentence commuted by the Governor, no execution shall be had; but in such cases, as well as when the sentence is executed, the Director of the Department of Corrections shall return the warrant and certificate with a statement of any such act and his proceedings endorsed thereon, together with a statement showing what disposition was made of the dead body of the convict, to the clerk of the court in which the sentence was passed, who shall record the warrant and return in the minutes of the court.

**Art. 43.24. Treatment of condemned.† [*Treatment of prisoner.*]**

No torture, or ill treatment, or unnecessary pain, shall be inflicted upon a prisoner to be executed under the sentence of the law.

**Art. 43.25. Body of convict.† [*Corpse of condemned.*]**

The body of a convict who has been legally executed shall be embalmed immediately and so directed by the Director of the Department of Corrections. If the body is not demanded or requested by a relative or bona fide friend within forty-eight hours after execution then it shall be delivered to the Anatomical Board of the State of Texas, if requested by the Board. If the body is requested by a relative, bona fide friend, or the Anatomical Board of the State of Texas, such recipient shall pay a fee of not to exceed twenty-five dollars to the mortician for his services in embalming the body for which the mortician shall issue to the recipient a written receipt. When such receipt is delivered to the Director of the Department of Corrections, the body of the deceased shall be delivered to the party named in the receipt or his authorized agent. If the body is not delivered to a relative, bona fide friend, or the Anatomical Board of the State of Texas, the Director of the Department of Corrections shall cause the body to be decently buried, and the fee for embalming shall be paid by the county in which the indictment which resulted in conviction was found.

**Art. 43.26. Preventing rescue.† [*Preventing rescue of prisoner.*]**

The sheriff may, when he supposes there will be a necessity, order such number of citizens of his county, or request any military or militia company, to aid in preventing the rescue of a prisoner.

## APPEAL AND WRIT OF ERROR

## CHAPTER 44. APPEAL AND WRIT OF ERROR

Article

## Art. 44.01. Appeal by state.† [*Appeal of order in criminal case by state.*]

(a) The state is entitled to appeal an order of a court in a criminal case if the order:

(1) dismisses an indictment, information, or complaint or any portion of an indictment, information, or complaint;

(2) arrests or modifies a judgment;

(3) grants a new trial;

(4) sustains a claim of former jeopardy; or

(5) grants a motion to suppress evidence, a confession, or an admission, if jeopardy has not attached in the case and if the prosecuting attorney certifies to the trial court that the appeal is not taken for the purpose of delay and that the evidence, confession, or admission is of substantial importance in the case.

(b) The state is entitled to appeal a sentence in a case on the ground that the sentence is illegal.

(c) The state is entitled to appeal a ruling on a question of law if the defendant is convicted in the case and appeals the judgment.

(d) The prosecuting attorney may not make an appeal under Subsection (a) or (b) of this article later than the 15th day after the date on which the order, ruling, or sentence to be appealed is entered by the court.

(e) The state is entitled to a stay in the proceedings pending the disposition of an appeal under Subsection (a) or (b) of this article.

(f) The court of appeals shall give precedence in its docket to an appeal filed under Subsection (a) or (b) of this article. The state shall pay all costs of appeal under Subsection (a) or (b) of this article, other than the cost of attorney's fees for the defendant.

(g) If the state appeals pursuant to this article and the defendant is on bail, he shall be permitted to remain at large on the existing bail. If the defendant is in custody, he is entitled to reasonable bail, as provided by law, unless the appeal is from an order which would terminate the prosecution, in which event the defendant is entitled to release on personal bond.

(h) The Texas Rules of Appellate Procedure apply to a petition by the state to the Court of Criminal Appeals for review of a decision of a court of appeals in a criminal case.

(i) In this article, "prosecuting attorney" means the county attorney, district attorney, or criminal district attorney who has the primary responsibility of prosecuting cases in the court hearing the case and does not include an assistant prosecuting attorney.

(j) Nothing in this article is to interfere with the defendant's right to appeal under the procedures of Article 44.02 of this code. The defendant's right to appeal under Article 44.02 may be prosecuted by the defendant where the punishment assessed is in accordance with Subsection (a),

Section 3d, Article 42.12 of this code, as well as any other punishment assessed in compliance with Article 44.02 of this code.

**Art. 44.02. Defendant may appeal.† [*Appeal by defendant.*]**

A defendant in any criminal action has the right of appeal under the rules hereinafter prescribed, provided, however, before the defendant who has been convicted upon either his plea of guilty or plea of nolo contendere before the court and the court, upon the election of the defendant, assesses punishment and the punishment does not exceed the punishment recommended by the prosecutor and agreed to by the defendant and his attorney may prosecute his appeal, he must have permission of the trial court, except on those matters which have been raised by written motion filed prior to trial. This article in no way affects appeals pursuant to Article 44.17 of this chapter.

**Art. 44.04. Bond pending appeal.† [*Release on bond pending appeal.*]**

(a) Pending the determination of any motion for new trial or the appeal from any misdemeanor conviction, the defendant is entitled to be released on reasonable bail, and if a defendant is charged with a misdemeanor is on bail, is convicted, and appeals that conviction, his bond is not discharged until his conviction is final or in the case of an appeal to a court where a trial de novo is held, he files an appeal bond as required by this code for appeal from the conviction.

(b) The defendant may not be released on bail pending the appeal from any felony conviction where the punishment equals or exceeds 10 years confinement or where the defendant has been convicted of an offense listed under Section 3g(a)(1), Article 42.12, but shall immediately be placed in custody and the bail discharged.

(c) Pending the appeal from any felony conviction other than a conviction described in Subsection (b) of this section, the trial court may deny bail and commit the defendant to custody if there then exists good cause to believe that the defendant would not appear when his conviction became final or is likely to commit another offense while on bail, permit the defendant to remain at large on the existing bail, or, if not then on bail, admit him to reasonable bail until his conviction becomes final. The court may impose reasonable conditions on bail pending the finality of his conviction. On a finding by the court on a preponderance of the evidence of a violation of a condition, the court may revoke the bail.

(d) After conviction, either pending determination of any motion for new trial or pending final determination of the appeal, the court in which trial was had may increase or decrease the amount of bail, as it deems proper, either upon its own motion or the motion of the State or of the defendant.

(e) Any bail entered into after conviction and the sureties on the bail must be approved by the court where trial was had. Bail is sufficient if it substantially meets the requirements of this code and may be entered into and given at any term of court.

(f) In no event shall the defendant and the sureties on his bond be released from their liability on such bond or bonds until the defendant is placed in the custody of the sheriff.

(g) The right of appeal to the Court of Appeals of this state is expressly accorded the defendant for a review of any judgment or order made hereunder, and said appeal shall be given preference by the appellate court.

(h) If a conviction is reversed by a decision of a Court of Appeals, the defendant, if in custody, is entitled to release on reasonable bail, regardless of the length of term of imprisonment, pending final determination of an appeal by the state or the defendant on a motion for discretionary review. If the defendant requests bail before a petition for discretionary review has been filed, the Court of Appeals shall determine the amount of bail. If the defendant requests bail after a petition for discretionary review has been filed, the Court of Criminal Appeals shall determine the amount of bail. The sureties on the bail must be approved by the court where the trial was had. The defendant's right to release under this subsection attaches immediately on the issuance of the Court of Appeals' final ruling as defined by Tex. Cr. App. R. 209(c).

*(Chgd. by L.1991, chap. 14(284(50)); L.1999, chap. 546(1), eff. 9/1/99.)*

**Art. 44.041. Conditions in lieu of bond.**

(a) If a defendant is confined in county jail pending appeal and is eligible for release on bond pending appeal but is financially unable to make bond, the court may release the defendant without bond pending the conclusion of the appeal only if the court determines that release under this article is reasonable given the circumstances of the defendant's offense and the sentence imposed.

(b) A court that releases a defendant under this article must require the defendant to participate in a program under Article 42.033, 42.034, 42.035, or 42.036 of this code during the pen-

dency of the appeal. The defendant may not receive credit toward completion of the defendant's sentence while participating in a program required by this subsection.
*(Added by L.1989, chap. 785(4.15), eff. 9/1/89.)*

**Art. 44.07. Right of appeal not abridged.**
The right of appeal, as otherwise provided by law, shall in no wise be abridged by any provision of this Chapter.

**Art. 44.10. Sheriff to report escape.† [*Sheriff shall report escape of prisoner.*]**
When any such escape occurs, the sheriff who had the prisoner in custody shall immediately report the fact under oath to the district or county attorney of the county in which the conviction was had, who shall forthwith forward such report to the State prosecuting attorney. Such report shall be sufficient evidence of the fact of such escape to authorize the dismissal of the appeal.

**Art. 44.12. Procedure as to bail pending appeal.† [*Determination of bail.*]**
The amount of any bail given in any felony or misdemeanor case to perfect an appeal from any court to the Court of Appeals shall be fixed by the court in which the judgment or order appealed from was rendered. The sufficiency of the security thereon shall be tested, and the same proceedings had in case of forfeiture, as in other cases regarding bail.

**Art. 44.13.** *(Repealed by L.1999, chap. 1545(75), eff. 9/1/99.)*

**Art. 44.14.** *(Redesignated to Chapter 45, Art. 45.0426 and chgd. by L.1999, chap. 1545(42), eff. 9/1/99.)*

**Art. 44.15. Appellate court may allow new bond.† [*New bond filed with appellate court.*]**
When an appeal is taken from any court of this State, by filing a bond within the time prescribed by law in such cases, and the court to which appeal is taken determines that such bond is defective in form or substance, such appellate court may allow the appellant to amend such bond by filing a new bond, on such terms as the court may prescribe.

**Art. 44.16. Appeal bond given within what time.† [*Time limit on appeal bond.*]**
If the defendant is not in custody, a notice of appeal as provided in Article 44.13 shall have no effect whatever until the required appeal bond has been given and approved. The appeal bond shall be given within ten days after the sentence of the court has been rendered, except as provided in Article 27.14 of this code.

**Art. 44.17. Appeal to county court, how conducted.† [*Procedure of appeal to county court.*]**
In all appeals to a county court from justice courts and municipal courts other than municipal courts of record, the trial shall be de novo in the trial in the county court, the same as if the prosecution had been originally commenced in that court. An appeal to the county court from a municipal court of record may be based only on errors reflected in the record.

**Art. 44.18. Original papers sent up.† [*Original papers required for appeal.*]**
In appeals from justice and corporation courts, all the original papers in the case, together with the appeal bond, if any, and together, with a certified transcript of all the proceedings had in the case before such court shall be delivered without delay to the clerk of the court to which the appeal was taken, who shall file the same and docket the case.

**Art. 44.181. Defect in complaint.**
(a) A court conducting a trial de novo based on an appeal from a justice or municipal court may dismiss the case because of a defect in the complaint only if the defendant objected to the defect before the trial began in the justice or municipal court.
(b) The attorney representing the state may move to amend a defective complaint before the trial de novo begins.
*(Added by L.1995, chap. 478(2); chgd. by L.1999, chap. 1545(4), eff. 9/1/99.)*

Printed in the U.S.A. Zt

**Art. 44.19. Witnesses not again summoned.† [*Responsibility of witnesses in appeal.*]**
In the cases mentioned in the preceding Article, the witnesses who have been summoned or attached to appear in the case before the court below, shall appear before the court to which the appeal is taken without further process. In case of their failure to do so, the same proceedings may be had as if they had been originally summoned or attached to appear before such court.

**Art. 44.20. Rules governing appeal bonds.† [*Appeal bond rules.*]**
The rules governing the taking and forfeiture of bail shall govern appeal bonds, and the forfeiture and collection of such appeal bonds shall be in the court to which such appeal is taken.

**Art. 44.25. Cases remanded.**
The courts of appeals or the Court of Criminal Appeals may reverse the judgment in a criminal action, as well upon the law as upon the facts.

Printed in the U.S.A. Zt

**Art. 44.251. Reformation of sentence in capital case.**
(a) The court of criminal appeals shall reform a sentence of death to a sentence of confinement in the institutional division of the Texas Department of Criminal Justice for life if the court finds that there is insufficient evidence to support an affirmative answer to an issue submitted to the jury under Section 2(b), Article 37.071, or Section 3(b), Article 37.0711, of this code or a negative answer to an issue submitted to a jury under Section 2(e), Article 37.071, or Section 3(e), Article 37.0711, of this code.

(b) The court of criminal appeals shall reform a sentence of death to a sentence of confinement in the institutional division of the Texas Department of Criminal Justice for life if:

(1) the court finds reversible error that affects the punishment stage of the trial other than a finding of insufficient evidence under Subsection (a) of this article; and

(2) within 30 days after the date on which the opinion is handed down, the date the court disposes of a timely request for rehearing, or the date that the United States Supreme Court disposes of a timely filed petition for writ of certiorari, whichever date is later, the prosecuting attorney files a motion requesting that the sentence be reformed to confinement for life.

(c) If the court of criminal appeals finds reversible error that affects the punishment stage of the trial only, as described by Subsection (b) of this article, and the prosecuting attorney does not file a motion for reformation of sentence in the period described by that subsection, the defendant shall receive a new sentencing trial in the manner required by Article 44.29(c) of this code. *(Chgd. by L.1991, chap. 838(3); L.1993, chap. 781(3), eff. 8/30/93.)*

**Art. 44.28. When misdemeanor is affirmed.† [*Affirmance in misdemeanor case.*]**
In misdemeanor cases where there has been an affirmance, no proceedings need be had after filing the mandate, except to forfeit the bond of the defendant, or to issue a capias for the defendant, or an execution against his property, to enforce the judgment of the court, as if no appeal had been taken.

**Art. 44.281. Disposition of fines and costs when misdemeanor affirmed.**
In misdemeanor cases affirmed on appeal from a municipal court, the fine imposed on appeal and the costs imposed on appeal shall be collected from the defendant, and the fine of the municipal court when collected shall be paid into the municipal treasury. *(Redesignated from Chap. 45, Art. 45.11 and chgd. by L.1999, chap. 1545(65), eff. 9/1/99.)*

**Art. 44.29. Effect of reversal.† [*Effect of reversal of conviction.*]**
(a) Where the court of appeals or the Court of Criminal Appeals awards a new trial to the defendant on the basis of an error in the guilt or innocence stage of the trial or on the basis of errors in both the guilt or innocence stage of the trial and the punishment stage of the trial, the cause shall stand as it would have stood in case the new trial had been granted by the court below.

(b) If the court of appeals or the Court of Criminal Appeals awards a new trial to a defendant other than a defendant convicted of an offense under Section 19.03, Penal Code, only on the basis of an error or errors made in the punishment stage of the trial, the cause shall stand as it would have stood in case the new trial had been granted by the court below, except that the court shall commence the new trial as if a finding of guilt had been returned and proceed to the punishment stage of the trial under Subsection (b), Section 2, Article 37.07, of this code. If the defendant elects, the court shall empanel a jury for the sentencing stage of the trial in the same manner as a jury is empaneled by the court for other trials before the court. At the new trial, the court shall allow both the state and the defendant to introduce evidence to show the circumstances of the offense and other evidence as permitted by Section 3 of Article 37.07 of this code.

(c) If any court sets aside or invalidates the sentence of a defendant convicted of an offense under Section 19.03, Penal Code, and sentenced to death on the basis of any error affecting punishment only, the court shall not set the conviction aside but rather shall commence a new punishment hearing under Article 37.071 or Article 37.0711 of this code, as appropriate, as if a finding of guilt had been returned. The court shall empanel a jury for the sentencing stage of the trial in the same manner as a jury is to be empaneled by the court in other trials before the court for offenses under Section 19.03, Penal Code. At the new punishment hearing, the court shall permit both the state and the defendant to introduce evidence as permitted by Article 37.071 or Article 37.0711 of this code.
*(Chgd. by L.1991, chap. 838(2); L.1993, chap. 781(4), eff. 8/30/93.)*

### Art. 44.33. Hearing in appellate court.† [*Procedure of hearing in appellate court.*]

(a) The Court of Criminal Appeals shall make rules of posttrial and appellate procedure as to the hearing of criminal actions not inconsistent with this Code. After the record is filed in the Court of Appeals or the Court of Criminal Appeals the parties may file such supplemental briefs as they may desire before the case is submitted to the court. Each party, upon filing any such supplemental brief, shall promptly cause true copy thereof to be delivered to the opposing party or to the latter's counsel. In every case at least two counsel for the defendant shall be heard in the Court of Appeals if such be desired by defendant. In every case heard by the Court of Criminal Appeals at least two counsel for the defendant shall be permitted oral argument if desired by the appellant.

(b) Appellant's failure to file his brief in the time prescribed shall not authorize a dismissal of the appeal by the Court of Appeals or the Court of Criminal Appeals, nor shall the Court of Appeals or the Court of Criminal Appeals, for such reason, refuse to consider appellant's case on appeal.



### Art. 44.35. Bail pending habeas corpus appeal.† [*Bail pending appeal on habeas corpus.*]

In any habeas corpus proceeding in any court or before any judge in this State where the defendant is remanded to the custody of an officer and an appeal is taken to an appellate court, the defendant shall be allowed bail by the court or judge so remanding the defendant, except in capital cases where the proof is evident. The fact that such defendant is released on bail shall not be grounds for a dismissal of the appeal except in capital cases where the proof is evident.

### Art. 44.39. Appellant detained by other than officer.† [*Habeas corpus appeal: detention of appellant.*]

If the appellant in a case of habeas corpus be detained by any person other than an officer, the sheriff receiving the mandate of the appellate court, shall immediately cause the person so held to be discharged; and the mandate shall be sufficient authority therefor.

### Art. 44.41. Who shall take bail bond.† [*Execution of bail bond.*]

When, by the judgment of the appellate court upon cases of habeas corpus, the applicant is ordered to give bail, such judgment shall be certified to the officer holding him in custody; and if such officer be the sheriff, the bail bond may be executed before him; if any other officer, he shall take the person detained before some magistrate, who may receive a bail bond, and shall file the same in the proper court of the proper county; and such bond may be forfeited and enforced as provided by law.

### Art. 44.42. Appeal on forfeitures.

An appeal may be taken by the defendant from every final judgment rendered upon a personal bond, bail bond or bond taken for the prevention or suppression of offenses, where such judgment is for twenty dollars or more, exclusive of costs, but not otherwise.

### Art. 44.43. Writ of error.

The defendant may also have any such judgment as is mentioned in the preceding Article, and which may have been rendered in courts other than the justice and corporation courts, reviewed upon writ of error.

### Art. 44.44. Rules of forfeitures.

In the cases provided for in the two preceding Articles, the proceeding shall be regulated by the same rules that govern civil actions where an appeal is taken or a writ of error sued out.

### Art. 44.45. Review by Court of Criminal Appeals.† [*Court of Criminal Appeals review.*]

(a) The Court of Criminal Appeals may review decisions of the court of appeals on its own motion. An order for review must be filed before the decision of the court of appeals becomes final as determined by Article 42.045.

(b) The Court of Criminal Appeals may review decisions of the court of appeals upon a petition for review.

(1) The state or a defendant in a case may petition the Court of Criminal Appeals for review of the decision of a court of appeals in that case.

(2) The petition shall be filed with the clerk of the court of appeals which rendered the decision within 30 days after the final ruling of the court of appeals.

(3) The petition for review shall be addressed to "The Court of Criminal Appeals of Texas," and shall state the name of the petitioning party and shall include a statement of the case and authorities and arguments in support of each ground for review.

(4) Upon filing a petition for review, the petitioning party shall cause a true copy to be delivered to the attorney representing the opposing party. The opposing party may file a reply to the petition with the Court of Criminal Appeals within 30 days after receipt of the petition from the petitioning party.

(5) Within 15 days after the filing of a petition for review, the clerk of the court of appeals shall note the filing on the record and forward the petition together with the original record and the opinion of the court of appeals to the Court of Criminal Appeals.

(6) The Court of Criminal Appeals shall either grant the petition and review the case or refuse the petition.

(7) Subsequent to granting the petition for review, the Court of Criminal Appeals may reconsider, set aside the order granting the petition, and refuse the petition as though the petition had never been granted.

(c) The Court of Criminal Appeals may promulgate rules pursuant to this article.

(d) Extensions of time for meeting the limits prescribed in Subdivisions (2) and (4) of Subsection (b) of this article may be granted by the Court of Criminal Appeals or a judge thereof for good cause shown on timely application to the Court of Criminal Appeals.

*(The Texas Court of Criminal Appeals, by order dated 12/18/85, effective 9/1/86, repealed the second sentence of subsec. (a), subds. (1) to (7) of subsec. (b), and subsec. (d). This order adopted the Texas Rules of Appellate Procedure, pursuant to Acts 1985, 69th Legislature, chap. 685(4).)*

### Art. 44.46. Reversal of conviction on the basis of service on jury by a disqualified juror.

A conviction in a criminal case may be reversed on appeal on the ground that a juror in the case was absolutely disqualified from service under Article 35.19 of this code only if:

(1) the defendant raises the disqualification before the verdict is entered; or

(2) the disqualification was not discovered or brought to the attention of the trial court until after the verdict was entered and the defendant makes a showing of significant harm by the service of the disqualified juror.

*(Added by L.1993, chap. 372(1), eff. 9/1/93.)*

### Art. 44.47. Appeal of transfer from juvenile court.

(a) A defendant may appeal an order of a juvenile court certifying the defendant to stand trial as an adult and transferring the defendant to a criminal court under Section 54.02, Family Code.

(b) A defendant may appeal a transfer under Subsection (a) only in conjunction with the appeal of a conviction of the offense for which the defendant was transferred to criminal court.

(c) An appeal under this section is a criminal matter and is governed by this code and the Texas Rules of Appellate Procedure that apply to a criminal case.

(d) An appeal under this article may include any claims under the law that existed before January 1, 1996, that could have been raised on direct appeal of a transfer under Section 54.02, Family Code.

*(Added by L.1995, chap. 262(85), eff. 1/1/96.)*

## JUSTICE AND MUNICIPAL COURTS

## CHAPTER 45. JUSTICE AND MUNICIPAL COURTS

*(Chgd. by L.1999, chap. 1545 (5), (6) to (65), (75), eff. 9/1/99.)*

### SUBCHAPTER A. GENERAL PROVISIONS

Article

45.001. Objectives of chapter.
45.002. Application of chapter.
45.003. Definition for certain prosecutions.

## SUBCHAPTER B. PROCEDURES FOR JUSTICE AND MUNICIPAL COURTS

45.011. Rules of evidence.
45.012. Electronically created records.
45.013. Filing with clerk by mail.
45.014. Warrant of arrest.
45.015. Defendant placed in jail.
45.016. Bail.
45.017. Criminal docket.
45.018. Complaint.
45.019. Requisites of complaint.
45.020. Appearance by counsel.
45.021. Pleadings.
45.0215. Plea by minor and appearance of parent.
45.022. Plea of guilty or nolo contendere.
45.023. Defendant's plea.
45.024. Defendant's refusal to plead.
45.025. Defendant may waive jury.
45.026. Jury trial; failure to appear.
45.027. Jury summoned.
45.028. Other jurors summoned.
45.029. Peremptory challenges.
45.030. Formation of jury.
45.031. Counsel for state not present.
45.032. Directed verdict.
45.033. Jury charge.
45.034. Jury kept together.
45.035. Mistrial.
45.036. Verdict.
45.037. Motion for new trial.
45.038. New trial granted.
45.039. Only one new trial granted.
45.040. State not entitled to new trial.
45.041. Judgment.
45.042. Appeal.
45.0425. Appeal bond.
45.0426. Filing bond perfects appeal.
45.043. Effect of appeal.
45.044. Forfeiture of cash bond in satisfaction of fine.
45.045. Capias pro fine.
45.046. Commitment.
45.047. Civil collection of fines after judgment.
45.048. Discharged from jail.
45.049. Community service in satisfaction of fine or costs.
45.050. Failure to pay fine; contempt: juveniles.
45.051. Suspension of sentence and deferral of final disposition.
45.0511. Deferred disposition procedures applicable to traffic offenses.
45.052. Dismissal of misdemeanor charge on completion of teen court program.
45.053. Dismissal of misdemeanor charge on commitment of chemically dependent person.

## SUBCHAPTER C. PROCEDURES IN JUSTICE COURT

45.101. Justice court prosecutions.
45.102. Offenses committed in another county.
45.103. Warrant without complaint.

## SUBCHAPTER D. PROCEDURES IN MUNICIPAL COURT

45.201. Municipal prosecutions.
45.202. Service of process.
45.203. Collection of fines, costs, and special expenses.

## SUBCHAPTER A. GENERAL PROVISIONS

*(Heading added by L.1999, chap. 1545(6), eff. 9/1/99.)*

### Art. 45.001. Objectives of chapter.

The purpose of this chapter is to establish procedures for processing cases that come within the criminal jurisdiction of the justice courts and municipal courts. This chapter is intended and shall be construed to achieve the following objectives:

(1) to provide fair notice to a person appearing in a criminal proceeding before a justice or municipal court and a meaningful opportunity for that person to be heard;

(2) to ensure appropriate dignity in court procedure without undue formalism;

(3) to promote adherence to rules with sufficient flexibility to serve the ends of justice; and

(4) to process cases without unnecessary expense or delay.

*(Added by L.1999, chap. 1545(6), eff. 9/1/99.)*



### Art. 45.002. Application of chapter.

Criminal proceedings in the justice and municipal courts shall be conducted in accordance with this chapter, including any other rules of procedure specifically made applicable to those proceedings by this chapter. If this chapter does not provide a rule of procedure governing any aspect of a case, the justice or judge shall apply the other general provisions of this code to the extent necessary to achieve the objectives of this chapter. *(Added by L.1999, chap. 1545(6), eff. 9/1/99.)*

### Art. 45.003. Definition for certain prosecutions.

For purposes of dismissing a charge under Section 502.407 or 548.605, Transportation Code, "day" does not include Saturday, Sunday, or a legal holiday. *(Added by L.1999, chap. 1545(6), eff. 9/1/99.)*

## SUBCHAPTER B. PROCEDURES FOR JUSTICE AND MUNICIPAL COURTS

*(Heading added by L.1999, chap. 1545(7), eff. 9/1/99.)*

### Art. 45.011. Rules of evidence.

The rules of evidence that govern the trials of criminal actions in the district court apply to a criminal proceeding in a justice or municipal court. *(Redesignated from Art. 45.38 and chgd. by L.1999, chap. 1545(8), eff. 9/1/99.)*

### Art. 45.012. Electronically created records.

(a) Notwithstanding any other provision of law, a document that is issued or maintained by a justice or municipal court or a notice or a citation issued by a law enforcement officer may be created by electronic means, including optical imaging, optical disk, digital imaging, or other electronic reproduction technique that does not permit changes, additions, or deletions to the originally created document.

(b) The court may use electronic means to:

(1) produce a document required by law to be written;

(2) record an instrument, paper, or notice that is permitted or required by law to be recorded or filed; or

(3) maintain a docket.

(c) The court shall maintain original documents as provided by law.

(d) An electronically recorded judgment has the same force and effect as a written signed judgment.

(e) A record created by electronic means is an original record or a certification of the original record.

(f) A printed copy of an optical image of the original record printed from an optical disk system is an accurate copy of the original record. *See other subsection (f) below.)*

(f) A statutory requirement that a document contain the signature of any person, including a judge, clerk of the court, or defendant, is satisfied if the document contains that signature as captured on an electronic device. *(Added by L.1999, chap. 701(2), eff. 6/18/99. See other subsection (f) above.)*

(g) A justice or municipal court shall have a court seal, the impression of which must be attached to all papers issued out of the court except subpoenas, and which must be used to authenticate the official acts of the clerk and of the recorder. A court seal may be created by electronic means, including optical imaging, optical disk, or other electronic reproduction technique that

does not permit changes, additions, or deletions to an original document created by the same type of system.
*(Chgd. by L.1999, chap. 701(2), eff. 6/18/99; redesignated from Art. 45.021 and chgd. by L.1999, chap. 1545(9), eff. 9/1/99.)*

### Art. 45.013. Filing with clerk by mail.

(a) Notwithstanding any other law, for the purposes of this chapter a document is considered timely filed with the clerk of a court if:

(1) the document is deposited with the United States Postal Service in a first class postage prepaid envelope properly addressed to the clerk on or before the date the document is required to be filed with the clerk; and

(2) the clerk receives the document not later than the 10th day after the date the document is required to be filed with the clerk.

(b) A legible postmark affixed by the United States Postal Service is prima facie evidence of the date the document is deposited with the United States Postal Service.

(c) In this article, "day" does not include Saturday, Sunday, or a legal holiday.
*(Added by L.1999, chap. 1545(10), eff. 9/1/99.)*

### Art. 45.014. Warrant of arrest.

(a) When a sworn complaint or affidavit based on probable cause has been filed before the justice or municipal court, the justice or judge may issue a warrant for the arrest of the accused and deliver the same to the proper officer to be executed.

(b) The warrant is sufficient if:

(1) it is issued in the name of "The State of Texas";

(2) it is directed to the proper peace officer or some other person specifically named in the warrant;

(3) it includes a command that the body of the accused be taken, and brought before the authority issuing the warrant, at the time and place stated in the warrant;

(4) it states the name of the person whose arrest is ordered, if known, or if not known, it describes the person as in the complaint;

(5) it states that the person is accused of some offense against the laws of this state, naming the offense; and

(6) it is signed by the justice or judge, naming the office of the justice or judge in the body of the warrant or in connection with the signature of the justice or judge.

(c) Chapter 15 applies to a warrant of arrest issued under this article, except as inconsistent or in conflict with this chapter.
*(Redesignated from Art. 45.18 and chgd. by L.1999, chap. 1545(11), eff. 9/1/99.)*

### Art. 45.015. Defendant placed in jail.

Whenever, by the provisions of this title, the peace officer is authorized to retain a defendant in custody, the peace officer may place the defendant in jail in accordance with this code or other law.
*(Redesignated from Art. 45.43 and chgd. by L.1999, chap. 1545(12), eff. 9/1/99.)*

### Art. 45.016. Bail.

The justice or judge may require the defendant to give bail to secure the defendant's appearance in accordance with this code. If the defendant fails to give bail, the defendant may be held in custody. *(Redesignated from Art. 45.41 and chgd. by L.1999, chap. 1545(13), eff. 9/1/99.)*

### Art. 45.017. Criminal docket.

(a) The justice or judge of each court, or, if directed by the justice or judge, the clerk of the court, shall keep a docket containing the following information:

(1) the style and file number of each criminal action;

(2) the nature of the offense charged;

(3) the plea offered by the defendant and the date the plea was entered;

(4) the date the warrant, if any, was issued and the return made thereon;

(5) the date the examination or trial was held, and if a trial was held, whether it was by a jury or by the justice or judge;

(6) the verdict of the jury, if any, and the date of the verdict;

(7) the judgment and sentence of the court, and the date each was given;

(8) the motion for new trial, if any, and the decision thereon; and

(9) whether an appeal was taken and the date of that action.



Zt

(b) The information in the docket may be processed and stored by the use of electronic data processing equipment, at the discretion of the justice of the peace or the municipal court judge. *(Redesignated from Art. 45.13 and chgd. by L.1999, chap. 1545(14), eff. 9/1/99.)*

### Art. 45.018. Complaint.

(a) For purposes of this chapter, a complaint is a sworn allegation charging the accused with the commission of an offense.

(b) A defendant is entitled to notice of a complaint against the defendant not later than the day before the date of any proceeding in the prosecution of the defendant under the complaint. The defendant may waive the right to notice granted by this subsection.
*(Added by L.1999, chap. 1545(15), eff. 9/1/99.)*

### Art. 45.019. Requisites of complaint.

(a) A complaint is sufficient, without regard to its form, if it substantially satisfies the following requisites:

(1) it must be in writing;

(2) it must commence "In the name and by the authority of the State of Texas";

(3) it must state the name of the accused, if known, or if unknown, must include a reasonably definite description of the accused;

(4) it must show that the accused has committed an offense against the law of this state, or state that the affiant has good reason to believe and does believe that the accused has committed an offense against the law of this state;

(5) it must state the date the offense was committed as definitely as the affiant is able to provide;

(6) it must bear the signature or mark of the affiant; and

(7) it must conclude with the words "Against the peace and dignity of the State" and, if the offense charged is an offense only under a municipal ordinance, it may also conclude with the words "Contrary to the said ordinance".

(b) A complaint filed in justice court must allege that the offense was committed in the county in which the complaint is made.

(c) A complaint filed in municipal court must allege that the offense was committed in the territorial limits of the municipality in which the complaint is made.

(d) A complaint may be sworn to before any officer authorized to administer oaths.

(e) A complaint in municipal court may be sworn to before:

(1) the municipal judge;

(2) the clerk of the court or a deputy clerk;

(3) the city secretary; or

(4) the city attorney or a deputy city attorney.

(f) If the defendant does not object to a defect, error, or irregularity of form or substance in a charging instrument before the date on which the trial on the merits commences, the defendant waives and forfeits the right to object to the defect, error, or irregularity. Nothing in this article prohibits a trial court from requiring that an objection to a charging instrument be made at an earlier time.
*(Redesignated from Art. 45.17 and chgd. by L.1999, chap. 1545(16), eff. 9/1/99.)*

### Art. 45.020. Appearance by counsel.

(a) The defendant has a right to appear by counsel as in all other cases.

(b) Not more than one counsel shall conduct either the prosecution or defense. State's counsel may open and conclude the argument.
*(Redesignated from Art. 45.37 and chgd. by L.1999, chap. 1545(17), eff. 9/1/99.)*

### Art. 45.021. Pleadings.

All pleading of the defendant in justice or municipal court may be oral or in writing as the court may direct. *(Redesignated from Art. 45.33 and chgd. by L.1999, chap. 1545(18), eff. 9/1/99.)*

### Art. 45.0215. Plea by minor and appearance of parent.

(a) If a defendant is younger than 17 years of age and has not had the disabilities of minority removed, the judge or justice:

(1) must take the defendant's plea in open court; and

(2) shall issue a summons to compel the defendant's parent, guardian, or managing conservator to be present during:

(A) the taking of the defendant's plea; and

(B) all other proceedings relating to the case.

(b) If the court is unable to secure the appearance of the defendant's parent, guardian, or managing conservator by issuance of a summons, the court may, without the defendant's parent, guardian, or managing conservator present, take the defendant's plea and proceed against the defendant.

(c) If the defendant resides in a county other than the county in which the alleged offense occurred, the defendant may, with leave of the judge of the court of original jurisdiction, enter the plea, including a plea under Article 45.052, before a judge in the county in which the defendant resides.
*(Redesignated from Art. 45.331 and chgd. by L.1999, chap. 1545(19), eff. 9/1/99.)*

**Art. 45.022. Plea of guilty or nolo contendere.**

Proof as to the offense may be heard upon a plea of guilty or a plea of nolo contendere and the punishment assessed by the court. *(Redesignated from Art. 45.34 and chgd. by L.1999, chap. 1545(20), eff. 9/1/99.)*

**Art. 45.023. Defendant's plea.**

After the jury is impaneled, or after the defendant has waived trial by jury, the defendant may:

(1) plead guilty or not guilty;

(2) enter a plea of nolo contendere; or

(3) enter the special plea of double jeopardy as described by Article 27.05.
*(Redesignated from Art. 45.31 and chgd. by L.1999, chap. 1545(21), eff. 9/1/99.)*

**Art. 45.024. Defendant's refusal to plead.**

The justice or judge shall enter a plea of not guilty if the defendant refuses to plead.
*(Redesignated from Art. 45.35 and chgd. by L.1999, chap. 1545(22), eff. 9/1/99.)*

**Art. 45.025. Defendant may waive jury.**

The accused may waive a trial by jury in writing. If the defendant waives a trial by jury, the justice or judge shall hear and determine the cause without a jury. *(Redesignated from Art. 45.24 and chgd. by L.1999, chap. 1545(23), eff. 9/1/99.)*

**Art. 45.026. Jury trial; failure to appear.**

(a) A justice or municipal court may order a party who does not waive a jury trial in a justice or municipal court and who fails to appear for the trial to pay the costs incurred for impaneling the jury.

(b) The justice or municipal court may release a party from the obligation to pay costs under this section for good cause.

(c) An order issued by a justice or municipal court under this section may be enforced by contempt as prescribed by Section 21.002(c), Government Code.
*(Redesignated from Art. 45.251 and chgd. by L.1999, chap. 1545(24), eff. 9/1/99.)*

**Art. 45.027. Jury summoned.**

(a) If the accused does not waive a trial by jury, the justice or judge shall issue a writ commanding the proper officer to summon a venire from which six qualified persons shall be selected to serve as jurors in the case.

(b) The jurors when so summoned shall remain in attendance as jurors in all cases that may come up for hearing until discharged by the court.

(c) Any person so summoned who fails to attend may be fined an amount not to exceed $100 for contempt.
*(Redesignated from Art. 45.25 and chgd. by L.1999, chap. 1545(25), eff. 9/1/99.)*

**Art. 45.028. Other jurors summoned.**

If, from challenges or any other cause, a sufficient number of jurors are not in attendance, the justice or judge shall order the proper officer to summon a sufficient number of qualified persons to form the jury. *(Redesignated from Art. 45.29 and chgd. by L.1999, chap. 1545(26), eff. 9/1/99.)*

**Art. 45.029. Peremptory challenges.**

In all jury trials in a justice or municipal court, the state and each defendant in the case is entitled to three peremptory challenges. *(Redesignated from Art. 45.28 and chgd. by L.1999, chap. 1545(27), eff. 9/1/99.)*

**Art. 45.030. Formation of jury.**

The justice or judge shall form the jury and administer the appropriate oath in accordance with Chapter 35. *(Redesignated from Art. 45.30 and chgd. by L.1999, chap. 1545(28), eff. 9/1/99.)*

**Art. 45.031. Counsel for state not present.**

If the state is not represented by counsel when the case is called for trial, the justice or judge may:

(1) postpone the trial to a date certain;
(2) appoint an attorney pro tem as provided by this code to represent the state; or
(3) proceed to trial.

*(Redesignated from Art. 45.36 and chgd. by L.1999, chap. 1545(29), eff. 9/1/99.)*

**Art. 45.032. Directed verdict.**

If, upon the trial of a case in a justice or municipal court, the state fails to prove a prima facie case of the offense alleged in the complaint, the defendant is entitled to a directed verdict of "not guilty." *(Redesignated from Art. 45.031 and chgd. by L.1999, chap. 1545(30), eff. 9/1/99.)*

**Art. 45.033. Jury charge.**

The judge shall charge the jury. The charge may be made orally or in writing, except that the charge shall be made in writing if required by law. *(Added by L.1999, chap. 1545(31), eff. 9/1/99.)*

**Art. 45.034. Jury kept together.**

The jury shall retire in charge of an officer when the cause is submitted to them, and be kept together until they agree to a verdict, are discharged, or the court recesses. *(Redesignated from Art. 45.39 and chgd. by L.1999, chap. 1545(32), eff. 9/1/99.)*

**Art. 45.035. Mistrial.**

A jury shall be discharged if it fails to agree to a verdict after being kept together a reasonable time. If a jury is discharged because it fails to agree to a verdict, the justice or judge may impanel another jury as soon as practicable to try such cause. *(Redesignated from Art. 45.40 and chgd. by L.1999, chap. 1545(33), eff. 9/1/99.)*

**Art. 45.036. Verdict.**

(a) When the jury has agreed on a verdict, the jury shall bring the verdict into court.

(b) The justice or judge shall see that the verdict is in proper form and shall render the proper judgment and sentence on the verdict.

*(Redesignated from Art. 45.42 and chgd. by L.1999, chap. 1545(34), eff. 9/1/99.)*

**Art. 45.037. Motion for new trial.**

A motion for a new trial must be made within one day after the rendition of judgment and sentence, and not afterward. *(Redesignated from Art. 45.45 and chgd. by L.1999, chap. 1545(35), eff. 9/1/99.)*

**Art. 45.038. New trial granted.**

(a) Not later than the 10th day after the date that the judgment is entered, a justice or judge may, for good cause shown, grant the defendant a new trial, whenever the justice or judge considers that justice has not been done the defendant in the trial of the case.

(b) If a motion for a new trial is not granted before the 11th day after the date that the judgment is entered, the motion shall be considered denied.

*(Redesignated from Art. 45.44 and chgd. by L.1999, chap. 1545(36), eff. 9/1/99.)*

**Art. 45.039. Only one new trial granted.**

Not more than one new trial shall be granted the defendant in the same case. When a new trial has been granted, the justice or judge shall proceed, as soon as practicable, to try the case again. *(Redesignated from Art. 45.46 and chgd. by L.1999, chap. 1545(37), eff. 9/1/99.)*

**Art. 45.040. State not entitled to new trial.**

In no case shall the state be entitled to a new trial. *(Redesignated from Art. 45.47 and chgd. by L.1999, chap. 1545(38), eff. 9/1/99.)*

### Art. 45.041. Judgment.

(a) The judgment and sentence, in case of conviction in a criminal action before a justice of the peace or municipal court judge, shall be that the defendant pay the amount of the fine and costs to the state.

(b) The justice or judge may direct the defendant:

(1) to pay:

(A) the entire fine and costs when sentence is pronounced;

(B) the entire fine and costs at some later date; or

(C) a specified portion of the fine and costs at designated intervals;

(2) if applicable, to make restitution to any victim of the offense in an amount not to exceed $500; and

(3) to satisfy any other sanction authorized by law.

(c) The justice or judge shall credit the defendant for time served in jail as provided by Article 42.03. The credit shall be applied to the amount of the fine and costs at the rate provided by Article 45.048.

(d) All judgments, sentences, and final orders of the justice or judge shall be rendered in open court.

*(Redesignated from Art. 45.50 and chgd. by L.1999, chap. 1545(39), eff. 9/1/99.)*

### Art. 45.042. Appeal.

(a) Appeals from a justice or municipal court, including appeals from final judgments in bond forfeiture proceedings, shall be heard by the county court except in cases where the county court has no jurisdiction, in which counties such appeals shall be heard by the proper court.

(b) Unless the appeal is taken from a municipal court of record and the appeal is based on error reflected in the record, the trial shall be de novo.

(c) In an appeal from the judgment and sentence of a justice or municipal court, if the defendant is in custody, the defendant is to be committed to jail unless the defendant gives bail.

*(Redesignated from Art. 45.10 and chgd. by L.1999, chap. 1545(40), eff. 9/1/99.)*

### Art. 45.0425. Appeal bond.

(a) If the court from whose judgment and sentence the appeal is taken is in session, the court must approve the bail. The amount of a bail bond may not be less than two times the amount of the fine and costs adjudged against the defendant, payable to the State of Texas. The bail may not in any case be for a sum less than $50. If the appeal bond otherwise meets the requirements of this code, the court without requiring a court appearance by the defendant shall approve the appeal bond in the amount the court under Article 27.14(b) notified the defendant would be approved.

(b) An appeal bond shall recite that in the cause the defendant was convicted and has appealed and be conditioned that the defendant shall make the defendant's personal appearance before the court to which the appeal is taken instanter, if the court is in session, or, if the court is not in session, at its next regular term, stating the time and place of that session, and there remain from day to day and term to term, and answer in the cause in the court.

*(Added by L.1999, chap. 1545(41), eff. 9/1/99.)*

### Art. 45.0426. Filing bond perfects appeal.

(a) When the appeal bond has been filed with the justice or judge who tried the case not later than the 10th day after the date the judgment was entered, the appeal in such case shall be held to be perfected.

(b) If an appeal bond is not timely filed, the appellate court does not have jurisdiction over the case and shall remand the case to the justice or municipal court for execution of the sentence.

(c) An appeal may not be dismissed because the defendant failed to give notice of appeal in open court. An appeal by the defendant or the state may not be dismissed on account of any defect in the transcript.

*(Redesignated from Chap. 44, Art. 44.14 and chgd. by L.1999, chap. 1545(42), eff. 9/1/99.)*

### Art. 45.043. Effect of appeal.

When a defendant files the appeal bond required by law with the justice or municipal court, all further proceedings in the case in the justice or municipal court shall cease. *(Redesignated from Art. 45.48 and chgd. by L.1999, chap. 1545(43), eff. 9/1/99.)*

### Art. 45.044. Forfeiture of cash bond in satisfaction of fine.

(a) A justice or judge may enter a judgment of conviction and forfeit a cash bond posted by the defendant in satisfaction of the defendant's fine and cost if the defendant:

(1) has entered a written and signed plea of nolo contendere and a waiver of jury trial; and

(2) fails to appear according to the terms of the defendant's release.

(b) A justice or judge who enters a judgment of conviction and forfeiture under Subsection (a) of this article shall immediately notify the defendant in writing, by regular mail addressed to the defendant at the defendant's last known address, that:

(1) a judgment of conviction and forfeiture of bond was entered against the defendant on a date certain and the forfeiture satisfies the defendant's fine and costs in the case; and

(2) the defendant has a right to a new trial in the case if the defendant applies for the new trial not later than the 10th day after the date of judgment and forfeiture.

(c) Notwithstanding Article 45.037 of this code, the defendant may file a motion for a new trial within the period provided by Subsection (b) of this article, and the court shall grant the motion if the motion is made within that period. On the new trial, the court shall permit the defendant to withdraw the previously entered plea of nolo contendere and waiver of jury trial.

*(Redesignated from Art. 45.231 and chgd. by L.1999, chap. 1545(44), eff. 9/1/99.)*

### Art. 45.045. Capias pro fine.

If the defendant is not in custody when the judgment is rendered or if the defendant fails to satisfy the judgment according to its terms, the court may order a capias pro fine issued for the defendant's arrest. The capias pro fine shall state the amount of the judgment and sentence, and command the appropriate peace officer to bring the defendant before the court or place the defendant in jail until the defendant can be brought before the court. *(Redesignated from Art. 45.51 and chgd. by L.1999, chap. 1545(45), eff. 9/1/99.)*

### Art. 45.046. Commitment.

(a) When a judgment and sentence have been entered against a defendant and the defendant defaults in the discharge of the judgment, the judge may order the defendant confined in jail until discharged by law if the judge determines that:

(1) the defendant intentionally failed to make a good faith effort to discharge the judgment; or

(2) the defendant is not indigent.

(b) A certified copy of the judgment, sentence, and order is sufficient to authorize such confinement.

*(Redesignated from Art. 45.52 and chgd. by L.1999, chap. 1545(46), eff. 9/1/99.)*

### Art. 45.047. Civil collection of fines after judgment.

If after a judgment and sentence is entered the defendant defaults in payment of a fine, the justice or judge may order the fine and costs collected by execution against the defendant's property in the same manner as a judgment in a civil suit. *(Added by L.1999, chap. 1545(47), eff. 9/1/99.)*

### Art. 45.048. Discharged from jail.

A defendant placed in jail on account of failure to pay the fine and costs shall be discharged on habeas corpus by showing that the defendant:

(1) is too poor to pay the fine and costs; or

(2) has remained in jail a sufficient length of time to satisfy the fine and costs, at the rate of not less than $100 for each day or part of a day of jail time served.

*(Redesignated from Art. 45.53 and chgd. by L.1999, chap. 1545(48), eff. 9/1/99.)*

### Art. 45.049. Community service in satisfaction of fine or costs.

(a) A justice or judge may require a defendant who fails to pay a previously assessed fine or costs, or who is determined by the court to have insufficient resources or income to pay a fine or costs, to discharge all or part of the fine or costs by performing community service. A defendant may discharge an obligation to perform community service under this article by paying at any time the fine and costs assessed.

(b) In the justice's or judge's order requiring a defendant to participate in community service work under this article, the justice or judge must specify the number of hours the defendant is required to work.

(c) The justice or judge may order the defendant to perform community service work under this article only for a governmental entity or a nonprofit organization that provides services to the general public that enhance social welfare and the general well-being of the community. A governmental entity or nonprofit organization that accepts a defendant under this article to perform community service must agree to supervise the defendant in the performance of the defendant's work and report on the defendant's work to the justice or judge who ordered the community service.

(d) A justice or judge may not order a defendant to perform more than 16 hours per week of community service under this article unless the justice or judge determines that requiring the defendant to work additional hours does not work a hardship on the defendant or the defendant's dependents.

(e) A defendant is considered to have discharged $100 of fines or costs for each eight hours of community service performed under this article.

(f) A sheriff, employee of a sheriff's department, county commissioner, county employee, county judge, justice of the peace, municipal court judge, or officer or employee of a political subdivision other than a county is not liable for damages arising from an act or failure to act in connection with manual labor performed by a defendant under this article if the act or failure to act:

(1) was performed pursuant to court order; and

(2) was not intentional, wilfully or wantonly negligent, or performed with conscious indifference or reckless disregard for the safety of others.

*(Rredesignated from Art. 45.521 and chgd. by L.1999, chap. 1545(49), eff. 9/1/99.)*

### Art. 45.050. Failure to pay fine; contempt: juveniles.

(a) A justice court or municipal court may not order the confinement of a person who is a child for the purposes of Title 3, Family Code, for the failure to pay all or any part of a fine or costs imposed for the conviction of an offense punishable by fine only.

(b) If a person who is a child under Section 51.02, Family Code, fails to obey an order of a justice or municipal court under circumstances that would constitute contempt of court, the justice or municipal court has jurisdiction to:

(1) hold the child in contempt of the justice or municipal court order as provided by Section 52.027(h), Family Code; or

(2) refer the child to the appropriate juvenile court for delinquent conduct for contempt of the justice or municipal court order.

*(Chgd. by L.1999, chap. 76(7), eff. 9/1/99; redesignated from Art. 45.522 and chgd. by L.1999, chap. 1545(49), eff. 9/1/99.)*

### Art. 45.051. Suspension of sentence and deferral of final disposition.

(a) On a plea of guilty or nolo contendere by a defendant or on a finding of guilt in a misdemeanor case punishable by fine only and payment of all court costs, the justice may defer further proceedings without entering an adjudication of guilt and place the defendant on probation for a period not to exceed 180 days.

(b) During the deferral period, the justice may require the defendant to:

(1) post a bond in the amount of the fine assessed to secure payment of the fine;

(2) pay restitution to the victim of the offense in an amount not to exceed the fine assessed;

(3) submit to professional counseling;

(4) submit to diagnostic testing for alcohol or a controlled substance or drug;

(5) submit to a psychosocial assessment;

(6) participate in an alcohol or drug abuse treatment or education program;

(7) pay the costs of any diagnostic testing, psychosocial assessment, or participation in a treatment or education program either directly or through the court as court costs; and

(8) comply with any other reasonable condition.

(c) At the conclusion of the deferral period, if the defendant presents satisfactory evidence that he has complied with the requirements imposed, the justice shall dismiss the complaint, and it shall be clearly noted in the docket that the complaint is dismissed and that there is not a final conviction. Otherwise, the justice may proceed with an adjudication of guilt. After an adjudication of guilt, the justice may reduce the fine assessed or may then impose the fine assessed, less any portion of the assessed fine that has been paid. If the complaint is dismissed, a special expense not to exceed the amount of the fine assessed may be imposed.

(d) If at the conclusion of the deferral period the defendant does not present satisfactory evidence that the defendant complied with the requirements imposed, the justice may impose the fine assessed or impose a lesser fine. The imposition of the fine or lesser fine constitutes a final conviction of the defendant.

(e) Records relating to a complaint dismissed as provided by this article may be expunged under Article 55.01 of this code. If a complaint is dismissed under this article, there is not a final conviction and the complaint may not be used against the person for any purpose.

*(Chgd. by L.1999, chaps. 62(3.06), 532(1), 1387(1), eff. 9/1/99; redesignated from Art. 45.54 and chgd. by L.1999, chap. 1545(50), eff. 9/1/99.)*

**Art. 45.0511. Deferred disposition procedures applicable to traffic offenses.**

(a) This article applies to an alleged offense involving the operation of a motor vehicle other than a commercial motor vehicle, as defined by Section 522.003, Transportation Code, and supplements Article 45.051.

(b) During the deferral period under Article 45.051, the justice:

(1) shall require the defendant to successfully complete a driving safety course approved by the Texas Education Agency if the defendant elects deferred disposition and the defendant has not completed an approved driving safety course or motorcycle operator training course, as appropriate, within the preceding 12 months; and

(2) may require the defendant to successfully complete a driving safety course approved by the Texas Education Agency if the defendant has completed an approved driving safety course within the preceding 12 months.

(c) Subsection (b)(1) applies only if:

(1) the person enters a plea in person or in writing of no contest or guilty and, before the answer date on the notice to appear:

(A) presents in person to the court an oral or written request to take a course; or

(B) sends to the court by certified mail, return receipt requested, postmarked on or before the answer date on the notice to appear, a written request to take a course;

(2) the court enters judgment on the person's plea of no contest or guilty at the time the plea is made but defers imposition of the judgment for 180 days;

(3) the person has a Texas driver's license or permit;

(4) the person is charged with an offense to which this article applies, other than speeding 25 miles per hour or more over the posted speed limit;

(5) the person provides evidence of financial responsibility as required by Chapter 601, Transportation Code;

(6) the defendant's driving record as maintained by the Texas Department of Public Safety shows the defendant has not completed an approved driving safety course or motorcycle operator training course, as appropriate, within the 12 months preceding the date of the offense; and

(7) the defendant files an affidavit with the court stating that the person is not taking a course under this section and has not completed a course that is not shown on the person's driving record within the 12 months preceding the date of the offense.

(d) Notwithstanding Subsection (c)(1), on a written motion submitted to the court before the final disposition of the case, the court may grant a request to take a driving safety course or a motorcycle operator training course under this article.

(e) A request to take a driving safety course made at or before the time and at the place at which a person is required to appear in court is an appearance in compliance with the person's promise to appear.

(f) The court may require a person requesting a driving safety course to pay a fee set by the court at an amount of not more than $10, including any other fee authorized by statute or municipal ordinance, to cover the cost of administering this article.

(g) A person who requests but does not take a course is not entitled to a refund of the fee.

(h) Fees collected by a municipal court shall be deposited in the municipal treasury. Fees collected by another court shall be deposited in the county treasury of the county in which the court is located.

(i) If a person requesting a driving safety course fails to furnish evidence of the successful completion of the course to the court, the court shall:

(1) notify the person in writing, mailed to the address appearing on the notice to appear, of that failure; and

(2) require the person to appear at the time and place stated in the notice to show cause why the evidence was not timely submitted to the court.

(j) A person who fails to appear at the time and place stated in the notice commits a misdemeanor punishable as provided by Section 543.009, Transportation Code.

(k) On a person's showing of good cause for failure to furnish evidence to the court, the court may allow an extension of time during which the person may present a uniform certificate of course completion as evidence that the person successfully completed the driving safety course.

(*l*) When a person complies with Subsection (b) and a uniform certificate of course completion is accepted by the court, the court shall:

(1) remove the judgment and dismiss the charge;

(2) report the fact that the person successfully completed a driving safety course and the date of completion to the Texas Department of Public Safety for inclusion in the person's driving record; and

(3) state in this report whether the course was taken under the procedure provided by this article to provide information necessary to determine eligibility to take a subsequent course under Subsection (b).

(m) The court may dismiss only one charge for each completion of a course.

(n) A charge that is dismissed under this article may not be part of a person's driving record or used for any purpose.

(*o*) An insurer delivering or issuing for delivery a motor vehicle insurance policy in this state may not cancel or increase the premium charged an insured under the policy because the insured completed a driving safety course or had a charge dismissed under this article.

(p) The court shall advise a person charged with a misdemeanor under Subtitle C, Title 7, Transportation Code, committed while operating a motor vehicle of the person's right under this article to successfully complete a driving safety course or, if the offense was committed while operating a motorcycle, a motorcycle operator training course. The right to complete a course does not apply to a person charged with a violation of Section 545.066, 545.401, 545.421, 550.022, or 550.023, Transportation Code, or serious traffic violation as defined by Section 522.003, Transportation Code.

**Note:** *L.1999, chap. 1387(2), eff. 9/1/99, adds as Art. 45.541 an identical Article as Art. 45.0511, with the exception of the following subsection:*

(q) Nothing in this article shall prevent a court from assessing a special expense for deferred disposition in the same manner as provided for in Article 45.14*. For a deferred disposition under Subsection (b)(1), the court may only collect a fee of up to $10 in addition to any other applicable court cost.

**See, now, Article 45.051.*

*(Added by L.1999, chap. 1545(51), eff. 9/1/99.)*

**Art. 45.052. Dismissal of misdemeanor charge on completion of teen court program.**

(a) A justice or municipal court may defer proceedings against a defendant who is under the age of 18 or enrolled full time in an accredited secondary school in a program leading toward a high school diploma for 90 days if the defendant:

(1) is charged with an offense that the court has jurisdiction of under Article 4.11 or 4.14, Code of Criminal Procedure;

(2) pleads nolo contendere or guilty to the offense in open court with the defendant's parent, guardian, or managing conservator present;

(3) presents to the court an oral or written request to attend a teen court program; and

(4) has not successfully completed a teen court program in the two years preceding the date that the alleged offense occurred.

(b) The teen court program must be approved by the court.

(c) The justice or municipal court shall dismiss the charge at the conclusion of the deferral period if the defendant presents satisfactory evidence that the defendant has successfully completed the teen court program.

(d) A charge dismissed under this article may not be part of the defendant's criminal record or driving record or used for any purpose. However, if the charge was for a traffic offense, the court shall report to the Department of Public Safety that the defendant successfully completed the teen court program and the date of completion for inclusion in the defendant's driving record.

(e) The justice or municipal court may require a person who requests a teen court program to pay a fee not to exceed $10 that is set by the court to cover the costs of administering this article. Fees collected by a municipal court shall be deposited in the municipal treasury. Fees collected by a justice court shall be deposited in the county treasury of the county in which the court is located. A person who requests a teen court program and fails to complete the program is not entitled to a refund of the fee.

(f) A court may transfer a case in which proceedings have been deferred under this section to a court in another county if the court to which the case is transferred consents. A case may not be transferred unless it is within the jurisdiction of the court to which it is transferred.

(g) In addition to the fee authorized by Subsection (e) of this article, the court may require a child who requests a teen court program to pay a $10 fee to cover the cost to the teen court for performing its duties under this article. The court shall pay the fee to the teen court program, and the teen court program must account to the court for the receipt and disbursal of the fee. A child who pays a fee under this subsection is not entitled to a refund of the fee, regardless of whether the child successfully completes the teen court program.

(h) A justice or municipal court may exempt a defendant for whom proceedings are deferred under this article from the requirement to pay a court cost or fee that is imposed by another statute.

*(Chgd. By L.1999, chap. 76(6), eff. 9/1/99; redesignated from Art. 45.55 by L.1999, chap. 1545(52), eff. 9/1/99.)*

**Art. 45.053. Dismissal of misdemeanor charge on commitment of chemically dependent person.**

(a) On a plea of guilty or nolo contendere by a defendant or on a finding of guilt in a misdemeanor case punishable by a fine only, a justice or municipal court may defer further proceedings for 90 days without entering an adjudication of guilt if:

(1) the court finds that the offense resulted from or was related to the defendant's chemical dependency; and

(2) an application for court-ordered treatment of the defendant is filed in accordance with Chapter 462, Health and Safety Code.

(b) At the end of the deferral period, the justice or municipal court shall dismiss the charge if satisfactory evidence is presented that the defendant was committed for and completed court-ordered treatment in accordance with Chapter 462, Health and Safety Code, and it shall be clearly noted in the docket that the complaint is dismissed and that there is not a final conviction.

(c) If at the conclusion of the deferral period satisfactory evidence that the defendant was committed for and completed court-ordered treatment in accordance with Chapter 462, Health and Safety Code, is not presented, the justice or municipal court may impose the fine assessed or impose a lesser fine. The imposition of a fine constitutes a final conviction of the defendant.

(d) Records relating to a complaint dismissed under this article may be expunged under Article 55.01 of this code. If a complaint is dismissed under this article, there is not a final conviction and the complaint may not be used against the person for any purpose.
*(Redesignated from Art. 45.56 by L.1999, chap. 1545(53), eff. 9/1/99.)*

## SUBCHAPTER C. PROCEDURES IN JUSTICE COURT

*(Heading added by L.1999, chap. 1545(54), eff. 9/1/99.)*

### Art. 45.101. Justice court prosecutions.

(a) All prosecutions in a justice court shall be conducted by the county or district attorney or a deputy county or district attorney.

(b) Except as otherwise provided by law, appeals from justice court may be prosecuted by the district attorney or a deputy district attorney with the consent of the county attorney.
*(Added by L.1999, chap. 1545(55), eff. 9/1/99.)*

### Art. 45.102. Offenses committed in another county.

Whenever complaint is made before any justice of the peace that a felony has been committed in any other than a county in which the complaint is made, the justice shall issue a warrant for the arrest of the accused, directed as in other cases, commanding that the accused be arrested and taken before any magistrate of the county where such felony is alleged to have been committed, forthwith, for examination as in other cases. *(Redesignated from Art. 45.21 and chgd. by L.1999, chap. 1545(56), eff. 9/1/99.)*

### Art. 45.103. Warrant without complaint.

If a criminal offense that a justice of the peace has jurisdiction to try is committed within the view of the justice, the justice may issue a warrant for the arrest of the offender. *(Redesignated from Art. 45.15 and chgd. by L.1999, chap. 1545(57), eff. 9/1/99.)*

## SUBCHAPTER D. PROCEDURES IN MUNICIPAL COURT

*(Heading added by L.1999, chap. 1545(58), eff. 9/1/99.)*

### Art. 45.201. Municipal prosecutions.

(a) All prosecutions in a municipal court shall be conducted by the city attorney of the municipality or by a deputy city attorney.

(b) The county attorney of the county in which the municipality is situated may, if the county attorney so desires, also represent the state in such prosecutions. In such cases, the county attorney is not entitled to receive any fees or other compensation for those services.

(c) With the consent of the county attorney, appeals from municipal court to a county court, county court at law, or any appellate court may be prosecuted by the city attorney or a deputy city attorney.

(d) It is the primary duty of a municipal prosecutor not to convict, but to see that justice is done.
*(Redesignated from Art. 45.03 and chgd. by L.1999, chap. 1545(59), eff. 9/1/99.)*

### Art. 45.202. Service of process.

(a) All process issuing out of a municipal court may be served and shall be served when directed by the court, by a peace officer or marshal of the municipality within which it is situated, under the same rules as are provided by law for the service by sheriffs and constables of process issuing out of the justice court, so far as applicable.

(b) The peace officer or marshal may serve all process issuing out of a municipal court anywhere in the county in which the municipality is situated. If the municipality is situated in more than one county, the peace officer or marshal may serve the process throughout those counties. *(Redesignated from Art. 45.04 and chgd. by L.1999, chap. 1545(60), eff. 9/1/99.)*

**Art. 45.203. Collection of fines, costs, and special expenses.**

(a) The governing body of each municipality shall by ordinance prescribe rules, not inconsistent with any law of this state, as may be proper to enforce the collection of fines imposed by a municipal court. In addition to any other method of enforcement, the municipality may enforce the collection of fines by:

(1) execution against the property of the defendant; or

(2) imprisonment of the defendant.

(b) The governing body of a municipality may adopt such rules and regulations, not inconsistent with any law of this state, concerning the practice and procedure in the municipal court as the governing body may consider proper.

(c) The governing body of each municipality may prescribe by ordinance the collection, after due notice, of a special expense, not to exceed $25 for the issuance and service of a warrant of arrest for an offense under Section 38.10, Penal Code, or Section 543.009, Transportation Code. Money collected from the special expense shall be paid into the municipal treasury for the use and benefit of the municipality.

(d) Costs may not be imposed or collected in criminal cases in municipal court by municipal ordinance.

*(Redesignated from Art. 45.06 and chgd. by L.1999, chap. 1545(61), eff. 9/1/99.)*

## MISCELLANEOUS PROCEEDINGS

## CHAPTER 46. INSANITY AS DEFENSE

Article



**Art. 46.01.** *(Repealed by L.1999, chap. 561(8), eff. 9/1/99.)*

**Art. 46.02. Incompetency to stand trial.† [*Incompetency to be tried.*]**

**Sec. 1. Definition.** In this article, "residential care facility" has the meaning assigned by Section 591.003, Health and Safety Code. *(Added by L.1999, chap. 561(1), eff. 9/1/99.)*

**Sec. 1A. Incompetency to stand trial.** (a) A person is incompetent to stand trial if the person does not have:

(1) sufficient present ability to consult with the person's lawyer with a reasonable degree of rational understanding; or

(2) a rational as well as factual understanding of the proceedings against the person.

(b) A defendant is presumed competent to stand trial and shall be found competent to stand trial unless proved incompetent by a preponderance of the evidence.

*(Redesignated from Sec. 1 by L.1999, chap. 561(1), eff. 9/1/99.)*

**Sec. 2.** (a) The issue of the defendant's incompetency to stand trial shall be determined in advance of the trial on the merits if the court determines there is evidence to support a finding of incompetency to stand trial on its own motion or on written motion by the defendant or his counsel filed prior to the date set for trial on the merits asserting that the defendant is incompetent to stand trial.

(b) If during the trial evidence of the defendant's incompetency is brought to the attention of the court from any source, the court must conduct a hearing out of the presence of the jury to determine whether or not there is evidence to support a finding of incompetency to stand trial.

**Sec. 3.** (a) At any time the issue of the defendant's incompetency to stand trial is raised, the court may, on its own motion or motion by the defendant, his counsel, or the prosecuting attorney, appoint disinterested experts experienced and qualified in mental health or mental retardation to examine the defendant with regard to his competency to stand trial and to testify at any trial or hearing on this issue.

(b) The court may order any defendant to submit to examination for the purposes described in this article. If the defendant is free on bail, the court in its discretion may order him to submit to examination. If the defendant fails or refuses to submit to examination, the court may order him to custody for examination for a reasonable period not to exceed 21 days. The court may not order a defendant to a facility operated by the Texas Department of Mental Health and Mental Retardation for examination without the consent of the head of that facility or for a period exceeding 21 days. If a defendant who has been ordered to a facility operated by Texas Department of Mental Health and Mental Retardation for examination remains in such facility for a period of time exceeding 21 days, the head of that facility shall cause the defendant to be immediately transported to the committing court and placed in the custody of the sheriff of the county in which the committing court is located. That county shall reimburse the Texas Department of Mental Health and Mental Retardation facility for the mileage and per diem expenses of the personnel required to transport the defendant calculated in accordance with the state travel regulations in effect at the time.

(c) The court shall advise any expert appointed pursuant to this section of the facts and circumstances of the offense with which the defendant is charged and the meaning of incompetency to stand trial.

(d) A written report of the examination shall be submitted to the court within 30 days of the order of examination, and the court shall furnish copies of the report to the defense counsel and the prosecuting attorney. The report shall include a description of the procedures used in the examination, the examiner's observations and findings pertaining to the defendant's competency to stand trial, and the recommended treatment. If the examiner concludes that the defendant is incompetent to stand trial, the report shall include the examiner's observations and findings about whether there is a substantial probability that the defendant will attain the competence to stand trial in the foreseeable future. The examiner shall also submit a separate report setting forth the examiner's observations and findings concerning:

(1) whether the defendant is a person with mental illness and meets the criteria for court-ordered inpatient mental health services under Subtitle C, Title 7, Health and Safety Code; or

(2) whether the defendant is a person with mental retardation and meets the criteria for commitment to a residential care facility under Subtitle D, Title 7, Health and Safety Code.

(e) If the examiner is a physician and concludes that the defendant is a person with mental illness, the examiner shall complete and submit to the court a Certificate of Medical Examination for Mental Illness. If the examiner is a physician or a licensed psychologist and determines that the defendant is a person with mental retardation and if the determination has been made in accordance with the standards established by Section 593.005, Health and Safety Code, the examiner shall submit to the court an affidavit setting forth the conclusions reached as a result of the examination.

(f) The appointed experts shall be paid by the county in which the indictment was returned or information was filed. A facility operated by the Texas Department of Mental Health and Mental Retardation which accepts a defendant for examination under Subsection (a) of this section shall be reimbursed by the county in which the indictment was returned or information was filed for such expenses incurred as are determined by the department to be reasonably necessary and incidental to the proper examination of the defendant.

(g) No statement made by the defendant during the examination or hearing on his competency to stand trial may be admitted in evidence against the defendant on the issue of guilt in any criminal proceeding.

(h) When a defendant wishes to be examined by a psychiatrist or other expert of his own choice, the court on timely request shall provide the examiner with reasonable opportunity to examine the defendant.

(i) The experts appointed under this section to examine the defendant with regard to his competency to stand trial also may be appointed by the court to examine the defendant with regard to the insanity defense pursuant to Section 3 of Article 46.03 of this code, but separate written reports concerning the defendant's competency to stand trial and the insanity defense shall be filed with the court.

*(Chgd. by L.1999, chap. 561(2), eff. 9/1/99.)*

**Sec. 4.** (a) If the court determines that there is evidence to support a finding of incompetency to stand trial, a jury shall be impaneled to determine the defendant's competency to stand trial. This determination shall be made by a jury that has not been selected to determine the guilt or innocence of the defendant. If the defendant is found incompetent to stand trial, a further hearing may be held to determine whether or not the defendant:

(1) is a person with mental illness and meets the criteria for court- ordered inpatient mental health services under Subtitle C, Title 7, Health and Safety Code; or

(2) is a person with mental retardation and meets the criteria for commitment to a residential care facility under Subtitle D, Title 7, Health and Safety Code.

(b) The defendant is entitled to counsel at the competency hearing. If the defendant is indigent and the court has not yet appointed counsel to represent the defendant, the court shall appoint counsel prior to the competency hearing.

(c) If the issue of incompetency to stand trial is raised other than by written motion in advance of trial pursuant to Subsection (a) of Section 2 of this article and the court determines that there is evidence to support a finding of incompetency to stand trial, the court shall set the issue for determination at any time prior to the sentencing of the defendant. If the competency hearing is delayed until after a verdict on the guilt or innocence of the defendant is returned, the competency hearing shall be held as soon thereafter as reasonably possible, but a competency hearing may be held only if the verdict in the trial on the merits is "guilty." If the defendant is found incompetent to stand trial after the beginning of the trial on the merits, the court shall declare a mistrial in the trial on the merits. A subsequent trial and conviction of the defendant for the same offense is not barred and jeopardy does not attach by reason of a mistrial under this section.

(d) Instructions submitting the issue of incompetency to stand trial shall be framed to require the jury to state in its verdict:

(1) whether the defendant is incompetent to stand trial; and

(2) if found incompetent to stand trial, whether there is no substantial probability that the defendant will attain the competency to stand trial within the foreseeable future.

(e) If the jury is unable to agree on a unanimous verdict after a reasonable opportunity to deliberate, the court shall declare a mistrial of the incompetency hearing, discharge the jury, and impanel another jury to determine the incompetency of the defendant to stand trial.

(f) If the defendant is found competent to stand trial, the court shall dismiss the jury that decided the issue and may continue the trial on the merits before the court or with the jury selected for that purpose.

(g) If the defendant is found incompetent to stand trial and it is determined that there is a substantial probability that he will attain the competency to stand trial within the foreseeable future, the court shall proceed under Section 5 of this article.

(h) If the defendant is found incompetent to stand trial and there is found no substantial probability that the defendant will become competent within the foreseeable future, and the court determines there is evidence that the defendant is a person with mental illness or mental retardation, and all charges pending against the defendant are not then dismissed, the court shall proceed under Section 6 of this article or shall release the defendant.

(i) If the defendant is found incompetent to stand trial and there is found no substantial probability that the defendant will become competent within the foreseeable future, and the court determines there is evidence that the defendant is a person with mental illness or mental retardation, and all charges pending against the defendant are then dismissed, the court shall proceed under Section 7 of this article or shall release the defendant.

*(Chgd. by L.1999, chap. 561(3), eff. 9/1/99.)*

**Sec. 5.** (a) When a defendant has been determined incompetent to stand trial for any felony or for a misdemeanor because of mental retardation, and absent a determination that there is no substantial probability that the defendant will attain competency to stand trial in the foreseeable future, the court shall enter an order committing the defendant to the maximum security unit of any facility designated by the Texas Department of Mental Health and Mental Retardation, to an agency of the United States operating a mental hospital, or to a Veterans Administration hospital for a period not to exceed 18 months. When a defendant has been determined incompetent to stand trial for a misdemeanor because of mental illness, and absent a determination that there is no substantial probability that the defendant will attain competency to stand trial in the foreseeable future, the court shall enter an order committing the defendant to the mental health facility designated by the Commissioner of Mental Health and Mental Retardation to serve the catchment area in which the committing court is located for a period not to exceed 18 months. An order issued under this subsection shall also place the defendant in the custody of the sheriff for transportation to the facility to be confined in the facility for further examination and treatment toward the specific objective of attaining competency to stand trial. The court shall order that a transcript of all medical testimony received by the jury be forthwith prepared by the court reporter and that the transcript, together with a statement of the facts and circumstances surrounding the alleged offense, shall accompany the patient to the facility.

(b) No person shall be committed to a mental health or residential care facility under this section except on competent medical or psychiatric testimony.

(c) The facility to which the defendant is committed shall develop an individual program of treatment and shall report on the defendant's progress toward achieving competency to the court at least every 90 days.

(d) Nothing in this section precludes the court from allowing the defendant to be released on bail if the court determines that the defendant can be adequately treated on an outpatient basis for the purpose of attaining competency to stand trial.

(e) If the charges pending against a defendant are dismissed, the committing court shall send a copy of the order of dismissal to the head of the facility in which the defendant is held and the defendant shall then be discharged.

(f) The head of a facility to which a person has been committed pursuant to Subsection (a) of this section shall promptly notify the committing court:

(1) when he is of the opinion that the defendant has attained competency to stand trial; or

(2) when he is of the opinion that there is no substantial probability that the defendant will attain the competency to stand trial in the foreseeable future; or

(3) when an 18-months commitment is due to expire, such notice to be given 14 days prior to such expiration.

(g) On notification to the committing court under Subsection (f) of this section, the sheriff of the county in which the committing court is located shall forthwith transport the defendant to the committing court; provided, however, that if the defendant remains in the maximum security unit of a facility of the Texas Department of Mental Health and Mental Retardation 14 days following receipt by the committing court of such notification, the head of that facility shall cause the defendant to be immediately transported to the committing court and placed in the custody of the sheriff of the county in which the committing court is located. That county shall reimburse the Texas Department of Mental Health and Mental Retardation facility for the mileage and per diem expenses of the personnel required to transport the defendant calculated in accordance with the state travel regulations in effect at the time.

(h) Upon the defendant's return to court, if he has no counsel and the court determines that the defendant is indigent, the court shall appoint counsel to represent him.

(i) When the head of a facility to which the defendant is committed discharges the defendant and the defendant is returned to court, a final report shall be filed with the court documenting the applicable reason for the discharge under Subsection (f) of this section, and the court shall furnish copies to the defense counsel and the prosecuting attorney. If the head of the facility is of the opinion that the defendant is a person with mental illness and meets the criteria for court-ordered inpatient mental health services under Subtitle C, Title 7, Health and Safety Code, the head of the facility shall cause to have completed and submitted to the court a Certificate of Medical Examination for Mental Illness. If the head of the facility is of the opinion that the defendant is a person with mental retardation, as defined by Section 591.003, Health and Safety Code, the head of the facility shall cause to be submitted to the court an affidavit setting forth the conclusions reached as a result of the examination. When the report is filed with the court, the court is authorized to make a determination based solely on the report with regard to the defendant's competency to stand trial, unless the prosecuting attorney or the defense counsel objects in writing or in open court to the findings of the report within 15 days from the time the report is served on the parties. In the event of objection, the issue shall be set for a hearing before the court or, on motion by the defendant, the defense counsel, the prosecuting attorney, or the court, the hearing shall be held before a jury. The hearing shall be held within 30 days following the date of objection unless continued for good cause.

(j) No defendant who has been committed to a facility under Subsection (a) of this section may be recommitted to a facility under that subsection in connection with the same offense.

(k) If the defendant is found competent to stand trial, criminal proceedings against him may be resumed.

(*l*) If the defendant is found incompetent to stand trial, and all charges pending against the defendant are not then dismissed, the court shall proceed under Section 6 of this article or shall release the defendant.

(m) If the defendant is found incompetent to stand trial, and all charges pending against the defendant are then dismissed, the court shall proceed under Section 7 of this article or shall release the defendant.

*(Chgd. by L.1999, chap. 561(4), eff. 9/1/99.)*

**Sec. 6. Civil commitment—charges pending.** (a) If a defendant is found incompetent to stand trial and there is found no substantial probability that the defendant will become competent in the foreseeable future, or if the defendant is found incompetent to stand trial and the defendant has been previously committed to a facility under Subsection (a) of Section 5 of this article in connection with the same offense, and, in either event, all charges pending against the defendant are not then dismissed, the court shall determine whether there is evidence to support findings that the defendant is a person with mental illness or a person with mental retardation and requires commitment to a mental health or residential care facility.

(b) If it appears to the court that the defendant may be a person with mental illness and there is on file with the court Certificates of Medical Examination for Mental Illness by two physicians, at least one of whom must not be employed by the Texas Department of Mental Health and Mental Retardation, who have examined the defendant within 30 days of the date of the commitment hearing, the court shall impanel a jury to determine whether the defendant shall be committed to a mental health facility or the hearing may be held before the jury impaneled to determine the defendant's competency to stand trial.

(1) If there has not been filed with the court the required Certificates of Medical Examination for Mental Illness, the judge shall appoint the necessary physicians, at least one of whom shall be a psychiatrist, if one is available in the county, to examine the defendant and file certificates with the court. The judge may order the defendant to submit to the examination.

(2) Proceedings for commitment of the defendant to a mental health facility are governed by Subtitle C, Title 7, Health and Safety Code, to the extent that subtitle applies and does not conflict with this article, except that the criminal court shall conduct the proceedings whether or not the criminal court is also the county court.

(3) If the defendant has not been under observation or treatment in a mental hospital for at least 60 days under Section 5(a) of this article or under an Order of Temporary Commitment under Subtitle C, Title 7, Health and Safety Code, within the 12 months immediately preceding the date of the hearing, the instructions submitting the issue shall be framed to require the jury to state in its verdict whether the defendant is a person with mental illness and whether the defendant meets the criteria for court-ordered inpatient mental health services under Subtitle C, Title 7, Health and Safety Code.

(4) If the jury finds under Subdivision (3) of this subsection that the defendant is not a person with mental illness or does not meet the criteria for court-ordered inpatient mental health services, the court shall order the immediate release of the defendant.

If the jury finds under Subdivision (3) of this subsection that the defendant is a person with mental illness and meets the criteria for court-ordered inpatient mental health services, the court shall order that the defendant be committed to a state mental hospital for inpatient care for a period not exceeding 90 days.

(5) If the defendant has been under observation or treatment in a mental hospital for at least 60 days under Section 5(a) of this article or under an Order of Temporary Commitment under Subtitle C, Title 7, Health and Safety Code, within the 12 months immediately preceding the date of the hearing, the instructions submitting the issue shall be framed to require the jury to state in its verdict whether the defendant is a person with mental illness and whether the defendant meets the criteria for court-ordered inpatient mental health services under Subtitle C, Title 7, Health and Safety Code.

(6) If the jury finds under Subdivision (5) of this subsection that the defendant is not a person with mental illness or that the defendant does not meet the criteria for court-ordered inpatient mental health services, the court shall enter an order discharging the defendant.

If the jury finds under Subdivision (5) of this subsection that the defendant is a person with mental illness and meets the criteria for court-ordered inpatient mental health services, the court shall order that the defendant be committed as a patient to a state mental hospital for inpatient care for a period not to exceed 12 months.

(7) If the court enters an order committing the defendant to a state mental hospital, the defendant shall be treated and released in conformity with Subtitle C, Title 7, Health and Safety Code, except as may be provided in this article.

(c) If it appears to the court that the defendant may be a person with mental retardation and there is on file with the court a determination of mental retardation made in accordance with the standards established by Section 593.005, Health and Safety Code, the court shall impanel a jury to determine whether the defendant is a person with mental retardation or the hearing may be held before the jury impaneled to determine the defendant's competency to stand trial.

(1) If that determination is not on file with the court, the judge shall arrange for the examination of the defendant by a facility of the Texas Department of Mental Health and Mental Retardation or by a local mental health and mental retardation authority approved by that department. The

judge may order the defendant to submit to the examination. The county shall reimburse the facility or authority that conducts the examination for the reasonable and necessary expenses incurred in conducting the examination.

(2) Proceedings for commitment of the defendant to a residential care facility are governed by Subtitle D, Title 7, Health and Safety Code, to the extent that subtitle applies and does not conflict with this article, except that the criminal court shall conduct the proceedings whether or not the criminal court is also a county court.

(3) The instructions submitting the issue of mental retardation to the jury shall be framed to require the jury to state in its verdict whether the defendant is a person with mental retardation as defined by Section 591.003, Health and Safety Code, and if so, whether the defendant meets the criteria for commitment to a residential care facility.

(4) If the jury finds that the defendant is not a person with mental retardation as defined by Section 591.003, Health and Safety Code, or that the defendant does not meet the criteria for commitment to a residential care facility, the court shall enter an order discharging the defendant.

(5) If the jury finds that the defendant is a person with mental retardation as defined by Section 591.003, Health and Safety Code, and meets the criteria for commitment to a residential care facility, the court shall enter an order declaring that fact and that the person is committed to a residential care facility of the Texas Department of Mental Health and Mental Retardation.

(6) If the court enters an order committing the defendant to a residential care facility of the Texas Department of Mental Health and Mental Retardation, the defendant shall be treated and released in accordance with Subtitle D, Title 7, Health and Safety Code, except as otherwise provided by this article.

(d) In the proceedings conducted under this section:

(1) an application for court-ordered temporary or extended mental health services or to have the defendant declared a person with mental retardation may not be required;

(2) the provisions of Subtitles C and D, Title 7, Health and Safety Code, relating to notice of hearing do not apply; and

(3) appeals from the criminal court proceedings under this section shall be to the court of appeals as in the proceedings for court-ordered inpatient mental health services under Subtitle C, Title 7, Health and Safety Code, or for commitment to a residential care facility under Subtitle D, Title 7, Health and Safety Code.

*(Chgd. by L.1999, chap. 561(5), eff. 9/1/99.)*

**Sec. 7. Civil commitment—charges dismissed.** If a defendant is found incompetent to stand trial and there is found no substantial probability that the defendant will become competent in the foreseeable future, or if the defendant is found incompetent to stand trial and the defendant has been previously committed to a facility under Section 5 of this article and all charges pending against the defendant are then dismissed, the court shall determine whether there is evidence to support a finding that the defendant is either a person with mental illness or a person with mental retardation. If it appears to the court that there is evidence to support either finding, the court shall enter an order transferring the defendant to the appropriate court for civil commitment proceedings, stating that all charges pending against the defendant in that court have been dismissed, and may order the defendant detained in jail or other suitable place pending the prompt initiation and prosecution by the attorney for the state or other person designated by the court of appropriate civil proceedings to determine whether the defendant will be committed to a mental health or residential care facility; provided, however, that a patient placed in a facility of the Texas Department of Mental Health and Mental Retardation pending civil hearing under this section may be detained in that facility only pursuant to an Order of Protective Custody issued under Subtitle C, Title 7, Health and Safety Code, and with the consent of the head of the facility, or the court may give the defendant into the care of a responsible person on satisfactory security being given for the defendant's proper care and protection; otherwise, the defendant shall be discharged. *(Chgd. by L.1999, chap. 561(6), eff. 9/1/99.)*

**Sec. 8. General.** (a) A person committed to a mental health or residential care facility as a result of the proceedings initiated pursuant to Section 6 or Section 7 of this article and who presently has felony charges pending against the person or has had felony charges against the person dismissed pursuant to Section 7 of this article shall be committed to the maximum security unit of any facility designated by the Texas Department of Mental Health and Mental Retardation. Within 60 days following arrival at the maximum security unit, the person shall be transferred to a nonsecurity unit or to a community program of a mental health or residential care facility or a community mental health and mental retardation center designated by the Texas Department of Mental Health and Mental Retardation unless the person is determined to be manifestly dangerous by a review board with the Texas Department of Mental Health and Mental Retardation. The Commissioner of Mental Health and Mental Retardation shall appoint a review board of five members, including one psychiatrist licensed to practice medicine in the State of Texas and two persons who work directly with persons with mental illness or mental retardation, to determine whether the person is manifestly dangerous and, as a result of the danger the person presents, requires continued placement in a maximum security unit. The review board shall make no determination as to the person's need for treatment. A finding that the person is not manifestly dangerous is not a medical determination that the person no longer meets the criteria for involuntary civil commitment under Subtitle C or D, Title 7, Health and Safety Code. If the superintendent of the facility at which the maximum security unit is located disagrees with the determination, then the matter will be referred to the Commissioner of Mental Health and Mental Retardation who will resolve the disagreement by deciding whether the person is manifestly dangerous. A person committed to a mental health facility as a result of the proceedings initiated pursuant to Section 6 or Section 7 of this article who presently has misdemeanor charges pending against the person or has had misdemeanor charges against the person dismissed pursuant to Section 7 of this article shall be committed to the mental health facility which is designated by the Commissioner of Mental Health and Mental Retardation to serve the catchment area in which the committing court is located. A person committed to a residential care facility as a result of the proceedings initiated pursuant to Section 6 or 7 of this article and who presently has misdemeanor charges pending against or has had misdemeanor charges against the person dismissed pursuant to Section 7 of this article shall be committed to the maximum security unit of any facility designated by the Texas Department of Mental Health and Mental Retardation for a maximum of 60 days pending placement in a nonsecurity facility.

(b) The court shall order that a transcript of all medical testimony received in both the criminal proceedings and the civil commitment proceedings be prepared forthwith by the court reporters and that the transcripts, together with a statement of the facts and circumstances surrounding the alleged offense, shall accompany the patient to the mental health or residential care facility.

(c) If the head of a mental health facility determines that a patient committed to a state mental hospital for a period not exceeding 90 days as a result of proceedings initiated pursuant to Section 6 or Section 7 of this article requires extended court-ordered inpatient mental health services, the head of the facility shall notify the court from which the patient was committed in writing at least 30 days prior to the expiration of the temporary commitment. The court from which the patient was committed shall order the sheriff of the county in which the court is located to return the patient for a hearing on court-ordered inpatient mental health services or shall make arrangements for the hearing to be held in an appropriate court of the county in which the patient is hospitalized. Provided, however, that if the patient has not received a hearing on court-ordered inpatient mental health services by the date on which the temporary commitment expires, the head of the facility in which the patient is hospitalized shall cause the patient to be immediately transported to the committing court and placed in the custody of the sheriff of the county in which the court is located. That county shall reimburse the facility of the Texas Department of Mental Health and Mental Retardation for the mileage and per diem expenses of the personnel required to transport the defendant calculated in accordance with the state travel regulations in effect at the time.

(d) The head of a mental health or residential care facility to which a person has been committed or transferred as a result of the proceedings initiated pursuant to Section 6 of this article and who has received written notice from a court or prosecuting attorney that criminal charges are pending against the person shall notify the court in writing at least 14 days prior to the discharge of the person unless the notice provided for in Subsection (c) of this section has been given. A written report as to the competency of the person to stand trial shall accompany the notice of discharge.

(e) On written notice by the head of a mental health or residential care facility that in the opinion of the head of the facility, a person who has been civilly committed to that facility and against whom criminal charges are pending is competent to stand trial, or on good cause shown by the defendant, the defense counsel, or the prosecuting attorney, the court in which the criminal charges are pending may hold a hearing to determine the competency of the defendant to stand trial. The hearing shall be before a jury unless waived by agreement of the parties. The order setting the hearing shall order the defendant placed in the custody of the sheriff for transportation to the court. The court may appoint disinterested experts to examine the defendant in accordance with the provisions of Section 3 of this article. If the defendant is found to be competent to stand trial, the proceedings on the criminal charges may be continued. If the defendant is found incompetent to stand trial and is under an order of commitment to a mental health or residential care facility, the court shall order the defendant placed in the custody of the sheriff for transportation to that facility. If the defendant is found incompetent to stand trial and has been discharged from a mental health or residential care facility, the court may civilly recommit the person under Subtitle C or D, Title 7,

Health and Safety Code. The recommitment shall be made to the facility from which the defendant was discharged if accomplished under Subtitle C, Title 7, Health and Safety Code, and to the Texas Department of Mental Health and Mental Retardation if accomplished under Subtitle D, Title 7, Health and Safety Code. Subsection (d) of this section shall again be followed prior to discharge of the committed person.
*(Chgd. by L.1999, chap. 561(7), eff. 9/1/99.)*

**Sec. 9.** The time a person charged with a criminal offense is confined in a mental health or mental retardation facility pending trial shall be credited to the term of his sentence on subsequent sentencing or resentencing.
*(Chgd. by L.1989, chap. 393(1)-(6), eff. 6/14/89.)*

### Art. 46.03. Insanity defense.

**Sec. 1.** (a) The insanity defense provided in Section 8.01 of the Penal Code shall be submitted to the jury only if supported by competent evidence.

(b) When the insanity defense is submitted, the trier of facts shall determine and include in the verdict or judgment or both whether the defendant is guilty, not guilty, or not guilty by reason of insanity.

(c) The trier of facts shall return a verdict of not guilty by reason of insanity if the prosecution has established beyond a reasonable doubt that the alleged conduct was committed and the defense has established by a preponderance of the evidence that the defendant was insane at the time of the alleged conduct.

(d) A defendant who has been found not guilty by reason of insanity shall stand acquitted of the offense charged and may not be considered a person charged with a criminal offense.

(e) The court, the attorney for the state, or the attorney for the defendant may not inform a juror or a prospective juror of the consequences to the defendant if a verdict of not guilty by reason of insanity is returned.

**Sec. 2.** (a) A defendant planning to offer evidence of the insanity defense shall file a notice of his intention to offer such evidence with the court and the prosecuting attorney:

(1) at least 10 days prior to the date the case is set for trial; or

(2) if the court sets a pretrial hearing before the 10-day period, the defendant shall give notice at the hearing; or

(3) if the defendant raises the issue of his incompetency to stand trial before the 10-day period, he shall at the same time file notice of his intention to offer evidence of the insanity defense.

(b) Unless notice is timely filed pursuant to Subsection (a) of this section, evidence on the insanity defense is not admissible unless the court finds that good cause exists for failure to give notice.

**Sec. 3.** (a) If notice of intention to raise the insanity defense is filed under Section 2 of this article, the court may, on its own motion or motion by the defendant, his counsel, or the prosecuting attorney, appoint disinterested experts experienced and qualified in mental health and mental retardation to examine the defendant with regard to the insanity defense and to testify thereto at any trial or hearing on this issue.

(b) The court may order any defendant to submit to examination for the purposes described in this article. If the defendant is free on bail, the court in its discretion may order him to submit to examination. If the defendant fails or refuses to submit to examination, the court may order him to custody for examination for a reasonable period not to exceed 21 days. The court may not order a defendant to a facility operated by the Texas Department of Mental Health and Mental Retardation for examination without the consent of the head of that facility or for a period exceeding 21 days. If a defendant who has been ordered to a facility operated by the Texas Department of Mental Health and Mental Retardation for examination remains in such facility for a period of time exceeding 21 days, the head of that facility shall cause the defendant to be immediately transported to the committing court and placed in the custody of the sheriff of the county in which the committing court is located. That county shall reimburse the Texas Department of Mental Health and Mental Retardation facility for the mileage and per diem expenses of the personnel required to transport the defendant calculated in accordance with the state travel regulations in effect at that time.

(c) The court shall advise any expert appointed pursuant to this section of the facts and circumstances of the offense with which the defendant is charged and the elements of the insanity defense.

(d) A written report of the examination shall be submitted to the court within 30 days of the order of examination, and the court shall furnish copies of the report to the defense counsel and the prosecuting attorney. The report shall include a description of the procedures used in the examination and the examiner's observations and findings pertaining to the insanity defense. The examiner shall also submit a separate report setting forth his observations and findings concerning:

(1) whether the defendant is presently mentally ill and requires court-ordered mental health services; or

(2) whether the defendant is a mentally retarded person as defined in the Mentally Retarded Persons Act of 1977 (Article 5547-300, Texas Civil Statutes).

(e) The appointed experts shall be paid by the county in which the indictment was returned or information was filed. A facility operated by the Texas Department of Mental Health and Mental Retardation which accepts a defendant for examination under Subsection (a) of this section shall be reimbursed by the county in which the indictment was returned or information was filed for such expenses incurred as are determined by the department to be reasonably necessary and incidental to the proper examination of the defendant.

(f) When a defendant wishes to be examined by a psychiatrist or other expert of his own choice, the court on timely request shall provide the examiner with reasonable opportunity to examine the defendant.

(g) The experts appointed under this section to examine the defendant with regard to the insanity defense also may be appointed by the court to examine the defendant with regard to his competency to stand trial pursuant to Section 3 of Article 46.02 of this code, provided that separate written reports concerning the defendant's competency to stand trial and the insanity defense shall be filed with the court.

**Sec. 4.** (a) Act Did Not Involve Serious Bodily Injury; Civil Commitment. If a defendant is found not guilty by reason of insanity in the trial of a criminal offense, the court shall determine whether the conduct committed by the defendant involved an act, attempt, or threat of serious bodily injury to another person. If the court determines that the defendant had not committed an act, attempt, or threat of serious bodily injury to another person, then the court shall further determine whether there is evidence to support findings that the defendant is either mentally ill or is a mentally retarded person. If the court determines that there is evidence to support either of such findings, the court shall transfer the defendant to the appropriate court for civil commitment proceedings and may order the defendant detained in jail or other suitable place pending the prompt initiation and prosecution by the attorney for the state or other person designated by the court of appropriate civil proceedings to determine whether the defendant shall be committed to a mental health or mental retardation facility; provided, however, that a patient placed in a facility of the Texas Department of Mental Health and Mental Retardation pending civil hearing under this section shall only be detained pursuant to the provisions for an Order of Protective Custody as set out in the Texas Mental Health Code and with the consent of the head of the facility, or the court may give the defendant into the care of a responsible person on satisfactory security being given for this proper care and protection; otherwise, the defendant shall be discharged.

(b) Commitment to Maximum Security Unit; Transfer to Nonsecurity Unit. A person committed to a mental health or mental retardation facility as a result of the proceedings initiated pursuant to Subsection (d) of this section shall be committed to the maximum security unit of any facility designated by the Texas Department of Mental Health and Mental Retardation. Within 60 days following arrival at the maximum security unit, the person shall be transferred to a nonsecurity unit of a mental health and mental retardation facility designated by the Texas Department of Mental Health and Mental Retardation unless the person is determined to be manifestly dangerous by a review board within the Texas Department of Mental Health and Mental Retardation. The Commissioner of Mental Health and Mental Retardation shall appoint a review board of five members, including one psychiatrist licensed to practice medicine in this state and two persons who work directly with mental health patients or mentally retarded clients, to determine whether the person is manifestly dangerous. If the superintendent of the facility at which the maximum security unit is located disagrees with the determination, then the matter will be referred to the Commissioner of Mental Health and Mental Retardation who will resolve the disagreement by deciding whether the person is manifestly dangerous.

(c) Transcript of all Medical Testimony. The court shall order that a transcript of all medical testimony received in both the criminal proceedings and the commitment proceedings be prepared forthwith by the court reporters and that such transcripts, together with a statement of the facts and circumstances surrounding the alleged offense, shall accompany the patient to the mental health or mental retardation facility.

(d) Act, Attempt, or Threat of Serious Bodily Injury; Special Commitment; Out-patient Supervision; Recommitment.

(1) Automatic Commitment for Evaluation. If a defendant is found not guilty by reason of insanity in the trial of a criminal offense and the court determines that the defendant committed an act, attempt, or threat of serious bodily injury to another person, the trial court shall retain jurisdiction over the person so acquitted and shall order such person to be committed to the maximum security unit of any facility designated by the Texas Department of Mental Health and Mental Retardation until such time as he is eligible for release pursuant to this subsection or is eligible for transfer to a nonsecurity facility pursuant to Subsection (b) of this section. The court shall order that an examination of the defendant's present mental condition be conducted and that a report be filed with the court.

(2) Hearing. A hearing shall take place not later than 30 days following the acquittal order to determine if the person acquitted by reason of insanity is presently mentally ill or mentally retarded and meets the criteria for involuntary commitment as provided in the Texas Mental Health Code (Article 5547-1 et seq., Texas Civil Statutes) or the Mentally Retarded Person's Act (Article 5547-300, Texas Civil Statutes). The hearing shall be conducted by the trial court in the same manner as a hearing on an application for involuntary commitment pursuant to the Mental Health Code or the Mentally Retarded Person's Act.

(3) Determination and Disposition. If, after the hearing, the court finds that the acquitted person meets the criteria for involuntary commitment, the court shall order that person to be committed to a mental hospital or other appropriate facility, as designated by the Texas Department of Mental Health and Mental Retardation, for a period not exceeding 90 days. The court may order the acquitted person to participate in a prescribed regimen of medical, psychiatric, or psychological care or treatment on an out-patient basis pursuant to the provisions of Subdivision (4) of this subsection. If the court finds that the person acquitted by reason of insanity does not meet the criteria for involuntary commitment, the court shall order that person's immediate release.

(4) Out-patient Supervision. If at the time of the evaluation as provided in Subdivision (1) of this subsection prior to the hearing on in voluntary commitment, the report of the defendant's present mental condition includes a recommendation that the person acquitted by reason of insanity meets the criteria for involuntary commitment but that such treatment or care can be provided on an out-patient basis provided he participates in a prescribed regimen of medical, psychiatric, or psychological care or treatment, and the court finds that the acquitted person does meet those criteria, the court may order the acquitted person to participate in that prescribed regimen of medical, psychiatric, or psychological care or treatment. The court may at any time modify or revoke the out-patient regimen of medical, psychiatric, or psychological care or treatment pursuant to the requirements of the Mental Health Code or the Mentally Retarded Person's Act. The court shall review the continuing need for such order at the completion of 90 days from the issuance of the initial out-patient order and no less often than once every 12 months for subsequent out-patient orders pursuant to the requirements of the Mental Health Code or Mentally Retarded Person's Act.

(5) Judicial Release. A person acquitted by reason of insanity and committed to a mental hospital or other appropriate facility pursuant to Subdivision (3) of this subsection may only be discharged by order of the committing court in accordance with the procedures specified in this subsection. If at any time prior to the expiration of a commitment order the superintendent of the facility to which the acquitted person is committed determines that the person has recovered from his mental condition to such an extent that he no longer meets the criteria for involuntary commitment or that he continues to meet those criteria but that treatment or care can be provided on an out-patient basis provided he participates in a prescribed regimen of medical, psychiatric, or psychological care and treatment, the director of the facility shall promptly file a certificate to that effect with the clerk of the court that ordered the commitment. If the superintendent of the facility intends to recommend release, out-patient care, or continued in-patient care upon the expiration of a commitment order, the superintendent shall file a certificate to that effect with the clerk of the court that ordered the commitment at least 14 days prior to the expiration of that order. The clerk shall notify the district or county attorney upon receipt of such certificate. Upon receipt of such certificate or upon the expiration of a commitment order, the court shall order the discharge of the acquitted person or on the motion of the district or county attorney or on its own motion shall hold a hearing, prior to the expiration of the commitment order, conducted pursuant to the provisions of the Mental Health Code or the Mentally Retarded Person's Act as appropriate, to determine if the acquitted person continues to meet the criteria for involuntary commitment and whether an order should be issued requiring the person to participate in a prescribed regimen of medical, psychiatric, or psychological care or treatment on an out-patient basis as provided in Subdivision (4) of this subsection. If the court determines that the acquitted person continues to meet the criteria for involuntary commitment and that out-patient supervision is not appropriate, the court shall order

that the person be returned to a mental hospital or other appropriate in-patient or residential facility. If the court finds that continued in-patient or residential care is required, the commitment will continue until the expiration of the original order, if one is still in effect, or the court shall issue a new commitment order of an appropriate duration as specified in the Mental Health Code or the Mentally Retarded Person's Act. If a hearing on a request for discharge or out-patient supervision has been held prior to the expiration of a commitment order, the court is not required to act on a subsequent request except upon the expiration of a commitment order or upon the expiration of 90 days following a hearing on a previous request. Commitment orders subsequent to an initial commitment order issued under this subsection shall be of an appropriate duration as specified in the Mental Health Code or the Mentally Retarded Person's Act, whichever is applicable.

(6) Modification or Revocation of Out-patient Supervision. The director of the facility or other individual responsible for administering a regimen of out-patient care or treatment imposed on an acquitted person pursuant to Subdivision (4) or (5) of this subsection shall notify the court ordering such out-patient care of any failure of the person to comply with that regimen or if the person's condition has so deteriorated that out-patient care is no longer appropriate. Upon such notice or upon other probable cause to believe that the person has failed to comply with the prescribed regimen of medical, psychiatric, or psychological care or treatment, the person may be taken into custody and brought without unnecessary delay before the court having jurisdiction over him. The court shall determine, after a hearing, whether the person should be remanded to a suitable facility for protective custody, pursuant to the provisions of the Mental Health Code or the Mentally Retarded Person's Act, pending a hearing on whether the person continues to meet the criteria for involuntary commitment and whether the out-patient order should be modified or revoked.

(7) In no event may a person acquitted by reason of insanity be committed to a mental hospital or other in-patient or residential facility pursuant to this subsection for a cumulative period of time which exceeds the maximum term provided by law for the crime for which the acquitted person was tried. Upon expiration of that maximum term, the acquitted person may be further confined in such a facility only pursuant to civil commitment proceedings.

*(Chgd. by L.1989, chap. 393(7)-(9), eff. 6/14/89.)*

### Art. 46.04. Competency to be executed.

(a) A person who is incompetent to be executed may not be executed.

(b) The trial court retains jurisdiction over motions filed by or for a defendant under this article.

(c) A motion filed under this article must identify the proceeding in which the defendant was convicted, give the date of the final judgment, set forth the fact that an execution date has been set if the date has been set, and clearly set forth alleged facts in support of the assertion that the defendant is presently incompetent to be executed. The defendant shall attach affidavits, records, or other evidence supporting the defendant's allegations or shall state why those items are not attached. The defendant shall identify any previous proceedings in which the defendant challenged the defendant's competency in relation to the conviction and sentence in question, including any challenge to the defendant's competency to be executed, competency to stand trial, or sanity at the time of the offense. The motion must be verified by the oath of some person on the defendant's behalf.

(d) On receipt of a motion filed under this article, the trial court shall determine whether the defendant has raised a substantial doubt of the defendant's competency to be executed on the basis of:

(1) the motion, any attached documents, and any responsive pleadings; and

(2) if applicable, the presumption of competency under Subsection (e).

(e) If a defendant is determined to have previously filed a motion under this article, and has previously been determined to be competent to be executed, the previous adjudication creates a presumption of competency and the defendant is not entitled to a hearing on the subsequent motion filed under this article, unless the defendant makes a prima facie showing of a substantial change in circumstances sufficient to raise a significant question as to the defendant's competency to be executed at the time of filing the subsequent motion under this article.

(f) If the trial court determines that the defendant has made a substantial showing of incompetency, the court shall order at least two mental health experts to examine the defendant using the standard described by Subsection (h) to determine whether the defendant is incompetent to be executed.

(g) If the trial court does not determine that the defendant has made a substantial showing of incompetency, the court shall deny the motion.

(h) A defendant is incompetent to be executed if the defendant does not understand:

(1) that he or she is to be executed and that the execution is imminent; and
(2) the reason he or she is being executed.

(i) Mental health experts who examine a defendant under this article shall provide within a time ordered by the trial court copies of their reports to the attorney representing the state, the attorney representing the defendant, and the court.

(j) By filing a motion under this article, the defendant waives any claim of privilege with respect to, and consents to the release of, all mental health and medical records relevant to whether the defendant is incompetent to be executed.

(k) If, on the basis of reports provided under Subsection (i), the motion, any attached documents, any responsive pleadings, and any evidence introduced in the final competency hearing, the trial court makes a finding by a preponderance of the evidence that the defendant is incompetent to be executed, the clerk shall send immediately to the court of criminal appeals in accordance with Section 8(d), Article 11.071, the appropriate documents for that court's determination of whether any existing execution date should be withdrawn and a stay of execution issued. If a stay of execution is issued by the court of criminal appeals, the trial court periodically shall order that the defendant be reexamined by mental health experts to determine whether the defendant is no longer incompetent to be executed.

(*l*) If the trial court does not make the finding as described by Subsection (k), the court may set an execution date as otherwise provided by law.

*(Added by L.1999, chap. 654(1), eff. 9/1/99. See other Art. 46.04 below.)*

## Art. 46.04. Transportation to a mental health facility or residential care facility

**Sec. 1. Persons accompanying transport.** (a) A patient transported from a jail or detention facility to a mental health facility or a residential care facility shall be transported by a special officer for mental health assignment certified under Section 415.037, Government Code, or by a sheriff or constable.

(b) The court ordering the transport shall require appropriate medical personnel to accompany the person transporting the patient, at the expense of the county from which the patient is transported, if there is reasonable cause to believe the patient will require medical assistance or will require the administration of medication during the transportation.

(c) A female patient must be accompanied by a female attendant.

**Sec. 2. Requirements for transport.** The transportation of a patient from a jail or detention facility to a mental health facility or residential care facility must meet the following requirements:

(1) the patient must be transported directly to the facility within a reasonable amount of time and without undue delay;

(2) a vehicle used to transport the patient must be adequately heated in cold weather and adequately ventilated in warm weather;

(3) a special diet or other medical precautions recommended by the patient's physician must be followed;

(4) the person transporting the patient shall give the patient reasonable opportunities to get food and water and to use a bathroom; and

(5) the patient may not be transported with a state prisoner.

*(Added by L.1999, chap. 1512(6), eff. 9/1/99. See other Art. 46.04 above.)*

# CHAPTER 46A. AIDS AND HIV TESTING IN COUNTY AND MUNICIPAL JAILS

Article



## Art. 46A.01. Testing; segregation; disclosure.

(a) In this article "AIDS" and "HIV" have the meanings assigned those terms by Section 81.101, Health and Safety Code.

(b) A county or municipality may test an inmate confined in the county or municipal jail or in a contract facility authorized by Article 5115d, Revised Statutes, or Article 5115e, Revised Statutes, to determine the proper medical treatment of the inmate or the proper social management of the inmate or other inmates in the jail or facility.

(c) If the county or municipality determines that an inmate has a positive test result for AIDS or HIV, the county or municipality may segregate the inmate from other inmates in the jail or facility.

(d) This article does not provide a duty to test for AIDS or HIV, and a cause of action does not arise under this article from a failure to test for AIDS or HIV.
*(Added by L.1989, chap. 1195(13); chgd. by L.1991, chap. 14(284(10)), eff. 9/1/91.)*

## CHAPTER 47. DISPOSITION OF STOLEN PROPERTY

Article


### Art. 47.01. Subject to order of court.

An officer who comes into custody of property alleged to have been stolen must hold it subject to the order of the proper court, except that if the officer recovers, within 14 days from the date it was reported stolen, property which is subject to Chapter 501, Transportation Code, the officer need not hold the property subject to the order of the proper court but may release the property to the owner, as shown on the certificate of title. *(Chgd. by L.1993, chap. 860(1); L.1999, chap. 62(3.07), eff. 9/1/99.)*

### Art. 47.01a. Restoration when no trial is pending.

(a) If a criminal action relating to allegedly stolen property is not pending, a district judge, county court judge, statutory county court judge, or justice of the peace having jurisdiction as a magistrate in the county in which the property is held or a municipal judge having jurisdiction as a magistrate in the municipality in which the property is being held may hold a hearing to determine the right to possession of the property, upon the petition of an interested person, a county, a city, or the state. Jurisdiction under this section is based solely on jurisdiction as a criminal magistrate under this code and not jurisdiction as a civil court. The court shall:

(1) order the property delivered to whoever has the superior right to possession, without conditions; or

(2) on the filing of a written motion before trial by an attorney representing the state, order the property delivered to whoever has the superior right to possession, subject to the condition that the property be made available to the prosecuting authority should it be needed in future prosecutions; or

(3) order the property awarded to the custody of the peace officer, pending resolution of criminal investigations regarding the property.

(b) If it is shown in a hearing that probable cause exists to believe that the property was acquired by theft or by another manner that makes its acquisition an offense and that the identity of the actual owner of the property cannot be determined, the court shall order the peace officer to:

(1) deliver the property to a government agency for official purposes;

(2) deliver the property to a person authorized by Article 18.17 of this code to receive and dispose of the property; or

(3) destroy the property.

(c) At a hearing under Subsection (a) of this article, any interested person may present evidence showing that the property was not acquired by theft or another offense or that the person is entitled to possess the property. At the hearing, hearsay evidence is admissible.

(d) Venue for a hearing under this article is in any justice, county, statutory county, or district court in the county in which the property is seized or in any municipal court in any municipality in which the property is seized, except that the court may transfer venue to a court in another county on the motion of any interested party.
*(Chgd. by L.1993, chap. 860(1); L.1995, chap. 184(3), eff. 5/23/95.)*

**Art. 47.02. Restored on trial.**

Upon the trial of any criminal action for theft, or for any other illegal acquisition of property which is by law a penal offense, the court trying the case shall order the property to be restored to the person appearing by the proof to be the owner of the same.

Likewise, the judge of any court in which the trial of any criminal action for theft or any other illegal acquisition of property which is by law a penal offense is pending may, upon hearing, if it is proved to the satisfaction of the judge of said court that any person is a true owner of the property alleged to have been stolen, and which is in possession of a peace officer, by written order, direct the property to be restored to such owner.

As to property subject to the Certificate of Title Act (Chapter 501, Transportation Code), any magistrate having jurisdiction in the county in which the criminal action is pending may hold a hearing to determine the right to possession of the property, even if a criminal action is pending, upon written consent of the prosecuting attorney.
*(Chgd. by L.1997, chap. 1415(1), eff. 9/1/97.)*

**Art. 47.03. Schedule.**

When an officer seizes property alleged to have been stolen, he shall immediately file a schedule of the same, and its value, with the court having jurisdiction of the case, certifying that the property has been seized by him, and the reason therefor. The officer shall notify the court of the names and addresses of each party known to the officer who has a claim to possession of the seized property. *(Chgd. by L.1993, chap. 860(1), eff. 8/30/93.)*

**Art. 47.04. Restored to owner.**

Upon an examining trial, if it is proven to the satisfaction of the court that any person is the true owner of property alleged to have been stolen, and which is in possession of a peace officer, the court may upon motion by the state, by written order direct the property to be restored to such owner subject to the conditions that such property shall be made available to the state or by order of any court having jurisdiction over the offense to be used for evidentiary purposes. *(Chgd. by L.1993, chap. 860(1), eff. 8/30/93.)*

**Art. 47.05. Bond required.**

If the court has any doubt as to the ownership of the property, the court may require a bond of the claimant for its re-delivery in case it should thereafter be shown not to belong to such claimant; or the court may, in its discretion, direct the property to be retained by the sheriff until further orders as to its possession. Such bond shall be in a sum equal to the value of the property, with sufficient security, payable to and approved by the county judge of the county in which the property is in custody. Such bond shall be filed in the office of the county clerk of such county, and in case of a breach thereof may be sued upon in such county by any claimant of the property; or by the county treasurer of such county. *(Chgd. by L.1993, chap. 860(1), eff. 8/30/93.)*

**Art. 47.06. Property sold.**

If the property is not claimed within 30 days from the conviction of the person accused of illegally acquiring it, the same procedure for its disposition as set out in Article 18.17 of this Code shall be followed.

**Art. 47.07. Owner may recover.**

The real owner of the property sold under the provisions of Article 47.06 may recover such property under the same terms as prescribed in Subsection (e) of Article 18.17 of this Code.

**Art. 47.08. Written instrument.**

If the property is a written instrument, it shall be deposited with the county clerk of the county where the proceedings are had, subject to the claim of any person who may establish his right thereto. The claimant of any such written instrument shall fire his written sworn claim thereto with the county judge. If such judge be satisfied that such claimant is the real owner of the written instrument, the same shall be delivered to him. The county judge may, in his discretion, require a bond of such claimant, as in other cases of property claimed under any provision of this Chapter, and may also before such delivery require the written instrument to be recorded in the minutes of his court.

**Art. 47.09. Claimant to pay charges.**

The claimant of the property, before he shall be entitled to have the same delivered to him, shall pay all reasonable charges for the safekeeping of the same while in the custody of the law, which charges shall be verified by the affidavit of the officer claiming the same, and determined by the court having jurisdiction thereof. If said charges are not paid, the property shall be sold as under execution; and the proceeds of sale, after the payment of said charges and costs of sale, paid to the owner of such property. *(Chgd. by L.1993, chap. 860(1), eff. 8/30/93.)*

### Art. 47.10. Charges of officer.

When property is sold, and the proceeds of sale are ready to be paid into the county treasury, the amount of expenses for keeping the same and the costs of sale shall be determined by the county judge. The account thereof shall be in writing and verified by the officer claiming the same, with the approval of the county judge thereto for the amount allowed and shall be filed in the office of the county treasurer at the time of paying into his hands the balance of the proceeds of such sale.

### Art. 47.11. Scope of chapter.† [*Extent of Chapter.*]

Each provision of this Chapter relating to stolen property applies as well to property acquired in any manner which makes the acquisition a penal offense.

### Art. 47.12. Appeal.

(a) Appeals from a hearing in a district court, county court, or statutory county court under Article 47.01a of this code shall be heard by a court of appeals. The appeal is governed by the applicable rules of procedure for appeals of civil cases to a court of appeals.

(b) Appeals from a hearing in a municipal court or justice court under Article 47.01a of this code shall be heard by a county court or statutory county court. The appeal is governed by the applicable rules of procedure for appeals for civil cases in justice courts to a county court or statutory county court.

(c) Only an interested person who appears at a hearing under this article may appeal, and such person must give an oral notice of appeal at the conclusion of the hearing and must post an appeal bond by the end of the next business day, exclusive of Saturdays, Sundays, and legal holidays.

(d) The court may require an appeal bond, in an amount determined appropriate by the court, but not to exceed twice the value of the property. The bond shall be made payable to the party who was awarded possession at the hearing, with sufficient sureties approved by the court, and conditioned that appellant will prosecute his appeal to conclusion.

*(Added by L.1993, chap. 860(2), eff. 8/30/93.)*

## CHAPTER 48. PARDON AND PAROLE

Article



### Art. 48.01. Governor may pardon.

In all criminal cases, except treason and impeachment, the Governor shall have power, after conviction, on the written signed recommendation and advice of the Board of Pardons and Paroles, or a majority thereof, to grant reprieves and commutations of punishments and pardons; and upon the written recommendation and advice of a majority of the Board of Pardons and Paroles, he shall have the power to remit fines and forfeitures. The Governor shall have the power to grant one reprieve in any capital case for a period not to exceed 30 days; and he shall have power to revoke conditional pardons. With the advice and consent of the Legislature, the Governor may grant reprieves, commutations of punishment and pardons in cases of treason. *(Chgd. by L.1995, chap. 321(2.019), eff. 9/1/95.)*

### Art. 48.02. Shall file reasons.† [*Must give justification.*]

When the Governor remits fines or forfeitures, or grants reprieves, commutation of punishment or pardons, he shall file in the office of the Secretary of State his reasons therefor.

### Art. 48.03. Governor's acts under seal.

All remissions of fines and forfeitures, and all reprieves, commutations of punishment and pardons, shall be signed by the Governor, and certified by the Secretary of State, under the state seal, and shall be forthwith obeyed by any officer to whom the same may be presented. *(Chgd. by L.1993, chap. 300(26), eff. 8/30/93.)*

**Art. 48.04. Power to remit fines and forfeitures.† [*Authority to remit fines and forfeitures.*]**

The Governor shall have the power to remit forfeitures of bail bonds.

**Art. 48.05. Restoration of civil rights.**

(a) An individual convicted of a federal offense other than an offense involving violence or the threat of violence or involving drugs or firearms may, except as provided by Subsection (b) of this article, submit an application for restoration of any civil rights forfeited under the laws of this state as a result of the conviction.

(b) An individual may not apply for restoration of civil rights under this article unless:

(1) the individual has completed the sentence for the federal offense;

(2) the conviction occurred three or more years before the date of application; and

(3) the individual has not been convicted at any other time of an offense under the laws of this state, another state, or the United States.

(c) An application for restoration of civil rights must contain:

(1) a completed application on a form adopted by the Board of Pardons and Paroles;

(2) three or more affidavits attesting to the good character of the applicant; and

(3) proof that the applicant has completed the sentence for the federal offense.

(d) The applicant must submit the application to:

(1) the sheriff of the county in which the applicant resides at the time of application or resided at the time of conviction of the federal offense, if the individual resided in this state at that time; or

(2) the Board of Pardons and Paroles.

(e) If an application is submitted to a sheriff, the sheriff shall review the application and recommend to the Board of Pardons and Paroles whether the individual's civil rights should be restored. If the sheriff recommends restoration of the individual's civil rights, the board may either:

(1) concur in the recommendation and forward the recommendation to the governor; or

(2) independently review the application to determine whether to recommend to the governor the restoration of the individual's civil rights.

(f) If the sheriff does not recommend the restoration of the individual's civil rights, the individual may apply directly to the Board of Pardons and Paroles.

(g) If an application is submitted to the Board of Pardons and Paroles without first being submitted to a sheriff, the board shall review the application and recommend to the governor as to whether the individual's civil rights should be restored.

(h) The Board of Pardons and Paroles may require or obtain additional information as necessary to perform a review under Subsection (e)(2) or Subsection (g) of this article.

(i) On receipt from the Board of Pardons and Paroles of a recommendation to restore the civil rights of an individual, the governor may either grant or deny the restoration of civil rights to the individual. If the governor grants the restoration of civil rights to the individual, the governor shall issue a certificate of restoration of civil rights.

(j) If an application under this article is denied by the Board of Pardons and Paroles or the governor, the individual may not file another application under this article before the first anniversary of the date of the denial.

(k) A restoration of civil rights under this article is a form of pardon that restores all civil rights under the laws of this state that an individual forfeits as a result of the individual's conviction of a federal offense, except as specifically provided in the certificate of restoration.
*(Added by L.1993, chap. 900(7.01), eff. 9/1/93.)*

## CHAPTER 49. INQUESTS UPON DEAD BODIES

### SUBCHAPTER A. DUTIES PERFORMED BY JUSTICES OF THE PEACE

Article

## SUBCHAPTER A. DUTIES PERFORMED BY JUSTICES OF THE PEACE

### Art. 49.01. Definitions.

In this article:

(1) "Autopsy" means a postmortem examination of the body of a person, including X-rays and an examination of the internal organs and structures after dissection, to determine the cause of death or the nature of any pathological changes that may have contributed to the death.

(2) "Inquest" means an investigation into the cause and circumstances of the death of a person, and a determination, made with or without a formal court hearing, as to whether the death was caused by an unlawful act or omission.

(3) "Inquest hearing" means a formal court hearing held to determine whether the death of a person was caused by an unlawful act or omission and, if the death was caused by an unlawful act or omission, to obtain evidence to form the basis of a criminal prosecution.

(4) "Institution" means any place where health care services are rendered, including a hospital, clinic, health facility, nursing home, extended-care facility, out-patient facility, foster-care facility, and retirement home.

(5) "Physician" means a practicing doctor of medicine or doctor of osteopathic medicine who is licensed by the Texas State Board of Medical Examiners under the Medical Practice Act (Article 4495b, Texas Civil Statutes).

*(Chgd. by L.1989, chap. 72(1), eff. 5/9/89.)*

### Art. 49.02. Applicability.† [*Where applicable.*]

This subchapter applies to the inquest into a death occurring in a county that does not have a medical examiner's office or that is not part of a medical examiner's district.

### Art. 49.03. Powers and duties.

The powers granted and duties imposed on a justice of the peace under this article are independent of the powers and duties of a law enforcement agency investigating a death.

### Art. 49.04. Deaths requiring an inquest.† [*Deaths where inquest required.*]

(a) A justice of the peace shall conduct an inquest into the death of a person who dies in the county served by the justice if:

(1) the person dies in prison under circumstances other than those described by Section 501.055(b), Government Code, or in jail;

(2) the person dies an unnatural death from a cause other than a legal execution;

(3) the body of a person is found, the cause or circumstances of death are unknown, and:

(A) the body is identified; or

(B) the body is unidentified;

(4) the circumstances of the death indicate that the death may have been caused by unlawful means;

(5) the pers‹ ı commits suicide or the circumstances of the death indicate that the death may have been caus‹ ‹ by suicide;

(6) the person dies without having been attended by a physician;

(7) the person dies while attended by a physician who is unable to certify the cause of death and who requests the justice of the peace to conduct an inquest; or

(8) the person is a child younger than six years of age and an inquest is required by Chapter 264, Family Code.

(b) Except as provided by Subsection (c) of this section, a physician who attends the death of a person and who is unable to certify the cause of death shall report the death to the justice of the peace of the precinct where the death occurred and request that the justice conduct an inquest.

(c) If a person dies in a hospital or other institution and an attending physician is unable to certify the cause of death, the superintendent or general manager of the hospital or institution shall report the death to the justice of the peace of the precinct where the hospital or institution is located.

(d) A justice of the peace investigating a death described by Subsection (a)(3)(B) shall report the death to the missing children and missing persons information clearinghouse of the Department of Public Safety and the national crime information center not later than the 10th working day after the date the investigation began.

*(Chgd. by L.1995, chaps. 255(3), 321(1.105), 878(2); L.1997, chap. 656(1); L.1999, chap. 785(2), eff. 9/1/99.)*

**Art. 49.041. Reopening an inquest.**

A justice of the peace may reopen an inquest if, based on information provided by a credible person or facts within the knowledge of the justice of the peace, the justice of the peace determines that reopening the inquest may reveal a different cause or different circumstances of death. *(Added by L.1997, chap. 897(1), eff. 9/1/97.)*

**Art. 49.05. Time and place of inquest; removal of property and body from place of death.† [*Timing and location of inquest; removal of property and remains from site of death.*]**

(a) A justice of the peace shall conduct an inquest immediately or as soon as practicable after the justice receives notification of the death.

(b) A justice of the peace may conduct an inquest:

(1) at the place where the death occurred;

(2) where the body was found; or

(3) at any other place determined to be reasonable by the justice.

(c) A justice of the peace may direct the removal of a body from the scene of death or move any part of the physical surroundings of a body only after a law enforcement agency is notified of the death and a peace officer has conducted an investigation or, if a law enforcement agency has not begun an investigation, a reasonable time has elapsed from the time the law enforcement agency was notified.

(d) A law enforcement agency that is notified of a death requiring an inquest under Article 49.04 of this code shall begin its investigation immediately or as soon as practicable after the law enforcement agency receives notification of the death.

(e) Except in emergency circumstances, a peace officer or other person conducting a death investigation for a law enforcement agency may not move the body or any part of the physical surroundings of the place of death without authorization from a justice of the peace.

(f) A person not authorized by law to move the body of a decedent or any part of the physical surroundings of the body commits an offense if the person tampers with a body that is subject to an inquest under Article 49.04 of this code or any part of the physical surroundings of the body. An offense under this section is punishable by a fine in an amount not to exceed $500.

**Art. 49.06. Hindering an inquest.† [*Impeding an inquest.*]**

(a) A person commits an offense if the person intentionally or knowingly hinders the entrance of a justice of the peace to a premises where a death occurred or a body is found.

(b) An offense under this article is a Class B misdemeanor.

**Art. 49.07. Notification of investigating official.† [*Informing the investigating official.*]**

(a) A physician or other person who has possession of a body of a person whose death requires an inquest under Article 49.04 of this code shall immediately notify the justice of the peace who serves the precinct in which the body was found.

(b) A peace officer who has been notified of the death of a person whose death requires an inquest under Article 49.04 of this code shall immediately notify the justice of the peace who serves the precinct in which the body was found.

(c) If the justice of the peace who serves the precinct in which the body was found is not available to conduct an inquest, a person required to give notice under this article shall notify the nearest available justice of the peace, municipal court judge, county judge, or judge of the county court at law of the county in which the death occurred or in which the body was found.

(d) A person commits an offense if the person is required by this article to give notice and intentionally or knowingly fails to give the notice. An offense under this subsection is a Class C misdemeanor.

*(Chgd. by L.1997, chap. 656(2), eff. 9/1/97.)*

### Art. 49.08. Information leading to an inquest.† [*Information resulting in an inquest.*]

A justice of the peace conducting an inquest may act on information the justice receives from any credible person or on facts within his knowledge.

### Art. 49.09. Body disinterred or cremated.† [*Remains unearthed or cremated.*]

(a) If a body subject to investigation under Article 49.04 of this code is interred and an authorized person has not conducted an inquest required under this subchapter, a justice of the peace may direct the disinterment of the body in order to conduct an inquest.

(b) A person may not cremate or direct the cremation of a body subject to investigation under Article 49.04 unless the body is identified and the person has received from the justice of the peace a certificate signed by the justice stating that:

(1) an autopsy was performed on the body under Article 49.10 of this code; or

(2) no autopsy was necessary.

(c) An owner or operator of a crematory shall retain a certificate received under Subsection (b) of this article for a period of 10 years from the date of cremation of the body named on the certificate.

(d) A person commits an offense if the person cremates or directs the cremation of a body without obtaining a certificate from a justice of the peace as required by Subsection (b) of this article. An offense under this section is a Class B misdemeanor.

(e) If the body of a deceased person is unidentified, a person may not cremate or direct the cremation of the body under this article. If the body is buried, the justice of the peace shall record and maintain for not less than 10 years all information pertaining to the body and the location of burial.

*(Chgd. by L.1997, chap. 656(3), eff. 9/1/97.)*

### Art. 49.10. Autopsies and tests.

(a) At his discretion, a justice of the peace may obtain the opinion of a county health officer or a physician concerning the necessity of obtaining an autopsy in order to determine or confirm the nature and cause of a death.

(b) The commissioners court of the county shall pay a reasonable fee for a consultation obtained by a justice of the peace under Subsection (a) of this article.

(c) Except as required by Section 264.514, Family Code, for each body that is the subject of an inquest by a justice of the peace, the justice, in the justice's discretion, shall:

(1) direct a physician to perform an autopsy; or

(2) certify that no autopsy is necessary.

(d) A justice of the peace may not order a person to perform an autopsy on the body of a deceased person whose death was caused by Asiatic cholera, bubonic plague, typhus fever, or smallpox.

(e) A justice of the peace shall order an autopsy performed on a body if:

(1) the justice determines that an autopsy is necessary to determine or confirm the nature and cause of death;

(2) the deceased was a child younger than six years of age and the death is determined under Section 264.514, Family Code, to be unexpected or the result of abuse or neglect; or

(3) directed to do so by the district attorney, criminal district attorney, or, if there is no district or criminal district attorney, the county attorney.

(f) A justice of the peace shall request a physician to perform the autopsy.

(g) The commissioners court shall pay a reasonable fee to a physician performing an autopsy on the order of a justice of the peace, if a fee is assessed.

(h) The commissioners court shall pay a reasonable fee for the transportation of a body to a place where an autopsy can be performed under this article if a justice of the peace orders the body to be transported to the place.

(i) If a justice of the peace determines that a complete autopsy is unnecessary to confirm or determine the cause of death, the justice may order a physician to take or remove from a body a sample of body fluids, tissues, or organs in order to determine the nature and cause of death. Except as provided by Subsection (j) of this article, a justice may not order any person other than a physician to take samples from the body of a deceased person.

(j) A justice of the peace may order a physician, qualified technician, paramedic, chemist, registered professional nurse, or licensed vocational nurse to take a specimen of blood from the body of a person who died as the result of a motor vehicle accident if the justice determines that circumstances indicate that the person may have been driving while intoxicated.

(k) A justice of the peace may order an investigative or laboratory test to determine the identity of a deceased person. After proper removal of a sample from a body, a justice may order any person specially trained in identification work to complete any tests necessary to determine the identity of the deceased person.

(*l*) A medical examination on an unidentified person shall include the following information to enable a timely and accurate identification of the person:

(1) all available fingerprints and palm prints;

(2) dental charts and radiographs (X-rays) of the person's teeth;

(3) frontal and lateral facial photographs with scale indicated;

(4) notation and photographs, with scale indicated, of a significant scar, mark, tattoo, or item of clothing or other personal effect found with or near the body;

(5) notation of antemortem medical conditions;

(6) notation of observations pertinent to the estimation of time of death; and

(7) precise documentation of the location of burial of the remains.

(m) A medical examination on an unidentified person may include the following information to enable a timely and accurate identification of the person:

(1) full body radiographs (X-rays); and

(2) hair specimens with roots.

(n) On discovering the body of a deceased person in the circumstances described by Article 49.04(a)(3)(B), the medical examiner may request the aid of a forensic anthropologist in the examination of the body. The forensic anthropologist must be board-certified by a nationally recognized association that accredits practitioners in the forensic sciences. The forensic anthropologist shall attempt to establish whether the body is of a human or animal, whether evidence of childbirth, injury, or disease exists, and the sex, race, age, stature, and physical anomalies of the body. The forensic anthropologist may also attempt to establish the cause, manner, and time of death. *(Chgd. by L.1995, chaps. 255(4), 878(3); L.1997, chaps. 656(4), 1022(102), 1301(1); L.1999, chaps. 1071(1), 1132(1), eff. 6/18/99, 9/1/99, respectively.)*

### Art. 49.11. Chemical analysis.† [*Biochemical testing.*]

(a) A justice of the peace may obtain a chemical analysis of a sample taken from a body in order to determine whether death was caused, in whole or in part, by the ingestion, injection, or introduction into the body of a poison or other chemical substance. A justice may obtain a chemical analysis under this article from a chemist, toxicologist, pathologist, or other medical expert.

(b) A justice of the peace shall obtain a chemical analysis under Subsection (a) of this article if requested to do so by the physician who performed an autopsy on the body.

(c) The commissioners court shall pay a reasonable fee to a person who conducts a chemical analysis at the request of a justice of the peace.

### Art. 49.12. Liability of person performing autopsy or test.† [*Liability of examiner.*]

A person who performs an autopsy or makes a test on a body on the order of a justice of the peace in the good faith belief that the order is valid is not liable for damages if the order is invalid.

### Art. 49.13. Consent to autopsy.† [*Permission to conduct autopsy.*]

(a) Consent for a physician to conduct an autopsy is sufficient if given by the following:

(1) if the deceased was married, the surviving spouse;

(2) if the deceased was married but not survived by a spouse, an adult child of the deceased;

(3) if the deceased was married but not survived by a spouse, and a child of the deceased is under the care of a guardian or a court, the guardian or court having care of the child; or

(4) if the deceased person was unmarried or is not survived by a spouse or a child, the following persons in the order stated:

(A) a parent;

(B) a guardian;

(C) the next of kin; or

(D) any person who assumes custody of and responsibility for the burial of the body.

(b) Notwithstanding Subsection (a), consent for a physician to conduct an autopsy is sufficient if given by the Texas Department of Criminal Justice or an authorized official of the department in accordance with Section 501.055, Government Code.
*(Chgd. by L.1997, chap. 1422(4), eff. 6/20/97.)*

## Art. 49.14. Inquest hearing.

(a) A justice of the peace conducting an inquest may hold an inquest hearing if the justice determines that the circumstances warrant the hearing. The justice shall hold an inquest hearing if requested to do so by a district attorney or a criminal district attorney who serves the county in which the body was found.

(b) An inquest hearing may be held with or without a jury unless the district attorney or criminal district attorney requests that the hearing be held with a jury.

(c) A jury in an inquest hearing is composed of six persons. Jurors shall be summoned in the same manner as are jurors for county court. A juror who is properly summoned and fails to appear, other than a juror exempted by law, commits an offense. An offense under this subsection is punishable by a fine not to exceed $100.

(d) A justice of the peace may hold a public or a private inquest hearing. If a person has been arrested and charged with causing the death of the deceased, the defendant and the defendant's counsel are entitled to be present at the inquest hearing, examine witnesses, and introduce evidence.

(e) A justice of the peace may issue a subpoena to enforce the attendance of a witness at an inquest hearing and may issue an attachment for a person who is subpoenaed and fails to appear at the time and place cited on the subpoena.

(f) A justice of the peace may require bail of a witness to secure the appearance of the witness at an inquest hearing or before a grand jury, examining court, or other court investigating a death.

(g) The justice of the peace shall swear witnesses appearing at an inquest hearing. The justice and an attorney representing the state may examine witnesses at an inquest hearing. The justice shall direct that all sworn testimony be reduced to writing and the justice shall subscribe the transcription.

(h) Only the justice of the peace, a person charged in the death under investigation, the counsel for the person charged, and an attorney representing the state may question a witness at an inquest hearing.

(i) A justice of the peace may hold a person who disrupts the proceedings of an inquest hearing in contempt of court. A person who is found in contempt of court under this subsection may be fined in an amount not to exceed $100 and removed from court by a peace officer.

## Art. 49.15. Inquest record.

(a) A justice of the peace or other person authorized under this subchapter to conduct an inquest shall make an inquest record for each inquest he conducts. The inquest record must include a report of the events, proceedings, findings, and conclusions of the inquest. The record must also include any autopsy prepared in the case and all other papers of the case. All papers of the inquest record must be marked with the case number and be clearly indexed and be maintained in the office of the justice of the peace and be made available to the appropriate officials upon request.

(b) As part of the inquest record, the justice of the peace shall make and keep complete and permanent records of all inquest hearings. The inquest hearing records must include:

(1) the name of the deceased person, or if the person is unidentified, a description of the body;
(2) the time, date, and place where the body was found;
(3) the time, date, and place where the inquest was held;
(4) the name of every witness who testified at the inquest;
(5) the name of every person who provided to the justice information pertinent to the inquest;
(6) the amount of bail set for each witness and person charged in the death;
(7) a transcript of the testimony given by each witness at the inquest hearing;
(8) the autopsy report, if an autopsy was performed; and
(9) the name of every person arrested as a suspect in the death who appeared at the inquest and the details of that person's arrest.

(c) The commissioners court shall pay a reasonable fee to a person who records or transcribes sworn testimony during an inquest hearing.

(d) The justice of the peace shall certify a copy of the inquest summary report and deliver the certified copy in a sealed envelope to the clerk of the district court. The clerk of the district court shall retain the summary report subject to an order by the district court.

### Art. 49.16. Orders and death certificates.

The justice of the peace or other person who conducts an inquest under this subchapter shall sign the death certificate and all orders made as a necessary part of the inquest.

### Art. 49.17. Evidence.

A justice of the peace shall preserve all tangible evidence that the justice accumulates in the course of an inquest that tends to show the real cause of death or identify the person who caused the death. The justice shall:

(1) deposit the evidence with the appropriate law enforcement agency to be stored in the agency's property room for safekeeping; or

(2) deliver the evidence to the district clerk for safekeeping subject to the order of the court.

### Art. 49.18. Death in custody.† [*Death while confined.*]

(a) If a person confined in a penal institution dies, the sheriff or other person in charge of the penal institution shall as soon as practicable inform the justice of the peace of the precinct where the penal institution is located of the death.

(b) If a person dies while in the custody of a peace officer or if a prisoner dies while confined in a jail or prison, the director of the law enforcement agency of which the officer is a member or of the facility in which the prisoner was confined shall investigate the death and file a written report of the cause of death with the attorney general no later than the 20th day after the date on which the person in custody or the prisoner died. The director shall make a good faith effort to obtain all facts relevant to the death and include those facts in the report. The attorney general shall make the report, with the exception of any portion of the report that the attorney general determines is privileged, available to any interested person.

(c) Subsection (a) does not apply to a death that occurs in a facility operated by or under contract with the Texas Department of Criminal Justice. Subsection (b) does not apply to a death that occurs in a facility operated by or under contract with the Texas Department of Criminal Justice if the death occurs under circumstances described by Section 501.055(b), Government Code.
*(Chgd. by L.1995, chap. 321(1.106); L.1997, chap. 1422(1), eff. 6/20/97.)*

### Art. 49.19. Warrant of arrest.† [*Arrest warrant.*]

(a) A justice of the peace who is conducting an inquest of a death under this subchapter may issue a warrant for the arrest of a person suspected of causing the death if:

(1) the justice has knowledge that the person caused the death of the deceased;

(2) the justice receives an affidavit stating that the person caused the death; or

(3) evidence is adduced at an inquest hearing that shows probable cause to believe the person caused the death.

(b) A peace officer who receives an arrest warrant issued by a justice of the peace shall:

(1) execute the warrant without delay; and

(2) detain the person arrested until the person's discharge is ordered by the justice of the peace or other proper authority.

(c) A person who is charged in a death and arrested under a warrant of a justice of the peace shall remain in the custody of the arresting peace officer and may not be removed from the peace officer's custody on the authority of a warrant from another magistrate. A person charged in a death who has not been arrested under a warrant of a justice of the peace may be arrested on the order of a magistrate other than the justice of the peace and examined by that magistrate while an inquest is pending.

### Art. 49.20. Requisites of warrant.† [*Requirements for warrant.*]

A warrant of arrest issued under Article 49.19 of this code is sufficient if it:

(1) is issued in the name of "The State of Texas";

(2) specifies the name of the person whose arrest is ordered or, if the person's name is unknown, reasonably describes the person;

(3) recites in plain language the offense with which the person is charged; and

(4) is signed and dated by a justice of the peace.

### Art. 49.21. Commitment of homicide suspect.

At the conclusion of an inquest, if a justice of the peace finds that a person who has been arrested in the case caused or contributed to the death of the deceased, the justice may:

(1) commit the person to jail; or

(2) require the person to execute a bail bond with security for the person's appearance before the proper court to answer for the offense.

### Art. 49.22. Sealing premises of deceased.† [*Closing of premises of deceased.*]

(a) If a body that is subject to an inquest under Article 49.04 of this code is found on premises that were under the sole control of the deceased, a justice of the peace or other person authorized under this subchapter to conduct an inquest may direct that the premises be locked and sealed to prohibit entrance by any person other than a peace officer conducting an investigation of the death.

(b) Rent, utility charges, taxes, and all other reasonable expenses accruing against the property of the deceased during the time the premises of the deceased are locked and sealed under this article may be charged against the estate of the deceased.

(c) A person other than a peace officer commits an offense if the person tampers with or removes a lock or seal placed on premises under this article.

(d) An offense under this article is a Class B misdemeanor.

*(Chgd. by L.1997, chap. 656(5), eff. 9/1/97.)*

### Art. 49.23. Office of death investigator.

(a) The commissioners court of a county may establish an office of death investigator and employ one or more death investigators to provide assistance to those persons in the county who conduct inquests. A death investigator employed under this article is entitled to receive compensation from the county in an amount set by the commissioners court. A death investigator serves at the will of the commissioners court and on terms and conditions set by the commissioners court.

(b) To be eligible for employment as a death investigator, a person must have experience or training in investigative procedures concerning the circumstances, manner, and cause of the death of a deceased person.

(c) At the request of and under the supervision of a justice of the peace or other person conducting an inquest, a death investigator may assist the person conducting the inquest to investigate the time, place, and manner of death and lock and seal the premises of the deceased. A death investigator who assists in an inquest under this subsection shall make a complete report of the death investigator's activities, findings, and conclusions to the justice of the peace or other person conducting the inquest not later than eight hours after the death investigator completes the investigation.

## SUBCHAPTER B. DUTIES PERFORMED BY MEDICAL EXAMINERS

### Art. 49.25. Medical examiners.

**Sec. 1. Office authorized.†** [***Office empowered.***] Subject to the provisions of this Act, the Commissioners Court of any county having a population of more than one million and not having a reputable medical school as defined in Articles 4501 and 4503, Revised Civil Statutes of Texas, shall establish and maintain the office of medical examiner, and the Commissioners Court of any county may establish and provide for the maintenance of the office of medical examiner. Population shall be according to the last preceding federal census.

**Sec. 1a. Multi-county district; joint office.** (a) The commissioners courts of two or more counties may enter into an agreement to create a medical examiners district and to jointly operate and maintain the office of medical examiner of the district. The district must include the entire area of all counties involved. The counties within the district must, when taken together, form a continuous area.

(b) There may be only one medical examiner in a medical examiners district, although he may employ, within the district, necessary staff personnel. When a county becomes a part of a medical examiners district, the effect is the same within the county as if the office of medical examiner had been established in that county alone. The district medical examiner has all the powers and duties within the district that a medical examiner who serves in a single county has within that county.

(c) The commissioners court of any county which has become a part of a medical examiners district may withdraw the county from the district, but twelve months' notice of withdrawal must be given to the commissioners courts of all other counties in the district.

**Sec. 2. Appointments and qualifications.** The commissioners court shall appoint the medical examiner, who shall serve at the pleasure of the commissioners court. No person shall be appointed medical examiner unless he is a physician licensed by the State Board of Medical Examiners. To the greatest extent possible, the medical examiner shall be appointed from persons having training and experience in pathology, toxicology, histology and other medico-legal sciences. The medical examiner shall devote so much of his time and energy as is necessary in the performance of the duties conferred by this Article.

**Sec. 3. Assistants.† [*Subordinates.*]** The medical examiner may, subject to the approval of the commissioners court, employ such deputy examiners, scientific experts, trained technicians, officers and employees as may be necessary to the proper performance of the duties imposed by this Article upon the medical examiner.

**Sec. 4. Salaries.† [*Earnings.*]** The commissioners court shall establish and pay the salaries and compensations of the medical examiner and his staff.

**Sec. 5. Offices.** The commissioners court shall provide the medical examiner and his staff with adequate office space and shall provide laboratory facilities or make arrangements for the use of existing laboratory facilities in the county, if so requested by the medical examiner.

**Sec. 6. Death investigations.** (a) Any medical examiner, or his duly authorized deputy, shall be authorized, and it shall be his duty, to hold inquests with or without a jury within his county, in the following cases:

1. When a person shall die within twenty-four hours after admission to a hospital or institution or in prison or in jail;

2. When any person is killed; or from any cause dies an unnatural death, except under sentence of the law; or dies in the absence of one or more good witnesses;

3. When the body of a person is found, the cause or circumstances of death are unknown, and:

(A) the body is identified; or

(B) the body is unidentified;

4. When the circumstances of the death of any person are such as to lead to suspicion that he came to his death by unlawful means;

5. When any person commits suicide, or the circumstances of his death are such as to lead to suspicion that he committed suicide;

6. When a person dies without having been attended by a duly licensed and practicing physician, and the local health officer or registrar required to report the cause of death under Section 193.005, Health and Safety Code, does not know the cause of death. When the local health officer or registrar of vital statistics whose duty it is to certify the cause of death does not know the cause of death, he shall so notify the medical examiner of the county in which the death occurred and request an inquest;

7. When the person is a child who is younger than six years of age and the death is reported under Chapter 264, Family Code; and

8. When a person dies who has been attended immediately preceding his death by a duly licensed and practicing physician or physicians, and such physician or physicians are not certain as to the cause of death and are unable to certify with certainty the cause of death as required by Section 193.004, Health and Safety Code. In case of such uncertainty the attending physician or physicians, or the superintendent or general manager of the hospital or institution in which the deceased shall have died, shall so report to the medical examiner of the county in which the death occurred, and request an inquest.

(b) The inquests authorized and required by this Article shall be held by the medical examiner of the county in which the death occurred.

(c) In making such investigations and holding such inquests, the medical examiner or an authorized deputy may administer oaths and take affidavits. In the absence of next of kin or legal representatives of the deceased, the medical examiner or authorized deputy shall take charge of the body and all property found with it.
*(Chgd. by L.1997, chap. 656(6), eff. 9/1/97.)*

**Sec. 6a. Organ transplant donors; notice; inquests.** (a) When death occurs to an individual designated a prospective organ donor for transplantation by a licensed physician under circumstances requiring the medical examiner of the county in which death occurred, or the medical examiner's authorized deputy, to hold an inquest, the medical examiner, or a member of his staff will be so notified by the administrative head of the facility in which the transplantation is to be performed.

(b) When notified pursuant to Subsection (a) of this Section, the medical examiner or the medical examiner's deputy shall perform an inquest on the deceased prospective organ donor.

**Sec. 7. Reports of Death.** (a) Any police officer, superintendent of institution, physician, or private citizen who shall become aware of a death under any of the circumstances set out in Section 6(a) of this Article, shall immediately report such death to the office of the medical examiner to the city or county police departments; any such report to a city or county police department shall be immediately transmitted to the office of the medical examiner.

(b) A person investigating a death described by Subdivision 3(B) of Section 6(a) shall report the death to the missing children and missing persons information clearinghouse of the Department of Public Safety and the national crime information center not later than the 10th working day after the date the investigation began.
*(Chgd. by L.1997, chap. 656(6), eff. 9/1/97.)*

**Sec. 8. Removal of bodies.† [*Removal of remains.*]** When any death under circumstances set out in Section 6 shall have occurred, the body shall not be disturbed or removed from the position in which it is found by any person without authorization from the medical examiner or authorized deputy, except for the purpose of preserving such body from loss or destruction or maintaining the flow of traffic on a highway, railroad or airport.

**Sec. 9. Autopsy.** (a) If the cause of death shall be determined beyond a reasonable doubt as a result of the investigation, the medical examiner shall file a report thereof setting forth specifically the cause of death with the district attorney or criminal district attorney, or in a county in which there is no district attorney or criminal district attorney with the county attorney, of the county in which the death occurred. If in the opinion of the medical examiner an autopsy is necessary, or if such is requested by the district attorney or criminal district attorney, or county attorney where there is no district attorney or criminal district attorney, the autopsy shall be immediately performed by the medical examiner or a duly authorized deputy. In those cases where a complete autopsy is deemed unnecessary by the medical examiner to ascertain the cause of death, the medical examiner may perform a limited autopsy involving the taking of blood samples or any other samples of body fluids, tissues or organs, in order to ascertain the cause of death or whether a crime has been committed. In the case of a body of a human being whose identity is unknown, the medical examiner may authorize such investigative and laboratory tests and processes as are required to determine its identity as well as the cause of death. In performing an autopsy the medical examiner or authorized deputy may use the facilities of any city or county hospital within the county or such other facilities as are made available. Upon completion of the autopsy, the medical examiner shall file a report setting forth the findings in detail with the office of the district attorney or criminal district attorney of the county, or if there is no district attorney or criminal district attorney, with the county attorney of the county.

(b) A medical examination on an unidentified person shall include the following information to enable a timely and accurate identification of the person:

(1) all available fingerprints and palm prints;

(2) dental charts and radiographs (X-rays) of the person's teeth;

(3) frontal and lateral facial photographs with scale indicated;

(4) notation and photographs, with scale indicated, of a significant scar, mark, tattoo, or item of clothing or other personal effect found with or near the body;

(5) notation of antemortem medical conditions;

(6) notation of observations pertinent to the estimation of time of death; and

(7) precise documentation of the location of burial of the remains.

(c) A medical examination on an unidentified person may include the following information to enable a timely and accurate identification of the person:

(1) full body radiographs (X-rays); and

(2) hair specimens with roots.

*(Chgd. by L.1997, chap. 656(6), eff. 9/1/97.)*

**Sec. 10. Disinterments and cremations.** When a body upon which an inquest ought to have been held has been interred, the medical examiner may cause it to be disinterred for the purpose of holding such inquest.

Before any body, upon which an inquest is authorized by the provisions of this Article, can be lawfully cremated, an autopsy shall be performed thereon as provided in this Article, or a certificate that no autopsy was necessary shall be furnished by the medical examiner. Before any dead body can be lawfully cremated, the owner or operator of the crematory shall demand and be furnished with a certificate, signed by the medical examiner of the county in which the death occurred showing that an autopsy was performed on said body or that no autopsy thereon was necessary. It shall be the duty of the medical examiner to determine whether or not, from all the circumstances surrounding the death, an autopsy is necessary prior to issuing a certificate under the provisions of this section. No autopsy shall be required by the medical examiner as a prerequisite to cremation in case death is caused by the pestilential diseases of Asiatic cholera, bubonic plague, typhus fever or smallpox. All certificates furnished to the owner or operator of a crematory by any medical examiner, under the terms of this Article, shall be preserved by such owner or operator of such crematory for a period of two years from the date of the cremation of said body.

**Sec. 10a. Waiting time between death and cremation.** The body of a deceased person shall not be cremated within forty-eight hours after the time of death as indicated on the regular death certificate, unless the death certificate indicates death was caused by the pestilential diseases of Asiatic cholera, bubonic plague, typhus fever, or smallpox, or unless the time requirement is waived in writing by the county medical examiner or, in counties not having a county medical examiner, a justice of the peace.

**Sec. 10b. Disposal of unidentified body.** If the body of a deceased person is unidentified, a person may not cremate or direct the cremation of the body under this article. If the body is buried, the investigating agency responsible for the burial shall record and maintain for not less than 10 years all information pertaining to the body and the location of burial. *(Added by L.1997, chap. 656(6), eff. 9/1/97.)*

**Sec. 11. Records.** The medical examiner shall keep full and complete records properly indexed, giving the name if known of every person whose death is investigated, the place where the body was found, the date, the cause and manner of death, and shall issue a death certificate. The full report and detailed findings of the autopsy, if any, shall be a part of the record. Copies of all records shall promptly be delivered to the proper district, county, or criminal district attorney in any case where further investigation is advisable. The records are subject to required public disclosure in accordance with Chapter 552, Government Code, except that a photograph or x-ray of a body taken during an autopsy is excepted from required public disclosure in accordance with Chapter 552, Government Code, but is subject to disclosure:

(1) under a subpoena or authority of other law; or

(2) if the photograph or x-ray is of the body of a person who died while in the custody of law enforcement.

*(Chgd. by L.1999, chap. 607(2), eff. 9/1/99.)*

**Sec. 12. Transfer of duties of justice of peace.† [*Shifting of responsibilities of justice of peace.*]** When the commissioners court of any county shall establish the office of medical examiner, all powers and duties of justices of the peace in such county relating to the investigation of deaths and inquests shall vest in the office of the medical examiner. Any subsequent General Law pertaining to the duties of justices of the peace in death investigations and inquests shall apply to the medical examiner in such counties as to the extent not inconsistent with this Article, and all laws or parts of laws otherwise in conflict herewith are hereby declared to be inapplicable to this Article.

**Sec. 13. Use of forensic anthropologist.** On discovering the body of a deceased person in the circumstances described by Subdivision 3(B) of Section 6(a), the medical examiner may request the aid of a forensic anthropologist in the examination of the body. The forensic anthropologist must be board-certified by a nationally recognized association that accredits practitioners in the forensic sciences. The forensic anthropologist shall attempt to establish whether the body is of a human or animal, whether evidence of childbirth, injury, or disease exists, and the sex, race, age, stature, and physical anomalies of the body. The forensic anthropologist may also attempt to establish the cause, manner, and time of death. *(Added by L.1997, chap. 656(6), eff. 9/1/97.)*

**Sec. 14. Penalty.** (a) A person commits an offense if the person knowingly violates this article.

(b) An offense under this section is a Class B misdemeanor.

*(Renumbered from Section 13 and chgd. by L.1997, chap. 656(6), eff. 9/1/97.)*
*(Chgd. by L.1989, chap. 1205(1); L.1991, chaps. 14(284(66), (67), (69)), 597(58); L.1995, chaps. 255(5), 878(4), eff. 9/1/95.)*

## CHAPTER 50. FIRE INQUESTS

Article

### Art. 50.01. Investigations.

When an affidavit is made by a credible person before any justice of the peace that there is ground to believe that any building has been unlawfully set or attempted to be set on fire, such justice shall cause the truth of such complaint to be investigated.

### Art. 50.02. Proceedings.

The proceedings in such case shall be governed by the laws relating to inquests upon dead bodies. The officer conducting such investigations shall have the same powers as are conferred upon justices of the peace in the preceding Articles of this Chapter.

### Art. 50.03. Verdict.

The jury after inspecting the place in question and after hearing the testimony, shall deliver to the justice holding such inquest its written signed verdict in which it shall find and certify how and in what manner such fire happened or was attempted, and all the circumstances attending the same, and who are guilty thereof, and in what manner. If such a jury is unable to so ascertain, it shall find and certify accordingly.

### Art. 50.04. Witnesses bound over.† [*Witness to appear.*]

If the jury finds that any building has been unlawfully set on fire or has been attempted so to be, the justice holding such inquest shall bind over the witnesses to appear and testify before the next grand jury of the county in which such offense was committed.

### Art. 50.05. Warrant for accused.† [*Warrant for suspect.*]

If the person charged with the offense, if any, be not in custody, the justice of the peace shall issue a warrant for his arrest, and when arrested, such person shall be dealt with as in other like cases.

### Art. 50.06. Testimony written down.† [*Testimony transcribed.*]

In all such investigations, the testimony of all witnesses examined before the jury shall be reduced to writing by or under the direction of the justice and signed by each witness. Such testimony together with the verdict and all bail bonds taken in the case shall be certified to and returned by the justice to the next district or criminal district court of his county.

### Art. 50.07. Compensation.

The pay of the officers and jury making such investigation shall be the same as that allowed for the holding of an inquest upon a dead body, so far as applicable, and shall be paid in like manner.

## CHAPTER 51. FUGITIVES FROM JUSTICE

Article



### Art. 51.01. Delivered up.

A person in any other State of the United States charged with treason or any felony who shall flee from justice and be found in this State, shall on demand of the executive authority of the State from which he fled, be delivered up, to be removed to the State having jurisdiction of the crime.

### Art. 51.02. To aid in arrest.† [*To assist arrest.*]

All peace officers of the State shall give aid in the arrest and detention of a fugitive from any other State that he may be held subject to a requisition by the Governor of the State from which he fled.

### Art. 51.03. Magistrate's warrant.

When a complaint is made to a magistrate that any person within his jurisdiction is a fugitive from justice from another State, he shall issue a warrant of arrest directing a peace officer to apprehend and bring the accused before him.

### Art. 51.04. Complaint.

The complaint shall be sufficient if it recites:

1. The name of the person accused;
2. The State from which he has fled;
3. The offense committed by the accused;
4. That he has fled to this State from the State where the offense was committed; and
5. That the act alleged to have been committed by the accused is a violation of the penal law of the State from which he fled.



### Art. 51.05. Bail or commitment.† [*Bail or confinement.*]

When the accused is brought before the magistrate, he shall hear proof, and if satisfied that the accused is charged in another State with the offense named in the complaint, he shall require of him bail with sufficient security, in such amount as the magistrate deems reasonable, to appear before such magistrate at a specified time. In default of such bail, he may commit the defendant to jail to await a requisition from the Governor of the State from which he fled. A properly certified transcript of an indictment against the accused is sufficient to show that he is charged with the crime alleged. One arrested under the provisions of this title shall not be committed or held to bail for a longer time than ninety days.

### Art. 51.06. Notice of arrest.

The magistrate who held or committed such fugitive shall immediately notify the Secretary of State and the district or county attorney of his county of such fact and the date thereof, stating the name of such fugitive, the State from which he fled, and the crime with which he is charged; and such officers so notified shall in turn notify the Governor of the proper State.

### Art. 51.07. Discharge.

A fugitive not arrested under a warrant from the Governor of this State before the expiration of ninety days from the day of his commitment or the date of the bail shall be discharged.

### Art. 51.08. Second arrest.

A person who has once been arrested under the provisions of this title and discharged under the provisions of the preceding Article or by habeas corpus shall not be again arrested upon a charge of the same offense, except by a warrant from the Governor of this State.

### Art. 51.09. Governor may demand fugitive.† [*Right of Governor to fugitive.*]

When the Governor deems it proper to demand a person who has committed an offense in this State and has fled to another State, he may commission any suitable person to take such requisition. The accused, if brought back to the State, shall be delivered up to the sheriff of the county in which it is alleged he has committed the offense.

### Art. 51.10. Pay of agent; traveling expenses.† [*Agent's compensation and travel expenses.*]

**Sec. 1.** The officer or person so commissioned shall receive as compensation the actual and necessary traveling expenses upon requisition of the Governor to be allowed by such Governor and to be paid out of the State Treasury upon a certificate of the Governor reciting the services rendered and the allowance therefor.

**Sec. 2.** The commissioners court of the county where an offense is committed may in its discretion, on the request of the sheriff and the recommendation of the district attorney, pay the actual and necessary traveling expenses of the officer or person so commissioned out of any fund or funds not otherwise pledged.

### Art. 51.11. Reward.

The Governor may offer a reward for the apprehension of one accused of a felony in this State who is evading arrest, by causing such offer to be published in such manner as he deems most likely to effect the arrest. The reward shall be paid out of the State Treasury to the person who becomes entitled to it upon a certificate of the Governor reciting the facts which entitle such person to receive it.

### Art. 51.12. Sheriff to report.

Each sheriff upon the close of any regular term of the district or criminal district court in his county, or within thirty days thereafter, shall make out and mail to the Director of the Department of Public Safety a certified list of all persons, who, after indictment for a felony, have fled from said county. Such lists shall contain the full name of each such fugitive, the offense with which he is charged, and a description giving his age, height, weight, color and occupation, the complexion of the skin and the color of eyes and hair, and any peculiarity in person, speech, manner or gait that may serve to identify such person so far as the sheriff may be able to give them. The Director of the Department of Public Safety shall prescribe and forward to all sheriffs the necessary blanks upon which are to be made the lists herein required.

### Art. 51.13. Uniform Criminal Extradition Act.

**Sec. 1. Definitions.** Where appearing in this Article, the term "Governor" includes any person performing the functions of Governor by authority of the laws of this State. The term "Executive Authority" includes the Governor, and any person performing the functions of Governor in a State other than this State, and the term "State", referring to a State other than this State, includes any other State organized or unorganized of the United States of America.

**Sec. 2. Fugitives from justice; duty of Governor.** Subject to the provisions of this Article, the provision of the Constitution of the United States controlling, and any and all Acts of Congress enacted in pursuance thereof, it is the duty of the Governor of this State to have arrested and delivered up to the Executive Authority of any other State of the United States any person charged in that State with treason, felony, or other crime, who has fled from justice and is found in this State.

**Sec. 3. Form of demand.** No demand for the extradition of a person charged with crime in another State shall be recognized by the Governor unless in writing, alleging, except in cases arising under Section 6, that the accused was present in the demanding State at the time of the commission of the alleged crime, and that thereafter he fled from the State, and accompanied by a copy of an indictment found or by information supported by affidavit in the State having jurisdiction of the crime, or by a copy of an affidavit before a magistrate there, together with a copy of any warrant which issued thereupon; or by a copy of a judgment of conviction or of a sentence imposed in execution thereof, together with a statement by the Executive Authority of the demanding State that the person claimed has escaped from confinement or has broken the terms of his bail, probation or parole. The indictment, information, or affidavit made before the magistrate must substantially charge the person demanded with having committed a crime under the law of that State; and the copy of indictment, information, affidavit, judgment of conviction or sentence must be authenticated by the Executive Authority making the demand; provided, however, that all such copies of the aforesaid instruments shall be in duplicate, one complete set of such instruments to be delivered to the defendant or to his attorney.

**Sec. 4. Governor may investigate case.** When a demand shall be made upon the Governor of this State by the Executive Authority of another State for the surrender of a person so charged with crime, the Governor may call upon the Secretary of State, Attorney General or any prosecuting officer in this State to investigate or assist in investigating the demand, and to report to him the situation and circumstances of the person so demanded, and whether he ought to be surrendered.

**Sec. 5. Extradition of persons imprisoned or awaiting trial in another State or who have left the demanding State under compulsion.** When it is desired to have returned to this State a person charged in this State with a crime, and such person is imprisoned or is held under criminal proceedings then pending against him in another State, the Governor of this State may agree with the Executive Authority of such other State for the extradition of such person before the conclusion of such proceedings or his term of sentence in such other State, upon condition that such person be returned to such other State at the expense of this State as soon as the prosecution in this State is terminated.

The Governor of this State may also surrender on demand of the Executive Authority of any other State any person in this State who is charged in the manner provided in Section 23 of this Act with having violated the laws of the State whose Executive Authority is making the demand, even though such person left the demanding State involuntarily.

**Sec. 6. Extradition of persons not present in demanding State at time of commission of crime.** The Governor of this State may also surrender, on demand of the Executive Authority of any other State, any person in this State charged in such other State in the manner provided in Section 3 with committing an act in this State, or in a third State, intentionally resulting in a crime in the State whose Executive Authority is making the demand, and the provisions of this Article not otherwise inconsistent, shall apply to such cases, even though the accused was not in that State at the time of the commission of the crime, and has not fled therefrom.

**Sec. 7. Issue of Governor's warrant of arrest; its recitals.** If the Governor decides that the demand should be complied with, he shall sign a warrant of arrest, which shall be sealed with the state seal and be directed to any peace officer or other person whom he may think fit to entrust with the execution thereof. The warrant must substantially recite the facts necessary to the validity of its issuance.



**Sec. 8. Manner and place of execution.** Such warrant shall authorize the peace officer or other person to whom directed to arrest the accused at any time and any place where he may be found within the State and to command the aid of all peace officers and other persons in the execution of the warrant, and to deliver the accused, subject to the provisions of this Article to the duly authorized agent of the demanding State.

**Sec. 9. Authority of arresting officer.** Every such peace officer or other person empowered to make the arrest, shall have the same authority, in arresting the accused, to command assistance therein, as peace officers have by law in the execution of any criminal process directed to them, with like penalties against those who refuse their assistance.

**Sec. 10. Rights of accused person; application for writ of habeas corpus.** No person arrested upon such warrant shall be delivered over to the agent whom the Executive Authority demanding him shall have appointed to receive him unless he shall first be taken forthwith before a judge of a court of record in this State, who shall inform him of the demand made for his surrender and of the crime with which he is charged, and that he has the right to demand and procure legal counsel; and if the prisoner or his counsel shall state that he or they desire to test the legality of his arrest, the judge of such court of record shall fix a reasonable time to be allowed him within which to apply for a writ of habeas corpus. When such a writ is applied for, notice thereof, and of the time and place of hearing thereon, shall be given to the prosecuting officer of the county in which the arrest is made and in which the accused is in custody, and to the said agent of the demanding State.

**Sec. 11. Penalty for non-compliance with preceding section.** Any officer who shall deliver to the agent for extradition of the demanding State a person in his custody under the Governor's warrant, in willful disobedience to Section 10 of this Act, shall be guilty of a misdemeanor and, on conviction, shall be fined not more than one thousand dollars or be imprisoned not more than six months, or both.

**Sec. 12. Confinement in jail, when necessary.** The officer or persons executing the Governor's warrant of arrest, or the agent of the demanding State to whom the prisoner may have been delivered may, when necessary, confine the prisoner in the jail of any county or city through which he may pass; and the keeper of such jail must receive and safely keep the prisoner until the officer or person having charge of him is ready to proceed on his route, such officer or person being chargeable with the expense of keeping.

The officer or agent of a demanding State to whom a prisoner may have been delivered following extradition proceedings in another State, or to whom a prisoner may have been delivered after waiving extradition in such other State, and who is passing through this State with such a prisoner for the purpose of immediately returning such prisoner to the demanding State may, when necessary, confine the prisoner in the jail of any county or city through which he may pass; and the keeper of such jail must receive and safely keep the prisoner until the officer or agent having charge of him is ready to proceed on his route, such officer or agent, however, being chargeable with the expense of keeping; provided, however, that such officer or agent shall produce and show to the keeper of such jail satisfactory written evidence of the fact that he is actually transporting such prisoner to the demanding State after a requisition by the Executive Authority of such demanding State. Such prisoner shall not be entitled to demand a new requisition while in this State.

**Sec. 13. Arrest prior to requisition.** Whenever any person within this State shall be charged on the oath of any credible person before any judge or magistrate of this State with the commission of any crime in any other State and except in cases arising under Section 6, with having fled from justice, or with having been convicted of a crime in that State and having escaped from confinement, or having broken the terms of his bail, probation or parole, or whenever complaint shall have been made before any judge or magistrate in this State setting forth on the affidavit of any credible person in another State that a crime has been committed in such other State and that the accused has been charged in such State with the commission of the crime, and except in cases arising under Section 6, has fled from justice, or with having been convicted of a crime in that State and having escaped from confinement, or having broken the terms of his bail, probation or parole and is believed to be in this State, the judge or magistrate shall issue a warrant directed to any peace officer commanding him to apprehend the person named therein, wherever he may be found in this State, and to bring him before the same or any other judge, magistrate or court who or which may be available in or convenient of access to the place where the arrest may be made, to answer the charge or complaint and affidavit, and a certified copy of the sworn charge or complaint and affidavit upon which the warrant is issued shall be attached to the warrant.

**Sec. 14. Arrest without a warrant.** The arrest of a person may be lawfully made also by any peace officer or private person, without a warrant upon reasonable information that the accused stands charged in the courts of a State with a crime punishable by death or imprisonment for a term exceeding one year, but when so arrested the accused must be taken before a judge or magistrate with all practicable speed and complaint must be made against him under oath setting forth the ground for the arrest as in the preceding section; and thereafter his answer shall be heard as if he had been arrested on a warrant.

**Sec. 15. Commitment to await requisition; bail.** If from the examination before the judge or magistrate it appears that the person held is the person charged with having committed the crime alleged and except in cases arising under Section 6, that he has fled from justice, the judge or magistrate must, by warrant reciting the accusation, commit him to the county jail for such time not exceeding thirty days and specified in the warrant, as will enable the arrest of the accused to be made under a warrant of the Governor on a requisition of the Executive Authority of the State having jurisdiction of the offense, unless the accused give bail as provided in the next section, or until he shall be legally discharged.

**Sec. 16. Bail; in what cases; conditions of bond.** Unless the offense with which the prisoner is charged is shown to be an offense punishable by death or life imprisonment under the laws of the State in which it was committed, a judge or magistrate in this State may admit the person arrested to bail by bond, with sufficient sureties and in such sum as he deems proper, conditioned for his appearance before him at a time specified in such bond, and for his surrender, to be arrested upon the warrant of the Governor in this State.

**Sec. 17. Extension of time of commitment; adjournment.** If the accused is not arrested under warrant of the Governor by the expiration of the time specified in the warrant or bond, a judge or magistrate may discharge him or may recommit him for a further period not to exceed sixty days, or a judge or magistrate may again take bail for his appearance and surrender, as provided in Section 16, but within a period not to exceed sixty days after the date of such new bond.

**Sec. 18. Forfeiture of bail.** If the prisoner is admitted to bail and fails to appear and surrender himself according to the conditions of his bond, the judge, or magistrate by proper order, shall declare the bond forfeited and order his immediate arrest without warrant if he be within this State. Recovery may be had on such bond in the name of the State as in the case of other bonds given by the accused in criminal proceedings within this State.

**Sec. 19. Persons under criminal prosecution in this State at the time of requisition.** If a criminal prosecution has been instituted against such person under the laws of this State and is still pending, the Governor, in his discretion, either may surrender him on demand of the Executive Authority of another State or hold him until he has been tried and discharged or convicted and punished in this State.

**Sec. 20. Guilt or innocence of accused, when inquired into.** The guilt or innocence of the accused as to the crime of which he is charged may not be inquired into by the Governor or in any proceeding after the demand for extradition accompanied by a charge of crime in legal form as above provided shall have been presented to the Governor, except as it may be involved in identifying the person held as the person charged with the crime.

**Sec. 21. Governor may recall warrant or issue alias.** The governor may recall his warrant of the arrest or may issue another warrant whenever he deems proper. Each warrant issued by the Governor shall expire and be of no force and effect when not executed within one year from the date thereof.

**Sec. 22. Fugitives from this State; duty of Governor.** Whenever the Governor of this State shall demand a person charged with crime or with escaping from confinement or breaking the terms of his bail, probation or parole in this State, from the Executive Authority of any other State, or from the Chief Justice or an Associate Justice of the Supreme Court of the District of Columbia authorized to receive such demand under the laws of the United States, he shall issue a warrant under the state seal, to some agent, commanding him to receive the person so charged if delivered to him and convey him to the proper officer of the county in this State in which the offense was committed, or in which the prosecution for such offense is then pending.

**Sec. 23. Application for issuance of requisition; by whom made; contents.** 1. When the return to this State of a person charged with crime in this State is required, the State's attorney shall present to the Governor his written motion for a requisition for the return of the person charged, in which motion shall be stated the name of the person so charged, the crime charged against him, the approximate time, place and circumstances of its commission, the State in which he is believed to be, including the location of the accused therein at the time the motion is made and certifying that, in the opinion of the said State's attorney the ends of justice require the arrest and return of the accused to this State for trial and that the proceeding is not instituted to enforce a private claim.

2. When the return to this State is required of a person who has been convicted of a crime in this State and has escaped from confinement, or broken the terms of his bail, probation or parole, the prosecuting attorney of the county in which the offense was committed, the parole board, or the warden of the institution or sheriff of the county, from which escape was made, shall present to the Governor a written application for a requisition for the return of such person, in which application shall be stated the name of the person, the crime of which he was convicted, the circumstances of his escape from confinement, or the circumstances of the breach of the terms of his bail, probation or parole, the State in which he is believed to be, including the location of the person therein at the time application is made.

3. The application shall be verified by affidavit, shall be executed in duplicate and shall be accompanied by two certified copies of the indictment returned, or information and affidavit filed, or of the complaint made to the judge or magistrate, stating the offense with which the accused is charged, or of the judgment of conviction or of the sentence. The prosecuting officer, parole board, warden or sheriff may also attach such further affidavits and other documents in duplicate as he shall deem proper to be submitted with such application. One copy of the application, with the action of the Governor indicated by endorsement thereon, and one of the certified copies of the indictment, complaint, information, and affidavits, or of the judgment of conviction or of the sentence shall be filed in the office of the Governor. The other copies of all papers shall be forwarded with the Governor's requisition.
*(Chgd. by L.1997, chap. 701(1), eff. 6/17/97.)*

**Sec. 24. Costs and expenses.** In all cases of extradition, the commissioners court of the county where an offense is alleged to have been committed, or in which the prosecution is then pending may in its discretion, on request of the sheriff and the recommendation of the prosecuting attorney, pay the actual and necessary expenses of the officer or person commissioned to receive the person charged, out of any county fund or funds not otherwise pledged.

**Sec. 25. Immunity from service of process in certain civil cases.** A person brought into this State by, or after waiver of, extradition based on a criminal charge shall not be subject to service of personal process in civil actions arising out of the same facts as the criminal proceeding to answer which he is being or has been returned, until he has been convicted in the criminal proceedings, or if acquitted, until he has had reasonable opportunity to return to the State from which he was extradited.

**Sec. 25a. Written waiver of extradition proceedings.** Any person arrested in this State charged with having committed any crime in another State or alleged to have escaped from confinement, or broken the terms of his bail, probation, or parole may waive the issuance and service of the warrant provided for in Sections 7 and 8 and all other procedure incidental to extradition proceedings, by executing or subscribing in the presence of a judge or any court of record within this State a writing which states that he consents to return to the demanding State; provided, however, that before such waiver shall be executed or subscribed by such person it shall be the duty of such judge to inform such person of his rights to the issuance and service of a warrant of extradition and to obtain a writ of habeas corpus as provided for in Section 10.

If and when such consent has been duly executed it shall forthwith be forwarded to the office of the Governor of this State and filed therein. The judge shall direct the officer having such person in custody to deliver forthwith such person to the duly accredited agent or agents of the demanding State, and shall deliver or cause to be delivered to such agent or agents a copy of such consent; provided, however, that nothing in this section shall be deemed to limit the rights of the accused person to return voluntarily and without formality to the demanding State, nor shall this waiver procedure be deemed to be an exclusive procedure or to limit the powers, rights or duties of the officers of the demanding State or of this State.

**Sec. 25b. Non-waiver by this State.** Nothing in this Act contained shall be deemed to constitute a waiver by this State of its right, power or privilege to try such demanded person for crime committed within this State, or of its right, power or privilege to regain custody of such person by extradition proceedings or otherwise for the purpose of trial, sentence or punishment for any crime committed within this State, nor shall any proceedings had under this Article which result, or fail to result in, extradition to be deemed a waiver by this State of any of its rights, privileges or jurisdiction in any way whatsoever.

**Sec. 26. No right of asylum, no immunity from other criminal prosecutions while in this State.** After a person has been brought back to this State by, or after waiver of extradition proceedings, he may be tried in this State for other crimes which he may be charged with having committed here as well as that specified in the requisition for his extradition.

**Sec. 27. Interpretation.** The provisions of this Article shall be interpreted and construed as to effectuate its general purposes to make uniform the law of those States which enact it.
*(Chgd. by L.1993, chap. 300(27), eff. 8/30/93.)*

## Art. 51.14. Interstate Agreement on Detainers.

This article may be cited as the "Interstate Agreement on Detainers Act." This agreement on detainers is hereby enacted into law and entered into by this state with all other jurisdictions legally joined therein in the form substantially as follows:

The contracting states solemnly agree that:

### ARTICLE I

The party states find that charges outstanding against a prisoner, detainers based on untried indictments, informations or complaints, and difficulties in securing speedy trial of persons already incarcerated in other jurisdictions, produce uncertainties which obstruct programs of prisoner treatment and rehabilitation. Accordingly, it is the policy of the party states and the purpose of this agreement to encourage the expeditious and orderly disposition of such charges and determination of the proper status of any and all detainers based on untried indictments, informations, or complaints. The party states also find that proceedings with reference to such charges and detainers, when emanating from another jurisdiction, cannot properly be had in the absence of cooperative procedures. It is the further purpose of this agreement to provide such cooperative procedures.

### ARTICLE II

As used in this agreement:

(a) "State" shall mean a state of the United States; the United States of America; a territory or possession of the United States; the District of Columbia; the Commonwealth of Puerto Rico.

Printed in the U.S.A. 21

(b) "Sending state" shall mean a state in which a prisoner is incarcerated at the time that he initiates a request for final disposition pursuant to Article III hereof or at the time that a request for custody or availability is initiated pursuant to Article IV hereof.

## ARTICLE III

(a) Whenever a person has entered upon a term of imprisonment in a penal or correctional institution of a party state, and whenever during the continuance of the term of imprisonment there is pending in any other party state any untried indictment, information, or complaint on the basis of which a detainer has been lodged against the prisoner, he shall be brought to trial within 180 days after he shall have caused to be delivered to the prosecuting officer and the appropriate court of the prosecuting officer's jurisdiction written notice of the place of his imprisonment and his request for a final disposition to be made of the indictment, information, or complaint; provided that for good cause shown in open court, the prisoner or his counsel being present, the court having jurisdiction of the matter may grant any necessary or reasonable continuance. The request of the prisoner shall be accompanied by a certificate of the appropriate official having custody of the prisoner, stating the term of commitment under which the prisoner is being held, the time already served, the time remaining to be served on the sentence, the amount of good time earned, the time of parole eligibility of the prisoner, and any decision of the state parole agency relating to the prisoner.

(b) The written notice and request for final disposition referred to in Paragraph (a) hereof shall be given or sent by the prisoner to the warden, commissioner of corrections, or other official having custody of him, who shall promptly forward it together with the certificate to the appropriate prosecuting official and court by registered or certified mail, return receipt requested.

(c) The warden, commissioner of corrections, or other official having custody of the prisoner shall promptly inform him of the source and contents of any detainer lodged against him and shall also inform him of his right to make a request for final disposition of the indictment, information, or complaint on which the detainer is based.

(d) Any request for final disposition made by a prisoner pursuant to Paragraph (a) hereof shall operate as a request for final disposition of all untried indictments, informations, or complaints on the basis of which detainers have been lodged against the prisoner from the state to whose prosecuting official the request for final disposition is specifically directed. The warden, commissioner of corrections, or other official having custody of the prisoner shall forthwith notify all appropriate prosecuting officers and courts in the several jurisdictions within the state to which the prisoner's request for final disposition is being sent of the proceeding being initiated by the prisoner. Any notification sent pursuant to this paragraph shall be accompanied by copies of the prisoner's written notice, request, and the certificate. If trial is not had on any indictment, information, or complaint contemplated hereby prior to the return of the prisoner to the original place of imprisonment, such indictment, information, or complaint shall not be of any further force or effect, and the court shall enter an order dismissing the same with prejudice.

(e) Any request for final disposition made by a prisoner pursuant to Paragraph (a) hereof shall also be deemed to be a waiver of extradition with respect to any charge or proceeding contemplated thereby or included therein by reason of Paragraph (d) hereof, and a waiver of extradition to the receiving state to serve any sentence there imposed upon him after completion of his term of imprisonment in the sending state. The request for final disposition shall also constitute a consent by the prisoner to the production of his body in any court where his presence may be required in order to effectuate the purposes of this agreement and a further consent voluntarily to be returned to the original place of imprisonment in accordance with the provisions of this agreement. Nothing in this paragraph shall prevent the imposition of a concurrent sentence if otherwise permitted by law.

(f) Escape from custody by the prisoner subsequent to his execution of the request for final disposition referred to in Paragraph (a) hereof shall void the request.

## ARTICLE IV

(a) The appropriate officer of the jurisdiction in which an untried indictment, information, or complaint is pending shall be entitled to have a prisoner against whom he has lodged a detainer and who is serving a term of imprisonment in any party state made available in accordance with Paragraph (a) of Article V hereof upon presentation of a written request for temporary custody or availability to the appropriate authorities of the state in which the prisoner is incarcerated; provided that the court having jurisdiction of such indictment, information, or complaint shall have duly approved, recorded, and transmitted the request; and provided further that there shall be a period of 30 days after receipt by the appropriate authorities before the request be honored, within which period the governor of the sending state may disapprove the request for temporary custody or availability, either upon his own motion or upon motion of the prisoner.

(b) Upon receipt of the officer's written request as provided in Paragraph (a) hereof, the appropriate authorities having the prisoner in custody shall furnish the officer with a certificate stating the term of commitment under which the prisoner is being held, the time already served, the time remaining to be served on the sentence, the amount of good time earned, the time of parole eligibility of the prisoner, and any decisions of the state parole agency relating to the prisoner. Said authorities simultaneously shall furnish all other officers and appropriate courts in the receiving state who have lodged detainers against the prisoner with similar certificates and with notices informing them of the request for custody or availability and of the reasons therefor.

(c) In respect of any proceeding made possible by this article, trial shall be commenced within 120 days of the arrival of the prisoner in the receiving state, but for good cause shown in open court, the prisoner or his counsel being present, the court having jurisdiction of the matter may grant any necessary or reasonable continuance.

(d) Nothing contained in this article shall be construed to deprive any prisoner of any right which he may have to contest the legality of his delivery as provided in Paragraph (a) hereof, but such delivery may not be opposed or denied on the ground that the executing authority of the sending state has not affirmatively consented to or ordered such delivery.

(e) If trial is not had on any indictment, information, or complaint contemplated hereby prior to the prisoner's being returned to the original place of imprisonment pursuant to Paragraph (e) of Article V hereof, such indictment, information, or complaint shall not be of any further force or effect, and the court shall enter an order dismissing the same with prejudice.

## ARTICLE V

(a) In response to a request made under Article III or Article IV hereof, the appropriate authority in a sending state shall offer to deliver temporary custody of such prisoner to the appropriate authority in the state where such indictment, information, or complaint is pending against such person in order that speedy and efficient prosecution may be had. If the request for final disposition is made by the prisoner, the offer of temporary custody shall accompany the written notice provided for in Article III of this agreement. In the case of a federal prisoner, the appropriate authority in the receiving state shall be entitled to temporary custody as provided by this agreement or to the prisoner's presence in federal custody at the place of trial, whichever custodial arrangement may be approved by the custodian.

(b) The officer or other representative of a state accepting an offer of temporary custody shall present the following upon demand:

(1) proper identification and evidence of his authority to act for the state into whose temporary custody this prisoner is to be given;

(2) a duly certified copy of the indictment, information, or complaint on the basis of which the detainer has been lodged and on the basis of which the request for temporary custody of the prisoner has been made.

(c) If the appropriate authority shall refuse or fail to accept temporary custody of said person, or in the event that an action on the indictment, information, or complaint on the basis of which the detainer has been lodged is not brought to trial within the period provided in Article III or Article IV hereof, the appropriate court of the jurisdiction where the indictment, information, or complaint has been pending shall enter an order dismissing the same with prejudice, and any detainer based thereon shall cease to be of any force or effect.

(d) The temporary custody referred to in this agreement shall be only for the purpose of permitting prosecution on the charge or charges contained in one or more untried indictments, informations, or complaints which form the basis of the detainer or detainers or for prosecution on any other charge or charges arising out of the same transaction. Except for his attendance at court and while being transported to or from any place at which his presence may be required, the prisoner shall be held in a suitable jail or other facility regularly used for persons awaiting prosecution.

(e) At the earliest practicable time consonant with the purposes of this agreement, the prisoner shall be returned to the sending state.

(f) During the continuance of temporary custody or while the prisoner is otherwise being made available for trial as required by this agreement, time being served on the sentence shall continue to run but good time shall be earned by the prisoner only if, and to the extent that, the law and practice of the jurisdiction which imposed the sentence may allow.

(g) For all purposes other than that for which temporary custody as provided in this agreement is exercised, the prisoner shall be deemed to remain in the custody of and subject to the jurisdiction of the sending state and any escape from temporary custody may be dealt with in the same manner as an escape from the original place of imprisonment or in any other manner permitted by law.

(h) From the time that a party state receives custody of a prisoner pursuant to this agreement until such prisoner is returned to the territory and custody of the sending state, the state in which the one or more untried indictments, informations, or complaints are pending or in which trial is being had shall be responsible for the prisoner and shall also pay all costs of transporting, caring for, keeping, and returning the prisoner. The provisions of this paragraph shall govern unless the states concerned shall have entered into a supplementary agreement providing for a different allocation of costs and responsibilities as between or among themselves. Nothing herein contained shall be construed to alter or affect any internal relationship among the departments, agencies, and officers of and in the government of a party state, or between a party state and its subdivisions, as to the payment of costs, or responsibilities therefor.

Printed in the U.S.A. Zt

## ARTICLE VI

(a) In determining the duration and expiration dates of the time periods provided in Articles III and IV of this agreement, the running of said time periods shall be tolled whenever and for as long as the prisoner is unable to stand trial, as determined by the court having jurisdiction of the matter.

(b) No provision of this agreement, and no remedy made available by this agreement shall apply to any person who is adjudged to be mentally ill.

## ARTICLE VII

Each state party to this agreement shall designate an officer who, acting jointly with like officers of other party states, shall promulgate rules and regulations to carry out more effectively the terms and provisions of this agreement, and who shall provide, within and without the state, information necessary to the effective operation of this agreement.

## ARTICLE VIII

This agreement shall enter into full force and effect as to a party state when such state has enacted the same into law. A state party to this agreement may withdraw herefrom by enacting a statute repealing the same. However, the withdrawal of any state shall not affect the status of any proceedings already initiated by inmates or by state officers at the time such withdrawal takes effect, nor shall it affect their rights in respect thereof.

## ARTICLE IX

(a) This agreement shall be liberally construed so as to effectuate its purposes. The provisions of this agreement shall be severable and if any phrase, clause, sentence, or provision of this agreement is declared to be contrary to the constitution of any party state or of the United States or the applicability thereof to any government, agency, person, or circumstance is held invalid, the validity of the remainder of this agreement and the applicability thereof to any government, agency, person, or circumstance shall not be affected thereby. If this agreement shall be held contrary to the constitution of any state party thereto, the agreement shall remain in full force and effect as to the remaining states and in full force and effect as to the state affected as to all severable matters.

(b) As used in this article, "appropriate court" means a court of record with criminal jurisdiction.

(c) All courts, departments, agencies, officers, and employees of this state and its political subdivisions are hereby directed to enforce this article and to cooperate with one another and with other party states in enforcing the agreement and effectuating its purpose.

(d) Any prisoner escapes from lawful custody while in another state as a result of the application of this article shall be punished as though such escape had occurred within this state.

(e) The governor is empowered to designate the officer who will serve as central administrator of and information agent for the agreement on detainers pursuant to the provisions of Article VII hereof.

(f) Copies of this article, upon its enactment, shall be transmitted to the governor of each state, the Attorney General and the Secretary of State of the United States, and the council of state governments.

## CHAPTER 52. COURT OF INQUIRY

Article



### Art. 52.01. Courts of Inquiry conducted by district judges.† [*Courts of Inquiry held by district judges.*]

(a) When a judge of any district court of this state, acting in his capacity as magistrate, has probable cause to believe that an offense has been committed against the laws of this state, he may request that the presiding judge of the administrative judicial district appoint a district judge to commence a Court of Inquiry. The judge, who shall be appointed in accordance with Subsection (b), may summon and examine any witness in relation to the offense in accordance with the rules hereinafter provided, which procedure is defined as a "Court of Inquiry".

(b)(1) Before requesting the presiding judge to appoint a district judge to commence a Court of Inquiry, a judge must enter into the minutes of his court a sworn affidavit stating the substantial facts establishing probable cause that a specific offense has been committed against the laws of this state.

(2) After the affidavit has been entered into the minutes of his court and a copy filed with the district clerk, the judge shall request the presiding judge of the administrative judicial district in which the affidavit is filed to appoint a judge to commence the Court of Inquiry. The judge appointed to commence the Court of Inquiry shall issue a written order commencing the Court of Inquiry and stating its scope. The presiding judge shall not name the judge who requests the Court of Inquiry to preside over the Court of Inquiry.

(c) The district or county attorney of the district or county in which the Court of Inquiry is held shall assist the district judge in conducting the Court of Inquiry. The attorney shall examine witnesses and evidence admitted before the court to determine if an offense has been committed and shall render other assistance to the judge as is necessary in the proceeding.

(d) If the Court of Inquiry pertains to the activities of the district or county attorney or to the attorney's office, deputies, or employees, or if the attorney is otherwise disqualified in the proceeding, the judge shall appoint one attorney pro tem to assist in the proceeding. In any other circumstance, the judge may appoint an attorney pro tem to assist in the proceeding.

(e) If more than one Court of Inquiry is commenced which pertains to the activities of a state governmental entity or public servant thereof, then, upon motion of the state governmental entity or public servant, made to the presiding judge or judges of the administrative judicial region or regions where the Courts of Inquiry have been commenced, the presiding judge or judges shall transfer the Courts of Inquiry to the presiding administrative judge of Travis County. The presiding administrative judge of Travis County shall consolidate the Courts of Inquiry for further proceedings and shall assign a district judge to preside over the consolidated Courts of Inquiry. *(Chgd. by L.1995, chap. 318(65), eff. 9/1/95.)*

### Art. 52.02. Evidence; deposition; affidavits.

At the hearing at a Court of Inquiry, evidence may be taken orally or by deposition, or, in the discretion of the judge, by affidavit. If affidavits are admitted, any witness against whom they may bear has the right to propound written interrogatories to the affiants or to file answering affidavits. The judge in hearing such evidence, at his discretion, may conclude not to sustain objections to all or to any portion of the evidence taken nor exclude same; but any of the witnesses or attorneys engaged in taking the testimony may have any objections they make recorded with the testimony and reserved for the action of any court in which such evidence is thereafter sought to be admitted, but such court is not confined to objections made at the taking of the testimony at the Court of Inquiry.

Printed in the U.S.A. Zt

Without restricting the foregoing, the judge may allow the introduction of any documentary or real evidence which he deems reliable, and the testimony adduced before any grand jury.

### Art. 52.03. Subpoenas.

The judge or his clerk has power to issue subpoenas which may be served within the same territorial limits as subpoenas issued in felony prosecutions or to summon witnesses before grand juries in this state.

### Art. 52.04. Rights of witnesses.

(a) All witnesses testifying in any Court of Inquiry have the same rights as to testifying as do defendants in felony prosecutions in this state. Before any witness is sworn to testify in any Court of Inquiry, he shall be instructed by the judge that he is entitled to counsel; that he cannot be forced to testify against himself; and that such testimony may be taken down and used against him in a later trial or trials ensuing from the instant Court of Inquiry. Any witness or his counsel has the right to fully cross-examine any of the witnesses whose testimony bears in any manner against him.

(b) If the Court of Inquiry pertains to the activities of a state governmental entity or its officers or employees, the officers and employees of that state governmental entity shall be indemnified for attorney's fees incurred as a result of exercising the employees' or officers' right to counsel under Subsection (a) if:

(1) the officer or employee is found not guilty after a trial or appeal or the complaint, information, or indictment is dismissed without a plea of guilty or nolo contendere being entered; and

(2) the judge commencing the Court of Inquiry, or the judge to whom the Court of Inquiry was transferred pursuant to Article 52.01(e), determines that the complaint, information, or indictment presented against the person was dismissed because:

(A) the presentment was made on mistake, false information, or other similar basis, indicating absence of probable cause to believe, at the time of dismissal, the person committed the offense; or

(B) the complaint, information, or indictment was void.

(c) The county in which the affidavit under Article 52.01 was filed shall be responsible for any attorney's fees awarded under Subsection (b).

*(Chgd. by L.1995, chap. 318(66), eff. 9/1/95.)*

### Art. 52.05. Witness must testify.† [*Witness must give testimony.*]

A person may be compelled to give testimony or produce evidence when legally called upon to do so at any Court of Inquiry; however, if any person refuses or declines to testify or produce evidence on the ground that it may incriminate him under the laws of this state, then the judge may, in his discretion, compel such person to testify or produce evidence but the person shall not be prosecuted or subjected to any penalty for forfeiture for, or on account of, any transaction, matter or thing concerning which he may be compelled to testify or produce evidence at such Court of Inquiry.

### Art. 52.06. Contempt.

Contempt of court in a Court of Inquiry may be punished by a fine not exceeding One Hundred Dollars ($100.00) and any witness refusing to testify may be attached and imprisoned until he does testify.

### Art. 52.07. Stenographic record; public hearing.

All evidence taken at a Court of Inquiry shall be transcribed by the court reporter and all proceedings shall be open to the public.

### Art. 52.08. Criminal prosecutions.

If it appear from a Court of Inquiry or any testimony adduced therein, that an offense has been committed, the Judge shall issue a warrant for the arrest of the offender as if complaint had been made and filed.

### Art. 52.09. Costs and attorney's fees.† [*Expenses; fees of attorneys.*]

(a) All costs incurred in conducting a Court of Inquiry, including compensation of an attorney pro tem, shall be borne by the county in which said Court of Inquiry is conducted; provided, however, that where the Attorney General of Texas has submitted a request in writing to the judge for the holding of such Court of Inquiry, then and in that event the costs shall be borne by the State of

Texas and shall be taxed to the attorney general and paid in the same manner and from the same funds as other court costs.

(b) Assistance by a county or district attorney to a Court of Inquiry is a duty of the attorney's office, and the attorney may not receive a fee for the service. A county is not liable for attorney's fees claimed for assistance in a Court of Inquiry by any attorney other than an attorney pro tem appointed under Article 52.01(d) of this code.

(c) An attorney pro tem appointed under Article 52.01(d) of this code is entitled to compensation in the same manner as an attorney pro tem appointed under Article 2.07 of this code. The district judge shall set the compensation of the attorney pro tem based on the sworn testimony of the attorney or other evidence that is given in open court.

## CHAPTER 53. COSTS AND FEES

*(Repealed by L.1987, chap. 167(4.01(b)), eff. 9/1/87.)*



**Art. 53.11.** *(Renumbered from Art. 53.08 by L.1987, chap. 167(5.01)(a)(10), eff. 9/1/87. See now Art. 102.006.)*



## CHAPTER 54. MISCELLANEOUS PROVISIONS



### Art. 54.01. Severability clause.

If any provision, section or clause of this Act or application thereof to any person or circumstances is held invalid, such invalidity shall not affect other provisions or applications hereof which can be given effect without the invalid provision, section or clause, and to this end the provisions of this Act are declared to be severable.

### Art. 54.02. Repealing clause.

**Sec. 1.** (a) Except as otherwise provided in this Article 54.02, all laws relating to criminal procedure in this State that are not embraced, incorporated, or included in this Act and that have not been enacted during the Regular Session of the 59th Legislature are repealed.

(b) None of the following articles of the Code of Criminal Procedure of Texas, 1925, in force on the effective date of this Act, is repealed: 52; 52-1 through 52-161, both inclusive; 367D through 367K, both inclusive; 781B-1, 781B-2; 944 through 951, both inclusive; 1009 through 1035, both inclusive; 1037 through 1056, both inclusive; 1058 through 1064, both inclusive; and 1075 through 1082, both inclusive.

**Sec. 2.** (a) All laws and parts of laws relating to criminal procedure omitted from this Act have been intentionally omitted, and all additions to and changes in such procedure have been intentionally made. This Act shall be construed to be an independent Act of the Legislature, enacted under its caption, and the articles contained in this Act, as revised, rewritten, changed, combined, and codified, may not be construed as a continuation of former laws except as otherwise provided in this Act. The existing statutes of the Revised Civil Statutes of Texas, 1925, as amended, and of the Penal Code of Texas, 1925, as amended, which contain special or specific provisions of criminal procedure covering specific instances are not repealed by this Act.

(b) A person under recognizance or bond on the effective date of this Act continues under such recognizance or bond pending final disposition of any action pending against him.

### Art. 54.03. Emergency clause.

The fact that the laws relating to criminal procedure in this State have not been completely revised and re-codified in more than a century past and the further fact that the administration of justice, in the field of criminal law, has undergone changes, through judicial construction and interpretation of constitutional provisions, which have been, in certain instances, modified or nullified, as the case may be, necessitates important changes requiring the revision or modernization of the laws relating to criminal procedure, and the further fact that it is desirous and desirable to strengthen, and to conform, various provisions in such laws to current interpretation and application, emphasizes the importance of this legislation and all of which, together with the crowded condition of the calendar in both Houses, create an emergency and an imperative public necessity that the Constitutional Rule requiring bills to be read on three several days be suspended, and said Rule is hereby suspended, and that this Act shall take effect and be in force and effect from and after 12 o'clock Meridian on the 1st day of January, Anno Domini, 1966, and it is so enacted.

## CHAPTER 55. EXPUNCTION OF CRIMINAL RECORDS

Article
55.01. Right to expunction.
55.02. Procedure for expunction.
55.03. Effect of expunction.
55.04. Violation of expunction order.† [*Violation of order.*]
55.05. Notice of right to expunction.† [*Notice of eligibility for expunction.*]
55.06. License suspensions and revocations.



### Art. 55.01. Right to expunction.

(a) A person who has been arrested for commission of either a felony or misdemeanor is entitled to have all records and files relating to the arrest expunged if:

(1) the person is tried for the offense for which the person was arrested and is:

(A) acquitted by the trial court, except as provided by Subsection (c) of this section; or

(B) convicted and subsequently pardoned; or

(2) each of the following conditions exist:

(A) an indictment or information charging the person with commission of a felony has not been presented against the person for an offense arising out of the transaction for which the person was arrested or, if an indictment or information charging the person with commission of a felony was presented, it has been dismissed and the court finds that it was dismissed because the presentment had been made because of mistake, false information, or other similar reason indicating absence of probable cause at the time of the dismissal to believe the person committed the offense or because it was void;

(B) the person has been released and the charge, if any, has not resulted in a final conviction and is no longer pending and there was no court ordered community supervision under Article 42.12 of this code; and

(C) the person has not been convicted of a felony in the five years preceding the date of the arrest.

(b) Except as provided by Subsection (c) of this section, a district court may expunge all records and files relating to the arrest of a person who has been arrested for commission of a felony or misdemeanor under the procedure established under Article 55.02 of this code if the person is:

(1) tried for the offense for which the person was arrested;

(2) convicted of the offense; and

(3) acquitted by the court of criminal appeals.

(c) A court may not order the expunction of records and files relating to an arrest for an offense for which a person is subsequently acquitted, whether by the trial court or the court of criminal appeals, if the offense for which the person was acquitted arose out of a criminal episode, as defined by Section 3.01, Penal Code, and the person was convicted of or remains subject to prosecution for at least one other offense occurring during the criminal episode.

*(Chgd. by L.1989, chap. 803(1); L.1991, chap. 14(284(53)); L.1993, chap. 900(7.02); L.1999, chap. 1236(1), eff. 6/18/99.)*

### Art. 55.02. Procedure for expunction.

**Sec. 1.** At the request of the defendant and after notice to the state and a hearing, the trial court presiding over the case in which the defendant was acquitted shall enter an order of expunction for a person entitled to expunction under Article 55.01(a)(1)(A) not later than the 30th day after the date of the acquittal. Upon acquittal, the court shall advise the defendant of the right to expunction. The defendant shall provide to the court all of the information required in a petition for expunction under Section 2(b).

**Sec. 2.** (a) A person who is entitled to expunction of records and files under Article 55.01(a)(1)(B) or 55.01(a)(2) or a person who is eligible for expunction of records and files under Article 55.01(b) may file an ex parte petition for expunction in a district court for the county in which the person was arrested or in the county where the offense was alleged to have occurred.

(b) The petition must be verified and shall include the following or an explanation for why one or more of the following is not included:

(1) the petitioner's:

(A) full name;

(B) sex;

(C) race;

(D) date of birth;

(E) driver's license number;

(F) social security number; and

(G) address at the time of the arrest;

(2) the offense charged against the petitioner;

(3) the date the offense charged against the petitioner was alleged to have been committed;

(4) the date the petitioner was arrested;

(5) the name of the county where the petitioner was arrested and if the arrest occurred in a municipality, the name of the municipality;

(6) the name of the agency that arrested the petitioner;

(7) the case number and court of offense; and

(8) a list of all law enforcement agencies, jails or other detention facilities, magistrates, courts, prosecuting attorneys, correctional facilities, central state depositories of criminal records, and other officials or agencies or other entities of this state or of any political subdivision of this state and of all central federal depositories of criminal records that the petitioner has reason to believe have records or files that are subject to expunction.

(c) The court shall set a hearing on the matter no sooner than thirty days from the filing of the petition and shall give reasonable notice of the hearing to each official or agency or other entity named in the petition by certified mail, return receipt requested, and such entity may be represented by the attorney responsible for providing such agency with legal representation in other matters.

(d) If the court finds that the petitioner is entitled to expunction of any records and files that are the subject of the petition, it shall enter an order directing expunction.

**Sec. 3.** (a) In an order of expunction issued under this article, the trial court shall require any state agency that sent information concerning the arrest to a central federal depository to request such depository to return all records and files subject to the order of expunction. The person who is the subject of the expunction order or an agency protesting the expunction may appeal the court's decision in the same manner as in other civil cases.

(b) The order of expunction entered by the trial court shall have attached and incorporate by reference a copy of the judgment of acquittal and shall include:

(1) the following information on the person who is the subject of the expunction order:

(A) full name;

(B) sex;

(C) race;

(D) date of birth;

(E) driver's license number; and

(F) social security number;

(2) the offense charged against the person who is the subject of the expunction order;

(3) the date the person who is the subject of the expunction order was arrested;

(4) the case number and court of offense; and

(5) the tracking incident number (TRN) assigned to the individual incident of arrest under Article 60.07(b)(1) by the Department of Public Safety.

(c) When the order of expunction is final, the clerk of the court shall send a certified copy of the order by certified mail, return receipt requested, to the Crime Records Service of the Department of Public Safety and to each official or agency or other entity of this state or of any political subdivision of this state designated by the person who is the subject of the order. The Department of Public Safety shall notify any central federal depository of criminal records by any means, including electronic transmission, of the order with an explanation of the effect of the order and a request that the records in possession of the depository, including any information with respect to the order, be destroyed or returned to the court.

(d) All returned receipts received by the clerk from notices of the hearing and copies of the order shall be maintained in the file on the proceedings under this chapter.

**Sec. 4.** (a) If the state establishes that the person who is the subject of an expunction order is still subject to conviction for an offense arising out of the transaction for which the person was ar-

Printed in the U.S.A. 21

rested because the statute of limitations has not run and there is reasonable cause to believe that the state may proceed against the person for the offense, the court may provide in its order that the law enforcement agency and the prosecuting attorney responsible for investigating the offense may retain any records and files that are necessary to the investigation. In the case of a person who is the subject of an expunction order on the basis of an acquittal, the court may provide in the expunction order that the law enforcement agency and the prosecuting attorney retain records and files if:

(1) the records and files are necessary to conduct a subsequent investigation and prosecution of a person other than the person who is the subject of the expunction order; or

(2) the state establishes that the records and files are necessary for use in:

(A) another criminal case, including a prosecution, motion to adjudicate or revoke community supervision, parole revocation hearing, mandatory supervision revocation hearing, punishment hearing, or bond hearing; or

(B) a civil case, including a civil suit or suit for possession of or access to a child.

(b) Unless the person who is the subject of the expunction order is again arrested for or charged with an offense arising out of the transaction for which the person was arrested or unless the court provides for the retention of records and files under Subsection (a) of this section, the provisions of Articles 55.03 and 55.04 of this code apply to files and records retained under this section.



**Sec. 5.** (a) On receipt of the order, each official or agency or other entity named in the order shall:

(1) return all records and files that are subject to the expunction order to the court or, if removal is impracticable, obliterate all portions of the record or file that identify the person who is the subject of the order and notify the court of its action; and

(2) delete from its public records all index references to the records and files that are subject to the expunction order.

(b) Except in the case of a person who is the subject of an expunction order on the basis of an acquittal, the court may give the person who is the subject of the order all records and files returned to it pursuant to its order.

(c) If an order of expunction is issued under this article, the court records concerning expunction proceedings are not open for inspection by anyone except the person who is the subject of the order unless the order permits retention of a record under Section 4 of this article and the person is again arrested for or charged with an offense arising out of the transaction for which the person was arrested or unless the court provides for the retention of records and files under Section 4(a) of this article. The clerk of the court issuing the order shall obliterate all public references to the proceeding and maintain the files or other records in an area not open to inspection.

(d) Except in the case of a person who is the subject of an expunction order on the basis of an acquittal, the clerk of the court shall destroy all the files or other records maintained under Subsection (c) of this section on the first anniversary of the date the order of expunction is issued unless the records or files were released under Subsection (b) of this section.

(e) The clerk shall certify to the court the destruction of files or other records under Subsection (d) of this section.

*(Chgd. by L.1989, chap. 803(2)-(4); L.1991, chap. 380(1); L.1999, chap. 1236(2), eff. 6/18/99.)*

## Art. 55.03. Effect of expunction.

After entry of an expunction order:

(1) the release, dissemination, or use of the expunged records and files for any purpose is prohibited;

(2) except as provided in Subdivision 3 of this article, the person arrested may deny the occurrence of the arrest and the existence of the expunction order; and

(3) the person arrested or any other person, when questioned under oath in a criminal proceeding about an arrest for which the records have been expunged, may state only that the matter in question has been expunged.

*(Chgd. by L.1999, chap. 1236(3), eff. 6/18/99.)*

## Art. 55.04. Violation of expunction order.† [*Violation of order.*]

**Sec. 1.** A person who acquires knowledge of an arrest while an officer or employee of the state or of any agency or other entity of the state or any political subdivision of the state and who knows of an order expunging the records and files relating to that arrest commits an offense if he knowingly releases, disseminates, or otherwise uses the records or files.

**Sec. 2.** A person who knowingly fails to return or to obliterate identifying portions of a record or file ordered expunged under this chapter commits an offense.

**Sec. 3.** An offense under this article is a Class B misdemeanor.

### Art. 55.05. Notice of right to expunction.† [*Notice of eligibility for expunction.*]

On release or discharge of an arrested person, the person responsible for the release or discharge shall give him a written explanation of his rights under this chapter and a copy of the provisions of this chapter.

### Art. 55.06. License suspensions and revocations.

Records relating to the suspension or revocation of a driver's license, permit, or privilege to operate a motor vehicle may not be expunged under this chapter except as provided in Section 524.015, Transportation Code, or Section 724.048 of that code. *(Added by L.1993, chap. 886(16); chgd. by L.1999, chap. 62(3.08), 1236(4), eff. 9/1/99, 6/18/99, respectively.)*

## CHAPTER 56. RIGHTS OF CRIME VICTIMS

### SUBCHAPTER A. CRIME VICTIMS' RIGHTS



### SUBCHAPTER B. CRIME VICTIMS' COMPENSATION

## SUBCHAPTER A. CRIME VICTIMS' RIGHTS

*(Subchapter heading added by L.1993, chap. 268(6), eff. 9/1/93.)*

### Art. 56.01. Definitions.

In this chapter:

(1) "Close relative of a deceased victim" means a person who was the spouse of a deceased victim at the time of the victim's death or who is a parent or adult brother, sister, or child of the deceased victim.

(2) "Guardian of a victim" means a person who is the legal guardian of the victim, whether or not the legal relationship between the guardian and victim exists because of the age of the victim or the physical or mental incompetency of the victim.

(3) "Victim" means a person who is the victim of sexual assault, kidnapping, or aggravated robbery or who has suffered bodily injury or death as a result of the criminal conduct of another.

### Art. 56.02. Crime victims' rights.† [*Rights of victims.*]

(a) A victim, guardian of a victim, or close relative of a deceased victim is entitled to the following rights within the criminal justice system:

(1) the right to receive from law enforcement agencies adequate protection from harm and threats of harm arising from cooperation with prosecution efforts;

(2) the right to have the magistrate take the safety of the victim or his family into consideration as an element in fixing the amount of bail for the accused;

(3) the right, if requested, to be informed of relevant court proceedings and to be informed if those court proceedings have been canceled or rescheduled prior to the event;

(4) the right to be informed, when requested, by a peace officer concerning the defendant's right to bail and the procedures in criminal investigations and by the district attorney's office concerning the general procedures in the criminal justice system, including general procedures in guilty plea negotiations and arrangements, restitution, and the appeals and parole process;

(5) the right to provide pertinent information to a probation department conducting a presentencing investigation concerning the impact of the offense on the victim and his family by testimony, written statement, or any other manner prior to any sentencing of the offender;

(6) the right to receive information regarding compensation to victims of crime as provided by Subchapter B, Chapter 56, including information related to the costs that may be compensated under that Act and the amount of compensation, eligibility for compensation, and procedures for application for compensation under that Act, the payment for a medical examination under Article 56.06 of this code for a victim of a sexual assault, and when requested, to referral to available social service agencies that may offer additional assistance; and

(7) the right to be informed, upon request, of parole procedures, to participate in the parole process, to be notified, if requested, of parole proceedings concerning a defendant in the victim's case, to provide to the Board of Pardons and Paroles for inclusion in the defendant's file information to be considered by the board prior to the parole of any defendant convicted of any crime subject to this Act, and to be notified, if requested, of the defendant's release;

(8) the right to be provided with a waiting area, separate or secure from other witnesses, including the offender and relatives of the offender, before testifying in any proceeding concerning the offender; if a separate waiting area is not available, other safeguards should be taken to minimize the victim's contact with the offender and the offender's relatives and witnesses, before and during court proceedings;

(9) the right to prompt return of any property of the victim that is held by a law enforcement agency or the attorney for the state as evidence when the property is no longer required for that purpose;

(10) the right to have the attorney for the state notify the employer of the victim, if requested, of the necessity of the victim's cooperation and testimony in a proceeding that may necessitate the absence of the victim from work for good cause; and

(11) the right to counseling, on request, regarding acquired immune deficiency syndrome (AIDS) and human immunodeficiency virus (HIV) infection and testing for acquired immune deficiency syndrome (AIDS), human immunodeficiency virus (HIV) infection, antibodies to HIV, or infection with any other probable causative agent of AIDS, if the offense is an offense under Section 21.11(a)(1), 22.011, or 22.021, Penal Code.

(b) A victim is entitled to the right to be present at all public court proceedings related to the offense, subject to the approval of the judge in the case.

(c) The office of the attorney representing the state, and the sheriff, police, and other law enforcement agencies shall ensure to the extent practicable that a victim, guardian of a victim, or close relative of a deceased victim is afforded the rights granted by Subsection (a) of this article and, on request, an explanation of those rights.

(d) A judge, attorney for the state, peace officer, or law enforcement agency is not liable for a failure or inability to provide a right enumerated in this article. The failure or inability of any person to provide a right or service enumerated in this article may not be used by a defendant in a criminal case as a ground for appeal, a ground to set aside the conviction or sentence, or a ground in a habeas corpus petition. A victim, guardian of a victim, or close relative of a deceased victim does not have standing to participate as a party in a criminal proceeding or to contest the disposition of any charge.

*(Chgd. by L.1989, chap. 996(1); L.1991, chap. 202(3); L.1993, chap. 811(3); L.1995, chap. 76(5.95(108)), eff. 9/1/95.)*



### Art. 56.03. Victim impact statement.

(a) The Texas Crime Victim Clearinghouse, with the participation of the Texas Adult Probation Commission and the Board of Pardons and Paroles, shall develop a form to be used by law enforcement agencies, prosecutors, and other participants in the criminal justice system to record the impact of an offense on a victim of the offense, guardian of a victim, or a close relative of a deceased victim and to provide the agencies, prosecutors, and participants with information needed to contact the victim, guardian, or relative if needed at any stage of a prosecution of a person charged with the offense. The Texas Crime Victim Clearinghouse, with the participation of the Texas Adult Probation Commission and the Board of Pardons and Paroles, shall also develop a victims' information booklet that provides a general explanation of the criminal justice system to victims of an offense, guardians of victims, and relatives of deceased victims.

(b) The victim impact statement must be in a form designed to inform a victim, guardian of a victim, or a close relative of a deceased victim with a clear statement of rights provided by Article 56.02 of this code and to collect the following information:

(1) the name of the victim of the offense or, if the victim has a legal guardian or is deceased, the name of a guardian or close relative of the victim;

(2) the address and telephone number of the victim, guardian, or relative through which the victim, guardian of a victim, or a close relative of a deceased victim, may by contacted;

(3) a statement of economic loss suffered by the victim, guardian, or relative as a result of the offense;

(4) a statement of any physical or psychological injury suffered by the victim, guardian, or relative as a result of the offense, as described by the victim, guardian, relative, or by a physician or counselor;

(5) a statement of any psychological services requested as a result of the offense;

(6) a statement of any change in the victim's, guardian's, or relative's personal welfare or familial relationship as a result of the offense;

(7) a statement as to whether or not the victim, guardian, or relative wishes to be notified in the future of any parole hearing for the defendant and an explanation as to the procedures by which the victim, guardian, or relative may obtain information concerning the release of the defendant from the Texas Department of Corrections; and

(8) any other information, other than facts related to the commission of the offense, related to the impact of the offense on the victim, guardian, or relative.

(c) The victim assistance coordinator, designated in Article 56.04(a) of this code, shall send to a victim, guardian of a victim, or close relative of a deceased victim a victim impact statement, a victims' information booklet, and an application for compensation under Subchapter B, Chapter 56, along with an offer to assist in completing those forms on request. The victim assistance coordinator, on request, shall explain the possible use and consideration of the victim impact statement at sentencing and future parole hearing of the offender.

(d) If a victim, guardian of a victim, or close relative of a deceased victim states on the victim impact statement that he wishes to be notified of parole proceedings, the victim, guardian, or relative is responsible for notifying the Board of Pardons and Paroles of any change of address.

(e) Prior to the imposition of a sentence by the court in a criminal case, the court, if it has received a victim impact statement, shall consider the information provided in the statement. Before sentencing the defendant, the court shall permit the defendant or his counsel a reasonable time to read the statement, comment on the statement, and, with the approval of the court, introduce testimony or other information alleging a factual inaccuracy in the statement. If the court sentences the defendant to a term of probation, the court shall forward any victim's impact statement received in the case to the probation department supervising the defendant, along with the papers in the case.

(f) The court may not inspect a victim impact statement until after a finding of guilt or until deferred adjudication is ordered and the contents of the statement may not be disclosed to any person unless:

(1) the defendant pleads guilty or nolo contendere or is convicted of the offense; or

(2) the defendant in writing authorizes the court to inspect the statement.

(g) A victim impact statement is subject to discovery under Article 39.14 of this code before the testimony of the victim is taken only if the court determines that the statement contains exculpatory material.

(h) Not later than December 1 of each odd-numbered year, the Texas Crime Victim Clearinghouse, with the participation of the Texas Adult Probation Commission and the Board of Pardons and Paroles, shall update the victim impact statement form and any other information provided by the commission to victims, guardians of victims, and relatives of deceased victims, if necessary, to reflect changes in law relating to criminal justice and the rights of victims and guardians and relatives of victims.

(i) In addition to the information described by Subsections (b)(1)-(8), the victim impact statement must be in a form designed to collect information on whether, if the victim is a child, there is an existing court order granting to the defendant possession of or access to the victim. If information collected under this subsection indicates the defendant is granted access or possession under court order and the defendant is subsequently confined by the Texas Department of Criminal Justice as a result of the commission of the offense, the victim services office of the department shall contact the court issuing the order before the defendant is released from the department on parole or mandatory supervision.

*(Chgd. by L.1989, chap. 996(2); L.1995, chap. 76(5.95(108)); L.1997, chap. 670(5), eff. 9/1/97.)*

## Art. 56.04. Victim assistance coordinator; crime victim liaison.

(a) The district attorney, criminal district attorney, or county attorney who prosecutes criminal cases shall designate a person to serve as victim assistance coordinator in that jurisdiction.

(b) The duty of the victim assistance coordinator is to ensure that a victim, guardian of a victim, or close relative of a deceased victim is afforded the rights granted victims, guardians, and relatives by Article 56.02 of this code. The victim assistance coordinator shall work closely with appropriate law enforcement agencies, prosecuting attorneys, the Board of Pardons and Paroles, and the judiciary in carrying out that duty.

(c) Each local law enforcement agency shall designate one person to serve as the agency's crime victim liaison. Each agency shall consult with the victim assistance coordinator in the office of the attorney representing the state to determine the most effective manner in which the crime victim liaison can perform the duties imposed on the crime victim liaison under this article.

(d) The duty of the crime victim liaison is to ensure that a victim, guardian of a victim, or close relative of a deceased victim is afforded the rights granted victims, guardians, or close relatives of deceased victims by Subdivisions (4), (6), and (9) of Article 56.02(a) of this code.

(e) The victim assistance coordinator shall send a copy of a victim impact statement to the court sentencing the defendant. If the court sentences the defendant to imprisonment in the Texas Department of Corrections, it shall attach the copy of the victim impact statement to the commitment papers.

*(Chgd. by L.1989, chap. 996(3); L.1991, chap. 202(4), eff. 9/1/91.)*

## Art. 56.05. Reports required.† [*Required reports.*]

(a) The Board of Pardons and Paroles, the Texas Adult Probation Commission, and the Texas Crime Victim Clearinghouse, designated as the planning body for the purposes of this article, shall develop a survey plan to maintain statistics on the numbers and types of persons to whom state and local agencies provide victim impact statements during each year.

(b) At intervals specified in the plan, the planning body may require any state or local agency to submit, in a form prescribed for the reporting of the information, statistical data on the numbers and types of persons to whom the agency provides victim impact statements and any other information required by the planning body. The form must be designed to protect the privacy of persons afforded rights under this chapter and to determine whether the selected agency or office is making a good faith effort to protect the rights of the persons served.

(c) The Texas Crime Victim Clearinghouse shall develop crime victim assistance standards and distribute those standards to law enforcement officers and attorneys representing the state to aid those officers and prosecutors in performing duties imposed by this chapter.
*(Chgd. by L.1989, chap. 996(4), eff. 9/1/89.)*

**Art. 56.06. Costs of medical examination.**

(a) A law enforcement agency that requests a medical examination of a victim of an alleged sexual assault for use in the investigation or prosecution of the offense shall pay all costs of the examination. A law enforcement agency or prosecuting attorney's office may pay all costs related to the testimony of a licensed health care professional in a criminal proceeding regarding the results of the medical examination or manner in which it was performed.

(b) This article does not require a law enforcement agency to pay any costs of treatment for injuries.
*(Added by L.1989, chap. 2(5.05(a)); chgd. by L.1991, chap. 75(1), eff. 9/1/91.)*

**Art. 56.07. Notification.**

At the initial contact or at the earliest possible time after the initial contact between the victim of a reported crime and the law enforcement agency having the responsibility for investigating that crime, that agency shall provide the victim a written notice containing:

(1) information about the availability of emergency and medical services, if applicable;

(2) notice that the victim has the right to receive information regarding compensation to victims of crime as provided by Subchapter B, Chapter 56, including information about:

(A) the costs that may be compensated under that Act and the amount of compensation, eligibility for compensation, and procedures for application for compensation under that Act;

(B) the payment for a medical examination for a victim of a sexual assault under Article 56.06 of this code; and

(C) referral to available social service agencies that may offer additional assistance;

(3) the name, address, and phone number of the law enforcement agency's victim assistance liaison;

(4) the address, phone number, and name of the crime victim assistance coordinator of the office of the attorney representing the state;

(5) the following statement:

"You may call the law enforcement agency's telephone number for the status of the case and information about victims' rights"; and

(6) the rights of crime victims under Article 56.02 of this code.
*(Added by L.1991, chap. 202(5); chgd. by L.1995, chap. 76(5.95(108)), eff. 9/1/95.)*

**Art. 56.08. Notification of rights by attorney representing the state.**

(a) Not later than the 10th day after the date that an indictment or information is returned against a defendant for an offense, the attorney representing the state shall give to each victim of the offense a written notice containing:

(1) a brief general statement of each procedural stage in the processing of a criminal case, including bail, plea bargaining, parole restitution, and appeal;

(2) notification of the rights and procedures under this chapter;

(3) suggested steps the victim may take if the victim is subjected to threats or intimidation;

(4) notification of the right to receive information regarding compensation to victims of crime as provided by Subchapter B of this chapter, including information about:

(A) the costs that may be compensated under Subchapter B of this chapter, eligibility for compensation, and procedures for application for compensation under Subchapter B of this chapter;

(B) the payment for a medical examination for a victim of a sexual assault under Article 56.06 of this code; and

(C) referral to available social service agencies that may offer additional assistance;

(5) the name, address, and phone number of the local victim assistance coordinator;

(6) the case number and assigned court for the case;

(7) the right to file a victim impact statement with the office of the attorney representing the state and the pardons and paroles division of the Texas Department of Criminal Justice; and

Printed in the U.S.A. 27

(8) notification of the right of a victim, guardian of a victim, or close relative of a deceased victim, as defined by Section 508.117, Government Code, to appear in person before a member of the Board of Pardons and Paroles as provided by Section 508.153, Government Code.

(b) If requested by the victim, the attorney representing the state, as far as reasonably practicable, shall give to the victim notice of any scheduled court proceedings, changes in that schedule, the filing of a request for continuance of a trial setting, and any plea agreements to be presented to the court.

(c) A victim who receives a notice under Subsection (a) of this article and who chooses to receive other notice under law about the same case must keep the following persons informed of the victim's current address and phone number;

(1) the attorney representing the state; and

(2) the pardons and paroles division of the Texas Department of Criminal Justice if after sentencing the defendant is confined in the institutional division.

(d) An attorney representing the state who receives information concerning a victim's current address and phone number shall immediately provide that information to the community supervision and corrections department supervising the defendant, if the defendant is placed on community supervision.

*(Added by L.1991, chap. 202(5); chgd. by L.1995, chaps. 76(5.95)(108)), 252(2), 253(2); L.1997, chap. 165(12.04), eff. 9/1/97.)*



## Art. 56.09. Victim's right to privacy.

As far as reasonably practical, the address of the victim may not be a part of the court file except as necessary to identify the place of the crime. The phone number of the victim may not be a part of the court file. *(Added by L.1991, chap. 202(5), eff. 9/1/91.)*

## Art. 56.10. Victims discovery attendance.

Unless absolutely necessary, victims or witnesses who are not incarcerated may not be required to attend depositions in a correctional facility. *(Added by L.1991, chap. 202(5), eff. 9/1/91.)*

## Art. 56.11. Notification to victim of release or escape of defendant.

(a) The Texas Department of Criminal Justice or the sheriff, whichever has custody of the defendant in the case of a felony, or the sheriff in the case of a misdemeanor, shall notify the victim of the offense whenever a person convicted of an offense described by Subsection (c):

(1) completes the person's sentence and is released; or

(2) escapes from a correctional facility.

(b) If the Texas Department of Criminal Justice is required by Subsection (a) to give notice to the victim of an offense, the department shall also give notice to local law enforcement officials in the county in which the victim resides.

(c) This article applies to a person convicted of an offense involving family violence, stalking, or violation of a protective order or magistrate's order.

(d) It is the responsibility of a victim desiring notification of the offender's release to provide the Texas Department of Criminal Justice or the sheriff, as appropriate, with the address and telephone number of the victim or other person through whom the victim may be contacted and to notify the department or the sheriff of any change of address or telephone number of the victim or other person. Information obtained and maintained by the Texas Department of Criminal Justice or a sheriff under this subsection is privileged and confidential.

(e) The Texas Department of Criminal Justice or the sheriff, as appropriate, shall make a reasonable attempt to give the notice required by Subsection (a):

(1) not later than the 30th day before the person completes the sentence and is released; or

(2) immediately if the person escapes from the correctional facility.

(f) An attempt by the Texas Department of Criminal Justice or the sheriff to give notice to the victim at the victim's last known address, as shown on the records of the department or agency, constitutes a reasonable attempt to give notice under this article.

(g) In this article:

(1) "Correctional facility" has the meaning assigned by Section 1.07, Penal Code.

(2) "Family violence" has the meaning assigned by Section 71.01, Family Code.

*(Added by L.1993, chap. 10(6); chgd. by L.1995, chap. 657(6); L.1997, chaps. 1(8), 670(6), eff. 1/28/97, 9/1/97, respectively.)*

## Art. 56.12. Notification of escape.

(a) The Texas Department of Criminal Justice shall immediately make a reasonable attempt to notify the victim of an offense, the victim's guardian, or the victim's close relative, if the victim is deceased, whenever the offender escapes from a facility operated by the institutional division of the Texas Department of Criminal Justice, if the victim, victim's guardian, or victim's close relative has notified the institutional division as provided by Subsection (b) of this article. An attempt by the Texas Department of Criminal Justice to give notice to the victim, the guardian of the victim, or a close relative of a deceased victim at the victim's, the guardian of the victim's, or a close relative of the deceased victim's last known telephone number or address as shown on the records of the department constitutes a reasonable attempt to give notice under this subsection.

(b) It is the responsibility of the victim, guardian, or close relative desiring notification of an offender's escape to notify the Texas Department of Criminal Justice of the desire for notification and any change of address.

*(Added by L.1995, chap. 251(1), eff. 5/29/95.)*

## SUBCHAPTER B. CRIME VICTIMS' COMPENSATION

*(Added by L.1993, chap. 268(6); chgd. by L.1995, chaps. 76(5.84), 779(1), eff. 9/1/95.)*

### Art. 56.31. Short title.

This subchapter may be cited as the Crime Victims' Compensation Act. *(Added by L.1993, chap. 268(6); redesignated as article by L.1995, chap. 76(5.84)(a), eff. 9/1/95; chgd. by L.1995, chap. 779(1), eff. 9/1/95.)*

### Art. 56.311. Legislative findings and intent.

The legislature recognizes that many innocent individuals suffer personal injury or death as a result of criminal acts. Crime victims and persons who intervene to prevent criminal acts often suffer disabilities, incur financial burdens, or become dependent on public assistance. The legislature finds that there is a need for the compensation of victims of crime and those who suffer personal injury or death in the prevention of crime or in the apprehension of criminals. It is the legislature's intent that the compensation of innocent victims of violent crime encourage greater public cooperation in the successful apprehension and prosecution of criminals. *(Added by L.1995, chap. 779(1), eff. 9/1/95.)*

### Art. 56.32. Definitions.

(a) In this subchapter:

(1) "Child" means an individual younger than 18 years of age who:

(A) is not married; or

(B) has not had the disabilities of minority removed for general purposes under Chapter 31, Family Code.

(2) "Claimant" means, except as provided by Subsection (b), any of the following individuals who is entitled to file or has filed a claim for compensation under this subchapter:

(A) an authorized individual acting on behalf of a victim;

(B) an individual who legally assumes the obligation or who voluntarily pays medical or burial expenses of a victim incurred as a result of the criminally injurious conduct of another;

(C) a dependent of a victim who died as a result of criminally injurious conduct;

(D) an immediate family member or household member of a victim who requires psychiatric care or counseling as a result of the criminally injurious conduct; or

(E) an authorized individual acting on behalf of an individual who is described by Subdivision (C) or (D) and who is a child.

(3) "Collateral source" means any of the following sources of benefits or advantages for pecuniary loss that a claimant or victim has received or that is readily available to the claimant or victim from:

(A) the offender under an order of restitution to the claimant or victim imposed by a court as a condition of community supervision;

(B) the United States, a federal agency, a state or any of its political subdivisions, or an instrumentality of two or more states, unless the law providing for the benefits or advantages makes them in excess of or secondary to benefits under this subchapter;

(C) social security, Medicare, or Medicaid;

(D) another state's or another country's crime victims' compensation program;

(E) workers' compensation;

(F) an employer's wage continuation program, not including vacation and sick leave benefits;

(G) proceeds of an insurance contract payable to or on behalf of the claimant or victim for loss that the claimant or victim sustained because of the criminally injurious conduct;

(H) a contract or self-funded program providing hospital and other health care services or benefits; or

(I) proceeds awarded to the claimant or victim as a result of third-party litigation.

(4) "Criminally injurious conduct" means conduct that:

(A) occurs or is attempted;

(B) poses a substantial threat of personal injury or death;

(C) is punishable by fine, imprisonment, or death, or would be punishable by fine, imprisonment, or death if the person engaging in the conduct possessed capacity to commit the conduct; and

(D) does not arise out of the ownership, maintenance, or use of a motor vehicle, aircraft, or water vehicle, unless the conduct is intended to cause personal injury or death or the conduct is in violation of Section 550.021, Transportation Code, or one or more of the following sections of the Penal Code:

(i) Section 19.04 (manslaughter);

(ii) Section 19.05 (criminally negligent homicide);

(iii) Section 22.02 (aggravated assault);

(iv) Section 49.04 (driving while intoxicated);

(v) Section 49.05 (flying while intoxicated);

(vi) Section 49.06 (boating while intoxicated);

(vii) Section 49.07 (intoxication assault); or

(viii) Section 49.08 (intoxication manslaughter).

(5) "Dependent" means:

(A) a surviving spouse;

(B) a person who is a dependent, within the meaning of the Internal Revenue Code, of a victim; and

(C) a posthumous child of a deceased victim.

(6) "Household member" means an individual who resided in the same permanent household as the victim at the time that the criminally injurious conduct occurred and who is related by consanguinity or affinity to the victim.

(7) "Immediate family member" means an individual who is related to a victim within the second degree by affinity or consanguinity.

(8) "Intervenor" means an individual who goes to the aid of another and is killed or injured in the good faith effort to prevent criminally injurious conduct, to apprehend a person reasonably suspected of having engaged in criminally injurious conduct, or to aid a peace officer.

(9) "Pecuniary loss" means the amount of expense reasonably and necessarily incurred as a result of personal injury or death for:

(A) medical, hospital, nursing, or psychiatric care or counseling, or physical therapy;

(B) actual loss of past earnings and anticipated loss of future earnings and necessary travel expenses because of:

(i) a disability resulting from the personal injury;

(ii) the receipt of medically indicated services related to the disability resulting from the personal injury; or

(iii) participation in or attendance at investigative, prosecutorial, or judicial processes related to the criminally injurious conduct and participation in or attendance at any postconviction or postadjudication proceeding relating to criminally injurious conduct;

(C) care of a child or dependent;

(D) funeral and burial expenses;

(E) loss of support to a dependent, consistent with Article 56.41(b)(5);

(F) reasonable and necessary costs of cleaning the crime scene;

(G) reasonable replacement costs for clothing, bedding, or property of the victim seized as evidence or rendered unusable as a result of the criminal investigation; and

(H) reasonable and necessary costs, as provided by Article 56.42(d), incurred by a victim of domestic violence for relocation and housing rental assistance payments.

(10) "Personal injury" means physical or mental harm.

(11) "Victim" means, except as provided by Subsection (c):

(A) an individual who:

(i) suffers personal injury or death as a result of criminally injurious conduct or as a result of actions taken by the individual as an intervenor, if the conduct or actions occurred in this state; and

(ii) is a resident of this state, another state of the United States, the District of Columbia, the Commonwealth of Puerto Rico, or a possession or territory of the United States;

(B) an individual who:

(i) suffers personal injury or death as a result of criminally injurious conduct or as a result of actions taken by the individual as an intervenor, if the conduct or actions occurred in a state or country that does not have a crime victims' compensation program that meets the requirements of Section 1403(b), Crime Victims Compensation Act of 1984 (42 U.S.C. Section 10602(b));

(ii) is a resident of this state; and

(iii) would be entitled to compensation under this subchapter if the criminally injurious conduct or actions had occurred in this state; or

(C) an individual who:

(i) suffers personal injury or death as a result of criminally injurious conduct caused by an act of international terrorism as defined by 18 U.S.C. Section 2331 committed outside of the United States; and

(ii) is a resident of this state.

(b) In this subchapter "claimant" does not include a service provider.

*(Added by L.1993, chap. 268(6); chgd. by L.1993, chap. 805(3), (4); redesignated as article and chgd. by L.1995, chap. 76(5.84); chgd. by L.1995, chaps. 76(9.55), (14.27); 779(1); L.1997, chap. 1434(1); L.1999, chap.1470(1), eff. 6/19/99.)*

## Art. 56.33. Administration; rules.

(a) The attorney general shall adopt rules consistent with this subchapter governing its administration, including rules relating to the method of filing claims and the proof of entitlement to compensation and the review of health care services subject to compensation under this chapter. Subchapters A and B, Chapter 2001, Government Code, except Sections 2001.004(3) and 2001.005, apply to the attorney general.

(b) The attorney general may delegate a power, duty, or responsibility given to the attorney general under this subchapter to a person in the attorney general's office.

*(Added by L.1993, chap. 268(6); redesignated as article and chgd. by L.1995, chap. 76(5.84), eff. 9/1/95; chgd. by L.1995, chap. 779(1), eff. 9/1/95.)*

## Art. 56.34. Compensation.

(a) The attorney general shall award compensation for pecuniary loss arising from criminally injurious conduct if the attorney general is satisfied by a preponderance of the evidence that the requirements of this subchapter are met.

(b) The attorney general, shall establish whether, as a direct result of criminally injurious conduct, a claimant or victim suffered personal injury or death that resulted in a pecuniary loss for which the claimant or victim is not compensated from a collateral source.

(c) The attorney general shall award compensation for health care services according to the medical fee guidelines prescribed by Subtitle A, Title 5, Labor Code.

(d) The attorney general, a claimant, or a victim is not liable for health care service charges in excess of the medical fee guidelines. A health care provider shall accept compensation from the attorney general as payment in full for the charges unless an investigation of the charges by the attorney general determines that there is a reasonable health care justification for the deviation from the guidelines.

(e) A claimant or victim is not liable for the balance of service charges left as a result of an adjustment of payment for the charges under Article 56.58.

(f) The compensation to victims of crime fund and the compensation to victims of crime auxiliary fund are the payers of last resort.

*(Added by L.1993, chap. 268(6); redesignated as article and chgd. by L.1995, chap. 76(5.84); chgd. by L.1995, chap. 779(1); L.1997, chap. 1434(1), eff. 9/1/97.)*

## Art. 56.35. Types of assistance.

If the attorney general approves an application for compensation under Article 56.41, the attorney general shall determine what type of state assistance will best aid the claimant or victim. The attorney general may do one or more of the following:

(1) authorize cash payment or payments to or on behalf of a claimant or victim for pecuniary loss;

(2) refer a claimant or victim to a state agency for vocational or other rehabilitative services; or

(3) provide counseling services for a claimant or victim or contract with a private entity to provide counseling services.

*(Added by L.1993, chap. 268(6); redesignated as article and chgd. by L.1995, chap. 76(5.84), eff. 9/1/95; chgd. by L.1995, chap. 779(1), eff. 9/1/95.)*

## Art. 56.36. Application.

(a) An applicant for compensation under this subchapter must apply in writing on a form prescribed by the attorney general.

(b) An application must be verified and must contain:

(1) the date on which the criminally injurious conduct occurred;

(2) a description of the nature and circumstances of the criminally injurious conduct;

(3) a complete financial statement, including:

(A) the cost of medical care or burial expenses and the loss of wages or support the claimant or victim has incurred or will incur; and

(B) the extent to which the claimant or victim has been indemnified for those expenses from a collateral source;

(4) if appropriate, a statement indicating the extent of a disability resulting from the injury incurred;

(5) an authorization permitting the attorney general to verify the contents of the application; and

(6) other information the attorney general requires.

*(Added by L.1993, chap. 268(6); redesignated as article and chgd. by L.1995, chap. 76(5.84); chgd. by L.1995, chap. 779(1); L.1997, chap. 1434(1), eff. 9/1/97.)*



## Art. 56.37. Time for filing.

(a) Except as otherwise provided by this article, a claimant or victim must file an application not later than three years from the date of the criminally injurious conduct.

(b) The attorney general may extend the time for filing for good cause shown by the claimant or victim.

(c) If the victim is a child, the application must be filed within three years from the date the claimant or victim is made aware of the crime but not after the child is 21 years of age.

(d) If a claimant or victim presents medically documented evidence of a physical or mental incapacity that was incurred by the claimant or victim as a result of the criminally injurious conduct and that reasonably prevented the claimant or victim from filing the application within the limitations period under Subsection (a), the period of the incapacity is not included.

*(Added by L.1993, chap. 268(6); chgd. by L.1993, chap. 805(10); redesignated as article and chgd. by L.1995, chap. 76(5.84); chgd. by L.1995, chap. 779(1); L.1997, chap. 1434(1), eff. 9/1/97.)*

## Art. 56.38. Review; verification.

(a) The attorney general shall appoint a clerk to review each application for compensation under Article 56.36 to ensure the application is complete. If an application is not complete, the clerk shall return it to the claimant or victim and give a brief statement showing the additional information required. Not later than the 30th day after receiving a returned application, a claimant or victim may:

(1) supply the additional information; or

(2) appeal the action to the attorney general, who shall review the application to determine whether it is complete.

(b) The attorney general may investigate an application.

(c) Incident to the attorney general's review, verification, and hearing duties under this subchapter, the attorney general may:

(1) subpoena witnesses and administer oaths to determine whether and the extent to which a claimant or victim qualifies for an award; and

(2) order a claimant or victim to submit to a mental or physical examination by a physician or psychologist or order an autopsy of a deceased victim as provided by Article 56.39, if the mental, physical, or emotional condition of a claimant or victim is material to a claim.

(d) On request by the attorney general and not later than the 14th business day after the date of the request, a law enforcement agency shall release to the attorney general all reports, including witness statements and criminal history record information, for the purpose of allowing the attorney general to determine whether a claimant or victim qualifies for an award and the extent of the qualification.

*(Added by L.1993, chap. 268(6); redesignated as article and chgd. by L.1995, chap. 76(5.84), eff. 9/1/95; chgd. by L.1995, chap. 779(1), eff. 9/1/95.)*

## Art. 56.385. Utilization review.

(a) The attorney general may adopt rules under which the attorney general may conduct or contract for a utilization review of applications for benefits or claims for pecuniary loss relating to psychological, psychiatric, or other mental health services.

(b) In this article, "utilization review" means a system for prospective, concurrent, or retrospective review of the necessity and appropriateness of services being provided or proposed to be provided to a victim.

*(Added by L.1995, chap. 76(5.85(a)), eff. 9/1/95. See other article 56.385 below.)*

## Art. 56.385. Review of health care services.

(a) The attorney general may review the actual or proposed health care services for which a claimant or victim seeks compensation in an application filed under Article 56.36.

(b) The attorney general may not compensate a claimant or victim for health care services that the attorney general determines are not medically necessary.

(c) The attorney general, a claimant, or a victim is not liable for a charge that is not medically necessary.

*(Added by L.1995, chap. 779(1), eff. 9/1/95. See other article 56.385 above.)*

## Art. 56.39. Mental or physical examination; autopsy.

(a) An order for a mental or physical examination or an autopsy as provided by Article 56.38(c)(3) may be made for good cause shown on notice to the individual to be examined and to all persons who have appeared.

(b) An order shall:

(1) specify the time, place, manner, conditions, and scope of the examination or autopsy;

(2) specify the person by whom the examination or autopsy is to be made; and

(3) require the person making the examination or autopsy to file with the attorney general a detailed written report of the examination or autopsy.

(c) A report shall set out the findings of the person making the examination or autopsy, including:

(1) the results of any tests made; and

(2) diagnoses, prognoses, and other conclusions and reports of earlier examinations of the same conditions.

(d) On request of the individual examined, the attorney general shall furnish the individual with a copy of the report. If the victim is deceased, the attorney general on request shall furnish the claimant with a copy of the report.

(e) A physician or psychologist making an examination or autopsy under this article shall be compensated from funds appropriated for the administration of this subchapter.

*(Added by L.1993, chap. 268(6); redesignated as article and chgd. by L.1995, chap. 76(5.84), eff. 9/1/95; chgd. by L.1995, chap. 779(1), eff. 9/1/95.)*

## Art. 56.40. Hearings.

(a) The attorney general shall determine whether a hearing on an application for compensation under this subchapter is necessary.

(b) If the attorney general determines that a hearing is not necessary, the attorney general may approve the application in accordance with the provisions of Article 56.41.

(c) If the attorney general determines that a hearing is necessary or if the claimant or victim requests a hearing, the attorney general shall consider the application at a hearing at a time and place of the attorney general's choosing. The attorney general shall notify all interested persons not less than 10 days before the date of the hearing.

(d) At the hearing the attorney general shall:

(1) review the application for assistance and the report prepared under Article 56.39 and any other evidence obtained as a result of the attorney general's investigation; and

(2) receive other evidence that the attorney general finds necessary or desirable to evaluate the application properly.

(e) The attorney general may appoint hearing officers to conduct hearings or prehearing conferences under this subchapter.

(f) A hearing or prehearing conference is open to the public unless in a particular case the hearing officer or attorney general determines that the hearing or prehearing conference or a part of it should be held in private because a criminal suspect has not been apprehended or because it is in the interest of the claimant or victim.

(g) The attorney general may suspend the proceedings pending disposition of a criminal prosecution that has been commenced or is imminent, but may make an emergency award under Article 56.50.

(h) Subchapters C through H, Chapter 2001, Government Code, do not apply to the attorney general or the attorney general's orders and decisions.

*(Added by L.1993, chap. 268(6); redesignated as article and chgd. by L.1995, chap. 76(5.84), eff. 9/1/95; chgd. by L.1995, chap. 779(1), eff. 9/1/95.)*

## Art. 56.41. Approval of claim.

(a) The attorney general shall approve an application for compensation under this subchapter if the attorney general finds by a preponderance of the evidence that grounds for compensation under this subchapter exist.

(b) The attorney general shall deny an application for compensation under this subchapter if:

(1) the criminally injurious conduct is not reported as provided by Article 56.46;

(2) the application is not made in the manner provided by Articles 56.36 and 56.37;

(3) the claimant or victim knowingly and willingly participated in the criminally injurious conduct;

(4) the claimant or victim is the offender or an accomplice of the offender;

(5) an award of compensation to the claimant or victim would benefit the offender or an accomplice of the offender;

(6) the claimant or victim was incarcerated in a penal institution, as defined by Section 1.07, Penal Code, at the time the offense was committed; or

(7) the claimant or victim knowingly or intentionally submits false or forged information to the attorney general.

(c) Except as provided by rules adopted by the attorney general to prevent the unjust enrichment of an offender, the attorney general may not deny an award otherwise payable to a claimant or victim because the claimant or victim:

(1) is an immediate family member of the offender; or

(2) resides in the same household as the offender.

*(Added by L.1993, chap. 268(6); redesignated as article and chgd. by L.1995, chap. 76(5.84); chgd. by L.1995, chaps. 76(14.28), 779(1); L.1997, chap. 1434(1), eff. 9/1/97.)*



## Art. 56.42. Limits on compensation.

(a) Except as otherwise provided by this article, awards payable to a victim and all other claimants sustaining pecuniary loss because of injury or death of that victim may not exceed $50,000 in the aggregate.

(b) In addition to an award payable under Subsection (a), the attorney general may award an additional $50,000 for extraordinary pecuniary losses, if the personal injury to a victim is catastrophic and results in a total and permanent disability to the victim, for lost wages and reasonable and necessary costs of:

(1) making a home or automobile accessible;

(2) obtaining job training and vocational rehabilitation;

(3) training in the use of special appliances; and

(4) receiving home health care.

(c) The attorney general may by rule establish limitations on any other pecuniary loss compensated for under this subchapter.

(d) A victim who is a victim of domestic violence may receive a onetime-only assistance payment in an amount not to exceed:

(1) $2,000 to be used for relocation expenses, including expenses for rental deposit, utility connections, expenses relating to the moving of belongings, motor vehicle mileage expenses, and for out-of-state moves, transportation, lodging, and meals; and

(2) $1,800 to be used for housing rental expenses.

*(Added by L.1993, chap. 268(6); redesignated as article and chgd. by L.1995, chap. 76(5.84); chgd. by L.1995, chap. 779(1); L.1997, chap. 1434(1); L.1999, chap. 1470(2), eff. 6/19/99.)*

## Art. 56.43. Attorney fees.

(a) As part of an order, the attorney general shall determine and award reasonable attorney's fees, commensurate with legal services rendered, to be paid by the state to the attorney representing the claimant or victim. Attorney fees shall not exceed 25 percent of the amount the attorney assisted the claimant or victim in obtaining. Where there is no dispute of the attorney general's determination of the amount of the award due to the claimant or victim and where no hearing is held, the attorney fee shall be the lesser of either 25 percent of the amount the attorney assisted the claimant or victim in obtaining or $300.

(b) Attorney fees may be denied on a finding that the claim or appeal is frivolous.

(c) An award of attorney fees is in addition to an award of compensation.

(d) An attorney may not contract for or receive an amount larger than that allowed under this article.

(e) Attorney fees may not be paid to an attorney of a claimant or victim unless an award is made to the claimant or victim.

*(Added by L.1993, chap. 268(6); chgd. by L.1993, chap. 805(9); redesignated as article and chgd. by L.1995, chap. 76(5.84), eff. 9/1/95; chgd. by L.1995, chap. 779(1), eff. 9/1/95.)*

## Art. 56.44. Payments.

(a) The attorney general may provide for the payment of an award in a lump sum or in installments. The attorney general shall provide that the part of an award equal to the amount of pecuniary loss accrued to the date of the award be paid in a lump sum. Except as provided in Subsection (b), the attorney general shall pay the part of an award for allowable expense that accrues after the award is made in installments.

(b) At the request of the claimant or victim, the attorney general may provide that an award for future pecuniary loss be paid in a lump sum if the attorney general finds that:

(1) paying the award in a lump sum will promote the interests of the claimant or victim; or

(2) the present value of all future pecuniary loss does not exceed $1,000.

(c) The attorney general may not provide for an award for future pecuniary loss payable in installments for a period for which the attorney general cannot reasonably determine the future pecuniary loss.

(d) The attorney general may make payments only to an individual who is a claimant or a victim or to a provider on the individual's behalf.

*(Added by L.1993, chap. 268(6); redesignated as article and chgd. by L.1995, chap. 76(5.84); chgd. by L.1995, chap. 779(1); L.1997, chap. 1434(1), eff. 9/1/97.)*

## Art. 56.45. Denial or reduction of award.

The attorney general may deny or reduce an award otherwise payable:

(1) if the claimant or victim has not substantially cooperated with an appropriate law enforcement agency;

(2) if the claimant or victim bears a share of the responsibility for the act or omission giving rise to the claim because of the claimant's or victim's behavior;

(3) to the extent that pecuniary loss is recouped from a collateral source; or

(4) if the claimant or victim was engaging in an activity that at the time of the criminally injurious conduct was prohibited by law or a rule made under law.

*(Added by L.1993, chap. 268(6); redesignated as article and chgd. by L.1995, chap. 76(5.84); chgd. by L.1995, chap. 779(1); L.1997, chap. 1434(1), eff. 9/1/97.)*

## Art. 56.46. Reporting of crime.

(a) Except as otherwise provided by this article, a claimant or victim may not file an application unless the victim reports the criminally injurious conduct to the appropriate state or local public safety or law enforcement agency within a reasonable period of time, but not so late as to interfere with or hamper the investigation and prosecution of the crime after the criminally injurious conduct is committed.

(b) The attorney general may extend the time for reporting the criminally injurious conduct if the attorney general determines that the extension is justified by extraordinary circumstances.

(c) Subsection (a) does not apply if the victim is a child.

*(Added by L.1993, chap. 268(6); redesignated as article and chgd. by L.1995, chap. 76(5.84); chgd. by L.1995, chap. 779(1); L.1997, chap. 1434(1), eff. 9/1/97.)*

## Art. 56.47. Reconsideration.

(a) The attorney general, on the attorney general's own motion or on request of a claimant or victim, may reconsider:

(1) a decision to make or deny an award; or

(2) the amount of an award.

(b) At least annually, the attorney general shall reconsider each award being paid in installments.

(c) An order on reconsideration may require a refund of an award if:

(1) the award was obtained by fraud or mistake; or

(2) newly discovered evidence shows the claimant or victim to be ineligible for the award under Article 56.41 or 56.45.
*(Added by L.1993, chap. 268(6); chgd. by L.1993, chap. 805(6); redesignated as article and chgd. by L.1995, chap. 76(5.84); chgd. by L.1995, chaps. 76(5.85(b)), 779(1); L.1997, chap. 1434(1), eff. 9/1/97.)*

## Art. 56.48. Judicial review.

(a) Not later than the 40th day after the attorney general renders a final decision, a claimant or victim may file with the attorney general a notice of dissatisfaction with the decision. Not later than the 40th day after the claimant or victim gives notice, the claimant or victim shall bring suit in the district court having jurisdiction in the county in which:

(1) the injury or death occurred;

(2) the victim resided at the time the injury or death occurred; or

(3) if the victim resided out of state at the time of the injury or death, in the county where the injury or death occurred or in a district court of Travis County.

(b) While judicial review of a decision by the attorney general is pending, the attorney general:

(1) shall suspend payments to the claimant or victim; and

(2) may not reconsider the award.

(c) The court shall determine the issues by trial de novo. The burden of proof is on the party who filed the notice of dissatisfaction.

(d) A court may award not more than 25 percent of the total recovery by the claimant or victim for attorney fees in the event of review.

(e) In computing a period under this article, if the last day is a legal holiday or Sunday, the last day is not counted, and the time is extended to include the next business day.
*(Added by L.1993, chap. 268(6); redesignated as article and chgd. by L.1995, chap. 76(5.84); chgd. by L.1995, chap. 779(1); L.1997, chap. 1434(1), eff. 9/1/97.)*

## Art. 56.49. Exemption; assignability.

(a) An award is not subject to execution, attachment, garnishment, or other process, except that an award is not exempt from a claim of a creditor to the extent that the creditor provided products, services, or accommodations, the costs of which are included in the award.

(b) An assignment or agreement to assign a right to benefits for loss accruing in the future is unenforceable except:

(1) an assignment of a right to benefits for loss of earnings is enforceable to secure payment of alimony, maintenance, or child support; and

(2) an assignment of a right to benefits is enforceable to the extent that the benefits are for the cost of products, services, or accommodations:

(A) made necessary by the injury or death on which the claim is based; and

(B) provided or to be provided by the assignee.
*(Added by L.1993, chap. 268(6); redesignated as article and chgd. by L.1995, chap. 76(5.84), eff. 9/1/95; chgd. by L.1995, chap. 779(1), eff. 9/1/95.)*

## Art. 56.50. Emergency award.

(a) The attorney general may make an emergency award if, before acting on an application for compensation under this subchapter, it appears likely that:

(1) a final award will be made; and

(2) the claimant or victim will suffer undue hardship if immediate economic relief is not obtained.

(b) An emergency award may not exceed $1,500.

(c) The amount of an emergency award shall be:

(1) deducted from the final award; or

(2) repaid by and recoverable from the claimant or victim to the extent the emergency award exceeds the final award.
*(Added by L.1993, chap. 268(6); redesignated as article and chgd. by L.1995, chap. 76(5.84), eff. 9/1/95; chgd. by L.1995, chap. 779(1), eff. 9/1/95.)*

## Art. 56.51. Subrogation.

If compensation is awarded under this subchapter, the state is subrogated to all the claimant's or victim's rights to receive or recover benefits for pecuniary loss to the extent compensation is awarded from a collateral source. *(Added by L.1993, chap. 268(6); redesignated as article and chgd. by L.1995, chap. 76(5.84), eff. 9/1/95; chgd. by L.1995, chap. 779(1), eff. 9/1/95.)*

**Art. 56.52. Notice of private action.**

(a) Before a claimant or victim may bring an action to recover damages related to criminally injurious conduct for which compensation under this subchapter is claimed or awarded, the claimant or victim must give the attorney general written notice of the proposed action. After receiving the notice, the attorney general shall promptly:

(1) join in the action as a party plaintiff to recover benefits awarded;

(2) require the claimant or victim to bring the action in the claimant's or victim's name as a trustee on behalf of the state to recover benefits awarded; or

(3) reserve the attorney general's rights and do neither in the proposed action.

(b) If the claimant or victim brings the action as trustee and recovers compensation awarded by the attorney general, the claimant or victim may deduct from the benefits recovered on behalf of the state the reasonable expenses of the suit, including attorney fees, expended in pursuing the recovery for the state. The claimant or victim must justify this deduction in writing to the attorney general on a form provided by the attorney general.

(c) A claimant or victim shall not settle or resolve any such action without written authorization to do so from the attorney general. No third party or agents, insurers, or attorneys for third parties shall participate in the settlement or resolution of such an action if they actually know, or should know, that the claimant or victim has received moneys from the fund and is subject to the subrogation provisions of this article. Any attempt by such third party, or agents, insurers, or attorneys of third parties to settle an action is void and shall result in no release from liability to the fund for any rights subrogated pursuant to this article. All such agents, insurers, and attorneys are personally liable to the fund for any moneys paid to a claimant or victim in violation of this subsection, up to the full amount of the fund's right to reimbursement. A claimant, victim, third party, or any agents, attorneys, or insurers of third parties who knowingly or intentionally fail to comply with the requirements of this chapter commits a Class B misdemeanor.

(d) A person adjudged guilty of a Class B misdemeanor shall be punished by:

(1) a fine not to exceed $500;

(2) confinement in jail for a term not to exceed 180 days; or

(3) both such fine and imprisonment.

*(Added by L.1993, chap. 268(6); chgd. by L.1993, chap. 805(11); redesignated as article and chgd. by L.1995, chap. 76(5.84), eff. 9/1/95; chgd. by L.1995, chap. 779(1), eff. 9/1/95.)*

**Art. 56.53. Annual report.**

Annually, the attorney general shall report to the governor and the legislature on the attorney general's activities, including a statistical summary of claims and awards made and denied. The reporting period is the state fiscal year. The attorney general shall file the report not later than the 100th day after the end of the fiscal year. *(Added by L.1993, chap. 268(6); redesignated as article and chgd. by L.1995, chap. 76(5.84), eff. 9/1/95; chgd. by L.1995, chap. 779(1), eff. 9/1/95.)*

**Art. 56.54. Funds.**

(a) The compensation to victims of crime fund and the compensation to victims of crime auxiliary fund are in the state treasury.

(b) Except as provided by Subsections (h) and (i), the compensation to victims of crime fund may be used by the attorney general only for the payment of compensation to claimants or victims under this subchapter, the operation of the Crime Victims' Institute created by Chapter 412, Government Code, and other expenses in administering this subchapter. *(Chgd. by L.1997, chap. 1434(1), eff. 9/1/97. See other subsection (b) below.)*

(b) Except as provided by Article 56.541, the compensation to victims of crime fund may be used only by the attorney general for the payment of compensation to claimants or victims under this subchapter and other expenses in administering this subchapter. *(Chgd. by L.1997, chap. 1042(2), eff. 9/1/97. See other subsection (b) above.)*

(c) Except as provided by Subsections (h) and (i), the compensation to victims of crime auxiliary fund may be used by the attorney general only for the payment of compensation to claimants or victims under this subchapter.

(d) The attorney general may not make compensation payments in excess of the amount of money available from the combined funds.

(e) General revenues may not be used for payments under this subchapter.

(f) The office of the attorney general is authorized to accept gifts, grants, and donations to be credited to the compensation to victims of crime fund and compensation to victims of crime auxiliary fund and shall file annually with the governor and the presiding officer of each house of the legislature a complete and detailed written report accounting for all gifts, grants, and donations re-

Printed in the U.S.A. 21

ceived and disbursed, used, or maintained by the office for the attorney general that are credited to these funds.

(g) Money in the compensation to victims of crime fund or in the compensation to victims of crime auxiliary fund may be used only as provided by this subchapter and is not available for any other purpose. Section 403.095, Government Code, does not apply to the fund.

(h) An amount of money deposited to the credit of the compensation to victims of crime fund not to exceed one-quarter of the amount disbursed from that fund in the form of compensation payments during a fiscal year shall be carried forward into the next succeeding fiscal year and applied toward the amount listed in the next succeeding fiscal year's method of financing. *(Added by L.1997, chap. 1434(1), eff. 9/1/97. See other subsection (h) below.)*

(h) In addition to the purposes provided by Subsection (b), the legislature may appropriate money in the compensation to victims of crime fund to state agencies that deliver or fund victim-related services or assistance. This subsection expires August 31, 1999. *(Added by L.1997, chap. 1042(1), eff. 6/19/97. Expires 8/31/99. See other subsection (h) above.)*

(i) If the sums available in the compensation to victims of crime fund are sufficient in a fiscal year to make all compensation payments, the attorney general may retain any portion of the fund that was deposited during the fiscal year that was in excess of compensation payments made during that fiscal year as an emergency reserve for the next fiscal year. Such emergency reserve may not exceed $10,000,000. The emergency reserve fund may be used only to make compensation awards in claims and for providing emergency relief and assistance, including crisis intervention, emergency housing, travel, food, or expenses and technical assistance expenses incurred in the implementation of this subsection in incidents resulting from an act of mass violence or from an act of international terrorism as defined by 18 U.S.C. Section 2331, occurring in the state or for Texas residents injured or killed in an act of terrorism outside of the United States.

(j) The legislature may appropriate money in the compensation to victims of crime fund to administer the associate judge program under Subchapter C, Chapter 201, Family Code.

*(Added by L.1993, chap. 268(6); chgd. by L.1993, chap. 805(1); redesignated as article and chgd. by L.1995, chap. 76(5.84); chgd. by L.1995, chap. 779(1); L.1997, chaps. 1042(1), (2); 1434(1); L.1999, chap. 1302(13), eff. 9/1/99.)*

## Art. 56.541. Appropriation of excess money for other crime victim assistance.

(a) Not later than December 15 of each even-numbered year, the attorney general, after consulting with the comptroller, shall prepare forecasts and certify estimates of:

(1) the amount of money that the attorney general anticipates will be received from deposits made to the credit of the compensation to victims of crime fund during the next state fiscal biennium, other than deposits of:

(A) gifts, grants, and donations; and

(B) money received from the United States;

(2) the amount of money from the fund that the attorney general anticipates will be obligated during the next state fiscal biennium to comply with this chapter; and

(3) the amount of money in the fund that the attorney general anticipates will remain unexpended at the end of the current state fiscal year and that is available for appropriation in the next state fiscal biennium.

(b) At the time the attorney general certifies the estimates made under Subsection (a), the attorney general shall also certify for the next state fiscal biennium the amount of excess money in the compensation to victims of crime fund for purposes of Subsection (c), calculated by multiplying the amount estimated under Subsection (a)(2) by 120 percent, and subtracting that product from the sum of the amounts estimated under Subsections (a)(1) and (a)(3).

(c) For a state fiscal biennium, the legislature may appropriate from the compensation to victims of crime fund the amount of excess money in the fund certified for the biennium under Subsection (b) to state agencies that deliver or fund victim-related services or assistance.

(d) The attorney general and the comptroller shall cooperate in determining the proper allocation of the various sources of revenue deposited to the credit of the compensation to victims of crime fund for purposes of this article.

(e) The attorney general may use money appropriated from the compensation to victims of crime fund for grants or contracts supporting victim-related services or assistance, including support for private Texas nonprofit corporations that provide victim-related civil legal services directly to victims, immediate family members of victims, or claimants. A grant supporting victim-related services or assistance is governed by Chapter 783, Government Code.

(f) The attorney general shall adopt rules necessary to carry out this article.

*(Added by L.1997, chap. 1042(3); chgd. by L.1999, chap. 1077(1), eff. 6/18/99.)*

## Art. 56.55. Court costs.

(a) A person shall pay:

(1) $45 as a court cost on conviction of a felony;

(2) $35 as a court cost on conviction of a violation of a municipal ordinance punishable by a fine of more than $200 or on conviction of a misdemeanor punishable by imprisonment or by a fine of more than $500; or

(3) $15 as a court cost on conviction of a violation of a municipal ordinance punishable by a fine of not more than $200 or on conviction of a misdemeanor punishable by a fine of not more than $500, other than a conviction of a misdemeanor offense or a violation of a municipal ordinance relating to pedestrians and the parking of motor vehicles.

(b) The court shall assess and make a reasonable effort to collect the cost due under this article whether any other court cost is assessed or collected.

(c) In this article, a person is considered to have been convicted if:

(1) a sentence is imposed;

(2) the defendant receives probation or deferred adjudication; or

(3) the court defers final disposition of the case.

(d) Court costs under this article are collected in the same manner as other fines or costs.

*(Added by L.1993, chap. 268(6); chgd. by L.1993, chap. 805(5); redesignated as article and chgd. by L.1995, chap. 76(5.84), eff. 9/1/95; chgd. by L.1995, chap. 779(1), eff. 9/1/95.)*

## Art. 56.56. Deposit and remittance of court costs.

(a) The officer collecting the costs in a municipal court case shall keep separate records of the funds collected as costs under Article 56.55 and shall deposit the funds in the municipal treasury. The officer collecting the costs in a justice, county, or district court case shall keep separate records of the funds collected as costs under Article 56.55 and shall deposit the funds in the county treasury.

(b) The custodian of a municipal or county treasury shall:

(1) keep records of the amount of funds on deposit collected under Article 56.55; and

(2) send to the comptroller before the last day of the first month following each calendar quarter the funds collected during the preceding quarter.

(c) A municipality or county may retain 10 percent of the funds collected under Article 56.55 as a collection fee if the custodian of the treasury:

(1) keeps records of the amount of funds on deposit collected under Article 56.55; and

(2) sends to the comptroller the funds within the period prescribed by Subsection (b)(2).

(d) If no funds due as costs under Article 56.55 are collected by a custodian of a municipal or county treasury in a quarter, the custodian shall file the report required for the quarter in the regular manner and must state that no funds were collected.

*(Added by L.1993, chap. 268(6); redesignated as article and chgd. by L.1995, chap. 76(5.84), eff. 9/1/95; chgd. by L.1995, chap. 779(1), eff. 9/1/95.)*

## Art. 56.57. Deposit by comptroller; audit.

(a) The comptroller shall deposit the funds received under Article 56.56 and all other moneys credited to the fund by any other provision of law in the compensation to victims of crime fund.

(b) Funds collected are subject to audit by the comptroller. Funds spent are subject to audit by the state auditor.

*(Added by L.1993, chap. 268(6); chgd. by L.1993, chap. 805(2); redesignated as article and chgd. by L.1995, chap. 76(5.84), eff. 9/1/95; chgd. by L.1995, chap. 779(1), eff. 9/1/95.)*

## Art. 56.58. Adjustment of awards and payments.

(a) The attorney general shall establish a policy to adjust awards and payments so that the total amount of awards granted in each calendar year does not exceed the amount of money credited to the fund during that year.

(b) If the attorney general establishes a policy to adjust awards under Subsection (a), the attorney general, the claimant, or the victim is not liable for the amount of charges incurred in excess of the adjusted amount for the service on which the adjusted payment is determined.

(c) A service provider who accepts a payment that has been adjusted by a policy established under Subsection (a) agrees to accept the adjusted payment as payment in full for the service and is barred from legal action against the claimant or victim for collection.

*(Added by L.1993, chap. 268(6); redesignated as article and chgd. by L.1995, chap. 76(5.84), eff. 9/1/95; chgd. by L.1995, chap. 779(1), eff. 9/1/95.)*

## Art. 56.59. Attorney general supervision of collection of costs; failure to comply.

(a) If the attorney general has reason to believe that a court has not been assessing costs due under Article 56.55 or has not been making a reasonable effort to collect those costs, the attorney general shall send a warning letter to the court or the governing body of the governmental unit in which the court is located.

(b) Within 60 days after receipt of a warning letter, the court or governing body shall respond in writing to the attorney general, specifically referring to the charges in the warning letter.

(c) If the court or governing body does not respond or if the attorney general considers the response inadequate, the attorney general may request the comptroller to audit the records of:

(1) the court;

(2) the officer charged with collecting the costs; or

(3) the treasury of the governmental unit in which the court is located.

(d) The comptroller shall give the attorney general the results of the audit.

(e) If, using the results of the audit and other evidence available, the attorney general finds that a court is not assessing costs due under Article 56.55 or is not making a reasonable effort to collect those costs, the attorney general may:

(1) refuse to award compensation under this subchapter to residents of the jurisdiction served by the court; or

(2) notify the State Commission on Judicial Conduct of the findings.

(f) The failure, refusal, or neglect of a judicial officer to comply with a requirement of Article 56.55:

(1) constitutes official misconduct; and

(2) is grounds for removal from office.

*(Added by L.1993, chap. 268(6); redesignated as article and chgd. by L.1995, chap. 76(5.84), eff. 9/1/95; chgd. by L.1995, chap. 779(1), eff. 9/1/95.)*

## Art. 56.60. Public notice.

(a) A hospital licensed under the laws of this state shall display prominently in its emergency room posters giving notification of the existence and general provisions of this subchapter. The attorney general shall set standards for the location of the display and shall provide posters, application forms, and general information regarding this subchapter to each hospital and physician licensed to practice in this state.

(b) Each local law enforcement agency shall inform a claimant or victim of criminally injurious conduct of the provisions of this subchapter and make application forms available. The attorney general shall provide application forms and all other documents that local law enforcement agencies may require to comply with this article. The attorney general shall set standards to be followed by local law enforcement agencies for this purpose and may require them to file with the attorney general a description of the procedures adopted by each agency to comply.

*(Added by L.1993, chap. 268(6); redesignated as article and chgd. by L.1995, chap. 76(5.84), eff. 9/1/95; chgd. by L.1995, chap. 779(1), eff. 9/1/95.)*

## Art. 56.61. Compensation for certain criminally injurious conduct prohibited.

The attorney general may not award compensation for economic loss arising from criminally injurious conduct that occurred before January 1, 1980. *(Added by L.1993, chap. 268(6); redesignated as article and chgd. by L.1995, chap. 76(5.84), eff. 9/1/95; chgd. by L.1995, chap. 779(1), eff. 9/1/95.)*

## Art. 56.62. Public letter of reprimand.

(a) The attorney general may issue a letter of reprimand against a person if the attorney general finds that the person has filed or has caused to be filed under this subchapter an application for benefits or claim for pecuniary loss that contains a statement or representation that the person knows to be false.

(b) The attorney general must give the person notice of the proposed action before issuing the letter.

(c) A proposal to issue a letter of reprimand is a contested case under Chapter 2001, Government Code.

(d) A letter of reprimand issued under this article is public information.

*(Added by L.1995, chap. 76(5.85(c)), eff. 9/1/95. See other article 56.62 below.)*

## Art. 56.62. Public letter of reprimand.

(a) The attorney general may issue a letter of reprimand against an individual if the attorney general finds that the person has filed or has caused to be filed under this subchapter an application for benefits or claim for pecuniary loss that contains a statement or representation that the person knows to be false.

(b) The attorney general must give the person notice of the proposed action before issuing the letter.

(c) A person may challenge the denial of compensation and the issuance of a letter of reprimand in a contested case hearing under Chapter 2001, Government Code (Administrative Procedure Act).

(d) A letter of reprimand issued under this article is public information.

*(Added by L.1995, chap. 779(1), eff. 9/1/95. See other article 56.62 above.)*

### Art. 56.63. Civil penalty.

(a) A person is subject to a civil penalty of not less than $2,500 or more than $25,000 for each application for benefits or claim for pecuniary loss that:

(1) the person files or causes to be filed under this subchapter; and

(2) contains a statement or representation that the person knows to be false.

(b) The attorney general shall institute and conduct the suit authorized by this article in the name of this state.

(c) A civil penalty recovered under this article shall be deposited to the credit of the compensation to victims of crime fund.

(d) The civil penalty authorized by this article is in addition to any other civil, administrative, or criminal penalty provided by law.

(e) In addition to the civil penalty authorized by this article, the attorney general may recover all expenses incurred by the attorney general in the investigation, institution, and prosecution of the suit, including investigative costs, witness fees, attorney's fees, and deposition expenses.

*(Added by L.1995, chap. 76(5.85(c)), eff. 9/1/95. See other article 56.63 below.)*

### Art. 56.63. Civil penalty.

(a) A person is subject to a civil penalty of not less than $2,500 or more than $25,000 for each application for compensation that:

(1) is filed under this subchapter by the person or is filed under this subchapter as a result of conduct of the person; and

(2) contains a material statement or representation that the person knows to be false.

(b) The attorney general shall institute and conduct the suit to collect the civil penalty authorized by this article on behalf of the state.

(c) A civil penalty recovered under this article shall be deposited to the credit of the compensation to victims of crime fund.

(d) The civil penalty authorized by this article is in addition to any other civil, administrative, or criminal penalty provided by law.

(e) In addition to the civil penalty authorized by this article, the attorney general may recover expenses incurred by the attorney general in the investigation, institution, and prosecution of the suit, including investigative costs, witness fees, attorney's fees, and deposition expenses.

*(Added by L.1995, chap. 779(1), eff. 9/1/95. See other article 56.63 above.)*

### Art. 56.64. Administrative penalty.

(a) A person who presents or causes to be presented to the attorney general an application for benefits or claim for pecuniary loss that contains a statement or representation the person knows to be false is liable to the attorney general for:

(1) the amount paid because of the false application for benefits or claim for pecuniary loss and interest on that amount determined at the rate provided by law for legal judgments and accruing from the date on which the payment was made;

(2) payment of an administrative penalty not to exceed twice the amount paid because of the false application for benefits or claim for pecuniary loss; and

(3) payment of an administrative penalty of not more than $10,000 for each item or service for which payment was claimed.

(b) In determining the amount of the penalty to be assessed under Subsection (a)(3), the attorney general shall consider:

(1) the seriousness of the violation;

(2) whether the person had previously submitted a false application for benefits or claim for pecuniary loss; and

(3) the amount necessary to deter the person from submitting future false applications for benefits or claims for pecuniary loss.

(c) If the attorney general determines that a violation has occurred, the attorney general may issue a report that states the facts on which the determination is made and the attorney general's recommendation on the imposition of a penalty, including a recommendation on the amount of the penalty.

(d) The attorney general shall give written notice of the report to the person. The notice may be given by certified mail. The notice must:

(1) include a brief summary of the alleged violation;

(2) include a statement of the amount of the recommended penalty; and

(3) inform the person that the person has a right to a hearing on the occurrence of the violation, the amount of the penalty, or both the occurrence of the violation and the amount of the penalty.

(e) Within 20 days after the date the person receives the notice, the person in writing may:

(1) accept the determination and recommended penalty of the attorney general; or

(2) make a written request for a hearing on the occurrence of the violation, the amount of the penalty, or both the occurrence of the violation and the amount of the penalty.

(f) If the person accepts the determination and recommended penalty of the attorney general, the attorney general by order shall approve the determination and impose the recommended penalty.

(g) If the person requests a hearing or fails to respond in a timely manner to the notice, the attorney general shall set a hearing and give notice of the hearing to the person. The administrative law judge shall make findings of fact and conclusions of law and promptly issue to the attorney general a proposal for a decision about the occurrence of the violation and the amount of a proposed penalty. According to the findings of fact, conclusions of law, and proposal for a decision, the attorney general by order may find that a violation has occurred and impose a penalty or may find that a violation has not occurred.

(h) The notice of the attorney general's order given to the person under Chapter 2001, Government Code, must include a statement of the right of the person to judicial review of the order.

(i) Within 30 days after the date the attorney general's order is final under Section 2001.144, Government Code, the person shall:

(1) pay the amount of the penalty;

(2) pay the amount of the penalty and file a petition for judicial review contesting the occurrence of the violation, the amount of the penalty, or both the occurrence of the violation and the amount of the penalty; or

(3) without paying the amount of the penalty, file a petition for judicial review contesting the occurrence of the violation, the amount of the penalty, or both the occurrence of the violation and the amount of the penalty.

(j) Within the 30-day period, a person who acts under Subsection (i)(3) may:

(1) stay enforcement of the penalty by:

(A) paying the amount of the penalty to the court for placement in an escrow account; or

(B) giving to the court a supersedeas bond approved by the court for the amount of the penalty and that is effective until all judicial review of the attorney general's order is final; or

(2) request the court to stay enforcement of the penalty by:

(A) filing with the court a sworn affidavit of the person stating that the person is financially unable to pay the amount of the penalty and is financially unable to give the supersedeas bond; and

(B) giving a copy of the affidavit to the attorney general by certified mail.

(k) On the attorney general's receipt of a copy of an affidavit under Subsection (j)(2), the attorney general may file with the court, within five days after the date the copy is received, a contest to the affidavit. The court shall hold a hearing on the facts alleged in the affidavit as soon as practicable and shall stay the enforcement of the penalty on finding that the alleged facts are true. The person who files an affidavit has the burden of proving that the person is financially unable to pay the amount of the penalty and to give a supersedeas bond.

(*l*) If the person does not pay the amount of the penalty and the enforcement of the penalty is not stayed, the attorney general may file suit for collection of the amount of the penalty.

(m) Judicial review of the order of the attorney general:

(1) is instituted by filing a petition as provided by Section 2001.176, Government Code; and

(2) is under the substantial evidence rule.

(n) If the court sustains the occurrence of the violation, the court may uphold or reduce the amount of the penalty and order the person to pay the full or reduced amount of the penalty. If the court does not sustain the occurrence of the violation, the court shall order that a penalty is not owed.

(*o*) When the judgment of the court becomes final, the court shall proceed under this subsection. If the person paid the amount of the penalty and if that amount is reduced or is not upheld by the court, the court shall order that the appropriate amount plus accrued interest be remitted to the person. The rate of the interest is the rate charged on loans to depository institutions by the New York Federal Reserve Bank, and the interest shall be paid for the period beginning on the date the penalty was paid and ending on the date the penalty is remitted. If the person gave a supersedeas bond and if the amount of the penalty is not upheld by the court, the court shall order the release of the bond. If the person gave a supersedeas bond and if the amount of the penalty is reduced, the court shall order the release of the bond after the person pays the amount.

(p) A penalty collected under this article shall be sent to the comptroller and deposited to the credit of the compensation to victims of crime fund.

(q) All proceedings under this article are subject to Chapter 2001, Government Code.

(r) In addition to the administrative penalty authorized by this article, the attorney general may recover all expenses incurred by the attorney general in the investigation, institution, and prosecution of the suit, including investigative costs, witness fees, attorney's fees, and deposition expenses.

*(Added by L.1995, chap. 76(5.85(c)), eff. 9/1/95. See other article 56.64 below.)*

**Art. 56.64. Administrative penalty.**

(a) A person who presents to the attorney general under this subchapter, or engages in conduct that results in the presentation to the attorney general under this subchapter of, an application for compensation under this subchapter that contains a statement or representation the person knows to be false is liable to the attorney general for:

(1) the amount paid in reliance on the application and interest on that amount determined at the rate provided by law for legal judgments and accruing from the date on which the payment was made;

(2) payment of an administrative penalty not to exceed twice the amount paid because of the false application for benefits or claim for pecuniary loss; and

(3) payment of an administrative penalty of not more than $10,000 for each item or service for which payment was claimed.

(b) In determining the amount of the penalty to be assessed under Subsection (a)(3), the attorney general shall consider:

(1) the seriousness of the violation;

(2) whether the person has previously submitted a false application for benefits or a claim for pecuniary loss; and

(3) the amount necessary to deter the person from submitting future false applications for benefits or claims for pecuniary loss.

(c) If the attorney general determines that a violation has occurred, the attorney general may issue a report that states the facts on which the determination is made and the attorney general's recommendation on the imposition of a penalty, including a recommendation on the amount of the penalty.

(d) The attorney general shall give written notice of the report to the person. Notice under this subsection may be given by certified mail and must:

(1) include a brief summary of the alleged violation;

(2) include a statement of the amount of the recommended penalty; and

(3) inform the person of the right to a hearing on:

(A) the occurrence of the violation;

(B) the amount of the penalty; or

(C) both the occurrence of the violation and the amount of the penalty.

(e) Not later than the 20th day after the date the person receives the notice, the person, in writing, may:

(1) accept the attorney general's determination and recommended penalty; or

(2) request in writing a hearing on:

(A) the occurrence of the violation;

(B) the amount of the penalty; or

(C) both the occurrence of the violation and the amount of the penalty.

(f) If the person accepts the determination and recommended penalty of the attorney general, the attorney general by order shall approve the determination and impose the recommended penalty.

(g) If the person requests a hearing as provided by Subsection (e) or fails to respond to the notice in a timely manner, the attorney general shall set a contested case hearing under Chapter 2001, Government Code (Administrative Procedure Act), and notify the person of the hearing. The administrative law judge shall make findings of facts and conclusions of law and promptly issue to the attorney general a proposal for a decision regarding the occurrence of the violation and the amount of a proposed penalty. Based on the findings of fact, conclusions of law, and proposal for a decision, the attorney general by order may:

(1) find that a violation has occurred and impose a penalty; or

(2) find that a violation has not occurred.

(h) Notice of the attorney general's order given to the person under Chapter 2001, Government Code, must include a statement of the right of the person to judicial review of the order.

(i) Not later than the 30th day after the date that the attorney general's order is final under Section 2001.144, Government Code, the person shall:

(1) pay the amount of the penalty;

(2) pay the amount of the penalty and file a petition for judicial review contesting:

(A) the occurrence of the violation;

(B) the amount of the penalty; or

(C) the occurrence of the violation and the amount of the penalty; or

(3) without paying the amount of the penalty, file a petition for judicial review contesting:

(A) the occurrence of the violation;

(B) the amount of the penalty; or

(C) the occurrence of the violation and the amount of the penalty.

(j) Within the 30-day period, a person who acts under Subsection (i)(3) may:

(1) stay enforcement of the penalty by:

(A) paying the amount of the penalty to the court for placement in an escrow account; or

(B) giving to the court a supersedeas bond that is approved by the court for the amount of the penalty and that is effective until all judicial review of the attorney general's order is final; or

(2) request the court to stay enforcement of the penalty by:

(A) filing with the court a sworn affidavit of the person stating that the person is financially unable to pay the amount of the penalty or to give the supersedeas bond; and

(B) delivering a copy of the affidavit to the attorney general by certified mail.

(k) On receipt by the attorney general of a copy of an affidavit under Subsection (j)(2), the attorney general may file with the court, not later than the fifth day after the date the copy is received, a contest to the affidavit. The court shall hold a hearing on the facts alleged in the affidavit as soon as practicable and shall stay the enforcement of the penalty on finding that the alleged facts are true. A person who files an affidavit under Subsection (j)(2) has the burden of proving that the person is financially unable to pay the amount of the penalty or to give a supersedeas bond.

(*l*) If the person does not pay the amount of the penalty and the enforcement of the penalty is not stayed, the attorney general may file suit for collection of the amount of the penalty.

(m) Judicial review of the order of the attorney general:

(1) is instituted by filing a petition as provided by Section 2001.176, Government Code; and

(2) is governed by the substantial evidence rule.

(n) If the court upholds the finding that a violation occurred, the court may order the person to pay the full or reduced amount of the penalty. If the court does not uphold the finding, the court shall order that no penalty is owed.

(*o*) If the person paid the amount of the penalty and if that amount is reduced or is not upheld by the court, the court shall order that the appropriate amount plus accrued interest be remitted to the person. The rate of the interest is the rate charged on loans to depository institutions by the New York Federal Reserve Bank, and the interest shall be paid for the period beginning on the date the penalty was paid and ending on the date the penalty is remitted. If the person gave a supersedeas bond and if the amount of the penalty is not upheld by the court, the court shall order the release of the bond. If the person gave a supersedeas bond and if the amount of the penalty is reduced, the court shall order the release of the bond after the person pays the amount.

(p) A penalty collected under this article shall be sent to the comptroller and deposited to the credit of the compensation to victims of crime fund.

(q) All proceedings under this article are subject to Chapter 2001, Government Code.

(r) In addition to the administrative penalty authorized by this article, the attorney general may recover all expenses incurred by the attorney general in the investigation, institution, and prosecution of the suit, including investigative costs, witness fees, attorney's fees, and deposition expenses.

*(Added by L.1995, chap. 779(1), eff. 9/1/95. See other article 56.64 above.)*

### Art. 56.65. Submission of contract for reenactment of crime to the attorney general.

A contract cannot be finally executed unless it is first submitted to the attorney general if:

(1) one of the parties to the contract is a person who is accused or convicted of a crime in this state, or the representative or assignee of that person; and

(2) the contract involves the reenactment of the crime in a movie, book, magazine article, tape recording, phonograph record, radio or television presentation, or live entertainment.
*(Added by L.1995, chap. 76(5.86(a)), eff. 9/1/95.)*

### Art. 56.66. Certain actions void.

An action taken by a person to defeat the purpose of this subchapter is void as against public policy, including the execution of a power of attorney or the creation of a corporate entity. *(Added by L.1995, chap. 76(5.86(a)), eff. 9/1/95.)*

### Art. 56.67. Victim first compensated from funds collected from perpetrator.

Notwithstanding this subchapter or any other law, the victim of a crime shall be the first one compensated from any revenue collected from the perpetrator of the crime for that purpose. *(Added by L.1995, chap. 76(5.86(a)), eff. 9/1/95.)*

## CHAPTER 57. CONFIDENTIALITY OF IDENTIFYING INFORMATION OF SEX OFFENSE VICTIMS

Article


### Art. 57.01. Definitions.

In this chapter:

(1) "Name" means the legal name of a person.

(2) "Pseudonym" means a set of initials or a fictitious name chosen by a victim to designate the victim in all public files and records concerning the offense, including police summary reports, press releases, and records of judicial proceedings.

(3) "Public servant" has the meaning assigned by Subsection (a), Section 1.07, Penal Code.

(4) "Victim" means a person who was the subject of an offense the commission of which leads to a reportable conviction or adjudication under Article 6252-13c.1, Revised Statutes.
*(Chgd. by L.1997, chap. 680(1), eff. 9/1/97.)*

### Art. 57.02. Confidentiality of files and records.† [*Confidentiality of documents.*]

(a) The Sexual Assault Prevention and Crisis Services Program of the Texas Department of Health shall develop and distribute to all law enforcement agencies of the state a pseudonym form to record the name, address, telephone number, and pseudonym of a victim.

(b) A victim may choose a pseudonym to be used instead of the victim's name to designate the victim in all public files and records concerning the offense, including police summary reports, press releases, and records of judicial proceedings. A victim who elects to use a pseudonym as provided by this article must complete a pseudonym form developed under this article and return the form to the law enforcement agency investigating the offense.

(c) A victim who completes and returns a pseudonym form to the law enforcement agency investigating the offense may not be required to disclose the victim's name, address, and telephone number in connection with the investigation or prosecution of the offense.

(d) A completed and returned pseudonym form is confidential and may not be disclosed to any person other than a defendant in the case or the defendant's attorney, except on an order of a court of competent jurisdiction. The court finding required by Subsection (g) of this article is not required to disclose the confidential pseudonym form to the defendant in the case or to the defendant's attorney.

(e) If a victim completes and returns a pseudonym form to a law enforcement agency under this article, the law enforcement agency receiving the form shall:

(1) remove the victim's name and substitute the pseudonym for the name on all reports, files, and records in the agency's possession;

(2) notify the attorney for the state of the pseudonym and that the victim has elected to be designated by the pseudonym; and

(3) maintain the form in a manner that protects the confidentiality of the information contained on the form.

(f) An attorney for the state who receives notice that a victim has elected to be designated by a pseudonym shall ensure that the victim is designated by the pseudonym in all legal proceedings concerning the offense.

(g) A court of competent jurisdiction may order the disclosure of a victim's name, address, and telephone number only if the court finds that the information is essential in the trial of the defendant for the offense or the identity of the victim is in issue.

### Art. 57.03. Offense.† [*Illegal disclosure.*]

(a) A public servant with access to the name, address, or telephone number of a victim who has chosen to be designated by a pseudonym commits an offense if the public servant intentionally or knowingly discloses the name, address, or telephone number of the victim to any person who is not assisting in the investigation or prosecution of the offense or to any person other than the defendant, the defendant's attorney, or the person specified in the order of a court of competent jurisdiction.

(b) An offense under this article is a Class C misdemeanor.

## CHAPTER 58. SEALING FILES AND RECORDS OF CHILDREN

*(Chapter 58 renumbered by L.1989, chap. 2(16.01)(11), eff. 8/28/89.)*

Article



### Art. 58.01. Sealing files and records of children.

A court in which a person under the age of 17 is prosecuted for an offense described by Section 8.07(a)(4) or (5), Penal Code, shall seal the person's files and records in the same manner and under the same conditions that Section 58.003, Family Code, requires a juvenile court to seal the files and records of a person adjudicated or taken into custody under Title 3, Family Code. *(Chgd. by L.1997, chap. 165(7.04), eff. 9/1/97.)*

## CHAPTER 59. FORFEITURE OF CONTRABAND

*(Added by L.1989, 1st C.S., chap. 12(1), eff. 10/18/89.)*

Article



### Art. 59.01. Definitions.

In this chapter:

(1) "Attorney representing the state" means the prosecutor with felony jurisdiction in the county in which a forfeiture proceeding is held under this chapter or, in a proceeding for forfeiture of contraband as defined under Subdivision (2)(B)(iv) of this article, the city attorney of a municipality if the property is seized in that municipality by a peace officer employed by that municipality and the governing body of the municipality has approved procedures for the city attorney acting in a forfeiture proceeding.

(2) "Contraband" means property of any nature, including real, personal, tangible, or intangible, that is:

(A) used in the commission of:

(i) any first or second degree felony under the Penal Code;

(ii) any felony under Section 38.04 or Chapters 29, 30, 31, 32, 33, 33A, or 35, Penal Code; or

(iii) any felony under The Securities Act (Article 581-1 et seq., Vernon's Texas Civil Statutes);

(B) used or intended to be used in the commission of:

(i) any felony under Chapter 481, Health and Safety Code (Texas Controlled Substances Act);

(ii) any felony under Chapter 483, Health and Safety Code;

(iii) a felony under Chapter 153, Finance Code;

(iv) any felony under Chapter 34, Penal Code;

(v) a Class A misdemeanor under Subchapter B, Chapter 365, Health and Safety Code, if the defendant has been previously convicted twice of an offense under that subchapter; or

(vi) any felony under Chapter 152, Finance Code;

(C) the proceeds gained from the commission of a felony listed in Paragraph (A) or (B) of this subdivision or a crime of violence; or

(D) acquired with proceeds gained from the commission of a felony listed in Paragraph (A) or (B) of this subdivision or a crime of violence.

(3) "Crime of violence" means:

(A) any criminal offense defined in the Penal Code or in a federal criminal law that results in a personal injury to a victim; or

(B) an act that is not an offense under the Penal Code involving the operation of a motor vehicle, aircraft, or water vehicle that results in injury or death sustained in an accident caused by a driver in violation of Section 550.021, Transportation Code.

*(See other subsection (3) below.)*

(3) "Crime of violence" has the meaning assigned by Article 56.32. *(See other subsection (3) above.)*

(4) "Interest holder" means the bona fide holder of a perfected lien or a perfected security interest in property.

(5) "Law enforcement agency" means an agency of the state or an agency of a political subdivision of the state authorized by law to employ peace officers.

(6) "Owner" means a person who claims an equitable or legal ownership interest in property.

(7) "Proceeds" includes income a person accused or convicted of a crime or the person's representative or assignee receives from a movie, book, magazine article, tape recording, phonographic record, radio or television presentation, or live entertainment in which the crime was reenacted.

(8) "Seizure" means the restraint of property by a peace officer under Article 59.03(a) or (b) of this code, whether the officer restrains the property by physical force or by a display of the officer's authority.

*(Added by L.1989, 1st C.S., chap. 12(1); chgd. by L.1991, chap. 102(2); L.1993, chaps. 761(5), 780(1), 828(1); L.1995, chaps. 76(5.91), (5.95(112)); 621(3); 708(2); L.1997, chap. 306(6); L.1999, chap. 62(3.09), (7.48), eff. 9/1/99.)*

## Art. 59.02. Forfeiture of contraband.

(a) Property that is contraband is subject to seizure and forfeiture under this chapter.

(b) Any property that is contraband other than property held as evidence in a criminal investigation or a pending criminal case, money, a negotiable instrument, or a security that is seized under this chapter may be replevied by the owner or interest holder of the property, on execution of a good and valid bond with sufficient surety in a sum equal to the appraised value of the property replevied. The bond may be approved as to form and substance by the court after the court gives notice of the bond to the authority holding the seized property. The bond must be conditioned:

(1) on return of the property to the custody of the state on the day of hearing of the forfeiture proceedings; and

(2) that the interest holder or owner of the property will abide by the decision that may be made in the cause.

(c) An owner or interest holder's interest in property may not be forfeited under this chapter if the owner or interest holder:

(1) acquired and perfected the interest before or during the act or omission giving rise to forfeiture or, if the property is real property, he acquired an ownership interest, security interest, or lien interest before a lis pendens notice was filed under Article 59.04(g) of this code; and

(2) did not know or should not reasonably have known of the act or omission giving rise to the forfeiture or that it was likely to occur at or before the time of acquiring and perfecting the interest or, if the property is real property, at or before the time of acquiring the ownership interest, security interest, or lien interest.

(d) On motion by any party or on the motion of the court, after notice in the manner provided by Article 59.04 of this code to all known owners and interest holders of property subject to forfeiture under this chapter, and after a hearing on the matter, the court may make appropriate orders to preserve and maintain the value of the property until a final disposition of the property is made under this chapter, including the sale of the property if that is the only method by which the value of the property may be preserved until final disposition.

(e) Any property that is contraband and has been seized by the institutional division of the Texas Department of Criminal Justice shall be forfeited to the institutional division under the same rules and conditions as for other forfeitures.

(f) An individual, firm, corporation, or other entity insured under a policy of title insurance may not assert a claim or cause of action on or because of the policy if the claim or cause of action is based on forfeiture under this chapter and, at or before the time of acquiring the ownership of real property, security interest in real property, or lien interest against real property, the insured knew or reasonably should have known of the act or omission giving rise to the forfeiture or that the act or omission was likely to occur.

(g) The forfeiture provisions of this chapter apply to contraband as defined by Article 59.01(2)(B)(iv) of this code only in a municipality with a population of 250,000 or more.
*(Added by L.1989, 1st C.S., chap. 12(1); chgd. by L.1993, chap. 828(2), eff. 9/1/93.)*

**Art. 59.03. Seizure of contraband.**

(a) Property subject to forfeiture under this chapter may be seized by any peace officer under authority of a search warrant.

(b) Seizure of property subject to forfeiture may be made without warrant if:

(1) the owner, operator, or agent in charge of the property knowingly consents;

(2) the seizure is incident to a search to which the owner, operator, or agent in charge of the property knowingly consents;

(3) the property subject to seizure has been the subject of a prior judgment in favor of the state in a forfeiture proceeding under this chapter; or

(4) the seizure was incident to a lawful arrest, lawful search, or lawful search incident to arrest.

(c) A peace officer who seizes property under this chapter has custody of the property, subject only to replevy under Article 59.02 of this code or an order of a court. A peace officer who has custody of property shall provide the attorney representing the state with a sworn statement that contains a schedule of the property seized, an acknowledgment that the officer has seized the property, and a list of the officer's reasons for the seizure. Not later than 72 hours after the seizure, the peace officer shall:

(1) place the property under seal;

(2) remove the property to a place ordered by the court; or

(3) require a law enforcement agency of the state or a political subdivision to take custody of the property and move it to a proper location.
*(Added by L.1989, 1st C.S., chap. 12(1), eff. 10/18/89.)*

**Art. 59.04. Notification of forfeiture proceeding.**

(a) If a peace officer seizes property under this chapter, the attorney representing the state shall commence proceedings under this section not later than the 30th day after the date of the seizure.

(b) A forfeiture proceeding commences under this chapter when the attorney representing the state files a notice of the seizure and intended forfeiture in the name of the state with the clerk of the district court in the county in which the seizure is made. The attorney representing the state must attach to the notice the peace officer's sworn statement under Article 59.03 of this code. Except as provided by Subsection (c) of this article, the attorney representing the state shall cause certified copies of the notice to be served on the following persons in the same manner as provided for the service of process by citation in civil cases:

(1) the owner of the property; and

(2) any interest holder in the property.

(c) If the property is a motor vehicle, and if there is reasonable cause to believe that the vehicle has been registered under the laws of this state, the attorney representing the state shall ask the Texas Department of Transportation to identify from its records the record owner of the vehicle and any interest holder. If the addresses of the owner and interest holder are not otherwise known, the attorney representing the state shall request citation be served on such persons at the address listed with the Texas Department of Transportation. If the citation issued to such address is returned unserved, the attorney representing the state shall cause a copy of the notice of the seizure and intended forfeiture to be posted at the courthouse door, to remain there for a period of not less than 30 days. If the owner or interest holder does not answer or appear after the notice has been so posted, the court shall enter a judgment by default as to the owner or interest holder, provided that the attorney representing the state files a written motion supported by affidavit setting forth the attempted service. An owner or interest holder whose interest is forfeited in this manner shall not be liable for court costs. If the person in possession of the vehicle at the time of the seizure is not the owner or the interest holder of the vehicle, notification shall be provided to the possessor in the same manner specified for notification to an owner or interest holder.

(d) If the property is a motor vehicle and is not registered in this state, the attorney representing the state shall attempt to ascertain the name and address of the person in whose name the vehicle is licensed in another state. If the vehicle is licensed in a state that has a certificate of title law, the attorney representing the state shall request the appropriate agency of that state to identify the record owner of the vehicle and any interest holder.

(e) If a financing statement is required by law to be filed to perfect a security interest affecting the property, and if there is reasonable cause to believe that a financing statement has been filed, the attorney representing the state who commences the proceedings shall ask the appropriate official designated by Chapter 9, Business & Commerce Code, to identify the record owner of the property and the person who is an interest holder.

(f) If the property is an aircraft or a part of an aircraft, and if there is reasonable cause to believe that a perfected security instrument affects the property, the attorney representing the state shall request an administrator of the Federal Aviation Administration to identify from the records of that agency the record owner of the property and the holder of the perfected security instrument. The attorney representing the state shall also notify the Department of Public Safety in writing of the fact that an aircraft has been seized and shall provide the department with a description of the aircraft.

(g) If the property is real property, the attorney representing the state, not later than the third day after the date proceedings are commenced, shall file a lis pendens notice describing the property with the county clerk of each county in which the property is located.

(h) For all other property subject to forfeiture, if there is reasonable cause to believe that a perfected security instrument affects the property, the attorney representing the state shall make a good faith inquiry to identify the holder of the perfected security instrument.

(i) Except as provided by Section (c) of this article, the attorney representing the state who commences the proceedings shall cause the owner and any interest holder to be named as a party and to be served with citation as provided by the Texas Rules of Civil Procedure.

(j) A person who was in possession of the property at the time it was seized shall be made a party to the proceeding.

(k) If no person was in possession of the property at the time it was seized, and if the owner of the property is unknown, the attorney representing the state shall file with the clerk of the court in which the proceedings are pending an affidavit stating that no person was in possession of the property at the time it was seized and that the owner of the property is unknown. The clerk of the court shall issue a citation for service by publication addressed to "The Unknown Owner of __________," filling in the blank space with a reasonably detailed description of the property subject to forfeiture. The citation must contain the other requisites prescribed by and be served as provided by Rules 114, 115, and 116, Texas Rules of Civil Procedure.

(*l*) Proceedings commenced under this chapter may not proceed to hearing unless the judge who is to conduct the hearing is satisfied that this article has been complied with and that the attorney representing the state will introduce into evidence at the hearing any answer received from an inquiry required by Subsections (c)-(h) of this article.

*(Added by L.1989, 1st C.S., chap. 12(1); chgd. by L.1991, chap. 14(282); L.1995, chaps. 165(22(25)), 533(1), eff. 9/1/95.)*

### Art. 59.05. Forfeiture hearing.

(a) All parties must comply with the rules of pleading as required in civil suits.

(b) All cases under this chapter shall proceed to trial in the same manner as in other civil cases. The state has the burden of proving by a preponderance of the evidence that property is subject to forfeiture.

(c) It is an affirmative defense to forfeiture under this chapter of property belonging to the spouse of a person whose acts gave rise to the seizure of community property that, because of an act of family violence, as defined by Section 71.01, Family Code, the spouse was unable to prevent the act giving rise to the seizure.

(d) A final conviction for an underlying offense is not a requirement for forfeiture under this chapter. An owner or interest holder may present evidence of a dismissal or acquittal of an underlying offense in a forfeiture proceeding, and evidence of an acquittal raises a presumption that the property or interest that is the subject of the hearing is nonforfeitable. This presumption can be rebutted by evidence that the owner or interest holder knew or should have known that the property was contraband.

(e) It is the intention of the legislature that asset forfeiture is remedial in nature and not a form of punishment. If the court finds that all or any part of the property is subject to forfeiture, the judge shall forfeit the property to the state, with the attorney representing the state as the agent for the state, except that if the court finds that the nonforfeitable interest of an interest holder in the property is valued in an amount greater than or substantially equal to the present value of the property, the court shall order the property released to the interest holder. If the court finds that the nonforfeitable interest of an interest holder is valued in an amount substantially less than the present value of the property and that the property is subject to forfeiture, the court shall order the property forfeited to the state with the attorney representing the state acting as the agent of the state, and making necessary orders to protect the nonforfeitable interest of the interest holder. On final judgment of forfeiture, the attorney representing the state shall dispose of the property in the manner required by Article 59.06 of this code.

(f) On forfeiture to the state of an amount greater than $2,500, the clerk of the court in which the forfeiture proceeding was held is entitled to court costs in that proceeding as in other civil proceedings unless the forfeiture violates federal requirements for multijurisdictional task force cases authorized under Chapter 362, Local Government Code. The procedure for collecting the costs is the procedure established under Subsections (a) and (c), Article 59.06.

*(Added by L.1989, 1st C.S., chap. 12(1); chgd. by L.1993, chap. 780(2); L.1995, chap. 533(2); L.1999, chap. 582(1), eff. 9/1/99.)*

### Art. 59.06. Disposition of forfeited property.

(a) Except as provided by Subsection (k), all forfeited property shall be administered by the attorney representing the state, acting as the agent of the state, in accordance with accepted accounting practices and with the provisions of any local agreement entered into between the attorney representing the state and law enforcement agencies. If a local agreement has not been executed, the property shall be sold on the 75th day after the date of the final judgment of forfeiture at public auction under the direction of the county sheriff, after notice of public auction as provided by law for other sheriff's sales. The proceeds of the sale shall be distributed as follows:

(1) to any interest holder to the extent of the interest holder's nonforfeitable interest; and

(2) the balance, if any, after the deduction of court costs to which a district court clerk is entitled under Article 59.05(f) and, after that deduction, the deduction of storage and disposal costs, to be deposited not later than the 30th day after the date of the sale in the state treasury to the credit of the general revenue fund.

(b) If a local agreement exists between the attorney representing the state and law enforcement agencies, the attorney representing the state may transfer the property to law enforcement agencies to maintain, repair, use, and operate the property for official purposes if the property is free of any interest of an interest holder. The agency receiving the forfeited property may purchase the interest of an interest holder so that the property can be released for use by the agency. The agency receiving the forfeited property may maintain, repair, use, and operate the property with money appropriated for current operations. If the property is a motor vehicle subject to registration under the motor vehicle registration laws of this state, the agency receiving the forfeited vehicle is considered to be the purchaser and the certificate of title shall issue to the agency. The agency at any time may transfer the property to a municipal or county law enforcement agency for the use of that agency.

(c) If a local agreement exists between the attorney representing the state and law enforcement agencies, all money, securities, negotiable instruments, stocks or bonds, or things of value, or proceeds from the sale of those items, shall be deposited, after the deduction of court costs to which a district court clerk is entitled under Article 59.05(f), according to the terms of the agreement into one or more of the following funds:

(1) a special fund in the county treasury for the benefit of the office of the attorney representing the state, to be used by the attorney solely for the official purposes of his office;

(2) a special fund in the municipal treasury if distributed to a municipal law enforcement agency, to be used solely for law enforcement purposes, such as salaries and overtime pay for officers, officer training, specialized investigative equipment and supplies, and items used by officers in direct law enforcement duties;

(3) a special fund in the county treasury if distributed to a county law enforcement agency, to be used solely for law enforcement purposes; or

(4) a special fund in the state law enforcement agency if distributed to a state law enforcement agency, to be used solely for law enforcement purposes.

(d) Proceeds awarded under this chapter to a law enforcement agency or to the attorney representing the state may be spent by the agency or the attorney after a budget for the expenditure of the proceeds has been submitted to the commissioners court or governing body of the municipality. The budget must be detailed and clearly list and define the categories of expenditures, but may not list details that would endanger the security of an investigation or prosecution. Expenditures are subject to audit provisions established under this article. A commissioners court or governing body of a municipality may not use the existence of an award to offset or decrease total salaries, expenses, and allowances that the agency or the attorney receives from the commissioners court or governing body at or after the time the proceeds are awarded. The head of the agency or attorney representing the state may not use the existence of an award to increase a salary, expense, or allowance for an employee of the attorney or agency who is budgeted by the commissioners court or governing body unless the commissioners court or governing body first approves the expenditure.

(e) On the sale of contraband under this article, the appropriate state agency shall issue a certificate of title to the recipient if a certificate of title is required for the property by other law.

(f) A final judgment of forfeiture under this chapter perfects the title of the state to the property as of the date that the contraband was seized or the date the forfeiture action was filed, whichever occurred first, except that if the property forfeited is real property, the title is perfected as of the date a notice of lis pendens is filed on the property.

(g) All law enforcement agencies and attorneys representing the state who receive proceeds or property under this chapter shall account for the seizure, forfeiture, receipt, and specific expenditure of all such proceeds and property in an audit, which is to be performed annually by the commissioners court or governing body of a municipality, as appropriate. The annual period of the audit for a law enforcement agency is the fiscal year of the appropriate county or municipality and the annual period for an attorney representing the state is the state fiscal year. The audit shall be completed on a form provided by the attorney general. Certified copies of the audit shall be delivered by the law enforcement agency or attorney representing the state to the comptroller's office and the attorney general not later than the 30th day after the date on which the annual period that is the subject of the audit ends.

(h) As a specific exception to the requirement of Subdivisions (1)-(3) of Subsection (c) of this article that the funds described by those subdivisions be used only for the official purposes of the attorney representing the state or for law enforcement purposes, on agreement between the attorney representing the state or the head of a law enforcement agency and the governing body of a political subdivision, the attorney representing the state or the head of the law enforcement agency shall comply with the request of the governing body to deposit not more than a total of 10 percent of the gross amount credited to the attorney's or agency's fund into the treasury of the political subdivision. The governing body of the political subdivision shall, by ordinance, order, or resolution, use funds received under this subsection for:

(1) nonprofit programs for the prevention of drug abuse;

(2) nonprofit chemical dependency treatment facilities licensed under Chapter 464, Health and Safety Code;

(3) nonprofit drug and alcohol rehabilitation or prevention programs administered or staffed by professionals designated as qualified and credentialed by the Texas Commission on Alcohol and Drug Abuse; or

(4) financial assistance as described by Subsection (*o*).

(i) The governing body of a political subdivision may not use funds received under this subchapter for programs or facilities listed under Subsections (h)(1)-(3) if an officer of or member of the Board of Directors of the entity providing the program or facility is related to a member of the governing body, the attorney representing the state, or the head of the law enforcement agency within the third degree by consanguinity or the second degree by affinity.

(j) As a specific exception to Subdivision (4) of Subsection (c) of this article, the director of a state law enforcement agency may use not more than 10 percent of the amount credited to the special fund of the agency under that subdivision for the prevention of drug abuse and the treatment of persons with drug-related problems.

(k) The attorney for the state shall transfer all forfeited property that is income from, or acquired with the income from, a movie, book, magazine article, tape recording, phonographic record, radio or television presentation, or live entertainment in which a crime is reenacted to the attorney general. The attorney general shall deposit the money or proceeds from the sale of the property into an escrow account. The money in the account is available to satisfy a judgment against the person who committed the crime in favor of a victim of the crime if the judgment is for damages incurred by the victim caused by the commission of the crime. The attorney general shall transfer the money in the account that has not been ordered paid to a victim in satisfaction of a judgment to the compensation to victims of crime fund on the fifth anniversary of the date the account was established. In this subsection, "victim" has the meaning assigned by Article 56.32.

(*l*) A law enforcement agency that, or an attorney representing the state who, does not receive proceeds or property under this chapter during an annual period as described by Subsection (g) shall, not later than the 30th day after the date on which the annual period ends, report to the attorney general that the agency or attorney, as appropriate, did not receive proceeds or property under this chapter during the annual period.

(m) As a specific exception to Subdivisions (1)-(3) of Subsection (c), a law enforcement agency or attorney representing the state may use proceeds received under this chapter to contract with a person or entity to prepare an audit as required by Subsection (g).

(n) As a specific exception to Subsection (c)(2) or (3), a local law enforcement agency may transfer not more than a total of 10 percent of the gross amount credited to the agency's fund to a separate special fund in the treasury of the political subdivision. The agency shall administer the separate special fund, and expenditures from the fund are at the sole discretion of the agency and may be used only for financial assistance as described by Subsection (*o*).

(*o*) The governing body of a political subdivision or a local law enforcement agency may provide financial assistance under Subsection (h)(4) or (n) only to a person who is a Texas resident, who plans to enroll or is enrolled at an institution of higher education in an undergraduate degree or certificate program in a field related to law enforcement, and who plans to return to that locality to work for the political subdivision or the agency in a field related to law enforcement. To ensure the promotion of a law enforcement purpose of the political subdivision or the agency, the governing body of the political subdivision or the agency shall impose other reasonable criteria related to the provision of this financial assistance, including a requirement that a recipient of the financial assistance work for a certain period of time for the political subdivision or the agency in a field related to law enforcement and including a requirement that the recipient sign an agreement to perform that work for that period of time. In this subsection, "institution of higher education" has the meaning assigned by Section 61.003, Education Code.

*(Added by L.1989, 1st C.S., chap. 12(1); chgd. by L.1991, chap. 312(1), (2); L.1993, chaps. 780(3), (4), 814(1); L.1995, chap. 76(5.95(112)); L.1997, chap. 975(1); L.1999, chaps. 481(1), (2), 582(2), 707(1), eff. 9/1/99.)*

## Art. 59.07. Immunity.

This chapter does not impose any additional liability on any authorized state, county, or municipal officer engaged in the lawful performance of the officer's duties. *(Added by L.1989, 1st C.S., chap. 12(1), eff. 10/18/89.)*

## Art. 59.08. Deposit of money pending disposition.

(a) If money that is contraband is seized, the attorney representing the state may deposit the money in an interest-bearing bank account in the jurisdiction of the attorney representing the state until a final judgment is rendered concerning the contraband.

(b) If a final judgment is rendered concerning contraband, money that has been placed in an interest-bearing bank account under Subsection (a) of this article shall be distributed in the same manner as proceeds are distributed under Article 59.06 of this code, with any interest being distributed in the same manner and used for the same purpose as the principal.

*(Added by L.1989, 1st C.S., chap. 12(1), eff. 10/18/89.)*

## Art. 59.09. Right to attorney not to be abridged.

This chapter is not intended to abridge an accused person's right to counsel in a criminal case. *(Added by L.1989, 1st C.S., chap. 12(1), eff. 10/18/89.)*

## Art. 59.10. Election of laws.

If property is subject to forfeiture under this chapter and under any other law of this state, the attorney representing the state may bring forfeiture proceedings under either law. *(Added by L.1989, 1st C.S., chap. 12(1), eff. 10/18/89.)*

## Art. 59.11. Report of seized and forfeited aircraft.

Not later than the 10th day after the last day of each quarter of the fiscal year, the Department of Public Safety shall report to the State Aircraft Pooling Board;

(1) a description of each aircraft that the department has received by forfeiture under this chapter during the preceding quarter and the purposes for which the department intends to use the aircraft; and

(2) a description of each aircraft the department knows to have been seized under this chapter during the preceding quarter and the purposes for which the department would use the aircraft if it were forfeited to the department.

*(Added by L.1991, chap. 14(283), eff. 9/1/91.)*

## CHAPTER 60. CRIMINAL HISTORY RECORD SYSTEM

*(Added by L.1989, chap. 785(6.01); chgd. by L.1990, 6th C.S., chap. 25(28), eff. 6/18/90.)*



### Art. 60.01. Definitions.

In this chapter:

(1) "Administration of criminal justice" means the performance of any of the following activities: detection, apprehension, detention, pretrial release, post-trial release, prosecution, adjudication, correctional supervision, or rehabilitation of an offender. The term includes criminal identification activities and the collection, storage, and dissemination of criminal record information.

(2) "Appeal" means the review of a decision of a lower court by a superior court other than by collateral attack.

(3) "Computerized criminal history system" means the data base containing arrest, disposition, and other criminal history maintained by the Department of Public Safety.

(4) "Corrections tracking system" means the data base maintained by the Texas Department of Criminal Justice on all offenders under its supervision.

(5) "Council" means the Criminal Justice Policy Council.

(6) "Criminal justice agency" means a federal or state agency that is engaged in the administration of criminal justice under a statute or executive order and allocate a substantial part of its annual budget to the administration of criminal justice.

(7) "Criminal justice information system" means the computerized criminal history system and the corrections tracking system.

(8) "Disposition" means an action that results in the termination, transfer to another jurisdiction, or indeterminate suspension of the prosecution of a criminal charge.

(9) "Incident number" means a unique number assigned to a specific person during a specific arrest.

(10) "Offender" means any person who is assigned an incident number.

(11) "Offense code" means a numeric code for each offense category.

(12) "Rejected case" means:

(A) a charge that, after the arrest of the offender, the prosecutor declines to include in an information or present to a grand jury; or

(B) an information or indictment that, after the arrest of the offender, the prosecutor refuses to prosecute.

(13) "Release" means the termination of jurisdiction over an individual by the criminal justice system.

(14) "State identification number" means a unique number assigned by the Department of Public Safety to each person whose name appears in the criminal justice information system.

(15) "Uniform incident fingerprint card" means a multiple part form containing a unique incident number with space for information relating to the charge or charges for which a person is being arrested, the person's fingerprints, and other information relevant to the arrest.

(16) "Electronic means" means the transmission of data between word processors, data processors, or similar automated information equipment over dedicated cables, commercial lines, or other similar methods of transmission.

*(Added by L.1989, chap. 785(6.01); chgd. by L.1990, 6th C.S., chap. 25(28); L.1993, chaps. 790(37), 1025(1), eff. 9/1/93.)*

## Art. 60.02. Information systems.

(a) The Texas Department of Criminal Justice is responsible for recording data and establishing and maintaining a data base for a corrections tracking system.

(b) The Department of Public Safety is responsible for recording data and maintaining a data base for a computerized criminal history system that serves as the record creation point for criminal history information maintained by the state.

(c) The criminal justice information system shall be established and maintained to supply the state with a system:

(1) that provides law enforcement officers with an accurate criminal history record depository;

(2) that provides criminal justice agencies with an accurate criminal history record depository for operational decision making;

(3) from which accurate criminal justice system modeling can be conducted;

(4) that improves the quality of data used to conduct impact analyses of proposed legislative changes in the criminal justice system; and

(5) that improves the ability of interested parties to analyze the functioning of the criminal justice system.

(d) The data bases must contain the information required by this chapter.

(e) The Department of Public Safety shall designate the offense codes and has the sole responsibility for designating the state identification number for each person whose name appears in the criminal justice information system.

(f) The Department of Public Safety and the Texas Department of Criminal Justice shall implement a system to link the computerized criminal history system and the corrections tracking system. Data received by the Texas Department of Criminal Justice that is required by the Department of Public Safety for the preparation of a criminal history record shall be made available to the computerized criminal history system not later than the seventh day after the date on which the Texas Department of Criminal Justice receives the request for the data from the Department of Public Safety.

(g) The Department of Public Safety is responsible for the operation of the computerized criminal history system and shall develop the necessary interfaces in the system to accommodate inquiries from a statewide automated fingerprint identification system, if such a system is implemented by the department.

(h) Whenever possible, the reporting of information relating to dispositions and subsequent offender processing data shall be conducted electronically.

(i) The Department of Public Safety and the Texas Department of Criminal Justice, with advice from the council and the Department of Information Resources, shall develop biennial plans to improve the reporting and accuracy of the criminal justice information system and to develop and maintain monitoring systems capable of identifying missing information.

(j) At least once during each five-year period the council shall coordinate an examination of the records and operations of the criminal justice information system to ensure the accuracy and completeness of information in the system and to ensure the promptness of information reporting. The state auditor, or other appropriate entity selected by the council, shall conduct the examination with the cooperation of the council, the Department of Public Safety, and the Texas Department of Criminal Justice. The Department of Public Safety, the council, and the Texas Department of Criminal Justice may examine the records of the agencies required to report information to the Department of Public Safety or the Texas Department of Criminal Justice. The examining entity shall submit to the legislature and the council a report that summarizes the findings of each examination and contains recommendations for improving the system.

(k) The council, the Department of Public Safety, the criminal justice division of the governor's office, and the Department of Information Resources cooperatively shall develop and adopt a grant program, to be implemented by the criminal justice division at a time and in a manner determined by the division, to aid local law enforcement agencies, prosecutors, and court personnel in obtaining equipment and training necessary to operate a telecommunications network capable of

(1) making inquiries to and receiving responses from the statewide automated fingerprint identification system and from the computerized criminal history system; and

(2) transmitting information to those systems.

*(Added by L.1989, chap. 785(6.01); chgd. by L.1990, 6th C.S., chap. 25(28); L.1991, chap. 362(1), eff. 8/26/91.)*

**Art. 60.03. Interagency cooperation; confidentiality.**

(a) Criminal justice agencies and the council are entitled to access to the data base of the Department of Public Safety and the Texas Department of Criminal Justice in accordance with applicable state or federal law or regulations. The access granted by this subsection does not grant an agency or the council the right to add, delete, or alter data maintained by another agency.

(b) The council may submit to the Department of Public Safety and the Texas Department of Criminal Justice an annual request for a data file containing data elements from the departments' systems. The Department of Public Safety and the Texas Department of Criminal Justice shall provide the council with that data file for the period requested. If the council submits data file requests other than the annual data file request, the director of the agency maintaining the requested records must approve the request.

(c) Neither a criminal justice agency nor the council may disclose to the public information in an individual's criminal history record if the record is protected by state or federal law or regulation.

*(Added by L.1989, chap. 785(6.01); chgd. by L.1990, 6th C.S., chap. 25(28), eff. 6/18/90.)*

**Art. 60.04. Compatibility of data.**

(a) Data supplied to the criminal justice information system must be compatible with the system and must contain both incident numbers and state identification numbers.

(b) A discrete submission of information under any article of this chapter must contain, in conjunction with information required, the defendant's name and state identification number.

*(Added by L.1989, chap. 785(6.01); chgd. by L.1990, 6th C.S., chap. 25(28), eff. 6/18/90.)*

**Art. 60.05. Types of information collected.**

The criminal justice information system must contain but is not limited to the following types of information for each arrest for a felony or a misdemeanor not punishable by fine only:

(1) information relating to offenders;

(2) information relating to arrests;

(3) information relating to prosecutions;

(4) information relating to the disposition of cases by courts;

(5) information relating to sentencing; and

(6) information relating to the handling of offenders received by a correctional agency, facility, or other institution.

*(Added by L.1989, chap. 785(6.01); chgd. by L.1990, 6th C.S., chap. 25(28), eff. 6/18/90.)*

**Art. 60.051. Information in computerized criminal history system.**

(a) Information in the computerized criminal history system relating to an offender must include:

(1) the offender's name, including other names by which the offender is known;

(2) the offender's date of birth;

(3) the offender's physical description, including sex, weight, height, race, ethnicity, eye color, hair color, scars, marks, and tattoos; and

(4) the offender's state identification number.

(b) Information in the computerized criminal history system relating to an arrest must include:

(1) the name of the offender;

(2) the offender's state identification number;

(3) the arresting agency;

(4) the arrest charge by offense code and incident number;

(5) whether the arrest charge is a misdemeanor or felony;

(6) the date of the arrest;

(7) the exact disposition of the case by a law enforcement agency following the arrest; and

(8) the date of disposition of the case by the law enforcement agency.

(c) Information in the computerized criminal history system relating to a prosecution must include:

(1) each charged offense by offense code and incident number;

(2) the level of the offense charged or the degree of the offense charged for each offense in Subdivision (1) of this subsection; and

(3) for a rejected case, the date of rejection, offense code, and incident number, and whether the rejection is a result of a successful pretrial diversion program.

(d) Information in the computerized criminal history system relating to the disposition of a case must include:

(1) the final pleading to each charged offense and the level of the offense;

(2) a listing of each charged offense disposed of by the court and:

(A) the date of disposition;

(B) the offense code for the disposed charge and incident number; and

(C) the type of disposition; and

(3) for a conviction that is appealed the final court decision and the final disposition of the offender on appeal.

(e) Information in the computerized criminal history system relating to sentencing must include for each sentence:

(1) the sentencing date;

(2) the sentence for each offense by offense code and incident number;

(3) if the offender was sentenced to confinement:

(A) the agency that receives custody of the offender;

(B) the length of sentence for each offense; and

(C) if multiple sentences were ordered, whether they were ordered to be served consecutively or concurrently;

(4) if the offender was sentenced to a fine, the amount of the fine;

(5) if a sentence to confinement or fine was ordered but was deferred, probated, suspended, or otherwise not imposed:

(A) the length of sentence or the amount of the fine that was deferred, probated, suspended, or otherwise not imposed; and

(B) the offender's name, offense code, and incident number; and

(6) if a sentence other than fine or confinement was ordered, a description of the sentence ordered.

(f) The department shall maintain in the computerized criminal history system any information the department maintains in the central database under Article 62.08.

*(Redesignated and chgd. by L.1990, 6th C.S., chap. 25(28); L.1993, chap. 1025(9); L.1995, chap. 258(14); L.1997, chap. 668(8), eff. 9/1/97.)*

## Art. 60.052. Information in corrections tracking system.

(a) Information in the corrections tracking system relating to a sentence to be served under the jurisdiction of the Texas Department of Criminal Justice must include:

(1) the offender's name;

(2) the offender's state identification number;

(3) the sentencing date;

(4) the sentence for each offense by offense code and incidence number;

(5) if the offender was sentenced to imprisonment

(A) the unit of imprisonment;

(B) the length of sentence for each offense; and

(C) if multiple sentences were ordered, whether they were ordered to be served consecutively or concurrently; and

(6) if a sentence other than a fine or imprisonment was ordered, a description of the sentence ordered.

(b) Sentencing information in the corrections tracking must also include the following information about each deferred adjudication, probation, or other alternative to imprisonment ordered:

(1) each conviction for which sentence was ordered but was deferred, probated, suspended, or otherwise not imposed, by offense code and incident number; and

(2) if a sentence or portion of a sentence of imprisonment was not deferred, probated, suspended, or otherwise imposed:

(A) the offense, the sentence, and the amount of the sentence deferred, probated, suspended, or otherwise not imposed;

(B) a statement of whether a return to confinement or other imprisonment was a condition of probation or an alternative sentence;

(C) the community supervision and corrections department exercising jurisdiction over the offender;

(D) the date the offender was received by a community supervision and corrections department;

(E) any program in which an offender is placed or has previously been placed and the level of supervision the offender is placed on while under the jurisdiction of a community supervision and corrections department;

(F) the date a program described by Paragraph (E) of this subdivision begins, the date the program ends, and whether the program was completed successfully;

(G) the date a level of supervision described by Paragraph (E) of this subdivision begins and the date the level of supervision ends;

(H) if the offender's probation is revoked:

(i) the reason for the revocation and the date of revocation by offense code and incident number; and

(ii) other current sentences of probation or other alternatives to confinement that have not been revoked, by offense code and incident number; and

(I) the date of the offender's release from the community supervision and corrections department.

(c) Information in the corrections tracking system relating to the handling of offenders must include the following information about each imprisonment, confinement, or execution of an offender:

(1) the date of the imprisonment or confinement;

(2) if the offender was sentenced to death:

(A) the date of execution; and

(B) if the death sentence was commuted, the sentence to which the sentence of death was commuted and the date of commutation;

(3) the date the offender was released from imprisonment or confinement and whether the release was a discharge or a release on parole or mandatory supervision; and

(4) if the offender is released on parole or mandatory supervision:

(A) the offense for which the offender was convicted by offense code and incident number;

(B) the date the offender was received by an office of the Board of Pardons and Paroles division;

(C) the county in which the offender resides while under supervision;

(D) any program in which an offender is placed or has been previously been placed and the level of supervision the offender is placed on while under the jurisdiction of the Board of Pardons and Paroles division;

(E) the date a program described by Paragraph (D) of this subdivision begins, the date the program ends, and whether the program was completed successfully;

(F) the date a level of supervision described by Paragraph (d) of this subdivision begins and the date the level of supervision ends;

(G) if the offender's release status is revoked, the reason for the revocation and the date of revocation;

(H) the expiration date of the sentence; and

(I) the date of the offender's release from the Board of Pardons and Paroles division or the date on which the offender is granted clemency; and

(5) if the offender is released under Section 6(a), Article 42.12, of this code, the date of the offender's release.

*(Redesignated and chgd. by L.1990, 6th C.S., chap. 25(28), eff. 6/18/90.)*

**Art. 60.06. Duties of agencies.**

(a) Each criminal justice agency shall:

(1) compile and maintain records needed for reporting data required by the Texas Department of Criminal Justice and the Department of Public Safety;

(2) transmit to the Texas Department of Criminal Justice and the Department of Public Safety, when and in the manner the Texas Department of Criminal Justice and the Department of Public Safety direct, all data required by the Texas Department of Criminal Justice and the Department of Public Safety;

(3) give the Department of Public Safety and the Texas Department of Criminal Justice or their accredited agents access to the agency for the purpose of inspection to determine the completeness and accuracy of data reported;

(4) cooperate with the Department of Public Safety and the Texas Department of Criminal Justice so that the Department of Public Safety and the Texas Department of Criminal Justice may properly and efficiently perform their duties under this chapter; and

(5) cooperate with the Department of Public Safety and the Texas Department of Criminal Justice to identify and eliminate redundant reporting of information to the criminal justice information system.

(b) Information on an individual that consists of an identifiable description and notation of an arrest, detention, indictment, information, or other formal criminal charge and a disposition of the charge, including sentencing, correctional supervision, and release that is collected and compiled by the Department of Public Safety and the Texas Department of Criminal Justice from criminal justice agencies and maintained in a central location is not subject to public disclosure except as authorized by federal or state law or regulation.

(c) Subsection (b) of this section does not apply to a document maintained by a criminal justice agency that is the source of information collected by the Department of Public Safety or the Texas Department of Criminal Justice. Each criminal justice agency shall retain documents described by this subsection.

(d) An optical disk or other technology may be used instead of microfilm as a medium to store information if allowed by the applicable state laws or regulations relating to the archiving of state agency information.

(e) An official of an agency may not intentionally conceal or destroy any record with intent to violate this section.

(f) The duties imposed on a criminal justice agency under this article are also imposed on district court and county court clerks.

*(Added by L.1989, chap. 785(6.01); chgd. by L.1990, 6th C.S., chap. 25(28); L.1995, chap. 750(1), eff. 8/28/95.)*

### Art. 60.061. Information on persons licensed by certain agencies.

(a) The Texas State Board of Medical Examiners, the Texas State Board of Podiatric Medical Examiners, the State Board of Dental Examiners, the Texas State Board of Pharmacy, and the State Board of Veterinary Medical Examiners shall provide to the Department of Public Safety through electronic means, magnetic tape, or disk, as specified by the department, a list including the name, date of birth, and any other personal descriptive information required by the department for each person licensed by the respective agency. Each agency shall update this information and submit to the Department of Public Safety the updated information quarterly.

(b) The Department of Public Safety shall perform at least quarterly a computer match of the licensing list against the convictions maintained in the computerized criminal history system. The Department of Public Safety shall report to the appropriate licensing agency for verification and administrative action, as considered appropriate by the licensing agency, the name of any person found to have a record of conviction, except a defendant whose prosecution is deferred during a period of community supervision without an adjudication or plea of guilt. The Department of Public Safety may charge the licensing agency a fee not to exceed the actual direct cost incurred by the department in performing a computer match and reporting to the agency.

(c) The transmission of information by electronic means under Subsection (a) of this article does not affect whether the information is subject to disclosure under Chapter 552, Government Code.

*(Added by L.1993, chap. 790(38); chgd. by L.1993, chaps. 790(38), 1025(2); L.1995, chaps. 76(3.21), (5.95(88)), 965(78); L.1999, chap. 1189(43), eff. 9/1/99.)*

### Art. 60.07. Uniform incident fingerprint card.

(a) The Department of Public Safety, in consultation with the council, shall design, print, and distribute to each law enforcement agency in the state a uniform incident fingerprint card.

(b) The incident card must:

(1) be serially numbered with an incident number in such a manner that the individual incident of arrest may be readily ascertained; and

(2) be a multiple part form that can be transmitted with the offender through the criminal justice process and that allows each agency to report required data to the Department of Public Safety or the Texas Department of Criminal Justice.

(c) Subject to available telecommunications capacity, the Department of Public Safety shall develop the capability to receive by electronic means from a law enforcement agency the information on the uniform incident fingerprint card. The information must be in a form that is compatible to the form required of data supplied to the criminal justice information system.

*(Added by L.1989, chap. 785(6.01); chgd. by L.1990, 6th C.S., chap. 25(28); L.1993, chaps. 790(39), 1025(3), eff. 9/1/93.)*

**Art. 60.08. Reporting.**

(a) The Department of Public Safety and the Texas Department of Criminal Justice shall, by rule, develop reporting procedures that:

(1) ensure that the offender processing data is reported from the time an offender is arrested until the time an offender is released; and

(2) provide measures and policies designed to identify and eliminate redundant reporting of information to the criminal justice information system.

(b) The arresting agency shall prepare a uniform incident fingerprint card and initiate the reporting process for each offender charged with a felony or a misdemeanor not punishable by fine only.

(c) The clerk of the court exercising jurisdiction over a case shall report the disposition of the case to the Department of Public Safety.

(d) Except as otherwise required by applicable state laws or regulations, information or data required by this chapter to be reported to the Texas Department of Criminal Justice or the Department of Public Safety shall be reported promptly but not later than the 30th day after the date on which the information or data is received by the agency responsible for reporting it except in the case of an arrest. An offender's arrest shall be reported to the Department of Public Safety not later than the seventh day after the date of the arrest.

(e) A court that orders the release of an offender under Section 6(a), Article 42.12, of this code at a time when the offender is under a bench warrant and not physically imprisoned in the institutional division shall report the release to the institutional division of the Texas Department of Criminal Justice not later than the seventh day after the date of the release.
*(Added by L.1989, chap. 785(6.01); chgd. by L.1990, 6th C.S., chap. 25(28); L.1995, chap. 750(2), eff. 8/28/95.)*

**Art. 60.09. Local data advisory boards.**

(a) The commissioners court of each county may create local data advisory boards to, among other duties:

(1) analyze the structure of local automated and manual data systems to identify redundant data entry and data storage;

(2) develop recommendations for the commissioners to improve the local data systems;

(3) develop recommendations, when appropriate, for the effective electronic transfer of required data from local agencies to state agencies; and

(4) perform any related duties to be determined by the commissioners court.

(b) Local officials responsible for collecting, storing, reporting, and using data may be appointed to the local data advisory board.

(c) The council and the Department of Public Safety shall, to the extent that resources allow, provide technical assistance and advice on the request of the local data advisory board.
*(Added by L.1989, chap. 785(6.01); chgd. by L.1990, 6th C.S., chap. 25(28), eff. 6/18/90.)*

**Art. 60.10. Expediting implementation.**

The requirements set out in Articles 60.11 through 60.17 of this code are established in order to expedite the implementation and continued improvement of the information systems established under this chapter. *(Added by L.1991, 2nd C.S., chap. 10(7.05), eff. 12/1/91.)*

**Art. 60.11. Operation date.**

The criminal justice information system must be in operation by a date not later than January 1, 1993, as determined by the Texas Department of Criminal Justice and the Department of Public Safety. *(Added by L.1991, 2nd C.S., chap. 10(7.05), eff. 12/1/91.)*

**Art. 60.12. Fingerprint and arrest information in computerized system.**

(a) The Department of Public Safety shall, when a jurisdiction transmits fingerprints and arrest information by a remote terminal accessing the statewide automated fingerprint identification system, use that transmission either to create a permanent record in the criminal justice information system or to create a temporary arrest record in the criminal justice information system to be maintained by the department until the department receives and processes the physical copy of the arrest information.

(b) The Department of Public Safety shall make available to a criminal justice agency making a background criminal inquiry any information contained in a temporary arrest record maintained

by the department, including a statement that a physical copy of the arrest information was not available at the time the information was entered in the system.
*(Added by L.1991, 2nd C.S., chap. 10(7.05); chgd. by L.1993, chaps. 790(40), 1025(4), eff. 9/1/93.)*

**Art. 60.13. Contracts for software development.**

If the Department of Public Safety is unable to hire qualified, full-time computer programmers to develop software for its computers, and the inability to hire the programmers will delay the development and implementation of the criminal justice information system established under this chapter, the department shall enter into contracts for the development of necessary software for the implementation of the criminal justice information system, based on open architecture readily accessible to other local and state branches of the criminal justice system. *(Added by L.1991, 2nd C.S., chap. 10(7.05), eff. 12/1/91.)*

**Art. 60.14. Allocation of grant program money for criminal justice programs.**

An agency of the state, before allocating money to a county from any federal or state grant program for the enhancement of criminal justice programs, shall certify that the county has taken or will take, using all or part of the allocated funds, all action necessary to provide the Texas Department of Criminal Justice and the Department of Public Safety any criminal history records maintained by the county in the manner specified for purposes of those departments. *(Added by L.1991, 2nd C.S., chap. 10(7.05), eff. 12/1/91.)*

**Art. 60.15. Timetable for system records.**

The Department of Public Safety shall establish a timetable and employ temporary personnel, if necessary, to ensure that all disposition records received by the department on or before June 1, 1992, are entered into the criminal justice information system by a date not later than September 1, 1992. *(Added by L.1991, 2nd C.S., chap. 10(7.05), eff. 12/1/91.)*

**Art. 60.16. Report.**

(a) The council shall, with the cooperation of the Department of Public Safety and the Texas Department of Criminal Justice, submit a report to the governor and the Legislative Criminal Justice Board no later than September 30, 1992, that proposes improvements to the criminal justice information system to take place during the biennium beginning September 1, 1993. The process of developing the report shall include a minimum of three regional public hearings to allow state and local law enforcement officers, prosecutors, and courts personnel to provide input on system development and design.

(b) The report must include:

(1) a proposed timetable and cost estimate for each recommended improvement;

(2) a plan to increase, if necessary, the level of detail contained in information uniformly available from the criminal justice information system, including information on parole, probation, and corrections classification levels and special programs for each individual in the criminal justice system;

(3) a plan to link, to the greatest extent practical, the criminal justice information system and the incident based reporting system, as implemented by the bureau of identification and records; and

(4) a plan to efficiently coordinate, to the extent practical, all county criminal history record systems with the criminal justice information system.
*(Added by L.1991, 2nd C.S., chap. 10(7.05), eff. 12/1/91.)*

**Art. 60.17. Coordination of implementation process.**

(a) The council, the Department of Information Resources, the Department of Public Safety, and the Texas Department of Criminal Justice shall establish a working group to expedite the implementation and continued improvement of the criminal justice information system. The council shall coordinate the activities of the working group.

(b) The working group shall:

(1) identify the status of the implementation of the criminal justice information system;

(2) determine from the text of this chapter and the legislative history of the enactment and amendments to this chapter the strategic goals of the criminal justice information system;

(3) translate strategic goals into specific project goals and objectives and shall give priorities to, schedule completion dates for, and identify the resources necessary to complete those goals

and objectives and report their findings to the Legislative Criminal Justice Board not later than January 1, 1992.
*(Added by L.1991, 2nd C.S., chap. 10(7.05), eff. 12/1/91.)*

### Art. 60.18. Information on subsequent arrest of certain individuals.

The Texas Department of Criminal Justice and the Department of Public Safety shall develop the capability to send to a community supervision and corrections department, district parole office, and county data processing department by electronic means information about the subsequent arrest of a person under the supervision of the office or department. *(Added by L.1993, chaps. 790(41), 1025(5), eff. 9/1/93.)*

### Art. 60.19. Information related to misused identity.

On receipt of a declaration under Section 411.0421, Government Code, or on receipt of information similar to that contained in a declaration, the department shall separate information maintained in the computerized criminal history system regarding an individual whose identity has been misused from information maintained in that system regarding the person who misused the identity. *(Added by L.1999, chap. 1334(2), eff. 9/1/99. Former Art. 60.19 expired 9/1/97.)*

## CHAPTER 61. COMPILATION OF INFORMATION PERTAINING TOCRIMINAL COMBINATIONS AND CRIMINAL STREET GANGS

*(Added by L.1995, chap. 671(1); heading chgd. by L.1999, chap. 1154(1), eff. 9/1/99.)*

Section


### Art. 61.01. Definitions.

In this chapter:

(1) "Combination" and "criminal street gang" have the meanings assigned by Section 71.01, Penal Code.

(2) "Child" has the meaning assigned by Section 51.02, Family Code.

(3) "Criminal information" means facts, material, photograph, or data reasonably related to the investigation or prosecution of criminal activity.

(4) "Criminal activity" means conduct that is subject to prosecution.

(5) "Criminal justice agency" has the meaning assigned by Article 60.01 and also means a municipal or county agency, or school district law enforcement agency, that is engaged in the administration of criminal justice under a statute or executive order.

(6) "Administration of criminal justice" has the meaning assigned by Article 60.01.

(7) "Department" means the Department of Public Safety of the State of Texas.

(8) "Intelligence database" means a collection or compilation of data organized for search and retrieval to evaluate, analyze, disseminate, or use intelligence information relating to a criminal combination or a criminal street gang for the purpose of investigating or prosecuting criminal offenses.

(9) "Law enforcement agency" does not include the Texas Department of Criminal Justice or the Texas Youth Commission.

*(Added by L.1995, chap. 671(1); chgd. by L.1999, chap. 1154(2), eff. 9/1/99.)*

**Art. 61.02. Criminal combination and criminal street gang intelligence database; submission criteria.**

(a) Subject to Subsection (b), a criminal justice agency may compile criminal information into an intelligence database for the purpose of investigating or prosecuting the criminal activities of criminal combinations or criminal street gangs. The information may be compiled on paper, by computer, or in any other useful manner.

(b) A law enforcement agency may compile and maintain criminal information relating to a criminal street gang as provided by Subsection (a) in a local or regional intelligence database only if the agency compiles and maintains the information in accordance with the criminal intelligence systems operating policies established under 28 C.F.R. Section 23.1 et seq. and the submission criteria established under Subsection (c).

(c) Criminal information collected under this chapter relating to a criminal street gang must:

(1) be relevant to the identification of an organization that is reasonably suspected of involvement in criminal activity; and

(2) consist of any two of the following:

(A) a self-admission by the individual of criminal street gang membership;

(B) an identification of the individual as a criminal street gang member by a reliable informant or other individual;

(C) a corroborated identification of the individual as a criminal street gang member by an informant or other individual of unknown reliability;

(D) evidence that the individual frequents a documented area of a criminal street gang, associates with known criminal street gang members, and uses criminal street gang dress, hand signals, tattoos, or symbols; or

(E) evidence that the individual has been arrested or taken into custody with known criminal street gang members for an offense or conduct consistent with criminal street gang activity.

*(Added by L.1995, chap. 671(1); chgd. by L.1999, chap. 1154(3), eff. 9/1/99.)*

**Art. 61.03. Release of information.**

(a) A criminal justice agency that maintains criminal information under this chapter may release the information on request to:

(1) another criminal justice agency;

(2) a court; or

(3) a defendant in a criminal proceeding who is entitled to the discovery of the information under Chapter 39.

(b) A criminal justice agency or court may use information received under this article only for the administration of criminal justice. A defendant may use information received under this article only for a defense in a criminal proceeding.

(c) If a local law enforcement agency compiles and maintains information under this chapter relating to a criminal street gang, the agency shall send the information to the department.

(d) The department shall establish an intelligence database and shall maintain information received from an agency under Subsection (c) in the database in accordance with the policies established under 28 C.F.R. Section 23.1 et seq. and the submission criteria under Article 61.02(c).

(e) The department shall designate a code to distinguish criminal information contained in the intelligence database relating to a child from criminal information contained in the database relating to an adult offender.

*(Added by L.1995, chap. 671(1); chgd. by L.1997, chap. 898(1); L.1999, chap. 1154(4), eff. 9/1/99.)*

**Art. 61.04. Criminal information relating to child.**

(a) Notwithstanding Chapter 58, Family Code, criminal information relating to a child associated with a combination or a criminal street gang may be compiled and released under this chapter regardless of the age of the child.

(b) A criminal justice agency that maintains information under this chapter may release the information to an attorney representing a child who is a party to a proceeding under Title 3, Family Code, if the juvenile court determines the information:

(1) is material to the proceeding; and

(2) is not privileged under law.

(c) An attorney may use information received under this article only for a child's defense in a proceeding under Title 3, Family Code.

(d) If a local law enforcement agency collects criminal information under this chapter relating to a criminal street gang, the governing body of the county or municipality served by the law

enforcement agency may adopt a policy to notify the parent or guardian of a child of the agency's observations relating to the child's association with a criminal street gang.
*(Added by L.1995, chap. 671(1); chgd. by L.1997, chaps. 165(7.05), 898(2); L.1999, chap. 1154(5), eff. 9/1/99.)*

**Art. 61.05. Unauthorized use or release of criminal information.**

(a) A person commits an offense if the person knowingly:
(1) uses criminal information obtained under this chapter for an unauthorized purpose; or
(2) releases the information to a person who is not entitled to the information.
(b) An offense under this article is a Class A misdemeanor.
*(Added by L.1995, chap. 671(1), eff. 8/28/95.)*

**Art. 61.06. Removal of records relating to an individual other than a child.**

(a) This article does not apply to information collected under this chapter by the Texas Department of Criminal Justice or the Texas Youth Commission.

(b) Subject to Subsection (c), information collected under this chapter relating to a criminal street gang must be removed from an intelligence database established under Article 61.02 and the intelligence database maintained by the department under Article 61.03 after three years if:

(1) the information relates to the investigation or prosecution of criminal activity engaged in by an individual other than a child; and

(2) the individual who is the subject of the information has not been arrested for criminal activity reported to the department under Chapter 60.

(c) In determining whether information is required to be removed from an intelligence database under Subsection (b), the three-year period does not include any period during which the individual who is the subject of the information is confined in the institutional division or the state jail division of the Texas Department of Criminal Justice.
*(Added by L.1995, chap. 671(1); chgd. by L.1997, chap. 898(3); L.1999, chap. 1154(6), eff. 9/1/99.)*

**Art. 61.07. Texas violent gang task force.**

(a) In this article, "task force" means the Texas Violent Gang Task Force.

(b) The purpose of the task force is to form a strategic partnership between state, federal, and local law enforcement agencies to better enable law enforcement and correctional agencies to take a proactive stance towards tracking gang activity and the growth and spread of gangs statewide.

(c) The task force shall focus its efforts on:

(1) developing a statewide networking system that will provide timely access to gang information;

(2) establishing communication between different law enforcement agencies, combining independent agency resources, and joining agencies together in a cooperative effort to focus on gang membership, gang activity, and gang migration trends; and

(3) forming a working group of law enforcement and correctional representatives from throughout the state to discuss specific cases and investigations involving gangs and other related gang activities.

(d) The task force may take any other actions as necessary to accomplish the purposes of this article.

(e) The Department of Public Safety shall support the task force to assist in coordinating statewide antigang initiatives.

(f) The task force shall consist of:

(1) a representative of the Department of Public Safety designated by the director of that agency;

(2) a representative of the Texas Department of Criminal Justice designated by the executive director of that agency;

(3) a representative of the Texas Youth Commission designated by the executive director of that agency;

(4) a representative of the Texas Juvenile Probation Commission designated by the executive director of that agency;

(5) a representative of the Criminal Justice Policy Council designated by the executive director of that agency;

(6) a representative of the office of the attorney general designated by the attorney general; and

(7) three local law enforcement or adult or juvenile community supervision personnel and a prosecuting attorney designated by the governor.
*(Added by L.1999, chap. 492(1), eff. 6/18/99. See other Art. 61.07 below.)*

## Art. 61.07. Removal of records relating to a child.

(a) This article does not apply to information collected under this chapter by the Texas Department of Criminal Justice or the Texas Youth Commission.

(b) Subject to Subsection (c), information collected under this chapter relating to a criminal street gang must be removed from an intelligence database established under Article 61.02 and the intelligence database maintained by the department under Article 61.03 after two years if:

(1) the information relates to the investigation or prosecution of criminal activity engaged in by a child; and

(2) the child who is the subject of the information has not been:

(A) arrested for criminal activity reported to the department under Chapter 60; or

(B) taken into custody for delinquent conduct reported to the department under Chapter 58, Family Code.

(c) In determining whether information is required to be removed from an intelligence database under Subsection (b), the two-year period does not include any period during which the child who is the subject of the information is:

(1) committed to the Texas Youth Commission for conduct that violates a penal law of the grade of felony; or

(2) confined in the institutional division or the state jail division of the Texas Department of Criminal Justice.
*(Added by L.1999, chap. 1154(7), eff. 9/1/99. See other Art. 61.07 above.)*

## Art. 61.08. Gang resource system.

(a) The office of the attorney general shall establish an electronic gang resource system to provide criminal justice agencies and juvenile justice agencies with information about criminal street gangs in the state. The system may include the following information with regard to any gang:

(1) gang name;
(2) gang identifiers, such as colors used, tattoos, and clothing preferences;
(3) criminal activities;
(4) migration trends;
(5) recruitment activities; and
(6) a local law enforcement contact.

(b) Upon request by the office of the attorney general, criminal justice agencies and juvenile justice agencies shall make a reasonable attempt to provide gang information to the office of the attorney general for the purpose of maintaining an updated, comprehensive gang resource system.

(c) The office of the attorney general shall cooperate with criminal justice agencies and juvenile justice agencies in collecting and maintaining the accuracy of the information included in the gang resource system.

(d) Information relating to the identity of a specific offender or alleged offender may not be maintained in the gang resource system.

(e) Information in the gang resource system may be used in investigating gang-related crimes but may be included in affidavits or subpoenas or used in connection with any other legal or judicial proceeding only if the information from the system is corroborated by information not provided or maintained in the system.

(f) Access to the gang resource system shall be limited to criminal justice agency personnel and juvenile justice agency personnel.

(g) Information in the gang resource system shall be accessible by:
(1) municipality or county; and
(2) gang name.

(h) The office of the attorney general may coordinate with the Texas Department of Criminal Justice to include information in the gang resource system regarding groups which have been identified by the Security Threat Group Management Office of the Texas Department of Criminal Justice.
*(Added by L.1999, chap. 491(1), eff. 6/18/99. See other Art. 61.08 below.)*

## Art. 61.08. Right to request review of criminal information.

(a) On receipt of a written request of a person or the parent or guardian of a child that includes a showing by the person or the parent or guardian that a law enforcement agency may have collected criminal information under this chapter relating to the person or child that is inaccurate or that does not comply with the submission criteria under Article 61.02(c), the head of the agency or the designee of the agency head shall review criminal information collected by the agency under this chapter relating to the person or child to determine if:

(1) reasonable suspicion exists to believe that the information is accurate; and

(2) the information complies with the submission criteria established under Article 61.02(c).

(b) If, after conducting a review of criminal information under Subsection (a), the agency head or designee determines that:

(1) reasonable suspicion does not exist to believe that the information is accurate or the information does not comply with the submission criteria, the agency shall:

(A) destroy all records containing the information; and

(B) notify the department and the person who requested the review of the agency's determination and the destruction of the records; or

(2) reasonable suspicion does exist to believe that the information is accurate and the information complies with the submission criteria, the agency shall notify the person who requested the review of the agency's determination and that the person is entitled to seek judicial review of the agency's determination under Article 61.09.

(c) On receipt of notice under Subsection (b), the department shall immediately destroy all records containing the information that is the subject of the notice in the intelligence database maintained by the department under Article 61.03.

(d) A person who is committed to the Texas Youth Commission or confined in the institutional division or the state jail division of the Texas Department of Criminal Justice does not while committed or confined have the right to request review of criminal information under this article.
*(Added by L.1999, chap. 1154(7), eff. 9/1/99. See other Art. 61.08 above.)*

**Art. 61.09. Judicial review.**

(a) A person who is entitled to seek judicial review of a determination made under Article 61.08(b)(2) may file a petition for review in district court in the county in which the person resides.

(b) On the filing of a petition for review under Subsection (a), the district court shall conduct an in camera review of the criminal information that is the subject of the determination to determine if:

(1) reasonable suspicion exists to believe that the information is accurate; and

(2) the information complies with the submission criteria under Article 61.02(c).

(c) If, after conducting an in camera review of criminal information under Subsection (b), the court finds that reasonable suspicion does not exist to believe that the information is accurate or that the information does not comply with the submission criteria, the court shall:

(1) order the law enforcement agency that collected the information to destroy all records containing the information; and

(2) notify the department of the court's determination and the destruction of the records.

(d) A petitioner may appeal a final judgment of a district court conducting an in camera review under this article.

(e) Information that is the subject of an in camera review under this article is confidential and may not be disclosed.
*(Added by L.1999, chap. 1154(7), eff. 9/1/99.)*

## CHAPTER 62. SEX OFFENDER REGISTRATION PROGRAM

*(Redesignated from Art. 6252-13c.1, Revised Statutes and chgd. by L.1997, chap. 668(1), eff. 9/1/97.)*

Article

**Art. 62.01. Definitions.**

In this chapter:

(1) "Department" means the Department of Public Safety.

(2) "Local law enforcement authority" means the chief of police of a municipality or the sheriff of a county in this state.

(3) "Penal institution" means a confinement facility operated by or under a contract with any division of the Texas Department of Criminal Justice, a confinement facility operated by or under contract with the Texas Youth Commission, or a juvenile secure pre-adjudication or post-adjudication facility operated by or under a local juvenile probation department, or a county jail.

(4) "Released" means discharged, paroled, placed in a nonsecure community program for juvenile offenders, or placed on juvenile probation, community supervision, or mandatory supervision.

(5) "Reportable conviction or adjudication" means a conviction or adjudication, regardless of the pendency of an appeal, that is:

(A) a conviction for a violation of Section 21.11 (Indecency with a child), 22.011 (Sexual assault), 22.021 (Aggravated sexual assault), or 25.02 (Prohibited sexual conduct), Penal Code;

(B) a conviction for a violation of Section 43.05 (Compelling prostitution), 43.25 (Sexual performance by a child), or 43.26 (Possession or promotion of child pornography), Penal Code;

(C) a conviction for a violation of Section 20.04(a)(4) (Aggravated kidnapping), Penal Code, if the defendant committed the offense with intent to violate or abuse the victim sexually;

(D) a conviction for a violation of Section 30.02 (Burglary), Penal Code, if the offense is punishable under Subsection (d) of that section and the defendant committed the offense with intent to commit a felony listed in Paragraph (A) or (C);

(E) a conviction for a violation of Section 20.02 (Unlawful restraint), 20.03 (Kidnapping), or 20.04 (Aggravated kidnapping), Penal Code, if the judgment in the case contains an affirmative finding under Article 42.015;

(F) the second conviction for a violation of Section 21.08 (Indecent exposure), Penal Code;

(G) a conviction for an attempt, conspiracy, or solicitation, as defined by Chapter 15, Penal Code, to commit an offense listed in Paragraph (A), (B), (C), (D), or (E);

(H) an adjudication of delinquent conduct:

(i) based on a violation of one of the offenses listed in Paragraph (A), (B), (C), (D), or (G) or, if the order in the hearing contains an affirmative finding that the victim or intended victim was younger than 17 years of age, one of the offenses listed in Paragraph (E); or

(ii) for which two violations of the offense listed in Paragraph (F) are shown;

(I) a deferred adjudication for an offense listed in:

(i) Paragraph (A), (B), (C), (D), or (G); or

(ii) Paragraph (E) if the papers in the case contain an affirmative finding that the victim or intended victim was younger than 17 years of age;

(J) a conviction under the laws of another state, federal law, or the Uniform Code of Military Justice for an offense containing elements that are substantially similar to the elements of an offense listed under Paragraph (A), (B), (C), (D), (E), or (G);

(K) an adjudication of delinquent conduct under the laws of another state or federal law based on a violation of an offense containing elements that are substantially similar to the elements of an offense listed under Paragraph (A), (B), (C), (D), (E), or (G);

(L) the second conviction under the laws of another state, federal law, or the Uniform Code of Military Justice for an offense containing elements that are substantially similar to the elements of the offense of indecent exposure; or

(M) the second adjudication of delinquent conduct under the laws of another state or federal law based on a violation of an offense containing elements that are substantially similar to the elements of the offense of indecent exposure.

(6) "Sexually violent offense" means any of the following offenses committed by a person 17 years of age or older:

(A) an offense under Section 21.11(a)(1) (Indecency with a child), 22.011 (Sexual assault), or 22.021 (Aggravated sexual assault), Penal Code;

(B) an offense under Section 43.25 (Sexual performance by a child), Penal Code;

(C) an offense under Section 20.04(a)(4) (Aggravated kidnapping), Penal Code, if the defendant committed the offense with intent to violate or abuse the victim sexually;

(D) an offense under Section 30.02 (Burglary), Penal Code, if the offense is punishable under Subsection (d) of that section and the defendant committed the offense with intent to commit a felony listed in Paragraph (A) or (C) of Subdivision (5); or

(E) an offense under the laws of another state, federal law, or the Uniform Code of Military Justice if the offense contains elements that are substantially similar to the elements of an offense listed under Paragraph (A), (B), (C), or (D).

(7) "Residence" includes a residence established in this state by a person described by Article 62.061(e).

*(Redesignated from Art. 6252-13c.1, Sec. 1, Revised Statutes, and chgd. by L.1997, chap. 668(1); chgd. by L.1999, chaps. 1193(4), 1415(7), (8), eff. 9/1/99.)*

### Art. 62.011. Workers or students.

(a) A person is employed or carries on a vocation for purposes of this chapter if the person works on a full-time or part-time basis for a consecutive period exceeding 14 days or for an aggregate period exceeding 30 days in a calendar year, whether the person works for compensation or for governmental or educational benefit.

(b) A person is a student for purposes of this chapter if the person enrolls in any educational facility, including:

(1) a public or private primary or secondary school, including a high school or alternative learning center; or

(2) a public or private institution of higher education, including a college, university, community college, or technical or trade institute.

*(Added by L.1999, chaps. 1193(8), 1415(9), eff. 9/1/99.)*

### Art. 62.02. Registration.

(a) A person who has a reportable conviction or adjudication or who is required to register as a condition of parole, release to mandatory supervision, or community supervision shall register or, if the person is a person for whom registration is completed under this chapter, verify registration as provided by Subsection (d), with the local law enforcement authority in any municipality where the person resides or intends to reside for more than seven days. If the person does not reside or intend to reside in a municipality, the person shall register or verify registration in any county where the person resides or intends to reside for more than seven days. The person shall satisfy the requirements of this subsection not later than the seventh day after the person's arrival in the municipality or county.

(b) The department shall provide the Texas Department of Criminal Justice, the Texas Youth Commission, the Juvenile Probation Commission, and each local law enforcement authority, county jail, and court with a form for registering persons required by this chapter to register. The registration form shall require:

(1) the person's full name, each alias, date of birth, sex, race, height, weight, eye color, hair color, social security number, driver's license number, shoe size, and home address;

(2) a photograph of the person and a complete set of the person's fingerprints;

(3) the type of offense the person was convicted of, the age of the victim, the date of conviction, and the punishment received;

(4) an indication as to whether the person is discharged, paroled, or released on juvenile probation, community supervision, or mandatory supervision; and

(5) any other information required by the department.

(c) Not later than the third day after a person's registering, the local law enforcement authority with whom the person registered shall send a copy of the registration form to the department.

(d) A person for whom registration is completed under this chapter shall report to the applicable local law enforcement authority to verify the information in the registration form received by the authority under this chapter. The authority shall require the person to produce proof of the person's identity and residence before the authority gives the registration form to the person for verification. If the information in the registration form is complete and accurate, the person shall verify registration by signing the form. If the information is not complete or not accurate, the person shall make any necessary additions or corrections before signing the form.

(e) A person who is required to register or verify registration under this chapter shall ensure that the person's registration form is complete and accurate with respect to each item of information required by the form in accordance with Subsection (b).

(f) If a person subject to registration under this chapter does not move to an intended residence by the end of the seventh day after the date on which the person is released or the date on which the person leaves a previous residence, the person shall:

(1) report to the juvenile probation officer, community supervision and corrections department officer, or parole officer supervising the person by not later than the seventh day after the date on which the person is released or the date on which the person leaves a previous residence, as applicable, and provide the officer with the address of the person's temporary residence; and

(2) continue to report to the person's supervising officer not less than weekly during any period of time in which the person has not moved to an intended residence and provide the officer with the address of the person's temporary residence.

(g) If the other state has a registration requirement for sex offenders, a person who has a reportable conviction or adjudication, who resides in this state, and who is employed, carries on a vocation, or is a student in another state shall, not later than the 10th day after the date on which the person begins to work or attend school in the other state, register with the law enforcement authority that is identified by the department as the authority designated by that state to receive registration information.

*(Redesignated from Art. 6252-13c.1, Sec. 2, Revised Statutes, and chgd. by L.1997, chap. 668(1); chgd. by L.1999, chaps. 444(1), 1193(5), 1415(10), eff. 9/1/99.)*

### Art. 62.021. Out-of-state registrants.

(a) This article applies to a person who is required to register as a sex offender under the laws of another state with which the department has entered into a reciprocal registration agreement and who is not otherwise required to register under this chapter because:

(1) the person does not have a reportable conviction for an offense under the laws of the other state containing elements that are substantially similar to an offense requiring registration under this chapter; or

(2) the person does not have a reportable adjudication of delinquent conduct based on a violation of an offense under the laws of the other state containing elements that are substantially similar to an offense requiring registration under this chapter.

(b) A person described by Subsection (a) is required to comply with the annual verification requirements of Article 62.06 in the same manner as a person who is required to verify registration on the basis of a reportable conviction or adjudication.

(c) The expiration of the duty to register for a person described by Subsection (a) expires on the date the person's duty to register would expire in the other state had the person remained in that state.

(d) The department may negotiate and enter into a reciprocal registration agreement with any other state to prevent residents of this state and residents of the other state from frustrating the public purpose of the registration of sex offenders by moving from one state to the other.

*(Added by L.1999, chaps. 444(2), 1415(11), eff. 9/1/99.)*

### Art. 62.03. Prerelease notification.

(a) Before a person who will be subject to registration under this chapter is due to be released from a penal institution, the risk assessment review committee established under Article 62.035 shall determine the person's level of risk to the community using the sex offender screening tool developed or selected under that article, assign to the person a numeric risk level to the penal institution from which the person is due to be released. On receiving notice under this subsection, an official of the penal institution shall:

(1) inform the person that:

(A) not later than the seventh day after the date on which the person is released or the date on which the person moves from a previous residence to a new residence in this state, the person must:

(i) register or verify registration with the local law enforcement authority in the municipality or county in which the person intends to reside; or

(ii) if the person has not moved to an intended residence, report to the juvenile probation officer, community supervision and corrections department officer, or parole officer supervising the person;

(B) not later than the seventh day before the date on which the person moves to a new residence in this state or another state, the person must report in person to the local law enforcement authority with whom the person last registered and to the juvenile probation officer, community supervision and corrections department officer, or parole officer supervising the person; [and]

(C) not later than the 10th day after the date on which the person arrives in another state in which the person intends to reside, the person must register with the law enforcement agency that is identified by the department as the agency designated by that state to receive registration information, if the other state has a registration requirement for sex offenders; *and*

*(D) not later than the 30th day after the date on which the person is released, the person must apply to the department in person for the issuance of an original or renewal driver's license or personal identification certificate and a failure to apply to the department as required by this paragraph results in the automatic revocation of any driver's license or personal identification certificate issued by the department to the person;*

(2) require the person to sign a written statement that the person was informed of the person's duties as described by Subdivision (1) or, if the person refuses to sign the statement, certify that the person was so informed;

(3) obtain the address where the person expects to reside on the person's release and other registration information, including a photograph and complete set of fingerprints; and

(4) complete the registration form for the person.

(b) On the seventh day before the date on which a person who will be subject to registration under this chapter is due to be released from a penal institution, or on receipt of notice by a penal institution that a person who will be subject to registration under this chapter is due to be released in less than seven days, an official of the penal institution shall send the person's completed registration form and numeric risk level to the department and to:

(1) the applicable local law enforcement authority in the municipality or county in which the person expects to reside, if the person expects to reside in this state; or

(2) the law enforcement agency that is identified by the department as the agency designated by another state to receive registration information, if the person expects to reside in that other state and that other state has a registration requirement for sex offenders.

(c) If a person who is subject to registration under this chapter receives an order deferring adjudication, placing the person on juvenile probation or community supervision, or imposing only a fine, the court pronouncing the order or sentence shall make a determination of the person's numeric risk level using the sex offender screening tool developed or selected under Article 62.035, assign to the person a numeric risk level of one or two, and ensure that the prerelease notification and registration requirements specified in this article are conducted on the day of entering the order or sentencing. If a community supervision and corrections department representative is available in court at the time a court pronounces a sentence of deferred adjudication or community supervision, the representative shall immediately obtain the person's numeric risk level from the court and conduct the prerelease notification and registration requirements specified in this article. In any other case in which the court pronounces a sentence under this subsection, the court shall designate another appropriate individual to obtain the person's numeric risk level from the court and conduct the prerelease notification and registration requirements specified in this article.

(d) If a person who has a reportable conviction described by Article 62.01(5)(J) or (L) is placed under the supervision of the pardons and paroles division of the Texas Department of Criminal Justice or a community supervision and corrections department under Article 42.11, the division or community supervision and corrections department shall conduct the prerelease notification and registration requirements specified in this article on the date the person is placed under the supervision of the division or community supervision and corrections department. If a person who has a reportable adjudication of delinquent conduct described by Article 62.01(5)(K) or (M) is, as permitted by Section 60.002, Family Code, placed under the supervision of the Texas Youth Commission, a public or private vendor operating under contract with the Texas Youth Commission, a local juvenile probation department, or a juvenile secure pre-adjudication or post-adjudication facility, the commission, vendor, probation department, or facility shall conduct the prerelease notification and registration requirements specified in this article on the date the person is placed under the supervision of the commission, vendor, probation department, or facility.

(e) Not later than the eighth day after receiving a registration form under Subsection (b), (c), or (d), the local law enforcement authority shall verify the age of the victim, the age of the person subject to registration, the basis on which the person is subject to registration under this chapter, and the person's numeric risk level. If the victim is a child younger than 17 years of age and the basis on which the person is subject to registration is not an adjudication of delinquent conduct and is not a conviction or a deferred adjudication for an offense under Section 25.02, Penal Code, the authority shall immediately publish notice in English and Spanish in the newspaper of greatest paid circulation in the county in which the person subject to registration intends to reside or, if there is no newspaper of paid circulation in that county, in the newspaper of greatest general circulation in the county. The authority shall publish a duplicate notice in the newspaper, with any necessary corrections, during the week immediately following the week of initial publication. If the victim is a child younger than 17 years of age or the person subject to registration is 17 years of age or older and a student enrolled in a public or private secondary school, regardless of the basis on which the person is subject to registration, the authority shall immediately provide notice to the superintendent of the public school district and to the administrator of any private primary or secondary school located in the public school district in which the person subject to registration intends to reside by mail to the office of the superintendent or administrator, as appropriate. On receipt of a notice under this subsection, the superintendent shall release the information contained in the notice to appropriate school district personnel, including peace officers and security personnel, principals, nurses, and counselors.

(f) The local law enforcement authority shall include in the notice by publication in a newspaper the following information only:

(1) the person's full name, age, and gender;

(2) a brief description of the offense for which the person is subject to registration;

(3) the municipality, numeric street address or physical address, if a numeric street address is not available, and zip code number where the person intends to reside; and

(4) either a recent photograph of the person or the Internet address of a website on which the person's photograph is accessible free of charge. *(Added by L.1999, chap. 1415(12), eff. 9/1/99. See other paragraph (4) below.)*

(4) the person's numeric risk level assigned under this chapter and the guidelines used to determine a person's risk level generally. *(Added by L.1999, chap. 1557(1), eff. 6/19/99. See other paragraph (4) above.)*

(g) The local law enforcement authority shall include in the notice to the superintendent of the public school district and to the administrator of any private primary or secondary school located in the public school district any information the authority determines is necessary to protect the public, except:

(1) the person's social security number, driver's license number, or telephone number; and

(2) any information that would identify the victim of the offense for which the person is subject to registration.

(h) Before a person who will be subject to registration under this chapter is due to be released from a penal institution in this state, an official of the penal institution shall inform the person that:

(1) if the person intends to reside in another state and to work or attend school in this state, the person must, not later than the seventh day after the date on which the person begins to work or attend school, register or verify registration with the local law enforcement authority in the municipality or county in which the person intends to work or attend school; and

(2) if the person intends to reside in this state and to work or attend school in another state and if the other state has a registration requirement for sex offenders, the person must, not later than the 10th day after the date on which the person begins to work or attend school in the other state, register with the law enforcement authority that is identified by the department as the authority designated by that state to receive registration information.

*(Redesignated from Art. 6252-13c.1, Sec. 3, Revised Statutes, and chgd. by L.1997, chaps. 667(5), 668(1), 1430(8); chgd. by L.1999, chaps. 444(3), 1193(6), (7), 1401(2), 1415(12), 1557(1), eff. 9/1/99, 9/1/99, 9/1/99, 9/1/2000, 9/1/99, 6/19/99, respectively. Matter in brackets eff. only until 9/1/2000. Matter in italics eff. 9/1/2000.)*

## Art. 62.035. Risk assessment review committee; sex offender screening tool.

(a) The Texas Department of Criminal Justice shall establish a risk assessment review committee composed of at least five members, each of whom is a state employee whose service on the review committee is in addition to the employee's regular duties. The review committee, to the extent feasible, should include at least:

(1) one member having experience in law enforcement;

(2) one member having experience working with juvenile sex offenders;

(3) one member having experience as a sex offender treatment provider; and

(4) one member having experience working with victims of sex offenses.

(b) The risk assessment review committee shall develop or select from among existing tools a sex offender screening tool to be used in determining the level of risk of a person subject to registration under this chapter. The sex offender screening tool must use an objective point system under which a person is assigned a designated number of points for each of various factors, such as the nature of the offense for which the person is subject to registration, the age of the victim, and the number of occasions on which the person has been convicted of or adjudicated for an offense for which a person is subject to registration under this chapter. In developing or selecting the sex offender screening tool, the risk assessment review committee shall use or shall select a screening tool that may be adapted to use the following general guidelines:

(1) level one:

(A) a designated number of points or higher on the sex offender screening tool; and

(B) a basis for concern that the person poses a serious danger to the community or will continue to engage in criminal sexual conduct;

(2) level two, either, but not both, of the following:

(A) a designated number of points or higher on the sex offender screening tool; or

(B) a basis for concern that the person poses a serious danger to the community or will continue to engage in criminal sexual conduct; and

(3) level three: no basis for concern that the person poses a serious danger to the community or will continue to engage in criminal sexual conduct.

(c) The risk assessment review committee may assign to a person a numeric risk level of three only on receipt of notice under Article 62.04 that the person intends to move to a new residence in this state and only if:

(1) the person was originally assigned a numeric risk level of two under Article 62.03;

(2) the committee considers any information available to the committee that was used by the committee or by the court at the time of assigning to the person a numeric risk level of two; and

(3) the basis on which the person is subject to registration is a conviction of or a grant of deferred adjudication for an offense under Section 21.11 or Section 22.011(a)(2), Penal Code, or an adjudication of delinquent conduct based on a violation of one of those offenses, committed against a victim who is of the opposite sex of the person and is not more than five years younger than the person.

*(Added by L.1999, chap. 1557(2), eff. 6/19/99.)*

## Art. 62.04. Change of address.

(a) If a person required to register intends to change address, regardless of whether the person intends to move to another state, the person shall, not later than the seventh day before the intended change, report in person to the local law enforcement authority with whom the person last registered and to the juvenile probation officer, community supervision and corrections department officer, or parole officer supervising the person and provide the authority and the officer with the person's anticipated move date and new address. If a person required to register changes address, the person shall, not later than the seventh day after changing the address, report in person to the local law enforcement authority in the municipality or county in which the person's new residence is located and provide the authority with proof of identity and proof of residence.

(b) Not later than the third day after receipt of notice under Subsection (a), the person's juvenile probation officer, community supervision and corrections department officer, or parole officer shall forward the information provided under Subsection (a) to the local law enforcement authority with whom the person last registered and, if the person intends to move to another municipality or county in this state, to the applicable local law enforcement authority in that municipality or county.

(c) If the person moves to another state that has a registration requirement for sex offenders, the person shall, not later than the 10th day after the date on which the person arrives in the other state, register with the law enforcement agency that is identified by the department as the agency designated by that state to receive registration information.

(d) Not later than the third day after receipt of information under Subsection (a) or (b), whichever is earlier, the local law enforcement authority shall forward this information to the department and, if the person intends to move to another municipality or county in this state, to the applicable local law enforcement authority in that municipality or county and, if the person meets the criteria described by Article 62.035(c)(3) to be reassigned a numeric risk level of three, to the risk assessment review committee established under that article. On receipt of information under this subsection, the risk assessment review committee shall determine whether the person meets the criteria to be reassigned a numeric risk level of three, assign to the person a numeric risk level of three, if the person meets that criteria, and immediately send a written notice of the person's risk level to the department and to the local law enforcement authority in the municipality or county where the person intends to reside.

(e) If a person who reports to a local law enforcement authority under Subsection (a) does not move on or before the anticipated move date or does not move to the new address provided to the authority, the person shall:

(1) report to the local law enforcement authority with whom the person last registered not later than the seventh day after the anticipated move date and provide an explanation to the authority regarding any changes in the anticipated move date and intended residence; and

(2) report to the juvenile probation officer, community supervision and corrections department officer, or parole officer supervising the person not less than weekly during any period in which the person has not moved to an intended residence.

(f) If the person moves to another municipality or county in this state, the department shall inform the applicable local law enforcement authority in the new area of the person's residence not later than the third day after the date on which the department receives information under Subsection (a). Not later than the eighth day after the date on which the local law enforcement authority is informed under Subsection (a) or under this subsection, the authority shall verify the age of the victim, the age of the person subject to registration, the basis on which the person is subject to registration under this chapter, and the person's numeric risk level. If the victim is a child younger than 17 years of age, the basis on which the person is subject to registration is not an adjudication of delinquent conduct and is not a conviction or a deferred adjudication for an offense under Section 25.02, Penal Code, and the person is not assigned a numeric risk level three, the authority shall immediately publish notice in English and Spanish in the newspaper of greatest paid circulation in the county in which the person subject to registration intends to reside or, if there is no newspaper of paid circulation in that county, in the newspaper of greatest general circulation in the county. The local law enforcement authority shall publish a duplicate notice in the newspaper, with any necessary corrections, during the week immediately following the week of initial publication. If the victim is a child younger than 17 years of age or the person subject to registration is 17 years of age or older and a student enrolled in a public or private secondary school, regardless of the basis on which the person is subject to registration or the person's numeric risk level, the authority shall immediately provide notice to the superintendent of the public school district and to the administrator of any private primary or secondary school located in the public school district in which the person subject to registration intends to reside by mail to the office of the superintendent or administrator, as appropriate. On receipt of a notice under this subsection, the superintendent shall release the information contained in the notice to appropriate school district personnel, including peace officers and security personnel, principals, nurses, and counselors.

(g) The local law enforcement authority shall include in the notice by publication in a newspaper the following information only:

(1) the person's full name, age, and gender;

(2) a brief description of the offense for which the person is subject to registration;

(3) the municipality, numeric street address or physical address, if a numeric street address is not available, and zip code number where the person intends to reside; and

(4) either a recent photograph of the person or the Internet address of a website on which the person's photograph is accessible free of charge. *(Added by L.1999, chap. 1415(13), eff. 9/1/99. See other paragraph (4) below.)*

(4) the person's numeric risk level assigned under this chapter and the guidelines used to determine a person's risk level generally. *(Added by L.1999, chap. 1557(1), eff. 6/19/99. See other paragraph (4) above.)*

(h) The local law enforcement authority shall include in the notice to the superintendent of the public school district and the administrator of any private primary or secondary school located in the public school district any information the authority determines is necessary to protect the public, except:

(1) the person's social security number, driver's license number, or telephone number; and

(2) any information that would identify the victim of the offense for which the person is subject to registration.

(i) If the person moves to another state, the department shall, immediately on receiving information under Subsection (d):

(1) inform the law enforcement agency that is designated by the other state to receive registration information, if that state has a registration requirement for sex offenders; and

(2) send to the Federal Bureau of Investigation a copy of the person's registration form, including the record of conviction and a complete set of fingerprints.

*(Redesignated from Art. 6252-13c.1, Sec. 4, Revised Statutes, and chgd. by L.1997, chap. 667(6), 668(1), 1430(9); chgd. by L.1999, chaps. 444(4), 1415(13), 1557(3), eff. 9/1/99, 9/1/99. 6/19/99, respectively.)*

**Art. 62.045. Additional public notice for certain offenders.**

(a) On receipt of notice under this chapter that a person subject to registration is due to be released from a penal institution, has been placed on community supervision or juvenile probation, or intends to move to a new residence in this state, the department shall verify the person's numeric risk level assigned under this chapter. If the person is assigned a numeric risk level one, the department shall, not later than the seventh day after the date on which the person is released or the 10th day after the date on which the person moves, provide written notice mailed or delivered to at least each residential address within a one-mile radius, in an area that has not been subdivided, or a three-block area, in an area that has been subdivided, of the place where the person intends to reside. In providing written notice under this subsection, the department shall use employees of the department whose duties in providing the notice are in addition to the employees' regular duties.

(b) The department shall include in the notice any information that is public information under this chapter. The department may not include any information that is not public information under this chapter.

(c) The department shall establish procedures for a person with respect to whom notice is provided under Subsection (a), other than a person subject to registration on the basis of an adjudication of delinquent conduct, to pay to the department all costs incurred by the department in providing the notice. The person shall pay those costs in accordance with the procedures established under this subsection.

(d) On receipt of notice under this chapter that a person subject to registration under this chapter is required to register or verify registration with a local law enforcement authority and has been assigned a numeric risk level of one, the local law enforcement authority may provide notice to the public in any manner determined appropriate by the local law enforcement authority, including holding a neighborhood meeting, posting notices in the area where the person intends to reside, distributing printed notices to area residents, or establishing a specialized local website. The local law enforcement authority may include in the notice any information that is public information under this chapter.

(e) An owner of a single-family residential property or the owner's agent has no duty to make a disclosure to a prospective buyer or tenant about registrants under this chapter.

*(Added by L.1999, chap. 1557(4), eff. 6/19/99.)*

**Art. 62.0451. Additional public notice for individuals subject to civil commitment.**

(a) On receipt of notice under this chapter that a person subject to registration who is civilly committed as a sexually violent predator is due to be released from a penal institution or intends to move to a new residence in this state, the department shall, not later than the seventh day after the date on which the person is released or the 10th day after the date on which the person moves, provide written notice mailed or delivered to at least each residential address within a one-mile radius, in an area that has not been subdivided, or a three-block area, in an area that has been subdivided, of the place where the person intends to reside.

(b) The department shall include in the notice any information that is public information under this chapter. The department may not include any information that is not public information under this chapter.

(c) The department shall establish procedures for a person with respect to whom notice is provided under this article to pay to the department all costs incurred by the department in providing the notice. The person shall pay those costs in accordance with the procedures established under this subsection.

(d) The department's duty to provide notice under this article in regard to a particular person ends on the date on which a court releases the person from all requirements of the civil commitment process.

*(Added by L.1999, chap. 444(5(a)), eff. 1/1/2000.)*

**Art. 62.05. Status report by supervising officer.**

(a) If the juvenile probation officer, community supervision and corrections department officer, or parole officer supervising a person subject to registration under this chapter receives information to the effect that the person's status has changed in any manner that affects proper supervision of the person, including a change in the person's physical health, job status, incarceration, or terms of release, the supervising officer shall promptly notify the appropriate local law enforcement authority or authorities of that change. If the person required to register intends to change address, the person's supervising officer shall notify the local law enforcement authorities designated by Article 62.04(b).

(b) If a person required to register is not supervised by an officer listed in Subsection (a), the person shall report to the local law enforcement authority any change in the person's physical health or job status not later than the seventh day after the date of the change. For purposes of this subsection, a person's job status changes if the person leaves employment for any reason, remains employed by an employer but changes the location at which the person works, or begins employment with a new employer. For purposes of this subsection, a person's health status changes if the person is hospitalized as a result of an illness.
*(Added by L.1997, chap. 668(1); chgd. by L.1999, chaps. 444(6), 1415(14), eff. 9/1/99.)*

### Art. 62.06. Law enforcement verification of registration information.

(a) A person subject to registration under this chapter who has for a sexually violent offense been convicted two or more times, received an order of deferred adjudication two or more times, or been convicted and received an order of deferred adjudication shall report to the local law enforcement authority with whom the person is required to register not less than once in each 90-day period following the date the person first registered under this chapter to verify the information in the registration form maintained by the authority for that person. A person subject to registration under this chapter who is not subject to the 90-day reporting requirement described by this subsection shall report to the local law enforcement authority with whom the person is required to register once each year not earlier than the 30th day before and not later than the 30th day after the anniversary of the person's date of birth to verify the information in the registration form maintained by the authority for that person. For purposes of this subsection, a person complies with a requirement that the person register within a 90-day period following a date if the person registers at any time on or after the 83rd day following that date but before the 98th day after that date.

(b) A local law enforcement authority with whom a person is required to register under this chapter may direct the person to report to the authority to verify the information in the registration form maintained by the authority for that person. The authority may direct the person to report under this subsection once in each 90-day period following the date the person first registered under this chapter, if the person is required to report not less than once in each 90-day period under Subsection (a) or once in each year not earlier than the 30th day before and not later than the 30th day after the anniversary of the person's date of birth, if the person is required to report once each year under Subsection (a). A local law enforcement authority may not direct a person to report to the authority under this subsection if the person is required to report under Subsection (a) and is in compliance with the reporting requirements of that subsection.

(c) A local law enforcement authority with whom a person reports under this article shall require the person to produce proof of the person's identity and residence before the authority gives the registration form to the person for verification. If the information in the registration form is complete and accurate, the person shall verify registration by signing the form. If the information is not complete or not accurate, the person shall make any necessary additions or corrections before signing the form.

(d) A local law enforcement authority with whom a person is required to register under this chapter may at any time mail a nonforwardable verification form to the last reported address of the person. Not later than the 21st day after receipt of a verification form under this subsection, the person shall:

(1) indicate on the form whether the person still resides at the last reported address and, if not, provide on the form the person's new address;

(2) complete any other information required by the form;

(3) sign the form; and

(4) return the form to the authority.

*(Added by L.1997, chap. 668(1); chgd. by L.1999, chaps. 444(7), 1415(15), eff. 9/1/99.)*

### Art. 62.061. Verification of individuals subject to commitment.

(a) Notwithstanding Article 62.06, if an individual subject to registration under this chapter is civilly committed as a sexually violent predator, the person shall report to the local law enforcement authority with whom the person is required to register not less than once in each 30-day period following the date the person first registered under this chapter to verify the information in the registration form maintained by the authority for that person. For purposes of this subsection, a person complies with a requirement that the person register within a 30-day period following a date if the person registers at any time on or after the 27th day following that date but before the 33rd day after that date.

(b) On the date that a court releases a person described by Subsection (a) from all requirements of the civil commitment process:

(1) the person's duty to verify registration as a sex offender is no longer imposed by this article; and

(2) the person is required to verify registration as provided by Article 62.06.

*(Added by L.1999, chap. 445(5(b)), eff. 1/1/2000. See other Art. 62.061 below.)*

**Art. 62.061. Registration of certain workers or students.**

(a) A person is subject to this article and, except as otherwise provided by this article, to the other articles of this chapter if the person:

(1) has a reportable conviction or adjudication;

(2) resides in another state; and

(3) is employed, carries on a vocation, or is a student in this state.

(b) A person described by Subsection (a) is subject to the registration and verification requirements of Articles 62.02 and 62.06 and to the change of address requirements of Article 62.04, except that the registration and verification and the reporting of a change of address are based on the municipality or county in which the person works or attends school. The person is subject to the school notification requirements of Articles 62.03 and 62.04, except that notice provided to the superintendent and any administrator is based on the public school district in which the person works or attends school.

(c) A person described by Subsection (a) is not subject to Article 62.12 and the newspaper publication requirements of Articles 62.03 and 62.04.

(d) The duty to register for a person described by Subsection (a) ends when the person no longer works or studies in this state, provides notice of that fact to the local law enforcement authority in the municipality or county in which the person works or attends school, and receives notice of verification of that fact from the authority. The authority must verify that the person no longer works or studies in this state and must provide to the person notice of that verification within a reasonable time.

(e) Notwithstanding Subsection (a), this article does not apply to a person who has a reportable conviction or adjudication, who resides in another state, and who is employed, carries on a vocation, or is a student in this state if the person establishes another residence in this state to work or attend school in this state. However, that person remains subject to the other articles of this chapter based on that person's residence in this state.

*(Added by L.1999, chaps. 1193(8), 1415(16), eff. 9/1/99. See other Art. 62.061 above.)*

**Art. 62.062. Registration of persons regularly visiting location.**

(a) A person subject to this chapter who on at least three occasions during any month spends more than 48 consecutive hours in a municipality or county in this state, other than the municipality or county in which the person is registered under this chapter, before the last day of that month shall report that fact to:

(1) the local law enforcement authority of the municipality in which the person is a visitor; or

(2) if the person is a visitor in a location that is not a municipality, the local law enforcement authority of the county in which the person is a visitor.

(b) A person described by Subsection (a) shall provide the local law enforcement authority with:

(1) all information the person is required to provide under Article 62.02(b);

(2) the address of any location in the municipality or county, as appropriate, at which the person was lodged during the month; and

(3) a statement as to whether the person intends to return to the municipality or county during the succeeding month.

(c) This article does not impose on a local law enforcement authority requirements of public notification or notification to schools relating to a person about whom the authority is not otherwise required by this chapter to make notifications.

*(Added by L.1999, chaps. 444(8), 1415(16), eff. 9/1/99.)*

**Art. 62.065. Requirements relating to driver's license or personal identification certificate.**

(a) A person subject to registration under this chapter shall apply to the department in person for the issuance of an original or renewal driver's license under Section 521.272, Transportation Code, or for a personal identification certificate under Section 521.103, Transportation Code, not later than the 30th day after the date:

(1) the person is released from a penal institution or is released by a court on juvenile probation or community supervision; or

(2) the department sends written notice to the person of the requirements of this article.

Printed in the U.S.A. ZI

(b) The person shall annually renew in person each driver's license or personal identification certificate issued by the department to the person, including each renewal, duplicate, or corrected license or certificate, until the person's duty to register under this chapter expires.

(c) The department shall determine from its records which persons required to register under this chapter are under the supervision and control of a juvenile probation office or an agency or entity operating under contract with a juvenile probation office, a community supervision and corrections department, or the pardons and paroles division of the Texas Department of Criminal Justice and shall provide written notice of the requirements of this article to each of those persons by not later than October 30, 2000. This subsection expires January 1, 2001. *(Subsection (c) expires 1/1/2001.)*

*(Added by L.1999, chap. 1401(3), eff. 9/1/2000.)*

### Art. 62.07. Remedies related to public notice.

A person subject to registration under this chapter may petition the district court for injunctive relief to restrain a local law enforcement authority from publishing notice in a newspaper as required by Article 62.03 or 62.04. The court may issue a temporary restraining order under this article before notice is served and a hearing is held on the matter. After a hearing on the matter, the court may grant any injunctive relief warranted by the facts, including a restraining order or a temporary or permanent injunction, if the person subject to registration under this chapter proves by a preponderance of the evidence specific facts indicating that newspaper publication under Article 62.03 or 62.04 would place the person's health and well-being in immediate danger. *(Redesignated from Art. 6252-13c.1, Sec. 4A, Revised Statutes, and chgd. by L.1997, chap. 668(1), eff. 9/1/97.)*



### Art. 62.08. Central database; public information.

(a) The department shall maintain a computerized central database containing only the information required for registration under this chapter.

(b) The information contained in the database is public information, with the exception of any information:

(1) regarding the person's social security number, driver's license number, or telephone number;

(2) that is required by the department under Article 62.02(b)(5); or

(3) that would identify the victim of the offense for which the person is subject to registration.

(c) A local law enforcement authority shall release public information described under Subsection (b) to any person who submits to the authority a written request for the information. The authority may charge the person a fee not to exceed the amount reasonably necessary to cover the administrative costs associated with the authority's release of information to the person under this subsection.

(d) On the written request of a licensing authority that identifies an individual and states that the individual is an applicant for or a holder of a license issued by the authority, the department shall release any information described by Subsection (a) to the licensing authority.

(e) For the purposes of Subsection (d):

(1) "License" means a license, certificate, registration, permit, or other authorization that:

(A) is issued by a licensing authority; and

(B) a person must obtain to practice or engage in a particular business, occupation, or profession.

(2) "Licensing authority" means a department, commission, board, office, or other agency of the state or a political subdivision of the state that issues a license.

*(Redesignated from Art. 6252-13c.1, Sec. 5, Revised Statutes, and chgd. by L.1997, chap. 668(1); chgd. by L.1999, chap. 1415(17), eff. 9/1/99.)*

### Art. 62.085. Information provided to peace officer.

The department shall establish a procedure by which a peace officer or employee of a law enforcement agency who provides the department with a driver's license, personal identification certificate, or license plate number is automatically provided information as to whether the person to whom the driver's license or personal identification certificate is issued is required to register under this chapter or whether the license plate number is entered in the computerized central database under Article 62.08 as assigned to a vehicle owned or driven by a person required to register under this chapter. *(Added by L.1999, chap. 1401(3), eff. 9/1/2000.)*

**Art. 62.09. Immunity for release of public information.**

(a) The department, a penal institution, or a local law enforcement authority may release to the public information regarding a person required to register if the information is public information under this chapter.

(b) An individual, agency, entity, or authority is not liable under Chapter 101, Civil Practice and Remedies Code, or any other law for damages arising from conduct authorized by Subsection (a).

(c) For purposes of determining liability, the release or withholding of information by an appointed or elected officer of an agency, entity, or authority is a discretionary act.

(d) A private primary or secondary school or administrator of a private primary or secondary school may release to the public information regarding a person required to register if the information is public information under this chapter and is released to the administrator under Article 62.03 or 62.04. A private primary or secondary school or administrator of a private primary or secondary school is not liable under any law for damages arising from conduct authorized by this subsection.

*(Redesignated from Art. 6252-13c.1, Sec. 5A, Revised Statutes, and chgd. by L.1997, chap. 668(1), eff. 9/1/97.)*

**Art. 62.10. Failure to comply with registration requirements.**

(a) A person commits an offense if the person is required to register and fails to comply with any requirement of this chapter.

(b) An offense under this article is:

(1) a state jail felony if the actor is a person whose duty to register expires under Article 62.12(b);

(2) a felony of the third degree if the actor is a person whose duty to register expires under Article 62.12(a) and who is required to verify registration once each year under Article 62.06; and

(3) a felony of the second degree if the actor is a person whose duty to register expires under Article 62.12(a) and who is required to verify registration once each 90-day period under Article 62.06.

(c) If it is shown at the trial of a person for an offense under this article that the person has previously been convicted of an offense under this article, the punishment for the offense is increased to the punishment for the next highest degree of felony.

*(Redesignated from Art. 6252-13c.1, Sec. 7, Revised Statutes, and chgd. by L.1997, chap. 668(1); chgd. by L.1999, chaps. 444(9), 1415(18), eff. 9/1/99.)*

**Art. 62.101. Failure to comply: individuals subject to commitment.**

(a) A person commits an offense if the person, after commitment as a sexually violent predator but before the person is released from all requirements of the civil commitment process, fails to comply with any requirement of this chapter.

(b) An offense under this section is a felony of the second degree.

*(Added by L.1999, chap. 444(5(c)), eff. 1/1/2000.)*

**Art. 62.11. Applicability.**

This chapter applies only to a reportable conviction or adjudication occurring on or after September 1, 1970, except that the provisions of Articles 62.03 and 62.04 of this chapter relating to the requirement of newspaper publication apply only to a reportable conviction or adjudication occurring on or after:

(1) September 1, 1997, if the conviction or adjudication relates to an offense under Section 43.05, Penal Code; or

(2) September 1, 1995, if the conviction or adjudication relates to any other offense listed in Article 62.01(5).

*(Redesignated from Art. 6252-13c.1, Sec. 8, Revised Statutes, and chgd. by L.1997, chap. 668(1), eff. 9/1/97.)*

**Art. 62.12. Expiration of duty to register.**

(a) The duty to register for a person with a reportable conviction or adjudication for a sexually violent offense or for an offense under Section 25.02, 43.05(a)(2), or 43.26, Penal Code, ends when the person dies.

(b) The duty to register for a person with a reportable conviction or adjudication for an offense other than an offense described by Subsection (a) ends:

(1) if the person's duty to register is based on an adjudication of delinquent conduct, on the 10th anniversary of the date on which the disposition is made or the person completes the terms of the disposition, whichever date is later; or

(2) if the person's duty to register is based on a conviction or on an order of deferred adjudication, on the 10th anniversary of the date on which the court dismisses the criminal proceedings against the person and discharges the person, the person is released from county jail, or the person discharges community supervision, whichever date is later.

(c) *(Repealed.)*

*(Redesignated from Art. 6252-13c.1, Sec. 9, Revised Statutes, and chgd. by L.1997, chap. 668(1); chgd. by L.1999, chap. 1415(25), eff. 9/1/99.)*

## CHAPTER 63. MISSING CHILDREN AND MISSING PERSONS

*(Transferred from Chapter 79, Human Resources Code, by L.1997, chap. 1427(1); renumbered from Chapter 62 by L.1999, chap. 62(19.01)(8(A)), eff. 9/1/99.)*

Article



### Art. 63.001. Definitions.

In this chapter:

(1) "Child" means a person under 18 years of age.

(2) "Missing person" means a person 18 years old or older whose disappearance is possibly not voluntary.

(3) "Missing child" means a child whose whereabouts are unknown to the child's legal custodian, the circumstances of whose absence indicate that:

(A) the child did not voluntarily leave the care and control of the custodian, and the taking of the child was not authorized by law;

(B) the child voluntarily left the care and control of his legal custodian without the custodian's consent and without intent to return; or

(C) the child was taken or retained in violation of the terms of a court order for possession of or access to the child.

(4) "Missing child" or "missing person" also includes a person of any age who is missing and:

(A) is under proven physical or mental disability or is senile, and because of one or more of these conditions is subject to immediate danger or is a danger to others;

(B) is in the company of another person or is in a situation the circumstances of which indicate that the missing child's or missing person's safety is in doubt; or

(C) is unemancipated as defined by the law of this state.

(5) "Missing child or missing person report" or "report" means information that is:

(A) given to a law enforcement agency on a form used for sending information to the national crime information center; and

(B) about a child or missing person whose whereabouts are unknown to the reporter and who is alleged in the form by the reporter to be missing.

(6) "Legal custodian of a child" means a parent of a child if no managing conservator or guardian of the person of the child has been appointed, the managing conservator of a child or a guardian of a child if a managing conservator or guardian has been appointed for the child, a possessory conservator of a child if the child is absent from the possessory conservator of the child at a time when the possessory conservator is entitled to possession of the child and the child is not believed to be with the managing conservator, or any other person who has assumed temporary care and control of a child if at the time of disappearance the child was not living with his parent, guardian, managing conservator, or possessory conservator.

(7) "Clearinghouse" means the missing children and missing persons information clearinghouse.

(8) "Law enforcement agency" means a police department of a city in this state, a sheriff of a county in this state, or the Department of Public Safety.

(9) "Possible match" occurs if the similarities between an unidentified body and a missing child or person would lead one to believe they are the same person.

(10) "City or state agency" means an employment commission, the Texas Department of Human Services, the Texas Department of Transportation, and any other agency that is funded or supported by the state or a city government.
*(Transferred from Section 79.001, Human Resources Code, and chgd. by L.1997, chap. 1427(1); renumbered from Art. 62.001 and chgd. by L.1999, chap. 62(3.10), (19.01)(8(A)), eff. 9/1/99.)*

### Art. 63.0015. Presumption regarding parentage.

For purposes of this chapter, a person named as a child's mother or father in the child's birth certificate is presumed to be the child's parent. *(Added as Art. 62.0015 by L.1999, chap. 685(2), eff. 9/1/99.)*

### Art. 63.002. Missing children and missing persons information clearinghouse.

(a) The missing children and missing persons information clearinghouse is established within the Department of Public Safety.

(b) The clearinghouse is under the administrative direction of the director of the department.

(c) The clearinghouse shall be used by all law enforcement agencies of the state.
*(Transferred from Section 79.002, Human Resources Code, by L.1997, chap. 1427(1); renumbered from Art. 62.002 by L.1999, chap. 62(19.01)(8(A)), eff. 9/1/99.)*

### Art. 63.003. Function of clearinghouse.

(a) The clearinghouse is a central repository of information on missing children and missing persons.

(b) The clearinghouse shall:

(1) establish a system of intrastate communication of information relating to missing children and missing persons;

(2) provide a centralized file for the exchange of information on missing children, missing persons, and unidentified dead bodies within the state;

(3) communicate with the national crime information center for the exchange of information on missing children and missing persons suspected of interstate travel;

(4) collect, process, maintain, and disseminate accurate and complete information on missing children and missing persons;

(5) provide a statewide toll-free telephone line for the reporting of missing children and missing persons and for receiving information on missing children and missing persons; and

(6) provide and disseminate to legal custodians, law enforcement agencies, and the Texas Education Agency information that explains how to prevent child abduction and what to do if a child becomes missing.
*(Transferred from Section 79.003, Human Resources Code, and chgd. by L.1997, chap. 1427(1); renumbered from Art. 62.003 by L.1999, chap. 62(19.01)(8(A)), eff. 9/1/99.)*

### Art. 63.004. Report forms.

(a) The Department of Public Safety shall distribute missing children and missing person report forms.

(b) A missing child or missing person report may be made to a law enforcement officer authorized by that department to receive reports in person or by telephone or other indirect method of communication and the officer may enter the information on the form for the reporting person. A report form may also be completed by the reporting person and delivered to a law enforcement officer.

*(Transferred from Section 79.004, Human Resources Code, by L.1997, chap. 1427(1); renumbered from Art. 62.004 by L.1999, chap. 62(19.01)(8(A)), eff. 9/1/99.)*

## Art. 63.005. Distribution of information.

(a) The clearinghouse shall print and distribute posters, flyers, and other forms of information containing descriptions of missing children.

(b) The clearinghouse shall also provide to the Texas Education Agency information about missing children who may be located in the school systems.

(c) The clearinghouse may also receive information about missing children from the Public Education Information Management System of the Texas Education Agency and from school districts.

*(Transferred from Section 79.005, Human Resources Code, and chgd. by L.1997, chap. 1427(1); renumbered from Art. 62.005 by L.1999, chap. 62(19.01)(8(A)), eff. 9/1/99.)*



## Art. 63.006. Release of dental records.

(a) At the time a report is made for a missing child, the person to whom the report is given shall give or mail to the reporter a dental record release form. The officer receiving the report shall endorse the form with the notation that a missing child report has been made in compliance with this chapter. When the form is properly completed by the reporter, and contains the endorsement, the form is sufficient to permit any dentist or physician in this state to release dental records relating to the child reported missing.

(b) At any time a report is made for a missing person the law enforcement officer taking the report shall complete a dental release form that states that the person is missing and that there is reason to believe that the person has not voluntarily relocated or removed himself from communications with others and that authorizes the bearer of the release to obtain dental information records from any dentist or physician in this state.

(c) Any person who obtains dental records through the use of the form authorized by this article shall send the records to the clearinghouse.

(d) The judge of any court of record of this state may for good cause shown authorize the release of dental records of a missing child or missing person.

(e) A dentist or physician who releases dental records to a person presenting a proper release executed or ordered under this article is immune from civil liability or criminal prosecution for the release of those records.

*(Transferred from Section 79.006, Human Resources Code, and chgd. by L.1997, chap. 1427(1); renumbered from Art. 62.006 by L.1999, chap. 62(19.01)(8(A)), eff. 9/1/99; chgd. by L.1999, chap. 685(3), eff. 9/1/99.)*

## Art. 63.007. Release of medical records.

(a) At the time a report is made for a missing child or adult, the law enforcement officer taking the report shall give a medical record release form to the parent, spouse, adult child, or legal guardian who is making the report. The officer receiving the report shall endorse the form with the notation that a missing child or missing adult report has been made in compliance with this chapter. When the form is properly completed by the parent, spouse, adult child, or legal guardian, and contains the endorsement, the form is sufficient to permit any physician, health care facility, or other licensed health care provider in this state to release to the law enforcement officer presenting the release dental records, blood type, height, weight, X rays, and information regarding scars, allergies, or any unusual illnesses suffered by the person who is reported missing. Except as provided by Subsection (d), a medical record of a missing child may be released only if the medical record release form is signed by a parent or legal guardian.

(b) At any time a report is made for an adult missing person, the law enforcement officer taking the report shall complete a medical release form that states that the person is missing and that there is reason to believe that the person has not voluntarily relocated or removed himself or herself from communications with others. A release under this subsection is not valid unless it is signed by the adult missing person's:

(1) spouse;

(2) adult child who is reasonably available;

(3) parent; or

(4) legal guardian.

(c) A law enforcement officer who obtains medical records under this article shall send a copy of the records to the clearinghouse. A law enforcement officer who obtains records under this article, a law enforcement agency using the records, and the clearinghouse are prohibited from disclosing the information contained in or obtained through the medical records unless permitted by law. Information contained in or obtained through medical records may be used only for purposes directly related to locating the missing person.

(d) The judge of any court of record of this state may for good cause shown authorize the release of pertinent medical records of a missing child or missing adult.

(e) A physician, health care facility, or other licensed health care provider releasing a medical record to a person presenting a proper release executed or ordered under this article is immune from civil liability or criminal prosecution for the release of the record.
*(Transferred from Section 79.0065, Human Resources Code, and chgd. by L.1997, chap. 1427(1); renumbered from Art. 62.007 by L.1999, chap. 62(19.01)(8(A)), eff. 9/1/99.)*



### Art. 63.008. Missing children program.

(a) The Texas Education Agency shall develop and administer a program for the location of missing children who may be enrolled within the Texas school system, including nonpublic schools, and for the reporting of children who may be missing or who may be unlawfully removed from schools.

(b) The program shall include the use of information received from the missing children and missing persons information clearinghouse and shall be coordinated with the operations of that information clearinghouse.

(c) The State Board of Education may adopt rules for the operation of the program and shall require the participation of all school districts and accredited private schools in this state.
*(Transferred from Section 79.007, Human Resources Code, and chgd. by L.1997, chap. 1427(1); renumbered from Art. 62.008 by L.1999, chap. 62(19.01)(8(A)), eff. 9/1/99.)*

### Art. 63.009. Law enforcement requirements.

(a) Local law enforcement agencies, on receiving a report of a missing child or a missing person, shall:

(1) if the subject of the report is a child and the well-being of the child is in danger or if the subject of the report is a person who is known by the agency to have or is reported to have chronic dementia, including Alzheimer's dementia, whether caused by illness, brain defect, or brain injury, immediately start an investigation in order to determine the present location of the child or person;

(2) if the subject of the report is a child or person other than a child or person described by Subdivision (1), start an investigation with due diligence in order to determine the present location of the child or person;

(3) immediately enter the name of the child or person into the clearinghouse, the national crime information center missing person file if the child or person meets the center's criteria, and the Alzheimer's Association Safe Return crisis number, if applicable, with all available identifying features such as dental records, fingerprints, other physical characteristics, and a description of the clothing worn when last seen, and all available information describing any person reasonably believed to have taken or retained the missing child or missing person; and

(4) inform the person who filed the report of the missing child or missing person that the information will be entered into the clearinghouse, the national crime information center missing person file, and the Alzheimer's Association Safe Return crisis number, if applicable,

(b) Information not immediately available shall be obtained by the agency and entered into the clearinghouse and the national crime information center file as a supplement to the original entry as soon as possible.

(c) All Texas law enforcement agencies are required to enter information about all unidentified bodies into the clearinghouse and the national crime information center unidentified person file. A law enforcement agency shall, not later than the 10th working day after the date the death is reported to the agency, enter all available identifying features of the unidentified body (fingerprints, dental records, any unusual physical characteristics, and a description of the clothing found on the body) into the clearinghouse and the national crime information center file. If an information entry into the national crime information center file results in an automatic entry of the information into the clearinghouse, the law enforcement agency is not required to make a direct entry of that information into the clearinghouse.

(d) If a local law enforcement agency investigating a report of a missing child or missing person obtains a warrant for the arrest of a person for taking or retaining the missing child or missing person, the local law enforcement agency shall immediately enter the name and other descriptive information of the person into the national crime information center wanted person file if the person meets the center's criteria. The local law enforcement agency shall also enter all available identifying features, including dental records, fingerprints, and other physical characteristics of the missing child or missing person. The information shall be cross-referenced with the information in the national crime information center missing person file.

(e) A local law enforcement agency that has access to the national crime information center database shall cooperate with other law enforcement agencies in entering or retrieving information from the national crime information center database.

(f) Immediately after the return of the missing child or missing person or the identification of an unidentified body, the local law enforcement agency having jurisdiction of the investigation shall cancel the entry in the national crime information center database.

(g) On determining the location of a child under Subsection (a)(1) or (2), other than a child who is subject to the continuing jurisdiction of a district court, an officer shall take possession of the child and shall deliver or arrange for the delivery of the child to a person entitled to possession of the child. If the person entitled to possession of the child is not immediately available, the law enforcement officer shall deliver the child to the Department of Protective and Regulatory Services.

*(Transferred from Section 79.008, Human Resources Code, and chgd. by L.1997, chap. 1427(1); renumbered from Art. 62.009 and chgd. by L.1999, chap. 62(3.11), (3.12), (19.01)(8(A)), eff. 9/1/99; chgd. by L.1999, chaps. 200(1), (2), 685(4), (5), eff. 9/1/99.)*



### Art. 63.010. Attorney general to require compliance.

The attorney general shall require each law enforcement agency to comply with this chapter and may seek writs of mandamus or other appropriate remedies to enforce this chapter. *(Transferred from Section 79.009, Human Resources Code, by L.1997, chap. 1427(1); renumbered from Art. 62.010 by L.1999, chap. 62(19.01)(8(A)), eff. 9/1/99.)*

### Art. 63.011. Missing children investigations.

On the written request made to a law enforcement agency by a parent, foster parent, managing or possessory conservator, guardian of the person or the estate, or other court-appointed custodian of a child whose whereabouts are unknown, the law enforcement agency shall request from the missing children and missing persons information clearinghouse information concerning the child that may aid the person making the request in the identification or location of the child. *(Transferred from Section 79.010, Human Resources Code, by L.1997, chap. 1427(1); renumbered from Art. 62.011 by L.1999, chap. 62(19.01)(8(A)), eff. 9/1/99.)*

### Art. 63.012. Report of inquiry.

A law enforcement agency to which a request has been made under Article 63.011 of this code shall report to the parent on the results of its inquiry within 14 days after the day that the written request is filed with the law enforcement agency. *(Transferred from Section 79.011, Human Resources Code, and chgd. by L.1997, chap. 1427(1); renumbered from Art. 62.012 and chgd. by L.1999, chap. 62(19.01)(8(A)), (19.02(1)), eff. 9/1/99.)*

### Art. 63.013. Information to clearinghouse.

Each law enforcement agency shall provide to the missing children and missing persons information clearinghouse any information that would assist in the location or identification of any missing child who has been reported to the agency as missing. *(Transferred from Section 79.012, Human Resources Code, by L.1997, chap. 1427(1); renumbered from Art. 62.013 by L.1999, chap. 62(19.01)(8(A)), eff. 9/1/99.)*

### Art. 63.014. Cross-checking and matching.

(a) The clearinghouse shall cross-check and attempt to match unidentified bodies with missing children or missing persons. When the clearinghouse discovers a possible match between an unidentified body and a missing child or missing person, the Department of Public Safety shall notify the appropriate law enforcement agencies.

(b) Those law enforcement agencies that receive notice of a possible match shall make arrangements for positive identification and complete and close out the investigation with notification to the clearinghouse.

*(Transferred from Section 79.013, Human Resources Code, by L.1997, chap. 1427(1); renumbered from Art. 62.014 by L.1999, chap. 62(19.01)(8(A)), eff. 9/1/99.)*

**Art. 63.015. Availability of information through other agencies.**

(a) On the request of any law enforcement agency, a city or state agency shall furnish the law enforcement agency with any information about a missing child or missing person that will assist in completing the investigation.

(b) The information given under Subsection (a) of this article is confidential and may not be released to any other person outside of the law enforcement agency.

*(Transferred from Section 79.014, Human Resources Code, and chgd. by L.1997, chap. 1427(1); renumbered from Art. 62.015 by L.1999, chap. 62(19.01)(8(A)), eff. 9/1/99.)*

**Art. 63.016. Donations.**

The Department of Public Safety may accept money donated from any source to assist in financing the activities and purposes of the missing children and missing persons information clearinghouse. *(Transferred from Section 79.015, Human Resources Code, by L.1997, chap. 1427(1); renumbered from Art. 62.016 by L.1999, chap. 62(19.01)(8(A)), eff. 9/1/99.)*

**Art. 63.017. Confidentiality of certain records.**

Clearinghouse records that relate to the investigation by a law enforcement agency of a missing child, a missing person, or an unidentified body and records or notations that the clearinghouse maintains for internal use in matters relating to missing children, missing persons, or unidentified bodies are confidential. *(Transferred from Section 79.016, Human Resources Code, by L.1997, chap. 1427(1); renumbered from Art. 62.017 by L.1999, chap. 62(19.01)(8(A)), eff. 9/1/99.)*

**Art. 63.018. Death certificates.**

A physician who performs a postmortem examination on the body of an unidentified person shall complete and file a death certificate in accordance with Chapter 193, Health and Safety Code. The physician shall note on the certificate the name of the law enforcement agency that submitted the body for examination and shall send a copy of the certificate to the clearinghouse not later than the 10th working day after the date the physician files the certificate. *(Added by L.1997, chap. 1427(1); renumbered from Art. 62.018 by L.1999, chap. 62(19.01)(8(A)), eff. 9/1/99.)*

**Art. 63.019. School records system.**

(a) On enrollment of a child under 11 years of age in a school for the first time at the school, the school shall:

(1) request from the person enrolling the child the name of each previous school attended by the child;

(2) request from each school identified in Subdivision (1), the school records for the child and, if the person enrolling the child provides copies of previous school records, request verification from the school of the child's name, address, birth date, and grades and dates attended; and

(3) notify the person enrolling the student that not later than the 30th day after enrollment, or the 90th day if the child was not born in the United States, the person must provide:

(A) a certified copy of the child's birth certificate; or

(B) other reliable proof of the child's identity and age and a signed statement explaining the person's inability to produce a copy of the child's birth certificate.

(b) If a person enrolls a child under 11 years of age in school and does not provide the valid prior school information or documentation required by this section, the school shall notify the appropriate law enforcement agency before the 31st day after the person fails to comply with this section. On receipt of notification, the law enforcement agency shall immediately check the clearinghouse to determine if the child has been reported missing. If the child has been reported missing, the law enforcement agency shall immediately notify other appropriate law enforcement agencies that the missing child has been located.

*(Transferred from Human Resources Code Section 79.017 by L.1999, chap. 62(19.01)(8(B)), eff. 9/1/99.)*

**Art. 63.020. Duty of schools and other entities to flag missing children's records.**

(a) When a report that a child under 11 years of age is missing is received by a law enforcement agency, the agency shall immediately notify each school and day care facility that the child attended or in which the child was enrolled as well as the bureau of vital statistics, if the child was born in the state, that the child is missing.

(b) On receipt of notice that a child under 11 years of age is missing, the bureau of vital statistics shall notify the appropriate municipal or county birth certificate agency that the child is missing.

(c) A school, day care facility, or birth certificate agency that receives notice concerning a child under this section shall flag the child's records that are maintained by the school, facility, or agency.

(d) The law enforcement agency shall notify the clearinghouse that the notification required under this section has been made. The clearinghouse shall provide the notice required under this section if the clearinghouse determines that the notification has not been made by the law enforcement agency.

(e) If a missing child under 11 years of age, who was the subject of a missing child report made in this state, was born in or attended a school or licensed day care facility in another state, the law enforcement agency shall notify law enforcement or the missing and exploited children clearinghouse in each appropriate state regarding the missing child and request the law enforcement agency or clearinghouse to contact the state birth certificate agency and each school or licensed day care facility the missing child attended to flag the missing child's records.

*(Transferred from Human Resources Code Section 79.018 by L.1999, chap. 62(19.01)(8(B)), eff. 9/1/99.)*



### Art. 63.021. System for flagging records.

(a) On receipt of notification by a law enforcement agency or the clearinghouse regarding a missing child under 11 years of age, the school, day care facility, or birth certificate agency shall maintain the child's records in its possession so that on receipt of a request regarding the child, the school, day care facility, or agency will be able to notify law enforcement or the clearinghouse that a request for a flagged record has been made.

(b) When a request concerning a flagged record is made in person, the school, day care facility, or agency may not advise the requesting party that the request concerns a missing child and shall:

(1) require the person requesting the flagged record to complete a form stating the person's name, address, telephone number, and relationship to the child for whom a request is made and the name, address, and birth date of the child;

(2) obtain a copy of the requesting party's driver's license or other photographic identification, if possible;

(3) if the request is for a birth certificate, inform the requesting party that a copy of a certificate will be sent by mail; and

(4) immediately notify the appropriate law enforcement agency that a request has been made concerning a flagged record and include a physical description of the requesting party, the identity and address of the requesting party, and a copy of the requesting party's driver's license or other photographic identification.

(c) After providing the notification required under Subsection (a)(4), the school, day care facility, or agency shall mail a copy of the requested record to the requesting party on or after the 21st day after the date of the request.

(d) When a request concerning a flagged record is made in writing, the school, day care facility, or agency may not advise the party that the request concerns a missing child and shall immediately notify the appropriate law enforcement agency that a request has been made concerning a flagged record and provide to the law enforcement agency a copy of the written request. After providing the notification under this subsection, the school, day care facility, or agency shall mail a copy of the requested record to the requesting party on or after the 21st day after the date of the request.

*(Transferred from Human Resources Code Section 79.019 by L.1999, chap. 62(19.01)(8(B)), eff. 9/1/99.)*

### Art. 63.022. Removal of flag from records.

(a) On the return of a missing child under 11 years of age, the law enforcement agency shall notify each school or day care facility that has maintained flagged records for the child and the bureau of vital statistics that the child is no longer missing. The law enforcement agency shall notify the clearinghouse that notification under this section has been made. The bureau of vital statistics shall notify the appropriate municipal or county birth certificate agency. The clearinghouse shall notify the school, day care facility, or bureau of vital statistics that the missing child is no longer missing if the clearinghouse determines that the notification was not provided by the law enforcement agency.

(b) On notification by the law enforcement agency or the clearinghouse that a missing child has been recovered, the school, day care facility, or birth certificate agency that maintained flagged records shall remove the flag from the records.

(c) A school, day care facility, or birth certificate agency that has reason to believe a missing child has been recovered may request confirmation that the missing child has been recovered from the appropriate law enforcement agency or the clearinghouse. If a response is not received after the 45th day after the date of the request for confirmation, the school, day care facility, or birth certificate agency may remove the flag from the record and shall inform the law enforcement agency or the clearinghouse that the flag has been removed.
*(Transferred from Human Resources Code Section 79.020 by L.1999, chap. 62(19.01)(8(B)), eff. 9/1/99.)*

**Art. 63.023.** *(Transferred from Human Resources Code Section 79.017 by L.1999, chap. 62(19.01)(8(C)), eff. 9/1/99; chgd. by L.1999, chap. 62(19.02(2)), eff. 9/1/99; repealed by L.1999, chap. 1081(8), eff. 9/1/99.)*

**Art. 63.024.** *(Transferred from Human Resources Code Section 79.018 by L.1999, chap. 62(19.01)(8(C)), eff. 9/1/99; chgd. by L.1999, chap. 62(19.02(3)), eff. 9/1/99; repealed by L.1999, chap. 1081(8), eff. 9/1/99.)*

# TITLE 2



## CHAPTER 101. GENERAL PROVISIONS



### Art. 101.001. Purpose of title.

(a) This title is enacted as a part of the state's continuing statutory revision program, begun by the Texas Legislative Council in 1963 as directed by the legislature in Chapter 448, Acts of the 58th Legislature, Regular Session, 1963 (Article 5429b-1, Texas Civil Statutes). The program contemplates a topic-by-topic revision of the state's general and permanent statute law without substantive change.

(b) Consistent with the objectives of the statutory revision program, the purpose of this title is to make the law encompassed by this title more accessible and understandable by:

(1) rearranging the statutes into a more logical order;

(2) employing a format and numbering system designed to facilitate citation of the law and to accommodate future expansion of the law;

(3) eliminating repealed, duplicative, unconstitutional, expired, executed, and other ineffective provisions, and;

(4) restating the law in modern American English to the greatest extent possible.

### Art. 101.002. Construction of titles.

The Code Construction Act (Article 5429b-2, Texas Civil Statutes) applies to the construction of each provision in this title, except as otherwise expressly provided by this title.

### Art. 101.003. Internal references.

In this title:

(1) a reference to a chapter or article without further identification is a reference to a chapter or article of this title; and

(2) a reference to a subchapter, article, subsection, subdivision, paragraph, or other numbered or lettered unit without further identification is a reference to a unit of the next larger unit of this title in which the reference appears.

Printed in the U.S.A. 17

# CHAPTER 102. COSTS PAID BY DEFENDANTS

## SUBCHAPTER A. GENERAL COSTS

Article


## SUBCHAPTER B. CRIMINAL JUSTICE PLANNING FUND



## SUBCHAPTER C. COURT COSTS AND FEES



## SUBCHAPTER D. COMPREHENSIVE REHABILITATION FUND



## SUBCHAPTER A. GENERAL COSTS

### Art. 102.001. Fees for services of peace officers.

(a) *(Repealed.)*

(b) In addition to fees provided by Subsection (a), a defendant required to pay fees under this article shall also pay 15 cents per mile for mileage required of an officer to perform a service listed in this subsection and to return from performing that service. If the service provided is the execution of a writ and the writ is directed to two or more persons or the officer executes more than one writ in a case, the defendant is required to pay only mileage actually and necessarily traveled. In calculating mileage, the officer must use the railroad or the most practical route by private conveyance. This subsection applies to:

(1) conveying a prisoner after conviction to the county jail;

(2) conveying a prisoner arrested on a warrant or capias issued in another county to the court or jail of the county in which the warrant or capias was issued; and

(3) traveling to execute criminal process, to summon or attach a witness, and to execute process not otherwise described by this article.

(c) to (e) *(Repealed.)*

(f) An officer who receives fees imposed under Subsection (a)(1) of this section in a municipal court shall keep separate records of the funds collected and shall deposit the funds in the municipal treasury. The officer collecting the fees under Subsection (a)(1) or (a)(2) of this article in a justice, county, or district court shall keep separate records of the funds collected and shall deposit the funds in the county treasury.

(g) *(Repealed.)*

(h) The custodian of a municipal or county treasury who receives fees under Subsection (a)(1) of this article for services performed by peace officers employed by the state shall remit all fees to the comptroller of public accounts in the manner directed by the comptroller. The custodian of a county treasury who receives fees under Subsection (a)(2) of this article for services performed by peace officers employed by the state may retain $2 of the fee for the county and shall forward the remainder to the comptroller in the manner directed by the comptroller. All custodians of municipal and county treasuries who receive fees under Subsection (a)(1) or (a)(2) of this article shall keep records of the amount of funds collected that are on deposit with them and, not later than the last day of the month following each calendar quarter, shall remit to the comptroller funds collected under Subsection (a)(1) or (a)(2) of this article during the preceding quarter in a manner directed by the comptroller. The municipality or county may retain all interest earned on those funds. The comptroller shall credit funds received under this subsection to the General Revenue Fund.

*(Chgd. by L.1989, chaps. 2(16.01(12)), 347(1), 826(2), eff. 8/28/89, 10/1/89, 9/1/89, respectively.)*

### Art. 102.002. Witness fees.

(a) *(Repealed by L.1999, chap. 580(11(a)), eff. 9/1/99.)*

(b) The justices of the peace and municipal courts shall maintain a record of and the clerks of district and county courts and county courts at law shall keep a book and record in the book:

(1) the number and style of each criminal action before the court;

(2) the name of each witness subpoenaed, attached, or recognized to testify in the action; and

(3) whether the witness was a witness for the state or for the defendant.

(c) Except as otherwise provided by this subsection, a defendant is liable on conviction for the fees provided by this article for witnesses in the defendant's case. If a defendant convicted of a misdemeanor does not pay the defendant's fines and costs, the county or municipality, as appropriate, is liable for the fees provided by this article for witnesses in the defendant's case.

*(Subsections (b) and (c) chgd. by L.1999, chap. 1545(63), eff. 9/1/99; repealed by L.1999, chap. 580(11(a)), eff. 9/1/99.)*

(d) if a person is subpoenaed as a witness in a criminal case and fails to appear, the person is liable for the costs of an attachment, unless he shows good cause to the court why he did not appear.

### Art. 102.003. *(Repealed by L.1995, chap. 122(4), eff. 9/1/95.)*

### Art. 102.004. Jury fee.

(a) A defendant convicted by a jury in a trial before a justice or municipal court shall pay a jury fee of $3. A defendant in a justice or municipal court who requests a trial by jury and who withdraws the request not earlier than 24 hours before the time of trial shall pay a jury fee of $3, if the defendant is convicted of the offense or final disposition of the defendant's case is deferred. A defendant convicted by a jury in a county court, a county court at law, or a district court shall pay a jury fee of $20.

(b) If two or more defendants are tried jointly in a justice or municipal court, only one jury fee of $3 may be imposed under this article. If the defendants sever and are tried separately, each defendant convicted shall pay a jury fee.

*(Chgd. by L.1989, chap. 1080(3); L.1995, chap. 122(2); L.1999, chap. 1545(64), eff. 9/1/99.)*

### Art. 102.005. Fees to clerks.

(a) A defendant convicted of an offense in a county court, a county court at law, or a district court shall pay for the services of the clerk of the court a fee of $40.

(b) In this article, a person is considered convicted if:

(1) a sentence is imposed on the person;

(2) the person receives community supervision, including deferred adjudication; or

(3) the court defers final disposition of the person's case.

(c) Except as provided by Subsection (d), the fee imposed under Subsection (a) is for all clerical duties performed by the clerk, including:

(1) filing a complaint or information;

(2) docketing the case;

(3) taxing costs against the defendant;

(4) issuing original writs and subpoenas;

(5) swearing in and impaneling a jury;

(6) receiving and recording the verdict;

(7) filing each paper entered in the case; and

(8) swearing in witnesses in the case.

(d) The fee imposed by law for issuing a certified or noncertified copy is in addition to the fee imposed by Subsection (a). The clerk may issue a copy only if a person requests the copy and pays the appropriate fee as required by Sections 118.011, 118.014, 118.0145, 118.052, 118.060, and 118.0605, Local Government Code, and Sections 51.318 and 51.319, Government Code.

(e) *(Repealed.)*

(f) A defendant convicted of an offense in a county court, a county court at law, or a district court shall pay a fee of $20 for records management and preservation services performed by the county as required by Chapter 203, Local Government Code. The fee shall be collected and distributed by the clerk of the court in the same manner as fees are collected and distributed under Section 51.317(c), Government Code. The fee received by a county shall be placed in a special fund to be called the records management and preservation fund. The fee shall be used only for records management and preservation purposes in the county as required by Chapter 203, Local Government Code. No expenditures may be made from this fund without prior approval of the commissioners court.

*(Chgd. by L.1989, chap. 1080(4); L.1993, chap. 675(6); L.1995, chap. 764(1); L.1999, chaps. 580(11(b)), 1031(1), eff. 9/1/99.)*



## Art. 102.006. Fees in expunction proceedings.

A petitioner seeking expunction of a criminal record shall pay the following fees:

(1) the fee charged for filing an ex parte petition in a civil action in district court;

(2) $1 plus postage for each certified mailing of notice of the hearing date; and

(3) $2 plus postage for each certified mailing of certified copies of an order of expunction.

## Art. 102.007. Fee for collecting and processing sight order.

(a) A county attorney, district attorney, or criminal district attorney may collect a fee if his office collects and processes a check or similar sight order if the check or similar sight order:

(1) has been issued or passed in a manner that makes the issuance or passing an offense under:

(A) Section 31.03, Penal Code;

(B) Section 31.04, Penal Code; or

(C) Section 32.41, Penal Code; or

(2) has been forged, as defined by Section 32.21, Penal Code.

(b) The county attorney, district attorney, or criminal district attorney may collect the fee from any person who is a party to the offense described in Subsection (a).

(c) The amount of the fee may not exceed:

(1) $10 if the face amount of the check or sight order does not exceed $10;

(2) $15 if the face amount of the check or sight order is greater than $10 but does not exceed $100;

(3) $30 if the face amount of the check or sight order is greater than $100 but does not exceed $300;

(4) $50 if the face amount of the check or sight order is greater than $300 but does not exceed $500; and

(5) $75 if the face amount of the check or sight order is greater than $500.

(d) If the person from whom the fee is collected was a party to the offense of forgery, as defined by Section 32.21, Penal Code, committed by altering the face amount of the check or sight order, the face amount as altered governs for the purposes of determining the amount of the fee.

(e) In addition to the collection fee specified in Subsection (c) of this article, the county attorney, district attorney, or criminal district attorney may collect the fee authorized by Article 9022, Texas Civil Statutes, for the benefit of the holder of a check or its assignee, agent, representative, or any other person retained by the holder to seek collection of the check.

(f) Fees collected under Subsection (c) of this article shall be deposited in the county treasury in a special fund to be administered by the county attorney, district attorney, or criminal district attorney. Expenditures from this fund shall be at the sole discretion of the attorney and may be used only to defray the salaries and expenses of the prosecutor's office, but in no event may the county attorney, district attorney, or criminal district attorney supplement his own salary from this fund.

*(Chgd. by L.1991, chap. 396(2); L.1997, chap. 256(1); L.1999, chap. 49(1), eff. 9/1/99.)*

## Art. 102.0071. Justice court dishonored check.

On conviction in justice court of an offense under Section 32.41, Penal Code, or an offense under Section 31.03 or 31.04, Penal Code, in which it is shown that the defendant committed the offense by issuing or passing a check that was subsequently dishonored, the court may collect from the defendant and pay to the holder of the check the fee permitted by Article 9022, Texas Civil Statutes. *(Added by L.1991, chap. 396(2), eff. 9/1/91.)*

**Art. 102.008. Fees for services of prosecutors.**

(a) Except as provided by Subsection (b), a defendant convicted of a misdemeanor or a gambling offense shall pay a fee of $25 for the trying of the case by the district or county attorney. If the court appoints an attorney to represent the state in the absence of the district or county attorney, the appointed attorney is entitled to the fee otherwise due.

(b) No fee for the trying of a case may be charged against a defendant prosecuted in a justice court for violation of a penal statute or of the Uniform Act Regulating Traffic on Highways (Article 6701d, Texas Civil Statutes).

(c) If two or more defendants are tried jointly, only one fee may be charged under this article. if the defendants sever and are tried separately, each defendant shall pay the fee.

(d) A defendant is liable for fees imposed by Subsection (a) if the defendant is convicted of an offense and:

(1) the defendant does not appeal the conviction; or

(2) the conviction is affirmed on appeal.

*(Chgd. by L.1989, chap. 1080(5), eff. 9/1/89.)*

**Art. 102.009. Court costs in certain counties.**

In counties with a population of two million or more according to the most recent federal census, the commissioners court may set court costs for persons convicted of a Class C misdemeanor in the justice courts. Court costs set as provided by this article may not exceed $7 for each conviction.

**Art. 102.011. Fees for services of peace officers in certain counties.**

(a) A defendant convicted of a felony or a misdemeanor shall pay the following fees for services performed in the case by a peace officer:

(1) $5 for issuing a written notice to appear in court following the defendant's violation of a traffic law, municipal ordinance, or penal law of this state, or for making an arrest without a warrant;

(2) $50 for executing or processing an issued arrest warrant or capias, with the fee imposed for the services of:

(A) the law enforcement agency that executed the arrest warrant or capias, if the agency requests of the court, not later than the 15th day after the date of the execution of the arrest warrant or capias, the imposition of the fee on conviction; or

(B) the law enforcement agency that processed the arrest warrant or capias, if the executing law enforcement agency failed to request the fee within the period required by Paragraph (A) of this subdivision;

(3) $5 for summoning a witness;

(4) $35 for serving a writ not otherwise listed in this article;

(5) $10 for taking and approving a bond and, if necessary, returning the bond to the courthouse;

(6) $5 for commitment or release;

(7) $5 for summoning a jury, if a jury is summoned; and

(8) $8 for each day's attendance of a prisoner in a habeas corpus case if the prisoner has been remanded to custody or held to bail.

(b) In addition to fees provided by Subsection (a) of this article, a defendant required to pay fees under this article shall also pay 29 cents per mile for mileage required of an officer to perform a service listed in this subsection and to return from performing that service. If the service provided is the execution of a writ and the writ is directed to two or more persons or the officer executes more than one writ in a case, the defendant is required to pay only mileage actually and necessarily traveled. In calculating mileage, the officer must use the railroad or the most practical route by private conveyance. The defendant shall also pay all necessary and reasonable expenses for meals and lodging incurred by the officer in the performance of services under this subsection, to the extent such expenses meet the requirements of Section 611.001, Government Code. This subsection applies to:

(1) conveying a prisoner after conviction to the county jail;

(2) conveying a prisoner arrested on a warrant or capias issued in another county to the court or jail of the county; and

(3) traveling to execute criminal process, to summon or attach a witness, and to execute process not otherwise described by this article.

(c) if an officer attaches a witness on the order of a court outside the county, the defendant shall pay $10 per day or part of a day spent by the officer conveying the witness and actual necessary expenses for travel by the most practical public conveyance. In order to receive expenses under this subsection, the officer must make a sworn statement of the expenses and the judge issuing the attachment must approve the statement.

(d) A defendant shall pay for the services of a sheriff or constable who serves process and attends an examining trial in a felony or a misdemeanor case the same fees allowed for those services in the trial of a felony or a misdemeanor, not to exceed $5.

(e) A fee under Subsection (a)(1) or (a)(2) of this article shall be assessed on conviction, regardless of whether the defendant was also arrested at the same time for another offense, and shall be assessed for each arrest made of a defendant arising out of the offense for which the defendant has been convicted.

(f) The custodian of a municipal or county treasury who receives fees imposed under this article for services performed by peace officers employed by the state shall forward the fees to the comptroller of public accounts by the last day of the month following each calendar quarter after deducting four-fifths of the amount of each fee received for a service performed under Subsection (a)(1) or (a)(2) of this article, in a manner directed by the comptroller. The municipality or county may retain all interest earned on those funds.

(g) The custodian of a municipal or county treasury shall keep a record of the amount of fees he collects under this article for services performed by peace officers employed by the state. If a custodian does not collect any fees described by this subsection during a calendar quarter, the custodian shall file a report with the comptroller of public accounts on the last day of that quarter stating that the custodian did not collect any fees described by this subsection during that quarter.

(h) The comptroller of public accounts shall credit fees received under Subsection (f) of this article to the general revenue fund.

(i) In addition to fees provided by Subsections (a) through (g) of this article, a defendant required to pay fees under this article shall also pay the costs of overtime paid to a peace officer for time spent testifying in the trial of the case or for traveling to or from testifying in the trial of the case.

*(Chgd. by L.1989, chap. 826(1); L.1991, chap. 575(1); L.1993, chap. 988(2.04); L.1995, chaps. 267(1), 560(1); L.1999, chap. 44(1), eff. 9/1/99.)*

## Art. 102.012. Fees for pretrial intervention programs.

A person in a pretrial intervention program established under Section 76.011, Government Code, may be assessed a fee that equals the actual cost to a community supervision and corrections department, not to exceed $500, for supervision of the defendant by the department or programs provided to the defendant by the department as part of the pretrial intervention program. *(Added by L.1990, 6th C.S., chap. 25(20); chgd. by L.1995, chap. 76(7.16), eff. 9/1/95.)*

## Art. 102.013. Court costs; crime stoppers assistance account.

(a) The legislature shall appropriate funds from the crime stoppers assistance account to the Criminal Justice Division of the Governor's Office. The Criminal Justice Division may use 10 percent of the funds for the operation of the toll-free telephone service under Section 414.012, Government Code, and shall distribute the remainder of the funds only to crime stoppers organizations. The Criminal Justice Division may adopt a budget and rules to implement the distribution of these funds.

(b) All funds distributed by the Criminal Justice Division under Subsection (a) of this article are subject to audit by the State auditor. All funds collected or distributed are subject to audit by the Governor's Division of Planning Coordination.

(c) In this article, "crime stoppers organization" has the meaning assigned by Section 414.001, Government Code.

*(Added by L.1990, 6th C.S., chap. 28(1); redesignated from Article 102.012 by L.1991, chap. 16(19.01(7)); chgd. by L.1991, chap. 727(2); L.1993, chap. 807(2); L.1997, chaps. 700(13), 1100(1), eff. 9/1/97.)*

## Art. 102.014. Court costs for child safety fund in municipalities.

(a) The governing body of a municipality with a population greater than 850,000 according to the most recent federal decennial census that has adopted an ordinance, regulation, or order regulating the stopping, standing, or parking of vehicles as allowed by Section 542.202, Transportation Code, or Chapter 682, Transportation Code, shall by order assess a court cost on each parking violation not less than $2 and not to exceed $5. The court costs under this subsection shall be collected in the same manner that other fines in the case are collected.

(b) The governing body of a municipality with a population less than 850,000 according to the most recent federal decennial census that has adopted an ordinance, regulation, or order regulating the stopping, standing, or parking of vehicles as allowed by Section 542.202, Transportation Code, or Chapter 682, Transportation Code, may by order assess a court cost on each parking violation not to exceed $5. The additional court cost under this subsection shall be collected in the same manner that other fines in the case are collected.

(c) A person convicted of an offense under Subtitle C, Title 7, Transportation Code, when the offense occurs within a school crossing zone as defined by Section 541.302 of that code, shall pay as court costs $25 in addition to other taxable court costs. A person convicted of an offense under Section 545.066, Transportation Code, shall pay as court costs $25 in addition to other taxable court costs. The additional court costs under this subsection shall be collected in the same manner that other fines and taxable court costs in the case are collected and shall be assessed only in a municipality with a population of 400,000 or more.

(d) A person convicted of an offense under Section 25.093, Education Code, or a child convicted of an offense under Section 25.094, Education Code, shall pay as taxable court costs $20 in addition to other taxable court costs. The additional court costs under this subsection shall be collected in the same manner that other fines and taxable court costs in the case are collected.

(e) In this article, a person is considered to have been convicted in a case if:

(1) a sentence is imposed;

(2) the defendant receives probation or deferred adjudication; or

(3) the court defers final disposition of the case.

(f) In a municipality with a population greater than 850,000 according to the most recent federal decennial census, the officer collecting the costs in a municipal court case shall deposit money collected under this article in the municipal child safety trust fund established as required by Chapter 106, Local Government Code.

(g) In a municipality with a population less than 850,000 according to the most recent federal decennial census, the money collected under this article in a municipal court case must be used for a school crossing guard program if the municipality operates one. If the municipality does not operate a school crossing guard program or if the money received from court costs from municipal court cases exceeds the amount necessary to fund the school crossing guard program, the municipality may either deposit the additional money in an interest-bearing account or expend it for programs designed to enhance child safety, health, or nutrition, including child abuse prevention and intervention and drug and alcohol abuse prevention.

(h) Money collected under this article in a justice, county, or district court shall be used to fund school crossing guard programs in the county where they are collected. If the county does not operate a school crossing guard program, the county may:

(1) remit fee revenues to school districts in its jurisdiction for the purpose of providing school crossing guard services;

(2) fund programs the county is authorized by law to provide which are designed to enhance child safety, health, or nutrition, including child abuse prevention and intervention and drug and alcohol abuse prevention;

(3) provide funding to the sheriff's department for school-related activities;

(4) provide funding to the county juvenile probation department; or

(5) deposit the money in the general fund of the county.

(i) Each collecting officer shall keep separate records of money collected under this article.

*(Added by L.1991, chap. 830(2); chgd. by L.1995, chap. 76(10.03); L.1997, chaps. 50(1), 165(6.05), 1384(1), eff. 9/1/97.)*

**Art. 102.015.** *(Repealed by L.1997, chap. 1100(6(2)), eff. 9/1/97.)*

**Art. 102.016. Costs for breath alcohol testing program.**

(a) The custodians of municipal and county treasuries may deposit funds collected under this article in interest-bearing accounts and retain for the municipality or county interest earned on the funds. The custodians shall keep records of funds received and disbursed under this article and shall provide a yearly report of all funds received and disbursed under this article to the comptroller, the Department of Public Safety, and to each agency in the county served by the court that participates in or maintains a certified breath alcohol testing program. The comptroller shall approve the form of the report.

(b) The custodian of a municipal or county treasury in a county that maintains a certified breath alcohol testing program but does not use the services of a certified technical supervisor employed by the department may, to defray the costs of maintaining and supporting a certified alcohol breath testing program, retain $22.50 of each court cost collected under Article 102.075 on conviction of an offense under Chapter 49, Penal Code, other than an offense that is a Class C misdemeanor.

(c) The legislature may appropriate money deposited to the credit of the breath alcohol testing account in the general revenue fund under this subsection to the Department of Public Safety for use by the department in the implementation, administration, and maintenance of the statewide certified breath alcohol testing program.

(d) The Department of Public Safety shall maintain a list of counties that do not use the services of a certified technical supervisor employed by the department.

*(Added by L.1991, 1st C.S., chap. 5(5.03(a)); chgd. by L.1993, chap. 900(3.03); L.1997, chap. 1100(2), eff. 9/1/97.)*

**Art. 102.017. Court costs; courthouse security fund; municipal court building security fund.**

(a) A defendant convicted of a felony offense in a district court shall pay a $5 security fee as a cost of court.

(b) A defendant convicted of a misdemeanor offense in a justice court, county court, county court at law, or district court shall pay a $3 security fee as a cost of court. The governing body of a municipality by ordinance may create a municipal court building security fund and may require a defendant convicted of a misdemeanor offense in a municipal court to pay a $3 security fee as a cost of court.

(c) In this article, a person is considered convicted if:

(1) a sentence is imposed on the person;

(2) the person receives community supervision, including deferred adjudication; or

(3) the court defers final disposition of the person's case.

(d) The clerks of the respective courts shall collect the costs and pay them to the county or municipal treasurer, as appropriate, or to any other official who discharges the duties commonly delegated to the county or municipal treasurer, as appropriate, for deposit in a fund to be known as the courthouse security fund or a fund to be known as the municipal court building security fund, as appropriate. A fund designated by this subsection may be used only to finance items when used for the purpose of providing security services for buildings housing a district, county, justice, or municipal court, as appropriate, including:

(1) the purchase or repair of X-ray machines and conveying systems;

(2) handheld metal detectors;

(3) walkthrough metal detectors;

(4) identification cards and systems;

(5) electronic locking and surveillance equipment;

(6) bailiffs, deputy sheriffs, deputy constables, or contract security personnel during times when they are providing appropriate security services;

(7) signage;

(8) confiscated weapon inventory and tracking systems;

(9) locks, chains, alarms, or similar security devices;

(10) the purchase or repair of bullet-proof glass; and

(11) continuing education on security issues for court personnel and security personnel.

(e) The courthouse security fund shall be administered by or under the direction of the commissioners court. The municipal court building fund shall be administered by or under the direction of the governing body of the municipality.

*(Added by L.1993, chap. 818(1); chgd. by L.1995, chap. 764(2); L.1997, chap. 12(1); L.1999, chap. 110(1), eff. 5/17/99.)*

**Art. 102.0171. Court costs: graffiti eradication funds.**

(a) A defendant convicted of an offense under Section 28.08, Penal Code, in a county court, county court at law, or district court shall pay a $5 graffiti eradication fee as a cost of court.

(b) In this article, a person is considered convicted if:

(1) a sentence is imposed on the person;

(2) the person receives community supervision, including deferred adjudication; or

(3) the court defers final disposition of the person's case.

(c) The clerks of the respective courts shall collect the costs and pay them to the county treasurer or to any other official who discharges the duties commonly delegated to the county treasurer for deposit in a fund to be known as the county graffiti eradication fund. A fund designated by this subsection may be used only to:

(1) repair damage caused by the commission of offenses under Section 28.08, Penal Code;

(2) provide educational and intervention programs designed to prevent individuals from committing offenses under Section 28.08, Penal Code; and

(3) provide to the public rewards for identifying and aiding in the apprehension and prosecution of offenders who commit offenses under Section 28.08, Penal Code.

(d) The county graffiti eradication fund shall be administered by or under the direction of the commissioners court.

*(Added by L.1997, chap. 593(2), eff. 9/1/97.)*

**Art. 102.0172. Court courts; municipal court technology fund.**

(a) The governing body of a municipality by ordinance may create a municipal court technology fund and may require a defendant convicted of a misdemeanor offense in a municipal court or municipal court of record to pay a technology fee not to exceed $4 as a cost of court.

(b) In this article, a person is considered convicted if:

(1) a sentenced is imposed on the person;

(2) the person is placed on community supervision, including deferred adjudication community supervision; or

(3) the court defers final disposition of the person's case.

(c) The municipal court clerk shall collect the costs and pay the funds to the municipal treasurer, or to any other official who discharges the duties commonly delegated to the municipal treasurer, for deposit in a fund to be known as the municipal court technology fund.

(d) A fund designated by this article may be used only to finance the purchase of technological enhancements for a municipal court or municipal court of record, including:

(1) computer systems;

(2) computer networks;

(3) computer hardware;

(4) computer software;

(5) imaging systems;

(6) electronic kiosks;

(7) electronic ticket writers; and

(8) docket management systems.

(e) The municipal court technology fund shall be administered by or under the direction of the governing body of the municipality.

(f) This article expires September 1, 2005.

*(Added by L.1999, chap. 285(1), eff. 9/1/99, expires 9/1/2005.)*

**Art. 102.018. Costs attendant to intoxication convictions.**

(a) Except as provided by Subsection (d) of this article, on conviction of an offense relating to the driving or operating of a motor vehicle under Section 49.04, Penal Code, the court shall impose a cost of $15 on a defendant if, subsequent to the arrest of the defendant, a law enforcement agency visually recorded the defendant with an electronic device. Costs imposed under this subsection are in addition to other court costs and are due whether or not the defendant is granted probation in the case. The court shall collect the costs in the same manner as other costs are collected in the case.

(b) Except as provided by Subsection (d) of this article, on conviction of an offense relating to the driving or operating of a motor vehicle punishable under Section 49.04(b), Penal Code, the court shall impose as a cost of court on the defendant an amount that is equal to the cost of an evaluation of the defendant performed under Section 13(a), Article 42.12, of this code. Costs imposed under this subsection are in addition to other court costs and are due whether or not the defendant is granted probation in the case, except that if the court determines that the defendant is indigent and unable to pay the cost, the court may waive the imposition of the cost.

(c)(1) Except as provided by Subsection (d) of this article, if a person commits an offense under Chapter 49, Penal Code, and as a direct result of the offense the person causes an incident resulting in an accident response by a public agency, the person is liable on conviction for the offense for the reasonable expense to the agency of the accident response. In this article, a person is considered to have been convicted in a case if:

(A) sentence is imposed;

(B) the defendant receives probation or deferred adjudication; or

(C) the court defers final disposition of the case.

(2) The liability authorized by this subsection may be established by civil suit; however, if a determination is made during a criminal trial that a person committed an offense under Chapter 49, Penal Code, and as a direct result of the offense the person caused an incident resulting in an accident response by a public agency, the court may include the obligation for the liability as part

of the judgment. A judgment that includes such an obligation is enforceable as any other judgment.

(3) The liability is a debt of the person to the public agency, and the public agency may collect the debt in the same manner as the public agency collects an express or implied contractual obligation to the agency.

(4) A person's liability under this subsection for the reasonable expense of an accident response may not exceed $1,000 for a particular incident. For the purposes of this subdivision, a reasonable expense for an accident response includes only those costs to the public agency arising directly from an accident response to a particular incident, such as the cost of providing police, fire-fighting, rescue, ambulance, and emergency medical services at the scene of the incident and the salaries of the personnel of the public agency responding to the incident.

(5) A bill for the expense of an accident response sent to a person by a public agency under this subsection must contain an itemized accounting of the components of the total charge. A bill that complies with this subdivision is prima facie evidence of the reasonableness of the costs incurred in the accident response to which the bill applies.

(6) A policy of motor vehicle insurance delivered, issued for delivery, or renewed in this state may not cover payment of expenses charged to a person under this subsection.

(7) In this subsection, "public agency" means the state, a county, a municipality district, or a public authority located in whole or in part in this state that provides police, fire-fighting, rescue, ambulance, or emergency medical services.

(d) Subsections (a), (b), and (c) of this article do not apply to an offense under Section 49.02 or 49.03, Penal Code.

*(Added by L.1993, chap. 900(1.07); renumbered by L.1995, chap. 76(17.01(4)), eff. 9/1/95.)*



**Art. 102.019. Costs on conviction for fugitive apprehension.**

(a) A person shall pay $5 as a court cost on conviction of:

(1) a felony; or

(2) a misdemeanor, including a criminal violation of a municipal ordinance, other than a conviction for an offense relating to pedestrians or the parking of a motor vehicle.

(b) The court shall assess and make a reasonable effort to collect the cost due under this article whether or not any other court cost is assessed or collected.

(c) For purposes of this article, a person is considered to have been convicted if:

(1) a sentence is imposed;

(2) the defendant receives community supervision or deferred adjudication; or

(3) the court defers final disposition of the case.

(d) Court costs under this article are collected in the same manner as other fines or costs. An officer collecting the costs shall keep separate records of the funds collected as costs under this article and shall deposit the funds in the county or municipal treasury, as appropriate.

(e) The custodian of a county or municipal treasury shall:

(1) keep records of the amount of funds on deposit collected under this article; and

(2) send to the comptroller before the last day of the first month following each calendar quarter the funds collected under this article during the preceding quarter.

(f) A county or municipality may retain 10 percent of the funds collected under this article by an officer of the county or municipality as a collection fee if the custodian of the county or municipal treasury complies with Subsection (e).

(g) If no funds due as costs under this article are deposited in a county or municipal treasury in a calendar quarter, the custodian of the treasury shall file the report required for the quarter in the regular manner and must state that no funds were collected.

(h) The comptroller shall deposit the funds received under this article to the credit of the fugitive apprehension account in the general revenue fund.

(i) Funds collected under this article are subject to audit by the comptroller.

*(Added by L.1997, chap. 1100(3), eff. 9/1/97.)*

## SUBCHAPTER B. CRIMINAL JUSTICE PLANNING FUND

**Arts. 102.051 to 102.55.** *(Repealed by L.1997, chap. 1100(6(3)), eff. 9/1/97.)*

**Art. 102.056. Distribution of funds.† [*Allocation of funds.*]**

(a) The legislature shall determine and appropriate the necessary amount from the criminal justice planning fund to the criminal justice division of the governor's office for expenditure for state and local criminal justice projects and for costs of administering the funds for the projects. The criminal justice division shall allocate not less than 20 percent of these funds to juvenile justice programs. The distribution of the funds to local units of government shall be in an amount equal at least to the same percentage as local expenditures for criminal justice activities are to total state and local expenditures for criminal justice activities for the preceding state fiscal year. Funds shall be a located among combinations of local units of government taking into consideration the population of the combination of local units of government as compared to the population of the state and the incidence of crime in the jurisdiction of the combination of local units of government as compared to the incidence of crime in the state. All funds collected are subject to audit by the comptroller of public accounts. All funds expended are subject to audit by the State Auditor. All funds collected or expended are subject to audit by the governor's division of planning coordination.

(b) The legislature may appropriate any unobligated balance of the criminal justice planning fund for any court-related purpose.

(c) Notwithstanding any other provision of this section, the criminal justice division shall allocate to a local unit of government or combination of local units of government located in an impacted region occurring as the result of the establishment of a significant new naval military facility an amount that exceeds by 10 percent the amount it would otherwise receive under this section.

(d) In this section "significant new naval military facility" and "impacted region" have the meanings assigned by Section 4, Article 1, National Defense Impacted Region Assistance Act of 1985.

*(Chgd. by L.1991, chap. 16(4.07(a)), eff. 8/26/91.)*

*(Editor's Note: Former Article 1083, Code of Criminal Procedure, as amended by L.1985, chap. 69(6(1)), is repealed by L.1991, chap. 16(4.07(b)), eff. 8/26/91.)*

## SUBCHAPTER C. COURT COSTS AND FEES

### Art. 102.071. Collection, allocation, and administration.

The comptroller of public accounts may require state court costs and fees in criminal cases to be reported in lump-sum amounts. The comptroller shall allocate the amounts received to the appropriate fund, with each fund receiving the same amount of money the fund would have received if the costs and fees had been reported individually. *(Added by L.1989, chap. 347(4), eff. 10/1/89.)*

### Art. 102.072. Administrative fee.

An officer listed in Article 103.003 or a community supervision and corrections department may assess an administrative fee for each transaction made by the officer or department relating to the collection of fines, fees, restitution, or other costs imposed by a court. The fee may not exceed $2 for each transaction. This article does not apply to a transaction relating to the collection of child support. *(Added by L.1995, chap. 217(2); L.1999, chap. 1345(1), eff. 9/1/99.)*

### Art. 102.075. Court costs for special services.

(a) Except as provided by Subsection (b), a person convicted of an offense shall pay, in addition to all other costs:

(1) $80 as a court cost on conviction of:

(A) a felony; or

(B) an offense punishable by imprisonment or confinement in jail for a term of more than one year;

(2) $40 as a court cost on conviction of:

(A) a Class A misdemeanor;

(B) a Class B misdemeanor;

(C) an offense punishable by confinement in jail for a term of not more than one year; or

(D) a municipal ordinance punishable by a fine of more than $500; or

(3) $17 as a court cost on conviction of any offense punishable by fine only, other than an offense described by Subdivision (2)(D) of this subsection.

(b) Subsection (a) does not apply to a person convicted under Subtitle C, Title 7, Transportation Code, if the person is convicted of a provision of that subtitle regulating pedestrians or the parking of a motor vehicle.

(c) An officer collecting a cost due under this article in a case in municipal court shall keep separate records of the money collected and shall deposit the money in the municipal treasury.

(d) An officer collecting a cost due under this article in a justice, county, or district court shall keep separate records of the money collected and shall deposit the money in the county treasury.

(e) An officer collecting a cost due under this article shall file the report required by Article 103.005. If no money due as a cost under this article is collected in any quarter, the report required for that quarter shall be filed in the regular manner, and the report shall state that no money due under this article was collected.

(f) The custodian of money in a municipal or county treasury may deposit money collected under this article in an interest-bearing account. The custodian shall:

(1) keep records of the amount of money collected under this article that is on deposit in the treasury; and

(2) not later than the last day of the month following each calendar quarter, remit to the comptroller money collected under this article during the preceding quarter, as required by the comptroller.

(g) A municipality or county may retain 10 percent of the money collected under this article as a service fee for the collection *if the municipality or county remits the funds to the comptroller within the period prescribed in Subsection (f)*. The municipality or county may retain any interest accrued on the money if the custodian of *the* money deposited in the treasury keeps records of the amount of money collected under this article that is on deposit in the treasury and remits the funds to the comptroller within the period prescribed in Subsection (f).

(h) The comptroller shall deposit money received under this article to the credit of the following accounts in the general revenue fund according to the specified percentages:

| NAME OF ACCOUNT | PERCENTAGE |
|---|---|
| abused children's counseling | 0.02% |
| crime stoppers assistance | 0.6% |
| breath alcohol testing | 1.28% |
| Bill Blackwood Law Enforcement Management Institute | 5.04% |
| law enforcement officers standards and education | 11.63% |
| comprehensive rehabilitation | 12.37% |
| operator's and chauffeur's license | 25.9% |
| criminal justice planning | 29.18% |

(i) Of each dollar credited to the law enforcement officers standards and education account under Subsection (h):

(1) $.333 may be used only to pay administrative expenses; and

(2) the remainder may be used only to pay expenses related to continuing education for persons licensed under Chapter 415, Government Code.

(j) Money collected under this article is subject to audit by the comptroller. Money spent is subject to audit by the state auditor.

(k) Except for a conviction in a municipal court or as otherwise provided by this article, Chapter 103 applies to the collection of a cost under this article.

(*l*) In this article:

(1) court costs are due from the person regardless of whether the person submitted a specimen of breath or blood for analysis; and

(2) a person is considered to have been convicted in a case if:

(A) a sentence is imposed;

(B) the person receives community supervision or deferred adjudication; or

(C) the court defers final disposition of the case.

(m) In addition to the cost on conviction imposed by Subsection (a), a person convicted of an offense described by Subsection (a) shall pay 25 cents on conviction of the offense. The comptroller shall deposit money received under this subsection to the credit of an account in the state treasury to be used only for the establishment and operation of the Center for the Study and Prevention of Juvenile Crime and Delinquency at Prairie View A&M University. Subsection (h) does not apply to money received under this subsection. *(Subsection (m) only eff. on date Act creating Center for the Study and Prevention of Juvenile Crime at Prairie View becomes effective.)*
*(Added by L.1997, chap. 1100(4); chgd. by L.1999, chap. 1467(2.01), eff. 10/1/99. Matter in italics eff. 10/1/99.)*

## SUBCHAPTER D. COMPREHENSIVE REHABILITATION FUND

*(Repealed by L.1997, chap. 1100(6(4)), eff. 9/1/97.)*

**Arts. 102.081 to 102.085.** *(Repealed by L.1997, chap. 1100(6(4)), eff. 9/1/97.)*

# CHAPTER 103. COLLECTION AND RECORDKEEPING

Article



 Zt

## Art. 103.001. Costs payable.† [*Expenses remittable.*]

A cost is not payable by the person charged with the cost until a written bill is produced or is ready to be produced, containing the items of cost, signed by the officer who charged the cost or the officer who is entitled to receive payment for the cost.

## Art. 103.002. Certain costs barred.† [*Certain expenses disallowed.*]

An officer may not impose a cost for a service not performed or for a service for which a cost is not expressly provided by law.

## Art. 103.003. Collection.

(a) District and county attorneys, clerks of district and county courts, sheriffs, constables, and justices of the peace may collect money payable under this title.

(b) A community supervision and corrections department serving a county with a population of 2.8 million or more may collect money payable under this title and as otherwise provided by law.

*(Chgd. by L.1995, chap. 217(3), eff. 5/23/95.)*

## Art. 103.0031. Collection contracts.

The commissioners court of a county may enter into a contract with a public or private vendor for the provision of collection services for fines, fees, restitution, and other costs ordered to be paid by a court serving the county. *(Added by L.1993, chap. 809(3), eff. 8/30/93.)*

## Art. 103.004. Disposition of collected money.

(a) Except as provided by Subsections (b) and (c), an officer who collects recognizances, bail bonds, fines, forfeitures, judgments, jury fees, and other obligations recovered in the name of the state under any provision of this title shall deposit the money in the county treasury not later than the next regular business day after the date that the money is collected. If it is not possible for the officer to deposit the money in the county treasury by that date, the officer shall deposit the money in the county treasury as soon as possible, but not later than the third regular business day after the date that the money is collected.

(b) The commissioners court of a county may authorize an officer who is required to deposit money under Subsection (a) to deposit the money in the county treasury not later than the seventh regular business day after the date that the money is collected.

(c) The commissioners court of a county with a population of less than 50,000 may authorize an officer who is required to deposit money under Subsection (a) to deposit the money in the county treasury not later than the 30th day after the date that the money is collected.

(d) The custodian of the county treasury shall deposit money received from fees imposed under Article 102.012 in the special fund of the county treasury for the community supervision and corrections department serving the county.

*(Chgd. by L.1990, 6th C.S., chap. 25(21); L.1999, chap. 1462(1), eff. 9/1/99.)*

## Art. 103.005. Report required.† [*Report necessary.*]

(a) An officer listed in Article 103.003 who collects money other than taxes for a county shall report to the commissioners court of the county for which the money was collected during each term of the court.

(b) An officer listed in Article 103.003 who collects money other than taxes for the state shall report to the district court having jurisdiction in the county the officer serves on the first day of each term of the court.

(c) The report must state for the reporting period:

(1) the amount of money collected by the officer;

(2) when and from whom the money was collected;

(3) the process by which the money was collected; and

(4) the disposition of the money.

(d) The report must be in writing and under the oath of the officer.

(e) If an officer has not collected money since the last report required to be filed with the court or the commissioners court, the officer shall report that fact to the court or commissioners court.

### Art. 103.006. Transfer of bill of costs.† [*Transfer of bill of expenses.*]

If a criminal action or proceeding is transferred from one court to another or is appealed, an officer of the court shall certify and sign a bill of costs stating the costs that have accrued and send the bill of costs to the court to which the action or proceeding is transferred or appealed.



### Art. 103.007. Additional costs after payment.† [*Additional expenses after remittal.*]

After a defendant has paid costs, no more costs may be charged against the defendant unless the court rules on a motion presented to the court that additional costs are due.

### Art. 103.008. Correction of costs.† [*Correction of expenses.*]

(a) On the filing of a motion by a defendant not later than one year after the date of the final disposition of a case in which costs were imposed, the court in which the case is pending or was last pending shall correct any error in the costs.

(b) The defendant must notify each person affected by the correction of costs in the same manner as notice of a similar motion is given in a civil action.

### Art. 103.009. Fee records.

(a) Each clerk of a court, county judge, justice of the peace, sheriff, constable, and marshal shall keep a fee record. The record must contain:

(1) a statement of each fee or item of cost charged for a service rendered in a criminal action or proceeding;

(2) the number and style of the action or proceeding; and

(3) the name of the officer or person who is entitled to receive the fee.

(b) Any person may inspect a fee record described by Subsection (a).

(c) A statement of an item of cost in a fee record is prima facie evidence of the correctness of the statement.

(d) The county shall provide to officers required to keep a fee record by this article equipment and supplies necessary to keep the record.

*(Chgd. by L.1993, chap. 988(2.05), eff. 9/1/93.)*

### Art. 103.010. Receipt book.

(a) Each county shall provide a receipt book to each officer collecting fines and fees in criminal cases for the county. The book must contain duplicate official receipts. Each receipt must bear a distinct number and a facsimile of the official seal of the county.

(b) An officer who collects fines or fees in a criminal case shall give the person paying the money a receipt from the receipt book. The receipt must show:

(1) the amount of money paid;

(2) the date the money was paid;

(3) the style and number of the case in which the costs were accrued;

(4) the item of costs;

(5) the name of the person paying the money; and

(6) the official signature of the officer receiving the money.

(c) Instead of a receipt book, each officer collecting fines or fees in criminal cases for the county may maintain the information listed in Subsections (b)(1)-(5) in a computer database. The officer shall provide a receipt to each person paying a fine or fee.

*(Chgd. by L.1999, chap. 412(1), eff. 6/18/99.)*

### Art. 103.011. Audit.

An officer shall deliver the receipt book or a copy of any receipt records contained in a computer database to the county auditor at the end of each month's business or at the end of each month shall allow the county auditor electronic access to receipt records contained in the computer database. The county auditor shall examine the receipt book or computer records and determine whether the money collected has been properly disposed of. If each receipt in a receipt book has been used, the county auditor shall keep the book. If any receipt in the book has not been used, the auditor shall return the book to the officer. The county auditor may keep a copy of computer generated receipt records delivered to the county auditor. Any person may inspect a receipt book or a computer generated receipt record kept by the county auditor. *(Chgd. by L.1999, chap. 412(2), eff. 6/18/99.)*

### Art. 103.012. Penalty.

(a) An officer commits an offense if the officer violates a provision of Article 103.010 or Article 103.011.

(b) An offense under this article is a Class C misdemeanor.

(c) An officer who violates a provision of Article 103.010 or Article 103.011 or whose deputy violates a provision of those articles may be removed from office on the petition of the county or district attorney.



## CHAPTER 104. CERTAIN EXPENSES PAID BY STATE OR COUNTY

Article



### Art. 104.001. Jury pay and expenses for jurors.† [*Jury compensation and costs for jurors.*]

(a) The sheriff of a county shall, with the approval of the commissioners court, provide food and lodging for jurors impaneled in a felony case tried in the county. A juror may pay his own expenses and draw his script.

(b) A juror in a felony case is entitled to receive as jury pay the amount authorized by Article 2122, Revised Statutes.

(c) The county treasurer shall pay a juror the amount due the juror for expenses under this article after receiving a certificate from a clerk of a court or justice of the peace stating the amount due the juror.

(d) A draft or certificate issued under this article may be transferred by delivery and, without further action of any authority except registration by the county treasurer, may be used at par to pay county taxes owed by the holder of the draft or certificate.

(e) If a defendant is indicted in one county and tried in another county after a change of venue, the county in which the defendant was indicted is liable for jury pay and expenses paid to jurors by the county trying the case.

(f) At each regular meeting of the commissioners court of a county, the court shall determine whether, since the last regular meeting of the court, a defendant described by Subsection (e) has been tried in the county. The commissioners court shall prepare an account against another county liable for jury pay and expenses under this article. The account must show the number of days the jury was impaneled in the case and the jury pay and expenses incurred by the county in the case.

(g) The county judge of the county in which the defendant was tried shall certify the correctness of the account and send the account to the county judge of the county in which the defendant was indicted. The county in which the defendant was indicted shall pay the account in the same manner required for payment of the expenses of transferred prisoners under Article 104.002.

### Art. 104.002. Expenses for prisoners.† [*Costs for prisoners.*]

(a) Except as otherwise provided by this article, a county is liable for all expenses incurred in the safekeeping of prisoners confined in the county jail or kept under guard by the county. If a prisoner is transferred to a county from another county on a change of venue, for safekeeping, or for a habeas corpus hearing, the county transferring the prisoner is liable for the expenses described by this article.

(b) If a county incurs expenses for the safekeeping of a prisoner from another county, the sheriff shall submit to the county judge an account of expenses incurred by the county for the prisoner. The county judge shall approve the amount he determines is a correct statement of the expenses and sign and date the account.

(c) The county judge shall submit to the commissioners court of the county for which the prisoner was kept, at a regular term of the court, his signed statement of the account described by Subsection (b). If the commissioners court determines that the account is in accordance with the law, it shall order the county treasurer to issue to the sheriff of the county submitting the statement a draft in an amount approved by the court.

(d) A person who is or was a prisoner in a county jail and received medical, dental, or health related services from a county or a hospital district shall be required to pay for such services when they are rendered. If such prisoner is an eligible county resident as defined in Section 61.002, Health and Safety Code, the county or hospital district providing the services has a right of subrogation to the prisoner's right of recovery from any source, limited to the cost of services provided. A prisoner, unless the prisoner fully pays for the cost of services received, shall remain obligated to reimburse the county or hospital district for any medical, dental, or health services provided, and the county or hospital district may apply for reimbursement in the manner provided by Chapter 61, Health and Safety Code. A county or hospital district shall have authority to recover the amount expended in a civil action.

*(Chgd. by L.1991, chaps. 14(284(19)), 434(1); L.1995, chap. 76(3.22), eff. 9/1/95.)*



**Art. 104.003. State payment of certain prosecution costs.**

(a) In a prosecution of a felony committed while the actor was a prisoner in the custody of the Texas Department of Corrections or a prosecution of an offense committed in the department by any person under Chapter 21, Acts of 55th Legislature, Regular Session, 1957 (Article 6184m, Texas Civil Statutes), or Chapter 481, Health and Safety Code, or Sections 485.031 through 485.035, Health and Safety Code, the state shall reimburse the county for expenses incurred by the county, in an amount that the court determines to be reasonable, for payment of:

(1) salaries and expenses of foreign language interpreters and interpreters for deaf persons whose services are necessary to the prosecution;

(2) consultation fees of experts whose assistance is directly related to the prosecution;

(3) travel expenses for witnesses;

(4) expenses for the food, lodging, and compensation of jurors;

(5) compensation of witnesses;

(6) the cost of preparation of a statement of facts and a transcript of the trial for purposes of appeal;

(7) if the death of a person is an element of the offense, expenses of an inquest relating to the death;

(8) food, lodging, and travel expenses incurred by the prosecutor's staff during travel essential to the prosecution of the offense;

(9) court reporter's fees; and

(10) the cost of special security officers.

(b) If there is a change of venue, the court may, in its discretion, determine that a special prosecutor should be hired for the prosecution of an offense described in Section (a), and the state shall reimburse the county for the salary and expenses of the special prosecutor if the court determines that the hiring of the special prosecutor was reasonable and necessary for effective prosecution. The amount of reimbursement may not exceed an amount that the court determines to be reasonable.

(c) The court shall certify the amount of reimbursement for expenses under Sections (a) and (b) on presentation by the county of an itemized and verified receipt for those expenses.

(d) The state shall reimburse the county for expenses incurred by the county for the investigation of an offense described in Section (a), whether or not the investigation results in the prosecution of an offense, and shall reimburse the county for reasonable operational expenses of the special prison prosecution unit, including educational activities for the staff and general expenses relating to its investigative and prosecutorial duties.

(e) The court shall certify the amount of reimbursement for expenses under Sections (a) and (b) to the comptroller. The comptroller shall issue a warrant in that amount to the commissioners court of the county or, if the comptroller determines that the amount certified by the court is unreasonable, in an amount that the comptroller determines to be reasonable.

(f) The commissioners court of the county shall certify the amount of reimbursement for expenses under Section (d) to the comptroller. The comptroller shall issue a warrant in that amount to the commissioners court or, if the comptroller determines that the amount certified by the commissioners court is unreasonable, in an amount that the comptroller determines to be reasonable.

(g) Notwithstanding any other provision of this article, the expenses submitted by the county for reimbursement may not exceed the amount the county would pay for the same activity or service, if that activity or service was not reimbursed by the state. The county judge shall certify compliance with this section on request by the comptroller.

*(Added by L.1989, chaps. 2(5.06(a)), 461(1); chgd. by L.1991, chap. 14(284(60)), eff. 9/1/91.)*

**Art. 104.004. Extraordinary costs of prosecution.**

(a) The criminal justice division of the governor's office may distribute money appropriated by the legislature for this purpose.

(b) A county is eligible to apply to the division for a distribution of money under this article if, during the preceding fiscal year:

(1) the total amount of expenditures of the county exceeded the total amount of funds received by the county from all sources and the county incurred expenses for the investigation or prosecution of an offense under Section 19.03, Penal Code; or

(2) the total amount of funds received by the county from all sources exceeded the total amount of expenditures of the county and the county incurred expenses for the investigation or prosecution of an offense under Section 19.03, Penal Code, that exceed five percent of the amount of that excess.

(c) The commissioners court must submit with an application under Subsection (b) a financial statement of the county that shows for the fiscal year for which application is made:

(1) the total amount of funds received by the county from all sources;

(2) the total amount of expenditures of the county; and

(3) the total amount of expenses incurred by the county for the investigation or prosecution of an offense under Section 19.03, Penal Code.

(d) The division may distribute money under this article only to an eligible county for the reimbursement of expenses incurred by the county during the fiscal year for which application is made for the investigation or prosecution of an offense under Section 19.03, Penal Code. The amount of the reimbursement to a county eligible under Subsection (b)(2) may not exceed an amount equal to five percent of the difference between the total amount of funds received by the county and the total amount of expenditures of the county during the fiscal year for which application is made.

(e) For each fiscal year, the division shall distribute at least 50 percent of the money distributed under this article during that year to eligible counties with a population of less than 50,000, except that if the total distributions applied for by those counties is less than 50 percent of the money distributed during that year, the division is only required to distribute to those counties the amount of money for which applications have been made.

(f) The division may adopt a budget and rules for the distribution of money under this article.

(g) All money distributed to a county under this subchapter and its expenditure by the county are subject to audit by the state auditor.

*(Added by L.1999, chap. 664(1), eff. 9/1/99.)*

*(Editor's Note: Former Article 1036, Code of Criminal Procedure, as amended by L.1985, chap. 269(5(2)), is repealed by L.1989, chap. 2(5.06(b)), eff. 8/28/89.)*

# TEXAS RULES OF EVIDENCE

*(Effective March 1, 1998.)*

## ARTICLE I. GENERAL PROVISIONS

Rule

101. Title and scope.
102. Purpose and construction.
103. Rulings of evidence.
104. Preliminary questions.
105. Limited admissibility.
106. Remainder of related writings or recorded statements.
107. Rule of optional completeness.

## ARTICLE II. JUDICIAL NOTICE

201. Judicial notice of adjudicative facts.
202. Determination of law of other states.
203. Determination of the laws of foreign countries.
204. Determination of Texas city and county ordinances, the contents of the Texas Register, the rules of agencies published in the Administrative Code.

## ARTICLE III. PRESUMPTIONS

*(Reserved.)*

## ARTICLE IV. RELEVANCY AND ITS LIMITS

401. Definition of "relevant evidence".
402. Relevant evidence generally admissible; irrelevant evidence inadmissible.
403. Exclusion of relevant evidence on special grounds.
404. Character evidence not admissible to prove conduct; exceptions; other crimes.
405. Methods of proving character.
406. Habit; routine practice.
407. Subsequent remedial measures; notification of defect.
408. Compromise and offers to compromise.
409. Payment of medical and similar expenses.
410. Inadmissibility of pleas, plea discussions and related statements.
411. Liability insurance.
412. Evidence of previous sexual conduct in criminal cases.

## ARTICLE V. PRIVILEGES

501. Privileges recognized only as provided.
502. Required reports privileged by statute.
503. Lawyer-client privilege.
504. Husband-wife privileges.
505. Communications to members of the clergy.
506. Political vote.
507. Trade secrets.
508. Identity of informer.
509. Physician-patient privilege.
510. Confidentiality of mental health information in civil cases.
511. Waiver of privilege by voluntary disclosure.
512. Privileged matter disclosed under compulsion or without opportunity to claim privilege.
513. Comment upon or inference from claim of privilege; instruction.

## ARTICLE VI. WITNESSES

601. Competency and incompetency of witnesses.
602. Lack of personal knowledge.

## ARTICLE VII. OPINIONS AND EXPERT TESTIMONY



## ARTICLE VIII. HEARSAY



## ARTICLE IX. AUTHENTICATION AND IDENTIFICATION



## ARTICLE X. CONTENTS OF WRITINGS, RECORDINGS, AND PHOTOGRAPHS



## ARTICLE I. GENERAL PROVISIONS

### Rule 101. Title and scope.

**(a) Title.** These rules shall be known and cited as the Texas Rules of Evidence.

**(b) Scope.** Except as otherwise provided by statute, these rules govern civil and criminal proceedings (including examining trials before magistrates) in all courts of Texas, except small claims courts.

**(c) Hierarchical governance in criminal proceedings.** Hierarchical governance shall be in the following order: the Constitution of the United States, those federal statutes that control states under the supremacy clause, the Constitution of Texas, the Code of Criminal Procedure and the Penal Code, civil statutes, these rules, and the common law. Where possible, inconsistency is to be removed by reasonable construction.

**(d) Special rules of applicability in criminal proceedings.**

(1) *Rules not applicable in certain proceedings.* These rules, except with respect to privileges, do not apply in the following situations:

(A) the determination of questions of fact preliminary to admissibility of evidence when the issue is to be determined by the court under Rule 104;

(B) proceedings before grand juries;

(C) proceedings in an application for habeas corpus in extradition, rendition, or interstate detainer;

(D) a hearing under Code of Criminal Procedure article 46.02, by the court out of the presence of a jury, to determine whether there is sufficient evidence of incompetency to require a jury determination of the question of incompetency;

(E) proceedings regarding bail except hearings to deny, revoke or increase bail;

(F) a hearing on justification for pretrial detention not involving bail;

(G) proceedings for the issuance of a search or arrest warrant; or

(H) proceedings in a direct contempt determination.

(2) *Applicability of privileges.* These rules with respect to privileges apply at all stages of all actions, cases, and proceedings.

(3) *Military justice hearings.* Evidence in hearings under the Texas Code of Military Justice, Tex. Gov't Code §432.001-432.195, shall be governed by that Code.

### Notes and Comments

Comment to 1998 change: "Criminal proceedings" rather than "criminal cases" is used since that was the terminology used in the prior Rules of Criminal Evidence. In subpart (b), the reference to "trials before magistrates" comes from prior Criminal Rule 1101(a). In the prior Criminal Rules, both Rule 101 and Rule 1101 dealt with the same thing — the applicability of the rules. Thus, Rules 101(c) and (d) have been written to incorporate the provisions of former Criminal Rule 1101 and that rule is omitted.

## Rule 102. Purpose and construction.

These rules shall be construed to secure fairness in administration, elimination of unjustifiable expense and delay, and promotion of growth and development of the law of evidence to the end that the truth may be ascertained and proceedings justly determined.

## Rule 103. Rulings on evidence.

**(a) Effect of erroneous ruling.** Error may not be predicated upon a ruling which admits or excludes evidence unless a substantial right of the party is affected, and

(1) *Objection.* In case the ruling is one admitting evidence, a timely objection or motion to strike appears of record, stating the specific ground of objection, if the specific ground was not apparent from the context. When the court hears objections to offered evidence out of the presence of the jury and rules that such evidence be admitted, such objections shall be deemed to apply to such evidence when it is admitted before the jury without the necessity of repeating those objections.

(2) *Offer of proof.* In case the ruling is one excluding evidence, the substance of the evidence was made known to the court by offer, or was apparent from the context within which questions were asked.

**(b) Record of offer and ruling.** The offering party shall, as soon as practicable, but before the court's charge is read to the jury, be allowed to make, in the absence of the jury, its offer of proof. The court may add any other or further statement which shows the character of the evidence, the form in which it was offered, the objection made, and the ruling thereon. The court may, or at the request of a party shall, direct the making of an offer in question and answer form.

**(c) Hearing of jury.** In jury cases, proceedings shall be conducted, to the extent practicable, so as to prevent inadmissible evidence from being suggested to the jury by any means, such as making statements or offers of proof or asking questions in the hearing of the jury.

**(d) Fundamental error in criminal cases.** In a criminal case, nothing in these rules precludes taking notice of fundamental errors affecting substantial rights although they were not brought to the attention of the court.

### Notes and Comments

Comment to 1998 change: The exception to the requirement of an offer of proof for matters that were apparent from the context within which questions were asked, found in paragraph (a)(2), is now applicable to civil as well as criminal cases.

## Rule 104. Preliminary questions.

**(a) Questions of admissibility generally.** Preliminary questions concerning the qualification of a person to be a witness, the existence of a privilege, or the admissibility of evidence shall be determined by the court, subject to the provisions of subdivision (b). In making its determination the court is not bound by the rules of evidence except those with respect to privileges.

**(b) Relevancy conditioned on fact.** When the relevancy of evidence depends upon the fulfillment of a condition of fact, the court shall admit it upon, or subject to, the introduction of evidence sufficient to support a finding of the fulfillment of the condition.

**(c) Hearing of jury.** In a criminal case, a hearing on the admissibility of a confession shall be conducted out of the hearing of the jury. All other civil or criminal hearings on preliminary matters shall be conducted out of the hearing of the jury when the interests of justice so require or in a criminal case when an accused is a witness and so requests.

**(d) Testimony by accused out of the hearing of the jury.** The accused in a criminal case does not, by testifying upon a preliminary matter out of the hearing of the jury, become subject to cross-examination as to other issues in the case.

**(e) Weight and credibility.** This rule does not limit the right of a party to introduce before the jury evidence relevant to weight or credibility.

## Rule 105. Limited admissibility.

**(a) Limiting instruction.** When evidence which is admissible as to one party or for one purpose but not admissible as to another party or for another purpose is admitted, the court, upon request, shall restrict the evidence to its proper scope and instruct the jury accordingly; but, in the absence of such request the court's action in admitting such evidence without limitation shall not be a ground for complaint on appeal.

**(b) Offering evidence for limited purpose.** When evidence referred to in paragraph (a) is excluded, such exclusion shall not be a ground for complaint on appeal unless the proponent expressly offers the evidence for its limited, admissible purpose or limits its offer to the party against whom it is admissible.

## Rule 106. Remainder of or related writings or recorded statements.

When a writing or recorded statement or part thereof is introduced by a party, an adverse party may at that time introduce any other part or any other writing or recorded statement which ought in fairness to be considered contemporaneously with it. "Writing or recorded statement" includes depositions.

## Rule 107. Rule of optional completeness.

When part of an act, declaration, conversation, writing or recorded statement is given in evidence by one party, the whole on the same subject may be inquired into by the other, and any other act, declaration, writing or recorded statement which is necessary to make it fully understood or to explain the same may also be given in evidence, as when a letter is read, all letters on the same subject between the same parties may be given. "Writing or recorded statement" includes depositions.

### Notes and Comments

Comment to 1998 change: This rule is the former Criminal Rule 107 except that the example regarding "when a letter is read" has been relocated in the rule so as to more accurately indicate the provision it explains. While this rule appeared only in the prior criminal rules, it is made applicable to civil cases because it accurately reflects the common law rule of optional completeness in civil cases.

# ARTICLE II. JUDICIAL NOTICE

## Rule 201. Judicial notice of adjudicative facts.

**(a) Scope of rule.** This rule governs only judicial notice of adjudicative facts.

**(b) Kinds of facts.** A judicially noticed fact must be one not subject to reasonable dispute in that it is either (1) generally known within the territorial jurisdiction of the trial court or (2) capable of accurate and ready determination by resort to sources whose accuracy cannot reasonably be questioned.

**(c) When discretionary.** A court may take judicial notice, whether requested or not.

**(d) When mandatory.** A court shall take judicial notice if requested by a party and supplied with the necessary information.

**(e) Opportunity to be heard.** A party is entitled upon timely request to an opportunity to be heard as to the propriety of taking judicial notice and the tenor of the matter noticed. In the absence of prior notification, the request may be made after judicial notice has been taken.

**(f) Time of taking notice.** Judicial notice may be taken at any stage of the proceeding.

**(g) Instructing jury.** In civil cases, the court shall instruct the jury to accept as conclusive any fact judicially noticed. In criminal cases, the court shall instruct the jury that it may, but is not required to, accept as conclusive any fact judicially noticed.

## Rule 202. Determination of law of other states.

A court upon its own motion may, or upon the motion of a party shall, take judicial notice of the constitutions, public statutes, rules, regulations, ordinances, court decisions, and common law of every other state, territory, or jurisdiction of the United States. A party requesting that judicial notice be taken of such matter shall furnish the court sufficient information to enable it properly to comply with the request, and shall give all parties such notice, if any, as the court may deem necessary, to enable all parties fairly to prepare to meet the request. A party is entitled upon timely request to an opportunity to be heard as to the propriety of taking judicial notice and the tenor of the matter noticed. In the absence of prior notification, the request may be made after judicial notice has been taken. Judicial notice of such matters may be taken at any stage of the proceeding. The court's determination shall be subject to review as a ruling on a question of law.

## Rule 203. Determination of the laws of foreign countries.

A party who intends to raise an issue concerning the law of a foreign country shall give notice in the pleadings or other reasonable written notice, and at least 30 days prior to the date of trial such party shall furnish all parties copies of any written materials or sources that the party intends to use as proof of the foreign law. If the materials or sources were originally written in a language other than English, the party intending to rely upon them shall furnish all parties both a copy of the foreign language text and an English translation. The court, in determining the law of a foreign nation, may consider any material or source, whether or not submitted by a party or admissible under the rules of evidence, including but not limited to affidavits, testimony, briefs, and treatises. If the court considers sources other than those submitted by a party, it shall give all parties notice and a reasonable opportunity to comment on the sources and to submit further materials for review by the court. The court, and not a jury, shall determine the laws of foreign countries. The court's determination shall be subject to review as a ruling on a question of law.

## Rule 204. Determination of Texas city and county ordinances, the contents of the Texas Register, and the rules of agencies published in the Administrative Code.

A court upon its own motion may, or upon the motion of a party shall, take judicial notice of the ordinances of municipalities and counties of Texas, of the contents of the Texas Register, and of the codified rules of the agencies published in the Administrative Code. Any party requesting that judicial notice be taken of such matter shall furnish the court sufficient information to enable it properly to comply with the request, and shall give all parties such notice, if any, as the court may deem necessary, to enable all parties fairly to prepare to meet the request. A party is entitled upon timely request to an opportunity to be heard as to the propriety of taking judicial notice and the tenor of the matter noticed. In the absence of prior notification, the request may be made after judicial notice has been taken. The court's determination shall be subject to review as a ruling on a question of law.

## ARTICLE III. PRESUMPTIONS

*(Reserved.)*

## ARTICLE IV. RELEVANCY AND ITS LIMITS

### Rule 401. Definition of "relevant evidence".

"Relevant evidence" means evidence having any tendency to make the existence of any fact that is of consequence to the determination of the action more probable or less probable than it would be without the evidence.

### Rule 402. Relevant evidence generally admissible; irrelevant evidence inadmissible.

All relevant evidence is admissible, except as otherwise provided by Constitution, by statute, by these rules, or by other rules prescribed pursuant to statutory authority. Evidence which is not relevant is inadmissible.

### Rule 403. Exclusion of relevant evidence on special grounds.

Although relevant, evidence may be excluded if its probative value is substantially outweighed by the danger of unfair prejudice, confusion of the issues, or misleading the jury, or by considerations of undue delay, or needless presentation of cumulative evidence.

### Rule 404. Character evidence not admissible to prove conduct; exceptions; other crimes.

**(a) Character evidence generally.**Evidence of a person's character or character trait is not admissible for the purpose of proving action in conformity therewith on a particular occasion, except:

(1) *Character of accused.* Evidence of a pertinent character trait offered:

(A) by an accused in a criminal case, or by the prosecution to rebut the same, or

(B) by a party accused in a civil case of conduct involving moral turpitude, or by the accusing party to rebut the same;

(2) *Character of victim.* In a criminal case and subject to Rule 412, evidence of a pertinent character trait of the victim of the crime offered by an accused, or by the prosecution to rebut the same, or evidence of peaceable character of the victim offered by the prosecution in a homicide case to rebut evidence that the victim was the first aggressor; or in a civil case, evidence of character for violence of the alleged victim of assaultive conduct offered on the issue of self-defense by a party accused of the assaultive conduct, or evidence of peaceable character to rebut the same;

(3) *Character of witness.* Evidence of the character of a witness, as provided in rules 607, 608 and 609.

**(b) Other crimes, wrongs or acts.** Evidence of other crimes, wrongs or acts is not admissible to prove the character of a person in order to show action in conformity therewith. It may, however, be admissible for other purposes, such as proof of motive, opportunity, intent, preparation, plan, knowledge, identity, or absence of mistake or accident, provided that upon timely request by the accused in a criminal case, reasonable notice is given in advance of trial of intent to introduce in the State's case-in-chief such evidence other than that arising in the same transaction.

### Rule 405. Methods of proving character.

**(a) Reputation or opinion.** In all cases in which evidence of a person's character or character trait is admissible, proof may be made by testimony as to reputation or by testimony in the form of an opinion. In a criminal case, to be qualified to testify at the guilt stage of trial concerning the character or character trait of an accused, a witness must have been familiar with the reputation, or with the underlying facts or information upon which the opinion is based, prior to the day of the offense. In all cases where testimony is admitted under this rule, on cross-examination inquiry is allowable into relevant specific instances of conduct.

**(b) Specific instances of conduct.** In cases in which a person's character or character trait is an essential element of a charge, claim or defense, proof may also be made of specific instances of that person's conduct.

### Rule 406. Habit; routine practice.

Evidence of the habit of a person or of the routine practice of an organization, whether corroborated or not and regardless of the presence of eyewitnesses, is relevant to prove that the conduct of the person or organization on a particular occasion was in conformity with the habit or routine practice.

### Rule 407. Subsequent remedial measures; notification of defect.

**(a) Subsequent remedial measures.** When, after an event, measures are taken which, if taken previously, would have made the event less likely to occur, evidence of the subsequent remedial measures is not admissible to prove negligence or culpable conduct in connection with the event. This rule does not require the exclusion of evidence of subsequent remedial measures when offered for another purpose, such as proving ownership, control or feasibility of precautionary measures, if controverted, or impeachment. Nothing in this rule shall preclude admissibility in products liability cases based on strict liability.

**(b) Notification of defect.** A written notification by a manufacturer of any defect in a product produced by such manufacturer to purchasers thereof is admissible against the manufacturer on the issue of existence of the defect to the extent that it is relevant.

### Rule 408. Compromise and offers to compromise.

Evidence of (1) furnishing or offering or promising to furnish or (2) accepting or offering or promising to accept, a valuable consideration in compromising or attempting to compromise a claim which was disputed as to either validity or amount is not admissible to prove liability for or invalidity of the claim or its amount. Evidence of conduct or statements made in compromise negotiations is likewise not admissible. This rule does not require the exclusion of any evidence otherwise discoverable merely because it is presented in the course of compromise negotiations. This rule also does not require exclusion when the evidence is offered for another purpose, such as proving bias or prejudice or interest of a witness or a party, negativing a contention of undue delay, or proving an effort to obstruct a criminal investigation or prosecution.

### Rule 409. Payment of medical and similar expenses.

Evidence of furnishing or offering or promising to pay medical, hospital, or similar expenses occasioned by an injury is not admissible to prove liability for the injury.

### Rule 410. Inadmissibility of pleas, plea discussions and related statements.

Except as otherwise provided in this rule, evidence of the following is not admissible against the defendant who made the plea or was a participant in the plea discussions:

(1) a plea of guilty that was later withdrawn;

(2) in civil cases, a plea of nolo contendere, and in criminal cases, a plea of nolo contendere that was later withdrawn;

(3) any statement made in the course of any proceedings under Rule 11 of the Federal Rules of Criminal Procedure or comparable state procedure regarding, in a civil case, either a plea of guilty that was later withdrawn or a plea of nolo contendere, or in a criminal case, either a plea of guilty that was later withdrawn or a plea of nolo contendere that was later withdrawn; or

(4) any statement made in the course of plea discussions with an attorney for the prosecuting authority, in a civil case, that do not result in a plea of guilty or that result in a plea of guilty later withdrawn, or in a criminal case, that do not result in a plea of guilty or a plea of nolo contendere or that results in a plea, later withdrawn, of guilty or nolo contendere.

However, such a statement is admissible in any proceeding wherein another statement made in the course of the same plea or plea discussions has been introduced and the statement ought in fairness be considered contemporaneously with it.

### Rule 411. Liability insurance.

Evidence that a person was or was not insured against liability is not admissible upon the issue whether the person acted negligently or otherwise wrongfully. This rule does not require the exclusion of evidence of insurance against liability when offered for another issue, such as proof of agency, ownership, or control, if disputed, or bias or prejudice of a witness.

### Rule 412. Evidence of previous sexual conduct in criminal cases.

**(a) Reputation or opinion evidence.** In a prosecution for sexual assault or aggravated sexual assault, or attempt to commit sexual assault or aggravated sexual assault, reputation or opinion evidence of the past sexual behavior of an alleged victim of such crime is not admissible.

**(b) Evidence of specific instances.** In a prosecution for sexual assault or aggravated sexual assault, or attempt to commit sexual assault or aggravated sexual assault, evidence of specific instances of an alleged victim's past sexual behavior is also not admissible, unless:

(1) such evidence is admitted in accordance with paragraphs (c) and (d) of this rule;

(2) it is evidence:

(A) that is necessary to rebut or explain scientific or medical evidence offered by the State;

(B) of past sexual behavior with the accused and is offered by the accused upon the issue of whether the alleged victim consented to the sexual behavior which is the basis of the offense charged;

(C) that relates to the motive or bias of the alleged victim;

(D) is admissible under Rule 609; or

(E) that is constitutionally required to be admitted; and

(3) its probative value outweighs the danger of unfair prejudice.

**(c) Procedure for offering evidence.** If the defendant proposes to introduce any documentary evidence or to ask any question, either by direct examination or cross-examination of any witness, concerning specific instances of the alleged victim's past sexual behavior, the defendant must inform the court out of the hearing of the jury prior to introducing any such evidence or asking any such question. After this notice, the court shall conduct an in camera hearing, recorded by the court reporter, to determine whether the proposed evidence is admissible under paragraph (b) of this rule. The court shall determine what evidence is admissible and shall accordingly limit the questioning. The defendant shall not go outside these limits or refer to any evidence ruled inadmissible in camera without prior approval of the court without the presence of the jury.

**(d) Record sealed.** The court shall seal the record of the in camera hearing required in paragraph (c) of this rule for delivery to the appellate court in the event of an appeal.

**(e) Sexual conduct of child as defense.** This rule does not limit the right of the accused to produce evidence of promiscuous sexual conduct of a child 14 years old or older as a defense to sexual assault, aggravated sexual assault, indecency with a child or an attempt to commit any of the foregoing crimes. If such evidence is admitted, the court shall instruct the jury as to the purpose of the evidence and as to its limited use.

## ARTICLE V. PRIVILEGES

### Rule 501. Privileges recognized only as provided.

Except as otherwise provided by Constitution, by statute, by these rules, or by other rules prescribed pursuant to statutory authority, no person has a privilege to:

(1) refuse to be a witness;

(2) refuse to disclose any matter;

(3) refuse to produce any object or writing; or

(4) prevent another from being a witness or disclosing any matter or producing any object or writing.

### Rule 502. Required reports privileged by statute.

A person, corporation, association, or other organization or entity, either public or private, making a return or report required by law to be made has a privilege to refuse to disclose and to prevent any other person from disclosing the return or report, if the law requiring it to be made so provides. A public officer or agency to whom a return or report is required by law to be made has a privilege to refuse to disclose the return or report if the law requiring it to be made so provides. No privilege exists under this rule in actions involving perjury, false statements, fraud in the return or report, or other failure to comply with the law in question.

### Rule 503. Lawyer-client privilege.

**(a) Definitions.** As used in this rule:

(1) A "client" is a person, public officer, or corporation, association, or other organization or entity, either public or private, who is rendered professional legal services by a lawyer, or who consults a lawyer with a view to obtaining professional legal services from that lawyer.

(2) A "representative of the client" is:

(A) a person having authority to obtain professional legal services, or to act on advice thereby rendered, on behalf of the client, or

(B) any other person who, for the purpose of effectuating legal representation for the client, makes or receives a confidential communication while acting in the scope of employment for the client.

(3) A "lawyer" is a person authorized, or reasonably believed by the client to be authorized, to engage in the practice of law in any state or nation.

(4) A "representative of the lawyer" is:

(A) one employed by the lawyer to assist the lawyer in the rendition of professional legal services; or

(B) an accountant who is reasonably necessary for the lawyer's rendition of professional legal services.

(5) A communication is "confidential" if not intended to be disclosed to third persons other than those to whom disclosure is made in furtherance of the rendition of professional legal services to the client or those reasonably necessary for the transmission of the communication.

**(b) Rules of privilege.**

(1) *General rule of privilege.* A client has a privilege to refuse to disclose and to prevent any other person from disclosing confidential communications made for the purpose of facilitating the rendition of professional legal services to the client:

(A) between the client or a representative of the client and the client's lawyer or a representative of the lawyer;

(B) between the lawyer and the lawyer's representative;

(C) by the client or a representative of the client, or the client's lawyer or a representative of the lawyer, to a lawyer or a representative of a lawyer representing another party in a pending action and concerning a matter of common interest therein;

(D) between representatives of the client or between the client and a representative of the client; or

(E) among lawyers and their representatives representing the same client.

(2) *Special rule of privilege in criminal cases.* In criminal cases, a client has a privilege to prevent the lawyer or lawyer's representative from disclosing any other fact which came to the knowledge of the lawyer or the lawyer's representative by reason of the attorney-client relationship.

**(c) Who may claim the privilege.** The privilege may be claimed by the client, the client's guardian or conservator, the personal representative of a deceased client, or the successor, trustee, or similar representative of a corporation, association, or other organization, whether or not in existence. The person who was the lawyer or the lawyer's representative at the time of the communication is presumed to have authority to claim the privilege but only on behalf of the client.

**(d) Exceptions.** There is no privilege under this rule:

(1) *Furtherance of crime or fraud.* If the services of the lawyer were sought or obtained to enable or aid anyone to commit or plan to commit what the client knew or reasonably should have known to be a crime or fraud;

(2) *Claimants through same deceased client.* As to a communication relevant to an issue between parties who claim through the same deceased client, regardless of whether the claims are by testate or intestate succession or by *inter vivos* transactions;

(3) *Breach of duty by a lawyer or client.* As to a communication relevant to an issue of breach of duty by a lawyer to the client or by a client to the lawyer;

(4) *Document attested by a lawyer.* As to a communication relevant to an issue concerning an attested document to which the lawyer is an attesting witness; or

(5) *Joint clients.* As to a communication relevant to a matter of common interest between or among two or more clients if the communication was made by any of them to a lawyer retained or consulted in common, when offered in an action between or among any of the clients.

### Notes and Comments

Comment to 1998 change: The addition of subsection (a)(2)(B) adopts a subject matter test for the privilege of an entity, in place of the control group test previously used. *See National Tank Co. v. Brotherton,* 851 S.W.2d 193, 197-198 (Tex. 1993).

## Rule 504. Husband-wife privileges.

**(a) Confidential communication privilege.**

(1) *Definition.* A communication is confidential if it is made privately by any person to the person's spouse and it is not intended for disclosure to any other person.

(2) *Rule of privilege.* A person, whether or not a party, or the guardian or representative of an incompetent or deceased person, has a privilege during marriage and afterwards to refuse to disclose and to prevent another from disclosing a confidential communication made to the person's spouse while they were married.

(3) *Who may claim the privilege.* The confidential communication privilege may be claimed by the person or the person's guardian or representative, or by the spouse on the person's behalf. The authority of the spouse to do so is presumed.

(4) *Exceptions.* There is no confidential communication privilege:

(A) *Furtherance of crime or fraud.* If the communication was made, in whole or in part, to enable or aid anyone to commit or plan to commit a crime or fraud.

(B) *Proceeding between spouses in civil cases.* In (A) a proceeding brought by or on behalf of one spouse against the other spouse, or (B) a proceeding between a surviving spouse and a person who claims through the deceased spouse, regardless of whether the claim is by testate or intestate succession or by *inter vivos* transaction.

(C) *Crime against spouse or minor child.* In a proceeding in which the party is accused of conduct which, if proved, is a crime against the person of the spouse, any minor child, or any member of the household of either spouse.

(D) *Commitment or similar proceeding.* In a proceeding to commit either spouse or otherwise to place that person or that person's property, or both, under the control of another because of an alleged mental or physical condition.

(E) *Proceeding to establish competence.* In a proceeding brought by or on behalf of either spouse to establish competence.

**(b) Privilege not to testify in criminal case.**

(1) *Rule of privilege.* In a criminal case, the spouse of the accused has a privilege not to be called as a witness for the state. This rule does not prohibit the spouse from testifying voluntarily for the state, even over objection by the accused. A spouse who testifies on behalf of an accused is subject to cross-examination as provided in rule 611(b).

(2) *Failure to call as witness.* Failure by an accused to call the accused's spouse as a witness, where other evidence indicates that the spouse could testify to relevant matters, is a proper subject of comment by counsel.

(3) *Who may claim the privilege.* The privilege not to testify may be claimed by the person or the person's guardian or representative but not by that person's spouse.

(4) *Exceptions.* The privilege of a person's spouse not to be called as a witness for the state does not apply:

(A) *Certain criminal proceedings.* In any proceeding in which the person is charged with a crime against the person's spouse, a member of the household of either spouse, or any minor.

(B) *Matters occurring prior to marriage.* As to matters occurring prior to the marriage.

### Notes and Comments

Comment to 1998 change: The rule eliminates the spousal testimonial privilege for prosecutions in which the testifying spouse is the alleged victim of a crime by the accused. This is intended to be consistent with Code of Criminal Procedure article 38.10, effective September 1, 1995.

## Rule 505. Communications to members of the clergy.

**(a) Definitions.** As used in this rule:

(1) A "member of the clergy" is a minister, priest, rabbi, accredited Christian Science Practitioner, or other similar functionary of a religious organization or an individual reasonably believed so to be by the person consulting with such individual.

(2) A communication is "confidential" if made privately and not intended for further disclosure except to other persons present in furtherance of the purpose of the communication.

**(b) General rule of privilege.** A person has a privilege to refuse to disclose and to prevent another from disclosing a confidential communication by the person to a member of the clergy in the member's professional character as spiritual adviser.

**(c) Who may claim the privilege.** The privilege may be claimed by the person, by the person's guardian or conservator, or by the personal representative of the person if the person is deceased. The member of the clergy to whom the communication was made is presumed to have authority to claim the privilege but only on behalf of the communicant.

## Rule 506. Political vote.

Every person has a privilege to refuse to disclose the tenor of the person's vote at a political election conducted by secret ballot unless the vote was cast illegally.

## Rule 507. Trade secrets.

A person has a privilege, which may be claimed by the person or the person's agent or employee, to refuse to disclose and to prevent other persons from disclosing a trade secret owned by the person, if the allowance of the privilege will not tend to conceal fraud or otherwise work injustice. When disclosure is directed, the judge shall take such protective measure as the interests of the holder of the privilege and of the parties and the furtherance of justice may require.

## Rule 508. Identity of informer.

**(a) Rule of privilege.** The United States or a state or subdivision thereof has a privilege to refuse to disclose the identity of a person who has furnished information relating to or assisting in an investigation of a possible violation of a law to a law enforcement officer or member of a legislative committee or its staff conducting an investigation.

**(b) Who may claim.** The privilege may be claimed by an appropriate representative of the public entity to which the information was furnished, except the privilege shall not be allowed in criminal cases if the state objects.

**(c) Exceptions.**

(1) *Voluntary disclosure; informer a witness.* No privilege exists under this rule if the identity of the informer or the informer's interest in the subject matter of the communication has been disclosed to those who would have cause to resent the communication by a holder of the privilege or by the informer's own action, or if the informer appears as a witness for the public entity.

(2) *Testimony on merits.* If it appears from the evidence in the case or from other showing by a party that an informer may be able to give testimony necessary to a fair determination of a material issue on the merits in a civil case to which the public entity is a party, or on guilt or innocence in a criminal case, and the public entity invokes the privilege, the court shall give the public entity an opportunity to show in camera facts relevant to determining whether the informer can, in fact, supply that testimony. The showing will ordinarily be in the form of affidavits, but the court may direct that testimony be taken if it finds that the matter cannot be resolved satisfactorily upon affidavit. If the court finds that there is a reasonable probability that the informer can give the testimony, and the public entity elects not to disclose the informer's identity, the court in a civil case may make any order that justice requires, and in a criminal case shall, on motion of the defendant, and may, on the court's own motion, dismiss the charges as to which the testimony would relate. Evidence submitted to the court shall be sealed and preserved to be made available to the appellate court in the event of an appeal, and the contents shall not otherwise be revealed without consent of the public entity. All counsel and parties shall be permitted to be present at every stage of proceedings under this subdivision except a showing in camera, at which no counsel or party shall be permitted to be present.

(3) *Legality of obtaining evidence.* If information from an informer is relied upon to establish the legality of the means by which evidence was obtained and the court is not satisfied that the information was received from an informer reasonably believed to be reliable or credible, it may require the identity of the informer to be disclosed. The court shall, on request of the public entity, direct that the disclosure be made in camera. All counsel and parties concerned with the issue of legality shall be permitted to be present at every stage of proceedings under this subdivision except a disclosure in camera, at which no counsel or party shall be permitted to be present. If disclosure of the identity of the informer is made in camera, the record thereof shall be sealed and preserved to be made available to the appellate court in the event of an appeal, and the contents shall not otherwise be revealed without consent of the public entity.

## Rule 509. Physician-patient privilege.

**(a) Definitions.** As used in this rule:

(1) A "patient" means any person who consults or is seen by a physician to receive medical care.

(2) A "physician" means a person licensed to practice medicine in any state or nation, or reasonably believed by the patient so to be.

(3) A communication is "confidential" if not intended to be disclosed to third persons other than those present to further the interest of the patient in the consultation, examination, or interview, or those reasonably necessary for the transmission of the communication, or those who are participating in the diagnosis and treatment under the direction of the physician, including members of the patient's family.

**(b) Limited privilege in criminal proceedings.** There is no physician-patient privilege in criminal proceedings. However, a communication to any person involved in the treatment or examination of alcohol or drug abuse by a person being treated voluntarily or being examined for admission to treatment for alcohol or drug abuse is not admissible in a criminal proceeding.

**(c) General rule of privilege in civil proceedings.** In a civil proceeding:

(1) Confidential communications between a physician and a patient, relative to or in connection with any professional services rendered by a physician to the patient are privileged and may not be disclosed.

(2) Records of the identity, diagnosis, evaluation, or treatment of a patient by a physician that are created or maintained by a physician are confidential and privileged and may not be disclosed.

(3) The provisions of this rule apply even if the patient received the services of a physician prior to the enactment of the Medical Liability and Insurance Improvement Act, Tex. Rev. Civ. Stat. art. 4590i.

**(d) Who may claim the privilege in a civil proceeding.** In a civil proceeding:

(1) The privilege of confidentiality may be claimed by the patient or by a representative of the patient acting on the patient's behalf.

(2) The physician may claim the privilege of confidentiality, but only on behalf of the patient. The authority to do so is presumed in the absence of evidence to the contrary.

**(e) Exceptions in a civil proceeding.** Exceptions to confidentiality or privilege in administrative proceedings or in civil proceedings in court exist:

(1) when the proceedings are brought by the patient against a physician, including but not limited to malpractice proceedings, and in any license revocation proceeding in which the patient is a complaining witness and in which disclosure is relevant to the claims or defense of a physician;

(2) when the patient or someone authorized to act on the patient's behalf submits a written consent to the release of any privileged information, as provided in paragraph (f);

(3) when the purpose of the proceedings is to substantiate and collect on a claim for medical services rendered to the patient;

(4) as to a communication or record relevant to an issue of the physical, mental or emotional condition of a patient in any proceeding in which any party relies upon the condition as a part of the party's claim or defense;

(5) in any disciplinary investigation or proceeding of a physician conducted under or pursuant to the Medical Practice Act, Tex. Rev. Civ. Stat. art. 4495b, or of a registered nurse under or pursuant to Tex. Rev. Civ. Stat. arts. 4525, 4527a, 4527b, and 4527c, provided that the board shall protect the identity of any patient whose medical records are examined, except for those patients covered under subparagraph (e)(1) or those patients who have submitted written consent to the release of their medical records as provided by paragraph (f);

(6) in an involuntary civil commitment proceeding, proceeding for court-ordered treatment, or probable cause hearing under Tex. Health & Safety Code ch. 462; tit. 7, subtit. C; and tit. 7, subtit. D;

(7) in any proceeding regarding the abuse or neglect, or the cause of any abuse or neglect, of the resident of an "institution" as defined in Tex. Health & Safety Code §242.002.

**(f) Consent.**

(1) Consent for the release of privileged information must be in writing and signed by the patient, or a parent or legal guardian if the patient is a minor, or a legal guardian if the patient has been adjudicated incompetent to manage personal affairs, or an attorney ad litem appointed for the patient, as authorized by Tex. Health & Safety Code tit. 7, subtits. C and D; Tex. Prob. Code ch. V; and Tex. Fam. Code §107.011; or a personal representative if the patient is deceased, provided that the written consent specifies the following:

(A) the information or medical records to be covered by the release;

(B) the reasons or purposes for the release; and

(C) the person to whom the information is to be released.

(2) The patient, or other person authorized to consent, has the right to withdraw consent to the release of any information. Withdrawal of consent does not affect any information disclosed prior to the written notice of the withdrawal.

(3) Any person who received information made privileged by this rule may disclose the information to others only to the extent consistent with the authorized purposes for which consent to release the information was obtained.

### Notes and Comments

Comment to 1998 change: This comment is intended to inform the construction and application of this rule. Prior Criminal Rules of Evidence 509 and 510 are now in subparagraph (b) of this Rule. This rule governs disclosures of patient-physician communications only in judicial or administrative proceedings. Whether a physician may or must disclose such communications in other circumstances is governed by Tex. Rev. Civ. Stat. Ann. art. 4495b, §5.08. Former subparagraph (d)(6) of the Civil Evidence Rules, regarding disclosures in a suit affecting the parent-child relationship, is omitted, not because there should be no exception to the privilege in suits affecting the parent-child relationship, but because the exception in such suits is properly considered under subparagraph (d)(4), as construed in *R.K. v. Ramirez*, 887 S.W.2d 836 (Tex. 1994). In determining the proper application of an exception in such suits, the trial court must ensure that the precise need for the information is not outweighed by legitimate privacy interests protected by the privilege. Subparagraph (d) does not except from the privilege information relating to a nonparty patient who is or may be a consulting or testifying expert in the suit.

## Rule 510. Confidentiality of mental health information in civil cases.

**(a) Definitions.** As used in this rule:

(1) "Professional" means any person:

(A) authorized to practice medicine in any state or nation;

(B) licensed or certified by the State of Texas in the diagnosis, evaluation or treatment of any mental or emotional disorder;

(C) involved in the treatment or examination of drug abusers; or

(D) reasonably believed by the patient to be included in any of the preceding categories.

(2) "Patient" means any person who:

(A) consults, or is interviewed by, a professional for purposes of diagnosis, evaluation, or treatment of any mental or emotional condition or disorder, including alcoholism and drug addiction; or

(B) is being treated voluntarily or being examined for admission to voluntary treatment for drug abuse.

(3) A representative of the patient is:

(A) any person bearing the written consent of the patient;

(B) a parent if the patient is a minor;

(C) a guardian if the patient has been adjudicated incompetent to manage the patient's personal affairs; or

(D) the patient's personal representative if the patient is deceased.

(4) A communication is "confidential" if not intended to be disclosed to third persons other than those present to further the interest of the patient in the diagnosis, examination, evaluation, or treatment, or those reasonably necessary for the transmission of the communication, or those who are participating in the diagnosis, examination, evaluation, or treatment under the direction of the professional, including members of the patient's family.

**(b) General rule of privilege.**

(1) Communication between a patient and a professional is confidential and shall not be disclosed in civil cases.

(2) Records of the identity, diagnosis, evaluation, or treatment of a patient which are created or maintained by a professional are confidential and shall not be disclosed in civil cases.

(3) Any person who received information from confidential communications or records as defined herein, other than a representative of the patient acting on the patient's behalf, shall not disclose in civil cases the information except to the extent that disclosure is consistent with the authorized purposes for which the information was first obtained.

(4) The provisions of this rule apply even if the patient received the services of a professional prior to the enactment of Tex. Rev. Civ. Stat. art. 5561h (Vernon Supp. 1984) (now codified as Tex. Health & Safety Code §§ 611.001-611.008).

**(c) Who may claim the privilege.**

(1) The privilege of confidentiality may be claimed by the patient or by a representative of the patient acting on the patient's behalf.

(2) The professional may claim the privilege of confidentiality but only on behalf of the patient. The authority to do so is presumed in the absence of evidence to the contrary.

**(d) Exceptions.** Exceptions to the privilege in court or administrative proceedings exist:

(1) when the proceedings are brought by the patient against a professional, including but not limited to malpractice proceedings, and in any license revocation proceedings in which the patient is a complaining witness and in which disclosure is relevant to the claim or defense of a professional;

(2) when the patient waives the right in writing to the privilege of confidentiality of any information, or when a representative of the patient acting on the patient's behalf submits a written waiver to the confidentiality privilege;

(3) when the purpose of the proceeding is to substantiate and collect on a claim for mental or emotional health services rendered to the patient;

(4) when the judge finds that the patient after having been previously informed that communications would not be privileged, has made communications to a professional in the course of a court-ordered examination relating to the patient's mental or emotional condition or disorder, providing that such communications shall not be privileged only with respect to issues involving the patient's mental or emotional health. On granting of the order, the court, in determining the extent to which any disclosure of all or any part of any communication is necessary, shall impose appropriate safeguards against unauthorized disclosure;

(5) as to a communication or record relevant to an issue of the physical, mental or emotional condition of a patient in any proceeding in which any party relies upon the condition as a part of the party's claim or defense;

(6) in any proceeding regarding the abuse or neglect, or the cause of any abuse or neglect, of the resident of an institution as defined in Tex. Health and Safety Code §242.002.

**Notes and Comments**

Comment to 1998 change: This comment is intended to inform the construction and application of this rule. This rule governs disclosures of patient-professional communications only in judicial or administrative proceedings. Whether a professional may or must disclose such communications in other circumstances is governed by Tex. Health & Safety Code §§611.001-611.008. Former subparagraph (d)(6) of the Civil Evidence Rules, regarding disclosures in a suit affecting the parent-child relationship, is omitted, not because there should be no exception to the privilege in suits affecting the parent-child relationship, but because the exception in such suits is properly considered under subparagraph (d)(5), as construed in *R.K. v. Ramirez*, 887 S.W.2d 836 (Tex. 1994). In determining the proper application of an exception in such suits, the trial court must ensure that the precise need for the information is not outweighed by legitimate privacy interests protected by the privilege. Subparagraph (d) does not except from the privilege information relating to a nonparty patient who is or may be a consulting or testifying expert in the suit.

## Rule 511. Waiver of privilege by voluntary disclosure.

A person upon whom these rules confer a privilege against disclosure waives the privilege if:

(1) the person or a predecessor of the person while holder of the privilege voluntarily discloses or consents to disclosure of any significant part of the privileged matter unless such disclosure itself is privileged; or

(2) the person or a representative of the person calls a person to whom privileged communications have been made to testify as to the person's character or character trait insofar as such communications are relevant to such character or character trait.

## Rule 512. Privileged matter disclosed under compulsion or without opportunity to claim privilege.

A claim of privilege is not defeated by a disclosure which was (1) compelled erroneously or (2) made without opportunity to claim the privilege.

## Rule 513. Comment upon or inference from claim of privilege; instruction.

**(a) Comment or inference not permitted.** Except as permitted in Rule 504(b)(2), the claim of a privilege, whether in the present proceeding or upon a prior occasion, is not a proper subject of comment by judge or counsel, and no inference may be drawn therefrom.

**(b) Claiming privilege without knowledge of jury.** In jury cases, proceedings shall be conducted, to the extent practicable, so as to facilitate the making of claims of privilege without the knowledge of the jury.

**(c) Claim of privilege against self-incrimination in civil cases.** Paragraphs (a) and (b) shall not apply with respect to a party's claim, in the present civil proceeding, of the privilege against self-incrimination.

**(d) Jury instruction.** Except as provided in Rule 504(b)(2) and in paragraph (c) of this Rule, upon request any party against whom the jury might draw an adverse inference from a claim of privilege is entitled to an instruction that no inference may be drawn therefrom.

**Notes and Comments**

Comment to 1998 change: Subdivision (d) regarding a party's entitlement to a jury instruction about a claim of privilege is made applicable to civil cases.

# ARTICLE VI. WITNESSES

## Rule 601. Competency and incompetency of witnesses.

**(a) General rule.** Every person is competent to be a witness except as otherwise provided in these rules. The following witnesses shall be incompetent to testify in any proceeding subject to these rules:

(1) *Insane persons.* Insane persons who, in the opinion of the court, are in an insane condition of mind at the time when they are offered as a witness, or who, in the opinion of the court, were in that condition when the events happened of which they are called to testify.

(2) *Children.* Children or other persons who, after being examined by the court, appear not to possess sufficient intellect to relate transactions with respect to which they are interrogated.

**(b) "Dead man's rule" in Civil Actions.** In civil actions by or against executors, administrators, or guardians, in which judgment may be rendered for or against them as such, neither party shall be allowed to testify against the others as to any oral statement by the testator, intestate or ward, unless that testimony to the oral statement is corroborated or unless the witness is called at the trial to testify thereto by the opposite party; and, the provisions of this article shall extend to and include all actions by or against the heirs or legal representatives of a decedent based in whole or in part on such oral statement. Except for the foregoing, a witness is not precluded from giving evidence of or concerning any transaction with, any conversations with, any admissions of, or statement by, a deceased or insane party or person merely because the witness is a party to the action or a person interested in the event thereof. The trial court shall, in a proper case, where this rule prohibits an interested party or witness from testifying, instruct the jury that such person is not permitted by the law to give evidence relating to any oral statement by the deceased or ward unless the oral statement is corroborated or unless the party or witness is called at the trial by the opposite party.

## Rule 602. Lack of personal knowledge.

A witness may not testify to a matter unless evidence is introduced sufficient to support a finding that the witness has personal knowledge of the matter. Evidence to prove personal knowledge may, but need not, consist of the testimony of the witness. This rule is subject to the provisions of Rule 703, relating to opinion testimony by expert witnesses.

## Rule 603. Oath or affirmation.

Before testifying, every witness shall be required to declare that the witness will testify truthfully, by oath or affirmation administered in a form calculated to awaken the witness' conscience and impress the witness' mind with the duty to do so.

## Rule 604. Interpreters.

An interpreter is subject to the provisions of these rules relating to qualification as an expert and the administration of an oath or affirmation to make a true translation.

## Rule 605. Competency of judge as a witness.

The judge presiding at the trial may not testify in that trial as a witness. No objection need be made in order to preserve the point.

## Rule 606. Competency of juror as a witness.

**(a) At the trial.** A member of the jury may not testify as a witness before that jury in the trial of the case in which the juror is sitting as a juror. If the juror is called so to testify, the opposing party shall be afforded an opportunity to object out of the presence of the jury.

**(b) Inquiry into validity of verdict or indictment.** Upon an inquiry into the validity of a verdict or indictment, a juror may not testify as to any matter or statement occurring during the jury's deliberations, or to the effect of anything on any juror's mind or emotions or mental processes, as influencing any juror's assent to or dissent from the verdict or indictment. Nor may a juror's affidavit or any statement by a juror concerning any matter about which the juror would be precluded from testifying be admitted in evidence for any of these purposes. However, a juror may testify: (1) whether any outside influence was improperly brought to bear upon any juror; or (2) to rebut a claim that the juror was not qualified to serve.

## Rule 607. Who may impeach.

The credibility of a witness may be attacked by any party, including the party calling the witness.

## Rule 608. Evidence of character and conduct of a witness.

**(a) Opinion and reputation evidence of character.** The credibility of a witness may be attacked or supported by evidence in the form of opinion or reputation, but subject to these limitations:

(1) the evidence may refer only to character for truthfulness or untruthfulness; and

(2) evidence of truthful character is admissible only after the character of the witness for truthfulness has been attacked by opinion or reputation evidence or otherwise.

**(b) Specific instances of conduct.** Specific instances of the conduct of a witness, for the purpose of attacking or supporting the witness' credibility, other than conviction of crime as provided in Rule 609, may not be inquired into on cross-examination of the witness nor proved by extrinsic evidence.

## Rule 609. Impeachment by evidence of conviction of crime.

**(a) General rule.** For the purpose of attacking the credibility of a witness, evidence that the witness has been convicted of a crime shall be admitted if elicited from the witness or established by public record but only if the crime was a felony or involved moral turpitude, regardless of punishment, and the court determines that the probative value of admitting this evidence outweighs its prejudicial effect to a party.

**(b) Time limit.** Evidence of a conviction under this rule is not admissible if a period of more than ten years has elapsed since the date of the conviction or of the release of the witness from the confinement imposed for that conviction, whichever is the later date, unless the court determines, in the interests of justice, that the probative value of the conviction supported by specific facts and circumstances substantially outweighs its prejudicial effect.

**(c) Effect of pardon, annulment, or certificate of rehabilitation.** Evidence of a conviction is not admissible under this rule if:

(1) based on the finding of the rehabilitation of the person convicted, the conviction has been the subject of a pardon, annulment, certificate of rehabilitation, or other equivalent procedure, and that person has not been convicted of a subsequent crime which was classified as a felony or involved moral turpitude, regardless of punishment;

(2) probation has been satisfactorily completed for the crime for which the person was convicted, and that person has not been convicted of a subsequent crime which was classified as a felony or involved moral turpitude, regardless of punishment; or

(3) based on a finding of innocence, the conviction has been the subject of a pardon, annulment, or other equivalent procedure.

**(d) Juvenile adjudications.** Evidence of juvenile adjudications is not admissible, except for proceedings conducted pursuant to Title III, Family Code, in which the witness is a party, under this rule unless required to be admitted by the Constitution of the United States or Texas.

**(e) Pendency of appeal.** Pendency of an appeal renders evidence of a conviction inadmissible.

**(f) Notice.** Evidence of a conviction is not admissible if after timely written request by the adverse party specifying the witness or witnesses, the proponent fails to give to the adverse party sufficient advance written notice of intent to use such evidence to provide the adverse party with a fair opportunity to contest the use of such evidence.

## Rule 610. Religious beliefs or opinions.

Evidence of the beliefs or opinions of a witness on matters of religion is not admissible for the purpose of showing that by reason of their nature the witness' credibility is impaired or enhanced.

### Notes and Comments

Comment to 1998 change: This is prior Rule of Criminal Evidence 615.

## Rule 611. Mode and order of interrogation and presentation.

**(a) Control by court.** The court shall exercise reasonable control over the mode and order of interrogating witnesses and presenting evidence so as to (1) make the interrogation and presentation effective for the ascertainment of the truth, (2) avoid needless consumption of time, and (3) protect witnesses from harassment or undue embarrassment.

**(b) Scope of cross-examination.** A witness may be cross-examined on any matter relevant to any issue in the case, including credibility.

**(c) Leading questions.** Leading questions should not be used on the direct examination of a witness except as may be necessary to develop the testimony of the witness. Ordinarily leading questions should be permitted on cross-examination. When a party calls a hostile witness, an adverse party, or a witness identified with an adverse party, interrogation may be by leading questions.

## Rule 612. Writing used to refresh memory.

If a witness uses a writing to refresh memory for the purpose of testifying either

(1) while testifying;

(2) before testifying, in civil cases, if the court in its discretion determines it is necessary in the interests of justice; or

(3) before testifying, in criminal cases;

an adverse party is entitled to have the writing produced at the hearing, to inspect it, to cross-examine the witness thereon, and to introduce in evidence those portions which relate to the testimony of the witness. If it is claimed that the writing contains matters not related to the subject matter of the testimony the court shall examine the writing in camera, excise any portion not so related, and order delivery of the remainder to the party entitled thereto. Any portion withheld over objections shall be preserved and made available to the appellate court in the event of an appeal. If a writing is not produced or delivered pursuant to order under this rule, the court shall make any order justice requires, except that in criminal cases when the prosecution elects not to comply, the order shall be one striking the testimony or, if the court in its discretion determines that the interests of justice so require, declaring a mistrial.

## Rule 613. Prior statements of witnesses: impeachment and support.

**(a) Examining witness concerning prior inconsistent statement.** In examining a witness concerning a prior inconsistent statement made by the witness, whether oral or written, and before further cross-examination concerning, or extrinsic evidence of, such statement may be allowed, the witness must be told the contents of such statement and the time and place and the person to whom it was made, and must be afforded an opportunity to explain or deny such statement. If written, the writing need not be shown to the witness at that time, but on request the same shall be shown to opposing counsel. If the witness unequivocally admits having made such statement, extrinsic evidence of same shall not be admitted. This provision does not apply to admissions of a party-opponent as defined in Rule 801(e)(2).

**(b) Examining witness concerning bias or interest.** In impeaching a witness by proof of circumstances or statements showing bias or interest on the part of such witness, and before further cross-examination concerning, or extrinsic evidence of, such bias or interest may be allowed, the circumstances supporting such claim or the details of such statement, including the contents and where, when and to whom made, must be made known to the witness, and the witness must be given an opportunity to explain or to deny such circumstances or statement. If written, the writing need not be shown to the witness at that time, but on request the same shall be shown to opposing counsel. If the witness unequivocally admits such bias or interest, extrinsic evidence of same shall not be admitted. A party shall be permitted to present evidence rebutting any evidence impeaching one of said party's witnesses on grounds of bias or interest.

**(c) Prior consistent statements of witnesses.** A prior statement of a witness which is consistent with the testimony of the witness is inadmissible except as provided in Rule 801(e)(1)(B).

## Rule 614. Exclusion of witnesses.

At the request of a party the court shall order witnesses excluded so that they cannot hear the testimony of other witnesses, and it may make the order of its own motion. This rule does not authorize exclusion of:

(1) a party who is a natural person or in civil cases the spouse of such natural person;

(2) an officer or employee of a party in a civil case or a defendant in a criminal case that is not a natural person designated as its representative by its attorney;

(3) a person whose presence is shown by a party to be essential to the presentation of the party's cause; or

(4) the victim in a criminal case, unless the victim is to testify and the court determines that the victim's testimony would be materially affected if the victim hears other testimony at the trial.

## Rule 615. Production of statements of witnesses in criminal cases.

**(a) Motion for production.** After a witness other than the defendant has testified on direct examination, the court, on motion of a party who did not call the witness, shall order the attorney for the state or the defendant and defendant's attorney, as the case may be, to produce, for the examination and use of the moving party, any statement of the witness that is in their possession and that relates to the subject matter concerning which the witness has testified.

**(b) Production of entire statement.** If the entire contents of the statement relate to the subject matter concerning which the witness has testified, the court shall order that the statement be delivered to the moving party.

**(c) Production of excised statement.** If the other party claims that the statement contains matter that does not relate to the subject matter concerning which the witness has testified, the court shall order that it be delivered to the court in camera. Upon inspection, the court shall excise the portions of the statement that do not relate to the subject matter concerning which the witness has testified, and shall order that the statement, with such material excised, be delivered to the moving party. Any portion withheld over objection shall be preserved and made available to the appellate court in the event of appeal.

**(d) Recess for examination of statement.** Upon delivery of the statement to the moving party, the court, upon application of that party, shall recess proceedings in the trial for a reasonable examination of such statement and for preparation for its use in the trial.

**(e) Sanction for failure to produce statement.** If the other party elects not to comply with an order to deliver a statement to the moving party, the court shall order that the testimony of the witness be stricken from the record and that the trial proceed, or, if it is the attorney for the state who elects not to comply, shall declare a mistrial if required by the interest of justice.

**(f) Definition.** As used in this rule, a "statement" of a witness means:

(1) a written statement made by the witness that is signed or otherwise adopted or approved by the witness;

(2) a substantially verbatim recital of an oral statement made by the witness that is recorded contemporaneously with the making of the oral statement and that is contained in a stenographic, mechanical, electrical, or other recording or a transcription thereof; or

(3) a statement, however taken or recorded, or a transcription thereof, made by the witness to a grand jury.

**Notes and Comments**

Comment to 1998 change: This is prior Rule of Criminal Evidence 614.

## ARTICLE VII. OPINIONS AND EXPERT TESTIMONY

### Rule 701. Opinion testimony by lay witnesses.

If the witness is not testifying as an expert, the witness' testimony in the form of opinions or inferences is limited to those opinions or inferences which are (a) rationally based on the perception of the witness and (b) helpful to a clear understanding of the witness' testimony or the determination of a fact in issue.

### Rule 702. Testimony by experts.

If scientific, technical, or other specialized knowledge will assist the trier of fact to understand the evidence or to determine a fact in issue, a witness qualified as an expert by knowledge, skill, experience, training, or education may testify thereto in the form of an opinion or otherwise.

### Rule 703. Bases of opinion testimony by experts.

The facts or data in the particular case upon which an expert bases an opinion or inference may be those perceived by, reviewed by, or made known to the expert at or before the hearing. If of a type reasonably relied upon by experts in the particular field in forming opinions or inferences upon the subject, the facts or data need not be admissible in evidence.

**Notes and Comments**

Comment to 1998 change: The former Civil Rule referred to facts or data "perceived by or reviewed by" the expert. The former Criminal Rule referred to facts or data "perceived by or made known to" the expert. The terminology is now conformed, but no change in meaning is intended.

### Rule 704. Opinion on ultimate issue.

Testimony in the form of an opinion or inference otherwise admissible is not objectionable because it embraces an ultimate issue to be decided by the trier of fact.

### Rule 705. Disclosure of facts or data underlying expert opinion.

**(a) Disclosure of facts or data.** The expert may testify in terms of opinion or inference and give the expert's reasons therefor without prior disclosure of the underlying facts or data, unless the court requires otherwise. The expert may in any event disclose on direct examination, or be required to disclose on cross-examination, the underlying facts or data.

**(b) Voir dire.** Prior to the expert giving the expert's opinion or disclosing the underlying facts or data, a party against whom the opinion is offered upon request in a criminal case shall, or in a civil case may, be permitted to conduct a voir dire examination directed to the underlying facts or data upon which the opinion is based. This examination shall be conducted out of the hearing of the jury.

**(c) Admissibility of opinion.** If the court determines that the underlying facts or data do not provide a sufficient basis for the expert's opinion under Rule 702 or 703, the opinion is inadmissible.

**(d) Balancing test; limiting instructions.** When the underlying facts or data would be inadmissible in evidence, the court shall exclude the underlying facts or data if the danger that they will be used for a purpose other than as explanation or support for the expert's opinion outweighs their value as explanation or support or are unfairly prejudicial. If otherwise inadmissible facts or data are disclosed before the jury, a limiting instruction by the court shall be given upon request.

**Notes and Comments**

Comment to 1998 change: Paragraphs (b), (c), and (d) are based on the former Criminal Rule and are made applicable to civil cases. This rule does not preclude a party in any case from conducting a voir dire examination into the qualifications of an expert.

### Rule 706. Audit in civil cases.

Despite any other evidence rule to the contrary, verified reports of auditors prepared pursuant to Rule of Civil Procedure 172, whether in the form of summaries, opinions, or otherwise, shall be admitted in evidence when offered by any party whether or not the facts or data in the reports are otherwise admissible and whether or not the reports embrace the ultimate issues to be decided by the trier of fact. Where exceptions to the reports have been filed, a party may contradict the reports by evidence supporting the exceptions.

## ARTICLE VIII. HEARSAY

### Rule 801. Definitions.

The following definitions apply under this article:

**(a) Statement.** A "statement" is (1) an oral or written verbal expression or (2) nonverbal conduct of a person, if it is intended by the person as a substitute for verbal expression.

**(b) Declarant.** A "declarant" is a person who makes a statement.

**(c) Matter asserted.** "Matter asserted" includes any matter explicitly asserted, and any matter implied by a statement, if the probative value of the statement as offered flows from declarant's belief as to the matter.

**(d) Hearsay.** "Hearsay" is a statement, other than one made by the declarant while testifying at the trial or hearing, offered in evidence to prove the truth of the matter asserted.

**(e) Statements which are not hearsay.** A statement is not hearsay if:

(1) *Prior statement by witness.* The declarant testifies at the trial or hearing and is subject to cross-examination concerning the statement, and the statement is:

(A) inconsistent with the declarant's testimony, and was given under oath subject to the penalty of perjury at a trial, hearing, or other proceeding except a grand jury proceeding in a criminal case, or in a deposition;

(B) consistent with the declarant's testimony and is offered to rebut an express or implied charge against the declarant of recent fabrication or improper influence or motive;

(C) one of identification of a person made after perceiving the person; or

(D) taken and offered in a criminal case in accordance with Code of Criminal Procedure article 38.071.

(2) *Admission by party-opponent.* The statement is offered against a party and is:

(A) the party's own statement in either an individual or representative capacity;

(B) a statement of which the party has manifested an adoption or belief in its truth;

(C) a statement by a person authorized by the party to make a statement concerning the subject;

(D) a statement by the party's agent or servant concerning a matter within the scope of the agency or employment, made during the existence of the relationship; or

(E) a statement by a co-conspirator of a party during the course and in furtherance of the conspiracy.

(3) *Depositions.* In a civil case, it is a deposition taken in the same proceeding, as same proceeding is defined in Rule of Civil Procedure 207. Unavailability of deponent is not a requirement for admissibility.

## Rule 802. Hearsay rule.

Hearsay is not admissible except as provided by statute or these rules or by other rules prescribed pursuant to statutory authority. Inadmissible hearsay admitted without objection shall not be denied probative value merely because it is hearsay.

## Rule 803. Hearsay exceptions; availability of declarant immaterial.

The following are not excluded by the hearsay rule, even though the declarant is available as a witness:

**(1) Present Sense Impression.** A statement describing or explaining an event or condition made while the declarant was perceiving the event or condition, or immediately thereafter.

**(2) Excited utterance.** A statement relating to a startling event or condition made while the declarant was under the stress of excitement caused by the event or condition.

**(3) Then existing mental, emotional, or physical condition.** A statement of the declarant's then existing state of mind, emotion, sensation, or physical condition (such as intent, plan, motive, design, mental feeling, pain, or bodily health), but not including a statement of memory or belief to prove the fact remembered or believed unless it relates to the execution, revocation, identification, or terms of declarant's will.

**(4) Statements for purposes of medical diagnosis or treatment.** Statements made for purposes of medical diagnosis or treatment and describing medical history, or past or present symptoms, pain, or sensations, or the inception or general character of the cause or external source thereof insofar as reasonably pertinent to diagnosis or treatment.

**(5) Recorded recollection.** A memorandum or record concerning a matter about which a witness once had personal knowledge but now has insufficient recollection to enable the witness to testify fully and accurately, shown to have been made or adopted by the witness when the matter was fresh in the witness' memory and to reflect that knowledge correctly, unless the circumstances of preparation cast doubt on the document's trustworthiness. If admitted, the memorandum or record may be read into evidence but may not itself be received as an exhibit unless offered by an adverse party.

**(6) Records of regularly conducted activity.** A memorandum, report, record, or data compilation, in any form, of acts, events, conditions, opinions, or diagnoses, made at or near the time by, or from information transmitted by, a person with knowledge, if kept in the course of a regularly conducted business activity, and if it was the regular practice of that business activity to make the memorandum, report, record, or data compilation, all as shown by the testimony of the custodian or other qualified witness, or by affidavit that complies with Rule 902(10), unless the source of information or the method or circumstances of preparation indicate lack of trustworthiness. "Business" as used in this paragraph includes any and every kind of regular organized activity whether conducted for profit or not.

**(7) Absence of entry in records kept in accordance with the provisions of paragraph (6).** Evidence that a matter is not included in the memoranda, reports, records, or data compilations, in any form, kept in accordance with the provisions of paragraph (6), to prove the nonoccurrence or nonexistence of the matter, if the matter was of a kind of which a memorandum, report, record, or data compilation was regularly made and preserved, unless the sources of information or other circumstances indicate lack of trustworthiness.

**(8) Public records and reports.** Records, reports, statements, or data compilations, in any form, of public offices or agencies setting forth:

(A) the activities of the office or agency;

(B) matters observed pursuant to duty imposed by law as to which matters there was a duty to report, excluding in criminal cases matters observed by police officers and other law enforcement personnel; or

(C) in civil cases as to any party and in criminal cases as against the state, factual findings resulting from an investigation made pursuant to authority granted by law;

unless the sources of information or other circumstances indicate lack of trustworthiness.

**(9) Records of vital statistics.** Records or data compilations, in any form, of births, fetal deaths, deaths, or marriages, if the report thereof was made to a public office pursuant to requirements of law.

**(10) Absence of public record or entry.** To prove the absence of a record, report, statement, or data compilation, in any form, or the nonoccurrence or nonexistence of a matter of which a record, report, statement, or data compilation, in any form, was regularly made and preserved by a public office or agency, evidence in the form of a certification in accordance with Rule 902, or testimony, that diligent search failed to disclose the record, report statement, or data compilation, or entry.

**(11) Records of religious organizations.** Statements of births, marriages, divorces, deaths, legitimacy, ancestry, relationship by blood or marriage, or other similar facts of personal or family history, contained in a regularly kept record of a religious organization.

**(12) Marriage, baptismal, and similar certificates.** Statements of fact contained in a certificate that the maker performed a marriage or other ceremony or administered a sacrament, made by a member of the clergy, public official, or other person authorized by the rules or practices of a religious organization or by law to perform the act certified, and purporting to have been issued at the time of the act or within a reasonable time thereafter.

**(13) Family records.** Statements of fact concerning personal or family history contained in family Bibles, genealogies, charts, engravings on rings, inscriptions on family portraits, engravings on urns, crypts, or tombstones, or the like.

**(14) Records of documents affecting an interest in property.** The record of a document purporting to establish or affect an interest in property, as proof of the content of the original recorded document and its execution and delivery by each person by whom it purports to have been executed, if the record is a record of a public office and an applicable statute authorizes the recording of documents of that kind in that office.

**(15) Statements in documents affecting an interest in property.** A statement contained in a document purporting to establish or affect an interest in property if the matter stated was relevant to the purpose of the document, unless dealings with the property since the document was made have been inconsistent with the truth of the statement or the purport of the document.

**(16) Statements in ancient documents.** Statements in a document in existence twenty years or more the authenticity of which is established.

**(17) Market reports, commercial publications.** Market quotations, tabulations, lists, directories, or other published compilations, generally used and relied upon by the public or by persons in particular occupations.

**(18) Learned treatises.** To the extent called to the attention of an expert witness upon cross-examination or relied upon by the expert in direct examination, statements contained in published treatises, periodicals, or pamphlets on a subject of history, medicine, or other science or art established as a reliable authority by the testimony or admission of the witness or by other expert testimony or by judicial notice. If admitted, the statements may be read into evidence but may not be received as exhibits.

**(19) Reputation concerning personal or family history.** Reputation among members of a person's family by blood, adoption, or marriage, or among a person's associates, or in the community, concerning a person's birth, adoption, marriage, divorce, death, legitimacy, relationship by blood, adoption, or marriage, ancestry, or other similar fact of personal or family history.

**(20) Reputation concerning boundaries or general history.** Reputation in a community, arising before the controversy, as to boundaries of or customs affecting lands in the community, and reputation as to events of general history important to the community or state or nation in which located.

**(21) Reputation as to character.** Reputation of a person's character among associates or in the community.

**(22) Judgment of previous conviction.** In civil cases, evidence of a judgment, entered after a trial or upon a plea of guilty (but not upon a plea of nolo contendere), judging a person guilty of a felony, to prove any fact essential to sustain the judgment of conviction. In criminal cases, evidence of a judgment, entered after a trial or upon a plea of guilty or nolo contendere, adjudging a person guilty of a criminal offense, to prove any fact essential to sustain the judgment of conviction, but not including, when offered by the state for purposes other than impeachment, judgments against persons other than the accused. In all cases, the pendency of an appeal renders such evidence inadmissible.

**(23) Judgment as to personal, family, or general history, or boundaries.** Judgments as proof of matters of personal, family or general history, or boundaries, essential to the judgment, if the same would be provable by evidence of reputation.

**(24) Statement against interest.** A statement which was at the time of its making so far contrary to the declarant's pecuniary or proprietary interest, or so far tended to subject the declarant to civil or criminal liability, or to render invalid a claim by the declarant against another, or to make the declarant an object of hatred, ridicule, or disgrace, that a reasonable person in declarant's position would not have made the statement unless believing it to be true. In criminal cases, a statement tending to expose the declarant to criminal liability is not admissible unless corroborating circumstances clearly indicate the trustworthiness of the statement.

## Rule 804. Hearsay exceptions; declarant unavailable.

**(a) Definition of unavailability.** "Unavailability as a witness" includes situations in which the declarant:

(1) is exempted by ruling of the court on the ground of privilege from testifying concerning the subject matter of the declarant's statement;

(2) persists in refusing to testify concerning the subject matter of the declarant's statement despite an order of the court to do so;

(3) testifies to a lack of memory of the subject matter of the declarant's statement;

(4) is unable to be present or to testify at the hearing because of death or then existing physical or mental illness or infirmity; or

(5) is absent from the hearing and the proponent of the declarant's statement has been unable to procure the declarant's attendance or testimony by process or other reasonable means.

A declarant is not unavailable as a witness if the declarant's exemption, refusal, claim of lack of memory, inability, or absence is due to the procurement or wrong-doing of the proponent of the declarant's statement for the purpose of preventing the witness from attending or testifying.

**(b) Hearsay exceptions.** The following are not excluded if the declarant is unavailable as a witness:

(1) *Former testimony.* In civil cases, testimony given as a witness at another hearing of the same or a different proceeding, or in a deposition taken in the course of another proceeding, if the party against whom the testimony is now offered, or a person with a similar interest, had an opportunity and similar motive to develop the testimony by direct, cross, or redirect examination. In criminal cases, testimony given as a witness at another hearing of the same or a different proceeding, if the party against whom the testimony is now offered had an opportunity and similar motive to develop the testimony by direct, cross, or redirect examination. In criminal cases the use of depositions is controlled by Chapter 39 of the Code of Criminal Procedure.

(2) *Dying declarations.* A statement made by a declarant while believing that the declarant's death was imminent, concerning the cause or circumstances of what the declarant believed to be impending death.

(3) *Statement of personal or family history.*

(A) A statement concerning the declarant's own birth, adoption, marriage, divorce, legitimacy, relationship by blood, adoption, or marriage, ancestry, or other similar fact of personal or family history even though declarant had no means of acquiring personal knowledge of the matter stated; or

(B) A statement concerning the foregoing matters, and death also, of another person, if the declarant was related to the other by blood, adoption, or marriage or was so intimately associated with the other's family as to be likely to have accurate information concerning the matter declared.

## Rule 805. Hearsay within hearsay.

Hearsay included within hearsay is not excluded under the hearsay rule if each part of the combined statements conforms with an exception to the hearsay rule provided in these rules.

## Rule 806. Attacking and supporting credibility of declarant.

When a hearsay statement, or a statement defined in Rule 801(e)(2)(C), (D), or (E), or in civil cases a statement defined in Rule 801(e)(3), has been admitted in evidence, the credibility of the declarant may be attacked, and if attacked may be supported by any evidence which would be admissible for those purposes if declarant had testified as a witness. Evidence of a statement or conduct by the declarant at any time, offered to impeach the declarant, is not subject to any requirement that the declarant may have been afforded an opportunity to deny or explain. If the party against whom a hearsay statement has been admitted calls the declarant as a witness, the party is entitled to examine the declarant on the statement as if under cross-examination.

# ARTICLE IX. AUTHENTICATION AND IDENTIFICATION

## Rule 901. Requirement of authentication or identification.

**(a) General provision.** The requirement of authentication or identification as a condition precedent to admissibility is satisfied by evidence sufficient to support a finding that the matter in question is what its proponent claims.

**(b) Illustrations.** By way of illustration only, and not by way of limitation, the following are examples of authentication or identification conforming with the requirements of this rule:

(1) *Testimony of witness with knowledge.* Testimony that a matter is what it is claimed to be.

(2) *Nonexpert opinion on handwriting.* Nonexpert opinion as to the genuineness of handwriting, based upon familiarity not acquired for purposes of the litigation.

(3) *Comparison by trier or expert witness.* Comparison by the trier of fact or by expert witness with specimens which have been found by the court to be genuine.

(4) *Distinctive characteristics and the like.* Appearance, contents, substance, internal patterns, or other distinctive characteristics, taken in conjunction with circumstances.

(5) *Voice identification.* Identification of a voice, whether heard firsthand or through mechanical or electronic transmission or recording, by opinion based upon hearing the voice at anytime under circumstances connecting it with the alleged speaker.

(6) *Telephone conversations.* Telephone conversations, by evidence that a call was made to the number assigned at the time by the telephone company to a particular person or business, if:

(A) in the case of a person, circumstances, including self-identification, show the person answering to be the one called; or

(B) in the case of a business, the call was made to a place of business and the conversation related to business reasonably transacted over the telephone.

(7) *Public records or reports.* Evidence that a writing authorized by law to be recorded or filed and in fact recorded or filed in a public office, or a purported public record, report, statement, or data compilation, in any form, is from the public office where items of this nature are kept.

(8) *Ancient documents or data compilation.* Evidence that a document or data compilation, in any form, (A) is in such condition as to create no suspicion concerning its authenticity, (B) was in a place where it, if authentic, would likely be, and (C) has been in existence twenty years or more at the time it is offered.

(9) *Process or system.* Evidence describing a process or system used to produce a result and showing that the process or system produces an accurate result.

(10) *Methods provided by statute or rule.* Any method of authentication or identification provided by statute or by other rule prescribed pursuant to statutory authority.

## Rule 902. Self-authentication.

Extrinsic evidence of authenticity as a condition precedent to admissibility is not required with respect to the following:

**(1) Domestic public documents under seal.** A document bearing a seal purporting to be that of the United States, or of any State, district, Commonwealth, territory, or insular possession thereof, or the Panama Canal Zone, or the Trust Territory of the Pacific Islands, or of a political subdivision, department, officer, or agency thereof, and a signature purporting to be an attestation or execution.

**(2) Domestic public documents not under seal.** A document purporting to bear the signature in the official capacity of an officer or employee of any entity included in paragraph (1) hereof, having no seal, if a public officer having a seal and having official duties in the district or political subdivision of the officer or employee certifies under seal that the signer has the official capacity and that the signature is genuine.

**(3) Foreign public documents.** A document purporting to be executed or attested in an official capacity by a person, authorized by the laws of a foreign country to make the execution or attestation, and accompanied by a final certification as to the genuineness of the signature and official position (A) of the executing or attesting person, or (B) of any foreign official whose certificate of genuineness of signature and official position relates to the execution or attestation or is in a chain of certificates of genuineness of signature and official position relating to the execution or attestation. A final certification may be made by a secretary of embassy or legation, consul general, consul, vice consul, or consular agent of the United States, or a diplomatic or consular official of the foreign country assigned or accredited to the United States. If reasonable opportunity has been given to all parties to investigate the authenticity and accuracy of official documents, the court may, for good cause shown, order that they be treated as presumptively authentic without final certification or permit them to be evidenced by an attested summary with or without final certification. The final certification shall be dispensed with whenever both the United States and the foreign country in which the official record is located are parties to a treaty or convention that abolishes or displaces such requirement, in which case the record and the attestation shall be certified by the means provided in the treaty or convention.

**(4) Certified copies of public records.** A copy of an official record or report or entry therein, or of a document authorized by law to be recorded or filed and actually recorded or filed in a public office, including data compilations in any form certified as correct by the custodian or other person authorized to make the certification, by certificate complying with paragraph (1), (2) or (3) of this rule or complying with any statute or other rule prescribed pursuant to statutory authority.

**(5) Official publications.** Books, pamphlets, or other publications purporting to be issued by public authority.

**(6) Newspapers and periodicals.** Printed materials purporting to be newspapers or periodicals.

**(7) Trade inscriptions and the like.** Inscriptions, signs, tags, or labels purporting to have been affixed in the course of business and indicating ownership, control, or origin.

**(8) Acknowledged documents.** Documents accompanied by a certificate of acknowledgment executed in the manner provided by law by a notary public or other officer authorized by law to take acknowledgments.

**(9) Commercial paper and related documents.** Commercial paper, signatures thereon, and documents relating thereto to the extent provided by general commercial law.

**(10) Business records accompanied by affidavit.**

(a) *Records or photocopies; admissibility; affidavit; filing.* Any record or set of records or photographically reproduced copies of such records, which would be admissible under Rule 803(6) or (7) shall be admissible in evidence in any court in this state upon the affidavit of the person who would otherwise provide the prerequisites of Rule 803(6) or (7), that such records attached to such affidavit were in fact so kept as required by Rule 803(6) or (7), provided further, that such record or records along with such affidavit are filed with the clerk of the court for inclusion with the papers in the cause in which the record or records are sought to be used as evidence at least fourteen days prior to the day upon which trial of said cause commences, and provided the other parties to said cause are given prompt notice by the party filing same of the filing of such record or records and affidavit, which notice shall identify the name and employer, if any, of the person making the affidavit and such records shall be made available to the counsel for other parties to the action or litigation for inspection and copying. The expense for copying shall be borne by the party, parties or persons who desire copies and not by the party or parties who file the records and serve notice of said filing, in compliance with this rule. Notice shall be deemed to have been promptly given if it is served in the manner contemplated by Rule of Civil Procedure 21a fourteen days prior to commencement of trial in said cause.

(b) *Form of affidavit.* A form for the affidavit of such person as shall make such affidavit as is permitted in paragraph (a) above shall be sufficient if it follows this form though this form shall not be exclusive, and an affidavit which substantially complies with the provisions of this rule shall suffice, to-wit:

No. ______________

| | | |
|---|---|---|
| John Doe | § | IN THE __________ |
| (Name of Plaintiff) | § | |
| v. | § | COURT IN AND FOR |
| | § | |
| John Roe | § | _________ COUNTY, |
| (Name of Defendant) | § | TEXAS |

AFFIDAVIT

Before me, the undersigned authority, personally appeared __________________, who, being by me duly sworn, deposed as follows:

My name is __________ __________, I am of sound mind, capable of making this affidavit, and personally acquainted with the facts herein stated:

I am the custodian of the records of __________________. Attached hereto are _____ pages of records from ________________. These said _____ pages of records are kept by ________________ in the regular course of business, and it was the regular course of business of __________________ for an employee or representative of __________________, with knowledge of the act, event, condition, opinion, or diagnosis, recorded to make the record or to transmit information thereof to be included in such record; and the record was made at or near the time or reasonably soon thereafter. The records attached hereto are the original or exact duplicates of the original.

______________________________
Affiant

SWORN TO AND SUBSCRIBED before me on the ________ day of _________, 19____.

______________________________
Notary Public, State of Texas

Notary's printed name:

______________________________

My commission expires:

______________

(11) **Presumptions under statutes or other rules.** Any signature, document, or other matter declared by statute or by other rules prescribed pursuant to statutory authority to be presumptively or prima facie genuine or authentic.

### Rule 903. Subscribing witness' testimony unnecessary.

The testimony of a subscribing witness is not necessary to authenticate a writing unless required by the laws of the jurisdiction whose laws govern the validity of the writing.

## ARTICLE X. CONTENTS OF WRITINGS, RECORDINGS, AND PHOTOGRAPHS

### Rule 1001. Definitions.

For purposes of this article the following definitions are applicable:

**(a) Writings and recordings.** "Writings" and "recordings" consist of letters, words, or numbers or their equivalent, set down by handwriting, typewriting, printing, photostating, photographing, magnetic impulse, mechanical or electronic recording, or other form of data compilation.

**(b) Photographs.** "Photographs" include still photographs, X-ray films, video tapes, and motion pictures.

**(c) Original.** An "original" of a writing or recording is the writing or recording itself or any counterpart intended to have the same effect by a person executing or issuing it. An "original" of a photograph includes the negative or any print therefrom. If data are stored in a computer or similar device, any printout or other output readable by sight, shown to reflect the data accurately, is an "original."

**(d) Duplicate.** A "duplicate" is a counterpart produced by the same impression as the original, or from the same matrix, or by means of photography, including enlargements and miniatures, or by mechanical or electronic re-recording, or by chemical reproduction, or by other equivalent techniques which accurately reproduce the original.

### Rule 1002. Requirement of originals.

To prove the content of a writing, recording, or photograph, the original writing, recording, or photograph is required except as otherwise provided in these rules or by law.

### Rule 1003. Admissibility of duplicates.

A duplicate is admissible to the same extent as an original unless (1) a question is raised as to the authenticity of the original or (2) in the circumstances it would be unfair to admit the duplicate in lieu of the original.

### Rule 1004. Admissibility of other evidence of contents.

The original is not required, and other evidence of the contents of a writing, recording, or photograph is admissible if:

**(a) Originals lost or destroyed.** All originals are lost or have been destroyed, unless the proponent lost or destroyed them in bad faith;

**(b) Original not obtainable.** No original can be obtained by any available judicial process or procedure;

**(c) Original outside the state.** No original is located in Texas;

**(d) Original in possession of opponent.** At a time when an original was under the control of the party against whom offered, that party was put on notice, by the pleadings or otherwise, that the content would be a subject of proof at the hearing, and that party does not produce the original at the hearing; or

**(e) Collateral matters.** The writing, recording or photograph is not closely related to a controlling issue.

## Rule 1005. Public records.

The contents of an official record or of a document authorized to be recorded or filed and actually recorded or filed, including data compilations in any form, if otherwise admissible, may be proved by copy, certified as correct in accordance with Rule 902 or testified to be correct by a witness who has compared it with the original. If a copy which complies with the foregoing cannot be obtained by the exercise of reasonable diligence, then other evidence of the contents may be given.

## Rule 1006. Summaries.

The contents of voluminous writings, recordings, or photographs, otherwise admissible, which cannot conveniently be examined in court may be presented in the form of a chart, summary, or calculation. The originals, or duplicates, shall be made available for examination or copying, or both, by other parties at a reasonable time and place. The court may order that they be produced in court.

## Rule 1007. Testimony or written admission of party.

Contents of writings, recordings, or photographs may be proved by the testimony or deposition of the party against whom offered or by that party's written admission, without accounting for the nonproduction of the original.

## Rule 1008. Functions of court and jury.

When the admissibility of other evidence of contents of writings, recordings, or photographs under these rules depends upon the fulfillment of a condition of fact, the question whether the condition has been fulfilled is ordinarily for the court to determine in accordance with the provisions of Rule 104. However, when an issue is raised (a) whether the asserted writing ever existed, or (b) whether another writing, recording, or photograph produced at the trial is the original, or (c) whether other evidence of contents correctly reflects the contents, the issue is for the trier of fact to determine as in the case of other issues of fact.

## Rule 1009. Translation of foreign language documents.

**(a) Translations.** A translation of foreign language documents shall be admissible upon the affidavit of a qualified translator setting forth the qualifications of the translator and certifying that the translation is fair and accurate. Such affidavit, along with the translation and the underlying foreign language documents, shall be served upon all parties at least 45 days prior to the date of trial.

**(b) Objections.** Any party may object to the accuracy of another party's translation by pointing out the specific inaccuracies of the translation and by stating with specificity what the objecting party contends is a fair and accurate translation. Such objection shall be served upon all parties at least 15 days prior to the date of trial.

**(c) Effect of failure to object or offer conflicting translation.** If no conflicting translation or objection is timely served, the court shall admit a translation submitted under paragraph (a) without need of proof, provided however that the underlying foreign language documents are otherwise admissible under the Texas Rules of Evidence. Failure to serve a conflicting translation under paragraph (a) or failure to timely and properly object to the accuracy of a translation under paragraph (b) shall preclude a party from attacking or offering evidence contradicting the accuracy of such translation at trial.

**(d) Effect of objections or conflicting translations.** In the event of conflicting translations under paragraph (a) or if objections to another party's translation are served under paragraph (b), the court shall determine whether there is a genuine issue as to the accuracy of a material part of the translation to be resolved by the trier of fact.

**(e) Expert testimony of translator.** Except as provided in paragraph (c), this Rule does not preclude the admission of a translation of foreign language documents at trial either by live testimony or by deposition testimony of a qualified expert translator.

**(f) Varying of time limits.** The court, upon motion of any party and for good cause shown, may enlarge or shorten the time limits set forth in this Rule.

**(g) Court appointment.** The court, if necessary, may appoint a qualified translator, the reasonable value of whose services shall be taxed as court costs.

### Notes and Comments

Comment to 1998 change: This is a new rule.

# TRANSPORTATION CODE

*(Added by L.1995, chap. 165(1), eff. 9/1/95.)*
*(See also Vehicle Laws, infra, for additional provisions and amendments to Texas Civil Statutes relating to transportation.)*

# TITLE 3. AVIATION

## CHAPTER 24. OPERATION OF AIRCRAFT

*(Selected Subchapters)*

### SUBCHAPTER B. OTHER FEDERAL REQUIREMENTS REGARDING AIRCRAFT



### SUBCHAPTER C. USE OF PUBLIC ROADS BY AIRCRAFT



### SUBCHAPTER B. OTHER FEDERAL REQUIREMENTS REGARDING AIRCRAFT

**§24.011. Failure to register aircraft; offense.**

(a) A person commits an offense if the person operates or navigates an aircraft that the person knows is not properly registered under Federal Aviation Administration aircraft registration regulations, 14 C.F.R. Part 47, as those regulations existed on September 1, 1985.

(b) An offense under Subsection (a) is a felony of the third degree.

*(Added by L.1995, chap. 165(1), eff. 9/1/95.)*

**§24.012. Aircraft identification numbers; offense.**

(a) The failure to have the aircraft identification numbers clearly displayed on an aircraft in compliance with federal aviation regulations is probable cause for a peace officer to further inspect the aircraft to determine the identity of the owner of the aircraft.

(b) A peace officer may inspect an aircraft under Subsection (a) if the aircraft is located on public property or on private property if the officer has the consent of the property owner.

(c) A person commits an offense if the person operates an aircraft that the person knows does not have aircraft identification numbers that comply with federal aviation regulations.

(d) An offense under Subsection (c) is a felony of the third degree.

(e) In this section, "federal aviation regulations" means the regulations adopted by the Federal Aviation Administration regarding identification and registration marking, 14 C.F.R. Part 45, as those regulations existed on September 1, 1985, except a regulation in existence on September 1, 1985, that is inconsistent with a regulation adopted after that date.

*(Added by L.1995, chap. 165(1), eff. 9/1/95.)*

**§24.013. Aircraft fuel containers; offense.**

(a) A person commits an offense if the person operates or intends to operate an aircraft equipped with:

(1) a fuel container that the person knows does not conform to federal aviation regulations or that has not been approved by the Federal Aviation Administration by inspection or special permit; or

(2) a pipe, hose, or auxiliary pump that is used or intended for transferring fuel to the primary fuel system of an aircraft from a fuel container that the person knows does not conform to federal

aviation regulations or that has not been approved by the Federal Aviation Administration by inspection or special permit.

(b) An offense under Subsection (a) is a felony of the third degree.

(c) A peace officer may seize an aircraft equipped with a fuel container that is the subject of an offense under Subsection (a).

(d) An aircraft seized under Subsection (c) may be forfeited to the Department of Public Safety in the same manner as property subject to forfeiture under Article 18.18, Code of Criminal Procedure.

(e) An aircraft forfeited under Subsection (d) is subject to Chapter 2205, Government Code.

(f) In this section:

(1) "Federal aviation regulations" means the following regulations adopted by the Federal Aviation Administration as those regulations existed on September 1, 1985, except a regulation in existence on September 1, 1985, that is inconsistent with a regulation adopted after that date:

(A) certification procedures for products and parts, 14 C.F.R. Part 21;

(B) maintenance, preventive maintenance, rebuilding, and alteration regulations, 14 C.F.R. Part 43; and

(C) general operating and flight rules, 14 C.F.R. Part 91.

(2) "Operate" means to use, cause to use, or authorize to use an aircraft for air navigation and includes:

(A) the piloting of an aircraft, with or without the right of legal control;

(B) the taxiing of an aircraft before takeoff or after landing; and

(C) the postflight or preflight inspection or starting of the engine of an aircraft.

*(Added by L.1995, chap. 165(1), eff. 9/1/95.)*

**§§24.014 to 24.020.** *(Reserved.)*

## SUBCHAPTER C. USE OF PUBLIC ROADS BY AIRCRAFT

### §24.021. Taking off, landing, or maneuvering aircraft on highways, roads, or streets; offense.

(a) A person commits an offense if the person takes off, lands, or maneuvers an aircraft, whether heavier or lighter than air, on a public highway, road, or street except:

(1) when necessary to prevent serious injury to a person or property;

(2) during or within a reasonable time after an emergency; or

(3) as provided by Section 24.022.

(b) An offense under Subsection (a) is a misdemeanor punishable by a fine of not less than $25 and not more than $200.

(c) The procedure prescribed by Section 543.003 applies to a violation of this section.

*(Added by L.1995, chap. 165(1); chgd. by L.1997, chap. 165(30.04), eff. 9/1/97.)*

### §24.022. Use of aircraft on county roads.

(a) A commissioners court of a county may enact ordinances to ensure the safe use of county roads by aircraft. An ordinance may:

(1) limit the kinds of aircraft that may use the roads;

(2) establish the procedure that a pilot shall follow before using a road, including requiring the pilot to furnish persons with flags at both ends of the road to be used; or

(3) establish other requirements considered necessary for the safe use of the roads by aircraft.

(b) A pilot who follows the ordinances adopted under Subsection (a):

(1) may land or take off in the aircraft on a county road; and

(2) is not subject to the traffic laws of this state during the landing or takeoff.

*(Added by L.1995, chap. 165(1), eff. 9/1/95.)*

# TITLE 6. ROADWAYS
*(Selected Subtitles)*

# SUBTITLE A. TEXAS DEPARTMENT OF TRANSPORTATION
*(Selected Chapter)*

## CHAPTER 201. GENERAL PROVISIONS AND ADMINISTRATION
*(Selected Subchapters)*

### SUBCHAPTER G. RECORDS
*(Selected Section)*

Section


### SUBCHAPTER K. ROAD AND HIGHWAY USE; SIGNS
*(Selected Sections)*



### SUBCHAPTER L. ELECTRONIC ISSUANCE OF LICENSES



### SUBCHAPTER G. RECORDS

#### §201.501. Reproduction of records.

(a) The department may photograph, microphotograph, or film any record that pertains to department operations.

(b) The department may create original records in micrographic form on media, such as computer output microfilm.

(c) The department shall provide an adequate number of microfilm readers and printers to allow the public convenient and inexpensive access to records created under Subsection (a). The department shall index the records alphabetically, by number, by subject matter, or by other appropriate references and shall provide the index to the public to promote convenient access.

(d) A photograph, microphotograph, or film of a record reproduced under Subsection (a) is equivalent to the original record for all purposes, including introduction as evidence in all courts and administrative agency proceedings. A certified or authenticated copy of such a photograph, microphotograph, or film is admissible as evidence equally with the original photograph, microphotograph, or film.

(e) The director or an authorized representative may certify the authenticity of a photograph, microphotograph, or film of a record reproduced under this section and shall charge a fee for the certified photograph, microphotograph, or film as provided by law.

(f) Certified records shall be furnished to any person who is authorized by law to receive them.

*(Added by L.1995, chap. 165(1), eff. 9/1/95.)*

## SUBCHAPTER K. ROAD AND HIGHWAY USE; SIGNS

### §201.901. Prohibiting use of highway or road.

(a) The commission may prohibit the use of any part of a highway or road under the control of the department by any vehicle that will unduly damage the highway or road when:

(1) because of wet weather or recent construction or repairs, the highway or road cannot be safely used without probable serious damage to it; or

(2) a bridge or culvert on the highway or road is unsafe.

(b) Before prohibiting the use of a highway or road under this section, the commission shall post notices that state the maximum load permitted and the time the use of the highway or road is prohibited. The notices must be posted at locations that enable drivers to detour to avoid the restricted highway or road.

(c) The commission may not prohibit the use of a highway or road under this section until a detour has been provided.

(d) If the owner or operator of a vehicle that is prohibited from using a highway or road under this section is aggrieved by the prohibition, the person may file with the county judge of the county in which the restricted highway or road is located a written complaint that sets forth the nature of the grievance. On the filing of the complaint the county judge immediately shall set the issue for a hearing to be held not later than the third day after the date on which the complaint is filed. The county judge shall give to the commission written notice of the day and purpose of each hearing.

(e) The county judge shall hear testimony offered by the parties. On conclusion of the hearing, the county judge shall sustain, revoke, or modify the commission's decision on the restriction. The county judge's judgment is final as to the issues raised.

(f) A person who violates a prohibition established under this section before or after it is approved by the county judge under Subsection (e) commits an offense. An offense under this section is a misdemeanor punishable by a fine not to exceed $200.

*(Added by L.1995, chap. 165(1), eff. 9/1/95.)*

### §201.903. Classification, designation, and marking of highways.

(a) The department may classify, designate, and mark state highways in this state.

(b) The department may provide a uniform system of marking and signing state highways under the control of the state. The system must correlate with and, to the extent possible, conform to the system adopted in other states.

*(Added by L.1995, chap. 165(1), eff. 9/1/95.)*

### §201.905. Traffic safety signs.

(a) The department may implement a traffic safety program that includes posting signs along the roadside at the 500 sites with the highest number of traffic fatalities. The signs shall be designed by the department and may contain the following information:

(1) the number of fatalities that occurred at that location in the last 10 years;

(2) the importance of driving safely and wearing seat belts;

(3) the importance of not drinking and driving; and

(4) any other information the department determines is necessary to promote safe driving.

(b) A program under this section may also include literature distributed to the public by the department.

*(Added by L.1997, chap. 1214(1), eff. 6/20/97.)*

## SUBCHAPTER L. ELECTRONIC ISSUANCE OF LICENSES

*(Added by L.1997, chap. 1171(1.15), eff. 9/1/97.)*

### §201.931. Definitions.

In this subchapter:

(1) "Digital signature" means an electronic identifier intended by the person using it to have the same force and effect as the use of a manual signature.

(2) "License" includes:

(A) a permit issued by the department that authorizes the operation of a vehicle and its load or a combination of vehicles and load exceeding size or weight limitations;

(B) motor carrier registration issued under Article 6675c, Revised Statutes;

(C) a vehicle storage facility license issued under Article 6687-9a, Revised Statutes;

(D) a license or permit for outdoor advertising issued under Chapter 391 or 394;

(E) a salvage motor vehicle dealer and agent license issued under Article 6687-1a, Revised Statutes;

(F) specially designated or specialized license plates issued under Subchapters E and F, Chapter 502; and

(G) an apportioned registration issued according to the International Registration Plan under Section 502.054.

*(Added by L.1997, chap. 1171(1.15), eff. 9/1/97.)*

### §201.932. Application for and issuance of license.

(a) The commission may by rule provide for the filing of a license application and the issuance of a license by electronic means.

(b) The commission may limit applicant eligibility under Subsection (a) if the rules include reasonable eligibility criteria.

*(Added by L.1997, chap. 1171(1.15), eff. 9/1/97.)*

### §201.933. Digital signature.

(a) A license application received by the department is considered signed if a digital signature is transmitted with the application and intended by the applicant to authenticate the license in accordance with Subsection (b).

(b) The department may only accept a digital signature used to authenticate a license application under procedures that:

(1) comply with any applicable rules of another state agency having jurisdiction over department use or acceptance of a digital signature; and

(2) provide for consideration of factors that may affect a digital signature's reliability, including whether a digital signature is:

(A) unique to the person using it;

(B) capable of independent verification;

(C) under the sole control of the person using it; and

(D) transmitted in a manner that will make it infeasible to change the data in the communication or digital signature without invalidating the digital signature.

*(Added by L.1997, chap. 1171(1.15), eff. 9/1/97.)*

### §201.934. Payment of fees.

The commission may adopt rules regarding the method of payment of a fee for a license issued under this subchapter. The rules may authorize the use of electronic funds transfer or a valid credit card issued by a financial institution chartered by a state or the federal government or by a nationally recognized credit organization approved by the department. The rules may require the payment of a discount or service charge for a credit card payment in addition to the fee. *(Added by L.1997, chap. 1171(1.15), eff. 9/1/97.)*

# SUBTITLE B. STATE HIGHWAY SYSTEM
*(Selected Chapter)*

## CHAPTER 224. ACQUISITION, CONSTRUCTION, AND MAINTENANCE
*(Selected Sections)*



### §224.155. Failure or refusal to pay toll charges.

Any motor vehicle other than a police or emergency vehicle that is driven or towed through a toll collection facility shall pay the proper toll. *(Added by L.1997, chap. 1171(1.24), eff. 9/1/97.)*

### §224.156. Administrative fee; notice.

(a) In the event of nonpayment of the proper toll, on issuance of proper notice of nonpayment, the registered owner of the nonpaying vehicle is legally bound to pay both the proper toll and an administrative fee.

(b) The commission by rule and a transportation corporation by order of its board of directors may respectively fix an administrative fee, not to exceed $100, to recover the cost of collecting an unpaid toll. The notice of nonpayment to the registered owner shall be sent by the department by first-class mail not later than 30 days after the date of the alleged failure to pay and may require payment not sooner than 30 days after the date the notice was mailed. The registered owner shall pay a separate toll and administrative fee for each event of nonpayment.

(c) If the registered owner of the vehicle fails to pay the proper toll and administrative fee within the time specified by the notice of nonpayment issued under this section, the registered owner shall be cited as for other traffic violations for the nonpayment, and the owner is legally bound to pay a fine, not to exceed $250, for each event of nonpayment. Neither the legal obligation to pay nor the actual payment of the fine affects the legal duty of the owner for any other fine or penalty prescribed by law.

*(Added by L.1997, chap. 1171(1.24), eff. 9/1/97.)*

### §224.158. Use and return of transponders.

(a) For purposes of this section, a "transponder" means a device, placed on or within a motor vehicle, that is capable of transmitting information used to assess or collect tolls. A transponder is "insufficiently funded" when there are no remaining funds in the account in connection with which the transponder was issued.

(b) Any law enforcement officer of the Department of Public Safety has the authority to seize a stolen or insufficiently funded transponder and to return it to the department or the transportation corporation, except that an insufficiently funded transponder may not be seized sooner than 30 days after the date the department or the transportation corporation has sent a notice of delinquency to the holder of the account.

(c) The following entities shall consider offering motor vehicle operators the option of using a transponder to pay tolls without stopping, to mitigate congestion at toll collection locations, to enhance traffic flow, and to otherwise increase efficiency of operations:

(1) the department;

(2) a regional tollway authority governed by Chapter 366;

(3) a transportation corporation;

(4) an entity to which a project authorized by this subchapter is transferred by an entity described by Subdivision (1), (2), or (3); or

(5) a third-party service provider under contract with an entity described by Subdivision (1), (2), (3), or (4).

*(Added by L.1997, chap. 1171(1.24), eff. 9/1/97.)*



## SUBTITLE C. COUNTY ROADS AND BRIDGES

## CHAPTER 251. GENERAL COUNTY AUTHORITY RELATING TO ROADS AND BRIDGES
*(Selected Subchapters)*

### SUBCHAPTER A. GENERAL PROVISIONS
*(Selected Sections)*

Section



### SUBCHAPTER E. COUNTY TRAFFIC REGULATIONS

## SUBCHAPTER A. GENERAL PROVISIONS

**§251.011. Detour roads.**

(a) The commissioners court of a county shall establish detour roads for the convenience of the public when a county road that is not part of the state highway system must be closed to traffic for road construction. When a county detour road is in use, the county has the same authority over the road as over an established public road.

(b) The commissioners court shall:

(1) post all signs necessary for the convenience and guidance of the public at each end of a county detour road; and

(2) maintain a county detour road so that it is reasonably adequate for normal traffic requirements.

*(Added by L.1995, chap. 165(1), eff. 9/1/95.)*

**§251.013. Road names and address numbers.**

(a) The commissioners court of a county by order may adopt uniform standards for naming public roads located wholly or partly in unincorporated areas of the county and for assigning address numbers to property located in unincorporated areas of the county. The standards apply to any new public road that is established.

(b) The commissioners court of a county by order may adopt a name for a public road located wholly or partly in an unincorporated area of the county and may assign address numbers to property located in an unincorporated area of the county for which there is no established address system.

(c) If an order adopted under this section conflicts with a municipal ordinance, the municipal ordinance prevails in the territory in which it is effective.

(d) A commissioners court may adopt an order under this section only after conducting a public hearing on the proposed order. The court shall give public notice of the hearing at least two weeks before the date of the hearing.

*(Added by L.1995, chap. 165(1), eff. 9/1/95.)*

**§251.016. General county authority over roads, highways, and bridges.**

The commissioners court of a county may exercise general control over all roads, highways, and bridges in the county. *(Added by L.1999, chap. 62(13.11(b)), eff. 9/1/99.)*

## SUBCHAPTER E. COUNTY TRAFFIC REGULATIONS

**§251.151. Authority of commissioners court.**

The commissioners court of a county may regulate traffic on a county road or on real property owned by the county that is under the jurisdiction of the commissioners court. *(Added by L.1995, chap. 165(1), eff. 9/1/95.)*

**§251.152. Public hearing required.**

(a) Except as provided by Section 251.159, before the commissioners court may issue a traffic regulation under this subchapter, the commissioners court must hold a public hearing on the proposed regulation.

(b) The commissioners court shall publish notice of the hearing in a newspaper of general circulation in the county. The notice must be published not later than the seventh or earlier than the 30th day before the date of the hearing.

*(Added by L.1995, chap. 165(1), eff. 9/1/95.)*

**§251.153. Load limits on county roads and bridges.**

(a) The commissioners court of a county may establish load limits for any county road or bridge.

(b) The commissioners court may authorize a county traffic officer, sheriff, deputy sheriff, constable, or deputy constable to weigh a vehicle to ascertain whether the vehicle's load exceeds the limit prescribed by the commissioners court.

*(Added by L.1995, chap. 165(1), eff. 9/1/95.)*

**§251.154. Maximum reasonable and prudent speeds on county roads.**

(a) The commissioners court of a county, by order entered on the minutes of the court, may determine and set a maximum reasonable and prudent speed for a vehicle travelling on any segment of a county road, including a road or highway intersection, railroad grade crossing, curve, or hill.

(b) In determining the maximum reasonable and prudent speed, the commissioners court shall consider all circumstances on the affected segment of the road, including the width and condition of the road surface and the usual traffic on the road.

(c) The maximum reasonable and prudent speed set by the commissioners court under this section may be lower than the maximum speed set by law for a vehicle travelling on a public highway.

(d) A speed limit set by the commissioners court under this section is effective when appropriate signs giving notice of the speed limit are installed on the affected segment of the county road.

*(Added by L.1995, chap. 165(1), eff. 9/1/95.)*

### §251.155. Restricted traffic zones.

(a) The commissioners court of a county may adopt regulations establishing a system of traffic control devices in restricted traffic zones on property described by Section 251.151.

(b) A system of traffic control devices adopted under this section must conform to the manual and specifications of the Texas Department of Transportation.

(c) The commissioners court by order entered on its minutes may install and maintain on property to which this section applies any traffic signal light, stop sign, or no-parking sign that the court considers necessary for public safety.

*(Added by L.1995, chap. 165(1), eff. 9/1/95.)*

Printed in the U.S.A. Zt

### §251.156. Parking restrictions.

The commissioners court of a county by order may have signs installed that prohibit or restrict the stopping, standing, or parking of a vehicle in a restricted traffic zone on property described by Section 251.151, if in the opinion of the court the stopping, standing, or parking:

(1) is dangerous to those using the road or property; or

(2) will unduly interfere with:

(A) the free movement of traffic; or

(B) the necessary control or use of the property.

*(Added by L.1995, chap. 165(1), eff. 9/1/95.)*

### §251.157. Prohibiting use of road.

(a) In this section, "road supervisor" means a person authorized to supervise roads in a county or in a district or precinct of a county.

(b) A road supervisor may prohibit the use of a road or a section of a road under the supervisor's control by any vehicle that will unduly damage the road when:

(1) because of wet weather or recent construction or repairs, the road cannot be safely used without probable serious damage to it; or

(2) a bridge or culvert on the road is unsafe.

(c) Before prohibiting the use of a road under this section, the road supervisor shall post notices that state the maximum load permitted and the time the use of the road is prohibited. The notices must be posted at locations that enable drivers to detour to avoid the restricted road.

(d) The road supervisor may not prohibit the use of a road under this section until a detour has been provided.

(e) If the owner or operator of a vehicle that is prohibited from using a road under this section is aggrieved by the prohibition, the person may file with the county judge of the county in which the restricted road is located a written complaint that sets forth the nature of the grievance. On the filing of the complaint the county judge promptly shall set the issue for a hearing to be held not later than the third day after the date on which the complaint is filed. The county judge shall give to the road supervisor written notice of the date and purpose of each hearing.

(f) The county judge shall hear testimony offered by the parties. On conclusion of the hearing, the county judge shall sustain, revoke, or modify the road supervisor's decision on the restriction. The county judge's judgment is final as to the issues raised.

*(Added by L.1995, chap. 165(1), eff. 9/1/95.)*

### §251.158. Temporary use of county road for festival or civic event.

(a) The commissioners court of a county by order may permit the temporary use of a county road located in an unincorporated area of the county for a civic event, including a festival.

(b) The court by order shall establish procedures for the temporary diversion of traffic from the road being used for the event.

*(Added by L.1995, chap. 165(1), eff. 9/1/95.)*

### §251.159. Delegation of commissioners' authority.

(a) This section applies only to a county with a population of more than 200,000.

(b) The commissioners court of a county may delegate to the county engineer or other county employee any function of the commissioners court under this subchapter, except as provided by Subsection (e). An action of the county engineer or other county employee under this section has the same effect as if the action were an action of the commissioners court.

(c) Before issuing a traffic regulation under this subchapter, the commissioners court, in lieu of publishing notice required by a law other than this subchapter, may give notice of the proposed regulation by posting a conspicuous sign in any location to be affected by the regulation.

(d) The commissioners court is not required to hold a public hearing on the proposed traffic regulation unless a resident of the county requests a public hearing. The request must be in writing and made before the eighth day after the later of:

(1) the date that the sign is posted; or

(2) the date that the notice under Section 251.152 is published.

(e) If a public hearing is requested, the commissioners court may not delegate the duty to hold the hearing.

*(Added by L.1995, chap. 165(1); chgd. by L.1999, chap. 885(1), eff. 6/18/99.)*

### §251.160. Liability of owner or operator for road damage.

(a) A person who operates or moves a vehicle or other object on a public road or bridge and the owner of the vehicle or other object are jointly and severally liable for damage sustained by the road or bridge as a result of the negligent operation or moving of the vehicle or other object or as a result of the operation or movement of the vehicle at a time prohibited by the officials with authority over the road.

(b) The county judge by appropriate legal action may recover damages for which liability is provided by this section. The county attorney shall represent the county in an action under this subsection. Damages collected under this subsection are for the use of the county to benefit the damaged road or bridge.

*(Added by L.1995, chap. 165(1), eff. 9/1/95.)*

### §251.161. Violations of subchapter; offense.

(a) A person commits a misdemeanor offense if the person:

(1) stops, stands, or parks a vehicle in violation of a restriction stated on a sign installed under Section 251.156;

(2) defaces, injures, knocks down, or removes a sign or traffic control device installed under an order of the commissioners court of a county issued under this subchapter;

(3) operates a motor vehicle in violation of an order of the commissioners court entered under this subchapter; or

(4) otherwise violates this subchapter.

(b) Except as provided by Subsections (c) and (d), an offense under this section is punishable by a fine not to exceed $50.

(c) If it is shown on the trial of an offense under this section that the person has previously been convicted one time of the offense, the offense is punishable by a fine not to exceed $200.

(d) If it is shown on the trial of an offense under this section that the person has previously been convicted two times of the offense, the offense is punishable by:

(1) a fine not to exceed $500;

(2) confinement in the county jail for a term not to exceed 60 days; or

(3) both the fine and the confinement.

*(Added by L.1995, chap. 165(1), eff. 9/1/95.)*

## CHAPTER 256. FUNDS AND TAXES FOR COUNTY ROADS

*(Selected Section)*

Section



### §256.007. Transfers of surplus registration fee revenue.

The commissioners court of a county that does not impose a tax for the construction and maintenance of roads and bridges may transfer surplus money derived from motor vehicle registration fees to any county fund that the court designates and may spend that money for any purpose authorized by Section 7-a, Article VIII, Texas Constitution. *(Added by L.1995, chap. 165(1), eff. 9/1/95.)*

# SUBTITLE D. ROAD LAWS RELATING TO PARTICULAR COUNTIES

*(Selected Chapters)*

# CHAPTER 284. CAUSEWAYS, BRIDGES, TUNNELS, TURNPIKES, AND HIGHWAYS IN CERTAIN COUNTIES

*(Selected Subchapter)*

## SUBCHAPTER D. UNAUTHORIZED USE OF TOLL ROADS IN CERTAIN COUNTIES





### §284.201. Applicability of subchapter.

This subchapter applies only to a county with a population of more than 2.2 million. *(Added by L.1997, chap. 165(30.18(a)), eff. 9/1/97.)*

### §284.202. Order prohibiting operation of motor vehicle on toll project.

(a) The commissioners court of a county by order may prohibit the operation of a motor vehicle on a county project described by Section 284.001(3) if:

(1) an operator of the vehicle has failed to pay a required toll or charge; and

(2) the county provides the registered owner of the vehicle with notice of the unpaid toll or charge.

(b) The notice required by Subsection (a)(2) must be mailed to the registered owner of the vehicle at least 10 days before the date the prohibition takes effect.

*(Added by L.1997, chap. 165(30.18(a)), eff. 9/1/97.)*

### §284.203. Violation of order; offense.

(a) A person commits an offense if the person operates a motor vehicle or causes or allows the operation of a motor vehicle in violation of an order adopted under Section 284.202(a).

(b) An offense under this section is a Class C misdemeanor.

*(Added by L.1997, chap. 165(30.18(a)), eff. 9/1/97.)*

### §284.204. Administrative adjudication hearing procedure.

(a) The commissioners court of a county may adopt an administrative adjudication hearing procedure for a person who is suspected of having violated an order adopted under Section 284.202(a) on at least two separate occasions within a 12-month period in connection with a toll to be paid by electronic means.

(b) A hearing procedure adopted under Subsection (a) must provide:

(1) a period for a person charged with violating the order:

(A) to pay the toll or charge plus administrative costs; or

(B) to request a hearing;

(2) for appointment of one or more hearing officers with authority to administer oaths and issue orders compelling the attendance of witnesses and the production of documents; and

(3) for the amount and disposition of civil fines, costs, and fees.

(c) An order issued under Subsection (b)(2) may be enforced by a justice of the peace.

*(Added by L.1997, chap. 165(30.18(a)), eff. 9/1/97.)*

**§284.205. Citation or summons.**

(a) A citation or summons issued under this subchapter must:

(1) inform the recipient of the time and place of the hearing; and

(2) notify the person charged with a violation that the person has the right of a hearing without delay.

(b) The original or any copy of the summons or citation is a record kept in the ordinary course of business of the county and is rebuttable proof of the facts it contains.
*(Added by L.1997, chap. 165(30.18(a)), eff. 9/1/97.)*

**§284.206. Administrative hearing: presumption; evidence of ownership.**

In an administrative adjudication hearing under this subchapter it is presumed that:

(1) the registered owner of the motor vehicle that is the subject of the hearing is the person who operated or allowed another person to operate the motor vehicle in violation of the order; and

(2) a computer record of the department of the registered vehicle owner is prima facie evidence of its contents.
*(Added by L.1997, chap. 165(30.18(a)), eff. 9/1/97.)*

**§284.207. Attendance on hearing.**

(a) The peace officer or toll road agent who alleges a violation is not required to attend the hearing.

(b) The failure of a person charged with an offense to appear at the hearing is considered an admission of liability for the violation.
*(Added by L.1997, chap. 165(30.18(a)), eff. 9/1/97.)*

**§284.208. Decision of hearing officer.**

(a) The hearing officer shall issue a decision stating:

(1) whether the person charged is liable for a violation of the order; and

(2) the amount of the fine and costs to be assessed against the person.

(b) The hearing officer shall file the decision with the county clerk.

(c) A decision of a hearing officer filed under Subsection (b) must be kept in a separate index and file. The decision may be recorded using a computer printout, microfilm, microfiche, or a similar data processing technique.
*(Added by L.1997, chap. 165(30.18(a)), eff. 9/1/97.)*

**§284.209. Enforcement of decision.**

A decision issued under Section 284.208(a) may be enforced by:

(1) placing a device that prohibits movement of a motor vehicle on the vehicle that is the subject of the decision;

(2) imposing an additional fine if the fine for the offense is not paid within a specified time; or

(3) refusing to allow the registration of the vehicle.
*(Added by L.1997, chap. 165(30.18(a)), eff. 9/1/97.)*

**§284.210. Appeal of hearing officer decision.**

(a) A person determined by a hearing officer to be in violation of an order may appeal the determination to a county court at law.

(b) To appeal, the person must file a petition with the court not later than the 30th day after the date the hearing officer's decision is filed with the county clerk. The petition must be accompanied by payment of the costs required by law for the court.
*(Added by L.1997, chap. 165(30.18(a)), eff. 9/1/97.)*

**§284.211. Hearing on appeal.**

The court in which an appeal petition is filed shall:

(1) schedule a hearing; and

(2) notify all parties of the date, time, and place of the hearing.
*(Added by L.1997, chap. 165(30.18(a)), eff. 9/1/97.)*

**§284.212. Effect of appeal.**

Service of notice of appeal does not stay the enforcement and collection of the decision of the hearing officer unless the person who files the appeal posts a bond with an agency designated by the county to accept payment for a violation. *(Added by L.1997, chap. 165(30.18(a)), eff. 9/1/97.)*

# CHAPTER 285. COUNTY REGULATION OF ROADSIDE VENDOR AND SOLICITOR IN CERTAIN COUNTIES

Section


### §285.001. Regulation of roadside vendor and solicitor.

To promote the public safety, the commissioners court of a county with a population of more than 1.4 million by order may regulate the following if they occur on a public highway or road in the unincorporated area of the county or in the right-of-way of the highway or road:

(1) the sale of items by a vendor of food or merchandise;

(2) the erection, maintenance, or placement of a structure by a vendor of food or merchandise; and

(3) the solicitation of money.

*(Added by L.1995, chap. 165(1), eff. 9/1/95.)*

### §285.002. Permit; removal of structure.

The commissioners court may:

(1) require a vendor or a person soliciting money to obtain a permit to sell the food or merchandise or to solicit money;

(2) charge a reasonable fee for the permit; and

(3) provide for the removal of a structure that is in violation of the regulations.

*(Added by L.1995, chap. 165(1), eff. 9/1/95.)*

### §285.003. Conflict with statute or state agency rule.

If a regulation adopted under this chapter conflicts with a statute or state agency rule, the statute or rule prevails to the extent of the conflict. *(Added by L.1995, chap. 165(1), eff. 9/1/95.)*

### §285.004. Violation of regulation; offense.

(a) A person commits an offense if the person knowingly:

(1) violates a regulation adopted under this chapter; or

(2) obstructs or threatens to obstruct the removal of a structure that is in violation of a regulation adopted under this chapter.

(b) Each day a violation continues is a separate offense.

(c) An offense under this section is a Class C misdemeanor.

*(Added by L.1995, chap. 165(1), eff. 9/1/95.)*

# SUBTITLE H. HIGHWAY BEAUTIFICATION

*(Selected Chapters)*

# CHAPTER 391. HIGHWAY BEAUTIFICATION ON INTERSTATE AND PRIMARY SYSTEMS

## SUBCHAPTER A. GENERAL PROVISIONS

Section

## SUBCHAPTER B. REGULATION OF OUTDOOR ADVERTISING GENERALLY



## SUBCHAPTER C. LICENSE AND PERMIT FOR OUTDOOR ADVERTISING



## SUBCHAPTER D. SPECIFIC INFORMATION LOGO SIGNS



## SUBCHAPTER E. REGULATION OF JUNKYARDS AND AUTOMOBILE GRAVEYARDS



## SUBCHAPTER F. ACQUISITION FOR SCENIC ENHANCEMENT OR PUBLIC ACCOMMODATION

## SUBCHAPTER G. ACQUISITIONS BY COMMISSION



## SUBCHAPTER H. REGULATION OF OUTDOOR ADVERTISING ON STATE HIGHWAY 288





## SUBCHAPTER A. GENERAL PROVISIONS

### §391.001. Definitions.

In this chapter:

(1) "Automobile graveyard" means an establishment that is maintained, used, or operated for storing, buying, or selling wrecked, scrapped, ruined, or dismantled motor vehicles or motor vehicle parts.

(2) "Eligible highway" means a highway that:

(A) is located outside an urbanized area with a population of 50,000 or more; and

(B) qualifies for a maximum speed limit of 65 miles per hour under 23 U.S.C. Section 154 or, if that law is repealed, qualified for a maximum speed limit of 65 miles per hour on the day before the effective date of the repeal.

(3) "Eligible urban highway" means an interstate highway that is located inside an urbanized area with a population of 200,000 or more.

(4) "Information logo sign" means a specific information logo sign or a major shopping area guide sign.

(5) "Interstate system" means that portion of the national system of interstate and defense highways that is located in this state and is designated officially by the commission and approved under Title 23, United States Code.

(6) "Junk" means:

(A) old or scrap copper, brass, rope, rags, batteries, paper, trash, rubber, debris, or waste;

(B) junked, dismantled, or wrecked automobiles or automobile parts; or

(C) iron, steel, and other old or scrap ferrous or nonferrous material.

(7) "Junkyard" means:

(A) an automobile graveyard;

(B) an establishment maintained, used, or operated for storing, buying, or selling junk or processing scrap metal; or

(C) a garbage dump or sanitary fill.

(8) "Major shopping area" means a geographic area that:

(A) consists of 30 acres or more of land; and

(B) includes an enclosed retail shopping mall that contains 1 million square feet or more of gross building area.

(9) "Major shopping area guide sign" means a rectangular guide sign panel imprinted with the name of a major shopping area, as it is commonly known to the public, and containing directional information to the major shopping area.

(10) "Outdoor advertising" means an outdoor sign, display, light, device, figure, painting, drawing, message, plaque, poster, billboard, or other thing designed, intended, or used to advertise or inform if any part of the advertising or information content is visible from the main-traveled way of the interstate or primary system. The term does not include a sign or marker giving information about the location of an underground electric transmission line, telegraph or telephone property or facility, pipeline, public sewer, or waterline.

(11) "Primary system" means that portion of connected main highways located in this state that is designated officially by the commission and approved under Title 23, United States Code.

(12) "Specific information logo sign" means a rectangular sign panel imprinted with the words "GAS," "FOOD," "LODGING," or "CAMPING," or with a combination of those words, and the specific brand names of commercial establishments offering those services.

(13) "Urban area" means an area defined by the commission in cooperation with local officials, subject to approval by the secretary of the United States Department of Transportation, that as a minimum includes an urban place as designated by the United States Bureau of the Census having a population of 5,000 or more and not located within an urbanized area.

(14) "Urbanized area" means an area defined by the commission in cooperation with local officials, subject to approval by the secretary of the United States Department of Transportation, that as a minimum includes an urbanized area as defined by the United States Bureau of the Census or that part of a multistate urbanized area located in this state.

*(Added by L.1995, chap. 165(1); chgd. by L.1997, chap. 165(30.22(a)), eff. 9/1/97.)*

### §391.002. Purpose.

(a) Subject to the availability of state and federal funds, it is the intent of the legislature to comply with the Highway Beautification Act of 1965 (23 U.S.C. Sections 131, 136, 319) to the extent that it is implemented by the United States Congress. This chapter is conditioned on that law.

(b) The legislature declares that it is necessary to regulate the erection and maintenance of outdoor advertising and the establishment, operation, and maintenance of junkyards in areas adjacent to the interstate and primary systems to:

(1) promote the health, safety, welfare, morals, convenience, and enjoyment of the traveling public; and

(2) protect the public investment in the interstate and primary systems.

(c) The legislature considers that the following are means of protecting and providing for the general welfare of the traveling public and promoting the safety of citizens using the highways of this state:

(1) landscaping and developing recreational areas;

(2) acquiring interests in and improving strips of real property within, adjacent to, or within view of the interstate or primary system that are necessary for the restoration, preservation, and enhancement of scenic beauty; and

(3) developing publicly owned and controlled rest and sanitary facilities in or adjacent to highway rights-of-way.

*(Added by L.1995, chap. 165(1), eff. 9/1/95.)*

### §391.003. Violation of rule; offense.

(a) A person commits an offense if the person wilfully violates a rule adopted by the commission under this chapter.

(b) An offense under this section is a misdemeanor punishable by a fine of not less than $500 or more than $1,000.

(c) Each day of a rule violation is a separate offense.

*(Added by L.1995, chap. 165(1), eff. 9/1/95.)*

### §391.004. Texas highway beautification fund account.

The Texas highway beautification fund account is an account in the general revenue fund. Money the commission receives under this chapter shall be deposited to the credit of the Texas highway beautification fund account. The commission shall use money in the Texas highway beautification fund account to administer this chapter. *(Added by L.1997, chap. 165(30.21), eff. 9/1/97.)*

### §391.005. Exemption.

This chapter does not apply to a sign erected solely for and relating to a public election if the sign:

(1) is on private property;

(2) is erected not earlier than the 90th day before the date of the election and is removed not later than the 10th day after the election date;

(3) is constructed of lightweight material; and

(4) has a surface area not larger than 50 square feet.

*(Added by L.1997, chap. 60(1), eff. the first day of the calendar month following the date the Texas Transportation Commission determines that the implementation of section 391.005 will not result in the loss of highway-related funds from the federal government.)*

**§§391.006 to 391.030.** *(Reserved.)*

## SUBCHAPTER B. REGULATION OF OUTDOOR ADVERTISING GENERALLY

### §391.031. Unlawful outdoor advertising; offense.

(a) A person commits an offense if the person wilfully erects or maintains outdoor advertising:

(1) within 660 feet of the nearest edge of a right-of-way if the advertising is visible from the main-traveled way of the interstate or primary system; or

(2) outside an urban area if the advertising is located more than 660 feet from the nearest edge of a right-of-way, is visible from the main-traveled way of the interstate or primary system, and is erected for the purpose of having its message seen from the main-traveled way of the interstate or primary system.

(b) A person does not commit an offense if the person erects or maintains in an area described by Subsection (a):

(1) directional or other official outdoor advertising authorized by law, including advertising pertaining to a natural wonder or a scenic or historic attraction;

(2) outdoor advertising for the sale or lease of the property on which it is located;

(3) outdoor advertising solely for activities conducted on the property on which it is located;

(4) outdoor advertising located within 660 feet of the nearest edge of a right-of-way in an area in which the land use:

(A) is designated industrial or commercial under authority of law; or

(B) is not designated industrial or commercial under authority of law but the land use is consistent with an area designated industrial or commercial;

(5) outdoor advertising that has as its purpose the protection of life and property; or

(6) outdoor advertising erected on or before October 22, 1965, that the commission, with the approval of the secretary of the United States Department of Transportation, determines to be a landmark of such historic or artistic significance that preservation is consistent with the purposes of this subchapter.

(c) The determination of whether an area is to be designated industrial or commercial must be made under criteria established by commission rule and according to actual land use.

(d) An offense under this section is a misdemeanor punishable by a fine of not less than $500 or more than $1,000. Each day of the proscribed conduct is a separate offense.
*(Added by L.1995, chap. 165(1), eff. 9/1/95.)*



### §391.032. Regulation of outdoor advertising in industrial or commercial area.

(a) The commission by rule may regulate the orderly and effective display of outdoor advertising consistent with the customary use of outdoor advertising in this state in an area in which the land use:

(1) is designated industrial or commercial under authority of law; and

(2) is not so designated but in which the land use is consistent with areas designated industrial or commercial in the manner provided by Section 391.031(c).

(b) The commission may agree with the secretary of the United States Department of Transportation to regulate the orderly and effective display of outdoor advertising in an area described by Subsection (a).
*(Added by L.1995, chap. 165(1), eff. 9/1/95.)*

### §391.033. Acquisition of outdoor advertising by commission.

(a) The commission may purchase or acquire by eminent domain outdoor advertising that is lawfully in existence on a highway in the interstate or primary system.

(b) If an acquisition is by eminent domain, the commission shall pay just compensation to:

(1) the owner for the right, title, leasehold, and interest in the outdoor advertising; and

(2) the owner or, if appropriate, the lessee of the real property on which the outdoor advertising is located for the right to erect and maintain the outdoor advertising.
*(Added by L.1995, chap. 165(1), eff. 9/1/95.)*

### §391.034. Removal of nuisance outdoor advertising by commission.

(a) Outdoor advertising that is erected or maintained in violation of this chapter:

(1) endangers the health, safety, welfare, morals, convenience, and enjoyment of the traveling public and the protection of the public investment in the interstate and primary highway systems; and

(2) is a public nuisance.

(b) On written notice by certified mail from the department, an owner of outdoor advertising that is a public nuisance under Subsection (a) shall remove the advertising. If the owner does not remove the outdoor advertising within 45 days of the date of the notice, the department may direct the attorney general to apply for an injunction to:

(1) prohibit the owner from maintaining the advertising; and

(2) require the removal of the advertising.

(c) The state is entitled to recover from the owner of outdoor advertising removed under an action brought under Subsection (b) all administrative and legal costs and expenses incurred to remove the advertising, including court costs and reasonable attorney's fees.
*(Added by L.1995, chap. 165(1), eff. 9/1/95.)*

### §391.035. Civil penalty.

(a) In addition to being subject to a criminal penalty or injunctive action, a person who intentionally violates this subchapter or Subchapter C is liable to the state for a civil penalty. The attorney general may sue to collect the penalty.

(b) The amount of the civil penalty is not less than $500 or more than $1,000 for each violation, depending on the seriousness of the violation. A separate penalty may be collected for each day a continuing violation occurs.

(c) A penalty collected under this section shall be deposited to the credit of the state highway fund.
*(Added by L.1995, chap. 165(1); chgd. by L.1999, chap. 442(1), eff. 6/18/99.)*

### §391.036. Scope of commission responsibility.

The commission's responsibility for the regulation of outdoor advertising is only on a federal-aid primary highway, interstate highway, state highway, or farm-to-market road. *(Added by L.1995, chap. 165(1), eff. 9/1/95.)*

### §§391.037 to 391.060. *(Reserved.)*

## SUBCHAPTER C. LICENSE AND PERMIT FOR OUTDOOR ADVERTISING

### §391.061. Outdoor advertising without license; offense.

(a) A person commits an offense if the person wilfully erects or maintains outdoor advertising in an area described by Section 391.031(a) without a license under this subchapter.

(b) An offense under this section is a misdemeanor punishable by a fine of not less than $500 or more than $1,000. Each day of the proscribed conduct is a separate offense.

(c) A person is not required to obtain a license to erect or maintain outdoor advertising described by Section 391.031(b)(2) or (3).
*(Added by L.1995, chap. 165(1), eff. 9/1/95.)*

### §391.062. Issuance and period of license.

(a) The commission shall issue a license to a person who:

(1) files with the commission a completed application form within the time specified by the commission;

(2) pays the appropriate license fee; and

(3) files with the commission a surety bond.

(b) A license may be issued for one year or longer.

(c) At least 30 days before the date on which a person's license expires, the commission shall notify the person of the impending expiration. The notice must be in writing and sent to the person's last known address according to the records of the commission.
*(Added by L.1995, chap. 165(1); chgd. by L.1997, chap. 1171(2.02), eff. 9/1/97.)*

### §391.063. License fee.

The commission may set the amount of a license fee according to a scale graduated by the number of units of outdoor advertising owned by a license applicant. *(Added by L.1995, chap. 165(1); chgd. by L.1999, chap. 62(17.03), eff. 9/1/99.)*

**§391.064. Surety bond.**

(a) The surety bond required of an applicant for a license under Section 391.062 must be:

(1) in the amount of $2,500 for each county in the state in which the person erects or maintains outdoor advertising; and

(2) payable to the commission for reimbursement for removal costs of outdoor advertising that the license holder unlawfully erects or maintains.

(b) A person may not be required to provide more than $10,000 in surety bonds.
*(Added by L.1995, chap. 165(1), eff. 9/1/95.)*

**§391.065. Rules; forms.**

(a) The commission may adopt rules to implement Sections 391.036, 391.061(a), 391.062, 391.063, 391.064, and 391.066.

(b) For the efficient management and administration of this chapter and to reduce the number of employees required to enforce this chapter, the commission shall adopt rules for issuing standardized forms that are for submission by license holders and applicants and that provide for an accurate showing of the number, location, or other information required by the commission for each license holder's or applicant's outdoor advertising.

(c) The commission may not adopt a rule under this chapter that restricts competitive bidding or advertising by the holder of a license issued under this chapter other than a rule to prohibit false, misleading, or deceptive practices. The limitation provided by this section applies only to rules relating to the occupation of outdoor advertiser and does not affect the commission's power to regulate the orderly and effective display of outdoor advertising under this chapter. A rule to prohibit false, misleading, or deceptive practices may not:

(1) restrict the use of:

(A) any legal medium for an advertisement;

(B) the license holder's advertisement under a trade name; or

(C) the license holder's personal appearance or voice in an advertisement, if the license holder is an individual; or

(2) relate to the size or duration of an advertisement by the license holder.
*(Added by L.1995, chap. 165(1); chgd. by L.1997, chap. 1171(2.01), eff. 9/1/97.)*



**§391.066. Revocation or suspension of license; appeal.**

(a) The commission may revoke or suspend a license issued under this subchapter or place on probation a license holder whose license is suspended if the license holder violates this chapter or a rule adopted under this chapter. If the suspension of the license is probated, the department may require the license holder to report regularly to the commission on any matter that is the basis of the probation.

(b) The judicial appeal of the revocation or suspension of a license must be initiated not later than the 15th day after the date of the commission's action.

(c) The commission may adopt rules for the reissuance of a revoked or suspended license and may set fees for the reissuance.
*(Added by L.1995, chap. 165(1); chgd. by L.1997, chap. 1171(2.03), eff. 9/1/97.)*

**§391.067. Outdoor advertising without permit; offense.**

(a) A person who has a license issued under this subchapter commits an offense if the person wilfully erects or maintains outdoor advertising for which a license is required under Section 391.061 unless that person also has a permit for the outdoor advertising.

(b) An offense under this section is a misdemeanor punishable by a fine of not less than $500 or more than $1,000. Each day of the proscribed conduct is a separate offense.
*(Added by L.1995, chap. 165(1), eff. 9/1/95.)*

**§391.068. Issuance of permit.**

(a) The commission shall issue a permit to a person with a license issued under this subchapter:

(1) whose license application complies with rules adopted under Section 391.065; and

(2) whose outdoor advertising, whether owned or leased, if erected would comply with this chapter and rules adopted under Section 391.032(a).

(b) The commission by rule shall prescribe:

(1) a reasonable fee for each permit;

(2) the time for and manner of applying for a permit; and

(3) the form and content of the permit application.

(c) A permit issued to regulate the erection and maintenance of outdoor advertising by a political subdivision of this state within that subdivision's jurisdiction shall be accepted in lieu of the permit required by this subchapter if the erection and maintenance of outdoor advertising complies with this subchapter and rules adopted under Section 391.032(a).
*(Added by L.1995, chap. 165(1), eff. 9/1/95.)*

### §391.069. Fee amounts.

The license and permit fees required by this subchapter may not exceed an amount reasonably necessary to cover the administrative costs incurred to enforce this chapter. *(Added by L.1995, chap. 165(1), eff. 9/1/95.)*

### §391.070. Exceptions for certain nonprofit organizations.

(a) The combined license and permit fees under this subchapter may not exceed $10 for outdoor advertising erected and maintained by a nonprofit organization in a municipality or a municipality's extraterritorial jurisdiction if the advertising relates to or promotes only the municipality or a political subdivision whose jurisdiction is wholly or partly concurrent with the municipality.

(b) The nonprofit organization is not required to file a bond as provided by Section 391.062(a)(3).
*(Added by L.1995, chap. 165(1), eff. 9/1/95.)*

### §§391.071 to 391.090. *(Reserved.)*

## SUBCHAPTER D. SPECIFIC INFORMATION LOGO SIGNS

### §391.091. Erection and maintenance of signs.

The commission shall contract with an individual, firm, group, or association in this state to erect and maintain specific information logo signs at appropriate locations along an eligible highway. *(Added by L.1995, chap. 165(1); L.1997, chap. 165(30.22(a)), eff. 9/1/97.)*

### §391.092. Regulation of signs generally.

(a) The commission shall:

(1) regulate the content, composition, placement, erection, and maintenance of specific information logo signs and supports on an eligible highway right-of-way; and

(2) adopt rules necessary to administer and enforce this subchapter.

(b) A specific information logo sign must:

(1) have a blue background with a white reflective border; and

(2) contain a principal legend equal in height to the directional legend.

(c) A specific information logo sign may not:

(1) contain a message, symbol, or trademark that resembles an official traffic-control device;

(2) contain more than six establishment names for each sign panel.
*(Added by L.1995, chap. 165(1); chgd. by L.1997, chap. 165(30.22(b)), eff. 9/1/97.)*

### §391.093. Eligibility for display on sign.

(a) A commercial establishment, to be eligible to have its name displayed on a specific information logo sign, must provide gas, food, lodging, or camping and be located not more than three miles from an interchange on an eligible highway. If no service participating or willing to participate in the specific information logo sign program is located within three miles of an interchange, the commission may grant permits for commercial establishments located not farther than:

(1) six miles from the interchange;

(2) nine miles from the interchange if no service participating or willing to participate in the program is located within six miles from the interchange;

(3) 12 miles from the interchange if no service participating or willing to participate in the program is located within nine miles of the interchange;

(4) 15 miles from the interchange if no service participating or willing to participate in the program is located within 12 miles of the interchange.

(b) An establishment that provides gas must operate continuously at least 12 hours each day and provide:

(1) vehicle services, including fuel, oil, and water;

(2) tire repair, unless the establishment is self-service;

(3) restroom facilities and drinking water; and

(4) a telephone for use by the public.

(c) An establishment that provides food must:

(1) have any required license or other evidence showing compliance with applicable public health or sanitation laws;

(2) operate continuously at least 12 hours a day and serve three meals a day; and

(3) provide:

(A) seating capacity for at least 16 persons;

(B) public restrooms; and

(C) a telephone for use by the public.

(d) An establishment that provides lodging must:

(1) have any required license or other evidence showing compliance with applicable laws regulating facilities providing lodging;

(2) provide at least 10 rooms; and

(3) provide a telephone for use by the public.

(e) An establishment that provides camping must:

(1) have any required license or other evidence showing compliance with applicable laws regulating camping facilities;

(2) provide adequate parking accommodations; and

(3) provide drinking water and modern sanitary facilities.

(f) The department shall by rule provide that an establishment that provides lodging is eligible to have its name displayed on a specific information logo sign if the establishment is:

(1) visible from an eligible highway or an interchange on an eligible highway; and

(2) located on a street that is not more than two turns off the access or frontage road to the eligible highway.

*(Added by L.1995, chap. 165(1); chgd. by L.1997, chap. 165(30.22(c)); L.1999, chap. 841(1), eff. 6/18/99.)*



### §391.0935. Major shopping area guide signs.

(a) Unless the commission determines there is a conflict with federal law, the commission shall establish a program that allows the erection and maintenance of major shopping area guide signs at appropriate locations along eligible urban highways.

(b) The commission shall adopt rules regulating the content, composition, placement, erection, and maintenance of major shopping area guide signs and supports within eligible urban highway rights-of-way. A major shopping area is entitled to have its name displayed on major shopping area guide signs if it is located not farther than three miles from an interchange on an eligible urban highway.

(c) A major shopping area that has its name displayed on a major shopping area guide sign shall reimburse the commission for all costs associated with the composition, placement, erection, and maintenance of the sign.

(d) Major shopping area guide signs may be included as part of exit direction signs, advance guide signs, and supplemental guide signs and must include guide signs for both directions of traffic on an eligible urban highway.

(e) Sections 391.093(b)-(e) do not apply to major shopping area guide signs.

*(Added by L.1997, chap. 165(30.22(d)), eff. 9/1/97.)*

### §391.094. Duty not to discriminate.

A commercial establishment identified on a specific information logo sign shall conform to all applicable laws concerning the provision of public accommodations without regard to race, religion, color, sex, or national origin. *(Added by L.1995, chap. 165(1), eff. 9/1/95.)*

### §391.095. Placement of signs.

(a) The contractor installing a specific information logo sign shall place the sign so that:

(1) the sign is at least 800 feet from the previous interchange and at least 800 feet from the exit direction sign at the interchange from which the services are available;

(2) two signs having the same legend are at least 800 feet apart, but are not excessively spaced;

(3) a motorist, after following the sign, can conveniently reenter the highway and continue in the original direction of travel.

(b) A specific information logo sign that is placed along a ramp or at a ramp terminal must be a duplicate of the corresponding establishment logo sign, except that the ramp sign must:

(1) be smaller;

(2) include the distance to the commercial establishment; and

(3) include directional arrows instead of directions shown in words.

(c) If the service facilities are not visible from an interchange ramp terminal, additional signs may be placed along the ramp or at the ramp terminal.
*(Added by L.1995, chap. 165(1); chgd. by L.1997, chap. 165(30.22(e)), eff. 9/1/97.)*

**§391.096. Disposition of funds.**
Funds received under this subchapter shall be deposited to the credit of the state highway fund.
*(Added by L.1995, chap. 165(1), eff. 9/1/95.)*

**§391.097. Major agricultural interest sign.**
(a) In this section:
(1) "Eligible rural highway" means a highway that:
(A) has noncontrolled access; and
(B) is outside the corporate limits of a municipality.
(2) "Major agricultural interest" means a farm, ranch, winery, nursery, greenhouse, or other facility that:
(A) sows or cultivates an agricultural product;
(B) devotes a minimum of five acres of land to the production of the agricultural product;
(C) markets the product on the premises as a retail sale of the product; and
(D) conducts public tours of the grounds or facilities.
(b) The commission shall enter into one or more contracts with an individual, firm, group, or association in this state to erect and maintain major agricultural interest signs at appropriate locations along eligible rural highways.
(c) A contract under this section shall provide for:
(1) the assessment of fees to be paid to a contractor by a commercial establishment of a major agricultural interest; and
(2) remittance to the department of a portion of the fees collected by the contractor in an amount sufficient to recover the department's costs of administering the program.
(d) To be eligible to have its name displayed on a major agricultural interest sign, a major agricultural interest must be located within five miles of an intersection with an eligible rural highway.
(e) A major agricultural interest sign must:
(1) have a brown background with a white reflective legend and border;
(2) not contain a corporate or trademark symbol; and
(3) not contain a message, symbol, or trademark that resembles an official traffic control device.
(f) The commission shall:
(1) regulate the content, composition, placement, erection, and maintenance of major agricultural interest signs and supports on an eligible rural highway right-of-way; and
(2) adopt rules necessary to administer and enforce this section.
*(Added by L.1997, chap. 1171(2.04), eff. 9/1/97.)*

**§391.098. Variances.**
(a) The commission shall authorize the director to grant variances, on a case-by-case basis, to the eligibility, location, or placement of specific logo signs, major agricultural interest signs, and major shopping area guide signs, including the highways along which a sign may be located. The commission may adopt rules prescribing conditions or guidelines the director should or must consider when determining whether to grant a variance.
(b) The director may grant a variance if the director determines that:
(1) the variance would promote traffic safety;
(2) the variance would improve traffic flow;
(3) an overpass, highway sign, or other highway structure unduly obstructs the visibility of an existing commercial sign; or
(4) the variance would satisfy other conditions or guidelines prescribed by commission rules authorizing the granting of variances.
(c) The director may not grant a variance to the requirements of this subchapter regarding supports, content, or composition of signs.
*(Added by L.1997, chap. 1171(2.04), eff. 9/1/97.)*

**§§391.099 to 391.120.** *(Reserved.)*

## SUBCHAPTER E. REGULATION OF JUNKYARDS AND AUTOMOBILE GRAVEYARDS

### §391.121. Prohibited junkyard; offense.

(a) A person commits an offense if:

(1) the person wilfully establishes, operates, or maintains a junkyard any portion of which is within 1,000 feet of the nearest edge of a right-of-way of a highway in the interstate or primary system; and

(2) the junkyard is not:

(A) screened by appropriate means, including natural objects, plantings, or fences, so that it is not visible from the main-traveled way of the interstate or primary highway; or

(B) located in an area that is a zoned or unzoned industrial area.

(b) The determination of whether an area is industrial must be made under criteria established by commission rule and according to actual land use.

(c) An offense under this section is a misdemeanor punishable by a fine of not less than $500 or more than $1,000. Each day of the proscribed conduct is a separate offense.

*(Added by L.1995, chap. 165(1), eff. 9/1/95.)*

17 Printed in the U.S.A.

### §391.122. Authority of commission to screen junkyard.

(a) The commission may screen with appropriate means, including natural objects, plantings, or fences, a lawfully existing junkyard that is within 1,000 feet of the nearest edge of a right-of-way of a highway in the interstate or primary system.

(b) The commission may acquire an area outside of a highway right-of-way so that a junkyard may be screened from the main-traveled way of a highway in the interstate or primary system.

*(Added by L.1995, chap. 165(1), eff. 9/1/95.)*

### §391.123. Rules relating to screening of junkyards.

The commission may adopt rules governing the location, planting, construction, and maintenance of the materials used in screening junkyards. *(Added by L.1995, chap. 165(1), eff. 9/1/95.)*

### §391.124. Compensation to owner of junkyard.

If the commission determines that the screening of a lawfully existing junkyard that is within 1,000 feet of the nearest edge of a right-of-way of a highway in the interstate or primary system is not feasible, the commission shall pay just compensation to:

(1) the owner of the junkyard for its relocation, removal, or disposal; and

(2) the owner or, if appropriate, the lessee of the real property on which the junkyard is located for the taking of the right to erect and maintain a junkyard.

*(Added by L.1995, chap. 165(1), eff. 9/1/95.)*

### §391.125. Injunction to require screening.

(a) On written notice by certified mail from the department, an owner of a junkyard that is established, operated, or maintained in violation of this subchapter or a rule adopted under this subchapter shall screen the junkyard in accordance with Section 391.121. If the owner does not screen the junkyard within 45 days of the date of the notice, the department may request the attorney general to apply for an injunction to require the screening of the junkyard.

(b) Under an action brought under Subsection (a), the state is entitled to recover from the owner of a junkyard all administrative and legal costs and expenses incurred to require the screening of the junkyard, including court costs and reasonable attorney's fees.

*(Added by L.1999, chap. 442(2), eff. 6/18/99.)*

### §391.126. Civil penalty.

(a) In addition to being subject to a criminal penalty or injunctive action, a person who intentionally violates this subchapter is liable to the state for a civil penalty. The attorney general may sue to collect the penalty.

(b) The amount of a civil penalty under this section is not less than $500 or more than $1,000 for each violation, depending on the seriousness of the violation. A separate penalty may be collected for each day a continuing violation occurs.

*(Added by L.1999, chap. 442(2), eff. 6/18/99.)*

### §391.127. Salvage vehicle dealer license.

The commission may revoke or suspend a license issued under Article 6687-1a, Revised Statutes, or place on probation a license holder whose license is suspended, if the license holder violates this chapter or a rule adopted under this chapter. *(Added by L.1999, chap. 442(2), eff. 6/18/99.)*

**§§391.128 to 391.150.** *(Reserved.)*

## SUBCHAPTER F. ACQUISITION FOR SCENIC ENHANCEMENT OR PUBLIC ACCOMMODATION

### §391.151. Acquisition for scenic enhancement.

The commission may acquire, improve, and maintain a strip of real property adjacent to a federal-aid highway in this state if the property is necessary to restore, preserve, or enhance scenic beauty. *(Added by L.1995, chap. 165(1), eff. 9/1/95.)*

### §391.152. Acquisition for public accommodation.

The commission may acquire and provide rest and recreation areas or sanitary and other facilities in or adjacent to a highway right-of-way if the area or facility is necessary to accommodate the traveling public. *(Added by L.1995, chap. 165(1), eff. 9/1/95.)*



**§§391.153 to 391.180.** *(Reserved.)*

## SUBCHAPTER G. ACQUISITIONS BY COMMISSION

### §391.181. Powers and methods of acquisition.

(a) The commission may acquire by gift, purchase, exchange, or condemnation any right or property interest that it considers necessary or convenient to implement this chapter.

(b) The exercise of the power of eminent domain authorized by this chapter is the same as that authorized by Subchapter D, Chapter 203.

(c) Real property owned by the state is subject to this chapter.

*(Added by L.1995, chap. 165(1), eff. 9/1/95.)*

### §391.182. State vouchers and warrants.

(a) On delivery to and acceptance by the commission of an instrument conveying to the state an interest described by Section 391.181(a), the commission shall prepare and transmit to the comptroller a voucher covering the commission's costs in acquiring the interest.

(b) The comptroller shall issue a warrant on the appropriate account covering the state's obligation as evidenced by the voucher.

*(Added by L.1995, chap. 165(1), eff. 9/1/95.)*

### §391.183. Recording of instruments.

(a) An instrument conveying an interest in real property to the state in connection with the implementation of this chapter must be recorded in the deed records of each county in which the property is situated.

(b) The state shall pay the fee for recording the instrument in the same manner as a fee is paid for the recording of a highway right-of-way instrument and in accordance with the law establishing the fee to be charged by the county clerk for recording a highway right-of-way instrument.

*(Added by L.1995, chap. 165(1), eff. 9/1/95.)*

### §391.184. Disposal of state real property.

An interest in real property acquired to implement this chapter that becomes surplus and is determined by the commission as no longer necessary to the state for the purpose for which it was acquired or for a highway purpose shall be disposed of in accordance with Subchapter B, Chapter 202. *(Added by L.1995, chap. 165(1), eff. 9/1/95.)*

**§§391.185 to 391.210.** *(Reserved.)*

## SUBCHAPTER H. REGULATION OF OUTDOOR ADVERTISING ON STATE HIGHWAY 288

### §391.211. Applicability of subchapter.

(a) This subchapter applies only to outdoor advertising that is erected on or after September 1, 1993.

(b) This subchapter does not limit any authority granted to the department under this chapter. *(Added by L.1995, chap. 165(1), eff. 9/1/95.)*

### §391.212. Regulation of certain outdoor advertising.

The department may license or otherwise regulate the erection of outdoor advertising that is located within 1,000 feet of the center line of that part of State Highway 288 in the unincorporated area of a county. *(Added by L.1995, chap. 165(1), eff. 9/1/95.)*

### §391.213. Violation of rule; offense.

(a) A person commits an offense if the person violates a rule adopted under this subchapter.

(b) An offense under this section is a Class C misdemeanor.

*(Added by L.1995, chap. 165(1), eff. 9/1/95.)*

## CHAPTER 392. HIGHWAY BEAUTIFICATION ON STATE HIGHWAY RIGHT-OF-WAY

*(Selected Subchapter)*

## SUBCHAPTER B. SIGNS ON STATE HIGHWAY RIGHT-OF-WAY





### §392.031. Definitions.

In this subchapter:

(1) "Sign" means an outdoor sign, display, light, device, figure, painting, drawing, message, plaque, poster, or other thing designed, intended, or used to advertise or inform.

(2) "State highway right-of-way" means the right-of-way of a highway designated as part of the state highway system.

*(Added by L.1995, chap. 165(1), eff. 9/1/95.)*

### §392.032. Offense.

(a) A person may not place or maintain a sign on a state highway right-of-way unless authorized by state law.

(b) A person commits an offense if the person violates this section.

(c) An offense under this section is a Class C misdemeanor.

*(Added by L.1995, chap. 165(1), eff. 9/1/95.)*

### §392.0325. Exception.

(a) A person may submit a request to the department for an exception to this subchapter for a sign that is attached to a building located on property other than a state highway right-of-way and that refers to a commercial activity or business located in the building if the sign:

(1) consists solely of the name of the establishment;

(2) identifies the establishment's principal product or services; or

(3) advertises the sale or lease of the property on which the sign is located.

(b) The department shall approve a request submitted under Subsection (a) if the department:

(1) determines that the sign will not constitute a safety hazard;

(2) determines that the sign will not interfere with the construction, reconstruction, operation, or maintenance of the highway facility; and

(3) obtains the approval of the Federal Highway Administration if approval is required under federal law.

*(Added by L.1999, chap. 442(3), eff. 6/18/99.)*

### §392.033. Removal and disposal of illegal sign.

(a) Except as provided by Section 392.034, the department, without prior notice to the owner of the sign, may remove a sign that is placed or maintained in violation of this subchapter.

(b) If the owner's identity and mailing address are displayed on the sign or are otherwise reasonably ascertainable, the department shall notify the owner in writing that the sign:

(1) has been removed; and

(2) may be disposed of unless the owner claims the sign on or before the 10th day after the removal date.

(c) If the owner of the sign does not claim the sign on or before the 10th day after the removal date, the department may dispose of the sign.

*(Added by L.1995, chap. 165(1), eff. 9/1/95.)*

### §392.034. Encroachment.

(a) The department shall give written notice of encroachment to the owner of a sign that:

(1) is on property other than a state highway right-of-way;

(2) is maintained under a written permit or agreement; and

(3) encroaches on the state highway right-of-way.

(b) If the owner of the sign does not correct the encroachment before the 31st day after the date of receipt of the notice, the department may remove the sign under Section 392.033.

*(Added by L.1995, chap. 165(1), eff. 9/1/95.)*

### §392.035. Removal costs.

(a) The owner of a sign removed by the department under Section 392.033 is liable to the department for removal costs.

(b) Removal costs received by the department under this section shall be deposited to the credit of the state highway fund.

*(Added by L.1995, chap. 165(1), eff. 9/1/95.)*

### §392.036. Defense.

It is a defense to prosecution for a violation under Section 392.032 that at the time of the alleged violation:

(1) the defendant is a candidate for elective public office; and

(2) the sign is placed:

(A) by a person other than the defendant;

(B) without the knowledge of the defendant; and

(C) in connection with a campaign for an elective public office by the defendant.

*(Added by L.1995, chap. 165(1), eff. 9/1/95.)*

### §392.037. Rules.

The commission may adopt rules to enforce this subchapter. *(Added by L.1995, chap. 165(1), eff. 9/1/95.)*

### §392.038. Effect of other law or ordinance.

If this subchapter conflicts with another law or a local ordinance, the more restrictive provision applies. *(Added by L.1995, chap. 165(1), eff. 9/1/95.)*

## SUBTITLE Z. MISCELLANEOUS ROADWAY PROVISIONS

## CHAPTER 471. RAILROAD AND ROADWAY CROSSINGS
*(Selected Sections)*

Section

### §471.003. Telephone service to report malfunctions of mechanical safety devices at crossings.

(a) The Department of Public Safety shall maintain a statewide toll-free telephone service to receive a report of a malfunction of a device, including a signal or crossbar, placed at an intersection of a railroad track and a public road to promote safety.

(b) At each intersection of a railroad track and a public road that is maintained by the state or a municipality and at which a mechanical safety device is placed, the Texas Department of Transportation shall affix on the crossbars of the device the telephone number, an explanation of its purpose, and the crossing number. At each intersection of a railroad track and a public road that is maintained by a political subdivision other than a municipality and at which a mechanical safety device is placed, the political subdivision shall affix on the crossbars of the device the telephone number, an explanation of its purpose, and the crossing number. The Texas Department of Transportation shall provide to the political subdivision the sign or label displaying the telephone number. A railway company shall permit personnel to affix the telephone number on the company's property as required by this subsection.

(c) The Department of Public Safety shall notify the identified railway company of each report of a malfunction received under Subsection (a).

(d) The Department of Public Safety shall maintain a computerized list of each intersection of a railroad track and a public road and of the railroad crossing safety equipment located at each intersection, using crossing numbers compiled by the Texas Department of Transportation.

(e) Not later than the fifth day after the date it places railroad crossing safety equipment in operation at an intersection subject to this section, a state agency or a political subdivision of the state other than a municipality shall notify the Department of Public Safety of:

(1) the location and type of the equipment installed; and

(2) the date it was placed in operation.

(f) The state, an agency or political subdivision of the state, or a railway company is not liable for damages caused by an action taken under this section or failure to perform a duty imposed by this section. Evidence may not be introduced in a judicial proceeding that the telephone service required by this section exists or that the state or railway company relies on the service.

(g) Except as provided by Subsection (d), a state agency is not required to make or retain a permanent record of information obtained in implementing this section.

*(Added by L.1995, chap. 165(1), eff. 9/1/95.)*



### §471.005. Dismantling of warning signals at railroad grade crossings; offense.

(a) A person may not dismantle a warning signal at a grade crossing on an active rail line, as defined by rule of the Texas Department of Transportation, if the cost of the warning signal was originally paid entirely or partly from public money unless the person:

(1) obtains a permit from the governmental entity that maintains the road or highway that intersects the rail line at the grade crossing; and

(2) pays that governmental entity an amount equal to the present salvage value of the warning signal, as determined by the governmental entity.

(b) The governmental entity shall grant the permit if:

(1) payment is received; and

(2) the entity finds that removal of the warning signal will not adversely affect public safety.

(c) Money received under Subsection (a)(2) shall be deposited in the state treasury.

(d) This section does not apply to a Class I or Class II railroad, as defined by Interstate Commerce Commission regulations.

(e) A person commits an offense if the person violates this section. An offense under this section is a Class C misdemeanor.

(f) The Texas Department of Transportation may adopt rules necessary to administer this section.

(g) In this section:

(1) "Grade crossing" has the meaning assigned by Section 472.004(f).

(2) "Warning signal" means a traffic control device that is activated by the approach or presence of a train, including a flashing light signal, an automatic gate, or a similar device that displays to motorists a warning of the approach or presence of a train.

*(Added by L.1995, chap. 165(1), eff. 9/1/95.)*

### §471.006. Use of bell and whistle or siren at crossings; offense.

(a) A railway company shall place on each locomotive:

(1) a bell weighing at least 30 pounds; and

(2) a steam whistle, air whistle, or air siren.

(b) The engineer in charge of the locomotive shall ring the bell and blow the whistle or siren at least one-quarter mile from the place where the railroad crosses a public road or street. The engineer shall continue to ring the bell until the locomotive has crossed the road or stopped.

(c) The railway company is liable for any damages sustained by a person because of a violation of Subsection (a) or (b).

(d) The engineer in charge of the locomotive commits an offense if the engineer violates Subsection (b). An offense under this subsection is a misdemeanor punishable by a fine of not less than $5 or more than $100.

(e) Notwithstanding Subsections (a) and (b), the governing body of a municipality having a population of at least 5,000 may regulate by ordinance the ringing of bells and blowing of whistles and sirens within its limits. Compliance with the ordinance is compliance with those subsections and a sufficient warning to the public at a crossing the ordinance affects.

*(Added by L.1995, chap. 165(1), eff. 9/1/95.)*

### §471.007. Obstructing railroad crossings; offense.

(a) A railway company commits an offense if a train of the railway company obstructs for more than 10 minutes a street, railroad crossing, or public highway.

(b) An offense under this section is a misdemeanor punishable by a fine of not less than $100 or more than $300.

(c) An officer charging a railway company for an offense under this section shall prepare in duplicate a citation to appear in court and attach one copy of the citation to the train or deliver the copy to an employee or other agent of the railway company. The citation must show:

(1) the name of the railway company;

(2) the offense charged; and

(3) the time and place that a representative of the railway company is to appear in court.

(d) It is a defense to prosecution under this section that the train obstructs the street, railroad crossing, or public highway because of an act of God or breakdown of the train.

(e) The hearing must be before a magistrate who has jurisdiction of the offense in the municipality or county in which the offense is alleged to have been committed.

(f) An appearance by counsel complies with the written promise to appear in court.

*(Added by L.1995, chap. 165(1); chgd. by L.1999, chap. 1023(1), eff. 9/1/99.)*



### §471.008. Franchise to obstruct street crossing.

(a) The governing body of a municipality by ordinance may grant a franchise to a railway company to obstruct a street crossing, other than a crossing of a designated state highway, by a passenger train for the purpose of receiving or discharging passengers, mail, express, or freight for a longer period than specified by Section 472.007.

(b) Section 471.007 does not apply to a street crossing named in an ordinance granting a franchise under this section.

(c) This section does not apply to a municipality having a special charter unless it amends its charter to adopt this section.

*(Added by L.1995, chap. 165(1), eff. 9/1/95.)*

## CHAPTER 472. MISCELLANEOUS PROVISIONS
*(Selected Subchapters)*

## SUBCHAPTER B. DEPARTMENT AUTHORITY TO REMOVE PROPERTY FROM STATE HIGHWAYS

Section

## SUBCHAPTER C. CRIMINAL OFFENSES AND PENALTIES REGARDING WARNING SIGNS AND BARRICADES



## SUBCHAPTER B. DEPARTMENT AUTHORITY TO REMOVE PROPERTY FROM STATE HIGHWAYS

### §472.011. Definition.

In this subchapter, "personal property" includes personal property of any kind or character, including:

(1) a vehicle, as defined by Section 502.001, that is damaged or disabled;
(2) spilled cargo;
(3) a hazardous material as defined by 49 U.S.C. App. Section 1802; and
(4) a hazardous substance as defined by Section 26.263, Water Code.
*(Added by L.1995, chap. 165(1); chgd. by L.1997, chap. 1171(1.43(a)), eff. 9/1/97.)*



### §472.012. Department authority generally.

(a) The department may remove personal property from the right-of-way or roadway of the state highway system if the department determines the property blocks the roadway or endangers public safety.

(b) The department may remove the personal property without the consent of the owner or carrier of the property.
*(Added by L.1995, chap. 165(1), eff. 9/1/95.)*

### §472.013. Owner and carrier responsible for costs of removal and disposition.

The owner and the carrier of personal property removed under this subchapter shall reimburse the department for the costs of removal and disposition. *(Added by L.1995, chap. 165(1), eff. 9/1/95.)*

### §472.014. Department not liable for damages.

Notwithstanding any other provision of law, the department and its officers and employees are not liable for:

(1) any damage to personal property resulting from its removal or disposal by the department unless the removal or disposal is carried out recklessly or in a grossly negligent manner; or
(2) any damage resulting from the failure to exercise authority granted under this subchapter.
*(Added by L.1995, chap. 165(1); chgd. by L.1997, chap. 1171(1.43(b)), eff. 9/1/97.)*

### §§472.015 to 472.020. *(Reserved.)*

## SUBCHAPTER C. CRIMINAL OFFENSES AND PENALTIES REGARDING WARNING SIGNS AND BARRICADES

### §472.021. Tampering with warning devices.

(a) A person commits an offense if the person tampers with, damages, or removes a barricade, flare pot, sign, flasher signal, or other device warning of construction, repair, or detour on or adjacent to a highway set out by the state, a political subdivision, a contractor, or a public utility.

(b) This section does not apply to a person acting within the scope and duty of employment if the person is:

(1) an officer, agent, independent contractor, employee, or trustee of the state or a political subdivision;
(2) a contractor; or
(3) a public utility.

(c) An offense under this section is a misdemeanor punishable by:

(1) a fine of not less than $25 or more than $1,000;
(2) confinement in a county jail for a term not to exceed two years; or
(3) both the fine and the confinement.

(d) In this section:

(1) "Contractor" means a person engaged in highway construction or repair under contract with this state or a political subdivision of this state.

(2) "Highway" means the entire width between the boundary lines of a publicly maintained way, any part of which is open to the public for vehicular travel or any part of which is under construction or repair and intended for public vehicular travel on completion. The term includes the space above or below the highway surface.

(3) "Person" means an individual, firm, association, or corporation and includes an officer, agent, independent contractor, employee, or trustee of that individual or entity.

(4) "Political subdivision" includes a county, municipality, local board, or other body of this state having authority to authorize highway construction or repair.

(5) "Public utility" means:

(A) a telegraph, telephone, water, gas, light, or sewage company or cooperative;

(B) a contractor of a company or cooperative described by Subdivision (A); or

(C) another business recognized by the legislature as a public utility.

*(Added by L.1995, chap. 165(1), eff. 9/1/95.)*

## §472.022. Obeying warning signs.

(a) A person commits an offense if the person disobeys the instructions, signals, warnings, or markings of a warning sign.

(b) This section does not apply to:

(1) a person who is following the directions of a police officer; or

(2) a person, including an employee of the department, a political subdivision of this state, or a contractor or subcontractor, whose duties require the person to go beyond or around a barricade.

(c) Each violation of this section is a separate offense.

(d) An offense under this section is a misdemeanor punishable by a fine of not less than $1 or more than $200, except that if the offense is committed in a construction or maintenance work zone when workers are present and any written notice to appear issued for the offense states on its face that workers were present when the offense was committed, the offense is a misdemeanor punishable by a fine of not less than $2 or more than $400.

(e) In this section:

(1) "Barricade" means an obstruction:

(A) placed on or across a road, street, or highway of this state by the department, a political subdivision of this state, or a contractor or subcontractor constructing or repairing the road, street, or highway under authorization of the department or a political subdivision of this state; and

(B) placed to prevent the passage of motor vehicles over the road, street, or highway during construction or repair.

(2) "Construction or maintenance work zone" means a portion of a highway or street:

(A) where highway construction or maintenance is being undertaken, other than mobile operations as defined by the Texas Manual on Uniform Traffic Control Devices; and

(B) that is marked by signs indicating that it is a construction or maintenance work zone and stating: "Fines double when workers present." *(Chgd. by L.1999, chap. 789(2), eff. 9/1/99. See other paragraph (B) below.)*

(B) that is marked by signs indicating that it is a construction or maintenance work zone and indicating where the zone begins and ends. *(Chgd. by L.1999, chap. 965(1), eff. 9/1/99. See other paragraph (B) above.)*

(3) "Warning sign" means a signal, marking, or device placed on a barricade or on a road, street, or highway under construction or repair by the department, a political subdivision of this state, or a contractor or subcontractor to warn or regulate motor vehicular traffic. The term includes a flagger deployed on a road, street, or highway by the department, a political subdivision of this state, or a contractor or subcontractor to direct traffic around or on the road, street, or highway under construction or repair.

(f) Article 45.54, Code of Criminal Procedure, does not apply to an offense under this section committed in a construction or maintenance work zone when workers are present.

*(Added by L.1995, chap. 165(1); chgd. by L.1997, chap. 674(1); L.1999, chaps. 789(1), (2), 965(1), 1088(1), eff. 9/1/99.)*

# TITLE 7. VEHICLES AND TRAFFIC
*(Complete Title)*

## SUBTITLE A. CERTIFICATES OF TITLE AND REGISTRATION OF VEHICLES

## CHAPTER 501. CERTIFICATE OF TITLE ACT

### SUBCHAPTER A. GENERAL PROVISIONS

Section




### SUBCHAPTER B. CERTIFICATE OF TITLE REQUIREMENTS



### SUBCHAPTER C. REFUSAL TO ISSUE AND REVOCATION OR SUSPENSION OF CERTIFICATE



### SUBCHAPTER D. SALES OF MOTOR VEHICLES AND TRANSFERS OF TITLE

## SUBCHAPTER E. NONREPAIRABLE AND SALVAGE MOTOR VEHICLES





## SUBCHAPTER F. SECURITY INTERESTS



## SUBCHAPTER G. ADMINISTRATIVE PROVISIONS



## SUBCHAPTER H. PENALTIES AND OTHER ENFORCEMENT PROVISIONS

## SUBCHAPTER A. GENERAL PROVISIONS

### §501.001. Short title.

This chapter may be cited as the Certificate of Title Act. *(Added by L.1995, chap. 165(1), eff. 9/1/95.)*



### §501.002. Definitions.

In this chapter:

(1) "Certificate of title" means an instrument issued under Section 501.021.

(2) "Dealer" means a person who purchases motor vehicles for sale at retail.

(3) "Department" means the Texas Department of Transportation.

(4) "Distributor" means a person engaged in the business of selling to a dealer motor vehicles purchased from a manufacturer.

(5) "First sale" means:

(A) the bargain, sale, transfer, or delivery of a motor vehicle that has not been previously registered or licensed, with intent to pass an interest in the motor vehicle, other than a lien, regardless of where the bargain, sale, transfer, or delivery occurred; and

(B) the registration or licensing of that vehicle.

(6) "House trailer" means a trailer designed for human habitation. The term does not include manufactured housing.

(7) "Importer" means a person, other than a manufacturer, that brings a used motor vehicle into this state for sale in this state.

(8) "Importer's certificate" means a certificate for a used motor vehicle brought into this state for sale in this state.

(9) "Lien" means:

(A) a lien provided for by the constitution or statute in a motor vehicle; or

(B) a security interest, as defined by Section 1.201, Business & Commerce Code, in a motor vehicle, other than an absolute title, created by any written security agreement, as defined by Section [9.105] *9.102*, Business & Commerce Code, including a lease, conditional sales contract, deed of trust, chattel mortgage, trust receipt, or reservation of title.

(10) "Manufactured housing" has the meaning assigned by the Texas Manufactured Housing Standards Act (Article 5221f, Texas Civil Statutes).

(11) "Manufacturer" means a person regularly engaged in the business of manufacturing or assembling new motor vehicles.

(12) "Manufacturer's permanent vehicle identification number" means the number affixed by the manufacturer to a motor vehicle in a manner and place easily accessible for physical examination and die-stamped or otherwise permanently affixed on one or more removable parts of the vehicle.

(13) "Motorcycle" means a motor vehicle, other than a tractor, designed to propel itself with not more than three wheels in contact with the ground.

(14) "Motor vehicle" means:

(A) any motor driven or propelled vehicle required to be registered under the laws of this state;

(B) a trailer or semitrailer, other than manufactured housing, that has a gross vehicle weight that exceeds 4,000 pounds;

(C) a house trailer;

(D) a four-wheel all-terrain vehicle designed by the manufacturer for off-highway use that is not required to be registered under the laws of this state; or

(E) a motorcycle, motor-driven cycle, or moped that is not required to be registered under the laws of this state, other than a motorcycle, motor-driven cycle, or moped designed for and used exclusively on a golf course.

(15) "New motor vehicle" means a motor vehicle that has not been the subject of a first sale.

(16) "Owner" includes a person, other than a manufacturer, importer, distributor, or dealer, claiming title to or having a right to operate under a lien a motor vehicle that has been subject to a first sale.

(17) "Semitrailer" means a vehicle that is designed or used with a motor vehicle so that part of the weight of the vehicle and its load rests on or is carried by another vehicle.

(18) "Serial number" means a vehicle identification number that is affixed to a part of a motor vehicle and that is:

(A) the manufacturer's permanent vehicle identification number;

(B) a derivative number of the manufacturer's permanent vehicle identification number;

(C) the motor number; or

(D) the vehicle identification number assigned by the department.

(19) "Steal" has the meaning assigned by Section 31.01, Penal Code.

(20) "Subsequent sale" means:

(A) the bargain, sale, transfer, or delivery of a motor vehicle that has been previously registered or licensed in this state or elsewhere, with intent to pass an interest in the vehicle, other than a lien, regardless of where the bargain, sale, transfer, or delivery occurs; and

(B) the registration of the vehicle if registration is required under the laws of this state.

(21) "Title receipt" means an instrument issued under Section 501.024.

(22) "Trailer" means a vehicle that:

(A) is designed or used to carry a load wholly on the trailer's own structure; and

(B) is drawn or designed to be drawn by a motor vehicle.

(23) "Used motor vehicle" means a motor vehicle that has been the subject of a first sale.

*(Added by L.1995, chap. 165(1); chgd. by L.1999, chap. 414(2.42), eff. 7/1/2001. Matter in brackets eff. only until 7/1/2001. Matter in italics eff. 7/1/2001.)*



## §501.003. Construction.

This chapter shall be liberally construed to lessen and prevent:

(1) the theft of motor vehicles;

(2) the importation into this state of and traffic in motor vehicles that are stolen; and

(3) the sale of an encumbered motor vehicle without the enforced disclosure to the purchaser of a lien secured by the vehicle.

*(Added by L.1995, chap. 165(1), eff. 9/1/95.)*

## §501.004. Applicability.

(a) This chapter applies to a motor vehicle owned by the state or a political subdivision of the state.

(b) This chapter does not apply to:

(1) a trailer or semitrailer used only for the transportation of farm products if the products are not transported for hire;

(2) the filing or recording of a lien that is created only on an automobile accessory, including a tire, radio, or heater;

(3) a motor vehicle while it is owned or operated by the United States; or

(4) a new motor vehicle on loan to a political subdivision of the state for use only in a driver education course approved by the Central Education Agency.

*(Added by L.1995, chap. 165(1), eff. 9/1/95.)*

## §501.005. Conflicts with Business & Commerce Code.

Chapters 1-9, Business & Commerce Code, control over a conflicting provision of this chapter. *(Added by L.1995, chap. 165(1), eff. 9/1/95.)*

## §§501.006 to 501.020. *(Reserved.)*

# SUBCHAPTER B. CERTIFICATE OF TITLE REQUIREMENTS

## §501.021. Certificate of title.

(a) A motor vehicle certificate of title is an instrument issued by the department that includes:

(1) the name and address of the purchaser and seller at the first sale or the transferee and transferor at a subsequent sale;

(2) the make of the motor vehicle;

(3) the body type of the vehicle;

(4) the manufacturer's permanent vehicle identification number of the vehicle or the vehicle's motor number if the vehicle was manufactured before the date that stamping a permanent identification number on a motor vehicle was universally adopted;

(5) the serial number for the vehicle;

(6) the number on the vehicle's current Texas license plates, if any;

(7) a statement:

(A) that no lien on the vehicle is recorded; or

(B) of the name and address of each lienholder and the date of each lien on the vehicle, listed in the chronological order in which the lien was recorded;

(8) a space for the signature of the owner of the vehicle;

(9) a statement indicating rights of survivorship under Section 501.031;

(10) if the vehicle has an odometer, the odometer reading indicated by the application for the certificate of title; and

(11) any other information required by the department.

(b) A certificate of title must bear the following statement on its face:

"UNLESS OTHERWISE AUTHORIZED BY LAW, IT IS A VIOLATION OF STATE LAW TO SIGN THE NAME OF ANOTHER PERSON ON A CERTIFICATE OF TITLE OR OTHERWISE GIVE FALSE INFORMATION ON A CERTIFICATE OF TITLE."

*(Added by L.1995, chap. 165(1); chgd. by L.1999, chap. 1423(1), eff. 9/1/99.)*



## §501.022. Certificate of title required.

(a) The owner of a motor vehicle registered in this state may not operate or permit the operation of the vehicle on a public highway until the owner obtains a certificate of title for the vehicle.

(b) A person may not operate a motor vehicle registered in this state on a public highway if the person knows or has reason to believe that the owner has not obtained a certificate of title for the vehicle.

(c) The owner of a motor vehicle that is required to be registered in this state must apply for a certificate of title of the vehicle before selling or disposing of the vehicle.

(d) Subsection (c) does not apply to a motor vehicle operated on a public highway in this state with a metal dealer's license plate or a dealer's or buyer's temporary cardboard tag attached to the vehicle as provided by Chapter 503.

*(Added by L.1995, chap. 165(1), eff. 9/1/95.)*

## §501.023. Application for certificate of title.

(a) The owner of a motor vehicle must apply for a certificate of title:

(1) to the county assessor-collector in the county in which:

(A) the owner is domiciled; or

(B) the motor vehicle is purchased or encumbered; and

(2) on a form prescribed by the department.

(b) The assessor-collector shall send the application to the department not later than 24 hours after receiving the application.

(c) The owner or a lessee of a commercial motor vehicle operating under the International Registration Plan or other agreement described by Section 502.054 that is applying for a certificate of title for purposes of registration only must be made directly to the department. Notwithstanding Section 501.138(a), an applicant for registration under this subsection shall pay the department the fee imposed by that section. The department shall send the fee to the appropriate county assessor-collector for distribution in the manner provided by Section 501.138.

*(Added by L.1995, chap. 165(1); chgd. by L.1999, chap. 1423(2), eff. 9/1/99.)*

## §501.0234. Duty of vehicle dealer on sale of certain vehicles.

(a) A person who sells at the first or a subsequent sale a motor vehicle and who holds a general distinguishing number issued under Chapter 503 or the Texas Motor Vehicle Commission Code (Article 4413(36), Vernon's Texas Civil Statutes) shall:

(1) in the time and manner provided by law, apply, in the name of the purchaser of the vehicle, for the registration of the vehicle, if the vehicle is to be registered, and a certificate of title for the vehicle and file with the appropriate designated agent each document necessary to transfer title to or register the vehicle; and at the same time

(2) remit any required motor vehicle sales tax.

(b) This section does not apply to a vehicle:

(1) that has been declared a total loss by an insurance company in the settlement or adjustment of a claim; or

(2) for which the certificate of title has been surrendered in exchange for:

(A) a salvage certificate of title issued under this chapter;

(B) a nonrepairable motor vehicle certificate of title issued under this chapter;

(C) a certificate of authority issued under Subchapter D, Chapter 683; or

(D) an ownership document issued by another state that is comparable to a document described by Paragraphs (A)-(C).

(c) Each duty imposed by this section on the seller of a motor vehicle is solely that of the seller.
*(Added by L.1997, chap. 165(30.37(a)); chgd. by L.1999, chap. 1423(3), eff. 9/1/99.)*

**§501.0235. Social security number of title applicant: automated registration and title system.**
(a) The department shall require an applicant for a certificate of title to provide the applicant's social security number to the department.
(b) The department or the county shall enter the applicant's social security number in the department's electronic database but may not print that number on the certificate of title.
(c) This section applies only in a county in which the department's automated registration and title system has been implemented.
*(Added by L.1997, chap. 165(30.38(a)), eff. 9/1/97.)*

**§501.024. Title receipt.**
(a) A county assessor-collector who receives an application for a certificate of title shall, after the requirements of this chapter are met, including the payment of the fees required under Section 501.138, issue a title receipt on which is noted information concerning the motor vehicle required for the certificate of title under Section 501.021, including a statement of the existence of each lien as disclosed on the application or a statement that no lien is disclosed.
(b) If a lien is not disclosed on the application for a certificate of title, the assessor-collector shall mark the title receipt "original" and deliver it to the applicant.
(c) If a lien is disclosed on the application for a certificate of title, the assessor-collector shall issue duplicate title receipts. The assessor-collector shall:
(1) mark one receipt "original" and mail or deliver it to the first lienholder disclosed on the application; and
(2) mark the second receipt "duplicate original" and mail or deliver it to the address of the applicant provided on the application.
(d) A title receipt authorizes the operation of the motor vehicle on a public highway in this state for 10 days or until the certificate of title is issued, whichever period is shorter. After that period, the receipt is not effective for any purpose, unless the receipt is renewed as provided by department rules.
*(Added by L.1995, chap. 165(1), eff. 9/1/95.)*

**§501.025. Title receipt required on first sale; manufacturer's certificate.**
A county assessor-collector may not issue a title receipt on the first sale of a motor vehicle unless the applicant for the certificate of title provides to the assessor-collector the application for a certificate of title and a manufacturer's certificate, on a form prescribed by the department, that:
(1) is assigned to the applicant by the manufacturer, distributor, or dealer shown on the manufacturer's certificate as the last transferee; and
(2) shows the transfer of the vehicle from its manufacturer to the purchaser, whether a distributor, dealer, or owner, and each subsequent transfer from distributor to dealer, dealer to dealer, and dealer to applicant.
*(Added by L.1995, chap. 165(1), eff. 9/1/95.)*

**§501.026. Importer's certificate.**
(a) A county assessor-collector may not issue a title receipt for a used motor vehicle imported into this state for the purpose of sale in this state unless the applicant for the certificate of title provides the assessor-collector with an importer's certificate properly assigned by the importer.
(b) An importer's certificate must be accompanied by evidence required by the department showing good title to the motor vehicle and the name and address of any lienholder on the vehicle.
*(Added by L.1995, chap. 165(1), eff. 9/1/95.)*

**§501.027. Issuance of certificate of title.**
(a) On the day that a county assessor-collector issues a title receipt, the assessor-collector shall mail to the department:
(1) a copy of the receipt; and
(2) the evidence of title delivered to the assessor-collector by the applicant.
(b) Not later than the fifth day after the date the department receives an application for a certificate of title and the department determines the requirements of this chapter are met, the department shall issue the certificate of title. If a lien is not disclosed on the application, the department

shall mark the certificate "original" and send it by first class mail to the applicant at the address provided on the application. If a lien is disclosed on the application, the department shall:

(1) issue the certificate of title in duplicate;

(2) mark one certificate of title "original" and send it by first class mail to the first lienholder as disclosed on the application; and

(3) mark the second certificate of title "duplicate original" and send it by first class mail to the applicant at the address provided on the application.

*(Added by L.1995, chap. 165(1), eff. 9/1/95.)*

## §501.0275. Issuance of title for unregistered vehicle.

(a) The department shall issue a certificate of title for a motor vehicle that complies with the other requirements for issuance of a certificate of title under this chapter except that:

(1) the vehicle is not registered for a reason other than a reason provided by Section 501.051(6); and

(2) the applicant does not provide evidence of financial responsibility that complies with Section 502.153.

(b) On application for a certificate of title under this section, the applicant must surrender any license plates issued for the motor vehicle and any registration insignia for validation of those plates to the department.

*(Added by L.1999, chap. 1423(4), eff. 9/1/99.)*



## §501.028. Owner's signature.

On receipt of a certificate of title, the owner of a motor vehicle shall write the owner's name in ink in the space provided on the certificate. *(Added by L.1995, chap. 165(1), eff. 9/1/95.)*

## §501.029. Use of duplicate title receipt or certificate.

A person may use a title receipt or certificate of title marked "Duplicate Original" only to evidence title to a motor vehicle and not to transfer an interest in or establish a lien on the vehicle. *(Added by L.1995, chap. 165(1), eff. 9/1/95.)*

## §501.030. Motor vehicles brought into state.

(a) Before a motor vehicle that was last registered or titled in another state or country may be titled in this state, the applicant must furnish the county assessor-collector with a verification form under Section 548.256.

(b) Before a motor vehicle that was not manufactured for sale or distribution in the United States may be titled in this state, the applicant must:

(1) provide to the assessor-collector:

(A) a bond release letter, with all attachments, issued by the United States Department of Transportation acknowledging:

(i) receipt of a statement of compliance submitted by the importer of the vehicle; and

(ii) that the statement meets the safety requirements of 19 C.F.R. 12.80(e);

(B) a bond release letter, with all attachments, issued by the United States Environmental Protection Agency stating that the vehicle has been tested and shown to conform to federal emission requirements; and

(C) a receipt or certificate issued by the United States Department of the Treasury showing that all gas guzzler taxes due on the vehicle under 26 U.S.C. Section 4064(a) have been paid; or

(2) provide to the assessor-collector proof satisfactory to the assessor-collector that the vehicle was not brought into the United States from outside of the country.

(c) Subsections (a) and (b) do not apply to a motor vehicle lawfully imported into the United States by a distributor or dealer from the vehicle's manufacturer.

(d) If a motor vehicle has not been titled or registered in the United States, the application for certificate of title must be accompanied by:

(1) a manufacturer's certificate of origin written in English issued by the vehicle manufacturer;

(2) the original documents that constitute valid proof of ownership in the country where the vehicle was originally purchased, with an English translation of the documents verified as to the accuracy of the translation by an affidavit of the translator; or

(3) if the vehicle was imported from a country that cancels the vehicle registration and title for export, the documents assigned to the vehicle after the registration and title were canceled, with an English translation of the documents verified as to the accuracy of the translation by an affidavit of the translator.

(e) Before a motor vehicle that is required to be registered in this state and that is brought into this state by a person other than a manufacturer or importer may be bargained, sold, transferred, or delivered with an intent to pass an interest in the vehicle or encumbered by a lien, the owner must apply for a certificate of title on a form prescribed by the department to the county assessor-collector for the county in which the transaction is to take place. The assessor-collector may not issue a title receipt unless the applicant delivers to the assessor-collector satisfactory evidence of title showing that the applicant is the owner of the vehicle and that the vehicle is free of any undisclosed liens.

(f) A county assessor-collector may not be held liable for civil damages arising out of the assessor-collector's failure to reflect on the title receipt a lien or encumbrance on a motor vehicle to which Subsection (e) applies unless the assessor-collector's failure constitutes wilful or wanton negligence.

(g) Until an applicant has complied with this section:

(1) a county assessor-collector may not accept an application for certificate of title; and

(2) the applicant is not entitled to an appeal as provided by Sections 501.052 and 501.053.

*(Added by L.1995, chap. 165(1), eff. 9/1/95.)*



## §501.031. Rights of survivorship agreement.

(a) The department shall include on each certificate of title a rights of survivorship agreement form. The form must:

(1) provide that if the agreement is signed by two or more eligible persons, the motor vehicle is held jointly by those persons with the interest of a person who dies to survive to the surviving person or persons; and

(2) provide blanks for the signatures of the persons.

(b) If the vehicle is registered in the name of one or more of the persons who signed the agreement, the certificate of title may contain a:

(1) rights of survivorship agreement signed by all the persons; or

(2) remark if a rights of survivorship agreement is surrendered with the application for certificate of title or otherwise on file with the department.

(c) Except as provided in Subsection (g), ownership of the vehicle may be transferred only:

(1) by all the persons acting jointly, if all the persons are alive; and

(2) on the death of one of the persons by the surviving person or persons by transferring the certificate of title, in the manner otherwise required by law for transfer of ownership of the vehicle, with a copy of the death certificate of the deceased person attached to the certificate of title application.

(d) A rights of survivorship agreement under this section may be revoked only by surrender of the certificate of title to the department and joint application by the persons who signed the agreement for a new title in the name of the person or persons designated in the application.

(e) A person is eligible to sign a rights of survivorship agreement under this section if the person:

(1) is married and the spouse of the signing person is the only other party to the agreement;

(2) is unmarried and attests to that unmarried status by affidavit; or

(3) is married and provides the department with an affidavit from the signing person's spouse that attests that the signing person's interest in the vehicle is the signing person's separate property.

(f) If the title is being issued in connection with the sale of the vehicle, the seller is not eligible to sign a rights of survivorship agreement under this section unless the seller is the child, grandchild, parent, grandparent, brother, or sister of each other person signing the agreement. A family relationship required by this subsection may be a relationship established by adoption.

(g) If an agreement, other than the agreement provided for in Subsection (a), providing for right of survivorship is signed by two or more persons, the department shall issue a new certificate of title to the surviving person or persons upon application accompanied by a copy of the death certificate of the deceased person. The department may develop for public use under this subsection an optional rights of survivorship agreement form.

*(Added by L.1995, chap. 165(1); chgd. by L.1997, chap. 165(30.39(a)); L.1999, chaps. 62(17.05), 241(1), eff. 9/1/99.)*

## §501.032. Assignment of serial number by department.

(a) On proper application, the department shall assign a serial number to a house trailer, a trailer or semitrailer that has a gross vehicle weight that exceeds 4,000 pounds, or an item of equipment, including a tractor, farm implement, unit of special mobile equipment, or unit of off-road construction equipment on which:

(1) a serial number was not die-stamped by the manufacturer; or

(2) the serial number die-stamped by the manufacturer has been lost, removed, or obliterated.

(b) The applicant shall die-stamp the assigned serial number at the place designated by the department on the house trailer, trailer, semitrailer, or equipment.

(c) The manufacturer's serial number or the serial number assigned by the department shall be affixed on the carriage or axle part of the house trailer, trailer, or semitrailer. The department shall use the number as the major identification of the vehicle in the issuance of a certificate of title.

*(Added by L.1995, chap. 165(1), eff. 9/1/95.)*

## §501.033. Assignment of identification number by department.

(a) A person determined by the department or a court to be the owner of a motor vehicle, a part of a motor vehicle, or an item of equipment including a tractor, farm implement, unit of special mobile equipment, or unit of off-road construction equipment that has had the serial number removed, altered, or obliterated may apply to the department for an assigned vehicle identification number.

(b) An application under this section must be on a form prescribed and furnished by the department and accompanied by the certificate of title for the vehicle or other valid evidence of ownership as required by the department if there is no certificate of title.

(c) A fee of $2 must accompany each application under this section to be deposited in the state highway fund.

(d) The assigned number shall be die-stamped or otherwise affixed to the motor vehicle, part, or item of equipment at the location and in the manner designated by the department.

*(Added by L.1995, chap. 165(1), eff. 9/1/95.)*

## §501.034. Issuance of title to government agency.

The department may issue a certificate of title to a government agency if a vehicle or part of a vehicle is:

(1) forfeited to the government agency;

(2) delivered by court order under the Code of Criminal Procedure to a government agency for official purposes; or

(3) sold as abandoned or unclaimed property under the Code of Criminal Procedure.

*(Added by L.1995, chap. 165(1), eff. 9/1/95.)*

## §501.035. Certificate of title for former military vehicle.

(a) Notwithstanding any other law, the department shall issue a certificate of title for a former military vehicle that is not registered under the laws of this state if all other requirements for issuance of a certificate of title are met.

(b) In this section, "former military vehicle" has the meaning assigned by Section 502.275(*o*).

*(Added by L.1997, chap. 165(30.40(a)), eff. 9/1/97.)*

## §§501.036 to 501.050. *(Reserved.)*

# SUBCHAPTER C. REFUSAL TO ISSUE AND REVOCATION OR SUSPENSION OF CERTIFICATE

## §501.051. Grounds for refusal to issue or for revocation or suspension of certificate.

The department shall refuse to issue a certificate of title or shall suspend or revoke a certificate of title if:

(1) the application for the certificate contains a false or fraudulent statement;

(2) the applicant failed to furnish required information requested by the department;

(3) the applicant is not entitled to a certificate of title;

(4) the department has reason to believe that the motor vehicle is stolen;

(5) the department has reason to believe that the issuance of a certificate of title would defraud the owner or a lienholder of the motor vehicle;

(6) the registration for the motor vehicle is suspended or revoked; or

(7) the required fee has not been paid.

*(Added by L.1995, chap. 165(1), eff. 9/1/95.)*

### §501.052. Hearing on refusal to issue or revocation or suspension of certificate of title; appeal.

(a) An interested person aggrieved by a refusal, suspension, or revocation under Section 501.051 may apply for a hearing to the county assessor-collector for the county in which the person is domiciled. On the day an assessor-collector receives the application, the assessor-collector shall notify the department of the date of the hearing.

(b) The assessor-collector shall hold the hearing not earlier than the 11th day and not later than the 15th day after the date the assessor-collector receives the application for a hearing.

(c) At the hearing, the applicant and the department may submit evidence.

(d) A determination of the assessor-collector is binding on the applicant and the department as to whether the department correctly refused to issue or correctly revoked or suspended the certificate of title.

(e) An applicant aggrieved by the determination under Subsection (d) may appeal to the county court of the county of the applicant's residence. An applicant must file an appeal not later than the fifth day after the date of the assessor-collector's determination. The county court judge shall try the appeal in the manner of other civil cases. All rights and immunities granted in the trial of a civil case are available to the interested parties. If the department's action is not sustained, the department shall promptly issue a certificate of title for the vehicle.

*(Added by L.1995, chap. 165(1), eff. 9/1/95.)*

### §501.053. Filing of bond as alternative to hearing.

(a) As an alternative to the procedure provided by Section 501.052, the person may file a bond with the department. On the filing of the bond the department may issue the certificate of title.

(b) The bond must be:

(1) in the form prescribed by the department;

(2) executed by the applicant;

(3) issued by a person authorized to conduct a surety business in this state;

(4) in an amount equal to one and one-half times the value of the vehicle as determined by the department; and

(5) conditioned to indemnify all prior owners and lienholders and all subsequent purchasers of the vehicle or persons who acquire a security interest in the vehicle, and their successors in interest, against any expense, loss, or damage, including reasonable attorney's fees, occurring because of the issuance of the certificate of title for the vehicle or for a defect in or undisclosed security interest on the right, title, or interest of the applicant to the vehicle.

(c) An interested person has a right of action to recover on the bond for a breach of the bond's condition. The aggregate liability of the surety to all persons may not exceed the amount of the bond.

(d) A bond under this section expires on the third anniversary of the date the bond became effective. The department shall return an expired bond to the person who filed the bond unless the department has been notified of a pending action to recover on the bond.

*(Added by L.1995, chap. 165(1), eff. 9/1/95.)*

### §§501.054 to 501.070. *(Reserved.)*

## SUBCHAPTER D. SALES OF MOTOR VEHICLES AND TRANSFERS OF TITLE

### §501.071. Sale of vehicle; transfer of title.

(a) A motor vehicle may not be the subject of a subsequent sale unless the owner designated in the certificate of title transfers the certificate of title at the time of the sale.

(b) The transfer of the certificate of title must be on a form prescribed by the department that includes a statement that:

(1) the signer is the owner of the vehicle; and

(2) there are no liens on the vehicle except as shown on the certificate of title or as fully described in the statement.

*(Added by L.1995, chap. 165(1), eff. 9/1/95.)*

### §501.072. Odometer disclosure statement.

(a) Except as provided by Subsection (c), the seller of a motor vehicle sold in this state shall provide to the buyer, on a form prescribed by the department, a written disclosure of the vehicle's odometer reading at the time of the sale. The form must include space for the signature and printed name of both the seller and buyer.

(b) When application for a certificate of title is made, the owner shall record the current odometer reading on the application. The written disclosure required by Subsection (a) must accompany the application.

(c) An odometer disclosure statement is not required for the sale of a motor vehicle that:

(1) has a manufacturer's rated carrying capacity of more than two tons;

(2) is not self-propelled;

(3) is 10 or more years old;

(4) is sold directly by the manufacturer to an agency of the United States government in conformity with contractual specifications; or

(5) is a new motor vehicle.

*(Added by L.1995, chap. 165(1), eff. 9/1/95.)*

### §501.073. Sales in violation of chapter.

A sale made in violation of this chapter is void and title may not pass until the requirements of this chapter are satisfied. *(Added by L.1995, chap. 165(1), eff. 9/1/95.)*

### §501.074. Transfer of vehicle by operation of law.

(a) The department shall issue a new certificate of title for a motor vehicle registered in this state for which the ownership is transferred by operation of law, including by inheritance, devise or bequest, bankruptcy, receivership, judicial sale, or other involuntary divestiture of ownership after receiving:

(1) a certified copy of the order appointing a temporary administrator or of the probate proceedings;

(2) letters testamentary or letters of administration;

(3) if administration of an estate is not necessary, an affidavit showing that administration is not necessary, identifying all heirs, and including a statement by the heirs of the name in which the certificate shall be issued;

(4) a court order; or

(5) the bill of sale from an officer making a judicial sale.

(b) If a lien is foreclosed by nonjudicial means, the department may issue a new certificate of title in the name of the purchaser at the foreclosure sale on receiving the affidavit of the lienholder of the fact of the nonjudicial foreclosure.

(c) If a constitutional or statutory lien is foreclosed, the department may issue a new certificate of title in the name of the purchaser at the foreclosure sale on receiving:

(1) the affidavit of the lienholder of the fact of the creation of the lien and of the divestiture of title according to law; and

(2) proof of notice as required by Sections 70.004 and 70.006, Property Code.

(d) *(Repealed by L.1997, chap. 165(30.41), eff. 9/1/97.)*

*(Added by L.1995, chap. 165(1), eff. 9/1/95.)*

### §501.075. Validity of documents not notarized.

A document necessary to transfer ownership of a motor vehicle is valid without regard to whether the document is executed before a notary public. *(Added by L.1995, chap. 165(1), eff. 9/1/95.)*

### §§501.076 to 501.090. *(Reserved.)*

## SUBCHAPTER E. NONREPAIRABLE AND SALVAGE MOTOR VEHICLES

*(Repealed and added by L.1997, chap. 165(30.43(a)), eff. 9/1/97.)*

### §§501.091 to 501.094. *(Repealed by L.1997, chap. 165(30.43(a)), eff. 9/1/97.)*

### §501.0911. Definitions.

(a) In this subchapter:

(1) "Actual cash value" means the market value of a motor vehicle as determined:

(A) from publications commonly used by the automotive and insurance industries to establish the values of motor vehicles; or

(B) if the entity determining the value is an insurance company, by any other procedure recognized by the insurance industry, including market surveys, that is applied by the company in a uniform manner.

(2) "Automobile recycler" means a person in the business of dealing in salvage motor vehicles for the purpose of dismantling the vehicles to sell used parts or a person otherwise engaged in the business of acquiring, selling, or dealing in salvage parts for reuse or resale as parts. The term includes a dealer in used motor vehicle parts.

(3) "Casual sale" means the sale at auction of not more than one nonrepairable motor vehicle or late model salvage motor vehicle to the same person during a calendar year.

(4) "Insurance company" means a person authorized to write automobile insurance in this state or an out-of-state insurance company that pays a loss claim for a motor vehicle in this state.

(5) "Late model motor vehicle" means a motor vehicle with the same model year as the current calendar year or one of the five calendar years preceding that calendar year.

(6) "Late model salvage motor vehicle" or "salvage motor vehicle" means a late model motor vehicle, other than a late model vehicle that is a nonrepairable motor vehicle, that is damaged to the extent that the total estimated cost of repairs, other than repairs related to hail damage but including parts and labor, is equal to or greater than an amount equal to 75 percent of the actual cash value of the vehicle in its predamaged condition.

(7) "Major component part" means one of the following parts of a motor vehicle:

(A) the engine;

(B) the transmission;

(C) the frame;

(D) the right or left front fender;

(E) the hood;

(F) a door allowing entrance to or egress from the passenger compartment of the vehicle;

(G) the front or rear bumper;

(H) the right or left quarter panel;

(I) the deck lid, tailgate, or hatchback;

(J) the cargo box of a pickup truck;

(K) the cab of a truck; or

(L) the body of a passenger vehicle.

(8) "Nonrepairable motor vehicle" means a late model motor vehicle that is damaged or missing a major component part to the extent that the total estimated cost of repairs to rebuild or reconstruct the vehicle, including parts and labor other than the costs of materials and labor for repainting the vehicle and excluding sales taxes on the total cost of the repairs, and excluding the cost of repairs to repair hail damage, is equal to or greater than an amount equal to 95 percent of the actual cash value of the vehicle in its predamaged condition.

(9) "Nonrepairable motor vehicle certificate of title" means a document issued by the department that evidences ownership of a nonrepairable motor vehicle.

(10) "Older model motor vehicle" means a motor vehicle that was manufactured in a model year before the sixth preceding model year, including the current model year.

(11) "Other negotiable evidence of ownership" means a document other than a Texas certificate of title or a salvage certificate of title that relates to a motor vehicle that the department considers sufficient to support issuance of a Texas certificate of title for the vehicle.

(12) "Out-of-state buyer" means a person licensed in an automotive business by another state or jurisdiction if the department has listed the holders of such a license as permitted purchasers of salvage motor vehicles or nonrepairable motor vehicles based on substantially similar licensing requirements and on whether salvage vehicle dealers licensed in Texas are permitted to purchase salvage motor vehicles or nonrepairable motor vehicles in the other state or jurisdiction.

(13) "Rebuilder" means a person who acquires and repairs, for operation on public highways, five or more late model salvage motor vehicles in any 12-month period.

(14) "Salvage motor vehicle certificate of title" means any document issued by the department that evidences ownership of a salvage motor vehicle.

(15) "Salvage vehicle dealer" has the meaning assigned by Section 1.01, Article 6687-1a, Revised Statutes.

(b) For purposes of this subchapter:

(1) the estimated cost of repair parts shall be determined by using a manual of repair costs or other instrument that is generally recognized and commonly used in the motor vehicle insurance industry to determine those costs or an estimate of the actual cost of the repair parts; and

(2) the estimated labor costs shall be computed by using the hourly rate and time allocations that are reasonable and commonly assessed in the repair industry in the community in which the repairs are performed.
*(Added by L.1997, chap. 165(30.43(a)), eff. 9/1/97.)*

### §501.0912. Insurance company to surrender certificates of title to certain late model salvage motor vehicles.

(a) An insurance company that is licensed to conduct business in this state and that acquires ownership of a late model salvage motor vehicle through payment of a claim shall surrender a properly assigned certificate of title to the department, on a form prescribed by the department.

(b) For a vehicle described by Section 501.0911(6) but not by Section 501.0911(8), the insurance company shall apply for a salvage motor vehicle certificate of title. For a vehicle described by Section 501.0911(8), the insurance company shall apply for a nonrepairable motor vehicle certificate of title.

(c) An insurance company may not sell a late model salvage motor vehicle to which this section applies unless the department has issued a salvage motor vehicle certificate of title or a nonrepairable motor vehicle certificate of title for the vehicle or a comparable ownership document has been issued by another state or jurisdiction for the vehicle.

(d) An insurance company may sell a late model salvage motor vehicle to which this section applies, or assign a salvage motor vehicle certificate of title or a nonrepairable motor vehicle certificate of title for the vehicle, only to a salvage vehicle dealer, an out-of-state buyer, a buyer in a casual sale at auction, or a person described by Subsection (g), Article 6687-2b, Revised Statutes. If the vehicle is not a late model salvage motor vehicle or a nonrepairable motor vehicle, the insurance company is not required to surrender the regular certificate of title for the vehicle or to be issued a salvage motor vehicle certificate of title or a nonrepairable motor vehicle certificate of title for the vehicle.
*(Added by L.1997, chap. 165(30.43(a)), eff. 9/1/97.)*

### §501.0913. Insurance company to deliver certificates of title to certain motor vehicles.

(a) If an insurance company acquires ownership of a motor vehicle other than a late model salvage motor vehicle or a nonrepairable motor vehicle through payment of a claim, the company shall, on delivery of the vehicle to a buyer of the vehicle, deliver the buyer a properly assigned certificate of title for the vehicle.

(b) An insurance company or other person who acquires ownership of a motor vehicle other than a late model salvage motor vehicle or a nonrepairable motor vehicle may voluntarily and on proper application obtain a salvage motor vehicle certificate of title or a nonrepairable motor vehicle certificate of title for the vehicle.
*(Added by L.1997, chap. 165(30.43(a)), eff. 9/1/97.)*

### §501.0914. Nonapplicability.

Sections 501.0912 and 501.0913 do not apply to a vehicle that has been stolen and recovered unless the damage to the vehicle causes the vehicle to be a salvage motor vehicle or a nonrepairable motor vehicle. *(Added by L.1997, chap. 165(30.43(a)), eff. 9/1/97.)*

### §501.0915. Insurance company to submit report to department.

(a) If after payment of a total loss claim on a late model salvage motor vehicle or a nonrepairable motor vehicle an insurance company does not acquire ownership of the vehicle, the insurance company shall submit to the department, before the 31st day after the date of the payment of the claim, on the form prescribed by the department, a report stating that:

(1) the insurance company has paid a total loss claim on the vehicle; and

(2) the insurance company has not acquired ownership of the vehicle.

(b) The owner of a late model salvage motor vehicle to which this section applies may not transfer ownership of the vehicle by sale or otherwise unless the department has issued a salvage motor vehicle certificate of title or a nonrepairable motor vehicle certificate of title for the vehicle or a comparable ownership document has been issued by another state or jurisdiction for the vehicle.
*(Added by L.1997, chap. 165(30.43(a)), eff. 9/1/97.)*

### §501.0916. Sale, transfer, or release of late model salvage motor vehicle.

(a) A person who owns a late model salvage motor vehicle may not sell, transfer, or release the vehicle to a person other than a salvage vehicle dealer, the former owner of the vehicle, a governmental entity, an out-of-state buyer, a buyer in a casual sale at auction, or a person described by Subsection (g), Article 6687-2b, Revised Statutes, and shall deliver to that person a properly assigned certificate of title for the vehicle.

(b) If the assigned certificate of title is not a salvage motor vehicle certificate of title, a nonrepairable motor vehicle certificate of title, or a comparable ownership document issued by another state or jurisdiction, the purchaser shall, not later than the 10th day after the date the purchaser receives the certificate of title from the owner:

(1) surrender the certificate of title to the department; and

(2) apply for a salvage motor vehicle certificate of title or a nonrepairable motor vehicle certificate of title for the vehicle, as appropriate.

(c) A salvage vehicle dealer that acquires ownership of a late model salvage motor vehicle or a nonrepairable motor vehicle for the purpose of dismantling, scrapping, or destroying the vehicle shall, before the 31st day after the date the dealer acquires the vehicle, submit to the department, on the form prescribed by the department, a report stating that the vehicle will be dismantled, scrapped, or destroyed, accompanied by a properly assigned regular certificate of title, salvage motor vehicle certificate of title, nonrepairable motor vehicle certificate of title, or comparable ownership document issued by another state or jurisdiction for the vehicle.

(d) On receipt of the report and the certificate of title, the department shall issue the salvage vehicle dealer a receipt for the certificate of title, salvage motor vehicle certificate of title, nonrepairable motor vehicle certificate of title, or comparable ownership document issued by another state or jurisdiction.

*(Added by L.1997, chap. 165(30.43(a)), eff. 9/1/97.)*

### §501.0917. Salvage vehicle dealer to submit report to department.

A salvage vehicle dealer that acquires an older model vehicle for the purpose of dismantling, scrapping, or destroying the vehicle and that receives a properly assigned certificate of title for the vehicle shall, before the 31st day after the date the dealer acquires the vehicle:

(1) submit to the department, on the form prescribed by the department, a report stating that the vehicle will be dismantled, scrapped, or destroyed, accompanied by the properly assigned regular certificate of title, salvage motor vehicle certificate of title, nonrepairable motor vehicle certificate of title, or comparable ownership document issued by another state or jurisdiction for the vehicle; and

(2) keep on the business premises of the dealer, until the third anniversary of the date the report on the vehicle is submitted to the department, a record of the vehicle.

*(Added by L.1997, chap. 165(30.43(a)), eff. 9/1/97.)*

### §501.0918. Person acquiring late model salvage motor vehicle to surrender certificate of title.

A person, other than a salvage vehicle dealer or an insurance company licensed to do business in this state, who acquires ownership of a late model salvage motor vehicle or a nonrepairable motor vehicle that has not been issued a salvage motor vehicle certificate of title, a nonrepairable motor vehicle certificate of title, or a comparable ownership document issued by another state or jurisdiction shall, before selling the vehicle, surrender the properly assigned certificate of title for the vehicle to the department and:

(1) if the vehicle is a vehicle described by Section 501.0911(6) but not by Section 501.0911(8), apply to the department for a salvage motor vehicle certificate of title for the vehicle; or

(2) if the vehicle is a vehicle described by Section 501.0911(8), apply to the department for a nonrepairable motor vehicle certificate of title for the vehicle.

*(Added by L.1997, chap. 165(30.43(a)), eff. 9/1/97.)*

### §501.0919. Sale of certain late model salvage motor vehicles.

The owner of a late model salvage motor vehicle that has been issued a salvage motor vehicle certificate of title or a nonrepairable motor vehicle certificate of title may sell the vehicle only to a salvage vehicle dealer in this state, an out-of-state buyer, a buyer in a casual sale at auction, or a person described by Subsection (g), Article 6687-2b, Revised Statutes. *(Added by L.1997, chap. 165(30.43(a)), eff. 9/1/97.)*

### §501.0920. Application for salvage motor vehicle certificate of title.

(a) An application for a salvage motor vehicle certificate of title or a nonrepairable motor vehicle certificate of title must:

(1) be made on a form prescribed by the department and accompanied by a fee established by the department, not to exceed an amount that is sufficient, when added to other fees collected under this chapter, to recover the actual costs to the department of issuing the certificate; and

(2) include, in addition to any other information required by the department:

(A) the name and current address of the owner;

(B) a description of the vehicle, including the make, style of body, model year, and vehicle identification number;

(C) a description of the damage to the vehicle;

(D) the estimated cost of repairs to the vehicle, including parts and labor; and

(E) the predamaged actual cash value of the vehicle.

(b) On receipt of a complete application and the prescribed application fee, the department shall, before the sixth business day after the date the department receives the application, issue the applicant a salvage motor vehicle certificate of title or a nonrepairable motor vehicle certificate of title, as appropriate.

(c) A nonrepairable motor vehicle certificate of title must state on its face that, except as provided by Sections 501.0925 and 501.0927, the vehicle:

(1) may not be issued a regular certificate of title or registered in this state; and

(2) may only be used for parts or scrap metal.

*(Added by L.1997, chap. 165(30.43(a)), eff. 9/1/97.)*

## §501.0921. Possession and operation of salvage motor vehicle.

(a) A person who holds a salvage motor vehicle certificate of title is entitled to possess the vehicle, record a lien on the vehicle, transport the vehicle, and transfer ownership of the vehicle.

(b) A vehicle for which a salvage motor vehicle certificate of title is the most current title may not be operated on a public highway.

*(Added by L.1997, chap. 165(30.43(a)), eff. 9/1/97.)*

## §501.0922. Application for regular certificate of title for salvage motor vehicle.

(a) A vehicle for which a salvage motor vehicle certificate of title has been issued may be issued a regular certificate of title only after application and, in addition to any other requirement of law, only if the application:

(1) describes each major component part used to repair the vehicle and shows the identification number required by federal law to be affixed to or inscribed on the part; and

(2) is accompanied by a written statement signed by a specially trained commissioned officer of the Department of Public Safety certifying to the department that:

(A) the vehicle identification numbers and parts identification numbers are accurate;

(B) the applicant has proof that the applicant owns the parts used to repair the vehicle; and

(C) the vehicle may be safely operated and complies with all applicable motor vehicle safety standards of this state.

(b) The Department of Public Safety may impose a fee, in an amount not to exceed the lesser of $200 or the actual cost to that department, for conducting an inspection and providing the written statement required by Subsection (a).

*(Added by L.1997, chap. 165(30.43(a)), eff. 9/1/97.)*

## §501.0923. Issuance of certificate of title for rebuilt salvage motor vehicle.

(a) On receipt of a complete application under Section 501.0922, accompanied by the peace officer's statement and the appropriate fee for the certificate of title, the department shall issue the applicant a certificate of title for the vehicle.

(b) A certificate of title issued under this section must:

(1) bear on its face the words "REBUILT SALVAGE"; and

(2) describe or disclose the vehicle's former condition in a manner understandable to a potential purchaser of the vehicle.

*(Added by L.1997, chap. 165(30.43(a)), eff. 9/1/97.)*

## §501.0924. Issuance of certificate of title to certain vehicles brought into state.

(a) On proper application by the owner of a vehicle brought into this state from another state or jurisdiction that has on any certificate of title issued by the other state or jurisdiction a "rebuilt," "salvage," "nonrepairable," or analogous notation, the department shall issue the applicant a certificate of title or other appropriate document for the vehicle.

(b) A certificate of title or other appropriate document issued under this section must show on its face:

(1) the date of issuance;

(2) the name and address of the owner;
(3) any registration number assigned to the vehicle;
(4) a description of the vehicle as determined by the department; and
(5) any notation the department considers necessary or appropriate.
*(Added by L.1997, chap. 165(30.43(a)), eff. 9/1/97.)*

### §501.0925. Rights of holder of nonrepairable motor vehicle certificate of title.

A person who holds a nonrepairable motor vehicle certificate of title for a vehicle:
(1) is entitled to possess the vehicle, dismantle, scrap, or destroy the vehicle, transport the vehicle or parts of the vehicle, or rebuild the vehicle;
(2) may not operate or permit the operation of the vehicle on a public highway; and
(3) may transfer ownership of the vehicle only as permitted by law.
*(Added by L.1997, chap. 165(30.43(a)), eff. 9/1/97.)*

### §501.0926. Offense.

Except as provided by Section 501.0927, a person commits an offense if the person:
(1) applies to the department for a certificate of title for a motor vehicle; and
(2) knows that the vehicle is a nonrepairable motor vehicle that has been rebuilt.
*(Added by L.1997, chap. 165(30.43(a)), eff. 9/1/97.)*

### §501.0927. Application for certificate of title by rebuilder of nonrepairable motor vehicle.

(a) A person who rebuilds a nonrepairable vehicle may apply to the department for a certificate of title for the vehicle if, in addition to any other requirement of law, the application:
(1) contains the information required by Section 501.0922(a)(1); and
(2) is accompanied by a written statement that complies with Section 501.0922(a)(2).

(b) The Department of Public Safety may impose a fee, in an amount not to exceed the lesser of $200 or the actual cost to that department, for conducting an inspection and providing the written statement required by Subsection (a).

(c) On receipt of a complete application under this section, accompanied by the appropriate fee for the certificate of title, the department shall issue the applicant a certificate of title for the vehicle that conforms to Section 501.0923(b).
*(Added by L.1997, chap. 165(30.43(a)), eff. 9/1/97.)*

### §501.0928. Department to print salvage and nonrepairable motor vehicle certificates of title.

(a) The department shall print salvage motor vehicle certificates of title and nonrepairable motor vehicle certificates of title in a color that distinguishes them from certificates of title and so that each document clearly shows that it is the ownership document for a late model salvage motor vehicle or a nonrepairable motor vehicle.

(b) A nonrepairable motor vehicle certificate of title for a vehicle that is nonrepairable because of damage caused exclusively by flood must bear an appropriate notation on its face.

(c) A salvage motor vehicle certificate of title for a vehicle that is a salvage motor vehicle because of damage caused exclusively by flood must bear an appropriate notation on its face.
*(Added by L.1997, chap. 165(30.43(a)), eff. 9/1/97.)*

### §501.0929. Rebuilder to possess certificate of title.

(a) A rebuilder must possess a certificate of title, a salvage motor vehicle certificate of title, a nonrepairable motor vehicle certificate of title, or a comparable ownership document issued by another state or jurisdiction for any motor vehicle that is:
(1) in the rebuilder's inventory; and
(2) being offered for resale.

(b) A person who rebuilds a late model salvage motor vehicle for which the department has issued a salvage motor vehicle certificate of title, or who assembles a late model salvage motor vehicle from component parts, may apply to the department for a certificate of title for the vehicle. A certificate of title issued by the department under this subsection must bear the words "REBUILT SALVAGE."
*(Added by L.1997, chap. 165(30.43(a)), eff. 9/1/97.)*

### §501.0930. Enforcement of subchapter.

(a) This subchapter shall be exclusively enforced by the department or any other governmental or law enforcement agency or its personnel, except as provided by this subchapter.

(b) The department, or an agent, officer, or employee of the department, is not liable to a person damaged or injured by an act or omission relating to the issuance of a certificate of title, salvage motor vehicle certificate of title, or nonrepairable motor vehicle certificate of title under this subchapter.
*(Added by L.1997, chap. 165(30.43(a)), eff. 9/1/97.)*

### §501.0931. Applicability of subchapter.

(a) This subchapter does not apply to, and does not preclude or prohibit a sale to, purchase by, or other transaction by or with, a person described by Subsection (g), Article 6687-2b, Revised Statutes, except as provided by Subsections (b) and (c).

(b) A person described by Subsection (g), Article 6687-2b, Revised Statutes, shall submit to the department the certificate of title or equivalent document that the person receives in conjunction with the purchase of a motor vehicle not later than the 60th day after the date the person receives the certificate of title or equivalent document.

(c) This subchapter applies to a transaction with a person described by Subsection (g), Article 6687-2b, Revised Statutes, in which a motor vehicle is sold or delivered to the person for the purpose of reuse or resale as a motor vehicle or as motor vehicle parts if the motor vehicle is so used.

(d) This subchapter does not:

(1) prohibit the owner of a late model salvage motor vehicle or a nonrepairable motor vehicle from selling the vehicle to any person, if the vehicle is so classified solely because of water damage caused by a flood; or

(2) limit the ability or authority of an insurance company to adjust or settle a claim for loss on a motor vehicle.
*(Added by L.1997, chap. 165(30.43(a)), eff. 9/1/97.)*

## SUBCHAPTER F. SECURITY INTERESTS

### §501.111. Perfection of security interest.

(a) Except as provided by Subsection (b), a person may perfect a security interest in a motor vehicle that is the subject of a first or subsequent sale only by recording the security interest on the certificate of title as provided by this chapter.

(b) A person may perfect a security interest in a motor vehicle held as inventory by a person in the business of selling motor vehicles only by complying with Chapter 9, Business & Commerce Code.
*(Added by L.1995, chap. 165(1), eff. 9/1/95.)*

### §501.112. Sale or security interest not created by certain vehicle leases.

Notwithstanding any other law, an agreement for the lease of a motor vehicle does not create a sale or security interest by merely providing that the rental price is permitted or required to be adjusted under the agreement as determined by the amount realized on the sale or other disposition of the vehicle. *(Added by L.1995, chap. 165(1), eff. 9/1/95.)*

### §501.113. Recordation of security interest.

(a) Recordation of a lien under this chapter is considered to occur when the county assessor-collector:

(1) is presented with an application for a certificate of title that discloses the lien with tender of the filing fee; or

(2) accepts the application.

(b) For purposes of Chapter 9, Business & Commerce Code, the time of recording a lien under this chapter is considered to be the time of filing the security interest.
*(Added by L.1995, chap. 165(1), eff. 9/1/95.)*

### §501.114. Assignment of lien.

(a) A lienholder may assign a lien recorded under Section 501.113 by:

(1) applying to the county assessor-collector for the assignment of the lien; and

(2) notifying the debtor of the assignment.

(b) A lienholder's failure to notify a debtor of an assignment does not create a cause of action against the lienholder.

(c) An application under Subsection (a) must be:

(1) signed by the person to whom the lien is assigned; and

(2) accompanied by:

(A) the applicable fee;

(B) a copy of the assignment agreement executed by the parties; and

(C) the certificate of title on which the lien to be assigned is recorded.

(d) On receipt of the completed application and fee, the department:

(1) may amend the department's records to substitute the subsequent lienholder for the previous lienholder; and

(2) shall issue a new certificate of title as provided by Section 501.027.

(e) The issuance of a certificate of title under Subsection (d) is recordation of the assignment. The time of the recordation of a lien assigned under this section is considered to be the time the lien was recorded under Section 501.113.

*(Added by L.1995, chap. 165(1), eff. 9/1/95.)*

### §501.115. Discharge of lien.

(a) When a debt or claim secured by a lien has been satisfied, the lienholder shall, within a reasonable time not to exceed the maximum time allowed by Section 348.408, Finance Code, execute and deliver to the owner, or the owner's designee, a discharge of the lien on a form prescribed by the department.

(b) The owner may present the discharge and certificate of title to the county assessor-collector with an application for a new certificate of title and the department shall issue a new certificate of title.

*(Added by L.1995, chap. 165(1); chgd. by L.1997, chap. 296(1); L.1999, chap. 268(1), eff. 5/28/99.)*

### §501.116. Cancellation of discharged lien.

The department may cancel a discharged lien that has been recorded on a certificate of title for six years or more if the recorded lienholder:

(1) does not exist; or

(2) cannot be located for the owner to obtain a release of the lien.

*(Added by L.1995, chap. 165(1), eff. 9/1/95.)*

### §§501.117 to 501.130. *(Reserved.)*

## SUBCHAPTER G. ADMINISTRATIVE PROVISIONS

### §501.131. Rules; forms.

(a) The department may adopt rules to administer this chapter.

(b) The department shall:

(1) in addition to the forms required by this chapter, prescribe forms for a title receipt, manufacturer's certificate, and importer's certificate, and other forms the department determines necessary; and

(2) provide each county assessor-collector with a sufficient supply of the forms.

*(Added by L.1995, chap. 165(1), eff. 9/1/95.)*

### §501.132. Duplicate title receipt or certificate.

Except as otherwise provided by department rule, the department may not issue a duplicate title receipt or duplicate certificate of title unless the original title receipt or certificate of title is surrendered. *(Added by L.1995, chap. 165(1), eff. 9/1/95.)*

### §501.133. Issuance of new certificate of title because of subsequent sales.

(a) If all of the forms of transfer on a certificate of title have been used because of subsequent sales, the certificate may be delivered to a county assessor-collector, who shall:

(1) provide a title receipt in the manner required for a first sale; and

(2) send the certificate of title to the department on the same day the certificate is received.

(b) On receipt of the certificate of title, the department shall issue a new certificate of title.

*(Added by L.1995, chap. 165(1), eff. 9/1/95.)*

### §501.134. Lost or destroyed certificate of title.

(a) If an original or duplicate original certificate of title is lost or destroyed, the owner or lienholder disclosed on the certificate may obtain, in the manner provided by this section and department rule, a certified copy of the lost or destroyed certificate of title directly from the department by applying on a form prescribed by the department and paying a fee of $2. A fee collected under this subsection shall be deposited to the credit of the state highway fund and may be spent only as provided by Section 501.138.

(b) If a lien is disclosed on a certificate of title, the department may issue a certified copy of the original certificate of title only to the first lienholder.

(c) The department must plainly mark "certified copy" on the face of a certified copy issued under this section, and each subsequent certificate issued for the motor vehicle until the vehicle is transferred. A subsequent purchaser or lienholder of the vehicle only acquires the rights, title, or interest in the vehicle held by the holder of the certified copy.

(d) A purchaser or lienholder of a motor vehicle having a certified copy issued under this section may at the time of the purchase or establishment of the lien require that the seller or owner indemnify the purchaser or lienholder and all subsequent purchasers of the vehicle against any loss the person may suffer because of a claim presented on the original certificate of title.

(e) If the original or duplicate original certificate of title is recovered, the owner of the vehicle shall promptly surrender the original or duplicate original certificate of title to the department for cancellation, and the department shall eliminate the words "certified copy" from any certificate of title issued for that vehicle after that date.

(f) Except as provided by Subsection (g), the department may not issue a certified copy of a certificate of title before the fourth business day after the date application is made.

(g) The department may issue a certified copy of a certificate of title before the fourth business day after the date application is made only if the applicant:

(1) is the registered owner of the vehicle, the holder of a recorded lien against the vehicle, or a verified agent of the owner or lienholder; and

(2) submits personal identification, including a photograph, issued by an agency of this state or the United States.

(h) If the applicant is the agent of the owner or lienholder of the vehicle and is applying on behalf of the owner or lienholder, the applicant must submit verifiable proof that the person is the agent of the owner or lienholder.

(i) If an applicant for a certified copy of a certificate of title is a person other than a person described by Subsection (g)(1), the department may issue a certified copy of the certificate of title only by mail.

*(Added by L.1995, chap. 165(1); chgd. by L.1997, chap. 165(30.42(a)), eff. 9/1/97.)*

## §501.135. Record of stolen or concealed motor vehicle.

(a) The department shall:

(1) make a record of each report to the department that a motor vehicle registered in this state has been stolen or concealed in violation of Section 32.33, Penal Code; and

(2) note the fact of the report in the department's records of the vehicle's certificate of title.

(b) A person who reports a motor vehicle as stolen or concealed under Subsection (a) shall notify the department promptly if the vehicle is recovered, and the department shall change its records accordingly.

*(Added by L.1995, chap. 165(1), eff. 9/1/95.)*

## §501.136. Acts by deputy county assessor-collector.

A deputy county assessor-collector, other than a limited service deputy appointed under Section 502.112, may perform the duties of an assessor-collector under this chapter. *(Added by L.1995, chap. 165(1), eff. 9/1/95.)*

## §501.137. Duty of county assessor-collector.

(a) Each county assessor-collector shall comply with this chapter.

(b) An assessor-collector who fails or refuses to comply with this chapter is liable on the assessor-collector's official bond for resulting damages suffered by any person.

*(Added by L.1995, chap. 165(1), eff. 9/1/95.)*

## §501.138. Collection and disposition of fees.

(a) An applicant for a certificate of title, other than the state or a political subdivision of the state, must pay the county assessor-collector a fee of $13.

(b) The county assessor-collector shall send:

(1) $5 of the fee to the county treasurer for deposit in the officers' salary fund; and

(2) $8 of the fee to the department:

(A) together with the application within the time prescribed by Section 501.023; or

(B) if the fee is deposited in an interest-bearing account or certificate in the county depository or invested in an investment authorized by Subchapter A, Chapter 2256, Government Code, not later than the 35th day after the date on which the fee is received.

(c) Of the amount received under Subsection (b)(2), the department shall deposit:

(1) $5 in the general revenue fund; and

(2) $3 to the credit of the state highway fund to recover the expenses necessary to administer this chapter.

(d) The county owns all interest earned on fees deposited or invested under Subsection (b)(2)(B). The county treasurer shall credit that interest to the county general fund.
*(Added by L.1995, chap. 165(1), eff. 9/1/95.)*

**§§501.139 to 501.150.** *(Reserved.)*

## SUBCHAPTER H. PENALTIES AND OTHER ENFORCEMENT PROVISIONS

### §501.151. Placement of serial number with intent to change identity.

(a) A person commits an offense if the person stamps or places a serial number on a vehicle or part of a vehicle with the intent of changing the identity of the vehicle.

(b) It is an affirmative defense to prosecution of an offense under this section that the person acted with respect to a number assigned by:

(1) a vehicle manufacturer and the person was an employee of the manufacturer acting within the course and scope of employment; or

(2) the department, and the person was:

(A) discharging official duties as an agent of the department; or

(B) complying with department rule as an applicant for a serial number assigned by the department.

(c) An offense under this section is a felony of the third degree.
*(Added by L.1995, chap. 165(1), eff. 9/1/95.)*

### §501.152. Sale or offer without title receipt or title.

(a) Except as provided by this section, a person commits an offense if the person:

(1) sells, offers to sell, or offers as security for an obligation a motor vehicle registered in this state; and

(2) does not possess the title receipt or certificate of title for the vehicle.

(b) It is not a violation of this section for the beneficial owner of a vehicle to sell or offer to sell a vehicle without having possession of the certificate of title to the vehicle if the sole reason he or she does not have possession of the certificate of title is that the title is in the possession of a lienholder who has not complied with the terms of Section 501.115(a) of this code.
*(Added by L.1995, chap. 165(1); chgd. by L.1997, chap. 296(2), eff. 5/26/97.)*

### §501.153. Application for title for stolen or concealed vehicle.

A person commits an offense if the person applies for a certificate of title for a motor vehicle that the person knows is stolen or concealed in violation of Section 32.33, Penal Code. *(Added by L.1995, chap. 165(1), eff. 9/1/95.)*

### §501.154. Alteration of certificate or receipt.

A person commits an offense if the person alters a manufacturer's or importer's certificate, a title receipt, or a certificate of title. *(Added by L.1995, chap. 165(1), eff. 9/1/95.)*

### §501.155. False name, false information, and forgery.

(a) A person commits an offense if the person knowingly provides false or incorrect information or without legal authority signs the name of another person on:

(1) an application for a certificate of title;

(2) an application for a certified copy of an original certificate of title;

(3) an assignment of title for a motor vehicle;

(4) a discharge of a lien on a title for a motor vehicle; or

(5) any other document required by the department or necessary to the transfer of ownership of a motor vehicle.

(b) An offense under this section is a felony of the third degree.
*(Added by L.1995, chap. 165(1), eff. 9/1/95.)*

### §501.156. Duty of transporters to determine right of possession; offense.

(a) The master or captain of a ship or airplane or a person who owns or controls the operation of a ship or airplane, in whole or part:

(1) may not take on board or allow to be taken on board the ship or airplane in this state for transport a motor vehicle without inquiring of the motor vehicle titles and registration division of the department as to the recorded ownership of the motor vehicle; and

(2) must make a reasonable inquiry as to the right of possession of a motor vehicle by the person delivering the vehicle for transport if the recorded owner of the vehicle is a person other than the person delivering the vehicle for transport.

(b) A person who violates this section commits an offense. An offense under this section is a misdemeanor punishable by a fine of not less than $50 or more than $500 for a first offense and, at the jury's discretion, not less than $100 or more than $1,000 for a subsequent offense.
*(Added by L.1995, chap. 165(1), eff. 9/1/95.)*

### §501.157. Penalties.

(a) Unless otherwise provided by this chapter, an offense under this chapter is a misdemeanor punishable by a fine of not less than $1 or more than $100 for the first offense. If a person is subsequently convicted of the same offense, at the jury's discretion, a person may be fined not less than $2 or more than $200.

(b) A person commits an offense if the person violates Subchapter E or a rule adopted under that subchapter. An offense under this subsection is a Class A misdemeanor.
*(Added by L.1995, chap. 165(1); chgd. by L.1997, chap. 165(30.43(b)), eff. 9/1/97.)*

### §501.158. Seizure of stolen vehicle or vehicle with altered serial number.

(a) A peace officer may seize a vehicle or part of a vehicle without a warrant if the officer has probable cause to believe that the vehicle or part:

(1) is stolen; or

(2) has had the serial number removed, altered, or obliterated.

(b) A vehicle or part seized under this section may be treated as stolen property for purposes of custody and disposition of the vehicle or part.
*(Added by L.1995, chap. 165(1), eff. 9/1/95.)*

### §501.159. Alias certificate of title.

On receipt of a written request approved by the executive administrator of a law enforcement agency, the department may issue a certificate of title for a vehicle in an alias for the law enforcement agency's use in a covert criminal investigation. *(Added by L.1995, chap. 165(1), eff. 9/1/95.)*

# CHAPTER 502. REGISTRATION OF VEHICLES

## SUBCHAPTER A. GENERAL PROVISIONS

Section



## SUBCHAPTER B. STATE ADMINISTRATION

## SUBCHAPTER C. COUNTY ADMINISTRATION



## SUBCHAPTER D. REGISTRATION PROCEDURES AND FEES

## SUBCHAPTER E. SPECIALLY DESIGNATED LICENSE PLATES; EXEMPTIONS FOR GOVERNMENTAL AND QUASI-GOVERNMENTAL VEHICLES



## SUBCHAPTER F. SPECIALIZED LICENSE PLATES; EXEMPTIONS FOR PRIVATELY OWNED VEHICLES

502.276. Certain farm vehicles and drilling and construction equipment.
502.2761. Texas agricultural products license plates.
502.277. Cotton vehicles.
502.278. Certain soil conservation equipment.
502.279. Certain log-loader vehicles.
502.280. Forestry vehicles.
502.281. Tow trucks.
502.282. Vehicles carrying mobile amateur radio equipment.
502.283. Parade vehicles owned by nonprofit service organizations.
502.284. Golf carts.
502.285. Manufactured housing.
502.286. Power sweepers.
502.287. Vehicles operated on public highway separating real property under vehicle owner's control.
502.288. Vehicles operated by certain nonresidents.
502.289. Peace officers wounded or killed in line of duty.
502.290. Foreign organization vehicles.
502.291. Animal friendly license plates.
502.292. Read to Succeed.
502.2921. Volunteer advocate program license plates.
502.293. Houston Livestock Show and Rodeo license plates.
502.2931. Girl Scout license plates.
502.294. Municipal and private buses.
502.295. State officials.
502.2951. County judges.
502.296. Members of congress.
502.297. State and federal judges.
502.298. Conservation license plates.
502.298. 100th football season of Stephen F. Austin High School.
502.299. Texas YMCA.
502.299. Texas Young Lawyers Association license plates.
502.299. Texas citrus industry.
502.300 to
502.302. *(Reserved.)*
502.303. Waterfowl and wetland conservation license plates.
502.304 to
502.350. *(Reserved.)*

## SUBCHAPTER G. TEMPORARY REGISTRATION

502.351. Farm vehicles: excess weight.
502.352. Foreign commercial vehicles.
502.353. Foreign commercial vehicles; annual permits; offense.
502.354. Single or 30-day trip permits; offense.
502.355. Nonresident-owned vehicles used to transport farm products; offense.
502.356 to
502.400. *(Reserved.)*

## SUBCHAPTER H. OFFENSES AND PENALTIES

502.401. General penalty.
502.402. Operation of unregistered motor vehicle.
502.403. Operation of vehicle under improper registration.
502.404. Operation of vehicle without license plate or registration insignia.
502.405. Operation of motorcycle without seal.
502.406. Operation of all-terrain vehicle without sticker.
502.407. Operation of vehicle with expired license plate.
502.408. Operation of vehicle with wrong license plate.
502.409. Wrong, fictitious, or unclean license plate.
502.410. Falsification or forgery.
502.411. Bribery of county officer or agent.
502.412. Operation of vehicle at weight greater than stated in registration application.

## SUBCHAPTER A. GENERAL PROVISIONS

### §502.001. Definitions.

In this chapter:

(1) "All-terrain vehicle" means a motor vehicle that is:

(A) equipped with a saddle for the use of the rider;

(B) designed to propel itself with three or four tires in contact with the ground;

(C) designed by the manufacturer for off-highway use by the operator only; and

(D) not designed by the manufacturer for farming or lawn care.

(2) "Commercial motor vehicle" means a motor vehicle, other than a motorcycle, designed or used primarily to transport property. The term includes a passenger car reconstructed and used primarily for delivery purposes. The term does not include a passenger car used to deliver the United States mail.

(3) "Department" means the Texas Department of Transportation.

(4) "Farm semitrailer" means a semitrailer designed and used primarily as a farm vehicle.

(5) "Farm tractor" means a motor vehicle designed and used primarily as a farm implement for drawing other implements of husbandry.

(6) "Farm trailer" means a trailer designed and used primarily as a farm vehicle.

(7) "Golf cart" means a motor vehicle designed by the manufacturer primarily for transporting persons on a golf course.

(8) "Implements of husbandry" means farm implements, machinery, and tools as used in tilling the soil, including self-propelled machinery specifically designed or adapted for applying plant food materials or agricultural chemicals but not specifically designed or adapted for the sole purpose of transporting the materials or chemicals. The term does not include a passenger car or truck.

(9) "Light truck" means a commercial motor vehicle that has a manufacturer's rated carrying capacity of one ton or less.

(10) "Moped" has the meaning assigned by Section 541.201.

(11) "Motor bus" includes every vehicle used to transport persons on the public highways for compensation, other than:

(A) a vehicle operated by muscular power; or

(B) a municipal bus.

(12) "Motorcycle" means a motor vehicle designed to propel itself with not more than three wheels in contact with the ground. The term does not include a tractor.

(13) "Motor vehicle" means a vehicle that is self-propelled.

(14) "Municipal bus" includes every vehicle, other than a passenger car, used to transport persons for compensation exclusively within the limits of a municipality or a suburban addition to the municipality.

(15) "Operate temporarily on the highways" means to travel between:

(A) different farms;

(B) a place of supply or storage and a farm; or

(C) an owner's farm and the place at which the owner's farm produce is prepared for market or is marketed.

(16) "Owner" means a person who:

(A) holds the legal title of a vehicle;

(B) has the legal right of possession of a vehicle; or

(C) has the legal right of control of a vehicle.

(17) "Passenger car" means a motor vehicle, other than a motorcycle, golf cart, light truck, or bus, designed or used primarily for the transportation of persons.

(18) "Public highway" includes a road, street, way, thoroughfare, or bridge:

(A) that is in this state;

(B) that is for the use of vehicles;

(C) that is not privately owned or controlled; and

(D) over which the state has legislative jurisdiction under its police power.

(19) "Public property" means property owned or leased by this state or a political subdivision of this state.

(20) "Road tractor" means a vehicle designed for the purpose of mowing the right-of-way of a public highway or a motor vehicle designed or used for drawing another vehicle or a load and not constructed to carry:

(A) an independent load; or

(B) a part of the weight of the vehicle and load to be drawn.

(21) "Semitrailer" means a vehicle designed or used with a motor vehicle so that part of the weight of the vehicle and its load rests on or is carried by another vehicle.

(22) "Trailer" means a vehicle that:

(A) is designed or used to carry a load wholly on its own structure; and

(B) is drawn or designed to be drawn by a motor vehicle.

(23) "Truck-tractor" means a motor vehicle:

(A) designed and used primarily for drawing another vehicle; and

(B) not constructed to carry a load other than a part of the weight of the vehicle and load to be drawn.

(24) "Vehicle" means a device in or by which a person or property is or may be transported or drawn on a public highway, other than a device used exclusively on stationary rails or tracks.
*(Added by L.1995, chap. 165(1); chgd. by L.1997, chap. 625(1), eff. 9/1/97.)*

## §502.002. Registration required; general rule.

(a) The owner of a motor vehicle, trailer, or semitrailer shall apply for the registration of the vehicle for:

(1) each registration year in which the vehicle is used or to be used on a public highway; and

(2) if the vehicle is unregistered for a registration year that has begun and that applies to the vehicle and if the vehicle is used or to be used on a public highway, the remaining portion of that registration year.

(b) The application must be made to the department through the county assessor-collector of the county in which the owner resides.

(c) A provision of this chapter that conflicts with this section prevails over this section to the extent of the conflict.

(d) A county assessor-collector, a deputy county assessor-collector, or a person acting on behalf of a county assessor-collector is not liable to any person for:

(2) registering a motor vehicle under this section.
*(Added by L.1995, chap. 165(1); chgd. by L.1997, chap. 165(30.44(a)), eff. 9/1/97.)*

## §502.0021. Rules and forms.

(a) The department may adopt rules to administer this chapter.

(b) The department shall:

(1) prescribe forms determined by the department to be necessary for the administration of this chapter; and

(2) provide each county assessor-collector with an adequate supply of each form necessary for the performance of a duty under this chapter by the assessor-collector.
*(Added by L.1997, chap. 625(2); renumbered from section 502.009 by L.1999, chap. 62(19.01(100)), eff. 9/1/99.)*

## §502.0025. Effect of certain military service on registration requirement.

(a) This section applies only to a motor vehicle that is owned by a person who:

(1) is a resident of this state;

(2) is on active duty in the armed forces of the United States;

(3) is stationed in or has been assigned to another nation under military orders; and

(4) has registered the vehicle or been issued a license for the vehicle under the applicable status of forces agreement by:

(A) the appropriate branch of the armed forces of the United States; or

(B) the nation in which the person is stationed or to which the person has been assigned.

(b) Unless the registration or license issued for a vehicle described by Subsection (a) is suspended, canceled, or revoked by this state as provided by law:

(1) Section 502.002(a) does not apply; and

(2) the registration or license issued by the armed forces or host nation remains valid and the motor vehicle may be operated in this state under that registration or license for a period of not more than 90 days after the date on which the vehicle returns to this state.
*(Added by L.1999, chap. 836(1), eff. 9/1/99.)*

## §502.003. Registration by political subdivision prohibited.

(a) Except as provided by Subsection (b), a political subdivision of this state may not require an owner of a motor vehicle to:

(1) register the vehicle;

(2) pay a motor vehicle registration fee; or

(3) pay an occupation tax or license fee in connection with a motor vehicle.

(b) This section does not affect the authority of a municipality to:

(1) license and regulate the use of motor vehicles for compensation within the municipal limits; and

(2) impose a permit fee or street rental charge for the operation of each motor vehicle used to transport passengers for compensation, other than a motor vehicle operating under a registration certificate from the department or a permit from the federal Surface Transportation Board.

(c) A fee or charge under Subsection (b) may not exceed two percent of the annual gross receipts from the vehicle.

(d) This section does not impair the payment provisions of an agreement or franchise between a municipality and the owners or operators of motor vehicles used to transport passengers for compensation.

*(Added by L.1995, chap. 165(1); chgd. by L.1997, chap. 165(30.45), eff. 9/1/97.)*

## §502.004. Collection of fees.

A person may not collect a registration fee under this chapter unless the person is:

(1) an officer or employee of the department; or

(2) a county assessor-collector or a deputy county assessor-collector.

*(Added by L.1995, chap. 165(1), eff. 9/1/95.)*

## §502.005. Refusal to register unsafe vehicle.

(a) The department may refuse to register a motor vehicle and may revoke a registration if the department determines that a motor vehicle is unsafe, improperly equipped, or otherwise unfit to be operated on a public highway.

(b) The department may refuse to register a motorcycle and may suspend or revoke the registration of a motorcycle if the department determines that the motorcycle's braking system does not comply with Section 547.408.

*(Added by L.1995, chap. 165(1), eff. 9/1/95.)*

## §502.006. All-terrain vehicles.

(a) Except as provided by Subsection (b), a person may not register an all-terrain vehicle, with or without design alterations, for operation on a public highway.

(b) The state, a county, or a municipality may register an all-terrain vehicle for operation on a public beach or highway to maintain public safety and welfare.

(c) The owner of an all-terrain vehicle that is not authorized to operate on a public beach or highway and that is used or to be used on public property shall apply each year to the department, through the assessor-collector of the county in which the person resides, for off-highway registration of the vehicle for the registration year in which the application is made or the succeeding registration year.

(d) For off-highway registration of an all-terrain vehicle, the department shall issue:

(1) a registration certificate; and

(2) a number decal or sticker of appropriate size and design as determined by the department, in lieu of a license plate.

(e) Section 502.172 does not apply to an all-terrain vehicle.

*(Added by L.1995, chap. 165(1); chgd. by L.1999, chap. 311(1), eff. 5/29/99.)*

## §502.007. Mopeds.

(a) For the registration purposes of this chapter, a moped is treated as if it were a motorcycle.

(b) A license plate issued for a moped must have a distinctive lettering designation and include the word "moped."

*(Added by L.1995, chap. 165(1), eff. 9/1/95.)*

## §502.008. Release of information in vehicle registration records.

(a) The department or a county may not release to any person information contained in vehicle registration records in response to a telephone inquiry by license number. The department or a county may release information only if the person:

(1) submits in writing a request that:

(A) provides the person's name and address; and

(B) states that the use of the information is for a lawful and legitimate purpose; or

(2) enters into a written service agreement with the department or county to receive the information.

(b) This section does not apply to the release of information to:

(1) a peace officer, as defined in Article 2.12, Code of Criminal Procedure, acting in an official capacity; or

(2) an official of this state or a political subdivision of this state if the official is requesting the information for:

(A) tax purposes; or

(B) the purpose of determining eligibility for a state public assistance program.

(c) The department shall provide a dedicated line to its vehicle registration record database for use by other state agencies. The access to or transmission of information under this subsection does not affect whether the information is subject to disclosure under Chapter 552, Government Code.

(d) This section does not authorize the release of information that is prohibited from disclosure under Chapter 730.

*(Added by L.1995, chap. 165(1); chgd. by L.1997, chaps. 165(30.46(a)), 1187(6), eff. 9/1/97.)*

**§502.009.** *(Renumbered to section 502.0021 by L.1999, chap. 62(19.01(100)), eff. 9/1/99.)*

**§§502.010 to 502.050.** *(Reserved.)*

## SUBCHAPTER B. STATE ADMINISTRATION

**§502.051. Deposit of registration fees in state highway fund.**

Except as otherwise provided by this chapter, the Texas Transportation Commission and the department shall deposit all money received from registration fees in the state treasury to the credit of the state highway fund. *(Added by L.1995, chap. 165(1), eff. 9/1/95.)*

**§502.052. Design of license plates and registration insignia; reflectorized material.**

(a) The department shall prepare the designs and specifications of license plates and devices selected by the Texas Transportation Commission to be used as the registration insignia.

(b) The department shall design each license plate to include a design at least one-half inch wide that represents in silhouette the shape of Texas and that appears between letters and numerals. The department may omit the silhouette of Texas from specially designed license plates.

(c) To promote highway safety, each license plate shall be made with a reflectorized material that provides effective and dependable brightness for the period for which the plate is issued. The purchase of reflectorized material shall be submitted to the General Services Commission for approval.

*(Added by L.1995, chap. 165(1), eff. 9/1/95.)*

**§502.053. Cost of manufacturing license plates or registration insignia.**

(a) The Texas Department of Transportation shall reimburse the institutional division of the Texas Department of Criminal Justice for the cost of manufacturing license plates or registration insignia as the license plates or insignia and the invoice for the license plates or insignia are delivered to the Texas Department of Transportation.

(b) When manufacturing is started, the General Services Commission shall set the price to be paid for each license plate or insignia. The price must be determined from:

(1) the cost of metal, paint, and other materials purchased;

(2) the inmate maintenance cost per day;

(3) overhead expenses;

(4) miscellaneous charges; and

(5) a previously approved amount of profit for the work.

(c) The annual profit received by the institutional division of the Texas Department of Criminal Justice from all contracts for the manufacturing of license plates or related manufacturing may not be less than the profit received by the Texas Department of Corrections for manufacturing license plates for use in 1974.

*(Added by L.1995, chap. 165(1), eff. 9/1/95.)*

**§502.054. Agreements with other jurisdictions; offense.**

(a) The department, through its director, may enter into an agreement with an authorized officer of another jurisdiction, including another state of the United States or a state, province, territory, or possession of a foreign country, to provide for:

(1) the registration of vehicles by residents of this state and nonresidents on an allocation or mileage apportionment plan, as under the International Registration Plan; and

(2) the exemption from payment of registration fees by nonresidents if residents of this state are granted reciprocal exemptions.

(b) The department may adopt and enforce rules to carry out the International Registration Plan or other agreement under this section.

(c) To carry out the International Registration Plan or other agreement under this section, the department shall direct that fees collected for other jurisdictions under the agreement be deposited to the credit of the proportional registration distributive fund in the state treasury and distributed to the appropriate jurisdiction through that fund.

(d) This section prevails to the extent of conflict with another law relating to the subject of this section.

(e) A person commits an offense if the person owns or operates a vehicle not registered in this state in violation of:

(1) an agreement under this section; or

(2) the applicable registration laws of this state, in the absence of an agreement under this section.

(f) An offense under Subsection (e) is a misdemeanor punishable by a fine not to exceed $200.

*(Added by L.1995, chap. 165(1), eff. 9/1/95.)*

## §502.055. Determination of weight.

(a) The weight, net weight, or gross weight of a vehicle, as determined by the department, is the correct weight for registration purposes, regardless of any other purported weight of the vehicle.

(b) The department may require an applicant for registration under this chapter to provide the department with evidence of:

(1) the manufacturer's rated carrying capacity for the vehicle;

(2) the nominal tonnage rating of the vehicle;

(3) the gross weight rating of the vehicle; or

(4) any combination of information described in Subdivisions (1)-(3).

*(Added by L.1995, chap. 165(1); chgd. by L.1997, chap. 625(3), eff. 9/1/97.)*

## §502.056. Disputed classification of vehicle.

In a disputed case, the department may determine:

(1) the classification to which a vehicle belongs; and

(2) the amount of the registration fee for the vehicle.

*(Added by L.1995, chap. 165(1), eff. 9/1/95.)*

## §§502.057 to 502.100. *(Reserved.)*

# SUBCHAPTER C. COUNTY ADMINISTRATION

## §502.101. Registration by mail or electronic means; service charge.

(a) A county assessor-collector may collect a service charge of $1 from each applicant registering a vehicle by mail. The service charge shall be used to pay the costs of handling and postage to mail the registration receipt and insignia to the applicant.

(b) With the approval of the commissioners court of a county, a county assessor-collector may contract with a private entity to enable an applicant for registration to use an electronic off-premises location. A private entity may charge an applicant not more than $1 for the service provided.

(c) The department may adopt rules to cover the timely application for and issuance of registration receipts and insignia by mail or through an electronic off-premises location.

*(Added by L.1995, chap. 165(1), eff. 9/1/95.)*

## §502.102. Disposition of fees generally.

(a) Except as provided by Sections 502.103 and 502.104, this section applies to all fees collected by a county assessor-collector under this chapter.

(b) Each Monday, a county assessor-collector shall credit to the county road and bridge fund an amount equal to the net collections made during the preceding week until the amount so credited for the calendar year equals the total of:

(1) $60,000;

(2) $350 for each mile of county road maintained by the county, according to the most recent information available from the department, not to exceed 500 miles;

(3) an amount equal to five percent of the tax and penalties collected by the assessor-collector under Chapter 152, Tax Code, in the preceding calendar year; and

(4) an amount equal to five percent of the tax and penalties collected by the comptroller under Section 152.047, Tax Code, in the preceding calendar year.

(c) After the credits to the county road and bridge fund equal the total computed under Subsection (b), each Monday the county assessor-collector shall:

(1) credit to the county road and bridge fund an amount equal to 50 percent of the net collections made during the preceding week, until the amount so credited for the calendar year equals $125,000; and

(2) send to the department an amount equal to 50 percent of those collections.

(d) After the credits to the county road and bridge fund equal the total amounts computed under Subsections (b) and (c)(1), each Monday the county assessor-collector shall send to the department all collections made during the preceding week.

(e) Each Monday the county assessor-collector shall send to the department a copy of each receipt issued the previous week for a registration fee under this chapter.
*(Added by L.1995, chap. 165(1), eff. 9/1/95.)*

### §502.103. Disposition of optional county road and bridge fee.

Each Monday a county assessor-collector shall apportion the collections for the preceding week for a fee imposed under Section 502.172 by:

(1) crediting an amount equal to 97 percent of the collections to the county road and bridge fund; and

(2) sending to the department an amount equal to three percent of the collections to defray the department's costs of administering Section 502.172.
*(Added by L.1995, chap. 165(1), eff. 9/1/95.)*

### §502.104. Disposition of certain special fees.

Each Monday a county assessor-collector shall send to the department an amount equal to collections for the preceding week for:

(1) each transfer fee collected under Section 502.175; and

(2) each fee collected under Section 502.169(b) or 502.279.
*(Added by L.1995, chap. 165(1), eff. 9/1/95.)*

### §502.105. Report of fees collected.

Together with each remittance of fees under Sections 502.102, 502.103, and 502.104, a county assessor-collector shall send to the department a complete report of the fees collected and the disposition of those fees. The department shall prescribe the form and the content requirements of the report. *(Added by L.1995, chap. 165(1), eff. 9/1/95.)*

### §502.106. Deposit of fees in interest-bearing account.

(a) Except as provided by Sections 502.103 and 502.104, a county assessor-collector may:

(1) deposit the fees in an interest-bearing account or certificate in the county depository; and

(2) send the fees to the department not later than the 34th day after the date the fees are due under Section 502.104.

(b) The county owns all interest earned on fees deposited under this section. The county treasurer shall credit the interest to the county general fund.
*(Added by L.1995, chap. 165(1), eff. 9/1/95.)*

### §502.107. Interest on fees.

(a) A fee required to be sent to the department under this chapter bears interest for the benefit of the state highway fund at an annual rate of 10 percent beginning on the 60th day after the date the county assessor-collector collects the fee.

(b) The department shall audit the registration and transfer fees collected and disbursed by each county assessor-collector and shall determine the exact amount of interest due on any fee not sent to the department.

(c) The state has a claim against a county assessor-collector and the sureties on the assessor-collector's official bond for the amount of interest due on a fee.
*(Added by L.1995, chap. 165(1), eff. 9/1/95.)*

**§502.108. Use of registration fees retained by county.**

(a) Money credited to the county road and bridge fund under Section 502.102 or 502.103 may not be used to pay the compensation of the county judge or a county commissioner. The money may be used only for the construction and maintenance of lateral roads in the county, under the supervision of the county engineer.

(b) If there is not a county engineer, the commissioners court of the county may require the services of the department's district engineer or resident engineer to supervise the construction and surveying of lateral roads in the county.

(c) A county may use money allocated to it under this chapter to:

(1) pay obligations issued in the construction or improvement of any roads, including state highways in the county;

(2) improve the roads in the county road system; or

(3) construct new roads.

(d) To the maximum extent possible, contracts for roads constructed by a county using funds provided under this chapter should be awarded by competitive bids.

(e) Registration fees that represent amounts of tax and penalties collected under Chapter 152, Tax Code, during the preceding year that are retained by a county may be used only for:

(1) county road construction, maintenance, and repair;

(2) bridge construction, maintenance, and repair;

(3) the purchase of right-of-way for road or highway purposes; or

(4) the relocation of utilities for road or highway purposes.

(f) *(Repealed by L.1997, chap. 165(30.47(a)), eff. 9/1/97.)*

*(Added by L.1995, chap. 165(1), eff. 9/1/95.)*

**§502.109. Compensation of assessor-collector.**

(a) A county assessor-collector shall receive a fee of $1.90 for each receipt issued under this chapter. If the assessor-collector may be compensated by fees, a fee received is compensation for services under this chapter. The assessor-collector shall deduct the fee weekly from the gross collections made under this chapter.

(b) A county assessor-collector who is compensated under this section shall pay the entire expense of issuing registration receipts and license plates under this chapter from the compensation allowed under this section.

*(Added by L.1995, chap. 165(1); chgd. by L.1997, chap. 165(30.44(b)), eff. 9/1/97.)*

**§502.110. Contingent provision for distribution of fees between state and counties.**

If the method of distributing vehicle registration fees collected under this chapter between the state and counties is declared invalid because of inequality of collection or distribution of those fees, 60 percent of each fee shall be distributed to the county collecting the fee and 40 percent shall be sent to the state in the manner provided by this chapter. *(Added by L.1995, chap. 165(1), eff. 9/1/95.)*

**§502.111. Branch offices.**

(a) The commissioners court of a county may authorize the county assessor-collector to:

(1) establish a suboffice or branch office for vehicle registration at one or more locations in the county other than the county courthouse; or

(2) appoint a deputy to register vehicles in the same manner and with the same authority as though done in the office of the assessor-collector.

(b) The report of vehicles registered through a suboffice or branch office shall be made through the office of the county assessor-collector.

*(Added by L.1995, chap. 165(1), eff. 9/1/95.)*

**§502.112. Deputy assessor-collectors.**

(a) A county assessor-collector, with the approval of the commissioners court of the county, may deputize an individual or business entity to:

(1) issue motor vehicle registration receipts as a limited-service deputy; or

(2) issue motor vehicle registration receipts and prepare or accept applications for title transfers as a full-service deputy.

(b) An individual or business entity is eligible to be deputized as a limited-service deputy if the person:

(1) is trained to issue registration receipts by the county assessor-collector; and

(2) posts a bond payable to the county assessor-collector:

(A) in an amount determined by the assessor-collector; and

(B) conditioned on the person's proper accounting and remittance of all fees the person collects.

(c) An individual or business entity is eligible to be deputized as a full-service deputy if the person:

(1) meets the requirements of Subsection (b); and

(2) has experience in title transfers.

(d) A person deputized under this section shall keep a separate account of the fees collected and a record of daily receipts.

*(Added by L.1995, chap. 165(1), eff. 9/1/95.)*

### §502.113. Limited-service deputies.

(a) A limited-service deputy appointed under Section 502.112 may only accept registration renewal cards provided by the department and may not prepare or accept an application for title transfer.

(b) The county assessor-collector may pay a limited-service deputy an amount not to exceed the fee the assessor-collector could collect under Section 502.109(a) for each registration receipt issued. The commissioners court of the county may permit a limited-service deputy to charge and retain an additional fee not to exceed $1 for each registration receipt issued.

*(Added by L.1995, chap. 165(1), eff. 9/1/95.)*

### §502.114. Full-service deputies.

(a) A full-service deputy appointed under Section 502.112 shall accept any application for registration, registration renewal, or title transfer that the county assessor-collector may accept.

(b) A full-service deputy may charge and retain an additional motor vehicle registration fee not to exceed $5 for each motor vehicle registration issued.

(c) A county assessor-collector may delegate to a full-service deputy, in the manner selected by the assessor-collector, the authority to use data processing equipment and software provided by the department for use in the titling and registration of motor vehicles. The department may not limit a county assessor-collector's ability to delegate the assessor-collector's functions regarding the titling and registration of motor vehicles to a qualified full-service deputy in the manner the assessor-collector considers appropriate.

*(Added by L.1995, chap. 165(1), eff. 9/1/95.)*

### §§502.115 to 502.150. *(Reserved.)*

## SUBCHAPTER D. REGISTRATION PROCEDURES AND FEES

### §502.151. Application for registration.

(a) An application for vehicle registration must:

(1) be made on a form furnished by the department;

(2) contain the full name and address of the owner of the vehicle;

(3) contain a brief description of the vehicle;

(4) contain any other information required by the department; and

(5) be signed by the owner.

(b) For a new motor vehicle, the description of the vehicle must include the vehicle's:

(1) trade name;

(2) year model;

(3) style and type of body;

(4) weight, if the vehicle is a passenger car;

(5) net carrying capacity and gross weight, if the vehicle is a commercial motor vehicle;

(6) vehicle identification number; and

(7) date of sale by the manufacturer or dealer to the applicant.

(c) An applicant for registration of a commercial motor vehicle, truck-tractor, trailer, or semitrailer must deliver to the county assessor-collector an affidavit showing the weight of the vehicle, the maximum load to be carried on the vehicle, and the gross weight for which the vehicle is to be registered. The assessor-collector shall keep the affidavit on file.

(d) In lieu of filing an application during a year as provided by Subsection (a), the owner of a vehicle registered in any state for that year or the preceding year may present the registration receipt and transfer receipt, if any. The county assessor-collector shall accept the receipt as an application for renewal of the registration if the receipt indicates the applicant owns the vehicle.

(e) If an owner or claimed owner has lost or misplaced the registration receipt or transfer receipt for the vehicle, the county assessor-collector shall register the vehicle on the person's furnishing to the assessor-collector satisfactory evidence, by affidavit or otherwise, that the person owns the vehicle.

(f) A county assessor-collector shall date each registration receipt issued for a vehicle with the date on which the application for registration is made.
*(Added by L.1995, chap. 165(1), eff. 9/1/95.)*

## §502.152. Certificate of title required for registration.

(a) The department may not register or renew the registration of a motor vehicle for which a certificate of title is required under Chapter 501 unless the owner:

(1) obtains a certificate of title for the vehicle; or

(2) presents satisfactory evidence that a certificate of title was previously issued to the owner by the department.

(b) This section does not apply to an automobile that was purchased new before January 1, 1936.
*(Added by L.1995, chap. 165(1), eff. 9/1/95.)*

## §502.153. Evidence of financial responsibility.

(a) Except as provided by Subsection (j), the owner of a motor vehicle, other than a trailer or semitrailer, for which evidence of financial responsibility is required by Section 601.051 or a person who represents the owner for purposes of registering a motor vehicle shall submit evidence of financial responsibility with the application for registration under Section 502.151. A county assessor-collector may not register the motor vehicle unless the owner or the owner's representative submits the evidence of financial responsibility.

(b) The county assessor-collector shall examine the evidence of financial responsibility to determine whether it complies with Subsection (c). After examining the evidence, the assessor-collector shall return the evidence unless it is in the form of a photocopy or an electronic submission.

(c) In this section, evidence of financial responsibility may be:

(1) a document listed under Section 601.053(a);

(2) a liability self-insurance or pool coverage document issued by a political subdivision or governmental pool under the authority of Chapter 791, Government Code, Chapter 119, Local Government Code, or other applicable law in at least the minimum amounts required by Chapter 601;

(3) a photocopy of a document described by Subdivision (1) or (2); or

(4) an electronic submission of a document or the information contained in a document described by Subdivision (1) or (2).

(d) A personal automobile policy used as evidence of financial responsibility under this section must comply with Article 5.06, Insurance Code.

(e) At the time of registration, the county assessor-collector shall provide to a person registering a motor vehicle a separate statement that the motor vehicle being registered may not be operated in this state unless:

(1) liability insurance coverage for the motor vehicle in at least the minimum amounts required by law remains in effect to insure against potential losses; or

(2) the motor vehicle is exempt from the insurance requirement because the person has established financial responsibility in a manner described by Section 601.051(2)-(5) or is exempt under Section 601.052.

(f) A county assessor-collector is not liable to any person for refusing to register a motor vehicle to which this section applies because of the person's failure to submit evidence of financial responsibility that complies with Subsection (c).

(g) A county, a county assessor-collector, a deputy county assessor-collector, a person acting for or on behalf of a county or a county assessor-collector, or a person acting on behalf of an owner for purposes of registering a motor vehicle is not liable to any person for registering a motor vehicle under this section.

(h) This section does not prevent a person from registering a motor vehicle by mail or through an electronic submission.

(i) To be valid under this section, an electronic submission must be in a format that is:

(1) submitted by electronic means, including a telephone, facsimile machine, or computer;

(2) approved by the department; and

(3) authorized by the commissioners court for use in the county.

(j) This section does not apply to a vehicle registered pursuant to Section 501.0234.
*(Added by L.1995, chap. 165(1); chgd. by L.1997, chap. 148(8); L.1999, chap. 260(1), eff. 5/28/99.)*

**§502.154. Report by county assessor-collector.**
A county assessor-collector shall submit an annual report to the Texas Natural Resource Conservation Commission and the department that shows:

(1) the number of registrations denied because of the applicant's failure to provide an original emissions inspection certificate or a valid waiver;

(2) the number of registrations denied because of the failure to provide proof of residency; and

(3) an itemized accounting of the costs to the county of administering Sections 502.002 and 502.006(a), (b), and (c).

*(Added by L.1995, chap. 165(1); chgd. by L.1997, chap. 165(30.44(c)), eff. 9/1/97.)*

**§502.155.** *(Repealed by L.1997, chap. 165(30.44(d)), eff. 9/1/97.)*

**§502.156. Statement required for rebuilt vehicles.**
A county assessor-collector shall require an applicant for registration of a rebuilt vehicle to provide a statement that the vehicle is rebuilt and that states the name of each person from whom the parts used in assembling the vehicle were obtained. *(Added by L.1995, chap. 165(1), eff. 9/1/95.)*

**§502.157. Initial registration.**
(a) Notwithstanding Section 502.002, when a motor vehicle must be registered before an application for a certificate of title will be accepted, the owner of the vehicle may concurrently apply for a certificate of title and for registration through the county assessor-collector of the county in which:

(1) the owner resides; or

(2) the vehicle is purchased or encumbered.

(b) The first time an owner applies for registration of a vehicle, the owner may demonstrate compliance with Section 502.153(a) as to the vehicle by showing proof of financial responsibility in any manner specified in Section 502.153(c) as to:

(1) any vehicle of the owner; or

(2) any vehicle used as part of the consideration for the purchase of the vehicle the owner applies to register.

*(Added by L.1995, chap. 165(1), eff. 9/1/95.)*

**§502.158. Registration year.**
(a) The department shall designate a vehicle registration year of 12 consecutive months to begin on the first day of a calendar month and end on the last day of the 12th calendar month.

(b) The department shall designate vehicle registration years so as to distribute the work of the department and the county assessor-collectors as uniformly as possible throughout the year. The department may establish separate registration years for any vehicle or classification of vehicle and may adopt rules to administer the year-round registration system.

(c) The department may designate a registration period of less than 12 months. The registration fee for a registration period of less than 12 months is computed at a rate of one-twelfth the annual registration fee multiplied by the number of months in the registration period. The department may not designate a registration period of more than 12 months, but:

(1) with the consent of the department, an owner may pay registration fees for a designated period of more than 12 months; and

(2) an owner of a passenger car or light truck that has not been previously registered in this or another state and is of the current or preceding model year may pay registration fees for a designated period of 12, 24, or 36 months.

(d) An application for registration shall be made during the two months preceding the date on which the registration expires.

(e) The fee to be paid for renewing a registration is the fee that will be in effect on the first day of the vehicle registration year.

(f) *(Repealed.)*

(g) The department shall issue the applicant for registration who pays registration fees for a designated period of 24 or 36 months a registration receipt and registration insignia that are valid until the expiration of the designated period.
*(Added by L.1995, chap. 165(1); chgd. by L.1997, chap. 433(1); L.1999, chap. 641(2), eff. 9/1/99.)*

**§502.1585. Registration period for truck-tractor or commercial motor vehicle transporting seasonal agricultural products.**

(a) The department shall provide for a monthly registration period for a truck-tractor or a commercial motor vehicle that:

(1) is used exclusively to transport a seasonal agricultural product; and

(2) would otherwise be registered for a vehicle registration year.

(b) The department shall adopt forms for registration under this section. An applicant must indicate the number of months registration is applied for.

(c) The department shall design, prescribe, and furnish a registration receipt and registration insignia that are valid until the expiration of the designated registration period.

(d) The registration fee for a registration under this section is computed at a rate of one-twelfth the annual registration fee under Section 502.162 or 502.167, as applicable, multiplied by the number of months in the registration period specified in the application for the registration.

(e) A person issued a registration under this section commits an offense if the person, during the registration period for the truck-tractor or commercial motor vehicle, uses the truck-tractor or commercial motor vehicle for a purpose other than to transport a seasonal agricultural product.

(f) A truck-tractor or commercial motor vehicle may not be registered under this section for a registration period that is less than one month or longer than six months.

(g) For purposes of this section, "to transport a seasonal agricultural product" includes any transportation activity necessary for the production, harvest, or delivery of an agricultural product that is produced seasonally.
*(Added by L.1999, chap. 732(1), eff. 9/1/99. See other section 502.1585 below.)*

**§502.1585. Designation of registration period by owner.**

(a) This section applies only to a person who owns more than one motor vehicle or trailer that is subject to registration under this chapter.

(b) Notwithstanding Section 502.158, the owner of a motor vehicle or a trailer may designate an initial or a renewal registration period for that vehicle so that the registration period for the vehicle or trailer expires on the same date as the registration period for another vehicle or trailer previously registered by that owner.

(c) A registration period designated under this section must begin on the first day of a calendar month and end on the last day of a calendar month and may not be for less than 12 months.

(d) The registration fee for a registration period designated under this section is computed at a rate of one-twelfth the annual registration fee multiplied by the number of months in the designated registration period.

(e) The department shall issue an applicant for registration who pays registration fees for a designated period under this section a registration receipt and registration insignia that are valid until the expiration of the designated period.
*(Added by L.1999, chap. 1197(1), eff. 9/1/99. See other section 502.1585 above.)*

**§502.159. Schedule of fees.**

The department shall compile and furnish to each county assessor-collector a complete schedule of registration fees to be collected on the various makes, models, and types of vehicles. *(Added by L.1995, chap. 165(1), eff. 9/1/95.)*

**§502.160. Fee: motorcycle.**

The fee for a registration year for registration of a motorcycle is $30. *(Added by L.1995, chap. 165(1), eff. 9/1/95.)*

**§502.161. Fee: passenger car, municipal bus, private bus.**

(a) The fee for a registration year for registration of a passenger car, a municipal bus, or a private bus that weighs 6,000 pounds or less is:

(1) $40.50 for a vehicle the model year of which is more than six years before the year in which the registration year begins;

(2) $50.50 for a vehicle the model year of which is more than three years but is six years or less before the year in which the registration year begins; or

(3) $58.50 for a vehicle the model year of which is three years or less before the year in which the registration year begins.

(b) The fee for a registration year for registration of a passenger car, a municipal bus, or a private bus that weighs more than 6,000 pounds is $25 plus 60 cents for each 100 pounds.

(c) For registration purposes, the weight of a passenger car, a municipal bus, or a private bus is the weight generally accepted as its correct shipping weight plus 100 pounds.

(d) In this section, "private bus" has the meaning assigned by Section 502.294.

*(Added by L.1995, chap. 165(1); chgd. by L.1997, chap. 625(4), eff. 9/1/97.)*

## §502.162. Fee: commercial motor vehicle or truck-tractor.

(a) The fee for a registration year for registration of a commercial motor vehicle or truck-tractor is $25 plus an amount determined according to the vehicle's gross weight and tire equipment, as follows:

| Gross weight in pounds | Fee for each 100 pounds or fraction of 100 pounds | |
|---|---|---|
| | Equipped with pneumatic tires | Equipped with solid tires |
| 1—6,000 | $0.44 | $0.55 |
| 6,001—8,000 | 0.495 | 0.66 |
| 8,001—10,000 | 0.605 | 0.77 |
| 10,001—17,000 | 0.715 | 0.88 |
| 17,001—24,000 | 0.77 | 0.99 |
| 24,001—31,000 | 0.88 | 1.10 |
| 31,001 and over | 0.99 | 1.32 |

(b) The gross weight of a vehicle is the actual weight of the vehicle, fully equipped with a body and other equipment, as certified by a public weigher or a license and weight inspector of the Department of Public Safety, plus its net carrying capacity.

(c) The net carrying capacity of a vehicle other than a bus is the heaviest net load to be carried on the vehicle, but not less than the manufacturer's rated carrying capacity.

(d) The net carrying capacity of a bus is computed by multiplying its seating capacity by 150 pounds. The seating capacity of a bus is:

(1) the manufacturer's rated seating capacity, excluding the operator's seat; or

(2) if the manufacturer has not rated the vehicle for seating capacity, a number computed by allowing one passenger for each 16 inches of seating on the bus, excluding the operator's seat.

*(Added by L.1995, chap. 165(1), eff. 9/1/95.)*

## §502.163. Fee: commercial motor vehicle used primarily for farm purposes; offense.

(a) The registration fee for a commercial motor vehicle as a farm vehicle is 50 percent of the applicable fee under Section 502.162 if the vehicle's owner will use the vehicle for commercial purposes only to transport:

(1) the person's own poultry, dairy, livestock, livestock products, timber in its natural state, or farm products to market or another place for sale or processing;

(2) laborers from their place of residence to the owner's farm or ranch; or

(3) without charge, materials, tools, equipment, or supplies from the place of purchase or storage to the owner's farm or ranch exclusively for the owner's use or for use on the farm or ranch.

(b) A commercial motor vehicle may be registered under this section despite its use for transporting without charge the owner or a member of the owner's family:

(1) to attend church or school;

(2) to visit a doctor for medical treatment or supplies; or

(3) for other necessities of the home or family.

(c) Subsection (b) does not permit the use of a vehicle registered under this section in connection with gainful employment other than farming or ranching.

(d) The department shall provide distinguishing license plates for a vehicle registered under this section.

(e) The owner of a commercial motor vehicle registered under this section commits an offense if the person uses or permits to be used the vehicle for a purpose other than one permitted by this section. Each use or permission for use in violation of this section is a separate offense.

(f) An offense under this section is a misdemeanor punishable by a fine of not less than $25 or more than $200.
*(Added by L.1995, chap. 165(1), eff. 9/1/95.)*

**§502.164. Fee: motor vehicle used exclusively to transport and spread fertilizer.**
The fee for a registration year for registration of a motor vehicle designed or modified and used exclusively to transport to the field and spread fertilizer, including agricultural limestone, is $75. *(Added by L.1995, chap. 165(1), eff. 9/1/95.)*

**§502.165. Fee: road tractor.**
The fee for a registration year for registration of a road tractor is $25 plus an amount determined according to the vehicle's weight as certified by a public weigher or a license and weight inspector of the Department of Public Safety, as follows:

| Gross weight in pounds | Fee for each 100 pounds or fraction of 100 pounds |
|---|---|
| 1—4,000 | $0.275 |
| 4,001—6,000 | 0.55 |
| 6,001—8,000 | 0.66 |
| 8,001—10,000 | 0.825 |
| 10,001 and over | 1.10 |

*(Added by L.1995, chap. 165(1), eff. 9/1/95.)*

**§502.166. Fee: trailer or semitrailer.**
(a) The fee for a registration year for registration of a trailer or semitrailer is $25 plus an amount determined according to the vehicle's gross weight and tire equipment, as follows:

| Gross weight in pounds | Fee for each 100 pounds or fraction of 100 pounds: Equipped with pneumatic tires | Equipped with solid tires |
|---|---|---|
| 1—6,000 | $0.33 | $0.44 |
| 6,001—8,000 | 0.44 | 0.55 |
| 8,001—10,000 | 0.55 | 0.66 |
| 10,001—17,000 | 0.66 | 0.88 |
| 17,001 and over | 0.715 | 0.99 |

(b) The gross weight of a trailer or semitrailer is the actual weight of the vehicle, as certified by a public weigher or a license and weight inspector of the Department of Public Safety, plus its net carrying capacity.
(c) The net carrying capacity of a vehicle is the heaviest net load to be carried on the vehicle, but not less than the manufacturer's rated carrying capacity.
(d) The department may issue specially designed license plates for rental trailers and travel trailers that include, as appropriate, the words "rental trailer" or "travel trailer."
(e) In this section:
(1) "Rental fleet" means five or more vehicles that are:
(A) owned by the same owner;
(B) offered for rent or rented without drivers; and
(C) designated by the owner in the manner prescribed by the department as a rental fleet.
(2) "Rental trailer" means a utility trailer that:
(A) has a gross weight of 4,000 pounds or less; and
(B) is part of a rental fleet.
(3) "Travel trailer" means a house trailer-type vehicle or a camper trailer that is:
(A) less than eight feet in width or 40 feet in length, exclusive of any hitch installed on the vehicle; and
(B) designed primarily for use as temporary living quarters in connection with recreational, camping, travel, or seasonal use and not as a permanent dwelling; provided that "travel trailer" shall not include a utility trailer, enclosed trailer, or other trailer not having human habitation as its primary purpose.
*(Added by L.1995, chap. 165(1); chgd. by L.1997, chap. 625(5), eff. 9/1/97.)*

**§502.167. Truck-tractor or commercial motor vehicle combination fee; semitrailer token fee.**

(a) This section applies only to a truck-tractor or commercial motor vehicle with a manufacturer's rated carrying capacity of more than one ton that is used or is to be used in combination with a semitrailer that has a gross weight of more than 6,000 pounds.

(b) Notwithstanding Section 502.162, the fee for a registration year for registration of a truck-tractor or commercial motor vehicle is $40 plus an amount determined according to the combined gross weight of the vehicles, as follows:

| Combined gross weight in pounds | Fee for each 100 pounds or fraction of 100 pounds |
|---|---|
| 18,000—36,000 | $0.60 |
| 36,001—42,000 | 0.75 |
| 42,001—62,000 | 0.90 |
| 62,001 and over | 1.00 |

(c) Notwithstanding Section 502.166, the fee for a registration year for registration of a semitrailer used in the manner described by Subsection (a), regardless of the date the semitrailer is registered, is:

(1) $30, for a semitrailer being propelled by a power unit for which a permit under Section 623.011 has been issued; or

(2) $15, for a semitrailer being propelled by a power unit for which a permit under Section 623.011 has not been issued.

(d) A registration made under Subsection (c) is valid only when the semitrailer is used in the manner described by Subsection (a).

(e) For registration purposes, a semitrailer converted to a trailer by means of an auxiliary axle assembly retains its status as a semitrailer.

(f) A combination of vehicles may not be registered under this section for a combined gross weight of less than 18,000 pounds.

(g) This section does not apply to:

(1) a combination of vehicles that includes a vehicle that has a distinguishing license plate under Section 502.276;

(2) a truck-tractor or commercial motor vehicle registered or to be registered with $5 distinguishing license plates for which the vehicle is eligible under this chapter;

(3) a truck-tractor or commercial motor vehicle used exclusively in combination with a semitrailer of the housetrailer type; or

(4) a vehicle registered or to be registered:

(A) with a temporary registration permit;

(B) under Section 502.163; or

(C) under Section 502.278.

(h) The department may adopt rules to administer this section.

(i) The department may issue specially designed license plates for token trailers.

(j) A person may register a semitrailer under this section for a registration period of five consecutive years if the person:

(1) owns 50 or more semitrailers at the time of the application;

(2) applies to the department for the five-year registration;

(3) provides proof of the person's eligibility to register the vehicle under this subsection as required by the department; and

(4) pays a fee of $15, plus any applicable fee under Section 502.172, for each year included in the registration period.

(k) If during the five-year registration period for a vehicle registered under Subsection (j) the amount of a fee imposed under that subsection is increased, the owner of the vehicle is liable to the department for the amount of the increase. If the amount of a fee is decreased, the owner of the vehicle is not entitled to a refund.

(*l*) In this section:

(1) "Combined gross weight" means the empty weight of the truck-tractor or commercial motor vehicle combined with the empty weight of the heaviest semitrailer used or to be used in combination with the truck-tractor or commercial motor vehicle plus the heaviest net load to be carried on the combination during the registration year.

(2) "Empty weight" means the unladen weight of the truck-tractor or commercial motor vehicle and semitrailer combination fully equipped, as certified by a public weigher or license and weight inspector of the Department of Public Safety.

(3) "Token trailer" means a semitrailer that:

(A) has a gross weight of more than 6,000 pounds; and

(B) is operated in combination with a truck or a truck-tractor that has been issued:

(i) an apportioned license plate;

(ii) a combination license plate; or

(iii) a forestry vehicle license plate.

(4) "Apportioned license plate" means a license plate issued in lieu of truck license plates or combination license plates to a motor carrier in this state who proportionally registers a vehicle owned by the carrier in one or more other states.

(5) "Combination license plate" means a license plate issued for a truck or truck-tractor that:

(A) has a manufacturer's rated carrying capacity of more than one ton; and

(B) is used or intended to be used in combination with a semitrailer that has a gross weight of more than 6,000 pounds.

*(Added by L.1995, chap. 165(1); chgd. by L.1997, chap. 625(6), eff. 9/1/97.)*



### §502.168. Fee: motor bus.

The fee for a registration year for registration of a motor bus is $25 plus an amount determined according to the vehicle's gross weight, as follows:

| Gross weight in pounds | Fee for each 100 pounds or fraction of 100 pounds |
|---|---|
| 1—6,000 | $0.44 |
| 6,001—8,000 | 0.495 |
| 8,001—10,000 | 0.605 |
| 10,001—17,000 | 0.715 |
| 17,001—24,000 | 0.77 |
| 24,001—31,000 | 0.88 |
| 31,001 and over | 0.99 |

*(Added by L.1995, chap. 165(1), eff. 9/1/95.)*

### §502.169. Fee: all-terrain vehicle.

(a) The fee for a registration year for off-highway registration of an all-terrain vehicle is $6.

(b) At the time of registration, the county assessor-collector shall also collect from the registered owner of the vehicle an annual all-terrain vehicle safety fee of $6.

*(Added by L.1995, chap. 165(1), eff. 9/1/95.)*

### §502.170. Additional fee for reflectorized license plates.

(a) In addition to the other registration fees for a license plate or set of license plates or other device used as the registration insignia, 30 cents shall be collected.

(b) The department shall use money collected under this section to purchase equipment and material for the production and manufacture of reflectorized license plates.

*(Added by L.1995, chap. 165(1), eff. 9/1/95.)*

### §502.1705. Additional fee for automated registration and title system.

(a) In addition to other registration fees for a license plate or set of license plates or other device used as the registration insignia, a fee of $1 shall be collected.

(b) The department may use money collected under this section to perform one or more of the following:

(1) enhancing the department's automated registration and title system;

(2) providing for the automated on-site production of registration insignia; or

(3) providing for automated on-premises and off-premises self-service registration.

(c) This section applies only in a county in which the department's automated registration and title system has been implemented and in which 50,000 or more motor vehicles were registered during the preceding year.

*(Added by L.1999, chap. 1455(1), eff. 9/1/99.)*

### §502.171. Additional fee for certain vehicles using diesel motor.

(a) The registration fee under this chapter for a motor vehicle other than a passenger car, a truck with a manufacturer's rated carrying capacity of two tons or less, or a vehicle registered in combination under Section 502.167 is increased by 11 percent if the vehicle has a diesel motor.

(b) A county assessor-collector shall show on the registration receipt for a motor vehicle, other than a passenger car or a truck with a manufacturer's rated carrying capacity of two tons or less, that the vehicle has a diesel motor.

(c) The department may adopt rules to administer this section.

*(Added by L.1995, chap. 165(1), eff. 9/1/95.)*

### §502.172. Optional county fee for road and bridge fund.

(a) The commissioners court of a county by order may impose an additional fee, not to exceed $10, for registering a vehicle in the county.

(b) A vehicle that may be registered under this chapter without payment of a registration fee may be registered in a county imposing a fee under this section without payment of the additional fee.

(c) A fee imposed under this section may take effect only on January 1 of a year. The county must adopt the order and notify the department not later than September 1 of the year preceding the year in which the fee takes effect.

(d) A fee imposed under this section may be removed. The removal may take effect only on January 1 of a year. A county may remove the fee only by:

(1) rescinding the order imposing the fee; and

(2) notifying the department not later than September 1 of the year preceding the year in which the removal takes effect.

(e) The county assessor-collector of a county imposing a fee under this section shall collect the additional fee for a vehicle when other fees imposed under this chapter are collected.

(f) The department shall collect the additional fee on a vehicle that is owned by a resident of a county imposing a fee under this section and that, under this chapter, must be registered directly with the department. The department shall send all fees collected for a county under this subsection to the county treasurer to be credited to the county road and bridge fund.

(g) The department shall adopt rules and develop forms necessary to administer registration by mail for a vehicle being registered in a county imposing a fee under this section.

*(Added by L.1995, chap. 165(1), eff. 9/1/95.)*

### §502.173. Optional county fee for child safety.

(a) The commissioners court of a county with a population greater than 1.18 million may impose by order an additional fee of not less than 50 cents or more than $1.50 for registering a vehicle in the county. The commissioners court of a county with a population less than 1.18 million may impose by order an additional fee of not more than $1.50 for registering a vehicle in the county.

(b) A vehicle that may be registered under this chapter without payment of a registration fee may be registered in a county imposing a fee under this section without payment of the additional fee.

(c) A fee imposed under this section may take effect only on January 1 of a year. The county must adopt the order and notify the department not later than September 10 of the year preceding the year in which the fee takes effect.

(d) A fee imposed under this section may be removed. The removal may take effect only on January 1 of a year. A county may remove the fee only by:

(1) rescinding the order imposing the fee; and

(2) notifying the department not later than September 1 of the year preceding the year in which the removal takes effect.

(e) The county assessor-collector of a county imposing a fee under this section shall collect the additional fee for a vehicle when other fees imposed under this chapter are collected.

(f) A county imposing a fee under this section may deduct for administrative costs an amount of not more than 10 percent of the revenue it receives from the fee. The county may also deduct from the fee revenue an amount proportional to the percentage of county residents who live in unincorporated areas of the county. After making the deductions provided for by this subsection, the county shall send the remainder of the fee revenue to the municipalities in the county according to their population.

(g) A municipality with a population greater than 850,000 shall deposit revenue from a fee imposed under this subsection to the credit of the child safety trust fund created under Section 106.001, Local Government Code. A municipality with a population less than 850,000 shall use revenue from a fee imposed under this section in accordance with Subsection (f), Article 102.014, Code of Criminal Procedure.

(h) After deducting administrative costs, a county may use revenue from a fee imposed under this section only for a purpose permitted by Subsection (g), Article 102.014, Code of Criminal Procedure.

*(Added by L.1995, chap. 165(1); chgd. by L.1997, chap. 165(30.48), eff. 9/1/97.)*

### §502.174. Voluntary assessment for young farmer loan guarantees.

(a) When a person registers a commercial motor vehicle under Section 502.163, the person shall pay a voluntary assessment of $5.

(b) The county assessor-collector shall send an assessment collected under this section to the comptroller, at the time and in the manner prescribed by the Texas Agricultural Finance Authority, for deposit in the Texas agricultural fund to the credit of the young farmer loan guarantee account.

(c) The Texas Agricultural Finance Authority shall prescribe procedures under which an assessment collected under this section may be refunded. The county assessor-collector of the county in which an assessment is collected shall:

(1) implement the refund procedures; and

(2) provide notice of those procedures to a person paying an assessment at the time of payment.

*(Added by L.1995, chap. 165(1); chgd. by L.1997, chap. 1423(18.04); L.1999, chap. 1459(15), eff. 6/19/99.)*

### §502.175. Transfer fee.

(a) A person other than a dealer who sells a vehicle subject to registration under this chapter shall indorse on the certificate of registration a written transfer of the vehicle.

(b) The purchaser of a motor vehicle to which Subsection (a) applies shall:

(1) pay a transfer fee of $1 to the county assessor-collector of the county in which the person resides; and

(2) provide the person's full name and address to the assessor-collector.

(c) On compliance with Subsection (b), a person is considered to be the owner of the vehicle and is subject to this chapter.

*(Added by L.1995, chap. 165(1), eff. 9/1/95.)*

### §502.176. Delinquent registration.

(a) A registration fee prescribed by this chapter for a vehicle becomes delinquent immediately if the vehicle is used on a public highway without the fee having been paid in accordance with this chapter.

(b) A county assessor-collector that determines that an applicant for registration for which payment of the registration fee is delinquent has provided evidence acceptable to the assessor-collector sufficient to establish good reason for delinquent registration and that the application complies with the other requirements for registration under this chapter shall register the vehicle for a 12-month period that ends on the last day of the 11th month after the month in which the registration occurs under this subsection. The registration period for vehicles registered in accordance with Sections 502.164, 502.167, 502.203, 502.255, 502.267, 502.277, 502.278, 502.293, as added by Chapter 1222, Acts of the 75th Legislature, Regular Session, 1997, and 502.295, as added by Chapter 625, Acts of the 75th Legislature, Regular Session, 1997, will end on the annual registration date, and the registration fees will be prorated.

(c) A county assessor-collector that determines that an applicant for registration that is delinquent has not provided evidence acceptable to the assessor-collector sufficient to establish good reason for delinquent registration but that the application complies with the other requirements for registration under this chapter shall register the vehicle for a 12-month period without changing the initial month of registration.

(d) A person who has been arrested or received a citation for a violation of Section 502.402 may register the vehicle being operated at the time of the offense with the county assessor-collector for a 12-month period without change to the initial month of registration only if the person:

(1) meets the other requirements for registration under this chapter; and

(2) pays an additional charge equal to 20 percent of the prescribed fee.

(e) The county assessor-collector shall adopt a list of evidentiary items sufficient to establish good reason for delinquent registration under Subsection (b) and provide for the forms of evidence that may be used to establish good reason under that subsection. The list of evidentiary items adopted under this section must allow for delinquent registration under Subsection (b) because of:

(1) extensive repairs on the vehicle;

(2) the absence of the owner of the vehicle from this country;

(3) seasonal use of the vehicle; or

(4) any other reason determined by the assessor-collector to be a valid explanation for the delinquent registration.

(f) The department by rule shall adopt procedures to implement this section in connection with the delinquent registration of a vehicle registered directly with the department.

*(Added by L.1995, chap. 165(1); L.1999, chap. 641(1), eff. 9/1/99.)*

### §502.177. Minimum registration fee.

Notwithstanding any other provision of this chapter and without regard to the month in which the application for registration is filed, the minimum registration fee for any vehicle may not be less than $5. *(Added by L.1995, chap. 165(1), eff. 9/1/95.)*

### §502.178. Registration receipt.

(a) The department shall issue or require to be issued to the owner of a vehicle registered under this chapter a registration receipt showing:

(1) the date of issuance;

(2) the license number assigned to the vehicle;

(3) the name and address of the owner; and

(4) other information as determined by the department.

(b) The registration receipt issued for a commercial motor vehicle, truck-tractor, trailer, or semitrailer must show the gross weight for which the vehicle is registered.

*(Added by L.1995, chap. 165(1), eff. 9/1/95.)*

### §502.179. Duplicate registration receipt.

(a) The owner of a vehicle for which the registration receipt has been lost or destroyed may obtain a duplicate receipt from the department or the county assessor-collector who issued the original receipt by paying a fee of $2.

(b) The office issuing a duplicate receipt shall retain the fee received as a fee of office.

*(Added by L.1995, chap. 165(1), eff. 9/1/95.)*

### §502.180. Issuance of license plate or registration insignia.

(a) On payment of the prescribed fee, the department shall issue to an applicant for motor vehicle registration a license plate or set of plates or a device that, when attached to the vehicle as prescribed by the department, is the registration insignia for the period for which it was issued.

(b) The department shall issue only one license plate or set of plates for a vehicle during a five-year period.

(c) On application and payment of the prescribed fee for a renewal of the registration of a vehicle for the first, second, third, or fourth registration year after the issuance of a license plate or set of plates for the vehicle, the department shall issue a registration insignia for the validation of the license plate or plates to be attached as provided by Subsection (d).

(d) Except as provided by Subsection (h), the registration insignia for validation of a license plate shall be attached to the inside of the vehicle's windshield, if the vehicle has a windshield, within six inches of the place where the motor vehicle inspection sticker is required to be placed. If the vehicle does not have a windshield, the owner, when applying for registration or renewal of registration, shall notify the department, and the department shall issue a distinctive device for attachment to the rear license plate of the vehicle.

(e) The department shall adopt rules for the issuance and use of license plates and registration insignia issued under this chapter. The rules may provide for the use of an automated registration process, including:

(1) the automated on-site production of registration insignia; and

(2) automated on-premises and off-premises self-service registration.

(f) Subsections (b)-(d) do not apply to:

(1) the issuance of specialized license plates as designated by the department, including state official license plates, exempt plates for governmental entities, and temporary registration plates; or

(2) the issuance or validation of replacement license plates, except as provided by Section 502.184.

(g) The department shall provide a separate and distinctive tab to be affixed to the license plate of an automobile, pickup, or recreational vehicle that is offered for rent, as a business, to any part of the public.

(h) The registration insignia for validation of a license plate shall be attached to the rear license plate of the vehicle, if the vehicle is:

(1) a motorcycle;

(2) machinery used exclusively to drill water wells or construction machinery for which a distinguishing license plate has been issued under Section 502.276; or

(3) oil well servicing, oil clean out, or oil well drilling machinery or equipment for which a distinguishing license plate has been issued under Subchapter G, Chapter 623.

*(Added by L.1995, chap. 165(1); chgd. by L.1997, chap. 165(30.49(a)); L.1999, chap. 1455(2), eff. 9/1/99.)*

**§502.181. Payment of registration fee by check drawn against insufficient funds.**

(a) A county assessor-collector who receives from any person a check or draft drawn on a bank or trust company in payment of a registration fee for a registration year that has not ended on a motor vehicle, trailer, or motorcycle sidecar that is returned unpaid because of insufficient funds or no funds in the bank or trust company to the credit of the drawer of the check or draft shall immediately certify the fact to the sheriff or a constable or highway patrol officer in the county. The certification must:

(1) be under the assessor-collector's official seal;

(2) include the name and address of the person who gave the assessor-collector the check or draft;

(3) include the license plate number and make of the vehicle; and

(4) be accompanied by the check or draft.

(b) On receiving a complaint under Subsection (a) from the county assessor-collector, the sheriff, constable, or highway patrol officer shall find the person who gave the assessor-collector the check or draft, if the person is in the county, and demand immediate redemption of the check or draft from the person. If the person fails or refuses to redeem the check or draft, the sheriff, constable, or highway patrol officer shall:

(1) seize and remove the license plates from the vehicle; and

(2) return the license plates to the county assessor-collector.

*(Added by L.1995, chap. 165(1), eff. 9/1/95.)*



**§502.182. Credit for registration fee paid on motor vehicle subsequently destroyed.**

(a) The owner of a motor vehicle that is destroyed to the extent that it cannot afterwards be operated on a public highway is entitled to a registration fee credit if the prorated portion of the registration fee for the remainder of the registration year is more than $15. The owner must claim the credit by:

(1) sending the registration fee receipt and the license plates for the vehicle to the department; and

(2) executing a statement on a form provided by the department showing that the license plates have been surrendered to the department.

(b) The department, on satisfactory proof that the vehicle is destroyed, shall issue a registration fee credit slip to the owner in an amount equal to the prorated portion of the registration fee for the remainder of the registration year. The owner, during the same or the next registration year, may use the registration fee credit slip as payment or part payment for the registration of another vehicle to the extent of the credit.

(c) A statement executed under Subsection (a)(2) shall be delivered to a purchaser of the destroyed vehicle. The purchaser may surrender the statement to the department in lieu of the vehicle license plates.

(d) The department shall adopt rules to administer this section.

*(Added by L.1995, chap. 165(1), eff. 9/1/95.)*

**§502.183. Refund of overcharged registration fee.**

(a) The owner of a motor vehicle that is required to be registered who pays an annual registration fee in excess of the statutory amount is entitled to a refund of the overcharge.

(b) The county assessor-collector who collects the excessive fee shall refund an overcharge on presentation to the assessor-collector of satisfactory evidence of the overcharge. The owner must make a claim for a refund of an overcharge not later than the fifth anniversary of the date the excessive registration fee was paid.

(c) A refund shall be paid from the fund in which the county's share of registration fees is deposited.

*(Added by L.1995, chap. 165(1), eff. 9/1/95.)*

**§502.184. Replacement of lost, stolen, or mutilated license plate or registration insignia.**

(a) The owner of a registered motor vehicle may obtain from the department through the county assessor-collector replacement license plates or a replacement registration insignia by:

(1) filing with the assessor-collector a statement:

(A) showing that one or both of the license plates or the registration insignia to be replaced has been lost, stolen, or mutilated; and

(B) stating that no license plate or registration insignia to be replaced will be used on any vehicle owned or operated by the person making the statement;

(2) paying a fee of $5 plus the fees required by Sections 502.170(a) and 502.1705(a) for each set of replacement license plates or each replacement registration insignia, except as provided by Subsection (b), (c), or (i); and

(3) returning to the assessor-collector each replaced plate or registration insignia in the owner's possession.

(b) The fee for replacement of certain specialized license plates is:

| License plates issued under: | Fee: |
|---|---|
| Section 502.254 | $1 |
| Section 502.255 or 502.257 | No fee |
| Section 502.256 or 502.267 | $2 |
| Section 502.268 | $9 |
| Section 502.273 | $30 |

(c) The fee for replacement of license plates issued under Section 502.280 is the amount prescribed by the department as necessary to recover the cost of providing the replacement plates.

(d) If license plates approved under Section 502.274(b) are lost, stolen, or mutilated, the owner of the vehicle may obtain approval of another set of license plates as provided by Section 502.274. The fee for approval of replacement license plates is $5.

(e) A county assessor-collector may not issue replacement license plates or a replacement registration insignia without complying with this section.

(f) A county assessor-collector shall retain $2.50 of each fee collected under this section and shall report and send the remainder to the department as provided by Sections 502.102 and 502.105.

(g) Replacement license plates may be used in the registration year in which the plates are issued and during each succeeding year of the five-year period as prescribed by Section 502.180(b) if the registration insignia is properly attached.

(h) Subsection (g) does not apply to the issuance of specialized license plates as designated by the department, including state official license plates, exempt plates for governmental entities, and temporary registration plates.

(i) The owner of a vehicle listed in Section 502.180(h) may obtain replacement plates and a replacement registration insignia by paying a fee of $5 plus the fees required by Sections 502.170(a) and 502.1705(a).

*(Added by L.1995, chap. 165(1); chgd. by L.1997, chap. 165(30.49(b), (c)); L.1999, chap. 1455(3), eff. 9/1/99.)*

## §502.185. Refusal to register vehicle in certain counties.

(a) A county assessor-collector or the department may refuse to register a motor vehicle if the assessor-collector or the department receives information that the owner of the vehicle owes the county money for a fine, fee, or tax that is past due.

(b) A county may contract with the department to provide information to the department necessary to make a determination under Subsection (a).

(c) A county that has a contract under Subsection (b) shall notify the department regarding a person for whom the county assessor-collector or the department has refused to register a motor vehicle on:

(1) the person's payment or other means of discharge of the past due fine, fee, or tax; or

(2) perfection of an appeal of the case contesting payment of the fine, fee, or tax.

(d) After notice is received under Subsection (c), the county assessor-collector or the department may not refuse to register the motor vehicle under Subsection (a).

(e) A contract under Subsection (b) must be entered into in accordance with Chapter 791, Government Code, and is subject to the ability of the parties to provide or pay for the services required under the contract.

(f) A county that has a contract under Subsection (b) may impose an additional fee to a person paying a fine, fee, or tax to the county after it is past due. The additional fee may be used only to reimburse the department for its expenses for providing services under the contract.

(g) In this section:

(1) a fine, fee, or tax is considered past due if it is unpaid 90 or more days after the date it is due; and

(2) registration of a motor vehicle includes renewal of the registration of the vehicle.

(h) This section does not apply to the registration of a motor vehicle under Section 501.0234.

*(Added by L.1997, chap. 192(1); chgd. by L.1999, chap. 97(1), eff. 5/17/99.)*

## §§502.186 to 502.200. *(Reserved.)*

## SUBCHAPTER E. SPECIALLY DESIGNATED LICENSE PLATES; EXEMPTIONS FOR GOVERNMENTAL AND QUASI-GOVERNMENTAL VEHICLES

### §502.201. License plates for exempt vehicles.

(a) Before license plates are issued or delivered to the owner of a vehicle that is exempt by law from payment of registration fees, the department must approve the application for registration. The department may not approve an application if there is the appearance that:

(1) the vehicle was transferred to the owner or purported owner:

(A) for the sole purpose of evading the payment of registration fees; or

(B) in bad faith; or

(2) the vehicle is not being used in accordance with the exemption requirements.

(b) The department shall revoke the registration of a vehicle issued license plates under this section and may recall the plates if the vehicle is no longer:

(1) owned and operated by the person whose ownership of the vehicle qualified the vehicle for the exemption; or

(2) used in accordance with the exemption requirements.

(c) The owner of a vehicle described by Subsection (b) shall return the license plates and registration receipt to the department for cancellation.

(d) The department shall provide by rule for the issuance of specially designated license plates for vehicles that are exempt by law. Except as provided by Subsection (g), the license plates must bear the word "exempt."

(e) A license plate under Subsection (d) is not issued annually, but remains on the vehicle until:

(1) the registration is revoked as provided by Subsection (b); or

(2) the plate is lost, stolen, or mutilated.

(f) A person who operates on a public highway a vehicle after the registration has been revoked is liable for the penalties for failing to register a vehicle.

(g) The department shall provide by rule for the issuance of regularly designed license plates not bearing the word "exempt" for a vehicle that is exempt by law and that is:

(1) a law enforcement vehicle, if the agency certifies to the department that the vehicle will be dedicated to law enforcement activities;

(2) a vehicle exempt from inscription requirements under a rule adopted as provided by Section 721.003; or

(3) a vehicle exempt from inscription requirements under an order or ordinance adopted by a governing body of a municipality or commissioners court of a county as provided by Section 721.005, if the applicant presents a copy of the order or ordinance.

*(Added by L.1995, chap. 165(1); chgd. by L.1997, chap. 485(1), eff. 9/1/97.)*

### §502.2015. Limitation on issuance of exempt license plates; seizure of certain vehicles.

(a) The department may not issue exempt license plates for a vehicle owned by the United States, this state, or a political subdivision of this state unless when application is made for registration of the vehicle, the person who under Section 502.202 has authority to certify to the department that the vehicle qualifies for registration under that section also certifies in writing to the department that there is printed on each side of the vehicle, in letters that are at least two inches high or in an emblem that is at least 100 square inches in size, the name of the agency, department, bureau, board, commission, or officer of the United States, this state, or the political subdivision of this state that has custody of the vehicle. The letters or emblem must be of a color sufficiently different from the body of the vehicle to be clearly legible from a distance of 100 feet.

(b) The department may not issue exempt license plates for a vehicle owned by a person other than the United States, this state, or a political subdivision of this state unless, when application is made for registration of the vehicle, the person who under Section 502.202 has authority to certify to the department that the vehicle qualifies for registration under that section also certifies in writing to the department that the name of the owner of the vehicle is printed on the vehicle in the manner prescribed by Subsection (a).

(c) A peace officer listed in Article 2.12, Code of Criminal Procedure, may seize a motor vehicle displaying exempt license plates if the vehicle is:

(1) operated on a public highway; and

(2) not identified in the manner prescribed by Subsection (a) or (b), unless the vehicle is covered by Subsection (f).

(d) A peace officer who seizes a motor vehicle under Subsection (c) may require that the vehicle be:

(1) moved to the nearest place of safety off the main-traveled part of the highway; or

(2) removed and placed in the nearest vehicle storage facility designated or maintained by the law enforcement agency that employs the peace officer.

(e) To obtain the release of the vehicle, in addition to any other requirement of law, the owner of a vehicle seized under Subsection (c) must:

(1) remedy the defect by identifying the vehicle as required by Subsection (a) or (b); or

(2) agree in writing with the law enforcement agency to provide evidence to that agency, before the 10th day after the date the vehicle is released, that the defect has been remedied by identifying the vehicle as required by Subsection (a) or (b).

(f) Subsections (a) and (b) do not apply to a vehicle to which Section 502.201(g) or 502.206 applies.

(g) For purposes of this section, an exempt license plate is a license plate issued by the department that is plainly marked with the word "exempt."

*(Added by L.1997, chaps. 165(30.50(a)), 485(2), eff. 9/1/97.)*

## §502.202. Government-owned vehicles; public school buses; fire-fighting vehicles; county marine law enforcement vehicles.

(a) The owner of a motor vehicle, trailer, or semitrailer may annually apply for registration under Section 502.201 and is exempt from the payment of a registration fee under this chapter if the vehicle is:

(1) owned by and used exclusively in the service of:

(A) the United States;

(B) this state; or

(C) a county, municipality, or school district in this state;

(2) owned by a commercial transportation company and used exclusively to provide public school transportation services to a school district under Section 34.008, Education Code;

(3) designed and used exclusively for fire fighting;

(4) owned by a volunteer fire department and used exclusively in the conduct of department business; or

(5) privately owned and used by a volunteer exclusively in county marine law enforcement activities, including rescue operations, under the direction of the sheriff's department.

(b) An application for registration under this section must be made by a person having the authority to certify that the vehicle meets the exemption requirements prescribed by Subsection (a). An application for registration under this section of a fire-fighting vehicle described by Subsection (a)(3) must include a reasonable description of the vehicle and of any fire-fighting equipment mounted on the vehicle. An application for registration under this section of a vehicle described by Subsection (a)(5) must include a statement signed by a person having the authority to act for a sheriff's department that the vehicle is used exclusively in marine law enforcement activities under the direction of the sheriff's department.

*(Added by L.1995, chap. 165(1); chgd. by L.1999, chap. 62(17.06), eff. 9/1/99.)*

## §502.203. Vehicles used by nonprofit disaster relief organizations.

(a) The owner of a commercial motor vehicle, trailer, or semitrailer may apply for registration under Section 502.201 and is exempt from the payment of the registration fee that would otherwise be required by this chapter if the vehicle is owned and used exclusively for emergencies by a nonprofit disaster relief organization.

(b) An application for registration under this section must include:

(1) a statement by the owner of the vehicle that the vehicle is used exclusively for emergencies;

(2) a statement by the sheriff of the county in which the vehicle is registered that the vehicle has not been used for any purpose other than emergencies; and

(3) a reasonable description of the vehicle and the emergency equipment included in the vehicle.

(c) An applicant for registration under this section must pay a fee of $5.

(d) A commercial motor vehicle registered under this section must display the name of the organization that owns it on each front door.

(e) A vehicle registered under this section must display at all times an appropriate license plate showing the vehicle's status.

(f) A vehicle registered under this section that is used for any purpose other than an emergency may not again be registered under this section.
*(Added by L.1995, chap. 165(1), eff. 9/1/95.)*

**§502.2035. Trailers and semitrailers owned by religious organizations.**

(a) A trailer or semitrailer may be registered without payment if the trailer or semitrailer is:

(1) owned by an organization that qualifies as a religious organization under Section 11.20, Tax Code; and

(2) used primarily for the purpose of transporting property in connection with the charitable activities and functions of the organization.

(b) An application for registration under this section must include a statement signed by an officer of the religious organization stating that the trailer or semitrailer qualifies for registration under this section.
*(Added by L.1999, chap. 1194(1), eff. 9/1/99.)*

**§502.204. Emergency services vehicles.**

(a) A vehicle may be registered without payment if:

(1) the vehicle is owned or leased by an emergency medical services provider that:

(A) is a nonprofit entity; or

(B) is created and operated by:

(i) a county;

(ii) a municipality; or

(iii) any combination of counties and municipalities through a contract, joint agreement, or other method provided by Chapter 791, Government Code, or other law authorizing counties and municipalities to provide joint programs; and

(2) the vehicle:

(A) is authorized under an emergency medical services provider license issued by the Texas Board of Health under Chapter 773, Health and Safety Code, and is used exclusively as an emergency medical services vehicle; or

(B) is an emergency medical services chief or supervisor vehicle and is used exclusively as an emergency services vehicle.

(b) A vehicle may be registered without payment of a registration fee if the vehicle:

(1) is owned by the Civil Air Patrol, Texas Wing; and

(2) is used exclusively as an emergency services vehicle by members of the Civil Air Patrol, Texas Wing.

(c) An application for registration under Subsection (a) must be accompanied by a copy of the license issued by the Texas Board of Health. An application for registration of an emergency medical services vehicle must include a statement signed by an officer of the emergency medical services provider that the vehicle is used exclusively as an emergency response vehicle and qualifies for registration under this section. An application for registration of an emergency medical services chief or supervisor vehicle must include a statement signed by an officer of the emergency medical services provider stating that the vehicle qualifies for registration under this section.

(d) An application for registration under Subsection (b) must include a statement signed by an officer of the Civil Air Patrol, Texas Wing, that the vehicle is used exclusively as an emergency services vehicle by members of the Civil Air Patrol, Texas Wing.

(e) The department must approve an application for registration under this section as provided by Section 502.201.
*(Added by L.1995, chap. 165(1), eff. 9/1/95.)*

**§502.205. All-terrain vehicles.**

(a) An all-terrain vehicle may be registered without payment of a registration fee if the vehicle:

(1) is owned by this state, a county, or a municipality; and

(2) is used exclusively to maintain public safety and welfare.

(b) An application for registration under this section must include a statement that is signed by an officer having the authority to certify for the agency, county, or municipality and that states that the vehicle is used exclusively to maintain the public safety and welfare.

(c) The department must approve an application for registration under this section as provided by Section 502.201.
*(Added by L.1995, chap. 165(1), eff. 9/1/95.)*

**§502.206. Registration of certain law enforcement vehicles under alias.**
On receipt of a written request approved by the executive administrator of a law enforcement agency, the department may issue exempt license plates for a vehicle and register the vehicle under an alias for the law enforcement agency's use in covert criminal investigations. *(Added by L.1995, chap. 165(1), eff. 9/1/95.)*

**§§502.207 to 502.250.** *(Reserved.)*

## SUBCHAPTER F. SPECIALIZED LICENSE PLATES; EXEMPTIONS FOR PRIVATELY OWNED VEHICLES

**§502.251. Personalized prestige license plates.**
(a) The department shall establish and issue personalized prestige license plates. The department may not issue identically lettered or numbered plates to more than one person.
(b) The department shall establish procedures for continuous application for and issuance of personalized prestige license plates. An owner must make a new application and pay a new fee for each registration period for which the owner seeks to obtain personalized prestige license plates. An owner who obtains personalized prestige license plates has first priority on those plates for each subsequent registration period for which the owner applies.
(c) The annual fee for personalized prestige license plates is $40, in addition to the registration fee otherwise prescribed by this chapter.
(d) The department may issue to an applicant only one set of personalized prestige license plates for a vehicle for a six-year period. The department may issue a new set of personalized prestige license plates within the six-year period if the applicant pays a fee of $50 in addition to the fees required by Subsection (c) for the registration period.
(e) On application and payment of the required fee for a registration period following the issuance of the plates, the department shall issue a registration insignia as provided by Section 502.180.
(f) Of each fee collected by the department under this section:
(1) $1.25 shall be deposited to the credit of the state highway fund to defray the cost of administering this section; and
(2) the remainder shall be deposited to the credit of the general revenue fund.
*(Added by L.1995, chap. 165(1), eff. 9/1/95.)*

**§502.252. Certain specialized plates available personalized.**
A person applying for license plates under Section 502.2555, 502.258, 502.259, 502.260, 502.261, 502.262, 502.263, 502.264, 502.265, 502.269, 502.270, 502.271, 502.272, 502.273, 502.2731, 502.274, 502.289, 502.291, or 502.294 may:
(1) have a license plate number assigned by the department; or
(2) apply for personalized prestige license plates under Section 502.251.
*(Added by L.1995, chap. 165(1); chgd. by L.1997, chaps. 165(30.51(a)), 625(7), 1258(2), eff. 9/1/97.)*

**§502.2525. Discontinuance of certain specialized license plates.**
(a) This section applies only to license plates authorized by:
(1) Section 502.269;
(2) Section 502.270;
(3) Section 502.2703;
(4) Section 502.271;
(5) Section 502.272;
(6) Section 502.2731;
(7) Section 502.291, as added by Chapter 165, Acts of the 75th Legislature, Regular Session, 1997;
(8) Section 502.291, as added by Chapter 657, Acts of the 75th Legislature, Regular Session, 1997;
(9) Section 502.292, as added by Chapter 61, Acts of the 75th Legislature, Regular Session, 1997;
(10) Section 502.292, as added by Chapter 397, Acts of the 75th Legislature, Regular Session, 1997;
(11) Section 502.293, as added by Chapter 511, Acts of the 75th Legislature, Regular Session, 1997;

Printed in the U.S.A. 21

(12) Section 502.293, as added by Chapter 1247, Acts of the 75th Legislature, Regular Session, 1997;

(13) Section 502.294, as added by Chapter 1222, Acts of the 75th Legislature, Regular Session, 1997; or

(14) Section 502.295, as added by Chapter 581, Acts of the 75th Legislature, Regular Session, 1997.

(b) Except as provided by Subsections (d) and (e), on or after September 1, 2004, the department may continue to issue license plates to which this section applies only if before that date at least:

(1) 3,500 sets of the license plates authorized by a section of this subchapter specified by Subsection (a) have been issued or presold;

(2) $15,000 has been received by the department from the issuance of license plates under that section; or

(3) $15,000 has been deposited with the department for the continued issuance of those license plates.

(c) If before September 1, 2004, one of the conditions described by Subsection (b) is not met for a type of license plate to which this section applies, the section of this subchapter that authorizes the issuance of that type of license plate expires on that date.

(d) On or after September 1, 2004, the department may continue to issue license plates under:

(1) Section 502.270 for a particular institution of higher education or private college or university only if before that date:

(A) 1,500 sets of license plates for the particular institution, college, or university have been issued or presold;

(B) $15,000 has been received by the department from the issuance of the license plates for that institution, college, or university; or

(C) $15,000 has been deposited with the department for the continued issuance of the license plates for that institution, college, or university; or

(2) Section 502.2703 for a particular professional sports team only if before that date:

(A) 5,000 sets of the license plates for that sports team have been issued or presold;

(B) $15,000 has been received by the department from the issuance of license plates for that sports team; or

(C) $15,000 has been deposited with the department for the continued issuance of license plates for that sports team.

(e) If before September 1, 2004, the department has not issued any license plates under Section 502.2703, that section expires on that date.

(f) Money deposited with the department under Subsection (b)(3), (d)(1)(C), or (d)(2)(C) shall be returned by the department to the person who made the deposit only after the requisite number of license plates under those subsections are issued or presold.

*(Added by L.1999, chap. 951(1), eff. 8/30/99.)*

### §502.2526. Specialized license plates authorized after January 1, 1999.

(a) This section applies only to specialized license plates that are authorized to be issued by a law that takes effect on or after January 1, 1999.

(b) The department may manufacture the specialized license plates only if a request for manufacture of the license plates is filed with the department. The request must be:

(1) made on a form adopted by the department;

(2) filed before the fifth anniversary of the effective date of the law that authorizes the issuance of the specialized license plates; and

(3) accompanied by:

(A) a deposit of $15,000; or

(B) applications for issuance of at least 3,500 sets of the license plates plus the fees for issuance of that number of sets.

(c) Money deposited with the department under Subsection (b)(3)(A) shall be returned to the person who made the deposit only if 3,500 sets of the applicable license plates are issued or presold.

(d) If a request is not filed with the department before the date specified by Subsection (b)(2), the law that authorizes the issuance of the specialized license plates expires on that date.

*(Added by L.1999, chap. 951(1), eff. 8/30/99.)*

### §502.253. Persons with disabilities.

(a) The department shall provide for the issuance of specially designed license plates for motorcycles, passenger cars, and light trucks regularly operated for noncommercial use by or for the transportation of a person with a permanent disability.

(b) In this section:

(1) "Disability" and "mobility problem that substantially impairs a person's ability to ambulate" have the meanings assigned by Section 681.001.

(2) "Legally blind" means a condition described by Section 681.001(2)(B) or (C).

(c) An owner of a motor vehicle regularly operated by or for the transportation of a person described by Subsection (b) may apply to the department for registration under this section.

(d) An application for registration under this section must:

(1) be on a form prescribed by the department;

(2) be submitted to the assessor-collector of the county in which the person resides; and

(3) be accompanied by the regular registration fee for the vehicle being registered.

(e) The first application for registration must be accompanied by a written statement of a physician licensed to practice medicine in this state or a state adjacent to this state, or authorized by applicable law to practice medicine in a hospital or other health facility of the Veterans Administration, certifying to the department that the person making the application or on whose behalf the application is made is legally blind or has a mobility problem that substantially impairs the person's ability to ambulate. The statement must include a certification of whether a mobility problem, if applicable, is temporary or permanent. A written statement from a physician is not required as acceptable medical proof if:

(1) the person with a disability:

(A) has had a limb, hand, or foot amputated; or

(B) must use a wheelchair; and

(2) the applicant and the county assessor-collector issuing the special license plates execute an affidavit attesting to the person's disability.

(f) A person with a disability may receive:

(1) one disabled parking placard under Section 681.002, if the person receives a set of special license plates under this section; or

(2) two disabled parking placards under Section 681.002, if the person does not receive a set of license plates under this section.

(g) A license plate issued under this section must include the symbol of access adopted by Rehabilitation International in 1969 at its Eleventh World Congress on Rehabilitation of the Disabled. The symbol must be the same size as the numbers on the license plates.

(h) A person entitled to register a vehicle under this section is entitled to a set of special license plates under this section for each motorcycle, passenger car, or light truck owned by the person that is equipped with special equipment that:

(1) is designed to allow a person who has lost the use of one or both of the person's legs to operate the vehicle; and

(2) is not standard equipment on that type of vehicle for use by a person who has use of both of the person's legs.

*(Added by L.1995, chap. 165(1); chgd. by L.1997, chaps. 165(30.52), 632(1); L.1999, chap. 1172(1), eff. 6/18/99.)*

### §502.2531. Issuance of disabled plates to certain institutions.

(a) The department shall provide for the issuance of the specially designed license plates under Section 502.253 for a van or bus operated by an institution, facility, or residential retirement community for the elderly in which a person described by Section 502.253(b) resides, including an institution licensed under Chapter 242, Health and Safety Code, and a facility licensed under Chapter 246 or 247 of that code.

(b) The application for registration must be made in the manner provided by Section 502.253(d) and be accompanied by a written statement signed by the administrator or manager of the institution, facility, or retirement community certifying to the department that the institution or facility regularly transports, as a part of the services that the institution, facility, or retirement community provides, one or more persons described by Section 502.253(b) who reside in the institution, facility, or retirement community. The department shall determine the eligibility of the institution, facility, or retirement community on the evidence the applicant provides.

*(Added by L.1999, chap. 513(1), eff. 9/1/99.)*

## §502.254. Veterans with disabilities.

(a) The department shall issue special license plates for passenger cars and light trucks that are owned by veterans of the United States armed forces. A veteran is entitled to register, for the person's own use, two passenger cars or light trucks under this section if the person:

(1) has suffered, as a result of military service:

(A) at least a 60 percent service-connected disability; or

(B) a 40 percent service-connected disability because of the amputation of a lower extremity; and

(2) receives compensation from the United States because of the disability.

(b) An organization may register a motor vehicle under this section if:

(1) the vehicle is used exclusively to transport veterans of the United States armed forces who have suffered, as a result of military service, a service-connected disability; and

(2) the veterans are not charged for the transportation.

(c) License plates issued under this section must include:

(1) the letters "DV" as a prefix or suffix to the numerals on the plate; and

(2) the words "DISABLED VET."

(d) An application for registration under this section must be on a form provided by the department and be accompanied by the fee prescribed by Subsection (g) and evidence required by the department that the applicant may register under this section.

(e) A statement by the veterans county service officer of the county in which a vehicle is registered or by the Veterans Administration that a vehicle is used exclusively to transport veterans with disabilities without charge to them is satisfactory evidence that an organization may register under Subsection (b).

(f) A license plate issued under this section becomes invalid and the owner shall return the license plate to the department for cancellation when:

(1) the owner disposes of the vehicle during the registration year; or

(2) the organization ceases to use the vehicle exclusively to transport veterans with disabilities.

(g) The fee for issuance of license plates under this section is:

(1) $3 for the first set of license plates; and

(2) the applicable annual fee prescribed by Section 502.161 for each additional set of license plates.

(h) If a plate is canceled under Subsection (f)(1), the owner may then register another vehicle under this section without charge.

(i) The department may adopt rules to administer this section.

*(Added by L.1995, chap. 165(1); chgd. by L.1997, chap. 370(1); L.1999, chap. 993(1), eff. 9/1/99.)*

## §502.255. Congressional Medal of Honor recipients.

(a) A recipient of a Congressional Medal of Honor awarded under Title 10, United States Code, is entitled to register, for the person's own use, one passenger car or light truck without payment of a registration fee or service charge.

(b) The department shall issue specially designed license plates for registration under this section. The department shall assign the license plate number.

(c) A person may apply to the department at any time for registration under this section on a form prescribed by the department. The department shall require an applicant to submit proof of eligibility for registration under this section.

(d) Registration under this section is valid for one year. A person who has registered a vehicle and obtained license plates under this section may renew the registration of the vehicle without charge by applying to the county assessor-collector of the county of the person's residence for an annual registration insignia.

(e) If the owner of a vehicle registered under this section disposes of the vehicle during the registration year, the owner shall return the special license plates to the department. The owner may then register another vehicle under this section without charge.

*(Added by L.1995, chap. 165(1), eff. 9/1/95.)*

## §502.2555. Air Force Cross or Distinguished Service Cross, Army Distinguished Service Cross, Navy Cross, or Medal of Honor recipients.

(a) The department shall issue specially designed license plates for passenger cars and light trucks owned by recipients of the Air Force Cross or Distinguished Service Cross, the Army Distinguished Service Cross, the Navy Cross, or the Medal of Honor.

(b) License plates issued under this section must include the words "Legion of Valor."

(c) The department shall issue license plates under this section to a person who:

(1) applies to the department on a form prescribed by the department;

(2) pays an annual fee of $3;

(3) submits proof that the person has been awarded the Air Force Cross or Distinguished Service Cross, the Army Distinguished Service Cross, the Navy Cross, or the Medal of Honor; and

(4) submits proof that the person is:

(A) an honorably discharged veteran of the United States armed forces; or

(B) a member of the United States armed forces on active duty.

(d) The department shall send 50 cents of each fee collected under this section to the county treasury of the county in which the applicant resides. The county treasurer shall credit money received under this section to the general fund of the county to pay the costs of administering this section.

(e) A vehicle for which license plates are issued under this section is exempt from the fee under Section 502.161.

(f) A person may be issued only one set of license plates under this section.

(g) If the owner of a vehicle registered under this section disposes of the vehicle during the registration year, the owner shall return the special license plates to the department. The owner may then apply for issuance of those plates to another vehicle.

*(Added by L.1997, chap. 165(30.53(a)), eff. 9/1/97.)*

## §502.256. Members of Texas National Guard, State Guard, or United States armed forces reserves.

(a) The department shall issue special license plates for passenger cars and light trucks owned by:

(1) active members of the Texas National Guard and Texas State Guard;

(2) retired members of the Texas National Guard and Texas State Guard who have completed 20 years of satisfactory federal service; or

(3) members of a reserve component of the United States armed forces.

(b) The department and the adjutant general must agree on the design and color of license plates issued under this section. The license plates must include the words "Texas Guard" or "Armed Forces Reserve," as applicable.

(c) A person may apply to the department at any time for registration under this section on a form prescribed by the department. The department shall require an applicant to submit proof of eligibility for registration under this section. A letter from the United States Department of Defense, the Department of the Army, or the Department of the Air Force stating that a retired guard member has 20 years of satisfactory federal service is proof of eligibility for registration under this section.

(d) The fee for registration under this section and issuance of the special license plates is the fee otherwise prescribed by this chapter for the vehicle.

(e) Registration under this section is valid for one registration year.

(f) The owner of a vehicle registered under this section shall return the special license plates to the department if the owner:

(1) disposes of the vehicle during the registration year;

(2) ceases to be an active member of the Texas National Guard or Texas State Guard; or

(3) ceases to be a member of a reserve component of the United States armed forces.

*(Added by L.1995, chap. 165(1), eff. 9/1/95.)*

## §502.257. Former prisoners of war.

(a) A person is entitled to register, for the person's own use, one passenger car or light truck without payment of a registration fee if the person:

(1) was captured and incarcerated by an enemy of the United States during a period of conflict with the United States; and

(2) was not discharged from the United States armed forces under conditions less than honorable.

(b) The department shall issue specially designed license plates for registration under this section. The license plates must show that the recipient is a former prisoner of war.

(c) A person may apply to the department at any time for registration under this section on a form prescribed by the department. The department shall require an applicant to submit proof of eligibility for registration under this section.

(d) The fee for issuance of license plates under this section is $3.

(e) Registration under this section is valid for one year. A person who has registered a vehicle and obtained license plates under this section may renew the registration of the vehicle by apply-

Printed in the U.S.A. 17

ing to the county assessor-collector of the county of the individual's residence for an annual registration insignia.

(f) If the owner of a vehicle registered under this section disposes of the vehicle during the registration year, the owner shall return the special license plates to the department. The owner may then register another vehicle under this section without charge.
*(Added by L.1995, chap. 165(1), eff. 9/1/95.)*

## §502.258. Members or former members of United States armed forces.

(a) The department shall issue specially designed license plates for passenger cars and light trucks owned by active, retired, or honorably discharged members of the United States armed forces.

(b) License plates issued under this section must include the designation of the appropriate branch of the United States armed forces.

(c) The department shall issue license plates under this section to a person who:

(1) applies to the department on a form prescribed by the department;

(2) pays the annual fee prescribed by Subsection (e), in addition to the fee prescribed by Section 502.161, and, if personalized prestige license plates are issued, in addition to the fee prescribed by Section 502.251; and

(3) submits proof that the person is eligible under this section.

(d) The department shall send 50 cents of each fee collected under this section to the county treasurer of the county in which the applicant resides. The county treasurer shall credit money received under this section to the general fund of the county to pay the costs of administering this section.

(e) The annual fee for issuance of license plates under this section is:

(1) $10 for the first set of license plates; and

(2) $15 for each additional set of license plates.

(f) If the owner of a vehicle registered under this section disposes of the vehicle during the registration year, the owner shall return the special license plates to the department. The owner may then apply for issuance of those plates to another vehicle.
*(Added by L.1995, chap. 165(1); chgd. by L.1997, chap. 165(30.54 (a), (b)), eff. 9/1/97.)*

## §502.2585. Persons retired from service in merchant marine of the United States.

(a) The department shall issue specially designed license plates for passenger cars and light trucks owned by persons retired from service in the merchant marine of the United States.

(b) License plates issued under this section must include the words "merchant marine."

(c) The department shall issue license plates under this section to a person who:

(1) applies to the department on a form prescribed by the department;

(2) pays an annual fee of $10 in addition to the fee prescribed by Section 502.161 and, if personalized prestige license plates are issued, in addition to the fee prescribed by Section 502.251; and

(3) submits proof that the person is eligible under this section.

(d) The department shall send 50 cents of each fee collected under this section to the county treasurer of the county in which the applicant resides. The county treasurer shall credit money received under this section to the general fund of the county to pay the costs of administering this section.

(e) A person may be issued only one set of license plates under this section.

(f) If the owner of a vehicle registered under this section disposes of the vehicle during the registration year, the owner shall return the special license plates to the department. The owner may then apply for issuance of those plates to another vehicle.
*(Added by L.1999, chap. 991(1), eff. 9/1/99.)*

## §502.259. Pearl Harbor survivors.

(a) The department shall issue specially designed license plates for passenger cars and light trucks owned by survivors of the attack on Pearl Harbor on December 7, 1941.

(b) License plates issued under this section must include the words "Pearl Harbor Survivor" and must be consecutively numbered.

(c) The department shall issue license plates under this section to a person who:

(1) applies to the department on a form prescribed by the department;

(2) pays an annual fee of:

(A) $3 for the first set of license plates issued under this section; and

(B) $15 for each additional set of license plates issued under this section; and

(3) submits proof that the person:

(A) served in the United States armed forces;
(B) was stationed in the Hawaiian Islands on December 7, 1941; and
(C) survived the attack on Pearl Harbor on December 7, 1941.

(d) The department shall send 50 cents of each fee collected under this section to the county treasurer of the county in which the applicant resides. The county treasurer shall credit money received under this section to the general fund of the county to pay the costs of administering this section.

(e) A person who registers one or more vehicles under this section is entitled to only one exemption from the fee under Section 502.161.

(f) If the owner of a vehicle registered under this section disposes of the vehicle during the registration year, the owner shall return the special license plates to the department. The owner may then apply for issuance of those plates to another vehicle.
*(Added by L.1995, chap. 165(1); chgd. by L.1997, chap. 165(30.54(c)), eff. 9/1/97.)*

## §502.260. Purple Heart recipients.

(a) The department shall issue specially designed license plates for passenger cars and light trucks owned by recipients of the Purple Heart.

(b) License plates issued under this section must include:
(1) the Purple Heart emblem;
(2) the words "Purple Heart" at the bottom of each plate; and
(3) the letters "PH" as a prefix or suffix to the numerals on the plate, if numbered plates are used.

(c) The department shall issue license plates under this section to a person who:
(1) applies to the department on a form prescribed by the department;
(2) pays an annual fee of:
(A) $3 for the first set of license plates issued under this section; and
(B) $15 for each additional set of license plates issued under this section; and
(3) submits proof that the person has been awarded the Purple Heart and is:
(A) an honorably discharged veteran of the United States armed forces;
(B) a member of the United States armed forces on active duty; or
(C) a civilian national of the United States who is an employee or a former employee of a branch of the United States armed forces.

(d) The department shall send 50 cents of each fee collected under this section to the county treasurer of the county in which the applicant resides. The county treasurer shall credit money received under this section to the general fund of the county to pay the costs of administering this section.

(e) A person who registers one or more vehicles under this section is entitled to only one exemption from the fee under Section 502.161.

(f) If the owner of a vehicle registered under this section disposes of the vehicle during the registration year, the owner shall return the special license plates to the department. The owner may then apply for issuance of those plates to another vehicle.
*(Added by L.1995, chap. 165(1); chgd. by L.1997, chaps. 165(30.54(d)), 625(8), eff. 9/1/97.)*

## §502.261. Members of United States armed forces auxiliaries.

(a) The department shall issue specially designed license plates for passenger cars and light trucks owned by members of:
(1) the United States Air Force Auxiliary, Civil Air Patrol;
(2) the United States Coast Guard Auxiliary; or
(3) the Marine Corps League or its auxiliary.

(b) License plates issued under this section to members of the Civil Air Patrol must include the words "Texas Wing Civil Air Patrol." License plates issued under this section to members of the Coast Guard Auxiliary must include the words "Coast Guard Auxiliary." License plates issued under this section to members of the Marine Corps League or its auxiliary must include the words "Marine Corps League" and the emblem of the Marine Corps League.

(c) The department shall issue license plates under this section to a person who:
(1) applies to the department on a form prescribed by the department;
(2) pays the annual fee prescribed by Subsection (e), in addition to the fee prescribed by Section 502.161, and, if personalized prestige license plates are issued, in addition to the fee prescribed by Section 502.251; and
(3) submits proof that the person is eligible under this section.

(d) The department shall send 50 cents of each fee collected under this section to the county treasurer of the county in which the applicant resides. The county treasurer shall credit money received under this section to the general fund of the county to pay the costs of administering this section.

(e) The annual fee for issuance of license plates under this section is:

(1) $10 for the first set of license plates; and

(2) $15 for each additional set of license plates.

(f) If the owner of a vehicle registered under this section disposes of the vehicle during the registration year, the owner shall return the special license plates to the department. The owner may then apply for issuance of those plates to another vehicle.

*(Added by L.1995, chap. 165(1); chgd. by L.1997, chap. 165(30.54(e)), eff. 9/1/97.)*

**§502.262. World war II veterans.**

(a) The department shall issue specially designed license plates for passenger cars and light trucks owned by persons who served in the United States armed forces after December 6, 1941, and before January 1, 1947.

(b) License plates issued under this section must include the words "WWII Veteran."

(c) The department shall issue license plates under this section to a person who:

(1) applies to the department on a form prescribed by the department;

(2) pays the fee prescribed by Section 502.161, and, if personalized prestige license plates are issued, the fee prescribed by Section 502.251; and

(3) submits proof that the person:

(A) served in the United States armed forces after December 6, 1941, and before January 1, 1947; and

(B) is an honorably discharged veteran of the United States armed forces.

(d) If the owner of a vehicle registered under this section disposes of the vehicle during the registration year, the owner shall return the special license plates to the department. The owner may then apply for issuance of those plates to another vehicle.

*(Added by L.1995, chap. 165(1); chgd. by L.1997, chap. 165(30.54(f)); L.1999, chap. 1249(1), eff. 9/1/99.)*

**§502.263. Korean War veterans.**

(a) The department shall issue specially designed license plates for passenger cars and light trucks owned by persons who served in the United States armed forces after June 26, 1950, and before February 1, 1955.

(b) License plates issued under this section must include the words "Korea Veteran."

(c) The department shall issue license plates under this section to a person who:

(1) applies to the department on a form prescribed by the department;

(2) pays the fee prescribed by Section 502.161, and, if personalized prestige license plates are issued, the fee prescribed by Section 502.251; and

(3) submits proof that the person:

(A) served in the United States armed forces after June 26, 1950, and before February 1, 1955; and

(B) is an honorably discharged veteran of the United States armed forces.

(d) If the owner of a vehicle registered under this section disposes of the vehicle during the registration year, the owner shall return the special license plates to the department. The owner may then apply for issuance of those plates to another vehicle.

*(Added by L.1995, chap. 165(1); chgd. by L.1997, chap. 165(30.54(g)); L.1999, chaps. 590(1), 1249(1), eff. 6/18/99, 9/1/99, respectively.)*

**§502.264. Vietnam veterans.**

(a) The department shall issue specially designed license plates for passenger cars and light trucks owned by persons who served in the United States armed forces after August 4, 1964, and before May 8, 1975.

(b) License plates issued under this section must include the words "Vietnam Veteran."

(c) The department shall issue license plates under this section to a person who:

(1) applies to the department on a form prescribed by the department;

(2) pays the fee prescribed by Section 502.161, and, if personalized prestige license plates are issued, the fee prescribed by Section 502.251; and

(3) submits proof that the person served in the United States armed forces after August 4, 1964, and before May 8, 1975, and is:

(A) an honorably discharged veteran of the United States armed forces; or

(B) a member of the United States armed forces on active duty.

(d) If the owner of a vehicle registered under this section disposes of the vehicle during the registration year, the owner shall return the special license plates to the department. The owner may then apply for issuance of those plates to another vehicle.

*(Added by L.1995, chap. 165(1); chgd. by L.1997, chap. 165(30.54(h)); L.1999, chap. 1249(1), eff. 9/1/99.)*

## §502.265. Desert Shield or Desert Storm veterans.

(a) The department shall issue specially designed license plates for passenger cars and light trucks owned by persons who served in the United States armed forces and were deployed to the Middle East, where they participated in Operation Desert Shield or Desert Storm.

(b) License plates issued under this section must include the words "Desert Storm."

(c) The department shall issue license plates under this section to a person who:

(1) applies to the department on a form prescribed by the department;

(2) pays the fee prescribed by Section 502.161, and, if personalized prestige license plates are issued, the fee prescribed by Section 502.251; and

(3) submits proof that the person:

(A) served in the United States armed forces and was deployed to the Middle East, where the person participated in Operation Desert Shield or Desert Storm; and

(B) is:

(i) an honorably discharged veteran of the United States armed forces or reserve component of the United States armed forces; or

(ii) a member of the United States armed forces, the Texas National Guard, or a reserve component of the United States armed forces.

(d) If the owner of a vehicle registered under this section disposes of the vehicle during the registration year, the owner shall return the special license plates to the department. The owner may then apply for issuance of those plates to another vehicle.

*(Added by L.1995, chap. 165(1); chgd. by L.1997, chap. 165(30.54(i)); L.1999, chap. 1249(1), eff. 9/1/99.)*

## §502.266. Surviving spouses of certain military veterans.

(a) The surviving spouse of a person who would be eligible for license plates under Section 502.254 is entitled to continue to register one motor vehicle under that section as long as the spouse remains unmarried.

(b) The surviving spouse of a person who would be eligible for license plates under Section 502.2555 is entitled to register one motor vehicle under that section as long as the spouse remains unmarried.

(c) The surviving spouse of a person who would be eligible for license plates under Section 502.257 is entitled to register one motor vehicle under that section as long as the spouse remains unmarried.

(d) The surviving spouse of a person who was killed in action while serving in the United States armed forces is entitled to register one or more motor vehicles under Section 502.258 as long as the spouse remains unmarried.

(e) The surviving spouse of a person who would be eligible for license plates under Section 502.259 or 502.260 is eligible to register one or more motor vehicles under that section as long as the spouse remains unmarried.

(f) The surviving spouse of a person who would be eligible for license plates under Section 502.264 is eligible to register one or more motor vehicles under that section.

(g) An applicant for registration under this section must submit proof of the eligibility of the applicant's deceased spouse for registration under Section 502.254, 502.2555, 502.257, 502.258, 502.259, 502.260, or 502.264, as applicable.

(h) The county assessor-collector shall require an applicant for registration under this section to make a statement that the spouse is unmarried. The statement must be sworn if the spouse renews a registration under Section 502.257, 502.259, or 502.260.

*(Added by L.1995, chap. 165(1); chgd. by L.1997, chaps. 165(30.54(j)), 625(9); L.1999, chap. 530(1), eff. 9/1/99.)*

## §502.2661. Gold Star Mothers.

(a) The department shall issue specially designed license plates for a passenger car or light truck owned by a mother of a person who died while serving in the United States armed forces.

(b) License plates issued under this section must include the words "Gold Star Mother" and a gold star.

(c) The department shall issue license plates under this section to a person who:

(1) applies to the department on a form prescribed by the department;

(2) pays an annual fee of $10, in addition to the fee prescribed by Section 502.161 or 502.162, and, if personalized prestige license plates are issued, in addition to the fee prescribed by Section 502.251; and

(3) submits proof that the person is eligible under this section.

(d) The department shall send 50 cents of each fee collected under this section to the county treasurer of the county in which the applicant resides. The county treasurer shall credit money received under this section to the general fund of the county to pay the costs of administering this section. The remainder of each fee collected under this section shall be deposited to the credit of the state highway fund.

(e) A person may be issued only one set of license plates under this section.

(f) If the owner of a vehicle registered under this section disposes of the vehicle during the registration year, the owner shall return the special license plates to the department. The owner may then apply for issuance of those plates to another vehicle.

*(Added by L.1997, chap. 1312(1); renumbered from section 502.292 by L.1999, chap. 62(19.01(103)), eff. 9/1/99.)*

## §502.2663. New millennium license plates.

(a) The department shall issue specially designed new millennium license plates for passenger cars and light trucks.

(b) The license plates must bear the words "New Millennium" and be of a color, quality, and design approved by the department from entries submitted by middle school students in a competition conducted by the department.

(c) The department shall issue license plates under this section to a person who:

(1) applies to the assessor-collector of the county in which the person resides on the form for original registration or annual renewal of registration provided by the department; and

(2) pays an annual fee in the amount set under Subsection (d), in addition to the fee prescribed by Section 502.161 and, if personalized prestige license plates are issued, in addition to the fee prescribed by Section 502.251.

(d) The department shall set the annual fee for license plates under this section at:

(1) an amount, not to exceed $5, necessary to administer this section; and

(2) an additional amount of:

(A) $25 for each set of plates, except as provided by Paragraph (B); or

(B) $15 for each set of plates, if the person is purchasing plates under this section for a fleet of 50 or more vehicles.

(e) The fee collected under Subsection (d)(1) may be used only to defray the cost of administering this section.

(f) The department shall deposit each fee collected under Subsection (d)(2) to the credit of an account in the general revenue fund to be known as the new millennium reading program account. Money from the account may be used only to make grants under Section 441.0092, Government Code. The account is composed of:

(1) money required to be deposited to the credit of the account under this subsection; and

(2) donations made to the account.

*(Added by L.1999, chap. 763(1), eff. 9/1/99.)*

## §502.267. Honorary consuls.

(a) The department shall issue special license plates for passenger cars and light trucks owned by persons who are honorary consuls authorized by the United States to perform consular duties.

(b) License plates issued under this section must include the words "Honorary Consul."

(c) A person may apply to the department at any time for registration under this section on a form prescribed by the department. The department shall require an applicant to submit proof of eligibility for registration under this section.

(d) The fee for registration under this section and issuance of the special license plates is the fee otherwise prescribed by this chapter for the vehicle plus an additional fee equal to the fee imposed under Section 502.251 for personalized prestige license plates.

(e) Registration under this section is valid for one registration year.

(f) The owner of a vehicle registered under this section shall return the special license plates to the department if the owner:

(1) disposes of the vehicle during the registration year; or

(2) ceases to be authorized to perform consular duties.

*(Added by L.1995, chap. 165(1), eff. 9/1/95.)*

### §502.268. Volunteer firefighters.

(a) The department shall issue specially designed license plates for passenger cars and light trucks owned by volunteer firefighters certified by:

(1) the Texas Commission on Fire Protection; or

(2) the State Firemen's and Fire Marshals' Association of Texas.

(b) A person may apply at any time for registration under this section to the department through the county assessor-collector of the county in which the person resides. The department shall prescribe the form of the application. The department shall require an applicant to submit satisfactory proof of eligibility under this section.

(c) The fee for registration under this section and issuance of the special license plates is the fee otherwise prescribed by this chapter for the vehicle plus an additional fee of $4. The county assessor-collector shall send the additional fee to the department to defray the cost of providing the special license plates.

(d) Registration under this section is valid for one registration year.

(e) A person may register, for the person's own use, only one vehicle under this section.

(f) The owner of a vehicle registered under this section shall return the special license plates to the department if the owner disposes of the vehicle during the registration year. The owner may then register another vehicle under this section.

*(Added by L.1995, chap. 165(1); chgd. by L.1999, chap. 818(1), eff. 9/1/99.)*

### §502.269. Texas Capitol license plates.

(a) The department shall issue specially designed license plates depicting the State Capitol for passenger cars and light trucks.

(b) The department shall issue license plates under this section to a person who:

(1) applies to the department on a form prescribed by the department; and

(2) pays an annual fee of $30, in addition to the fee prescribed by Section 502.161, and, if personalized prestige license plates are issued, in addition to the fee prescribed by Section 502.251.

(c) The department shall send 50 cents of each fee collected under this section to the county treasurer of the county in which the applicant resides. The county treasurer shall credit money received under this section to the general fund of the county to pay the costs of administering this section.

(d) The department shall deposit $25 of each fee collected under this section in the general revenue fund.

*(Added by L.1995, chap. 165(1), eff. 9/1/95.)*

### §502.270. Collegiate license plates.

(a) The department shall issue for passenger cars and light trucks specially designed license plates that include the name and insignia of:

(1) an institution of higher education as defined by Section 61.003(8), Education Code; or

(2) a private college or university described by Section 61.222, Education Code.

(b) The department may not issue a license plate under this section for a particular institution unless the institution:

(1) certifies to the department that it has determined that at least 1,500 persons will apply for the plates; and

(2) approves the design of the license plates, including the name, insignia, color, and quality.

(c) Except as provided by Subsection (b), the department shall issue license plates under this section to a person who:

(1) applies to the county assessor-collector of the county in which the person resides on a form provided by the department; and

(2) pays an annual fee of $30, in addition to the fee prescribed by Section 502.161, and, if personalized prestige license plates are issued, in addition to the fee prescribed by Section 502.251.

(d) The department shall send $25 of each fee collected under this section to the comptroller for deposit in the general revenue fund. If the fee is for the issuance of license plates described by Subsection (a)(1), the money shall be deposited to the credit of the institution of higher education designated on the license plates. If the fee is for the issuance of license plates described by Subsection (a)(2), the money shall be deposited to the credit of the Texas Higher Education Coordinating Board.

(e) Money deposited under Subsection (d) may be used only for scholarships to students who demonstrate a need for financial assistance under Texas Higher Education Coordinating Board rule.

(f) Money deposited for the issuance of license plates described by Subsection (a)(1) is supplementary and is not income for purposes of reducing general revenue appropriations to the institution of higher education designated on the license plates.

(g) Money deposited for the issuance of license plates described by Subsection (a)(2):

(1) shall be allocated to students at the college or university designated on the plates; and

(2) is in addition to other money that the board may allocate to that college or university.

(h) If the owner of a vehicle registered under this section disposes of the vehicle during the registration year, the owner shall return the special license plates to the department.

*(Added by L.1995, chap. 165(1); chgd. by L.1997, chap. 165(30.55), eff. 9/1/97.)*

## §502.2703. Professional sports team license plates.

(a) The department shall issue for passenger cars and light trucks specially designed license plates that include the name and insignia of a professional sports team located in this state.

(b) The department may not issue a license plate under this section for a particular professional sports team unless that team:

(1) certifies to the department that it has determined that at least 5,000 persons will apply for the plates; and

(2) plays its home games in a facility constructed or operated, in whole or in part, with public funds.

(c) Except as provided by Subsection (b), the department shall issue license plates under this section to a person who:

(1) applies to the county assessor-collector of the county in which the person resides on a form provided by the department; and

(2) pays an annual fee of $35, in addition to the fee prescribed by Section 502.161 and, if personalized prestige license plates are issued, in addition to the fee prescribed by Section 502.251.

(d) Of each fee collected under this section, the department shall:

(1) send $25 to the public entity that provided public funds for the construction or renovation of the facility in which the professional sports team plays its home games or that provides public funds for the operation of that facility; and

(2) deposit $10 to the credit of the state highway fund.

(e) Funds distributed to a public entity under Subsection (d)(1) shall be deposited to the credit of the venue project fund, if the public entity has created a venue project fund under Section 334.042 or 335.072, Local Government Code. If the public entity has not created a venue project fund, funds distributed to a public entity under Subsection (d)(1) must first be used to retire any public debt incurred by the public entity in the construction or acquisition of the facility in which the professional sports team plays its home games. After that debt is retired, funds distributed to the public entity may be spent only for maintenance or improvement of the facility.

(f) If the owner of a vehicle registered under this section disposes of the vehicle during the registration year, the owner shall return the special license plates to the department.

(g) In this section:

(1) "Public entity" includes a municipality, county, industrial development corporation, or special district that is authorized to plan, acquire, establish, develop, construct, or renovate a facility in which a professional sports team plays its home games.

(2) "Professional sports team" means a sports team that is a member or an affiliate of a member of the National Football League, National Basketball Association, or National Hockey League or a major league baseball team.

*(Added by L.1997, chap. 1171(1.44), eff. 9/1/97. If, before September 1, 2004, the department has not issued any license plates under Section 502.2703, this section expires on that date. See Section 502.2526.)*

## §502.2704. United States Olympic Committee license plates.

(a) The department shall issue specially designed United States Olympic Committee license plates for passenger cars and light trucks.

(b) The license plates must include the words "United States Olympic Committee" and be of a color, quality, and design approved by the United States Olympic Committee.

(c) The department shall issue license plates under this section to a person who:

(1) applies to the assessor-collector of the county in which the person resides on a form provided by the department; and

(2) pays an annual fee of $20, in addition to the fee prescribed by Section 502.161, and, if personalized prestige license plates are issued, in addition to the fee prescribed by Section 502.251.

(d) Of each fee collected under this section, the department shall deposit $10 to the credit of the state highway fund.

(e) If the owner of a vehicle registered under this section disposes of the vehicle during the registration year, the owner shall return the special license plates to the department.
*(Added by L.1997, chap. 165(30.62(a)); renumbered from section 502.291 by L.1999, chap. 62(19.01(101)), eff. 9/1/99.)*

### §502.271. Texas Aerospace Commission license plates.

(a) The department shall issue specially designed Texas Aerospace Commission license plates for passenger cars and light trucks.

(b) The license plates must include the name "Texas Aerospace Commission" and be of a color, quality, and design approved by the Texas Aerospace Commission.

(c) The department shall issue license plates under this section to a person who:

(1) applies to the county assessor-collector of the county in which the person resides on a form provided by the department; and

(2) pays an annual fee of $30, in addition to the fee prescribed by Section 502.161, and, if personalized prestige license plates are issued, in addition to the fee prescribed by Section 502.251.

(d) Of each fee collected under this section, the department shall deposit $25 under this section to the credit of the general revenue fund and $5 to the credit of the state highway fund.

(e) If the owner of a vehicle registered under this section disposes of the vehicle during the registration year, the owner shall return the special license plates to the department.
*(Added by L.1995, chap. 165(1), eff. 9/1/95.)*

### §502.272. Texas Commission on the Arts license plates.

(a) The department shall issue specially designed Texas Commission on the Arts license plates for passenger cars and light trucks.

(b) The license plates must include the words "State of the Arts" and be of a color, quality, and design approved by the Texas Commission on the Arts.

(c) The department shall issue license plates under this section to a person who:

(1) applies to the county assessor-collector of the county in which the person resides on a form provided by the department; and

(2) pays an annual fee of $25, in addition to the fee prescribed by Section 502.161, and, if personalized prestige license plates are issued, in addition to the fee prescribed by Section 502.251.

(d) The department shall deposit $20 of each fee collected under this section to the credit of the Texas Commission on the Arts operating fund established under Section 444.027, Government Code.

(e) The remainder of each fee collected under this section, after deposit as provided by Subsection (d), may be used only to defray the cost of administering this section.

(f) If the owner of a vehicle registered under this section disposes of the vehicle during the registration year, the owner shall return the special license plates to the department.
*(Added by L.1995, chap. 165(1), eff. 9/1/95.)*

### §502.2721. Texas Commission on Alcohol and Drug Abuse license plates.

(a) The department shall issue specially designed Texas Commission on Alcohol and Drug Abuse license plates for passenger cars and light trucks.

(b) The department shall design the license plates in consultation with the Boy Scouts of America.

(c) The department shall issue license plates under this section to a person who:

(1) applies to the county assessor-collector of the county in which the person resides on a form provided by the department; and

(2) pays an annual fee of $30, in addition to the fee prescribed by Section 502.161, and, if personalized prestige license plates are issued, in addition to the fee prescribed by Section 502.251.

(d) Of each fee collected under this section, the department shall deposit $20 to the credit of the general revenue fund and $10 to the credit of the state highway fund.

(e) Money deposited to the credit of the general revenue fund under Subsection (d) may be appropriated only to the Texas Commission on Alcohol and Drug Abuse for drug-abuse prevention programs provided by nonprofit organizations that primarily serve children. In selecting a program provider under this subsection, it is the intent of the legislature that to the extent permissible, a preference be given to a provider whose membership substantially consists of persons who purchase the specially designed license plates under this section.

(f) If the owner of a vehicle registered under this section disposes of the vehicle during the registration year, the owner shall return the special license plates to the department.
*(Added by L.1997, chaps. 1247(1), 1225(5); renumbered from sections 502.293 and 502.294 by L.1999, chap. 62(19.01(105)), eff. 9/1/99.)*

### §502.273. Private nonprofit organizations.

(a) The department shall issue specially designed license plates for passenger cars and light trucks owned by persons who are members of a private nonprofit organization that:

(1) has a statewide membership of at least 7,500 individuals;

(2) requests, through an authorized representative of the organization's governing body in the state, the issuance of license plates under this section;

(3) deposits $15,000 with the department; and

(4) provides the department with the names, addresses, and counties of residence of 750 members of the organization for whom the deposit may be credited to obtain the special license plates.

(b) The department shall design the license plate in consultation with the organization's governing body.

(c) The deposit made under Subsection (a)(3) shall be credited toward the purchase of license plates by the persons named under Subsection (a)(4).

(d) A person at any time after specialized license plates are authorized under this section may apply to the department through the county assessor-collector of the county in which the person resides for registration under this section. The department shall prescribe the form of the application. An applicant must submit to the assessor-collector proof of eligibility under this section that meets standards prescribed by the department.

(e) The annual fee for issuance of special license plates under this section is $25, in addition to the fee prescribed by Section 502.161, and, if personalized prestige license plates are issued, in addition to the fee prescribed by Section 502.251. The county assessor-collector shall send the additional fee to the department.

(f) Registration under this section is valid for one year.

(g) A person may register, for the person's own use, only one vehicle under this section.

(h) The owner of a vehicle registered under this section shall return the special license plates to the department if the owner disposes of the vehicle during the registration year.
*(Added by L.1995, chap. 165(1), eff. 9/1/95.)*

### §502.2731. Keep Texas Beautiful license plates.

(a) The department shall issue specially designed "Keep Texas Beautiful" license plates for passenger cars and light commercial motor vehicles having a manufacturer's rated carrying capacity of one ton or less. The license plates must include the words "Keep Texas Beautiful."

(b) The department shall design the license plate in consultation with Keep Texas Beautiful, Inc.

(c) The department shall issue license plates under this section to a person who:

(1) applies to the county assessor-collector of the county in which the person resides on a form provided by the department; and

(2) pays an annual fee of $25, in addition to the fee prescribed by Section 502.161 or Section 502.162 and, if personalized prestige license plates are issued, in addition to the fee prescribed by Section 502.251.

(d) The department shall deposit fees collected under this section in the state treasury to the credit of the state highway fund.

(e) Twenty dollars of each fee collected under Subsection (c)(2) may be used by the department only for the purposes of supporting the department's litter prevention and community beautification programs. The remainder of each fee collected may be used by the department only to defray the cost of administering this section.

(f) If license plates issued under this section are lost, stolen, or mutilated, the owner of the vehicle for which the license plates were issued may obtain replacement license plates from the department by paying a replacement fee of $5. If the owner of a vehicle for which license plates were issued under this section disposes of the vehicle during a registration year, the person shall return the special license plates to the department.

(g) There is no limit to the number of passenger cars and light commercial motor vehicles for which the person may apply for the issuance of license plates under this section.
*(Added by L.1997, chap. 1258(1); chgd. by L.1999, chap. 951(2), eff. 8/30/99.)*

### §502.2732. Big Bend National Park license plates.

(a) Except as provided by Subsection (b), the department shall issue specially designed license plates for passenger cars and light trucks to support the activities of a nonprofit organization designated by the Parks and Wildlife Department that has as its principal purpose the improvement or preservation of Big Bend National Park.

(b) The department is not required to issue license plates under this section unless the designated organization can establish a commitment for the purchase of at least 1,000 sets of the license plates.

(c) The license plates must bear one or more graphic images of significant features of Big Bend National Park designed by the Parks and Wildlife Department in consultation with the designated organization.

(d) The department shall issue license plates under this section to a person who:

(1) applies to the county assessor-collector of the county in which the person resides on a form provided by the department; and

(2) pays a fee of $50 for an original issuance of license plates under this section or $40 for a renewal of issuance of license plates under this section, in addition to the fee prescribed by Section 502.161 or 502.162, and, if personalized prestige license plates are issued, in addition to the fee prescribed by Section 502.251.

(e) The fee for replacement of a lost, stolen, or mutilated plate issued under this section is $35, in addition to the fee prescribed by Section 502.184(a).

(f) Of each fee collected under this section, $5 may be used to defray the cost of administering this section by the department and the Parks and Wildlife Department. The department shall deposit the remainder of each fee collected under this section to the credit of the Big Bend National Park account in the state treasury. Money in the account may be used only by the Parks and Wildlife Department to support the activities of a designated nonprofit organization whose primary purpose is the improvement or preservation of Big Bend National Park. The Parks and Wildlife Department shall establish reporting and other mechanisms necessary to ensure that the money is expended for purposes for which it is dedicated.

(g) If the owner of a vehicle registered under this section disposes of the vehicle during the registration year, the owner shall return the special license plates to the department.

*(Added by L.1997, chap. 581(1); renumbered from section 502.295 by L.1999, chap. 62(19.01(106)), eff. 9/1/99.)*

## §502.2733. Texas. It's Like A Whole Other Country license plates.

(a) The department shall issue specially designed "Texas. It's Like A Whole Other Country" license plates for passenger cars and light trucks.

(b) The license plates must include the trademarked Texas patch and the words "Texas. It's Like A Whole Other Country" and be of a color, quality, and design approved by the Texas Department of Economic Development.

(c) The department shall issue license plates under this section to a person who:

(1) applies to the county assessor-collector of the county in which the person resides on a form provided by the department; and

(2) pays an annual fee of $30, in addition to the fee prescribed by Section 502.161 and, if personalized prestige license plates are issued, in addition to the fee prescribed by Section 502.251.

(d) Of each fee collected under this section:

(1) $25 shall be deposited to the credit of the tourism account in the general revenue fund to finance the Texas Department of Economic Development's tourism activities; and

(2) $5 shall be deposited to the credit of the state highway fund to defray the cost of administering this section.

(e) If the owner of a vehicle registered under this section disposes of the vehicle during the registration year, the owner shall return the special license plates to the department.

*(Added by L.1999, chap. 1220(1), eff. 9/1/99.)*

## §502.274. Classic motor vehicles.

(a) The department shall issue specially designed license plates for passenger cars, motorcycles, and light trucks that are at least 25 years old. The license plates must include the words "Classic Auto," "Classic Motorcycle," or "Classic Truck," as appropriate.

(b) In lieu of license plates described by Subsection (a), a person applying for registration may under this section use license plates that:

(1) were issued by this state in the same year as the model year of the vehicle; and

(2) are approved by the department.

(c) The department shall register a vehicle under this section if the owner:

(1) applies to the county assessor-collector of the county in which the person resides on a form provided by the department; and

(2) pays an annual fee of $15, in addition to the fee prescribed by Section 502.161, and, if personalized prestige license plates are issued, in addition to the fee prescribed by Section 502.251.

(d) The department may require the attachment of a registration insignia to a license plate approved under Subsection (b) in a manner that does not affect the display of information originally inscribed on the license plate.

(e) Registration under this section is valid for one registration year.

(f) If the owner of a vehicle registered under this section disposes of the vehicle during the registration year, the owner shall return the special license plates issued under this section to the department.

*(Added by L.1995, chap. 165(1); chgd. by L.1997, chap. 1222(1), eff. 6/20/97.)*

## §502.275. Certain exhibition vehicles; offense.

(a) The department shall issue specially designed license plates for a passenger car, truck, motorcycle, or former military vehicle that:

(1) is at least 25 years old, if the vehicle is a passenger car, truck, or motorcycle;

(2) is a collector's item;

(3) is used exclusively for exhibitions, club activities, parades, and other functions of public interest, and is not used for regular transportation; and

(4) does not carry advertising.

(b) Special license plates issued under Subsection (a) must include the words "Antique Auto," "Antique Truck," "Antique Motorcycle," or "Military Vehicle," as appropriate.

(c) In lieu of issuing plates under Subsection (a), the department may approve for use license plates presented by the owner that were issued by this state in the same year as the model year of a vehicle described by Subsection (a). The department shall approve for use on a passenger car license plates that were issued for a passenger car or for a truck and shall approve for use on a truck license plates that were issued for a truck or for a passenger car. If the department approves license plates under this subsection, the department shall issue a symbol for attachment to one of the license plates, as determined by the department, showing the year in which the vehicle was registered under this section.

(d) License plates issued under Subsection (a) or approved under Subsection (c) are valid for a maximum period of five years.

(e) The department shall issue license plates under Subsection (a) or approve license plates under Subsection (c) and shall issue a registration receipt to a person who:

(1) files a sworn written application with the county assessor-collector of the county in which the person resides that:

(A) is on a form provided by the department;

(B) if the vehicle is a passenger car, truck, or motorcycle, contains the make, body style, motor number, and age of the vehicle;

(C) states any other information required by the department; and

(D) states that the vehicle and the use of the vehicle comply with Subsection (a); and

(2) pays a fee of:

(A) $10 for each year or portion of a year remaining in the five-year registration period, if the vehicle was manufactured in 1921 or a later year; or

(B) $8 for each year or portion of a year remaining in the five-year registration period, if the vehicle was manufactured before 1921.

(f) Notwithstanding any other provision of this section, the department may exempt a former military vehicle from the requirement to display license plates or any symbol, tab, or other device indicating registration of the vehicle if the department determines that the exemption is necessary to maintain the vehicle's accurate military design or markings. *(Added by L.1997, chap. 1222(2), eff. 6/20/97. See other subsection (f) below.)*

(f) The department shall issue a registration receipt to a person who:

(1) files a sworn written application for registration of a former military vehicle with the county assessor-collector of the county in which the person resides that:

(A) is on a form provided by the department;

(B) contains the information required by the department, including;

(i) the vehicle's year of manufacture; and

(ii) a description of the vehicle as required by the department; and

(C) states that the vehicle and the use of the vehicle comply with Subsection (a) (2)-(4); and

(2) pays the fee required by Subsection (e) (2).

*(Added by L.1997, chap. 165(30.56(a)), eff. 9/1/97. See other subsection (f) above.)*

(g) A vehicle registered under this section is exempt from the registration fee otherwise prescribed by this chapter.

(h) Registration under this section is valid without renewal for the period for which the vehicle was registered if the vehicle is owned by the same person.

(i) A county assessor-collector may not renew the registration of a vehicle under this section until the registered owner surrenders to the assessor-collector any license plates or symbol and the registration receipt issued for the vehicle for the previous period.

(j) If a vehicle registered under this section is transferred to another owner or is junked, is destroyed, or otherwise ceases to exist, the registration receipt and any license plates or symbol are immediately void and the license plates or symbol issued under this section shall be sent immediately to the department.

(k) A former military vehicle operated on a public highway is not required to display license plates or registration insignia if:

(1) proof of current registration for the vehicle, in the form prescribed by the department, is carried in the vehicle; and

(2) the vehicle displays in a prominent location on the vehicle a registration mark prescribed by the department.

(*l*) The department shall allow use of a unique identification mark on a former military vehicle that is similar to the mark assigned the vehicle by the armed force in which the vehicle was used. If such a mark is not used, the department shall designate a registration mark for the vehicle. A registration mark designated by the department must consist of numbers or letters, or both numbers and letters, that are at least two inches high. *(Added by L.1997, chap. 165(30.56(a)), eff. 9/1/97. See other subsection (l) below.)*

(*l*) Notwithstanding any other section of this code, a vehicle issued plates under Subsection (a) shall be required to display only one license plate, which is to be attached to the rear of the vehicle. *(Added by L.1997, chap. 1222(2), eff. 6/20/97. See other subsection (l) above.)*

(m) To the extent possible, the location and design of a registration mark for a former military vehicle registered under this section must conform to the vehicle's official military design and markings. *(Added by L.1997, chap. 165(30.56(a)), eff. 9/1/97. See other subsection (m) below.)*

(m) In this section, "former military vehicle" means a vehicle, including a trailer, regardless of the vehicle's size, weight, or year of manufacture, that:

(1) was manufactured for use in any country's military forces; and

(2) is maintained to accurately represent its military design and markings.

*(Added by L.1997, chap. 1222(1), eff. 6/20/97. See other subsection (m) above.)*

(n) An owner of a vehicle registered under this section who violates this section commits an offense. An offense under this section is a misdemeanor punishable by a fine of not less than $5 or more than $200.

(*o*) In this section, "former military vehicle" means a vehicle that:

(1) has been, but is not currently used by the armed forces of a national government; and

(2) displays markings indicating it was a military vehicle.

*(Added by L.1995, chap. 165(1); chgd. by L.1997, chaps. 165(30.56(a)), 1222(2), eff. 9/1/97, 6/20/97, respectively.)*

### §502.276. Certain farm vehicles and drilling and construction equipment.

(a) An owner is not required to register a farm tractor, a farm trailer or farm semitrailer that has a gross weight of 4,000 pounds or less, or an implement of husbandry, if the vehicle is operated only temporarily on the highways.

(b) A vehicle owner may obtain a distinguishing license plate from the department by:

(1) applying to the department through the county assessor-collector of the county in which the person resides on a form provided by the department; and

(2) paying a fee of $5 for each year or portion of a year.

(c) A vehicle that has a distinguishing license plate issued under Subsection (b) may be operated temporarily on the highways if the vehicle is:

(1) a farm trailer or farm semitrailer with a gross weight of more than 4,000 pounds but not more than 34,000 pounds that is used exclusively to transport:

(A) seasonally harvested agricultural products or livestock from the place of production to the place of processing, market, or storage; or

(B) farm supplies from the place of loading to the farm;

(2) machinery used exclusively for the purpose of drilling water wells; or

(3) construction machinery that is not designed to transport persons or property on a public highway.

(d) This section applies to:

(1) a farm trailer or farm semitrailer owned by a cotton gin and used exclusively to transport agricultural products without charge from the place of production to the place of processing, market, or storage;

(2) a trailer used exclusively to transport fertilizer without charge from a place of supply or storage to a farm; or

(3) a trailer used exclusively to transport cottonseed without charge from a place of supply or storage to a farm or place of processing.

(e) A vehicle described by Subsection (c) is exempt from the inspection requirements of Subchapters B and F, Chapter 548.

(f) This section does not apply to a farm trailer or farm semitrailer that:

(1) is used for hire;

(2) has metal tires operating in contact with the highway;

(3) is not equipped with an adequate hitch pinned or locked so that it will remain securely engaged to the towing vehicle while in motion; or

(4) is not operated and equipped in compliance with all other law.

(g) A vehicle to which this section applies that is operated on a public highway in violation of this section is considered to be operated while unregistered and is immediately subject to the registration fees and penalties otherwise prescribed by this chapter.

(h) In this section, the "gross weight" of a trailer or semitrailer is the combined weight of the vehicle and the load carried on the highway.

*(Added by L.1995, chap. 165(1); chgd. by L.1997, chap. 165(30.57); L.1999, chap. 572(1), eff. 9/1/99.)*

## §502.2761 Texas agricultural products license plates.

(a) The department shall issue specially designed license plates for passenger cars and light trucks to support the promotion of Texas agricultural products.

(b) The license plates must include the words "Go Texan" and the "Go Texan" logo of the Department of Agriculture and must be of a color, quality, and design approved by the commissioner of agriculture.

(c) The department shall issue license plates under this section to a person who:

(1) applies to the county assessor-collector of the county in which the person resides on the form provided by the department; and

(2) pays an annual fee of $30, in addition to the fee prescribed by Section 502.161 or Section 502.162 and, if personalized prestige license plates are issued, in addition to the fee prescribed by Section 502.251.

(d) The department shall deposit $25 of each fee collected under Subsection (c) to the credit of the "Go Texan" partner program account established by Section 46.008, Agriculture Code.

(e) The remainder of each fee collected under this section, after deposit as provided by Subsection (d), shall be deposited to the credit of the state highway fund and may be used only to defray the cost of administering this section.

(f) If the owner of a vehicle registered under this section disposes of the vehicle during the registration year, the owner shall return the special license plates to the department.

*(Added by L.1999, chap. 186(3), eff. 9/1/99 if a specific appropriation for the implementation of this Act is provided in H.B. No. 1 (General Appropriations Act), Act of the 76th Legislature, Regular Session 1999. If no specific appropriation is provided in H.B. No. 1, the General Appropriations Act, this act has no effect.)*

## §502.277. Cotton vehicles.

(a) The department shall issue specially designed license plates for single motor vehicles that:

(1) are used only to transport seed cotton modules, cotton, cotton burrs, or equipment used in transporting or processing cotton; and

(2) are not more than 10 feet in width.

(b) License plates issued under this section must include the words "Cotton Vehicle."

(c) A person may apply to the department at any time for registration under this section on a form prescribed by the department. The department may require an applicant to submit proof of eligibility for registration under this section.

(d) The fee for the initial issuance of the special license plates is $8, in addition to the fee prescribed by Section 502.162 and, if applicable, the fee prescribed by Section 502.172. The additional fee may be appropriated only to the department to defray the cost of providing the special license plates.

(e) Registration under this section is valid for one registration year.

(f) A person who has registered a vehicle under this section and received license plates may renew the registration by applying to the county assessor-collector in the county in which the per-

son resides for an annual registration insignia. On renewal, the person must pay only the fee prescribed by Section 502.162 and, if applicable, the fee prescribed by Section 502.172.
*(Added by L.1995, chap. 165(1); chgd. by L.1997, chap. 848(1), eff. 6/18/97.)*

**§502.278. Certain soil conservation equipment.**

(a) The owner of a truck-tractor, semitrailer, or low-boy trailer used on a highway exclusively to transport the owner's soil conservation machinery or equipment used in clearing real property, terracing, or building farm ponds, levees, or ditches may register the vehicle for a fee equal to 50 percent of the fee otherwise prescribed by this chapter for the vehicle.

(b) An owner may register only one truck-tractor and only one semitrailer or low-boy trailer under this section.

(c) An owner applying for registration under this section must submit a statement that the vehicle is to be used only as provided by Subsection (a).

(d) The registration receipt issued for a vehicle registered under this section shall state the nature of the operation for which the vehicle may be used. The receipt must be carried at all times in or on the vehicle to permit ready inspection.

(e) A vehicle to which this section applies that is operated on a public highway in violation of this section is considered to be operated while unregistered and is immediately subject to the registration fees and penalties otherwise prescribed by this chapter.
*(Added by L.1995, chap. 165(1), eff. 9/1/95.)*

**§502.279. Certain log-loader vehicles.**

(a) An owner who obtains a distinguishing license plate from the department may without payment of the registration fee otherwise prescribed by this chapter temporarily operate on a public highway, during daylight hours only, a vehicle on which is mounted machinery used only for loading logs on other vehicles.

(b) An owner may obtain the distinguishing license plate under Subsection (a) by:

(1) applying to the department through the county assessor-collector of the county in which the owner resides; and

(2) paying a fee of $62.50 for each registration year or portion of a registration year.

(c) A vehicle having a distinguishing license plate under Subsection (a) is exempt from the inspection requirements of Chapter 548.

(d) This section does not apply to a vehicle used to haul logs.

(e) A vehicle to which this section applies that is operated on the public highways in violation of this section is considered to be operated or moved while unregistered and is immediately subject to the fees and penalties otherwise prescribed by this chapter.
*(Added by L.1995, chap. 165(1), eff. 9/1/95.)*

**§502.280. Forestry vehicles.**

(a) The department shall issue specially designed license plates for forestry vehicles.

(b) License plates issued under this section must include the words "forestry vehicle."

(c) The department shall issue license plates under this section to a person who:

(1) applies to the department on a form prescribed by the department;

(2) pays a fee in an amount prescribed by the department as necessary to recover the costs of administering this section, in addition to the registration fee otherwise prescribed by this chapter; and

(3) submits proof that the person is eligible to receive the license plates.

(d) The department shall collect any additional fee that a county imposes under this chapter for registration of a forestry vehicle and shall send the fee to the appropriate county for disposition as provided by this chapter.

(e) In this section, "forestry vehicle" means a vehicle used exclusively for transporting forest products in their natural state, including logs, debarked logs, untreated ties, stave bolts, plywood bolts, pulpwood billets, wood chips, stumps, sawdust, moss, bark, wood shavings, and property used in production of those products.
*(Added by L.1995, chap. 165(1); chgd. by L.1997, chap. 165(30.58(a)), eff. 9/1/97.)*

**§502.281. Tow trucks.**

(a) The department shall issue specially designed license plates for commercial motor vehicles used as tow trucks.

(b) License plates issued under this section must include the words "Tow Truck."

(c) The department shall issue license plates under this section to a person engaged in the business of using a tow truck who:

(1) applies on a form prescribed by the department to the county assessor-collector of the county in which the person resides;

(2) pays a fee of $15, in addition to the fee prescribed by Section 502.162; and

(3) submits a certified copy of the registration certificate issued by the department for the tow truck.

(d) Registration under this section is valid for one registration year.

(e) In this section, "tow truck" means a motor vehicle adapted or used to tow, winch, or otherwise move another motor vehicle.

*(Added by L.1995, chap. 165(1); chgd. by L.1997, chap. 165(30.59), eff. 9/1/97.)*

## §502.282. Vehicles carrying mobile amateur radio equipment.

(a) A resident of this state who holds an amateur radio station license issued by the Federal Communications Commission and who operates receiving and transmitting mobile amateur radio equipment in a passenger car or a light truck commonly known as a pickup truck may obtain specially designed license plates that may include the person's amateur call letters as assigned by the Federal Communications Commission. A person may register more than one vehicle equipped with mobile amateur radio equipment under this section, and the department shall issue license plates that include the same amateur call letters for each vehicle.

(b) An applicant for license plates under this section must:

(1) apply to the department;

(2) pay a fee of $2 for the first year of registration or $1 for each subsequent year of registration as applicable, in addition to the fee otherwise prescribed by this chapter;

(3) submit proof that the person owns the amateur radio station license; and

(4) furnish the applicant's call letters to the department.

(c) The department shall furnish license plates that include the applicant's call letters to the appropriate county assessor-collector. The assessor-collector shall:

(1) keep on file a copy of the registration receipt issued to the applicant; and

(2) give the license plates and registration receipt to the applicant for the registration year.

(d) If the owner of a vehicle registered under this section disposes of the vehicle during the registration year, the owner shall return the special license plates to the county assessor-collector and receive replacement plates for a fee prescribed by law.

*(Added by L.1995, chap. 165(1), eff. 9/1/95.)*



## §502.283. Parade vehicles owned by nonprofit service organizations.

(a) A motor vehicle owned and operated by a nonprofit service organization and designed, constructed, and used primarily for parade purposes is subject to registration as provided by this chapter but is exempt from the fee otherwise prescribed by this chapter.

(b) Subsection (a) does not apply to a vehicle for which a registration fee has been paid under other law.

*(Added by L.1995, chap. 165(1), eff. 9/1/95.)*

## §502.284. Golf carts.

(a) An owner of a golf cart is not required to register the golf cart if:

(1) the operation of the golf cart occurs in the daytime, as defined by Section 541.401; and

(2) the operation:

(A) does not exceed a distance of two miles from the point of origin to the destination if driven to and from a golf course;

(B) occurs entirely within a master planned community with a uniform set of restrictive covenants that has had a plat approved by a county or a municipality; or

(C) occurs on a public or private beach.

(b) If an owner of a golf cart resides on real property that is owned or under the control of the United States Corps of Engineers and is required by that agency to register the owner's golf cart under this chapter, the fee for registering the golf cart is $10. This subsection applies only to an owner of a golf cart who resides in a county that borders another state and has a population of more than 95,000 but less than 100,000.

(c) Subsection (b) does not authorize the operation of a golf cart on a public road where otherwise prohibited by law.

*(Added by L.1995, chap. 165(1); chgd. by L.1997, chaps. 896(1), 1128(1); L.1999, chap. 780(1), eff. 9/1/99.)*

### §502.285. Manufactured housing.

Manufactured housing, as defined by the Texas Manufactured Housing Standards Act (Article 5221f, Texas Civil Statutes), is not a vehicle subject to this chapter. *(Added by L.1995, chap. 165(1), eff. 9/1/95.)*

### §502.286. Power sweepers.

(a) An owner of a power sweeper is not required to register the power sweeper.

(b) In this section, "power sweeper" means an implement, with or without motive power, designed for the removal by broom, vacuum, or regenerative air system of debris, dirt, gravel, litter, or sand from asphaltic concrete or cement concrete surfaces, including surfaces of parking lots, roads, streets, highways, and warehouse floors. The term includes a vehicle on which the implement is permanently mounted if the vehicle is used only as a power sweeper.
*(Added by L.1995, chap. 165(1), eff. 9/1/95.)*

### §502.287. Vehicles operated on public highway separating real property under vehicle owner's control.

Where a public highway separates real property under the control of the owner of a motor vehicle, the operation of the motor vehicle by the owner or the owner's agent or employee across the highway is not a use of the motor vehicle on the public highway. *(Added by L.1995, chap. 165(1), eff. 9/1/95.)*



### §502.288. Vehicles operated by certain nonresidents.

(a) A nonresident owner of a motor vehicle, trailer, or semitrailer that is registered in the state or country in which the person resides may operate the vehicle to transport persons or property for compensation without being registered in this state, if the person does not exceed two trips in a calendar month and each trip does not exceed four days.

(b) A nonresident owner of a privately owned vehicle that is not registered in this state may not make more than five occasional trips in any calendar month into this state using the vehicle. Each occasional trip into this state may not exceed five days.

(c) A nonresident owner of a privately owned passenger car that is registered in the state or country in which the person resides and that is not operated for compensation may operate the car in this state for the period in which the car's license plates are valid. In this subsection, "nonresident" means a resident of a state or country other than this state whose presence in this state is as a visitor and who does not engage in gainful employment or enter into business or an occupation, except as may otherwise be provided by any reciprocal agreement with another state or country.

(d) This chapter does not prevent:

(1) a nonresident owner of a motor vehicle from operating the vehicle in this state for the sole purpose of marketing farm products raised exclusively by the person; or

(2) a resident of an adjoining state or country from operating in this state a privately owned and registered vehicle to go to and from the person's place of regular employment and to make trips to purchase merchandise, if the vehicle is not operated for compensation.

(e) The privileges provided by this section may be allowed only if, under the laws of the appropriate state or country, similar privileges are granted to vehicles registered under the laws of and owned by residents of this state.

(f) This chapter does not affect the right or status of a vehicle owner under any reciprocal agreement between this state and another state or country.
*(Added by L.1995, chap. 165(1), eff. 9/1/95.)*

### §502.289. Peace officers wounded or killed in line of duty.

(a) The department shall issue specially designed licensed plates for a vehicle owned by:

(1) a person wounded in the line of duty as a peace officer; or

(2) a surviving spouse, parent, or adult child of a person killed in the line of duty as a peace officer.

(b) License plates issued under this section must include the words "To Protect and Serve" above an insignia depicting a yellow rose superimposed over the outline of a badge.

(c) The department shall issue license plates under this section to a person who:

(1) applies to the department on a form prescribed by the department;

(2) pays an annual fee of $20, in addition to the fee prescribed by Section 502.160 or 502.161, and, if personalized prestige license plates are issued, in addition to the fee prescribed by Section 502.251; and

(3) submits proof acceptable to the department that the person is eligible under this section.

(d) If the owner of a vehicle registered under this section disposes of the vehicle during the registration year, the owner shall return the special license plates to the department.

(e) The department shall deposit each fee collected under this section to the credit of the state highway fund.

(f) In this section, "peace officer" has the meaning assigned by Section 1.07, Penal Code. *(Added by L.1997, chap. 165(30.51(b)), eff. 9/1/97.)*

## §502.290. Foreign organization vehicles.

(a) The department shall issue specially designed license plates for passenger cars and light trucks owned by an instrumentality established by a foreign government recognized by the United States before January 1, 1979, that is without official representation or diplomatic relations with the United States.

(b) A vehicle for which license plates are issued under this section is exempt from the fee under Section 502.161.

(c) License plates issued under this section must include the words "Foreign Organization." *(Added by L.1997, chap. 165(30.60(a)), eff. 9/1/97.)*



## §502.291. Animal friendly license plates.

(a) The department shall issue specially designed license plates for passenger cars and light trucks that include the words "Animal Friendly."

(b) The department shall issue license plates under this section to a person who:

(1) applies to the county assessor-collector of the county in which the person resides on a form provided by the department; and

(2) pays an annual fee of $25, in addition to the fee prescribed by Section 502.161, and, if personalized prestige license plates are issued, in addition to the fee prescribed by Section 502.251.

(c) Of each fee collected under this section, the department shall deposit:

(1) $20 to the credit of the animal friendly account established by Section 828.014, Health and Safety Code; and

(2) $5 to the credit of the state highway fund.

(d) If the owner of a vehicle registered under this section disposes of the vehicle during the registration year, the owner shall return the special license plates to the department. *(Added by L.1997, chap. 657(2), eff. 9/1/97. Repealed 9/1/2004 if at least $500,000 has not been deposited to the credit of the animal revenue account in the general revenue fund, as chgd. by L.1999, chap. 952(5), eff. 8/30/99.)*

## §502.292. Read to Succeed.

(a) The department shall issue specially designed "Read to Succeed" license plates for passenger cars and light trucks.

(b) The department shall issue license plates under this section to a person who:

(1) applies to the county assessor-collector of the county in which the person resides on the form for original registration or annual renewal of registration provided by the department; and

(2) pays an annual fee in the amount set under Subsection (c), in addition to the fee prescribed by Section 502.161 and, if personalized prestige license plates are issued, in addition to the fee prescribed by Section 502.251.

(c) The department shall set the annual fee for license plates under this section at:

(1) an amount, not to exceed $5, necessary to administer this section; and

(2) an additional amount of:

(A) $25 for each set of plates, except as provided by Paragraph (B); or

(B) $15 for each set of plates, if the person is purchasing plates under this section for a fleet of 50 or more vehicles.

(d) The fee collected under Subsection (c)(1) may be used only to defray the cost of administering this section.

(e) The department shall deposit each fee collected under Subsection (c)(2) to the credit of an account in the general revenue fund to be known as the "Read to Succeed" account. Money from the account may be used only for the purpose of providing educational materials for public school libraries. The account is composed of:

(1) money required to be deposited to the credit of the account under this subsection; and

(2) donations made to the account.

*(Added by L.1997, chap. 397(1); chgd. by L.1999, chap. 1108(1), eff. 9/1/99.)*

**§502.2921. Volunteer advocate program license plates.**

(a) In recognition of children, the department shall issue specially designed volunteer advocate program license plates for passenger cars and light trucks.

(b) The license plates must be of a color, quality, and design approved by the attorney general in consultation with the department.

(c) The department shall issue license plates under this section to a person who:

(1) applies to the county assessor-collector of the county in which the person resides on a form provided by the department; and

(2) pays an annual fee of $30, in addition to the fee prescribed by Section 502.161, and, if personalized prestige license plates are issued, in addition to the fee prescribed by Section 502.251.

(d) Of each fee collected under this section, the department shall deposit $25 under this section to the credit of the attorney general volunteer advocate program account in the general revenue fund and $5 to the credit of the state highway fund.

(e) Money deposited to the credit of the volunteer advocate program account under Subsection (d) may be used only by the attorney general to fund a contract entered into by the attorney general under Section 264.602, Family Code.

(f) If the owner of a vehicle registered under this section disposes of the vehicle during the registration year, the owner shall return the special license plates to the department.

*(Added by L.1997, chap. 61(1); renumbered from section 502.292 by L.1999, chap. 62(19.01(102)), eff. 9/1/99.)*

**§502.293. Houston Livestock Show and Rodeo license plates.**

(a) The department shall issue specially designed Houston Livestock Show and Rodeo license plates for passenger cars and light trucks.

(b) The license plates must include the words "Houston Livestock Show and Rodeo" and be of a color, quality, and design approved by the Houston Livestock Show and Rodeo.

(c) The department shall issue license plates under this section to a person who:

(1) applies to the county assessor-collector of the county in which the person resides on a form provided by the department; and

(2) pays an annual fee of $30, in addition to the fee prescribed by Section 502.161 or Section 502.162, and, if personalized prestige license plates are issued, in addition to the fee prescribed by Section 502.251.

(d) The department shall deposit $20 of each fee collected under this section to the credit of the Houston Livestock Show and Rodeo scholarship account in the state treasury. Money in the account may be used only by the Texas Higher Education Coordinating Board in making grants to benefit the Houston Livestock Show and Rodeo.

(e) The remainder of each fee collected under this section, after deposit as provided by Subsection (d), shall be deposited to the credit of the state highway fund and may be used only to defray the cost of administering this section.

(f) If the owner of a vehicle registered under this section disposes of the vehicle during the registration year, the owner shall return the special license plates to the department.

*(Added by L.1997, chap. 511(1), eff. 9/1/97.)*

**§502.2931. Girl Scout license plates.**

(a) The department shall issue specially designed Girl Scout license plates for passenger cars and light trucks.

(b) The license plates must include the words "Girl Scouts."

(c) The department shall design the license plates in consultation with the Girl Scout Councils of Texas.

(d) The department shall issue license plates under this section to a person who:

(1) applies to the county assessor-collector of the county in which the person resides on a form provided by the department; and

(2) pays an annual fee of $30, in addition to the fee prescribed by Section 502.161 or Section 502.162, and, if personalized prestige license plates are issued, in addition to the fee prescribed by Section 502.251.

(e) The department shall deposit $20 of each fee collected under this section to the credit of the Girl Scout account in the state treasury. Money in the account may be used by the Texas Higher Education Coordinating Board in making grants to benefit educational projects sponsored by the Girl Scout Councils of Texas.

(f) The remainder of each fee collected under this section, after deposit as provided by Subsection (e), shall be deposited to the credit of the state highway fund and may be used only to defray the cost of administering this section.

(g) If license plates issued under this section are lost, stolen, or mutilated, the owner of the vehicle for which the license plates were issued may obtain replacement license plates from the department by paying a replacement fee of $5. If the owner of a vehicle registered under this section disposes of the vehicle during the registration year, the owner shall return the special license plates to the department.
*(Added by L.1999, chap. 550(1), eff. 9/1/99.)*

## §502.294. Municipal and private buses.

(a) The department shall issue specially designed license plates for municipal buses and private buses.

(b) License plates issued under this section must include the words "city bus" or "private bus," as appropriate.

(c) The department shall issue license plates under this section to a person who:

(1) applies on a form prescribed by the department to the county assessor-collector of the county in which the person resides; and

(2) pays the fee prescribed by Section 502.161.

(d) Registration under this section is valid for one registration year.

(e) In this section, "private bus" means a bus that:

(1) is not operated for hire; and

(2) is not classified as a municipal bus or a motor bus.
*(Added by L.1997, chap. 625(10), eff. 9/1/97.)*



## §502.295. State officials.

(a) The department shall issue specially designed license plates for a passenger car or light truck owned by a state official.

(b) License plates issued under this section must include the words "state official."

(c) The department shall issue license plates under this section to a person who:

(1) applies to the department on a form prescribed by the department;

(2) furnishes evidence acceptable to the department that the person is eligible to register the vehicle under this section; and

(3) pays the fee prescribed by Section 502.161.

(d) A person may be issued three sets of license plates under this section.

(e) A registration under this section is for a registration period of 12 consecutive months or until March 31, whichever period is shorter.

(f) If the owner of a vehicle registered under this section disposes of the vehicle during the registration period, the owner shall surrender the special license plates to the department.

(g) In this section, "state official" means:

(1) a member of the legislature;

(2) the governor;

(3) the lieutenant governor;

(4) a justice of the supreme court;

(5) a judge of the court of criminal appeals;

(6) the attorney general;

(7) the Commissioner of the General Land Office;

(8) the comptroller;

(9) a member of the Railroad Commission of Texas;

(10) the commissioner of agriculture;

(11) the secretary of state; or

(12) a member of the State Board of Education.
*(Added by L.1997, chap. 625(10), eff. 9/1/97.)*

## §502.2951. County judges.

(a) The department shall design and provide for the issuance of special license plates for passenger cars and light trucks that are owned by persons who are county judges of this state.

(b) License plates issued to county judges under this section shall bear the words "County Judge."

(c) The department shall issue license plates under this section to a person who:

(1) applies to the county tax collector in the county of the person's residence on a form prescribed by the department;

(2) pays the fee prescribed by Subsection (d); and

(3) submits with the application proof that the person is a county judge of this state.

(d) The fee for registration under this section and issuance of the special license plates is the fee otherwise prescribed by this chapter for the vehicle.

(e) Registration under this section is valid for one year and expires in the same manner as do regular motor vehicle registrations, except as provided by Subsection (f).

(f) Registration under this section expires when the owner of the vehicle for which the special plates were issued ceases to be a county judge. The judge shall return the special license plates to the department.

(g) If the owner of a vehicle for which plates are issued under this section disposes of the vehicle during a registration year, the person shall return the special plates to the department, and at that time may apply for issuance of those plates to another vehicle.

(h) If license plates issued under this section are lost, stolen, or mutilated, the owner of the vehicle for which the plates were issued may obtain replacement plates from the department by paying a replacement fee of $5.

(i) In this section, "county judge" means the judge of the county court established by Section 15, Article V, Texas Constitution.

*(Added by L.1997, chap. 1222(3); renumbered from section 502.293 by L.1999, chap. 62(19.01(104)), eff. 9/1/99.)*

### §502.296. Members of congress.

(a) The department shall issue specially designed license plates for a passenger car or light truck owned by a member of congress.

(b) License plates issued under this section must include the words "U.S. Congress."

(c) The department shall issue license plates under this section to a person who:

(1) applies to the department on a form prescribed by the department;

(2) furnishes evidence acceptable to the department that the person is eligible to register the vehicle under this section; and

(3) pays the fee prescribed by Section 502.161.

(d) A person may be issued three sets of license plates under this section.

(e) A registration under this section is for a registration period of 12 consecutive months or until March 31, whichever period is shorter.

(f) If the owner of a vehicle registered under this section disposes of the vehicle during the registration period, the owner shall surrender the special license plates to the department.

*(Added by L.1997, chap. 625(10), eff. 9/1/97.)*

### §502.297. State and federal judges.

(a) The department shall issue specially designed license plates for a passenger car or light truck owned by a state or federal judge or a retired state or federal judge.

(b) License plates issued under this section must include the words "state judge" or "U.S. judge," as appropriate.

(c) The department shall issue license plates under this section to a person who:

(1) applies to the department on a form prescribed by the department;

(2) furnishes evidence acceptable to the department that the person is eligible to register the vehicle under this section; and

(3) pays the fee prescribed by Section 502.161.

(d) A person may be issued three sets of license plates under this section.

(e) A registration under this section is for a registration period of 12 consecutive months or until March 31, whichever period is shorter.

(f) If the owner of a vehicle registered under this section disposes of the vehicle during the registration period, the owner shall surrender the special license plates to the department.

(g) In this section:

(1) "Federal judge" means:

(A) a judge of the Fifth Circuit Court of Appeals;

(B) a judge or a magistrate of a United States district court; or

(C) a judge of a United States bankruptcy court.

(2) "State judge" means:

(A) a judge of a court of appeals;

(B) a district court judge;

(C) a presiding judge of an administrative judicial district; or

(D) a statutory county court judge.

*(Added by L.1997, chap. 625(10), eff. 9/1/97.)*

## §502.298. Conservation license plates.

(a) The department shall issue one or more specially designed conservation license plates for passenger cars and light trucks to support Texas Parks and Wildlife Department activities.

(b) Each of the license plates must be of a color, quality, and design approved by the Parks and Wildlife Department.

(c) The department shall issue license plates under this section to a person who:

(1) applies to the county assessor-collector of the county in which the person resides on an original or renewal registration application form provided by the department; and

(2) pays an annual fee of $25, in addition to the fee prescribed by Section 502.161, and, if personalized prestige license plates are issued, in addition to the fee prescribed by Section 502.251.

(d) Of each $25 fee collected under Subsection (c) or (e), the department shall deposit $20 to the credit of the Texas parks and wildlife capital account established by Section 11.043, Parks and Wildlife Code. The remaining $5 of the fee may be used by the department to defray the cost of administering this section.

(e) The fee for replacement of a lost, stolen, or mutilated license plate issued under this section is $25, in addition to the fee prescribed by Section 502.184(a).

(f) If the owner of a vehicle registered under this section disposes of the vehicle during the registration year, the owner shall return the license plates to the department.

(g) There is no limit to the number of passenger cars or light trucks for which a person may apply for the issuance of license plates under this section.

(h) Money deposited in the Texas parks and wildlife capital account under this section is supplementary and is not income for the purposes of reducing general revenue appropriations to the Texas Parks and Wildlife Department.

*(Added by L.1999, chap. 862(1), eff. 9/1/99. See other section 502.298 below.)*

## §502.298. 100th football season of Stephen F. Austin High School.

(a) The department shall issue specially designed license plates for passenger cars and light trucks in honor of the 100th football season of Stephen F. Austin High School in Austin.

(b) The license plates must be of a color, quality, and design approved by the principal of Stephen F. Austin High School in consultation with the department.

(c) The department shall issue license plates under this section to a person who:

(1) applies to the county assessor-collector of the county in which the person resides on a form provided by the department; and

(2) pays an annual fee of $50, in addition to the fee prescribed by Section 502.161, and, if personalized prestige license plates are issued, in addition to the fee prescribed by Section 502.251.

(d) Of each fee collected under this section, the department shall send $35 to the Texas Education Agency for distribution to the Austin Independent School District to be used only for the benefit of the Austin High School Athletic Department. The remainder of each fee collected under this section shall be deposited to the credit of the state highway fund.

(e) This section expires September 1, 2004.

*(Added by L.1999, chap. 951(4), eff. 8/30/99, expires 9/1/2004. See other section 502.298 above.)*

## §502.299. Texas YMCA.

(a) The department shall issue specially designed license plates for passenger cars and light trucks in honor of the Young Men's Christian Association (YMCA).

(b) The department shall issue license plates under this section to a person who:

(1) applies to the county assessor-collector of the county in which the person resides on a form provided by the department; and

(2) pays the annual fee established by the department under Subsection (c), in addition to the fee prescribed by Section 502.161, and, if personalized prestige license plates are issued, in addition to the fee prescribed by Section 502.251.

(c) The department by rule shall establish the annual fee for registration under this section in an amount that, when added to the other fees collected by the department, does not exceed the amount sufficient to recover the actual cost to the department of issuing license plates under this section.

*(Added by L.1999, chap. 433(1), eff. 9/1/99. See two other sections 502.299 below.)*

## §502.299. Texas Young Lawyers Association license plates.

(a) The department shall issue specially designed Texas Young Lawyers Association license plates for passenger cars and light trucks.

(b) The license plates must bear the words "And Justice For All" and be of a color, quality, and design approved by the Texas Young Lawyers Association in consultation with the department.

(c) The department shall issue license plates under this section to a person who:

(1) applies to the county assessor-collector of the county in which the person resides on a form provided by the department; and

(2) pays an annual fee of $30, in addition to the fee prescribed by Section 502.161, and, if personalized prestige license plates are issued, in addition to the fee prescribed by Section 502.251.

(d) Of each fee collected under this section, the department shall deposit $25 to the credit of the basic civil legal services account established under Section 51.903, Government Code, as added by Chapter 699, Acts of the 75th Legislature, Regular Session, 1997. The remainder of the fee may be used only by the department to defray the cost of administering this section.

(e) If the owner of a vehicle registered under this section disposes of the vehicle during the registration year, the owner shall return the special license plates to the department.

*(Added by L.1999, chap. 634(1), eff. 9/1/99. See two other sections 502.299 above and below.)*

### §502.299. Texas citrus industry.

(a) The department shall issue specially designed license plates for passenger cars and light trucks in honor of the citrus industry in this state.

(b) The department shall issue license plates under this section to a person who:

(1) applies to the county assessor-collector of the county in which the person resides on a form provided by the department; and

(2) pays an annual fee of $30, in addition to the fee prescribed by Section 502.161, and, if personalized prestige license plates are issued, in addition to the fee prescribed by Section 502.251.

(c) Of each fee collected under this section, the department shall deposit $25 to the credit of an account in the general revenue fund that may be appropriated only to Texas A&M University—Kingsville to provide financial assistance to graduate students in the College of Agriculture and Human Sciences. The remainder of the fee may be used only by the department to defray the cost of administering this section.

*(Added by L.1999, chap. 1230(1), eff. 9/1/99. See two other sections 502.299 above.)*

### §§502.300 to 502.302. *(Reserved.)*

### §502.303. Waterfowl and wetland conservation license plates.

(a) Except as provided by Subsection (b), the department shall issue specially designed license plates for passenger cars and light trucks to support the activities of a nonprofit organization designated by the Parks and Wildlife Department that has as its principal purpose the conservation of waterfowl and wetland.

(b) The license plates must bear one or more graphic images designed by the Parks and Wildlife Department in consultation with the designated organization.

(c) The department shall issue license plates under this section to a person who:

(1) applies to the county assessor-collector of the county in which the person resides on a form provided by the department; and

(2) pays a fee of $50 for an original issuance of license plates under this section or $40 for a renewal of issuance of license plates under this section, in addition to the fee prescribed by Section 502.161 or 502.162, and, if personalized prestige license plates are issued, in addition to the fee prescribed by Section 502.251.

(d) The fee for replacement of a lost, stolen, or mutilated plate issued under this section is $35, in addition to the fee prescribed by Section 502.184(a).

(e) Of each fee collected under this section, $5 may be used to defray the cost of administering this section by the department and the Parks and Wildlife Department. The department shall deposit the remainder of each fee collected under this section to the credit of an account in the state treasury. Money in the account may be used only by the Parks and Wildlife Department to support the activities of a designated nonprofit organization whose primary purpose is the conservation of waterfowl and wetland. The Parks and Wildlife Department shall establish reporting and other mechanisms necessary to ensure that the money is spent for purposes for which it is dedicated.

(f) If the owner of a vehicle registered under this section disposes of the vehicle during the registration year, the owner shall return the special license plates to the department.

*(Added by L.1999, chap. 951(3), eff. 9/1/99.)*

### §§502.304 to 502.350. *(Reserved.)*

## SUBCHAPTER G. TEMPORARY REGISTRATION

### §502.351. Farm vehicles: excess weight.

(a) The owner of a registered commercial motor vehicle, truck-tractor, trailer, or semitrailer may obtain a short-term permit to haul loads of a weight more than that for which the vehicle is registered by paying an additional fee before the additional weight is hauled to transport:

(1) the person's own seasonal agricultural products to market or another point for sale or processing;

(2) seasonal laborers from their place of residence to a farm or ranch; or

(3) materials, tools, equipment, or supplies, without charge, from the place of purchase or storage to a farm or ranch exclusively for use on the farm or ranch.

(b) A permit may not be issued under this section for a period that is less than one month or that:

(1) is greater than one year; or

(2) extends beyond the expiration of the registration year for the vehicle.

(c) A permit issued under this section for a quarter must be for a calendar quarter.

(d) The fee for a permit under this section is a percentage of the difference between the registration fee otherwise prescribed by this chapter for the vehicle and the annual fee for the desired weight, as follows:

| | |
|---|---|
| One month (30 consecutive days) | 10 percent |
| One quarter | 30 percent |
| Two quarters | 60 percent |
| Three quarters | 90 percent |

(e) The department shall design, prescribe, and furnish a sticker, plate, or other means of indicating the additional weight and the registration period for each vehicle registered under this section.

*(Added by L.1995, chap. 165(1), eff. 9/1/95.)*

### §502.352. Foreign commercial vehicles.

(a) The department may issue a temporary permit for a commercial motor vehicle, trailer, semitrailer, or motor bus that:

(1) is owned by a resident of the United States, Canada, or the United Mexican States;

(2) is subject to registration in this state; and

(3) is not authorized to travel on a public highway because of the lack of registration in this state or the lack of reciprocity with the state or province in which the vehicle is registered.

(b) A permit issued under this section:

(1) is in lieu of registration; and

(2) is valid for the period stated on the permit, effective from the date and time shown on the receipt issued as evidence of registration under this section.

(c) A person may obtain a permit under this section by:

(1) applying to the county assessor-collector, the department, or the department's wire service agent, if the department has a wire service agent;

(2) paying a fee of $25 for a 72-hour permit or $50 for a 144-hour permit:

(A) in cash;

(B) by postal money order;

(C) by certified check;

(D) by wire transfer through the department's wire service agent, if any;

(E) by an escrow account; or

(F) where the service is provided, by a credit card issued by:

(i) a financial institution chartered by a state or the United States; or

(ii) a nationally recognized credit organization approved by the Texas Transportation Commission;

(3) paying a discount or service charge for a credit card payment or escrow account, in addition to the fee; and

(4) furnishing to the county assessor-collector, the department, or the department's wire service agent, evidence of financial responsibility for the vehicle that complies with Sections 502.153(c) and 601.168(a) and is written by an insurance company or surety company authorized to write motor vehicle liability insurance in this state.

(d) A county assessor-collector shall report and send a fee collected under this section in the manner provided by Sections 502.102 and 502.105. Each week, a wire service agent shall send to the department a report of all permits issued by the agent during the previous week. The department by rule shall prescribe the form and content of a report required by this subsection.

(e) The department may:

(1) adopt rules to administer this section; and

(2) prescribe an application for a permit and other forms under this section.

(f) A vehicle issued a permit under this section is subject to Subchapters B and F, Chapter 548, unless the vehicle:

(1) is registered in another state of the United States, in a province of Canada, or in a state of the United Mexican States; or

(2) is mobile drilling or servicing equipment used in the production of gas, crude petroleum, or oil, including a mobile crane or hoisting equipment, mobile lift equipment, forklift, or tug.

(g) A commercial motor vehicle, trailer, semitrailer, or motor bus apprehended for violating a registration law of this state:

(1) may not be issued a permit under this section; and

(2) is immediately subject to registration in this state.

(h) A person who operates a commercial motor vehicle, trailer, or semitrailer with an expired permit issued under this section is considered to be operating an unregistered vehicle subject to each penalty prescribed by law.

(i) The department may establish one or more escrow accounts in the state highway fund for the prepayment of a 72-hour permit or a 144-hour permit. Any fee established by the department for the administration of this subsection shall be administered as required by an agreement entered into by the department.

*(Added by L.1995, chap. 165(1); chgd. by L.1997, chaps. 165(30.61(a)), 625(11), eff. 9/1/97.)*

## §502.353. Foreign commercial vehicles; annual permits; offense.

(a) The department may issue an annual permit to a foreign commercial motor vehicle, trailer, or semitrailer that:

(1) is subject to registration in this state; and

(2) is not authorized to travel on a public highway because of the lack of registration in this state or the lack of reciprocity with the state or country in which the vehicle is registered.

(b) A permit issued under this section:

(1) is in lieu of registration; and

(2) is valid for a vehicle registration year to begin on the first day of a calendar month designated by the department and end on the last day of the last calendar month of the registration year.

(c) A permit may not be issued under this section for the importation of citrus fruit into this state from a foreign country except for foreign export or processing for foreign export.

(d) A person may obtain a permit under this section by:

(1) applying to the department;

(2) paying a fee in the amount required by Subsection (e) in cash or by postal money order or certified check; and

(3) furnishing evidence of financial responsibility for the motor vehicle that complies with Sections 502.153(c) and 601.168(a), the policies to be written by an insurance company or surety company authorized to write motor vehicle liability insurance in this state.

(e) The fee for a permit under this section is the fee that would be required for registering the vehicle under Section 502.162 or 502.167, except as provided by Subsection (f).

(f) A vehicle registered under this section is exempt from the token fee and is not required to display the associated distinguishing license plate if the vehicle:

(1) is a semitrailer that has a gross weight of more than 6,000 pounds; and

(2) is used or intended to be used in combination with a truck tractor or commercial motor vehicle with a manufacturer's rated carrying capacity of more than one ton.

(g) A vehicle registered under this section is not subject to the fee required by Section 502.172 or 502.173.

(h) The department may:

(1) adopt rules to administer this section; and

(2) prescribe an application for a permit and other forms under this section.

(i) A person who violates this section commits an offense. An offense under this section is a misdemeanor punishable by a fine not to exceed $200.

*(Added by L.1995, chap. 165(1); chgd. by L.1997, chap. 165(30.63(a)), eff. 9/1/97.)*

## §502.354. Single or 30-day trip permits; offense.

(a) The department may issue a temporary permit for a vehicle that:

(1) is subject to registration in this state; and

(2) is not authorized to travel on a public highway because of the lack of registration in this state or the lack of reciprocity with the state or country in which the vehicle is registered.

(b) A permit issued under this section:

(1) is in lieu of registration; and

(2) is valid for:

(A) one trip, as provided by Subsection (c); or

(B) 30 days, as provided by Subsection (d).

(c) A one-trip permit is valid for one trip between the points of origin and destination and those intermediate points specified in the application and registration receipt. Unless the vehicle is a bus operating under charter that is not covered by a reciprocity agreement with the state or country in which the bus is registered, a one-trip permit is for the transit of the vehicle only, and the vehicle may not be used for the transportation of any passenger or property. A one-trip permit may not be valid for longer than 15 days from the effective date of registration.

(d) A 30-day permit may be issued only to a passenger vehicle, a private bus, a trailer or semitrailer with a gross weight of not more than 10,000 pounds, a light truck, or a light commercial vehicle with a manufacturer's rated carrying capacity of more than one ton that will operate unladen. A person may obtain multiple 30-day permits. The department may issue a single registration receipt to apply to all of the periods for which the vehicle is registered.

(e) A person may obtain a permit under this section by:

(1) applying on a form provided by the department to:

(A) the county assessor-collector of the county in which the vehicle will first be operated on a public highway; or

(B) the department in Austin or at one of the department's vehicle title and registration regional offices;

(2) paying a fee, in cash or by postal money order or certified check, of:

(A) $5 for a one-trip permit; or

(B) $25 for each 30-day period; and

(3) furnishing evidence of financial responsibility for the vehicle in a form listed under Section 502.153(c).

(f) A registration receipt and temporary tag shall be issued on forms provided by the department. The temporary tag must contain all pertinent information required by this section and must be displayed in the rear window of the vehicle so that the tag is clearly visible and legible when viewed from the rear of the vehicle. If the vehicle does not have a rear window, the temporary tag must be attached on or carried in the vehicle to allow ready inspection. The registration receipt must be carried in the vehicle at all times during the period in which it is valid.

(g) The department may refuse and may instruct a county assessor-collector to refuse to issue a temporary registration for any vehicle if, in the department's opinion, the vehicle or the owner of the vehicle has been involved in operations that constitute an abuse of the privilege granted by this section. A registration issued after notice to a county assessor-collector under this subsection is void.

(h) A person issued a temporary registration under this section who operates a vehicle in violation of Subsection (f) commits an offense. An offense under this subsection is a Class C misdemeanor.

(i) The department may:

(1) adopt rules to administer this section; and

(2) prescribe an application for a permit and other forms under this section.

*(Added by L.1995, chap. 165(1); chgd. by L.1997, chap. 1092(1), eff. 6/19/97.)*

### §502.355. Nonresident-owned vehicles used to transport farm products; offense.

(a) The department may issue to a nonresident owner a permit for a truck, truck-tractor, trailer, or semitrailer that:

(1) is registered in the owner's home state or country; and

(2) will be used to transport:

(A) farm products produced in this state from the place of production to a place of market or storage or a railhead that is not more than 75 miles from the place of production;

(B) machinery used to harvest farm products produced in this state; or

(C) farm products produced outside this state from the point of entry into this state to a place of market, storage, or processing or a railhead or seaport that is not more than 80 miles from the point of entry.

(b) The department shall issue a distinguishing insignia for a vehicle issued a permit under this section. The insignia must be attached to the vehicle in lieu of regular license plates and must show the permit expiration date. A permit issued under this section is valid until the earlier of:

(1) the date the vehicle's registration in the owner's home state or country expires; or

(2) the 30th day after the date the permit is issued.

(c) A person may obtain a permit under this section by:

(1) applying to the department on a form prescribed by the department;

(2) paying a fee equal to 1/12 the registration fee prescribed by this chapter for the vehicle;

(3) furnishing satisfactory evidence that the motor vehicle is insured under an insurance policy that complies with Section 601.072 and that is written by:

(A) an insurance company or surety company authorized to write motor vehicle liability insurance in this state; or

(B) with the department's approval, a surplus lines insurer that meets the requirements of Article 1.14-2, Insurance Code, and rules adopted by the commissioner of insurance under that article, if the applicant is unable to obtain insurance from an insurer described by Paragraph (A); and

(4) furnishing evidence that the vehicle has been inspected as required under Chapter 548.

(d) A nonresident owner may not obtain more than three permits under this section during a registration year.

(e) A vehicle for which a permit is issued under this section may not be operated in this state after the permit expires unless the owner:

(1) obtains another temporary permit; or

(2) registers the vehicle under Section 502.162, 502.165, 502.166, or 502.167, as appropriate, for the remainder of the registration year.

(f) A vehicle for which a permit is issued under this section may not be registered under Section 502.163.

(g) A mileage referred to in this section is a state highway mileage.

(h) A person operating a vehicle under a permit issued under this section commits an offense if the person:

(1) transports farm products to a place of market, storage, or processing or a railhead or seaport that is farther from the place of production or point of entry, as appropriate, than the distance provided for in the permit; or

(2) follows a route other than that prescribed by the Texas Transportation Commission.

(i) An offense under Subsection (h) is a misdemeanor punishable by a fine of not less than $25 or more than $200.

*(Added by L.1995, chap. 165(1), eff. 9/1/95.)*

### §§502.356 to 502.400. *(Reserved.)*

## SUBCHAPTER H. OFFENSES AND PENALTIES

### §502.401. General penalty.

(a) A person commits an offense if the person violates a provision of this chapter and no other penalty is prescribed for the violation.

(b) This section does not apply to a violation of Section 502.003, 502.101, 502.109, 502.112, 502.113, 502.114, 502.152, 502.164, or 502.282.

(c) An offense under this section is a misdemeanor punishable by a fine not to exceed $200.

*(Added by L.1995, chap. 165(1), eff. 9/1/95.)*

### §502.402. Operation of unregistered motor vehicle.

(a) A person commits an offense if the person operates a motor vehicle that has not been registered as required by law. An offense under this subsection is a misdemeanor punishable by a fine not to exceed $200.

(b), (c) *(Repealed by L.1997, chap. 165(30.64), eff. 9/1/97.)*

*(Added by L.1995, chap. 165(1), eff. 9/1/95.)*

### §502.403. Operation of vehicle under improper registration.

(a) A person commits an offense if the person operates on a public highway a motor vehicle registered for a class other than that to which the vehicle belongs.

(b) An offense under this section is a misdemeanor punishable by a fine not to exceed $200.

*(Added by L.1995, chap. 165(1), eff. 9/1/95.)*

### §502.404. Operation of vehicle without license plate or registration insignia.

(a) A person commits an offense if the person operates on a public highway during a registration period a passenger car or commercial motor vehicle that does not display two license plates, at the front and rear of the vehicle, that have been:

(1) assigned by the department for the period; or

(2) validated by a registration insignia issued by the department that establishes that the vehicle is registered for the period.

(b) A person commits an offense if the person operates on a public highway during a registration period a passenger car or commercial motor vehicle, other than a vehicle assigned license plates for the registration period, that does not properly display the registration insignia issued by the department that establishes that the license plates have been validated for the period.

(c) A person commits an offense if the person operates on a public highway during a registration period a road tractor, motorcycle, trailer, or semitrailer that does not display a license plate, attached to the rear of the vehicle, that has been:

(1) assigned by the department for the period; or

(2) validated by a registration insignia issued by the department that establishes that the vehicle is registered for the period.

(d) Subsections (a) and (b) do not apply to a dealer operating a vehicle as provided by law.

(e) An offense under this section is a misdemeanor punishable by a fine not to exceed $200.

*(Added by L.1995, chap. 165(1), eff. 9/1/95.)*



## §502.405. Operation of motorcycle without seal.

(a) A person commits an offense if the person operates, or as the owner permits another to operate, on a public highway during a registration period a motorcycle that does not have attached a registration seal for the period.

(b) An offense under this section is a misdemeanor punishable by a fine not to exceed $200.

*(Added by L.1995, chap. 165(1), eff. 9/1/95.)*

## §502.406. Operation of all-terrain vehicle without sticker.

(a) A person commits an offense if the person operates on public property during a registration period an all-terrain vehicle, other than a vehicle owned by a nonresident and registered under the laws of the owner's home state, that does not have a number sticker or decal that is valid for the period attached to the vehicle at the location specified by the department.

(b) This section does not apply to the operation of an all-terrain vehicle owned by this state, a county, or a municipality by a person authorized to operate the vehicle.

(c) An offense under this section is a Class C misdemeanor.

*(Added by L.1995, chap. 165(1), eff. 9/1/95.)*

## §502.407. Operation of vehicle with expired license plate.

(a) A person commits an offense if, after the fifth working day after the date the registration for the vehicle expires:

(1) the person operates on a public highway during a registration period a motor vehicle, trailer, or semitrailer that has attached to it a license plate for the preceding period; and

(2) the license plate has not been validated by the attachment of a registration insignia for the registration period in effect.

(b) A justice of the peace or municipal court judge having jurisdiction of the offense may:

(1) dismiss a charge of driving with an expired motor vehicle registration if the defendant:

(A) remedies the defect not later than the 10th working day after the date of the offense; and

(B) establishes that the fee prescribed by Section 502.176 has been paid; and

(2) assess an administrative fee not to exceed $10 when the charge is dismissed.

(c) An offense under this section is a misdemeanor punishable by a fine not to exceed $200.

*(Added by L.1995, chap. 165(1); chgd. by L.1999, chap. 207(1), eff. 9/1/99.)*

## §502.408. Operation of vehicle with wrong license plate.

(a) A person commits an offense if the person operates, or as the owner permits another to operate, on a public highway a motor vehicle that has attached to it a number plate or registration insignia issued for a different vehicle. An offense under this subsection is a misdemeanor punishable by a fine not to exceed $200.

(b)-(d) *(Repealed by L.1997, chap. 165(30.65), eff. 9/1/97.)*

*(Added by L.1995, chap. 165(1), eff. 9/1/95.)*

## §502.409. Wrong, fictitious, or unclean license plate.

(a) A person commits an offense if the person attaches to or displays on a motor vehicle a number plate or registration insignia that:

(1) is assigned to a different motor vehicle;

(2) is assigned to the vehicle under any other motor vehicle law other than by the department;

(3) is assigned for a registration period other than the registration period in effect;

(4) is fictitious;

(5) has letters, numbers, or other identification marks that because of blurring matter are not plainly visible at all times during daylight;

(6) is a sticker, decal, or other insignia that is not authorized by law and that interferes with the readability of the letters or numbers on the plate; or

(7) has a coating, covering, or protective material that distorts angular visibility or detectability.

(b) Except as provided by Subsection (f), an offense under Subsection (a) is a misdemeanor punishable by a fine of not more than $200, unless it is shown at the trial of the offense that the owner knowingly altered or made illegible the letters, numbers, and other identification marks, in which case the offense is a Class B misdemeanor.

(c)-(e) *(Repealed by L.1997, chap. 165(30.66), eff. 9/1/97.)*

(f) An offense under Subsection (a)(4) is a Class B misdemeanor.

*(Added by L.1995, chap. 165(1); chgd. by L.1997, chap. 851(1); L.1999, chap. 1189(17), eff. 9/1/99.)*

### §502.410. Falsification or forgery.

(a) A person commits an offense if the person knowingly provides false or incorrect information or without legal authority signs the name of another person on a statement or application filed or given as required by this chapter.

(b) Subsection (a) does not apply to a statement or application filed or given under Section 502.184, 502.253, 502.267, 502.281, 502.352, 502.353, 502.354, or 502.355.

(c) An offense under this section is a felony of the third degree.

*(Added by L.1995, chap. 165(1); chgd. by L.1997, chap. 165(30.67(a)), eff. 9/1/97.)*

### §502.411. Bribery of county officer or agent.

(a) A person commits an offense if the person directly or indirectly agrees with the commissioners court of a county or an officer or agent of the commissioners court or county that the person will register or cause to be registered a motor vehicle, trailer, or semitrailer in that county in consideration of:

(1) the use by the county of the funds derived from the registration in the purchase of property; or

(2) an act to be performed by the commissioners court or an agent or officer of the commissioners court or the county.

(b) The registration of each separate vehicle in violation of Subsection (a) is a separate offense. The agreement or conspiracy to register is a separate offense.

(c) A person who makes or seeks to make an agreement prohibited by Subsection (a) shall be restrained by injunction on application by the district or county attorney of the county in which the vehicle is registered or the attorney general.

(d) An offense under this section is punishable in the same manner as an offense under Section 36.02, Penal Code.

*(Added by L.1995, chap. 165(1), eff. 9/1/95.)*

### §502.412. Operation of vehicle at weight greater than stated in registration application.

(a) A person commits an offense if the person operates, or permits to be operated, a motor vehicle registered under this chapter that has a weight greater than that stated in the person's application for registration. Each use of the vehicle is a separate offense.

(b) Venue for a prosecution under this section is in any county in which the motor vehicle is operated with a gross weight greater than that stated in the person's application for registration.

(c) An offense under this section is a misdemeanor punishable by a fine not to exceed $200.

*(Added by L.1995, chap. 165(1), eff. 9/1/95.)*

## CHAPTER 503. DEALER'S AND MANUFACTURER'S VEHICLE LICENSE PLATES

## SUBCHAPTER A. GENERAL PROVISIONS

Section

## SUBCHAPTER B. GENERAL DISTINGUISHING NUMBER



## SUBCHAPTER C. LICENSE PLATES AND TAGS



## SUBCHAPTER D. ENFORCEMENT

## SUBCHAPTER A. GENERAL PROVISIONS

### §503.001. Definitions.

In this chapter:

(1) "Commission" means the Texas Transportation Commission.

(2) "Dealer" means a person who regularly and actively buys, sells, or exchanges vehicles at an established and permanent location. The term includes a franchised motor vehicle dealer, an independent motor vehicle dealer, and a wholesale motor vehicle dealer.

(3) "Department" means the Texas Department of Transportation.

(4) "Drive-a-way operator" means a person who transports and delivers a vehicle in this state from the manufacturer or another point of origin to a location in this state using the vehicle's own power or using the full-mount method, the saddle-mount method, the tow-bar method, or a combination of those methods.

(5) "Franchise" has the meaning assigned by the Texas Motor Vehicle Commission Code (Article 4413(36), Texas Civil Statutes).

(6) "Franchised motor vehicle dealer" means a person engaged in the business of buying, selling, or exchanging new motor vehicles at an established and permanent place of business under a franchise in effect with a motor vehicle manufacturer or distributor.

(7) "Independent motor vehicle dealer" means a dealer other than a franchised motor vehicle dealer or a wholesale motor vehicle dealer.

(8) "Manufacturer" means a person who manufactures, distributes, or assembles new vehicles.

(9) "Motorcycle" has the meaning assigned by Section 502.001.

(10) "Motor vehicle" has the meaning assigned by Section 502.001.

(11) "Semitrailer" has the meaning assigned by Section 502.001.

(12) "Trailer" has the meaning assigned by Section 502.001.

(13) "Vehicle" means a motor vehicle, motorcycle, house trailer, trailer, or semitrailer.

(14) "Wholesale motor vehicle auction" means the offering of a motor vehicle for sale to the highest bidder during a transaction that is one of a series of regular periodic transactions that occur at a permanent location.

(15) "Wholesale motor vehicle dealer" means a dealer who sells motor vehicles only to a person who is:

(A) the holder of a dealer's general distinguishing number; or

(B) a foreign dealer authorized by a law of this state or interstate reciprocity agreement to purchase a vehicle in this state without remitting the motor vehicle sales tax.

*(Added by L.1995, chap. 165(1); chgd. by L.1997, chap. 165(30.69(a)), eff. 9/1/97.)*

### §503.002. Rules.

The commission may adopt rules for the administration of this chapter. *(Added by L.1995, chap. 165(1), eff. 9/1/95.)*

### §503.003. Display or sale of nonmotorized vehicle or trailer.

This chapter does not prohibit the display or sale of a nonmotorized vehicle or trailer at a regularly scheduled vehicle or boat show with multiple vendors in accordance with commission rules. *(Added by L.1995, chap. 165(1), eff. 9/1/95.)*

### §503.004. Buying, selling, exchanging, or manufacturing vehicles.

This chapter does not prohibit a person from entering into the business of buying, selling, or exchanging new or used vehicles at wholesale or retail or from manufacturing vehicles. *(Added by L.1995, chap. 165(1), eff. 9/1/95.)*

### §503.005. Notice of sale or transfer.

(a) A manufacturer or dealer shall immediately notify the department if the manufacturer or dealer transfers, including by sale or lease, a motor vehicle, trailer, or semitrailer to a person other than a manufacturer or dealer.

(b) The notice must be in writing using the form provided by the department and must include:

(1) the date of the transfer;

(2) the names and addresses of the transferrer and transferee; and

(3) a description of the vehicle.

*(Added by L.1995, chap. 165(1), eff. 9/1/95.)*

Printed in the U.S.A. Zt

**§503.006. Notice of change of address.**

A dealer or manufacturer who has been issued dealer's or manufacturer's license plates shall notify the department of a change to the dealer's or manufacturer's address not later than the 10th day after the date the change occurs. *(Added by L.1995, chap. 165(1), eff. 9/1/95.)*

**§503.007. Fees for general distinguishing number.**

(a) The fee for an original general distinguishing number is $500.

(b) The fee for the renewal of a general distinguishing number is $200.

(c) The registration fee for a drive-a-way in-transit license is $50.

(d) A fee collected under this section shall be deposited to the credit of the state highway fund. *(Added by L.1995, chap. 165(1); chgd. by L.1997, chap. 165(30.69(b)), eff. 9/1/97.)*

**§503.008. Fees for license plates.**

(a) The fee for a metal dealer's license plate is $20.

(b) The fee for a manufacturer's license plate is $40.

(c) The fee for an additional set of drive-a-way in-transit license plates is $5.

(d) A fee collected under this section shall be deposited to the credit of the state highway fund.

*(Added by L.1995, chap. 165(1); chgd. by L.1997, chap. 165(30.69(c)), eff. 9/1/97.)*



**§§503.009 to 503.020.** *(Reserved.)*

## SUBCHAPTER B. GENERAL DISTINGUISHING NUMBER

**§503.021. Dealer general distinguishing number.**

A person may not engage in business as a dealer, directly or indirectly, including by consignment, without a dealer general distinguishing number in one of the six categories described by Section 503.029(a)(6) for each location from which the person conducts business as a dealer. *(Added by L.1995, chap. 165(1); chgd. by L.1997, chap. 165(30.69(d)), eff. 9/1/97.)*

**§503.022. Wholesale motor vehicle auction general distinguishing number.**

A person may not engage in the business of conducting a wholesale motor vehicle auction without a wholesale motor vehicle auction general distinguishing number for each location from which the person conducts business. *(Added by L.1995, chap. 165(1), eff. 9/1/95.)*

**§503.023. Drive-a-way operator license.**

A person may not engage in business as a drive-a-way operator without a drive-a-way in-transit license. *(Added by L.1995, chap. 165(1), eff. 9/1/95.)*

**§503.024. Exclusions for dealer.**

(a) A person is not required to obtain a dealer general distinguishing number if the person:

(1) sells or offers to sell during a calendar year fewer than five vehicles of the same type that are owned and registered in that person's name; or

(2) is a federal, state, or local governmental agency.

(b) For the purposes of Section 503.021, a person is not engaging in business as a dealer by:

(1) selling or offering to sell a vehicle the person acquired for personal or business use to a person other than a retail buyer if the sale or offer is not made to avoid a requirement of this chapter;

(2) selling, in a manner provided by law for the forced sale of vehicles, a vehicle in which the person holds a security interest;

(3) acting under a court order as a receiver, trustee, administrator, executor, guardian, or other appointed person;

(4) selling a vehicle the person acquired from the vehicle's owner as a result of paying an insurance claim if the person is an insurance company;

(5) selling an antique passenger car or truck that is at least 25 years of age; or

(6) selling a special interest vehicle that is at least 12 years of age if the person is a collector.

(c) For the purposes of Section 503.021, a domiciliary of another state who holds a dealer license and bond, if applicable, issued by the other state is not engaging in business as a dealer by buying a vehicle from, selling a vehicle to, or exchanging a vehicle with a person who:

(1) holds a general distinguishing number issued by the department, if the transaction is not intended to avoid a requirement of this chapter; or

(2) is a domiciliary of another state who holds a dealer license and bond, if applicable, issued by the other state and the transaction is not intended to avoid a requirement of this chapter.

(d) For the purposes of Section 503.021, a licensed auctioneer is not engaging in business as a dealer by, as a bid caller, selling or offering to sell property to the highest bidder at a bona fide auction if:

(1) legal or equitable title does not pass to the auctioneer;

(2) the auction is not held to avoid a requirement of this chapter; and

(3) for an auction of vehicles owned legally or equitably by a person who holds a general distinguishing number, the auction is conducted at the location for which the general distinguishing number was issued.

(e) In this section, "special interest vehicle" has the meaning assigned by Section 683.077(b). *(Added by L.1995, chap. 165(1), eff. 9/1/95.)*

### §503.025. Wholesale motor vehicle auction exception.

A person exempt under Section 503.024(d) is not required to obtain a wholesale motor vehicle auction general distinguishing number. *(Added by L.1995, chap. 165(1), eff. 9/1/95.)*

### §503.026. Requirement for each type of dealer vehicle.

A person must obtain a dealer general distinguishing number for each type of vehicle the person intends to sell. *(Added by L.1995, chap. 165(1); chgd. by L.1997, chap. 871(1), eff. 9/1/97.)*

### §503.027. Requirements relating to dealer location.

(a) If a person consigns for sale more than five vehicles in a calendar year from a location other than the location for which the person holds a wholesale motor vehicle auction general distinguishing number or a dealer general distinguishing number, the location to which the person consigns the vehicles must have a general distinguishing number for that location.

(b) If a person is not otherwise prohibited from doing business as a dealer at more than one location in the territory of a municipality, a person may buy, sell, or exchange a vehicle of the type for which the person holds a dealer general distinguishing number from more than one location in the territory of the municipality without obtaining an additional dealer general distinguishing number. Each location must comply with the requirements prescribed by this chapter and commission rules relating to an established and permanent place of business.
*(Added by L.1995, chap. 165(1), eff. 9/1/95.)*

### §503.028. Requirements relating to wholesale motor vehicle auction location.

(a) Except as provided by Subsection (b), the department may not issue more than one general distinguishing number for a location for which the wholesale motor vehicle auction general distinguishing number has been issued.

(b) The department may issue to a person who holds a wholesale motor vehicle auction general distinguishing number a dealer general distinguishing number for the location for which the wholesale motor vehicle auction general distinguishing number is issued. The provisions of this subchapter relating to the application for and issuance of a dealer general distinguishing number apply to an application for and issuance of a dealer general distinguishing number issued under this subsection.
*(Added by L.1995, chap. 165(1), eff. 9/1/95.)*

### §503.029. Application for dealer general distinguishing number.

(a) An applicant for an original or renewal dealer general distinguishing number must submit to the department a written application on a form that:

(1) is provided by the department;

(2) contains the information required by the department;

(3) contains information that demonstrates the person meets the requirements prescribed by Section 503.032;

(4) contains information that demonstrates the applicant has complied with all applicable state laws and municipal ordinances;

(5) states that the applicant agrees to allow the department to examine during working hours the ownership papers for each registered or unregistered vehicle in the applicant's possession or control; and

(6) specifies whether the applicant proposes to be a:

(A) franchised motor vehicle dealer;

(B) independent motor vehicle dealer;

(C) wholesale motor vehicle dealer;

(D) motorcycle dealer;
(E) house trailer dealer; or
(F) trailer or semitrailer dealer.

(b) The applicant must swear to the truth of the information contained in the application before an officer authorized to administer oaths.

(c) A renewal application must be:
(1) submitted before the date the general distinguishing number expires; and
(2) accompanied by the appropriate fee prescribed by Section 503.007.

*(Added by L.1995, chap. 165(1); chgd. by L.1997, chaps. 165(30.69(e)), 871(2), eff. 9/1/97.)*

### §503.030. Application for wholesale motor vehicle auction general distinguishing number.

(a) An applicant for an original or renewal wholesale motor vehicle auction general distinguishing number must submit to the department an application that contains:
(1) the information required by the department;
(2) information that demonstrates the person meets the requirements prescribed by Section 503.032; and
(3) information that demonstrates the applicant has complied with all applicable state laws and municipal ordinances.

(b) The applicant must swear to the truth of the information contained in the application.

*(Added by L.1995, chap. 165(1), eff. 9/1/95.)*

### §503.031. Application for drive-a-way in-transit license.

(a) An applicant for a drive-a-way in-transit license must submit to the commission an application containing the information required by the commission.

(b) The license application must be accompanied by the registration fee prescribed by Section 503.007(c).

*(Added by L.1995, chap. 165(1), eff. 9/1/95.)*

### §503.032. Established and permanent place of business.

(a) An applicant for a dealer general distinguishing number or wholesale motor vehicle auction general distinguishing number must demonstrate that the location for which the applicant requests the number is an established and permanent place of business. A location is considered to be an established and permanent place of business if the applicant:
(1) owns the real property on which the business is situated or has a written lease for the property that has a term of not less than one year;
(2) maintains on the location:
(A) a permanent furnished office that is equipped as required by the department for the sale of the vehicles of the type specified in the application; and
(B) a conspicuous sign with letters at least six inches high showing the name of the applicant's business; and
(3) has sufficient space on the location to display at least five vehicles of the type specified in the application.

(b) An applicant for a general distinguishing number as a wholesale motor vehicle dealer is not required to maintain display space in accordance with Subsection (a)(3).

(c) The applicant must demonstrate that:
(1) the applicant intends to remain regularly and actively engaged in the business specified in the application for at least one year at the location specified in the application; and
(2) the applicant or a bona fide employee of the applicant will be:
(A) at the location to buy, sell, lease, or exchange vehicles; and
(B) available to the public or the department at that location during reasonable and lawful business hours.

*(Added by L.1995, chap. 165(1); chgd. by L.1997, chap. 165(30.69(f)), eff. 9/1/97.)*

### §503.033. Security requirement.

(a) The department may not issue or renew a motor vehicle dealer general distinguishing number or a wholesale motor vehicle auction general distinguishing number unless the applicant provides to the department:
(1) satisfactory proof that the applicant has purchased a properly executed surety bond in the amount of $25,000 with a good and sufficient surety approved by the department; or
(2) other security under Subsection (c).

(b) The surety bond must be:

(1) in a form approved by the attorney general;

(2) conditioned on:

(A) the payment by the applicant of all valid bank drafts, including checks, drawn by the applicant to buy motor vehicles; and

(B) the transfer by the applicant of good title to each motor vehicle the applicant offers for sale.

(c) In lieu of the surety bond, the department may accept and receive for the surety obligation:

(1) a pledge of cash;

(2) a cash deposit;

(3) a certificate of deposit; or

(4) another instrument the department determines to be adequate security.

(d) A person may recover against a surety bond or other security if the person obtains against a person issued a motor vehicle dealer general distinguishing number or a wholesale motor vehicle auction general distinguishing number a judgment assessing damages and reasonable attorney's fees based on an act or omission on which the bond is conditioned that occurred during the term for which the general distinguishing number was valid.

(e) The liability imposed on a surety is limited to:

(1) the amount:

(A) of the valid bank drafts, including checks, drawn by the applicant to buy motor vehicles; or

(B) paid to the applicant for a motor vehicle for which the applicant did not deliver good title; and

(2) attorney's fees that are incurred in the recovery of the judgment and that are reasonable in relation to the work performed.

(f) The liability of a surety may not exceed the face value of the surety bond. A surety is not liable for successive claims in excess of the bond amount regardless of the number of claims made against the bond or the number of years the bond remains in force.

(g) This section does not apply to a person licensed as a franchised motor vehicle dealer by the department's Motor Vehicle Board.

*(Added by L.1995, chap. 165(1); chgd. by L.1997, chap. 755(1), eff. 6/17/97.)*

### §503.034. Issuance and renewal or denial of dealer or wholesale motor vehicle auction general distinguishing number.

(a) The department shall deny an application for the issuance or renewal of a dealer general distinguishing number or a wholesale motor vehicle auction general distinguishing number if the department is satisfied from the application or from other information before it that:

(1) information in the application is not true; or

(2) the applicant is guilty of conduct that would result in the cancellation of the general distinguishing number under Section 503.038.

(b) The department may not issue a dealer general distinguishing number until the applicant complies with the requirements of this chapter.

(c) A dealer's general distinguishing number expires on March 31 of each year, unless provided otherwise by law or rule of the department's Motor Vehicle Board.

*(Added by L.1995, chap. 165(1); chgd. by L.1997, chap. 165(30.69(g)), eff. 9/1/97.)*

### §503.035. Issuance and renewal of drive-a-way in-transit license.

The department shall issue to an applicant on the filing of the application and the payment of the fee an annual drive-a-way in-transit license and in-transit license plates. *(Added by L.1995, chap. 165(1); chgd. by L.1997, chap. 871(3), eff. 9/1/97.)*

### §503.036. Reassignment of evidence of ownership; dealer categories.

(a) The holder of a franchised motor vehicle dealer's general distinguishing number may buy, sell, or exchange new or used motor vehicles and reassign a manufacturer's certificate of origin, certificate of title, or other basic evidence of ownership of any type of vehicle owned by the dealer that the dealer is not otherwise prohibited by law from selling or offering for sale.

(b) The holder of an independent motor vehicle dealer's general distinguishing number may reassign a certificate of title or other basic evidence of ownership of any type of vehicle owned by the dealer that the dealer is not otherwise prohibited by law from selling or offering for sale.

(c) The holder of a wholesale motor vehicle dealer's general distinguishing number may sell or offer to sell motor vehicles to no person except:

(1) a person who holds a general distinguishing number; or

(2) a person who is legally recognized as and duly licensed or otherwise qualified as a dealer under the laws of another state or foreign jurisdiction.
*(Added by L.1995, chap. 165(1); chgd. by L.1997, chaps. 755(2), eff. 6/17/97. See other section 503.036 below.)*

## §503.036 Rights of dealer.

(a) Except as provided by Subsections (b), (c), and (d), a dealer may reassign any basic evidence of ownership, including a manufacturer's certificate of origin or a certificate of title, for a vehicle owned the dealer that the dealer is not otherwise prohibited by law from selling only if the dealer:

(1) is licensed by the department's Motor Vehicle Board; or

(2) has filed security as required by Section 503.033.

(b) A person who holds a franchised motor vehicle dealer's general distinguishing number may buy, sell, or exchange a new or used motor vehicle and may reassign a manufacturer's certificate of title, or other basic evidence of ownership for a vehicle owned by the person that the person is not otherwise prohibited by law from selling.

(c) A person who holds an independent motor vehicle dealer's general distinguishing number may reassign a basic evidence of ownership, including a certificate of title, for a vehicle owned by the person is not otherwise prohibited by law from selling.

(d) A person who holds a wholesale motor vehicle dealer's general distinguishing number may sell a motor vehicle only to a person who is:

(1) a dealer who holds a general distinguishing number; or

(2) a foreign dealer authorized by a law of this state or interstate reciprocity agreement to purchase a vehicle in this state without remitting the motor vehicle sales tax.
*(Added by L.1995, chap. 165(1); chgd. by L.1997, chap. 165(30.69(h)), eff. 9/1/97. See other section 503.036 above.)*

## §503.037. Rights of wholesale motor vehicle auction.

(a) A person who holds a wholesale motor vehicle auction general distinguishing number may accept on consignment one or more motor vehicles to auction. The person may offer a motor vehicle for sale only at the location for which the general distinguishing number is issued and only by bid to the highest bidder. The title to a motor vehicle may be in the name in which the general distinguishing number is issued.

(b) Except as provided by Subsection (d), a person who holds a wholesale motor vehicle auction general distinguishing number may not sell a motor vehicle to a person other than a person who:

(1) is a dealer; or

(2) has a license and, if applicable, a bond issued by the appropriate authority of another state or nation.

(c) A person who holds a wholesale motor vehicle auction general distinguishing number may not allow another person to use the auction's facilities or general distinguishing number to sell or auction a motor vehicle.

(d) Subsection (b) does not prohibit a person who holds a wholesale motor vehicle auction general distinguishing number from offering for sale a motor vehicle to a person who is not a dealer or who does not have a license issued by the appropriate authority of another state, if the motor vehicle is owned by:

(1) this state or a department, agency, or subdivision of this state; or

(2) the United States.
*(Added by L.1995, chap. 165(1); chgd. by L.1997, chap. 165(30.70(a)), eff. 9/1/97.)*

## §503.038. Cancellation of general distinguishing number.

(a) The department may cancel a dealer's general distinguishing number if the dealer:

(1) falsifies or forges a title document, including an affidavit making application for a certified copy of a title;

(2) files a false or forged tax document, including a sales tax affidavit;

(3) fails to take assignment of any basic evidence of ownership, including a certificate of title or manufacturer's certificate, for a vehicle the dealer acquires;

(4) fails to assign any basic evidence of ownership, including a certificate of title or manufacturer's certificate, for a vehicle the dealer sells;

(5) uses or permits the use of a metal dealer's license plate or a dealer's temporary cardboard tag on a vehicle that the dealer does not own or control or that is not in stock and offered for sale;

(6) makes a material misrepresentation in an application or other information filed with the department;

(7) fails to maintain the qualifications for a general distinguishing number;

(8) fails to provide to the department within 30 days after the date of demand by the department satisfactory and reasonable evidence that the person is regularly and actively engaged in business as a wholesale or retail dealer;

(9) has been licensed for at least 12 months and has not assigned at least five vehicles during the previous 12-month period;

(10) has failed to demonstrate compliance with Sections 23.12, 23.121, and 23.122, Tax Code;

(11) uses or allows the use of the dealer's general distinguishing number or the location for which the general distinguishing number is issued to avoid the requirements of this chapter;

(12) misuses or allows the misuse of a temporary cardboard tag authorized under this chapter;

(13) refuses to show on a buyer's temporary cardboard tag the date of sale or other reasonable information required by the department; or

(14) otherwise violates this chapter or a rule adopted under this chapter.

(b) The department shall cancel a dealer's general distinguishing number if the dealer obtains the number by submitting false or misleading information.

(c) A person whose general distinguishing number is canceled under this chapter shall surrender to a representative of the department each license plate, temporary cardboard tag, sticker, and receipt issued under this chapter not later than the 10th day after the date the general distinguishing number is canceled. The department shall direct any peace officer to secure and return to the department any plate, tag, sticker, or receipt of a person who does not comply with this subsection.

(d) A person whose general distinguishing number is canceled automatically loses any benefits and privileges afforded under Chapter 501 to the person as a dealer.

*(Added by L.1995, chap. 165(1); chgd. by L.1997, chaps. 165(30.69(i)), 871(4), eff. 9/1/97.)*

**§§503.039 to 503.060.** *(Reserved.)*

## SUBCHAPTER C. LICENSE PLATES AND TAGS

### §503.061. Dealer's license plates.

Instead of registering under Chapter 502 a vehicle that the dealer owns, operates, or permits to be operated on a public street or highway, the dealer may apply for, receive, and attach metal dealer's license plates to the vehicle if it is the type of vehicle:

(1) that the dealer sells; and

(2) for which the dealer has been issued a general distinguishing number.

*(Added by L.1995, chap. 165(1), eff. 9/1/95.)*

### §503.0615. Personalized prestige dealer's license plates.

(a) The department shall establish and issue personalized prestige dealer's license plates. The department may not issue identically lettered or numbered dealer's plates to more than one dealer.

(b) The department shall establish procedures for continuous application for and issuance of personalized prestige dealer's license plates. A dealer must make a new application and pay a new fee for each registration period for which the dealer seeks to obtain personalized prestige dealer's license plates. A dealer who obtains personalized prestige dealer's license plates has first priority on those plates for each subsequent registration period for which the dealer applies.

(c) The annual fee for personalized prestige dealer's license plates is $40, in addition to any fee otherwise prescribed by this chapter.

(d) The department may issue to an applicant only one set of personalized prestige dealer's license plates for a vehicle for a six-year period. The department may issue a new set of personalized prestige dealer's license plates within the six-year period if the applicant pays a fee of $50 in addition to the fees required by Subsection (c).

(e) On application and payment of the required fee for a registration period following the issuance of the plates, the department shall issue a registration insignia.

(f) Of each fee collected by the department under this section:

(1) $1.25 shall be deposited to the credit of the state highway fund to defray the cost of administering this section; and

(2) the remainder shall be deposited to the credit of the general revenue fund.

*(Added by L.1997, chap. 871(5), eff. 9/1/97.)*

Printed in the U.S.A. Zt

### §503.0618. Converter's license plates.

(a) In this section, "converter" means a person who holds a converter's license issued under the Texas Motor Vehicle Commission Code (Article 4413(36), Vernon's Texas Civil Statutes).

(b) Instead of registering under Chapter 502 a vehicle that a converter operates or permits to be operated on a public street or highway, the converter may apply for, receive, and attach metal converter's license plates to the vehicle if it is the type of vehicle that the converter is engaged in the business of assembling or modifying.

(c) The fee for a metal converter's license plate is $20.

(d) The department shall prescribe the form of an application under this section.

*(Added by L.1999, chap. 964(1), eff. 9/1/99.)*

### §503.062. Dealer's temporary cardboard tags.

(a) A dealer may issue a temporary cardboard tag for use on an unregistered vehicle by the dealer or the dealer's employees only to:

(1) demonstrate or cause to be demonstrated to a prospective buyer the vehicle for sale purposes only;

(2) convey or cause to be conveyed the vehicle:

(A) from one of the dealer's places of business in this state to another of the dealer's places of business in this state;

(B) from the dealer's place of business to a place the vehicle is to be repaired, reconditioned, or serviced;

(C) from the state line or a location in this state where the vehicle is unloaded to the dealer's place of business;

(D) from the dealer's place of business to a place of business of another dealer;

(E) from the point of purchase by the dealer to the dealer's place of business; or

(F) to road test the vehicle; or

(3) use the vehicle for or allow its use by a charitable organization.

(b) Subsection (a)(1) does not prohibit a dealer from permitting a prospective buyer to operate a vehicle while the vehicle is being demonstrated.

(c) A vehicle being conveyed under this section is exempt from the inspection requirements of Chapter 548.

(d) The department may not issue a dealer temporary cardboard tag or contract for the issuance of a dealer temporary cardboard tag but shall prescribe:

(1) the specifications, form, and color of a dealer temporary cardboard tag; and

(2) the period for which a tag may be used for or by a charitable organization.

(e) For purposes of this section, "charitable organization" means an organization organized to relieve poverty, to advance education, religion, or science, to promote health, governmental, or municipal purposes, or for other purposes beneficial to the community without financial gain.

*(Added by L.1995, chap. 165(1); chgd. by L.1997, chap. 871(6), eff. 9/1/97.)*

### §503.0625. Converter's temporary cardboard tags.

(a) In this section, "converter" means a person who holds a converter's license issued under the Texas Motor Vehicle Commission Code (Article 4413(36), Vernon's Texas Civil Statutes).

(b) A converter may issue a temporary cardboard tag for use on an unregistered vehicle by the converter or the converter's employees only to:

(1) demonstrate or cause to be demonstrated to a prospective buyer who is an employee of a franchised motor vehicle dealer the vehicle; or

(2) convey or cause to be conveyed the vehicle:

(A) from one of the converter's places of business in this state to another of the converter's places of business in this state;

(B) from the converter's place of business to a place the vehicle is to be assembled, repaired, reconditioned, modified, or serviced;

(C) from the state line or a location in this state where the vehicle is unloaded to the converter's place of business;

(D) from the converter's place of business to a place of business of a franchised motor vehicle dealer; or

(E) to road test the vehicle.

(c) Subsection (b)(1) does not prohibit a converter from permitting a prospective buyer who is an employee of a franchised motor vehicle dealer to operate a vehicle while the vehicle is being demonstrated.

(d) A vehicle being conveyed while displaying a temporary tag issued under this section is exempt from the inspection requirements of Chapter 548.

(e) The department may not issue a converter temporary cardboard tag or contract for the issuance of a converter temporary cardboard tag but shall prescribe the specifications, form, and color of a converter temporary cardboard tag.

(f) A converter or employee of a converter may not use a temporary cardboard tag issued under this section as authorization to operate a vehicle for the converter's or the employee's personal use.

*(Added by L.1999, chap. 964(2), eff. 9/1/99.)*

### §503.063. Buyer's temporary cardboard tags.

(a) Except as provided by this section, a dealer may issue to a person who buys an unregistered vehicle one temporary cardboard buyer's tag for the vehicle.

(b) Except as provided by this section, the buyer's tag is valid for the operation of the vehicle until the earlier of:

(1) the date on which the vehicle is registered; or

(2) the 21st day after the date of purchase.

(c) The dealer:

(1) must show in ink on the buyer's tag the actual date of sale and any other required information; and

(2) is responsible for displaying the tag.

(d) The dealer is responsible for the safekeeping and distribution of each buyer's tag the dealer obtains.

(e) The department may not issue a buyer's tag or contract for the issuance of a buyer's tag but shall prescribe the specifications, color, and form of a buyer's tag.

(f) A dealer may issue an additional temporary cardboard buyer's tag to a person after the expiration of 21 days after the issue of a temporary cardboard buyer's tag, and the person may operate the vehicle for which the tag was issued on the additional temporary cardboard buyer's tag if the dealer has been unable to obtain on behalf of the vehicle's owner the necessary documents to obtain permanent metal license plates because the documents are in the possession of a lienholder who has not complied with the terms of Section 501.115(a) of this code. An additional tag issued under the terms of this subsection is valid for a maximum of 21 days after the date of issue.

*(Added by L.1995, chap. 165(1); chgd. by L.1997, chaps. 296(3), 871(7), eff. 5/26/97, 9/1/97, respectively.)*

### §503.064. Manufacturer's license plates.

(a) Instead of registering a new vehicle that a manufacturer intends to test on a public street or highway or to loan to a consumer for the purpose described by Section 6.07(d), Texas Motor Vehicle Commission Code (Article 4413(36), Texas Civil Statutes), the manufacturer may apply for, receive, and attach manufacturer's license plates to the vehicle.

(b) If the vehicle to which the manufacturer's license plates are attached is a commercial motor vehicle, the vehicle may not carry a load.

*(Added by L.1995, chap. 165(1), eff. 9/1/95.)*

### §503.065. Buyer's out-of-state license plates.

(a) The department may issue or cause to be issued to a person a temporary license plate made of cardboard or similar material authorizing the person to operate a new unregistered vehicle on a public highway of this state if the person:

(1) buys the vehicle from a dealer outside this state and intends to drive the vehicle from the dealer's place of business; or

(2) buys the vehicle from a dealer in this state but intends to drive the vehicle from the manufacturer's place of business outside this state.

(b) The department may not issue a temporary license plate under this section to a manufacturer or dealer of a motor vehicle, trailer, or semitrailer or to a representative of such a dealer.

(c) A person may not use a temporary license plate issued under this section on a vehicle transporting property.

(d) A temporary license plate issued under this section expires not later than the 30th day after the date on which it is issued. The department shall place or cause to be placed on the license plate at the time of issuance the date of expiration and the type of vehicle for which the license plate is issued.

(e) The fee for a temporary license plate issued under this section is $3. Only one license plate may be issued for each vehicle.

*(Added by L.1995, chap. 165(1), eff. 9/1/95.)*

## §503.066. Application for dealer's or manufacturer's license plates.

(a) An applicant for one or more original or renewal dealer's or manufacturer's license plates must submit to the department a written application on a form that:

(1) is provided by the department; and

(2) contains a statement that the applicant agrees to allow the department to examine during working hours the ownership papers for each registered or unregistered vehicle in the applicant's possession or control.

(b) The applicant must swear to the truth of the information contained in the application before an officer authorized to administer oaths.

(c) An application must be:

(1) submitted before the date the plate expires; and

(2) accompanied by the appropriate fee prescribed by Section 503.008.

(d) License plates shall be mailed to qualified applicants during February and March.

(e) A license plate issued under this section expires on March 31 of the year after the year of issuance, unless provided otherwise by law or rule of the department's Motor Vehicle Board.
*(Added by L.1995, chap. 165(1); chgd. by L.1997, chaps. 165(30.69(j)), 871(8), eff. 9/1/97.)*

## §503.067. Unauthorized reproduction of temporary cardboard tags.

(a) A person other than a dealer may not produce or reproduce a buyer's or dealer's temporary cardboard tag.

(b) A person may not operate a vehicle that displays an unauthorized temporary cardboard tag.
*(Added by L.1995, chap. 165(1), eff. 9/1/95.)*

## §503.068. Limitation on use of dealer's license plates and tags.

(a) A dealer or an employee of a dealer may not use a dealer's temporary cardboard tag as authorization to operate a vehicle for the dealer's or the employee's personal use.

(b) A person may not use a metal dealer's license plate or dealer's temporary cardboard tag on:

(1) a service or work vehicle; or

(2) a commercial vehicle that is carrying a load.

(c) For purposes of this section, a boat trailer carrying a boat is not a commercial vehicle carrying a load. A dealer complying with this chapter may affix to the rear of a boat trailer the dealer owns or sells a metal dealer's license plate or temporary cardboard tag issued under Section 503.061, 503.062, or 503.063.

(d) This section does not prohibit the operation or conveyance of an unregistered vehicle using the full-mount method, saddle-mount method, tow-bar method, or a combination of those methods in accordance with Section 503.062 or 503.063.
*(Added by L.1995, chap. 165(1), eff. 9/1/95.)*

## §503.069. Display of license plates and tags.

(a) A license plate, other than an in-transit license plate, or a temporary cardboard tag issued under this chapter shall be displayed in accordance with commission rules.

(b) A drive-a-way operator who has been issued a drive-a-way in-transit license shall display the operator's in-transit license plates on each transported motor vehicle from the vehicle's point of origin to its point of destination in this state in accordance with the laws relating to the operation of a vehicle on a public highway.
*(Added by L.1995, chap. 165(1), eff. 9/1/95.)*

## §503.070. Removal of out-of-state license plates.

(a) A dealer who purchases a vehicle that displays an out-of-state license plate must remove the plate within a reasonable time.

(b) A dealer who purchases a vehicle for resale may not operate the vehicle on a public street or highway in this state while the vehicle displays an out-of-state license plate.
*(Added by L.1995, chap. 165(1), eff. 9/1/95.)*

## §503.071. Notice of driving or towing from out of state.

(a) A motor vehicle that is manufactured outside this state and is driven or towed from the place of manufacture to this state for sale in this state must have affixed to it a sticker stating that the vehicle is being driven or towed from the place it was manufactured.

(b) The sticker must be at least three inches in diameter and must be affixed to the windshield or front of the motor vehicle in plain view.

(c) The sticker must remain on the motor vehicle until the vehicle is sold by a dealer.
*(Added by L.1995, chap. 165(1), eff. 9/1/95.)*

### §§503.072 to 503.090. *(Reserved.)*

## SUBCHAPTER D. ENFORCEMENT

### §503.091. Enforcement agreement.

The department may agree with an authorized official of another jurisdiction to regulate activities and exchange information relating to the wholesale operations of nonresident vehicle dealers. *(Added by L.1995, chap. 165(1), eff. 9/1/95.)*

### §503.092. Action to enforce chapter.

(a) The attorney general or a district, county, or city attorney may enforce this chapter and bring an enforcement action in the county in which a violation of this chapter is alleged to have occurred.

(b) A justice court has concurrent original jurisdiction with the county court or a county court at law over an action to enforce this chapter.
*(Added by L.1995, chap. 165(1), eff. 9/1/95.)*

### §503.093. Action to enforce subchapter.

(a) The department or any interested person may bring an action, including an action for an injunction, to:

(1) enforce a provision of Subchapter B; or

(2) prohibit a person from operating in violation of the person's application for a general distinguishing number.

(b) A plaintiff other than the department may recover the plaintiff's attorney's fees.
*(Added by L.1995, chap. 165(1); chgd. by L.1997, chap. 871(9), eff. 9/1/97.)*

### §503.094. Criminal penalty.

(a) A person commits an offense if the person violates this chapter.

(b) An offense under this section is a misdemeanor punishable by a fine of not less than $50 or more than $5,000.

(c) If the trier of fact finds that the person committed the violation wilfully or with conscious indifference to law, the court may treble the fine otherwise due as a penalty for the violation.
*(Added by L.1995, chap. 165(1), eff. 9/1/95.)*

### §503.095. Civil penalty.

(a) In addition to any other penalty prescribed by this chapter, a person who violates this chapter or a rule adopted under this chapter is subject to a civil penalty of not less than $50 or more than $1,000.

(b) For purposes of this section, each act in violation of this chapter and each day of a continuing violation is a separate violation.
*(Added by L.1995, chap. 165(1), eff. 9/1/95.)*

## CHAPTERS 504 to 519. *(Reserved.)*

## CHAPTER 520. MISCELLANEOUS PROVISIONS

## SUBCHAPTER A. GENERAL PROVISIONS

## SUBCHAPTER B. MOTOR NUMBER RECORD REQUIREMENTS



## SUBCHAPTER C. GENERAL REQUIREMENTS RELATING TO TRANSFERS OF USED MOTOR VEHICLES





## SUBCHAPTER D. TRANSFER OF TITLE AND REGISTRATION OF USED VEHICLE



## SUBCHAPTER E. MOTOR VEHICLE TITLE SERVICES



## SUBCHAPTER A. GENERAL PROVISIONS

### §520.001. Definition.

In this chapter, "department" means the Texas Department of Transportation. *(Added by L.1995, chap. 165(1), eff. 9/1/95.)*

### §520.002. Lease of additional computer equipment.

(a) This section applies only to the lease of equipment to a county for the operation of the automated registration and title system in addition to the equipment provided by the department at no cost to the county under a formula prescribed by the department.

(b) On the request of the tax assessor-collector of a county, the department may enter into an agreement with the commissioners court of that county under which the department leases additional equipment to the county for the use of the tax assessor-collector in operating the automated registration and title system in that county.

(c) A county may install equipment leased under this section at offices of the county or of an agent of the county.

(d) Equipment leased under this section:

(1) remains the property of the department; and

(2) must be used primarily for the automated registration and title system.

(e) Under the agreement, the department shall charge the county an amount not less than the amount of the cost to the department to provide the additional equipment and any related services under the lease. All money collected under the lease shall be deposited to the credit of the state highway fund.
*(Added by L.1999, chap. 876(1), eff. 6/18/99.)*

**§§520.003 to 520.010.** *(Reserved.)*

## SUBCHAPTER B. MOTOR NUMBER RECORD REQUIREMENTS

### §520.011. Motor number required for vehicle registration; penalty.

(a) A person may not apply to the county assessor-collector for the registration of a motor vehicle from which the original motor number has been removed, erased, or destroyed until the motor vehicle bears the motor number assigned by the department.

(b) A person commits an offense if the person violates this section. An offense under this subsection is a misdemeanor punishable by a fine of not less than $50 and not more than $100.
*(Added by L.1995, chap. 165(1), eff. 9/1/95.)*

### §520.012. Application for motor number record; record; penalty.

(a) To obtain a motor number assigned by the department, the owner of a motor vehicle that has had the original motor number removed, erased, or destroyed must file a sworn application with the department.

(b) The department shall maintain a separate register for recording each motor number assigned by the department. For each motor number assigned by the department, the record must indicate:

(1) the motor number assigned by the department;

(2) the name and address of the owner of the motor vehicle; and

(3) the make, model, and year of manufacture of the motor vehicle.

(c) A person who fails to comply with this section commits an offense. An offense under this subsection is a misdemeanor punishable by a fine of not less than $10 and not more than $100.
*(Added by L.1995, chap. 165(1), eff. 9/1/95.)*

### §520.013. Presentation of motor number receipt required; penalty.

(a) A person who receives a motor number from the department shall present the receipt received from the department for the assignment of the motor number to the county assessor-collector when the person applies for the registration of the motor vehicle.

(b) A person commits an offense if the person violates this section. An offense under this subsection is a misdemeanor punishable by a fine of not less than $10 and not more than $50.
*(Added by L.1995, chap. 165(1), eff. 9/1/95.)*

### §520.014. Violation by county assessor-collector; penalty.

(a) A county assessor-collector commits an offense if the county assessor-collector knowingly accepts an application for the registration of a motor vehicle that:

(1) has had the original motor number removed, erased, or destroyed; and

(2) does not bear a motor number assigned by the department.

(b) An offense under this section is a misdemeanor punishable by a fine of not less than $10 and not more than $50.
*(Added by L.1995, chap. 165(1), eff. 9/1/95.)*

**§§520.015 to 520.020.** *(Reserved.)*

## SUBCHAPTER C. GENERAL REQUIREMENTS RELATING TO TRANSFERS OF USED MOTOR VEHICLES

### §520.021. Current registration required.

A person, whether acting for that person or another, may not sell, trade, or otherwise transfer a used vehicle required to be registered under the law of this state unless at the time of delivery the vehicle is registered in this state. *(Added by L.1995, chap. 165(1), eff. 9/1/95.)*

### §520.022. Delivery of receipt and title to transferee; penalty.

(a) A person, whether acting for that person or another, who sells, trades, or otherwise transfers a used motor vehicle shall deliver to the transferee at the time of delivery of the vehicle:

(1) the license receipt issued by the department for registration of the vehicle, if the vehicle was required to be registered at the time of the delivery; and

(2) a properly assigned certificate of title or other evidence of title as required under Chapter 501.

(b) A person commits an offense if the person violates this section. An offense under this subsection is a misdemeanor punishable by a fine not to exceed $200.

*(Added by L.1995, chap. 165(1); chgd. by L.1999, chap. 1423(5), eff. 9/1/99.)*

### §520.0225. Persons on active duty in armed forces of United States.

(a) This section applies only to a used motor vehicle that is owned by a person who:

(1) is on active duty in the armed forces of the United States;

(2) is stationed in or has been assigned to another nation under military orders; and

(3) has registered the vehicle or been issued a license for the vehicle under the applicable status of forces agreement by:

(A) the appropriate branch of the armed forces of the United States; or

(B) the nation in which the person is stationed or to which the person has been assigned.

(b) The requirement in Section 520.021 that a used vehicle be registered under the law of this state does not apply to a vehicle described by Subsection (a). In lieu of delivering the license receipt to the transferee of the vehicle, as required by Section 520.022, the person selling, trading, or otherwise transferring a used motor vehicle described by Subsection (a) shall deliver to the transferee:

(1) a letter written on official letterhead by the owner's unit commander attesting to the registration of the vehicle under Subsection (a)(3); or

(2) the registration receipt issued by the appropriate branch of the armed forces or host nation.

(c) A registration receipt issued by a host nation that is not written in the English language must be accompanied by:

(1) a written translation of the registration receipt in English; and

(2) an affidavit, in English and signed by the person translating the registration receipt, attesting to the person's ability to translate the registration receipt into English.

*(Added by L.1999, chap. 836(2), eff. 9/1/99.)*

### §520.023. Powers and duties of department on transfer of used vehicle.

(a) On receipt of a written notice of transfer from the transferor of a motor vehicle, the department shall indicate the transfer on the motor vehicle records maintained by the department.

(b) The department may design the written notice of transfer to be part of the certificate of title for the vehicle. The form shall be provided by the department and must include a place for the transferor to state:

(1) the vehicle identification number of the vehicle;

(2) the number of the license plate issued to the vehicle, if any;

(3) the full name and address of the transferor;

(4) the full name and address of the transferee;

(5) the date the transferor delivered possession of the vehicle to the transferee;

(6) the signature of the transferor; and

(7) the date the transferor signed the form.

(c) After the date of the transfer of the vehicle shown on the records of the department, the transferee of the vehicle shown on the records is rebuttably presumed to be:

(1) the owner of the vehicle; and

(2) subject to civil and criminal liability arising out of the use, operation, or abandonment of the vehicle, to the extent that ownership of the vehicle subjects the owner of the vehicle to criminal or civil liability under another provision of law.

(d) The department may adopt:

(1) rules to implement this section; and

(2) a fee for filing a notice of transfer under this section in an amount not to exceed the lesser of the actual cost to the department of implementing this section or $5.

(e) This section does not impose or establish civil or criminal liability on the owner of a motor vehicle who transfers ownership of the vehicle but does not disclose the transfer to the department.

(f) This section does not require the department to issue a certificate of title to a person shown on a notice of transfer as the transferee of a motor vehicle. The department may not issue a certificate of title for the vehicle until the transferee applies to the county assessor-collector as provided by Chapter 501.
*(Added by L.1995, chap. 165(1); chgd. by L.1997, chap. 165(30.71(a)), eff. 9/1/97.)*

**§§520.024 to 520.030.** *(Reserved.)*

## SUBCHAPTER D. TRANSFER OF TITLE AND REGISTRATION OF USED VEHICLE

**§520.031. Filing by transferee; application for transfer of title and registration.**
(a) Not later than the 20th working day after the date of receiving the documents under Section 520.022 or 520.0225, the transferee of the used motor vehicle shall file with the county assessor-collector:
(1) each document received under that section; or
(2) if appropriate, a document described by Section 520.0225(b)(1) or (2) and the certificate of title or other evidence of title.
(b) The filing under Subsection (a) is an application for transfer of title as required under Chapter 501 and, if the license receipt is filed, an application for transfer of the registration of the motor vehicle.
(c) In this section, "working day" means any day other than a Saturday, a Sunday, or a holiday on which county offices are closed.
*(Added by L.1995, chap. 165(1); chgd. by L.1999, chaps. 836(3), 1423(6), eff. 9/1/99.)*

**§520.032. Transfer fee; late fee.**
(a) The transferee of a used motor vehicle shall pay, in addition to any fee required under Chapter 501 for the transfer of title, a transfer fee of $2.50 for the transfer of the registration of the motor vehicle.
(b) If the transferee does not file the application during the period provided by Section 520.031, the transferee is liable for a $10 late fee to be paid to the county assessor-collector when the application is filed.
(c) The county assessor-collector and the surety on the county assessor-collector's bond are liable for the late fee if the county assessor-collector does not collect the late fee.
*(Added by L.1995, chap. 165(1), eff. 9/1/95.)*

**§520.033. Allocation of fees.**
(a) The county assessor-collector may retain as commission for services provided under this subchapter half of each transfer fee collected and half of each late fee collected under Section 520.032.
(b) The county assessor-collector shall report and remit the balance of the fees collected to the department on Monday of each week as other registration fees are required to be reported and remitted.
*(Added by L.1995, chap. 165(1), eff. 9/1/95.)*

**§520.034. Processing of application; rules.**
(a) On receipt of an application for the transfer of a certificate of title and registration, the county assessor-collector shall process the application for transfer of title as provided under Chapter 501, and the department shall issue a transfer of registration receipt when the department receives the application for transfer of registration.
(b) The department may adopt rules and prescribe forms to implement this subchapter.
*(Added by L.1995, chap. 165(1), eff. 9/1/95.)*

**§520.035. Execution of transfer documents; penalty.**
(a) A person who transfers a motor vehicle in this state shall execute in full and date as of the date of the transfer all documents relating to the transfer of registration or certificate of title. A person who transfers a vehicle commits an offense if the person fails to execute the documents in full.
(b) A person commits an offense if the person:
(1) accepts a document described by Subsection (a) that does not contain all of the required information; or
(2) alters or mutilates such a document.

(c) An offense under this section is a misdemeanor punishable by a fine of not less than $50 and not more than $200.
*(Added by L.1995, chap. 165(1), eff. 9/1/95.)*

### §520.036. General penalty.

(a) A person commits an offense if the person violates this subchapter in a manner for which a specific penalty is not provided.

(b) An offense under this section is a misdemeanor punishable by a fine of not less than $50 and not more than $200.
*(Added by L.1995, chap. 165(1), eff. 9/1/95.)*

## SUBCHAPTER E. MOTOR VEHICLE TITLE SERVICES

*(Added by L.1999, chap. 1478(2), eff. 9/1/99.)*

### §520.051. Definitions.

In this subchapter:

(1) "Motor vehicle" has the meaning assigned by Section 501.002.

(2) "Motor vehicle title service" means any person that for compensation directly or indirectly assists other persons in obtaining title documents by submitting, transmitting, or sending applications for title documents to the appropriate government agencies.

(3) "Title documents" means motor vehicle title applications, motor vehicle registration renewal applications, motor vehicle mechanic's lien title applications, motor vehicle storage lien title applications, motor vehicle temporary registration permits, motor vehicle title application transfers occasioned by the death of the title holder, or notifications under Chapter 683 of this code or Chapter 70, Property Code.

(4) "Title service license holder" means a person who holds a motor vehicle title service license or a title service runner's license.

(5) "Title service record" means the written record for each transaction in which a motor vehicle title service receives compensation.

(6) "Title service runner" means any person employed by a licensed motor vehicle title service to submit or present title documents to the county tax assessor-collector.
*(Added by L.1999, chap. 1478(2), eff. 9/1/99.)*

### §520.052. Applicability.

This subchapter applies to any motor vehicle title service operating in a county that has a population of more than 2.8 million. *(Added by L.1999, chap. 1478(2), eff. 9/1/99.)*

### §520.053. License required.

A person may not act as a motor vehicle title service or act as an agent for that business unless that person holds a license issued under this subchapter. *(Added by L.1999, chap. 1478(2), eff. 9/1/99.)*

### §520.054. General license application requirements.

(a) An applicant for a motor vehicle title service license must apply on a form prescribed by the county tax assessor-collector. The application form must be signed by the applicant and accompanied by the application fee.

(b) An application must include:

(1) the applicant's name, business address, and business telephone number;

(2) the name under which the applicant will do business;

(3) the physical address of each office from which the applicant will conduct business;

(4) a statement indicating whether the applicant has previously applied for a license under this subchapter, the result of the previous application, and whether the applicant has ever been the holder of a license under this subchapter that was revoked or suspended;

(5) information from the applicant as required by the county tax assessor-collector to establish the business reputation and character of the applicant;

(6) the applicant's federal tax identification number;

(7) the applicant's state sales tax number; and

(8) any other information required by rules adopted under this subchapter.
*(Added by L.1999, chap. 1478(2), eff. 9/1/99.)*

## §520.055. Application requirements: corporation.

In addition to the information required in Section 520.054, an applicant for a motor vehicle title service license that intends to engage in business as a corporation shall submit the following information:

(1) the state of incorporation;

(2) the name, address, date of birth, and social security number of each of the principal owners and directors of the corporation;

(3) information about each officer and director as required by the county tax assessor-collector to establish the business reputation and character of the applicant; and

(4) a statement indicating whether an employee, officer, or director has been refused a motor vehicle title service license or a title service runner's license or has been the holder of a license that was revoked or suspended.

*(Added by L.1999, chap. 1478(2), eff. 9/1/99.)*

## §520.056. Application requirements: partnership.

In addition to the information required in Section 520.054, a motor vehicle title service license applicant that intends to engage in business as a partnership shall submit an application that includes the following information:

(1) the name, address, date of birth, and social security number of each partner;

(2) information about each partner as required by the county tax assessor-collector to establish the business reputation and character of the applicant; and

(3) a statement indicating whether a partner or employee has been refused a motor vehicle title service license or a title service runner's license or has been the holder of a license that was revoked or suspended.

*(Added by L.1999, chap. 1478(2), eff. 9/1/99.)*

## §520.057. Records.

(a) A holder of a motor vehicle title service license shall maintain records as required by this section on a form prescribed and made available by the county tax assessor-collector for each transaction in which the license holder receives compensation. The records shall include:

(1) the date of the transaction;

(2) the name, age, address, sex, driver's license number, and a legible photocopy of the driver's license for each customer; and

(3) the license plate number, vehicle identification number, and a legible photocopy of proof of financial responsibility for the motor vehicle involved.

(b) A motor vehicle title service shall keep:

(1) two copies of all records required under this section for at least two years after the date of the transaction;

(2) legible photocopies of any documents submitted by a customer; and

(3) legible photocopies of any documents submitted to the county tax assessor-collector.

*(Added by L.1999, chap. 1478(2), eff. 9/1/99.)*

## §520.058. Inspection of records.

A motor vehicle title service license holder or any of its employees shall allow an inspection of records required under Section 520.057 by a peace officer on the premises of the motor vehicle title service at any reasonable time to verify, check, or audit the records. *(Added by L.1999, chap. 1478(2), eff. 9/1/99.)*

## §520.059. Denial, suspension, or revocation of license.

(a) The county tax assessor-collector may deny, suspend, revoke, or reinstate a license issued under this subchapter.

(b) The county tax assessor-collector shall adopt rules that establish grounds for the denial, suspension, revocation, or reinstatement of a license and rules that establish procedures for disciplinary action. Procedures issued under this subchapter are subject to Chapter 2001, Government Code.

(c) A person whose license is revoked may not apply for a new license before the first anniversary of the date of the revocation.

(d) A license may not be issued under a fictitious name that is similar to or may be confused with the name of a governmental entity or that is deceptive or misleading to the public.

*(Added by L.1999, chap. 1478(2), eff. 9/1/99.)*

## §520.060. License renewal.

(a) A license issued under this subchapter expires on the first anniversary of the date of issuance and may be renewed annually on or before the expiration date on payment of the required renewal fee.

(b) A person who is otherwise eligible to renew a license may renew an unexpired license by paying to the county tax assessor-collector before the expiration date of the license the required renewal fee. A person whose license has expired may not engage in activities that require a license until the license has been renewed under this section.

(c) If a person's license has been expired for 90 days or less, the person may renew the license by paying to the county tax assessor-collector 1-1/2 times the required renewal fee.

(d) If a person's license has been expired for longer than 90 days but less than one year, the person may renew the license by paying to the county tax assessor-collector two times the required renewal fee.

(e) If a person's license has been expired for one year or longer, the person may not renew the license. The person may obtain a new license by complying with the requirements and procedures for obtaining an original license.

(f) Notwithstanding Subsection (e), if a person was licensed in this state, moved to another state, and has been doing business in the other state for the two years preceding application, the person may renew an expired license. The person must pay to the county tax assessor-collector a fee that is equal to two times the required renewal fee for the license.

(g) Before the 30th day preceding the date on which a person's license expires, the county tax assessor-collector shall notify the person of the impending expiration. The notice must be in writing and sent to the person's last known address according to the records of the county tax assessor-collector.

*(Added by L.1999, chap. 1478(2), eff. 9/1/99.)*

## §520.061. Criminal penalty.

(a) A person commits an offense if the person violates this subchapter or a rule adopted by the county tax assessor-collector under this subchapter.

(b) An offense under this section is a Class A misdemeanor.

*(Added by L.1999, chap. 1478(2), eff. 9/1/99.)*

## §520.062. Injunction.

(a) A district attorney of the county in which the motor vehicle title service is located may bring an action to enjoin the operation of a motor vehicle title service if the motor vehicle title service license holder or a runner of the motor vehicle title service while in the scope of the runner's employment is convicted of more than one offense under this subchapter.

(b) If the court grants relief under Subsection (a), the court may:

(1) enjoin the person from maintaining or participating in the business of a motor vehicle title service for a period of time as determined by the court; or

(2) declare the place where the person's business is located to be closed for any use relating to the business of the motor vehicle title service for as long as the person is enjoined from participating in that business.

*(Added by L.1999, chap. 1478(2), eff. 9/1/99.)*

## §520.063. Exemptions.

The following persons and their agents are exempt from the licensing and other requirements established by this subchapter:

(1) a franchised motor vehicle dealer or independent motor vehicle dealer who holds a general distinguishing number issued by the department under Chapter 503;

(2) a motor vehicle lessor holding a license issued by the Motor Vehicle Board under the Texas Motor Vehicle Commission Code (Article 4413(36), Vernon's Texas Civil Statutes) or a trust or other entity that is specifically not required to obtain a lessor license under Section 4.01(a) of that Act; and

(3) a lease facilitator holding a license issued by the Motor Vehicle Board under the Texas Motor Vehicle Commission Code (Article 4413(36), Vernon's Texas Civil Statutes).

*(Added by L.1999, chap. 1478(2), eff. 9/1/99.)*

# SUBTITLE B. DRIVER'S LICENSES AND PERSONAL IDENTIFICATION CARDS

## CHAPTER 521. DRIVER'S LICENSES AND CERTIFICATES

### SUBCHAPTER A. GENERAL PROVISIONS



### SUBCHAPTER B. GENERAL LICENSE REQUIREMENTS



### SUBCHAPTER C. DEPARTMENT LICENSE RECORDS



### SUBCHAPTER D. CLASSIFICATION OF DRIVER'S LICENSES

## SUBCHAPTER E. CLASSIFICATION OF CERTIFICATES



## SUBCHAPTER F. APPEARANCE OF DRIVER'S LICENSE



## SUBCHAPTER G. LICENSE APPLICATION REQUIREMENTS



## SUBCHAPTER H. EXAMINATION REQUIREMENTS



## SUBCHAPTER I. ISSUANCE OF DRIVER'S LICENSE



## SUBCHAPTER J. PERSONS INELIGIBLE FOR LICENSE

## SUBCHAPTER K. RESTRICTED LICENSES



## SUBCHAPTER L. OCCUPATIONAL LICENSE



## SUBCHAPTER M. LICENSE EXPIRATION, RENEWAL AND NUMBER CHANGE



## SUBCHAPTER N. GENERAL PROVISIONS RELATING TO LICENSE DENIAL, SUSPENSION, OR REVOCATION

*(Effective only until 9/1/2000.)*

## SUBCHAPTER N. GENERAL PROVISIONS RELATING TO LICENSE DENIAL, SUSPENSION, OR REVOCATION

*(Effective 9/1/2000.)*



## SUBCHAPTER O. AUTOMATIC SUSPENSION

521.3465. Automatic suspension on conviction of certain offenses involving fictitious motor vehicle license plates, registration insignia, or safety inspection certificates.
521.3466. Automatic revocation for offense involving certain fraudulent governmental records.
521.347. Reports; recommended suspension.
521.348. Automatic revocation for certain sex offenders.
521.349 to
521.370. *(Reserved.)*

## SUBCHAPTER P. AUTOMATIC SUSPENSION FOR CERTAIN DRUG OFFENSES

521.371. Definitions.
521.372. Automatic suspension; license denial.
521.373. Reinstatement requirements.
521.374. Educational program.
521.375. Joint adoption of rules.
521.376. Duties of Texas Commission on Alcohol and Drug Abuse; application and renewal fees.
521.377. License reinstatement.
521.378 to
521.400. *(Reserved.)*

## SUBCHAPTER Q. ANATOMICAL GIFTS

521.401. Statement of gift.
521.402. Revocation of statement of gift.
521.403. Information provided to hospital.
521.404. Notification to procurement organization.
521.405. Determination; request; removal of certain organs.
521.406 to
521.420. *(Reserved.)*

## SUBCHAPTER R. FEES

521.421. License fees; examination fees.
521.422. Personal identification certificate fee.
521.423. Fee for disability certificate or health condition certificate.
521.424. Duplicate license or certificate fee.
521.425. Remittance of fees and charges.
521.426. Disabled veteran exemption.
521.427. Method of payment of fees.
521.428 to
521.450. *(Reserved.)*

## SUBCHAPTER S. MISCELLANEOUS OFFENSES

521.451. General violation.
521.452. Alias driver's license for law enforcement purposes.
521.453. Fictitious license or certificate.
521.454. False application.
521.455. Use of illegal license or certificate.
521.456. Delivery or manufacture of counterfeit instrument.
521.457. Driving while license invalid.
521.458. Permitting unauthorized person to drive.
521.459. Employment of unlicensed driver.
521.460. Motor vehicle rentals.
521.461. General criminal penalty.

## SUBCHAPTER A. GENERAL PROVISIONS

### §521.001. Definitions.

(a) In this chapter:

(1) "Department" means the Department of Public Safety.

(2) "Director" means the public safety director.

(3) "Driver's license" means an authorization issued by the department for the operation of a motor vehicle. The term includes:

(A) a temporary license or instruction permit; and

(B) an occupational license.

(4) "Gross combination weight rating" has the meaning assigned by Section 522.003.

(5) "Gross vehicle weight rating" has the meaning assigned by Section 522.003.

(6) "License" means an authorization to operate a motor vehicle that is issued under or granted by the laws of this state. The term includes:

(A) a driver's license;

(B) the privilege of a person to operate a motor vehicle regardless of whether the person holds a driver's license; and

(C) a nonresident's operating privilege.

(7) "Nonresident" means a person who is not a resident of this state.

(8) "State" means a state, territory, or possession of the United States, the District of Columbia, or the Commonwealth of Puerto Rico.

(b) A word or phrase that is not defined by this chapter but is defined by Subtitle C has the meaning in this chapter that is assigned by that subtitle.

*(Added by L.1995, chap. 165(1), eff. 9/1/95.)*



### §521.002. Convenience to public.

The department shall implement its duties under this chapter in the manner that provides the greatest convenience to the public. *(Added by L.1995, chap. 165(1), eff. 9/1/95.)*

### §521.003. Enrollment and attendance verification.

The Central Education Agency shall design a standard form for use by public and private schools to verify a student's enrollment and attendance for purposes of this chapter. The form must be approved by the department. *(Added by L.1995, chap. 165(1), eff. 9/1/95.)*

### §521.004. Penal Code references.

In this chapter:

(1) a reference to an offense under Section 49.04, Penal Code, includes an offense under Article 6701*l*-1, Revised Statutes, as that law existed immediately before September 1, 1994;

(2) a reference to an offense under Section 49.07, Penal Code:

(A) means only an offense under that section involving the operation of a motor vehicle; and

(B) includes an offense under Section 6701*l*-1, Revised Statutes, as that law existed immediately before September 1, 1994; and

(3) a reference to an offense under Section 49.08, Penal Code:

(A) means only an offense under that section involving the operation of a motor vehicle; and

(B) includes an offense under Section 19.05(a)(2), Penal Code, as that law existed immediately before September 1, 1994.

*(Added by L.1995, chap. 165(1), eff. 9/1/95.)*

### §521.005. Rulemaking authority.

The department may adopt rules necessary to administer this chapter. *(Added by L.1997, chap. 165(30.72), eff. 9/1/97.)*

### §521.006. Advertising in driver's handbook.

(a) Except as provided by Subsection (c), the department may sell advertising in any driver's handbook that the department publishes.

(b) The department shall deposit the proceeds from the advertising to the credit of the driver's handbook advertising account. The driver's handbook advertising account is an account in the general revenue fund that may be appropriated only for the purpose of administration of this chapter.

(c) The department may not include in the driver's handbook advertising for an alcoholic beverage or a product promoting alcoholic beverages.

*(Added by L.1999, chap. 1258(1), eff. 8/30/99.)*

**§§521.007 to 521.020.** *(Reserved.)*

## SUBCHAPTER B. GENERAL LICENSE REQUIREMENTS

### §521.021. License required.

A person, other than a person expressly exempted under this chapter, may not operate a motor vehicle on a highway in this state unless the person holds a driver's license issued under this chapter. *(Added by L.1995, chap. 165(1), eff. 9/1/95.)*

### §521.022. Restrictions on operators of certain school buses.

(a) A person under 18 years of age may not operate a school bus for the transportation of students.

(b) A person who is 18 years of age or older may not operate a school bus unless the person holds an appropriate class of driver's license for the vehicle being operated.

(c) A person may not operate a school bus for the transportation of students unless the person meets the mental and physical capability requirements the department establishes by rule and has passed an examination approved by the department to determine the person's mental and physical capabilities to operate a school bus safely. A physician, advanced practice nurse, or physician assistant may conduct the examination. An ophthalmologist, optometrist, or therapeutic optometrist may conduct the part of the examination relating to the person's vision. Each school bus operator must pass the examination annually.

(d) A person may not operate a school bus for the transportation of students unless the person's driving record is acceptable according to minimum standards adopted by the department. A check of the person's driving record shall be made with the department annually.

(e) A person may not operate a school bus for the transportation of students unless the person is certified in school bus safety education or has enrolled in a school bus safety education class under provisions adopted by the department. Effective on the date and under provisions determined by the department, a school bus operator must have in the operator's possession a card that states that the operator is enrolled in or has completed a driver education course approved by the department in school bus safety education. The card is valid for three years.

(f) Before a person is employed to operate a school bus to transport students, the employer must obtain a criminal history record check. A school district, school, service center, or shared services arrangement, or a commercial transportation company under contract with a school district, that obtains information that a person has been convicted of a felony or misdemeanor involving moral turpitude may not employ the person to drive a school bus on which students are transported unless the employment is approved by the board of trustees of the school district or the board's designee.

(g) This section does not affect the right of an otherwise qualified person with a hearing disability to be licensed, certified, and employed as a bus operator for vehicles used to transport hearing-impaired students.

(h) This section does not apply to the operation of a vehicle owned by a public institution of higher education to transport students of a school district that operates within that institution if:

(1) the person operating the vehicle is approved by the institution to operate the vehicle; and

(2) the transportation is for a special event, including a field trip.

(i) For purposes of this section, "school bus" includes a school activity bus as defined by Section 541.201.

*(Added by L.1995, chap. 165(1); chgd. by L.1997, chaps. 165(30.73(a), (b)), 1438(7); L.1999, chaps. 663(3), 786(1), eff. 6/18/99.)*

### §521.023. Junior college buses.

(a) A person who is 18 years of age or older and who is licensed by the department to operate a motor vehicle as a school bus may operate the motor vehicle for the transportation of junior college students and employees to and from school or official school activities.

(b) A school bus operated by a junior college may also be used to transport public school students if it is convenient. If students of a local public school district are transported to and from school on a bus operated by a junior college and the operator is under 21 years of age, the selection of the operator must be approved by the principal of the public school whose students are transported on that bus.

(c) This section does not apply to the operator of a vehicle operated under a registration certificate issued under Chapter 643.

*(Added by L.1995, chap. 165(1); chgd. by L.1997, chap. 165(30.74), eff. 9/1/97.)*

### §521.024. Restrictions on certain common carriers.

(a) A person under 18 years of age may not operate a motor vehicle while that vehicle is in use as a public or common carrier of persons unless the person is licensed to operate the vehicle.

(b) A person may not operate a taxicab unless the person is at least 18 years of age.

*(Added by L.1995, chap. 165(1), eff. 9/1/95.)*

### §521.025. License to be carried and exhibited on demand; criminal penalty.

(a) A person required to hold a license under Section 521.021 shall:

(1) have in the person's possession while operating a motor vehicle the class of driver's license appropriate for the type of vehicle operated; and

(2) display the license on the demand of a magistrate, court officer, or peace officer.

(b) A peace officer may stop and detain a person operating a motor vehicle to determine if the person has a driver's license as required by this section.

(c) A person who violates this section commits an offense. An offense under this subsection is a misdemeanor punishable by a fine not to exceed $200, except that:

(1) for a second conviction within one year after the date of the first conviction, the offense is a misdemeanor punishable by a fine of not less than $25 or more than $200; and

(2) for a third or subsequent conviction within one year after the date of the second conviction the offense is a misdemeanor punishable by:

(A) a fine of not less than $25 or more than $500;

(B) confinement in the county jail for not less than 72 hours or more than six months; or

(C) both the fine and confinement.

(d) It is a defense to prosecution under this section if the person charged produces in court a driver's license:

(1) issued to that person;

(2) appropriate for the type of vehicle operated; and

(3) valid at the time of the arrest for the offense.

(e) The judge of each court shall report promptly to the department each conviction obtained in the court under this section.

*(Added by L.1995, chap. 165(1), eff. 9/1/95.)*



### §521.026. Dismissal of expired license charge.

(a) A judge may dismiss a charge of driving with an expired license if the defendant remedies this defect within 10 working days.

(b) The judge may assess the defendant an administrative fee not to exceed $10 when the charge of driving with an expired driver's license is dismissed under Subsection (a).

*(Added by L.1995, chap. 165(1), eff. 9/1/95.)*

### §521.027. Persons exempt from license requirement.

The following persons are exempt from the license requirement imposed under this chapter:

(1) a person in the service of the state military forces or the United States while the person is operating an official motor vehicle in the scope of that service;

(2) a person while the person is operating a road machine, farm tractor, or implement of husbandry on a highway, unless the vehicle is a commercial motor vehicle under Section 522.003;

(3) a nonresident on active duty in the armed forces of the United States who holds a license issued by the person's state or Canadian province of residence; and

(4) a person who is the spouse or dependent child of a nonresident exempt under Subdivision (3) and who holds a license issued by the person's state or Canadian province of residence.

*(Added by L.1995, chap. 165(1), eff. 9/1/95.)*

### §521.028. Effect of military service on license requirement.

(a) Unless the license is suspended, canceled, or revoked as provided by law, a driver's license issued by this state that is held by a person who is on active duty in the armed forces of the United States and is absent from this state, notwithstanding the expiration date of the license, remains valid while the person is absent from this state. If the person is honorably discharged from active duty, the license remains valid until the earlier of:

(1) the 91st day after the date of the discharge; or

(2) the date on which the person returns to this state.

(b) A person on active duty in the armed forces of the United States who has in the person's possession a license issued in a foreign country by the armed forces of the United States may oper-

ate a motor vehicle in this state for a period of not more than 90 days after the date on which the person returns to the United States.
*(Added by L.1995, chap. 165(1), eff. 9/1/95.)*

**§521.029. Operation of motor vehicle by new state residents.**

(a) A person who enters this state as a new resident may operate a motor vehicle in this state for no more than 30 days after the date on which the person enters this state if the person:

(1) is 16 years of age or older; and

(2) has in the person's possession a driver's license issued to the person by the person's state or country of previous residence.

(b) If a person subject to this section is prosecuted for operating a motor vehicle without a driver's license, the prosecution alleges that the person has resided in this state for more than 30 days, and the person claims to have been covered by Subsection (a), the person must prove by the preponderance of the evidence that the person has not resided in this state for more than 30 days.
*(Added by L.1995, chap. 165(1), eff. 9/1/95.)*

**§521.030. Reciprocal license.**

(a) A nonresident who is 18 years of age or older and who has in the person's possession a license issued to the person by the person's state or country of residence that is similar to a Class A or Class B driver's license issued under this chapter is not required to hold a Class A or Class B driver's license issued under this chapter if that state or country of residence recognizes such a license issued by this state and exempts the holder from securing a license issued by the state or foreign country.

(b) A nonresident who is 16 years of age or older and who has in the person's possession a driver's license issued to the person by the person's state or Canadian province of residence may operate a type of motor vehicle that is permitted to be operated with a Class C or Class M driver's license in this state if the license held by the nonresident permits operation of that type of vehicle in the person's state or province of residence.
*(Added by L.1995, chap. 165(1), eff. 9/1/95.)*

**§521.031. License from other authority.**

A person holding a driver's license under this chapter is not required to obtain a license for the operation of a motor vehicle from another state authority or department. *(Added by L.1995, chap. 165(1), eff. 9/1/95.)*

**§§521.032 to 521.040.** *(Reserved.)*

## SUBCHAPTER C. DEPARTMENT LICENSE RECORDS

**§521.041. Application records; records of denial, suspension, cancellation, or revocation.**

(a) The department shall record each driver's license application received by the department.

(b) The department shall maintain suitable indexes, in alphabetical or numerical order, that contain:

(1) each denied application and the reasons for the denial;

(2) each application that is granted; and

(3) the name of each license holder whose license has been suspended, canceled, or revoked and the reasons for that action.

(c) The department shall maintain the application records for personal identification certificates in the manner required for license applications under this section.
*(Added by L.1995, chap. 165(1), eff. 9/1/95.)*

**§521.042. Accident and conviction reports; individual records.**

(a) Except as provided by this section, the department shall record each accident report and abstract of the court record of a conviction received by the department under a law of this state.

(b) The records must enable the department to consider, on receipt of a renewal application and at other suitable times, the record of each license holder that shows any:

(1) conviction of that license holder; and

(2) traffic accident in which the license holder has been involved.

(c) The record of a license holder who is employed as a peace officer, fire fighter, or emergency medical services employee of this state, a political subdivision of this state, or a special purpose district may not include information relating to a traffic accident that occurs during an

 Zt

emergency while the peace officer, fire fighter, or emergency medical services employee is driving an official vehicle in the course and scope of the license holder's official duties.

(d) Before issuing or renewing a license, the department shall examine the record of the applicant for information relating to a conviction of a traffic violation or involvement in a traffic accident. The department may not issue or renew a license if the department determines that the issuance or renewal of the license would be inimical to the public safety.

(e) The director may maintain records required under this subchapter on microfilm or computer.

*(Added by L.1995, chap. 165(1), eff. 9/1/95.)*



## §521.043. Elimination of certain unnecessary records.

The department is not required to maintain records relating to a person if the director decides that the records are no longer necessary, except that the department shall maintain a record of a conviction as long as the record may be used:

(1) as grounds for a license cancellation, suspension, revocation, or denial; or

(2) in conjunction with other records of convictions, to establish that a person is a frequent violator of traffic laws.

*(Added by L.1995, chap. 165(1), eff. 9/1/95.)*

## §521.044. Use of social security number information for child support collection.

(a) Information provided on a driver's license application that relates to the applicant's social security number may be used only by the department or disclosed only to:

(1) the child support enforcement division of the attorney general's office; or

(2) another state entity responsible for enforcing the payment of child support.

(b) The department shall enter an applicant's social security number in the department's electronic database but may not print the number on the applicant's driver's license.

(c) On the request of a state entity responsible for investigating or enforcing the payment of child support, the department shall disclose information regarding an applicant's social security number.

(d) Information disclosed under this section may be used by a state entity responsible for enforcing the payment of child support only to implement the duties of the state entity.

(e) The department shall include in the department's legislative appropriations requests and budgets, in quarterly performance reports, and in audits of the department's local offices performance measures on the percentage of complete and correct social security numbers on driver's licenses.

(f) This section does not prohibit the department from requiring an applicant for a driver's license to provide the applicant's social security number.

*(Added by L.1995, chap. 165(1); chgd. by L.1997, chap. 420(28); L.1999, chap. 556(77), 1189(18), eff. 9/1/99.)*

## §521.0445. Notice regarding suspension of license for nonpayment of child support.

The department shall include in each notice sent to a driver's license holder a statement advising a holder who is delinquent in the payment of child support to make satisfactory arrangements with the office of the attorney general to correct the delinquency and that failure to contact the attorney general or to make satisfactory arrangements may result in the commencement by the attorney general of procedures to suspend the holder's driver's license. *(Added by L.1997, chap. 420(29), eff. 9/1/97.)*

## §521.045. Disclosure of certain information relating to individual operator.

On receipt of a written request and payment of a $4 fee, the department may disclose information relating to an individual's date of birth, current license status, and most recent address, as shown in the department's records, to a person who:

(1) is eligible to receive the information under Chapter 730; and

(2) submits to the department the individual's driver's license number or the individual's full name and date of birth.

*(Added by L.1995, chap. 165(1); chgd. by L.1997, chap. 1187(7), eff. 9/1/97.)*

## §521.046. Disclosure of accident and conviction information.

(a) In addition to the information authorized to be released under Section 521.045, on receipt of a written request and payment of a $6 fee, the department may disclose that information and information regarding each reported motor vehicle moving violation, as defined by department rule, resulting in a traffic law conviction and each motor vehicle accident in which the individual received a citation, by date and location, within the three years preceding the date of the request, to a person who:

(1) is eligible to receive the information under Chapter 730; and

(2) submits to the department the individual's driver's license number or the individual's full name and date of birth.

(b) If the department receives requests for information under this section in quantities of 100 or more from a single person at one time and on data processing request forms acceptable to the department, the department may reduce the fee to $5 for each individual request.
*(Added by L.1995, chap. 165(1); chgd. by L.1997, chaps. 356(1), 1187(8), eff. 9/1/97.)*

### §521.047. Disclosure of information to license holder.

(a) The department may disclose information relating to a license holder to that license holder on receipt of a written request that includes the individual's driver's license number or the individual's full name and date of birth, and payment of a $7 fee.

(b) The department may disclose information as recorded in department records that relates to:

(1) the individual's date of birth;

(2) the current license status of the individual;

(3) the individual's most recent address;

(4) the completion of an approved driver education course by the individual;

(5) the fact of, but not the reason for, completion of a driver safety course by the individual; and

(6) each of the individual's reported traffic law violations and motor vehicle accidents, by date and location.
*(Added by L.1995, chap. 165(1), eff. 9/1/95.)*

### §521.048. Certified information.

The department may disclose information under Section 521.046 or 521.047 that is certified by the custodian of records on payment of a $10 fee for each individual request. *(Added by L.1995, chap. 165(1), eff. 9/1/95.)*

### §521.049. Information supplied to certain governmental entities.

(a) The department shall disclose information relating to the name, date of birth, and most recent address as shown in department records to the Texas Department of Health during an emergency or epidemic declared by the commissioner of health to notify individuals of the need to receive certain immunizations.

(b) The department may not charge a fee for information disclosed to a law enforcement agency or other governmental agency for an official purpose, except that the department may charge its regular fees for information provided to those governmental agencies in bulk for research projects.

(c) The department may make information from driver's license record files, including class-type listings, available to an official of the United States, the state, or a political subdivision of this state for government purposes only.
*(Added by L.1995, chap. 165(1), eff. 9/1/95.)*

### §521.050. Sale of license information.

(a) In addition to the provisions of this subchapter relating to the disclosure of driver's license information on an individual, the department may provide a purchaser with a magnetic tape of the names, addresses, and dates of birth of all license holders that are contained in the department's basic driver's license record file if the purchaser certifies in writing that the purchaser is eligible to receive the information under Chapter 730.

(b) A magnetic tape provided under this section may contain only the names, addresses, and dates of birth of individuals who have not prohibited the disclosure of personal information relating to those individuals under Section 521.052 and Chapter 730.

(c) The department may also periodically provide to the purchaser of the information any addition to that file.

(d) Before the department may provide information under Subsection (a), the purchaser must agree to delete the name, address, and date of birth of an individual whose name is also included on the mail or telephone preference list maintained by a recognized trade association that is used to

remove the name of an individual who has requested that the individual's name not be made available for solicitation purposes.
*(Added by L.1995, chap. 165(1); chgd. by L.1997, chap. 1187(9), eff. 9/1/97.)*

## §521.051. Disclosure of certain information prohibited.

The department may not disclose class-type listings from the basic driver's license record file to any person except as provided by Section 521.049(c), regardless of whether the requestor is eligible to receive the information under Chapter 730. *(Added by L.1995, chap. 165(1); chgd. by L.1997, chap. 1187(10), eff. 9/1/97.)*

## §521.052. Disclosure of individual information prohibited.

(a) Except as provided by Sections 521.045, 521.046, 521.049(c), and 521.050 and by Chapter 730, the department may not disclose information from the department's files that relates to personal information, as that term is defined by Section 730.003.

(b) The department shall provide written notice to each applicant for an original or renewal license or personal identification certificate, or a duplicate or corrected license or certificate, that the applicant is entitled to prohibit disclosure of personal information under Chapter 730 and is entitled to execute a statement that prohibits public access to personal information relating to the applicant.

(c) An individual may at any time revoke a statement executed under Subsection (a) or (b). Revocation of an executed statement must be in writing in the manner prescribed by the department.
*(Added by L.1995, chap. 165(1); chgd. by L.1997, chap. 1187(11), eff. 9/1/97.)*



## §521.053. Commercial driver's license information.

(a) The department may provide to any person the information specified by Section 521.045, 521.046, or 521.047 and by Section 601.022, for the fee required by those sections, that relate to the holder of or applicant for a commercial driver's license under Chapter 522 if the person is eligible to receive the information under Chapter 730.

(b) If the information is provided through the commercial driver license information system, the fee for this service is the fee specified in the applicable section plus $2.
*(Added by L.1995, chap. 165(1); chgd. by L.1997, chap. 1187(12), eff. 9/1/97.)*

## §521.054. Notice of change of address or name.

(a) This section applies to a person who:

(1) after applying for the license or certificate moves from the address stated in the person's application for a license or certificate;

(2) moves from the address shown on the license or certificate held by the person; or

(3) changes the person's name by marriage or otherwise.

(b) A person subject to this section shall notify the department of the change not later than the 30th day after the date on which the change takes effect and, except as provided by Subsection (d), shall apply for a duplicate license or certificate as provided by Section 521.146.

(c) A person changing the person's address shall notify the department of the old and new addresses and the number of the license or certificate held by the person. A person changing the person's name shall notify the department of the former and new names and the number of the license or certificate held by the person.

(d) In lieu of applying for a duplicate license or certificate, a person who moves from the address shown on the person's license or certificate may:

(1) submit a written notice to the department on a form approved by the department that contains the information required under Subsection (c); and

(2) request that the department furnish the person with a sticker to affix to or a certificate to carry with the license or certificate that indicates that a change of address has been filed with the department.

(e) On receipt of a request under Subsection (d) and payment of a $10 fee, the department shall provide a sticker or certificate to the requestor.

(f) The department shall make the forms required under Subsection (d) available in public places in addition to driver's license offices.
*(Added by L.1995, chap. 165(1), eff. 9/1/95.)*

## §521.055. Establishment of interactive system.

(a) The department may establish a system, separate from the department's mainframe computer, that will allow interactive access to certain driver's license record information.

(b) The system may provide for the release of the following information:

(1) the status check described in Section 521.045; and

(2) the three-year driving record under Section 521.046.

(c) The fee for a status check under Subsection (b)(1) is $2.50. The fee for a three-year driving record under Subsection (b)(2) is $4.50.

(d) Fifty cents of each fee collected under Subsection (c) shall be deposited in a special account in the general revenue fund that may be appropriated only to the department for administration of this chapter.

(e) The department may contract with private vendors as necessary to implement this section.

(f) The department may adopt rules as necessary to administer this section.

*(Added by L.1997, chap. 1365(1), eff. 6/20/97.)*

## §521.056. National Driver Register.

(a) The department may process file check requests under the National Driver Register on behalf of current or prospective employers of individuals employed or seeking employment as operators of motor vehicles or railway locomotive operators if the individual:

(1) has given written consent to the release of the information; and

(2) has a license in this state.

(b) The fee for a request under Subsection (a) is $4.

(c) The department shall forward a request made under Subsection (a) directly to the current or prospective employer.

(d) The department shall assist and provide procedures for an individual to obtain information from the National Driver Register on the individual's own driving record. The department may by rule establish a reasonable fee for this service, in conformity with the policies of the National Driver Register.

(e) The department may adopt forms and rules as necessary to carry out the purposes of this section and comply with the policies of the National Driver Register.

*(Added by L.1997, chap. 1365(1), eff. 6/20/97.)*

## §521.057. Information regarding certain sex offenders.

(a) On receipt of a court order issued under Article 42.016, Code of Criminal Procedure, the department shall ensure that any driver's license record or personal identification certificate record maintained by the department for the person includes an indication that the person is subject to the registration requirements of Chapter 62, Code of Criminal Procedure, as added by Chapter 668, Acts of the 75th Legislature, Regular Session, 1997.

(b) The department shall include the indication required by Subsection (a) in any driver's license record or personal identification certificate record maintained by the department for the person until the expiration of the person's duty to register under Chapter 62, Code of Criminal Procedure, as added by Chapter 668, Acts of the 75th Legislature, Regular Session, 1997.

*(Added by L.1999, chap. 1401(4), eff. 9/1/2000.)*

## §§521.058 to 521.080. *(Reserved.)*

# SUBCHAPTER D. CLASSIFICATION OF DRIVER'S LICENSES

## §521.081. Class A license.

A Class A driver's license authorizes the holder of the license to operate:

(1) a vehicle with a gross vehicle weight rating of 26,001 pounds or more; or

(2) a combination of vehicles that has a gross combination weight rating of 26,001 pounds or more, if the gross vehicle weight rating of any vehicle or vehicles in tow is more than 10,000 pounds.

*(Added by L.1995, chap. 165(1), eff. 9/1/95.)*

## §521.082. Class B license.

(a) A Class B driver's license authorizes the holder of the license to operate:

(1) a vehicle with a gross vehicle weight rating that is more than 26,000 pounds;

(2) a vehicle with a gross vehicle weight rating of 26,000 pounds or more towing:

(A) a vehicle, other than a farm trailer, with a gross vehicle weight rating that is not more than 10,000 pounds; or

(B) a farm trailer with a gross vehicle weight rating that is not more than 20,000 pounds; and

(3) a bus with a seating capacity of 24 passengers or more.

(b) For the purposes of Subsection (a)(3), seating capacity is computed in accordance with Section 502.162, except that the operator's seat is included in the computation.
*(Added by L.1995, chap. 165(1), eff. 9/1/95.)*

### §521.083. Class C license.

A Class C driver's license authorizes the holder of the license to operate:

(1) a vehicle or combination of vehicles not described by Section 521.081 or 521.082; and

(2) a vehicle with a gross vehicle weight rating of less than 26,001 pounds towing a farm trailer with a gross vehicle weight rating that is not more than 20,000 pounds.
*(Added by L.1995, chap. 165(1), eff. 9/1/95.)*

### §521.084. Class M license.

A Class M driver's license authorizes the holder of the license to operate a motorcycle or moped. *(Added by L.1995, chap. 165(1), eff. 9/1/95.)*

### §521.085. Type of vehicle authorized.

Unless prohibited by Chapter 522, the license holder may operate any vehicle of the type for which that class of license is issued and any lesser type of vehicle other than a motorcycle or moped. *(Added by L.1995, chap. 165(1), eff. 9/1/95.)*

### §§521.086 to 521.100. *(Reserved.)*



## SUBCHAPTER E. CLASSIFICATION OF CERTIFICATES

### §521.101. Personal identification certificate.

(a) The department shall issue personal identification certificates.

(b) A personal identification certificate must be similar in form to, but distinguishable in color from, a driver's license.

(c) The department shall indicate "UNDER 21" on the face of a personal identification certificate issued to a person under 21 years of age.

(d) The department may require each applicant for an original, renewal, or duplicate personal identification certificate to furnish to the department the information required by Section 521.142.

(e) The department may cancel and require surrender of a personal identification certificate after determining that the holder was not entitled to the certificate or gave incorrect or incomplete information in the application for the certificate.

(f) A certificate expires on a date specified by the department, except that a certificate issued to a person 60 years of age or older does not expire.

(g) An individual, corporation, or association may not deny the holder of a personal identification certificate access to goods, services, or facilities, except as provided by Section 521.460 or in regard to the operation of a motor vehicle, because the holder has a personal identification certificate rather than a driver's license.

*(h) The department shall automatically revoke each personal identification certificate issued by the department to a person who:*

*(1) is subject to the registration requirements of Chapter 62, Code of Criminal Procedure, as added by Chapter 668, Acts of the 75th Legislature, Regular Session, 1997; and*

*(2) fails to apply to the department for renewal of the personal identification certificate as required by Article 62.065, Code of Criminal Procedure.*

*(i) The department may issue a personal identification certificate to a person whose certificate is revoked under Subsection (h) only if the person applies for an original or renewal certificate under Section 521.103.*
*(Added by L.1995, chap. 165(1); chgd. by L.1997, chaps. 165(30.75(a)), 1372(1); L.1999, chap. 1401(5), eff. 9/1/2000. Matter in italics eff. 9/1/2000.)*

### §521.102. Disability or health condition certificate.

(a) The department may issue a notated personal identification certificate to a person who has a physical disability or health condition that may cause unconsciousness, incoherence, or an inability to communicate. The department may indicate the disability or condition on the certificate by word, symbol, or code.

(b) An application for an original or renewal disability or health condition certificate must:

(1) be submitted on a form prescribed by the department; and

(2) include the information required by the department.
*(Added by L.1995, chap. 165(1), eff. 9/1/95.)*

### §521.103. Renewal by mail or electronic means.

The department by rule may provide that the holder of a personal identification certificate may renew the certificate by mail, by telephone, over the Internet, or by other electronic means. A rule adopted under this section may prescribe eligibility standards for renewal under this section.
*(Added by L.1999, chap. 1189(19), eff. 9/1/99. See other section 521.103 below.)*

### §521.103. Expiration and renewal requirements for certain sex offenders.

(a) The department may issue an original or renewal personal identification certificate to a person whose driver's license or personal identification certificate record indicates that the person is subject to the registration requirements of Chapter 62, Code of Criminal Procedure, as added by Chapter 668, Acts of the 75th Legislature, Regular Session, 1997, only if the person:

(1) applies in person for the issuance of a certificate under this section; and

(2) pays a fee of $20.

(b) A personal identification certificate issued under this section, including a renewal, duplicate, or corrected certificate, expires on the first birthday of the certificate holder occurring after the date of application, except that the initial certificate issued under this section expires on the second birthday of the certificate holder occurring after the date of application.
*(Added by L.1999, chap. 1401(6), eff. 9/1/2000. See other section 521.103 above.)*

### §§521.104 to 521.120. *(Reserved.)*

## SUBCHAPTER F. APPEARANCE OF DRIVER'S LICENSE

### §521.121. General information on driver's license.

(a) The driver's license must include:

(1) a distinguishing number assigned by the department to the license holder;

(2) a color photograph of:

(A) the entire face of the holder; or

(B) the profile of the holder if the license is a provisional license;

(3) the full name, date of birth, and residence address of the holder; and

(4) a brief description of the holder.

(b) The driver's license must include a facsimile of the license holder's signature or a space on which the holder shall write the holder's usual signature in ink immediately on receipt of the license. A license is not valid until it complies with this subsection.
*(Added by L.1995, chap. 165(1), eff. 9/1/95.)*

### §521.122. Type of vehicle required to be indicated on license.

(a) The department shall show on each driver's license the general type of vehicle that the license holder is authorized to operate.

(b) The department may include on the driver's license an authorization to operate a motorcycle or moped if the license holder has met all requirements for a Class M license.
*(Added by L.1995, chap. 165(1), eff. 9/1/95.)*

### §521.123. Designator on license issued to person under 21 years of age.

The department shall:

(1) designate and clearly mark as a provisional license each original driver's license issued by the department to a person who is under 18 years of age; and

(2) indicate "UNDER 21" on the face of each original, renewed, or duplicate license issued to a person who is under 21 years of age.
*(Added by L.1995, chap. 165(1), eff. 9/1/95.)*

### §521.124. Temporary license; issued without photograph.

(a) The department may issue a temporary license without a photograph of the license holder:

(1) to an applicant who is out of state or a member of the armed forces of the United States; or

(2) if the department otherwise determines that a temporary license is necessary.

(b) A temporary license is valid only until the applicant has time to appear and be photographed and a license with a photograph is issued.
*(Added by L.1995, chap. 165(1), eff. 9/1/95.)*

### §521.125. Medical and emergency information on license.

On the reverse side of a driver's license, the department shall:

(1) print:

(A) "Allergic Reaction to Drugs:_______";
(B) "Directive to physician has been filed at tel. #"; and
(C) "Emergency contact tel. #";

(2) include to the right of the statements under Subdivisions (1)(B) and (C) a surface on which the license holder may write the appropriate telephone number; and

(3) include to the left of each of the statements under Subdivisions (1)(B) and (C) a box that the license holder may use to indicate for what purpose the telephone number applies.
*(Added by L.1995, chap. 165(1); chgd. by L.1999, chap. 1189(20), eff. 9/1/99.)*

**§521.126. Electronically readable information.**

(a) The department may not include any information on a driver's license, commercial driver's license, or identification certificate in an electronically readable form other than the information printed on the license and a physical description of the licensee.

(b) The department shall take necessary steps to ensure that the information is used only for law enforcement or governmental purposes.

(c) Unauthorized use of the information is a Class A misdemeanor.
*(Added by L.1999, chap. 1340(1), eff. 9/1/99.)*

**§§521.127 to 521.140.** *(Reserved.)*

## SUBCHAPTER G. LICENSE APPLICATION REQUIREMENTS

**§521.141. General application requirements.**

(a) An applicant for an original or renewal of a driver's license must apply in a manner prescribed by the department.

(b) An application for an original license must be verified by the applicant before a person authorized to administer oaths. An officer or employee of the department may administer the oath. An officer or employee of this state may not charge for the administration of the oath.

(c) The application must be accompanied by the required fee and must be submitted to the department before the department may administer an examination.
*(Added by L.1995, chap. 165(1); chgd. by L.1999, chap. 1189(21), eff. 9/1/99.)*

**§521.142. Application for original license.**

(a) An application for an original license must state the applicant's full name and place and date of birth. This information must be verified by presentation of proof of identity satisfactory to the department.

(b) The application must include:

(1) the thumbprints of the applicant or, if thumbprints cannot be taken, the index fingerprints of the applicant; and

(2) a brief description of the applicant.

(c) The application must state:

(1) the sex of the applicant;
(2) the residence address of the applicant;
(3) whether the applicant has been licensed to drive a motor vehicle before;
(4) if previously licensed, when and by what state or country;
(5) whether that license has been suspended or revoked or a license application denied;
(6) the date and reason for the suspension, revocation, or denial;
(7) whether the applicant is a citizen of the United States; and
(8) the county of residence of the applicant.

(d) If the applicant is under 25 years of age, the application must state whether the applicant has completed a driver education course approved by the department.

(e) The application must include any other information the department requires to determine the applicant's identity, competency, and eligibility.

(f) Information supplied to the department relating to an applicant's medical history is for the confidential use of the department and may not be disclosed to any person or used as evidence in a legal proceeding other than a proceeding under Subchapter N.

(g) The department may require an applicant to provide the applicant's social security number only for a purpose permitted by Section 521.044.
*(Added by L.1995, chap. 165(1); chgd. by L.1999, chaps. 556(78(a)), 640(3), 1189(22), eff. 9/1/99.)*

**§521.1425. Information required to be furnished to department.**

(a) Except as provided by Subsection (b), the department may require each applicant for an original, renewal, or duplicate driver's license to furnish to the department the information required by Section 521.142.

(b) The department shall require each applicant for an original, renewal, or duplicate driver's license to furnish to the department the information required by Sections 521.142(c)(7) and (8).

*(Added by L.1997, chap. 165(30.76(a)); chgd. by L.1999, chap. 640(4), eff. 9/1/99.)*

**§521.143. Evidence of financial responsibility required.**

(a) An application for an original driver's license must be accompanied by evidence of financial responsibility or a statement that the applicant does not own a motor vehicle for which evidence of financial responsibility is required under Chapter 601. The department may require an application for a renewal of a driver's license to be accompanied by evidence of financial responsibility or a statement that the applicant does not own a motor vehicle for which evidence of financial responsibility is required under Chapter 601.

(b) Evidence of financial responsibility presented under this section must be in at least the minimum amounts required by Section 601.072 and must cover each motor vehicle owned by the applicant for which the applicant is required to maintain evidence of financial responsibility. The evidence may be shown in the manner provided by Section 601.053(a).

(c) A personal automobile insurance policy used as evidence of financial responsibility under this section must comply with Article 5.06, Insurance Code.

(d) A statement that an applicant does not own a motor vehicle to which the evidence of financial responsibility requirement applies must be sworn to and signed by the applicant.

*(Added by L.1995, chap. 165(1); chgd. by L.1999, chap. 1189(23), eff. 9/1/99.)*

**§521.144. Application by new state resident.**

(a) A new resident of this state who applies for a driver's license must submit with the application:

(1) evidence that each motor vehicle owned by the person is registered under Chapter 502; or

(2) an affidavit that the applicant does not own a motor vehicle required to be registered under Chapter 502.

(b) The department may not issue a driver's license to a new resident who fails to comply with Subsection (a).

(c) A registration receipt issued by the county assessor-collector of the county in which the new resident resides is satisfactory evidence that a motor vehicle is registered under Chapter 502.

*(Added by L.1995, chap. 165(1), eff. 9/1/95.)*

**§521.145. Application by person under 18 years of age.**

(a) The application of an applicant under 18 years of age must be signed by:

(1) the parent or guardian who has custody of the applicant; or

(2) if the applicant has no parent or guardian:

(A) the applicant's employer; or

(B) the county judge of the county in which the applicant resides.

(b) The department shall provide the applicant and the cosigner with information concerning state laws relating to driving while intoxicated, driving by a minor with alcohol in the minor's system, and implied consent. The applicant and cosigner must acknowledge receipt of this information.

*(Added by L.1995, chap. 165(1); chgd. by L.1997, chap. 1013(19), eff. 9/1/97.)*

**§521.146. Application for duplicate license or certificate.**

(a) If a driver's license or certificate issued under this chapter is lost or destroyed, or there is a change in pertinent information, the person to whom the license or certificate was issued may obtain a duplicate or corrected version.

(b) An applicant for a duplicate or corrected driver's license or certificate must submit to the department the required fee, accompanied by:

(1) proof satisfactory to the department that the driver's license or certificate was lost or destroyed; or

(2) the required information that has changed with proof satisfactory to the department that supports the change.

*(Added by L.1995, chap. 165(1), eff. 9/1/95.)*

**§§521.147 to 521.160.** *(Reserved.)*

## SUBCHAPTER H. EXAMINATION REQUIREMENTS

### §521.161. Examination of license applicants.

(a) Except as otherwise provided by this subchapter, the department shall examine each applicant for a driver's license. The examination shall be held in the county in which the applicant resides or applies not later than the 10th day after the date on which the application is made.

(b) The examination must include:

(1) a test of the applicant's:

(A) vision;

(B) ability to identify and understand highway signs in English that regulate, warn, or direct traffic; and

(C) knowledge of the traffic laws of this state;

(2) a demonstration of the applicant's ability to exercise ordinary and reasonable control in the operation of a motor vehicle of the type that the applicant will be licensed to operate; and

(3) any additional examination the department finds necessary to determine the applicant's fitness to operate a motor vehicle safely.

(c) The department shall give each applicant the option of taking the traffic law and highway sign part of the examination in writing in addition to or instead of through a mechanical, electronic, or other testing method. If the applicant takes that part of the examination in writing in addition to another testing method, the applicant is considered to have passed that part of the examination if the applicant passes either version of the examination. The department shall inform each person taking the examination of the person's rights under this subsection.

(d) On payment of the required fee, an applicant is entitled to three examinations of each element under Subsection (b) for each application to qualify for a driver's license. If the applicant has not qualified after the third examination, the applicant must submit a new application accompanied by the required fee.

(e) The department may not issue a driver's license to a person who has not passed each examination required under this chapter.

*(Added by L.1995, chap. 165(1); chgd. by L.1997, chap. 165(30.77(a)), eff. 9/1/97.)*

### §521.162. Alternate examination in Spanish.

(a) The department shall design and administer in each county of this state an alternate examination for Spanish-speaking applicants who are unable to take the regular examination in English.

(b) The alternate examination must be identical to the examination administered to other applicants under Section 521.161 except that all directions and written material, other than the text of highway signs, must be in Spanish. The text of highway signs must be in English.

*(Added by L.1995, chap. 165(1), eff. 9/1/95.)*

### §521.163. Reexamination.

(a) The director may require the holder of a license to be reexamined if the director determines that the holder is incapable of safely operating a motor vehicle.

(b) The reexamination shall be conducted in the license holder's county of residence unless the holder and the director agree to a different location.

*(Added by L.1995, chap. 165(1), eff. 9/1/95.)*

### §521.164. Exemption from certain examination requirements for licensed nonresidents.

(a) The department by rule may provide that a holder of a driver's license issued to the person by another state or Canadian province and who is otherwise qualified may, after passing the vision test and paying the required fees, be issued a driver's license without the complete examination required under Section 521.161.

(b) A license issued under this section must be of the class of license equivalent to the license issued by the other jurisdiction.

*(Added by L.1995, chap. 165(1), eff. 9/1/95.)*

### §521.165. Testing by other entities.

(a) The director may certify and set standards for the certification of certain employers, government agencies, and other appropriate organizations to allow those persons to train and test for the ability to operate certain types of vehicles.

(b) The department shall set the standards for the training and testing of driver's license applicants under Subsection (a).

(c) In issuing a driver's license for certain types of vehicles, the director may waive a driving test for an applicant who has successfully completed and passed the training and testing conducted by a person certified under Subsection (a).
*(Added by L.1995, chap. 165(1), eff. 9/1/95.)*

### §521.1655. Testing by driver education school.

(a) A driver education school licensed under the Texas Driver and Traffic Safety Education Act (Article 4413(29c), Texas Civil Statutes) may administer to a student of that school the vision, highway sign, and traffic law parts of the examination required by Section 521.161.

(b) An examination administered under this section complies with the examination requirements of this subchapter as to the parts of the examination administered.
*(Added by L.1997, chap. 165(30.77(a)), eff. 9/1/97.)*

### §521.166. Motorcycle road test requirements.

(a) An applicant required to submit to a motorcycle road test must provide a passenger vehicle and a licensed driver to convey the license examiner during the road test.

(b) The department may refuse to administer any part of the road test to an applicant who fails to comply with Subsection (a).
*(Added by L.1995, chap. 165(1), eff. 9/1/95.)*

### §§521.167 to 521.180. *(Reserved.)*

## SUBCHAPTER I. ISSUANCE OF DRIVER'S LICENSE

### §521.181. Issuance of driver's license.

On payment of the required fee, the department shall issue to each qualifying applicant a driver's license of the class for which the applicant has applied. *(Added by L.1995, chap. 165(1), eff. 9/1/95.)*

### §521.182. Surrender of license issued by other jurisdiction.

(a) A person is not entitled to receive a driver's license until the person surrenders to the department each driver's license in the person's possession that was issued by this state or another state or Canadian province.

(b) The department shall send to the state or province that issued the license:

(1) the surrendered license or a notification that the license has been surrendered; and

(2) a statement that the person holds a driver's license issued by this state.
*(Added by L.1995, chap. 165(1), eff. 9/1/95.)*

### §§521.183 to 521.200. *(Reserved.)*

## SUBCHAPTER J. PERSONS INELIGIBLE FOR LICENSE

### §521.201. License ineligibility in general.

The department may not issue any license to a person who:

(1) is under 15 years of age;

(2) is under 18 years of age unless the person complies with the requirements imposed by Section 521.204;

(3) is shown to be addicted to the use of alcohol, a controlled substance, or another drug that renders a person incapable of driving;

(4) holds a driver's license issued by this state or another state or country that is revoked, canceled, or under suspension;

(5) has been determined by a judgment of a court to be totally incapacitated or incapacitated to act as the operator of a motor vehicle unless the person has, by the date of the license application, been:

(A) restored to capacity by judicial decree; or

(B) released from a hospital for the mentally incapacitated on a certificate by the superintendent or administrator of the hospital that the person has regained capacity;

(6) the department determines to be afflicted with a mental or physical disability or disease that prevents the person from exercising reasonable and ordinary control over a motor vehicle while operating the vehicle on a highway, except that a person may not be refused a license be-

cause of a physical defect if common experience shows that the defect does not incapacitate a person from safely operating a motor vehicle;

(7) has been reported by a court under Section 729.003 for failure to appear or for default in payment of a fine unless the court has filed an additional report on final disposition of the case; or

(8) has been reported by a court for failure to appear or default in payment of a fine for a misdemeanor that is not covered under Subdivision (7) and that is punishable by a fine only, including a misdemeanor under a municipal ordinance, committed by a person who was under 17 years of age at the time of the alleged offense, unless the court has filed an additional report on final disposition of the case.

*(Added by L.1995, chap. 165(1); chgd. by L.1997, chap. 560(1); L.1999, chap. 1080(1), eff. 9/1/99.)*

### §521.202. Ineligibility for license based on certain convictions.

(a) Unless the period of suspension that would have applied if the person held a license at the time of the conviction has expired, the department may not issue a license to a person convicted of an offense:

(1) described by Section 49.04, 49.07, or 49.08, Penal Code; or

(2) to which Section 521.342(a) applies.

(b) Until the period specified in the juvenile court order has expired, the department may not issue a license to a person if the department has been ordered by a juvenile court under Section 54.042, Family Code, to deny the person a license.

(c) A person does not have a privilege to operate a vehicle in this state during a period of suspension under Subsection (a) or (b) if the department is prohibited from issuing a license to that person.

*(Added by L.1995, chap. 165(1), eff. 9/1/95.)*

### §521.203. Restrictions on Class A and B licenses.

The department may not issue a Class A or Class B driver's license to a person who:

(1) is under 17 years of age;

(2) is under 18 years of age unless the person has completed a driver training course approved by the Central Education Agency; or

(3) has not provided the department with an affidavit, on a form prescribed by the department, that states that no vehicle that the person will drive that requires a Class A or Class B license is a commercial motor vehicle as defined by Section 522.003.

*(Added by L.1995, chap. 165(1), eff. 9/1/95.)*

### §521.204. Restrictions on minor.

The department may issue a Class C driver's license to an applicant under 18 years of age only if the applicant:

(1) is 16 years of age or older;

(2) has submitted to the department a driver education certificate issued under Section 9A, Texas Driver and Traffic Safety Education Act (Article 4413(29c), Texas Civil Statutes), that states that the person has completed and passed a driver education course approved by the department under Section 521.205 or by the Texas Education Agency;

(3) has obtained a high school diploma or its equivalent or is a student:

(A) enrolled in a public school, home school, or private school who attended school for at least 80 days in the fall or spring semester preceding the date of the driver's license application; or

(B) who has been enrolled for at least 45 days, and is enrolled as of the date of the application, in a program to prepare persons to pass the high school equivalency exam; and

(4) has passed the examination required by Section 521.161.

*(Added by L.1995, chap. 165(1); chgd. by L.1997, chap. 165(30.78(a)), eff. 9/1/97.)*

### §521.205. Department-approved courses.

(a) The department by rule shall provide for approval of a driver education course conducted by the parent, stepparent, legal guardian, step-grandparent, or grandparent of a person who is required to complete a driver education course to obtain a Class C license. The rules must provide that:

(1) the person conducting the course be a licensed driver;

(2) the student driver spend a minimum number of hours in:

(A) classroom instruction; and

(B) behind-the-wheel instruction;

(3) the person conducting the course not be convicted of:

(A) criminally negligent homicide; or
(B) driving while intoxicated; and
(4) the person conducting the course not be disabled because of mental illness.

(b) The department may not approve a course unless it determines that the course materials are at least equal to those required in a course approved by the Texas Education Agency, except that the department may not require that:

(1) the classroom instruction be provided in a room with particular characteristics or equipment; or

(2) the vehicle used for the behind-the-wheel instruction have equipment other than the equipment otherwise required by law for operation of the vehicle on a highway while the vehicle is not being used for driver training.

(c) The rules must provide a method by which:
(1) approval of a course is obtained; and
(2) an applicant submits proof of completion of the course.

(d) Completion of a driver education course approved under this section has the same effect under this chapter as completion of a driver education course approved by the Texas Education Agency.
*(Added by L.1997, chap. 165(30.79(a)); chgd. by L.1999, chap. 721(1), eff. 9/1/99.)*

### §§521.206 to 521.220. *(Reserved.)*

## SUBCHAPTER K. RESTRICTED LICENSES

### §521.221. Imposition of special restrictions and endorsements.

(a) For good cause the department may impose a restriction or require an endorsement suitable to the driver's license holder's driving ability. The restriction or endorsement may relate to:

(1) the type of motor vehicle that the holder may operate;

(2) a special mechanical control device required on a motor vehicle that the holder may operate;

(3) mechanical attachments, including glasses or an artificial limb, required on the person of the holder;

(4) an area, location, road, or highway in this state on which the holder is permitted to drive a motor vehicle;

(5) the time of day that the holder is permitted to operate a motor vehicle; and

(6) any other condition the department determines to be appropriate to ensure the safe operation of a motor vehicle by the holder.

(b) The department may issue a special restricted license or state the applicable restriction on the regular license.

(c) A person commits an offense if the person operates a motor vehicle in violation of a restriction imposed or without the endorsement required on the license issued to that person. An offense under this subsection is a misdemeanor punishable under Section 521.461.
*(Added by L.1995, chap. 165(1), eff. 9/1/95.)*

### §521.222. Instruction permit.

(a) The department or a driver education school licensed under the Texas Driver and Traffic Safety Education Act (Article 4413(29c), Texas Civil Statutes) may issue an instruction permit, including a Class A or Class B driver's license instruction permit, to a person who:

(1) is 15 years of age or older but under 18 years of age;

(2) has satisfactorily completed and passed the classroom phase of an approved driver education course, which may be a course approved under Section 521.205;

(3) meets the requirements imposed under Section 521.204(3); and

(4) has passed each examination required under Section 521.161 other than the driving test.

(b) The department may issue an instruction permit to a person 18 years of age or older who has successfully passed all parts of the driver's examination required under Section 521.161 other than the driving test.

(c) A driver education school may issue an instruction permit to a person 18 years of age or older who has successfully passed:

(1) a six-hour adult classroom driver education course approved by the Texas Education Agency; and

(2) each part of the driver's examination required by Section 521.161 other than the driving test.

(d) An instruction permit entitles the holder to operate a type of motor vehicle on a highway while:

(1) the permit is in the holder's possession; and

(2) the holder is accompanied by a person occupying the seat by the operator who:

(A) holds a license that qualifies the operator to operate that type of vehicle;

(B) is 18 years of age or older; and

(C) has at least one year of driving experience.

(e) An instruction permit is not required to include a photograph.

*(Added by L.1995, chap. 165(1); chgd. by L.1997, chap. 165(30.80(a)), eff. 9/1/97.)*

## §521.223. Hardship license.

(a) The department may issue a license to a person who complies with the requirements of Subsection (b) if the department finds that:

(1) the failure to issue the license will result in an unusual economic hardship for the family of the applicant;

(2) the license is necessary because of the illness of a member of the applicant's family; or

(3) the license is necessary because the applicant is enrolled in a vocational education program and requires a driver's license to participate in the program.

(b) An applicant for a license under Subsection (a) must be 15 years of age or older and must:

(1) have passed a driver education course approved by the department, which may be a course approved under Section 521.205; and

(2) pass the examination required by Section 521.161.

(c) To be eligible to take the driver training course, the person must be at least 14 years of age.

(d) If the department determines that an applicant must assist in the responsibilities imposed by a family illness, disability, death-related emergency, or economic emergency, it may waive the driver training course requirement and may issue a temporary license. A temporary license issued under this subsection is valid for 60 days after the date of issuance and may be renewed for additional 60-day periods as long as the condition continues.

(e) A person who is refused a driver's license under this section may appeal to the county court of the county in which the person resides. The court may try the matter on the request of the petitioner or respondent.

(f) In the manner provided by Subchapter N, the department may suspend a license issued under this section if the holder of the license is convicted of a moving violation.

*(Added by L.1995, chap. 165(1); chgd. by L.1997, chap. 165(30.81(a)), (30.82), eff. 9/1/97.)*



## §521.224. Restricted Class M license.

(a) In this section, "motorcycle" includes a motor driven cycle.

(b) The department may issue a special restricted Class M license that authorizes the holder to operate only a motorcycle that has not more than a 250 cubic centimeter piston displacement.

(c) A person is eligible for a restricted motorcycle license if the person:

(1) is 15 years of age or older but under 18 years of age;

(2) has completed and passed a motorcycle operator training course approved by the department; and

(3) has met the requirements imposed under Section 521.145.

(d) The department shall make the motorcycle operator training course available.

(e) On the 16th birthday of a holder of a special restricted Class M license, the department shall remove the 250 cubic centimeter restriction from the license without completion by the holder of an additional motorcycle operator training course.

(f) An applicant for the special restricted license must apply in accordance with Subchapter G. The applicant is subject to the requirements of Section 521.161 and to other provisions of this chapter in the same manner as an applicant for another license. The department shall prescribe the form of the license.

*(Added by L.1995, chap. 165(1); chgd. by L.1999, chap. 797(1), eff. 9/1/99.)*

## §521.225. Moped license.

(a) A person may not operate a moped unless the person holds a driver's license. An applicant for a moped license must be 15 years of age or older.

(b) The department shall administer to an applicant for a moped license a written examination relating to the traffic laws applicable to the operation of mopeds. A test involving the operation of the vehicle is not required.

(c) An applicable provision of this chapter relating to a restricted Class M license applies also to a moped license, including a provision relating to the application, issuance, duration, suspension, cancellation, or revocation of that license.

(d) The department shall certify whether a vehicle alleged to be a moped is a moped. The department shall:

(1) by rule establish the procedure for determining whether a vehicle is a moped;

(2) compile a list of mopeds certified by the department; and

(3) make the list available to the public on request.

*(Added by L.1995, chap. 165(1); chgd. by L.1999, chap. 797(2), eff. 9/1/99.)*

### §521.226. *(Repealed by L.1999, chap. 797(4), eff. 9/1/99.)*

### §521.227. Inspection by peace officer.

Any peace officer may stop and detain a motorcycle, motor driven cycle, or moped to determine if the vehicle is of a model and make certified by the department. *(Added by L.1995, chap. 165(1), eff. 9/1/95.)*

### §§521.228 to 521.240. *(Reserved.)*

## SUBCHAPTER L. OCCUPATIONAL LICENSE

### §521.241. Definitions.

In this subchapter:

(1) "Essential need" means a need of a person for the operation of a motor vehicle:

(A) in the performance of an occupation or trade or for transportation to and from the place at which the person practices the person's occupation or trade;

(B) for transportation to and from an educational facility in which the person is enrolled; or

(C) in the performance of essential household duties.

(2) "Ignition interlock device" means a device that uses a deep-lung breath analysis mechanism to make impractical the operation of a motor vehicle if ethyl alcohol is detected in the breath of the operator of the vehicle.

*(Added by L.1995, chap. 165(1), eff. 9/1/95.)*

### §521.242. Petition.

(a) A person whose license has been suspended for a cause other than a physical or mental disability or impairment or a conviction under Section 49.04, Penal Code, may apply for an occupational license by filing a verified petition with the clerk of the county court or district court with jurisdiction in the county in which:

(1) the person resides; or

(2) the offense occurred for which the license was suspended.

(b) A person may apply for an occupational license by filing a verified petition only with the clerk of the county court or district court in which the person was convicted if:

(1) the person's license has been automatically suspended or canceled under this chapter or Chapter 522 for a conviction of an offense under the laws of this state; and

(2) the person has not been issued, in the 10 years preceding the date of the filing of the petition, more than one occupational license after a conviction under the laws of this state.

(c) A petition filed under this section must set forth in detail the person's essential need.

(d) A petition filed under Subsection (b) must state that the petitioner was convicted in that court for an offense under the laws of this state.

(e) The clerk of the court shall file the petition as in any other civil matter.

*(Added by L.1995, chap. 165(1); chgd. by L.1997, chaps. 165(30.83(a)), 1289(1), (2), eff. 9/1/97.)*

### §521.243. Notice to state; presentation of evidence.

(a) The clerk of the court shall send by certified mail to the attorney representing the state a copy of the petition and notice of the hearing if the petitioner's license was suspended following a conviction for:

(1) an offense under Section 19.05, 49.04, 49.07, or 49.08, Penal Code; or

(2) an offense to which Section 521.342 applies.

(b) A person who receives a copy of a petition under Subsection (a) may attend the hearing and may present evidence at the hearing against granting the petition.

*(Added by L.1995, chap. 165(1), eff. 9/1/95.)*

## §521.244. Hearing; order; determination of essential need.

(a) The judge who hears the petition shall sign an order finding whether an essential need exists.

(b) In determining whether an essential need exists, the judge shall consider:

(1) the petitioner's driving record; and

(2) any evidence presented by a person under Section 521.243(b).

(c) If the judge finds that there is an essential need, the judge also, as part of the order, shall:

(1) determine the actual need of the petitioner to operate a motor vehicle; and

(2) require the petitioner to provide evidence of financial responsibility in accordance with Chapter 601.

(d) Except as provided by Section 521.243(b), the hearing on the petition may be ex parte.

*(Added by L.1995, chap. 165(1), eff. 9/1/95.)*

## §521.245. Required counseling.

(a) If the petitioner's license has been suspended under Chapter 524 or 724, the court shall require the petitioner to attend a program approved by the court that is designed to provide counseling and rehabilitation services to persons for alcohol dependence. This requirement shall be stated in the order granting the occupational license.

(b) The program required under Subsection (a) may not be the program provided by Section 521.344 or by Section 13, Article 42.12, Code of Criminal Procedure.

(c) The court may require the person to report periodically to the court to verify that the person is attending the required program.

(d) On finding that the person is not attending the program as required, the court may revoke the order granting the occupational license. The court shall send a certified copy of the order revoking the license to the department.

(e) On receipt of the copy under Subsection (d), the department shall suspend the person's occupational license for:

(1) 60 days, if the original driver's license suspension was under Chapter 524; or

(2) 120 days, if the original driver's license suspension was under Chapter 724.

(f) A suspension under Subsection (e):

(1) takes effect on the date on which the court signs the order revoking the occupational license; and

(2) is cumulative of the original suspension.

(g) A person is not eligible for an occupational license during a period of suspension under Subsection (e).

*(Added by L.1995, chap. 165(1), eff. 9/1/95.)*



## §521.246. Ignition interlock device requirement.

(a) If the person's license has been suspended after a conviction under Section 49.04, 49.07, or 49.08, Penal Code, the judge, before signing an order, shall determine from the criminal history record information maintained by the department whether the person has any previous conviction under those laws.

(b) As part of the order the judge may restrict the person to the operation of a motor vehicle equipped with an ignition interlock device if the judge determines that the person's license has been suspended following a conviction under Section 49.04, 49.07, or 49.08, Penal Code. As part of the order, the judge shall restrict the person to the operation of a motor vehicle equipped with an ignition interlock device if the judge determines that:

(1) the person has two or more convictions under any combination of Section 49.04, 49.07, or 49.08, Penal Code; or

(2) the person's license has been suspended after a conviction under Section 49.04, Penal Code, for which the person has been punished under Section 49.09, Penal Code.

(c) The person shall obtain the ignition interlock device at the person's own expense unless the court finds that to do so is not in the best interest of justice and enters that finding in the record. If the court determines that the person is unable to pay for the device, the court may impose a reasonable payment schedule for a term not to exceed twice the period of the court's order.

(d) The court shall order the ignition interlock device to remain installed for at least half of the period of supervision.

(e) A person to whom this section applies may operate a motor vehicle without the installation of an approved ignition interlock device if:

(1) the person is required to operate a motor vehicle in the course and scope of the person's employment;

(2) the vehicle is owned by the person's employer;

(3) the employer is not owned or controlled by the person whose driving privilege is restricted;

(4) the employer is notified of the driving privilege restriction; and

(5) proof of that notification is with the vehicle.

(f) A previous conviction may not be used for purposes of restricting a person to the operation of a motor vehicle equipped with an interlock ignition device under this section if:

(1) the previous conviction was a final conviction under Section 49.04, 49.07, or 49.08, Penal Code, and was for an offense committed more than 10 years before the instant offense for which the person was convicted; and

(2) the person has not been convicted of an offense under Section 49.04, 49.07, or 49.08 of that code committed within 10 years before the date on which the instant offense for which the person was convicted.

*(Added by L.1995, chap. 165(1); chgd. by L.1997, chap. 165(30.84(a)); L.1999, chap. 1105(1), eff. 9/1/99.)*

### §521.2465. Restricted license.

(a) On receipt of notice that a person has been restricted to the use of a motor vehicle equipped with an ignition interlock device, the department shall notify that person that the person's driver's license expires on the 30th day after the date of the notice. On application by the person and payment of a fee of $10, the department shall issue a special restricted license that authorizes the person to operate only a motor vehicle equipped with an ignition interlock device.

(b) On receipt of a copy of a court order removing the restriction, the department shall issue the person a driver's license without the restriction.

*(Added by L.1997, chap. 165(30.85(a)), eff. 9/1/97.)*

### §521.247. Approval of ignition interlock devices by department.

(a) The department shall adopt rules for the approval of ignition interlock devices used under this subchapter.

(b) The department by rule shall establish general standards for the calibration and maintenance of the devices. The manufacturer or an authorized representative of the manufacturer is responsible for calibrating and maintaining the device.

(c) If the department approves a device, the department shall notify the manufacturer of that approval in writing. Written notice from the department to a manufacturer is admissible in a civil or criminal proceeding in this state. The manufacturer shall reimburse the department for any cost incurred by the department in approving the device.

(d) The department is not liable in a civil or criminal proceeding that arises from the use of an approved device.

*(Added by L.1995, chap. 165(1); chgd. by L.1997, chap. 165(30.84(b)), eff. 9/1/97.)*

### §521.2475. Ignition interlock device evaluation.

(a) On January 1 of each year, the department shall issue an evaluation of each ignition interlock device approved under Section 521.247 using guidelines established by the National Highway Traffic Safety Administration, including:

(1) whether the device provides accurate detection of alveolar air;

(2) the moving retest abilities of the device;

(3) the use of tamper-proof blood alcohol content level software by the device;

(4) the anticircumvention design of the device;

(5) the recalibration requirements of the device; and

(6) the breath action required by the operator.

(b) The department shall assess the cost of preparing the evaluation equally against each manufacturer of an approved device.

*(Added by L.1997, chap. 165(30.86(a)), eff. 9/1/97.)*

### §521.2476. Minimum standards for vendors of ignition interlock devices.

(a) The department by rule shall establish:

(1) minimum standards for vendors of ignition interlock devices who conduct business in this state; and

(2) procedures to ensure compliance with those standards, including procedures for the inspection of a vendor's facilities.

(b) The minimum standards shall require each vendor to:

(1) be authorized by the department to do business in this state;

(2) install a device only if the device is approved under Section 521.247;

(3) obtain liability insurance providing coverage for damages arising out of the operation or use of devices in amounts and under the terms specified by the department;

(4) install the device and activate any anticircumvention feature of the device within a reasonable time after the vendor receives notice that installation is ordered by a court;

(5) install and inspect the device in accordance with any applicable court order;

(6) repair or replace a device not later than 48 hours after receiving notice of a complaint regarding the operation of the device;

(7) submit a written report of any violation of a court order to that court and to the person's supervising officer, if any, not later than 48 hours after the vendor discovers the violation;

(8) maintain a record of each action taken by the vendor with respect to each device installed by the vendor, including each action taken as a result of an attempt to circumvent the device, until at least the fifth anniversary after the date of installation;

(9) make a copy of the record available for inspection by or send a copy of the record to any court, supervising officer, or the department on request; and

(10) annually provide to the department a written report of each service and ignition interlock device feature made available by the vendor.

(c) The department may revoke the department's authorization for a vendor to do business in this state if the vendor or an officer or employee of the vendor violates:

(1) any law of this state that applies to the vendor; or

(2) any rule adopted by the department under this section or another law that applies to the vendor.

(d) A vendor shall reimburse the department for the reasonable cost of conducting each inspection of the vendor's facilities under this section.

(e) In this section, "offense relating to the operating of a motor vehicle while intoxicated" has the meaning assigned by Section 49.09, Penal Code.
*(Added by L.1999, chap. 1105(2), eff. 9/1/99.)*

### §521.248. Order requirements.

(a) An order granting an occupational license must specify:

(1) the hours of the day and days of the week during which the person may operate a motor vehicle;

(2) the reasons for which the person may operate a motor vehicle; and

(3) areas or routes of travel permitted.

(b) The person may not operate a motor vehicle for more than four hours in any 24-hour period, except that on a showing of necessity the court may allow the person to drive for any period determined by the court that does not exceed 12 hours in any 24-hour period.

(c) An order granting an occupational license remains valid until the end of the period of suspension of the person's regular driver's license.
*(Added by L.1995, chap. 165(1), eff. 9/1/95.)*

### §521.249. Notice to department; issuance of occupational license.

(a) The court shall send a certified copy of the petition and the court order setting out the judge's findings and restrictions to the department. The person may use a copy of the order as a restricted license until the 31st day after the date on which the order takes effect.

(b) On receipt of the copy under this section and after compliance with Chapter 601, the department shall issue an occupational license to the person. The license must refer on its face to the court order.
*(Added by L.1995, chap. 165(1), eff. 9/1/95.)*

### §521.250. Court order in operator's possession.

A person who is issued an occupational license shall have in the person's possession a certified copy of the court order granting the license while operating a motor vehicle. The person shall allow a peace officer to examine the order on request. *(Added by L.1995, chap. 165(1), eff. 9/1/95.)*

### §521.251. Effective date of occupational license.

(a) If a person's license is suspended under Chapter 524 or 724 and the person has not had a prior suspension arising from an alcohol-related or drug-related enforcement contact in the five years preceding the date of the person's arrest, an order under this subchapter granting the person an occupational license takes effect immediately. However, the court shall order the person to comply with the counseling and rehabilitation program required under Section 521.245.

(b) If the person's driver's license has been suspended as a result of an alcohol-related or drug-related enforcement contact during the five years preceding the date of the person's arrest, the order may not take effect before the 91st day after the effective date of the suspension.

(c) If the person's driver's license has been suspended as a result of a conviction under Section 49.04, 49.07, or 49.08, Penal Code, during the five years preceding the date of the person's arrest, the order may not take effect before the 181st day after the effective date of the suspension.

(d) For the purposes of this section, "alcohol-related or drug-related enforcement contact" has the meaning assigned by Section 524.001.

*(Added by L.1995, chap. 165(1), eff. 9/1/95.)*

### §521.252. License revocation.

(a) The court that signs an order granting an occupational license may issue at any time an order revoking the license for good cause.

(b) The court shall send a certified copy of the order to the department.

*(Added by L.1995, chap. 165(1), eff. 9/1/95.)*

### §521.253. Criminal penalty.

(a) A person who holds an occupational license commits an offense if the person:

(1) operates a motor vehicle in violation of a restriction imposed on the license; or

(2) fails to have in the person's possession a certified copy of the court order as required under Section 521.250.

(b) An offense under this section is a Class B misdemeanor.

(c) On conviction of an offense under this section, the occupational license and the order granting that license are revoked.

*(Added by L.1995, chap. 165(1), eff. 9/1/95.)*

### §§521.254 to 521.270. *(Reserved.)*

## SUBCHAPTER M. LICENSE EXPIRATION, RENEWAL, AND NUMBER CHANGE

*(Subchapter heading chgd. by L.1999, chaps. 709(1), 1189(25), eff. 9/1/99.)*

### §521.271. License expiration.

(a) Each original driver's license and provisional license expires as follows:

(1) a driver's license expires on the first birthday of the license holder occurring after the sixth anniversary of the date of the application;

(2) a provisional license expires on the earlier of:

(A) the 18th birthday of the license holder; or

(B) the first birthday of the license holder occurring after the date of the application;

(3) an instruction permit expires on the first birthday of the license holder occurring after the date of the application; and

(4) an occupational license expires on the first anniversary of the court order granting the license.

(b) A driver's license that is renewed expires on the sixth anniversary of the expiration date before renewal.

*(Added by L.1995, chap. 165(1); chgd. by L.1997, chap. 1372(2), eff. 9/1/97.)*

### §521.272. Renewal of license issued to certain sex offenders.

(a) The department may issue an original or renewal driver's license to a person whose driver's license or personal identification certificate record indicates that the person is subject to the registration requirements of Chapter 62, Code of Criminal Procedure, as added by Chapter 668, Acts of the 75th Legislature, Regular Session, 1997, only if the person:

(1) applies in person for the issuance of a license under this section; and

(2) pays a fee of $20.

(b) Notwithstanding Section 521.143, a person is not required to provide proof of financial responsibility to receive the person's initial driver's license under this section.

(c) Notwithstanding Section 521.271, a driver's license issued under this section, including a renewal, duplicate, or corrected license, expires on the first birthday of the license holder occurring after the date of application, except that the initial license issued under this section expires on the second birthday of the license holder occurring after the date of application.

*(Added by L.1999, chap. 1401(7), eff. 9/1/2000.)*

### §521.273. Renewal examinations.

(a) The department may require and prescribe the procedure and standards for an examination for the renewal of a driver's license.

(b) A license holder who fails to obtain a renewal license as provided by this subchapter may be required to take any examination required for the original license.

*(Added by L.1995, chap. 165(1), eff. 9/1/95.)*

### §521.274. Renewal by mail or electronic means.

The department by rule may provide that the holder of a driver's license may renew the license by mail, by telephone, over the Internet, or by other electronic means. A rule adopted under this section may prescribe eligibility standards for renewal under this section.

**Note:** *L.1999, chap. 1401(8), eff. 9/1/2000, amends former subsection (b) as follows:*

(b) A rule adopted under this subsection may not permit renewal by mail of:

(1) a provisional license;

(2) an occupational license; or

(3) a driver's license if the license holder's:

(A) driving record as maintained by the department shows that the holder, within the four years preceding the date of the renewal application, has been convicted of:

(i) a moving violation, as defined by department rule, in this state; or

(ii) an offense described by Subchapter O; or

(B) driver's license record or personal identification certificate record indicates that the holder is subject to the registration requirements of Chapter 62, Code of Criminal Procedure, as added by Chapter 668, Acts of the 75th Legislature, Regular Session, 1997.

*(Added by L.1995, chap. 165(1); chgd. by L.1999, chaps. 1189(24), 1401(8), eff. 9/1/99, 9/1/2000, respectively.)*



### §521.275. Change of driver's license or personal identification certificate number.

(a) The department shall issue to a person a new driver's license number or personal identification certificate number on the person's showing a court order stating that the person has been the victim of domestic violence.

(b) The department may require each applicant to furnish the information required by Section 521.142. If the applicant's name has changed, the department may require evidence identifying the applicant by both the former and new name.

(c) Except as provided by Sections 521.049(c), 730.005, and 730.006, the department may not disclose:

(1) the changed license or certificate number; or

(2) the person's name or any former name.

*(Added by L.1999, chaps. 709(2), 1189(26), eff. 9/1/99.)*

### §§521.276 to 521.290. *(Reserved.)*

## SUBCHAPTER N. GENERAL PROVISIONS RELATING TO LICENSE DENIAL, SUSPENSION, OR REVOCATION

*(Effective only until 9/1/2000. See other Subchapter N, infra, eff. 9/1/2000.)*

### §521.291. Authority to suspend or revoke license; notice; hearing.

(a) If the director determines under Section 521.163 that a license holder is incapable of safely operating a motor vehicle, or if the department receives information about a license holder in accordance with a contract under Chapter 702, the director may notify the license holder of that fact and may summon the license holder to appear at a hearing.

(b) The notice may be sent by first class mail to the license holder's address as shown on the holder's driver's license.

*(Added by L.1995, chap. 165(1); chgd. by L.1999, chap. 1409(1), eff. 9/1/99. Effective only until 9/1/2000. See other section 521.291, infra, eff. 9/1/2000.)*

### §521.292. Written charges required.

The hearing must be based on written charges. Except as otherwise provided by this subchapter, a copy of the charges must be given to the license holder not later than the 10th day before the date of the hearing. *(Added by L.1995, chap. 165(1), eff. 9/1/95. Effective only until 9/1/2000. See other section 521.292, infra, eff. 9/1/2000.)*

### §521.293. Jurisdiction; presiding officer.

(a) A hearing under this subchapter must be presided over by a hearing officer, a municipal court judge, or a justice of the peace in the county in which the license holder resides.

(b) The presiding officer may receive a fee for hearing the case if a fee is approved and set by the commissioners court of the county in which the license holder resides. The fee may not exceed $5 and shall be paid from the general revenue fund of the county.

(c) The presiding officer may administer oaths and issue subpoenas to compel the attendance of witnesses and the production of relevant books and documents.

(d) The hearing shall be conducted not less than 10 days after the date of the notification required by Section 521.291. The presiding officer shall set the case for hearing at the earliest practical time.

*(Added by L.1995, chap. 165(1); chgd. by L.1997, chap. 165(30.88), eff. 9/1/97. Effective only until 9/1/2000. See other section 521.293, infra, eff. 9/1/2000.)*

### §521.294. Suspension; revocation.

(a) The issue to be determined at the hearing is whether the license should be suspended or revoked.

(b) The presiding officer shall determine whether a person's license should be suspended or revoked, and the period of a suspension, because the person:

(1) has operated a motor vehicle on a highway while the person's license was suspended, canceled, disqualified, or revoked, or without a license after an application for a license was denied;

(2) has been responsible as an operator for any accident resulting in death;

(3) is a habitually reckless or negligent operator of a motor vehicle;

(4) is a habitual violator of the traffic laws;

(5) has permitted the unlawful or fraudulent use of the person's license;

(6) has committed an offense in another state or Canadian province that, if committed in this state, would be grounds for suspension or revocation;

(7) has violated a restriction or an endorsement imposed on the use of the license;

(8) has been responsible as a driver for any accident resulting in serious personal injury or serious property damage;

(9) is the holder of a provisional license issued under Section 521.123 and has been convicted of two or more moving violations committed within a 12-month period; or

(10) has committed an offense under Section 545.421.

(c) The period of a suspension may not exceed one year. If the hearing results in an affirmative finding that the person has engaged in conduct proscribed by Subsection (b)(1), the period of suspension is extended for an additional period of the lesser of:

(1) the term of the original suspension; or

(2) one year.

(d) The presiding officer shall determine whether a person's license should be revoked because the person:

(1) is incapable of safely operating a motor vehicle;

(2) has not complied with the terms of a citation issued by a jurisdiction that is a party to the Nonresident Violator Compact of 1977 for a traffic violation to which that compact applies;

(3) has failed to provide medical records or has failed to undergo medical or other examinations as required by a panel of the medical advisory board;

(4) has failed to pass an examination required by the director under this chapter;

(5) has been reported by a court under Section 729.003 for failure to appear or for default in payment of a fine unless the court files an additional report on final disposition of the case; or

(6) has been reported by a justice or municipal court for failure to appear or for a default in payment of a fine for a misdemeanor punishable only by fine, other than a failure or default reported under Section 729.003, committed by a person younger than 17 years of age when the offense was committed, unless the court files an additional report on final disposition of the case.

(e) The presiding officer shall report the officer's determination to the department.

(f) The director may suspend the person's license for the recommended period or revoke the license in accordance with the presiding officer's determination.

(g) The license holder or department may appeal the ruling of the presiding officer by filing a petition in the manner provided by Section 521.302.

(h) For the purposes of this subchapter, a person is a "habitual violator" if the person has four or more convictions that arise out of different transactions in 12 consecutive months, or seven or more convictions that arise out of different transactions in 24 months, if the convictions are for moving violations of the traffic laws of any state, Canadian province, or political subdivision, other than a violation under:

(1) Section 621.101, 621.201, or 621.203-621.207;

(2) Subchapter B or C, Chapter 623; or

(3) Section 545.413.

*(Added by L.1995, chap. 165(1); chgd. by L.1997, chap. 165(30.89(a), (d)), eff. 9/1/97. Effective only until 9/1/2000. See other section 521.294, infra, eff. 9/1/2000.)*

**§521.295.** *(Repealed by L.1999, chap. 1409(9), eff. 9/1/99. See other section 521.295, infra, eff. 9/1/2000.)*

**§521.296. Cancellation of minor's license on cosigner's request; release from liability.**

(a) The person who cosigned a minor's application for a driver's license under Section 521.145 may file with the department a request that the department cancel the license. The request must be in writing and acknowledged.

(b) On receipt of a request under Subsection (a), the department shall cancel the minor's license. On cancellation, the person who cosigned the application is released from liability based on the person's signing of the application for any subsequent negligence or wilful misconduct of the minor in operating a motor vehicle.

*(Added by L.1995, chap. 165(1), eff. 9/1/95. Effective only until 9/1/2000. See other section 521.296, infra, eff. 9/1/2000.)*



**§521.297. Cancellation of minor's license on death of cosigner.**

On receipt of information satisfactory to the department of the death of a person who cosigned a minor's application for a driver's license under Section 521.145, the department shall cancel the license if the license holder is under 18 years of age and the department may not issue a new license until the minor files a new application that complies with this chapter. *(Added by L.1995, chap. 165(1), eff. 9/1/95. Effective only until 9/1/2000. See other section 521.297, infra, eff. 9/1/2000.)*

**§521.298.** *(Repealed by L.1997, chap. 1013(41), eff. 9/1/97. See other section 521.298, infra, eff. 9/1/2000.)*

**§521.299. Effect of conduct in other jurisdiction; suspension under driver's license compact.**

(a) The department may suspend or revoke the license of a resident or the operating privilege of a nonresident to operate a motor vehicle in this state on receipt of notice of a conviction of the individual in another state or a Canadian province of an offense that, if committed in this state, would be grounds for the suspension or revocation of a driver's license.

(b) The department may give the same effect to the conduct of a resident of this state that occurs in another state or Canadian province that the department may give to conduct that occurs in this state under state law.

(c) The department may seek the suspension of the license of a person who has failed to comply with the terms of a citation to which Chapter 523 applies.

*(Added by L.1995, chap. 165(1), eff. 9/1/95. Effective only until 9/1/2000. See other section 521.299, infra, eff. 9/1/2000.)*

**§521.300. Suspension of certain provisional licenses.**

(a) On the recommendation of a juvenile court with jurisdiction over the holder of a provisional license, the department shall suspend a provisional license if it is found by the juvenile court that the provisional license holder has committed:

(1) an offense that would be classified as a felony if the license holder were an adult; or

(2) a misdemeanor in which a motor vehicle was used to travel to or from the scene of the offense, other than an offense specified by Chapter 729.

(b) The department shall suspend the license for the period set by the juvenile court but not to exceed one year.

(c) The court shall report its recommendation promptly to the department in the manner and form prescribed by the department.

*(Added by L.1995, chap. 165(1), eff. 9/1/95. Effective only until 9/1/2000. See other section 521.300, infra, eff. 9/1/2000.)*

### §521.301. Order binding.

A suspension, cancellation, or revocation order of the department is binding on the person to whom it pertains unless the person appeals the order as provided by Section 521.303 or unless the person establishes that a hearing was timely requested under Section 521.344(g) but was not held. *(Added by L.1995, chap. 165(1), eff. 9/1/95. Effective only until 9/1/2000. See other section 521.301, infra, eff. 9/1/2000.)*

### §521.302. Appeal; judicial review.

(a) A person whose driver's license has been suspended under this subchapter, whose license suspension has been probated under Section 521.303, or who is denied a license or whose driver's license has been canceled or revoked by the department may appeal the action unless the suspension, cancellation, or revocation is automatic under this chapter or Chapter 522.

(b) To appeal the action, the person must file a petition not later than the 30th day after the date on which the department order was entered in the county court at law of the county in which the person resides, or, if there is no county court at law, in the county court. The person must send a copy of the petition, certified by the clerk of the court in which the petition is filed, to the department by certified mail.

(c) The court shall notify the department of the hearing not later than the 31st day before the date the court sets for the hearing.

(d) The court shall take testimony, examine the facts of the case, and determine whether the petitioner is entitled to a license or is subject to the cancellation, denial, suspension, or revocation of a license under this chapter.

(e) A trial on appeal is a trial de novo, and the license holder has the right to trial by jury.

(f) The filing of a petition of appeal as provided by this section stays an order of cancellation, suspension, probated suspension, or revocation until the trial is completed and final judgment is rendered.

*(Added by L.1995, chap. 165(1), eff. 9/1/95. Effective only until 9/1/2000. See other section 521.302, infra, eff. 9/1/2000.)*

### §521.303. Probation of suspension.

(a) On determining that a license shall be suspended, the presiding officer who conducts a hearing under Section 521.291, or the court that tries an appeal under Section 521.302, may recommend that the suspension be probated on any terms and conditions considered necessary or proper by the officer or court, if it appears that justice and the best interests of the public and the defendant will be served by the probation.

(b) The report to the department of the results of the hearing must include any terms and conditions of the probation.

(c) If probation is recommended, the department shall probate the suspension.

(d) If a presiding officer or a court probates a suspension of a driver's license or privilege under this section, the probationary period shall be for a term of not less than 90 days or more than two years.

*(Added by L.1995, chap. 165(1), eff. 9/1/95. Effective only until 9/1/2000. See other section 521.303, infra, eff. 9/1/2000.)*

### §521.304. Probation violation.

(a) If the director believes that a license holder who has been placed on probation under Section 521.303 has violated a term or condition of the probation, the director shall notify the holder and summon the holder to appear at a hearing in the court or before the officer that recommended that the suspension be probated, after notice as provided by Section 521.291.

(b) The issue at the hearing under this section is whether a term or condition of the probation has been violated. The officer or judge presiding at the hearing shall report the finding to the department. If the finding is that a term or condition of the probation has been violated, the department shall suspend the license as determined in the original hearing.

*(Added by L.1995, chap. 165(1), eff. 9/1/95. Effective only until 9/1/2000. See other section 521.304, infra, eff. 9/1/2000.)*

### §521.305. Effective date of order.

A decision under this subchapter takes effect on the 11th day after the date on which an order is rendered. *(Added by L.1995, chap. 165(1), eff. 9/1/95. Effective only until 9/1/2000. See other section 521.305, infra, eff. 9/1/2000.)*

### §521.306. Period of suspension or revocation.

(a) Revocation of a license is for an indefinite period and may not be probated.

(b) Except as provided by Subsection (c) of this section and Subchapter O, the department may not suspend a license for a period that exceeds one year.

(c) The department may not reinstate a license suspended under Section 521.294(d)(5) until the court that filed the report for which the license was suspended files an additional report on final disposition of the case.

(d) The department may not reinstate a license suspended or revoked under this subchapter unless the person whose license was suspended or revoked applies to the department for reinstatement of the license and pays a $100 reinstatement fee to the department.
*(Added by L.1995, chap. 165(1); chgd. by L.1997, chap. 165(30.90); L.1999, chap. 1189(27), eff. 9/1/99. Effective only until 9/1/2000. See other section 521.306, infra, eff. 9/1/2000.)*

### §521.307. Cancellation authority.

The department may cancel a license or certificate if it determines that the holder:

(1) was not entitled to the license or certificate; or

(2) failed to give required information in the application for the license or certificate.
*(Added by L.1995, chap. 165(1), eff. 9/1/95. Effective only until 9/1/2000. See other section 521.307, infra, eff. 9/1/2000.)*



### §521.308. Surrender of license; return.

(a) On the suspension or revocation of a license by the department, the department may require the holder to surrender the license to the department.

(b) The department may return a suspended license to the holder on the expiration of the suspension period.
*(Added by L.1995, chap. 165(1); chgd. by chap. 884(1), eff. 9/1/99. Effective only until 9/1/2000. See other section 521.308, infra, eff. 9/1/2000.)*

### §521.309. Suspended foreign license.

A person whose driver's license or privilege to operate a vehicle in this state is suspended or revoked under this chapter may not operate a motor vehicle in this state under a license, permit, or registration certificate issued by any other state or Canadian province during the suspension period or after the revocation until a new license is obtained as provided by this chapter. *(Added by L.1995, chap. 165(1), eff. 9/1/95. Effective only until 9/1/2000. See other section 521.309, infra, eff. 9/1/2000.)*

### §521.310. Denial of license renewal after warning.

The department may deny the renewal of the driver's license of a person about whom the department has received information under Section 706.004 until the date the department receives a notification from the political subdivision under Section 706.005 that there is no cause to deny the renewal based on the person's previous failure to appear for a complaint, citation, or court order to pay a fine involving a violation of a traffic law. *(Added by L.1995, chap. 165(1); chgd. by L.1997, chap. 165(30.91(a)), eff. 9/1/97. Effective only until 9/1/2000. See other section 521.310, infra, eff. 9/1/2000.)*

### §521.311. Nonresidents.

(a) The department may suspend or revoke a nonresident's operating privilege in the same manner and for the same causes as a driver's license issued under this chapter.

(b) On receipt of a record of conviction of a nonresident in this state under the motor vehicle laws of this state, the department may forward a certified copy of the record to the motor vehicle administrator of the state or Canadian province of which the convicted person is a resident.
*(Added by L.1995, chap. 165(1), eff. 9/1/95. Effective only until 9/1/2000. See other section 521.311, infra, eff. 9/1/2000.)*

### §521.312. Revocation for medical reasons.

(a) A person may not operate a motor vehicle if the person:

(1) is a chemically dependent person who:

(A) is likely to cause serious harm to the person or to others; or

(B) will, if not treated, continue to suffer abnormal mental, emotional, or physical distress, or to deteriorate in ability to function independently; or

(2) has been determined by a judgment of a court to be totally incapacitated or incapacitated to act as the operator of a motor vehicle.

(b) The driver's license of a person is revoked on:

(1) the judgment of a court that the person is totally incapacitated or incapacitated to act as the operator of a motor vehicle; or

(2) the order of a court of involuntary treatment of the person under Subchapter D, Chapter 462, Health and Safety Code.

(c) If the person has not been issued a driver's license, the judgment or order of a court under Subsection (b) automatically prohibits the department from issuing a driver's license to the person.

(d) The clerk of the court that renders a judgment or enters an order under Subsection (b) shall notify the department of the court's judgment or order before the 10th day after the date the court renders the judgment or enters the order.

(e) The revocation of a driver's license under Subsection (b) or the prohibition against the issuance of a driver's license under Subsection (c) expires on the date on which:

(1) the person is:

(A) restored to capacity by judicial decree; or

(B) released from a hospital for the mentally incapacitated on a certificate of the superintendent or administrator that the person has regained capacity; or

(2) the order of involuntary treatment of the chemically dependent person expires.

(f) Before the 10th day after the date under Subsection (e)(1)(A) or (2), the clerk of the appropriate court shall notify the department that:

(1) the person has been restored to capacity by judicial decree; or

(2) the order of involuntary treatment has expired or has been terminated under Section 462.080(d), Health and Safety Code.

(g) Before the 10th day after the date under Subsection (e)(1)(B), the superintendent or administrator of the hospital shall notify the department that the person has been released from the hospital on a certificate that the person has regained capacity.

(h) In this section:

(1) "Chemically dependent person" means a person with chemical dependency.

(2) "Chemical dependency" and "treatment" have the meanings assigned those terms by Section 462.001, Health and Safety Code.

*(Added by L.1995, chap. 165(1); chgd. by L.1997, chap. 165(30.92(a)), eff. 9/1/97. Effective only until 9/1/2000. See other section 521.312, infra, eff. 9/1/2000.)*

### §521.314. Suspension for certain criminal mischief; license denial.

(a) A court may order the department to suspend a person's driver's license on conviction of an offense under Section 28.08, Penal Code.

(b) A court may order the department to deny an application for reinstatement or issuance of a driver's license to a person convicted of an offense under Section 28.08, Penal Code, who, on the date of the conviction, did not hold a driver's license.

(c) The period of suspension under this section is one year after the date of a final conviction. The period of license denial is one year after the date the person applies to the department for reinstatement or issuance of a driver's license.

(d) The department may not reinstate a driver's license suspended under Subsection (a) unless the person whose license was suspended applies to the department for reinstatement.

(e) A person whose license is suspended under Subsection (a) remains eligible to receive an occupational license under Subchapter L.

(f) For the purposes of this section, a person is convicted of an offense regardless of whether sentence is imposed or the person is placed on community supervision for the offense under Article 42.12, Code of Criminal Procedure.

*(Added by L.1997, chap. 593(5), eff. 9/1/97. Effective only until 9/1/2000. See other section 521.314, infra, eff. 9/1/2000.)*

### §§521.315 to 521.340. *(Reserved.)*

## SUBCHAPTER N. GENERAL PROVISIONS RELATING TO LICENSE DENIAL, SUSPENSION, OR REVOCATION

*(Effective 9/1/2000. See other Subchapter N, supra, eff. only until 9/1/2000.)*

### §521.291. Rules.

The department shall adopt rules to administer this subchapter. *(Repealed and added by L.1999, chap. 1117(1), eff. 9/1/2000. See other section 521.291, supra, eff. only until 9/1/2000.)*

### §521.292. Department's determination for license suspension.

(a) The department shall suspend the person's license if the department determines that the person:

(1) has operated a motor vehicle on a highway while the person's license was suspended, canceled, disqualified, or revoked, or without a license after an application for a license was denied;

(2) is a habitually reckless or negligent operator of a motor vehicle;

(3) is a habitual violator of the traffic laws;

(4) has permitted the unlawful or fraudulent use of the person's license;

(5) has committed an offense in another state or Canadian province that, if committed in this state, would be grounds for suspension;

(6) has violated a restriction or an endorsement imposed on the use of the license;

(7) has been convicted of two or more separate offenses of a violation of a restriction imposed on the use of the license;

(8) has been responsible as a driver for any accident resulting in serious personal injury or serious property damage;

(9) is the holder of a provisional license issued under Section 521.123 and has been convicted of two or more moving violations committed within a 12-month period; or

(10) has committed an offense under Section 545.421.

(b) For purposes of Subsection (a)(3), a person is a "habitual violator" if the person has four or more convictions that arise out of different transactions in 12 consecutive months, or seven or more convictions that arise out of different transactions in 24 months, if the convictions are for moving violations of the traffic laws of any state, Canadian province, or political subdivision, other than a violation under:

(1) Section 621.101, 621.201, or 621.203-621.207;

(2) Subchapter B or C, Chapter 623; or

(3) Section 545.413.

*(Repealed and added by L.1999, chap. 1117(1), eff. 9/1/2000. See other section 521.292, supra, eff. only until 9/1/2000.)*

### §521.293. Period of suspension under section 521.292.

(a) Except as provided by Subsection (b), if the person does not request a hearing, the period of license suspension under Section 521.292 is 90 days.

(b) If the department determines that the person engaged in conduct described by Section 521.292(a)(1), the period of license suspension is extended for an additional period of the lesser of:

(1) the term of the original suspension; or

(2) one year.

*(Repealed and added by L.1999, chap. 1117(1), eff. 9/1/2000. See other section 521.293, supra, eff. only until 9/1/2000.)*

### §521.294. Department's determination for license revocation.

The department shall revoke the person's license if the department determines that the person:

(1) is incapable of safely operating a motor vehicle;

(2) has not complied with the terms of a citation issued by a jurisdiction that is a party to the Nonresident Violator Compact of 1977 for a traffic violation to which that compact applies;

(3) has failed to provide medical records or has failed to undergo medical or other examinations as required by a panel of the medical advisory board;

(4) has failed to pass an examination required by the director under this chapter;

(5) has been reported by a court under Section 729.003 for failure to appear or for default in payment of a fine unless the court files an additional report on final disposition of the case;

(6) has been reported within the preceding two years by a justice or municipal court for failure to appear or for a default in payment of a fine for a misdemeanor punishable only by fine, other than a failure or default reported under Section 729.003, committed by a person who is at least 14 years of age but younger than 17 years of age when the offense was committed, unless the court files an additional report on final disposition of the case; or

(7) has committed an offense in another state or Canadian province that, if committed in this state, would be grounds for revocation.

*(Repealed and added by L.1999, chap. 1117(1), eff. 9/1/2000. See other section 521.294, supra, eff. only until 9/1/2000.)*

### §521.295. Notice of department's determination.

(a) If the department suspends a person's license under Section 521.292 or revokes a person's license under Section 521.294, the department shall send a notice of suspension or revocation by first class mail to the person's address in the records of the department.

(b) Notice is considered received on the fifth day after the date the notice is mailed.

*(Repealed and added by L.1999, chap. 1117(1), eff. 9/1/2000. See other section 521.295, supra, eff. only until 9/1/2000.)*

### §521.296. Notice of suspension or revocation.

A notice of suspension under Section 521.292 or revocation under Section 521.294 must state:

(1) the reason and statutory grounds for the suspension or revocation;

(2) the effective date of the suspension or revocation;

(3) the right of the person to a hearing;

(4) how to request a hearing; and

(5) the period in which the person must request a hearing.

*(Added by L.1999, chap. 1117(1), eff. 9/1/2000. See other section 521.296, supra, eff. only until 9/1/2000.)*

### §521.297. Suspension or revocation effective date.

A license suspension under Section 521.292 or revocation under Section 521.294 takes effect on the 40th day after the date the person is considered to have received notice of the suspension or revocation under Section 521.295(b). *(Added by L.1999, chap. 1117(1), eff. 9/1/2000. See other section 521.297, supra, eff. only until 9/1/2000.)*

### §521.298. Hearing request.

If, not later than the 15th day after the date on which the person is considered to have received notice of the suspension or revocation under Section 521.295(b), the department receives at its headquarters in Austin, in writing, including a facsimile transmission, or by another manner prescribed by the department, a request that a hearing be held, a hearing shall be held as provided by Sections 521.295-521.303. *(Added by L.1999, chap. 1117(1), eff. 9/1/2000. See other section 521.298, supra, eff. only until 9/1/2000.)*

### §521.299. Hearing date; rescheduling.

(a) A hearing requested under Section 521.298 shall be held not earlier than the 11th day after the date on which the person requesting the hearing is notified of the hearing. The hearing shall be set for the earliest practical date.

(b) A hearing may be continued on a motion of the person, the department, both parties, or as necessary to accommodate the docket of the presiding officer.

(c) A request for a hearing stays suspension or revocation of a person's license until the date of the final decision of the presiding officer.

*(Added by L.1999, chap. 1117(1), eff. 9/1/2000. See other section 521.299, supra, eff. only until 9/1/2000.)*

### §521.300. Hearing: location; presiding officer.

(a) A hearing under this subchapter shall be conducted in a municipal court or a justice court in the county in which the person resides. The judge of the municipal court or the justice is designated as the presiding officer.

(b) The presiding officer is entitled to receive a fee for hearing the case if a fee is approved and set by the commissioners court of the county in which the person resides. The fee may not exceed $5 and shall be paid from the general revenue fund of the county.

(c) The presiding officer may administer oaths and issue subpoenas to compel the attendance of witnesses and the production of relevant books and documents.

*(Added by L.1999, chap. 1117(1), eff. 9/1/2000. See other section 521.300, supra, eff. only until 9/1/2000.*

### §521.301. Issue at hearing.

(a) The issue that must be proved at the hearing by a preponderance of the evidence is whether the grounds for suspension or revocation stated in the notice are true.

(b) If the presiding officer finds in the affirmative on that issue, the suspension or revocation is sustained.

(c) If the presiding officer sustains a suspension, the department shall suspend the person's license for the period specified by the presiding officer, which may not be less than 30 days or more than one year.

(d) If the presiding officer does not find in the affirmative on that issue, the department may not suspend or revoke the person's license.

(e) The decision of the presiding officer is final when issued and signed.

*(Repealed and added by L.1999, chap. 1117(1), eff. 9/1/2000. See other section 521.301, supra, eff. only until 9/1/2000.)*

### §521.302. Failure to appear.

A person who requests a hearing under this subchapter and fails to appear without just cause waives the right to a hearing and the department's determination is final. *(Added by L.1999, chap. 1117(1), eff. 9/1/2000. See other section 521.302, supra, eff. only until 9/1/2000.)*



### §521.303. Continuance.

A continuance under Section 521.299 stays the suspension or revocation of a license until the date of the final decision of the presiding officer. *(Added by L.1999, chap. 1117(1), eff. 9/1/2000. See other section 521.303, supra, eff. only until 9/1/2000.)*

### §521.304. Cancellation of minor's license on cosigner's request; release from liability.

(a) The person who cosigned a minor's application for a driver's license under Section 521.145 may file with the department a request that the department cancel the license. The request must be in writing and acknowledged.

(b) On receipt of a request under Subsection (a), the department shall cancel the minor's license. On cancellation, the person who cosigned the application is released from liability based on the person's signing of the application for any subsequent negligence or wilful misconduct of the minor in operating a motor vehicle.

*(Renumbered from section 521.296 by L.1999, chap. 1117(1), eff. 9/1/2000. See other section 521.304, supra, eff. only until 9/1/2000.)*

### §521.305. Cancellation of minor's license on death of cosigner.

On receipt of information satisfactory to the department of the death of a person who cosigned a minor's application for a driver's license under Section 521.145, the department shall cancel the license if the license holder is under 18 years of age and the department may not issue a new license until the minor files a new application that complies with this chapter. *(Renumbered from section 521.297 by L.1999, chap. 1117(1), eff. 9/1/2000. See other section 521.305, supra, eff. only until 9/1/2000.)*

### §521.306. Effect of conduct in other jurisdiction; suspension under driver's license compact.

(a) The department may suspend or revoke the license of a resident or the operating privilege of a nonresident to operate a motor vehicle in this state on receipt of notice of a conviction of the individual in another state or a Canadian province of an offense that, if committed in this state, would be grounds for the suspension or revocation of a driver's license.

(b) The department may give the same effect to the conduct of a resident of this state that occurs in another state or Canadian province that the department may give to conduct that occurs in this state under state law.

(c) The department may seek the suspension of the license of a person who has failed to comply with the terms of a citation to which Chapter 523 applies.

*(Renumbered from section 521.299 by L.1999, chap. 1117(1), eff. 9/1/2000. See other section 521.306, supra, eff. only until 9/1/2000.)*

### §521.307. Suspension of certain provisional licenses.

(a) On the recommendation of a juvenile court with jurisdiction over the holder of a provisional license, the department shall suspend a provisional license if it is found by the juvenile court that the provisional license holder has committed:

(1) an offense that would be classified as a felony if the license holder were an adult; or

(2) a misdemeanor in which a motor vehicle was used to travel to or from the scene of the offense, other than an offense specified by Chapter 729.

(b) The department shall suspend the license for the period set by the juvenile court but not to exceed one year.

(c) The court shall report its recommendation promptly to the department in the manner and form prescribed by the department.
*(Renumbered from section 521.300 by L.1999, chap. 1117(1), eff. 9/1/2000. See other section 521.307, supra, eff. only until 9/1/2000.)*

### §521.308. Appeal; judicial review.

(a) A person whose driver's license suspension or revocation has been sustained by a presiding officer under this subchapter may appeal the decision of the presiding officer.

(b) To appeal the decision of the presiding officer, the person must file a petition not later than the 30th day after the date on which the department order was entered in the county court at law of the county in which the person resides, or, if there is no county court at law, in the county court. The person must send a file-stamped copy of the petition, certified by the clerk of the court in which the petition is filed, to the department by certified mail.

(c) The court shall notify the department of the hearing not later than the 31st day before the date the court sets for the hearing.

(d) The court shall take testimony, examine the facts of the case, and determine whether the petitioner is subject to the suspension or revocation of a license under this subchapter.

(e) A trial on appeal is a trial de novo, and the person has the right to trial by jury.

(f) The filing of a petition of appeal as provided by this section stays an order of suspension, probated suspension, or revocation until the earlier of the 91st day after the date the appeal petition is filed or the date the trial is completed and final judgment is rendered.

(g) On expiration of the stay, the department shall impose the suspension, probated suspension, or revocation. The stay may not be extended, and an additional stay may not be granted.
*(Renumbered from section 521.302 and chgd. by L.1999, chap. 1117(1), eff. 9/1/2000. See other section 521.308, supra, eff. only until 9/1/2000.)*



### §521.309. Probation of suspension.

(a) On determining that a license shall be suspended, the presiding officer who conducts a hearing under this subchapter, or the court that tries an appeal under this subchapter, may recommend that the suspension be probated on any terms and conditions considered necessary or proper by the presiding officer or court, if it appears that justice and the best interests of the public and the person will be served by the probation.

(b) The revocation of a license may not be probated.

(c) The report to the department of the results of the hearing must include any terms and conditions of the probation.

(d) If probation is recommended, the department shall probate the suspension.

(e) If a presiding officer or a court probates a suspension of a license under this section, the probationary period shall be for a term of not less than 90 days or more than two years.
*(Renumbered from section 521.303 and chgd. by L.1999, chap. 1117(1), eff. 9/1/2000. See other section 521.309, supra, eff. only until 9/1/2000.)*

### §521.310. Probation violation.

(a) If the director believes that a person who has been placed on probation under Section 521.309 has violated a term or condition of the probation, the director shall notify the person and summon the person to appear at a hearing in the court or before the presiding officer or judge who recommended that the person be placed on probation after notice as provided by Sections 521.295 and 521.296.

(b) The issue at the hearing under this section is whether a term or condition of the probation has been violated. The presiding officer or judge presiding at the hearing shall report the finding to the department. If the finding is that a term or condition of the probation has been violated, the department shall take the action as determined in the original hearing.
*(Renumbered from section 521.304 and chgd. by L.1999, chap. 1117(1), eff. 9/1/2000. See other section 521.310, supra, eff. only until 9/1/2000.)*

### §521.311. Effective date of order.

Except as provided by another section of this subchapter to the contrary, a decision under this subchapter takes effect on the 11th day after the date on which an order is rendered. *(Renumbered from section 521.305 and chgd. by L.1999, chap. 1117(1), eff. 9/1/2000. See other section 521.311, supra, eff. only until 9/1/2000.)*

### §521.312. Period of suspension or revocation; reinstatement of license.

(a) Revocation of a license is for an indefinite period.

(b) Except as provided by Subsection (c), Section 521.293(b), or Subchapter O, the department may not suspend a license for a period that exceeds one year.

(c) The department may not reinstate a license revoked under Section 521.294(5) until the court that filed the report for which the license was revoked files an additional report on final disposition of the case.

*(Renumbered from section 521.306 and chgd. by L.1999, chap. 1117(1), eff. 9/1/2000. See other section 521.312, supra, eff. only until 9/1/2000.)*

### §521.313. Reinstatement and reissuance; fee.

(a) A license suspended or revoked under this subchapter may not be reinstated or another license issued to the person until the person pays the department a fee of $100 in addition to any other fee required by law.

(b) The payment of a reinstatement fee is not required if a suspension or revocation under this subchapter is:

(1) rescinded by the department; or

(2) not sustained by a presiding officer or a court.

*(Added by L.1999, chap. 1117(1), eff. 9/1/2000.)*

### §521.314. Cancellation authority.

The department may cancel a license or certificate if it determines that the holder:

(1) was not entitled to the license or certificate; or

(2) failed to give required information in the application for the license or certificate.

*(Renumbered from section 521.307 by L.1999, chap. 1117(1), eff. 9/1/2000. See other section 521.314, supra, eff. only until 9/1/2000.)*

### §521.315. Surrender of license; return.

(a) On the suspension or revocation of a license by the department, the department may require the holder to surrender the license to the department.

(b) The department shall return a suspended license to the holder on the expiration of the suspension period.

*(Renumbered from section 521.308 and chgd. by L.1999, chap. 1117(1), eff. 9/1/2000.)*

### §521.316. Suspended foreign license.

A person whose driver's license or privilege to operate a vehicle in this state is suspended or revoked under this chapter may not operate a motor vehicle in this state under a license, permit, or registration certificate issued by any other state or Canadian province during the suspension period or after the revocation until a new license is obtained as provided by this chapter. *(Renumbered from section 521.309 by L.1999, chap. 1117(1), eff. 9/1/2000.)*

### §521.317. Denial of license renewal after warning.

The department may deny the renewal of the driver's license of a person about whom the department has received information under Section 706.004 until the date the department receives a notification from the political subdivision under Section 706.005 that there is no cause to deny the renewal based on the person's previous failure to appear for a complaint, citation, or court order to pay a fine involving a violation of a traffic law. *(Renumbered from section 521.310 by L.1999, chap. 1117(1), eff. 9/1/2000.)*

### §521.318. Nonresidents.

(a) The department may suspend or revoke a nonresident's operating privilege in the same manner and for the same causes as a driver's license issued under this chapter.

(b) On receipt of a record of conviction of a nonresident in this state under the motor vehicle laws of this state, the department may forward a certified copy of the record to the motor vehicle administrator of the state or Canadian province of which the convicted person is a resident.

*(Renumbered from section 521.311 by L.1999, chap. 1117(1), eff. 9/1/2000.)*

### §521.319. Revocation for medical reasons.

(a) A person may not operate a motor vehicle if the person:

(1) is a chemically dependent person who:

(A) is likely to cause serious harm to the person or to others; or

(B) will, if not treated, continue to suffer abnormal mental, emotional, or physical distress, or to deteriorate in ability to function independently; or

(2) has been determined by a judgment of a court to be totally incapacitated or incapacitated to act as the operator of a motor vehicle.

(b) The driver's license of a person is revoked on:

(1) the judgment of a court that the person is totally incapacitated or incapacitated to act as the operator of a motor vehicle; or

(2) the order of a court of involuntary treatment of the person under Subchapter D, Chapter 462, Health and Safety Code.

(c) If the person has not been issued a driver's license, the judgment or order of a court under Subsection (b) automatically prohibits the department from issuing a driver's license to the person.

(d) The clerk of the court that renders a judgment or enters an order under Subsection (b) shall notify the department of the court's judgment or order before the 10th day after the date the court renders the judgment or enters the order.

(e) The revocation of a driver's license under Subsection (b) or the prohibition against the issuance of a driver's license under Subsection (c) expires on the date on which:

(1) the person is:

(A) restored to capacity by judicial decree; or

(B) released from a hospital for the mentally incapacitated on a certificate of the superintendent or administrator that the person has regained capacity; or

(2) the order of involuntary treatment of the chemically dependent person expires.

(f) Before the 10th day after the date under Subsection (e)(1)(A) or (2), the clerk of the appropriate court shall notify the department that:

(1) the person has been restored to capacity by judicial decree; or

(2) the order of involuntary treatment has expired or has been terminated under Section 462.080(d), Health and Safety Code.

(g) Before the 10th day after the date under Subsection (e)(1)(B), the superintendent or administrator of the hospital shall notify the department that the person has been released from the hospital on a certificate that the person has regained capacity.

(h) In this section:

(1) "Chemically dependent person" means a person with chemical dependency.

(2) "Chemical dependency" and "treatment" have the meanings assigned by Section 462.001, Health and Safety Code.

*(Renumbered from section 521.312 and chgd. by L.1999, chap. 1117(1), eff. 9/1/2000.)*

### §521.320. Suspension for certain criminal mischief; license denial.

(a) A court may order the department to suspend a person's driver's license on conviction of an offense under Section 28.08, Penal Code.

(b) A court may order the department to deny an application for reinstatement or issuance of a driver's license to a person convicted of an offense under Section 28.08, Penal Code, who, on the date of the conviction, did not hold a driver's license.

(c) The period of suspension under this section is one year after the date of a final conviction. The period of license denial is one year after the date the person applies to the department for reinstatement or issuance of a driver's license.

(d) The department may not reinstate a driver's license suspended under Subsection (a) unless the person whose license was suspended applies to the department for reinstatement.

(e) A person whose license is suspended under Subsection (a) remains eligible to receive an occupational license under Subchapter L.

(f) For the purposes of this section, a person is convicted of an offense regardless of whether sentence is imposed or the person is placed on community supervision for the offense under Article 42.12, Code of Criminal Procedure.

*(Renumbered from section 521.314 by L.1999, chap. 1117(1), eff. 9/1/2000.)*

## SUBCHAPTER O. AUTOMATIC SUSPENSION

### §521.341. Requirements for automatic license suspension.

Except as provided by Sections 521.344(d)-(i), a license is automatically suspended on final conviction of the license holder of:

(1) an offense under Section 19.05, Penal Code, committed as a result of the holder's criminally negligent operation of a motor vehicle;

(2) an offense under Section 38.04, Penal Code;

(3) an offense under Section 49.04 or 49.08, Penal Code;

(4) an offense under Section 49.07, Penal Code, if the person used a motor vehicle in the commission of the offense;

(5) an offense punishable as a felony under the motor vehicle laws of this state;

(6) an offense under Section 550.021; or

(7) an offense under Section 521.451 or 521.453.

*(Added by L.1995, chap. 165(1); chgd. by L.1997, chap. 165(30.93(a)), eff. 9/1/97.)*

### §521.342. Person under 21 years of age.

(a) Except as provided by Section 521.344, the license of a person who was under 21 years of age at the time of the offense, other than an offense classified as a misdemeanor punishable by fine only, is automatically suspended on conviction of:

(1) an offense under Section 49.04 or 49.07, Penal Code, committed as a result of the introduction of alcohol into the body;

(2) an offense under the Alcoholic Beverage Code, other than an offense to which Section 106.071 of that code applies, involving the manufacture, delivery, possession, transportation, or use of an alcoholic beverage;

(3) a misdemeanor offense under Chapter 481, Health and Safety Code, for which Subchapter P does not require the automatic suspension of the license;

(4) an offense under Chapter 483, Health and Safety Code, involving the manufacture, delivery, possession, transportation, or use of a dangerous drug; or

(5) an offense under Chapter 484, Health and Safety Code, involving the manufacture, delivery, possession, transportation, or use of a volatile chemical.

(b) The department shall suspend for one year the license of a person who is under 21 years of age and is convicted of an offense under Section 49.04, 49.07, or 49.08, Penal Code, regardless of whether the person is required to attend an educational program under Section 13(h), Article 42.12, Code of Criminal Procedure, that is designed to rehabilitate persons who have operated motor vehicles while intoxicated, unless the person is placed under community supervision under that article and is required as a condition of the community supervision to not operate a motor vehicle unless the vehicle is equipped with the device described by Section 13(i) of that article. If the person is required to attend such a program and does not complete the program before the end of the person's suspension, the department shall suspend the person's license or continue the suspension, as appropriate, until the department receives proof that the person has successfully completed the program. On the person's successful completion of the program, the person's instructor shall give notice to the department and to the community supervision and corrections department in the manner provided by Section 13(h), Article 42.12, Code of Criminal Procedure.

(c) A person whose license is suspended under Subsection (a) remains eligible to receive an occupational license under Subchapter L. Suspension under Subsection (a) is not a suspension for physical or mental disability or impairment for purposes of eligibility to apply for an occupational license under Subchapter L.

*(Added by L.1995, chap. 165(1); chgd. by L.1997, chaps. 165(30.94(a)), (30.95(a)); 1013(20); L.1999, chap. 580(9), eff. 9/1/99.)*

### §521.343. Period of suspension; extension.

(a) Except as provided by Sections 521.342(b), 521.344(a), (b), (d), (e), (f), (g), (h), and (i), 521.345, 521.346, and 521.3465, a suspension under this subchapter is for one year.

(b) If a license is suspended under this subchapter for a subsequent period, the subsequent suspension is for 18 months except as otherwise provided by a section listed in Subsection (a).

(c) If the license holder is convicted of operating a motor vehicle while the license to operate a motor vehicle is cancelled, disqualified, suspended, revoked, or denied, the period is extended for the same term as the original suspension or disqualification, in addition to any penalty assessed under this chapter or Chapter 522.

*(Added by L.1995, chap. 165(1); chgd. by L.1997, chap. 851(3), eff. 9/1/97.)*

### §521.344. Suspension for offenses related to use of alcohol.

(a) Except as provided by Sections 521.342(b) and 521.345, and by Subsections (d)-(i), if a person is convicted of an offense under Section 49.04 or 49.07, Penal Code, that is committed as a result of the introduction of alcohol into the body, the license suspension:

(1) begins on a date set by the court that is not earlier than the date of the conviction or later than the 30th day after the date of the conviction, as determined by the court; and

(2) continues for a period set by the court according to the following schedule:

(A) not less than 90 days or more than one year if the person is punished under Section 49.04 or 49.07, Penal Code; or

(B) not less than 180 days or more than two years, if the person is punished under Section 49.09, Penal Code.

(b) Except as provided by Section 521.342(b), if a person is convicted of an offense under Section 49.08, Penal Code, the license suspension begins:

(1) on a date set by the court that is not earlier than the date of the conviction or later than the 30th day after the date of the conviction, as determined by the court; and

(2) continues for a period set by the court of not less than 180 days or more than two years.

(c) The court shall credit toward the period of suspension a suspension imposed on the person for refusal to give a specimen under Chapter 724 if the refusal followed an arrest for the same offense for which the court is suspending the person's license under this chapter. The court may not extend the credit to a person:

(1) who has been previously convicted of an offense under Section 49.04, 49.07, or 49.08, Penal Code; or

(2) whose period of suspension is governed by Section 521.342(b).

(d) Except as provided by Subsection (e) and Section 521.342(b), during a period of probation the department may not revoke the person's license if the person is required under Section 13(h) or (j), Article 42.12, Code of Criminal Procedure, to successfully complete an educational program designed to rehabilitate persons who have operated motor vehicles while intoxicated. The department may not revoke the license of a person:

(1) for whom the jury has recommended that the license not be revoked under Section 13(g), Article 42.12, Code of Criminal Procedure; or

(2) who is placed under community supervision under that article and is required as a condition of community supervision to not operate a motor vehicle unless the vehicle is equipped with the device described by Section 13(i) of that article.

(e) After the date has passed, according to department records, for successful completion of the educational program designed to rehabilitate persons who operated motor vehicles while intoxicated, the director shall revoke the license of a person who does not successfully complete the program or, if the person is a resident without a license to operate a motor vehicle in this state, shall issue an order prohibiting the person from obtaining a license.

(f) After the date has passed, according to department records, for successful completion of an educational program for repeat offenders as required by Section 13, Article 42.12, Code of Criminal Procedure, the director shall suspend the license of a person who does not successfully complete the program or, if the person is a resident without a license, shall issue an order prohibiting the person from obtaining a license.

(g) A revocation, suspension, or prohibition order under Subsection (e) or (f) remains in effect until the department receives notice of successful completion of the educational program. The director shall promptly send notice of a revocation or prohibition order issued under Subsection (e) or (f) by first class mail to the person at the person's most recent address as shown in the records of the department. The notice must include the date of the revocation or prohibition order, the reason for the revocation or prohibition, and a statement that the person has the right to request in writing that a hearing be held on the revocation or prohibition. Notice is considered received on the fifth day after the date the notice is mailed. A revocation or prohibition under Subsection (e) or (f) takes effect on the 30th day after the date the notice is mailed. The person may request a hearing not later than the 20th day after the date the notice is mailed. If the department receives a request under this subsection, the department shall set the hearing for the earliest practical time and the revocation or prohibition does not take effect until resolution of the hearing.

(h) The hearing shall be held in a municipal or justice court in the county of the person's residence in the manner provided for a suspension hearing under *Subchapter N* [Section 521.291]. The issues to be determined at the hearing are whether the person has successfully completed a required educational program and whether the period for completion of the program has passed. If the presiding officer determines that the educational program has not been completed and the period for completion has passed, the officer shall confirm the revocation or prohibition and shall notify the department of that fact. The director may not revoke or prohibit the license if the officer finds that the program has been completed, that, before the hearing, the court that originally imposed the requirement to attend an educational program has granted an extension that has not expired, or that the period for completion has not passed. If the person or the person's agent fails to appear at the hearing, the department shall revoke the person's license until the department receives notice of successful completion of the educational program.

(i) On the date that a suspension order under Section 521.343(c) is to expire, the period of suspension or the corresponding period in which the department is prohibited from issuing a license

is automatically increased to two years unless the department receives notice of successful completion of the educational program as required by Section 13, Article 42.12, Code of Criminal Procedure. At the time a person is convicted of an offense under Section 49.04, Penal Code, the court shall warn the person of the effect of this subsection. On the person's successful completion of the program, the person's instructor shall give notice to the department and to the community supervision and corrections department in the manner required by Section 13, Article 42.12, Code of Criminal Procedure. If the department receives proof of completion after a period has been extended under this subsection, the department shall immediately end the suspension or prohibition.
*(Added by L.1995, chap. 165(1); chgd. by L.1997, chap. 165(30.96(a)); L.1999, chaps. 580(10), 1117(2), 1409(2), eff. 9/1/99, 9/1/2000, 9/1/99, respectively. Matter in brackets eff. only until 9/1/2000. Matter in italics eff. 9/1/2000.)*

**§521.345. Suspension on order of juvenile court or on order of court based on alcoholic beverage violation by minor.**

(a) The department shall suspend the license of a person on receipt of an order to suspend the license that is issued by:

(1) a juvenile court under Section 54.042, Family Code; or

(2) a court under Section 106.115, Alcoholic Beverage Code.

(b) The period of suspension is for the period specified in the order.

*(Added by L.1995, chap. 165(1); chgd. by L.1997, chap. 165(30.97(a)), eff. 9/1/97.)*

**§521.346. Suspension on conviction of certain fraudulent activities.**

(a) If an individual is convicted of an offense under Section 521.451 or 521.453, the period of suspension shall be for the period set by the court of not less than 90 days or more than one year.

(b) If the court does not set the period, the department shall suspend the license for one year.

*(Added by L.1995, chap. 165(1), eff. 9/1/95.)*

**§521.3465. Automatic suspension on conviction of certain offenses involving fictitious motor vehicle license plates, registration insignia, or safety inspection certificates.**

(a) A license is automatically suspended on final conviction of the license holder of:

(1) an offense under Section 502.409(a)(4); or

(2) an offense under Section 548.603(a)(1) that involves a fictitious safety inspection certificate.

(b) A suspension under this section is for 180 days.

(c) If the person is a resident of this state without a driver's license to operate a motor vehicle, the director shall issue an order prohibiting the person from being issued a driver's license before the 181st day after the date of the conviction.

*(Added by L.1997, chap. 851(4), eff. 9/1/97.)*

**§521.3466. Automatic revocation for offense involving certain fraudulent governmental records.**

(a) A license is automatically revoked on final conviction of the license holder of an offense under Section 37.10, Penal Code, if the governmental record was a motor vehicle license plate or registration insignia, within the meaning of Chapter 502, or a safety inspection certificate, within the meaning of Chapter 548.

(b) If the person is a resident of this state without a driver's license to operate a motor vehicle, the director shall issue an order prohibiting the person from being issued a driver's license until the second anniversary of the date of the conviction.

(c) Section 521.347 applies to a conviction under Section 37.10, Penal Code, in the same manner that section applies to a conviction of an offense that requires automatic suspension of a person's driver's license.

(d) The department may not issue a driver's license to the person before the second anniversary of the date of the conviction. The department may issue a driver's license to the person only if the person:

(1) applies to the department for the license;

(2) is otherwise qualified for the license; and

(3) pays, in addition to the fee required by Section 521.421, a fee of $100.

*(Added by L.1997, chap. 851(4), eff. 9/1/97.)*

### §521.347. Reports; recommended suspension.

(a) The court in which a person is convicted of an offense for which this chapter or Chapter 522 requires automatic suspension of the person's driver's license may require the person to surrender to the court each driver's license held by the person. Not later than the 10th day after the date on which the license is surrendered to the court, the clerk of the court shall send to the department:

(1) the license; and

(2) a record of the conviction that states whether the vehicle involved in the offense was a commercial motor vehicle as defined by Chapter 522 or was involved in the transport of hazardous materials.

(b) Each court with jurisdiction of an offense under this chapter or another law of this state regulating the operation of a motor vehicle on a highway shall send to the department a record of conviction of any person convicted in the court of such a violation. The court may recommend the suspension of the person's driver's license as provided by Subchapter N.

(c) For purposes of this section, "conviction" means a final conviction. A conviction is a final conviction regardless of whether any portion of the sentence for the conviction was suspended or probated but is not a final conviction if the defendant receives a deferred adjudication in the case or if the court defers final disposition of the case, unless the court subsequently proceeds with an adjudication of guilt and imposes a sentence on the defendant. For purposes of this section, a final judgment of forfeiture of bail or collateral deposited to secure a defendant's appearance in court is a conviction if the forfeiture is not vacated.

*(Added by L.1995, chap. 165(1); chgd. by L.1999, chaps. 581(1), 884(2), eff. 6/18/99, 9/1/99, respectively.)*

### §521.348. Automatic revocation for certain sex offenders.

(a) A driver's license is automatically revoked if the holder of the license:

(1) is subject to the registration requirements of Chapter 62, Code of Criminal Procedure, as added by Chapter 668, Acts of the 75th Legislature, Regular Session, 1997; and

(2) fails to apply to the department for renewal of the license as required by Article 62.065, Code of Criminal Procedure.

(b) The department may issue a driver's license to a person whose license is revoked under this section only if the person:

(1) applies for an original or renewal license under Section 521.272; and

(2) is otherwise qualified for the license.

*(Added by L.1999, chap. 1401(9), eff. 9/1/2000.)*

### §§521.349 to 521.370. *(Reserved.)*

## SUBCHAPTER P. AUTOMATIC SUSPENSION FOR CERTAIN DRUG OFFENSES

*(Heading chgd. by L.1997, chap. 165(30.101), eff. 9/1/97.)*

### §521.371. Definitions.

In this subchapter:

(1) "Controlled Substances Act" means the federal Controlled Substances Act (21 U.S.C. Sec. 801 et seq.).

(2) "Convicted" includes an adjudication under juvenile proceedings.

(3) "Drug offense" has the meaning assigned under 23 U.S.C. Section 159(c) and includes an offense under Section 49.04, 49.07, or 49.08, Penal Code, that is committed as a result of the introduction into the body of any substance the possession of which is prohibited under the Controlled Substances Act.

*(Added by L.1995, chap. 165(1), eff. 9/1/95.)*

### §521.372. Automatic suspension; license denial.

(a) A person's driver's license is automatically suspended on final conviction of:

(1) an offense under the Controlled Substances Act;

(2) a drug offense; or

(3) a felony under Chapter 481, Health and Safety Code, that is not a drug offense.

(b) The department may not issue a driver's license to a person convicted of an offense specified in Subsection (a) who, on the date of the conviction, did not hold a driver's license.

(c) Except as provided by Section 521.374(b), the period of suspension under this section is the 180 days after the date of a final conviction, and the period of license denial is the 180 days after the date the person applies to the department for reinstatement or issuance of a driver's license.
*(Added by L.1995, chap. 165(1), eff. 9/1/95.)*

## §521.373. Reinstatement requirements.

(a) The department may not reinstate a driver's license suspended under Section 521.372 unless the person whose license was suspended applies to the department for reinstatement.

(b) The department may not reinstate the driver's license of a person convicted of an offense specified by Section 521.372(a) if the driver's license was under suspension on the date of the conviction.
*(Added by L.1995, chap. 165(1), eff. 9/1/95.)*

## §521.374. Educational program.

(a) A person whose license is suspended under Section 521.372 may attend an educational program, approved by the Texas Commission on Alcohol and Drug Abuse under rules adopted by the commission and the department, that is designed to educate persons on the dangers of drug abuse.

(b) The period of suspension or prohibition under Section 521.372(c) continues for an indefinite period until the individual successfully completes the educational program.
*(Added by L.1995, chap. 165(1), eff. 9/1/95.)*

## §521.375. Joint adoption of rules.

(a) The Texas Commission on Alcohol and Drug Abuse and the department shall jointly adopt rules for the qualification and approval of providers of educational programs under Section 521.374.

(b) The Texas Commission on Alcohol and Drug Abuse shall publish the jointly adopted rules.
*(Added by L.1995, chap. 165(1), eff. 9/1/95.)*

## §521.376. Duties of Texas Commission on Alcohol and Drug Abuse; application and renewal fees.

The Texas Commission on Alcohol and Drug Abuse:

(1) shall monitor, coordinate, and provide training to persons who provide educational programs under Section 521.374;

(2) shall administer the approval of those educational programs; and

(3) may charge a nonrefundable application fee for:

(A) initial certification of approval; and

(B) renewal of the certification.
*(Added by L.1995, chap. 165(1); chgd. by L.1997, chap. 577(19), eff. 9/1/97.)*

## §521.377. License reinstatement.

(a) The department, on payment of the applicable fee, shall reinstate a person's license or, if the person otherwise qualifies for a license, issue the license, if:

(1) the department receives notification from the clerk of the court in which the person was convicted that the person has successfully completed an educational program under this subchapter; and

(2) the person's driver's license has been suspended or license application denied for at least the period provided by Section 521.372(c).

(b) A person whose license is suspended under Section 521.372 remains eligible to receive an occupational license under Subchapter L. Suspension under Section 521.372 is not a suspension for physical or mental disability or impairment for purposes of eligibility to apply for an occupational license under Subchapter L.
*(Added by L.1995, chap. 165(1), eff. 9/1/95.)*

## §§521.378 to 521.400. *(Reserved.)*

## SUBCHAPTER Q. ANATOMICAL GIFTS

### §521.401. Statement of gift.

(a) A person who wishes to be an eye, tissue, or organ donor may execute a statement of gift.

(b) The statement of gift may be shown by a card designed to be carried by the donor to evidence the donor's intentions with respect to organ, tissue, and eye donation. A donor card signed by the donor shall be given effect as if executed pursuant to Section 692.003(d), Health and Safety Code.

(c) Donor cards shall be provided to the department by qualified organ or tissue procurement organizations or eye banks, as those terms are defined in Section 692.002, Health and Safety Code. The department shall provide a means to distribute donor cards to interested individuals in each office authorized to issue driver's licenses or personal identification certificates. The department and other appropriate state agencies, in cooperation with qualified organ, tissue, and eye bank organizations shall pursue the development of a combined statewide database of donors.

(d) Effective September 1, 1997, a statement of gift on driver's licenses or personal identification certificates shall have no force and effect, provided, however, that an affirmative statement of gift on a person's driver's license or personal identification certificate executed prior to September 1, 1997, shall be conclusive evidence of a decedent's status as a donor and serve as consent for organ, tissue, and eye removal.

*(Added by L.1995, chap. 165(1); chgd. by L.1997, chap. 225(1), eff. 9/1/97.)*

### §521.402. Revocation of statement of gift.

(a) To revoke an affirmative statement of gift on a person's driver's license or personal identification certificate made prior to September 1, 1997, a person must apply to the department for an amendment to the license or certificate.

(b) The fee for an amendment is the same as the fee for a duplicate license.

*(Added by L.1995, chap. 165(1); chgd. by L.1997, chap. 225(1), eff. 9/1/97.)*

### §521.403. Information provided to hospital.

The donor card of a person who is involved in an accident or other trauma shall accompany the person to the hospital or other health care facility. The driver's license or personal identification certificate issued prior to September 1, 1997, indicating an affirmative statement of gift of a person who is involved in an accident or other trauma, shall accompany the person to the hospital or health care facility if the person does not have a donor card. *(Added by L.1995, chap. 165(1); chgd. by L.1997, chap. 225(1), eff. 9/1/97.)*

### §521.404. Notification to procurement organization.

If the person meets the medical criteria for organ or tissue donation, the receiving hospital or facility shall immediately notify a qualified organ or tissue procurement organization as soon as brain death or cardiac death occurs. *(Added by L.1995, chap. 165(1), eff. 9/1/95.)*

### §521.405. Determination; request; removal of certain organs.

(a) The qualified organ or tissue procurement organization shall immediately determine if the deceased is a declared donor. If the deceased is not a declared donor, the organization shall make the required request of a person listed in Section 692.004, Health and Safety Code, according to the priority established under that section. The organization may authorize the hospital or facility or the hospital's or facility's agent to make the request.

(b) If a person listed in Section 692.004, Health and Safety Code, is not contacted within four hours after death is pronounced, the medical examiner may permit the removal of the heart, lung, kidney, liver, or other organ or tissue that requires a patient support system to maintain the viability of the organ or tissue.

(c) A person who performs an action authorized by this section is not civilly or criminally liable because of that action. Each medical examiner is encouraged to permit organ and tissue removal at the earliest possible time consistent with the examiner's duties regarding the cause and manner of death.

*(Added by L.1995, chap. 165(1), eff. 9/1/95.)*

### §§521.406 to 521.420. *(Reserved.)*

## SUBCHAPTER R. FEES

### §521.421. License fees; examination fees.

(a) The fee for issuance or renewal of a license not otherwise provided for by this section is $24.

(b) The fee for renewal of a Class M license or for renewal of a license that includes authorization to operate a motorcycle is $32.

(c) The fee for issuance or renewal of a provisional license or instruction permit is $5.

(d) The fee for issuance or renewal of an occupational license is $10.

(e) An applicant who changes from a lower to a higher class of license or who adds a type of vehicle other than a motorcycle to the license shall pay a $10 fee for the required examination.

(f) The department shall collect an additional fee of $1 for the issuance or renewal of a license to fund the Blindness Education, Screening, and Treatment Program established under Section 91.027, Human Resources Code, if the person applying for or renewing a license opts to pay the additional fee. *(Added by L.1997, chap. 510(2), eff. 9/1/97. See other subsections (f) below.)*

(f) If a Class A, B, or C driver's license includes an authorization to operate a motorcycle or moped, the fee for the driver's license is increased by $8. *(Added by L.1997, chap. 1372(3), eff. 9/1/97. See other subsections (f) above and below.)*

(f) An applicant applying for additional authorization to operate a motorcycle shall pay a $15 fee for the required application. *(Added by L.1997, chap. 1156(1), eff. 9/1/97. See other subsections (f) above.)*

(g) The department shall collect an additional fee of $1 for the issuance or renewal of a license to fund the anatomical gift educational program established under Chapter 46, Health and Safety Code, if the person applying for or renewing a license opts to pay the additional fee. The department shall remit fees collected under this subsection to the comptroller, who shall maintain the identity of the source of the fees.

*(Added by L.1995, chap. 165(1); chgd. by L.1997, chaps. 510(2), 1156(1), 1372(3); L.1999, chap. 1516(2), eff. 9/1/99.)*

### §521.422. Personal identification certificate fee.

(a) The fee for a personal identification certificate is:

(1) $15 for a person under 60 years of age; and

(2) $5 for a person 60 years of age or older.

(b) The department shall collect an additional fee of $1 for the issuance or renewal of a personal identification card to fund the Blindness Education, Screening, and Treatment Program established under Section 91.027, Human Resources Code, if the person applying for or renewing a personal identification card opts to pay the additional fee.

(c) The department shall collect an additional fee of $1 for the issuance or renewal of a personal identification card to fund the anatomical gift educational program established under Chapter 46, Health and Safety Code, if the person applying for or renewing a personal identification card opts to pay the additional fee. The department shall remit fees collected under this subsection to the comptroller, who shall maintain the identity of the source of the fees.

*(Added by L.1995, chap. 165(1); chgd. by L.1997, chaps. 510(3), 1372(4); L.1999, chap. 1516(3), eff. 9/1/99.)*

### §521.423. Fee for disability certificate or health condition certificate.

The fee for a disability certificate or a health condition certificate is $5. *(Added by L.1995, chap. 165(1), eff. 9/1/95.)*

### §521.424. Duplicate license or certificate fee.

(a) The fee for a duplicate driver's license or duplicate personal identification certificate is $10.

(b) The fee for a duplicate disability certificate or duplicate health condition certificate is $5. *(Added by L.1995, chap. 165(1), eff. 9/1/95.)*

### §521.425. Remittance of fees and charges.

Each fee or charge required by this chapter and collected by an officer or agent of the department shall be sent without deduction to the department in Austin. *(Added by L.1995, chap. 165(1), eff. 9/1/95.)*

### §521.426. Disabled veteran exemption.

(a) A veteran of service in the armed forces of the United States is exempt from the payment of fees under this chapter for the issuance of a driver's license if the veteran:

(1) was honorably discharged;

(2) has a service-related disability of at least 60 percent; and

(3) receives compensation from the United States because of the disability.

(b) The department shall adopt rules relating to the proof of entitlement to this exemption.

*(Added by L.1995, chap. 165(1), eff. 9/1/95.)*

### §521.427. Method of payment of fees.

(a) The department may adopt rules regarding the method of payment of a fee for a license, personal identification card, or license record issued under this chapter.

(b) The rules may authorize payment, under circumstances prescribed by the department:

(1) in person, by mail, by telephone, or over the Internet;

(2) by means of electronic funds transfer; or

(3) by means of a valid credit card issued by a financial institution chartered by a state or the federal government or by a nationally recognized credit organization approved by the department.

(c) The rules may require the payment of a discount or service charge for a credit card payment in addition to the fee.

*(Added by L.1999, chap. 1189(28), eff. 9/1/99.)*

### §§521.428 to 521.450. *(Reserved.)*

## SUBCHAPTER S. MISCELLANEOUS OFFENSES

### §521.451. General violation.

(a) Except as provided by Section 521.452, a person may not:

(1) display, cause or permit to be displayed, or have in the person's possession a driver's license or certificate that the person knows is fictitious or has been canceled, revoked, suspended, or altered;

(2) lend the person's driver's license or certificate to another person or knowingly permit another person to use the person's driver's license or certificate;

(3) display or represent as the person's own a driver's license or certificate not issued to the person;

(4) fail or refuse to surrender to the department on demand a driver's license or certificate that has been canceled, suspended, or revoked;

(5) possess more than one currently valid driver's license or more than one currently valid certificate; or

(6) in an application for an original, renewal, or duplicate driver's license or certificate:

(A) provide a false name, false address, or a counterfeit document; or

(B) knowingly make a false statement, conceal a material fact, or otherwise commit fraud.

(b) An offense under this section is a Class B misdemeanor.

*(Added by L.1995, chap. 165(1); chgd. by L.1999, chap. 659(3), eff. 9/1/99.)*

### §521.452. Alias driver's license for law enforcement purposes.

(a) After written approval by the director, the department may issue to a law enforcement officer an alias driver's license to be used in supervised activities involving a criminal investigation.

(b) An application for, or possession or use of, an alias driver's license for a purpose described by this section by the officer to whom the license is issued is not a violation of this subchapter unless the department has canceled, suspended, or revoked the license.

*(Added by L.1995, chap. 165(1), eff. 9/1/95.)*

### §521.453. Fictitious license or certificate.

(a) Except as provided by Subsection (f), a person under the age of 21 years commits an offense if the person possesses, with the intent to represent that the person is 21 years of age or older, a document that is deceptively similar to a driver's license or a personal identification certificate unless the document displays the statement "NOT A GOVERNMENT DOCUMENT" diagonally printed clearly and indelibly on both the front and back of the document in solid red capital letters at least one-fourth inch in height.

(b) For purposes of this section, a document is deceptively similar to a driver's license or personal identification certificate if a reasonable person would assume that it was issued by the department, another agency of this state, another state, or the United States.

(c) A peace officer listed in Article 2.12, Code of Criminal Procedure, may confiscate a document that:

(1) is deceptively similar to a driver's license or personal identification certificate; and

(2) does not display the statement required under Subsection (a).

(d) For purposes of this section, an offense under Subsection (a) is a Class C misdemeanor.

(e) The attorney general, district attorney, or prosecuting attorney performing the duties of the district attorney may bring an action to enjoin a violation or threatened violation of this section. The action must be brought in a court in the county in which the violation or threatened violation occurs.

(f) Subsection (a) does not apply to:

(1) a government agency, office, or political subdivision that is authorized to produce or sell personal identification certificates; or

(2) a person that provides a document similar to a personal identification certificate to an employee of the person for a business purpose.

(g) In this section:

(1) "Driver's license" includes a driver's license issued by another state or by the United States.

(2) "Personal identification certificate" means a personal identification certificate issued by the department, by another agency of this state, by another state, or by the United States.

(h) In addition to the punishment provided by Subsection (d), a court, if the court is located in a municipality or county that has established a community service program, may order a person younger than 21 years of age who commits an offense under this section to perform eight hours of community service unless the person is shown to have previously committed an offense under this section, in which case the court may order the person to perform 12 hours of community service.

(i) If the person ordered to perform community service under Subsection (h) is younger than 17 years of age, the community service shall be performed as if ordered by a juvenile court under Section 54.044(a), Family Code, as a condition of probation under Section 54.04(d), Family Code.

*(Added by L.1995, chap. 165(1); chgd. by L.1997, chaps. 823(1), 1358(1), eff. 9/1/97.)*

## §521.454. False application.

(a) A person commits an offense if the person knowingly swears to or affirms falsely before a person authorized to take statements under oath any matter, information, or statement required by the department in an application for an original, renewal, or duplicate driver's license or certificate issued under this chapter.

(b) An information or indictment for a violation of Subsection (a) that alleges that the declarant has made inconsistent statements under oath, both of which cannot be true, need not allege which statement is false and the prosecution is not required to prove which statement is false.

(c) An offense under this section is a Class A misdemeanor.

*(Added by L.1995, chap. 165(1); chgd. by L.1999, chap. 658(1), eff. 9/1/99.)*

## §521.455. Use of illegal license or certificate.

(a) A person commits an offense if the person intentionally or knowingly uses a driver's license or certificate obtained in violation of Section 521.451 or 521.454 to harm or defraud another.

(b) An offense under this section is a Class A misdemeanor.

*(Added by L.1995, chap. 165(1), eff. 9/1/95.)*

## §521.456. Delivery or manufacture of counterfeit instrument.

(a) A person commits an offense if the person possesses with the intent to sell, distribute, or deliver a forged or counterfeit instrument that is not printed, manufactured, or made by or under the direction of, or issued, sold, or circulated by or under the direction of, a person, board, agency, or authority authorized to do so under this chapter or under the laws of the United States, another state, or a Canadian province. An offense under this subsection is a Class A misdemeanor.

(b) A person commits an offense if the person manufactures or produces with the intent to sell, distribute, or deliver a forged or counterfeit instrument that the person knows is not printed, manufactured, or made by or under the direction of, or issued, sold, or circulated by or under the direction of, a person, board, agency, or authority authorized to do so under this chapter or under the laws of the United States, another state, or a Canadian province. An offense under this subsection is a felony of the third degree.

(c) A person commits an offense if the person possesses with the intent to use, circulate, or pass a forged or counterfeit instrument that is not printed, manufactured, or made by or under the direction of, or issued, sold, or circulated by or under the direction of, a person, board, agency, or authority authorized to do so under this chapter or under the laws of the United States, another state, or a Canadian province. An offense under this subsection is a Class C misdemeanor.

(d) For purposes of this section, "instrument" means a driver's license, driver's license form, personal identification certificate, stamp, permit, license, official signature, certificate, evidence of fee payment, or any other instrument.

*(Added by L.1995, chap. 165(1); chgd. by L.1997, chaps. 165(30.99), 823(2), eff. 9/1/97.)*

## §521.457. Driving while license invalid.

(a) A person commits an offense if the person operates a motor vehicle on a highway:

(1) after the person's driver's license has been canceled under this chapter if the person does not have a license that was subsequently issued under this chapter;

(2) during a period that the person's driver's license or privilege is suspended or revoked under:

(A) this chapter;

(B) Chapter 524;

(C) Chapter 724;

(D) Section 106.071, Alcoholic Beverage Code; or

(E) Article 42.12, Code of Criminal Procedure;

(3) while the person's driver's license is expired if the license expired during a period of suspension imposed under:

(A) this chapter;

(B) Chapter 524;

(C) Chapter 724;

(D) Section 106.071, Alcoholic Beverage Code; or

(E) Article 42.12, Code of Criminal Procedure; or

(4) after renewal of the person's driver's license has been denied under Chapter 706, if the person does not have a driver's license subsequently issued under this chapter.

(b) A person commits an offense if the person is the subject of an order issued under this chapter or Chapter 724 that prohibits the person from obtaining a driver's license and the person operates a motor vehicle on a highway.

(c) It is not a defense to prosecution under this section that the person did not receive actual notice of a suspension imposed as a result of a conviction for an offense under Section 521.341.

(d) Except as provided by Subsection (c), it is an affirmative defense to prosecution of an offense, other than an offense under Section 521.341, that the person did not receive actual notice of a cancellation, suspension, revocation, or prohibition order relating to the person's license. For purposes of this section, actual notice is presumed if the notice was mailed in accordance with law.

(e) Except as provided by Subsection (f), an offense under this section is a misdemeanor punishable by:

(1) a fine of not less than $100 or more than $500; and

(2) confinement in county jail for a term of not less than 72 hours or more than six months.

(f) If it is shown on the trial of an offense under this section that the person has previously been convicted of an offense under this section or Section 601.371(a), the offense is a Class A misdemeanor.

(g) For purposes of this section, a conviction for an offense that involves operation of a motor vehicle after August 31, 1987, is a final conviction, regardless of whether the sentence for the conviction is probated.

*(Added by L.1995, chap. 165(1); chgd. by L.1997, chap. 165(30.98(a)); L.1999, chap. 1207(6), eff. 9/1/99.)*

## §521.458. Permitting unauthorized person to drive.

(a) A person may not knowingly permit or cause the person's child or ward who is under 18 years of age to operate a motor vehicle on a highway in violation of this chapter.

(b) A person may not authorize or knowingly permit a motor vehicle owned by or under the control of the person to be operated on a highway by any person in violation of this chapter.

*(Added by L.1995, chap. 165(1), eff. 9/1/95.)*

## §521.459. Employment of unlicensed driver.

(a) Before employing a person as an operator of a motor vehicle used to transport persons or property, an employer shall request from the department:

(1) a list of convictions for traffic violations contained in the department records on the potential employee; and

(2) a verification that the person has a license.

(b) A person may not employ a person as an operator of a motor vehicle used to transport persons or property who does not hold the appropriate driver's license to operate the vehicle as provided by this chapter.
*(Added by L.1995, chap. 165(1), eff. 9/1/95.)*

### §521.460. Motor vehicle rentals.

(a) A person may not rent a motor vehicle to any other person unless the other person holds a driver's license under this chapter or, if a nonresident, holds a license issued under the laws of the state or Canadian province in which the person resides, unless that state or province does not require that the operator of a motor vehicle hold a license.

(b) A person may not rent a motor vehicle to another person until inspecting the driver's license of the renter and comparing and verifying the signature on the renter's driver's license with the renter's signature written in the person's presence.

(c) Each person who rents a motor vehicle to another shall maintain a record of:

(1) the number of the license plate issued for the motor vehicle;
(2) the name and address of the person to whom the vehicle is rented;
(3) the license number of the person to whom the vehicle is rented;
(4) the date the license was issued; and
(5) the place where the license was issued.

(d) The record maintained under Subsection (c) may be inspected by any police officer or officer or employee of the department.
*(Added by L.1995, chap. 165(1), eff. 9/1/95.)*

### §521.461. General criminal penalty.

(a) A person who violates a provision of this chapter for which a specific penalty is not provided commits an offense.

(b) An offense under this section is a misdemeanor punishable by a fine not to exceed $200.
*(Added by L.1995, chap. 165(1), eff. 9/1/95.)*

## CHAPTER 522. COMMERCIAL DRIVER'S LICENSES

## SUBCHAPTER A. GENERAL PROVISIONS

Section


## SUBCHAPTER B. LICENSE OR PERMIT REQUIRED



## SUBCHAPTER C. LICENSE OR PERMIT APPLICATION AND ISSUANCE

## SUBCHAPTER D. CLASSIFICATION, ENDORSEMENT, OR RESTRICTION OF LICENSE



## SUBCHAPTER E. EXPIRATION AND RENEWAL OF LICENSE OR PERMIT



## SUBCHAPTER F. NOTIFICATION OF CONVICTION, ADMINISTRATIVE ACTION, OR PREVIOUS EMPLOYMENT



## SUBCHAPTER G. UNAUTHORIZED DRIVING



## SUBCHAPTER H. DISQUALIFICATION FROM DRIVING COMMERCIAL MOTOR VEHICLE

## SUBCHAPTER I. DRIVING WHILE HAVING ALCOHOL, CONTROLLED SUBSTANCE, OR DRUG IN SYSTEM



## SUBCHAPTER A. GENERAL PROVISIONS

### §522.001. Short title.

This chapter may be cited as the Texas Commercial Driver's License Act. *(Added by L.1995, chap. 165(1), eff. 9/1/95.)*

### §522.002. Construction.

This chapter is a remedial law that shall be liberally construed to promote the public health, safety, and welfare. *(Added by L.1995, chap. 165(1), eff. 9/1/95.)*

### §522.003. Definitions.

In this chapter:

(1) "Alcohol" means:

(A) beer, ale, port, stout, sake, or any other similar fermented beverages or products containing one-half of one percent or more of alcohol by volume, brewed or produced wholly or in part from malt or a malt substitute;

(B) wine containing one-half of one percent or more of alcohol by volume; or

(C) distilled spirits, including ethyl alcohol, ethanol, and spirits of wine in any form, and all dilutions and mixtures of distilled spirits from whatever source or by whatever process produced.

(2) "Alcohol concentration" means the number of grams of alcohol for each:

(A) 100 milliliters of blood;

(B) 210 liters of breath; or

(C) 67 milliliters of urine.

(3) "Commercial driver's license" means a license issued to an individual that authorizes the individual to drive a class of commercial motor vehicle.

(4) "Commercial driver learner's permit" means a commercial driver's license that restricts the holder to driving a commercial motor vehicle as provided by Section 522.011(a)(2)(B).

(5) "Commercial motor vehicle" means a motor vehicle or combination of motor vehicles used to transport passengers or property that:

(A) has a gross combination weight rating of 26,001 or more pounds, including a towed unit with a gross vehicle weight rating of more than 10,000 pounds;

(B) has a gross vehicle weight rating of 26,001 or more pounds;

(C) is designed to transport 16 or more passengers, including the driver; or

(D) is transporting hazardous materials and is required to be placarded under 49 C.F.R. Part 172, Subpart F.

(6) "Controlled substance" means a substance classified as a controlled substance under:

(A) Section 102(6), Controlled Substances Act (21 U.S.C. Section 802(6)), including Schedules I-V of 21 C.F.R. Part 1308; or

(B) Chapter 481, Health and Safety Code.

(7) "Conviction" means:

(A) an adjudication of guilt, an unvacated forfeiture of bail or collateral deposited to secure the person's appearance in court, the payment of a fine or court costs, or the violation of a condition of release without bail, in a court, regardless of whether the penalty is suspended, probated, or rebated; or

(B) a determination by a court, an authorized administrative tribunal or officer, or the department as authorized by this chapter that:

(i) the person has refused to give a specimen to determine the person's alcohol concentration or the presence in the person's body of a controlled substance or drug while driving a commercial motor vehicle; or

(ii) the person has driven a commercial motor vehicle while the person's alcohol concentration was 0.04 or more.

(8) "Department" means the Department of Public Safety.

(9) "Disqualify" means to withdraw the privilege to drive a commercial motor vehicle, including to suspend, cancel, or revoke that privilege under a state or federal law.

(10) "Domicile" means the place where a person has the person's true, fixed, and permanent home and principal residence and to which the person intends to return whenever absent.

(11) "Drive" means to operate or be in physical control of a motor vehicle.

(12) "Driver's license" means a license issued by a state to an individual that authorizes the individual to drive a motor vehicle.

(13) "Drug" has the meaning assigned by Section 481.002, Health and Safety Code.

(14) "Employer" means a person who owns or leases a commercial motor vehicle or assigns a person to drive a commercial motor vehicle.

(15) "Federal act" means the Commercial Motor Vehicle Safety Act of 1986 (49 U.S.C. App. Section 2701 et seq.).

(16) "Foreign jurisdiction" means a jurisdiction other than a state.

(17) "Gross combination weight rating" means the value specified by the manufacturer as the loaded weight of a combination or articulated vehicle or, if the manufacturer has not specified a value, the sum of the gross vehicle weight rating of the power unit and the total weight of the towed unit or units and any load on a towed unit.

(18) "Gross vehicle weight rating" means the value specified by the manufacturer as the loaded weight of a single vehicle.

(19) "Hazardous materials" has the meaning assigned by the Hazardous Materials Transportation Act (49 U.S.C. Section 1801 et seq.).

(20) "Highway administration" means the United States Department of Transportation, Federal Highway Administration.

(21) "Motor vehicle" means a vehicle, machine, tractor, trailer, or semitrailer propelled or drawn by mechanical power and used on a highway. The term does not include a vehicle, machine, tractor, trailer, or semitrailer operated exclusively on a rail.

(22) "Nonresident commercial driver's license" means a commercial driver's license issued by a state to an individual who resides in a foreign jurisdiction.

(23) "Out-of-service order" means:

(A) a temporary prohibition against driving a commercial motor vehicle issued under Section 522.101, the law of another state, or 49 C.F.R. Section 383.5; or

(B) a declaration by the highway administration or an authorized enforcement officer of a state or local jurisdiction that a driver, commercial motor vehicle, or motor carrier operation is out of service under 49 C.F.R. Section 383.5.

(24) "Secretary" means the United States secretary of transportation.

(25) "Serious traffic violation" means a conviction arising from the driving of a commercial motor vehicle, other than a parking, vehicle weight, or vehicle defect violation, for:

(A) excessive speeding, involving a single charge of driving 15 miles per hour or more above the posted speed limit;

(B) reckless driving, as defined by state or local law;

(C) a violation of a state or local law related to motor vehicle traffic control, including a law regulating the operation of vehicles on highways, arising in connection with a fatal accident;

(D) improper or erratic traffic lane change; or

(E) following the vehicle ahead too closely.

(26) "State" means a state of the United States or the District of Columbia.

*(Added by L.1995, chap. 165(1), eff. 9/1/95.)*

## §522.004. Applicability.

(a) This chapter does not apply to:

(1) a vehicle that is controlled and operated by a farmer and:

(A) used to transport agricultural products, farm machinery, or farm supplies to or from a farm;

(B) used within 150 miles of the person's farm; and

(C) not used in the operations of a common or contract motor carrier;

(2) a fire-fighting or emergency vehicle necessary to the preservation of life or property or the execution of emergency governmental functions, whether operated by an employee of a political subdivision or by a volunteer fire fighter;

(3) a military vehicle, when operated for military purposes by military personnel, including:

(A) active duty military personnel; and

(B) members of the reserves and national guard on active duty, including personnel on full-time national guard duty, personnel engaged in part-time training, and national guard military technicians;

(4) a recreational vehicle that is driven for personal use;

(5) a vehicle that is owned, leased, or controlled by an air carrier, as defined by Section 21.155, and that is driven or operated exclusively by an employee of the air carrier only on the premises of an airport, as defined by Section 22.001, on service roads to which the public does not have access; or

(6) a vehicle used exclusively to transport seed cotton modules or cotton burrs.

(b) In this section, "recreational vehicle" means a motor vehicle primarily designed as temporary living quarters for recreational camping or travel use. The term includes a travel trailer, camping trailer, truck camper, and motor home.

*(Added by L.1995, chap. 165(1); chgd. by L.1997, chap. 1061(13), eff. 9/1/97.)*

### §522.005. Rulemaking authority.

The department may adopt rules necessary to carry out this chapter and the federal act. *(Added by L.1995, chap. 165(1), eff. 9/1/95.)*

### §522.006. Contracting authority.

The department may enter into a contract to carry out this chapter, including a contract with an agency of another state or with another organization. *(Added by L.1995, chap. 165(1), eff. 9/1/95.)*

### §522.007. Exemption for neighboring states.

(a) The public safety director shall enter negotiations with an appropriate person or entity of a state bordering this state for the purpose of applying the exemption contained in Section 522.004(a)(1) to residents of that state.

(b) The public safety director may enter an agreement to apply the exemption contained in Section 522.004(a)(1) to residents of a bordering state only if that state extends a similar exemption to residents of this state.

*(Added by L.1997, chap. 1061(14), eff. 9/1/97.)*

### §§522.008 to 522.010. *(Reserved.)*

## SUBCHAPTER B. LICENSE OR PERMIT REQUIRED

### §522.011. License or permit required; offense.

(a) A person may not drive a commercial motor vehicle unless:

(1) the person:

(A) has in the person's immediate possession a commercial driver's license issued by the department appropriate for the class of vehicle being driven; and

(B) is not disqualified or subject to an out-of-service order;

(2) the person:

(A) has in the person's immediate possession a commercial driver learner's permit issued by the department; and

(B) is accompanied by the holder of a commercial driver's license issued by the department appropriate for the class of vehicle being driven, and the license holder:

(i) occupies a seat beside the permit holder for the purpose of giving instruction in driving the vehicle; and

(ii) is not disqualified or subject to an out-of-service order; or

(3) the person is authorized to drive the vehicle under Section 522.015.

(b) A person commits an offense if the person violates Subsection (a).

(c) An offense under this section is a Class C misdemeanor.

*(Added by L.1995, chap. 165(1), eff. 9/1/95.)*

### §522.012. Restricted license.

(a) If the department is authorized under the federal act to grant the waiver, the department by rule may waive the knowledge and skills tests required by Section 522.022 and issue a restricted commercial driver's license to an employee of a farm-related service industry.

(b) In granting a waiver under this section, the department is subject to any condition or requirement established for the waiver by the secretary or the highway administration.

(c) In addition to any restriction or limitation imposed by this chapter or the department, a restricted commercial driver's license issued under this section is subject to any restriction or limitation imposed by the secretary or the highway administration.

(d) In this section, "farm-related service industry" has the meaning assigned by the secretary or the highway administration under the federal act.
*(Added by L.1995, chap. 165(1), eff. 9/1/95.)*

### §522.013. Nonresident license.

(a) The department may issue a nonresident commercial driver's license to a resident of a foreign jurisdiction if the secretary has determined that the commercial motor vehicle testing and licensing standards in the foreign jurisdiction do not meet the testing standards established by 49 C.F.R. Part 383.

(b) An applicant must surrender any nonresident commercial driver's license issued by another state.

(c) Before issuing a nonresident commercial driver's license, the department must establish the practical capability of disqualifying the person under the conditions applicable to a commercial driver's license issued to a resident of this state.

(d) "Nonresident" must appear on the face of a nonresident commercial driver's license.
*(Added by L.1995, chap. 165(1), eff. 9/1/95.)*

Printed in the U.S.A.

### §522.014. Permit.

The department may issue a commercial driver learner's permit to an individual who has passed the vision and written tests required for a Texas driver's license appropriate for the class of vehicle to be driven. *(Added by L.1995, chap. 165(1), eff. 9/1/95.)*

### §522.015. License or permit issued by other jurisdiction.

A person may drive a commercial motor vehicle in this state if:

(1) the person has a commercial driver's license or commercial driver learner's permit issued by:

(A) another state in accordance with the minimum federal standards for the issuance of a commercial motor vehicle driver's license; or

(B) a foreign jurisdiction the testing and licensing standards of which the United States Department of Transportation has determined meet the requirements of the federal act;

(2) the person's license or permit is appropriate for the class of vehicle being driven;

(3) the person is not disqualified from driving a commercial motor vehicle and is not subject to an out-of-service order; and

(4) the person has not had a domicile in this state for more than 30 days.
*(Added by L.1995, chap. 165(1), eff. 9/1/95.)*

### §§522.016 to 522.020. *(Reserved.)*

## SUBCHAPTER C. LICENSE OR PERMIT APPLICATION AND ISSUANCE

### §522.021. Application; offense.

(a) An application for a commercial driver's license or commercial driver learner's permit must include:

(1) the full name and current residence and mailing address of the applicant;

(2) a physical description of the applicant, including sex, height, and eye color;

(3) the applicant's date of birth;

(4) the applicant's social security number, unless the application is for a nonresident commercial driver's license;

(5) certifications, including those required by 49 C.F.R. Section 383.71(a); and

(6) any other information required by the department.

(b) The application must be sworn to and signed by the applicant. An officer or employee of the department may administer the oath. An officer or employee of this state may not charge for administering the oath.

(c) The application must meet the requirements of an application under Section 521.141 and must be accompanied by the fee required under Section 522.029. The department may require documentary evidence to verify the information required by Subsection (a).

(d) A person who knowingly falsifies information or a certification required by Subsection (a) commits an offense and is subject to a 60-day cancellation of the person's commercial driver's

license, commercial driver learner's permit, or application. An offense under this subsection is a Class C misdemeanor.
*(Added by L.1995, chap. 165(1), eff. 9/1/95.)*

### §522.022. License requirements.

The department may not issue a commercial driver's license other than a nonresident license to a person unless the person:

(1) has a domicile in this state;

(2) has passed knowledge and skills tests for driving a commercial motor vehicle that comply with minimal federal standards established by 49 C.F.R. Part 383, Subparts G and H; and

(3) has satisfied the requirements imposed by the federal act, federal regulation, or state law.
*(Added by L.1995, chap. 165(1), eff. 9/1/95.)*

### §522.023. Tests.

(a) The tests required by Section 522.022 must be prescribed by the department.

(b) The knowledge test must be conducted by the department. The department shall provide each applicant who has a reading impairment an opportunity to take the knowledge test orally or, at the applicant's option, the applicant may have the questions read to the applicant and may answer in writing.

(c) Except as provided by Subsection (d), the department must conduct the skills test.

(d) The department may authorize a person, including an agency of this or another state, an employer, a private driver training facility or other private institution, or a department, agency, or instrumentality of local government, to administer the skills test specified by this section if:

(1) the test is the same that would be administered by the department; and

(2) the person has entered into an agreement with the department that complies with 49 C.F.R. Section 383.75.

(e) The skills test must be taken in a commercial motor vehicle that is representative of the type of vehicle the person drives or expects to drive.

(f) The department may waive the skills test for an applicant who meets the requirements of 49 C.F.R. Section 383.77.

(g) The department shall test the applicant's ability to understand highway traffic signs and signals that are written in English.
*(Added by L.1995, chap. 165(1), eff. 9/1/95.)*

### §522.0235. Waiver of visual standards for intrastate driver.

(a) Except as provided by Subsection (b), the department by rule may provide for a waiver of the visual standards for a commercial driver's license in 49 C.F.R. Part 391, Subpart E, if the person who is applying for a commercial driver's license or who has been issued a commercial driver's license is a person who drives a commercial motor vehicle only in this state.

(b) Subsection (a) does not apply to standards for distant binocular acuity.
*(Added by L.1997, chap. 165(30.100(a)), eff. 9/1/97.)*

### §522.024. Additional testing.

To ensure compliance with the federal act and to promote the systematic conversion to commercial driver's licenses, the department may require the commercial driver's license testing of a person to whom the department has previously issued a driver's license that authorizes the driving of a vehicle that may be subject to this chapter. The testing may be required before the expiration of an existing license. *(Added by L.1995, chap. 165(1), eff. 9/1/95.)*

### §522.025. Limitations on issuance of license or permit.

(a) The department may not issue a commercial driver's license or commercial driver learner's permit to a person who is disqualified from driving a commercial motor vehicle or while the person's driver's license or driving privilege is suspended, revoked, or canceled in any state.

(b) The department may not issue a commercial driver's license to a person who has a driver's license, commercial driver's license, or commercial driver learner's permit issued by another state unless the person surrenders the license or permit. The department shall return a surrendered license or permit to the issuing state for cancellation.
*(Added by L.1995, chap. 165(1), eff. 9/1/95.)*

### §522.026. Limitation on number of driver's licenses; offense.

(a) A person commits an offense if the person drives a commercial motor vehicle and has more than one driver's license.

(b) It is an affirmative defense to prosecution of an offense under this section that the offense occurred during the 10-day period beginning on the date the person was issued a driver's license.

(c) An offense under this section is a Class C misdemeanor.

*(Added by L.1995, chap. 165(1), eff. 9/1/95.)*

### §522.027. Minimum age.

The department may not issue a commercial driver's license or a commercial driver learner's permit to a person who is younger than 18 years of age. *(Added by L.1995, chap. 165(1), eff. 9/1/95.)*

### §522.028. Check of driving record.

Before issuing a commercial driver's license, the department shall check the applicant's driving record as required by 49 C.F.R. Section 383.73. *(Added by L.1995, chap. 165(1), eff. 9/1/95.)*

### §522.029. Fees.

(a) The fee for a commercial driver's license or commercial driver learner's permit issued by the department is $60, except as provided by Subsection (f).

(b) The fee for a commercial driver's license or commercial driver learner's permit shall be reduced by $4 for each remaining year of validity of a driver's license, other than a commercial driver's license or commercial driver learner's permit issued by the department to the applicant.

(c) The fee for a duplicate commercial driver's license or commercial driver learner's permit is $10.

(d) An applicant who is changing a class of license, endorsement, or restriction or who is adding a class of vehicle other than a motorcycle to the license must pay a fee of $10 for the examination, except for a renewal or original issuance of a commercial driver's license.

(e) The fees required by this chapter and collected by an officer or agent of the department shall be remitted without deduction to the department.

(f) The fee for renewal of a commercial driver's license or a commercial driver learner's permit that includes authorization to operate a motorcycle is $45. *(Added by L.1997, chap. 1156(2), eff. 9/1/97. See other subsection (f) below.)*

(f) If a commercial driver's license or commercial driver learner's permit includes an authorization to operate a motorcycle or moped, the fee for the driver's license or permit is increased by $8. *(Added by L.1997, chap. 1372(5), eff. 9/1/97. See other subsection (f) above.)*

(g) An applicant who is applying for additional authorization to operate a motorcycle shall pay a fee of $15 for the examination.

*(Added by L.1995, chap. 165(1); chgd. by L.1997, chaps. 1156(2), 1372(5), eff. 9/1/97.)*

### §522.030. Content of license.

A commercial driver's license must:

(1) be marked "Commercial Driver License" or "CDL";

(2) be, to the extent practicable, tamper-proof; and

(3) include:

(A) the name and mailing address of the person to whom it is issued;

(B) the person's color photograph;

(C) a physical description of the person, including sex, height, and eye color;

(D) the person's date of birth;

(E) a number or identifier the department considers appropriate;

(F) the person's signature;

(G) each class of commercial motor vehicle that the person is authorized to drive, with any endorsements or restrictions;

(H) the name of this state; and

(I) the dates between which the license is valid.

*(Added by L.1995, chap. 165(1), eff. 9/1/95.)*

### §522.031. Notification of license issuance.

(a) After issuing a commercial driver's license, the department shall notify the commercial driver's license information system of that fact and provide the information required to ensure identification of the person.

(b) In this section, "commercial driver's license information system" means the information system established under the federal act as a clearinghouse for locating information related to the licensing and identification of commercial motor vehicle drivers.
*(Added by L.1995, chap. 165(1), eff. 9/1/95.)*

**§522.032. Change of name or address of license or permit holder; offense.**

(a) The holder of a commercial driver's license or commercial driver learner's permit who changes the holder's name or mailing address must apply for a duplicate license or permit not later than the 30th day after the date of the change in the manner provided by Section 521.054.

(b) The holder of a commercial driver's license or commercial driver learner's permit who changes the holder's residence address shall notify the department not later than the 30th day after the date of the change.

(c) A person commits an offense if the person violates this section. An offense under this section is a Class C misdemeanor.
*(Added by L.1995, chap. 165(1), eff. 9/1/95.)*

**§§522.033 to 522.040.** *(Reserved.)*

## SUBCHAPTER D. CLASSIFICATION, ENDORSEMENT, OR RESTRICTION OF LICENSE

**§522.041. Classifications.**

(a) The department may issue a Class A, Class B, or Class C commercial driver's license.

(b) Class A covers a combination of vehicles with a gross combination weight rating of 26,001 pounds or more, if the gross vehicle weight rating of the towed vehicle or vehicles exceeds 10,000 pounds.

(c) Class B covers:

(1) a single vehicle with a gross vehicle weight rating of 26,001 pounds or more;

(2) a single vehicle with a gross vehicle weight rating of 26,001 pounds or more towing a vehicle with a gross vehicle weight rating of 10,000 pounds or less; and

(3) a vehicle designed to transport 24 passengers or more, including the driver.

(d) Class C covers a single vehicle or combination of vehicles not described by Subsection (b) or (c) that is:

(1) designed to transport 16-23 passengers, including the driver; or

(2) used in the transportation of hazardous materials that require the vehicle to be placarded under 49 C.F.R. Part 172, Subpart F.

(e) The holder of a commercial driver's license may drive any vehicle in the class for which the license is issued and lesser classes of vehicles except a motorcycle or moped. The holder may drive a motorcycle only if authorization to drive a motorcycle is shown on the commercial driver's license and the requirements for issuance of a motorcycle license have been met.
*(Added by L.1995, chap. 165(1), eff. 9/1/95.)*

**§522.042. Endorsements; offense.**

(a) The department may issue a commercial driver's license with endorsements:

(1) authorizing the driving of a vehicle transporting hazardous materials;

(2) authorizing the towing of a double or triple trailer or a trailer over a specified weight;

(3) authorizing the driving of a vehicle carrying passengers;

(4) authorizing the driving of a tank vehicle; or

(5) representing a combination of hazardous materials and tank vehicle endorsements.

(b) The holder of a commercial driver's license may not drive a vehicle that requires an endorsement unless the proper endorsement appears on the license.

(c) A person commits an offense if the person violates Subsection (b). An offense under this section is a Class C misdemeanor.
*(Added by L.1995, chap. 165(1), eff. 9/1/95.)*

**§522.043. Restrictions; offense.**

(a) On issuing a commercial driver's license, the department for good cause may impose one or more restrictions suitable to the license holder's driving ability and limitations, including restrictions:

(1) prohibiting the license holder from driving a vehicle equipped with air brakes; and

(2) as provided by 49 C.F.R. Part 391, prohibiting driving a commercial vehicle in interstate commerce by a person who:

(A) is under 21 years of age;

(B) does not meet applicable physical guidelines; or

(C) cannot sufficiently read and speak the English language.

(b) For purposes of this section, the department may not administer examinations or tests relating to the applicant's proficiency in the English language, but if an applicant cannot speak English sufficiently to communicate to department personnel the applicant's need for a commercial driver's license, the department may issue to the person a commercial driver's license restricted to operation in intrastate commerce.

(c) A person commits an offense if the person drives a commercial motor vehicle in violation of a restriction. An offense under this section is a Class C misdemeanor.
*(Added by L.1995, chap. 165(1), eff. 9/1/95.)*

### §§522.044 to 522.050. *(Reserved.)*

## SUBCHAPTER E. EXPIRATION AND RENEWAL OF LICENSE OR PERMIT

### §522.051. Expiration of license or permit.

(a) An original commercial driver's license or commercial driver learner's permit expires six years after the applicant's next birthday.

(b) A commercial driver's license or commercial driver learner's permit issued to a person holding a Texas Class A, B, C, or M license that would expire one year or more after the date of issuance of the commercial driver's license or commercial driver learner's permit expires six years after the applicant's next birthday.

(c) A commercial driver's license or commercial driver learner's permit issued to a person holding a Texas Class A, B, C, or M license that would expire less than one year after the date of issuance of the commercial driver's license or commercial driver learner's permit or that has been expired for less than one year expires six years after the expiration date shown on the Class A, B, C, or M license.

(d) A commercial driver's license or commercial driver learner's permit issued to a person holding a Texas Class A, B, C, or M license that has been expired for at least one year but not more than two years expires six years after the applicant's last birthday.

(e) For purposes of this section, a person's "last birthday" is the birthday that occurs on or before the date of issuance, and a person's "next birthday" is the birthday that occurs on or after the date of issuance.
*(Added by L.1995, chap. 165(1); chgd. by L.1997, chap. 1372(6), eff. 9/1/97.)*

### §522.052. Renewal of license.

(a) A commercial driver's license issued by the department may be renewed in the year preceding the expiration date.

(b) A renewal of a commercial driver's license that has been expired for less than one year expires six years after the expiration date shown on the commercial driver's license.

(c) A renewal of a commercial driver's license that has been expired for at least one year but not more than two years expires six years after the applicant's last birthday.

(d) If a commercial driver's license has been expired for more than two years, the person must make an application and meet the requirements for original issuance of a commercial driver's license.

(e) A commercial driver learner's permit may not be renewed.

(f) For purposes of this section, a person's "last birthday" is the birthday that occurs on or before the date of issuance.
*(Added by L.1995, chap. 165(1); chgd. by L.1997, chap. 1372(7), eff. 9/1/97.)*

### §522.053. License renewal procedures.

(a) A person applying for renewal of a commercial driver's license must complete the application form required by the department, including updated information and required certifications.

(b) To retain a hazardous materials endorsement, an applicant must pass the written test for that endorsement.

(c) The department may require an examination, including a vision test, for the renewal of a commercial driver's license.

(d) Before renewing a commercial driver's license, the department shall check the applicant's driving record as required by 49 C.F.R. Section 383.73.
*(Added by L.1995, chap. 165(1), eff. 9/1/95.)*

### §§522.054 to 522.060. *(Reserved.)*

## SUBCHAPTER F. NOTIFICATION OF CONVICTION, ADMINISTRATIVE ACTION, OR PREVIOUS EMPLOYMENT

### §522.061. Notification of conviction to department or employer.

(a) A person who holds or is required to hold a commercial driver's license under this chapter and who is convicted in another state of violating a state law or local ordinance relating to motor vehicle traffic control shall notify the department in the manner specified by the department not later than the 30th day after the date of conviction.

(b) A person who holds or is required to hold a commercial driver's license under this chapter and who is convicted in this state or another state of violating a state law or local ordinance relating to motor vehicle traffic control, including a law regulating the operation of vehicles on highways, shall notify the person's employer in writing of the conviction not later than the 30th day after the date of conviction.

(c) A notification to the department or an employer must be in writing and must contain:

(1) the driver's full name;

(2) the driver's license number;

(3) the date of conviction;

(4) the nature of the violation;

(5) a notation of whether the violation was committed in a commercial motor vehicle;

(6) the location where the offense was committed; and

(7) the driver's signature.

(d) This section does not apply to a parking violation.

*(Added by L.1995, chap. 165(1), eff. 9/1/95.)*

### §522.062. Notification of conviction to licensing authority in other state.

(a) Not later than the 10th day after the date the department receives a report of a conviction of a person who has a domicile in another state or in a foreign jurisdiction for a violation of a state law or local ordinance relating to motor vehicle traffic control, including a law regulating the operation of vehicles on highways, that was committed in a commercial motor vehicle, the department shall notify the driver's licensing authority in the licensing state of the conviction.

(b) This section does not apply to a parking violation.

*(Added by L.1995, chap. 165(1), eff. 9/1/95.)*

### §522.063. Notification of disqualification.

A person who is denied the privilege of driving a commercial motor vehicle in a state for any period, who is disqualified from driving a commercial motor vehicle, or who is subject to an out-of-service order shall notify the person's employer of that fact before the end of the first business day after the date the person receives notice of that fact. *(Added by L.1995, chap. 165(1), eff. 9/1/95.)*

### §522.064. Notification of previous employment and offenses.

(a) A person who applies for employment as a commercial motor vehicle driver shall provide the employer, at the time of the application, with the following information for the 10 years preceding the date of application:

(1) a list of the names and addresses of the applicant's previous employers for which the applicant drove a commercial motor vehicle;

(2) the dates between which the applicant drove for each employer;

(3) the reason for leaving the employment of each employer; and

(4) each specific criminal offense or serious traffic violation of which the applicant has been convicted and each suspension, revocation, or cancellation of driving privileges that resulted from the conviction.

(b) The applicant must certify that the information furnished is true and complete. An employer may require an applicant to provide additional information. Before an application is submitted, the employer shall inform the applicant that the information provided by the applicant under this section may be used, and the applicant's previous employers may be contacted, to investigate the applicant's work history.

(c) An employer shall require each applicant to provide the information specified by Subsections (a) and (b).

*(Added by L.1995, chap. 165(1), eff. 9/1/95.)*

### §§522.065 to 522.070. *(Reserved.)*

## SUBCHAPTER G. UNAUTHORIZED DRIVING

### §522.071. Driving while disqualified prohibited.

(a) A person commits an offense if the person drives a commercial motor vehicle on a highway:

(1) after the person has been denied the issuance of a license, unless the person has a driver's license appropriate for the class of vehicle being driven that was subsequently issued;

(2) during a period that a disqualification of the person's driver's license or privilege is in effect;

(3) while the person's driver's license is expired, if the license expired during a period of disqualification;

(4) during a period that the person was subject to an order prohibiting the person from obtaining a driver's license; or

(5) during a period in which the person is subject to an out-of-service order.

(b) It is not a defense to prosecution that the person had not received notice of a disqualification imposed as a result of a conviction that results in an automatic disqualification of the person's driver's license or privilege.

(c) Except as provided by Subsection (b), it is an affirmative defense to prosecution of an offense under this section that the person had not received notice of a denial, disqualification, prohibition order, or out-of-service order concerning the person's driver's license, permit, or privilege to operate a motor vehicle. For purposes of this subsection, notice is presumed if the notice was sent by first class mail to the last known address of the person as shown by the records of the department or licensing authority of another state.

(d) An offense under this section is a misdemeanor punishable as provided for an offense under Section 521.457.

*(Added by L.1995, chap. 165(1); chgd. by L.1999, chap. 1409(3), eff. 9/1/99.)*

### §522.072. Permitting unauthorized driving prohibited.

(a) An employer may not knowingly permit a person to drive a commercial motor vehicle during a period in which the person:

(1) has been denied the privilege of driving a commercial motor vehicle;

(2) is disqualified from driving a commercial motor vehicle;

(3) is subject to an out-of-service order in a state; or

(4) has more than one commercial driver's license, except during the 10-day period beginning on the date the person is issued a driver's license.

(b) In addition to any penalty imposed under this chapter, an employer who violates Subsection (a) or an out-of-service order may be penalized or disqualified under 49 C.F.R. Part 383.

*(Added by L.1995, chap. 165(1), eff. 9/1/95.)*

### §§522.073 to 522.080. *(Reserved.)*

## SUBCHAPTER H. DISQUALIFICATION FROM DRIVING COMMERCIAL MOTOR VEHICLE

### §522.081. Disqualification.

(a) A person is disqualified from driving a commercial motor vehicle for 60 days if convicted of two serious traffic violations, or 120 days if convicted of three serious traffic violations, committed in a commercial motor vehicle arising from separate incidents occurring within a three-year period.

(b) A person is disqualified from driving a commercial motor vehicle for one year on first conviction of:

(1) driving a commercial motor vehicle under the influence of alcohol or a controlled substance, including a violation of Section 49.04 or 49.07, Penal Code;

(2) driving a commercial motor vehicle while the person's alcohol concentration was 0.04 or more;

(3) intentionally leaving the scene of an accident involving a commercial motor vehicle driven by the person;

(4) using a commercial motor vehicle in the commission of a felony, other than a felony described by Subsection (d)(2); or

(5) refusing to submit to a test to determine the person's alcohol concentration or the presence in the person's body of a controlled substance or drug while driving a commercial motor vehicle.

(c) If a violation listed in Subsection (b) occurred while the person was transporting a hazardous material required to be placarded, the person is disqualified for three years.

(d) A person is disqualified from driving a commercial motor vehicle for life if the person:

(1) is convicted of two or more violations of an offense specified by Subsection (b), or a combination of those offenses, arising from two or more separate incidents; or

(2) uses a commercial motor vehicle in the commission of a felony involving:

(A) the manufacture, distribution, or dispensing of a controlled substance; or

(B) possession with intent to manufacture, distribute, or dispense a controlled substance.

(e) In this section, "felony" means an offense under state or federal law that is punishable by death or imprisonment for a term of more than one year.

*(Added by L.1995, chap. 165(1), eff. 9/1/95.)*

### §522.082. Reinstatement following disqualification for life.

(a) The department may adopt rules establishing guidelines, including conditions, under which a person disqualified for life under Section 522.081(d)(1) may apply to the department for reinstatement of the person's commercial driver's license, if authorized under federal law.

(b) A person is not eligible for reinstatement unless the person has been disqualified for at least 10 years and meets the department's conditions for reinstatement.

(c) If a reinstated driver is subsequently convicted of another disqualifying offense as specified by Section 522.081(b), the person is permanently disqualified and is not eligible for reinstatement.

*(Added by L.1995, chap. 165(1), eff. 9/1/95.)*



### §522.083. Update of records.

After disqualifying a person, the department shall update its records to reflect that action.

*(Added by L.1995, chap. 165(1), eff. 9/1/95.)*

### §522.084. Notification to other jurisdiction.

After disqualifying a person who has a domicile in another state or in a foreign jurisdiction, the department shall give notice of that fact to the licensing authority of the state that issued the person's commercial driver's license or commercial driver learner's permit. *(Added by L.1995, chap. 165(1), eff. 9/1/95.)*

### §522.085. Probation of disqualification prohibited.

Notwithstanding Section 521.303, if a person is disqualified under this chapter, the disqualification may not be probated. *(Added by L.1995, chap. 165(1), eff. 9/1/95.)*

### §522.086. Issuance of essential need or occupational driver's license prohibited.

A person who is disqualified from operating a commercial motor vehicle may not be granted an essential need or occupational driver's license that would authorize operation of a commercial motor vehicle. *(Added by L.1995, chap. 165(1), eff. 9/1/95.)*

### §522.087. Procedures applicable to disqualification.

(a) A person is automatically disqualified under Section 522.081(b)(1), (3), or (4) or Section 522.081(d)(2). An appeal may not be taken from the disqualification.

(b) Disqualifying a person under Section 522.081(a) or (d)(1) is subject to the notice and hearing procedures of [Section 521.304] *Sections 521.295-521.303*. An appeal of the disqualification is subject to Section [521.302] *521.308*.

*(Added by L.1995, chap. 165(1); chgd. by L.1999, chap. 1117(3), eff. 9/1/2000. Matter in brackets eff. only until 9/1/2000. Matter in italics eff. 9/1/2000.)*

### §522.088. Applicability of other law.

Section 521.344 of this code and Section 13, Article 42.12, Code of Criminal Procedure, do not apply to a person disqualified under this chapter. *(Added by L.1995, chap. 165(1), eff. 9/1/95.)*

### §522.089. Effect of suspension, revocation, cancellation, or denial of license under other law.

(a) A suspension, revocation, cancellation, or denial of a driver's license or privilege under Chapter 521 or another law of this state disqualifies the person under this chapter.

(b) If this chapter disqualifies a person for a longer period than the other law, the person is disqualified for the longer period.

*(Added by L.1995, chap. 165(1), eff. 9/1/95.)*

### §522.090. Additional penalty.

In addition to any penalty imposed under this chapter, a person convicted of an offense under Section 522.071(a)(5) may be penalized or disqualified under 49 C.F.R. Part 383. *(Added by L.1995, chap. 165(1), eff. 9/1/95.)*

### §522.091. Recognition of action taken by other state.

(a) The department shall give an out-of-state conviction, disqualification, or denial full faith and credit and treat it for sanctioning purposes under this chapter as if it occurred in this state.

(b) The department may include the conviction, disqualification, or denial on the person's driving record.

*(Added by L.1995, chap. 165(1), eff. 9/1/95.)*

### §522.092. Suspension, revocation, cancellation, or denial of driver's license under other laws.

A person subject to disqualification under this chapter may also have the person's driver's license suspended, revoked, canceled, or denied under one or more of the following, if the conduct that is a ground for disqualification is also a ground for the suspension, revocation, cancellation, or denial of a driver's license suspension under:

(1) Chapter 521;
(2) Chapter 524;
(3) Chapter 601; or
(4) Chapter 724.

*(Added by L.1995, chap. 165(1), eff. 9/1/95.)*

### §§522.093 to 522.100. *(Reserved.)*

## SUBCHAPTER I. DRIVING WHILE HAVING ALCOHOL, CONTROLLED SUBSTANCE, OR DRUG IN SYSTEM

### §522.101. Driving while having alcohol in system prohibited.

(a) Notwithstanding any other law of this state, a person may not drive a commercial motor vehicle in this state while having a measurable or detectable amount of alcohol in the person's system.

(b) A person who violates Subsection (a) or who refuses to submit to an alcohol test under Section 522.102 shall be placed out of service for 24 hours.

(c) A peace officer may issue an out-of-service order based on probable cause that the person has violated this section. The order must be on a form approved by the department. The peace officer shall submit the order to the department.

*(Added by L.1995, chap. 165(1), eff. 9/1/95.)*

### §522.102. Implied consent to taking of specimen.

(a) A person who drives a commercial motor vehicle in this state is considered to have consented, subject to Chapter 724, to the taking of one or more specimens of the person's breath, blood, or urine for the purpose of analysis to determine the person's alcohol concentration or the presence in the person's body of a controlled substance or drug.

(b) Notwithstanding Chapter 724, one or more specimens may be taken at the request of a peace officer who, after stopping or detaining a person driving a commercial motor vehicle, has probable cause to believe that the person was driving the vehicle while having alcohol, a controlled substance, or a drug in the person's system.

*(Added by L.1995, chap. 165(1), eff. 9/1/95.)*

### §522.103. Warning by peace officer.

A peace officer requesting a person to submit a specimen under Section 522.102 shall warn the person that a refusal to submit a specimen will result in the person's being immediately placed out of service for 24 hours and being disqualified from driving a commercial motor vehicle for at least one year under Section 522.081. *(Added by L.1995, chap. 165(1), eff. 9/1/95.)*

### §522.104. Submission of report to department.

If a person driving a commercial motor vehicle refuses to give a specimen or submits a specimen that discloses an alcohol concentration of 0.04 or more, the peace officer shall submit to the department a sworn report, on a form approved by the department, certifying that the specimen was requested under Section 522.102 and that the person refused to submit a specimen or submitted a specimen that disclosed an alcohol concentration of 0.04 or more. *(Added by L.1995, chap. 165(1), eff. 9/1/95.)*

### §522.105. Disqualification of driver.

(a) On receipt of a report under Section 522.104, the department shall disqualify the person from driving a commercial motor vehicle under Section 522.081.

(b) Except as provided by Subsection (c), the procedure for notice and disqualification under this section is that specified by Subchapters C and D, Chapter 724, or Chapter 524.

(c) The department shall disqualify the person from driving a commercial motor vehicle for the period authorized by this chapter if, in a hearing held under this section, the court finds that:

(1) probable cause existed that the person was driving a commercial motor vehicle while having alcohol, a controlled substance, or a drug in the person's system;

(2) the person was offered an opportunity to give a specimen under this chapter; and

(3) the person submitted a specimen that disclosed an alcohol concentration of 0.04 or more or refused to submit a specimen.

(d) An appeal of a disqualification under this section is subject to Sections 524.041-524.044. *(Added by L.1995, chap. 165(1), eff. 9/1/95.)*

### §522.106. Affidavit by certified breath test technical supervisor.

(a) In a proceeding under this chapter, the certified breath test technical supervisor responsible for maintaining and directing the operation of the breath test instruments in compliance with department rules, in lieu of appearing in court, may attest by affidavit to:

(1) the reliability of the instrument used to take or analyze a specimen of a person's breath to determine alcohol concentration; and

(2) the validity of the results of the analysis.

(b) An affidavit submitted under this section must contain statements regarding:

(1) the reliability of the instrument and the analytical results; and

(2) compliance with state law in the administration of the program.

(c) A certified copy of an affidavit prepared in accordance with this section is admissible only if the department serves a copy of the affidavit on the person or the person's attorney not later than the seventh day before the date on which the hearing begins.
*(Added by L.1995, chap. 165(1), eff. 9/1/95.)*

## CHAPTER 523. DRIVER'S LICENSE COMPACT OF 1993

Section



### §523.001. Enactment.

The Driver's License Compact of 1993 is enacted and entered into. *(Added by L.1995, chap. 165(1), eff. 9/1/95.)*

### §523.002. Findings and declaration of policy.

(a) The states find that:

(1) the safety of their streets and highways is materially affected by the degree of compliance with state laws and local ordinances relating to the operation of motor vehicles;

(2) violation of such a law or ordinance is evidence that the violator engages in conduct which is likely to endanger the safety of persons and property; and

(3) the continuance in force of a license to drive is predicated on compliance with laws and ordinances relating to the operation of motor vehicles in whichever jurisdiction the vehicle is operated.

(b) It is the policy of each of the states to:

(1) promote compliance with the laws, ordinances, and administrative rules and regulations relating to the operation of motor vehicles by their operators in each of the jurisdictions where the operators drive motor vehicles; and

(2) make the reciprocal recognition of licenses to drive and eligibility therefor more just and equitable by considering the overall compliance with motor vehicle laws, ordinances, and administrative rules and regulations as a condition precedent to the continuance or issuance of any license by reason of which the licensee is authorized or permitted to operate a motor vehicle in any of the states.
*(Added by L.1995, chap. 165(1), eff. 9/1/95.)*

## §523.003. Definitions.

In this compact:

(1) "Conviction" has the same meaning as provided in Section 522.003.

(2) "Executive director" means the director of the Department of Public Safety or the equivalent officer of another state.

(3) "Home state" means the state which has issued a license or permit and has the power to suspend or revoke use of the license or permit to operate a motor vehicle.

(4) "License" means a license or permit to operate a motor vehicle issued by a state.

(5) "Licensing authority" means the Department of Public Safety or the equivalent agency of another state.

(6) "State" means a state, territory, or possession of the United States, the District of Columbia, or the commonwealth of Puerto Ricò.

(7) "Violation" means the commission of an offense related to the use or operation of a motor vehicle, even if there has been no conviction. A suspension by reason of a violation includes a suspension for failure to appear in court or comply with a court order or suspension for violating an implied consent law.
*(Added by L.1995, chap. 165(1), eff. 9/1/95.)*

## §523.004. Reports of convictions.

The licensing authority of a state shall report each conviction of a person from another state occurring within its jurisdiction to the licensing authority of the home state of the licensee. Such report shall clearly identify the person convicted; describe the violation specifying the section of the statute, code, or ordinance violated; identify the court in which action was taken; indicate whether a plea of guilty or not guilty was entered or the conviction was a result of the forfeiture of bail, bond, or other security; and include any special findings made in connection with the conviction. A conviction or judicial or administrative action of a federal or military court or tribunal may be reported to this state subject to this chapter. *(Added by L.1995, chap. 165(1); chgd. by L.1999, chap. 1257(1), eff. 9/1/99.)*

## §523.005. Effect of conviction.

(a) The licensing authority in the home state, for the purpose of suspension, revocation, cancellation, denial, disqualification, or limitation of the privilege to operate a motor vehicle, shall give the same effect to the conduct reported pursuant to Section 523.004 as it would if such conduct had occurred in the home state in the case of conviction for:

(1) manslaughter or negligent homicide resulting from the operation of a motor vehicle;

(2) driving a motor vehicle while under the influence of alcoholic beverages or a narcotic to a degree which renders the driver incapable of safely driving a motor vehicle;

(3) any felony in the commission of which a motor vehicle is used; or

(4) failure to stop and render aid or information in the event of a motor vehicle accident resulting in the death or personal injury of another.

(b) As to other convictions reported pursuant to this compact, the licensing authority in the home state shall give such effect to the conduct as is provided by the laws of the home state.

(c) If the laws of a state do not provide for offenses or violations denominated or described in precisely the words employed in Subsection (a), those offenses or violations of a substantially similar nature and the laws of that state shall be understood to contain such provisions as may be necessary to ensure that full force and effect is given to this compact.
*(Added by L.1995, chap. 165(1), eff. 9/1/95.)*

## §523.006. Applications for new licenses.

On receiving an application for a license to drive, the licensing authority in a state shall ascertain whether the applicant has ever held or is the holder of a license to drive issued by any other state. The licensing authority in the state where application is made shall not issue a license to the applicant if the applicant:

(1) has held a license but the license has been suspended by reason, in whole or in part, of a violation and the suspension period has not terminated;

(2) has held a license but the license has been revoked by reason, in whole or in part, of a violation and the revocation has not terminated, except that after the expiration of one year from the date the license was revoked the person may apply for a new license if permitted by law; the licensing authority may refuse to issue a license to any such applicant if, after investigation, the licensing authority determines that it will not be safe to grant the person the privilege of driving a motor vehicle on the public highways; or

(3) is the holder of a license issued by another state currently in force unless the applicant surrenders such license or provides an affidavit prescribed by the licensing authority that such license is no longer in the person's possession.

*(Added by L.1995, chap. 165(1), eff. 9/1/95.)*



### §523.007. Applicability of other laws.

Except as expressly required by provisions of this compact, nothing contained herein shall be construed to affect the right of any state to apply any of its other laws relating to licenses to drive to any person or circumstance nor to invalidate or prevent any driver's license agreement or other cooperative arrangement between a member state and a nonmember state. *(Added by L.1995, chap. 165(1), eff. 9/1/95.)*

### §523.008. Compact administrator and interchange of information and compensation of expenses.

(a) The compact administrator shall be appointed by the executive director of the licensing authority. A compact administrator may provide for the discharge of his duties and the performance of his position by an alternate. The administrators, acting jointly, shall have the power to formulate all necessary and proper procedures for the exchange of information under this compact.

(b) The administrator of each state shall furnish to the administrator of each other state any information or documents reasonably necessary to facilitate the administration of this compact.

(c) The compact administrator provided for in this compact shall not be entitled to any additional compensation on account of his service as such administrator but shall be entitled to expenses incurred in connection with his duties and responsibilities as such administrator in the same manner as for expenses incurred in connection with any other duties or responsibilities of his office or employment.

*(Added by L.1995, chap. 165(1), eff. 9/1/95.)*

### §523.009. Effective date; withdrawal from compact.

(a) This compact shall enter into force and become effective as to any state when it has enacted the compact into law.

(b) Any member state may withdraw from this compact by enacting a statute repealing the compact, but no such withdrawal shall take effect until six months after the executive director of the withdrawing state has given notice of the withdrawal to the executive directors of all other member states. No withdrawal shall affect the validity or applicability by the licensing authorities of states remaining party to the compact of any report of conviction occurring prior to the withdrawal.

*(Added by L.1995, chap. 165(1), eff. 9/1/95.)*

### §523.010. Rulemaking authority.

The licensing authority may adopt any rules and regulations deemed necessary by the executive director to administer and enforce the provisions of this compact. *(Added by L.1995, chap. 165(1), eff. 9/1/95.)*

### §523.011. Construction and severability.

This compact shall be liberally construed so as to effectuate the purposes thereof. The provisions of this compact shall be severable; if any phrase, clause, sentence, or provision of this compact is declared to be contrary to the constitution of any state or of the United States or the applicability thereof to any government, agency, person, or circumstance is held invalid, the validity of the remainder of this compact and the applicability thereof to any government, agency, person, or circumstance shall not be affected thereby. If this compact is held contrary to the constitution of any state party thereto, the compact shall remain in full force and effect in the remaining states and in full force and effect in the state affected with regard to all severable matters. *(Added by L.1995, chap. 165(1), eff. 9/1/95.)*

# CHAPTER 524. ADMINISTRATIVE SUSPENSION OF DRIVER'S LICENSE FOR FAILURE TO PASS TEST FOR INTOXICATION

## SUBCHAPTER A. GENERAL PROVISIONS

Section


## SUBCHAPTER B. SUSPENSION DETERMINATION AND NOTICE



## SUBCHAPTER C. SUSPENSION PROVISIONS



## SUBCHAPTER D. HEARING AND APPEAL



## SUBCHAPTER E. REINSTATEMENT AND REISSUANCE OF DRIVER'S LICENSE



## SUBCHAPTER A. GENERAL PROVISIONS

### §524.001. Definitions.

In this chapter:

(1) "Adult" means an individual 21 years of age or older.

(2) "Alcohol concentration" has the meaning assigned by Section 49.01, Penal Code.

(3) "Alcohol-related or drug-related enforcement contact" means a driver's license suspension, disqualification, or prohibition order under the laws of this state or another state resulting from:

(A) a conviction of an offense prohibiting the operation of a motor vehicle while:

(i) intoxicated;

(ii) under the influence of alcohol; or

(iii) under the influence of a controlled substance;

(B) a refusal to submit to the taking of a breath or blood specimen following an arrest for an offense prohibiting the operation of a motor vehicle while:

(i) intoxicated;

(ii) under the influence of alcohol; or

(iii) under the influence of a controlled substance; or

(C) an analysis of a breath or blood specimen showing an alcohol concentration of a level specified by Section 49.01, Penal Code, following an arrest for an offense prohibiting the operation of a motor vehicle while intoxicated.

(4) "Arrest" includes the taking into custody of a child, as defined by Section 51.02, Family Code.

(5) "Conviction" includes an adjudication under Title 3, Family Code.

(6) "Criminal charge" includes a charge that may result in a proceeding under Title 3, Family Code.

(7) "Criminal prosecution" includes a proceeding under Title 3, Family Code.

(8) "Department" means the Department of Public Safety.

(9) "Director" means the public safety director of the department.

(10) "Driver's license" has the meaning assigned by Section 521.001.

(11) "Minor" means an individual under 21 years of age.

(12) "Public place" has the meaning assigned by Section 1.07(a), Penal Code.

*(Added by L.1995, chap. 165(1); chgd. by L.1997, chap. 1013(21), eff. 9/1/97.)*

### §524.002. Rules; application of Administrative Procedure Act.

(a) The department and the State Office of Administrative Hearings shall adopt rules to administer this chapter.

(b) Chapter 2001, Government Code, applies to a proceeding under this chapter to the extent consistent with this chapter.

(c) The State Office of Administrative Hearings may adopt a rule that conflicts with Chapter 2001, Government Code, if a conflict is necessary to expedite the hearings process within the time required by this chapter and applicable federal funding guidelines.

*(Added by L.1995, chap. 165(1), eff. 9/1/95.)*

### §§524.003 to 524.010. *(Reserved.)*

## SUBCHAPTER B. SUSPENSION DETERMINATION AND NOTICE

### §524.011. Officer's duties for driver's license suspension.

(a) An officer arresting a person shall comply with Subsection (b) if:

(1) the person is arrested for an offense under Section 49.04, Penal Code, or an offense under Section 49.07 or 49.08 of that code involving the operation of a motor vehicle, submits to the taking of a specimen of breath or blood and an analysis of the specimen shows the person had an alcohol concentration of a level specified by Section 49.01(2)(B), Penal Code; or

(2) the person is a minor arrested for an offense under Section 106.041, Alcoholic Beverage Code, or Section 49.04, Penal Code, or an offense under Section 49.07 or 49.08, Penal Code, involving the operation of a motor vehicle and:

(A) the minor is not requested to submit to the taking of a specimen; or

(B) the minor submits to the taking of a specimen and an analysis of the specimen shows that the minor had an alcohol concentration of greater than .00 but less than the level specified by Section 49.01(2)(B), Penal Code.

(b) A peace officer shall:

(1) serve or, if a specimen is taken and the analysis of the specimen is not returned to the arresting officer before the person is admitted to bail, released from custody, delivered as provided by Title 3, Family Code, or committed to jail, attempt to serve notice of driver's license suspension by delivering the notice to the arrested person; and

(2) send to the department not later than the fifth business day after the date of the arrest:

(A) a copy of the driver's license suspension notice; and

(B) a sworn report of information relevant to the arrest.

(c) The report required under Subsection (b)(2)(B) must:

(1) identify the arrested person;

(2) state the arresting officer's grounds for believing the person committed the offense;

(3) give the analysis of the specimen if any; and

(4) include a copy of the criminal complaint filed in the case, if any.

(d) A peace officer shall make the report on a form approved by the department and in the manner specified by the department.

(e) The department shall develop a form for the notice of driver's license suspension that shall be used by all state and local law enforcement agencies.

*(Added by L.1995, chap. 165(1); chgd. by L.1997, chaps. 609(1), 1013(22), eff. 9/1/97.)*

## §524.012. Department's determination for driver's license suspension.

(a) On receipt of a report under Section 524.011, if the officer did not serve a notice of suspension of driver's license at the time the results of the analysis of a breath or blood specimen were obtained, the department shall determine from the information in the report whether to suspend the person's driver's license.

(b) The department shall suspend the person's driver's license if the department determines that:

(1) the person had an alcohol concentration of a level specified by Section 49.01(2)(B), Penal Code, while operating a motor vehicle in a public place; or

(2) the person is a minor and had any detectable amount of alcohol in the minor's system while operating a motor vehicle in a public place.

(c) The department may not suspend a person's driver's license if:

(1) the person is an adult and the analysis of the person's breath or blood specimen determined that the person had an alcohol concentration of a level below that specified by Section 49.01(2)(B), Penal Code, at the time the specimen was taken; or

(2) the person is a minor and the department does not determine that the minor had any detectable amount of alcohol in the minor's system when the minor was arrested.

(d) A determination under this section is final unless a hearing is requested under Section 524.031.

(e) A determination under this section:

(1) is a civil matter;

(2) is independent of and is not an estoppel to any matter in issue in an adjudication of a criminal charge arising from the occurrence that is the basis for the suspension; and

(3) does not preclude litigation of the same or similar facts in a criminal prosecution.

*(Added by L.1995, chap. 165(1); chgd. by L.1997, chaps. 165(30.102), 1013(23), eff. 9/1/97.)*

## §524.013. Notice of department's determination.

(a) If the department suspends a person's driver's license, the department shall send a notice of suspension by first class mail to the person's address:

(1) in the records of the department; or

(2) in the peace officer's report if it is different from the address in the department's records.

(b) Notice is considered received on the fifth day after the date the notice is mailed.

(c) If the department determines not to suspend a person's driver's license, the department shall notify the person of that determination and shall rescind any notice of driver's license suspension served on the person.

*(Added by L.1995, chap. 165(1); chgd. by L.1999, chap. 1409(4), eff. 9/1/99.)*

## §524.014. Notice of suspension.

A notice of suspension under Section 524.013 must state:

(1) the reason and statutory grounds for the suspension;

(2) the effective date of the suspension;

(3) the right of the person to a hearing;

(4) how to request a hearing; and

(5) the period in which the person must request a hearing.

*(Added by L.1995, chap. 165(1), eff. 9/1/95.)*

## §524.015. Effect of disposition of criminal charge on driver's license suspension.

(a) Except as provided by Subsection (b), the disposition of a criminal charge does not affect a driver's license suspension under this chapter and does not bar any matter in issue in a driver's license suspension proceeding under this chapter.

(b) A suspension may not be imposed under this chapter on a person who is acquitted of a criminal charge under Section 49.04, 49.07, or 49.08, Penal Code, or Section 106.041, Alcoholic Beverage Code, arising from the occurrence that was the basis for the suspension. If a suspension was imposed before the acquittal, the department shall rescind the suspension and shall remove any reference to the suspension from the person's computerized driving record.
*(Added by L.1995, chap. 165(1); chgd. by L.1997, chap. 1013(24), eff. 9/1/97.)*

**§§524.016 to 524.020.** *(Reserved.)*

## SUBCHAPTER C. SUSPENSION PROVISIONS

### §524.021. Suspension effective date.

(a) A driver's license suspension under this chapter takes effect on the 40th day after the date the person:

(1) receives a notice of suspension under Section 524.011; or

(2) is presumed to have received notice of suspension under Section 524.013.

(b) A suspension under this chapter may not be probated.
*(Added by L.1995, chap. 165(1), eff. 9/1/95.)*



### §524.022. Period of suspension.

(a) A period of suspension under this chapter for an adult is:

(1) 60 days if the person's driving record shows no alcohol-related or drug-related enforcement contact during the five years preceding the date of the person's arrest;

(2) 120 days if the person's driving record shows one or more alcohol-related or drug-related enforcement contacts, as defined by Section 524.001(2)(B) or (C), during the five years preceding the date of the person's arrest; or

(3) 180 days if the person's driving record shows one or more alcohol-related or drug-related enforcement contacts, as defined by Section 524.001(2)(A), during the five years preceding the date of the person's arrest.

(b) A period of suspension under this chapter for a minor is:

(1) 60 days if the minor has not been previously convicted of an offense under Section 106.041, Alcoholic Beverage Code, or Section 49.04, Penal Code, or an offense under Section 49.07 or 49.08, Penal Code, involving the operation of a motor vehicle;

(2) 120 days if the minor has been previously convicted once of an offense listed by Subdivision (1); or

(3) 180 days if the minor has been previously convicted twice or more of an offense listed by Subdivision (1).

(c) For the purposes of determining whether a minor has been previously convicted of an offense described by Subsection (b)(1):

(1) an adjudication under Title 3, Family Code, that the minor engaged in conduct described by Subsection (b)(1) is considered a conviction under that provision; and

(2) an order of deferred adjudication for an offense alleged under a provision described by Subsection (b)(1) is considered a conviction of an offense under that provision.

(d) A minor whose driver's license is suspended under this chapter is not eligible for an occupational license under Subchapter L, Chapter 521, for:

(1) the first 30 days of a suspension under Subsection (b)(1);

(2) the first 90 days of a suspension under Subsection (b)(2); or

(3) the entire period of a suspension under Subsection (b)(3).
*(Added by L.1995, chap. 165(1); chgd. by L.1997, chap. 1013(25), eff. 9/1/97.)*

### §524.023. Application of suspension under other laws.

(a) If a person is convicted of an offense under Section 106.041, Alcoholic Beverage Code, or Section 49.04, 49.07, or 49.08, Penal Code, and if any conduct on which that conviction is based is a ground for a driver's license suspension under this chapter and Section 106.041, Alcoholic Beverage Code, Subchapter O, Chapter 521, or Subchapter H, Chapter 522, each of the suspensions shall be imposed.

(b) The court imposing a driver's license suspension under Section 106.041, Alcoholic Beverage Code, or Chapter 521 or 522 as required by Subsection (a) shall credit a period of suspension imposed under this chapter toward the period of suspension required under Section 106.041, Alcoholic Beverage Code, or Subchapter O, Chapter 521, or Subchapter H, Chapter 522, unless the person was convicted of an offense under Article 6701*l*-1, Revised Statutes, as that law existed before September 1, 1994, Section 19.05(a)(2), Penal Code, as that law existed before September 1,

1994, Section 49.04, 49.07, or 49.08, Penal Code, or Section 106.041, Alcoholic Beverage Code, before the date of the conviction on which the suspension is based, in which event credit may not be given.
*(Added by L.1995, chap. 165(1); chgd. by L.1997, chap. 1013(26), eff. 9/1/97.)*

**§§524.024 to 524.030.** *(Reserved.)*

## SUBCHAPTER D. HEARING AND APPEAL

### §524.031. Hearing request.

If, not later than the 15th day after the date on which the person receives notice of suspension under Section 524.011 or is presumed to have received notice under Section 524.013, the department receives at its headquarters in Austin, in writing, including a facsimile transmission, or by another manner prescribed by the department, a request that a hearing be held, a hearing shall be held as provided by this subchapter. *(Added by L.1995, chap. 165(1), eff. 9/1/95.)*

### §524.032. Hearing date; rescheduling.

(a) A hearing requested under this subchapter shall be held not earlier than the 11th day after the date on which the person requesting the hearing is notified of the hearing unless the parties agree to waive this requirement. The hearing shall be held before the effective date of the suspension.

(b) A hearing shall be rescheduled if, before the fifth day before the date scheduled for the hearing, the department receives a request for a continuance from the person who requested the hearing. Unless both parties agree otherwise, the hearing shall be rescheduled for a date not earlier than the fifth day after the date the department receives the request for the continuance.

(c) A person who requests a hearing under this chapter may obtain only one continuance under this section unless the person shows that a medical condition prevents the person from attending the rescheduled hearing, in which event one additional continuance may be granted for a period not to exceed 10 days.

(d) A request for a hearing stays suspension of a person's driver's license until the date of the final decision of the administrative law judge.
*(Added by L.1995, chap. 165(1), eff. 9/1/95.)*

### §524.033. State Office of Administrative Hearings.

(a) A hearing under this subchapter shall be heard by an administrative law judge employed by the State Office of Administrative Hearings.

(b) The State Office of Administrative Hearings shall provide for the stenographic or electronic recording of the hearing.
*(Added by L.1995, chap. 165(1), eff. 9/1/95.)*

### §524.034. Hearing location.

A hearing under this subchapter shall be held:

(1) at a location designated by the State Office of Administrative Hearings:

(A) in the county of arrest if the arrest occurred in a county with a population of 300,000 or more; or

(B) in the county in which the person is alleged to have committed the offense for which the person was arrested or not more than 75 miles from the county seat of the county in which the person was arrested; or

(2) with the consent of the person and the department, by telephone conference call.
*(Added by L.1995, chap. 165(1), eff. 9/1/95.)*

### §524.035. Hearing.

(a) The issues that must be proved at a hearing by a preponderance of the evidence are:

(1) whether:

(A) the person had an alcohol concentration of a level specified by Section 49.01(2)(B), Penal Code, while operating a motor vehicle in a public place; or

(B) the person is a minor and had any detectable amount of alcohol in the minor's system while operating a motor vehicle in a public place; and

(2) whether reasonable suspicion to stop or probable cause to arrest the person existed.

(b) If the administrative law judge finds in the affirmative on each issue in Subsection (a), the suspension is sustained.

(c) If the administrative law judge does not find in the affirmative on each issue in Subsection (a), the department shall:

(1) reinstate the person's driver's license; and

(2) rescind an order prohibiting the issuance of a driver's license to the person.

(d) An administrative law judge may not find in the affirmative on the issue in Subsection (a)(1) if:

(1) the person is an adult and the analysis of the person's breath or blood determined that the person had an alcohol concentration of a level below that specified by Section 49.01, Penal Code, at the time the specimen was taken; or

(2) the person is a minor and the administrative law judge does not find that the minor had any detectable amount of alcohol in the minor's system when the minor was arrested.

(e) The decision of the administrative law judge is final when issued and signed.

*(Added by L.1995, chap. 165(1); chgd. by L.1997, chap. 1013(27), eff. 9/1/97.)*



## §524.036. Failure to appear.

A person who requests a hearing and fails to appear without just cause waives the right to a hearing and the department's determination is final. *(Added by L.1995, chap. 165(1), eff. 9/1/95.)*

## §524.037. Continuance.

(a) A continuance under Section 524.032 stays the suspension of a driver's license until the date of the final decision of the administrative law judge.

(b) A suspension order may not go into effect pending a final decision of the administrative law judge as a result of a continuance granted under Section 524.039.

*(Added by L.1995, chap. 165(1), eff. 9/1/95.)*

## §524.038. Instrument reliability and analysis validity.

(a) The reliability of an instrument used to take or analyze a specimen of a person's breath to determine alcohol concentration and the validity of the results of the analysis may be attested to in a proceeding under this subchapter by affidavit from the certified breath test technical supervisor responsible for maintaining and directing the operation of breath test instruments in compliance with department rule.

(b) An affidavit submitted under Subsection (a) must contain statements on:

(1) the reliability of the instrument and the analytical results; and

(2) compliance with state law in the administration of the program.

(c) An affidavit of an expert witness contesting the reliability of the instrument or the results is admissible.

(d) An affidavit from a person whose presence is timely requested under this section is inadmissible if the person fails to appear at a hearing without a showing of good cause. Otherwise, an affidavit under this section may be submitted in lieu of an appearance at the hearing by the breath test operator, breath test technical supervisor, or expert witness.

*(Added by L.1995, chap. 165(1), eff. 9/1/95.)*

## §524.039. Appearance of technicians at hearing.

(a) Notwithstanding Section 524.038, if not later than the fifth day before the date of a scheduled hearing the department receives from the person who requested a hearing written notice, including a facsimile transmission, requesting the presence at the hearing of the breath test operator who took the specimen of the person's breath to determine alcohol concentration or the certified breath test technical supervisor responsible for maintaining and directing the operation of the breath test instrument used to analyze the specimen of the person's breath, or both, each requested person must appear at the hearing.

(b) The department may reschedule a hearing once not less than 48 hours before the hearing if the person requested to attend under Subsection (a) is unavailable. The department may also reschedule the hearing on showing good cause that the person requested under Subsection (a) is not available at the time of the hearing.

*(Added by L.1995, chap. 165(1), eff. 9/1/95.)*

## §524.040. Notice requirements.

(a) Notice required to be provided by the department under this subchapter may be given by telephone or other electronic means. If notice is given by telephone or other electronic means, written notice must also be provided.

(b) Notice by mail is considered received on the fifth day after the date the notice is deposited with the United States Postal Service.
*(Added by L.1995, chap. 165(1), eff. 9/1/95.)*

## §524.041. Appeal from administrative hearing.

(a) A person whose driver's license suspension is sustained may appeal the decision by filing a petition not later than the 30th day after the date the administrative law judge's decision is final. The administrative law judge's final decision is immediately appealable without the requirement of a motion for rehearing.

(b) A petition under Subsection (a) must be filed in a county court at law in the county in which the person was arrested or, if there is not a county court at law in the county, in the county court. If the county judge is not a licensed attorney, the county judge shall transfer the case to a district court for the county on the motion of either party or of the judge.

(c) A person who files an appeal under this section shall send a copy of the petition by certified mail to the department and to the State Office of Administrative Hearings at each agency's headquarters in Austin. The copy must be certified by the clerk of the court in which the petition is filed.

(d) The department's right to appeal is limited to issues of law.

(e) A district or county attorney may represent the department in an appeal.
*(Added by L.1995, chap. 165(1), eff. 9/1/95.)*



## §524.042. Stay of suspension on appeal.

(a) A suspension of a driver's license under this chapter is stayed on the filing of an appeal petition only if:

(1) the person's driver's license has not been suspended as a result of an alcohol-related or drug-related enforcement contact during the five years preceding the date of the person's arrest; and

(2) the person has not been convicted during the 10 years preceding the date of the person's arrest of an offense under:

(A) Article 6701*l*-1, Revised Statutes, as that law existed before September 1, 1994;

(B) Section 19.05(a)(2), Penal Code, as that law existed before September 1, 1994;

(C) Section 49.04, Penal Code;

(D) Section 49.07 or 49.08, Penal Code, if the offense involved the operation of a motor vehicle; or

(E) Section 106.041, Alcoholic Beverage Code.

(b) A stay under this section is effective for not more than 90 days after the date the appeal petition is filed. On the expiration of the stay, the department shall impose the suspension. The department or court may not grant an extension of the stay or an additional stay.
*(Added by L.1995, chap. 165(1); chgd. by L.1997, chap. 1013(28), eff. 9/1/97.)*

## §524.043. Review; additional evidence.

(a) Review on appeal is on the record certified by the State Office of Administrative Hearings with no additional testimony.

(b) On appeal, a party may apply to the court to present additional evidence. If the court is satisfied that the additional evidence is material and that there were good reasons for the failure to present it in the proceeding before the administrative law judge, the court may order that the additional evidence be taken before an administrative law judge on conditions determined by the court.

(c) There is no right to a jury trial in an appeal under this section.

(d) An administrative law judge may change a finding or decision as to whether the person had an alcohol concentration of a level specified in Section 49.01, Penal Code, or whether a minor had any detectable amount of alcohol in the minor's system because of the additional evidence and shall file the additional evidence and any changes, new findings, or decisions with the reviewing court.

(e) A remand under this section does not stay the suspension of a driver's license.
*(Added by L.1995, chap. 165(1); chgd. by L.1997, chap. 1013(29), eff. 9/1/97.)*

## §524.044. Transcript of administrative hearing.

(a) To obtain a transcript of an administrative hearing, the party who appeals the administrative law judge's decision must apply to the State Office of Administrative Hearings.

(b) On payment of a fee not to exceed the actual cost of preparing the transcript, the State Office of Administrative Hearings shall promptly furnish both parties with a transcript of the administrative hearing.
*(Added by L.1995, chap. 165(1), eff. 9/1/95.)*

### §§524.045 to 524.050. *(Reserved.)*

## SUBCHAPTER E. REINSTATEMENT AND REISSUANCE OF DRIVER'S LICENSE

### §524.051. Reinstatement and reissuance.

(a) A driver's license suspended under this chapter may not be reinstated or another driver's license issued to the person until the person pays the department a fee of $100 in addition to any other fee required by law.

(b) The payment of a reinstatement fee is not required if a suspension under this chapter is:

(1) rescinded by the department; or

(2) not sustained by an administrative law judge, or a court.
*(Added by L.1995, chap. 165(1), eff. 9/1/95.)*



## CHAPTER 525. MOTORCYCLE AND BICYCLE AWARENESS

Section


### §525.001. Motorcycle and bicycle awareness.

(a) In this section, "motorcycle" has the meaning assigned that term by Section 502.001, and includes a motorcycle equipped with a sidecar.

(b) The Department of Public Safety shall include motorcycle and bicycle awareness information in any edition of the Texas driver's handbook published after the department exhausts the supply of the handbook that the department had on September 1, 1993.
*(Added by L.1995, chap. 165(1), eff. 9/1/95.)*

## CHAPTERS 526 to 540. *(Reserved.)*

# SUBTITLE C. RULES OF THE ROAD

## CHAPTER 541. DEFINITIONS

## SUBCHAPTER A. PERSONS AND GOVERNMENTAL AUTHORITIES

Section


## SUBCHAPTER B. PROPERTY AREAS

## SUBCHAPTER C. VEHICLES, RAIL TRANSPORTATION, AND EQUIPMENT



## SUBCHAPTER D. TRAFFIC, TRAFFIC AREAS, AND TRAFFIC CONTROL



## SUBCHAPTER E. MISCELLANEOUS TERMS





## SUBCHAPTER A. PERSONS AND GOVERNMENTAL AUTHORITIES

### §541.001. Persons.

In this subtitle:

(1) "Operator" means, as used in reference to a vehicle, a person who drives or has physical control of a vehicle.

(2) "Owner" means, as used in reference to a vehicle, a person who has a property interest in or title to a vehicle. The term:

(A) includes a person entitled to use and possess a vehicle subject to a security interest; and

(B) excludes a lienholder and a lessee whose lease is not intended as security.

(3) "Pedestrian" means a person on foot.

(4) "Person" means an individual, firm, partnership, association, or corporation.

(5) "School crossing guard" means a responsible person who is at least 18 years of age and is designated by a local authority to direct traffic in a school crossing zone for the protection of children going to or leaving a school.

*(Added by L.1995, chap. 165(1); chgd. by L.1997, chap. 165(30.103), eff. 9/1/97.)*

### §541.002. Governmental authorities.

In this subtitle:

(1) "Department" means the Department of Public Safety acting directly or through its authorized officers and agents.

(2) "Director" means the public safety director.

(3) "Local authority" means:

(A) a county, municipality, or other local entity authorized to enact traffic laws under the laws of this state; or

(B) a school district created under the laws of this state only when it is designating school crossing guards for schools operated by the district.

(4) "Police officer" means an officer authorized to direct traffic or arrest persons who violate traffic regulations.

(5) "State" has the meaning assigned by Section 311.005, Government Code, and includes a province of Canada.

*(Added by L.1995, chap. 165(1), eff. 9/1/95.)*

### §§541.003 to 541.100. *(Reserved.)*

## SUBCHAPTER B. PROPERTY AREAS

### §541.101. Metropolitan area.

In this subtitle, "metropolitan area" means an area that:

(1) contains at least one municipality with a population of at least 100,000; and

(2) includes the adjacent municipalities and unincorporated urban districts.

*(Added by L.1995, chap. 165(1), eff. 9/1/95.)*

### §541.102. Restricted districts.

In this subtitle:

(1) "Business district" means the territory adjacent to and including a highway if buildings used for business or industrial purposes, including a building used as a hotel, bank, office building, public building, or railroad station:

(A) are located within a 600-foot segment along the highway; and

(B) within that segment the buildings occupy at least 300 feet of frontage:

(i) on one side of the highway; or

(ii) collectively on both sides of the highway.

(2) "Residence district" means the territory, other than a business district, adjacent to and including a highway, if at least 300 feet of the highway frontage is primarily improved with:

(A) residences; or

(B) buildings used for business purposes and residences.

(3) "Urban district" means the territory adjacent to and including a highway, if the territory:

(A) is not in a municipality; and

(B) is improved with structures that are used for business, industry, or dwelling houses and located at intervals of less than 100 feet for a distance of at least one-quarter mile on either side of the highway.

*(Added by L.1995, chap. 165(1), eff. 9/1/95.)*



### §§541.103 to 541.200. *(Reserved.)*

## SUBCHAPTER C. VEHICLES, RAIL TRANSPORTATION, AND EQUIPMENT

### §541.201. Vehicles.

In this subtitle:

(1) "Authorized emergency vehicle" means:

(A) a fire department or police vehicle;

(B) a public or private ambulance operated by a person who has been issued a license by the Texas Department of Health;

(C) a municipal department or public service corporation emergency vehicle that has been designated or authorized by the governing body of a municipality;

(D) a private vehicle of a volunteer firefighter or a certified emergency medical services employee or volunteer when responding to a fire alarm or medical emergency;

(E) an industrial emergency response vehicle, including an industrial ambulance, when responding to an emergency, but only if the vehicle is operated in compliance with criteria in effect September 1, 1989, and established by the Texas Industrial Fire Training Board of the State Firemen's and Fire Marshals' Association of Texas; or

(F) a vehicle of a blood bank or tissue bank, accredited or approved under the laws of this state or the United States, when making emergency deliveries of blood, drugs, medicines, or organs.

(2) "Bicycle" means a device that a person may ride and that is propelled by human power and has two tandem wheels at least one of which is more than 14 inches in diameter.

(3) "Bus" means:

(A) a motor vehicle used to transport persons and designed to accommodate more than 10 passengers, including the operator; or

(B) a motor vehicle, other than a taxicab, designed and used to transport persons for compensation.

(4) "Farm tractor" means a motor vehicle designed and used primarily as a farm implement to draw an implement of husbandry, including a plow or a mowing machine.

(5) "House trailer" means a trailer or semitrailer, other than a towable recreational vehicle, that:

(A) is transportable on a highway in one or more sections;

(B) is less than 40 feet in length, excluding tow bar, while in the traveling mode;

(C) is built on a permanent chassis;

(D) is designed to be used as a dwelling or for commercial purposes if connected to required utilities; and

(E) includes plumbing, heating, air-conditioning, and electrical systems.

(6) "Implement of husbandry" means a vehicle, other than a passenger car or truck, that is designed and adapted for use as a farm implement, machinery, or tool for tilling the soil.

(7) "Light truck" means a truck, including a pickup truck, panel delivery truck, or carryall truck, that has a manufacturer's rated carrying capacity of 2,000 pounds or less.

(8) "Moped" means a motor-driven cycle that cannot attain a speed in one mile of more than 30 miles per hour and the engine of which:

(A) cannot produce more than two-brake horsepower; and

(B) if an internal combustion engine, has a piston displacement of 50 cubic centimeters or less and connects to a power drive system that does not require the operator to shift gears.

(9) "Motorcycle" means a motor vehicle, other than a tractor, that is equipped with a rider's saddle and designed to have when propelled not more than three wheels on the ground.

(10) "Motor-driven cycle" means a motorcycle equipped with a motor that has an engine piston displacement of 250 cubic centimeters or less.

(11) "Motor vehicle" means a self-propelled vehicle or a vehicle that is propelled by electric power from overhead trolley wires.

(12) "Passenger car" means a motor vehicle, other than a motorcycle, used to transport persons and designed to accommodate 10 or fewer passengers, including the operator.

(13) "Pole trailer" means a vehicle without motive power:

(A) designed to be drawn by another vehicle and secured to the other vehicle by pole, reach, boom, or other security device; and

(B) ordinarily used to transport a long or irregularly shaped load, including poles, pipes, or structural members, generally capable of sustaining themselves as beams between the supporting connections.

(14) "Road tractor" means a motor vehicle designed and used to draw another vehicle but not constructed to carry a load independently or a part of the weight of the other vehicle or its load.

(15) "School activity bus" means a bus designed to accommodate more than 15 passengers, including the operator, that is owned, operated, rented, or leased by a school district, county school, open-enrollment charter school, regional education service center, or shared services arrangement and that is used to transport public school students on a school-related activity trip, other than on routes to and from school. The term does not include a chartered bus, a bus operated by a mass transit authority, or a school bus.

(16) "School bus" means a motor vehicle that was manufactured in compliance with the federal motor vehicle safety standards for school buses in effect on the date of manufacture and that is used to transport pre-primary, primary, or secondary students on a route to or from school or on a school-related activity trip other than on routes to and from school. The term does not include a school-chartered bus or a bus operated by a mass transit authority.

(17) "Semitrailer" means a vehicle with or without motive power, other than a pole trailer:

(A) designed to be drawn by a motor vehicle and to transport persons or property; and

(B) constructed so that part of the vehicle's weight and load rests on or is carried by another vehicle.

(18) "Special mobile equipment" means a vehicle that is not designed or used primarily to transport persons or property and that is only incidentally operated on a highway. The term:

(A) includes ditchdigging apparatus, well boring apparatus, and road construction and maintenance machinery, including an asphalt spreader, bituminous mixer, bucket loader, tractor other than a truck tractor, ditcher, levelling grader, finishing machine, motor grader, road roller, scarifier, earth-moving carryall and scraper, power shovel or dragline, or self-propelled crane and earth-moving equipment; and

(B) excludes a vehicle that is designed to transport persons or property and that has machinery attached, including a house trailer, dump truck, truck-mounted transit mixer, crane, and shovel.

(19) "Towable recreational vehicle" means a nonmotorized vehicle that:

(A) is designed:

(i) to be towable by a motor vehicle; and

(ii) for temporary human habitation for uses including recreational camping or seasonal use;

(B) is permanently built on a single chassis;

(C) may contain one or more life-support systems; and

(D) may be used permanently or temporarily for advertising, selling, displaying, or promoting merchandise or services, but is not used for transporting property for hire or for distribution by a private carrier.

(20) "Trailer" means a vehicle, other than a pole trailer, with or without motive power:

(A) designed to be drawn by a motor vehicle and to transport persons or property; and

(B) constructed so that no part of the vehicle's weight and load rests on the motor vehicle.

(21) "Truck" means a motor vehicle designed, used, or maintained primarily to transport property.

(22) "Truck tractor" means a motor vehicle designed and used primarily to draw another vehicle but not constructed to carry a load other than a part of the weight of the other vehicle and its load.

(23) "Vehicle" means a device that can be used to transport or draw persons or property on a highway. The term does not include:

(A) a device exclusively used on stationary rails or tracks; or

(B) manufactured housing as that term is defined by the Texas Manufactured Housing Standards Act (Article 5221f, Vernon's Texas Civil Statutes).

*(Added by L.1995, chap. 165(1); chgd. by L.1997, chaps. 1020(1), 1438(8); L.1999, chaps. 663(1), 797(3), eff. 6/18/99, 9/1/99, respectively.)*



### §541.202. Rail transportation.

In this subtitle:

(1) "Railroad" means a carrier that operates cars, other than streetcars, on stationary rails to transport persons or property.

(2) "Railroad train" means a steam engine or electric or other motor with or without an attached car operated on rails, other than a streetcar.

(3) "Streetcar" means a car, other than a railroad train, used to transport persons or property and operated on rails located primarily within a municipality.

*(Added by L.1995, chap. 165(1), eff. 9/1/95.)*

### §541.203. Equipment.

In this subtitle:

(1) "Exhaust emission system" means a motor vehicle engine modification designed to control or reduce the emission of substances from a motor vehicle or motor vehicle engine, of a model year of 1968 or later, and installed on or incorporated in a motor vehicle or motor vehicle engine in compliance with requirements imposed by the Motor Vehicle Air Pollution Control Act (42 U.S.C. Section 1857 et seq.) or other applicable law.

(2) "Metal tire" includes a tire the surface of which in contact with the highway is wholly or partly made of metal or other hard, nonresilient material.

(3) "Muffler" means a device that reduces noise using:

(A) a mechanical design, including a series of chambers or baffle plates, to receive exhaust gas from an internal combustion engine; or

(B) turbine wheels to receive exhaust gas from a diesel engine.

(4) "Solid tire" includes only a tire that:

(A) is made of rubber or another resilient material; and

(B) does not use compressed air to support its load.

*(Added by L.1995, chap. 165(1), eff. 9/1/95.)*

### §§541.204 to 541.300. *(Reserved.)*

## SUBCHAPTER D. TRAFFIC, TRAFFIC AREAS, AND TRAFFIC CONTROL

### §541.301. Traffic.

In this subtitle "traffic" means pedestrians, ridden or herded animals, and conveyances, including vehicles and streetcars, singly or together while using a highway for the purposes of travel. *(Added by L.1995, chap. 165(1), eff. 9/1/95.)*

### §541.302. Traffic areas.

In this subtitle:

(1) "Alley" means a street that:

(A) is not used primarily for through traffic; and

(B) provides access to rear entrances of buildings or lots along a street.

(2) "Crosswalk" means:

(A) the portion of a roadway, including an intersection, designated as a pedestrian crossing by surface markings, including lines; or

(B) the portion of a roadway at an intersection that is within the connections of the lateral lines of the sidewalks on opposite sides of the highway measured from the curbs or, in the absence of curbs, from the edges of the traversable roadway.

(3) "Freeway" means a divided, controlled-access highway for through traffic.

(4) "Freeway main lane" means a freeway lane having an uninterrupted flow of through traffic.

(5) "Highway or street" means the width between the boundary lines of a publicly maintained way any part of which is open to the public for vehicular travel.

(6) "Improved shoulder" means a paved shoulder.

(7) "Laned roadway" means a roadway that is divided into at least two clearly marked lanes for vehicular travel.

(8) "Limited-access or controlled-access highway" means a highway or roadway to which:

(A) persons, including owners or occupants of abutting real property, have no right of access; and

(B) access by persons to enter or exit the highway or roadway is restricted under law except at a place and in the manner determined by the authority that has jurisdiction over the highway or roadway.

(9) "Private road or driveway" means a privately owned way or place used for vehicular travel and used only by the owner and persons who have the owner's express or implied permission.

(10) "Ramp" means an interconnecting roadway of a traffic interchange, or a connecting roadway between highways at different levels or between parallel highways, that allows a vehicle to enter or exit a roadway.

(11) "Roadway" means the portion of a highway, other than the berm or shoulder, that is improved, designed, or ordinarily used for vehicular travel. If a highway includes at least two separate roadways, the term applies to each roadway separately.

(12) "Safety zone" means the area in a roadway officially designated for exclusive pedestrian use and that is protected or so marked or indicated by adequate signs as to be plainly visible at all times while so designated.

(13) "School crossing zone" means a reduced-speed zone designated on a street by a local authority to facilitate safe crossing of the street by children going to or leaving a public or private elementary or secondary school during the time the reduced speed limit applies.

(14) "School crosswalk" means a crosswalk designated on a street by a local authority to facilitate safe crossing of the street by children going to or leaving a public or private elementary or secondary school.

(15) "Shoulder" means the portion of a highway that is:

(A) adjacent to the roadway;

(B) designed or ordinarily used for parking;

(C) distinguished from the roadway by different design, construction, or marking; and

(D) not intended for normal vehicular travel.

(16) "Sidewalk" means the portion of a street that is:

(A) between a curb or lateral line of a roadway and the adjacent property line; and

(B) intended for pedestrian use.

*(Added by L.1995, chap. 165(1), eff. 9/1/95.)*

## §541.303. Intersection.

(a) In this subtitle, "intersection" means the common area at the junction of two highways, other than the junction of an alley and a highway.

(b) The dimensions of an intersection include only the common area:

(1) within the connection of the lateral curb lines or, in the absence of curb lines, the lateral boundary lines of the roadways of intersecting highways that join at approximate right angles; or

(2) at the place where vehicles could collide if traveling on roadways of intersecting highways that join at any angle other than an approximate right angle.

(c) Each junction of each roadway of a highway that includes two roadways at least 30 feet apart with the roadway of an intersecting highway, including each roadway of an intersecting highway that includes two roadways at least 30 feet apart, is a separate intersection.

*(Added by L.1995, chap. 165(1), eff. 9/1/95.)*

### §541.304. Traffic control.

In this subtitle:

(1) "Official traffic-control device" means a sign, signal, marking, or device that is:

(A) consistent with this subtitle;

(B) placed or erected by a public body or officer having jurisdiction; and

(C) used to regulate, warn, or guide traffic.

(2) "Railroad sign or signal" means a sign, signal, or device erected by a railroad, public body, or public officer to notify traffic of railroad tracks or an approaching railroad train.

(3) "Traffic-control signal" means a manual, electric, or mechanical device that alternately directs traffic to stop and to proceed.

*(Added by L.1995, chap. 165(1), eff. 9/1/95.)*

### §§541.305 to 541.400. *(Reserved.)*



## SUBCHAPTER E. MISCELLANEOUS TERMS

### §541.401. Miscellaneous terms.

In this subtitle:

(1) "Daytime" means the period beginning one-half hour before sunrise and ending one-half hour after sunset.

(2) "Explosive" means a chemical compound or mechanical mixture that:

(A) is commonly intended for use or used to produce an explosion; and

(B) contains ingredients, which may include oxidizing or combustive units, in packing, proportions, or quantities that, if ignited by fire, friction, concussion, percussion, or detonator, could suddenly generate highly heated gases that could damage surrounding objects or destroy life or limb.

(3) "Flammable liquid" means a liquid that has a flash point of not more than 70 degrees Fahrenheit as determined by a tagliabue or equivalent closed-cup test device.

(4) "Gross vehicle weight" means the weight of a vehicle and the weight of its load.

(5) "Nighttime" means the period beginning one-half hour after sunset and ending one-half hour before sunrise.

(6) "Park" or "parking" means to stand an occupied or unoccupied vehicle, other than temporarily while loading or unloading merchandise or passengers.

(7) "Personal injury" means an injury to any part of the human body and that requires treatment.

(8) "Right-of-way" means the right of one vehicle or pedestrian to proceed in a lawful manner in preference to another vehicle or pedestrian that is approaching from a direction, at a speed, and within a proximity that could cause a collision unless one grants precedence to the other.

(9) "Stand" or "standing" means to halt an occupied or unoccupied vehicle, other than temporarily while receiving or discharging passengers.

(10) "Stop" or "stopping" means:

(A) when required, to completely cease movement; and

(B) when prohibited, to halt, including momentarily halting, an occupied or unoccupied vehicle, unless necessary to avoid conflict with other traffic or to comply with the directions of a police officer or a traffic-control sign or signal.

*(Added by L.1995, chap. 165(1), eff. 9/1/95.)*

# CHAPTER 542. GENERAL PROVISIONS

## SUBCHAPTER A. APPLICABILITY

Section

## SUBCHAPTER B. UNIFORMITY AND INTERPRETATION OF TRAFFIC LAWS



## SUBCHAPTER C. OFFENSES



## SUBCHAPTER D. PENALTIES AND COSTS OF COURT



## SUBCHAPTER E. MISCELLANEOUS



## SUBCHAPTER A. APPLICABILITY

### §542.001. Vehicles on highways.

A provision of this subtitle relating to the operation of a vehicle applies only to the operation of a vehicle on a highway unless the provision specifically applies to a different place. *(Added by L.1995, chap. 165(1), eff. 9/1/95.)*

### §542.002. Government vehicles.

A provision of this subtitle applicable to an operator of a vehicle applies to the operator of a vehicle owned or operated by the United States, this state, or a political subdivision of this state, except as specifically provided otherwise by this subtitle for an authorized emergency vehicle. *(Added by L.1995, chap. 165(1), eff. 9/1/95.)*

### §542.003. Animals and animal-drawn vehicles.

A person riding an animal on a roadway or operating a vehicle drawn by an animal on a roadway has the rights and duties applicable to the operator of a vehicle under this subtitle, except a right or duty that by its nature cannot apply to a person riding an animal or operating a vehicle drawn by an animal. *(Added by L.1995, chap. 165(1), eff. 9/1/95.)*

### §542.004. Persons and equipment engaged in work on highway surface.

This subtitle does not apply to a person, team, motor vehicle, or other equipment engaged in work on a highway unless the provision is specifically made applicable, but does apply to those persons and vehicles while traveling to or from that work. *(Added by L.1995, chap. 165(1), eff. 9/1/95.)*

### §542.005. Rules on private property.

This subtitle does not prevent an owner of private property that is a private road from:

(1) regulating or prohibiting use of the property by the public for vehicular travel; or

(2) requiring conditions different from or in addition to those specified by this subtitle.

*(Added by L.1995, chap. 165(1), eff. 9/1/95.)*

### §542.006. Speed restrictions on private roads.

(a) The owners of a majority of the parcels of real property abutting a private road may petition the Texas Transportation Commission to extend the speed restrictions of this subtitle to the portion of the road in a subdivision or across adjacent subdivisions if:

(1) the road is not in a municipality;

(2) the total number of residents in the subdivision and subdivisions adjacent to the subdivision is at least 400; and

(3) a plat for the subdivision and each adjacent subdivision included to determine the number of residents under Subdivision (2) has been filed in the deed records of the county.

(b) After the commission receives a petition and verifies the property ownership of its signers, the commission may issue an order extending the speed restrictions to the private road if the commission finds the order is in the interests of the area residents and the public generally.

(c) If the commission rejects the petition, the commission shall hold a public hearing on the advisability of making the speed restrictions applicable. The hearing must be held in the county in which the portion of the road that is the subject of the petition is located. The commission shall publish notice of the hearing in a newspaper of general circulation in that county at least 10 days before the date of the hearing.

(d) At the hearing, if the commission finds that it would be in the interests of the area residents and the public generally, the commission shall issue an order extending the speed restrictions to the private road.

(e) After the commission issues an order under this section, the private road is a public highway for purposes of setting and enforcing speed restrictions under this subtitle, and the commission shall post speed limit signs on property abutting the private road with the consent of the owner of the property on which a sign is placed.

*(Added by L.1995, chap. 165(1); chgd. by L.1999, chap. 308(1), eff. 5/29/99.)*



### §542.007. Traffic regulations: private subdivision in certain counties.

(a) This section applies only to a subdivision that is located in the unincorporated area of a county with a population of 10,000 or less.

(b) On petition of 25 percent of the property owners residing in a subdivision in which the roads are privately maintained or on the request of the governing body of the entity that maintains those roads, the commissioners court of the county by order may extend any traffic rules that apply to a county road to the roads of the subdivision if the commissioners court finds the order in the interest of the county generally. The petition must specify the traffic rules that are sought to be extended. The court order may extend any or all of the requested traffic rules.

(c) As a condition of extending a traffic rule under Subsection (b), the commissioners court may require that owners of the property in the subdivision pay all or part of the cost of extending and enforcing the traffic rules in the subdivision. The commissioners court shall consult with the sheriff to determine the cost of enforcing traffic rules in the subdivision.

(d) On issuance of an order under this section, the private roads in the subdivision are considered to be county roads for purposes of the application and enforcement of the specified traffic rules. The commissioners court may place official traffic control devices on property abutting the private roads if:

(1) those devices relate to the specified traffic rule; and

(2) the consent of the owner of that property is obtained.

*(Added by L.1999, chap. 1393(1), eff. 9/1/99.)*

### §§542.008 to 542.200. *(Reserved.)*

## SUBCHAPTER B. UNIFORMITY AND INTERPRETATION OF TRAFFIC LAWS

### §542.201. General rule of uniformity.

This subtitle applies uniformly throughout this state. A local authority may not enact or enforce an ordinance or rule that conflicts with this subtitle unless expressly authorized by this subtitle. However, a local authority may regulate traffic in a manner that does not conflict with this subtitle. *(Added by L.1995, chap. 165(1), eff. 9/1/95.)*

### §542.202. Powers of local authorities.

(a) This subtitle does not prevent a local authority, with respect to a highway under its jurisdiction and in the reasonable exercise of the police power, from:

(1) regulating traffic by police officers or traffic-control devices;

(2) regulating the stopping, standing, or parking of a vehicle;

(3) regulating or prohibiting a procession or assemblage on a highway;

(4) regulating the operation and requiring registration and licensing of a bicycle, including payment of a registration fee;

(5) regulating the time, place, and manner in which a roller skater may use a highway;

(6) regulating the speed of a vehicle in a public park;

(7) regulating or prohibiting the turning of a vehicle or specified type of vehicle at an intersection;

(8) designating an intersection as a stop intersection or a yield intersection and requiring each vehicle to stop or yield at one or more entrances to the intersection;

(9) designating a highway as a through highway;

(10) designating a highway as a one-way highway and requiring each vehicle on the highway to move in one specific direction;

(11) designating school crossing guards and school crossing zones;

(12) altering a speed limit as authorized by this subtitle; or

(13) adopting other traffic rules specifically authorized by this subtitle.

(b) In this section:

(1) "Roller skater" means a person wearing footwear with a set of wheels attached.

(2) "Through highway" means a highway or a portion of a highway on which:

(A) vehicular traffic is given preferential right-of-way; and

(B) vehicular traffic entering from an intersecting highway is required by law to yield right-of-way in compliance with an official traffic-control device.

*(Added by L.1995, chap. 165(1), eff. 9/1/95.)*



### §542.203. Limitation on local authorities.

(a) A local authority may not erect or maintain a traffic-control device to direct the traffic on a state highway, including a farm-to-market or ranch-to-market road, to stop or yield before entering or crossing an intersecting highway unless permitted by agreement between the local authority and the Texas Department of Transportation under Section 221.002.

(b) An ordinance or rule of a local authority is not effective until signs giving notice are posted on or at the entrance to the highway or part of the highway, as may be most appropriate. This subsection applies only to an ordinance or rule that:

(1) regulates the speed of a vehicle in a public park;

(2) alters a speed limit as authorized by this subtitle;

(3) designates an intersection as a stop intersection or a yield intersection; or

(4) designates a highway as a one-way highway or a through highway.

(c) An ordinance or rule of a local authority regulating the time, place, and manner in which a roller skater may use a highway may not alter the local authority's standard of care or liability with regard to construction, design, or maintenance of a highway.

*(Added by L.1995, chap. 165(1), eff. 9/1/95.)*

### §542.204. Powers related to intersections.

The Texas Transportation Commission and a local authority may, in a matter of highway or traffic engineering design, consider the separate intersections of divided highways with medians at least 30 feet apart as components of a single intersection. *(Added by L.1995, chap. 165(1), eff. 9/1/95.)*

### §542.205. Conflict between this subtitle and an order, rule, or regulation of certain agencies.

(a) If this subtitle conflicts with an order, rule, regulation, or requirement of the federal Surface Transportation Board or the department relating to a vehicle safety requirement, including a requirement relating to vehicle equipment, compliance by the owner or operator of the vehicle with the order, rule, regulation, or requirement of the federal Surface Transportation Board or the department is compliance with this subtitle.

(b) The owner or operator of a vehicle shall comply with any requirement of this subtitle that is in addition to, but not in conflict with, a requirement of the federal Surface Transportation Board or the department.
*(Added by L.1995, chap. 165(1); chgd. by L.1997, chap. 165(30.104), eff. 9/1/97.)*

### §542.206. Effect of speed limits in a civil action.

A provision of this subtitle declaring a maximum or minimum speed limit does not relieve the plaintiff in a civil action from the burden of proving negligence of the defendant as the proximate cause of an accident. *(Added by L.1995, chap. 165(1), eff. 9/1/95.)*

### §§542.207 to 542.300. *(Reserved.)*

## SUBCHAPTER C. OFFENSES

### §542.301. General offense.

(a) A person commits an offense if the person performs an act prohibited or fails to perform an act required by this subtitle.

(b) Except as otherwise provided, an offense under this subtitle is a misdemeanor.
*(Added by L.1995, chap. 165(1), eff. 9/1/95.)*

### §542.302. Offense by person owning or controlling vehicle.

A person who owns a vehicle or employs or otherwise directs the operator of a vehicle commits an offense if the person requires or knowingly permits the operator of the vehicle to operate the vehicle in a manner that violates law. *(Added by L.1995, chap. 165(1), eff. 9/1/95.)*

### §542.303. Inchoate offense.

(a) A person who attempts to commit or conspires to commit an act declared by this subtitle to be an offense is guilty of the offense.

(b) A person who falsely, fraudulently, or wilfully permits another to violate this subtitle is guilty of the violation.
*(Added by L.1995, chap. 165(1), eff. 9/1/95.)*

### §§542.304 to 542.400. *(Reserved.)*

## SUBCHAPTER D. PENALTIES AND COSTS OF COURT

### §542.401. General penalty.

A person convicted of an offense that is a misdemeanor under this subtitle for which another penalty is not provided shall be punished by a fine of not less than $1 or more than $200. *(Added by L.1995, chap. 165(1), eff. 9/1/95.)*

### §542.402. Disposition of fines.

(a) A municipality or county shall use a fine collected for a violation of a highway law in this title to:

(1) construct and maintain roads, bridges, and culverts in the municipality or county;

(2) enforce laws regulating the use of highways by motor vehicles; and

(3) defray the expense of county traffic officers.

(b) In each fiscal year, a municipality having a population of less than 5,000 may retain, from fines collected for violations of this title and from special expenses collected under Article 45.051, Code of Criminal Procedure, in cases in which a violation of this title is alleged, an amount equal to 30 percent of the municipality's revenue for the preceding fiscal year from all sources, other than federal funds and bond proceeds, as shown by the audit performed under Section 103.001, Local Government Code. After a municipality has retained that amount, the municipality shall send to the comptroller any portion of a fine or a special expense collected that exceeds $1.

(c) The comptroller shall enforce Subsection (b).

(d) In a fiscal year in which a municipality retains from fines and special expenses collected for violations of this title an amount equal to at least 20 percent of the municipality's revenue for the preceding fiscal year from all sources other than federal funds and bond proceeds, not later than the 120th day after the last day of the municipality's fiscal year, the municipality shall send to the comptroller:

(1) a copy of the municipality's financial statement for that fiscal year filed under Chapter 103, Local Government Code; and

(2) a report that shows the total amount collected for that fiscal year from fines and special expenses under Subsection (b).

(e) If an audit is conducted by the comptroller under Subsection (c) and it is determined that the municipality is retaining more than 20 percent of the amounts under Subsection (b) and has not complied with Subsection (d), the municipality shall pay the costs incurred by the comptroller in conducting the audit.
*(Added by L.1995, chap. 165(1); chgd. by L.1997, chap. 165(30.105(a)); L.1999, chaps. 1336(1), 1545(72), eff. 9/1/99.)*

### §542.403. Court costs.

(a) In addition to other costs, a person convicted of a misdemeanor under this subtitle shall pay $3 as a cost of court.

(b) The officer who collects a cost under this section shall:

(1) deposit in the municipal treasury a cost collected in a municipal court case; and

(2) deposit in the county treasury a cost collected in a justice court case or in a county court case, including a case appealed from a justice or municipal court.
*(Added by L.1995, chap. 165(1), eff. 9/1/95.)*

### §542.404. Fine for offense in construction or maintenance work zone.

(a) If an offense under this subtitle, other than an offense under Chapter 548 or 552 or Section 545.412 or 545.413, is committed in a construction or maintenance work zone when workers are present and any written notice to appear issued for the offense states on its face that workers were present when the offense was committed:

(1) the minimum fine applicable to the offense is twice the minimum fine that would be applicable to the offense if it were committed outside a construction or maintenance work zone; and

(2) the maximum fine applicable to the offense is twice the maximum fine that would be applicable to the offense if it were committed outside a construction or maintenance work zone.

(b) In this section, "construction or maintenance work zone" has the meaning assigned by Section 472.022.
*(Added by L.1997, chap. 674(2); chgd. by L.1999, chap. 789(3), eff. 9/1/99.)*

### §§542.405 to 542.500. *(Reserved.)*

## SUBCHAPTER E. MISCELLANEOUS

### §542.501. Obedience required to police officers and to school crossing guards.

A person may not wilfully fail or refuse to comply with a lawful order or direction of:

(1) a police officer; or

(2) a school crossing guard who:

(A) is performing crossing guard duties in a school crosswalk to stop and yield to a pedestrian; or

(B) has been trained under Section 600.004 and is directing traffic in a school crossing zone.
*(Added by L.1995, chap. 165(1); chgd. by L.1999, chap. 724(1), eff. 6/18/99.)*

# CHAPTER 543. ARREST AND PROSECUTION OF VIOLATORS

## SUBCHAPTER A. ARREST AND CHARGING PROCEDURES; NOTICES AND PROMISES TO APPEAR

Section

## SUBCHAPTER B. DISMISSAL OF CERTAIN MISDEMEANOR CHARGES ON COMPLETING DRIVING SAFETY COURSE





## SUBCHAPTER C. RECORDS AND INFORMATION MAINTAINED BY DEPARTMENT



## SUBCHAPTER A. ARREST AND CHARGING PROCEDURES; NOTICES AND PROMISES TO APPEAR

### §543.001. Arrest without warrant authorized.

Any peace officer may arrest without warrant a person found committing a violation of this subtitle. *(Added by L.1995, chap. 165(1), eff. 9/1/95.)*

### §543.002. Person arrested to be taken before magistrate.

(a) A person arrested for a violation of this subtitle punishable as a misdemeanor shall be immediately taken before a magistrate if:

(1) the person is arrested on a charge of failure to stop in the event of an accident causing damage to property; or

(2) the person demands an immediate appearance before a magistrate or refuses to make a written promise to appear in court as provided by this subchapter.

(b) The person must be taken before a magistrate who:

(1) has jurisdiction of the offense;

(2) is in the county in which the offense charged is alleged to have been committed; and

(3) is nearest or most accessible to the place of arrest.

*(Added by L.1995, chap. 165(1), eff. 9/1/95.)*

### §543.003. Notice to appear required: person not taken before magistrate.

An officer who arrests a person for a violation of this subtitle punishable as a misdemeanor and who does not take the person before a magistrate shall issue a written notice to appear in court showing the time and place the person is to appear, the offense charged, the name and address of the person charged, and, if applicable, the license number of the person's vehicle. *(Added by L.1995, chap. 165(1); chgd. by L.1999, chap. 701(3), eff. 6/18/99.)*

### §543.004. Notice to appear required: certain offenses.

(a) An officer shall issue a written notice to appear if:

(1) the offense charged is speeding or a violation of the open container law, Section 49.03, Penal Code; and

(2) the person makes a written promise to appear in court as provided by Section 543.005.

(b) If the person is a resident of or is operating a vehicle licensed in a state or country other than this state, Subsection (a) applies only as provided by Chapter 703.

(c) The offenses specified by Subsection (a) are the only offenses for which issuance of a written notice to appear is mandatory.
*(Added by L.1995, chap. 165(1); chgd. by L.1999, chap. 62(17.07), eff. 9/1/99.)*

### §543.005. Promise to appear; release.

To secure release, the person arrested must make a written promise to appear in court by signing the written notice prepared by the arresting officer. The signature may be obtained on a duplicate form or on an electronic device capable of creating a copy of the signed notice. The arresting officer shall retain the paper or electronic original of the notice and deliver the copy of the notice to the person arrested. The officer shall then promptly release the person from custody. *(Added by L.1995, chap. 165(1); chgd. by L.1999, chap. 701(4), eff. 6/18/99.)*

### §543.006. Time and place of appearance.

(a) The time specified in the notice to appear must be at least 10 days after the date of arrest unless the person arrested demands an earlier hearing.

(b) The place specified in the notice to appear must be before a magistrate having jurisdiction of the offense who is in the municipality or county in which the offense is alleged to have been committed.
*(Added by L.1995, chap. 165(1), eff. 9/1/95.)*

### §543.007. Notice to appear: commercial vehicle or license.

A notice to appear issued to the operator of a commercial motor vehicle or holder of a commercial driver's license or commercial driver learner's permit, for the violation of a law regulating the operation of vehicles on highways, must contain the information required by department rule, to comply with Chapter 522 and the federal Commercial Motor Vehicle Safety Act of 1986 (Title 49, U.S.C. Section 2701 et seq.). *(Added by L.1995, chap. 165(1); chgd. by L.1999, chap. 701(5), eff. 6/18/99.)*

### §543.008. Violation by officer.

A violation by an officer of a provision of Sections 543.003-543.007 is misconduct in office and the officer is subject to removal from the officer's position. *(Added by L.1995, chap. 165(1), eff. 9/1/95.)*

### §543.009. Compliance with or violation of promise to appear.

(a) A person may comply with a written promise to appear in court by an appearance by counsel.

(b) A person who wilfully violates a written promise to appear in court, given as provided by this subchapter, commits a misdemeanor regardless of the disposition of the charge on which the person was arrested.
*(Added by L.1995, chap. 165(1), eff. 9/1/95.)*

### §543.010. Specifications of speeding charge.

The complaint and the summons or notice to appear on a charge of speeding under this subtitle must specify:

(1) the maximum or minimum speed limit applicable in the district or at the location; and

(2) the speed at which the defendant is alleged to have driven.
*(Added by L.1995, chap. 165(1), eff. 9/1/95.)*

### §§543.011 to 543.100. *(Reserved.)*

## SUBCHAPTER B. DISMISSAL OF CERTAIN MISDEMEANOR CHARGES ON COMPLETING DRIVING SAFETY COURSE

### §543.101. Statement of right provided on notice to appear.

(a) A notice to appear issued for an offense to which this subchapter applies must state: "You may be able to require that this charge be dismissed by taking a driving safety course. However, you will lose that right if you do not provide written notice to the court on or before your appearance date of your desire to do so."

(b) If this statement is not supplied, the person may continue to exercise the right described until the person is informed as provided by Subsection (a) or until the disposal of the case.
*(Added by L.1995, chap. 165(1), eff. 9/1/95.)*

**§§543.102 to 543.110.** *(Repealed by L.1999, chaps. 1387(3), 1545(75(b)), eff. 9/1/99.)*

### §543.111. Regulation by certain state agencies.

(a) The State Board of Education shall enter into a memorandum of understanding with the Texas Department of Insurance for the interagency development of a curriculum for driving safety courses.

(b) The Texas Education Agency shall:

(1) adopt and administer comprehensive rules governing driving safety courses; and

(2) investigate options to develop and implement procedures to electronically transmit information pertaining to driving safety courses to municipal and justice courts.
*(Added by L.1995, chap. 165(1); chgd. by L.1997, chap. 165(30.106(d)), eff. 9/1/97.)*



### §543.112. Standards for uniform certificate of course completion.

(a) The Texas Education Agency by rule shall provide for the design and distribution of uniform certificates of course completion so as to prevent to the greatest extent possible the unauthorized production or misuse of the certificates.

(b) The uniform certificate of course completion must include an identifying number by which the Texas Education Agency, the court, or the department may verify its authenticity with the course provider and must be in a form adopted by the Texas Education Agency.

(c) The Texas Education Agency shall issue duplicate uniform certificates of course completion. The State Board of Education by rule shall determine the amount of the fee to be charged for issuance of a duplicate certificate.

(d) A driving safety course provider shall electronically submit data identified by the Texas Education Agency pertaining to issued uniform certificates of course completion to the agency as directed by the agency.
*(Added by L.1995, chap. 165(1); chgd. by L.1997, chap. 165(30.106(e)), eff. 9/1/97.)*

### §543.113. Fees for printing and supplying certificate.

(a) The Texas Education Agency shall print the uniform certificates and supply them to persons who are licensed providers of courses approved under the Texas Driver and Traffic Safety Education Act (Article 4413(29c), Texas Civil Statutes). The agency may charge a fee for each certificate. The fee may not exceed $4.

(b) A course provider shall charge an operator a fee equal to the fee paid to the agency for a certificate.

(c) Money collected by the Texas Education Agency under this section may be used only to pay monetary awards for information relating to abuse of uniform certificates that leads to the conviction or removal of an approval, license, or authorization.
*(Added by L.1995, chap. 165(1); chgd. by L.1997, chap. 165(30.106(f)), eff. 9/1/97.)*

### §543.114. Distribution of written information on provider.

(a) A person may not distribute written information to advertise a provider of a driving safety course within 500 feet of a court having jurisdiction over an offense to which this subchapter applies. A violation of this section by a provider or a provider's agent, employee, or representative results in loss of the provider's status as a provider of a course approved under the Texas Driver and Safety Education Act (Article 4413(29c), Texas Civil Statutes).

(b) This section does not apply to distribution of information:

(1) by a court;

(2) to a court to obtain approval of the course; or

(3) to a court to advise the court of the availability of the course.
*(Added by L.1995, chap. 165(1), eff. 9/1/95.)*

### §543.115. Fees for driving safety course.

(a) A driving safety course may not be provided to a student for less than $25.

(b) A course provider shall charge each student a fee for course materials and for overseeing and administering the course. The fee may not be less than $3.
*(Added by L.1997, chap. 165(30.106(g)), eff. 9/1/97.)*

### §543.116. Delivery of uniform certificate of course completion.

(a) A driving safety course provider shall mail an issued uniform certificate of course completion to a person who successfully completes the course.

(b) The certificate must be mailed not later than the 15th working day after the date a person successfully completes the course.

*(Added by L.1997, chap. 165(30.106(g)), eff. 9/1/97.)*

### §543.117. Offense in construction or maintenance work zone.

A charge may not be dismissed under this subchapter for an offense to which Section 542.404 or 729.004 applies except upon motion of the attorney representing the state. *(Added by L.1999, chap. 1088(2), eff. 9/1/99.)*

### §§543.118 to 543.200. *(Reserved.)*

## SUBCHAPTER C. RECORDS AND INFORMATION MAINTAINED BY DEPARTMENT

### §543.201. Conviction reported to department.

Each magistrate or judge of a court not of record and each clerk of a court of record shall keep a record of each case in which a person is charged with a violation of law regulating the operation of vehicles on highways. *(Added by L.1995, chap. 165(1), eff. 9/1/95.)*

### §543.202. Form of record.

The record must be made on a form or by a data processing method acceptable to the department and must include:

(1) the name, address, physical description, date of birth, and driver's license number of the person charged;

(2) the registration number of the vehicle involved;

(3) whether the vehicle was a commercial motor vehicle as defined by Chapter 522 or was involved in transporting hazardous materials;

(4) the person's social security number, if the person was operating a commercial motor vehicle or was the holder of a commercial driver's license or commercial driver learner's permit;

(5) the date and nature of the offense, including whether the offense was a serious traffic violation as defined by Chapter 522;

(6) the plea, the judgment, and whether bail was forfeited;

(7) the date of conviction; and

(8) the amount of the fine or forfeiture.

*(Added by L.1995, chap. 165(1), eff. 9/1/95.)*

### §543.203. Submitting record to department.

Not later than the 30th day after the date of conviction or forfeiture of bail of a person on a charge of violating a law regulating the operation of a vehicle on a highway or conviction of a person of negligent homicide or a felony in the commission of which a vehicle was used, the magistrate, judge, or clerk of the court in which the conviction was had or bail was forfeited shall immediately submit to the department a written record of the case containing the information required by Section 543.202. *(Added by L.1995, chap. 165(1), eff. 9/1/95.)*

### §543.204. Submission of record prohibited.

(a) A justice of the peace or municipal judge who defers further proceedings, suspends all or part of the imposition of the fine, and places a defendant on probation under Article 45.051, Code of Criminal Procedure, or a county court judge who follows that procedure under Article 42.111, Code of Criminal Procedure, may not submit a written record to the department, except that if the justice or judge subsequently adjudicates the defendant's guilt, the justice or judge shall submit the record not later than the 30th day after the date on which the justice or judge adjudicates guilt.

(b) The department may not keep a record for which submission is prohibited by this section.

(c) The department may receive a record prepared by a department employee from court records.

*(Added by L.1995, chap. 165(1); chgd. by L.1999, chap. 1545(73), eff. 9/1/99.)*

### §543.205. Record received at main office.

The department shall receive all records under Section 543.204(a) at its main office. *(Added by L.1995, chap. 165(1), eff. 9/1/95.)*

### §543.206. Violation.

A violation by a judicial officer of this subchapter may constitute misconduct in office and may be grounds for removal from the officer's position. *(Added by L.1995, chap. 165(1), eff. 9/1/95.)*

## CHAPTER 544. TRAFFIC SIGNS, SIGNALS, AND MARKINGS

Section





### §544.001. Adoption of sign manual for state highways.

The Texas Transportation Commission shall adopt a manual and specifications for a uniform system of traffic-control devices consistent with this chapter that correlates with and to the extent possible conforms to the system approved by the American Association of State Highway and Transportation Officials. *(Added by L.1995, chap. 165(1), eff. 9/1/95.)*

### §544.002. Placing and maintaining traffic-control device.

(a) To implement this subtitle, the Texas Department of Transportation may place and maintain a traffic-control device on a state highway as provided by the manual and specifications adopted under Section 544.001. The Texas Department of Transportation may provide for the placement and maintenance of the device under Section 221.002.

(b) To implement this subtitle or a local traffic ordinance, a local authority may place and maintain a traffic-control device on a highway under the authority's jurisdiction. The traffic-control device must conform to the manual and specifications adopted under Section 544.001.

(c) A local authority may not place or maintain a traffic-control device on a highway under the jurisdiction of the Texas Department of Transportation without that department's permission. *(Added by L.1995, chap. 165(1), eff. 9/1/95.)*

### §544.003. Authority to designate through highway and stop and yield intersections.

(a) The Texas Transportation Commission may:

(1) designate a state or county highway as a through highway and place a stop or yield sign at a specified entrance; or

(2) designate an intersection on a state or county highway as a stop intersection or a yield intersection and place a sign at one or more entrances to the intersection.

(b) A local authority may:

(1) designate a highway under its jurisdiction as a through highway and place a stop or yield sign at a specified entrance; or

(2) designate an intersection on a highway under its jurisdiction as a stop intersection or a yield intersection and place a sign at one or more entrances to the intersection.

(c) The stop or yield sign indicating the preferential right-of-way must:

(1) conform to the manual and specifications adopted under Section 544.001; and

(2) be located:

(A) as near as practicable to the nearest line of the crosswalk; or

(B) in the absence of a crosswalk, at the nearest line of the roadway.

*(Added by L.1995, chap. 165(1), eff. 9/1/95.)*

### §544.004. Compliance with traffic-control device.

(a) The operator of a vehicle or streetcar shall comply with an applicable official traffic-control device placed as provided by this subtitle unless the person is:

(1) otherwise directed by a traffic or police officer; or

(2) operating an authorized emergency vehicle and is subject to exceptions under this subtitle.

(b) A provision of this subtitle requiring an official traffic-control device may not be enforced against an alleged violator if at the time and place of the alleged violation the device is not in proper position and sufficiently legible to an ordinarily observant person. A provision of this sub-

title that does not require an official traffic-control device is effective regardless of whether a device is in place.
*(Added by L.1995, chap. 165(1), eff. 9/1/95.)*

**§544.005. Interference with traffic-control device or railroad sign or signal.**
A person may not, without lawful authority, alter, injure, knock down, or remove or attempt to alter, injure, knock down, or remove:
(1) an official traffic-control device or railroad sign or signal;
(2) an inscription, shield, or insignia on an official traffic-control device or railroad sign or signal; or
(3) another part of an official traffic-control device or railroad sign or signal.
*(Added by L.1995, chap. 165(1), eff. 9/1/95.)*

**§544.006. Display of unauthorized signs, signals, or markings.**
(a) A person may not place, maintain, or display on or in view of a highway an unauthorized sign, signal, marking, or device that:
(1) imitates or resembles an official traffic-control device or railroad sign or signal;
(2) attempts to direct the movement of traffic; or
(3) hides from view or hinders the effectiveness of an official traffic-control device or railroad sign or signal.
(b) A person may not place or maintain on a highway, and a public authority may not permit on a highway, a traffic sign or signal bearing commercial advertising.
(c) A person may not place or maintain a flashing light or flashing electric sign within 1,000 feet of an intersection except under a permit issued by the Texas Transportation Commission.
(d) This section does not prohibit a person from placing on private property adjacent to a highway a sign that gives useful directional information and that cannot be mistaken for an official sign.
(e) A sign, signal, light, or marking prohibited under this section is a public nuisance. The authority with jurisdiction over the highway may remove that sign, signal, light, or marking without notice.
*(Added by L.1995, chap. 165(1), eff. 9/1/95.)*

**§544.007. Traffic-control signals in general.**
(a) A traffic-control signal displaying different colored lights or colored lighted arrows successively or in combination may display only green, yellow, or red and applies to operators of vehicles as provided by this section.
(b) An operator of a vehicle facing a circular green signal may proceed straight or turn right or left unless a sign prohibits the turn. The operator shall yield the right-of-way to other vehicles and to pedestrians lawfully in the intersection or an adjacent crosswalk when the signal is exhibited.
(c) An operator of a vehicle facing a green arrow signal, displayed alone or with another signal, may cautiously enter the intersection to move in the direction permitted by the arrow or other indication shown simultaneously. The operator shall yield the right-of-way to a pedestrian lawfully in an adjacent crosswalk and other traffic lawfully using the intersection.
(d) An operator of a vehicle facing only a steady red signal shall stop at a clearly marked stop line. In the absence of a stop line, the operator shall stop before entering the crosswalk on the near side of the intersection. A vehicle that is not turning shall remain standing until an indication to proceed is shown. After stopping, standing until the intersection may be entered safely, and yielding right-of-way to pedestrians lawfully in an adjacent crosswalk and other traffic lawfully using the intersection, the operator may:
(1) turn right; or
(2) turn left, if the intersecting streets are both one-way streets and a left turn is permissible.
(e) An operator of a vehicle facing a steady yellow signal is warned by that signal that:
(1) movement authorized by a green signal is being terminated; or
(2) a red signal is to be given.
(f) The Texas Transportation Commission, a municipal authority, or the commissioners court of a county may prohibit within the entity's jurisdiction a turn by an operator of a vehicle facing a steady red signal by posting notice at the intersection that the turn is prohibited.
(g) This section applies to an official traffic-control signal placed and maintained at a place other than an intersection, except for a provision that by its nature cannot apply. A required stop shall be made at a sign or marking on the pavement indicating where the stop shall be made. In the absence of such a sign or marking, the stop shall be made at the signal.
(h) The obligations imposed by this section apply to an operator of a streetcar in the same manner they apply to the operator of a vehicle.
*(Added by L.1995, chap. 165(1), eff. 9/1/95.)*

### §544.008. Flashing signals.

(a) The operator of a vehicle facing a flashing red signal shall stop at a clearly marked stop line. In the absence of a stop line, the operator shall stop before entering the crosswalk on the near side of the intersection. In the absence of a crosswalk, the operator shall stop at the place nearest the intersecting roadway where the operator has a view of approaching traffic on the intersecting roadway. The right to proceed is subject to the rules applicable after stopping at a stop sign.

(b) The operator of a vehicle facing a flashing yellow signal may proceed through an intersection or past the signal only with caution.

(c) This section does not apply at a railroad crossing.
*(Added by L.1995, chap. 165(1), eff. 9/1/95.)*

### §544.009. Lane-direction-control signals.

If a lane-direction-control signal is placed over an individual lane of a highway, a vehicle may travel in a lane over which a green signal is shown but may not enter or travel in a lane over which a red signal is shown. *(Added by L.1995, chap. 165(1), eff. 9/1/95.)*



### §544.010. Stop signs and yield signs.

(a) Unless directed to proceed by a police officer or traffic-control signal, the operator of a vehicle or streetcar approaching an intersection with a stop sign shall stop as provided by Subsection (c).

(b) If safety requires, the operator of a vehicle approaching a yield sign shall stop as provided by Subsection (c).

(c) An operator required to stop by this section shall stop before entering the crosswalk on the near side of the intersection. In the absence of a crosswalk, the operator shall stop at a clearly marked stop line. In the absence of a stop line, the operator shall stop at the place nearest the intersecting roadway where the operator has a view of approaching traffic on the intersecting roadway.
*(Added by L.1995, chap. 165(1), eff. 9/1/95.)*

### §544.011. Lane use signs.

If, on a highway having more than one lane with vehicles traveling in the same direction, the Texas Department of Transportation or a local authority places a sign that directs slower traffic to travel in a lane other than the farthest left lane, the sign must read "left lane for passing only."
*(Added by L.1997, chap. 628(1); chgd. by L.1999, chap. 62(17.08), eff. 9/1/99.)*

# CHAPTER 545. OPERATION AND MOVEMENT OF VEHICLES

## SUBCHAPTER A. GENERAL PROVISIONS

Section


## SUBCHAPTER B. DRIVING ON RIGHT SIDE OF ROADWAY AND PASSING

## SUBCHAPTER C. TURNING AND SIGNALS FOR STOPPING AND TURNING





Zt

## SUBCHAPTER D. RIGHT-OF-WAY



## SUBCHAPTER E. STREETCARS



## SUBCHAPTER F. SPECIAL STOPS AND SPEED RESTRICTIONS



## SUBCHAPTER G. STOPPING, STANDING, AND PARKING

## SUBCHAPTER H. SPEED RESTRICTIONS





## SUBCHAPTER I. MISCELLANEOUS RULES



## SUBCHAPTER A. GENERAL PROVISIONS

### §545.001. Definition.

In this chapter, "pass" or "passing" used in reference to a vehicle means to overtake and proceed past another vehicle moving in the same direction as the passing vehicle or to attempt that maneuver. *(Added by L.1995, chap. 165(1), eff. 9/1/95.)*

### §545.002. Operator.

In this chapter, a reference to an operator includes a reference to the vehicle operated by the operator if the reference imposes a duty or provides a limitation on the movement or other operation of that vehicle. *(Added by L.1995, chap. 165(1), eff. 9/1/95.)*

### §§545.003 to 545.050. *(Reserved.)*

## SUBCHAPTER B. DRIVING ON RIGHT SIDE OF ROADWAY AND PASSING

### §545.051. Driving on right side of roadway.

(a) An operator on a roadway of sufficient width shall drive on the right half of the roadway, unless:

(1) the operator is passing another vehicle;

(2) an obstruction necessitates moving the vehicle left of the center of the roadway and the operator yields the right-of-way to a vehicle that:

(A) is moving in the proper direction on the unobstructed portion of the roadway; and

(B) is an immediate hazard;

(3) the operator is on a roadway divided into three marked lanes for traffic; or

(4) the operator is on a roadway restricted to one-way traffic.

(b) An operator of a vehicle on a roadway moving more slowly than the normal speed of other vehicles at the time and place under the existing conditions shall drive in the right-hand lane available for vehicles, or as close as practicable to the right-hand curb or edge of the roadway, unless the operator is:

(1) passing another vehicle; or

(2) preparing for a left turn at an intersection or into a private road or driveway.

(c) An operator on a roadway having four or more lanes for moving vehicles and providing for two-way movement of vehicles may not drive left of the center line of the roadway except:

(1) as authorized by an official traffic-control device designating a specified lane to the left side of the center of the roadway for use by a vehicle not otherwise permitted to use the lane;

(2) under the conditions described by Subsection (a)(2); or

(3) in crossing the center line to make a left turn into or out of an alley, private road, or driveway.

*(Added by L.1995, chap. 165(1), eff. 9/1/95.)*



### §545.052. Driving past vehicle moving in opposite direction.

An operator moving in the opposite direction of the movement of another operator shall:

(1) move to or remain to the right; and

(2) on a roadway wide enough for not more than one line of vehicle movement in each direction, give the other operator:

(A) at least one-half of the main traveled portion of the roadway; or

(B) if complying with Paragraph (A) is not possible, as much of the roadway as possible.

*(Added by L.1995, chap. 165(1), eff. 9/1/95.)*

### §545.053. Passing to the left; return; being passed.

(a) An operator passing another vehicle:

(1) shall pass to the left of the other vehicle at a safe distance; and

(2) may not move back to the right side of the roadway until safely clear of the passed vehicle.

(b) An operator being passed by another vehicle:

(1) shall, on audible signal, move or remain to the right in favor of the passing vehicle; and

(2) may not accelerate until completely passed by the passing vehicle.

(c) Subsection (b) does not apply when passing to the right is permitted.

*(Added by L.1995, chap. 165(1), eff. 9/1/95.)*

### §545.054. Passing to the left: safe distance.

(a) An operator may not drive on the left side of the center of the roadway in passing another vehicle unless:

(1) driving on the left side of the center of the roadway is authorized by this subtitle; and

(2) the left side is clearly visible and free of approaching traffic for a distance sufficient to permit passing without interfering with the operation of the passed vehicle or a vehicle approaching from the opposite direction.

(b) An operator passing another vehicle shall return to an authorized lane of travel:

(1) before coming within 200 feet of an approaching vehicle, if a lane authorized for vehicles approaching from the opposite direction is used in passing; or otherwise

(2) as soon as practicable.

*(Added by L.1995, chap. 165(1), eff. 9/1/95.)*

### §545.055. Passing to the left: passing zones.

(a) An operator shall obey the directions of a sign or marking in Subsection (c) or (d) if the sign or marking is in place and clearly visible to an ordinarily observant person.

(b) An operator may not drive on the left side of the roadway in a no-passing zone or on the left side of any pavement striping designed to mark a no-passing zone. This subsection does not prohibit a driver from crossing pavement striping, or the center line in a no-passing zone marked by signs only, to make a left turn into or out of an alley or private road or driveway.

(c) The Texas Transportation Commission, on a state highway under the jurisdiction of the commission, may:

(1) determine those portions of the highway where passing or driving to the left of the roadway would be especially hazardous; and

(2) show the beginning and end of each no-passing zone by appropriate signs or markings on the roadway.

(d) A local authority, on a highway under the jurisdiction of the local authority, may:

(1) determine those portions of the highway where passing or driving to the left of the roadway would be especially hazardous; and

(2) show the beginning and end of each no-passing zone by appropriate signs or markings on the roadway.

*(Added by L.1995, chap. 165(1), eff. 9/1/95.)*



### §545.056. Driving to left of center of roadway: limitations other than passing.

(a) An operator may not drive to the left side of the roadway if the operator is:

(1) approaching within 100 feet of an intersection or railroad grade crossing in a municipality;

(2) approaching within 100 feet of an intersection or railroad grade crossing outside a municipality and the intersection or crossing is shown by a sign or marking in accordance with Section 545.055;

(3) approaching within 100 feet of a bridge, viaduct, or tunnel; or

(4) awaiting access to a ferry operated by the Texas Transportation Commission.

(b) The limitations in Subsection (a) do not apply:

(1) on a one-way roadway; or

(2) to an operator turning left into or from an alley or private road or driveway.

(c) The Texas Transportation Commission shall post signs along the approach to a ferry operated by the commission notifying operators that passing is prohibited if there is a standing line of vehicles awaiting access to the ferry.

*(Added by L.1995, chap. 165(1), eff. 9/1/95.)*

### §545.057. Passing to the right.

(a) An operator may pass to the right of another vehicle only if conditions permit safely passing to the right and:

(1) the vehicle being passed is making or about to make a left turn; and

(2) the operator is:

(A) on a highway having unobstructed pavement not occupied by parked vehicles and sufficient width for two or more lines of moving vehicles in each direction; or

(B) on a one-way street or on a roadway having traffic restricted to one direction of movement and the roadway is free from obstructions and wide enough for two or more lines of moving vehicles.

(b) An operator may not pass to the right by leaving the main traveled portion of a roadway except as provided by Section 545.058.

*(Added by L.1995, chap. 165(1), eff. 9/1/95.)*

### §545.058. Driving on improved shoulder.

(a) An operator may drive on an improved shoulder to the right of the main traveled portion of a roadway if that operation is necessary and may be done safely, but only:

(1) to stop, stand, or park;

(2) to accelerate before entering the main traveled lane of traffic;

(3) to decelerate before making a right turn;

(4) to pass another vehicle that is slowing or stopped on the main traveled portion of the highway, disabled, or preparing to make a left turn;

(5) to allow another vehicle traveling faster to pass;

(6) as permitted or required by an official traffic-control device; or

(7) to avoid a collision.

(b) An operator may drive on an improved shoulder to the left of the main traveled portion of a divided or limited-access or controlled-access highway if that operation may be done safely, but only:

(1) to slow or stop when the vehicle is disabled and traffic or other circumstances prohibit the safe movement of the vehicle to the shoulder to the right of the main traveled portion of the roadway;

(2) as permitted or required by an official traffic-control device; or

(3) to avoid a collision.

(c) A limitation in this section on driving on an improved shoulder does not apply to:

(1) an authorized emergency vehicle responding to a call;

(2) a police patrol; or

(3) a bicycle.

*(Added by L.1995, chap. 165(1), eff. 9/1/95.)*

### §545.059. One-way roadways and rotary traffic islands.

(a) The Texas Transportation Commission may designate a highway or separate roadway under the jurisdiction of the commission for one-way traffic and shall erect appropriate signs giving notice of the designation.

(b) On a roadway that is designated and on which signs are erected for one-way traffic, an operator shall drive only in the direction indicated.

(c) An operator moving around a rotary traffic island shall drive only to the right of the island.

*(Added by L.1995, chap. 165(1), eff. 9/1/95.)*

### §545.060. Driving on roadway laned for traffic.

(a) An operator on a roadway divided into two or more clearly marked lanes for traffic:

(1) shall drive as nearly as practical entirely within a single lane; and

(2) may not move from the lane unless that movement can be made safely.

(b) If a roadway is divided into three lanes and provides for two-way movement of traffic, an operator on the roadway may not drive in the center lane except:

(1) if passing another vehicle and the center lane is clear of traffic within a safe distance;

(2) in preparing to make a left turn; or

(3) where the center lane is designated by an official traffic-control device for movement in the direction in which the operator is moving.

(c) Without regard to the center of the roadway, an official traffic-control device may be erected directing slow-moving traffic to use a designated lane or designating lanes to be used by traffic moving in a particular direction.

(d) Official traffic-control devices prohibiting the changing of lanes on sections of roadway may be installed.

*(Added by L.1995, chap. 165(1), eff. 9/1/95.)*

### §545.061. Driving on multiple-lane roadway.

On a roadway divided into three or more lanes and providing for one-way movement of traffic, an operator entering a lane of traffic from a lane to the right shall yield the right-of-way to a vehicle entering the same lane of traffic from a lane to the left. *(Added by L.1995, chap. 165(1), eff. 9/1/95.)*

### §545.062. Following distance.

(a) An operator shall, if following another vehicle, maintain an assured clear distance between the two vehicles so that, considering the speed of the vehicles, traffic, and the conditions of the highway, the operator can safely stop without colliding with the preceding vehicle or veering into another vehicle, object, or person on or near the highway.

(b) An operator of a truck or of a motor vehicle drawing another vehicle who is on a roadway outside a business or residential district and who is following another truck or motor vehicle drawing another vehicle shall, if conditions permit, leave sufficient space between the vehicles so that a vehicle passing the operator can safely enter and occupy the space. This subsection does not prohibit a truck or a motor vehicle drawing another vehicle from passing another vehicle.

(c) An operator on a roadway outside a business or residential district driving in a caravan of other vehicles or a motorcade shall allow sufficient space between the operator and the vehicle preceding the operator so that another vehicle can safely enter and occupy the space. This subsection does not apply to a funeral procession.
*(Added by L.1995, chap. 165(1), eff. 9/1/95.)*

## §545.063. Driving on divided highway.

(a) On a highway having two or more roadways separated by a space, physical barrier, or clearly indicated dividing section constructed to impede vehicular traffic, an operator shall drive on the right roadway unless directed or permitted to use another roadway by an official traffic-control device or police officer.

(b) An operator may not drive over, across, or in a dividing space, physical barrier, or section constructed to impede vehicular traffic except:

(1) through an opening in the physical barrier or dividing section or space; or

(2) at a crossover or intersection established by a public authority.
*(Added by L.1995, chap. 165(1), eff. 9/1/95.)*



## §545.064. Restricted access.

An operator may not drive on or from a limited-access or controlled-access roadway except at an entrance or exit that is established by a public authority. *(Added by L.1995, chap. 165(1), eff. 9/1/95.)*

## §545.065. State and local regulation of limited-access or controlled-access highways.

(a) The Texas Transportation Commission by resolution or order recorded in its minutes may prohibit the use of a limited-access or controlled-access highway under the jurisdiction of the commission by a parade, funeral procession, pedestrian, bicycle, motor-driven cycle, or nonmotorized traffic.

(b) If the commission adopts a rule under Subsection (a), the commission shall erect and maintain official traffic-control devices on the portions of the limited-access or controlled-access highway to which the rule applies.

(c) A local authority by ordinance may prohibit the use of a limited-access or controlled-access roadway under the jurisdiction of the authority by a parade, funeral procession, pedestrian, bicycle, motor-driven cycle, or nonmotorized traffic.

(d) If a local authority adopts an ordinance under Subsection (c), the authority shall erect and maintain official traffic-control devices on the portions of the limited-access or controlled-access roadway to which the ordinance applies.
*(Added by L.1995, chap. 165(1), eff. 9/1/95.)*

## §545.0651. Municipal restriction on use of highway.

(a) In this section:

(1) "Department" means the Texas Department of Transportation.

(2) "Highway" means a public roadway that:

(A) is in the designated state highway system;

(B) is designated a controlled access facility; and

(C) has a minimum of three travel lanes, excluding access or frontage roads, in each direction of traffic.

(b) A municipality by ordinance may restrict, by class of vehicle, through traffic to two designated lanes of a highway in the municipality.

(c) An ordinance under Subsection (b) must:

(1) be in effect only during peak traffic hours of a workday; and

(2) allow a restricted vehicle to use any lane of the highway to pass another vehicle and to enter and exit the highway.

(d) Before adopting an ordinance under this section, the municipality shall submit to the department a description of the proposed restriction. The municipality may not enforce the restrictions unless:

(1) the department's executive director or the executive director's designee has approved the restrictions; and

(2) the appropriate traffic control devices are in place.

(e) Department approval under Subsection (d) must:

(1) be based on a traffic study performed by the department to evaluate the effect of the proposed restriction; and

(2) to the greatest extent practicable, ensure a systems approach to preclude the designation of inconsistent lane restrictions among adjacent municipalities.

(f) The department's executive director or the executive director's designee may suspend or rescind approval under this section for one or more of the following reasons:

(1) a change in pavement conditions;

(2) a change in traffic conditions;

(3) a geometric change in roadway configuration;

(4) construction or maintenance activity; or

(5) emergency or incident management.

(g) The department shall erect and maintain official traffic control devices necessary to implement and enforce an ordinance adopted and approved under this section.

*(Added by L.1997, chap. 384(1), eff. 5/28/97.)*

### §545.066. Passing a school bus; offense.

(a) An operator on a highway, when approaching from either direction a school bus stopped on the highway to receive or discharge a student:

(1) shall stop before reaching the school bus when the bus is operating a visual signal as required by Section 547.701; and

(2) may not proceed until:

(A) the school bus resumes motion;

(B) the operator is signaled by the bus driver to proceed; or

(C) the visual signal is no longer actuated.

(b) An operator on a highway having separate roadways is not required to stop:

(1) for a school bus that is on a different roadway; or

(2) if on a controlled-access highway, for a school bus that is stopped:

(A) in a loading zone that is a part of or adjacent to the highway; and

(B) where pedestrians are not permitted to cross the roadway.

(c) An offense under this section is a misdemeanor punishable by a fine of not less than $200 or more than $1,000.

(d) The court may order that the driver's license of a person convicted of a second or subsequent offense under this section be suspended for not longer than six months beginning on the date of conviction. In this subsection, "driver's license" has the meaning assigned by Chapter 521.

(e) If a person does not pay the previously assessed fine or costs on a conviction under this section, or is determined by the court to have insufficient resources or income to pay a fine or costs on a conviction under this section, the court may order the person to perform community service. The court shall set the number of hours of service under this subsection.

(f) For the purposes of this section:

(1) a highway is considered to have separate roadways only if the highway has roadways separated by an intervening space on which operation of vehicles is not permitted, a physical barrier, or a clearly indicated dividing section constructed to impede vehicular traffic; and

(2) a highway is not considered to have separate roadways if the highway has roadways separated only by a left turn lane.

*(Added by L.1995, chap. 165(1); chgd. by L.1997, chap. 1438(9), eff. 9/1/97.)*

### §§545.067 to 545.100. *(Reserved.)*

## SUBCHAPTER C. TURNING AND SIGNALS FOR STOPPING AND TURNING

### §545.101. Turning at intersection.

(a) To make a right turn at an intersection, an operator shall make both the approach and the turn as closely as practicable to the right-hand curb or edge of the roadway.

(b) To make a left turn at an intersection, an operator shall:

(1) approach the intersection in the extreme left-hand lane lawfully available to a vehicle moving in the direction of the vehicle; and

(2) after entering the intersection, turn left, leaving the intersection so as to arrive in a lane lawfully available to traffic moving in the direction of the vehicle on the roadway being entered.

(c) On a street or roadway designated for two-way traffic, the operator turning left shall, to the extent practicable, turn in the portion of the intersection to the left of the center of the intersection.

(d) To turn left, an operator who is approaching an intersection having a roadway designated for one-way traffic and for which signs are posted from a roadway designated for one-way traffic and for which signs are posted shall make the turn as closely as practicable to the left-hand curb or edge of the roadway.

(e) The Texas Transportation Commission or a local authority, with respect to a highway in its jurisdiction, may:

(1) authorize the placement of an official traffic-control device in or adjacent to an intersection; and

(2) require a course different from that specified in this section for movement by vehicles turning at an intersection.

*(Added by L.1995, chap. 165(1), eff. 9/1/95.)*

### §545.102. Turning on curve or crest of grade.

An operator may not turn the vehicle to move in the opposite direction when approaching a curve or the crest of a grade if the vehicle is not visible to the operator of another vehicle approaching from either direction within 500 feet. *(Added by L.1995, chap. 165(1), eff. 9/1/95.)*



### §545.103. Safely turning.

An operator may not turn the vehicle to enter a private road or driveway, otherwise turn the vehicle from a direct course, or move right or left on a roadway unless movement can be made safely. *(Added by L.1995, chap. 165(1), eff. 9/1/95.)*

### §545.104. Signaling turns; use of turn signals.

(a) An operator shall use the signal authorized by Section 545.106 to indicate an intention to turn, change lanes, or start from a parked position.

(b) An operator intending to turn a vehicle right or left shall signal continuously for not less than the last 100 feet of movement of the vehicle before the turn.

(c) An operator may not light the signals on only one side of the vehicle on a parked or disabled vehicle or use the signals as a courtesy or "do pass" signal to the operator of another vehicle approaching from the rear.

*(Added by L.1995, chap. 165(1), eff. 9/1/95.)*

### §545.105. Signaling stops.

An operator may not stop or suddenly decrease the speed of the vehicle without first giving a stop signal as provided by this subchapter to the operator of a vehicle immediately to the rear when there is an opportunity to give the signal. *(Added by L.1995, chap. 165(1), eff. 9/1/95.)*

### §545.106. Signals by hand and arm or by signal lamp.

(a) Except as provided by Subsection (b), an operator required to give a stop or turn signal shall do so by:

(1) using the hand and arm; or

(2) lighting signal lamps approved by the department.

(b) A motor vehicle in use on a highway shall be equipped with signal lamps, and the required signal shall be given by lighting the lamps, if:

(1) the distance from the center of the top of the steering post to the left outside limit of the body, cab, or load of the motor vehicle is more than two feet; or

(2) the distance from the center of the top of the steering post to the rear limit of the body or load, including the body or load of a combination of vehicles, is more than 14 feet.

*(Added by L.1995, chap. 165(1), eff. 9/1/95.)*

### §545.107. Method of giving hand and arm signals.

An operator who is permitted to give a hand and arm signal shall give the signal from the left side of the vehicle as follows:

(1) to make a left turn signal, extend hand and arm horizontally;

(2) to make a right turn signal, extend hand and arm upward, except that a bicycle operator may signal from the right side of the vehicle with the hand and arm extended horizontally; and

(3) to stop or decrease speed, extend hand and arm downward.

*(Added by L.1995, chap. 165(1), eff. 9/1/95.)*

### §§545.108 to 545.150. *(Reserved.)*

## SUBCHAPTER D. RIGHT-OF-WAY

### §545.151. Vehicle approaching or entering intersection.

(a) An operator approaching an intersection:

(1) shall stop, yield, and grant immediate use of the intersection in obedience to an official traffic-control device, including a stop sign or yield right-of-way sign; and

(2) after stopping, may proceed when the intersection can be safely entered without interference or collision with traffic using a different street or roadway.

(b) An operator on a single-lane or two-lane street or roadway who approaches an intersection that is not controlled by an official traffic-control device and that is located on a divided highway or on a street or roadway divided into three or more marked traffic lanes:

(1) shall stop, yield, and grant immediate use of the intersection to a vehicle on the other street or roadway that is within the intersection or approaching the intersection in such proximity as to be a hazard; and

(2) after stopping, may proceed when the intersection can be safely entered without interference or collision with traffic using a different street or roadway.

(c) An operator on an unpaved street or roadway approaching an intersection of a paved street or roadway:

(1) shall stop, yield, and grant immediate use of the intersection to a vehicle on the paved street or roadway that is within the intersection or approaching the intersection in such proximity as to be a hazard; and

(2) after stopping, may proceed when the intersection can be safely entered without interference or collision with traffic using the paved street or roadway.

(d) Except as provided in Subsection (e), an operator approaching an intersection of a street or roadway that is not controlled by an official traffic-control device:

(1) shall stop, yield, and grant immediate use of the intersection to a vehicle that has entered the intersection from the operator's right or is approaching the intersection from the operator's right in a proximity that is a hazard; and

(2) after stopping, may proceed when the intersection can be safely entered without interference or collision with traffic using a different street or roadway.

(e) An operator approaching an intersection of a street or roadway from a street or roadway that terminates at the intersection and that is not controlled by an official traffic-control device or controlled as provided by Subsection (b) or (c):

(1) shall stop, yield, and grant immediate use of the intersection to another vehicle that has entered the intersection from the other street or roadway or is approaching the intersection on the other street or roadway in a proximity that is a hazard; and

(2) after stopping, may proceed when the intersection can be safely entered without interference or collision with the traffic using the other street or roadway.

(f) An operator who is required by this section to stop and yield the right-of-way at an intersection to another vehicle and who is involved in a collision or interferes with other traffic at the intersection to whom right-of-way is to be given is presumed not to have yielded the right-of-way. *(Added by L.1995, chap. 165(1), eff. 9/1/95.)*



### §545.152. Vehicle turning left.

To turn left at an intersection or into an alley or private road or driveway, an operator shall yield the right-of-way to a vehicle that is approaching from the opposite direction and that is in the intersection or in such proximity to the intersection as to be an immediate hazard. *(Added by L.1995, chap. 165(1), eff. 9/1/95.)*

### §545.153. Vehicle entering stop or yield intersection.

(a) Preferential right-of-way at an intersection may be indicated by a stop sign or yield sign as authorized in Section 544.003.

(b) Unless directed to proceed by a police officer or official traffic-control device, an operator approaching an intersection on a roadway controlled by a stop sign, after stopping as required by Section 544.010, shall yield the right-of-way to a vehicle that has entered the intersection from another highway or that is approaching so closely as to be an immediate hazard to the operator's movement in or across the intersection.

(c) An operator approaching an intersection on a roadway controlled by a yield sign shall:

(1) slow to a speed that is reasonable under the existing conditions; and

(2) yield the right-of-way to a vehicle in the intersection or approaching on another highway so closely as to be an immediate hazard to the operator's movement in or across the intersection.

(d) If an operator is required by Subsection (c) to yield and is involved in a collision with a vehicle in an intersection after the operator drove past a yield sign without stopping, the collision is prima facie evidence that the operator failed to yield the right-of-way.
*(Added by L.1995, chap. 165(1), eff. 9/1/95.)*

### §545.154. Vehicle entering or leaving limited-access or controlled-access highway.

An operator on an access or feeder road of a limited-access or controlled-access highway shall yield the right-of-way to a vehicle entering or about to enter the access or feeder road from the highway or leaving or about to leave the access or feeder road to enter the highway. *(Added by L.1995, chap. 165(1), eff. 9/1/95.)*

### §545.155. Vehicle entering highway from private road or driveway.

An operator about to enter or cross a highway from an alley, building, or private road or driveway shall yield the right-of-way to a vehicle approaching on the highway to be entered. *(Added by L.1995, chap. 165(1), eff. 9/1/95.)*



### §545.156. Vehicle approached by authorized emergency vehicle.

(a) On the immediate approach of an authorized emergency vehicle using audible and visual signals that meet the requirements of Sections 547.305 and 547.702, or of a police vehicle lawfully using only an audible signal, an operator, unless otherwise directed by a police officer, shall:

(1) yield the right-of-way;

(2) immediately drive to a position parallel to and as close as possible to the right-hand edge or curb of the roadway clear of any intersection; and

(3) stop and remain standing until the authorized emergency vehicle has passed.

(b) This section does not exempt the operator of an authorized emergency vehicle from the duty to drive with due regard for the safety of all persons using the highway.
*(Added by L.1995, chap. 165(1), eff. 9/1/95.)*

### §§545.157 to 545.200. *(Reserved.)*

## SUBCHAPTER E. STREETCARS

### §545.201. Passing streetcar to left.

(a) An operator may not pass to the left or drive on the left side of a streetcar moving in the same direction, even if the streetcar is temporarily at rest, unless the operator:

(1) is directed to do so by a police officer;

(2) is on a one-way street; or

(3) is on a street on which the location of the tracks prevents compliance with this section.

(b) An operator when lawfully passing to the left of a streetcar that has stopped to receive or discharge a passenger:

(1) shall reduce speed;

(2) may proceed only on exercising due caution for pedestrians; and

(3) shall accord a pedestrian the right-of-way as required by this subtitle.
*(Added by L.1995, chap. 165(1), eff. 9/1/95.)*

### §545.202. Passing streetcar to right.

(a) An operator passing to the right of a streetcar stopped or about to stop to receive or discharge a passenger shall:

(1) stop the vehicle at least five feet to the rear of the nearest running board or door of the streetcar; and

(2) remain standing until all passengers have entered the streetcar or, on leaving, have reached a place of safety.

(b) An operator is not required to stop before passing a streetcar to the right if a safety zone has been established and may proceed past the streetcar at a reasonable speed and with due caution for the safety of pedestrians.
*(Added by L.1995, chap. 165(1), eff. 9/1/95.)*

### §545.203. Driving on streetcar tracks.

(a) An operator on a streetcar track in front of a streetcar shall move the operator's vehicle off the track as soon as possible after a signal from the operator of the streetcar.

(b) An operator may not drive on or cross a streetcar track in an intersection in front of a streetcar crossing the intersection.

(c) An operator who is passing a streetcar may not turn in front of the streetcar so as to interfere with or impede its movement.
*(Added by L.1995, chap. 165(1), eff. 9/1/95.)*

### §545.204. Streetcar approached by authorized emergency vehicle.

(a) On the immediate approach of an authorized emergency vehicle using audible and visual signals that meet the requirements of Sections 547.305 and 547.702, or of a police vehicle lawfully using only an audible signal, the operator of a streetcar shall immediately stop the streetcar clear of any intersection and remain there until the authorized emergency vehicle has passed, unless otherwise directed by a police officer.

(b) This section does not exempt the operator of an authorized emergency vehicle from the duty to drive with due regard for the safety of all persons using the highway.
*(Added by L.1995, chap. 165(1), eff. 9/1/95.)*

### §545.205. Crossing fire hose.

An operator of a streetcar may not, without the consent of the fire department official in command, drive over an unprotected hose of a fire department when the hose is on a streetcar track and intended for use at a fire or alarm of fire. *(Added by L.1995, chap. 165(1), eff. 9/1/95.)*

### §545.206. Obstruction of operator's view or driving mechanism.

A passenger in a streetcar may not ride in a position that interferes with the operator's view ahead or to the side or with control over the driving mechanism of the streetcar. *(Added by L.1995, chap. 165(1), eff. 9/1/95.)*

### §§545.207 to 545.250. *(Reserved.)*

## SUBCHAPTER F. SPECIAL STOPS AND SPEED RESTRICTIONS

### §545.251. Obedience to signal indicating approach of train.

(a) An operator approaching a railroad grade crossing shall stop not closer than 15 feet or farther than 50 feet from the nearest rail if:

(1) a clearly visible railroad signal warns of the approach of a train;

(2) a crossing gate is lowered, or a flagger warns of the approach or passage of a railroad train;

(3) a railroad engine approaching within approximately 1,500 feet of the highway crossing emits a signal audible from that distance and the engine is an immediate hazard because of its speed or proximity to the crossing;

(4) an approaching railroad train is plainly visible to the operator and is in hazardous proximity to the crossing; or

(5) the operator is required to stop by:

(A) other law;

(B) a rule adopted under a statute;

(C) an official traffic-control device; or

(D) a traffic-control signal.

(b) An operator of a vehicle required by Subsection (a) to stop shall remain stopped until permitted to proceed and may not proceed until it is safe to do so. *(Chgd. by L.1997, chap. 165(30.107(a)), eff. 9/1/97. See other subsection (b) below.)*

(b) An operator of a vehicle required by Subsection (a) to stop shall remain stopped until it is safe to proceed. *(Chgd. by L.1997, chap. 1097(1), eff. 9/1/97. See other subsection (b) above.)*

(c) An operator commits an offense if the operator drives around, under, or through a crossing gate or a barrier at a railroad crossing while the gate or barrier is closed, being closed, or being opened. *(Chgd. by L.1997, chap. 165(30.107(a)), eff. 9/1/97. See other subsection (c) below.)*

(c) An operator of a vehicle who approaches a railroad grade crossing equipped with railroad crossbuck signs without automatic, electric, or mechanical signal devices, crossing gates, or a flagger warning of the approach or passage of a train shall yield the right-of-way to a train in hazardous proximity to the crossing, and proceed at a speed that is reasonable for the existing conditions. If required for safety, the operator shall stop at a clearly marked stop line before the grade crossing or, if no stop line exists, not closer than 15 feet or farther than 50 feet from the nearest rail. *(Chgd. by L.1997, chap. 1097(1), eff. 9/1/97. See other subsection (c) above.)*

(d) In a prosecution under Subsection (a)(4), proof that at the time of the offense a railroad train was approaching the grade crossing and that the train was visible from the crossing is prima facie evidence that it was not safe for the operator to proceed. *(Chgd. by L.1997, chap. 165(30.107(a)), eff. 9/1/97. See other subsection (d) below.)*

(d) An operator commits an offense if the operator drives around, under, or through a crossing gate or a barrier at a railroad crossing while the gate or barrier is closed, being closed, or being opened. *(Chgd. by L.1997, chap. 1097(1), eff. 9/1/97. See other subsection (d) above.)*

(e) In a prosecution under this section, proof that at the time of the offense a train was in hazardous proximity to the crossing and that the train was plainly visible to the operator is prima facie evidence that it was not safe for the operator to proceed. *(Chgd. by L.1997, chap. 1097(1), eff. 9/1/97.)*

(f) An offense under this section is punishable by a fine of not less than $50 or more than $200.

*(Added by L.1995, chap. 165(1); chgd. by L.1997, chaps. 165(30.107(a)), 1097(1), eff. 9/1/97.)*

## §545.252. All vehicles to stop at certain railroad grade crossings.

(a) The Texas Department of Transportation or a local authority, with respect to a highway in its jurisdiction, may:

(1) designate a railroad grade crossing as particularly dangerous; and

(2) erect a stop sign or other official traffic-control device at the grade crossing.

(b) An operator approaching a stop sign or other official traffic-control device that requires a stop and that is erected under Subsection (a) shall stop not closer than 15 feet or farther than 50 feet from the nearest rail of the railroad and may proceed only with due care.

(c) The costs of installing and maintaining a mechanically operated grade crossing safety device, gate, sign, or signal erected under this section shall be apportioned and paid on the same percentage ratio and in the same proportionate amounts by this state and all participating political subdivisions of this state as costs are apportioned and paid between the state and the United States.

(d) An offense under this section is punishable by a fine of not less than $50 or more than $200.

*(Added by L.1995, chap. 165(1); chgd. by L.1997, chap. 165(30.107(b)), eff. 9/1/97.)*

## §545.253. Buses to stop at all railroad grade crossings.

(a) Except as provided by Subsection (c), the operator of a motor bus carrying passengers for hire, before crossing a railroad grade crossing:

(1) shall stop the vehicle not closer than 15 feet or farther than 50 feet from the nearest rail of the railroad;

(2) while stopped, shall listen and look in both directions along the track for an approaching train and signals indicating the approach of a train; and

(3) may not proceed until it is safe to do so.

(b) After stopping as required by Subsection (a), an operator described by Subsection (a) shall proceed without manually shifting gears while crossing the track.

(c) A vehicle is not required to stop at the crossing if a police officer or a traffic-control signal directs traffic to proceed.

(d) This section does not apply at a railway grade crossing in a business or residence district.

(e) An offense under this section is punishable by a fine of not less than $50 or more than $200.

*(Added by L.1995, chap. 165(1); chgd. by L.1997, chaps. 165(30.107(c)), 1061(15), 1438(10), eff. 9/1/97.)*

## §545.2535. School buses to stop at all railroad grade crossings.

(a) Except as provided by Subsection (c), the operator of a school bus, before crossing a track at a railroad grade crossing:

(1) shall stop the vehicle not closer than 15 feet or farther than 50 feet from the track;

(2) while stopped, shall listen and look in both directions along the track for an approaching train and signals indicating the approach of a train; and

(3) may not proceed until it is safe to do so.

(b) After stopping as required by Subsection (a), the operator may proceed in a gear that permits the vehicle to complete the crossing without a change of gears. The operator may not shift gears while crossing the track.

(c) An operator is not required to stop at:

(1) an abandoned railroad grade crossing that is marked with a sign reading "tracks out of service"; or

(2) an industrial or spur line railroad grade crossing that is marked with a sign reading "exempt."

(d) A sign under Subsection (c) may be erected only by or with the consent of the appropriate state or local governmental official.
*(Added by L.1997, chaps. 1061(16), 1438(11), eff. 9/1/97.)*

## §545.254. Vehicles carrying explosive substances or flammable liquids.

(a) Before crossing a railroad grade crossing, an operator of a vehicle that has an explosive substance or flammable liquid as the vehicle's principal cargo and that is moving at a speed of more than 20 miles per hour:

(1) shall reduce the speed of the vehicle to 20 miles per hour or less before coming within 200 feet of the nearest rail of the railroad;

(2) shall listen and look in both directions along the track for an approaching train and for signals indicating the approach of a train; and

(3) may not proceed until the operator determines that the course is clear.

(b) The operator of a vehicle that has an explosive substance or flammable liquid as the vehicle's principal cargo, before crossing a railroad grade crossing on a highway in a municipality:

(1) shall stop the vehicle not closer than 15 feet or farther than 50 feet from the nearest rail of the railroad;

(2) while stopped, shall listen and look in both directions along the track for an approaching train and for signals indicating the approach of a train; and

(3) may not proceed until the operator determines that the course is clear.

(c) Subsections (a) and (b) do not apply:

(1) if a police officer, crossing flagger, or traffic-control signal directs traffic to proceed;

(2) where a railroad flashing signal is installed and does not indicate an approaching train;

(3) to an abandoned or exempted grade crossing that is clearly marked by or with the consent of the state, if the markings can be read from the operator's location;

(4) at a streetcar crossing in a business or residential district of a municipality; or

(5) to a railroad track used exclusively for industrial switching purposes in a business district.

(d) This section does not exempt the operator from compliance with Section 545.251 or 545.252.

(e) An offense under this section is punishable by a fine of not less than $50 or more than $200.
*(Added by L.1995, chap. 165(1); chgd. by L.1997, chap. 165(30.107(d)), eff. 9/1/97.)*

## §545.255. Moving heavy equipment at railroad grade crossings.

(a) This section applies only to:

(1) a crawler-type tractor, steam shovel, derrick, or roller; and

(2) any other equipment or structure with:

(A) a normal operating speed of 10 miles per hour or less; or

(B) a vertical body or load clearance of less than one-half inch per foot of the distance between two adjacent axles or less than nine inches measured above the level surface of a roadway.

(b) An operator of a vehicle or equipment may not move on or across a track at a railroad grade crossing unless the operator has given notice to a station agent of the railroad and given the railroad reasonable time to provide proper protection at the crossing.

(c) To move a vehicle or equipment on or across a track at a railroad grade crossing, the operator:

(1) shall stop the vehicle or equipment not closer than 15 feet or farther than 50 feet from the nearest rail of the railroad;

(2) while stopped, shall listen and look in both directions along the track for an approaching train and for signals indicating the approach of a train; and

(3) may not proceed until it is safe to cross the track.

(d) An operator of a vehicle or equipment may not cross a railroad grade crossing when warning of the immediate approach of a railroad car or train is given by automatic signal, crossing gates, a flagger, or otherwise. If a flagger is provided by the railroad, the operator shall move the vehicle or equipment over the crossing at the flagger's direction.

(e) An offense under this section is punishable by a fine of not less than $50 or more than $200.
*(Added by L.1995, chap. 165(1); chgd. by L.1997, chap. 165(30.107(e)), eff. 9/1/97.)*

## §545.2555. Report and investigation of certain railroad crossing violations.

(a) A person who on site observes a violation of Section 545.251, 545.252, 545.253, 545.254, or 545.255 may file a report of the violation if the person:

(1) is an on-engine employee of a railroad; and

(2) observes the violation while on a moving engine.

(b) A report under this section must:

(1) be made:

(A) on a form approved by the department; and

(B) not later than 72 hours after the violation;

(2) be filed with:

(A) an office of the department located in the county in which the violation occurred;

(B) the sheriff of the county in which the violation occurred, if the violation occurred in the unincorporated area of the county; or

(C) the police department of a municipality, if the violation occurred in the municipality; and

(3) contain, in addition, to any other required information:

(A) the date, time, and location of the violation;

(B) the license plate number and a description of the vehicle involved in the violation;

(C) a description of the operator of the vehicle involved in the violation; and

(D) the name, address, and telephone number of the person filing the report.

(c) A peace officer may:

(1) before the seventh day after the date a report under this section is filed, initiate an investigation of the alleged violation; and

(2) request the owner of the reported vehicle, as shown by the vehicle registration records of the Texas Department of Transportation, to disclose the name and address of the individual operating that vehicle at the time of the violation alleged in the report.

(d) Unless the owner of the reported vehicle believes that to provide the peace officer with the name and address of the individual operating the vehicle at the time of the violation alleged would incriminate the owner, the owner shall, to the best of the owner's ability, disclose that individual's name and address.

(e) An investigating peace officer who has probable cause to believe that a charge against an individual for a violation of Section 545.251, 545.252, 545.253, 545.254, or 545.255 is justified may:

(1) prepare a written notice to appear in court that complies with Sections 543.003, 543.006, and 543.007; and

(2) deliver the notice to the individual named in the notice in person or by certified mail.
*(Added by L.1997, chap. 165(30.108(a)), eff. 9/1/97.)*

### §545.256. Emerging from an alley, driveway, or building.

An operator emerging from an alley, driveway, or building in a business or residence district shall:

(1) stop the vehicle before moving on a sidewalk or the sidewalk area extending across an alley or driveway;

(2) yield the right-of-way to a pedestrian to avoid collision; and

(3) on entering the roadway, yield the right-of-way to an approaching vehicle.
*(Added by L.1995, chap. 165(1), eff. 9/1/95.)*

### §§545.257 to 545.300. *(Reserved.)*

## SUBCHAPTER G. STOPPING, STANDING, AND PARKING

### §545.301. Stopping, standing, or parking outside a business or residence district.

(a) An operator may not stop, park, or leave standing an attended or unattended vehicle on the main traveled part of a highway outside a business or residence district unless:

(1) stopping, parking, or leaving the vehicle off the main traveled part of the highway is not practicable;

(2) a width of highway beside the vehicle is unobstructed and open for the passage of other vehicles; and

(3) the vehicle is in clear view for at least 200 feet in each direction on the highway.

(b) This section does not apply to an operator of a vehicle that is disabled while on the paved or main traveled part of a highway if it is impossible to avoid stopping and temporarily leaving the vehicle on the highway.
*(Added by L.1995, chap. 165(1), eff. 9/1/95.)*

### §545.302. Stopping, standing, or parking prohibited in certain places.

(a) An operator may not stop, stand, or park a vehicle:

(1) on the roadway side of a vehicle stopped or parked at the edge or curb of a street;

(2) on a sidewalk;
(3) in an intersection;
(4) on a crosswalk;
(5) between a safety zone and the adjacent curb or within 30 feet of a place on the curb immediately opposite the ends of a safety zone, unless the governing body of a municipality designates a different length by signs or markings;
(6) alongside or opposite a street excavation or obstruction if stopping, standing, or parking the vehicle would obstruct traffic;
(7) on a bridge or other elevated structure on a highway or in a highway tunnel;
(8) on a railroad track; or
(9) where an official sign prohibits stopping.

(b) An operator may not, except momentarily to pick up or discharge a passenger, stand or park an occupied or unoccupied vehicle:
(1) in front of a public or private driveway;
(2) within 15 feet of a fire hydrant;
(3) within 20 feet of a crosswalk at an intersection;
(4) within 30 feet on the approach to a flashing signal, stop sign, yield sign, or traffic-control signal located at the side of a roadway;
(5) within 20 feet of the driveway entrance to a fire station and on the side of a street opposite the entrance to a fire station within 75 feet of the entrance, if the entrance is properly marked with a sign; or
(6) where an official sign prohibits standing.

(c) An operator may not, except temporarily to load or unload merchandise or passengers, park an occupied or unoccupied vehicle:
(1) within 50 feet of the nearest rail of a railroad crossing; or
(2) where an official sign prohibits parking.

(d) A person may stop, stand, or park a bicycle on a sidewalk if the bicycle does not impede the normal and reasonable movement of pedestrian or other traffic on the sidewalk.

(e) A municipality may adopt an ordinance exempting a private vehicle operated by an elevator constructor responding to an elevator emergency from Subsections (a)(1), (a)(5), (a)(6), (a)(9), (b), and (c).

(f) Subsections (a), (b), and (c) do not apply if the avoidance of conflict with other traffic is necessary or if the operator is complying with the law or the directions of a police officer or official traffic-control device.

(g) If the governing body of a municipality determines that it is necessary to improve the economic development of the municipality's central business district and that it will not adversely affect public safety, the governing body may adopt an ordinance regulating the standing, stopping, or parking of a vehicle at a place described by Subsection (a)(1), other than a road or highway in the state highway system, in the central business district of the municipality as defined in the ordinance. To the extent of any conflict between the ordinance and Subsection (a)(1), the ordinance controls.

*(Added by L.1995, chap. 165(1); chgd. by L.1999, chap. 814(1), eff. 6/18/99.)*

## §545.303. Additional parking regulations.

(a) An operator who stops or parks on a two-way roadway shall do so with the right-hand wheels of the vehicle parallel to and within 18 inches of the right-hand curb or edge of the roadway.

(b) An operator who stops or parks on a one-way roadway shall stop or park the vehicle parallel to the curb or edge of the roadway in the direction of authorized traffic movement with the right-hand wheels within 18 inches of the right-hand curb or edge of the roadway or the left-hand wheels within 18 inches of the left-hand curb or edge of the roadway. This subsection does not apply where a local ordinance otherwise regulates stopping or parking on the one-way roadway.

(c) A local authority by ordinance may permit angle parking on a roadway. This subsection does not apply to a federal-aid or state highway unless the director of the Texas Department of Transportation determines that the roadway is wide enough to permit angle parking without interfering with the free movement of traffic.

(d) The Texas Department of Transportation, on a highway under the jurisdiction of that department, may place signs prohibiting or restricting the stopping, standing, or parking of a vehicle on the highway where the director of the Texas Department of Transportation determines that stopping, standing, or parking is dangerous to, or would unduly interfere with, the free movement of traffic on the highway.

(c) To the extent of any conflict between Subsection (a) or (b) and a municipal ordinance adopted under Section 545.302(g), the ordinance controls.
*(Added by L.1995, chap. 165(1); chgd. by L.1999, chap. 814(2), eff. 6/18/99.)*

### §545.304. Moving the vehicle of another; unlawful parking.

A person may not move a vehicle that is not lawfully under the person's control:

(1) into an area where a vehicle is prohibited under Section 545.302; or

(2) away from a curb a distance that is unlawful under Section 545.303.
*(Added by L.1995, chap. 165(1), eff. 9/1/95.)*

### §545.305. Removal of unlawfully stopped vehicle.

(a) A peace officer listed under Article 2.12, Code of Criminal Procedure, or a license and weight inspector of the department may remove or require the operator or a person in charge of a vehicle to move a vehicle from a highway if the vehicle:

(1) is unattended on a bridge, viaduct, or causeway or in a tube or tunnel and the vehicle is obstructing traffic;

(2) is unlawfully parked and blocking the entrance to a private driveway;

(3) has been reported as stolen;

(4) is identified as having been stolen in a warrant issued on the filing of a complaint;

(5) is unattended and the officer has reasonable grounds to believe that the vehicle has been abandoned for longer than 48 hours;

(6) is disabled so that normal operation is impossible or impractical and the owner or person in charge of the vehicle is:

(A) incapacitated and unable to provide for the vehicle's removal or custody; or

(B) not in the immediate vicinity of the vehicle;

(7) is disabled so that normal operation is impossible or impractical and the owner or person in charge of the vehicle does not designate a particular towing or storage company;

(8) is operated by a person an officer arrests for an alleged offense and the officer is required by law to take the person into custody; or

(9) is, in the opinion of the officer, a hazard, interferes with a normal function of a governmental agency, or because of a catastrophe, emergency, or unusual circumstance is imperiled.

(b) An officer acting under Subsection (a) may require that the vehicle be taken to:

(1) the nearest garage or other place of safety;

(2) a garage designated or maintained by the governmental agency that employs the officer; or

(3) a position off the paved or main traveled part of the highway.

(c) A law enforcement agency other than the department that removes an abandoned vehicle in an unincorporated area shall notify the sheriff.

(d) The owner of a vehicle that is removed or stored under this section is liable for all reasonable towing and storage fees incurred.

(e) In this section:

(1) "Towing company" means an individual, corporation, partnership, or other association engaged in the business of towing vehicles on a highway for compensation or with the expectation of compensation for the towing or storage of the vehicles and includes the owner, operator, employee, or agent of a towing company.

(2) "Storage company" means an individual, corporation, partnership, or other association engaged in the business of storing or repairing vehicles for compensation or with the expectation of compensation for the storage or repair of vehicles and includes the owner, operator, employee, or agent of a storage company.
*(Added by L.1995, chap. 165(1), eff. 9/1/95.)*

### §545.306. Regulation of towing companies in certain counties.

(a) The commissioners court of a county with a population of 2.2 million or more shall by ordinance provide for the licensing of or the granting of a permit to a person to remove or store a vehicle authorized by Section 545.305 to be removed in an unincorporated area of the county. The ordinance must include rules to ensure the protection of the public and the safe and efficient operation of towing and storage services in the county. The sheriff shall determine the rules included in the ordinance with the review and consent of the commissioners court.

(b) The commissioners court shall set the fee for the license or permit in an amount that reasonably offsets the costs of enforcing the ordinance. The commissioners court shall use each license or permit fee to pay salaries and expenses of the sheriff's office for conducting inspections

to determine compliance with the ordinance and laws relating to dealers in scrap metal and salvage.
*(Added by L.1995, chap. 165(1), eff. 9/1/95.)*

### §545.307. Overnight parking of commercial motor vehicle in residential subdivision.

(a) In this section:

(1) "Commercial motor vehicle" means:

(A) a commercial motor vehicle, as defined by Section 522.003, and includes a vehicle meeting that definition regardless of whether the vehicle is used for a commercial purpose; or

(B) a road tractor, truck tractor, pole trailer, or semitrailer, as those terms are defined by Section 541.201.

(2) "Residential subdivision" means a subdivision in a county with a population greater than 220,000:

(A) for which a plat is recorded in the county real property records; and

(B) in which the majority of lots are subject to deed restrictions limiting the lots to residential use.

(b) After 10 p.m. and before 6 a.m., a person may not park a commercial motor vehicle or leave the vehicle parked on a street of a residential subdivision for which signs are posted as provided by Subsection (c) unless the commercial motor vehicle:

(1) is transporting persons or property to or from the residential subdivision or performing work in the subdivision; and

(2) remains parked in the subdivision only for the period necessary to complete the transportation or work.

(c) The residents of a residential subdivision may petition a county or municipality in which the subdivision is located for the posting of signs prohibiting the overnight parking of a commercial motor vehicle in the subdivision. The petition must be signed by at least 25 percent of the owners or tenants of residences in the subdivision. Not more than one person for each residence may sign the petition, and each person signing must be at least 18 years of age. Promptly after the filing of a petition meeting the requirements of this subsection and subject to Subsection (d), the county or municipality receiving the petition shall post the signs. The signs must:

(1) be posted at each entrance of the subdivision through which a commercial motor vehicle may enter the subdivision or within the subdivision if there is not defined entrance to the subdivision; and

(2) state, in letters at least two inches in height, that overnight parking of a commercial motor vehicle is prohibited in the subdivision.

(d) A county or municipality receiving a petition under Subsection (c) may condition the posting of the signs on payment by the residents of the residential subdivision of the cost of providing the signs.

(e) A person commits an offense if the person parks a commercial motor vehicle in violation of Subsection (b).

(f) This section does not limit the power of a municipality to regulate the parking of commercial motor vehicles.

(g) For the purposes of this section, contiguous subdivisions that are developed by the same entity or a successor to that entity and that are given the same public name or a variation of the same public name are considered one subdivision. Separation of one of the subdivisions from another by a road, stream, greenbelt, or similar barrier does not make the subdivisions noncontiguous.
*(Added by L.1997, chap. 173(1); chgd. by L.1999, chaps. 731(1), 1419(1), eff. 9/1/99, 6/19/99, respectively.)*

### §§545.308 to 545.350. *(Reserved.)*

## SUBCHAPTER H. SPEED RESTRICTIONS

### §545.351. Maximum speed requirement.

(a) An operator may not drive at a speed greater than is reasonable and prudent under the circumstances then existing.

(b) An operator:

(1) may not drive a vehicle at a speed greater than is reasonable and prudent under the conditions and having regard for actual and potential hazards then existing; and

(2) shall control the speed of the vehicle as necessary to avoid colliding with another person or vehicle that is on or entering the highway in compliance with law and the duty of each person to use due care.

(c) An operator shall, consistent with Subsections (a) and (b), drive at an appropriate reduced speed if:

(1) the operator is approaching and crossing an intersection or railroad grade crossing;

(2) the operator is approaching and going around a curve;

(3) the operator is approaching a hill crest;

(4) the operator is traveling on a narrow or winding roadway; and

(5) a special hazard exists with regard to traffic, including pedestrians, or weather or highway conditions.

*(Added by L.1995, chap. 165(1); chgd. by L.1997, chap. 165(30.109), eff. 9/1/97.)*

## §545.352. Prima facie speed limits.

(a) A speed in excess of the limits established by Subsection (b) or under another provision of this subchapter is prima facie evidence that the speed is not reasonable and prudent and that the speed is unlawful.

(b) Unless a special hazard exists that requires a slower speed for compliance with Section 545.351(b), the following speeds are lawful:

(1) 30 miles per hour in an urban district on a street other than an alley and 15 miles per hour in an alley;

(2) 70 miles per hour in daytime and 65 miles per hour in nighttime if the vehicle is a passenger car, motorcycle, passenger car or light truck towing a trailer bearing a vessel, as defined by Section 31.003, Parks and Wildlife Code, that is less than 26 feet in length, passenger car or light truck towing a trailer or semitrailer designed and used primarily to transport a motorcycle, or passenger car or light truck towing a trailer or semitrailer designed and used primarily to transport dogs or livestock, on a highway numbered by this state or the United States outside an urban district, including a farm-to-market or ranch-to-market road; *(Chgd. By L.1999, chap. 739(1), eff. 9/199. See other paragraph (2) below.)*

(2) 70 miles per hour in daytime and 65 milers per hour in nighttime if the vehicle is on a highway numbered by this state or the United States outside an urban district, including a farm-to-market or ranch-to-market road, except as provided by Subdivision (4); *(Chgd. By L.1999, chap. 1346(1), eff. 9/1/99. See other paragraph (2) above,)*

(3) 60 miles per hour in daytime and 55 miles per hour in nighttime if the vehicle is on a highway that is outside an urban district and not a highway numbered by this state or the United States;

(4) outside an urban district:

(A) 60 miles per hour if the vehicle is a school bus that has passed a commercial motor vehicle inspection under Section 548.201 and is on a highway numbered by the United States or this state, including a farm-to-market road;

(B) 50 miles per hour if the vehicle is a school bus that:

(i) has not passed a commercial motor vehicle inspection under Section 548.201; or

(ii) is traveling on a highway not numbered by the United States or this state; or

(C) 60 miles per hour in daytime and 55 miles per hour in nighttime if:

(i) the vehicle is a truck, other than a light truck, or if the vehicle is a truck tractor, trailer, or semitrailer other than a trailer described by Subdivision (2); and

(ii) the vehicle is on a farm-to-market or ranch-to-market road;

(5) on a beach, 15 miles per hours; or

(6) on a county road adjacent to a public beach, 15 miles per hour, if declared by the commissioners court of the county.

(c) The speed limits for a bus or other vehicle engaged in the business of transporting passengers for compensation or hire, for a commercial vehicle used as a highway post office vehicle for highway post office service in the transportation of United States mail, for a light truck, and for a school activity bus are the same as required for a passenger car at the same time and location.

(d) In this section:

(1) "Interstate highway" means a segment of the national system of interstate and defense highways that is:

(A) located in this state;

(B) officially designated by the Texas Transportation Commission; and

(C) approved under Title 23, United States Code.

(2) "Light truck" means a truck with a manufacturer's rated carrying capacity of not more than 2,000 pounds, including a pick-up truck, panel delivery truck, and carry-all truck.

(3) "Urban district" means the territory adjacent to and including a highway, if the territory is improved with structures that are used for business, industry, or dwelling houses and are located at

intervals of less than 100 feet for a distance of at least one-quarter mile on either side of the highway.

*(Added by L.1995, chap. 165(1); chgd. by L.1997, chaps. 165(30.110(a)), 1020(2); L.1999, chaps. 663(2), 739(1), 1346(1), eff. 6/18/99, 9/1/99, 9/1/99, respectively.)*

### §545.353. Authority of Texas Transportation Commission to alter speed limits.

(a) If the Texas Transportation Commission determines from the results of an engineering and traffic investigation that a prima facie speed limit in this subchapter is unreasonable or unsafe on a part of the highway system, the commission, by order recorded in its minutes, and except as provided in Subsection (d), may determine and declare:

(1) a reasonable and safe prima facie speed limit; and

(2) another reasonable and safe speed because of wet or inclement weather.

(b) In determining whether a prima facie speed limit on a part of the highway system is reasonable and safe, the commission shall consider the width and condition of the pavement, the usual traffic at the affected area, and other circumstances.

(c) A prima facie speed limit that is declared by the commission under this section is effective when the commission erects signs giving notice of the new limit. A new limit that is enacted for a highway under this section is effective at all times or at other times as determined.

(d) The commission may not:

(1) modify the rules established by Section 545.351(b);

(2) establish a speed limit of more than 70 miles per hour; or

(3) increase the speed limit for a vehicle described by Section 545.352(b)(5).

(e) The commission, in conducting the engineering and traffic investigation specified by Subsection (a), shall follow the "Procedure for Establishing Speed Zones" as adopted by the commission. The commission may revise the procedure to accommodate technological advancement in traffic operation, the design and construction of highways and motor vehicles, and the safety of the motoring public.

(f) The commission's authority to alter speed limits applies:

(1) to any part of a highway officially designated or marked by the commission as part of the state highway system; and

(2) both inside and outside the limits of a municipality, including a home-rule municipality, for a limited-access or controlled-access highway.

(g) For purposes of this section, "wet or inclement weather" means a condition of the roadway that makes driving on the roadway unsafe and hazardous and that is caused by precipitation, including water, ice, and snow.

*(Added by L.1995, chap. 165(1); chgd. by L.1997, chap. 165(30.111), eff. 9/1/97.)*

### §545.3535. Authority of Texas Transportation Commission to alter speed limits on certain roads.

(a) The commissioners court of a county by resolution may request the Texas Transportation Commission to determine and declare a reasonable and safe prima facie speed limit that is lower than a speed limit established by Section 545.352 on any part of a farm-to-market or a ranch-to-market road of the highway system that is located in that county and is without improved shoulders.

(b) The commission shall give consideration to local public opinion and may determine and declare a lower speed limit on any part of the road without an engineering and traffic investigation, but the commission must use sound and generally accepted traffic engineering practices in determining and declaring the lower speed limit.

(c) The commission by rule shall establish standards for determining lower speed limits within a set range.

*(Added by L.1997, chap. 1171(1.45); chgd. by L.1999, chap. 1346(2), eff. 9/1/99.)*

### §545.354. Authority of Texas Turnpike Authority and regional tollway authorities to alter speed limits on turnpike projects.

(a)(1) In this section, "authority" means the Texas Turnpike Authority or a regional tollway authority governed by Chapter 366.

(2) If an authority determines from the results of an engineering and traffic investigation that a prima facie speed limit described in this subchapter is unreasonable or unsafe on a part of a turnpike constructed and maintained by the authority, the authority by order recorded in its minutes shall determine and declare a reasonable and safe prima facie speed limit for vehicles or classes of vehicles on the turnpike.

Printed in the U.S.A. 71

(b) In determining whether a prima facie speed limit on a part of a turnpike constructed and maintained by the authority is reasonable or safe, the authority shall consider the width and condition of the pavement, the usual traffic on the turnpike, and other circumstances.

(c) A prima facie speed limit that is declared by the authority in accordance with this section is effective when the authority erects signs giving notice of the new limit. A new limit that is adopted for a turnpike project constructed and maintained by the authority in accordance with this section is effective at all times or at other times as determined.

(d) The authority's power to alter prima facie speed limits is effective and exclusive on any part of a turnpike project constructed and maintained by the authority inside and outside the limits of a municipality, including a home-rule municipality.

(e) Sections 545.353 and 545.355-545.359 do not apply to any part of a turnpike project constructed and maintained by the authority and covered under Subsection (d) unless a turnpike constructed by the authority becomes part of the state highway system, in which event the Texas Transportation Commission has the sole authority to alter prima facie speed limits on the turnpike project.

(f) The authority may not:

(1) alter the general rule established by Section 545.351(a); or

(2) establish a speed limit of more than 70 miles per hour.

(g) The authority, in conducting the engineering and traffic investigation specified by Subsection (a), shall follow the procedure for establishing speed zones adopted by the Texas Department of Transportation.

*(Added by L.1995, chap. 165(1); chgd. by L.1999, chap. 576(3), eff. 9/1/99.)*



### §545.355. Authority of county commissioners court to alter speed limits.

(a) The commissioners court of a county, for a county road or highway outside the limits of the right-of-way of an officially designated or marked highway or road of the state highway system and outside a municipality, has the same authority to increase prima facie speed limits from the results of an engineering and traffic investigation as the Texas Transportation Commission on an officially designated or marked highway of the state highway system, and may declare a lower speed limit of not less than 30 miles per hour on a county road or highway to which this section applies, if the commissioners court determines that the prima facie speed limit on the road or highway is unreasonable or unsafe. The commissioners court may not modify the rule established by Section 545.351(a) or establish a speed limit of more than 60 miles per hour.

(b) The commissioners court may modify a prima facie speed limit in accordance with this section only by an order entered on its records.

(c) The commissioners court of a county with a population of more than 2.8 million may establish from the results of an engineering and traffic investigation a speed limit of not more than 70 miles per hour on any part of a highway of that county that is a limited-access or controlled-access highway, regardless of the location of the part of the highway.

*(Added by L.1995, chap. 165(1); chgd. by L.1997, chaps. 58(1), 833(1), eff. 5/9/97, 6/18/97, respectively.)*

### §545.356. Authority of municipality to alter speed limits.

(a) The governing body of a municipality, for a highway or part of a highway in the municipality, including a highway of the state highway system, has the same authority to alter by ordinance prima facie speed limits from the results of an engineering and traffic investigation as the Texas Transportation Commission on an officially designated or marked highway of the state highway system. The governing body of a municipality may not modify the rule established by Section 545.351(a) or establish a speed limit of more than 60 miles per hour.

(b) The governing body of a municipality, for a highway or part of a highway in the municipality, including a highway of the state highway system, has the same authority to alter prima facie speed limits from the results of an engineering and traffic investigation as the commission for an officially designated or marked highway of the state highway system, when the highway or part of the highway is under repair, construction, or maintenance. A municipality may not modify the rule established by Section 545.351(a) or establish a speed limit of more than 60 miles per hour.

(c) A prima facie speed limit that is altered by the governing body of a municipality under Subsection (b) is effective when the governing body erects signs giving notice of the new limit and at all times or at other times as determined.

*(Added by L.1995, chap. 165(1), eff. 9/1/95.)*

**§545.357. Public hearing to consider speed limits where certain schools are located.**

(a) The governing body of a municipality in which a public or private elementary or secondary school or an institution of higher education as defined by Section 61.003(8) or (15), Education Code, is located shall on request hold a public hearing at least once each calendar year to consider prima facie speed limits on a highway in the municipality, including a highway of the state highway system, near the school or institution of higher education.

(b) If a county road outside the state highway system is located within 500 feet of a public or private elementary or secondary school or an institution of higher education that is not in a municipality, the commissioners court of the county on request shall hold a public hearing at least once each calendar year to consider the prima facie speed limit on the road near the school or institution of higher education.

(c) A municipal governing body or commissioners court on request may hold one public hearing for all public and private elementary and secondary schools and institutions of higher education in its jurisdiction.

(d) The Texas Transportation Commission, on request, shall hold a public hearing at least once each calendar year to consider prima facie speed limits on highways in the state highway system that are near public or private elementary or secondary schools or institutions of higher education. *(Added by L.1995, chap. 165(1); chgd. by L.1997, chap. 350(1), eff. 9/1/97.)*

**§545.358. Authority of commanding officer of United States military reservation to alter speed limits.**

The commanding officer of a United States military reservation, for a highway or part of a highway in the military reservation, including a highway of the state highway system, has the same authority by order to alter prima facie speed limits from the results of an engineering and traffic investigation as the Texas Transportation Commission for an officially designated or marked highway of the state highway system. A commanding officer may not modify the rule established by Section 545.351(a) or establish a speed limit of more than 60 miles per hour. *(Added by L.1995, chap. 165(1), eff. 9/1/95.)*

**§545.359. Conflicting designated speed limits.**

An order of the Texas Transportation Commission declaring a speed limit on a part of a designated or marked route of the state highway system made under Section 545.353 or 545.362 supersedes any conflicting designated speed established under Sections 545.356 and 545.358. *(Added by L.1995, chap. 165(1), eff. 9/1/95.)*

**§545.360. Duty of Texas Transportation Commission and State Board of Education to provide information and assistance.**

The chairman of the Texas Transportation Commission and the chairman of the State Board of Education shall provide assistance and information relevant to consideration of speed limits to commissioners courts, municipal governing bodies, and other interested persons. *(Added by L.1995, chap. 165(1), eff. 9/1/95.)*

**§545.361. Special speed limitations.**

(a) An operator of a motor-driven cycle may not drive at a speed of more than 35 miles per hour during the time specified by Section 547.302(a) unless the cycle is equipped with a headlamp or lamps that reveal a person or vehicle 300 feet ahead.

(b) An operator of a vehicle equipped with solid rubber or cushion tires may not drive at a speed of more than 10 miles per hour.

(c) An operator driving over a bridge or other elevated structure that is a part of a highway may not drive at a speed of more than the maximum speed that can be maintained with safety to the bridge or structure, when signs are posted as provided by this section.

(d) An operator of self-propelled machinery designed or adapted for applying plant food materials or agricultural chemicals and not designed or adapted for the sole purpose of transporting the materials or chemicals may not drive at a speed of more than 30 miles per hour unless the machinery is registered under Chapter 502.

(e) The Texas Transportation Commission, for a state highway, the Texas Turnpike Authority, for any part of a turnpike constructed and maintained by the authority, and a local authority for a highway under the jurisdiction of the local authority, may investigate a bridge or other elevated structure that is a part of a highway. If after conducting the investigation the commission, turnpike authority, or local authority finds that the structure cannot safely withstand vehicles traveling at a

Printed in the U.S.A.

speed otherwise permissible under this subtitle, the commission, turnpike authority, or local authority shall:

(1) determine and declare the maximum speed of vehicles that the structure can safely withstand; and

(2) post and maintain signs before each end of the structure stating the maximum speed.
*(Added by L.1995, chap. 165(1), eff. 9/1/95.)*

**§545.362. Temporary speed limits.**

(a) Subject to Subsection (c), the Texas Transportation Commission may enter an order establishing prima facie speed limits of not more than 70 miles per hour applicable to all highways, including a turnpike under the authority of the Texas Turnpike Authority or a highway under the control of a municipality or county. An order entered under this section does not have the effect of increasing a speed limit on any highway.

(b) The limits established under this section:

(1) are prima facie prudent and reasonable speed limits enforceable in the same manner as prima facie limits established under other provisions of this subchapter; and

(2) supersede any other established speed limit that would permit a person to operate a motor vehicle at a higher rate of speed.

(c) An order may be issued under Subsection (a) only if the commission finds and states in the order that:

(1) a severe shortage of motor fuel or other petroleum product exists, the shortage was caused by war, national emergency, or other circumstances, and a reduction of speed limits will foster conservation and safety; or

(2) the failure to alter state speed limits will prevent the state from receiving money from the United States for highway purposes.

(d) Unless a specific speed limit is required by federal law or directive under threat of loss of highway money of the United States, the commission may not set prima facie speed limits under this section of all vehicles at less than 60 miles per hour, except on a divided highway of at least four lanes, for which the commission may not set prima facie speed limits of all vehicles at less than 65 miles per hour.

(e) Before the commission may enter an order establishing a prima facie speed limit, it must hold a public hearing preceded by the publication in at least three newspapers of general circulation in the state of a notice of the date, time, and place of the hearing and of the action proposed to be taken. The notice must be published at least 12 days before the date of the hearing. At the hearing, all interested persons may present oral or written testimony regarding the proposed order.

(f) If the commission enters an order under this section, it shall file the order in the office of the governor. The governor shall then make an independent finding of fact and determine the existence of the facts in Subsection (c). Before the 13th day after the date the order is filed in the governor's office, the governor shall conclude the finding of fact, issue a proclamation stating whether the necessary facts exist to support the issuance of the commission's order, and file copies of the order and the proclamation in the office of the secretary of state.

(g) If the governor's proclamation states that the facts necessary to support the issuance of the commission's order exist, the order takes effect according to Subsection (h). Otherwise, the order has no effect.

(h) In an order issued under this section, the commission may specify the date the order takes effect, but that date may not be sooner than the eighth day after the date the order is filed with the governor. If the order does not have an effective date, it takes effect on the 21st day after the date it is filed with the governor. Unless the order by its own terms expires earlier, it remains in effect until a subsequent order adopted by the procedure prescribed by this section amends or repeals it, except that an order adopted under this section expires when this section expires. The procedure for repealing an order is the same as for adopting an order, except that the commission and the governor must find that the facts required to support the issuance of an order under Subsection (c) no longer exist.

(i) If an order is adopted in accordance with this section, the commission and all governmental authorities responsible for the maintenance of highway speed limit signs shall take appropriate action to conceal or remove all signs that give notice of a speed limit of more than the one contained in the order and to erect appropriate signs. All governmental entities responsible for administering traffic safety programs and enforcing traffic laws shall use all available resources to notify the public of the effect of the order. To accomplish this purpose, the governmental entities shall request the cooperation of all news media in the state.

Printed in the U.S.A. Zt

(j) A change in speed limits under this section is effective until the commission makes a finding that the conditions in Subsection (c) require or authorize an additional change in those speed limits or in the highway or sections of highway to which those speed limits apply.

(k) This section expires when the national maximum speed limits are repealed.

*(Added by L.1995, chap. 165(1), eff. 9/1/95.)*

**§545.3625. Confidentiality of violation information: fuel conservation speed limit.**

(a) If a person violates a maximum prima facie speed limit imposed under Section 545.362, as that law existed immediately before December 8, 1995, and the person was not traveling at a speed, as alleged in the citation, if not contested by the person, or, if contested by the person, as alleged in the complaint and found by the court, that is greater than the maximum prima facie speed limit for the location that has been established under this chapter, other than under Section 545.362, information in the custody of the department concerning the violation is confidential.

(b) The department may not release the information to any person or to another state governmental entity.

*(Added by L.1997, chap. 165(30.112(a)), eff. 9/1/97.)*

**§545.363. Minimum speed regulations.**

(a) An operator may not drive so slowly as to impede the normal and reasonable movement of traffic, except when reduced speed is necessary for safe operation or in compliance with law.

(b) When the Texas Transportation Commission, the Texas Turnpike Authority, the commissioners court of a county, or the governing body of a municipality, within the jurisdiction of each, as applicable, as specified in Sections 545.353-545.357, determines from the results of an engineering and traffic investigation that slow speeds on a part of a highway consistently impede the normal and reasonable movement of traffic, the commission, authority, county commissioners court, or governing body may determine and declare a minimum speed limit on the highway.

(c) If appropriate signs are erected giving notice of a minimum speed limit adopted under this section, an operator may not drive a vehicle more slowly than that limit except as necessary for safe operation or in compliance with law.

*(Added by L.1995, chap. 165(1), eff. 9/1/95.)*

**§545.364.** *(Repealed by L.1999, chap. 1346(3), eff. 9/1/99.)*

**§545.365. Speed limit exception for emergencies; municipal regulation.**

(a) The regulation of the speed of a vehicle under this subchapter does not apply to:

(1) an authorized emergency vehicle responding to a call;

(2) a police patrol; or

(3) a physician or ambulance responding to an emergency call.

(b) A municipality by ordinance may regulate the speed of:

(1) an ambulance;

(2) an emergency medical services vehicle; or

(3) an authorized vehicle operated by a blood or tissue bank.

*(Added by L.1995, chap. 165(1), eff. 9/1/95.)*

**§§545.366 to 545.400.** *(Reserved.)*

## SUBCHAPTER I. MISCELLANEOUS RULES

**§545.401. Reckless driving; offense.**

(a) A person commits an offense if the person drives a vehicle in wilful or wanton disregard for the safety of persons or property.

(b) An offense under this section is a misdemeanor punishable by:

(1) a fine not to exceed $200;

(2) confinement in county jail for not more than 30 days; or

(3) both the fine and the confinement.

(c) Notwithstanding Section 542.001, this section applies to:

(1) a private access way or parking area provided for a client or patron by a business, other than a private residential property or the property of a garage or parking lot for which a charge is made for the storing or parking of motor vehicles; and

(2) a highway or other public place.

(d) Notwithstanding Section 542.004, this section applies to a person, a team, or motor vehicles and other equipment engaged in work on a highway surface.
*(Added by L.1995, chap. 165(1), eff. 9/1/95.)*

### §545.402. Moving a parked vehicle.

An operator may not begin movement of a stopped, standing, or parked vehicle unless the movement can be made safely. *(Added by L.1995, chap. 165(1), eff. 9/1/95.)*

### §545.403. Driving through safety zone.

An operator may not drive through or in a safety zone. *(Added by L.1995, chap. 165(1), eff. 9/1/95.)*

### §545.404. Unattended motor vehicle.

An operator may not leave the vehicle unattended without:

(1) stopping the engine;

(2) locking the ignition;

(3) removing the key from the ignition;

(4) setting the parking brake effectively; and

(5) if standing on a grade, turning the front wheels to the curb or side of the highway.

*(Added by L.1995, chap. 165(1), eff. 9/1/95.)*



### §545.405. Driving on mountain highway.

An operator moving through a defile or canyon or on a mountain highway shall:

(1) hold the vehicle under control and as near the right-hand edge of the highway as possible; and

(2) on approaching a curve that obstructs the view of the highway for 200 feet, give warning with the horn of the motor vehicle.

*(Added by L.1995, chap. 165(1), eff. 9/1/95.)*

### §545.406. Coasting.

(a) An operator moving on a downgrade may not coast with the gears or transmission of the vehicle in neutral.

(b) An operator of a truck, tractor, or bus moving on a downgrade may not coast with the clutch disengaged.

*(Added by L.1995, chap. 165(1), eff. 9/1/95.)*

### §545.407. Following or obstructing fire apparatus or ambulance.

(a) An operator, unless on official business, may not follow closer than 500 feet a fire apparatus responding to a fire alarm or drive into or park the vehicle in the block where the fire apparatus has stopped to answer a fire alarm.

(b) An operator may not:

(1) follow closer than 500 feet an ambulance that is flashing red lights unless the operator is on official business; or

(2) drive or park the vehicle where an ambulance has been summoned for an emergency call in a manner intended to interfere with the arrival or departure of the ambulance.

*(Added by L.1995, chap. 165(1), eff. 9/1/95.)*

### §545.408. Crossing fire hose.

An operator may not, without the consent of the fire department official in command, drive over an unprotected hose of a fire department if the hose is on a street or private driveway and is intended for use at a fire or alarm of fire. *(Added by L.1995, chap. 165(1), eff. 9/1/95.)*

### §545.409. Drawbars and trailer hitches; saddle-mount towing.

(a) The drawbar or other connection between a vehicle drawing another vehicle and the drawn vehicle:

(1) must be strong enough to pull all weight drawn; and

(2) may not exceed 15 feet between the vehicles except for a connection between two vehicles transporting poles, pipe, machinery, or other objects of structural nature that cannot readily be dismembered.

(b) An operator drawing another vehicle and using a chain, rope, or cable to connect the vehicles shall display on the connection a white flag or cloth not less than 12 inches square.

(c) A motor vehicle may not draw more than three motor vehicles attached to it by the triple saddle-mount method. In this subsection, "triple saddle-mount method" means the mounting of

the front wheels of trailing vehicles on the bed of another vehicle while leaving the rear wheels only of the trailing vehicles in contact with the roadway.
*(Added by L.1995, chap. 165(1), eff. 9/1/95.)*

### §545.410. Towing safety chains.

(a) An operator of a passenger car or light truck may not draw a trailer, semitrailer, house trailer, or another motor vehicle unless safety chains of a type approved by the department are attached in a manner approved by the department from the trailer, semitrailer, house trailer, or drawn motor vehicle to the drawing vehicle. This subsection does not apply to the drawing of a trailer or semitrailer used for agricultural purposes.

(b) The department shall adopt rules prescribing the type of safety chains required to be used according to the weight of the trailer, semitrailer, house trailer, or motor vehicle being drawn. The rules shall:

(1) require safety chains to be strong enough to maintain the connection between the trailer, semitrailer, house trailer, or drawn motor vehicle and the drawing vehicle; and

(2) show the proper method to attach safety chains between the trailer, semitrailer, house trailer, or drawn motor vehicle and the drawing vehicle.

(c) Subsection (b) does not apply to trailers, semitrailers, or house trailers that are equipped with safety chains installed by the original manufacturer before the effective date of the rules.

(d) This section does not apply to a trailer, semitrailer, house trailer, or drawn motor vehicle that is operated in compliance with the federal motor carrier safety regulations.

(e) In this section, "safety chains" means flexible tension members connected from the front of a drawn vehicle to the rear of the drawing vehicle to maintain connection between the vehicles if the primary connecting system fails.
*(Added by L.1995, chap. 165(1); chgd. by L.1997, chap. 165(30.113(a)); L.1999, chap. 1357(1), eff. 9/1/99.)*

### §545.411. Use of rest area: offense.

(a) A person commits an offense if the person remains at a rest area for longer than 24 hours or erects a tent, shelter, booth, or structure at the rest area and the person:

(1) has notice while conducting the activity that the activity is prohibited; or

(2) receives notice that the activity is prohibited but does not depart or remove the structure within eight hours after receiving notice.

(b) For purposes of this section, a person:

(1) has notice if a sign stating the prohibited activity and penalty is posted on the premises; or

(2) receives notice if a peace officer orally communicates to the person the prohibited activity and penalty for the offense.

(c) It is an exception to Subsection (a) if a nonprofit organization erects a temporary structure at a rest area to provide food services, food, or beverages to travelers and the Texas Department of Transportation:

(1) finds that the services would constitute a public service for the benefit of the traveling public; and

(2) issues a permit to the organization.

(d) In this section, "rest area" means public real property designated as a rest area, comfort station, picnic area, roadside park, or scenic overlook by the Texas Department of Transportation.
*(Added by L.1995, chap. 165(1), eff. 9/1/95.)*

### §545.412. Child passenger safety seat systems; offense.

(a) A person commits an offense if the person operates a passenger car or light truck and:

(1) transports a child younger than two years of age and does not keep the child secured during the operation of the vehicle in a child passenger safety seat system according to the instructions of the manufacturer of the safety seat system; or

(2) transports a child who is at least two years of age but younger than four years of age and does not keep the child secured during the operation of the vehicle:

(A) in a child passenger safety seat system according to the instructions of the manufacturer of the safety seat system; or

(B) by a safety belt.

(b) An offense under this section is a misdemeanor punishable by a fine of not less than $25 or more than $50.

(c) It is a defense to prosecution under this section that the person was operating the vehicle in an emergency or for a law enforcement purpose.

Printed in the U.S.A. Zt

(d) Use or nonuse of a child passenger safety seat system is not admissible evidence in a civil trial, other than a proceeding under Subtitle A or B, Title 5, Family Code.

(e) This section does not apply to a person:

(1) operating a vehicle transporting passengers for hire; or

(2) transporting a child in a vehicle in which all seating positions equipped with child passenger safety seat systems or safety belts are occupied.

(f) In this section, "child passenger safety seat system" means an infant or child passenger restraint system that meets the federal standards for crash-tested restraint systems as set by the National Highway Traffic Safety Administration.

*(Added by L.1995, chap. 165(1); chgd. by L.1997, chap. 165(30.114(a)), eff. 9/1/97.)*

## §545.413. Safety belts; offense.

(a) A person commits an offense if the person:

(1) is at least 15 years of age;

(2) is riding in the front seat of a passenger car while the vehicle is being operated;

(3) is occupying a seat that is equipped with a safety belt; and

(4) is not secured by a safety belt.

(b) A person commits an offense if the person:

(1) operates a passenger car or light truck that is equipped with safety belts; and

(2) allows a child who is at least four years of age but younger than 15 years of age to ride in the vehicle without requiring the child to be secured by a safety belt, provided the child is occupying a seat that is equipped with a safety belt.

(c) A passenger car or a seat in a passenger car is considered to be equipped with a safety belt if the vehicle is required under Section 547.601 to be equipped with safety belts.

(d) An offense under this section is a misdemeanor punishable by a fine of not less than $25 or more than $50.

(e) It is a defense to prosecution under this section that:

(1) the person possesses a written statement from a licensed physician stating that for a medical reason the person should not wear a safety belt;

(2) the person presents to the court, not later than the 10th day after the date of the offense, a statement from a licensed physician stating that for a medical reason the person should not wear a safety belt;

(3) the person is employed by the United States Postal Service and performing a duty for that agency that requires the operator to service postal boxes from a vehicle or that requires frequent entry into and exit from a vehicle;

(4) the person is engaged in the actual delivery of newspapers from a vehicle or is performing newspaper delivery duties that require frequent entry into and exit from a vehicle; or

(5) the person is employed by a public or private utility company and is engaged in the reading of meters or performing a similar duty for that company requiring the operator to frequently enter into and exit from a vehicle.

(f) The department shall develop and implement an educational program to encourage the wearing of safety belts and to emphasize:

(1) the effectiveness of safety belts and other restraint devices in reducing the risk of harm to passengers in motor vehicles; and

(2) the requirements of this section and the penalty for noncompliance.

(g) Use or nonuse of a safety belt is not admissible evidence in a civil trial, other than a proceeding under Subtitle A or B, Title 5, Family Code.

(h) In this section:

(1) "Passenger car" includes a truck with a manufacturer's rated carrying capacity of not more than 1,500 pounds.

(2) "Safety belt" means a lap belt and any shoulder straps included as original equipment on or added to a vehicle.

*(Added by L.1995, chap. 165(1); chgd. by L.1997, chap. 165(30.115(a)); L.1999, chaps. 316(1), 515(1), eff. 9/1/99.)*

## §545.414. Riding in open beds; offense.

(a) A person commits an offense if the person operates an open-bed pickup truck or an open flatbed truck or draws an open flatbed trailer at a speed of more than 35 miles per hour when a child younger than 12 years of age is occupying the bed of the truck or trailer.

(b) An offense under this section is a misdemeanor punishable by a fine of not less than $25 or more than $200.

(c) It is a defense to prosecution under this section that the person was operating or towing the vehicle in an emergency.
*(Added by L.1995, chap. 165(1), eff. 9/1/95.)*

### §545.415. Backing a vehicle.

(a) An operator may not back the vehicle unless the movement can be made safely and without interference with other traffic.

(b) An operator may not back the vehicle on a shoulder or roadway of a limited-access or controlled-access highway.
*(Added by L.1995, chap. 165(1), eff. 9/1/95.)*

### §545.416. Riding on motorcycle.

(a) An operator of a motorcycle shall ride on the permanent and regular seat attached to the motorcycle.

(b) An operator may not carry another person on the motorcycle, and a person who is not operating the motorcycle may not ride on the motorcycle, unless the motorcycle is designed to carry more than one person.

(c) If the motorcycle is designed to carry more than one person, a passenger may ride only on the permanent and regular seat, if designed for two persons, or on another seat firmly attached to the motorcycle behind or to the side of the operator.
*(Added by L.1995, chap. 165(1), eff. 9/1/95.)*

### §545.417. Obstruction of operator's view or driving mechanism.

(a) An operator may not drive a vehicle when it is loaded so that, or when the front seat has a number of persons, exceeding three, so that:

(1) the view of the operator to the front or sides of the vehicle is obstructed; or

(2) there is interference with the operator's control over the driving mechanism of the vehicle.

(b) A passenger in a vehicle may not ride in a position that interferes with the operator's view to the front or sides or control over the driving mechanism of the vehicle.
*(Added by L.1995, chap. 165(1), eff. 9/1/95.)*

### §545.418. Opening vehicle doors.

A person may not:

(1) open the door of a motor vehicle on the side available to moving traffic, unless the door may be opened in reasonable safety without interfering with the movement of other traffic; or

(2) leave a door on the side of a vehicle next to moving traffic open for longer than is necessary to load or unload a passenger.
*(Added by L.1995, chap. 165(1), eff. 9/1/95.)*

### §545.419. Riding in house trailer.

A person may not occupy a house trailer while it is being moved. *(Added by L.1995, chap. 165(1), eff. 9/1/95.)*

### §545.420. Racing on highway.

(a) A person may not participate in any manner in:

(1) a race;

(2) a vehicle speed competition or contest;

(3) a drag race or acceleration contest;

(4) a test of physical endurance of the operator of a vehicle; or

(5) an exhibition of vehicle speed or acceleration or to make a vehicle speed record.

(b) In this section:

(1) "Drag race" means the operation of:

(A) two or more vehicles from a point side by side at accelerating speeds in a competitive attempt to outdistance each other; or

(B) one or more vehicles over a common selected course, from the same place to the same place, for the purpose of comparing the relative speeds or power of acceleration of the vehicle or vehicles in a specified distance or time.

(2) "Race" means the use of one or more vehicles in an attempt to:

(A) outgain or outdistance another vehicle or prevent another vehicle from passing;

(B) arrive at a given destination ahead of another vehicle or vehicles; or

(C) test the physical stamina or endurance of an operator over a long-distance driving route.
*(Added by L.1995, chap. 165(1), eff. 9/1/95.)*

### §545.421. Fleeing or attempting to elude police officer; offense.

(a) A person commits an offense if the person operates a motor vehicle and wilfully fails or refuses to bring the vehicle to a stop or flees, or attempts to elude, a pursuing police vehicle when given a visual or audible signal to bring the vehicle to a stop.

(b) A signal under this section that is given by a police officer pursuing a vehicle may be by hand, voice, emergency light, or siren. The officer giving the signal must be in uniform and prominently display the officer's badge of office. The officer's vehicle must be appropriately marked as an official police vehicle.

(c) Except as provided by Subsection (d), an offense under this section is a Class B misdemeanor.

(d) An offense under this section is a Class A misdemeanor if the person, during the commission of the offense, recklessly engages in conduct that places another in imminent danger of serious bodily injury.

(e) A person is presumed to have recklessly engaged in conduct placing another in imminent danger of serious bodily injury under Subsection (d) if the person while intoxicated knowingly operated a motor vehicle during the commission of the offense. In this subsection, "intoxicated" has the meaning assigned by Section 49.01, Penal Code.

*(Added by L.1995, chap. 165(1), eff. 9/1/95.)*



### §545.422. Crossing sidewalk or hike and bike trail.

(a) A person may not drive a motor vehicle on a sidewalk, sidewalk area, or hike and bike trail except on a permanent or authorized temporary driveway.

(b) Subsection (a) does not prohibit the operation of a motor vehicle on a hike and bike trail in connection with maintenance of the trail.

(c) In this section, "hike and bike trail" means a trail designed for the exclusive use of pedestrians, bicyclists, or both.

*(Added by L.1995, chap. 165(1); chgd. by L.1997, chap. 165(30.116(a)), eff. 9/1/97.)*

### §545.423. Crossing property.

(a) An operator may not cross a sidewalk or drive through a driveway, parking lot, or business or residential entrance without stopping the vehicle.

(b) An operator may not cross or drive in or on a sidewalk, driveway, parking lot, or business or residential entrance at an intersection to turn right or left from one highway to another highway.

*(Added by L.1995, chap. 165(1), eff. 9/1/95.)*

# CHAPTER 546. OPERATION OF AUTHORIZED EMERGENCY VEHICLES AND CERTAIN OTHER VEHICLES

## SUBCHAPTER A. AUTHORIZED EMERGENCY VEHICLES

Section



## SUBCHAPTER B. OPERATION OF CERTAIN FIRE-FIGHTING EQUIPMENT



## SUBCHAPTER A. AUTHORIZED EMERGENCY VEHICLES

### §546.001. Permissible conduct.

In operating an authorized emergency vehicle the operator may:

(1) park or stand, irrespective of another provision of this subtitle;

(2) proceed past a red or stop signal or stop sign, after slowing as necessary for safe operation;

(3) exceed a maximum speed limit, except as provided by an ordinance adopted under Section 545.365, as long as the operator does not endanger life or property; and

(4) disregard a regulation governing the direction of movement or turning in specified directions.

*(Added by L.1995, chap. 165(1), eff. 9/1/95.)*

### §546.002. When conduct permissible.

Section 546.001 applies only when the operator is:

(1) responding to an emergency call;

(2) pursuing an actual or suspected violator of the law; or

(3) responding to but not returning from a fire alarm.

*(Added by L.1995, chap. 165(1), eff. 9/1/95.)*

### §546.003. Audible or visual signals required.

Except as provided by Section 546.004, the operator of an authorized emergency vehicle engaging in conduct permitted by Section 546.001 shall use, at the discretion of the operator in accordance with policies of the department or the local government that employs the operator, audible or visual signals that meet the pertinent requirements of Sections 547.305 and 547.702.

*(Added by L.1995, chap. 165(1), eff. 9/1/95.)*

### §546.004. Exceptions to signal requirement.

(a) A volunteer fire fighter who operates a private vehicle as an authorized emergency vehicle may engage in conduct permitted by Section 546.001 only when the fire fighter is using visual signals meeting the pertinent requirements of Sections 547.305 and 547.702.

(b) An authorized emergency vehicle that is operated as a police vehicle is not required to be equipped with or display a red light visible from the front of the vehicle.

(c) A police officer may operate an authorized emergency vehicle for a law enforcement purpose without using the audible or visual signals required by Section 546.003 if the officer is:

(1) responding to an emergency call or pursuing a suspected violator of the law with probable cause to believe that:

(A) knowledge of the presence of the officer will cause the suspect to:

(i) destroy or lose evidence of a suspected felony;

(ii) end a suspected continuing felony before the officer has obtained sufficient evidence to establish grounds for arrest; or

(iii) evade apprehension or identification of the suspect or the suspect's vehicle; or

(B) because of traffic conditions on a multilaned roadway, vehicles moving in response to the audible or visual signals may:

(i) increase the potential for a collision; or

(ii) unreasonably extend the duration of the pursuit; or

(2) complying with a written regulation relating to the use of audible or visible signals adopted by the local government that employs the officer or by the department.

*(Added by L.1995, chap. 165(1), eff. 9/1/95.)*

### §546.005. Duty of care.

This chapter does not relieve the operator of an authorized emergency vehicle from:

(1) the duty to operate the vehicle with appropriate regard for the safety of all persons; or

(2) the consequences of reckless disregard for the safety of others.

*(Added by L.1995, chap. 165(1), eff. 9/1/95.)*

### §§546.006 to 546.020. *(Reserved.)*

## SUBCHAPTER B. OPERATION OF CERTAIN FIRE-FIGHTING EQUIPMENT

### §546.021. Mutual aid organizations.

(a) Two or more businesses whose activities require the maintenance of fire-fighting equipment may form a mutual aid organization in which the member businesses agree to assist each other during an emergency by supplying fire-fighting equipment or services.

(b) The presiding officer or director of an organization formed under this section shall deliver a list to the county fire marshal, or to the commissioners court of a county if the county does not have a fire marshal, in each county in which a member business is located. The list must contain the name of the registered owner and license plate number of each motor vehicle that each member intends to use in supplying fire-fighting equipment or services.

(c) If the county fire marshal or commissioners court determines that the operation of the vehicles on the list is in the public interest and not a threat to public safety, the marshal or court shall approve the list.

(d) On approval of the list by the county fire marshal or commissioners court, a person operating a listed motor vehicle in response to a call for emergency fire-fighting assistance from a member has the rights and restrictions placed by this subtitle on the operator of an authorized emergency vehicle.

(e) A county is not liable for damage to a person or property caused by a person approved by the county under this section to operate a motor vehicle for emergency fire-fighting assistance. *(Added by L.1995, chap. 165(1), eff. 9/1/95.)*

# CHAPTER 547. VEHICLE EQUIPMENT

## SUBCHAPTER A. GENERAL PROVISIONS

Section



## SUBCHAPTER B. ADOPTION OF RULES AND STANDARDS



## SUBCHAPTER C. PROVISIONS RELATING TO THE OFFER, DISTRIBUTION, AND SALE OF VEHICLE EQUIPMENT



## SUBCHAPTER D. GENERAL PROVISIONS REGARDING LIGHTING REQUIREMENTS

## SUBCHAPTER E. GENERAL LIGHTING REQUIREMENTS FOR VEHICLES

547.321. Headlamps required.
547.3215. Use of federal standard.
547.322. Taillamps required.
547.323. Stoplamps required.
547.324. Turn signal lamps required.
547.325. Reflectors required.
547.326. Minimum lighting equipment required.
547.327. Spotlamps permitted.
547.328. Fog lamps permitted.
547.329. Auxiliary passing lamps permitted.
547.330. Auxiliary driving lamps permitted.
547.331. Hazard lamps permitted.
547.332. Other lamps permitted.
547.333. Multiple-beam lighting equipment required.
547.334. Single-beam lighting equipment permitted.
547.335. Alternative road lighting equipment permitted.
547.336 to
547.350. *(Reserved.)*

## SUBCHAPTER F. ADDITIONAL LIGHTING REQUIREMENTS FOR CERTAIN LARGE VEHICLES

547.351. Applicability.
547.352. Additional lighting equipment requirements.
547.353. Color requirements.
547.354. Mounting requirements.
547.355. Visibility requirements.
547.356 to
547.370. *(Reserved.)*

## SUBCHAPTER G. ALTERNATIVE LIGHTING REQUIREMENTS FOR FARM TRACTORS, FARM EQUIPMENT, AND IMPLEMENTS OF HUSBANDRY

547.371. General lighting equipment requirements.
547.372. Lighting requirements for combination vehicles.
547.373 to
547.380. *(Reserved.)*

## SUBCHAPTER H. LIGHTING REQUIREMENTS IN SPECIAL CIRCUMSTANCES

547.381. Obstructed lights on combination vehicles.
547.382. Lighting equipment on projecting loads.
547.383. Lighting requirements on parked vehicles.
547.384 to
547.400. *(Reserved.)*

## SUBCHAPTER I. PROVISIONS RELATING TO BRAKE REQUIREMENTS ON VEHICLES

547.401. Brakes required.
547.402. Operation and maintenance of brakes.
547.403. Service brakes required.
547.404. Parking brakes required.

## SUBCHAPTER J. PROVISIONS RELATING TO WARNING DEVICE REQUIREMENTS ON VEHICLES



## SUBCHAPTER K. PROVISIONS RELATING TO OTHER VEHICLE EQUIPMENT



## SUBCHAPTER L. ADDITIONAL EQUIPMENT REQUIREMENTS FOR SCHOOL BUSES, AUTHORIZED EMERGENCY VEHICLES, AND SLOW-MOVING VEHICLES



## SUBCHAPTER M. ADDITIONAL OR ALTERNATIVE EQUIPMENT REQUIREMENTS FOR MOTORCYCLES AND MOTOR-DRIVEN CYCLES

## SUBCHAPTER A. GENERAL PROVISIONS

### §547.001. Definitions.

In this chapter:

(1) "Air-conditioning equipment" means mechanical vapor compression refrigeration equipment used to cool a motor vehicle passenger or operator compartment.

(2) "Explosive cargo vehicle" means a motor vehicle used to transport explosives or a cargo tank truck used to transport a flammable liquid or compressed gas.

(3) "Light transmission" means the ratio of the amount of light that passes through a material to the amount of light that falls on the material and the glazing.

(4) "Luminous reflectance" means the ratio of the amount of light that is reflected by a material to the amount of light that falls on the material.

(5) "Multipurpose vehicle" means a motor vehicle that is:

(A) designed to carry 10 or fewer persons; and

(B) constructed on a truck chassis or with special features for occasional off-road use.

(6) "Safety glazing material" includes only a glazing material that is constructed, treated, or combined with another material to reduce substantially, as compared to ordinary sheet or plate glass, the likelihood of injury to persons by an external object or by cracked or broken glazing material.

(7) "Slow-moving vehicle" means:

(A) a motor vehicle designed to operate at a maximum speed of 25 miles per hour or less; or

(B) a vehicle, implement of husbandry, or machinery, including road construction machinery, that is towed by:

(i) an animal; or

(ii) a motor vehicle designed to operate at a maximum speed of 25 miles per hour or less.

(8) "Slow-moving-vehicle emblem" means a triangular emblem that conforms to standards and specifications adopted by the director under Section 547.104.

(9) "Sunscreening device" means a film, material, or device that meets the department's standards for reducing effects of the sun.

(10) "Vehicle equipment" means:

(A) a system, part, or device that is manufactured or sold as original or replacement equipment or as a vehicle accessory; or

(B) a device or apparel manufactured or sold to protect a vehicle operator or passenger.

*(Added by L.1995, chap. 165(1), eff. 9/1/95.)*

### §547.002. Applicability.

Unless a provision is specifically made applicable, this chapter and the rules of the department adopted under this chapter do not apply to:

(1) an implement of husbandry;

(2) road machinery;

(3) a road roller;

(4) a farm tractor;

(5) a bicycle, a bicyclist, or bicycle equipment; or

(6) a golf cart not required to be registered under Section 502.284.

*(Added by L.1995, chap. 165(1); chgd. by L.1997, chap. 896(2), eff. 9/1/97.)*

### §547.003. Equipment not affected.

This chapter does not prohibit and the department by rule may not prohibit the use of:

(1) equipment required by an agency of the United States; or

(2) a part or accessory not inconsistent with this chapter or a rule adopted under this chapter.

*(Added by L.1995, chap. 165(1), eff. 9/1/95.)*

### §547.004. General offenses.

(a) A person commits an offense that is a misdemeanor if the person operates or moves or, as an owner, knowingly permits another to operate or move, a vehicle that:

(1) is unsafe so as to endanger a person;

(2) is not equipped in a manner that complies with the vehicle equipment standards and requirements established by this chapter; or

(3) is equipped in a manner prohibited by this chapter.

(b) A person commits an offense that is a misdemeanor if the person operates a vehicle equipped with an item of vehicle equipment that the person knows has been determined in a compliance proceeding under Section 547.206 to not comply with a department standard.

*(Added by L.1995, chap. 165(1), eff. 9/1/95.)*

**§547.005. Offense relating to violation of special-use provisions.**

(a) A person may not use a slow-moving-vehicle emblem on a stationary object or a vehicle other than a slow-moving vehicle.

(b) A person may not operate a motor vehicle bearing the words "school bus" unless the vehicle is used primarily to transport persons to or from school or a school-related activity. In this subsection, "school" means a privately or publicly supported elementary or secondary school, day-care center, preschool, or institution of higher education and includes a church if the church is engaged in providing formal education.

*(Added by L.1995, chap. 165(1), eff. 9/1/95.)*

**§§547.006 to 547.100.** *(Reserved.)*

## SUBCHAPTER B. ADOPTION OF RULES AND STANDARDS

**§547.101. Rules and standards in general.**

(a) The department may adopt rules necessary to administer this chapter.

(b) The department may adopt standards for vehicle equipment to:

(1) protect the public from unreasonable risk of death or injury; and

(2) enforce safety standards of the United States as permitted under the federal motor vehicle act.

(c) A department standard must:

(1) duplicate a standard of the United States that applies to the same aspect of vehicle equipment performance as the department standard; or

(2) if there is no standard of the United States for the same aspect of vehicle equipment performance as the department standard, conform as closely as possible to a relevant standard of the United States, similar standards established by other states, and a standard issued or endorsed by recognized national standard-setting organizations or agencies.

(d) The department may not adopt a vehicle equipment standard inconsistent with a standard provided by this chapter.

*(Added by L.1995, chap. 165(1), eff. 9/1/95.)*

**§547.102. School bus equipment standards.**

The department may adopt standards and specifications that:

(1) supplement the standards and specifications provided by this chapter;

(2) apply to lighting and warning device equipment required for a school bus; and

(3) at the time adopted, correlate with and conform as closely as possible to specifications approved by the Society of Automotive Engineers.

*(Added by L.1995, chap. 165(1), eff. 9/1/95.)*

**§547.103. Air-conditioning equipment standards.**

The department may adopt safety requirements, rules, and specifications that:

(1) apply to air-conditioning equipment; and

(2) correlate with and conform as closely as possible to recommended practices or standards approved by the Society of Automotive Engineers.

*(Added by L.1995, chap. 165(1), eff. 9/1/95.)*

**§547.104. Slow-moving-vehicle emblem standards.**

The director shall adopt standards and specifications that:

(1) apply to the color, size, and mounting position of a slow-moving-vehicle emblem; and

(2) at the time adopted, correlate with and conform as closely as practicable to the standards and specifications adopted or approved by the American Society of Agricultural Engineers for a uniform emblem to identify a slow-moving vehicle.

*(Added by L.1995, chap. 165(1), eff. 9/1/95.)*

**§547.105. Maintenance and service equipment lighting standards.**

(a) The Texas Department of Transportation shall adopt standards and specifications that:

(1) apply to lamps on highway maintenance and service equipment, including snow-removal equipment; and

(2) correlate with and conform as closely as possible to standards and specifications approved by the American Association of State Highway and Transportation Officials.

(b) The Texas Department of Transportation may adopt standards and specifications for lighting that permit the use of flashing lights for identification purposes on highway maintenance and service equipment, including snow-removal equipment.

(c) The standards and specifications adopted under this section are in lieu of the standards and specifications otherwise provided by this chapter for lamps on vehicles.
*(Added by L.1995, chap. 165(1), eff. 9/1/95.)*

**§§547.106 to 547.200.** *(Reserved.)*

## SUBCHAPTER C. PROVISIONS RELATING TO THE OFFER, DISTRIBUTION, AND SALE OF VEHICLE EQUIPMENT

### §547.201. Offenses relating to the offer, distribution, and sale of vehicle equipment.

(a) A person may not offer or distribute for sale or sell an item of vehicle equipment for which a standard is prescribed by this chapter or the department and that does not comply with the standard. It is an affirmative defense to prosecution under this subsection that the person did not have reason to know in the exercise of due care that the item did not comply with the applicable standard.

(b) A person may not offer or distribute for sale or sell an item of vehicle equipment for which a standard is prescribed by this chapter or the department, unless the item or its package:

(1) bears the manufacturer's trademark or brand name; or

(2) complies with each applicable identification requirement established by an agency of the United States or the department.
*(Added by L.1995, chap. 165(1), eff. 9/1/95.)*

### §547.202. Department certification or approval of vehicle equipment.

(a) When or after an item of vehicle equipment is sold in this state, the department shall determine whether a department standard is prescribed for the item. If a department standard is prescribed, the department shall determine whether the item complies with the standard.

(b) If a standard of an agency of the United States or of the department is not prescribed, the department by rule may require departmental approval before the sale of the item.
*(Added by L.1995, chap. 165(1), eff. 9/1/95.)*

### §547.203. Vehicle equipment testing: department standards.

(a) The department shall prescribe standards for and approve testing facilities to:

(1) review test data submitted by a manufacturer to show compliance with a department standard; and

(2) test an item of vehicle equipment independently in connection with a proceeding to determine compliance with a department standard.

(b) The department may not impose a product certification or approval fee, including a fee for testing facility approval.

(c) The department may:

(1) by rule, require a manufacturer of an item of vehicle equipment sold in this state to submit adequate test data to show that the item complies with department standards;

(2) periodically require a manufacturer to submit revised test data to demonstrate continuing compliance;

(3) purchase an item of vehicle equipment at retail for the purpose of review and testing under Subsection (a); and

(4) enter into cooperative arrangements with other states and interstate agencies to reduce duplication of testing and to facilitate compliance with rules under Subsection (c)(1).
*(Added by L.1995, chap. 165(1), eff. 9/1/95.)*

### §547.204. Vehicle equipment testing: federal standards.

(a) For a vehicle or item of vehicle equipment subject to a motor vehicle safety standard of the United States, the department may, on or after the first sale of the vehicle or item of vehicle equipment:

(1) require the manufacturer to submit adequate test data to show that the vehicle or item of vehicle equipment complies with standards of the United States;

(2) review the manufacturer's laboratory test data and the qualifications of the laboratory; and

(3) independently test the vehicle or item of vehicle equipment.

(b) The department may not require certification or approval of an item of vehicle equipment subject to a motor vehicle safety standard of the United States.

(c) The department may not require a manufacturer of a vehicle or of an item of vehicle equipment subject to a motor vehicle safety standard of the United States to use an outside laboratory or a specified laboratory.
*(Added by L.1995, chap. 165(1), eff. 9/1/95.)*

## §547.205. Initiation of compliance proceeding.

(a) The department may initiate a proceeding to determine whether an item of vehicle equipment complies with a department standard if the department reasonably believes that the item is being offered or distributed for sale or sold in violation of the standard.

(b) The department shall send written notice of the proceeding to the manufacturer of the item by certified mail, return receipt requested.

(c) The notice required by Subsection (b) must:

(1) cite the standard that the item allegedly violates; and

(2) state that the manufacturer must file a written request with the department for a hearing not later than the 30th day after the date the notice is received to obtain a hearing on the issue of compliance.

(d) When the department sends notice under Subsection (b), the department shall require the manufacturer to submit to the department, not later than the 30th day after the date the notice is received, the names and addresses of the persons the manufacturer knows to be offering the item for sale to retail merchants.

(e) On receipt under Subsection (d) of the names and addresses, the department shall send by certified mail, return receipt requested, written notice of the compliance proceeding to those persons.

(f) The notice must:

(1) cite the standard that the item allegedly violates;

(2) state that the manufacturer of the item has been notified and may request a hearing on the issue of compliance before a stated date;

(3) state that if the manufacturer or another person requests a hearing, the person may appear at the hearing;

(4) state that if the manufacturer does not request a hearing, the person may request a hearing by filing a written request with the department not later than the 30th day after the date notice is received; and

(5) state that the person may determine from the department whether a hearing will be held and the time and place of the hearing.
*(Added by L.1995, chap. 165(1), eff. 9/1/95.)*



## §547.206. Compliance proceeding hearing.

The department shall conduct a hearing on the issue of compliance if a person required by Section 547.205 to be notified requests a hearing in the manner and within the time specified by that section. *(Added by L.1995, chap. 165(1), eff. 9/1/95.)*

## §547.207. Compliance proceeding issues.

(a) In a hearing under Section 547.206 or in the absence of a request for a hearing, the department may make a determination of the following issues only:

(1) whether an item of vehicle equipment has been offered, distributed, or sold in violation of a department standard;

(2) whether the manufacturer did not submit test data required by the department under Section 547.203; and

(3) whether an item of vehicle equipment has been offered, distributed, or sold without the identification required by Section 547.201.

(b) The department by order shall prohibit the manufacture, offer for sale, distribution for sale, or sale of the item if the department finds affirmatively on at least one of the issues.

(c) After entering its order, the department shall send written notice by certified mail, return receipt requested, to each person the department notified under Section 547.205.
*(Added by L.1995, chap. 165(1), eff. 9/1/95.)*

## §547.208. Judicial review and judicial enforcement.

(a) A person may appeal an order entered under Section 547.207 to a district court in Travis County only if a hearing was held by the department and the person:

(1) is aggrieved by the order; and

(2) appeared at the hearing on compliance.

(b) The department may bring suit in a district court of Travis County for an injunction to prohibit the manufacture, offer, distribution, or sale of an item of vehicle equipment that is the subject of a department order entered under Section 547.207. The attorney general shall represent the department in the suit.
*(Added by L.1995, chap. 165(1), eff. 9/1/95.)*

### §§547.209 to 547.300. *(Reserved.)*

## SUBCHAPTER D. GENERAL PROVISIONS REGARDING LIGHTING REQUIREMENTS

### §547.301. General provisions relating to measurements.

(a) Unless expressly stated otherwise, a visibility distance requirement imposed by this chapter for a lamp or device applies when a lighted lamp or device is required and is measured as if the vehicle were unloaded and on a straight, level, unlighted highway under normal atmospheric conditions.

(b) A mounted height requirement imposed by this chapter for a lamp or device is measured as if the vehicle were unloaded and on level ground and is measured from the center of the lamp or device to the ground.
*(Added by L.1995, chap. 165(1), eff. 9/1/95.)*

### §547.302. Duty to display lights.

(a) A vehicle shall display each lighted lamp and illuminating device required by this chapter to be on the vehicle:

(1) at nighttime; and

(2) when light is insufficient or atmospheric conditions are unfavorable so that a person or vehicle on the highway is not clearly discernible at a distance of 1,000 feet ahead.

(b) A signaling device, including a stoplamp or a turn signal lamp, shall be lighted as prescribed by this chapter.

(c) At least one lighted lamp shall be displayed on each side of the front of a motor vehicle.

(d) Not more than four of the following may be lighted at one time on the front of a motor vehicle:

(1) a headlamp required by this chapter; or

(2) a lamp, including an auxiliary lamp or spotlamp, that projects a beam with an intensity brighter than 300 candlepower.
*(Added by L.1995, chap. 165(1), eff. 9/1/95.)*

### §547.303. Color requirements.

(a) Unless expressly provided otherwise, a lighting device or reflector mounted on the rear of a vehicle must be or reflect red.

(b) A signaling device mounted on the rear of a vehicle may be red, amber, or yellow.
*(Added by L.1995, chap. 165(1), eff. 9/1/95.)*

### §547.304. Applicability.

(a) A provision of this chapter that requires a vehicle to be equipped with fixed electric lights does not apply to a farm trailer or fertilizer trailer registered under Section 502.276 or a boat trailer with a gross weight of 3,000 pounds or less if the trailer is not operated at a time or under a condition specified by Section 547.302(a).

(b) Except for Sections 547.323 and 547.324, a provision of this chapter that requires a vehicle to be equipped with fixed electric lights does not apply to a boat trailer with a gross weight of less than 4,500 pounds if the trailer is not operated at a time or under a condition specified by Section 547.302(a).

(c) Except for Sections 547.323 and 547.324, a provision of this chapter that requires a vehicle to be equipped with lamps, reflectors, and lighting equipment does not apply to a mobile home if the mobile home:

(1) is moved under a permit issued by the Texas Department of Transportation under Subchapter D, Chapter 623; and

(2) is not moved at a time or under a condition specified by Section 547.302(a).

(d) A mobile home lighted as provided by this section may be moved only during daytime.
*(Added by L.1995, chap. 165(1), eff. 9/1/95.)*

## §547.305. Restrictions on use of lights.

(a) A motor vehicle lamp or illuminating device, other than a headlamp, spotlamp, auxiliary lamp, turn signal lamp, or emergency vehicle or school bus warning lamp, that projects a beam with an intensity brighter than 300 candlepower shall be directed so that no part of the high-intensity portion of the beam strikes the roadway at a distance of more than 75 feet from the vehicle.

(b) Except as expressly authorized by law, a person may not operate or move equipment or a vehicle, other than a police vehicle, with a lamp or device that displays a red light visible from directly in front of the center of the equipment or vehicle.

(c) A person may not operate a motor vehicle equipped with a red, white, or blue beacon, flashing, or alternating light unless the equipment is:

(1) used as specifically authorized by this chapter; or

(2) a running lamp, headlamp, taillamp, backup lamp, or turn signal lamp that is used as authorized by law.

(d) A vehicle may be equipped with alternately flashing lighting equipment described by Section 547.701 or 547.702 only if the vehicle is:

(1) a school bus;

(2) an authorized emergency vehicle;

(3) a church bus that has the words "church bus" printed on the front and rear of the bus so as to be clearly discernable to other vehicle operators;

(4) a tow truck while under the direction of a law enforcement officer at the scene of an accident or while hooking up to a disabled vehicle on a roadway; or

(5) a tow truck with a mounted light bar which has turn signals and stop lamps in addition to those required by Sections 547.322, 547.323, and 547.324, Transportation Code.

(e) A person may not operate highway maintenance or service equipment, including snow-removal equipment, that is not equipped with lamps or that does not display lighted lamps as required by the standards and specifications adopted by the Texas Department of Transportation.

(f) In this section "tow truck" means a motor vehicle or mechanical device that is adapted or used to tow, winch, or move a disabled vehicle.

*(Added by L.1995, chap. 165(1); chgd. by L.1999, chap. 380(1), eff. 7/1/99.)*

## §§547.306 to 547.320. *(Reserved.)*

# SUBCHAPTER E. GENERAL LIGHTING REQUIREMENTS FOR VEHICLES

## §547.321. Headlamps required.

(a) A motor vehicle shall be equipped with at least two headlamps.

(b) At least one headlamp shall be mounted on each side of the front of the vehicle.

(c) Each headlamp shall be mounted at a height from 24 to 54 inches.

*(Added by L.1995, chap. 165(1), eff. 9/1/95.)*

## §547.3215. Use of federal standard.

Unless specifically prohibited by this chapter, lighting, reflective devices, and associated equipment on a vehicle or motor vehicle must comply with:

(1) the current federal standards in 49 C.F.R. Section 571.108; or

(2) the federal standards in that section in effect, if any, at the time the vehicle or motor vehicle was manufactured.

*(Added by L.1997, chap. 324(1), eff. 9/1/97.)*

## §547.322. Taillamps required.

(a) Except as provided by Subsection (b), a motor vehicle, trailer, semitrailer, pole trailer, or vehicle that is towed at the end of a combination of vehicles shall be equipped with at least two taillamps.

(b) A passenger car or truck that was manufactured or assembled before the model year 1960 shall be equipped with at least one taillamp.

(c) Taillamps shall be mounted on the rear of the vehicle:

(1) at a height from 15 to 72 inches; and

(2) at the same level and spaced as widely apart as practicable if a vehicle is equipped with more than one lamp.

(d) A taillamp shall emit a red light plainly visible at a distance of 1,000 feet from the rear of the vehicle.

(e) If vehicles are traveling in combination, only the taillamps on the rearmost vehicle are required to emit a light for the distance specified in Subsection (d).

(f) A taillamp or a separate lamp shall be constructed and mounted to emit a white light that:

(1) illuminates the rear license plate; and

(2) makes the plate clearly legible at a distance of 50 feet from the rear.

(g) A taillamp, including a separate lamp used to illuminate a rear license plate, must emit a light when a headlamp or auxiliary driving lamp is lighted.

*(Added by L.1995, chap. 165(1), eff. 9/1/95.)*

## §547.323. Stoplamps required.

(a) Except as provided by Subsection (b), a motor vehicle, trailer, semitrailer, or pole trailer shall be equipped with at least two stoplamps.

(b) A passenger car manufactured or assembled before the model year 1960 shall be equipped with at least one stoplamp.

(c) A stoplamp shall be mounted on the rear of the vehicle.

(d) A stoplamp shall emit a red or amber light, or a color between red and amber, that is:

(1) visible in normal sunlight at a distance of at least 300 feet from the rear of the vehicle; and

(2) displayed when the vehicle service brake is applied.

(e) If vehicles are traveling in combination, only the stoplamps on the rearmost vehicle are required to emit a light for the distance specified in Subsection (d).

(f) A stoplamp may be included as a part of another rear lamp.

*(Added by L.1995, chap. 165(1), eff. 9/1/95.)*

## §547.324. Turn signal lamps required.

(a) Except as provided by Subsection (b), a motor vehicle, trailer, semitrailer, or pole trailer shall be equipped with electric turn signal lamps that indicate the operator's intent to turn by displaying flashing lights to the front and rear of a vehicle or combination of vehicles and on that side of the vehicle or combination toward which the turn is to be made.

(b) Subsection (a) does not apply to a passenger car or truck less than 80 inches wide manufactured or assembled before the model year 1960.

(c) Turn signal lamps:

(1) shall be mounted at the same level and spaced as widely apart as practicable on the front and on the rear of the vehicle; and

(2) may be included as a part of another lamp on the vehicle.

(d) A turn signal lamp shall emit:

(1) a white or amber light, or a color between white and amber, if the lamp is mounted on the front of the vehicle; or

(2) a red or amber light, or a color between red and amber, if the lamp is mounted on the rear of the vehicle.

(e) A turn signal lamp must be visible in normal sunlight at a distance of:

(1) at least 500 feet from the front and rear of the vehicle if the vehicle is at least 80 inches wide; and

(2) at least 300 feet from the front and rear of the vehicle if the vehicle is less than 80 inches wide.

*(Added by L.1995, chap. 165(1), eff. 9/1/95.)*

## §547.325. Reflectors required.

(a) Except as provided by Subchapter F, a motor vehicle, trailer, semitrailer, or pole trailer shall be equipped with at least two red reflectors on the rear of the vehicle. A red reflector may be included as a part of a taillamp.

(b) A reflector shall be:

(1) mounted at a height from 15 to 60 inches; and

(2) visible at night at all distances:

(A) from 100 to 600 feet when directly in front of lawful lower beams of headlamps; or

(B) from 100 to 350 feet when directly in front of lawful upper beams of headlamps if the vehicle was manufactured or assembled before January 1, 1972.

*(Added by L.1995, chap. 165(1), eff. 9/1/95.)*

## §547.326. Minimum lighting equipment required.

(a) A vehicle that is not specifically required to be equipped with lamps or other lighting devices shall be equipped at the times specified in Section 547.302(a) with at least one lamp that emits a white light visible at a distance of at least 1,000 feet from the front and:

(1) two lamps that emit a red light visible at a distance of at least 1,000 feet from the rear; or

(2) one lamp that emits a red light visible at a distance of at least 1,000 feet from the rear and two red reflectors visible when illuminated by the lawful lower beams of headlamps at all distances from 100 to 600 feet to the rear.

(b) This section also applies to an animal-drawn vehicle and a vehicle exempted from this chapter by Section 547.002.

*(Added by L.1995, chap. 165(1), eff. 9/1/95.)*

### §547.327. Spotlamps permitted.

(a) A motor vehicle may be equipped with not more than two spotlamps.

(b) A spotlamp shall be aimed so that no part of the high-intensity portion of the beam strikes the windshield, window, mirror, or occupant of another vehicle in use.

*(Added by L.1995, chap. 165(1), eff. 9/1/95.)*

### §547.328. Fog lamps permitted.

(a) A motor vehicle may be equipped with not more than two fog lamps.

(b) A fog lamp shall be:

(1) mounted on the front of the vehicle at a height from 12 to 30 inches; and

(2) aimed so that no part of the high-intensity portion of the beam from a lamp mounted to the left of center on a vehicle projects a beam of light at a distance of 25 feet that is higher than four inches below the level of the center of the lamp.

(c) Lighted fog lamps may be used with lower headlamp beams as specified by Section 547.333.

*(Added by L.1995, chap. 165(1), eff. 9/1/95.)*



### §547.329. Auxiliary passing lamps permitted.

(a) A motor vehicle may be equipped with no more than two auxiliary passing lamps.

(b) An auxiliary passing lamp shall be mounted on the front of the vehicle at a height from 24 to 42 inches.

(c) An auxiliary passing lamp may be used with headlamps as specified by Section 547.333.

*(Added by L.1995, chap. 165(1), eff. 9/1/95.)*

### §547.330. Auxiliary driving lamps permitted.

(a) A motor vehicle may be equipped with no more than two auxiliary driving lamps.

(b) An auxiliary driving lamp shall be mounted on the front of the vehicle at a height from 16 to 42 inches.

(c) Auxiliary driving lamps may be used with headlamps as specified by Section 547.333.

*(Added by L.1995, chap. 165(1), eff. 9/1/95.)*

### §547.331. Hazard lamps permitted.

(a) A vehicle may be equipped with lamps to warn other vehicle operators of a vehicular traffic hazard that requires unusual care in approaching, overtaking, or passing.

(b) The lamps shall be:

(1) mounted at the same level and spaced as widely apart as practicable on the front and on the rear of the vehicle; and

(2) visible at a distance of at least 500 feet in normal sunlight.

(c) The lamps shall display simultaneously flashing lights that emit:

(1) a white or amber light, or a color between white and amber, if the lamp is mounted on the front of the vehicle; or

(2) a red or amber light, or a color between red and amber, if the lamp is mounted on the rear of the vehicle.

*(Added by L.1995, chap. 165(1), eff. 9/1/95.)*

### §547.332. Other lamps permitted.

A motor vehicle may be equipped with:

(1) not more than two side cowl or fender lamps that emit an amber or white light without glare;

(2) not more than two running board courtesy lamps, one on each side of the vehicle, that emit an amber or white light without glare; and

(3) one or more backup lamps that:

(A) emit an amber or white light only when the vehicle is not moving forward; and

(B) may be displayed separately or in combination with another lamp.
*(Added by L.1995, chap. 165(1), eff. 9/1/95.)*

### §547.333. Multiple-beam lighting equipment required.

(a) Unless provided otherwise, a headlamp, auxiliary driving lamp, auxiliary passing lamp, or combination of those lamps mounted on a motor vehicle, other than a motorcycle or motor-driven cycle:

(1) shall be arranged so that the operator can select at will between distributions of light projected at different elevations; and

(2) may be arranged so that the operator can select the distribution automatically.

(b) A lamp identified by Subsection (a) shall produce:

(1) an uppermost distribution of light or composite beam that is aimed and emits light sufficient to reveal a person or vehicle at a distance of at least 450 feet ahead during all conditions of loading; and

(2) a lowermost distribution of light or composite beam that:

(A) is aimed and emits light sufficient to reveal a person or vehicle at a distance of at least 150 feet ahead; and

(B) is aimed so that no part of the high-intensity portion of the beam on a vehicle that is operated on a straight, level road under any condition of loading projects into the eyes of an approaching vehicle operator.

(c) A person who operates a vehicle on a roadway or shoulder shall select a distribution of light or composite beam that is aimed and emits light sufficient to reveal a person or vehicle at a safe distance ahead of the vehicle, except that:

(1) an operator approaching an oncoming vehicle within 500 feet shall select:

(A) the lowermost distribution of light or composite beam, regardless of road contour or condition of loading; or

(B) a distribution aimed so that no part of the high-intensity portion of the lamp projects into the eyes of an approaching vehicle operator; and

(2) an operator approaching a vehicle from the rear within 300 feet may not select the uppermost distribution of light.

(d) A motor vehicle of a model year of 1948 or later, other than a motorcycle or motor-driven cycle, that has multiple-beam lighting equipment shall be equipped with a beam indicator that is:

(1) designed and located so that the lighted indicator is visible without glare to the vehicle operator; and

(2) lighted only when the uppermost distribution of light is in use.
*(Added by L.1995, chap. 165(1), eff. 9/1/95.)*

### §547.334. Single-beam lighting equipment permitted.

(a) In lieu of the multiple-beam lighting equipment required by Section 547.333, a headlamp system that provides a single distribution of light and meets the requirements of Subsection (b) is permitted for:

(1) a farm tractor; or

(2) a motor vehicle manufactured and sold before September 4, 1948.

(b) The headlamp system specified by Subsection (a) shall:

(1) emit a light sufficient to reveal a person or vehicle at a distance of at least 200 feet; and

(2) be aimed so that no part of the high-intensity portion of the lamp projects a beam:

(A) higher than five inches below the level of the center of the lamp at a distance of 25 feet ahead; or

(B) higher than 42 inches above the ground at a distance of 75 feet ahead.
*(Added by L.1995, chap. 165(1), eff. 9/1/95.)*

### §547.335. Alternative road lighting equipment permitted.

In lieu of the multiple-beam or single-beam lighting equipment otherwise required by this subchapter, a motor vehicle that is operated at a speed of not more than 20 miles per hour under the conditions specified in Section 547.302(a) may be equipped with two lighted lamps:

(1) mounted on the front of the vehicle; and

(2) capable of revealing a person or vehicle 100 feet ahead.
*(Added by L.1995, chap. 165(1), eff. 9/1/95.)*

### §§547.336 to 547.350. *(Reserved.)*

## SUBCHAPTER F. ADDITIONAL LIGHTING REQUIREMENTS FOR CERTAIN LARGE VEHICLES

### §547.351. Applicability.

The color, mounting, and visibility requirements in this subchapter apply only to equipment on a vehicle described by Section 547.352. *(Added by L.1995, chap. 165(1), eff. 9/1/95.)*

### §547.352. Additional lighting equipment requirements.

In addition to other equipment required by this chapter:

(1) a bus, truck, trailer, or semitrailer that is at least 80 inches wide shall be equipped with:

(A) two clearance lamps on the front, one at each side;

(B) two clearance lamps on the rear, one at each side;

(C) four side marker lamps, one on each side at or near the front and one on each side at or near the rear;

(D) four reflectors, one on each side at or near the front and one on each side at or near the rear; and

(E) hazard lamps that meet the requirements of Section 547.331;

(2) a bus or truck that is at least 30 feet long shall be equipped with hazard lamps that meet the requirements of Section 547.331;

(3) a trailer or semitrailer that is at least 30 feet long shall be equipped with:

(A) two side marker lamps, one centrally mounted on each side with respect to the length of the vehicle;

(B) two reflectors, one centrally mounted on each side with respect to the length of the vehicle; and

(C) hazard lamps that meet the requirements of Section 547.331;

(4) a pole trailer shall be equipped with:

(A) two side marker lamps, one at each side at or near the front of the load;

(B) one reflector at or near the front of the load;

(C) one combination marker lamp that:

(i) emits an amber light to the front and a red light to the rear and side; and

(ii) is mounted on the rearmost support for the load to indicate the maximum width of the trailer; and

(D) hazard lamps that meet the requirements of Section 547.331, if the pole trailer is at least 30 feet long or at least 80 inches wide;

(5) a truck-tractor shall be equipped with:

(A) two clearance lamps, one at each side on the front of the cab; and

(B) hazard lamps that meet the requirements of Section 547.331, if the truck-tractor is at least 30 feet long or at least 80 inches wide; and

(6) a vehicle at least 80 inches wide may be equipped with:

(A) not more than three front identification lamps without glare; and

(B) not more than three rear identification lamps without glare.

*(Added by L.1995, chap. 165(1), eff. 9/1/95.)*

### §547.353. Color requirements.

(a) A clearance lamp, identification lamp, side marker lamp, or reflector mounted on the front, on the side near the front, or in the center of the vehicle must be or reflect amber.

(b) A clearance lamp, identification lamp, side marker lamp, or reflector mounted on the rear or the side near the rear of the vehicle must be or reflect red.

*(Added by L.1995, chap. 165(1), eff. 9/1/95.)*

### §547.354. Mounting requirements.

(a) A reflector shall be mounted:

(1) at a height from 24 to 60 inches; or

(2) as high as practicable on the permanent structure of the vehicle if the highest part of the permanent structure is less than 24 inches.

(b) A rear reflector may be:

(1) included as a part of a taillamp if the reflector meets each other requirement of this subchapter; and

(2) mounted on each side of the bolster or load, if the vehicle is a pole trailer.

(c) A clearance lamp shall be mounted, if practicable, on the permanent structure of the vehicle to indicate the extreme height and width of the vehicle, except that:

(1) a clearance lamp on a truck-tractor shall be mounted to indicate the extreme width of the cab; and

(2) a front clearance lamp may be mounted at a height that indicates, as near as practicable, the extreme width of the trailer if mounting of the lamp as otherwise provided by this section would not indicate the extreme width of the trailer.

(d) A clearance lamp and side marker lamp may be mounted in combination if each lamp complies with the visibility requirements of Section 547.355.
*(Added by L.1995, chap. 165(1), eff. 9/1/95.)*

### §547.355. Visibility requirements.

(a) A clearance lamp, identification lamp, or side marker lamp shall be visible and recognizable under normal atmospheric conditions at all distances from 50 to 500 feet from the vehicle on the side, front, or rear where the lamp is mounted.

(b) A reflector required by this chapter mounted on a vehicle subject to this subchapter shall be visible from the rear, if a rear reflector, or from the applicable side, if a side reflector, at nighttime at all distances from 100 to 600 feet from the vehicle when the reflector is directly in front of:

(1) lawful lower beams of headlamps; or

(2) lawful upper beams of headlamps on a vehicle manufactured or assembled before January 1, 1972.
*(Added by L.1995, chap. 165(1), eff. 9/1/95.)*

### §§547.356 to 547.370. *(Reserved.)*

## SUBCHAPTER G. ALTERNATIVE LIGHTING REQUIREMENTS FOR FARM TRACTORS, FARM EQUIPMENT, AND IMPLEMENTS OF HUSBANDRY

### §547.371. General lighting equipment requirements.

(a) Except as provided by Subsection (b), a farm tractor, self-propelled unit of farm equipment, or implement of husbandry shall be equipped with:

(1) at least two headlamps that comply with Section 547.333, 547.334, or 547.335;

(2) at least one red lamp visible at a distance of at least 1,000 feet from the rear and mounted as far to the left of the center of the vehicle as practicable;

(3) at least two red reflectors visible at all distances from 100 to 600 feet from the rear when directly in front of lawful lower beams of headlamps; and

(4) hazard lamps as described in Section 547.331, which shall be lighted and visible in normal sunlight at a distance of at least 1,000 feet from the front and rear.

(b) A farm tractor, self-propelled unit of farm equipment, or implement of husbandry manufactured or assembled on or before January 1, 1972, is required to be equipped as provided by Subsection (a) only at the times specified by Section 547.302(a), and hazard lamps are not required.
*(Added by L.1995, chap. 165(1), eff. 9/1/95.)*

### §547.372. Lighting requirements for combination vehicles.

(a) If a unit of farm equipment or implement of husbandry is towed by a farm tractor and the towed object or its load extends more than four feet to the rear of the tractor or obscures a light on the tractor, the towed object shall be equipped at the times specified by Section 547.302(a) with at least two rear red reflectors that are:

(1) visible at all distances from 100 to 600 feet when directly in front of lawful lower beams of headlamps; and

(2) mounted to indicate, as nearly as practicable, the extreme width of the vehicle or combination of vehicles.

(b) If a unit of farm equipment or implement of husbandry is towed by a farm tractor and extends more than four feet to the left of the centerline of the tractor, the towed object shall be equipped at the times specified by Section 547.302(a) with a front amber reflector that is:

(1) visible at all distances from 100 to 600 feet when directly in front of lawful lower beams of headlamps; and

(2) mounted to indicate, as nearly as practicable, the extreme left projection of the towed object.

(c) Reflective tape or paint may be used as an alternative to the reflectors required by this section if the alternative complies with the other requirements of this section.
*(Added by L.1995, chap. 165(1), eff. 9/1/95.)*

**§§547.373 to 547.380.** *(Reserved.)*

## SUBCHAPTER H. LIGHTING REQUIREMENTS IN SPECIAL CIRCUMSTANCES

### §547.381. Obstructed lights on combination vehicles.

(a) A motor vehicle when operated in combination with another vehicle is not required to display a lighted lamp, other than a taillamp, if the lamp is obscured because of its location by another vehicle in the combination of vehicles.

(b) Subsection (a) is not an exception for the lighting as provided by this chapter of:

(1) front clearance lamps on the frontmost vehicle in the combination; or

(2) rear lamps on the rearmost vehicle in the combination.

*(Added by L.1995, chap. 165(1), eff. 9/1/95.)*



### §547.382. Lighting equipment on projecting loads.

(a) A vehicle transporting a load that extends to the rear at least four feet beyond the bed or body of the vehicle shall display on the extreme end of the load at the times specified in Section 547.302(a):

(1) two red lamps visible at a distance of at least 500 feet from the rear;

(2) two red reflectors that indicate the maximum width and are visible at nighttime at all distances from 100 to 600 feet from the rear when directly in front of lawful lower beams of head lamps; and

(3) two red lamps, one on each side, that indicate the maximum overhang and are visible at a distance of at least 500 feet from the side.

(b) At all other times, a vehicle transporting a load that extends beyond the vehicle's sides or more than four feet beyond the vehicle's rear shall display red flags that:

(1) are at least 12 inches square;

(2) mark the extremities of the load; and

(3) are placed where a lamp is required by this section.

*(Added by L.1995, chap. 165(1), eff. 9/1/95.)*

### §547.383. Lighting requirements on parked vehicles.

(a) A vehicle, other than a motor-driven cycle, shall be equipped with at least one lamp, or a combination of lamps, that:

(1) emits a white or amber light visible at a distance of 1,000 feet from the front and a red light visible at a distance of 1,000 feet from the rear; and

(2) is mounted so that at least one lamp is installed as near as practicable to the side of the vehicle that is closest to passing traffic.

(b) A vehicle, other than a motor-driven cycle, that is parked or stopped on a roadway or shoulder at a time specified in Section 547.302(a) shall display a lamp that complies with Subsection (a).

(c) A vehicle that is lawfully parked on a highway is not required to display lights at night-time if there is sufficient light to reveal a person or vehicle on the highway at a distance of 1,000 feet.

(d) A lighted headlamp on a parked vehicle shall be dimmed.

*(Added by L.1995, chap. 165(1), eff. 9/1/95.)*

**§§547.384 to 547.400.** *(Reserved.)*

## SUBCHAPTER I. PROVISIONS RELATING TO BRAKE REQUIREMENTS ON VEHICLES

### §547.401. Brakes required.

(a) Except as provided by Subsection (b), a motor vehicle, trailer, semitrailer, pole trailer, or combination of those vehicles shall be equipped with brakes that comply with this chapter.

(b) A trailer, semitrailer, or pole trailer is not required to have brakes if:

(1) its gross weight is 4,500 pounds or less; or

(2) its gross weight is heavier than 4,500 pounds but not heavier than 15,000 pounds, and it is drawn at a speed of not more than 30 miles per hour.

*(Added by L.1995, chap. 165(1), eff. 9/1/95.)*

## §547.402. Operation and maintenance of brakes.

(a) Required brakes shall operate on each wheel of a vehicle except:

(1) special mobile equipment;

(2) a vehicle that is towed as a commodity when at least one set of the towed vehicle's wheels is on the roadway, if the combination of vehicles complies with the performance requirements of this chapter; and

(3) a trailer, semitrailer, or pole trailer with a gross weight heavier than 4,500 pounds but not heavier than 15,000 pounds drawn at a speed of more than 30 miles per hour, if the brakes operate on both wheels of the rear axle.

(b) A truck or truck-tractor that has at least three axles is not required to have brakes on the front wheels, but must have brakes that:

(1) operate on the wheels of one steerable axle if the vehicle is equipped with at least two steerable axles; and

(2) comply with the performance requirements of this chapter.

(c) A trailer or semitrailer that has a gross weight of 15,000 pounds or less may use surge or inertia brake systems to satisfy the requirements of Subsection (a).

(d) Brakes shall be maintained in good working order and adjusted to operate on wheels on each side of the vehicle as equally as practicable.

*(Added by L.1995, chap. 165(1), eff. 9/1/95.)*



Zt

## §547.403. Service brakes required.

(a) A vehicle required to have brakes by this subchapter, other than special mobile equipment, shall be equipped with service brakes that:

(1) comply with the performance requirements of this subchapter; and

(2) are adequate to control the movement of the vehicle, including stopping and holding, under all loading conditions and when on any grade on which the vehicle is operated.

(b) A vehicle required to have brakes by this subchapter shall be equipped so that one control device operates the service brakes. This subsection does not prohibit an additional control device that may be used to operate brakes on a towed vehicle. A vehicle that tows another vehicle as a commodity when at least one set of the towed vehicle's wheels is on the roadway is not required to comply with this requirement unless the brakes on the towing and towed vehicles are designed to be operated by a single control on the towing vehicle.

*(Added by L.1995, chap. 165(1), eff. 9/1/95.)*

## §547.404. Parking brakes required.

(a) A vehicle required to have brakes by this subchapter, other than a motorcycle or motor-driven cycle, shall be equipped with parking brakes adequate to hold the vehicle:

(1) on any grade on which the vehicle is operated;

(2) under all loading conditions; and

(3) on a surface free from snow, ice, or loose material.

(b) The parking brakes shall be:

(1) designed to operate continuously as required once applied, despite a leakage or an exhaustion of power source; and

(2) activated by the vehicle operator's muscular effort, by spring action, or by equivalent means.

(c) The parking brakes may be assisted by the service brakes or by another power source, unless a failure in the power source would prevent the parking brakes from operating as required by this section.

(d) The same brake drums, brake shoes and lining assemblies, brake shoe anchors, and mechanical brake shoe actuation mechanism normally associated with wheel brake assemblies may be used for the parking brakes and service brakes.

(e) If the means of applying the parking brakes and service brakes are connected, the brake system shall be constructed so that the failure of one part will not cause the vehicle to be without operative brakes.

*(Added by L.1995, chap. 165(1), eff. 9/1/95.)*

## §547.405. Emergency brakes required.

(a) A vehicle used to tow another vehicle equipped with air-controlled brakes shall be equipped with the following means, together or separate, for applying the trailer brakes in an emergency:

(1) an automatic device that applies the brakes to a fixed pressure from 20 to 45 pounds per square inch if the towing vehicle's air supply is reduced; and

(2) a manual device to apply and release the brakes that is readily operable by a person seated in the operator's seat and arranged so that:

(A) its emergency position or method of operation is clearly indicated; and

(B) its use does not prevent operation of the automatic brakes.

(b) In addition to the single control device required by Section 547.403, a vehicle used to tow another vehicle equipped with vacuum brakes shall be equipped with a second control device that:

(1) is used to operate the brakes on a towed vehicle in an emergency;

(2) is independent of brake air, hydraulic, or other pressure and independent of other controls, unless the braking system is arranged to automatically apply the towed vehicle's brakes if the pressure for the second control device on the towing vehicle fails; and

(3) is not required to provide modulated braking.

(c) Subsections (a) and (b) do not apply to a vehicle that tows another vehicle as a commodity when at least one set of wheels of the towed vehicle is on the roadway.

(d) A trailer, semitrailer, or pole trailer that is equipped with air or vacuum brakes or that has a gross weight heavier than 3,000 pounds shall be equipped with brakes that:

(1) operate on all wheels; and

(2) are promptly applied automatically and remain applied for at least 15 minutes in case of a breakaway from the towing vehicle.

(e) A motor vehicle used to tow a trailer, semitrailer, or pole trailer equipped with brakes shall be equipped with service brakes arranged so that, in case of a breakaway of the towed vehicle, the towing vehicle is capable of stopping by use of its service brakes.

*(Added by L.1995, chap. 165(1), eff. 9/1/95.)*



## §547.406. Brake reservoir or reserve capacity required.

(a) A bus, truck, or truck-tractor equipped with air brakes shall be equipped with at least one reservoir that:

(1) is sufficient to ensure that the service brakes can be fully applied without lowering the reservoir pressure, if fully charged to the maximum pressure as regulated by the air compressor governor cut-out setting, by more than 20 percent; and

(2) has a means for readily draining accumulated oil or water.

(b) A truck with at least three axles that is equipped with vacuum brakes or a truck-tractor or truck used to tow a vehicle equipped with vacuum brakes shall be equipped with a reserve capacity or a vacuum reservoir sufficient to ensure that, with the reserve capacity or vacuum reservoir fully charged and with the engine stopped, the service brakes can be fully applied without depleting the vacuum supply by more than 40 percent.

(c) A motor vehicle, trailer, semitrailer, or pole trailer that is equipped with an air or vacuum reservoir or reserve capacity shall be equipped with a check valve or equivalent device to prevent depletion of the air or vacuum supply by failure or leakage.

(d) An air brake system installed on a trailer shall be designed to prevent a backflow of air from the supply reservoir through the supply line.

*(Added by L.1995, chap. 165(1), eff. 9/1/95.)*

## §547.407. Brake warning devices required.

(a) A bus, truck, or truck-tractor that uses air to operate its brakes or the brakes of a towed vehicle shall be equipped with:

(1) a warning signal, other than a pressure gauge, that is readily audible or visible to the vehicle operator and that shows when the air reservoir pressure is below 50 percent of the air compressor governor cut-out pressure; and

(2) a pressure gauge visible to the vehicle operator that shows in pounds per square inch the pressure available for braking.

(b) A truck-tractor or truck used to tow a vehicle equipped with vacuum brakes, or a truck with at least three axles that is equipped with vacuum brakes, shall be equipped with a warning signal, other than a gauge showing vacuum, that is readily audible or visible to the vehicle operator and that shows when the vacuum in the reservoir or reserve capacity is less than eight inches of mercury. This subsection does not apply to an operation in which a motor vehicle, trailer, or semitrailer is transported as a commodity when at least one set of the vehicle's wheels is on the roadway.

(c) If a vehicle required to be equipped with a warning device is equipped with air and vacuum power to operate its brakes or the brakes on a towed vehicle, the warning devices required may be combined into a single device that is not a pressure or vacuum gauge.

*(Added by L.1995, chap. 165(1), eff. 9/1/95.)*

**§547.408. Performance requirements for brakes.**

(a) A motor vehicle or combination of vehicles shall be equipped with service brakes capable of:

(1) developing a braking force that is not less than:

(A) 52.8 percent of the gross weight of the vehicle for a passenger vehicle; or

(B) 43.5 percent of the gross weight of the vehicle for a vehicle other than a passenger vehicle;

(2) decelerating to a stop from 20 miles per hour or less at not less than:

(A) 17 feet per second per second for a passenger vehicle; or

(B) 14 feet per second per second for other vehicles; and

(3) stopping from a speed of 20 miles per hour in a distance, measured from the location where the service brake pedal or control is activated, of not more than:

(A) 25 feet for a passenger vehicle;

(B) 30 feet for a motorcycle, motor-driven cycle, or single unit vehicle with a manufacturer's gross vehicle weight rating of 10,000 pounds or less;

(C) 40 feet for:

(i) a single unit vehicle with a manufacturer's gross weight rating of more than 10,000 pounds;

(ii) a two-axle towing vehicle and trailer combination with a weight of 3,000 pounds or less;

(iii) a bus that does not have a manufacturer's gross weight rating; and

(iv) the combination of vehicles in an operation exempted by Section 547.407(b); and

(D) 50 feet for other vehicles.

(b) A test for deceleration or stopping distance shall be performed on a dry, smooth, hard surface that:

(1) is free of loose material; and

(2) does not exceed plus or minus one percent grade.

(c) In this section, "passenger vehicle" means a vehicle that has a maximum seating capacity of 10 persons, including the operator, and that does not have a manufacturer's gross vehicle weight rating.

*(Added by L.1995, chap. 165(1), eff. 9/1/95.)*

**§§547.409 to 547.500.** *(Reserved.)*

## SUBCHAPTER J. PROVISIONS RELATING TO WARNING DEVICE REQUIREMENTS ON VEHICLES

**§547.501. Audible warning devices.**

(a) A motor vehicle shall be equipped with a horn in good working condition that emits a sound audible under normal conditions at a distance of at least 200 feet.

(b) A vehicle may not be equipped with and a person may not use on a vehicle a siren, whistle, or bell unless the vehicle is:

(1) a commercial vehicle that is equipped with a theft alarm signal device arranged so that the device cannot be used as an ordinary warning signal; or

(2) an authorized emergency vehicle that is equipped with a siren, whistle, or bell that complies with Section 547.702.

(c) A motor vehicle operator shall use a horn to provide audible warning only when necessary to insure safe operation.

(d) A warning device, including a horn, may not emit an unreasonably loud or harsh sound or a whistle.

*(Added by L.1995, chap. 165(1), eff. 9/1/95.)*

**§547.502. Visible warning devices required.**

(a) Except as provided by Subsection (b), a person who operates, outside an urban district or on a divided highway, a truck, bus, or truck-tractor or a motor vehicle towing a house trailer shall carry in the vehicle:

(1) at daytime:

(A) at least two red flags at least 12 inches square; and

(B) standards to support the flags; and

(2) at nighttime:

(A) at least three flares and at least three red-burning fusees;

(B) at least three red electric lanterns; or

(C) at least three portable red emergency reflectors.

(b) A person who operates an explosive cargo vehicle at nighttime:

(1) shall carry in the vehicle three red electric lanterns or three portable red emergency reflectors; and

(2) may not carry in the vehicle a flare, fusee, or signal produced by flame.

(c) A flare, electric lantern, or portable reflector must be visible and distinguishable at a distance of at least 600 feet at night under normal atmospheric conditions.

(d) A portable reflector unit must be designed and constructed to reflect a red light clearly visible at all distances from 100 to 600 feet under normal atmospheric conditions at night when directly in front of lawful lower beams of headlamps.

(e) A flare, fusee, electric lantern, portable reflector, or warning flag must be a type approved by the department.

*(Added by L.1995, chap. 165(1), eff. 9/1/95.)*

## §547.503. Display of hazard lamps.

(a) The operator of a vehicle that is described by Subsection (b) and that is stopped on a roadway or shoulder shall immediately display vehicular hazard warning lamps that comply with Section 547.331, unless the vehicle:

(1) is parked lawfully in an urban district;

(2) is stopped lawfully to receive or discharge a passenger;

(3) is stopped to avoid conflict with other traffic;

(4) is stopped to comply with a direction of a police officer or an official traffic-control device; or

(5) displays other warning devices as required by Sections 547.504-547.507.

(b) This section applies to a truck, bus, truck-tractor, trailer, semitrailer, or pole trailer at least 80 inches wide or at least 30 feet long.

*(Added by L.1995, chap. 165(1), eff. 9/1/95.)*

## §547.504. Display of devices when lighted lamps required.

(a) Unless sufficient light exists to reveal a person or vehicle at a distance of 1,000 feet, the operator of a vehicle described by Section 547.503(b) or an explosive cargo vehicle shall display warning devices that comply with the requirements of Section 547.502:

(1) when lighted lamps are required; and

(2) under the conditions stated in this section.

(b) Except as provided by Section 547.506 and Subsection (d), the operator of a vehicle described by Section 547.503(b) or an explosive cargo vehicle that is disabled, or stopped for more than 10 minutes, on a roadway outside an urban district shall:

(1) immediately place a lighted red electric lantern or a portable red emergency reflector at the traffic side of the vehicle in the direction of the nearest approaching traffic; and

(2) place in the following order and as soon as practicable within 15 minutes one lighted red electric lamp or portable red emergency reflector:

(A) in the center of the lane occupied by the vehicle toward approaching traffic approximately 100 feet from the vehicle; and

(B) in the center of the lane occupied by the vehicle in the opposite direction approximately 100 feet from the vehicle.

(c) Except as provided by Section 547.506 and Subsection (d), the operator of a vehicle described by Section 547.503(b) or an explosive cargo vehicle that is disabled, or stopped for more than 10 minutes, on a roadway of a divided highway shall place the warning devices described by Subsection (b):

(1) in the center of the lane occupied by the vehicle toward approaching traffic approximately 200 feet from the vehicle;

(2) in the center of the lane occupied by the vehicle toward approaching traffic approximately 100 feet from the vehicle; and

(3) at the traffic side approximately 10 feet from the vehicle in the direction of the nearest approaching traffic.

(d) As an alternative to the use of electric lamps or red reflectors and except as provided by Subsection (e), the operator of a vehicle described by Section 547.503(b) may display a lighted fusee to comply with the requirements of Subsection (b)(1) or liquid-burning flares to comply with the requirements of Subsections (b)(2) and (c). If the operator uses liquid-burning flares to comply with Subsection (b)(2), the operator shall also, after complying with Subsection (b)(2)(B), place a liquid-burning flare at the traffic side of the vehicle at least 10 feet in the direction of the nearest approaching traffic. If a fusee is used to comply with Subsection (b)(1), the operator shall comply with Subsection (b)(2) within the burning period of the fusee.

(c) The operator of an explosive cargo vehicle may not display as a warning device a flare, fusee, or signal produced by flame.
*(Added by L.1995, chap. 165(1), eff. 9/1/95.)*

## §547.505. Display of devices when lighted lamps are not required.

(a) The operator of a vehicle described by Section 547.503(b) or an explosive cargo vehicle that is disabled, or stopped for more than 10 minutes, on a roadway outside an urban district or on a roadway of a divided highway when lighted lamps are not required shall display two red flags that comply with Section 547.502.

(b) If traffic on the roadway moves in two directions, one flag shall be placed approximately 100 feet to the rear and one approximately 100 feet ahead of the vehicle in the center of the lane occupied by the vehicle.

(c) If traffic on the roadway moves in one direction, one flag shall be placed approximately 100 feet and one approximately 200 feet to the rear of the vehicle in the center of the lane occupied by the vehicle.
*(Added by L.1995, chap. 165(1), eff. 9/1/95.)*

## §547.506. Display of devices: vehicles off roadway.

The operator of a vehicle described by Section 547.503(b) or an explosive cargo vehicle that is stopped entirely on the shoulder at a time and in a place referred to in this subchapter shall place required warning devices on the shoulder as close as practicable to the edge of the roadway.
*(Added by L.1995, chap. 165(1), eff. 9/1/95.)*

## §547.507. Display of devices when view of vehicle obstructed.

Unless sufficient light exists to reveal a person or vehicle at a distance of 1,000 feet, the operator of a vehicle described by Section 547.503(b) or an explosive cargo vehicle that is disabled, or stopped for more than 10 minutes, within 500 feet of a curve, hillcrest, or other obstruction to view shall place the required warning device for the direction of the obstruction from 100 to 500 feet from the vehicle so as to provide ample warning to other traffic. *(Added by L.1995, chap. 165(1), eff. 9/1/95.)*

## §547.508. Offense relating to warning devices.

(a) Except as provided by Subsection (b), a person may not remove, damage, destroy, misplace, or extinguish a warning device required under Sections 547.502-547.507 when the device is being displayed or used as required.

(b) This section does not apply to:

(1) an owner of a vehicle or the owner's authorized agent or employee; or

(2) a peace officer acting in an official capacity.
*(Added by L.1995, chap. 165(1), eff. 9/1/95.)*

## §§547.509 to 547.600. *(Reserved.)*

# SUBCHAPTER K. PROVISIONS RELATING TO OTHER VEHICLE EQUIPMENT

## §547.601. Safety belts required.

A motor vehicle required by Chapter 548 to be inspected shall be equipped with front safety belts if safety belt anchorages were part of the manufacturer's original equipment on the vehicle.
*(Added by L.1995, chap. 165(1), eff. 9/1/95.)*

## §547.602. Mirrors required.

A motor vehicle, including a motor vehicle used to tow another vehicle, shall be equipped with a mirror located to reflect to the operator a view of the highway for a distance of at least 200 feet from the rear of the vehicle. *(Added by L.1995, chap. 165(1), eff. 9/1/95.)*

## §547.603. Windshield wipers required.

A motor vehicle shall be equipped with a device that is operated or controlled by the operator of the vehicle and that cleans moisture from the windshield. The device shall be maintained in good working condition. *(Added by L.1995, chap. 165(1), eff. 9/1/95.)*

### §547.604. Muffler required.

(a) A motor vehicle shall be equipped with a muffler in good working condition that continually operates to prevent excessive or unusual noise.

(b) A person may not use a muffler cutout, bypass, or similar device on a motor vehicle. *(Added by L.1995, chap. 165(1), eff. 9/1/95.)*

### §547.605. Emission systems required.

(a) The engine and power mechanism of a motor vehicle shall be equipped and adjusted to prevent the escape of excessive smoke or fumes.

(b) A motor vehicle or motor vehicle engine, of a model year after 1967, shall be equipped to prevent the discharge of crankcase emissions into the ambient atmosphere.

(c) The owner or operator of a motor vehicle or motor vehicle engine, of a model year after 1967, that is equipped with an exhaust emission system:

(1) shall maintain the system in good working condition;

(2) shall use the system when the motor vehicle or motor vehicle engine is operated; and

(3) may not remove the system or a part of the system or intentionally make the system inoperable in this state, unless the owner or operator removes the system or part to install another system or part intended to be equally effective in reducing atmospheric emissions. *(Added by L.1995, chap. 165(1), eff. 9/1/95.)*

### §547.606. Safety guards or flaps required.

(a) A road tractor, truck, trailer, truck-tractor in combination with a semitrailer, or semitrailer in combination with a towing vehicle that has at least four tires on the rearmost axle of the vehicle or the rearmost vehicle in the combination shall be equipped with safety guards or flaps that:

(1) are of a type prescribed by the department; and

(2) are located and suspended behind the rearmost wheels of the vehicle or the rearmost vehicle in the combination within eight inches of the surface of the highway.

(b) This section does not apply to a truck-tractor operated alone or a pole trailer. *(Added by L.1995, chap. 165(1), eff. 9/1/95.)*

### §547.607. Fire extinguisher required.

A school bus or a motor vehicle that transports passengers for hire or lease shall be equipped with at least one quart of chemical-type fire extinguisher in good condition and located for immediate use. *(Added by L.1995, chap. 165(1), eff. 9/1/95.)*

### §547.608. Safety glazing material required.

(a) Except as provided by Subsection (b), a person who sells or registers a new passenger-type motor vehicle, including a passenger bus and school bus, shall equip the vehicle doors, windows, and windshield with safety glazing material of a type approved by the department.

(b) The requirements of Subsection (a) do not apply to a glazing material in a compartment of a truck, including a truck-tractor, that is not designed and equipped for a person to ride in.

(c) A person may not replace or require the replacement of glass in a door, window, or windshield of any motor vehicle if the replacement is not made with safety glazing material.

(d) A person who sells or attaches to a motor vehicle a camper manufactured or assembled after January 1, 1972, shall equip the camper doors and windows with safety glazing material of a type approved by the department. In this subsection "camper" means a structure designed to:

(1) be loaded on or attached to a motor vehicle; and

(2) provide temporary living quarters for recreation, travel, or other use.

(e) A person who sells imperfect safety glass for a door, window, or windshield of a motor vehicle shall:

(1) label the glass "second," "imperfect," or by a similar term in red letters at least one inch in size to indicate to the consumer the quality of the glass;

(2) orally notify the consumer of each imperfection and the possible result of using imperfect glass; and

(3) deliver written notice at the time of purchase notifying the consumer of each imperfection and the possible result of using imperfect glass. *(Added by L.1995, chap. 165(1), eff. 9/1/95.)*

### §547.609. Sunscreening devices permitted.

A sunscreening device must have a label that:

(1) is legible;

(2) contains information required by the department on light transmission and luminous reflectance of the device; and

(3) is permanently installed between the material and the surface to which the material is applied.

*(Added by L.1995, chap. 165(1), eff. 9/1/95.)*

### §547.610. Safe air-conditioning equipment required; sale of noncomplying vehicle.

(a) Air-conditioning equipment:

(1) shall be manufactured, installed, and maintained to ensure the safety of the vehicle occupants and the public; and

(2) may not contain any refrigerant that is flammable or is toxic to persons.

(b) A person may not possess or offer for sale, sell, or equip a motor vehicle with air-conditioning equipment that does not comply with the requirements of this section and Section 547.103.

*(Added by L.1995, chap. 165(1), eff. 9/1/95.)*

### §547.611. Television receivers permitted.

(a) A motor vehicle may be equipped with video receiving equipment, including a television and similar equipment, only if the equipment is located so that the video display is not visible from the operator's seat.

(b) A motor vehicle specially designed as a mobile unit used by a licensed television station may have video receiving equipment located so that the video display is visible from the operator's side, but the receiver may be used only when the vehicle is stopped.

(c) This section does not prohibit the use of:

(1) equipment used:

(A) exclusively for receiving digital information for commercial purposes;

(B) exclusively for a safety or law enforcement purpose, if each installation is approved by the department; or

(C) in a remote television transmission truck; or

(2) a monitoring device that:

(A) produces an electronic display; and

(B) is used exclusively in conjunction with a mobile navigation system installed in the vehicle.

*(Added by L.1995, chap. 165(1); chgd. by L.1997, chap. 165(30.117(a)), eff. 9/1/97.)*

### §547.612. Restrictions on use and sale of tires.

(a) A solid rubber tire used on a vehicle must have rubber on the traction surface that extends above the edge of the flange of the periphery.

(b) A person may not operate or move a motor vehicle, trailer, or semitrailer that has a metal tire in contact with the roadway, unless:

(1) the vehicle is a farm wagon or farm trailer that has a gross weight of less than 5,000 pounds; and

(2) the owner is transporting farm products to market, for processing, or from farm to farm.

(c) A tire used on a moving vehicle may not have on its periphery a block, stud, flange, cleat, or spike or other protuberance of a material other than rubber that projects beyond the tread of the traction surface, unless the protuberance:

(1) does not injure the highway; or

(2) is a tire chain of reasonable proportion that is used as required for safety because of a condition that might cause the vehicle to skid.

(d) The Texas Transportation Commission and a local authority within its jurisdiction may issue a special permit that authorizes a person to operate a tractor or traction engine that has movable tracks with transverse corrugations on the periphery or a farm tractor or other farm machinery.

(e) A person commits an offense if the person offers for sale or sells a private passenger automobile tire that is regrooved. An offense under this section is a misdemeanor punishable by a fine of not less than $500 or more than $2,000.

*(Added by L.1995, chap. 165(1), eff. 9/1/95.)*

### §547.613. Restrictions on windows.

(a) Except as provided by Subsection (b), a person commits an offense that is a misdemeanor:

(1) if the person operates a motor vehicle that has an object or material that is placed on or attached to the windshield or side or rear window and that obstructs or reduces the operator's clear view; or

(2) if a person, including an installer or manufacturer, places on or attaches to the windshield or side or rear window of a motor vehicle a transparent material that alters the color or reduces the light transmission.

(b) This section does not apply to:

(1) a windshield that has a sunscreening device that:

(A) has a light transmission of 33 percent or more;

(B) has a luminous reflectance of 35 percent or less;

(C) is not red or amber; and

(D) does not extend downward beyond the AS-1 line or more than five inches from the top of the windshield, whichever is closer to the top of the windshield;

(2) a front side wing vent or window, a side window to the rear of the vehicle operator, or a rear window that has a sunscreening device that has a light transmission of 35 percent or more and a luminous reflectance of 35 percent or less;

(3) a rear window, if the motor vehicle is equipped with an outside mirror on each side of the vehicle that reflects to the vehicle operator a view of the highway for a distance of at least 200 feet from the rear;

(4) a rearview mirror;

(5) an adjustable nontransparent sun visor that is mounted in front of a side window and not attached to the glass;

(6) a direction, destination, or termination sign on a passenger common carrier motor vehicle, if the sign does not interfere with the vehicle operator's view of approaching traffic;

(7) a rear window wiper motor;

(8) a rear trunk lid handle or hinge;

(9) a luggage rack attached to the rear trunk;

(10) a side window that is to the rear of the vehicle operator on a multipurpose vehicle;

(11) a window that has a United States, state, or local certificate placed on or attached to it as required by law;

(12) a motor vehicle that is not registered in this state;

(13) a motor vehicle with a manufacturer's model year before 1988;

(14) a vehicle that is:

(A) used regularly to transport passengers for a fee; and

(B) authorized to operate under license or permit by a local authority; or

(15) a vehicle that is maintained by a law enforcement agency and used for law enforcement purposes.

(c) A manufacturer shall certify to the department that the device made or assembled by the manufacturer complies with the light transmission and luminous reflectance specifications established by Subsection (b).

(d) The department may determine that a window that has a sunscreening device is exempt under Subsection (b)(2) if the light transmission or luminous reflectance varies by no more than three percent from the standard established in that subsection.

(e) It is a defense to prosecution under this section that the defendant or a passenger in the vehicle at the time of the violation is required for a medical reason to be shielded from direct rays of the sun.

(f) It is not an offense under this section for a person to offer for sale or sell a motor vehicle with a windshield or window that does not comply with this section.

(g) In this section:

(1) "Installer" means a person who fabricates, laminates, or tempers a safety glazing material to incorporate, during the installation process, the capacity to reflect light or reduce light transmission.

(2) "Manufacturer" means a person who:

(A) manufactures or assembles a sunscreening device; or

(B) fabricates, laminates, or tempers safety glazing material to incorporate, during the manufacturing process, the capacity to reflect light or reduce light transmission.

*(Added by L.1995, chap. 165(1); chgd. by L.1997, chap. 165(30.118(a)), eff. 9/1/97.)*

**§§547.614 to 547.700.** *(Reserved.)*

## SUBCHAPTER L. ADDITIONAL EQUIPMENT REQUIREMENTS FOR SCHOOL BUSES, AUTHORIZED EMERGENCY VEHICLES, AND SLOW-MOVING VEHICLES

### §547.701. Additional equipment requirements for school buses.

(a) A school bus shall be equipped with:

(1) a convex mirror or other device that reflects to the school bus operator a clear view of the area immediately in front of the vehicle that would otherwise be hidden from view; and

(2) signal lamps that:

(A) are mounted as high and as widely spaced laterally as practicable;

(B) display four alternately flashing red lights, two located on the front at the same level and two located on the rear at the same level; and

(C) emit a light visible at a distance of 500 feet in normal sunlight.

(b) A school bus may be equipped with:

(1) rooftop warning lamps:

(A) that conform to and are placed on the bus in accordance with specifications adopted under Section 34.002, Education Code; and

(B) that are operated under rules adopted by the school district; and

(2) movable stop arms:

(A) that conform to regulations adopted under Section 34.002, Education Code; and

(B) that may be operated only when the bus is stopped to load or unload students.

(c) When a school bus is being stopped or is stopped on a highway to permit students to board or exit the bus, the operator of the bus shall activate all flashing warning signal lights and other equipment on the bus designed to warn other drivers that the bus is stopping to load or unload children. A person may not operate such a light or other equipment except when the bus is being stopped or is stopped on a highway to permit students to board or exit the bus.

(d) The exterior of a school bus may not bear advertising or another paid announcement directed at the public if the advertising or announcement distracts from the effectiveness of required safety warning equipment. The department shall adopt rules to implement this subsection. A school bus that violates this section or rules adopted under this section shall be placed out of service until it complies.

*(Added by L.1995, chap. 165(1); chgd. by L.1997, chap. 1438(12); L.1999, chap. 183(1), eff. 9/1/99.)*

### §547.7011. Additional equipment requirements for other buses.

(a) A bus, other than a school bus, that provides public transportation and that was acquired on or after September 1, 1997, shall be equipped with two or more hazard lamps that:

(1) are mounted at the same level on the rear of the bus;

(2) are visible at a distance of 500 feet in normal sunlight;

(3) flash; and

(4) emit amber light.

(b) An operator of a bus to which this section applies shall activate the hazard lamps if the bus stops to load or unload a person under 18 years of age.

(c) A bus to which this section applies must bear a sign on the rear of the bus stating: "Caution—children may be exiting".

*(Added by L.1997, chap. 1131(1), eff. 9/1/97.)*

### §547.7015. Rules relating to school buses.

(a) The General Services Commission, with the advice of the department, shall adopt and enforce rules governing the design, color, lighting and other equipment, construction, and operation of a school bus for the transportation of schoolchildren that is:

(1) owned and operated by a school district in this state; or

(2) privately owned and operated under a contract with a school district in this state.

(b) In adopting rules under this section, the General Services Commission shall emphasize:

(1) safety features; and

(2) long-range, maintenance-free factors.

(c) Rules adopted under this section:

(1) apply to each school district, the officers and employees of a district, and each person employed under contract by a school district; and

(2) shall by reference be made a part of any contract that is entered into by a school district in this state for the transportation of schoolchildren on a privately owned school bus.

*(Added by L.1997, chap. 165(30.119(a)), eff. 9/1/97.)*

**§547.702. Additional equipment requirements for authorized emergency vehicles.**

(a) An authorized emergency vehicle may be equipped with a siren, exhaust whistle, or bell:

(1) of a type approved by the department; and

(2) that emits a sound audible under normal conditions at a distance of at least 500 feet.

(b) The operator of an authorized emergency vehicle shall use the siren, whistle, or bell when necessary to warn other vehicle operators or pedestrians of the approach of the emergency vehicle.

(c) Except as provided by this section, an authorized emergency vehicle shall be equipped with signal lamps that:

(1) are mounted as high and as widely spaced laterally as practicable;

(2) display four alternately flashing red lights, two located on the front at the same level and two located on the rear at the same level; and

(3) emit a light visible at a distance of 500 feet in normal sunlight.

(d) A private vehicle operated by a volunteer firefighter responding to a fire alarm or a medical emergency may, but is not required to, be equipped with signal lamps that comply with the requirements of Subsection (c).

(e) A private vehicle operated by a volunteer firefighter responding to a fire alarm or a medical emergency may be equipped with a signal lamp that is temporarily attached to the vehicle roof and flashes a red light visible at a distance of at least 500 feet in normal sunlight.

(f) A police vehicle may, but is not required to, be equipped with signal lamps that comply with Subsection (c).

*(Added by L.1995, chap. 165(1), eff. 9/1/95.)*



**§547.703. Additional equipment requirements for slow-moving vehicles.**

(a) Except as provided by Subsection (b), a slow-moving vehicle shall display a slow-moving-vehicle emblem that:

(1) has a reflective surface designed to be clearly visible in daylight or at night from the light of standard automobile headlamps at a distance of at least 500 feet;

(2) is mounted base down on the rear of the vehicle at a height from three to five feet above the road surface; and

(3) is maintained in a clean, reflective condition.

(b) Subsection (a) does not apply to a vehicle that is used in construction or maintenance work and is traveling in a construction area that is marked as required by the Texas Transportation Commission.

(c) If a motor vehicle displaying a slow-moving-vehicle emblem tows machinery, including an implement of husbandry, and the visibility of the emblem is not obstructed, the towed unit is not required to display a slow-moving-vehicle emblem.

(d) A golf cart as defined by Section 502.001 is required to display a slow-moving-vehicle emblem only when it is operated on an arterial street.

(e) In this section, "arterial street" means:

(1) a roadway assigned a number by this state or the United States;

(2) a controlled-access highway; or

(3) a major radial or circumferential street or highway that is in the territory of a local authority and designated by the authority as part of a major arterial system of streets or highways.

*(Added by L.1995, chap. 165(1), eff. 9/1/95.)*

**§§547.704 to 547.800.** *(Reserved.)*

## SUBCHAPTER M. ADDITIONAL OR ALTERNATIVE EQUIPMENT REQUIREMENTS FOR MOTORCYCLES AND MOTOR-DRIVEN CYCLES

**§547.801. Lighting equipment.**

(a) A motorcycle, including a motor-driven cycle, shall be equipped with:

(1) not more than two headlamps mounted at a height from 24 to 54 inches;

(2) at least one taillamp mounted at a height from 20 to 72 inches;

(3) a taillamp or separate lamp to illuminate the rear license plate that complies with the requirements of Sections 547.322(f) and (g);

(4) at least one stoplamp that complies with the requirements of Section 547.323(d); and

(5) at least one rear red reflector that complies with the requirements of Section 547.325(b) and may be included as a part of the taillamp.

(b) A motorcycle, other than a motor-driven cycle, shall be equipped with multiple-beam lighting equipment that produces:

(1) an uppermost distribution of light that reveals a person or vehicle at a distance of at least 300 feet ahead; and

(2) a lowermost distribution of light that:

(A) reveals a person or vehicle at a distance of at least 150 feet ahead; and

(B) is aimed so that no part of the high-intensity portion of the beam on the motorcycle that is on a straight and level road under any condition of loading projects into the eyes of an approaching vehicle operator.

(c) A motor-driven cycle shall be equipped with:

(1) multiple-beam lighting equipment that complies with the requirements of Subsection (b); or

(2) single-beam lighting equipment that:

(A) emits light sufficient to reveal a person or vehicle:

(i) at a distance of at least 100 feet when the cycle is operated at a speed less than 25 miles per hour;

(ii) at a distance of at least 200 feet when the cycle is operated at a speed of 25 miles per hour or more; and

(iii) at a distance of at least 300 feet when the cycle is operated at a speed of 35 miles per hour or more; and

(B) is aimed so that no part of the high-intensity portion of the beam from the lamp on a loaded cycle projects a beam higher than the level center of the lamp for a distance of 25 feet ahead.

(d) A motorcycle may not be operated at any time unless at least one headlamp on the motorcycle is illuminated. This subsection does not apply to a motorcycle manufactured before the model year 1975.

*(Added by L.1995, chap. 165(1); chgd. by L.1997, chap. 782(1); L.1999, chap. 1022(1), eff. 9/1/99.)*

### §547.802. Brake equipment.

(a) If a motorcycle, including a motor-driven cycle, complies with the performance requirements of Section 547.408, brakes are not required on the wheel of a sidecar attached to the cycle.

(b) If a motor-driven cycle complies with the performance standards of Section 547.408, brakes are not required on the front wheel of the cycle.

(c) The director may require an inspection of a motor-driven cycle braking system and may disapprove a system that:

(1) does not comply with the brake performance requirements in Section 547.408; or

(2) is not designed or constructed to ensure reasonable and reliable performance during actual use.

*(Added by L.1995, chap. 165(1), eff. 9/1/95.)*

# CHAPTER 548. COMPULSORY INSPECTION OF VEHICLES

## SUBCHAPTER A. GENERAL PROVISIONS

Section



## SUBCHAPTER B. VEHICLES AND EQUIPMENT SUBJECT TO INSPECTION AND REINSPECTION

## SUBCHAPTER C. PERIODS OF INSPECTION; PREREQUISITES TO ISSUANCE OF INSPECTION CERTIFICATE





## SUBCHAPTER D. INSPECTION OF COMMERCIAL MOTOR VEHICLES



## SUBCHAPTER E. ISSUANCE, RECORDING, AND PROOF OF INSPECTION CERTIFICATES AND VERIFICATION FORMS



## SUBCHAPTER F. MOTOR VEHICLE EMISSIONS INSPECTION AND MAINTENANCE



## SUBCHAPTER G. CERTIFICATION OF INSPECTION STATION OR INSPECTOR

## SUBCHAPTER H. INSPECTION AND CERTIFICATION FEES



## SUBCHAPTER I. VIOLATIONS AND OFFENSES



## SUBCHAPTER A. GENERAL PROVISIONS

### §548.001. Definitions.

In this chapter:

(1) "Commercial motor vehicle" means a self-propelled or towed vehicle, other than a farm vehicle with a gross weight, registered weight, or gross weight rating of less than 48,000 pounds, that is used on a public highway to transport passengers or cargo if:

(A) the vehicle, including a school activity bus as defined in Section 541.201, or combination of vehicles has a gross weight, registered weight, or gross weight rating of more than 26,000 pounds;

(B) the vehicle, including a school activity bus as defined in Section 541.201, is designed to transport more than 15 passengers, including the driver; or

(C) the vehicle is used to transport hazardous materials in a quantity requiring placarding by a regulation issued under the Hazardous Materials Transportation Act (49 U.S.C. Section 1801 et seq.).

(2) "Commission" means the Public Safety Commission.

(3) "Conservation commission" means the Texas Natural Resource Conservation Commission.

(4) "Department" means the Department of Public Safety.

(5) "Farm vehicle" has the meaning assigned by the federal motor carrier safety regulations.

(6) "Federal motor carrier safety regulation" has the meaning assigned by Section 644.001.

(7) "Inspection station" means a facility certified to conduct inspections of vehicles under this chapter.

(8) "Inspector" means an individual certified to conduct inspections of vehicles under this chapter.

(9) "Nonattainment area" means an area so designated within the meaning of Section 107(d) of the Clean Air Act (42 U.S.C. Section 7407).

*(Added by L.1995, chap. 165(1); chgd. by L.1997, chaps. 165(30.120), (30.122(a)); 1061(17); 1069(4); L.1999, chap. 663(4), eff. 6/18/99.)*

### §548.002. Department rules.

The department may adopt rules to administer and enforce this chapter. *(Added by L.1995, chap. 165(1), eff. 9/1/95.)*

**§548.003. Department certification and supervision of inspection stations.**

(a) The department may certify inspection stations to carry out this chapter and may instruct and supervise the inspection stations and mechanics for the inspection of vehicles and equipment subject to this chapter.

(b) The department shall certify at least one inspection station for each county.

*(Added by L.1995, chap. 165(1), eff. 9/1/95.)*

**§548.004. Department certification of inspection stations for political subdivisions and state agencies.**

(a) The department may certify a vehicle maintenance facility owned and operated by a political subdivision or agency of this state as an inspection station.

(b) An inspection station certified under this section is subject to the requirements of this chapter applicable to another inspection station, except as otherwise provided by this chapter.

(c) The facility may inspect only a vehicle owned by the political subdivision or state agency. An officer, employee, or inspector of the subdivision or agency may not place an inspection certificate received from the department under this section on a vehicle not owned by the subdivision or agency.

*(Added by L.1995, chap. 165(1), eff. 9/1/95.)*

**§548.005. Inspection only by state-certified and supervised inspection station.**

A compulsory inspection under this chapter may be made only by an inspection station, except that the department may:

(1) permit inspection to be made by an inspector under terms and conditions the department prescribes; and

(2) authorize the acceptance in this state of a certificate of inspection and approval issued in another state having a similar inspection law.

*(Added by L.1995, chap. 165(1), eff. 9/1/95.)*

**§§548.006 to 548.050.** *(Reserved.)*

## SUBCHAPTER B. VEHICLES AND EQUIPMENT SUBJECT TO INSPECTION AND REINSPECTION

**§548.051. Vehicles and equipment subject to inspection.**

(a) A motor vehicle, trailer, semitrailer, pole trailer, or mobile home, registered in this state, must have the following items inspected at an inspection station or by an inspector:

(1) tires;
(2) wheel assembly;
(3) safety guards or flaps, if required by Section 547.606;
(4) brake system, including power brake unit;
(5) steering system, including power steering;
(6) lighting equipment;
(7) horns and warning devices;
(8) mirrors;
(9) windshield wipers;
(10) sunscreening devices, unless the vehicle is exempt from sunscreen device restrictions under Section 547.613;
(11) front seat belts in vehicles on which seat belt anchorages were part of the manufacturer's original equipment;
(12) tax decal, if required by Section 548.104(d)(1);
(13) exhaust system;
(14) exhaust emission system;
(15) fuel tank cap, using pressurized testing equipment approved by department rule; and
(16) emissions control equipment as designated by department rule.

(b) A moped is subject to inspection in the same manner as a motorcycle, except that the only items of equipment required to be inspected are the brakes, headlamps, rear lamps, and reflectors, which must comply with the standards prescribed by Sections 547.408 and 547.801.

*(Added by L.1995, chap. 165(1); chgd. by L.1999, chap. 1189(29), eff. 9/1/99.)*

### §548.052. Vehicles not subject to inspection.

This chapter does not apply to:

(1) a trailer, semitrailer, pole trailer, or mobile home moving under or bearing a current factory-delivery license plate or current in-transit license plate;

(2) a vehicle moving under or bearing a paper dealer in-transit tag, machinery license, disaster license, parade license, prorate tab, one-trip permit, antique license, temporary 24-hour permit, or permit license;

(3) a trailer, semitrailer, pole trailer, or mobile home having an actual gross weight or registered gross weight of 4,500 pounds or less;

(4) farm machinery, road-building equipment, a farm trailer, or a vehicle required to display a slow-moving-vehicle emblem under Section 547.703;

(5) a former military vehicle, as defined by Section 502.275(*o*); or

(6) a vehicle qualified for a tax exemption under Section 152.092, Tax Code. *(Added by L.1999, chap. 963(1), eff. 6/18/99. See other subdivision (6) below.)*

(6) a vehicle for which a certificate of title has been issued but that is not required to be registered. *(Added by L.1999, chap. 1423(7), eff. 9/1/99. See other subdivision (6) above.)*
*(Added by L.1995, chap. 165(1); chgd. by L.1997, chap. 165(30.121(a)); L.1999, chaps. 963(1), 1423(7), eff. 6/18/99, 9/1/99, respectively.)*



### §548.053. Reinspection of vehicle requiring adjustment, correction, or repair.

(a) If an inspection discloses the necessity for adjustment, correction, or repair, an inspection station or inspector may not issue an inspection certificate until the adjustment, correction, or repair is made. The owner of the vehicle may have the adjustment, correction, or repair made by a qualified person of the owner's choice, subject to reinspection. The vehicle shall be reinspected once free of charge within 15 days after the date of the original inspection, not including the date the original inspection is made, at the same inspection station after the adjustment, correction, or repair is made.

(b) A vehicle that is inspected and is subsequently involved in an accident affecting the safe operation of an item of inspection must be reinspected following repair. The reinspection must be at an inspection station and shall be treated and charged as an initial inspection.

(c) If a vehicle subject to this chapter is damaged to the apparent extent that it would require repair before passing inspection, the investigating officer shall remove the inspection certificate from the vehicle windshield and give the operator of the vehicle a dated receipt. The vehicle must be reinspected not later than the 30th day after the date shown on the receipt.
*(Added by L.1995, chap. 165(1), eff. 9/1/95.)*

### §§548.054 to 548.100. *(Reserved.)*

## SUBCHAPTER C. PERIODS OF INSPECTION; PREREQUISITES TO ISSUANCE OF INSPECTION CERTIFICATE

### §548.101. General one-year inspection period.

Except as provided by Section 548.102, the department shall require an annual inspection. The department shall set the periods of inspection and may make rules with respect to those periods. *(Added by L.1995, chap. 165(1), eff. 9/1/95.)*

### §548.102. Two-year initial inspection period for passenger car or light truck.

(a) The initial inspection period is two years for a passenger car or light truck that:

(1) is sold in this state;

(2) has not been previously registered in this or another state; and

(3) on the date of sale is of the current or preceding model year.

(b) This section does not affect a requirement that a motor vehicle emission inspection be conducted during an initial inspection period in a county covered by an inspection and maintenance program approved by the United States Environmental Protection Agency under Section 548.301 and the Clean Air Act (42 U.S.C. Section 7401 et seq.).
*(Added by L.1995, chap. 165(1), eff. 9/1/95.)*

### §548.103. Extended inspection period for certain vehicles.

The department may extend the time within which the resident owner of a vehicle that is not in this state when an inspection is required must obtain an inspection certificate in this state. *(Added by L.1995, chap. 165(1), eff. 9/1/95.)*

### §548.104. Equipment-related prerequisites to issuance of inspection certificate.

(a) The commission shall adopt uniform standards of safety applicable to each item required to be inspected by Section 548.051. The standards and the list of items to be inspected shall be posted in each inspection station.

(b) An inspection station or inspector may issue an inspection certificate only if the vehicle is inspected and found to be in proper and safe condition and to comply with this chapter and the rules adopted under this chapter.

(c) An inspection station or inspector may inspect only the equipment required to be inspected by Section 548.051 and may not:

(1) falsely and fraudulently represent to an applicant that equipment required to be inspected must be repaired, adjusted, or replaced before the vehicle will pass inspection; or

(2) require an applicant to have another part of the vehicle or other equipment inspected as a prerequisite for issuance of an inspection certificate.

(d) An inspection station or inspector may not issue an inspection certificate for a vehicle equipped with:

(1) a carburetion device permitting the use of liquefied gas alone or interchangeably with another fuel, unless a valid liquefied gas tax decal issued by the comptroller is attached to the lower right-hand corner of the front windshield of the vehicle on the passenger side; or

(2) a sunscreening device prohibited by Section 547.613, except that the department by rule shall provide procedures for issuance of an inspection certificate for a vehicle exempt under Section 547.613(c).

(e) The department shall adopt rules relating to inspection of and issuance of an inspection certificate for a moped.

*(Added by L.1995, chap. 165(1), eff. 9/1/95.)*



### §548.105. Evidence of financial responsibility as prerequisite to issuance of inspection certificate.

(a) An inspection station or inspector may not issue an inspection certificate for a vehicle unless the owner or operator furnishes evidence of financial responsibility at the time of inspection. Evidence of financial responsibility may be shown in the manner specified under Section 601.053(a). A personal automobile insurance policy used as evidence of financial responsibility must be written for a term of 30 days or more as required by Article 5.06, Insurance Code.

(b) An inspection station is not liable to a person, including a third party, for issuing an inspection certificate in reliance on evidence of financial responsibility furnished to the station. An inspection station that is the seller of a motor vehicle may rely on an oral insurance binder.

*(Added by L.1995, chap. 165(1), eff. 9/1/95.)*

### §§548.106 to 548.200. *(Reserved.)*

## SUBCHAPTER D. INSPECTION OF COMMERCIAL MOTOR VEHICLES

### §548.201. Commercial motor vehicle inspection program.

(a) The commission shall establish an inspection program for commercial motor vehicles that:

(1) meets the requirements of federal motor carrier safety regulations; and

(2) requires a commercial motor vehicle registered in this state to pass an annual inspection of all safety equipment required by the federal motor carrier safety regulations.

(b) A program under this section also applies to any:

(1) vehicle or combination of vehicles with a gross weight rating of more than 10,000 pounds that is operated in interstate commerce and registered in this state;

(2) school activity bus, as defined in Section 541.201, that has a gross weight, registered weight, or gross weight rating of more than 26,000 pounds, or is designed to transport more than 15 passengers, including the driver; and

(3) school bus that will operate at a speed authorized by Section 545.352(b)(5)(A).

*(Added by L.1995, chap. 165(1); chgd. by L.1997, chap. 1061(18); L.1999, chap. 663(5), eff. 6/18/99.)*

### §548.202. General applicability of chapter to commercial motor vehicles.

This chapter applies to a commercial motor vehicle inspection program established under Section 548.201 except as otherwise provided. *(Added by L.1995, chap. 165(1), eff. 9/1/95.)*

### §548.203. Exemptions.

The commission by rule may exempt a type of commercial motor vehicle from the application of this subchapter if the vehicle:

(1) was manufactured before September 1, 1995;

(2) is operated only temporarily on a highway of this state and at a speed of less than 30 miles per hour; and

(3) complies with Section 548.051 and each applicable provision in Title 49, Code of Federal Regulations.

*(Added by L.1997, chap. 165(30.122(b)), eff. 9/1/97.)*

### §§548.204 to 548.250. *(Reserved.)*

## SUBCHAPTER E. ISSUANCE, RECORDING, AND PROOF OF INSPECTION CERTIFICATES AND VERIFICATION FORMS

### §548.251. Department to provide inspection certificates and verification forms.

The department shall provide serially numbered inspection certificates and verification forms to inspection stations. The department may issue a unique inspection certificate for:

(1) a commercial motor vehicle inspected under Section 548.201; or

(2) a vehicle inspected under Subchapter F. *(Chgd. by L.1997, chap. 1069(5), eff. 6/19/97. See other paragraph (2) below.)*

(2) a vehicle inspected under Section 548.301(a) or (b). *(Chgd. by L.1997, chap. 165(30.123(c)), eff. 9/1/97. See other paragraph (2) above.)*

*(Added by L.1995, chap. 165(1); chgd. by L.1997, chaps. 165(30.123(c)), 1069(5), eff. 9/1/97, 6/19/97, respectively.)*

### §548.252. Safekeeping and control of inspection certificates and verification forms.

On being licensed, an inspector or owner of an inspection station shall:

(1) provide for the safekeeping of inspection certificates and verification forms;

(2) safeguard the certificates and forms against theft, loss, or damage;

(3) control the sequence of issuance of the certificates and forms; and

(4) ensure that the certificates and forms are issued in accordance with department rules.

*(Added by L.1995, chap. 165(1), eff. 9/1/95.)*

### §548.253. Information to be recorded on issuance of inspection certificate and verification form.

An inspection station or inspector, on issuing an inspection certificate and verification form, shall:

(1) make a record and report as prescribed by the department of the inspection and certificate issued; and

(2) include in the inspection certificate and verification form the information required by the department for the type of vehicle inspected.

*(Added by L.1995, chap. 165(1), eff. 9/1/95.)*

### §548.254. Validity of inspection certificate.

An inspection certificate is invalid after the end of the 12th month following the month in which the certificate is issued. An unused inspection certificate representing a previous inspection period may not be issued after the beginning of the next period. *(Added by L.1995, chap. 165(1), eff. 9/1/95.)*

### §548.255. Attachment or production of inspection certificate.

(a) An inspection certificate shall be attached to or produced for a vehicle in the manner required by department rule.

(b) The department shall:

(1) require that a certificate for a motorcycle be attached to the rear of the motorcycle near the license plate; and

(2) adopt rules with respect to display of an inspection certificate for a moped.

*(Added by L.1995, chap. 165(1), eff. 9/1/95.)*

### §548.256. Verification form required to register vehicle.

(a) Before a vehicle that is brought into this state by a person other than a manufacturer or importer may be registered, the owner must have the vehicle inspected and have the inspection station record the following information on a verification form prescribed and provided by the department:

(1) the vehicle identification number;

(2) the number appearing on the odometer of the vehicle at the time of the inspection, if the vehicle has an odometer; and

(3) other information the department requires.

(b) An inspection station may not issue the verification form unless the vehicle complies with the inspection requirements of this chapter.

(c) *(Repealed by L.1997, chap. 1069(19(2)), eff. 6/19/97.)*

*(Added by L.1995, chap. 165(1); chgd. by L.1997, chap. 165(30.123(a)); L.1999, chaps. 1423(8), (9), eff. 9/1/99.)*



### §§548.257 to 548.300. *(Reserved.)*

## SUBCHAPTER F. MOTOR VEHICLE EMISSIONS INSPECTION AND MAINTENANCE

### §548.301. Commission to establish program.

(a) The commission shall establish a motor vehicle emissions inspection and maintenance program for vehicles covered by the Texas air quality state implementation plan authorized by Section 382.0371, Health and Safety Code, or otherwise specified by the department at the direction of the governor as required by any law of the United States or the state's air quality state implementation plan.

(b) The commission by rule may establish a motor vehicle emissions inspection and maintenance program for vehicles specified by the conservation commission at the direction of the governor in a county for which the conservation commission has adopted a resolution requesting the commission to establish such a program and for which the county and the municipality with the largest population in the county by resolution have formally requested a proactive air quality plan consisting of such a program.

(c) A program established under Subsection (b) may not include reregistration-based enforcement unless the county by resolution requests reregistration-based enforcement.

(d) A vehicle emissions inspection under this section may be performed by the same facility that performs a safety inspection if the facility is authorized and certified by the department to perform the vehicle emissions inspection and certified by the department to perform the safety inspection.

*(Added by L.1995, chap. 165(1); chgd. by L.1997, chaps. 165(30.123(d)), 1069(6), eff. 9/1/97, 6/19/97, respectively.)*

### §548.302. Commission to adopt standards and requirements.

The commission shall:

(1) adopt standards for emissions-related inspection criteria consistent with requirements of the United States and the conservation commission applicable to a county in which a program is established under this subchapter; and

(2) develop and impose requirements necessary to ensure that an inspection certificate is not issued to a vehicle subject to a program established under this subchapter unless the vehicle has passed a motor vehicle emissions inspection at a facility authorized and certified by the department.

*(Added by L.1995, chap. 165(1); chgd. by L.1997, chaps. 165(30.123(e)), 1069(7), eff. 9/1/97, 6/19/97, respectively.)*

### §548.303. Program administration.

(a) The commission shall administer the motor vehicle emissions inspection and maintenance program under this subchapter until the vehicle emissions inspection program administered by the department is suspended or discontinued at the direction of the governor under Section 382.037(a-1), Health and Safety Code.

(b) The department may reestablish a program under Section 548.301 or otherwise as directed by the governor under Section 382.037(a-1), Health and Safety Code.

*(Added by L.1995, chap. 165(1); chgd. by L.1997, chap. 165(30.123(f)), eff. 9/1/97. See other section 548.303 below.)*

### §548.303. Program administration.

The commission shall administer the motor vehicle emissions inspection and maintenance program under this subchapter. *(Added by L.1995, chap. 165(1); chgd. by L.1997, chap. 1069(8), eff. 6/19/97. See other section 548.303 above.)*

### §548.304. Stations licensed to conduct emissions inspections.

(a) The department may authorize and certify inspection stations as necessary to implement the emissions-related inspection requirements of the motor vehicle emissions inspection and maintenance program established under Section 382.0371, Health and Safety Code, and this subchapter if the station meets the department's certification requirements.

(b) The department shall provide inspection certificates for distribution and issuance at decentralized inspection stations certified by the department.

(c) The department shall authorize a vehicle emissions inspection facility authorized and licensed under Subsection (a) to issue a unique inspection certificate for a vehicle that passes an inspection under Section 548.301 and Subchapter B.

(d) *(Repealed by L.1997, chap. 1069(9), eff. 6/19/97.)*

*(Added by L.1995, chap. 165(1); chgd. by L.1997, chaps. 165(30.123(g)), 1069(9), eff. 9/1/97, 6/19/97, respectively.)*

### §548.3045. Appointment of decentralized facility.

(a) The department may issue an inspection station certificate to a decentralized facility authorized and licensed by the department under Section 548.304 if the facility meets the certification requirements of that section and the department.

(b) A decentralized facility issued a certificate under Subsection (a) is authorized to perform an inspection under this subchapter or Subchapter B.

*(Added by L.1997, chap. 165(30.123(h)), eff. 9/1/97.)*

### §548.305. *(Repealed by L.1997, chap. 1069(19(2)), eff. 6/19/97.)*

### §548.306. Excessive motor vehicle emissions.

(a) This section applies to a motor vehicle registered in:

(1) a county or a portion of a county designated by department rule in accordance with standards provided by the United States Environmental Protection Agency; or

(2) one of the following areas:

(A) the part of the Dallas/Fort Worth ozone nonattainment area that consists of Collin, Dallas, Denton, and Tarrant counties;

(B) the part of the El Paso ozone nonattainment area that consists of El Paso County; or

(C) the part of the Houston/Galveston ozone nonattainment area that consists of Brazoria, Chambers, Fort Bend, Galveston, Harris, Liberty, Montgomery, and Waller counties.

(b) The registered owner of a motor vehicle commits an offense if the vehicle, in an area described by Subsection (a), emits:

(1) hydrocarbons, carbon monoxide, or nitrogen oxide in an amount that is excessive under United States Environmental Protection Agency standards or standards provided by department rule;

(2) another vehicle-related pollutant that is listed by a department rule adopted to comply with Part A, National Emission Standards Act (42 U.S.C. Sections 7602-7619), or rules of the United States Environmental Protection Agency in an amount identified as excessive under that rule; or

(3) visible smoke that remains suspended in the air 10 or more seconds before fully dissipating.

(c) The department shall provide a notice of violation to the registered owner of a vehicle that is detected violating Subsection (b). The notice of violation must be made by personal delivery to the registered owner or by mailing the notice to the registered owner at the last known address of the owner. The department shall include in the notice the date and location of the violation detected and instructions for the registered owner explaining how the owner must proceed to obtain and pass a verification emissions inspection and to make any repair to the vehicle necessary to pass the inspection and explaining any extension or assistance that may be available to the owner for making any necessary repair. Notice by mail is presumed delivered on the 10th day after the date the notice is deposited in the mail.

(d) The department shall provide notice under Subsection (c) to the registered owner of a vehicle in violation of Subsection (b)(3) as soon as is practicable after the department receives notice that a peace officer in this state has issued the driver of the vehicle an informative citation for the violation. The department shall adopt rules governing the procedures for a peace officer or police department to provide notice of informative citations issued for violations of Subsection (b)(3). The rules must include a requirement that, for each citation issued, the peace officer or police department inform the department of the date and location of the violation.

(e) A peace officer who has probable cause to believe an offense under Subsection (b)(3) has been committed may issue the driver of the vehicle an informative citation that indicates that an offense under Subsection (b)(3) may have been committed and that explains that the registered owner of the vehicle may receive in the mail a notice under Subsection (c).

(f) A registered owner of a vehicle commits an offense if:

(1) notice is delivered to the owner under Subsection (c); and

(2) the owner fails to comply with any provision of the notice before the 31st day after the date the notice is delivered.

(g) An offense under this section is a misdemeanor punishable by a fine of not less than $1 and not more than $350. If a person has previously been convicted of an offense under this section, an offense under this section is a misdemeanor punishable by a fine of not less than $200 and not more than $1,000.

(h) It is an affirmative defense to an offense under this section that the registered owner of the vehicle, before the 31st day after the date the owner receives a notice of violation:

(1) after a verification emissions inspection indicated that the vehicle did not comply with applicable emissions standards, repaired the vehicle as necessary and passed another verification emissions inspection; and

(2) has complied with rules of the department concerning a violation under this section.

(i) The department may contract with a private person to implement this section. The person must comply with terms, policies, rules, and procedures the department adopts to administer this section.

(j) The Texas Department of Transportation may deny reregistration of a vehicle if the registered owner of the vehicle has received notification under Subsection (c) and the vehicle has not passed a verification emissions inspection.

(k) A hearing for a citation issued under this section shall be heard by a justice of the peace of any precinct in the county in which the vehicle is registered.

(*l*) Enforcement of the remote sensing component of the vehicle emissions inspection and maintenance program may not involve any method of screening in which the registered owner of a vehicle found to have allowable emissions by remote sensing technology is charged a fee.

(m) The department by rule may require that a vehicle determined by on-road testing to have excessive emissions be assessed an on-road emissions testing fee not to exceed the emissions testing fee charged by a certified emissions testing facility.

(n) The department by rule may establish procedures for reimbursing a fee for a verification test required by Subsection (c) if the owner demonstrates to the department's satisfaction that:

(1) the vehicle passed the verification emissions test not later than the 30th day after the date the vehicle owner received notice that the vehicle was detected as having excessive emissions; and

(2) the vehicle was not repaired between the date of detection and the date of the verification emissions test.

*(Added by L.1997, chap. 1069(10); chgd. by L.1999, chap. 1189(30), eff. 9/1/99.)*

**§§548.307 to 548.400.** *(Reserved.)*

## SUBCHAPTER G. CERTIFICATION OF INSPECTION STATION OR INSPECTOR

### §548.401. Certification generally.

A person may perform an inspection or issue an inspection certificate only if certified to do so by the department under rules adopted by the department. *(Added by L.1995, chap. 165(1), eff. 9/1/95.)*

### §548.402. Application for certification as inspection station.

(a) To operate as an inspection station, a person must apply to the department for certification. The application must:

(1) be filed with the department on a form prescribed and provided by the department; and

(2) state:

(A) the name of the applicant;

(B) if the applicant is an association, the names and addresses of the persons constituting the association;

(C) if the applicant is a corporation, the names and addresses of its principal officers;

(D) the name under which the applicant transacts or intends to transact business;

(E) the location of the applicant's place of business in the state; and

(F) other information required by the department, including information required by the department for identification.

(b) The application must be signed and sworn or affirmed by:

(1) if the applicant is an individual, the owner; or

(2) if the applicant is a corporation, an executive officer or person specifically authorized by the corporation to sign the application, to which shall be attached written evidence of the person's authority.

(c) An applicant who has or intends to have more than one place of business in this state must file a separate application for each place of business.

*(Added by L.1995, chap. 165(1), eff. 9/1/95.)*



### §548.403. Approval and certification as inspection station.

(a) The department may approve an application for certification as an inspection station only if:

(1) the location complies with department requirements; and

(2) the applicant complies with department rules.

(b) On approval of an application, the department shall issue to the applicant an inspection station certificate. The certificate is valid for each person in whose name the certificate is issued and for the transaction of business at the location designated in the certificate. A certificate is not assignable.

(c) An inspection station certificate shall be conspicuously displayed at the station for which the certificate was issued.

*(Added by L.1995, chap. 165(1), eff. 9/1/95.)*

### §548.404. Application for certification as inspector.

An application for certification as an inspector shall:

(1) be made on a form prescribed and provided by the department; and

(2) state:

(A) the name of the applicant;

(B) the address of the applicant's residence and place of employment;

(C) the applicant's driver's license number; and

(D) other information required by the department.

*(Added by L.1995, chap. 165(1), eff. 9/1/95.)*

### §548.405. Denial, revocation, or suspension of certificate.

(a) The department may deny a person's application for a certificate, revoke or suspend the certificate of a person, inspection station, or inspector, place on probation a person who holds a suspended certificate, or reprimand a person who holds a certificate if:

(1) the station or inspector conducts an inspection, fails to conduct an inspection, or issues a certificate:

(A) in violation of this chapter or a rule adopted under this chapter; or

(B) without complying with the requirements of this chapter or a rule adopted under this chapter;

(2) the person, station, or inspector commits an offense under this chapter or violates this chapter or a rule adopted under this chapter;

(3) the applicant or certificate holder does not meet the standards for certification under this chapter or a rule adopted under this chapter;

(4) the station or inspector does not maintain the qualifications for certification or does not comply with a certification requirement under Subchapter G;

(5) the certificate holder or the certificate holder's agent, employee, or representative commits an act or omission that would cause denial, revocation, or suspension of a certificate to an individual applicant or certificate holder;

(6) the station or inspector does not pay a fee required by Subchapter H; or

(7) the inspector or owner of an inspection station is convicted of a:

(A) felony or Class A or Class B misdemeanor;

(B) similar crime under the jurisdiction of another state or the federal government that is punishable to the same extent as a felony or a Class A or Class B misdemeanor in this state; or

(C) crime under the jurisdiction of another state or the federal government that would be a felony or a Class A or Class B misdemeanor if the crime were committed in this state.

(b) For purposes of Subsection (a)(7), a person is convicted of an offense if a court enters against the person an adjudication of the person's guilt, including an order of probation or deferred adjudication.

(c) If the department suspends a certificate because of a violation of Subchapter F, the suspension must be for a period of not less than six months. The suspension may not be probated or deferred.

(d) Until an inspector or inspection station whose certificate is suspended or revoked receives a new certificate, has the certificate reinstated, or has the suspension expire, the inspector or station may not be directly or indirectly involved in an inspection operation.
*(Added by L.1995, chap. 165(1); chgd. by L.1997, chap. 1069(11); L.1999, chap. 1189(31), eff. 9/1/99.)*



### §548.406. Certificate holder on probation may be required to report.

The director may require the holder of a suspended certificate who is placed on probation to report regularly to the department on a matter that is the basis of the probation. *(Added by L.1995, chap. 165(1), eff. 9/1/95.)*

### §548.407. Hearing on denial, revocation, or suspension of certificate.

(a) Before an application for certification as an inspection station or inspector is denied, the director or a person the director designates shall give the person written notification of:

(1) the proposed denial;

(2) each reason for the proposed denial; and

(3) the person's right to an administrative hearing to determine whether the evidence warrants the denial.

(b) Before a certificate of appointment as an inspector or inspection station is revoked or suspended, the director or a person the director designates shall give written notification to the inspector or inspection station of the revocation or the period of suspension. The notice shall include:

(1) the effective date of the revocation or the period of the suspension, as applicable;

(2) each reason for the revocation or suspension; and

(3) a statement explaining the person's right to an administrative hearing to determine whether the evidence warrants the revocation or suspension.

(c) Notice under Subsection (a) or (b) must be made by personal delivery or by mail to the last address given to the department by the person.

(d) The department may provide that a revocation or suspension takes effect on receipt of notice under Subsection (b) if the department finds that the action is necessary to prevent or remedy a threat to public health, safety, or welfare. Violations that present a threat to public health, safety, or welfare include:

(1) issuing an inspection certificate with knowledge that the issuance is in violation of this chapter or rules adopted under this chapter;

(2) falsely or fraudulently representing to the owner or operator of a vehicle that equipment inspected or required to be inspected must be repaired, adjusted, or replaced for the vehicle to pass an inspection;

(3) issuing an inspection certificate:

(A) without authorization to issue the certificate; or

(B) without inspecting the vehicle;

(4) issuing an inspection certificate for a vehicle with knowledge that the vehicle has not been repaired, adjusted, or corrected after an inspection has shown a repair, adjustment, or correction to be necessary;

(5) knowingly issuing an inspection certificate:

(A) for a vehicle without conducting an inspection of each item required to be inspected; or

(B) for a vehicle that is missing an item required to be inspected or that has an item required to be inspected that is not in compliance with state law or department rules;

(6) refusing to allow a vehicle's owner to have a qualified person of the owner's choice make a required repair, adjustment, or correction;

(7) charging for an inspection an amount greater than the authorized fee;

(8) a violation of Subchapter F;

(9) a violation of Section 548.603; or

(10) a conviction of a felony or a Class A or B misdemeanor that directly relates to or affects the duties or responsibilities of a vehicle inspection station or inspector or a conviction of a similar crime under the jurisdiction of another state or the federal government.

(e) For purposes of Subsection (d)(10), a person is convicted of an offense if a court enters against the person an adjudication of the person's guilt, including an order of probation or deferred adjudication.

(f) To obtain an administrative hearing on a denial, suspension, or revocation under this section, a person must submit a written request for a hearing to the director not later than the 20th day after the date notice is delivered personally or is mailed.

(g) If the director receives a timely request under Subsection (f), the director shall provide the person with an opportunity for a hearing as soon as practicable. A hearing on a revocation or suspension under Subsection (d) that takes effect on receipt of the notice must be held not later than 14 days after the department receives the request for hearing. The revocation or suspension continues in effect until the hearing is completed if the hearing is continued beyond the 14-day period:

(1) at the request of the inspector or inspection station; or

(2) on a finding of good cause by a judge, administrative law judge, or hearing officer.

(h) If the director does not receive a timely request under Subsection (f), the director may deny the application, revoke or suspend a certificate, or sustain the revocation or suspension of a certificate without a hearing.

(i) Except as provided by Subsection (g), the hearing must be held not earlier than the 11th day after the date written notice of the hearing and a copy of the charges is given to the person by personal service or by certified mail to the last address given to the department by the person.

(j) The director or a person designated by the director shall conduct the hearing and may administer oaths and issue subpoenas for the attendance of witnesses and the production of relevant books, papers, or documents. If the hearing is conducted by a person designated by the director, the director may take action under this section on a recommendation of the designated person.

(k) On the basis of the evidence submitted at the hearing, the director may deny the application or revoke or suspend the certificate.

(*l*) If an administrative law judge of the State Office of Administrative Hearings conducts a hearing under this section and the proposal for decision supports the position of the department, the proposal for decision may recommend a denial of an application or a revocation or suspension of a certificate only. The proposal may not recommend a reprimand or a probated or otherwise deferred disposition of the denial, revocation, or suspension. If the administrative law judge makes a proposal for a decision to deny an application or to suspend or revoke a certificate, the administrative law judge shall include in the proposal a finding of the costs, fees, expenses, and reasonable and necessary attorney's fees the state incurred in bringing the proceeding. The director may adopt the finding for costs, fees, and expenses and make the finding a part of the final order entered in the proceeding. Proceeds collected from a finding made under this subsection shall be paid to the department.

*(Added by L.1995, chap. 165(1); chgd. by L.1997, chap. 1069(12); L.1999, chap. 1189(32), eff. 9/1/99.)*

## §548.408. Judicial review of administrative action.

(a) A person dissatisfied with the action of the director may appeal the action by filing a petition in district court in the county where the person resides or in Travis County. The petition must be filed not later than the 30th day after the date the action is taken.

(b) The district or county attorney or the attorney general shall represent the director in the appeal, except that an attorney who is a full-time employee of the department may represent the director in the appeal with the approval of the attorney general.

(c) The court in which the appeal is filed shall:

(1) set the matter for hearing after 10 days' written notice to the director and the attorney representing the director; and

(2) determine whether an action of the director shall be suspended pending hearing and enter an order for the suspension.

(d) The court order takes effect when served on the director.

(e) The director shall provide a copy of the petition and court order to the attorney representing the director.

(f) A stay under this section may not be effective for more than 90 days after the date the petition for appeal is filed. On the expiration of the stay, the director's action shall be reinstated or imposed. The department or court may not extend the stay or grant an additional stay.

*(Added by L.1995, chap. 165(1); chgd. by L.1999, chap. 1189(33), eff. 9/1/99.)*

§§548.409 to 548.500. *(Reserved.)*

## SUBCHAPTER H. INSPECTION AND CERTIFICATION FEES

### §548.501. Inspection fees generally.

(a) Except as provided by Sections 548.503 and 548.504, the fee for inspection of a motor vehicle other than a moped is $12.50. The fee for inspection of a moped is $5.75. The fee for a verification form issued as required by Section 548.256 is $1.

(b) An inspection station shall pay to the department $5.50 of each fee for an inspection. The department may require the station to make an advance payment of $5.50 for each inspection certificate provided to the station. If advance payment is made:

(1) no further payment may be required on issuance of a certificate;

(2) the inspection station may waive the fee due from the owner of an inspected vehicle who is issued a certificate to which the advance payment applies;

(3) the department shall refund to the inspection station $5.50 for each unissued certificate that the station returns to the department in accordance with department rules; and

(4) the conservation commission shall pay to the department $2 for each unissued certificate that the station returns to the department.

*(Added by L.1995, chap. 165(1); chgd. by L.1999, chap. 1189(34), eff. 9/1/99.)*



### §548.502. Inspection by political subdivision or state agency.

A political subdivision or state agency for which the department certifies an inspection station under Section 548.004:

(1) shall pay to the department an advance payment of $5.50 for each inspection certificate provided to it; and

(2) may not be required to pay the compulsory inspection fee.

*(Added by L.1995, chap. 165(1), eff. 9/1/95.)*

### §548.503. Initial two-year inspection of passenger car or light truck.

(a) The fee for inspection of a passenger car or light truck under Section 548.102 shall be set by the department by rule on or before September 1 of each year. A fee set by the department under this subsection must be based on the costs of producing certificates, providing inspections, and administering the program, but may not be less than $21.75.

(b) The department shall require an inspection station to make an advance payment of $14.75 for a certificate to be issued under this section. Additional payment may not be required of the station for the certificate. The inspection station may waive the fee due from the owner of the vehicle inspected. A refund for an unissued certificate shall be made in the same manner as provided for other certificate refunds.

*(Added by L.1995, chap. 165(1); chgd. by L.1999, chap. 1189(35), eff. 9/1/99.)*

### §548.504. Inspection of commercial motor vehicle.

(a) The fee for inspection of a commercial motor vehicle under the program established under Section 548.201 is $50.

(b) The inspection station shall pay to the department $10 of each fee for inspection of a commercial motor vehicle. The department may require the station to make an advance payment of $10 for a certificate to be issued under this section. If advance payment is made:

(1) no additional payment may be required of the station for the certificate; and

(2) a refund for an unissued certificate shall be made in the same manner as provided for other certificate refunds.

*(Added by L.1995, chap. 165(1), eff. 9/1/95.)*

### §548.505. Emissions-related inspection fee.

(a) The department by rule may impose an inspection fee for a vehicle inspected under Section 548.301(a) in addition to the fee provided by Section 548.501, 548.502, 548.503, or 548.504. A fee imposed under this subsection must be based on the costs of:

(1) producing certificates;

(2) providing inspections; and

(3) administering the program.

(b) The department may provide a maximum fee for an inspection under this subchapter. The department may not set a minimum fee for an inspection under this subchapter.

(c) If an inspection under Section 548.101 or Section 548.102 is not performed when an inspection is performed under Section 548.301(a), the only fee due is the fee authorized by this section.

(d) The decentralized inspection stations shall pay to the department an amount equal to the cost of producing certificates provided to the decentralized inspection stations under Section 548.304.

(e) The conservation commission shall implement procedures governing the tracking of certificates and the refunding of the cost of unissued certificates provided to inspection stations.

(f) The department may establish a maximum fee for an inspection under Section 548.301. The department may not establish a minimum fee for inspection.
*(Added by L.1995, chap. 165(1); chgd. by L.1997, chaps. 165(30.123(i)), 1069(13), eff. 9/1/97, 6/19/97, respectively.)*

### §548.506. Fee for certification as inspector.

An applicant for certification as an inspector must submit with the applicant's first application a fee of $10 for certification until August 31 of the even-numbered year following the date of certification. To be certified after August 31 of that year, the applicant must pay $10 as a certificate fee for each subsequent two-year period. *(Added by L.1995, chap. 165(1), eff. 9/1/95.)*

### §548.507. Fee for certification as inspection station.

When an applicant for certification as an inspection station is notified that the application will be approved, the applicant shall pay a fee of $30 for certification until August 31 of the odd-numbered year after the date of appointment. To be certified after August 31 of that year, the applicant must pay a fee of $30 for certification for each subsequent two-year period. *(Added by L.1995, chap. 165(1), eff. 9/1/95.)*

### §§548.508 to 548.600. *(Reserved.)*

## SUBCHAPTER I. VIOLATIONS AND OFFENSES

### §548.601. Offense generally.

(a) A person, including an inspector or an inspection station, commits an offense if the person:

(1) issues an inspection certificate with knowledge that the issuance is in violation of this chapter or rules adopted under this chapter;

(2) falsely or fraudulently represents to the owner or operator of a vehicle that equipment inspected or required to be inspected must be repaired, adjusted, or replaced for the vehicle to pass an inspection;

(3) misrepresents:

(A) material information in an application in violation of Section 548.402 or 548.403; or

(B) information filed with the department under this chapter or as required by department rule;

(4) issues an inspection certificate:

(A) without authorization to issue the certificate; or

(B) without inspecting the vehicle;

(5) issues an inspection certificate for a vehicle with knowledge that the vehicle has not been repaired, adjusted, or corrected after an inspection has shown a repair, adjustment, or correction to be necessary;

(6) knowingly issues an inspection certificate:

(A) for a vehicle without conducting an inspection of each item required to be inspected; or

(B) for a vehicle that is missing an item required to be inspected or that has an item required to be inspected that is not in compliance with state law or department rules;

(7) refuses to allow a vehicle's owner to have a qualified person of the owner's choice make a required repair, adjustment, or correction;

(8) charges for an inspection an amount greater than the authorized fee; or

(9) performs an act prohibited by or fails to perform an act required by this chapter or a rule adopted under this chapter.

(b) Unless otherwise specified in this chapter, an offense under this section is a Class C misdemeanor.

(c) A designated representative of the department may issue a notice of an offense or a notice to appear to a person, including an inspector or inspection station, who violates this chapter or a rule adopted under this chapter.

*(Added by L.1995, chap. 165(1); chgd. by L.1997, chap. 1069(14); L.1999, chap. 1189(36), eff. 9/1/99.)*

## §548.602. Failure to display inspection certificate.

(a) After the fifth day after the date of expiration of the period designated for inspection, a person may not operate:

(1) a motor vehicle registered in this state unless a current and appropriate inspection certificate is displayed on the vehicle; or

(2) a commercial motor vehicle registered in this state unless it is equipped as required by federal motor carrier safety regulations and displays an inspection certificate issued under the program established under Section 548.201.

(b) A peace officer who exhibits a badge or other sign of authority may stop a vehicle not displaying an inspection certificate on the windshield and require the owner or operator to produce an inspection certificate for the vehicle.

(c) It is a defense to prosecution under Subsection (a)(1) that an inspection certificate for the vehicle is in effect at the time of the arrest.

*(Added by L.1995, chap. 165(1); chgd. by L.1997, chap. 1069(15); L.1999, chap. 1189(37), eff. 9/1/99.)*



## §548.603. Fictitious or counterfeit inspection certificate or insurance document.

(a) A person commits an offense if the person:

(1) displays or causes or permits to be displayed an inspection certificate or insurance document knowing that the certificate or document is counterfeit, tampered with, altered, fictitious, issued for another vehicle, issued for a vehicle failing to meet all emissions inspection requirements, or issued in violation of:

(A) this chapter, rules adopted under this chapter, or other law of this state; or

(B) a law of another state, the United States, the United Mexican States, a state of the United Mexican States, Canada, or a province of Canada;

(2) transfers an inspection certificate from a windshield or location to another windshield or location;

(3) with intent to circumvent the emissions inspection requirements seeks an inspection of a vehicle at a station not certified to perform an emissions inspection if the person knows that the vehicle is required to be inspected under Section 548.301;

(4) knowingly does not comply with an emissions inspection requirement for a vehicle; or

(5) displays on a vehicle an inspection certificate that was obtained knowing that the vehicle does not meet all emissions inspection requirements for the vehicle.

(b) A person commits an offense if the person:

(1) makes or possesses, with the intent to sell, circulate, or pass, a counterfeit inspection certificate or insurance document; or

(2) possesses any part of a stamp, dye, plate, negative, machine, or other device that is used or designated for use in making a counterfeit inspection certificate or insurance document.

(c) The owner of a vehicle commits an offense if the owner knowingly allows the vehicle to be registered or operated while the vehicle displays an inspection certificate in violation of Subsection (a).

(d) An offense under Subsection (a) or (c) is a Class B misdemeanor. An offense under Subsection (b) is a third degree felony unless the person acts with the intent to defraud or harm another person, in which event the offense is a second degree felony.

(e) In this section:

(1) "Counterfeit" means an imitation of a document that is printed, engraved, copied, photographed, forged, or manufactured by a person not authorized to take that action under:

(A) this chapter, rules adopted under this chapter, or other law of this state; or

(B) a law of another state, the United States, the United Mexican States, a state of the United Mexican States, Canada, or a province of Canada.

(2) "Inspection certificate" means a document that is printed, manufactured, or made by the department or an authorized agent of the department for issuance after a vehicle passes an inspection performed under this chapter.

(3) "Insurance document" means a standard proof of motor vehicle insurance coverage that is:

(A) in a form prescribed by the Texas Department of Insurance or by a similarly authorized board, agency, or authority of another state; and

(B) issued by an insurer or insurer's agent who is authorized to write motor vehicle insurance coverage.

(4) "Person" includes an inspection station or inspector.

(f) A motor vehicle on which a vehicle emissions inspection certificate is displayed in violation of Subsection (a) and that is operated or parked on a public roadway may be impounded by a peace officer or other authorized employee of this state or a political subdivision of this state in which the vehicle is operated or parked. *(Chgd. by L.1997, chap. 1069(16), eff. 6/19/97. See other subsection (f) below.)*

(f) Notwithstanding Subsection (c), an offense under Subsection (a)(1) that involves a fictitious inspection certificate is a Class B misdemeanor. *(Added by L.1997, chap. 851(2), eff. 9/1/97. See other subsection (f) above.)*

*(Added by L.1995, chap. 165(1); chgd. by L.1997, chaps. 165(30.123(j), (k)), 851(2), 1069(16), eff. 9/1/97, 9/1/97, 6/19/97, respectively.)*



### §548.604. Penalty for certain violations.

(a) A person commits an offense if the person operates or moves a motor vehicle, trailer, semitrailer, pole trailer, or mobile home, or a combination of those vehicles, that is:

(1) equipped in violation of this chapter or a rule adopted under this chapter; or

(2) in a mechanical condition that endangers a person, including the operator or an occupant, or property.

(b) An offense under this section is a misdemeanor punishable by a fine not to exceed $200.

*(Added by L.1995, chap. 165(1), eff. 9/1/95.)*

### §548.605. Dismissal of charge; administrative fee.

(a) In this section, "working day" means any day other than a Saturday, a Sunday, or a holiday on which county offices are closed.

(b) The court shall:

(1) dismiss a charge of driving with an expired inspection certificate if:

(A) the defendant remedies the defect within 10 working days; and

(B) the inspection certificate has not been expired for more than 60 days; and

(2) assess an administrative fee not to exceed $10 when the charge of driving with an expired inspection certificate has been remedied.

(c) Notwithstanding Subsection (b)(1)(B), the court may dismiss a charge of driving with an expired inspection certificate that has been expired for more than 60 days.

*(Added by L.1995, chap. 165(1); chgd. by L.1999, chap. 688(1), eff. 9/1/99.)*

## CHAPTER 549. MOTOR CARRIER SAFETY STANDARDS

*(Repealed by L.1997, chap. 165(30.124), eff. 9/1/97.)*

## CHAPTER 550. ACCIDENTS AND ACCIDENT REPORTS

## SUBCHAPTER A. GENERAL PROVISIONS

Section



## SUBCHAPTER B. DUTIES FOLLOWING ACCIDENT

## SUBCHAPTER C. INVESTIGATION OF ACCIDENT



## SUBCHAPTER D. WRITTEN ACCIDENT REPORT



## SUBCHAPTER E. OTHER REPORTS





## SUBCHAPTER A. GENERAL PROVISIONS

### §550.001. Applicability of chapter.

This chapter applies only to:

(1) a road owned and controlled by a water control and improvement district;

(2) a private access way or parking area provided for a client or patron by a business, other than a private residential property, or the property of a garage or parking lot for which a charge is made for storing or parking a motor vehicle; and

(3) a highway or other public place.

*(Added by L.1995, chap. 165(1), eff. 9/1/95.)*

### §§550.002 to 550.020. *(Reserved.)*

## SUBCHAPTER B. DUTIES FOLLOWING ACCIDENT

### §550.021. Accident involving personal injury or death.

(a) The operator of a vehicle involved in an accident resulting in injury to or death of a person shall:

(1) immediately stop the vehicle at the scene of the accident or as close to the scene as possible;

(2) immediately return to the scene of the accident if the vehicle is not stopped at the scene of the accident; and

(3) remain at the scene of the accident until the operator complies with the requirements of Section 550.023.

(b) An operator of a vehicle required to stop the vehicle by Subsection (a) shall do so without obstructing traffic more than is necessary.

(c) A person commits an offense if the person does not stop or does not comply with the requirements of this section. An offense under this section is punishable by:

(1) imprisonment in the institutional division of the Texas Department of Criminal Justice for not more than five years or confinement in the county jail for not more than one year;

(2) a fine not to exceed $5,000; or

(3) both the fine and the imprisonment or confinement.

*(Added by L.1995, chap. 165(1), eff. 9/1/95.)*

## §550.022. Accident involving damage to vehicle.

(a) Except as provided by Subsection (b), the operator of a vehicle involved in an accident resulting only in damage to a vehicle that is driven or attended by a person shall:

(1) immediately stop the vehicle at the scene of the accident or as close as possible to the scene of the accident without obstructing traffic more than is necessary;

(2) immediately return to the scene of the accident if the vehicle is not stopped at the scene of the accident; and

(3) remain at the scene of the accident until the operator complies with the requirements of Section 550.023.

(b) If an accident occurs on a main lane, ramp, shoulder, median, or adjacent area of a freeway in a metropolitan area and each vehicle involved can be normally and safely driven, each operator shall move the operator's vehicle as soon as possible to a designated accident investigation site, if available, a location on the frontage road, the nearest suitable cross street, or other suitable location to complete the requirements of Section 550.023 and minimize interference with freeway traffic.

(c) A person commits an offense if the person does not stop or does not comply with the requirements of this section. An offense under this section is:

(1) a Class C misdemeanor, if the damage to all vehicles is less than $200; or

(2) a Class B misdemeanor, if the damage to all vehicles is $200 or more.

(d) In this section, a vehicle can be normally and safely driven only if the vehicle:

(1) does not require towing; and

(2) can be operated under its own power and in its usual manner, without additional damage or hazard to the vehicle, other traffic, or the roadway.

*(Added by L.1995, chap. 165(1), eff. 9/1/95.)*

## §550.023. Duty to give information and render aid.

The operator of a vehicle involved in an accident resulting in the injury or death of a person or damage to a vehicle that is driven or attended by a person shall:

(1) give the operator's name and address, the registration number of the vehicle the operator was driving, and the name of the operator's motor vehicle liability insurer to any person injured or the operator or occupant of or person attending a vehicle involved in the collision;

(2) if requested and available, show the operator's driver's license to a person described by Subdivision (1); and

(3) provide any person injured in the accident reasonable assistance, including transporting or making arrangements for transporting the person to a physician or hospital for medical treatment if it is apparent that treatment is necessary, or if the injured person requests the transportation.

*(Added by L.1995, chap. 165(1), eff. 9/1/95.)*

## §550.024. Duty on striking unattended vehicle.

(a) The operator of a vehicle that collides with and damages an unattended vehicle shall immediately stop and:

(1) locate the operator or owner of the unattended vehicle and give that person the name and address of the operator and the owner of the vehicle that struck the unattended vehicle; or

(2) leave in a conspicuous place in, or securely attach in a plainly visible way to, the unattended vehicle a written notice giving the name and address of the operator and the owner of the vehicle that struck the unattended vehicle and a statement of the circumstances of the collision.

(b) A person commits an offense if the person violates Subsection (a). An offense under this section is:

(1) a Class C misdemeanor, if the damage to all vehicles involved is less than $200; or

(2) a Class B misdemeanor, if the damage to all vehicles involved is $200 or more.

*(Added by L.1995, chap. 165(1), eff. 9/1/95.)*

## §550.025. Duty on striking fixture or highway landscaping.

(a) The operator of a vehicle involved in an accident resulting only in damage to a fixture or landscaping legally on or adjacent to a highway shall:

(1) take reasonable steps to locate and notify the owner or person in charge of the property of the accident and of the operator's name and address and the registration number of the vehicle the operator was driving;

(2) if requested and available, show the operator's driver's license to the owner or person in charge of the property; and

(3) report the accident if required by Section 550.061.

(b) A person commits an offense if the person violates Subsection (a). An offense under this section is:

(1) a Class C misdemeanor, if the damage to all fixtures and landscaping is less than $200; or

(2) a Class B misdemeanor, if the damage to all fixtures and landscaping is $200 or more.

*(Added by L.1995, chap. 165(1), eff. 9/1/95.)*

### §550.026. Immediate report of accident.

(a) The operator of a vehicle involved in an accident resulting in injury to or death of a person or damage to a vehicle to the extent that it cannot be normally and safely driven shall immediately by the quickest means of communication give notice of the accident to the:

(1) local police department if the accident occurred in a municipality;

(2) local police department or the sheriff's office if the accident occurred not more than 100 feet outside the limits of a municipality; or

(3) sheriff's office or the nearest office of the department if the accident is not required to be reported under Subdivision (1) or (2).

(b) If a section of road is within 100 feet of the limits of more than one municipality, the municipalities may agree regarding the maintenance of reports made under Subsection (a)(2). A county may agree with municipalities in the county regarding the maintenance of reports made under Subsection (a)(2). An agreement under this subsection does not affect the duty to report an accident under Subsection (a).

*(Added by L.1995, chap. 165(1), eff. 9/1/95.)*



### §§550.027 to 550.040. *(Reserved.)*

## SUBCHAPTER C. INVESTIGATION OF ACCIDENT

### §550.041. Investigation by peace officer.

(a) A peace officer who is notified of a motor vehicle accident resulting in injury to or death of a person or property damage to an apparent extent of at least $500 may investigate the accident and file justifiable charges relating to the accident without regard to whether the accident occurred on property to which this chapter applies.

(b) This section does not apply to:

(1) a privately owned residential parking area; or

(2) a privately owned parking lot where a fee is charged for parking or storing a vehicle.

*(Added by L.1995, chap. 165(1), eff. 9/1/95.)*

### §§550.042 to 550.060. *(Reserved.)*

## SUBCHAPTER D. WRITTEN ACCIDENT REPORT

### §550.061. Operator's accident report.

(a) The operator of a vehicle involved in an accident shall make a written report of the accident if the accident is not investigated by a law enforcement officer and the accident resulted in injury to or the death of a person or damage to the property of any one person to an apparent extent of $500 or more.

(b) The report required by Subsection (a) must be filed with the department not later than the 10th day after the date of the accident.

(c) A person commits an offense if the person does not file the report with the department as required by this section.

(d) Venue for the prosecution of an offense under this section is in the county in which the accident occurred.

(e) The department may require:

(1) the operator of a vehicle involved in an accident in which a report is required by this section to file a supplemental report if the department considers the original report insufficient; and

(2) a witness of an accident to make a report with the department.

*(Added by L.1995, chap. 165(1), eff. 9/1/95.)*

### §550.062. Officer's accident report.

(a) A law enforcement officer who in the regular course of duty investigates a motor vehicle accident shall make a written report of the accident if the accident resulted in injury to or the death of a person or damage to the property of any one person to the apparent extent of $500 or more.

(b) The report required by Subsection (a) must be filed with the department not later than the 10th day after the date of the accident.

(c) This section applies without regard to whether the officer investigates the accident at the location of the accident and immediately after the accident or afterwards by interviewing those involved in the accident or witnesses to the accident.
*(Added by L.1995, chap. 165(1), eff. 9/1/95.)*

### §550.063. Report on appropriate form.

A person who is required to file a written accident report shall report on the appropriate form approved by the department and shall disclose all information required by the form unless the information is not available. *(Added by L.1995, chap. 165(1), eff. 9/1/95.)*

### §550.064. Accident report forms.

(a) The department shall prepare and when requested supply to police departments, coroners, sheriffs, garages, and other suitable agencies or individuals the accident report forms appropriate for the persons required to make a report and appropriate for the purposes to be served by those reports.

(b) An accident report form prepared by the department must:

(1) require sufficiently detailed information to disclose the cause and conditions of and the persons and vehicles involved in an accident if the form is for the report to be made by a person involved in or investigating the accident;

(2) include a way to designate and identify a peace officer, firefighter, or emergency medical services employee who during an emergency is involved in an accident while driving a law enforcement vehicle, fire department vehicle, or emergency medical services vehicle while performing the person's duties;

(3) require a statement by a person described by Subdivision (2) as to the nature of the emergency; and

(4) include a way to designate whether an individual involved in an accident wants to be contacted by a person seeking to obtain employment as a professional described by Section 38.01(12), Penal Code.
*(Added by L.1995, chap. 165(1); chgd. by L.1997, chap. 750(3), eff. 9/1/97.)*

### §550.065. Release of accident reports.

(a) This section applies to an accident report required by this chapter or by Section 601.004.

(b) Except as provided by Subsection (c), an accident report made by a person involved in an accident, by a garage, or by a peace officer is:

(1) without prejudice to the individual making the report; and

(2) privileged and for the confidential use of:

(A) the department; and

(B) an agency of the United States, this state, or a local government of this state that has use for the report for accident prevention purposes.

(c) On written request and payment of any required fee, the department or the law enforcement agency that employs the peace officer who makes an accident report shall release a copy of the report to:

(1) an agency described by Subsection (b)(2)(B);

(2) the law enforcement agency that employs the peace officer who investigated the accident and sent the information to the department;

(3) the court in which a case involving a person involved in the accident is pending if the report is subpoenaed; or

(4) a person who provides the department or law enforcement agency with two or more of the following:

(A) the date of the accident; or

(B) the name of any person involved in the accident; or

(C) the specific location of the accident.

(d) The department or law enforcement agency shall request information on a written form adopted by the department or the agency to determine whether the person or entity requesting an accident report is entitled to receive the report under Subsection (c).

(e) The fee for a copy of the peace officer's report is $4. The copy may be certified by the department or a law enforcement agency for an additional fee of $2. The department may issue a certification that no report is on file for a fee of $4.
*(Added by L.1995, chap. 165(1); chgd. by L.1997, chap. 165(30.125(a)), eff. 9/1/97. See other section 550.065 below.)*

**§550.065. Release of accident reports and certain information relating to accidents.**

(a) This section applies only to information that is held by the department or another governmental entity and relates to a motor vehicle accident, including:

(1) information reported under this chapter, Section 601.004, or Chapter 772, Health and Safety Code;

(2) information contained in a dispatch log, towing record, or a record of a 9-1-1 service provider; and

(3) the part of any other record that includes information relating to the date of the accident, the name of any person involved in the accident, or the specific location of the accident.

(b) Except as provided by Subsection (c), the information is privileged and for the confidential use of:

(1) the department; and

(2) an agency of the United States, this state, or a local government of this state that has use for the information for accident prevention purposes.

(c) On written request and payment of any required fee, the department or the governmental entity shall release the information to:

(1) an entity described by Subsection (b);

(2) the law enforcement agency that employs the peace officer who investigated the accident and sent the information to the department;

(3) the court in which a case involving a person involved in the accident is pending if the report is subpoenaed; or

(4) a person who provides the department or governmental entity with the name of any person involved in the accident and one or more of the following:

(A) the date of the accident; or

(B) the specific address or the highway or street where the accident occurred.

(d) The department or governmental entity shall request information on a written form adopted by the department or the entity to determine whether the person or entity requesting the information is entitled to receive the information under Subsection (c).

(e) The fee for a copy of the peace officer's report is $4. The copy may be certified by the department or a law enforcement agency for an additional fee of $2. The department may issue a certification that no report is on file for a fee of $4.

(f) If the person or entity requesting the information is entitled to receive the information under Subsection (c), Subchapter F, Chapter 552, Government Code, applies in connection with:

(1) making the information available to that person or entity if the information exists in a paper record;

(2) providing that person or entity access to the information if the information exists in an electronic medium or in an electronic form; and

(3) providing a copy of the information to that person or entity.

*(Added by L.1995, chap. 165(1); chgd. by L.1997, chap. 1187(13), eff. 9/1/97. See other section 550.065 above.)*

**§550.066. Admissibility of certain accident report information.**

An individual's response to the information requested on an accident report form as provided by Section 550.064(b)(4) is not admissible evidence in a civil trial. *(Added by L.1995, chap. 165(1), eff. 9/1/95.)*

**§550.067. Municipal authority to require accident reports.**

(a) A municipality by ordinance may require the operator of a vehicle involved in an accident to file with a designated municipal department:

(1) a report of the accident, if the accident results in injury to or the death of a person or the apparent total property damage is $25 or more; or

(2) a copy of a report required by this chapter to be filed with the department.

(b) A report filed under Subsection (a) is for the confidential use of the municipal department and subject to the provisions of Section 550.065.

(c) A municipality by ordinance may require the person in charge of a garage or repair shop where a motor vehicle is brought if the vehicle shows evidence of having been involved in an accident requiring a report to be filed under Section 550.061 or 550.062 or shows evidence of having been struck by a bullet to report to a department of the municipality within 24 hours after the garage or repair shop receives the motor vehicle, giving the engine number, registration number, and the name and address of the owner or operator of the vehicle.

*(Added by L.1995, chap. 165(1), eff. 9/1/95.)*

**§550.068. Changing accident report.**

(a) Except as provided by Subsection (b), a change in or a modification of a written report of a motor vehicle accident prepared by a peace officer or the operator of a vehicle involved in an accident that alters a material fact in the report may be made only by the peace officer or person who prepared the report.

(b) A change in or a modification of the written report of the accident may be made by a person other than the peace officer or the operator of the vehicle if:

(1) the change is made by a written supplement to the report; and

(2) the written supplement clearly indicates the name of the person who originated the change.

*(Added by L.1997, chap. 214(1), eff. 9/1/97.)*

**§§550.069 to 550.080.** *(Reserved.)*

## SUBCHAPTER E. OTHER REPORTS

**§550.081. Coroner's report.**

A coroner or other officer performing similar functions shall, not later than the 10th day of each month:

(1) report in writing to the department the death of a person within the officer's jurisdiction during the preceding calendar month as the result of a traffic accident; and

(2) include in the report the time, place, and circumstances of the accident.

*(Added by L.1995, chap. 165(1), eff. 9/1/95.)*

# CHAPTER 551. OPERATION OF BICYCLES, MOPEDS, AND PLAY VEHICLES

## SUBCHAPTER A. APPLICATION OF CHAPTER

Section



## SUBCHAPTER B. REGULATION OF OPERATION



## SUBCHAPTER A. APPLICATION OF CHAPTER

**§551.001. Persons affected.**

This chapter applies only to a person operating a bicycle on:

(1) a highway; or

(2) a path set aside for the exclusive operation of bicycles.

*(Added by L.1995, chap. 165(1), eff. 9/1/95.)*

**§551.002. Moped included.**

A provision of this subtitle applicable to a bicycle also applies to a moped, other than a provision that by its nature cannot apply to a moped. *(Added by L.1995, chap. 165(1), eff. 9/1/95.)*

**§§551.003 to 551.100.** *(Reserved.)*

## SUBCHAPTER B. REGULATION OF OPERATION

### §551.101. Rights and duties.

(a) A person operating a bicycle has the rights and duties applicable to a driver operating a vehicle under this subtitle, unless:

(1) a provision of this chapter alters a right or duty; or

(2) a right or duty applicable to a driver operating a vehicle cannot by its nature apply to a person operating a bicycle.

(b) A parent of a child or a guardian of a ward may not knowingly permit the child or ward to violate this subtitle.

*(Added by L.1995, chap. 165(1), eff. 9/1/95.)*

### §551.102. General operation.

(a) A person operating a bicycle shall ride only on or astride a permanent and regular seat attached to the bicycle.

(b) A person may not use a bicycle to carry more persons than the bicycle is designed or equipped to carry.

(c) A person operating a bicycle may not use the bicycle to carry an object that prevents the person from operating the bicycle with at least one hand on the handlebars of the bicycle.

(d) A person operating a bicycle, coaster, sled, or toy vehicle or using roller skates may not attach either the person or the bicycle, coaster, sled, toy vehicle, or roller skates to a streetcar or vehicle on a roadway.

*(Added by L.1995, chap. 165(1), eff. 9/1/95.)*

### §551.103. Operation on roadway.

(a) Except as provided by Subsection (b), a person operating a bicycle on a roadway who is moving slower than the other traffic on the roadway shall ride as near as practicable to the right curb or edge of the roadway, unless:

(1) the person is passing another vehicle moving in the same direction;

(2) the person is preparing to turn left at an intersection or onto a private road or driveway; or

(3) a condition on or of the roadway, including a fixed or moving object, parked or moving vehicle, pedestrian, animal, surface hazard, or substandard width lane, prevents the person from safely riding next to the right curb or edge of the roadway.

(b) A person operating a bicycle on a one-way roadway with two or more marked traffic lanes may ride as near as practicable to the left curb or edge of the roadway.

(c) Persons operating bicycles on a roadway may ride two abreast. Persons riding two abreast on a laned roadway shall ride in a single lane. Persons riding two abreast may not impede the normal and reasonable flow of traffic on the roadway. Persons may not ride more than two abreast unless they are riding on a part of a roadway set aside for the exclusive operation of bicycles.

(d) In this section, "substandard width lane" means a lane that is too narrow for a bicycle and a motor vehicle to safely travel in the lane side by side.

*(Added by L.1995, chap. 165(1), eff. 9/1/95.)*

### §551.104. Safety equipment.

(a) A person may not operate a bicycle unless the bicycle is equipped with a brake capable of making a braked wheel skid on dry, level, clean pavement.

(b) A person may not operate a bicycle at nighttime unless the bicycle is equipped with:

(1) a lamp on the front of the bicycle that emits a white light visible from a distance of at least 500 feet in front of the bicycle; and

(2) a red reflector on the rear of the bicycle that is:

(A) of a type approved by the department; and

(B) visible when directly in front of lawful upper beams of motor vehicle headlamps from all distances from 50 to 300 feet to the rear of the bicycle.

(c) In addition to the reflector required by Subsection (b), a person operating a bicycle at nighttime may use a lamp on the rear of the bicycle that emits a red light visible from a distance of 500 feet to the rear of the bicycle.

*(Added by L.1995, chap. 165(1), eff. 9/1/95.)*

### §551.105. Competitive racing.

(a) In this section, "bicycle" means a nonmotorized vehicle propelled by human power.

(b) A sponsoring organization may hold a competitive bicycle race on a public road only with the approval of the appropriate local law enforcement agencies.

Printed in the U.S.A. Zt

(c) The local law enforcement agencies and the sponsoring organization may agree on safety regulations governing the movement of bicycles during a competitive race or during training for a competitive race, including the permission for bicycle operators to ride abreast.
*(Added by L.1995, chap. 165(1), eff. 9/1/95.)*

# CHAPTER 552. PEDESTRIANS

Section




## §552.001. Traffic control signals.

(a) A traffic control signal displaying green, red, and yellow lights or lighted arrows applies to a pedestrian as provided by this section unless the pedestrian is otherwise directed by a special pedestrian control signal.

(b) A pedestrian facing a green signal may proceed across a roadway within a marked or unmarked crosswalk unless the sole green signal is a turn arrow.

(c) A pedestrian facing a steady red signal alone or a steady yellow signal may not enter a roadway.
*(Added by L.1995, chap. 165(1), eff. 9/1/95.)*

## §552.002. Pedestrian right-of-way if control signal present.

(a) A pedestrian control signal displaying "Walk," "Don't Walk," or "Wait" applies to a pedestrian as provided by this section.

(b) A pedestrian facing a "Walk" signal may proceed across a roadway in the direction of the signal, and the operator of a vehicle shall yield the right-of-way to the pedestrian.

(c) A pedestrian may not start to cross a roadway in the direction of a "Don't Walk" signal or a "Wait" signal. A pedestrian who has partially crossed while the "Walk" signal is displayed shall proceed to a sidewalk or safety island while the "Don't Walk" signal or "Wait" signal is displayed.
*(Added by L.1995, chap. 165(1), eff. 9/1/95.)*

## §552.003. Pedestrian right-of-way at crosswalk.

(a) The operator of a vehicle shall yield the right-of-way to a pedestrian crossing a roadway in a crosswalk if:

(1) no traffic control signal is in place or in operation; and

(2) the pedestrian is:

(A) on the half of the roadway in which the vehicle is traveling; or

(B) approaching so closely from the opposite half of the roadway as to be in danger.

(b) Notwithstanding Subsection (a), a pedestrian may not suddenly leave a curb or other place of safety and proceed into a crosswalk in the path of a vehicle so close that it is impossible for the vehicle operator to yield.

(c) The operator of a vehicle approaching from the rear of a vehicle that is stopped at a crosswalk to permit a pedestrian to cross a roadway may not pass the stopped vehicle.
*(Added by L.1995, chap. 165(1), eff. 9/1/95.)*

## §552.004. Pedestrian to keep to right.

A pedestrian shall proceed on the right half of a crosswalk if possible. *(Added by L.1995, chap. 165(1), eff. 9/1/95.)*

## §552.005. Crossing at point other than crosswalk.

(a) A pedestrian shall yield the right-of-way to a vehicle on the highway if crossing a roadway at a place:

(1) other than in a marked crosswalk or in an unmarked crosswalk at an intersection; or

(2) where a pedestrian tunnel or overhead pedestrian crossing has been provided.

(b) Between adjacent intersections at which traffic control signals are in operation, a pedestrian may cross only in a marked crosswalk.

(c) A pedestrian may cross a roadway intersection diagonally only if and in the manner authorized by a traffic control device.

*(Added by L.1995, chap. 165(1), eff. 9/1/95.)*

### §552.006. Use of sidewalk.

(a) A pedestrian may not walk along and on a roadway if an adjacent sidewalk is provided.

(b) If a sidewalk is not provided, a pedestrian walking along and on a highway shall if possible walk on:

(1) the left side of the roadway; or

(2) the shoulder of the highway facing oncoming traffic.

(c) The operator of a vehicle emerging from or entering an alley, building, or private road or driveway shall yield the right-of-way to a pedestrian approaching on a sidewalk extending across the alley, building entrance or exit, road, or driveway.

*(Added by L.1995, chap. 165(1), eff. 9/1/95.)*



### §552.007. Solicitation by pedestrians.

(a) A person may not stand in a roadway to solicit a ride, contribution, employment, or business from an occupant of a vehicle, except that a person may stand in a roadway to solicit a charitable contribution if authorized to do so by the local authority having jurisdiction over the roadway.

(b) A person may not stand on or near a highway to solicit the watching or guarding of a vehicle parked or to be parked on the highway.

(c) In this section, "charitable contribution" means a contribution to an organization defined as charitable by the standards of the United States Internal Revenue Service.

*(Added by L.1995, chap. 165(1), eff. 9/1/95.)*

### §552.008. Drivers to exercise due care.

Notwithstanding another provision of this chapter, the operator of a vehicle shall:

(1) exercise due care to avoid colliding with a pedestrian on a roadway;

(2) give warning by sounding the horn when necessary; and

(3) exercise proper precaution on observing a child or an obviously confused or incapacitated person on a roadway.

*(Added by L.1995, chap. 165(1), eff. 9/1/95.)*

### §552.009. Ordinances relating to pedestrians.

A local authority may by ordinance:

(1) require pedestrians to comply strictly with the directions of an official traffic control signal; and

(2) prohibit pedestrians from crossing a roadway in a business district or a designated highway except in a crosswalk.

*(Added by L.1995, chap. 165(1), eff. 9/1/95.)*

## CHAPTER 553. ENACTMENT AND ENFORCEMENT OF CERTAIN TRAFFIC LAWS IN CERTAIN MUNICIPALITIES

Section



### §553.001. Applicability.

This chapter applies only to a municipality with a population of less than 2,500 in a county with a population of 250,000 or more. *(Added by L.1995, chap. 165(1), eff. 9/1/95.)*

### §553.002. Traffic signals or signs in municipality.

(a) A municipality may not enact an ordinance governing the erection or operation of a traffic signal or sign in the municipality on a state highway funded in whole or in part by the state without prior approval by the Texas Department of Transportation.

(b) A municipality intending to erect or operate a traffic signal or sign described by Subsection (a) must apply in writing to the Texas Department of Transportation. After the application is filed, the Texas Department of Transportation shall designate an employee to investigate the application and shall grant or refuse the application not later than the 90th day after the date of the designation.

(c) In granting an application, the Texas Department of Transportation:

(1) may prescribe the conditions under which the municipality may erect and operate the signal or sign and all other aspects of the signal or sign; and

(2) shall consider the convenience of the traveling public in raising speed limits in noncongested areas and the control of traffic for the protection of schoolchildren and other inhabitants of small communities where there are areas of congestion and cross-traffic.

*(Added by L.1995, chap. 165(1), eff. 9/1/95.)*

### §553.003. Injunction against unauthorized signal or sign.

(a) If a municipality erects or maintains a traffic signal or sign without meeting the requirements of this chapter, the district or county attorney of the county where the signal or sign is located shall bring a suit to enjoin the erection and maintenance of the signal or sign.

(b) If the district or county attorney does not institute a suit under Subsection (a) within 15 days after the date a request to do so is received from a resident of the state, any state resident may institute and prosecute the suit.

*(Added by L.1995, chap. 165(1), eff. 9/1/95.)*

## CHAPTERS 554 to 599. *(Reserved.)*

## CHAPTER 600. MISCELLANEOUS PROVISIONS

Section



### §600.001. Removing material from highway.

(a) A person who drops or permits to be dropped or thrown on a highway destructive or injurious material shall immediately remove the material or cause it to be removed.

(b) A person who removes a wrecked or damaged vehicle from a highway shall remove glass or another injurious substance dropped on the highway from the vehicle.

*(Added by L.1995, chap. 165(1), eff. 9/1/95.)*

### §600.002. Identification required for vehicle near Mexican border.

On demand of a peace officer within 250 feet of the Mexican border at a checkpoint authorized by Section 411.0095, Government Code, as added by Chapter 497, Acts of the 73rd Legislature, Regular Session, 1993, the driver of a vehicle shall produce a driver's license and proof of compliance with Chapter 601. *(Added by L.1995, chap. 165(1), eff. 9/1/95.)*

### §600.003. Enforcement of certain traffic laws by private institutions of higher education.

(a) In this section, "private or independent institution of higher education" has the meaning assigned by Section 61.003(15), Education Code.

(b) A private or independent institution of higher education may enforce a traffic law of this state under Chapter 545 restricting or prohibiting the operation or movement of vehicles on a road of the institution if:

(1) the road of the institution is open to the public at the time the traffic law is enforced;

(2) the governing body of the institution adopts a regulation to enforce the traffic law; and

(3) the restriction or prohibition on the operation and movement of vehicles adopted by the institution:

(A) is posted by means of a sign, marking, signal, or other device visible to and, if it contains writing, able to be read by an operator of a vehicle to whom the restriction or prohibition applies in the same manner as a similar restriction or prohibition on the operation and movement of vehicles would be posted by a municipality; and

(B) has been approved by:

(i) the commissioners court of the county in which the applicable road of the institution is located, if the road is located in the unincorporated area of a county; or

Printed in the U.S.A. Zt

(ii) the governing body of the municipality in which the applicable road of the institution is located, if the road is located in a municipality.

(c) Campus security personnel of the institution commissioned under Section 51.212, Education Code, are authorized to enforce the provisions of this section and have the authority to issue and use traffic tickets and summons in a form prescribed by the Texas Department of Public Safety to enforce this chapter only on the property of the institution that commissioned the campus security personnel under Section 51.212, Education Code.

(d) The same procedures that apply to a traffic ticket or summons by a commissioned peace officer of an institution of higher education under Sections 51.206 and 51.210, Education Code, also apply to a ticket or summons issued under this section.

(e) The governing body of the municipality or the commissioners court of the county that approves the enforcement of traffic laws under Subsection (b) shall also determine the disposition of funds collected under this section from any fees or fines from the enforcement of a traffic law of this state.

*(Added by L.1997, chap. 620(1), eff. 9/1/97.)*



### §600.004. Training of school crossing guard.

(a) A local authority may authorize a school crossing guard to direct traffic in a school crossing zone if the guard successfully completes a training program in traffic direction as defined by the basic peace officer course curriculum established by the Commission on Law Enforcement Standards and Education.

(b) A school crossing guard trained under this section:

(1) is not a peace officer; and

(2) may not carry a weapon while directing traffic in a school crossing zone.

*(Added by L.1999, chap. 724(2), eff. 6/18/99.)*

## SUBTITLE D. MOTOR VEHICLE SAFETY RESPONSIBILITY

## CHAPTER 601. TEXAS MOTOR VEHICLE SAFETY RESPONSIBILITY ACT

### SUBCHAPTER A. GENERAL PROVISIONS



### SUBCHAPTER B. ADMINISTRATION BY DEPARTMENT



### SUBCHAPTER C. FINANCIAL RESPONSIBILITY; REQUIREMENTS

601.054. Owner may provide evidence of financial responsibility for others.
601.055. Substitution of evidence of financial responsibility.
601.056. Cancellation, return, or waiver of evidence of financial responsibility.
601.057. Evidence that does not fulfill requirements; suspension.
601.058 to
601.070. *(Reserved.)*

## SUBCHAPTER D. ESTABLISHMENT OF FINANCIAL RESPONSIBILITY THROUGH MOTOR VEHICLE LIABILITY INSURANCE

601.071. Motor vehicle liability insurance; requirements.
601.072. Minimum coverage amounts.
601.073. Required policy terms.
601.074. Optional terms.
601.075. Prohibited terms.
601.076. Required terms: owner's policy.
601.077. Required terms: operator's policy.
601.078. Additional coverage.
601.079. Multiple policies.
601.080. Insurance binder.
601.081. Standard proof of motor vehicle liability insurance form.
601.082. Motor vehicle liability insurance; certification.
601.083. Certificate of motor vehicle liability insurance.
601.084. Nonresident certificate.
601.085. Termination of certified policy.
601.086. Response of insurance company if policy not in effect.
601.087. *(Repealed.)*
601.088. Effect on certain other policies.
601.089 to
601.120. *(Reserved.)*

## SUBCHAPTER E. ALTERNATIVE METHODS OF ESTABLISHING FINANCIAL RESPONSIBILITY

601.121. Surety bond.
601.122. Deposit of cash or securities with comptroller.
601.123. Deposit of cash or cashier's check with county judge.
601.124. Self-insurance.
601.125 to
601.150. *(Reserved.)*

## SUBCHAPTER F. SECURITY FOLLOWING ACCIDENT

601.151. Applicability of subchapter.
601.152. Suspension of driver's license and vehicle registration or privilege.
601.153. Deposit of security; evidence of financial responsibility.
601.154. Department determination of probability of liability.
601.155. Notice of determination.
601.156. Setting of hearing.
601.157. Hearing procedures.
601.158. Appeal.
601.159. Procedures for suspension of driver's license and vehicle registration or privilege.
601.160. Suspension stayed pending hearing or appeal.
601.161. Notice of suspension.
601.162. Duration of suspension.
601.163. Form of security.
601.164. Reduction in security.
601.165. Custody of cash security.
601.166. Payment of cash security.
601.167. Return of cash security.
601.168. Insurance policy or bond; limits.

601.169. Reasonable probability not admissible in civil suit.
601.170. Department acting on erroneous information.
601.171 to
601.190. *(Reserved.)*

## SUBCHAPTER G. FAILURE TO MAINTAIN MOTOR VEHICLE LIABILITY INSURANCE OR OTHERWISE ESTABLISH FINANCIAL RESPONSIBILITY; CRIMINAL PENALTIES

601.191. Operation of motor vehicle in violation of motor vehicle liability insurance requirement; offense.
601.192. *(Repealed.)*
601.193. Defense: financial responsibility in effect at time of alleged offense.
601.194. Defense: possession of motor vehicle for maintenance or repair.
601.195. Operation of motor vehicle in violation of requirement to establish financial responsibility; offense.
601.196. *(Repealed.)*
601.197 to
601.230. *(Reserved.)*

## SUBCHAPTER H. FAILURE TO MAINTAIN EVIDENCE OF FINANCIAL RESPONSIBILITY; SUSPENSION OF DRIVER'S LICENSE AND MOTOR VEHICLE REGISTRATION

601.231. Suspension of driver's license and vehicle registration.
601.232. Notice of suspension.
601.233. Notice of potential suspension.
601.234. Issuance or continuation of vehicle registration.
601.235 to
601.260. *(Reserved.)*

## SUBCHAPTER I. FAILURE TO MAINTAIN EVIDENCE OF FINANCIAL RESPONSIBILITY; IMPOUNDMENT OF MOTOR VEHICLE

601.261. Impoundment of motor vehicle.
601.262. Duration of impoundment.
601.263. Cost for impoundment.
601.264. Penalties cumulative.
601.265. Transfer of title of impounded motor vehicle.
601.266. Release on involuntary transfer of title of impounded motor vehicle.
601.267. Release of impounded motor vehicle by sheriff.
601.268 to
601.290. *(Reserved.)*

## SUBCHAPTER J. IMPOUNDMENT OF MOTOR VEHICLE NOT REGISTERED IN THIS STATE

601.291. Applicability of subchapter.
601.292. Duty to provide evidence of financial responsibility to investigating officer.
601.293. Failure to provide evidence of financial responsibility; magistrate's inquiry and order.
601.294. Impoundment of motor vehicle.
601.295. Duration of impoundment; release.
601.296. Certificate of release.
601.297. Liability for cost of impoundment.
601.298 to
601.330. *(Reserved.)*

## SUBCHAPTER K. EVIDENCE OF FINANCIAL RESPONSIBILITY FOLLOWING JUDGMENT, CONVICTION, PLEA, OR FORFEITURE OR FOLLOWING SUSPENSION OR REVOCATION



## SUBCHAPTER L. EFFECT OF SUSPENSION



## SUBCHAPTER M. APPEAL OF DEPARTMENT ACTION



## SUBCHAPTER A. GENERAL PROVISIONS

### §601.001. Short title.

This chapter may be cited as the Texas Motor Vehicle Safety Responsibility Act. *(Added by L.1995, chap. 165(1), eff. 9/1/95.)*

### §601.002. Definitions.

In this chapter:

(1) "Department" means the Department of Public Safety.

(2) "Driver's license" has the meaning assigned by Section 521.001.

(3) "Financial responsibility" means the ability to respond in damages for liability for an accident that:

(A) occurs after the effective date of the document evidencing the establishment of the financial responsibility; and

(B) arises out of the ownership, maintenance, or use of a motor vehicle.

(4) "Highway" means the entire width between property lines of a road, street, or way in this state that is not privately owned or controlled and:

(A) some part of which is open to the public for vehicular traffic; and

(B) over which the state has legislative jurisdiction under its police power.

(5) "Motor vehicle" means a self-propelled vehicle designed for use on a highway, a trailer or semitrailer designed for use with a self-propelled vehicle, or a vehicle propelled by electric power from overhead wires and not operated on rails. The term does not include:

(A) a traction engine;

(B) a road roller or grader;

(C) a tractor crane;

(D) a power shovel;

(E) a well driller; or

(F) an implement of husbandry.

(6) "Nonresident" means a person who is not a resident of this state.

(7) "Nonresident's operating privilege" means the privilege conferred on a nonresident by the laws of this state relating to the operation of a motor vehicle in this state by the nonresident or the use in this state of a motor vehicle owned by the nonresident.

(8) "Operator" means the person in actual physical control of a motor vehicle.

(9) "Owner" means:

(A) the person who holds legal title to a motor vehicle;

(B) the purchaser or lessee of a motor vehicle subject to an agreement for the conditional sale or lease of the vehicle, if the person has:

(i) the right to purchase the vehicle on performing conditions stated in the agreement; and

(ii) an immediate right to possess the vehicle; or

(C) a mortgagor of a motor vehicle who is entitled to possession of the vehicle.

(10) "Person" means an individual, firm, partnership, association, or corporation.

(11) "State" means:

(A) a state, territory, or possession of the United States; or

(B) the District of Columbia.

(12) "Vehicle registration" means:

(A) a registration certificate, registration receipt, or number plate issued under Chapter 502; or

(B) a dealer's license plate or temporary cardboard tag issued under Chapter 503.

*(Added by L.1995, chap. 165(1), eff. 9/1/95.)*

### §601.003. Judgment; satisfied judgment.

(a) For purposes of this chapter, judgment refers only to a final judgment that is no longer appealable or has been finally affirmed on appeal and that was rendered by a court of any state, a province of Canada, or the United States on a cause of action:

(1) for damages for bodily injury, death, or damage to or destruction of property arising out of the ownership, maintenance, or use of a motor vehicle; or

(2) on an agreement of settlement for damages for bodily injury, death, or damage to or destruction of property arising out of the ownership, maintenance, or use of a motor vehicle.

(b) For purposes of this chapter, a judgment is considered to be satisfied as to the appropriate part of the judgment set out by this subsection if:

(1) the total amount credited on one or more judgments for bodily injury to or death of one person resulting from one accident equals or exceeds the amount required under Section 601.072(a)(1) to establish financial responsibility;

(2) the total amount credited on one or more judgments for bodily injury to or death of two or more persons resulting from one accident equals or exceeds the amount required under Section 601.072(a)(2) to establish financial responsibility; or

(3) the total amount credited on one or more judgments for damage to or destruction of property of another resulting from one accident equals or exceeds the amount required under Section 601.072(a)(3) to establish financial responsibility.

(c) In determining whether a judgment is satisfied under Subsection (b), a payment made in settlement of a claim for damages for bodily injury, death, or damage to or destruction of property is considered to be an amount credited on a judgment.

(d) For purposes of this section:

(1) damages for bodily injury or death include damages for care and loss of services; and

(2) damages for damage to or destruction of property include damages for loss of use.

*(Added by L.1995, chap. 165(1), eff. 9/1/95.)*

### §601.004. Accident report.

(a) The operator of a motor vehicle that is involved in an accident in this state shall report the accident to the department not later than the 10th day after the date of the accident if:

(1) the accident is not investigated by a law enforcement officer; and

(2) at least one person, including the operator, sustained:

(A) bodily injury or death; or

(B) property damage to an apparent extent of at least $500.

(b) If the operator is physically incapable of making the report, the owner of the motor vehicle shall make the report not later than the 10th day after the date the owner learns of the accident.

(c) The report must be made in writing in the form prescribed by the department and must contain information as necessary to enable the department to determine if the requirements for the deposit of security under Subchapter F do not apply because of the existence of insurance or an exception specified in this chapter. The operator or owner shall provide additional information as required by the department.

(d) A written report of an accident made to the department under Section 550.061 or 550.062 complies with this section if that report contains the information required by this section.

(e) The department may rely on the accuracy of information contained in the report unless the department has reason to believe that the information is erroneous.

(f) An accident report that is released for insurance purposes, other than investigation of a specific accident, may show only an accident for which the insured was issued a citation for a violation of Subtitle C.

(g) The department shall suspend the driver's license or nonresident's operating privilege of a person who fails to make a report as required by this section if another person sustained bodily injury, death, or property damage to the extent described by Subsection (a)(2)(B). The suspension continues until a date set by the department that is not earlier than the date the report is filed and not later than the 30th day after the date the report is filed.

(h) A person commits an offense if the person fails to report an accident as required by this section. An offense under this subsection is a misdemeanor punishable by a fine not to exceed $25.

(i) A person commits an offense if the person provides information under this section that the person knows or has reason to believe is false. An offense under this subsection is a misdemeanor punishable by:

(1) a fine not to exceed $1,000;

(2) confinement in county jail for a term not to exceed one year; or

(3) both the fine and the confinement.

*(Added by L.1995, chap. 165(1), eff. 9/1/95.)*

### §601.005. Evidence in civil suit.

On the filing of a report under Section 601.004, a person at a trial for damages may not refer to or offer as evidence of the negligence or due care of a party:

(1) an action taken by the department under this chapter;

(2) the findings on which that action is based; or

(3) the security or evidence of financial responsibility filed under this chapter.

*(Added by L.1995, chap. 165(1), eff. 9/1/95.)*

### §601.006. Applicability to certain owners and operators.

If an owner or operator of a motor vehicle involved in an accident in this state does not have a driver's license or vehicle registration or is a nonresident, the person may not be issued a driver's license or registration until the person has complied with this chapter to the same extent that would be necessary if, at the time of the accident, the person had a driver's license or registration. *(Added by L.1995, chap. 165(1), eff. 9/1/95.)*

### §601.007. Applicability of chapter to government vehicles.

(a) This chapter does not apply to a government vehicle.

(b) The provisions of this chapter, other than Section 601.004, do not apply to an officer, agent, or employee of the United States, this state, or a political subdivision of this state while operating a government vehicle in the course of that person's employment.

(c) The provisions of this chapter, other than Sections 601.004 and 601.054, do not apply to a motor vehicle that is subject to Chapter 643.

(d) In this section, "government vehicle" means a motor vehicle owned by the United States, this state, or a political subdivision of this state.

*(Added by L.1995, chap. 165(1); chgd. by L.1997, chap. 165(30.126(a)), eff. 9/1/97.)*

### §601.008. Violation of chapter; offense.

(a) A person commits an offense if the person violates a provision of this chapter for which a penalty is not otherwise provided.

(b) An offense under this section is a misdemeanor punishable by:

(1) a fine not to exceed $500;

(2) confinement in county jail for a term not to exceed 90 days; or

(3) both the fine and the confinement.

*(Added by L.1995, chap. 165(1), eff. 9/1/95.)*

### §601.009. Report from other state or Canada.

(a) On receipt of a certification by the department that the operating privilege of a resident of this state has been suspended or revoked in another state or a province of Canada under a financial responsibility law, the department shall contact the official who issued the certification to request information relating to the specific nature of the resident's failure to comply.

(b) Except as provided by Subsection (c), the department shall suspend the resident's driver's license and vehicle registrations if the evidence shows that the resident's operating privilege was suspended in the other state or the province for violation of a financial responsibility law under circumstances that would require the department to suspend a nonresident's operating privilege had the accident occurred in this state.

(c) The department may not suspend the resident's driver's license and registration if the alleged failure to comply is based on the failure of the resident's insurance company or surety company to:

(1) obtain authorization to write motor vehicle liability insurance in the other state or the province; or

(2) execute a power of attorney directing the appropriate official in the other state or the province to accept on the company's behalf service of notice or process in an action under the policy arising out of an accident.

(d) Suspension of a driver's license and vehicle registrations under this section continues until the resident furnishes evidence of compliance with the financial responsibility law of the other state or the province.

(e) In this section, "financial responsibility law" means a law authorizing suspension or revocation of an operating privilege for failure to:

(1) deposit security for the payment of a judgment;

(2) satisfy a judgment; or

(3) file evidence of financial responsibility.

*(Added by L.1995, chap. 165(1), eff. 9/1/95.)*

### §§601.010 to 601.020. *(Reserved.)*

## SUBCHAPTER B. ADMINISTRATION BY DEPARTMENT

### §601.021. Department powers and duties; rules.

The department shall:

(1) administer and enforce this chapter; and

(2) provide for hearings on the request of a person aggrieved by an act of the department under this chapter.

*(Added by L.1995, chap. 165(1), eff. 9/1/95.)*

### §601.022. Department to provide operating record.

(a) The department, on request and receipt of the required fee, shall provide any person a certified abstract of the record of conviction of a person subject to this chapter for violation of a law relating to the operation of a motor vehicle or the record of any injury or damage caused by the person's operation of a motor vehicle if the requestor is eligible to receive the information under Chapter 730.

(b) If a record described by Subsection (a) does not exist, the department shall certify that fact.

(c) A request for a certified abstract under this section must be accompanied by a $20 fee for each abstract.

*(Added by L.1995, chap. 165(1); chgd. by L.1997, chap. 1187(14), eff. 9/1/97.)*

**§601.023. Payment of statutory fees.**

The department may pay:

(1) a statutory fee required by the Texas Department of Transportation for a certified abstract or in connection with suspension of a vehicle registration; or

(2) a statutory fee payable to the comptroller for issuance of a certificate of deposit required by Section 601.122.

*(Added by L.1995, chap. 165(1); chgd. by L.1997, chap. 1423(18.05), eff. 9/1/97.)*

**§§601.024 to 601.050.** *(Reserved.)*

## SUBCHAPTER C. FINANCIAL RESPONSIBILITY; REQUIREMENTS

**§601.051. Requirement of financial responsibility.**

A person may not operate a motor vehicle in this state unless financial responsibility is established for that vehicle through:

(1) a motor vehicle liability insurance policy that complies with Subchapter D;

(2) a surety bond filed under Section 601.121;

(3) a deposit under Section 601.122;

(4) a deposit under Section 601.123; or

(5) self-insurance under Section 601.124.

*(Added by L.1995, chap. 165(1), eff. 9/1/95.)*

**§601.052. Exceptions to financial responsibility requirement.**

(a) Section 601.051 does not apply to:

(1) the operation of a motor vehicle that:

(A) is a former military vehicle or is at least 25 years old;

(B) is used only for exhibitions, club activities, parades, and other functions of public interest and not for regular transportation; and

(C) for which the owner files with the department an affidavit, signed by the owner, stating that the vehicle is a collector's item and used only as described by Paragraph (B);

(2) the operation of a golf cart not required to be registered under Section 502.284; or

(3) a volunteer fire department for the operation of a motor vehicle the title of which is held in the name of a volunteer fire department.

(b) Subsection (a)(3) does not exempt from the requirement of Section 601.051 a person who is operating a vehicle described by that subsection.

(c) In this section:

(1) "Former military vehicle" has the meaning assigned by Section 502.275(*o*).

(2) "Volunteer fire department" means a company, department, or association that is:

(A) organized in an unincorporated area to answer fire alarms and extinguish fires or to answer fire alarms, extinguish fires, and provide emergency medical services; and

(B) composed of members who:

(i) do not receive compensation; or

(ii) receive only nominal compensation.

*(Added by L.1995, chap. 165(1); chgd. by L.1997, chaps. 165(30.127(a)), 896(3), eff. 9/1/97.)*

**§601.053. Evidence of financial responsibility.**

(a) As a condition of operating in this state a motor vehicle to which Section 601.051 applies, the operator of the vehicle on request shall provide to a peace officer, as defined by Article 2.12, Code of Criminal Procedure, or a person involved in an accident with the operator evidence of financial responsibility by exhibiting:

(1) a motor vehicle liability insurance policy covering the vehicle that satisfies Subchapter D or a photocopy of the policy;

(2) a standard proof of motor vehicle liability insurance form prescribed by the Texas Department of Insurance under Section 601.081 and issued by a liability insurer for the motor vehicle;

(3) an insurance binder that confirms the operator is in compliance with this chapter;

(4) a surety bond certificate issued under Section 601.121;

(5) a certificate of a deposit with the comptroller covering the vehicle issued under Section 601.122;

(6) a copy of a certificate of a deposit with the appropriate county judge covering the vehicle issued under Section 601.123; or

(7) a certificate of self-insurance covering the vehicle issued under Section 601.124 or a photocopy of the certificate.

(b) An operator who does not exhibit evidence of financial responsibility under Subsection (a) is presumed to have operated the vehicle in violation of Section 601.051.
*(Added by L.1995, chap. 165(1); chgd. by L.1997, chap. 1423(18.06), eff. 9/1/97.)*

**§601.054. Owner may provide evidence of financial responsibility for others.**

(a) The department shall accept evidence of financial responsibility from an owner for another person required to establish evidence of financial responsibility if the other person is:

(1) an operator employed by the owner; or

(2) a member of the owner's immediate family or household.

(b) The evidence of financial responsibility applies to a person who becomes subject to Subsection (a)(1) or (2) after the effective date of that evidence.

(c) Evidence of financial responsibility accepted by the department under Subsection (a) is a substitute for evidence by the other person and permits the other person to operate a motor vehicle for which the owner has provided evidence of financial responsibility.

(d) The department shall designate the restrictions imposed by this section on the face of the other person's driver's license.
*(Added by L.1995, chap. 165(1), eff. 9/1/95.)*



**§601.055. Substitution of evidence of financial responsibility.**

(a) If a person who has filed evidence of financial responsibility substitutes other evidence of financial responsibility that complies with this chapter, and the department accepts the other evidence, the department shall:

(1) consent to the cancellation of a bond or certificate of insurance filed as evidence of financial responsibility; or

(2) direct the comptroller to return money or securities deposited with the comptroller as evidence of financial responsibility to the person entitled to the return of the money or securities.

(b) The comptroller shall return money or securities deposited with the comptroller in accordance with the direction of the department under Subsection (a)(2).
*(Added by L.1995, chap. 165(1); chgd. by L.1997, chap. 1423(18.07), eff. 9/1/97.)*

**§601.056. Cancellation, return, or waiver of evidence of financial responsibility.**

(a) As provided by this section, the department, on request, shall:

(1) consent to the cancellation of a bond or certificate of insurance filed as evidence of financial responsibility;

(2) direct the comptroller to return money or securities deposited with the comptroller as evidence of financial responsibility to the person entitled to the return of the money or securities; or

(3) waive the requirement of filing evidence of financial responsibility.

(b) Evidence of financial responsibility may be canceled, returned, or waived under Subsection (a) if:

(1) the department, during the two years preceding the request, has not received a record of a conviction or a forfeiture of bail that would require or permit the suspension or revocation of the driver's license, vehicle registration, or nonresident's operating privilege of the person by or for whom the evidence was provided;

(2) the person for whom the evidence of financial responsibility was provided dies or has a permanent incapacity to operate a motor vehicle; or

(3) the person for whom the evidence of financial responsibility was provided surrenders the person's license and vehicle registration to the department.

(c) A cancellation, return, or waiver under Subsection (b)(1) may be made only after the second anniversary of the date the evidence of financial responsibility was required.

(d) The comptroller shall return the money or securities as directed by the department under Subsection (a)(2).

(e) The department may not act under Subsection (a)(1) or (2) if:

(1) an action for damages on a liability covered by the evidence of financial responsibility is pending;

(2) a judgment for damages on a liability covered by the evidence of financial responsibility is not satisfied; or

(3) the person for whom the bond has been filed or for whom money or securities have been deposited has, within the two years preceding the request for cancellation or return of the evidence of financial responsibility, been involved as an operator or owner in a motor vehicle accident resulting in bodily injury to, or property damage to the property of, another person.

(f) In the absence of evidence to the contrary in the records of the department, the department shall accept as sufficient an affidavit of the person requesting action under Subsection (a) stating that:

(1) the facts described by Subsection (e) do not exist; or

(2) the person has been released from the liability or has been finally adjudicated as not liable for bodily injury or property damage described by Subsection (e)(3).

(g) A person whose evidence of financial responsibility has been canceled or returned under Subsection (b)(3) may not be issued a new driver's license or vehicle registration unless the person establishes financial responsibility for the remainder of the two-year period beginning on the date the evidence of financial responsibility was required.
*(Added by L.1995, chap. 165(1); chgd. by L.1997, chap. 1423(18.08), eff. 9/1/97.)*

### §601.057. Evidence that does not fulfill requirements; suspension.

If evidence filed with the department does not continue to fulfill the purpose for which it was required, the department shall suspend the driver's license and all vehicle registrations or nonresident's operating privilege of the person who filed the evidence pending the filing of other evidence of financial responsibility. *(Added by L.1995, chap. 165(1), eff. 9/1/95.)*

### §§601.058 to 601.070. *(Reserved.)*

## SUBCHAPTER D. ESTABLISHMENT OF FINANCIAL RESPONSIBILITY THROUGH MOTOR VEHICLE LIABILITY INSURANCE

### §601.071. Motor vehicle liability insurance; requirements.

For purposes of this chapter, a motor vehicle liability insurance policy must be an owner's or operator's policy that:

(1) except as provided by Section 601.083, is issued by an insurance company authorized to write motor vehicle liability insurance in this state;

(2) is written to or for the benefit of the person named in the policy as the insured; and

(3) meets the requirements of this subchapter.
*(Added by L.1995, chap. 165(1), eff. 9/1/95.)*

### §601.072. Minimum coverage amounts.

(a) The minimum amounts of motor vehicle liability insurance coverage required to establish financial responsibility under this chapter are:

(1) $20,000 for bodily injury to or death of one person in one accident;

(2) $40,000 for bodily injury to or death of two or more persons in one accident, subject to the amount provided by Subdivision (1) for bodily injury to or death of one of the persons; and

(3) $15,000 for damage to or destruction of property of others in one accident.

(b) The coverage required under Subsection (a) may exclude, with respect to one accident:

(1) the first $250 of liability for bodily injury to or death of one person;

(2) the first $500 of liability for bodily injury to or death of two or more persons, subject to the amount provided by Subdivision (1) for bodily injury to or death of one of the persons; and

(3) the first $250 of liability for property damage to or destruction of property of others.
*(Added by L.1995, chap. 165(1), eff. 9/1/95.)*

### §601.073. Required policy terms.

(a) A motor vehicle liability insurance policy must state:

(1) the name and address of the named insured;

(2) the coverage provided under the policy;

(3) the premium charged for the policy;

(4) the policy period; and

(5) the limits of liability.

(b) The policy must contain an agreement or endorsement that the insurance coverage provided under the policy is:

(1) provided in accordance with the coverage required by this chapter for bodily injury, death, and property damage; and

(2) subject to this chapter.

(c) The liability of the insurance company for the insurance required by this chapter becomes absolute at the time bodily injury, death, or damage covered by the policy occurs. The policy may not be canceled as to this liability by an agreement between the insurance company and the insured that is entered into after the occurrence of the injury or damage. A statement made by or on behalf of the insured or a violation of the policy does not void the policy.

(d) The policy may not require the insured to satisfy a judgment for bodily injury, death, or property damage as a condition precedent under the policy to the right or duty of the insurance company to make payment for the injury, death, or damage.

(e) The insurance company may settle a claim covered by the policy. If the settlement is made in good faith, the amount of the settlement is deductible from the amounts specified in Section 601.072.

(f) The policy, any written application for the policy, and any rider or endorsement that does not conflict with this chapter constitute the entire contract between the parties.

(g) Subsections (c)-(f) apply to the policy without regard to whether those provisions are stated in the policy.

*(Added by L.1995, chap. 165(1), eff. 9/1/95.)*



## §601.074. Optional terms.

(a) A motor vehicle liability insurance policy may provide that the insured shall reimburse the insurance company for a payment that, in the absence of this chapter, the insurance company would not have been obligated to make under the terms of the policy.

(b) A policy may allow prorating of the insurance provided under the policy with other collectible insurance.

*(Added by L.1995, chap. 165(1), eff. 9/1/95.)*

## §601.075. Prohibited terms.

A motor vehicle liability insurance policy may not insure against liability:

(1) for which the insured or the insured's insurer may be held liable under a workers' compensation law;

(2) for bodily injury to or death of an employee of the insured while engaged in the employment, other than domestic, of the insured, or in domestic employment if benefits for the injury are payable or required to be provided under a workers' compensation law; or

(3) for injury to or destruction of property owned by, rented to, in the care of, or transported by the insured.

*(Added by L.1995, chap. 165(1), eff. 9/1/95.)*

## §601.076. Required terms: owner's policy.

An owner's motor vehicle liability insurance policy must:

(1) cover each motor vehicle for which coverage is to be granted under the policy; and

(2) pay, on behalf of the named insured or another person who, as insured, uses a covered motor vehicle with the express or implied permission of the named insured, amounts the insured becomes obligated to pay as damages arising out of the ownership, maintenance, or use of the motor vehicle in the United States or Canada, subject to the amounts, excluding interest and costs, and exclusions of Section 601.072.

*(Added by L.1995, chap. 165(1), eff. 9/1/95.)*

## §601.077. Required terms: operator's policy.

An operator's motor vehicle liability insurance policy must pay, on behalf of the named insured, amounts the insured becomes obligated to pay as damages arising out of the use by the insured of a motor vehicle the insured does not own, subject to the same territorial limits, payment limits, and exclusions as for an owner's policy under Section 601.076. *(Added by L.1995, chap. 165(1), eff. 9/1/95.)*

## §601.078. Additional coverage.

(a) An insurance policy that provides the coverage required for a motor vehicle liability insurance policy may also provide lawful coverage in excess of or in addition to the required coverage.

(b) The excess or additional coverage is not subject to this chapter.

(c) In the case of a policy that provides excess or additional coverage, the term "motor vehicle liability insurance policy" applies only to that part of the coverage that is required under this subchapter.

*(Added by L.1995, chap. 165(1), eff. 9/1/95.)*

**§601.079. Multiple policies.**
The requirements for a motor vehicle liability insurance policy may be satisfied by a combination of policies of one or more insurance companies if the policies in combination meet the requirements. *(Added by L.1995, chap. 165(1), eff. 9/1/95.)*

**§601.080. Insurance binder.**
A binder issued pending the issuance of a motor vehicle liability insurance policy satisfies the requirements for such a policy. *(Added by L.1995, chap. 165(1), eff. 9/1/95.)*

**§601.081. Standard proof of motor vehicle liability insurance form.**
A standard proof of motor vehicle liability insurance form prescribed by the Texas Department of Insurance must include:

(1) the name of the insurer;
(2) the insurance policy number;
(3) the policy period;
(4) the name and address of each insured;
(5) the policy limits or a statement that the coverage of the policy complies with the minimum amounts of motor vehicle liability insurance required by this chapter; and
(6) the make and model of each covered vehicle.

*(Added by L.1995, chap. 165(1), eff. 9/1/95.)*

 Zt

**§601.082. Motor vehicle liability insurance; certification.**
If evidence of financial responsibility is required to be filed with the department under this chapter, a motor vehicle liability insurance policy that is to be used as evidence must be certified under Section 601.083 or 601.084. *(Added by L.1995, chap. 165(1), eff. 9/1/95.)*

**§601.083. Certificate of motor vehicle liability insurance.**
(a) A person may provide evidence of financial responsibility by filing with the department the certificate of an insurance company authorized to write motor vehicle liability insurance in this state certifying that a motor vehicle liability insurance policy for the benefit of the person required to provide evidence of financial responsibility is in effect.

(b) The certificate must state the effective date of the policy, which must be the same date as the effective date of the certificate.

(c) The certificate must cover each motor vehicle owned by the person required to provide the evidence of financial responsibility, unless the policy is issued to a person who does not own a motor vehicle.

(d) A motor vehicle may not be registered in the name of a person required to provide evidence of financial responsibility unless the vehicle is covered by a certificate.

(e) If a person files a certificate of insurance to establish financial responsibility under Section 601.153, the certificate must state that the requirements of Section 601.153(b) are satisfied.
*(Added by L.1995, chap. 165(1); chgd. by L.1997, chap. 178(1), eff. 9/1/97.)*

**§601.084. Nonresident certificate.**
(a) Subject to Subsection (c), a nonresident owner of a motor vehicle that is not registered in this state may provide evidence of financial responsibility by filing with the department the certificate of an insurance company authorized to transact business in the state in which the vehicle is registered certifying that a motor vehicle liability insurance policy for the benefit of the person required to provide evidence of financial responsibility is in effect.

(b) Subject to Subsection (c), a nonresident who does not own a motor vehicle may provide evidence of financial responsibility by filing with the department the certificate of an insurance company authorized to transact business in the state in which the nonresident resides.

(c) The department shall accept the certificate of an insurer not authorized to transact business in this state if the certificate otherwise complies with this chapter and the insurance company:

(1) executes a power of attorney authorizing the department to accept on its behalf service of notice or process in an action arising out of a motor vehicle accident in this state; and

(2) agrees in writing that its policies will be treated as conforming to the laws of this state relating to the terms of a motor vehicle liability insurance policy.

(d) The department may not accept a certificate of an insurance company not authorized to transact business in this state during the period that the company is in default in any undertaking or agreement under this section.
*(Added by L.1995, chap. 165(1), eff. 9/1/95.)*

### §601.085. Termination of certified policy.

(a) If an insurer has certified a policy under Section 601.083 or 601.084, the policy may not be terminated before the sixth day after the date a notice of the termination is received by the department except as provided by Subsection (b).

(b) A policy that is obtained and certified terminates a previously certified policy on the effective date of the certification of a subsequent policy.

*(Added by L.1995, chap. 165(1), eff. 9/1/95.)*

### §601.086. Response of insurance company if policy not in effect.

An insurance company that is notified by the department of an accident in connection with which an owner or operator has reported a motor vehicle liability insurance policy with the company shall advise the department if a policy is not in effect as reported. *(Added by L.1995, chap. 165(1), eff. 9/1/95.)*



### §601.087. *(Repealed by L.1999, chap. 659(4), eff. 9/1/99.)*

### §601.088. Effect on certain other policies.

(a) This chapter does not apply to or affect a policy of motor vehicle liability insurance required by another law of this state. If that policy contains an agreement or is endorsed to conform to the requirements of this chapter, the policy may be certified as evidence of financial responsibility under this chapter.

(b) This chapter does not apply to or affect a policy that insures only the named insured against liability resulting from the maintenance or use of a motor vehicle that is not owned by the insured by persons who are:

(1) employed by the insured; or

(2) acting on the insured's behalf.

*(Added by L.1995, chap. 165(1), eff. 9/1/95.)*

### §§601.089 to 601.120. *(Reserved.)*

## SUBCHAPTER E. ALTERNATIVE METHODS OF ESTABLISHING FINANCIAL RESPONSIBILITY

### §601.121. Surety bond.

(a) A person may establish financial responsibility by filing with the department a bond:

(1) with at least two individual sureties, each of whom owns real property in this state that is not exempt from execution under the constitution or laws of this state;

(2) conditioned for payment in the amounts and under the same circumstances as required under a motor vehicle liability insurance policy;

(3) that is not cancelable before the sixth day after the date the department receives written notice of the cancellation;

(4) accompanied by the fee required by Subsection (e); and

(5) approved by the department.

(b) The real property required by Subsection (a)(1) must be described in the bond approved by a judge of a court of record. The assessor-collector of the county in which the property is located must certify the property as free of any tax lien. The sureties in combination must have equity in the property in an amount equal to at least twice the amount of the bond.

(c) The bond is a lien in favor of the state on the real property described in the bond. The lien exists in favor of a person who holds a final judgment against the person who filed the bond.

(d) On filing of a bond, the department shall issue to the person who filed the bond a certificate of compliance with this section.

(e) The department shall file notice of the bond in the office of the county clerk of the county in which the real property is located. The notice must include a description of the property described in the bond. The county clerk or the county clerk's deputy, on receipt of the notice, shall acknowledge the notice and record it in the lien records. The recording of the notice is notice in accordance with statutes governing the recordation of a lien on real property.

(f) If a judgment rendered against the person who files a bond under this section is not satisfied before the 61st day after the date the judgment becomes final, the judgment creditor, for the judgment creditor's own use and benefit and at the judgment creditor's expense, may bring an action in the name of the state against the sureties on the bond, including an action to foreclose a lien on the real property of a surety. The foreclosure action must be brought in the same manner as, and is subject to the law applicable to, an action to foreclose a mortgage on real property.

(g) Cancellation of a bond filed under this section does not prevent recovery for a right or cause of action arising before the date of the cancellation.
*(Added by L.1995, chap. 165(1), eff. 9/1/95.)*

### §601.122. Deposit of cash or securities with comptroller.

(a) A person may establish financial responsibility by depositing $55,000 with the comptroller in:

(1) cash; or

(2) securities that:

(A) are of the type that may legally be purchased by savings banks or trust funds; and

(B) have a market value equal to the required amount.

(b) On receipt of the deposit, the comptroller shall issue to the person making the deposit a certificate stating that a deposit complying with this section has been made.

(c) The comptroller may not accept the deposit and the department may not accept the certificate unless the deposit or certificate is accompanied by evidence that an unsatisfied judgment of any character against the person making the deposit does not exist in the county in which the person making the deposit resides.

(d) The comptroller shall hold a deposit made under this section to satisfy, in accordance with this chapter, an execution on a judgment issued against the person making the deposit for damages that:

(1) result from the ownership, maintenance, use, or operation of a motor vehicle after the date the deposit was made; and

(2) are for:

(A) bodily injury to or death of any person, including damages for care and loss of services; or

(B) damage to or destruction of property, including the loss of use of the property.

(e) Money or securities deposited under this section are not subject to attachment or execution unless the attachment or execution arises out of a suit for damages described by Subsection (d).
*(Added by L.1995, chap. 165(1); chgd. by L.1997, chap. 1423(18.09), eff. 9/1/97.)*

### §601.123. Deposit of cash or cashier's check with county judge.

(a) A person may establish financial responsibility by making a deposit with the county judge of the county in which the motor vehicle is registered.

(b) The deposit must be made in cash or a cashier's check in the amount of at least $55,000.

(c) On receipt of the deposit, the county judge shall issue to the person making the deposit a certificate stating that a deposit complying with this section has been made. The certificate must be acknowledged by the sheriff of that county and filed with the department.
*(Added by L.1995, chap. 165(1), eff. 9/1/95.)*

### §601.124. Self-insurance.

(a) A person in whose name more than 25 motor vehicles are registered may qualify as a self-insurer by obtaining a certificate of self-insurance issued by the department as provided by this section.

(b) The department may issue a certificate of self-insurance to a person if:

(1) the person applies for the certificate; and

(2) the department is satisfied that the person has and will continue to have the ability to pay judgments obtained against the person.

(c) The self-insurer must supplement the certificate with an agreement that, for accidents occurring while the certificate is in force, the self-insurer will pay the same judgments in the same amounts as an insurer would be obligated to pay under an owner's motor vehicle liability insurance policy issued to the self-insurer if such policy were issued.

(d) The department for cause may cancel a certificate of self-insurance after a hearing. The self-insurer must receive at least five days' notice of the hearing. Cause includes failure to pay a judgment before the 31st day after the date the judgment becomes final.
*(Added by L.1995, chap. 165(1), eff. 9/1/95.)*

### §§601.125 to 601.150. *(Reserved.)*

## SUBCHAPTER F. SECURITY FOLLOWING ACCIDENT

### §601.151. Applicability of subchapter.

(a) This subchapter applies only to a motor vehicle accident in this state that results in bodily injury or death or in damage to the property of one person of at least $1,000.

(b) This subchapter does not apply to:

(1) an owner or operator who has in effect at the time of the accident a motor vehicle liability insurance policy that covers the motor vehicle involved in the accident;

(2) an operator who is not the owner of the motor vehicle, if a motor vehicle liability insurance policy or bond for the operation of a motor vehicle the person does not own is in effect at the time of the accident;

(3) an owner or operator whose liability for damages resulting from the accident, in the judgment of the department, is covered by another liability insurance policy or bond;

(4) an owner or operator, if there was not bodily injury to or damage of the property of a person other than the owner or operator;

(5) the owner or operator of a motor vehicle that at the time of the accident was legally parked or legally stopped at a traffic signal;

(6) the owner of a motor vehicle that at the time of the accident was being operated without the owner's express or implied permission or was parked by a person who had been operating the vehicle without that permission; or

(7) a person qualifying as a self-insurer under Section 601.124 or a person operating a motor vehicle for a self-insurer.

*(Added by L.1995, chap. 165(1), eff. 9/1/95.)*



### §601.152. Suspension of driver's license and vehicle registration or privilege.

(a) Subject to Section 601.153, the department shall suspend the driver's license and vehicle registrations of the owner and operator of a motor vehicle if:

(1) the vehicle is involved in any manner in an accident; and

(2) the department finds that there is a reasonable probability that a judgment will be rendered against the person as a result of the accident.

(b) If the owner or operator is a nonresident, the department shall suspend the person's nonresident operating privilege and the privilege of use of any motor vehicle owned by the nonresident.

*(Added by L.1995, chap. 165(1), eff. 9/1/95.)*

### §601.153. Deposit of security; evidence of financial responsibility.

(a) The department may not suspend a driver's license, vehicle registration, or nonresident's privilege under this subchapter if the owner or operator:

(1) deposits with the department security in an amount determined to be sufficient under Section 601.154 or 601.157 as appropriate; and

(2) files evidence of financial responsibility as required by this chapter.

(b) If the owner or operator chooses to establish financial responsibility under Subsection (a)(2) by filing evidence of motor vehicle liability insurance, the owner or operator must file a certificate of insurance for a policy that has a policy period of at least six months and for which the premium for the entire policy period is paid in full.

(c) Notwithstanding Section 601.085, coverage for a motor vehicle under a motor vehicle liability policy for which a person files with the department a certificate of insurance under Subsection (b) may not be canceled unless:

(1) the person no longer owns the motor vehicle;

(2) the person dies;

(3) the person has a permanent incapacity that renders the person unable to drive the motor vehicle; or

(4) the person surrenders to the department the person's driver's license and the vehicle registration for the motor vehicle.

*(Added by L.1995, chap. 165(1); chgd. by L.1997, chap. 178(2), eff. 9/1/97.)*

### §601.154. Department determination of probability of liability.

(a) Subject to Subsection (d), if the department finds that there is a reasonable probability that a judgment will be rendered against an owner or operator as a result of an accident, the department shall determine the amount of security sufficient to satisfy any judgment for damages resulting from the accident that may be recovered from the owner or operator.

(b) The department may not require security in an amount:

(1) less than $1,000; or
(2) more than the limits prescribed by Section 601.072.

(c) In determining whether there is a reasonable probability that a judgment will be rendered against the person as a result of an accident and the amount of security that is sufficient under Subsection (a), the department may consider:

(1) a report of an investigating officer;
(2) an accident report of a party involved; and
(3) an affidavit of a person who has knowledge of the facts.

(d) The department shall make the determination required by Subsection (a) only if the department has not received, before the 21st day after the date the department receives a report of a motor vehicle accident, satisfactory evidence that the owner or operator has:

(1) been released from liability;
(2) been finally adjudicated not to be liable; or
(3) executed an acknowledged written agreement providing for the payment of an agreed amount in installments for all claims for injuries or damages resulting from the accident.

*(Added by L.1995, chap. 165(1), eff. 9/1/95.)*

### §601.155. Notice of determination.

(a) The department shall notify the affected person of a determination made under Section 601.154.

(b) The notice must state that:

(1) the person's driver's license and vehicle registration or the person's nonresident's operating privilege will be suspended unless the person, not later than the 20th day after the date the notice was personally served or mailed, establishes that:

(A) this subchapter does not apply to the person, and the person has previously provided this information to the department; or

(B) there is no reasonable probability that a judgment will be rendered against the person as a result of the accident; and

(2) the person is entitled to a hearing under this subchapter if a written request for a hearing is delivered or mailed to the department not later than the 20th day after the date the notice was personally served or mailed.

(c) Notice under this section that is mailed must be mailed to the person's last known address, as shown by the department's records.

(d) For purposes of this section, notice is presumed to be received if the notice was mailed to the person's last known address, as shown by the department's records.

*(Added by L.1995, chap. 165(1); chgd. by L.1997, chap. 1395(1), eff. 9/1/97.)*

### §601.156. Setting of hearing.

(a) A hearing under this subchapter *is subject to the notice and hearing procedures of Sections 521.295-521.303 and* shall be heard by a judge of a municipal court or *a* [the] justice of the peace of the *county* [precinct] in which the person requesting the hearing resides. A party is not entitled to a jury.

(b) The court shall set a date for the hearing. The hearing must be held at the earliest practical time after notice is given to the person requesting the hearing.

(c) The department shall summon the person requesting the hearing to appear at the hearing. Notice under this subsection shall be delivered through personal service or mailed by first class mail to the person's last known address, as shown by the department's records. The notice must include written charges issued by the department.

*(Added by L.1995, chap. 165(1); chgd. by L.1999, chaps. 1117(4), 1409(6), eff. 9/1/2000, 9/1/99, respectively. Matter in brackets eff. only until 9/1/200. Matter in italics eff. 9/1/2000.)*

### §601.157. Hearing procedures.

(a) The judge may administer oaths and issue subpoenas for the attendance of witnesses and the production of relevant books and papers.

(b) The judge at the hearing shall determine:

(1) whether there is a reasonable probability that a judgment will be rendered against the person requesting the hearing as a result of the accident; and

(2) if there is a reasonable probability that a judgment will be rendered, the amount of security sufficient to satisfy any judgment for damages resulting from the accident.

(c) The amount of security under Subsection (b)(2) may not be less than the amount specified as a minimum by Section 601.154.

(d) The judge shall report the judge's determination to the department.

(e) The judge may receive a fee to be paid from the general revenue fund of the county for holding a hearing under this subchapter. The fee must be approved by the commissioners court of the county and may not be more than $5 for each hearing.
*(Added by L.1995, chap. 165(1), eff. 9/1/95.)*

### §601.158. Appeal.

(a) If, after a hearing under this subchapter, the judge determines that there is a reasonable probability that a judgment will be rendered against the person requesting the hearing as a result of the accident, the person may appeal the determination.

[(b) An appeal under this section is by trial de novo to the county court of the county in which the hearing was held.]

*(b) To appeal a determination under Subsection (a), the person must file a petition not later than the 30th day after the date of the determination in the county court at law of the county in which the person resides, or, if there is no county court at law, in the county court of the county.*

*(c) A person who files an appeal under this section shall send a file-stamped copy of the petition by certified mail to the department at the department's headquarters in Austin. The copy must be certified by the clerk of the court in which the petition is filed.*

*(d) The filing of a petition of appeal as provided by this section stays an order of suspension until the earlier of the 91st day after the date the appeal petition is filed or the date the trial is completed and final judgment is rendered.*

*(e) On expiration of the stay, the department shall impose the suspension. The stay may not be extended, and an additional stay may not be granted.*

*(f) A trial on appeal is de novo.*

*(Added by L.1995, chap. 165(1); chgd. by L.1999, chap. 1117(5), eff. 9/1/2000. Matter in brackets eff. only until 9/1/2000. Matter in italics eff. 9/1/2000.)*

### §601.159. Procedures for suspension of driver's license and vehicle registration or privilege.

The department shall suspend the driver's license and each vehicle registration of an owner or operator or the nonresident's operating privilege of an owner or operator unless:

(1) if a hearing is not requested, the person, not later than the 20th day after the date the notice under Section 601.155 was personally served or mailed:

(A) delivers or mails to the department a written request for a hearing;

(B) shows that this subchapter does not apply to the person; or

(C) complies with Section 601.153; or

(2) the person complies with Section 601.153 not later than the 20th day after:

(A) the date of the expiration of the period in which an appeal may be brought, if the determination at a hearing is rendered against the owner or operator and the owner or operator does not appeal; or

(B) the date of a decision against the person following the appeal.

*(Added by L.1995, chap. 165(1), eff. 9/1/95.)*

### §601.160. Suspension stayed pending hearing or appeal.

The department may not suspend a driver's license, vehicle registration, or nonresident's operating privilege pending the outcome of a hearing and any appeal under this subchapter. *(Added by L.1995, chap. 165(1), eff. 9/1/95.)*

### §601.161. Notice of suspension.

Not later than the 11th day before the effective date of a suspension under Section 601.159, the department shall send notice of the suspension to each affected owner or operator. The notice must state the amount required as security under Section 601.153 and the necessity for the owner or operator to file evidence of financial responsibility with the department. *(Added by L.1995, chap. 165(1), eff. 9/1/95.)*

### §601.162. Duration of suspension.

(a) The suspension of a driver's license, vehicle registration, or nonresident's operating privilege under this subchapter remains in effect, the license, registration, or privilege may not be renewed, and a license or vehicle registration may not be issued to the holder of the suspended license, registration, or privilege, until:

(1) the date the person, or a person acting on the person's behalf, deposits security and files evidence of financial responsibility under Section 601.153;

(2) the second anniversary of the date of the accident, if evidence satisfactory to the department is filed with the department that, during the two-year period, an action for damages arising out of the accident has not been instituted; or

(3) the date evidence satisfactory to the department is filed with the department of:

(A) a release from liability for claims arising out of the accident;

(B) a final adjudication that the person is not liable for claims arising out of the accident; or

(C) an installment agreement described by Section 601.154(d)(3).

(b) If a suspension is terminated under Subsection (a)(3)(C), on notice of a default in the payment of an installment under the agreement, the department shall promptly suspend the driver's license and vehicle registration or nonresident's operating privilege of the person defaulting. A suspension under this subsection continues until:

(1) the person deposits and maintains security in accordance with Section 601.153 in an amount determined by the department at the time of suspension under this subsection and files evidence of financial responsibility in accordance with Section 601.153; or

(2) the second anniversary of the date security was deposited under Subdivision (1) if, during that period, an action on the agreement has not been instituted in a court in this state.
*(Added by L.1995, chap. 165(1), eff. 9/1/95.)*



## §601.163. Form of security.

(a) The security required under this subchapter shall be made:

(1) by cash deposit;

(2) through a bond that complies with Section 601.168; or

(3) in another form as required by the department.

(b) A person depositing security shall specify in writing the person on whose behalf the deposit is made. A single deposit of security is applicable only on behalf of persons required to provide security because of the same accident and the same motor vehicle.

(c) The person depositing the security may amend in writing the specification of the person on whose behalf the deposit is made to include an additional person. This amendment may be made at any time the deposit is in the custody of the department or the comptroller.
*(Added by L.1995, chap. 165(1); chgd. by L.1997, chap. 1423(18.10), eff. 9/1/97.)*

## §601.164. Reduction in security.

(a) The department may reduce the amount of security ordered in a case within six months after the date of the accident if, in the department's judgment, the amount is excessive.

(b) The amount of security originally deposited that exceeds the reduced amount shall be returned promptly to the depositor or the depositor's personal representative.
*(Added by L.1995, chap. 165(1), eff. 9/1/95.)*

## §601.165. Custody of cash security.

The department shall place cash deposited in compliance with this subchapter in the custody of the comptroller. *(Added by L.1995, chap. 165(1); chgd. by L.1997, chap. 1423(18.11), eff. 9/1/97.)*

## §601.166. Payment of cash security.

(a) Cash security may be applied only to the payment of:

(1) a judgment rendered against the person on whose behalf the deposit is made for damages arising out of the accident; or

(2) a settlement, agreed to by the depositor, of a claim arising out of the accident.

(b) For payment under Subsection (a), the action under which the judgment was rendered must have been instituted before the second anniversary of the later of:

(1) the date of the accident; or

(2) the date of the deposit, in the case of a deposit of security under Section 601.162(b).
*(Added by L.1995, chap. 165(1), eff. 9/1/95.)*

## §601.167. Return of cash security.

Cash security or any balance of the security shall be returned to the depositor or the depositor's personal representative when:

(1) evidence satisfactory to the department is filed with the department that there has been:

(A) a release of liability;

(B) a final adjudication that the person on whose behalf the deposit is made is not liable; or

(C) an agreement as described by Section 601.154(d)(3);

(2) reasonable evidence is provided to the department after the second anniversary of the date of the accident that no action arising out of the accident is pending and no judgment rendered in such an action is unpaid; or

(3) in the case of a deposit of security under Section 601.162(b), reasonable evidence is provided to the department after the second anniversary of the date of the deposit that no action arising out of the accident is pending and no unpaid judgment rendered in such an action is unpaid. *(Added by L.1995, chap. 165(1), eff. 9/1/95.)*

### §601.168. Insurance policy or bond; limits.

(a) A bond or motor vehicle liability insurance policy under this subchapter must:

(1) be issued by a surety company or insurance company:

(A) authorized to write motor vehicle liability insurance in this state; or

(B) that complies with Subsection (b); and

(2) cover the amounts, excluding interest and costs, required to establish financial responsibility under Section 601.072.

(b) A bond or motor vehicle liability insurance policy issued by a surety company or insurance company that is not authorized to do business in this state is effective under this subchapter only if:

(1) the bond or policy is issued for a motor vehicle that:

(A) is not registered in this state; or

(B) was not registered in this state on the effective date of the most recent renewal of the policy; and

(2) the surety company or insurance company executes a power of attorney authorizing the department to accept on the company's behalf service of notice or process in an action arising out of the accident on the bond or policy.

(c) The bond must be filed with and approved by the department.

*(Added by L.1995, chap. 165(1), eff. 9/1/95.)*



### §601.169. Reasonable probability not admissible in civil suit.

A determination under Section 601.154 or 601.157 that there is a reasonable probability that a judgment will be rendered against a person as a result of an accident may not be introduced in evidence in a suit for damages arising from that accident. *(Added by L.1995, chap. 165(1), eff. 9/1/95.)*

### §601.170. Department acting on erroneous information.

If the department is given erroneous information relating to a matter covered by Section 601.151(b)(1) or (b)(2) or to a person's status as an employee of the United States acting within the scope of the person's employment, the department shall take appropriate action as provided by this subchapter not later than the 60th day after the date the department receives correct information. *(Added by L.1995, chap. 165(1), eff. 9/1/95.)*

### §§601.171 to 601.190. *(Reserved.)*

## SUBCHAPTER G. FAILURE TO MAINTAIN MOTOR VEHICLE LIABILITY INSURANCE OR OTHERWISE ESTABLISH FINANCIAL RESPONSIBILITY; CRIMINAL PENALTIES

### §601.191. Operation of motor vehicle in violation of motor vehicle liability insurance requirement; offense.

(a) A person commits an offense if the person operates a motor vehicle in violation of Section 601.051.

(b) Except as provided by Subsections (c) and (d), an offense under this section is a misdemeanor punishable by a fine of not less than $175 or more than $350.

(c) If a person has been previously convicted of an offense under this section, an offense under this section is a misdemeanor punishable by a fine of not less than $350 or more than $1,000.

(d) If the court determines that a person who has not been previously convicted of an offense under this section is economically unable to pay the fine, the court may reduce the fine to less than $175.

*(Added by L.1995, chap. 165(1), eff. 9/1/95.)*

### §601.192. *(Repealed by L.1997, chap. 1100(6(5)), eff. 9/1/97.)*

## §601.193. Defense: financial responsibility in effect at time of alleged offense.

(a) It is a defense to prosecution under Section 601.191 or 601.195 that the person charged produces to the court one of the documents listed in Section 601.053(a) that was valid at the time that the offense is alleged to have occurred.

(b) After the court verifies a document produced under Subsection (a), the court shall dismiss the charge.

*(Added by L.1995, chap. 165(1); chgd. by L.1997, chap. 844(1); L.1999, chap. 961(1), eff. 9/1/99.)*

## §601.194. Defense: possession of motor vehicle for maintenance or repair.

It is a defense to prosecution of an offense under Section 601.191 that the motor vehicle operated by the person charged:

(1) was in the possession of that person for the sole purpose of maintenance or repair; and

(2) was not owned in whole or in part by that person.

*(Added by L.1995, chap. 165(1), eff. 9/1/95.)*

## §601.195. Operation of motor vehicle in violation of requirement to establish financial responsibility; offense.

(a) A person commits an offense if the person:

(1) is required to establish financial responsibility under Subchapter F or K;

(2) does not maintain evidence of financial responsibility; and

(3) during the period evidence of financial responsibility must be maintained:

(A) operates on a highway a motor vehicle owned by the person; or

(B) knowingly permits another person, who is not otherwise permitted to operate a vehicle under this chapter, to operate on a highway a motor vehicle owned by the person.

(b) An offense under this section is a misdemeanor punishable by:

(1) a fine not to exceed $500;

(2) confinement in county jail for a term not to exceed six months; or

(3) both the fine and the confinement.

*(Added by L.1995, chap. 165(1), eff. 9/1/95.)*

**§601.196.** *(Repealed by L.1999, chap. 659(4), eff. 9/1/99.)*

**§§601.197 to 601.230.** *(Reserved.)*

# SUBCHAPTER H. FAILURE TO MAINTAIN EVIDENCE OF FINANCIAL RESPONSIBILITY; SUSPENSION OF DRIVER'S LICENSE AND MOTOR VEHICLE REGISTRATION

## §601.231. Suspension of driver's license and vehicle registration.

(a) If a person is convicted of an offense under Section 601.191 and a prior conviction of that person under that section has been reported to the department by a magistrate or the judge or clerk of a court, the department shall suspend the driver's license and vehicle registrations of the person unless the person files and maintains evidence of financial responsibility with the department until the second anniversary of the date of the subsequent conviction.

(b) The department may waive the requirement of maintaining evidence of financial responsibility under Subsection (a) if satisfactory evidence is filed with the department showing that at the time of arrest the person was in compliance with the financial responsibility requirement of Section 601.051 or was exempt from that section under Section 601.007 or 601.052(a)(3).

*(Added by L.1995, chap. 165(1), eff. 9/1/95.)*

## §601.232. Notice of suspension.

(a) The department shall mail in a timely manner a notice to each person whose driver's license and vehicle registrations are suspended under Section 601.231.

(b) The notice must state that the person's driver's license and registration are suspended and that the person may apply for reinstatement of the license and vehicle registration or issuance of a new license and registration as provided by Sections 601.162 and 601.376.

*(Added by L.1995, chap. 165(1), eff. 9/1/95.)*

### §601.233. Notice of potential suspension.

(a) A citation for an offense under Section 601.191 issued as a result of Section 601.053 must include, in type larger than other type on the citation, the following statement:

> "A second or subsequent conviction of an offense under the Texas Motor Vehicle Safety Responsibility Act will result in the suspension of your driver's license and motor vehicle registration unless you file and maintain evidence of financial responsibility with the Department of Public Safety for two years from the date of conviction. The department may waive the requirement to file evidence of financial responsibility if you file satisfactory evidence with the department showing that at the time this citation was issued, the vehicle was covered by a motor vehicle liability insurance policy or that you were otherwise exempt from the requirements to provide evidence of financial responsibility."

(b) A judge presiding at a trial at which a person is convicted of an offense under Section 601.191 shall notify the person that the person's driver's license is subject to suspension if the person fails to provide to the department evidence of financial responsibility as required by Section 601.231.

*(Added by L.1995, chap. 165(1), eff. 9/1/95.)*



### §601.234. Issuance or continuation of vehicle registration.

A motor vehicle may not be registered in the name of a person required to file evidence of financial responsibility unless evidence of financial responsibility is furnished for the vehicle. *(Added by L.1995, chap. 165(1), eff. 9/1/95.)*

### §§601.235 to 601.260. *(Reserved.)*

## SUBCHAPTER I. FAILURE TO MAINTAIN EVIDENCE OF FINANCIAL RESPONSIBILITY; IMPOUNDMENT OF MOTOR VEHICLE

### §601.261. Impoundment of motor vehicle.

On a second or subsequent conviction for an offense under Section 601.191, the court shall order the sheriff of the county in which the court has jurisdiction to impound the motor vehicle operated by the defendant at the time of the offense if the defendant:

(1) was an owner of the motor vehicle at the time of the offense; and

(2) is an owner on the date of that conviction.

*(Added by L.1995, chap. 165(1), eff. 9/1/95.)*

### §601.262. Duration of impoundment.

(a) The duration of an impoundment under Section 601.261 is 180 days.

(b) The court may not order the release of the vehicle unless the defendant applies to the court for the vehicle's release and provides evidence of financial responsibility that complies with Section 601.053 and this section.

(c) The evidence of financial responsibility must cover the two-year period immediately following the date the defendant applies for release of the impounded vehicle.

(d) If an insurance binder is offered as evidence of financial responsibility under this section, the binder must confirm to the court's satisfaction that the defendant is in compliance with this chapter for the period required by Subsection (c).

*(Added by L.1995, chap. 165(1), eff. 9/1/95.)*

### §601.263. Cost for impoundment.

The court shall impose against the defendant a cost of $15 a day for each day of impoundment of the defendant's vehicle. *(Added by L.1995, chap. 165(1), eff. 9/1/95.)*

### §601.264. Penalties cumulative.

Impoundment of a motor vehicle under this subchapter is in addition to any other punishment imposed under this chapter. *(Added by L.1995, chap. 165(1), eff. 9/1/95.)*

### §601.265. Transfer of title of impounded motor vehicle.

(a) To transfer title to a motor vehicle impounded under Section 601.261, the owner must apply to the court for permission.

(b) If the court finds that the transfer is being made in good faith and is not being made to circumvent this chapter, the court shall approve the transfer.
*(Added by L.1995, chap. 165(1), eff. 9/1/95.)*

### §601.266. Release on involuntary transfer of title of impounded motor vehicle.

(a)* Notwithstanding Section 601.262, the court shall order the release of a motor vehicle impounded under Section 601.261 if, while the vehicle is impounded, title to the vehicle is transferred by:

(1) foreclosure;
(2) sale on execution;
(3) cancellation of a conditional sales contract; or
(4) judicial order.

**So in original. No subsection (b) has been enacted.*
*(Added by L.1995, chap. 165(1), eff. 9/1/95.)*

### §601.267. Release of impounded motor vehicle by sheriff.

A sheriff who impounds a motor vehicle shall release the vehicle:

(1) on presentation of an order of release from the court and payment of the fee for the impoundment by the defendant or a person authorized by the owner; or

(2) to a person who is shown as a lienholder on the vehicle's certificate of title on presentation of the certificate of title and an accompanying affidavit from an officer of the lienholder establishing that the debt secured by the vehicle is in default or has matured.
*(Added by L.1995, chap. 165(1), eff. 9/1/95.)*

### §§601.268 to 601.290. *(Reserved.)*

## SUBCHAPTER J. IMPOUNDMENT OF MOTOR VEHICLE NOT REGISTERED IN THIS STATE

### §601.291. Applicability of subchapter.

This subchapter applies only to the owner or operator of a motor vehicle that:

(1) is not registered in this state; and

(2) is involved in a motor vehicle accident in this state that results in bodily injury, death, or damage to the property of one person to an apparent extent of at least $500.
*(Added by L.1995, chap. 165(1), eff. 9/1/95.)*

### §601.292. Duty to provide evidence of financial responsibility to investigating officer.

A person to whom this subchapter applies shall provide evidence of financial responsibility to a law enforcement officer of this state or a political subdivision of this state who is conducting an investigation of the accident. *(Added by L.1995, chap. 165(1), eff. 9/1/95.)*

### §601.293. Failure to provide evidence of financial responsibility; magistrate's inquiry and order.

(a) A person to whom this subchapter applies who fails to provide evidence under Section 601.292 shall be taken before a magistrate as soon as practicable.

(b) The magistrate shall conduct an inquiry on the issues of negligence and liability for bodily injury, death, or property damage sustained in the accident.

(c) If the magistrate determines that there is a reasonable possibility that a judgment will be rendered against the person for bodily injury, death, or property damage sustained in the accident, the magistrate shall order the person to provide:

(1) evidence of financial responsibility for the bodily injury, death, or property damage; or
(2) evidence that the person is exempt from the requirement of Section 601.051.

(d) A determination of negligence or liability under Subsection (c) does not act as collateral estoppel on an issue in a criminal or civil adjudication arising from the accident.
*(Added by L.1995, chap. 165(1), eff. 9/1/95.)*

### §601.294. Impoundment of motor vehicle.

If a person to whom this subchapter applies does not provide evidence required under Section 601.293(c), the magistrate shall enter an order directing the sheriff of the county or the chief of police of the municipality to impound the motor vehicle owned or operated by the person that was involved in the accident. *(Added by L.1995, chap. 165(1), eff. 9/1/95.)*

### §601.295. Duration of impoundment; release.

(a) A motor vehicle impounded under Section 601.294 remains impounded until the owner, operator, or person authorized by the owner presents to the person authorized to release the vehicle:

(1) a certificate of release obtained from the department; and

(2) payment for the cost of impoundment.

(b) On presentation of the items described by Subsection (a), the person authorized to release an impounded motor vehicle shall release the vehicle.

*(Added by L.1995, chap. 165(1), eff. 9/1/95.)*

### §601.296. Certificate of release.

(a) The department shall issue a certificate of release of an impounded motor vehicle to the owner, operator, or person authorized by the owner on submission to the department of:

(1) evidence of financial responsibility under Section 601.053 that shows that at the time of the accident the vehicle was in compliance with Section 601.051 or was exempt from the requirement of Section 601.051;

(2) a release executed by each person damaged in the accident other than the operator of the vehicle for which the certificate of release is requested; or

(3) security in a form and amount determined by the department to secure the payment of damages for which the operator may be liable.

(b) A person may satisfy the requirement of Subsection (a)(1) or (2) by submitting a photocopy of the item required.

(c) The department shall adopt the form, content, and procedures for issuance of a certificate of release.

(d) Security provided under this section is subject to Sections 601.163–601.167.

*(Added by L.1995, chap. 165(1), eff. 9/1/95.)*

### §601.297. Liability for cost of impoundment.

The owner of an impounded vehicle is liable for the costs of the impoundment. *(Added by L.1995, chap. 165(1), eff. 9/1/95.)*

### §§601.298 to 601.330. *(Reserved.)*

## SUBCHAPTER K. EVIDENCE OF FINANCIAL RESPONSIBILITY FOLLOWING JUDGMENT, CONVICTION, PLEA, OR FORFEITURE OR FOLLOWING SUSPENSION OR REVOCATION

### §601.331. Report of unsatisfied judgment or conviction, plea, or forfeiture of bail; nonresident.

(a) If a person does not satisfy a judgment before the 61st day after the date of the judgment, the clerk of the court, on the written request of a judgment creditor or a judgment creditor's attorney, immediately shall send a certified copy of the judgment to the department.

(b) The clerk of the court immediately shall send to the department a certified copy of the action of the court in relation to:

(1) a conviction for a violation of a motor vehicle law; or

(2) a guilty plea or forfeiture of bail by a person charged with violation of a motor vehicle law.

(c) A certified copy sent to the department under Subsection (b) is prima facie evidence of the conviction, plea, forfeiture, or other action.

(d) If the court does not have a clerk, the judge of the court shall send the certified copy required by this section.

(e) If the defendant named in a judgment reported to the department is a nonresident, the department shall send a certified copy of the judgment to the official in charge of issuing driver's licenses and vehicle registrations of the state, province of Canada, or state of Mexico in which the defendant resides.

*(Added by L.1995, chap. 165(1); chgd. by L.1997, chap. 75(1), eff. 9/1/97.)*

**§601.332. Suspension of driver's license and vehicle registration or nonresident's operating privilege for unsatisfied judgment.**

(a) Except as provided by Sections 601.333, 601.334, and 601.336, on receipt of a certified copy of a judgment under Section 601.331, the department shall suspend the judgment debtor's:

(1) driver's license and vehicle registrations; or

(2) nonresident's operating privilege.

(b) Subject to Sections 601.333, 601.334, and 601.336, the suspension continues, and the person's driver's license, vehicle registrations, or nonresident's operating privilege may not be renewed or the person issued a driver's license or registration in the person's name, until:

(1) the judgment is stayed or satisfied; and

(2) the person provides evidence of financial responsibility.

*(Added by L.1995, chap. 165(1), eff. 9/1/95.)*

**§601.333. Relief from suspension: motor vehicle liability insurance.**

(a) A person whose driver's license, vehicle registrations, or nonresident's operating privilege has been suspended or is subject to suspension under Section 601.332 may file with the department:

(1) evidence that there was a motor vehicle liability insurance policy covering the motor vehicle involved in the accident out of which the judgment arose in effect at the time of the accident;

(2) an affidavit stating that the person was insured at the time of the accident, that the insurance company is liable to pay the judgment, and the reason, if known, that the insurance company has not paid the judgment;

(3) the original policy of insurance or a certified copy of the policy, if available; and

(4) any other documents required by the department to show that the loss, injury, or damage for which the judgment was rendered was covered by the insurance.

(b) The department may not suspend the driver's license, vehicle registrations, or nonresident's operating privilege, and shall reinstate a license, registration, or privilege that has been suspended, if it is satisfied from the documents filed under Subsection (a) that:

(1) there was a motor vehicle liability insurance policy in effect for the vehicle at the time of the accident;

(2) the insurance company that issued the policy was authorized to issue the policy in this state at the time the policy was issued; and

(3) the insurance company is liable to pay the judgment to the extent and for the amounts required by this chapter.

*(Added by L.1995, chap. 165(1), eff. 9/1/95.)*

**§601.334. Relief from suspension: consent of judgment creditor.**

(a) The department may allow a judgment debtor's driver's license and vehicle registrations or nonresident's operating privilege to continue, notwithstanding Section 601.332, if:

(1) the judgment creditor consents to the continuation in writing in the form prescribed by the department; and

(2) the judgment debtor provides evidence of financial responsibility to the department.

(b) Continuation of a judgment debtor's driver's license and vehicle registrations or nonresident's operating privilege expires on the later of:

(1) the date the consent of the judgment creditor is revoked in writing; or

(2) the expiration of six months after the effective date of the consent.

(c) Subsection (b) applies notwithstanding default in the payment of the judgment or any installments to be made under Section 601.335.

*(Added by L.1995, chap. 165(1), eff. 9/1/95.)*

**§601.335. Installment payments authorized.**

(a) A judgment debtor, on notice to the judgment creditor, may apply to the court in which judgment was rendered to pay the judgment in installments.

(b) The court may order payment in installments and may establish the amounts and times of the payments.

(c) An order issued under this section is issued without prejudice to any other legal remedy that the judgment creditor has.

*(Added by L.1995, chap. 165(1), eff. 9/1/95.)*

### §601.336. Relief from suspension: installment payments; default.

(a) Subject to Subsection (c), the department may not suspend a judgment debtor's driver's license, vehicle registration, or nonresident's operating privilege under Section 601.332 if the judgment debtor:

(1) files evidence of financial responsibility with the department; and

(2) obtains an order under Section 601.335 permitting the payment of the judgment in installments.

(b) Subject to Subsection (c), the department shall restore a judgment debtor's driver's license, vehicle registrations, or nonresident's operating privilege that was suspended following nonpayment of a judgment if the judgment debtor complies with Subsections (a)(1) and (2).

(c) On notice that a judgment debtor has failed to pay an installment as specified in an order issued under Section 601.335, the department shall suspend the judgment debtor's driver's license, vehicle registrations, or nonresident's operating privilege. The suspensions continue until the judgment is satisfied as provided by this chapter.

*(Added by L.1995, chap. 165(1), eff. 9/1/95.)*



### §601.337. Effect of bankruptcy.

A discharge in bankruptcy after a judgment is rendered relieves the judgment debtor from the requirements of this chapter, except for financial responsibility requirements arising after the date of the discharge. *(Added by L.1995, chap. 165(1), eff. 9/1/95.)*

### §601.338. Evidence of financial responsibility or suspension of driver's license and vehicle registration of owner of motor vehicle.

(a) The department shall suspend the driver's license and vehicle registrations of the owner of a motor vehicle that was used with the owner's consent by another person at the time of an offense resulting in conviction or a plea of guilty, if under state law the department:

(1) suspends or revokes the driver's license of the other person on receipt of a record of a conviction; or

(2) suspends the vehicle registration of the other person on receipt of a record of a plea of guilty.

(b) The department may not suspend the driver's license and vehicle registration of an owner under this section if the owner files and maintains evidence of financial responsibility with the department for each motor vehicle registered in the name of the owner.

*(Added by L.1995, chap. 165(1), eff. 9/1/95.)*

### §601.339. Evidence of financial responsibility following conviction, plea, or forfeiture.

(a) Except as provided by Subsection (c), the department may not issue a driver's license to a person who does not hold a driver's license and who:

(1) enters a plea of guilty to an offense or is convicted by a final order or a judgment that:

(A) requires the suspension or revocation of a driver's license;

(B) is imposed for operating a motor vehicle on a highway without a driver's license; or

(C) is imposed for operating an unregistered motor vehicle on a highway; or

(2) forfeits bail or collateral deposited to secure an appearance for trial for an offense described by Subdivision (1).

(b) Except as described by Subsection (c), a motor vehicle may not be registered in the name of a person described by Subsection (a).

(c) Notwithstanding Subsections (a) and (b), a driver's license may be issued or a motor vehicle may be registered if the person files and maintains evidence of financial responsibility with the department.

*(Added by L.1995, chap. 165(1), eff. 9/1/95.)*

### §601.340. Evidence of financial responsibility or suspension of vehicle registration following suspension or revocation of driver's license.

(a) Except as provided by Subsection (b) or (c), the department shall suspend the registration of each motor vehicle registered in the name of a person if the department:

(1) under any state law, other than Section 521.341(6), suspends or revokes the person's driver's license on receipt of a record of a conviction or a forfeiture of bail; or

(2) receives a record of a guilty plea of the person entered for an offense for which the department would be required to suspend the driver's license of a person convicted of the offense.

(b) The department, unless otherwise required by law, may not suspend a registration under Subsection (a) if the person files and maintains evidence of financial responsibility with the department for each motor vehicle registered in the name of the person.

(c) This section does not apply to a suspension of a driver's license for an offense under Chapter 106, Alcoholic Beverage Code, other than an offense that includes confinement as an authorized sanction.

*(Added by L.1995, chap. 165(1); chgd. by L.1997, chaps. 165(30.128), 1013(30), eff. 9/1/97.)*

### §601.341. Evidence of financial responsibility; termination of penalty.

Unless a person whose driver's license or vehicle registration has been suspended or revoked under this subchapter files and maintains evidence of financial responsibility with the department:

(1) the suspension or revocation may not be terminated;

(2) the driver's license or registration may not be renewed;

(3) a new driver's license may not be issued to the person; or

(4) a motor vehicle may not be registered in the name of the person.

*(Added by L.1995, chap. 165(1); chgd. by L.1997, chap. 165(30.129), eff. 9/1/97.)*

### §601.342. Evidence of financial responsibility following suspension or revocation of nonresident's operating privilege.

The department may not terminate the suspension or revocation of a nonresident's operating privilege suspended or revoked under this subchapter because of a conviction, forfeiture of bail, or guilty plea unless the person files and maintains evidence of financial responsibility with the department. *(Added by L.1995, chap. 165(1); chgd. by L.1997, chap. 165(30.129), eff. 9/1/97.)*

### §§601.343 to 601.370. *(Reserved.)*

## SUBCHAPTER L. EFFECT OF SUSPENSION

### §601.371. Operation of motor vehicle in violation of suspension; offense.

(a) A person commits an offense if the person operates a motor vehicle on a highway:

(1) during a period that a suspension of the person's driver's license or nonresident's operating privilege is in effect under this chapter; or

(2) while the person's driver's license is expired, if the license expired during a period of suspension imposed under this chapter.

(b) A person commits an offense if the person, during a period that a suspension of the person's vehicle registration is in effect under this chapter, knowingly permits a motor vehicle owned by the person to be operated on a highway.

(c) It is an affirmative defense to prosecution under this section that the person had not received notice of a suspension order concerning the person's driver's license, nonresident's operating privilege, or vehicle registration. For purposes of this subsection, notice is presumed to be received if the notice was mailed in accordance with this chapter to the last known address of the person as shown by department records.

(d) Except as provided by Subsection (e), an offense under this section is a misdemeanor punishable by:

(1) a fine of not less than $100 or more than $500; and

(2) confinement in county jail for a term of not less than 72 hours or more than six months.

(e) If it is shown on the trial of an offense under this section that the person has previously been convicted of an offense under this section or under Section 521.457, the offense is punishable as a Class A misdemeanor.

(f) In this section, a conviction for an offense that involves operation of a motor vehicle after August 31, 1987, is a final conviction, whether the sentence for the conviction is imposed or probated.

*(Added by L.1995, chap. 165(1), eff. 9/1/95.)*

### §601.372. Return of driver's license and vehicle registration to department.

(a) The department shall give written notice of a suspension of a driver's license and vehicle registration to a person who is required to maintain a motor vehicle liability insurance policy or bond under this chapter and whose policy or bond is canceled or terminated or who does not provide other evidence of financial responsibility on the request of the department.

(b) The notice must be by personal delivery to the person or by deposit in the United States mail addressed to the person at the last address supplied to the department by the person. Notice by mail is presumed to be received on the 10th day after the date the notice is mailed.

(c) The department by rule may require the person to send the person's driver's license and vehicle registrations not later than the 10th day after the date the person receives written notice from the department.

(d) Proof of the notice may be made by the certificate of a department employee stating that:

(1) the notice was prepared in the regular course of business and placed in the United States mail as part of the regular organized activity of the department; or

(2) the employee delivered the notice in person.

(e) A certificate under Subsection (d)(2) must specify the name of the person to whom the notice was given and the time, place, and manner of the delivery of the notice.

*(Added by L.1995, chap. 165(1); chgd. by L.1999, chap. 884(3), eff. 9/1/99.)*

**§601.373. Failure to return driver's license or vehicle registration; offense.**

(a) A person commits an offense if the person wilfully fails to send a driver's license or vehicle registration as required by Section 601.372. An offense under this subsection is a misdemeanor punishable by a fine not to exceed $200.

(b) The department may direct a department employee to obtain and send to the department the driver's license and vehicle registration of a person who fails to send the person's license or registration in accordance with Section 601.372. The director of the department or the person designated by the director may file a complaint against a person for an offense under Subsection (a).

*(Added by L.1995, chap. 165(1); chgd. by L.1999, chap. 884(4), eff. 9/1/99.)*

**§601.374. Transfer of vehicle registration prohibited.**

(a) An owner whose vehicle registration has been suspended under this chapter may not:

(1) transfer the registration unless the transfer is authorized under Subsection (b); or

(2) register in another name the motor vehicle to which the registration applies.

(b) The department may authorize the transfer of vehicle registration if the department is satisfied that the transfer is proposed in good faith and not to defeat the purposes of this chapter.

(c) This section does not affect the rights of a conditional vendor or lessor of, or person with a security interest in, a motor vehicle owned by a person who is subject to this section if the vendor, lessor, or secured party is not the registered owner of the vehicle.

*(Added by L.1995, chap. 165(1), eff. 9/1/95.)*

**§601.375. Cooperation with other state or Canada.**

(a) The department shall send a certified copy of the record of the department's action suspending a nonresident's operating privilege under Subchapter F or under Sections 601.332, 601.333, and 601.334 to the official in charge of issuing driver's licenses and vehicle registrations of the state or province of Canada in which the nonresident resides.

(b) Subsection (a) applies only if the law of the other state or the province provides for action similar to the action required by Section 601.009.

*(Added by L.1995, chap. 165(1), eff. 9/1/95.)*

**§601.376. Reinstatement fee.**

(a) A driver's license, vehicle registration, or nonresident's operating privilege that has been suspended under this chapter may not be reinstated and a new license or registration may not be issued to the holder of the suspended license, registration, or privilege until the person:

(1) pays to the department a fee of $100; and

(2) complies with the other requirements of this chapter.

(b) The fee imposed by this section is in addition to other fees imposed by law.

(c) A person is required to pay only one fee under this section, without regard to the number of driver's licenses and vehicle registrations to be reinstated for or issued to the person in connection with the payment.

*(Added by L.1995, chap. 165(1); chgd. by L.1999, chap. 1189(38), eff. 9/1/99.)*

**§§601.377 to 601.400.** *(Reserved.)*

## SUBCHAPTER M. APPEAL OF DEPARTMENT ACTION

**§601.401. Department *actions* [acts] subject to review.**

*(a)* An *action* [act] of the department under this chapter may be appealed, *unless:*

*(1) an order of suspension by the department is based on an existing unsatisfied final judgment rendered against a person by a court in this state arising out of the use of a motor vehicle in this state; or*

*(2) the suspension is automatic under Section 601.231(a).*

*(b) To appeal an action of the department, the person must file a petition not later than the 30th day after the date of the action* [by a person in interest] in[:]

[(1)] the county court at law in the county in which the person resides *or*[;]

[(2)] the county court of the county in which the person resides, if the county does not have a county court at law[; or]

[(3) the district court of the county in which the person resides if:

(A) the county does not have a county court at law; and

(B) the county court does not have the civil jurisdiction provided by general law for a county court.].

*(c) A person who files an appeal under this section shall send a file-stamped copy of the petition by certified mail to the department at the department's headquarters in Austin. The copy must be certified by the clerk of the court in which the petition is filed.*

*(d) The filing of a petition of appeal as provided by this section stays an order of suspension until the earlier of the 91st day after the date the appeal petition is filed or the date the trial is completed and final judgment is rendered.*

*(e) On expiration of the stay, the department shall impose the suspension. The stay may not be extended, and an additional stay may not be granted.*

*(f) A trial on appeal is de novo.*

*(Added by L.1995, chap. 165(1); chgd. by L.1999, chap. 1117(6), eff. 9/1/2000. Matter in brackets eff. only until 9/1/2000. Matter in italics eff. 9/1/2000.)*

## §601.402. Time for appeal.

An appeal under Section 601.401 must be brought not later than the 30th day after the date of notice of the act or may be brought, for good cause shown, on a later date. *(Added by L.1995, chap. 165(1); repealed by L.1999, chap. 1117(9), eff. 9/1/2000.)*

## §601.403. Trial.

(a) Trial of an appeal under this subchapter is de novo, with the burden of proof on the department. The appeal shall be tried without regard to a prior holding of fact or law by the department, the substantial evidence rule does not apply, and judgment may be entered only on the evidence offered at the trial by the court.

(b) The court shall grant a trial by jury on proper application.

*(Added by L.1995, chap. 165(1); repealed by L.1999, chap. 1117(9), eff. 9/1/2000.)*

## §601.404. Stay of act on appeal.

(a) The court shall determine whether the filing of an appeal under Section 601.401 stays an act of the department that is the subject of the appeal.

(b) The court may not stay an order of suspension by the department based on an existing unsatisfied final judgment that is rendered against a person by a court in this state and that arises out of the use of a motor vehicle in this state.

(c) Except as provided by Section 601.405 or 601.406 an appeal does not stay an act of the department if:

(1) the person aggrieved by the act was the operator of a motor vehicle involved in an accident;

(2) the person was charged with a violation of a law of this state or a political subdivision of this state; and

(3) a complaint or indictment is pending at the time the appeal is filed.

*(Added by L.1995, chap. 165(1); repealed by L.1999, chap. 1117(9), eff. 9/1/2000.)*

## §601.405. Filing of evidence of financial responsibility; effect on appeal.

An appeal stays an act of the department in the circumstances described by Section 601.404(c) if the person aggrieved by the act:

(1) files evidence of financial responsibility with the department; and

(2) maintains evidence of financial responsibility until the complaint or indictment is dismissed or for the period specified by Section 601.409.

*(Added by L.1995, chap. 165(1); repealed by L.1999, chap. 1117(9), eff. 9/1/2000.)*

## §601.406. Temporary stay of department's order on filing of affidavit.

(a) A person who is required to file evidence of financial responsibility under Sections 601.404(c) and 601.405 and who, at the time of appeal, files with the court and the department an affidavit setting forth specific facts that would entitle the person to an acquittal of the offense alleged in the complaint or indictment, is entitled to a stay of the order of the department without filing evidence of financial responsibility.

(b) On the filing of an affidavit under Subsection (a), the cause shall be set on the docket in the court in which the complaint or indictment is pending. If the complaint or indictment is not tried before the 46th day after the date the complaint or indictment was filed, it may be transferred to the county or district court of an adjoining county on motion of the person who filed the affidavit.

(c) If, not later than the 90th day after the date of the original suspension or order of the department, the department does not receive a certified copy of a judgment of a court acquitting the person, the department shall suspend the person's driver's license and the registration of all motor vehicles registered in the person's name.

(d) An appeal does not stay an order of suspension under Subsection (c) unless the person files and maintains evidence of financial responsibility with the department:

(1) until the complaint or indictment is dismissed; or

(2) if the person pleads guilty or is convicted, for the period required by Section 601.409.

*(Added by L.1995, chap. 165(1); repealed by L.1999, chap. 1117(9), eff. 9/1/2000.)*



### §601.407. Stay after plea or conviction.

(a) A person may obtain a stay from an act of the department after the person has entered a plea of guilty or has been finally convicted if the person files and maintains evidence of financial responsibility with the department for the period required by Section 601.409.

(b) This section does not apply if the person applied for a stay before entering a plea of guilty or before a final conviction.

*(Added by L.1995, chap. 165(1); repealed by L.1999, chap. 1117(9), eff. 9/1/2000.)*

### §601.408. Stay after acquittal or dismissal.

If the person aggrieved by the act of the department is acquitted of the offense alleged in a complaint or indictment, or if the complaint or indictment is dismissed:

(1) the person may not be required to file evidence of financial responsibility with the department to obtain a stay of the act; and

(2) the person may withdraw evidence of financial responsibility previously filed to obtain a stay of an act of the department.

*(Added by L.1995, chap. 165(1); repealed by L.1999, chap. 1117(9), eff. 9/1/2000.)*

### §601.409. Maintenance of evidence of financial responsibility.

A person who is convicted of or pleads guilty to a violation of a law of this state or any political subdivision of this state in connection with a motor vehicle accident and who is required to file evidence of financial responsibility to obtain a stay of an act of the department must maintain the evidence of financial responsibility with the department until the second anniversary of the date of the conviction or plea of guilty. *(Added by L.1995, chap. 165(1); repealed by L.1999, chap. 1117(9), eff. 9/1/2000.)*

### §601.410. Limit on courts.

A provision of this subchapter that restricts the granting of a stay in an appeal in which the person making the appeal has been charged with violation of a law of this state or a political subdivision of this state limits a court in an original action brought against the department to enjoin or order the enforcement of an order of the department issued under this chapter. *(Added by L.1995, chap. 165(1); repealed by L.1999, chap. 1117(9), eff. 9/1/2000.)*

## CHAPTERS 602 to 620. *(Reserved.)*

## SUBTITLE E. VEHICLE SIZE AND WEIGHT

## CHAPTER 621. GENERAL PROVISIONS RELATING TO VEHICLE SIZE AND WEIGHT

## SUBCHAPTER A. GENERAL PROVISIONS

Section

## SUBCHAPTER B. WEIGHT LIMITATIONS



## SUBCHAPTER C. SIZE LIMITATIONS



## SUBCHAPTER D. LOCAL REGULATIONS



## SUBCHAPTER E. FEES



## SUBCHAPTER F. ENFORCEMENT

## SUBCHAPTER G. OFFENSES AND PENALTIES



## SUBCHAPTER A. GENERAL PROVISIONS

### §621.001. Definitions.

In this chapter:

(1) "Commercial motor vehicle" means a motor vehicle, other than a motorcycle, designed or used for:

(A) the transportation of property; or

(B) delivery purposes.

(2) "Commission" means the Texas Transportation Commission.

(3) "Department" means the Texas Department of Transportation.

(4) "Director" means the executive director of the Texas Department of Transportation.

(5) "Motor vehicle" means a vehicle that is self-propelled.

(6) "Semitrailer" means a vehicle without motive power that is designed, or used with a motor vehicle, so that some of its weight and the weight of its load rests on or is carried by the motor vehicle.

(7) "Trailer" means a vehicle without motive power that is:

(A) designed or used to carry property or passengers on its own structure exclusively; and

(B) drawn by a motor vehicle.

(8) "Truck-tractor" means a motor vehicle designed or used primarily for drawing another vehicle:

(A) that is not constructed to carry a load other than a part of the weight of the vehicle and load being drawn; or

(B) that is engaged with a semitrailer in the transportation of automobiles or boats and that transports the automobiles or boats on part of the truck-tractor.

(9) "Vehicle" means a mechanical device, other than a device moved by human power or used exclusively upon stationary rails or tracks, in, on, or by which a person or property can be transported on a public highway. The term includes a motor vehicle, commercial motor vehicle, truck-tractor, trailer, or semitrailer but does not include manufactured housing as defined by the Texas Manufactured Housing Standards Act (Article 5221f, Texas Civil Statutes).

*(Added by L.1995, chap. 165(1), eff. 9/1/95.)*

### §621.002. Vehicle registration receipt for certain heavy vehicles.

(a) A copy of the registration receipt issued under Section 502.178 for a commercial motor vehicle, truck-tractor, trailer, or semitrailer shall be:

(1) carried on the vehicle when the vehicle is on a public highway; and

(2) presented to an officer authorized to enforce this chapter on request of the officer.

(b) A copy of the registration receipt is:

(1) admissible in evidence in any cause in which the gross registered weight of the vehicle is an issue; and

(2) prima facie evidence of the gross weight for which the vehicle is registered.

*(Added by L.1995, chap. 165(1), eff. 9/1/95.)*

### §621.003. Reciprocal agreement with another state for issuance of permits.

(a) The commission by rule may authorize the director to enter into with the proper authority of another state an agreement that authorizes:

(1) the authority of the other state to issue on behalf of the department to the owner or operator of a vehicle, or combination of vehicles, that exceeds the weight or size limits allowed by this state a permit that authorizes the operation or transportation on a highway in this state of the vehicle or combination of vehicles; and

(2) the department to issue on behalf of the authority of the other state to the owner or operator of a vehicle, or combination of vehicles, that exceeds the weight or size limits allowed by that state

a permit that authorizes the operation or transportation on a highway of that state of the vehicle or combination of vehicles.

(b) A permit issued by the authority of another state under an agreement entered into under this section has the same validity in this state as a permit issued by the department.

(c) The holder of a permit issued by the authority of another state under an agreement entered into under this section is subject to all applicable laws of this state and rules of the department.

(d) The department may contract with a third party to act as the department's agent in the processing of a permit application and the distribution of a permit issued by the department under this section.

(e) An agreement entered into under this section may provide for a third party to act as the agent of each state in the processing of a permit application and the distribution of a permit issued by a state under this section.
*(Added by L.1995, chap. 165(1); chgd. by L.1997, chap. 515(1), eff. 9/1/97.)*

### §621.004. Admissibility of certificate of vertical clearance.

In each civil or criminal proceeding in which a violation of this chapter may be an issue, a certificate of the vertical clearance of a structure, including a bridge or underpass, signed by the director is admissible in evidence for all purposes. *(Added by L.1995, chap. 165(1), eff. 9/1/95.)*

### §621.005. Effect of increased limits by United States.

If the United States prescribes or adopts vehicle size or weight limits greater than those prescribed by 23 U.S.C. Section 127 on March 18, 1975, for the national system of interstate and defense highways, the increased limits apply to the national system of interstate and defense highways in this state. *(Added by L.1995, chap. 165(1), eff. 9/1/95.)*

### §621.006. Restricted operation on certain holidays.

The department by rule may impose restrictions on the weight and size of vehicles to be operated on state highways on the following holidays only:

(1) New Year's Day;
(2) Memorial Day;
(3) Independence Day;
(4) Labor Day;
(5) Thanksgiving Day; and
(6) Christmas Day.

*(Added by L.1995, chap. 165(1), eff. 9/1/95.)*

### §§621.007 to 621.100. *(Reserved.)*

## SUBCHAPTER B. WEIGHT LIMITATIONS

### §621.101. Maximum weight of load.

(a) A vehicle or combination of vehicles may not be operated over or on a public highway outside the territory of a municipality, over or on a state-maintained public highway inside the territory of a municipality, or at a port-of-entry between Texas and the United Mexican States if the vehicle or combination has:

(1) an axle that carries a load heavier than:

(A) 16,000 pounds on high-pressure tires; or

(B) 20,000 pounds on low-pressure tires, including all enforcement tolerances;

(2) a tandem axle weight heavier than 34,000 pounds, including all enforcement tolerances;

(3) an overall gross weight on a group of two or more consecutive axles heavier than the weight computed using the following formula and rounding the result to the nearest 500 pounds:

$W = 500((LN/(N - 1)) + 12N + 36)$

where:

"W" is maximum overall gross weight on the group;

"L" is distance in feet between the axles of the group that are the farthest apart; and

"N" is number of axles in the group;

(4) a weight heavier than:

(A) 600 pounds for each inch of tire width concentrated on the surface of the highway on a wheel using high-pressure tires; or

(B) 650 pounds for each inch of tire width concentrated on the surface of the highway on a wheel using low-pressure tires; or

(5) a wheel that carries a load heavier than:

(A) 8,000 pounds on high-pressure tires; or

(B) 10,000 pounds on low-pressure tires.

(b) Notwithstanding Subsection (a)(3), two consecutive sets of tandem axles may carry a gross load of not more than 34,000 pounds each if the overall distance between the first and last axles of the consecutive sets is 36 feet or more. The overall gross weight on a group of two or more consecutive axles may not be heavier than 80,000 pounds, including all enforcement tolerances.

(c) This section does not:

(1) authorize size or weight limits on the national system of interstate and defense highways in this state greater than those permitted under 23 U.S.C. Section 127; or

(2) prohibit the operation of a vehicle or combination of vehicles that could be lawfully operated on a highway or road of this state on December 16, 1974.

(d) For the purposes of this section, the load carried on an axle is the total load transmitted to the road by all wheels the centers of which can be included between two parallel transverse vertical planes 40 inches apart, extending across the full width of the vehicle.

*(Added by L.1995, chap. 165(1); chgd. by L.1999, chap. 601(1), eff. 9/1/99.)*

### §621.102. Commission's authority to set maximum weights.

(a) The commission may set the maximum gross weight of a vehicle and its load, maximum gross weight of a combination of vehicles and loads, maximum axle load, or maximum wheel load that may be moved over a state highway or a farm or ranch road if the commission finds that heavier maximum weight would rapidly deteriorate or destroy the road or a bridge or culvert along the road. A maximum weight or load set under this subsection may not exceed the maximum set by statute for that weight or load.

(b) The commission must set a maximum weight under this section by order entered in its minutes.

(c) The commission must make the finding under this section on an engineering and traffic investigation and in making the finding shall consider the width, condition, and type of pavement structures and other circumstances on the road.

(d) A maximum weight or load set under this section becomes effective on a highway or road when appropriate signs giving notice of the maximum weight or load are erected on the highway or road under order of the commission.

(e) This section does not affect a law that authorizes or provides for a special permit for a weight heavier than the maximum weight provided by law.

(f) For the purpose of this section, a farm or ranch road is a state highway that is shown in the records of the commission to be a farm-to-market or ranch-to-market road.

(g) This section does not apply to a vehicle delivering groceries, farm products, or liquefied petroleum gas.

*(Added by L.1995, chap. 165(1); chgd. by L.1997, chap. 165(30.131), eff. 9/1/97.)*

### §§621.103 to 621.200. *(Reserved.)*

## SUBCHAPTER C. SIZE LIMITATIONS

### §621.201. Maximum width.

(a) The total width of a vehicle operated on a public highway other than a vehicle to which Subsection (b) applies, including a load on the vehicle but excluding any safety device determined by the United States Department of Transportation or the Texas Department of Public Safety to be necessary for the safe and efficient operation of motor vehicles of that type, may not be greater than 102 inches.

(b) The total width of a passenger vehicle and its load may not be greater than eight feet. This subsection does not apply to a motor bus or trolley bus operated exclusively in the territory of a municipality, in suburbs contiguous to the municipality, or in the county in which the municipality is located.

(c) A passenger vehicle may not carry a load extending more than three inches beyond the left side line of its fenders or more than six inches beyond the right side line of its fenders.

*(Added by L.1995, chap. 165(1), eff. 9/1/95.)*

### §621.202. Commission's authority to set maximum width.

(a) To comply with safety and operational requirements of federal law, the commission by order may set the maximum width of a vehicle, including the load on the vehicle, at eight feet for a designated highway or segment of a highway if the results of an engineering and traffic study that includes an analysis of structural capacity of bridges and pavements, traffic volume, unique climatic conditions, and width of traffic lanes support the change.

(b) An order under this section becomes effective on the designated highway or segment when appropriate signs giving notice of the limitations are erected.

(c) This section is intended to comply with the Surface Transportation Assistance Act of 1982 (23 U.S.C. Section 101 et seq.) and is conditioned on that Act and federal regulations implementing that Act.

*(Added by L.1995, chap. 165(1), eff. 9/1/95.)*

## §621.203. Maximum length of motor vehicle.

(a) A motor vehicle, other than a truck-tractor, may not be longer than 45 feet.

(b) A motor bus as defined by Section 502.001 that is longer than 35 feet but not longer than 45 feet may be operated on a highway if the motor bus is equipped with air brakes and has either three or more axles or a minimum of four tires on the rear axle.

(c) The limitation prescribed by Subsection (a) does not apply to a house trailer or towable recreational vehicle or a combination of a house trailer or towable recreational vehicle and a motor vehicle. A house trailer or towable recreational vehicle and motor vehicle combination may not be longer than 65 feet.

(d) In this section, "house trailer" and "towable recreational vehicle" have the meanings assigned by Section 541.201.

*(Added by L.1995, chap. 165(1); chgd. by L.1997, chap. 1020(3), eff. 9/1/97.)*

## §621.204. Maximum length of semitrailer or trailer.

(a) A semitrailer that is operated in a truck-tractor and semitrailer combination may not be longer than 59 feet.

(b) A semitrailer or trailer that is operated in a truck-tractor, semitrailer, and trailer combination may not be longer than 28-½ feet.

(c) The limitations prescribed by this section do not include any safety device determined by regulation of the United States Department of Transportation or by rule of the Department of Public Safety to be necessary for the safe and efficient operation of motor vehicles.

(d) The limitations prescribed by this section do not apply to a semitrailer or trailer that has the dimensions of a semitrailer or trailer, as appropriate, that was being operated lawfully in this state on December 1, 1982.

*(Added by L.1995, chap. 165(1), eff. 9/1/95.)*

## §621.205. Maximum length of vehicle combinations.

(a) Except as provided by this section, a combination of not more than three vehicles, including a truck and semitrailer, truck and trailer, truck-tractor and semitrailer and trailer, or a truck-tractor and two trailers, may be coupled together if the combination of vehicles, other than a truck-tractor combination, is not longer than 65 feet.

(b) A passenger car or another motor vehicle that has an unloaded weight of less than 2,500 pounds may not be coupled with more than one other vehicle or towing device at one time. This subsection does not apply to the towing of a disabled vehicle to the nearest intake place for repair.

(c) A motor vehicle, including a passenger car, that has an unloaded weight of 2,500 pounds or more may be coupled with a towing device and one other vehicle.

(d) In this section:

(1) "Passenger car" means a motor vehicle designed to transport 10 or fewer persons simultaneously.

(2) "Towing device" means a device used to tow a vehicle behind a motor vehicle by supporting one end of the towed vehicle above the surface of the road and permitting the wheels at the other end of the towed vehicle to remain in contact with the road.

*(Added by L.1995, chap. 165(1), eff. 9/1/95.)*

## §621.206. Maximum extended length of load.

*A vehicle or combination of vehicles may not carry a load that extends more than three feet beyond its front or, except as permitted by other law, more than four feet beyond its rear.

**So in original. Probably should be designated subsection (a).*

(b) *(Repealed by L.1997, chap. 165(30.132), eff. 9/1/97.)*

(c) Subsection (a) does not apply to vehicles collecting garbage, rubbish, refuse, or recyclable materials which are equipped with front-end loading attachments and containers provided that the vehicle is actively engaged in the collection of garbage, rubbish, refuse, or recyclable materials.

*(Added by L.1995, chap. 165(1); chgd. by L.1997, chaps. 25(1), 165(30.132), eff. 9/1/97.)*

### §621.2061. Exception to maximum extended length of load: certain motor vehicles.

Notwithstanding Section 621.206, a trailer may carry a load that extends more than four feet beyond the rear of the trailer if the load consists of a motor vehicle that:

(1) is designed and intended to be carried at the rear of the trailer;

(2) is used or intended to be used to load or unload a commodity on or off the trailer;

(3) does not extend more than seven feet beyond the rear of the trailer; and

(4) complies with each applicable federal motor carrier safety regulation.

*(Added by L.1997, chap. 25(2), eff. 9/1/97.)*

### §621.207. Maximum height.

(a) A vehicle and its load may not be higher than 14 feet.

(b) The operator of a vehicle that is higher than 13 feet 6 inches shall ensure that the vehicle will pass through each vertical clearance of a structure in its path without touching the structure.

(c) Any damage to a bridge, underpass, or similar structure that is caused by the height of a vehicle is the responsibility of the owner of the vehicle.

*(Added by L.1995, chap. 165(1), eff. 9/1/95.)*



### §§621.208 to 621.300. *(Reserved.)*

## SUBCHAPTER D. LOCAL REGULATIONS

### §621.301. County's authority to set maximum weights.

(a) The commissioners court of a county may establish load limits for any county road or bridge.

(b) The commissioners court may limit the maximum weights to be moved on or over a county road, bridge, or culvert by exercising its authority under this subsection in the same manner and under the same conditions provided by Section 621.102 for the commission to limit maximum weights on highways and roads to which that section applies.

(c) The commissioners court shall record an action under Subsection (b) in its minutes.

(d) A maximum weight set under this section becomes effective on a road when appropriate signs giving notice of the maximum weight are erected on the road under order of the commissioners court.

(e) This section does not affect a law that authorizes or provides for special permits for a weight heavier than the maximum weight provided by law.

*(Added by L.1995, chap. 165(1), eff. 9/1/95.)*

### §621.302. Exception to county's weight limitations.

A maximum weight set under Section 621.301 does not apply to a vehicle delivering groceries or farm products to a destination requiring travel over a road for which the maximum is set. *(Added by L.1995, chap. 165(1), eff. 9/1/95.)*

### §621.303. Municipal regulation of loads and equipment.

The governing body of any municipality may regulate the movement and operation on a public road, other than a state highway in the territory of the municipality, of:

(1) an overweight, oversize, or overlength commodity that cannot reasonably be dismantled; and

(2) superheavy or oversize equipment for the transportation of an overweight, oversize, or overlength commodity that cannot be reasonably dismantled.

*(Added by L.1995, chap. 165(1), eff. 9/1/95.)*

### §§621.304 to 621.350. *(Reserved.)*

## SUBCHAPTER E. FEES

### §621.351. Escrow account for prepayment of permit fees.

(a) The department may establish one or more escrow accounts in the state highway fund for the prepayment of a fee for a permit issued by the department that authorizes the operation of a vehicle and its load or a combination of vehicles and load exceeding size or weight limitations.

(b) The fees and any fees established by the department for the administration of this section shall be administered in accordance with an agreement containing terms and conditions agreeable to the department.

(c) The department shall deposit each fee established under this section to the credit of the state highway fund. The fees may be appropriated only to the department for purposes of administering this section.
*(Added by L.1995, chap. 165(1), eff. 9/1/95.)*

### §621.352. Fees for permits issued under reciprocal agreement.

(a) The commission by rule may establish fees for the administration of Section 621.003 in an amount that, when added to the other fees collected by the department, does not exceed the amount sufficient to recover the actual cost to the department of administering that section. An administrative fee collected under this section shall be sent to the comptroller for deposit to the credit of the state highway fund and may be appropriated only to the department for the administration of Section 621.003.

(b) A permit fee collected by the department under Section 621.003 for another state shall be sent to the comptroller for deposit to the credit of the permit distributive account in the general revenue fund. The comptroller shall distribute money in the permit distributive account only to the proper authorities of other states and only as directed by the department.
*(Added by L.1995, chap. 165(1); chgd. by L.1997, chap. 1423(18.12), eff. 9/1/97.)*

### §621.353. Distribution of fee for permit for excess weight.

(a) The comptroller shall send $50 of each base fee collected under Section 623.011 for an excess weight permit to the counties of the state, with each county receiving an amount determined according to the ratio of the total number of miles of county roads maintained by the county to the total number of miles of county roads maintained by all of the counties of this state. The comptroller shall deposit $25 of each base fee, plus each fee collected under Section 623.0112, to the credit of the state highway fund. Money deposited to the credit of that fund under this subsection may be appropriated only to the department to administer this section and Sections 623.011, 623.0111, and 623.0112.

(b) The comptroller shall send the amount due each county under Subsection (a) to the county treasurer or officer performing the function of that office at least twice each fiscal year.

(c) The comptroller shall send each fee collected under Section 623.0112 for an excess weight permit to the counties designated on the application for the permit, with each county shown on the application receiving an amount determined according to the ratio of the total number of miles of county roads maintained by the county to the total number of miles of county roads maintained by all of the counties designated on the application.

(d) The county treasurer or officer shall deposit amounts received under this section to the credit of the county road and bridge fund. Money deposited to the credit of that fund under this subsection may be used only for a purpose authorized by Section 256.001(a).
*(Added by L.1995, chap. 165(1); chgd. by L.1997, chaps. 165(30.133(a)), 1423(18.13), eff. 9/1/97.)*

### §621.354. Disposition of fees for permit for movement of cylindrical hay bales.

The department shall deposit each fee collected under Section 623.017 in the state treasury to the credit of the state highway fund. *(Added by L.1995, chap. 165(1), eff. 9/1/95.)*

### §621.355. Distribution of fees for registration of additional weight.

(a) If an operator or owner is required to pay for registration of additional weight under Section 621.406 in a county other than the county in which the owner resides, the assessor-collector of the county in which the payment is made shall send the amount collected to the department for deposit to the credit of the state highway fund.

(b) The department shall send the county's share of the amount collected under Section 621.406 to the county in which the owner resides.
*(Added by L.1995, chap. 165(1), eff. 9/1/95.)*

### §621.356. Form of payment.

The commission may adopt rules prescribing the method for payment of a fee for a permit issued by the department that authorizes the operation of a vehicle and its load or a combination of vehicles and load exceeding size or weight limitations. The rules may:

(1) authorize the use of electronic funds transfer or a credit card issued by:

(A) a financial institution chartered by a state or the federal government; or

(B) a nationally recognized credit organization approved by the commission; and

(2) require the payment of a discount or service charge for a credit card payment in addition to the fee.
*(Added by L.1997, chap. 515(2), eff. 9/1/97.)*

**§§621.357 to 621.400.** *(Reserved.)*

## SUBCHAPTER F. ENFORCEMENT

### §621.401. Definition.

In this subchapter, "weight enforcement officer" means:

(1) a license and weight inspector of the Department of Public Safety;

(2) a highway patrol officer;

(3) a sheriff or sheriff's deputy;

(4) a municipal police officer in a municipality with a population of:

(A) 100,000 or more; or

(B) 74,000 or more in a county with a population of more than 1.5 million; or

(5) a police officer certified under Section 644.101.

*(Added by L.1995, chap. 165(1); chgd. by L.1997, chap. 364(3); L.1999, chaps. 62(17.09), 1523(1), eff. 9/1/99.)*



### §621.402. Weighing loaded vehicle.

(a) A weight enforcement officer who has reason to believe that the gross weight or axle load of a loaded motor vehicle is unlawful may:

(1) weigh the vehicle using portable or stationary scales furnished or approved by the Department of Public Safety; or

(2) require the vehicle to be weighed by a public weigher.

(b) The officer may require that the vehicle be driven to the nearest available scales.

*(Added by L.1995, chap. 165(1), eff. 9/1/95.)*

### §621.403. Unloading vehicle if gross weight exceeded.

(a) If the gross weight of a motor vehicle weighed under Section 621.402 is heavier than the weight equal to the maximum gross weight authorized by law for that vehicle plus a tolerance allowance equal to five percent of that maximum weight, the weight enforcement officer shall require the operator or owner of the vehicle to unload a part of the load necessary to decrease the gross weight of the vehicle to a gross weight that is not heavier than the weight equal to the vehicle's maximum gross weight plus the applicable tolerance allowance.

(b) The operator or owner of the vehicle immediately shall unload the vehicle to the extent necessary to reduce the gross weight as required by Subsection (a), and the vehicle may not be operated further over a public highway or road of this state until the gross weight has been reduced as required by Subsection (a).

### §621.404. Unloading vehicle if axle load exceeded.

(a) If the axle load of a motor vehicle weighed under Section 621.402 is heavier than the maximum axle load authorized by law for the vehicle plus a tolerance allowance equal to five percent of that maximum load, the weight enforcement officer shall require the operator or owner of the vehicle to rearrange the vehicle's cargo, if possible, to bring the vehicle's axles within the maximum axle load allowed by law for that vehicle. If the requirement cannot be satisfied by rearrangement of cargo, a part of the vehicle's load shall be unloaded to decrease the axle load to a weight that is not heavier than the maximum axle load allowed by law for the vehicle plus the applicable tolerance allowance.

(b) The vehicle may not be operated further over the public highways or roads of the state until the axle load of the vehicle has been reduced as required by Subsection (a).

*(Added by L.1995, chap. 165(1), eff. 9/1/95.)*

### §621.405. Unloading exceptions.

(a) The operator or owner of a vehicle is not required to unload any part of the vehicle's load under Section 621.403 or 621.404 if the vehicle is:

(1) a motor vehicle loaded with timber, pulp wood, or agricultural products in their natural state being transported from the place of production to the place of marketing or first processing; or

(2) a vehicle crossing a highway as provided by Subchapter C, Chapter 623.

(b) The operator of a motor vehicle may proceed to the vehicle's destination without unloading the vehicle as required by Section 621.403 or 621.404 if:

(1) the vehicle is loaded with livestock; and

(2) the vehicle's destination is in this state.

*(Added by L.1995, chap. 165(1), eff. 9/1/95.)*

### §621.406. Additional gross weight registration.

(a) If the gross weight of the motor vehicle is not heavier than the maximum gross weight allowed for the vehicle but is heavier than the registered gross weight for the vehicle, the weight enforcement officer shall require the operator or owner of the vehicle to apply to the nearest available county assessor-collector to increase the gross weight for which the vehicle is registered to a weight equal to or heavier than the gross weight of the vehicle before the operator or owner may proceed.

(b) The vehicle may not be operated further over the public highways or roads of the state until the registered gross weight of the vehicle has been increased as required by Subsection (a) unless the load consists of livestock or perishable merchandise, in which event the operator or owner may proceed with the vehicle in the direction of the vehicle's destination to the nearest practical location at which the vehicle's load can be protected from damage or destruction before increasing the registered weight.

(c) If an operator or owner is found to be carrying a load that is heavier than the load allowed for the registered gross weight of the vehicle, the operator or owner shall pay for the registration of the additional weight for the entire period for which the vehicle is registered without regard to whether the owner or operator has been carrying similar loads from the date of purchase of the vehicle's current license registration for that registration period.
*(Added by L.1995, chap. 165(1), eff. 9/1/95.)*



### §621.407. Forms; accounting procedures.

The department shall prescribe all forms and accounting procedures necessary to carry out Sections 621.401—621.406. *(Added by L.1995, chap. 165(1), eff. 9/1/95.)*

### §621.408. Powers of weight enforcement officers.

Except for the authority granted to a port-of-entry supervisor or inspector by Section 621.409, weight enforcement officers have exclusive authority:

(1) to enforce this subchapter in any area of this state other than in the territory of a municipality with a population of more than:

(A) 100,000; or

(B) 74,000 in a county with a population of more than 1.5 million; and

(2) to enforce all weight limitations for a vehicle on a state-maintained public highway or at a port-of-entry between Texas and the United Mexican States.
*(Added by L.1995, chap. 165(1); chgd. by L.1999, chaps. 601(2), 1523(2), eff. 9/1/99.)*

### §621.409. Weighing of loaded vehicles by port-of-entry supervisors, inspectors, or weight enforcement officers.

(a) A port-of-entry supervisor, an inspector employed by the Alcoholic Beverage Commission, or a weight enforcement officer who has reason to believe that the gross weight or axle load of a loaded motor vehicle is unlawful may weigh the vehicle using portable or stationary scales furnished or approved by the Department of Public Safety.

(b) If the vehicle exceeds the maximum gross weight authorized by law, plus the tolerance allowance provided by Section 621.403, the supervisor, inspector, or weight enforcement officer may prohibit the vehicle from proceeding farther into the state.
*(Added by L.1995, chap. 165(1); chgd. by L.1997, chap. 364(4), eff. 5/27/97.)*

### §§621.410 to 621.500. *(Reserved.)*

## SUBCHAPTER G. OFFENSES AND PENALTIES

### §621.501. Failure to carry or present vehicle license receipt.

(a) A person commits an offense if the person fails in violation of Section 621.002 to carry or present a vehicle registration receipt.

(b) An offense under this section is a misdemeanor punishable by a fine not to exceed $200.
*(Added by L.1995, chap. 165(1), eff. 9/1/95.)*

### §621.502. Prohibitions on size and weight; restrictions on construction and equipment.

(a) A person may not operate or move a vehicle on a highway if:

(1) the vehicle's size is larger than the applicable maximum size authorized for that vehicle by this subtitle;

(2) the vehicle's weight, axle load, or wheel load is greater than the applicable weight or load authorized for that vehicle by this subtitle; or

(3) the vehicle is not constructed or equipped as required by this chapter.

(b) The owner of a vehicle the size of which or the weight, axle load, or wheel load of which is greater than the applicable maximum size, weight, or load authorized for that vehicle by this subtitle or a vehicle that is not constructed or equipped as required by this chapter may not cause or allow the vehicle to be operated or moved on a highway.

(c) A person may not transport on a vehicle a load the size or weight of which is more than the applicable maximum size, weight, or load authorized for that vehicle by this subtitle.

(d) Intent to operate a vehicle at a weight that is heavier than the weight authorized by a permit issued under Section 623.011 is presumed if:

(1) the vehicle is operated at a weight that is heavier than the applicable weight plus the tolerance allowance provided by Section 623.011(a); and

(2) a permit to operate at that weight has not been issued for the vehicle.

*(Added by L.1995, chap. 165(1), eff. 9/1/95.)*



### §621.503. Prohibition of loading more than weight limitation.

(a) A person may not load, or cause to be loaded, a vehicle for operation on a public highway of this state that exceeds the weight limitations for operation of that vehicle provided by Section 621.101.

(b) Intent to violate a limitation is presumed if the weight of the loaded vehicle is heavier than the applicable gross vehicular weight limit or axle load limit by 15 percent or more.

(c) This section does not apply to the loading of an agricultural or a forestry commodity before the commodity is changed in processing from its natural state.

*(Added by L.1995, chap. 165(1); chgd. by L.1997, chap. 364(5), eff. 5/27/97.)*

### §621.504. Bridge or underpass clearance.

A person may not operate or attempt to operate a vehicle over or on a bridge or through an underpass or similar structure unless the height of the vehicle, including load, is less than the vertical clearance of the structure as shown by the records of the department. *(Added by L.1995, chap. 165(1), eff. 9/1/95.)*

### §621.505. Maximum size and weight of containers.

A person may not operate or move over a highway of this state, or an owner may not cause to be operated or moved over a highway of this state, a motor vehicle or combination of motor vehicles that has a product, commodity, good, ware, or merchandise that is in a container or binding that contains more than 30 cubic feet and weighs more than 500 pounds if:

(1) more than 14 of those containers or bindings are being carried as a load on that vehicle or combination; or

(2) the load on the vehicle or combination exceeds 7,000 pounds.

*(Added by L.1995, chap. 165(1), eff. 9/1/95.)*

### §621.506. Offense of operating or loading overweight vehicle; penalty; defense.

(a) A person commits an offense if the person:

(1) operates a vehicle or combination of vehicles in violation of Section 621.101; or

(2) loads a vehicle or causes a vehicle to be loaded in violation of Section 621.503.

(b) An offense under this section is a misdemeanor punishable:

(1) by a fine of not less than $100 and not more than $150;

(2) on conviction of an offense involving a vehicle having a gross weight that is more than 5,000 but not more than 10,000 pounds heavier than the vehicle's allowable gross weight, by a fine of not less than $300 or more than $500;

(3) on conviction of an offense involving a vehicle having a gross weight that is more than 10,000 pounds heavier than the vehicle's allowable gross weight, by a fine of not less than $500 or more than $1,000; or

(4) on conviction before the first anniversary of the date of a previous conviction under this section, by a fine in an amount that is twice the amount specified by Subdivision (1), (2), or (3).

(c) On conviction of a violation of an axle load limitation, the court may assess a fine less than the applicable minimum amount prescribed by Subsection (b) if the court finds that when the violation occurred:

(1) the vehicle was registered to carry the maximum gross weight authorized for that vehicle under Section 621.101; and

(2) the gross weight of the vehicle did not exceed that maximum gross weight.

(d) A judge or justice shall promptly report to the Department of Public Safety each conviction obtained in the judge's or the justice's court under this section. The Department of Public Safety shall keep a record of each conviction reported to it under this subsection.

(e) If a corporation fails to pay the fine assessed on conviction of an offense under this section, the district or county attorney in the county in which the conviction occurs may file suit against the corporation to collect the fine.

(f) A justice court has jurisdiction of an offense under this section. A municipal court has jurisdiction of an offense under this section for which the fine does not exceed $500.

(g) A governmental entity that collects a fine under this section for an offense involving a vehicle having a gross weight that is more than 5,000 pounds heavier than the vehicle's allowable gross weight shall send an amount equal to 50 percent of the fine to the comptroller unless the offense occurred within 20 miles of an international border in which event the entire amount of the fine shall be deposited for the purposes of road maintenance in:

(1) the municipal treasury, if the fine was imposed by a municipal court; or

(2) the county treasury, if the fine was imposed by a justice court.

*(Added by L.1995, chap. 165(1); chgd. by L.1997, chap. 165(30.133(b)); L.1999, chap. 1101(1), eff. 9/1/99.)*



## §621.507. General offense; penalty.

(a) A person commits an offense if the person violates a provision of this subchapter for which an offense is not specified by another section of this subchapter.

(b) An offense under this section is a misdemeanor punishable:

(1) by a fine not to exceed $200;

(2) on conviction before the first anniversary of the date of a previous conviction under this section:

(A) by a fine not to exceed $500, by confinement in a county jail for not more than 60 days, or by both the fine and confinement; or

(B) if the convicted person is a corporation, by a fine not to exceed $1,000; or

(3) on a conviction before the first anniversary of the date of a previous conviction under this section that was punishable under Subdivision (2) or this subdivision:

(A) by a fine not to exceed $1,000, by confinement in the county jail for not more than six months, or by both the fine and confinement; or

(B) if the convicted person is a corporation, by a fine not to exceed $2,000.

*(Added by L.1995, chap. 165(1), eff. 9/1/95.)*

## §621.508. Affirmative defense for operating vehicle with heavy axle load.

It is an affirmative defense to prosecution of, or an action under Subchapter F for, the offense of operating a vehicle with an axle load heavier than the axle load authorized by law that at the time of the offense the vehicle:

(1) had an axle weight that was not heavier than the axle load authorized by law plus 12 percent;

(2) was loaded with timber, pulp wood, wood chips, cotton, or agricultural products in their natural state; and

(3) was not being operated on a portion of the national system of interstate and defense highways.

*(Added by L.1995, chap. 165(1), eff. 9/1/95.)*

# CHAPTER 622. SPECIAL PROVISIONS AND EXCEPTIONS FOR OVERSIZE OR OVERWEIGHT VEHICLES

## SUBCHAPTER A. GENERAL PROVISIONS

## SUBCHAPTER B. VEHICLES TRANSPORTING READY-MIXED CONCRETE

622.011. Definition; designation as perishable.
622.012. Axle-load restrictions.
622.013. Surety bond.
622.014. Local regulation.
622.015. Local surety bond.
622.016. Interstate and defense highways.
622.017. Penalties.
622.018 to
622.030. *(Reserved.)*

## SUBCHAPTER C. VEHICLES TRANSPORTING MILK

622.031. Length and axle-load restrictions.
622.032. Interstate and defense highways.
622.033. Penalties.
622.034 to
622.040. *(Reserved.)*

## SUBCHAPTER D. VEHICLES TRANSPORTING TIMBER OR TIMBER PRODUCTS

622.041. Length limitation.
622.042. Time of operation; display of flag, cloth, or strobe light.
622.043. Conformity with general provisions relating to vehicle size and weight.
622.0435. Vehicles transporting raw wood products.
622.044. Extension of load beyond rear of vehicle.
622.045 to
622.050. *(Reserved.)*

## SUBCHAPTER E. VEHICLES TRANSPORTING ELECTRIC POWER TRANSMISSION POLES

622.051. Length limitation; fee.
622.052. Time of operation; speed; lighting requirements.
622.053. Conformity with general provisions relating to vehicle size and weight.
622.054 to
622.060. *(Reserved.)*

## SUBCHAPTER F. VEHICLES TRANSPORTING POLES OR PIPE

622.061. Length limitation.
622.062. Time of operation; lighting requirements.
622.063. Conformity with general provisions relating to vehicle size and weight.
622.064 to
622.070. *(Reserved.)*

## SUBCHAPTER G. SPECIAL MOBILE EQUIPMENT

622.071. Definition.
622.072. Identification markings on special mobile equipment; offense.
622.073. Transportation of special mobile equipment; offense.
622.074. Nonapplicability of subchapter.
622.075 to
622.080. *(Reserved.)*

## SUBCHAPTER H. VEHICLES TRANSPORTING LUMBER



## SUBCHAPTER I. VEHICLES TRANSPORTING COTTON OR COTTON PROCESSING EQUIPMENT



## SUBCHAPTER J. CERTAIN VEHICLES TRANSPORTING RECYCLABLE MATERIALS



## SUBCHAPTER Y. MISCELLANEOUS SIZE EXCEPTIONS



## SUBCHAPTER Z. MISCELLANEOUS WEIGHT EXCEPTIONS



## SUBCHAPTER A. GENERAL PROVISIONS

### §622.001. Definition.

In this chapter, "department" means the Texas Department of Transportation. *(Added by L.1995, chap. 165(1), eff. 9/1/95.)*

### §§622.002 to 622.010. *(Reserved.)*

## SUBCHAPTER B. VEHICLES TRANSPORTING READY-MIXED CONCRETE

### §622.011. Definition; designation as perishable.

(a) In this subchapter, "ready-mixed concrete truck" means:

(1) a vehicle designed exclusively to transport or manufacture ready-mixed concrete and includes a vehicle designed exclusively to transport and manufacture ready-mixed concrete; or

(2) a concrete pump truck.

(b) Ready-mixed concrete is a perishable product.

*(Added by L.1995, chap. 165(1); chgd. by L.1997, chap. 165(30.134(a)), eff. 9/1/97.)*

### §622.012. Axle-load restrictions.

(a) A ready-mixed concrete truck may be operated on a public highway of this state only if the tandem axle load is not heavier than 46,000 pounds and the single axle load is not heavier than 23,000 pounds.

(b) A truck may be operated at a weight that exceeds the maximum single axle or tandem axle load limitation by not more than 10 percent if the gross load is not heavier than 69,000 pounds. *(Added by L.1995, chap. 165(1); chgd. by L.1997, chap. 165(30.135), eff. 9/1/97.)*

**§622.013. Surety bond.**

(a) The owner of a ready-mixed concrete truck with a tandem axle load heavier than 34,000 pounds shall before operating the vehicle on a public highway of this state file with the department a surety bond subject to the approval of the department in the principal amount set by the department not to exceed $15,000 for each truck.

(b) The bond must be conditioned that the owner of the truck will pay to the state, within the limit of the bond, any damage to a highway caused by the operation of the truck.

*(Added by L.1995, chap. 165(1), eff. 9/1/95.)*

**§622.014. Local regulation.**

(a) The governing body of a county or municipality that determines a public highway under its jurisdiction is insufficient to carry a load authorized by Section 622.012 may prescribe, by order or ordinance, rules governing the operation of a ready-mixed concrete truck over a public highway maintained by the county or municipality.

(b) The rules may include weight limitations on a truck with:

(1) a tandem axle load that is heavier than 36,000 pounds;

(2) a single axle load that is heavier than 12,000 pounds; or

(3) a gross load that is heavier than 48,000 pounds.

*(Added by L.1995, chap. 165(1), eff. 9/1/95.)*

**§622.015. Local surety bond.**

The governing body of a county or municipality may require the owner of a ready-mixed concrete truck to file a surety bond in an amount not to exceed $15,000 and conditioned that the owner of the truck will pay to the county or municipality any damage to a highway caused by the operation of the truck with a tandem axle load that is heavier than 34,000 pounds. *(Added by L.1995, chap. 165(1), eff. 9/1/95.)*

**§622.016. Interstate and defense highways.**

(a) This subchapter does not authorize the operation on the national system of interstate and defense highways in this state of a vehicle of a size or weight greater than that authorized by 23 U.S.C. Section 127, as amended.

(b) If the United States authorizes the operation on the national system of interstate and defense highways of a vehicle of a size or weight greater than that authorized on January 1, 1977, the new limit automatically takes effect on the national system of interstate and defense highways in this state.

*(Added by L.1995, chap. 165(1), eff. 9/1/95.)*

**§622.017. Penalties.**

(a) A person commits an offense if the person violates this subchapter.

(b) Except as provided by Subsection (c), an offense under this section is a misdemeanor punishable:

(1) by a fine of not more than $200;

(2) on conviction within one year after the date of a prior conviction under this section that was punishable under Subdivision (1), by a fine of not more than $500, by confinement in the county jail for not more than 60 days, or by both the fine and the confinement; or

(3) on conviction within one year after the date of a prior conviction under this section that was punishable under Subdivision (2) or this subdivision, by a fine of not more than $1,000, by confinement in the county jail for not more than six months, or by both the fine and the confinement.

(c) A corporation is not subject to confinement for an offense under this section, but two times the maximum fine provided for in the applicable subdivision of Subsection (b) may be imposed against the corporation.

*(Added by L.1995, chap. 165(1), eff. 9/1/95.)*

**§§622.018 to 622.030.** *(Reserved.)*

## SUBCHAPTER C. VEHICLES TRANSPORTING MILK

### §622.031. Length and axle-load restrictions.

A vehicle used exclusively to transport milk may be operated on a public highway of this state only if:

(1) the distance between the front wheel of the forward tandem axle and the rear wheel of the rear tandem axle, measured longitudinally, is 28 feet or more; and

(2) the load carried on any group of axles is not heavier than 68,000 pounds.

*(Added by L.1995, chap. 165(1), eff. 9/1/95.)*

### §622.032. Interstate and defense highways.

(a) This subchapter does not authorize the operation on the national system of interstate and defense highways in this state of a vehicle of a size or weight greater than that authorized by 23 U.S.C. Section 127, as amended.

(b) If the United States authorizes the operation on the national system of interstate and defense highways of a vehicle of a size or weight greater than that authorized by 23 U.S.C. Section 127 on August 29, 1977, the new limit takes effect on the national system of interstate and defense highways in this state.

*(Added by L.1995, chap. 165(1), eff. 9/1/95.)*

### §622.033. Penalties.

(a) A person commits an offense if the person violates this subchapter.

(b) Except as provided by Subsection (c), an offense under this section is a misdemeanor punishable:

(1) by a fine of not more than $200;

(2) on conviction within one year after the date of a prior conviction under this section that was punishable under Subdivision (1), by a fine of not more than $500, by confinement in the county jail for not more than 60 days, or by both the fine and the confinement; or

(3) on conviction within one year after the date of a prior conviction under this section that was punishable under Subdivision (2) or this subdivision, by a fine of not more than $1,000, by confinement in the county jail for not more than six months, or by both the fine and the confinement.

(c) A corporation is not subject to confinement for an offense under this section, but two times the maximum fine provided for in the applicable subdivision of Subsection (b) may be imposed against the corporation.

*(Added by L.1995, chap. 165(1), eff. 9/1/95.)*

### §§622.034 to 622.040. *(Reserved.)*

## SUBCHAPTER D. VEHICLES TRANSPORTING TIMBER OR TIMBER PRODUCTS

### §622.041. Length limitation.

(a) A person may operate over a highway or road of this state a vehicle or combination of vehicles that is used exclusively for transporting poles, piling, or unrefined timber from the point of origin of the timber (the forest where the timber is felled) to a wood processing mill if:

(1) the vehicle, or combination of vehicles, is not longer than 90 feet, including the load; and

(2) the distance from the point of origin to the destination or delivery point does not exceed 125 miles.

(b) The limitation in Subsection (a)(1) does not apply to a truck-tractor or truck-tractor combination transporting poles, piling, or unrefined timber.

*(Added by L.1995, chap. 165(1), eff. 9/1/95.)*

### §622.042. Time of operation; display of flag, cloth, or strobe light.

(a) A vehicle subject to this subchapter may be operated only during daytime.

(b) In this section, "daytime" has the meaning assigned by Section 541.401.

(c) A red flag or cloth not less than 12 inches square or a strobe light must be displayed at the rear of the load carried on the vehicle so that the light or the entire area of the flag or cloth is visible to the driver of a vehicle approaching from the rear.

*(Added by L.1995, chap. 165(1); chgd. by L.1997, chap. 165(30.134(b)); L.1999, chap. 749(1), eff. 9/1/99.)*

### §622.043. Conformity with general provisions relating to vehicle size and weight.

The width, height, and gross weight of a vehicle or combination of vehicles subject to this subchapter shall conform to Chapter 621. *(Added by L.1995, chap. 165(1), eff. 9/1/95.)*

### §622.0435. Vehicles transporting raw wood products.

(a) The width, height, and gross weight of a vehicle or combination of vehicles subject to this subchapter that is transporting raw wood products shall conform to Chapters 621 and 623, except that when it is necessary to transport the load, the distance between axles on a vehicle may be shortened by not more than 12 feet for gross weight determinations.

(b) Notwithstanding any other provision of law, Subsection (a) does not authorize the operation of a vehicle or combination of vehicles subject to this subchapter that is transporting raw wood products on a bridge with a load limitation at a weight that exceeds that limitation.
*(Added by L.1997, chap. 1106(1), eff. 9/1/97.)*

### §622.044. Extension of load beyond rear of vehicle.

Section 621.206(a) does not apply to a vehicle to which this subchapter applies to the extent that section prescribes a limit on the extension of the load beyond the rear of the vehicle. *(Added by L.1995, chap. 165(1), eff. 9/1/95.)*

### §§622.045 to 622.050. *(Reserved.)*



## SUBCHAPTER E. VEHICLES TRANSPORTING ELECTRIC POWER TRANSMISSION POLES

### §622.051. Length limitation; fee.

(a) A person may operate over a highway or road of this state a vehicle or combination of vehicles that is used exclusively for transporting poles required for the maintenance of electric power transmission and distribution lines if:

(1) the vehicle, or combination of vehicles, is not longer than 75 feet, including the load; and

(2) the operator of the vehicle, or combination of vehicles, pays to the department $120 each calendar year.

(b) The limitation in Subsection (a)(1) does not apply to a truck-tractor or truck-tractor combination transporting poles for the maintenance of electric power transmission or distribution lines.
*(Added by L.1995, chap. 165(1), eff. 9/1/95.)*

### §622.052. Time of operation; speed; lighting requirements.

(a) A vehicle to which this subchapter applies may be operated only:

(1) between sunrise and sunset as defined by law; and

(2) at a speed not to exceed 50 miles per hour.

(b) A vehicle to which this subchapter applies shall display on the extreme end of the load:

(1) two red lamps visible at a distance of at least 500 feet from the rear;

(2) two red reflectors that indicate the maximum width and are visible, when light is insufficient or atmospheric conditions are unfavorable, at all distances from 100 to 600 feet from the rear when directly in front of lawful lower beams of headlamps; and

(3) two red lamps, one on each side, that indicate the maximum overhang and are visible at a distance of at least 500 feet from the side.

(c) The limitation in Subsection (a)(1) does not apply to a vehicle being operated to prevent interruption or impairment of electric service or to restore electric service that has been interrupted.
*(Added by L.1995, chap. 165(1); chgd. by L.1999, chap. 749(2), (3), eff. 9/1/99.)*

### §622.053. Conformity with general provisions relating to vehicle size and weight.

The width, height, and gross weight of a vehicle or combination of vehicles to which this subchapter applies shall conform to Chapter 621. *(Added by L.1995, chap. 165(1), eff. 9/1/95.)*

### §§622.054 to 622.060. *(Reserved.)*

## SUBCHAPTER F. VEHICLES TRANSPORTING POLES OR PIPE

### §622.061. Length limitation.

(a) A person may operate over a highway or road of this state a vehicle or combination of vehicles exclusively for the transportation of poles or pipe if the vehicle or combination of vehicles is not longer than 65 feet, including the load.

(b) The limitation in Subsection (a) does not apply to a truck-tractor or truck-tractor combination transporting poles or pipe.

*(Added by L.1995, chap. 165(1), eff. 9/1/95.)*

### §622.062. Time of operation; lighting requirements.

(a) A vehicle to which this subchapter applies may be operated only during daytime.

(b) A vehicle to which this subchapter applies shall display on the extreme end of the load:

(1) two red lamps visible at a distance of at least 500 feet from the rear;

(2) two red reflectors that indicate the maximum width and are visible, when light is insufficient or atmospheric conditions are unfavorable, at all distances from 100 to 600 feet from the rear when directly in front of lawful lower beams of headlamps; and

(3) two red lamps, one on each side, that indicate the maximum overhang and are visible at a distance of at least 500 feet from the side.

(c) In this section, "daytime" has the meaning assigned by Section 541.401.

*(Added by L.1995, chap. 165(1); chgd. by L.1997, chaps. 165(30.134(c)), 1106(2); L.1999, chap. 749(4), (5), eff. 9/1/99.)*



### §622.063. Conformity with general provisions relating to vehicle size and weight.

A vehicle or combination of vehicles to which this subchapter applies shall conform to the length, width, height, and weight requirements of Chapter 621. *(Added by L.1995, chap. 165(1), eff. 9/1/95.)*

### §§622.064 to 622.070. *(Reserved.)*

## SUBCHAPTER G. SPECIAL MOBILE EQUIPMENT

### §622.071. Definition.

In this subchapter, "special mobile equipment" has the meaning assigned by Section 541.201. *(Added by L.1995, chap. 165(1), eff. 9/1/95.)*

### §622.072. Identification markings on special mobile equipment; offense.

(a) Before the 31st day after the date a person becomes the owner of a unit of special mobile equipment, the person shall mark in a conspicuous place on the main chassis the manufacturer's serial number, an operation identification number recognized by law enforcement agencies, or a company identification number in a manner that is visible from not less than 50 feet.

(b) A person commits an offense if the person:

(1) owns a unit of special mobile equipment; and

(2) fails to mark the unit as provided by this section.

(c) An offense under this section is a misdemeanor punishable by a fine of not less than $10 or more than $100 for each unit.

*(Added by L.1995, chap. 165(1), eff. 9/1/95.)*

### §622.073. Transportation of special mobile equipment; offense.

(a) A person commits an offense if the person transports on a public road or highway a unit of special mobile equipment that is not marked as required by Section 622.072.

(b) Except as provided by Subsection (c), an offense under this section is a misdemeanor punishable by a fine of not less than $25 or more than $200.

(c) An offense under this section is a misdemeanor punishable by a fine of not less than $200 or more than $500, confinement in the county jail for a term of not less than 60 days or more than 180 days, or both the fine and the confinement if:

(1) the person committing the offense fails or refuses to exhibit, on demand of a peace officer, a document that contains:

(A) the name, address, and telephone number of the owner of the unit of special mobile equipment;

(B) the place of origin of the unit, including the address of and telephone number at that point and the date the unit was picked up;

(C) the destination of the unit, including the address or telephone number;

(D) a description of the unit being transported, including the manufacturer's serial number and other identification numbers;

(E) a description of the motor vehicle transporting the unit; and

(F) the name, address, and telephone number of the person operating the motor vehicle transporting the unit;

(2) the person committing the offense exhibits a false or forged document purporting to contain the information described by Subdivision (1); or

(3) on inspection by the peace officer, the peace officer determines that the identification number of the unit of special mobile equipment has been removed, covered, or altered.

(d) For purposes of Subsection (c)(3), a peace officer has probable cause to inspect a unit of special mobile equipment to determine the identification numbers of the unit if:

(1) the person operating the motor vehicle transporting the unit fails or refuses to exhibit on demand a document described by Subsection (c)(1); or

(2) the unit is not marked as required by Section 622.072.

*(Added by L.1995, chap. 165(1), eff. 9/1/95.)*



### §622.074. Nonapplicability of subchapter.

This subchapter does not apply to:

(1) farm equipment used for a purpose other than construction;

(2) special mobile equipment owned by a dealer or distributor;

(3) a vehicle used to propel special mobile equipment that is registered as a farm vehicle as defined by Section 502.163; or

(4) equipment while being used by a commercial hauler to transport special mobile equipment under hire of a person who derives $500 in gross receipts annually from a farming or ranching enterprise.

*(Added by L.1995, chap. 165(1), eff. 9/1/95.)*

### §§622.075 to 622.080. *(Reserved.)*

## SUBCHAPTER H. VEHICLES TRANSPORTING LUMBER

### §622.081. Weight of lumber.

The weights in the schedule of "average weights of Southern Pine Association" issued in 1933 shall be used to determine the weight of lumber carried by a truck engaged in transporting lumber over a highway in this state. *(Added by L.1995, chap. 165(1), eff. 9/1/95.)*

### §§622.082 to 622.100. *(Reserved.)*

## SUBCHAPTER I. VEHICLES TRANSPORTING COTTON OR COTTON PROCESSING EQUIPMENT

### §622.101. Vehicle transporting cotton or processing equipment.

A single motor vehicle used exclusively to transport seed cotton modules, cotton, cotton burrs, or equipment used to transport or process cotton, including a burr spreader, may not be operated on a highway or road if the vehicle is:

(1) wider than 10 feet and the highway has not been designated by the commission under Section 621.202 if the vehicle is registered under Section 502.277;

(2) longer than 48 feet; or

(3) higher than 14 feet 6 inches.

*(Added by L.1995, chap. 165(1); chgd. by L.1997, chap. 848(2), eff. 6/18/97.)*

## SUBCHAPTER J. CERTAIN VEHICLES TRANSPORTING RECYCLABLE MATERIALS

*(Added by L.1997, chaps. 165(30.136(a)), 436(1), eff. 9/1/97, 7/15/97, respectively.)*

### §622.131. Definition.

In this subchapter, "recyclable material" has the meaning assigned by Section 361.421, Health and Safety Code. *(Added by L.1997, chaps. 165(30.136(a)), 436(1), eff. 9/1/97, 7/15/97, respectively.)*

### §622.132. Applicability of subchapter.

This subchapter applies only to a vehicle other than a tractor-trailer combination, only if equipped with a container roll-off unit or a front-end loader. *(Added by L.1997, chap. 436(1), eff. 7/15/97. See other section 622.132 below.)*

### §622.132 Applicability of subchapter.

(a) This subchapter applies only to a vehicle equipped with one or more container roll-off units.

(b) This subchapter does not apply to a tractor-trailer combination.

*(Added by L.1997, chap. 165(30.136(a)), eff. 9/1/97. See other section 622.132 above.)*

### §622.133. Axle-load restrictions.

A vehicle used exclusively to transport recyclable materials may be operated on a public highway only if the tandem axle load is not heavier than 44,000 pounds, a single axle load is not heavier than 21,000 pounds, and the gross load is not heavier than 64,000 pounds. *(Added by L.1997, chaps. 165(30.136(a)), 436(1), eff. 9/1/97, 7/15/97, respectively.)*

### §622.134. Surety bond.

(a) Except as provided by Subsection (c), the owner of a vehicle covered by this subchapter with a tandem axle load heavier than 34,000 pounds shall before operating the vehicle on a public highway of this state file with the department a surety bond subject to the approval of the department in the principal amount set by the department not to exceed $15,000 for each vehicle.

(b) The bond must be conditioned that the owner of the vehicle will pay, within the limits of the bond, to the state any damage to a highway, to a county any damage to a county road, and to a municipality any damage to a municipal street caused by the operation of the vehicle.

(c) Subsection (a) does not apply to a vehicle owned by a municipality or a county.

*(Added by L.1997, chaps. 165(30.136(a)), 436(1), eff. 9/1/97, 7/15/97, respectively.)*

### §622.135. Interstate and defense highways.

(a) This subchapter does not authorize the operation on the national system of interstate and defense highways in this state of a vehicle of a size or weight greater than authorized in 23 U.S.C. Section 127, as amended.

(b) If the United States government authorizes the operation on the national system of interstate and defense highways of vehicles of a size or weight greater than those authorized on January 1, 1983, the new limit automatically takes effect on the national system of interstate and defense highways in this state.

*(Added by L.1997, chaps. 165(30.136(a)), 436(1), eff. 9/1/97, 7/15/97, respectively.)*

### §622.136. Penalties.

(a) A person commits an offense if the person violates this subchapter.

(b) Except as provided by Subsection (c), an offense under this section is a misdemeanor punishable:

(1) by a fine not to exceed $200;

(2) on conviction within one year after the date of a prior conviction under this section that was punishable under Subdivision (1), by a fine not to exceed $500, by confinement in the county jail for not more than 60 days, or by both the fine and confinement; or

(3) on conviction within one year after the date of a prior conviction under this section that was punishable under Subdivision (2), by a fine not to exceed $1,000, by confinement in the county jail for not more than six months, or by both the fine and confinement.

(c) A corporation is not subject to confinement for an offense under this section, but two times the maximum fine provided for in the applicable subdivision of Subsection (b) may be imposed against the corporation.

*(Added by L.1997, chaps. 165(30.136(a)), 436(1), eff. 9/1/97, 7/15/97, respectively.)*

## SUBCHAPTER Y. MISCELLANEOUS SIZE EXCEPTIONS

### §622.901. Width exceptions.

The width limitation provided by Section 621.201 does not apply to:

(1) highway building or maintenance machinery that is traveling:

(A) during daylight on a public highway other than a highway that is part of the national system of interstate and defense highways; or

(B) for not more than 50 miles on a highway that is part of the national system of interstate and defense highways;

(2) a vehicle traveling during daylight on a public highway other than a highway that is part of the national system of interstate and defense highways or traveling for not more than 50 miles on a highway that is part of the national system of interstate and defense highways if the vehicle is:

(A) a farm tractor or implement of husbandry; or

(B) a vehicle on which a farm tractor or implement of husbandry, other than a tractor or implement being transported from one dealer to another, is being moved by the owner of the tractor or implement or by an agent or employee of the owner:

(i) to deliver the tractor or implement to a new owner;

(ii) to transport the tractor or implement to or from a mechanic for maintenance or repair; or

(iii) in the course of an agricultural operation;

(3) machinery that is used solely for drilling water wells, including machinery that is a unit or a unit mounted on a conventional vehicle or chassis, and that is traveling:

(A) during daylight on a public highway other than a highway that is part of the national system of interstate and defense highways; or

(B) for not more than 50 miles on a highway that is part of the national system of interstate and defense highways;

(4) a vehicle owned or operated by a public, private, or volunteer fire department; or

(5) a vehicle registered under Section 502.164.

*(Added by L.1995, chap. 165(1), eff. 9/1/95.)*



### §622.902. Length exceptions.

The length limitations provided by Sections 621.203 to 621.205 do not apply to:

(1) machinery used exclusively for drilling water wells, including machinery that is itself a unit or that is a unit mounted on a conventional vehicle or chassis;

(2) a vehicle owned or operated by a public, private, or volunteer fire department;

(3) a vehicle or combination of vehicles operated exclusively in the territory of a municipality or to a combination of vehicles operated by a municipality in a suburb adjoining the municipality in which the municipality has been using the equipment or similar equipment in connection with an established service to the suburb;

(4) a truck-tractor, truck-tractor combination, or truck-trailer combination exclusively transporting machinery, materials, and equipment used in the construction, operation, and maintenance of facilities, including pipelines, that are used for the discovery, production, and processing of natural gas or petroleum;

(5) a drive-away saddlemount vehicle transporter combination or a drive-away saddlemount with fullmount vehicle transporter combination, as defined by 23 C.F.R. Part 658 or its successor, if:

(A) the overall length of the combination is not longer than 75 feet; and

(B) the combination does not have more than three saddlemounted vehicles if the combination does not include more than one fullmount vehicle;

(6) the combination of a tow truck and another vehicle or vehicle combination if:

(A) the other vehicle or vehicle combination cannot be normally or safely driven or was abandoned on a highway; and

(B) the tow truck is towing the other vehicle or vehicle combination directly to the nearest authorized place of repair, terminal, or destination of unloading; or

(7) a vehicle or combination of vehicles used to transport a combine that is used in farm custom harvesting operations on a farm if the overall length of the vehicle or combination is not longer than 75 feet.

*(Added by L.1995, chap. 165(1); chgd. by L.1997, chaps. 165(30.137(a)), 1144(1), eff. 9/1/97, 6/19/97, respectively.)*

### §§622.903 to 622.950. *(Reserved.)*

## SUBCHAPTER Z. MISCELLANEOUS WEIGHT EXCEPTIONS

### §622.951. Oil field service equipment.

(a) A limitation relating to a vehicle's total gross weight or the weight on a vehicle's axle or group of axles does not apply to a motor vehicle that is used exclusively for transporting fixed load oil field service equipment used in connection with servicing oil and gas wells that are not more than 50 highway miles from the equipment's point of origin.

(b) The total gross weight of a vehicle to which this section applies may not be heavier than 58,000 pounds.
*(Added by L.1995, chap. 165(1), eff. 9/1/95.)*

### §622.952. Fire department vehicle.

(a) The weight limitations of Section 621.101 do not apply to a vehicle owned or operated by a public, private, or volunteer fire department.

(b) The weight of a fire department's vehicle may not be heavier than the manufacturer's gross vehicle weight capacity or axle design rating.
*(Added by L.1995, chap. 165(1), eff. 9/1/95.)*

### §622.953. Vehicle transporting seed cotton modules.

(a) The weight limitations of Section 621.101 do not apply to a vehicle or combination of vehicles used exclusively to transport seed cotton modules.

(b) The overall gross weight of a vehicle or combination to which this section applies may not be heavier than 59,400 pounds.

(c) The owner of a vehicle or combination to which this section applies that has a gross weight of more than 59,400 pounds is liable to the state, county, or municipality for any damage to a highway, street, road, or bridge caused by the weight of the load.

(d) A vehicle or combination to which this section applies may not be operated on the national system of interstate and defense highways if the vehicle exceeds the maximum weight authorized by 23 U.S.C. Section 127.
*(Added by L.1995, chap. 165(1), eff. 9/1/95.)*

# CHAPTER 623. PERMITS FOR OVERSIZE OR OVERWEIGHT VEHICLES

## SUBCHAPTER A. GENERAL PROVISIONS



## SUBCHAPTER B. GENERAL PERMITS



## SUBCHAPTER C. CONTRACTS FOR CROSSING ROADS

## SUBCHAPTER D. HEAVY EQUIPMENT

623.071. Permit to move certain heavy equipment.
623.072. Designated route in municipality.
623.073. *(Repealed.)*
623.074. Application.
623.075. Bond.
623.076. Permit fee.
623.077. Highway maintenance fee.
623.078. Vehicle supervision fee.
623.079. Registration of equipment.
623.080. Contents of permit.
623.081. Permit issued by telephone.
623.082. Penalties.
623.083 to
623.090. *(Reserved.)*

## SUBCHAPTER E. MANUFACTURED AND INDUSTRIALIZED HOUSING

623.091. Definition.
623.092. Permit requirement.
623.093. Contents of application and permit.
623.094. Installer's permit issuance.
623.095. Permit types.
623.096. Permit fee.
623.097. Duration of permit.
623.098. Caution lights.
623.099. Escort flag vehicle.
623.100. Times and days of movement.
623.101. Speed limit.
623.102. Equipment.
623.103. Liability insurance.
623.104. Civil and criminal penalties.
623.105 to
623.120. *(Reserved.)*

## SUBCHAPTER F. PORTABLE BUILDING UNITS

623.121. Permit to move portable building unit.
623.122. Designated route in municipality.
623.123. Application.
623.124. Fee.
623.125. *(Repealed.)*
623.126. Form of permit.
623.127. Duration of permit.
623.128. Time of movement.
623.129. Escort flag vehicle.
623.130. Compatible cargo.
623.131 to
623.140. *(Reserved.)*

## SUBCHAPTER G. OIL WELL SERVICING AND DRILLING MACHINERY

623.141. Optional procedure.
623.142. Permit to move oil well servicing or drilling machinery.
623.143. Designated route in municipality.
623.144. Registration of vehicle.
623.145. Rules; forms and procedures; fees.
623.146. Violation of rule.
623.147. Deposit of fee in state highway fund.

## SUBCHAPTER H. VEHICLES TRANSPORTING SOLID WASTE



## SUBCHAPTER I. UNLADEN LIFT EQUIPMENT MOTOR VEHICLES; ANNUAL PERMIT



## SUBCHAPTER J. UNLADEN LIFT EQUIPMENT MOTOR VEHICLES; TRIP PERMITS



## SUBCHAPTER K. PORT AUTHORITY PERMITS



## SUBCHAPTER A. GENERAL PROVISIONS

**§623.001. Definition.**

In this chapter, "department" means the Texas Department of Transportation. *(Added by L.1995, chap. 165(1), eff. 9/1/95.)*

**§§623.002 to 623.010.** *(Reserved.)*

## SUBCHAPTER B. GENERAL PERMITS

### §623.011. Permit for excess axle or gross weight.

(a) The department may issue a permit that authorizes the operation of a commercial motor vehicle, trailer, semitrailer, or combination of those vehicles, or a truck-tractor or combination of a truck-tractor and one or more other vehicles:

(1) at an axle weight that is not heavier than the weight equal to the maximum allowable axle weight for the vehicle or combination plus a tolerance allowance of 10 percent of that allowable weight; and

(2) at a gross weight that is not heavier than the weight equal to the maximum allowable gross weight for the vehicle or combination plus a tolerance allowance of five percent.

(b) To qualify for a permit under this section:

(1) the vehicle must be registered under Chapter 502 for the maximum gross weight applicable to the vehicle under Section 621.101, not to exceed 80,000 pounds;

(2) the security requirement of Section 623.012 must be satisfied; and

(3) a base permit fee of $75, any additional fee required by Section 623.0111, and any additional fee set by the department under Section 623.0112 must be paid.

(c) A permit issued under this section:

(1) is valid for one year;

(2) must be carried in the vehicle for which it is issued; and

(3) does not authorize the operation on the national system of interstate and defense highways in this state of vehicles with a weight greater than authorized by federal law.

(d) When the department issues a permit under this section, the department shall issue a sticker to be placed on the front windshield of the vehicle above the inspection certificate issued to the vehicle. The department shall design the form of the sticker to aid in the enforcement of weight limits for vehicles.

(e) The sticker must:

(1) indicate the expiration date of the permit; and

(2) be removed from the vehicle when:

(A) the permit for operation of the vehicle expires;

(B) a lease of the vehicle expires; or

(C) the vehicle is sold.

(f) A person commits an offense if the person fails to display the sticker in the manner required by Subsection (d). An offense under this subsection is a Class C misdemeanor. Section 623.019(g) applies to an offense under this subsection.

(g) A vehicle operating under a permit issued under this section may exceed the maximum allowable gross weight tolerance allowance by not more than five percent, regardless of the weight of any one axle or tandem axle, if no axle or tandem axle exceeds the tolerance permitted by Subsection (a).

*(Added by L.1995, chap. 165(1); chgd. by L.1997, chap. 165(30.138(a)), eff. 9/1/97.)*

### §623.0111. Additional fee for operation of vehicle under permit.

(a) When a person applies for a permit under Section 623.011, the person must:

(1) designate in the application each county in which the vehicle will be operated; and

(2) pay in addition to other fees an annual fee in an amount determined according to the following table:

| Number of Counties Designated | Fee |
|---|---|
| 1-20 | $125 |
| 21-40 | $345 |
| 41-60 | $565 |
| 61-80 | $785 |
| 81-100 | $1,005 |
| 101-254 | $2,000 |

(b) A permit issued under Section 623.011 does not authorize the operation of the vehicle in a county that is not designated in the application.

*(Added by L.1997, chap. 165(30.138(b)), eff. 9/1/97.)*

### §623.0112. Additional administrative fee.

When a person applies for a permit under Section 623.011, the person must pay in addition to other fees an administrative fee adopted by department rule in an amount not to exceed the direct and indirect cost to the department of:

(1) issuing a sticker under Section 623.011(d);

(2) distributing fees under Section 621.353; and

(3) notifying counties under Section 623.013.

*(Added by L.1997, chap. 165(30.138(b)), eff. 9/1/97.)*

### §623.012. Security for permit.

(a) An applicant for a permit under Section 623.011, other than a permit to operate a vehicle loaded with timber or pulp wood, wood chips, cotton, or agricultural products in their natural state, shall file with the department:

(1) a blanket bond; or

(2) an irrevocable letter of credit issued by a financial institution the deposits of which are guaranteed by the Federal Deposit Insurance Corporation.

(b) The bond or letter of credit must:

(1) be in the amount of $15,000 payable to the department and the counties of this state;

(2) be conditioned that the applicant will pay the department for any damage to a state highway, and a county for any damage to a road or bridge of the county, caused by the operation of the vehicle for which the permit is issued at a heavier weight than the maximum weights authorized by Subchapter B of Chapter 621 or Section 621.301; and

(3) provide that the issuer is to notify the department and the applicant in writing promptly after a payment is made by the issuer on the bond or letter of credit.

(c) If an issuer of a bond or letter of credit pays under the bond or letter of credit, the permit holder shall file with the department before the 31st day after the date on which the payment is made:

(1) a replacement bond or letter of credit in the amount prescribed by Subsection (b) for the original bond or letter of credit; or

(2) a notification from the issuer of the existing bond or letter of credit that the bond or letter of credit has been restored to the amount prescribed by Subsection (b).

(d) If the filing is not made as required by Subsection (c), each permit held by the permit holder under Section 623.011 automatically expires on the 31st day after the date on which the payment is made on the bond or letter of credit.

*(Added by L.1995, chap. 165(1), eff. 9/1/95.)*

### §623.013. Department's notice to county.

(a) Not later than the 14th day after the date the department issues a permit under Section 623.011, the department shall notify the county clerk of each county listed in the application for the permit. The notice must include:

(1) the name and address of the person for whom a permit was issued; and

(2) the vehicle identification number and license plate number of the vehicle.

(b) The department shall send a copy of the permit and the bond or letter of credit required for the permit with the notice required by this section.

*(Added by L.1995, chap. 165(1); chgd. by L.1997, chap. 165(30.138(c)), eff. 9/1/97.)*

### §623.014. Transfer of permit.

(a) A permit issued under Section 623.011 may not be transferred.

(b) If the vehicle for which a permit was issued is destroyed or permanently inoperable, a person may apply to the department for a credit for the remainder of the permit period.

(c) The department shall issue the prorated credit if the person:

(1) pays the fee adopted by the department; and

(2) provides the department with:

(A) the original permit; or

(B) if the original permit does not exist, written evidence in a form approved by the department that the vehicle has been destroyed or is permanently inoperable.

(d) The fee adopted by the department under Subsection (c)(1) may not exceed the cost of issuing the credit.

(e) A credit issued under Subsection (c) may be used only toward the payment of a permit fee under this subchapter.

*(Added by L.1995, chap. 165(1); chgd. by L.1997, chap. 165(30.138(d)), eff. 9/1/97.)*

### §623.015. Liability for damage.

(a) The liability of a holder of a permit issued under Section 623.011 for damage to a state road or highway or a county road is not limited to the amount of the bond or letter of credit required for the issuance of the permit.

(b) The holder of a permit issued under Section 623.011 who has filed the bond or letter of credit required for the permit and who has filed the notice required by Section 623.013 is liable to the county only for the actual damage to a county road, bridge, or culvert with a load limitation established under Subchapter B of Chapter 621 or Section 621.301 caused by the operation of the vehicle in excess of the limitation. If a county judge, county commissioner, county road supervisor, or county traffic officer requires the vehicle to travel over a designated route, it is presumed that the designated route, including a bridge or culvert on the route, is of sufficient strength and design to carry and withstand the weight of the vehicle traveling over the designated route.
*(Added by L.1995, chap. 165(1), eff. 9/1/95.)*

### §623.0155. Indemnification from motor carrier prohibited.

(a) A person may not require indemnification from a motor carrier as a condition to:

(1) the transportation of property for compensation or hire by the carrier; or

(2) entrance on property by the carrier for the purpose of loading, unloading, or transporting property for compensation or hire.

(b) Subsection (a)(2) does not apply to a claim arising from damage or loss from a wrongful or negligent act or omission of the carrier.
*(Added by L.1997, chap. 165(30.139(a)), eff. 9/1/97. See other section 623.0155 below.)*



### §623.0155. Indemnification from motor carrier prohibited.

(a) A person may not require indemnification from a motor carrier as a condition to:

(1) the transportation of property for compensation or hire by the carrier;

(2) entrance on property by the carrier for the purpose of loading, unloading, or transporting property for compensation or hire; or

(3) a service incidental to an activity described by Subdivision (1) or (2), including storage of property.

(b) Subsection (a) does not apply to:

(1) a claim arising from damage or loss from a wrongful or negligent act or omission of the carrier; or

(2) services or goods other than those described by Subsection (a).

(c) In this section, "motor carrier" means a common carrier, specialized carrier, or contract carrier that transports property for hire. The term does not include a person who transports property as an incidental activity of a nontransportation business activity regardless of whether the person imposes a separate charge for the transportation.

(d) A provision that is contrary to Subsection (a) is not enforceable.
*(Added by L.1997, chap. 1061(19), eff. 9/1/97. See other section 623.0155 above.)*

### §623.016. Recovery on permit security.

(a) The department or a county may recover on the bond or letter of credit required for a permit issued under Section 623.011 only by a suit against the permit holder and the issuer of the bond or letter of credit.

(b) Venue for a suit by the department is in a district court in:

(1) the county in which the defendant resides;

(2) the county in which the defendant has its principal place of business in this state if the defendant is a corporation or partnership; or

(3) Travis County if the defendant is a corporation or partnership that does not have a principal place of business in this state.

(c) Venue for a suit by a county is in district court in:

(1) the county in which the defendant resides;

(2) the county in which the defendant has its principal place of business in this state if the defendant is a corporation or partnership; or

(3) the county in which the damage occurred if the defendant is a corporation or partnership that does not have a principal place of business in this state.
*(Added by L.1995, chap. 165(1), eff. 9/1/95.)*

### §623.017. Permit for movement of cylindrical hay bales.

(a) The department may issue an annual permit to authorize the movement of a vehicle that is used to carry cylindrical bales of hay and that is wider than the maximum allowable vehicle width but not wider than 12 feet.

(b) A $10 permit fee must accompany an application for a permit under this section.
*(Added by L.1995, chap. 165(1), eff. 9/1/95.)*

## §623.018. County permit.

(a) The commissioners court of a county, through the county judge, may issue a permit for:

(1) the transportation over highways of that county, other than state highways and public roads in the territory of a municipality, of an overweight, oversize, or overlength commodity that cannot be reasonably dismantled; or

(2) the operation over a highway of that county other than a state highway or public road in the territory of a municipality of:

(A) superheavy or oversize equipment for the transportation of an overweight, oversize, or overlength commodity that cannot be reasonably dismantled; or

(B) vehicles or combinations of vehicles that exceed the weights authorized under Subchapter B, Chapter 621, or Section 621.301.

(b) A permit under Subsection (a) may not be issued for longer than 90 days.

(c) The commissioners court of a county, through the county judge, may issue an annual permit to a dealer in implements of husbandry to allow the dealer to use vehicles that exceed the width limitations provided by this chapter to transport an implement on a highway. The county judge may exercise authority under this subsection independently of the commissioners court until the commissioners court takes action on the request.

(d) If a vehicle has a permit issued under Section 623.011, a commissioners court may not:

(1) issue a permit under this section or charge an additional fee for or otherwise regulate or restrict the operation of the vehicle because of weight; or

(2) require the owner or operator to execute or comply with a road use agreement or indemnity agreement, to make a filing or application, or to provide a bond or letter of credit other than the bond or letter of credit prescribed by Section 623.012.

(e) The commissioners court may require a bond to be executed by an applicant in an amount sufficient to guarantee the payment of any damage to a road or bridge sustained as a consequence of the transportation authorized by the permit.

*(Added by L.1995, chap. 165(1), eff. 9/1/95.)*

## §623.019. Violations of subchapter; offenses.

(a) A person who holds a permit issued under Section 623.011 commits an offense if:

(1) the person:

(A) operates or directs the operation of the vehicle for which the permit was issued on a public highway or road; and

(B) is criminally negligent with regard to the operation of the vehicle at a weight heavier than the weight limit authorized by Section 623.011; or

(2) the person operates or directs the operation of the vehicle for which the permit was issued:

(A) in a county not designated in the person's application under Section 623.0111; and

(B) at a weight heavier than a weight limit established under:

(i) Subchapter E, Chapter 251;

(ii) Chapter 621 or 622; or

(iii) this chapter.

(b) Except as provided by Subsections (c) and (d), an offense under Subsection (a) is a misdemeanor punishable by a fine of not less than $100 or more than $150.

(c) An offense under Subsection (a) is a misdemeanor and, except as provided by Subsection (d), is punishable by a fine of:

(1) not less than $300 or more than $500 if the offense involves a vehicle having a gross weight that is heavier than 5,000 but not heavier than 10,000 pounds over the vehicle's allowable gross weight; or

(2) not less than $500 or more than $1,000 if the offense involves a vehicle having a gross weight that is at least 10,000 pounds heavier than the vehicle's allowable gross weight.

(d) On conviction before the first anniversary of the date of a previous conviction under Subsection (a), an offense is punishable by a fine in an amount that is twice the amount specified by Subsection (c).

(e) A governmental entity collecting a fine under Subsection (c) shall send an amount equal to 50 percent of the fine to the comptroller.

(f) A justice of the peace has jurisdiction of any offense under this section. A municipal court has jurisdiction of an offense under this section in which the fine does not exceed $500.

(g) A justice or judge who renders a conviction under this section shall report the conviction to the Department of Public Safety. The Department of Public Safety shall keep a record of each conviction reported under this subsection.

*(Added by L.1997, chap. 165(30.139(c)), eff. 9/1/97.)*

Printed in the U.S.A. Zt

**§§623.020 to 623.050.** *(Reserved.)*

## SUBCHAPTER C. CONTRACTS FOR CROSSING ROADS

### §623.051. Contract allowing oversize or overweight vehicle to cross road; surety bond.

(a) A person may operate a vehicle that cannot comply with one or more of the restrictions of Subchapter C of Chapter 621 or Section 621.101 to cross the width of any road or highway under the jurisdiction of the department, other than a controlled access highway as defined by Section 203.001, from private property to other private property if the person contracts with the commission to indemnify the department for the cost of maintenance and repair of the part of the highway crossed by the vehicle.

(b) The commission shall adopt rules relating to the forms and procedures to be used under this section and other matters that the commission considers necessary to carry out this section.

(c) To protect the safety of the traveling public, minimize any delays and inconveniences to the operators of vehicles in regular operation, and assure payment for the added wear on the highways in proportion to the reduction of service life, the commission, in adopting rules under this section, shall consider:

(1) the safety and convenience of the general traveling public;

(2) the suitability of the roadway and subgrade on the road or highway to be crossed, variation in soil grade prevalent in the different regions of the state, and the seasonal effects on highway load capacity, the highway shoulder design, and other highway geometrics; and

(3) the state's investment in its highway system.

(d) Before exercising any right under a contract under this section, a person must execute with a corporate surety authorized to do business in this state a surety bond in an amount determined by the commission to compensate for the cost of maintenance and repairs as provided by this section. The bond must be approved by the comptroller and the attorney general and must be conditioned on the person fulfilling the obligations of the contract.

(e) *(Repealed by L.1997, chap. 165(30.140), eff. 9/1/97.)*

*(Added by L.1995, chap. 165(1); chgd. by L.1997, chap. 1423(18.14), eff. 9/1/97.)*

### §623.052. Contract allowing overweight vehicle with commodities or products to cross highway; surety bond.

(a) A person may operate a vehicle that exceeds the overall gross weight limits provided by Section 621.101 to cross the width of a highway from private property to other private property if:

(1) the vehicle is transporting grain, sand, or another commodity or product and the vehicle's overall gross weight is not heavier than 110,000 pounds; or

(2) the vehicle is an unlicensed vehicle that is transporting sand, gravel, stones, rock, caliche, or a similar commodity.

(b) Before a person may operate a vehicle under this section, the person must:

(1) contract with the department to indemnify the department for the cost of the maintenance and repair for damage caused by a vehicle crossing that part of the highway; and

(2) execute an adequate surety bond to compensate for the cost of maintenance and repair, approved by the comptroller and the attorney general, with a corporate surety authorized to do business in this state, conditioned on the person fulfilling each obligation of the agreement.

*(Added by L.1995, chap. 165(1); chgd. by L.1997, chap. 1423(18.15), eff. 9/1/97.)*

**§§623.053 to 623.070.** *(Reserved.)*

## SUBCHAPTER D. HEAVY EQUIPMENT

### §623.071. Permit to move certain heavy equipment.

(a) The department may issue a permit to a person to operate over a state highway superheavy or oversize equipment that:

(1) is used to transport cylindrically shaped bales of hay or a commodity that cannot reasonably be dismantled; and

(2) has a gross weight or size that exceeds the limits allowed by law to be transported over a state highway.

(b) The department may issue a permit to a person to operate over a farm-to-market or ranch-to-market road superheavy or oversize equipment that:

(1) is used to transport oilfield drill pipe or drill collars stored in a pipe box; and

(2) has a gross weight or size that exceeds the limits allowed by law to be transported over a state highway.

(c) The department may issue an annual permit to allow the operation on a state highway of equipment that exceeds weight and size limits provided by law for the movement of:

(1) an implement of husbandry by a dealer;

(2) water well drilling machinery and equipment or harvesting equipment being moved as part of an agricultural operation; or

(3) superheavy or oversize equipment that:

(A) cannot reasonably be dismantled; and

(B) does not exceed:

(i) 12 feet in width;

(ii) 14 feet in height;

(iii) 110 feet in length; or

(iv) 120,000 pounds gross weight.

(d) The department may issue an annual permit to a motor carrier, as defined by Section 643.001, that allows the motor carrier to operate on a state highway two or more vehicles for the movement of superheavy or oversize equipment described by Subsection (c)(3). An application under this subsection must be on the form prescribed by the department and include a description of each vehicle to be operated by the motor carrier under the permit. A permit issued under this subsection:

(1) may not authorize the operation of more than one vehicle at the same time; and

(2) must be carried in the vehicle that is being operated to move the superheavy or oversize equipment under the permit.

(e) The department may not issue a permit under this section unless the equipment may be operated without material damage to the highway.

(f) In this section, "pipe box" means a container specifically constructed to safely transport and handle oilfield drill pipe and drill collars.

(g) A single trip permit that increases the height or width limits established in Subsection (c)(3)(B)(i) or (ii) may be issued by the department and used in conjunction with an annual permit issued under Subsection (c).

*(Added by L.1995, chap. 165(1); chgd. by L.1997, chap. 568(1); L.1999, chap. 807(1), eff. 9/1/99.)*

## §623.072. Designated route in municipality.

(a) A municipality having a state highway in its territory shall designate to the department the route in the municipality to be used by equipment described by Section 623.071 operating over the state highway. The department shall show the designated route on each map routing the equipment.

(b) If a municipality does not designate a route, the department shall determine the route of the equipment and the commodity on each state highway in the municipality.

(c) A municipality may not require a fee, permit, or license for movement of superheavy or oversize equipment on the route of a state highway designated by the municipality or department.

*(Added by L.1995, chap. 165(1), eff. 9/1/95.)*

## §623.073. *(Repealed by L.1997, chap. 515(3), eff. 9/1/97.)*

## §623.074. Application.

(a) The department may issue a permit under this subchapter on the receipt of an application for the permit.

(b) The application must:

(1) be in writing;

(2) state the kind of equipment to be operated;

(3) describe the equipment;

(4) give the weight and dimensions of the equipment;

(5) give the width, height, and length of the equipment;

(6) state the kind of commodity to be transported and the weight of the total load; and

(7) be dated and signed by the applicant.

(c) An application for a permit under Section 623.071(a) or (b) must also state:

(1) each highway over which the equipment is to be operated, if the permit is for a single trip; or

(2) the region or area, as required by rule, over which the equipment is to be operated, if the permit is for other than a single trip.

(d) The department may by rule authorize an applicant to submit an application electronically. An electronically submitted application shall be considered signed if a digital signature is transmitted with the application and intended by the applicant to authenticate the application. For purposes of this subsection, "digital signature" means an electronic identifier intended by the person using it to have the same force and effect as the use of a manual signature.
*(Added by L.1995, chap. 165(1); chgd. by L.1997, chaps. 515(4), 568(2), 1171(1.30), eff. 9/1/97, 6/2/97, 9/1/97, respectively.)*

### §623.075. Bond.

(a) Before the department may issue a permit under this subchapter, the applicant shall file with the department a bond in an amount set by the department, payable to the department, and conditioned that the applicant will pay to the department any damage that might be sustained to the highway because of the operation of the equipment for which a permit is issued.

(b) Venue of a suit for recovery on the bond is in Travis County.

(c) This section applies to the delivery of farm equipment to a farm equipment dealer. This section does not apply to:

(1) the driving or transporting of farm equipment that is being used for an agricultural purpose and is driven or transported by or under the authority of the owner of the equipment; or

(2) a vehicle or equipment operated by a motor carrier registered under Chapter 643 or Chapter 645.
*(Added by L.1995, chap. 165(1); chgd. by L.1997, chap. 165(30.141(a)), eff. 9/1/97.)*



### §623.076. Permit fee.

(a) An application for a permit under this subchapter must be accompanied by a permit fee of:

(1) $30 for a single-trip permit;

(2) $60 for a permit that is valid for a period not exceeding 30 days;

(3) $90 for a permit that is valid for a period of 31 days or more but not exceeding 60 days;

(4) $120 for a permit that is valid for a period of 61 days or more but not exceeding 90 days; or

(5) $135 for a permit issued under Section 623.071(c)(1) or (2).

(b) The Texas Transportation Commission may adopt rules for the payment of a fee under Subsection (a). The rules may:

(1) authorize the use of electronic funds transfer;

(2) authorize the use of a credit card issued by:

(A) a financial institution chartered by a state or the United States; or

(B) a nationally recognized credit organization approved by the Texas Transportation Commission; and

(3) require the payment of a discount or service charge for a credit card payment in addition to the fee prescribed by Subsection (a).

(c) An application for a permit under Section 623.071(c)(3) or (d) must be accompanied by the permit fee established by the commission for the permit, not to exceed $3,500. Of each fee collected under this subsection, the department shall send:

(1) the first $1,000 to the comptroller for deposit to the credit of the general revenue fund; and

(2) any amount in excess of $1,000 to the comptroller for deposit to the credit of the state highway fund.
*(Added by L.1995, chap. 165(1); chgd. by L.1997, chaps. 515(5), 568(3); L.1999, chap. 807(2), eff. 9/1/99.)*

### §623.077. Highway maintenance fee.

(a) An applicant for a permit under this subchapter, other than a permit under Section 623.071(c)(3), must also pay a highway maintenance fee in an amount determined according to the following table:

| Vehicle Weight in Pounds | Fee |
|---|---|
| 80,001 to 120,000 | $ 50 |
| 120,001 to 160,000 | $ 75 |
| 160,001 to 200,000 | $100 |
| 200,001 and above | $125 |

(b) The department shall send each fee collected under Subsection (a) to the comptroller for deposit to the credit of the state highway fund.
*(Added by L.1995, chap. 165(1); chgd. by L.1997, chaps. 568(4), 1423(18.16), eff. 6/2/97, 9/1/97, respectively.)*

**§623.078. Vehicle supervision fee.**

(a) Each applicant for a permit under this subchapter for a vehicle that is heavier than 200,000 pounds must also pay a vehicle supervision fee in an amount determined by the department and designed to recover the direct cost of providing safe transportation of the vehicle over the state highway system, including the cost of:

(1) bridge structural analysis;

(2) the monitoring of the trip process; and

(3) moving traffic control devices.

(b) The department shall send each fee collected under Subsection (a) to the comptroller for deposit to the credit of the state highway fund.

*(Added by L.1995, chap. 165(1); chgd. by L.1997, chap. 1423(18.17), eff. 9/1/97.)*

**§623.079. Registration of equipment.**

A permit under this subchapter may be issued only if the equipment to be operated under the permit is registered under Chapter 502 for maximum gross weight applicable to the vehicle under Section 621.101 that is not heavier than 80,000 pounds overall gross weight. *(Added by L.1995, chap. 165(1), eff. 9/1/95.)*

**§623.080. Contents of permit.**

(a) Except as provided by Subsection (b), a permit under this subchapter must include:

(1) the name of the applicant;

(2) the date of issuance;

(3) the signature of the director of the department or of a division engineer;

(4) a statement of the kind of equipment to be transported over the highway, the weight and dimensions of the equipment, and the kind and weight of each commodity to be transported; and

(5) a statement of any condition on which the permit is issued.

(b) A permit issued under Section 623.071(a) or (b) must also state:

(1) each highway over which the equipment is to be transported, if the permit is for a single trip; or

(2) the region or area, as required by rule, over which the equipment is to be operated, if the permit is for other than a single trip.

*(Added by L.1995, chap. 165(1); chgd. by L.1997, chap. 515(6), eff. 9/1/97.)*

**§623.081. Permit issued by telephone.**

(a) The department shall provide for issuing a permit by telephone for the operation of an overweight or oversize motor vehicle over a state highway.

(b) The department shall issue a permit under this section for a period and at the rate provided by Section 623.076(a).

(c) An applicant for a permit under this section must provide by telephone to the department:

(1) the information required for a permit issued under Section 623.071(a) or (b), other than the applicant's signature; and

(2) the account number of a credit card approved by the department.

(d) On granting a permit under this section, the agent shall:

(1) issue to the applicant an approval number; and

(2) provide to the applicant the agent's name, designation, and office address.

(e) After receiving an approval number, the applicant shall prepare, on a form provided by the department, a permit with the information provided to the agent under Subsection (c) and the information received under Subsection (d).

(f) The applicant shall keep the permit in the vehicle for which the permit was issued until the day after the date the permit expires.

*(Added by L.1995, chap. 165(1); chgd. by L.1997, chap. 515(7), eff. 9/1/97.)*

**§623.082. Penalties.**

(a) A person commits an offense if the person violates this subchapter.

(b) Except as provided by Subsection (c), an offense under this section is a misdemeanor punishable:

(1) by a fine of not more than $200;

(2) on conviction within one year after the date of a prior conviction under this section that was punishable under Subdivision (1), by a fine of not more than $500, by confinement in the county jail for not more than 60 days, or by both the fine and the confinement; or

(3) on conviction within one year after the date of a prior conviction under this section that was punishable under Subdivision (2) or this subdivision, by a fine of not more than $1,000, by

confinement in the county jail for not more than six months, or by both the fine and the confinement.

(c) A corporation is not subject to confinement for an offense under this section, but two times the maximum fine provided for in the applicable subdivision of Subsection (b) may be imposed against the corporation.

(d) The judge shall report a conviction under this section to the Department of Public Safety. The Department of Public Safety shall keep a record of each conviction.

(e) If a corporation does not pay a fine assessed under this section, the district or county attorney for the county in which the conviction was obtained may file suit to collect the fine. *(Added by L.1995, chap. 165(1), eff. 9/1/95.)*

### §§623.083 to 623.090. *(Reserved.)*

## SUBCHAPTER E. MANUFACTURED AND INDUSTRIALIZED HOUSING



### §623.091. Definition.

In this subchapter, "manufactured house" means "industrialized building" as defined by Article 5221f-1, Revised Statutes, "industrialized housing" as defined by Article 5221f-1, Revised Statutes, or "manufactured home" as defined by the Texas Manufactured Housing Standards Act (Article 5221f, Texas Civil Statutes). The term includes a temporary chassis system or returnable undercarriage used for the transportation of a manufactured house and a transportable section of a manufactured house that is transported on a chassis system or returnable undercarriage and that is constructed so that it cannot, without dismantling or destruction, be transported within the legal size limits for a motor vehicle. *(Added by L.1995, chap. 165(1), eff. 9/1/95.)*

### §623.092. Permit requirement.

(a) A manufactured house in excess of legal size limits for a motor vehicle may not be moved over a highway, road, or street in this state except in accordance with a permit issued by the department.

(b) A county or municipality may not require a permit, bond, fee, or license, in addition to that required by state law, for the movement of a manufactured house. *(Added by L.1995, chap. 165(1), eff. 9/1/95.)*

### §623.093. Contents of application and permit.

(a) The application for a permit and the permit must be in the form prescribed by the department. The permit must show:

(1) the length, width, and height of the manufactured house and the towing vehicle in combination;

(2) the complete identification or serial number, the Department of Housing and Urban Development label number, or the state seal number of the house;

(3) the name of the owner of the house;

(4) the location from which the house is being transported;

(5) the location to which the house is being transported; and

(6) the route for the transportation of the house.

(b) The length of the manufactured house and the towing vehicle in combination includes the length of the hitch or towing device. The height is measured from the roadbed to the highest elevation of the manufactured house. The width of the house or section includes any roof or eave extension or overhang on either side.

(c) The route must be the shortest distance from the place where the transportation begins in this state to the place where the transportation ends in this state and include divided and interstate systems, except where construction is in progress or bridge or overpass width or height creates a safety hazard. A county or municipality may designate to the department the route to be used inside the territory of the county or municipality.

(d) If the manufactured home is being moved from or to a site in this state where it has been, or will be, occupied as a dwelling, the permit must also show:

(1) the complete serial or identification number;

(2) the HUD label or state seal number;

(3) the name of the owner of the home; and

(4) the location from which the home is being moved and the location to which the home is being delivered.

(e) If the permit shows the additional information required by Subsection (d), the department shall send on a quarterly basis a copy of the permit, or furnish the essential information in the permit, to the tax assessor-collector and the chief appraiser of the appraisal district for each county in which the movement begins or ends.

(f) Each quarter the department shall send a copy of each permit for the transportation of a manufactured house that begins or ends in this state, or provide the essential information in the permit, to the chief appraiser of the appraisal district in each county in which the transportation begins or ends.

*(Added by L.1995, chap. 165(1); chgd. by L.1997, chaps. 165(30.142(a)), 791(19); L.1999, chap. 62(19.01(107)), eff. 9/1/99.)*

## §623.094. Installer's permit issuance.

(a) Except as authorized by Section 623.095, the department may issue a permit only to:

(1) a person licensed by the Texas Department of Housing and Community Affairs as a manufacturer, retailer, or installer; or

(2) motor carriers registered with the department.

(b) The license or registration number of the person to whom the permit is issued shall be affixed to the rear of the manufactured house during transportation and have letters and numbers that are at least eight inches high. *(Chgd. by L.1997, chap. 791(20), eff. 9/1/97. See other subsection (b) below.)*

(b) The registration number or the motor carrier number of the person to whom the permit is issued shall be affixed to the rear of the manufactured house during transportation and have letters and numbers that are at least eight inches high. *(Chgd. by L.1997, chap. 165(30.143(a)), eff. 9/1/97. See other subsection (b) above.)*

*(Added by L.1995, chap. 165(1); chgd. by L.1997, chaps. 165(30.143(a)), 791(20), eff. 9/1/97.)*



## §623.095. Permit types.

(a) The department may issue a single-trip permit for the transportation of a manufactured house to:

(1) the owner of a manufactured house if:

(A) the title to the manufactured house and the title to the towing vehicle show that the owner of the manufactured house and the owner of the towing vehicle are the same person; or

(B) a lease shows that the owner of the manufactured house and the lessee of the towing vehicle are the same person;

(2) a person authorized to be issued permits by Section 623.094; or

(3) a motor carrier registered under Chapter 643.

(b) A person or owner, motor carrier, must have proof of the insurance coverage required by Section 623.103.

(c) In lieu of a single-trip permit, the department may issue an annual permit to any person authorized to be issued permits by Section 623.094 for the transportation of new manufactured homes from a manufacturing facility to a temporary storage location not to exceed 20 miles from the point of manufacture. A copy of the permit must be carried in the vehicle transporting a manufactured home from the manufacturer to temporary storage. The department may adopt rules concerning requirements for a permit issued under this subsection.

*(Added by L.1995, chap. 165(1); chgd. by L.1997, chaps. 165(30.143(b)), 791(21), eff. 9/1/97.)*

## §623.096. Permit fee.

(a) The department shall collect a fee of $20 for each permit issued under this subchapter. Of each fee, 30 cents shall be deposited to the credit of the state highway fund.

(b) The department shall adopt rules concerning fees for each annual permit issued under Section 623.095(c) at a cost not to exceed $1,500. Two percent of any fee adopted shall be deposited to the credit of the state highway fund.

(c) The department may establish an escrow account for the payment of permit fees.

*(Added by L.1995, chap. 165(1); chgd. by L.1997, chaps. 165(30.144(a)), 791(22), eff. 9/1/97)*

## §623.097. Duration of permit.

A permit is valid for a five-day period. *(Added by L.1995, chap. 165(1), eff. 9/1/95.)*

## §623.098. Caution lights.

(a) A manufactured house that is wider than 12 feet must have one rotating amber beacon of not less than eight inches mounted at the rear of the manufactured house on the roof or one flashing amber light mounted at each rear corner of the manufactured house approximately six feet above ground level. In addition, the towing vehicle must have one rotating amber beacon of not less than eight inches mounted on top of the cab.

(b) Each beacon shall be operated during a move under a permit and while on a highway, road, or street in this state.

*(Added by L.1995, chap. 165(1); chgd. by L.1997, chap. 165(30.145(a)), eff. 9/1/97.)*

### §623.099. Escort flag vehicle.

(a) A manufactured house that is wider than 16 feet, but is not wider than 18 feet, must have one escort flag vehicle that must:

(1) precede the house on a two-lane roadway; or

(2) follow the house on a roadway of four or more lanes.

(b) A manufactured house that is wider than 18 feet must be preceded and followed by escort flag vehicles while moving over a highway, road, or street in this state.

(c) An escort flag vehicle must have:

(1) on top of the vehicle and visible from the front and rear:

(A) two lights flashing simultaneously; or

(B) one rotating amber beacon of not less than eight inches;

(2) four red 16-inch square flags mounted on the four corners of the vehicle so that one flag is on each corner; and

(3) signs that:

(A) are mounted on the front and rear of the vehicle; and

(B) have a yellow background and black letters at least eight inches high stating "wide load."

(d) Two transportable sections of a multisection manufactured house or two single-section manufactured houses towed in convoy are considered one house for purposes of the escort flag vehicle requirements of this section if the distance between the two does not exceed 1,000 feet.

(e) The department shall publish and annually revise a map or list of the bridges or overpasses that because of height or width require an escort flag vehicle to stop oncoming traffic while a manufactured house crosses the bridge or overpass.

(f) An escort flag vehicle may not be required under this subchapter except as expressly provided by this section.

*(Added by L.1995, chap. 165(1); chgd. by L.1997, chap. 487(1), eff. 9/1/97.)*



### §623.100. Times and days of movement.

(a) Movement authorized by a permit issued under this subchapter may be made on any day, except a national holiday, but shall be made only during daylight hours.

(b) The department may limit the hours for travel on certain routes because of heavy traffic conditions.

(c) The department shall publish the limitation on movements prescribed by this section and the limitations adopted under Subsection (b) and shall make the publications available to the public. Each limitation adopted by the department must be made available to the public before it takes effect.

*(Added by L.1995, chap. 165(1), eff. 9/1/95.)*

### §623.101. Speed limit.

(a) A manufactured house or house trailer may not be towed in excess of the posted speed limit or 55 miles per hour, whichever is less.

(b) In this section, "house trailer" has the meaning assigned by Section 541.201.

*(Added by L.1995, chap. 165(1); chgd. by L.1997, chap. 1020(4), eff. 9/1/97.)*

### §623.102. Equipment.

(a) The brakes on a towing vehicle and a manufactured house must be capable of stopping the vehicle and house from an initial velocity of 20 miles per hour in not more than 40 feet.

(b) Each manufactured house must be equipped with a wiring harness during transportation over a roadway to provide on the rear of the house:

(1) right-turn and left-turn signal lights;

(2) braking or stopping lights; and

(3) parking lights.

*(Added by L.1995, chap. 165(1), eff. 9/1/95.)*

### §623.103. Liability insurance.

A vehicle towing a manufactured house shall be covered by liability insurance of not less than $300,000 combined single limit. *(Added by L.1995, chap. 165(1), eff. 9/1/95.)*

## §623.104. Civil and criminal penalties.

(a) A person commits an offense if the person violates this subchapter. An offense under this subsection is a Class C misdemeanor.

(b) A person convicted of an offense under Subsection (a) may also be assessed a civil penalty of not less than $200 or more than $500 for failure to:

(1) obtain a permit;

(2) have a required rotating amber beacon on the manufactured house or towing vehicle;

(3) provide a required escort flag vehicle; or

(4) have the required insurance.

(c) The civil penalty:

(1) may be awarded by a court having jurisdiction over a Class C misdemeanor; and

(2) shall be paid to the county in which the person was convicted.

*(Added by L.1995, chap. 165(1), eff. 9/1/95.)*

## §§623.105 to 623.120. *(Reserved.)*

# SUBCHAPTER F. PORTABLE BUILDING UNITS

## §623.121. Permit to move portable building unit.

(a) The department may issue a permit to a person to operate equipment to move over a state highway one or more portable building units that in combination with the towing vehicle are in excess of the length or width limitations provided by law but less than 80 feet in length.

(b) The length limitation in this section does not apply to a truck-tractor or truck-tractor combination towing or carrying the portable building units.

(c) In this section, "portable building unit" means the prefabricated structural and other components incorporated and delivered by the manufacturer as a complete inspected unit with a distinct serial number. The term includes a fully assembled configuration, a partially assembled configuration, or a kit or unassembled configuration, when loaded for transport.

*(Added by L.1995, chap. 165(1); chgd. by L.1997, chap. 165(30.146(a)), eff. 9/1/97.)*

## §623.122. Designated route in municipality.

(a) A municipality having a state highway in its territory shall designate to the department the route in the municipality to be used by equipment described by Section 623.121 moving over the state highway. The department shall show the designated route on each map routing the equipment.

(b) If a municipality does not designate a route, the department shall determine the route to be used by the equipment on the state highway within the municipality.

(c) A municipality may not require a fee or license for movement of a portable building unit on the route of a state highway designated by the department or the municipality.

*(Added by L.1995, chap. 165(1), eff. 9/1/95.)*

## §623.123. Application.

The application for a permit under Section 623.121 must:

(1) be in writing;

(2) state the make and model of the portable building unit or units;

(3) state the length and width of the portable building unit or units;

(4) state the make and model of the towing vehicle;

(5) state the length and width of the towing vehicle;

(6) state the length and width of the combined portable building unit or units and towing vehicle;

(7) state each highway over which the portable building unit or units are to be moved;

(8) indicate the point of origin and destination; and

(9) be dated and signed by the applicant.

*(Added by L.1995, chap. 165(1), eff. 9/1/95.)*

## §623.124. Fee.

An application for a permit must be accompanied by a fee of $7.50. *(Added by L.1995, chap. 165(1), eff. 9/1/95.)*

## §623.125. *(Repealed by L.1997, chap. 515(8), eff. 9/1/97.)*

### §623.126. Form of permit.

(a) A permit issued under this subchapter must:

(1) contain the name of the applicant;

(2) be dated and signed by the director of the department, a division engineer, or a designated agent;

(3) state the make and model of the portable building unit or units to be transported over the highways;

(4) state the make and model of the towing vehicle;

(5) state the combined length and width of the portable building unit or units and towing vehicle; and

(6) state each highway over which the portable building unit or units are to be moved.

(b) A permit is valid if it is substantially in the form provided by this section.
*(Added by L.1995, chap. 165(1), eff. 9/1/95.)*



### §623.127. Duration of permit.

A permit issued under this subchapter is effective for a 10-day period and valid only for a single continuous movement. *(Added by L.1995, chap. 165(1), eff. 9/1/95.)*

### §623.128. Time of movement.

Movement authorized by a permit issued under this subchapter shall be made only during daylight hours. *(Added by L.1995, chap. 165(1), eff. 9/1/95.)*

### §623.129. Escort flag vehicle.

The escort flag vehicle requirements provided by Section 623.099 apply to the movement of portable building units and compatible cargo under this subchapter as if such building units and cargo were a manufactured house. *(Added by L.1997, chap. 487(2), eff. 9/1/97.)*

### §623.130. Compatible cargo.

(a) A permit issued under this subchapter may authorize the movement of cargo, other than a portable building unit, manufactured, assembled, or distributed by a portable building unit manufacturer, as an authorized distributor if:

(1) the movement is conducted by employees of the manufacturer or by independent drivers and equipment under exclusive contract to the manufacturer during the movement;

(2) the movement is to or from a location where the manufacturer's building units may be legally stored, sold, or delivered; and

(3) the cargo is compatible with the movement of portable building units in that:

(A) the cargo does not cause the load to exceed applicable height or weight limits; and

(B) the cargo is loaded to properly distribute weight, width, and height to maximize safety and economy without exceeding size or weight limits authorized for movement of portable building units.

(b) If cargo moved under this section exceeds any width limit that would apply to the cargo if it were moved in a manner not governed by this section, the department shall collect an amount equal to any fee that would apply to movement of the cargo if the cargo were moved in a manner not governed by this section in addition to the fee required under this subchapter.
*(Added by L.1997, chap. 487(2), eff. 9/1/97.)*

### §§623.131 to 623.140. *(Reserved.)*

## SUBCHAPTER G. OIL WELL SERVICING AND DRILLING MACHINERY

### §623.141. Optional procedure.

This subchapter provides an optional procedure for the issuance of a permit for the movement of oversize or overweight oil well servicing or oil well drilling machinery and equipment. *(Added by L.1995, chap. 165(1), eff. 9/1/95.)*

### §623.142. Permit to move oil well servicing or drilling machinery.

(a) The department may, on application, issue a permit for the movement over a road or highway under the jurisdiction of the department of a vehicle that:

(1) is a piece of fixed-load mobile machinery or equipment used to service, clean out, or drill an oil well; and

(2) cannot comply with the restrictions set out in Subchapter C of Chapter 621 and Section 621.101.

(b) The department may not issue a permit under this section unless the vehicle may be moved without material damage to the highway or serious inconvenience to highway traffic.
*(Added by L.1995, chap. 165(1), eff. 9/1/95.)*

### §623.143. Designated route in municipality.

(a) A municipality having a state highway in its territory may designate to the department the route in the municipality to be used by a vehicle described by Section 623.142 operating over the state highway. When the route is designated, the department shall show the route on each map routing the vehicles.

(b) If a municipality does not designate a route, the department shall determine the route to be used by a vehicle on a state highway in the municipality.

(c) A municipality may not require a fee, permit, or license for movement of vehicles on the route of a state highway designated by the municipality or department.
*(Added by L.1995, chap. 165(1), eff. 9/1/95.)*

### §623.144. Registration of vehicle.

A permit under this subchapter may be issued only if the vehicle is registered under Chapter 502 for the maximum gross weight applicable to the vehicle under Section 621.101 or has the distinguishing license plates as provided by Section 502.276 if applicable to the vehicle. *(Added by L.1995, chap. 165(1), eff. 9/1/95.)*

### §623.145. Rules; forms and procedures; fees.

(a) The Texas Transportation Commission by rule shall provide for the issuance of permits under this subchapter. The rules must include each matter the commission determines necessary to implement this subchapter and:

(1) requirements for forms and procedures used in applying for a permit;

(2) conditions with regard to route and time of movement;

(3) requirements for flags, flaggers, and warning devices;

(4) the fee for a permit; and

(5) standards to determine whether a permit is to be issued for one trip only or for a period established by the commission.

(b) In adopting a rule or establishing a fee, the commission shall consider and be guided by:

(1) the state's investment in its highway system;

(2) the safety and convenience of the general traveling public;

(3) the registration or license fee paid on the vehicle for which the permit is requested;

(4) the fees paid by vehicles operating within legal limits;

(5) the suitability of roadways and subgrades on the various classes of highways of the system;

(6) the variation in soil grade prevalent in the different regions of the state;

(7) the seasonal effects on highway load capacity;

(8) the highway shoulder design and other highway geometrics;

(9) the load capacity of the highway bridges;

(10) administrative costs;

(11) added wear on highways; and

(12) compensation for inconvenience and necessary delays to highway users.
*(Added by L.1995, chap. 165(1), eff. 9/1/95.)*

### §623.146. Violation of rule.

A permit under this subchapter is void on the failure of an owner or the owner's representative to comply with a rule of the commission or with a condition placed on the permit, and immediately on the violation, further movement over the highway of an oversize or overweight vehicle violates the law regulating the size or weight of a vehicle on a public highway. *(Added by L.1995, chap. 165(1), eff. 9/1/95.)*

### §623.147. Deposit of fee in state highway fund.

A fee collected under this subchapter shall be deposited to the credit of the state highway fund. *(Added by L.1995, chap. 165(1), eff. 9/1/95.)*

**§623.148. Liability for damage to highways.**

(a) By issuing a permit under this subchapter, the department does not guarantee that a highway can safely accommodate the movement.

(b) The owner of a vehicle involved in the movement of an oversize or overweight vehicle, even if a permit has been issued for the movement, is strictly liable for any damage the movement causes the highway system or any of its structures or appurtenances.

*(Added by L.1995, chap. 165(1), eff. 9/1/95.)*

**§623.149. Determination whether vehicle subject to registration or eligible for distinguishing license plate.**

(a) The department may establish criteria to determine whether oil well servicing, oil well clean out, or oil well drilling machinery or equipment is subject to registration under Chapter 502 or eligible for the distinguishing license plate provided by Section 502.276.

(b) Notwithstanding Subsection (a), a vehicle authorized by the department before August 22, 1963, to operate without registration under Chapter 502 may not be required to register under that chapter.

(c) In this section, "oil well servicing, oil well clean out, or oil well drilling machinery or equipment" means a vehicle constructed as a machine used solely for servicing, cleaning out, or drilling an oil well and consisting in general of a mast, an engine for power, a draw works, and a chassis permanently constructed or assembled for one or more of those purposes.

*(Added by L.1995, chap. 165(1), eff. 9/1/95.)*



**§623.150. Nonapplicability of subchapter.**

This subchapter does not apply to a person issued a registration certificate under Chapter 643, even if not all the operations of the person are performed under that certificate. *(Added by L.1995, chap. 165(1); chgd. by L.1997, chap. 165(30.147), eff. 9/1/97.)*

**§§623.151 to 623.160.** *(Reserved.)*

## SUBCHAPTER H. VEHICLES TRANSPORTING SOLID WASTE

**§623.161. Definition.**

In this subchapter, "solid waste" has the meaning assigned by Chapter 361, Health and Safety Code, except that it does not include hazardous waste. *(Added by L.1995, chap. 165(1), eff. 9/1/95.)*

**§623.162. Axle-load restrictions.**

A vehicle used exclusively to transport solid waste may be operated on a public highway of this state only if the tandem axle load is not heavier than 44,000 pounds, the single axle load is not heavier than 21,000 pounds, and the gross load is not heavier than 64,000 pounds. *(Added by L.1995, chap. 165(1), eff. 9/1/95.)*

**§623.163. Surety bond.**

(a) The owner of a vehicle used exclusively to transport solid waste with a tandem axle load heavier than 34,000 pounds shall before operating the vehicle on a public highway of this state file with the department a surety bond subject to the approval of the department in the principal amount set by the department not to exceed $15,000 for each vehicle.

(b) The bond must be conditioned that the owner of the vehicle will pay to the state and to any municipality in which the vehicle is operated on a municipal street, within the limit of the bond, any damages to a highway or municipal street caused by the operation of the vehicle.

(c) This section does not apply to a vehicle owned by a municipality.

*(Added by L.1995, chap. 165(1), eff. 9/1/95.)*

**§623.164. Interstate and defense highways.**

(a) This subchapter does not authorize the operation on the national system of interstate and defense highways in this state of a vehicle of a size or weight greater than that authorized by 23 U.S.C. Section 127, as amended.

(b) If the United States authorizes the operation on the national system of interstate and defense highways of a vehicle of a size or weight greater than that authorized on January 1, 1983, the new limit automatically takes effect on the national system of interstate and defense highways in this state.

*(Added by L.1995, chap. 165(1), eff. 9/1/95.)*

### §623.165. Penalties.

(a) A person commits an offense if the person violates this subchapter.

(b) Except as provided by Subsection (c), an offense under this section is a misdemeanor punishable:

(1) by a fine of not more than $200;

(2) on conviction within one year after the date of a prior conviction under this section that was punishable under Subdivision (1), by a fine of not more than $500, by confinement in the county jail for not more than 60 days, or by both the fine and the confinement; or

(3) on conviction within one year after the date of a prior conviction under this section that was punishable under Subdivision (2) or this subdivision, by a fine of not more than $1,000, by confinement in the county jail for not more than six months, or by both the fine and the confinement.

(c) A corporation is not subject to confinement for an offense under this section, but two times the maximum fine provided for in the applicable subdivision of Subsection (b) may be imposed against the corporation.
*(Added by L.1995, chap. 165(1), eff. 9/1/95.)*

### §§623.166 to 623.180. *(Reserved.)*

## SUBCHAPTER I. UNLADEN LIFT EQUIPMENT MOTOR VEHICLES; ANNUAL PERMIT

### §623.181. Annual permit.

(a) The department may issue an annual permit for the movement over a highway or road of this state of an unladen lift equipment motor vehicle that because of its design for use as lift equipment exceeds the maximum weight or width limitations prescribed by statute.

(b) The department may issue a permit on receipt of an application for the permit.
*(Added by L.1995, chap. 165(1), eff. 9/1/95.)*

### §623.182. Permit fee.

The fee for a permit under this subchapter is $50. *(Added by L.1995, chap. 165(1), eff. 9/1/95.)*

### §§623.183 to 623.190. *(Reserved.)*

## SUBCHAPTER J. UNLADEN LIFT EQUIPMENT MOTOR VEHICLES; TRIP PERMITS

### §623.191. Optional procedure.

This subchapter provides an optional procedure for the issuance of a permit for the movement of an unladen lift equipment motor vehicle that because of its design for use as lift equipment exceeds the maximum weight and width limitations prescribed by statute. *(Added by L.1995, chap. 165(1), eff. 9/1/95.)*

### §623.192. Permit to move unladen lift equipment motor vehicles.

(a) The department may, on application, issue a permit to a person to move over a road or highway under the jurisdiction of the department an unladen lift equipment motor vehicle that cannot comply with the restrictions set out in Subchapter C of Chapter 621 and 621.101.

(b) The department may not issue a permit under this section unless the vehicle may be moved without material damage to the highway or serious inconvenience to highway traffic.
*(Added by L.1995, chap. 165(1), eff. 9/1/95.)*

### §623.193. Designated route in municipality.

(a) A municipality having a state highway in its territory may designate to the department the route in the municipality to be used by a vehicle described by Section 623.192 operating over the state highway. The department shall show the designated route on each map routing the vehicle.

(b) If a municipality does not designate a route, the department shall determine the route of the vehicle on each state highway in the municipality.

(c) A municipality may not require a fee, permit, or license for movement of the vehicles on the route of a state highway designated by the municipality or department.
*(Added by L.1995, chap. 165(1), eff. 9/1/95.)*

### §623.194. Registration of vehicle.

A permit under this subchapter may be issued only if the vehicle to be moved is registered under Chapter 502 for the maximum gross weight applicable to the vehicle under Section 621.101 or has the distinguishing license plates as provided by Section 502.276 if applicable to the vehicle. *(Added by L.1995, chap. 165(1), eff. 9/1/95.)*

### §623.195. Rules; forms and procedures; fees.

(a) The Texas Transportation Commission by rule shall provide for the issuance of a permit under this subchapter. The rules must include each matter the commission determines necessary to implement this subchapter and:

(1) requirements for forms and procedures used in applying for a permit;

(2) conditions with regard to route and time of movement;

(3) requirements for flags, flaggers, and warning devices;

(4) the fee for a permit; and

(5) standards to determine whether a permit is to be issued for one trip only or for a period established by the commission.

(b) In adopting a rule or establishing a fee, the commission shall consider and be guided by:

(1) the state's investment in its highway system;

(2) the safety and convenience of the general traveling public;

(3) the registration or license fee paid on the vehicle for which the permit is requested;

(4) the fees paid by vehicles operating within legal limits;

(5) the suitability of roadways and subgrades on the various classes of highways of the system;

(6) the variation in soil grade prevalent in the different regions of the state;

(7) the seasonal effects on highway load capacity;

(8) the highway shoulder design and other highway geometrics;

(9) the load capacity of highway bridges;

(10) administrative costs;

(11) added wear on highways; and

(12) compensation for inconvenience and necessary delays to highway users.

*(Added by L.1995, chap. 165(1), eff. 9/1/95.)*



### §623.196. Violation of rule.

A permit under this subchapter is void on the failure of an owner or the owner's representative to comply with a rule of the commission or with a condition placed on the permit, and immediately on the violation, further movement over a highway of an oversize or overweight vehicle violates the law regulating the size or weight of a vehicle on a public highway. *(Added by L.1995, chap. 165(1), eff. 9/1/95.)*

### §623.197. Deposit of fee in state highway fund.

A fee collected under this subchapter shall be deposited to the credit of the state highway fund. *(Added by L.1995, chap. 165(1), eff. 9/1/95.)*

### §623.198. Liability for damage to highways.

(a) By issuing a permit under this subchapter, the department does not guarantee that a highway can safely accommodate the movement.

(b) The owner of a vehicle involved in the movement of an oversize or overweight vehicle, even if a permit has been issued for the movement, is strictly liable for any damage the movement causes the highway system or any of its structures or appurtenances.

*(Added by L.1995, chap. 165(1), eff. 9/1/95.)*

### §623.199. Determination whether vehicle subject to registration or eligible for distinguishing license plate.

(a) The department may establish criteria to determine whether an unladen lift equipment motor vehicle that because of its design for use as lift equipment exceeds the maximum weight and width limitations prescribed by statute is subject to registration under Chapter 502 or eligible for the distinguishing license plate provided by Section 502.276.

(b) Notwithstanding Subsection (a), a vehicle authorized by the department before June 11, 1985, to operate without registration under Chapter 502 may not be required to register under that chapter.

*(Added by L.1995, chap. 165(1), eff. 9/1/95.)*

### §623.200. Nonapplicability of subchapter.

This subchapter does not apply to a person issued a registration certificate under Chapter 643, even if not all the operations of the person are performed under that certificate. *(Added by L.1995, chap. 165(1); L.1997, chap. 165(30.147), eff. 9/1/97.)*

## SUBCHAPTER K. PORT AUTHORITY PERMITS

*(Added by L.1997, chap. 1194(1), eff. 9/1/97, expires 3/1/2005.)*

### §623.210. Optional procedure.

This subchapter provides an optional procedure for the issuance of a permit for the movement of oversize or overweight vehicles carrying cargo on state highways located in counties contiguous to the Gulf of Mexico or a bay or inlet opening into the gulf and bordering the United Mexican States. *(Added by L.1997, chap. 1194(1), eff. 9/1/97, expires 3/1/2005.)*

### §623.211. Definition.

In this subchapter, "port authority" means a port authority created or operating under Section 52, Article III, or Section 59, Article XVI, Texas Constitution. *(Added by L.1997, chap. 1194(1), eff. 9/1/97, expires 3/1/2005.)*

### §623.212. Permits by port authority.

The department may authorize a port authority to issue permits for the movement of oversize or overweight vehicles carrying cargo on state highways located in counties contiguous to the Gulf of Mexico or a bay or inlet opening into the gulf and bordering the United Mexican States. *(Added by L.1997, chap. 1194(1), eff. 9/1/97, expires 3/1/2005.)*

### §623.213. Maintenance contracts.

A port authority issuing permits under this subchapter shall make payments to the department to provide funds for the maintenance of state highways subject to this subchapter. *(Added by L.1997, chap. 1194(1), eff. 9/1/97, expires 3/1/2005.)*

### §623.214. Permit fees.

(a) A port authority may collect a fee for permits issued under this subchapter. Such fees shall not exceed $80 per trip.

(b) Fees collected under Subsection (a) shall be used solely to provide funds for the payments provided for under Section 623.213 less administrative costs which shall not exceed 15 percent of the fees collected. Such fees shall be deposited in State Highway Fund 6.

*(Added by L.1997, chap. 1194(1), eff. 9/1/97, expires 3/1/2005; chgd. by L.1999, chap. 624(1), eff. 6/18/99.)*

### §623.215. Permit requirements.

(a) A permit issued under this subchapter must include:

(1) the name of the applicant;

(2) the date of issuance;

(3) the signature of the director of the port authority;

(4) a statement of the kind of cargo being transported over State Highways 48 and 4 between the Gateway International Bridge and the entrance to the Port of Brownsville, or over State Highways 48 and 4 and United States Highways 77 and 83 between Veterans International Bridge at Los Tomates and the entrance to the Port of Brownsville, the maximum weight and dimensions of the equipment, and the kind and weight of each commodity to be transported provided the gross weight of such equipment and commodities shall not exceed 125,000 pounds;

(5) a statement of any condition on which the permit is issued;

(6) a statement that the cargo shall be transported over the most direct route from the Gateway International Bridge or the Veterans International Bridge at Los Tomates to the entrance of the Port of Brownsville using State Highways 48 and 4 or United States Highways 77 and 83;

(7) the name of the driver of the vehicle in which the cargo is to be transported; and

(8) the location where the cargo was loaded.

(b) A port authority shall report to the department all permits issued under this subchapter.

*(Added by L.1997, chap. 1194(1), eff. 9/1/97, expires 3/1/2005; chgd. by L.1999, chap. 624(2), eff. 6/18/99.)*

### §623.216. Time of movement.

A permit issued under this subchapter shall specify the time in which movement authorized by the permit is allowed. *(Added by L.1997, chap. 1194(1), eff. 9/1/97, expires 3/1/2005.)*

### §623.217. Speed limit.

Movement authorized by a permit issued under this subchapter shall not exceed the posted speed limit or 55 miles per hour, whichever is less. Violation of this provision shall constitute a moving violation. *(Added by L.1997, chap. 1194(1), eff. 9/1/97, expires 3/1/2005.)*

### §623.218. Enforcement.

The Department of Public Safety shall have authority to enforce the provisions of this subchapter. *(Added by L.1997, chap. 1194(1), eff. 9/1/97, expires 3/1/2005.)*

### §623.219. Expiration.

This Act expires March 1, 2005. *(Added by L.1997, chap. 1194(1), eff. 9/1/97, expires 3/1/2005; chgd. by L.1999, chap. 624(3), eff. 6/18/99.)*



## CHAPTERS 624 to 640. *(Reserved.)*

## SUBTITLE F. COMMERCIAL MOTOR VEHICLES

## CHAPTER 641. OPERATION OF LEASED COMMERCIAL MOTOR VEHICLES AND TRUCK-TRACTORS

*(Repealed by L.1997, chap. 165(30.148), eff. 9/1/97.)*

## CHAPTER 642. IDENTIFYING MARKINGS ON COMMERCIAL MOTOR VEHICLES

Section


### §642.001. Definitions.

In this chapter:

(1) "Motor vehicle" means a motor vehicle, other than a motorcycle, that is designed or used primarily for the transportation of persons or property.

(2) "Operator" means the person who is in actual physical control of a motor vehicle.

(3) "Owner" means a person who has:

(A) legal title to a motor vehicle; or

(B) the right to possess or control the vehicle.

(4) "Road-tractor" means a motor vehicle that is:

(A) used for towing manufactured housing; or

(B) designed and used for drawing other vehicles and not constructed so as to carry any load independently or as a part of the weight of a vehicle or load it is drawing.

(5) "Truck-tractor" means a motor vehicle that:

(A) transports passenger cars loaded on the vehicle while the vehicle is engaged with a semitrailer transporting passenger cars; or

(B) is designed or used primarily for pulling other vehicles and constructed to carry only a part of the weight of a vehicle it is pulling.

(6) "Tow truck" has the meaning assigned that term by Section 643.001.

*(Added by L.1995, chap. 165(1); chgd. by L.1997, chap. 1171(4.12(a)), eff. 9/1/97.)*

### §642.002. Identifying markings on certain vehicles required; offense; penalty.

(a) A person commits an offense if:

(1) the person operates on a public street, road, or highway:

(A) a commercial motor vehicle that has three or more axles;

(B) a truck-tractor;

(C) a road-tractor; or

(D) a tow truck; and

(2) the vehicle does not have on each side of the power unit identifying markings that comply with the identifying marking requirements specified by 49 C.F.R. Section 390.21 or that:

(A) show the name of the owner or operator of the vehicle;

(B) have clearly legible letters and numbers of a height of at least two inches; and

(C) show the motor carrier registration number in clearly legible letters and numbers, if the vehicle is required to be registered under this chapter.

(b) A person commits an offense if the person operates on a public street, road, or highway a tow truck that does not show on each side of the power unit, in addition to the markings required by Subsection (a)(2), the city in which the owner or operator maintains its place of business and the telephone number, including area code, at that place of business in clearly legible letters and numbers.

(c) The owner of a vehicle commits an offense if the owner or operator permits another to operate a vehicle in violation of Subsection (a) or (b).

(d) The Texas Department of Transportation by rule may prescribe additional requirements regarding the form of the markings required by Subsection (a)(2) that are not inconsistent with that subsection.

(e) An offense under this section is a Class C misdemeanor.

*(Added by L.1995, chap. 165(1); chgd. by L.1997, chap. 1171(4.12(b)); L.1999, chap. 566(1), eff. 6/18/99.)*

### §642.003. Nonapplicability.

Section 642.002 does not apply to a commercial motor vehicle, road-tractor, or truck-tractor that is:

(1) registered under Section 502.163;

(2) required to be registered under Section 113.131, Natural Resources Code;

(3) operated in private carriage that is subject to Title 49, Code of Federal Regulations, Part 397.21;

(4) operated under the direct control, supervision, or authority of a public utility, as recognized by the legislature, that is otherwise visibly marked; or

(5) transporting timber products in their natural state from first point of production or harvest to first point of processing.

*(Added by L.1995, chap. 165(1); chgd. by L.1997, chap. 165(30.149(a)), eff. 9/1/97.)*

## CHAPTER 643. MOTOR CARRIER REGISTRATION

*(Added by L.1997, chap. 165(30.150(a)), eff. 9/1/97.)*

## SUBCHAPTER A. GENERAL PROVISIONS

Section



## SUBCHAPTER B. REGISTRATION

## SUBCHAPTER C. INSURANCE





## SUBCHAPTER D. ECONOMIC REGULATION



## SUBCHAPTER E. TOW TRUCKS



## SUBCHAPTER F. ENFORCEMENT



## SUBCHAPTER A. GENERAL PROVISIONS

### §643.001. Definitions.

In this chapter:

(1) "Department" means the Texas Department of Transportation.

(2) "Director" means:

(A) the executive director of the department; or

(B) an employee of the department who:

(i) is a division or special office director or holds a higher rank; and

(ii) is designated by the director.

(3) "Hazardous material" has the meaning assigned by 49 U.S.C. Section 5102.

(4) "Household goods" has the meaning assigned by 49 U.S.C. Section 13102.

(5) "Insurer" means a person, including a surety, authorized in this state to write lines of insurance coverage required by this chapter.

(6) "Motor carrier" means an individual, association, corporation, or other legal entity that controls, operates, or directs the operation of one or more vehicles that transport persons or cargo over a road or highway in this state.

(7) "Tow truck" means a motor vehicle, including a wrecker, equipped with a mechanical device used to tow, winch, or otherwise move another motor vehicle.

(8) "Vehicle requiring registration" means a vehicle described by Section 643.051.
*(Added by L.1997, chap. 165(30.150(a)), eff. 9/1/97.)*

### §643.002. Exemptions.

This chapter does not apply to:

(1) a motor vehicle registered under the single state registration system established under 49 U.S.C. Section 14504(c) when operating exclusively in interstate or international commerce;

(2) a motor vehicle registered as a cotton vehicle under Section 502.277;

(3) a motor vehicle the department by rule exempts because the vehicle is subject to comparable registration and a comparable safety program administered by another governmental entity;

(4) a motor vehicle used to transport passengers operated by an entity whose primary function is not the transportation of passengers, such as a vehicle operated by a hotel, day-care center, public or private school, nursing home, or similar organization;

(5) a vehicle operating under a private carrier permit issued under Chapter 42, Alcoholic Beverage Code; or

(6) a vehicle operated by a governmental entity.

*(Added by L.1997, chap. 165(30.150(a)); chgd. by L.1999, chaps. 62(17.10(a)), 603(1), eff. 9/1/99, 6/18/99, respectively.)*

### §643.003. Rules.

The department may adopt rules to administer this chapter. *(Added by L.1997, chap. 165(30.150(a)), eff. 9/1/97.)*

### §643.004. Payment of fees.

(a) The department may adopt rules on the method of payment of a fee under this chapter, including:

(1) authorizing the use of:

(A) escrow accounts described by Subsection (b); and

(B) electronic funds transfer or a credit card issued by a financial institution chartered by a state or the United States or by a nationally recognized credit organization approved by the department; and

(2) requiring the payment of a discount or service charge for a credit card payment in addition to the fee.

(b) The department may establish one or more escrow accounts in the state highway fund for the prepayment of a fee under this chapter. Prepaid fees and any fees established by the department for the administration of this section shall be:

(1) administered under an agreement approved by the department; and

(2) deposited to the credit of the state highway fund to be appropriated only to the department for the purposes of administering this chapter.

*(Added by L.1997, chap. 165(30.150(a)); chgd. by L.1999, chap. 62(17.11(a)), eff. 9/1/99.)*

### §§643.005 to 643.050. *(Reserved.)*

## SUBCHAPTER B. REGISTRATION

### §643.051. Registration required.

A motor carrier may not operate a commercial motor vehicle, as defined by Section 548.001, or a tow truck on a road or highway of this state unless the carrier registers with the department under this subchapter. *(Added by L.1997, chap. 165(30.150(a)), eff. 9/1/97.)*

### §643.052. Application.

To register under this subchapter a motor carrier must submit to the department an application on a form prescribed by the department. The application must include:

(1) the name of the owner and the principal business address of the motor carrier;

(2) the name and address of the legal agent for service of process on the carrier in this state, if different;

(3) a description of each vehicle requiring registration the carrier proposes to operate, including the motor vehicle identification number, make, and unit number;

(4) a statement as to whether the carrier proposes to transport household goods or a hazardous material;

(5) a declaration that the applicant has knowledge of all laws and rules relating to motor carrier safety, including this chapter, Chapter 644, and Subtitle C; and

(6) any other information the department by rule determines is necessary for the safe operation of a motor carrier under this chapter.
*(Added by L.1997, chap. 165(30.150(a)), eff. 9/1/97.)*

### §643.053. Filing of application.

An application under Section 643.052 must be filed with the department and accompanied by:

(1) an application fee of $100 plus a $10 fee for each vehicle requiring registration the motor carrier proposes to operate;

(2) evidence of insurance or financial responsibility as required by Section 643.103(a); and

(3) any insurance filing fee required under Section 643.103(c).
*(Added by L.1997, chap. 165(30.150(a)), eff. 9/1/97.)*

### §643.054. Department approval; issuance of certificate.

(a) The department shall register a motor carrier under this subchapter if the carrier complies with Sections 643.052 and 643.053. The department may deny a registration if the applicant has had a registration revoked under Section 643.252.

(b) The department shall issue a certificate containing a single registration number to a motor carrier, regardless of the number of vehicles requiring registration the carrier operates.

(c) To avoid multiple registrations of a single motor carrier, the department shall adopt simplified procedures for the registration of motor carriers transporting household goods as agents for carriers required to register under this chapter.
*(Added by L.1997, chap. 165(30.150(a)); chgd. by L.1999, chap. 62(17.12(a)), eff. 9/1/99.)*



### §643.055. Conditional acceptance.

(a) The department may conditionally accept an incomplete application for registration under this subchapter if the motor carrier complies with Section 643.053.

(b) The department shall notify a motor carrier that an application is incomplete and inform the carrier of the information required for completion. If the motor carrier fails to provide the information before the 46th day after the date the department provides the notice, the application is considered withdrawn, and the department shall retain each fee required by Section 643.053(1).
*(Added by L.1997, chap. 165(30.150(a)), eff. 9/1/97.)*

### §643.056. Supplemental registration.

(a) A motor carrier required to register under this subchapter shall supplement the carrier's application for registration before:

(1) the carrier transports a hazardous material or household goods if the carrier has not provided notice of the transportation to the department in the carrier's initial or a supplemental application for registration;

(2) the carrier operates a vehicle requiring registration that is not described on the carrier's initial or a supplemental application for registration; or

(3) the carrier changes the carrier's principal business address, legal agent, ownership, or name.

(b) The department shall prescribe the form of a supplemental application for registration under Subsection (a).
*(Added by L.1997, chap. 165(30.150(a)), eff. 9/1/97.)*

### §643.057. Additional vehicles and fees.

(a) A motor carrier may not operate an additional vehicle requiring registration unless the carrier pays a registration fee of $10 for each additional vehicle and shows the department evidence of insurance or financial responsibility for the vehicle in an amount at least equal to the amount set by the department under Section 643.101.

(b) A motor carrier is not required to pay the $10 registration fee for a vehicle that replaces a vehicle for which the fee has been paid.

(c) A registered motor carrier may not transport household goods or a hazardous material unless the carrier shows the department evidence of insurance or financial responsibility in an amount at least equal to the amount set by the department under Section 643.101 for a vehicle carrying household goods or a hazardous material.

(d) The department may not collect more than $10 in equipment registration fees for a vehicle registered under both this subchapter and Chapter 645.
*(Added by L.1997, chap. 165(30.150(a)), eff. 9/1/97.)*

## §643.058. Renewal of registration.

(a) Except as provided in Section 643.061, a registration issued under this subchapter is valid for one year. The department may adopt a system under which registrations expire at different times during the year.

(b) At least 30 days before the date on which a motor carrier's registration expires, the department shall notify the carrier of the impending expiration. The notice must be in writing and sent to the motor carrier's last known address according to the records of the department.

(c) A motor carrier may renew a registration under this subchapter by:

(1) supplementing the application with any new information required under Section 643.056;

(2) paying a $10 fee for each vehicle requiring registration the carrier operates; and

(3) providing the department evidence of continuing insurance or financial responsibility in an amount at least equal to the amount set by the department under Section 643.101.

*(Added by L.1997, chap. 165(30.150(a)); chgd. by L.1999, chaps. 62(17.13(a)), 603(2), eff. 9/1/99, 6/18/99, respectively.)*

## §643.059. Cab cards.

(a) The department shall issue a cab card for each vehicle requiring registration. A cab card must:

(1) show the registration number of the certificate issued under Section 643.054(b);

(2) show the vehicle unit number;

(3) show the vehicle identification number; and

(4) contain a statement that the vehicle is registered to operate under this subchapter.

(b) The department shall issue cab cards at the time a motor carrier pays a registration fee under this subchapter. The department may charge a fee of $1 for each cab card.

(c) A motor carrier required to register under this subchapter must keep the cab card in the cab of each vehicle requiring registration the carrier operates.

(d) The department may order a motor carrier to surrender a cab card if the carrier's registration is suspended or revoked under Section 643.252.

(e) If the department determines that the cab card system described by Subsections (a)-(c) is not an efficient means of enforcing this subchapter, the department by rule may adopt an alternative method that is accessible by law enforcement personnel in the field and provides for the enforcement of the registration requirements of this subchapter.

(f) A cab card or a vehicle registration issued under the alternative method described in Subsection (e) must be valid for the same duration of time as a motor carrier's certificate issued under Section 643.054(b) or Section 643.061(c)(1).

*(Added by L.1997, chap. 165(30.150(a)); chgd. by L.1999, chap. 603(3), eff. 6/18/99.)*

## §643.060. Temporary registration of international motor carrier.

The department by rule may provide for the temporary registration of an international motor carrier that provides evidence of insurance as required for a domestic motor carrier. The department may charge a fee for a temporary registration in an amount not to exceed the cost of administering this section. *(Added by L.1997, chap. 165(30.150(a)), eff. 9/1/97.)*

## §643.061 Length of registration period.

The department may vary the registration period under this subchapter by adopting rules that provide for:

(1) an optional two-year registration; and

(2) the issuance of a temporary registration permit that is valid for less than one year.

*(Added by L.1999, chap. 62(17.14(a)) eff. 9/1/99.)*

## §643.061 Optional registration periods.

(a) The department may vary the registration period under this subchapter by adopting rules that provide for:

(1) an optional two-year registration; and

(2) an optional temporary registration that is valid for less than one year.

(b) A motor carrier applying for registration under this section must pay:

(1) a $20 fee for each vehicle registered under Subsection (a)(1);

(2) a $10 fee for each vehicle registered under Subsection (a)(2); and

(3) application and insurance filing fees the department by rule adopts in an amount not to exceed $100 each.

(c) The department shall issue to a motor carrier registering under this section:

(1) a motor carrier's certificate, in the manner provided by Section 643.054; and

(2) a cab card or the equivalent of a cab card, in the manner provided by Section 643.059. *(Added by L.1999, chap. 603(4), eff. 6/18/99.)*

### §643.062 Limitation on international motor carrier.

(a) A foreign-based international motor carrier required to register under this chapter or registered under Chapter 645 may not transport persons or cargo in intrastate commerce in this state.

(b) A person may not assist a foreign-based international motor carrier in violating Subsection (a).

*(Added by L.1999, chaps. 62(17.14(a)), 603(4), eff. 9/1/99, 6/18/99, respectively.)*

### §643.063 Vehicles operated under short-term lease and substitute vehicles.

(a) In this section:

(1) "Leasing business" means a person that leases vehicles requiring registration.

(2) "Short-term lease" means a lease of 30 days or less.



(b) A vehicle requiring registration operated under a short-term lease is exempt from the registration requirements of Sections 643.052-643.059. The department shall adopt rules providing for the operation of these vehicles under flexible procedures. A vehicle requiring registration operated under a short-term lease is not required to carry a cab card or other proof of registration if a copy of the lease agreement is carried in the cab of the vehicle.

(c) A motor carrier may operate a substitute vehicle without notifying the department in advance if the substitute is a temporary replacement because of maintenance, repair, or other unavailability of the vehicle originally leased. A substitute vehicle is not required to carry a cab card or other proof of registration if a copy of the lease agreement for the vehicle originally leased is carried in the cab of the substitute.

(d) Instead of the registration procedures described by Sections 643.052-643.059, the department shall adopt rules that allow a leasing business to report annually to the department on the number of vehicles requiring registration that the leasing business actually operated in the previous 12 months. The rules may not require the vehicles operated to be described with particularity. The registration fee for each vehicle operated may be paid at the time the report is filed.

(e) A leasing business that registers its vehicles under Subsection (d) may comply with the liability insurance requirements of Subchapter C by filing evidence of a contingency liability policy satisfactory to the department.

(f) Rules adopted by the department under this section:

(1) must be designed to avoid requiring a vehicle to be registered more than once in a calendar year; and

(2) may allow a leasing business to register a vehicle on behalf of a lessee.

*(Added by L.1999, chap. 62(17.15(a)), eff. 9/1/99.)*

### §§643.064 to 643.100. *(Reserved.)*

## SUBCHAPTER C. INSURANCE

### §643.101. Amount required.

(a) A motor carrier required to register under Subchapter B shall maintain liability insurance in an amount set by the department for each vehicle requiring registration the carrier operates.

(b) The department by rule may set the amount of liability insurance required at an amount that does not exceed the amount required for a motor carrier under a federal regulation adopted under 49 U.S.C. Section 13906(a)(1). In setting the amount the department shall consider:

(1) the class and size of the vehicle; and

(2) the persons or cargo being transported.

(c) A motor carrier required to register under Subchapter B that transports household goods shall maintain cargo insurance in the amount required for a motor carrier transporting household goods under federal law.

*(Added by L.1997, chap. 165(30.150(a)), eff. 9/1/97.)*

### §643.102. Self-insurance.

A motor carrier may comply with Section 643.101 through self-insurance if the carrier demonstrates to the department that it can satisfy its obligations for liability for bodily injury or property damage. In the interest of public safety, the department by rule shall provide for a responsible system of self-insurance for a motor carrier. *(Added by L.1997, chap. 165(30.150(a)), eff. 9/1/97.)*

### §643.103. Filing; evidence of insurance; fees.

(a) A motor carrier that is required to register under Subchapter B must file with the department evidence of insurance in the amounts required by Section 643.101, or evidence of financial responsibility as described by Section 643.102, in a form prescribed by the department. The form must be filed:

(1) at the time of the initial registration;

(2) at the time of a subsequent registration if the motor carrier was required to be continuously registered under Subchapter B and the carrier failed to maintain continuous registration;

(3) at the time a motor carrier changes insurers; and

(4) at the time a motor carrier changes ownership, as determined by rules adopted by the department.

(b) A motor carrier shall keep evidence of insurance in a form approved by the department in the cab of each vehicle requiring registration the carrier operates.

(c) The department may charge a fee of $100 for a filing under Subsection (a).

*(Added by L.1997, chap. 165(30.150(a)), eff. 9/1/97.)*

### §643.104. Termination of insurance coverage.

(a) An insurer may not terminate coverage provided to a motor carrier registered under Subchapter B unless the insurer provides the department with notice at least 30 days before the date the termination takes effect.

(b) Notice under Subsection (a) must be in a form approved by the department and the Texas Department of Insurance. The department shall notify the Department of Public Safety of each notice filed under Subsection (a).

*(Added by L.1997, chap. 165(30.150(a)), eff. 9/1/97.)*

### §643.105. Insolvency of insurer.

If an insurer for a motor carrier becomes insolvent, is placed in receivership, or has its certificate of authority suspended or revoked and if the carrier no longer has insurance coverage as required by this subchapter, the carrier shall file with the department, not later than the 10th day after the date the coverage lapses:

(1) evidence of insurance as required by Section 643.103; and

(2) an affidavit that:

(A) indicates that an accident from which the carrier may incur liability did not occur while the coverage was not in effect; or

(B) contains a plan acceptable to the department indicating how the carrier will satisfy claims of liability against the carrier for an accident that occurred while the coverage was not in effect.

*(Added by L.1997, chap. 165(30.150(a)), eff. 9/1/97.)*

### §643.106. Insurance for employees.

(a) Notwithstanding any provision of any law or regulation, a motor carrier that is required to register under Subchapter B and whose primary business is transportation for compensation or hire between two or more municipalities shall protect its employees by obtaining:

(1) workers' compensation insurance coverage as defined under Subtitle A, Title 5, Labor Code; or

(2) accidental insurance coverage approved by the department from:

(A) a reliable insurance company authorized to write accidental insurance policies in this state; or

(B) a surplus lines insurer under Article 1.14-2, Insurance Code.

(b) The department shall determine the amount of insurance coverage under Subsection (a)(2). The amount may not be less than:

(1) $300,000 for medical expenses for at least 104 weeks;

(2) $100,000 for accidental death and dismemberment;

(3) 70 percent of an employee's pre-injury income for at least 104 weeks when compensating for loss of income; and

(4) $500 for the maximum weekly benefit.

*(Added by L.1997, chap. 165(30.150(a)); chgd. by L.1999, chaps. 62(17.17(a)), 886(1), eff. 9/1/99, 6/18/99, respectively.)*

### §§643.107 to 643.150. *(Reserved.)*

## SUBCHAPTER D. ECONOMIC REGULATION

### §643.151. Prohibition.

Except as provided by this subchapter, the department may not regulate the prices, routes, or services provided by a motor carrier. *(Added by L.1997, chap. 165(30.150(a)), eff. 9/1/97.)*

### §643.152. Voluntary standards.

The department may establish voluntary standards for uniform cargo liability, uniform bills of lading or receipts for cargo being transported, and uniform cargo credit. A standard adopted under this section must be consistent with Subtitle IV, Title 49, United States Code, or a regulation adopted under that law. *(Added by L.1997, chap. 165(30.150(a)), eff. 9/1/97.)*

### §643.153. Motor carrier transporting household goods.

(a) The department shall adopt rules to protect a consumer using the service of a motor carrier who is transporting household goods for compensation.

(b) The department may adopt rules necessary to ensure that a customer of a motor carrier transporting household goods is protected from deceptive or unfair practices and unreasonably hazardous activities. The rules must:

(1) establish a formal process for resolving a dispute over a fee or damage;

(2) require a motor carrier to indicate clearly to a customer whether an estimate is binding or nonbinding and disclose the maximum price a customer could be required to pay;

(3) create a centralized process for making complaints about a motor carrier that also allows a customer to inquire about a carrier's complaint record;

(4) require a motor carrier transporting household goods to list a place of business with a street address in this state and the carrier's registration number issued under this article in any print advertising published in this state;

(5) require motor carriers that are required to register under Subsection (c) to file proof of cargo insurance in amounts to be determined by the department that do not exceed the amount required for a motor carrier transporting household goods under federal law and allow alternative evidence of financial responsibility, through surety bonds, letters of credit, or other means satisfactory to the department, for contractual obligations to customers that do not exceed $5,000 aggregate loss or damage to total cargo shipped at any one time;

(6) require motor carriers that are required to register under Subsection (c) to conspicuously advise consumers concerning limitation of any carrier liability for loss or damage as determined under Subdivision (7); and

(7) determine reasonable provisions governing limitation of liability for loss or damage of motor carriers required to register under Subsection (c), not to exceed 60 cents per pound per article.

(c) The department shall require motor carriers that are not required to register under Subchapter B to register their operations before transporting household goods for compensation. The department shall determine the forms and procedures for registration required under this subsection. The department shall charge a motor carrier who registers under this subsection a fee that does not exceed the total of the fees imposed in Subchapter B.

(d) A motor carrier that is required to register under Subchapter B and that transports household goods shall file a tariff with the department that establishes maximum charges for transportation between two or more municipalities. A motor carrier may comply with this requirement by filing a copy of the carrier's tariff governing interstate transportation services on a highway between two or more municipalities. The department shall make tariffs filed under this subsection available for public inspection at the department.

(e) The department may not adopt rules regulating the rates, except as provided by this section, or routes of a motor carrier transporting household goods.

(f) The unauthorized practice of the insurance business under Article 1.14-1, Insurance Code, does not include the offer of insurance by a household goods motor carrier, or its agent, that transports goods for up to the full value of a customer's property transported or stored, if the offer is authorized by a rule adopted under Subsection (b).

(g) A motor carrier may designate an association or an agent of an association as its collective maximum ratemaking association for the purpose of the filing of a tariff under Subsection (d). *(Added by L.1997, chap. 165(30.150(a)); chgd. by L.1999, chaps. 62(17.19(a)), 603(5), eff. 9/1/99, 6/18/99, respectively.)*

## §643.154. Antitrust exemption.

(a) Chapter 15, Business & Commerce Code, does not apply to a discussion or agreement between a motor carrier that is required to register under Subchapter B and that transports household goods and an agent of the carrier involving:

(1) the following matters if they occur under the authority of the principal carrier:

(A) a rate for the transportation of household goods;

(B) an access, terminal, storage, or other charge incidental to the transportation of household goods; or

(C) an allowance relating to the transportation of household goods; or

(2) ownership of the carrier by the agent or membership on the board of directors of the carrier by the agent.

(b) An agent under Subsection (a) may itself be a motor carrier required to register under Subchapter B.

(c) The department by rule may exempt a motor carrier required to register under Subchapter B from Chapter 15, Business & Commerce Code, for an activity relating to the establishment of a joint line rate, route, classification, or mileage guide.

(d) A motor carrier that is required to register under Subchapter B and that transports household goods, or an agent of the carrier, may enter into a collective ratemaking agreement with another motor carrier of household goods or an agent of that carrier concerning the establishment and filing of maximum rates, classifications, rules, or procedures. The agreement must be submitted to the department for approval.

(e) The department shall approve an agreement submitted under Subsection (d) if the agreement provides that each meeting of parties to the agreement is open to the public and that notice of each meeting must be given to customers who are multiple users of the services of a motor carrier that is a party to the agreement. The department may withhold approval of the agreement if it determines, after notice and hearing, that the agreement fails to comply with this subsection.

(f) Unless disapproved by the department, an agreement made under Subsection (d) is valid, and Chapter 15, Business & Commerce Code, does not apply to a motor carrier that is a party to the agreement.

*(Added by L.1997, chap. 165(30.150(a)), eff. 9/1/97.)*



## §643.155. Rules advisory committee.

(a) The department shall appoint a rules advisory committee consisting of representatives of motor carriers transporting household goods using small, medium, and large equipment, the public, and the department.

(b) Members of the committee serve at the pleasure of the department and are not entitled to compensation or reimbursement of expenses for serving on the committee. The department may adopt rules to govern the operations of the advisory committee.

(c) The committee shall:

(1) examine the rules adopted by the department under Sections 643.153(a) and (b) and make recommendations to the department on modernizing and streamlining the rules;

(2) conduct a study of the feasibility and necessity of requiring any vehicle liability insurance for household goods carriers required to register under Section 643.153(c); and

(3) recommend a maximum level of liability limitation under Section 643.153(b)(7) that does not exceed 60 cents per pound.

*(Repealed and added by L.1999, chap. 62(17.19(b)), eff. 9/1/99.)*

## §643.156. Regulation of advertising.

(a) The department may not by rule restrict competitive bidding or advertising by a motor carrier except to prohibit false, misleading, or deceptive practices.

(b) A rule to prohibit false, misleading, or deceptive practices may not:

(1) restrict the use of:

(A) any medium for an advertisement;

(B) a motor carrier's advertisement under a trade name; or

(C) a motor carrier's personal appearance or voice in an advertisement, if the motor carrier is an individual; or

(2) relate to the size or duration of an advertisement by a motor carrier.

*(Added by L.1999, chap. 62(17.20(a)), eff. 9/1/99.)*

## §§643.157 to 643.200. *(Reserved.)*

## SUBCHAPTER E. TOW TRUCKS

### §643.201. Tow truck regulation by municipality.

(a) In addition to the registration requirements of Subchapter B, a municipality may regulate the operation of a tow truck to the extent allowed by federal law.

(b) A municipality may not require the registration of a tow truck that performs consent tows in the municipality unless the owner of the tow truck has a place of business in the territory of the municipality.

(c) A municipality may require the registration of a tow truck that performs a nonconsent tow in the municipality, regardless of whether the owner of the tow truck has a place of business in the territory of the municipality.

(d) A municipality may not require a person who holds a driver's license or commercial driver's license to obtain a license or permit for operating a tow truck unless the person performs nonconsent tows in the territory of the municipality. A fee charged for a license or permit may not exceed $15.

(e) In this section:

(1) "Commercial driver's license" has the meaning assigned by Section 522.003.

(2) "Consent tow" means the towing of a vehicle with the consent of the owner or operator of the vehicle.

(3) "Driver's license" has the meaning assigned by Section 521.001.

(4) "Nonconsent tow" means the towing of a vehicle without the consent of the owner or operator of the vehicle.

*(Added by L.1997, chap. 165(30.150(a)), eff. 9/1/97.)*



### §643.202. Rules advisory committee.

(a) The department shall appoint a rules advisory committee to advise the department on adoption of rules regarding:

(1) the application of this chapter to tow trucks; and

(2) the administration by the department of the Vehicle Storage Facility Act (Article 6687-9a, Revised Statutes).

(b) The department shall determine the size of the committee, but the committee must include one member who represents each of the following:

(1) tow truck operators;

(2) vehicle storage facility operators;

(3) owners of property having parking facilities;

(4) law enforcement agencies or municipalities;

(5) insurance companies; and

(6) the general public.

(c) Members of the committee serve at the pleasure of the department. A member of the committee is not entitled to compensation or reimbursement of expenses for serving as a member.

(d) The department may adopt rules to govern the operations of the committee.

*(Added by L.1997, chap. 165(30.150(a)), eff. 9/1/97.)*

### §§643.203 to 643.250. *(Reserved.)*

## SUBCHAPTER F. ENFORCEMENT

### §643.251. Administrative penalty.

(a) The department may impose an administrative penalty against a motor carrier required to register under Subchapter B that violates Subchapter B or C or Section 643.151, 643.152, 643.153(a)-(f), or 643.155 or a rule or order adopted under those provisions or Section 643.003. The department shall designate one or more employees to investigate violations and administer penalties under this section.

(b) Except as provided by this section, the amount of an administrative penalty may not exceed $5,000. If it is found that the motor carrier knowingly committed the violation, the penalty may not exceed $15,000. If it is found that the motor carrier knowingly committed multiple violations, the aggregate penalty for the multiple violations may not exceed $30,000. Each day a violation continues or occurs is a separate violation for purposes of imposing a penalty.

(c) The amount of the penalty shall be based on:

(1) the seriousness of the violation, including the nature, circumstances, extent, and gravity of any prohibited act, and the hazard or potential hazard created to the health, safety, or economic welfare of the public;

(2) the economic harm to property or the environment caused by the violation;
(3) the history of previous violations;
(4) the amount necessary to deter future violations;
(5) efforts to correct the violation; and
(6) any other matter that justice may require.

(d) If the department determines that a violation has occurred, it may issue to the director a report that states the facts on which the determination is based and a recommendation on the imposition and amount of any penalty.

(e) Before the 15th day after the date the report is issued, the department shall give written notice of the report to the motor carrier. The notice may be given by certified mail. The notice must include a brief summary of the alleged violation and a statement of the amount of the recommended penalty and must inform the motor carrier that the carrier has a right to a hearing on the occurrence of the violation, the amount of the penalty, or both the occurrence of the violation and the amount of the penalty.

(f) Before the 21st day after the date the motor carrier receives the notice, the carrier in writing may accept the determination and recommended penalty of the department or may make a written request for a hearing on the occurrence of the violation, the amount of the penalty, or both the occurrence of the violation and the amount of the penalty. The department may, on the request of the person, hold an informal hearing to discuss a penalty recommended under this section. The department may modify a recommendation for a penalty at the conclusion of the informal hearing.

(g) If the motor carrier accepts the determination and recommended penalty of the department, the director by order shall approve the determination and impose the recommended penalty.

(h) If the motor carrier requests a hearing or fails to respond timely to the notice, the department shall set a hearing and give notice of the hearing to the carrier. The hearing shall be held by an administrative law judge of the State Office of Administrative Hearings. The administrative law judge shall make findings of fact and conclusions of law and promptly issue to the director a proposal for a decision about the occurrence of the violation and the amount of a proposed penalty. Based on the findings of fact, conclusions of law, and proposal for a decision, the director by order may find that a violation has occurred and impose a penalty or may find that no violation occurred. The director may increase or decrease the amount of the penalty recommended by an administrative law judge within the limits prescribed by Subsection (b).

(i) The notice of the director's order given to the motor carrier under Chapter 2001, Government Code, must include a statement of the right of the carrier to judicial review of the order.

(j) Before the 31st day after the date the director's order becomes final as provided by Section 2001.144, Government Code, the motor carrier shall:

(1) pay the amount of the penalty;

(2) pay the amount of the penalty and file a petition for judicial review contesting the occurrence of the violation, the amount of the penalty, or both the occurrence of the violation and the amount of the penalty; or

(3) without paying the amount of the penalty, file a petition for judicial review contesting the occurrence of the violation, the amount of the penalty, or both the occurrence of the violation and the amount of the penalty.

(k) Within the 30-day period, a motor carrier that acts under Subsection (j)(3) may:

(1) stay enforcement of the penalty by:

(A) paying the amount of the penalty to the court for placement in an escrow account; or

(B) giving to the court a supersedeas bond that is approved by the court for the amount of the penalty and that is effective until all judicial review of the director's order is final; or

(2) request the court to stay enforcement of the penalty by:

(A) filing with the court a sworn affidavit of the person stating that the person is financially unable to pay the amount of the penalty and is financially unable to give the supersedeas bond; and

(B) giving a copy of the affidavit to the director by certified mail.

(*l*) If the department receives a copy of an affidavit under Subsection (k)(2), it may file with the court, before the sixth day after the date the copy is received, a contest to the affidavit. The court shall hold a hearing on the facts alleged in the affidavit as soon as practicable and shall stay the enforcement of the penalty if the court finds that the alleged facts are true. The motor carrier that files an affidavit has the burden of proving that the carrier is financially unable to pay the amount of the penalty and to give a supersedeas bond.

(m) If the motor carrier does not pay the amount of the penalty and the enforcement of the penalty is not stayed, the director may refer the matter to the attorney general for collection of the amount of the penalty.

(n) Judicial review of the order of the director:

(1) is instituted by filing a petition as provided by Subchapter G, Chapter 2001, Government Code; and

(2) is under the substantial evidence rule.

(*o*) If the court sustains the occurrence of the violation, the court may uphold or reduce the amount of the penalty and order the motor carrier to pay the full or reduced amount of the penalty. If the court does not sustain the occurrence of the violation, the court shall order that no penalty is owed.

(p) When the judgment of the court becomes final, the court shall proceed under this subsection. If the motor carrier paid the amount of the penalty and if that amount is reduced or is not upheld by the court, the court shall order that the appropriate amount plus accrued interest be remitted to the person. The rate of the interest is the rate charged on loans to depository institutions by the New York Federal Reserve Bank, and the interest shall be paid for the period beginning on the date the penalty was paid and ending on the date the penalty is remitted. If the motor carrier gave a supersedeas bond and if the penalty is not upheld by the court, the court shall order the release of the bond. If the motor carrier gave a supersedeas bond and if the amount of the penalty is reduced, the court shall order the release of the bond after the carrier pays the amount.

(q) All proceedings under this section are subject to Chapter 2001, Government Code.

(r) In addition to a penalty proposed by an administrative law judge under Subsection (h), the administrative law judge shall include in the proposal for a decision a finding setting out costs, fees, expenses, and reasonable and necessary attorney's fees incurred by the state in bringing the proceeding. The director may adopt the finding and make it a part of a final order entered in the proceeding.

*(Added by L.1997, chap. 165(30.150(a)), eff. 9/1/97.)*



### §643.252. Suspension and revocation of registration.

(a) The department may suspend or revoke a registration issued under this chapter or place on probation a motor carrier whose registration is suspended if a motor carrier:

(1) fails to maintain insurance or evidence of financial responsibility as required by Section 643.101(a), (b), or (c) or 643.153(b);

(2) fails to keep evidence of insurance in the cab of each vehicle as required by Section 643.103(b);

(3) fails to register a vehicle requiring registration;

(4) knowingly provides false information on any form filed with the department under this chapter; or

(5) violates a rule adopted under Section 643.063.

(b) The Department of Public Safety may request that the department suspend or revoke a registration issued under this chapter or place on probation a motor carrier whose registration is suspended if a motor carrier has:

(1) an unsatisfactory safety rating under 49 C.F.R. Part 385; or

(2) multiple violations of Chapter 644, a rule adopted under that chapter, or Subtitle C.

(c) Except as provided by Subsection (d), a suspension or revocation or the imposition of probation made under Subsection (a) or (b) is a contested case under Chapter 2001, Government Code.

(d) The department may suspend or revoke a registration issued under this chapter or place on probation a motor carrier whose registration is suspended without a hearing under Chapter 2001, Government Code, if:

(1) the department provides notice to the motor carrier of:

(A) the proposed suspension or revocation; and

(B) the right of the carrier to request a hearing under Chapter 2001, Government Code; and

(2) the motor carrier fails to provide the department with a written request for a hearing before the 11th day after the date the carrier receives the notice described in Subdivision (1).

(e) If the suspension of a motor carrier's registration is probated, the department may require the carrier to report regularly to the department on any matter that is the basis of the probation.

*(Added by L.1997, chap. 165(30.150(a)); chgd. by L.1999, chap. 62(17.21(a)), eff. 9/1/99.)*

### §643.253. Criminal penalty.

(a) A person commits an offense if the person fails to:

(1) register as required by Subchapter B or Section 643.153(c);

(2) maintain insurance or evidence of financial responsibility as required by Subchapter C or Section 643.153; or

(3) keep a cab card in the cab of a vehicle as required by Section 643.059.

(b) A person commits an offense if the person solicits the transportation of household goods for compensation and is not registered as required by Subchapter B or Section 643.153.

(c) An offense under this section is a Class C misdemeanor.

*(Added by L.1997, chap. 165(30.150(a)); chgd. by L.1999, chap. 62(17.22(a)), eff. 9/1/99.)*

**§643.254. Inspection of documents.**

(a) To investigate an alleged violation of Subchapter B, C, or D, an officer or employee of the department who has been certified for the purpose by the director may enter a motor carrier's premises to copy or verify the correctness of a document, including an operation log or insurance certificate.

(b) The officer or employee may conduct the inspection:

(1) at a reasonable time;

(2) after stating the purpose of the inspection; and

(3) by presenting to the motor carrier:

(A) appropriate credentials; and

(B) a written statement from the department to the motor carrier indicating the officer's or employee's authority to inspect.

(c) A motor carrier domiciled outside this state must:

(1) designate a location in the state for inspection of records concerning the alleged violation; or

(2) request that an officer or employee of the department conduct the inspection at an office of the motor carrier located outside this state.

(d) A motor carrier requesting an out-of-state inspection will be responsible for payment of actual expenses incurred by the department in conducting the inspection.

*(Added by L.1997, chap. 165(30.150(a)); chgd. by L.1999, chap. 603(6), eff. 6/18/99.)*

# CHAPTER 644. COMMERCIAL MOTOR VEHICLE SAFETY STANDARDS

*(Added by L.1997, chap. 165(30.151(a)), eff. 9/1/97.)*

## SUBCHAPTER A. GENERAL PROVISIONS

Section



## SUBCHAPTER B. ADOPTION OF RULES



## SUBCHAPTER C. ADMINISTRATIVE ENFORCEMENT

## SUBCHAPTER D. OFFENSES, PENALTIES, AND JUDICIAL ENFORCEMENT



## SUBCHAPTER E. ROUTING OF HAZARDOUS MATERIALS





## SUBCHAPTER A. GENERAL PROVISIONS

### §644.001. Definitions.

In this chapter:

(1) "Commercial motor vehicle" means a motor vehicle described by Section 548.001.

(2) "Department" means the Department of Public Safety.

(3) "Director" means the public safety director.

(4) "Federal hazardous material regulation" means a federal regulation in 49 C.F.R. Parts 101-199.

(5) "Federal motor carrier safety regulation" means a federal regulation in Subchapter B, Chapter III, Subtitle B, Title 49, Code of Federal Regulations.

(6) "Federal safety regulation" means a federal hazardous material regulation or a federal motor carrier safety regulation.

*(Added by L.1997, chap. 165(30.151(a)); chgd. by L.1999, chap. 62(17.24(a)), (17.25(a)), eff. 9/1/99.)*

### §644.002. Conflicts of law.

(a) A federal motor carrier safety regulation prevails over a conflicting provision of this chapter or a rule adopted by the director under this chapter.

(b) A safety rule adopted under this chapter prevails over a conflicting rule adopted by a local government, authority, or state agency or officer, other than a conflicting rule adopted by the Railroad Commission of Texas under Chapter 113, Natural Resources Code.

*(Added by L.1997, chap. 165(30.151(a)), eff. 9/1/97.)*

### §644.003. Rules.

The department may adopt rules to administer this chapter. *(Added by L.1997, chap. 165(30.151(a)), eff. 9/1/97.)*

### §644.004. Applicability to foreign commercial motor vehicles.

Except as otherwise provided by law, this chapter also applies to a foreign commercial motor vehicle, as defined by Section 648.001. *(Added by L.1999, chap. 62(17.26(a)), eff. 9/1/99.)*

### §§644.005 to 644.050. *(Reserved.)*

## SUBCHAPTER B. ADOPTION OF RULES

### §644.051. Authority to adopt rules.

(a) The director shall, after notice and a public hearing, adopt rules regulating:

(1) the safe transportation of hazardous materials; and

(2) the safe operation of commercial motor vehicles.

(b) A rule adopted under this chapter must be consistent with federal regulations, including federal safety regulations.

(c) The director may adopt all or part of the federal safety regulations by reference.

(d) Rules adopted under this chapter must ensure that:

(1) a commercial motor vehicle is safely maintained, equipped, loaded, and operated;

(2) the responsibilities imposed on a commercial motor vehicle's operator do not impair the operator's ability to operate the vehicle safely; and

(3) the physical condition of a commercial motor vehicle's operator enables the operator to operate the vehicle safely.

(e) A motor carrier safety rule adopted by a local government, authority, or state agency or officer must be consistent with corresponding federal regulations.

*(Added by L.1997, chap. 165(30.151(a)), eff. 9/1/97.)*

## §644.052. Applicability of rules.

(a) Notwithstanding an exemption provided in the federal safety regulations, other than an exemption relating to intracity or commercial zone operations provided in 49 C.F.R. Part 395, a rule adopted by the director under this chapter applies uniformly throughout this state.

(b) A rule adopted under this chapter applies to a vehicle that requires a hazardous material placard.

(c) A rule adopted under this chapter may not apply to a vehicle that is operated intrastate and that is:

(1) a machine generally consisting of a mast, engine, draw works, and chassis permanently constructed or assembled to be used and used in oil or water well servicing or drilling;

(2) a mobile crane that is an unladen, self-propelled vehicle constructed as a machine to raise, shift, or lower weight; or

(3) a vehicle transporting a seed cotton module.

*(Added by L.1997, chap. 165(30.151(a)), eff. 9/1/97.)*



## §644.053. Limitations of rules.

(a) A rule adopted under this chapter may not:

(1) prevent an intrastate operator from operating a vehicle up to 12 hours following eight consecutive hours off;

(2) require a person to meet the medical standards provided in the federal motor carrier safety regulations if the person:

(A) was regularly employed in this state as a commercial motor vehicle operator in intrastate commerce before August 28, 1989; and

(B) is not transporting property that requires a hazardous material placard;

(3) require a person to maintain a government form, separate company form, operator's record of duty status, or operator's daily log for operations within a 150-mile radius of the normal work-reporting location if a general record of an operator's hours of service can be compiled from:

(A) business records maintained by the owner that provide the date, time, and location of the delivery of a product or service; or

(B) documents required to be maintained by law, including delivery tickets or sales invoices, that provide the date of delivery and the quantity of merchandise delivered; or

(4) impose during a planting or harvesting season maximum driving and on-duty times on an operator of a vehicle transporting an agricultural commodity in intrastate commerce for agricultural purposes from the source of the commodity to the first place of processing or storage or the distribution point for the commodity, if the place is located within 150 air miles of the source.

(b) For purposes of Subsection (a)(3)(A), an owner's business records must generally include:

(1) the time an operator reports for duty each day;

(2) the number of hours an operator is on duty each day;

(3) the time an operator is released from duty each day; and

(4) an operator's signed statement in compliance with 49 C.F.R. Section 395.8(j)(2).

(c) In this section, "agricultural commodity" means an agricultural, horticultural, viticultural, silvicultural, or vegetable product, bees or honey, planting seed, cottonseed, rice, livestock or a livestock product, or poultry or a poultry product that is produced in this state, either in its natural form or as processed by the producer, including woodchips.

(d) A rule adopted by the director under this chapter that relates to hours of service, an operator's record of duty status, or an operator's daily log, for operations outside a 150-mile radius of the normal work-reporting location, also applies to and must be complied with by a motor carrier of household goods not using a commercial motor vehicle. In this subsection:

(1) "commercial motor vehicle" has the meaning assigned by Section 548.001; and

(2) "motor carrier" has the meaning assigned by Section 643.001.

*(Added by L.1997, chap. 165(30.151(a)); chgd. by L.1999, chap. 62(17.27(a), (b)), eff. 9/1/99.)*

### §644.054. Regulation of contract carriers of certain passengers.

(a) This section applies only to a contract carrier that transports an operating employee of a railroad on a road or highway of this state in a vehicle designed to carry 15 or fewer passengers.

(b) The department shall adopt rules regulating the operation of a contract carrier to which this section applies. The rules must:

(1) prohibit a person from operating a vehicle for more than 12 hours in a day;

(2) require a person who operates a vehicle for the number of consecutive hours or days the department determines is excessive to rest for a period determined by the department;

(3) require a contract carrier to keep a record of all hours a vehicle subject to regulation under this section is operated; and

(4) be determined by the department to be necessary to protect the safety of a passenger being transported or the general public.

*(Added by L.1999, chap. 62(17.28(a)), eff. 9/1/99.)*

### §§644.055 to 644.100. *(Reserved.)*

## SUBCHAPTER C. ADMINISTRATIVE ENFORCEMENT

### §644.101. Certification of municipal peace officers.

(a) The department shall establish procedures, including training, for the certification of municipal police officers to enforce this chapter.

(b) A police officer of any of the following municipalities is eligible to apply for certification under this section:

(1) a municipality with a population of 100,000 or more;

(2) a municipality with a population of 25,000 or more any part of which is located in a county with a population of 2.4 million or more;

(3) a municipality with a population of less than 25,000:

(A) any part of which is located in a county with a population of 2.4 million; and

(B) that contains or is adjacent to an international port; or

(4) a municipality any part of which is located in a county bordering the United Mexican States.

(c) The department by rule shall establish reasonable fees sufficient to recover from a municipality the cost of certifying its police officers under this section.

*(Added by L.1997, chap. 165(30.151(a)); chgd. by L.1999, chaps. 62(17.29(a)), 1189(39), eff. 9/1/99.)*

### §644.102. Municipal enforcement requirements.

(a) The department by rule shall establish uniform standards for municipal enforcement of this chapter.

(b) A municipality that engages in enforcement under this chapter:

(1) shall pay all costs relating to the municipality's enforcement;

(2) may not be considered, in the context of a federal grant related to this chapter:

(A) a party to a federal grant agreement; or

(B) a grantee under a federal grant to the department; and

(3) must comply with the standards established under Subsection (a).

(c) Municipal enforcement under Section 644.103(b) is not considered departmental enforcement for purposes of maintaining levels of effort required by a federal grant.

(d) In each fiscal year, a municipality may retain fines from the enforcement of this chapter in an amount not to exceed 110 percent of the municipality's actual expenses for enforcement of this chapter in the preceding fiscal year, as determined by the comptroller after reviewing the most recent municipal audit conducted under Section 103.001, Local Government Code. If there are no actual expenses for enforcement of this chapter in the most recent municipal audit, a municipality may retain fines in an amount not to exceed 110 percent of the amount the comptroller estimates would be the municipality's actual expenses for enforcement of this chapter during the year.

(e) A municipality shall send to the comptroller the proceeds of all fines that exceed the limit imposed by Subsection (d).

(f) The department shall revoke or rescind the certification of any municipal police officer who fails to comply with any standard established under Subsection (a).

*(Added by L.1997, chap. 165(30.151(a)); chgd. by L.1999, chap. 292(1), eff. 9/1/99.)*

## §644.103. Detention of vehicles.

(a) An officer of the department may enter or detain on a highway or at a port of entry a motor vehicle that is subject to this chapter.

(b) A police officer who is certified under Section 644.101 may detain on a highway or at a port of entry within the territory of the municipality a motor vehicle that is subject to this chapter.

(c) An officer who detains a vehicle under this section may prohibit the further operation of the vehicle on a highway if the vehicle or operator of the vehicle is in violation of a federal safety regulation or a rule adopted under this chapter.

(d) A noncommissioned employee of the department who is certified for the purpose by the director and who is supervised by an officer of the department may, at a fixed-site facility, enter a motor vehicle that is subject to this chapter. If the employee's inspection shows that an enforcement action, such as the issuance of a citation, is warranted, the supervising officer must take the action.

(e) The department's training and other requirements for certification of a noncommissioned employee of the department under this section must be the same as the training and requirements, other than the training and requirements for becoming and remaining a peace officer, for officers who enforce this chapter.

*(Added by L.1997, chap. 165(30.151(a)); chgd. by L.1999, chap. 62(17.31(a)), 1189(40), eff. 9/1/99.)*

## §644.104. Inspection of premises.

(a) An officer or employee of the department who has been certified for the purpose by the director may enter a motor carrier's premises to:

(1) inspect real property, including a building, or equipment; or

(2) copy or verify the correctness of documents, including records or reports, required to be kept or made by rules adopted under this chapter.

(b) The officer or employee may conduct the inspection:

(1) at a reasonable time;

(2) after stating the purpose of the inspection; and

(3) by presenting to the motor carrier:

(A) appropriate credentials; and

(B) a written statement from the department to the motor carrier indicating the officer's or employee's authority to inspect.

(c) The department may use an officer to conduct an inspection under this section if the inspection involves a situation that the department determines to reasonably require the use or presence of an officer to accomplish the inspection.

(d) The department's training and other requirements for certification of a noncommissioned employee of the department under this section must be the same as the training and requirements, other than the training and requirements for becoming and remaining a peace officer, for officers who enforce this chapter.

*(Added by L.1997, chap. 165(30.151(a)); chgd. by L.1999, chap. 1189(41), eff. 9/1/99.)*

## §§644.105 to 644.150. *(Reserved.)*

# SUBCHAPTER D. OFFENSES, PENALTIES, AND JUDICIAL ENFORCEMENT

## §644.151. Criminal offense.

(a) A person commits an offense if the person:

(1) violates a rule adopted under this chapter; or

(2) does not permit an inspection authorized under Section 644.104.

(b) An offense under this section is a Class C misdemeanor.

(c) Each day a violation continues under Subsection (a)(1) or each day a person refuses to allow an inspection described under Subsection (a)(2) is a separate offense.

*(Added by L.1997, chap. 165(30.151(a)), eff. 9/1/97.)*

## §644.152. Civil penalty.

(a) A person who does not permit an inspection authorized by Section 644.104 is liable to the state for a civil penalty in an amount not to exceed $1,000.

(b) The attorney general may sue to collect the penalty in:

(1) the county in which the violation is alleged to have occurred; or

(2) Travis County.

(c) The penalty provided by this section is in addition to the penalty provided by Section 644.151.

(d) Each day a person refuses to permit an inspection described by Subsection (a) is a separate violation for purposes of imposing a penalty.

*(Added by L.1997, chap. 165(30.151(a)), eff. 9/1/97.)*

### §644.153. Administrative penalty.

(a) The department may impose an administrative penalty against a person who violates:

(1) a rule adopted under this chapter; or

(2) a provision of Subtitle C that the department by rule subjects to administrative penalties.

(b) To be designated as subject to an administrative penalty under Subsection (a)(2), a provision must relate to the safe operation of a commercial motor vehicle.

(c) A penalty under this section:

(1) may not exceed the maximum penalty provided for a violation of a similar federal safety regulation; and

(2) shall be administered in the same manner as a penalty under Section 643.251, except that the amount of a penalty shall be determined under Subdivision (1).

(d) A person who is subject to an administrative penalty imposed by the department under this subchapter is required to pay the administrative penalties or respond to the department within 20 days of receipt of the department's notice of claim.

(e) A person who fails to pay, or becomes delinquent in the payment of, the administrative penalties imposed by the department under this subchapter shall not operate or direct the operation of a commercial motor vehicle on the highways of this state until such time as the administrative penalties have been remitted to the department.

(f) The department shall impound any commercial motor vehicle owned or operated by a person in violation of Subsection (e) after the department has first served the person with a notice of claim. Service of the notice may be by certified mail, registered mail, personal delivery, or any other manner of delivery showing receipt of the notice.

(g) A commercial motor vehicle impounded by the department under this section shall remain impounded until such time as the administrative penalties imposed against the person are remitted to the department.

(h) All costs associated with the towing and storage of the vehicle and load shall be the responsibility of the person and not the department or the State of Texas.

*(Added by L.1997, chap. 165(30.151(a)); chgd. by L.1999, chap. 292(2), eff. 9/1/99.)*



### §644.154. Suit for injunction.

(a) The attorney general shall sue to enjoin a violation or a threatened violation of a rule adopted under this chapter on request of the director.

(b) The suit must be brought in the county in which the violation or threat is alleged to have occurred.

(c) The court may grant the director, without bond or other undertaking:

(1) a prohibitory or mandatory injunction, including a temporary restraining order; or

(2) after notice and hearing, a temporary or permanent injunction.

*(Added by L.1997, chap. 165(30.151(a)), eff. 9/1/97.)*

### §644.155. Safety audit program.

The department shall implement and enforce a safety audit program similar to the federal program established under 49 C.F.R. Part 385 for any person who owns or operates a commercial motor vehicle that is domiciled in this state. *(Added by L.1997, chap. 165(30.151(a)); chgd. by L.1999, chap. 292(3), eff. 9/1/99.)*

## SUBCHAPTER E. ROUTING OF HAZARDOUS MATERIALS

*(Added by L.1999, chap. 62(17.32(a)), eff. 9/1/99.)*

### §644.201. Adoption of rules.

(a) The Texas Transportation Commission shall adopt rules under this subchapter consistent with 49 C.F.R. Part 397 for the routing of nonradioactive hazardous materials.

(b) Rules concerning signage, public participation, and procedural requirements may impose more stringent requirements than provided by 49 C.F.R. Part 397.

(c) The rules must provide for consultation with a political subdivision when a route is being proposed within the jurisdiction of the political subdivision.

*(Added by L.1999, chap. 62(17.32(a)), eff. 9/1/99.)*

### §644.202. Designation of route.

(a) A political subdivision of this state or a state agency may designate a route for the transportation of nonradioactive hazardous materials over a public road or highway in this state only if the Texas Department of Transportation approves the route.

(b) A municipality with a population of more than 750,000 shall develop a route for commercial motor vehicles carrying hazardous materials on a road or highway in the municipality and submit the route to the Texas Department of Transportation for approval. If the Texas Department of Transportation determines that the route complies with all applicable federal and state regulations regarding the transportation of hazardous materials, the Texas Department of Transportation shall approve the route and notify the municipality of the approved route.

(c) The Texas Transportation Commission may designate a route for the transportation of nonradioactive hazardous materials over any public road or highway in this state. The designation may include a road or highway that is not a part of the state highway system only on the approval of the governing body of the political subdivision that maintains the road or highway.
*(Added by L.1999, chap. 62(17.32(a)), eff. 9/1/99.)*

### §644.203. Signs.

(a) The Texas Department of Transportation shall provide signs for a designated route under Section 644.202(c) over a road or highway that is not part of the state highway system. Notwithstanding Section 222.001, the Texas Department of Transportation may use money in the state highway fund to pay for the signs.

(b) The political subdivision that maintains the road or highway shall bear the costs for installation and maintenance of the signs.
*(Added by L.1999, chap. 62(17.32(a)), eff. 9/1/99.)*



## CHAPTER 645. SINGLE STATE REGISTRATION

*(Added by L.1997, chap. 165(30.152(a)), eff. 9/1/97.)*

Section


### §645.001. Single state registration.

The Texas Department of Transportation shall, to the fullest extent practicable, participate in the single state registration system established under 49 U.S.C. Section 14504. *(Added by L.1997, chap. 165(30.152(a)), eff. 9/1/97.)*

### §645.002. Fees.

(a) The department may charge a motor carrier holding a permit issued under Subtitle IV, Title 49, United States Code, a fee for filing proof of insurance consistent with 49 U.S.C. Section 14504 not to exceed the maximum fee established under federal law.

(b) The department may adopt rules regarding the method of payment of a fee under this chapter. The rules may:

(1) authorize the use of an escrow account described by Subsection (c), an electronic funds transfer, or a valid credit card issued by a financial institution chartered by a state or the United States or by a nationally recognized credit organization approved by the department; and

(2) require the payment of a discount or service charge for a credit card payment in addition to the fee.

(c) The department may establish one or more escrow accounts in the state highway fund for the prepayment of a fee under this chapter. A prepaid fee or any fee established by the department for the administration of this section shall be:

(1) administered under an agreement approved by the department; and

(2) deposited to the credit of the state highway fund to be appropriated only to the department for the purposes of administering this chapter.
*(Added by L.1997, chap. 165(30.152(a)); chgd. by L.1999, chap. 62(17.33(a)), eff. 9/1/99.)*

### §645.003. Enforcement rules.

The department shall adopt rules that are consistent with federal law providing for:

(1) administrative penalties in the same manner as Section 643.251; and

(2) suspension and revocation of registration in the same manner as Section 643.252.
*(Added by L.1997, chap. 165(30.152(a)), eff. 9/1/97.)*

### §645.004. Criminal offense.

(a) A person commits an offense if the person:

(1) violates a rule adopted under this chapter; or

(2) fails to register a vehicle required to be registered under this chapter.

(b) An offense under this section is a Class C misdemeanor.

(c) Each day a violation of a rule occurs is a separate offense under this section.
*(Added by L.1997, chap. 165(30.152(a)), eff. 9/1/97.)*

## CHAPTER 646. MOTOR TRANSPORTATION BROKERS

*(Added by L.1997, chap. 165(30.153(a)), eff. 9/1/97.)*

Section



### §646.001. Definition.

In this chapter, "motor transportation broker" means a person who:

(1) sells, offers for sale, provides, or negotiates for the transportation of cargo by a motor carrier operated by another person; or

(2) aids or abets a person in performing an act described by Subdivision (1).
*(Added by L.1997, chap. 165(30.153(a)), eff. 9/1/97.)*

### §646.002. Exception.

This chapter does not apply to a motor transportation broker who:

(1) is registered as a motor carrier under Chapter 643; or

(2) holds a permit issued under Subtitle IV, Title 49, United States Code.
*(Added by L.1997, chap. 165(30.153(a)), eff. 9/1/97.)*

### §646.003. Bond required.

(a) A person may not act as a motor transportation broker unless the person provides a bond to the Texas Department of Transportation.

(b) The bond must be in an amount of at least $10,000 and must be:

(1) executed by a bonding company authorized to do business in this state;

(2) payable to this state or a person to whom the motor transportation broker provides services; and

(3) conditioned on the performance of the contract for transportation services between the broker and the person for whom services are provided.

(c) The department may charge the broker a bond review fee in an amount not to exceed the cost of reviewing the bond.

(d) The department may adopt rules regarding the method of payment of a fee under this chapter. The rules may:

(1) authorize the use of electronic funds transfer or a credit card issued by a financial institution chartered by a state or the United States or by a nationally recognized credit organization approved by the department; and

(2) require the payment of a discount or service charge for a credit card payment in addition to the fee.
*(Added by L.1997, chap. 165(30.153(a)), eff. 9/1/97.)*

### §646.004. Criminal offense.

(a) A person commits an offense if the person fails to provide the bond required by Section 646.003.

(b) An offense under this section is a Class C misdemeanor.
*(Added by L.1997, chap. 165(30.153(a)), eff. 9/1/97.)*

# CHAPTER 647. MOTOR TRANSPORTATION OF MIGRANT AGRICULTURAL WORKERS

*(Added by L.1999, chap. 62(17.34(a)), eff. 9/1/99.)*



## §647.001. Definitions.

In this chapter:

(1) "Bus" means a motor vehicle that is designed, constructed, and used to transport passengers. The term does not include a passenger automobile or a station wagon other than a taxicab.

(2) "Highway" has the meaning assigned by Section 541.302.

(3) "Migrant agricultural worker" means a person who:

(A) performs or seeks to perform farm labor of a seasonal nature, including labor necessary to process an agricultural food product; and

(B) occupies living quarters other than the individual's permanent home during the period of employment.

(4) "Motor vehicle" means any vehicle, machine, tractor, trailer, or semitrailer propelled or drawn by mechanical power and used on a highway to transport passengers or property or both. The term does not include:

(A) a vehicle, locomotive, or car that operates exclusively on one or more rails; or

(B) a trolley bus that operates on electricity generated from a fixed overhead wire and that provides local passenger transportation in street-railway service.

(5) "Operator" means a person who operates a motor vehicle.

(6) "Semitrailer" has the meaning assigned by Section 541.201.

(7) "Truck" has the meaning assigned by Section 541.201.

(8) "Truck tractor" has the meaning assigned by Section 541.201.

*(Added by L.1999, chap. 62(17.34(a)), eff. 9/1/99.)*

## §647.002. Application of chapter.

(a) This chapter applies to any carrier, including a carrier under contract, who at any time uses a motor vehicle to transport to or from a place of employment in this state at least five migrant agricultural workers for a total distance of more than 50 miles.

(b) This chapter does not apply if:

(1) the carrier is a common carrier;

(2) the motor vehicle used is a station wagon or passenger automobile; or

(3) the carrier is a migrant agricultural worker transporting the worker or a member of the worker's immediate family.

*(Added by L.1999, chap. 62(17.34(a)), eff. 9/1/99.)*

## §647.003. Type of vehicle allowed.

(a) A carrier may transport migrant agricultural workers only in a:

(1) bus;

(2) truck to which a trailer is not attached; or

(3) semitrailer attached to a truck tractor.

(b) A carrier may not:

(1) attach a trailer to a semitrailer described by Subsection (a)(3); or

(2) use a closed van that does not have windows or a method to ensure ventilation.

*(Added by L.1999, chap. 62(17.34(a)), eff. 9/1/99.)*

### §647.004. Compliance with requirements of chapter.

(a) A carrier shall comply with the requirements and specifications of this chapter.

(b) An officer, agent, representative, or employee of a carrier who operates a motor vehicle used to transport migrant agricultural workers or who hires, supervises, trains, assigns, or dispatches operators of those motor vehicles shall comply with the requirements of Sections 647.006, 647.007, and 647.008.

(c) An officer, agent, representative, operator, or employee of a carrier who is directly involved in the management, maintenance, or operation of a motor vehicle used to transport migrant agricultural workers shall comply with the requirements of Sections 647.003, 647.005, 647.009, 647.010, 647.011, 647.012, 647.014, 647.016, and 647.017. The carrier shall instruct its officers, agents, representatives, and operators with the requirements of those sections and shall take necessary measures to ensure compliance with those requirements.

(d) An officer, agent, representative, operator, or employee of a carrier who is directly involved with the installation or maintenance of equipment and accessories of a motor vehicle used to transport migrant agricultural workers shall comply with the requirements and specifications of Sections 647.012, 647.013, 647.014, 647.015, and 647.016. A carrier may not operate a motor vehicle transporting migrant agricultural workers or cause or permit the vehicle to be operated unless the vehicle is equipped as required by those sections.

(e) A carrier shall systematically inspect and maintain each motor vehicle used to transport migrant agricultural workers and their accessories subject to its control to ensure that the vehicle and its accessories are in safe and proper operating condition.

*(Added by L.1999, chap. 62(17.34(a)), eff. 9/1/99.)*

### §647.005. Operation in accordance with law.

If this chapter imposes a greater affirmative obligation or restraint on the operation of a motor vehicle transporting migrant agricultural workers than the laws, ordinances, and regulations of the jurisdiction in which the vehicle is operated, the operator shall comply with this chapter. *(Added by L.1999, chap. 62(17.34(a)), eff. 9/1/99.)*

### §647.006. Operator age and experience requirements.

A person may not operate a motor vehicle transporting migrant agricultural workers and a carrier may not permit or require a person to operate the motor vehicle unless the person:

(1) is at least 18 years of age;

(2) has at least one year of experience in operating any type of motor vehicle, including a private automobile, during the different seasons;

(3) is familiar with the law relating to operating a motor vehicle; and

(4) is authorized by law to operate that type of motor vehicle.

*(Added by L.1999, chap. 62(17.34(a)), eff. 9/1/99.)*

### §647.007. Operator physical requirements.

(a) A person may not operate a motor vehicle transporting migrant agricultural workers and a carrier may not permit or require a person to operate the motor vehicle if the person:

(1) is missing a foot, leg, hand, or arm;

(2) has a mental, nervous, organic, or functional disorder that is likely to interfere with the person's ability to safely operate the motor vehicle;

(3) is missing fingers, has impaired use of a foot, leg, finger, hand, or arm, or has another structural defect or limitation likely to interfere with the person's ability to safely operate the motor vehicle;

(4) has a visual acuity of less than 20/40 (Snellen) in each eye either without glasses or with corrective lenses;

(5) has a form field of vision in the horizontal median of less than a total of 140 degrees;

(6) cannot distinguish the colors red, green, and yellow;

(7) has hearing ability of less than 10/20 in the better ear for conversational tones without the use of a hearing aid; or

(8) is addicted to alcohol, narcotics, or habit-forming drugs.

(b) An operator who requires corrective lenses for vision shall use properly prescribed corrective lenses when operating the motor vehicle.

*(Added by L.1999, chap. 62(17.34(a)), eff. 9/1/99.)*

### §647.008. Physical examination requirement.

(a) A person may not operate a motor vehicle transporting migrant agricultural workers and a carrier may not permit or require a person to operate the motor vehicle unless:

(1) the person has been physically examined by a licensed doctor of medicine or osteopathy during the preceding 36 months; and

(2) the doctor certifies that the person is physically qualified in accordance with Section 647.007.

(b) The doctor's certificate must state:

"Doctor's Certificate

(Operator of Migrant Agricultural Workers)

This is to certify that I have this day examined ______________________________ in accordance with the Texas law governing physical qualifications of operators of migrant agricultural workers and that I find ______________________________

Qualified under that law
Qualified only when wearing glasses or corrective lenses

I have kept on file in my office a completed examination. ______________________________
(Signature of Examining Doctor)

______________ (Date) ______________ (Place)

______________________________
(Address of Doctor)

Signature of Operator ______________________________
Address of Operator ______________________________"

(c) A carrier shall keep in its files at the carrier's principal place of business a legible doctor's certificate or a legible photographically reproduced copy of the doctor's certificate for each operator it employs or uses.

(d) An operator shall carry the operator's legible doctor's certificate or a legible photographically reproduced copy of the doctor's certificate when operating the motor vehicle.
*(Added by L.1999, chap. 62(17.34(a)), eff. 9/1/99.)*

### §647.009. Limitation on operation of motor vehicle.

(a) Except in an emergency, a person assigned to operate a motor vehicle transporting migrant workers may not allow another person to operate the motor vehicle without the carrier's authorization.

(b) A person may not operate a motor vehicle if the person's alertness or ability to operate the vehicle is impaired for any reason, including fatigue or illness, to the extent that it is not safe for the person to begin or to continue. This subsection does not apply if there is a grave emergency in which failure to operate a motor vehicle would result in a greater hazard to passengers. However, the person may operate the motor vehicle only to the nearest location at which the passengers' safety is ensured.

(c) A carrier may not permit or require a person to operate a motor vehicle from one location to another in a period that would necessitate the operation of the vehicle at a speed in excess of the applicable speed limit.

(d) An operator shall make a meal stop of not less than 30 minutes at least every six hours. The carrier shall provide for reasonable rest stops at least once between each meal stop.

(e) The operator of a truck transporting migrant agricultural workers for more than 500 miles shall stop for at least eight hours to provide rest for the operator and passengers either before or at the completion of each 500 miles.

(f) A person may not operate and a carrier may not permit or require the person to operate a motor vehicle for more than 10 hours in the aggregate, excluding meal and rest stops, during any 24-hour period unless the person rests for at least eight consecutive hours at the end of the 10-hour period. For purposes of this subsection, the 24-hour period begins at the time the operator reports for duty.
*(Added by L.1999, chap. 62(17.34(a)), eff. 9/1/99.)*

### §647.010. Required stop at railroad crossing.

(a) An operator transporting migrant agricultural workers who approaches a railroad grade crossing:

(1) shall stop the motor vehicle not less than 15 feet or more than 50 feet from the nearest rail of the crossing; and

(2) may proceed only after the operator determines that the course is clear.

(b) An operator is not required to stop at:

(1) a streetcar crossing that is in a municipal business or residential district;

(2) a railroad grade crossing at which a police officer or traffic-control signal other than a railroad flashing signal directs traffic to proceed; or

(3) a grade crossing that the proper state authority has clearly marked as being abandoned or exempted if the marking can be read from the operator's position.

(c) The motor vehicle must display a sign on the rear of the vehicle that states: "This Vehicle Stops at Railroad Crossings."

*(Added by L.1999, chap. 62(17.34(a)), eff. 9/1/99.)*

### §647.011. Fuel restrictions.

(a) An operator or carrier employee fueling a motor vehicle used to transport migrant agricultural workers may not:

(1) fuel the motor vehicle while the engine is running unless running the engine is required to fuel the vehicle;

(2) smoke or expose any open flame in the vicinity of the motor vehicle;

(3) fuel the motor vehicle when the nozzle of the fuel hose is not in continuous contact with the intake pipe of the fuel tank; or

(4) permit any other person to engage in an activity that would likely result in a fire or explosion.

(b) A person may carry fuel on the motor vehicle for use in the motor vehicle or an accessory only in a properly mounted fuel tank.

*(Added by L.1999, chap. 62(17.34(a)), eff. 9/1/99.)*



### §647.012. Required vehicle equipment; use of required equipment.

(a) A motor vehicle used to transport migrant agricultural workers must be equipped with:

(1) at least one properly mounted fire extinguisher;

(2) road warning devices, including at least one red-burning fusee and at least three red flares, red electric lanterns, or red emergency reflectors;

(3) coupling devices as prescribed by Subsection (c), if the vehicle is a truck tractor or dolly; and

(4) tires as prescribed by Subsection (d).

(b) A person may not operate a motor vehicle unless the person is satisfied that the equipment required under Subsection (a) and the following equipment is in good working order:

(1) the brakes, including service brakes, trailer brake connections, and hand parking brakes;

(2) lighting devices and reflectors;

(3) the steering mechanism;

(4) the horn;

(5) each windshield wiper; and

(6) each rearview mirror.

(c) Adequate means must be provided positively to prevent the shifting of the lower half of each fifth wheel attached to the frame of a truck tractor or dolly. The lower half of each fifth wheel must be securely fastened to the frame by U-bolts that are of adequate size and are securely tightened. Another method may be used if the method provides equivalent security. A U-bolt may not be of welded construction and must be installed so as not to crack, warp, or deform the frame. The upper half of each fifth wheel must be fastened with at least the security required for the lower half. A locking means must be provided in each fifth wheel mechanism, including adapters when used, so that the upper and lower half will not separate without the use of a positive manual release, such as a release mechanism that the operator uses from the cab. If the fifth wheel is designed and constructed to be readily separable, the requirement for a fifth wheel coupling device applies to a vehicle manufactured after December 31, 1952.

(d) Vehicle tires must be of adequate capacity to support the vehicle's gross weight. Each tire must have a tread configuration on the part of the tire that is in contact with the road and may not be so smooth as to expose any tread fabric. A tire may not have a defect likely to cause failure. A front tire may not be regrooved, recapped, or retreaded.

(e) An operator shall use required equipment as necessary.

*(Added by L.1999, chap. 62(17.34(a)), eff. 9/1/99.)*

### §647.013. Passenger safety provisions on motor vehicle other than bus.

(a) A motor vehicle other than a bus transporting migrant agricultural workers must have a passenger compartment in accordance with this section.

(b) The floor of the passenger compartment must be substantially smooth and without cracks or holes. Except as necessary to secure the seats or other devices attached to the floor, the floor may not have any object that protrudes more than two inches in height.

(c) The side walls and ends of the passenger compartment must extend at least 60 inches from the floor. If necessary, sideboards may be attached to the body of the motor vehicle. Stake body construction meets the requirements of this subsection only if the space six inches or larger between any two stakes is suitably closed to prevent the passengers from falling off the vehicle.

(d) The floor and interior of the sides and ends of the passenger compartment must be free of protruding nails, screws, splinters, or any other protruding object that is likely to injure a passenger or the passenger's clothes.

(e) The motor vehicle must have an adequate means of exiting and entering the passenger compartment from the rear or from the right side of the vehicle. Each exit and entrance must have a gate or door that has at least one latch or fastening device that will keep the gate or door securely closed during transportation. The latch or fastening device must be readily operative without the use of tools. An exit or entrance must:

(1) be at least 18 inches wide;

(2) have a top and clear opening of at least 60 inches or as high as the passenger compartment side wall if the side wall is less than 60 inches high; and

(3) have a bottom that is at the floor of the passenger compartment.

(f) If the motor vehicle has a permanently attached roof, the vehicle must have at least one emergency exit on a side or rear of the vehicle that does not have a regular exit or entrance. The exit must have a gate or door and a latch and hold as prescribed by Subsection (e).

(g) If necessary, a ladder or steps shall be used to enter and exit the passenger compartment. The maximum vertical spacing of footholds may not exceed 12 inches and the lowest step may not be more than 18 inches above the ground when the vehicle is empty.

(h) The motor vehicle must include handholds or other devices that will enable passengers to enter and exit the vehicle without hazard.

(i) The motor vehicle must have a way for passengers to communicate with the operator, including a telephone, speaker tube, buzzer, pull cord, or other mechanical or electrical device.

*(Added by L.1999, chap. 62(17.34(a)), eff. 9/1/99.)*



## §647.014. Passenger seating.

One seat must be provided for each passenger. Passengers shall remain seated while the vehicle is in motion.

*(Added by L.1999, chap. 62(17.34(a)), eff. 9/1/99.)*

## §647.015. Passenger seating requirements for certain trips.

(a) A motor vehicle transporting migrant agricultural workers for a total distance of 100 miles or more must have a passenger compartment in accordance with this section.

(b) Each passenger seat must:

(1) be securely attached to the vehicle during use;

(2) be not less than 16 or more than 19 inches above the floor;

(3) be at least 13 inches deep;

(4) be equipped with backrests that extend at least 36 inches above the floor;

(5) have at least 24 inches of space between the backrests or the edges of the opposite seats when positioned face to face;

(6) provide at least 18 inches of seat area for each passenger;

(7) not have any cracks that are more than one-fourth inch wide;

(8) not have any cracks in the backrests, if slatted, that are more than two inches wide; and

(9) have any exposed wood surfaces planed or sanded smooth and free of splinters.

*(Added by L.1999, chap. 62(17.34(a)), eff. 9/1/99.)*

## §647.016. Passenger protection from weather.

(a) If necessary to protect passengers from inclement weather, including rain, snow, or sleet, the passenger compartment must be equipped with a top that is at least 80 inches above the floor and with a means of closing the sides and ends. A tarpaulin or other removable protective device may be used if secured in place.

(b) The motor vehicle must have a safe method of protecting the passengers from cold or undue exposure. A motor vehicle may not have a heater that:

(1) conducts engine exhaust gases or engine compartment air into or through a space occupied by an individual;

(2) uses a flame that is not completely enclosed;

(3) might spill or leak fuel if the vehicle is tilted or overturned;

(4) uses heated or unheated air that comes from or through the engine compartment or from direct contact with any part of the exhaust system unless the heater ducts prevent contamination of the air from the exhaust or engine compartment gases; or

(5) is not securely fastened to the motor vehicle.

*(Added by L.1999, chap. 62(17.34(a)), eff. 9/1/99.)*

### §647.017. Operational requirements.

(a) A person may not operate a motor vehicle transporting migrant agricultural workers that is loaded or that has a load that is distributed or secured in a manner that prevents the vehicle's safe operation.

(b) A person may not operate a motor vehicle if:

(1) a tailgate, tailboard, tarpaulin, door, fastening device, or equipment or rigging is not securely in place;

(2) an object:

(A) obscures the operator's view in any direction;

(B) interferes with the free movement of the operator's arms or legs;

(C) obstructs the operator's access to emergency accessories; or

(D) obstructs a person's entrance or exit from the cab or operator's compartment; or

(3) property on the vehicle is stowed so that it:

(A) restricts the operator's freedom of motion in properly operating the vehicle;

(B) obstructs a person's exit from the vehicle; or

(C) does not provide adequate protection to passengers and others from injury resulting from a falling or displaced article.

(c) An operator who leaves a motor vehicle unattended shall securely set the parking brake, chock the wheels, and take all reasonable precautions to prevent the vehicle from moving.

*(Added by L.1999, chap. 62(17.34(a)), eff. 9/1/99.)*

### §647.018. Certificate of compliance.

A carrier is considered to be in compliance with this chapter if the carrier holds a certificate of compliance with the United States Department of Transportation regulations governing transportation of migrant agricultural workers in interstate commerce. *(Added by L.1999, chap. 62(17.34(a)), eff. 9/1/99.)*

### §647.019. Penalty.

(a) A carrier who violates this chapter commits an offense.

(b) An offense under this section is a misdemeanor punishable by a fine of not less than $5 or more than $50.

*(Added by L.1999, chap. 62(17.34(a)), eff. 9/1/99.)*

## CHAPTER 648. FOREIGN COMMERCIAL MOTOR TRANSPORTATION

*(Added by L.1999, chap. 62(17.35(a)), eff. 9/1/99.)*

## SUBCHAPTER A. GENERAL PROVISIONS



## SUBCHAPTER B. BORDER COMMERCIAL ZONE

## SUBCHAPTER C. REGULATION OF OPERATION OF FOREIGN COMMERCIAL MOTOR VEHICLES



## SUBCHAPTER A. GENERAL PROVISIONS

### §648.001. Definitions.

In this chapter:

(1) "Border" means the border between this state and the United Mexican States.

(2) "Border commercial zone" means a commercial zone established under 49 C.F.R. Part 372, Subpart B, any portion of which is contiguous to the border in this state.

(3) "Commercial motor vehicle" includes a foreign commercial motor vehicle.

(4) "Foreign commercial motor vehicle" means a commercial motor vehicle, as defined by 49 C.F.R. Section 390.5, that is owned or controlled by a person or entity that is domiciled in or a citizen of a country other than the United States.

(5) "Motor carrier" includes a foreign motor carrier and a foreign motor private carrier, as defined in 49 U.S.C. Sections 13102(6) and (7).

*(Added by L.1999, chap. 62(17.35(a)), eff. 9/1/99.)*

### §648.002. Rules.

In addition to rules required by this chapter, the Texas Department of Transportation, the Department of Public Safety, and the Texas Department of Insurance may adopt other rules to carry out this chapter. *(Added by L.1999, chap. 62(17.35(a)), eff. 9/1/99.)*

### §648.003. Reference to federal statute or regulation.

A reference in this chapter to a federal statute or regulation includes any subsequent amendment or redesignation of the statute or regulation. *(Added by L.1999, chap. 62(17.35(a)), eff. 9/1/99.)*

### §§648.004 to 648.050. *(Reserved.)*

## SUBCHAPTER B. BORDER COMMERCIAL ZONE

### §648.051. Border commercial zone exclusive; boundaries.

(a) A law or agreement of less than statewide application that is adopted by an agency or political subdivision of this state and that regulates motor carriers or commercial motor vehicles or the operation of those carriers or vehicles in the transportation of cargo across the border or within an area adjacent to the border by foreign commercial motor vehicles has no effect unless the law or agreement applies uniformly to an entire border commercial zone and only in a border commercial zone.

(b) This subchapter supersedes that portion of any paired city, paired state, or similar understanding governing foreign commercial motor vehicles or motor carriers entered into under Section 502.054 or any other law.

*(Added by L.1999, chap. 62(17.35(a)), eff. 9/1/99.)*

### §648.052. Modification of zone boundaries.

The boundaries of a border commercial zone may be modified or established only as provided by federal law. *(Added by L.1999, chap. 62(17.35(a)), eff. 9/1/99.)*

### §§648.053 to 648.100. *(Reserved.)*

Printed in the U.S.A. 12

## SUBCHAPTER C. REGULATION OF OPERATION OF FOREIGN COMMERCIAL MOTOR VEHICLES

### §648.101. Registration exemption in border commercial zone.

(a) A foreign commercial motor vehicle is exempt from Chapter 502 and any other law of this state requiring the vehicle to be registered in this state, including a law providing for a temporary registration permit, if:

(1) the vehicle is engaged solely in transportation of cargo across the border into or from a border commercial zone;

(2) for each load of cargo transported the vehicle remains in this state:

(A) not more than 24 hours; or

(B) not more than 48 hours, if:

(i) the vehicle is unable to leave this state within 24 hours because of circumstances beyond the control of the motor carrier operating the vehicle; and

(ii) all financial responsibility requirements applying to the vehicle are satisfied;

(3) the vehicle is registered and licensed as required by the law of another state or country as evidenced by a valid metal license plate attached to the front or rear of the exterior of the vehicle; and

(4) the country in which the person that owns or controls the vehicle is domiciled or is a citizen provides a reciprocal exemption for commercial motor vehicles owned or controlled by residents of this state.

(b) A foreign commercial motor vehicle operating under the exemption provided by this section and the vehicle's driver may be considered unregistered if the vehicle is operated in this state outside a border commercial zone or in violation of United States law.
*(Added by L.1999, chap. 62(17.35(a)), eff. 9/1/99.)*



### §648.102. Financial responsibility.

(a) The Texas Department of Transportation shall adopt rules that conform with 49 C.F.R. Part 387 requiring motor carriers operating foreign commercial motor vehicles in this state to maintain financial responsibility.

(b) This chapter prevails over any other requirement of state law relating to financial responsibility for operation of foreign commercial motor vehicles in this state.
*(Added by L.1999, chap. 62(17.35(a)), eff. 9/1/99.)*

### §648.103. Domestic transportation.

A foreign motor carrier or foreign motor private carrier may not transport persons or cargo in intrastate commerce in this state unless the carrier is authorized to conduct operations in interstate and foreign commerce domestically between points in the United States under federal law or international agreement. *(Added by L.1999, chap. 62(17.35(a)), eff. 9/1/99.)*

## CHAPTERS 649 to 660. *(Reserved.)*

# SUBTITLE G. MOTORCYCLES AND ALL-TERRAIN VEHICLES

## CHAPTER 661. PROTECTIVE HEADGEAR FOR MOTORCYCLE OPERATORS AND PASSENGERS

Section


### §661.001. Definitions.

In this chapter:

(1) "Motorcycle" means a motor vehicle designed to propel itself with not more than three wheels in contact with the ground, and having a saddle for the use of the rider. The term does not include a tractor or a three-wheeled vehicle equipped with a cab, seat, and seat belt and designed to contain the operator in the cab.

(2) "Department" means the Department of Public Safety.
*(Added by L.1995, chap. 165(1), eff. 9/1/95.)*

**§661.002. Department to prescribe minimum safety standards for protective headgear.**

(a) To provide for the safety and welfare of motorcycle operators and passengers, the department shall prescribe minimum safety standards for protective headgear used by motorcyclists in this state.

(b) The department may adopt any part or all of the American National Standards Institute's standards for protective headgear for vehicular users.

(c) On request of a manufacturer of protective headgear, the department shall make the safety standards prescribed by the department available to the manufacturer.
*(Added by L.1995, chap. 165(1), eff. 9/1/95.)*

**§661.003. Offenses relating to not wearing protective headgear.**

(a) A person commits an offense if the person:

(1) operates or rides as a passenger on a motorcycle on a public street or highway; and

(2) is not wearing protective headgear that meets safety standards adopted by the department.

(b) A person commits an offense if the person carries on a motorcycle on a public street or highway a passenger who is not wearing protective headgear that meets safety standards adopted by the department.

(c) It is an exception to the application of Subsection (a) or (b) that at the time the offense was committed, the person required to wear protective headgear was at least 21 years old and had successfully completed a motorcycle operator training and safety course under Chapter 662 or was covered by a health insurance plan providing the person with at least $10,000 in medical benefits for injuries incurred as a result of an accident while operating or riding on a motorcycle.

(d) The department shall issue a sticker to a person who:

(1) applies to the department on a form provided by the department;

(2) provides the department with evidence satisfactory to the department showing that the person:

(A) is the owner of a motorcycle that is currently registered in this state; and

(B) has successfully completed the training and safety course described by Subsection (c) or has the insurance coverage described by that subsection; and

(3) pays a fee of $5 for the sticker.

(e) The medical exemption is permanent if the physician attests that the person's medical condition is permanent. *(Chgd. by L.1997, chap. 165(30.154(a)), eff. 9/1/97. See other subsection (e) below.)*

(e) A person may apply to the department for a sticker for each motorcycle owned by the applicant. *(Chgd. by L.1997, chap. 1156(3); L.1999, chap. 62(17.36). eff. 9/1/99. See other subsection (e) above.)*

(f) A sticker issued by the department under Subsection (d) expires on the third anniversary of the date of issuance.

(g) A person operating or riding as a passenger on a motorcycle that displays on the license plate of the motorcycle or the license plate mounting bracket a sticker issued by the department under Subsection (d) is presumed to have successfully completed the training and safety course described by Subsection (c) or to have the insurance coverage described by that subsection.

(h) An offense under this section is a misdemeanor punishable by a fine of not less than $10 or more than $50.

(i) In this section, "health insurance plan" means an individual, group, blanket, or franchise insurance policy, insurance agreement, evidence of coverage, group hospital services contract, health maintenance organization membership, or employee benefit plan that provides benefits for health care services or for medical or surgical expenses incurred as a result of an accident.
*(Added by L.1995, chap. 165(1); chgd. by L.1997, chaps. 165(30.154(a)), 1156(3); chgd. by L.1999, chap. 62(17.36), eff. 9/1/99.)*

**§661.004. Authority of peace officer to inspect protective headgear.**

Any peace officer may stop and detain a person who is a motorcycle operator or passenger to inspect the person's protective headgear for compliance with the safety standards prescribed by the department. *(Added by L.1995, chap. 165(1), eff. 9/1/95.)*

# CHAPTER 662. MOTORCYCLE OPERATOR TRAINING AND SAFETY

Section

662.011. Motorcycle education fund account.



## §662.001. Designated state agency.

The governor shall designate a state agency to establish and administer a motorcycle operator training and safety program. *(Added by L.1995, chap. 165(1), eff. 9/1/95.)*

## §662.002. Purpose of program; curriculum.

(a) The purpose of the motorcycle operator training and safety program is:

(1) to make available to motorcycle operators:

(A) information relating to the operation of motorcycles; and

(B) courses in knowledge, skills, and safety relating to the operation of motorcycles; and

(2) to provide information to the public on sharing roadways with motorcycles.

(b) The program shall include curricula developed by the Motorcycle Safety Foundation. *(Added by L.1995, chap. 165(1), eff. 9/1/95.)*

## §662.003. Program director.

The designated state agency shall employ as program director a person who is certified as a chief instructor by the Motorcycle Safety Foundation. *(Added by L.1995, chap. 165(1), eff. 9/1/95.)*

## §662.004. Motorcycle safety coordinator.

(a) The designated state agency shall employ a motorcycle safety coordinator.

(b) The coordinator shall supervise the motorcycle operator training and safety program and shall determine:

(1) locations at which courses will be provided;

(2) fees for the courses;

(3) qualifications for instructors;

(4) instructor certification requirements; and

(5) eligibility requirements for program sponsors.

(c) The program must include instructor certification requirements developed by the Motorcycle Safety Foundation.

*(Added by L.1995, chap. 165(1), eff. 9/1/95.)*

## §662.005. Contracts.

The designated state agency may license or contract with qualified persons to administer or operate the motorcycle operator training and safety program. *(Added by L.1995, chap. 165(1), eff. 9/1/95.)*

## §662.006. Unauthorized training prohibited.

A person may not offer training in motorcycle operation for a consideration unless the person is licensed by or contracts with the designated state agency. *(Added by L.1995, chap. 165(1), eff. 9/1/95.)*

## §662.007. Fee for course.

A person may charge, for a course under the motorcycle operator training and safety program, a fee that is reasonably related to the costs of administering the course. *(Added by L.1995, chap. 165(1), eff. 9/1/95.)*

### §662.008. Denial, suspension, or cancellation of approval.

(a) The designated state agency may deny, suspend, or cancel its approval for a program sponsor to conduct or for an instructor to teach a course offered under this chapter if the applicant, instructor, or sponsor:

(1) does not satisfy the requirements established under this chapter to receive or retain approval;

(2) permits fraud or engages in a fraudulent practice with reference to an application to the agency;

(3) induces or countenances fraud or a fraudulent practice by a person applying for a driver's license or permit;

(4) permits fraud or engages in a fraudulent practice in an action between the applicant or license holder and the public; or

(5) fails to comply with rules of the state agency.

(b) Before the designated state agency may deny, suspend, or cancel the approval of a program sponsor or an instructor, notice and opportunity for a hearing must be given as provided by:

(1) Chapter 2001, Government Code;

(2) Article 6252-13c, Revised Statutes; and

(3) Sections 2 through 5, Chapter 267, Acts of the 67th Legislature, Regular Session, 1981 (Article 6252-13d, Texas Civil Statutes).

*(Added by L.1995, chap. 165(1), eff. 9/1/95.)*

### §662.009. Rules.

The designated state agency may adopt rules to administer this chapter. *(Added by L.1995, chap. 165(1), eff. 9/1/95.)*

### §662.010. Nonapplicability of certain other law.

Chapter 332, Acts of the 60th Legislature, Regular Session, 1967 (Article 4413(29c), Texas Civil Statutes), does not apply to training offered under this chapter. *(Added by L.1995, chap. 165(1), eff. 9/1/95.)*

### §662.011. Motorcycle education fund account.

(a) The motorcycle education fund account is an account in the general revenue fund.

(b) Of each fee for renewal of a Class M license, the Department of Public Safety shall send $5 to the comptroller for deposit to the credit of the motorcycle education fund account.

(c) Money deposited to the credit of the motorcycle education fund account may be used only to defray the cost of administering the motorcycle operator training and safety program, except as provided by Subsection (d).

(d) The unspent and unencumbered balance in the motorcycle education fund account at the end of each fiscal year may be appropriated for:

(1) the motorcycle operator training and safety program; or

(2) any other purpose relating to:

(A) maintaining or policing highways; or

(B) supervising traffic or promoting safety on highways.

*(Added by L.1997, chap. 165(30.155), eff. 9/1/97. See other section 662.011 below.)*

### §662.011. Motorcycle education fund account.

(a) Of each fee collected under Sections 521.421(b) and (f), Sections 522.029(f) and (g), and Section 661.003(d), the Department of Public Safety shall send $5 to the comptroller for deposit to the credit of the motorcycle education fund account.

(b) Money deposited to the credit of the motorcycle education fund account may be used only to defray the cost of administering the motorcycle operator training and safety program.

*(Added by L.1997, chap. 1156(4), eff. 9/1/97. See other section 662.011 above.)*

## CHAPTER 663. ALL-TERRAIN VEHICLES

## SUBCHAPTER A. GENERAL PROVISIONS

Section

## SUBCHAPTER B. ALL-TERRAIN VEHICLE OPERATOR EDUCATION AND CERTIFICATION





## SUBCHAPTER C. OPERATION OF ALL-TERRAIN VEHICLES



## SUBCHAPTER A. GENERAL PROVISIONS

### §663.001. Definitions.

In this chapter:

(1) "All-terrain vehicle" means a motor vehicle that is:

(A) equipped with a saddle for the use of the rider;

(B) designed to propel itself with three or four tires in contact with the ground;

(C) designed by the manufacturer for off-highway use by the operator only; and

(D) not designed by the manufacturer for farming or lawn care.

(2) "Public property" means property owned or leased by the state or a political subdivision of the state.

*(Added by L.1995, chap. 165(1), eff. 9/1/95.)*

### §663.002. Nonapplicability of certain other laws.

(a) Chapter 521 does not apply to the operation or ownership of an all-terrain vehicle registered for off-highway operation.

(b) Chapter 332, Acts of the 60th Legislature, Regular Session, 1967 (Article 4413(29c), Texas Civil Statutes), does not apply to instruction in the operation of an all-terrain vehicle provided under the operator education and certification program established by this chapter.

*(Added by L.1995, chap. 165(1), eff. 9/1/95.)*

### §§663.003 to 663.010. *(Reserved.)*

## SUBCHAPTER B. ALL-TERRAIN VEHICLE OPERATOR EDUCATION AND CERTIFICATION

### §663.011. Designated division or state agency.

The governor shall designate a division of the governor's office or a state agency to establish and administer an all-terrain vehicle operator education and certification program. *(Added by L.1995, chap. 165(1), eff. 9/1/95.)*

### §663.012. Purpose of program.

The purpose of the all-terrain vehicle operator education and certification program is to make available courses in basic training and safety skills relating to the operation of all-terrain vehicles and to issue safety certificates to operators who successfully complete the educational program requirements or pass a test established under the program. *(Added by L.1995, chap. 165(1), eff. 9/1/95.)*

### §663.013. All-terrain vehicle safety coordinator.

(a) The designated division or state agency shall employ an all-terrain vehicle safety coordinator.

(b) The coordinator shall supervise the all-terrain vehicle operator education and certification program and shall determine:

(1) locations at which courses will be offered;

(2) fees for the courses;

(3) qualifications of instructors;

(4) course curriculum; and

(5) standards for operator safety certification.

(c) In establishing standards for instructors, curriculum, and operator certification, the coordinator shall consult and be guided by standards established by recognized all-terrain vehicle safety organizations.

*(Added by L.1995, chap. 165(1), eff. 9/1/95.)*

### §663.014. Contracts.

To administer the education program and certify all-terrain vehicle operators, the designated division or state agency may contract with nonprofit safety organizations, nonprofit educational organizations, or agencies of local governments. *(Added by L.1995, chap. 165(1), eff. 9/1/95.)*

### §663.015. Teaching and testing methods.

(a) If the all-terrain vehicle safety coordinator determines that vehicle operation is not feasible in a program component or at a particular program location, the operator education and certification program for persons who are at least 14 years of age may use teaching or testing methods that do not involve the actual operation of an all-terrain vehicle.

(b) An operator safety certificate may not be issued to a person younger than 14 years of age unless the person has successfully completed a training course that involves the actual operation of an all-terrain vehicle.

*(Added by L.1995, chap. 165(1), eff. 9/1/95.)*

### §663.016. Fee for course.

A person may charge, for a course under the all-terrain vehicle operator education and certification program, a fee that is reasonably related to the costs of administering the course. *(Added by L.1995, chap. 165(1), eff. 9/1/95.)*

### §663.017. Denial, suspension, or cancellation of approval.

(a) The designated division or state agency may deny, suspend, or cancel its approval for a program sponsor to conduct or for an instructor to teach a course offered under this chapter if the applicant, sponsor, or instructor:

(1) does not satisfy the requirements established under this chapter to receive or retain approval;

(2) permits fraud or engages in fraudulent practices with reference to an application to the division or agency;

(3) induces or countenances fraud or fraudulent practices by a person applying for a driver's license or permit;

(4) permits or engages in a fraudulent practice in an action between the applicant or license holder and the public; or

(5) fails to comply with rules of the division or agency.

(b) Before the designated division or agency may deny, suspend, or cancel the approval of a program sponsor or an instructor, notice and opportunity for a hearing must be given as provided by:

(1) Chapter 2001, Government Code;

(2) Article 6252-13c, Revised Statutes; and

(3) Sections 2 through 5, Chapter 267, Acts of the 67th Legislature, Regular Session, 1981 (Article 6252-13d, Texas Civil Statutes).

*(Added by L.1995, chap. 165(1), eff. 9/1/95.)*

### §663.018. Rules.

The designated division or state agency may adopt rules to administer this chapter. *(Added by L.1995, chap. 165(1), eff. 9/1/95.)*

### §663.019. Exemptions.

The designated division or state agency by rule may temporarily exempt the residents of any county from Section 663.015 or from Section 663.031(a)(1) until the appropriate education and certification program is established at a location that is reasonably accessible to the residents of that county. *(Added by L.1995, chap. 165(1), eff. 9/1/95.)*

### §§663.020 to 663.030. *(Reserved.)*

## SUBCHAPTER C. OPERATION OF ALL-TERRAIN VEHICLES



### §663.031. Safety certificate required.

(a) A person may not operate an all-terrain vehicle on public property unless the person:

(1) holds a safety certificate issued under this chapter or under the authority of another state;

(2) is taking a safety training course under the direct supervision of a certified all-terrain vehicle safety instructor; or

(3) is under the direct supervision of an adult who holds a safety certificate issued under this chapter or under the authority of another state.

(b) A person to whom a safety certificate required by Subsection (a) has been issued shall:

(1) carry the certificate when the person operates an all-terrain vehicle on public property; and

(2) display the certificate at the request of any law enforcement officer.

*(Added by L.1995, chap. 165(1), eff. 9/1/95.)*

### §663.032. Operation by person younger than 14.

A person younger than 14 years of age who is operating an all-terrain vehicle must be accompanied by and be under the direct supervision of:

(1) the person's parent or guardian; or

(2) an adult who is authorized by the person's parent or guardian.

*(Added by L.1995, chap. 165(1), eff. 9/1/95.)*

### §663.033. Required equipment; display of lights.

(a) An all-terrain vehicle that is operated on public property must be equipped with:

(1) a brake system maintained in good operating condition;

(2) an adequate muffler system in good working condition; and

(3) a United States Forest Service qualified spark arrester.

(b) An all-terrain vehicle that is operated on public property must display a lighted headlight and taillight:

(1) during the period from one-half hour after sunset to one-half hour before sunrise; and

(2) at any time when visibility is reduced because of insufficient light or atmospheric conditions.

(c) A person may not operate an all-terrain vehicle on public property if:

(1) the vehicle has an exhaust system that has been modified with a cutout, bypass, or similar device; or

(2) the spark arrester has been removed or modified, unless the vehicle is being operated in a closed-course competition event.

(d) The coordinator may exempt all-terrain vehicles that are participating in certain competitive events from the requirements of this section.

*(Added by L.1995, chap. 165(1), eff. 9/1/95.)*

### §663.034. Safety apparel required.

A person may not operate, ride, or be carried on an all-terrain vehicle on public property unless the person wears:

(1) a safety helmet that complies with United States Department of Transportation standards; and

(2) eye protection.

*(Added by L.1995, chap. 165(1), eff. 9/1/95.)*

### §663.035. Reckless or careless operation prohibited.

A person may not operate an all-terrain vehicle on public property in a careless or reckless manner that endangers, injures, or damages any person or property. *(Added by L.1995, chap. 165(1), eff. 9/1/95.)*

### §663.036. Passengers prohibited.

A person may not carry a passenger on an all-terrain vehicle operated on public property. *(Added by L.1995, chap. 165(1), eff. 9/1/95.)*

### §663.037. Operation on public roadway prohibited.

(a) A person may not operate an all-terrain vehicle on a public street, road, or highway except as provided by this section.

(b) The operator of an all-terrain vehicle may drive the vehicle across a public street, road, or highway that is not an interstate or limited-access highway, if the operator:

(1) brings the vehicle to a complete stop before crossing the shoulder or main traveled way of the roadway;

(2) yields the right-of-way to oncoming traffic that is an immediate hazard; and

(3) makes the crossing:

(A) at an angle of approximately 90 degrees to the roadway;

(B) at a place where no obstruction prevents a quick and safe crossing; and

(C) with the vehicle's headlights and taillights lighted.

(c) The operator of an all-terrain vehicle may drive the vehicle across a divided highway other than an interstate or limited access highway only at an intersection of the highway with another public street, road, or highway.

(d) This section does not apply to the operation of an all-terrain vehicle that is owned by the state, a county, or a municipality by a person who is an authorized operator of the vehicle.
*(Added by L.1995, chap. 165(1), eff. 9/1/95.)*

### §663.038. Violation of chapter; offense.

(a) A person commits an offense if the person violates a provision of this chapter.

(b) Except as otherwise provided by Title 6 or this title, an offense under this section is a Class C misdemeanor.
*(Added by L.1995, chap. 165(1), eff. 9/1/95.)*

## CHAPTERS 664 to 679. *(Reserved.)*

## CHAPTER 680. MISCELLANEOUS PROVISIONS

## SUBCHAPTER A. SALE OF MOTORCYCLE WITHOUT SERIAL NUMBERS

Section


## SUBCHAPTER B. TOLLS FOR MOTORCYCLE; USE OF PREFERENTIAL LANE BY MOTORCYCLE

## SUBCHAPTER A. SALE OF MOTORCYCLE WITHOUT SERIAL NUMBERS

### §680.001. Definitions.

In this subchapter:

(1) "Department" means the Department of Public Safety.

(2) "Motorcycle" has the meaning assigned that term by Section 661.001.

(3) "Person" means an individual, partnership, firm, corporation, association, or other private entity.

*(Added by L.1995, chap. 165(1), eff. 9/1/95.)*

### §680.002. Sale of motorcycle without serial numbers.

A person may not sell a motorcycle manufactured after January 1, 1976, unless:

(1) the serial number of the frame and the serial number of the engine are affixed so that they may not be removed without defacing the frame or engine; and

(2) the manufacturer has filed with the department a statement that:

(A) identifies the part to which each number is affixed;

(B) gives the exact dimensions of the part; and

(C) gives the location on the part to which the number is affixed.

*(Added by L.1995, chap. 165(1), eff. 9/1/95.)*



### §680.003. Offense; penalty.

(a) An individual who violates Section 680.002 commits an offense.

(b) An offense under this section is a misdemeanor punishable by:

(1) a fine not to exceed $200;

(2) confinement in county jail for a term not to exceed 30 days; or

(3) both the fine and confinement.

(c) Each sale of a motorcycle in violation of this subchapter is a separate offense.

*(Added by L.1995, chap. 165(1), eff. 9/1/95.)*

### §680.004. Civil penalty.

A partnership, firm, corporation, or association that violates Section 680.002 is liable to the state for a civil penalty of not more than $500 for each offense. *(Added by L.1995, chap. 165(1), eff. 9/1/95.)*

### §680.005. Director to adopt rules and develop forms.

The director of the department shall adopt rules and develop forms to administer this subchapter. *(Added by L.1995, chap. 165(1), eff. 9/1/95.)*

### §§680.006 to 680.010. *(Reserved.)*

## SUBCHAPTER B. TOLLS FOR MOTORCYCLE; USE OF PREFERENTIAL LANE BY MOTORCYCLE

### §680.011. Definitions.

In this subchapter:

(1) "Motorcycle" has the meaning assigned by Section 502.001 and includes a motorcycle equipped with a sidecar.

(2) "Preferential lane" means a traffic lane on a street or highway where motor vehicle usage is limited to:

(A) buses;

(B) vehicles occupied by a minimum number of persons; or

(C) car pool vehicles.

*(Added by L.1995, chap. 165(1), eff. 9/1/95.)*

### §680.012. Toll for motorcycle.

A person who operates a toll road, toll bridge, or turnpike may not impose a toll for the operation of a motorcycle on the road, bridge, or turnpike that is greater than the toll imposed for the operation of a passenger car on the road, bridge, or turnpike. *(Added by L.1995, chap. 165(1), eff. 9/1/95.)*

### §680.013. Use of preferential lane by motorcycle.

A motorcycle may be operated in a preferential lane that is not closed to all vehicular traffic. *(Added by L.1995, chap. 165(1), eff. 9/1/95.)*

# SUBTITLE H. PARKING, TOWING, AND STORAGE OF VEHICLES

## CHAPTER 681. PRIVILEGED PARKING

Section



### §681.001. Definitions.

In this chapter:

(1) "Department" means the Texas Department of Transportation.

(2) "Disability" means a condition in which a person has:

(A) mobility problems that substantially impair the person's ability to ambulate;

(B) visual acuity of 20/200 or less in the better eye with correcting lenses; or

(C) visual acuity of more than 20/200 but with a limited field of vision in which the widest diameter of the visual field subtends an angle of 20 degrees or less.

(3) "Disabled parking placard" means a placard issued under Section 681.002.

(4) "International symbol of access" means the symbol adopted by Rehabilitation International in 1969 at its Eleventh World Congress on Rehabilitation of the Disabled.

(5) "Mobility problem that substantially impairs a person's ability to ambulate" means that the person:

(A) cannot walk 200 feet without stopping to rest;

(B) cannot walk without the use of or assistance from an assistance device, including a brace, a cane, a crutch, another person, or a prosthetic device;

(C) cannot ambulate without a wheelchair or similar device;

(D) is restricted by lung disease to the extent that the person's forced respiratory expiratory volume for one second, measured by spirometry, is less than one liter, or the arterial oxygen tension is less than 60 millimeters of mercury on room air at rest;

(E) uses portable oxygen;

(F) has a cardiac condition to the extent that the person's functional limitations are classified in severity as Class III or Class IV according to standards set by the American Heart Association;

(G) is severely limited in the ability to walk because of an arthritic, neurological, or orthopedic condition; or

(H) has another debilitating condition that, in the opinion of a physician licensed to practice medicine in this state or a state adjacent to this state, or authorized by applicable law to practice medicine in a hospital or other health facility of the Veterans Administration, limits or impairs the person's ability to walk.

*(Added by L.1995, chap. 165(1); chgd. by L.1997, chap. 165(30.156(a)); L.1999, chap. 1172(2), eff. 6/18/99.)*

### §681.002. Disabled parking placard.

(a) The department shall provide for the issuance of a disabled parking placard to a person with a disability.

(b) A disabled parking placard must be two-sided and hooked and include on each side:

(1) the international symbol of access, which must be at least three inches in height, be centered on the placard, and be:

(A) white on a blue shield for a placard issued to a person with a mobility disability described by Section 681.001(5)(B) or (C); or

(B) white on a red shield for a placard issued to a person with any other permanent or temporary disability;

(2) an identification number;

(3) an expiration date at least three inches in height; and

(4) the seal or other identification of the department.

(c) The department shall furnish the disabled parking placards to each county assessor-collector.

(d) A disabled parking placard must bear a hologram designed to prevent the reproduction of the placard or the production of a counterfeit placard.

(e) In addition to the expiration date included on a disabled parking placard under Subsection (b), the expiration date must be indicated on the placard by a month and year hole-punch system.
*(Added by L.1995, chap. 165(1); chgd. by L.1997, chap. 1353(1); L.1999, chap. 1362(1), eff. 9/1/99.)*



## §681.003. Parking placard application.

(a) An owner of a motor vehicle regularly operated by or for the transportation of a person with a disability may apply for a disabled parking placard.

(b) An application for a disabled parking placard must be:

(1) on a form furnished by the department;

(2) submitted to the county assessor-collector of the county in which the person with the disability resides; and

(3) accompanied by a fee of $5.

(c) The first application must be accompanied by a notarized written statement or written prescription of a physician licensed to practice medicine in this state or a state adjacent to this state, or authorized by applicable law to practice medicine in a hospital or other health facility of the Veterans Administration, certifying and providing evidence acceptable to the department that the person making the application or on whose behalf the application is made is legally blind or has a mobility problem that substantially impairs the person's ability to ambulate. The statement or prescription must include a certification of whether the disability is temporary or permanent and information acceptable to the department to determine the type of disabled parking placard for which the applicant is eligible. The department shall determine a person's eligibility based on evidence provided by the applicant establishing legal blindness or mobility impairment.

(d) Information concerning the name or address of a person to whom a disabled parking placard is issued or in whose behalf a disabled parking placard is issued is confidential and not subject to disclosure under Chapter 552, Government Code.
*(Added by L.1995, chap. 165(1); chgd. by L.1997, chaps. 165(30.156(b)), 1353(2); L.1999, chaps. 1172(3), 1362(2), eff. 6/18/99, 9/1/99, respectively.)*

## §681.0031. Applicant's driver's license or personal identification card number.

(a) The applicant shall include on the application the applicant's driver's license number or the number of a personal identification card issued to the applicant under Chapter 521. The department shall provide for this information in prescribing the application form.

(b) The county assessor-collector shall record the number on any disabled parking placard issued to the applicant.
*(Added by L.1997, chap. 1353(3), eff. 9/1/97.)*

## §681.0032. Issuance of disabled parking placards to certain institutions.

(a) The department shall provide for the issuance of disabled parking placards described by Section 681.002 for a van or bus operated by an institution, facility, or residential retirement community for the elderly in which a person described by Section 502.253(b) resides, including an institution licensed under Chapter 242, Health and Safety Code, and a facility licensed under Chapter 246 or 247 of that code.

(b) The application for a disabled parking placard must be made in the manner provided by Section 681.003(b) and be accompanied by a written statement signed by the administrator or manager of the institution, facility, or retirement community certifying to the department that the institution, facility, or retirement community regularly transports, as a part of the services that the institution, facility, or retirement community provides, one or more persons described by Section 502.253(b) who reside in the institution, facility, or retirement community. The department shall

determine the eligibility of the institution, facility, or retirement community on the evidence the applicant provides.
*(Added by L.1999, chap. 513(2), eff. 9/1/99.)*

## §681.004. Issuance of parking placard; expiration.

(a) A person with a permanent disability may receive:

(1) two disabled parking placards, if the person does not receive a set of special license plates under Section 502.253; or

(2) one disabled parking placard, if the person receives a set of special license plates under Section 502.253.

(b) A person with a temporary disability may receive two disabled parking placards.

(c) A disabled parking placard issued to a person with a permanent disability is valid for a period of four years and shall be replaced or renewed on request of the person to whom the initial card was issued without presentation of evidence of eligibility.

(d) A disabled parking placard issued to a person with a temporary disability expires after the period set by the department and may be renewed at the end of that period if the disability remains as evidenced by a physician's statement or prescription submitted as required for a first application under Section 681.003(c).
*(Added by L.1995, chap. 165(1); chgd. by L.1997, chap. 1353(4), eff. 9/1/97.)*

## §681.005. Duties of county assessor-collector.

Each county assessor-collector shall send to the department:

(1) each fee collected under Section 681.003, to be deposited in the state highway fund to defray the cost of providing the disabled parking placard; and

(2) a copy of each application for a disabled parking placard.
*(Added by L.1995, chap. 165(1), eff. 9/1/95.)*

## §681.006. Parking privileges: persons with disabilities.

(a) Subject to Section 681.009(e), a vehicle may be parked for an unlimited period in a parking space or area that is designated specifically for persons with physical disabilities if:

(1) the vehicle is being operated by or for the transportation of a person with a disability; and

(2) there are:

(A) displayed on the vehicle special license plates issued under Section 502.253; or

(B) placed on the rearview mirror of the vehicle's front windshield a disabled parking placard.

(b) The owner of a vehicle is exempt from the payment of a fee or penalty imposed by a governmental unit for parking at a meter if:

(1) the vehicle is being operated by or for the transportation of a person with a disability; and

(2) there are:

(A) displayed on the vehicle special license plates issued under Section 502.253; or

(B) placed on the rearview mirror of the vehicle's front windshield a disabled parking placard.

(c) The exemption provided by Subsection (b) or (e) does not apply to a fee or penalty:

(1) imposed by a branch of the United States government; or

(2) imposed by a governmental unit for parking at a meter, in a parking garage or lot, or in a space located within the boundaries of a municipal airport.

(d) This section does not permit a vehicle to be parked at a time when or a place where parking is prohibited.

(e) A governmental unit may provide by ordinance or order that the exemption provided by Subsection (b) also applies to payment of a fee or penalty imposed by the governmental unit for parking in a parking garage or lot or in a space with a limitation on the length of time for parking.
*(Added by L.1995, chap. 165(1); chgd. by L.1997, chaps. 165(30.156(c)), 804(1), 1353(5); L.1999, chap. 1362(3), eff. 9/1/99.)*

## §681.007. Parking privileges: vehicles displaying international symbol of access.

A vehicle may be parked and is exempt from the payment of a fee or penalty in the same manner as a vehicle that has displayed on the vehicle special license plates issued under Section 502.253 or a disabled parking placard as provided by Section 681.006 if there is displayed on the vehicle a license plate or placard that:

(1) bears the international symbol of access; and

(2) is issued by a state or by a state or province of a foreign country to the owner or operator of the vehicle for the transportation of a person with a disability.
*(Added by L.1995, chap. 165(1), eff. 9/1/95.)*

**§681.008. Parking privileges: certain veterans.**

(a) A vehicle may be parked for an unlimited period in a parking space or area that is designated specifically for persons with physical disabilities if:

(1) the vehicle is being operated by or for the transportation of:

(A) the person who registered the vehicle under Section 502.254(a); or

(B) a person described by Section 502.254(b) if the vehicle is registered under that subsection; and

(2) there are displayed on the vehicle special license plates issued under Section 502.254.

(b) A vehicle on which license plates issued under Section 502.254, 502.255, 502.257, 502.259, 502.260 are displayed is exempt from the payment of a parking fee collected through a parking meter charged by a governmental authority other than a branch of the federal government, when being operated by or for the transportation of:

(1) the person who registered the vehicle under Section 502.254(a), 502.255, 502.257, 502.259, 502.260; or

(2) a person described in Section 502.254(b) if the vehicle is registered under that subsection.
*(Chgd. By L.1999, chaps. 738(1), 1195(1), eff. 9/1/99, 6/18/99, respectively. See other subsection (b) below.)*

(b) A governmental unit may provide by ordinance or order that the exemption provided by Subsection (a) also applies to payment of a fee or penalty imposed by the governmental unit for parking in a parking garage or lot or in a space with a limitation on the length of time for parking.
*(Chgd. by L.1999, chap. 1362(4), eff. 9/1/99. See other subsection (b) above.)*

(c) This section does not permit a vehicle to be parked at a time when or a place where parking is prohibited.
*(Added by L.1995, chap. 165(1); chgd. by L.1999, chaps. 738(1), 1195(1), 1362(4), eff. 9/1/99, 6/18/99, 9/1/99, respectively.)*

**§681.009. Designation of parking spaces by political subdivision or private property owner.**

(a) A political subdivision or a person who owns or controls property used for parking may designate one or more parking spaces or a parking area for the exclusive use of vehicles transporting persons with disabilities.

(b) A political subdivision must designate a parking space or area by conforming to the standards and specifications adopted by the Texas Commission of Licensing and Regulation under Section 5(i), Article 9102, Revised Statutes, relating to the identification and dimensions of parking spaces for persons with disabilities. A person who owns or controls private property used for parking may designate a parking space or area without conforming to those standards and specifications, unless required to conform by law.

(c) A political subdivision may require a private property owner or a person who controls property used for parking:

(1) to designate one or more parking spaces or a parking area for the exclusive use of vehicles transporting persons with disabilities; or

(2) to conform to the standards and specifications referred to in Subsection (b) when designating a parking space or area for persons with disabilities.

(d) The department shall provide at cost a design and stencil for use by a political subdivision or person who owns or controls property used for parking to designate spaces as provided by this section.

(e) A private property owner or private person who controls property used for parking and who designates one or more uncovered parking spaces for the exclusive use of vehicles transporting persons with disabilities shall assign at least half of those spaces for the exclusive use of vehicles displaying a white on blue shield disabled parking placard, except that if an odd number of spaces is designated, only the number of spaces that is the largest whole number less than half of the number of designated spaces must be assigned for the exclusive use of vehicles displaying a white on blue shield placard. Van-accessible parking spaces shall be counted as assigned spaces under this subsection. These assigned spaces must be the spaces located closest to an accessible route to an entrance accessible to a person with a disability. The remaining designated parking spaces may be used by vehicles displaying a white on blue shield disabled parking placard, a white on red shield disabled parking placard, or license plates issued under Section 502.253. This subsection applies only to property used for parking that serves a building or other facility:

(1) that state law requires to be accessible to persons with disabilities; and

Printed in the U.S.A. Zt

(2) for which construction or an alteration of the building or other facility is completed on or after September 1, 1999.
*(Added by L.1995, chap. 165(1); chgd. by L.1999, chaps. 1246(9), 1362(5), eff. 9/1/99.)*

## §681.010. Enforcement.

(a) A peace officer or a person designated by a political subdivision to enforce parking regulations may file a charge against a person who commits an offense under this chapter at a parking space or area designated as provided by Section 681.009.

(b) A security officer commissioned under the Private Investigators and Private Security Agencies Act (Article 4413(29bb), Texas Civil Statutes) and employed by the owner of private property may file a charge against a person who commits an offense under this chapter at a parking space or area designated by the owner of the property as provided by Section 681.009.
*(Added by L.1995, chap. 165(1), eff. 9/1/95.)*

## §681.0101. Enforcement by certain appointed persons.

(a) A political subdivision may appoint a person to have authority to file a charge against a person who commits an offense under this chapter.

(b) A person appointed under this section must:

(1) be a United States citizen of good moral character who has not been convicted of a felony;

(2) take and subscribe to an oath of office that the political subdivision prescribes; and

(3) successfully complete a training program developed by the political subdivision.

(c) A person appointed under this section:

(1) is not a peace officer;

(2) has no authority other than the authority applicable to a citizen to enforce a law other than this chapter; and

(3) may not carry a weapon while performing duties under this section.

(d) A person appointed under this section is not entitled to compensation for performing duties under this section or to indemnification from the political subdivision or the state for injury or property damage the person sustains or liability the person incurs in performing duties under this section.

(e) The political subdivision and the state are not liable for any damage arising from an act or omission of a person appointed under Subsection (a) in performing duties under this section.
*(Added by L.1997, chaps. 165(30.156(d)), 1353(6), eff. 9/1/97.)*

## §681.011. Offenses; presumption.

(a) A person commits an offense if:

(1) the person parks a vehicle on which are displayed license plates issued under Section 502.253 or 502.254 or a disabled parking placard in a parking space or area designated specifically for persons with disabilities by:

(A) a political subdivision; or

(B) a person who owns or controls private property used for parking as to which a political subdivision has provided for the application of this section under Subsection (f); and

(2) the parking of the vehicle in that parking space or area is not authorized by Section 681.006, 681.007, or 681.008.

(b) A person commits an offense if the person:

(1) parks a vehicle on which license plates issued under Section 502.253 or 502.254 are not displayed and a disabled parking placard is not displayed in a parking space or area designated specifically for individuals with disabilities by:

(A) a political subdivision; or

(B) a person who owns or controls private property used for parking as to which a political subdivision has provided for the application of this section under Subsection (f); or

(2) parks a vehicle displaying a white on red shield disabled parking placard or license plates issued under Section 502.253 in a space designated under Section 681.009(e) for the exclusive use of vehicles displaying a white on blue shield disabled parking placard.

(c) A person commits an offense if the person parks a vehicle so that the vehicle blocks an architectural improvement designed to aid persons with disabilities, including an access or curb ramp.

(d) A person commits an offense if the person lends a disabled parking placard issued to the person to a person who uses the placard in violation of this section.

(e) In a prosecution under this section, it is presumed that the registered owner of the motor vehicle is the person who parked the vehicle at the time and place the offense occurred.

(f) A political subdivision may provide that this section applies to a parking space or area for persons with disabilities on private property that is designated in compliance with the identification requirements referred to in Section 681.009(b).

(g) Except as provided by Subsections (h)-(k), an offense under this section is a misdemeanor punishable by a fine of not less than $250 or more than $500.

(h) If it is shown on the trial of an offense under this section that the person has been previously convicted one time of an offense under this section, the offense is punishable by a fine of not less than $300 or more than $600.

(i) If it is shown on the trial of an offense under this section that the person has been previously convicted two times of an offense under this section, the offense is punishable by:

(1) a fine of not less than $300 or more than $600; and

(2) not less than 10 or more than 20 hours of community service.

(j) If it is shown on the trial of an offense under this section that the person has been previously convicted three times of an offense under this section, the offense is punishable by:

(1) a fine of not less than $500 or more than $1,000; and

(2) not less than 20 or more than 50 hours of community service.

(k) If it is shown on the trial of an offense under this section that the person has been previously convicted four times of an offense under this section, the offense is punishable by a fine of $1,000 and 50 hours of community service.

*(l) (Repealed.)*

(m) A person commits an offense if the person:

(1) parks a vehicle on which are displayed license plates issued under Section 502.253 or a disabled parking placard in a parking space or area for which this chapter creates an exemption from payment of a fee or penalty imposed by a governmental unit;

(2) does not have a disability;

(3) is not transporting a person with a disability; and

(4) does not pay any applicable fee related to parking in the space or area imposed by a governmental unit or exceeds a limitation on the length of time for parking in the space or area.

*(Added by L.1995, chap. 165(1); chgd. by L.1997, chap. 165(30.156(e)); L.1999, chaps. 738(2), 1362(6),(7), eff. 9/1/99.)*

### §681.012. Seizure and revocation of placard.

(a) A law enforcement officer who believes that an offense under Section 681.011(a) or (d) has occurred in the officer's presence shall seize any disabled parking placard involved in the offense. Not later than 48 hours after the seizure, the officer shall determine whether probable cause existed to believe that the offense was committed. If the officer does not find that probable cause existed, the officer shall promptly return each placard to the person from whom it was seized. If the officer finds that probable cause existed, the officer, not later than the fifth day after the date of the seizure, shall submit each seized placard to the department.

(b) On submission to the department under Subsection (a), a placard is revoked. On request of the person from whom the placard was seized, the department shall conduct a hearing and determine whether the revocation should continue or the placard should be returned to the person and the revocation rescinded.

*(Added by L.1997, chap. 1353(7), eff. 9/1/97.)*

## CHAPTER 682. ADMINISTRATIVE ADJUDICATION OF VEHICLE PARKING AND STOPPING OFFENSES

*(Heading chgd. by L.1999, chap. 156(1), eff. 5/21/99.)*

Section

### §682.001. Applicability.

This chapter applies only to:

(1) a municipality that:

(A) has a population greater than 30,000; and

(2) an airport operated by a joint board to which Section 22.074(d) applies.

*(Added by L.1995, chap. 165(1); chgd. by L.1999, chaps. 156(2), 310(1), eff. 5/21/99, 5/29/99, respectively.)*

### §682.002. Civil offense.

(a) A municipality may declare the violation of a municipal ordinance relating to parking or stopping a vehicle to be a civil offense.

(b) A joint board to which Section 22.074(d) applies may declare the violation of a resolution, rule, or order of the joint board relating to parking or stopping a vehicle to be a civil offense.

*(Added by L.1995, chap. 165(1); chgd. by L.1999, chap. 156(2), eff. 5/21/99.)*

### §682.003. Adoption of hearing procedure.

A municipality may by ordinance or a joint board may by resolution, rule, or order establish an administrative adjudication hearing procedure under which a civil fine may be imposed. *(Added by L.1995, chap. 165(1); chgd. by L.1999, chap. 156(2), eff. 5/21/99.)*

### §682.004. Content of ordinance.

An ordinance, resolution, rule, or order adopted under this chapter must provide that a person charged with violating a parking or stopping ordinance, resolution, rule, or order is entitled to a hearing and provide for:

(1) the period during which a hearing must be held;

(2) the appointment of a hearing officer with authority to administer oaths and issue orders compelling the attendance of witnesses and the production of documents; and

(3) the amount and disposition of civil fines, costs, and fees.

*(Added by L.1995, chap. 165(1); chgd. by L.1999, chap. 156(2), eff. 5/21/99.)*

### §682.005. Enforcement of order concerning witnesses and documents.

A municipal court may enforce an order of the hearing officer compelling the attendance of a witness or the production of a document. *(Added by L.1995, chap. 165(1), eff. 9/1/95.)*

### §682.006. Citation or summons.

(a) A citation or summons issued for a vehicle parking or stopping civil offense under this chapter must:

(1) provide information as to the time and place of an administrative adjudication hearing; and

(2) contain a notification that the person charged with the civil offense has the right to an instanter hearing.

(b) The original or any copy of the summons or citation shall be kept as a record in the ordinary course of business of the municipality and is rebuttable proof of the facts it contains.

*(Added by L.1995, chap. 165(1), eff. 9/1/95.)*

### §682.007. Appearance at hearing.

(a) A person charged with a civil offense who fails to appear at an administrative adjudication hearing authorized under this chapter is considered to admit liability for the offense charged.

(b) The person who issued the citation or summons is not required to attend an instanter hearing.

*(Added by L.1995, chap. 165(1), eff. 9/1/95.)*

### §682.008. Presumptions.

In an administrative adjudication hearing under this chapter:

(1) it is presumed that the registered owner of the motor vehicle is the person who parked or stopped the vehicle at the time and place of the offense charged; and

(2) the Texas Department of Transportation's computer-generated record of the registered vehicle owner is prima facie evidence of the contents of the record.

*(Added by L.1995, chap. 165(1), eff. 9/1/95.)*

### §682.009. Order.

(a) The hearing officer at an administrative adjudication hearing under this chapter shall issue an order stating:

(1) whether the person charged with the violation is liable for the violation; and

(2) the amount of any fine, cost, or fee assessed against the person.

(b) The order issued under Subsection (a) may be filed with the clerk or secretary of the municipality or a person designated by the joint board. The clerk, secretary, or designated person shall keep the order in a separate index and file. The order may be recorded using microfilm, microfiche, or data processing techniques.

*(Added by L.1995, chap. 165(1); chgd. by L.1999, chap. 156(3), eff. 5/21/99.)*

### §682.010. Enforcement.

An order filed under Section 682.009 may be enforced by:

(1) impounding the vehicle if the offender has committed three or more vehicle parking or stopping offenses in a calendar year;

(2) placing a device on the vehicle that prohibits movement of the motor vehicle;

(3) imposing an additional fine if the original fine is not paid within a specified time; or

(4) denying issuance of or revoking a parking or operating permit, as applicable.

*(Added by L.1995, chap. 165(1); chgd. by L.1999, chap. 156(4), eff. 5/21/99.)*

### §682.011. Appeal.

(a) A person whom the hearing officer determines to be in violation of a vehicle parking or stopping ordinance may appeal the determination by filing a petition with the clerk of a municipal court and paying the costs required by law for municipal court not later than the 30th day after the date on which the order is filed.

(b) The municipal court clerk shall schedule a hearing and notify each party of the date, time, and place of the hearing.

(c) An appeal does not stay enforcement and collection of the judgment unless the person, before appealing, posts bond with, as applicable:

(1) the agency of the municipality designated by ordinance to accept payment for a violation of a parking or stopping ordinance; or

(2) the agency of the joint board designated by the resolution, rule, or order to accept payment for a violation of a parking or stopping resolution, rule, or order.

*(Added by L.1995, chap. 165(1); chgd. by L.1999, chap. 156(5), eff. 5/21/99.)*

## CHAPTER 683. ABANDONED MOTOR VEHICLES

## SUBCHAPTER A. GENERAL PROVISIONS

Section



## SUBCHAPTER B. ABANDONED MOTOR VEHICLES: SEIZURE AND AUCTION

## SUBCHAPTER C. VEHICLE ABANDONED IN STORAGE FACILITY



## SUBCHAPTER D. DEMOLITION OF ABANDONED MOTOR VEHICLES



## SUBCHAPTER E. JUNKED VEHICLES: PUBLIC NUISANCE; ABATEMENT



## SUBCHAPTER A. GENERAL PROVISIONS

### §683.001. Definitions.

In this chapter:

(1) "Department" means the Texas Department of Transportation.

(2) "Garagekeeper" means an owner or operator of a storage facility.

(3) "Law enforcement agency" means:

(A) the Department of Public Safety;

(B) the police department of a municipality;

(C) the police department of an institution of higher education; or

(D) a sheriff or a constable.

(4) "Motor vehicle" means a vehicle that is subject to registration under Chapter 501*.

(5) "Motor vehicle demolisher" means a person in the business of:

(A) converting motor vehicles into processed scrap or scrap metal; or

(B) wrecking or dismantling motor vehicles.

(6) "Outboard motor" means an outboard motor subject to registration under Chapter 31, Parks and Wildlife Code.

(7) "Storage facility" includes a garage, parking lot, or establishment for the servicing, repairing, or parking of motor vehicles.

(8) "Watercraft" means a vessel subject to registration under Chapter 31, Parks and Wildlife Code.

**So in original. Probably should be "Chapter 502".*
*(Added by L.1995, chap. 165(1), eff. 9/1/95.)*

### §683.002. Abandoned motor vehicle.

(a) For the purposes of this chapter, a motor vehicle is abandoned if the motor vehicle:

(1) is inoperable, is more than five years old, and has been left unattended on public property for more than 48 hours;

(2) has remained illegally on public property for more than 48 hours;

(3) has remained on private property without the consent of the owner or person in charge of the property for more than 48 hours;

(4) has been left unattended on the right-of-way of a designated county, state, or federal highway for more than 48 hours; or

(5) has been left unattended for more than 24 hours on the right-of-way of a turnpike project constructed and maintained by the Texas Turnpike Authority or a controlled access highway.

(b) In this section, "controlled access highway" has the meaning assigned by Section 541.302.

*(Added by L.1995, chap. 165(1); chgd. by L.1997, chap. 165(30.157(a)), eff. 9/1/97.)*

### §683.003. Conflict of laws; effect on other laws.

(a) Sections 683.051-683.055 may not be read as conflicting with Sections 683.074-683.078.

(b) This chapter does not affect a law authorizing the immediate removal of a vehicle left on public property that is an obstruction to traffic.

*(Added by L.1995, chap. 165(1), eff. 9/1/95.)*

### §§683.004 to 683.010. *(Reserved.)*

## SUBCHAPTER B. ABANDONED MOTOR VEHICLES: SEIZURE AND AUCTION

### §683.011. Authority to take abandoned motor vehicle into custody.

(a) A law enforcement agency may take into custody an abandoned motor vehicle, watercraft, or outboard motor found on public or private property.

(b) A law enforcement agency may use agency personnel, equipment, and facilities or contract for other personnel, equipment, and facilities to remove, preserve, and store an abandoned motor vehicle, watercraft, or outboard motor taken into custody by the agency under this subchapter.

*(Added by L.1995, chap. 165(1), eff. 9/1/95.)*

### §683.012. Taking abandoned motor vehicle into custody: notice.

(a) A law enforcement agency shall send notice of abandonment to:

(1) the last known registered owner of each motor vehicle, watercraft, or outboard motor taken into custody by the agency or for which a report is received under Section 683.031; and

(2) each lienholder recorded under Chapter 501 for the motor vehicle or under Chapter 31, Parks and Wildlife Code, for the watercraft or outboard motor.

(b) The notice under Subsection (a) must:

(1) be sent by certified mail not later than the 10th day after the date the agency:

(A) takes the abandoned motor vehicle, watercraft, or outboard motor into custody; or

(B) receives the report under Section 683.031;

(2) specify the year, make, model, and identification number of the item;

(3) give the location of the facility where the item is being held;

(4) inform the owner and lienholder of the right to claim the item not later than the 20th day after the date of the notice on payment of:

(A) towing, preservation, and storage charges; or

(B) garagekeeper's charges and fees under Section 683.032; and

(5) state that failure of the owner or lienholder to claim the item during the period specified by Subdivision (4) is:

(A) a waiver by that person of all right, title, and interest in the item; and

(B) consent to the sale of the item at a public auction.

(c) Notice by publication in one newspaper of general circulation in the area where the motor vehicle, watercraft, or outboard motor was abandoned is sufficient notice under this section if:

(1) the identity of the last registered owner cannot be determined;

(2) the registration has no address for the owner; or

(3) the determination with reasonable certainty of the identity and address of all lienholders is impossible.

(d) Notice by publication:

(1) must be published in the same period that is required by Subsection (b) for notice by certified mail and contain all of the information required by that subsection; and

(2) may contain a list of more than one abandoned motor vehicle, watercraft, or outboard motor.
*(Added by L.1995, chap. 165(1), eff. 9/1/95.)*

### §683.013. Storage fees.

A law enforcement agency or the agent of a law enforcement agency that takes into custody an abandoned motor vehicle, watercraft, or outboard motor is entitled to reasonable storage fees:

(1) for not more than 10 days, beginning on the day the item is taken into custody and ending on the day the required notice is mailed; and

(2) beginning on the day after the day the agency mails notice and ending on the day accrued charges are paid and the vehicle, watercraft, or outboard motor is removed.
*(Added by L.1995, chap. 165(1), eff. 9/1/95.)*

### §683.014. Auction or use of abandoned items; waiver of rights.

(a) If an abandoned motor vehicle, watercraft, or outboard motor is not claimed under Section 683.012:

(1) the owner or lienholder:

(A) waives all rights and interests in the item; and

(B) consents to the sale of the item by public auction; and

(2) the law enforcement agency may sell the item at a public auction or use the item as provided by Section 683.016.

(b) Proper notice of the auction shall be given. A garagekeeper who has a garagekeeper's lien shall be notified of the time and place of the auction.

(c) The purchaser of a motor vehicle, watercraft, or outboard motor:

(1) takes title free and clear of all liens and claims of ownership;

(2) shall receive a sales receipt from the law enforcement agency; and

(3) is entitled to register the motor vehicle, watercraft, or outboard motor and receive a certificate of title.
*(Added by L.1995, chap. 165(1), eff. 9/1/95.)*

### §683.015. Auction proceeds.

(a) A law enforcement agency is entitled to reimbursement from the proceeds of the sale of an abandoned motor vehicle, watercraft, or outboard motor for:

(1) the cost of the auction;

(2) towing, preservation, and storage fees resulting from the taking into custody; and

(3) the cost of notice or publication as required by Section 683.012.

(b) After deducting the reimbursement allowed under Subsection (a), the proceeds of the sale shall be held for 90 days for the owner or lienholder of the vehicle.

(c) After the period provided by Subsection (b), proceeds unclaimed by the owner or lienholder shall be deposited in an account that may be used for the payment of auction, towing, preservation, storage, and notice and publication fees resulting from taking other vehicles, watercraft, or outboard motors into custody if the proceeds from the sale of the other items are insufficient to meet those fees.

(d) A municipality or county may transfer funds in excess of $1,000 from the account to the municipality's or county's general revenue account to be used by the law enforcement agency.
*(Added by L.1995, chap. 165(1), eff. 9/1/95.)*

### §683.016. Law enforcement agency use of certain abandoned motor vehicles.

(a) The law enforcement agency that takes an abandoned motor vehicle into custody that is not claimed under Section 683.012 may use the vehicle for agency purposes.

(b) The law enforcement agency shall auction the vehicle as provided by this subchapter if the agency discontinues use of the vehicle.

(c) This section does not apply to an abandoned vehicle on which there is a garagekeeper's lien.

(d) This section does not apply to a vehicle that is:

(1) taken into custody by a law enforcement agency located in a county with a population of 2.4 million or more; and

(2) removed to a privately owned storage facility.
*(Added by L.1995, chap. 165(1), eff. 9/1/95.)*

### §§683.017 to 683.030. *(Reserved.)*

## SUBCHAPTER C. VEHICLE ABANDONED IN STORAGE FACILITY

### §683.031. Garagekeeper's duty: abandoned motor vehicles.

(a) A motor vehicle is abandoned if the vehicle is left in a storage facility operated for commercial purposes after the 10th day after the date on which:

(1) the garagekeeper gives notice by registered or certified mail, return receipt requested, to the last known registered owner of the vehicle and to each lienholder of record of the vehicle under Chapter 501 to remove the vehicle;

(2) a contract for the vehicle to remain on the premises of the facility expires; or

(3) the vehicle was left in the facility, if the vehicle was left by a person other than the registered owner or a person authorized to have possession of the vehicle under a contract of use, service, storage, or repair.

(b) If notice sent under Subsection (a)(1) is returned unclaimed by the post office, substituted notice is sufficient if published in one newspaper of general circulation in the area where the vehicle was left.

(c) The garagekeeper shall report the abandonment of the motor vehicle to a law enforcement agency and shall pay a $5 fee to be used by the law enforcement agency for the cost of the notice required by this subchapter or other cost incurred in disposing of the vehicle. A fee paid to the Department of Public Safety shall be used to administer this chapter.

(d) The garagekeeper shall retain custody of an abandoned motor vehicle until the law enforcement agency takes the vehicle into custody under Section 683.034.

*(Added by L.1995, chap. 165(1), eff. 9/1/95.)*

### §683.032. Garagekeeper's fees and charges.

(a) A garagekeeper who acquires custody of a motor vehicle for a purpose other than repair is entitled to towing, preservation, and notification charges and reasonable storage fees, in addition to storage fees earned under a contract, for each day:

(1) not to exceed five days, until the notice described by Section 683.031(a) is mailed; and

(2) after notice is mailed, until the vehicle is removed and all accrued charges are paid.

(b) A garagekeeper who fails to report an abandoned motor vehicle to a law enforcement agency within seven days after the date it is abandoned may not claim reimbursement for storage of the vehicle.

(c) This subchapter does not impair any lien that a garagekeeper has on a vehicle except for the termination or limitation of claim for storage for the failure to report the vehicle to the law enforcement agency.

*(Added by L.1995, chap. 165(1); chgd. by L.1997, chap. 165(30.158(a)), eff. 9/1/97.)*

### §683.033. Unauthorized storage fee; offense.

(a) A person commits an offense if the person charges a storage fee for a period for which the fee is not authorized by Section 683.032.

(b) An offense under this subsection is a misdemeanor punishable by a fine of not less than $200 or more than $1,000.

*(Added by L.1995, chap. 165(1), eff. 9/1/95.)*

### §683.034. Disposal of vehicle abandoned in storage facility.

(a) A law enforcement agency shall take into custody an abandoned vehicle left in a storage facility that has not been claimed in the period provided by the notice under Section 683.012.

(b) The law enforcement agency may use the vehicle as authorized by Section 683.016 or sell the vehicle at auction as provided by Section 683.014. If a vehicle is sold, the proceeds of the sale shall first be applied to a garagekeeper's charges for service, storage, and repair of the vehicle.

(c) As compensation for expenses incurred in taking the vehicle into custody and selling it, the law enforcement agency shall retain:

(1) two percent of the gross proceeds of the sale of the vehicle; or

(2) all the proceeds if the gross proceeds of the sale are less than $10.

(d) Surplus proceeds shall be distributed as provided by Section 683.015.

(e) If the law enforcement agency does not take the vehicle into custody before the 31st day after the date notice is sent under Section 683.012:

(1) the law enforcement agency may not take the vehicle into custody; and

(2) the storage facility may dispose of the vehicle under Chapter 70, Property Code, except that notice under Section 683.012 satisfies the notice requirements of that chapter.

*(Added by L.1995, chap. 165(1); chgd. by L.1997, chap. 165(30.158(b)), eff. 9/1/97.)*

**§§683.035 to 683.050.** *(Reserved.)*

## SUBCHAPTER D. DEMOLITION OF ABANDONED MOTOR VEHICLES

### §683.051. Application for authorization to dispose of certain motor vehicles.

A person may apply to the department for authority:

(1) to sell, give away, or dispose of a motor vehicle to a motor vehicle demolisher if:

(A) the person owns the motor vehicle and the certificate of title to the vehicle is lost, destroyed, or faulty; or

(B) the vehicle is an abandoned motor vehicle and is:

(i) in the possession of the person; or

(ii) located on property owned by the person; or

(2) to dispose of a motor vehicle to a motor vehicle demolisher for demolition, wrecking, or dismantling if:

(A) the abandoned motor vehicle:

(i) is in the possession of the person;

(ii) is more than eight years old;

(iii) either has no motor or is otherwise totally inoperable or does not comply with all applicable air pollution emissions control related requirements included in: (aa) the vehicle inspection requirements under Chapter 548, as evidenced by a current inspection certificate affixed to the vehicle windshield; or (bb) the vehicle emissions inspection and maintenance requirements contained in the Public Safety Commission's motor vehicle emissions inspection and maintenance program under Subchapter F, Chapter 548, or the state's air quality state implementation plan; and

(iv) was authorized to be towed by a law enforcement agency; and

(B) the law enforcement agency approves the application.

*(Added by L.1995, chap. 165(1); chgd. by L.1999, chap. 612(1), eff. 9/1/99.)*

### §683.052. Contents of application; application fee.

(a) An application under Section 683.051 must:

(1) contain the name and address of the applicant;

(2) state the year, make, model, and vehicle identification number of the vehicle, if ascertainable, and any other identifying feature of the vehicle; and

(3) include:

(A) a concise statement of facts about the abandonment;

(B) a statement that the certificate of title is lost or destroyed; or

(C) a statement of the reasons for the defect in the owner's certificate of title for the vehicle.

(b) An application under Section 683.051(2) must also include an affidavit containing a statement of the facts that make that subdivision applicable.

(c) The applicant shall make an affidavit stating that:

(1) the facts stated in the application are true; and

(2) no material fact has been withheld.

(d) The application must be accompanied by a fee of $2, unless the application is made by a unit of government. Fees collected under this subsection shall be deposited to the credit of the state highway fund.

*(Added by L.1995, chap. 165(1), eff. 9/1/95.)*

### §683.053. Department to provide notice.

Except as provided by Section 683.054(b), the department shall give notice as provided by Section 683.012 if it determines that an application under Section 683.051 is:

(1) executed in proper form; and

(2) shows that:

(A) the abandoned motor vehicle is in the possession of the applicant or has been abandoned on the applicant's property; or

(B) the vehicle is not an abandoned motor vehicle and the applicant appears to be the owner of the vehicle.

*(Added by L.1995, chap. 165(1), eff. 9/1/95.)*

### §683.054. Certificate of authority to dispose of vehicle.

(a) The department shall issue the applicant a certificate of authority to dispose of the vehicle to a motor vehicle demolisher for demolition, wrecking, or dismantling if notice under Section 683.053 was given and the vehicle was not claimed as provided by the notice.

(b) Without giving the notice required by Section 683.053, the department may issue to an applicant under Section 683.051(2) a certificate of authority to dispose of the motor vehicle to a demolisher if the vehicle meets the requirements of Sections 683.051(2)(A)(ii) and (iii).

(c) A motor vehicle demolisher shall accept the certificate of authority in lieu of a certificate of title for the vehicle.

*(Added by L.1995, chap. 165(1); chgd. by L.1999, chap. 612(2), eff. 9/1/99.)*

### §683.055. Rules and forms.

The department may adopt rules and prescribe forms to implement Sections 683.051-683.054.

*(Added by L.1995, chap. 165(1), eff. 9/1/95.)*

### §683.056. Demolisher's duty.

(a) A motor vehicle demolisher who acquires a motor vehicle for dismantling or demolishing shall obtain from the person delivering the vehicle:

(1) the motor vehicle's certificate of title;

(2) a sales receipt for the motor vehicle;

(3) a transfer document for the vehicle as provided by Subchapter B or Subchapter E; or

(4) a certificate of authority for the disposal of the motor vehicle.

(b) A demolisher is not required to obtain a certificate of title for the vehicle in the demolisher's name.

(c) On the department's demand, the demolisher shall surrender for cancellation the certificate of title or certificate of authority.

(d) The department shall adopt rules and forms necessary to regulate the surrender of auction sales receipts and certificates of title.

*(Added by L.1995, chap. 165(1), eff. 9/1/95.)*



### §683.057. Demolisher's records; offense.

(a) A motor vehicle demolisher shall keep a record of a motor vehicle that is acquired in the course of business.

(b) The record must contain:

(1) the name and address of the person from whom the vehicle was acquired; and

(2) the date of acquisition of the vehicle.

(c) The demolisher shall keep the record until the first anniversary of the date of acquisition of the vehicle.

(d) The record shall be open to inspection by the department or any law enforcement agency at any time during normal business hours.

(e) A motor vehicle demolisher commits an offense if the demolisher fails to keep a record as provided by this section.

(f) An offense under Subsection (e) is a misdemeanor punishable by:

(1) a fine of not less than $100 or more than $1,000;

(2) confinement in the county jail for a term of not less than 10 days or more than six months; or

(3) both the fine and confinement.

*(Added by L.1995, chap. 165(1), eff. 9/1/95.)*

### §§683.058 to 683.070. *(Reserved.)*

## SUBCHAPTER E. JUNKED VEHICLES: PUBLIC NUISANCE; ABATEMENT

### §683.071. Definition.

In this subchapter, "junked vehicle" means a vehicle that is self-propelled and:

(1) does not have lawfully attached to it:

(A) an unexpired license plate; or

(B) a valid motor vehicle inspection certificate;

(2) is wrecked, dismantled or partially dismantled, or discarded; or

(3) is inoperable and has remained inoperable for more than:

(A) 72 consecutive hours, if the vehicle is on public property; or

(B) 30 consecutive days, if the vehicle is on private property.

*(Added by L.1995, chap. 165(1); chgd. by L.1999, chap. 746(1), eff. 9/1/99.)*

## §683.072. Junked vehicle declared to be public nuisance.

A junked vehicle, including a part of a junked vehicle, that is visible from a public place or public right-of-way:

(1) is detrimental to the safety and welfare of the public;

(2) tends to reduce the value of private property;

(3) invites vandalism;

(4) creates a fire hazard;

(5) is an attractive nuisance creating a hazard to the health and safety of minors;

(6) produces urban blight adverse to the maintenance and continuing development of municipalities; and

(7) is a public nuisance.

*(Added by L.1995, chap. 165(1), eff. 9/1/95.)*

## §683.073. Offense.

(a) A person commits an offense if the person maintains a public nuisance described by Section 683.072.

(b) An offense under this section is a misdemeanor punishable by a fine not to exceed $200.

(c) The court shall order abatement and removal of the nuisance on conviction.

*(Added by L.1995, chap. 165(1), eff. 9/1/95.)*

## §683.074. Authority to abate nuisance; procedures.

(a) A municipality or county may adopt procedures that conform to this subchapter for the abatement and removal from private or public property or a public right-of-way of a junked vehicle or part of a junked vehicle as a public nuisance.

(b) The procedures must:

(1) prohibit a vehicle from being reconstructed or made operable after removal;

(2) require a public hearing before removal of the public nuisance; and

(3) require that notice identifying the vehicle or part of the vehicle be given to the department not later than the fifth day after the date of removal.

(c) An appropriate court of the municipality or county may issue necessary orders to enforce the procedures.

(d) Procedures for abatement and removal of a public nuisance must be administered by regularly salaried, full-time employees of the municipality or county, except that any authorized person may remove the nuisance.

(e) A person authorized to administer the procedures may enter private property to examine a public nuisance, to obtain information to identify the nuisance, and to remove or direct the removal of the nuisance.

(f) On receipt of notice of removal under Subsection (b)(3), the department shall immediately cancel the certificate of title issued for the vehicle.

(g) The procedures may provide that the relocation of a junked vehicle that is a public nuisance to another location in the same municipality or county after a proceeding for the abatement and removal of the public nuisance has commenced has no effect on the proceeding if the junked vehicle constitutes a public nuisance at the new location.

*(Added by L.1995, chap. 165(1); chgd. by L.1999, chap. 1226(1), eff. 6/18/99.)*

## §683.075. Notice.

(a) The procedures for the abatement and removal of a public nuisance under this subchapter must provide not less than 10 days' notice of the nature of the nuisance and must be sent by certified mail with a five-day return requested to:

(1) the last known registered owner of the nuisance;

(2) each lienholder of record of the nuisance; and

(3) the owner or occupant of:

(A) the property on which the nuisance is located; or

(B) if the nuisance is located on a public right-of-way, the property adjacent to the right-of-way.

(b) The notice must state that:

(1) the nuisance must be abated and removed not later than the 10th day after the date on which the notice was mailed; and

(2) any request for a hearing must be made before that 10-day period expires.

(c) If the post office address of the last known registered owner of the nuisance is unknown, notice may be placed on the nuisance or, if the owner is located, hand delivered.

(d) If notice is returned undelivered, action to abate the nuisance shall be continued to a date not earlier than the 11th day after the date of the return.
*(Added by L.1995, chap. 165(1), eff. 9/1/95.)*

## §683.076. Hearing.

(a) The governing body of the municipality or county or a board, commission, or official designated by the governing body shall conduct hearings under the procedures adopted under this subchapter.

(b) If a hearing is requested by a person for whom notice is required under Section 683.075(a)(3), the hearing shall be held not earlier than the 11th day after the date of the service of notice.

(c) At the hearing, the junked motor vehicle is presumed, unless demonstrated otherwise by the owner, to be inoperable.

(d) If the information is available at the location of the nuisance, a resolution or order requiring removal of the nuisance must include the vehicle's:

(1) description;

(2) vehicle identification number; and

(3) license plate number.

*(Added by L.1995, chap. 165(1), eff. 9/1/95.)*



## §683.077. Inapplicability of subchapter.

(a) Procedures adopted under Section 683.074 may not apply to a vehicle or vehicle part:

(1) that is completely enclosed in a building in a lawful manner and is not visible from the street or other public or private property; or

(2) that is stored or parked in a lawful manner on private property in connection with the business of a licensed vehicle dealer or junkyard, or that is an antique or special interest vehicle stored by a motor vehicle collector on the collector's property, if the vehicle or part and the outdoor storage area, if any, are:

(A) maintained in an orderly manner;

(B) not a health hazard; and

(C) screened from ordinary public view by appropriate means, including a fence, rapidly growing trees, or shrubbery.

(b) In this section:

(1) "Antique vehicle" means a passenger car or truck that is at least 35 years old.

(2) "Motor vehicle collector" means a person who:

(A) owns one or more antique or special interest vehicles; and

(B) acquires, collects, or disposes of an antique or special interest vehicle or part of an antique or special interest vehicle for personal use to restore and preserve an antique or special interest vehicle for historic interest.

(3) "Special interest vehicle" means a motor vehicle of any age that has not been changed from original manufacturer's specifications and, because of its historic interest, is being preserved by a hobbyist.

*(Added by L.1995, chap. 165(1), eff. 9/1/95.)*

## §683.078. Junked vehicle disposal.

(a) A junked vehicle, including a part of a junked vehicle, may be removed to a scrapyard, a motor vehicle demolisher, or a suitable site operated by a municipality or county.

(b) A municipality or county may operate a disposal site if its governing body determines that commercial disposition of junked vehicles is not available or is inadequate. A municipality or county may:

(1) finally dispose of a junked vehicle or vehicle part; or

(2) transfer it to another disposal site if the disposal is scrap or salvage only.

*(Added by L.1995, chap. 165(1), eff. 9/1/95.)*

# CHAPTER 684. REMOVAL OF UNAUTHORIZED VEHICLES FROM PARKING FACILITY OR PUBLIC ROADWAY

## SUBCHAPTER A. GENERAL PROVISIONS



## SUBCHAPTER B. UNAUTHORIZED VEHICLES



## SUBCHAPTER C. SIGNS PROHIBITING UNAUTHORIZED VEHICLES AND DESIGNATING RESTRICTED AREAS



## SUBCHAPTER D. REGULATION OF PARKING ON CERTAIN PUBLIC ROADWAY AREAS



## SUBCHAPTER E. REGULATION OF TOWING COMPANIES AND PARKING FACILITY OWNERS

## SUBCHAPTER F. MISCELLANEOUS PROVISIONS



## SUBCHAPTER A. GENERAL PROVISIONS

### §684.001. Definitions.

In this chapter:

(1) "Parking facility" means public or private property used, in whole or in part, for restricted or paid vehicle parking. The term includes:

(A) a restricted space on a portion of an otherwise unrestricted parking facility; and

(B) a commercial parking lot, a parking garage, and a parking area serving or adjacent to a business, church, school, home, apartment complex, property governed by a property owners' association, or government-owned property leased to a private person, including:

(i) a portion of the right-of-way of a public roadway that is leased by a governmental entity to the parking facility owner; and

(ii) the area between the facility's property line abutting a county or municipal public roadway and the center line of the roadway's drainageway or the curb of the roadway, whichever is farther from the facility's property line.

(2) "Parking facility owner" means:

(A) an owner or operator of a parking facility, including a lessee, employee, or agent of an owner or operator;

(B) a property owners' association having control under a dedicatory instrument over assigned or unassigned parking areas; or

(C) a property owner having an exclusive right under a dedicatory instrument to use a parking space.

(3) "Property owners' association" and "dedicatory instrument" have the meanings assigned by Section 202.001, Property Code.

(4) "Public roadway" means a public street, alley, road, right-of-way, or other public way, including paved and unpaved portions of the right-of-way.

(5) "Towing company" means a person operating a tow truck registered under Chapter 1135, Acts of the 70th Legislature, Regular Session, 1987 (Article 6687-9b, Texas Civil Statutes). The term includes the owner, operator, employee, or agent of a towing company, but does not include a political subdivision of the state.

(6) "Unauthorized vehicle" means a vehicle parked, stored, or located on a parking facility without the consent of the parking facility owner.

(7) "Vehicle" means a device in, on, or by which a person or property may be transported on a public roadway. The term includes an operable or inoperable automobile, truck, motorcycle, recreational vehicle, or trailer, but does not include a device moved by human power or used exclusively on a stationary rail or track.

(8) "Vehicle storage facility" means a facility operated by a person licensed under Article 6687-9a, Revised Statutes.

*(Added by L.1995, chap. 165(1), eff. 9/1/95.)*

### §§684.002 to 684.010. *(Reserved.)*

## SUBCHAPTER B. UNAUTHORIZED VEHICLES

### §684.011. Prohibition against unattended vehicles in certain areas.

(a) The owner or operator of a vehicle may not leave unattended on a parking facility a vehicle that:

(1) is in or obstructs a vehicular traffic aisle, entry, or exit of the parking facility;

(2) prevents a vehicle from exiting a parking space in the facility;

(3) is in or obstructs a fire lane marked according to Subsection (c); or

(4) does not display the special license plates issued under Section 502.253 or the disabled parking placard issued under Chapter 681 for a vehicle transporting a disabled person and is in a parking space that is designated for the exclusive use of a vehicle transporting a disabled person.

(b) Subsection (a) does not apply to an emergency vehicle that is owned by, or the operation of which is authorized by, a governmental entity.

(c) If a government regulation governing the marking of a fire lane applies to a parking facility, a fire lane in the facility must be marked as provided by the regulation. If a government regulation on the marking of a fire lane does not apply to the parking facility, all curbs of fire lanes must be painted red and be conspicuously and legibly marked with the warning "FIRE LANE—TOW AWAY ZONE" in white letters at least three inches tall, at intervals not exceeding 50 feet.
*(Added by L.1995, chap. 165(1), eff. 9/1/95.)*

## §684.012. Removal and storage of unauthorized vehicle.

(a) A parking facility owner may, without the consent of the owner or operator of an unauthorized vehicle, cause the vehicle and any property on or in the vehicle to be removed and stored at a vehicle storage facility at the vehicle owner's or operator's expense if:

(1) signs that comply with Subchapter C prohibiting unauthorized vehicles are located on the parking facility at the time of towing and for the preceding 24 hours and remain installed at the time of towing;

(2) the owner or operator of the vehicle has received actual notice from the parking facility owner that the vehicle will be towed at the vehicle owner's or operator's expense if it is in or not removed from an unauthorized space;

(3) the parking facility owner gives notice to the owner or operator of the vehicle under Subsection (b); or

(4) the vehicle is:

(A) left in violation of Section 684.011; or

(B) in or obstructing a portion of a paved driveway or abutting public roadway used for entering or exiting the facility.

(b) A parking facility owner is considered to have given notice under Subsection (a)(3) if:

(1) a conspicuous notice has been attached to the vehicle's front windshield or, if the vehicle has no front windshield, to a conspicuous part of the vehicle stating:

(A) that the vehicle is in a parking space in which the vehicle is not authorized to be parked;

(B) a description of all other unauthorized areas in the parking facility;

(C) that the vehicle will be towed at the expense of the owner or operator of the vehicle if it remains in an unauthorized area of the parking facility; and

(D) a telephone number that is answered 24 hours a day to enable the owner or operator of the vehicle to locate the vehicle; and

(2) a notice is mailed after the notice is attached to the vehicle as provided by Subdivision (1) to the owner of the vehicle by certified mail, return receipt requested, to the last address shown for the owner according to the vehicle registration records of the Texas Department of Transportation, or if the vehicle is registered in another state, the appropriate agency of that state.

(c) The notice under Subsection (b)(2) must:

(1) state that the vehicle is in a space in which the vehicle is not authorized to park;

(2) describe all other unauthorized areas in the parking facility;

(3) contain a warning that the unauthorized vehicle will be towed at the expense of the owner or operator of the vehicle if it is not removed from the parking facility before the 15th day after the postmark date of the notice; and

(4) state a telephone number that is answered 24 hours a day to enable the owner or operator to locate the vehicle.

(d) The mailing of a notice under Subsection (b)(2) is not required if after the notice is attached under Subsection (b)(1) the owner or operator of the vehicle leaves the vehicle in another location where parking is unauthorized for the vehicle according to the notice.
*(Added by L.1995, chap. 165(1), eff. 9/1/95.)*

## §684.013. Limitation on parking facility owner's authority to remove unauthorized vehicle.

A parking facility owner may not have an unauthorized vehicle removed from the facility except:

(1) as provided by this chapter or a municipal ordinance that complies with Section 684.101; or

(2) under the direction of a peace officer or the owner or operator of the vehicle.
*(Added by L.1995, chap. 165(1), eff. 9/1/95.)*

## §684.014. Towing company's authority to remove and store unauthorized vehicle.

(a) A towing company that is insured as provided by Subsection (c) may, without the consent of an owner or operator of an unauthorized vehicle, remove and store the vehicle at a vehicle storage facility at the expense of the owner or operator of the vehicle if:

(1) the towing company has received written verification from the parking facility owner that:

(A) the parking facility owner has installed the signs required by Section 684.012(a)(1); or

(B) the owner or operator received notice under Section 684.012(a)(2) or the parking facility owner gave notice complying with Section 684.012(a)(3); or

(2) the vehicle is:

(A) left in violation of Section 684.011; or

(B) in or obstructing a portion of a paved driveway or abutting public roadway used for entering or exiting the facility.

(b) A towing company may not remove an unauthorized vehicle except under:

(1) this chapter;

(2) a municipal ordinance that complies with Section 684.101; or

(3) the direction of a peace officer or the owner or operator of the vehicle.

(c) Only a towing company that is insured against liability for property damage incurred in towing a vehicle may remove and store an unauthorized vehicle under this section.

*(Added by L.1995, chap. 165(1), eff. 9/1/95.)*



### §684.015. Vehicle storage facility's duty to report after accepting unauthorized vehicle.

(a) A vehicle storage facility accepting a vehicle that is towed under this chapter shall within two hours after receiving the vehicle report to the police department of the municipality in which the parking facility is located, or, if the parking facility is not located in a municipality having a police department, to the sheriff of the county in which the parking facility is located:

(1) a general description of the vehicle;

(2) the state and number of the vehicle's license plate, if any;

(3) the vehicle identification number of the vehicle, if it can be ascertained;

(4) the location from which the vehicle was towed; and

(5) the name and location of the vehicle storage facility where the vehicle is being stored.

(b) The report required by this section must be made by telephone or delivered personally or by facsimile.

*(Added by L.1995, chap. 165(1), eff. 9/1/95.)*

### §§684.016 to 684.030. *(Reserved.)*

## SUBCHAPTER C. SIGNS PROHIBITING UNAUTHORIZED VEHICLES AND DESIGNATING RESTRICTED AREAS

### §684.031. General requirements for sign prohibiting unauthorized vehicles.

(a) Except as provided by Subsection (a)(2)(B) and Section 684.034 or 684.035 an unauthorized vehicle may not be towed under Section 684.012(a)(1) unless a sign prohibiting unauthorized vehicles on a parking facility is:

(1) facing and conspicuously visible to the driver of a vehicle that enters the facility;

(2) located:

(A) on the right or left side of each driveway or curb-cut through which a vehicle can enter the facility, including an entry from an alley abutting the facility; or

(B) at intervals along the entrance so that no entrance is farther than 25 feet from a sign if:

(i) curbs, access barriers, landscaping, or driveways do not establish definite vehicle entrances onto a parking facility from a public roadway other than an alley; and

(ii) the width of an entrance exceeds 35 feet;

(3) permanently mounted on a pole, post, permanent wall, or permanent barrier;

(4) installed on the parking facility; and

(5) installed so that the bottom edge of the sign is no lower than five feet and no higher than eight feet above ground level.

(b) Except as provided by Section 684.035, an unauthorized vehicle may be towed under Section 684.012(a)(1) only if each sign prohibiting unauthorized vehicles:

(1) is made of weather-resistant material;

(2) is at least 18 inches wide and 24 inches tall;

(3) contains the international symbol for towing vehicles;

(4) contains a statement describing who may park in the parking facility and prohibiting all others;

(5) bears the words "Unauthorized Vehicles Will Be Towed at Owner's or Operator's Expense";

(6) contains a statement of the days and hours of towing enforcement; and

(7) contains a number, including the area code, of a telephone that is answered 24 hours a day to enable an owner or operator of a vehicle to locate the vehicle.
*(Added by L.1995, chap. 165(1), eff. 9/1/95.)*

## §684.032. Color, layout, and lettering height requirements.

(a) Except as provided by Section 684.035, each sign required by this chapter must comply with the color, layout, and lettering height requirements of this section.

(b) A bright red international towing symbol, which is a solid silhouette of a tow truck towing a vehicle on a generally rectangular white background, at least four inches in height, must be on the uppermost portion of a sign or on a separate sign placed immediately above the sign.

(c) The portion of the sign immediately below the international towing symbol must contain the words "Towing Enforced" or the information provided by Section 684.031(b)(4) in lettering at least two inches in height. The lettering on this portion of the sign must consist of white letters on a bright red background.

(d) Except as provided by Subsection (e), the next lower portion of the sign must contain the remaining information required by Section 684.031(b) displayed in bright red letters at least one inch in height on a white background.

(e) The bottommost portion of the sign must contain the telephone number required by Section 684.031(b), in lettering at least one inch in height and may, if the facility owner chooses or if an applicable municipal ordinance requires, include the name and address of the storage facility to which an unauthorized vehicle will be removed. The lettering on this portion of the sign must consist of white letters on a bright red background.

(f) *(Expired 1/1/96.)*
*(Added by L.1995, chap. 165(1), eff. 9/1/95.)*

## §684.033. Telephone number for locating towed vehicle required.

If a parking facility owner posts a sign described by Sections 684.031 and 684.032, the owner of a vehicle that is towed from the facility under this chapter must be able to locate the vehicle by calling the telephone number on the sign. *(Added by L.1995, chap. 165(1), eff. 9/1/95.)*

## §684.034. Designation of restricted parking spaces on otherwise unrestricted parking facility.

A parking facility owner may designate one or more spaces as restricted parking spaces on a portion of an otherwise unrestricted parking facility. Instead of installing a sign at each entrance to the parking facility as provided by Section 684.031(a)(2), an owner may place a sign that prohibits unauthorized vehicles from parking in designated spaces and that otherwise complies with Sections 684.031 and 684.032:

(1) at the right or left side of each entrance to a designated area or group of parking spaces located on the restricted portion of the parking facility; or

(2) at the end of a restricted parking space so that the sign, the top of which must not be higher than seven feet above the ground, is in front of a vehicle that is parked in the space and the rear of which is at the entrance of the space.
*(Added by L.1995, chap. 165(1), eff. 9/1/95.)*

## §684.035. Individual parking restrictions in restricted area.

(a) A parking facility owner who complies with Sections 684.031 and 684.032 may impose further specific parking restrictions in an area to which the signs apply for individual spaces by installing or painting a weather-resistant sign or notice on a curb, pole, post, permanent wall, or permanent barrier so that the sign is in front of a vehicle that is parked in the space and the rear of which is at the entrance of the space.

(b) The top of the sign or notice may not be higher than seven feet above the ground.

(c) The sign or notice must include an indication that the space is reserved for a particular unit number, person, or type of person.

(d) The letters on the sign or notice must be at least two inches in height and must contrast to the color of the curb, wall, or barrier so they can be read during the day and at night. The letters are not required to be illuminated or made of reflective material.
*(Added by L.1995, chap. 165(1), eff. 9/1/95.)*

## §§684.036 to 684.050. *(Reserved.)*

## SUBCHAPTER D. REGULATION OF PARKING ON CERTAIN PUBLIC ROADWAY AREAS

### §684.051. Removal of unauthorized vehicle from leased right-of-way.

Unless prohibited by the lease, a parking facility owner or towing company may remove an unauthorized vehicle parked in a leased area described by Section 684.001(1)(B)(i) if the owner or towing company gives notice under Section 684.012(a)(1), (2), or (3) and otherwise complies with this chapter. *(Added by L.1995, chap. 165(1), eff. 9/1/95.)*

### §684.052. Removal of unauthorized vehicle from area between parking facility and public roadway.

Unless prohibited by a municipal ordinance, a parking facility owner or towing company may remove an unauthorized vehicle any part of which is in an area described by Section 684.001(1)(B)(ii) if notice provided by Section 684.012(a)(2) or (3) is given and the owner or towing company has otherwise complied with this chapter. *(Added by L.1995, chap. 165(1), eff. 9/1/95.)*



### §684.053. Removal under governmental entity's authority of unauthorized vehicle parked in right-of-way.

(a) A governmental entity that has jurisdiction over a public roadway and that has posted one or more signs in the right-of-way stating that parking is prohibited in the right-of-way may:

(1) remove or contract with a towing company to remove an unauthorized vehicle parked in the right-of-way of the public roadway; or

(2) grant written permission to an abutting parking facility owner to:

(A) post one or more "No parking in R.O.W." signs along a common property line of the facility and the roadway; and

(B) remove vehicles from the right-of-way of the public roadway under this chapter.

(b) A sign under Subsection (a)(2) must:

(1) state that a vehicle parked in the right-of-way may be towed at the expense of the owner or operator of the vehicle;

(2) be placed facing the public roadway:

(A) on the parking facility owner's property not more than two feet from the common boundary line; and

(B) at intervals so that no point in the boundary line is less than 25 feet from a sign posted under this subsection; and

(3) in all other respects comply with Subchapter C.

(c) After signs have been posted under Subsection (b), the parking facility owner or a towing company may remove an unauthorized vehicle from the right-of-way subject to the governmental entity's written permission given under Subsection (a)(2).

*(Added by L.1995, chap. 165(1), eff. 9/1/95.)*

### §684.054. Authority for removal of vehicle from public roadway.

A parking facility owner or towing company may not remove a vehicle from a public roadway except under:

(1) this chapter or a municipal ordinance that complies with Section 684.101; or

(2) the direction of a peace officer or the owner or operator of the vehicle.

*(Added by L.1995, chap. 165(1), eff. 9/1/95.)*

### §§684.055 to 684.080. *(Reserved.)*

## SUBCHAPTER E. REGULATION OF TOWING COMPANIES AND PARKING FACILITY OWNERS

### §684.081. Parking facility owner prohibited from receiving financial gain from towing company.

(a) A parking facility owner may not directly or indirectly accept anything of value from a towing company in connection with the removal of a vehicle from a parking facility.

(b) A parking facility owner may not have a direct or indirect monetary interest in a towing company that for compensation removes unauthorized vehicles from a parking facility in which the parking facility owner has an interest.

*(Added by L.1995, chap. 165(1), eff. 9/1/95.)*

**§684.082. Towing company prohibited from financial involvement with parking facility owner.**

(a) A towing company may not directly or indirectly give anything of value to a parking facility owner in connection with the removal of a vehicle from a parking facility.

(b) A towing company may not have a direct or indirect monetary interest in a parking facility from which the towing company for compensation removes unauthorized vehicles.
*(Added by L.1995, chap. 165(1), eff. 9/1/95.)*

**§684.083. Limitation on liability of parking facility owner for removal or storage of unauthorized vehicle.**

A parking facility owner who causes the removal of an unauthorized vehicle is not liable for damages arising from the removal or storage of the vehicle if the vehicle:

(1) was removed in compliance with this chapter; and

(2) is:

(A) removed by a towing company insured against liability for property damage incurred in towing a vehicle; and

(B) stored by a vehicle storage facility insured against liability for property damage incurred in storing a vehicle.
*(Added by L.1995, chap. 165(1), eff. 9/1/95.)*

**§684.084. Civil liability of towing company or parking facility owner for violation of chapter.**

(a) A towing company or parking facility owner who violates this chapter is liable to the owner or operator of the vehicle that is the subject of the violation for:

(1) damages arising from the removal or storage of the vehicle; and

(2) towing or storage fees assessed in connection with the vehicle's removal or storage.

(b) A vehicle's owner or operator is not required to prove negligence of a parking facility owner or towing company to recover under Subsection (a).

(c) A towing company or parking facility owner who intentionally, knowingly, or recklessly violates this chapter is liable to the owner or operator of the vehicle that is the subject of the violation for $300 plus three times the amount of fees assessed in the vehicle's removal, towing, or storage.

(d) In a suit brought under this chapter, the prevailing party is entitled to recover reasonable attorney's fees.
*(Added by L.1995, chap. 165(1), eff. 9/1/95.)*

**§684.085. Violation of chapter; fine.**

A violation of this chapter is punishable by a fine of not less than $200 or more than $500.
*(Added by L.1995, chap. 165(1), eff. 9/1/95.)*

**§684.086. Violation of chapter; injunction.**

A violation of this chapter may be enjoined under Subchapter E, Chapter 17, Business & Commerce Code. *(Added by L.1995, chap. 165(1), eff. 9/1/95.)*

**§684.087. Minor sign or lettering height variations.**

A minor variation of a required or minimum height of a sign or lettering is not a violation of this chapter. *(Added by L.1995, chap. 165(1), eff. 9/1/95.)*

**§§684.088 to 684.100.** *(Reserved.)*

## SUBCHAPTER F. MISCELLANEOUS PROVISIONS

**§684.101. Municipal ordinance regulating unauthorized vehicles.**

A municipality may adopt an ordinance that is identical to this chapter or that imposes additional requirements that exceed the minimum standards of this chapter but may not adopt an ordinance conflicting with this chapter. *(Added by L.1995, chap. 165(1), eff. 9/1/95.)*

# CHAPTER 685. RIGHTS OF OWNERS AND OPERATORS OF STORED VEHICLES

*(Heading chgd. by L.1997, chap. 165(30.159(a)), eff. 9/1/97.)*

Section




## §685.001. Definitions.

In this chapter:

(1) "Vehicle storage facility" has the meaning assigned by the Vehicle Storage Facility Act, Article 6687-9a, Revised Statutes.

(2) "Parking facility," "towing company," and "vehicle" have the meanings assigned by Section 684.001.

*(Added by L.1995, chap. 165(1); chgd. by L.1997, chap. 165(30.159(a)), eff. 9/1/97.)*

## §685.002. Payment of cost of removal and storage of vehicle.

(a) If in a hearing held under this chapter the court finds that a person or law enforcement agency authorized, with probable cause, the removal and storage in a vehicle storage facility of a vehicle, the person who requested the hearing shall pay the costs of the removal and storage.

(b) If in a hearing held under this chapter the court does not find that a person or law enforcement agency authorized, with probable cause, the removal and storage in a vehicle storage facility of a vehicle, the person or law enforcement agency that authorized the removal shall:

(1) pay the costs of the removal and storage; or

(2) reimburse the owner or operator for the cost of the removal and storage paid by the owner or operator.

*(Added by L.1995, chap. 165(1); chgd. by L.1997, chap. 165(30.159(a)), eff. 9/1/97.)*

## §685.003. Right of owner or operator of vehicle to hearing.

The owner or operator of a vehicle that has been removed and placed in a vehicle storage facility without the consent of the owner or operator of the vehicle is entitled to a hearing on whether probable cause existed for the removal and placement. *(Added by L.1995, chap. 165(1), chgd. by L.1997, chap. 165(30.159(a)) eff. 9/1/97.)*

## §685.004. Jurisdiction.

(a) A hearing under this chapter is before the justice of the peace or a magistrate in whose jurisdiction is the location from which the vehicle was removed, except as provided by Subsection (b).

(b) In a municipality with a population of 1,200,000 or more, a hearing under this chapter is before a judge of a municipal court in whose jurisdiction is the location from which the vehicle was removed.

*(Added by L.1995, chap. 165(1); chgd. by L.1997, chap. 165(30.159(a)), eff. 9/1/97.)*

## §685.005. Notice to vehicle owner or operator.

(a) If before a hearing held under this chapter the owner or operator of a vehicle pays the costs of the vehicle's removal or storage, the towing company or vehicle storage facility that received the payment shall at the time of payment give the owner or operator written notice of the person's rights under this chapter.

(b) The operator of a vehicle storage facility that sends a notice under Section 13, Vehicle Storage Facility Act (Article 6687-9a, Revised Statutes), shall include with that notice a notice of the person's rights under this chapter.

*(Added by L.1997, chap. 165(30.159(a)), eff. 9/1/97. Former section 685.005 renumbered to 685.007 by L.1997, chap. 165(30.159(a)), eff. 9/1/97.)*

### §685.006. Contents of notice.

(a) The notice under Section 685.005 must include:

(1) a statement of:

(A) the person's right to submit a request within 14 days for a court hearing to determine whether probable cause existed to remove the vehicle;

(B) the information that a request for a hearing must contain; and

(C) any filing fee for the hearing;

(2) the name, address, and telephone number of the towing company that removed the vehicle;

(3) the name, address, and telephone number of the vehicle storage facility in which the vehicle was placed; and

(4) the name, address, and telephone number of one or more of the appropriate magistrates as determined under Subsection (b).

(b) The notice must include the name, address, and telephone number of:

(1) the municipal court of the municipality, if the towing company that removed the vehicle or the vehicle storage facility in which the vehicle was placed is located in a municipality; or

(2) the justice of the peace of the precinct in which the towing company or the vehicle storage facility is located, if the towing company that removed the vehicle or the vehicle storage facility in which the vehicle was placed is not located in a municipality.

*(Added by L.1997, chap. 165(30.159(a)), eff. 9/1/97. Former section 685.006 renumbered to 685.008 by L.1997, chap. 165(30.159(a)), eff. 9/1/97.)*



### §685.007. Request for hearing.

(a) Except as provided by Subsection (c), a person entitled to a hearing under this chapter must deliver a written request for the hearing to the court before the 14th day after the date the vehicle was removed and placed in the vehicle storage facility, excluding Saturdays, Sundays, and legal holidays.

(b) A request for a hearing must contain:

(1) the name, address, and telephone number of the owner or operator of the vehicle;

(2) the location from which the vehicle was removed;

(3) the date when the vehicle was removed;

(4) the name, address, and telephone number of the person or law enforcement agency that authorized the removal;

(5) the name, address, and telephone number of the vehicle storage facility in which the vehicle was placed;

(6) the name, address, and telephone number of the towing company that removed the vehicle;

(7) a copy of any receipt or notification that the owner or operator received from the towing company or the vehicle storage facility; and

(8) if the vehicle was removed from a parking facility:

(A) one or more photographs that show the location and text of any sign posted at the facility restricting parking of vehicles; or

(B) a statement that no sign restricting parking was posted at the parking facility.

(c) If notice was not given under Section 685.005, the 14-day deadline for requesting a hearing under Subsection (a) does not apply, and the owner or operator of the vehicle may deliver a written request for a hearing at any time.

(d) A person who fails to deliver a request in accordance with Subsection (a) waives the right to a hearing.

*(Added by L.1995, chap. 165(1); renumbered from 685.005 and chgd. by L.1997, chap. 165(30.159(a)), eff. 9/1/97.)*

### §685.008. Filing fee authorized.

The court may charge a filing fee of $10 for a hearing under this chapter. *(Added by L.1995, chap. 165(1); renumbered from 685.006 by L.1997, chap. 165(30.159(a)), eff. 9/1/97.)*

### §685.009. Hearing.

(a) A hearing under this chapter shall be held before the seventh working day after the date the court receives the request for the hearing.

(b) The court shall notify the person who requested the hearing and the person or law enforcement agency that authorized the removal of the vehicle of the date, time, and place of the hearing.

(c) The sole issue in a hearing under this chapter is whether probable cause existed for the removal and placement of the vehicle.

(d) The court shall make written findings of fact and a conclusion of law.

(e) The court may award:

(1) court costs to the prevailing party; and

(2) the reasonable cost of photographs submitted under Section 685.007(b)(8) to a vehicle owner or operator who is the prevailing party.

*(Added by L.1995, chap. 165(1); renumbered from 685.007 and chgd. by L.1997, chap. 165(30.159(a)), eff. 9/1/97.)*

## CHAPTERS 686 to 700. *(Reserved.)*

# SUBTITLE I. ENFORCEMENT OF TRAFFIC LAWS

## CHAPTER 701. COUNTY TRAFFIC OFFICERS



Section



### §701.001. Authorization.

(a) Acting in conjunction with the sheriff of the county, the commissioners court of a county may employ not more than five regular deputies as county traffic officers.

(b) The commissioners court may employ not more than two additional deputies as county traffic officers to aid the regular officers in special emergencies.

*(Added by L.1995, chap. 165(1), eff. 9/1/95.)*

### §701.002. Power to act; guidance.

(a) A county traffic officer:

(1) must be deputized by the sheriff or a constable of the county in which the officer is employed;

(2) must give a bond and take an oath of office as other deputy sheriffs;

(3) must work under the direction of the sheriff; and

(4) has the same right and duty as a deputy sheriff to arrest a person who violates a law.

(b) The district engineer of a Texas Department of Transportation district in which an officer operates shall advise the officer on enforcement of the state laws that regulate traffic on highways.

*(Added by L.1995, chap. 165(1), eff. 9/1/95.)*

### §701.003. Duties.

(a) A county traffic officer shall:

(1) be a motorcycle rider when practicable;

(2) cooperate with the police department of each municipality in the county to enforce state traffic laws in that municipality and in the county;

(3) enforce state laws that regulate the operation of a motor vehicle on a highway, street, or alley; and

(4) remain on and patrol the highway at all times when performing the officer's duties.

(b) An officer may leave a highway only in pursuit of an offender the officer is unable to apprehend on the highway.

*(Added by L.1995, chap. 165(1), eff. 9/1/95.)*

### §701.004. Compensation.

(a) The compensation to be paid a county traffic officer shall be set before the officer is employed.

(b) Salary paid to the officer is independent of a salary paid to the sheriff and sheriff's deputies who do not act as highway officers. Compensation for an officer may not be included in the sheriff's settlement in accounting for a fee of office or as salary paid to the sheriff or a sheriff's deputy.

(c) The commissioners court may provide necessary equipment for the officer at the county's expense. An officer's equipment may include a motorcycle and maintenance of that motorcycle. *(Added by L.1995, chap. 165(1), eff. 9/1/95.)*

### §701.005. Fees.

A fee may not be charged for a service of a county traffic officer. *(Added by L.1995, chap. 165(1), eff. 9/1/95.)*

### §701.006. Complaint; hearing; dismissal.

(a) If a county traffic officer fails to perform the officer's duty to enforce the law, the district engineer of the Texas Department of Transportation district in which the officer operates may send a written, signed complaint to the commissioners court.

(b) On receipt of the complaint, the commissioners court shall hold a hearing and summon the officer to appear before it.

(c) If the commissioners court determines at the hearing that the officer has not performed the officer's duty, the commissioners court shall immediately discharge the officer and promptly employ another officer.

(d) The commissioners court on its own initiative, or on recommendation of the sheriff, may dismiss a county traffic officer if the officer is no longer needed or if the officer's service is unsatisfactory.

*(Added by L.1995, chap. 165(1), eff. 9/1/95.)*



## CHAPTER 702. CONTRACTS FOR ENFORCEMENT OF CERTAIN ARREST WARRANTS

Section



### §702.001. Definitions.

In this chapter:

(1) "Department" means the Texas Department of Transportation.

(2) "Registration" of a motor vehicle includes a renewal of the registration of that vehicle.

(3) "Traffic law" means a statute or ordinance, a violation of which is a misdemeanor punishable by a fine not to exceed $200, that regulates, on a street, road, or highway of this state:

(A) the conduct or condition of a person while operating a motor vehicle; or

(B) the condition of a motor vehicle being operated.

*(Added by L.1995, chap. 165(1); chgd. by L.1997, chap. 165(30.160(a)), eff. 9/1/97.)*

### §702.002. Application.

This chapter applies only to a home-rule municipality. *(Added by L.1995, chap. 165(1); chgd. by L.1999, chap. 744(1), eff. 6/18/99.)*

### §702.003. Refusal to register vehicle.

(a) A county assessor-collector or the department may refuse to register a motor vehicle if the assessor-collector or the department receives under a contract information from a municipality that the owner of the vehicle has an outstanding warrant from that municipality for failure to appear or failure to pay a fine on a complaint that involves the violation of a traffic law.

(b) A municipality may contract with a county in which the municipality is located or the department to provide information to the county or department necessary to make a determination under Subsection (a).

(c) A municipality that has a contract under Subsection (b) shall notify the county or the department regarding a person for whom the county assessor-collector or the department has refused to register a motor vehicle on:

(1) entry of a judgment against the person and the person's payment to the court of the fine for the violation and of all court costs;

(2) perfection of an appeal of the case for which the arrest warrant was issued; or

(3) dismissal of the charge for which the arrest warrant was issued.

(d) After notice is received under Subsection (c), the county assessor-collector or the department may not refuse to register the motor vehicle under Subsection (a).

(e) A contract under Subsection (b) must be entered into in accordance with Chapter 791, Government Code, and is subject to the ability of the parties to provide or pay for the services required under the contract.
*(Added by L.1995, chap. 165(1); chgd. by L.1997, chap. 165(30.160(b)), eff. 9/1/97.)*

### §702.004. Warning; citation.

(a) A peace officer authorized to issue citations in a municipality that has a contract under Section 702.003 shall issue a written warning to each person to whom the officer issues a citation for a violation of a traffic law in the municipality.

(b) The warning must state that if the person fails to appear in court as provided by law for the prosecution of the offense or fails to pay a fine for the violation, the person might not be permitted to register a motor vehicle in this state.

(c) The warning required by this section may be printed on the citation.
*(Added by L.1995, chap. 165(1); renumbered from 702.005 and chgd. by L.1997, chap. 165(30.160(d)), eff. 9/1/97. Former section 702.004 repealed by L.1997, chap. 165(30.160(c)), eff. 9/1/97.)*



## CHAPTER 703. NONRESIDENT VIOLATOR COMPACT OF 1977

Section


### §703.001. Definitions.

In this chapter:

(1) "Citation" and "motorist" have the meanings assigned by Article II, Section (b), Nonresident Violator Compact of 1977.

(2) "Department" and "licensing authority" mean the Department of Public Safety.
*(Added by L.1995, chap. 165(1), eff. 9/1/95.)*

### §703.002. Enactment; terms of compact.

The Nonresident Violator Compact of 1977 is enacted and entered into as follows:

## NONRESIDENT VIOLATOR COMPACT OF 1977

## Art. I. FINDINGS, DECLARATION OF POLICY, AND PURPOSE

(a) The party jurisdictions find that:

(1) In most instances, a motorist who is cited for a traffic violation in a jurisdiction other than his home jurisdiction:

(i) Must post collateral or bond to secure appearance for trial at a later date; or

(ii) If unable to post collateral or bond, is taken into custody until the collateral or bond is posted; or

(iii) Is taken directly to court for his trial to be held.

(2) In some instances, the motorist's driver's license may be deposited as collateral to be returned after he has complied with the terms of the citation.

(3) The purpose of the practices described in paragraphs (1) and (2) above is to ensure compliance with the terms of a traffic citation by the motorist who, if permitted to continue on his way after receiving the traffic citation, could return to his home jurisdiction and disregard his duty under the terms of the traffic citation.

(4) A motorist receiving a traffic citation in his home jurisdiction is permitted, except for certain violations, to accept the citation from the officer at the scene of the violation and to immediately continue on his way after promising or being instructed to comply with the terms of the citation.

(5) The practice described in paragraph (1) above causes unnecessary inconvenience and, at times, a hardship for the motorist who is unable at the time to post collateral, furnish a bond, stand trial, or pay the fine, and thus is compelled to remain in custody until some arrangement can be made.

(6) The deposit of a driver's license as a bail bond, as described in paragraph (2) above, is viewed with disfavor.

(7) The practices described herein consume an undue amount of law enforcement time.

(b) It is the policy of the party jurisdictions to:

(1) Seek compliance with the laws, ordinances, and administrative rules and regulations relating to the operation of motor vehicles in each of the jurisdictions.

(2) Allow motorists to accept a traffic citation for certain violations and proceed on their way without delay whether or not the motorist is a resident of the jurisdiction in which the citation was issued.

(3) Extend cooperation to its fullest extent among the jurisdictions for obtaining compliance with the terms of a traffic citation issued in one jurisdiction to a resident of another jurisdiction.

(4) Maximize effective utilization of law enforcement personnel and assist court systems in the efficient disposition of traffic violations.

(c) The purpose of this compact is to:

(1) Provide a means through which the party jurisdictions may participate in a reciprocal program to effectuate the policies enumerated in paragraph (b) above in a uniform and orderly manner.

(2) Provide for the fair and impartial treatment of traffic violators operating within party jurisdictions in recognition of the motorist's right of due process and the sovereign status of a party jurisdiction.



## Art. II. DEFINITIONS

(a) In the Nonresident Violator Compact, the following words have the meaning indicated, unless the context requires otherwise.

(b)(1) "Citation" means any summons, ticket, or other official document issued by a police officer for a traffic violation containing an order which requires the motorist to respond.

(2) "Collateral" means any cash or other security deposited to secure an appearance for trial, following the issuance by a police officer of a citation for a traffic violation.

(3) "Court" means a court of law or traffic tribunal.

(4) "Driver's license" means any license or privilege to operate a motor vehicle issued under the laws of the home jurisdiction.

(5) "Home jurisdiction" means the jurisdiction that issued the driver's license of the traffic violator.

(6) "Issuing jurisdiction" means the jurisdiction in which the traffic citation was issued to the motorist.

(7) "Jurisdiction" means a state, territory, or possession of the United States, the District of Columbia, or the Commonwealth of Puerto Rico.

(8) "Motorist" means a driver of a motor vehicle operating in a party jurisdiction other than the home jurisdiction.

(9) "Personal recognizance" means an agreement by a motorist made at the time of issuance of the traffic citation that he will comply with the terms of that traffic citation.

(10) "Police officer" means any individual authorized by the party jurisdiction to issue a citation for a traffic violation.

(11) "Terms of the citation" means those options expressly stated upon the citation.

## Art. III. PROCEDURE FOR ISSUING JURISDICTION

(a) When issuing a citation for a traffic violation, a police officer shall issue the citation to a motorist who possesses a driver's license issued by a party jurisdiction and shall not, subject to the exceptions noted in paragraph (b) of this article, require the motorist to post collateral to secure appearance, if the officer receives the motorist's personal recognizance that he or she will comply with the terms of the citation.

(b) Personal recognizance is acceptable only if not prohibited by law. If mandatory appearance is required, it must take place immediately following issuance of the citation.

(c) Upon failure of a motorist to comply with the terms of a traffic citation, the appropriate official shall report the failure to comply to the licensing authority of the jurisdiction in which the traffic citation was issued. The report shall be made in accordance with procedures specified by the issuing jurisdiction and shall contain information as specified in the Compact Manual as minimum requirements for effective processing by the home jurisdiction.

(d) Upon receipt of the report, the licensing authority of the issuing jurisdiction shall transmit to the licensing authority in the home jurisdiction of the motorist the information in a form and content as contained in the Compact Manual.

(e) The licensing authority of the issuing jurisdiction may not suspend the privilege of a motorist for whom a report has been transmitted.

(f) The licensing authority of the issuing jurisdiction shall not transmit a report on any violation if the date of transmission is more than six months after the date on which the traffic citation was issued.

(g) The licensing authority of the issuing jurisdiction shall not transmit a report on any violation where the date of issuance of the citation predates the most recent of the effective dates of entry for the two jurisdictions affected.

## Art. IV. PROCEDURE FOR HOME JURISDICTION

(a) Upon receipt of a report of a failure to comply from the licensing authority of the issuing jurisdiction, the licensing authority of the home jurisdiction shall notify the motorist and initiate a suspension action, in accordance with the home jurisdiction's procedures, to suspend the motorist's driver's license until satisfactory evidence of compliance with the terms of the traffic citation has been furnished to the home jurisdiction licensing authority. Due process safeguards will be accorded.

(b) The licensing authority of the home jurisdiction shall maintain a record of actions taken and make reports to issuing jurisdictions as provided in the Compact Manual.



## Art. V. APPLICABILITY OF OTHER LAWS

Except as expressly required by provisions of this compact, nothing contained herein shall be construed to affect the right of any party jurisdiction to apply any of its other laws relating to licenses to drive to any person or circumstance, or to invalidate or prevent any driver license agreement or other cooperative arrangement between a party jurisdiction and a nonparty jurisdiction.

## Art. VI. COMPACT ADMINISTRATOR PROCEDURES

(a) For the purpose of administering the provisions of this compact and to serve as a governing body for the resolution of all matters relating to the operation of this compact, a Board of Compact Administrators is established. The board shall be composed of one representative from each party jurisdiction to be known as the compact administrator. The compact administrator shall be appointed by the jurisdiction executive and will serve and be subject to removal in accordance with the laws of the jurisdiction he represents. A compact administrator may provide for the discharge of his duties and the performance of his functions as a board member by an alternate. An alternate may not be entitled to serve unless written notification of his identity has been given to the board.

(b) Each member of the Board of Compact Administrators shall be entitled to one vote. No action of the board shall be binding unless taken at a meeting at which a majority of the total number of votes on the board are cast in favor. Action by the board shall be only at a meeting at which a majority of the party jurisdictions are represented.

(c) The board shall elect annually, from its membership, a chairman and a vice chairman.

(d) The board shall adopt bylaws, not inconsistent with the provisions of this compact or the laws of a party jurisdiction, for the conduct of its business and shall have the power to amend and rescind its bylaws.

(e) The board may accept for any of its purposes and functions under this compact any and all donations, and grants of money, equipment, supplies, materials, and services, conditional or otherwise, from any jurisdiction, the United States, or any other governmental agency, and may receive, utilize, and dispose of the same.

(f) The board may contract with, or accept services or personnel from, any governmental or intergovernmental agency, person, firm, or corporation, or any private nonprofit organization or institution.

(g) The board shall formulate all necessary procedures and develop uniform forms and documents for administering the provisions of this compact. All procedures and forms adopted pursuant to board action shall be contained in the Compact Manual.

## Art. VII. ENTRY INTO COMPACT AND WITHDRAWAL

(a) This compact shall become effective when it has been adopted by at least two jurisdictions.

(b)(1) Entry into the compact shall be made by a Resolution of Ratification executed by the authorized officials of the applying jurisdiction and submitted to the chairman of the board.

(2) The resolution shall be in a form and content as provided in the Compact Manual and shall include statements that in substance are as follows:

(i) A citation of the authority by which the jurisdiction is empowered to become a party to this compact.

(ii) Agreement to comply with the terms and provisions of the compact.

(iii) That compact entry is with all jurisdictions then party to the compact and with any jurisdiction that legally becomes a party to the compact.

(3) The effective date of entry shall be specified by the applying jurisdiction, but it shall not be less than 60 days after notice has been given by the chairman of the Board of Compact Administrators or by the secretariat of the board to each party jurisdiction that the resolution from the applying jurisdiction has been received.

(c) A party jurisdiction may withdraw from this compact by official written notice to the other party jurisdictions, but a withdrawal shall not take effect until 90 days after notice of withdrawal is given. The notice shall be directed to the compact administrator of each member jurisdiction. No withdrawal shall affect the validity of this compact as to the remaining party jurisdictions.

## Art. VIII. EXCEPTIONS

The provisions of this compact shall not apply to offenses which mandate personal appearance, moving traffic violations which alone carry a suspension, equipment violations, inspection violations, parking or standing violations, size and weight limit violations, violations of law governing the transportation of hazardous materials, motor carrier violations, lease law violations, and registration law violations.



## Art. IX. AMENDMENTS TO THE COMPACT

(a) This compact may be amended from time to time. Amendments shall be presented in resolution form to the chairman of the Board of Compact Administrators and may be initiated by one or more party jurisdictions.

(b) Adoption of an amendment shall require endorsement of all party jurisdictions and shall become effective 30 days after the date of the last endorsement.

(c) Failure of a party jurisdiction to respond to the compact chairman within 120 days after receipt of the proposed amendment shall constitute endorsement.

## Art. X. CONSTRUCTION AND SEVERABILITY

This compact shall be liberally construed so as to effectuate the purposes stated herein. The provisions of this compact shall be severable and if any phrase, clause, sentence, or provision of this compact is declared to be contrary to the constitution of any party jurisdiction or of the United States or the applicability thereof to any government, agency, person, or circumstance, the compact shall not be affected thereby. If this compact shall be held contrary to the constitution of any jurisdiction party thereto, the compact shall remain in full force and effect as to the remaining jurisdictions and in full force and effect as to the jurisdiction affected as to all severable matters.

## Art. XI. TITLE

This compact shall be known as the Nonresident Violator Compact of 1977.
*(Added by L.1995, chap. 165(1), eff. 9/1/95.)*

### §703.003. Nonresident violator compact administrator.

(a) The office of nonresident violator compact administrator is created.

(b) The governor shall appoint the compact administrator with the advice and consent of the senate to a two-year term that expires on February 1 of each odd-numbered year.

(c) The compact administrator is entitled to compensation and reimbursement for expenses as provided by legislative appropriation.
*(Added by L.1995, chap. 165(1), eff. 9/1/95.)*

### §703.004. Reports of failure to comply with citation.

(a) The department shall report the failure of a motorist to comply with the terms of a citation.

(b) The department shall establish procedures for making the reports required by Subsection (a).
*(Added by L.1995, chap. 165(1), eff. 9/1/95.)*

# CHAPTER 704. FORFEITURE OF CERTAIN MOTOR VEHICLES

Section





## §704.001. Grounds for forfeiture; notice.

(a) A motor vehicle is subject to forfeiture if the vehicle is owned and operated at the time of an offense under Section 49.04, Penal Code, or an offense under Section 49.07 or 49.08 of that code involving the operation of a motor vehicle, by a person who:

(1) at the time of arrest was under community supervision for an offense under:

(A) Section 49.08, Penal Code; or

(B) Section 19.05(a)(2), Penal Code, as that law existed before September 1, 1994; or

(2) has previously been finally convicted three or more times of:

(A) an offense under Section 49.04, Penal Code;

(B) an offense under Section 49.07, Penal Code, that involves operation of a motor vehicle;

(C) an offense under Section 49.08, Penal Code;

(D) an offense under Article 6701*l*-1, Revised Statutes, as that law existed before September 1, 1994;

(E) an offense under Article 6701*l*-2, Revised Statutes, as that law existed before January 1, 1984;

(F) an offense under Section 19.05(a)(2), Penal Code, as that law existed before September 1, 1994; or

(G) any combination of offenses under the statutes listed in Paragraphs (A)-(F).

(b) The officer who arrests a person described by Subsection (a) shall immediately notify the district or county attorney of that fact.

(c) A vehicle forfeited under this chapter is forfeited to the county in which the offense occurred.

*(Added by L.1995, chap. 165(1), eff. 9/1/95.)*

## §704.002. Temporary restraining order prohibiting disposition of vehicle pending trial of offense.

(a) The district or county attorney may seek a temporary restraining order prohibiting a person described by Section 704.001(a) from selling or disposing of a vehicle described by that subsection and may, not later than the 20th day after the date of the arrest, request a hearing in a county court or district court in the county to determine whether the vehicle is subject to forfeiture.

(b) The court in which the hearing is to be held shall set the cause for a hearing to be held not later than the 20th day after the date on which the district or county attorney requests the hearing. The court shall serve notice of the hearing in the manner provided for service of process by citation in a civil case to the owner of the vehicle and to any lienholder or other secured party whose interest in the vehicle is registered as provided by law.

(c) If, at a hearing requested under Subsection (a), the person arrested fails to file a denial stating that the vehicle is not subject to forfeiture, the court shall find that the vehicle is subject to forfeiture. If the person files a denial stating that the vehicle is not subject to forfeiture, the court shall hear evidence to determine whether the vehicle is subject to forfeiture.

(d) If the court determines that the vehicle is subject to forfeiture, the court shall enter an order enjoining the person from selling or disposing of the vehicle pending the outcome of the prosecution of the person for the offense for which the person was arrested. The court shall specify in the order that if the person is acquitted of the offense for which the person was arrested, the injunction expires on the date of the acquittal. If, after the court has issued an order under this subsection, the person proves by document or other evidence satisfactory to the court that prosecution for the offense has been dismissed, the court shall terminate the injunction.

*(Added by L.1995, chap. 165(1), eff. 9/1/95.)*

## §704.003. Forfeiture of vehicle following conviction.

(a) If a person described by Section 704.001(a) is convicted at the trial for the offense for which the person is arrested, the court sentencing the person may forfeit the vehicle:

(1) on the motion of the district or county attorney;

(2) after notice and hearing; and

(3) on a showing that a court has determined that the vehicle is subject to forfeiture.

(b) If proof at sentencing discloses that a person, including a lienholder or secured party, holds a security interest in the vehicle that is greater than or equal to the present value of the vehicle, the court shall order the vehicle released to the person holding the security interest. If that interest is less than the present value of the vehicle, the court may forfeit the vehicle.
*(Added by L.1995, chap. 165(1), eff. 9/1/95.)*

### §704.004. Sale of forfeited vehicle; certificate of title.

(a) A vehicle that has been forfeited under this chapter shall be sold at a public auction under the direction of the sheriff after notice of public auction as provided by law for other sheriff's sales.

(b) The proceeds of the sale shall be delivered to the county clerk and shall be paid to any party holding a security interest in the vehicle, including a lienholder or secured party, to the extent of the interest. The balance, if any, shall be deposited in the county treasury.

(c) The Texas Department of Transportation shall issue a certificate of title to a person who purchases a vehicle under this section and who complies with Chapter 501.
*(Added by L.1995, chap. 165(1), eff. 9/1/95.)*



## CHAPTER 705. ALLOWING DANGEROUS DRIVER TO BORROW MOTOR VEHICLE

Section


### §705.001. Allowing dangerous driver to borrow motor vehicle; offense.

(a) A person commits an offense if the person:
(1) knowingly permits another to operate a motor vehicle owned by the person; and
(2) knows that at the time permission is given the other person's license has been suspended as a result of a:
(A) conviction of an offense under:
(i) Section 49.04, Penal Code;
(ii) Section 49.07, Penal Code, if the offense involved operation of a motor vehicle; or
(iii) Article 6701*l*-1, Revised Statutes, as that law existed before September 1, 1994; or
(B) failure to give a specimen under:
(i) Chapter 724; or
(ii) Chapter 434, Acts of the 61st Legislature, Regular Session, 1969 (Article 6701*l*-5, Texas Civil Statutes), as that law existed before September 1, 1995.
(b) An offense under this section is a Class C misdemeanor.
*(Added by L.1995, chap. 165(1), eff. 9/1/95.)*

## CHAPTER 706. DENIAL OF RENEWAL OF LICENSE FOR FAILURE TO APPEAR

*(Added by L.1997, chap. 165(30.161(a)), eff. 9/1/97.)*

Section


### §706.001. Definitions.

In this chapter:
(1) "Complaint" means a notice of an offense as described by Article 27.14(d) or 45.019, Code of Criminal Procedure.
(2) "Department" means the Department of Public Safety.
(3) "Driver's license" has the meaning assigned by Section 521.001.

(4) "Highway or street" has the meaning assigned by Section 541.302.

(5) "Motor vehicle" has the meaning assigned by Section 541.201.

(6) "Operator" has the meaning assigned by Section 541.001.

(7) "Political subdivision" means a municipality or county.

(8) "Public place" has the meaning assigned by Section 1.07, Penal Code.

(9) "Traffic law" means a statute or ordinance, a violation of which is a misdemeanor punishable by a fine in an amount not to exceed $1,000, that:

(A) regulates an operator's conduct or condition while operating a motor vehicle on a highway or street or in a public place;

(B) regulates the condition of a motor vehicle while it is being operated on a highway or street;

(C) relates to the driver's license status of an operator while operating a motor vehicle on a highway or street; or

(D) relates to the registration status of a motor vehicle while it is being operated on a highway or street.

*(Added by L.1997, chap. 165(30.161(a)); chgd. by L.1999, chaps. 62(17.37(a)), 1545(74), eff. 9/1/99.)*

## §706.002. Contract with department.

(a) A political subdivision may contract with the department to provide information necessary for the department to deny renewal of the driver's license of a person who fails to appear for a complaint, citation, or court order to pay a fine involving:

(1) a violation of a traffic law;

(2) an offense under Section 543.009(b) or 543.107(b);

(3) an offense under Section 38.10, Penal Code, if the underlying offense is a traffic offense; or

(4) any other offense that a justice or municipal court has jurisdiction of under Article 4.11 or 4.14, Code of Criminal Procedure.

(b) A contract under this section:

(1) must be made in accordance with Chapter 791, Government Code; and

(2) is subject to the ability of the parties to provide or pay for the services required under the contract.

*(Added by L.1997, chap. 165(30.161(a)); chgd. by L.1999, chaps. 62(17.37(b)), 999(1), eff. 9/1/99.)*

## §706.003. Warning; citation.

(a) If a political subdivision has contracted with the department, a peace officer authorized to issue a citation in the jurisdiction of the political subdivision shall issue a written warning to each person to whom the officer issues a citation for a violation of a traffic law in the jurisdiction of the political subdivision.

(b) The warning under Subsection (a):

(1) is in addition to any other warning required by law;

(2) must state in substance that if the person fails to appear in court as provided by law for the prosecution of the offense, the person may be denied renewal of the person's driver's license; and

(3) may be printed on the same instrument as the citation.

*(Added by L.1997, chap. 165(30.161(a)), eff. 9/1/97.)*

## §706.004. Denial of renewal of driver's license.

(a) If a political subdivision has contracted with the department, on receiving the necessary information from the political subdivision the department may deny renewal of the person's driver's license for failure to appear based on a complaint, citation, or court order to pay a fine involving a violation of a traffic law or an offense described by Section 706.002(a)(2), (3), or (4).

(b) The information must include:

(1) the name, date of birth, and driver's license number of the person;

(2) the nature and date of the alleged violation;

(3) a statement that the person failed to appear as required by law for a traffic violation or an offense described by Section 706.002(a)(2), (3), or (4); and

(4) any other information required by the department.

*(Added by L.1997, chap. 165(30.161(a)); chgd. by L.1999, chaps. 62(17.37(c)), 999(2), eff. 9/1/99.)*

## §706.005. Notice to department.

A political subdivision shall notify the department that there is no cause to continue to deny renewal of a person's driver's license based on the person's previous failure to appear for a traffic violation or an offense described by Section 706.002(a)(2), (3), or (4), on payment of a fee as provided by Section 706.006 and:

(1) the entry of a judgment against the person;

(2) the perfection of an appeal of the case for which the warrant of arrest was issued;
(3) the dismissal of the charge for which the warrant of arrest was issued;
(4) the acquittal of the charge on which the person failed to appear;
(5) the posting of bond or the giving of other security to reinstate the charge for which the warrant was issued; or
(6) the payment of the fine owed on an outstanding court order to pay a fine.
*(Added by L.1997, chap. 165(30.161(a)); chgd. by L.1999, chaps. 62(17.37(c)), 999(2), eff. 9/1/99.)*

### §706.006. Administrative fee.

(a) Unless a person has been acquitted of the offense for which the person failed to appear for a complaint, citation, or court order to pay a fine involving a violation of a traffic law or an offense described by Section 706.002(a)(2), (3), or (4), the political subdivision shall require the person to pay an administrative fee of $30 for each violation for which the person failed to appear.
(b) The fee required by Subsection (a) is in addition to any other fee required by law.
*(Added by L.1997, chap. 165(30.161(a)); chgd. by L.1999, chaps. 62(17.37(d)), 999(3), eff. 9/1/99.)*

### §706.007. Records relating to fees; disposition of fees.

(a) An officer collecting a fee under Section 706.006 shall:
(1) keep separate records of the money; and
(2) deposit the money in the appropriate municipal or county treasury.
(b) The custodian of the municipal or county treasury may:
(1) deposit each fee collected under Section 706.006 in an interest-bearing account; and
(2) retain for the municipality or county the interest earned on money in the account.
(c) The custodian shall keep records of money received and disbursed under this section and shall provide an annual report, in the form approved by the comptroller, of all money received and disbursed under this section to:
(1) the comptroller;
(2) the department; and
(3) another entity as provided by interlocal contract.
(d) Of each fee collected under Section 706.006, the custodian of a municipal or county treasury shall:
(1) send $20 to the comptroller on or before the last day of each calendar quarter; and
(2) deposit the remainder to the credit of the general fund of the municipality or county.
(e) Of each $20 received by the comptroller, the comptroller shall deposit $10 to the credit of the department to implement this chapter.
*(Added by L.1997, chap. 165(30.161(a)), eff. 9/1/97.)*

### §706.008. Contract with private vendor; compensation.

(a) The department may contract with a private vendor to implement this chapter.
(b) The vendor performing the contract may be compensated by each political subdivision that has contracted with the department.
(c) Except for an action based on a citation issued by a peace officer employed by the department, the vendor may not be compensated with state money.
*(Added by L.1997, chap. 165(30.161(a)), eff. 9/1/97.)*

### §706.009. Vendor to provide customer support services.

(a) A vendor must establish and maintain customer support services as directed by the department, including a toll-free telephone service line to answer and resolve questions from persons who are denied renewal of a driver's license under this chapter.
(b) The vendor shall comply with terms, policies, and rules adopted by the department to administer this chapter.
*(Added by L.1997, chap. 165(30.161(a)), eff. 9/1/97.)*

### §706.010. Use of information collected by vendor.

Information collected under this chapter by a vendor may not be used by a person other than the department, the political subdivision, or a vendor as provided by this chapter. *(Added by L.1997, chap. 165(30.161(a)), eff. 9/1/97.)*

Printed in the U.S.A. Zt

### §706.011. Liability of state or political subdivision.

(a) An action for damages may not be brought against the state or a political subdivision based on an act or omission under this chapter, including the denial of renewal of a driver's license.

(b) The state or a political subdivision may not be held liable in damages based on an act or omission under this chapter, including the denial of renewal of a driver's license.
*(Added by L.1997, chap. 165(30.161(a)), eff. 9/1/97.)*

### §706.012. Rules.

The department may adopt rules to implement this chapter. *(Added by L.1997, chap. 165(30.161(a)), eff. 9/1/97.)*

## CHAPTERS 707 to 719. *(Reserved.)*



## CHAPTER 720. MISCELLANEOUS PROVISIONS



### §720.001. Badge of sheriff, constable, or deputy.

(a) A sheriff, constable, or deputy sheriff or deputy constable may not arrest or accost a person for driving a motor vehicle on a highway in violation of a law relating to motor vehicles unless the sheriff, constable, or deputy displays a badge showing the sheriff's, constable's, or deputy's title.

(b) A person commits an offense if the person violates this section. An offense under this section is a misdemeanor punishable in the same manner as an offense under Section 86.011, Local Government Code.

(c) An officer charged by law to take or prosecute a complaint under this section shall be removed from office if the officer refuses to do so.
*(Added by L.1995, chap. 165(1), eff. 9/1/95.)*

### §720.002. Prohibition on traffic-offense quotas.

(a) A political subdivision or an agency of this state may not establish or maintain, formally or informally, a plan to evaluate, promote, compensate, or discipline:

(1) a peace officer according to the officer's issuance of a predetermined or specified number of any type or combination of types of traffic citations; or

(2) a justice of the peace or a judge of a county court, statutory county court, municipal court, or municipal court of record according to the amount of money the justice or judge collects from persons convicted of a traffic offense.

(b) A political subdivision or an agency of this state may not require or suggest to a peace officer, a justice of the peace, or a judge of a county court, statutory county court, municipal court, or municipal court of record:

(1) that the peace officer is required or expected to issue a predetermined or specified number of any type or combination of types of traffic citations within a specified period; or

(2) that the justice or judge is required or expected to collect a predetermined amount of money from persons convicted of a traffic offense within a specified period.

(c) Subsection (a) does not prohibit a municipality from considering the source and amount of money collected from a municipal court or a municipal court of record when evaluating the performance of a judge employed by the municipality.

(d) This section does not prohibit a municipality from obtaining budgetary information from a municipal court or a municipal court of record, including an estimate of the amount of money the court anticipates will be collected in a budget year.

(e) A violation of this section by an elected official is misconduct and a ground for removal from office. A violation of this section by a person who is not an elected official is a ground for removal from the person's position.

(f) In this section:

(1) "Conviction" means the rendition of an order by a court imposing a punishment of incarceration or a fine.

(2) "Traffic offense" means an offense under:

(A) Chapter 521; or

(B) Subtitle C.

*(Added by L.1995, chap. 165(1), eff. 9/1/95.)*

# SUBTITLE J. MISCELLANEOUS PROVISIONS

## CHAPTER 721. INSCRIPTION REQUIRED ON STATE, MUNICIPAL, AND COUNTY MOTOR VEHICLES



### §721.001. Definition.

In this chapter, "state agency" means a department, bureau, board, commission, or office of state government. *(Added by L.1995, chap. 165(1), eff. 9/1/95.)*

### §721.002. Inscription required on state-owned motor vehicles.

(a) The official having control of a state-owned motor vehicle shall have printed on each side of the vehicle the word "Texas," followed by the title of the state agency having custody of the vehicle.

(b) The inscription must be in a color sufficiently different from the body of the motor vehicle so that the lettering is plainly legible at a distance of not less than 100 feet.

(c) The title of the state agency must be in letters not less than two inches high.

*(Added by L.1995, chap. 165(1), eff. 9/1/95.)*

### §721.003. Exemption from inscription requirement for certain state-owned motor vehicles.

(a) The governing bodies of the following state agencies or divisions by rule may exempt from the requirements of Section 721.002 a motor vehicle that is under the control and custody of the agency or division:

(1) Texas Commission on Fire Protection;

(2) Texas State Board of Pharmacy;

(3) Texas Department of Mental Health and Mental Retardation;

(4) Department of Public Safety of the State of Texas;

(5) the institutional division or the pardons and paroles division of the Texas Department of Criminal Justice;

(6) Board of Pardons and Paroles;

(7) Parks and Wildlife Department;

(8) Railroad Commission of Texas;

(9) Texas Alcoholic Beverage Commission;

(10) Banking Department of Texas;

(11) Savings and Loan Department of Texas;

(12) Texas Juvenile Probation Commission;

(13) Texas Natural Resource Conservation Commission;

(14) Texas Youth Commission; and

(15) an agency that receives an appropriation under an article of the General Appropriations Act that appropriates money to the legislature.

(b) The attorney general by rule may exempt from the requirements of Section 721.002 a motor vehicle that is under the control and custody of the attorney general's health services providers integrity and Medicaid fraud division.

(c) A rule adopted under this section must specify:

(1) the purpose served by not printing on the motor vehicle the inscription required by Section 721.002; and

(2) the primary use of the motor vehicle.

(d) A rule adopted under this section is not effective until the rule is filed with the secretary of state.

*(Added by L.1995, chap. 165(1), eff. 9/1/95.)*

**§721.004. Inscription required on municipal and county-owned motor vehicles and heavy equipment.**

(a) The office having control of a motor vehicle or piece of heavy equipment owned by a municipality or county shall have printed on each side of the vehicle or equipment the name of the municipality or county, followed by the title of the department or office having custody of the vehicle or equipment.

(b) The inscription must be in a color sufficiently different from the body of the vehicle or equipment so that the lettering is plainly legible.

(c) The title of the department or office must be in letters plainly legible at a distance of not less than 100 feet.

*(Added by L.1995, chap. 165(1), eff. 9/1/95.)*

**§721.005. Exemption from inscription requirement for certain municipal and county-owned motor vehicles.**

(a) The governing body of a municipality may exempt from the requirements of Section 721.004 an automobile when used to perform an official duty by a:

(1) police department;

(2) magistrate as defined by Article 2.09, Code of Criminal Procedure; or

(3) medical examiner.

(b) The commissioners court of a county may exempt from the requirements of Section 721.004:

(1) an automobile when used to perform an official duty by a:

(A) police department;

(B) sheriff's office;

(C) constable's office;

(D) criminal district attorney's office;

(E) district attorney's office;

(F) county attorney's office;

(G) magistrate as defined by Article 2.09, Code of Criminal Procedure;

(H) county fire marshal's office; or

(I) medical examiner; or

(2) a juvenile probation department vehicle used to transport children, when used to perform an official duty.

(c) An exemption provided under this section does not apply to a contract deputy.

*(Added by L.1995, chap. 165(1); chgd. by L.1997, chaps. 46(1), 355(1); L.1999, chap. 62(17.38), eff. 9/1/99.)*

**§721.006. Operation of vehicle in violation of chapter; offense.**

(a) A person commits an offense if the person:

(1) operates on a municipal street or on a highway a motor vehicle or piece of equipment that does not have the inscription required by this chapter; or

(2) uses a motor vehicle that is exempt by rule under Section 721.003, and that use is not expressly specified by the rule.

(b) An offense under this section is a misdemeanor punishable by a fine of not less than $25 or more than $100.

*(Added by L.1995, chap. 165(1), eff. 9/1/95.)*

## CHAPTER 722. AUTOMOBILE CLUB SERVICES

Section

## §722.001. Short title.

This chapter may be cited as the Automobile Club Services Act. *(Added by L.1995, chap. 165(1), eff. 9/1/95.)*

## §722.002. Definitions.

In this chapter:

(1) "Agent" means a salesman or other individual appointed by an automobile club to sell memberships in the club to the public.

(2) "Automobile club" means a person who, for consideration, promises the membership assistance in matters relating to travel, and to the operation, use, or maintenance of a motor vehicle, by supplying services such as services related to:

(A) community traffic safety;
(B) travel and touring;
(C) theft prevention or rewards;
(D) maps;
(E) towing;
(F) emergency road assistance;
(G) bail bonds and legal fee reimbursement in the defense of traffic offenses; and
(H) purchase of accidental injury and death benefits insurance coverage from an authorized insurance company.

*(Added by L.1995, chap. 165(1), eff. 9/1/95.)*

## §722.003. Certificate of authority required.

(a) A person may not engage in business as an automobile club unless the person meets the requirements of this chapter and obtains an automobile club certificate of authority from the secretary of state.

(b) A person may not solicit or aid in the solicitation of another person to purchase a service contract or membership issued by an automobile club that does not hold an automobile club certificate of authority.

*(Added by L.1995, chap. 165(1), eff. 9/1/95.)*

## §722.004. Application.

(a) Each applicant for an automobile club certificate of authority must file an application with the secretary of state in the form and manner prescribed by the secretary. The secretary shall adopt the forms necessary for an applicant to comply with this chapter and shall furnish those forms on request to an applicant for a certificate of authority.

(b) An application must be executed under oath by the club president or other principal club officer and must be accompanied by:

(1) the first year's annual fee for the certificate of authority;

(2) a certificate by the secretary of state stating that the applicant has complied with the corporation laws of this state, if the applicant is a corporation;

(3) a list of each person who holds an ownership interest in the applicant and each officer of the applicant, if the applicant is not incorporated;

(4) a copy of any operating agreement or management agreement affecting the club and a list of each party to the agreement if the applicant is not incorporated; and

(5) proof of security in a manner that complies with Section 722.005.

(c) The secretary of state shall issue the automobile club certificate of authority or deny the application not later than the 15th day after the day the secretary receives the application, certificate, or security. Failure to issue the certificate of authority within the prescribed time entitles the applicant to a refund of all money and security deposited with the application.

*(Added by L.1995, chap. 165(1), eff. 9/1/95.)*

## §722.005. Security requirements.

(a) An applicant for an automobile club certificate of authority may provide the security required for that certificate by depositing with the state or pledging in the form prescribed by the secretary of state:

(1) $25,000 in securities approved by the secretary;
(2) $25,000 in cash; or
(3) a $25,000 bond in the form prescribed by the secretary that is:

(A) payable to the state;

(B) executed by a corporate surety licensed to do business in this state; and

(C) conditioned on the faithful performance of the automobile club in selling or providing club services and the payment of any fines or penalties levied against the club for failure to comply with this chapter.

(b) The aggregate liability of the surety for all breaches of the bond conditions and for payment of all fines and penalties may not exceed the amount of the bond.

(c) The required security shall be maintained as long as the automobile club has any liability or obligation in this state. On showing to the satisfaction of the secretary of state that the club has ceased to do business and that all liabilities and obligations of the club have been satisfied, the secretary may return the security to the club or deliver the security in accordance with a court order. *(Added by L.1995, chap. 165(1), eff. 9/1/95.)*



### §722.006. Renewal.

(a) An automobile club certificate of authority expires annually on August 31. The certificate may be renewed by filing a renewal application in the manner prescribed by the secretary of state and paying the annual fee.

(b) The secretary of state may adopt forms for the renewal application. *(Added by L.1995, chap. 165(1), eff. 9/1/95.)*

### §722.007. Annual fee.

The annual fee for an automobile club certificate of authority is $150. *(Added by L.1995, chap. 165(1), eff. 9/1/95.)*

### §722.008. Certificate revocation or suspension.

(a) After a public hearing, the secretary of state shall revoke or suspend an automobile club's certificate of authority if the secretary determines, for good cause shown, that:

(1) the club:

(A) has violated this chapter;

(B) is not acting as an automobile club;

(C) is insolvent or has assets valued at less than its liabilities;

(D) has refused to submit to an examination by the secretary; or

(E) is transacting business in a fraudulent manner; or

(2) an owner, officer, or manager of the club is not of good moral character.

(b) The secretary of state shall give public notice of the suspension or revocation in the manner the secretary considers appropriate. *(Added by L.1995, chap. 165(1), eff. 9/1/95.)*

### §722.009. Service contract; membership information.

(a) Each automobile club operating under this chapter shall furnish to the membership a service contract or membership card that includes the following information:

(1) the club's name;

(2) the street address of the club's home office and of its usual place of business in this state; and

(3) a description of the services or benefits to which the members are entitled.

(b) For purposes of this chapter, the completed application for an automobile club certificate of authority and the description of services listed under Subsection (a) constitute the service contract. *(Added by L.1995, chap. 165(1), eff. 9/1/95.)*

### §722.010. Filing of information.

(a) Each automobile club shall file a certified copy of its service contract with the secretary of state.

(b) If an automobile club provides participation in a group accidental injury or death policy, the club shall file with the service contract a copy of the certificate of participation.

(c) An automobile club shall file with the secretary of state any change to the service contract. *(Added by L.1995, chap. 165(1), eff. 9/1/95.)*

### §722.011. Agent registration.

(a) An automobile club that operates in this state under an automobile club certificate of authority shall file with the secretary of state a notice of appointment of each agent not later than the 30th day after the date on which that agent is employed by the club.

(b) The notice of appointment must be in the form prescribed by the secretary of state and must contain:

(1) the name, address, age, sex, and social security number of the agent; and

(2) proof satisfactory to the secretary that the agent is of good moral character.

(c) Registration under this section is valid for one year from the date of the initial registration and may be renewed on each anniversary of that date. The annual registration fee is $10.

(d) Each automobile club shall notify the secretary of state of the termination of an agent's employment by the club not later than the 30th day after the date of the termination.
*(Added by L.1995, chap. 165(1), eff. 9/1/95.)*

**§722.012. Advertising restrictions.**

An automobile club operating under this chapter may not:

(1) refer to its certificate of authority or to approval by the secretary of state in any advertising, contract, or membership card; or

(2) advertise or describe its services in a manner that would lead the public to believe that the services include automobile insurance.
*(Added by L.1995, chap. 165(1), eff. 9/1/95.)*

**§722.013.** *(Repealed by L.1999, chap. 1530(5.02), eff. 9/1/99.)*

**§722.014. Criminal penalty.**

(a) A person commits an offense if the person violates this chapter.

(b) An offense under this section is a misdemeanor punishable by:

(1) a fine not to exceed $500; and

(2) confinement in the county jail for a term not to exceed six months.
*(Added by L.1995, chap. 165(1), eff. 9/1/95.)*

## CHAPTER 723. TEXAS TRAFFIC SAFETY ACT

### SUBCHAPTER A. GENERAL PROVISIONS



### SUBCHAPTER B. PREPARATION AND ADMINISTRATION OF TRAFFIC SAFETY PROGRAM



### SUBCHAPTER C. GIFTS, GRANTS, DONATIONS, GRANTS-IN-AID, AND PAYMENTS



### SUBCHAPTER A. GENERAL PROVISIONS

**§723.001. Short title.**

This chapter may be cited as the Texas Traffic Safety Act. *(Added by L.1995, chap. 165(1), eff. 9/1/95.)*

## §723.002. Governmental purpose.

The establishment, development, and maintenance of a traffic safety program is a vital governmental purpose and function of the state and its legal and political subdivisions. *(Added by L.1995, chap. 165(1), eff. 9/1/95.)*

## §723.003. Traffic safety fund account.

(a) The traffic safety fund account is an account in the general revenue fund. Money received from any source to implement this chapter shall be:

(1) deposited to the credit of the traffic safety fund account; and

(2) spent with other state money spent to implement this chapter in the manner in which the other state money is spent.

(b) A payment from the traffic safety fund account shall be made in compliance with this chapter and rules adopted by the governor.

*(Added by L.1997, chap. 165(30.162(a)), eff. 9/1/97.)*



## §§723.004 to 723.010. *(Reserved.)*

# SUBCHAPTER B. PREPARATION AND ADMINISTRATION OF TRAFFIC SAFETY PROGRAM

## §723.011. Governor's responsibility for program.

(a) The governor shall:

(1) prepare and administer a statewide traffic safety program designed to reduce traffic accidents and the death, injury, and property damage that result from traffic accidents;

(2) adopt rules for the administration of this chapter, including rules, procedures, and policy statements governing grants-in-aid and contractual relations;

(3) receive on the state's behalf for the implementation of this chapter money made available by the United States under federal law; and

(4) allocate money appropriated by the legislature in the General Appropriations Act to implement this chapter.

(b) In preparing and administering the traffic safety program, the governor may:

(1) cooperate with the United States or a legal or political subdivision of the state in research designed to aid in traffic safety;

(2) accept federal money available for research relating to traffic safety; and

(3) employ personnel necessary to administer this chapter.

*(Added by L.1995, chap. 165(1), eff. 9/1/95.)*

## §723.012. Traffic safety program.

The statewide traffic safety program must include:

(1) a driver education and training program administered by the governor through appropriate agencies that complies with Section 723.013;

(2) plans for improving:

(A) driver licensing;

(B) accident records;

(C) vehicle inspection, registration, and titling;

(D) traffic engineering;

(E) personnel;

(F) police traffic supervision;

(G) traffic courts;

(H) highway design; and

(I) uniform traffic laws; and

(3) plans for local traffic safety programs by legal and political subdivisions of this state that may be implemented if the programs:

(A) are approved by the governor; and

(B) conform with uniform standards adopted under the Highway Safety Act of 1966 (23 U.S.C. Sec. 401 et seq.).

*(Added by L.1995, chap. 165(1), eff. 9/1/95.)*

## §723.013. Driver education and training program.

(a) The statewide driver education and training program required by Section 723.012 shall provide for:

(1) rules that permit controlled innovation and experimentation and that set minimum standards for:

(A) classroom instruction;

(B) driving skills training;

(C) instructor qualifications;

(D) program content; and

(E) supplementary materials and equipment;

(2) a method for continuing evaluation of approved driver education and training programs to identify the practices most effective in preventing traffic accidents; and

(3) contracts between the governing bodies of centrally located independent school districts or other appropriate public or private agencies and the state to provide approved driver education and training programs.

(b) Instruction offered under a contract authorized by this section must be offered to any applicant who is over 15 years of age.

*(Added by L.1995, chap. 165(1), eff. 9/1/95.)*





### §723.014. Cooperation of state agencies, officers, and employees.

On the governor's request, a state agency or institution, state officer, or state employee shall cooperate in an activity of the state that is consistent with:

(1) this chapter; and

(2) the agency's, institution's, officer's, or employee's official functions.

*(Added by L.1995, chap. 165(1), eff. 9/1/95.)*

### §723.015. Participation in program by legal or political subdivision.

A legal or political subdivision of this state may:

(1) cooperate and contract with the state, another legal or political subdivision of this state, or a private person in establishing, developing, and maintaining a statewide traffic safety program;

(2) spend money from any source for an activity related to performing a part of the traffic safety program; and

(3) contract and pay for a personal service or property to be used in the traffic safety program or for an activity related to the program.

*(Added by L.1995, chap. 165(1), eff. 9/1/95.)*

### §§723.016 to 723.030. *(Reserved.)*

## SUBCHAPTER C. GIFTS, GRANTS, DONATIONS, GRANTS-IN-AID, AND PAYMENTS

### §723.031. Gifts, grants, and donations.

To implement this chapter, the state may accept and spend a gift, grant, or donation of money or other property from a private source. *(Added by L.1995, chap. 165(1), eff. 9/1/95.)*

### §723.032. Grants-in-aid and contractual payments.

(a) A grant-in-aid for a governmental purpose or a contractual payment may be made to a legal or political subdivision of this state to carry out a duty or activity that is part of the statewide traffic safety program.

(b) To implement this chapter, a contractual payment may be made from money in the traffic safety fund account for a service rendered or property furnished by a private person or an agency that is not a legal or political subdivision of this state.

*(Added by L.1995, chap. 165(1); chgd. by L.1997, chap. 165(30.162(b)), eff. 9/1/97.)*

# CHAPTER 724. IMPLIED CONSENT

## SUBCHAPTER A. GENERAL PROVISIONS

## SUBCHAPTER B. TAKING AND ANALYSIS OF SPECIMEN





## SUBCHAPTER C. SUSPENSION OR DENIAL OF LICENSE ON REFUSAL OF SPECIMEN



## SUBCHAPTER D. HEARING



## SUBCHAPTER E. ADMISSIBILITY OF EVIDENCE



## SUBCHAPTER A. GENERAL PROVISIONS

### §724.001. Definitions.

In this chapter:

(1) "Alcohol concentration" has the meaning assigned by Section 49.01, Penal Code.

(2) "Arrest" includes the taking into custody of a child, as defined by Section 51.02, Family Code.

(3) "Controlled substance" has the meaning assigned by Section 481.002, Health and Safety Code.

(4) "Criminal charge" includes a charge that may result in a proceeding under Title 3, Family Code.

(5) "Criminal proceeding" includes a proceeding under Title 3, Family Code.

(6) "Dangerous drug" has the meaning assigned by Section 483.001, Health and Safety Code.

(7) "Department" means the Department of Public Safety.

(8) "Drug" has the meaning assigned by Section 481.002, Health and Safety Code.

(9) "Intoxicated" has the meaning assigned by Section 49.01, Penal Code.
(10) "License" has the meaning assigned by Section 521.001.
(11) "Operate" means to drive or be in actual control of a motor vehicle or watercraft.
(12) "Public place" has the meaning assigned by Section 1.07, Penal Code.
*(Added by L.1995, chap. 165(1); chgd. by L.1997, chap. 1013(31), eff. 9/1/97.)*

### §724.002. Applicability.

The provisions of this chapter that apply to suspension of a license for refusal to submit to the taking of a specimen (Sections 724.013, 724.015, and 724.048 and Subchapters C and D) apply only to a person arrested for an offense involving the operation of a motor vehicle. *(Added by L.1995, chap. 165(1), eff. 9/1/95.)*

### §724.003. Rulemaking.

The department and the State Office of Administrative Hearings shall adopt rules to administer this chapter. *(Added by L.1995, chap. 165(1), eff. 9/1/95.)*

### §§724.004 to 724.010. *(Reserved.)*

## SUBCHAPTER B. TAKING AND ANALYSIS OF SPECIMEN

### §724.011. Consent to taking of specimen.

(a) If a person is arrested for an offense arising out of acts alleged to have been committed while the person was operating a motor vehicle in a public place, or a watercraft, while intoxicated, or an offense under Section 106.041, Alcoholic Beverage Code, the person is deemed to have consented, subject to this chapter, to submit to the taking of one or more specimens of the person's breath or blood for analysis to determine the alcohol concentration or the presence in the person's body of a controlled substance, drug, dangerous drug, or other substance.

(b) A person arrested for an offense described by Subsection (a) may consent to submit to the taking of any other type of specimen to determine the person's alcohol concentration.
*(Added by L.1995, chap. 165(1); chgd. by L.1997, chap. 1013(32), eff. 9/1/97.)*

### §724.012. Taking of specimen.

(a) One or more specimens of a person's breath or blood may be taken if the person is arrested and at the request of a peace officer having reasonable grounds to believe the person:

(1) while intoxicated was operating a motor vehicle in a public place, or a watercraft; or

(2) was in violation of Section 106.041, Alcoholic Beverage Code.

(b) A peace officer shall require the taking of a specimen of the person's breath or blood if:

(1) the officer arrests the person for an offense under Chapter 49, Penal Code, involving the operation of a motor vehicle or a watercraft;

(2) the person was the operator of a motor vehicle or a watercraft involved in an accident that the officer reasonably believes occurred as a result of the offense;

(3) at the time of the arrest the officer reasonably believes that a person has died or will die as a direct result of the accident; and

(4) the person refuses the officer's request to submit to the taking of a specimen voluntarily.

(c) The peace officer shall designate the type of specimen to be taken.
*(Added by L.1995, chap. 165(1); chgd. by L.1997, chap. 1013(33), eff. 9/1/97.)*

### §724.013. Prohibition on taking specimen if person refuses; exception.

Except as provided by Section 724.012(b), a specimen may not be taken if a person refuses to submit to the taking of a specimen designated by a peace officer. *(Added by L.1995, chap. 165(1), eff. 9/1/95.)*

### §724.014. Person incapable of refusal.

(a) A person who is dead, unconscious, or otherwise incapable of refusal is considered not to have withdrawn the consent provided by Section 724.011.

(b) If the person is dead, a specimen may be taken by:

(1) the county medical examiner or the examiner's designated agent; or

(2) a licensed mortician or a person authorized under Section 724.016 or 724.017 if there is not a county medical examiner for the county.

(c) If the person is alive but is incapable of refusal, a specimen may be taken by a person authorized under Section 724.016 or 724.017.
*(Added by L.1995, chap. 165(1), eff. 9/1/95.)*

### §724.015. Information provided by officer before requesting specimen.

Before requesting a person to submit to the taking of a specimen, the officer shall inform the person orally and in writing that:

(1) if the person refuses to submit to the taking of the specimen, that refusal may be admissible in a subsequent prosecution;

(2) if the person refuses to submit to the taking of the specimen, the person's license to operate a motor vehicle will be automatically suspended, whether or not the person is subsequently prosecuted as a result of the arrest, for:

(A) not less than 90 days if the person is 21 years of age or older; or

(B) not less than 120 days if the person is younger than 21 years of age;

(3) if the person is 21 years of age or older and submits to the taking of a specimen designated by the officer and an analysis of the specimen shows the person had an alcohol concentration of a level specified by Chapter 49, Penal Code, the person's license to operate a motor vehicle will be automatically suspended for not less than 60 days, whether or not the person is subsequently prosecuted as a result of the arrest;

(4) if the person is younger than 21 years of age and has any detectable amount of alcohol in the person's system, the person's license to operate a motor vehicle will be automatically suspended for not less than 60 days even if the person submits to the taking of the specimen, but that if the person submits to the taking of the specimen and an analysis of the specimen shows that the person had an alcohol concentration less than the level specified by Chapter 49, Penal Code, the person may be subject to criminal penalties less severe than those provided under that chapter;

(5) if the officer determines that the person is a resident without a license to operate a motor vehicle in this state, the department will deny to the person the issuance of a license, whether or not the person is subsequently prosecuted as a result of the arrest, under the same conditions and for the same periods that would have applied to a revocation of the person's driver's license if the person had held a driver's license issued by this state; and

(6) the person has a right to a hearing on the suspension or denial if, not later than the 15th day after the date on which the person receives the notice of suspension or denial or on which the person is considered to have received the notice by mail as provided by law, the department receives, at its headquarters in Austin, a written demand, including a facsimile transmission, or a request in another form prescribed by the department for the hearing.

*(Added by L.1995, chap. 165(1); chgd. by L.1997, chap. 1013(34), eff. 9/1/97.)*

### §724.016. Breath specimen.

(a) A breath specimen taken at the request or order of a peace officer must be taken and analyzed under rules of the department by an individual possessing a certificate issued by the department certifying that the individual is qualified to perform the analysis.

(b) The department may:

(1) adopt rules approving satisfactory analytical methods; and

(2) ascertain the qualifications of an individual to perform the analysis.

(c) The department may revoke a certificate for cause.

*(Added by L.1995, chap. 165(1), eff. 9/1/95.)*

### §724.017. Blood specimen.

(a) Only a physician, qualified technician, chemist, registered professional nurse, or licensed vocational nurse may take a blood specimen at the request or order of a peace officer under this chapter. The blood specimen must be taken in a sanitary place.

(b) The person who takes the blood specimen under this chapter, or the hospital where the blood specimen is taken, is not liable for damages arising from the request or order of the peace officer to take the blood specimen as provided by this chapter if the blood specimen was taken according to recognized medical procedures. This subsection does not relieve a person from liability for negligence in the taking of a blood specimen.

(c) In this section, "qualified technician" does not include emergency medical services personnel.

*(Added by L.1995, chap. 165(1), eff. 9/1/95.)*

### §724.018. Furnishing information concerning test results.

On the request of a person who has given a specimen at the request of a peace officer, full information concerning the analysis of the specimen shall be made available to the person or the person's attorney. *(Added by L.1995, chap. 165(1), eff. 9/1/95.)*

### §724.019. Additional analysis by request.

(a) A person who submits to the taking of a specimen of breath, blood, urine, or another bodily substance at the request or order of a peace officer may, on request and within a reasonable time not to exceed two hours after the arrest, have a physician, qualified technician, chemist, or registered professional nurse selected by the person take for analysis an additional specimen of the person's blood.

(b) The person shall be allowed a reasonable opportunity to contact a person specified by Subsection (a).

(c) A peace officer or law enforcement agency is not required to transport for testing a person who requests that a blood specimen be taken under this section.

(d) The failure or inability to obtain an additional specimen or analysis under this section does not preclude the admission of evidence relating to the analysis of the specimen taken at the request or order of the peace officer.

(e) A peace officer, another person acting for or on behalf of the state, or a law enforcement agency is not liable for damages arising from a person's request to have a blood specimen taken.
*(Added by L.1995, chap. 165(1), eff. 9/1/95.)*

### §§724.020 to 724.030. *(Reserved.)*

## SUBCHAPTER C. SUSPENSION OR DENIAL OF LICENSE ON REFUSAL OF SPECIMEN

### §724.031. Statement requested on refusal.

If a person refuses the request of a peace officer to submit to the taking of a specimen, the peace officer shall request the person to sign a statement that:

(1) the officer requested that the person submit to the taking of a specimen;

(2) the person was informed of the consequences of not submitting to the taking of a specimen; and

(3) the person refused to submit to the taking of a specimen.
*(Added by L.1995, chap. 165(1), eff. 9/1/95.)*

### §724.032. Issuance by officer of notice of suspension or denial of license; written refusal report.

(a) If a person refuses to submit to the taking of a specimen, whether expressly or because of an intentional failure of the person to give the specimen, the peace officer shall:

(1) serve notice of license suspension or denial on the person; and

(2) make a written report of the refusal to the director of the department.

(b) The director must approve the form of the refusal report. The report must:

(1) show the grounds for the officer's belief that the person had been operating a motor vehicle while intoxicated; and

(2) contain a copy of:

(A) the refusal statement requested under Section 724.031; or

(B) a statement signed by the officer that the person refused to:

(i) submit to the taking of the requested specimen; and

(ii) sign the requested statement under Section 724.031.

(c) The officer shall forward to the department a copy of the notice of suspension or denial and the refusal report not later than the fifth business day after the date of the arrest.

(d) The department shall develop forms for notices of suspension or denial that shall be used by all state and local law enforcement agencies.
*(Added by L.1995, chap. 165(1), eff. 9/1/95.)*

### §724.033. Issuance by department of notice of suspension or denial of license.

(a) On receipt of a report of a peace officer under Section 724.032, if the officer did not serve notice of suspension or denial of a license at the time of refusal to submit to the taking of a specimen, the department shall mail notice of suspension or denial, by first class mail, to the address of the person shown by the records of the department or to the address given in the peace officer's report, if different.

(b) Notice is considered received on the fifth day after the date it is mailed.
*(Added by L.1995, chap. 165(1); chgd. by L.1999, chap. 1409(5), eff. 9/1/99.)*

### §724.034. Contents of notice of suspension or denial of license.

A notice of suspension or denial of a license must state:

(1) the reason and statutory grounds for the action;
(2) the effective date of the suspension or denial;
(3) the right of the person to a hearing;
(4) how to request a hearing; and
(5) the period in which a request for a hearing must be received by the department.
*(Added by L.1995, chap. 165(1), eff. 9/1/95.)*

**§724.035. Suspension or denial of license.**
(a) If a person refuses the request of a peace officer to submit to the taking of a specimen, the department shall:
(1) suspend the person's license to operate a motor vehicle on a public highway for 90 days if the person is 21 years of age or older or 120 days if the person is younger than 21 years of age; or
(2) if the person is a resident without a license, issue an order denying the issuance of a license to the person for 90 days if the person is 21 years of age or older or 120 days if the person is younger than 21 years of age.
(b) The period of suspension or denial is 180 days if the person is 21 years of age or older or 240 days if the person is younger than 21 years of age and the person's driving record shows one or more alcohol-related or drug-related enforcement contacts, as defined by Section 524.001(3)(B) or (C), during the five years preceding the date of the person's arrest.
(c) The period of suspension or denial is one year if the person's driving record shows one or more alcohol-related or drug-related enforcement contacts, as defined by Section 524.001(3)(A), during the five years preceding the date of the person's arrest.
(d) A suspension or denial takes effect on the 40th day after the date on which the person:
(1) receives notice of suspension or denial under Section 724.032(a); or
(2) is considered to have received notice of suspension or denial under Section 724.033.
*(Added by L.1995, chap. 165(1); chgd. by L.1997, chaps. 165(30.163), 1013(35), eff. 9/1/97.)*

**§§724.036 to 724.040.** *(Reserved.)*

## SUBCHAPTER D. HEARING

**§724.041. Hearing on suspension or denial.**
(a) If, not later than the 15th day after the date on which the person receives notice of suspension or denial under Section 724.032(a) or is considered to have received notice under Section 724.033, the department receives at its headquarters in Austin, in writing, including a facsimile transmission, or by another manner prescribed by the department, a request that a hearing be held, the State Office of Administrative Hearings shall hold a hearing.
(b) A hearing shall be held not earlier than the 11th day after the date the person is notified, unless the parties agree to waive this requirement, but before the effective date of the notice of suspension or denial.
(c) A request for a hearing stays the suspension or denial until the date of the final decision of the administrative law judge.
(d) A hearing shall be held by an administrative law judge employed by the State Office of Administrative Hearings.
(e) A hearing shall be held:
(1) at a location designated by the State Office of Administrative Hearings:
(A) in the county of arrest if the county has a population of 300,000 or more; or
(B) in the county in which the person was alleged to have committed the offense for which the person was arrested or not more than 75 miles from the county seat of the county of arrest if the population of the county of arrest is less than 300,000; or
(2) with the consent of the person requesting the hearing and the department, by telephone conference call.
(f) The State Office of Administrative Hearings shall provide for the stenographic or electronic recording of a hearing under this subchapter.
(g) An administrative hearing under this section is governed by Sections 524.032(b) and (c), 524.035(e), 524.037(a), and 524.040.
*(Added by L.1995, chap. 165(1); chgd. by L.1997, chap. 165(30.164), eff. 9/1/97.)*

**§724.042. Issues at hearing.**
The issues at a hearing under this subchapter are whether:
(1) reasonable suspicion or probable cause existed to stop or arrest the person;

(2) probable cause existed to believe that the person was operating a motor vehicle in a public place while intoxicated;

(3) the person was placed under arrest by the officer and was requested to submit to the taking of a specimen; and

(4) the person refused to submit to the taking of a specimen on request of the officer.

*(Added by L.1995, chap. 165(1), eff. 9/1/95.)*

### §724.043. Findings of administrative law judge.

(a) If the administrative law judge finds in the affirmative on each issue under Section 724.042, the suspension order is sustained. If the person is a resident without a license, the department shall continue to deny to the person the issuance of a license for the applicable period provided by Section 724.035.

(b) If the administrative law judge does not find in the affirmative on each issue under Section 724.042, the department shall reinstate the person's license or rescind any order denying the issuance of a license because of the person's refusal to submit to the taking of a specimen under Section 724.032(a).

*(Added by L.1995, chap. 165(1), eff. 9/1/95.)*

### §724.044. Waiver of right to hearing.

A person waives the right to a hearing under this subchapter and the department's suspension or denial is final and may not be appealed if the person:

(1) fails to request a hearing under Section 724.041; or

(2) requests a hearing and fails to appear, without good cause.

*(Added by L.1995, chap. 165(1), eff. 9/1/95.)*

### §724.045. Prohibition on probation of suspension.

A suspension under this chapter may not be probated. *(Added by L.1995, chap. 165(1), eff. 9/1/95.)*

### §724.046. Reinstatement of license or issuance of new license.

(a) A license suspended under this chapter may not be reinstated or a new license issued until the person whose license has been suspended pays to the department a fee of $100 in addition to any other fee required by law. A person subject to a denial order issued under this chapter may not obtain a license after the period of denial has ended until the person pays to the department a fee of $100 in addition to any other fee required by law.

(b) If a suspension or denial under this chapter is rescinded by the department, an administrative law judge, or a court, payment of the fee under this section is not required for reinstatement or issuance of a license.

*(Added by L.1995, chap. 165(1), eff. 9/1/95.)*

### §724.047. Appeal.

Chapter 524 governs an appeal from an action of the department, following an administrative hearing under this chapter, in suspending or denying the issuance of a license. *(Added by L.1995, chap. 165(1), eff. 9/1/95.)*

### §724.048. Relationship of administrative proceeding to criminal proceeding.

(a) The determination of the department or administrative law judge:

(1) is a civil matter;

(2) is independent of and is not an estoppel as to any matter in issue in an adjudication of a criminal charge arising from the occurrence that is the basis for the suspension or denial; and

(3) does not preclude litigation of the same or similar facts in a criminal prosecution.

(b) Except as provided by Subsection (c), the disposition of a criminal charge does not affect a license suspension or denial under this chapter and is not an estoppel as to any matter in issue in a suspension or denial proceeding under this chapter.

(c) If a criminal charge arising from the same arrest as a suspension under this chapter results in an acquittal, the suspension under this chapter may not be imposed. If a suspension under this chapter has already been imposed, the department shall rescind the suspension and remove references to the suspension from the computerized driving record of the individual.

*(Added by L.1995, chap. 165(1); chgd. by L.1997, chap. 1013(36), eff. 9/1/97.)*

### §§724.049 to 724.060. *(Reserved.)*

## SUBCHAPTER E. ADMISSIBILITY OF EVIDENCE

**§724.061. Admissibility of refusal of person to submit to taking of specimen.**

A person's refusal of a request by an officer to submit to the taking of a specimen of breath or blood, whether the refusal was express or the result of an intentional failure to give the specimen, may be introduced into evidence at the person's trial. *(Added by L.1995, chap. 165(1), eff. 9/1/95.)*

**§724.062. Admissibility of refusal of request for additional test.**

The fact that a person's request to have an additional analysis under Section 724.019 is refused by the officer or another person acting for or on behalf of the state, that the person was not provided a reasonable opportunity to contact a person specified by Section 724.019(a) to take the specimen, or that reasonable access was not allowed to the arrested person may be introduced into evidence at the person's trial. *(Added by L.1995, chap. 165(1), eff. 9/1/95.)*

**§724.063. Admissibility of alcohol concentration or presence of substance.**

Evidence of alcohol concentration or the presence of a controlled substance, drug, dangerous drug, or other substance obtained by an analysis authorized by Section 724.014 is admissible in a civil or criminal action. *(Added by L.1995, chap. 165(1); chgd. by L.1997, chap. 165(30.165), eff. 9/1/97.)*

**§724.064. Admissibility in criminal proceeding of specimen analysis.**

On the trial of a criminal proceeding arising out of an offense under Chapter 49, Penal Code, involving the operation of a motor vehicle or a watercraft, or an offense under Section 106.041, Alcoholic Beverage Code, evidence of the alcohol concentration or presence of a controlled substance, drug, dangerous drug, or other substance as shown by analysis of a specimen of the person's blood, breath, or urine or any other bodily substance taken at the request or order of a peace officer is admissible. *(Added by L.1995, chap. 165(1); chgd. by L.1997, chap. 1013(37), eff. 9/1/97.)*

# CHAPTER 725. TRANSPORTATION OF LOOSE MATERIALS

## SUBCHAPTER A. GENERAL PROVISIONS



## SUBCHAPTER B. REQUIREMENTS FOR TRANSPORTING LOOSE MATERIALS



## SUBCHAPTER A. GENERAL PROVISIONS

**§725.001. Definitions.**

In this chapter:

(1) "Load" means a load of loose material.

(2) "Loose material" means material that can be blown or spilled from a vehicle because of movement or exposure to air, wind currents, or other weather. The term includes dirt, sand, gravel, and wood chips but excludes an agricultural product in its natural state.

(3) "Motor vehicle" has the meaning assigned by Section 621.001.

(4) "Public highway" includes a public road or street.

(5) "Semitrailer" has the meaning assigned by Section 621.001.

(6) "Trailer" has the meaning assigned by Section 621.001.

(7) "Vehicle" has the meaning assigned by Section 621.001.

*(Added by L.1995, chap. 165(1), eff. 9/1/95.)*

### §725.002. Applicability.

This chapter applies to any motor vehicle, trailer, or semitrailer operated on a public highway except:

(1) a vehicle or construction or mining equipment that is:

(A) moving between construction barricades on a public works project; or

(B) crossing a public highway; or

(2) a vehicle that is operated at a speed less than 30 miles per hour.

*(Added by L.1995, chap. 165(1), eff. 9/1/95.)*

### §725.003. Offense; penalty.

(a) A person or the person's agent or employee may not load or transport loose material in violation of this chapter.

(b) A person, excluding this state or a political subdivision of this state but including an agent or employee of this state or a political subdivision of this state, commits an offense if the person violates Subsection (a).

(c) An offense under this section is a misdemeanor punishable by a fine of:

(1) not less than $25 or more than $200 for a first conviction; and

(2) not less than $200 or more than $500 for a second or subsequent conviction.

*(Added by L.1995, chap. 165(1), eff. 9/1/95.)*

### §§725.004 to 725.020. *(Reserved.)*

## SUBCHAPTER B. REQUIREMENTS FOR TRANSPORTING LOOSE MATERIALS

### §725.021. Containing loose materials.

(a) A vehicle subject to this chapter shall be equipped and maintained as required by this section to prevent loose material from escaping by blowing or spilling.

(b) A vehicle bed carrying a load:

(1) may not have a hole, crack, or other opening through which loose material can escape; and

(2) shall be enclosed:

(A) on both sides by side panels;

(B) on the front by a panel or the vehicle cab; and

(C) on the rear by a tailgate or panel.

(c) The load shall be covered and the covering firmly secured at the front and back, unless the load:

(1) is completely enclosed by the load-carrying compartment; or

(2) does not blow or spill over the top of the load-carrying compartment.

(d) The tailgate of the vehicle shall be securely closed to prevent spillage during transportation.

*(Added by L.1995, chap. 165(1), eff. 9/1/95.)*

### §725.022. Maintaining non-load-carrying vehicle parts.

(a) Loose material that is spilled because of loading on a vehicle part that does not carry the load shall be removed before the vehicle is operated on a public highway.

(b) After the vehicle is unloaded and before the vehicle is operated on a public highway, residue of transported loose material on a vehicle part that does not carry the load shall be removed from the vehicle part.

*(Added by L.1995, chap. 165(1), eff. 9/1/95.)*

## CHAPTER 726. TESTING AND INSPECTION OF MOTOR VEHICLES BY CERTAIN MUNICIPALITIES

Section

### §726.001. Applicability.

(a) This chapter applies only to a municipality with a population of more than 290,000.

(b) This section or an ordinance adopted under this section does not apply to a motor vehicle, trailer, or semitrailer operated under a registration certificate issued under Chapter 643.
*(Added by L.1995, chap. 165(1); chgd. by L.1997, chap. 165(30.166), eff. 9/1/97.)*

### §726.002. Testing and inspection of motor vehicles.

A municipality may adopt an ordinance:

(1) requiring each resident of the municipality, including a corporation having its principal office or place of business in the municipality, who owns a motor vehicle used for the transportation of persons or property and each person operating a motor vehicle on the public thoroughfares of the municipality to have each motor vehicle owned or operated, as appropriate, tested and inspected not more than four times in each calendar year;

(2) requiring each motor vehicle involved in an accident to be tested and inspected before it may be operated on the public thoroughfares of the municipality; or

(3) requiring that a motor vehicle operated on the public thoroughfares of the municipality be tested, inspected, and approved by the testing and inspecting authority.
*(Added by L.1995, chap. 165(1), eff. 9/1/95.)*

### §726.003. Motor vehicle testing stations; testing and inspection fee.

(a) A municipality may acquire, establish, improve, operate, and maintain motor vehicle testing stations and pay for the stations from fees charged for testing and inspecting motor vehicles.

(b) A municipality may impose a fee for the testing and inspecting of a motor vehicle. The fee may not exceed $1 a year. Fees collected under this subsection shall be placed in a separate fund from which may be paid the costs in connection with automotive and safety education programs and the acquisition, establishment, improvement, operation, and maintenance of the testing stations.
*(Added by L.1995, chap. 165(1), eff. 9/1/95.)*

### §726.004. Financing of motor vehicle testing stations.

(a) A municipality may borrow money to finance all or part of the cost of the acquisition, establishment, improvement, or repair of motor vehicle testing stations and may pledge all or part of the fees or other receipts derived from the operation of the stations for payment of principal and interest on the loan.

(b) A municipality may encumber a testing station, including things acquired pertaining to the station, to secure the payment of funds to construct all or part of the station or to improve, operate, or maintain the station. An encumbrance is not a debt of the municipality but is solely a charge on the property encumbered and may not be considered in determining the power of the municipality to issue bonds.
*(Added by L.1995, chap. 165(1), eff. 9/1/95.)*

## CHAPTER 727. MODIFICATION OF, TAMPERING WITH, AND EQUIPMENT OF MOTOR VEHICLES

Section


### §727.001. Minimum road clearance of certain vehicles; offense.

(a) A person commits an offense if the person operates on a public roadway a passenger or commercial vehicle that has been modified from its original design or weighted so that the clearance between any part of the vehicle other than the wheels and the surface of the level roadway is less than the clearance between the roadway and the lowest part of the rim of any wheel in contact with the roadway.

(b) An offense under this section is a misdemeanor punishable by a fine not to exceed $50.
*(Added by L.1995, chap. 165(1), eff. 9/1/95.)*

### §727.002. Tampering with odometer; offense.

(a) A person commits an offense if the person, with intent to defraud, disconnects or resets an odometer to reduce the number of miles indicated on the odometer.

(b) Except as provided by Subsection (c), an offense under this section is punishable by:
(1) confinement in the county jail for not more than two years;
(2) a fine not to exceed $1,000; or
(3) both the confinement and fine.

(c) If it is shown on the trial of an offense under this section that the person has previously been convicted of an offense under this section, the offense is punishable by:
(1) confinement in the county jail for not less than 30 days or more than two years; and
(2) a fine not to exceed $2,000.

(d) In this section, "odometer" means an instrument for measuring and recording the distance a motor vehicle travels while in operation but does not include an auxiliary odometer designed to be reset by the operator to record mileage on trips.

*(Added by L.1995, chap. 165(1), eff. 9/1/95.)*

### §727.003. Tire equipment of motor vehicle, trailer, or tractor; offense.

(a) A person commits an offense if the person operates or permits to be operated on a public highway a motor vehicle, trailer, semitrailer, or tractor equipped with:
(1) solid rubber tires less than one inch in thickness at any point from the surface to the rim; or
(2) pneumatic tires, one or more of which has been removed.

(b) An offense under this section is a misdemeanor punishable by a fine not to exceed $200.

*(Added by L.1995, chap. 165(1), eff. 9/1/95.)*

### §727.004. Rim or tire width; offense.

(a) A person commits an offense if the person sells or offers for sale a road vehicle, including a wagon, that has a rim or tire width less than:
(1) three inches, if the vehicle has an intended carrying capacity of more than 2,000 pounds and not more than 4,500 pounds; or
(2) four inches, if the vehicle has an intended carrying capacity of more than 4,500 pounds.

(b) This section does not apply to an individual who sells or offers for sale a road vehicle purchased for the individual's use.

(c) An offense under this section is punishable by a fine of not less than $100 or more than $1,000.

*(Added by L.1995, chap. 165(1), eff. 9/1/95.)*

## CHAPTER 728. SALE OR TRANSFER OF MOTOR VEHICLES AND MASTER KEYS

## SUBCHAPTER A. SALE OF MOTOR VEHICLES ON CONSECUTIVE SATURDAY AND SUNDAY

Section


## SUBCHAPTER B. SALE OF MASTER KEY FOR MOTOR VEHICLE IGNITIONS

## SUBCHAPTER C. TRANSFER OF OWNERSHIP OF CERTAIN EMERGENCY VEHICLES



## SUBCHAPTER A. SALE OF MOTOR VEHICLES ON CONSECUTIVE SATURDAY AND SUNDAY

### §728.001. Definitions.

In this subchapter:

(1) "Employer" means a person who:

(A) owns a facility that sells or offers for sale motor vehicles; or

(B) has the authority to determine the hours of operation of the facility.

(2) "Motor vehicle" means a self-propelled vehicle of two or more wheels designed to transport a person or property.

*(Added by L.1995, chap. 165(1), eff. 9/1/95.)*

### §728.002. Sale of motor vehicles on consecutive Saturday and Sunday prohibited.

(a) A person may not, on consecutive days of Saturday and Sunday:

(1) sell or offer for sale a motor vehicle; or

(2) compel an employee to sell or offer for sale a motor vehicle.

(b) Each day a motor vehicle is offered for sale is a separate violation. Each sale of a motor vehicle is a separate violation.

(c) This section does not prohibit the occasional sale of a motor vehicle by a person not in a business that includes the sale of motor vehicles.

*(Added by L.1995, chap. 165(1), eff. 9/1/95.)*

### §728.003. Civil penalty.

(a) A person who violates Section 728.002 is subject to a civil penalty of:

(1) not more than $500 for a first violation;

(2) not less than $500 or more than $1,000 for a second violation; or

(3) not less than $1,000 or more than $5,000 for a third or subsequent violation.

(b) On a finding by the trier of fact that a person wilfully or with conscious indifference violated Section 728.002, the court may triple the penalty due under Subsection (a).

*(Added by L.1995, chap. 165(1), eff. 9/1/95.)*

### §728.004. Enforcement; injunction.

(a) The attorney general or a district, county, or municipal attorney may enforce this subchapter and may bring an action in the county in which a violation is alleged.

(b) The operation of a business in violation of this subchapter is a public nuisance. Any person, including a district, county, or municipal attorney, may obtain an injunction restraining a violation of this subchapter. A person who obtains an injunction under this subsection may recover the person's costs, including court costs and reasonable attorney's fees.

(c) An employer is a necessary party to an action brought against its employee under this section. An employer is strictly liable for all amounts, including civil penalties, damages, costs, and attorney's fees, resulting from a violation of Section 728.002 by its employee.

*(Added by L.1995, chap. 165(1), eff. 9/1/95.)*

### §§728.005 to 728.010. *(Reserved.)*

## SUBCHAPTER B. SALE OF MASTER KEY FOR MOTOR VEHICLE IGNITIONS

### §728.011. Sale of master key for motor vehicle ignitions.

(a) A person commits an offense if the person sells or offers to sell a master key knowingly designed to fit the ignition switch on more than one motor vehicle.

(b) An offense under this section is a misdemeanor punishable by a fine of not less than $25 or more than $200.

*(Added by L.1995, chap. 165(1), eff. 9/1/95.)*

**§§728.012 to 728.020.** *(Reserved.)*

## SUBCHAPTER C. TRANSFER OF OWNERSHIP OF CERTAIN EMERGENCY VEHICLES

### §728.021. Transfer of ownership of certain emergency vehicles; offense.

(a) The owner of an authorized emergency vehicle that is used to transport sick or injured persons commits an offense if the owner transfers ownership of the vehicle without:

(1) removing from the vehicle any vehicle equipment, including a light, siren, or device, that under Subtitle C only an authorized emergency vehicle may be equipped with; and

(2) removing or obliterating any emblem or marking on the vehicle that identifies the vehicle as an authorized emergency vehicle.

(b) Subsection (a) does not apply if the owner of the vehicle transfers ownership of the vehicle to a person:

(1) who holds a license as an emergency medical services provider under Chapter 773, Health and Safety Code;

(2) who is in the business of buying and selling used vehicles in this state and who specializes in authorized emergency vehicles; or

(3) described by Section 541.201 or a similar person operating in a foreign country.

(c) An offense under this section is a Class C misdemeanor.

(d) In this section:

(1) "Authorized emergency vehicle" has the meaning assigned by Section 541.201.

(2) "Vehicle equipment" has the meaning assigned by Section 547.001.

*(Added by L.1995, chap. 165(1), eff. 9/1/95.)*

## CHAPTER 729. OPERATION OF MOTOR VEHICLE BY MINOR

Section


### §729.001. Operation of motor vehicle by minor in violation of traffic laws; offense.

(a) A person who is younger than 17 years of age commits an offense if the person operates a motor vehicle on a public road or highway, a street or alley in a municipality, or a public beach in violation of any traffic law of this state, including:

(1) Chapter 502, other than Section 502.282 or 502.412;

(2) Chapter 521;

(3) Subtitle C, other than an offense under Section 550.021, 550.022, or 550.024;

(4) Chapter 601;

(5) Chapter 621;

(6) Chapter 661; and

(7) Chapter 681.

(b) In this section, "beach" means a beach bordering on the Gulf of Mexico that extends inland from the line of mean low tide to the natural line of vegetation bordering on the seaward shore of the Gulf of Mexico, or the larger contiguous area to which the public has acquired a right of use or easement to or over by prescription, dedication, or estoppel, or has retained a right by virtue of continuous right in the public since time immemorial as recognized by law or custom.

(c) An offense under this section is punishable by the fine or other sanction, other than confinement or imprisonment, authorized by statute for violation of the traffic law listed under Subsection (a) that is the basis of the prosecution under this section.

*(Added by L.1995, chap. 165(1); chgd. by L.1997, chaps. 165(30.167), 822(1), 1086(40); L.1999, chap. 1477(36), eff. 9/1/99.)*

### §729.002. Operation of motor vehicle by minor without license.

(a) A person who is younger than 17 years of age commits an offense if the person operates a motor vehicle without a driver's license authorizing the operation of a motor vehicle on a:

(1) public road or highway;

(2) street or alley in a municipality; or

(3) public beach as defined by Section 729.001.

(b) An offense under this section is punishable in the same manner as if the person was 17 years of age or older and operated a motor vehicle without a license as described by Subsection (a), except that an offense under this section is not punishable by confinement or imprisonment.
*(Added by L.1995, chap. 165(1); chgd. by L.1997, chap. 1086(43); L.1999, chap. 1477(37), eff. 9/1/99.)*

### §729.003. Procedure and jurisdiction in cases involving minors.

(a) A person may not plead guilty to an offense under Section 729.001 or 729.002 or to a violation of a motor vehicle traffic ordinance of an incorporated city or town except in open court before a judge. A person may not be convicted of an offense or fined as provided by this chapter or under a municipal traffic ordinance except in the presence of one or both parents or guardians having legal custody of the person. The court shall summon one or both parents or guardians to appear in court and shall require one or both of them to be present during all proceedings in the case. The court may waive the requirement of the presence of parents or guardians if, after diligent effort, the court cannot locate them or compel their presence.

(b) The provisions of the Code of Criminal Procedure relating to release of a defendant on bail apply to a person charged with a traffic offense under this chapter.

(c) A person detained for an offense under this chapter shall be detained in a facility that complies with Section 51.12, Family Code.

(d) A court shall report to the Department of Public Safety a person charged with a traffic offense under this chapter who does not appear before the court as required by law. In addition to any other action or remedy provided by law, the department may deny renewal of the person's driver's license under Section 521.310 or Chapter 706. The court also shall report to the department on final disposition of the case.

(e) A person may not be committed to a jail in default of payment of a fine imposed under this chapter, but the court imposing the fine shall report the default to the Department of Public Safety. The court also shall report to the department on final disposition of the case.

(f) The court may order a person convicted of an offense under this chapter to perform a specified number of hours of community service in lieu of a fine.

(g) An offense under this chapter is within the jurisdiction of the courts regularly empowered to try misdemeanors carrying the penalty provided by this chapter and is not within the jurisdiction of a juvenile court. This chapter does not otherwise affect the powers and duties of juvenile courts.
*(Added by L.1995, chap. 165(1); chgd. by L.1997, chaps. 165(30.168(a)), 1086(44), eff. 9/1/97.)*

### §729.004. Fine for offense in construction or maintenance work zone.

(a) This section applies to an offense under Section 729.001 for a violation of Subtitle C, other than Chapter 548 or 552 or Section 545.412 or 545.413.

(b) If an offense to which this section applies is committed in a construction or maintenance work zone when workers are present and any written notice to appear issued for the offense states on its face that workers were present when the offense was committed:

(1) the minimum fine applicable to the offense is twice the minimum fine that would be applicable to the offense if it were committed outside a construction or maintenance work zone; and

(2) the maximum fine applicable to the offense is twice the maximum fine that would be applicable to the offense if it were committed outside a construction or maintenance work zone.

(c) In this section, "construction or maintenance work zone" has the meaning assigned by Section 472.022.
*(Added by L.1997, chap. 674(3); chgd. by L.1999, chap. 789(4), eff. 9/1/99.)*

## CHAPTER 730. MOTOR VEHICLE RECORDS DISCLOSURE ACT

*(Added by L.1997, chap. 1187(1), eff. 9/1/97.)*

Section

### §730.001. Short title.

This chapter may be cited as the Motor Vehicle Records Disclosure Act. *(Added by L.1997, chap. 1187(1), eff. 9/1/97.)*

### §730.002. Purpose.

The purpose of this chapter is to implement 18 U.S.C. Chapter 123 and to protect the interest of an individual in the individual's personal privacy by prohibiting the disclosure and use of personal information contained in motor vehicle records, except as authorized by the individual or by law. *(Added by L.1997, chap. 1187(1), eff. 9/1/97.)*

### §730.003. Definitions.

In this chapter:

(1) "Agency" includes any agency of this state, or an authorized agent or contractor of an agency of this state, that compiles or maintains motor vehicle records.

(2) "Disclose" means to make available or make known personal information contained in a motor vehicle record about a person to another person, by any means of communication.

(3) "Individual record" means a motor vehicle record obtained by an agency containing personal information about an individual who is the subject of the record as identified in a request.

(4) "Motor vehicle record" means a record that pertains to a motor vehicle operator's or driver's license or permit, motor vehicle registration, motor vehicle title, or identification document issued by an agency of this state or a local agency authorized to issue an identification document. The term does not include a record that pertains to a motor carrier.

(5) "Person" means an individual, organization, or entity but does not include this state or an agency of this state.

(6) "Personal information" means information that identifies a person, including an individual's photograph or computerized image, social security number, driver identification number, name, address, but not the zip code, telephone number, and medical or disability information. The term does not include information on vehicle accidents, driving or equipment-related violations, or driver's license or registration status.

(7) "Record" includes any book, paper, photograph, photostat, card, film, tape, recording, electronic data, printout, or other documentary material regardless of physical form or characteristics.

*(Added by L.1997, chap. 1187(1), eff. 9/1/97.)*

### §730.004. Prohibition on disclosure and use of personal information from motor vehicle records.

Notwithstanding any other provision of law to the contrary, including Chapter 552, Government Code, except as provided by Sections 730.005-730.008, an agency may not disclose personal information about any person obtained by the agency in connection with a motor vehicle record. *(Added by L.1997, chap. 1187(1), eff. 9/1/97.)*

### §730.005. Required disclosure.

Personal information obtained by an agency in connection with a motor vehicle record shall be disclosed for use in connection with any matter of:

(1) motor vehicle or motor vehicle operator safety;

(2) motor vehicle theft;

(3) motor vehicle emissions;

(4) motor vehicle product alterations, recalls, or advisories;

(5) performance monitoring of motor vehicles or motor vehicle dealers by a motor vehicle manufacturer; or

(6) removal of nonowner records from the original owner records of a motor vehicle manufacturer to carry out the purposes of:

(A) the Automobile Information Disclosure Act, 15 U.S.C. Section 1231 et seq.;

(B) 49 U.S.C. Chapters 301, 305, 323, 325, 327, 329, and 331;

(C) the Anti Car Theft Act of 1992, 18 U.S.C. Sections 553, 981, 982, 2119, 2312, 2313, and 2322, 19 U.S.C. Sections 1646b and 1646c, and 42 U.S.C. Section 3750a et seq., all as amended;

(D) the Clean Air Act, 42 U.S.C. Section 7401 et seq., as amended; and

(E) any other statute or regulation enacted or adopted under or in relation to a law included in Paragraphs (A)-(D).

*(Added by L.1997, chap. 1187(1), eff. 9/1/97.)*

## §730.006. Required disclosure with consent.

Personal information obtained by an agency in connection with a motor vehicle record shall be disclosed to a requestor who demonstrates, in such form and manner as the agency requires, that the requestor has obtained the written consent of the person who is the subject of the information.

*(Added by L.1997, chap. 1187(1), eff. 9/1/97.)*

## §730.007. Permitted disclosures.

(a) Personal information obtained by an agency in connection with a motor vehicle record may be disclosed to any requestor by an agency if the requestor:

(1) provides the requestor's name and address and any proof of that information required by the agency; and

(2) represents that the use of the personal information will be strictly limited to:

(A) use by:

(i) a government agency, including any court or law enforcement agency, in carrying out its functions; or

(ii) a private person or entity acting on behalf of a government agency in carrying out the functions of the agency;

(B) use in connection with a matter of:

(i) motor vehicle or motor vehicle operator safety;

(ii) motor vehicle theft;

(iii) motor vehicle product alterations, recalls, or advisories;

(iv) performance monitoring of motor vehicles, motor vehicle parts, or motor vehicle dealers;

(v) motor vehicle market research activities, including survey research; or

(vi) removal of nonowner records from the original owner records of motor vehicle manufacturers;

(C) use in the normal course of business by a legitimate business or an agent, employee, or contractor of the business, but only:

(i) to verify the accuracy of personal information submitted by the individual to the business or an agent, employee, or contractor of the business; and

(ii) if the information as submitted is not correct or is no longer correct, to obtain the correct information, for the sole purpose of preventing fraud by, pursuing a legal remedy against, or recovering on a debt or security interest against the individual;

(D) use in conjunction with a civil, criminal, administrative, or arbitral proceeding in any court or government agency or before any self-regulatory body, including service of process, investigation in anticipation of litigation, execution or enforcement of a judgment or order, or under an order of any court;

(E) use in research or in producing statistical reports, but only if the personal information is not published, redisclosed, or used to contact any individual;

(F) use by an insurer or insurance support organization, or by a self-insured entity, or an agent, employee, or contractor of the entity, in connection with claims investigation activities, antifraud activities, rating, or underwriting;

(G) use in providing notice to an owner of a towed or impounded vehicle;

(H) use by a licensed private investigator agency or licensed security service for a purpose permitted under this section;

(I) use by an employer or an agent or insurer of the employer to obtain or verify information relating to a holder of a commercial driver's license that is required under 49 U.S.C. Chapter 313;

(J) use in connection with the operation of a private toll transportation facility;

(K) use for bulk distribution for surveys, marketing, or solicitations, but only if the agency has implemented procedures to ensure that:

(i) persons are provided an opportunity, in a clear and conspicuous manner, to opt out and prohibit those uses; and

(ii) the information will be used, rented, or sold solely for bulk distribution for surveys, marketing, or solicitations, and that surveys, marketing, or solicitations will not be directed at any individual who has timely requested that the material not be directed at that individual; and

(L) use for any other purpose specifically authorized by law that relates to the operation of a motor vehicle or to public safety.

(b) The only personal information an agency may release under this section is the individual's:

(1) name and address;

(2) date of birth; and

(3) driver's license number.

*(Added by L.1997, chap. 1187(1), eff. 9/1/97.)*

### §730.008. Disclosure of individual record.

(a) Personal information obtained by an agency in connection with a motor vehicle record that is contained in an individual record may be disclosed to a requestor without regard to intended use if the Department of Public Safety has:

(1) provided, in a clear and conspicuous manner on forms for issuance or renewal of an operator's or driver's license, registration, title, or identification document, notice that personal information collected by the Department of Public Safety may be disclosed to any person making a request for an individual record; and

(2) provided in a clear and conspicuous manner on that form an opportunity for each person who is the subject of the record to prohibit that disclosure.

(b) An agency may include the notice described by Subsection (a)(1) on forms used by members of the general public.

*(Added by L.1997, chap. 1187(1), eff. 9/1/97.)*

### §730.009. Requests to prohibit disclosure.

Each agency shall distinguish between a request by a person under Section 730.008 to prohibit disclosure of personal information in the person's individual record and a request under Section 730.007(a)(2)(K) by a person to prohibit disclosure of that information. *(Added by L.1997, chap. 1187(1), eff. 9/1/97.)*

### §730.010. Disclosure of thumb or finger images prohibited.

Notwithstanding any other provision of this chapter, if an agency obtains an image of an individual's thumb or finger in connection with the issuance of a license, permit, or certificate to the individual, the agency may:

(1) use the image only in connection with the issuance of the license, permit, or certificate; and

(2) disclose the image only if disclosure is expressly authorized by law.

*(Added by L.1997, chap. 1187(1), eff. 9/1/97.)*

### §730.011. Fees.

Unless a fee is imposed by law, an agency that has obtained information in connection with a motor vehicle may adopt reasonable fees for disclosure of that personal information under this chapter. *(Added by L.1997, chap. 1187(1), eff. 9/1/97.)*

### §730.012. Additional conditions.

(a) In addition to the payment of a fee adopted under Section 730.011, an agency may require a requestor to provide reasonable assurance:

(1) as to the identity of the requestor; and

(2) that use of the personal information will be only as authorized or that the consent of the person who is the subject of the information has been obtained.

(b) An agency may require the requestor to make or file a written application in the form and containing any certification requirement the agency may prescribe.

*(Added by L.1997, chap. 1187(1), eff. 9/1/97.)*

### §730.013. Resale or redisclosure.

(a) An authorized recipient of personal information, other than a recipient under Section 730.007(a)(2)(K)(ii) or Section 730.008, may resell or redisclose the information for any use permitted under Section 730.007, other than a use described by Section 730.007(a)(2)(K)(ii).

(b) An authorized recipient of an individual record under Section 730.008 may resell or redisclose personal information for any purpose.

(c) An authorized recipient of personal information for bulk distribution for surveys, marketing, or solicitations under Section 730.007(a)(2)(K)(ii) may resell or redisclose personal information only in compliance with the terms of that section.

(d) Any authorized recipient who resells or rediscloses personal information obtained from an agency shall be required by that agency to:

(1) maintain for a period of not less than five years records as to any person or entity receiving that information and the permitted use for which it was obtained; and

(2) make those records available for inspection by the agency on request.

*(Added by L.1997, chap. 1187(1), eff. 9/1/97.)*

### §730.014. Agency rules; organization of records.

(a) Each agency may adopt rules to implement and administer this chapter.

(b) An agency that maintains motor vehicle records in relation to motor vehicles is not required to also maintain those records in relation to the individuals named in those records.

*(Added by L.1997, chap. 1187(1), eff. 9/1/97.)*

### §730.015. Penalty for false representation.

(a) A person who requests the disclosure of personal information from an agency's records under this chapter and misrepresents the person's identity or who makes a false statement to the agency on an application required by the agency under this chapter commits an offense.

(b) An offense under Subsection (a) is a Class A misdemeanor.

*(Added by L.1997, chap. 1187(1), eff. 9/1/97.)*



## CHAPTER 731. DISCLOSURE OF PERSONAL INFORMATION FROM MOTOR VEHICLE RECORDS

*(Added by L.1997, chap. 1187(2), eff. 9/1/97.)*

Section



### §731.001. Definitions.

In this chapter:

(1) "Agency" means an agency of this state that compiles or maintains motor vehicle records. The term includes the Department of Public Safety and the Texas Department of Transportation.

(2) "Internet" means the international computer network of federal and nonfederal interoperable packet switched data networks or a similar computer bulletin board or computer network accessible to the public.

(3) "Motor vehicle record" means a record that pertains to a motor vehicle operator's or driver's license or permit, motor vehicle registration, motor vehicle title, or identification document issued by an agency or a local governmental entity authorized to issue an identification document. The term includes a driver record maintained by the Department of Public Safety.

(4) "Personal information" means information that identifies an individual, including an individual's photograph or computerized photographic image, social security number, driver identification number, personal identification certificate number, name, address other than the postal routing code, telephone number, and medical or disability information. The term does not include information on vehicular accidents, driving violations, or driver's license status.

*(Added by L.1997, chap. 1187(2), eff. 9/1/97.)*

### §731.002. Release of personal information by agency.

Notwithstanding any other law, including Chapter 501, 502, 521, or 522 of this code and Chapter 552, Government Code, an agency is prohibited from providing a person with personal information from the agency's motor vehicle records unless the person receiving the information is the individual to whom the information pertains or that individual's agent or the person agrees in writing with the agency that the person will not:

(1) disseminate or publish the information on the internet; or

(2) permit another to disseminate or publish the information on the internet.
*(Added by L.1997, chap. 1187(2), eff. 9/1/97.)*

### §731.003. Publication or disclosure of personal information on internet.

A person may not publish or disclose on the internet personal information from a motor vehicle record that has been obtained directly or indirectly from an agency without the consent of the individual to whom the information pertains. *(Added by L.1997, chap. 1187(2), eff. 9/1/97.)*

### §731.004. Civil enforcement.

A district or county attorney or the attorney general may file suit in a district court to enjoin a violation of this chapter or to compel compliance with this chapter. *(Added by L.1997, chap. 1187(2), eff. 9/1/97.)*

### §731.005. Civil cause of action.

(a) A person who knowingly discloses or uses personal information from an agency's motor vehicle records in violation of this chapter is liable for damages caused by the disclosure or use in an action brought in a district court by the individual to whom the information relates.

(b) A person who brings a suit under Subsection (a) may recover:

(1) actual damages or, if actual damages are less than $2,500, actual damages and liquidated damages of not less than $2,500;

(2) punitive damages, on proof of wilful or reckless disregard of the law;

(3) reasonable attorney's fees and litigation costs; and

(4) other equitable and preliminary relief that the court finds appropriate.

*(Added by L.1997, chap. 1187(2), eff. 9/1/97.)*

### §731.006. False statement to agency; penalty.

(a) A person commits an offense if the person makes a false statement or representation to an agency to obtain personal information pertaining to any individual from the agency's motor vehicle records.

(b) An offense under this section is a Class A misdemeanor.

*(Added by L.1997, chap. 1187(2), eff. 9/1/97.)*

### §731.007. Dissemination or publication of personal information on internet prohibited; penalty.

(a) A person commits an offense if the person:

(1) has access to or is in possession of personal information obtained from an agency's motor vehicle records; and

(2) disseminates or publishes the information on the internet without the consent of the individual to whom the information pertains.

(b) An offense under Subsection (a) is a Class A misdemeanor.

*(Added by L.1997, chap. 1187(2), eff. 9/1/97.)*

### §731.008. Affirmative defense to civil action or prosecution.

It is an affirmative defense to an action brought under Section 731.005 or to a prosecution brought under Section 731.007 that the person disclosed or used the personal information of the individual in compliance with and for a purpose authorized by the federal Driver's Privacy Protection Act of 1994 (18 U.S.C. Section 2721 et seq.). *(Added by L.1997, chap. 1187(2), eff. 9/1/97.)*

### §731.009. Rules.

Each agency to which this chapter applies shall adopt rules to implement and enforce this chapter. *(Added by L.1997, chap. 1187(2), eff. 9/1/97.)*

## CHAPTERS 730 to 749. *(Reserved.)*

## CHAPTER 750. MISCELLANEOUS PROVISIONS

Section

**§750.001.** *(Repealed by L.1997, chap. 165(30.169), eff. 9/1/97.)*

**§750.002. Speed of vehicle in park in county bordering Gulf of Mexico.**

(a) A person commits an offense if the person drives a vehicle at a speed greater than 30 miles per hour within the boundaries of a county park located in a county that borders on the Gulf of Mexico, other than on a beach as that term is defined by Section 61.012, Natural Resources Code, in the park.

(b) An offense under this section is a misdemeanor punishable by a fine of not less than $1 or more than $200.

*(Added by L.1995, chap. 165(1), eff. 9/1/95.)*

## TITLE 8. REGULATION OF MOTOR CARRIERS

*(Repealed by L.1997, chap. 165(30.170), eff. 9/1/97.)*

# VEHICLE LAWS

*(See also Transportation Code, supra, for newly codified provisions.)*

# CIVIL STATUTES

*(Selected Articles)*

## LAWS RELATING TO COMMERCIAL DRIVER-TRAINING SCHOOLS AND INSTRUCTORS—LICENSING

4413(29c). Texas Driver and Traffic Safety Education Act.
5221f.
  Sec. 18(f). Texas Manufactured Housing Standards Act.
6419a. Railroads—engineer's operator permits.† [*Railroads—engineer's operator permit.*]
6419b. Duty to stop and render aid.† [*Duty to stop at accidents.*]

## LAWS RELATING TO REGISTRATION OF VEHICLES

6675c. *(Repealed.)*
6675c-1. *(Repealed.)*
6675c-2. *(Repealed.)*
6675-d. *(Repealed.)*

## LAWS RELATING TO DRIVER'S LICENSE

6687d. *(Repealed.)*

## LAWS RELATING TO CERTIFICATE OF TITLE

6687-1a. Salvage vehicle dealers.
6687-2. Vehicle salvage dealers.
6687-2a. Injunction; salvage vehicle dealers.
6687-2b. Hours of operation of motor vehicle salvage yard in populous counties.
6687-7. Repaired vehicle records.† [*Records of vehicle repairs.*]
6687-9a. Vehicle Storage Facility Act.

## LAWS RELATING TO SAFETY RESPONSIBILITY

6701j-2. Railroad and highway grade crossing safety instruction.

## LAWS RELATING TO FUEL MIXTURES

8614. Sales of certain fuel mixtures.

## LAWS RELATING TO COMMERCIAL DRIVER-TRAINING SCHOOLS AND INSTRUCTORS—LICENSING

### Art. 4413(29c). Texas Driver and Traffic Safety Education Act.

**Sec. 1. Short title.** This Act may be cited as the Texas Driver and Traffic Safety Education Act.

**Sec. 2. Purpose and objectives.** Traffic crashes in Texas annually take the lives of thousands of people and cause billions of dollars in economic losses. These alarming facts make safe driving a concern for all citizens of the state. Deaths, injuries, and property damage must be reduced. The attitudes and skills of drivers must be improved through effective driver education and training. It is a matter of vital public importance to identify and implement all reasonable means to reduce the toll in human suffering and property loss that is inflicted by vehicle crashes. The purpose of this Act is to improve driver knowledge and skills through the licensing and regulation by the Central Education Agency of driver training schools and driver training instructors in Texas. It is additionally intended that state agency rules affecting schools that qualify as small businesses be established and administered so as to have the least possible adverse economic effect on those establishments.

**Sec. 3. Definitions.** In this Act:

(1) "Agency" means the Central Education Agency, acting directly or through its authorized officers and agents.

(2) "Board" means the State Board of Education.

(3) "Commissioner" means the commissioner of education or a person knowledgeable in the administration of regulating driver training schools and designated by the commissioner to administer this Act.

(4) "Driver education" means a nonvocational course of instruction that provides the knowledge and hands-on experience to prepare persons for written and practical driving tests that lead to authorization to operate a vehicle.

(5) "Driver training" means driver education provided by a driver education school and driving safety training provided by a driving safety school.

(6) "Driving safety course" means a course of instruction intended to improve a driver's knowledge, perceptions, and attitudes about driving.

(7) "School" means a driver education school or driving safety school.

(8) "Operator" means a person approved by a driving safety course owner or consignee to conduct an approved driving safety course.

(9) "Owner" means:

(A) in the case of a school owned by an individual, the individual;

(B) in the case of a school owned by a partnership, all full, silent, or limited partners; or

(C) in the case of a school owned by a corporation, the corporation, its directors, officers, and each shareholder owning at least 10 percent of the total of the issued and outstanding shares.

(10) "Person" means an individual, firm, partnership, association, corporation, or other private entity or combination of persons.

(11) "School employee" means any person, other than an owner, who directly or indirectly receives compensation from the school for instructional or other services rendered.

(12) "Support" means the primary source and means by which a school derives revenue.

(13) "Suspension of enrollment" means a ruling by the commissioner that restricts a school from accepting enrollments or reenrollments, advertising, soliciting, or directly or indirectly advising prospective students of its program or course offerings.

(14) "Uniform certificate of completion" means a document that is printed, administered, and supplied by the agency to owners or primary consignees for issuance to students who successfully complete an approved driving safety course and that meets the requirements of Section 143A, Uniform Act Regulating Traffic on Highways (Article 6701d, Texas Civil Statutes).

(15) "Instructor" means an individual who has been licensed by the agency for the type of instruction being given.

(16) "Approved driving safety course" means a driving safety course approved by the board.

(17) "Course provider" means an enterprise that maintains a place of business or solicits business in this state, that is operated by an individual, association, partnership, or corporation, and that is a driving safety course owner or primary consignee.

(18) "Driver education school" means an enterprise that maintains a place of business or solicits business in this state, that is operated by an individual, association, partnership, or corporation for the education and training of persons at a primary or branch location in driver education or driver education instructor development, and that is not specifically exempted by this Act.

(19) "Driver education school owner" means a person who has been approved by the commissioner to own and operate a driver education school.

(20) "Driving safety course owner" means an enterprise that is operated by an individual, association, partnership, or corporation that has received an approval for a driving safety course from the board.

(21) "Driving safety school" means an enterprise that maintains a place of business or solicits business in this state, that is operated by an individual, association, partnership, or corporation for the education and training of persons in driving safety, and that is not specifically exempted by this Act. A driving safety school may use multiple classroom locations to teach a driving safety course if each location is approved by the parent school and the agency and bears the same name and has the same ownership as the parent school.

(22) "Primary consignee" means any enterprise that is operated by an individual, association, partnership, or corporation that has been designated by a driving safety course owner to conduct business and represent the course owner in this state.

(23) "Drug and alcohol driving awareness program" means a course with particular emphasis on curricula designed to prevent or deter misuse and abuse of controlled substances.
*(Chgd. by L.1999, chap. 1489(1), eff. 9/1/99.)*

**Sec. 4. General powers and duties.** (a) The agency shall exercise jurisdiction and control of the system of schools, and the commissioner shall administer this Act and enforce minimum standards for schools under this Act.

(b) The agency shall enter into a memorandum of understanding with the Texas Rehabilitation Commission and the Department of Public Safety for the interagency development of curricula and licensing criteria for hospital and rehabilitation facilities that teach driver education. The agency shall administer comprehensive rules governing driver education courses adopted by mutual agreement between the board, the Texas Rehabilitation Commission, and the Department of Public Safety. The agency shall file the rules with the secretary of state.

(c) The agency by rule shall require that information relating to alcohol awareness and the effect of alcohol on the effective operation of a motor vehicle be included in the curriculum of any driver education or driving safety course that is governed by this article. The agency shall consult with the Department of Public Safety in developing those rules.
*(Chgd. by L.1999, chap. 762(1), eff. 6/18/99.)*

**Sec. 4A. Drug and alcohol driving awareness programs.** (a) The agency shall develop standards for a separate school certification and approve educational curricula under this Act for drug and alcohol driving awareness programs. The programs may include one or more courses. Except as provided by rules adopted by the agency, the programs must be offered in the same manner as driving safety courses offered in compliance with this Act.

(b) The agency and the Texas Commission on Alcohol and Drug Abuse shall enter into a memorandum of understanding for the interagency approval of the educational curricula required by Subsection (a) of this section, in accordance with Section 461.013(b), Health and Safety Code.

(c) The standards adopted by the agency for drug and alcohol driving awareness programs may require the course provider to evaluate procedures, projects, techniques, and controls conducted as part of the educational programs.

(d) The board may establish fees in connection with drug and alcohol driving awareness programs in lieu of the fees established under Section 13 of this Act. The fees established under this subsection shall be in amounts reasonable and necessary to implement and administer this Act in connection with drug and alcohol driving awareness programs.
*(Added by L.1999, chap. 1489(2), eff. 9/1/99.)*

**Sec. 5.** *(Repealed by L.1993, chap. 771(19)(6), eff. 9/1/93.)*

**Sec. 6. Duties of commissioner.** (a) The commissioner shall carry out the policies of this Act, adopt rules necessary to implement this Act, enforce rules adopted by the commissioner, and certify those schools and course providers meeting the requirements for a driver education school license, driving safety school license, or both, or for a course provider license. A reference in another provision of this Act to a rule adopted by the board means a rule adopted by the commissioner.

(b) The commissioner by rule shall establish the curriculum and designate the textbooks that must be used in a driver education course.

(c) The commissioner by rule shall require that information relating to litter prevention be included in the curriculum of each driver education and driving safety course. The commissioner shall consult the Department of Public Safety in developing rules under this subsection.
*(Chgd. by L.1999, chap. 604(1), eff. 6/18/99.)*

**Sec. 7. Exemptions.** (a) An organization is exempt from this Act if it has 50,000 or more members, qualifies for a tax exemption under Section 501(a), Internal Revenue Code of 1986 (26 U.S.C. Section 501(a)), based on being listed under Section 501(c) (4), Internal Revenue Code of 1986 (26 U.S.C. Section 501(c) (4)), and conducts for its members and other individuals who are at least 50 years of age a driving safety course that is not used for purposes of Section 143A, Uniform Act Regulating Traffic on Highways (Article 6701d, Texas Civil Statutes).

(b) Classes of a nonexempt course that are taught without providing a uniform certificate of completion to graduates of the course are exempt from this Act.

(c) A driver education course is exempt from this Act, except Section 9A of this Act, if it is:

(1) a vocational driver training school operated to train or prepare a person for a field of endeavor in a business, trade, technical, or industrial occupation;

(2) a school or training program that offers only instruction of purely avocational or recreational subjects as determined by the commissioner;

(3) a course of instruction or study sponsored by an employer for the training of its own employees, and no tuition is charged to a student;

(4) a course of study or instruction sponsored by a recognized trade, business, or professional organization for the instruction of the members of the organization with a closed membership; or

(5) a school that is otherwise regulated and approved under any other state law.

**Sec. 8. Competitive bidding; advertising.** (a) The board may not adopt rules to restrict competitive bidding or advertising by a driver training school except to prohibit false, misleading, or deceptive competitive bidding or advertising practices. Specifically, no rule may restrict:

(1) the use of an advertising medium;

(2) the outside dimensions of a printed advertisement or outdoor display;

(3) the duration of an advertisement; or

(4) advertisement under a trade name.

(b) The board may adopt rules to restrict advertising by a branch location of a school so that the branch location adequately identifies its primary driver training school in any solicitation.



**Sec. 9. Prohibitions.** A person may not:

(1) operate a school that provides a driver education course without a driver education school license issued by the commissioner;

(2) operate a school that provides driving safety courses without a driving safety school license issued by the commissioner;

(3) operate as a course provider without a course provider license issued by the commissioner;

(4) utilize advertising designed to mislead or deceive a prospective student;

(5) fail to notify the commissioner of the discontinuance of the operation of any school within three working days after cessation of classes and make available accurate records as required by this Act;

(6) issue, sell, trade, or transfer a uniform certificate of completion or driver education certificate to any person or school not authorized to possess it;

(7) issue, sell, trade, or transfer:

(A) a uniform certificate of completion to a person who has not successfully completed an approved, six-hour driving safety course; or

(B) a driver education certificate to a person who has not successfully completed a board-approved driver education course;

(8) negotiate any promissory instrument received as payment of tuition or other charge before completion of 75 percent of the course, except that before that time, the instrument may be assigned to a purchaser who will be subject to all the defenses available against the school named as payee;

(9) conduct any part of an approved driver education or driving safety course without an instructor who is physically present in appropriate proximity to the student for the type of instruction being given; or

(10) violate any provision of this Act.

**Sec. 9A. Driver education certificates.** The agency shall print and supply to licensed and exempt driver education schools serially numbered driver education certificates to be used for certifying completion of an approved driver education course for the purposes of Section 7(a), Chapter 173, Acts of the 47th Legislature, Regular Session, 1941 (Article 6687b, Texas Civil Statutes). The agency by rule shall provide for the design and distribution of the certificates in a manner that to the greatest extent possible prevents the unauthorized reproduction or misuse of the certificates. The agency may charge a fee of not more than $4 for each certificate.

**Sec. 10. License required for driver training school.** A person may not operate a driver training school unless a driver training school license for the school has been secured.

**Sec. 10A. Branch locations.** A driver education school that teaches a driver education course at one or more branch locations other than the main business location of the school must obtain a driver education school license for the main business location of the school and a driver education school license for each branch location. A branch location of a branch location is not permitted.

**Sec. 10B. Course at public or private school.** A licensed driver training school may conduct a driver training course at a public or private school for students of the public or private school as provided by an agreement with the public or private school. The course is subject to all requirements of law applicable to a course conducted at the main business location of the driver training school.

**Sec. 11. Locations authorized for instruction.** Driving safety courses complying with Section 143A, Uniform Act Regulating Traffic on Highways (Article 6701d, Texas Civil Statutes), may be taught at a driving safety school if the entity is approved by the agency. If the commissioner determines that an approved driving safety course can be taught by an alternative delivery method that does not require the students to be present in a classroom and that includes testing and security measures that are at least as secure as the measures available in a usual classroom, the commissioner may approve the alternative method. On approval, the alternative delivery method is considered to satisfy the requirements of this Act for a driving safety course, and the school may use the alternative delivery method. A location at which a person taking the course by the alternative method receives supplies or equipment for the course is considered a classroom of the school providing the course.



**Sec. 12. Application for school license.** (a) To operate or do business in this state, a school must make written application to the commissioner for a driver education or driving safety school license. The application must be verified, be in the form prescribed by the board, and include all information required. A driving safety school shall obtain approval from the agency for any multiple classroom locations.

(b) A school may not maintain, advertise, solicit for, or conduct any course of instruction in this state before the later of:

(1) the 30th day after the date the school applies for a driver training school license; or

(2) the date the school receives a driver training school license from the commissioner.

(c) Any contract entered into with any person for a course of instruction by or on behalf of any person operating any school to which a driver training school license has not been issued under this Act is unenforceable.

**Sec. 13. Requisites for license.** (a) The commissioner shall approve the application of a driver education school when the school is found, on investigation at the premises of the school, to meet the following criteria:

(1) the courses, curriculum, and instruction are of such quality, content, and length as may reasonably and adequately achieve the stated objective for which the courses, curriculum, and instruction are offered;

(2) there are in the school, and in the provision for behind-the-wheel instruction, adequate space, equipment, instructional material, and instructors to provide training of good quality;

(3) educational and experience qualifications of directors, instructors, and administrators are adequate;

(4) a copy of the schedule of tuition, fees, refund policy, and other charges, regulations pertaining to absence, grading policy, and rules of operation and conduct, and the name, mailing address, and telephone number of the agency for the purpose of directing complaints to the agency is furnished to each student before enrollment;

(5) on completion of training, each student is given a certificate by the school indicating the course name and satisfactory completion;

(6) adequate records as prescribed by the commissioner are kept to show attendance and progress or grades, and satisfactory standards relating to attendance, progress, and conduct are enforced;

(7) the school complies with all county, municipal, state, and federal regulations, including fire, building, and sanitation codes and assumed name registration;

(8) the school is financially sound and capable of fulfilling its commitments for training;

(9) the school's administrators, directors, owners, and instructors are of good reputation and character;

(10) the school has, maintains, and publishes as part of its student enrollment contract the proper policy for the refund of the unused portion of tuition, fees, and other charges if a student enrolled by the school fails to take the course or withdraws or is discontinued from the school at any time before completion;

(11) the school does not use erroneous or misleading advertising, either by actual statement, omission, or intimation, as determined by the board;

(12) the school does not use a name like or similar to the name of another existing school or tax-supported educational establishment in this state, unless specifically approved in writing by the commissioner;

(13) the school submits to the agency for approval the applicable course hour lengths and curriculum content for each course offered by the school;

(14) the school does not owe a civil penalty under this Act; and

(15) additional criteria as may be required by the agency.

(a-1) The commissioner shall approve the application of a driving safety school if on investigation the agency finds that:

(1) the school presents the driving safety course, curriculum, and instruction in a quality, content, and length that reasonably and adequately achieve the stated objective for which the course, curriculum, and instruction are developed by the course provider;

(2) the school has adequate space, equipment, instructional material, and instructors to provide training of good quality;

(3) the school's instructors and administrators have adequate educational and experience qualifications;

(4) the school keeps and maintains adequate records as prescribed by the commissioner to show attendance and progress of grades and that satisfactory standards relating to attendance, progress, and conduct are enforced;

(5) the school complies with all county, municipal, state, and federal law, including fire, building, and sanitation codes and assumed name registration;

(6) the school's administrators, owners, and instructors are of good reputation and character;

(7) the school does not use erroneous or misleading advertising, either by actual statement, omission, or intimation, as determined by the board;

(8) the school does not use a name like or similar to the name of another existing school or tax-supported educational establishment in this state unless specifically approved in writing by the commissioner;

(9) the school has, maintains, and uses the approved contract and policies developed by the course provider;

(10) the school does not owe a civil penalty under this Act;

(11) the school will not provide a driving safety course to any person for a cost less than $25; and

(12) the school meets additional criteria required by the board.

(a-2) The commissioner shall approve the application of a person to be a course provider if on investigation the agency finds that:

(1) the course provider has an approved course;

(2) the course provider can show evidence that there is at least one licensed driving safety school that is willing to offer the course;

(3) the course provider has adequate educational and experience qualifications;

(4) the course provider will develop and provide to driving safety schools that offer the approved course a refund policy, regulations pertaining to absence, grading policy, rules of operation, and conduct, and the name, mailing address, and telephone number of the agency for the purpose of directing complaints to the agency and that copies of these will be furnished to each student by the schools before enrollment;

(5) not later than the 15th working day after the date of completion of the course by a person, the course provider mails a uniform certificate of completion to the person indicating the course name and successful completion;

(6) the course provider keeps and maintains adequate records as prescribed by the commissioner to show attendance and progress or grades and that satisfactory standards relating to attendance, progress, and conduct are enforced;

(7) the course provider complies with all county, municipal, state, and federal law, including assumed name registration and other applicable requirements;

(8) the course provider is financially sound and capable of fulfilling its commitments for training;

(9) the course provider is of good reputation and character;

(10) the course provider has, maintains, and publishes as a part of its student enrollment contract the proper policy for the refund of the unused portion of tuition, fees, and other charges if a person enrolled by the school fails to take the course or withdraws or is discontinued from the school at any time before completion;

(11) the course provider does not use erroneous or misleading advertising, either by actual statement, omission, or intimation, as determined by the board;

(12) the course provider does not use a name like or similar to the name of another existing school or tax-supported educational establishment in this state unless specifically approved in writing by the commissioner;

(13) the course provider does not owe a civil penalty under this Act; and

(14) the course provider meets additional criteria required by the board.

(b)(1) License, application, and registration fees shall be collected by the commissioner and deposited with the comptroller. Fees shall be sufficient to cover administrative costs and may not be subject to refund. Fees shall be as follows:

(A)(i) the initial fee for a driver education school license is $1,000 plus $850 for each branch location;

(ii) the initial fee for a driving safety school license is an appropriate amount established by the board not to exceed $200; and

(iii) the initial fee for a course provider license is an appropriate amount established by the board not to exceed $2,000, except that this fee may be waived by the agency if revenue received by the agency from the course provider is sufficient to fund the cost of licensing the course provider;

(B) the annual renewal fee for a course provider, driving safety school, driver education school, and branch school is an appropriate amount established by the board not to exceed $200, but may be waived by the agency if revenue generated by the issuance of uniform certificates of completion and driver education certificates is sufficient to fund the cost of administering this Act and Subchapter B, Chapter 543, Transportation Code;

(C) the fee for a change of address of a driver education school is $180 and of a driving safety school or course provider is $50;

(D) the fee for a change of name of:

(i) a driver education school or course provider or an owner of a driver education school or course provider is $100; and

(ii) a driving safety school or owner of a driving safety school is $50;

(E) the application fee for each additional driver education or driving safety course at a school is $25;

(F) the application fee for each director is $30, and for each assistant director, or administrative staff member is $15;

(G) each application for approval of a driving safety course that has not been evaluated by the board shall be accompanied by a nonrefundable fee of $9,000;

(H) each application for an original driver education or driving safety instructor's license shall be accompanied by a processing fee of $50 and an annual license fee of $25, except that the commissioner may not collect the processing fee from an applicant for a driver education instructor license who is currently teaching a driver education course in a public school in this state; and

(I) the fee for a duplicate license, which may be issued if the original is lost or destroyed and an affidavit of that fact is filed with the agency, shall be set by the board.

(2) A driver education instructor who teaches driver education courses in a county having a population of 50,000 or less, according to the most recent federal census, and who has no more than 200 students annually, shall be regulated by the agency as a school. An instructor described by this subdivision shall submit a school application or renewal form plus all required documentation and information to the agency. The commissioner may waive initial school fees, annual school renewal fees, or director's or administrative staff member's fees. An instructor described by this subdivision is not exempt from licensing requirements or fees.

(3) The commissioner shall periodically review and recommend adjustments in the level of fees to the board and legislature.

(4) The fee for an investigation of a school or course provider to resolve a complaint filed against the school or course provider shall be set by the commissioner and approved by the board. The complaint investigation fee may be charged only if:

(A) the complaint could not have been resolved solely by telephone or written correspondence;

(B) a representative of the agency visited the school or course provider as a part of the complaint resolution process; and

(C) the school or course provider is found to be at fault.

(5) The agency shall print and supply to licensed course providers serially numbered uniform certificates of course completion. The agency may charge a fee of not more than $4 for each certificate. A course provider shall charge an operator a fee equal to the fee paid to the agency for a cer-

Printed in the U.S.A. Zt

tificate. The course provider shall charge and retain a user fee of not less than $3 a student for the use of course materials, oversight, and administration of the course.

(6) Fees collected under this subsection shall be deposited in the state treasury in a special account in the General Revenue Fund. Money in the account may be appropriated only for payment of monetary awards for information concerning abuse of the driver education or uniform certificates of completion that leads to the conviction or removal of an approval, license, or authorization and for the administration of this Act and Subchapter B, Chapter 543, Transportation Code. This dedication is exempt from the application of Sections 403.094 and 403.095, Government Code.

(7) Duplicate uniform certificates of completion shall be issued by the agency. An appropriate fee for issuing duplicate certificates shall be determined by board rule.

(c) The cost of administration of this Act shall be included in the state budget allowance for the board.

(d)(1) The commissioner, on review of an application for a driver education school, driving safety school, or course provider license that is submitted in accordance with this Act and that meets the requirements of this Act, shall issue a license to the applicant. Each license shall be in a form determined by the commissioner and approved by the board and shall show in a clear and conspicuous manner at least the following:

(A) the date of issuance, effective date, and term of approval;

(B) the name and address of the school or course provider;

(C) the authority for approval and conditions of approval;

(D) the signature of the commissioner; and

(E) any other fair and reasonable representations that are consistent with this Act and considered necessary by the commissioner.

(2) The term for which a driver education school, driving safety school, or course provider license is issued may not exceed one year.

(3)(A) A driver education school, driving safety school, or course provider license issued to an owner of the applicant school or course provider is nontransferable and is the property of the state. In the event of a change in ownership of the school or course provider, a new owner shall, at least 30 days before the date of the change in ownership, apply for a new driver education school, driving safety school, or course provider license. Instead of the fees required by Subsection (b) of this section, the fee for a new driver education school or course provider license required under this subdivision is $500, plus $200 for each branch location, if the purchasing entity is substantially similar to the transferring entity and there is no significant change in the management or control of the driver education school or course provider.

(B) The commissioner is not required to reinspect a school or a branch location after a change of its ownership.

(4) At least 30 days before the expiration of a driver education school, driving safety school, or course provider license, the school or course provider shall forward to the commissioner an application for renewal. The commissioner may reexamine a driver education school's premises. The commissioner shall renew or cancel the driver education school, driving safety school, or course provider license. If a school or course provider fails to file a complete application for renewal at least 30 days before the expiration date of the driver education school, driving safety school, or course provider license, the school or course provider shall pay as a condition of renewal and in addition to any annual renewal fee a late renewal fee in an amount established by board rule of at least $100, subject to Subsection (b) of this section.

(5) The commissioner shall visit a school or course provider and reexamine the school or course provider for compliance with the criteria adopted under this Act.

(e)(1) If the commissioner determines the applicant for a driver education school, driving safety school, or course provider license to be unacceptable, the commissioner shall state the reasons for denial, in writing, to the applicant.

(2) Any applicant whose driver education school, driving safety school, or course provider license is denied has the right of appeal under Section 17 of this Act.

(f)(1) The commissioner may revoke a driver education school, driving safety school, or course provider license or may place reasonable conditions on the continued approval represented by the license. On revocation or imposition of conditions on a driver education school, driving safety school, or course provider license, the commissioner shall notify the licensee, in writing, of the impending action and state the grounds for the proposed action. The commissioner may reexamine a school or course provider two or more times during any year in which a notice relating to the school or course provider has been issued or conditions have been imposed on the school under this subsection.

(2) A driver education school, driving safety school, or course provider license may be revoked or be made conditional if the commissioner has reasonable cause to believe that the school or course provider is guilty of a violation of this Act or any rule adopted under this Act.

(g)(1) Before a driver education school license may be issued under this Act, a bond shall be provided by the school for the period for which the license is to be issued, and the obligation of the bond shall be that neither a provision of this Act nor any rule adopted under this Act shall be violated by the school or any of its officers, agents, or employees. A driver education school shall submit a bond in the amount of $10,000 for its primary driver education school and $5,000 for each branch location of the school. A bond must be a corporate surety bond issued by a company authorized to do business in the state, be payable to the state, and be used only for payment of a refund due to a student or potential student. The bond shall be filed with the commissioner and shall be in such form as shall be approved by the commissioner. Posting of these bond amounts shall satisfy the requirements for financial stability for driver education schools under this Act.

(2) A driving safety school is not required to post a surety bond.

(3) Before a course provider license may be issued under this Act, a bond shall be provided by the course provider for the period for which the license is to be issued, and the obligation of the bond shall be that no provision of this Act or the Uniform Act Regulating Traffic on Highways (Article 6701d, Texas Civil Statutes) and no rule adopted under this Act may be violated by the course provider or any of its officers, agents, or employees. A course provider shall submit the bond in the amount of $25,000. The bond must be a corporate surety bond issued by a company authorized to do business in this state, payable to the state, and used:

(A) for payment of a refund due to any student of the course provider's approved course;

(B) to cover the payment of any unpaid fees, penalties, and fines assessed by the agency; and

(C) to recover the cost of any uniform certificates of completion demanded by the agency to be returned or any cost associated with the certificates.

(4) Instead of the bond required by Subdivision (1) of this subsection, the school may provide another form of security that is:

(A) approved by the commissioner; and

(B) in the amount required for a comparable bond under Subdivision (1) or (3) of this subsection.

(h)(1) As a condition for the granting of a driver education school or course provider license, a school or course provider must maintain a cancellation and settlement policy that provides a full refund of all money paid by a student if:

(A) the student cancels the enrollment agreement or contract before midnight of the third day, excluding Saturdays, Sundays, and legal holidays, after the date the enrollment contract is signed by the prospective student, unless the student has successfully completed the course or received a failing grade on the course examination; or

(B) the enrollment of the student was procured as a result of any misrepresentation in advertising, promotional materials of the school or course provider, or representation made by an owner or employee of the school or course provider.

(2) As a condition for granting a driver education school license, a school shall maintain a policy for the refund of the unused portion of driver education tuition, fees, and other charges if a student, after expiration of the cancellation period described by Subdivision (1) of this subsection, fails to enter the course, withdraws, or is discontinued from the course at any time before completion, and the policy must provide that:

(A) refunds are based on the period of enrollment computed on the basis of course time expressed in clock hours;

(B) the effective date of the termination for refund purposes is the earliest of the following:

(i) the last day of attendance, if the student's enrollment is terminated by the school;

(ii) the date of receipt of written notice from the student; or

(iii) the 10th school day following the last day of attendance;

(C) if tuition is collected in advance of entrance and if, after expiration of the cancellation period described by Subdivision (1) of this subsection, a student does not enter the school, terminates enrollment, or withdraws, the school may retain up to $50 as administrative expenses and, from the remainder, shall refund that portion of the classroom tuition and fees and behind-the-wheel tuition and fees for services not previously received by the student;

(D) refunds of items of extra expense to the student, including instructional supplies, books, laboratory fees, service charges, rentals, deposits, and all other such ancillary miscellaneous charges, will be made within 30 days after the effective date of enrollment termination, if these items are separately stated and shown in the data furnished the student before enrollment and the student returns any school property in the student's possession to the school; and

(E) refunds will be completed within 30 days after the effective date of enrollment termination.

(3) If the course of instruction is discontinued by the school or course provider, preventing a student from completing the course, all tuition and fees paid are then due and refundable.

(4) If a refund is not made within the period required by this subsection, the school or course provider shall pay interest on the refund for the interval beginning with the first day following the expiration of the refund period and ending with the day immediately preceding the date the refund is made. The commissioner annually shall establish the rate of interest at a rate sufficient to provide a deterrent to the retention of student funds. The agency may except a school or course provider from the payment of the interest if the school or course provider makes a good-faith effort to refund tuition but is unable to locate the student to whom the refund is owed. The school or course provider shall provide on request of the agency documentation of the effort to locate a student. *(Chgd. by L.1997, chap. 1423(21.42), eff. 9/1/97.)*

**Sec. 13A. Course provider responsibilities.** (a) An issued uniform certificate of completion shall be mailed to the student not later than the 15th working day after the date of completion of an approved driving safety course only by the course provider or authorized personnel at the course provider's facilities.

(b) Data identified by the agency pertaining to issued uniform certificates of completion shall be submitted electronically by each course provider to the agency in a manner determined by the agency.

(c) The agency shall investigate options to develop and implement procedures to provide information pertaining to driving safety courses by electronic transmission to the state municipal and justice courts.

(d) A course provider shall conduct driving safety instructor development courses for its approved driving safety course.

(e) The board may adopt additional rules to ensure integrity of the course and enhance program quality.

(f) A course provider license entitles a provider to purchase uniform certificates of completion for only one approved driving safety course.

**Sec. 14. Withholding records.** A school may withhold a student's diploma or certificate of completion until the student has fulfilled the student's financial obligation to the school.

**Sec. 15. License required for instructor.** (a) A person may not teach or give driving safety training, either as an individual or in a driving safety school, or any phase of driving safety education, unless a driving safety instructor license has been secured from the agency, except that an instructor of a driving safety course that does not provide a uniform certificate of completion to its graduates is exempt from this section. A person may not teach or give driver education, either as an individual or in a driver education school, or any phase of driver education unless a driver education instructor license has been secured from the agency.

(b) A license issued to a driver education or driving safety instructor expires not more than 12 months after the date of issue, unless sooner suspended or revoked. License renewal applications must include evidence of completion of continuing education and shall be postmarked at least 30 days before the date of expiration or a late renewal fee of $25 will be imposed. The continuing education must be in courses approved by the commissioner and be for a certain number of hours determined by the commissioner.

(c) A driver education instructor license shall be carried by the instructor at all times while instructing driver education courses. A driving safety instructor license shall be carried by the instructor at all times while instructing driving safety courses. Each license shall be signed by the commissioner and issued under the seal of the board.

**Sec. 15A. Driver education instructor training.** (a) With approval of the board, the commissioner shall establish standards for certification of professional and paraprofessional personnel who conduct driver education programs in driver education schools.

(b) A driver education instructor license may not be issued authorizing a person to teach or give driver education in-car training unless the person has successfully completed six semester hours of driver and traffic safety education or a program of study in driver education approved by the board from an approved driver education school. A person holding a driver education instructor license authorizing in-car training may be approved to assist classroom instructors in the classroom phase of driver education if the person successfully completes the additional three semester hours of training required for a classroom instructor or a program of study in driver education approved by the board.

(c) Except as provided by Subsection (f) of this section, a driver education instructor license may not be issued authorizing a person to teach or give classroom driver education training unless the person:

(1) has completed nine semester hours of driver and traffic safety education or a program of study in driver education approved by the board from an approved driver education school; and

(2) holds a teaching certificate and any additional certification required to teach driver education.

(d) A driver education instructor who has completed the educational requirements for a classroom driver education instructor under Subsection (c)(1) of this section may be approved to teach instructor training classes after successfully completing a supervising instructor development program consisting of at least six additional semester hours or a program of study in driver education approved by the board that includes administering driver education programs and supervising and administering traffic safety education.

(e) A driver education school may submit for agency approval a curriculum for an instructor development program for driver education instructors. The program must be taught by a person who has successfully completed a supervising instructor development program under Subsection (d) of this section and must satisfy the requirements of this section for the particular program or type of training to be provided.

(f) A temporary, nonrenewable driver education instructor license valid for a six-month period may be issued authorizing a person to teach or give classroom driver education training if the person:

(1) has completed the educational requirements for a classroom driver education instructor prescribed under Subsection (c)(1) of this section;

(2) holds a Texas teaching certificate with an effective date before February 1, 1986;

(3) meets all requirements for licensure, other than successful completion of the examination required under rules adopted by the State Board for Educator Certification to revalidate the teaching certificate; and

(4) demonstrates, in a manner prescribed by the commissioner, the intention to comply with the examination requirement at the first available opportunity.

*(Chgd. by L.1999, chap. 1166(1), eff. 6/18/99.)*

**Sec. 16. Denial, suspension, revocation grounds.** (a) The agency may deny, suspend, or revoke the license of any instructor on any one or more of the following grounds:

(1) when the agency is satisfied that the applicant or licensee fails to meet the requirements to receive or hold a license under this Act;

(2) when the applicant or licensee permits fraud or engages in fraudulent practices with reference to the application to the agency, induces or countenances fraud or fraudulent practices on the part of any applicant for a driver's license or permit, or permits or engages in any other fraudulent practice in any action between the applicant or licensee and the public; or

(3) when the applicant or licensee fails to comply with the rules of the agency regarding the instruction of drivers in this state or fails to comply with any section of this Act.

(b) Not later than the 10th day after the date of a decision under this section the agency shall notify the applicant or license holder by certified mail of the decision.

**Sec. 17. Hearing.** (a) A person aggrieved by the denial, suspension, or revocation of a license may appeal the decision and request a hearing before the commissioner. The request must be submitted not later than the 15th day after the date of receipt of notice of a decision made under Section 16 of this Act. On receipt of a request for a hearing, the commissioner shall set a time and place for the hearing and send notice to the person of the time and place. A hearing shall be held within 30 days after the date of receipt of the request. At the hearing, an applicant or licensee may appear in person or by counsel and present evidence. Any interested person may appear and present oral or documentary evidence.

(b) Except as provided by Subsection (c), the commissioner shall conduct the administrative hearing and is authorized to administer oaths and issue subpoenas for the attendance of witnesses and the production of relevant books, papers, and documents. On the basis of the evidence submitted at the hearing, the commissioner shall take whatever action the commissioner deems necessary in denying the application or suspending or revoking the license. Not later than the 10th day after the date of the hearing the commissioner shall notify the applicant or license holder by certified mail of the commissioner's decision on the appeal.

(c) The agency may contract with another entity for the conducting of a hearing required under this Act.

**Sec. 18. Judicial review.** (a) The commissioner's decision on the appeal may be appealed to a district court in Travis County.

(b) Unless stayed by the court on showing of good cause, the commissioner's decision may not be superseded during appeal.

(c) On filing of the lawsuit, citation shall be served on the commissioner, who shall cause to be made a complete record of all proceedings had before the commissioner and certify a copy of the proceedings to the court. Trial before the court shall be on the basis of the record made before the commissioner, and the court shall make its decision based on the record. The commissioner's decision shall be affirmed by the court if the court finds substantial evidence in the record to justify the decision, unless the court finds the denial of the license to be:

(1) arbitrary and capricious;

(2) in violation of the constitution or laws of the United States or this state; or

(3) in violation of rules adopted by the board under this Act.

(d) A decision of the trial court is subject to appeal in the same manner as is any civil lawsuit.

(e) An appeal concerning suspension or revocation of any license shall be prosecuted in the same manner and under the same provisions as provided by this Act for appeals from denial of licenses.

**Sec. 19. Class action suits.** Any person who is injured by an act taken or permitted in violation of this Act may, on behalf of the person and others similarly situated, maintain an action in any district court of competent jurisdiction, regardless of the amount in controversy, for temporary or permanent injunctive relief, declaratory relief, or other relief, including damages, in accordance with Rule 42, Texas Rules of Civil Procedure. Venue for any action under this section is in Travis County. A party filing an action under this section shall give prompt notice to the attorney general, who shall be permitted to join, on application within 30 days after the date of filing, as a party plaintiff.

**Sec. 20. Notice.** In any class action permitted under this Act, the court shall direct the defendant to serve on each member of the class the best practicable notice. The court may direct that individual notice be served on each member of the class who can be identified through reasonable efforts. The notice shall inform the recipient that the person is thought to be a member of the class, and, if so, the person may enter an appearance and join in the suit.

**Sec. 21. Judgment and costs.** The court shall enter judgment in a class action brought under this Act in such form as may be justified. Damages shall be awarded only to those members of the class joined as parties plaintiff, but all other relief granted by the court shall inure to the benefit of all members of the class. Should a plaintiff prevail in a class action, the plaintiff shall be awarded court costs and reasonable attorney fees. A legal aid society or legal services program that represents a plaintiff or plaintiffs shall be awarded a service fee in lieu of attorney fees.

**Sec. 22. Surrender of license.** On the revocation or suspension of any license, the licensee shall within five days after the date of revocation or suspension surrender the license or licenses to the agency; failure of a licensee to do so shall be a violation of this Act and upon conviction shall be subject to the penalties hereinafter set forth. The agency may restore a suspended license to the former licensee upon full compliance with the provisions of this Act. No suspension invoked hereunder shall be for a period less than 30 days nor longer than one year.

**Sec. 23. Injunction.** (a) If the commissioner believes that any school has committed any act in violation of this Act, the commissioner shall apply to a court of competent jurisdiction for an injunction restraining the commission of the act.

(b) An action under this section shall be brought in Travis County.

**Sec. 24. Civil penalty.** (a) A person who violates this Act or a rule adopted under this Act is liable for a civil penalty in an amount assessed by the commissioner after an opportunity for a hearing in addition to any injunctive relief or other remedy provided by law. A civil penalty may not exceed $1,000 a day for each violation.

(b) The attorney general, at the request of the agency, may bring a civil action to collect a civil penalty.

(c) Civil penalties shall be deposited in the state treasury to the credit of the General Revenue Fund.

**Sec. 25. Sanctions.** (a) If the agency believes that a driver education school or instructor has violated this Act or a rule adopted under this Act, the agency may, without notice:

(1) order a peer review;

(2) suspend the enrollment of students in the school or the offering of instruction by the instructor; or

(3) suspend the right to purchase driver education certificates of completion.

(b) If the agency believes that a course provider, driving safety school, or driving safety instructor has violated this Act or the Uniform Act Regulating Traffic on Highways (Article 6701d, Texas Civil Statutes) or a rule adopted under one of those Acts, the agency may, without notice:

(1) order a peer review of the course provider, driving safety school, or driving safety instructor;

(2) suspend the enrollment of students in the school or the offering of instruction by the instructor; or

(3) suspend the right to purchase uniform certificates of completion.

(c) A peer review ordered under this section shall be conducted by a peer review team composed of knowledgeable persons selected by the agency. The team shall provide the agency with an objective assessment of the content of the school's or course provider's curriculum and its application. The costs of providing a peer review team shall be paid by the school or course provider, as appropriate.

**Sec. 26. Proceedings through the attorney general.** If any person violates any of the provisions of this Act, the commissioner shall, in the name of the State of Texas through the Attorney General of the State of Texas, apply in any district court of competent jurisdiction for an order enjoining such violation or for an order enforcing compliance with this Act. Upon the filing of a verified petition to the court, if the court or any judge thereof is satisfied by affidavit or otherwise that the person has violated this Act, it may issue a temporary injunction without notice or bond enjoining such continued violation, and if after a hearing it is established that the person violated or is violating this Act the court or any judge thereof may enter a decree perpetually enjoining the violation of or enforcing compliance with this Act. In case of violation of any order or decree issued under the provisions of this section, the court or any judge thereof may try and punish the offender for contempt of court. Proceedings under this section shall be in addition to and not in lieu of all other remedies and penalties provided by this Act.

**Sec. 27. Penalties.** Any person who violates any provision of this Act commits an offense and, except as otherwise provided by law, upon conviction thereof shall be punished by a fine of not less than $100 nor more than $20,000, or by imprisonment in the county jail for a term of not to exceed six months, or both.

**Sec. 27A. Unauthorized transfer of certificate.** (a) A person who knowingly sells, trades, issues, or otherwise transfers, or possesses with intent to sell, trade, issue, or otherwise transfer, a uniform certificate of completion or driver education certificate to an individual, firm, or corporation not authorized to possess it commits an offense.

(b) A person who knowingly possesses a uniform certificate of completion or driver education certificate and who is not authorized to possess the certificate commits an offense.

(c) A person adjudged guilty of an offense under this section shall be punished by imprisonment in the institutional division of the Texas Department of Criminal Justice for a term of not more than five years.

(d) The agency shall contract with the Department of Public Safety to provide undercover and investigative assistance in the enforcement of the prohibition provided by Subsection (a) of this section.

*(Chgd. by L.1991, chaps. 867(1), (2), 835(1); L.1993, chaps. 771(16), (19)(6), 954(1)-(5); L.1995, chaps. 165(15), 1009(3)-(24), eff. 9/1/95.)*

## Art. 5221f. Texas Manufactured Housing Standards Act.

**Sec. 18.** (f) Notwithstanding any provisions of any other statute, regulation, or ordinance to the contrary, a licensed retailer or licensed installer is not required to secure any permit, certificate, or license or pay any fee for the transportation of manufactured housing to the place where it is to be installed except as required by the department or by the Texas Department of Transportation pursuant to Subchapter E, Chapter 623, Transportation Code. The department shall cooperate with the Texas Department of Transportation by providing current lists of licensed manufactured housing manufacturers, retailers, and installers. *(Chgd. by L.1995, chaps. 165(22)(13), 978(12); L.1997, chap. 791(15), eff. 9/1/97.)*

**Art. 6419a. Railroads—engineer's operator permits.† [*Railroads—engineer's operator permit.*]**

**Sec. 1. Issuance of permit.** (a) A railroad company shall issue to each person that it employs to operate or permits to operate a railroad locomotive in this state an engineer's operator permit. A permit must include the engineer's name, address, physical description, photograph, and date of birth.

(b) A railroad company shall issue to each person that it employs to operate or permits to operate a train in this state, other than a person issued a permit under Subsection (a) of this section, a trainman's permit. A permit must include the trainman's name, address, physical description, photograph, and date of birth.

**Sec. 2. Operation of locomotive.† [*Operation of locomotive or train.*]** (a) A person operating a railroad locomotive in this state shall have in his or her immediate possession an engineer's operator permit issued under this Act.

(b) A person operating a train in this state, other than a person issued a permit under Section 1(a) of this Act, shall have in his or her immediate possession a trainman's permit issued under this Act.

**Sec. 3. Proof of identification.** A person who operates a railroad locomotive or train and who is required by a peace officer to show proof of identification in connection with the person's operation of a locomotive or train shall display the person's permit issued under this Act and may not be required to display an operator's, commercial operator's, or chauffeur's driver's license issued under Chapter 173, Acts of the 47th Legislature, Regular Session, 1941, as amended (Article 6687b, Texas Civil Statutes).

**Sec. 4. Records relating to accidents or violations.** If a person operating a railroad locomotive or train is involved in an accident with another train or a motor vehicle or is arrested for violation of a law relating to the person's operation of a locomotive or train, the number or other identifying information about the person's operator's, commercial operator's, or chauffeur's driver's license may not be included in any report of the accident or violation, and the person's involvement in the accident or violation may not be recorded in the person's individual driving record maintained by the Department of Public Safety.
*(Article 6419a chgd. by L.1991, chap. 340(1), eff. 1/1/92.)*

**Art. 6419b. Duty to stop and render aid.† [*Duty to stop at accidents.*]**

**Sec. 1. Stop after accident.† [*Stop at accidents.*]** The person assigned by a railroad corporation to be responsible for the operation of the train who is involved, while operating a locomotive, in an accident resulting in injury to or death of any person or damage to any vehicle that is driven or attended by a person shall immediately stop the locomotive at the scene of the accident.

**Sec. 2. Rendering of aid.† [*Rendering aid.*]** The person responsible for the operation of the train shall render to any person injured in the accident reasonable assistance, including the carrying, or the making of arrangements for the carrying, of the person to a physician, surgeon, or hospital for medical or surgical treatment if it is apparent that treatment is necessary or if the carrying is requested by the injured person.

**Sec. 3. Offense.** A person who violates this article commits an offense. An offense under this article is a Class C misdemeanor.

## LAWS RELATING TO REGISTRATION OF VEHICLES

**Art. 6675c.** *(Repealed by L.1997, chap. 165(30.150(b)), eff. 9/1/97.)*

**Sec. 2.** *(Chgd. by L.1997, chap. 1061(1); repealed by L.1999, chaps. 62(17.10(b)), 603(7(a)), eff. 9/1/99, 6/18/99, respectively.)*

**Sec. 3.** *(Repealed by L.1999, chaps. 62(17.12(b)), (17.13(b)), (17.14(b)), 603(7(a)), eff. 9/1/99, 9/1/99, 9/1/99, 6/18/99, respectively.)*

**Sec. 3A.** *(Added by L.1997, chap. 1061(3); repealed by L.1999, chap. 62(17.15(b)), eff. 9/1/99.)*

**Sec. 4.** *(Repealed by L.1999, chap. 62(17.16), (17.17(b)), eff. 9/1/99.)*

**Sec. 6.** *(Repealed by L.1999, chap. 62(17.18), eff. 9/1/99.)*

**Sec. 7.** *(Chgd. by L.1997, chaps. 858(3), 1061(6), 1171(4.02); repealed by L.1999, chap. 62(17.21(b)), eff. 9/1/99.)*

**Sec. 8.** *(Chgd. by L.1997, chaps. 858(4); 1171(4.03), (4.06); repealed by L.1999, chap. 62(17.19(c)), (17.20(b)), eff. 9/1/99.)*

**Sec. 10.** *(Chgd. by L.1997, chaps. 858(5), 1171(4.07); repealed by L.1999, chap. 62(17.22(b)), eff. 9/1/99.)*

**Sec. 13.** *(Chgd. by L.1997, chap. 1061(7); repealed by L.1999, chap. 62(17.23), eff. 9/1/99.)*

**Sec. 15.** *(Chgd. by L.1997, chap. 1061(8); repealed by L.1999, chap. 62(17.11(b)), eff. 9/1/99.)*

**Art. 6675c-1.** *(Repealed by L.1997, chap. 165(30.152(b)); chgd. by L.1997, chap. 1061(9); repealed by L.1999, chap. 62(17.33(b)), eff. 9/1/99.)*

**Art. 6675c-2.** *(Added by L.1997, chap. 1171(4.11(a)); repealed by L.1999, chap. 62(17.35(b)), eff. 9/1/99.)*

**Art. 6675d.** *(Repealed by L.1997, chap. 165(30.151(b)), eff. 9/1/97.)*

**Sec. 1.** *(Chgd. by L.1997, chap. 1061(12); repealed by L.1999, chap. 62(17.24(b)), (17.25(b)), eff. 9/1/99.)*

**Sec. 3A.** *(Added by L.1997, chap. 157(1); repealed by L.1999, chap. 62(17.32(b)), eff. 9/1/99.)*

**Sec. 3A.** *(Added by L.1997, chap. 476(1); repealed by L.1999, chap. 62(17.28(b)), eff. 9/1/99.)*

**Sec. 5.** *(Chgd. by L.1997, chaps. 858(7), 1061(10), 1171(4.09); repealed by L.1999, chap. 62(17.27(c)), eff. 9/1/99.)*

**Sec. 6.** *(Chgd. by L.1997, chaps. 364(1), 1061(11); repealed by L.1999, chap. 62(17.29(b)), eff. 9/1/99.)*

**Sec. 7.** *(Chgd. by L.1997, chaps. 1364(1), 1423 (21.66); repealed by L.1999, chap. 62(17.30), (17.32(b)), eff. 9/1/99.)*

**Sec. 8.** *(Chgd. by L.1997, chap. 364(2); repealed by L.1999, chap. 62(17.31(b)), eff. 9/1/99.)*

**Sec. 16.** *(Added by L.1997, chap. 1171(4.11(b)); repealed by L.1999, chap. 62(17.26(b)), eff. 9/1/99.)*

## LAWS RELATING TO DRIVER'S LICENSE

**Art. 6687d.** *(Repealed by L.1997, chap. 165(30.161(b)), eff. 9/1/97.)*

**Sec. 1.** *(Repealed by L.1999, chap. 62(17.37(e)), eff. 9/1/99.)*

**Sec. 2.** *(Repealed by L.1999, chap. 62(17.37(e)), eff. 9/1/99.)*

**Sec. 4.** *(Repealed by L.1999, chap. 62(17.37(e)), eff. 9/1/99.)*

# LAWS RELATING TO CERTIFICATE OF TITLE

## Art. 6687-1a. Salvage vehicle dealers.

## PART 1. GENERAL PROVISIONS

**Sec. 1.01. Definitions.** In this article:

(1) "Actual cash value" means the market value of a motor vehicle as determined:

(A) from publications that are commonly used in the automotive and insurance industries to establish the value of motor vehicles; or

(B) if the entity determining the value is an insurance company, by any other procedure recognized by the insurance industry, including market surveys, that is applied by the company in a uniform manner.

(2) "Automobile recycler" means a person who engages in the business of dealing in salvage vehicles for the purpose of dismantling the vehicles to sell used parts and the resulting scrap metal or a person otherwise engaged in the business of acquiring, selling, or dealing in salvage parts. The term includes a dealer in used motor vehicle parts.

(3) "Casual sale" means the sale at auction of not more than one nonrepairable motor vehicle or late model salvage motor vehicle to the same person during a calendar year.

(4) "Commission" means the Texas Transportation Commission.

(5) "Department" means the Texas Department of Transportation.

(6) "Late model motor vehicle" means a motor vehicle with a model year equal to the then current calendar year or one of the five preceding calendar years.

(7) "Major component part" means one of the following parts of a vehicle:

(A) the engine;

(B) the transmission;

(C) the frame;

(D) the right or left front fender;

(E) the hood;

(F) a door allowing entrance to or egress from the passenger compartment of the vehicle;

(G) the front or rear bumper;

(H) the right or left quarter panel;

(I) the deck lid, tailgate, or hatchback;

(J) the cargo box of a pickup truck;

(K) the cab of a truck; or

(L) the body of a passenger vehicle.

(8) "Motor vehicle" has the meaning assigned by the Uniform Act Regulating Traffic on Highways (Article 6701d, Texas Civil Statutes).

(9) "Nonrepairable vehicle" means:

(A) a late model vehicle that is damaged or missing a major component part to the extent that the total estimated cost of repairs to rebuild or reconstruct the vehicle, including parts and labor other than the cost of materials and labor for repainting the vehicle but excluding sales taxes on the total cost of the repairs, and excluding the cost of repairs to repair hail damage, is equal to or greater than an amount equal to 95 percent of the actual cash value of the vehicle in its predamaged condition; or

(B) a vehicle that comes into this state with a nonrepairable vehicle certificate of title or other comparable certificate of title.

(10) "Nonrepairable vehicle certificate of title" means any document issued by the department that evidences ownership of a nonrepairable vehicle.

(11) "Out-of-state buyer" means a person licensed by another state or jurisdiction in an automotive business if the department has listed the holders of such license as permitted purchasers of salvage motor vehicles or nonrepairable motor vehicles based on substantially similar licensing requirements and on whether salvage vehicle dealers licensed in Texas are permitted to purchase salvage motor vehicles or nonrepairable motor vehicles in the other state or jurisdiction.

(12) "Person" means an individual, partnership, corporation, trust, association, or other private legal entity.

(13) "Salvage part" means a major component part of a late model salvage vehicle that is serviceable to the extent that it can be reused.

(14) "Salvage vehicle" or "late model salvage vehicle" means:

(A) a late model motor vehicle with a major component part that is damaged or missing to the extent that the total estimated cost of repairs to rebuild or reconstruct the vehicle, including parts and labor, but excluding the cost of repairs to repair hail damage, is equal to or greater than an amount equal to 75 percent of the actual cash value of the vehicle in its predamaged condition; or

(B) a damaged vehicle that comes into this state under a salvage vehicle certificate of title or other comparable certificate of title.

(15) "Salvage vehicle agent" means a person employed by a licensed salvage vehicle dealer to acquire, sell, or otherwise deal in late model salvage vehicles or salvage parts in this state.

(16) "Salvage vehicle certificate of title" means any document issued by the department that evidences ownership of a salvage vehicle.

(17) "Salvage vehicle dealer" means a person who is engaged in this state in the business of acquiring, selling, or otherwise dealing in salvage vehicles or vehicle parts of a type required to be covered by a salvage vehicle certificate of title or nonrepairable vehicle certificate of title under a license issued by the department that allows the holder of the license to acquire, sell, dismantle, repair, or otherwise deal in salvage vehicles.

(18) "Salvage pool operator" means a person who engages in the business of selling nonrepairable vehicles or salvage vehicles at auction, including wholesale auction, or otherwise.

(19) "Salvage vehicle record" means the record of sales and purchases for each salvage vehicle handled by a salvage vehicle dealer.



**Sec. 1.02. Powers and duties of commission.** (a) The Texas Transportation Commission shall adopt rules as necessary to administer this article and may take other action as necessary to enforce this article.

(b) The commission shall set application fees, license fees, renewal fees, and other fees as required to implement this article. The commission shall set the fees in amounts reasonable and necessary to implement this article.

(c) The commission may not adopt a rule under this article that restricts competitive bidding or advertising by a person who holds a license issued under this article other than a rule to prohibit false, misleading, or deceptive practices. A rule to prohibit false, misleading, or deceptive practices may not:

(1) restrict the use of:

(A) any medium for an advertisement;

(B) the license holder's advertisement under a trade name; or

(C) the license holder's personal appearance or voice in an advertisement, if the license holder is an individual; or

(2) relate to the size or duration of an advertisement by the license holder.

*(Chgd. by L.1997, chap. 1171(5.01), eff. 9/1/97.)*

**Sec. 1.03. Determination of estimated cost of repair.** (a) The estimated cost of repair parts shall be determined by using a manual of repair costs or other instrument that is generally recognized and commonly used in the motor vehicle insurance industry to determine those costs or an estimate of the actual cost of the repair parts.

(b) The estimated labor costs shall be computed by using the hourly rate and time allocations that are reasonable and commonly assessed in the repair industry in the community in which the repairs are performed.

## PART 2. LICENSE REQUIREMENTS

**Sec. 2.01. License required; exemptions.** (a) A person may not act as an automobile recycler or salvage vehicle dealer, including storing or displaying vehicles as an agent or escrow agent of an insurance company, unless the person holds a salvage vehicle dealer license issued under this article.

(b) A person may not act as a salvage vehicle agent unless the person holds a salvage vehicle agent license issued under this article.

(c) This article does not apply to an insurance company authorized to engage in the business of insurance in this state.

(d) This article does not apply to, and does not preclude or prohibit any sales to, purchases by, or other transactions by or with, a person described by Subsection (g), Article 6687-2b, Revised Statutes, except as provided by Subsection (e) or (f) of this section.

(e) A person described by Subsection (g), Article 6687-2b, Revised Statutes, shall submit to the department the certificate of title or equivalent document that the person receives in conjunction with the purchase of a motor vehicle not later than the 60th day after the date of receipt of the certificate of title or equivalent document.

(f) This article applies to a transaction with a person described by Subsection (g), Article 6687-2b, Revised Statutes, in which a motor vehicle is sold or delivered to the person for the purpose of reuse or resale as a motor vehicle or as motor vehicle parts if the motor vehicle is so used.

(g) Except as otherwise provided by this subsection, this article does not apply to a person who purchases a nonrepairable vehicle or salvage vehicle from a salvage pool operator in a casual sale. The commission shall adopt rules as necessary to regulate casual sales and to enforce this subsection. A salvage vehicle pool operator that sells a vehicle in a casual sale shall comply with each rule adopted by the commission regarding that sale.

(h) This article does not prohibit the sale to any person of a vehicle that is classified as a late model salvage vehicle or a nonrepairable vehicle solely because of water damage caused by flood conditions.

*(Section 2.01 eff. 3/1/96.)*



**Sec. 2.02. License application.** (a) An applicant for a salvage vehicle dealer license must apply on a form prescribed by the department. The application form must be signed by the applicant and accompanied by the application fee. The application must include:

(1) the name, business address, and business telephone number of the applicant;

(2) the name under which the applicant will do business;

(3) the location, by number, street, and municipality, of each office from which the applicant will conduct business;

(4) a statement indicating whether the applicant has previously applied for a license under this article, the result of the previous application, and whether the applicant has ever been the holder of a license under this article that was revoked or suspended;

(5) a statement of the previous history, record, and associations of the applicant to the extent sufficient to establish, to the satisfaction of the department, the business reputation and character of the applicant;

(6) the applicant's federal tax identification number, if any;

(7) the applicant's state sales tax number; and

(8) other information as required by rules adopted under this article.

(b) A license may not be issued in a fictitious name that may be confused with or is similar to that of a governmental entity or that is otherwise deceptive or misleading to the public.

**Sec. 2.03. Additional requirements for corporate or partnership license.** (a) If a salvage vehicle dealer license applicant intends to engage in business through a corporation, the license application must include, in addition to the information required under Section 2.02 of this article:

(1) the state of incorporation;

(2) the name, address, date of birth, and social security number of each of the principal officers and directors of the corporation;

(3) a statement of the previous history, record, and associations of each officer and director to the extent sufficient to establish, to the satisfaction of the department, the business reputation and character of the applicant; and

(4) a statement showing whether an employee, officer, or director has been refused a license as a salvage vehicle dealer or has been the holder of a license that was revoked or suspended.

(b) If the license applicant intends to engage in business through a partnership, the license application must include, in addition to the information required under Section 2.02 of this article:

(1) the name, address, date of birth, and social security number of each owner or partner;

(2) a statement of the previous history, record, and associations of each owner and partner to the extent sufficient to establish, to the satisfaction of the department, the business reputation and character of the applicant; and

(3) a statement showing whether a partner, owner, or employee has been refused a license as a salvage vehicle dealer or has been the holder of a license that was revoked or suspended.

**Sec. 2.04. Classification of license endorsements.** (a) The department shall classify salvage vehicle dealers according to the type of activity performed by the dealers. A salvage vehicle dealer may not engage in activities of a particular classification as provided by this article unless the salvage vehicle dealer holds a license endorsement under that classification.

(b) An applicant may apply for a salvage vehicle dealer license with an endorsement in one or more of the following classifications:

(1) new automobile dealer;

(2) used automobile dealer;

(3) used vehicle parts dealer;

(4) salvage vehicle pool operator;

(5) salvage vehicle broker; or
(6) salvage vehicle rebuilder.

**Sec. 2.05. Investigation.** (a) The department may not grant a license under this article until the department completes an investigation of the applicant's qualifications under this article.

(b) The department shall conduct the investigation not later than the 15th day after the date on which the application is received by the department and shall report the results of the investigation to the applicant.

**Sec. 2.06. License issuance.** The department shall issue a license to an applicant who meets the license qualifications adopted under this article and pays the required fees.

**Sec. 2.07. License Renewal.** (a) A license issued under this article expires on the first anniversary of the date of issuance and may be renewed annually on or before the expiration date on payment of the required renewal fee.

(b) A person who is otherwise eligible to renew a license may renew an unexpired license by paying to the department before the expiration date of the license the required renewal fee. A person whose license has expired may not engage in the activities that require a license until the license has been renewed under the provisions of this section.

(c) If a person's license has been expired for 90 days or less, the person may renew the license by paying to the department one and one-half times the required renewal fee.

(d) If a person's license has been expired for longer than 90 days but less than one year, the person may renew the license by paying to the department two times the required renewal fee.

(e) If a person's license has been expired for one year or longer, the person may not renew the license. The person may obtain a new license by complying with the requirements and procedures for obtaining an original license. If the person was licensed in this state, moved to another state, and has been doing business in the other state for the two years preceding application, the person may renew an expired license. The person must pay to the department a fee that is equal to two times the required renewal fee for the license.

(f) At least 30 days before the date on which a person's license expires, the department shall notify the person of the impending expiration. The notice must be in writing and sent to the person's last known address according to the records of the department.

*(Chgd. by L.1997, chap. 1171(5.02), eff. 9/1/97.)*

**Sec. 2.08. Registration of business locations.** (a) A license applicant who intends to operate as a salvage vehicle dealer at more than one location must list in the application each location at which business is to be conducted.

(b) Before moving a place of business or opening an additional place of business, a salvage vehicle dealer must register the new location with the department.

## PART 3. DUTIES OF LICENSE HOLDER

**Sec. 3.01. Certificate of title.** (a) If a salvage vehicle dealer acquires ownership of a late model salvage vehicle from an owner, the dealer must receive an assigned certificate of title. If the assigned certificate of title is not a salvage vehicle certificate of title, a nonrepairable vehicle certificate of title, or comparable ownership document issued by another state or jurisdiction, the licensed salvage vehicle dealer shall, not later than the 10th day after the date of receipt of the title, surrender the assigned certificate of title to the department and apply for a salvage vehicle certificate of title or a nonrepairable vehicle certificate of title, as appropriate.

(b) If a late model salvage vehicle or nonrepairable vehicle is to be dismantled, scrapped, or destroyed, the salvage vehicle dealer shall surrender an assigned certificate of title, salvage vehicle certificate of title, nonrepairable vehicle certificate of title, or comparable ownership document issued by another state or jurisdiction to the department in the manner prescribed by the department not later than the 30th day after the date the vehicle is acquired and report to the department that the vehicle was dismantled, scrapped, or destroyed.

(c) If the holder of a salvage vehicle dealer license acquires ownership of an older model vehicle from an owner and receives an assigned certificate of title and the vehicle is to be dismantled, scrapped, or destroyed, the license holder shall surrender the assigned certificate of title to the department on a form prescribed by the department not later than the 30th day after the date on which the title is received and present evidence that the vehicle was dismantled, scrapped, or destroyed. The license holder shall keep a record of the vehicle.

**Sec. 3.02. Records.** Each holder of a salvage vehicle dealer license shall maintain records of each salvage vehicle and any salvage parts purchased by the license holder and shall maintain sales records as required by this article.

**Sec. 3.03. Authorized sale.** A person may not sell, transfer, or release a late model salvage vehicle or a nonrepairable motor vehicle to anyone other than:

(1) a governmental entity;
(2) the vehicle's former owner;
(3) a licensed salvage vehicle dealer;
(4) an out-of-state buyer;
(5) a buyer in a casual sale at auction; or
(6) a person described by Subsection (g), Article 6687-2b, Revised Statutes.

**Sec. 3.04. Agents.** The holder of a salvage vehicle dealer license may authorize not more than five persons to operate as salvage vehicle agents under the dealer's license. An agent may acquire, sell, or otherwise deal in late model salvage vehicles, nonrepairable vehicles, or salvage parts as directed by the dealer. An agent authorized to operate under this section is entitled to a salvage vehicle agent license on application to the department and payment of the required fee.



## PART 4. DISCIPLINARY ACTIONS AND PENALTIES

**Sec. 4.01. Denial, suspension, or revocation of license.** (a) The department may deny, suspend, revoke, or reinstate a license issued under this article.

(b) The commission shall adopt rules establishing the grounds for the denial, suspension, revocation, or reinstatement of a license and establishing procedures for disciplinary actions. A rule adopted under this subsection may not conflict with a rule adopted by the State Office of Administrative Hearings.

(c) Proceedings relating to the denial, suspension, or revocation of a license issued under this article are subject to Chapter 2001, Government Code.

(d) A person whose license is revoked may not apply for a new license before the first anniversary of the date of the revocation.

*(Chgd. by L.1997, chap. 1171(5.03), eff. 9/1/97.)*

**Sec. 4.02. Criminal penalty.** (a) A person commits an offense if the person acts as a salvage vehicle dealer without a salvage vehicle dealer license issued under this article.

(b) A person commits an offense if the person acts as a salvage vehicle agent without a salvage vehicle agent license issued under this article.

(c) A person commits an offense if the person violates a provision of this article, other than Subsection (a) or (b) of this section, or a rule adopted by the commission under this article.

(d) An offense under this section is a Class A misdemeanor.

*(Section 4.02 eff. 3/1/96.)*

## PART 5. EFFECT ON LOCAL REGULATION

**Sec. 5.01. Cumulative effect; effect on municipal licenses.** (a) This article is cumulative of municipal ordinances relating to the regulation of persons who deal in salvage vehicles.

(b) This article does not prohibit, and may not be construed as prohibiting, the enforcement of a requirement of a municipal license or permit that is related to an activity regulated under this article.

*(Added by L.1995, chap. 404(1), eff. 9/1/95, except sections 2.01 and 4.02, eff. 3/1/96.)*

### Art. 6687-2. Salvage vehicle dealers.

**Sec. 1. Salvage vehicle dealers.** (a) In this section:

(1) "Salvage vehicle dealer" has the meaning assigned by Article 6687-1a, Revised Statutes.

(2) "Component part" means the front end assembly or tail section of a motor vehicle, the cab of a truck (light or heavy), the bed of a one ton or lighter truck, an interior component part of a motor vehicle, a special accessory part, or a vehicle part that contains or should contain a federal safety sticker, motor number, serial number, manufacturer's permanent vehicle identification number, or a derivative of a vehicle identification number.

(3) "Front-end assembly" means the hood, right or left front fender, grill, bumper, radiator, or radiator support, if two or more such parts are assembled together as one unit.

(4) "Tail section" means the roof, floor pan, right or left rear quarter panel, deck lid, or rear bumper, if two or more of such parts are assembled together as one unit.

(5) "Federal safety sticker" means a sticker, label, or tag required by 49 U.S.C. Section 30115 or rules adopted under that section.

(6) "Interior component part" means the front or rear seat or radio of a motor vehicle.

(7) "Special accessory part" means the tire, wheel, tailgate, or removable glass top of a motor vehicle.

(8) "Motor vehicle" has the meaning given by Subsection (b), Section 2, Uniform Act Regulating Traffic on Highways (Article 6701d, Texas Civil Statutes).

(b) A salvage vehicle dealer with an endorsement as a used vehicle parts dealer may not receive a motor vehicle unless the dealer first obtains a certificate of authority, sales receipt, or transfer document under Chapter 683, Transportation Code, or a Certificate of Title showing that there are no liens on the vehicle or that all recorded liens have been released. On receipt of a vehicle, a salvage vehicle dealer shall immediately remove any unexpired license plates from the motor vehicle and place them in a secure, locked place. An inventory list of such plates showing the license number, the make, the motor number, and the vehicle identification number of the motor vehicle from which such plates were removed shall be maintained on forms to be furnished by the Texas Department of Transportation. Upon demand and if required, the Certificate of Title or authority, the sales receipt, or transfer document, license plates, and inventory lists shall be surrendered to the Texas Department of Transportation for cancellation. It is further provided that all Certificates of Title covering such motor vehicles shall, if required, be surrendered to the Texas Department of Transportation for cancellation. It shall thereafter be the duty of the Texas Department of Transportation to furnish a signed receipt for the surrendered license plates and Certificates of Title.

(c) A salvage vehicle dealer shall keep an accurate and legible inventory of each used component part purchased by or delivered to the dealer, as follows:

(1) date of purchase or delivery;

(2) name, age, address, sex, and driver's license number of the seller and a legible photocopy of the seller's driver's license;

(3) the license number of the motor vehicle used to deliver the used component part;

(4) a complete description of the item purchased, including the type of material and, if applicable, the make, model, color, and size of the item; and

(5) the vehicle identification number of the motor vehicle from which the used component part was removed.

(d) A salvage vehicle dealer is not required to keep records under Subsection (c) of this section of:

(1) interior used component parts or special accessory parts on a motor vehicle more than 10 years of age; or

(2) used component parts delivered by commercial freight lines or commercial carriers.

(e) In lieu of the requirements contained in Subsection (c) of this section, a salvage vehicle dealer may record the name of the business that the motor vehicle or motor vehicle part is purchased from and the Texas Certificate of Inventory number or federal taxpayer identification number.

(f) A salvage vehicle dealer shall keep all records required to be kept by this article for one year after the date of sale or disposal of the item, and he shall allow an inspection of the records by a peace officer at any reasonable time. A peace officer may inspect the inventory on the premises of the salvage vehicle dealer at any reasonable time in order to verify, check, or audit the records. A salvage vehicle dealer or an employee of the dealer shall allow and shall not interfere with a full and complete inspection by a peace officer of the inventory, premises and inventory records of the dealer.

(g)(1) Except as provided by Subdivision (3) of this subsection, a salvage vehicle dealer shall:

(A) assign a unique inventory number to each transaction in which the dealer purchases or takes delivery of one or more component parts;

(B) attach the unique inventory number to each component part the dealer obtains in the transaction; and

(C) retain each component part in its original condition on the business premises of the salvage vehicle dealer who originally purchased the part for at least three calendar days, excluding Sundays, after the date on which the dealer obtains the part.

(2) A unique inventory number attached to a component part as required by Subdivision (1) of this subsection may not be removed while the part remains in the inventory of the salvage vehicle dealer. If a component part does not have a vehicle identification number or the vehicle identification number has been removed or the vehicle identification number of the vehicle from which the

component part was removed is not available, a motor vehicle salvage dealer shall record the component part or component parts on an affidavit bill of sale. The form of the affidavit bill of sale shall be prescribed and made available by the Texas Department of Transportation.

(3) Subdivisions (1) and (2) of this subsection do not apply to the purchase by a salvage vehicle dealer of a nonoperable engine, transmission, or rear axle assembly from another motor vehicle salvage dealer or an automotive-related business.

(h) A salvage vehicle dealer shall keep a record required to be kept by this section on a form prescribed by the Texas Department of Transportation. The dealer shall maintain two copies of each record for one year after the date of sale or disposal of the item. On demand of a peace officer, the dealer shall give a copy of a record to the officer.

(i) The Texas Department of Transportation shall:

(1) prescribe the form to be used as required by Subsection (c) of this section; and

(2) make the form available to salvage vehicle dealers.

(j) A salvage vehicle dealer or an employee of the dealer shall allow an inspection of the dealer's required inventory records and affidavit bills of sale by a peace officer at any reasonable time. A peace officer may inspect the inventory on the premises of the dealer at any reasonable time in order to verify, check, or audit the records. The dealer or the employee shall allow and shall not interfere with a full and complete inspection by a peace officer of the inventory, premises, and required inventory records and affidavit bills of sale of the dealer.

(k) A peace officer may seize, hold, and dispose of according to the Code of Criminal Procedure a motor vehicle or part thereof which has been stolen or which has been altered so as to remove, change, mutilate, or obliterate a permanent vehicle identification number, derivative number, motor number, serial number, or federal safety sticker.

(*l*) Except as provided by Subsections (m) and (*o*) of this section, a person who fails to comply with any provision of this section or violates a provision of this section commits a Class A misdemeanor.

(m) A person commits an offense if the person commits theft as defined by Section 31.03, Penal Code, and the person fails to comply with any provision of this section or violates a provision of this section in conjunction with the commission of the theft.

(n) Except as provided by Subsection (*o*) of this section, an offense under Subsection (m) of this section is a Class A misdemeanor.

(*o*) If it is shown on the trial of an offense under Subsection (m) of this section that the defendant has previously been convicted of an offense under that subsection, the offense is punishable as a felony of the third degree.

*(Chgd. by L.1989, chaps. 610(1), 965(1); L.1991, chap. 14(284(82)); L.1995, chaps. 165(22(19)), 404(2), eff. 9/1/95.)*



## Art. 6687-2a. Injunction; salvage vehicle dealers.

(a) If a salvage vehicle dealer or an employee of the dealer acting in the course of his employment is convicted of more than one offense under Section 1, Chapter 506, Acts of the 57th Legislature, Regular Session, 1961 (Article 6687-2, Texas Civil Statutes), a district attorney of the county in which the dealer's salvage business is located may bring an action in the county to enjoin the dealer's business operations. The proceedings must be brought in the name of the state.

(b) If judgment is in favor of the petitioner, the court shall grant an injunction enjoining the dealer from maintaining or participating in the business of a salvage vehicle dealer for a definite period of time or indefinitely, as determined by the court. The judgment must order that the place where the dealer's business is located be closed for the same period of time.

*(Added by L.1989, chap. 610(2); chgd. by L.1995, chap. 404(3), eff. 9/1/95.)*

## Art. 6687-2b. Hours of operation of motor vehicle salvage yard in populous counties.

(a) A salvage vehicle dealer may not operate heavy machinery in a motor vehicle salvage yard between the hours of 7 p.m. of one day and 7 a.m. of the following day.

(b) *(Repealed by L.1995, chap. 404(5), eff. 9/1/95.)*

(c) This article applies only to a motor vehicle salvage yard located in a county with a population of 2.8 million or more, according to the most recent federal decennial census.

(d) A person who violates this article commits a Class C misdemeanor.

(e) The prosecutor in the county where the salvage yard is located or the city attorney in the municipality where the salvage yard is located may bring suit to enjoin a violation of this article.

(f) In this article, "salvage vehicle dealer" has the meaning assigned by Article 6687-1a, Revised Statutes.

(g) This article excludes sales and purchases by a person who:

(1) is predominately engaged in the business of obtaining ferrous or nonferrous metals that have served their original economic purpose in order to convert such metals, or to sell such metals for conversion, into raw material products consisting of prepared grades and having an existing or potential economic value;

(2) has facilities for performing the process by which ferrous or nonferrous metals are converted into raw material products consisting of prepared grades and having an existing or potential economic value, other than by the exclusive use of hand tools, by methods including, without limitation, the processing, sorting, cutting, classifying, cleaning, baling, wrapping, shredding, shearing, or changing the physical form or chemical content thereof; and

(3) is selling or purchasing such ferrous or nonferrous metals solely for purposes of use in the form of raw materials in the production of new products.

*(Added by L.1993, chap. 1019(1); chgd. by L.1995, chap. 404(4), eff. 9/1/95.)*

## Art. 6687-7. Repaired vehicle records.† [*Records of vehicle repairs.*]

Every person, firm or corporation engaged in the business of operating a repair shop or garage of every kind, within this State, where the repairing, rebuilding or repainting of automobiles is carried on, or electrical work in connection with the repair of automobiles is done and performed, and every person, firm or corporation engaged in the business of the purchase and sale of secondhand or used automobiles within this State, shall keep a well bound book in the office or place of business where said work is carried on, or said business conducted, in which shall be kept, in a clear and intelligent manner, a register of each repair or change in any automobile of every description so repaired or dealt in by any party mentioned in this law. Repairs of a value not exceeding one dollar ($1.00) are hereby excepted.

Said register shall contain a substantially complete and accurate description of each car upon which there is performed said repairs, or upon which there is installed any new parts or accessories of any character, and where the said car is bought or sold as a used car, the said register shall particularly show in each of the cases mentioned, the make of the automobile, the number of cylinders, motor number, passenger capacity, model, and also the name, apparent age and sex and any special identifying physical characteristics of the party or parties claiming to be the owner or owners of the automobile, his or their usual place of address, and the State register number of such automobile. In case of the sale of a used or secondhand car by any dealer, or the owner or proprietor of any garage, a like register shall be made as to the name and address and description of said purchaser, the character and description of said car and the state register thereof. Said registers shall be kept in a secure place and be subject at all times to the inspection of any peace officer desiring to examine the same or any party or parties interested in tracing or locating stolen automobiles.

All records required to be kept by the requirements of this article shall be preserved for one year after the date recorded and shall be open to the inspection of the public at all reasonable hours. Whoever shall fail to comply with any provision of this article shall be fined not less than ten ($10.00) dollars nor more than one hundred dollars ($100.00).

## Art. 6687-9a. Vehicle Storage Facility Act.

**Sec. 1. Short title.** This article may be cited as the Vehicle Storage Facility Act.

**Sec. 2. Definitions.** In this article:

(1) "Commission" means the Texas Transportation Commission.

(2) "Department" means the Texas Department of Transportation.

(3) "Director" means the executive director of the department or a person designated by the executive director who is not below the rank of division or special office director.

(4) "Vehicle storage facility" means a garage, parking lot, or any type of facility owned by a person other than a governmental entity, except as provided by Section 14(f) of this article, for storing or parking 10 or more vehicles a year.

(5) "Vehicle" means a motor vehicle subject to registration under Chapter 501, Transportation Code, or any other device designed to be self-propelled or transported on a public highway.

(6) "Owner of a vehicle" means:

(A) a person in whose name the vehicle is registered under Chapter 501, Transportation Code;

(B) a person in whose name the vehicle is registered under Chapter 502, Transportation Code, or a member of the person's immediate family;

(C) a person who holds the vehicle through a valid lease agreement; or

(D) an unrecorded lienholder whose right to possess the vehicle exists through a chattel mortgage.

(7) "Person" means an individual, corporation, organization, business trust, estate, trust, partnership, association, or other legal entity.

(8) "Principal" means an individual who:

(A) holds personally or as a beneficiary of a trust or by other constructive method:

(i) 10 percent of a corporation's outstanding stock; or

(ii) more than $25,000 of the fair market value of a business;

(B) has the controlling interest in a business;

(C) has a participating interest of more than 10 percent in the profits, proceeds, or capital gains of a business, regardless of whether the interest is direct or indirect, is through shares, stock, or any other manner, or includes voting rights;

(D) is a member of the board of directors or other governing body of a business; or

(E) serves as an elected officer of a business.

(9) "Impoundment" means an action taken by or at the direction of the owner or operator of a vehicle storage facility that is necessary to preserve, protect, or service a vehicle stored or parked at the facility.

*(Chgd. by L.1997, chaps. 187(1), 969(1), eff. 5/21/97, 6/18/97, respectively.)*



**Sec. 3. Exception.** This article does not apply to a vehicle parked or stored at a vehicle storage facility with the consent of the vehicle's owner. This article does not apply to a vehicle storage facility operated by a person licensed pursuant to the Texas Motor Vehicle Commission Code.

**Sec. 4. Authority.** (a) The department may issue licenses to operate vehicle storage facilities.

(b) The commission shall adopt rules establishing requirements for the licensing of persons to operate vehicle storage facilities to ensure that licensed storage facilities maintain adequate standards for the care of stored vehicles.

(c) The department may impose and collect a fee for a license in an amount sufficient to recover the department's costs of administering this Act. Fees collected under this subsection shall be deposited in the general revenue fund. The commission may adopt rules regarding the method of payment of a fee under this Act. The rules may authorize the use of electronic funds transfer or a valid credit card issued by a financial institution chartered by a state or the federal government or by a nationally recognized credit organization approved by the department. The rules may require the payment of a discount or a service charge for a credit card payment in addition to the fee.

(d) The commission may not adopt a rule under this Act that restricts competitive bidding or advertising by a person who holds a license issued under this Act other than a rule to prohibit false, misleading, or deceptive practices. A rule to prohibit false, misleading, or deceptive practices may not:

(1) restrict the use of:

(A) any medium for an advertisement;

(B) the license holder's advertisement under a trade name; or

(C) the license holder's personal appearance or voice in an advertisement, if the license holder is an individual; or

(2) relate to the size or duration of an advertisement by the license holder.

*(Chgd. by L.1997, chaps. 969(2), 1171(6.01), eff. 6/18/97, 9/1/97, respectively.)*

**Sec. 5. Prohibition.** A person may not operate a vehicle storage facility unless the person holds a current license to operate a vehicle storage facility issued to the person by the department. *(Chgd. by L.1997, chap. 969(3), eff. 6/18/97.)*

**Sec. 6. Application.** (a) The commission by rule shall determine the types of information to be supplied on an application for a license under this article, but the rules must require that an application be made under oath and list:

(1) each conviction of a felony, or a misdemeanor for which the maximum punishment is by confinement in jail or by a fine exceeding $200, that was obtained against the applicant or a partner or officer of the applicant in the three years immediately preceding the date of the application;

(2) the name and address of each partner, if the applicant is a partnership; and

(3) the name and address of the president, secretary, and treasurer of the corporation, if the applicant is a corporation.

(b) The application of a corporation must be signed and sworn to by the president and secretary of the corporation.

(c) *(Repealed by L.1989, chap. 1039(5.01(3)), eff. 9/1/89.)*

**Sec. 7. Approval.** The department shall approve an application that is submitted as provided by Section 6 of this article for a license to operate a vehicle storage facility unless the department determines that:

(1) the applicant knowingly supplied false or incomplete information on the application;

(2) the applicant, one of the applicant's partners, a principal or the general manager of the applicant, or one of the applicant's officers has been convicted of a felony, or a misdemeanor for which the maximum punishment is by confinement in jail or by a fine exceeding $500, in the three years preceding the date of the application; or

(3) the vehicle storage facility for which the license is sought does not meet the standards for storage facilities established by the rules of the commission.

*(Chgd. by L.1997, chap. 969(4), eff. 6/18/97.)*

**Sec. 8. Notice of denial.** If the department denies an application for a license under this article, the department shall send written notice of the decision to the applicant, at the address shown on the application, by certified mail, return receipt requested. The notice shall state the reason for the department's decision and that the applicant is entitled to a hearing before the department under Section 11 of this article. The notice may state that the decision is temporary pending compliance by the applicant. If the decision is temporary and the applicant complies with the requirements of this article and rules of the commission before the 15th day after the date the applicant receives the notice, the department shall then approve the application. *(Chgd. by L.1997, chap. 969(5), eff. 6/18/97.)*

**Sec. 9. Term of license.** (a) A license issued under this article is valid for the period set by the department. At least 30 days before the date on which a person's license expires, the commission shall notify the person of the impending expiration. The notice must be in writing and sent to the person's last known address according to the records of the commission.

(b) A person may apply to the department to renew the license on an application form approved by the department. An application for renewal of a license must be accompanied by a nonrefundable fee.

(c) If an application for renewal of a license is not submitted before the date of expiration of the license, the license may not be renewed.

(d) A person whose license expires and is not renewed under this section may apply for a new license under Section 6 of this article.

*(Chgd. by L.1997, chaps. 969(5), 1171(6.02), eff. 6/18/97, 9/1/97, respectively.)*

**Sec. 10. Sanctions.** (a) The commission shall adopt rules relating to the administrative sanctions that may be enforced against a licensee. If a licensee, a partner of a licensee, a principal in the licensee's business, or an employee of the licensee violates, with the knowledge of the licensee, this article or a rule or order adopted under this article, the department may:

(1) issue a written warning to the licensee specifying the violations;

(2) deny, revoke, or suspend an application or license under this article;

(3) place on probation a person whose license has been suspended; or

(4) assess an administrative penalty in an amount not to exceed $1,000 for each violation, with each violation considered a separate offense.

(b) The department may revoke or suspend a license issued under this article or place on probation a person whose license has been suspended if the department determines that a licensee, a partner of the licensee, a principal in the licensee's business, or an employee of the licensee has been finally convicted of:

(1) a felony; or

(2) a misdemeanor that:

(A) is punishable by confinement or by a fine that exceeds $500; and

(B) directly relates to a duty or responsibility of an operator of a vehicle storage facility.

(c) If it appears that a person is in violation of or is threatening to violate this article or a rule or order adopted under this article, the department or the attorney general at the department's request may institute an action for injunctive relief, to recover a civil penalty not to exceed $1,000 for each violation, or for both injunctive relief and the civil penalty. If the department or the attorney general prevails in an action under this subsection, the department or the attorney general is entitled to recover reasonable attorney's fees and court costs.

(d) A peace officer or license and weight inspector for the Department of Public Safety may make an arrest for a violation of a rule adopted under this article.

(e) If the commission places a person on probation under this section, the commission may require the person to report regularly to the commission on any matter that is the basis of the probation.

(f) If the commission proposes to take an action under Subsection (a) or (b) of this section, the person is entitled to a hearing conducted by the State Office of Administrative Hearings. Proceedings for a disciplinary action are governed by the administrative procedure law, Chapter 2001, Government Code. Rules of practice adopted by the commission under Section 2001.004, Government Code, applicable to the proceedings for a disciplinary action may not conflict with rules adopted by the State Office of Administrative Hearings.
*(Chgd. by L.1997, chaps. 969(7), 1171(6.03), eff. 6/18/97, 9/1/97, respectively.)*

**Sec. 10A. Administrative penalties.** (a) In addition to sanctions that may be imposed under Sections 10(c) and 17 of this article, a person who violates Section 5 of this article may be assessed by the department an administrative penalty in an amount not to exceed $10,000 for each violation. Each day a violation continues or occurs is a separate violation for purposes of imposing a penalty.

(b) In determining the amount of the penalty, the department shall consider:

(1) the seriousness of the violation, including the nature, circumstances, extent, and gravity of any prohibited acts, and the hazard or potential hazard created to the health, safety, or economic welfare of the public;

(2) the economic harm to property or the environment caused by the violation;

(3) the history of previous violations;

(4) the amount necessary to deter future violations;

(5) efforts to correct the violation; and

(6) any other matter that justice may require.

(c) An administrative penalty may be assessed under this section only after the person charged with a violation has been given an opportunity for an administrative hearing.

(d) If the person charged requests a hearing or fails to respond timely to notice, the department shall set a hearing and give notice of the hearing to the person charged. The hearing shall be held by an administrative law judge of the State Office of Administrative Hearings. The administrative law judge shall make findings of fact and conclusions of law and issue to the director a proposal for a decision as to the occurrence of the violation.

(e) Based on the findings of fact, conclusions of law, and proposal for a decision, the director by order may find that a violation has occurred and impose a penalty or may find that a violation has not occurred. The director may increase or decrease the amount of the penalty recommended by the administrative law judge.

(f) If the person charged with a violation does not appear for the hearing, the director may assess a penalty and issue an order that the penalty be paid after the department has determined that a violation occurred.

(g) A hearing under this section is an exhaustion of administrative remedies, and an appeal from a hearing is to the district court in Travis County.

(h) Within 30 days after the date the director's order becomes final as provided by Section 2001.144, Government Code, the person charged with the penalty shall:

(1) pay the penalty in full;

(2) stay enforcement of the penalty by:

(A) forwarding the amount of the penalty to the department for placement in an escrow account pending judicial review of the matter; or

(B) posting with the department a supersedeas bond for the amount of the penalty until judicial review is final; or

(3) request the court to stay enforcement of the penalty by:

(A) filing with the court a sworn affidavit of the person stating that the person is financially unable to pay the amount of the penalty and is financially unable to give the supersedeas bond; and

(B) giving a copy of the affidavit to the department by certified mail.

(i) If the department receives a copy of an affidavit under Subsection (h)(3) of this section, the department may file with the court, within five days after the date the copy is received, a contest to the affidavit. The court shall hold a hearing on the facts alleged in the affidavit as soon as practicable and shall stay the enforcement of the penalty on finding that the alleged facts are true. The person who files an affidavit has the burden of proving that the person is financially unable to pay the penalty and to give a supersedeas bond.

(j) Failure to comply with Subsection (h) of this section is a waiver of the right to contest the order.

Printed in the U.S.A. 12

(k) If a court determines that a violation has not occurred or that the amount of the penalty should be reduced or not assessed, the department shall remit the appropriate amount to the person with interest or execute release of the bond.

(*l*) An administrative penalty owed under this section may be recovered in a civil action brought by the attorney general at the request of the department.
*(Added by L.1997, chap. 969(8), eff. 6/18/97.)*

**Sec. 11. Hearing.** (a) A person whose application for a license to operate a storage facility has been denied, whose license has been revoked, or whose application to renew a license has been denied may, before the 15th day after the date the person receives notice of the revocation or denial, request in writing an administrative hearing on the revocation or denial.

(b) The provisions of Chapter 2001, Government Code, relating to notice and hearings on contested cases, apply to notice and hearings on denial, revocation, and renewal of licenses under this article.

(c) A hearing under this section shall be held by an administrative law judge of the State Office of Administrative Hearings. The administrative law judge shall make findings of fact and conclusions of law and promptly issue to the director a proposal for a decision about revocation or denial. Based on the findings of fact, conclusions of law, and proposal for a decision, the director by order may revoke or deny a license.

(d) A hearing under this section is an exhaustion of administrative remedies, and an appeal from a hearing is to the district court in Travis County.
*(Chgd. by L.1997, chap. 969(9), eff. 6/18/97.)*

**Sec. 12. Validity of license.** (a) A license issued under this article is not valid for any person other than the person who applied for the license.

(b) A license issued under this article applies only to a single vehicle storage facility named on the license.

**Sec. 13. Notification of owner.** (a) The operator of a vehicle storage facility who receives a vehicle that is registered in this state and has been towed to the facility for storage shall, not later than the fifth day but not before 24 hours after the date the operator receives the vehicle, send a written notice to the registered owner and the primary lienholder of the vehicle.

(b) The operator of a vehicle storage facility who receives a vehicle that is registered outside this state or the United States shall send a written notice to the vehicle's last registered owner and all recorded lienholders not later than the 14th day but not before 24 hours after the date the operator receives the vehicle.

(c) It is a defense to an action initiated by the department for a violation of this section that the facility has attempted in writing to obtain information from the governmental entity in which the vehicle is registered but was unsuccessful.

(d) The notice must be correctly addressed, with sufficient postage, sent by certified mail, return receipt requested, and must contain:

(1) the date the vehicle was accepted for storage;

(2) the first day for which a storage fee is assessed;

(3) the daily storage rate;

(4) the type and amount of all other charges to be paid when the vehicle is claimed;

(5) the full name, street address, and telephone number of the facility;

(6) the hours during which the owner may claim the vehicle; and

(7) the facility license number preceded by "Texas Department of Transportation Vehicle Storage Facility License Number."

(e) Notice by publication in a newspaper of general circulation in the county in which the vehicle is stored may be used if:

(1) the vehicle is registered in another state;

(2) the operator of the storage facility submits a written request that is correctly addressed, with sufficient postage, and is sent by certified mail, return receipt requested, to the governmental entity in which the vehicle is registered requesting information relating to the identity of the last known registered owner and any lienholder of record;

(3) the identity of the last known registered owner cannot be determined;

(4) the registration does not contain an address for the last known registered owner; and

(5) the operator of the storage facility cannot reasonably determine the identity and address of each lienholder.

(f) Notice by publication under Subsection (e) of this section is not required if all correctly addressed notices sent with sufficient postage under Subsection (a) or (b) of this section are returned because:

(1) the notices were unclaimed or refused; or

(2) the addressees moved without leaving a forwarding address.

(g) Notice by publication must contain all of the information required by this section. The publication may contain a list of more than one vehicle, watercraft, or outboard motor.

(h) Notice under Subsection (a) or (b) of this section is considered to have been given on the date indicated on the postmark and is considered to be timely filed if the postmark shows that it was mailed within the period provided by Subsection (a) or (b) of this section, as applicable, or if publication was made as authorized by Subsection (e) of this section.

(i) The operator of the storage facility may charge the owner of the vehicle a reasonable fee for giving the notice required by this section.

(j) If a vehicle for which notice was given under this section has not, before the 41st day after the date notice was mailed or published, been claimed by a person permitted to claim the vehicle or been taken into custody by a law enforcement agency under Chapter 683, Transportation Code, the operator of the vehicle storage facility shall send a second notice to the registered owner and primary lienholder. The second notice must contain:

(1) the information required under Subsection (d) of this section;

(2) a statement of the right of the facility to dispose of the vehicle under Section 14B of this article; and

(3) a statement that the failure of the owner or lienholder to claim the vehicle before the 30th day after the date the second notice was mailed is:

(A) a waiver by that person of all right, title, and interest in the vehicle; and

(B) a consent to the sale of the vehicle at a public sale.

*(Chgd. by L.1997, chap. 24(1); L.1999, chap. 1376(1), eff. 9/1/99.)*



**Sec. 14. Fees; charges.** (a) The operator of a vehicle storage facility may not charge an owner more than $25 for notification under Section 13 of this article.

(b) The operator of a vehicle storage facility is entitled to charge an owner $10 for any action taken by or at the direction of the operator or owner of the vehicle storage facility necessary to preserve, protect, or service a vehicle stored or parked at the facility.

(c) The operator of a vehicle storage facility may not charge less than $5 or more than $15 for each day or part of a day for storage of a vehicle. A daily storage fee may be charged for a day regardless of whether the vehicle is stored for 24 hours of the day, except that a daily storage fee may not be charged for more than one day if the vehicle remains at the vehicle storage facility less than 12 hours. For the purposes of this subsection, a day is considered to begin and end at midnight.

(d) The operator of a vehicle storage facility may charge a fee under Subsection (c):

(1) for not more than five days before the date notice described by Section 13 of this article is mailed or published; and

(2) after the date notice is mailed or published, for each day the vehicle is in storage until the vehicle is removed and all accrued charges are paid.

(e) The operator of a vehicle storage facility may not charge any additional fees that are similar to notification, impoundment, or administrative fees.

(f) This section controls over any conflicting municipal ordinance or charter provision.

(g) For the purposes of this section, "vehicle storage facility" includes a garage, parking lot, or any type of facility owned by a governmental entity for storing or parking 10 or more vehicles.

*(Chgd. by L.1997, chaps. 187(2), 969(10); L.1999, chap. 1376(3), eff. 9/1/99.)*

**Sec. 14A. Payment by lienholder or insurance company.** A lienholder who repossesses a vehicle, or an insurance company that pays a claim of total loss involving an owner of a vehicle in a vehicle storage facility, is liable to the operator of a vehicle storage facility for all unpaid amounts owed the operator in relation to the delivery of the vehicle to or the storage of the vehicle in the vehicle storage facility regardless of whether an amount accrued before the lienholder repossessed the vehicle or the insurance company paid the claim.

**Sec. 14B. Disposal of certain abandoned vehicles.** (a) The operator of a vehicle storage facility may dispose of a vehicle for which notice was given under Section 13(j) of this article as provided by this section if, before the 30th day after the date the notice was mailed, the vehicle has not been:

(1) claimed by a person entitled to claim the vehicle; or

(2) taken into custody by a law enforcement agency under Chapter 683, Transportation Code.

(b) An operator entitled to dispose of a vehicle under this section may sell the vehicle at a public sale without being required to obtain a release or discharge of any lien on the vehicle. The proceeds from the sale of the vehicle shall be applied to the charges incurred for the vehicle under Section 14 of this article. The operator shall pay excess proceeds, if any, to the person entitled to them.
*(Added by L.1997, chap. 24(2); chgd. by L.1999, chap. 1376(2), eff. 9/1/99.)*

**Sec. 15. Use of fees.** The department shall remit all fees collected under this article for deposit in the general revenue fund. *(Chgd. by L.1997, chap. 969(11), eff. 6/18/97. See other section 15 below.)*

**Sec. 15. Use of fees.** The commission shall remit all fees collected under this article to the Comptroller for deposit in the State Treasury to the credit of the general revenue fund. *(Chgd. by L.1997, chap. 1423(21.67), eff. 9/1/97. See other section 15 above.)*

**Sec. 16.** *(Repealed by L.1997, chap. 969(12), eff. 6/18/97.)*

**Sec. 17. Offenses; penalties.** (a) A person commits an offense if the person:

(1) operates a vehicle storage facility that does not have a valid license issued under this article; or

(2) violates any rule adopted by the commission under this article.

(b) A person convicted of an offense under this section shall be punished by a fine of not less than $200 and not more than $500.

(c) A person commits a separate offense for each day the person acts in violation of this section.
*(Chgd. by L.1989, chap. 1039(2.38), (2.39), (2.41)-(2.49); L.1993, chaps. 401(1), (2), 629(2), 710(4)-(10), 763(1); L.1995, chaps. 705(18)-(21), 940(1), eff. 9/1/95.)*



## LAWS RELATING TO SAFETY RESPONSIBILITY

### Art. 6701j-2. Railroad and highway grade crossing safety instruction.

(a) All driving safety courses approved by the Department of Public Safety or by a court as authorized by law must include instruction on railroad and highway grade crossing safety.

(b) The Department of Public Safety shall by rule provide minimum standards of course content relating to operation of vehicles at railroad and highway grade crossings.
*(Added by L.1989, chap. 466(1), eff. 9/1/89.)*

## LAWS RELATING TO FUEL MIXTURES

### Art. 8614. Sales of certain fuel mixtures.

**Sec. 1. Definitions.** In this Act:

(1) "Automotive fuel rating" has the meaning assigned by 15 U.S.C. Section 2821.

(2) "Dealer" means a person who is the operator of a service station or other retail outlet and who delivers motor fuel into the fuel tanks of motor vehicles or motor boats.

(3) "Motor fuel" has the meaning given that term by Section 153.001, Tax Code.

**Sec. 2. Testing.** In order to determine compliance with the standards and for the enforcement of rules adopted under Sections 3, 3A, 3B, 4, and 5 of this Act, the commissioner of agriculture or an authorized representative of the commissioner may test any motor fuel sold in this state, with or without a complaint about the fuel. Nothing under this section shall prohibit the commissioner from adopting rules relating to the frequency of testing motor fuels. In adopting such rules the commissioner shall consider the nature of the violation, history of past violations, and funds available as provided by Subsection (e), Section 9 of this Act.

**Sec. 3. Posting notice of sale of alcohol and motor fuel mixture.** (a) A motor fuel dealer in this state may not sell or offer for sale any motor fuel from a motor fuel pump that is supplied by a storage tank into which motor fuel containing ethanol in a mixture in which one percent or more of the mixture measured by volume is ethanol or into which motor fuel containing methanol in a mixture in which one percent or more of the mixture measured by volume is methanol has been delivered within the 60-day period preceding the day of sale or offer of sale, unless the dealer prominently displays on the pump from which the mixture is sold a sign that complies with the requirements of Subsection (b) of this section.

(b)(1) The sign required under Subsection (a) of this section must be displayed on each face of the motor fuel pump on which the price of the motor fuel mixture sold from the pump is displayed. The sign must state "Contains Ethanol" or "Contains Methanol," as applicable. The sign must appear in contrasting colors with block letters at least one-half inch in height and one-fourth inch in width and shall be displayed in a clear, conspicuous, and prominent manner, visible to customers using either side of the pump.

(2) In addition to the requirements of Subsection (b)(1) of this section, if a motor fuel pump is supplied by a storage tank into which motor fuel containing 10 percent or more ethanol by volume or five percent or more methanol by volume has been delivered within the 60-day period preceding the day of the sale or offer of sale, the sign shall state the percentage of ethanol or methanol by volume, to the nearest whole percent, of the motor fuel having the highest percentage of ethanol or methanol delivered into that storage tank within the 60-day period. This subsection does not prohibit the posting of other alcohol or additive information, the information and posting being subject to regulations by the commissioner of agriculture.



**Sec. 3A. Sale of motor fuel with automotive fuel rating lower than rating posted on pump label.** A motor fuel dealer in this state may not sell or offer for sale motor fuel from a motor fuel pump if the motor fuel contains an automotive fuel rating that is lower than the automotive fuel rating for that motor fuel posted on the motor fuel pump.

**Sec. 3B. Delivery of motor fuel with automotive fuel rating lower than rating certified by transfer.** A distributor or supplier of motor fuel, as those persons are defined by Section 153.001, Tax Code, may not deliver or transfer motor fuel to a motor fuel dealer in this state if the fuel contains an automotive fuel rating that is lower than the certification of the automotive fuel rating the distributor or supplier is required to make to the motor fuel dealer under federal law.

**Sec. 4. Documentation of motor fuel mixture sales.** (a) A distributor, supplier, wholesaler, or jobber of motor fuel, as those persons are defined by Section 153.001, Tax Code, may not make a delivery of motor fuel containing ethanol or methanol if the ethanol or methanol in the motor fuel mixture exceeds one percent by volume, other than a delivery made into the fuel supply tanks of a motor vehicle, to any outlet in this state unless the person delivers to the outlet receiving the delivery at the time of the delivery of the mixture:

(1) the sign described in Section 3 of this Act in sufficient quantities for the dealer receiving the motor fuel mixture to comply with the requirements of this Act; and

(2) a manifest, bill of sale, bill of lading, or any other document evidencing delivery of the motor fuel containing ethanol or methanol, which shall include a statement showing the percentage of ethanol or methanol contained in the mixture delivered, and the types and percentages of associated cosolvents, if any, contained in the mixture delivered. The document shall also show delivery of the sign or signs, as applicable, required to be delivered by this subsection.

(b) On the request of any motor fuel user, a dealer must reveal the percentage of ethanol contained in motor fuel being sold, the percentage of methanol contained in motor fuel being sold, and, if the motor fuel contains methanol, the types and percentages of associated cosolvents contained in the motor fuel being sold.

(c) The commissioner of agriculture by rule may prescribe the form of the statement required by Subsection (a) of this section.

(d) The signs required to be posted by a motor fuel dealer under Section 3 of this Act and delivered to a motor fuel dealer under this section shall be obtained from the commissioner of agriculture.

(e) If the commissioner of agriculture determines that certain types of motor fuel, such as diesel or liquefied petroleum gas, are not sold in this state as mixtures with alcohol in sufficient quantities to warrant regulation of those deliveries under this Act, the commissioner may limit the application of Section 3 of this Act and this section to motor fuels sold in sufficient quantity to warrant regulation.

**Sec. 5. Dealer and delivery documents.** (a) Each motor fuel dealer in this state shall keep for one year a copy of each manifest, bill of sale, bill of lading, or any other document required to be delivered to the dealer by Section 4 of this Act. During the first 60 days following delivery of a fuel mixture covered by this Act, the dealer shall keep at the station or retail outlet where the motor fuel was delivered a copy of each manifest, bill of sale, bill of lading, or any other document required to be delivered to the dealer by Section 4 of this Act. Each distributor, supplier, wholesaler, or jobber of motor fuel shall keep for one year at the principal place of business a copy of each manifest, bill of sale, bill of lading, or any other document required to be delivered to the dealer by

Section 4 of this Act. The documents are subject to inspection by the commissioner of agriculture or an authorized representative of the commissioner.

(b) The commissioner of agriculture by rule may prescribe the manner of filing documents required to be kept under Subsection (a) of this section, and the time, place, and manner of inspection of the documents.

**Sec. 5A. Documents relating to postings or certification of automotive fuel ratings.** (a) Each motor fuel dealer in this state shall keep for at least one year a copy of:

(1) each delivery ticket or letter of certification on which the motor fuel dealer based a posting of the automotive fuel rating of motor fuel contained in a motor fuel pump;

(2) records of any automotive fuel rating determination made by the motor fuel dealer under 16 C.F.R. Part 306; and

(3) each delivery ticket or letter of certification that is required to be delivered to the dealer under 16 C.F.R. Part 306.

(b) Each distributor or supplier shall keep for at least one year at the principal place of business a copy of each delivery ticket or letter of certification required to be delivered by the distributor or supplier to a motor fuel dealer in this state under 16 C.F.R. Part 306.

(c) A document required to be kept under this section is subject to inspection by the commissioner of agriculture or an authorized representative of the commissioner.

**Sec. 6. Civil Action.** (a) If a motor fuel dealer or a distributor, supplier, wholesaler, or jobber of motor fuel violates Section 3, 3A, 3B, 4, 5, or 5A of this Act, any motor fuel user who has purchased the fuel and who has suffered damages or has a complaint about the product may maintain a civil action against the motor fuel dealer or the distributor, supplier, wholesaler, or jobber of motor fuel. The action may be brought, without regard to any specific amount in damages, in the district court in any county in which the motor fuel dealer, distributor, supplier, wholesaler, or jobber is doing business or in which the motor fuel dealer resides.

(b) In any action under this section, the court shall award to the motor fuel user who prevails the amount of actual damages and grant such equitable relief as the court determines is necessary to remedy the effects of the motor fuel dealer's violation or the distributor, supplier, wholesaler, or jobber's violation of the provisions of Section 3, 3A, 3B, 4, 5, or 5A of this Act, including declaratory judgment, permanent injunctive relief, and temporary injunctive relief. In addition, the court shall award to the motor fuel user who prevails in an action brought hereunder court costs and attorney's fees that are reasonable in relation to the amount of work expended.

(c) In addition to the remedies provided in Subsection (b) of this section, if the trier of fact finds that a violation of Section 3, 4, or 5 of this Act was committed wilfully or knowingly by the defendant, the trier of fact shall award not more than three times the amount of actual damages.

(d) A violation of Section 3, 3A, 3B, 4, 5, or 5A of this Act is also a deceptive trade practice under Subchapter E, Chapter 17, Business & Commerce Code.

(e) Any action alleging a violation of Section 3, 3A, 3B, 4, 5, or 5A of this Act shall be commenced and prosecuted within two years after the date the cause of action accrued.

**Sec. 7. Civil Penalty.** A motor fuel dealer or a distributor, supplier, wholesaler, or jobber of motor fuel who violates a provision of Section 3, 3A, 3B, 4, 5, or 5A of this Act forfeits to the state a civil penalty of not less than $200 nor more than $10,000.

**Sec. 7A. Administrative penalty.** (a) The commissioner of agriculture may impose an administrative penalty against a person licensed or regulated under this Act who violates this Act or a rule or order adopted under this Act.

(b) The penalty for a violation may be in an amount not to exceed $500. Each day a violation continues or occurs is a separate violation for purposes of imposing a penalty.

(c) The amount of the penalty shall be based on:

(1) the seriousness of the violation, including the nature, circumstances, extent, and gravity of any prohibited acts, and the hazard or potential hazard created to the health, safety, or economic welfare of the public;

(2) the economic harm to property or the environment caused by the violation;

(3) the history of previous violations;

(4) the amount necessary to deter future violations;

(5) efforts to correct the violation; and

(6) any other matter that justice may require.

(d) An employee of the Department of Agriculture designated by the commissioner of agriculture to act under this section who determines that a violation has occurred may issue to the commissioner of agriculture a report that states the facts on which the determination is based and the designated employee's recommendation on the imposition of a penalty, including a recommendation on the amount of the penalty.

(e) Within 14 days after the date the report is issued, the designated employee shall give written notice of the report to the person. The notice may be given by certified mail. The notice must include a brief summary of the alleged violation and a statement of the amount of the recommended penalty and must inform the person that the person has a right to a hearing on the occurrence of the violation, the amount of the penalty, or both the occurrence of the violation and the amount of the penalty.

(f) Within 20 days after the date the person receives the notice, the person in writing may accept the determination and recommended penalty of the designated employee or may make a written request for a hearing on the occurrence of the violation, the amount of the penalty, or both the occurrence of the violation and the amount of the penalty.

(g) If the person accepts the determination and recommended penalty of the designated employee, the commissioner of agriculture by order shall approve the determination and impose the recommended penalty.

(h) If the person requests a hearing or fails to respond timely to the notice, the designated employee shall set a hearing and give notice of the hearing to the person. The hearing shall be held by an administrative law judge of the State Office of Administrative Hearings. The administrative law judge shall make findings of fact and conclusions of law and promptly issue to the commissioner of agriculture a proposal for a decision about the occurrence of the violation and the amount of a proposed penalty. Based on the findings of fact, conclusions of law, and proposal for a decision, the commissioner of agriculture by order may find that a violation has occurred and impose a penalty or may find that no violation occurred.

(i) The notice of the commissioner of agriculture's order given to the person under Chapter 2001, Government Code, must include a statement of the right of the person to judicial review of the order.

(j) Within 30 days after the date the commissioner of agriculture's order becomes final as provided by Section 2001.144, Government Code, the person shall:

(1) pay the amount of the penalty;

(2) pay the amount of the penalty and file a petition for judicial review contesting the occurrence of the violation, the amount of the penalty, or both the occurrence of the violation and the amount of the penalty; or

(3) without paying the amount of the penalty, file a petition for judicial review contesting the occurrence of the violation, the amount of the penalty, or both the occurrence of the violation and the amount of the penalty.

(k) Within the 30-day period, a person who acts under Subsection (j)(3) of this section may:

(1) stay enforcement of the penalty by:

(A) paying the amount of the penalty to the court for placement in an escrow account; or

(B) giving to the court a supersedeas bond that is approved by the court for the amount of the penalty and that is effective until all judicial review of the commissioner of agriculture's order is final; or

(2) request the court to stay enforcement of the penalty by:

(A) filing with the court a sworn affidavit of the person stating that the person is financially unable to pay the amount of the penalty and is financially unable to give the supersedeas bond; and

(B) giving a copy of the affidavit to the designated employee by certified mail.

(*l*) A designated employee who receives a copy of an affidavit under Subsection (k)(2) of this section may file with the court, within five days after the date the copy is received, a contest to the affidavit. The court shall hold a hearing on the facts alleged in the affidavit as soon as practicable and shall stay the enforcement of the penalty on finding that the alleged facts are true. The person who files an affidavit has the burden of proving that the person is financially unable to pay the amount of the penalty and to give a supersedeas bond.

(m) If the person does not pay the amount of the penalty and the enforcement of the penalty is not stayed, the designated employee may refer the matter to the attorney general for collection of the amount of the penalty.

(n) Judicial review of the order of the commissioner of agriculture:

(1) is instituted by filing a petition as provided by Subchapter G, Chapter 2001, Government Code; and

(2) is under the substantial evidence rule.

(*o*) If the court sustains the occurrence of the violation, the court may uphold or reduce the amount of the penalty and order the person to pay the full or reduced amount of the penalty. If the court does not sustain the occurrence of the violation, the court shall order that no penalty is owed.

(p) When the judgment of the court becomes final, the court shall proceed under this subsection. If the person paid the amount of the penalty and if that amount is reduced or is not upheld by the court, the court shall order that the appropriate amount plus accrued interest be remitted to the person. The rate of the interest is the rate charged on loans to depository institutions by the New York Federal Reserve Bank, and the interest shall be paid for the period beginning on the date the penalty was paid and ending on the date the penalty is remitted. If the person gave a supersedeas bond and if the amount of the penalty is not upheld by the court, the court shall order the release of the bond. If the person gave a supersedeas bond and if the amount of the penalty is reduced, the court shall order the release of the bond after the person pays the amount.

(q) A penalty collected under this section shall be remitted to the comptroller for deposit in the general revenue fund.

(r) All proceedings under this section are subject to Chapter 2001, Government Code, except as provided by Subsections (s) and (t) of this section.

(s) Notwithstanding Section 2001.058, Government Code, the commissioner of agriculture may change a finding of fact or conclusion of law made by the administrative law judge if the commissioner of agriculture:

(1) determines that the administrative law judge:

(A) did not properly apply or interpret applicable law, department rules or policies, or prior administrative decisions; or

(B) issued a finding of fact that is not supported by a preponderance of the evidence; or

(2) determines that a department policy or a prior administrative decision on which the administrative law judge relied is incorrect or should be changed.

(t) The commissioner of agriculture shall state in writing the specific reason and legal basis for a determination under Subsection (s) of this section.

**Sec. 8. Criminal offenses and penalties.**

(a) A person commits an offense if the person intentionally or knowingly violates Section 3, 3A, 3B, 4, 5, or 5A of this Act or any rule of the commissioner of agriculture prescribed to enforce or implement those sections of this Act.

(b) A person commits an offense if the person intentionally or knowingly:

(1) refuses to permit a person authorized by Section 2 of this Act to test any motor fuel sold or held for sale in this state;

(2) refuses to permit inspection of any document required to be kept or delivered by this Act upon request of a person authorized to inspect such documents by Section 5 or 5A of this Act; or

(3) mutilates, destroys, secretes, forges, or falsifies any document, record, report, or sign required to be delivered, kept, filed, or posted by this Act or any rule prescribed by the commissioner of agriculture for the enforcement of this Act.

(c) An offense under Subsection (a) of this section is a Class C misdemeanor.

(d) An offense under Subsection (b) of this section is a Class B misdemeanor.

(e) The commissioner of agriculture or the authorized representative of the commissioner may request the appropriate prosecuting attorney to prosecute a violation of a provision of this Act.

**Sec. 9. Rules and fees.** (a) The commissioner of agriculture may adopt rules not inconsistent with this Act for the regulation of the sale of motor fuels containing ethanol and methanol.

(b) The comptroller by rule may impose fees for testing, inspection, statement or record forms, sale of signs, or the performance of other services provided as determined necessary by the commissioner of agriculture in the administration of this Act.

(c) In addition to the fees authorized by Subsection (b) of this section, the comptroller by rule may impose a fee to be collected on a periodic basis determined by the comptroller from each distributor, supplier, wholesaler, and jobber who deals in a motor fuel, without regard to whether the motor fuel is subject to regulation under this Act, as determined necessary by the commissioner of agriculture. The comptroller by rule shall prescribe the form for reporting and remitting the fees imposed by and under this section.

(d) The fees and penalties imposed by this Act or by a rule of the comptroller made pursuant to this Act shall be subject to the provisions of Chapter 111 and Sections 153.006, 153.007, and 153.401, Tax Code, except to the extent those sections are in conflict with this Act.

(e) The total amount of the fees collected annually under this Act may not exceed the lesser of:

(1) the costs of administering and enforcing the provisions of this Act as determined necessary by the commissioner of agriculture; or

(2) $500,000.

(f) The fees collected under this section may be used only:

(1) by the comptroller to defray the cost of collecting the fees and penalties imposed by this Act but may not exceed $25,000 annually; or

(2) by the commissioner of agriculture for the administration and enforcement of this Act.

**Sec. 10. Contracting for Enforcement.** The commissioner of agriculture may contract for the enforcement of this Act after due notice.

**Sec. 11. Delivery of Documents to Federal Government.** The commissioner of agriculture, an authorized representative of the commissioner, or the attorney general may make a copy of any manifest, bill of sale, bill of lading, delivery ticket, letter of certification, or other document the commissioner or attorney general is entitled to inspect under this Act. The commissioner, an authorized representative of the commissioner, or the attorney general may deliver the copy of a document described by this section to the federal government for purposes of prosecuting persons for violations of federal law relating to the sale or transfer of motor fuel.
*(Chgd. by L.1997, chap. 1036(1) through (13), eff. 9/1/97.)*



## COMMERCIAL VEHICLE REGISTRATION DATA

This data has been prepared to assist the Tax Collectors and the general public in the proper and legal registration of commercial vehicles and combinations of commercial vehicles. All the data and illustrations are based upon the approximate maximum load the vehicle can carry and the approximate maximum that the vehicles can be registered for under our statutes. The distribution between the two units on combinations is based upon the statutory axle load limitations and the distance in feet between the extremes of any group of axles. The purpose of this distribution is to prevent either unit from being over its registered weight so long as the load does not exceed the maximum load permitted under the scientific load law. It should be understood that the weights applied to the front axles are only approximate as there is no way in determining the actual weight except by weighing the vehicles. Variations should be made on the front axles in accordance with the size and design of the vehicle.

Vehicles that will not transport the maximum load they are equipped to transport should be registered in the following manner: For single units, the empty weight plus the heaviest net load to be carried. For combinations the net load should be divided between the 2 units to conform with the usual distribution of actual load. No commercial vehicle or combination of vehicles may be registered for a gross weight less than the empty weight plus the manufacturer's rated carrying capacity.

Fig. No. 1

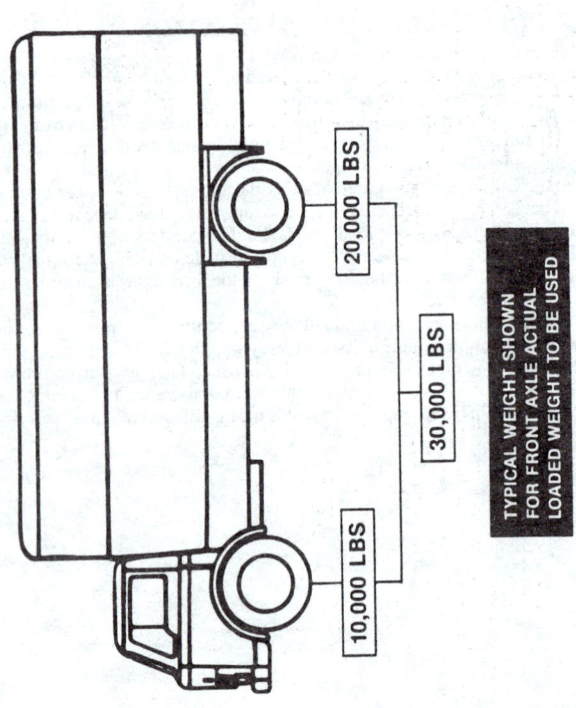
10,000 LBS
20,000 LBS
30,000 LBS
TYPICAL WEIGHT SHOWN
FOR FRONT AXLE ACTUAL
LOADED WEIGHT TO BE USED

Zt

Fig. No. 2

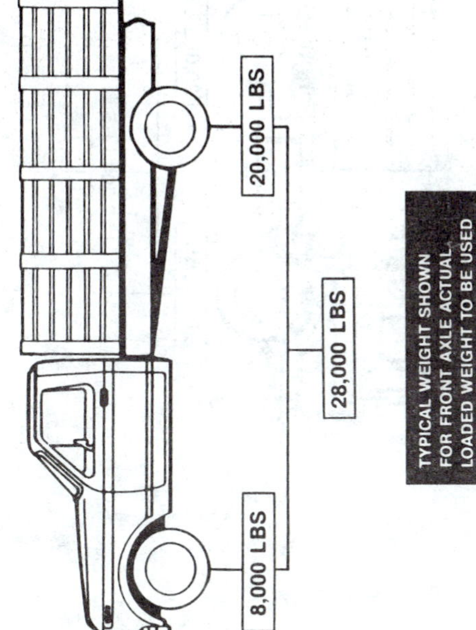
8,000 LBS
20,000 LBS
28,000 LBS
TYPICAL WEIGHT SHOWN
FOR FRONT AXLE ACTUAL
LOADED WEIGHT TO BE USED

Fig. No. 3

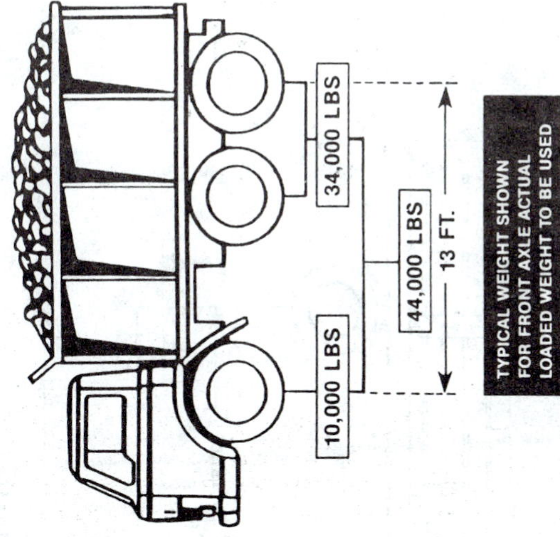
10,000 LBS
34,000 LBS
44,000 LBS
13 FT.
TYPICAL WEIGHT SHOWN
FOR FRONT AXLE ACTUAL
LOADED WEIGHT TO BE USED

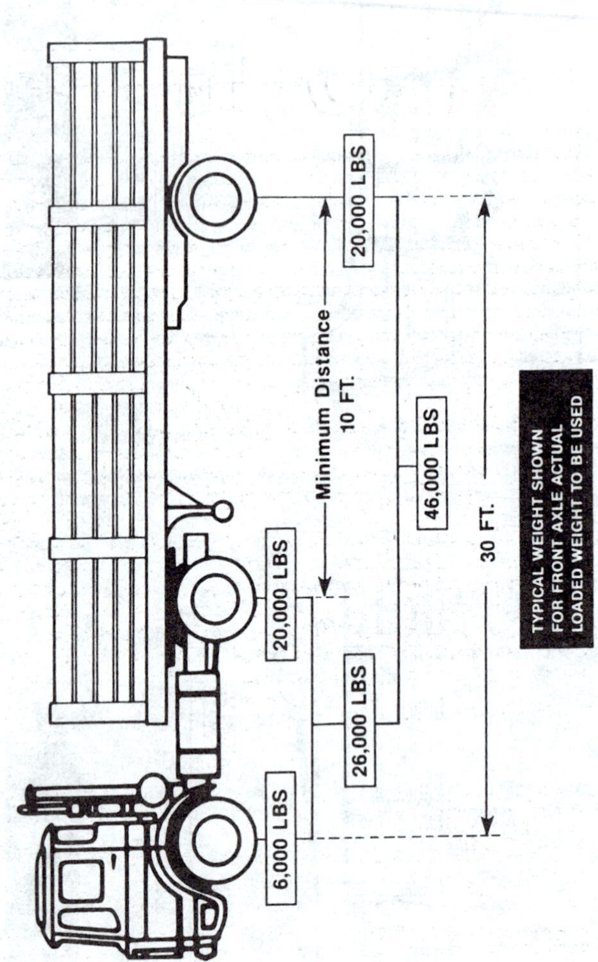
6,000 LBS
20,000 LBS
26,000 LBS
Minimum Distance
10 FT.
20,000 LBS
46,000 LBS
30 FT.
TYPICAL WEIGHT SHOWN
FOR FRONT AXLE ACTUAL
LOADED WEIGHT TO BE USED

Fig. No. 4

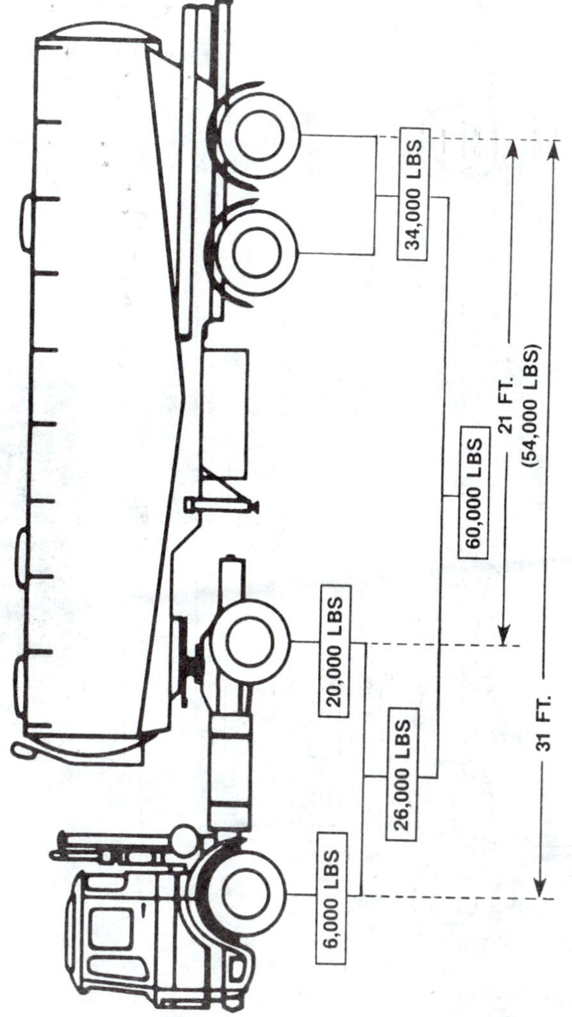


Fig. No. 5

TYPICAL WEIGHT SHOWN FOR FRONT AXLE ACTUAL LOADED WEIGHT TO BE USED

Fig. No. 6

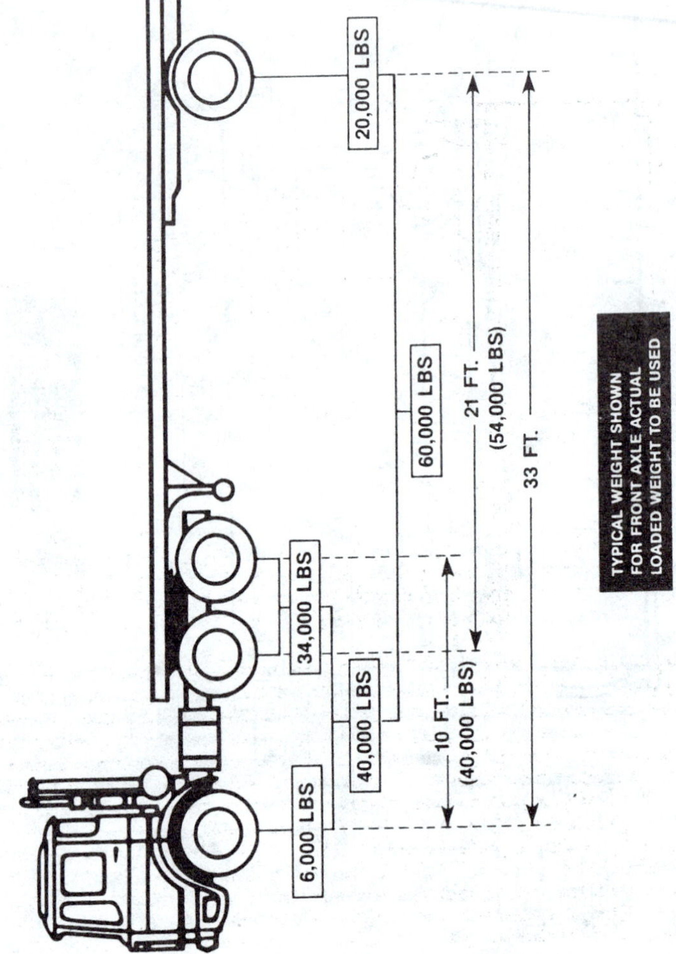
20,000 LBS
60,000 LBS
34,000 LBS
40,000 LBS
6,000 LBS
10 FT.
(40,000 LBS)
21 FT.
(54,000 LBS)
33 FT.
TYPICAL WEIGHT SHOWN
FOR FRONT AXLE ACTUAL
LOADED WEIGHT TO BE USED

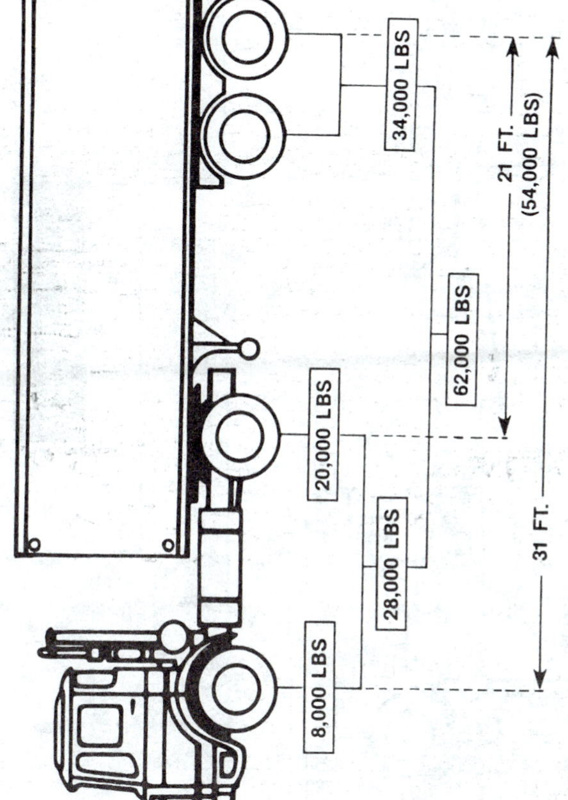

34,000 LBS
21 FT.
(54,000 LBS)
62,000 LBS
20,000 LBS
28,000 LBS
8,000 LBS
31 FT.
TYPICAL WEIGHT SHOWN
FOR FRONT AXLE ACTUAL
LOADED WEIGHT TO BE USED


Fig. No. 7

Fig. No. 8

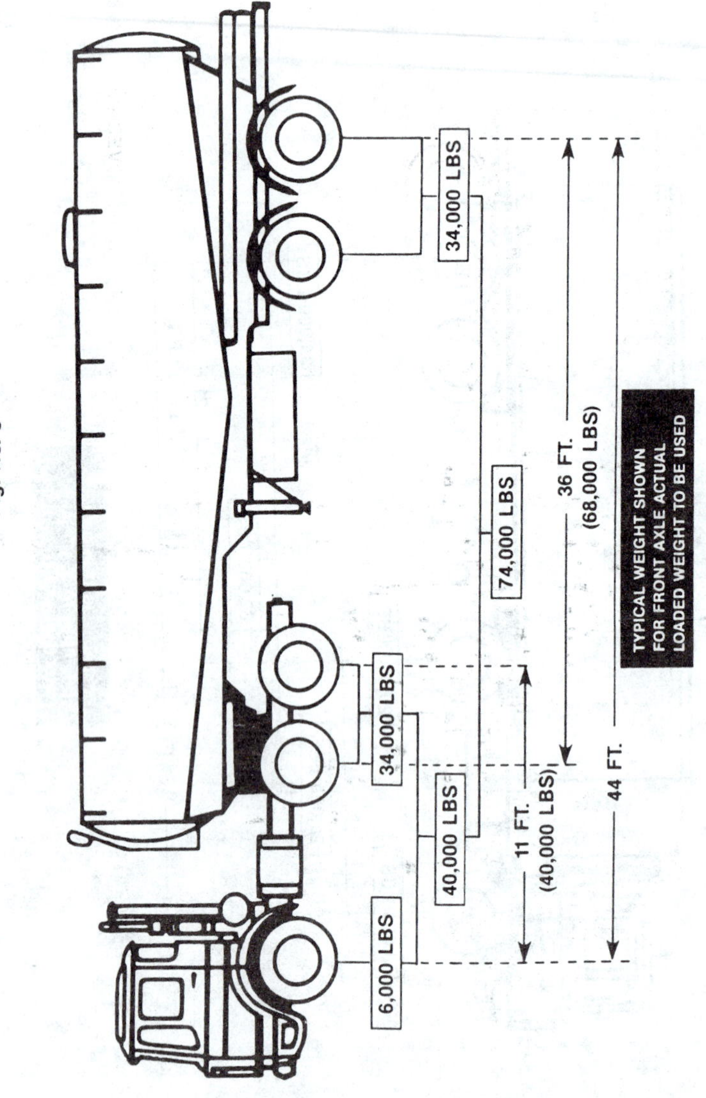


Printed in the U.S.A.

Fig. No. 9

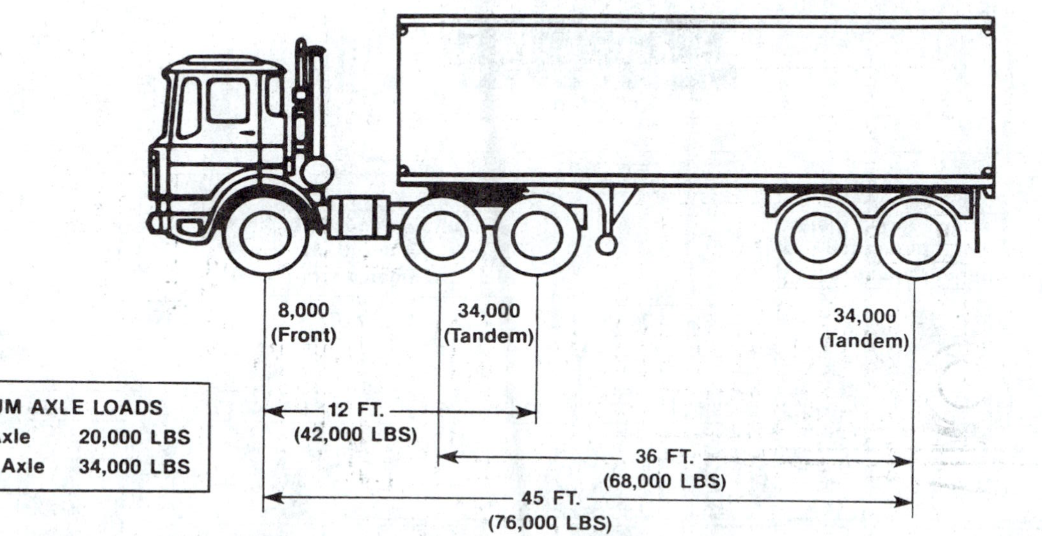


(MINIMUM DISTANCE IN FEET BETWEEN EXTREMES OF CONSECUTIVE TANDEM AXLE GROUPS AND OVERALL AXLE DISTANCE)

TYPICAL WEIGHT SHOWN FOR FRONT AXLE ACTUAL LOADED WEIGHT TO BE USED

Fig. No. 10

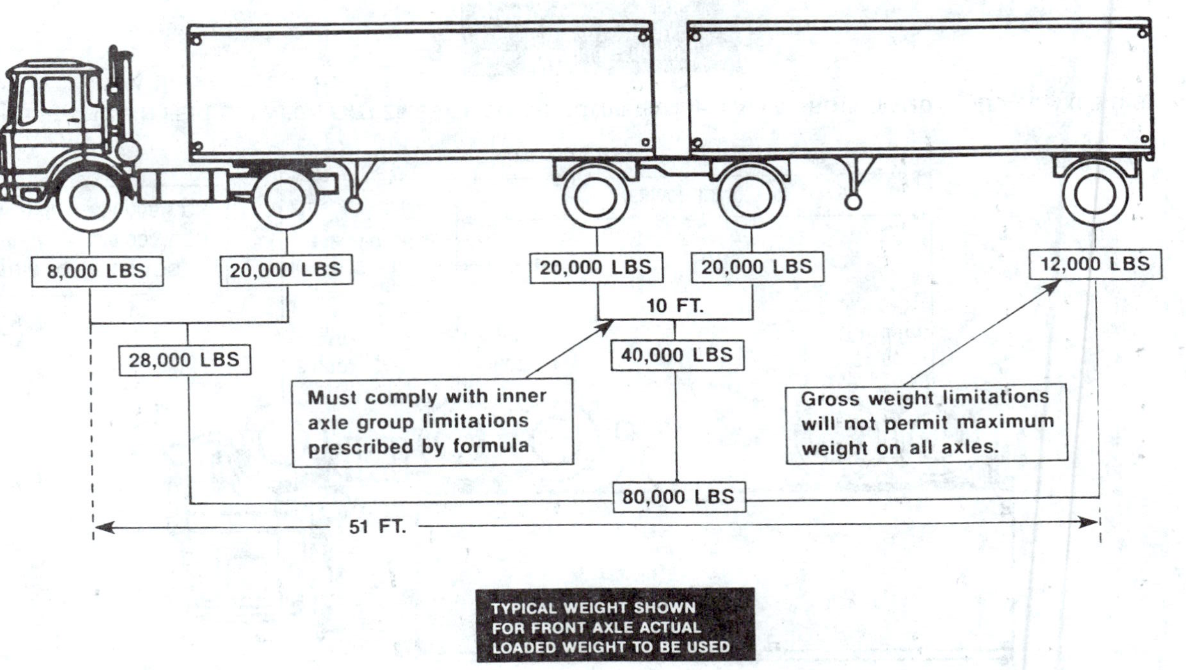
8,000 LBS
20,000 LBS
20,000 LBS
20,000 LBS
12,000 LBS
10 FT.
28,000 LBS
40,000 LBS
Must comply with inner axle group limitations prescribed by formula
Gross weight limitations will not permit maximum weight on all axles.
80,000 LBS
51 FT.
TYPICAL WEIGHT SHOWN FOR FRONT AXLE ACTUAL LOADED WEIGHT TO BE USED

**Fig. No. 11**
**LENGTH LIMITS AS THEY APPLY TO MOTOR VEHICLES OTHER THAN TRUCK TRACTORS**

**TRUCK**

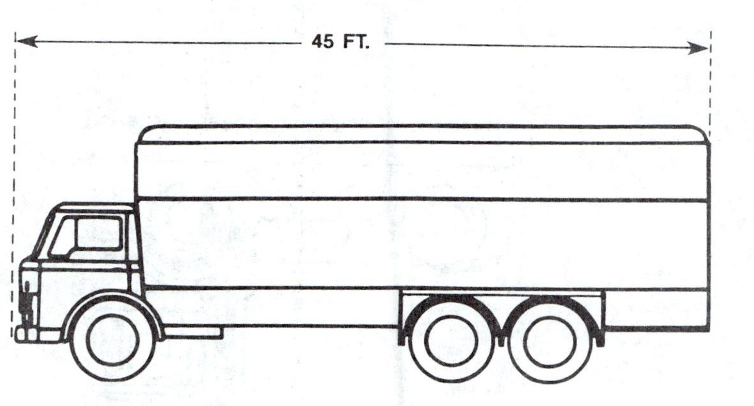


**No motor vehicle other than a truck tractor shall exceed a length of 45 feet.**

Fig. No. 12

LENGTH REQUIREMENTS FOR TRACTOR

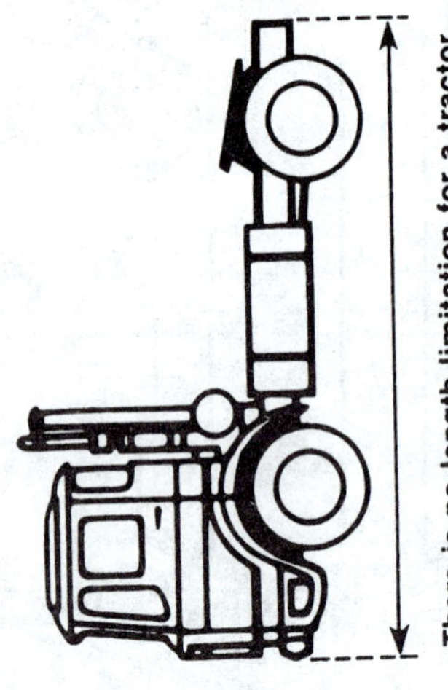

There is no length limitation for a tractor.

Fig. No. 13
TRUCK TRACTOR, SEMITRAILER COMBINATION

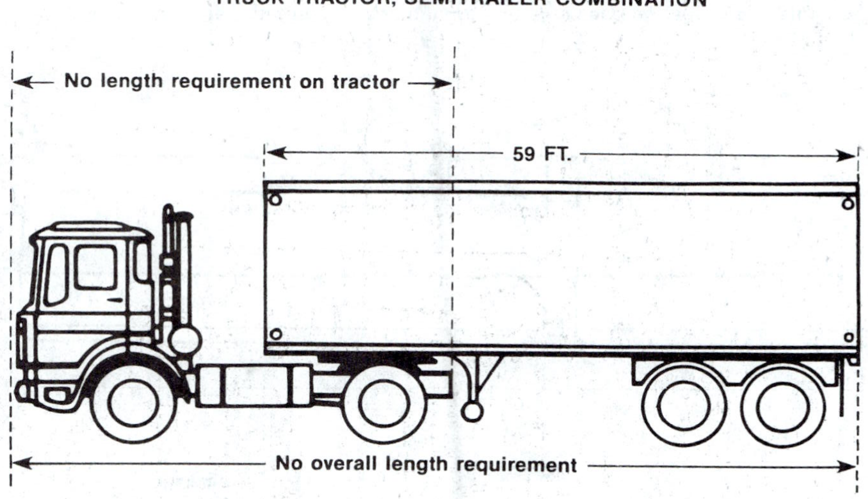


A semitrailer operated in a truck tractor, semitrailer combination would be limited to 59 feet. There is no length limitation for a truck tractor or overall length limitation for this combination.

Fig. No. 14
TRUCK AND TRAILER COMBINATION

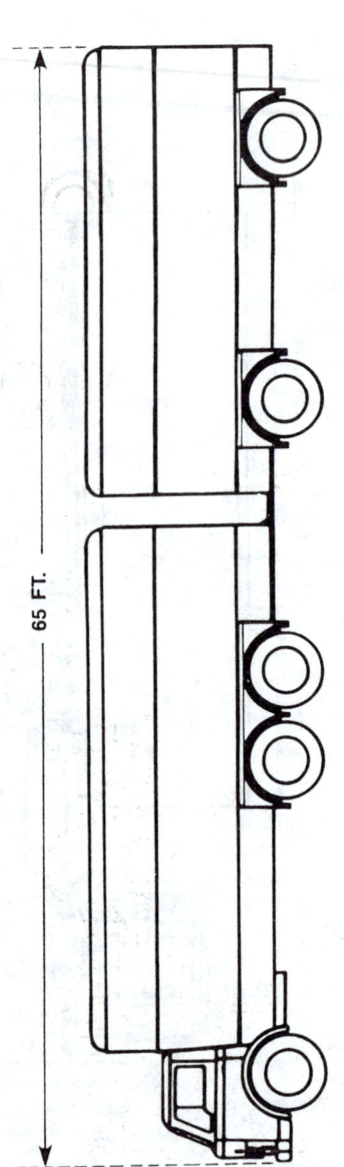


No truck and trailer operated in combination shall exceed 65 feet in overall length.

Printed in the U.S.A.

Fig. No. 15
TRUCK AND SEMITRAILER COMBINATION

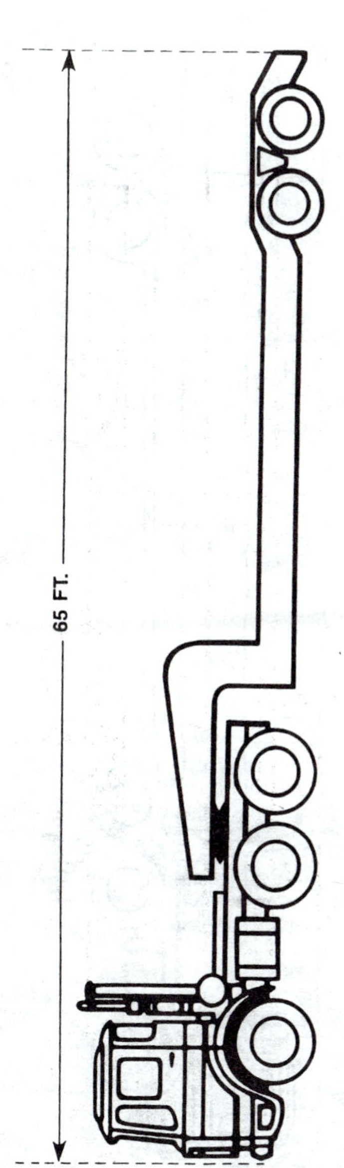


No truck and semitrailer shall exceed a total length of 65 feet.

Printed in the U.S.A. Zt

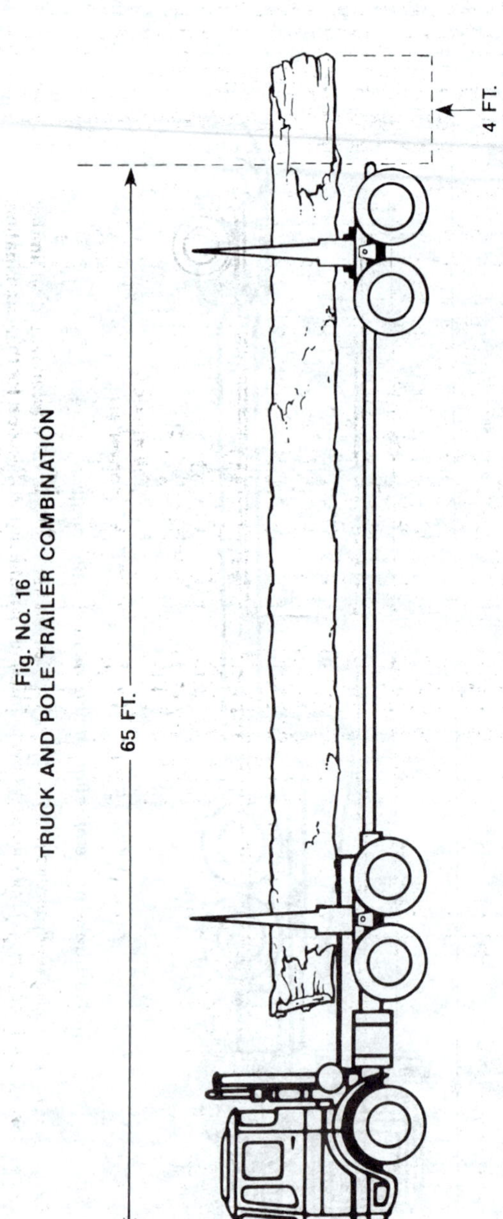


Fig. No. 16
TRUCK AND POLE TRAILER COMBINATION

No truck and pole trailer combaintion shall exceed a total length of 65 feet.

Fig. No. 17

TRUCK TRACTOR, SEMITRAILER, TRAILER AXLE CONVERTER AND SEMITRAILER COMBINATION

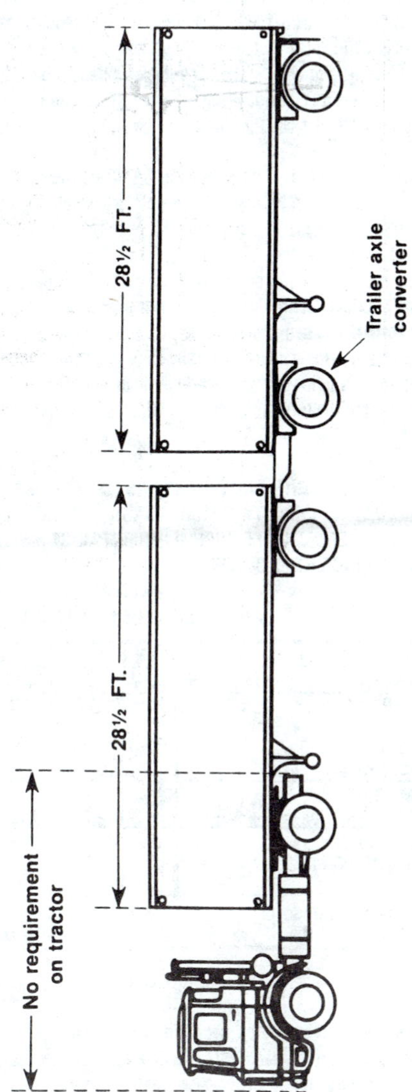


Each semitrailer and trailer operated in a truck-tractor, semitrailer, trailer combination would be limited to 28½ feet. There is no length limitation for a truck tractor or overall length limitation for this combination.

# COMMERCIAL VEHICLE LIGHTING AND REFLECTOR REQUIREMENTS

**TURN SIGNAL LAMPS REGULATIONS**—Reference: TRC §§545.016 and 547.324. Every motor vehicle, trailer, semitrailer and pole trailer shall be equipped with electric turn signal lamps, except that passenger cars and trucks less than 80 inches in width, manufactured or assembled prior to model year 1960, need not be equipped with electric turn signal lamps, unless the body or load of the vehicle or combination of vehicles extends to the side more than 24 inches from the center of the top of the steering wheel post, or the rear limit of the body or load exceeds more than 14 feet from the center of the top of the steering wheel post.

**VEHICULAR HAZARD WARNING SIGNALS REGULATIONS**—Reference: TRC §§547.352 and 547.331. After January 1, 1972, every bus, truck, truck-tractor, trailer, semitrailer or pole trailer eighty (80) inches or more in overall width or thirty (30) feet or more in overall length shall be equipped with hazard warning lamps. The lamps used to display such warning to the front shall be mounted at the same level and as widely spaced laterally as practicable, and shall display simultaneously flashing white or amber lights, or any shade of color between white and amber. The lamps used to display such warning to the rear shall be mounted at the same level and as widely spaced laterally as practicable, and shall show simultaneously flashing amber or red lights, or any shade of color between amber and red. (The use of a flasher switch causing the turn signal lamps to flash simultaneously may be used to comply with this section.)

TRAILERS OF THE TYPE, WEIGHT, AND DIMENSIONS LISTED BELOW, OPERATED ONLY DURING DAYTIME AND WHEN VISIBILITY IS MORE THAN 1,000 FEET, ARE PARTIALLY EXEMPT FROM THE LAMP AND REFLECTOR REQUIREMENTS BUT MUST DISPLAY LAMP AND REFLECTOR EQUIPMENT AS INDICATED BELOW.

DAYTIME OPERATION
AND WHEN VISIBILITY IS MORE THAN 1,000′

| WIDTH | LESS THAN 80″ | | 80″ OR MORE | |
|---|---|---|---|---|
| LENGTH | UNDER 30′ | 30′ AND OVER | UNDER 30′ | 30′ AND OVER |
| TRAILER TYPE | | SEE REQUIREMENTS BELOW | | |
| Boat Trailer 0 to 3,000 lbs. gross weight | E | B,E | A,C,E | A,B,C,E |
| Boat Trailer 3,000 lbs. but less than 4,500 lbs. | D,E,F | B,D,E,F | A,C,D,E,F | A,B,C,D,E,F |
| Farm & Fertilizer Trailers not exceeding 15,000 lbs. gross weight | E | B,E | A,C,E | A,B,C,E |
| Mobile Home operated under permit issued by T.H.D. | D,F | D,F | D,F | D,F |

**REQUIREMENTS**

A—Two amber reflectors, one on each side near front.
B—One amber reflector on each side, centrally located on body of trailer.
C—Two red reflectors, one on each side near the rear.
D—Two red stop lamps on the rear, one on each side.
E—Two red reflectors on the rear, one on each side.
F—Electric turn signal lamps on rear.

TEXAS DEPARTMENT OF PUBLIC SAFETY

# COMMERCIAL VEHICLE LIGHTING AND REFLECTOR REQUIREMENTS

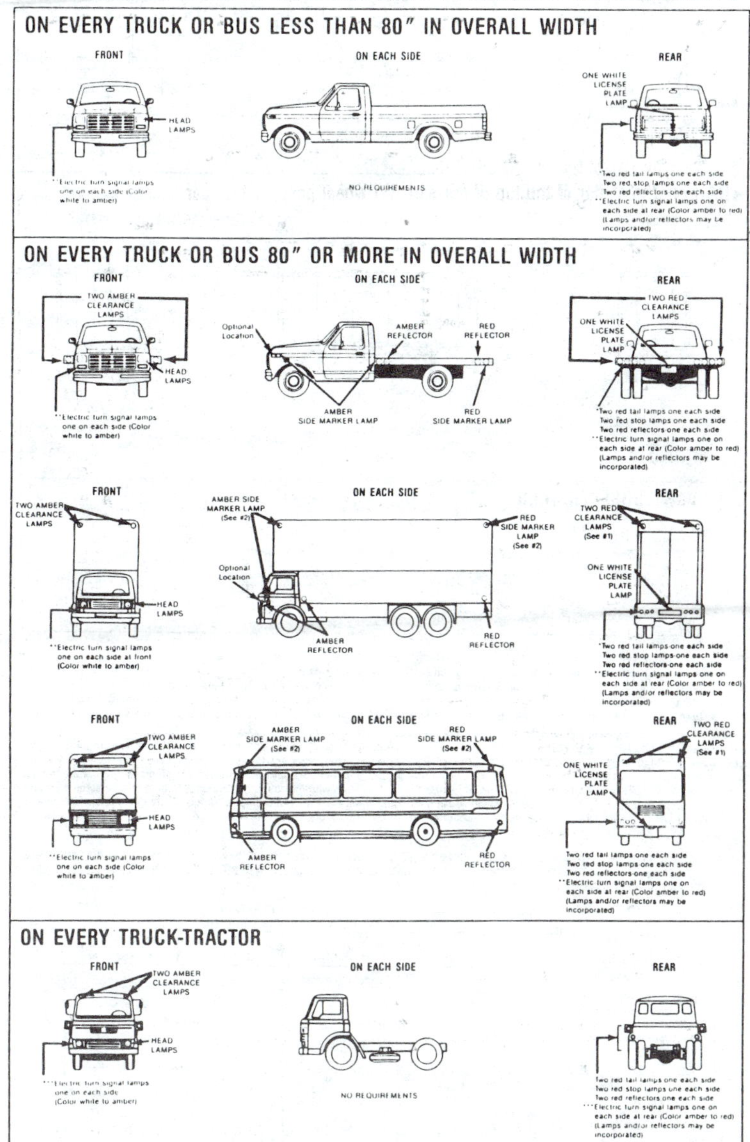


1. Identification lamps are not required, but if present, rear clearance lamps may be mounted at an optional height.
2. Front and rear side marker lamps may be mounted at optional height.

*Trucks manufactured or assembled prior to model year 1960 required to have at least one tail lamp

**See turn signal regulations on back of this sheet.

***Turn signal lamps on truck tractors may be incorporated into one double-faced lamp mounted on each side of vehicle provided signal is visible to front and rear when truck tractor is operated as single unit.

If two license plates are issued rear plate must be illuminated.

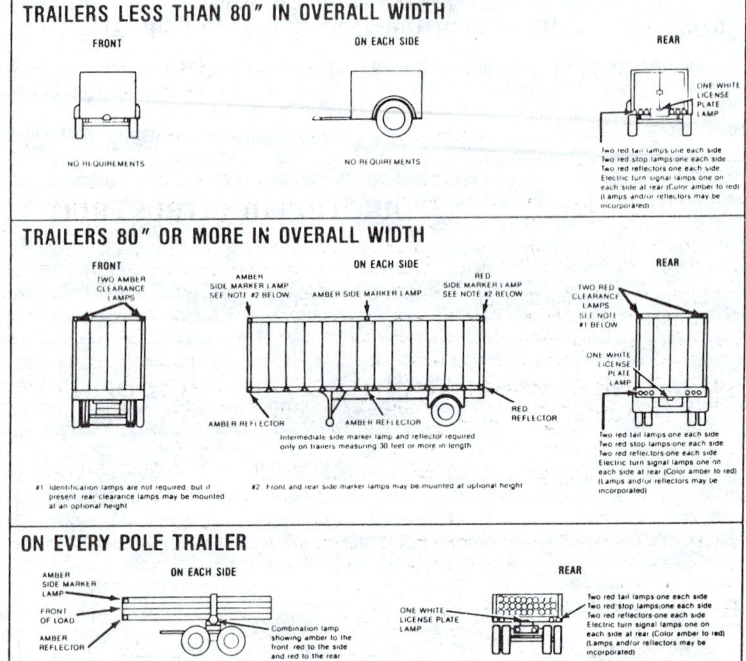


TURN SIGNAL LAMPS REGULATIONS · Reference: TRC §§545.106 and 547.325
Every motor vehicle, trailer, semitrailer and pole trailer shall be equipped with electric turn signal lamps, except that passenger cars and trucks less than 80 inches in width, manufactured or assembled prior to model year 1960, need not be equipped with electric turn signal lamps, unless the body or load of the vehicle or combination of vehicles extends to the side more than 24 inches from the center of the top of the steering wheel post, or the rear limit of the body or load exceeds more than 14 feet from the center of the top of the steering wheel post.

VEHICULAR HAZARD WARNING SIGNALS REGULATIONS · Reference: TRC §§547.352 and 547.331
After January 1, 1972, every bus, truck, truck-tractor, trailer, semitrailer or pole trailer eighty (80) inches or more in overall width or thirty (30) feet or more in overall length shall be equipped with hazard warning lamps. The lamps used to display such warning to the front shall be mounted at the same level and as widely spaced laterally as practicable, and shall display simultaneously flashing white or amber lights, or any shade of color between white and amber. The lamps used to display such warning to the rear shall be mounted at the same level and as widely spaced laterally as practicable, and shall show simultaneously flashing amber or red lights, or any shade of color between amber and red. (The use of a flasher switch causing the turn signal lamps to flash simultaneously may be used to comply with this section.)

TRAILERS OF THE TYPE, WEIGHT, AND DIMENSIONS LISTED BELOW, OPERATED ONLY DURING DAYTIME AND WHEN VISIBILITY IS MORE THAN 1,000 FEET, ARE PARTIALLY EXEMPT FROM THE LAMP AND REFLECTOR REQUIREMENTS BUT MUST DISPLAY LAMP AND REFLECTOR EQUIPMENT AS INDICATED BELOW.

DAYTIME OPERATION
AND WHEN VISIBILITY IS MORE THAN 1,000'

| Width | Less than 80" | | 80" or More | |
|---|---|---|---|---|
| Length | Under 30' | 30' and Over | Under 30' | 30' and Over |
| Trailer Type | See Requirements Below | | | |
| Boat Trailer 0 to 3,000 lbs. gross weight | E | B, E | A, C, E | A, B, C, E |
| Boat Trailer 3,000 lbs. but less than 4,500 lbs. | D, E, F | B, D, E, F | A, C, D, E, F | A, B, C, D, E, F |
| Farm & Fertilizer Trailers not exceeding 20,000 lbs. gross weight | E | B, E | A C, E | A, B, C, E |
| Mobile Home operated under permit issued by T.H.D. | D, F | D, F | D, F | D, F |

REQUIREMENTS

A · Two amber reflectors, one on each side near front.
B · One amber reflector on each side, centrally located on body of trailer.
C · Two red reflectors, one on each side near the rear.
D · Two red stop lamps on the rear, one on each side.
E · Two red reflectors on the rear, one on each side.
F · Electric turn signal lamps on rear.

# AGRICULTURE CODE

## CHAPTER 102. HANDLING AND MARKETING OF CITRUS FRUIT
*(Selected Sections)*

## SUBCHAPTER A. REGULATION OF CITRUS FRUIT DEALERS



## SUBCHAPTER B. TRANSPORTATION OF CITRUS FRUIT





## SUBCHAPTER A. REGULATION OF CITRUS FRUIT DEALERS
*(Repealed by L.1999, chap. 358(27), eff. 9/1/99.)*

**§102.0195.** *(Added by L.1989, chap. 230(116); repealed by L.1999, chap. 358(27), eff. 9/1/99.)*

## SUBCHAPTER B. TRANSPORTATION OF CITRUS FRUIT

### §102.101. Identification signs.† [*Identification; vehicle.*]

(a) A motor vehicle, including a truck or tractor, that hauls citrus fruit in bulk or in open containers for commercial purposes on the highways of this state must be identified by signs showing:

(1) the name of the person who owns the vehicle; or

(2) the name of the person who leases or operates the vehicle.

(b) If a person licensed under Subchapter A of this chapter is the owner or operator of the vehicle, each identification sign must also show "Licensed Citrus Fruit Dealer" under the name of the person.

(c) The lettering on each identification sign must be at least three inches in height.

(d) An identification sign must appear on both sides of the vehicle or on both the front and the rear and must be affixed permanently or in another manner in which it may not easily be removed. If both a tractor and a trailer or two units are used in hauling the citrus fruit, both the tractor and the trailer or both units must be labeled with identification signs in the manner required by this subsection.

### §102.102. Certificate.† [*Identification; operator.*]

A person who operates a motor vehicle, including a truck or tractor, or a motor vehicle and a trailer for hauling citrus fruit in bulk or in open containers for commercial purposes on the highways of this state shall, when operating the vehicle, have on his or her person a certificate or other document showing:

(1) the approximate amount of citrus fruit being hauled;

(2) the name of the owner of the citrus fruit; and

(3) the origin of the citrus fruit.

### §102.103. Exception.† [*Exceptions.*]

This subchapter does not apply to citrus fruit being hauled from the farm or grove to market or the place of first processing by the producer of the citrus fruit operating the producer's vehicle or by an employee of the producer operating a vehicle owned by the producer.

### §102.104. Penalty.† [*Offenses.*]

(a) A person commits an offense if the person:

(1) operates a motor vehicle or a motor vehicle and trailer not identified in accordance with Section 102.101 of this code; or

(2) operates a motor vehicle or motor vehicle and trailer without a certificate or document required by Section 102.102 of this code.

(b) An offense under this section is a Class B misdemeanor.

*(Chgd. by L.1989, chap. 230(118), eff. 9/1/89.)*

### §102.1045. Civil penalty; injunction.

(a) A person who violates this subchapter or a rule adopted under this subchapter is liable to the state for a civil penalty not to exceed $500 for each violation. Each day a violation continues may be considered a separate violation for purposes of a civil penalty assessment.

(b) On request of the department, the attorney general or the county attorney or district attorney of the county in which the violation is alleged to have occurred shall file suit to collect the penalty.

(c) A civil penalty collected under this section shall be deposited in the state treasury to the credit of the General Revenue Fund. All civil penalties recovered in suits first instituted by a local government or governments under this section shall be equally divided between the State of Texas and the local government or governments with 50 percent of the recovery to be paid to the General Revenue Fund and the other 50 percent equally to the local government or governments first instituting the suit.

(d) The department is entitled to appropriate injunctive relief to prevent or abate a violation of this subchapter or a rule adopted under this subchapter. On request of the department, the attorney general or the county or district attorney of the county in which the alleged violation is threatened or is occurring shall file suit for the injunctive relief. Venue is in the county in which the alleged violation is threatened or is occurring.

*(Added by L.1989, chap. 230(119), eff. 9/1/89.)*



## CHAPTER 143. ANIMALS AT LARGE ON HIGHWAYS
*(Selected Sections)*

Section



### §143.101. Definition.

In this subchapter, "highway" means a U.S. highway or a state highway in this state, but does not include a numbered farm-to-market road. The term includes the portion of Recreation Road Number 255 that is located in Newton County between State Highway Number 87 and the boundary line with Jasper County.

### §143.102. Running at large on highway prohibited.† [*Animals at large on highways prohibited.*]

A person who owns or has responsibility for the control of a horse, mule, donkey, cow, bull, steer, hog, sheep, or goat may not knowingly permit the animal to traverse or roam at large, unattended, on the right-of-way of a highway.

### §143.103. Immunity for liability.† [*Driver immunity from liability.*]

A person whose vehicle strikes, kills, injures, or damages an unattended animal running at large on a highway is not liable for damages to the animal except on a finding of:

(1) gross negligence in the operation of the vehicle; or

(2) wilful intent to strike, kill, injure, or damage the animal.

### §143.104. Herding of livestock along highway.† [*Herding livestock on highways.*]

This subchapter does not prevent the movement of livestock from one location to another by herding, leading, or driving the livestock on, along, or across a highway.

### §143.106. Enforcement.

Each state highway patrolman or county or local law enforcement officer shall enforce this subchapter and may enforce it without the use of a written warrant.

### §143.107. Conflict with other law.† [*Procedure over other provisions.*]

This subchapter prevails to the extent of any conflict with another provision of this chapter.

### §143.108. Penalty.† [*Offenses.*]

(a) A person commits an offense if the person violates Section 143.102 of this code.

(b) An offense under this section is a Class C misdemeanor.

(c) A person commits a separate offense for each day that an animal is permitted to roam at large in violation of Section 143.102 of this code.

## CHAPTER 146. SALE AND SHIPMENT OF LIVESTOCK
*(Selected Sections)*

Section





### §146.005. Permits to transport animals.† [*Permit to transport livestock.*]

(a) A person who drives a vehicle, including a truck or an automobile, containing livestock, domestic fowl, slaughtered livestock or domestic fowl, or butchered portions of livestock or domestic fowl on a highway, public street, or thoroughfare or on property owned or leased by a person other than the driver shall obtain a permit authorizing the movement.

(b) A permit must be signed by the owner or caretaker of the shipment or by the owner or person in control of the land from which the driver began movement. In addition, the permit must state the following information:

(1) the point of origin of the shipment, including the name of the ranch or other place;

(2) the point of destination of the shipment, including the name of the ranch, market center, packinghouse, or other place;

(3) the number of living animals, slaughtered animals, or butchered portions; and

(4) the description of the shipment, including the kind, breed, color, and marks and brands of living or slaughtered animals.

(c) On demand of a peace officer or any other person, the driver shall exhibit the permit required by this section or shall provide a signed, written statement containing all of the information required for a permit under this section.

(d) Failure or refusal of a driver to exhibit a permit or provide a statement in accordance with this section is probable cause for a search of the vehicle to determine if it contains stolen property and for detaining the shipment a reasonable length of time to make that determination.

### §146.008. Penalty for transporting animals without permit or with fraudulent permit.† [*Offenses: transporting without permit.*]

(a) A person commits an offense if, under Section 146.005 of this code, the person:

(1) transports living animals, slaughtered animals, or butchered portions of animals without possessing a permit;

(2) fails to exhibit a permit or provide a statement on demand;

(3) transports living animals, slaughtered animals, or butchered portions of animals that are not covered by a permit;

(4) possesses a false or forged permit; or

(5) provides a false written statement.

(b) An offense under Subsection (a)(1) or (a)(2) of this section is a misdemeanor punishable by a fine of not less than $25 nor more than $200 for each animal in the shipment.

(c) An offense under Subsection (a)(3) of this section is a misdemeanor punishable by a fine of not less than $25 nor more than $200 for each animal that is not covered by the permit.

(d) An offense under Subsection (a)(4) or (a)(5) of this section is a misdemeanor punishable by:

(1) a fine of not less than $200 nor more than $500;

(2) confinement in county jail for not less than 60 days nor more than 6 months; or

(3) both fine and confinement under this subsection.

# ALCOHOLIC BEVERAGE CODE

## TITLE 1. GENERAL PROVISIONS

### CHAPTER 1. GENERAL PROVISIONS
*(Selected Sections)*

Section


**§1.03. Public policy.† [*Statement of policy.*]**
This code is an exercise of the police power of the state for the protection of the welfare, health, peace, temperance, and safety of the people of the state. It shall be liberally construed to accomplish this purpose.

**§1.04. Definitions.**
In this code:
(1) "Alcoholic beverage" means alcohol, or any beverage containing more than one-half of one percent of alcohol by volume, which is capable of use for beverage purposes, either alone or when diluted.
(2) "Consignment sale" means:
(A) the delivery of alcoholic beverages under an agreement, arrangement, condition, or system by which the person receiving the beverages has the right at any time to relinquish possession to them or to return them to the shipper and in which title to the beverages remains in the shipper;
(B) the delivery of alcoholic beverages under an agreement, arrangement, condition, or system by which the person designated as the receiver merely acts as an intermediary for the shipper or seller and the actual receiver;
(C) the delivery of alcoholic beverages to a factor or broker;
(D) any method employed by a shipper or seller by which a person designated as the purchaser of alcoholic beverages does not in fact purchase the beverages;
(E) any method employed by a shipper or seller by which a person is placed in actual or constructive possession of an alcoholic beverage without acquiring title to the beverage; or
(F) any other type of transaction which may legally be construed as a consignment sale.
(3) "Distilled spirits" means alcohol, spirits of wine, whiskey, rum, brandy, gin, or any liquor produced in whole or in part by the process of distillation, including all dilutions or mixtures of them, and includes spirit coolers that may have an alcoholic content as low as four percent alcohol by volume and that contain plain, sparkling, or carbonated water and may also contain one or more natural or artificial blending or flavoring ingredients.
(4) "Illicit beverage" means an alcoholic beverage:
(A) manufactured, distributed, bought, sold, bottled, rectified, blended, treated, fortified, mixed, processed, warehoused, stored, possessed, imported, or transported in violation of this code;
(B) on which a tax imposed by the laws of this state has not been paid and to which the tax stamp, if required, has not been affixed; or
(C) possessed, kept, stored, owned, or imported with intent to manufacture, sell, distribute, bottle, rectify, blend, treat, fortify, mix, process, warehouse, store, or transport in violation of this code.
(5) "Liquor" means any alcoholic beverage containing alcohol in excess of four percent by weight, unless otherwise indicated. Proof that an alcoholic beverage is alcohol, spirits of wine, whiskey, liquor, wine, brandy, gin, rum, ale, malt liquor, tequila, mescal, habanero or barreteago, is prima facie evidence that it is liquor.
(6) "Person" means a natural person or association of natural persons, trustee, receiver, partnership, corporation, organization, or the manager, agent, servant, or employee of any of them.
(7) "Wine and vinous liquor" means the product obtained from the alcoholic fermentation of juice of sound ripe grapes, fruits, berries, or honey, and includes wine coolers.
(8) "Hotel" means the premises of an establishment:
(A) where, in consideration of payment, travelers are furnished food and lodging;
(B) in which are located at least 10 adequately furnished completely separate rooms with adequate facilities so comfortably disposed that persons usually apply for and receive overnight ac-

commodations in the establishment, either in the course of usual and regular travel or as a residence; and

(C) which operates a regular dining room constantly frequented by customers each day.

(9) "Applicant" means a person who submits or files an original or renewal application with the county judge, commission, or administrator for a license or permit.

(10) "Commission" means the Texas Alcoholic Beverage Commission.

(11) "Permittee" means a person who is the holder of a permit provided for in this code, or an agent, servant, or employee of that person.

(12) "Ale" or "malt liquor" means a malt beverage containing more than four percent of alcohol by weight.

(13) "Mixed beverage" means one or more servings of a beverage composed in whole or part of an alcoholic beverage in a sealed or unsealed container of any legal size for consumption on the premises where served or sold by the holder of a mixed beverage permit, the holder of a daily temporary mixed beverage permit, the holder of a caterer's permit, the holder of a mixed beverage late hours permit, the holder of a private club registration permit, or the holder of a private club late hours permit.

(14) "Barrel" means, as a standard of measure, a quantity of beer equal to 31 standard gallons.

(15) "Beer" means a malt beverage containing one-half of one percent or more of alcohol by volume and not more than four percent of alcohol by weight, and does not include a beverage designated by label or otherwise by a name other than beer.

(16) "Licensee" means a person who is the holder of a license provided in this code, or any agent, servant, or employee of that person.

(17) "Manufacturer" means a person engaged in the manufacture or brewing of beer, whether located inside or outside the state.

(18) "Original package," as applied to beer, means a container holding one barrel, one-half barrel, one-quarter barrel, or one-eighth barrel of beer in bulk, or any box, crate, carton, or other device used in packing beer that is contained in bottles or other containers.

(19) "Premises" has the meaning given it in Section 11.49 of this code.

(20) "Citizen of Texas" and "citizen of this state" mean a person who is a citizen of both the United States and Texas.

(21) "Minibar" means a closed container in a hotel guestroom with access to the interior of the container restricted by a locking device which requires the use of a key, magnetic card, or similar device.

(22) "Minibar key" means the key, magnetic card, or similar device which permits access to the interior of a minibar.

(23) "Guestroom" means a sleeping room, including any adjacent private living area, in a hotel which is rented to guests for their use as an overnight accommodation.

(24) "Wine cooler" means an alcoholic beverage consisting of vinous liquor plus plain, sparkling, or carbonated water and which may also contain one or more natural or artificial blending or flavoring ingredients. A wine cooler may have an alcohol content as low as one-half of one percent by volume.

*(Chgd. by L.1989, chaps. 532(1), 692(1); L.1993, chap. 934(1), eff. 9/1/93.)*

## §1.05. General penalty.† [*Violations; penalty.*]

(a) A person who violates a provision of this code for which a specific penalty is not provided is guilty of a misdemeanor and on conviction is punishable by a fine of not less than $100 nor more than $1,000 or by confinement in the county jail for not more than one year or by both.

(b) The term "specific penalty," as used in this section, means a penalty which might be imposed as a result of a criminal prosecution.

## §1.08. Criminal negligence defined.

For purposes of this code, a person acts with criminal negligence if the person acts with a mental state that would constitute criminal negligence under Chapter 6, Penal Code, if the act were an offense. *(Added by L.1993, chap. 437(1), eff. 9/1/93. See other section 1.08 below.)*

## §1.08. Criminal negligence standard for administrative action.

For the purposes of administrative actions under this code, a person acts with criminal negligence if the person acts with a mental state that would constitute criminal negligence under Chapter 6, Penal Code, if the act were offense. *(Added by L.1993, chap. 934(2), eff. 9/1/93. See other section 1.08 above.)*

# TITLE 2. ADMINISTRATION OF CODE
*(Selected Chapter)*

## CHAPTER 5. ALCOHOLIC BEVERAGE COMMISSION
*(Selected Section)*



### §5.36. Investigation of violations.† [*Violations; investigation.*]

(a) The commission shall investigate violations of this code and of other laws relating to alcoholic beverages, and shall cooperate in the prosecution of offenders before any court of competent jurisdiction. The commission may seize alcoholic beverages manufactured, sold, kept, imported, or transported in violation of this code and apply for the confiscation of the beverages if required to do so by this code.

(b) *(Repealed by L.1993, chap. 790(46(2)), eff. 9/1/93.)*

# TITLE 3. LICENSES AND PERMITS
*(Selected Chapters)*

## CHAPTER 11. PROVISIONS GENERALLY APPLICABLE TO PERMITS
*(Selected Sections)*



### §11.09. Expiration or suspension of permit.

(a) A permit issued under this code expires one year after the date it is issued except as otherwise provided by this code.

(b) A secondary permit which requires the holder of the permit to first obtain another permit, including a late hours permit or temporary permit, expires on the same date the basic or primary permit expires. The commission may not prorate or refund any part of the fee for the secondary permit if the application of this section results in the expiration of the permit in less than one year.

(c) An action by the commission resulting in the suspension of a basic or primary permit also acts to suspend any secondary permit held by the holder of the basic or primary permit.
*(Chgd. by L.1999, chap. 517(1), eff. 9/1/99.)*

### §11.46. General grounds for refusal.† [*Grounds for refusal.*]

(a) The commission or administrator may refuse to issue an original or renewal permit with or without a hearing if it has reasonable grounds to believe and finds that any of the following circumstances exists:

(1) the applicant has been convicted in a court of competent jurisdiction of the violation of any provision of this code during the two years immediately preceding the filing of his application;

(2) three years have not elapsed since the termination, by pardon or otherwise, of a sentence imposed on the applicant for the conviction of a felony;

(3) within the six-month period immediately preceding his application the applicant violated or caused to be violated a provision of this code or a rule or regulation of the commission which involves moral turpitude, as distinguished from a technical violation of this code or of the rule;

(4) the applicant failed to answer or falsely or incorrectly answered a question in an original or renewal application;

(5) the applicant is indebted to the state for any taxes, fees, or payment of penalty imposed by this code or by rule of the commission;

(6) the applicant is not of good moral character or his reputation for being a peaceable, law-abiding citizen in the community where he resides is bad;

(7) the applicant is a minor;

(8) the place or manner in which the applicant may conduct his business warrants the refusal of a permit based on the general welfare, health, peace, morals, and safety of the people and on the public sense of decency;

(9) the applicant is in the habit of using alcoholic beverages to excess or is physically or mentally incapacitated;

(10) the applicant will sell liquor unlawfully in a dry area or in a manner contrary to law or will knowingly permit an agent, servant, or employee to do so;

(11) the applicant is not a United States citizen or has not been a citizen of Texas for a period of one year immediately preceding the filing of his application, unless he was issued a permit or renewal permit on or before September 1, 1948, and has at some time been a United States citizen;

(12) the applicant does not provide an adequate building available at the address for which the permit is sought before conducting any activity authorized by the permit;

(13) the applicant is residentially domiciled with a person whose permit or license has been cancelled for cause within the 12 months immediately preceding the date of his present application;

(14) the applicant has failed or refused to furnish a true copy of his application to the commission's district office in the district in which the premises for which the permit is sought are located; or

(15) during the six months immediately preceding the filing of the application the premises for which the permit is sought have been operated, used, or frequented for a purpose or in a manner that is lewd, immoral, or offensive to public decency.

(b) The commission or administrator shall refuse to issue an original permit authorizing the retail sale of alcoholic beverages unless the applicant for the permit files with the application a certificate issued by the comptroller of public accounts stating that the applicants holds, or has applied for and satisfies all legal requirements for the issuance of, a sales tax permit, if required, for the place of business for which the alcoholic beverage permit is sought.

(c) The commission or administrator shall refuse to issue for a period of one year after cancellation a mixed beverage permit or private club registration permit for a premises where a license or permit has been canceled during the preceding 12 months as a result of a shooting, stabbing, or other violent act, or as a result of an offense involving drugs.

*(Chgd. by L.1993, chap. 934(21), eff. 9/1/93.)*

### §11.49. Premises defined; designation of licensed premises.† [*Designation of licensed premises.*]

(a) In this code, "premises" means the grounds and all buildings, vehicles, and appurtenances pertaining to the grounds, including any adjacent premises if they are directly or indirectly under the control of the same person.

(b)(1) Subject to the approval of the commission or the administrator, and except as provided in Subsection (c) of this section, an applicant for a permit or license may designate a portion of the grounds, buildings, vehicles, and appurtenances to be excluded from the licensed premises.

(2) If such a designation has been made and approved as to the holder of a license or permit authorizing the sale of alcoholic beverages at retail or as to a private club registration permit, the sharing of space, employees, business facilities, and services with another business entity (including the permittee's lessor, which, if a corporation, may be a domestic or foreign corporation, but excluding a business entity holding any type of winery permit, a manufacturer's license, or a general, local, or branch distributor's license), does not constitute a subterfuge or surrender of exclusive control in violation of Section 109.53 of this code or the use or display of the license for the benefit of another in violation of Subdivision (15) of Subsection (a) of Section 61.71 of this code. This subsection shall not apply to original or renewal package store permits, wine only package store permits, local distributor's permits, or any type of wholesaler's permits.

(c) An applicant for an original or renewal package store permit, wine only package store permit, local distributor's permit, or any type of wholesaler's permit may not take advantage of the right conferred by Subsection (b) of this section except as permitted in Section 11.50 or 109.53 of this code.

(d) Any package store, wine only package store, wholesaler's, or local distributor's permittee who is injured in his business or property by another person (other than a person in his capacity as the holder of a wine and beer retailer's permit, wine and beer retailer's off-premise permit, private club registration permit, or mixed beverage permit or any person in the capacity of lessor of the holder of such a permit) by reason of anything prohibited in this section or Section 109.53 of this code is entitled to the same remedies available to a package store permittee under Section 109.53 of this code. Except for actions brought against a person in his capacity as the holder of or as the lessor of the holder of a wine and beer retailer's permit, wine and beer retailer's off-premise permit, mixed beverage permit, or private club registration permit, the statute of limitations for any action brought under this section or Section 109.53 of this code for any cause of action arising after the effective date of this Act is four years unless a false affidavit has been filed with the commission in which event the statute of limitations is 10 years for all purposes.

(e) When a designation under Subsection (b) of this section is made by a wine and beer retailer or a beer retailer, selling primarily for off-premise consumption, or by a wine and beer retailer's off-premise permittee, no more than 20 percent of the retail floor and display space of the entire premises may be included in the licensed premises, and all the retail floor and display space in the licensed premises must be compact and contiguous and may not be gerrymandered. However, the retail floor and display space included in the licensed premises may be in two separate locations within the retail premises if the total retail floor and display space included in the licensed premises does not exceed 20 percent of the floor and display space of the entire premises and each of the two portions of floor and display space included in the licensed premises is itself compact and contiguous and not gerrymandered. In addition to the one or two separate locations of retail floor and display space on the premises, the licensed premises may include the cash register and check-out portions of the premises provided that (1) no alcoholic beverages are displayed in the check-out or cash register portion of the premises, and (2) the area of the check-out and cash register portions of the premises are counted towards the total of 20 percent of the retail floor and display space that may be dedicated to the sale and display of wine and beer. A storage area that is not accessible or visible to the public may be included in the licensed premises but shall not be considered retail floor and display space for purposes of this section. The commission or administrator shall adopt rules to implement this subsection and to prevent gerrymandering.

### §11.493. Supplemental or amended designation of premises.

(a) Subject to the limitations imposed by Section 11.49 of this code on designating a portion of a building or premises where alcoholic beverages may be sold or served, a licensee or permittee may submit an amended or supplemental designation at the time of renewal of the license or permit or at any other time, provided the license or permit is not under suspension at the time the amended or supplemental designation is submitted.

(b) If the amended or supplemental designation is submitted with an application for renewal, there is no charge for processing the document. If the amended or supplemental designation is submitted at any other time, the commission may charge a fee for processing the document. *(Added by L.1991, chap. 1(1), eff. 8/23/91.)*

### §11.61. Cancellation or suspension of permit.† [*Permit: cancellation, suspension.*]

(a) As used in Subsection (b) of this section, the word "permittee" also includes each member of a partnership or association and, with respect to a corporation, each officer and the owner or owners of a majority of the corporate stock. This section shall not be construed as prohibiting anything permitted under Section 22.06, 24.05, or 102.05 of this code.

(b) The commission or administrator may suspend for not more than 60 days or cancel an original or renewal permit if it is found, after notice and hearing, that any of the following is true:

(1) the permittee has been finally convicted of a violation of this code;

(2) the permittee violated a provision of this code or a rule of the commission;

(3) the permittee was finally convicted of a felony while holding an original or renewal permit;

(4) the permittee made a false or misleading statement in connection with his original or renewal application, either in the formal application itself or in any other written instrument relating to the application submitted to the commission, its officers, or employees;

(5) the permittee is indebted to the state for taxes, fees, or payment of penalties imposed by this code, by a rule of the commission, or by Chapter 183, Tax Code;

(6) the permittee is not of good moral character or his reputation for being a peaceable and law-abiding citizen in the community where he resides is bad;

(7) the place or manner in which the permittee conducts his business warrants the cancellation or suspension of the permit based on the general welfare, health, peace, morals, and safety of the people and on the public sense of decency;

(8) the permittee is not maintaining an acceptable bond;

(9) the permittee maintains a noisy, lewd, disorderly, or unsanitary establishment or has supplied impure or otherwise deleterious beverages;

(10) the permittee is insolvent or mentally or physically unable to carry on the management of his establishment;

(11) the permittee is in the habit of using alcoholic beverages to excess;

(12) the permittee knowingly misrepresented to a customer or the public any liquor sold by him;

(13) the permittee was intoxicated on the licensed premises;

(14) the permittee sold or delivered an alcoholic beverage to an intoxicated person;

(15) the permittee possessed on the licensed premises an alcoholic beverage that he was not authorized by his permit to purchase and sell;

(16) a package store or wine only package store permittee transported or shipped liquor, or caused it to be transported or shipped, into a dry state or a dry area within this state;

(17) the permittee is residentially domiciled with a person who has a financial interest in an establishment engaged in the business of selling beer at retail, other than a mixed beverage establishment, except as authorized by Section 22.06, 24.05, or 102.05 of this code;

(18) the permittee is residentially domiciled with a person whose permit or license was cancelled for cause within the 12-month period preceding his own application;

(19) the permittee is not a citizen of the United States or has not been a citizen of Texas for a period of one year immediately preceding the filing of his application, unless he was issued an original or renewal permit on or before September 1, 1948, and has been a United States citizen at some time;

(20) the permittee permitted a person to open a container of alcoholic beverage or possess an open container of alcoholic beverage on the licensed premises unless a mixed beverage permit has been issued for the premises; or

(21) the permittee failed to promptly report to the commission a breach of the peace occurring on the permittee's licensed premises.

(c) The commission or administrator may refuse to renew or, after notice and hearing, suspend for not more than 60 days or cancel a permit if the commission or administrator finds that the permittee:

(1) no longer holds a sales tax permit, if required, for the place of business covered by the alcoholic beverage permit; or

(2) is shown on the records of the comptroller of public accounts as being subject to a final determination of taxes due and payable under the Limited Sales, Excise and Use Tax Act (Chapter 151, Tax Code), or is shown on the records of the comptroller of public accounts as being subject to a final determination of taxes due and payable under Chapter 321, Tax Code.

(d) The commission or administrator without a hearing may for investigative purposes summarily suspend a mixed beverage permit or a wine and beer retailer's permit for not more than seven days if the commission or administrator finds that a shooting, stabbing, or murder has occurred on the licensed premises which is likely to result in a subsequent act of violence. Notice of the order suspending the permit shall be given to the permittee personally within 24 hours of the time the violent act occurs. If the permittee cannot be located, notice shall be provided by posting a copy of the order on the front door of the licensed premises.

(e) Except as provided by Subsection (f), the commission or administrator shall cancel an original or renewal permit if it is found, after notice and hearing, that the permittee knowingly allowed a person to possess a firearm in a building on the licensed premises. This subsection does not apply to a person:

(1) who holds a security officer commission issued by the Texas Board of Private Investigators and Private Security Agencies, if:

(A) the person is engaged in the performance of the person's duties as a security officer;

(B) the person is wearing a distinctive uniform; and

(C) the weapon is in plain view;

(2) who is a peace officer;

(3) who is a permittee or an employee of a permittee if the person is supervising the operation of the premises; or

(4) who possesses a concealed handgun of the same category the person is licensed to carry under Subchapter H, Chapter 411, Government Code, unless the person is on the premises of a business described by Section 46.035(b)(1), Penal Code.

(f) The commission may adopt a rule allowing:

(1) a gun or firearm show on the premises of a permit holder, if the premises is owned or leased by a governmental entity or a nonprofit civic, religious, charitable, fraternal, or veterans' organization;

(2) the holder of a permit for the sale of alcoholic beverages for off-premises consumption to also hold a federal firearms license; or

(3) the ceremonial display of firearms on the premises of the permit holder.

*(Chgd. by L.1993, chap. 934(24); L.1995, chaps. 998(1), 1001(5), 1060(3); L.1997, chaps. 1001(1), 1261(17); L.1999, chap. 62(9.19), eff. 9/1/99.)*

## CHAPTER 26. WINE AND BEER RETAILER'S OFF-PREMISE PERMIT

*(Selected Section)*



### §26.05. Warning sign required.† [*Warning sign.*]

(a) Each holder of a wine and beer retailer's off-premise permit shall display in a prominent place on his premises a sign stating in letters at least two inches high: IT IS A CRIME (MISDEMEANOR) TO CONSUME LIQUOR OR BEER ON THESE PREMISES. The commission or administrator may require the holder of the permit to also display the sign in a language other than English if it can be observed or determined that a substantial portion of the expected customers speak the other language as their familiar language.

(b) A permittee who fails to comply with this section commits a misdemeanor punishable by a fine of not more than $25.



## CHAPTER 28. MIXED BEVERAGE PERMIT

*(Selected Section)*



### §28.13. Issuance of permit for certain boats.† [*Mixed beverage permit for boats.*]

(a) A mixed beverage permit may be issued for a boat if:

(1) the boat:

(A) carries at least 350 passengers;

(B) weighs at least 90 gross tons; and

(C) is at least 80 feet long; and

(2) the home port of the boat is in an area where the sale of mixed beverages is legal.

(b) For purposes of Section 11.38 of this code, the home port of the boat is treated as the location of the licensed premises.

(c) A permit for a boat is inoperative in a dry area.

## CHAPTER 30. DAILY TEMPORARY MIXED BEVERAGE PERMIT

*(Selected Section)*



### §30.01. Authorized activities.† [*Daily temporary mixed beverage permit: authorized activities.*]

The holder of a daily temporary mixed beverage permit may sell mixed beverages for consumption on the premises for which the permit is issued.

## CHAPTER 32. PRIVATE CLUB REGISTRATION PERMIT

*(Selected Sections)*

### §32.01. Authorized activities.

(a) A private club registration permit authorizes alcoholic beverages belonging to members of the club to be:

(1) stored, possessed, and mixed on the club premises; and

(2) served for on-premises consumption only to members of the club and their families and guests, by the drink or in sealed, unsealed, or broken containers of any legal size.

(b) An applicant for or the holder of a private club registration permit may apply to the commission to have the activities authorized under the permit restricted to the storage and service of wine, beer, and malt liquor for members of the club. Except as otherwise provided by this chapter, an applicant for or the holder of a permit that is restricted under this subsection is subject to all the requirements of this chapter. The commission may adopt rules as necessary to implement this subsection.

*(Chgd. by L.1993, chap. 290(1), eff. 9/1/93.)*

### §32.04. Application for permit; renewals.† [*Private club registration permit: applications, renewals.*]

(a) A private club which meets the requirements set forth in Section 32.03 of this code may apply for a private club registration permit on forms furnished by the commission and containing all information necessary to insure compliance with the provisions of this code.

(b) Each applicant shall furnish a true copy of his application to the commission's district office in the district in which the premises sought to be covered by the permit are located prior to the filing of the original application with the commission at Austin.

(c) Applications for a renewal permit shall be filed with the commission within 30 days prior to the expiration of the current permit.

### §32.05. Locker system.† [*Private club registration permit: locker system.*]

The locker system of storage is a system whereby the club rents a locker to a member in which he may store alcoholic beverages for consumption by himself and his guests. All alcoholic beverages stored at a club under the locker system must be purchased and owned by the member individually.

### §32.06. Pool system.† [*Private club registration permit: pool system.*]

(a) The pool system of storage may be used in any area. Under this system all members of a pool participate equally in the original purchase of all alcoholic beverages. The replacement of all alcoholic beverages shall be paid for either by money assessed equally from each member and collected in advance or by the establishment of an alcoholic beverages replacement account in which a designated percentage of each charge for the service of alcoholic beverages, as determined by the club's governing body, is deposited.

(b) If an alcoholic beverages replacement account is used:

(1) each service check shall have printed on it the percentage of the service charge that is to be deposited in the alcoholic beverages replacement account;

(2) no money other than the designated percentage of service charges may be deposited in the replacement account;

(3) the replacement of alcoholic beverages may be paid for only from money in the replacement account;

(4) the club's governing body may transfer from the replacement account to the club's general operating account any portion of the replacement account that the governing body determines is in excess of the amount that will be needed to purchase replacement alcoholic beverages, but it may make only one transfer in a calendar month; and

(5) the club shall maintain a monthly record of the total amount of alcoholic beverage service charges collected, the amount deposited in the replacement account, the amount used to purchase alcoholic beverages, and the amount transferred to the club's general operating account.

## §32.09. Temporary members.† [*Temporary club members.*]

(a) The manager or other person in charge of the club premises may allow a person to enter the club if he possesses a valid temporary membership card which has no erasures or changes and which has the temporary dates in a prominent position on the card. A temporary member may enjoy the club's services and privileges for a period of not more than three days per invitation. A temporary member may bring not more than three guests to the club and must remain in their presence while they are at the club.

(b) At the time of his admission the temporary member shall pay the club a fee of $3, which shall represent the fee payable by the permittee to the state. All fees and payments from temporary members shall be collected in cash or through credit cards approved by the commission or administrator.

(c) Temporary memberships shall be governed by rules promulgated by the commission consistent with the provisions of this section.

## §32.10. Guests.

(a) Guests shall be limited to those who accompany a member or temporary member onto the premises or for whom a member, other than a temporary member, has made prior arrangements with the management of the club.

(b) Except as provided in Subsection (c) of this section no guest shall be permitted to pay, by cash or otherwise, for any service of alcoholic beverages. Any charge for a service rendered to a guest by the club must be billed by the club to the member or temporary member sponsoring the guest. A club shall bill a member other than a temporary member for the service of guests in the club's regular billing cycle.

(c) The manager of a hotel who is a member of a private club located within the hotel building may issue a guest card to a patron of the hotel who is staying in the hotel overnight or longer. The holder of the guest card may be served alcoholic beverages in the club or the holder's hotel room. The guest may not be allowed to pay, by cash or otherwise, at the time of service in the private club. The charge for service shall be billed to the hotel manager's account in the hotel and shall be collected by the hotel manager along with other hotel charges, including the charge for using the hotel room, when the patron leaves the hotel. The hotel records shall be available for inspection at the request of the commission. If the club operates under the locker system a guest shall be served from the locker rented to the manager of the hotel.

(d) The commission shall promulgate rules necessary to implement the provisions of this section.

## §32.11. Fraternal and veterans organizations.

(a) In this section:

(1) "Fraternal organization" means:

(A) any chapter, aerie, parlor, lodge, or other local unit of an American national fraternal organization or Texas state fraternal organization that, as the owner, lessee, or occupant, has operated an establishment for fraternal purposes for at least one year. If an American national fraternal organization, it must actively operate in not fewer than 31 states and have at least 300 local units in those 31 states, and must have been in active, continuous existence for at least 20 years. If a Texas state fraternal organization, it must actively operate in at least two counties of the state and have at least 10 local units in those two counties, and must have been in active, continuous existence for at least five years;

(B) a hall association or building association of a local unit described in Paragraph (A), all the capital stock of which is owned by the local unit or the members of the local unit, and which operates the clubroom facilities of the local unit;

(C) a building association not owned by a local unit described in Paragraph (A) but one that is composed wholly of members appointed by a county commissioners court to administer, manage, and control an exposition center containing an exhibition area of not less than 100,000 square feet and an arena with not less than 6,000 fixed seats, situated on property with an area of not less than 50 acres that is owned, together with all buildings, appurtenances, and parking areas, by a county; or

(D) a chapter or other local unit of an American national fraternal organization that promotes physical fitness and provides classes in athletics to children and that, as owner, lessee, or occupant, has operated an establishment for fraternal purposes for at least one year. The fraternal organization must:

(i) actively operate in not fewer than 12 states;

(ii) have at least six local units in this state; and

(iii) have at least one unit in this state that has been in active, continuous existence for at least 75 years.

(2) "Veterans organization" means an organization composed of members or former members of the armed forces of the United States which is organized for patriotic and public service purposes, including the American Legion, Veterans of Foreign Wars, Disabled American Veterans, Jewish War Veterans, American GI Forum, Catholic War Veterans, or any veterans organization chartered by the United States Congress.

(b) The permit fee imposed by Section 32.02 of this code and the provisions of Section 32.03 and 32.10 of this code requiring regular food service and prohibiting guests from paying in cash do not apply to a fraternal or veterans organization. Those organizations are also exempt from Sections 32.05 and 32.06 of this code, and the members of the organization may use any club funds owned by them jointly, including revenue from the service of alcoholic beverages, to replenish their joint stock of alcoholic beverages.

(c) The requirement that the fraternal or veterans organization hold a private club registration permit is satisfied by the issuance of a certificate by the commission that states that the organization meets the requirements of this section.

(d) All other provisions of this code apply to fraternal and veterans organizations.

*(Chgd. by L.1995, chap. 338(1), eff. 9/1/95.)*



### §32.12. Inspection of premises.† [*Premises: inspection.*]

The acceptance of a private club registration permit constitutes an express agreement and consent on the part of the private club that any authorized representative of the commission or any peace officer has the right and privilege to freely enter the club premises at any time to conduct an investigation or to inspect the premises for the purpose of performing a duty imposed by this code.

### §32.14. Unregistered clubs; prohibited activities.† [*Prohibited activities of unregistered clubs.*]

(a) No permittee, licensee, or any other person shall deliver, transport, or carry an alcoholic beverage to, into, or on the premises of any establishment, location, room, or place purporting to be a club, or holding itself out to the public or any person as a club or private club, unless the club holds a private club registration permit.

(b) No person may store, possess, mix, or serve by the drink or in broken or unsealed containers an alcoholic beverage on the premises of any establishment, location, room, or place purporting to be a club or private club unless the club holds a private club registration permit.

(c) An alcoholic beverage stored or possessed on the premises of any establishment, location, room, or place purporting to be a club, or holding itself out to the public or any person as a club or private club, is declared to be an illicit beverage and subject to seizure without a warrant unless a private club registration permit has been issued for the premises, location, room, or place.

### §32.15. Removal of beverages from premises.

A private club, irrespective of location or system of storage of alcoholic beverages, may not permit any person to remove any alcoholic beverages from the club premises, except as authorized by Subsection (b) of Section 28.10 of this code.

### §32.17. Cancellation or suspension of permit; grounds.† [*Grounds for cancellation or suspension of permit.*]

(a) The commission or administrator may cancel or suspend for a period of time not exceeding 60 days, after notice and hearing, an original or renewal private club registration permit on finding that the permittee club has:

(1) sold, offered for sale, purchased, or held title to any alcoholic beverage so as to constitute an open saloon;

(2) refused to allow an authorized agent or representative of the commission or a peace officer to come on the club premises for the purposes of inspecting alcoholic beverages stored on the premises or investigating compliance with the provisions of this code;

(3) refused to furnish the commission or its agent or representative when requested any information pertaining to the storage, possession, serving, or consumption of alcoholic beverages on club premises;

(4) permitted or allowed any alcoholic beverages stored on club premises to be served or consumed at any place other than on the club premises;

(5) failed to maintain an adequate building at the address for which the private club registration permit was issued;

(6) caused, permitted, or allowed any member of a club in a dry area to store any liquor on club premises except under the locker system;

(7) caused, permitted, or allowed any person to consume or be served any alcoholic beverage on the club premises:

(A) at any time on Sunday between the hours of 1:15 a.m. and 10 a.m. or on any other day at any time between the hours of 12:15 a.m. and 7 a.m., if the club does not have a private club late hours permit, except that an alcoholic beverage served to a customer between 10 a.m. and 12 noon on Sunday must be provided during the service of food to the customer; or

(B) at any time on Sunday between the hours of 2 a.m. and 10 a.m. or on any other day at any time between the hours of 2 a.m. and 7 a.m., if the club has a private club late hours permit, except that an alcoholic beverage served to a customer between 10 a.m. and 12 noon on Sunday must be provided during the service of food to the customer; or

(8) violated or assisted, aided or abetted the violation of any provision of this code.

(b) As used in Subsection (a)(1) of this section, the term "open saloon" means any place where an alcoholic beverage is sold or offered for sale for beverage purposes by the drink or in broken or unsealed containers, or a place where any alcoholic beverage is sold or offered for sale for on-premises consumption.

(c) After notice and an opportunity for a hearing, the commission or administrator may cancel or suspend the private club registration permit of a permit holder who has restricted the holder's authorized activities under the permit as provided by Section 32.01(b) of this code on a determination that the permit holder is storing or serving alcoholic beverages to club members other than, or in addition to, wine, beer, and malt liquor.

*(Chgd. by L.1993, chaps. 290(3), 934(41); L.1997, chap. 1002(2), eff. 9/1/97.)*

Printed in the U.S.A.

## CHAPTER 33. OTHER PRIVATE CLUB PERMITS
*(Selected Section)*

Section


### §33.01. Authorized activities.† [*Other private club permits: authorized activities.*]

The holder of a private club late hours permit may allow persons to consume or be served alcoholic beverages on club premises on Sunday between the hours of 1:00 a.m. and 2 a.m. and on any other day between the hours of 12 midnight and 2 a.m. if the licensed premises are in an area where consumption or service of alcoholic beverages in a public place during those hours is authorized by this code.

## CHAPTER 61. PROVISIONS GENERALLY APPLICABLE TO LICENSES
*(Selected Sections)*

Section


### §61.03. Expiration or suspension of license.

(a) Except as provided by Subsection (b), a license may not be issued for a term longer than one year. Any license except a branch, importer's, importer's carrier's, or temporary license expires one year after the date on which it is issued.

(b) A secondary license which requires the holder of the license to first obtain another license, including a late hours license or temporary license, expires on the same date the basic or primary license expires. The commission may not prorate or refund any part of the fee for the secondary license if the application of this section results in the expiration of the license in less than one year.

(c) An action by the commission resulting in the suspension of a basic or primary license also acts to suspend any secondary license held by the holder of the basic or primary license.

*(Chgd. by L.1999, chap. 517(3), eff. 9/1/99.)*

## §61.11. Warning sign required.

(a) Each holder of a license who is not otherwise required to display a sign under Section 411.204, Government Code, shall display in a prominent place on the license holder's premises a sign giving notice that it is unlawful for a person to carry a weapon on the premises unless the weapon is a concealed handgun of the same category the person is licensed to carry under Subchapter H, Chapter 411, Government Code.

(b) The sign must be at least 6 inches high and 14 inches wide, must appear in contrasting colors, and shall be displayed in a conspicuous manner clearly visible to the public. The commission or administrator may require the holder of the license to also display the sign in a language other than English if it can be observed or determined that a substantial portion of the expected customers speak the other language as their familiar language.

*(Chgd. by L.1997, chap. 1261(18); L.1999, chap. 62(9.20), eff. 9/1/99.)*

## §61.71. Grounds for cancellation or suspension: retail dealer.† [*Retail dealer license: grounds for cancellation or suspension.*]



(a) The commission or administrator may suspend for not more than 60 days or cancel an original or renewal retail dealer's on-or off-premise license if it is found, after notice and hearing, that the licensee:

(1) violated a provision of this code or a rule of the commission during the existence of the license sought to be cancelled or suspended or during the immediately preceding license period;

(2) was finally convicted for violating a penal provision of this code;

(3) was finally convicted of a felony while holding an original or renewal license;

(4) made a false statement or a misrepresentation in his original application or a renewal application;

(5) with criminal negligence sold, served, or delivered an alcoholic beverage to a minor;

(6) sold, served, or delivered an alcoholic beverage to an intoxicated person;

(7) sold, served, or delivered an alcoholic beverage at a time when its sale is prohibited;

(8) entered or offered to enter an agreement, condition, or system which would constitute the sale or possession of alcoholic beverages on consignment;

(9) possessed on the licensed premises, or on adjacent premises directly or indirectly under his control, an alcoholic beverage not authorized to be sold on the licensed premises, or permitted an agent, servant, or employee to do so, except as permitted by Section 22.06, 24.05, or 102.05 of this code;

(10) does not have at his licensed premises running water, if it is available, and separate toilets for both sexes which are properly identified;

(11) permitted a person on the licensed premises to engage in conduct which is lewd, immoral, or offensive to public decency;

(12) employed a person under 18 years of age to sell, handle, or dispense beer, or to assist in doing so, in an establishment where beer is sold for on-premises consumption;

(13) conspired with a person to violate Section 101.41-101.43, 101.68, 102.11-102.15, 104.04, 108.01, or 108.04-108.06 of this code, or a rule promulgated under Section 5.40 of this code, or accepted a benefit from an act prohibited by any of these sections or rules;

(14) refused to permit or interfered with an inspection of the licensed premises by an authorized representative of the commission or a peace officer;

(15) permitted the use or display of his license in the conduct of a business for the benefit of a person not authorized by law to have an interest in the license;

(16) maintained blinds or barriers at his place of business in violation of this code;

(17) conducted his business in a place or manner which warrants the cancellation or suspension of the license based on the general welfare, health, peace, morals, safety, and sense of decency of the people;

(18) consumed an alcoholic beverage or permitted one to be consumed on the licensed premises at a time when the consumption of alcoholic beverages is prohibited by this code;

(19) purchased beer for the purpose of resale from a person other than the holder of a manufacturer's or distributor's license;

(20) acquired an alcoholic beverage for the purpose of resale from another retail dealer of alcoholic beverages;

(21) owned an interest of any kind in the business or premises of the holder of a distributor's license;

(22) purchased, sold, offered for sale, distributed, or delivered an alcoholic beverage, or consumed an alcoholic beverage or permitted one to be consumed on the licensed premises while his license was under suspension;

(23) purchased, possessed, stored, sold, or offered for sale beer in or from an original package bearing a brand or trade name of a manufacturer other than the brand or trade name shown on the container;

(24) habitually uses alcoholic beverages to excess, is mentally incompetent, or is physically unable to manage his establishment;

(25) imported beer into this state except as authorized by Section 107.07 of this code;

(26) occupied premises in which the holder of a manufacturer's or distributor's license had an interest of any kind;

(27) knowingly permitted a person who had an interest in a permit or license which was cancelled for cause to sell, handle, or assist in selling or handling alcoholic beverages on the licensed premises within one year after the cancellation;

(28) was financially interested in a place of business engaged in the selling of distilled spirits or permitted a person having an interest in that type of business to have a financial interest in the business authorized by his license, except as permitted by Section 22.06, 24.05, or 102.05 of this code;

(29) is residentially domiciled with or related to a person engaged in selling distilled spirits, except as permitted by Section 22.06, 24.05, or 102.05 of this code, so that there is a community of interests which the commission or administrator finds contrary to the purposes of this code;

(30) is residentially domiciled with or related to a person whose license has been cancelled within the preceding 12 months so that there is a community of interests which the commission or administrator finds contrary to the purposes of this code; or

(31) failed to promptly report to the commission a breach of the peace occurring on the licensee's licensed premises.

(b) Subdivisions (9), (28), (29), and (30) of Subsection (a) of this section do not apply to a licensee whose business is located in a hotel in which an establishment authorized to sell distilled spirits in unbroken packages is also located if the licensed premises of the businesses do not coincide or overlap.

(c) The grounds listed in Subsection (a) of this section, except the ground contained in Subdivision (2), also apply to each member of a partnership or association and, as to a corporation, to the president, manager, and owner of the majority of the corporate stock. This subsection shall not be construed as prohibiting anything permitted by Section 22.06, 24.05, or 102.05 of this code.

(d) The grounds set forth in Subdivisions (1), (4)-(14), (16), (18), (19), (21), (23), and (26), of Subsection (a) of this section, also apply to an agent, servant, or employee of the licensee.

(e) The commission or administrator without a hearing may for investigative purposes summarily suspend a retail dealer's on-premise license for not more than seven days if the commission or administrator finds that a shooting, stabbing, or murder has occurred on the licensed premises which is likely to result in a subsequent act of violence. Notice of the order suspending the license shall be given to the licensee personally within 24 hours of the time the violent act occurs. If the licensee cannot be located, notice shall be provided by posting a copy of the order on the front door of the licensed premises.

(f) Except as provided by Subsection (g), the commission or administrator shall cancel an original or renewal dealer's on-premises or off-premises license if it is found, after notice and hearing, that the licensee knowingly allowed a person to possess a firearm in a building on the licensed premises. This subsection does not apply to a person:

(1) who holds a security officer commission issued by the Texas Board of Private Investigators and Private Security Agencies, if:

(A) the person is engaged in the performance of the person's duties as a security officer;

(B) the person is wearing a distinctive uniform; and

(C) the weapon is in plain view;

(2) who is a peace officer;

(3) who is a licensee or an employee of a licensee if the person is supervising the operation of the premises; or

(4) who possesses a concealed handgun of the same category the person is licensed to carry under Subchapter H, Chapter 411, Government Code, unless the person is on the premises of a business described by Section 46.035(b)(1), Penal Code.

(g) The commission may adopt a rule allowing:

(1) a gun or firearm show on the premises of a license holder, if the premises is owned or leased by a governmental entity or a nonprofit civic, religious, charitable, fraternal, or veterans' organization;

(2) the holder of a license for the sale of alcoholic beverages for off-premises consumption to also hold a federal firearms license; or

(3) the ceremonial display of firearms on the premises of the license holder.
*(Chgd. by L.1993, chaps. 437(2), 934(53); L.1995, chap. 998(2); L.1997, chaps. 1001(2), 1138(1), 1261(19); L.1999, chap. 62(9.21), eff. 9/1/99.)*

### §61.721. Cancellation of permit or license in certain municipalities.

The commission or administrator may cancel an original or a renewal wine and beer retailer's permit or retail dealer's on-premise license and may refuse to issue any new alcoholic beverage permit or license for the same premises for one year after the date of cancellation if:

(1) the chief of police of the city or the sheriff of the county in which the premises are located has submitted a sworn statement to the commission stating specific allegations that the place or manner in which the permittee or licensee conducts its business endangers the general welfare, health, peace, morals, or safety of the community and further stating that there is a reasonable likelihood that such conduct would continue at the same location under another licensee or permittee; and

(2) the commission or administrator finds, after notice and hearing within the county where the premises are located, that the place or manner in which the permittee or licensee conducts its business does in fact endanger the general welfare, health, peace, morals, or safety of the community and that there is a reasonable likelihood that such conduct would continue at the same location under another licensee or permittee.
*(Added by L.1993, chap. 139(1), eff. 5/16/93.)*



## CHAPTER 69. RETAIL DEALER'S ON-PREMISE LICENSE
*(Selected Sections)*

Section


### §69.12. Possession of certain beverages prohibited.† [*Possession of unauthorized beverages prohibited.*]

No retail dealer's on-premise licensee, nor the licensee's officer, agent, servant, or employee, may possess on the licensed premises an alcoholic beverage which is not authorized to be sold on the premises.

### §69.13. Breach of peace: retail establishment.† [*Breach of peace: cancellation, suspension of license.*]

The commission or administrator may suspend or cancel the license of a retail beer dealer after giving the licensee notice and the opportunity to show compliance with all requirements of law for retention of the license if it finds that a breach of the peace has occurred on the licensed premises or on premises under the licensee's control and that the breach of the peace was not beyond the control of the licensee and resulted from his improper supervision of persons permitted to be on the licensed premises or on premises under his control.

### §69.14. Seating area required.

A retail dealer's on-premise licensee must have an area designated on the premises for the permittee's customers to sit if they wish to consume beverages sold by the licensee on the premises.

## CHAPTER 70. RETAIL DEALER'S ON-PREMISE LATE HOURS LICENSE

*(Selected Section)*

Section
70.01. Authorized activities.† [*Retail dealer's on-premise late hours license: authorized activities.*]

### §70.01. Authorized activities.† [*Retail dealer's on-premise late hours license: authorized activities.*]

The holder of a retail dealer's on-premise late hours license may sell beer for consumption on the premises on Sunday between the hours of 1:00 a.m. and 2 a.m. and on any other day between the hours of 12 p.m. and 2 a.m. if the premises covered by the license are in an area where the sale of beer during the hours is authorized by this code.

## CHAPTER 71. RETAIL DEALER'S OFF-PREMISE LICENSE

*(Selected Sections)*

Section
71.01. Authorized activities.† [*Retail dealer's off-premise license: authorized activities.*]
71.06. Storing and possessing beer off premises prohibited.† [*Storage and possession of beer: restrictions.*]
71.10. Warning sign required.

### §71.01. Authorized activities.† [*Retail dealer's off-premise license: authorized activities.*]

The holder of a retail dealer's off-premise license may sell beer in lawful containers to consumers, but not for resale and not to be opened or consumed on or near the premises where sold.

### §71.06. Storing and possessing beer off premises prohibited.† [*Storage and possession of beer: restrictions.*]

No holder of a retail dealer's off-premise license may own, possess, or store beer for the purpose of resale except on the licensed premises.

### §71.10. Warning sign required.

(a) Each holder of a retail dealer's off-premise license shall display in a prominent place on his premises a sign stating in letters at least two inches high: IT IS A CRIME (MISDEMEANOR) TO CONSUME LIQUOR OR BEER ON THESE PREMISES.

(b) A licensee who fails to comply with this section commits a misdemeanor punishable by a fine of not more than $25.

# TITLE 4. REGULATORY AND PENAL PROVISIONS

## CHAPTER 101. GENERAL CRIMINAL PROVISIONS

*(Selected Sections)*

Section
101.01. Restraining orders and injunctions.
101.02. Arrest without warrant.† [*Peace officer may arrest without warrant.*]
101.03. Search and seizure.
101.04. Consent to inspect.† [*Licensee's consent to inspection.*]
101.07. Duty of peace officers.† [*Peace officers: duties.*]
101.10. Wholesale or retail sale: prima facie evidence.† [*Prima facie evidence of type of sale.*]
101.31. Alcoholic beverages in dry areas.† [*Alcoholic beverages in dry areas: prohibitions.*]
101.32. Prima facie evidence of intent to sell.† [*Intent to sell: prima facie evidence.*]
101.62. Offensive noise on premises.
101.63. Sale to certain persons.† [*Prohibited sale of alcohol.*]
101.64. Indecent graphic material.† [*Indecent material on premises.*]

101.66. Beverages of certain alcohol content prohibited.
101.70. Common nuisance.
101.71. Inspection of vehicle.
101.72. Consumption of alcoholic beverage on premises licensed for off-premises consumption.† [*Premises licensed for off-premises consumption: consumption of alcoholic beverage.*]
101.73. Expungement of conviction for consumption on premises licensed for off-premises consumption.
101.75. Consumption of alcoholic beverages near schools.

## §101.01. Restraining orders and injunctions.

(a) If a credible person by affidavit informs the attorney general or a county or district attorney that a person is violating or is about to violate a provision of this code, or that a permit or license was wrongfully issued, the attorney general or county or district attorney shall begin proceedings in district court to restrain the person from violating the code or operating under the permit or license.

(b) The court may issue a restraining order without a hearing, and on notice and hearing may grant an injunction, to prevent the threatened or further violation or operation. The court may require the complaining party to file a bond in an amount and with the conditions the court finds necessary.

(c) If the court finds that a person has violated a restraining order or injunction issued under this section, it shall enter a judgment to that effect. The judgment operates to cancel without further proceedings any license or permit held by the person. The district clerk shall notify the county judge of the county where the premises covered by the permit or license are located and shall notify the commission when a judgment is entered that operates to cancel a license or permit.

(d) No license or permit may be issued to a person whose license or permit is cancelled under Subsection (c) of this section for one year after the cancellation.

## §101.02. Arrest without warrant.† [*Peace officer may arrest without warrant.*]

A peace officer may arrest without a warrant any person he observes violating any provision of this code or any rule or regulation of the commission. The officer shall take possession of all illicit beverages the person has in his possession or on his premises as provided in Chapter 103 of this code.

## §101.03. Search and seizure.

(a) A search warrant may issue under Chapter 18, Code of Criminal Procedure, 1965, as amended, to search for, seize, and destroy or otherwise dispose of in accordance with this code:

(1) an illicit beverage;

(2) any equipment or instrumentality used, or capable or designed to be used, to manufacture an illicit beverage;

(3) a vehicle or instrumentality used or to be used for the illegal transportation of an illicit beverage;

(4) unlawful equipment or materials used or to be used in the illegal manufacturing of an illicit beverage;

(5) a forged or counterfeit stamp, die, plate, official signature, certificate, evidence of tax payment, license, permit, or other instrument pertaining to this code; or

(6) any instrumentality or equipment, or parts of either of them, used or to be used, or designed or capable of use, to manufacture, print, etch, indite, or otherwise make a forged or counterfeit instrument covered by Subdivision (5) of this subsection.

(b) Any magistrate may issue a search warrant on the affidavit of a credible person, setting forth the name or description of the owner or person in charge of the premises (or stating that the name and description are unknown), the address or description of the premises, and showing that the described premises is a place where this code has been or is being violated. If the place to be searched is a private dwelling occupied as such and no part of it is used as a store, shop, hotel, boarding house, or for any other purpose except as a private residence, the affidavit must be made by two credible persons.

(c) All provisions of Chapter 18, Code of Criminal Procedure, 1965, as amended, apply to the application, issuance, and execution of the warrant except those that conflict with this section.

(d) The officer executing the warrant shall seize all items described in Subsection (a) of this section, and those items may not be taken from his custody by a writ of replevin or any other process. The officer shall retain the items pending final judgment in the proceedings.

(e) This section does not require a peace officer to obtain a search warrant to search premises covered by a license or permit.

**§101.04. Consent to inspect.†** ***[Licensee's consent to inspection.]***

By accepting a license or permit, the holder consents that the commission, an authorized representative of the commission, or a peace officer may enter the licensed premises at any time to conduct an investigation or inspect the premises for the purpose of performing any duty imposed by this code.

**§101.07. Duty of peace officers.†** ***[Peace officers: duties.]***

All peace officers in the state, including those of cities, counties, and state, shall enforce the provisions of this code and cooperate with and assist the commission in detecting violations and apprehending offenders.

**§101.10. Wholesale or retail sale: prima facie evidence.†** ***[Prima facie evidence of type of sale.]***

(a) Proof that a retail permittee sold or delivered more than three gallons of distilled spirits to a person in a single or continuous transaction is prima facie evidence that the sale was at wholesale.

(b) Proof that a permittee authorized to sell distilled spirits at wholesale sold or delivered less than three gallons of distilled spirits in a single transaction is prima facie evidence that the sale was a retail sale.

(c) The presumption created by Subsection (b) of this section does not apply to the lawful delivery of 2.4 gallons or more of distilled spirits under the authority of a local distributor's permit.

**§101.31. Alcoholic beverages in dry areas.†** ***[Alcoholic beverages in dry areas: prohibitions.]***

Except as otherwise provided in this code, no person in a dry area may manufacture, distill, brew, sell, import into the state, export from the state, transport, distribute, warehouse, store, solicit or take orders for, or possess with intent to sell an alcoholic beverage.

**§101.32. Prima facie evidence of intent to sell.†** ***[Intent to sell: prima facie evidence.]***

(a) Possession of more than one quart of liquor in a dry area is prima facie evidence that it is possessed with intent to sell.

(b) Possession in a dry area of more than 24 twelve-ounce bottles of beer, or an equivalent amount, is prima facie evidence of possession with intent to sell.

**§101.62. Offensive noise on premises.**

No licensee or permittee, on premises under his control, may maintain or permit a radio, television, amplifier, piano, phonograph, music machine, orchestra, band, singer, speaker, entertainer, or other device or person that produces, amplifies, or projects music or other sound that is loud, vociferous, vulgar, indecent, lewd, or otherwise offensive to persons on or near the licensed premises.

**§101.63. Sale to certain persons.†** ***[Prohibited sale of alcohol.]***

(a) A person commits an offense if he knowingly sells an alcoholic beverage to an habitual drunkard or an intoxicated or insane person.

(b) Except as provided in Subsection (c) of this section, a violation of this section is a misdemeanor punishable by a fine of not less than $100 nor more than $500, by confinement in jail for not more than one year, or by both.

(c) If a person has been previously convicted of a violation of this section or of Section 106.03 of this code, a violation is a misdemeanor punishable by a fine of not less than $500 nor more than $1,000, by confinement in jail for not more than one year, or by both.

**§101.64. Indecent graphic material.†** ***[Indecent material on premises.]***

No holder of a license or permit may possess or display on the licensed premises a card, calendar, placard, picture, or handbill that is immoral, indecent, lewd, or profane.

**§101.66. Beverages of certain alcohol content prohibited.**

No person may manufacture, sell, barter, or exchange a beverage that contains alcohol in excess of one-half of one percent by volume and not more than four percent of alcohol by weight, except beer, wine coolers, and spirit coolers. *(Chgd. by L.1993, chap. 934(60), eff. 9/1/93.)*

## §101.70. Common nuisance.

(a) A room, building, boat, structure, or other place where alcoholic beverages are sold, bartered, manufactured, stored, possessed, or consumed in violation of this code or under circumstances contrary to the purposes of this code, the beverages themselves, and all property kept or used in the place, are a common nuisance. A person who maintains or assists in maintaining the nuisance commits an offense.

(b) The county or district attorney in the county where the nuisance exists or the attorney general may sue in the name of the state for an injunction to abate and temporarily and permanently enjoin it. Except as otherwise provided in this section, the proceeding is conducted as other similar proceedings.

(c) The plaintiff is not required to give a bond. The final judgment is a judgment in rem against the property and a judgment against the defendant. If the court finds against the defendant, on final judgment it shall order that the place where the nuisance exists be closed for one year or less and until the owner, lessee, tenant, or occupant gives bond with sufficient surety as approved by the court in the penal sum of at least $1,000. The bond must be payable to the state and conditioned:

(1) that this code will not be violated;

(2) that no person will be permitted to resort to the place to drink alcoholic beverages in violation of this code; and

(3) that the defendant will pay all fines, costs, and damages assessed against him for any violation of this code.

(d) On appeal, the judgment may not be superseded except on filing an appeal bond in the penal sum of not more than $500, in addition to the bond for costs of the appeal. That bond must be approved by the trial court and must be posted before the judgment of the court may be superseded on appeal. The bond must be conditioned that if the judgment of the trial court is finally affirmed it may be forfeited in the same manner and for any cause for which a bond required on final judgment may be forfeited for an act committed during the pendency of an appeal.



## §101.71. Inspection of vehicle.

No holder of a permit issued under Title 3, Subtitle A, of this code, may refuse to allow the commission or its authorized representative or a peace officer, on request, to make a full inspection, investigation, or search of any vehicle.

## §101.72. Consumption of alcoholic beverage on premises licensed for off-premises consumption.† [*Premises licensed for off-premises consumption: consumption of alcoholic beverage.*]

(a) A person commits an offense if the person knowingly consumes liquor or beer on the premises of a holder of a wine and beer retailer's off-premise permit or a retail dealer's off-premise license.

(b) A person is presumed to have knowingly violated Subsection (a) of this section if the warning sign required by either Section 26.05 or 71.10 of this code is displayed on the premises.

(c) Except as provided in Subsection (d) of this section, a violation of this section is a misdemeanor punishable by a fine of not less than $25 nor more than $200.

(d) If a person has been convicted of a violation of this section occurring within a year of a subsequent violation, the subsequent violation is a misdemeanor punishable by a fine of not less than $100 nor more than $200.

## §101.73. Expungement of conviction for consumption on premises licensed for off-premises consumption.

(a) A person convicted of not more than one violation of Section 101.72 of this code within 12 months, after the first anniversary of the conviction, may apply to the court in which he was convicted to have the conviction expunged.

(b) The application shall contain the applicant's sworn statement that he was not convicted of an additional violation of Section 101.72 of this code during the previous 12 months.

(c) If the court finds that the applicant was not convicted of another violation of Section 101.72 of this code during the preceding 12 months, the court shall order the conviction, together with all complaints, verdicts, fines, and other documents relating to the offense, to be expunged from the applicant's record. After entry of the order, the applicant is released from all disabilities resulting from the conviction, and the conviction may not be shown or made known for any purpose.

### §101.75. Consumption of alcoholic beverages near schools.

(a) A person commits an offense if the person possesses an open container or consumes an alcoholic beverage on a public street, public alley, or public sidewalk within 1,000 feet of the property line of a facility that is a public or private school that provides all or any part of kindergarten through twelfth grade.

(b) This section does not apply to the possession of an open container or the consumption at an event duly authorized by appropriate authorities and held in compliance with all other applicable provisions of this code.

(c) An offense under this section is a Class C misdemeanor.

(d) In this section, "open container" has the meaning assigned in Section 109.35.

*(Added by L.1993, chap. 934(63); chgd. by L.1995, chap. 260(6), eff. 5/30/95.)*

## CHAPTER 103. ILLICIT BEVERAGES

*(Selected Sections)*



### §103.01. Illicit beverages prohibited.

No person may possess, manufacture, transport, or sell an illicit beverage.

### §103.02. Equipment or material for manufacture of illicit beverages.† [*Possession of equipment or material for manufacture of illicit beverages.*]

No person may possess equipment or material designed for, capable of use for, or used in manufacturing an illicit beverage.

### §103.03. Seizure of illicit beverages, etc.† [*Peace officer may seize illicit beverages.*]

A peace officer may seize without a warrant:

(1) any illicit beverage, its container, and its packaging;

(2) any vehicle, including an aircraft or watercraft, used to transport an illicit beverage;

(3) any equipment designed for use in or used in manufacturing an illicit beverage; or

(4) any material to be used in manufacturing an illicit beverage.

### §103.04. Arrest of person in possession.† [*Peace officer may arrest persons possessing illicit beverage.*]

A peace officer may arrest without a warrant any person found in possession of:

(1) an illicit beverage;

(2) any equipment designed for use in or used in manufacturing an illicit beverage; or

(3) any material to be used in manufacturing an illicit beverage.

Printed in the U.S.A. Zt

### §103.05. Report of seizure.† [*Seizure of illicit beverage: report.*]

(a) A peace officer who makes a seizure under Section 103.03 of this code shall make a report in triplicate which lists each item seized and the place and name of the owner, operator, or other person from whom it is seized. One copy of the report shall be verified by oath.

(b) The verified copy shall be retained in the permanent files of the commission or other agency making the seizure. The copy is subject to inspection by any member of the legislature or by any authorized law enforcement agency of the state.

(c) One copy of the report shall be delivered to the person from whom the seizure is made.

(d) A peace officer who makes a false report of the property seized commits a felony punishable by confinement in the penitentiary for not less than two years and not more than five years.

(e) A peace officer who fails to file the reports of a seizure as required by this section commits a misdemeanor punishable by a fine of not less than $50 nor more than $100 or by confinement in jail for not less than 10 nor more than 90 days or by both. The commission shall insure that the reports are made by peace officers.

### §103.06. Beverage delivered to commission.† [*Seized beverage: delivery to commission.*]

Any alcoholic beverage, its container, and its packaging which has been seized by a peace officer, as provided in Section 103.03 of this code, may not be replevied and shall be delivered to the commission for immediate public or private sale in the manner the commission considers best.

### §103.14. Institution of suit for forfeiture.† [*Attorney general may institute suit for forfeiture.*]

(a) The attorney general or the county or district attorney in the county in which a seizure is made shall institute a suit for forfeiture of the property or the proceeds in escrow from any sale of illicit beverages, or both, when notified by the commission, or by the seizing officer that a seizure has been made under Section 103.03 of this code.

(b) The forfeiture suit shall be brought in the name of the State of Texas against the property or the proceeds in escrow, or both, and shall be brought in a court of competent jurisdiction in the county in which the seizure was made.

### §103.15. Notice of forfeiture suit.† [*Forfeiture suit: notice.*]

(a) Notice of the pendency of a suit for forfeiture under this chapter shall be served in the manner prescribed by law on any person in possession of the property at the time of seizure.

(b) If no person was in possession at the time of seizure or if the location of anyone who was in possession is unknown, notice of the suit shall be posted for 20 consecutive days immediately preceding the date of the suit at the courthouse door in the county in which the seizure was made.

### §103.16. Forfeiture of a seized vehicle.† [*Seized vehicle: forfeiture.*]

(a) In a suit for forfeiture of a vehicle seized under Section 103.03 of this code, the state shall have the burden of proving that the vehicle was used to transport an illicit beverage and that all intervenors under Subsection (b) of this section, if any, knowingly violated some provision of this code.

(b) Any person with an ownership or security interest in the vehicle may intervene in the suit for forfeiture to establish his rights. An intervenor under the provisions of this section has the burden of proving that he has a valid ownership or security interest in the vehicle.

(c) If the state fails to prove that the vehicle was used to transport an illicit beverage, the court shall render judgment returning the vehicle to the owner.

(d) If the state proves that the vehicle was used to transport an illicit beverage and that all intervenors, if any, knowingly violated some provision of this code, the court shall render judgment forfeiting the vehicle to the state.

(e) If the state proves that the vehicle was used to transport an illicit beverage but fails to prove that any intervenor knowingly violated some provision of this code, the court shall render judgment delivering possession of the vehicle to the innocent intervenor with the highest priority to possession of the vehicle.

### §103.17. Forfeiture of other seized property.

(a) In any suit for forfeiture of proceeds in escrow from a sale of illicit beverages or of property other than vehicles, or both, seized under Section 103.03 of this code, the state shall have the burden of proving that:

(1) the alcoholic beverages were illicit;

(2) the equipment is designed to be used on or is used in manufacturing an illicit beverage; or

(3) the material is to be used in manufacturing an illicit beverage.

(b) If the state fails to prove the facts necessary for forfeiture, the court shall render judgment returning possession of the property or of the proceeds in escrow to the owner or the person in possession at the time of seizure.

(c) If the state proves the facts necessary for forfeiture, the court shall render judgment forfeiting the property or the proceeds in escrow, or both, to the state and ordering disposal in accordance with the provisions of Section 103.20 or Section 103.18(c) of this code.

### §103.18. Intervention by secured creditors.† [*Secured creditors: intervention.*]

(a) In any suit for forfeiture of proceeds in escrow from any sale of illicit beverages or of property other than vehicles, or both, seized under Section 103.03 of this code, any person who has a security interest in any of the seized property may intervene to establish his rights.

(b) An intervenor under the provisions of this section shall have the burden of proving that he has a valid security interest in the property and that he had no knowledge that the property in which he has a security interest had been used or was to be used in violation of this code at the time the security interest was created.

(c) If an intervenor under this section establishes a security interest and a lack of knowledge of unlawful use of the property, the court, in the judgment forfeiting the property, shall issue an order of sale directed to the sheriff or any constable of the county in which the property was seized. The order shall command the sheriff or constable to conduct a sale at the courthouse door of all or part of the property, whichever the court considers proper, in the same manner as personal property is sold under execution.

(d) The proceeds of a sale under Subsection (c) of this section shall be applied first to the payment of the costs of suit and the expenses incident to the sale. After the costs of suit and expenses of sale have been approved by the court that tried the suit, any remaining proceeds shall be applied toward payment of creditors secured by the property, according to their priorities. After all secured creditors are satisfied, any remaining proceeds shall be paid to the commission to be allocated in accordance with the provisions of Section 103.23 of this code.

(e) If all intervenors under this section fail to establish a valid security interest or lack of knowledge of unlawful use of the property, the court, in the judgment forfeiting the property, shall order disposal of the property in accordance with the provisions of Section 103.20 of this code.

### §103.19. Transfer of security interests.

All security interests in property sold under this chapter shall be transferred to the proceeds of the sale.

### §103.20. Disposition of forfeited property.† [*Forfeited property: disposition.*]

(a) The commission may sell property, other than proceeds in escrow, forfeited to the state at a public or private sale in the manner the commission considers best.

(b) If in the opinion of the commission or the administrator the property is needed for the use of the commission, the commission may retain and use the property until it is no longer needed, at which time it shall be sold in accordance with Subsection (a) of this section.

### §103.21. Bill of sale to purchaser.† [*Purchaser bill of sale.*]

When executing a sale under this chapter, the commission or the sheriff or constable shall issue a bill of sale to each purchaser of property. The bill of sale shall convey a valid and unimpaired title in the property to the purchaser.

### §103.22. Cost of forfeiture suits.† [*Forfeiture suits: costs.*]

The commission shall pay all costs of forfeiture suits out of the confiscated liquor fund or any other fund available to the commission for that purpose.

### §103.23. Allocation of proceeds of sale.† [*Proceeds of sale: allocation.*]

Proceeds from a forfeiture sale and proceeds in escrow which are forfeited to the state in a forfeiture suit shall be disposed of by depositing 35 percent of the proceeds in a separate fund in the state treasury designated as the confiscated liquor fund and depositing 65 percent of the proceeds in the general revenue fund. The confiscated liquor fund may be appropriated to the commission to defray the expenses of accumulating evidence pertaining to violations of this code; assembling, storing, transporting, selling, and accounting for confiscated alcoholic beverages, containers, devices, and property; and any other purposes deemed necessary by the commission in administering and enforcing this code. Any unexpended balance in the confiscated liquor fund at the end of a biennium shall remain in the fund subject to further appropriation for the same purposes.

## CHAPTER 104. REGULATION OF RETAILERS
*(Selected Section)*



### §104.01. Lewd, immoral, indecent conduct.† [*Prohibited conduct.*]

No person authorized to sell beer at retail, nor his agent, servant, or employee, may engage in or permit conduct on the premises of the retailer which is lewd, immoral, or offensive to public decency, including, but not limited to, any of the following acts:

(1) the use of loud and vociferous or obscene, vulgar, or indecent language, or permitting its use;

(2) the exposure of person or permitting a person to expose his person;

(3) rudely displaying or permitting a person to rudely display a pistol or other deadly weapon in a manner calculated to disturb persons in the retail establishment;

(4) solicitation of any person to buy drinks for consumption by the retailer or any of his employees;

(5) being intoxicated on the licensed premises;

(6) permitting lewd or vulgar entertainment or acts;

(7) permitting solicitations of persons for immoral or sexual purposes;

(8) failing or refusing to comply with state or municipal health or sanitary laws or ordinances; or

(9) possession of a narcotic or any equipment used or designed for the administering of a narcotic or permitting a person on the licensed premises to do so.



## CHAPTER 105. HOURS OF SALE AND CONSUMPTION



### §105.01. Hours of sale: liquor.† [*Liquor: hours of sale.*]

(a) Except as provided in Sections 105.02, 105.03, and 105.04 of this code, no person may sell, offer for sale, or deliver any liquor:

(1) on New Year's Day, Thanksgiving Day, or Christmas Day.

(2) on Sunday; or

(3) before 10 a.m. or after 9 p.m. on any other day.

(b) When Christmas Day or New Year's Day falls on a Sunday, Subsection (a) of this section applies to the following Monday.

### §105.02. Hours of sale: wholesalers and local distributors to retailers.† [*Wholesalers and local distributors to retailers: hours of sale.*]

(a) Except as provided by Subsection (b) of this section, a wholesaler or a local distributor's permittee may sell, offer for sale, or deliver liquor to a retailer between 5 a.m. and 9 p.m. on any day except Sunday and Christmas Day.

(b) A local distributor's permittee may not sell, offer for sale, or deliver any liquor on a day on which a package store permittee is prohibited from selling liquor.
*(Chgd. by L.1993, chap. 934(69), eff. 9/1/93.)*

### §105.03. Hours of sale: mixed beverages.† [*Mixed beverages: hours of sale.*]

(a) No person may sell or offer for sale mixed beverages at any time not permitted by this section.

(b) A mixed beverage permittee may sell and offer for sale mixed beverages between 7 a.m. and midnight on any day except Sunday. On Sunday he may sell mixed beverages between midnight and 1:00 a.m. and between 10 a.m. and midnight, except that an alcoholic beverage served to

a customer between 10 a.m. and 12 noon on Sunday must be provided during the service of food to the customer.

(c) In a county having a population of 500,000 or more, according to the last preceding federal census, a holder of a mixed beverage late hours permit may also sell and offer for sale mixed beverages between midnight and 2 a.m. on any day.

(d) In a county having a population of less than 500,000, according to the last preceding federal census, the extended hours prescribed in Subsection (c) of this section are effective for the sale of mixed beverages and the offer to sell them by a holder of a mixed beverages late hours permit:

(1) in the unincorporated areas of the county if the extended hours are adopted by an order of the commissioners court; and

(2) in an incorporated city or town if the extended hours are adopted by an ordinance of the governing body of the city or town.

(e) A violation of a city ordinance or order of a commissioners court adopted pursuant to Subsection (d) of this section is a violation of this code.
*(Chgd. by L.1993, chaps. 923(2), 934(70), eff. 9/1/93.)*

## §105.04. Hours of sale: wine and beer retailer.

The hours of sale and delivery for alcoholic beverages sold under a wine and beer retailer's permit or a wine and beer retailer's off-premise permit are the same as those prescribed for the sale of beer under Section 105.05 of this code, except that no sale shall be allowed between 2 a.m. and noon on Sunday. *(Chgd. by L.1993, chap. 934(71), eff. 9/1/93.)*

## §105.05. Hours of sale: beer.† [*Beer: hours of sale.*]

(a) No person may sell, offer for sale, or deliver beer at any time not permitted by this section.

(b) A person may sell, offer for sale, or deliver beer between 7 a.m. and midnight on any day except Sunday. On Sunday he may sell beer between midnight and 1:00 a.m. and between noon and midnight, except that permittees or licensees authorized to sell for on-premise consumption may sell beer between 10:00 a.m. and noon if the beer is served to a customer during the service of food to the customer.

(c) In a county having a population of 500,000 or more, according to the last preceding federal census, a holder of a retail dealer's on-premise late hours license may also sell, offer for sale, and deliver beer between midnight and 2 a.m. on any day.

(d) In a county having a population of less than 500,000, according to the last preceding federal census, the extended hours prescribed in Subsection (c) of this section or any part of the extended hours prescribed in Subsection (c) of this section are effective for the sale, offer to sell, and delivery of beer by a holder of a retail dealer's on-premise late hours license:

(1) in the unincorporated areas of the county if the extended hours are adopted by an order of the commissioners court; and

(2) in an incorporated city or town if the extended hours are adopted by an ordinance of the governing body of the city or town.

(e) A violation of a city ordinance or order of a commissioners court adopted pursuant to Subsection (d) of this section is a violation of this code.
*(Chgd. by L.1993, chaps. 923(1), 934(72), (73), eff. 9/1/93.)*

## §105.051. Sale of beer by distributor's licensee.

In addition to the hours specified for the sale of beer in Section 105.05(b) of this code, the holder of a general, local, or branch distributor's license may sell, offer for sale, or deliver beer beginning at 5 a.m. on any day except Sunday. *(Added by L.1993, chap. 934(74), eff. 9/1/93.)*

## §105.06. Hours of consumption.

(a) In this section:

(1) "Extended hours area" means an area subject to the extended hours of sale provided in Section 105.03 or 105.05 of this code.

(2) "Standard hours area" means an area which is not an extended hours area.

(b) In a standard hours area, a person commits an offense if he consumes or possesses with intent to consume an alcoholic beverage in a public place at any time on Sunday between 1:15 a.m. and 12 noon or on any other day between 12:15 a.m. and 7 a.m.

(c) In an extended hours area, a person commits an offense if he consumes or possesses with intent to consume an alcoholic beverage in a public place at any time on Sunday between 2:15 a.m. and 12 noon and on any other day between 2:15 a.m. and 7 a.m.

Printed in the U.S.A. Zt

(d) Proof that an alcoholic beverage was possessed with intent to consume in violation of this section requires evidence that the person consumed an alcoholic beverage on that day in violation of this section.

(e) An offense under this section is a misdemeanor punishable by a fine of not more than $50.
*(Chgd. by L.1993, chap. 923(3), eff. 9/1/93.)*

# CHAPTER 106. PROVISIONS RELATING TO AGE

Section




## §106.01. Definition.

In this code, "minor" means a person under 21 years of age.

## §106.02. Purchase of alcohol by a minor.

(a) A minor commits an offense if the minor purchases an alcoholic beverage. A minor does not commit an offense if the minor purchases an alcoholic beverage under the immediate supervision of a commissioned peace officer engaged in enforcing the provisions of this code.

(b) An offense under this section is punishable as provided by Section 106.071.
*(Chgd. by L.1991, chap. 163(1); L.1993, chap. 934(75); L.1997, chaps. 1013(1), 1139(1), eff. 9/1/97, 6/19/97, respectively.)*

## §106.025. Attempt to purchase alcohol by a minor.

(a) A minor commits an offense if, with specific intent to commit an offense under Section 106.02 of this code, the minor does an act amounting to more than mere preparation that tends but fails to effect the commission of the offense intended.

(b) An offense under this section is punishable as provided by Section 106.071.
*(Added by L.1993, chap. 934(76); chgd. by L.1997, chap. 1013(2), eff. 9/1/97.)*

## §106.03. Sale to minors.

(a) A person commits an offense if with criminal negligence he sells an alcoholic beverage to a minor.

(b) A person who sells a minor an alcoholic beverage does not commit an offense if the minor falsely represents himself to be 21 years old or older by displaying an apparently valid Texas driver's license or an identification card issued by the Texas Department of Public Safety, containing a physical description consistent with his appearance for the purpose of inducing the person to sell him an alcoholic beverage.

(c) An offense under this section is a Class A misdemeanor.
*(Chgd. by L.1997, chap. 1013(3), eff. 9/1/97.)*

## §106.04. Consumption of alcohol by a minor.

(a) A minor commits an offense if he consumes an alcoholic beverage.

(b) It is an affirmative defense to prosecution under this section that the alcoholic beverage was consumed in the visible presence of the minor's adult parent, guardian, or spouse.

(c) An offense under this section is punishable as provided by Section 106.071.

(d) A minor who commits an offense under this section and who has been previously convicted twice or more of offenses under this section is not eligible for deferred disposition. For the purposes of this subsection:

(1) an adjudication under Title 3, Family Code, that the minor engaged in conduct described by this section is considered a conviction of an offense under this section; and

(2) an order of deferred disposition for an offense alleged under this section is considered a conviction of an offense under this section.

*(Chgd. by L.1991, chap. 163(2); L.1993, chap. 934(77); L.1997, chap. 1013(4); L.1999, chap. 1207(1), eff. 9/1/99.)*

## §106.041. Driving under the influence of alcohol by minor.

(a) A minor commits an offense if the minor operates a motor vehicle in a public place while having any detectable amount of alcohol in the minor's system.

(b) Except as provided by Subsection (c), an offense under this section is a Class C misdemeanor.

(c) If it is shown at the trial of the defendant that the defendant is a minor who is not a child and who has been previously convicted at least twice of an offense under this section, the offense is punishable by:

(1) a fine of not less than $500 or more than $2,000;

(2) confinement in jail for a term not to exceed 180 days; or

(3) both the fine and confinement.

(d) In addition to any fine and any order issued under Section 106.115, the court shall order a minor convicted of an offense under this section to perform community service for:

(1) not less than 20 or more than 40 hours, if the minor has not been previously convicted of an offense under this section; or

(2) not less than 40 or more than 60 hours, if the minor has been previously convicted of an offense under this section.

(e) Community service ordered under this section must be related to education about or prevention of misuse of alcohol.

(f) A minor who commits an offense under this section and who has been previously convicted twice or more of offenses under this section is not eligible for deferred disposition.

(g) An offense under this section is not a lesser included offense under Section 49.04, Penal Code.

(h) For the purpose of determining whether a minor has been previously convicted of an offense under this section:

(1) an adjudication under Title 3, Family Code, that the minor engaged in conduct described by this section is considered a conviction under this section; and

(2) an order of deferred disposition for an offense alleged under this section is considered a conviction of an offense under this section.

(i) A peace officer who is charging a minor with committing an offense under this section is not required to take the minor into custody but may issue a citation to the minor that contains written notice of the time and place the minor must appear before a magistrate, the name and address of the minor charged, and the offense charged.

(j) In this section:

(1) "Child" has the meaning assigned by Section 51.02, Family Code.

(2) "Motor vehicle" has the meaning assigned by Section 32.34(a), Penal Code.

(3) "Public place" has the meaning assigned by Section 1.07, Penal Code.

*(Added by L.1997, chap. 1013(5); chgd. by L.1999, chap. 1207(2), eff. 9/1/99.)*

## §106.05. Possession of alcohol by a minor.

(a) Except as provided in Subsection (b) of this section, a minor commits an offense if he possesses an alcoholic beverage.

(b) A minor may possess an alcoholic beverage:

(1) while in the course and scope of the minor's employment if the minor is an employee of a licensee or permittee and the employment is not prohibited by this code;

(2) if the minor is in the visible presence of his adult parent, guardian, or spouse, or other adult to whom the minor has been committed by a court; or

Printed in the U.S.A. 17

(3) if the minor is under the immediate supervision of a commissioned peace officer engaged in enforcing the provisions of this code.

(c) An offense under this section is punishable as provided by Section 106.071.

*(Chgd. by L.1991, chap. 163(3); L.1993, chap. 934(78); L.1997, chaps. 1013(6), 1139(2), eff. 9/1/97, 6/19/97, respectively.)*

## §106.06. Purchase of alcohol for a minor; furnishing alcohol to a minor.

(a) Except as provided in Subsection (b) of this section, a person commits an offense if he purchases an alcoholic beverage for or gives or with criminal negligence makes available an alcoholic beverage to a minor with criminal negligence.

(b) A person may purchase an alcoholic beverage for or give an alcoholic beverage to a minor if he is the minor's adult parent, guardian or spouse, or an adult in whose custody the minor has been committed by a court, and he is visibly present when the minor possesses or consumes the alcoholic beverage.

(c) An offense under this section is a Class B misdemeanor.

*(Chgd. by L.1993, chaps. 437(4), 934(79); L.1997, chap. 1013(7), eff. 9/1/97.)*



## §106.07. Misrepresentation of age by a minor.

(a) A minor commits an offense if he falsely states that he is 21 years of age or older or presents any document that indicates he is 21 years of age or older to a person engaged in selling or serving alcoholic beverages.

(b) An offense under this section is punishable as provided by Section 106.071.

*(Chgd. by L.1997, chap. 1013(8), eff. 9/1/97.)*

## §106.071. Punishment for alcohol-related offense by minor.

(a) This section applies to an offense under Section 106.02, 106.025, 106.04, 106.05, or 106.07.

(b) Except as provided by Subsection (c), an offense to which this section applies is a Class C misdemeanor.

(c) If it is shown at the trial of the defendant that the defendant is a minor who is not a child and who has been previously convicted at least twice of an offense to which this section applies, the offense is punishable by:

(1) a fine of not less than $250 or more than $2,000;

(2) confinement in jail for a term not to exceed 180 days; or

(3) both the fine and confinement.

(d) In addition to any fine and any order issued under Section 106.115:

(1) the court shall order a minor placed on deferred disposition for or convicted of an offense to which this section applies to perform community service for:

(A) not less than eight or more than 12 hours, if the minor has not been previously convicted of an offense to which this section applies; or

(B) not less than 20 or more than 40 hours, if the minor has been previously convicted once of an offense to which this section applies; and

(2) the court shall order the Department of Public Safety to suspend the driver's license or permit of a minor convicted of an offense to which this section applies or, if the minor does not have a driver's license or permit, to deny the issuance of a driver's license or permit for:

(A) 30 days, if the minor has not been previously convicted of an offense to which this section applies;

(B) 60 days, if the minor has been previously convicted once of an offense to which this section applies; or

(C) 180 days, if the minor has been previously convicted twice or more of an offense to which this section applies.

(e) Community service ordered under this section must be related to education about or prevention of misuse of alcohol if programs or services providing that education are available in the community in which the court is located. If programs or services providing that education are not available, the court may order community service that it considers appropriate for rehabilitative purposes.

(f) For the purpose of determining whether a minor has been previously convicted of an offense to which this section applies:

(1) an adjudication under Title 3, Family Code, that the minor engaged in conduct described by this section is considered a conviction under this section; and

(2) an order of deferred disposition for an offense alleged under this section is considered a conviction of an offense under this section.

(g) In this section, "child" has the meaning assigned by Section 51.02, Family Code.

(h) A driver's license suspension under this section takes effect on the 11th day after the date the minor is convicted.

(i) A defendant who is not a child and who has been previously convicted at least twice of an offense to which this section applies is not eligible to receive a deferral of final disposition of a subsequent offense.

*(Added by L.1997, chap. 1013(9); chgd. by L.1999, chaps. 76(4), 1207(3), eff. 9/1/99.)*

### §106.08. Importation by a minor.† [*Importation of alcoholic beverage by a minor.*]

No minor may import into this state or possess with intent to import into this state any alcoholic beverage.

### §106.09. Employment of minors.

(a) Except as provided in Subsections (b) and (c) of this section, no person may employ a person under 18 years of age to sell, prepare, serve, or otherwise handle liquor, or to assist in doing so.

(b) A holder of a wine only package store permit may employ a person 16 years old or older to work in any capacity.

(c) A holder of a mixed beverage permit may employ a person under 18 years of age to work in any capacity other than the actual selling, preparing, or serving of mixed beverages.

(d) The fact that a person is 18, 19, or 20 years of age is not a ground for refusal of an original or renewal permit or license issued under Chapter 35 or 73 of this code, provided that such a person to whom a permit or license is issued may carry out the activities authorized by those chapters only while in the actual course and scope of the person's employment.



### §106.10. Plea of guilty by a minor.† [*Minor: guilty plea.*]

No minor may plead guilty to an offense under this chapter except in open court before a judge.

### §106.11. Parent or guardian at trial.

(a) Except as provided in Subsection (d) of this section, no person under 18 years of age may be convicted of an offense under this chapter unless his parent or legal guardian is present in court.

(b) If the parent or legal guardian of a person under 18 years of age accused of a violation of this chapter resides within the jurisdiction of the court before whom the case is to be heard, the court shall summon the parent or legal guardian to appear in court and shall require him to be present at all proceedings in the case.

(c) If the parent or legal guardian of a person under 18 years of age accused of a violation of this chapter resides outside the jurisdiction of the court before whom the case is to be heard, the court shall give written notice of the charge against the person to the parent or legal guardian.

(d) If the court is unable to locate or compel the presence of the person's parent or legal guardian after diligent effort, the court may waive the requirement of presence of a parent or legal guardian.

### §106.115. Attendance at alcohol awareness course; license suspension.

(a) On the placement of a minor on deferred disposition for an offense under Section 49.02, Penal Code, or under Section 106.02, 106.025, 106.04, 106.041, 106.05, or 106.07, the court shall require the defendant to attend an alcohol awareness program approved by the Texas Commission on Alcohol and Drug Abuse. On conviction of a minor of an offense under one or more of those sections, the court, in addition to assessing a fine as provided by those sections, shall require a defendant who has not been previously convicted of an offense under one of those sections to attend the alcohol awareness program. If the defendant has been previously convicted once or more of an offense under one or more of those sections, the court may require the defendant to attend the alcohol awareness program. If the defendant is younger than 18 years of age, the court may require the parent or guardian of the defendant to attend the program with the defendant. The Texas Commission on Alcohol and Drug Abuse:

(1) is responsible for the administration of the certification of approved alcohol awareness programs;

(2) may charge a nonrefundable application fee for:

(A) initial certification of the approval; or

(B) renewal of the certification;

(3) shall adopt rules regarding alcohol awareness programs approved under this section; and

(4) shall monitor, coordinate, and provide training to a person who provides an alcohol awareness program.

(b) When requested, an alcohol awareness program may be taught in languages other than English.

(c) The court shall require the defendant to present to the court, within 90 days of the date of final conviction, evidence in the form prescribed by the court that the defendant, as ordered by the court, has satisfactorily completed an alcohol awareness program or performed the required hours of community service. For good cause the court may extend this period by not more than 90 days. If the defendant presents the required evidence within the prescribed period, the court may reduce the assessed fine to an amount equal to no less than one-half of the amount of the initial fine.

(d) If the defendant does not present the required evidence within the prescribed period, the court:

(1) shall order the Department of Public Safety to suspend the defendant's driver's license or permit for a period not to exceed six months or, if the defendant does not have a license or permit, to deny the issuance of a license or permit to the defendant for that period; and

(2) may order the defendant or the parent, managing conservator, or guardian of the defendant to do any act or refrain from doing any act if the court determines that doing the act or refraining from doing the act will increase the likelihood that the defendant will present evidence to the court that the defendant has satisfactorily completed an alcohol awareness program or performed the required hours of community service.

(e) The Department of Public Safety shall send notice of the suspension or prohibition order issued under Subsection (d) by first class mail to the defendant. The notice must include the date of the suspension or prohibition order, the reason for the suspension or prohibition, and the period covered by the suspension or prohibition.
*(Added by L.1991, chap. 163(4); chgd. by L.1993, chap. 934(80); L.1995, chap. 615(1); L.1997, chaps. 577(17), 1013(10); L.1999, chaps. 62(2.01), 76(5), 1207(4), 1409(7), eff. 9/1/99.)*



## §106.116. Reports of court to commission.

Unless the clerk is otherwise required to include the information in a report submitted under Section 101.09, the clerk of a court, including a justice court, municipal court, or juvenile court, shall furnish to the commission on request a notice of a conviction of an offense under this chapter or an adjudication under Title 3, Family Code, for conduct that constitutes an offense under this chapter. The report must be in the form prescribed by the commission. *(Added by L.1997, chap. 1013(11), eff. 9/1/97.)*

## §106.117. Report of court to Department of Public Safety.

(a) Each court, including a justice court, municipal court, or juvenile court, shall furnish to the Department of Public Safety a notice of each:

(1) adjudication under Title 3, Family Code, for conduct that constitutes an offense under this chapter;

(2) conviction of an offense under this chapter;

(3) order of deferred disposition for an offense alleged under this chapter; and

(4) acquittal of an offense under Section 106.041.

(b) The notice must be in a form prescribed by the Department of Public Safety and must contain the driver's license number of the defendant, if the defendant holds a driver's license.

(c) The Department of Public Safety shall maintain appropriate records of information in the notices and shall provide the information to law enforcement agencies and courts as necessary to enable those agencies and courts to carry out their official duties. The information is admissible in any action in which it is relevant. A person who holds a driver's license having the same number that is contained in a record maintained under this section is presumed to be the person to whom the record relates. The presumption may be rebutted only by evidence presented under oath.

(d) The information maintained under this section is confidential and may not be disclosed except as provided by this section. A provision of Chapter 58, Family Code, or other law limiting collection or reporting of information on a juvenile or other minor or requiring destruction of that information does not apply to information reported and maintained under this section.
*(Added by L.1997, chap. 1013(11); chgd. by L.1999, chap. 1207(5), eff. 9/1/99.)*

## §106.12. Expungement of conviction of a minor.

(a) Any person convicted of not more than one violation of this code while a minor, on attaining the age of 21 years, may apply to the court in which he was convicted to have the conviction expunged.

(b) The application shall contain the applicant's sworn statement that he was not convicted of any violation of this code while a minor other than the one he seeks to have expunged.

(c) If the court finds that the applicant was not convicted of any other violation of this code while he was a minor, the court shall order the conviction, together with all complaints, verdicts, sentences, and other documents relating to the offense, to be expunged from the applicant's record. After entry of the order, the applicant shall be released from all disabilities resulting from the conviction, and the conviction may not be shown or made known for any purpose.

### §106.13. Sanctions against retailer.

(a) Except as provided in Subsections (b) and (c) of this section, the commission or administrator may cancel or suspend for not more than 60 days a retail license or permit or a private club registration permit if it is found, on notice and hearing, that the licensee or permittee with criminal negligence sold, served, dispensed, or delivered an alcoholic beverage to a minor or with criminal negligence permitted a minor to violate Section 106.04 or 106.05 of this code on the licensed premises.

(b) For a second offense the commission or administrator may cancel the license or permit or suspend it for not more than three months. For a third offense within a period of 36 consecutive months the commission or administrator may cancel the permit or suspend it for not more than 12 months.

(c) The commission or administrator may relax the provisions of this section concerning suspension and cancellation and assess a sanction the commission or administrator finds just under the circumstances if, at a hearing, the licensee or permittee establishes to the satisfaction of the commission or administrator:

(1) that the violation could not reasonably have been prevented by the permittee or licensee by the exercise of due diligence;

(2) that the permittee or licensee was entrapped; or

(3) that an agent, servant, or employee of the permittee or licensee violated this code without the knowledge of the permittee or licensee.

*(Chgd. by L.1993, chaps. 437(5), 934(81); L.1997, chap. 798(1), eff. 9/1/97.)*

### §106.14. Actions of employee.

(a) For purposes of this chapter and any other provision of this code relating to the sales, service, dispensing, or delivery of alcoholic beverages to a minor or an intoxicated person or the consumption of alcoholic beverages by a minor or an intoxicated person, the actions of an employee shali not be attributable to the employer if:

(1) the employer requires its employees to attend a commission-approved seller training program;

(2) the employee has actually attended such a training program; and

(3) the employer has not directly or indirectly encouraged the employee to violate such law.

(b) The commission shall adopt rules or policies establishing the minimum requirements for approved seller training programs. Upon application, the commission shall approve seller training programs meeting such requirements that are sponsored either privately, by public community colleges, or by public or private institutions of higher education that offer a four-year undergraduate program and a degree or certificate in hotel or motel management, restaurant management, or travel or tourism management. The commission may charge an application fee to be set by the commission in such amount as is necessary to defray the expense of processing the application.

(c) The commission may approve under this section a seller training program sponsored by a licensee or permittee for the purpose of training its employees whether or not such employees are located at the same premises. This subsection shall only apply to licensees or permittees who employ at least 150 persons at any one time during the license or permit year who sell, serve, or prepare alcoholic beverages.

(d) The commission may approve under this section a seller training program conducted by a hotel management company or a hotel operating company for the employees of five or more hotels operated or managed by the company if:

(1) the seller training program is administered through the corporate offices of the company; and

(2) the hotels employ a total of at least 200 persons at one time during the license or permit year who sell, serve, or prepare alcoholic beverages.

*(Chgd. by L.1989, chap. 477(1); L.1993, chap. 934(82); L.1995, chap. 270(1), eff. 9/1/95.)*

### §106.15. Prohibited activities by persons younger than 18.

(a) A permittee or licensee commits an offense if he employs, authorizes, permits, or induces a person younger than 18 years of age to dance with another person in exchange for a benefit, as defined by Section 1.07, Penal Code, on the premises covered by the permit or license.

(b) An offense under Subsection (a) is a Class A misdemeanor.

(c) In addition to a penalty imposed under Subsection (b), the commission or administrator shall:

(1) suspend for a period of five days the license or permit of a person convicted of a first offense under Subsection (a);

(2) suspend for a period of 60 days the license or permit of a person convicted of a second offense under Subsection (a); and

(3) cancel the license or permit of a person convicted of a third offense under Subsection (a).

(d) This section does not apply to a gift or benefit given for a dance at a wedding, anniversary, or similar event.

(e) A person does not commit an offense under Subsection (a) if the person younger than 18 years of age falsely represents the person's age to be at least 18 years of age by displaying an apparently valid Texas driver's license or an identification card issued by the Department of Public Safety containing a physical description consistent with the person's appearance.

*(Added by L.1999, chap. 80(2), eff. 9/1/99.)*



## CHAPTER 107. TRANSPORTATION AND IMPORTATION
*(Selected Sections)*



### §107.01. Transportation of liquor: statement required.

(a) No person may transport liquor into this state or on a public highway, street, or alley in this state unless the person accompanying or in charge of the shipment has with him, available for exhibition and inspection, a written statement furnished and signed by the shipper showing the name and address of the consignor and the consignee, the origin and destination of the shipment, and any other information required by rule or regulation of the commission.

(b) The person in charge of the shipment while it is being transported shall exhibit the statement to the commission, an authorized representative of the commission, or a peace officer on demand, and it is a violation of this code to fail or refuse to do so. The representative or officer shall accept the written statement as prima facie evidence of the legal right to transport the liquor.

### §107.02. Transportation of beer: statement required.

(a) It is lawful for a person to transport beer from any place where its sale, manufacture, or distribution is authorized to another place in the state where its sale, manufacture, or distribution is authorized, or from the state boundary to a place where its sale, manufacture, or distribution is authorized, even though the route of transportation may cross a dry area.

(b) A shipment of beer must be accompanied by a written statement furnished and signed by the shipper showing:

(1) the name and address of the consignor and consignee;

(2) the origin and destination of the shipment; and

(3) any other information required by the commission or administrator.

(c) The person in charge of the shipment while it is being transported shall exhibit the written statement to any representative of the commission or peace officer who demands to see it. The statement shall be accepted by the representative or peace officer as prima facie evidence of the legal right to transport the beer.

(d) A person who transports beer not accompanied by the required statement, or who fails to exhibit the statement after a lawful demand, violates this code.

### §107.06. Importation of beer.

(a) No person may import beer into the state except the holder of a manufacturer's or general, local, or branch distributor's license.

(b) No person may transport beer into this state unless it is consigned and delivered to one of the licensees named in Subsection (a) of this section.

(c) This section does not apply to the importation or transportation of military beer consigned to a military installation or to the importation of beer as authorized under Section 107.07 of this code.

### §107.08. Transportation of beverages for personal consumption.

A person who purchases an alcoholic beverage for his own consumption may transport it from a place where its sale is legal to a place where its possession is legal without holding a license or permit.

# TITLE 6. LOCAL OPTION ELECTIONS

## CHAPTER 251. LOCAL OPTION ELECTIONS
*(Selected Section)*



### §251.71. Wet and dry areas.

(a) An area is a "dry area" as to an alcoholic beverage of a particular type and alcohol content if the sale of that beverage is unlawful in the area. An area is a "wet area" as to an alcoholic beverage of a particular type and alcoholic content if the sale of that beverage is lawful in the area.

(b) Those areas that are wet or dry when this code takes effect retain that status until the status of the area is changed as provided in this code.

(c) All trial courts of this state shall take judicial notice of the wet or dry status of an area in a criminal prosecution.

(d) In an information, complaint, or indictment, an allegation that an area is a dry area as to a particular type of alcoholic beverage is sufficient, but a different status of the area may be urged and proved as a defense.

# BUSINESS AND COMMERCE CODE

## CHAPTER 17. DECEPTIVE TRADE PRACTICES
*(Selected Sections)*



### §17.08. Private use of state seal.

(a) In this section:

(1) "Commercial purpose" means a purpose that is intended to result in a profit or other tangible benefit but does not include:

(A) official use of the state seal or a representation of the state seal in a state function;

(B) use of the state seal or a representation of the state seal for a political purpose by an elected official of this state;

(C) use of the state seal or a representation of the state seal in an encyclopedia, dictionary, book, journal, pamphlet, periodical, magazine, or newspaper incident to a description or history of seals, coats of arms, heraldry, or this state;

(D) use of the state seal or a representation of the state seal in a library, museum, or educational facility incident to descriptions or exhibits relating to seals, coats of arms, heraldry, or this state;

(E) use of the state seal or a representation of the state seal in a theatrical, motion-picture, television, or similar production for a historical, educational, or newsworthy purpose; or

(F) use of the state seal or a representation of the state seal for another historical, educational, or newsworthy purpose if authorized in writing by the secretary of state.

(2) "Representation of the state seal" includes a nonexact representation that the secretary of state determines is deceptively similar to the state seal.

(3) "Official use" means the use of the state seal by an officer or employee of this state in performing a state function.

(4) "State function" means a state governmental activity authorized or required by law.

(5) "State seal" means the state seal, the reverse of the state seal, and the state arms as defined by Article 6139f, Revised Statutes.

(b) Except as otherwise provided by this section, a person may not use a representation of the state seal:

(1) to advertise or publicize tangible personal property or a commercial undertaking; or

(2) for another commercial purpose.

(c) A person may use a representation of the state seal for a commercial purpose if the person obtains a license from the secretary of state for that use. The secretary of state, under the authority vested in the secretary as custodian of the seal under Article IV, Section 19, of the Texas Constitution, shall issue a license to a person who applies for a license on a form provided by the secretary of state and who pays the fees required under this section if the secretary of state determines that the use is in the best interests of the state and not detrimental to the image of the state. A license issued under this section expires one year after the date of issuance and may be renewed.

(d) The secretary of state shall adopt rules relating to the use of the state seal by a person licensed under this section. The secretary of state shall adopt the rules in the manner provided by Chapter 2001, Government Code.

(e) The application fee for a license under this section is $35. The license fee for an original or renewal license is $250. In addition to those fees, each licensee shall pay an amount equal to three percent of the licensee's annual gross receipts related to the licensed use in excess of $5,000 to the state as a royalty fee.

(f) A person licensed under this section shall maintain records relating to the licensee's use of the state seal in the manner required by the rules of the secretary of state. The secretary of state may examine the records during reasonable business hours to determine the licensee's compliance with this section. Each licensee shall display the license in a conspicuous manner in the licensee's office or place of business.

(g) The secretary of state may suspend or revoke a license issued under this section for failure to comply with this section or the rules adopted under this section. The secretary of state may bring a civil action to enjoin a violation of this section or the rules adopted under this section.

(h) A person who reproduces an official document bearing the state seal does not violate Subsection (b) of this section if the document is:

(1) reproduced in complete form; and

(2) used for a purpose related to the purpose for which the document was issued by the state.

(i) A person who violates a provision of Subsection (b) of this section commits an offense. An offense under this section is a Class C misdemeanor.

(j) A person who violates Subsection (b) of this section commits a separate offense each day that the person violates a provision of that subsection.

*(Chgd. by L.1993, chap. 300(8); L.1995, chap. 76(5.95(49)), eff. 9/1/95.)*

### §17.461. Pyramid promotional scheme.

(a) In this section:

(1) "Compensation" means payment of money, a financial benefit, or another thing of value. The term does not include payment based on sale of a product to a person, including a participant, who purchases the product for actual use or consumption.

(2) "Consideration" means the payment of cash or the purchase of a product. The term does not include:

(A) a purchase of a product furnished at cost to be used in making a sale and not for resale;

(B) a purchase of a product subject to a repurchase agreement that complies with Subsection (b); or

(C) time and effort spent in pursuit of a sale or in a recruiting activity.

(3) "Participate" means to contribute money into a pyramid promotional scheme without promoting, organizing, or operating the scheme.

(4) "Product" means a good, a service, or intangible property of any kind.

(5) "Promoting a pyramid promotional scheme" means:

(A) inducing or attempting to induce one or more other persons to participate in a pyramid promotional scheme; or

(B) assisting another person in inducing or attempting to induce one or more other persons to participate in a pyramid promotional scheme, including by providing references.

(6) "Pyramid promotional scheme" means a plan or operation by which a person gives consideration for the opportunity to receive compensation that is derived primarily from a person's introduction of other persons to participate in the plan or operation rather than from the sale of a product by a person introduced into the plan or operation.

(b) To qualify as a repurchase agreement for the purposes of Subsection (a)(2)(B), an agreement must be an enforceable agreement by the seller to repurchase, on written request of the purchaser and not later than the first anniversary of the purchaser's date of purchase, all unencumbered products that are in an unused, commercially resalable condition at a price not less than 90 percent of the amount actually paid by the purchaser for the products being returned, less any consideration received by the purchaser for purchase of the products being returned. A product that is no longer marketed by the seller is considered resalable if the product is otherwise in an unused, commercially resalable condition and is returned to the seller not later than the first anniversary of the purchaser's date of purchase, except that the product is not considered resalable if before the purchaser purchased the product it was clearly disclosed to the purchaser that the product was sold as a nonreturnable, discontinued, seasonal, or special promotion item.

(c) A person commits an offense if the person contrives, prepares, establishes, operates, advertises, sells, or promotes a pyramid promotional scheme. An offense under this subsection is a state jail felony.

(d) It is not a defense to prosecution for an offense under this section that the pyramid promotional scheme involved both a franchise to sell a product and the authority to sell additional franchises if the emphasis of the scheme is on the sale of additional franchises.

*(Added by L.1995, chap. 463(2), eff. 9/1/95.)*

## CHAPTER 35. MISCELLANEOUS
*(Selected Sections)*

Section


### §35.46. Attaching motor vehicle dealer's name to vehicle.

(a) In this section:

(1) "Motor vehicle" has the meaning assigned by Section 541.201, Transportation Code.

(2) "Center high-mounted stop lamp" means a device that is mounted on the rear center line of a motor vehicle either in or on the rear window or within six inches from the rear of the window of the vehicle for the purpose of emitting a light when the vehicle's brakes are applied.

(3) "Overlay" means a transparent or semi-transparent covering placed over a center high-mounted stop lamp on which is impressed or imprinted a name, trade name, or other message that can be read by a person behind the vehicle when the lamp is illuminated.

(b) A person in the business of selling motor vehicles may not sell a motor vehicle with a center high-mounted stop lamp over which an overlay has been placed.

(c) A person who violates this section commits an offense. An offense under this section is a Class C misdemeanor.

*(Chgd. by L.1997, chap. 165(30.178), eff. 9/1/97.)*

**§35.54. Use of crime victim information for certain purposes prohibited.† [*Use of crime victim or motor vehicle accident information for certain purposes prohibited.*]**

(a) In this section:

(1) "Crime victim information" means information that is collected or prepared by a law enforcement agency that identifies or serves to identify a person who, according to the records of the law enforcement agency, may have been the victim of a crime in which physical injury to the person occurred or was attempted or in which the offender entered or attempted to enter the dwelling of the person.

(2) "Motor vehicle accident information" means information that is collected or prepared by a law enforcement agency that identifies or serves to identify a person who, according to the records of the law enforcement agency, may have been involved in a motor vehicle accident.

(b) A person who has possession of crime victim or motor vehicle accident information that the person obtained or knows was obtained from a law enforcement agency may not use the information to contact directly a person who is a crime victim or who was involved in a motor vehicle accident or a member of the person's family for the purpose of soliciting business from the person or family member and may not sell the information to another person for financial gain.

(c) The attorney general may bring an action against a person who violates Subsection (b) of this section pursuant to Section 17.47 of this code.

(d) A person who violates Subsection (b) of this section commits an offense. An offense under this subsection is a Class C misdemeanor unless the defendant has been previously convicted under this subsection more than two times, in which event the offense is a felony of the third degree.

*(Chgd. by L.1991, chap. 860(1), eff. 9/1/91.)*

# CIVIL PRACTICE AND REMEDIES CODE

## CHAPTER 7. LIABILITY OF COURT OFFICERS
*(Selected Section)*



### §7.003. Liability regarding execution of writs.† [*Writs.*]

(a) Except as provided by Section 34.061, an officer is not liable for damages resulting from the execution of a writ issued by a court of this state if the officer:

(1) in good faith executes the writ as provided by law and by the Texas Rules of Civil Procedure; and

(2) uses reasonable diligence in performing his official duties.

(b) An officer shall execute a writ issued by a court of this state without requiring that bond be posted for the indemnification of the officer.



## CHAPTER 22. WITNESSES
*(Selected Section)*



### §22.011. Privilege from arrest.

(a) A witness is privileged from arrest while attending, going to, and returning from court.

(b) The privilege provided by this section extends for a period computed by allowing one day of travel for each 150 miles of the distance from the courthouse to the witness's residence.

(c) This section does not apply to an arrest for a felony, treason, or breach of the peace. *(Chgd. by L.1993, chap. 103(1), eff. 1/1/94.)*

## CHAPTER 34. EXECUTION OF JUDGMENTS
*(Selected Sections)*



### §34.021. Recovery of property before sale.† [*Recovery of seized property; before sale.*]

A person is entitled to recover his property that has been seized through execution of a writ issued by a court if the judgment on which execution is issued is reversed or set aside and the property has not been sold at execution.

### §34.022. Recovery of property value after sale.† [*Recovery of seized property; after sale.*]

(a) A person is entitled to recover from the judgment creditor the market value of the person's property that has been seized through execution of a writ issued by a court if the judgment on which execution is issued is reversed or set aside but the property has been sold at execution.

(b) The amount of recovery is determined be the market value at the time of sale of the property sold.

## CHAPTER 74. GOOD SAMARITAN LAW



### §74.001. Liability for emergency care.

(a) A person who in good faith administers emergency care, including using an automated external defibrillator, at the scene of an emergency but not in a hospital or other health care facility or means of medical transport is not liable in civil damages for an act performed during the emergency unless the act is wilfully or wantonly negligent.

(b) This section does not apply to care administered:

(1) for or in expectation of remuneration; or

(2) by a person who was at the scene of the emergency because he or a person he represents as an agent was soliciting business or seeking to perform a service for remuneration.

(c) If the scene of an emergency is in a hospital or other health care facility or means of medical transport, a person who in good faith administers emergency care is not liable in civil damages for an act performed during the emergency unless the act is wilfully or wantonly negligent, provided that this subsection does not apply to care administered:

(1) by a person who regularly administers care in a hospital emergency room unless such person is at the scene of the emergency for reasons wholly unrelated to the person's work in administering health care; or

(2) by an admitting or attending physician of the patient or a treating physician associated by the admitting or attending physician of the patient in question.

(d) For purposes of Subsections (b)(1) and (c)(1), a person who would ordinarily receive or be entitled to receive a salary, fee, or other remuneration for administering care under such circumstances to the patient in question shall be deemed to be acting for or in expectation of remuneration even if the person waives or elects not to charge or receive remuneration on the occasion in question.

(e) This section does not apply to a person whose negligent act or omission was a producing cause of the emergency for which care is being administered.
*(Chgd. by L.1993, chap. 960(1); L.1999, chap. 679(2), eff. 9/1/99.)*



### §74.002. Unlicensed medical personnel.

Persons not licensed in the healing arts who in good faith administer emergency care as emergency medical service personnel are not liable in civil damages for an act performed in administering the care unless the act is wilfully or wantonly negligent. This section applies without regard to whether the care is provided for or in expectation of remuneration.

## CHAPTER 83. USE OF DEADLY FORCE IN DEFENSE OF PERSON

*(Added by L.1995, chap. 235(2), eff. 9/1/95.)*



### §83.001. Affirmative defense.

It is an affirmative defense to a civil action for damages for personal injury or death that the defendant, at the time the cause of action arose, was justified in using deadly force under Section 9.32, Penal Code, against a person who at the time of the use of force was committing an offense of unlawful entry in the habitation of the defendant. *(Added by L.1995, chap. 235(2), eff. 9/1/95.)*

## CHAPTER 124. PRIVILEGE TO INVESTIGATE THEFT

*(Selected Section)*



### §124.001. Detention.

A person who reasonably believes that another has stolen or is attempting to steal property is privileged to detain that person in a reasonable manner and for a reasonable time to investigate ownership of the property.

## CHAPTER 125. COMMON AND PUBLIC NUISANCES

*(Selected Sections)*

## SUBCHAPTER A. SUIT TO ABATE CERTAIN COMMON NUISANCES

## SUBCHAPTER B. SUIT TO ABATE CERTAIN PUBLIC NUISANCES



## SUBCHAPTER C. ADDITIONAL NUISANCE REMEDIES



## SUBCHAPTER D. ORGANIZED CRIMINAL ACTIVITY*

## SUBCHAPTER D. MEMBERSHIP IN CRIMINAL STREET GANG*



**Two subchapter headings created by separate amendments. See text for citation.*



## SUBCHAPTER A. SUIT TO ABATE CERTAIN COMMON NUISANCES

### §125.001. Common nuisance.

(a) A person who knowingly maintains a place to which persons habitually go for the following purposes maintains a common nuisance:

(1) prostitution or gambling in violation of the Penal Code;

(2) discharge of a firearm in a public place in violation of Section 42.01(a)(9), Penal Code;

(3) reckless discharge of a firearm as described by Section 42.12, Penal Code;

(4) engaging in organized criminal activity as a member of a combination as described by Section 71.02, Penal Code; or

(5) delivery, possession, manufacture, or use of a controlled substance in violation of Chapter 481, Health and Safety Code.

(b) A person maintains a common nuisance if the person:

(1) knowingly maintains a multiunit residential property described by Subsection (c) to which persons habitually go to commit the following acts:

(A) aggravated assault as described by Section 22.02, Penal Code;

(B) sexual assault as described by Section 22.011, Penal Code;

(C) aggravated sexual assault as described by Section 22.021, Penal Code;

(D) robbery as described by Section 29.02, Penal Code;

(E) aggravated robbery as described by Section 29.03, Penal Code; or

(F) unlawfully carrying a weapon as described by Section 46.02, Penal Code; and

(2) has failed to make reasonable attempts to abate such acts.

(c) Subsection (b) applies only to a multiunit residential property, as that term is defined by Section 125.041, that is located in a municipality.

*(Chgd. by L.1991, chap. 14(284(42)); L.1993, chaps. 857(2), 968(1); L.1995, chaps. 76(14.03), 318(25), 663(2); L.1997, chap. 1181(1); L.1999, chap. 1161(1), eff. 9/1/99.)*

## SUBCHAPTER B. SUIT TO ABATE CERTAIN PUBLIC NUISANCES

### §125.021. Public nuisance.

The habitual use or the threatened or contemplated habitual use of any place for any of the following purposes is a public nuisance:

(1) gambling, gambling promotion, or communicating gambling information prohibited by law;

(2) promotion or aggravated promotion of prostitution;

(3) compelling prostitution;

(4) commercial manufacture, commercial distribution, or commercial exhibition of obscene material;

(5) commercial exhibition of live dances or other acts depicting real or simulated sexual intercourse or deviate sexual intercourse;

(6) engaging in a voluntary fight between a man and a bull if the fight is for a thing of value or a championship, if a thing of value is wagered on the fight, or if an admission fee for the fight is directly or indirectly charged, as prohibited by law;

(7) discharge of a firearm in a public place in violation of Section 42.01(a)(9), Penal Code;

(8) reckless discharge of a firearm as described by Section 42.12, Penal Code;

(9) engaging in organized criminal activity as a member of a combination as described in Section 71.02, Penal Code; or

(10) delivering or using a controlled substance in violation of Chapter 481, Health and Safety Code.

*(Chgd. by L.1991, chap. 14(284(42)); L.1993, chap. 857(2); L.1993, chap. 968(1); L.1995, chaps. 76(14.07), 318(28), 663(5), eff. 9/1/95.)*



## SUBCHAPTER C. ADDITIONAL NUISANCE REMEDIES

### §125.041. Public nuisance.

For the purposes of this subchapter, a public nuisance is considered to exist at a place if one or more of the following acts occurs at that place on a regular basis:

(1) gambling, gambling promotion, or communication of gambling information, as prohibited by Chapter 47, Penal Code;

(2) promotion or aggravated promotion of prostitution, as prohibited by Chapter 43, Penal Code;

(3) compelling prostitution, as prohibited by Chapter 43, Penal Code;

(4) commercial manufacture, commercial distribution, or commercial exhibition of material that is obscene, as defined by Section 43.21, Penal Code;

(5) commercial exhibition of a live dance or other act in which a person engages in real or simulated sexual intercourse or deviate sexual intercourse, as defined by Section 43.01, Penal Code;

(6) discharge of a firearm in violation of Section 42.01(a)(9), Penal Code;

(7) reckless discharge of a firearm as described by Section 42.12, Penal Code;

(8) engaging in organized criminal activity as a member of a combination as described by Section 71.02, Penal Code; or

(9) manufacture, delivery, or use of a controlled substance in violation of Chapter 481, Health and Safety Code.

*(Chgd. by L.1991, chap. 14(284(42)); L.1993, chap. 857(2); L.1993, chap. 968(1); L.1995, chaps. 76(14.08), 318(29), 663(6), eff. 9/1/95. See other section 125.041 below.)*

### §125.041. Definitions.

In this subchapter:

(1) "Common nuisance" is a nuisance described by Section 125.001.

(2) "Public nuisance" is a nuisance described by Section 125.021.

(3) "Multiunit residential property" means improved real property with at least three dwelling units, including an apartment building or condominium. The term does not include:

(A) a property in which each dwelling unit is occupied by the owner of the property; or

(B) a single-family home or duplex.

*(Chgd. by L.1991, chap. 14(284(42)); L.1993, chap. 857(2); L.1993, chap. 968(1); L.1995, chap. 818(1), eff. 8/28/95. See other section 125.041 above.)*

## SUBCHAPTER D. ORGANIZED CRIMINAL ACTIVITY

*(Subchapter heading chgd. by L.1995, chap. 76(14.09), eff. 9/1/95. See other heading below.)*

## SUBCHAPTER D. MEMBERSHIP IN CRIMINAL STREET GANG

*(Subchapter heading chgd. by L.1995, chap. 318(30), eff. 9/1/95. See other heading above.)*

### §125.061. Definitions.

In this subchapter, "combination" has the meaning assigned by Section 71.01, Penal Code. *(Added by L.1993, chap. 968(3); chgd. by L.1995, chap. 76(14.10), eff. 9/1/95. See other section 125.061 below.)*

### §125.061. Definitions.

In this subchapter, "combination" and "criminal street gang" have the meanings assigned by Section 71.01, Penal Code. *(Added by L.1993, chap. 968(3); chgd. by L.1995, chap. 318(31), eff. 9/1/95. See other section 125.061 above.)*

### §125.062. Public nuisance; combination.

A combination that continuously or regularly associates in organized criminal activities as described by Section 71.02, Penal Code, is a public nuisance. *(Added by L.1993, chap. 968(3); chgd. by L.1995, chap. 76(14.11), eff. 9/1/95. See other section 125.062 below.)*

### §125.062. Public nuisance; combination or criminal street gang.

A combination or criminal street gang that continuously or regularly associates in organized criminal activities as described by Section 71.02, Penal Code, is a public nuisance. *(Added by L.1993, chap. 968(3); chgd. by L.1995, chap. 318(32), eff. 9/1/95. See other section 125.062 above.)*

### §125.063. Public nuisance; use of place.

The habitual use of a place for engaging in organized criminal activity as described by Section 71.02, Penal Code, is a public nuisance. *(Added by L.1993, chap. 968(3), eff. 8/30/93.)*

### §125.064. Suit to abate nuisance.

(a) A district, county, or city attorney, the attorney general, or a resident of the state may sue to enjoin a public nuisance under this subchapter.

(b) Any person who habitually associates with others to engage in organized criminal activity as a member of a combination may be made a defendant in the suit. Any person who owns or is responsible for maintaining a place that is habitually used for engaging in organized criminal activity as described by Section 71.02, Penal Code, may be made a defendant in the suit. *(See other subsection (b) below.)*

(b) Any person who habitually associates with others to engage in organized criminal activity as a member of a combination or criminal street gang may be made a defendant in the suit. Any person who owns or is responsible for maintaining a place that is habitually used for engaging in organized criminal activity as described by Section 71.02, Penal Code, may be made a defendant in the suit. *(See other subsection (b) above.)*

(c) If the suit is brought by the state, the petition does not require verification.

(d) If the suit is brought by a resident, the resident is not required to show personal injury. *(Added by L.1993, chap. 968(3); chgd. by L.1995, chaps. 76(14.12), 318(33), eff. 9/1/95.)*

### §125.065. Court order.

(a) If the court finds that a combination constitutes a public nuisance, the court may enter an order enjoining a defendant in the suit from engaging in the organized criminal activities of the combination. *(See other subsection (a) below.)*

(a) If the court finds that a combination or criminal street gang constitutes a public nuisance, the court may enter an order enjoining a defendant in the suit from engaging in the organized criminal activities of the combination or gang. *(See other subsection (a) above.)*

(b) If the court finds that a place is habitually used in a manner that constitutes a public nuisance, the court may include in its order reasonable requirements to prevent the use of the place for organized criminal activity.

*(Added by L.1993, chap. 968(3); chgd. by L.1995, chaps. 76(14.13), 318(34), eff. 9/1/95.)*

### §125.066. Violation of court order.

A person who violates a temporary or permanent injunctive order under this subchapter is subject to the following sentences for civil contempt:

(1) a fine of not less than $1,000 nor more than $10,000;

(2) confinement in jail for a term of not less than 10 nor more than 30 days; or

(3) both fine and confinement.

*(Added by L.1993, chap. 968(3), eff. 8/30/93.)*

### §125.067. Continuation of activities pending trial or appeal; appeal.

(a) A person may not continue the enjoined activity pending trial or appeal on the merits of an injunctive order in a suit brought under this subchapter.

(b) Not later than the 90th day after the date of the injunctive order, an appropriate court of appeals shall hear and decide an appeal taken by a person enjoined under this subchapter.

(c) If an appeal is not taken by a person temporarily enjoined under this subchapter, the person is entitled to a trial on the merits not later than the 90th day after the date of the temporary injunctive order.

*(Added by L.1993, chap. 968(3), eff. 8/30/93.)*



### §125.068. Attorney's fees.

In an action brought under this subchapter, the court may award a prevailing party reasonable attorney's fees and costs. *(Added by L.1993, chap. 968(3), eff. 8/30/93.)*

### §125.069. Use of place; evidence.

In an action brought under this subchapter, proof that organized criminal activity by a member of a combination as described by Section 71.02, Penal Code, is frequently committed at a place or proof that a place is frequently used for engaging in organized criminal activity by a member of a combination as described by Section 71.02, Penal Code, is prima facie evidence that the proprietor knowingly permitted the act, unless, the act constitutes conspiring to commit an offense as described by Section 71.02. *(Added by L.1993, chap. 968(3); chgd. by L.1995, chap. 76(14.14), eff. 9/1/95. See other section 125.069 below.)*

### §125.069. Use of place; evidence.

In an action brought under this subchapter, proof that organized criminal activity by a member of a combination or a criminal street gang as described by Section 71.02, Penal Code, is frequently committed at a place or proof that a place is frequently used for engaging in organized criminal activity by a member of a combination or a criminal street gang as described by Section 71.02, Penal Code, is prima facie evidence that the proprietor knowingly permitted the act, unless, the act constitutes conspiring to commit an offense as described by Section 71.02. *(Added by L.1993, chap. 968(3); chgd. by L.1995, chap. 318(35), eff. 9/1/95. See other section 125.069 above.)*

# CIVIL STATUTES
## *(Selected Articles)*





Zt

## Art. 179e. Texas Racing Act.

## ARTICLE 1. GENERAL PROVISIONS

**Sec. 1.01. Short title.** This Act may be cited as the Texas Racing Act.

**Sec. 1.02. Purpose.** The purpose of this Act is to provide for the strict regulation of horse racing and greyhound racing and the control of pari-mutuel wagering in connection with that racing.

**Sec. 1.03. Definitions.** In this Act:

(1) "Person" includes any individual or entity capable of holding a legal or beneficial interest in property.

(2) "Association" means a person licensed under this Act to conduct a horse race meeting or a greyhound race meeting with pari-mutuel wagering.

(3) "Commission" means the Texas Racing Commission.

(4) "Comptroller" means the comptroller of public accounts.

(5) "Executive secretary" means the executive secretary of the Texas Racing Commission.

(6) "Horse race meeting" means the conducting of horse races on a day or during a period of consecutive or nonconsecutive days.

(7) "Thoroughbred horse" means a horse that is registered by the Jockey Club.

(8) "Thoroughbred racing" means the form of horse racing in which Thoroughbred horses mounted by jockeys engage in a race.

(9) "Quarter horse" means a horse that is registered by the American Quarter Horse Association.

(10) "Quarter horse racing" means the form of horse racing in which quarter horses mounted by jockeys engage in a race.

(11) "Appaloosa horse" means a horse that is registered by the Appaloosa Horse Club.

(12) "Appaloosa racing" means the form of horse racing in which Appaloosa horses mounted by jockeys engage in a race.

(13) "Arabian horse" means a horse that is registered by the Arabian Horse Registry of America or by the Canadian Arabian Horse Registry.

(14) "Arabian racing" means the form of horse racing in which Arabian horses sanctioned for racing by the Texas Arabian Breeders Association, while mounted by jockeys, engage in a race.

(15) "Paint horse" means a horse that is registered by The American Paint Horse Association.

(16) "Paint horse racing" means the form of horse racing in which paint horses mounted by jockeys engage in a race.

(17) "Enclosure" means all areas of a racing association's grounds, including the parking area, to which admission ordinarily can be obtained only on payment of an admission fee or presentation of official credentials.

(18) "Pari-mutuel wagering" means the form of wagering on the outcome of greyhound or horse racing in which those who wager purchase tickets of various denominations on an animal or animals and all wagers for each race are pooled and held by the racing association for distribution of the total amount, less the deductions authorized by this Act, to holders of tickets on the winning animals.

(19) "Pari-mutuel pool" means the total amount of money wagered by patrons on the result of a particular race or combination of races, the total being divided into separate mutuel pools for win, place, show, or combinations.

(20) "Breakage" means the odd cents by which the amount payable on each dollar wagered exceeds a multiple of 10 cents, except in the event a minus pool occurs, in which case the breakage shall be in multiples of five cents.

(21) "Texas-bred horse" means a horse that is sired by a stallion standing in Texas at the time of conception and foaled by a mare in Texas, except that a mare may be bred outside Texas and brought into Texas to foal and all foals sired and foaled under those conditions in the mare's lifetime shall be considered "Texas-bred" if the mare is bred back to a stallion standing in Texas. In all instances any foai must qualify under the rules of the commission.

(22) "Accredited Texas-bred horse" means a Texas-bred horse that meets the accreditation requirements of the state breed registry of that breed of horse.

(23) "Mixed racing" means a race in which different breeds of horses participate.

(24) "State horse breed registry" means a designated association administering accredited Texas-bred requirements for its specific breed of horses.

(25) "Racetrack" means a facility that is licensed under this Act for the conduct of pari-mutuel wagering on greyhound racing or horse racing.

(26) "Horse racing day" means the 24-hour period ending at 12 midnight.

(27) "Clerk of scales" means a racetrack official who is responsible for weighing a jockey before and after a race.

(28) "Jockey" or "apprentice jockey" means a professional rider licensed by the commission to ride horse races.

(29) *(Repealed by L.1991, chap. 386(74(a)), eff. 8/26/91.)*

(30) "Official starter" means a racetrack official who is in charge of the start of a race.

(31) "Paddock judge" means a racetrack official who supervises animals entered in a race while the animals are assembled before the beginning of a race in an enclosure on the grounds of a racetrack.

(32) "Patrol judge" means a racetrack official who is stationed at a set point along the racetrack to monitor the running of a race.

(33) "Placing official" means a racetrack official who records the order of the finish of a race.

(34) "Stable foreman" means the person in charge of the building in which horses are lodged and fed.

(35) "Steward" means a racing official with general authority and supervision over:

(A) the conduct of a licensed race meeting; and

(B) all licensees at a racetrack during a race meeting.

(36) "Trainer" means a person who is licensed by the commission to train racehorses.

(37) "Handicapper" means a person who predicts the winner of a horse race.

(38) "Authorized agent" means a person appointed by an owner of a horse to represent the owner. The term is limited to a person who is appointed by a written instrument that is acknowledged and approved by the commission.

(39) "Horseshoe inspector" means a racetrack official who inspects the shoes of the horses entered in a race.

(40) "Jockey room custodian" means a person who maintains the premises of a room in which jockeys prepare for a race.

(41) "Timer" means a racetrack official who times the running of a race.

(42) "Veterinarian" means a person licensed under The Veterinary Licensing Act (Article 7465a, Vernon's Texas Civil Statutes).

(43) "Concessionaire" means a person licensed by the commission to sell refreshments or souvenirs at a racetrack.

(44) "Combination" means a combination of races.

(45) "Regular wagering" means wagering on a single horse or greyhound in a single race. The term includes wagering on the win pool, the place pool, or the show pool.

(46) "Multiple wagering" means wagering on two or more animals in one race or on one or more animals in more than one race. "Multiple two wagering" means wagering on two animals in one or more races. "Multiple three wagering" means wagering on three or more animals in one or more races.

(47) "Greyhound" means a purebred greyhound dog registered by the National Greyhound Association.

(48) "Greyhound racing" means any race in which two or more greyhounds engage in a contest of speed or endurance or pursue a mechanical lure.

(49) "Enclosure—public" means the areas of the grounds of an association to which a member of the public is admitted by payment of an admission fee or on presentation of authorized credentials, but excludes restricted areas such as the racetrack, the receiving area, and the area in which the animals are housed.

(50) "Greyhound racing days" means days on which a permitted association conducts greyhound racing. "One racing day" means a period commencing at noon and ending at 2 a.m. the next calendar day, except in the case of days on which there are matinee races.

(51) "Greyhound matinee race" means any performance starting between 10 a.m. and 5 p.m. on any day other than Sunday.

(52) "Performance" means the consecutive running of not more than 13 greyhound races.

(53) "Judge" means an executive official of a greyhound racetrack.

(54) "Nonprofit corporation" means a corporation organized under Subdivision 7, Article 1302, Revised Statutes, or organized under the Texas Non-Profit Corporation Act (Article 1396-1.01 et seq., Vernon's Texas Civil Statutes) that:

(A) does not distribute any of its income to its members, officers, or governing body, other than as reasonable compensation for services;

(B) has a governing body or officers elected by a vote of members or by a vote of delegates elected by the members; and

(C) has obtained an exemption under Section 501 of the Internal Revenue Code (26 U.S.C. Section 501).

(55) "Mixed meet" means a live horse race meeting that includes races by more than one breed of horse.

(56) "Texas-owned horse" means a horse owned by a bona fide resident of this state as determined by the rules of the commission.

(57) "National historic district" means a district included in or eligible for inclusion in the National Register of Historic Places created under the National Historic Preservation Act, 16 U.S.C. Section 470 et seq.

(58) "Corporation" means an incorporated entity, either for profit or not for profit.

(59) "Applicant" means a person with a legal, equitable, or beneficial interest in a license application.

(60) "Maiden" means a horse that has never won a race at a race meeting authorized by the commission or by another racing jurisdiction.

(61) "Simulcast" means the telecast or other transmission of live audio and visual signals of a race, transmitted from a sending track to a receiving location, for the purpose of wagering conducted on the race at the receiving location.

(62) "Live pari-mutuel pool" means the total amount of money wagered by patrons on the result of a particular live race or combination of live races within the enclosure of the racetrack association where the race is being run.

(63) "Simulcast pari-mutuel pool" means the total amount of money wagered by patrons at a licensed racetrack association in Texas on the result of a particular simulcast race or combination of simulcast races.

(64) "Receiving location" means a licensed racetrack association in this state that has been allocated live and simulcast race dates or a facility not located in this state that is authorized to conduct wagering under the law of the jurisdiction in which it is located.

(65) "Credential" means any license, certificate, identification card, or other document indicating or representing authority or permission under this Act.

(66) "Sending track" means any licensed track for racing in this state or out-of-state from which a race is transmitted.

(67) "Racetrack facility" means a facility operated by an association within its enclosure for the purpose of presenting races for pari-mutuel wagering.

(68) "Child" means a person younger than 16 years of age.

(69) "Minor" means a person younger than 21 years of age.

(70) "Contraband" means:

(A) any item or thing the possession of which is unlawful under this Act, a commission rule, or other law;

(B) any item or thing that might reasonably have the effect of unnaturally depressing, stimulating, or exciting an animal during a race in a manner contrary to this Act or commission rule, including a prohibited device or substance; or

(C) a document, including a credential or forged ticket, possessed by an individual or used by an individual in violation of this Act or a commission rule.

(71) "Prohibited device" means:

(A) a spur or an electrical or other device prohibited by a commission rule regulating the unlawful influence of a race; or

(B) a device specifically designed, made, or adapted to influence or affect the outcome of a race in a manner contrary to this Act or a commission rule.

(72) "Prohibited substance" means a drug, chemical, or other substance that:

(A) in its use or intended use, is reasonably capable of influencing or affecting the outcome of a race in a manner contrary to this Act or a commission rule; and

(B) is prohibited by a commission rule regulating the unlawful influence of a race.

(73) "Unlawful touting" means an offense described by Section 14.01 of this Act or a similar offense under the laws of another state.

(74) "Race" includes a live audio and visual signal of a race.

(75) "Outstanding ticket" means a pari-mutuel ticket not presented for payment before the end of the greyhound racing or horse racing day for which the ticket was purchased.

(76) "Pari-mutuel voucher" means a bearer instrument issued by a pari-mutuel wagering machine that represents money owned by a wagering patron and held by an association, including winnings from a pari-mutuel wager.

(77) "Horsemen's organization" means an organization recognized by the commission that represents horse owners and trainers in negotiating and contracting with associations on subjects relating to racing and in representing and advocating the interests of horse owners and trainers before administrative, legislative, and judicial forums.

(78) "Cross-species simulcast signal" means a simulcast signal of a horse race at a greyhound racetrack facility or a simulcast signal of a greyhound race at a horse racetrack facility.



## ARTICLE 2. TEXAS RACING COMMISSION

**Sec. 2.01. Creation.** The Texas Racing Commission is created.

**Sec. 2.02. Membership.** (a) The commission consists of six members appointed by the governor with the advice and consent of the senate and two ex officio members who shall have the right to vote. The ex officio members are:

(1) the chairman of the Public Safety Commission or a member of the Public Safety Commission designated by the chairman of the Public Safety Commission; and

(2) the comptroller of public accounts or the comptroller's designee.

(b) Appointments to the commission shall be made without regard to the race, color, disability, sex, religion, age, or national origin of the appointees.

(c) In making appointments to the commission, the governor shall attempt to reflect the minority groups found in the state's general populace.

**Sec. 2.03. Term of office.** (a) Appointed members hold office for staggered terms of six years with two members' terms expiring February 1 of each odd-numbered year. A member holds office until that member's successor is appointed and qualifies.

(b) The ex officio members hold office on the commission for the time for which they hold their other offices.

**Sec. 2.04. Residence requirement.** An appointed member is not eligible to be a member of the commission unless that appointee has been a resident of this state for at least 10 consecutive years immediately before appointment.

**Sec. 2.05. Eligibility.** (a) Four of the appointed members of the commission must be representatives of the general public and have general knowledge of business or agribusiness. One additional appointed member must have special knowledge or experience related to greyhound racing and one additional appointed member must have special knowledge or experience related to horse racing. A person is not eligible for appointment as a member of the commission if the person or the person's spouse:

(1) is licensed by the commission, except as a commissioner;

(2) is employed by the commission or participates in the management of a business entity or other organization regulated by the commission or receiving funds from or through the commission;

(3) owns or controls, directly or indirectly, more than a 10 percent interest in a business entity or other organization regulated by the commission or receiving funds from or through the commission; or

(4) uses or receives a substantial amount of tangible goods, services, or funds from or through the commission, other than compensation or reimbursement authorized by law for commission membership, attendance, or expenses.

(b) In addition to the eligibility requirements of Subsection (a), a person is not eligible to be an appointed member of the commission if that person owns any financial interest in a racetrack or its operation or if that person is related within the second degree by affinity or the third degree by consanguinity, as determined under Subchapter B, Chapter 573, Government Code, to a person who owns any financial interest in a racetrack or its operation.

(c) Each person appointed to or employed by the commission is subject to all background checks and qualification criteria required to hold a racetrack license or other license under this Act.

(d) A person who has been convicted of a felony or of any crime involving moral turpitude is not eligible for appointment to the commission.

**Sec. 2.06. Financial statement.** Each appointed member of the commission and the executive secretary of the commission is an "appointed officer of a major state agency" within the meaning of Chapter 421, Acts of the 63rd Legislature, Regular Session, 1973 (Article 6252-9b, Vernon's Texas Civil Statutes). An appointee shall also file a detailed financial statement with the secretary of state of the type required by The Banking Department of Texas in the application for charter for state banks. The financial statement is a public record under Chapter 424, Acts of the 63rd Legislature, Regular Session, 1973 (Article 6252-17a, Vernon's Texas Civil Statutes).

**Sec. 2.07.** *(Repealed by L.1997, chap. 1275(54), eff. 9/1/97.)*

**Sec. 2.071. Conflict of interest.** (a) An officer, employee, or paid consultant of a Texas trade association in the field of horse or greyhound racing or breeding may not be a member of the commission or an employee of the commission who is exempt from the state's position classification plan or is compensated at or above the amount prescribed by the General Appropriations Act for step 1, salary group 17, of the position classification salary schedule.

(b) A person who is the spouse of an officer, manager, or paid consultant of a Texas trade association in the field of horse or greyhound racing or breeding may not be a member of the commission and may not be an employee of the commission who is exempt from the state's position classification plan or is compensated at or above the amount prescribed by the General Appropriations Act for step 1, salary group 17, of the position classification salary schedule.

(c) For the purposes of this section, a Texas trade association is a nonprofit association of business or professional competitors in this state designed to assist its members and its industry or profession in dealing with mutual business or professional problems and in promoting their common interest.

**Sec. 2.072. Lobbyist restriction.** A person may not serve as a member of the commission or act as the general counsel to the commission if the person is required to register as a lobbyist under Chapter 305, Government Code, because of the person's activities for compensation on behalf of a profession related to the operation of the commission.

**Sec. 2.073. Grounds for removal.** (a) It is a ground for removal from the commission if a member:

(1) does not have at the time of appointment the qualifications required by Section 2.02, 2.04, or 2.05 of this Act;

(2) does not maintain during service on the commission the qualifications required by Section 2.02 or 2.05 of this Act;

(3) violates a prohibition established by Section 2.05, 2.071, or 2.072 of this Act;

(4) cannot because of illness or disability discharge the member's duties for a substantial part of the term for which the member is appointed; or

(5) is absent from more than half of the regularly scheduled commission meetings that the member is eligible to attend during a calendar year.

(b) The validity of an action of the commission is not affected by the fact that it is taken when a ground for removal of a commission member exists.

(c) If the executive secretary has knowledge that a potential ground for removal exists, the executive secretary shall notify the presiding officer of the commission of the potential ground. The presiding officer shall then notify the governor and the attorney general that a potential ground for removal exists. If the potential ground for removal involves the presiding officer, the executive secretary shall notify the next highest officer of the commission, who shall notify the governor and the attorney general that a potential ground for removal exists.

**Sec. 2.074. Member training.** (a) To be eligible to take office as a member of the commission, a person appointed to the commission must complete at least one course of a training program that complies with this section.

(b) The training program must provide information to the person regarding:

(1) the enabling legislation that created the commission;

(2) the programs operated by the commission;

(3) the role and functions of the commission;

(4) the rules of the commission with an emphasis on the rules that relate to disciplinary and investigatory authority;

(5) the current budget for the commission;

(6) the results of the most recent formal audit of the commission;

(7) the requirements of the:

(A) open meetings law, Chapter 551, Government Code;

(B) open records law, Chapter 552, Government Code; and

(C) administrative procedure law, Chapter 2001, Government Code;

(8) the requirements of the conflict of interests laws and other laws relating to public officials; and

(9) any applicable ethics policies adopted by the commission or the Texas Ethics Commission.

(c) A person appointed to the commission is entitled to reimbursement for travel expenses incurred in attending the training program, as provided by the General Appropriations Act and as if the person were a member of the commission.

**Sec. 2.08. Expenses.** Each appointed member of the commission is entitled to a per diem in an amount prescribed by legislative appropriation for each day spent in performing the duties of the office and is entitled to reimbursement for actual and necessary expenses incurred in performing those duties. Reimbursement for expenses under this section is subject to any applicable limitation in the General Appropriations Act. The ex officio members are entitled to reimbursement for expenses from their respective agencies as provided by law for expenses incurred in the performance of their other official duties.

**Sec. 2.09. Offices.** The commission shall maintain its general office in the City of Austin. The commission may also establish branch offices.

**Sec. 2.10. Presiding officer.** The governor shall designate a public member of the commission as the presiding officer of the commission to serve in that capacity at the pleasure of the governor.

**Sec. 2.11. Meetings of commission.** (a) The commission shall hold at least six regular meetings each year on dates fixed by the commission. The commission shall adopt rules providing for the holding of special meetings.

(b) A majority of the commission constitutes a quorum.

(c) The commission shall keep at its general office a public record of every vote.

(d) The commission shall, by rule, develop and implement policies that provide the public with a reasonable opportunity to appear before the commission and to speak on any issue under the jurisdiction of the commission.

**Sec. 2.12. Executive secretary; employees.** (a) The commission shall employ an executive secretary and other employees as necessary to administer this Act.

(b) The commission may not employ or continue to employ a person:

(1) who owns or controls a financial interest in a licensee of the commission;

(2) who is employed by or serves as a paid consultant to a licensee of the commission, an official breed registry, or a Texas trade association, as defined by Section 2.071(c) of this Act, in the field of horse or greyhound racing or breeding;

(3) who owns or leases a race animal that participates in pari-mutuel racing in this state; or

(4) who accepts or is entitled to any part of the purse or Texas-bred incentive award to be paid on a greyhound or a horse in a race conducted in this state.

(c) The commission may not employ or continue to employ a person who is residentially domiciled with or related within the first degree by affinity or consanguinity to a person who is subject to a disqualification prescribed by Subsection (b) of this section.

(d) The commission shall employ the executive secretary and other employees to reflect the diversity of the population of the state as regards race, color, handicap, sex, religion, age, and national origin.

**Sec. 2.13. Executive secretary; duties.** The executive secretary shall keep the records of the commission and shall perform other duties as required by the commission. The executive secretary serves at the pleasure of the commission on a full-time basis and may not hold other employment.

**Sec. 2.14. Legal representation.** The attorney general shall designate at least one member of the attorney general's staff to counsel and advise the commission and to represent the commission in legal proceedings. The attorney general shall make available to the appropriate prosecuting attorneys any information obtained regarding violations of this Act.

**Sec. 2.15. Records.** All records of the commission that are not made confidential by other law are open to inspection by the public during regular office hours. All applications for a license under this Act shall be maintained by the commission and shall be available for public inspection during regular office hours. The contents of the investigatory files of the commission, however, are not public records and are confidential except in a criminal proceeding, in a hearing conducted by the commission, on court order, or with the consent of the party being investigated.

**Sec. 2.16. Department of public safety records.** (a) Except as otherwise provided by this Act, the files, records, information, compilations, documents, photographs, reports, summaries, and reviews of information and related matters that are collected, retained, or compiled by the Department of Public Safety in the discharge of its duties under this Act are confidential and are not subject to public disclosure, but are subject to discovery by a person that is the subject of the files, records, information, compilations, documents, photographs, reports, summaries, and reviews of information and related matters that are collected, retained, or compiled by the Department of Public Safety in the discharge of its duties under this Act.

(b) An investigation report or other document submitted by the Department of Public Safety to the commission becomes part of the investigative files of the commission and is subject to discovery by a person that is the subject of the investigation report or other document submitted by the Department of Public Safety to the commission that is part of the investigative files of the commission.

(c) Information that is in a form available to the public is not privileged or confidential under this section and is subject to public disclosure.

**Sec. 2.17. Annual accounting.** The commission shall prepare annually a complete and detailed written report accounting for all funds received and disbursed by the commission during the preceding fiscal year. The annual report must meet the reporting requirements applicable to financial reporting provided in the General Appropriations Act.

**Sec. 2.18. Funds paid to commission.** All money paid to the commission under this Act is subject to Subchapter F, Chapter 404, Government Code.

**Sec. 2.19. Employment practices.** (a) The executive secretary or the executive secretary's designee shall develop an intra-agency career ladder program that addresses opportunities for mobility and advancement for employees within the commission. The program shall require intra-agency posting of all positions concurrently with any public posting.

(b) The executive secretary or the executive secretary's designee shall develop a system of annual performance evaluations that are based on documented employee performance. All merit pay for commission employees must be based on the system established under this subsection.

(c) The executive secretary or the executive secretary's designee shall prepare and maintain a written policy statement to assure implementation of a program of equal employment opportunity under which all personnel transactions are made without regard to race, color, disability, sex, religion, age, or national origin. The policy statement must include:

(1) personnel policies, including policies relating to recruitment, evaluation, selection, appointment, training, and promotion of personnel that are in compliance with the requirements of Chapter 21, Labor Code;

(2) a comprehensive analysis of the commission workforce that meets federal and state laws, rules, regulations, and instructions directly promulgated from those laws, rules, and regulations;

(3) procedures by which a determination can be made about the extent of underuse in the commission workforce of all persons for whom federal or state laws, rules, regulations, and instructions directly promulgated from those laws, rules, and regulations encourage a more equitable balance; and

(4) reasonable methods to appropriately address those areas of underuse.

(d) A policy statement prepared under Subsection (c) of this section must cover an annual period, be updated annually and reviewed by the Texas Commission on Human Rights for compliance with Subsection (c)(1) of this section, and be filed with the governor's office.

(e) The governor's office shall deliver a biennial report to the legislature based on the information received under Subsection (d) of this section. The report may be made separately or as a part of other biennial reports made to the legislature.



**Sec. 2.20. Standards of conduct.** The executive secretary or the executive secretary's designee shall provide to members of the commission and to agency employees, as often as necessary, information regarding their qualification for office or employment under this Act and their responsibilities under applicable laws relating to standards of conduct for state officers or employees.

**Sec. 2.21. Division of responsibility.** The commission shall, by rule, develop and implement policies that clearly separate the policymaking responsibilities of the commission and the management responsibilities of the executive secretary and the staff of the commission.

**Sec. 2.22. Program and facility accessibility.** The commission shall comply with federal and state laws related to program and facility accessibility. The executive secretary shall also prepare and maintain a written plan that describes how a person who does not speak English can be provided reasonable access to the commission's programs and services.

**Sec. 2.23. Information to public.** (a) The commission shall prepare information of public interest describing the functions of the commission and the procedures by which complaints are filed with and resolved by the commission. The commission shall make the information available to the public and appropriate state agencies.

(b) The commission by rule shall establish methods by which racetrack patrons are notified of the name, mailing address, and telephone number of the commission for the purpose of directing complaints to the commission. The commission may provide for that notification:

(1) on every race performance program provided by each racetrack association; or

(2) on signs prominently displayed in the common public areas on the premises of each racetrack association.

**Sec. 2.24. Complaint handling.** (a) The commission shall keep information about each complaint filed with the commission. The information shall include:

(1) the date the complaint is received;

(2) the name of the complainant;

(3) the subject matter of the complaint;

(4) a record of all persons contacted in relation to the complaint;

(5) a summary of the results of the review or investigation of the complaint; and

(6) for complaints for which the agency took no action, an explanation of the reason the complaint was closed without action.

(b) The commission shall keep a file about each written complaint filed with the commission that the agency has authority to resolve. The commission shall provide to the person filing the complaint and the persons or entities complained about the commission's policies and procedures pertaining to complaint investigation and resolution. The commission, at least quarterly and until final disposition of the complaint, shall notify the person filing the complaint and the persons or entities complained about of the status of the complaint unless the notice would jeopardize an undercover investigation.

## ARTICLE 3. POWERS AND DUTIES OF COMMISSION

**Sec. 3.01.** *(Repealed by L.1997, chap. 1275(54), eff. 9/1/97.)*

**Sec. 3.02. Regulation and supervision.** (a) The commission shall regulate and supervise every race meeting in this state involving wagering on the result of greyhound or horse racing. All persons and things relating to the operation of those meetings are subject to regulation and supervision by the commission. The commission shall adopt rules for conducting greyhound or horse racing in this state involving wagering and shall adopt other rules to administer this Act that are consistent with this Act. The commission shall also make rules, issue licenses, and take any other necessary action relating exclusively to horse racing or to greyhound racing.

(b) The commission may establish separate sections to review or propose rules of the commission.

(c) The commission or a section of the commission shall hold a meeting on any proposed rule before the commission publishes the proposed rule in the Texas Register.

(d) The commission shall post notice of a meeting under Subsection (c) of this section at each racetrack facility. The notice shall include an agenda of the meeting and a summary of the proposed rule.

(e) A copy of a proposed rule published in the Texas Register shall also be posted concurrently at each racetrack facility.

(f) The commission or a section of the commission may appoint a committee of experts, members of the public, or other interested parties to advise the commission or section of the commission about a proposed rule of the commission.

(g) The commission, in adopting rules and in the supervision and conduct of racing, shall consider the effect of a proposed commission action on the state's agricultural, horse breeding, horse training, greyhound breeding, and greyhound training industry.



**Sec. 3.021. Regulation by commission.** (a) Any provision in this Act to the contrary notwithstanding, the commission may license and regulate all aspects of greyhound racing and horse racing in this state, whether or not that racing involves pari-mutuel wagering.

(b) To protect the health, safety, and welfare of race animals and participants in racing, to safeguard the interest of the general public, and to promote the orderly conduct of racing within the state, the commission may adopt rules for the licensing and regulation of races and workouts at racetracks that do not offer pari-mutuel wagering and for workouts at training facilities to secure past performances and workouts.

(c) The commission may charge an annual fee for licensing and regulating a racetrack that does not offer pari-mutuel wagering or a training facility in a reasonable amount that may not exceed the actual cost of enforcing rules adopted for the licensing and regulation of races and workouts at such a facility.

(d) The commission may not adopt rules restricting competitive bidding or advertising by a licensee except to prohibit false, misleading, or deceptive practices. In its rules to prohibit false, misleading, or deceptive practices, the commission may not include a rule that:

(1) restricts the use of any medium for advertising;
(2) restricts the use of a licensee's personal appearance or voice in an advertisement;
(3) relates to the size or duration of an advertisement by the licensee; or
(4) restricts the licensee's advertisement under a trade name.

**Sec. 3.03. Power of entry.** A member of the commission, an authorized agent of the commission, a commissioned officer of the Department of Public Safety, or a peace officer of the local jurisdiction in which the association maintains a place of business may enter any part of the racetrack facility or any other place of business of an association at any time for the purpose of enforcing and administering this Act.

**Sec. 3.04. Requirement of books and records; financial statements.** The commission shall require associations, managers, totalisator licensees, and concessionaires to keep books and records and to submit financial statements to the commission. The commission shall adopt reasonable rules relating to those matters.

**Sec. 3.05. Subpoena power.** (a) A member of the commission, or a duly appointed agent of the commission, while involved in carrying out functions under this Act, may take testimony and may require by subpoena the attendance of witnesses and the production of books, records, papers, correspondence, and other documents that the commission considers advisable. Subpoenas shall be issued under the signature of the commission or its duly appointed agent and shall be served by any person designated by the commission. A member of the commission, or a duly appointed agent of the commission, may administer oaths or affirmations to witnesses appearing before the commission or its agents.

(b) If a subpoena issued under this section is disobeyed, the commission or its duly appointed agent may invoke the aid of a Travis County district court in requiring compliance with the subpoena. A Travis County district court may issue an order requiring the person to appear and testify and to produce books, records, papers, correspondence, and documents. Failure to obey the order of the court shall be punished by the court as contempt.

**Sec. 3.06. Certified documents.** Instead of requiring an affidavit or other sworn statement in any application or other document required to be filed with the commission, the commission may require a certification of the document under penalty of perjury in the form the commission may prescribe.

**Sec. 3.07. Officials of race meetings.** (a) The commission shall employ all of the judges and all of the stewards for the supervision of a horse race or greyhound race meeting. Each horse race or greyhound race meeting shall be supervised by three stewards for horse racing or by three judges for greyhound racing. The commission shall designate one of the stewards or judges as the presiding steward or judge for each race meeting. The association, following the completion of the race meeting, may submit written comments to the commission regarding the job performance of the stewards and judges for the commission's review. Comments received are not binding, in any way, on the commission. For each race meeting, the commission shall employ at least one state veterinarian. The commission may, by rule, impose a fee on an association to offset the costs of compensating the stewards, judges, and state veterinarians. The amount of the fee for the compensation of stewards, judges, and state veterinarians must be reasonable according to industry standards for the compensation of those officials at other racetracks and may not exceed the actual cost to the commission for compensating the officials. All other racetrack officials shall be appointed by the association, with the approval of the commission. Compensation for those officials not compensated by the commission shall be determined by the association.

(b) The commission shall make rules specifying the authority and the duties of each official, including the power of stewards or judges to impose penalties for unethical practices or violations of racing rules. A penalty imposed by the stewards or judges may include a fine of not more than $5,000, a suspension for not more than one year, or both a fine and suspension. Before imposing a penalty under this subsection, the stewards and judges shall conduct a hearing that is consistent with constitutional due process. A hearing conducted by a steward or judge under this subsection is not subject to Chapter 2001, Government Code. If, in the opinion of the stewards or judges, the allowable penalties are not sufficient, the stewards or judges may refer the case to the commission for further action.

(c) The commission shall require each steward or judge to take and pass both a written examination and a medical examination annually. The commission by rule shall prescribe the methods and procedures for taking the examinations and the standards for passing. Failure to pass an examination is a ground for refusal to issue an original or renewal license to a steward or judge or for suspension or revocation of such a license.

(d) Medication or drug testing performed on a race animal under this Act shall be conducted by a laboratory selected by the commission on a yearly basis by competitive bidding submitted to the commission for final approval. The commission's decision shall be based on cost and integrity. The Texas Veterinary Medical Diagnostic Laboratory may aid the commission in its selection. Medication or drug testing performed on a human under this Act shall be conducted by a laboratory approved by the commission. Charges for services performed under this section shall be forwarded to the commission for approval as to the reasonableness of the charges for the services. Charges may include but are not limited to expenses incurred for travel, lodging, testing, and processing of test results. The reasonable charges associated with medication or drug testing conducted under this Act shall be paid by the association that receives the services. The commission shall adopt rules for the procedures for approving and paying laboratory charges under this section. On the approval of the charges as reasonable, in relation to industry standards for testing charges, the commission shall forward a copy of the charges to the association that receives the services for immediate payment.

(e) To pay the charges associated with the medication or drug testing, an association may use the money held by the association to pay outstanding tickets and pari-mutuel vouchers. If additional amounts are needed to pay the charges, the association shall pay those additional amounts.

If the amount held exceeds the amount needed to pay the charges, the association shall pay the excess to the commission in accordance with Section 11.08 of this Act.

(f) The association is responsible for the cost of approved charges for animal drug testing services under this section. The commission shall adopt rules to allocate responsibility for the costs of human drug testing of a licensee.

(g) A steward or judge may exercise the supervisory authority granted the steward or judge under this Act or commission rule, including the performance of supervisory acts requiring the exercise of discretion, on any day.

**Sec. 3.08. Appeal from decision of stewards or judges.** (a) Except as provided by Subsection (b) of this section, a final decision of the stewards or judges may be appealed to the commission in the manner provided for a contested case under the Administrative Procedure and Texas Register Act (Article 6252-13a, Vernon's Texas Civil Statutes).

(b) A decision of the stewards or judges on a disqualification for a foul in a race or on a finding of fact regarding the running of a race is final and may not be appealed.



**Sec. 3.09. Funding.** (a) The comptroller shall deposit the state's share of each pari-mutuel pool from horse racing and greyhound racing in the General Revenue Fund.

(b) The commission shall deposit the money it collects under this Act in the State Treasury to the credit of a special fund to be known as the Texas Racing Commission fund. The Texas Racing Commission fund may be appropriated only for the administration and enforcement of this Act. Any unappropriated money remaining in that special fund at the close of each fiscal biennium shall be transferred to the General Revenue Fund and may be appropriated for any legal purpose. The legislature may also appropriate money from the General Revenue Fund for the administration and enforcement of this Act. Any amount of general revenue appropriated for the administration and enforcement of this Act in excess of the cumulative amount deposited in the Texas Racing Commission fund shall be reimbursed from the Texas Racing Commission fund not later than one year after the date on which the general revenue funds are appropriated, with 12 percent interest per year until August 31, 1993, and 6 3/4 percent interest thereafter with all payments first attributable to interest.

**Sec. 3.10. Annual report.** The commission shall make a report to the governor, lieutenant governor, and speaker of the house of representatives not later than January 31 of each year. The report shall cover the operations of the commission and the condition of horse breeding and racing and greyhound breeding and racing during the previous year. The commission shall also obtain from the Department of Public Safety a comprehensive report of any organized crime activities in this state which the department may wish to report and information concerning any and all illegal gambling which may be known to exist in the state and shall include the report by the department in its report and shall include any recommendations it considers appropriate.

**Sec. 3.11. Cooperation with peace officers.** The commission shall cooperate with all district attorneys, criminal district attorneys, county attorneys, the Department of Public Safety, the attorney general, and all peace officers in enforcing this Act. Under its authority to conduct criminal history information record checks under Section 5.04 of this Act, the commission shall maintain and exchange pertinent intelligence data with other states and agencies.

**Sec. 3.12. Reporting of violations.** The commission's rules shall allow anonymous reporting of violations of this Act or of rules adopted by the commission.

**Sec. 3.13. Recognition of organization.** (a) The commission by rule shall adopt criteria to recognize an organization to represent members of a segment of the racing industry, including owners, breeders, trainers, kennel operators, or other persons involved in the racing industry, in any interaction between the members of the organization and an association or the commission.

(b) The commission may recognize an organization that meets the requirements of Subsection (a) of this section.

**Sec. 3.14. Disciplinary actions.** The commission shall revoke, suspend, or refuse to renew a license, place on probation a person whose license has been suspended, or reprimand a licensee for a violation of this Act or a rule of the commission. If a license suspension is probated, the commission may require the licensee to report regularly to the commission on matters that are the basis of the probation.

**Sec. 3.15. Hearing requirements.** If the commission proposes to suspend, revoke, or refuse to renew a person's license, the person is entitled to a hearing conducted by the State Office of Administrative Hearings. Proceedings for a disciplinary action, other than those conducted by racing stewards or judges, are governed by Chapter 2001, Government Code. Rules of practice adopted by the commission under Section 2001.004, Government Code, applicable to the proceedings for a disciplinary action, other than those conducted by racing stewards or judges, may not conflict with rules adopted by the State Office of Administrative Hearings.

**Sec. 3.16. Rules relating to unlawful influences on racing.** (a) The commission shall adopt rules prohibiting a person from unlawfully influencing or affecting the outcome of a race, including rules relating to the use of a prohibited device or prohibited substance at a racetrack or training facility.

(b) The commission may require prerace testing and shall require postrace testing to determine whether a prohibited substance has been used. The testing may be by an invasive or noninvasive method. The commission's rules shall require state-of-the-art testing methods.

(c) Following the discovery of a prohibited device or a return of a test showing the presence of a prohibited substance, a steward or judge may summarily suspend a person who has used or administered the prohibited device or prohibited substance until a hearing before the stewards and judges. The steward or judge may also disqualify an animal as provided by a commission rule adopted under this section.

(d) Except as otherwise provided, a person may appeal a ruling of the stewards or judges to the commission. The commission may stay a suspension during the period the matter is before the commission.

(e) The commission may require urine samples to be frozen for a period necessary to allow any follow-up testing to detect and identify a prohibited substance. Any other specimen shall be maintained for testing purposes in a manner required by commission rule.

(f) If a test sample or specimen shows the presence of a prohibited substance, the entire sample, including any split portion remaining in the custody of the commission, shall be maintained until final disposition of the matter.

(g) A licensee whose animal test shows the presence of a prohibited substance is entitled to have a split portion of the test sample or specimen tested at a testing facility authorized to perform drug testing under this Act and selected by the licensee. The commission shall adopt rules relating to split testing procedures.

(h) The licensed trainer of an animal is:

(1) considered by law to be the absolute ensurer that no prohibited substance has been administered to the animal; and

(2) responsible for ensuring that no prohibited substance is administered to the animal.

(i) The commission shall adopt rules relating to the drug testing of licensees.

(j) A person who violates a rule adopted under this section may:

(1) have any license issued to the person by the commission revoked or suspended; or

(2) be barred for life or any other period from applying for or receiving a license issued by the commission or entering any portion of a racetrack facility.

**Sec. 3.17. Security for fees and charges.** The commission may require an association to post security in an amount and form determined by the commission to adequately ensure the payment of any fees or charges due to the state or the commission relating to pari-mutuel racing, including charges for drug testing.

**Sec. 3.18. Cease and desist order.** (a) The executive secretary may issue a cease and desist order if the executive secretary reasonably believes an association or other licensee is engaging or is likely to engage in conduct that violates this Act or a commission rule.

(b) On issuance of a cease and desist order, the executive secretary shall serve on the association or other licensee by personal delivery or registered or certified mail, return receipt requested, to the person's last known address, a proposed cease and desist order. The proposed order must state the specific acts or practices alleged to violate this Act or a commission rule. The proposed order must state its effective date. The effective date may not be before the 21st day after the date the proposed order is mailed or delivered. If the person against whom the proposed order is directed requests, in writing, a hearing before the effective date of the proposed order, the order is automatically stayed pending final adjudication of the order. Unless the person against whom the proposed order is directed requests, in writing, a hearing before the effective date of the proposed order, the order takes effect and is final and nonappealable as to that person.

(c) On receiving a request for a hearing, the executive secretary shall serve notice of the time and place of the hearing by personal delivery or registered or certified mail, return receipt requested. At a hearing, the commission has the burden of proof and must present evidence in support of the order. Each person against whom the order is directed may cross-examine and show cause why the order should not be issued.

(d) After the hearing, the commission shall issue or decline to issue a cease and desist order. The proposed order may be modified as necessary to conform to the findings at the hearing. An order issued under this section is final for purposes of enforcement and appeal and shall require the person to immediately cease and desist from the conduct that violates this Act or a commission rule.

(e) A person affected by a cease and desist order issued, affirmed, or modified after a hearing may file a petition for judicial review in a district court of Travis County under Chapter 2001, Government Code. A petition for judicial review does not stay or vacate the order unless the court, after hearing, specifically stays or vacates the order.

**Sec. 3.19. Emergency cease and desist order.** (a) The executive secretary may issue an emergency cease and desist order if the executive secretary reasonably believes an association or other licensee is engaged in a continuing activity that violates this Act or a commission rule in a manner that threatens immediate and irreparable public harm.

(b) After issuing an emergency cease and desist order, the executive secretary shall serve on the association or other licensee by personal delivery or registered or certified mail, return receipt requested, to the person's last known address, an order stating the specific charges and requiring the person immediately to cease and desist from the conduct that violates this Act or a commission rule. The order must contain a notice that a request for hearing may be filed under this section.

(c) An association or other licensee that is the subject of an emergency cease and desist order may request a hearing. The request must be filed with the executive secretary not later than the 10th day after the date the order was received or delivered. A request for a hearing must be in writing and directed to the executive secretary and must state the grounds for the request to set aside or modify the order. Unless a person who is the subject of the emergency order requests a hearing in writing before the 11th day after the date the order is received or delivered, the emergency order is final and nonappealable as to that person.

(d) On receiving a request for a hearing, the executive secretary shall serve notice of the time and place of the hearing by personal delivery or registered or certified mail, return receipt requested. The hearing must be held not later than the 10th day after the date the executive secretary receives the request for a hearing unless the parties agree to a later hearing date. At the hearing, the commission has the burden of proof and must present evidence in support of the order. The person requesting the hearing may cross-examine witnesses and show cause why the order should not be affirmed. Section 2003.021(b), Government Code, does not apply to hearings conducted under this section.

(e) An emergency cease and desist order continues in effect unless the order is stayed by the executive secretary. The executive secretary may impose any condition before granting a stay of the order.

(f) After the hearing, the executive secretary shall affirm, modify, or set aside in whole or part the emergency cease and desist order. An order affirming or modifying the emergency cease and desist order is final for purposes of enforcement and appeal.

**Sec. 3.20. Violation of final cease and desist order.** (a) If the executive secretary reasonably believes that a person has violated a final and enforceable cease and desist order, the executive secretary may:

(1) initiate administrative penalty proceedings under Article 15 of this Act;

(2) refer the matter to the attorney general for enforcement by injunction and any other available remedy; or

(3) pursue any other action, including suspension of the person's license, that the executive secretary considers appropriate.

(b) If the attorney general prevails in an action brought under Subsection (a)(2) of this section, the attorney general is entitled to recover reasonable attorney's fees.

**Sec. 3.21. Injunction.** The commission may institute an action in its own name to enjoin the violation of this Act. An action for an injunction is in addition to any other action, proceeding, or remedy authorized by law.



Zt

**Sec. 3.22. Enforcement regarding horsemen's account.** (a) The commission, by rule, shall develop a system for monitoring the activities of managers and employees of an association relating to the horsemen's account. The monitoring system may include review of the financial operations of the association, including inspections of records at the association's offices, at any racetrack, or at any other place the association transacts business.

(b) The executive secretary may issue an order prohibiting the association from making any transfer from a bank account held by the association for the conduct of its business under this Act, pending commission review of the records of the account, if the executive secretary reasonably believes that the association has failed to maintain the proper amount of money in the horsemen's account. The executive secretary shall provide in the order a procedure for the association to pay certain expenses necessary for the operation of the racetrack, subject to the executive secretary's approval. An order issued under this section may be made valid for a period not to exceed 14 days.

(c) The executive secretary may issue an order requiring the appropriate transfers to or from the horsemen's account if, after reviewing the association's records of its bank accounts, the executive secretary determines there is an improper amount of money in the horsemen's account.



## ARTICLE 4. POWERS AND DUTIES OF COMPTROLLER

**Sec. 4.01. Books and records.** All books, records, and financial statements required by the commission under Section 3.04 of this Act are open to inspection by the comptroller. The comptroller by rule may specify the form and manner in which the books, records, and statements are to be kept and reports are to be filed that relate to the state's share of a pari-mutuel pool.

**Sec. 4.02. Power of entry.** The comptroller and the authorized agents of the comptroller may enter the office, racetrack, or other place of business of an association or totalisator licensee at any time to inspect books, records, or financial statements or to inspect and test the totalisator system to determine the accuracy of totalisator-generated reports and calculations pertaining to the state share of the pari-mutuel pool.

**Sec. 4.03. Rules.** The comptroller may adopt rules for the enforcement of the comptroller's powers and duties under this Act.

**Sec. 4.04. Collection of state's portion of pari-mutuel pool.** (a) The comptroller may prescribe by rule procedures for the collection and deposit of the state's portion of each pari-mutuel pool. The state's portion of each pool shall be deposited by the association at the time and in the manner that the comptroller prescribes by rule.

(b) The comptroller by rule may require each association to post security in an amount estimated to be sufficient to cover the amount of state money that will be collected and held by an association between bank deposits to ensure payment of the state's portion of the pari-mutuel pool. Cash, cashier's checks, surety bonds, irrevocable bank letters of credit, United States Treasury bonds that are readily convertible to cash, or irrevocable assignments of federally insured accounts in banks, savings and loan institutions, and credit unions are acceptable as security for purposes of this section.

**Sec. 4.05. Compliance.** (a) If an association or totalisator company does not comply with a rule adopted by the comptroller under this article, refuses to allow access to or inspection of any of its required books, records, or financial statements, refuses to allow access to or inspection of the totalisator system, or becomes delinquent for the state's portion of the pari-mutuel pool or for any other tax collected by the comptroller, the comptroller shall certify that fact to the commission.

(b) With regard to the state's portion of the pari-mutuel pool and any penalties related to the state's portion, the comptroller, acting independently of the commission, may take any collection or enforcement actions authorized under the Tax Code against a delinquent or dilatory taxpayer. Administrative appeals related to the state's portion of the pari-mutuel pool or late reporting or deposit of the state's portion shall be to the comptroller and then to the courts as under Title 2, Tax Code. All other administrative appeals shall be to the commission and then to the courts.

**Sec. 4.06. Penalties for delayed reports and payments.** An association incurs a penalty for the late payment of the state's portion of the pari-mutuel pool or reports related to the payment of that portion at the rate of five percent of the total amount due or $1,000, whichever is greater, for a report or payment not filed on or before the time it is due. An additional penalty equal to one percent of the amount of the state's portion that is unpaid shall be added for each business day that the required report or payment is late up to a maximum penalty of 12 percent. The penalty may be waived in situations in which penalties would be waived under Section 111.103, Tax Code.

## ARTICLE 5. GENERAL LICENSE PROVISIONS

**Sec. 5.01. Form; certificate; fees.** (a) The commission shall prescribe forms for applications for licenses and shall provide each occupational licensee with a license certificate or credentials.

(b) The commission shall annually prescribe reasonable license fees for each category of license issued under this Act.

(c) The operation of a racetrack and the participation in racing are privileges, not rights, granted only by the commission by license and subject to reasonable and necessary conditions set by the commission.

**Sec. 5.02. Judicial review.** (a) Judicial review of an order of the commission is under the substantial evidence rule.

(b) Venue for judicial review of an order of the commission is in a district court in Travis County.

**Sec. 5.03. Fingerprints.** (a) An applicant for any license under this Act must, except as allowed under Section 7.10 of this Act, submit to the commission a complete set of fingerprints of the individual natural person applying for the license or, if the applicant is not an individual natural person, a complete set of fingerprints of each officer or director and of each person owning an interest of at least five percent in the applicant. The Department of Public Safety may request any person owning any interest in an applicant for a racetrack license to submit a complete set of fingerprints.

(b) If a complete set of fingerprints is required by the commission, the commission shall, not later than the next day after receiving the prints, forward the prints to the Department of Public Safety or the Federal Bureau of Investigation. If the prints are forwarded to the Department of Public Safety, the department shall classify the prints and check them against its fingerprint files and shall report to the commission its findings concerning the criminal record of the applicant or the lack of such a record. A racetrack license may not be issued until the report is made to the commission. A temporary occupational license may be issued before a report is made to the commission.

(c) A peace officer of this or any other state, or any district office of the commission, shall take the fingerprints of an applicant for a license on forms approved and furnished by the Department of Public Safety and shall immediately deliver them to the commission.

**Sec. 5.04. Access to criminal history records.** (a) The commission is authorized to obtain any criminal history record information that relates to each applicant for employment by the commission and to each applicant for a license issued by the commission and that is maintained by the Department of Public Safety or the Federal Bureau of Investigation Identification Division. The commission may refuse to recommend an applicant who fails to provide a complete set of fingerprints.

(b) *(Repealed by L.1993, chap. 790(46(8)), eff. 9/1/93.)*

(c) *(Repealed by L.1993, chap. 790(46(8)), eff. 9/1/93.)*

**Sec. 5.05. Cost of criminal history check.** (a) The commission shall, in determining the amount of a license fee, set the fee in an amount that will cover, at least, the cost of conducting a criminal history check on the applicant for a license.

(b) The commission shall reimburse the Department of Public Safety for the cost of conducting a criminal history check under this article.

## ARTICLE 6. RACETRACK LICENSES

**Sec. 6.01. License required.** A person may not conduct wagering on a greyhound race or a horse race meeting without first obtaining a racetrack license from the commission. A person who violates this section commits an offense.

**Sec. 6.02. Classification of horse-racing tracks.** (a) Horse-racing tracks are classified as class 1 racetracks, class 2 racetracks, class 3 racetracks, and class 4 racetracks.

(b) A class 1 racetrack is a racetrack on which live racing is conducted for a number of days in a calendar year, the number of days and the actual dates to be determined by the commission under Article 8 of this Act. A class 1 racetrack may operate only in a county with a population of not less than 750,000, according to the most recent federal census, or in a county adjacent to a county with such a population. Not more than three class 1 racetracks may be licensed and operated in this state.

(c) A class 2 racetrack is a racetrack on which live racing is conducted for a number of days to be determined by the commission under Article 8 of this Act. A class 2 racetrack is entitled to conduct 60 days of live racing in a calendar year. An association may request additional or fewer days of live racing. If after receipt of a request from an association the commission determines additional or fewer days to be economically feasible and in the best interest of the state and the racing industry, the commission shall grant the additional or fewer days. The commission may permit an association that holds a class 2 racetrack license and that is located in a national historic district to conduct horse races for more than 60 days in a calendar year.

(d) A class 3 racetrack is a racetrack operated by a county or a nonprofit fair under Article 12 of this Act. An association that holds a class 3 racetrack license and that conducted horse races in 1986 may conduct live races for a number of days not to exceed 16 days in a calendar year on the dates selected by the association.

(e) For purposes of this section live race dates are counted separately from the dates on which the association presents simulcast races.

(f) The number of race dates allowed under this section relates only to live race dates. A racetrack may present simulcast races on other dates as approved by the commission.

(g) A class 4 racetrack is a racetrack operated by a county fair under Section 12.03 of this Act. An association that holds a class 4 racetrack license may conduct live races for a number of days not to exceed five days in a calendar year on dates selected by the association and approved by the commission.

**Sec. 6.03. Application.** (a) The commission shall require each applicant for an original racetrack license to pay the required application fee and to submit an application, on a form prescribed by the commission, containing the following information:

(1) if the applicant is an individual, the full name of the applicant, the applicant's date of birth, a physical description of the applicant, the applicant's current address and telephone number, and a statement by the applicant disclosing any arrest or conviction for a felony or for a misdemeanor, except a misdemeanor under the Uniform Act Regulating Traffic on Highways (Article 6701d, Vernon's Texas Civil Statutes) or a similar misdemeanor traffic offense;

(2) if the applicant is a corporation:

(A) the state in which it is incorporated, the names and addresses of the corporation's agents for service of process in this state, the names and addresses of its officers and directors, the names and addresses of its stockholders, and, for each individual named under this subdivision, the individual's date of birth, current address and telephone number, and physical description, and a statement disclosing any arrest or conviction for a felony or for a misdemeanor, except a misdemeanor under the Uniform Act Regulating Traffic on Highways (Article 6701d, Vernon's Texas Civil Statutes) or a similar misdemeanor traffic offense; and

(B) identification of any other beneficial owner of shares in the applicant that bear voting rights, absolute or contingent, any other person that directly or indirectly exercises any participation in the applicant, and any other ownership interest in the applicant that the applicant making its best effort is able to identify;

(3) if the applicant is an unincorporated business association:

(A) the names and addresses of each of its members and, for each individual named under this subdivision, the individual's date of birth, current address and telephone number, and physical description, and a statement disclosing any arrest or conviction for a felony or for a misdemeanor, except a misdemeanor under the Uniform Act Regulating Traffic on Highways (Article 6701d, Vernon's Texas Civil Statutes) or a similar misdemeanor traffic offense; and

(B) identification of any other person that exercises voting rights in the applicant or that directly or indirectly exercises any participation in the applicant and any other ownership interest in the applicant that the applicant making its best effort is able to identify;

(4) the exact location at which a race meeting is to be conducted;

(5) if the racing facility is in existence, whether it is owned by the applicant and, if leased to the applicant, the name and address of the owner and, if the owner is a corporation or unincorporated business association, the names and addresses of its officers and directors, its stockholders and members, if any, and its agents for service of process in this state;

(6) if construction of the racing facility has not been initiated, whether it is to be owned by the applicant and, if it is to be leased to the applicant, the name and address of the prospective owner and, if the owner is a corporation or unincorporated business association, the names and addresses of its officers and directors, the names and addresses of its stockholders, the names and addresses of its members, if any, and the names and addresses of its agents for service of process in this state;

(7) identification of any other beneficial owner of shares that bear voting rights, absolute or contingent, in the owner or prospective owner of the racing facility, or any other person that directly or indirectly exercises any participation in the owner or prospective owner and all other ownership interest in the owner or prospective owner that the applicant making its best effort is able to identify;

(8) a detailed statement of the assets and liabilities of the applicant;

(9) the kind of racing to be conducted and the dates requested;

(10) proof of residency as required by Section 6.06 of this Act;

(11) a copy of each management, concession, and totalisator contract dealing with the proposed license at the proposed location in which the applicant has an interest for inspection and review by the commission; the applicant or licensee shall advise the commission of any change in any management, concession, or totalisator contract; all management, concession, and totalisator contracts must have prior approval of the commission; the same fingerprint, criminal records history, and other information required of license applicants pursuant to Sections 5.03 and 5.04 and Subdivisions (1) through (3) of this subsection shall be required of proposed totalisator firms, concessionaires, and managers and management firms; and

(12) any other information required by the commission.

(b) When the commission receives a plan for the security of a racetrack facility, or a copy of a management, concession, or totalisator contract for review under Subdivision (11) of Subsection (a) of this section, the commission shall review the contract or security plan in an executive session. Documents submitted to the commission under this section by an applicant are subject to discovery in a suit brought under this Act but are not public records and are not subject to Chapter 424, Acts of the 63rd Legislature, Regular Session, 1973 (Article 6252-17a, Vernon's Texas Civil Statutes). In reviewing and approving contracts under this subsection, the commission shall attempt to ensure the involvement of minority owned businesses whenever possible.

(c) The application must be sworn to by the applicant or, if a corporation or association, by its chief executive officer.

(d) The application for an original racetrack license must be accompanied by an application fee in the form of a cashier's check or certified check.

(e) The minimum application fee for a horse racing track is $15,000 for a class 1 racetrack, $7,500 for a class 2 racetrack, $2,500 for a class 3 racetrack, and $1,500 for a class 4 racetrack. The minimum application fee for a greyhound racing track is $20,000. Using the minimum fees, the commission by rule shall establish a schedule of application fees for the various types and sizes of racing facilities. The commission shall set the application fees in amounts that are reasonable and necessary to cover the costs of administering this Act.

(f) If the applicant is a nonprofit corporation, only directors and officers of the corporation must disclose the information required under Subdivision (2) of Subsection (a) of this section.

(g) The burden of proof is on the applicant to show compliance with this Act and with the rules of the commission. An applicant who does not show the necessary compliance is not eligible for a license under this article.

(h) In considering an application for a horse racetrack license under this section, the commission shall give additional weight to evidence concerning an applicant who has experience operating a horse racetrack licensed under this Act.

(i) Notwithstanding this section, if a licensed track petitions for an upgrade in the classification of the track, the fees and charges imposed shall be the difference between the fees and charges previously paid and the fees and charges for the upgraded facility classification.

**Sec. 6.031. Background check.** The commission shall require a complete personal, financial, and business background check of the applicant or any person owning an interest in or exercising control over an applicant for a racetrack license, the partners, stockholders, concessionaires, management personnel, management firms, and creditors and shall refuse to issue or renew a license or approve a concession or management contract if, in the sole discretion of the commission, the background checks reveal anything which might be detrimental to the public interest or the racing industry. The commission may not hold a hearing on the application, or any part of the application, of an applicant for a racetrack license before the completed background check of the applicant has been on file with the commission for at least 14 days.

**Sec. 6.04. Issuance of license; bond.** (a) The commission may issue a racetrack license to a qualified person if it finds that the conduct of race meetings at the proposed track and location will be in the public interest, complies with all zoning laws, and complies with this Act and the rules adopted by the commission and if the commission finds by clear and convincing evidence that the applicant will comply with all criminal laws of this state. In determining whether to grant or deny an application for any class of racetrack license, the commission may consider the following factors:

(1) the applicant's financial stability;
(2) the applicant's resources for supplementing the purses for races for various breeds;
(3) the location of the proposed track;
(4) the effect of the proposed track on traffic flow;
(5) facilities for patrons and occupational licensees;
(6) facilities for race animals;
(7) availability to the track of support services and emergency services;
(8) the experience of the applicant's employees;
(9) the potential for conflict with other licensed race meetings;
(10) the anticipated effect of the race meeting on the greyhound or horse breeding industry in this state; and
(11) the anticipated effect of the race meeting on the state and local economy from tourism, increased employment, and other sources.

(b) Before issuance of a license under this article, an applicant for a racetrack license must post security in an amount determined by the commission to adequately ensure the association's compliance with this Act and the rules of the commission. Cash, cashier's checks, surety bonds, irrevocable bank letters of credit, United States Treasury bonds that are readily convertible to cash, or irrevocable assignments of federally insured deposits in banks, savings and loan institutions, and credit unions are acceptable as security for purposes of this section. The security shall be conditioned on compliance with this Act and the rules adopted under this Act and shall be returned after the conditions of the security are met.

(c) The commission shall not issue licenses for more than three greyhound racetracks in this state. Those racetracks must be located in counties that border the Gulf of Mexico.

(d) In considering an application for a class 4 racetrack license, the commission may waive or defer compliance with the commission's standards regarding the physical facilities or operations of a horse racetrack. The commission may not waive or defer compliance with standards that relate to the testing of horses or licensees for the presence of a prohibited drug, chemical, or other substance. If the commission defers compliance, the commission shall, when granting the application, establish a schedule under which the licensee must comply with the standards.

**Sec. 6.05.** *(Repealed by L.1991, chap. 386(74(a)), eff. 8/26/91.)*

**Sec. 6.06. Racetrack licenses; grounds for denial, revocation, and suspension.** (a) To preserve and protect the public health, welfare, and safety, the commission shall adopt rules relating to license applications, the financial responsibility, moral character, and ability of applicants, and all matters relating to the planning, construction, and operation of racetracks. The commission may refuse to issue a racetrack license or may revoke or suspend a license if, after notice and hearing, it has reasonable grounds to believe and finds that:

(1) the applicant has been convicted in a court of competent jurisdiction of a violation of this Act or any rule adopted by the commission or that the applicant has aided, abetted, or conspired with any person to commit such a violation;

(2) the applicant has been convicted of a felony or of any crime involving moral turpitude, including convictions for which the punishment received was a suspended sentence, probation, or a nonadjudicated conviction, that is reasonably related to the applicant's present fitness to hold a license under this Act;

(3) the applicant has violated or has caused to be violated this Act or a rule of the commission in a manner that involves moral turpitude, as distinguished from a technical violation of this Act or of a rule;

(4) the applicant is unqualified, by experience or otherwise, to perform the duties required of a licensee under this Act;

(5) the applicant failed to answer or falsely or incorrectly answered a question in an application;

(6) the applicant fails to disclose the true ownership or interest in a greyhound or horse as required by the rules of the commission;

(7) the applicant is indebted to the state for any fees or for the payment of a penalty imposed by this Act or by a rule of the commission;

(8) the applicant is not of good moral character or the applicant's reputation as a peaceable, law-abiding citizen in the community where the applicant resides is bad;

(9) the applicant has not yet attained the minimum age necessary to purchase alcoholic beverages in this state;

(10) the applicant is in the habit of using alcoholic beverages to an excess or uses a controlled substance as defined in Chapter 481, Health and Safety Code, or a dangerous drug as defined in Chapter 483, Health and Safety Code, or is mentally incapacitated;

(11) the applicant may be excluded from a track enclosure under this Act;

(12) the applicant has not been a United States citizen residing in this state for the period of 10 consecutive years immediately preceding the filing of the application;

(13) the applicant has improperly used a license certificate, credential, or identification card issued under this Act;

(14) the applicant is residentially domiciled with a person whose license has been revoked for cause within the 12 months immediately preceding the date of the present application;

(15) the applicant has failed or refused to furnish a true copy of the application to the commission's district office in the district in which the premises for which the permit is sought are located;

(16) the applicant is engaged or has engaged in activities or practices that the commission finds are detrimental to the best interests of the public and the sport of greyhound racing or horse racing; or

(17) the applicant fails to fully disclose the true owners of all interests, beneficial or otherwise, in a proposed racetrack facility.

(b) Subsection (a) of this section applies to a corporation, partnership, limited partnership, or any other organization or group whose application is comprised of more than one person if a shareholder, partner, limited partner, director, or officer is disqualified under Subsection (a) of this section.

(c) A license for operation of a class 1 or class 2 racetrack or a greyhound racetrack may not be issued to a corporation unless the corporation is incorporated under the laws of this state and a majority of the stock, if any, of the corporation is owned at all times by individuals who meet the residency qualifications prescribed by this section for individual applicants.

(d) The majority ownership of a partnership, firm, or association applying for or holding a license must be held by citizens who meet the residency qualifications enumerated in this section for individual applicants. A corporation holding a license to operate a racetrack under this Act that violates this subsection is subject to forfeiture of its charter, and the attorney general, on receipt of information relating to such a violation, shall file suit in a district court of Travis County for cancellation of the charter and revocation of the license issued under this Act. Subterfuge in the ownership and operation of a racetrack shall be prevented, and this Act shall be liberally construed to carry out this intent.

(e) The commission may condition the issuance of a license under this article on the observance of its rules. The commission may amend the rules at any time and may condition the continued holding of the license on compliance with the rules as amended.

(f) The commission may refuse to issue a license or may suspend or revoke a license of a licensee under this article who knowingly or intentionally allows access to an enclosure where greyhound races or horse races are conducted to a person who has engaged in bookmaking, touting, or illegal wagering, whose income is from illegal activities or enterprises, or who has been convicted of a violation of this Act.

(g) A person awarded a management contract to operate a racetrack must meet all of the requirements of this section.

(h) A person may not own more than a five percent interest in more than two racetracks licensed under this Act.

(i) Subsections (a)(12), (c), and (d) of this section do not apply to an applicant for or the holder of a racetrack license if the applicant, the license holder, or the license holder's parent company is a publicly traded company.

**Sec. 6.061. Regulation of inappropriate or unsafe conditions.** (a) The commission shall adopt rules implementing this section, including rules:

(1) requiring the report of and correction of:

(A) an inappropriate condition on the premises of a racetrack facility, including a failure to properly maintain the facility, that interferes with the administration of this Act; or

(B) a condition on the premises of a racetrack facility that makes the facility unsafe for a race participant, patron, or animal; and

(2) determining the methods and manner in which the executive secretary may determine and remedy inappropriate conditions or unsafe facilities on the premises of a racetrack facility, including the methods and manner in which the executive secretary may conduct inspections of the racetrack facility and remedy emergency situations.

(b) The executive secretary shall issue a notice of violation to a racetrack facility on a finding that an inappropriate or unsafe condition exists.

(c) If the executive secretary determines that an inappropriate or unsafe condition exists at the racetrack facility, the executive secretary shall order the racetrack facility to take action within a specified period to remedy the inappropriate condition or unsafe condition. In determining the period for compliance, the executive secretary shall consider the nature and severity of the problem and the threat to the health, safety, and welfare of the race participants, patrons, or animals.

(d) The commission shall adopt rules requiring the reporting of any corrective action taken by a racetrack facility in response to an order of the executive secretary under Subsection (c) of this section.

(e) If a racetrack facility fails to take any action as required under Subsection (c) of this section, the executive secretary shall initiate an enforcement action against the racetrack facility. The executive secretary may rescind any live or simulcast race date of any racetrack association that does not take corrective action within the period set by the executive secretary.

(f) The commission shall adopt rules relating to the commission's review of an action taken under this section by the executive secretary. A review procedure adopted under this subsection must be consistent with Chapter 2001, Government Code.

**Sec. 6.062. Supervision of changes to premises.** (a) The commission shall adopt a method of supervising and approving the construction, renovation, or maintenance of any building or improvement on the premises of a racetrack facility.

(b) The commission shall adopt rules relating to:

(1) the approval of plans and specifications;

(2) the contents of plans and specifications;

(3) the maintenance of records to ensure compliance with approved plans and specifications;

(4) the content and filing of construction progress reports by the racetrack facility to the commission;

(5) the inspection by the commission or others;

(6) the method for making a change or amendment to an approved plan or specification; and

(7) any other method of supervision or oversight necessary.

(c) If the commission has grounds to believe that an association has failed to comply with the requirements of this section, a representative of the association shall appear before the commission to consider the issue of compliance with the rules adopted under this section.

(d) Before a building or improvement may be used by the association, the commission shall determine whether the construction, renovation, or maintenance of the building or improvement was completed in accordance with the approved plans and specifications and whether other requirements of the commission were met.

(e) If the commission determines that the association failed to comply with a requirement of this section or rule adopted under this section, the commission shall initiate an enforcement action against the association. In addition to any other authorized enforcement action, the commission may rescind any live or simulcast race date of any association that has failed to comply with the requirement of this section.

**Sec. 6.063. Summary suspension.** (a) The commission may summarily suspend a racetrack license if the commission determines that a racetrack at which races or pari-mutuel wagering are conducted under the license is being operated in a manner that constitutes an immediate threat to the health, safety, or welfare of the participants in racing or the patrons.

(b) After issuing a summary suspension order, the executive secretary shall serve on the association by personal delivery or registered or certified mail, return receipt requested, to the licensee's last known address, an order stating the specific charges and requiring the licensee immediately to cease and desist from all conduct permitted by the license. The order must contain a notice that a request for hearing may be filed under this section.

(c) An association that is the subject of a summary suspension order may request a hearing. The request must be filed with the executive secretary not later than the 10th day after the date the order was received or delivered. A request for a hearing must be in writing and directed to the executive secretary and must state the grounds for the request to set aside or modify the order. Unless a licensee who is the subject of the order requests a hearing in writing before the 11th day after the date the order is received or delivered, the order is final and nonappealable as to that licensee.

(d) On receiving a request for a hearing, the executive secretary shall serve notice of the time and place of the hearing by personal delivery or registered or certified mail, return receipt requested. The hearing must be held not later than the 10th day after the date the executive secretary receives the request for a hearing unless the parties agree to a later hearing date. At the hearing, the commission has the burden of proof and must present evidence in support of the order. The licensee requesting the hearing may cross examine witnesses and show cause why the order should not be affirmed. Section 2003.021(b), Government Code, does not apply to hearings conducted under this section.

(e) A summary suspension order continues in effect unless the order is stayed by the executive secretary. The executive secretary may impose any condition before granting a stay of the order.

(f) After the hearing, the executive secretary shall affirm, modify, or set aside in whole or part the summary suspension order. An order affirming or modifying the summary suspension order is final for purposes of enforcement and appeal.

**Sec. 6.07. Lease.** (a) The commission may adopt rules to authorize an association, as lessee, to contract for the lease of a racetrack and the surrounding structures.

(b) The commission may not approve a lease if:

(1) it appears that the lease is a subterfuge to evade compliance with Section 6.05 or 6.06 of this Act;

(2) the racetrack and surrounding structures do not conform to the rules adopted under this Act; or

(3) the lessee, prospective lessee, or lessor is disqualified from holding a racetrack license.

(c) Each lessor and lessee under this section must comply with the disclosure requirements of Subdivision (1) of Subsection (a) of Section 6.03 of this Act. The commission may not approve a lease if the lessor and lessee do not provide the required information.

**Sec. 6.08. Special provisions relating to horse racing: deductions from pool; allocations of shares and breakage.** (a) An amount shall be deducted from each wagering pool to be distributed as provided by Subsections (b) through (e) of this section. The total maximum deduction from a regular wagering pool is 18 percent. The total maximum deduction from a multiple two wagering pool is 21 percent. The total maximum deduction from a multiple three wagering pool is 25 percent.

(b)(1) A horse racing association shall set aside for purses an amount not less than seven percent of a live regular wagering pool or live multiple two wagering pool and not less than 8.5 percent of a live multiple three wagering pool.

(2) A horse racing association, after January 1, 1999, shall set aside from simulcast pools for purses not less than the following amounts from the takeout of the sending racetrack:

(A) 38.8 percent of the regular wagering pool;

(B) 33.3 percent of the multiple two wagering pool; and

(C) 34 percent of the multiple three wagering pool.

If the cost of the simulcast signal exceeds five percent of the simulcast handle, the receiving horse racing association shall split the cost of the signal in excess of five percent evenly with the horsemen's organization by allocating the cost against the purse money derived from that simulcast signal.

(3) The horse racing association shall transfer the amount set aside for purses from any live and simulcast pools and shall deposit the amounts in purse accounts maintained by breed by the horsemen's organization in one or more federally insured depositories. Legal title to purse accounts is vested in the horsemen's organization. The horsemen's organization may contract with an association to manage and control the purse accounts and to make disbursements from the purse accounts:

(A) to an owner whose horse won a purse;

(B) to the horsemen's organization for its expenses; or

(C) for other disbursements as provided by contract between the horsemen's organization and the association.

(4) An association, after January 1, 1999, may pay a portion of the revenue set aside under this subsection to an organization recognized under Section 3.13 of this Act, as provided by a contract approved by the commission.

(c) *(Repealed by L.1997, chap. 1275(54), eff. 9/1/97.)*

(d) A horse racing association shall set aside for the Texas-bred program as provided by Subsection (f) of this section an amount equal to one percent of a live multiple two wagering pool and a live multiple three wagering pool.

(e) The remainder of the amount deducted under Subsection (a) of this section from a regular wagering pool, a multiple two wagering pool, or a multiple three wagering pool, after allocation of the amounts specified in Subsections (b), (c), and (d) of this section, shall be retained by the association as its commission.

(f) The amount of a multiple two wagering pool or a multiple three wagering pool set aside under Subsection (d) of this section for the Texas-bred program is in addition to any money received from the breakage. Of the amount set aside under Subsection (d) of this section, two percent shall be set aside for deposit in the equine research account under Subchapter F, Chapter 88, Education Code, and, of the remaining 98 percent, 10 percent may be used by the appropriate breed registry for administration and the remaining 90 percent shall be used for awards.

(g) The commission shall adopt rules relating to the accounting, audit, and distribution of all amounts set aside for the Texas-bred program under this section.

(h) Two percent of the breakage shall be allocated to the equine research account under Subchapter F, Chapter 51, Education Code. The remaining 98 percent of the breakage shall constitute "total breakage" and shall be allocated pursuant to Subsections (i) and (j) of this section.

(i) Ten percent of the total breakage from a live pari-mutuel pool or a simulcast pari-mutuel pool is to be paid to the commission for use by the appropriate state horse breed registry, subject to rules promulgated by the commission. The appropriate breed registry for Thoroughbred horses is the Texas Thoroughbred Breeders Association, for quarter horses is the Texas Quarter Horse Association, for Appaloosa horses is the Texas Appaloosa Horse Club, for Arabian horses is the Texas Arabian Breeders Association, and for paint horses is the Texas Paint Horse Breeders Association.

(j) Ten percent of the total breakage from a live pari-mutuel pool or a simulcast pari-mutuel pool is to be retained by the association to be used in stakes races restricted to accredited Texas-bred horses. The appropriate state horse breed registry shall pay out the remaining 80 percent of the total breakage as follows:

(1) 40 percent of the remaining breakage is allocated to the owners of the accredited Texas-bred horses that finish first, second, or third;

(2) 40 percent is allocated to the breeders of the accredited Texas-bred horses that finish first, second, or third; and

(3) 20 percent is allocated to the owner of the stallion standing in this state at the time of conception whose Texas-bred get finish first, second, or third.

(k) For purposes of this section:

(1) "Horse owner" means a person who is owner of record of an accredited Texas-bred horse at the time of a race;

(2) "Breeder" means a person who, according to the rules of the appropriate state horse breed registry, is the breeder of the accredited Texas-bred horse; and

(3) "Stallion owner" means a person who is owner of record, at the time of conception, of the stallion that sired the accredited Texas-bred horse.

(*l*) An association may not make a deduction or withhold any percentage of a purse from the account into which the purse paid to a horse owner is deposited for membership payments, dues, assessments, or any other payments to an organization except an organization of the horse owner's choice.

(m) If a share of the breakage cannot be distributed to the person who is entitled to a share, the appropriate breed registry shall retain that share.

**Sec. 6.09. Disposition of pari-mutuel pools at greyhound races.** (a) Every association authorized under this Act to conduct pari-mutuel wagering at a greyhound race meeting on races run shall distribute all sums deposited in any pari-mutuel pool to the holders of the winning tickets if those tickets are presented for payment within 60 days after the closing day of the race meeting at which the pool was formed, less an amount paid as a commission of 18 percent of the total deposits in pools resulting from regular win, place, and show wagering, and an amount not to exceed 21 percent of the total deposits in pools resulting from multiple two wagering and an amount not to exceed 25 percent of the total deposits in pools resulting from multiple three wagering.

(b) *(Repealed by L.1997, chap. 1275(54), eff. 9/1/97.*

(c) On each racing day, the association shall pay:

(1) the fee due the state to the comptroller; and

(2) the 50 percent of the breakage due the state to the commission.

(d) Fifty percent of the breakage is to be paid to the appropriate state greyhound breeding registry. Of that portion of the breakage 25 percent of that breakage is to be used in stakes races and 25 percent of that total breakage from a live pari-mutuel pool or a simulcast pari-mutuel pool is to be paid to the commission for the use by the state greyhound breed registry, subject to rules promulgated by the commission.

(e) The deductions and allocations made pursuant to this section are applicable to live pari-mutuel pools.

(f) The commission in adopting rules relating to money paid to the commission for use by the state greyhound breed registry under Subsection (d) of this section shall require the award of a grant in an amount equal to two percent of the amount paid to the commission for use by the state greyhound breed registry to a person for the rehabilitation of greyhounds or to locate homes for greyhounds.

**Sec. 6.091. Distribution of deductions from simulcast pari-mutuel pool.** (a) An association shall distribute from the total amount deducted as provided by Sections 6.08(a) and 6.09(a) of this Act from each simulcast pari-mutuel pool and each simulcast cross-species pool the following shares:

(1)(A) until January 1, 1999, an amount equal to 0.25 percent of each simulcast pari-mutuel pool and each simulcast cross-species simulcast pool as the amount set aside to reimburse the general revenue fund for amounts that are appropriated for the administration and enforcement of this Act and that are in excess of the cumulative amount of funds deposited in the Texas Racing Commission fund, until the excess amount and interest on the excess amount are fully reimbursed;

(B) an amount equal to one percent of each simulcast pool as the amount set aside for the state; and

(C) an amount equal to 1.25 percent of each cross-species simulcast pool as the amount set aside for the state;

(2) an amount equal to 0.25 percent of each pool set aside to reimburse the general revenue fund for amounts that are appropriated for the administration and enforcement of this Act and that are in excess of the cumulative amount of funds deposited in the Texas Racing Commission fund, until the excess amount and interest on the excess amount are fully reimbursed;

(3) if the association is a horse racing association, an amount equal to one percent of a multiple two wagering pool or multiple three wagering pool as the amount set aside for the Texas-bred program to be used as provided by Section 6.08(f) of this Act;

(4) if the association is a greyhound association, an amount equal to one percent of a multiple two wagering pool or a multiple three wagering pool as the amount set aside for the Texas-bred program for greyhound races, to be distributed and used in accordance with rules of the commission adopted to promote greyhound breeding in this state; and

(5) the remainder as the amount set aside for purses, expenses, the sending association, and the receiving location pursuant to a contract approved by the commission between the sending association and the receiving location.

(b) Section 6.09(b)(1) of this Act does not apply to amounts deducted from a simulcast pari-mutuel pool in a greyhound race.

(c) A greyhound racetrack association that receives an interstate cross-species simulcast signal shall distribute the following amounts from the total amount deducted as provided by Subsection (a) of this section from each pool wagered on the signal at the facility:

(1) a fee of 1.5 percent to be paid to the racetrack facility in this state sending the signal;

(2) a purse in the amount of 0.75 percent to be paid to the official state breed registry for thoroughbred horses for use as purses at racetracks in this state;

(3) a purse in the amount of 0.75 percent to be paid to the official state breed registry for quarter horses for use as purses at racetracks in this state; and

(4) a purse of 4.5 percent to be escrowed with the commission for purses in the manner set forth in Subsection (e) of this section.

(d) A horse racetrack association receiving an interstate cross-species simulcast signal shall distribute the following amounts from the total amount deducted as provided by Subsection (a) of this section from each pool wagered on the signal at the facility:

(1) a fee of 1.5 percent to be paid to the racetrack facility in this state sending the signal; and

(2) a purse in the amount of 5.5 percent to be paid to the official state breed registry for greyhounds for use at racetracks in this state. The breed registry may use not more than 20 percent of this amount to administer this subdivision.

(e) The purse set aside under Subsection (c)(4) of this section shall be deposited into an escrow account in the registry of the commission. Any horse racetrack association in this state may apply to the commission for receipt of all or part of the escrowed purse account for use as purses. The commission shall determine to which horse racetracks the escrowed purse account shall be allocated and in what percentages, taking into consideration purse levels, racing opportunities, and the financial status of the requesting racetrack. The first distribution of the escrowed purse account allocated to a racetrack under this section may not be made before October 1, 1998.

(f) After October 15, 1998, a horse racetrack association that is located not more than 75 miles from a greyhound racetrack facility that offers wagering on a cross-species simulcast signal may apply to the commission for an additional allocation of up to 20 percent of the funds in the escrowed purse account that is attributable to the wagering on a cross-species simulcast signal at the greyhound racetrack facility, if the horse racetrack facility sends the cross-species simulcast signal to the greyhound racetrack. If the applying horse racetrack can prove to the commission's satisfaction that a decrease in the racetrack's handle has occurred that is directly due to wagering on an interstate cross-species simulcast signal at a greyhound racetrack facility that is located not more than 75 miles from the applying racetrack, the commission shall allocate the amounts from the escrowed purse account as the commission considers appropriate to compensate the racetrack for the decrease, but the amount allocated may not exceed 20 percent of the funds in the escrowed purse account that are attributable to the wagering on the interstate cross-species simulcast signal at the greyhound racetrack facility. Any amount allocated by the commission under this subsection may be used by the racetrack facility for any purpose.

(g) If a racing association purchases an interstate simulcast signal and the cost of the signal is more than five percent of the pari-mutuel pool, the commission shall reimburse the racing association an amount equal to one-half of the signal cost that is more than five percent of the pari-mutuel pool from the escrowed purse account under Subsection (c)(4) of this section.

(h) A racetrack facility offering wagering on an intrastate cross-species simulcast signal shall send the purse amount specified under Subsection (c)(4) or (d)(2) of this section, as appropriate, to the racetrack facility conducting the live race that is being simulcast.

(i) A racing facility conducting a live race that is being simulcast may charge the receiving racetrack facility a host fee in addition to the amounts described in this section.

(j) The commission shall adopt rules relating to this section and the oversight of amounts allocated under Subsections (c) and (d) of this section.

**Sec. 6.092. Oversight of use of funds generated by pari-mutuel racing.** (a) The commission shall adopt reporting, monitoring, and auditing requirements or other appropriate performance measures for any funds distributed to or used by or any function or service provided by the expenditure of any funds distributed to or used by any organization that receives funds generated by live or simulcast pari-mutuel racing.

(b) The commission shall adopt the requirements or performance measures after consultation with the affected organization. In adopting the rules, the commission shall give consideration to the concerns of the affected organization.

(c) An organization receiving funds generated by live or simulcast pari-mutuel racing shall annually file with the commission a copy of an audit report prepared by an independent certified public accountant. The audit shall include a verification of any performance report sent to or required by the commission.

(d) The commission may review any records or books of an organization that submits an independent audit to the commission as the commission determines necessary to confirm or further investigate the findings of an audit or report.

(e) The commission by rule may suspend or withhold funds from an organization that:

(1) it determines has failed to comply with the requirements or performance measures adopted under Subsection (a) of this section; or

(2) has, following an independent audit or other report to the commission, material questions raised on the use of funds by the organization.

**Sec. 6.093. Deductions from live pari-mutuel pool.** (a)(1) A horse racing association, until January 1, 1999, shall set aside for the state:

(A) an amount equal to one percent of each live pari-mutuel pool from the first $100 million of the total amount of all live pari-mutuel pools of the association in a calendar year;

(B) an amount equal to two percent of each live pari-mutuel pool from the next $100 million of the total amount of all live pari-mutuel pools of the association in a calendar year;

(C) an amount equal to three percent of the next $100 million of the total amount of all live pari-mutuel pools of the association in a calendar year;

(D) an amount equal to four percent of the next $100 million of the total amount of all live pari-mutuel pools of the association in a calendar year; and

(E) an amount equal to five percent of each live pari-mutuel pool from the amount of all live pari-mutuel pools of the association in a calendar year not covered by Paragraphs (A) through (D) of this subdivision.

(2) A greyhound racing association, until January 1, 1999, shall set aside for the state:

(A) an amount equal to two percent of each live pari-mutuel pool from the first $100 million of the total amount of all live pari-mutuel pools of the association in a calendar year;

(B) an amount equal to three percent of each live pari-mutuel pool from the next $100 million of the total amount of all live pari-mutuel pools of the association in a calendar year;

(C) an amount equal to four percent of each live pari-mutuel pool from the next $100 million of the total amount of all live pari-mutuel pools of the association in a calendar year;

(D) an amount equal to five percent of each live pari-mutuel pool from the total amount of all live pari-mutuel pools of the association in a calendar year not covered by Paragraphs (A) through (C) of this subdivision; and

(E) 50 percent of the breakage.

(3) All amounts set aside by the association for the state in Subdivisions (1) and (2) of this subsection shall be applied to the reimbursement of all amounts of general revenue appropriated for the administration and enforcement of this Act in excess of the cumulative amount deposited to the Texas Racing Commission fund until the earlier of:

(A) the excesses together with interest thereon are reimbursed in full; or

(B) January 1, 1999.

(b) On or after January 1, 1999, a horse or greyhound racing association shall set aside for the state from the live pari-mutuel pool at the association:

(1) an amount equal to one percent of each live pari-mutuel pool from the total amount of all live pari-mutuel pools of the association in a calendar year in excess of $100 million but less than $200 million;

(2) an amount equal to two percent of each live pari-mutuel pool from the total amount of all live pari-mutuel pools of the association in a calendar year in excess of $200 million but less than $300 million;

(3) an amount equal to three percent of each live pari-mutuel pool from the total amount of all live pari-mutuel pools of the association in a calendar year in excess of $300 million but less than $400 million;

(4) an amount equal to four percent of each live pari-mutuel pool from the total amount of all live pari-mutuel pools of the association in a calendar year in excess of $400 million but less than $500 million; and

(5) an amount equal to five percent of each live pari-mutuel pool from the total amount of all live pari-mutuel pools of the association in a calendar year in excess of $500 million.

**Sec. 6.10. Application of Tax Code.** Unless inconsistent with the provisions of this Act, Chapters 111 through 113, Tax Code, including without limitation provisions relating to the assessment of penalty and interest, apply to the collection of the state's share under this Act. In applying those provisions of the Tax Code for purposes of this section, the state's share under this Act is treated as if it were a tax. For purposes of collecting the state's share under this Act, the comptroller may use any procedure authorized under Title 2, Tax Code.

**Sec. 6.11. Allocation of purse.** (a) In no event shall the purse in a greyhound race be less than a minimum of 4.7 percent of the total deposited in each pool.

(b) Thirty-five percent of the portion of a purse allocated to a greyhound shall be paid directly to its owner. The balance shall be paid to its contract kennel as provided by the rules of the commission.

**Sec. 6.12. Not transferable.** (a) A racetrack license is not transferable.

(b) In the event of the death of any person whose death causes a violation of the licensing provisions of this Act, the commission may issue a temporary license for a period not to exceed one year under rules adopted by the commission.

**Sec. 6.13. Financial disclosure.** (a) The commission by rule shall require that each association holding a license for a class 1 racetrack, class 2 racetrack, or greyhound racetrack must annually file with the commission a detailed financial statement that:

(1) contains the names and addresses of all stockholders, members and owners of any interest in the racetrack facility;

(2) indicates compliance during the filing period with Section 6.06 of this Act; and

(3) includes any other information required by the commission.

(b) Each transaction that involves an acquisition or a transfer of a pecuniary interest in the association must receive prior approval from the commission. A transaction that changes the ownership of the association requires submission of updated information of the type required to be disclosed under Subsection (a) of Section 6.03 of this Act.

**Sec. 6.14. Racing restricted to designated place.** (a) An association may not conduct greyhound or horse racing at any place other than the place designated in the license except as provided by this section or by Section 6.15 of this Act. However, if the racetrack or enclosure designated in the license becomes unsuitable for racing because of fire, flood, or other catastrophe, the affected association, with the prior approval of the commission, may conduct a race meeting or any remaining portion of a meeting temporarily at any other racetrack licensed by the commission to conduct the same type of racing as may be conducted by the affected association if the licensee of the other racetrack also consents to the usage.

(b) The commission shall not issue more than three racetrack licenses for greyhound racing.

(c) Each greyhound racetrack licensed under this Act must be located in a county that has a population of more than 190,000, according to the most recent federal census, and that includes all or part of an island that borders the Gulf of Mexico.

(d) On request of an association, the commission shall amend a racetrack license to change the location of the racetrack if the commission finds that:

(1) the conduct of race meetings at the proposed track at the new location will be in the public interest;

(2) there was not a competing applicant for the original license; and

(3) the association's desire to change location is not the result of a subterfuge in the original licensing proceeding.

**Sec. 6.15. Racing at temporary location.** After an association has been granted a license to operate a racetrack and before the completion of construction at the designated place for which the license was issued, the commission may, on application by the association, issue a temporary license that permits the association to conduct races at a location in the same county for a period expiring two years after the date of issuance of the temporary license or on the completion of the permanent facility, whichever occurs first. The commission may set the conditions and standards for issuance of a temporary license and allocation of appropriate race days. An applicant for a temporary license must pay the application fees and must post the bonds required of other licensees before the issuance of a temporary license. After a temporary license has expired, no individual, corporation, or association, nor any individual belonging to a corporation or association which has been granted a temporary license, may get an extension of the temporary license or a new temporary license.

**Sec. 6.16. Employment of former commission members or employees.** (a) An association may not employ any person who has been a member of the commission, the executive secretary of the commission, or an employee employed by the commission in a position in the state employment classification plan of grade 12 or above, or any person related within the second degree by affinity or the third degree by consanguinity, as determined under Article 5996h, Revised Statutes, to such a member or employee, during the two-year period immediately preceding the employment by the association.

(b) A person may not seek or accept employment with an association if the association would violate this section by employing the person.

(c) An association or person who violates this section commits an offense.

**Sec. 6.17. City and county fees.** (a) A commissioners court may collect a fee not to exceed 15 cents as an admission fee to a licensed racetrack located within the county. If the racetrack is located within an incorporated city or town, the governing body of the city or town may collect a fee not to exceed 15 cents as an admission fee to a licensed racetrack located within the city or town. If the racetrack is not located within an incorporated city or town, the court may collect an additional fee not to exceed 15 cents as an admission fee to a licensed racetrack located within the county for allocation among the incorporated cities or towns in the county. If the racetrack is not located in an incorporated city or town, the court shall collect the additional fee if requested to do so by the governing bodies of a majority of the incorporated cities and towns in the county. Allocation of the fees shall be based on the population within the county of the cities or towns.

(b) If the racetrack is a class 1 racetrack, the commissioners court of each county with a population of not less than 750,000 adjacent to the county in which the racetrack is located may each collect fees equal to the fees authorized by Subsection (a) of this section.

(c) The commissioners court by order may establish procedures for the collection of the fees under Subsection (a) of this section. The procedures may require a person holding a racetrack license to keep records and file reports as considered necessary by the commissioners court.

(d) A county or municipality may not assess or collect any other license fee, privilege tax, excise tax, or racing fee on admissions to, or wagers placed at, a licensed racetrack.

(e) *(Repealed by L.1991, chap. 386(74(a)), eff. 8/26/91.)*

**Sec. 6.18. Term of license; restrictions on racetracks.** (a) A racetrack license issued under this article is perpetual. The commission may suspend or revoke a license as provided by this Act.

(b) The commission may prescribe a reasonable annual fee to be paid by each racetrack licensee. The fee must be in an amount sufficient to provide that the total amount of fees imposed under this section, together with the license fees prescribed under Section 5.01(b) of this Act, is sufficient to pay the costs of administering and enforcing this Act.

**Sec. 6.19. Reinstatement of certain licenses.** (a) A class 2 racetrack license revoked by the commission before September 1, 1991, for the licensee's failure to demonstrate financial responsibility may be reinstated as provided by this section.

(b) A licensee to which this section applies must apply for reinstatement not later than January 1, 1992. The commission may not require the licensee to pay an application or renewal fee.

(c) A county or nonprofit fair that desires to use any racetrack facilities constructed, used, or leased by a licensee to which this section applies, with the written consent of the licensee, may apply for reinstatement of the license as a class 3 racetrack license in the name of the county or nonprofit fair.

(d) The commission shall reinstate the license and may not revoke or suspend the license before the second anniversary of the date that it is reinstated unless it finds that:

(1) material grounds that cannot be cured, other than the licensee's inability to demonstrate financial responsibility, exist for denial, revocation, or suspension of the license;

(2) the licensee is or has been the subject of a voluntary or involuntary proceeding under the Bankruptcy Code (Title 11 U.S.C.); or

(3) another person has obtained a racetrack license for the racetrack facility for which the licensee obtained the license.

(e) A license reinstated under this section expires on the second anniversary of the date that it is reinstated. The commission shall convert a reinstated license to a perpetual license if the commission finds that, on the date the reinstated license will expire, construction or renovation of the racetrack proposed by the association has been financed.

## ARTICLE 7. OTHER LICENSES

**Sec. 7.01. License required.** A person may not participate in racing with pari-mutuel wagering without first obtaining a license from the commission.

**Sec. 7.02. Licensed activities.** (a) Each person, other than a spectator or person placing a wager, involved in any capacity with racing with pari-mutuel wagering under this Act must obtain a license under this article.

(b) The commission shall adopt categories of licenses for the various occupations licensed under this article and shall specify by rule the qualifications and experience required for licensing in each category that requires specific qualifications or experience.

(c) If an examination is required for the issuance of a license under this article, not later than the 30th day after the date on which a licensing examination is administered under this Act, the commission shall notify each examinee of the results of the examination.

(d) If requested in writing by a person who fails a licensing examination administered under this Act, the commission shall furnish the person with an analysis of the person's performance on the examination.

(e) The commission may not approve a management contract to operate or manage a racetrack owned by a governmental entity unless the racetrack license holder is an owner of the entity that proposes to manage the racetrack.

**Sec. 7.03. Issuance.** The commission shall issue a license to a qualified person on application and payment of the license fee.

**Sec. 7.04. Licenses; grounds for denial, revocation, and suspension.** The commission, after notice and hearing, may refuse to issue any original or renewal license under this article or may revoke or suspend the license if it has reasonable grounds to believe and finds that:

(1) the applicant has been convicted in a court of competent jurisdiction of a violation of this Act or of any rule adopted by the commission or has aided, abetted, or conspired with any person to commit such a violation;

(2) the applicant has been convicted of a felony or of any crime involving moral turpitude that is reasonably related to the applicant's present fitness to hold a license under this Act;

(3) the applicant has violated or has caused to be violated this Act or a rule of the commission in a manner that involves moral turpitude, as distinguished from a technical violation of this Act or of a rule;

(4) the applicant is unqualified, by experience or otherwise, to perform the duties required of a licensee under this Act;

(5) the applicant failed to answer or has falsely or incorrectly answered a question in an original or renewal application;

(6) the applicant fails to disclose the true ownership or interest in a greyhound or horse as required by the rules of the commission;

(7) the applicant is indebted to the state for any fees or for the payment of a penalty imposed by this Act or by a rule of the commission;

(8) the applicant is not of good moral character or the applicant's reputation as a peaceable, law-abiding citizen in the community where the applicant resides is bad;

(9) the applicant is in the habit of using alcoholic beverages to an excess or uses a controlled substance as defined in Chapter 481, Health and Safety Code, or a dangerous drug as defined in Chapter 483, Health and Safety Code, or is mentally incapacitated;

(10) the applicant may be excluded from a track enclosure under this Act;

(11) the commission determines that the applicant has improperly used a temporary pass, license certificate, credential, or identification card issued under this Act;

(12) the applicant is residentially domiciled with a person whose license has been revoked for cause within the 12 months immediately preceding the date of the present application;

(13) the applicant has failed or refused to furnish a true copy of the application to the commission's district office in the district in which the premises for which the permit is sought are located; or

(14) the applicant is engaged or has engaged in activities or practices that are detrimental to the best interests of the public and the sport of horse racing or greyhound racing.

**Sec. 7.05. License fees.** (a) The commission shall adopt by rule a fee schedule for licenses issued under this article.

(b) The commission shall base the license fees on the relative or comparative incomes or property interests of the various categories of licensees, with the lower income category of licensees being charged nearer the minimum fee and the higher income category of licensees charged nearer the maximum fee.

(c) In setting the fee schedule under Subsection (a) of this section, the commission shall include the cost of criminal history checks determined under Section 5.05 of this Act. The commission may determine the best method for recouping this cost and complying with the other provisions of this section, including collecting the costs over an extended period.

**Sec. 7.06. Form of license.** The commission shall issue a license certificate under this article in the form of an identification card with a photograph and other information as prescribed by the commission.

**Sec. 7.07. Term of license.** (a) A license issued under this article is valid for a period set by the commission not to exceed 36 months following the date of its issuance. It is renewable on application and payment of the fee in accordance with the rules of the commission.

(b) The commission by rule may adopt a system under which licenses expire on various dates during the year. For the year in which the license expiration date is changed, license fees shall be prorated on a monthly basis so that each licensee pays only that portion of the license fee that is allocable to the number of months during which the license is valid. On renewal of the license on the new expiration date, the total license renewal fee is payable.

**Sec. 7.08. Valid throughout state.** A license issued under this article is valid, as determined by the commission, at all race meetings conducted in this state.

**Sec. 7.09. Temporary licenses.** Pending investigation of an applicant's qualifications to receive an original or renewal license, the commission may issue a temporary license to an applicant under this article whose application appears to comply with the requirements of law and who has paid the necessary fee. The temporary license is valid for a period not to exceed 120 days from the date of issuance.

**Sec. 7.10. Reciprocal licenses; out-of-state applicants.** (a) The commission may waive any prerequisite to obtaining a license for an applicant, including any requirement to submit a set of fingerprints, after reviewing the applicant's credentials and determining that the applicant holds a valid license from another state that has license requirements substantially equivalent to those of this state.

(b) The commission may waive any prerequisite to obtaining a license, including any requirement to submit a set of fingerprints, for an applicant with a valid license from another state with which the State of Texas has a reciprocity agreement. The commission may enter into reciprocal agreements with other states to allow for licensing by reciprocity.

## ARTICLE 8. ALLOCATION OF RACING DAYS—HORSES

**Sec. 8.01. Allocation.** The commission shall allocate the live and simulcast racing days for the conduct of live and simulcast racing at each racetrack licensed under this Act. Each racetrack shall accord reasonable access to races for all breeds of horses as determined by the racetrack through negotiations with the representative state breed registry with the final approval of the commission. In granting approval, the commission shall consider the factors of availability of competitive horses, economic feasibility, and public interest. In allocating race dates under this section, the commission shall consider live race dates separately from simulcast race dates. The commission may prohibit Sunday racing unless the prohibition would conflict with another provision of this Act.

**Sec. 8.02. Charity days.** (a) The commission shall grant additional racing days to each association during a race meeting to be conducted as charity days. The commission shall grant at least two and not more than five additional days to each class 1 racetrack and to each class 2 racetrack. Each class 1 and class 2 racetrack shall conduct charity race days in accordance with this section.

(b) The commission shall adopt rules relating to the conduct of charity days. The commission shall insure that the races held by an association on a charity day are comparable in all respects, including the generation of revenue, to the races held by that association on any other racing day.

## ARTICLE 9. HORSE REGISTRATION; RACING

**Sec. 9.01. Texas-bred horses.** Subject to this Act or any rule of the commission, the state horse breed registries shall make reasonable rules to establish the qualifications of accredited Texas-bred horses to promote, develop, and improve the breeding of horses in this state. Rules adopted by a registry are subject to commission approval.

**Sec. 9.02. Breed registries.** The officially designated state horse breed registries for accredited Texas-bred horses are the Texas Thoroughbred Breeders Association for Thoroughbred horses, the Texas Quarter Horse Association for quarter horses, the Texas Appaloosa Horse Club for Appaloosa horses, the Texas Arabian Breeders Association for Arabian horses, and the Texas Paint Horse Breeders Association for paint horses.

**Sec. 9.03. Texas-bred race.** An association shall provide for the running of races limited to accredited Texas-bred horses, each to be known as a Texas-bred race. Unless otherwise provided by this section, on every racing day, an association shall provide for the running of at least two races limited to accredited Texas-bred horses, one of which shall be restricted to maidens. Before January 1, 1994, if on any day not enough horses are entered in an accredited Texas-bred race to provide sufficient competition, an association shall provide for the running of two races in which accredited Texas-bred horses are preferred. An association may defer, in accordance with commission rule, the running of one or both of the two races required by this section for each racing day, but the association must provide that the total number of accredited Texas-bred races in a race meeting is equal to twice the total number of race dates in the race meeting. To encourage the breeding of horses in this state, any accredited Texas-bred horse finishing first, second, or third in any race in this state except a stakes race shall receive a purse supplement. The appropriate state breed registry shall act in an advisory capacity to the association and the commission for the purpose of administering the provisions of this section.

**Sec. 9.04. Funds for awards.** Funds for the purse supplements shall be derived from the breakage as provided by Section 6.08 of this Act.

**Sec. 9.05. Types of racing.** When a horse racing association conducts a race meeting for more than one breed of horse at one racetrack, the number of races to be run by each breed on each day shall be equitable as determined by the commission under Section 8.01 of this Act. The commission, by rule or by order, may allow an exception if there are not enough horses of a breed available to provide sufficient competition.

**Sec. 9.06. Stabling.** When a horse racing association conducts a race meeting for more than one breed of horse at one racetrack, on-track stalls shall be provided on an equitable basis as determined by the commission under Section 8.01 of this Act.

**Sec. 9.07. Security.** The horse racing association shall provide security at its track that is adequate to ensure the safety of the spectators, employees, and animals.

## ARTICLE 10. ALLOCATION OF RACING DAYS—GREYHOUNDS; KENNELS

**Sec. 10.01. Number of racing days.** Any greyhound racing licensee shall be entitled to have 300 evening and 150 matinee performances in a calendar year. The commission shall grant at least five additional racing days during a race meeting to be conducted as charity days. The commission shall adopt rules relating to the conduct of charity days. The commission shall insure that the races held by an association on a charity day are comparable in all respects, including the generation of revenue, to the races held by that association on any other racing day.

**Sec. 10.02. Substitute racing days or additional races.** If for a reason beyond the licensee's control and not caused by the licensee's fault or neglect it is impossible for the licensee to hold or conduct a race or races on a day authorized by the commission, the commission in its discretion and at the request of the licensee, as a substitute for the race or races, may specify another day for the holding or conducting of racing by the licensee or may add additional races to already programmed events.

**Sec. 10.03. Kennels.** Each greyhound racetrack must contract for a maximum of 18 kennels and shall provide free kennel rent and schooling.

**Sec. 10.04. Texas-bred greyhounds.** (a) Subject to this Act or any rule of the commission, the state greyhound breed registry shall make reasonable rules to establish the qualifications of accredited Texas-bred greyhounds to promote, develop, and improve the breeding of greyhounds in this state. Rules adopted by the registry are subject to commission approval.

(b) The commission shall adopt standards relating to the operation of greyhound farms or other facilities where greyhounds are raised for pari-mutuel racing.

**Sec. 10.05. Breed registry; breakage distributions.** The officially designated state greyhound breed registry for accredited Texas-bred greyhounds is the Texas Greyhound Association. The state breed registry shall adopt rules to provide for the use of breakage received by it under Section 6.09(d) of this Act. An association shall pay the breakage due the breed registry to the appropriate state greyhound breed registry at least every 30 days.

**Sec. 10.06. Texas kennels.** (a) In contracting with kennel owners for a racetrack, an association shall ensure that at least 50 percent of the kennels with which the association contracts are wholly owned by Texas residents.

(b) In this section, "Texas resident" means an individual who has resided in Texas for the five-year period preceding the date the kennel contract is signed.

## ARTICLE 11. WAGERING

**Sec. 11.01. Pari-mutuel wagering; rules.** (a) The commission shall adopt rules to regulate wagering on greyhound races and horse races under the system known as pari-mutuel wagering. Wagering may be conducted only by an association within its enclosure. The commission may commission as many investigators as the commission determines necessary to enforce this Act and the rules of the commission. Each investigator shall take the constitutional oath of office and file it with the commission. Each commissioned investigator has the powers of a peace officer, and shall make and execute a bond as required by the commission.

(b) The commission's rules adopted under this section and this Act shall be written and updated to ensure their maximum enforceability within existing constitutional guidelines.

**Sec. 11.011. Simulcast races.** (a) The commission shall adopt rules to license and regulate pari-mutuel wagering on:

(1) races conducted in this state and simulcast to licensed racetrack associations in this state or to out-of-state receiving locations; and

(2) races conducted out-of-state and simulcast to licensed racetrack associations in this state.

(b) With approval of the commission, wagers accepted on a simulcast race by any out-of-state receiving location may be included in the pari-mutuel pool for the race at the sending racetrack association in this state.

(c) With approval of the commission, wagers accepted by a licensed racetrack association in this state on a race simulcast from out-of-state may be included in the pari-mutuel pools for the race at the out-of-state sending racetrack.

(d) The commission may adopt rules necessary to facilitate the interstate commingling of pari-mutuel pools as provided by Subsections (b) and (c) of this section.

(e) If intrastate wagering pools are combined between tracks, the track where the race originates is responsible for the state's share of the pari-mutuel pool regardless of whether a shortage or error occurred at the originating track or receiving track.

(f) Nothing in this Act is to be construed to allow wagering in Texas on simulcast races at any location other than a racetrack licensed under this Act that has been granted live race dates by the commission.

(g) Nothing in this Act is to be construed to prohibit wagering on a simulcast horse race at a greyhound racetrack in this state, or to prohibit wagering on a simulcast greyhound race at a horse racetrack in this state. A horse racetrack may not be required to accept a greyhound simulcast signal, nor may a greyhound racetrack be required to accept a horse simulcast signal.

(h) Except as provided by this section, a horse racetrack facility that offers wagering on interstate greyhound race simulcast signals must do so as provided by a contract with the nearest greyhound racetrack. If an agreement between the racetracks cannot be reached by October 1 of the year preceding the calendar year in which the simulcasting is to occur, the horse racetrack may purchase and offer wagering on greyhound race simulcast signals and shall pay the amounts specified under Section 6.091(d)(1) of this Act to the nearest greyhound racetrack.

(i) Except as provided by this section, a greyhound racetrack facility that offers wagering on interstate horse race simulcast signals must do so as provided by a contract with the nearest Class 1 horse racetrack. If an agreement between the racetracks cannot be reached by October 1 of the year preceding the calendar year in which the simulcasting is to occur, the greyhound racetrack may purchase and offer wagering on interstate horse race simulcast signals and shall pay the amounts specified in Section 6.091(c)(1) of this Act to the nearest Class 1 horse racetrack.

(j) A horse racetrack that offers wagering on interstate greyhound simulcast races must offer wagering on all Texas greyhound races made available for simulcast wagering. A greyhound racetrack that offers wagering on interstate horse simulcast races must offer wagering on all Texas horse races made available for simulcast wagering.

(k) Wagering on a simulcast greyhound race at a horse racetrack that conducts its inaugural meet within 12 months of September 1, 1997, or at an operational horse racetrack within 60 miles of such racetrack may be conducted only pursuant to an agreement between said racetracks.

(*l*) Notwithstanding other provisions of law, a greyhound racing association and the state greyhound breed registry shall by contract agree that each simulcast contract to which the greyhound racing association is a party, including a simulcast contract with a horse racing association or a simulcast contract with another greyhound racing association, include terms that provide adequately for the development of greyhound racing, breeding, purses, and any actual or potential loss of live racing handle based on the association's historical live racing schedule and handle in this state. If a greyhound racing association and the state greyhound breed registry fail to reach an agreement, the racing association or the breed registry may submit the contract negotiations for binding arbitration under Chapter 171, Civil Practice and Remedies Code, and rules adopted by the commission. The arbitration must be conducted by a board of three arbitrators. The greyhound racing association shall appoint one arbitrator. The state greyhound breed registry shall appoint one arbitrator. The arbitrators appointed by the greyhound racing association and the state greyhound breed registry shall appoint the third arbitrator. A greyhound racing association and the state greyhound breed registry shall each pay its own arbitration expenses. The greyhound racing association and the state greyhound breed registry shall equally pay the arbitrator fees and costs. This subsection does not apply to a contract that was in effect before September 2, 1997.

(m) The commission shall not approve wagering on an interstate simulcast race unless the receiving location consents to wagering on interstate simulcast races at all other receiving locations in this state.

**Sec. 11.02. Computation of wagering.** The wagering may be calculated only by state-of-the-art computational equipment that is approved by the commission. The commission may not require the use of a particular make of equipment.

**Sec. 11.03. Information on ticket.** The commission shall by rule prescribe the information to be printed on each pari-mutuel ticket.

**Sec. 11.04. Wagering inside enclosure.** (a) Only a person inside the enclosure where both live and simulcast race meetings are authorized may wager on the result of a live or simulcast race presented by the association in accordance with commission rules. The commission shall adopt rules to prohibit wagering by employees of the commission and to regulate wagering by persons licensed under this Act.

(b) The commission shall adopt rules prohibiting an association from accepting wagers by telephone.

(c) The commission shall adopt rules prohibiting an association from accepting a wager made on credit and shall adopt rules providing for the use of automatic banking machines within the enclosure. The commission shall limit the use of an automatic banking machine to:

(1) allow a person to have access to only the person's checking account at a bank or other financial institution; and

(2) deliver no more than $200.

(d) *(Repealed by L.1997, chap. 1275(54), eff. 9/1/97.)*

(e) An association that allows a machine in an enclosure as provided by Subsection (c) shall collect a fee of $1 for each transaction under Subsection (c). The commission shall adopt rules providing for collection, reporting, and auditing of the transaction fee. The association shall forward the fee to the commission. The commission shall deposit the fee to the credit of the general revenue fund.

**Sec. 11.05. Unlawful wagering.** A person shall not wager on the result of a greyhound race or horse race in this state except as permitted by this Act.

**Sec. 11.06. Minors.** The commission shall adopt rules to prohibit wagering by a minor and to prohibit a child from entering the viewing section of a racetrack unless accompanied by the child's parent or guardian. The rules may except any conduct described as an affirmative defense by Section 14.13 of this Act.

**Sec. 11.07. Claim after race meeting.** (a) A person who claims to be entitled to any part of a distribution from a pari-mutuel pool and who fails to claim the money due the person before the completion of the race meeting at which the pool was formed may, not later than the 60th day after the closing day of the meeting, file with the association a claim for the money together with a substantial portion of the pari-mutuel ticket sufficient to identify the association, race, and horse or greyhound involved and sufficient to show the amount wagered and the type of ticket.

(b) If the claimant satisfactorily establishes a right to distribution from the pool, the association shall pay the amount due the claimant. If the association refuses to pay a claimant who has established satisfactorily a right to distribution from the pool, the claimant may appeal to the commission under procedures prescribed by commission rule.

**Sec. 11.08. Money not claimed.** Not later than the 61st day after the closing day of a race meeting, an association shall pay to the commission all distributable money that is subject to payment under Section 11.07 of this Act but that is not successfully claimed and that is not spent on drug testing under the provisions of this Act.

**Sec. 11.09. No liability to prosecution.** The defense to prosecution under Chapter 47, Penal Code, that the conduct was authorized under this Act is available only to a person who is:

(1) lawfully conducting or participating in the conduct of pari-mutuel wagering in connection with horse racing or greyhound racing; or

(2) permitting the lawful conduct of an activity described by Subdivision (1) of this section on any racetrack facility.

**Sec. 11.10. Automobile racing facility.** No automobile racing facility may be located within 10,000 feet of a horse or greyhound racetrack licensed under this Act that is located in a county with a population of 1,800,000 or more, according to the most recent federal census.

## ARTICLE 12. FAIRS, STOCK SHOWS, AND EXPOSITIONS

**Sec. 12.01. County stock shows.** Subject to the licensing requirements and other provisions of this Act, a county may conduct an annual race meeting, not to exceed 16 racing days, in connection with a livestock show or exhibit that is held under Chapter 319, Local Government Code. The race meetings may be conducted by an agent selected by the commissioners court under Section 319.004, Local Government Code, if the agent is qualified to hold a license under this Act. This Act does not prohibit a county from exercising any right otherwise granted to any person by this Act.

**Sec. 12.02. Fairs.** Subject to the licensing requirements and other provisions of this Act, a nonprofit corporation organized under the Texas Non-Profit Corporation Act (Article 1396-1.01 et seq., Vernon's Texas Civil Statutes) for the purpose of encouraging agriculture through the operation of public fairs and livestock exhibitions may conduct a race meeting, not to exceed 16 racing days.

**Sec. 12.03. County fairs.** (a) A county that holds a class 4 racetrack license may conduct an annual race meeting not to exceed five racing days in connection with a livestock show or exhibition held under Chapter 319, Local Government Code. A race meeting must be conducted on a day when general fair activities are conducted.

(b) A county that holds a class 4 racetrack license may contract with an agent to conduct any portion of a race meeting. An agent must hold a license issued under this Act that is appropriate for the service the agent provides.

## ARTICLE 13. EXCLUSION OR EJECTION FROM RACETRACK

**Sec. 13.01. Regulation by commission.** The commission shall adopt rules providing for the exclusion or ejection from an enclosure where greyhound races or horse races are conducted, or from specified portions of an enclosure, of a person:

(1) who has engaged in bookmaking, touting, or illegal wagering;

(2) whose income is from illegal activities or enterprises;

(3) who has been convicted of a violation of this Act;

(4) who has been convicted of theft;

(5) who has been convicted under the penal law of another jurisdiction for committing an act that would have constituted a violation of any of the rules mentioned in this section;

(6) who has committed a corrupt or fraudulent act in connection with greyhound racing or horse racing or pari-mutuel wagering or who has committed any act tending or intended to corrupt greyhound racing or horse racing or pari-mutuel wagering in this state or elsewhere;

(7) who is under suspension or ruled off a racetrack by the commission or a steward in this state or by a corresponding authority in another state because of fraudulent or corrupt practices or other acts detrimental to racing;

(8) who has submitted a forged pari-mutuel ticket or has altered or forged a pari-mutuel ticket for cashing or who has cashed or caused to be cashed an altered, raised, or forged pari-mutuel ticket;

(9) who has been convicted of committing a lewd or lascivious act or other crime involving moral turpitude;

(10) who is guilty of boisterous or disorderly conduct while inside a racing enclosure;

(11) who is an agent or habitual associate of a person excludable under this section; or

(12) who has been convicted of a felony.

**Sec. 13.02. Hearing; appeal; exclusion or expulsion from an enclosure.** (a) A person who is excluded or ejected from an enclosure under a rule of the commission may apply to the commission for a hearing on the question of the applicability of the rule to that person.

(b) Such an application constitutes a contested case under the Administrative Procedure and Texas Register Act (Article 6252-13a, Vernon's Texas Civil Statutes). If, after a hearing as provided under Section 13 of that Act, the commission determines that the exclusion or ejection was proper, it shall make and enter an order to that effect in its minutes, and the person shall continue to be excluded from each association.

(c) The person excluded or ejected may appeal an adverse decision of the commission by filing a petition for judicial review in the manner provided by Section 19 of the Administrative Procedure and Texas Register Act (Article 6252-13a, Vernon's Texas Civil Statutes). Judicial review under this subsection is subject to the substantial evidence rule. Venue for the review is in a district court in Travis County.

(d) The judgment of the court may be appealed as in other civil cases. The person appealing the commission's ruling under this article shall continue to be excluded from all enclosures in this state during the pendency of the appeal.



**Sec. 13.03. Criminal tresspass*.** A person, for the purposes of Section 30.05, Penal Code, is presumed to have received notice that entry to an enclosure was forbidden if the person:

(1) was excluded or ejected from the enclosure under this Act;

(2) possessed, displayed, or used in the enclosure a credential that the person was not authorized to use; or

(3) entered the enclosure using a falsified credential.

**So in original. Probably should be "trespass".*

**Sec. 13.04. Exclusion by association.** Nothing in this article shall prohibit an association from evicting or excluding a person from its enclosure for any lawful reason.

## ARTICLE 14. CRIMINAL OFFENSES

**Sec. 14.01. Touting.** (a) A person commits an offense if, with an intent to deceive and an intent to obtain a benefit, the person knowingly makes a false statement or offers, agrees to convey, or conveys false information about a greyhound race or horse race to another.

(b) Except as provided by Subsection (c) of this section, an offense under this section is a Class A misdemeanor.

(c) An offense under this section is a state jail felony if:

(1) the actor is a licensee under this Act or an employee or member of the commission and the actor knowingly represents that a member or employee of the commission or a person licensed by the commission is the source of the false information; or

(2) the false statement or information was contained in racing selection information provided to the public.

**Sec. 14.02. Unlawful possession or use of credential.** (a) A person commits an offense if the person knowingly or intentionally possesses or displays a credential or false credential that identifies the person as the holder of the credential and the person knows:

(1) that the credential is not issued to the person; or

(2) the person is not a licensee.

(b) An offense under this section is a Class C misdemeanor.

**Sec. 14.03.** *(Repealed by L.1997, chap. 1275(43), eff. 9/1/97.)*

**Sec. 14.04. Illegal access.** (a) A person commits an offense if the person is a licensee and the person knowingly or intentionally permits, facilitates, or allows access, to an enclosure where races are conducted, to another person who the person knows:

(1) has engaged in bookmaking, touting, or illegal wagering;

(2) derives income from illegal activities or enterprises;

(3) has been convicted of a violation of this Act; or

(4) is excluded by the commission from entering a racetrack facility.

(b) An offense under this section is a Class B misdemeanor.

**Sec. 14.05. Races conducted on certain Indian lands.** (a) A person who is subject to this section commits an offense if the person intentionally or knowingly wagers on the result of a greyhound race or horse race conducted in this state that:

(1) is held on an American Indian reservation or on American Indian trust land located in this state; and

(2) is not held under the supervision of the commission under rules adopted under this Act.

(b) An offense under this section is a felony of the third degree.

(c) It is an exception to the application of this section that the person is a member of a recognized Texas Indian tribe who lives on a reservation or on trust lands located in this state.

**Sec. 14.06. False statements.** (a) A person commits an offense if the person knowingly makes a material and false, incorrect, or deceptive statement to another who is conducting an investigation or exercising discretion under this Act or a rule adopted under this Act.

(b) In this section, the term "statement" means a representation of fact and includes:

(1) a written or oral statement; or

(2) a sworn or unsworn statement.

(c) An offense under this section is a state jail felony unless the statement was material in a commission action relating to a racetrack license, in which event the offense is a felony of the third degree.

**Sec. 14.07. Hindering of entry.** (a) A person commits an offense if the person with criminal negligence refuses, denies, or hinders entry to another who is exercising or attempting to exercise a power of entry under this Act or a commission rule.

(b) A person commits an offense if the person with criminal negligence refuses, denies, hinders, interrupts, disrupts, impedes, or otherwise interferes with a search by a person exercising or attempting to exercise a power to search under this Act or a commission rule.

(c) An offense under this section is a Class B misdemeanor.

**Sec. 14.08. Forging pari-mutuel ticket.** (a) A person commits an offense if the person intentionally or knowingly forges a pari-mutuel ticket with the intent to defraud or harm another.

(b) In this section, "forge" has the meaning assigned by Section 32.21, Penal Code.

(c) An offense under this section is a felony of the third degree.

**Sec. 14.09. Impersonating a licensee.** (a) A person commits an offense if the person impersonates a licensee with the intent to induce another person to submit to the actor's purported authority as a licensee or to rely on the actor's actions as an alleged licensee.

(b) An offense under this section is a Class A misdemeanor.

**Sec. 14.10. Unlawful influence on racing.** (a) A person commits an offense if the person possesses a prohibited device or prohibited substance on a racetrack facility, in an enclosure, or at a training facility.

(b) An offense under Subsection (a) of this section is a Class A misdemeanor, unless the actor possessed the device or substance with the intent to influence or affect the outcome of a horse or greyhound race in a manner contrary to this Act or a commission rule, in which event it is a state jail felony.

(c) A person commits an offense if, with the intent to influence or affect a horse or greyhound race in a manner contrary to this Act or a commission rule, the person:

(1) uses or offers to use a prohibited device; or

(2) uses or offers to use a prohibited substance.

(d) An offense under Subsection (c) of this section is a felony of the third degree.

**Sec. 14.11. Bribery and corupt* influence.** (a) A person commits an offense if, with the intent to influence or affect the outcome of a race in a manner contrary to this Act or a commission rule, the person offers, confers, agrees to confer on another, or solicits, accepts, or agrees to accept from another person any benefit as consideration for the actions of a person who receives the benefit relating to the conduct, decision, opinion, recommendation, vote, or exercise of discretion as a licensee or other person associated with or interested in any stable, kennel, horse, greyhound, or horse or greyhound race.

**So in original. Probably should be "corrupt".*

(b) An offense under this section is a state jail felony, unless the recipient of the benefit is a steward, judge, or other racetrack official exercising authority over a horse or greyhound race that the person providing or offering the benefit intended to influence, in which event it is a felony of the third degree.

**Sec. 14.12. Criminal conflict of interest.** A person who is a member of the commission commits an offense if the person:

(1) accepts, directly or indirectly, employment or remuneration from a racetrack facility, association, or other licensee, including a facility, association, or licensee located or residing in another state;

(2) wagers or causes a wager to be placed on the outcome of a horse or greyhound race conducted in this state; or

(3) accepts or is entitled to any part of a purse to be paid to an animal in a race conducted in this state.

**Sec. 14.13. Offenses involving a minor.** (a) A person commits an offense if the person with criminal negligence permits, facilitates, or allows:

(1) wagering by a minor at a racetrack facility; or

(2) entry by a child to the viewing section of a racetrack facility.

(b) An offense under Subsection (a) of this section is a Class B misdemeanor.

(c) A person commits an offense if the person is a minor and intentionally or knowingly engages in wagering at a racetrack.

(d) An offense under Subsection (c) of this section is a Class C misdemeanor.

(e) It is an affirmative defense to prosecution of an offense under Subsection (a)(2) that a child was accompanied by and was in the physical presence of a parent, guardian, or spouse who was 21 years of age or older.

(f) It is an affirmative defense to prosecution of an offense under Subsection (a) of this section that the minor falsely represented the minor's age by displaying to the person an apparently valid Texas driver's license or identification card issued by the Department of Public Safety that contains a physical description consistent with the minor's appearance.

**Sec. 14.14. Unlawful racing.** A person commits an offense if:

(1) the person participates, permits, or conducts a greyhound or horse race at a licensed racetrack facility;

(2) the person wagers on the partial or final outcome of the greyhound or horse race or knows or reasonably should know that another is betting on the partial or final outcome of the race; and

(3) the race is not part of a performance or meeting conducted under this Act or commission rule.

**Sec. 14.15. Pari-mutuel racing without a license.** (a) A person commits an offense if, without a license, the person participates or is otherwise involved in, in any capacity, greyhound racing or horse racing with pari-mutuel wagering.

(b) It is an affirmative defense to prosecution under Subsection (a) of this section that the actor was a spectator or a person placing a wager.

(c) An offense under Subsection (a) of this section is a Class A misdemeanor, unless the actor was required by this Act to obtain a racetrack license, in which event it is a state jail felony.

**Sec. 14.16. Racing without a license.** (a) A person commits an offense if the person:

(1) conducts a greyhound or horse race without a racetrack license; and

(2) knows or reasonably should know that another person is betting on the final or partial outcome of the race.

(b) An offense under this section is a felony of the third degree.

**Sec. 14.17. Failure to display credential.** (a) A person commits an offense if the person intentionally or knowingly:

(1) fails or refuses to display a credential to another after a lawful request; or

(2) fails or refuses to give the person's name, residence address, or date of birth to another after a lawful request.

(b) In this section, "lawful request" means a request from the commission, an authorized agent of the commission, the director or a commissioned officer of the Department of Public Safety, a peace officer, or a steward or judge at any time and any restricted location that:

(1) is on a racetrack facility; and

(2) is not a public place.

(c) Except as provided by Subsection (d) of this section, an offense under this section is a Class B misdemeanor.

(d) At the punishment stage of a trial for an offense under Subsection (a)(1) of this section, the defendant may raise an issue as to whether the defendant was a licensee at the time of the offense. If the defendant proves the issue, the offense is a Class C misdemeanor.

**Sec. 14.18. Search and seizure.** (a) A person consents to a search at a time and location described in Subsection (b) of this section for a prohibited device, prohibited substance, or other contraband if the person:

(1) accepts a license or other credential issued under this Act; or

(2) enters a racetrack facility under the authority of a license or other credential alleged to have been issued under this Act.

(b) A search may be conducted by a commissioned officer of the Department of Public Safety or a peace officer, including a peace officer employed by the commission, at any time and at any location that is on a racetrack facility, except a location:

(1) excluded by commission rule from searches under this section; or

(2) provided by an association under commission rule for private storage of personal items belonging to a licensee entering a racetrack facility.

(c) A person conducting a search under Subsection (b) of this section may seize any prohibited device, prohibited substance, or other contraband discovered during the search.

Printed in the U.S.A. Zt

**Sec. 14.19. Prosecution.** A person who is subject to prosecution for a penal offense under this Act and another law may be prosecuted under either law.

**Sec. 14.20. Commission authority.** This article may not be construed to restrict the commission's administrative authority to enforce this Act or commission rules to the fullest extent authorized by this Act.

**Sec. 14.21. Venue for criminal prosecution.** The venue for the prosecution of a criminal offense under this Act is in Travis County or in a county where an element of the offense occurred.

## ARTICLE 15. GENERAL PENALTY PROVISIONS

**Sec. 15.01. General penalty.** If no specific penalty is provided for a provision of this Act that is a penal offense, a person who violates the provision commits a state jail felony.

**Sec. 15.02.** *(Repealed by L.1997, chap. 1275(54), eff. 9/1/97.)*

**Sec. 15.03. Administrative penalty.** (a) If the commission determines that a person regulated under this Act has violated this Act or a rule or order adopted under this Act in a manner that constitutes a ground for a disciplinary action under this Act, the commission may assess an administrative penalty against that person as provided by this section.

(b) The commission may assess the administrative penalty in an amount not to exceed $10,000 for each violation. In determining the amount of the penalty, the commission shall consider the seriousness of the violation.

(c) If, after examination of a possible violation and the facts relating to that possible violation, the commission determines that a violation has occurred, the commission shall issue a preliminary report that states the facts on which the conclusion is based, the fact that an administrative penalty is to be imposed, and the amount to be assessed. Not later than the 10th day after the date on which the commission issues the preliminary report, the commission shall send a copy of the report to the person charged with the violation, together with a statement of the right of the person to a hearing relating to the alleged violation and the amount of the penalty.

(d) Not later than the 20th day after the date on which the commission sends the preliminary report, the person charged may make a written request for a hearing or may remit the amount of the administrative penalty to the commission. Failure to request a hearing or to remit the amount of the administrative penalty within the period prescribed by this subsection results in a waiver of a right to a hearing under this Act. If the person charged requests a hearing, the hearing shall be conducted in the manner provided for a contested case hearing under the Administrative Procedure and Texas Register Act (Article 6252-13a, Vernon's Texas Civil Statutes). If it is determined after the hearing that the person has committed the alleged violation, the commission shall give written notice to the person of the findings established by the hearing and the amount of the penalty and shall enter an order requiring the person to pay the penalty.

(e) Not later than the 30th day after the date on which the notice is received, the person charged shall pay the administrative penalty in full or exercise the right to appeal either the amount of the penalty or the fact of the violation. If a person exercises a right of appeal either as to the amount of the penalty or the fact of the violation, the amount of the penalty is not required to be paid until the 30th day after the date on which all appeals have been exhausted and the commission's decision has been upheld.

**Sec. 15.04. Complaints.** Complaints alleging violations of this Act may be instituted by the Department of Public Safety, the commission, or the attorney general. Such complaints shall be adjudicated by the commission pursuant to the provisions for a contested case proceeding under the Administrative Procedure and Texas Register Act (Article 6252-13a, Vernon's Texas Civil Statutes).

## ARTICLE 16. LOCAL OPTION ELECTION



**Sec. 16.01. Condition precedent.** (a) The commission shall not issue a racetrack license or accept an application for a license for a racetrack to be located in a county until the commissioners court has certified to the secretary of state that the qualified voters of the county have approved the legalization of pari-mutuel wagering on horse races or greyhound races in the county at an election held under this article. A local option election may not be held under this article before January 1, 1987.

(b) A racetrack may not be located within a home-rule city unless a majority of the votes cast in the city in the election held under this article that legalized pari-mutuel wagering on horse races in the county were in favor of legalization. This subsection does not apply to a licensed racetrack that was located outside the boundaries of the city when it was first licensed and has continuously held a license since the original license was issued.

**Sec. 16.02. Methods for initiating election.** The commissioners court on its own motion by a majority vote of its members may order an election to approve the legalization of pari-mutuel wagering on horse races or greyhound races, and it shall order an election on presentation of a petition meeting the requirements of this article.

**Sec. 16.021. Approval of simulcast races.** The commissioners court of a county in which there is a racetrack conducting live racing, on its own motion by a majority vote of its members, may order an election to approve pari-mutuel wagering on simulcast greyhound or horse races.

**Sec. 16.03. Application for petition; issuance.** If petitioned to do so by written application of 10 or more registered voters of the county, the county clerk shall issue to the applicants a petition to be circulated among registered voters for their signatures.

**Sec. 16.04. Contents of application.** To be valid, an application must contain:

(1) a heading, in the following words: "Application for a Petition for a Local Option Election to Approve the Legalization of Pari-mutuel Wagering on Horse Races" or "Application for a Petition for a Local Option Election to Approve the Legalization of Pari-mutuel Wagering on Greyhound Races," as appropriate;

(2) a statement of the issue to be voted on, in the following words: "Legalizing pari-mutuel wagering on horse races in __________ County" or "Legalizing pari-mutuel wagering on greyhound races in __________ County," as appropriate;

(3) a statement immediately above the signatures of the applicants, reading as follows: "It is the hope, purpose, and intent of the applicants whose signatures appear below that pari-mutuel wagering on horse races be legalized in __________ County" or "It is the hope, purpose, and intent of the applicants whose signatures appear below that pari-mutuel wagering on greyhound races be legalized in __________ County," as appropriate; and

(4) the printed name, signature, residence address, and voter registration certificate number of each applicant.

**Sec. 16.05. Contents of petition.** To be valid, a petition must contain:

(1) a heading, in the following words: "Petition for a Local Option Election to Approve the Legalization of Pari-mutuel Wagering on Horse Races" or "Petition for a Local Option Election to Approve the Legalization of Pari-mutuel Wagering on Greyhound Races," as appropriate;

(2) a statement of the issue to be voted on, in the same words used in the application;

(3) a statement immediately above the signatures of the petitioners, reading as follows: "It is the hope, purpose, and intent of the petitioners whose signatures appear below that pari-mutuel wagering on horse races be legalized in __________ County" or "It is the hope, purpose, and intent of the petitioners whose signatures appear below that pari-mutuel wagering on greyhound races be legalized in __________ County," as appropriate;

(4) lines and spaces for the names, signatures, addresses, and voter registration certificate numbers of the petitioners; and

(5) the date of issuance, the serial number, and the seal of the county clerk on each page.

**Sec. 16.06. Copies.** The county clerk shall keep the application and a copy of the petition in the files of that office. The clerk shall issue to the applicants as many copies as they request.

**Sec. 16.07. Filing of petition; number of signatures.** To form the basis for the ordering of an election, the petition must be filed with the county clerk not later than the 30th day after the date of its issuance, and it must contain a number of signatures of registered voters of the county equal to five percent of the number of votes cast in the county for all candidates for governor in the most recent gubernatorial general election.

**Sec. 16.08. Review by county clerk.** (a) The county clerk shall, on request of any person, check each name on the petition to determine whether the signer is a registered voter of the county. The person requesting this verification by the county clerk shall pay the county clerk a sum equal to 20 cents per name before commencement of the verification.

(b) The county clerk may not count a signature if there is reason to believe that:

(1) it is not the actual signature of the purported signer;

(2) the voter registration certificate number is not correct;

(3) it is a duplication either of a name or of handwriting used in any other signature on the petition;

(4) the residence address of the signer is not correct; or

(5) the name of the voter is not signed exactly as it appears on the official copy of the current list of registered voters for the voting year in which the petition is issued.

**Sec. 16.09. Certification.** Not later than the 40th day after the date the petition is filed, excluding Saturdays, Sundays, and legal holidays, the county clerk shall certify to the commissioners court the number of registered voters signing the petition.

**Sec. 16.10. Order of election.** (a) The commissioners court shall record on its minutes the date the petition is filed and the date it is certified by the county clerk.

(b) If the petition contains the required number of signatures and is in proper order, the commissioners court shall, at its next regular session after the certification by the county clerk, order an election to be held at the regular polling place in each county election precinct in the county on the next uniform election date authorized by Section 41.001, Election Code, that occurs at least 20 days after the date of the order. The commissioners court shall state in the order the issue to be voted on in the election. The order is prima facie evidence of compliance with all provisions necessary to give it validity.

**Sec. 16.11. Application of Election Code.** (a) The election shall be held and the returns shall be prepared and canvassed in conformity with the Election Code.

(b) The ballots shall be printed to permit voting for or against the proposition: "Legalizing pari-mutuel wagering on horse races in __________ County," "Legalizing pari-mutuel wagering on greyhound races in __________ County," or "Authorizing pari-mutuel wagering on simulcast races in _____ County," as appropriate.

**Sec. 16.12. Results of election.** (a) If a majority of the votes cast in the election are for the legalization of pari-mutuel wagering on horse races or greyhound races in the county, or for the authorization of pari-mutuel wagering on simulcast races in the county, as appropriate, the commissioners court shall certify that fact to the secretary of state not later than the 10th day after the date of the canvass of the returns.

(b) No other election may be held in the county under this Act until five years have elapsed since the date of the preceding election.

**Sec. 16.13. Contest of election.** (a) Not later than the 30th day after the date the result of the election is declared, any qualified voter of the county may contest the election by filing a petition in the district court of the county. Any person who is licensed or who has made application to the commission to be licensed in any capacity under this Act may become a named party to the proceedings by pleading to the petition on or before the time set for hearing and trial as provided by Subsection (c) of this section or thereafter by intervention on leave of court.

(b) The proceedings in the suit shall be conducted in the manner prescribed by Title 14, Election Code, for contesting an election held for a purpose other than the election of an officer or officers. Unless otherwise provided by this Act, the applicable Texas Rules of Civil Procedure and all applicable statutes govern the proceedings and appeals held and conducted under this Act.

(c) At or after the time for hearing and trial, the judge shall hear and determine all questions of law and fact in the proceedings and may enter orders as to the proceedings that will enable the judge to try and determine the questions and to render a final judgment with the least possible delay.

**Sec. 16.14. Contest of election; bond.** At any time prior to the entry of a final judgment in the proceedings, any party may ask the court to dismiss the contestant's action unless the contestant posts a bond with sufficient surety, approved by the court, payable to the movant for the payment of all damages and costs that may accrue by reason of the delay that will be occasioned by the continued participation of the contestant in the proceedings in the event that the contestant fails to finally prevail and obtain substantially the judgment prayed for in the petition. The court shall then issue an order directed to the contestant, which order, together with a copy of the motion, shall be served on all parties, or on their attorney of record, personally or by registered mail, requiring the contestant to appear at the time and place, not sooner than five nor later than 10 days after receipt of the order and motion, as the court may direct, and show cause why the motion should not be granted. The maximum bond that the court may set is $10,000 for contests of elections for tracks to be located in a county with a population of less than 1.18 million, according to the most recent federal census. The maximum bond that the court may set is $100,000 for contests of elections for tracks to be located in a county with a population of 1.18 million or more, according to the most recent federal census. Motions with respect to more than one contestant may be heard together if so directed by the court. Unless at the hearing on the motion the contestant establishes facts that in the judgment of the court would entitle the contestant to a temporary injunction against the issuance of licenses on the basis of the election in question, the court shall grant the motion of the movant and in its order the court shall fix the amount of the bond to be posted by the contestant in an amount found by the court to be sufficient to cover all damages and costs that may accrue by reason of the delay that will be occasioned by the continued participation of the contestant in the proceedings in the event that the contestant fails to prevail and obtain substantially the judgment prayed for in its petition.

**Sec. 16.15. Contest of election; appeal.** Any party to the cause who is dissatisfied with an order or judgment entered under Section 16.13 of this Act may appeal to the appropriate court of appeals after the entry of the order or judgment; otherwise the order or judgment becomes final. If such a party does not file an appeal not later than the 30th day after the date on which the result of the election is declared, it is presumed that the election is valid. Any appeal has priority over all other cases, causes, or matters pending in the court of appeals, except habeas corpus, and the court of appeals shall assure the priority and act on the matter and render its final order or judgment with the least possible delay. The supreme court may review by writ of error or other authorized procedure all questions of law arising out of the orders and judgments of the court of appeals in the manner, time, and form applicable in other civil causes in which a decision of the court of appeals is not final, but the review has priority over all other cases, causes, or matters pending in the supreme court, except habeas corpus, and the supreme court shall assure the priority and review and act on the matter and render its final order or judgment with the least possible delay.

**Sec. 16.16. Suit to have precedence.** The court shall accelerate the disposition of any action brought under this Act.

**Sec. 16.17. Contestee.** (a) The county attorney is the contestee of a suit brought under Section 16.13 of this Act. If there is no county attorney of the county, then the criminal district attorney or district attorney is the contestee.

(b) Costs of the election contest may not be adjudged against the contestee or against the county, and neither may be required to give bond on appeal.

**Sec. 16.18. Rescission election.** (a) The commissioners court of a county that elects to approve the legalization of racing with pari-mutuel wagering in that county may hold an election on the question of rescinding that approval. The court shall order such an election on the presentation of a petition that requests such a rescission. The election may not be held earlier than two years after the date of the election conducted under Section 16.10 of this Act at which the legalization of pari-mutuel wagering was approved. The petition must meet the requirements imposed under this article for a petition to request a local option election on the question of the legalization of racing with pari-mutuel wagering. An election to rescind legalization of racing shall be conducted in the manner provided for the original local option election under this article. The ballots shall be printed to permit voting for or against the proposition: "Rescinding the legalization of pari-mutuel wagering on horse races in __________ County" or "Rescinding the legalization of pari-mutuel wagering on greyhound races in __________ County," as appropriate.

(b) If the majority of the votes cast in an election under this section favor the rescission, racing with pari-mutuel wagering may not be conducted in that county except as provided by Subsection (c) of this section.

(c) An association located in a county that elects to rescind the legalization of racing and that has outstanding long-term liabilities may continue to operate on a temporary basis as provided by Section 18.01 of this Act.

## ARTICLE 17. STATEWIDE REFERENDUM

**Secs. 17.01 to 17.06.** *(Repealed by L.1991, chap. 386(74(b)), eff. 8/26/91.)*

## ARTICLE 18. MISCELLANEOUS PROVISIONS

**Sec. 18.01. Application of Sunset Act.** (a) The Texas Racing Commission is subject to Chapter 325, Government Code (Texas Sunset Act). Unless continued in existence as provided by that chapter, and except as provided by Subsections (b) and (c) of this section, the commission is abolished and this Act expires September 1, 2005.

(b) If, at the time that the commission would be abolished under Subsection (a) of this section, an association created under this Act has outstanding long-term liabilities:

(1) the association may continue to operate for a period not to exceed one year after those liabilities are satisfied; and

(2) the commission and this Act are continued in effect for the purpose of regulating that association under this Act.

(c) If the commission and this Act are continued in effect under Subsection (b) of this section, the commission is abolished and this Act expires on the first day of the fiscal year following the fiscal year in which the commission certifies to the secretary of state that no associations are operating under the terms of Subsection (b) of this section.

(d) An association that continues to operate under Subsection (b) of this section may not incur any new liabilities without the approval of the commission. At the beginning of that period, the commission shall review the outstanding liabilities of the association and shall set a specific date by which the association must retire its outstanding liabilities. Notwithstanding any contrary contract provisions, an association regulated under this Act may prepay any debt incurred by the association in conducting racing under this Act.

**Sec. 18.02.** *(Repealed by L.1997, chap. 1275(54), eff. 9/1/97.)*

**Sec. 18.03. Other lawful businesses.** An association may conduct other lawful business on the association's grounds.

**Sec. 18.04. Suit to have precedence.** The courts shall accelerate the disposition of any action brought under this Act.

**Sec. 18.05. Fee in lieu of state taxes.** A fee or payment collected by the state under this Act is in lieu of any other fee, payment, or tax levied by the state. This section does not preclude the application of the sales tax or any increase thereof to the sale or purchase of taxable items by a person or association licensed under this Act or the application of the franchise tax to a person or association licensed under this Act.

**Sec. 18.06. Release of liability.** A member of the commission, an employee of the commission, a steward or judge, an association, a horsemen's organization, or any other person regulated under this Act is not liable to any individual, corporation, business association, or other entity for a cause of action that arises out of that person's performance or exercise of discretion in the implementation or enforcement of this Act or a rule adopted under this Act if the person has acted in good faith.

**Sec. 18.07. Past performance of association.** In considering a pleading of a racetrack association, the commission shall take into account the operating experience of the racetrack association in Texas, which includes, but is not limited to, the financial condition of the track, regulatory compliance and conduct, and any other relevant matters concerning the operation of a track.

**Sec. 18.08. Distance learning.** The commission may provide assistance to members of the racing industry who are attempting to develop or implement adult, youth, or continuing education programs that use distance learning.
*(Chgd. by L.1997, chap. 1275(1-50), (54), eff. 9/1/97.)*

**Art. 179f.** *(Added by L.1989, chap. 1030(5); repealed by L.1999, chap. 388(6(a)), eff. 9/1/99.)*

**Art. 4413(29ee).** *(Repealed by L.1997, chap. 165(10.01(b)), eff. 9/1/97. See now Government Code Chapter 411, Subchapter H, sections 411.171 to 411.208.)*

**Sec. 1.** *(Chgd. by L.1997, chap. 1261(1), (31); repealed by L.1999, chap. 62(9.01(b)), eff. 9/1/99.)*

**Sec. 2.** *(Chgd. by L.1997, chaps. 1261(3), 1423(21.44); repealed by L.1999, chap. 62(9.03(b)), (9.04(b)), eff. 9/1/99.)*

**Sec. 3.** *(Chgd. by L.1997, chap. 1261(4); repealed by L.1999, chap. 62(9.06(b)), eff. 9/1/99.)*

**Sec. 5.** *(Chgd. by L.1997, chap. 1261(5); repealed by L.1999, chap. 62(9.07(b)), eff. 9/1/99.)*

**Sec. 6.** *(Chgd. by L.1997, chap. 1261(6), (7); repealed by L.1999, chap. 62(9.08(b)), (9.17(b)), eff. 9/1/99.)*

Printed in the U.S.A.

**Sec. 12.** *(Chgd. by L.1997, chap. 1261(8); repealed by L.1999, chap. 62(9.09(a)), eff. 9/1/99.)*

**Sec. 13.** *(Chgd. by L.1997, chap. 1261(9); repealed by L.1999, chap. 62(9.10(b)), eff. 9/1/99.)*

**Sec. 16.** *(Chgd. by L.1997, chap. 1261(10); repealed by L.1999, chap. 62(9.11(b)), eff. 9/1/99.)*

**Sec. 17.** *(Chgd. by L.1997, chap. 1261(11); repealed by L.1999, chap. 62(9.12(b)), eff. 9/1/99.)*

**Sec. 18.** *(Chgd. by L.1997, chap. 1261(12); repealed by L.1999, chap. 62(9.13(b)), eff. 9/1/99.)*

**Sec. 28.** *(Chgd. by L.1997, chap. 1261(13); repealed by L.1999, chap. 62(9.15(b)), eff. 9/1/99.)*

**Sec. 28A.** *(Chgd. by L.1997, chap. 1261(13); repealed by L.1999, chap. 62(9.15(b)), eff. 9/1/99.)*

**Sec. 31.** *(Chgd. by L.1997, chap. 1261(14); repealed by L.1999, chap. 62(9.16(b)), eff. 9/1/99.)*

**Sec. 35.** *(Chgd. by L.1997, chap. 1261(15); repealed by L.1999, chap. 62(9.05(b)), eff. 9/1/99.)*

**Art. 4495b.** *(Repealed by L.1999, chap. 388(6(a)), eff. 9/1/99. See Occupations Code sections 158.001 to 158.003.)*

## Art. 4495c. Intractable Pain Treatment Act.

**Sec. 1. Short title.** This article may be cited as the Intractable Pain Treatment Act.

**Sec. 2. Definitions.** For the purposes of this Act:

(1) "Board" means the Texas State Board of Medical Examiners.

(2) "Physician" means a licensee of the Texas State Board of Medical Examiners.

(3) "Intractable pain" means a pain state in which the cause of the pain cannot be removed or otherwise treated and which in the generally accepted course of medical practice no relief or cure of the cause of the pain is possible or none has been found after reasonable efforts.

**Sec. 3. [*Prescription or administration of drugs by physicians.*]** Notwithstanding any other provision of law, a physician may prescribe or administer dangerous drugs or controlled substances to a person in the course of the physician's treatment of a person for intractable pain.

**Sec. 4. Restriction by hospital or health care facility of prescribed drug use prohibited.** No hospital or health care facility may forbid or restrict the use of dangerous drugs or controlled substances when prescribed or administered by a physician having staff privileges at that hospital or health care facility for a person diagnosed and treated by a physician for intractable pain.

**Sec. 5. Disciplinary action against physician for prescribing or administering drug treatment prohibited.** No physician may be subject to disciplinary action by the board for prescribing or administering dangerous drugs or controlled substances in the course of treatment of a person for intractable pain.

**Sec. 6. Application of act to chemically dependent persons.** (a) Except as provided by Subsection (c) of this section, the provisions of this Act shall not apply to those persons being treated by the physician for chemical dependency because of their use of dangerous drugs or controlled substances.

(b) The provisions of this Act provide no authority to a physician to prescribe or administer dangerous drugs or controlled substances to a person for other than legitimate medical purposes as defined by the board and who the physician knows or should know to be using drugs for nontherapeutic purposes.

(c) The provisions of this Act authorize a physician to treat a patient who develops an acute or chronic painful medical condition with a dangerous drug or a controlled substance to relieve the patient's pain using appropriate doses, for an appropriate length of time, and for as long as the pain persists. A patient under this subsection includes a person who:

(1) is a current drug abuser;

(2) is not currently abusing drugs but has a history of drug abuse; or

(3) lives in an environment that poses a risk for drug misuse or diversion of the drug to illegitimate use.

(d) A physician who treats a patient under Subsection (c) of this section shall monitor the patient to ensure the prescribed dangerous drug or controlled substance is used only for the treatment of the patient's painful medical condition. To ensure that the prescribed dangerous drug or controlled substance is not being diverted to another use and the appropriateness of the treatment of the patient's targeted symptoms, the physician shall:

(1) specifically document:

(A) the understanding between the physician and patient about the patient's prescribed treatment;

(B) the name of the drug prescribed;

(C) the dosage and method of taking the prescribed drug;

(D) the number of dose units prescribed; and

(E) the frequency of prescribing and dispensing the drug; and

(2) consult with a psychologist, psychiatrist, expert in the treatment of addictions, or other health care professional, as appropriate.

*(Chgd. by L.1997, chap. 233(1), eff. 9/1/97.)*



**Sec. 7. Cancellation, revocation or suspension of physician's license.** Nothing in this Act shall deny the right of the Texas State Board of Medical Examiners to cancel, revoke, or suspend the license of any physician who:

(1) prescribes, administers, or dispenses a drug or treatment for other than legitimate medical purposes as defined by the board and that is nontherapeutic in nature or nontherapeutic in the manner the drug or treatment is administered or prescribed;

(2) fails to keep complete and accurate records of purchases and disposals of drugs listed in the Texas Controlled Substances Act (Chapter 481, Health and Safety Code), or of controlled substances scheduled in the federal Comprehensive Drug Abuse Prevention and Control Act of 1970, 21 U.S.C. Section 801 et seq. (Public Law 91-513), including records of:

(A) the date of purchase;

(B) the sale or disposal of the drugs by the physician;

(C) the name and address of the person receiving the drugs; and

(D) the reason for the disposal of or the dispensing of the drugs to the person;

(3) writes false or fictitious prescriptions for dangerous drugs as defined by Chapter 483, Health and Safety Code, for controlled substances scheduled in the Texas Controlled Substances Act (Chapter 481, Health and Safety Code), or for controlled substances scheduled in the federal Comprehensive Drug Abuse Prevention and Control Act of 1970, 21 U.S.C. Section 801 et seq. (Public Law 91-513); or

(4) prescribes, administers, or dispenses in a manner not consistent with public health and welfare dangerous drugs as defined by Chapter 483, Health and Safety Code, controlled substances scheduled in the Texas Controlled Substances Act (Chapter 481, Health and Safety Code), or controlled substances scheduled in the federal Comprehensive Drug Abuse Prevention and Control Act of 1970, 21 U.S.C. Section 801 et seq. (Public Law 91-513).

*(Chgd. by L.1997, chap. 233(2), eff. 9/1/97.)*

**Sec. 8. Illegal substances.** This Act is not intended nor shall it be interpreted to allow for the prescription of any illegal substance to any patient or person at any time in violation of federal law.

*(Added by L.1997, chap. 233(3), eff. 9/1/97.)*

*(Article 4495c added by L.1989, 1st C.S., chap. 5(1), eff. 11/1/89.)*

*(Editor's Note: The following paragraphs of Art. 4542a-1, Texas Civil Statutes, were repealed by the 1999 State Legislature, although paragraph (f) was enacted by L.1999, chap. 428(3), eff. 9/1/99.)*

## Art. 4542a-1. Texas Pharmacy Act.

**Sec. 33. Administration and provision of dangerous drugs (rural areas).† [*Administration and provision of dangerous drugs.*]** (a) through (e). *(Repealed.)*

(f) A person who is a licensed vocational nurse or has an education equivalent to or greater than that required for a licensed vocational nurse may be designated by the practitioner to communicate prescriptions of an advanced practice nurse or physician assistant authorized by the practitioner to sign prescription drug orders under Section 3.06(d)(5) or (6), Medical Practice Act (Article 4495b, Vernon's Texas Civil Statutes). *(Added by L.1999, chap. 428(3), eff. 9/1/99.)* *(Art. 4542a-1 repealed by L.1999, chap. 388(6(a)), eff. 9/1/99. See now Occupations Code, sections 563.001 to 563.053)*

**Art. 6252-13c.1.** *(Redesignated to Code of Criminal Procedure Chapter 62 and chgd. by L.1997, chap. 668(1), eff. 9/1/97.)*

**Art. 9003.** *(Repealed by L.1999, chap. 388(6(a)), eff. 9/1/99. See now Occupation Code sections 2104.001 et seq.)*

**Art. 9009. Secondhand metal dealers; records and reports of purchases and sales of copper and brass materials.† [*Copper and brass materials: sale, purchase, records, reports.*]**

**Sec. 1. Definitions.** As used in this Act:

(1) "Aluminum material" means a product made from aluminum, an aluminum alloy, or an aluminum by-product. The term includes an aluminum beer keg, but does not otherwise include an aluminum can used to contain a food or beverage.

(2) "Bronze material" means:

(A) a cemetery vase, receptacle, or memorial made from bronze;

(B) bronze statuary; or

(C) material that is readily identifiable as bronze.

(3) "Copper or brass material" means insulated or noninsulated copper wire or cable of the type used by public utilities or common carriers that consists of at least 50 percent copper, copper or brass items of a type commonly used in construction or by public utilities, or any combination consisting only of those items.

(4) "Passport" means a passport issued by the United States or issued by another country and recognized by the United States.

(5) "Personal identification certificate" means a personal identification card issued by the Department of Public Safety under Section 14A, Chapter 173, Acts of the 47th Legislature, Regular Session, 1941 Article 6687b, Texas Civil Statutes), or an analogous card or certificate issued by another state.

(6) "Regulated material" means aluminum material, bronze material, or copper or brass material.

(7) "Secondhand metal dealer" means an auto wrecker, a scrap metal processor, or any other person or organization purchasing, gathering, collecting, soliciting, or traveling about from place to place procuring regulated material, or any person operating, carrying on, conducting, or maintaining a scrap metal yard or other place where scrap metal or cast-off regulated material of any kind is gathered together or kept for shipment, sale, or transfer.

**Sec. 2. Duty to maintain record; exhibition; form and contents.** (a) Each secondhand metal dealer in this state shall keep an accurate and legible written record of any purchase made in the course of the dealer's business from an individual of:

(1) copper or brass material in excess of 50 pounds;

(2) bronze material; or

(3) aluminum material in excess of 40 pounds.

(b) The record must be in English and must include:

(1) the place and date of each purchase;

(2) the name and address of each individual from whom the regulated material is purchased or obtained;

(3) the identifying number of the seller's driver's license, military identification card, passport, or personal identification certificate;

(4) a description made in accordance with the custom of the trade of the type of regulated material purchased, and the quantity of the material; and

(5) a signed statement by the seller that states the seller's right of legal ownership or right to sell the regulated material offered for sale.

(c) A person attempting to sell a regulated material to a secondhand metal dealer must:

(1) display to the secondhand metal dealer the person's driver's license, military identification card, passport, or personal identification certificate or, if the seller does not have a driver's license, military card, passport, or personal identification certificate, a statement signed by the seller that states that the seller does not possess any of these types of identification; and

(2) sign a written statement provided by the secondhand metal dealer that states that the person is the legal owner of, or is lawfully entitled to sell, the regulated material offered for sale.

(d) If a person is required by a municipality to prepare a signed statement consisting of the same information required by Subsection (c)(1) or (2) of this section, the person may use the statement required by the municipality to comply with the requirements of Subsection (c)(1) or (2) of this section.

(e) The secondhand metal dealer or the dealer's agent shall visually verify the accuracy of the identification presented by the seller at the time of the purchase of a regulated material.

(f) A person commits an offense if that person, with the intent to deceive:

(1) makes a material and false statement or representation to a secondhand metal dealer in connection with the dealer's efforts to obtain the information required under Section 2(b) of this Act;

(2) displays to a secondhand metal dealer a false of invalid driver's license, military identification card, passport, or personal identification certificate in connection with the person's attempted sale of any regulated material; or

(3) makes a material and false statement or representation to a secondhand metal dealer in connection with that person's execution of a written statement required by Section 2 (c)(1) or (2) of this Act.

**Sec. 3. Preservation of records.** Each secondhand metal dealer shall preserve the records required by Section 2 of this Act for a period of at least three years.

**Sec. 4. Reports; mailing.** (a) On request, a secondhand metal dealer shall permit any peace officer of this state to inspect, during the usual and customary business hours of the dealer, a record compiled under Section 2 of this Act, and any regulated materials in the possession of the dealer. The inspecting officer shall identify himself as a peace officer.

(b) Except as provided by Subsection (c) of this section, not later than seven days after the purchase or other acquisition of any material required to be recorded under Section 2 of this Act, a secondhand metal dealer must mail to or file with the Department of Public Safety a report containing the information required to be recorded in Section 2 of this Act.

(c) If a secondhand metal dealer purchases any bronze material that is a cemetery vase, receptacle, memorial, or statuary or any aluminum irrigation pipe that can reasonably be identified as aluminum irrigation pipe from a person other than the manufacturer or fabricator of the material, a seller bearing a bill of sale for the material, or the owner of the material, the dealer shall provide oral notification to the Department of Public Safety not later than the close of business on the dealer's next working day following the date of the purchase and, not later than the fifth day after the date of the purchase, shall mail to or file with the Department of Public Safety a report containing the information required to be recorded in Section 2 of this Act.

**Sec. 5. Violations; penalties.** (a) If a peace officer has reasonable suspicion to believe that certain items consisting or composed of regulated materials and in the possession of a secondhand metal dealer are stolen, the peace officer may place the items on hold as provided by this section. If the officer places the items on hold, the officer shall issue a hold notice to the dealer.

(b) The hold notice must be in writing, and must:

(1) specifically identify the items alleged to be stolen and subject to the hold; and

(2) inform the dealer of the requirements imposed under Subsection (c) of this section.

(c) On receipt of a hold notice under this section, a secondhand metal dealer may not process or remove from the dealer's premises the items subject to the hold, or any part of those items, until the expiration of the 10th day after the date on which the notice is issued, unless the hold is released at an earlier time in writing by a peace officer of this state or an order of a court of competent jurisdiction. At the expiration of the holding period, the hold is automatically released and the dealer may dispose of the regulated material unless another disposition of the material has been ordered by a court of competent jurisdiction.

**Sec. 6. Exempt purchases and sales.** (a) A secondhand metal dealer must at all times maintain in a prominent place in the dealer's place of business, in open view to a seller of a regulated material, a notice in two-inch lettering that:

(1) includes the following language:
"A PERSON ATTEMPTING TO SELL ANY REGULATED MATERIAL MUST PRESENT SUFFICIENT IDENTIFICATION REQUIRED BY STATE LAW."
"WARNING: STATE LAW PROVIDES A CRIMINAL PENALTY FOR A PERSON WHO INTENTIONALLY PROVIDES A FALSE DOCUMENT OF IDENTIFICATION OR OTHER FALSE INFORMATION TO A SECONDHAND METAL DEALER WHILE ATTEMPTING TO SELL ANY REGULATED MATERIAL.";
and

(2) states the secondhand metal dealer's usual business hours.

(b) The notice required by this section may be contained on a sign that contains another notice if the secondhand metal dealer is required to display another notice under applicable law.

**Sec. 7. [*Violations; penalties.*]** (a) A person who knowingly or intentionally violates any provision of this Act commits an offense.

(b) Except as provided by Subsection (c) of this section, an offense under this section is a Class B misdemeanor.

(c) An offense under this section is a Class A misdemeanor if a person:

(1) knowingly or intentionally violates a provision of this Act; and

(2) has been convicted for a violation of this Act within the 36 months preceding the date of the offense.

(d) In addition to the penalties imposed under this section, a court, on the conviction of a secondhand metal dealer for an offense under Subsection (c) of this section, may order that the dealer cease from engaging in business as a secondhand metal dealer for a period not to exceed 30 days from the date of the order for each violation that forms the basis of the conviction.

**Sec. 8. [*Purchases and sales; exempt.*]** This Act does not apply to a purchase of a regulated material from a manufacturing, industrial, or other commercial vendor that sells regulated materials in the ordinary course of the vendor's business.
*(Chgd. by L.1991, chap. 398(1), eff. 9/1/91.)*

## Art. 9009a. Crafted precious metals—purchases and disposition—dealers.† [*Purchase and disposition of crafted precious metals.*]

**Sec. 1 Definitions.** In this Act:

(1) "Crafted precious metals" includes jewelry, silverware, art objects, or any other thing or object made, in whole or in part, from gold, silver, platinum, palladium, iridium, rhodium, osmium, ruthenium, or their alloys, excluding coins and commemorative medallions.

(2) "Dealer" means a person who engages in the business of purchasing and selling crafted precious metals.

(3) "Department" means the Department of Public Safety of the State of Texas.

(4) "Person" means an individual, association, corporation, or any other legal entity.

(5) "Temporary location" means a place where business is conducted for a period shorter than 90 days.

**Sec. 2. Purchases from minor.† [*Parent must consent to sale of item by minor.*]** (a) A dealer may not purchase crafted precious metals from a person under 18 years of age unless the seller delivers to the dealer before the purchase a written statement from a parent or legal guardian of the seller consenting to the transaction. The dealer shall preserve the statement with the records required to be kept under this Act. The dealer may destroy the statement one year from date of purchase or until the item is sold, whichever occurs later.

(b) A person who fails to obtain or keep a statement as required by this section commits a Class B misdemeanor.

**Sec. 3. Report of purchasing.† [*Dealer must report purchase.*]** (a) Not later than 48 hours after the time it is received, each dealer shall report in accordance with Section 4 of this Act all identifiable crafted precious metal that the dealer purchases, takes in trade, accepts for sale on consignment, or accepts for auction.

(b) Each dealer, before the time any crafted precious metal is offered for sale or exchange, shall notify each person intending to sell or exchange the crafted precious metal that the person must file with the dealer, before the dealer may accept any of the person's property, a list describing all of the person's crafted precious metal to be accepted by the dealer. The list must set forth:

(1) the name and address of the proposed seller;

(2) a complete and accurate description of the crafted precious metal;

(3) a certification by the proposed seller that the information is true and complete; and

(4) the driver's license number or DPS identification card number of the seller, as recorded by the dealer upon being physically presented the driver's license or DPS identification card by the seller.

(c) On demand the dealer shall provide the list required by Subsection (b) of this section to any peace officer and shall mail or deliver a complete copy of each list to the chief of police or to the sheriff in accordance with Section 4 of this Act not later than 48 hours after it is filed with the dealer.

(d) A dealer who fails to make or permit inspection of a report as required by this section commits a Class B misdemeanor.

**Sec. 4. Form of report; filing.†** [*Filing of report.*] (a) Each report required by this Act must be filed in accordance with this section unless a similar report is required by other state law or by a city ordinance. If such a report is required, the report must comply with and be submitted in accordance with the applicable law or ordinance.

(b) If a transaction regulated by this Act takes place inside an incorporated municipality, any report required by this Act shall be submitted to the chief of police of the municipality. If the transaction takes place outside an incorporated city or inside an incorporated city that does not maintain a police department, the report shall be submitted to the sheriff of the county where the transaction takes place.

(c) In the absence of other state law, or a city ordinance, that requires reporting of property acquired by a dealer in a transaction enumerated by Section 3(a) of this Act, the report shall be submitted on forms prescribed by the district attorney or person performing the duties of district attorney of the county where the transaction occurs.

(d) The original report and a copy shall be submitted by the dealer in accordance with Subsection (b) of this section. The dealer shall retain a copy of the report until the third anniversary of the date on which the report is filed.

(e) A dealer who fails to make or permit inspection of a report as required by this section commits a Class B misdemeanor.

**Sec. 4A. Retention of property.†** [***Dealer shall retain item for 11 days.***] (a) A dealer may not melt, deface, alter, or dispose of crafted precious metal for which a report is required under this Act before the 11th day after the day on which the report is filed unless:

(1) the peace officer to whom the report is submitted, for some good cause, authorizes disposition of that crafted precious metal;

(2) the dealer obtains the name, address, and description of the buyer and retains this information record, which shall be made available for inspection by any peace officer; or

(3) the dealer is a pawnbroker and the disposition is the redemption of pledged property by the pledgor.

(b) A person who disposes of property or who fails to make a record available for inspection by a peace officer as required by this section commits a Class B misdemeanor.

**Sec. 5. Inspection of property.** (a) The purchased property must be made available by the dealer for inspection by any police officer during regular business hours while the property is in the dealer's possession.

(b) Information obtained under this section is confidential except for use in a criminal investigation or prosecution or a civil court proceeding.

**Sec. 6. Purchases at temporary locations.†** [***Dealer purchase of items: temporary location.***] (a) A dealer who conducts business from a temporary location may not engage in business of buying precious metal or used items made of precious metal unless the person has filed a registration statement with the department within a 12-month period at least 30 days preceding the date on which each purchase is made and the person has filed within the same period, a copy of the registration statement with the local law enforcement agency of the municipality in which the temporary location is situated or, if the temporary location is not situated in a municipality, with the local law enforcement agency of the county in which the temporary location is situated. A registration statement must set forth:

(1) the name and address of the person;

(2) the location where business is to be conducted; and

(3) other relevant information required by the department.

(b) If the dealer is an association or corporation, the statement must set forth the name and address of each member of the association or each officer and director of the corporation, respectively.

(c) A dealer who fails to file a registration statement in violation of this section commits a Class B misdemeanor.

**Sec. 7. Purchase of melted items.†** [*Unlawful purchase: melted items.*] (a) A dealer, in the course of business, may not purchase an object that is formed as the result of the melting of crafted precious metal unless the object is purchased from a manufacturer of or a regular dealer in crafted precious metal.

(b) A person who purchases an object in violation of this section commits a Class B misdemeanor.

**Sec. 8. Necessity of compliance with other law or ordinance.†** [***Dealer must comply with local or state law.***] Nothing in this Act excuses noncompliance with another state law or city ordinance covering the reporting, holding, or releasing of crafted precious metal.

**Sec. 9. Effect of Act upon enactment, amendment, or enforcement of local ordinance.** This Act does not prohibit enactment, amendment, or enforcement by any city of any local ordinance relating to a dealer and does not supersede any city ordinance except to the extent that an ordinance does not require any reporting for transactions involving crafted precious metal.

**Sec. 10. Application of Act.** (a) This Act applies only to the crafted precious metals that have been sold or used primarily for personal, family, or household purposes. This Act does not apply to any person whose purchases and sales of precious metals and products made thereof are merely incidental to its business of extracting, recovering, or salvaging precious metals from industrial by-products and industrial waste products nor does this Act apply to dental, pharmaceutical, or medical applications of crafted precious metals.

(b) This Act does not apply to crafted precious metal that has been:

(1) acquired in good faith in a transaction involving the stock in trade of another dealer who previously made the reports required by this Act concerning the crafted precious metal included in the transaction if:

(A) the selling dealer delivers to the acquiring dealer a written document that states that the reports have been made;

(B) the acquiring dealer submits a copy of the statement to the chief of police of the city or the sheriff of the county where the selling dealer is located; and

(C) each dealer involved in the transaction retains a copy of the statement required by this subdivision until the third anniversary of the date of the transaction;

(2) acquired in a nonjudicial sale, transfer, assignment, assignment for the benefit of creditors, or consignment of the assets or stock in trade, in bulk, or a substantial part of those assets, of an industrial or commercial enterprise, other than dealer, for the voluntary dissolution or liquidation of the seller's business, or for disposing of an excessive quantity of personal property, or property that has been acquired in a nonjudicial sale or transfer from an owner other than a dealer, his entire household of personal property, or a substantial part of that property, if:

(A) the dealer gives written notice to the chief of police of the city or the sheriff of the county where the dealer's business is located that exemption from reporting is being claimed under this subdivision; and

(B) the dealer retains in his place of business, until the third anniversary of the date of the transaction, a copy of the bill of sale, receipt, inventory list, or other transfer document as a record which shall be made available for inspection by any peace officer;

(3) acquired in a sale made by any public officer in his official capacity as a trustee in bankruptcy, executor, administrator, receiver, or public official acting under judicial process or authority, or acquired in a sale made on the execution of, or by virtue of, any process issued by a court;

(4) acquired in good faith as part or complete payment for other crafted precious metal by a person, partnership, firm, or corporation whose principal business is primarily that of selling directly to the consumer crafted precious metal that has not been subject to a prior sale;

(5) acquired as surplus property from the United States or a state, subdivision of a state, or municipal corporation; or

(6) reported by a dealer as an acquisition or a purchase, or reported as destroyed or otherwise disposed of, to:

(A) a state agency in accordance with another law of this state; or

(B) a city or county officer or agency in accordance with another law of this state or a city ordinance.

(7) acquired by a person licensed and regulated under the Texas Pawnshop Act (Article 5069-51.01 et seq., Texas Civil Statutes).

**Art. 9023.** *(Repealed by L.1999, chap. 388(6(a)), eff. 9/1/99.)*

**Art. 9023c.** *(Added by L.1993, chap. 920(1)-(16); chgd. by L.1995, chap. 532(1), (2); repealed by L.1999, chap. 388(6(a)), eff. 9/1/99. See now Occupations Code, sections 1803.001 et seq.)*

**Art. 9028. Motor vehicle repair facilities.† [*Registration of motor vehicle repair facilities; penalties.*]**

**Sec. 1. Definitions.** In this Act:

(1) "Person" means an individual human being, corporation, partnership, firm, or other legal entity.

(2) "Commission" means the Texas Water Commission.

(3) "Executive director" means the executive director of the commission.

(4) "Motor vehicle" means a self-propelled device with at least four wheels by which a person or property may be transported or drawn on a public street or highway, except a device exclusively on stationary rails or tracks.

(5) "Repair facility" means a person that engages in the business of repairing or replacing the nonmechanical exterior or interior body parts of a damaged motor vehicle.

(6) "Registrant" means a person registered under the terms of this Act.

**Sec. 2. Registration required.** A repair facility shall register with the commission as provided by this Act and by rules promulgated by the commission. The repair facility shall renew the registration annually in the manner prescribed by the commission.

**Sec. 3. Information disclosed in registration.** (a) The commission by rule shall promulgate a form for application for the registration required by this Act and for application for renewal of the registration required by this Act. The commission by rule shall determine the information to be disclosed on the application. The application shall be sworn and shall set forth at least the following:

(1) each conviction of a felony, or misdemeanor for which the maximum punishment is by confinement in jail or by a fine exceeding $200, that was obtained against the applicant or a partner or officer of the applicant in the three-year period immediately preceding the date of the application;

(2) the name and street address, and the mailing address if different from the street address, of each location at which the applicant operates a repair facility;

(3) the name and address of each owner, partner, officer, director, or shareholder holding 10 percent or more of the outstanding shares if the applicant is a corporation;

(4) a statement setting forth each identification number assigned by, or other evidence of compliance with the requirements of, each of the following, if applicable:

(A) the United States Environmental Protection Agency;

(B) the United States Occupational Safety and Health Administration;

(C) the Texas Water Commission;

(D) the Texas Department of Health;

(E) the Texas Air Control Board;

(F) the comptroller of public accounts; and

(G) a municipal ordinance or county regulation.

(b) A registration or a renewal of a registration shall be accompanied by a fee of $50.

**Sec. 4. Certificate of registration; expiration.** On receipt of the form required by Section 3 of this Act, the executive director shall issue a certificate of registration to the applicant. A certificate of registration:

(1) shall bear a unique number;

(2) is valid for one year from the date of issuance;

(3) may be renewed upon application to the executive director on a form provided by the executive director;

(4) is not transferrable; and

(5) is applicable only to the person whose name appears on the certificate or an employee of that person.

**Sec. 5. Renewal.** Within 30 days prior to the expiration of a certificate of registration, the registrant shall apply for renewal of the license in the manner provided by this Act.

**Sec. 6. Expiration; termination; surrender.** (a) The executive director may suspend or revoke a certificate of registration prior to its expiration date according to the procedures and on the grounds established pursuant to Section 7 of this Act. A certificate of registration may be terminated at any time by voluntary surrender by the registrant.

(b) Upon the expiration, termination, or surrender of a certificate of registration, the registrant shall deliver the certificate to the executive director who shall cancel the certificate or endorse the date of expiration, termination, or surrender on the certificate.

(c) If a certificate of registration is lost or destroyed, the registrant shall file an affidavit to that effect, and the commissioner shall, on receipt of a $25 replacement fee, issue a replacement certificate clearly identified as such on the certificate and in the records of the commission.

**Sec. 7. Revocation; suspension; rules.** (a) The commission shall adopt rules establishing the grounds for suspension, revocation, or reinstatement of a certificate of registration and establishing the procedures for disciplinary actions.

(b) Proceedings relating to the suspension or revocation of a certificate of registration issued under this Act are subject to the Administrative Procedure and Texas Register Act (Article 6252-13a, Texas Civil Statutes).

**Sec. 8. Registration applications and certificates: maintenance of records.** The executive director shall maintain, in convenient form and open to the public, all applications for registration and copies of certificates of registration and shall annually publish a list of names and addresses of persons registered with the commission under this Act, the names of all persons whose registration has been revoked, suspended, or surrendered during the period, and the specific time that the suspension, revocation, or surrender became effective.

**Sec. 9. Public display of certificate of registration.** A registrant shall publicly display its current certificate of registration in its place of business in a location readily visible to a customer paying for repairs. A registrant shall also include the registrant's registration number on repair estimates, repair orders, and correspondence.

**Sec. 10. Advertising; repair charges.** (a) A registrant shall include the number of its certificate assigned by the commission as provided by this Act as a part of an advertisement for motor vehicle repairs.

(b) A registrant may not make any false or fraudulent statement in connection with any repair or attempt to collect for a repair.

**Sec. 11. Records.** (a) A registrant shall maintain a record of each motor vehicle that enters the registrant's premises for the purpose of obtaining repairs. Except as provided by Subsection (b) of this section, the registrant shall include in that record at least the following information:

(1) a description of the vehicle;

(2) the vehicle identification number;

(3) the date the vehicle entered the registrant's premises;

(4) the odometer reading at the time the vehicle is received;

(5) the name and address of the person from whom the vehicle was received; and

(6) a signed authorization for the work to be performed on the vehicle.

(b) The record required by Subsection (a) of this section shall be kept in a convenient place and, along with the premises of the registrant's place of business, may be inspected at any time by the executive director or an employee of the commission.

(c) In the case of a vehicle that was towed to the registrant's repair facility without the consent of the owner of the vehicle, the information that the registrant shall maintain is the information provided by the law enforcement agency that initiated the towing process.

**Sec. 12. Violations; penalty.** (a) A repair facility that fails to register as provided by this Act shall pay a civil penalty of $250. The executive director shall waive the penalty if the repair facility files proper registration within 10 days after notice of the violation.

(b) A registrant that violates a provision of this Act is subject to a civil penalty not to exceed $100.

**Sec. 13. Applicability.** This Act does not apply to a repair facility located within a county with a population of 50,000 or fewer.
*(Added by L.1993, chap. 956(1)-(13), eff. 1/1/94.)*

# EDUCATION CODE

# TITLE 2. PUBLIC SCHOOLS

## CHAPTER 25. ADMISSION, TRANSFER, AND ATTENDANCE

*(Added by L.1995, chap. 260(1), eff. 5/30/95.)*
*(Selected Sections)*

## SUBCHAPTER C. OPERATION OF SCHOOLS AND SCHOOL ATTENDANCE

Section


## SUBCHAPTER C. OPERATION OF SCHOOLS AND SCHOOL ATTENDANCE

### §25.085. Compulsory school attendance.

(a) A child who is required to attend school under this section shall attend school each school day for the entire period the program of instruction is provided.

(b) Unless specifically exempted by Section 25.086, a child who is at least six years of age, or who is younger than six years of age and has previously been enrolled in first grade, and who has not yet reached the child's 18th birthday shall attend school.

(c) On enrollment in prekindergarten or kindergarten, a child shall attend school.

(d) Unless specifically exempted by Section 25.086, a student enrolled in a school district must attend:

(1) an extended-year program for which the student is eligible that is provided by the district for students identified as likely not to be promoted to the next grade level or tutorial classes required by the district under Section 29.084;

(2) an accelerated reading instruction program to which the student is assigned under Section 28.006(g);

(3) an accelerated instruction program to which the student is assigned under Section 28.0211; or

(4) a basic skills program to which the student is assigned under Section 29.086.

(e) A person who voluntarily enrolls in school or voluntarily attends school after the person's 18th birthday shall attend school each school day for the entire period the program of instruction is offered. A school district may revoke for the remainder of the school year the enrollment of a person who has more than five absences in a semester that are not excused under Section 25.087. A person whose enrollment is revoked under this subsection may be considered an unauthorized person on school district grounds for purposes of Section 37.107.

*(Added by L.1995, chap. 260(1); chgd. by L.1997, chap. 1019(2); L.1999, chaps. 396(2.10), 711(1), eff. 9/1/99, 6/18/99, respectively.)*

### §25.086. Exemptions.

(a) A child is exempt from the requirements of compulsory school attendance if the child:

(1) attends a private or parochial school that includes in its course a study of good citizenship;

(2) is eligible to participate in a school district's special education program under Section 29.003 and cannot be appropriately served by the resident district;

(3) has a physical or mental condition of a temporary and remediable nature that makes the child's attendance infeasible and holds a certificate from a qualified physician specifying the temporary condition, indicating the treatment prescribed to remedy the temporary condition, and covering the anticipated period of the child's absence from school for the purpose of receiving and recuperating from that remedial treatment;

(4) is expelled in accordance with the requirements of law in a school district that does not participate in a mandatory juvenile justice alternative education program under Section 37.011;

(5) is at least 17 years of age and:

(A) is attending a course of instruction to prepare for the high school equivalency examination, and:

(i) has the permission of the child's parent or guardian to attend the course;

(ii) is required by court order to attend the course;

(iii) has established a residence separate and apart from the child's parent, guardian, or other person having lawful control of the child; or

(iv) is homeless as defined by 42 U.S.C. Section 11302; or

(B) has received a high school diploma or high school equivalency certificate;

(6) is at least 16 years of age and is attending a course of instruction to prepare for the high school equivalency examination, if:

(A) the child is recommended to take the course of instruction by a public agency that has supervision or custody of the child under a court order; or

(B) the child is enrolled in a Job Corps training program under the Job Training Partnership Act (29 U.S.C. Section 1501 et seq.), and its subsequent amendments;

(7) is enrolled in the Texas Academy of Mathematics and Science;

(8) is enrolled in the Texas Academy of Leadership in the Humanities; or

(9) is specifically exempted under another law.

(b) This section does not relieve a school district in which a child eligible to participate in the district's special education program resides of its fiscal and administrative responsibilities under Subchapter A, Chapter 29, or of its responsibility to provide a free appropriate public education to a child with a disability.

*(Added by L.1995, chap. 260(1); chgd. by L.1997, chaps. 1015(1), 1019(3); L.1999, chap. 1282(2), eff. 6/18/99.)*



## §25.093. Thwarting compulsory attendance law.

(a) If any parent of a child required to attend school fails to require the child to attend school as required by law, the school attendance officer shall warn the parent in writing that attendance is immediately required.

(b) If, after a warning under Subsection (a), the parent with criminal negligence fails to require the child to attend school as required by law and the child has unexcused voluntary absences for the amount of time specified under Section 51.03(b)(2), Family Code, the parent commits an offense.

(c) The attendance officer shall file a complaint against the parent in the county court, in a justice court in the county in which the parent resides or in which the school is located, or in a municipal court of the municipality in which the parent resides or in which the school is located. The attendance officer shall file a complaint under this section in the court to which the parent's child has been referred for engaging in conduct described in Section 51.03(b)(2), Family Code, if a referral has been made for the child. If a referral has not been made, the attendance officer shall refer the child to the county juvenile probation department for action as engaging in conduct indicating a need for supervision under that section.

(d) A court in which a complaint is filed under this section shall give preference to a hearing on the complaint over other cases before the court.

(e) An offense under this section is a Class C misdemeanor. Each day the child remains out of school after the warning has been given or the child has been ordered to attend school by the juvenile court may constitute a separate offense. Two or more offenses under this section may be consolidated and prosecuted in a single action. If the court probates the sentence, the court may require the defendant to render personal services to a charitable or educational institution as a condition of probation.

(f) A fine collected under this section shall be deposited as follows:

(1) one-half shall be deposited to the credit of the operating fund of the school district in which the child attends school or of the juvenile justice alternative education program that the child has been ordered to attend, as applicable; and

(2) one-half shall be deposited to the credit of:

(A) the general fund of the county, if the complaint is filed in the county court or justice court; or

(B) the general fund of the municipality, if the complaint is filed in municipal court.

(g) At the trial of any person charged with violating this section, the attendance records of the child may be presented in court by any authorized employee of the school district.

(h) The court in which a conviction for an offense under this section occurs may order the defendant to attend a class for parents of students with unexcused absences that provides instruction designed to assist those parents in identifying problems that contribute to the students' unexcused absences and in developing strategies for resolving those problems if the school district in which the person resides offers such a class.

(i) In this section, "parent" includes a person standing in parental relation.
*(Added by L.1995, chap. 260(1); chgd. by L.1997, chap. 865(2); L.1999, chap. 1403(1), eff. 9/1/99.)*

### §25.094. Failure to attend school.

(a) A child commits an offense if the child:

(1) is required to attend school under Section 25.085; and

(2) fails to attend school for the amount of time specified under Section 51.03(b)(2), Family Code, and is not excused under Section 25.087.

(b) An offense under this section may be prosecuted in a justice court in the county in which the child resides or in which the school is located or in a municipal court in the municipality in which the child resides or in which the school is located.

(c) On a finding by the justice or municipal court that the child has committed an offense under Subsection (a), the court may enter an order that includes one or more of the requirements listed in Section 54.021(d), Family Code.

(d) If the justice or municipal court finds that a child has violated an order issued under Subsection (c), the court shall transfer the complaint against the child, together with all pleadings and orders, to a juvenile court for the county in which the child resides. The juvenile court shall conduct an adjudication hearing as provided by Section 54.03, Family Code. The adjudication hearing shall be de novo.

(e) Pursuant to an order of the justice or municipal court, a peace officer may take a child into custody if there are reasonable grounds to believe that the child has committed an offense under this section. A peace officer taking a child into custody under this subsection shall:

(1) promptly notify the child's parent, guardian, or custodian of the officer's action and the reason for that action; and

(2) without unnecessary delay:

(A) release the child to the child's parent, guardian, or custodian or to another responsible adult, if the person promises to bring the child to the justice or municipal court as requested by the court; or

(B) bring the child to the justice of the peace of the court having jurisdiction over the child.

(f) An offense under this section is a Class C misdemeanor.

(g) Any person convicted of not more than one violation under this section while a minor, on attaining the age of 18 years, may apply to the court in which the person was convicted to have the conviction expunged.

(h) The application must contain the applicant's sworn statement that the person was not convicted of any violation of this section while a minor other than the one the person seeks to have expunged.

(i) If the court finds that the applicant was not convicted of any other violation of this section while the person was a minor, the court shall order the conviction, together with all complaints, verdicts, sentences, and other documents relating to the offense, to be expunged from the applicant's record. After entry of the order, the applicant shall be released from all disabilities resulting from the conviction, and the conviction may not be shown or made known for any purpose.
*(Added by L.1995, chap. 260(1); chgd. by L.1997, chap. 865(2), eff. 9/1/97.)*



## CHAPTER 34. TRANSPORTATION

*(Added by L.1995, chap. 260(1), eff. 5/30/95.)*
*(Selected Sections)*

Section


### §34.003. Operation of school buses or mass transit authority vehicles.

(a) School buses or mass transit authority motor buses shall be used for the transportation of students to and from schools on routes having 10 or more students. On those routes having fewer than 10 students, passenger cars may be used for the transportation of students to and from school.
*(Chgd. by L.1997, chap. 1438(3), eff. 9/1/97. See subsection (a) below.)*

(a) School buses or mass transit authority vehicles shall be used for the transportation of students to and from schools on routes having 10 or more students. On those routes having fewer than 10 students, passenger cars may be used for the transportation of students to and from school.
*(Chgd. by L.1997, chap. 1061(20), eff. 9/1/97. See subsection (a) above.)*

(b) To transport students in connection with school activities other than on routes to and from school:

(1) only school buses, mass transit authority vehicles, or motor buses may be used to transport 15 or more students in any one vehicle; and

(2) passenger cars or passenger vans may be used to transport fewer than 15 students.

(c) In all circumstances in which passenger cars or passenger vans are used to transport students, the operator of the vehicle shall ensure that the number of passengers in the vehicle does not exceed the designed capacity of the vehicle and that each passenger is secured by a safety belt.

(d) In this section, "passenger van" means a motor vehicle, other than a motorcycle or passenger car, used to transport persons and designed to transport 15 or fewer passengers, including the driver.

(e) "Motor bus" means a vehicle designed to transport more than 15 passengers, including the driver.

*(Added by L.1995, chap. 260(1); chgd. by L.1997, chaps. 1029(1), 1061(20), 1438(3), eff. 6/19/97, 9/1/97, 9/1/97, respectively.)*



### §34.004. Standing children.

A school district may not require or allow a child to stand on a school bus or passenger van that is in motion. *(Added by L.1995, chap. 260(1); chgd. by L.1997, chaps. 1029(2), 1061(21), 1438(4), eff. 6/19/97, 9/1/97, 9/1/97, respectively.)*

## CHAPTER 37. DISCIPLINE; LAW AND ORDER

*(Added by L.1995, chap. 260(1), eff. 5/30/95.)*

*(Selected Sections)*

## SUBCHAPTER A. ALTERNATIVE SETTINGS FOR BEHAVIOR MANAGEMENT

Section



## SUBCHAPTER C. LAW AND ORDER



## SUBCHAPTER D. PROTECTION OF BUILDINGS AND GROUNDS



## SUBCHAPTER E. PENAL PROVISIONS

## SUBCHAPTER F. HAZING



## SUBCHAPTER A. ALTERNATIVE SETTINGS FOR BEHAVIOR MANAGEMENT

### §37.006. Removal for certain conduct.

(a) Except as provided by Section 37.007(a)(3) or (b), a student shall be removed from class and placed in an alternative education program as provided by Section 37.008 if the student commits the following on or within 300 feet of school property, as measured from any point on the school's real property boundary line, or while attending a school-sponsored or school-related activity on or off of school property:

(1) engages in conduct punishable as a felony;

(2) engages in conduct that contains the elements of the offense of assault under Section 22.01(a)(1), Penal Code, or terroristic threat under Section 22.07, Penal Code;

(3) sells, gives, or delivers to another person or possesses or uses or is under the influence of:

(A) marihuana or a controlled substance, as defined by Chapter 481, Health and Safety Code, or by 21 U.S.C. Section 801 et seq.; or

(B) a dangerous drug, as defined by Chapter 483, Health and Safety Code;

(4) sells, gives, or delivers to another person an alcoholic beverage, as defined by Section 1.04, Alcoholic Beverage Code, commits a serious act or offense while under the influence of alcohol, or possesses, uses, or is under the influence of an alcoholic beverage;

(5) engages in conduct that contains the elements of an offense relating to abusable glue or aerosol paint under Sections 485.031 through 485.035, Health and Safety Code, or relating to volatile chemicals under Chapter 484, Health and Safety Code; or

(6) engages in conduct that contains the elements of the offense of public lewdness under Section 21.07, Penal Code, or indecent exposure under Section 21.08, Penal Code.

(b) Except as provided by Section 37.007(d), a student shall be removed from class and placed in an alternative education program under Section 37.008 if the student engages in conduct that contains the elements of the offense of retaliation under Section 36.06, Penal Code, against any school employee.

(c) In addition to Subsection (a), a student shall be removed from class and placed in an alternative education program under Section 37.008 based on conduct occurring off campus and while the student is not in attendance at a school-sponsored or school-related activity if:

(1) the student receives deferred prosecution under Section 53.03, Family Code, for conduct defined as a felony offense in Title 5, Penal Code;

(2) a court or jury finds that the student has engaged in delinquent conduct under Section 54.03, Family Code, for conduct defined as a felony offense in Title 5, Penal Code; or

(3) the superintendent or the superintendent's designee has a reasonable belief that the student has engaged in a conduct defined as a felony offense in Title 5, Penal Code.

(d) In addition to Subsection (a), a student may be removed from class and placed in an alternative education program under Section 37.008 based on conduct occurring off campus and while the student is not in attendance at a school-sponsored or school-related activity if:

(1) the superintendent or the superintendent's designee has a reasonable belief that the student has engaged in conduct defined as a felony offense other than those defined in Title 5, Penal Code; and

(2) the continued presence of the student in the regular classroom threatens the safety of other students or teachers or will be detrimental to the educational process.

(e) In determining whether there is a reasonable belief that a student has engaged in conduct defined as a felony offense by the Penal Code, the superintendent or the superintendent's designee may consider all available information, including the information furnished under Article 15.27, Code of Criminal Procedure.

(f) Subject to Section 37.007(e), a student who is younger than 10 years of age shall be removed from class and placed in an alternative education program under Section 37.008 if the student engages in conduct described by Section 37.007. An elementary school student may not be placed in an alternative education program with any other student who is not an elementary school student.

(g) The terms of a placement under this section must prohibit the student from attending or participating in a school-sponsored or school-related activity.

(h) On receipt of notice under Article 15.27(g), Code of Criminal Procedure, the superintendent or the superintendent's designee shall review the student's placement in the alternative education program. The student may not be returned to the regular classroom pending the review. The superintendent or the superintendent's designee shall schedule a review of the student's placement with the student's parent or guardian not later than the third class day after the superintendent or superintendent's designee receives notice from the office or official designated by the court. After reviewing the notice and receiving information from the student's parent or guardian, the superintendent or the superintendent's designee may continue the student's placement in the alternative education program if there is reason to believe that the presence of the student in the regular classroom threatens the safety of other students or teachers.

(i) The student or the student's parent or guardian may appeal the superintendent's decision under Subsection (h) to the board of trustees. The student may not be returned to the regular classroom pending the appeal. The board shall, at the next scheduled meeting, review the notice provided under Article 15.27(g), Code of Criminal Procedure, and receive information from the student, the student's parent or guardian, and the superintendent or superintendent's designee and confirm or reverse the decision under Subsection (h). The board shall make a record of the proceedings. If the board confirms the decision of the superintendent or superintendent's designee, the board shall inform the student and the student's parent or guardian of the right to appeal to the commissioner under Subsection (j).



(j) Notwithstanding Section 7.057(e), the decision of the board of trustees under Subsection (i) may be appealed to the commissioner as provided by Sections 7.057(b), (c), (d), and (f). The student may not be returned to the regular classroom pending the appeal.

(k) Subsections (h), (i), and (j) do not apply to placements made in accordance with Subsection (a).

(*l*) Notwithstanding any other provision of this code, a student who is younger than six years of age may not be removed from class and placed in an alternative education program.

*(Added by L.1995, chap. 260(1); chgd. by L.1997, chap. 1015(3); L.1999, chap. 396(2.15), eff. 9/1/99.)*

## §37.007. Expulsion for serious offenses.

(a) A student shall be expelled from a school if the student, on school property or while attending a school-sponsored or school-related activity on or off of school property:

(1) uses, exhibits, or possesses:

(A) a firearm as defined by Section 46.01(3), Penal Code;

(B) an illegal knife as defined by Section 46.01(6), Penal Code, or by local policy;

(C) a club as defined by Section 46.01(1), Penal Code; or

(D) a weapon listed as a prohibited weapon under Section 46.05, Penal Code;

(2) engages in conduct that contains the elements of the offense of:

(A) aggravated assault under Section 22.02, Penal Code, sexual assault under Section 22.011, Penal Code, or aggravated sexual assault under Section 22.021, Penal Code;

(B) arson under Section 28.02, Penal Code;

(C) murder under Section 19.02, Penal Code, capital murder under Section 19.03, Penal Code, or criminal attempt, under Section 15.01, Penal Code, to commit murder or capital murder;

(D) indecency with a child under Section 21.11, Penal Code; or

(E) aggravated kidnapping under Section 20.04, Penal Code; or

(3) engages in conduct specified by Section 37.006(a)(3) or (4), if the conduct is punishable as a felony.

(b) A student may be expelled if the student, while on school property or while attending a school-sponsored or school-related activity on or off of school property:

(1) sells, gives, or delivers to another person or possesses, uses, or is under the influence of any amount of:

(A) marihuana or a controlled substance, as defined by Chapter 481, Health and Safety Code, or by 21 U.S.C. Section 801 et seq.;

(B) a dangerous drug, as defined by Chapter 483, Health and Safety Code; or

(C) an alcoholic beverage, as defined by Section 1.04, Alcoholic Beverage Code;

(2) engages in conduct that contains the elements of an offense relating to abusable glue or aerosol paint under Sections 485.031 through 485.035, Health and Safety Code, or relating to volatile chemicals under Chapter 484, Health and Safety Code; or

(3) engages in conduct that contains the elements of an offense under Section 22.01(a)(1), Penal Code, against a school district employee or a volunteer as defined by Section 22.053.

(c) A student may be expelled if the student, while placed in an alternative education program for disciplinary reasons, continues to engage in serious or persistent misbehavior that violates the district's student code of conduct.

(d) A student shall be expelled if the student engages in conduct that contains the elements of any offense listed in Subsection (a), and may be expelled if the student engages in conduct that contains the elements of any offense listed in Subsection (b)(3), against any employee or volunteer in retaliation for or as a result of the person's employment or association with a school district, without regard to whether the conduct occurs on or off of school property or while attending a school-sponsored or school-related activity on or off of school property.

(e) In accordance with federal law, a local educational agency, including a school district, home-rule school district, or open-enrollment charter school, shall expel a student who brings a firearm, as defined by 18 U.S.C. Section 921, to school. The student must be expelled from the student's regular campus for a period of at least one year, except that:

(1) the superintendent or other chief administrative officer of the school district or of the other local educational agency, as defined by 20 U.S.C. Section 2891, may modify the length of the expulsion in the case of an individual student;

(2) the district or other local educational agency shall provide educational services to an expelled student in an alternative education program as provided by Section 37.008 if the student is younger than 10 years of age on the date of expulsion; and

(3) the district or other local educational agency may provide educational services to an expelled student who is older than 10 years of age in an alternative education program as provided in Section 37.008.

(f) A student who engages in conduct that contains the elements of the offense of criminal mischief under Section 28.03, Penal Code, may be expelled at the district's discretion if the conduct is punishable as a felony under that section. The student shall be referred to the authorized officer of the juvenile court regardless of whether the student is expelled.

(g) A school district shall inform each teacher of the conduct of a student who has engaged in any violation listed in this section. A teacher shall keep the information received in this subsection confidential. The State Board for Educator Certification may revoke or suspend the certification of a teacher who intentionally violates this subsection.

(h) Subject to Subsection (e), notwithstanding any other provision of this section, a student who is younger than 10 years of age may not be expelled for engaging in conduct described by this section.

*(Added by L.1995, chap. 260(1); chgd. by L.1997, chap. 1015(5); L.1999, chap. 542(1), eff. 6/18/99.)*

## §37.015. Reports to local law enforcement; liability.

(a) The principal of a public or private primary or secondary school, or a person designated by the principal under Subsection (d), shall notify any school district police department and the police department of the municipality in which the school is located or, if the school is not in a municipality, the sheriff of the county in which the school is located if the principal has reasonable grounds to believe that any of the following activities occur in school, on school property, or at a school-sponsored or school-related activity on or off school property, whether or not the activity is investigated by school security officers:

(1) conduct that may constitute an offense listed under Section 508.149, Government Code;

(2) deadly conduct under Section 22.05, Penal Code;

(3) a terroristic threat under Section 22.07, Penal Code;

(4) the use, sale, or possession of a controlled substance, drug paraphernalia, or marihuana under Chapter 481, Health and Safety Code;

(5) the possession of any of the weapons or devices listed under Sections 46.01(1)-(14) or Section 46.01(16), Penal Code; or

(6) conduct that may constitute a criminal offense under Section 71.02, Penal Code.

(b) A person who makes a notification under this section shall include the name and address of each student the person believes may have participated in the activity.

(c) A notification is not required under Subsection (a) if the person reasonably believes that the activity does not constitute a criminal offense.

(d) The principal of a public or private primary or secondary school may designate a school employee who is under the supervision of the principal to make the reports required by this section.

Printed in the U.S.A. Zt

(e) The person who makes the notification required under Subsection (a) shall also notify each instructional or support employee of the school who has regular contact with a student whose conduct is the subject of the notice.

(f) A person is not liable in civil damages for reporting in good faith as required by this section.

*(Added by L.1995, chap. 260(1); chgd. by L.1997, chap. 165(12.05), eff. 9/1/97.)*

### §37.016. Report of drug offenses; liability.

A teacher, school administrator, or school employee is not liable in civil damages for reporting to a school administrator or governmental authority, in the exercise of professional judgment within the scope of the teacher's, administrator's, or employee's duties, a student whom the teacher suspects of using, passing, or selling, on school property:

(1) marihuana or a controlled substance, as defined by Chapter 481, Health and Safety Code;

(2) a dangerous drug, as defined by Chapter 483, Health and Safety Code;

(3) an abusable glue or aerosol paint, as defined by Chapter 485, Health and Safety Code, or a volatile chemical, as listed in Chapter 484, Health and Safety Code, if the substance is used or sold for the purpose of inhaling its fumes or vapors; or

(4) an alcoholic beverage, as defined by Section 1.04, Alcoholic Beverage Code.

*(Added by L.1995, chap. 260(1), eff. 5/30/95.)*



## SUBCHAPTER C. LAW AND ORDER

### §37.081. School district peace officers and security personnel.

(a) The board of trustees of any school district may employ security personnel and may commission peace officers to carry out this subchapter. If a board of trustees authorizes a person employed as security personnel to carry a weapon, the person must be a commissioned peace officer. The jurisdiction of a peace officer or security personnel under this section shall be determined by the board of trustees and may include all territory in the boundaries of the school district and all property outside the boundaries of the district that is owned, leased, or rented by or otherwise under the control of the school district and the board of trustees that employ the peace officer or security personnel.

(b) In a peace officer's jurisdiction, a peace officer commissioned under this section:

(1) has the powers, privileges, and immunities of peace officers;

(2) may enforce all laws, including municipal ordinances, county ordinances, and state laws; and

(3) may, in accordance with Chapter 52, Family Code, take a juvenile into custody.

(c) A school district peace officer may provide assistance to another law enforcement agency. A school district may contract with a political subdivision for the jurisdiction of a school district peace officer to include all territory in the jurisdiction of the political subdivision.

(d) A school district peace officer shall perform administrative and law enforcement duties for the school district as determined by the board of trustees of the school district. Those duties must include protecting:

(1) the safety and welfare of any person in the jurisdiction of the peace officer; and

(2) the property of the school district.

(e) The board of trustees of the district shall determine the scope of the on-duty and off-duty law enforcement activities of school district peace officers. A school district must authorize in writing any off-duty law enforcement activities performed by a school district peace officer.

(f) The chief of police of the school district police department shall be accountable to the superintendent and shall report to the superintendent or the superintendent's designee. School district police officers shall be supervised by the chief of police of the school district or the chief of police's designee and shall be licensed by the Commission on Law Enforcement Officer Standards and Education.

(g) A school district police department and the law enforcement agencies with which it has overlapping jurisdiction shall enter into a memorandum of understanding that outlines reasonable communication and coordination efforts between the department and the agencies.

(h) A peace officer assigned to duty and commissioned under this section shall take and file the oath required of peace officers and shall execute and file a bond in the sum of $1,000, payable to the board of trustees, with two or more sureties, conditioned that the peace officer will fairly, impartially, and faithfully perform all the duties that may be required of the peace officer by law. The bond may be sued on in the name of any person injured until the whole amount of the bond is recovered. Any peace officer commissioned under this section must meet all minimum standards

for peace officers established by the Commission on Law Enforcement Officer Standards and Education.
*(Added by L.1995, chap. 260(1), eff. 5/30/95.)*

### §37.082. Possession of paging devices.

(a) The board of trustees of a school district may adopt a policy prohibiting a student from possessing a paging device while on school property or while attending a school-sponsored or school-related activity on or off school property. The policy may establish disciplinary measures to be imposed for violation of the prohibition and may provide for confiscation of the paging device.

(b) The policy may provide for the district to:

(1) dispose of a confiscated paging device in any reasonable manner after having provided the student's parent and the company whose name and address or telephone number appear on the device 30 days' prior notice of its intent to dispose of that device. The notice shall include the serial number of the device and may be made by telephone, telegraph, or in writing; and

(2) charge the owner of the device or the student's parent an administrative fee not to exceed $15 before it releases the device.

(c) In this section, "paging device" means a telecommunications device that emits an audible signal, vibrates, displays a message, or otherwise summons or delivers a communication to the possessor.
*(Added by L.1995, chap. 260(1), eff. 5/30/95.)*





## SUBCHAPTER D. PROTECTION OF BUILDINGS AND GROUNDS

### §37.101. Applicability of criminal laws.

The criminal laws of the state apply in the areas under the control and jurisdiction of the board of trustees of any school district in this state. *(Added by L.1995, chap. 260(1), eff. 5/30/95.)*

### §37.102. Rules; penalty.

(a) The board of trustees of a school district may adopt rules for the safety and welfare of students, employees, and property and other rules it considers necessary to carry out this subchapter and the governance of the district, including rules providing for the operation and parking of vehicles on school property. The board may adopt and charge a reasonable fee for parking and for providing traffic control.

(b) A law or ordinance regulating traffic on a public highway or street applies to the operation of a vehicle on school property, except as modified by this subchapter.

(c) A person who violates this subchapter or any rule adopted under this subchapter commits an offense. An offense under this section is a Class C misdemeanor.
*(Added by L.1995, chap. 260(1), eff. 5/30/95.)*

### §37.103. Enforcement of rules.

Notwithstanding any other provision of this subchapter, the board of trustees of a school district may authorize any officer commissioned by the board to enforce rules adopted by the board. This subchapter is not intended to restrict the authority of each district to adopt and enforce appropriate rules for the orderly conduct of the district in carrying out its purposes and objectives or the right of separate jurisdiction relating to the conduct of its students and personnel. *(Added by L.1995, chap. 260(1), eff. 5/30/95.)*

### §37.104. Courts having jurisdiction.

The judge of a municipal court of a municipality in which, or any justice of the peace of a county in which, property under the control and jurisdiction of a school district is located may hear and determine criminal cases involving violations of this subchapter or rules adopted under this subchapter. *(Added by L.1995, chap. 260(1), eff. 5/30/95.)*

### §37.105. Unauthorized persons: refusal of entry, ejection, identification.

The board of trustees of a school district or its authorized representative may refuse to allow a person without legitimate business to enter on property under the board's control and may eject any undesirable person from the property on the person's refusal to leave peaceably on request. Identification may be required of any person on the property. *(Added by L.1995, chap. 260(1), eff. 5/30/95.)*

### §37.107. Trespass on school grounds.

An unauthorized person who trespasses on the grounds of any school district of this state commits an offense. An offense under this section is a Class C misdemeanor. *(Added by L.1995, chap. 260(1), eff. 5/30/95.)*

## SUBCHAPTER E. PENAL PROVISIONS

### §37.121. Fraternities, sororities, secret societies, and gangs.

(a) A person commits an offense if the person:

(1) is a member of, pledges to become a member of, joins, or solicits another person to join or pledge to become a member of a public school fraternity, sorority, secret society, or gang; or

(2) is not enrolled in a public school and solicits another person to attend a meeting of a public school fraternity, sorority, secret society, or gang or a meeting at which membership in one of those groups is encouraged.

(b) A school district board of trustees or an educator shall recommend placing in an alternative education program any student under the person's control who violates Subsection (a).

(c) An offense under this section is a Class C misdemeanor.

(d) In this section, "public school fraternity, sorority, secret society, or gang" means an organization composed wholly or in part of students of public primary or secondary schools that seeks to perpetuate itself by taking in additional members from the students enrolled in school on the basis of the decision of its membership rather than on the free choice of a student in the school who is qualified by the rules of the school to fill the special aims of the organization. The term does not include an agency for public welfare, including Boy Scouts, Hi-Y, Girl Reserves, DeMolay, Rainbow Girls, Pan-American Clubs, scholarship societies, or other similar educational organizations sponsored by state or national education authorities.

*(Added by L.1995, chap. 260(1), eff. 5/30/95.)*



### §37.122. Possession of intoxicants on public school grounds.

(a) A person commits an offense if the person possesses an intoxicating beverage for consumption, sale, or distribution while:

(1) on the grounds or in a building of a public school; or

(2) entering or inside any enclosure, field, or stadium where an athletic event sponsored or participated in by a public school of this state is being held.

(b) An officer of this state who sees a person violating this section shall immediately seize the intoxicating beverage and, within a reasonable time, deliver it to the county or district attorney to be held as evidence until the trial of the accused possessor.

(c) An offense under this section is a Class C misdemeanor.

*(Added by L.1995, chap. 260(1), eff. 5/30/95.)*

### §37.123. Disruptive activities.

(a) A person commits an offense if the person, alone or in concert with others, intentionally engages in disruptive activity on the campus or property of any private or public school.

(b) For purposes of this section, disruptive activity is:

(1) obstructing or restraining the passage of persons in an exit, entrance, or hallway of a building without the authorization of the administration of the school;

(2) seizing control of a building or portion of a building to interfere with an administrative, educational, research, or other authorized activity;

(3) preventing or attempting to prevent by force or violence or the threat of force or violence a lawful assembly authorized by the school administration so that a person attempting to participate in the assembly is unable to participate due to the use of force or violence or due to a reasonable fear that force or violence is likely to occur;

(4) disrupting by force or violence or the threat of force or violence a lawful assembly in progress; or

(5) obstructing or restraining the passage of a person at an exit or entrance to the campus or property or preventing or attempting to prevent by force or violence or by threats of force or violence the ingress or egress of a person to or from the property or campus without the authorization of the administration of the school.

(c) An offense under this section is a Class B misdemeanor.

(d) Any person who is convicted the third time of violating this section is ineligible to attend any institution of higher education receiving funds from this state before the second anniversary of the third conviction.

(e) This section may not be construed to infringe on any right of free speech or expression guaranteed by the constitution of the United States or of this state.
*(Added by L.1995, chap. 260(1), eff. 5/30/95.)*

### §37.124. Disruption of classes.

(a) A person commits an offense if the person, on school property or on public property within 500 feet of school property, alone or in concert with others, intentionally disrupts the conduct of classes or other school activities.

(b) An offense under this section is a Class C misdemeanor.

(c) In this section:

(1) "Disrupting the conduct of classes or other school activities" includes:

(A) emitting noise of an intensity that prevents or hinders classroom instruction;

(B) enticing or attempting to entice a student away from a class or other school activity that the student is required to attend;

(C) preventing or attempting to prevent a student from attending a class or other school activity that the student is required to attend; and

(D) entering a classroom without the consent of either the principal or the teacher and, through either acts of misconduct or the use of loud or profane language, disrupting class activities.

(2) "Public property" includes a street, highway, alley, public park, or sidewalk.

(3) "School property" includes a public school campus or school grounds on which a public school is located and any grounds or buildings used by a school for an assembly or other school-sponsored activity.
*(Added by L.1995, chap. 260(1), eff. 5/30/95.)*



### §37.125. Exhibition of firearms.

(a) A person commits an offense if the person, by exhibiting, using, or threatening to exhibit or use a firearm, interferes with the normal use of a building or portion of a campus or of a school bus being used to transport children to or from school-sponsored activities of a private or public school.

(b) An offense under this section is a third degree felony.
*(Added by L.1995, chap. 260(1), eff. 5/30/95.)*

### §37.126. Disruption of transportation.

(a) Except as provided by Section 37.125, a person commits an offense if the person intentionally disrupts, prevents, or interferes with the lawful transportation of children to or from school or an activity sponsored by a school on a vehicle owned or operated by a county or independent school district.

(b) An offense under this section is a Class C misdemeanor.
*(Added by L.1995, chap. 260(1), eff. 5/30/95.)*

## SUBCHAPTER F. HAZING

### §37.151. Definitions.

In this subchapter:

(1) "Educational institution" includes a public or private high school.

(2) "Pledge" means any person who has been accepted by, is considering an offer of membership from, or is in the process of qualifying for membership in an organization.

(3) "Pledging" means any action or activity related to becoming a member of an organization.

(4) "Student" means any person who:

(A) is registered in or in attendance at an educational institution;

(B) has been accepted for admission at the educational institution where the hazing incident occurs; or

(C) intends to attend an educational institution during any of its regular sessions after a period of scheduled vacation.

(5) "Organization" means a fraternity, sorority, association, corporation, order, society, corps, club, or service, social, or similar group, whose members are primarily students.

(6) "Hazing" means any intentional, knowing, or reckless act, occurring on or off the campus of an educational institution, by one person alone or acting with others, directed against a student, that endangers the mental or physical health or safety of a student for the purpose of pledging, being initiated into, affiliating with, holding office in, or maintaining membership in an organization. The term includes:

(A) any type of physical brutality, such as whipping, beating, striking, branding, electronic shocking, placing of a harmful substance on the body, or similar activity;

(B) any type of physical activity, such as sleep deprivation, exposure to the elements, confinement in a small space, calisthenics, or other activity that subjects the student to an unreasonable risk of harm or that adversely affects the mental or physical health or safety of the student;

(C) any activity involving consumption of a food, liquid, alcoholic beverage, liquor, drug, or other substance that subjects the student to an unreasonable risk of harm or that adversely affects the mental or physical health or safety of the student;

(D) any activity that intimidates or threatens the student with ostracism, that subjects the student to extreme mental stress, shame, or humiliation, that adversely affects the mental health or dignity of the student or discourages the student from entering or remaining registered in an educational institution, or that may reasonably be expected to cause a student to leave the organization or the institution rather than submit to acts described in this subdivision; and

(E) any activity that induces, causes, or requires the student to perform a duty or task that involves a violation of the Penal Code.

*(Added by L.1995, chap. 260(1), eff. 5/30/95.)*



## §37.152. Personal hazing offense.

(a) A person commits an offense if the person:

(1) engages in hazing;

(2) solicits, encourages, directs, aids, or attempts to aid another in engaging in hazing;

(3) recklessly permits hazing to occur; or

(4) has firsthand knowledge of the planning of a specific hazing incident involving a student in an educational institution, or has firsthand knowledge that a specific hazing incident has occurred, and knowingly fails to report that knowledge in writing to the dean of students or other appropriate official of the institution.

(b) The offense of failing to report is a Class B misdemeanor.

(c) Any other offense under this section that does not cause serious bodily injury to another is a Class B misdemeanor.

(d) Any other offense under this section that causes serious bodily injury to another is a Class A misdemeanor.

(e) Any other offense under this section that causes the death of another is a state jail felony.

(f) Except if an offense causes the death of a student, in sentencing a person convicted of an offense under this section, the court may require the person to perform community service, subject to the same conditions imposed on a person placed on community supervision under Section 11, Article 42.12, Code of Criminal Procedure, for an appropriate period of time in lieu of confinement in county jail or in lieu of a part of the time the person is sentenced to confinement in county jail.

*(Added by L.1995, chap. 260(1), eff. 5/30/95.)*

## §37.153. Organization hazing offense.

(a) An organization commits an offense if the organization condones or encourages hazing or if an officer or any combination of members, pledges, or alumni of the organization commits or assists in the commission of hazing.

(b) An offense under this section is a misdemeanor punishable by:

(1) a fine of not less than $5,000 nor more than $10,000; or

(2) if the court finds that the offense caused personal injury, property damage, or other loss, a fine of not less than $5,000 nor more than double the amount lost or expenses incurred because of the injury, damage, or loss.

*(Added by L.1995, chap. 260(1), eff. 5/30/95.)*

## §37.154. Consent not a defense.

It is not a defense to prosecution of an offense under this subchapter that the person against whom the hazing was directed consented to or acquiesced in the hazing activity. *(Added by L.1995, chap. 260(1), eff. 5/30/95.)*

## §37.155. Immunity from prosecution available.

In the prosecution of an offense under this subchapter, the court may grant immunity from prosecution for the offense to each person who is subpoenaed to testify for the prosecution and who does testify for the prosecution. Any person reporting a specific hazing incident involving a student in an educational institution to the dean of students or other appropriate official of the institution is immune from civil or criminal liability that might otherwise be incurred or imposed as a result of the report. Immunity extends to participation in any judicial proceeding resulting from the report. A person reporting in bad faith or with malice is not protected by this section. *(Added by L.1995, chap. 260(1), eff. 5/30/95.)*

### §37.156. Offenses in addition to other penal provisions.

This subchapter does not affect or repeal any penal law of this state. This subchapter does not limit or affect the right of an educational institution to enforce its own penalties against hazing. *(Added by L.1995, chap. 260(1), eff. 5/30/95.)*

### §37.157. Reporting by medical authorities.

A doctor or other medical practitioner who treats a student who may have been subjected to hazing activities:

(1) may report the suspected hazing activities to police or other law enforcement officials; and

(2) is immune from civil or other liability that might otherwise be imposed or incurred as a result of the report, unless the report is made in bad faith or with malice.

*(Added by L.1995, chap. 260(1), eff. 5/30/95.)*



## CHAPTER 38. HEALTH AND SAFETY

*(Added by L.1995, chap. 260(1), eff. 5/30/95.)*

*(Selected Sections)*

Section



### §38.004. Child abuse reporting and programs.

(a) The agency shall develop a policy governing the child abuse reports required by Chapter 261, Family Code, of school districts and their employees. The policy must provide for cooperation with law enforcement child abuse investigations without the consent of the child's parents if necessary, including investigations by the Department of Protective and Regulatory Services. Each school district shall adopt the policy.

(b) Each school district shall provide child abuse antivictimization programs in elementary and secondary schools.

*(Added by L.1995, chap. 260(1), eff. 5/30/95.)*

### §38.008. Posting of steroid law notice.

Each school in a school district in which there is a grade level of seven or higher shall post in a conspicuous location in the school gymnasium and each other place in a building where physical education classes are conducted the following notice:

> Anabolic steroids are for medical use only. State law prohibits possessing, dispensing, delivering, or administering an anabolic steroid in any manner not allowed by state law. State law provides that body building, muscle enhancement, or the increase of muscle bulk or strength through the use of an anabolic steroid or human growth hormone by a person who is in good health is not a valid medical purpose. Only a medical doctor may prescribe an anabolic steroid or human growth hormone for a person. A violation of state law concerning anabolic steroids or human growth hormones is a criminal offense punishable by confinement in jail or imprisonment in the institutional division of the Texas Department of Criminal Justice.

*(Added by L.1995, chap. 260(1), eff. 5/30/95.)*

## CHAPTER 51. PROVISIONS GENERALLY APPLICABLE TO HIGHER EDUCATION

*(Selected Sections)*

Section

### §51.921. Posting of steroid law notice.

Each public institution of higher education shall post in a conspicuous location in each gymnasium at the institution the following notice:

> Anabolic steroids and growth hormones are for medical use only. State law prohibits the possession, dispensing, delivery, or administering of an anabolic steroid or growth hormone in any manner not allowed by state law. State law provides that body building, muscle enhancement, or increasing muscle bulk or strength through the use of an anabolic steroid by a person who is in good health is not a valid medical purpose. Only a medical doctor may prescribe an anabolic steroid or human growth hormone for a person. A violation of state law concerning anabolic steroids or human growth hormones is a criminal offense punishable by confinement in jail or imprisonment in the Texas Department of Corrections.

*(Added by L.1989, chap. 403(8), eff. 9/1/89.)*



### §51.935. Disruptive activities.

(a) A person commits an offense if the person, alone or in concert with others, intentionally engages in disruptive activity on the campus or property of an institution of higher education.

(b) For purposes of this section, disruptive activity is activity described by Section 37.123(b).

(c) An offense under this section is a Class B misdemeanor.

(d) Any person who is convicted the third time of violating this section is ineligible to attend any institution of higher education receiving funds from this state before the second anniversary of the third conviction.

(e) This section may not be construed to infringe on any right of free speech or expression guaranteed by the Constitution of the United States or of this state.

*(Added by L.1995, chap. 260(18), eff. 5/30/95.)*

### §51.936. Hazing.

(a) Subchapter F, Chapter 37, applies to hazing at an educational institution under this section.

(b) For purposes of this section, in Subchapter F, Chapter 37, "educational institution" means an institution of higher education.

(c) Each postsecondary educational institution shall distribute to each student during the first three weeks of each semester:

(1) a summary of the provisions of Subchapter F, Chapter 37; and

(2) a list of organizations that have been disciplined for hazing or convicted for hazing on or off the campus of the institution during the preceding three years.

(d) If the institution publishes a general catalogue, student handbook, or similar publication, it shall publish a summary of the provisions of Subchapter F, Chapter 37, in each edition of the publication.

*(Added by L.1995, chap. 260(18), eff. 5/30/95.)*

This page intentionally left blank.

# ELECTION CODE
*(Selected Chapters)*

## CHAPTER 20. VOTER REGISTRATION AGENCIES
*(Added by L.1995, chap. 797(33), eff. 9/1/95.)*
*(Selected Subchapter)*

## SUBCHAPTER C. DEPARTMENT OF PUBLIC SAFETY

Section




### §20.061. Applicability of other provisions.

The other provisions of this chapter apply to the Department of Public Safety except provisions that conflict with this subchapter. *(Added by L.1995, chap. 797(33), eff. 9/1/95.)*

### §20.062. Department forms and procedure.

(a) The Department of Public Safety shall prescribe and use a form and procedure that combines the department's application form for a license or card with an officially prescribed voter registration application form.

(b) The department shall prescribe and use a change of address form and procedure that combines department and voter registration functions. The form must allow a licensee or cardholder to indicate whether the change of address is also to be used for voter registration purposes.

(c) The design, content, and physical characteristics of the department forms must be approved by the secretary of state.

*(Added by L.1995, chap. 797(33), eff. 9/1/95.)*

### §20.063. Registration procedures.

(a) The Department of Public Safety shall provide to each person who applies in person at the department's offices for an original or renewal of a driver's license, a personal identification card, or a duplicate or corrected license or card an opportunity to complete a voter registration application form.

(b) When the department processes a license or card for renewal by mail, the department shall deliver to the applicant by mail a voter registration application form.

(c) A change of address that relates to a license or card and that is submitted to the department in person or by mail serves as a change of address for voter registration unless the licensee or cardholder indicates that the change is not for voter registration purposes. The date of submission of a change of address to a department employee is considered to be the date of submission to the voter registrar for the purpose of determining the effective date of registration only.

(d) If a completed voter registration application submitted to a department employee does not include the applicant's correct driver's license number or personal identification card number, a department employee shall enter the appropriate information on the application. If a completed application does not include the applicant's correct residence address or mailing address, a department employee shall obtain the appropriate information from the applicant and enter the information on the application.

*(Added by L.1995, chap. 797(33); chgd. by L.1997, chap. 454(9), eff. 9/1/97.)*

### §20.064. Declination form not required.

The Department of Public Safety is not required to comply with the procedures prescribed by this chapter relating to the form for a declination of voter registration. *(Added by L.1995, chap. 797(33), eff. 9/1/95.)*

### §20.065. Delivery of applications and changes of address.

At the end of each day a Department of Public Safety office is regularly open for business, the manager of the office shall deliver by mail or in person to the voter registrar of the county in which the office is located each completed voter registration application and applicable change of address submitted to a department employee. *(Added by L.1995, chap. 797(33), eff. 9/1/95.)*

# TITLE 16. MISCELLANEOUS PROVISIONS
*(Selected Chapter)*

## CHAPTER 276. MISCELLANEOUS OFFENSES AND OTHER PROVISIONS
*(Selected Section)*



### §276.005. Voter's privilege from arrest.

A voter may not be arrested during the voter's attendance at an election and while going to and returning from a polling place except for treason, a felony, or a breach of peace.

# FAMILY CODE

## TITLE 1. THE MARRIAGE RELATIONSHIP

*(Added by L.1997, chap. 7(1), eff. 4/17/97. Former Title 1 repealed by L.1997, chap. 7(3), eff. 4/17/97.)*

## SUBTITLE C. DISSOLUTION OF MARRIAGE

## CHAPTER 6. SUIT FOR DISSOLUTION OF MARRIAGE

### SUBCHAPTER E. FILING SUIT

*(Selected Section)*





**§6.405. Protective order.**

(a) The petition in a suit for dissolution of a marriage must state whether a protective order under Title 4 is in effect or if an application for a protective order is pending with regard to the parties to the suit.

(b) The petitioner shall attach to the petition a copy of each protective order issued under Title 4 in which one of the parties to the suit was the applicant and the other party was the respondent without regard to the date of the order. If a copy of the protective order is not available at the time of filing, the petition must state that a copy of the order will be filed with the court before any hearing. *(Added by L.1997, chap. 7(1); chgd. by L.1999, chap. 62(6.04), eff. 9/1/99.)*

### SUBCHAPTER F. TEMPORARY ORDERS

*(Selected Sections)*



**§6.501. Temporary restraining order.**

(a) After the filing of a suit for dissolution of a marriage, on the motion of a party or on the court's own motion, the court may grant a temporary restraining order without notice to the adverse party for the preservation of the property and for the protection of the parties as necessary, including an order prohibiting one or both parties from:

(1) intentionally communicating by telephone or in writing with the other party by use of vulgar, profane, obscene, or indecent language or in a coarse or offensive manner, with intent to annoy or alarm the other;

(2) threatening the other, by telephone or in writing, to take unlawful action against any person, intending by this action to annoy or alarm the other;

(3) placing a telephone call, anonymously, at an unreasonable hour, in an offensive and repetitious manner, or without a legitimate purpose of communication with the intent to annoy or alarm the other;

(4) intentionally, knowingly, or recklessly causing bodily injury to the other or to a child of either party;

(5) threatening the other or a child of either party with imminent bodily injury;

(6) intentionally, knowingly, or recklessly destroying, removing, concealing, encumbering, transferring, or otherwise harming or reducing the value of the property of the parties or either party with intent to obstruct the authority of the court to order a division of the estate of the parties in a manner that the court deems just and right, having due regard for the rights of each party and any children of the marriage;

(7) intentionally falsifying a writing or record relating to the property of either party;

(8) intentionally misrepresenting or refusing to disclose to the other party or to the court, on proper request, the existence, amount, or location of any property of the parties or either party;

(9) intentionally or knowingly damaging or destroying the tangible property of the parties or either party; or

(10) intentionally or knowingly tampering with the tangible property of the parties or either party and causing pecuniary loss or substantial inconvenience to the other.

(b) A temporary restraining order under this subchapter may not include a provision:

(1) the subject of which is a requirement, appointment, award, or other order listed in Section 64.104, Civil Practice and Remedies Code; or

(2) that:

(A) excludes a spouse from occupancy of the residence where that spouse is living except as provided in a protective order made in accordance with Title 4;

(B) prohibits a party from spending funds for reasonable and necessary living expenses; or

(C) prohibits a party from engaging in acts reasonable and necessary to conduct that party's usual business and occupation.

*(Added by L.1997, chap. 7(1); chgd. by L.1999, chap. 1081(6), eff. 9/1/99.)*

### §6.504. Protective orders.

On the motion of a party to a suit for dissolution of a marriage, the court may render a protective order as provided by Subtitle B, Title 4. *(Added by L.1997, chap. 7(1), eff. 4/17/97; chgd. by L.1997, chap. 1193(1), eff. 9/1/97.)*

### §6.506. Contempt.

The violation of a temporary restraining order, temporary injunction, or other temporary order issued under this subchapter is punishable as contempt. *(Added by L.1997, chap. 7(1), eff. 4/17/97.)*



# TITLE 2. PARENT AND CHILD

*(Repealed by L.1995, chap. 20(2), eff. 4/20/95. See other title 2 below.)*

## CHAPTER 17. EMERGENCY PROCEDURES IN SUIT BY GOVERNMENTAL ENTITY

*(Selected Section)*



*(Editor's Note: The following subsection of Section 17.03, Family Code, was amended by the 1995 State Legislature, although such section was repealed by L.1995, chap. 20(2), eff. 4/20/95.)*

### §17.03. Taking possession of a child without a court order.† [*Taking custody of child without a court order.*] *(Subsection (a) only.)*

(a) An authorized representative of the Department of Protective and Regulatory Services, a law enforcement officer, or a juvenile probation officer may take possession of a child without a court order under the following conditions and no others:

(1) upon discovery of a child in a situation of danger to the child's physical health or safety when the sole purpose is to deliver the child without unnecessary delay to the parent, managing conservator, possessory conservator, guardian, caretaker, or custodian who is presently entitled to possession of the child;

(2) upon the voluntary delivery of the child by the parent, managing conservator, possessory conservator, guardian, caretaker, or custodian who is currently entitled to possession of the child;

(3) upon personal knowledge of facts which would lead a person of ordinary prudence and caution to believe that there is an immediate danger to the physical health or safety of the child and that there is no time to obtain a temporary restraining order or attachment under Section 17.02 of this code;

(4) upon information furnished by another which has been corroborated by personal knowledge of facts and all of which taken together would lead a person of ordinary prudence and caution to believe that there is an immediate danger to the physical health or safety of the child and that there is no time to obtain a temporary restraining order or attachment under Section 17.02 of this code;

(5) upon personal knowledge of facts that would lead a person of ordinary prudence and caution to believe that the child has been the victim of sexual abuse and that there is no time to obtain a temporary restraining order or attachment under Section 17.02 of this code; or

(6) upon information furnished by another that has been corroborated by personal knowledge of facts and all of which taken together would lead a person of ordinary prudence and caution to

believe that the child has been the victim of sexual abuse and that there is no time to obtain a temporary restraining order or attachment under Section 17.02 of this code.
*(Chgd. by L.1995, chap. 76(8.062), eff. 9/1/95.)*
*(Section 17.03 repealed by L.1995, chap. 20(2), eff. 4/20/95.)*

# CHAPTER 34. REPORT OF CHILD ABUSE

## SUBCHAPTER A. GENERAL PROVISIONS
*(Selected Sections)*





*(Editor's Note: The following subsections of Section 34.02, Family Code, were amended by the 1995 State Legislature, although such section was repealed by L.1995, chap. 20(2), eff. 4/20/95.)*

**§34.02. Contents of report: to whom made.† [*Contents of report.*]** *(Subsections (a) and (c) only.)*

(a) Nonaccusatory reports reflecting the reporter's belief that a child has been or will be abused or neglected, or has died of abuse or neglect, has violated the compulsory school attendance laws on three or more occasions, or has, on three or more occasions, been voluntarily absent from his home without the consent of his parent or guardian for a substantial length of time or without the intent to return shall be made to:

(1) any local or state law enforcement agency;

(2) the Department of Protective and Regulatory Services;

(3) the state agency that operates, licenses, certifies, or registers the facility in which the alleged abuse or neglected occurred; or

(4) the agency designated by the court to be responsible for the protection of children.

(c) All reports received by any local or state law enforcement agency that involve a person responsible for a child's care, custody, or welfare shall be referred to the Department of Protective and Regulatory Services or to the agency designated by the court to be responsible for the protection of children. The department or designated agency immediately shall notify the appropriate state or local law enforcement agency of any report it receives, other than from a law enforcement agency, that concerns the suspected abuse or neglect of a child or death of a child from abuse or neglect. If the report relates to a child in a facility operated, licensed, certified, or registered by a state agency, the department shall also refer the report to the agency for investigation. If the department initiates an investigation and determines that the abuse or neglect does not involve a person responsible for the child's care, custody or welfare, the department shall refer to report to a law enforcement agency for further investigation.
*(Chgd. by L.1995, chap. 76(8.066), eff. 9/1/95.)*
*(Section 34.02 repealed by L.1995, chap. 20(2), eff. 4/20/95.)*

*(Editor's Note: The following subsection of Section 34.05, Family Code, was amended by the 1995 State Legislature, although such section was repealed by L.1995, chap. 20(2), eff. 4/20/95.)*

**§34.05. Investigation and report of receiving agency.** *(Subsection (a) only.)*

(a) Unless the report alleges that the abuse or neglect occurred in a facility operated, licensed, certified, or registered by another state agency, the Department of Protective and Regulatory Services or the agency designated by the court to be responsible for the protection of children shall make a thorough investigation promptly after receiving either the oral or written report of child abuse or neglect by a person responsible for a child's care, custody, or welfare. If the report is anonymous, the department shall make the investigation after determining that there is some evidence to corroborate the report as prescribed by Section 34.053 of this code. If the report alleges that the abuse or neglect occurred in a facility operated, licensed, certified, or registered by another state agency, that agency shall investigate the report as prescribed by Subchapter B of this chapter. If the report alleges child abuse or neglect in a location other than a facility operated, licensed, certified, or registered by a state agency and by a person other than a person responsible for a child's care, custody, or welfare, the department is not required to investigate the report. The appropriate state or local law enforcement agency shall investigate that report if that agency

determines an investigation should be conducted. The department may assign priorities to investigations based on the severity and immediacy of the alleged harm to the child. If the department establishes a priority system, the department shall adopt the system by rule. The primary purpose of the investigation shall be the protection of the child.
*(Chgd. by L.1995, chap. 76(8.067), eff. 9/1/95.)*
*(Section 34.05 repealed by L.1995, chap. 20(2), eff. 4/20/95.)*

*(Editor's Note: The following Section 34.055, Family Code, was amended by the 1995 State Legislature, although such section was repealed by L.1995, chap. 20(2), eff. 4/20/95.)*

### §34.055. Notice of interview or examination.

If during an investigation under this subchapter a representative of the Department of Protective and Regulatory Services or of the agency designated by the court to be responsible for the protection of children conducts an interview with or an examination of a child, the department or other agency must make a reasonable effort within 24 hours after the interview or examination to notify each parent of the child and the child's legal guardian if one has been appointed that the interview or examination was conducted. *(Chgd. by L.1995, chap. 76(8.071), eff. 9/1/95.)*
*(Section 34.055 repealed by L.1995, chap. 20(2), eff. 4/20/95)*



# TITLE 2. CHILD IN RELATION TO THE FAMILY

*(Added by L.1995, chap. 20(1), eff. 4/20/95.*
*See other title 2, above.)*

## SUBTITLE A. LIMITATIONS OF MINORITY

## CHAPTER 32. CONSENT TO TREATMENT OF CHILD BY NON-PARENT OR CHILD

## SUBCHAPTER A. CONSENT TO MEDICAL, DENTAL, PSYCHOLOGICAL, AND SURGICAL TREATMENT



### §32.001. Consent by non-parent.

(a) The following persons may consent to medical, dental, psychological, and surgical treatment of a child when the person having the right to consent as otherwise provided by law cannot be contacted and that person has not given actual notice to the contrary:

(1) a grandparent of the child;

(2) an adult brother or sister of the child;

(3) an adult aunt or uncle of the child;

(4) an educational institution in which the child is enrolled that has received written authorization to consent from a person having the right to consent;

(5) an adult who has actual care, control, and possession of the child and has written authorization to consent from a person having the right to consent;

(6) a court having jurisdiction over a suit affecting the parent-child relationship of which the child is the subject;

(7) an adult responsible for the actual care, control, and possession of a child under the jurisdiction of a juvenile court or committed by a juvenile court to the care of an agency of the state or county; or

(8) a peace officer who has lawfully taken custody of a minor, if the peace officer has reasonable grounds to believe the minor is in need of immediate medical treatment.

(b) The Texas Youth Commission may consent to the medical, dental, psychological, and surgical treatment of a child committed to it under Title 3 when the person having the right to consent has been contacted and that person has not given actual notice to the contrary.

(c) This section does not apply to consent for the immunization of a child.

(d) A person who consents to the medical treatment of a minor under Subsection (a)(7) or (8) is immune from liability for damages resulting from the examination or treatment of the minor, except to the extent of the person's own acts of negligence. A physician or dentist licensed to practice in this state, or a hospital or medical facility at which a minor is treated is immune from liability for damages resulting from the examination or treatment of a minor under this section, except to the extent of the person's own acts of negligence.
*(Added by L.1995, chap. 20(1), eff. 4/20/95; chgd. by L.1995, chap. 751(5), eff. 9/1/95.)*

## §32.002. Consent form.

Consent to medical treatment under Sections 35.01 and 35.011 of this code shall be in writing, signed by the person giving consent, and given to the doctor, hospital, or other medical facility that administers the treatment.

(b) The consent must include:

(1) the name of the child;

(2) the name of one or both parents, if known, and the name of any managing conservator or guardian of the child;

(3) the name of the person giving consent and the person's relationship to the child;

(4) a statement of the nature of the medical treatment to be given; and

(5) the date the treatment is to begin.

*(Chgd. by L.1995, chap. 20(1), 123(4), eff. 4/20/95, 9/1/95, respectively).*



## §32.003. Consent to treatment by child.

(a) A child may consent to medical, dental, psychological, and surgical treatment for the child by a licensed physician or dentist if the child:

(1) is on active duty with the armed services of the United States of America;

(2) is:

(A) 16 years of age or older and resides separate and apart from the child's parents, managing conservator, or guardian, with or without the consent of the parents, managing conservator, or guardian and regardless of the duration of the residence; and

(B) managing the child's own financial affairs, regardless of the source of the income;

(3) consents to the diagnosis and treatment of an infectious, contagious, or communicable disease that is required by law or a rule to be reported by the licensed physician or dentist to a local health officer or the Texas Department of Health, including all diseases within the scope of Section 81.041, Health and Safety Code;

(4) is unmarried and pregnant and consents to hospital, medical, or surgical treatment, other than abortion, related to the pregnancy;

(5) consents to examination and treatment for drug or chemical addiction, drug or chemical dependency, or any other condition directly related to drug or chemical use; or

(6) is unmarried and has actual custody of the child's biological child and consents to medical, dental, psychological, or surgical treatment for the child.

(b) Consent by a child to medical, dental, psychological, and surgical treatment under this section is not subject to disaffirmance because of minority.

(c) Consent of the parents, managing conservator, or guardian of a child is not necessary in order to authorize hospital, medical, surgical, or dental care under this section.

(d) A licensed physician, dentist, or psychologist may, with or without the consent of a child who is a patient, advise the parents, managing conservator, or guardian of the child of the treatment given to or needed by the child.

(e) A physician, dentist, psychologist, hospital, or medical facility is not liable for the examination and treatment of a child under this section except for the provider's or the facility's own acts of negligence.

(f) A physician, dentist, psychologist, hospital, or medical facility may rely on the written statement of the child containing the grounds on which the child has capacity to consent to the child's medical treatment.

*(Added by L.1995, chap. 20(1), eff. 4/20/95; chgd. by L.1995, chap. 751(6), eff. 9/1/95.)*

## §32.004. Consent to counseling.

(a) A child may consent to counseling for:

(1) suicide prevention;

(2) chemical addiction or dependency; or

(3) sexual, physical, or emotional abuse.

(b) A licensed or certified physician, psychologist, counselor, or social worker having reasonable grounds to believe that a child has been sexually, physically, or emotionally abused, is contemplating suicide, or is suffering from a chemical or drug addiction or dependency may:

(1) counsel the child without the consent of the child's parents or, if applicable, managing conservator or guardian;

(2) with or without the consent of the child who is a client, advise the child's parents or, if applicable, managing conservator or guardian of the treatment given to or needed by the child; and

(3) rely on the written statement of the child containing the grounds on which the child has capacity to consent to the child's own treatment under this section.

(c) Unless consent is obtained as otherwise allowed by law, a physician, psychologist, counselor, or social worker may not counsel a child if consent is prohibited by a court order.

(d) A physician, psychologist, counselor, or social worker counseling a child under this section is not liable for damages except for damages resulting from the person's negligence or wilful misconduct.

(e) A parent, or, if applicable, managing conservator or guardian, who has not consented to counseling treatment of the child is not obligated to compensate a physician, psychologist, counselor, or social worker for counseling services rendered under this section.
*(Added by L.1995, chap. 20(1), eff. 4/20/95.)*



### §32.005. Examination without consent of abuse or neglect of child.

(a) Except as provided by Subsection (c), a physician, dentist, or psychologist having reasonable grounds to believe that a child's physical or mental condition has been adversely affected by abuse or neglect may examine the child without the consent of the child, the child's parents, or other person authorized to consent to treatment under this subchapter.

(b) An examination under this section may include X-rays, blood tests, and penetration of tissue necessary to accomplish those tests.

(c) Unless consent is obtained as otherwise allowed by law, a physician, dentist, or psychologist may not examine a child:

(1) 16 years of age or older who refuses to consent; or

(2) for whom consent is prohibited by a court order.

(d) A physician, dentist, or psychologist examining a child under this section is not liable for damages except for damages resulting from the physician's or dentist's negligence.
*(Added by L.1995, chap. 20(1), eff. 4/20/95.)*

## SUBTITLE B. PARENTAL LIABILITY

## CHAPTER 41. LIABILITY OF PARENTS FOR CONDUCT OF CHILD

*(Selected Sections)*

Section



### §41.001. Liability.

A parent or other person who has the duty of control and reasonable discipline of a child is liable for any property damage proximately caused by:

(1) the negligent conduct of the child if the conduct is reasonably attributable to the negligent failure of the parent or other persons to exercise that duty; or

(2) the wilful and malicious conduct of a child who is at least 12 years of age but under 18 years of age.
*(Added by L.1995, chap. 20(1), eff. 4/20/95.)*

### §41.002. Limit of damages.

Recovery for damage caused by wilful and malicious conduct is limited to actual damages, not to exceed $25,000 per occurrence, plus court costs and reasonable attorney's fees. *(Chgd. by L.1997, chap. 783(1), eff. 9/1/97.)*

### §41.0025. Liability for property damage to an inn or hotel.

(a) Notwithstanding Section 41.002, recovery of damages by an inn or hotel for wilful and malicious conduct is limited to actual damages, not to exceed $25,000 per occurrence, plus court costs and reasonable attorney's fees.

(b) In this section "occurrence" means one incident on a single day in one hotel room. The term does not include incidents in separate rooms or incidents that occur on different days.
*(Added by L.1997, chap. 40(1), eff. 9/1/97.)*

## SUBTITLE C. CHANGE OF NAME

## CHAPTER 45. CHANGE OF NAME





### §45.101. Who may file; venue.

An adult may file a petition requesting a change of name in the county of the adult's place of residence. *(Chgd. by L.1995, chap. 20(1), eff. 4/20/95.)*

### Sec. 45.102. Requirements of petition.

(a) A petition to change the name of an adult must be verified and include:

(1) the present name and place of residence of the petitioner;

(2) the full name requested for the petitioner;

(3) the reason the change in name is requested; and

(4) whether the petitioner has been the subject of a final felony conviction.

(b) The petition must include each of the following or a reasonable explanation why the required information is not included:

(1) the petitioner's:

(A) full name;

(B) sex;

(C) race;

(D) date of birth;

(E) driver's license number for any driver's license issued in the 10 years preceding the date of the petition;

(F) social security number; and

(G) assigned FBI number, state identification number, if known, or any other reference number in a criminal history record system that identifies the petitioner;

(2) any offense above the grade of Class C misdemeanor for which the petitioner has been charged; and

(3) the case number and the court if a warrant was issued or a charging instrument was filed or presented for an offense listed in Subsection (b)(2).
*(Chgd. by L.1995, chap. 20(1), eff. 4/20/95.)*

### §45.103. Order.

(a) The court shall order a change of name under this subchapter for a person other than a person with a final felony conviction if the change is in the interest or to the benefit of the petitioner and in the interest of the public.

(b) A court may order a change of name under this subchapter for a person with a final felony conviction if, in addition to the requirements of Subsection (a), the person has:

(1) received a certificate of discharge by the pardons and paroles division of the Texas Department of Criminal Justice or completed a period of probation ordered by a court and not less than two years have passed from the date of the receipt of discharge or completion of probation; or

(2) been pardoned.
*(Chgd. by L.1995, chap. 20(1), eff. 4/20/95.)*

### §45.104. Liabilities and rights unaffected.

A change of name under this subchapter does not release a person from liability incurred in that person's previous name or defeat any right the person had in the person's previous name. *(Chgd. by L.1995, chap. 20(1), eff. 4/20/95.)*

# TITLE 3. JUVENILE JUSTICE CODE

*(Heading chgd. by L.1995, chap. 262(1), eff. 1/1/96.)*

## CHAPTER 51. GENERAL PROVISIONS

| Section | |
|---|---|
| 51.01. | Purpose and interpretation. |
| 51.02. | Definitions. |
| 51.03. | Delinquent conduct; conduct indicating a need for supervision.† [*Delinquent conduct: conduct suggesting a need for supervision.*] |
| 51.031. | Habitual felony conduct. |
| 51.04. | Jurisdiction. |
| 51.041. | Jurisdiction after appeal. |
| 51.0411. | Jurisdiction for transfer or release hearing. |
| 51.042. | Objection to jurisdiction because of age of the child. |
| 51.045. | Juries in county courts at law. |
| 51.05. | Court sessions and facilities. |
| 51.06. | Venue. |
| 51.07. | Transfer to another county.† [*Transfer between counties.*] |
| 51.08. | Transfer from criminal court. |
| 51.09. | Waiver of rights. |
| 51.095. | Admissibility of a statement of a child. |
| 51.10. | Right to assistance of attorney; compensation.† [*Right to attorney's assistance; payment.*] |
| 51.11. | Guardian ad litem. |
| 51.115. | Attendance at hearing; parent or other guardian. |
| 51.116. | Right to reemployment. |
| 51.12. | Place and conditions of detention. |
| 51.13. | Effect of adjudication or disposition. |
| 51.14, 51.15. | *(Repealed.)* |
| 51.151. | Polygraph examination.† [*Polygraph test.*] |
| 51.16. | *(Repealed.)* |
| 51.17. | Procedure and evidence. |
| 51.18. | Election between juvenile court and alternate juvenile court. |
| 51.19. | Limitation periods. |
| 51.20. | Physical or mental examination. |

### §51.01. Purpose and interpretation.

This title shall be construed to effectuate the following public purposes:

(1) to provide for the protection of the public and public safety;

(2) consistent with the protection of the public and public safety:

(A) to promote the concept of punishment for criminal acts;

(B) to remove, where appropriate, the taint of criminality from children committing certain unlawful acts; and

(C) to provide treatment, training, and rehabilitation that emphasizes the accountability and responsibility of both the parent and the child for the child's conduct;

(3) to provide for the care, the protection, and the wholesome moral, mental, and physical development of children coming within its provisions;

(4) to protect the welfare of the community and to control the commission of unlawful acts by children;

(5) to achieve the foregoing purposes in a family environment whenever possible, separating the child from the child's parents only when necessary for the child's welfare or in the interest of public safety and when a child is removed from the child's family, to give the child the care that should be provided by parents; and

(6) to provide a simple judicial procedure through which the provisions of this title are executed and enforced and in which the parties are assured a fair hearing and their constitutional and other legal rights recognized and enforced.
*(Chgd. by L.1995, chap. 262(2), eff. 1/1/96.)*

## §51.02. Definitions.

In this title:

(1) "Aggravated controlled substance felony" means an offense under Subchapter D, Chapter 481, Health and Safety Code, that is punishable by:

(A) a minimum term of confinement that is longer than the minimum term of confinement for a felony of the first degree; or

(B) a maximum fine that is greater than the maximum fine for a felony of the first degree.

(2) "Child" means a person who is:

(A) ten years of age or older and under 17 years of age; or

(B) seventeen years of age or older and under 18 years of age who is alleged or found to have engaged in delinquent conduct or conduct indicating a need for supervision as a result of acts committed before becoming 17 years of age.

(3) "Custodian" means the adult with whom the child resides.

(4) "Guardian" means the person who, under court order, is the guardian of the person of the child or the public or private agency with whom the child has been placed by a court.

(5) "Judge" or "juvenile court judge" means the judge of a juvenile court.

(6) "Juvenile court" means a court designated under Section 51.04 of this code to exercise jurisdiction over proceedings under this title.

(7) "Law-enforcement officer" means a peace officer as defined by Article 2.12, Code of Criminal Procedure.

(8) "Nonoffender" means a child who:

(A) is subject to jurisdiction of a court under abuse, dependency, or neglect statutes under Title 5 for reasons other than legally prohibited conduct of the child; or

(B) has been taken into custody and is being held solely for deportation out of the United States.

(9) "Parent" means the mother, the father whether or not the child is legitimate, or an adoptive parent, but does not include a parent whose parental rights have been terminated.

(10) "Party" means the state, a child who is the subject of proceedings under this subtitle, or the child's parent, spouse, guardian, or guardian ad litem.

(11) "Prosecuting attorney" means the county attorney, district attorney, or other attorney who regularly serves in a prosecutory capacity in a juvenile court.

(12) "Referral to juvenile court" means the referral of a child or a child's case to the office or official, including an intake officer or probation officer, designated by the juvenile court to process children within the juvenile justice system.

(13) "Secure correctional facility" means any public or private residential facility, including an alcohol or other drug treatment facility, that:

(A) includes construction fixtures designed to physically restrict the movements and activities of juveniles or other individuals held in lawful custody in the facility; and

(B) is used for the placement of any juvenile who has been adjudicated as having committed an offense, any nonoffender, or any other individual convicted of a criminal offense.

(14) "Secure detention facility" means any public or private residential facility that:

(A) includes construction fixtures designed to physically restrict the movements and activities of juveniles or other individuals held in lawful custody in the facility; and

(B) is used for the temporary placement of any juvenile who is accused of having committed an offense, any nonoffender, or any other individual accused of having committed a criminal offense.

(15) "Status offender" means a child who is accused, adjudicated, or convicted for conduct that would not, under state law, be a crime if committed by an adult, including:

(A) truancy under Section 51.03(b)(2);

(B) running away from home under Section 51.03(b)(3);

(C) a fineable only offense under Section 51.03(b)(1) transferred to the juvenile court under Section 51.08(b), but only if the conduct constituting the offense would not have been criminal if engaged in by an adult;

(D) failure to attend school under Section 25.094, Education Code;

(E) a violation of standards of student conduct as described by Section 51.03(b)(5);

(F) a violation of a juvenile curfew ordinance or order;

(G) a violation of a provision of the Alcoholic Beverage Code applicable to minors only; or

(H) a violation of any other fineable only offense under Section 8.07(a)(4) or (5), Penal Code, but only if the conduct constituting the offense would not have been criminal if engaged in by an adult.

(16) "Traffic offense" means:

(A) a violation of a penal statute cognizable under Chapter 729, Transportation Code, except for:

(i) conduct constituting an offense under Section 550.021, Transportation Code;

(ii) conduct constituting an offense punishable as a Class B misdemeanor under Section 550.022, Transportation Code; or

(iii) conduct constituting an offense punishable as a Class B misdemeanor under Section 550.024, Transportation Code; or

(B) a violation of a motor vehicle traffic ordinance of an incorporated city or town in this state.

(17) "Valid court order" means a court order entered under Section 54.04 concerning a child adjudicated to have engaged in conduct indicating a need for supervision as a status offender. *(Chgd. by L.1995, chap. 262(3); L.1997, chaps. 165(6.06), (30.182); 822(2); 1013(13); 1086(41), (47), eff. 9/1/97, 6/18/97, 9/1/97, 9/1/97, respectively.)*



### §51.03. Delinquent conduct; conduct indicating a need for supervision.† [*Delinquent conduct: conduct suggesting a need for supervision.*]

(a) Delinquent conduct is:

(1) conduct, other than a traffic offense, that violates a penal law of this state or of the United States punishable by imprisonment or by confinement in jail;

(2) conduct that violates a reasonable and lawful order of a juvenile court entered under Section 54.04 or 54.05 of this code, except an order prohibiting the following conduct:

(A) a violation of the penal laws of this state of the grade of misdemeanor that is punishable by fine only or a violation of the penal ordinances of any political subdivision of this state;

(B) the unexcused voluntary absence of a child from school; or

(C) the voluntary absence of a child from his home without the consent of his parent or guardian for a substantial length of time or without intent to return;

(3) conduct that violates a lawful order of a municipal court or justice court under circumstances that would constitute contempt of that court;

(4) conduct that violates Section 49.04, 49.05, 49.06, 49.07, or 49.08, Penal Code; or

(5) conduct that violates Section 106.041, Alcoholic Beverage Code, relating to driving under the influence of alcohol by a minor.

(b) Conduct indicating a need for supervision is:

(1) subject to Subsection (f) of this section, conduct, other than a traffic offense, that violates:

(A) the penal laws of this state of the grade of misdemeanor that are punishable by fine only; or

(B) the penal ordinances of any political subdivision of this state;

(2) the unexcused voluntary absence of a child on 10 or more days or parts of days within a six-month period or three or more days or parts of days within a four-week period from school without the consent of his parents;

(3) the voluntary absence of a child from his home without the consent of his parent or guardian for a substantial length of time or without intent to return;

(4) conduct prohibited by city ordinance or by state law involving the inhalation of the fumes or vapors of paint and other protective coatings or glue and other adhesives and the volatile chemicals itemized in Section 484.002, Health and Safety Code;

(5) an act that violates a school district's previously communicated written standards of student conduct for which the child has been expelled under Section 37.007(c), Education Code; or

(6) conduct that violates a reasonable and lawful order of a court entered under Section 264.305.

(c) Nothing in this title prevents criminal proceedings against a child for perjury.

(d) For the purpose of Subsection (b)(2) of this section an absence is excused when the absence results from:

(1) illness of the child;

(2) illness or death in the family of the child;

(3) quarantine of the child and family;

(4) weather or road conditions making travel dangerous;

(5) an absence approved by a teacher, principal, or superintendent of the school in which the child is enrolled; or

(6) circumstances found reasonable and proper.

(e) For the purposes of Subdivisions (2) and (3) of Subsection (b) of this section, "child" does not include a person who is married, divorced, or widowed.

(f) Conduct described under Subsection (b)(1) of this section, other than conduct that violates Section 49.02, Penal Code, prohibiting public intoxication, does not constitute conduct indicating a need for supervision unless the child has been referred to the juvenile court under Section 51.08(b) of this code.

*(Chgd. by L.1989, chaps. 1100(3.02), 1245(1), (4); L.1991, chaps. 14(284)(35), 16(7.02), 169(1); L.1993, chap. 46(1); L.1995, chaps. 76(14.30), 262(4); L.1997, chaps. 165(6.07), 1013(14), 1015(15), 1086(1), eff. 9/1/97, 9/1/97, 6/19/97, 9/1/97, respectively.)*

## §51.031. Habitual felony conduct.

(a) Habitual felony conduct is conduct violating a penal law of the grade of felony, other than a state jail felony, if:

(1) the child who engaged in the conduct has at least two previous final adjudications as having engaged in delinquent conduct violating a penal law of the grade of felony;

(2) the second previous final adjudication is for conduct that occurred after the date the first previous adjudication became final; and

(3) all appeals relating to the previous adjudications considered under Subdivisions (1) and (2) have been exhausted.

(b) For purposes of this section, an adjudication is final if the child is placed on probation or committed to the Texas Youth Commission.

(c) An adjudication based on conduct that occurred before January 1, 1996, may not be considered in a disposition made under this section.

*(Added by L.1995, chap. 262(5); chgd. by L.1997, chap. 1086(2), eff. 9/1/97.)*



## §51.04. Jurisdiction.

(a) This title covers the proceedings in all cases involving the delinquent conduct or conduct indicating a need for supervision engaged in by a person who was a child within the meaning of this title at the time he engaged in the conduct, and the juvenile court has exclusive original jurisdiction over proceedings under this title.

(b) In each county, the county's juvenile board shall designate one or more district, criminal district, domestic relations, juvenile, or county courts or county courts at law as the juvenile court, subject to Subsections (c) and (d) of this section.

(c) If the county court is designated as a juvenile court, at least one other court shall be designated as the juvenile court. A county court does not have jurisdiction of a proceeding involving a petition approved by a grand jury under Section 53.045 of this code.

(d) If the judge of a court designated in Subsection (b) or (c) of this section is not an attorney licensed in this state, there shall also be designated an alternate court, the judge of which is an attorney licensed in this state.

(e) A designation made under Subsection (b) or (c) of this section may be changed from time to time by the authorized boards or judges for the convenience of the people and the welfare of children. However, there must be at all times a juvenile court designated for each county. It is the intent of the legislature that in selecting a court to be the juvenile court of each county, the selection shall be made as far as practicable so that the court designated as the juvenile court will be one which is presided over by a judge who has a sympathetic understanding of the problems of child welfare and that changes in the designation of juvenile courts be made only when the best interest of the public requires it.

(f) If the judge of the juvenile court or any alternate judge named under Subsection (b) or (c) is not in the county or is otherwise unavailable, any magistrate may make a determination under Section 53.02(f) or may conduct the detention hearing provided for in Section 54.01.

(g) The juvenile board, or if there is no juvenile board, the juvenile court, may appoint a referee to make determinations under Section 53.02(f) or to conduct hearings under this title. The referee shall be an attorney licensed to practice law in this state and shall comply with Section 54.10. Payment of any referee services shall be provided from county funds.

*(Chgd. by L.1993, chap. 168(4); L.1999, chap. 232(2), eff. 9/1/99.)*

## §51.041. Jurisdiction after appeal.

The court retains jurisdiction over a person, without regard to the age of the person, for conduct engaged in by the person before becoming 17 years of age if, as a result of an appeal by the person under Chapter 56 of an order of the court, the order is reversed or modified and the case remanded to the court by the appellate court. *(Added by L.1995, chap. 262(6), eff. 1/1/96.)*

## §51.0411. Jurisdiction for transfer or release hearing.

The court retains jurisdiction over a person, without regard to the age of the person, who is referred to the court under Section 54.11 for transfer to the Texas Department of Criminal Justice or release under supervision. *(Added by L.1997, chap. 1086(3), eff. 9/1/97.)*

## §51.042. Objection to jurisdiction because of age of the child.

(a) A child who objects to the jurisdiction of the court over the child because of the age of the child must raise the objection at the adjudication hearing or discretionary transfer hearing, if any.

(b) A child who does not object as provided by Subsection (a) waives any right to object to the jurisdiction of the court because of the age of the child at a later hearing or on appeal.
*(Added by L.1995, chap. 262(6), eff. 1/1/96.)*

## §51.045. Juries in county courts at law.

If a provision of this title requires a jury of 12 persons, that provision prevails over any other law that limits the number of members of a jury in a particular county court at law. The state and the defense are entitled to the same number of peremptory challenges allowed in a district court.

## §51.05. Court sessions and facilities.

(a) The juvenile court shall be deemed in session at all times. Suitable quarters shall be provided by the commissioners court of each county for the hearing of cases and for the use of the judge, the probation officer, and other employees of the court.

(b) The juvenile court and the juvenile board shall report annually to the commissioners court on the suitability of the quarters and facilities of the juvenile court and may make recommendations for their improvement.

## §51.06. Venue.

(a) A proceeding under this title shall be commenced in

(1) the county in which the alleged delinquent conduct or conduct indicating a need for supervision occurred; or

(2) the county in which the child resides at the time the petition is filed, but only if:

(A) the child was under probation supervision in that county at the time of the commission of the delinquent conduct or conduct indicating a need for supervision;

(B) it cannot be determined in which county the delinquent conduct or conduct indicating a need for supervision occurred; or

(C) the county in which the child resides agrees to accept the case for prosecution, in writing, prior to the case being sent to the county of residence for prosecution.

(b) An application for a writ of habeas corpus brought by or on behalf of a person who has been committed to an institution under the jurisdiction of the Texas Youth Commission and which attacks the validity of the judgment of commitment shall be brought in the county in which the court that entered the judgment of commitment is located.
*(Chgd. by L.1995, chap. 262(7); L.1999, chap. 488(1), eff. 9/1/99.)*

## §51.07. Transfer to another county.† [*Transfer between counties.*]

(a) When a child has been found to have engaged in delinquent conduct or conduct indicating a need for supervision under Section 54.03 of this code, the juvenile court, with the consent of the child and appropriate adult given in accordance with Section 51.09 of this code, may transfer the case and transcripts of records and documents to the juvenile court of the county where the child resides for disposition of the case under Section 54.04 of this code.

(b) When a child who is on probation moves with his family from one county to another, the juvenile court may transfer the case to the juvenile court in the county of the child's new residence if the transfer is in the best interest of the child. In all other cases of transfer, consent of the receiving court is required. The transferring court shall forward transcripts of records and documents in the case to the judge of the receiving court.

## §51.08. Transfer from criminal court.

(a) If the defendant in a criminal proceeding is a child who is charged with an offense other than perjury, a traffic offense, a misdemeanor punishable by fine only other than public intoxication, or a violation of a penal ordinance of a political subdivision, unless he has been transferred to criminal court under Section 54.02 of this code, the court exercising criminal jurisdiction shall transfer the case to the juvenile court, together with a copy of the accusatory pleading and other papers, documents, and transcripts of testimony relating to the case, and shall order that the child be taken to the place of detention designated by the juvenile court, or shall release him to the custody of his parent, guardian, or custodian, to be brought before the juvenile court at a time designated by that court.

(b) A court in which there is pending a complaint against a child alleging a violation of a misdemeanor offense punishable by fine only other than a traffic offense of public intoxication or a violation of a penal ordinance of a political subdivision other than a traffic offense:

(1) shall waive its original jurisdiction and refer a child to juvenile court if the child has previously been convicted of:

(A) two or more misdemeanors punishable by fine only other than a traffic offense or public intoxication;

(B) two or more violations of a penal ordinance of a political subdivision other than a traffic offense; or

(C) one or more of each of the types of misdemeanors described in Paragraph (A) or (B) of this subdivision; and

(2) may waive its original jurisdiction and refer a child to juvenile court if the child:

(A) has not previously been convicted of a misdemeanor punishable by fine only other than a traffic offense or public intoxication or a violation of a penal ordinance of a political subdivision other than a traffic offense; or

(B) has previously been convicted of fewer than two misdemeanors punishable by fine only other than a traffic offense or public intoxication or two violations of a penal ordinance of a political subdivision other than a traffic offense.

(c) A court in which there is pending a complaint against a child alleging a violation of a misdemeanor offense punishable by fine only other than a traffic offense or public intoxication or a violation of a penal ordinance of a political subdivision other than a traffic offense shall notify the juvenile court of the county in which the court is located of the pending complaint and shall furnish to the juvenile court a copy of the final disposition of any matter for which the court does not waive its original jurisdiction under Subsection (b) of this section.

*(Chgd. by L.1989, chap. 1245(2); L.1991, chap. 169(2), eff. 9/1/91.)*

## §51.09. Waiver of rights.

Unless a contrary intent clearly appears elsewhere in this title, any right granted to a child by this title or by the constitution or laws of this state or the United States may be waived in proceedings under this title if:

(1) the waiver is made by the child and the attorney for the child;

(2) the child and the attorney waving the right are informed of and understand the right and the possible consequences of waiving it;

(3) the waiver is voluntary; and

(4) the waiver is made in writing or in court proceedings that are recorded.

*(Chgd. by L.1997, chap. 1086(4), eff. 9/1/97.)*

## §51.095. Admissibility of a statement of a child.

(a) Notwithstanding Section 51.09, the statement of a child is admissible in evidence in any future proceeding concerning the matter about which the statement was given if:

(1) the statement is made in writing under a circumstance described by Subsection (d) and:

(A) the statement shows that the child has at some time before the making of the statement received from a magistrate a warning that:

(i) the child may remain silent and not make any statement at all and that any statement that the child makes may be used in evidence against the child;

(ii) the child has the right to have an attorney present to advise the child either prior to any questioning or during the questioning;

(iii) if the child is unable to employ an attorney, the child has the right to have an attorney appointed to counsel with the child before or during any interviews with peace officers or attorneys representing the state; and

(iv) the child has the right to terminate the interview at any time;

(B) and:

(i) the statement must be signed in the presence of a magistrate by the child with no law enforcement officer or prosecuting attorney present, except that a magistrate may require a bailiff or a law enforcement officer if a bailiff is not available to be present if the magistrate determines that the presence of the bailiff or law enforcement officer is necessary for the personal safety of the magistrate or other court personnel, provided that the bailiff or law enforcement officer may not carry a weapon in the presence of the child; and

(ii) the magistrate must be fully convinced that the child understands the nature and contents of the statement and that the child is signing the same voluntarily, and if a statement is taken, the magistrate must sign a written statement verifying the foregoing requisites have been met;

(C) the child knowingly, intelligently, and voluntarily waives these rights before and during the making of the statement and signs the statement in the presence of a magistrate; and

(D) the magistrate certifies that the magistrate has examined the child independent of any law enforcement officer or prosecuting attorney, except as required to ensure the personal safety of the magistrate or other court personnel, and has determined that the child understands the nature and contents of the statement and has knowingly, intelligently, and voluntarily waived these rights;

(2) the statement is made orally and the child makes a statement of facts or circumstances that are found to be true, which conduct tends to establish the child's guilt, such as the finding of secreted or stolen property, or the instrument with which the child states the offense was committed;

(3) the statement was res gestae of the delinquent conduct or the conduct indicating a need for supervision or of the arrest;

(4) the statement is made:

(A) in open court at the child's adjudication hearing;

(B) before a grand jury considering a petition, under Section 53.045, that the child engaged in delinquent conduct; or

(C) at a preliminary hearing concerning the child held in compliance with this code, other than at a detention hearing under Section 54.01; or

(5) the statement is made orally under a circumstance described by Subsection (d) and the statement is recorded by an electronic recording device, including a device that records images, and:

(A) before making the statement, the child is given the warning described by Subdivision (1)(A) by a magistrate, the warning is a part of the recording, and the child knowingly, intelligently, and voluntarily waives each right stated in the warning;

(B) the recording device is capable of making an accurate recording, the operator of the device is competent to use the device, the recording is accurate, and the recording has not been altered;

(C) each voice on the recording is identified; and

(D) not later than the 20th day before the date of the proceeding, the attorney representing the child is given a complete and accurate copy of each recording of the child made under this subdivision.

(b) This section and Section 51.09 do not preclude the admission of a statement made by the child if:

(1) the statement does not stem from interrogation of the child under a circumstance described by Subsection (d); or

(2) without regard to whether the statement stems from interrogation of the child under a circumstance described by Subsection (d), the statement is voluntary and has a bearing on the credibility of the child as a witness.

(c) An electronic recording of a child's statement made under Subsection (a)(5) shall be preserved until all juvenile or criminal matters relating to any conduct referred to in the statement are final, including the exhaustion of all appeals, or barred from prosecution.

(d) Subsections (a)(1) and (a)(5) apply to the statement of a child made:

(1) while the child is in a detention facility or other place of confinement;

(2) while the child is in the custody of an officer; or

(3) during or after the interrogation of the child by an officer if the child is in the possession of the Department of Protective and Regulatory Services and is suspected to have engaged in conduct that violates a penal law of this state.

*(Added by L.1999, chap. 982(1), eff. 9/1/99. See other subsection (d) below.)*

(d) A juvenile law referee or master may perform the duties imposed on a magistrate under this section without the approval of the juvenile court if the juvenile board of the county in which the statement of the child is made has authorized a referee or master to perform the duties of a magistrate under this section. *(Added by L.1999, chap. 1477(1), eff. 9/1/99. See other subsection (d) above.)*

*(Chgd. by L.1989, chap. 84(1); L.1991, chaps. 64(1), 429(1), 557(1), 593(1); L.1995, chap. 262(8), (9); L.1997, redesignated from §51.09(b), (c) and chgd. by L.1997, chap. 1086(4); chgd. by L.1999, chaps. 982(1), 1477(1), eff. 9/1/99.)*

### §51.10. Right to assistance of attorney; compensation.† [*Right to attorney's assistance; payment.*]

(a) A child may be represented by an attorney at every stage of proceedings under this title, including:

(1) the detention hearing required by Section 54.01 of this code;

(2) the hearing to consider transfer to criminal court required by Section 54.02 of this code;

(3) the adjudication hearing required by Section 54.03 of this code;

(4) the disposition hearing required by Section 54.04 of this code;

(5) the hearing to modify disposition required by Section 54.05 of this code;

(6) hearings required by Chapter 55 of this code;

(7) habeas corpus proceedings challenging the legality of detention resulting from action under this title; and

(8) proceedings in a court of civil appeals or the Texas Supreme Court reviewing proceedings under this title.

(b) The child's right to representation by an attorney shall not be waived in:

(1) a hearing to consider transfer to criminal court as required by Section 54.02 of this code;

(2) an adjudication hearing as required by Section 54.03 of this code;

(3) a disposition hearing as required by Section 54.04 of this code;

(4) a hearing prior to commitment to the Texas Youth Commission as a modified disposition in accordance with Section 54.05(f) of this code; or

(5) hearings required by Chapter 55 of this code.

(c) If the child was not represented by an attorney at the detention hearing required by Section 54.01 of this code and a determination was made to detain the child, the child shall immediately be entitled to representation by an attorney. The court shall order the retention of an attorney according to Subsection (d) or appoint an attorney according to Subsection (f).

(d) The court shall order a child's parent or other person responsible for support of the child to employ an attorney to represent the child if:

(1) the child is not represented by an attorney;

(2) after giving the appropriate parties an opportunity to be heard, the court determines that the parent or other person responsible for support of the child is financially able to employ an attorney to represent the child; and

(3) the child's right to representation by an attorney:

(A) has not been waived under Section 51.09 of this code; or

(B) may not be waived under Subsection (b) of this section.

(e) The court may enforce orders under Subsection (c) of this section by proceedings under Section 54.07 of this code or by appointing counsel and ordering the parent or other person responsible for support of the child to pay a reasonable attorney's fee set by the court. The order may be enforced under Section 54.07 of this code.

(f) The court shall appoint an attorney to represent the interest of a child entitled to representation by an attorney, if:

(1) the child is not represented by an attorney;

(2) the court determines that the child's parent or other person responsible for support of the child is financially unable to employ an attorney to represent the child; and

(3) the child's right to representation by an attorney:

(A) has not been waived under Section 51.09 of this code; or

(B) may not be waived under Subsection (b) of this section.

(g) The juvenile court may appoint an attorney in any case in which it deems representation necessary to protect the interest of the child.

(h) Any attorney representing a child in proceedings under this title is entitled to 10 days to prepare for any adjudication or transfer hearing under this title.

(i) Except as provided in Subsection (d) of this section, an attorney appointed under this section to represent the interest of a child shall be paid from the general fund of the county in which the proceedings were instituted according to the schedule in Article 26.05 of the Texas Code of Criminal Procedure, 1965. For this purpose, a bona fide appeal to a court of civil appeals or proceedings on the merits in the Texas Supreme Court are considered the equivalent of a bona fide appeal to the Texas Court of Criminal Appeals.

*(Chgd. by L.1995, chap. 262(11), eff. 1/1/96.)*

### §51.11. Guardian ad litem.

(a) If a child appears before the juvenile court without a parent or guardian, the court shall appoint a guardian ad litem to protect the interests of the child. The juvenile court need not appoint a guardian ad litem if a parent or guardian appears with the child.

(b) In any case in which it appears to the juvenile court that the child's parent or guardian is incapable or unwilling to make decisions in the best interest of the child with respect to proceedings under this title, the court may appoint a guardian ad litem to protect the interests of the child in the proceedings.

(c) An attorney for a child may also be his guardian ad litem. A law-enforcement officer, probation officer, or other employee of the juvenile court may not be appointed guardian ad litem.

## §51.115. Attendance at hearing: parent or other guardian.

(a) Each parent of a child, each managing and possessory conservator of a child, each court-appointed custodian of a child, and a guardian of the person of the child shall attend each hearing affecting the child held under:

(1) Section 54.02 (waiver of jurisdiction and discretionary transfer to criminal court);
(2) Section 54.03 (adjudication hearing);
(3) Section 54.04 (disposition hearing);
(4) Section 54.05 (hearing to modify disposition); and
(5) Section 54.11 (release or transfer hearing).

(b) Subsection (a) does not apply to:

(1) a person for whom, for good cause shown, the court waives attendance;
(2) a person who is not a resident of this state; or
(3) a parent of a child for whom a managing conservator has been appointed and the parent is not a conservator of the child.

(c) A person required under this section to attend a hearing is entitled to reasonable written or oral notice that includes a statement of the place, date, and time of the hearing and that the attendance of the person is required. The notice may be included with or attached to any other notice required by this chapter to be given the person. Separate notice is not required for a disposition hearing that convenes on the adjournment of an adjudication hearing. If a person required under this section fails to attend a hearing, the juvenile court may proceed with the hearing.

(d) A person who is required by Subsection (a) to attend a hearing, who receives the notice of the hearing, and who fails to attend the hearing may be punished by the court for contempt by a fine of not less than $100 and not more than $1,000. In addition to or in lieu of contempt, the court may order the person to receive counseling or to attend an educational course on the duties and responsibilities of parents and skills and techniques in raising children.

*(Added by L.1995, chap. 262(10), eff. 1/1/96.)*

## §51.116. Right to reemployment.

(a) An employer may not terminate the employment of a permanent employee because the employee is required under Section 51.115 to attend a hearing.

(b) An employee whose employment is terminated in violation of this section is entitled to return to the same employment that the employee held when notified of the hearing if the employee, as soon as practical after the hearing, gives the employer actual notice that the employee intends to return.

(c) A person who is injured because of a violation of this section is entitled to reinstatement to the person's former position and to damages, but the damages may not exceed an amount equal to six months' compensation at the rate at which the person was compensated when required to attend the hearing.

(d) The injured person is also entitled to reasonable attorney's fees in an amount approved by the court.

(e) It is a defense to an action brought under this section that the employer's circumstances changed while the employee attended the hearing so that reemployment was impossible or unreasonable. To establish a defense under this subsection, an employer must prove that the termination of employment was because of circumstances other than the employee's attendance at the hearing.

*(Added by L.1995, chap. 262(10), eff. 1/1/96.)*

## §51.12. Place and conditions of detention.† [*Detention: location; conditions.*]

(a) Except as provided by Subsection (h), a child may be detained only in a:

(1) juvenile processing office in compliance with Section 52.025;
(2) place of nonsecure custody in compliance with Section 52.027;
(3) certified juvenile detention facility that complies with the requirements of Subsection (f);
(4) secure detention facility as provided by Subsection (j); or
(5) county jail or other facility as provided by Subsection (*l*).

(b) The proper authorities in each county shall provide a suitable place of detention for children who are parties to proceedings under this title, but the juvenile court shall control the conditions and terms of detention and detention supervision and shall permit visitation with the child at all reasonable times.

(c) In each county, each judge of the juvenile court and the members of the juvenile board shall personally inspect the juvenile pre-adjudication secure detention facilities and any public or private juvenile secure correctional facilities used for post-adjudication confinement that are located in the county and operated under authority of the juvenile board at least annually and shall certify in writing to the authorities responsible for operating and giving financial support to the facilities and to the Texas Juvenile Probation Commission that they are suitable or unsuitable for the detention of children in accordance with:

(1) the requirements of Subsections (a), (f), and (g); and

(2) minimum professional standards for the detention of children in pre-adjudication or post-adjudication secure confinement promulgated by the Texas Juvenile Probation Commission or, at the election of the juvenile board, the current standards promulgated by the American Correctional Association.

(d) Except as provided by Subsections (j) and (*l*), a child may not be placed in a facility that has not been certified under Subsection (c) as suitable for the detention of children and registered under Subsection (i). Except as provided by Subsections (j) and (*l*), a child detained in a facility that has not been certified under Subsection (c) as suitable for the detention of children or that has not been registered under Subsection (i) shall be entitled to immediate release from custody in that facility.

(e) If there is no certified place of detention in the county in which the petition is filed, the designated place of detention may be in another county.

(f) A child detained in a building that contains a jail, lockup, or other place of secure confinement, including an alcohol or other drug treatment facility, shall be separated by sight and sound from adults detained in the same building. Children and adults are separated by sight and sound only if they are unable to see each other and conversation between them is not possible. The separation must extend to all areas of the facility, including sally ports and passageways, and those areas used for admission, counseling, sleeping, toileting, showering, dining, recreational, educational, or vocational activities, and health care. The separation may be accomplished through architectural design.

(g) Except for a child detained in a juvenile processing office, a place of nonsecure custody, a secure detention facility as provided by Subsection (j), or a facility as provided by Subsection (*l*), a child detained in a building that contains a jail or lockup may not have any contact with:

(1) part-time or full-time security staff, including management, who have contact with adults detained in the same building; or

(2) direct-care staff who have contact with adults detained in the same building.

(h) This section does not apply to a person:

(1) after transfer to criminal court for prosecution under Section 54.02; or

(2) who is at least 17 years of age and who has been taken into custody after having:

(A) escaped from a juvenile facility operated by or under contract with the Texas Youth Commission; or

(B) violated a condition of release under supervision of the Texas Youth Commission.

(i) Except for a facility operated or certified by the Texas Youth Commission or a facility as provided by Subsection (*l*), a governmental unit or private entity that operates or contracts for the operation of a juvenile pre-adjudication secure detention facility or a juvenile post-adjudication secure correctional facility in this state shall:

(1) register the facility annually with the Texas Juvenile Probation Commission; and

(2) adhere to all applicable minimum standards for the facility.

(j) After being taken into custody, a child may be detained in a secure detention facility until the child is released under Section 53.01, 53.012, or 53.02 or until a detention hearing is held under Section 54.01(a), regardless of whether the facility has been certified under Subsection (c), if:

(1) a certified juvenile detention facility is not available in the county in which the child is taken into custody;

(2) the detention facility complies with:

(A) the short-term detention standards adopted by the Texas Juvenile Probation Commission; and

(B) the requirements of Subsection (f); and

(3) the detention facility has been designated by the county juvenile board for the county in which the facility is located.

(k) If a child who is detained under Subsection (j) or (*l*) is not released from detention at the conclusion of the detention hearing for a reason stated in Section 54.01(e), the child may be detained after the hearing only in a certified juvenile detention facility.

(*l*) A child who is taken into custody and required to be detained under Section 53.02(f) may be detained in a county jail or other facility until the child is released under Section 53.02(f) or until a detention hearing is held as required by Section 54.01(p), regardless of whether the facility complies with the requirements of this section, if:

(1) a certified juvenile detention facility or a secure detention facility described by Subsection (j) is not available in the county in which the child is taken into custody or in an adjacent county;

(2) the facility has been designated by the county juvenile board for the county in which the facility is located;

(3) the child is separated by sight and sound from adults detained in the same facility through architectural design or time-phasing;

(4) the child does not have any contact with management or direct-care staff that has contact with adults detained in the same facility on the same work shift;

(5) the county in which the child is taken into custody is not located in a metropolitan statistical area as designated by the United States Bureau of the Census; and

(6) each judge of the juvenile court and the members of the juvenile board of the county in which the child is taken into custody have personally inspected the facility at least annually and have certified in writing to the Texas Juvenile Probation Commission that the facility complies with the requirements of Subdivisions (3) and (4).

*(Chgd. by L.1995, chap. 262(12); L.1997, chaps. 772(1), 1374(1); L.1999, chaps. 62(6.07), 232(3), 1477(2), eff. 9/1/99.)*

## §51.13. Effect of adjudication or disposition.

(a) Except as provided by Subsection (d), an order of adjudication or disposition in a proceeding under this title is not a conviction of crime. Except as provided by Chapter 841, Health and Safety Code, an order of adjudication or disposition does not impose any civil disability ordinarily resulting from a conviction or operate to disqualify the child in any civil service application or appointment.

(b) The adjudication or disposition of a child or evidence adduced in a hearing under this title may be used only in subsequent:

(1) proceedings under this title in which the child is a party;

(2) sentencing proceedings in criminal court against the child to the extent permitted by the Texas Code of Criminal Procedure, 1965; or

(3) civil commitment proceedings under Chapter 841, Health and Safety Code.

(c) A child may not be committed or transferred to a penal institution or other facility used primarily for the execution of sentences of persons convicted of crime, except:

(1) for temporary detention in a jail or lockup pending juvenile court hearing or disposition under conditions meeting the requirements of Section 51.12 of this code;

(2) after transfer for prosecution in criminal court under Section 54.02 of this code; or

(3) after transfer from the Texas Youth Commission under Section 61.084, Human Resources Code.

(d) An adjudication under Section 54.03 that a child engaged in conduct that occurred on or after January 1, 1996, and that constitutes a felony offense resulting in commitment to the Texas Youth Commission under Section 54.04(d)(2), (d)(3), or (m) or 54.05(f) is a final felony conviction only for the purposes of Sections 12.42(a)-(c) and (e), Penal Code.

*(Chgd. by L.1993, chap. 799(1); L.1995, chap. 262(13); L.1997, chap. 1086(5); L.1999, chap. 1188(4.02), eff. 9/1/99.)*

## §§51.14, 51.15. *(Repealed by L.1995, chap. 262(100), eff. 1/1/96.)*

## §51.151. Polygraph examination.† [*Polygraph test.*]

If a child is taken into custody under Section 52.01 of this code, a person may not administer a polygraph examination to the child without the consent of the child's attorney or the juvenile court unless the child is transferred to criminal court for prosecution under Section 54.02 of this code.

## §51.16. *(Repealed by L.1995, chap. 262(100), eff. 1/1/96; L.1997, chap. 165(10.05(b)), eff. 9/1/97.)*

## §51.17. Procedure and evidence.

(a) Except for the burden of proof to be borne by the state in adjudicating a child to be delinquent or in need of supervision under Section 54.03(f) or otherwise when in conflict with a provision of this title, the Texas Rules of Civil Procedure govern proceedings under this title.

Printed in the U.S.A. 17

(b) Discovery in a proceeding under this title is governed by the Code of Criminal Procedure and by case decisions in criminal cases.

(c) Except as otherwise provided by this title, the Texas Rules of Evidence applicable to criminal cases and Chapter 38, Code of Criminal Procedure, apply in a judicial proceeding under this title. *(Chgd. by L.1995, chap. 262(14); L.1999, chap. 1477(3), eff. 9/1/99.)*

### §51.18. Election between juvenile court and alternate juvenile court.

(a) This section applies only to a child who has a right to a trial before a juvenile court the judge of which is not an attorney licensed in this state.

(b) On any matter that may lead to an order appealable under Section 56.01 of this code, a child may be tried before either the juvenile court or the alternate juvenile court.

(c) The child may elect to be tried before the alternate juvenile court only if the child files a written notice with that court not later than 10 days before the date of the trial. After the notice is filed, the child may be tried only in the alternate juvenile court. If the child does not file a notice as provided by this subsection, the child may be tried only in the juvenile court.

(d) If the child is tried before the juvenile court, the child is not entitled to a trial de novo before the alternate juvenile court.

(e) The child may appeal any order of the juvenile court or alternate juvenile court only as provided by Section 56.01 of this code.

*(Chgd. by L.1993, chap. 168(3), eff. 8/30/93.)*

### §51.19. Limitation periods.

(a) The limitation periods and the procedures for applying the limitation periods under Chapter 12, Code of Criminal Procedure, and other statutory law apply to proceedings under this title.

(b) For purposes of computing a limitation period, a petition filed in juvenile court for a transfer or an adjudication hearing is equivalent to an indictment or information and is treated as presented when the petition is filed in the proper court.

(c) The limitation period is two years for an offense or conduct that is not given a specific limitation period under Chapter 12, Code of Criminal Procedure, or other statutory law.

*(Added by L.1997, chap. 1086(6), eff. 9/1/97.)*

### §51.20. Physical or mental examination.

(a) At any stage of the proceedings under this title, the juvenile court may order a child who is referred to the juvenile court or who is alleged by a petition or found to have engaged in delinquent conduct or conduct indicating a need for supervision to be examined by an appropriate expert, including a physician, psychiatrist, or psychologist.

(b) If, after conducting an examination of a child ordered under Subsection (a) and reviewing any other relevant information, there is reason to believe that the child has a mental illness or mental retardation, the probation department shall refer the child to the local mental health or mental retardation authority for evaluation and services, unless the prosecuting attorney has filed a petition under Section 53.04.

*(Added by L.1999, chap. 1477(4), eff. 9/1/99.)*

## CHAPTER 52. PROCEEDINGS BEFORE AND INCLUDING REFERRAL TO JUVENILE COURT



Printed in the U.S.A.

**§52.01. Taking into custody; issuance of warning notice.† [*Taking into custody; delivery of warning notice.*]**

(a) A child may be taken into custody:

(1) pursuant to an order of the juvenile court under the provisions of this subtitle;

(2) pursuant to the laws of arrest;

(3) by a law-enforcement officer, including a school district peace officer commissioned under Section 37.081, Education Code, if there is probable cause to believe that the child has engaged in:

(A) conduct that violates a penal law of this state or a penal ordinance of any political subdivision of this state; or

(B) delinquent conduct or conduct indicating a need for supervision;

(4) by a probation officer if there is probable cause to believe that the child has violated a condition of probation imposed by the juvenile court; or

(5) pursuant to a directive to apprehend issued as provided by Section 52.015.

(b) The taking of a child into custody is not an arrest except for the purpose of determining the validity of taking him into custody or the validity of a search under the laws and constitution of this state or of the United States.

(c) A law-enforcement officer authorized to take a child into custody under Subdivisions (2) and (3) of Subsection (a) of this section may issue a warning notice to the child in lieu of taking him into custody if:

(1) guidelines for warning disposition have been issued by the law-enforcement agency in which the officer works;

(2) the guidelines have been approved by the juvenile court of the county in which the disposition is made;

(3) the disposition is authorized by the guidelines;

(4) the warning notice identifies the child and describes his alleged conduct;

(5) a copy of the warning notice is sent to the child's parent, guardian, or custodian as soon as practicable after disposition; and

(6) a copy of the warning notice is filed with the law-enforcement agency and the office or official designated by the juvenile court.

(d) A warning notice filed with the office or official designated by the juvenile court may be used as the basis of further action if necessary.

*(Chgd. by L.1993, chap. 115(2); L.1995, chap. 262(15); L.1997, chap. 165(6.08), eff. 9/1/97.)*

**§52.015. Directive to apprehend.**

(a) On the request of a law-enforcement or probation officer, a juvenile court may issue a directive to apprehend a child if the court finds there is probable cause to take the child into custody under the provisions of this title.

(b) On the issuance of a directive to apprehend, any law-enforcement or probation officer shall take the child into custody.

(c) An order under this section is not subject to appeal.

*(Added by L.1995, chap. 262(16), eff. 1/1/96.)*

**§52.02. Release or delivery to court.**

(a) Except as provided by Subsection (c), a person taking a child into custody, without unnecessary delay and without first taking the child to any place other than a juvenile processing office designated under Section 52.025, shall do one of the following:

(1) release the child to a parent, guardian, custodian of the child, or other responsible adult upon that person's promise to bring the child before the juvenile court as requested by the court;

(2) bring the child before the office or official designated by the juvenile court if there is probable cause to believe that the child engaged in delinquent conduct or conduct indicating a need for supervision;

(3) bring the child to a detention facility designated by the juvenile court;

(4) bring the child to a secure detention facility as provided by Section 51.12(j);

(5) bring the child to a medical facility if the child is believed to suffer from a serious physical condition or illness that requires prompt treatment; or

(6) dispose of the case under Section 52.03.

(b) A person taking a child into custody shall promptly give notice of his action and a statement of the reason for taking the child into custody, to

(1) the child's parent, guardian, or custodian; and

(2) the office of or official designated by the juvenile court.

(c) A person who takes a child into custody and who has reasonable grounds to believe that the child has been operating a motor vehicle in a public place while having any detectable amount of alcohol in the child's system may, before complying with Subsection (a):

(1) take the child to a place to obtain a specimen of the child's breath or blood as provided by Chapter 724, Transportation Code; and

(2) perform intoxilyzer processing and videotaping of the child in an adult processing office of a law enforcement agency.

(d) Notwithstanding Section 51.09(a), a child taken into custody as provided by Subsection (c) may submit to the taking of a breath specimen or refuse to submit to the taking of a breath specimen without the concurrence of an attorney, but only if the request made of the child to give the specimen and the child's response to that request is videotaped. A videotape made under this subsection must be maintained until the disposition of any proceeding against the child relating to the arrest is final and be made available to an attorney representing the child during that period.
*(Chgd. by L.1991, chap. 495(1); L.1997, chaps. 1013(15), 1374(2); L.1999, chaps. 62(6.08), 1477(5), eff. 9/1/99.)*



## §52.025. Designation of juvenile processing office.

(a) The juvenile court may designate an office or a room, which may be located in a police facility or sheriff's offices, as the juvenile processing office for the temporary detention of a child taken into custody under Section 52.01 of this code. The office may not be a cell or holding facility used for detentions other than detentions under this section. The juvenile court by written order may prescribe the conditions of the designation and limit the activities that may occur in the office during the temporary detention.

(b) A child may be detained in a juvenile processing office only for:

(1) the return of a child to the custody of a person under Section 52.02(a)(1);

(2) the completion of essential forms and records required by the juvenile court or this title;

(3) the photographing and fingerprinting of the child if otherwise authorized at the time of temporary detention by this title;

(4) the issuance of warnings to the child as required or permitted by this title; or

(5) the receipt of a statement by the child under Section 51.095(a)(1), (2), (3), or (5).

(c) A child may not be left unattended in a juvenile processing office and is entitled to be accompanied by the child's parent, guardian, or other custodian or by the child's attorney.

(d) A child may not be detained in a juvenile processing office for longer than six hours.
*(Added by L.1991, chap. 495(2); chgd. by L.1997, chap. 1086(48), eff. 9/1/97.)*

## §52.026. Responsibility for transporting juvenile offenders.

(a) It shall be the duty of the law enforcement officer who has taken a child into custody to transport the child to the appropriate detention facility if the child is not released to the parent, guardian, or custodian of the child.

(b) If the juvenile detention facility is located outside the county in which the child is taken into custody, it shall be the duty of the sheriff of that county to transport the child to the appropriate juvenile detention facility unless the child is:

(1) detained in a secure detention facility under Section 51.12(j); or

(2) released to the parent, guardian, or custodian of the child.
*(Chgd. by L.1999, chap. 62(6.09), eff. 9/1/99. See other section (b) below.)*

(b) If the juvenile detention facility is located outside the county in which the child is taken into custody, it shall be the duty of the law enforcement officer who has taken the child into custody or, if authorized by the commissioners court of the county, the sheriff of that county to transport the child to the appropriate juvenile detention facility unless the child is:

(1) detained in a secure detention facility under Section 51.12(i); or

(2) released to the parent, guardian, or custodian of the child.
*(Chgd. by L.1999, chap. 1082(1), eff. 6/18/99. See other section (b) above.)*

(c) On adoption of an order by the juvenile board and approval of the juvenile board's order by record vote of the commissioners court, it shall be the duty of the sheriff of the county in which the child is taken into custody to transport the child to and from all scheduled juvenile court proceedings and appearances and other activities ordered by the juvenile court.
*(Added by L.1993, chap. 411(1); chgd. by L.1997, chap. 1374(3); L.1999, chaps. 62(6.09), 1082(1), eff. 9/1/99, 6/18/99, respectively.)*

**§52.027. Children taken into custody for traffic offenses, other fineable only offenses, or as a status offender.**

(a) A child may be released to the child's parent, guardian, custodian, or other responsible adult as provided in Section 52.02(a)(1) if the child is taken into custody:

(1) for an offense that a justice or municipal court has jurisdiction of under Article 4.11 or 4.14, Code of Criminal Procedure, other than public intoxication; or

(2) as a status offender or nonoffender.

(b) A child described by Subsection (a) must be taken only to a place previously designated by the head of the law enforcement agency with custody of the child as an appropriate place of nonsecure custody for children unless the child:

(1) is released under Section 52.02(a)(1);

(2) is taken before a municipal court or justice court; or

(3) for truancy or running away, is taken to a juvenile detention facility, or a secure detention facility, as authorized by Sections 51.12(a)(3) and (4), respectively, for the detention of the child as provided by Section 54.011.

(c) A place of nonsecure custody for children must be an unlocked, multipurpose area. A lobby, office, or interrogation room is suitable if the area is not designated, set aside, or used as a secure detention area and is not part of a secure detention area. A place of nonsecure custody may be a juvenile processing office designated under Section 52.025 if the area is not locked when it is used as a place of nonsecure custody.

(d) The following procedures shall be followed in a place of nonsecure custody for children:

(1) a child may not be secured physically to a cuffing rail, chair, desk, or other stationary object;

(2) the child may be held in the nonsecure facility only long enough to accomplish the purpose of identification, investigation, processing, release to parents, or the arranging of transportation to the appropriate juvenile court, juvenile detention facility, secure detention facility, municipal court, or justice court;

(3) residential use of the area is prohibited; and

(4) the child shall be under continuous visual supervision by a law enforcement officer or facility staff person during the time the child is in nonsecure custody.

(e) Notwithstanding any other provision of this section, a child may not, under any circumstances, be detained in a place of nonsecure custody for more than six hours.

(f) A child taken into custody for an offense that a justice or municipal court has jurisdiction of under Article 4.11 or 4.14, Code of Criminal Procedure, other than public intoxication, may be presented or detained in a detention facility designated by the juvenile court under Section 52.02(a)(3) only if:

(1) the child's non-traffic case is transferred to the juvenile court by a municipal court or justice court under Section 51.08(b); or

(2) the child is referred to the juvenile court by a municipal court or justice court for contempt of court under Subsection (h).

(g) A law enforcement officer may issue a field release citation, as provided by Article 14.06, Code of Criminal Procedure, in place of taking a child into custody for a traffic offense or an offense, other than public intoxication, punishable by fine only.

(h) If a child intentionally or knowingly fails to obey a lawful order of disposition after an adjudication of guilt of an offense that a justice or municipal court has jurisdiction of under Article 4.11 or 4.14, Code of Criminal Procedure, the municipal court or justice court may: *(Chgd. by L.1999, chap. 76(1), eff. 9/1/99. See other paragraph (h) below.)*

(h) If a child intentionally or knowingly fails to obey a lawful order of disposition after an adjudication of guilt of a traffic offense or other offense punishable by fine only, the municipal court or justice court may: *(Chgd. by L.1999, chap. 1545(66), eff. 9/1/99. See other paragraph (h) above.)*

(1) except as provided by Subsection (j), hold the child in contempt of the municipal court or justice court order and order the child to pay a fine not to exceed $500; or

(2) refer the child to the appropriate juvenile court for delinquent conduct for contempt of the municipal court or justice court order.

(i) In this section, "child" means a person who:

(1) is at least 10 years of age and younger than 17 years of age and who is charged with or convicted of an offense that a justice or municipal court has jurisdiction of under Article 4.11 or 4.14, Code of Criminal Procedure, other than public intoxication; or

(2) is at least 10 years of age and younger than 18 years of age and who:

(A) is a status offender and was taken into custody as a status offender for conduct engaged in before becoming 17 years of age; or

(B) is a nonoffender and became a nonoffender before becoming 17 years of age.

(j) A municipal or justice court may not order a child to a term of confinement or imprisonment for contempt of a municipal or justice court order under Subsection (h).
*(Added by L.1995, chap. 262(17); chgd. by L.1997, chaps. 822(3), 1374(4); L.1999, chaps. 76(1), 1545(66), eff. 9/1/99.)*

### §52.028. Children taken into custody for violation of juvenile curfew ordinance or order.

(a) A peace officer taking into custody a person under 17 years of age for violation of a juvenile curfew ordinance of a municipality or order of the commissioners court of a county shall, without unnecessary delay:

(1) release the person to the person's parent, guardian, or custodian;

(2) take the person before a municipal or justice court to answer the charge; or

(3) take the person to a place designated as a juvenile curfew processing office by the head of the law enforcement agency having custody of the person.

(b) A juvenile curfew processing office must observe the following procedures:

(1) the office must be an unlocked, multipurpose area that is not designated, set aside, or used as a secure detention area or part of a secure detention area;

(2) the person may not be secured physically to a cuffing rail, chair, desk, or stationary object;

(3) the person may not be held longer than necessary to accomplish the purposes of identification, investigation, processing, release to parents, guardians, or custodians, and arrangement of transportation to school or court;

(4) a juvenile curfew processing office may not be designated or intended for residential purposes;

(5) the person must be under continuous visual supervision by a peace officer or other person during the time the person is in the juvenile curfew processing office; and

(6) a person may not be held in a juvenile curfew processing office for more than six hours.

(c) A place designated under this section as a juvenile curfew processing office is not subject to the approval of the juvenile board having jurisdiction where the governmental entity is located.
*(Added by L.1995, chap. 262(17), eff. 5/31/95.)*

### §52.03. Disposition without referral to court.

(a) A law-enforcement officer authorized by this title to take a child into custody may dispose of the case of a child taken into custody without referral to juvenile court, if:

(1) guidelines for such disposition have been adopted by the juvenile board of the county in which the disposition is made as required by Section 52.032;

(2) the disposition is authorized by the guidelines; and

(3) the officer makes a written report of the officer's disposition to the law-enforcement agency, identifying the child and specifying the grounds for believing that the taking into custody was authorized.

(b) No disposition authorized by this section may involve:

(1) keeping the child in law-enforcement custody; or

(2) requiring periodic reporting of the child to a law-enforcement officer, law-enforcement agency, or other agency.

(c) A disposition authorized by this section may involve:

(1) referral of the child to an agency other than the juvenile court;

(2) a brief conference with the child and his parent, guardian, or custodian; or

(3) referral of the child and the child's parent, guardian, or custodian for services under Section 264.302.

(d) Statistics indicating the number and kind of dispositions made by a law-enforcement agency under the authority of this section shall be reported at least annually to the office or official designated by the juvenile court, as ordered by the court.
*(Chgd. by L.1995, chap. 262(18); L.1999, chap. 48(1), eff. 9/1/99.)*

### §52.031. First offender program.

(a) A juvenile board may establish a first offender program under this section for the referral and disposition of children taken into custody for:

(1) conduct indicating a need for supervision; or

(2) delinquent conduct other than conduct that constitutes:

(A) a felony of the first, second, or third degree, an aggravated controlled substance felony, or a capital felony; or

(B) a state jail felony or misdemeanor involving violence to a person or the use or possession of a firearm, illegal knife, or club, as those terms are defined by Section 46.01, Penal Code, or a prohibited weapon, as described by Section 46.05, Penal Code.

(b) Each juvenile board in the county in which a first offender program is established shall designate one or more law enforcement officers and agencies, which may be law enforcement agencies, to process a child under the first offender program.

(c) The disposition of a child under the first offender program may not take place until guidelines for the disposition have been adopted by the juvenile board of the county in which the disposition is made as required by Section 52.032.

(d) A law enforcement officer taking a child into custody may refer the child to the law enforcement officer or agency designated under Subsection (b) for disposition under the first offender program and not refer the child to juvenile court only if:

(1) the child has not previously been adjudicated as having engaged in delinquent conduct;

(2) the referral complies with guidelines for disposition under Subsection (c); and

(3) the officer reports in writing the referral to the agency, identifying the child and specifying the grounds for taking the child into custody.

(e) A child referred for disposition under the first offender program may not be detained in law enforcement custody.

(f) The parent, guardian, or other custodian of the child must receive notice that the child has been referred for disposition under the first offender program. The notice must:

(1) state the grounds for taking the child into custody;

(2) identify the law enforcement officer or agency to which the child was referred;

(3) briefly describe the nature of the program; and

(4) state that the child's failure to complete the program will result in the child being referred to the juvenile court.

(g) The child and the parent, guardian, or other custodian of the child must consent to participation by the child in the first offender program.

(h) Disposition under a first offender program may include:

(1) voluntary restitution by the child or the parent, guardian, or other custodian of the child to the victim of the conduct of the child;

(2) voluntary community service restitution by the child;

(3) educational, vocational training, counseling, or other rehabilitative services; and

(4) periodic reporting by the child to the law enforcement officer or agency to which the child has been referred.

(i) The case of a child who successfully completes the first offender program is closed and may not be referred to juvenile court, unless the child is taken into custody under circumstances described by Subsection (j)(3).

(j) The case of a child referred for disposition under the first offender program shall be referred to juvenile court if:

(1) the child fails to complete the program;

(2) the child or the parent, guardian, or other custodian of the child terminates the child's participation in the program before the child completes it; or

(3) the child completes the program but is taken into custody under Section 52.01 before the 90th day after the date the child completes the program for conduct other than the conduct for which the child was referred to the first offender program.

(k) A statement made by a child to a person giving advice or supervision or participating in the first offender program may not be used against the child in any proceeding under this title or any criminal proceeding.

(*l*) The law enforcement agency must report to the juvenile board in December of each year the following:

(1) the last known address of the child, including the census tract;

(2) the gender and ethnicity of the child referred to the program; and

(3) the offense committed by the child.

*(Added by L.1995, chap. 262(19); chgd. by L.1999, chap. 48(2), eff. 9/1/99.)*

## §52.032. Informal disposition guidelines.

The juvenile board of each county, in cooperation with each law enforcement agency in the county, shall adopt guidelines for the disposition of a child under Section 52.03 or 52.031. The guidelines adopted under this section shall not be considered mandatory. *(Added by L.1999, chap. 48(3), eff. 9/1/99.)*

### §52.04. Referral to juvenile court.

(a) The following shall accompany referral of a child or a child's case to the office or official designated by the juvenile court or be provided as quickly as possible after referral:

(1) all information in the possession of the person or agency making the referral pertaining to the identity of the child and his address, the name and address of the child's parent, guardian, or custodian, the names and addresses of any witness, and the child's present whereabouts;

(2) a complete statement of the circumstances of the alleged delinquent conduct or conduct indicating a need for supervision;

(3) when applicable, a complete statement of the circumstances of taking the child into custody; and

(4) when referral is by an officer of a law-enforcement agency, a complete statement of all prior contacts with the child by officers of that law-enforcement agency.

(b) The office or official designated by the juvenile court may refer the case to a law-enforcement agency for the purpose of conducting an investigation to obtain necessary information.

(c) If the office of the prosecuting attorney is designated by the juvenile court to conduct the preliminary investigation under Section 53.01, the referring entity shall first transfer the child's case to the juvenile probation department for statistical reporting purposes only. On the creation of a statistical record or file for the case, the probation department shall within three business days forward the case to the prosecuting attorney for review under Section 53.01.

*(Chgd. by L.1997, chap. 1091(1), eff. 6/19/97.)*



### §52.041. Referral of child to juvenile court after expulsion.

(a) A school district that expels a child shall refer the child to juvenile court in the county in which the child resides.

(b) The board of the school district or a person designated by the board shall deliver a copy of the order expelling the student and any other information required by Section 52.04 on or before the second working day after the date of the expulsion hearing to the authorized officer of the juvenile court.

(c) Within five working days of receipt of an expulsion notice under this section by the office or official designated by the juvenile court, a preliminary investigation and determination shall be conducted as required by Section 53.01.

(d) The office or official designated by the juvenile court shall within two working days notify the school district that expelled the child if:

(1) a determination was made under Section 53.01 that the person referred to juvenile court was not a child within the meaning of this title;

(2) a determination was made that no probable cause existed to believe the child engaged in delinquent conduct or conduct indicating a need for supervision;

(3) no deferred prosecution or formal court proceedings have been or will be initiated involving the child;

(4) the court or jury finds that the child did not engage in delinquent conduct or conduct indicating a need for supervision and the case has been dismissed with prejudice; or

(5) the child was adjudicated but no disposition was or will be ordered by the court.

(e) In any county where a juvenile justice alternative education program is operated, no student shall be expelled without written notification by the board of the school district or its designated agent to the juvenile board's designated representative. The notification shall be made not later than two business days following the board's determination that the student is to be expelled. Failure to timely notify the designated representative of the juvenile board shall result in the child's duty to continue attending the school district's educational program, which shall be provided to that child until such time as the notification to the juvenile board's designated representative is properly made.

*(Added by L.1995, chap. 262(20); chgd. by L.1997, chap. 1015(16), eff. 6/19/97.)*

## CHAPTER 53. PROCEEDINGS PRIOR TO JUDICIAL PROCEEDINGS

Section

### §53.01. Preliminary investigation and determinations; notice to parents.† [*Initial investigation and determinations; notice to parents.*]

(a) On referral of a person believed to be a child or on referral of the person's case to the office or official designated by the juvenile court, the intake officer, probation officer, or other person authorized by the court shall conduct a preliminary investigation to determine whether:

(1) the person referred to juvenile court is a child within the meaning of this title; and

(2) there is probable cause to believe the person engaged in delinquent conduct or conduct indicating a need for supervision.

(b) If it is determined that the person is not a child or there is no probable cause, the person shall immediately be released.

(c) When custody of a child is given to the office or official designated by the juvenile court, the intake officer, probation officer, or other person authorized by the court shall promptly give notice of the whereabouts of the child and a statement of the reason he was taken into custody to the child's parent, guardian, or custodian unless the notice given under Section 52.02(b) of this code provided fair notice of the child's present whereabouts.

(d) Unless the juvenile board approves a written procedure proposed by the office of prosecuting attorney and chief juvenile probation officer which provides otherwise, if it is determined that the person is a child and, regardless of a finding of probable cause, or a lack thereof, there is an allegation that the child engaged in delinquent conduct of the grade of felony, or conduct constituting a misdemeanor offense involving violence to a person or the use or possession of a firearm, illegal knife, or club, as those terms are defined by Section 46.01, Penal Code, or prohibited weapon, as described by Section 46.05, Penal Code, the case shall be promptly forwarded to the office of the prosecuting attorney, accompanied by:

(1) all documents that accompanied the current referral; and

(2) a summary of all prior referrals of the child to the juvenile court, juvenile probation department, or a detention facility.

(e) If a juvenile board adopts an alternative referral plan under Subsection (d), the board shall register the plan with the Texas Juvenile Probation Commission.

(f) A juvenile board may not adopt an alternate referral plan that does not require the forwarding of a child's case to the prosecuting attorney as provided by Subsection (d) if probable cause exists to believe that the child engaged in delinquent conduct that violates Section 19.03, Penal Code (capital murder), or Section 19.02, Penal Code (murder).

*(Chgd. by L.1995, chap. 262(21); L.1997, chap. 1374(5), eff. 9/1/97.)*

### §53.012. Review by prosecutor.

(a) The prosecuting attorney shall promptly review the circumstances and allegations of a referral made under Section 53.01 for legal sufficiency and the desirability of prosecution and may file a petition without regard to whether probable cause was found under Section 53.01.

(b) If the prosecuting attorney does not file a petition requesting the adjudication of the child referred to the prosecuting attorney, the prosecuting attorney shall:

(1) terminate all proceedings, if the reason is for lack of probable cause; or

(2) return the referral to the juvenile probation department for further proceedings.

(c) The juvenile probation department shall promptly refer a child who has been returned to the department under Subsection (b)(2) and who fails or refuses to participate in a program of the department to the prosecuting attorney for review of the child's case and determination of whether to file a petition.

*(Added by L.1995, chap. 262(22), eff. 1/1/96.)*

### §53.013. Progressive sanctions program.

(a) Each juvenile board may adopt a progressive sanctions program using the guidelines for progressive sanctions in Chapter 59.

(b) A juvenile court or probation department that deviates from the guidelines under Section 59.003 shall state in writing the reasons for the deviation and submit the statement to the juvenile board regardless of whether the juvenile board has adopted a progressive sanctions program.
*(Added by L.1995, chap. 262(22); chgd. by L.1997, chap. 1086(7), eff. 9/1/97.)*

### §53.02. Release from detention.

(a) If a child is brought before the court or delivered to a detention facility as authorized by Sections 51.12(a)(3) and (4), the intake or other authorized officer of the court shall immediately make an investigation and shall release the child unless it appears that his detention is warranted under Subsection (b). The release may be conditioned upon requirements reasonably necessary to insure the child's appearance at later proceedings, but the conditions of the release must be in writing and filed with the office or official designated by the court and a copy furnished to the child.

(b) A child taken into custody may be detained prior to hearing on the petition only if:

(1) the child is likely to abscond or be removed from the jurisdiction of the court;

(2) suitable supervision, care, or protection for the child is not being provided by a parent, guardian, custodian, or other person;

(3) the child has no parent, guardian, custodian, or other person able to return the child to the court when required;

(4) the child may be dangerous to himself or herself or the child may threaten the safety of the public if released;

(5) the child has previously been found to be a delinquent child or has previously been convicted of a penal offense punishable by a term in jail or prison and is likely to commit an offense if released; or

(6) the child's detention is required under Subsection (f).

(c) If the child is not released, a request for detention hearing shall be made and promptly presented to the court, and an informal detention hearing as provided in Section 54.01 of this code shall be held promptly, but not later than the time required by Section 54.01 of this code.

(d) A release of a child to an adult under Subsection (a) must be conditioned on the agreement of the adult to be subject to the jurisdiction of the juvenile court and to an order of contempt by the court if the adult, after notification, is unable to produce the child at later proceedings.

(e) Unless otherwise agreed in the memorandum of understanding under Section 37.011, Education Code, in a county with a population greater than 125,000, if a child being released under this section is expelled under Section 37.007, Education Code, the release shall be conditioned on the child's attending a juvenile justice alternative education program pending a deferred prosecution or formal court disposition of the child's case.

(f) A child who is alleged to have engaged in delinquent conduct and to have used, possessed, or exhibited a firearm, as defined by Section 46.01, Penal Code, in the commission of the offense shall be detained until the child is released at the direction of the judge of the juvenile court, a substitute judge authorized by Section 51.04(f), or a referee appointed under Section 51.04(g), including an oral direction by telephone, or until a detention hearing is held as required by Section 54.01.
*(Chgd. by L.1995, chap. 262(23); L.1997, chaps. 1015(17), 1374(6); L.1999, chap. 232(1), eff. 9/1/99.)*

### §53.03. Deferred prosecution.

(a) Subject to Subsections (e) and (g), if the preliminary investigation required by Section 53.01 of this code results in a determination that further proceedings in the case are authorized, the probation officer or other designated officer of the court, subject to the direction of the juvenile court, may advise the parties for a reasonable period of time not to exceed six months concerning deferred prosecution and rehabilitation of a child if:

(1) deferred prosecution would be in the interest of the public and the child;

(2) the child and his parent, guardian, or custodian consent with knowledge that consent is not obligatory; and

(3) the child and his parent, guardian, or custodian are informed that they may terminate the deferred prosecution at any point and petition the court for a court hearing in the case.

(b) Except as otherwise permitted by this title, the child may not be detained during or as a result of the deferred prosecution process.

(c) An incriminating statement made by a participant to the person giving advice and in the discussions or conferences incident thereto may not be used against the declarant in any court hearing.

(d) The court may adopt a fee schedule for deferred prosecution services and rules for the waiver of a fee for financial hardship in accordance with guidelines that the Texas Juvenile

Probation Commission shall provide. The maximum fee is $15 a month. If the court adopts a schedule and rules for waiver, the probation officer or other designated officer of the court shall collect the fee authorized by the schedule from the parent, guardian, or custodian of a child for whom a deferred prosecution is authorized under this section or waive the fee in accordance with the rules adopted by the court. The officer shall deposit the fees received under this section in the county treasury to the credit of a special fund that may be used only for juvenile probation or community-based juvenile corrections services or facilities in which a juvenile may be required to live while under court supervision. If the court does not adopt a schedule and rules for waiver, a fee for deferred prosecution services may not be imposed.

(e) A prosecuting attorney may defer prosecution for any child. A probation officer or other designated officer of the court:

(1) may not defer prosecution for a child for a case that is required to be forwarded to the prosecuting attorney under Section 53.01(d); and

(2) may defer prosecution for a child who has previously been adjudicated for conduct that constitutes a felony only if the prosecuting attorney consents in writing.

(f) The probation officer or other officer designated by the court supervising a program of deferred prosecution for a child under this section shall report to the juvenile court any violation by the child of the program.

(g) Prosecution may not be deferred for a child alleged to have engaged in conduct that:

(1) is an offense under Section 49.04, 49.05, 49.06, 49.07, or 49.08, Penal Code; or

(2) is a third or subsequent offense under Section 106.04 or 106.041, Alcoholic Beverage Code.

(h) If the child is alleged to have engaged in delinquent conduct or conduct indicating a need for supervision that violates Section 28.08, Penal Code, deferred prosecution under this section may include:

(1) voluntary attendance in a class with instruction in self-responsibility and empathy for a victim of an offense conducted by a local juvenile probation department, if the class is available; and

(2) voluntary restoration of the property damaged by the child by removing or painting over any markings made by the child, if the owner of the property consents to the restoration.
*(Chgd. by L.1995, chap. 262(24); L.1997, chaps. 593(6), 1013(16); L.1999, chap. 62(19.01(17)), eff. 9/1/99.)*

## §53.035. Grand jury referral.

(a) The prosecuting attorney may, before filing a petition under Section 53.04, refer an offense to a grand jury in the county in which the offense is alleged to have been committed.

(b) The grand jury has the same jurisdiction and powers to investigate the facts and circumstances concerning an offense referred to the grand jury under this section as it has to investigate other criminal activity.

(c) If the grand jury votes to take no action on an offense referred to the grand jury under this section, the prosecuting attorney may not file a petition under Section 53.04 concerning the offense unless the same or a successor grand jury approves the filing of the petition.

(d) If the grand jury votes for approval of the prosecution of an offense referred to the grand jury under this section, the prosecuting attorney may file a petition under Section 53.04.

(e) The approval of the prosecution of an offense by a grand jury under this section does not constitute approval of a petition by a grand jury for purposes of Section 53.045.
*(Added by L.1999, chap. 1477(6), eff. 9/1/99.)*

## §53.04. Court petition; answer.† [*Court petition; response.*]

(a) If the preliminary investigation, required by Section 53.01 of this code results in a determination that further proceedings are authorized and warranted, a petition for an adjudication or transfer hearing of a child alleged to have engaged in delinquent conduct or conduct indicating a need for supervision may be made as promptly as practicable by a prosecuting attorney who has knowledge of the facts alleged or is informed and believes that they are true.

(b) The proceedings shall be styled "In the matter of ______________."

(c) The petition may be on information and belief.

(d) The petition must state:

(1) with reasonable particularity the time, place, and manner of the acts alleged and the penal law or standard of conduct allegedly violated by the acts;

(2) the name, age, and residence address, if known, of the child who is the subject of the petition;

(3) the names and residence addresses, if known, of the parent, guardian, or custodian of the child and of the child's spouse, if any;

(4) if the child's parent, guardian, or custodian does not reside or cannot be found in the state, or if their places of residence are unknown, the name and residence address of any known adult relative residing in the county or, if there is none, the name and residence address of the known adult relative residing nearest to the location of the court; and

(5) if the child is alleged to have engaged in habitual felony conduct, the previous adjudications in which the child was found to have engaged in conduct violating penal laws of the grade of felony.

(e) An oral or written answer to the petition may be made at or before the commencement of the hearing. If there is no answer, a general denial of the alleged conduct is assumed.
*(Chgd. by L.1995, chap. 262(25), eff. 1/1/96.)*

## §53.045. Violent or habitual offenders.

(a) Except as provided by Subsection (e), the prosecuting attorney may refer the petition to the grand jury of the county in which the court in which the petition is filed presides if the petition alleges that the child engaged in delinquent conduct that constitutes habitual felony conduct as described by Section 51.031 or that included the violation of any of the following provisions:

(1) Section 19.02, Penal Code (murder);

(2) Section 19.03, Penal Code (capital murder);

(3) Section 20.04, Penal Code (aggravated kidnapping);

(4) Section 22.011, Penal Code (sexual assault) or Section 22.021, Penal Code (aggravated sexual assault);

(5) Section 22.02, Penal Code (aggravated assault);

(6) Section 29.03, Penal Code (aggravated robbery);

(7) Section 22.04, Penal Code (injury to a child, elderly individual, or disabled individual), if the offense is punishable as a felony, other than a state jail felony;

(8) Section 22.05(b), Penal Code (felony deadly conduct involving discharging a firearm);

(9) Subchapter D, Chapter 481, Health and Safety Code, if the conduct constitutes a felony of the first degree or an aggravated controlled substance felony (certain offenses involving controlled substances);

(10) Section 15.03, Penal Code (criminal solicitation);

(11) Section 21.11(a)(1), Penal Code (indecency with a child);

(12) Section 15.031, Penal Code (criminal solicitation of a minor);

(13) Section 15.01, Penal Code (criminal attempt), if the offense attempted was an offense under Section 19.02, Penal Code (murder) or Section 19.03, Penal Code (capital murder), or an offense listed by Section 3g(a)(1), Article 42.12, Code of Criminal Procedure; or

(14) Section 28.02, Penal Code (arson), if bodily injury or death is suffered by any person by reason of the commission of the conduct.

(b) A grand jury may approve a petition submitted to it under this section by a vote of nine members of the grand jury in the same manner that the grand jury votes on the presentment of an indictment.

(c) The grand jury has all the powers to investigate the facts and circumstances relating to a petition submitted under this section as it has to investigate other criminal activity but may not issue an indictment unless the child is transferred to a criminal court as provided by Section 54.02 of this code.

(d) If the grand jury approves of the petition, the fact of approval shall be certified to the juvenile court, and the certification shall be entered in the record of the case. For the purpose of the transfer of a child to the Texas Department of Corrections as provided by Section 61.084(c), Human Resources Code, a juvenile court petition approved by a grand jury under this section is an indictment presented by the grand jury.

(e) The prosecuting attorney may not refer a petition that alleges the child engaged in conduct that violated Section 22.011(a)(2), Penal Code, or Sections 22.021(a)(1)(B) and (2)(B), Penal Code, unless the child is more than three years older than the victim of the conduct.
*(Chgd. by L.1991, chap. 574(1); L.1995, chap. 262(26), (27); L.1997, chap. 1086(8), eff. 9/1/97.)*

## §53.05. Time set for hearing.† [*Time selected for hearing.*]

(a) After the petition has been filed, the juvenile court shall set a time for the hearing.

(b) The time set for the hearing shall not be later than 10 working days after the day the petition was filed if:

(1) the child is in detention; or

(2) the child will be taken into custody under Section 53.06(d) of this code.
*(Chgd. by L.1995, chap. 262(28), eff. 1/1/96.)*

### §53.06. Summons.

(a) The juvenile court shall direct issuance of a summons to:

(1) the child named in the petition;

(2) the child's parent, guardian, or custodian;

(3) the child's guardian ad litem; and

(4) any other person who appears to the court to be a proper or necessary party to the proceeding.

(b) The summons must require the persons served to appear before the court at the time set to answer the allegations of the petition. A copy of the petition must accompany the summons.

(c) The court may endorse on the summons an order directing the person having the physical custody or control of the child to bring the child to the hearing. A person who violates an order entered under this subsection may be proceeded against under Section 53.08 or 54.07 of this code.

(d) If it appears from an affidavit filed or from sworn testimony before the court that immediate detention of the child is warranted under Section 53.02(b) of this code, the court may endorse on the summons an order that a law-enforcement officer shall serve the summons and shall immediately take the child into custody and bring him before the court.

(e) A party, other than the child, may waive service of summons by written stipulation or by voluntary appearance at the hearing.

*(Chgd. by L.1995, chap. 262(29), eff. 1/1/96.)*

### §53.07. Service of summons.† [*Delivery of summons.*]

(a) If a person to be served with a summons is in this state and can be found, the summons shall be served upon him personally at least two days before the day of the adjudication hearing. If he is in this state and cannot be found, but his address is known or can with reasonable diligence be ascertained, the summons may be served on him by mailing a copy by registered or certified mail, return receipt requested, at least five days before the day of the hearing. If he is outside this state but he can be found or his address is known, or his whereabouts or address can with reasonable diligence be ascertained, service of the summons may be made either by delivering a copy to him personally or mailing a copy to him by registered or certified mail, return receipt requested, at least five days before the day of the hearing.

(b) The juvenile court has jurisdiction of the case if after reasonable effort a person other than the child cannot be found nor his post-office address ascertained, whether he is in or outside this state.

(c) Service of the summons may be made by any suitable person under the direction of the court.

(d) The court may authorize payment from the general funds of the county of the costs of service and of necessary travel expenses incurred by persons summoned or otherwise required to appear at the hearing.

(e) Witnesses may be subpoenaed in accordance with the Texas Code of Criminal Procedure, 1965.

### §53.08. Writ of attachment.

(a) The juvenile court may issue a writ of attachment for a person who violates an order entered under Section 53.06(c).

(b) A writ of attachment issued under this section is executed in the same manner as in a criminal proceeding as provided by Chapter 24, Code of Criminal Procedure.

*(Added by L.1995, chap. 262(30), eff. 1/1/96.)*

## CHAPTER 54. JUDICIAL PROCEEDINGS

Section

## §54.01. Detention hearing.† [*Hearing on detention.*]

(a) Except as provided by Subsection (p), if the child is not released under Section 53.02, a detention hearing without a jury shall be held promptly, but not later than the second working day after the child is taken into custody; provided, however, that when a child is detained on a Friday or Saturday, then such detention hearing shall be held on the first working day after the child is taken into custody.

(b) Reasonable notice of the detention hearing, either oral or written, shall be given, stating the time, place, and purpose of the hearing. Notice shall be given to the child and, if they can be found, to his parents, guardian, or custodian. Prior to the commencement of the hearing, the court shall inform the parties of the child's right to counsel and to appointed counsel if they are indigent and of the child's right to remain silent with respect to any allegations of delinquent conduct or conduct indicating a need for supervision.

(c) At the detention hearing, the court may consider written reports from probation officers, professional court employees, or professional consultants in addition to the testimony of witnesses. Prior to the detention hearing, the court shall provide the attorney for the child with access to all written matter to be considered by the court in making the detention decision. The court may order counsel not to reveal items to the child or his parent, guardian, or guardian ad litem if such disclosure would materially harm the treatment and rehabilitation of the child or would substantially decrease the likelihood of receiving information from the same or similar sources in the future.

(d) A detention hearing may be held without the presence of the child's parents if the court has been unable to locate them. If no parent or guardian is present, the court shall appoint counsel or a guardian ad litem for the child.

(e) At the conclusion of the hearing, the court shall order the child released from detention unless it finds that:

(1) he is likely to abscond or be removed from the jurisdiction of the court;

(2) suitable supervision, care, or protection for him is not being provided by a parent, guardian, custodian, or other person;

(3) he has no parent, guardian, custodian, or other person able to return him to the court when required;

(4) he may be dangerous to himself or may threaten the safety of the public if released; or

(5) he has previously been found to be a delinquent child or has previously been convicted of a penal offense punishable by a term in jail or prison and is likely to commit an offense if released.

(f) Unless otherwise agreed in the memorandum of understanding under Section 37.011, Education Code, a release may be conditioned on requirements reasonably necessary to insure the child's appearance at later proceedings, but the conditions of the release must be in writing and a copy furnished to the child. In a county with a population greater than 125,000, if a child being released under this section is expelled under Section 37.007, Education Code, the release shall be conditioned on the child's attending a juvenile justice alternative education program pending a deferred prosecution or formal court disposition of the child's case.

(g) No statement made by the child at the detention hearing shall be admissible against the child at any other hearing.

(h) A detention order extends to the conclusion of the disposition hearing, if there is one, but in no event for more than 10 working days. Further detention orders may be made following subsequent detention hearings. The initial detention hearing may not be waived but subsequent detention hearings may be waived in accordance with the requirements of Section 51.09. Each subsequent detention order shall extend for no more than 10 working days, except that in a county that does not have a certified juvenile detention facility, as described by Section 51.12(a)(3), each subsequent detention order shall extend for no more than 15 working days.

(i) A child in custody may be detained for as long as 10 days without the hearing described in Subsection (a) of this section if:

(1) a written request for shelter in detention facilities pending arrangement of transportation to his place of residence in another state or country or another county of this state is voluntarily executed by the child not later than the next working day after he was taken into custody;

(2) the request for shelter contains:

(A) a statement by the child that he voluntarily agrees to submit himself to custody and detention for a period of not longer than 10 days without a detention hearing;

(B) an allegation by the person detaining the child that the child has left his place of residence in another state or country or another county of this state, that he is in need of shelter, and that an effort is being made to arrange transportation to his place of residence; and

(C) a statement by the person detaining the child that he has advised the child of his right to demand a detention hearing under Subsection (a) of this section; and

(3) the request is signed by the juvenile court judge to evidence his knowledge of the fact that the child is being held in detention.

(j) The request for shelter may be revoked by the child at any time, and on such revocation, if further detention is necessary, a detention hearing shall be held not later than the next working day in accordance with Subsections (a) through (g) of this section.

(k) Notwithstanding anything in this title to the contrary, the child may sign a request for shelter without the concurrence of an adult specified in Section 51.09 of this code.

(*l*) The juvenile board or, if there is none, the juvenile court, may appoint a referee to conduct the detention hearing. The referee shall be an attorney licensed to practice law in this state. Such payment or additional payment as may be warranted for referee services shall be provided from county funds. Before commencing the detention hearing, the referee shall inform the parties who have appeared that they are entitled to have the hearing before the juvenile court judge or a substitute judge authorized by Section 51.04(f) of this code. If a party objects to the referee conducting the detention hearing, an authorized judge shall conduct the hearing within 24 hours. At the conclusion of the hearing, the referee shall transmit written findings and recommendations to the juvenile court judge or substitute judge. The juvenile court judge or substitute judge shall adopt, modify, or reject the referee's recommendations not later than the next working day after the day that the judge receives the recommendations. Failure to act within that time results in release of the child by operation of law. A recommendation that the child be released operates to secure his immediate release, subject to the power of the juvenile court judge or substitute judge to reject or modify that recommendation. The effect of an order detaining a child shall be computed from the time of the hearing before the referee.

(m) The detention hearing required in this section may be held in the county of the designated place of detention where the child is being held even though the designated place of detention is outside the county of residence of the child or the county in which the alleged delinquent conduct or conduct indicating a need for supervision occurred.

(n) An attorney appointed by the court under Section 51.10(c) because a determination was made under this section to detain a child who was not represented by an attorney may request on behalf of the child and is entitled to a de novo detention hearing under this section. The attorney must make the request not later than the 10th working day after the date the attorney is appointed. The hearing must take place not later than the second working day after the date the attorney filed a formal request with the court for a hearing.

(*o*) The court or referee shall find whether there is probable cause to believe that a child taken into custody without an arrest warrant or a directive to apprehend has engaged in delinquent conduct or conduct indicating a need for supervision. The court or referee must make the finding within 48 hours, including weekends and holidays, of the time the child was taken into custody. The court or referee may make the finding on any reasonably reliable information without regard to admissibility of that information under the Texas Rules of Criminal Evidence. A finding of probable cause is required to detain a child after the 48th hour after the time the child was taken into custody. If a court or referee finds probable cause, additional findings of probable cause are not required in the same cause to authorize further detention.

(p) If a child is detained in a county jail or other facility as provided by Section 51.12(*l*) and the child is not released under Section 53.02(f), a detention hearing without a jury shall be held promptly, but not later than the 24th hour, excluding weekends and holidays, after the time the child is taken into custody. *(Added by L.1999, chap. 232(4), eff. 9/1/99. See other subsection (p) below.)*

(p) If a child has not been released under Section 53.02 or this section and a petition has not been filed under Section 53.04 concerning the child, the court shall order the child released from detention not later than:

(1) the 30th working day after the date the initial detention hearing is held, if the child is alleged to have engaged in conduct constituting a capital felony, an aggravated controlled substance felony, or a felony of the first degree; or

(2) the 15th working day after the date the initial detention hearing is held, if the child is alleged to have engaged in conduct constituting an offense other than an offense listed in Subdivision (1).

*(Added by L.1999, chap. 1477(7), eff. 9/1/99. See other subsection (p) above.)*
*(Chgd. by L.1995, chap. 262(31); L.1997, chaps. 922(1), 1015(18), 1086(9); L.1999, chaps. 232(4), 1477(7), eff. 9/1/99.)*

### §54.011. Detention hearings for status offenders and nonoffenders.

(a) The detention hearing for a status offender or nonoffender who has not been released administratively under Section 53.02 shall be held before the 24th hour after the time the child arrived at a detention facility, excluding hours of a weekend or a holiday. Except as otherwise provided by this section, the judge or referee conducting the detention hearing shall release the status offender or nonoffender from secure detention.

(b) The judge or referee may order a child in detention accused of the violation of a valid court order as defined by Section 51.02 detained not longer than 72 hours after the time the detention order was entered, excluding weekends and holidays, if:

(1) the judge or referee finds at the detention hearing that there is probable cause to believe the child violated the valid court order; and

(2) the detention of the child is justified under Section 54.01(e)(1), (2), or (3).

(c) Except as provided by Subsection (d), a detention order entered under Subsection (b) may be extended for one additional 72-hour period, excluding weekends and holidays, only on a finding of good cause by the juvenile court.

(d) A detention order for a child under this section may be extended on the demand of the child's attorney only to allow the time that is necessary to comply with the requirements of Section 51.10(h), entitling the attorney to 10 days to prepare for an adjudication hearing.

(e) A status offender may be detained for a necessary period, not to exceed five days, to enable the child's return to the child's home in another state under Chapter 60.

*(Added by L.1995, chap. 262(32); chgd. by L.1997, chap. 1374(7), eff. 9/1/97.)*

### §54.012. Interactive video recording of detention hearing.

(a) A detention hearing under Section 54.01, other than the first detention hearing, may be held using interactive video equipment if:

(1) the child and the child's attorney agree to the video hearing; and

(2) the parties to the proceeding have the opportunity to cross-examine witnesses.

(b) A detention hearing may not be held using video equipment unless the video equipment for the hearing provides for a two-way communication of image and sound among the child, the court, and other parties at the hearing.

(c) A recording of the communications shall be made. The recording shall be preserved until the earlier of:

(1) the 91st day after the date on which the recording is made if the child is alleged to have engaged in conduct constituting a misdemeanor;

(2) the 120th day after the date on which the recording is made if the child is alleged to have engaged in conduct constituting a felony; or

(3) the date on which the adjudication hearing ends.

(d) An attorney for the child may obtain a copy of the recording on payment of the reasonable costs of reproducing the copy.

*(Added by L.1995, chap. 262(33), eff. 1/1/96.)*

Printed in the U.S.A. 17

**§54.02. Waiver of jurisdiction and discretionary transfer to criminal court.† [*Waiver of jurisdiction and discretionary move to criminal court.*]**

(a) The juvenile court may waive its exclusive original jurisdiction and transfer a child to the appropriate district court or criminal district court for criminal proceedings if:

(1) the child is alleged to have violated a penal law of the grade of felony;

(2) the child was:

(A) 14 years of age or older at the time he is alleged to have committed the offense, if the offense is a capital felony, an aggravated controlled substance felony, or a felony of the first degree, and no adjudication hearing has been conducted concerning that offense; or

(B) 15 years of age or older at the time the child is alleged to have committed the offense, if the offense is a felony of the second or third degree or a state jail felony, and no adjudication hearing has been conducted concerning that offense; and

(3) after a full investigation and a hearing, the juvenile court determines that there is probable cause to believe that the child before the court committed the offense alleged and that because of the seriousness of the offense alleged or the background of the child the welfare of the community requires criminal proceedings.

(b) The petition and notice requirements of Sections 53.04, 53.05, 53.06, and 53.07 of this code must be satisfied, and the summons must state that the hearing is for the purpose of considering discretionary transfer to criminal court.

(c) The juvenile court shall conduct a hearing without a jury to consider transfer of the child for criminal proceedings.

(d) Prior to the hearing, the juvenile court shall order and obtain a complete diagnostic study, social evaluation, and full investigation of the child, his circumstances, and the circumstances of the alleged offense.

(e) At the transfer hearing the court may consider written reports from probation officers, professional court employees, or professional consultants in addition to the testimony of witnesses. At least one day prior to the transfer hearing, the court shall provide the attorney for the child with access to all written matter to be considered by the court in making the transfer decision. The court may order counsel not to reveal items to the child or his parent, guardian, or guardian ad litem if such disclosure would materially harm the treatment and rehabilitation of the child or would substantially decrease the likelihood of receiving information from the same or similar sources in the future.

(f) In making the determination required by Subsection (a) of this section, the court shall consider, among other matters:

(1) whether the alleged offense was against person or property, with greater weight in favor of transfer given to offenses against the person;

(2) the sophistication and maturity of the child;

(3) the record and previous history of the child; and

(4) the prospects of adequate protection of the public and the likelihood of the rehabilitation of the child by use of procedures, services, and facilities currently available to the juvenile court.

(g) If the petition alleges multiple offenses that constitute more than one criminal transaction, the juvenile court shall either retain or transfer all offenses relating to a single transaction. A child is not subject to criminal prosecution at any time for any offense arising out of a criminal transaction for which the juvenile court retains jurisdiction.

(h) If the juvenile court waives jurisdiction, it shall state specifically in the order its reasons for waiver and certify its action, including the written order and findings of the court, and shall transfer the person to the appropriate court for criminal proceedings and cause the results of the diagnostic study of the person ordered under Subsection (d), including psychological information, to be transferred to the appropriate criminal prosecutor. On transfer of the person for criminal proceedings, the person shall be dealt with as an adult and in accordance with the Code of Criminal Procedure. The transfer of custody is an arrest.

(i) A waiver under this section is a waiver of jurisdiction over the child and the criminal court may not remand the child to the jurisdiction of the juvenile court.

(j) The juvenile court may waive its exclusive original jurisdiction and transfer a person to the appropriate district court or criminal district court for criminal proceedings if:

(1) the person is 18 years of age or older;

(2) the person was:

(A) 10 years of age or older and under 17 years of age at the time the person is alleged to have committed a capital felony or an offense under Section 19.02, Penal Code;

(B) 14 years of age or older and under 17 years of age at the time the person is alleged to have committed an aggravated controlled substance felony or a felony of the first degree other than an offense under Section 19.02, Penal Code; or

(C) 15 years of age or older and under 17 years of age at the time the person is alleged to have committed a felony of the second or third degree or a state jail felony;

(3) no adjudication concerning the alleged offense has been made or no adjudication hearing concerning the offense has been conducted;

(4) the juvenile court finds from a preponderance of the evidence that:

(A) for a reason beyond the control of the state it was not practicable to proceed in juvenile court before the 18th birthday of the person; or

(B) after due diligence of the state it was not practicable to proceed in juvenile court before the 18th birthday of the person because:

(i) the state did not have probable cause to proceed in juvenile court and new evidence has been found since the 18th birthday of the person;

(ii) the person could not be found; or

(iii) a previous transfer order was reversed by an appellate court or set aside by a district court; and

(5) the juvenile court determines that there is probable cause to believe that the child before the court committed the offense alleged.

(k) The petition and notice requirements of Sections 53.04, 53.05, 53.06, and 53.07 of this code must be satisfied, and the summons must state that the hearing is for the purpose of considering waiver of jurisdiction under Subsection (j) of this section.

(*l*) The juvenile court shall conduct a hearing without a jury to consider waiver of jurisdiction under Subsection (j) of this section.

(m) Notwithstanding any other provision of this section, the juvenile court shall waive its exclusive original jurisdiction and transfer a child to the appropriate district court or criminal court for criminal proceedings if:

(1) the child has previously been transferred to a district court or criminal district court for criminal proceedings under this section, unless:

(A) the child was not indicted in the matter transferred by the grand jury;

(B) the child was found not guilty in the matter transferred;

(C) the matter transferred was dismissed with prejudice; or

(D) the child was convicted in the matter transferred, the conviction was reversed on appeal, and the appeal is final; and

(2) the child is alleged to have violated a penal law of the grade of felony.

(n) A mandatory transfer under Subsection (m) may be made without conducting the study required in discretionary transfer proceedings by Subsection (d). The requirements of Subsection (b) that the summons state that the purpose of the hearing is to consider discretionary transfer to criminal court does not apply to a transfer proceeding under Subsection (m). In a proceeding under Subsection (m), it is sufficient that the summons provide fair notice that the purpose of the hearing is to consider mandatory transfer to criminal court.

(*o*) If a respondent is taken into custody for possible discretionary transfer proceedings under Subsection (j), the juvenile court shall hold a detention hearing in the same manner as provided by Section 54.01, except that the court shall order the respondent released unless it finds that the respondent:

(1) is likely to abscond or be removed from the jurisdiction of the court;

(2) may be dangerous to himself or herself or may threaten the safety of the public if released; or

(3) has previously been found to be a delinquent child or has previously been convicted of a penal offense punishable by a term of jail or prison and is likely to commit an offense if released.

(p) If the juvenile court does not order a respondent released under Subsection (*o*), the court shall, pending the conclusion of the discretionary transfer hearing, order that the respondent be detained in:

(1) a certified juvenile detention facility as provided by Subsection (q); or

(2) an appropriate county facility for the detention of adults accused of criminal offenses.

(q) The detention of a respondent in a certified juvenile detention facility must comply with the detention requirements under this title, except that, to the extent practicable, the person shall be kept separate from children detained in the same facility.

(r) If the juvenile court orders a respondent detained in a county facility under Subsection (p), the county sheriff shall take custody of the respondent under the juvenile court's order. The juvenile court shall set or deny bond for the respondent as required by the Code of Criminal Procedure and other law applicable to the pretrial detention of adults accused of criminal offenses.

*(Chgd. by L.1995, chap. 262(34); L.1999, chap. 1477(8), eff. 9/1/99.)*

**§54.021. Justice or municipal court: truancy.**

(a) The juvenile court may waive its exclusive original jurisdiction and transfer a child to an appropriate justice or municipal court, with the permission of the justice or municipal court, for disposition in the manner provided by Subsection (b) of this section if the child is alleged to have engaged in conduct described in Section 51.03(b)(2) of this code. A waiver of jurisdiction under this subsection may be for an individual case or for all cases in which a child is alleged to have engaged in conduct described in Section 51.03(b)(2) of this code. The waiver of a juvenile court's exclusive original jurisdiction for all cases in which a child is alleged to have engaged in conduct described in Section 51.03(b)(2) of this code is effective for a period of one year.

(b) A justice or municipal court may exercise jurisdiction over a person alleged to have engaged in conduct indicating a need for supervision by engaging in conduct described in Section 51.03(b)(2) in a case where the juvenile court has waived its original jurisdiction under this section. A justice or municipal court may exercise jurisdiction under this section without regard to whether the justice of the peace or municipal judge for the court is a licensed attorney or the hearing for a case is before a jury consisting of six persons.

(c) On a finding that a person has engaged in conduct described by Section 51.03(b)(2) or conduct that violates Section 25.094, Education Code, the justice or municipal court shall enter an order appropriate to the nature of the conduct.

(d) On a finding by the justice or municipal court that the person has engaged in truant conduct described in Section 51.03(b)(2) or conduct that violates Section 25.094, Education Code, the court has jurisdiction to enter an order that includes one or more of the following provisions requiring that:

(1) the person do either or both of the following:

(A) attend a preparatory class for the high school equivalency examination provided under Section 7.111, Education Code, if the court determines that the person is too old to do well in a formal classroom environment; or

(B) if the person is at least 16 years of age, take the high school equivalency examination provided under Section 7.111, Education Code;

(2) the person attend a special program that the court determines to be in the best interests of the person, including:

(A) an alcohol and drug abuse program;

(B) rehabilitation;

(C) counseling, including self-improvement counseling;

(D) training in self-esteem and leadership;

(E) work and job skills training;

(F) training in parenting, including parental responsibility;

(G) training in manners;

(H) training in violence avoidance;

(I) sensitivity training; and

(J) training in advocacy and mentoring;

(3) the person and the person's parents, managing conservator, or guardian attend a class for students at risk of dropping out of school designed for both the person and the person's parents, managing conservator, or guardian;

(4) the person complete reasonable community service requirements;

(5) the person's driver's license be suspended in the manner provided by Section 54.042;

(6) the person attend school without unexcused absences; or

(7) the person participate in a tutorial program provided by the school attended by the person in the academic subjects in which the person is enrolled for a total number of hours ordered by the court.

(e) An order under Subsection (d)(3) that requires the parent, managing conservator, or guardian of a person to attend a class for students at risk of dropping out of school is enforceable in the justice court by contempt.

(f) A school attendance officer may refer a person alleged to have engaged in conduct described in Section 51.03(b)(2) of this code to a justice court in the county where the person resides or where the person's school is located or to a municipal court of the municipality where the person resides or where the person's school is located if the juvenile court having exclusive original jurisdiction has waived its jurisdiction as provided by Subsection (a) of this section for all cases involving conduct described by Section 51.03(b)(2) of this code.

(g) A court having jurisdiction under this section shall endorse on the summons issued to the parent, guardian, or custodian of the person who is the subject of the hearing an order directing the parent, guardian, or custodian to appear personally at the hearing and directing the person having custody of the person to bring the person to the hearing.

(h) A person commits an offense if the person is a parent, guardian, or custodian who fails to attend a hearing under this section after receiving notice under Subsection (g) of this section that the person's attendance was required. An offense under this subsection is a Class C misdemeanor.
*(Added by L.1991, chap. 741(1); chgd. by L.1993, chap. 358(1); L.1995, chaps. 260(24), 262(35); L.1997, chap. 865(1); L.1999, chap. 76(2), eff. 9/1/99.)*

## §54.022. Justice or municipal court: certain misdemeanors.

(a) On a finding by a justice or municipal court that a child committed an offense that the court has jurisdiction of under Article 4.11 or 4.14, Code of Criminal Procedure, other than a traffic offense or public intoxication, the court has jurisdiction to enter an order:

(1) referring the child or the child's parents, managing conservators, or guardians for services under Section 264.302;

(2) requiring that the child attend a special program that the court determines to be in the best interest of the child and, if the program involves the expenditure of county funds, that is approved by the county commissioners court, including a rehabilitation, counseling, self-esteem and leadership, work and job skills training, job interviewing and work preparation, self-improvement, parenting, manners, violence avoidance, tutoring, sensitivity training, parental responsibility, community service, restitution, advocacy, or mentoring program; or

(3) if the court finds the parent, managing conservator, or guardian, by act or omission, contributed to, caused, or encouraged the child's conduct, requiring that the child's parent, managing conservator, or guardian do any act or refrain from doing any act that the court determines will increase the likelihood that the child will comply with the orders of the court and that is reasonable and necessary for the welfare of the child, including:

(A) attend a parenting class or parental responsibility program; and

(B) attend the child's school classes or functions.

(b) The justice or municipal court may order the parents, managing conservator, or guardian of a child required to attend a program under Subsection (a) to pay an amount not greater than $100 to pay for the costs of the program.

(c) A justice or municipal court may require a child, parent, managing conservator, or guardian required to attend a program, class, or function under this section to submit proof of attendance to the court.

(d) A justice or municipal court shall endorse on the summons issued to a parent, managing conservator, or a guardian an order to appear personally at the hearing with the child. The summons must include a warning that the failure of the parent, managing conservator, or guardian to appear may be punishable as a Class C misdemeanor.

(e) An order under this section involving a child is enforceable under Section 51.03(a)(3) by referral to the juvenile court.

(f) A person commits an offense if the person is a parent, managing conservator, or guardian who fails to attend a hearing under this section after receiving an order under Subsection (d). An offense under this subsection is a Class C misdemeanor.

(g) Any other order under this section is enforceable by the justice or municipal court by contempt.
*(Added by L.1995, chap. 262(36); chgd. by L.1997, chap. 713(1); L.1999, chap. 76(3), eff. 9/1/99.)*

## §54.03. Adjudication hearing.

(a) A child may be found to have engaged in delinquent conduct or conduct indicating a need for supervision only after an adjudication hearing conducted in accordance with the provisions of this section.

(b) At the beginning of the adjudication hearing, the juvenile court judge shall explain to the child and his parent, guardian, or guardian ad litem:

(1) the allegations made against the child;

(2) the nature and possible consequences of the proceedings, including the law relating to the admissibility of the record of a juvenile court adjudication in a criminal proceeding;

(3) the child's privilege against self-incrimination;

(4) the child's right to trial and to confrontation of witnesses;

(5) the child's right to representation by an attorney if he is not already represented; and

(6) the child's right to trial by jury.

(c) Trial shall be by jury unless jury is waived in accordance with Section 51.09 of this code. If the hearing is on a petition that has been approved by the grand jury under Section 53.045 of this code, the jury must consist of 12 persons. Jury verdicts under this title must be unanimous.

(d) Except as provided by Section 54.031, only material, relevant, and competent evidence in accordance with the Texas Rules of Evidence applicable to criminal cases and Chapter 38, Code of Criminal Procedure, may be considered in the adjudication hearing. Except in a detention or discretionary transfer hearing, a social history report or social service file shall not be viewed by the court before the adjudication decision and shall not be viewed by the jury at any time.

(e) A child alleged to have engaged in delinquent conduct or conduct indicating a need for supervision need not be a witness against nor otherwise incriminate himself. An extrajudicial statement which was obtained without fulfilling the requirements of this title or of the constitution of this state or the United States, may not be used in an adjudication hearing. A statement made by the child out of court is insufficient to support a finding of delinquent conduct or conduct indicating a need for supervision unless it is corroborated in whole or in part by other evidence. An adjudication of delinquent conduct or conduct indicating a need for supervision cannot be had upon the testimony of an accomplice unless corroborated by other evidence tending to connect the child with the alleged delinquent conduct or conduct indicating a need for supervision; and the corroboration is not sufficient if it merely shows the commission of the alleged conduct. Evidence illegally seized or obtained is inadmissible in an adjudication hearing.

(f) At the conclusion of the adjudication hearing, the court or jury shall find whether or not the child has engaged in delinquent conduct or conduct indicating a need for supervision. The finding must be based on competent evidence admitted at the hearing. The child shall be presumed to be innocent of the charges against the child and no finding that a child has engaged in delinquent conduct or conduct indicating a need for supervision may be returned unless the state has proved such beyond a reasonable doubt. In all jury cases the jury will be instructed that the burden is on the state to prove that a child has engaged in delinquent conduct or is in need of supervision beyond a reasonable doubt. A child may be adjudicated as having engaged in conduct constituting a lesser included offense as provided by Articles 37.08 and 37.09, Code of Criminal Procedure.

(g) If the court or jury finds that the child did not engage in delinquent conduct or conduct indicating a need for supervision, the court shall dismiss the case with prejudice.

(h) If the finding is that the child did engage in delinquent conduct or conduct indicating a need for supervision, the court or jury shall state which of the allegations in the petition were found to be established by the evidence. The court shall also set a date and time for the disposition hearing.

(i) In order to preserve for appellate or collateral review the failure of the court to provide the child the explanation required by Subsection (b), the attorney for the child must comply with Rule 52(a), Texas Rules of Appellate Procedure, before testimony begins or, if the adjudication is uncontested, before the child pleads to the petition or agrees to a stipulation of evidence.

(j) When the state and the child agree to the disposition of the case, in whole or in part, the prosecuting attorney shall inform the court of the agreement between the state and the child. The court shall inform the child that the court is not required to accept the agreement. The court may delay a decision on whether to accept the agreement until after reviewing a report filed under Section 54.04(b). If the court decides not to accept the agreement, the court shall inform the child of the court's decision and give the child an opportunity to withdraw the plea or stipulation of evidence. If the court rejects the agreement, no document, testimony, or other evidence placed before the court that relates to the rejected agreement may be considered by the court in a subsequent hearing in the case. A statement made by the child before the court's rejection of the agreement to a person writing a report to be filed under Section 54.04(b) may not be admitted into evidence in a subsequent hearing in the case. If the court accepts the agreement, the court shall make a disposition in accordance with the terms of the agreement between the state and the child.

*(Chgd. by L.1995, chap. 262(37); L.1997, chap. 1086(10); L.1999, chap. 1477(9), eff. 9/1/99.)*

**§54.031. Hearsay statement of child abuse victim.† [*Hearsay statement by victim of child abuse.*]**

(a) This section applies to a hearing under this title in which a child is alleged to be a delinquent child on the basis of a violation of any of the following provisions of the Penal Code, if a child 12 years of age or younger is the alleged victim of the violation:

(1) Chapter 21 (Sexual Offenses) or 22 (Assaultive Offenses);

(2) Section 25.02 (Prohibited Sexual Conduct); or

(3) Section 43.25 (Sexual Performance by a Child).

(b) This section applies only to statements that describe the alleged violation that:

(1) were made by the child who is the alleged victim of the violation; and

(2) were made to the first person, 18 years of age or older, to whom the child made a statement about the violation.

(c) A statement that meets the requirements of Subsection (b) of this section is not inadmissible because of the hearsay rule if:

(1) on or before the 14th day before the date the hearing begins, the party intending to offer the statement:

(A) notifies each other party of its intention to do so;

(B) provides each other party with the name of the witness through whom it intends to offer the statement; and

(C) provides each other party with a written summary of the statement;

(2) the juvenile court finds, in a hearing conducted outside the presence of the jury, that the statement is reliable based on the time, content, and circumstances of the statement; and

(3) the child who is the alleged victim testifies or is available to testify at the hearing in court or in any other manner provided by law.

*(Chgd. by L.1995, chap. 76(14.31), eff. 9/1/95.)*

### §54.032. Deferral of adjudication and dismissal of certain cases on completion of teen court program.

(a) A juvenile court may defer adjudication proceedings under Section 54.03 of this code for 90 days if the child:

(1) is alleged to have engaged in conduct indicating a need for supervision that violated a penal law of this state of the grade of misdemeanor that is punishable by fine only or a penal ordinance of a political subdivision of this state;

(2) waives, under Section 51.09 of this code, the privilege against self-incrimination and testifies under oath that the allegations are true;

(3) presents to the court an oral or written request to attend a teen court program; and

(4) has not successfully completed a teen court program for the violation of the same penal law or ordinance in the two years preceding the date that the alleged conduct occurred.

(b) The teen court program must be approved by the court.

(c) The court shall dismiss the case with prejudice at the conclusion of the deferral period if the child presents satisfactory evidence that the child has successfully completed the teen court program.

(d) A case dismissed under this section may not be part of the child's records for any purpose.

(e) The court may require a child who requests a teen court program to pay a fee not to exceed $10 that is set by the court to cover the costs of administering this section. The court shall deposit the fee in the county treasury of the county in which the court is located. A child who requests a teen court program and does not complete the program is not entitled to a refund of the fee.

(f) A court may transfer a case in which proceedings have been deferred as provided by this section to a court in a contiguous county if the court to which the case is transferred consents. A case may not be transferred unless it is within the jurisdiction of the court to which it is transferred.

(g) In addition to the fee authorized by Subsection (e), the court may require a child who requests a teen court program to pay a $10 fee to cover the cost to the teen court for performing its duties under this section. The court shall pay the fee to the teen court program, and the teen court program must account to the court for the receipt and disbursal of the fee. A child who pays a fee under this subsection is not entitled to a refund of the fee, regardless of whether the child successfully completes the teen court program.

*(Added by L.1989, chap. 1031(2); chgd. by L.1995, chap. 748(1), eff. 9/1/95.)*

### §54.033. Sexually transmitted disease, AIDS, and HIV testing.

(a) A child found at the conclusion of an adjudication hearing under Section 54.03 of this code to have engaged in delinquent conduct that included a violation of Sections 21.11(a)(1), 22.011, or 22.021, Penal Code, shall undergo a medical procedure or test at the direction of the juvenile court designed to show or help show whether the child has a sexually transmitted disease, acquired immune deficiency syndrome (AIDS), human immunodeficiency virus (HIV) infection, antibodies to HIV, or infection with any other probable causative agent of AIDS. The court may direct the child to undergo the procedure or test on the court's own motion or on the request of the victim of the delinquent conduct.

(b) If the child or another person who has the power to consent to medical treatment for the child refuses to submit voluntarily or consent to the procedure or test, the court shall require the child to submit to the procedure or test.

(c) The person performing the procedure or test shall make the test results available to the local health authority. The local health authority shall be required to notify the victim of the delinquent conduct and the person found to have engaged in the delinquent conduct of the test result.

(d) The state may not use the fact that a medical procedure or test was performed on a child under this section or use the results of the procedure or test in any proceeding arising out of the delinquent conduct.

(e) Testing under this section shall be conducted in accordance with written infectious disease control protocols adopted by the Texas Board of Health that clearly establish procedural guidelines that provide criteria for testing and that respect the rights of the child and the victim of the delinquent conduct.

(f) Nothing in this section allows a court to release a test result to anyone other than a person specifically authorized under this section. Section 81.103(d), Health and Safety Code, may not be construed to allow the disclosure of test results under this section except as provided by this section.

*(Added by L.1993, chap. 811(2), eff. 9/1/93.)*

## §54.034. Limited right to appeal: warning.

Before the court may accept a child's plea or stipulation of evidence in a proceeding held under this title, the court shall inform the child that if the court accepts the plea or stipulation and the court makes a disposition in accordance with the agreement between the state and the child regarding the disposition of the case, the child may not appeal an order of the court entered under Section 54.03, 54.04, or 54.05, unless:

(1) the court gives the child permission to appeal; or

(2) the appeal is based on a matter raised by written motion filed before the proceeding in which the child entered the plea or agreed to the stipulation of evidence.

*(Added by L.1999, chap. 74(1), eff. 9/1/99.)*

## §54.04. Disposition hearing.† [*Hearing on disposition.*]

(a) The disposition hearing shall be separate, distinct, and subsequent to the adjudication hearing. There is no right to a jury at the disposition hearing unless the child is in jeopardy of a determinate sentence under Subsection (d)(3) or (m) of this section, in which case, the child is entitled to a jury of 12 persons to determine the sentence.

(b) At the disposition hearing, the juvenile court may consider written reports from probation officers, professional court employees, or professional consultants, in addition to the testimony of witnesses. Prior to the disposition hearing, the court shall provide the attorney for the child with access to all written matter to be considered in disposition. The court may order counsel not to reveal items to the child or his parent, guardian, or guardian ad litem if such disclosure would materially harm the treatment and rehabilitation of the child or would substantially decrease the likelihood of receiving information from the same or similar sources in the future.

(c) No disposition may be made under this section unless the child is in need of rehabilitation or the protection of the public or the child requires that disposition be made. If the court or jury does not so find, the court shall dismiss the child and enter a final judgment without any disposition. No disposition placing the child on probation outside the child's home may be made under this section unless the court or jury finds that the child, in the child's home, cannot be provided the quality of care and level of support and supervision that the child needs to meet the conditions of the probation.

(d) If the court or jury makes the finding specified in Subsection (c) allowing the court to make a disposition in the case:

(1) the court or jury may, in addition to any order required or authorized under Section 54.041 or 54.042, place the child on probation on such reasonable and lawful terms as the court may determine:

(A) in his own home or in the custody of a relative or other fit person; or

(B) subject to the finding under Subsection (c) on the placement of the child outside the child's home, in:

(i) a suitable foster home; or

(ii) a suitable public or private institution or agency, except the Texas Youth Commission;

(2) if the court or jury found at the conclusion of the adjudication hearing that the child engaged in delinquent conduct that violates a penal law of this state or the United States of the grade of felony or, if the requirements of Subsection (q) are met, of the grade of misdemeanor, and if the petition was not approved by the grand jury under Section 53.045, the court may commit the child to the Texas Youth Commission without a determinate sentence;

(3) if the court or jury found at the conclusion of the adjudication hearing that the child engaged in delinquent conduct that included a violation of a penal law listed in Section 53.045(a) and if the petition was approved by the grand jury under Section 53.045, the court or jury may sentence the child to commitment in the Texas Youth Commission with a possible transfer to the institutional division or the pardons and paroles division of the Texas Department of Criminal Justice for a term of:

(A) not more than 40 years if the conduct constitutes:
(i) a capital felony;
(ii) a felony of the first degree; or
(iii) an aggravated controlled substance felony;
(B) not more than 20 years if the conduct constitutes a felony of the second degree; or
(C) not more than 10 years if the conduct constitutes a felony of the third degree;
(4) the court may assign the child an appropriate sanction level and sanctions as provided by the assignment guidelines in Section 59.003; or
(5) if applicable, the court or jury may make a disposition under Subsection (m).

(e) The Texas Youth Commission shall accept a person properly committed to it by a juvenile court even though the person may be 17 years of age or older at the time of commitment.

(f) The court shall state specifically in the order its reasons for the disposition and shall furnish a copy of the order to the child. If the child is placed on probation, the terms of probation shall be written in the order.

(g) If the court orders a disposition under Subsection (d)(3) or (m) of this section and there is an affirmative finding that the defendant used or exhibited a deadly weapon during the commission of the conduct or during immediate flight from commission of the conduct, the court shall enter the finding in the order. If there is an affirmative finding that the deadly weapon was a firearm, the court shall enter that finding in the order.

(h) At the conclusion of the dispositional hearing, the court shall inform the child of:
(1) the child's right to appeal, as required by Section 56.01 of this code; and
(2) the procedures for the sealing of the child's records under Section 58.003 of this code.

(i) If the court places the child on probation outside the child's home or commits the child to the Texas Youth Commission, the court shall include in its order its determination that:
(1) it is in the child's best interests to be placed outside the child's home;
(2) reasonable efforts were made to prevent or eliminate the need for the child's removal from the home and to make it possible for the child to return to the child's home; and
(3) the child, in the child's home, cannot be provided the quality of care and level of support and supervision that the child needs to meet the conditions of probation.

(j) If the court or jury found that the child engaged in delinquent conduct that included a violation of a penal law of the grade of felony, the court:
(1) shall require that the child's thumbprint be affixed to the order; and
(2) may require that a photograph of the child be attached to the order.

(k) Except as provided by Subsection (m), the period to which a court or jury may sentence a person to commitment to the Texas Youth Commission with a transfer to the Texas Department of Criminal Justice under Subsection (d)(3) of this section applies without regard to whether the person has previously been adjudicated as having engaged in delinquent conduct.

(*l*) Except as provided by Subsection (q), a court or jury may place a child on probation under Subsection (d)(1) for any period, except that probation may not continue on or after the child's 18th birthday. Except as provided by Subsection (q), the court may, before the period of probation ends, extend the probation for any period, except that the probation may not extend to or after the child's 18th birthday.

(m) The court or jury may sentence a child adjudicated for habitual felony conduct as described by Section 51.031 to a term prescribed by Subsection (d)(3) and applicable to the conduct adjudicated in the pending case if:
(1) a petition was filed and approved by a grand jury under Section 53.045 alleging that the child engaged in habitual felony conduct; and
(2) the court or jury finds beyond a reasonable doubt that the allegation described by Subdivision (1) in the grand jury petition is true.

(n) A court may order a disposition of secure confinement of a status offender adjudicated for violating a valid court order only if:
(1) before the order is issued, the child received the full due process rights guaranteed by the Constitution of the United States or the Texas Constitution; and
(2) the juvenile probation department in a report authorized by Subsection (b):
(A) reviewed the behavior of the child and the circumstances under which the child was brought before the court;
(B) determined the reasons for the behavior that caused the child to be brought before the court; and
(C) determined that all dispositions, including treatment, other than placement in a secure detention facility or secure correctional facility, have been exhausted or are clearly inappropriate.

(*o*) A status offender may not, under any circumstances, be committed to the Texas Youth Commission for engaging in conduct that would not, under state or local law, be a crime if committed by an adult.

(p) Except as provided by Subsection (*l*), a court that places a child on probation under Subsection (d)(1) for conduct described by Section 54.0405(b) and punishable as a felony shall specify a minimum probation period of two years.

(q) If the judge orders a disposition under this section and there is an affirmative finding that the victim or intended victim was younger than 17 years of age at the time of the conduct, the judge shall enter the finding in the order. *(Added by L.1999, chaps. 1193(9), 1415(19), eff. 9/1/99. See two other subsections (q) below.)*

(q) The court may make a disposition under Subsection (d)(2) for delinquent conduct that violates a penal law of the grade of misdemeanor if:

(1) the child has been adjudicated as having engaged in delinquent conduct violating a penal law of the grade of felony or misdemeanor on at least two previous occasions;

(2) of the previous adjudications, the conduct that was the basis for one of the adjudications occurred after the date of another previous adjudication; and

(3) the conduct that is the basis of the current adjudication occurred after the date of at least two previous adjudications.

*(Added by L.1999, chap. 1448(1), eff. 9/1/99. See two other subsections (q) above and below.)*

(q) If a court or jury sentences a child to commitment in the Texas Youth Commission under Subsection (d)(3) for a term of not more than 10 years, the court or jury may place the child on probation under Subsection (d)(1) as an alternative to making the disposition under Subsection (d)(3). The court shall prescribe the period of probation ordered under this subsection for a term of not more than 10 years. The court may, before the sentence of probation expires, extend the probationary period under Section 54.05, except that the sentence of probation and any extension may not exceed 10 years. The court may, before the child's 18th birthday, discharge the child from the sentence of probation. If a sentence of probation ordered under this subsection and any extension of probation ordered under Section 54.05 will continue after the child's 18th birthday, the court shall discharge the child from the sentence of probation on the child's 18th birthday unless the court transfers the child to an appropriate district court under Section 54.051. *(Added by L.1999, chap. 1477(10), eff. 9/1/99. See two other subsections (q) above.)*

*(Chgd. by L.1989, chaps. 2(16.01(17)), 80(1); L.1991, chaps. 557(2), 574(2), 784(8); L.1993, chap. 1048(1); L.1995, chap. 262(38); L.1997, chaps. 669(2), 1086(11); L.1999, chaps. 1193(9), 1415(19), 1448(1), 1477(10), eff. 9/1/99.)*

**§54.0405. Child placed on probation for conduct constituting sexual offense.**

(a) If a court or jury makes a disposition under Section 54.04 in which a child described by Subsection (b) is placed on probation and the court determines that the victim of the offense was a child as defined by Section 22.011(c), Penal Code, the court may require as a condition of probation that the child:

(1) attend psychological counseling sessions for sex offenders as provided by Subsection (e); and

(2) submit to a polygraph examination as provided by Subsection (f) for purposes of evaluating the child's treatment progress.

(b) This section applies to a child placed on probation for conduct constituting an offense:

(1) under Section 21.08, 21.11, 22.011, 22.021, or 25.02, Penal Code;

(2) under Section 20.04(a)(4), Penal Code, if the child engaged in the conduct with the intent to violate or abuse the victim sexually; or

(3) under Section 30.02, Penal Code, punishable under Subsection (d) of that section, if the child engaged in the conduct with the intent to commit a felony listed in Subdivision (1) or (2) of this subsection.

(c) Psychological counseling required as a condition of probation under Subsection (a) must be with an individual or organization that:

(1) provides sex offender treatment or counseling;

(2) is specified by the local juvenile probation department supervising the child; and

(3) meets minimum standards of counseling established by the local juvenile probation department.

(d) A polygraph examination required as a condition of probation under Subsection (a) must be administered by an individual who is:

(1) specified by the local juvenile probation department supervising the child; and

(2) licensed as a polygraph examiner under the Polygraph Examiners Act (Article 4413(29cc), Texas Civil Statutes).

Printed in the U.S.A. Zt

(e) A local juvenile probation department that specifies a sex offender treatment provider under Subsection (c) to provide counseling to a child shall:

(1) establish with the cooperation of the treatment provider the date, time, and place of the first counseling session between the child and the treatment provider;

(2) notify the child and the treatment provider, not later than the 21st day after the date the order making the disposition placing the child on probation under Section 54.04 becomes final, of the date, time, and place of the first counseling session between the child and the treatment provider; and

(3) require the treatment provider to notify the department immediately if the child fails to attend any scheduled counseling session.

(f) A local juvenile probation department that specifies a polygraph examiner under Subsection (d) to administer a polygraph examination to a child shall arrange for a polygraph examination to be administered to the child:

(1) not later than the 60th day after the date the child attends the first counseling session established under Subsection (e); and

(2) after the initial polygraph examination, as required by Subdivision (1), on the request of the treatment provider specified under Subsection (c).

(g) A court that requires as a condition of probation that a child attend psychological counseling under Subsection (a) may order the parent or guardian of the child to:

(1) attend four sessions of instruction with an individual or organization specified by the court relating to:

(A) sexual offenses;

(B) family communication skills;

(C) sex offender treatment;

(D) victims' rights;

(E) parental supervision; and

(F) appropriate sexual behavior; and

(2) during the period the child attends psychological counseling, participate in monthly treatment groups conducted by the child's treatment provider relating to the child's psychological counseling.

(h) A court that orders a parent or guardian of a child to attend instructional sessions and participate in treatment groups under Subsection (g) shall require:

(1) the individual or organization specified by the court under Subsection (g) to notify the court immediately if the parent or guardian fails to attend any scheduled instructional session; and

(2) the child's treatment provider specified under Subsection (c) to notify the court immediately if the parent or guardian fails to attend a session in which the parent or guardian is required to participate in a scheduled treatment group.

(i) A court that requires as a condition of probation that a child attend psychological counseling under Subsection (a) may, before the date the probation period ends, extend the probation for any additional period necessary to complete the required counseling as determined by the treatment provider, except that the probation may not be extended to a date after the date of the child's 18th birthday.

*(Added by L.1997, chap. 669(1), eff. 9/1/97.)*

## §54.0406. Child placed on probation for conduct involving a handgun.

(a) If a court or jury places a child on probation under Section 54.04(d) for conduct that violates a penal law that includes as an element of the offense the possession, carrying, using, or exhibiting of a handgun, as defined by Section 46.01, Penal Code, and if at the adjudication hearing the court or jury affirmatively finds that the child personally possessed, carried, used, or exhibited the handgun, the court shall require as a condition of probation that the child, not later than the 30th day after the date the court places the child on probation, notify the juvenile probation officer who is supervising the child of the manner in which the child acquired the handgun, including the date and place of and any person involved in the acquisition.

(b) On receipt of information described by Subsection (a), a juvenile probation officer shall promptly notify the appropriate local law enforcement agency of the information.

(c) Information provided by a child to a juvenile probation officer as required by Subsection (a) and any other information derived from that information may not be used as evidence against the child in any juvenile or criminal proceeding.

*(Added by L.1999, chap. 1446(1), eff. 9/1/99.)*

**§54.041. Orders affecting parents and others.† [*Orders with impact on parents and others.*]**

(a) When a child has been found to have engaged in delinquent conduct or conduct indicating a need for supervision and the juvenile court has made a finding that the child is in need of rehabilitation or that the protection of the public or the child requires that disposition be made, the juvenile court, on notice by any reasonable method to all persons affected, may:

(1) order any person found by the juvenile court to have, by a wilful act or omission, contributed to, caused, or encouraged the child's delinquent conduct or conduct indicating a need for supervision to do any act that the juvenile court determines to be reasonable and necessary for the welfare of the child or to refrain from doing any act that the juvenile court determines to be injurious to the welfare of the child;

(2) enjoin all contact between the child and a person who is found to be a contributing cause of the child's delinquent conduct or conduct indicating a need for supervision; or

(3) after notice and a hearing of all persons affected order any person living in the same household with the child to participate in social or psychological counseling to assist in the rehabilitation of the child and to strengthen the child's family environment.

(b) If a child is found to have engaged in delinquent conduct or conduct indicating a need for supervision arising from the commission of an offense in which property damage or loss or personal injury occurred, the juvenile court, on notice to all persons affected and on hearing, may order the child or a parent to make full or partial restitution to the victim of the offense. The program of restitution must promote the rehabilitation of the child, be appropriate to the age and physical, emotional, and mental abilities of the child, and not conflict with the child's schooling. When practicable and subject to court supervision, the court may approve a restitution program based on a settlement between the child and the victim of the offense. An order under this subsection may provide for periodic payments by the child or a parent of the child for the period specified in the order but that period may not extend past the date of the 18th birthday of the child or past the date the child is no longer enrolled in an accredited secondary school in a program leading toward a high school diploma, whichever date is later.

(c) Restitution under this section is cumulative of any other remedy allowed by law and may be used in addition to other remedies; except that a victim of an offense is not entitled to receive more than actual damages under a juvenile court order.

(d) A person subject to an order proposed under Subsection (a) of this section is entitled to a hearing on the order before the order is entered by the court.

(e) An order made under this section may be enforced as provided by Section 54.07 of this code.

(f) If a child is found to have engaged in conduct indicating a need for supervision described under Section 51.03(b)(2) of this code, the court may order the child's parents or guardians to attend a class described by Section 25.093(h), Education Code, if the school district in which the child's parents or guardians reside offers a class under that section.

(g) On a finding by the court that a child's parents or guardians have made a reasonable good faith effort to prevent the child from engaging in delinquent conduct or engaging in conduct indicating a need for supervision and that, despite the parents' or guardians' efforts, the child continues to engage in such conduct, the court shall waive any requirement for restitution that may be imposed on a parent under this section.

*(Chgd. by L.1989, chap. 1170(3); L.1995, chap. 262(39); L.1997, chap. 165(6.09), eff. 9/1/97.)*

**§54.0411. Juvenile probation diversion fund.**

(a) If a disposition hearing is held under Section 54.04 of this code, the juvenile court, after giving the child, parent, or other person responsible for the child's support a reasonable opportunity to be heard, shall order the child, parent, or other person, if financially able to do so, to pay a fee as costs of court of $20.

(b) Orders for the payment of fees under this section may be enforced as provided by Section 54.07 of this code.

(c) An officer collecting costs under this section shall keep separate records of the funds collected as costs under this section and shall deposit the funds in the county treasury.

(d) Each officer collecting court costs under this section shall file the reports required under Article 103.005, Code of Criminal Procedure. If no funds due as costs under this section have been collected in any quarter, the report required for each quarter shall be filed in the regular manner, and the report must state that no funds due under this section were collected.

(e) The custodian of the county treasury may deposit the funds collected under this section in interest-bearing accounts. The custodian shall keep records of the amount of funds on deposit collected under this section and not later than the last day of the month following each calendar quarter shall send to the comptroller of public accounts the funds collected under this section during the preceding quarter. A county may retain 10 percent of the funds as a service fee and may retain the interest accrued on the funds if the custodian of a county treasury keeps records of the amount of funds on deposit collected under this section and remits the funds to the comptroller within the period prescribed under this subsection.

(f) Funds collected are subject to audit by the comptroller and funds expended are subject to audit by the State Auditor.

(g) The comptroller shall deposit the funds in a special fund to be known as the juvenile probation diversion fund.

(h) The legislature shall determine and appropriate the necessary amount from the juvenile probation diversion fund to the Texas Juvenile Probation Commission for the purchase of services the commission considers necessary for the diversion of any juvenile who is at risk of commitment to the Texas Youth Commission. The Texas Juvenile Probation Commission shall develop guidelines for the use of the fund. The commission may not purchase the services if a person responsible for the child's support or a local juvenile probation department is financially able to provide the services.

*(Chgd. by L.1989, chap. 347(8), eff. 10/1/89.)*



### §54.042. License suspension.

(a) A juvenile court, in a disposition hearing under Section 54.04, shall:

(1) order the Department of Public Safety to suspend a child's driver's license or permit, or if the child does not have a license or permit, to deny the issuance of a license or permit to the child if the court finds that the child has engaged in conduct that violates a law of this state enumerated in Section 521.342(a), Transportation Code; or

(2) notify the Department of Public Safety of the adjudication, if the court finds that the child has engaged in conduct that violates a law of this state enumerated in Section 521.372(a), Transportation Code.

(b) A juvenile court, in a disposition hearing under Section 54.04, may order the Department of Public Safety to suspend a child's driver's license or permit or, if the child does not have a license or permit, to deny the issuance of a license or permit to the child, if the court finds that the child has engaged in conduct that violates Section 28.08, Penal Code.

(c) The order under Subsection (a)(1) shall specify a period of suspension or denial that is until the child reaches the age of 19 or for a period of 365 days, whichever is longer.

(d) The order under Subsection (b) shall specify a period of suspension or denial that is:

(1) for a period not to exceed 365 days; or

(2) if the court finds the child has been previously adjudicated as having engaged in conduct violating Section 28.08, Penal Code, until the child reaches the age of 19 or for a period not to exceed 365 days, whichever is longer.

(e) A child whose driver's license or permit has been suspended or denied pursuant to this section may, if the child is otherwise eligible for, and fulfils the requirements for issuance of, a provisional driver's license or permit under Chapter 521, Transportation Code, apply for and receive an occupational license in accordance with the provisions of Subchapter L, Chapter 521, Transportation Code.

(f) A juvenile court, in a disposition hearing under Section 54.04, may order the Department of Public Safety to suspend a child's driver's license or permit or, if the child does not have a license or permit, to deny the issuance of a license or permit to the child for a period not to exceed 12 months if the court finds that the child has engaged in conduct in need of supervision or delinquent conduct other than the conduct described by Subsection (a).

(g) A juvenile court that places a child on probation under Section 54.04 may require as a reasonable condition of the probation that if the child violates the probation, the court may order the Department of Public Safety to suspend the child's driver's license or permit or, if the child does not have a license or permit, to deny the issuance of a license or permit to the child for a period not to exceed 12 months. The court may make this order if a child that is on probation under this condition violates the probation. A suspension under this subsection is cumulative of any other suspension under this section.

(h) If a child is adjudicated for conduct that violates Section 49.04, 49.07, or 49.08, Penal Code, and if any conduct on which that adjudication is based is a ground for a driver's license suspension under Chapter 524 or 724, Transportation Code, each of the suspensions shall be imposed. The court imposing a driver's license suspension under this section shall credit a period of

suspension imposed under Chapter 524 or 724, Transportation Code, toward the period of suspension required under this section, except that if the child was previously adjudicated for conduct that violates Section 49.04, 49.07, or 49.08, Penal Code, credit may not be given.
*(Chgd. by L. 1991, chaps. 14(284(42)), 784(7); L.1993, chap. 491(3); L.1995, chaps. 76(14.32), 262(40); chgd. by L.1997, chaps. 165(30.183), 593(3), 1013(17); L.1999, chap. 62(19.01(18)), eff. 9/1/99.)*

### §54.043. Monitoring school attendance.

If the court places a child on probation under Section 54.04(d) and requires as a condition of probation that the child attend school, the probation officer charged with supervising the child shall monitor the child's school attendance and report to the court if the child is voluntarily absent from school. *(Added by L.1993, chap. 347(6.02), eff. 9/1/93.)*

### §54.044. Community service.

(a) If the court places a child on probation under Section 54.04(d), the court shall require as a condition of probation that the child work a specified number of hours at a community service project approved by the court and designated by the juvenile board as provided by Subsection (e), unless the court determines and enters a finding on the order placing the child on probation that:

(1) the child is physically or mentally incapable of participating in the project;

(2) participating in the project will be a hardship on the child or the family of the child; or

(3) the child has shown good cause that community service should not be required.

(b) The court may also order under this section that the child's parent perform community service with the child.

(c) The court shall order that the child and the child's parent perform a total of not more than 500 hours of community service under this section.

(d) A municipality or county that establishes a program to assist children and their parents in rendering community service under this section may purchase insurance policies protecting the municipality or county against claims brought by a person other than the child or the child's parent for a cause of action that arises from an act of the child or parent while rendering community service. The municipality or county is not liable under this section to the extent that damages are recoverable under a contract of insurance or under a plan of self-insurance authorized by statute. The liability of the municipality or county for a cause of action that arises from an action of the child or the child's parent while rendering community service may not exceed $100,000 to a single person and $300,000 for a single occurrence in the case of personal injury or death, and $10,000 for a single occurrence of property damage. Liability may not extend to punitive or exemplary damages. This subsection does not waive a defense, immunity, or jurisdictional bar available to the municipality or county or its officers or employees, nor shall this section be construed to waive, repeal, or modify any provision of Chapter 101, Civil Practice and Remedies Code.

(e) For the purposes of this section, a court may submit to the juvenile probation department a list of organizations or projects approved by the court for community service. The juvenile probation department may:

(1) designate an organization or project for community service only from the list submitted by the court; and

(2) reassign or transfer a child to a different organization or project on the list submitted by the court under this subsection without court approval.

(f) A person subject to an order proposed under Subsection (a) or (b) is entitled to a hearing on the order before the order is entered by the court.

(g) On a finding by the court that a child's parents or guardians have made a reasonable good faith effort to prevent the child from engaging in delinquent conduct or engaging in conduct indicating a need for supervision and that, despite the parents' or guardians' efforts, the child continues to engage in such conduct, the court shall waive any requirement for community service that may be imposed on a parent under this section.

(h) An order made under this section may be enforced as provided by Section 54.07.

(i) In a disposition hearing under Section 54.04 in which the court finds that a child engaged in conduct violating Section 521.453, Transportation Code, the court, in addition to any other order authorized under this title and if the court is located in a municipality or county that has established a community service program, may order the child to perform eight hours of community service as a condition of probation under Section 54.04(d) unless the child is shown to have previously engaged in conduct violating Section 521.453, Transportation Code, in which case the court may order the child to perform 12 hours of community service.
*(Added by L.1995, chap. 262(41); chgd. by L.1997, chap. 1358(2), eff. 9/1/97.)*

## §54.045. Admission of unadjudicated conduct.

(a) During a disposition hearing under Section 54.04, a child may:

(1) admit having engaged in delinquent conduct or conduct indicating a need for supervision for which the child has not been adjudicated; and

(2) request the court to take the admitted conduct into account in the disposition of the child.

(b) If the prosecuting attorney agrees in writing, the court may take the admitted conduct into account in the disposition of the child.

(c) A court may take into account admitted conduct over which exclusive venue lies in another county only if the court obtains the written permission of the prosecuting attorney for that county.

(d) A child may not be adjudicated by any court for having engaged in conduct taken into account under this section, except that, if the conduct taken into account included conduct over which exclusive venue lies in another county and the written permission of the prosecuting attorney of that county was not obtained, the child may be adjudicated for that conduct, but the child's admission under this section may not be used against the child in the adjudication.

*(Added by L.1995, chap. 262(41), eff. 1/1/96.)*



## §54.046. Conditions of probation for damaging property with graffiti.

(a) If a juvenile court places on probation under Section 54.04(d) a child adjudicated as having engaged in conduct in violation of Section 28.08, Penal Code, in addition to other conditions of probation, the court may, with consent of the owner of the property, order the child as a condition of probation to restore the property by removing or painting over any markings made by the child on the property.

(b) In addition to a condition imposed under Subsection (a), the court may require the child as a condition of probation to attend a class with instruction in self-responsibility and empathy for a victim of an offense conducted by a local juvenile probation department.

*(Added by L.1997, chap. 593(7), eff. 9/1/97.)*

## §54.0461. Payment of graffiti eradication fees.

(a) If a child is adjudicated as having engaged in delinquent conduct that violates Section 28.08, Penal Code, the juvenile court shall order the child, parent, or other person responsible for the child's support to pay to the court a $5 graffiti eradication fee as a cost of court.

(b) The court shall deposit fees received under this section to the credit of the county graffiti eradication fund provided for under Article 102.0171, Code of Criminal Procedure.

(c) If the court finds that a child, parent, or other person responsible for the child's support is unable to pay the graffiti eradication fee required under Subsection (a), the court shall enter into the child's case records a statement of that finding. The court may waive a fee under this section only if the court makes the finding under this subsection.

*(Added by L.1999, chap. 174(1), eff. 9/1/99.)*

## §54.047. Alcohol-related offense.

If the court or jury finds at an adjudication hearing for a child that the child engaged in conduct indicating a need for supervision or delinquent conduct that violates the alcohol-related offenses in Section 106.02, 106.025, 106.04, 106.05, or 106.07, Alcoholic Beverage Code, or Section 49.02, Penal Code, the court shall, subject to a finding under Section 54.04(c), order, in addition to any other order authorized by this title, that, in the manner provided by Section 106.071(d), Alcoholic Beverage Code:

(1) the child perform community service; and

(2) the child's driver's license or permit be suspended or that the child be denied issuance of a driver's license or permit.

*(Added by L.1997, chap. 1013(18); renumbered from section 54.046 by L.1999, chap. 62(19.01(19)), eff. 9/1/99.)*

## §54.05. Hearing to modify disposition.† [*Hearing to alter disposition.*]

(a) Any disposition, except a commitment to the Texas Youth Commission, may be modified by the juvenile court as provided in this section until

(1) the child reaches his 18th birthday; or

(2) the child is earlier discharged by the court or operation of law.

(b) Except for a commitment to the Texas Youth Commission, all dispositions automatically terminate when the child reaches his 18th birthday.

(c) There is no right to a jury at a hearing to modify disposition.

(d) A hearing to modify disposition shall be held on the petition of the child and his parent, guardian, guardian ad litem, or attorney, or on the petition of the state, a probation officer, or the court itself. Reasonable notice of a hearing to modify disposition shall be given to all parties. When the petition to modify is filed under Section 51.03(a)(2) of this code, the court must hold an adjudication hearing and make an affirmative finding prior to considering any written reports under Subsection (e) of this section.

(e) After the hearing on the merits of facts, the court may consider written reports from probation officers, professional court employees, or professional consultants in addition to the testimony of other witnesses. Prior to the hearing to modify disposition, the court shall provide the attorney for the child with access to all written matter to be considered by the court in deciding whether to modify disposition. The court may order counsel not to reveal items to the child or his parent, guardian, or guardian ad litem if such disclosure would materially harm the treatment and rehabilitation of the child or would substantially decrease the likelihood of receiving information from the same or similar sources in the future.

(f) Except as provided by Subsection (j), a disposition based on a finding that the child engaged in delinquent conduct that violates a penal law of this state or the United States of the grade of felony or, if the requirements of Subsection (j) are met, of the grade of misdemeanor, may be modified so as to commit the child to the Texas Youth Commission if the court after a hearing to modify disposition finds by a preponderance of the evidence that the child violated a reasonable and lawful order of the court. A disposition based on a finding that the child engaged in habitual felony conduct as described by Section 51.031 or in delinquent conduct that included a violation of a penal law listed in Section 53.045(a) may be modified to commit the child to the Texas Youth Commission with a possible transfer to the institutional division or the pardons and paroles division of the Texas Department of Criminal Justice for a definite term prescribed by Section 54.04(d)(3) if the original petition was approved by the grand jury under Section 53.045 and if after a hearing to modify the disposition the court finds that the child violated a reasonable and lawful order of the court.

(g) Except as provided by Subsection (j), a disposition based solely on a finding that the child engaged in conduct indicating a need for supervision may not be modified to commit the child to the Texas Youth Commission. A new finding in compliance with Section 54.03 must be made that the child engaged in delinquent conduct that meets the requirements for commitment under Section 54.04.

(h) A hearing shall be held prior to commitment to the Texas Youth Commission as a modified disposition. In other disposition modifications, the child and the child's parent, guardian, guardian ad litem, or attorney may waive hearing in accordance with Section 51.09.

(i) The court shall specifically state in the order its reasons for modifying the disposition and shall furnish a copy of the order to the child.

(j) The court may modify a disposition under Subsection (f) that is based on a finding that the child engaged in delinquent conduct that violates a penal law of the grade of misdemeanor if:

(1) the child has been adjudicated as having engaged in delinquent conduct violating a penal law of the grade of felony or misdemeanor on at least two previous occasions; and

(2) of the previous adjudications, the conduct that was the basis for the adjudications occurred after the date of another previous adjudication.

*(Added by L.1999, chap. 1448(2), eff. 9/1/99. See other subsection (j) below.)*

(j) If, after conducting a hearing to modify disposition without a jury, the court finds by a preponderance of the evidence that a child violated a reasonable and lawful condition of probation ordered under Section 54.04(q), the court may modify the disposition to commit the child to the Texas Youth Commission under Section 54.04(d)(3) for a term that does not exceed the original sentence assessed by the court or jury. *(Added by L.1999, chap. 1477(11), eff. 9/1/99. See other subsection (j) above.)*

*(Chgd. by L.1991, chap. 557(3); L.1995, chap. 262(42); L.1999, chaps. 1448(2), 1477(11), eff. 9/1/99.)*

## §54.051. Transfer of determinate sentence probation to appropriate district court.

(a) On motion of the state concerning a child who is placed on probation under Section 54.04(q) for a period, including any extension ordered under Section 54.05, that will continue after the child's 18th birthday, the juvenile court shall hold a hearing to determine whether to transfer the child to an appropriate district court or discharge the child from the sentence of probation.

(b) The hearing must be conducted before the child's 18th birthday and in the same manner as a hearing to modify disposition under Section 54.05.

(c) If, after a hearing, the court determines to discharge the child, the court shall specify a date on or before the child's 18th birthday to discharge the child from the sentence of probation.

(d) If, after a hearing, the court determines to transfer the child, the court shall transfer the child to an appropriate district court on the child's 18th birthday.

(e) A district court that exercises jurisdiction over a child transferred under Subsection (d) shall place the child on community supervision under Article 42.12, Code of Criminal Procedure, for the remainder of the child's probationary period and under conditions consistent with those ordered by the juvenile court. If a child who is placed on community supervision under this subsection violates a condition of that supervision or if the child violated a condition of probation ordered under Section 54.04(q) and that probation violation was not discovered by the state before the child's 18th birthday, the district court shall dispose of the violation of community supervision or probation, as appropriate, in the same manner as if the court had originally exercised jurisdiction over the case. The time that a child serves on probation ordered under Section 54.04(q) is the same as time served on community supervision ordered under this subsection for purposes of determining the child's eligibility for early discharge from community supervision under Section 20, Article 42.12, Code of Criminal Procedure.

(f) The juvenile court may transfer a child to an appropriate district court as provided by this section without a showing that the child violated a condition of probation ordered under Section 54.04(q).

*(Added by L.1999, chap. 1477(12), eff. 9/1/99.)*



## §54.06. Judgments for support.

(a) At any stage of the proceeding, when a child has been placed outside the child's home, the juvenile court, after giving the parent or other person responsible for the child's support a reasonable opportunity to be heard, shall order the parent or other person to pay in a manner directed by the court a reasonable sum for the support in whole or in part of the child or the court shall waive the payment by order. The court shall order that the payment for support be made to the local juvenile probation department to be used only for residential care and other support for the child unless the child has been committed to the Texas Youth Commission, in which case the court shall order that the payment be made to the Texas Youth Commission for deposit in a special account in the general revenue fund that may be appropriated only for the care of children committed to the commission.

(b) At any stage of the proceeding, when a child has been placed outside the child's home and the parent of the child is obligated to pay support for the child under a court order under Title 5, the juvenile court shall order that the person entitled to receive the support assign the person's right to support for the child placed outside the child's home to the local juvenile probation department to be used for residential care and other support for the child unless the child has been committed to the Texas Youth Commission, in which event the court shall order that the assignment be made to the Texas Youth Commission.

(c) A court may enforce an order for support under this section by ordering garnishment of the wages of the person ordered to pay support or by any other means available to enforce a child support order under Title 5.

(d) An order for support may be enforced as provided in Section 54.07 of this code.

(e) The court shall apply the child support guidelines under Subchapter C, Chapter 154, in an order requiring the payment of child support under this section. The court shall also require in an order to pay child support under this section that health insurance be provided for the child. Subchapter D, Chapter 154, applies to an order requiring health insurance for a child under this section.

(f) An order under this section prevails over any previous child support order issued with regard to the child to the extent of any conflict between the orders.

*(Chgd. by L.1993, chaps. 798(23), 1048(2); L.1995, chap. 262(43); L.1997, chap. 165(7.11), eff. 9/1/97.)*

## §54.061. Payment of probation fees.† [*Remittal of probation fees.*]

(a) If a child is placed on probation under Section 54.04(d)(1) of this code, the juvenile court, after giving the child, parent, or other person responsible for the child's support a reasonable opportunity to be heard, shall order the child, parent, or other person, if financially able to do so, to pay to the court a fee of not more than $15 a month during the period that the child continues on probation.

(b) Orders for the payment of fees under this section may be enforced as provided by Section 54.07 of this code.

(c) The court shall deposit the fees received under this section in the county treasury to the credit of a special fund that may be used only for juvenile probation or community-based juvenile corrections services or facilities in which a juvenile may be required to live while under court supervision.

(d) If the court finds that a child, parent, or other person responsible for the child's support is financially unable to pay the probation fee required under Subsection (a), the court shall enter into the records of the child's case a statement of that finding. The court may waive a fee under this section only if the court makes the finding under this subsection.
*(Chgd. by L.1995, chap. 262(44), eff. 1/1/96.)*

### §54.07. Enforcement of order.

(a) Any order of the juvenile court may be enforced by contempt.

(b) The juvenile court may enforce its order for support or for the payment of restitution or probation fees by civil contempt proceedings after 10 days' notice to the defaulting person of his failure or refusal to carry out the terms of the order.

(c) On the motion of the juvenile court or any person or agency entitled to receive restitution or probation payments or payments for the benefit of a child, the juvenile court may render judgment against a defaulting person for any amount unpaid and owing after 10 days' notice to the defaulting person of his failure or refusal to carry out the terms of the order. The judgment may be enforced by any means available for the enforcement of judgments for other debts.

### §54.08. Public access to court hearings.

(a) Except as provided by this section, the court shall open hearings under this title to the public unless the court, for good cause shown, determines that the public should be excluded.

(b) The court may not prohibit a person who is a victim of the conduct of a child, or the person's family, from personally attending a hearing under this title relating to the conduct by the child unless the victim or member of the victim's family is to testify in the hearing or any subsequent hearing relating to the conduct and the court determines that the victim's or family member's testimony would be materially affected if the victim or member of the victim's family hears other testimony at trial.

(c) If a child is under the age of 14 at the time of the hearing, the court shall close the hearing to the public unless the court finds that the interests of the child or the interests of the public would be better served by opening the hearing to the public.

(d) In this section, "family" has the meaning assigned by Section 71.003.
*(Chgd. by L.1995, chap. 262(45); L.1997, chap. 1086(12), eff. 9/1/97.)*

### §54.09. Recording of proceedings.

All judicial proceedings under this chapter except detention hearings shall be recorded by stenographic notes or by electronic, mechanical, or other appropriate means. Upon request of any party, a detention hearing shall be recorded.

### §54.10. Hearings before referee.

(a) Except as provided by Subsection (e), a hearing under Section 54.03, 54.04, or 54.05, including a jury trial, a hearing under Chapter 55, including a jury trial, or a hearing under Article IV, Article V, and Article VI of the Uniform Interstate Compact on Juveniles (Chapter 60) may be held by a referee appointed in accordance with Section 51.04(g) or a master appointed under Chapter 54, Government Code, provided:

(1) the parties have been informed by the referee or master that they are entitled to have the hearing before the juvenile court judge; and

(2) after each party is given an opportunity to object, no party objects to holding the hearing before the referee or master.

(b) The determination under Section 53.02(f) whether to release a child may be made by a referee appointed in accordance with Section 51.04(g) if:

(1) the child has been informed by the referee that the child is entitled to have the determination made by the juvenile court judge or a substitute judge authorized by Section 51.04(f); or

(2) the child and the attorney for the child have in accordance with Section 51.09 waived the right to have the determination made by the juvenile court judge or a substitute judge.

(c) If a child objects to a referee making the determination under Section 53.02(f), the juvenile court judge or a substitute judge authorized by Section 51.04(f) shall make the determination.

(d) At the conclusion of the hearing or immediately after making the determination, the referee shall transmit written findings and recommendations to the juvenile court judge. The juvenile court judge shall adopt, modify, or reject the referee's recommendations not later than the next working day after the day that the judge receives the recommendations. Failure to act within that time results in release of the child by operation of law and a recommendation that the child be released operates to secure the child's immediate release subject to the power of the juvenile court judge to modify or reject that recommendation.

(e) The hearings provided by Sections 54.03, 54.04, and 54.05 may not be held before a referee if the grand jury has approved of the petition and the child is subject to a determinate sentence.

*(Chgd. by L.1991, chap. 74(1); L.1997, chap. 1086(13); L.1999, chaps. 232(5), 1477(13), eff. 9/1/99.)*

## §54.11. Release or transfer hearing.

(a) On receipt of a referral under Section 61.079(a), Human Resources Code, for the transfer to the institutional division of the Texas Department of Criminal Justice of a person committed to the Texas Youth Commission under Section 54.04(d)(3), 54.04(m), or 54.05(f), or on receipt of a request by the commission under Section 61.081(g), Human Resources Code, for approval of the release under supervision of a person committed to the commission under Section 54.04(d)(3), 54.04(m), or 54.05(f), the court shall set a time and place for a hearing on the release of the person.

(b) The court shall notify the following of the time and place of the hearing:

(1) the person to be transferred or released under supervision;

(2) the parents of the person;

(3) any legal custodian of the person, including the Texas Youth Commission;

(4) the office of the prosecuting attorney that represented the state in the juvenile delinquency proceedings;

(5) the victim of the offense that was included in the delinquent conduct that was a ground for the disposition, or a member of the victim's family; and

(6) any other person who has filed a written request with the court to be notified of a release hearing with respect to the person to be transferred or released under supervision.

(c) Except for the person to be transferred or released under supervision and the prosecuting attorney, the failure to notify a person listed in Subsection (b) of this section does not affect the validity of a hearing conducted or determination made under this section if the record in the case reflects that the whereabouts of the persons who did not receive notice were unknown to the court and a reasonable effort was made by the court to locate those persons.

(d) At a hearing under this section the court may consider written reports from probation officers, professional court employees, or professional consultants, in addition to the testimony of witnesses. At least one day before the hearing, the court shall provide the attorney for the person to be transferred or released under supervision with access to all written matter to be considered by the court.

(e) At the hearing, the person to be transferred or released under supervision is entitled to an attorney, to examine all witnesses against him, to present evidence and oral argument, and to previous examination of all reports on and evaluations and examinations of or relating to him that may be used in the hearing.

(f) A hearing under this section is open to the public unless the person to be transferred or released under supervision waives a public hearing with the consent of his attorney and the court.

(g) A hearing under this section must be recorded by a court reporter or by audio or video tape recording, and the record of the hearing must be retained by the court for at least two years after the date of the final determination on the transfer or release of the person by the court.

(h) The hearing on a person who is referred for transfer under Section 61.079(a), Human Resources Code, shall be held not later than the 60th day after the date the court receives the referral.

(i) On conclusion of the hearing on a person who is referred for transfer under Section 61.079(a), Human Resources Code, the court may order:

(1) the return of the person to the Texas Youth Commission; or

(2) the transfer of the person to the custody of the institutional division of the Texas Department of Criminal Justice for the completion of the person's sentence.

(j) On conclusion of the hearing on a person who is referred for release under supervision under Section 61.081(f), Human Resources Code, the court may order the return of the person to the Texas Youth Commission:

(1) with approval for the release of the person under supervision; or

(2) without approval for the release of the person under supervision.

(k) In making a determination under this section, the court may consider the experiences and character of the person before and after commitment to the youth commission, the nature of the penal offense that the person was found to have committed and the manner in which the offense was committed, the abilities of the person to contribute to society, the protection of the victim of

the offense or any member of the victim's family, the recommendations of the youth commission and prosecuting attorney, the best interests of the person, and any other factor relevant to the issue to be decided.
*(Chgd. by L.1991, chap. 574(3); L.1995, chap. 262(46), eff. 1/1/96.)*

# CHAPTER 55. PROCEEDINGS CONCERNING CHILDREN WITH MENTAL ILLNESS OR MENTAL RETARDATION

*(Chgd. by L.1995, chap. 262(47); L.1999, chap. 1477(14), eff. 9/1/99.)*

## SUBCHAPTER A. GENERAL PROVISIONS



## SUBCHAPTER B. CHILD WITH MENTAL ILLNESS



## SUBCHAPTER C. CHILD UNFIT TO PROCEED AS A RESULT OF MENTAL ILLNESS OR MENTAL RETARDATION



## SUBCHAPTER D. LACK OF RESPONSIBILITY FOR CONDUCT AS A RESULT OF MENTAL ILLNESS OR MENTAL RETARDATION

## SUBCHAPTER A. GENERAL PROVISIONS

*(Added by L.1999, chap. 1477(14), eff. 9/1/99.)*

### §55.01. Meaning of "having a mental illness."

For purposes of this chapter, a child who is described as having a mental illness means a child who suffers from mental illness as defined by Section 571.003, Health and Safety Code. *(Repealed and added by L.1999, chap. 1477(14), eff. 9/1/99.)*



### §55.02. Mental health and mental retardation jurisdiction.

For the purpose of initiating proceedings to order mental health or mental retardation services for a child or for commitment of a child as provided by this chapter, the juvenile court has jurisdiction of proceedings under Subtitle C or D, Title 7, Health and Safety Code. *(Added by L.1999, chap. 1477(14), eff. 9/1/99.)*

### §55.03. Standards of care.

(a) Except as provided by this chapter, a child for whom inpatient mental health services is ordered by a court under this chapter shall be cared for as provided by Subtitle C, Title 7, Health and Safety Code.

(b) Except as provided by this chapter, a child who is committed by a court to a residential care facility for mental retardation shall be cared for as provided by Subtitle D, Title 7, Health and Safety Code.

*(Chgd. by L.1997, chap. 1086(14); repealed and added by L.1999, chap. 1477(14), eff. 9/1/99.)*

### §§55.04 to 55.10. *(Reserved.)*

## SUBCHAPTER B. CHILD WITH MENTAL ILLNESS

*(Added by L.1999, chap. 1477(14), eff. 9/1/99.)*

### §55.11. Mental illness determination; examination.

(a) On a motion by a party, the juvenile court shall determine whether probable cause exists to believe that a child who is alleged by petition or found to have engaged in delinquent conduct or conduct indicating a need for supervision has a mental illness. In making its determination, the court may:

(1) consider the motion, supporting documents, professional statements of counsel, and witness testimony; and

(2) make its own observation of the child.

(b) If the court determines that probable cause exists to believe that the child has a mental illness, the court shall temporarily stay the juvenile court proceedings and immediately order the child to be examined under Section 51.20. The information obtained from the examination must include expert opinion as to whether the child has a mental illness and whether the child meets the commitment criteria under Subtitle C, Title 7, Health and Safety Code. If ordered by the court, the information must also include expert opinion as to whether the child is unfit to proceed with the juvenile court proceedings.

(c) After considering all relevant information, including information obtained from an examination under Section 51.20, the court shall:

(1) if the court determines that evidence exists to support a finding that the child has a mental illness and that the child meets the commitment criteria under Subtitle C, Title 7, Health and Safety Code, proceed under Section 55.12; or

(2) if the court determines that evidence does not exist to support a finding that the child has a mental illness or that the child meets the commitment criteria under Subtitle C, Title 7, Health and Safety Code, dissolve the stay and continue the juvenile court proceedings.

*(Added by L.1999, chap. 1477(14), eff. 9/1/99.)*

## §55.12. Initiation of commitment proceedings.

If, after considering all relevant information, the juvenile court determines that evidence exists to support a finding that a child has a mental illness and that the child meets the commitment criteria under Subtitle C, Title 7, Health and Safety Code, the court shall:

(1) initiate proceedings as provided by Section 55.13 to order temporary or extended mental health services, as provided in Subchapter C, Chapter 574, Health and Safety Code; or

(2) refer the child's case as provided by Section 55.14 to the appropriate court for the initiation of proceedings in that court for commitment of the child under Subchapter C, Chapter 574, Health and Safety Code.

*(Added by L.1999, chap. 1477(14), eff. 9/1/99.)*

## §55.13. Commitment proceedings in juvenile court.

(a) If the juvenile court initiates proceedings for temporary or extended mental health services under Section 55.12(1), the prosecuting attorney or the attorney for the child may file with the juvenile court an application for court-ordered mental health services under Section 574.001, Health and Safety Code. The juvenile court shall:

(1) set a date for a hearing and provide notice as required by Sections 574.005 and 574.006, Health and Safety Code; and

(2) conduct the hearing in accordance with Subchapter C, Chapter 574, Health and Safety Code.

(b) The burden of proof at the hearing is on the party who filed the application.

(c) The juvenile court shall appoint the number of physicians necessary to examine the child and to complete the certificates of medical examination for mental illness required under Section 574.009, Health and Safety Code.

(d) After conducting a hearing on an application under this section, the juvenile court shall:

(1) if the criteria under Section 574.034, Health and Safety Code, are satisfied, order temporary mental health services for the child; or

(2) if the criteria under Section 574.035, Health and Safety Code, are satisfied, order extended mental health services for the child.

*(Added by L.1999, chap. 1477(14), eff. 9/1/99.)*

## §55.14. Referral for commitment proceedings.

(a) If the juvenile court refers the child's case to the appropriate court for the initiation of commitment proceedings under Section 55.12(2), the juvenile court shall:

(1) send all papers relating to the child's mental illness to the clerk of the court to which the case is referred;

(2) send to the office of the appropriate county attorney or, if a county attorney is not available, to the office of the appropriate district attorney, copies of all papers sent to the clerk of the court under Subdivision (1); and

(3) if the child is in detention:

(A) order the child released from detention to the child's home or another appropriate place;

(B) order the child detained in an appropriate place other than a juvenile detention facility; or

(C) if an appropriate place to release or detain the child as described by Paragraph (A) or (B) is not available, order the child to remain in the juvenile detention facility subject to further detention orders of the court.

(b) The papers sent to the clerk of a court under Subsection (a)(1) constitute an application for mental health services under Section 574.001, Health and Safety Code.

*(Added by L.1999, chap. 1477(14), eff. 9/1/99.)*

## §55.15. Standards of care; expiration of court order for mental health services.

If the juvenile court or a court to which the child's case is referred under Section 55.12(2) orders mental health services for the child, the child shall be cared for, treated, and released in conformity to Subtitle C, Title 7, Health and Safety Code, except:

(1) a court order for mental health services for a child automatically expires on the 120th day after the date the child becomes 18 years of age; and

(2) the administrator of a mental health facility shall notify, in writing, by certified mail, return receipt requested, the juvenile court that ordered mental health services or the juvenile court that referred the case to a court that ordered the mental health services of the intent to discharge the child at least 10 days prior to discharge.

*(Added by L.1999, chap. 1477(14), eff. 9/1/99.)*

### §55.16. Order for mental health services; stay of proceedings.

(a) If the court to which the child's case is referred under Section 55.12(2) orders temporary or extended inpatient mental health services for the child, the court shall immediately notify in writing the referring juvenile court of the court's order for mental health services.

(b) If the juvenile court orders temporary or extended inpatient mental health services for the child or if the juvenile court receives notice under Subsection (a) from the court to which the child's case is referred, the proceedings under this title then pending in juvenile court shall be stayed.

*(Added by L.1999, chap. 1477(14), eff. 9/1/99.)*

### §55.17. Mental health services not ordered; dissolution of stay.

(a) If the court to which a child's case is referred under Section 55.12(2) does not order temporary or extended inpatient mental health services for the child, the court shall immediately notify in writing the referring juvenile court of the court's decision.

(b) If the juvenile court does not order temporary or extended inpatient mental health services for the child or if the juvenile court receives notice under Subsection (a) from the court to which the child's case is referred, the juvenile court shall dissolve the stay and continue the juvenile court proceedings.

*(Added by L.1999, chap. 1477(14), eff. 9/1/99.)*



### §55.18. Discharge from mental health facility before reaching 18 years of age.

If the child is discharged from the mental health facility before reaching 18 years of age, the juvenile court may:

(1) dismiss the juvenile court proceedings with prejudice; or

(2) continue with proceedings under this title as though no order of mental health services had been made.

*(Added by L.1999, chap. 1477(14), eff. 9/1/99.)*

### §55.19. Transfer to criminal court on 18th birthday.

(a) The juvenile court shall transfer all pending proceedings from the juvenile court to a criminal court on the 18th birthday of a child for whom the juvenile court or a court to which the child's case is referred under Section 55.12(2) has ordered inpatient mental health services if:

(1) the child is not discharged or furloughed from the inpatient mental health facility before reaching 18 years of age; and

(2) the child is alleged to have engaged in delinquent conduct that included a violation of a penal law listed in Section 53.045 and no adjudication concerning the alleged conduct has been made.

(b) The juvenile court shall send notification of the transfer of a child under Subsection (a) to the inpatient mental health facility. The criminal court shall, within 90 days of the transfer, institute proceedings under Article 46.02, Code of Criminal Procedure. If those or any subsequent proceedings result in a determination that the defendant is competent to stand trial, the defendant may not receive a punishment for the delinquent conduct described by Subsection (a)(2) that results in confinement for a period longer than the maximum period of confinement the defendant could have received if the defendant had been adjudicated for the delinquent conduct while still a child and within the jurisdiction of the juvenile court.

*(Added by L.1999, chap. 1477(14), eff. 9/1/99.)*

### §§55.20 to 55.30. *(Reserved.)*

## SUBCHAPTER C. CHILD UNFIT TO PROCEED AS A RESULT OF MENTAL ILLNESS OR MENTAL RETARDATION

*(Added by L.1999, chap. 1477(14), eff. 9/1/99.)*

### §55.31. Unfitness to proceed determination; examination.

(a) A child alleged by petition or found to have engaged in delinquent conduct or conduct indicating a need for supervision who as a result of mental illness or mental retardation lacks capacity to understand the proceedings in juvenile court or to assist in the child's own defense is unfit to proceed and shall not be subjected to discretionary transfer to criminal court, adjudication, disposition, or modification of disposition as long as such incapacity endures.

(b) On a motion by a party, the juvenile court shall determine whether probable cause exists to believe that a child who is alleged by petition or who is found to have engaged in delinquent conduct or conduct indicating a need for supervision is unfit to proceed as a result of mental illness or mental retardation. In making its determination, the court may:

(1) consider the motion, supporting documents, professional statements of counsel, and witness testimony; and

(2) make its own observation of the child.

(c) If the court determines that probable cause exists to believe that the child is unfit to proceed, the court shall temporarily stay the juvenile court proceedings and immediately order the child to be examined under Section 51.20. The information obtained from the examination must include expert opinion as to whether the child is unfit to proceed as a result of mental illness or mental retardation.

(d) After considering all relevant information, including information obtained from an examination under Section 51.20, the court shall:

(1) if the court determines that evidence exists to support a finding that the child is unfit to proceed, proceed under Section 55.32; or

(2) if the court determines that evidence does not exist to support a finding that the child is unfit to proceed, dissolve the stay and continue the juvenile court proceedings.

*(Added by L.1999, chap. 1477(14), eff. 9/1/99.)*

## §55.32. Hearing on issue of fitness to proceed.

(a) If the juvenile court determines that evidence exists to support a finding that a child is unfit to proceed as a result of mental illness or mental retardation, the court shall set the case for a hearing on that issue.

(b) The issue of whether the child is unfit to proceed as a result of mental illness or mental retardation shall be determined at a hearing separate from any other hearing.

(c) The court shall determine the issue of whether the child is unfit to proceed unless the child or the attorney for the child demands a jury before the 10th day before the date of the hearing.

(d) Unfitness to proceed as a result of mental illness or mental retardation must be proved by a preponderance of the evidence.

(e) If the court or jury determines that the child is fit to proceed, the juvenile court shall continue with proceedings under this title as though no question of fitness to proceed had been raised.

(f) If the court or jury determines that the child is unfit to proceed as a result of mental illness or mental retardation, the court shall:

(1) stay the juvenile court proceedings for as long as that incapacity endures; and

(2) proceed under Section 55.33.

(g) The fact that the child is unfit to proceed as a result of mental illness or mental retardation does not preclude any legal objection to the juvenile court proceedings which is susceptible of fair determination prior to the adjudication hearing and without the personal participation of the child.

*(Added by L.1999, chap. 1477(14), eff. 9/1/99.)*

## §55.33. Proceedings following finding of unfitness to proceed.

(a) If the juvenile court or jury determines under Section 55.32 that a child is unfit to proceed with the juvenile court proceedings for delinquent conduct, the court shall:

(1) if the unfitness to proceed is a result of mental illness or mental retardation:

(A) provided that the child meets the commitment criteria under Subtitle C or D, Title 7, Health and Safety Code, order the child placed with the Texas Department of Mental Health and Mental Retardation for a period of not more than 90 days, which order may not specify a shorter period, for placement in a facility designated by the department; or

(B) on application by the child's parent, guardian, or guardian ad litem, order the child placed in a private psychiatric inpatient facility for a period of not more than 90 days, which order may not specify a shorter period, but only if the placement is agreed to in writing by the administrator of the facility; or

(2) if the unfitness to proceed is a result of mental illness and the court determines that the child may be adequately treated in an alternative setting, order the child to receive treatment for mental illness on an outpatient basis for a period of not more than 90 days, which order may not specify a shorter period.

(b) If the court orders a child placed in a private psychiatric inpatient facility under Subsection (a)(1)(B), the state or a political subdivision of the state may be ordered to pay any costs associated with the child's placement, subject to an express appropriation of funds for the purpose.

*(Added by L.1999, chap. 1477(14), eff. 9/1/99.)*

### §55.34. Transportation to and from facility.

(a) If the court issues a placement order under Section 55.33(a)(1), the court shall order the probation department or sheriff's department to transport the child to the designated facility.

(b) On receipt of a report from a facility to which a child has been transported under Subsection (a), the court shall order the probation department or sheriff's department to transport the child from the facility to the court. If the child is not transported to the court before the 11th day after the date of the court's order, an authorized representative of the facility shall transport the child from the facility to the court.

(c) The county in which the juvenile court is located shall reimburse the facility for the costs incurred in transporting the child to the juvenile court as required by Subsection (b).
*(Added by L.1999, chap. 1477(14), eff. 9/1/99.)*

### §55.35. Information required to be sent to facility; report to court.

(a) If the juvenile court issues a placement order under Section 55.33(a), the court shall order the probation department to send copies of any information in the possession of the department and relevant to the issue of the child's mental illness or mental retardation to the public or private facility or outpatient center, as appropriate.

(b) Not later than the 75th day after the date the court issues a placement order under Section 55.33(a), the public or private facility or outpatient center, as appropriate, shall submit to the court a report that:

(1) describes the treatment of the child provided by the facility or center; and

(2) states the opinion of the director of the facility or center as to whether the child is fit or unfit to proceed.

(c) The court shall provide a copy of the report submitted under Subsection (b) to the prosecuting attorney and the attorney for the child.
*(Added by L.1999, chap. 1477(14), eff. 9/1/99.)*



### §55.36. Report that child is fit to proceed; hearing on objection.

(a) If a report submitted under Section 55.35(b) states that a child is fit to proceed, the juvenile court shall find that the child is fit to proceed unless the child's attorney objects in writing or in open court not later than the second day after the date the attorney receives a copy of the report under Section 55.35(c).

(b) On objection by the child's attorney under Subsection (a), the juvenile court shall promptly hold a hearing to determine whether the child is fit to proceed, except that the hearing may be held after the date that the placement order issued under Section 55.33(a) expires. At the hearing, the court shall determine the issue of the fitness of the child to proceed unless the child or the child's attorney demands in writing a jury before the 10th day before the date of the hearing.

(c) If, after a hearing, the court or jury finds that the child is fit to proceed, the court shall dissolve the stay and continue the juvenile court proceedings as though a question of fitness to proceed had not been raised.

(d) If, after a hearing, the court or jury finds that the child is unfit to proceed, the court shall proceed under Section 55.37.
*(Added by L.1999, chap. 1477(14), eff. 9/1/99.)*

### §55.37. Report that child is unfit to proceed as a result of mental illness; initiation of commitment proceedings.

If a report submitted under Section 55.35(b) states that a child is unfit to proceed as a result of mental illness and that the child meets the commitment criteria for civil commitment under Subtitle C, Title 7, Health and Safety Code, the director of the public or private facility or outpatient center, as appropriate, shall submit to the court two certificates of medical examination for mental illness. On receipt of the certificates, the court shall:

(1) initiate proceedings as provided by Section 55.38 in the juvenile court for commitment of the child under Subtitle C, Title 7, Health and Safety Code; or

(2) refer the child's case as provided by Section 55.39 to the appropriate court for the initiation of proceedings in that court for commitment of the child under Subtitle C, Title 7, Health and Safety Code.
*(Added by L.1999, chap. 1477(14), eff. 9/1/99.)*

### §55.38. Commitment proceedings in juvenile court for mental illness.

(a) If the juvenile court initiates commitment proceedings under Section 55.37(1), the prosecuting attorney may file with the juvenile court an application for court-ordered mental health services under Section 574.001, Health and Safety Code. The juvenile court shall:

(1) set a date for a hearing and provide notice as required by Sections 574.005 and 574.006, Health and Safety Code; and

(2) conduct the hearing in accordance with Subchapter C, Chapter 574, Health and Safety Code.

(b) After conducting a hearing under Subsection (a)(2), the juvenile court shall:

(1) if the criteria under Section 574.034, Health and Safety Code, are satisfied, order temporary mental health services; or

(2) if the criteria under Section 574.035, Health and Safety Code, are satisfied, order extended mental health services.

*(Added by L.1999, chap. 1477(14), eff. 9/1/99.)*

## §55.39. Referral for commitment proceedings for mental illness.

(a) If the juvenile court refers the child's case to an appropriate court for the initiation of commitment proceedings under Section 55.37(2), the juvenile court shall:

(1) send all papers relating to the child's unfitness to proceed, including the verdict and judgment of the juvenile court finding the child unfit to proceed, to the clerk of the court to which the case is referred;

(2) send to the office of the appropriate county attorney or, if a county attorney is not available, to the office of the appropriate district attorney, copies of all papers sent to the clerk of the court under Subdivision (1); and

(3) if the child is in detention:

(A) order the child released from detention to the child's home or another appropriate place;

(B) order the child detained in an appropriate place other than a juvenile detention facility; or

(C) if an appropriate place to release or detain the child as described by Paragraph (A) or (B) is not available, order the child to remain in the juvenile detention facility subject to further detention orders of the court.

(b) The papers sent to a court under Subsection (a)(1) constitute an application for mental health services under Section 574.001, Health and Safety Code.

*(Added by L.1999, chap. 1477(14), eff. 9/1/99.)*

## §55.40. Report that child is unfit to proceed as a result of mental retardation.

If a report submitted under Section 55.35(b) states that a child is unfit to proceed as a result of mental retardation and that the child meets the commitment criteria for civil commitment under Subtitle D, Title 7, Health and Safety Code, the director of the residential care facility shall submit to the court an affidavit stating the conclusions reached as a result of the diagnosis. On receipt of the affidavit, the court shall:

(1) initiate proceedings as provided by Section 55.41 in the juvenile court for commitment of the child under Subtitle D, Title 7, Health and Safety Code; or

(2) refer the child's case as provided by Section 55.42 to the appropriate court for the initiation of proceedings in that court for commitment of the child under Subtitle D, Title 7, Health and Safety Code.

*(Added by L.1999, chap. 1477(14), eff. 9/1/99.)*

## §55.41. Commitment proceedings in juvenile court for mental retardation.

(a) If the juvenile court initiates commitment proceedings under Section 55.40(1), the prosecuting attorney may file with the juvenile court an application for placement under Section 593.041, Health and Safety Code. The juvenile court shall:

(1) set a date for a hearing and provide notice as required by Sections 593.047 and 593.048, Health and Safety Code; and

(2) conduct the hearing in accordance with Sections 593.049-593.056, Health and Safety Code.

(b) After conducting a hearing under Subsection (a)(2), the juvenile court may order commitment of the child to a residential care facility if the commitment criteria under Section 593.052, Health and Safety Code, are satisfied.

*(Added by L.1999, chap. 1477(14), eff. 9/1/99.)*

## §55.42. Referral for commitment proceedings for mental retardation.

(a) If the juvenile court refers the child's case to an appropriate court for the initiation of commitment proceedings under Section 55.40(2), the juvenile court shall:

(1) send all papers relating to the child's mental retardation to the clerk of the court to which the case is referred;

(2) send to the office of the appropriate county attorney or, if a county attorney is not available, to the office of the appropriate district attorney, copies of all papers sent to the clerk of the court under Subdivision (1); and

(3) if the child is in detention:

(A) order the child released from detention to the child's home or another appropriate place;

(B) order the child detained in an appropriate place other than a juvenile detention facility; or

(C) if an appropriate place to release or detain the child as described by Paragraph (A) or (B) is not available, order the child to remain in the juvenile detention facility subject to further detention orders of the court.

(b) The papers sent to a court under Subsection (a)(1) constitute an application for placement under Section 593.041, Health and Safety Code.

*(Added by L.1999, chap. 1477(14), eff. 9/1/99.)*

### §55.43. Restoration hearing.



(a) The prosecuting attorney may file with the juvenile court a motion for a restoration hearing concerning a child if:

(1) the child is found unfit to proceed as a result of mental illness or mental retardation; and

(2) the child:

(A) is not:

(i) ordered by a court to receive inpatient mental health services;

(ii) committed by a court to a residential care facility; or

(iii) ordered by a court to receive treatment on an outpatient basis; or

(B) is discharged or furloughed from a mental health facility or outpatient center before the child reaches 18 years of age.

(b) At the restoration hearing, the court shall determine the issue of whether the child is fit to proceed.

(c) The restoration hearing shall be conducted without a jury.

(d) The issue of fitness to proceed must be proved by a preponderance of the evidence.

(e) If, after a hearing, the court finds that the child is fit to proceed, the court shall continue the juvenile court proceedings.

(f) If, after a hearing, the court finds that the child is unfit to proceed, the court shall dismiss the motion for restoration.

*(Added by L.1999, chap. 1477(14), eff. 9/1/99.)*

### §55.44. Transfer to criminal court on 18th birthday of child.

(a) The juvenile court shall transfer all pending proceedings from the juvenile court to a criminal court on the 18th birthday of a child for whom the juvenile court or a court to which the child's case is referred has ordered inpatient mental health services or residential care for persons with mental retardation if:

(1) the child is not discharged or furloughed from the facility before reaching 18 years of age; and

(2) the child is alleged to have engaged in delinquent conduct that included a violation of a penal law listed in Section 53.045 and no adjudication concerning the alleged conduct has been made.

(b) The juvenile court shall send notification of the transfer of a child under Subsection (a) to the facility. The criminal court shall, before the 91st day after the date of the transfer, institute proceedings under Article 46.02, Code of Criminal Procedure. If those or any subsequent proceedings result in a determination that the defendant is competent to stand trial, the defendant may not receive a punishment for the delinquent conduct described by Subsection (a)(2) that results in confinement for a period longer than the maximum period of confinement the defendant could have received if the defendant had been adjudicated for the delinquent conduct while still a child and within the jurisdiction of the juvenile court.

*(Added by L.1999, chap. 1477(14), eff. 9/1/99.)*

### §§55.45 to 55.50. *(Reserved.)*

## SUBCHAPTER D. LACK OF RESPONSIBILITY FOR CONDUCT AS A RESULT OF MENTAL ILLNESS OR MENTAL RETARDATION

*(Added by L.1999, chap. 1477(14), eff. 9/1/99.)*

### §55.51. Lack of responsibility for conduct determination; examination.

(a) A child alleged by petition to have engaged in delinquent conduct or conduct indicating a need for supervision is not responsible for the conduct if at the time of the conduct, as a result of mental illness or mental retardation, the child lacks substantial capacity either to appreciate the wrongfulness of the child's conduct or to conform the child's conduct to the requirements of law.

(b) On a motion by a party in which it is alleged that a child may not be responsible as a result of mental illness or mental retardation for the child's conduct, the court shall order the child to be examined under Section 51.20. The information obtained from the examinations must include expert opinion as to whether the child is not responsible for the child's conduct as a result of mental illness or mental retardation.

(c) The issue of whether the child is not responsible for the child's conduct as a result of mental illness or mental retardation shall be tried to the court or jury in the adjudication hearing.

(d) Lack of responsibility for conduct as a result of mental illness or mental retardation must be proved by a preponderance of the evidence.

(e) In its findings or verdict the court or jury must state whether the child is not responsible for the child's conduct as a result of mental illness or mental retardation.

(f) If the court or jury finds the child is not responsible for the child's conduct as a result of mental illness or mental retardation, the court shall proceed under Section 55.52.

(g) A child found to be not responsible for the child's conduct as a result of mental illness or mental retardation shall not be subject to proceedings under this title with respect to such conduct, other than proceedings under Section 55.52.
*(Added by L.1999, chap. 1477(14), eff. 9/1/99.)*



### §55.52. Proceedings following finding of lack of responsibility for conduct.

(a) If the court or jury finds that a child is not responsible for the child's conduct under Section 55.51, the court shall:

(1) if the lack of responsibility is a result of mental illness or mental retardation:

(A) provided that the child meets the commitment criteria under Subtitle C or D, Title 7, Health and Safety Code, order the child placed with the Texas Department of Mental Health and Mental Retardation for a period of not more than 90 days, which order may not specify a shorter period, for placement in a facility designated by the department; or

(B) on application by the child's parent, guardian, or guardian ad litem, order the child placed in a private psychiatric inpatient facility for a period of not more than 90 days, which order may not specify a shorter period, but only if the placement is agreed to in writing by the administrator of the facility; or

(2) if the child's lack of responsibility is a result of mental illness and the court determines that the child may be adequately treated in an alternative setting, order the child to receive treatment on an outpatient basis for a period of not more than 90 days, which order may not specify a shorter period.

(b) If the court orders a child placed in a private psychiatric inpatient facility under Subsection (a)(1)(B), the state or a political subdivision of the state may be ordered to pay any costs associated with the child's placement, subject to an express appropriation of funds for the purpose.
*(Added by L.1999, chap. 1477(14), eff. 9/1/99.)*

### §55.53. Transportation to and from facility.

(a) If the court issues a placement order under Section 55.52(a)(1), the court shall order the probation department or sheriff's department to transport the child to the designated facility.

(b) On receipt of a report from a facility to which a child has been transported under Subsection (a), the court shall order the probation department or sheriff's department to transport the child from the facility to the court. If the child is not transported to the court before the 11th day after the date of the court's order, an authorized representative of the facility shall transport the child from the facility to the court.

(c) The county in which the juvenile court is located shall reimburse the facility for the costs incurred in transporting the child to the juvenile court as required by Subsection (b).
*(Added by L.1999, chap. 1477(14), eff. 9/1/99.)*

### §55.54. Information required to be sent to facility; report to court.

(a) If the juvenile court issues a placement order under Section 55.52(a), the court shall order the probation department to send copies of any information in the possession of the department and relevant to the issue of the child's mental illness or mental retardation to the public or private facility or outpatient center, as appropriate.

(b) Not later than the 75th day after the date the court issues a placement order under Section 55.52(a), the public or private facility or outpatient center, as appropriate, shall submit to the court a report that:

(1) describes the treatment of the child provided by the facility or center; and

(2) states the opinion of the director of the facility or center as to whether the child is mentally ill or mentally retarded.

(c) The court shall send a copy of the report submitted under Subsection (b) to the prosecuting attorney and the attorney for the child.

*(Added by L.1999, chap. 1477(14), eff. 9/1/99.)*



### §55.55. Report that child is not mentally ill or mentally retarded; hearing on objection.

(a) If a report submitted under Section 55.54(b) states that a child does not have a mental illness or mental retardation, the juvenile court shall discharge the child unless:

(1) an adjudication hearing was conducted concerning conduct that included a violation of a penal law listed in Section 53.045(a) and a petition was approved by a grand jury under Section 53.045; and

(2) the prosecuting attorney objects in writing not later than the second day after the date the attorney receives a copy of the report under Section 55.54(c).

(b) On objection by the prosecuting attorney under Subsection (a), the juvenile court shall hold a hearing without a jury to determine whether the child has a mental illness or mental retardation and whether the child meets the commitment criteria for civil commitment under Subtitle C or D, Title 7, Health and Safety Code.

(c) At the hearing, the burden is on the state to prove by clear and convincing evidence that the child has a mental illness or mental retardation and that the child meets the commitment criteria for civil commitment under Subtitle C or D, Title 7, Health and Safety Code.

(d) If, after a hearing, the court finds that the child does not have a mental illness or mental retardation and that the child does not meet the commitment criteria under Subtitle C or D, Title 7, Health and Safety Code, the court shall discharge the child.

(e) If, after a hearing, the court finds that the child has a mental illness or mental retardation and that the child meets the commitment criteria under Subtitle C or D, Title 7, Health and Safety Code, the court shall issue an appropriate commitment order.

*(Added by L.1999, chap. 1477(14), eff. 9/1/99.)*

### §55.56. Report that child has mental illness; initiation of commitment proceedings.

If a report submitted under Section 55.54(b) states that a child has a mental illness and that the child meets the commitment criteria for civil commitment under Subtitle C, Title 7, Health and Safety Code, the director of the public or private facility or outpatient center, as appropriate, shall submit to the court two certificates of medical examination for mental illness. On receipt of the certificates, the court shall:

(1) initiate proceedings as provided by Section 55.57 in the juvenile court for commitment of the child under Subtitle C, Title 7, Health and Safety Code; or

(2) refer the child's case as provided by Section 55.58 to the appropriate court for the initiation of proceedings in that court for commitment of the child under Subtitle C, Title 7, Health and Safety Code.

*(Added by L.1999, chap. 1477(14), eff. 9/1/99.)*

### §55.57. Commitment proceedings in juvenile court for mental illness.

(a) If the juvenile court initiates commitment proceedings under Section 55.56(1), the prosecuting attorney may file with the juvenile court an application for court-ordered mental health services under Section 574.001, Health and Safety Code. The juvenile court shall:

(1) set a date for a hearing and provide notice as required by Sections 574.005 and 574.006, Health and Safety Code; and

(2) conduct the hearing in accordance with Subchapter C, Chapter 574, Health and Safety Code.

(b) After conducting a hearing under Subsection (a)(2), the juvenile court shall:

(1) if the criteria under Section 574.034, Health and Safety Code, are satisfied, order temporary mental health services; or

(2) if the criteria under Section 574.035, Health and Safety Code, are satisfied, order extended mental health services.

*(Added by L.1999, chap. 1477(14), eff. 9/1/99.)*

## §55.58. Referral for commitment proceedings for mental illness.

(a) If the juvenile court refers the child's case to an appropriate court for the initiation of commitment proceedings under Section 55.56(2), the juvenile court shall:

(1) send all papers relating to the child's mental illness, including the verdict and judgment of the juvenile court finding that the child was not responsible for the child's conduct, to the clerk of the court to which the case is referred;

(2) send to the office of the appropriate county attorney or, if a county attorney is not available, to the office of the district attorney, copies of all papers sent to the clerk of the court under Subdivision (1); and

(3) if the child is in detention:

(A) order the child released from detention to the child's home or another appropriate place;

(B) order the child detained in an appropriate place other than a juvenile detention facility; or

(C) if an appropriate place to release or detain the child as described by Paragraph (A) or (B) is not available, order the child to remain in the juvenile detention facility subject to further detention orders of the court.

(b) The papers sent to a court under Subsection (a)(1) constitute an application for mental health services under Section 574.001, Health and Safety Code.

*(Added by L.1999, chap. 1477(14), eff. 9/1/99.)*

## §55.59. Report that child has mental retardation; initiation of commitment proceedings.

If a report submitted under Section 55.54(b) states that a child has mental retardation and that the child meets the commitment criteria for civil commitment under Subtitle D, Title 7, Health and Safety Code, the director of the residential care facility shall submit to the court an affidavit stating the conclusions reached as a result of the diagnosis. On receipt of an affidavit, the juvenile court shall:

(1) initiate proceedings in the juvenile court as provided by Section 55.60 for commitment of the child under Subtitle D, Title 7, Health and Safety Code; or

(2) refer the child's case to the appropriate court as provided by Section 55.61 for the initiation of proceedings in that court for commitment of the child under Subtitle D, Title 7, Health and Safety Code.

*(Added by L.1999, chap. 1477(14), eff. 9/1/99.)*

## §55.60. Commitment proceedings in juvenile court for mental retardation.

(a) If the juvenile court initiates commitment proceedings under Section 55.59(1), the prosecuting attorney may file with the juvenile court an application for placement under Section 593.041, Health and Safety Code. The juvenile court shall:

(1) set a date for a hearing and provide notice as required by Sections 593.047 and 593.048, Health and Safety Code; and

(2) conduct the hearing in accordance with Sections 593.049-593.056, Health and Safety Code.

(b) After conducting a hearing under Subsection (a)(2), the juvenile court may order commitment of the child to a residential care facility only if the commitment criteria under Section 593.052, Health and Safety Code, are satisfied.

*(Added by L.1999, chap. 1477(14), eff. 9/1/99.)*

## §55.61. Referral for commitment proceedings for mental retardation.

(a) If the juvenile court refers the child's case to an appropriate court for the initiation of commitment proceedings under Section 55.59(2), the juvenile court shall:

(1) send all papers relating to the child's mental retardation to the clerk of the court to which the case is referred;

(2) send to the office of the appropriate county attorney or, if a county attorney is not available, to the office of the appropriate district attorney, copies of all papers sent to the clerk of the court under Subdivision (1); and

(3) if the child is in detention:

(A) order the child released from detention to the child's home or another appropriate place;

(B) order the child detained in an appropriate place other than a juvenile detention facility; or

(C) if an appropriate place to release or detain the child as described by Paragraph (A) or (B) is not available, order the child to remain in the juvenile detention facility subject to further detention orders of the court.

(b) The papers sent to a court under Subsection (a)(1) constitute an application for placement under Section 593.041, Health and Safety Code.
*(Added by L.1999, chap. 1477(14), eff. 9/1/99.)*

## CHAPTER 57. RIGHTS OF VICTIMS

*(Added by L.1989, chap. 633(1), eff. 6/14/89.)*

Section




### §57.001. Definitions.

In this chapter:

(1) "Close relative of a deceased victim" means a person who was the spouse of a deceased victim at the time of the victim's death or who is a parent or adult brother, sister, or child of the deceased victim.

(2) "Guardian of a victim" means a person who is the legal guardian of the victim, whether or not the legal relationship between the guardian and victim exists because of the age of the victim or the physical or mental incompetency of the victim.

(3) "Victim" means a person who as the result of the delinquent conduct of a child suffers a pecuniary loss or personal injury or harm.
*(Added by L.1989, chap. 633(1); chgd. by L.1995, chap. 262(49); L.1997, chap. 368(1), eff. 9/1/97.)*

### §57.002. Victim's rights.

A victim, guardian of a victim, or close relative of a deceased victim is entitled to the following rights within the juvenile justice system:

(1) the right to receive from law enforcement agencies adequate protection from harm and threats of harm arising from cooperation with prosecution efforts;

(2) the right to have the court or person appointed by the court take the safety of the victim or the victim's family into consideration as an element in determining whether the child should be detained before the child's conduct is adjudicated;

(3) the right, if requested, to be informed of relevant court proceedings, including appellate proceedings, and to be informed in a timely manner if those court proceedings have been canceled or rescheduled;

(4) the right to be informed, when requested, by the court or a person appointed by the court concerning the procedures in the juvenile justice system, including general procedures relating to:

(A) the preliminary investigation and deferred prosecution of a case; and

(B) the appeal of the case;

(5) the right to provide pertinent information to a juvenile court conducting a disposition hearing concerning the impact of the offense on the victim and the victim's family by testimony, written statement, or any other manner before the court renders its disposition;

(6) the right to receive information regarding compensation to victims as provided by Subchapter B, Chapter 56, Code of Criminal Procedure, including information related to the costs that may be compensated under that Act and the amount of compensation, eligibility for compensation, and procedures for application for compensation under that Act, the payment of medical expenses under Section 56.06, Code of Criminal Procedure, for a victim of a sexual assault, and when requested, to referral to available social service agencies that may offer additional assistance;

(7) the right to be informed, upon request, of procedures for release under supervision or transfer of the person to the custody of the pardons and paroles division of the Texas Department

of Criminal Justice for parole, to participate in the release or transfer for parole process, to be notified, if requested, of release or transfer for parole proceedings concerning the person, to provide to the Texas Youth Commission for inclusion in the person's file information to be considered by the commission before the release under supervision or transfer for parole of the person, and to be notified, if requested, of the person's release or transfer for parole;

(8) the right to be provided with a waiting area, separate or secure from other witnesses, including the child alleged to have committed the conduct and relatives of the child, before testifying in any proceeding concerning the child, or, if a separate waiting area is not available, other safeguards should be taken to minimize the victim's contact with the child and the child's relatives and witnesses, before and during court proceedings;

(9) the right to prompt return of any property of the victim that is held by a law enforcement agency or the attorney for the state as evidence when the property is no longer required for that purpose;

(10) the right to have the attorney for the state notify the employer of the victim, if requested, of the necessity of the victim's cooperation and testimony in a proceeding that may necessitate the absence of the victim from work for good cause;

(11) the right to be present at all public court proceedings related to the conduct of the child as provided by Section 54.08, subject to that section; and

(12) any other right appropriate to the victim that a victim of criminal conduct has under Article 56.02, Code of Criminal Procedure.

*(Added by L.1989, chap. 633(1); chgd. by L.1995, chaps. 76(5.95)(110), 262(50), eff. 9/1/95, 1/1/96, respectively.)*





## §57.003. Duty of juvenile board.

(a) The juvenile board shall ensure to the extent practicable that a victim, guardian of a victim, or close relative of a deceased victim is afforded the rights granted by Section 57.002 and, on request, an explanation of those rights.

(b) The juvenile board may designate a person to serve as victim assistance coordinator in the juvenile board's jurisdiction for victims of juvenile offenders.

(c) The victim assistance coordinator shall ensure that a victim, or close relative of a deceased victim, is afforded the rights granted victims, guardians, and relatives by Section 57.002 and, on request, an explanation of those rights. The victim assistance coordinator shall work closely with appropriate law enforcement agencies, prosecuting attorneys, the Texas Juvenile Probation Commission, and the Texas Youth Commission in carrying out that duty.

(d) The victim assistance coordinator shall ensure that at a minimum, a victim, guardian of a victim, or close relative of a deceased victim receives:

(1) a written notice of the rights outlined in Section 57.002;

(2) an application for compensation under the Crime Victims' Compensation Act (Subchapter B, Chapter 56, Code of Criminal Procedure); and

(3) a victim impact statement with information explaining the possible use and consideration of the victim impact statement at detention, adjudication, and release proceedings involving the juvenile.

(e) The victim assistance coordinator shall, on request, offer to assist a person receiving a form under Subsection (d) to complete the form.

(f) The victim assistance coordinator shall send a copy of the victim impact statement to the court conducting a disposition hearing involving the juvenile.

*(Added by L.1989, chap. 633(1); chgd. by L.1995, chap. 262(51), eff. 1/1/96.)*

## §57.0031. Notification of rights of victims of juveniles.

At the initial contact or at the earliest possible time after the initial contact between the victim of a reported crime and the juvenile probation office having the responsibility for the disposition of the juvenile, the office shall provide the victim a written notice:

(1) containing information about the availability of emergency and medical services, if applicable;

(2) stating that the victim has the right to receive information regarding compensation to victims of crime as provided by the Crime Victims' Compensation Act (Subchapter B, Chapter 56, Code of Criminal Procedure), including information about:

(A) the costs that may be compensated and the amount of compensation, eligibility for compensation, and procedures for application for compensation;

(B) the payment for a medical examination for a victim of a sexual assault; and

(C) referral to available social service agencies that may offer additional assistance;

(3) stating the name, address, and phone number of the victim assistance coordinator for victims of juveniles;

(4) containing the following statement: "You may call the crime victim assistance coordinator for the status of the case and information about victims' rights."

(5) stating the rights of victims of crime under Section 57.002;

(6) summarizing each procedural stage in the processing of a juvenile case, including preliminary investigation, detention, informal adjustment of a case, disposition hearings, release proceedings, restitution, and appeals;

(7) suggesting steps the victim may take if the victim is subjected to threats or intimidation;

(8) stating the case number and assigned court for the case; and

(9) stating that the victim has the right to file a victim impact statement and to have it considered in juvenile proceedings.

*(Added by L.1995, chap. 262(51), eff. 1/1/96.)*



### §57.004. Notification.

A court, a person appointed by the court, or the Texas Youth Commission is responsible for notifying a victim, guardian of a victim, or close relative of a deceased victim of a proceeding under this chapter only if the victim, guardian of a victim, or close relative of a deceased victim requests the notification in writing and provides a current address to which the notification is to be sent. *(Added by L.1989, chap. 633(1), eff. 6/14/89.)*

### §57.005. Liability.

The Texas Youth Commission, a juvenile board, a court, a person appointed by a court, an attorney for the state, a peace officer, or a law enforcement agency is not liable for a failure or inability to provide a right listed under Section 57.002 of this code. *(Added by L.1989, chap. 633(1), eff. 6/14/89.)*

### §57.006. Appeal.

The failure or inability of any person to provide a right or service listed under Section 57.002 of this code may not be used by a child as a ground for appeal or for a post conviction writ of habeas corpus. *(Added by L.1989, chap. 633(1), eff. 6/14/89.)*

### §57.007. Standing.

A victim, guardian of a victim, or close relative of a victim does not have standing to participate as a party in a juvenile proceeding or to contest the disposition of any case. *(Added by L.1989, chap. 633(1), eff. 6/14/89.)*

### §57.008. Court order for protection from juveniles.

(a) A court may issue an order for protection from juveniles directed against a child to protect a victim of the child's conduct who, because of the victim's participation in the juvenile justice system, risks further harm by the child.

(b) In the order, the court may prohibit the child from doing specified acts or require the child to do specified acts necessary or appropriate to prevent or reduce the likelihood of further harm to the victim by the child.

*(Added by L.1995, chap. 262(52), eff. 1/1/96.)*

## CHAPTER 58. RECORDS; JUVENILE JUSTICE INFORMATION SYSTEM

*(Added by L.1995, chap. 262(53), eff. 1/1/96.)*

## SUBCHAPTER A. RECORDS

Section

## SUBCHAPTER B. JUVENILE JUSTICE INFORMATION SYSTEM





## SUBCHAPTER A. RECORDS

### §58.001. Collection of records of children.

(a) Law enforcement officers and other juvenile justice personnel shall collect information described by Section 58.104 as a part of the juvenile justice information system created under Subchapter B.

(b) The information is available as provided by Subchapter B.

(c) A law enforcement agency shall forward information, including fingerprints, relating to a child who has been taken into custody under Section 52.01 by the agency to the Department of Public Safety for inclusion in the juvenile justice information system created under Subchapter B, but only if the child is referred to juvenile court on or before the 10th day after the date the child is taken into custody under Section 52.01. If the child is not referred to juvenile court within that time, the law enforcement agency shall destroy all information, including photographs and fingerprints, relating to the child unless the child is placed in a first offender program under Section 52.031 or on informal disposition under Section 52.03. The law enforcement agency may not forward any information to the Department of Public Safety relating to the child while the child is in a first offender program under Section 52.031, or during the 90 days following successful completion of the program or while the child is on informal disposition under Section 52.03. Except as provided by Subsection (f), after the date the child completes an informal disposition under Section 52.03 or after the 90th day after the date the child successfully completes a first offender program under Section 52.031, the law enforcement agency shall destroy all information, including photographs and fingerprints, relating to the child.

(d) If information relating to a child is contained in a document that also contains information relating to an adult and a law enforcement agency is required to destroy all information relating to the child under this section, the agency shall alter the document so that the information relating to the child is destroyed and the information relating to the adult is preserved.

(e) The deletion of a computer entry constitutes destruction of the information contained in the entry.

(f) A law enforcement agency may maintain information relating to a child after the 90th day after the date the child successfully completes a first offender program under Section 52.031 only to determine the child's eligibility to participate in a first offender program.

*(Added by L.1995, chap. 262(53); chgd. by L.1997, chap. 1086(16); L.1999, chap. 1477(16), eff. 9/1/99.)*

### §58.002. Photographs and fingerprints of children.

(a) Except as provided by Chapter 79, Human Resources Code, a child may not be photographed or fingerprinted without the consent of the juvenile court unless the child is taken into custody or referred to the juvenile court for conduct that constitutes a felony or a misdemeanor punishable by confinement in jail.

(b) On or before December 31 of each year, the head of each municipal or county law enforcement agency located in a county shall certify to the juvenile board for that county that the photographs and fingerprints required to be destroyed under Section 58.001 have been destroyed. The juvenile board shall conduct an audit of the records of the law enforcement agency to verify the destruction of the photographs and fingerprints and the law enforcement agency shall make its records available for this purpose. If the audit shows that the certification provided by the head of the law enforcement agency is false, that person is subject to prosecution for perjury under Chapter 37, Penal Code.

(c) This section does not prohibit a law enforcement officer from photographing or fingerprinting a child who is not in custody if the child's parent or guardian voluntarily consents in writing to the photographing or fingerprinting of the child.

(d) This section does not apply to fingerprints that are required or authorized to be submitted or obtained for an application for a driver's license or personal identification card.

*(Added by L.1995, chap. 262(53); chgd. by L.1997, chap. 1086(17); L.1999, chap. 1477(17), eff. 9/1/99.)*



## §58.003. Sealing of records.

(a) Except as provided by Subsections (b) and (c), on the application of a person who has been found to have engaged in delinquent conduct or conduct indicating a need for supervision, or a person taken into custody to determine whether the person engaged in delinquent conduct or conduct indicating a need for supervision, on the juvenile court's own motion or on receipt of a certification from the Department of Public Safety of the State of Texas that the records of a person are eligible for sealing under this section, the court shall order the sealing of the records in the case if the court finds that:

(1) two years have elapsed since final discharge of the person or since the last official action in the person's case if there was no adjudication; and

(2) since the time specified in Subdivision (1), the person has not been convicted of a felony or a misdemeanor involving moral turpitude or found to have engaged in delinquent conduct or conduct indicating a need for supervision and no proceeding is pending seeking conviction or adjudication.

(b) A court may not order the sealing of the records of a person who has received a determinate sentence for engaging in delinquent conduct that violated a penal law listed in Section 53.045 or engaging in habitual felony conduct as described by Section 51.031.

(c) Subject to Subsection (b), a court may order the sealing of records concerning a person adjudicated as having engaged in delinquent conduct that violated a penal law of the grade of felony only if:

(1) the person is 21 years of age or older;

(2) the person was not transferred by a juvenile court under Section 54.02 to a criminal court for prosecution;

(3) the records have not been used as evidence in the punishment phase of a criminal proceeding under Section 3(a), Article 37.07, Code of Criminal Procedure; and

(4) the person has not been convicted of a penal law of the grade of felony after becoming age 17.

(d) The court may grant the relief authorized in Subsection (a) at any time after final discharge of the person or after the last official action in the case if there was no adjudication. If the child is referred to the juvenile court for conduct constituting any offense and at the adjudication hearing the child is found to be not guilty of each offense alleged, the court shall immediately order the sealing of all files and records relating to the case.

(e) Reasonable notice of the hearing shall be given to:

(1) the person who made the application or who is the subject of the records named in the motion;

(2) the prosecuting attorney for the juvenile court;

(3) the authority granting the discharge if the final discharge was from an institution or from parole;

(4) the public or private agency or institution having custody of records named in the application or motion; and

(5) the law enforcement agency having custody of files or records named in the application or motion.

(f) A copy of the sealing order shall be sent to each agency or official named in the order.

(g) On entry of the order:

(1) all law enforcement, prosecuting attorney, clerk of court, and juvenile court records ordered sealed shall be sent before the 61st day after the date the order is received to the court issuing the order;

(2) all records of a public or private agency or institution ordered sealed shall be sent before the 61st day after the date the order is received to the court issuing the order;

(3) all index references to the records ordered sealed shall be deleted before the 61st day after the date the order is received, and verification of the deletion shall be sent before the 61st day after the date of the deletion to the court issuing the order;

(4) the juvenile court, clerk of court, prosecuting attorney, public or private agency or institution, and law enforcement officers and agencies shall properly reply that no record exists with respect to the person on inquiry in any matter; and

(5) the adjudication shall be vacated and the proceeding dismissed and treated for all purposes other than a subsequent capital prosecution, including the purpose of showing a prior finding of delinquent conduct, as if it had never occurred.

(h) Inspection of the sealed records may be permitted by an order of the juvenile court on the petition of the person who is the subject of the records and only by those persons named in the order.

(i) On the final discharge of a child or on the last official action in the case if there is no adjudication, the child shall be given a written explanation of the child's rights under this section and a copy of the provisions of this section.

(j) A person whose records have been sealed under this section is not required in any proceeding or in any application for employment, information, or licensing to state that the person has been the subject of a proceeding under this title and any statement that the person has never been found to be a delinquent child shall never be held against the person in any criminal or civil proceeding.

(k) A prosecuting attorney may, on application to the juvenile court, reopen at any time the files and records of a person adjudicated as having engaged in delinquent conduct that violated a penal law of the grade of felony sealed by the court under this section for the purposes of Sections 12.42(a)-(c) and (e), Penal Code.

(*l*) On the motion of a person in whose name records are kept or on the court's own motion, the court may order the destruction of records that have been sealed under this section if:

(1) the records relate to conduct that did not violate a penal law of the grade of felony or a misdemeanor punishable by confinement in jail;

(2) five years have elapsed since the person's 16th birthday; and

(3) the person has not been convicted of a felony.

(m) On request of the Department of Public Safety, a juvenile court shall reopen and allow the department to inspect the files and records of the juvenile court relating to an applicant for a license to carry a concealed handgun under Subchapter H, Chapter 411, Government Code.

(n) A record created or maintained under Article 6252-13c.1, Revised Statutes, may not be sealed under this section if the person who is the subject of the record has a continuing obligation to register under that article.

(*o*) An agency or official named in the order that cannot seal the records because there is incorrect or insufficient information in the order shall notify the court issuing the order before the 61st day after the date the agency or official receives the order. The court shall notify the person who made the application or who is the subject of the records named in the motion, or the attorney for that person, before the 61st day after the date the court receives the notice that the agency or official cannot seal the records because there is incorrect or insufficient information in the order.
*(Added by L.1995, chap. 262(53); chgd. by L.1997, chaps. 165(10.05(a)), 1086(18); L.1999, chaps. 62(19.01(20)), 147(1), eff. 9/1/99.)*

**§58.004.** *(Repealed by L.1997, chap. 1086(49(a), (c)), eff. 9/1/97.)*

**§58.005. Confidentiality of records.**

(a) Information obtained for the purpose of diagnosis, examination, evaluation, or treatment or for making a referral for treatment of a child by a public or private agency or institution providing supervision of a child by arrangement of the juvenile court or having custody of the child under order of the juvenile court may be disclosed only to:

(1) the professional staff or consultants of the agency or institution;

(2) the judge, probation officers, and professional staff or consultants of the juvenile court;

(3) an attorney for the child;

(4) a governmental agency if the disclosure is required or authorized by law;

(5) a person or entity to whom the child is referred for treatment or services if the agency or institution disclosing the information has entered into a written confidentiality agreement with the person or entity regarding the protection of the disclosed information;

(6) the Texas Department of Criminal Justice and the Texas Juvenile Probation Commission for the purpose of maintaining statistical records of recidivism and for diagnosis and classification; or

(7) with leave of the juvenile court, any other person, agency, or institution having a legitimate interest in the proceeding or in the work of the court.

(b) This section does not apply to information collected under Section 58.104.
*(Added by L.1995, chap. 262(53), eff. 1/1/96.)*

## §58.0051. Interagency sharing of records.

(a) Within each county, a district school superintendent and the juvenile probation department may enter into a written interagency agreement to share information about juvenile offenders. The agreement must specify the conditions under which summary criminal history information is to be made available to appropriate school personnel and the conditions under which school records are to be made available to appropriate juvenile justice agencies.

(b) Information disclosed under this section by a school district must relate to the juvenile system's ability to serve, before adjudication, the student whose records are being released.

(c) A juvenile justice agency official who receives educational information under this section shall certify in writing that the institution or individual receiving the personally identifiable information has agreed not to disclose it to a third party, other than another juvenile justice agency.

(d) A juvenile justice agency that receives educational information under this section shall destroy all information when the child is no longer under the jurisdiction of a juvenile court.

*(Added by L.1999, chap. 217(1), eff. 5/24/99.)*



## §58.006. Destruction of certain records.

The court shall order the destruction of the records relating to the conduct for which a child is taken into custody, including records contained in the juvenile justice information system, if:

(1) a determination that no probable cause exists to believe the child engaged in the conduct is made under Section 53.01 and the case is not referred to a prosecutor for review under Section 53.012; or

(2) a determination that no probable cause exists to believe the child engaged in the conduct is made by a prosecutor under Section 53.012.

*(Added by L.1995, chap. 262(53), eff. 1/1/96.)*

## §58.007. Physical records or files.

(a) This section applies only to the inspection and maintenance of a physical record or file concerning a child and the storage of information, by electronic means or otherwise, concerning the child from which a physical record or file could be generated and does not affect the collection, dissemination, or maintenance of information as provided by Subchapter B. This section does not apply to a record or file relating to a child that is:

(1) required or authorized to be maintained under the laws regulating the operation of motor vehicles in this state;

(2) maintained by a municipal or justice court; or

(3) subject to disclosure under Chapter 62, Code of Criminal Procedure, as added by Chapter 668, Acts of the 75th Legislature, Regular Session, 1997.

(b) Except as provided by Article 15.27, Code of Criminal Procedure, the records and files of a juvenile court, a clerk of court, a juvenile probation department, or a prosecuting attorney relating to a child who is a party to a proceeding under this title are open to inspection only by:

(1) the judge, probation officers, and professional staff or consultants of the juvenile court;

(2) a juvenile justice agency as that term is defined by Section 58.101;

(3) an attorney for a party to the proceeding;

(4) a public or private agency or institution providing supervision of the child by arrangement of the juvenile court, or having custody of the child under juvenile court order; or

(5) with leave of the juvenile court, any other person, agency, or institution having a legitimate interest in the proceeding or in the work of the court.

(c) Except as provided by Subsection (d), law enforcement records and files concerning a child and information stored, by electronic means or otherwise, concerning the child from which a record or file could be generated may not be disclosed to the public and shall be:

(1) if maintained on paper or microfilm, kept separate from adult files and records;

(2) if maintained electronically in the same computer system as records or files relating to adults, be accessible under controls that are separate and distinct from controls to access electronic data concerning adults; and

(3) maintained on a local basis only and not sent to a central state or federal depository, except as provided by Subchapter B.

(d) The law enforcement files and records of a person who is transferred from the Texas Youth Commission to the institutional division or the pardons and paroles division of the Texas Department of Criminal Justice may be transferred to a central state or federal depository for adult records on or after the date of transfer.

(e) Law enforcement records and files concerning a child may be inspected by a juvenile justice agency as that term is defined by Section 58.101 and a criminal justice agency as that term is defined by Section 411.082, Government Code.

(f) If a child has been reported missing by a parent, guardian, or conservator of that child, information about the child may be forwarded to and disseminated by the Texas Crime Information Center and the National Crime Information Center.

(g) For the purpose of offering a record as evidence in the punishment phase of a criminal proceeding, a prosecuting attorney may obtain the record of a defendant's adjudication that is admissible under Section 3(a), Article 37.07, Code of Criminal Procedure, by submitting a request for the record to the juvenile court that made the adjudication. If a court receives a request from a prosecuting attorney under this subsection, the court shall, if the court possesses the requested record of adjudication, certify and provide the prosecuting attorney with a copy of the record.

(h) The juvenile court may disseminate to the public the following information relating to a child who is the subject of a directive to apprehend or a warrant of arrest and who cannot be located for the purpose of apprehension:

(1) the child's name, including other names by which the child is known;

(2) the child's physical description, including sex, weight, height, race, ethnicity, eye color, hair color, scars, marks, and tattoos;

(3) a photograph of the child; and

(4) a description of the conduct the child is alleged to have committed, including the level and degree of the alleged offense.

*(Added by L.1995, chap. 262(53); chgd. by L.1997, chap. 1086(19), (20); L.1999, chaps. 815(1), eff. 6/18/99, 1415(20), 1477(18), eff. 9/19/99.)*

### §§58.008 to 58.100. *(Reserved.)*

## SUBCHAPTER B. JUVENILE JUSTICE INFORMATION SYSTEM

### §58.101. Definitions.

In this subchapter:

(1) "Criminal justice agency" has the meaning assigned by Section 411.082, Government Code.

(2) "Department" means the Department of Public Safety of the State of Texas.

(3) "Disposition" means an action that results in the termination, transfer of jurisdiction, or indeterminate suspension of the prosecution of a juvenile offender.

(4) "Incident number" means a unique number assigned to a child during a specific custodial or detention period or for a specific referral to the office or official designated by the juvenile court, if the juvenile offender was not taken into custody before the referral.

(5) "Juvenile justice agency" means an agency that has custody or control over juvenile offenders.

(6) "Juvenile offender" means a child who has been assigned an incident number.

(7) "State identification number" means a unique number assigned by the department to a child in the juvenile justice information system.

(8) "Uniform incident fingerprint card" means a multiple-part form containing a unique incident number with space for information relating to the conduct for which a child has been taken into custody, detained, or referred, the child's fingerprints, and other relevant information.

*(Added by L.1995, chap. 262(53), eff. 1/1/96.)*

### §58.102. Juvenile justice information system.

(a) The department is responsible for recording data and maintaining a database for a computerized juvenile justice information system that serves:

(1) as the record creation point for the juvenile justice information system maintained by the state; and

(2) as the control terminal for entry of records, in accordance with federal law, rule, and policy, into the federal records system maintained by the Federal Bureau of Investigation.

(b) The department shall develop and maintain the system with the cooperation and advice of the:

(1) Texas Youth Commission;

(2) Texas Juvenile Probation Commission;

(3) Criminal Justice Policy Council; and

(4) juvenile courts and clerks of juvenile courts.

(c) The department may not collect or retain information relating to a juvenile if this chapter prohibits or restricts the collection or retention of the information.

(d) The database must contain the information required by this subchapter.

(e) The department shall designate the offense codes and has the sole responsibility for designating the state identification number for each juvenile whose name appears in the juvenile justice system.
*(Added by L.1995, chap. 262(53), eff. 1/1/96.)*

### §58.103. Purpose of system.

The purpose of the juvenile justice information system is to:

(1) provide agencies and personnel within the juvenile justice system accurate information relating to children who come into contact with the juvenile justice system of this state;

(2) provide, where allowed by law, adult criminal justice agencies accurate and easily accessible information relating to children who come into contact with the juvenile justice system;

(3) provide an efficient conversion, where appropriate, of juvenile records to adult criminal records;

(4) improve the quality of data used to conduct impact analyses of proposed legislative changes in the juvenile justice system; and

(5) improve the ability of interested parties to analyze the functioning of the juvenile justice system.
*(Added by L.1995, chap. 262(53), eff. 1/1/96.)*



### §58.104. Types of information collected.

(a) Subject to Subsection (f), the juvenile justice information system shall consist of information relating to delinquent conduct committed by a juvenile offender that, if the conduct had been committed by an adult, would constitute a criminal offense other than an offense punishable by a fine only, including information relating to:

(1) the juvenile offender;

(2) the intake or referral of the juvenile offender into the juvenile justice system;

(3) the detention of the juvenile offender;

(4) the prosecution of the juvenile offender;

(5) the disposition of the juvenile offender's case, including the name and description of any program to which the juvenile offender is referred; and

(6) the probation or commitment of the juvenile offender.

(b) To the extent possible and subject to Subsection (a), the department shall include in the juvenile justice information system the following information for each juvenile offender taken into custody, detained, or referred under this title for delinquent conduct:

(1) the juvenile offender's name, including other names by which the juvenile offender is known;

(2) the juvenile offender's date and place of birth;

(3) the juvenile offender's physical description, including sex, weight, height, race, ethnicity, eye color, hair color, scars, marks, and tattoos;

(4) the juvenile offender's state identification number, and other identifying information, as determined by the department;

(5) the juvenile offender's fingerprints;

(6) the juvenile offender's last known residential address, including the census tract number designation for the address;

(7) the name and identifying number of the agency that took into custody or detained the juvenile offender;

(8) the date of detention or custody;

(9) the conduct for which the juvenile offender was taken into custody, detained, or referred, including level and degree of the alleged offense;

(10) the name and identifying number of the juvenile intake agency or juvenile probation office;

(11) each disposition by the juvenile intake agency or juvenile probation office;

(12) the date of disposition by the juvenile intake agency or juvenile probation office;

(13) the name and identifying number of the prosecutor's office;

(14) each disposition by the prosecutor;

(15) the date of disposition by the prosecutor;

(16) the name and identifying number of the court;

(17) each disposition by the court, including information concerning custody of a juvenile offender by a juvenile justice agency or probation;

(18) the date of disposition by the court;

(19) any commitment or release under supervision by the Texas Youth Commission;

(20) the date of any commitment or release under supervision by the Texas Youth Commission; and

(21) a description of each appellate proceeding.

(c) The department may designate codes relating to the information described by Subsection (b).

(d) The department shall designate a state identification number for each juvenile offender.

(e) This subchapter does not apply to a disposition that represents an administrative status notice of an agency described by Section 58.102(b).

(f) Records maintained by the department in the depository are subject to being sealed under Section 58.003. The department shall send to the appropriate juvenile court its certification of records that the department determines, according to the department's records, are eligible for sealing under Section 58.003(a).

*(Added by L.1995, chap. 262(53); chgd. by L.1997, chap. 1086(21), eff. 9/1/97.)*

## §58.105. Duties of juvenile board.

Each juvenile board shall provide for:

(1) the compilation and maintenance of records and information needed for reporting information to the department under this subchapter;

(2) the transmittal to the department, in the manner provided by the department, of all records and information required by the department under this subchapter; and

(3) access by the department to inspect records and information to determine the completeness and accuracy of information reported.

*(Added by L.1995, chap. 262(53), eff. 1/1/96.)*



## §58.106. Confidentiality.

(a) Except as otherwise provided by this section, information contained in the juvenile justice information system is confidential information for the use of the department and may not be disseminated by the department except:

(1) with the permission of the juvenile offender, to military personnel of this state or the United States;

(2) to a person or entity to which the department may grant access to adult criminal history records as provided by Section 411.083, Government Code;

(3) to a juvenile justice agency; and

(4) to the Criminal Justice Policy Council, the Texas Youth Commission, and the Texas Juvenile Probation Commission for analytical purposes.

(b) Subsection (a) does not apply to a document maintained by a juvenile justice agency that is the source of information collected by the department.

(c) The department may, if necessary to protect the welfare of the community, disseminate to the public the following information relating to a juvenile who has escaped from the custody of the Texas Youth Commission or from another secure detention or correctional facility:

(1) the juvenile's name, including other names by which the juvenile is known;

(2) the juvenile's physical description, including sex, weight, height, race, ethnicity, eye color, hair color, scars, marks, and tattoos;

(3) a photograph of the juvenile; and

(4) a description of the conduct for which the juvenile was committed to the Texas Youth Commission or detained in the secure detention or correctional facility, including the level and degree of the alleged offense.

(d) The department may, if necessary to protect the welfare of the community, disseminate to the public the information listed under Subsection (c) relating to a juvenile offender when notified by a law enforcement agency of this state that the law enforcement agency has been issued a directive to apprehend the offender or an arrest warrant for the offender or that the law enforcement agency is otherwise authorized to arrest the offender and that the offender is suspected of having:

(1) committed a felony offense under the following provisions of the Penal Code:

(A) Title 5;

(B) Section 29.02; or

(C) Section 29.03; and

(2) fled from arrest or apprehension for commission of the offense.

*(Added by L.1995, chap. 262(53); chgd. by L.1997, chap. 380(1); L.1999, chaps. 407(1), 1477(19), eff. 9/1/99.)*

### §58.107. Compatibility of data.

Data supplied to the juvenile justice information system must be compatible with the system and must contain both incident numbers and state identification numbers. *(Added by L.1995, chap. 262(53), eff. 1/1/96.)*

### §58.108. Duties of agencies and courts.

(a) A juvenile justice agency and a clerk of a juvenile court shall:

(1) compile and maintain records needed for reporting data required by the department;

(2) transmit to the department in the manner provided by the department data required by the department;

(3) give the department or its accredited agents access to the agency or court for the purpose of inspection to determine the completeness and accuracy of data reported; and

(4) cooperate with the department to enable the department to perform its duties under this chapter.

(b) A juvenile justice agency and clerk of a court shall retain documents described by this section.

*(Added by L.1995, chap. 262(53), eff. 1/1/96.)*



### §58.109. Uniform incident fingerprint card.

(a) The department may provide for the use of a uniform incident fingerprint card in the maintenance of the juvenile justice information system.

(b) The department shall design, print, and distribute to each law enforcement agency and juvenile intake agency uniform incident fingerprint cards.

(c) The incident cards must:

(1) be serially numbered with an incident number in a manner that allows each incident of referral of a juvenile offender who is the subject of the incident fingerprint card to be readily ascertained; and

(2) be multiple-part forms that can be transmitted with the juvenile offender through the juvenile justice process and that allow each agency to report required data to the department.

(d) Subject to available telecommunications capacity, the department shall develop the capability to receive by electronic means from a law enforcement agency the information on the uniform incident fingerprint card. The information must be in a form that is compatible to the form required of data supplied to the juvenile justice information system.

*(Added by L.1995, chap. 262(53), eff. 1/1/96.)*

### §58.110. Reporting.

(a) The department by rule shall develop reporting procedures that ensure that the juvenile offender processing data is reported from the time a juvenile offender is initially taken into custody, detained, or referred until the time a juvenile offender is released from the jurisdiction of the juvenile justice system.

(b) The law enforcement agency or the juvenile intake agency that initiates the entry of the juvenile offender into the juvenile justice information system for a specific incident shall prepare a uniform incident fingerprint card and initiate the reporting process for each incident reportable under this subchapter.

(c) The clerk of the court exercising jurisdiction over a juvenile offender's case shall report the disposition of the case to the department. A clerk of the court who violates this subsection commits an offense. An offense under this subsection is a Class C misdemeanor.

(d) In each county, the reporting agencies may make alternative arrangements for reporting the required information, including combined reporting or electronic reporting, if the alternative reporting is approved by the juvenile board and the department.

(e) Except as otherwise required by applicable state laws or regulations, information required by this chapter to be reported to the department shall be reported promptly. The information shall be reported not later than the 30th day after the date the information is received by the agency responsible for reporting the information, except that a juvenile offender's custody, detention, or referral without previous custody shall be reported to the department not later than the seventh day after the date of the custody, detention, or referral.

(f) Subject to available telecommunications capacity, the department shall develop the capability to receive by electronic means the information required under this section to be reported to the department. The information must be in a form that is compatible to the form required of data to be reported under this section.

*(Added by L.1995, chap. 262(53), eff. 1/1/96.)*

### §58.111. Local data advisory boards.

The commissioners court of each county may create a local data advisory board to perform the same duties relating to the juvenile justice information system as the duties performed by a local data advisory board in relation to the criminal history record system under Article 60.09, Code of Criminal Procedure. *(Added by L.1995, chap. 262(53), eff. 1/1/96.)*

### §58.112. Report to legislature.

Not later than January 15 of each year, the Criminal Justice Policy Council shall submit to the lieutenant governor, the speaker of the house of representatives, and the governor a report that contains the following statistical information relating to children referred to a juvenile court during the preceding year:

(1) the ages, races, and counties of residence of the children transferred to a district court or criminal district court for criminal proceedings; and

(2) the ages, races, and counties of residence of the children committed to the Texas Youth Commission, placed on probation, or discharged without any disposition.
*(Added by L.1995, chap. 262(53), eff. 1/1/96.)*

### §58.113. Warrants.

The department shall maintain in a computerized database that is accessible by the same entities that may access the juvenile justice information system information relating to a warrant of arrest, as that term is defined by Article 15.01, Code of Criminal Procedure, or a directive to apprehend under Section 52.015 for any child, without regard to whether the child has been taken into custody. *(Added by L.1995, chap. 262(53), eff. 1/1/96.)*

## CHAPTER 60. UNIFORM INTERSTATE COMPACT ON JUVENILES

*(Added by L.1995, chap. 262(53), eff. 1/1/96.)*

Section


### §60.001. Short title.

This chapter may be cited as the Uniform Interstate Compact on Juveniles. *(Added by L.1995, chap. 262(53), eff. 1/1/96.)*

### §60.002. Execution of interstate compact.

The governor shall execute a compact on behalf of the state with any other state or states legally joining in it in substantially the following form:

#### INTERSTATE COMPACT ON JUVENILES

The contracting states solemnly agree:

#### Article I
#### FINDINGS AND PURPOSE

That juveniles who are not under proper supervision and control, or who have absconded, escaped, or run away are likely to endanger their own health, morals, and welfare, and the health, morals, and welfare of others. The cooperation of the states party to this compact is therefore necessary to provide for the welfare and protection of juveniles and of the public with respect to (1) cooperative supervision of delinquent juveniles on probation or parole; (2) the return, from one state to another, of delinquent juveniles who have escaped or absconded; (3) the return, from one state to another, of nondelinquent juveniles who have run away from home; and (4) additional measures for the protection of juveniles and of the public, which any two or more of the party states may find desirable to undertake cooperatively. In carrying out the provisions of this compact the party states shall be guided by the noncriminal, reformative, and protective policies which guide their laws concerning delinquent, neglected, or dependent juveniles generally. It shall be the policy of the states party to this compact to cooperate and observe their respective responsibilities for the prompt return and acceptance of juveniles and delinquent juveniles who become subject to the provisions of this compact. The provisions of this compact shall be reasonably and liberally construed to accomplish the foregoing purposes.

### Article II
### EXISTING RIGHTS AND REMEDIES

That all remedies and procedures provided by this compact shall be in addition to and not in substitution for other rights, remedies, and procedures, and shall not be in derogation of parental rights and responsibilities.

### Article III
### DEFINITIONS

That, for the purpose of this compact, "delinquent juvenile" means any juvenile who has been adjudged delinquent and who, at the time the provisions of this compact are invoked, is still subject to the jurisdiction of the court that has made such adjudication or to the jurisdiction or supervision of an agency or institution pursuant to an order of such court; "probation or parole" means any kind of conditional release of juveniles authorized under the laws of the states party hereto; "court" means any court having jurisdiction over delinquent, neglected, or dependent children; "state" means any state, territory, or possessions of the United States, the District of Columbia, and the Commonwealth of Puerto Rico; and "residence" or any variant thereof means a place at which a home or regular place of abode is maintained.



### Article IV
### RETURN OF RUNAWAYS

(a) That the parent, guardian, person, or agency entitled to legal custody of a juvenile who has not been adjudged delinquent but who has run away without the consent of such parent, guardian, person, or agency may petition the appropriate court in the demanding state for the issuance of a requisition for his return. The petition shall state the name and age of the juvenile, the name of the petitioner, and the basis of entitlement to the juvenile's custody, the circumstances of his running away, his location if known at the time application is made, and such other facts as may tend to show that the juvenile who has run away is endangering his own welfare or the welfare of others and is not an emancipated minor. The petition shall be verified by affidavit, shall be executed in duplicate, and shall be accompanied by two certified copies of the document or documents on which the petitioner's entitlement to the juvenile's custody is based, such as birth certificates, letters of guardianship, or custody decrees. Such further affidavits and other documents as may be deemed proper may be submitted with such petition. The judge of the court to which this application is made may hold a hearing thereon to determine whether for the purposes of this compact the petitioner is entitled to the legal custody of the juvenile, whether or not it appears that the juvenile has in fact run away without consent, whether or not he is an emancipated minor, and whether or not it is in the best interest of the juvenile to compel his return to the state. If the judge determines, either with or without a hearing, that the juvenile should be returned, he shall present to the appropriate court or to the executive authority of the state where the juvenile is alleged to be located a written requisition for the return of such juvenile. Such requisition shall set forth the name and age of the juvenile, the determination of the court that the juvenile has run away without the consent of a parent, guardian, person, or agency entitled to his legal custody, and that it is in the best interest and for the protection of such juvenile that he be returned. In the event that a proceeding for the adjudication of the juvenile as a delinquent, neglected, or dependent juvenile is pending in the court at the time when such juvenile runs away, the court may issue a requisition for the return of such juvenile upon its own motion, regardless of the consent of the parent, guardian, person, or agency entitled to legal custody, reciting therein the nature and circumstances of the pending proceeding. The requisition shall in every case be executed in duplicate and shall be signed by the judge. One copy of the requisition shall be filed with the compact administrator of the demanding state, there to remain on file subject to the provisions of law governing records of such court. Upon the receipt of a requisition demanding the return of a juvenile who has run away, the court or the executive authority to whom the requisition is addressed shall issue an order to any peace officer or other appropriate person directing him to take into custody and detain such juvenile. Such detention order must substantially recite the facts necessary to the validity of its issuance hereunder. No juvenile detained upon such order shall be delivered over to the officer whom the court demanding him shall have appointed to receive him unless he shall first be taken forthwith before a judge of a court in the state, who shall inform him of the demand made for his return, and who may appoint counsel or guardian ad litem for him. If the judge of such court shall find that the requisition is in order, he shall deliver such juvenile over to the officer whom the court demanding him shall have appointed to receive him. The judge, however, may fix a reasonable time to be allowed for the purpose of testing the legality of the proceeding.

Upon reasonable information that a person is a juvenile who has run away from another state party to this compact without the consent of a parent, guardian, person, or agency entitled to his legal custody, such juvenile may be taken into custody without a requisition and brought forthwith before a judge of the appropriate court who may appoint counsel or guardian ad litem for such juvenile and who shall determine after a hearing whether sufficient cause exists to hold the person, subject to the order of the court, for his own protection and welfare, for such a time not exceeding 90 days as will enable his return to another state party to this compact pursuant to a requisition for his return from a court of that state. If, at the time when a state seeks the return of a juvenile who has run away, there is pending in the state wherein he is found any criminal charge, or any proceeding to have him adjudicated a delinquent juvenile for an act committed in such state, or if he is suspected of having committed within such state a criminal offense or an act of juvenile delinquency, he shall not be returned without the consent of such state until discharged from prosecution or other form of proceeding, imprisonment, detention, or supervision for such offense of juvenile delinquency. The duly accredited officers of any state party to this compact, upon the establishment of their authority and the identity of the juvenile being returned, shall be permitted to transport such juvenile through any and all states party to this compact, without interference. Upon his return to the state from which he ran away, the juvenile shall be subject to such further proceedings as may be appropriate under the laws of that state.

(b) That the state to which a juvenile is returned under this article shall be responsible for payment of the transportation costs of such return.

(c) That "juvenile" as used in this article means any person who is a minor under the law of the state of residence of the parent, guardian, person, or agency entitled to the legal custody of such minor.

## Article V
## RETURN OF ESCAPEES AND ABSCONDERS

(a) That the appropriate person or authority from whose probation or parole supervision a delinquent juvenile has absconded or from whose institutional custody he has escaped shall present to the appropriate court or to the executive authority of the state where the delinquent juvenile is alleged to be located a written requisition for the return of such delinquent juvenile. Such requisition shall state the name and age of the delinquent juvenile, the particulars of his adjudication as a delinquent juvenile, the circumstances of the breach of the terms of his probation or parole or of his escape from an institution or agency vested with his legal custody or supervision, and the location of such delinquent juvenile, if known, at the time the requisition is made. The requisition shall be verified by affidavit, shall be executed in duplicate, and shall be accompanied by two certified copies of the judgment, formal adjudication, or order of commitment which subjects such delinquent juvenile to probation or parole or to the legal custody of the institution or agency concerned. Such further affidavits and other documents as may be deemed proper may be submitted with such requisition. One copy of the requisition shall be filed with the compact administrator of the demanding state, there to remain on file subject to the provisions of law governing records of the appropriate court. Upon the receipt of a requisition demanding the return of a delinquent juvenile who has absconded or escaped, the court or the executive authority to whom the requisition is addressed shall issue an order to any peace officer or other appropriate person directing him to take into custody and detain such delinquent juvenile. Such detention order must substantially recite the facts necessary to the validity of its issuance hereunder. No delinquent juvenile detained upon such order shall be delivered over to the officer whom the appropriate person or authority demanding him shall have appointed to receive him unless he shall first be taken forthwith before a judge of an appropriate court in the state, who shall inform him of the demand made for his return and who may appoint counsel or guardian ad litem for him. If the judge of such court shall find that the requisition is in order, he shall deliver such delinquent juvenile over to the officer whom the appropriate person or authority demanding him shall have appointed to receive him. The judge, however, may fix a reasonable time to be allowed for the purpose of testing the legality of the proceeding.

Upon reasonable information that a person is a delinquent juvenile who has absconded while on probation or parole, or escaped from an institution or agency vested with this legal custody or supervision in any state party to this compact, such person may be taken into custody in any other state party to this compact without a requisition. But in such event, he must be taken forthwith before a judge of the appropriate court, who may appoint counsel or guardian ad litem for such person and who shall determine, after a hearing, whether sufficient cause exists to hold the person subject to the order of the court for such a time, not exceeding 90 days, as will enable his detention under a detention order issued on a requisition pursuant to this article. If, at the time when a state seeks the return of a delinquent juvenile who has either absconded while on probation or parole or escaped from an institution or agency vested with his legal custody or supervision, there is pending in the state wherein he is detained any criminal charge or any proceeding to have him adjudicated a delinquent juvenile for an act committed in such state, or if he is suspected of having committed within such state a criminal offense or an act of juvenile delinquency, he shall not be returned without the consent of such state until discharged from prosecution or other form of proceeding, imprisonment, detention, or supervision for such offense of juvenile delinquency. The duly accredited officers of any state party to this compact, upon the establishment of their authority and the identity of the delinquent juvenile being returned, shall be permitted to transport such delinquent juvenile through any and all states party to this compact, without interference. Upon his return to the state from which he escaped or absconded, the delinquent juvenile shall be subject to such further proceedings as may be appropriate under the laws of that state.

(b) That the state to which a delinquent juvenile is returned under this article shall be responsible for the payment of the transportation costs of such return.

## Article VI
## VOLUNTARY RETURN PROCEDURE

That any delinquent juvenile who has absconded while on probation or parole, or escaped from an institution or agency vested with his legal custody or supervision in any state party to this compact, and any juvenile who has run away from any state party to this compact, who is taken into custody without a requisition in another state party to this compact under the provisions of Article IV(a) or of Article V(a), may consent to his immediate return to the state from which he absconded, escaped, or ran away. Such consent shall be given by the juvenile or delinquent juvenile and his counsel or guardian ad litem, if any, by executing or subscribing in writing, in the presence of a judge of the appropriate court, which states that the juvenile or delinquent juvenile and his counsel or guardian ad litem, if any, consent to his return to the demanding state. Before such consent shall be executed or subscribed, however, the judge, in the presence of counsel or guardian ad litem, if any, shall inform the juvenile or delinquent juvenile of his rights under this compact. When the consent has been duly executed, it shall be forwarded to and filed with the compact administrator of the state in which the court is located and the judge shall direct the officer having the juvenile or delinquent juvenile in custody to deliver him to the duly accredited officer or officers of the state demanding his return, and shall cause to be delivered to such officer or officers a copy of the consent. The court may, however, upon the request of the state to which the juvenile or delinquent juvenile is being returned, order him to return unaccompanied to such state and shall provide him with a copy of such court order; in such event a copy of the consent shall be forwarded to the compact administrator of the state to which said juvenile or delinquent juvenile is ordered to return.

## Article VII
## COOPERATIVE SUPERVISION OF PROBATIONERS AND PAROLEES

(a) That the duly constituted judicial and administrative authorities of a state party to this compact (herein called "sending state") may permit any delinquent juvenile within such state, placed on probation or parole, to reside in any other state party to this compact (herein called "receiving state") while on probation or parole, and the receiving state shall accept such delinquent juvenile, if the parent, guardian, or person entitled to the legal custody of such delinquent juvenile is residing or undertakes to reside within the receiving state. Before granting such permission, opportunity shall be given to the receiving state to make such investigations as it deems necessary. The authorities of the sending state shall send to the authorities of the receiving state copies of pertinent court orders, social case studies, and all other available information which may be of value to and assist the receiving state in supervising a probationer or parolee under this compact. A receiving state, in its discretion, may agree to accept supervision of a probationer or parolee in cases where the parent, guardian, or person entitled to the legal custody of the delinquent juvenile is not a resident of the receiving state, and if so accepted the sending state may transfer supervision accordingly.

(b) That each receiving state will assume the duties of visitation and of supervision over any such delinquent juvenile and in the exercise of those duties will be governed by the same standards of visitation and supervision that prevail for its own delinquent juveniles released on probation or parole.

(c) That, after consultation between the appropriate authorities of the sending state and of the receiving state as to the desirability and necessity of returning such a delinquent juvenile, the duly accredited officers of a sending state may enter a receiving state and there apprehend and retake any such delinquent juvenile on probation or parole. For that purpose, no formalities will be required, other than establishing the authority of the officer and the identity of the delinquent juvenile to be retaken and returned. The decision of the sending state to retake a delinquent juvenile on probation or parole shall be conclusive upon and not reviewable within the receiving state, but if, at the time the sending state seeks to retake a delinquent juvenile on probation or parole, there is pending against him within the receiving state any criminal charge or any proceedings to have him adjudicated a delinquent juvenile for any act committed in such state or if he is suspected of having committed within such state a criminal offense or an act of juvenile delinquency, he shall not be returned without the consent of the receiving state until discharged from prosecution or other form of proceeding, imprisonment, detention, or supervision for such offense of juvenile delinquency. The duly accredited officers of the sending state shall be permitted to transport delinquent juveniles being so returned through any and all states party to this compact, without interference.

(d) That the sending state shall be responsible under this article for paying the costs of transporting any delinquent juvenile to the receiving state or of returning any delinquent juvenile to the sending state.

## Article VIII
## RESPONSIBILITY FOR COSTS

(a) That the provisions of Articles IV(b), V(b), and VII(d) of this compact shall not be construed to alter or affect any internal relationship among the departments, agencies, and officers of and in the government of a party state, or between a party state and its subdivisions, as to the payment of costs, or responsibilities therefor.

(b) That nothing in this compact shall be construed to prevent any party state or subdivision thereof from asserting any right against any person, agency, or other entity in regard to costs for which such party state or subdivision thereof may be responsible pursuant to Articles IV(b), V(b), or VII(d) of this compact.

## Article IX
## DETENTION PRACTICES

That, to every extent possible, it shall be the policy of states party to this compact that no juvenile or delinquent juvenile shall be placed or detained in any prison, jail, or lockup nor be detained or transported in association with criminal, vicious, or dissolute persons.

## Article X
## SUPPLEMENTARY AGREEMENTS

That the duly constituted administrative authorities of a state party to this compact may enter into supplementary agreements with any other state or states party hereto for the cooperative care, treatment, and rehabilitation of delinquent juveniles whenever they shall find that such agreements will improve the facilities or programs available for such care, treatment, and rehabilitation. Such care, treatment, and rehabilitation may be provided in an institution located within any state entering into such supplementary agreement. Such supplementary agreements shall (1) provide the rates to be paid for the care, treatment, and custody of such delinquent juveniles, taking into consideration the character of facilities, services, and subsistence furnished; (2) provide that the delinquent juvenile shall be given a court hearing prior to his being sent to another state for care, treatment, and custody; (3) provide that the state receiving such a delinquent juvenile in one of its institutions shall act solely as agent for the state sending such delinquent juvenile; (4) provide that the sending state shall at all times retain jurisdiction over delinquent juveniles sent to an institution in another state; (5) provide for reasonable inspection of such institutions by the sending state; (6) provide that the consent of the parent, guardian, person, or agency entitled to the legal custody of said delinquent juvenile shall be secured prior to his being sent to another state; and (7) make provision for such other matters and details as shall be necessary to protect the rights and equities of such delinquent juveniles and of the cooperating states.

## Article XI
## ACCEPTANCE OF FEDERAL AND OTHER AID

That any state party to this compact may accept any and all donations, gifts, and grants of money, equipment, and services from the federal or any local government, or any agency thereof and from any person, firm, or corporation, for any of the purposes and functions of this compact, and may receive and utilize the same, subject to the terms, conditions, and regulations governing such donations, gifts, and grants.

**Article XII**
**COMPACT ADMINISTRATORS**

That the governor of each state party to this compact shall designate an officer who, acting jointly with like officers of other party states, shall promulgate rules and regulations to carry out more effectively the terms and provisions of this compact.

**Article XIII**
**EXECUTION OF COMPACT**

That this compact shall become operative immediately upon its execution by any state as between it and any other state or states so executing. When executed it shall have the full force and effect of law within such state, the form or execution to be in accordance with the laws of the executing state.

**Article XIV**
**RENUNCIATION**

That this compact shall continue in force and remain binding upon each executing state until renounced by it. Renunciation of this compact shall be by the same authority which executed it, by sending six months notice in writing of its intention to withdraw from the compact to the other states party hereto. The duties and obligations of a renouncing state under Article VII hereof shall continue as to parolees and probationers residing therein at the time of withdrawal until retaken or finally discharged. Supplementary agreements entered into under Article X hereof shall be subject to renunciation as provided by such supplementary agreements, and shall not be subject to the six months renunciation notice of the present article.

**Article XV**
**SEVERABILITY**

That the provisions of this compact shall be severable and if any phrase, clause, sentence, or provision of this compact is declared to be contrary to the constitution of any participating state or of the United States or the applicability thereof to any government, agency, person, or circumstance is held invalid, the validity of the remainder of this compact and the applicability thereof to any government, agency, person, or circumstances shall not be affected thereby. If this compact shall be held contrary to the constitution of any state participating therein, the compact shall remain in full force and effect as to the remaining states and in full force and effect as to the state affected as to all severable matters.
*(Added by L.1995, chap. 262(53), eff. 1/1/96.)*

## §60.003. Execution of additional article.

The governor shall also execute on the behalf of the state with any other state or states legally joining in it, an additional article to the Interstate Compact on Juveniles in substantially the following form:

**Article XVI**
**ADDITIONAL ARTICLE**

That this article shall provide additional remedies, and shall be binding only as among and between those party states which specifically execute the same.

For the purposes of this article, "child," as used herein, means any minor within the jurisdictional age limits of any court in the home state.

When any child is brought before a court of a state of which such child is not a resident, and such state is willing to permit such child's return to the home state of such child, such home state, upon being so advised by the state in which such proceeding is pending, shall immediately institute proceedings to determine the residence and jurisdictional facts as to such child in such home state, and upon finding that such child is in fact a resident of said state and subject to the jurisdiction of the court thereof shall within five days authorize the return of such child to the home state, and to the parent or custodial agency legally authorized to accept such custody in such home state, and at the expense of such home state, to be paid from such funds as such home state may procure, designate, or provide, prompt action being of the essence.
*(Added by L.1995, chap. 262(53), eff. 1/1/96.)*

## §60.004. Execution of amendment.

The governor shall also execute on the behalf of the state with any other state or states legally joining in it, an amendment to the Interstate Compact on Juveniles in substantially the following form:

**RENDITION AMENDMENT**

(a) This amendment shall provide additional remedies, and shall be binding only as among and between those party states which specifically execute the same.

(b) All provisions and procedures of Articles V and VI of the Interstate Compact on Juveniles shall be construed to apply to any juvenile charged with being a delinquent by reason of a violation of any criminal law. Any juvenile charged with being a delinquent by reason of violating any criminal law shall be returned to the requesting state upon a requisition to the state where the juvenile may be found. A petition in such case shall be filed in a court of competent jurisdiction in the requesting state where the violation of criminal law is alleged to have been committed. The petition may be filed regardless of whether the juvenile has left the state before or after the filing of the petition. The requisition described in Article V of the compact shall be forwarded by the judge of the court in which the petition has been filed.

*(Added by L.1995, chap. 262(53), eff. 1/1/96.)*

## §60.005. Juvenile compact administrator.

Under the compact, the governor may designate an officer as the compact administrator. The administrator, acting jointly with like officers of other party states, shall adopt regulations to carry out more effectively the terms of the compact. The compact administrator serves at the pleasure of the governor. The compact administrator shall cooperate with all departments, agencies, and officers of and in the government of this state and its subdivisions in facilitating the proper administration of the compact or of a supplementary agreement entered into by this state. *(Added by L.1995, chap. 262(53), eff. 1/1/96.)*

## §60.006. Supplementary agreements.

A compact administrator may make supplementary agreements with appropriate officials of other states pursuant to the compact. If a supplementary agreement requires or contemplates the use of an institution or facility of this state or requires or contemplates the provision of a service of this state, the supplementary agreement has no force or effect until approved by the head of the department or agency under whose jurisdiction the institution is operated, or whose department or agency is charged with performing the service. *(Added by L.1995, chap. 262(53), eff. 1/1/96.)*

## §60.007. Financial arrangements.

The compact administrator may make or arrange for the payments necessary to discharge the financial obligations imposed upon this state by the compact or by a supplementary agreement made under the compact, subject to legislative appropriations. *(Added by L.1995, chap. 262(53), eff. 1/1/96.)*

## §60.008. Enforcement.

The courts, departments, agencies, and officers of this state and its subdivisions shall enforce this compact and shall do all things appropriate to effectuate its purposes and intent which are within their respective jurisdictions. *(Added by L.1995, chap. 262(53), eff. 1/1/96.)*

## §60.009. Additional procedures not precluded.

In addition to the procedures provided in Articles IV and VI of the compact for the return of a runaway juvenile, the particular states, the juvenile, or his parents, the courts, or other legal custodian involved may agree upon and adopt any plan or procedure legally authorized under the laws of this state and the other respective party states for the return of the runaway juvenile. *(Added by L.1995, chap. 262(53), eff. 1/1/96.)*

Printed in the U.S.A.

# TITLE 4. PROTECTIVE ORDERS AND FAMILY VIOLENCE

*(Added by L.1997, chap. 34(1), eff. 5/5/97, Former Title 4 repealed by L.1997, chap. 34(2), eff. 5/5/97.)*

## SUBTITLE A. GENERAL PROVISIONS

## CHAPTER 71. DEFINITIONS





### §71.001. Applicability of definitions.

(a) Definitions in this chapter apply to this title.

(b) If, in another part of this title, a term defined by this chapter has a meaning different from the meaning provided by this chapter, the meaning of that other provision prevails.

(c) Except as provided by this chapter, the definitions in Chapter 101 apply to terms used in this title.

*(Added by L.1997, chap. 34(1), eff. 5/5/97.)*

### §71.002. Court.

"Court" means the district court, court of domestic relations, juvenile court having the jurisdiction of a district court, statutory county court, constitutional county court, or other court expressly given jurisdiction under this title. *(Added by L.1997, chap. 34(1), eff. 5/5/97; chgd. by L.1997, chap. 1220(1), eff. 9/1/97.)*

### §71.003. Family.

"Family" includes individuals related by consanguinity or affinity, as determined under Sections 573.022 and 573.024, Government Code, individuals who are former spouses of each other, individuals who are the biological parents of the same child, without regard to marriage, and a foster child and foster parent, without regard to whether those individuals reside together. *(Added by L.1997, chap. 34(1), eff. 5/5/97.)*

### §71.004. Family violence.

"Family violence" means:

(1) an act by a member of a family or household against another member of the family or household that is intended to result in physical harm, bodily injury, assault, or sexual assault or that is a threat that reasonably places the member in fear of imminent physical harm, bodily injury, assault, or sexual assault, but does not include defensive measures to protect oneself; or

(2) abuse, as that term is defined by Sections 261.001(1)(C), (E), and (G) by a member of a family or household toward a child of the family or household.

*(Added by L.1997, chap. 34(1), eff. 5/5/97.)*

### §71.005. Household.

"Household" means a unit composed of persons living together in the same dwelling, without regard to whether they are related to each other. *(Added by L.1997, chap. 34(1), eff. 5/5/97.)*

### §71.006. Member of a household.

"Member of a household" includes a person who previously lived in a household. *(Added by L.1997, chap. 34(1), eff. 5/5/97.)*

**§71.007. Prosecuting attorney.**

"Prosecuting attorney" means the attorney, determined as provided in this title, who represents the state in a district or statutory county court in the county in which venue of the application for a protective order is proper. *(Added by L.1997, chap. 34(1), eff. 5/5/97.)*

**§71.008. Protective order from another jurisdiction.**

"Protective order from another jurisdiction" means a protective order rendered by a military court or a court of another state, tribe, or territory related to protecting an individual from domestic or family violence and that meets the following requirements:

(1) the order is rendered by a court that has jurisdiction over the parties and the matter under the law of the military, state, tribe, or territory; and

(2) the respondent is given notice and an opportunity to be heard consistent with due process either:

(A) before the date the order was rendered; or

(B) in the case of an ex parte order, within the time required by the jurisdiction rendering the order after the date the order is rendered, but not later than a reasonab'e time.

*(Added by L.1997, chap. 1193(2), eff. 9/1/97.)*

*Editor's Note: The following sections of former Title 4, Chapter 71 were amended despite its repeal by L.1997, chap. 34(2), eff. 5/5/97.)*

**§71.01. Definitions.** *(Subsections (a), (b)(2) only.)*

(a) Except as provided by Subsection (b) of this section, the definitions in Chapter 101 apply to terms in used in this chapter. *(Chgd. by L.1997, chap. 165(7.12), eff. 9/1/97.)*

(b)(2) "Family violence" means:

(a) an act by a member of a family or household against another member of the family or household that is intended to result in physical harm, bodily injury, assault, or sexual assault or that is a threat that reasonably places the member in fear of imminent physical harm, bodily injury, assault, or sexual assault, but does not include defensive measures to protect oneself; or

(B) abuse, as that term is defined by Sections 261.001(1)(C), (E), and (G), by a member of a family or household toward a child of the family or household.

*(Chgd. by L.1997, chap. 165(7.13), eff. 9/1/97.)*

**§71.05. Contents of application.** *(Subsection (c) only.)*

(c) If an application requests a protective order for a child who is subject to the continuing jurisdiction of a court under Title 5 or alleges that a child who is subject to the continuing jurisdiction of a court under Title 5 has committed family violence:

(1) a copy of the court orders affecting the conservatorship, possession, and support of or the access to the child must be filed with the application; or

(2) the application must state that the orders affecting the child are unavailable to the applicant and that a copy of the orders will be filed with the court before the hearing on the application.

*(Chgd. by L.1997, chap. 165(7.14), eff. 9/1/97.)*

**§71.09.** *(Chgd. by L.1997, chap. 752(4); repealed by L.1999, chap. 62(6.10(b)), eff. 9/1/99.)*

**§71.11. Protective order.** *(Subsection (a)(3) only.)*

(a) In a protective order the court may:

(3) provide for the possession of and access to a child of a party if the person receiving possession of or access to the child is a parent, as that term is defined by Section 101.024, of the child;

*(Chgd. by L.1997, chap. 165(7.15), eff. 9/1/97.)*

**§71.15. Temporary orders.** *(Subsection (f) only.)*

(f) During the period of its validity, a temporary ex parte order prevails over any other court order made under Title 5, except that on a motion to vacate the temporary ex parte order, the court shall vacate those portions of the temporary order shown to be in conflict with any other court order under Title 5. *(Chgd. by L.1997, chap. 165(7.16), eff. 9/1/97.)*

# SUBTITLE B. PROTECTIVE ORDERS

## CHAPTER 81. GENERAL PROVISIONS



Printed in the U.S.A. Zt

### §81.001. Entitlement to protective order.

A court shall render a protective order as provided by Section 85.001(b) if the court finds that family violence has occurred and is likely to occur in the future. *(Added by L.1997, chap. 34(1), eff. 5/5/97.)*

### §81.002. No fee for applicant.

An applicant for a protective order or an attorney representing an applicant may not be assessed a fee, cost, charge, or expense by a district or county clerk of the court or a sheriff, constable, or other public official or employee in connection with the filing, serving, or entering of a protective order or for any other service described by this subsection, including:

(1) a fee to dismiss, modify, or withdraw a protective order;
(2) a fee for certifying copies;
(3) a fee for comparing copies to originals;
(4) a court reporter fee;
(5) a judicial fund fee;
(6) a fee for any other service related to a protective order; or
(7) a fee to transfer a protective order.

*(Added by L.1997, chap. 34(1), eff. 5/5/97; chgd. by L.1997, chap. 1193(3), eff. 9/1/97.)*

### §81.003. Fees and costs paid by party found to have committed family violence.

(a) Except on a showing of good cause or of the indigence of a party found to have committed family violence, the court shall require in a protective order that the party against whom the order is rendered pay the $16 protective order fee, the standard fees charged by the clerk of the court in a general civil proceeding for the cost of serving the order, the costs of court, and all other fees, charges, or expenses incurred in connection with the protective order.

(b) The court may order a party against whom an agreed protective order is rendered under Section 85.005 to pay the fees required in Subsection (a).

*(Added by L.1997, chap. 34(1), eff. 5/5/97; chgd. by L.1997, chap. 1193(4), eff. 9/1/97.)*

### §81.004. Contempt for nonpayment of fee.

(a) A party who is ordered to pay fees and costs and who does not pay before the date specified by the order may be punished for contempt of court as provided by Section 21.002, Government Code.

(b) If a date is not specified by the court under Subsection (a), payment of costs is required before the 60th day after the date the order was rendered.

*(Added by L.1997, chap. 34(1), eff. 5/5/97; chgd. by L.1997, chap. 1193(5), eff. 9/1/97.)*

### §81.005. Attorney's fees.

(a) The court may assess reasonable attorney's fees against the party found to have committed family violence or a party against whom an agreed protective order is rendered under Section 85.005 as compensation for the services of a private or prosecuting attorney or an attorney employed by the Department of Protective and Regulatory Services.

(b) In setting the amount of attorney's fees, the court shall consider the income and ability to pay of the person against whom the fee is assessed.

*(Added by L.1997, chap. 34(1), eff. 5/5/97; chgd. by L.1997, chap. 1193(6), eff. 9/1/97.)*

### §81.006. Payment of attorney's fees.

The amount of fees collected under this chapter as compensation for the fees:

(1) of a private attorney shall be paid to the private attorney who may enforce the order for fees in the attorney's own name;

(2) of a prosecuting attorney shall be paid to the credit of the county fund from which the salaries of the employees of the prosecuting attorney are paid or supplemented; and

(3) of an attorney employed by the Department of Protective and Regulatory Services shall be deposited in the general revenue fund to the credit of the Department of Protective and Regulatory Services.

*(Added by L.1997, chap. 34(1), eff. 5/5/97.)*

### §81.007. Prosecuting attorney.

(a) The county attorney or the criminal district attorney is the prosecuting attorney responsible for filing applications under this subtitle unless the district attorney assumes the responsibility by giving notice of that assumption to the county attorney.

(b) The prosecuting attorney responsible for filing an application under this subtitle shall provide notice of that responsibility to all law enforcement agencies in the jurisdiction of the prosecuting attorney.

(c) The prosecuting attorney shall comply with Article 5.06, Code of Criminal Procedure, in filing an application under this subtitle.

*(Added by L.1997, chap. 34(1), eff. 5/5/97.)*

### §81.0075. Representation by prosecuting attorney in certain subsequent actions.

A prosecuting attorney who represents a party in a proceeding under this subtitle is not precluded from representing the Department of Protective and Regulatory Services in a subsequent action involving the party. *(Added by L.1997, chap. 1193(7), eff. 9/1/97.)*

### §81.008. Relief cumulative.

Except as provided by this subtitle, the relief and remedies provided by this subtitle are cumulative of other relief and remedies provided by law. *(Added by L.1997, chap. 34(1), eff. 5/5/97.)*

## CHAPTER 82. APPLYING FOR PROTECTIVE ORDER

## SUBCHAPTER A. APPLICATION FOR PROTECTIVE ORDER

Section



## SUBCHAPTER B. PLEADINGS BY RESPONDENT

## SUBCHAPTER C. NOTICE OF APPLICATION FOR PROTECTIVE ORDER



## SUBCHAPTER A. APPLICATION FOR PROTECTIVE ORDER

### §82.001. Application.

A proceeding under this subtitle is begun by filing "An Application for a Protective Order" with the clerk of the court. *(Added by L.1997, chap. 34(1), eff. 5/5/97.)*



### §82.002. Who may file application.

(a) An application for a protective order to protect the applicant or any other member of the applicant's family or household may be filed by:

(1) an adult member of the family or household; or

(2) any adult for the protection of a child.

(b) In addition, an application may be filed for the protection of any person alleged to be a victim of family violence by:

(1) a prosecuting attorney; or

(2) the Department of Protective and Regulatory Services.

(c) The person alleged to be the victim of family violence in an application filed under Subsection (b) is considered to be the applicant for a protective order under this subtitle.
*(Added by L.1997, chap. 34(1), eff. 5/5/97; chgd. by L.1997, chap. 1193(8), eff. 9/1/97.)*

### §82.003. Venue.

An application may be filed in:

(1) the county in which the applicant resides; or

(2) the county in which the respondent resides.
*(Added by L.1997, chap. 34(1), eff. 5/5/97.)*

### §82.004. Contents of application.

An application must state:

(1) the name and county of residence of each applicant;

(2) the name, address, and county of residence of each individual alleged to have committed family violence;

(3) the relationships between the applicants and the individual alleged to have committed family violence; and

(4) a request for one or more protective orders.
*(Added by L.1997, chap. 34(1), eff. 5/5/97.)*

### §82.005. Application filed during suit for dissolution of marriage or suit affecting parent-child relationship.

A person who wishes to apply for a protective order with respect to the person's spouse and who is a party to a suit for the dissolution of a marriage or a suit affecting the parent-child relationship that is pending in a court must file the application as required by Subchapter D, Chapter 85.
*(Added by L.1997, chap. 34(1), eff. 5/5/97; chgd. by L.1997, chap. 1193(9), eff. 9/1/97.)*

### §82.006. Application filed after dissolution of marriage.

If an applicant for a protective order is a former spouse of the individual alleged to have committed family violence, the application must include:

(1) a copy of the decree dissolving the marriage; or

(2) a statement that the decree is unavailable to the applicant and that a copy of the decree will be filed with the court before the hearing on the application.
*(Added by L.1997, chap. 34(1), eff. 5/5/97.)*

### §82.007. Application filed for child subject to continuing jurisdiction.

An application that requests a protective order for a child who is subject to the continuing exclusive jurisdiction of a court under Title 5 or alleges that a child who is subject to the continuing exclusive jurisdiction of a court under Title 5 has committed family violence must include:

(1) a copy of each court order affecting the conservatorship, support, and possession of or access to the child; or

(2) a statement that the orders affecting the child are unavailable to the applicant and that a copy of the orders will be filed with the court before the hearing on the application.
*(Added by L.1997, chap. 34(1), eff. 5/5/97.)*

### §82.008. Application filed after expiration of former protective order.

(a) An application for a protective order that is filed after a previously rendered protective order has expired must include:

(1) a copy of the expired protective order attached to the application or, if a copy of the expired protective order is unavailable, a statement that the order is unavailable to the applicant and that a copy of the order will be filed with the court before the hearing on the application;

(2) a description of either:

(A) the violation of the expired protective order, if the application alleges that the respondent violated the expired protective order by committing an act prohibited by that order before the order expired; or

(B) the threatened harm that reasonably places the applicant in fear of imminent physical harm, bodily injury, assault, or sexual assault; and

(3) if a violation of the expired order is alleged, a statement that the violation of the expired order has not been grounds for any other order protecting the applicant that has been issued or requested under this subtitle.

(b) The procedural requirements for an original application for a protective order apply to a protective order requested under this section.
*(Added by L.1997, chap. 34(1); chgd. by L.1999, chap. 1160(1), eff. 9/1/99.)*

### §82.0085. Application filed before expiration of previously rendered protective order.

(a) If an application for a protective order alleges that an unexpired protective order applicable to the respondent is due to expire not later than the 30th day after the date the application was filed, the application for the subsequent protective order must include:

(1) a copy of the previously rendered protective order attached to the application or, if a copy of the previously rendered protective order is unavailable, a statement that the order is unavailable to the applicant and that a copy of the order will be filed with the court before the hearing on the application; and

(2) a description of the threatened harm that reasonably places the applicant in fear of imminent physical harm, bodily injury, assault, or sexual assault.

(b) The procedural requirements for an original application for a protective order apply to a protective order requested under this section.
*(Added by L.1999, chap. 1160(2), eff. 9/1/99.)*

### §82.009. Application for temporary ex parte order.

An application that requests the issuance of a temporary ex parte order under Chapter 83 must:

(1) contain a detailed description of the facts and circumstances concerning the alleged family violence and the need for the immediate protective order; and

(2) be signed by each applicant under an oath that the facts and circumstances contained in the application are true to the best knowledge and belief of each applicant.
*(Added by L.1997, chap. 34(1), eff. 5/5/97.)*

### §§82.010 to 82.020. *(Reserved.)*

## SUBCHAPTER B. PLEADINGS BY RESPONDENT

### §82.021. Answer.

A respondent to an application for a protective order who is served with notice of an application for a protective order may file an answer at any time before the hearing. A respondent is not required to file an answer to the application. *(Added by L.1997, chap. 34(1), eff. 5/5/97.)*

### §82.022. Request by respondent for protective order.

To apply for a protective order, a respondent to an application for a protective order must file a separate application. *(Added by L.1997, chap. 34(1), eff. 5/5/97.)*

### §§82.023 to 82.040. *(Reserved.)*

## SUBCHAPTER C. NOTICE OF APPLICATION FOR PROTECTIVE ORDER

### §82.041. Contents of notice of application.

(a) A notice of an application for a protective order must:

(1) be styled "The State of Texas";

(2) be signed by the clerk of the court under the court's seal;

(3) contain the name and location of the court;

(4) show the date the application was filed;

(5) show the date notice of the application for a protective order was issued;

(6) show the date, time, and place of the hearing;

(7) show the file number;

(8) show the name of each applicant and each person alleged to have committed family violence;

(9) be directed to each person alleged to have committed family violence;

(10) show the name and address of the attorney for the applicant or the mailing address of the applicant, if the applicant is not represented by an attorney; and

(11) contain the address of the clerk of the court.

(b) The notice of an application for a protective order must state: "An application for a protective order has been filed in the court stated in this notice alleging that you have committed family violence. You may employ an attorney to defend you against this allegation. You or your attorney may, but are not required to, file a written answer to the application. Any answer must be filed before the hearing on the application. If you receive this notice within 48 hours before the time set for the hearing, you may request the court to reschedule the hearing not later than 14 days after the date set for the hearing. If you do not attend the hearing, a default judgment may be taken and a protective order may be issued against you."

*(Added by L.1997, chap. 34(1), eff. 5/5/97; chgd. by L.1997, chap. 1193(10), eff. 9/1/97.)*

### §82.042. Issuance of notice of application.

(a) On the filing of an application, the clerk of the court shall issue a notice of an application for a protective order and deliver the notice as directed by the applicant.

(b) On request by the applicant, the clerk of the court shall issue a separate or additional notice of an application for a protective order.

*(Added by L.1997, chap. 34(1), eff. 5/5/97.)*

### §82.043. Service of notice of application.

(a) Each respondent to an application for a protective order is entitled to service of notice of an application for a protective order.

(b) An applicant for a protective order shall furnish the clerk with a sufficient number of copies of the application for service on each respondent.

(c) Notice of an application for a protective order must be served in the same manner as citation under the Texas Rules of Civil Procedure, except that service by publication is not authorized.

(d) Service of notice of an application for a protective order is not required before the issuance of a temporary ex parte order under Chapter 83.

(e) The requirements of service of notice under this subchapter do not apply if the application is filed as a motion in a suit for dissolution of a marriage. Notice for the motion is given in the same manner as any other motion in a suit for dissolution of a marriage.

*(Added by L.1997, chap. 34(1), eff. 5/5/97.)*

## CHAPTER 83. TEMPORARY EX PARTE ORDERS

Section

### §83.001. Requirements for temporary ex parte order.

(a) If the court finds from the information contained in an application for a protective order that there is a clear and present danger of family violence, the court, without further notice to any other member of the family or household and without a hearing, may enter a temporary ex parte order for the protection of the applicant or any other member of the family or household of the applicant.

(b) In a temporary ex parte order, the court may direct a respondent to do or refrain from doing specified acts.

*(Added by L.1997, chap. 34(1), eff. 5/5/97.)*

### §83.002. Duration of order; extension.

(a) A temporary ex parte order is valid for the period specified in the order, not to exceed 20 days.

(b) On the request of an applicant or on the court's own motion, a temporary ex parte order may be extended for additional 20-day periods.

*(Added by L.1997, chap. 34(1), eff. 5/5/97.)*

### §83.003. Bond not required.

The court, at the court's discretion, may dispense with the necessity of a bond for a temporary ex parte order. *(Added by L.1997, chap. 34(1), eff. 5/5/97.)*

### §83.004. Motion to vacate.

Any member of the family or household affected by a temporary ex parte order may file a motion at any time to vacate the order. On the filing of the motion to vacate, the court shall set a date for hearing the motion as soon as possible. *(Added by L.1997, chap. 34(1), eff. 5/5/97.)*

### §83.005. Conflicting orders.

During the time the order is valid, a temporary ex parte order prevails over any other court order made under Title 5 to the extent of any conflict between the orders. *(Added by L.1997, chap. 34(1), eff. 5/5/97; chgd. by L.1997, chap. 1193(11), eff. 9/1/97.)*

### §83.006. Exclusion of party from residence.

(a) Subject to the limitations of Section 85.021(2), a person may only be excluded from the occupancy of the person's residence by a temporary ex parte order under this chapter if the applicant:

(1) files a sworn affidavit that provides a detailed description of the facts and circumstances requiring the exclusion of the person from the residence; and

(2) appears in person to testify at a temporary ex parte hearing to justify the issuance of the order without notice.

(b) Before the court may render a temporary ex parte order excluding a person from the person's residence, the court must find from the required affidavit and testimony that:

(1) the applicant requesting the excluding order either resides on the premises or has resided there within 30 days before the date the application was filed;

(2) the person to be excluded has within the 30 days before the date the application was filed committed family violence against a member of the household; and

(3) there is a clear and present danger that the person to be excluded is likely to commit family violence against a member of the household.

*(Added by L.1997, chap. 34(1), eff. 5/5/97.)*

### §83.007. Recess of hearing to contact respondent.

The court may recess the hearing on a temporary ex parte order to contact the respondent by telephone and provide the respondent the opportunity to be present when the court resumes the hearing. Without regard to whether the respondent is able to be present at the hearing, the court shall resume the hearing before the end of the working day. *(Added by L.1997, chap. 34(1), eff. 5/5/97.)*

# CHAPTER 84. HEARING

Section


### §84.001. Time set for hearing.

(a) On the filing of an application for a protective order, the court shall set a date and time for the hearing unless a later date is requested by the applicant. Except as provided by Section 84.002, the court may not set a date later than the 14th day after the date the application is filed.

(b) The court may not delay a hearing on an application in order to consolidate it with a hearing on a subsequently filed application.
*(Added by L.1997, chap. 34(1), eff. 5/5/97.)*



### §84.002. Extended time for hearing in district court in certain counties.

(a) On the request of the prosecuting attorney in a county with a population of more than 1.5 million or in a county in a judicial district that is composed of more than one county, the district court shall set the hearing on a date and time not later than 20 days after the date the application is filed or 20 days after the date a request is made to reschedule a hearing under Section 84.003.

(b) The district court shall grant the request of the prosecuting attorney for an extended time in which to hold a hearing on a protective order either on a case-by-case basis or for all cases filed under this subtitle.
*(Added by L.1997, chap. 34(1), eff. 5/5/97; chgd. by L.1997, chap. 1193(12), eff. 9/1/97.)*

### §84.003. Hearing rescheduled for failure of service.

(a) If a hearing set under this chapter is not held because of the failure of a respondent to receive service of notice of an application for a protective order, the applicant may request the court to reschedule the hearing.

(b) Except as provided by Section 84.002, the date for a rescheduled hearing shall be not later than 14 days after the date the request is made.
*(Added by L.1997, chap. 34(1), eff. 5/5/97.)*

### §84.004. Hearing rescheduled for insufficient notice.

(a) If a respondent receives service of notice of an application for a protective order within 48 hours before the time set for the hearing, on request by the respondent, the court shall reschedule the hearing for a date not later than 14 days after the date set for the hearing.

(b) The respondent is not entitled to additional service for a hearing rescheduled under this section.
*(Added by L.1997, chap. 34(1), eff. 5/5/97.)*

### §84.005. Legislative continuance.

If a proceeding for which a legislative continuance is sought under Section 30.003, Civil Practice and Remedies Code, includes an application for a protective order, the continuance is discretionary with the court. *(Added by L.1999, chap. 62(6.10(a)), eff. 9/1/99.)*

# CHAPTER 85. ISSUANCE OF PROTECTIVE ORDER

## SUBCHAPTER A. FINDINGS AND ORDERS

Section

## SUBCHAPTER B. CONTENTS OF PROTECTIVE ORDER



## SUBCHAPTER C. DELIVERY OF PROTECTIVE ORDER



## SUBCHAPTER D. RELATIONSHIP BETWEEN PROTECTIVE ORDER AND SUIT FOR DISSOLUTION OF MARRIAGE AND SUIT AFFECTING PARENT-CHILD RELATIONSHIP



## SUBCHAPTER A. FINDINGS AND ORDERS

### §85.001. Required findings and orders.

(a) At the close of a hearing on an application for a protective order, the court shall find whether:

(1) family violence has occurred; and

(2) family violence is likely to occur in the future.

(b) If the court finds that family violence has occurred and that family violence is likely to occur in the future, the court:

(1) shall render a protective order as provided by Section 85.022 applying only to a person found to have committed family violence; and

(2) may render a protective order as provided by Section 85.021 applying to both parties that is in the best interest of the family or household or member of the family or household.

(c) A protective order that requires the first applicant to do or refrain from doing an act under Section 85.022 shall include a finding that the first applicant has committed family violence and is likely to commit family violence in the future.
*(Added by L.1997, chap. 34(1), eff. 5/5/97.)*

### §85.002. Exception for violation of expired protective order.

If the court finds that a respondent violated a protective order by committing an act prohibited by the order as provided by Section 85.022, that the order was in effect at the time of the violation, and that the order has expired after the date that the violation occurred, the court, without the necessity of making the findings described by Section 85.001(a), shall render a protective order as provided by Section 85.022 applying only to the respondent and may render a protective order as provided by Section 85.021. *(Added by L.1997, chap. 34(1), eff. 5/5/97; chgd. by L.1997, chap. 1193(13), eff. 9/1/97.)*

### §85.003. Separate protective orders required.

(a) A court that renders separate protective orders that apply to both parties and require both parties to do or refrain from doing acts under Section 85.022 shall render two distinct and separate protective orders in two separate documents that reflect the appropriate conditions for each party.

(b) A court that renders protective orders that apply to both parties and require both parties to do or refrain from doing acts under Section 85.022 shall render the protective orders in two separate documents. The court shall provide one of the documents to the applicant and the other document to the respondent.

(c) A court may not render one protective order under Section 85.022 that applies to both parties.

*(Added by L.1997, chap. 34(1), eff. 5/5/97.)*

### §85.004. Protective order in suit for dissolution of marriage.

A protective order in a suit for dissolution of a marriage must be in a separate document entitled "PROTECTIVE ORDER." *(Added by L.1997, chap. 34(1), eff. 5/5/97.)*



### §85.005. Agreed order.

(a) To facilitate settlement, the parties to a proceeding may agree in writing to the terms of a protective order as provided by Section 85.021. An agreement under this subsection is subject to the approval of the court.

(b) To facilitate settlement, a respondent may agree in writing to the terms of a protective order as provided by Section 85.022, subject to the approval of the court. The court may not approve an agreement that requires the applicant to do or refrain from doing an act under Section 85.022.

(c) If the court approves an agreement between the parties, the court shall render an agreed protective order that is in the best interest of the applicant, the family or household, or a member of the family or household.

(d) An agreed protective order is not enforceable as a contract.

(e) An agreed protective order expires on the date the court order expires.

*(Added by L.1997, chap. 34(1), eff. 5/5/97.)*

### §85.006. Default order.

(a) A court may render a protective order that is binding on a respondent who does not attend a hearing if the respondent received service of the application and notice of the hearing.

(b) If the court reschedules the hearing under Chapter 84, a protective order may be rendered if the respondent does not attend the rescheduled hearing.

*(Added by L.1997, chap. 34(1), eff. 5/5/97.)*

### §85.007. Confidentiality of certain information.

(a) On request by a member of a family or household, the court may exclude from a protective order the address and telephone number of:

(1) a person protected by the order, in which case the order shall state the county in which the person resides;

(2) the place of employment or business of a person protected by the order; or

(3) the child-care facility or school a child protected by the order attends or in which the child resides.

(b) On granting a request for confidentiality under this section, the court shall order the clerk to:

(1) strike the information described by Subsection (a) from the public records of the court; and

(2) maintain a confidential record of the information for use only by the court.

*(Added by L.1997, chap. 34(1), eff. 5/5/97.)*

**§85.008.** *(Added by L.1997, chap. 34(1), eff. 5/5/97; repealed by L.1997, chap. 1193(24), eff. 9/1/97.)*

### §85.009. Order valid until superseded.

A protective order rendered under this chapter is valid and enforceable pending further action by the court that rendered the order until the order is properly superseded by another court with jurisdiction over the order. *(Added by L.1997, chap. 34(1), eff. 5/5/97.)*

**§§85.010 to 85.020.** *(Reserved.)*

## SUBCHAPTER B. CONTENTS OF PROTECTIVE ORDER

### §85.021. Requirements of order applying to any party.

In a protective order, the court may:

(1) prohibit a party from:

(A) removing a child who is a member of the family or household from:

(i) the possession of a person named in the order; or

(ii) the jurisdiction of the court; or

(B) transferring, encumbering, or otherwise disposing of property, other than in the ordinary course of business, that is mutually owned or leased by the parties;

(2) grant exclusive possession of a residence to a party and, if appropriate, direct one or more parties to vacate the residence if the residence:

(A) is jointly owned or leased by the party receiving exclusive possession and a party being denied possession;

(B) is owned or leased by the party retaining possession; or

(C) is owned or leased by the party being denied possession and that party has an obligation to support the party or a child of the party granted possession of the residence;

(3) provide for the possession of and access to a child of a party if the person receiving possession of or access to the child is a parent of the child;

(4) require the payment of support for a party or for a child of a party if the person required to make the payment has an obligation to support the other party or the child; or

(5) award to a party the use and possession of specified property that is community property or jointly owned or leased property.

*(Added by L.1997, chap. 34(1), eff. 5/5/97.)*

### §85.022. Requirements of order applying to person who committed family violence.

(a) In a protective order, the court may order the person found to have committed family violence to:

(1) complete a battering intervention and prevention program as provided by Article 42.141, Code of Criminal Procedure, and that meets the guidelines adopted by the community justice assistance division of the Texas Department of Criminal Justice if a program is available;

(2) counsel with a social worker, family service agency, physician, psychologist, licensed therapist, or licensed professional counselor if a program under Subdivision (1) is not available; or

(3) perform acts specified by the court that the court determines are necessary or appropriate to prevent or reduce the likelihood of family violence.

(b) In a protective order, the court may prohibit the person found to have committed family violence from:

(1) committing family violence;

(2) communicating:

(A) directly with a member of the family or household in a threatening or harassing manner;

(B) a threat through any person to a member of the family or household; and

(C) if the court finds good cause, in any manner with a member of the family or household except through the party's attorney or a person appointed by the court;

(3) going to or near the residence or place of employment or business of a member of the family or household;

(4) going to or near the residence, child-care facility, or school a child protected under the order normally attends or in which the child normally resides; and

(5) engaging in conduct directed specifically toward a person who is a member of the family or household, including following the person, that is reasonably likely to harass, annoy, alarm, abuse, torment, or embarrass the person.

(c) In an order under Subsection (b)(3) or (4), the court shall specifically describe each prohibited location and the minimum distances from the location, if any, that the party must maintain. This subsection does not apply to an order in which Section 85.007 applies.

(d) In a protective order, the court may suspend a license to carry a concealed handgun issued under Section 411.177, Government Code, that is held by a person found to have committed family violence.

*(Added by L.1997, chap. 34(1); chgd. by L.1997, chap. 1193(14); L.1999, chap. 1412(3), eff. 9/1/99.)*

### §85.023. Effect on property rights.

A protective order or an agreement approved by the court under this subtitle does not affect the title to real property. *(Added by L.1997, chap. 34(1), eff. 5/5/97.)*

### §85.024. Enforcement of counseling requirement.

(a) A person found to have engaged in family violence who is ordered to attend a program or counseling under Section 85.022(a)(1) or (2) shall file with the court an affidavit before the 60th day after the date the order was rendered stating either that the person has begun the program or counseling or that a program or counseling is not available within a reasonable distance from the person's residence. A person who files an affidavit that the person has begun the program or counseling shall file with the court before the date the protective order expires a statement that the person completed the program or counseling not later than the 30th day before the expiration date of the protective order. An affidavit under this subsection must be accompanied by a letter, notice, or certificate from the program or counselor that verifies the person's completion of the program or counseling. A person who fails to comply with this subsection may be punished for contempt of court under Section 21.002, Government Code.

(b) A protective order under Section 85.022 must specifically advise the person subject to the order of the requirement of this section and the possible punishment if the person fails to comply with the requirement.

*(Added by L.1997, chap. 34(1), eff. 5/5/97; chgd. by L.1997, chap. 1193(15), eff. 9/1/97.)*

### §85.025. Duration of protective order.

(a) Except as provided by Subsection (b) or (c), an order under this subtitle is effective:

(1) for the period stated in the order, not to exceed two years; or

(2) if a period is not stated in the order, until the second anniversary of the date the order was issued.

(b) A person who is the subject of a protective order may file a motion not earlier than the first anniversary of the date on which the order was rendered requesting that the court review the protective order and determine whether there is a continuing need for the order. After a hearing on the motion, if the court finds there is a continuing need for the protective order, the protective order remains in effect until the date the order expires under this section. If the court finds there is no continuing need for the protective order, the court shall order that the protective order expires on a date set by the court.

(c) If a person who is the subject of a protective order is confined or imprisoned on the date the protective order would expire under Subsection (a), the period for which the order is effective is extended, and the order expires on the first anniversary of the date the person is released from confinement or imprisonment.

*(Added by L.1997, chap. 34(1); chgd. by L.1999, chap. 1160(3), eff. 9/1/99.)*

### §85.026. Warning on protective order.

(a) Each protective order issued under this subtitle, including a temporary ex parte order, must contain the following prominently displayed statements in boldfaced type, capital letters, or underlined:

"A PERSON WHO VIOLATES THIS ORDER MAY BE PUNISHED FOR CONTEMPT OF COURT BY A FINE OF AS MUCH AS $500 OR BY CONFINEMENT IN JAIL FOR AS LONG AS SIX MONTHS, OR BOTH.

"NO PERSON, INCLUDING A PERSON WHO IS PROTECTED BY THIS ORDER, MAY GIVE PERMISSION TO ANYONE TO IGNORE OR VIOLATE ANY PROVISION OF THIS ORDER. DURING THE TIME IN WHICH THIS ORDER IS VALID, EVERY PROVISION OF THIS ORDER IS IN FULL FORCE AND EFFECT UNLESS A COURT CHANGES THE ORDER.

"IT IS UNLAWFUL FOR ANY PERSON WHO IS SUBJECT TO A PROTECTIVE ORDER TO POSSESS A FIREARM OR AMMUNITION."

*(As amended by by L.1999, chaps. 1160(4), 9/1/99. See other (a) below.)*

(a) Each protective order issued under this subtitle, including a temporary ex parte order, must contain the following prominently displayed statements in boldfaced type, capital letters, or underlined:

"A PERSON WHO VIOLATES THIS ORDER MAY BE PUNISHED FOR CONTEMPT OF COURT BY A FINE OF AS MUCH AS $500 OR BY CONFINEMENT IN JAIL FOR AS LONG AS SIX MONTHS, OR BOTH.

*(As amended by by L.1999, chaps. 178(3), 5/21/99. See other (a) above.)*

(b) Each protective order issued under this subtitle, except for a temporary ex parte order, must contain the following prominently displayed statement in boldfaced type, capital letters, or underlined:

"A VIOLATION OF THIS ORDER BY COMMISSION OF AN ACT PROHIBITED BY THE ORDER MAY BE PUNISHABLE BY A FINE OF AS MUCH AS $4,000 OR BY CONFINEMENT IN JAIL FOR AS LONG AS ONE YEAR, OR BOTH. AN ACT THAT RESULTS IN FAMILY VIOLENCE MAY BE PROSECUTED AS A SEPARATE MISDEMEANOR OR FELONY OFFENSE. IF THE ACT IS PROSECUTED AS A SEPARATE FELONY OFFENSE, IT IS PUNISHABLE BY CONFINEMENT IN PRISON FOR AT LEAST TWO YEARS."

(c) Each protective order issued under this subtitle, including a temporary ex parte order, must contain the following prominently displayed statement in boldfaced type, capital letters, or underlined:

"NO PERSON, INCLUDING A PERSON WHO IS PROTECTED BY THIS ORDER, MAY GIVE PERMISSION TO ANYONE TO IGNORE OR VIOLATE ANY PROVISION OF THIS ORDER. DURING THE TIME IN WHICH THIS ORDER IS VALID, EVERY PROVISION OF THIS ORDER IS IN FULL FORCE AND EFFECT UNLESS A COURT CHANGES THE ORDER."

*(As amended by L.1999, chaps. 178(3), eff. 5/21/99.)*
*(Added by L.1997, chap. 34(1); chgd. by L.1999, chaps. 178(3), 1160(4), eff. 5/21/99, 9/1/99, respectively.)*

**§§85.027 to 85.040.** *(Reserved.)*

## SUBCHAPTER C. DELIVERY OF PROTECTIVE ORDER

### §85.041. Delivery to respondent.

(a) A protective order rendered under this subtitle shall be:

(1) delivered to the respondent as provided by Rule 21a, Texas Rules of Civil Procedure;

(2) served in the same manner as a writ of injunction; or

(3) served in open court at the close of the hearing as provided by this section.

(b) The court shall serve an order in open court to a respondent who is present at the hearing by giving to the respondent a copy of the order, reduced to writing and signed by the judge or master. A certified copy of the signed order shall be given to the applicant at the time the order is given to the respondent. If the applicant is not in court at the conclusion of the hearing, the clerk of the court shall mail a certified copy of the order to the applicant not later than the third business day after the date the hearing is concluded.

(c) If the order has not been reduced to writing, the court shall give notice orally to a respondent who is present at the hearing of the part of the order that contains prohibitions under Section 85.022 or any other part of the order that contains provisions necessary to prevent further family violence. The clerk of the court shall mail a copy of the order to the respondent and a certified copy of the order to the applicant not later than the third business day after the date the hearing is concluded.

(d) If the respondent is not present at the hearing and the order has been reduced to writing at the conclusion of the hearing, the clerk of the court shall immediately provide a certified copy of the order to the applicant and mail a copy of the order to the respondent not later than the third business day after the date the hearing is concluded.

*(Added by L.1997, chap. 34(1), eff. 5/5/97.)*

### §85.042. Delivery of order to other persons.

(a) The clerk of the court issuing an original or modified protective order under this subtitle shall send a copy of the order, along with the information provided by the applicant or the applicant's attorney that is required under Section 411.042(b)(5), Government Code, to the chief of police of the municipality in which the member of the family or household protected by the order resides, if the person resides in a municipality, or to the appropriate constable and the sheriff of the county in which the person resides, if the person does not reside in a municipality. The chief of police or constable and sheriff shall enter the information into the statewide law enforcement information system.

(b) If a protective order made under this chapter prohibits a respondent from going to or near a child-care facility or school, the clerk of the court shall send a copy of the order to the child-care facility or school.

Printed in the U.S.A. 47

(c) The clerk of a court that vacates an original or modified protective order under this subtitle shall notify the chief of police or constable and sheriff who received a copy of the original or modified order that the order is vacated.

(d) The applicant or the applicant's attorney shall provide to the clerk of the court:

(1) the name and address of each law enforcement agency, child-care facility, and school to which the clerk is required to mail a copy of the order under this section; and

(2) any other information required under Section 411.042(b)(5), Government Code.

(e) The clerk of the court issuing an original or modified protective order under Section 85.022 that suspends a license to carry a concealed handgun shall send a copy of the order to the appropriate division of the Department of Public Safety at its Austin headquarters. On receipt of the order suspending the license, the department shall:

(1) record the suspension of the license in the records of the department;

(2) report the suspension to local law enforcement agencies, as appropriate; and

(3) demand surrender of the suspended license from the license holder.

*(Added by L.1997, chap. 34(1), eff. 5/5/97; chgd. by L.1997, chap. 614(3); L.1999, chap. 1412(4), eff. 9/1/99.)*



## SUBCHAPTER D. RELATIONSHIP BETWEEN PROTECTIVE ORDER AND SUIT FOR DISSOLUTION OF MARRIAGE AND SUIT AFFECTING PARENT-CHILD RELATIONSHIP

*(Added by L.1997, chap. 1193(16), eff. 9/1/97.)*

### §85.061. Dismissal of application prohibited; subsequently filed suit for dissolution of marriage or suit affecting parent-child relationship.

If an application for a protective order is pending, a court may not dismiss the application or delay a hearing on the application on the grounds that a suit for dissolution of marriage or suit affecting the parent-child relationship is filed after the date the application was filed. *(Added by L.1997, chap. 1193(16), eff. 9/1/97.)*

### §85.062. Application filed while suit for dissolution of marriage or suit affecting parent-child relationship pending.

(a) If a suit for dissolution of a marriage or suit affecting the parent-child relationship is pending, a party to the suit may apply for a protective order against another party to the suit by filing an application:

(1) in the court in which the suit is pending; or

(2) in a court in the county in which the applicant resides if the applicant resides outside the jurisdiction of the court in which the suit is pending.

(b) An applicant subject to this section shall inform the clerk of the court that renders a protective order that a suit for dissolution of a marriage or a suit affecting the parent-child relationship is pending in which the applicant is party.

(c) If a final protective order is rendered by a court other than the court in which a suit for dissolution of a marriage or a suit affecting the parent-child relationship is pending, the clerk of the court that rendered the protective order shall:

(1) inform the clerk of the court in which the suit is pending that a final protective order has been rendered; and

(2) forward a copy of the final protective order to the court in which the suit is pending.

(d) A protective order rendered by a court in which an application is filed under Subsection (a)(2) is subject to transfer under Section 85.064.

*(Added by L.1997, chap. 1193(16), eff. 9/1/97.)*

### §85.063. Application filed after final order rendered in suit for dissolution of marriage or suit affecting parent-child relationship.

(a) If a final order has been rendered in a suit for dissolution of marriage or suit affecting the parent-child relationship, an application for a protective order by a party to the suit against another party to the suit filed after the date the final order was rendered, and that is:

(1) filed in the county in which the final order was rendered, shall be filed in the court that rendered the final order; and

(2) filed in another county, shall be filed in a court having jurisdiction to render a protective order under this subtitle.

(b) A protective order rendered by a court in which an application is filed under Subsection (a)(2) is subject to transfer under Section 85.064.
*(Added by L.1997, chap. 1193(16), eff. 9/1/97.)*

### §85.064. Transfer of protective order.

(a) If a protective order was rendered before the filing of a suit for dissolution of marriage or suit affecting the parent-child relationship or while the suit is pending as provided by Section 85.062, the court that rendered the order may, on the motion of a party or on the court's own motion, transfer the protective order to the court having jurisdiction of the suit if the court makes the finding prescribed by Subsection (c).

(b) If a protective order that affects a party's right to possession of or access to a child is rendered after the date a final order was rendered in a suit affecting the parent-child relationship, on the motion of a party or on the court's own motion, the court may transfer the protective order to the court of continuing, exclusive jurisdiction if the court makes the finding prescribed by Subsection (c).

(c) A court may transfer a protective order under this section if the court finds that the transfer is:

(1) in the interest of justice; or

(2) for the safety or convenience of a party or a witness.

(d) The transfer of a protective order under this section shall be conducted according to the procedures provided by Section 155.207.

(e) Except as provided by Section 81.002, the fees or costs associated with the transfer of a protective order shall be paid by the movant.
*(Added by L.1997, chap. 1193(16), eff. 9/1/97.)*

### §85.065. Effect of transfer.

(a) A protective order transferred under Section 85.064 has the same effect as if the order remained in the court that rendered the order. The protective order may be enforced by the court that receives the order in the same manner as if the court originally rendered the order.

(b) A protective order that is transferred is enforceable by contempt or by any other means by which the court that rendered the order could enforce the order. The court that receives the protective order may punish a violation of the order regardless of whether the violation occurred before or after the date of the transfer.

(c) A protective order that is transferred is subject to modification by the court that receives the order to the same extent modification is permitted under Chapter 87 by a court that rendered the order.
*(Added by L.1997, chap. 1193(16), eff. 9/1/97.)*

## CHAPTER 86. LAW ENFORCEMENT DUTIES RELATING TO PROTECTIVE ORDERS

Section


### §86.001. Adoption of procedures by law enforcement agency.

(a) To ensure that law enforcement officers responding to calls are aware of the existence and terms of protective orders issued under this subtitle, each law enforcement agency shall establish procedures in the agency to provide adequate information or access to information for law enforcement officers of the names of each person protected by an order issued under this subtitle and of each person against whom protective orders are directed.

(b) A law enforcement agency may enter a protective order in the agency's computer records of outstanding warrants as notice that the order has been issued and is currently in effect. On receipt of notification by a clerk of court that the court has vacated or dismissed an order, the law enforcement agency shall remove the order from the agency's computer record of outstanding warrants.
*(Added by L.1997, chap. 34(1), eff. 5/5/97.)*

**§86.002. Duty to provide information to firearms dealers.**

(a) On receipt of a request for a law enforcement information system record check of a prospective transferee by a licensed firearms dealer under the Brady Handgun Violence Prevention Act, 18 U.S.C. Section 922, the chief law enforcement officer shall determine whether the Department of Public Safety has in the department's law enforcement information system a record indicating the existence of an active protective order directed to the prospective transferee.

(b) If the department's law enforcement information system indicates the existence of an active protective order directed to the prospective transferee, the chief law enforcement officer shall immediately advise the dealer that the transfer is prohibited.

*(Added by L.1997, chap. 34(1), eff. 5/5/97.)*

**§86.003. Court order for law enforcement assistance under temporary order.**

On request by an applicant obtaining a temporary ex parte protective order that excludes the respondent from the respondent's residence, the court granting the temporary order shall render a written order to the sheriff, constable, or chief of police to provide a law enforcement officer from the department of the chief of police, constable, or sheriff to:

(1) accompany the applicant to the residence covered by the order;

(2) inform the respondent that the court has ordered that the respondent be excluded from the residence;

(3) protect the applicant while the applicant takes possession of the residence; and

(4) protect the applicant if the respondent refuses to vacate the residence while the applicant takes possession of the applicant's necessary personal property.

*(Added by L.1997, chap. 34(1), eff. 5/5/97; chgd. by L.1997, chap. 852(1), eff. 6/18/97.)*

**§86.004. Court order for law enforcement assistance under final order.**

On request by an applicant obtaining a final protective order that excludes the respondent from the respondent's residence, the court granting the final order shall render a written order to the sheriff, constable, or chief of police to provide a law enforcement officer from the department of the chief of police, constable, or sheriff to:

(1) accompany the applicant to the residence covered by the order;

(2) inform the respondent that the court has ordered that the respondent be excluded from the residence;

(3) protect the applicant while the applicant takes possession of the residence and the respondent takes possession of the respondent's necessary personal property; and

(4) if the respondent refuses to vacate the residence:

(A) remove the respondent from the residence; and

(B) arrest the respondent for violating the court order.

*(Added by L.1997, chap. 34(1), eff. 5/5/97; chgd. by L.1997, chap. 852(2), eff. 6/18/97.)*

**§86.005. Protective order from another jurisdiction.**

(a) To ensure that law enforcement officers responding to calls are aware of the existence and terms of a protective order from another jurisdiction, each law enforcement agency shall establish procedures in the agency to provide adequate information or access to information for law enforcement officers regarding the name of each person protected by an order rendered in another jurisdiction and of each person against whom the protective order is directed.

(b) Unless a law enforcement officer knows that the protective order has expired, the officer shall rely on:

(1) a copy of a protective order from another jurisdiction that has been provided to the officer by any source; and

(2) the statement by a person protected by the order that the order remains in effect.

(c) A law enforcement officer acting in good faith is not subject to civil or criminal liability for any action arising in connection with the enforcement of a protective order issued in another jurisdiction that a court later determines was not entitled to full faith and credit under Chapter 88.

*(Added by L.1997, chap. 1193(17), eff. 9/1/97.)*

## CHAPTER 87. MODIFICATION OF PROTECTIVE ORDERS

Section

### §87.001. Modification of protective order.

On the motion of any party, the court, after notice and hearing, may modify an existing protective order to:

(1) exclude any item included in the order; or

(2) include any item that could have been included in the order.

*(Added by L.1997, chap. 34(1), eff. 5/5/97.)*

### §87.002. Modification may not extend duration of order.

A protective order may not be modified to extend the period of the order's validity beyond the second anniversary of the date the original order was rendered or beyond the date the order expires under Section 85.025(c), whichever date occurs later. *(Added by L.1997, chap. 34(1); chgd. by L.1999, chap. 1160(5), eff. 9/1/99.)*

### §87.003. Notification of motion to modify.

Notice of a motion to modify a protective order is sufficient if delivery of the motion is attempted on the respondent at the respondent's last known address by registered or certified mail as provided by Rule 21a, Texas Rules of Civil Procedure. *(Added by L.1997, chap. 34(1), eff. 5/5/97.)*

### §87.004. Change of address or telephone number.

(a) If a protective order contains the address or telephone number of a person protected by the order, of the place of employment or business of the person, or of the child-care facility or school of a child protected by the order and that information is not confidential under Section 85.007, the person protected by the order may file a notification of change of address or telephone number with the court that rendered the order to modify the information contained in the order.

(b) The clerk of the court shall attach the notification of change to the protective order and shall deliver a copy of the notification to the respondent by registered or certified mail as provided by Rule 21a, Texas Rules of Civil Procedure.

(c) The filing of a notification of change of address or telephone number and the attachment of the notification to a protective order does not affect the validity of the order.

*(Added by L.1997, chap. 1193(18), eff. 9/1/97.)*



## CHAPTER 88. PROTECTIVE ORDER FROM ANOTHER JURISDICTION

*(Added by L.1997, chap. 1193(19), eff. 9/1/97.)*

Section



### §88.001. Full faith and credit of protective order from another jurisdiction.

(a) Except as provided by Subsection (b), a protective order from another jurisdiction shall be accorded full faith and credit by the courts of this state and enforced as if the order were rendered by a court in this state.

(b) A protective order from another jurisdiction rendered against both the applicant and respondent is not enforceable against the applicant in this state unless:

(1) the respondent filed a cross or counter petition, complaint, or other written pleading seeking a protective order against the applicant; and

(2) the issuing court determined that each party was entitled to a protective order.

*(Added by L.1997, chap. 1193(19), eff. 9/1/97.)*

### §88.002. Presumption of validity.

A protective order from another jurisdiction is presumed to be valid if the order appears authentic on the order's face. *(Added by L.1997, chap. 1193(19), eff. 9/1/97.)*

### §88.003. Affirmative defense.

It is an affirmative defense in any action seeking enforcement of a protective order rendered in another jurisdiction that the respondent was not given reasonable notice and an opportunity to be heard consistent with due process either:

(1) before the date the order was rendered; or

(2) in the case of an ex parte order, within the time required by the jurisdiction rendering the order after the date the order was rendered, but not later than a reasonable time.
*(Added by L.1997, chap. 1193(19), eff. 9/1/97.)*

### §88.004. Enforcement of an order.

A protective order from another jurisdiction may be enforced even if the order is not entered into the state law enforcement information system maintained by the Department of Public Safety.
*(Added by L.1997, chap. 1193(19), eff. 9/1/97.)*

# SUBTITLE C. REPORTING FAMILY VIOLENCE

## CHAPTER 91. REPORTING FAMILY VIOLENCE

Section




### §91.001. Definitions.

In this subtitle:

(1) "Family violence" has the meaning assigned by Section 71.004.

(2) "Medical professional" means a licensed doctor, nurse, physician assistant, or emergency medical technician.
*(Added by L.1997, chap. 34(1), eff. 5/5/97.)*

### §91.002. Reporting by witnesses encouraged.

A person who witnesses family violence is encouraged to report the family violence to a local law enforcement agency. *(Added by L.1997, chap. 34(1), eff. 5/5/97.)*

### §91.003. Information provided by medical professionals.

A medical professional who treats a person for injuries that the medical professional has reason to believe were caused by family violence shall:

(1) immediately provide the person with information regarding the nearest family violence shelter center;

(2) document in the person's medical file:

(A) the fact that the person has received the information provided under Subdivision (1); and

(B) the reasons for the medical professional's belief that the person's injuries were caused by family violence; and

(3) give the person a written notice in substantially the following form, completed with the required information, in both English and Spanish:

**"NOTICE TO ADULT VICTIMS OF FAMILY VIOLENCE**

"It is a crime for any person to cause you any physical injury or harm even if that person is a member or former member of your family or household.

"You may report family violence to a law enforcement officer by calling the following telephone numbers: _______________.

"If you, your child, or any other household resident has been injured or if you feel you are going to be in danger after a law enforcement officer investigating family violence leaves your residence or at a later time, you have the right to:

"Ask the local prosecutor to file a criminal complaint against the person committing family violence; and

"Apply to a court for an order to protect you. You may want to consult with a legal aid office, a prosecuting attorney, or a private attorney. A court can enter an order that:

"(1) prohibits the abuser from committing further acts of violence;

"(2) prohibits the abuser from threatening, harassing, or contacting you at home;

"(3) directs the abuser to leave your household; and

"(4) establishes temporary custody of the children or any property.

"A VIOLATION OF CERTAIN PROVISIONS OF COURT-ORDERED PROTECTION MAY BE A FELONY.

"CALL THE FOLLOWING VIOLENCE SHELTERS OR SOCIAL ORGANIZATIONS IF YOU NEED PROTECTION: _______________."
*(Added by L.1997, chap. 34(1), eff. 5/5/97.)*

### §91.004. Application of subtitle.

This subtitle does not affect a duty to report child abuse under Chapter 261. *(Added by L.1997, chap. 34(1), eff. 5/5/97.)*

## CHAPTER 92. IMMUNITY



### §92.001. Immunity.

(a) Except as provided by Subsection (b), a person who reports family violence under Section 91.002 or provides information under Section 91.003 is immune from civil liability that might otherwise be incurred or imposed.

(b) A person who reports the person's own conduct or who otherwise reports family violence in bad faith is not protected from liability under this section.
*(Added by L.1997, chap. 34(1), eff. 5/5/97.)*



# TITLE 5. THE PARENT-CHILD RELATIONSHIP AND THE SUIT AFFECTING THE PARENT-CHILD RELATIONSHIP

*(Added by L.1995, chap. 20(1), eff. 4/20/95.)*

## SUBTITLE A. GENERAL PROVISIONS

## CHAPTER 105. SETTINGS, HEARINGS, AND ORDERS

*(Selected Section)*



### §105.001. Temporary orders before final order.

(a) In a suit, the court may make a temporary order, including the modification of a prior temporary order, for the safety and welfare of the child, including an order:

(1) for the temporary conservatorship of the child;

(2) for the temporary support of the child;

(3) restraining a party from molesting or disturbing the peace of the child or another party;

(4) prohibiting a person from removing the child beyond a geographical area identified by the court; or

(5) for payment of reasonable attorney's fees and expenses.

(b) Except as provided by Subsection (c), temporary restraining orders and temporary injunctions under this section shall be granted without the necessity of an affidavit or verified pleading stating specific facts showing that immediate and irreparable injury, loss, or damage will result before notice can be served and a hearing can be held. Except as provided by Subsection (h), an order may not be rendered under Subsection (a)(1), (2), or (5) except after notice and a hearing. A temporary restraining order or temporary injunction granted under this section need not:

(1) define the injury or state why it is irreparable;

(2) state why the order was granted without notice; or

(3) include an order setting the cause for trial on the merits with respect to the ultimate relief requested.

(c) Except on a verified pleading or an affidavit in accordance with the Texas Rules of Civil Procedure, an order may not be rendered:

(1) attaching the body of the child;

(2) taking the child into the possession of the court or of a parent designated by the court; or

(3) excluding a parent from possession of or access to a child.

(d) In a suit, the court may dispense with the necessity of a bond in connection with temporary orders on behalf of the child.

(e) Temporary orders rendered under this section are not subject to interlocutory appeal.

(f) The violation of a temporary restraining order, temporary injunction, or other temporary order rendered under this section is punishable by contempt and the order is subject to and enforceable under Chapter 157.

(g) The rebuttable presumptions established in favor of the application of the guidelines for a child support order and for the standard possession order under Chapters 153 and 154 apply to temporary orders. The presumptions do not limit the authority of the court to render other temporary orders.

(h) An order under Subsection (a)(1) may be rendered without notice and an adversary hearing if the order is an emergency order sought by a governmental entity under Chapter 262.

*(Added by L.1995, chap. 20(1); chgd. by L.1997, chap. 575(5); L.1999, chap. 1390(3), eff. 9/1/99.)*



## SUBTITLE B. SUITS AFFECTING THE PARENT-CHILD RELATIONSHIP

## CHAPTER 151. THE PARENT-CHILD RELATIONSHIP

*(Selected Section)*

### SUBCHAPTER A. GENERAL PROVISIONS

Section



### SUBCHAPTER A. GENERAL PROVISIONS

**§151.003. Rights and duties of parent.**

(a) A parent of a child has the following rights and duties:

(1) the right to have physical possession, to direct the moral and religious training, and to establish the residence of the child;

(2) the duty of care, control, protection, and reasonable discipline of the child;

(3) the duty to support the child, including providing the child with clothing, food, shelter, medical and dental care, and education;

(4) the duty, except when a guardian of the child's estate has been appointed, to manage the estate of the child, including the right as an agent of the child to act in relation to the child's estate if the child's action is required by a state, the United States, or a foreign government;

(5) the right to the services and earnings of the child;

(6) the right to consent to the child's marriage, enlistment in the armed forces of the United States, medical and dental care, and psychiatric, psychological, and surgical treatment;

(7) the right to represent the child in legal action and to make other decisions of substantial legal significance concerning the child;

(8) the right to receive and give receipt for payments for the support of the child and to hold or disburse funds for the benefit of the child;

(9) the right to inherit from and through the child;

(10) the right to make decisions concerning the child's education; and

(11) any other right or duty existing between a parent and child by virtue of law.

(b) The duty of a parent to support his or her child exists while the child is an unemancipated minor and continues as long as the child is fully enrolled in an accredited secondary school in a program leading toward a high school diploma until the end of the school year in which the child graduates.

(c) A parent who fails to discharge the duty of support is liable to a person who provides necessaries to those to whom support is owed.

(d) The rights and duties of a parent are subject to:

(1) a court order affecting the rights and duties;

(2) an affidavit of relinquishment of parental rights; and

(3) an affidavit by the parent designating another person or agency to act as managing conservator.

*(Added by L.1995, chap. 20(1), eff. 4/20/95; chgd. by L.1995, chap. 751(23), eff. 9/1/95.)*

# CHAPTER 153. CONSERVATORSHIP, POSSESSION, AND ACCESS
*(Selected Sections)*

## SUBCHAPTER A. GENERAL PROVISIONS



## SUBCHAPTER B. PARENT APPOINTED AS CONSERVATOR: IN GENERAL



## SUBCHAPTER A. GENERAL PROVISIONS

### §153.013. False report of child abuse.

(a) If a party to a pending suit affecting the parent-child relationship makes a report alleging child abuse by another party to the suit that the reporting party knows lacks a factual foundation, the court shall deem the report to be a knowingly false report.

(b) Evidence of a false report of child abuse is admissible in a suit between the involved parties regarding the terms of conservatorship of a child.

(c) If the court makes a finding under Subsection (a), the court shall impose a civil penalty not to exceed $500.

*(Added by L.1995, chap. 751(28); chgd. by L.1997, chap. 786(2), eff. 9/1/97.)*

## SUBCHAPTER B. PARENT APPOINTED AS CONSERVATOR: IN GENERAL

### §153.074. Rights and duties during period of possession.

Unless limited by court order, a parent appointed as a conservator of a child has the following rights and duties during the period that the parent has possession of the child:

(1) the duty of care, control, protection, and reasonable discipline of the child;

(2) the duty to support the child, including providing the child with clothing, food, shelter, and medical and dental care not involving an invasive procedure;

(3) the right to consent for the child to medical and dental care not involving an invasive procedure;

(4) the right to consent for the child to medical, dental, and surgical treatment during an emergency involving immediate danger to the health and safety of the child; and

(5) the right to direct the moral and religious training of the child.

*(Added by L.1995, chap. 20(1), eff. 4/20/95; chgd. by L.1995, chap. 751(30), eff. 9/1/95.)*

# CHAPTER 156. MODIFICATION
*(Selected Section)*

## SUBCHAPTER A. GENERAL PROVISIONS



## SUBCHAPTER A. GENERAL PROVISIONS

### §156.006. Temporary orders.

(a) Except as provided by Subsection (b), the court may render a temporary order in a suit for modification.

(b) While a suit for modification is pending, the court may not render a temporary order that has the effect of changing the designation of a sole or joint managing conservator appointed in a final order unless:

(1) the order is necessary because the child's present living environment may endanger the child's physical health or significantly impair the child's emotional development;

(2) the child's managing conservator has voluntarily relinquished the actual care, control, and possession of the child for more than six months and the temporary order is in the best interest of the child; or

(3) the child is 10 years of age or older and has filed with the court in writing the name of the person who is the child's choice for managing conservator and the temporary order naming that person as managing conservator is in the best interest of the child.

*(Added by L.1995, chap. 20(1); chgd. by L.1999, chap. 1390(15), eff. 9/1/99.)*

# CHAPTER 157. ENFORCEMENT
*(Selected Sections)*

## SUBCHAPTER B. PROCEDURE

Section


## SUBCHAPTER C. FAILURE TO APPEAR; BOND OR SECURITY



## SUBCHAPTER B. PROCEDURE

### §157.066. Failure to appear.

If a respondent who has been personally served with notice to appear at a hearing does not appear at the designated time, place, and date to respond to a motion for enforcement of an existing court order, regardless of whether the motion is joined with other claims or remedies, the court may not hold the respondent in contempt but may, on proper proof, grant a default judgment for the relief sought and issue a capias for the arrest of the respondent. *(Added by L.1995, chap. 20(1), eff. 4/20/95; chgd. by L.1995, chap. 751(50), eff. 9/1/95.)*

## SUBCHAPTER C. FAILURE TO APPEAR; BOND OR SECURITY

### §157.101. Bond or security for release of respondent.

(a) When the court orders the issuance of a capias as provided in this chapter, the court shall also set an appearance bond or security, payable to the obligee or to a person designated by the court, in a reasonable amount.

(b) An appearance bond or security in the amount of $1,000 or a cash bond in the amount of $250 is presumed to be reasonable. Evidence that the respondent has attempted to evade service of process, has previously been found guilty of contempt, or has accrued arrearages over $1,000 is sufficient to rebut the presumption. If the presumption is rebutted, the court shall set a reasonable bond.

*(Added by L.1995, chap. 20(1), eff. 4/20/95.)*

### §157.102. Capias; duty of law enforcement officials.

Law enforcement officials shall treat the capias in the same manner as an arrest warrant for a criminal offense and shall enter the capias in the computer records for outstanding warrants maintained by the local police, sheriff, and Department of Public Safety. The capias shall be forwarded to and disseminated by the Texas Crime Information Center and the National Crime Information Center. *(Added by L.1995, chap. 20(1); chgd. by L.1997, chap. 702(3); L.1999, chap. 556(16), eff. 9/1/99.)*

### §157.103. Capias fee.

(a) The fee for issuing a capias as provided in this chapter is the same as the fee for issuance of a writ of attachment.

(b) The fee for serving a capias is the same as the fee for service of a writ in civil cases generally.

*(Added by L.1995, chap. 20(1), eff. 4/20/95.)*

### §157.104. Conditional release.

If the respondent is taken into custody and released on bond, the court shall condition the bond on the respondent's promise to appear in court for a hearing as required by the court without the necessity of further personal service of notice on the respondent. *(Added by L.1995, chap. 20(1), eff. 4/20/95.)*

### §157.105. Release hearing.

(a) If the respondent is taken into custody and not released on bond, the respondent shall be brought before the court that issued the capias on or before the first working day after the arrest. The court shall determine whether the respondent's appearance in court at a designated time and place can be assured by a method other than by posting the bond or security previously established.

(b) If the respondent is released without posting bond or security, the court shall set a hearing on the alleged contempt at a designated date, time, and place and give the respondent notice of hearing in open court. No other notice to the respondent is required.

(c) If the court is not satisfied that the respondent's appearance in court can be assured and the respondent remains in custody, a hearing on the alleged contempt shall be held as soon as practicable, but not later than the fifth day after the date that the respondent was taken into custody, unless the respondent and the respondent's attorney waive the accelerated hearing.

*(Added by L.1995, chap. 20(1), eff. 4/20/95.)*

### §157.106. Cash bond as support.

(a) If the respondent has posted a cash bond and is found to be in arrears in the payment of court-ordered child support, the court shall order that the proceeds of the cash bond be paid to the child support obligee or to a person designated by the court, not to exceed the amount of child support arrearages determined to exist.

(b) This section applies without regard to whether the respondent appears at the hearing.

*(Added by L.1995, chap. 20(1), eff. 4/20/95.)*

### §157.107. Appearance bond or security other than cash bond as support.

(a) If the respondent fails to appear at the hearing as directed, the court shall order that the appearance bond or security be forfeited and that the proceeds of any judgment on the bond or security, not to exceed the amount of child support arrearages determined to exist, be paid to the obligee or to a person designated by the court.

(b) The obligee may file suit on the bond.

*(Added by L.1995, chap. 20(1), eff. 4/20/95.)*

### §157.108. Cash bond as property of respondent.

A court shall treat a cash bond posted for the benefit of the respondent as the property of the respondent. A person who posts the cash bond does not have recourse in relation to an order regarding the bond other than against the respondent. *(Added by L.1995, chap. 20(1), eff. 4/20/95.)*

### §157.114. Failure to appear.

The court may order a capias to be issued for the arrest of the respondent if:

(1) the motion for enforcement requests contempt;

(2) the respondent was personally served; and

(3) the respondent fails to appear.

*(Added by L.1995, chap. 20(1), eff. 4/20/95.)*

### §157.115. Default judgment.

(a) The court may render a default order for the relief requested if the respondent:

(1) has been personally served, has filed an answer, or has entered an appearance; and

(2) does not appear at the designated time, place, and date to respond to the motion.

(b) If the respondent fails to appear, the court may not hold the respondent in contempt but may order a capias to be issued.

*(Added by L.1995, chap. 20(1), eff. 4/20/95; chgd. by L.1995, chap. 751(51), eff. 9/1/95.)*

## SUBTITLE C. JUDICIAL RESOURCES AND SERVICES
*(Selected Chapter)*

## CHAPTER 203. DOMESTIC RELATIONS OFFICES
*(Selected Section)*



### §203.007. Access to records; offense.

(a) A domestic relations office may obtain the records described by Subsections (b) and (c) that relate to a person who has:

(1) been ordered to pay child support;

(2) been designated as a possessory conservator or managing conservator of a child;

(3) been designated to be the father of a child; or

(4) executed a statement of paternity.

(b) A domestic relations office is entitled to obtain from the Department of Public Safety records that relate to:

(1) a person's date of birth;

(2) a person's most recent address;

(3) a person's current driver's license status;

(4) motor vehicle accidents involving a person; and

(5) reported traffic-law violations of which a person has been convicted.

(c) A domestic relations office is entitled to obtain from the Texas Employment Commission records that relate to:

(1) a person's address;

(2) a person's employment status and earnings;

(3) the name and address of a person's current or former employer; and

(4) unemployment compensation benefits received by a person.

(d) An agency required to provide records under this section may charge a domestic relations office a fee for providing the records in an amount that does not exceed the amount paid for those records by the agency responsible for Title IV-D cases.

(e) The Department of Public Safety, the Texas Employment Commission, or the office of the secretary of state may charge a domestic relations office a fee not to exceed the charge paid by the Title IV-D agency for furnishing records under this section.

(f) Information obtained by a domestic relations office under this section that is confidential under a constitution, statute, judicial decision, or rule is privileged and may be used only by that office.

(g) A person commits an offense if the person releases or discloses confidential information obtained under this section without the consent of the person to whom the information relates. An offense under this subsection is a Class C misdemeanor.

(h) A domestic relations office is entitled to obtain from the office of the secretary of state the following information about a registered voter to the extent that the information is available:

(1) complete name;

(2) current and former street and mailing address;

(3) sex;

(4) date of birth;

(5) social security number; and

(6) telephone number.

*(Added by L.1995, chap. 20(1); renumbered from Section 203.012 and amended by L.1995, chap. 475(1); chgd. by L.1995, chap. 803(1); L.1997, chap. 165(7.18), eff. 9/1/97.)*

## SUBTITLE D. ADMINISTRATIVE SERVICES

## CHAPTER 232. SUSPENSION OF LICENSE FOR FAILURE TO PAY CHILD SUPPORT OR COMPLY WITH SUBPOENA

## §232.001. Definitions.

In this chapter:

(1) "License" means a license, certificate, registration, permit, or other authorization that:

(A) is issued by a licensing authority;

(B) is subject before expiration to suspension, revocation, forfeiture, or termination by the issuing licensing authority; and

(C) a person must obtain to:

(i) practice or engage in a particular business, occupation, or profession;

(ii) operate a motor vehicle; or

(iii) engage in any other regulated activity, including hunting, fishing, or other recreational activity for which a license or permit is required.

(2) "Licensing authority" means a department, commission, board, office, or other agency of the state or a political subdivision of the state that issues a license.

(3) "Order suspending license" means an order issued by the Title IV-D agency or a court directing a licensing authority to suspend a license.

(4) "Subpoena" means a subpoena issued in a parentage determination or child support proceeding under this title.

*(Added by L.1995, chaps. 655(5.03), 751(85); chgd. by L.1997, chap. 911(82), eff. 9/1/97.)*

## §232.002. Licensing authorities subject to chapter.

The following are licensing authorities subject to this chapter:

(1) Department of Agriculture;
(2) Texas Commission on Alcohol and Drug Abuse;
(3) Texas Alcoholic Beverage Commission;
(4) Texas Appraiser Licensing and Certification Board;
(5) Texas Board of Architectural Examiners;
(6) State Board of Barber Examiners;
(7) Texas Board of Chiropractic Examiners;
(8) Comptroller of Public Accounts;
(9) Texas Cosmetology Commission;
(10) Court Reporters Certification Board;
(11) State Board of Dental Examiners;
(12) Texas State Board of Examiners of Dietitians;
(13) Texas Funeral Service Commission;
(14) Texas Department of Health;
(15) Texas Department of Human Services;
(16) Texas Board of Professional Land Surveying;
(17) Texas Department of Licensing and Regulation;
(18) Texas State Board of Examiners of Marriage and Family Therapists;
(19) Texas State Board of Medical Examiners;
(20) Midwifery Board;
(21) Texas Natural Resource Conservation Commission;
(22) Board of Nurse Examiners;
(23) Texas Board of Occupational Therapy Examiners;
(24) Texas Optometry Board;
(25) Parks and Wildlife Department;
(26) Texas State Board of Examiners of Perfusionists;
(27) Texas State Board of Pharmacy;
(28) Texas Board of Physical Therapy Examiners;
(29) Texas State Board of Plumbing Examiners;

(30) Texas State Board of Podiatric Medical Examiners;
(31) Polygraph Examiners Board;
(32) Texas Board of Private Investigators and Private Security Agencies;
(33) Texas State Board of Examiners of Professional Counselors;
(34) Texas Board of Professional Engineers;
(35) Department of Protective and Regulatory Services;
(36) Texas State Board of Examiners of Psychologists;
(37) Texas State Board of Public Accountancy;
(38) Department of Public Safety of the State of Texas;
(39) Public Utility Commission of Texas;
(40) Railroad Commission of Texas;
(41) Texas Real Estate Commission;
(42) State Bar of Texas;
(43) Texas State Board of Social Worker Examiners;
(44) State Board of Examiners for Speech-Language Pathology and Audiology;
(45) Texas Structural Pest Control Board;
(46) Board of Tax Professional Examiners;
(47) Secretary of State;
(48) Supreme Court of Texas;
(49) Texas Transportation Commission;
(50) State Board of Veterinary Medical Examiners;
(51) Board of Vocational Nurse Examiners;
(52) Texas Ethics Commission;
(53) Advisory Board of Athletic Trainers;
(54) State Committee of Examiners in the Fitting and Dispensing of Hearing Instruments;
(55) Texas Board of Licensure for Professional Medical Physicists;
(56) Texas Department of Insurance;
(57) Texas Board of Orthotics and Prosthetics; and
(58) savings and loan commissioner.

*(Added by L.1995, chaps. 655(5.03), 751(85); chgd. by L.1997, chaps. 165(7.22), 1280(1.02), 1288(2); L.1999, chap. 1254(4), eff. 9/1/99. See other section 232.002 below.)*



### §232.002. Licensing authorities subject to chapter.

The following state agencies are licensing authorities subject to this chapter:
(1) Department of Agriculture;
(2) Texas Commission on Alcohol and Drug Abuse;
(3) Texas Alcoholic Beverage Commission;
(4) Texas Appraiser Licensing and Certification Board;
(5) Texas Board of Architectural Examiners;
(6) State Board of Barber Examiners;
(7) Texas Board of Chiropractic Examiners;
(8) Comptroller of Public Accounts;
(9) Texas Cosmetology Commission;
(10) Court Reporters Certification Board;
(11) State Board of Dental Examiners;
(12) Texas State Board of Examiners of Dietitians;
(13) Texas Funeral Service Commission;
(14) Texas Department of Health;
(15) Texas Department of Human Services;
(16) Texas Board of Professional Land Surveying;
(17) Texas Department of Licensing and Regulation;
(18) Texas State Board of Examiners of Marriage and Family Therapists;
(19) Texas State Board of Medical Examiners;
(20) Midwifery Board;
(21) Texas Natural Resource Conservation Commission;
(22) Board of Nurse Examiners;
(23) Texas Board of Occupational Therapy Examiners;
(24) Texas Optometry Board;
(25) Parks and Wildlife Department;
(26) Texas State Board of Examiners of Perfusionists;
(27) Texas State Board of Pharmacy;
(28) Texas Board of Physical Therapy Examiners;

(29) Texas State Board of Plumbing Examiners;
(30) Texas State Board of Podiatric Medical Examiners;
(31) Polygraph Examiners Board;
(32) Texas Board of Private Investigators and Private Security Agencies;
(33) Texas State Board of Examiners of Professional Counselors;
(34) State Board of Registration for Professional Engineers;
(35) Department of Protective and Regulatory Services;
(36) Texas State Board of Examiners of Psychologists;
(37) Texas State Board of Public Accountancy;
(38) Department of Public Safety of the State of Texas;
(39) Public Utility Commission of Texas;
(40) Railroad Commission of Texas;
(41) Texas Real Estate Commission;
(42) State Bar of Texas;
(43) Texas State Board of Social Worker Examiners;
(44) State Board of Examiners for Speech-Language Pathology and Audiology;
(45) Texas Structural Pest Control Board;
(46) Board of Tax Professional Examiners;
(47) Secretary of State;
(48) Supreme Court of Texas;
(49) Texas Transportation Commission;
(50) State Board of Veterinary Medical Examiners;
(51) Board of Vocational Nurse Examiners;
(52) Texas Ethics Commission;
(53) Advisory Board of Athletic Trainers;
(54) State Committee of Examiners in the Fitting and Dispensing of Hearing Instruments;
(55) Texas Board of Licensure for Professional Medical Physicists;
(56) Texas Department of Insurance;
(57) Texas Board of Orthotics and Prosthetics; and
(58) Texas Juvenile Probation Commission.

*(Added by L.1995, chaps. 655(5.03), 751(85); chgd. by L.1997, chaps. 165(7.22), 1280(1.02), 1288(2); L.1999, chap. 1477(23), eff. 9/1/99. See other section 232.002 above.)*



## §232.003. Suspension of license.

(a) A court or the Title IV-D agency may issue an order suspending a license as provided by this chapter if an individual who is an obligor:

(1) has a child support arrearage equal to or greater than the total support due for 90 days under a support order;

(2) has been provided an opportunity to make payments toward the child support arrearage under a court order or an agreed repayment schedule; and

(3) has failed to comply with the repayment schedule.

(b) A court or the Title IV-D agency may issue an order suspending license as provided by this chapter if an individual has failed, after receiving appropriate notice, to comply with a subpoena.

*(Added by L.1995, chaps. 655(5.03), 751(85); chgd. by L.1997, chaps. 420(22), (23), 911(83); L.1999, chap. 556(59), eff. 9/1/99.)*

## §232.004. Petition for suspension of license.

(a) A child support agency or obligee may file a petition to suspend, as provided by this chapter, a license of an obligor who has an arrearage equal to or greater than the total support due for 90 days under a support order.

(b) In a Title IV-D case, the petition shall be filed with the Title IV-D agency, the court of continuing jurisdiction, or the tribunal in which a child support order has been registered under Chapter 159. The tribunal in which the petition is filed obtains jurisdiction over the matter.

(c) In a case other than a Title IV-D case, the petition shall be filed in the court of continuing jurisdiction or the court in which a child support order has been registered under Chapter 159.

(d) A proceeding in a case filed with the Title IV-D agency under this chapter is governed by the contested case provisions of Chapter 2001, Government Code, except that Section 2001.054 does not apply to the proceeding. The director of the Title IV-D agency or the director's designee may render a final decision in a contested case proceeding under this chapter.

*(Added by L.1995, chaps. 655(5.03), 751(85); chgd. by L.1997, chap. 420(24), 911(84); L.1999, chap. 556(60), eff. 9/1/99.)*

### §232.005. Contents of petition.

(a) A petition under this chapter must state that license suspension is required under Section 232.003 and allege:

(1) the name and, if known, social security number of the individual;

(2) the type, and if known, number of any license the individual is believed to hold and the name of the licensing authority that issued the license; and

(3) the amount of arrearages owed under the child support order or the facts associated with the individual's failure to comply with a subpoena.

(b) A petition under this chapter may include as an attachment a copy of:

(1) the record of child support payments maintained by the Title IV-D registry or local registry; or

(2) the subpoena with which the individual has failed to comply, together with proof of service of the subpoena.

*(Added by L.1995, chaps. 655(5.03), 751(85); chgd. by L.1997, chap. 911(85), eff. 9/1/97.)*



### §232.006. Notice.

(a) On the filing of a petition under Section 232.004, the clerk of the court or the Title IV-D agency shall deliver to the individual:

(1) notice of the individual's right to a hearing before the court or agency;

(2) notice of the deadline for requesting a hearing; and

(3) a hearing request form if the proceeding is in a Title IV-D case.

(b) Notice under this section may be served as in civil cases generally.

(c) The notice must contain the following prominently displayed statement in boldfaced type, capital letters, or underlined:

"AN ACTION TO SUSPEND ONE OR MORE LICENSES ISSUED TO YOU HAS BEEN FILED. YOU MAY EMPLOY AN ATTORNEY TO REPRESENT YOU IN THIS ACTION. IF YOU OR YOUR ATTORNEY DO NOT REQUEST A HEARING BEFORE THE 21ST DAY AFTER THE DATE OF SERVICE OF THIS NOTICE, AN ORDER OF LICENSE SUSPENSION MAY BE RENDERED."

*(Added by L.1995, chaps. 655(5.03), 751(85); chgd. by L.1997, chaps. 911(86), 976(7); L.1999, chap. 178(11), eff. 5/21/99.)*

### §232.007. Hearing on petition to suspend license.

(a) A request for a hearing and motion to stay suspension must be filed with the court or Title IV-D agency by the individual not later than the 20th day after the date of service of the notice under Section 232.006.

(b) If a request for a hearing is filed, the court or Title IV-D agency shall:

(1) promptly schedule a hearing;

(2) notify each party of the date, time, and location of the hearing; and

(3) stay suspension pending the hearing.

(c) In a case involving support arrearages, a record of child support payments made by the Title IV-D agency or a local registry is evidence of whether the payments were made. A copy of the record appearing regular on its face shall be admitted as evidence at a hearing under this chapter, including a hearing on a motion to revoke a stay. Either party may offer controverting evidence.

(d) In a case in which an individual has failed to comply with a subpoena, proof of service is evidence of delivery of the subpoena.

*(Added by L.1995, chaps. 655(5.03), 751(85); chgd. by L.1997, chap. 911(87), eff. 9/1/97.)*

### §232.008. Order suspending license for failure to pay child support.

(a) On making the findings required by Section 232.003, the court or Title IV-D agency shall render an order suspending the license unless the individual:

(1) proves that all arrearages and the current month's support have been paid;

(2) shows good cause for failure to comply with the subpoena; or

(3) establishes an affirmative defense as provided by Section 157.008(c).

(b) The court or Title IV-D agency may stay an order suspending a license conditioned on the individual's compliance with:

(1) a reasonable repayment schedule that is incorporated in the order; or

(2) the requirements of a reissued and delivered subpoena.

(c) An order suspending a license with a stay of the suspension may not be served on the licensing authority unless the stay is revoked as provided by this chapter.

(d) A final order suspending license rendered by a court or the Title IV-D agency shall be forwarded to the appropriate licensing authority by the clerk of the court or Title IV-D agency. The clerk shall collect from an obligor a fee of $5 for each order mailed.

(e) If the court or Title IV-D agency renders an order suspending license, the individual may also be ordered not to engage in the licensed activity.

(f) If the court or Title IV-D agency finds that the petition for suspension should be denied, the petition shall be dismissed without prejudice, and an order suspending license may not be rendered.

*(Added by L.1995, chaps. 655(5.03), 751(85); chgd. by L.1997, chaps. 911(88), 976(8); L.1999, chap. 556(61), eff. 9/1/99.)*

## §232.009. Default Order.

The court or Title IV-D agency shall consider the allegations of the petition for suspension to be admitted and shall render an order suspending the license of an obligor without the requirement of a hearing if the court or Title IV-D agency determines that the individual failed to:

(1) respond to a notice issued under Section 232.006;

(2) request a hearing; or

(3) appear at a hearing.

*(Added by L.1995, chaps. 655(5.03), 751(85); chgd. by L.1997, chaps. 420(25), 911(89), eff. 9/1/97.)*



## §232.010. Review of final administrative order.

An order issued by a Title IV-D agency under this chapter is a final agency decision and is subject to review under the substantial evidence rule as provided by Chapter 2001, Government Code. *(Added by L.1995, chaps. 655(5.03), 751(85), eff. 9/1/95.)*

## §232.011. Action by licensing authority.

(a) On receipt of a final order suspending license, the licensing authority shall immediately determine if the authority has issued a license to the individual named on the order and, if a license has been issued:

(1) record the suspension of the license in the licensing authority's records;

(2) report the suspension as appropriate; and

(3) demand surrender of the suspended license if required by law for other cases in which a license is suspended.

(b) A licensing authority shall implement the terms of a final order suspending license without additional review or hearing. The authority may provide notice as appropriate to the license holder or to others concerned with the license.

(c) A licensing authority may not modify, remand, reverse, vacate, or stay an order suspending license issued under this chapter and may not review, vacate, or reconsider the terms of a final order suspending license.

(d) An individual who is the subject of a final order suspending license is not entitled to a refund for any fee or deposit paid to the licensing authority.

(e) An individual who continues to engage in the business, occupation, profession, or other licensed activity after the implementation of the order suspending license by the licensing authority is liable for the same civil and criminal penalties provided for engaging in the licensed activity without a license or while a license is suspended that apply to any other license holder of that licensing authority.

(f) A licensing authority is exempt from liability to a license holder for any act authorized under this chapter performed by the authority.

(g) Except as provided by this chapter, an order suspending license or dismissing a petition for the suspension of a license does not affect the power of a licensing authority to grant, deny, suspend, revoke, terminate, or renew a license.

(h) The denial or suspension of a driver's license under this chapter is governed by this chapter and not by the general licensing provisions of Chapter 521, Transportation Code.

*(Added by L.1995, chaps. 655(5.03), 751(85); chgd. by L.1997, chaps. 165(30.184), 911(90), eff. 9/1/97.)*

## §232.012. Motion to revoke stay.

(a) The obligee, support enforcement agency, court, or Title IV-D agency may file a motion to revoke the stay of an order suspending license if the individual who is subject of an order suspending license does not comply with:

(1) the terms of a reasonable repayment plan entered into by the individual; or

(2) the requirements of a reissued subpoena.

(b) Notice to the individual of a motion to revoke stay under this section may be given by personal service or by mail to the address provided by the individual, if any, in the order suspending license. The notice must include a notice of hearing. The notice must be provided to the individual not less than 10 days before the date of the hearing.

(c) A motion to revoke stay must allege the manner in which the individual failed to comply with the repayment plan or the reissued subpoena.

(d) If the court or Title IV-D agency finds that the individual is not in compliance with the terms of the repayment plan or reissued subpoena, the court or agency shall revoke the stay of the order suspending license and render a final order suspending license.
*(Added by L.1995, chaps. 655(5.03), 751(85); chgd. by L.1997, chap. 911(91), eff. 9/1/97.)*

## §232.013. Vacating or Staying Order Suspending License.

(a) The court or Title IV-D agency may render an order vacating or staying an order suspending license if the individual has:

(1) paid all delinquent child support or has established a satisfactory payment record; or

(2) complied with the requirements of a reissued subpoena.

(b) The clerk of the court or Title IV-D agency shall promptly deliver an order vacating or staying an order suspending license to the appropriate licensing authority. The clerk shall collect from an obligor a fee of $5 for each order mailed.

(c) On receipt of an order vacating or staying an order suspending license, the licensing authority shall promptly issue the affected license to the individual if the individual is otherwise qualified for the license.

(d) An order rendered under this section does not affect the right of the child support agency or obligee to any other remedy provided by law, including the right to seek relief under this chapter. An order rendered under this section does not affect the power of a licensing authority to grant, deny, suspend, revoke, terminate, or renew a license as otherwise provided by law.
*(Added by L.1995, chaps. 655(5.03), 751(85); chgd. by L.1997, chaps. 911(92), 976(9), eff. 9/1/97.)*



## §232.014. Fee by licensing authority.

A licensing authority may charge a fee to an individual who is the subject of an order suspending license in an amount sufficient to recover the administrative costs incurred by the authority under this chapter. *(Added by L.1995, chaps. 655(5.03), 751(85); chgd. by L.1997, chap. 911(93), eff. 9/1/97.)*

## §232.015. Cooperation between licensing authorities and Title IV-D agency.

(a) The Title IV-D agency may request from each licensing authority the name, address, social security number, license renewal date, and other identifying information for each individual who holds, applies for, or renews a license issued by the authority.

(b) A licensing authority shall provide the requested information in the manner agreed to by the Title IV-D agency and the licensing authority.

(c) The Title IV-D agency may enter into a cooperative agreement with a licensing authority to administer this chapter in a cost-effective manner.

(d) The Title IV-D agency may adopt a reasonable implementation schedule for the requirements of this section.

(e) The Title IV-D agency, the comptroller, and the Texas Alcoholic Beverage Commission shall by rule specify additional prerequisites for the suspension of licenses relating to state taxes collected under Title 2, Tax Code. The joint rules must be adopted not later than March 1, 1996.
*(Added by L.1995, chap. 751(85), eff. 9/1/95.*

## §232.016. Rules, forms, and procedures.

The Title IV-D agency by rule shall prescribe forms and procedures for the implementation of this chapter. *(Added by L.1995, chap. 655(5.03), 751(85), eff. 9/1/95.)*

# SUBTITLE E. PROTECTION OF THE CHILD

## CHAPTER 261. INVESTIGATION OF REPORT OF CHILD ABUSE OR NEGLECT

*(Selected Sections)*

### SUBCHAPTER A. GENERAL PROVISIONS

Section
261.001. Definitions.

### SUBCHAPTER B. REPORT OF ABUSE OR NEGLECT; IMMUNITIES

261.101. Persons required to report; time to report.
261.102. Matters to be reported.
261.103. Report made to appropriate agency.
261.104. Contents of report.
261.105. Referral of report by department or law enforcement.
261.1055. Notification of district attorneys.
261.106. Immunities.
261.107. False report; penalty.
261.108. Frivolous claims against person reporting.
261.109. Failure to report; penalty.
261.110 to 261.200. *(Reserved.)*

### SUBCHAPTER C. CONFIDENTIALITY AND PRIVILEGED COMMUNICATION

261.201. Confidentiality and disclosure of information.
261.202. Privileged communication.
261.203 to 261.300. *(Reserved.)*

### SUBCHAPTER D. INVESTIGATIONS

261.301. Investigation of report.
261.3015. Flexible response system.
261.3019. Pilot programs for investigations of child abuse.
261.302. Conduct of investigation.
261.303. Interference with investigation; court order.
261.304. Investigation of anonymous report.
261.305. Access to mental health records.
261.306. Removal of child from state.
261.307. Information relating to investigation procedure.
261.308. Submission of investigation report.
261.309. Review of department investigations.
261.310. Investigation standards.
261.311. Notice of report.
261.312. Review teams; offense.
261.3125. Investigations coordinator.
261.313. *(Reserved.)*
261.314. Testing.
261.315. Exemption from fees for medical records.
261.315. Removal of certain investigation information from records.
261.316. Exemption from fees for medical records.
261.317 to 261.400. *(Reserved.)*

## SUBCHAPTER E. INVESTIGATIONS OF ABUSE OR NEGLECT IN CERTAIN FACILITIES





## SUBCHAPTER A. GENERAL PROVISIONS
*(Selected Section)*

### §261.001. Definitions.

In this chapter:

(1) "Abuse" includes the following acts or omissions by a person:

(A) mental or emotional injury to a child that results in an observable and material impairment in the child's growth, development, or psychological functioning;

(B) causing or permitting the child to be in a situation in which the child sustains a mental or emotional injury that results in an observable and material impairment in the child's growth, development, or psychological functioning;

(C) physical injury that results in substantial harm to the child, or the genuine threat of substantial harm from physical injury to the child, including an injury that is at variance with the history or explanation given and excluding an accident or reasonable discipline by a parent, guardian, or managing or possessory conservator that does not expose the child to a substantial risk of harm;

(D) failure to make a reasonable effort to prevent an action by another person that results in physical injury that results in substantial harm to the child;

(E) sexual conduct harmful to a child's mental, emotional, or physical welfare;

(F) failure to make a reasonable effort to prevent sexual conduct harmful to a child;

(G) compelling or encouraging the child to engage in sexual conduct as defined by Section 43.01, Penal Code;

(H) causing, permitting, encouraging, engaging in, or allowing the photographing, filming, or depicting of the child if the person knew or should have known that the resulting photograph, film, or depiction of the child is obscene as defined by Section 43.21, Penal Code, or pornographic;

(I) the current use by a person of a controlled substance as defined by Chapter 481, Health and Safety Code, in a manner or to the extent that the use results in physical, mental, or emotional injury to a child; or

(J) causing, expressly permitting, or encouraging a child to use a controlled substance as defined by Chapter 481, Health and Safety Code.

(2) "Department" means the Department of Protective and Regulatory Services.

(3) "Designated agency" means the agency designated by the court as responsible for the protection of children.

(4) "Neglect" includes:

(A) the leaving of a child in a situation where the child would be exposed to a substantial risk of physical or mental harm, without arranging for necessary care for the child, and the demonstration of an intent not to return by a parent, guardian, or managing or possessory conservator of the child;

(B) the following acts or omissions by a person:

(i) placing a child in or failing to remove a child from a situation that a reasonable person would realize requires judgment or actions beyond the child's level of maturity, physical condition, or mental abilities and that results in bodily injury or a substantial risk of immediate harm to the child;

(ii) failing to seek, obtain, or follow through with medical care for a child, with the failure resulting in or presenting a substantial risk of death, disfigurement, or bodily injury or with the failure resulting in an observable and material impairment to the growth, development, or functioning of the child;

(iii) the failure to provide a child with food, clothing, or shelter necessary to sustain the life or health of the child, excluding failure caused primarily by financial inability unless relief services had been offered and refused; or

(iv) placing a child in or failing to remove the child from a situation in which the child would be exposed to a substantial risk of sexual conduct harmful to the child; or

(C) the failure by the person responsible for a child's care, custody, or welfare to permit the child to return to the child's home without arranging for the necessary care for the child after the child has been absent from the home for any reason, including having been in residential placement or having run away.

(5) "Person responsible for a child's care, custody, or welfare" means a person who traditionally is responsible for a child's care, custody, or welfare, including:

(A) a parent, guardian, managing or possessory conservator, or foster parent of the child;

(B) a member of the child's family or household as defined by Chapter 71;

(C) a person with whom the child's parent cohabits;

(D) school personnel or a volunteer at the child's school; or

(E) personnel or a volunteer at a public or private child-care facility that provides services for the child or at a public or private residential institution or facility where the child resides.

(6) "Report" means a report that alleged or suspected abuse or neglect of a child has occurred or may occur.

(7) "Board" means the Board of Protective and Regulatory Services.

(8) "Born addicted to alcohol or a controlled substance" means a child:

(A) who is born to a mother who during the pregnancy used a controlled substance, as defined by Chapter 481, Health and Safety Code, other than a controlled substance legally obtained by prescription, or alcohol; and

(B) who, after birth as a result of the mother's use of the controlled substance or alcohol:

(i) experiences observable withdrawal from the alcohol or controlled substance;

(ii) exhibits observable or harmful effects in the child's physical appearance or functioning; or

(iii) exhibits the demonstrable presence of alcohol or a controlled substance in the child's bodily fluids.

*(Added by L.1995, chap. 20(1); chgd. by L.1995, chap. 751(86); L.1997, chaps. 575(10), 1022(63); L.1999, chap. 62(19.01(26)), eff. 9/1/99.)*

## SUBCHAPTER B. REPORT OF ABUSE OR NEGLECT; IMMUNITIES

### §261.101. Persons required to report; time to report.

(a) A person having cause to believe that a child's physical or mental health or welfare has been adversely affected by abuse or neglect by any person shall immediately make a report as provided by this subchapter.

(b) If a professional has cause to believe that a child has been abused or neglected or may be abused or neglected or that a child is a victim of an offense under Section 21.11, Penal Code, the professional shall make a report not later than the 48th hour after the hour the professional first suspects that the child has been or may be abused or neglected or is a victim of an offense under Section 21.11, Penal Code. A professional may not delegate to or rely on another person to make the report. In this subsection, "professional" means an individual who is licensed or certified by the state or who is an employee of a facility licensed, certified, or operated by the state and who, in the normal course of official duties or duties for which a license or certification is required, has direct contact with children. The term includes teachers, nurses, doctors, day-care employees, employees of a clinic or health care facility that provides reproductive services, juvenile probation officers, and juvenile detention or correctional officers.

(c) The requirement to report under this section applies without exception to an individual whose personal communications may otherwise be privileged, including an attorney, a member of the clergy, a medical practitioner, a social worker, a mental health professional, and an employee of a clinic or health care facility that provides reproductive services.

(d) Unless waived in writing by the person making the report, the identity of an individual making a report under this chapter is confidential and may be disclosed only:

(1) as provided by Section 261.201; or

(2) to a law enforcement officer for the purposes of conducting a criminal investigation of the report.

*(Added by L.1995, chap. 20(1); chgd. by L.1995, chap. 751(87); L.1997, chaps. 162(1), 575(11), 1022(65); L.1999, chaps. 62(6.29), 1150(2), 1390(21), eff. 9/1/99.)*

### §261.102. Matters to be reported.

A report should reflect the reporter's belief that a child has been or may be abused or neglected or has died of abuse or neglect. *(Added by L.1995, chap. 20(1), eff. 4/20/95; chgd. by L.1995, chap. 751(88), eff. 9/1/95.)*

### §261.103. Report made to appropriate agency.

(a) Except as provided by Subsection (b), a report shall be made to:

(1) any local or state law enforcement agency;

(2) the department if the alleged or suspected abuse involves a person responsible for the care, custody, or welfare of the child;

(3) the state agency that operates, licenses, certifies, or registers the facility in which the alleged abuse or neglect occurred; or

(4) the agency designated by the court to be responsible for the protection of children.

(b) A report may be made to the Texas Youth Commission instead of the entities listed under Subsection (a) if the report is based on information provided by a child while under the supervision of the commission concerning the child's alleged abuse of another child.

*(Added by L.1995, chap. 20(1); chgd. by L.1995, chap. 751(89); L.1999, chap. 1477(24), eff. 9/1/99.)*



### §261.104. Contents of report.

The person making a report shall identify, if known:

(1) the name and address of the child;

(2) the name and address of the person responsible for the care, custody, or welfare of the child; and

(3) any other pertinent information concerning the alleged or suspected abuse or neglect.

*(Added by L.1995, chap. 20(1), eff. 4/20/95; chgd. by L.1995, chap. 751(90), eff. 9/1/95.)*

### §261.105. Referral of report by department or law enforcement.

(a) All reports received by a local or state law enforcement agency that allege abuse or neglect by a person responsible for a child's care, custody, or welfare shall be referred immediately to the department or the designated agency.

(b) The department or designated agency shall immediately notify the appropriate state or local law enforcement agency of any report it receives, other than a report from a law enforcement agency, that concerns the suspected abuse or neglect of a child or death of a child from abuse or neglect.

(c) In addition to notifying a law enforcement agency, if the report relates to a child in a facility operated, licensed, certified, or registered by a state agency, the department shall refer the report to the agency for investigation.

(d) If the department initiates an investigation and determines that the abuse or neglect does not involve a person responsible for the child's care, custody, or welfare, the department shall refer the report to a law enforcement agency for further investigation.

(e) In cooperation with the department, the Texas Youth Commission by rule shall adopt guidelines for identifying a report made to the commission under Section 261.103(b) that is appropriate to refer to the department or a law enforcement agency for investigation. Guidelines adopted under this subsection must require the commission to consider the severity and immediacy of the alleged abuse or neglect of the child victim.

*(Added by L.1995, chap. 20(1); chgd. by L.1997, chap. 1022(66); L.1999, chap. 1477(25), eff. 9/1/99.)*

### §261.1055. Notification of district attorneys.

(a) A district attorney may inform the department or designated agency that the district attorney wishes to receive notification of some or all reports of suspected abuse or neglect of children who were in the county at the time the report was made or who were in the county at the time of the alleged abuse or neglect.

(b) If the district attorney makes the notification under this section, the department or designated agency shall, on receipt of a report of suspected abuse or neglect, immediately notify the district attorney as requested and the department or designated agency shall forward a copy of the reports to the district attorney on request.

*(Added by L.1997, chap. 1022(67), eff. 9/1/97.)*

## §261.106. Immunities.

(a) A person acting in good faith who reports or assists in the investigation of a report of alleged child abuse or neglect or who testifies or otherwise participates in a judicial proceeding arising from a report, petition, or investigation of alleged child abuse or neglect is immune from civil or criminal liability that might otherwise be incurred or imposed.

(b) Immunity from civil and criminal liability extends to an authorized volunteer of the department or a law enforcement officer who participates at the request of the department in an investigation of alleged or suspected abuse or neglect or in an action arising from an investigation if the person was acting in good faith and in the scope of the person's responsibilities.

(c) A person who reports the person's own abuse or neglect of a child or who acts in bad faith or with malicious purpose in reporting alleged child abuse or neglect is not immune from civil or criminal liability.

*(Added by L.1995, chap. 20(1), eff. 4/20/95; chgd. by L.1995, chap. 751(91), eff. 9/1/95.)*

## §261.107. False report; penalty.

(a) A person commits an offense if the person knowingly or intentionally makes a report as provided in this chapter that the person knows is false or lacks factual foundation. An offense under this section is a Class A misdemeanor unless it is shown on the trial of the offense that the person has previously been convicted under this section, in which case the offense is a state jail felony.

(b) A finding by a court in a suit affecting the parent-child relationship that a report made under this chapter before or during the suit was false or lacking factual foundation may be grounds for the court to modify an order providing for possession of or access to the child who was the subject of the report by restricting further access to the child by the person who made the report.

(c) The appropriate county prosecuting attorney shall be responsible for the prosecution of an offense under this section.

*(Added by L.1995, chap. 20(1); chgd. by L.1995, chap. 751(92); L.1997, chaps. 575(2), 1022(68); reenacted by L.1999, chap. 62(6.30), eff. 9/1/99.)*

 Zt

## §261.108. Frivolous claims against person reporting.

(a) In this section:

(1) "Claim" means an action or claim by a party, including a plaintiff, counterclaimant, cross-claimant, or third-party plaintiff, requesting recovery of damages.

(2) "Defendant" means a party against whom a claim is made.

(b) A court shall award a defendant reasonable attorney's fees and other expenses related to the defense of a claim filed against the defendant for damages or other relief arising from reporting or assisting in the investigation of a report under this chapter or participating in a judicial proceeding resulting from the report if:

(1) the court finds that the claim is frivolous, unreasonable, or without foundation because the defendant is immune from liability under Section 261.106; and

(2) the claim is dismissed or judgment is rendered for the defendant.

(c) To recover under this section, the defendant must, at any time after the filing of a claim, file a written motion stating that:

(1) the claim is frivolous, unreasonable, or without foundation because the defendant is immune from liability under Section 261.106; and

(2) the defendant requests the court to award reasonable attorney's fees and other expenses related to the defense of the claim.

*(Added by L.1995, chap. 20(1), eff. 4/20/95.)*

## §261.109. Failure to report; penalty.

(a) A person commits an offense if the person has cause to believe that a child's physical or mental health or welfare has been or may be adversely affected by abuse or neglect and knowingly fails to report as provided in this chapter.

(b) An offense under this section is a Class B misdemeanor.

*(Added by L.1995, chap. 20(1), eff. 4/20/95.)*

## §§261.110 to 261.200. *(Reserved.)*

## SUBCHAPTER C. CONFIDENTIALITY AND PRIVILEGED COMMUNICATION

### §261.201. Confidentiality and disclosure of information.

(a) The following information is confidential, is not subject to public release under Chapter 552, Government Code, and may be disclosed only for purposes consistent with this code and applicable federal or state law or under rules adopted by an investigating agency:

(1) a report of alleged or suspected abuse or neglect made under this chapter and the identity of the person making the report; and

(2) except as otherwise provided in this section, the files, reports, records, communications, audiotapes, videotapes, and working papers used or developed in an investigation under this chapter or in providing services as a result of an investigation.

(b) A court may order the disclosure of information that is confidential under this section if:

(1) a motion has been filed with the court requesting the release of the information;

(2) a notice of hearing has been served on the investigating agency and all other interested parties; and

(3) after hearing and an in camera review of the requested information, the court determines that the disclosure of the requested information is:

(A) essential to the administration of justice; and

(B) not likely to endanger the life or safety of:

(i) a child who is the subject of the report of alleged or suspected abuse or neglect;

(ii) a person who makes a report of alleged or suspected abuse or neglect; or

(iii) any other person who participates in an investigation of reported abuse or neglect or who provides care for the child.

(c) In addition to Subsection (b), a court, on its own motion, may order disclosure of information that is confidential under this section if:

(1) the order is rendered at a hearing for which all parties have been given notice;

(2) the court finds that disclosure of the information is:

(A) essential to the administration of justice; and

(B) not likely to endanger the life or safety of:

(i) a child who is the subject of the report of alleged or suspected abuse or neglect;

(ii) a person who makes a report of alleged or suspected abuse or neglect; or

(iii) any other person who participates in an investigation of reported abuse or neglect or who provides care for the child; and

(3) the order is reduced to writing or made on the record in open court.

(d) The adoptive parents of a child who was the subject of an investigation and an adult who was the subject of an investigation as a child are entitled to examine and make copies of any report, record, working paper, or other information in the possession, custody, or control of the state that pertains to the history of the child. The department may edit the documents to protect the identity of the biological parents and any other person whose identity is confidential.

(e) Before placing a child who was the subject of an investigation, the department shall notify the prospective adoptive parents of their right to examine any report, record, working paper, or other information in the possession, custody, or control of the state that pertains to the history of the child.

(f) The department shall provide prospective adoptive parents an opportunity to examine information under this section as early as practicable before placing a child.

(g) Notwithstanding Subsection (b), the department, on request and subject to department rule, shall provide to the parent, managing conservator, or other legal representative of a child who is the subject of reported abuse or neglect information concerning the reported abuse or neglect that would otherwise be confidential under this section if the department has edited the information to protect the confidentiality of the identity of the person who made the report and any other person whose life or safety may be endangered by the disclosure.

(h) This section does not apply to an investigation of child abuse or neglect in a home or facility regulated under Chapter 42, Human Resources Code.

*(Added by L.1995, chap. 20(1); chgd. by L.1995, chap. 751(93); L.1997, chap. 575(12), 1022(69); L.1999, chaps. 1150(3), 1390(22), eff. 9/1/99.)*

### §261.202. Privileged communication.

In a proceeding regarding the abuse or neglect of a child, evidence may not be excluded on the ground of privileged communication except in the case of communications between an attorney and client. *(Added by L.1995, chap. 20(1), eff. 4/20/95.)*

### §§261.203 to 261.300. *(Reserved.)*

## SUBCHAPTER D. INVESTIGATIONS

### §261.301. Investigation of report.

(a) With assistance from the appropriate state or local law enforcement agency, the department or designated agency shall make a prompt and thorough investigation of a report of child abuse or neglect allegedly committed by a person responsible for a child's care, custody, or welfare. The investigation shall be conducted without regard to any pending suit affecting the parent-child relationship.

(b) A state agency shall investigate a report that alleges abuse or neglect occurred in a facility operated, licensed, certified, or registered by that agency as provided by Subchapter E. In conducting an investigation for a facility operated, licensed, certified, registered, or listed by the department, the department shall perform the investigation as provided by:

(1) Subchapter E; and

(2) the Human Resources Code.

(c) The department is not required to investigate a report that alleges child abuse or neglect by a person other than a person responsible for a child's care, custody, or welfare. The appropriate state or local law enforcement agency shall investigate that report if the agency determines an investigation should be conducted.

(d) The department may by rule assign priorities and prescribe investigative procedures for investigations based on the severity and immediacy of the alleged harm to the child. The primary purpose of the investigation shall be the protection of the child.

(e) As necessary to provide for the protection of the child, the department or designated agency shall determine:

(1) the nature, extent, and cause of the abuse or neglect;

(2) the identity of the person responsible for the abuse or neglect;

(3) the names and conditions of the other children in the home;

(4) an evaluation of the parents or persons responsible for the care of the child;

(5) the adequacy of the home environment;

(6) the relationship of the child to the persons responsible for the care, custody, or welfare of the child; and

(7) all other pertinent data.

(f) An investigation of a report to the department of serious physical or sexual abuse of a child shall be conducted jointly by an investigator from the appropriate local law enforcement agency and the department or agency responsible for conducting an investigation under Subchapter E.

(g) The inability or unwillingness of a local law enforcement agency to conduct a joint investigation under Subsection (f) does not constitute grounds to prevent or prohibit the department from performing its duties under this subtitle. The department shall document any instance in which a law enforcement agency is unable or unwilling to conduct a joint investigation under Subsection (f).

*(Added by L.1995, chap. 20(1); chgd. by L.1995, chaps. 751(94), 943(2); L.1997, chaps. 1022(70), 1137(1); L.1999, chaps. 1150(4), 1390(23), eff. 9/1/99.)*

### §261.3015. Flexible response system.

(a) In assigning priorities and prescribing investigative procedures based on the severity and immediacy of the alleged harm to a child under Section 261.301(d), the board by rule shall establish a flexible response system to allow the department to allocate resources by investigating serious cases of abuse and neglect and providing assessment and family preservation services in less serious cases.

(b) The classification under the flexible response system of a case may be changed as warranted by the circumstances.

(c) The department may implement the flexible response system by establishing a pilot program in a single department service region. The department shall study the results of the system in the region in determining the method by which to implement the system statewide.

*(Added by L.1997, chap. 1022(71), eff. 9/1/97.)*

### §261.3019. Pilot programs for investigations of child abuse.

(a) On or after September 1, 1997, but not later than March 1, 1998, the department shall enter into two agreements, one with a sheriff of a county with a population of not less than 500,000 and if necessary for jurisdictional purposes any other law enforcement agency, and one with a sheriff of a county with a population of 25,000 or less and if necessary for jurisdictional purposes any other law enforcement agency, under which the sheriff or law enforcement agency shall conduct investigations of reports of abuse. The commissioners court of a county that is eligible to establish a pilot program and that intends to do so shall inform the department of the county's interest.

(b) An agreement under this section shall:

(1) specify the respective roles of law enforcement and department staff in the investigative process;

(2) provide for the department to assist in the removal of a child under Chapter 262 as necessary for the protection of the child;

(3) provide for the use of any available children's advocacy center or multidisciplinary team under Subchapter E, Chapter 264;

(4) include provisions for the reimbursement by the department from available state and federal funds of the costs incurred by the sheriff or law enforcement agency in conducting an investigation of a report of abuse;

(5) develop a plan for the transfer of calls received by the state child abuse hotline to the local law enforcement agency;

(6) develop a plan to be submitted to the department that specifies the manner in which the county's law enforcement agency shall handle investigations, investigator training, and the processing of reports made to the local agency;

(7) permit an additional contract with other appropriate local law enforcement agencies, if necessary for jurisdictional purposes, to implement the pilot program; and

(8) contain provisions the department and the sheriff and law enforcement determine to be necessary and appropriate.

(c) The department may provide advice and technical assistance to the county to ensure that the county complies with state and federal law in implementing and operating the pilot program.

(d) Under each pilot program, the department shall provide to a participating county law enforcement agency:

(A) information regarding:

(i) the average number of child abuse cases that are typically investigated; and

(ii) staff and investigator training; and

(B) other assistance necessary to adequately implement and fund the pilot program.

(e) Under the pilot program, the commissioners court shall establish an independent local citizens review board composed of seven volunteers who represent the community, including members who have experience in matters relating to child abuse and including one member who is licensed as a psychologist, one member licensed as a medical or health professional, and one member who is a licensed or ordained priest, rabbi, or officer of a religious organization. A member of a review board may not be an employee of or contract with any participating law enforcement agency or the department. The citizens review board shall prepare and make available to the public on an annual basis a report containing a summary of the activities of the board.

(f) The commissioners court may apply for any grants and research other sources of funding for the county's participation in the pilot program.

(g) An agreement under Subsection (a) is not required to provide for:

(1) the investigation of abuse alleged to have occurred in a facility or home regulated by the department under Chapter 42, Human Resources Code; or

(2) an investigation conducted under Section 261.404.

(h) The state auditor shall perform an audit and evaluation of the pilot program under this section. In preparing the evaluation, the auditor shall consider any report prepared by a citizens review board established under Subsection (e). The auditor shall report, not later than March 1, 2001, the results of the audit and evaluation to the presiding officers of both houses of the 77th Legislature and to the governor. The report must include an evaluation of the strengths and weaknesses of the pilot program and a recommendation about the feasibility of expanding the pilot program statewide.

(i) The department shall adopt rules necessary to perform the department's duties under this section.

(j) This section expires September 1, 2001.

*(Added by L.1997, chap. 1022(72), eff. 9/1/97 until 9/1/2001; chgd. by L.1999, chap. 907(38), eff. 9/1/99.)*

## §261.302. Conduct of investigation.

(a) The investigation may include:

(1) a visit to the child's home, unless the alleged abuse or neglect can be confirmed or clearly ruled out without a home visit; and

(2) an interview with and examination of the subject child, which may include a medical, psychological, or psychiatric examination.

(b) The interview with and examination of the child may:

(1) be conducted at any reasonable time and place, including the child's home or the child's school;

(2) include the presence of persons the department or designated agency determines are necessary; and

(3) include transporting the child for purposes relating to the interview or investigation.

(c) The investigation may include an interview with the child's parents and an interview with and medical, psychological, or psychiatric examination of any child in the home.

(d) If, before an investigation is completed, the investigating agency believes that the immediate removal of a child from the child's home is necessary to protect the child from further abuse or neglect, the investigating agency shall file a petition or take other action under Chapter 262 to provide for the temporary care and protection of the child.

(e) An interview with a child alleged to be a victim of physical abuse or sexual abuse shall be audiotaped or videotaped unless the investigating agency determines that good cause exists for not audiotaping or videotaping the interview in accordance with rules of the agency. Good cause may include, but is not limited to, such considerations as the age of the child and the nature and seriousness of the allegations under investigation. Nothing in this subsection shall be construed as prohibiting the investigating agency from audiotaping or videotaping an interview of a child on any case for which such audiotaping or videotaping is not required under this subsection. The fact that the investigating agency failed to audiotape or videotape an interview is admissible at the trial of the offense that is the subject of the interview.

*(Added by L.1995, chap. 20(1); chgd. by L.1995, chap. 751(95); L.1997, chaps. 575(13), (14); 1022(73), eff. 9/1/97.)*



## §261.303. Interference with investigation; court order.

(a) A person may not interfere with an investigation of a report of child abuse or neglect conducted by the department or designated agency.

(b) If admission to the home, school, or any place where the child may be cannot be obtained, then for good cause shown the court having family law jurisdiction shall order the parent, the person responsible for the care of the children, or the person in charge of any place where the child may be to allow entrance for the interview, examination, and investigation.

(c) If a parent or person responsible for the child's care does not consent to release of the child's prior medical, psychological, or psychiatric records or to a medical, psychological, or psychiatric examination of the child that is requested by the department or designated agency, the court having family law jurisdiction shall, for good cause shown, order the records to be released or the examination to be made at the times and places designated by the court.

(d) A person, including a medical facility, that makes a report under Subchapter B shall release to the department or designated agency, as part of the required report under Section 261.103, records that directly relate to the suspected abuse or neglect without requiring parental consent or a court order.

*(Added by L.1995, chap. 20(1); chgd. by L.1995, chap. 751(96); L.1999, chaps. 1150(5), 1390(24), eff. 9/1/99.)*

## §261.304. Investigation of anonymous report.

(a) If the department receives an anonymous report of child abuse or neglect by a person responsible for a child's care, custody, or welfare, the department shall conduct a preliminary investigation to determine whether there is any evidence to corroborate the report.

(b) An investigation under this section may include a visit to the child's home and an interview with and examination of the child and an interview with the child's parents. In addition, the department may interview any other person the department believes may have relevant information.

(c) Unless the department determines that there is some evidence to corroborate the report of abuse, the department may not conduct the thorough investigation required by this chapter or take any action against the person accused of abuse.

*(Added by L.1995, chap. 20(1), eff. 4/20/95.)*

## §261.305. Access to mental health records.

(a) An investigation may include an inquiry into the possibility that a parent or a person responsible for the care of a child who is the subject of a report under Subchapter B has a history of medical or mental illness.

(b) If the parent or person does not consent to an examination or allow the department or designated agency to have access to medical or mental health records requested by the department or agency, the court having family law jurisdiction, for good cause shown, shall order the examination to be made or that the department or agency be permitted to have access to the records under terms and conditions prescribed by the court.

(c) If the court determines that the parent or person is indigent, the court shall appoint an attorney to represent the parent or person at the hearing. The fees for the appointed attorney shall be paid as provided by Chapter 107.

(d) A parent or person responsible for the child's care is entitled to notice and a hearing when the department or designated agency seeks a court order to allow a medical, psychological, or psychiatric examination or access to medical or mental health records.

(e) This access does not constitute a waiver of confidentiality.

*(Added by L.1995, chap. 20(1); chgd. by L.1997, chap. 575(15); L.1999, chaps. 1150(6), 1390(25), eff. 9/1/99.)*



### §261.306. Removal of child from state.

(a) If the department or designated agency has reason to believe that a person responsible for the care, custody, or welfare of the child may remove the child from the state before the investigation is completed, the department or designated agency may file an application for a temporary restraining order in a district court without regard to continuing jurisdiction of the child as provided in Chapter 155.

(b) The court may render a temporary restraining order prohibiting the person from removing the child from the state pending completion of the investigation if the court:

(1) finds that the department or designated agency has probable cause to conduct the investigation; and

(2) has reason to believe that the person may remove the child from the state.

*(Added by L.1995, chap. 20(1), eff. 4/20/95.)*

### §261.307. Information relating to investigation procedure.

As soon as possible after initiating an investigation of a parent or other person having legal custody of a child, the department shall provide to the person a brief and easily understood summary of:

(1) the department's procedures for conducting an investigation of alleged child abuse or neglect, including:

(A) a description of the circumstances under which the department would request to remove the child from the home through the judicial system; and

(B) an explanation that the law requires the department to refer all reports of alleged child abuse or neglect to a law enforcement agency for a separate determination of whether a criminal violation occurred;

(2) the person's right to file a complaint with the department or to request a review of the findings made by the department in the investigation;

(3) the person's right to review all records of the investigation unless the review would jeopardize an ongoing criminal investigation;

(4) the person's right to seek legal counsel;

(5) references to the statutory and regulatory provisions governing child abuse and neglect and how the person may obtain copies of those provisions; and

(6) the process the person may use to acquire access to the child if the child is removed from the home.

*(Added by L.1995, chap. 20(1), eff. 4/20/95.)*

### §261.308. Submission of investigation report.

(a) The department or designated agency shall make a complete written report of the investigation.

(b) If sufficient grounds for filing a suit exist, the department or designated agency shall submit the report, together with recommendations, to the court, the district attorney, and the appropriate law enforcement agency.

(c) On receipt of the report and recommendations, the court may direct the department or designated agency to file a petition requesting appropriate relief as provided in this title.

*(Added by L.1995, chap. 20(1), eff. 4/20/95; chgd. by L.1995, chap. 751(97), eff. 9/1/95.)*

### §261.309. Review of department investigations.

(a) The department shall by rule establish policies and procedures to resolve complaints relating to and conduct reviews of child abuse or neglect investigations conducted by the department.

(b) If a person under investigation for allegedly abusing or neglecting a child requests clarification of the status of the person's case or files a complaint relating to the conduct of the department's staff or to department policy, the department shall conduct an informal review to clarify the person's status or resolve the complaint. The immediate supervisor of the employee who conducted the child abuse or neglect investigation or against whom the complaint was filed shall conduct the informal review as soon as possible but not later than the 14th day after the date the request or complaint is received.

(c) If, after the department's investigation, the person who is alleged to have abused or neglected a child disputes the department's determination of whether child abuse or neglect occurred, the person may request an administrative review of the findings. A department employee in administration who was not involved in or did not directly supervise the investigation shall conduct the review. The review must sustain, alter, or reverse the department's original findings in the investigation.

(d) Unless a civil or criminal court proceeding or an ongoing criminal investigation relating to the alleged abuse or neglect investigated by the department is pending, the department employee shall conduct the review prescribed by Subsection (c) as soon as possible but not later than the 45th day after the date the department receives the request. If a civil or criminal court proceeding or an ongoing criminal investigation is pending, the department may postpone the review until the court proceeding is completed.

(e) A person is not required to exhaust the remedies provided by this section before pursuing a judicial remedy provided by law.

(f) This section does not provide for a review of an order rendered by a court.
*(Added by L.1995, chap. 20(1), eff. 4/20/95.)*



## §261.310. Investigation standards.

(a) The department shall by rule develop and adopt voluntary standards for persons who investigate suspected child abuse or neglect at the state or local level. The standards shall encourage professionalism and consistency in the investigation of suspected child abuse or neglect.

(b) The standards must provide for a minimum number of hours of annual professional training for interviewers and investigators of suspected child abuse or neglect.

(c) The professional training curriculum developed under this section shall include information concerning:

(1) physical abuse and neglect, including distinguishing physical abuse from ordinary childhood injuries;

(2) psychological abuse and neglect;

(3) available treatment resources; and

(4) the incidence and types of reports of child abuse and neglect that are received by the investigating agencies, including information concerning false reports.

(d) The standards shall recommend:

(1) that videotaped and audiotaped interviews with a suspected victim be uninterrupted;

(2) a maximum number of interviews with and examinations of a suspected victim;

(3) procedures to preserve evidence, including the original notes, videotapes, and audiotapes; and

(4) that an investigator of suspected child abuse or neglect make a reasonable effort to locate and inform each parent of a child of any report of abuse or neglect relating to the child.
*(Added by L.1995, chap. 20(1), eff. 4/20/95.)*

## §261.311. Notice of report.

(a) When during an investigation of a report of suspected child abuse or neglect a representative of the department or the designated agency conducts an interview with or an examination of a child, the department or designated agency shall make a reasonable effort before 24 hours after the time of the interview or examination to notify each parent of the child and the child's legal guardian, if one has been appointed, of the nature of the allegation and of the fact that the interview or examination was conducted.

(b) If a report of suspected child abuse or neglect is administratively closed by the department or designated agency as a result of a preliminary investigation that did not include an interview or examination of the child, the department or designated agency shall make a reasonable effort before the expiration of 24 hours after the time the investigation is closed to notify each parent and legal guardian of the child of the disposition of the investigation.

(c) The notice required by Subsection (a) or (b) is not required if the department or agency determines that the notice is likely to endanger the safety of the child who is the subject of the report, the person who made the report, or any other person who participates in the investigation of the report.

(d) The notice required by Subsection (a) or (b) may be delayed at the request of a law enforcement agency if notification during the required time would interfere with an ongoing criminal investigation.
*(Added by L.1995, chap. 20(1); chgd. by L.1997, chap. 1022(74), eff. 9/1/97.)*

## §261.312. Review Teams; Offense.

(a) The department shall establish review teams to evaluate department casework and decision-making related to investigations by the department of child abuse or neglect. The department may create one or more review teams for each region of the department for child protective services. A review team is a citizen review panel or a similar entity for the purposes of federal law relating to a state's child protection standards.

(b) A review team consists of five members who serve staggered two-year terms. Review team members are appointed by the director of the department and consist of community representatives and private citizens who live in the region for which the team is established. Each member must be a parent who has not been convicted of or indicted for an offense involving child abuse or neglect, has not been determined by the department to have engaged in child abuse or neglect, or is not under investigation by the department for child abuse or neglect. A member of a review team is a department volunteer for the purposes of Section 411.114, Government Code.

(c) A review team conducting a review of an investigation may conduct the review by examining the facts of the case as outlined by the department caseworker and law enforcement personnel. A review team member acting in the member's official capacity may receive information made confidential under Section 40.005, Human Resources Code, or Section 261.201.

(d) A review team shall report to the department the results of the team's review of an investigation. The review team's report may not include confidential information. The findings contained in a review team's report are subject to disclosure under Chapter 552, Government Code. This section does not require a law enforcement agency to divulge information to a review team that the agency believes would compromise an ongoing criminal case, investigation, or proceeding.

(e) A member of a review team commits an offense if the member discloses confidential information. An offense under this subsection is a Class C misdemeanor.
*(Added by L.1995, chap. 943(3); chgd. by L.1997, chap. 575(16), eff. 9/1/97.)*



## §261.3125. Investigations coordinator.

(a) The department shall employ in each region of the department for child protective services at least one child protective services investigations coordinator. The job responsibilities of the investigations coordinator must focus only on child abuse and neglect investigation issues, including reports of child abuse required by Section 261.101, to achieve a greater compliance with that section, and on assessing and improving the effectiveness of the department in providing for the protection of children in the region.

(b) The duties of a child protective services investigations coordinator must include the duty to:

(1) conduct staff reviews and evaluations of cases determined to involve a high risk to the health or safety of a child, including cases of abuse reported under Section 261.101;

(2) monitor cases in which there have been multiple referrals to the department of child abuse or neglect involving the same family, child, or person alleged to have committed the abuse or neglect; and

(3) approve decisions and assessments related to investigations of cases of child abuse or neglect that involve a high risk to the health or safety of a child.
*(Added by L.1999, chap. 1490(1), eff. 9/1/99.)*

## §261.313. *(Reserved.)*

## §261.314. Testing.

(a) The department shall provide testing as necessary for the welfare of a child who the department believes, after an investigation under this chapter, has been sexually abused, including human immunodeficiency virus (HIV) testing of a child who was abused in a manner by which HIV may be transmitted.

(b) Except as provided by Subsection (c), the results of a test under this section are confidential.

(c) If requested, the department shall report the results of a test under this section to:

(1) a court having jurisdiction of a proceeding involving the child or a proceeding involving a person suspected of abusing the child;

(2) a person responsible for the care and custody of the child as a foster parent; and
(3) a person seeking to adopt the child.
*(Added by L.1995, chap. 943(7, eff. 9/1/95.)*

**§261.315. Exemption from fees for medical records.**
The department is exempt from the payment of a fee otherwise required or authorized by law to obtain a medical record from a hospital or health care provider if the request for a record is made in the course of an investigation by the department. *(Added by L.1997, chap. 575(17), eff. 9/1/97. See other section 261.315 below.)*

**§261.315. Removal of certain investigation information from records.**
(a) At the conclusion of an investigation in which the department determines that the person alleged to have abused or neglected a child did not commit abuse or neglect, the department shall notify the person of the person's right to request the department to remove information about the person's alleged role in the abuse or neglect report from the department's records.

(b) On request under Subsection (a) by a person whom the department has determined did not commit abuse or neglect, the department shall remove information from the department's records concerning the person's alleged role in the abuse or neglect report.

(c) The board shall adopt rules necessary to administer this section.
*(Added by L.1997, chap. 1022(75), eff. 9/1/97. See other section 261.315 above.)*



**§261.316. Exemption from fees for medical records.**
The department is exempt from the payment of a fee otherwise required or authorized by law to obtain a medical record from a hospital or health care provider if the request for a record is made in the course of an investigation by the department. *(Added by L.1997, chap. 575(17); renumbered from section 261.315 by L.1999, chap. 62(19.01(27)), eff. 9/1/99.)*

**§§261.317 to 261.400.** *(Reserved.)*

## SUBCHAPTER E. INVESTIGATIONS OF ABUSE OR NEGLECT IN CERTAIN FACILITIES

**§261.401. Agency investigation.**
(a) A state agency that operates, licenses, certifies, or registers a facility in which children are located shall make a prompt, thorough investigation of a report that a child has been or may be abused or neglected in the facility. The primary purpose of the investigation shall be the protection of the child.

(b) A state agency shall adopt rules relating to the investigation and resolution of reports received as provided by this subchapter. The Health and Human Services Commission shall review and approve the rules to ensure that all agencies implement appropriate standards for the conduct of investigations and that uniformity exists among agencies in the investigation and resolution of reports.
*(Added by L.1995, chap. 20(1), eff. 4/20/95; chgd. by L.1995, chap. 751(98), eff. 9/1/95.)*

**§261.402. Investigative Reports.**
(a) A state agency shall prepare and keep on file a complete written report of each investigation conducted by the agency under this subchapter.

(b) A state agency shall immediately notify the appropriate state or local law enforcement agency of any report the agency receives, other than a report from a law enforcement agency, that concerns the suspected abuse or neglect of a child or the death of a child from abuse or neglect. If the state agency finds evidence indicating that a child may have been abused or neglected, the agency shall report the evidence to the appropriate law enforcement agency.

(d) A state agency that licenses, certifies, or registers a facility in which children are located shall compile, maintain, and make available statistics on the incidence of child abuse and neglect in the facility.

(e) A state agency shall compile, maintain, and make available statistics on the incidence of child abuse and neglect in a facility operated by the state agency.
*(Added by L.1995, chap. 20(1), eff. 4/20/95; chgd. by L.1995, chap. 751(99), eff. 9/1/95.)*

## §261.403. Complaints.

(a) If a state agency receives a complaint relating to an investigation conducted by the agency concerning a facility operated by that agency in which children are located, the agency shall refer the complaint to the agency's board.

(b) The board of a state agency that operates a facility in which children are located shall ensure that the procedure for investigating abuse and neglect allegations and inquiries in the agency's facility is periodically reviewed under the agency's internal audit program required by Chapter 2102, Government Code.
*(Added by L.1995, chap. 20(1), eff. 4/20/95.)*

## §261.404. Investigations in facilities under Department of Mental Health and Mental Retardation.

(a) The department shall investigate a report of abuse, neglect, or exploitation of a child receiving services:

(1) in a facility operated by the Texas Department of Mental Health and Mental Retardation;

(2) in or from a community center, a local mental health authority, or a local mental retardation authority; or

(3) through a program providing services to that child by contract with a facility operated by the Texas Department of Mental Health and Mental Retardation, a community center, a local mental health authority, or a local mental retardation authority.

(b) The department shall investigate the report under rules developed jointly between the department and the Texas Department of Mental Health and Mental Retardation.

(c) The definitions of "abuse" and "neglect" prescribed by Section 261.001 do not apply to an investigation under this section.

(d) In this section, "community center," "local mental health authority," and "local mental retardation authority" have the meanings assigned by Section 531.002, Health and Safety Code.
*(Added by L.1995, chap. 751(100); chgd. by L.1999, chap. 907(39), eff. 9/1/99.)*



## §261.405. Investigations in county detention facilities involving children.

A report of alleged abuse or neglect in a county juvenile detention facility or other secure detention facility in which a child is placed shall be made to a local law enforcement agency for investigation. *(Added by L.1995, chap. 751(100); chgd. by L.1997, chap. 1374(8), eff. 9/1/97. See other sections 261.405 below.)*

## §261.405. Investigations in pre-adjudication and post-adjudication secure juvenile facilities.

A report of alleged abuse or neglect in a public or private juvenile pre-adjudication secure detention facility, including hold-over facilities, or public or private juvenile post-adjudication secure correctional facility, except for a facility operated solely for children committed to the Texas Youth Commission, shall be made to a local law enforcement agency for investigation. The local law enforcement agency shall immediately notify the Texas Juvenile Probation Commission of any report the agency receives. *(Added by L.1995, chap. 751(100); chgd. by L.1997, chap. 162(2), 1374(8); reenacted by L.1999, chaps. 1150(7), 1390(26), eff. 9/1/99. See other sections 261.405 above and below.)*

## §261.405. Investigations in juvenile justice programs and facilities.

(a) A report of alleged abuse or neglect in a public or private juvenile pre-adjudication secure detention facility, including hold-over facilities, or public or private juvenile post-adjudication secure correctional facility, except for a facility operated solely for children committed to the Texas Youth Commission, shall be made to a local law enforcement agency for investigation. The local law enforcement agency shall immediately notify the Texas Juvenile Probation Commission of any report the agency receives.

(b) The Texas Juvenile Probation Commission shall conduct an investigation as provided by this chapter if the commission receives a report of alleged abuse or neglect in any program, including a juvenile justice alternative education program, operated wholly or partly by:

(1) a local juvenile probation department; or

(2) a private vendor operating under the authority of a county juvenile board in accordance with the standards adopted by the commission.

(c) In an investigation required under this section, the investigating agency shall have access to medical and mental health records as provided by Subchapter D.
*(Added by L.1995, chap. 751(100); chgd. by L.1997, chap. 162(2), 1374(8); reenacted and amended by L.1999, chap. 1477(26), eff. 9/1/97. See other sections 261.405 above.)*

### §261.406. Investigations in schools.

(a) On receipt of a report of alleged or suspected abuse or neglect of a child in a public or private school under the jurisdiction of the Texas Education Agency, the department shall perform an investigation as provided by this chapter.

(b) The department shall send a written report of the department's investigation, as appropriate, to the Texas Education Agency, the agency responsible for teacher certification, the local school board or the school's governing body, and the school principal or director, unless the principal or director is alleged to have committed the abuse or neglect, for appropriate action. On request, the department shall provide a copy of the report of investigation to the parent, managing conservator, or legal guardian of a child who is the subject of the investigation and to the person alleged to have committed the abuse or neglect. The report of investigation shall be edited to protect the identity of the persons who made the report of abuse or neglect. Section 261.201(b) applies to the release of confidential information relating to the investigation of a report of abuse or neglect under this section and to the identity of the person who made the report of abuse or neglect.

(c) Nothing in this section may prevent a law enforcement agency from conducting an investigation of a report made under this section.

(d) The Board of Protective and Regulatory Services shall adopt rules necessary to implement this section.

*(Added by L.1995, chap. 751(100); chgd. by L.1997, chap. 575(18); L.1999, chaps. 1150(8), 1390(27), eff. 9/1/99.)*



# CHAPTER 262.
# PROCEDURES IN SUIT BY GOVERNMENTAL ENTITY TO PROTECT HEALTH AND SAFETY OF CHILD

*(Heading chgd. by L.1999, chaps. 1150(9), 1390(28), eff. 9/1/99.)*

*(Selected Sections)*

## SUBCHAPTER A. GENERAL PROVISIONS

Section



## SUBCHAPTER B. TAKING POSSESSION OF CHILD

## SUBCHAPTER A. GENERAL PROVISIONS

### §262.001. Authorized actions by governmental entity.

(a) A governmental entity with an interest in the child may file a suit affecting the parent-child relationship requesting an order or take possession of a child without a court order as provided by this chapter.

(b) In determining the reasonable efforts that are required to be made with respect to preventing or eliminating the need to remove a child from the child's home or to make it possible to return a child to the child's home, the child's health and safety is the paramount concern.
*(Added by L.1995, chap. 20(1); chgd. by L.1999, chaps. 1150(10), 1390(29), eff. 9/1/99.)*

### §262.002. Jurisdiction.

A suit brought by a governmental entity requesting an order under this chapter may be filed in a court with jurisdiction to hear the suit in the county in which the child is found. *(Added by L.1995, chap. 20(1); chgd. by L.1999, chaps. 1150(11), 1390(30), eff. 9/1/99.)*



### §262.003. Civil liability.

A person who takes possession of a child without a court order is immune from civil liability if, at the time possession is taken, there is reasonable cause to believe there is an immediate danger to the physical health or safety of the child. *(Added by L.1995, chap. 20(1), eff. 4/20/95.)*

### §262.004. Accepting voluntary delivery of possession of child.

A law enforcement officer or a juvenile probation officer may take possession of a child without a court order on the voluntary delivery of the child by the parent, managing conservator, possessory conservator, guardian, caretaker, or custodian who is presently entitled to possession of the child. *(Added by L.1995, chap. 20(1), eff. 4/20/95; chgd. by L.1995, chap. 751(101), eff. 9/1/95.)*

### §262.005. Filing petition after accepting voluntary delivery of possession of child.

When possession of the child has been acquired through voluntary delivery of the child to a law enforcement officer or juvenile probation officer, the law enforcement officer or juvenile probation officer taking the child into possession shall cause a suit to be filed not later than the 60th day after the date the child is taken into possession. *(Added by L.1995, chap. 20(1), eff. 4/20/95; chgd. by L. 1995, chap. 751(102), eff. 9/1/95.)*

### §262.006. Living child after abortion.

(a) An authorized representative of the Department of Protective and Regulatory Services may assume the care, control, and custody of a child born alive as the result of an abortion as defined by Chapter 161.

(b) The department shall file a suit and request an emergency order under this chapter.

(c) A child for whom possession is assumed under this section need not be delivered to the court except on the order of the court.
*(Added by L.1995, chap. 20(1), eff. 4/20/95.)*

### §262.007. Possession and delivery of missing child.

(a) A law enforcement officer who, during a criminal investigation relating to a child's custody, discovers that a child is a missing child and believes that a person may flee with or conceal the child shall take possession of the child and provide for the delivery of the child as provided by Subsection (b).

(b) An officer who takes possession of a child under Subsection (a) shall deliver or arrange for the delivery of the child to a person entitled to possession of the child.

(c) If a person entitled to possession of the child is not immediately available to take possession of the child, the law enforcement officer shall deliver the child to the Department of Protective and Regulatory Services. Until a person entitled to possession of the child takes possession of the child, the department may, without a court order, retain possession of the child not longer than five days after the date the child is delivered to the department. While the department retains possession of a child under this subsection, the department may place the child in foster home care. If a parent or other person entitled to possession of the child does not take possession of the child before the sixth day after the date the child is delivered to the department, the department shall proceed under this chapter as if the law enforcement officer took possession of the child under Section 262.104.
*(Added by L.1995, chap. 776(1); chgd. by L.1999, chaps. 685(6), 1150(12), 1390(31), eff. 9/1/99.)*

**§262.008. Abandoned children.**

(a) An authorized representative of the Department of Protective and Regulatory Services may assume the care, control, and custody of a child:

(1) who is abandoned without identification or a means for identifying the child; and

(2) whose identity cannot be ascertained by the exercise of reasonable diligence.

(b) The department shall immediately file a suit to terminate the parent-child relationship of a child under Subsection (a).

(c) A child for whom possession is assumed under this section need not be delivered to the court except on the order of the court.

*(Added by L.1997, chap. 600(4), eff. 1/1/98.)*

**§§262.009 to 262.100.** *(Reserved.)*

## SUBCHAPTER B. TAKING POSSESSION OF CHILD

*(Heading chgd. by L.1999, chaps. 1150(13), 1390(32), eff. 9/1/99.)*



**§262.101. Filing petition before taking possession of child.**

An original suit filed by a governmental entity that requests permission to take possession of a child without prior notice and a hearing must be supported by an affidavit sworn to by a person with personal knowledge and stating facts sufficient to satisfy a person of ordinary prudence and caution that:

(1) there is an immediate danger to the physical health or safety of the child or the child has been a victim of neglect or sexual abuse and that continuation in the home would be contrary to the child's welfare; and

(2) there is no time, consistent with the physical health or safety of the child, for an adversary hearing or to make reasonable efforts to prevent or eliminate the need for the removal of the child.

*(Added by L.1995, chap. 20(1); chgd. by L.1995, chap. 751(103); L.1997, chap. 752(1); L.1999, chaps. 1150(14), 1390(33), eff. 9/1/99.)*

**§262.1015. Removal of alleged perpetrator; offense.**

(a) If the department determines after an investigation that child abuse has occurred and that the child would be protected in the child's home by the removal of the alleged perpetrator of the abuse, the department shall file a petition for the removal of the alleged perpetrator from the residence of the child rather than attempt to remove the child from the residence.

(b) A court may issue a temporary restraining order in a suit by the department for the removal of an alleged perpetrator under Subsection (a) if the department's petition states facts sufficient to satisfy the court that:

(1) there is an immediate danger to the physical health or safety of the child or the child has been a victim of sexual abuse;

(2) there is no time, consistent with the physical health or safety of the child, for an adversary hearing;

(3) the child is not in danger of abuse from a parent or other adult with whom the child will continue to reside in the residence of the child; and

(4) the issuance of the order is in the best interest of the child.

(c) The order shall be served on the alleged perpetrator and on the parent or other adult with whom the child will continue to reside.

(d) A temporary restraining order under this section expires not later than the 14th day after the date the order was rendered.

(e) A temporary restraining order under this section and any other order requiring the removal of an alleged perpetrator from the residence of a child shall require that the parent or other adult with whom the child will continue to reside in the child's home make a reasonable effort to monitor the residence and report to the department and the appropriate law enforcement agency any attempt by the alleged perpetrator to return to the residence.

(f) The court shall order the removal of an alleged perpetrator if the court finds that the child is not in danger of abuse from a parent or other adult with whom the child will continue to reside in the child's residence and that:

(1) the presence of the alleged perpetrator in the child's residence constitutes a continuing danger to the physical health or safety of the child; or

(2) the child has been the victim of sexual abuse and there is a substantial risk that the child will be the victim of sexual abuse in the future if the alleged perpetrator remains in the residence.

(g) A person commits an offense if the person is a parent or other person with whom a child resides, the person is served with an order containing the requirement specified by Subsection (e), and the person fails to make a reasonable effort to monitor the residence of the child or to report to the department and the appropriate law enforcement agency an attempt by the alleged perpetrator to return to the residence. An offense under this section is a Class A misdemeanor.

(h) A person commits an offense if, in violation of a court order under this section, the person returns to the residence of the child the person is alleged to have abused. An offense under this subsection is a Class A misdemeanor, except that the offense is a felony of the third degree if the person has previously been convicted under this subsection.
*(Added by L.1995, chap. 943(4); chgd. by L.1997, chap. 575(19), eff. 9/1/97.)*

## §262.102. Emergency order authorizing possession of child.

(a) Before a court may, without prior notice and a hearing, issue a temporary restraining order or attachment of a child in a suit brought by a governmental entity, the court must find that:

(1) there is an immediate danger to the physical health or safety of the child or the child has been a victim of neglect or sexual abuse and that continuation in the home would be contrary to the child's welfare; and

(2) there is no time, consistent with the physical health or safety of the child and the nature of the emergency, to hold an adversary hearing or to make reasonable efforts to prevent or eliminate the need for removal of the child.

(b) In determining whether there is an immediate danger to the physical health or safety of a child, the court may consider whether the child's household includes a person who has:

(1) abused or neglected another child in a manner that caused serious injury to or the death of the other child; or

(2) sexually abused another child.

(c) If, based on the recommendation of or a request by the department, the court finds that child abuse or neglect has occurred and that the child requires protection from family violence by a member of the child's family or household, the court shall render a temporary order under Chapter 71 for the protection of the child. In this subsection, "family violence" has the meaning assigned by Section 71.01.
*(Added by L.1995, chap. 20(1); chgd. by L.1995, chap. 751(104); L.1997, chap. 752(2); L.1999, chaps. 1150(15), 1390(34), eff. 9/1/99.)*

## §262.103. Duration of temporary restraining order and attachment.

A temporary restraining order or attachment of the child issued under this chapter expires not later than 14 days after the date it is issued unless it is extended as provided by the Texas Rules of Civil Procedure. *(Added by L.1995, chap. 20(1), eff. 4/20/95.)*

## §262.104. Taking possession of a child in emergency without a court order.

If there is no time to obtain a temporary restraining order or attachment before taking possession of a child consistent with the health and safety of that child, an authorized representative of the Department of Protective and Regulatory Services, a law enforcement officer, or a juvenile probation officer may take possession of a child without a court order under the following conditions, only:

(1) on personal knowledge of facts that would lead a person of ordinary prudence and caution to believe that there is an immediate danger to the physical health or safety of the child;

(2) on information furnished by another that has been corroborated by personal knowledge of facts and all of which taken together would lead a person of ordinary prudence and caution to believe that there is an immediate danger to the physical health or safety of the child;

(3) on personal knowledge of facts that would lead a person of ordinary prudence and caution to believe that the child has been the victim of sexual abuse;

(4) on information furnished by another that has been corroborated by personal knowledge of facts and all of which taken together would lead a person of ordinary prudence and caution to believe that the child has been the victim of sexual abuse; or

(5) on information furnished by another that has been corroborated by personal knowledge of facts and all of which taken together would lead a person of ordinary prudence and caution to believe that the parent or person who has possession of the child is currently using a controlled substance as defined by Chapter 481, Health and Safety Code, and the use constitutes an immediate danger to the physical health or safety of the child.
*(Added by L.1995, chap. 20(1); chgd. by L.1997, chap. 575(20), eff. 9/1/97.)*

### §262.105. Filing petition after taking possession of child in emergency.

When a child is taken into possession without a court order, the person taking the child into possession, without unnecessary delay, shall:

(1) file a suit affecting the parent-child relationship;

(2) request the court to appoint an attorney ad litem for the child; and

(3) request an initial hearing to be held by no later than the first working day after the date the child is taken into possession.

*(Added by L.1995, chap. 20(1), eff. 4/20/95.)*

### §262.106. Initial hearing after taking possession of child in emergency without court order.

(a) The court in which a suit has been filed after a child has been taken into possession without a court order by a governmental entity shall hold an initial hearing on or before the first working day after the date the child is taken into possession. The court shall render orders that are necessary to protect the physical health and safety of the child. If the court is unavailable for a hearing on the first working day, then, and only in that event, the hearing shall be held no later than the first working day after the court becomes available, provided that the hearing is held no later than the third working day after the child is taken into possession.

(b) The initial hearing may be ex parte and proof may be by sworn petition or affidavit if a full adversary hearing is not practicable.

(c) If the initial hearing is not held within the time required, the child shall be returned to the parent, managing conservator, possessory conservator, guardian, caretaker, or custodian who is presently entitled to possession of the child.

(d) For the purpose of determining under Subsection (a) the first working day after the date the child is taken into possession, the child is considered to have been taken into possession by the Department of Protective and Regulatory Services on the expiration of the five-day period permitted under Section 262.007(c) or 262.110(b), as appropriate.

*(Added by L.1995, chap. 20(1); chgd. by L.1999, chaps. 1150(16), 1390(35), eff. 9/1/99.)*

### §262.107. Standard for decision at initial hearing after taking possession of child without a court order in emergency.

(a) The court shall order the return of the child at the initial hearing regarding a child taken in possession without a court order by a governmental entity unless the court is satisfied that:

(1) there is a continuing danger to the physical health or safety of the child if the child is returned to the parent, managing conservator, possessory conservator, guardian, caretaker, or custodian who is presently entitled to possession of the child or the evidence shows that the child has been the victim of sexual abuse on one or more occasions and that there is a substantial risk that the child will be the victim of sexual abuse in the future; and

(2) the nature of the emergency and the continuing danger to the welfare of the child make efforts to allow the child to remain with or return to the person entitled to possession of the child impossible or unreasonable.

(b) In determining whether there is a continuing danger to the physical health or safety of a child, the court may consider whether the household to which the child would be returned includes a person who has:

(1) abused or neglected another child in a manner that caused serious injury to or the death of the other child; or

(2) sexually abused another child.

*(Added by L.1995, chap. 20(1), eff. 4/20/95; chgd. by L.1995, chap. 751(105), eff. 9/1/95.)*

### §262.108. Unacceptable facilities for housing child.

When a child is taken into possession under this chapter, that child may not be held in isolation or in a jail, juvenile detention facility, or other secure detention facility. *(Added by L.1995, chap. 20(1); chgd. by L.1997, chap. 1374(9), eff. 9/1/97.)*

### §262.109. Notice to parent, conservator, or guardian.

(a) The department or other agency must give written notice as prescribed by this section to each parent of the child or to the child's conservator or legal guardian when a representative of the Department of Protective and Regulatory Services or other agency takes possession of a child under this chapter.

(b) The written notice must be given as soon as practicable, but in any event not later than the first working day after the date the child is taken into possession.

(c) The written notice must include:

(1) the reasons why the department or agency is taking possession of the child and the facts that led the department to believe that the child should be taken into custody;

(2) the name of the person at the department or agency that the parent, conservator, or other custodian may contact for information relating to the child or a legal proceeding relating to the child;

(3) a summary of legal rights of a parent, conservator, guardian, or other custodian under this chapter and an explanation of the probable legal procedures relating to the child; and

(4) a statement that the parent, conservator, or other custodian has the right to hire an attorney.

(d) The written notice may be waived by the court at the initial hearing:

(1) on a showing that the parents, conservators, or other custodians of the child could not be located; or

(2) for other good cause.

*(Added by L.1995, chap. 20(1); chgd. by L.1997, chap. 1022(76); L.1999, chaps. 1150(17), 1390(36), eff. 9/1/99.)*



**§262.110. Taking possession of child in emergency with intent to return home.**

(a) An authorized representative of the Department of Protective and Regulatory Services, a law enforcement officer, or a juvenile probation officer may take temporary possession of a child without a court order on discovery of a child in a situation of danger to the child's physical health or safety when the sole purpose is to deliver the child without unnecessary delay to the parent, managing conservator, possessory conservator, guardian, caretaker, or custodian who is presently entitled to possession of the child.

(b) Until a parent or other person entitled to possession of the child takes possession of the child, the department may retain possession of the child without a court order for not more than five days. On the expiration of the fifth day, if a parent or other person entitled to possession does not take possession of the child, the department shall take action under this chapter as if the department took possession of the child under Section 262.104.

*(Added by L.1995, chap. 20(1); chgd. by L.1999, chaps. 1150(18), 1390(37), eff. 9/1/99.)*

**§262.111. Finding that child cannot remain in or be returned to home.**

In the absence of a specific finding to the contrary, the issuance of a temporary restraining order or attachment pending a full adversary hearing or the issuance of an order after a full adversary hearing constitutes a finding by the court that for the child to remain in the home is contrary to the child's welfare or safety and that the emergency made efforts to prevent or eliminate the need for the removal of the child impossible or unreasonable. *(Added by L.1995, chap. 751(106), eff. 9/1/95.)*

**§262.112. Expedited hearing and appeal.**

(a) The Department of Protective and Regulatory Services is entitled to an expedited hearing under this chapter in any proceeding in which a hearing is required if the department determines that a child should be removed from the child's home because of an immediate danger to the physical health of safety of the child.

(b) In any proceeding in which an expedited hearing is held under Subsection (a), the department, parent, guardian, or other party to the proceeding is entitled to an expedited appeal on a ruling by a court that the child may not be removed from the child's home.

(c) If a child is returned to the child's home after a removal in which the department was entitled to an expedited hearing under this section and the child is the subject of a subsequent allegation of abuse or neglect, the department or any other interested party is entitled to an expedited hearing on the removal of the child from the child's home in the manner provided by Subsection (a) and to an expedited appeal in the manner provided by Subsection (b).

*(Renunbered from section 262.111 by L.1997, chap. 165(31.01(20)), eff. 9/1/97.)*

**§262.113. Filing suit without taking possession of child.**

An original suit filed by a governmental entity that requests to take possession of a child after notice and a hearing must be supported by an affidavit sworn to by a person with personal knowledge and stating facts sufficient to satisfy a person of ordinary prudence and caution that:

(1) reasonable efforts have been made to prevent or eliminate the need to remove the child from the child's home; and

(2) allowing the child to remain in the home would be contrary to the child's welfare.

*(Added by L.1999, chaps. 1150(19), 1390(38), eff. 9/1/99.)*

**§§262.114 to 262.200.** *(Reserved.)*

# CHAPTER 264. CHILD WELFARE SERVICES
*(Selected Section)*

## SUBCHAPTER F. CHILD FATALITY REVIEW AND INVESTIGATION*

## SUBCHAPTER F. CHILD FATALITY REVIEW*


**Two subchapter headings created by separate amendments. See text for citation.*

## SUBCHAPTER F. CHILD FATALITY REVIEW AND INVESTIGATION
*(Added by L.1995, chap. 255(2), eff. 9/1/95.*
*See other subchapter F heading below.)*

## SUBCHAPTER F. CHILD FATALITY REVIEW
*(Added by L.1995, chap. 878(1), eff. 9/1/95.*
*See other subchapter F heading above.)*

### §264.513. Report of death of child.

(a) A person who knows of the death of a child younger than six years of age shall immediately report the death to the medical examiner of the county in which the death occurs or, if the death occurs in a county that does not have a medical examiner's office or that is not part of a medical examiner's district, to a justice of the peace in that county.

(b) The requirement of this section is in addition to any other reporting requirement imposed by law, including any requirement that a person report child abuse or neglect under this code.

(c) A person is not required to report a death under this section that is the result of a motor vehicle accident. This subsection does not affect a duty imposed by another law to report a death that is the result of a motor vehicle accident.

*(Added by L.1995, chaps. 255(2), 878(1), eff. 9/1/95.)*

# FINANCE CODE

# TITLE 5. PROTECTION OF CONSUMERS OF FINANCIAL SERVICES

## CHAPTER 391. FURNISHING FALSE CREDIT INFORMATION

*(Added by L.1997, chap. 1008(1), eff. 9/1/97.)*



### §391.001. Definition.

In this chapter, "credit reporting bureau" means a person who engages in the practice of assembling or reporting credit information about individuals for the purpose of furnishing the information to a third party. (C.S. Art. 9016, Sec. 1). *(Added by L.1997, chap. 1008(1), eff. 9/1/97.)*

### §391.002. Furnishing false information; penalty.

(a) A person commits an offense if the person knowingly furnishes false information about another person's creditworthiness, credit standing, or credit capacity to a credit reporting bureau.

(b) A credit reporting bureau commits an offense if the credit reporting bureau knowingly furnishes false information about a person's creditworthiness, credit standing, or credit capacity to a third party.

(c) An offense under this section is a misdemeanor punishable by a fine of not more than $200. (C.S. Art. 9016, Secs. 2, 3.).
*(Added by L.1997, chap. 1008(1), eff. 9/1/97.)*

This page intentionally left blank.

# GOVERNMENT CODE

## TITLE 2. JUDICIAL BRANCH

## CHAPTER 27. JUSTICE COURTS
*(Selected Section)*



### §27.031. Jurisdiction.

(a) In addition to the jurisdiction and powers provided by the constitution and other law, the justice court has original jurisdiction of:

(1) civil matters in which the exclusive jurisdiction is not in the district or county court and in which the amount in controversy is not more than $5,000, exclusive of interest;

(2) cases of forcible entry and detainer; and

(3) foreclosure of mortgages and enforcement of liens on personal property in cases in which the amount in controversy is otherwise within the justice court's jurisdiction.

(b) A justice court does not have jurisdiction of:

(1) a suit in behalf of the state to recover a penalty, forfeiture, or escheat;

(2) a suit for divorce;

(3) a suit to recover damages for slander or defamation of character;

(4) a suit for trial of title to land; or

(5) a suit for the enforcement of a lien on land.

*(Chgd. by L.1991, chap. 776(2), eff. 9/1/91.)*



## CHAPTER 28. SMALL CLAIMS COURTS
*(Selected Section)*



### §28.003. Jurisdiction.

(a) The small claims court has concurrent jurisdiction with the justice court in actions by any person for the recovery of money in which the amount involved, exclusive of costs, does not exceed $5,000.

(b) An action may not be brought in small claims court by:

(1) an assignee of the claim or other person seeking to bring an action on an assigned claim;

(2) a person primarily engaged in the business of lending money at interest; or

(3) a collection agency or collection agent.

(c) A person may be represented by an attorney in small claims court.

(d) This section does not prevent a legal heir from bringing an action on a claim or account otherwise within the jurisdiction of the court.

(e) A corporation need not be represented by an attorney in small claims court.

*(Chgd. by L.1989, chaps. 501(1), 802(4),(5); L.1991, chap. 776(4), eff. 9/1/91.)*

## CHAPTER 29. MUNICIPAL COURTS

## SUBCHAPTER A. GENERAL PROVISIONS

## SUBCHAPTER B. MUNICIPAL COURTS IN CERTAIN CITIES





## SUBCHAPTER A. GENERAL PROVISIONS

### §29.001. Definition.† [*"Municipality" defined.*]

In this chapter, "municipality" means an incorporated city, town, or village.

### §29.002. Creation.† [*Municipal court; creation.*]

A municipal court is created in each municipality. A reference in state law to a "corporation court" means a "municipal court."

### §29.003. Jurisdiction.

(a) A municipal court, including a municipal court of record, shall have exclusive original jurisdiction within the municipality's territorial limits and property owned by the municipality located in the municipality's extraterritorial jurisdiction in all criminal cases that:

(1) arise under:

(A) the ordinances of the municipality; or

(B) a resolution, rule, or order of a joint board operating an airport under Section 22.074, Transportation Code; and

(2) are punishable by a fine not to exceed:

(A) $2,000 in all cases arising under municipal ordinances or resolutions, rules, or orders of a joint board that govern fire safety, zoning, or public health and sanitation, including dumping of refuse; or

(B) $500 in all other cases arising under a municipal ordinance or a resolution, rule, or order of a joint board.

(b) The municipal court has concurrent jurisdiction with the justice court of a precinct in which the municipality is located in all criminal cases arising under state law that:

(1) arise within the municipality's territorial limits or property owned by the municipality located in the municipality's extraterritorial jurisdiction and are punishable only by a fine, as defined in Subsection (c); or

(2) arise under Chapter 106, Alcoholic Beverage Code, and do not include confinement as an authorized sanction.

(c) In this section, an offense which is punishable by "fine only" is defined as an offense that is punishable by fine and such sanctions, if any, as authorized by statute not consisting of confinement in jail or imprisonment.

(d) The fact that a conviction in a municipal court has as a consequence the imposition of a penalty or sanction by an agency or entity other than the court, such as a denial, suspension, or revocation of a privilege, does not affect the original jurisdiction of the municipal court.

(e) The municipal court has jurisdiction in the forfeiture and final judgment of all bail bonds and personal bonds taken in criminal cases of which the court has jurisdiction.

(f) This section does not affect the powers given exclusively to a joint board operating an airport under Section 22.074(d), Transportation Code.

*(Chgd. by L.1991, chap. 108(7); L.1995, chap. 449(2); L.1997, chaps. 533(3), 1013(40); L.1999, chaps. 611(1), 660(1), eff. 9/1/99, 6/18/99, respectively.)*

**§29.004. Judge.† [*Selection; commencement of term; judge of the municipal court.*]**

(a) The judge and alternate judges of the municipal court in a home-rule city are selected under the municipality's charter provisions relating to the election or appointment of judges. The judge shall be known as the "judge of the municipal court" unless the municipality by charter provides for another title.

(b) In a general-law city, the mayor is ex officio judge of the municipal court unless the municipality by ordinance authorizes the election of the judge or provides for the appointment and qualifications of the judge. If the municipality authorizes an election, the judge shall be elected in the manner and for the same term as the mayor. If the municipality authorizes the appointment, the mayor ceases to be judge on the enactment of the ordinance. The first elected or appointed judge serves until the expiration of the mayor's term.

(c) If a general-law municipality changes the method of judicial selection from election to appointment, the first appointee takes office on the expiration of the term of the previously elected judge.

(d) A reference in the laws of this state to a "recorder" means a "judge of the municipal court."



**§29.005. Term of office.**

The judge of a municipal court serves for a term of office of two years unless the municipality provides for a longer term pursuant to Article XI, Section 11, of the Texas Constitution. A municipal court judge who is not reappointed by the 91st day following the expiration of a term of office shall, absent action by the appointing authority, continue to serve for another term of office beginning on the date the previous term of office expired. *(Chgd. by L.1993, chap 764(1), eff. 1/1/94.)*

**§29.006. Temporary replacement in general-law municipalities.† [*Temporary replacement; municipal court judge.*]**

If a municipal judge of a municipality incorporated under the general laws of this state is temporarily unable to act, the governing body may appoint one or more persons meeting the qualifications for the position to sit for the regular municipal judge. The appointee has all powers and duties of the office and is entitled to compensation set by the governing body.

**§29.007. Municipal court panels or divisions; temporary judges.† [*Panels, divisions; municipal court.*]**

(a) A home-rule city by charter or by ordinance may divide the municipal court into two or more panels or divisions, one of which shall be presided over by a presiding judge. Each additional panel or division shall be presided over by an associate judge, who is a magistrate with the same powers as the presiding judge.

(b) The panels or divisions may hold concurrent or continuous sessions either day or night.

(c) Each panel or division may exercise municipal court jurisdiction and has concurrent jurisdiction with the other panels or divisions.

(d) Except as otherwise provided by the charter, the municipality by ordinance may establish:

(1) the qualifications for appointment as a judge;

(2) the ability of a judge to transfer cases, exchange benches, and preside over any of the panels or divisions;

(3) the office of the municipal court clerk, who shall serve as clerk of all the panels or divisions with the assistance of deputy clerks as needed; and

(4) a system for the filing of complaints with the municipal court clerk so that the case load is equally distributed among the panels or divisions.

(e) Except as modified by this section, procedure before a panel or division and appeal from the decision of a panel or division is governed by general law applicable to municipal courts.

(f) If the municipality has established the office of municipal court clerk, the clerk shall keep minutes of the proceedings of the municipal court and its panels or divisions, administer oaths, issue process, and generally perform the duties for the municipal court that a county clerk performs for a county court.

(g) The municipality may provide by character or by ordinance for the appointment of one or more temporary judges to serve if the regular judge, the presiding judge, or an associate judge is temporarily unable to act. A temporary judge must have the same qualifications as the judge he replaces and has the same powers and duties as that judge.

**§§29.008, 29.009.** *(Repealed.)*

### §29.010. Clerk.† [*Municipal court clerk.*]

(a) In a municipality that provides for the election of a municipal judge, the municipal court clerk is elected in the same manner unless by ordinance the city secretary serves as clerk. A city secretary who serves as clerk may be authorized to appoint a deputy clerk.

(b) The clerk serves a two-year term of office unless the municipality provides for a longer term pursuant to Article XI, Section 11, of the Texas Constitution. If the city secretary serves as clerk, that person serves as clerk during the term as city secretary.

(c) The clerk shall keep minutes of the proceedings of the court, issue process, and generally perform the duties for the municipal court that a county clerk performs for a county court.

(d) Subsection (a) does not apply to a home-rule municipality that provides by charter for the appointment of the clerk.

*(Chgd. by L.1991, chap. 774(1), eff. 9/1/91.)*

### §29.011. Vacancy.† [*Vacancies filled; balance of term only.*]

The governing body of the municipality shall by appointment fill a vacancy in the office of municipal judge or clerk for the remainder of the unexpired term of office only.

### §29.012. Sitting for disqualified or recused judge.

(a) If the judge of a municipal court is disqualified or recused in a pending case, the judge of another municipal court located in an adjacent municipality may sit in the case.

(b) A municipal court judge may not sit in a case for another municipal court judge under this section if either party objects to the judge. An objection under this subsection must be filed before the first hearing or trial, including pretrial hearings, over which the judge is to preside.

*(Added by L.1999, chap. 912(1), eff. 9/1/99.)*



## SUBCHAPTER B. MUNICIPAL COURTS IN CERTAIN CITIES

### §29.101. Municipality of more than 250,000.† [*Population of more than 250,000.*]

(a) A municipality with a population of more than 250,000 may by ordinance establish two municipal courts. With the confirmation of the governing body of the municipality, the mayor may appoint two or more judges for the courts and may designate the seniority of the judges.

(b) Either or both of the courts may hold concurrent or continuous sessions either day or night.

(c) Each court may exercise municipal court jurisdiction and has concurrent jurisdiction with the other municipal courts.

(d) The municipality by ordinance may establish:

(1) the qualifications for appointment as a municipal judge;

(2) the ability of a judge to transfer cases, exchange benches, and preside over any of the municipal courts;

(3) the office of the municipal court clerk, who shall serve as clerk of all the municipal courts with the assistance of deputy clerks as needed; and

(4) a system for the filing of complaints with the municipal court clerk so that the case load is equally distributed among the courts.

(e) Except as modified by this section, procedure before each of the courts and appeal from a decision of either of the courts are governed by general law applicable to municipal courts.

(f) This section supersedes any municipal charter provision that conflicts with this section.

### §29.102. Municipality of 130,001 to 285,000.† [*Population between 130,001 and 285,000.*]

(a) An incorporated municipality with a population of 130,001 to 285,000 by ordinance may establish up to four additional municipal courts. The judge of each additional court must meet the same qualifications and be selected in the same manner as provided in the city charter for the judges of the existing municipal courts. If the charter provides for the election of municipal judges, the governing body of the municipality may appoint a person to serve as judge in each newly created court until the next regular city election.

(b) The courts may hold concurrent or continuous sessions either day or night.

(c) Each court may exercise municipal court jurisdiction and has concurrent jurisdiction with the other municipal courts.

(d) Except as otherwise provided by the charter, the governing body by ordinance may establish:

(1) the qualifications for appointment as a municipal judge;

(2) the ability of a judge to transfer cases, exchange benches, and preside over any of the municipal courts;

(3) the office of the municipal court clerk, who shall serve as clerk of all the municipal courts with the assistance of deputy clerks as needed; and

(4) a system for the filing of complaints with the municipal court clerk so that the case load is equally distributed among the courts.

(e) Except as modified by this section, procedure before each of the courts and appeal from a decision of any of the courts are governed by general law applicable to municipal courts.

### §29.103. Municipal courts in El Paso.† [*El Paso; municipal courts.*]

(a) The City of El Paso by ordinance may establish additional municipal courts as needed. The judge of each additional court must meet the same qualifications and be selected in the same manner as provided in the city charter for the judges of the existing municipal courts. If the charter provides for the election of municipal judges, the governing body of the municipality may appoint a person to serve as judge in each newly created court until the next regular city election.

(b) The courts may hold concurrent or continuous sessions either day or night.

(c) Each court may exercise municipal court jurisdiction and has concurrent jurisdiction with the other municipal courts.

(d) Except as otherwise provided by the charter, the governing body may by ordinance establish:

(1) the qualifications for appointment as a municipal judge;

(2) the ability of a judge to transfer cases, exchange benches, and preside over any of the municipal courts;

(3) the office of the municipal court clerk, who shall serve as clerk of all the municipal courts with the assistance of deputy clerks as needed; and

(4) a system for the filing of complaints with the municipal court clerk so that the case load is equally distributed among the courts.

(e) Except as modified by this section, procedure before each of the courts and appeal from a decision of any of the courts are governed by general law applicable to municipal courts.

### §29.104. Municipal court proceeding outside corporate limits.† [*Population of 700 or less; municipal court in adjacent municipality.*]

The municipal court of a municipality with a population of 700 or less may conduct its proceedings within the corporate limits of a contiguous incorporated municipality.

### §29.105. Municipal court proceedings in municipality participating in police department contract.

A municipality that contracts with one or more municipalities for the operation of a joint police department may conduct its municipal court proceedings within the municipal limits of any municipality that is a party to the contract. *(Added by L.1995, chap. 741(1), eff. 6/15/95.)*

# SUBTITLE E. JURIES

## CHAPTER 62. PETIT JURIES

## SUBCHAPTER A. GENERAL PROVISIONS
*(Selected Section)*

Section



### §62.001. Jury source; reconstitution of jury wheel.

(a) The jury wheel must be reconstituted by using, as the source:

(1) the names of all persons on the current voter registration lists from all the precincts in the county; and

(2) all names on a current list to be furnished by the Department of Public Safety, showing the citizens of the county who:

(A) hold a valid Texas driver's license or a valid personal identification card or certificate issued by the department; and

(B) are not disqualified from jury service under Section 62.102(1), (2), or (7).

(b) Notwithstanding Subsection (a), the names of persons listed on a register of persons exempt from jury service may not be placed in the jury wheel, as provided by Sections 62.108 and 62.109.

(c) Each year not later than the third Tuesday in November or the date provided by Section 16.032, Election Code, for the cancellation of voter registrations, whichever is earlier, the voter registrar of each county shall furnish to the secretary of state a current voter registration list from all the precincts in the county that, except as provided by Subsection (d), includes:

(1) the complete name, mailing address, date of birth, voter registration number, and precinct number for each voter;

(2) if available, the Texas driver's license number or personal identification card or certificate number and social security number for each voter; and

(3) any other information included on the voter registration list of the county.

(d) The list required by Subsection (c) may exclude, at the option of the voter registrar of each county, the names of persons on the suspense list maintained under Section 15.081, Election Code.

(e) The voter registrar shall send a list of the names of persons excluded to the secretary of state with the list required by Subsection (c).

(f) The Department of Public Safety shall furnish a list to the secretary of state that shows the names required under Subsection (a)(2) and that contains any of the information enumerated in Subsection (c) that is available to the department, including citizenship status and county of residence. The list shall exclude the names of convicted felons, persons who are not citizens of the United States, persons residing outside the county, and the duplicate name of any registrant. The department shall furnish the list to the secretary of state on or before the first Monday in October of each year.

(g) The secretary of state shall accept the lists furnished as provided by Subsections (c) through (f). The secretary of state shall combine the lists, eliminate duplicate names, and send the combined list to each county on or before December 31 of each year or as may be required under a plan developed in accordance with Section 62.011. The district clerk of a county that has adopted a plan under Section 62.011 shall give the secretary of state notice not later than the 90th day before the date the list is required. The list furnished the county must be in a format, electronic or printed copy, as requested by the county and must be certified by the secretary of state stating that the list contains the names required by Subsections (c) through (f), eliminating duplications. The secretary of state shall furnish the list free of charge.

(h) If the secretary of state is unable to furnish the list as provided in this section because of the failure of the voter registrar to furnish the county voter registration list to the secretary of state, the county tax assessor-collector, sheriff, county clerk, and district clerk in the county shall meet at the county courthouse between January 1 and January 15 of the following year and shall reconstitute the jury wheel for the county, except as provided under a plan adopted under Section 62.011. The deadlines included in the plan control for preparing the list and reconstituting the wheel. The secretary of state shall send the list furnished by the Department of Public Safety as provided by Subsection (f) to the voter registrar, who shall combine the lists as described in this section for use as the juror source and certify the combined list as required of the secretary of state under Subsection (g).

(i) The commissioners court may, instead of using the method provided by Subsections (c) through (h), contract with another governmental unit or a private person to combine the voter registration list with the list furnished by the Department of Public Safety. Subsections (c) through (h) do not apply to a county in which the commissioners court has contracted with another governmental unit or a private person under this subsection. The Department of Public Safety may not charge a fee for furnishing a list under this subsection. Each list must contain the name, date of birth, address, county of residence, and citizenship status of each person listed. If practical, each list must contain any other information useful in determining if the person is qualified to serve as a juror.

(j) Notwithstanding Subsection (a), in a county with a population of 250,000 or more, the names of persons who are summoned for jury service in the county and who appear for service must be removed from the jury wheel and may not be maintained in the jury wheel until the third anniversary of the date the person appeared for service or until the next date the jury wheel is reconstituted, whichever date occurs earlier. This subsection applies regardless of whether the person served on a jury as a result of the summons.

*(Chgd. by L.1999, chap. 640(1), eff. 9/1/99.)*

# CHAPTER 76. COMMUNITY SUPERVISION AND CORRECTIONS DEPARTMENTS

*(Added by L.1995, chap. 76(7.11), eff. 9/1/95.)*



## §76.001. Definitions.

In this chapter:

(1) "Board" means the Texas Board of Criminal Justice.

(2) "Community supervision" has the meaning assigned by Section 2, Article 42.12, Code of Criminal Procedure.

(3) "Council" means a community justice council.

(4) "Department" means a community supervision and corrections department established under this chapter.

(5) "Division" means the community justice assistance division of the Texas Department of Criminal Justice.

*(Added by L.1995, chap. 76(7.11), eff. 9/1/95.)*

## §76.002. Establishment of departments.

(a) The district judge or district judges trying criminal cases in each judicial district shall:

(1) establish a community supervision and corrections department; and

(2) employ district personnel as necessary to conduct presentence investigations, supervise and rehabilitate defendants placed on community supervision, enforce the conditions of community supervision, and staff community corrections facilities.

(b) The district judges trying criminal cases and judges of statutory county courts trying criminal cases that are served by a community supervision and corrections department are entitled to participate in the management of the department.

(c) Except as provided by Subsection (d), one department serves all courts and counties in a judicial district if:

(1) two or more judicial districts serve a county; or

(2) a district includes more than one county.

(d) The board may adopt rules to allow more than one department to serve a judicial district that includes more than one county if providing more than one department will promote administrative convenience or economy or improve services.

(e) The board may adopt rules allowing departments to contract with one another for services or facilities.

*(Added by L.1995, chap. 76(7.11), eff. 9/1/95.)*

## §76.003. Community justice council.

(a) A community justice council must be established by the district judge or district judges in each jurisdiction served by a department, unless a board or council that was in existence on September 1, 1991, is performing duties substantially similar to those imposed on a community justice council under this section. The council shall provide continuing policy guidance and direction for the development of community justice plans and community corrections facilities and programs.

(b) A council should consist of the following persons or their designees:

(1) a sheriff of a county served by the department, chosen by the sheriffs of the counties to be served by the department;

(2) a county commissioner or a county judge from a county served by the department, chosen by the county commissioners and county judges of the counties served by the department;

(3) a city council member of the most populous municipality in a county served by the department, chosen by the members of the city councils of cities served by the department;

(4) not more than two state legislators elected from a county served by the department, or in a county with a population of one million or more to be served by the department, not more than one state senator and one state representative elected from the county, chosen by the state legislators elected from the county or counties served by the department;

(5) the presiding judge from a judicial district served by the department, chosen by the district judges from the judicial districts served by the department;

(6) a judge of a statutory county court exercising criminal jurisdiction in a county served by the department, chosen by the judges of statutory county courts with criminal jurisdiction in the counties served by the department;

(7) a county attorney with criminal jurisdiction from a county served by the department, chosen by the county attorneys with criminal jurisdiction from the counties served by the department;

(8) a district attorney or criminal district attorney from a judicial district served by the department, chosen by the district attorneys or criminal district attorneys from the judicial districts served by the department; and

(9) an elected member of the board of trustees of an independent school district in a county served by the department, chosen by the members of the boards of trustees of independent school districts located in counties served by the department.

(c) The community justice council shall appoint a community justice task force to provide support staff for the development of a community justice plan. The task force may consist of any number of members, but should include:

(1) the county or regional director of the Texas Department of Human Services with responsibility for the area served by the department;

(2) the chief of police of the most populous municipality served by the department;

(3) the chief juvenile probation officer of the juvenile probation office serving the most populous area served by the department;

(4) the superintendent of the most populous school district served by the department;

(5) the supervisor of the Department of Public Safety region closest to the department, or the supervisor's designee;

(6) the county or regional director of the Texas Department of Mental Health and Mental Retardation with responsibility for the area served by the department;

(7) a substance abuse treatment professional appointed by the Council of Governments serving the area served by the department;

(8) the department director;

(9) the local or regional representative of the pardons and paroles division of the Texas Department of Criminal Justice with responsibility for the area served by the department;

(10) the representative of the Texas Workforce Commission with responsibility for the area served by the department;

(11) the representative of the Texas Rehabilitation Commission with responsibility for the area served by the department;

(12) a licensed attorney who practices in the area served by the department and whose practice consists primarily of criminal law;

(13) a court administrator, if one serves the area served by the department;

(14) a representative of a community service organization that provides adult treatment, educational, or vocational services to the area served by the department;

(15) a representative of an organization in the area served by the department that is actively involved in issues relating to defendants' rights, chosen by the county commissioners and county judges of the counties served by the department; and

(16) an advocate for rights of victims of crime and awareness of issues affecting victims.

*(Added by L.1995, chap. 76(7.11); chgd. by L.1997, chaps. 165(9.02(a)), (9.03(a)), eff. 9/1/97.)*

## §76.004. Department director.

(a) The district judge or judges shall appoint a department director who must meet, at a minimum, the eligibility requirements for officers established under Section 76.005.

(b) The department director shall employ a sufficient number of officers and other employees to perform the professional and clerical work of the department.

*(Added by L.1995, chap. 76(7.11), eff. 9/1/95.)*

### §76.005. Standards for officers.

(a) An officer appointed by the department director must comply with a code of ethics developed by the division.

(b) To be eligible for appointment as an officer who supervises defendants placed on community supervision a person must have acquired a bachelor's degree conferred by an institution of higher education accredited by an accrediting organization recognized by the Texas Higher Education Coordinating Board.

(c) A person employed as a peace officer is not eligible for appointment as an officer under this section.

(d) The division may establish a waiver procedure for departments unable to hire persons meeting the requirements under Subsection (b)(2).

*(Added by L.1995, chap. 76(7.11); chgd. by L.1997, chap. 108(1), eff. 5/15/97.)*

### §76.0051. Authorization to carry weapon.

An officer is authorized to carry a weapon while engaged in the actual discharge of the officer's duties only if:

(1) the officer possesses a certificate of firearms proficiency issued by the Commission on Law Enforcement Officer Standards and Education under Section 415.038; and

(2) the director of the department and the judges participating in the management of the department agree to the authorization.

*(Added by L.1997, chap. 1261(29), eff. 9/1/97.)*

### §76.006. Employee status and benefits.

(a) Except as provided by Subsection (c), department employees are not state employees. The department shall contract for all employee benefits with one county served by the department and designated for that purpose by the district judge or judges, and the employees are governed by personnel policies and benefits equal to personnel policies for and benefits of other employees of that county.

(b) The judicial districts served by a department shall pay the salaries of department employees.

(c) Department employees are state employees for the purposes of Chapter 104, Civil Practice and Remedies Code, and Chapter 501, Labor Code.

(d) The attorney general has the duty to defend a department for suits for injunctive, declaratory, or monetary relief brought against it for any action not covered by an indemnification policy, except any action brought by the state or another political subdivision. The attorney general shall not defend a department or its employees in cases in which a person under supervision challenges the fact or duration of the supervision.

(e) The department shall provide information requested by the attorney general that the attorney general considers necessary for the defense or prosecution of any case brought under this section.

(f) The department shall provide transportation or automobile allowances for officers who supervise defendants placed on community supervision.

(g) A document evaluating the performance of an officer of the department who supervises defendants placed on community supervision is confidential.

(h) If under Subsection (a) the district judge or judges change the designation of the county providing employee benefits, the district judge or judges may not subsequently change that designation before the 10th anniversary of the date on which the previous designation was made.

*(Added by L.1995, chap. 76(7.11); chgd. by L.1997, chaps. 987(1), 1240(1); L.1999, chaps. 62(19.01)(29), 875(1), eff. 9/1/99, 6/18/99, respectively.)*

### §76.007. Public funds, grants, and gifts.

A department may accept public funds and grants and gifts from any source for the purpose of financing programs and facilities. A municipality, county, or other political subdivision may make grants to a department for those purposes. *(Added by L.1995, chap. 76(7.11), eff. 9/1/95.)*

### §76.008. Financial responsibilities of counties.

(a) The county or counties served by a department shall provide physical facilities, equipment, and utilities for a department. The division shall monitor the support a county provides under this section and determine whether a county provides support that meets the standards for minimum support established by the division. If the division determines that a county's support is insufficient, the division may impose on the department a sanction authorized by Section 509.012.

(b) If a department serves two or more counties, those counties may enter into an agreement for the distribution of the expenses of facilities, equipment, and utilities.
*(Added by L.1995, chap. 76(7.11), eff. 9/1/95.)*

### §76.009. Financial responsibilities of districts.

(a) The district judge or judges may expend district funds in order to provide expanded facilities, equipment, and utilities if:

(1) the department needs to increase its personnel in order to provide more effective services or to meet workload requirements established under Chapter 509;

(2) the county or counties certify to the judge or judges that they have neither adequate space in county-owned buildings nor adequate funds to lease additional physical facilities, purchase additional equipment, or pay for additional utilities required by the department; and

(3) the county or counties provide facilities, equipment, and utilities at or above the levels required by the division.

(b) The division shall set as the level of contribution a county or counties must meet or exceed to receive district funds under Subsection (a) a level not lower than the average level provided by the county or counties during the fiscal year in which the funds are to be received and the four fiscal years immediately preceding that year.
*(Added by L.1995, chap. 76(7.11), eff. 9/1/95.)*

### §76.010. State funds or guarantees for corrections facilities.

(a) In this section:

(1) "Community corrections facility" has the meaning assigned by Section 509.001.

(2) "State jail felony facility" means a facility operated or contracted for by the state jail division of the Texas Department of Criminal Justice under Subchapter A, Chapter 507.

(b) A department, county, municipality, or a combination involving more than one of those entities may establish a community corrections facility and are specifically encouraged to purchase or enter into a contract for the use of abandoned or underutilized public facilities, such as former military bases and rural hospitals, for the purpose of providing community corrections facilities.

(c) The district judge or judges may authorize expenditures of funds provided by the division to the department for the purposes of providing facilities, equipment, and utilities for community corrections facilities or state jail felony facilities if:

(1) the community justice council recommends the expenditures; and

(2) the division, or the state jail division in the case of a state jail felony facility, provides funds for the purpose of assisting in the establishment or improvement of the facilities.

(d) A department may acquire, hold title to, and own real property for the purpose of establishing a community corrections facility or a state jail felony facility.

(e) A department, county, municipality, or a combination involving more than one of those entities may not use a facility or real property purchased, acquired, or improved with state funds unless the division, or the state jail division in the case of a state jail felony facility, first approves the use.

(f) The division or the state jail division, in the case of a state jail felony facility, is entitled to reimbursement from an entity described by Subsection (e) of all state funds used by the entity without division approval as required by Subsection (e).
*(Added by L.1995, chap. 76(7.11), eff. 9/1/95.)*

### §76.011. Pretrial services.

(a) The department may operate programs for the supervision and rehabilitation of persons in pretrial intervention programs. Programs may include testing for controlled substances. A person in a pretrial intervention program may be supervised for a period not to exceed one year.

(b) The department may use money deposited in the special fund of the county treasury for the department under Article 103.004(b), Code of Criminal Procedure, only for the same purposes for which state aid may be used under this chapter.
*(Added by L.1995, chap. 76(7.11), eff. 9/1/95.)*

### §76.012. Reporting and management services.

A department may enter into a contract with a public or private vendor to provide telephone reporting, automated caseload management, and collection services for fines, fees, restitution, and other costs ordered to be paid by a court or fees imposed by a department. *(Added by L.1995, chap. 76(7.11), eff. 9/1/95.)*

## §76.013. Restitution.

(a) If a judge requires a defendant to make restitution to a victim of the defendant's offense, and a payment is received by a department from the defendant for transmittal to a victim of the offense, the department that receives the payment for disbursement to the victim shall immediately deposit the payment in an interest-bearing account in the county treasury as required by Section 140.003(f), Local Government Code.

(b) If an initial restitution payment is received by a department, the department immediately shall notify the victim of that fact by certified mail, mailed to the last known address of the victim. If a victim then makes a claim for payment, the department promptly shall remit the payment to the victim. A department is obligated to make a good faith effort to locate and notify a victim that an unclaimed payment exists. The department satisfies the good faith requirement under this subsection by sending to the victim by certified mail on any one occasion during the period the defendant is required to make payments a notice that the victim is entitled to an unclaimed payment. Not earlier than the fifth anniversary of the date on which the department mails notice under this subsection, if the victim has not made a claim for payment, the department shall transfer from the interest-bearing account to the comptroller all payments received. After making an initial transfer of payments to the comptroller under this subsection, the department, not later than the 121st day after the date the department receives a subsequent payment, shall transfer the subsequent payment to the comptroller. The department shall deduct five percent of the payment or subsequent payment as a collection fee and deduct any interest accrued on the payment or subsequent payment before transferring the payment to the comptroller under this subsection. The comptroller shall deposit the payment in the state treasury to the credit of the compensation to victims of crime auxiliary fund.

(c) The collection fee under Subsection (b) and the accrued interest under Subsections (a) and (b) shall be deposited in the special fund of the county treasury provided by Section 509.011 to be used for the same purposes for which state aid may be used under that section. The department has a maximum of 121 days after the five-year expiration date to transfer the funds to the comptroller's office. Failure to comply with the 121-day deadline will result in a five percent collection fee penalty calculated from the total deposit and all interest attributable to the unclaimed funds.

(d) If the victim of the offense claims the payment during the five- year period in which the payment is held in the interest-bearing account, the department shall pay the victim the amount of the original payment, less any interest earned while holding the payment. After the payment has been transferred to the comptroller, the department has no liability in regard to the payment, and any claim for the payment must be made to the comptroller. If the victim makes a claim to the comptroller, the comptroller shall pay the victim the amount of the original payment, less the collection fee, from the compensation to victims of crime auxiliary fund.

*(Added by L.1995, chap. 76(7.11); chgd. by L.1997, chaps. 165(9.04(a)), 796(1(a)), eff. 9/1/97.)*

## §76.014. Assessment and enhancement of defendant's educational skills.

(a) A department, with the assistance of the Texas Workforce Commission, the Council on Workforce and Economic Competitiveness, local workforce development boards, and other appropriate public and private entities, may establish a developmental program for a defendant under the supervision of the department on the basis of information obtained in the presentence investigation report prepared for the defendant.

(b) The developmental program may provide the defendant with the educational and vocational training necessary to:

(1) meet the average skill level of students who have completed the sixth grade in public schools in this state; and

(2) maintain employment while under the supervision of the department, to lessen the likelihood that the defendant will commit additional offenses.

(c) To decrease expenditures by departments for the educational and vocational skills assessment and enhancement program established under this section, the Texas Department of Commerce shall provide information to departments, the Texas Workforce Commission, the Council on Workforce and Economic Competitiveness, local workforce development boards, and other appropriate public and private entities for obtaining financial assistance through programs under Chapter 301, Labor Code, and other applicable programs of public or private entities.

*(Added by L.1995, chap. 76(7.11); chgd. by L.1997, chap. 165(9.05(a)), eff. 9/1/97.)*

## §76.015. Administrative fee.

(a) A department may collect money from an individual as ordered by a court served by the department regardless of whether the individual is under the department's supervision.

(b) A department that collects money under this section shall promptly transfer the money collected to the appropriate county or state officer.

(c) A department may assess a reasonable administrative fee of not less than $25 and not more than $40 per month on an individual who participates in a department program or receives department services and who is not paying a monthly fee under Section 19, Article 42.12, Code of Criminal Procedure.

(d) This section applies only to a county with a population of 2.8 million or more.
*(Added by L.1997, chaps. 165(9.07(a)), 983(1(a)), eff. 9/1/97.)*

**§76.016. Victim notification.**

(a) A department, using the name and address provided by the attorney representing the state under Article 56.08(d), Code of Criminal Procedure, shall make a reasonable effort to notify a victim of the defendant's crime or, if the victim has a guardian or is deceased, to notify the guardian of the victim or close relative of the deceased victim of:

(1) the fact that the defendant has been placed on community supervision;

(2) the conditions of community supervision imposed on the defendant by the court; and

(3) the date, time, and location of any hearing or proceeding at which the conditions of the defendant's community supervision may be modified or the defendant's placement on community supervision may be revoked or terminated.

(b) An attempt by the department to give notice to the victim, the guardian of the victim, or a close relative of a deceased victim at the victim's, the guardian of the victim's, or a close relative of a deceased victim's last known telephone number or address as shown on the records of the department constitutes a reasonable attempt to give notice under this section.

(c) In this section, "close relative of a deceased victim," "guardian of a victim," and "victim" have meanings assigned by Article 56.01, Code of Criminal Procedure.
*(Added by L.1997, chap. 165(9.08(a)), eff. 9/1/97.)*

**§76.017. Treatment alternative to incarceration program.**

(a) A department may establish a treatment alternative to incarceration program in each county served by the department according to standards adopted by the division. A department may enter into an interlocal cooperation agreement with one or more other departments in order to establish this program on a regional basis.

(b) The program must:

(1) include automatic screening and evaluation of a person arrested for an offense, other than a Class C misdemeanor, in which an element of the offense is the use or possession of alcohol or the use, possession, or sale of a controlled substance or marihuana;

(2) include automatic screening and evaluation of a person arrested for an offense, other than a Class C misdemeanor, in which the use of alcohol or drugs is suspected to have significantly contributed to the offense for which the individual has been arrested;

(3) coordinate the evaluation and referral to treatment services; and

(4) make referrals for the appropriate treatment of a person determined to be in need of treatment.

(c) A program administered under this section must use a screening and evaluation procedure developed or approved by the division.

(d) After a person is screened and evaluated, a representative of the department shall meet with the participating criminal justice and treatment agencies to review the person's case and to determine if the person should be referred for treatment. If a person is considered appropriate for referral, the person may be referred to community-based treatment in accordance with applicable law or any other treatment program deemed appropriate. A magistrate may order a person to participate in a treatment program recommended under this section as a condition of bond or condition of pretrial release.

(e) A department may contract for the provision of treatment services. The department may pay for services only if other adequate public or private sources of payment are not available. A person is responsible for the payment of any treatment program recommended under this section if it is determined that a person referred for treatment is able to pay for the costs of treatment or if the person has insurance that will pay for the treatment. If a person is able to pay for treatment or if the person has insurance that will pay for the treatment, the payment may be made a condition for receiving treatment.

(f) An employee of a department or treatment provider either administering this program or providing services under this section may exchange or otherwise disclose information regarding the assessment, evaluation, or treatment of a person participating in this program to:

(1) another employee of the department;
(2) an officer in the court that has jurisdiction over the person's case;
(3) a county sheriff or jail administrator;
(4) an employee of the Texas Department of Criminal Justice; or
(5) any employee in a facility, institution, or halfway house in which a person may be confined in accordance with a disposition of the criminal charges in the case.
*(Added by L.1997, chaps. 165(9.09(a)), 1269(1), eff. 9/1/97, 6/20/97.)*

**§76.018. Application of law relating to free exercise of religion.**

For purposes of Chapter 110, Civil Practice and Remedies Code, an ordinance, rule, order, decision, or practice that applies to a person in the custody of a correctional facility operated by or under a contract with a community supervision and corrections department is presumed to be in furtherance of a compelling governmental interest and the least restrictive means of furthering that interest. The presumption may be rebutted.
*(Added by L.1999, chap. 399(3), eff. 6/10/99.)*

Printed in the U.S.A. 17

# TITLE 3. LEGISLATIVE BRANCH

## CHAPTER 311. CODE CONSTRUCTION ACT
*(Selected Section)*



**§311.005. General definitions.** *(Subsection (2) only.)*

The following definitions apply unless the statute or context in which the word or phrase is used requires a different definition:

(2) "Person" includes corporation, organization, government or governmental subdivision or agency, business trust, estate, trust, partnership, association, and any other legal entity.

# TITLE 4. EXECUTIVE BRANCH

## SUBTITLE B. LAW ENFORCEMENT AND PUBLIC PROTECTION

## CHAPTER 411. DEPARTMENT OF PUBLIC SAFETY OF THE STATE OF TEXAS
*(Selected Sections)*

### SUBCHAPTER A. GENERAL PROVISIONS AND ADMINISTRATION



### SUBCHAPTER B. TEXAS RANGERS

## SUBCHAPTER C. TEXAS HIGHWAY PATROL

411.032. Powers and duties of officers.

## SUBCHAPTER D. ADMINISTRATIVE DIVISION

411.047. Reporting related to concealed handgun incidents.

## SUBCHAPTER F. CRIMINAL HISTORY RECORD INFORMATION

411.135. Access to criminal history record information: State Bar of Texas.
411.135. Access to certain information by public.

## SUBCHAPTER H. LICENSE TO CARRY A CONCEALED HANDGUN

411.171. Definitions.
411.172. Eligibility.
411.173. Nonresident license.
411.174. Application.
411.175. Request for application materials.
411.176. Review of application materials.
411.177. Issuance or denial of license.
411.178. Notice to local law enforcement.
411.179. Form of license.
411.180. Notification of denial, revocation, or suspension of license; review.
411.181. Notice of change of address or name.
411.182. Notice.
411.183. Expiration.
411.184. Modification.
411.185. Renewal.
411.186. Revocation.
411.187. Suspension of license.
411.188. Handgun proficiency requirement.
411.189. Handgun proficiency certificate.
411.190. Qualified handgun instructors.
411.191. Review of denial, revocation, or suspension of certification as qualified handgun instructor.
411.192. Confidentiality of records.
411.193. Statistical report.
411.194. Reduction of fees due to indigency.
411.195. Reduction of fees for senior citizens.
411.196. Method of payment.
411.197. Rules.
411.198. Law enforcement officer alias handgun license.
411.199. Honorably retired peace officers.
411.1991. Active peace officers.
411.200. Application to licensed security officers.
411.201. Active and retired judicial officers.
411.202. License a benefit.
411.203. Rights of employers.
411.204. Notice required on certain premises.
411.205. Displaying license; penalty.
411.206. Seizure of handgun and license.
411.207. Authority of peace officer to disarm.
411.208. Limitation of liability.

## SUBCHAPTER A. GENERAL PROVISIONS AND ADMINISTRATION

### §411.0085. Driver's license facilities: personnel.

The department may not assign more than 123 commissioned officers plus supervising personnel to driver's license facilities. *(Added by L.1995, chap. 165(4), eff. 9/1/95.)*

### §411.0086. *(Expired 9/1/96.)*

### §411.0098. Sex offender compliance unit.

(a) The director shall create a sex offender compliance unit to be operated by the department.

(b) The sex offender compliance unit shall investigate and arrest individuals determined to have committed a sexually violent offense, as defined by Article 62.01, Code of Criminal Procedure.

(c) The legislature may appropriate funds to the department from the fugitive apprehension account for the purpose of paying the costs to the department of implementing this section.

(d) The department may adopt rules as necessary to implement this section.

*(Added by L.1999, chap. 150(1), eff. 9/1/99, if specific appropriation is provided in H.B. No. 1, 76th Legislature, 1999. See other section 411.0098 below.)*



### §411.0098. Coordination with Department of Transportation.

(a) The department and the Texas Department of Transportation shall establish procedures to ensure effective coordination of the development of transportation infrastructure projects that affect both agencies.

(b) Procedures established under this section shall:

(1) allow each agency to provide comments and advice to the other agency on an ongoing basis regarding statewide transportation planning efforts that affect traffic law enforcement;

(2) define the role of each agency in transportation infrastructure efforts; and

(3) require the department and the Texas Department of Transportation to develop a plan for applying for and using federal funds to address infrastructure needs that affect enforcement efforts.

(c) The department and the Texas Department of Transportation shall:

(1) update and revise the procedures established under this section as necessary; and

(2) file not later than January 15 of each odd-numbered year with the presiding officer of each house of the legislature a report that describes the procedures established under this section and their implementation.

*(Added by L.1999, chap. 1189(7), eff. 9/1/99. See other section 411.0098 above.)*

### §411.017. Unauthorized acts involving department name, insignia, or division name.

(a) A person commits an offense if, without the director's authorization, the person:

(1) manufactures, sells, or possesses a badge, identification card, or other item bearing a department insignia or an insignia deceptively similar to the department's;

(2) makes a copy or likeness of a badge, identification card, or department insignia, with intent to use or allow another to use the copy or likeness to produce an item bearing the department insignia or an insignia deceptively similar to the department's; or

(3) uses the term "Texas Department of Public Safety," "Department of Public Safety," "Texas Ranger," or "Texas Highway Patrol" in connection with an object, with the intent to create the appearance that the object belongs to or is being used by the department.

(b) In this section, "department insignia" means an insignia or design prescribed by the director for use by officers and employees of the department in connection with their official activities. An insignia is deceptively similar to the department's if it is not prescribed by the department but a reasonable person would presume that it was prescribed by the department.

(c) A district or county court, on application of the attorney general or of the district attorney or prosecuting attorney performing the duties of district attorney for the district in which the court is located, may enjoin a violation or threatened violation of this section on a showing that a violation has occurred or is likely to occur.

(d) It is an affirmative defense to a prosecution under this section that the object is used exclusively:

(1) for decorative purposes, maintained or preserved in a decorative state, and not offered for sale; or

(2) in an artistic or dramatic presentation, and before the use of the object the producer of the presentation notifies the director in writing of the intended use, the location where the use will occur, and the period during which the use will occur.

(e) An offense under this section is a Class A misdemeanor, unless the object is shipped by United States mail or by any type of commercial carrier from a point outside the State of Texas to a point inside the state if the shipper or his agent has been sent notification by registered United States mail of this section prior to the shipment, in which event the offense is a felony of the third degree.

### §411.0175. Accident reports.

The department shall:

(1) tabulate and analyze the motor vehicle accident reports it receives;

(2) annually or more frequently publish statistical information derived from the accident reports as to the number, cause, and location of highway accidents; and

(3) provide an abstract of the statistical information for each preceding biennium to the governor and the legislature, with its conclusions and findings and recommendations for decreasing highway accidents and increasing highway safety.

*(Added by L.1995, chap. 165(5), eff. 9/1/95.)*

### §411.019. Toll-free number.

(a) The department shall provide a 24-hour toll-free telephone number for use by the public in reporting traffic offenses, including driving while intoxicated, suspected criminal activity, and traffic accidents and other emergencies.

(b) On receiving a report of an offense, the department shall contact the law enforcement agency of the jurisdiction where the reported suspected driver or incident was observed or shall dispatch department officers.

### §411.0201. Reproduction of records.

(a) Except as provided by Subsection (b), the department may photograph, microphotograph, or film any record in connection with the issuance of a driver's license or commercial driver's license and any record of any division of the department.

(b) None of the following may be photographed or filmed to dispose of the original record:

(1) an original fingerprint card;

(2) any evidence submitted in connection with a criminal case; or

(3) a confession or statement made by the defendant in a criminal case.

(c) The department may create original records in micrographic form on media, such as computer output microfilm.

(d) A photograph, microphotograph, or film of a record reproduced under Subsection (a) is equivalent to the original record for all purposes, including introduction as evidence in all courts and administrative agency proceedings. A certified or authenticated copy of such a photograph, microphotograph, or film is admissible as evidence equally with the original photograph, microphotograph, or film.

(e) The director or an authorized representative may certify the authenticity of a photograph, microphotograph, or film of a record reproduced under this section and shall charge a fee for the certified photograph, microphotograph, or film as provided by law.

(f) Certified records shall be furnished to any person who is authorized by law to receive them.

*(Added by L.1995, chap. 165(6); chgd. by L.1997, chap. 1187(3), eff. 9/1/97.)*

## SUBCHAPTER B. TEXAS RANGERS

### §411.022. Authority of officers.

(a) An officer of the Texas Rangers is governed by the law regulating and defining the powers and duties of sheriffs performing similar duties, except that the officer may make arrests, execute process in a criminal case in any county and, if specially directed by the judge of a court of record, execute process in a civil case.

(b) An officer of the Texas Rangers who arrests a person charged with a criminal offense shall immediately convey the person to the proper officer of the county where the person is charged and shall obtain a receipt. The state shall pay all necessary expenses incurred under this subsection.

## SUBCHAPTER C. TEXAS HIGHWAY PATROL

### §411.032. Powers and duties of officers.

In addition to the powers and duties provided by law for the officers, noncommissioned officers, and enlisted persons of the Texas Highway Patrol, they have the powers and authority provided by law for members of the Texas Rangers force.

## SUBCHAPTER D. ADMINISTRATIVE DIVISION

### §411.047. Reporting related to concealed handgun incidents.

(a) The department shall maintain statistics related to responses by law enforcement agencies to incidents in which a person licensed to carry a handgun under Subchapter H is convicted of an offense under Section 46.035, Penal Code.

(b) The department by rule shall adopt procedures for local law enforcement to make reports to the department described by Subsection (a).

*(Added by L.1995, chap. 229(6); chgd. by L.1997, chap. 165(10.06); L.1999, chap. 1189(12), eff. 9/1/99.)*



## SUBCHAPTER F. CRIMINAL HISTORY RECORD INFORMATION

### §411.135. Access to criminal history record information: State Bar of Texas.

(a) The general counsel of the State Bar of Texas is entitled to obtain from the department criminal history record information maintained by the department that relates to a person who is:

(1) a person licensed by the state bar and who is the subject of or involved in an investigation of:

(A) professional misconduct relating to a grievance filed under the disciplinary rules of the state bar; or

(B) barratry, the unauthorized practice of law, or falsely holding oneself out as a lawyer, in violation of Section 38.12, 38.122, or 38.123, Penal Code;

(2) a witness in any disciplinary action or proceeding conducted by the state bar, the Board of Disciplinary Appeals, or any court; or

(3) an applicant for reinstatement to practice law.

(b) Information received by the state bar is confidential and may be disseminated only in a disciplinary action or proceeding conducted by the state bar, the Board of Disciplinary Appeals, or any court.

(c) The state bar shall destroy criminal history record information obtained under this section promptly after a final determination is made in the matter for which the information was obtained.

*(Added by L.1997, chap. 440(1). See other section 411.135 below.)*

### §411.135. Access to certain information by public.

(a) Any person is entitled to obtain from the department:

(1) any information described as public information under Chapter 62, Code of Criminal Procedure, as added by Chapter 668, Acts of the 75th Legislature, Regular Session, 1997, including, to the extent available, a recent photograph of each person subject to registration under that chapter; and

(2) criminal history record information maintained by the department that relates to the conviction of or a grant of deferred adjudication to a person for any criminal offense, including arrest information that relates to the conviction or grant of deferred adjudication.

(b) The department by rule shall design and implement a system to respond to electronic inquiries and other inquiries for information described by Subsection (a).

(c) A person who obtains information from the department under Subsection (a) may:

(1) use the information for any purpose; or

(2) release the information to any other person.

*(Added by L.1997, chap. 747(2); chgd. by L.1999, chap. 1415(21), eff. 9/1/99. See other section 411.135 above.)*

## SUBCHAPTER H. LICENSE TO CARRY A CONCEALED HANDGUN

*(Added by L.1997, chap. 165(10.01(a)), eff. 9/1/97.)*

### §411.171. Definitions.

In this subchapter:

(1) "Action" means single action, revolver, or semi-automatic action.

(2) "Chemically dependent person" means a person who frequently or repeatedly becomes intoxicated by excessive indulgence in alcohol or uses controlled substances or dangerous drugs so as to acquire a fixed habit and an involuntary tendency to become intoxicated or use those substances as often as the opportunity is presented.

(3) "Concealed handgun" means a handgun, the presence of which is not openly discernible to the ordinary observation of a reasonable person.

(4) "Convicted" means an adjudication of guilt or an order of deferred adjudication entered against a person by a court of competent jurisdiction whether or not the imposition of the sentence is subsequently probated and the person is discharged from community supervision. The term does not include an adjudication of guilt or an order of deferred adjudication that has been subsequently:

(A) expunged; or

(B) pardoned under the authority of a state or federal official.

(5) "Handgun" has the meaning assigned by Section 46.01, Penal Code.

(6) "Intoxicated" has the meaning assigned by Section 49.01, Penal Code.

(7) "Qualified handgun instructor" means a person who is certified to instruct in the use of handguns by the department.

(8) *(Repealed by L.1999, chap. 62(9.02)(a), eff. 9/1/99.)*

*(Added by L.1997, chap. 165(10.01(a)); chgd. by L.1999, chap. 62(9.01)(a), (9.02)(a), eff. 9/1/99.)*

### §411.172. Eligibility.

(a) A person is eligible for a license to carry a concealed handgun if the person:

(1) is a legal resident of this state for the six-month period preceding the date of application under this subchapter or is otherwise eligible for a license under Section 411.173(a);

(2) is at least 21 years of age;

(3) has not been convicted of a felony;

(4) is not charged with the commission of a Class A or Class B misdemeanor or an offense under Section 42.01, Penal Code, or of a felony under an information or indictment;

(5) is not a fugitive from justice for a felony or a Class A or Class B misdemeanor;

(6) is not a chemically dependent person;

(7) is not incapable of exercising sound judgment with respect to the proper use and storage of a handgun;

(8) has not, in the five years preceding the date of application, been convicted of a Class A or Class B misdemeanor or an offense under Section 42.01, Penal Code;

(9) is fully qualified under applicable federal and state law to purchase a handgun;

(10) has not been finally determined to be delinquent in making a child support payment administered or collected by the attorney general;

(11) has not been finally determined to be delinquent in the payment of a tax or other money collected by the comptroller, the tax collector of a political subdivision of the state, or any agency or subdivision of the state;

(12) has not been finally determined to be in default on a loan made under Chapter 57, Education Code;

(13) is not currently restricted under a court protective order or subject to a restraining order affecting the spousal relationship, other than a restraining order solely affecting property interests;

(14) has not, in the 10 years preceding the date of application, been adjudicated as having engaged in delinquent conduct violating a penal law of the grade of felony; and

(15) has not made any material misrepresentation, or failed to disclose any material fact, in an application submitted pursuant to Section 411.174 or in a request for application submitted pursuant to Section 411.175.

(b) For the purposes of this section, an offense under the laws of this state, another state, or the United States is:

(1) a felony if the offense is so designated by law or if confinement for one year or more in a penitentiary is affixed to the offense as a possible punishment; and

(2) a Class A misdemeanor if the offense is not a felony and confinement in a jail other than a state jail felony facility is affixed as a possible punishment.

(c) An individual who has been convicted two times within the 10-year period preceding the date on which the person applies for a license of an offense of the grade of Class B misdemeanor or greater that involves the use of alcohol or a controlled substance as a statutory element of the offense is a chemically dependent person for purposes of this section and is not qualified to receive a license under this subchapter. This subsection does not preclude the disqualification of an individual for being a chemically dependent person if other evidence exists to show that the person is a chemically dependent person.

(d) For purposes of Subsection (a)(7), a person is incapable of exercising sound judgment with respect to the proper use and storage of a handgun if the person:

(1) has been diagnosed by a licensed physician as suffering from a psychiatric disorder or condition that causes or is likely to cause substantial impairment in judgment, mood, perception, impulse control, or intellectual ability;

(2) suffers from a psychiatric disorder or condition described by Subdivision (1) that:

(A) is in remission but is reasonably likely to redevelop at a future time; or

(B) requires continuous medical treatment to avoid redevelopment;

(3) has been diagnosed by a licensed physician or declared by a court to be incompetent to manage the person's own affairs; or

(4) has entered in a criminal proceeding a plea of not guilty by reason of insanity.

(e) The following constitutes evidence that a person has a psychiatric disorder or condition described by Subsection (d)(1):

(1) involuntary psychiatric hospitalization in the preceding five-year period;

(2) psychiatric hospitalization in the preceding two-year period;

(3) inpatient or residential substance abuse treatment in the preceding five-year period;

(4) diagnosis in the preceding five-year period by a licensed physician that the person is dependent on alcohol, a controlled substance, or a similar substance; or

(5) diagnosis at any time by a licensed physician that the person suffers or has suffered from a psychiatric disorder or condition consisting of or relating to:

(A) schizophrenia or delusional disorder;

(B) bipolar disorder;

(C) chronic dementia, whether caused by illness, brain defect, or brain injury;

(D) dissociative identity disorder;

(E) intermittent explosive disorder; or

(F) antisocial personality disorder.

(f) Notwithstanding Subsection (d), a person who has previously been diagnosed as suffering from a psychiatric disorder or condition described by Subsection (d) or listed in Subsection (e) is not because of that disorder or condition incapable of exercising sound judgment with respect to the proper use and storage of a handgun if the person provides the department with a certificate from a licensed physician whose primary practice is in the field of psychiatry stating that the psychiatric disorder or condition is in remission and is not reasonably likely to develop at a future time.

*(Added by L.1997, chap. 165(10.01(a)); chgd. by L.1999, chap. 62(9.03)(a), (9.04)(a), eff. 9/1/99.)*

### §411.173. Nonresident license.

(a) The department by rule shall establish a procedure for a person who is a legal resident of a state that does not provide for the issuance of a license to carry a concealed handgun and who meets the eligibility requirements of this subchapter other than the residency requirement established by Section 411.172(a)(1) to obtain a license under this subchapter. The procedure must include payment of a fee in an amount sufficient to recover the average cost to the department of obtaining a criminal history record check and investigation on a nonresident applicant.

(b) The department shall negotiate an agreement with any other state that provides for the issuance of a license to carry a concealed handgun under which a license issued by the other state is recognized in this state if the department determines that:

(1) the eligibility requirements imposed by the other state include background check requirements that meet or exceed background check requirements imposed by federal law as a condition of receiving a handgun; and

(2) the other state recognizes a license issued in this state.

*(Added by L.1997, chap. 165(10.01(a)); chgd. by L.1999, chap. 62(9.05)(a), eff. 9/1/99.)*

**§411.174. Application.**

(a) An applicant for a license to carry a concealed handgun must submit to the director's designee described by Section 411.176:

(1) a completed application on a form provided by the department that requires only the information listed in Subsection (b);

(2) two recent color passport photographs of the applicant;

(3) a certified copy of the applicant's birth certificate or certified proof of age;

(4) proof of residency in this state;

(5) two complete sets of legible and classifiable fingerprints of the applicant taken by a person appropriately trained in recording fingerprints who is employed by a law enforcement agency or by a private entity designated by a law enforcement agency as an entity qualified to take fingerprints of an applicant for a license under this subchapter;

(6) a nonrefundable application and license fee of $140 paid to the department;

(7) a handgun proficiency certificate described by Section 411.189;

(8) an affidavit signed by the applicant stating that the applicant:

(A) has read and understands each provision of this subchapter that creates an offense under the laws of this state and each provision of the laws of this state related to use of deadly force; and

(B) fulfills all the eligibility requirements listed under Section 411.172; and

(9) a form executed by the applicant that authorizes the director to make an inquiry into any noncriminal history records that are necessary to determine the applicant's eligibility for a license under Section 411.172(a).

(b) An applicant must provide on the application a statement of the applicant's:

(1) full name and place and date of birth;

(2) race and sex;

(3) residence and business addresses for the preceding five years;

(4) hair and eye color;

(5) height and weight;

(6) driver's license number or identification certificate number issued by the department;

(7) criminal history record information of the type maintained by the department under this chapter, including a list of offenses for which the applicant was arrested, charged, or under an information or indictment and the disposition of the offenses; and

(8) history during the preceding five years, if any, of treatment received by, commitment to, or residence in:

(A) a drug or alcohol treatment center licensed to provide drug or alcohol treatment under the laws of this state or another state; or

(B) a psychiatric hospital.

(c) The department shall distribute on request a copy of this subchapter and application materials.

*(Added by L.1997, chap. 165(10.01(a)); chgd. by L.1999, chap. 62(9.06)(a), eff. 9/1/99.)*

**§411.175. Request for application materials.**

(a) A person applying for a license to carry a concealed handgun must apply by obtaining a request for application materials from a handgun dealer, the department, or any other person or entity approved by the department. The request for application materials must include the applicant's full name, address, race, sex, height, date of birth, and driver's license number and such other identifying information as required by department rule. The department shall prescribe the form of the request and make the form available to interested parties. An individual who desires to receive application materials must complete the request for application materials and forward it to the department at its Austin address. The department shall review all requests for application materials and make a preliminary determination as to whether or not the individual is qualified to receive a handgun license. If an individual is not disqualified to receive a handgun license, the department shall forward to the individual the appropriate application materials. The applicant must complete the application materials and forward the completed materials to the department at its Austin address.

(b) If a preliminary review indicates that an individual will not be qualified to receive a handgun license, the department shall send written notification to that individual. The notice shall provide the reason that the preliminary review indicates that the individual is not entitled to receive a handgun license. The department shall give the individual an opportunity to correct whatever defect may exist.

*(Added by L.1997, chap. 165(10.01(a)), eff. 9/1/97.)*

## §411.176. Review of application materials.

(a) On receipt of the application materials by the department at its Austin headquarters, the department shall conduct the appropriate criminal history record check of the applicant through its computerized criminal history system. Not later than the 30th day after the date the department receives the application materials, the department shall forward the materials to the director's designee in the geographical area of the applicant's residence so that the designee may conduct the investigation described by Subsection (b).

(b) The director's designee as needed shall conduct an additional criminal history record check of the applicant and an investigation of the applicant's local official records to verify the accuracy of the application materials. The scope of the record check and the investigation are at the sole discretion of the department, except that the director's designee shall complete the record check and investigation not later than the 60th day after the date the department receives the application materials. The department shall send a fingerprint card to the Federal Bureau of Investigation for a national criminal history check of the applicant. On completion of the investigation, the director's designee shall return all materials and the result of the investigation to the appropriate division of the department at its Austin headquarters. The director's designee may submit to the appropriate division of the department, at the department's Austin headquarters, along with the application materials a written recommendation for disapproval of the application, accompanied by an affidavit stating personal knowledge or naming persons with personal knowledge of a ground for denial under Section 411.172. The director's designee in the appropriate geographical area may also submit the application and the recommendation that the license be issued. On receipt at the department's Austin headquarters of the application materials and the result of the investigation by the director's designee, the department shall conduct any further record check or investigation the department determines is necessary if a question exists with respect to the accuracy of the application materials or the eligibility of the applicant, except that the department shall complete the record check and investigation not later than the 180th day after the date the department receives the application materials from the applicant.

*(Added by L.1997, chap. 165(10.01(a)); chgd. by L.1999, chap. 62(9.07)(a), eff. 9/1/99.)*

## §411.177. Issuance or denial of license.

(a) The department shall issue a license to carry a concealed handgun to an applicant if the applicant meets all the eligibility requirements and submits all the application materials. The department may issue a license to carry handguns only of the categories indicated on the applicant's certificate of proficiency issued under Section 411.189. The department shall administer the licensing procedures in good faith so that any applicant who meets all the eligibility requirements and submits all the application materials shall receive a license. The department may not deny an application on the basis of a capricious or arbitrary decision by the department.

(b) The department shall, not later than the 60th day after the date of the receipt by the director's designee of the completed application materials:

(1) issue the license;

(2) notify the applicant in writing that the application was denied:

(A) on the grounds that the applicant failed to qualify under the criteria listed in Section 411.172;

(B) based on the affidavit of the director's designee submitted to the department under Section 411.176(b); or

(C) based on the affidavit of the qualified handgun instructor submitted to the department under Section 411.189(c); or

(3) notify the applicant in writing that the department is unable to make a determination regarding the issuance or denial of a license to the applicant within the 60-day period prescribed by this subsection and include in that notification an explanation of the reason for the inability and an estimation of the amount of time the department will need to make the determination.

(c) Failure of the department to issue or deny a license for a period of more than 30 days after the department is required to act under Subsection (b) constitutes denial.

(d) A license issued under this subchapter is effective from the date of issuance.

*(Added by L.1997, chap. 165(10.01(a)); chgd. by L.1999, chap. 62(9.08)(a), eff. 9/1/99.)*

## §411.178. Notice to local law enforcement.

On request of a local law enforcement agency, the department shall notify the agency of the licenses that have been issued to license holders who reside in the county in which the agency is located. *(Added by L.1997, chap. 165(10.01(a)); chgd. by L.1999, chap. 1189(14), eff. 9/1/99.)*

### §411.179. Form of license.

(a) The department by rule shall adopt the form of the license. A license must include:

(1) a number assigned to the license holder by the department;

(2) a statement of the period for which the license is effective;

(3) a statement of the category or categories of handguns the license holder may carry as provided by Subsection (b);

(4) a color photograph of the license holder; and

(5) the license holder's full name, date of birth, residence address, hair and eye color, height, weight, signature, and the number of a driver's license or an identification certificate issued to the license holder by the department.

(b) A category of handguns contains handguns that are not prohibited by law and are of certain actions. The categories of handguns are:

(1) SA: any handguns, whether semi-automatic or not; and

(2) NSA: handguns that are not semi-automatic.

*(Added by L.1997, chap. 165(10.01(a)), eff. 9/1/97.)*

### §411.180. Notification of denial, revocation, or suspension of license; review.

(a) The department shall give written notice to each applicant for a handgun license of any denial, revocation, or suspension of that license. Not later than the 30th day after the notice is received by the applicant, according to the records of the department, the applicant or license holder may request a hearing on the denial, revocation, or suspension. The applicant must make a written request for a hearing addressed to the department at its Austin address. The request for hearing must reach the department in Austin prior to the 30th day after the date of receipt of the written notice. On receipt of a request for hearing from a license holder or applicant, the department shall promptly schedule a hearing in the appropriate justice court in the county of residence of the applicant or license holder. The justice court shall conduct a hearing to review the denial, revocation, or suspension of the license. In a proceeding under this section, a justice of the peace shall act as an administrative hearing officer. A hearing under this section is not subject to Chapter 2001 (Administrative Procedure Act). A district attorney or county attorney, the attorney general, or a designated member of the department may represent the department.

(b) The department, on receipt of a request for hearing, shall file the appropriate petition in the justice court selected for the hearing and send a copy of that petition to the applicant or license holder at the address contained in departmental records. A hearing under this section must be scheduled within 30 days of receipt of the request for a hearing. The hearing shall be held expeditiously but in no event more than 60 days after the date that the applicant or license holder requested the hearing. The date of the hearing may be reset on the motion of either party, by agreement of the parties, or by the court as necessary to accommodate the court's docket.

(c) The justice court shall determine if the denial, revocation, or suspension is supported by a preponderance of the evidence. Both the applicant or license holder and the department may present evidence. The court shall affirm the denial, revocation, or suspension if the court determines that denial, revocation, or suspension is supported by a preponderance of the evidence. If the court determines that the denial, revocation, or suspension is not supported by a preponderance of the evidence, the court shall order the department to immediately issue or return the license to the applicant or license holder.

(d) A proceeding under this section is subject to Chapter 105, Civil Practice and Remedies Code, relating to fees, expenses, and attorney's fees.

(e) A party adversely affected by the court's ruling following a hearing under this section may appeal the ruling by filing within 30 days after the ruling a petition in a county court at law in the county in which the applicant or license holder resides or, if there is no county court at law in the county, in the county court of the county. A person who appeals under this section must send by certified mail a copy of the person's petition, certified by the clerk of the court in which the petition is filed, to the appropriate division of the department at its Austin headquarters. The trial on appeal shall be a trial de novo without a jury. A district or county attorney or the attorney general may represent the department.

(f) A suspension of a license may not be probated.

(g) If an applicant or a license holder does not petition the justice court, a denial becomes final and a revocation or suspension takes effect on the 30th day after receipt of written notice.

(h) The department may use and introduce into evidence certified copies of governmental records to establish the existence of certain events that could result in the denial, revocation, or suspension of a license under this subchapter, including records regarding convictions, judicial findings regarding mental competency, judicial findings regarding chemical dependency, or other matters that may be established by governmental records that have been properly authenticated.

(i) This section does not apply to a suspension of a license under Section 85.022, Family Code, or Article 17.292, Code of Criminal Procedure.
*(Added by L.1997, chap. 165(10.01(a)); chgd. by L.1999, chap. 1412(5), eff. 9/1/99.)*

### §411.181. Notice of change of address or name.

(a) If a person who is a current license holder moves from the address stated on the license or if the name of the person is changed by marriage or otherwise, the person shall, not later than the 30th day after the date of the address or name change, notify the department and provide the department with the number of the person's license and the person's:

(1) former and new addresses; or

(2) former and new names.

(b) If the name of the license holder is changed by marriage or otherwise, the person shall apply for a duplicate license.

(c) If a license holder moves from the address stated on the license, the person shall apply for a duplicate license.

(d) The department shall charge a license holder a fee of $25 for a duplicate license.

(e) The department shall make the forms available on request.

(f) On request of a local law enforcement agency, the department shall notify the agency of changes made under Subsection (a) by license holders who reside in the county in which the agency is located.

(g) If a license is lost, stolen, or destroyed, the license holder shall apply for a duplicate license not later than the 30th day after the date of the loss, theft, or destruction of the license.

(h) If a license holder is required under this section to apply for a duplicate license and the license expires not later than the 60th day after the date of the loss, theft, or destruction of the license, the applicant may renew the license with the modified information included on the new license. The applicant must pay only the nonrefundable renewal fee.
*(Added by L.1997, chap. 165(10.01(a)); chgd. by L.1999, chap. 1189(15), eff. 9/1/99.)*

### §411.182. Notice.

(a) For the purpose of a notice required by this subchapter, the department may assume that the address currently reported to the department by the applicant or license holder is the correct address.

(b) A written notice meets the requirements under this subchapter if the notice is sent by certified mail to the current address reported by the applicant or license holder to the department.

(c) If a notice is returned to the department because the notice is not deliverable, the department may give notice by publication once in a newspaper of general interest in the county of the applicant's or license holder's last reported address. On the 31st day after the date the notice is published, the department may take the action proposed in the notice.
*(Added by L.1997, chap. 165(10.01(a)), eff. 9/1/97.)*

### §411.183. Expiration.

(a) A license issued under this subchapter expires on the first birthday of the license holder occurring after the fourth anniversary of the date of issuance.

(b) A renewed license expires on the license holder's birthdate, four years after the date of the expiration of the previous license.

(c) A duplicate license expires on the date the license that was duplicated would have expired.

(d) A modified license expires on the date the license that was modified would have expired.

(e) Notwithstanding Subsection (a), the department by rule may adopt a system to implement staggered and evenly distributed license expiration dates over the four-year period beginning January 1, 1996. The department may not issue a license that is effective for less than two years. A license that is effective for less than four years and is renewed expires as provided by Subsection (b). Notwithstanding Section 411.174(a)(6), the department by rule shall prorate the nonrefundable application and license fee for applicants who receive licenses that are effective for less than four years under this subsection. This subsection expires January 1, 2005.
*(Added by L.1997, chap. 165(10.01(a)), eff. 9/1/97.)*

### §411.184. Modification.

(a) To modify a license to allow a license holder to carry a handgun of a different category than the license indicates, the license holder must:

(1) complete a proficiency examination as provided by Section 411.188(e);

(2) obtain a handgun proficiency certificate under Section 411.189 not more than six months before the date of application for a modified license; and

(3) submit to the department:

(A) an application for a modified license on a form provided by the department;

(B) a copy of the handgun proficiency certificate;

(C) payment of a modified license fee of $25; and

(D) two recent color passport photographs of the license holder.

(b) The director by rule shall adopt a modified license application form requiring an update of the information on the original completed application.

(c) The department may modify the license of a license holder who meets all the eligibility requirements and submits all the modification materials. Not later than the 45th day after receipt of the modification materials, the department shall issue the modified license or notify the license holder in writing that the modified license application was denied.

(d) On receipt of a modified license, the license holder shall return the previously issued license to the department.

*(Added by L.1997, chap. 165(10.01(a)), eff. 9/1/97.)*

## §411.185. Renewal.

(a) To renew a license, a license holder must:

(1) complete a continuing education course in handgun proficiency under Section 411.188(c) not more than six months before the date of application for renewal;

(2) obtain a handgun proficiency certificate under Section 411.189 not more than six months before the date of application for renewal; and

(3) submit to the department:

(A) an application for renewal on a form provided by the department;

(B) a copy of the handgun proficiency certificate;

(C) payment of a nonrefundable renewal fee as set by the department; and

(D) two recent color passport photographs of the applicant.

(b) The director by rule shall adopt a renewal application form requiring an update of the information on the original completed application. The director by rule shall set the renewal fee in an amount that is sufficient to cover the actual cost to the department to renew a license. Not later than the 60th day before the expiration date of the license, the department shall mail to each license holder a written notice of the expiration of the license and a renewal form.

(c) The department shall renew the license of a license holder who meets all the eligibility requirements and submits all the renewal materials. Not later than the 45th day after receipt of the renewal materials, the department shall issue the renewal or notify the license holder in writing that the renewal application was denied.

(d) The director by rule shall adopt a procedure by which a license holder who satisfies the eligibility criteria may renew a license by mail. The materials for renewal by mail must include a form to be signed and returned to the department by the applicant that describes state law regarding:

(1) the use of deadly force; and

(2) the places where it is unlawful for the holder of a license issued under this subchapter to carry a concealed handgun.

*(Added by L.1997, chap. 165(10.01(a)), eff. 9/1/97.)*

## §411.186. Revocation.

(a) A license may be revoked under this section if the license holder:

(1) was not entitled to the license at the time it was issued;

(2) gave false information on the application;

(3) subsequently becomes ineligible for a license under Section 411.172, unless the sole basis for the ineligibility is that the license holder is charged with the commission of a Class A or Class B misdemeanor or an offense under Section 42.01, Penal Code, or of a felony under an information or indictment;

(4) is convicted of an offense under Section 46.035, Penal Code; or

(5) is determined by the department to have engaged in conduct constituting a reason to suspend a license listed in Section 411.187(a) after the person's license has been previously suspended twice for the same reason.

(b) If a peace officer believes a reason listed in Subsection (a) to revoke a license exists, the officer shall prepare an affidavit on a form provided by the department stating the reason for the revocation of the license and giving the department all of the information available to the officer at the time of the preparation of the form. The officer shall attach the officer's reports relating to the license holder to the form and send the form and attachments to the appropriate division of the department at its Austin headquarters not later than the fifth working day after the date the form is prepared. The officer shall send a copy of the form and the attachments to the license holder. If the license holder has not surrendered the license or the license was not seized as evidence, the license holder shall surrender the license to the appropriate division of the department not later than the 10th day after the date the license holder receives the notice of revocation from the department, unless the license holder requests a hearing from the department. The license holder may request that the justice court in the justice court precinct in which the license holder resides review the revocation as provided by Section 411.180. If a request is made for the justice court to review the revocation and hold a hearing, the license holder shall surrender the license on the date an order of revocation is entered by the justice court.

(c) A license holder whose license is revoked for a reason listed in this section may reapply as a new applicant for the issuance of a license under this subchapter after the second anniversary of the date of the revocation if the cause for revocation does not exist on the date of the second anniversary. If the cause for revocation exists on the date of the second anniversary after the date of revocation, the license holder may not apply for a new license until the cause for revocation no longer exists and has not existed for a period of two years.

*(Added by L.1997, chap. 165(10.01(a)); chgd. by L.1999, chap. 62(9.09)(a), eff. 9/1/99.)*



### §411.187. Suspension of license.

(a) A license may be suspended under this section if the license holder:

(1) is charged with the commission of a Class A or Class B misdemeanor or an offense under Section 42.01, Penal Code, or of a felony under an information or indictment;

(2) fails to display a license as required by Section 411.205;

(3) fails to notify the department of a change of address or name as required by Section 411.181;

(4) carries a concealed handgun under the authority of this subchapter of a different category than the license holder is licensed to carry;

(5) fails to return a previously issued license after a license is modified as required by Section 411.184(d);

(6) commits an act of family violence and is the subject of an active protective order rendered under Title 4, Family Code; or

(7) is arrested for an offense involving family violence or an offense under Section 42.072, Penal Code, and is the subject of an order for emergency protection issued under Article 17.292, Code of Criminal Procedure.

(b) If a peace officer believes a reason listed in Subsection (a) to suspend a license exists, the officer shall prepare an affidavit on a form provided by the department stating the reason for the suspension of the license and giving the department all of the information available to the officer at the time of the preparation of the form. The officer shall attach the officer's reports relating to the license holder to the form and send the form and the attachments to the appropriate division of the department at its Austin headquarters not later than the fifth working day after the date the form is prepared. The officer shall send a copy of the form and the attachments to the license holder. If the license holder has not surrendered the license or the license was not seized as evidence, the license holder shall surrender the license to the appropriate division of the department not later than the 10th day after the date the license holder receives the notice of suspension from the department unless the license holder requests a hearing from the department. The license holder may request that the justice court in the justice court precinct in which the license holder resides review the suspension as provided by Section 411.180. If a request is made for the justice court to review the suspension and hold a hearing, the license holder shall surrender the license on the date an order of suspension is entered by the justice court.

(c) A license may be suspended under this section:

(1) for 30 days, if the person's license is subject to suspension for a reason listed in Subsection (a)(3), (4), or (5), except as provided by Subdivision (3);

(2) for 90 days, if the person's license is subject to suspension for a reason listed in Subsection (a)(2), except as provided by Subdivision (3);

(3) for not less than one year and not more than three years if the person's license is subject to suspension for a reason listed in Subsection (a), other than the reason listed in Subsection (a)(1), and the person's license has been previously suspended for the same reason;

(4) until dismissal of the charges if the person's license is subject to suspension for the reason listed in Subsection (a)(1); or

(5) for the duration of or the period specified by:

(A) the protective order issued under Title 4, Family Code, if the person's license is subject to suspension for the reason listed in Subsection (a)(6); or

(B) the order for emergency protection issued under Article 17.292, Code of Criminal Procedure, if the person's license is subject to suspension for the reason listed in Subsection (a)(7).
*(Added by L.1997, chap. 165(10.01(a)); chgd. by L.1999, chaps. 62(9.10)(a), 1412(6), eff. 9/1/99.)*

## §411.188. Handgun proficiency requirement.

(a) The director by rule shall establish minimum standards for handgun proficiency and shall develop a course to teach handgun proficiency and examinations to measure handgun proficiency. The course to teach handgun proficiency must contain training sessions divided into two parts. One part of the course must be classroom instruction and the other part must be range instruction and an actual demonstration by the applicant of the applicant's ability to safely and proficiently use the category of handgun for which the applicant seeks certification. An applicant may not be certified unless the applicant demonstrates, at a minimum, the degree of proficiency that is required to effectively operate a handgun of .32 caliber or above. The department shall distribute the standards, course requirements, and examinations on request to any qualified handgun instructor.

(b) Only a qualified handgun instructor may administer a handgun proficiency course. The handgun proficiency course must include at least 10 hours and not more than 15 hours of instruction on:

(1) the laws that relate to weapons and to the use of deadly force;

(2) handgun use, proficiency, and safety;

(3) nonviolent dispute resolution; and

(4) proper storage practices for handguns with an emphasis on storage practices that eliminate the possibility of accidental injury to a child.

(c) The department by rule shall develop a continuing education course in handgun proficiency for a license holder who wishes to renew a license. Only a qualified handgun instructor may administer the continuing education course. The course must include:

(1) at least four hours of instruction on one or more of the subjects listed in Subsection (b); and

(2) other information the director determines is appropriate.

(d) Only a qualified handgun instructor may administer the proficiency examination to obtain or to renew a license. The proficiency examination must include:

(1) a written section on the subjects listed in Subsection (b); and

(2) a physical demonstration of proficiency in the use of one or more handguns of specific categories and in handgun safety procedures.

(e) Only a qualified handgun instructor may administer the proficiency examination to modify a license. The proficiency examination must include a physical demonstration of the proficiency in the use of one or more handguns of specific categories and in handgun safety procedures.

(f) The department shall develop and distribute directions and materials for course instruction, test administration, and recordkeeping. All test results shall be sent to the department, and the department shall maintain a record of the results.

(g) A person who wishes to obtain or renew a license to carry a concealed handgun must apply in person to a qualified handgun instructor to take the appropriate course in handgun proficiency, demonstrate handgun proficiency, and obtain a handgun proficiency certificate as described by Section 411.189.

(h) A license holder who wishes to modify a license to allow the license holder to carry a handgun of a different category than the license indicates must apply in person to a qualified handgun instructor to demonstrate the required knowledge and proficiency to obtain a handgun proficiency certificate in that category as described by Section 411.189.

(i) A certified firearms instructor of the department may monitor any class or training presented by a qualified handgun instructor. A qualified handgun instructor shall cooperate with the department in the department's efforts to monitor the presentation of training by the qualified handgun instructor. A qualified handgun instructor shall make available for inspection to the department any and all records maintained by a qualified handgun instructor under this subchapter. The qualified handgun instructor shall keep a record of all certificates of handgun proficiency issued by the qualified handgun instructor and other information required by department rule.
*(Added by L.1997, chap. 165(10.01(a)); chgd. by L.1999, chap. 62(9.11)(a), eff. 9/1/99.)*

## §411.189. Handgun proficiency certificate.

(a) The department shall develop a sequentially numbered handgun proficiency certificate and distribute the certificate to qualified handgun instructors who administer the handgun proficiency examination described in Section 411.188. The department by rule may set a fee not to exceed $5 to cover the cost of the certificates.

Printed in the U.S.A. 2t

(b) If a person successfully completes the proficiency requirements as described in Section 411.188, the instructor shall endorse a certificate of handgun proficiency provided by the department. An applicant must successfully complete both classroom and range instruction to receive a certificate. The certificate must indicate the category of any handgun for which the applicant demonstrated proficiency during the examination.

(c) A qualified handgun instructor may submit to the department a written recommendation for disapproval of the application for a license, renewal, or modification of a license, accompanied by an affidavit stating personal knowledge or naming persons with personal knowledge of facts that lead the instructor to believe that an applicant is not qualified for handgun proficiency certification. The department may use a written recommendation submitted under this subsection as the basis for denial of a license only if the department determines that the recommendation is made in good faith and is supported by a preponderance of the evidence. The department shall make a determination under this subsection not later than the 45th day after the date the department receives the written recommendation. The 60-day period in which the department must take action under Section 411.177(b) is extended one day for each day a determination is pending under this subsection.

*(Added by L.1997, chap. 165(10.01(a)); chgd. by L.1999, chap. 62(9.12)(a), eff. 9/1/99.)*

## §411.190. Qualified handgun instructors.

(a) The director may certify as a qualified handgun instructor a person who:

(1) is certified by the Commission on Law Enforcement Officer Standards and Education or the Texas Board of Private Investigators and Private Security Agencies to instruct others in the use of handguns;

(2) regularly instructs others in the use of handguns and has graduated from a handgun instructor school that uses a nationally accepted course designed to train persons as handgun instructors; or

(3) is certified by the National Rifle Association of America as a handgun instructor.

(b) In addition to the qualifications described by Subsection (a), a qualified handgun instructor must be qualified to instruct persons in:

(1) the laws that relate to weapons and to the use of deadly force;

(2) handgun use, proficiency, and safety;

(3) nonviolent dispute resolution; and

(4) proper storage practices for handguns, including storage practices that eliminate the possibility of accidental injury to a child.

(c) In the manner applicable to a person who applies for a license to carry a concealed handgun, the department shall conduct a background check of a person who applies for certification as a qualified handgun instructor. If the background check indicates that the applicant for certification would not qualify to receive a handgun license, the department may not certify the applicant as a qualified handgun instructor. If the background check indicates that the applicant for certification would qualify to receive a handgun license, the department shall provide handgun instructor training to the applicant. The applicant shall pay a fee of $100 to the department for the training. The applicant must take and successfully complete the training offered by the department and pay the training fee before the department may certify the applicant as a qualified handgun instructor. The department shall issue a license to carry a concealed handgun under the authority of this subchapter to any person who is certified as a qualified handgun instructor and who pays to the department a fee of $100 in addition to the training fee. The department by rule may prorate or waive the training fee for an employee of another governmental entity.

(d) The certification of a qualified handgun instructor expires on the second anniversary after the date of certification. To renew a certification, the qualified handgun instructor must pay a fee of $100 and take and successfully complete the retraining courses required by department rule.

(e) After certification, a qualified handgun instructor may conduct training for applicants for a license under this subchapter.

(f) If the department determines that a reason exists to revoke, suspend, or deny a license to carry a concealed handgun with respect to a person who is a qualified handgun instructor or an applicant for certification as a qualified handgun instructor, the department shall take that action against the person's:

(1) license to carry a concealed handgun if the person is an applicant for or the holder of a license issued under this subchapter; and

(2) certification as a qualified handgun instructor.

*(Added by L.1997, chap. 165(10.01(a)); chgd. by L.1999, chaps. 62(9.13)(a), 199(1), eff. 9/1/99.)*

### §411.191. Review of denial, revocation, or suspension of certification as qualified handgun instructor.

The procedures for the review of a denial, revocation, or suspension of a license under Section 411.180 apply to the review of a denial, revocation, or suspension of certification as a qualified handgun instructor. The notice provisions of this subchapter relating to denial, revocation, or suspension of handgun licenses apply to the proposed denial, revocation, or suspension of a certification of a qualified handgun instructor or an applicant for certification as a qualified handgun instructor. *(Added by L.1997, chap. 165(10.01(a)), eff. 9/1/97.)*

### §411.192. Confidentiality of records.

The department shall disclose to a criminal justice agency information contained in its files and records regarding whether a named individual or any individual named in a specified list is licensed under this subchapter. The department shall, on written request and payment of a reasonable fee to cover costs of copying, disclose to any other individual whether a named individual or any individual whose full name is listed on a specified written list is licensed under this subchapter. Information on an individual subject to disclosure under this section includes the individual's name, date of birth, gender, race, and zip code. Except as otherwise provided by this section and by Section 411.193, all other records maintained under this subchapter are confidential and are not subject to mandatory disclosure under the open records law, Chapter 552, except that the applicant or license holder may be furnished a copy of disclosable records on request and the payment of a reasonable fee. The department shall notify a license holder of any request that is made for information relating to the license holder under this section and provide the name of the person or agency making the request. This section does not prohibit the department from making public and distributing to the public at no cost lists of individuals who are certified as qualified handgun instructors by the department. *(Added by L.1997, chap. 165(10.01(a)), eff. 9/1/97.)*

### §411.193. Statistical report.

The department shall make available, on request and payment of a reasonable fee to cover costs of copying, a statistical report that includes the number of licenses issued, denied, revoked, or suspended by the department during the preceding month, listed by age, gender, race, and zip code of the applicant or license holder. *(Added by L.1997, chap. 165(10.01(a)), eff. 9/1/97.)*

### §411.194. Reduction of fees due to indigency.

(a) Notwithstanding any other provision of this subchapter, the department shall reduce by 50 percent any fee required for the issuance of an original, duplicate, modified, or renewed license under this subchapter if the department determines that the applicant is indigent.

(b) The department shall require an applicant requesting a reduction of a fee to submit proof of indigency with the application materials.

(c) For purposes of this section, an applicant is indigent if the applicant's income is not more than 100 percent of the applicable income level established by the federal poverty guidelines. *(Added by L.1997, chap. 165(10.01(a)), eff. 9/1/97.)*

### §411.195. Reduction of fees for senior citizens.

Notwithstanding any other provision of this subchapter, the department shall reduce by 50 percent any fee required for the issuance of an original, duplicate, or modified license under this subchapter if the applicant for the license is 60 years of age or older. *(Added by L.1997, chap. 165(10.01(a)), eff. 9/1/97.)*

### §411.196. Method of payment.

A person may pay a fee required by this subchapter only by cashier's check, money order made payable to the "Texas Department of Public Safety," or any other method approved by the department. A fee received by the department under this subchapter is nonrefundable. *(Added by L.1997, chap. 165(10.01(a)), eff. 9/1/97.)*

### §411.197. Rules.

The director shall adopt rules to administer this subchapter. *(Added by L.1997, chap. 165(10.01(a)), eff. 9/1/97.)*

### §411.198. Law enforcement officer alias handgun license.

(a) On written approval of the director, the department may issue to a law enforcement officer an alias license to carry a concealed handgun to be used in supervised activities involving criminal investigations.

Printed in the U.S.A. 42

(b) It is a defense to prosecution under Section 46.035, Penal Code, that the actor, at the time of the commission of the offense, was the holder of an alias license issued under this section.
*(Added by L.1997, chap. 165(10.01(a)), eff. 9/1/97.)*

### §411.199. Honorably retired peace officers.

(a) A person who is licensed as a peace officer under Chapter 415 and who has been employed full-time as a peace officer by a law enforcement agency may apply for a license under this subchapter at any time after retirement.

(b) The person shall submit two complete sets of legible and classifiable fingerprints and a sworn statement from the head of the law enforcement agency employing the applicant. A head of a law enforcement agency may not refuse to issue a statement under this subsection. If the applicant alleges that the statement is untrue, the department shall investigate the validity of the statement. The statement must include:

(1) the name and rank of the applicant;

(2) the status of the applicant before retirement;

(3) whether or not the applicant was accused of misconduct at the time of the retirement;

(4) the physical and mental condition of the applicant;

(5) the type of weapons the applicant had demonstrated proficiency with during the last year of employment;

(6) whether the applicant would be eligible for reemployment with the agency, and if not, the reasons the applicant is not eligible; and

(7) a recommendation from the agency head regarding the issuance of a license under this subchapter.

(c) The department may issue a license under this subchapter to an applicant under this section if the applicant is honorably retired and physically and emotionally fit to possess a handgun. In this subsection, "honorably retired" means the applicant:

(1) did not retire in lieu of any disciplinary action;

(2) was employed as a full-time peace officer for not less than 10 years by one agency; and

(3) is entitled to receive a pension or annuity for service as a law enforcement officer.

(d) An applicant under this section must pay a fee of $25 for a license issued under this subchapter.

(e) A retired peace officer who obtains a license under this subchapter must maintain, for the category of weapon licensed, the proficiency required for a peace officer under Section 415.035. The department or a local law enforcement agency shall allow a retired peace officer of the department or agency an opportunity to annually demonstrate the required proficiency. The proficiency shall be reported to the department on application and renewal.

(f) A license issued under this section expires as provided by Section 411.183.

(g) A retired officer of the United States who was eligible to carry a firearm in the discharge of the officer's official duties is eligible for a license under this section. An applicant described by this subsection may submit the application at any time after retirement. The applicant shall submit with the application proper proof of retired status by presenting the following documents prepared by the agency from which the applicant retired:

(1) retirement credentials; and

(2) a letter from the agency head stating the applicant retired in good standing.

*(Added by L.1997, chap. 165(10.01(a)); chgd. by L.1999, chaps. 25(1), 62(9.14), eff. 5/3/99, 9/1/99, respectively.)*

### §411.1991. Active peace officers.

(a) A person who is licensed as a peace officer under Chapter 415 and is employed full- time as a peace officer by a law enforcement agency may apply for a license under this subchapter. The person shall submit to the department two complete sets of legible and classifiable fingerprints and a sworn statement of the head of the law enforcement agency employing the applicant. A head of a law enforcement agency may not refuse to issue a statement under this subsection. If the applicant alleges that the statement is untrue, the department shall investigate the validity of the statement. The statement must include:

(1) the name and rank of the applicant;

(2) whether the applicant has been accused of misconduct at any time during the applicant's period of employment with the agency and the disposition of that accusation;

(3) a description of the physical and mental condition of the applicant;

(4) a list of the types of weapons the applicant has demonstrated proficiency with during the preceding year; and

(5) a recommendation from the agency head that a license be issued to the person under this subchapter.

(b) The department may issue a license under this subchapter to an applicant under this section if the statement from the head of the law enforcement agency employing the applicant complies with Subsection (a) and indicates that the applicant is qualified and physically and mentally fit to carry a handgun.

(c) An applicant under this section shall pay a fee of $25 for a license issued under this subchapter.

(d) A license issued under this section expires as provided by Section 411.183.
*(Added by L.1999, chap. 62(9.15)(a), eff. 9/1/99.)*

### §411.200. Application to licensed security officers.

This subchapter does not exempt a license holder who is also employed as a security officer and licensed under the Private Investigators and Private Security Agencies Act (Article 4413(29bb), Texas Civil Statutes) from the duty to comply with that Act or Section 46.02, Penal Code. *(Added by L.1997, chap. 165(10.01(a)), eff. 9/1/97.)*

### §411.201. Active and retired judicial officers.

(a) In this section:

(1) "Active judicial officer" means a person serving as a judge or justice of the supreme court, the court of criminal appeals, a court of appeals, a district court, a criminal district court, a constitutional county court, a statutory county court, a justice court, or a municipal court.

(2) "Retired judicial officer" means:

(A) a special judge appointed under Section 26.023 or 26.024; or

(B) a senior judge designated under Section 75.001 or a judicial officer as designated or defined by Section 75.001, 831.001, or 836.001.

(b) Notwithstanding any other provision of this subchapter, the department shall issue a license under this subchapter to an active or retired judicial officer who meets the requirements of this section.

(c) An active judicial officer is eligible for a license to carry a concealed handgun under the authority of this subchapter. A retired judicial officer is eligible for a license to carry a concealed handgun under the authority of this subchapter if the officer:

(1) has not been convicted of a felony;

(2) has not, in the five years preceding the date of application, been convicted of a Class A or Class B misdemeanor;

(3) is not charged with the commission of a Class A or Class B misdemeanor or of a felony under an information or indictment;

(4) is not a chemically dependent person; and

(5) is not a person of unsound mind.

(d) An applicant for a license who is an active or retired judicial officer must submit to the department:

(1) a completed application on a form prescribed by the department;

(2) two recent color passport photographs of the applicant;

(3) a handgun proficiency certificate issued to the applicant as evidence that the applicant successfully completed the proficiency requirements of this subchapter;

(4) a nonrefundable application and license fee set by the department in an amount reasonably designed to cover the administrative costs associated with issuance of a license to carry a concealed handgun under this subchapter; and

(5) if the applicant is a retired judicial officer:

(A) two complete sets of legible and classifiable fingerprints of the applicant taken by a person employed by a law enforcement agency who is appropriately trained in recording fingerprints; and

(B) a form executed by the applicant that authorizes the department to make an inquiry into any noncriminal history records that are necessary to determine the applicant's eligibility for a license under this subchapter.

(e) On receipt of all the application materials required by this section, the department shall:

(1) if the applicant is an active judicial officer, issue a license to carry a concealed handgun under the authority of this subchapter; or

(2) if the applicant is a retired judicial officer, conduct an appropriate background investigation to determine the applicant's eligibility for the license and, if the applicant is eligible, issue a license to carry a concealed handgun under the authority of this subchapter.

(f) Except as otherwise provided by this subsection, an applicant for a license under this section must satisfy the handgun proficiency requirements of Section 411.188. The classroom instruction part of the proficiency course for an active judicial officer is not subject to a minimum hour requirement. The instruction must include instruction only on:

(1) handgun use, proficiency, and safety; and

(2) proper storage practices for handguns with an emphasis on storage practices that eliminate the possibility of accidental injury to a child.

(g) A license issued under this section expires as provided by Section 411.183 and, except as otherwise provided by this subsection, may be renewed in accordance with Section 411.185 of this subchapter. An active judicial officer is not required to attend the classroom instruction part of the continuing education proficiency course to renew a license.

(h) The department shall issue a license to carry a concealed handgun under the authority of this subchapter to an elected attorney representing the state in the prosecution of felony cases who meets the requirements of this section for an active judicial officer. The department shall waive any fee required for the issuance of an original, duplicate, or renewed license under this subchapter for an applicant who is an attorney elected or employed to represent the state in the prosecution of felony cases.

*(Added by L.1997, chap. 165(10.01(a)), eff. 9/1/97.)*

## §411.202. License a benefit.

The issuance of a license under this subchapter is a benefit to the license holder for purposes of those sections of the Penal Code to which the definition of "benefit" under Section 1.07, Penal Code, applies. *(Added by L.1997, chap. 165(10.01(a)), eff. 9/1/97.)*

## §411.203. Rights of employers.

This subchapter does not prevent or otherwise limit the right of a public or private employer to prohibit persons who are licensed under this subchapter from carrying a concealed handgun on the premises of the business. *(Added by L.1997, chap. 165(10.01(a)), eff. 9/1/97.)*

## §411.204. Notice required on certain premises.

(a) A business that has a permit or license issued under Chapter 25, 28, 32, 69, or 74, Alcoholic Beverage Code, and that derives 51 percent or more of its income from the sale of alcoholic beverages for on-premises consumption as determined by the Texas Alcoholic Beverage Commission under Section 104.06, Alcoholic Beverage Code, shall prominently display at each entrance to the business premises a sign that complies with the requirements of Subsection (c).

(b) A hospital licensed under Chapter 241, Health and Safety Code, or a nursing home licensed under Chapter 242, Health and Safety Code, shall prominently display at each entrance to the hospital or nursing home, as appropriate, a sign that complies with the requirements of Subsection (c) other than the requirement that the sign include on its face the number "51".

(c) The sign required under Subsections (a) and (b) must give notice in both English and Spanish that it is unlawful for a person licensed under this subchapter to carry a handgun on the premises. The sign must appear in contrasting colors with block letters at least one inch in height and must include on its face the number "51" printed in solid red at least five inches in height. The sign shall be displayed in a conspicuous manner clearly visible to the public.

(d) A business that has a permit or license issued under the Alcoholic Beverage Code and that is not required to display a sign under this section may be required to display a sign under Section 11.041 or 61.11, Alcoholic Beverage Code.

(e) This section does not apply to a business that has a food and beverage certificate issued under the Alcoholic Beverage Code.

*(Added by L.1997, chap. 165(10.01(a)); chgd. by L.1999, chaps. 62(9.16)(a), 523(1), eff. 9/1/99, 6/18/99, respectively.)*

## §411.205. Displaying license; penalty.

(a) If a license holder is carrying a handgun on or about the license holder's person when a magistrate or a peace officer demands that the license holder display identification, the license holder shall display both the license holder's driver's license or identification certificate issued by the department and the license holder's handgun license. A person who fails or refuses to display the license and identification as required by this subsection is subject to suspension of the person's license as provided by Section 411.187.

(b) A person commits an offense if the person fails or refuses to display the license and identification as required by Subsection (a) after previously having had the person's license suspended for a violation of that subsection. An offense under this subsection is a Class B misdemeanor. *(Added by L.1997, chap. 165(10.01(a)); chgd. by L.1999, chap. 62(9.17)(a), eff. 9/1/99.)*

### §411.206. Seizure of handgun and license.

(a) If a peace officer arrests and takes into custody a license holder who is carrying a handgun under the authority of this subchapter, the officer shall seize the license holder's handgun and license as evidence.

(b) The provisions of Article 18.19, Code of Criminal Procedure, relating to the disposition of weapons seized in connection with criminal offenses, apply to a handgun seized under this subsection.

(c) Any judgment of conviction entered by any court for an offense under Section 46.035, Penal Code, must contain the handgun license number of the convicted license holder. A certified copy of the judgment is conclusive and sufficient evidence to justify revocation of a license under Section 411.186(a)(4).
*(Added by L.1997, chap. 165(10.01(a)), eff. 9/1/97.)*

### §411.207. Authority of peace officer to disarm.

A peace officer who is acting in the lawful discharge of the officer's official duties may disarm a license holder at any time the officer reasonably believes it is necessary for the protection of the license holder, officer, or another individual. The peace officer shall return the handgun to the license holder before discharging the license holder from the scene if the officer determines that the license holder is not a threat to the officer, license holder, or another individual and if the license holder has not violated any provision of this subchapter or committed any other violation that results in the arrest of the license holder. *(Added by L.1997, chap. 165(10.01(a)), eff. 9/1/97.)*

### §411.208. Limitation of liability.

(a) A court may not hold the state, an agency or subdivision of the state, an officer or employee of the state, a peace officer, or a qualified handgun instructor liable for damages caused by:

(1) an action authorized under this subchapter or a failure to perform a duty imposed by this subchapter; or

(2) the actions of an applicant or license holder that occur after the applicant has received a license or been denied a license under this subchapter.

(b) A cause of action in damages may not be brought against the state, an agency or subdivision of the state, an officer or employee of the state, a peace officer, or a qualified handgun instructor for any damage caused by the actions of an applicant or license holder under this subchapter.

(c) The department is not responsible for any injury or damage inflicted on any person by an applicant or license holder arising or alleged to have arisen from an action taken by the department under this subchapter.

(d) The immunities granted under Subsections (a), (b), and (c) do not apply to an act or a failure to act by the state, an agency or subdivision of the state, an officer of the state, or a peace officer if the act or failure to act was capricious or arbitrary.
*(Added by L.1997, chap. 165(10.01(a)), eff. 9/1/97.)*

## CHAPTER 414. CRIME STOPPERS ADVISORY COUNCIL
*(Selected Section)*



### §414.009. Misuse of information.

(a) A person who is a member or employee of the council or who accepts a report of criminal activity on behalf of a crime stoppers organization commits an offense if the person intentionally or knowingly divulges to a person not employed by a law enforcement agency the content of a report of a criminal act or the identity of the person who made the report without the consent of the person who made the report.

(b) An offense under this section is a Class A misdemeanor, except that an offense under this section is a third degree felony if the offense is committed with intent to obtain monetary gain or other benefit.

(c) A person convicted of an offense under this section is not eligible for state employment during the five-year period following the date that the conviction becomes final.
*(Chgd. by L.1999, chap. 1560(1), eff. 6/19/99.)*

## CHAPTER 415. COMMISSION ON LAW ENFORCEMENT OFFICER STANDARDS AND EDUCATION

*(Repealed by L.1999, chap. 388(5)(b)(1), eff. 9/1/99. See, now, Occupations Code, Chapter 1701.)*

# SUBTITLE C. STATE MILITARY FORCES AND VETERANS

## CHAPTER 431. STATE MILITIA

### SUBCHAPTER F. SERVICE AND DUTIES



**§431.086. Exemption from arrest.**

(a) A member of the state military forces may not be arrested, except for treason, felony, or breach of the peace, while the person is going to or coming from a place that the person was required to be for military duty.

(b) This section does not prevent a peace officer from issuing a traffic summons or citation to appear in court at a later date that does not conflict with the member's duty hours.

# SUBTITLE E. OTHER EXECUTIVE AGENCIES AND PROGRAMS

*(Heading chgd. by L.1993, chap. 107(4.03)(a), eff. 8/30/93.)*

## CHAPTER 466. STATE LOTTERY

*(Added by L.1993, chap. 107(4.03)(b), eff. 8/30/93.)*
*(Selected Sections)*

### SUBCHAPTER F. REGULATION OF GAMES



### SUBCHAPTER G. OFFENSES

## SUBCHAPTER I. PRIZES

466.409. Treatment of prize payable on ticket purchased by ineligible person.

## SUBCHAPTER F. REGULATION OF GAMES

**§466.253.** *(Renumbered to §§466.3051, 466.409, by L.1995, chap. 76(6.31), eff. 9/1/95.)*

**§466.254. Purchase of ticket by or payment of prize to certain persons.**

A person may not purchase a ticket or claim, collect, or receive a lottery prize or a share of a lottery prize if the person is:

(1) a member, officer, or employee of a person that has a contract with the commission to sell or lease goods or services used in the operation of the lottery, and the member, officer, or employee is directly involved in selling or leasing the goods or performing the services that are the subject of the contract with the commission;

(2) a member, officer, or employee of a lottery operator;

(3) an officer or employee of the commission; or

(4) a spouse, child, brother, sister, or parent residing as a member of the same household in the principal place of residence of a person described by Subdivision (1), (2), or (3).

*(Added by L.1993, chap. 107(4.03)(b); chgd. by L.1995, chap. 76(6.32); L.1999, chap. 678(2), eff. 9/1/99.)*

**§466.255.** *(Renumbered to §§466.3052, 466.3053 by L.1995, chap. 76(6.33), eff. 9/1/95.)*

**§466.256. Representations by person claiming lottery prize.**

A person claiming or attempting to claim a lottery prize or a share of a lottery prize represents that the ticket or other item showing that the person is entitled to the prize or share was lawfully obtained, is not stolen, forged, or altered, and has not previously been redeemed. *(Added by L.1995, chap. 76(6.34), eff. 9/1/95.)*

## SUBCHAPTER G. OFFENSES

**§466.302. Sale of ticket at price greater than fixed price.**

(a) A person commits an offense if the person intentionally or knowingly sells a ticket at a price the person knows is greater than that fixed by the commission or by the lottery operator authorized to set that price.

(b) An offense under this section is a Class A misdemeanor.

*(Added by L.1993, chap. 107(4.03)(b); chgd. by L.1995, chap. 76(6.36), eff. 9/1/95.)*

**§466.303. Sale of ticket by unauthorized person.**

(a) Except as provided by Subsection (b), a person who is not a sales agent or an employee of a sales agent commits an offense if the person intentionally or knowingly sells a ticket.

(b) A lottery operator may sell tickets to a sales agent. A person who is not a sales agent may distribute tickets as premiums to customers, employees, or other persons who deal with the person if no purchase is required to entitle the recipient to the ticket. A qualified organization as defined in Section 2, Charitable Raffle Enabling Act (Article 179f, Revised Statutes, as added by Chapter 957, Acts of the 71st Legislature, Regular Session, 1989), may distribute tickets as a prize in a raffle authorized by that Act.

(c) An offense under this section is a felony of the third degree.

*(Added by L.1993, chap. 107(4.03)(b); chgd. by L.1995, chap. 76(6.37), eff. 9/1/95.)*

**§466.304. Sale of ticket at unauthorized location.**

(a) A person commits an offense if the person sells a ticket at a location other than the location of a sales agency.

(b) An offense under this section is a Class A misdemeanor.

*(Added by L.1993, chap. 107(4.03)(b), eff. 8/30/93.)*

## §466.305. Sale of ticket on credit.

(a) A sales agent or an employee of a sales agent commits an offense if the person intentionally or knowingly sells a ticket to another person by extending credit or lending money to the person to enable the person to purchase the ticket.

(b) An offense under this section is a Class C misdemeanor.

*(Added by L.1993, chap. 107(4.03)(b), eff. 8/30/93.)*

## §466.3051. Sale of ticket to person younger than 18 years.

(a) A sales agent or an employee of a sales agent commits an offense if the person intentionally or knowingly sells or offers to sell a ticket to an individual that the person knows is younger than 18 years of age.

(b) A person 18 years of age or older may purchase a ticket to give as a gift to another person, including an individual younger than 18 years of age.

(c) An offense under this section is a Class C misdemeanor.

*(Added by L.1993, chap. 107(4.03)(b); renumbered from §466.253 and chgd. by L.1995, chap. 76(6.31), eff. 9/1/95.)*

## §466.3052. Purchase and sale of tickets.

(a) A person commits an offense if the person intentionally or knowingly sells a ticket and the person accepts anything other than the following as payment for the ticket:

(1) United States currency;

(2) a negotiable instrument in the form of a check that meets the requirements of Section 3.104, Business & Commerce Code;

(3) a debit made through a financial institution debit card;

(4) a coupon or voucher issued by the commission for purposes of purchasing a lottery ticket; or

(5) a mail order subscription on a mail order subscription form authorized by the commission

(b) An offense under this section is a Class C misdemeanor.

*(Added by L.1993, chap. 107(4.03)(b); renumbered from §466.255 and chgd. by L.1995, chap. 76(6.33); chgd. by L.1999, chap. 687(1), eff. 9/1/99.)*

## §466.3053. Purchase of ticket with proceeds of AFDC check or food stamps.

(a) A person commits an offense if the person intentionally or knowingly purchases a ticket with:

(1) the proceeds of a check issued as a payment under the Aid to Families with Dependent Children program administered under Chapter 31, Human Resources Code; or

(2) a food stamp coupon issued under the food stamp program administered under Chapter 33, Human Resources Code.

(b) An offense under this section is a Class C misdemeanor.

*(Renumbered from §466.255 and chgd. by L.1995, chap. 76(6.33), eff. 9/1/95.)*

## §466.3054. Group purchase arrangements.

(a) A person commits an offense if, for financial gain, the person establishes or promotes a group purchase or pooling arrangement under which tickets are purchased on behalf of the group or pool and any prize is divided among the members of the group or pool, and the person intentionally or knowingly:

(1) uses any part of the funds solicited or accepted for a purpose other than purchasing tickets on behalf of the group or pool; or

(2) retains a share of any prize awarded as compensation for establishing or promoting the group purchase or pooling arrangement.

(b) An offense under this section is a felony of the third degree.

*(Added by L.1995, chap. 76(6.38), eff. 9/1/95.)*

## §466.306. Forgery; alteration of ticket.

(a) A person commits an offense if the person intentionally or knowingly alters or forges a ticket.

(b) An offense under this section is a felony of the third degree unless it is shown on the trial of the offense that the prize alleged to be authorized by the ticket forged or altered is greater that $10,000, in which event the offense is a felony of the second degree.

*(Added by L.1993, chap. 107(4.03)(b), eff. 8/30/93.)*

**§466.307. Influencing selection of winner.**

(a) A person commits an offense if the person intentionally or knowingly influences or attempts to influence the selection of the winner of a lottery game.

(b) An offense under this section is a felony of the third degree unless it is shown on the trial of the offense that a prize in the game influenced or attempted to be influenced is greater that $10,000, in which event the offense is a felony of the second degree.

*(Added by L.1993, chap. 107(4.03)(b), eff. 8/30/93.)*

**§466.308. Claiming lottery prize by fraud.**

(a) A person commits an offense if the person intentionally or knowingly:

(1) claims a lottery prize or a share of a lottery prize by means of fraud, deceit, or misrepresentation; or

(2) aids or agrees to aid another person or persons to claim a lottery prize or a share of a lottery prize by means of fraud, deceit, or misrepresentation.

(b) In this section, "claim" includes an attempt to claim, without regard to whether the attempt is successful.

(c) An offense under this section is a Class A misdemeanor unless it is shown on the trial of the offense that:

(1) the amount claimed is greater than $200 but not more than $10,000, in which event the offense is a felony of the third degree;

(2) the amount claimed is greater than $10,000, in which event the offense is a felony of the second degree; or

(3) the person has previously been convicted of an offense under Section 466.306, 466.307, 466.309, 466.310, or this section, in which event the offense is a felony of the third degree, unless the offense is designated as a felony of the second degree under Subdivision (2).

*(Added by L.1993, chap. 107(4.03)(b); chgd. by L.1995, chap. 76(6.39), eff. 9/1/95.)*

**§466.309. Tampering with lottery equipment.**

(a) A person commits an offense if the person intentionally or knowingly tampers with, damages, defaces, or renders inoperable any vending machine, electronic computer terminal, or other mechanical device used in a lottery game.

(b) An offense under this section is a felony of the third degree.

*(Added by L.1993, chap. 107(4.03)(b), eff. 8/30/93.)*

**§466.310. Certain transfers of claims.**

(a) A person commits an offense if the person:

(1) induces another person to assign or transfer a right to claim a prize;

(2) offers for sale the right to claim a prize; or

(3) offers, for compensation, to claim the prize of another person.

(b) An offense under this section is a felony of the third degree, unless it is shown on the trial of the offense that the prize involved is greater that $10,000, in which event the offense is a felony of the second degree.

*(Added by L.1993, chap. 107(4.03)(b), eff. 8/30/93.)*

**§466.311. Reporting and record violations.**

(a) A person commits an offense if the person, in a license application, in a book or record required to be maintained by this chapter or a rule adopted under this chapter, or in a report required to be submitted by this chapter or a rule adopted under this chapter:

(1) intentionally or knowingly makes a statement or entry that the person knows to be false or misleading; or

(2) fails to maintain or make an entry the person knows is required to be maintained or made.

(b) A person commits an offense if the person knowingly refuses to produce for inspection by the director, executive director, commission, or state auditor a book, record, or document required to be maintained or made by this chapter or a rule adopted under this chapter.

(c) An offense under this section is a Class A misdemeanor.

*(Added by L.1993, chap. 107(4.03)(b); chgd. by L.1995, chap. 76(6.40), eff. 9/1/95.)*

**§466.312. False, incorrect, or deceptive statement.**

(a) A person commits an offense if the person intentionally or knowingly makes a material and false, incorrect, or deceptive statement to a person conducting an investigation or exercising discretion under this chapter or a rule adopted under this chapter.

(b) In this section, "statement" includes:
(1) a written or oral statement; and
(2) a sworn or unsworn statement.
(c) An offense under this section is a Class A misdemeanor.
*(Added by L.1993, chap. 107(4.03)(b); chgd. by L.1995, chap. 76(6.41), eff. 9/1/95.)*

**§466.313. Conspiracy.**

(a) A person commits an offense of conspiracy if, with intent that an offense under this chapter be committed:

(1) the person agrees with one or more other persons that they or one or more of them engage in conduct that would constitute the offense; and

(2) one or more of the persons agreeing under Subdivision (1) performs an overt act in pursuance of the agreement.

(b) An agreement constituting a conspiracy may be inferred from acts of the parties.

(c) It is no defense to prosecution for conspiracy under this section that:

(1) one or more of the coconspirators is not criminally responsible for the object offense;

(2) one or more of the coconspirators has been acquitted, so long as at least two coconspirators have not been acquitted;

(3) one or more of the coconspirators has not been prosecuted or convicted, has been convicted of a different offense, or is immune from prosecution;

(4) the actor belongs to a class of persons that by definition of the object offense is legally incapable of committing the object offense in an individual capacity; or

(5) the object offense was not actually committed.

(d) An offense under this section is one category lower than the most serious offense under this chapter that is the object of the conspiracy, and if the most serious offense under this chapter that is the object of the conspiracy is a felony of the third degree, the offense is a Class A misdemeanor.

*(Added by L.1993, chap. 107(4.03)(b), eff. 8/30/93.)*



## SUBCHAPTER I. PRIZES

**§466.409. Treatment of prize payable on ticket purchased by ineligible person.**

If an individual listed in Section 466.254 purchases a ticket or claims or otherwise attempts to collect or receive a lottery prize or a share of a lottery prize or an individual younger than 18 years of age directly purchases a ticket, the individual is not eligible to receive a prize or share of a prize, and the prize or share of a prize otherwise payable on the ticket is treated as an unclaimed prize as provided by Section 466.408. *(Renumbered from §466.253 and chgd. by L.1995, chap. 76(6.31), eff. 9/1/95.)*

# SUBTITLE G. CORRECTIONS

# CHAPTER 500. MISCELLANEOUS DISCIPLINARY MATTERS

*(Heading chgd. by L.1995, chap. 321(1.102), eff. 9/1/95.)*

**§500.004.** *(Repealed by L.1991, 2nd C.S., chap. 10(5.02), eff. 10/1/91. See now Penal Code section 38.11.)*

# CHAPTER 508. PAROLE AND MANDATORY SUPERVISION

*(Added by L.1997, chap. 165(12.01), eff. 9/1/97.)*

## SUBCHAPTER A. GENERAL PROVISIONS

## SUBCHAPTER B. BOARD OF PARDONS AND PAROLES





## SUBCHAPTER C. REPRESENTATION OF INMATES



## SUBCHAPTER D. PARDONS AND PAROLES DIVISION



## SUBCHAPTER E. PAROLE AND MANDATORY SUPERVISION; RELEASE PROCEDURES

## SUBCHAPTER F. MANDATORY CONDITIONS OF PAROLE OR MANDATORY SUPERVISION



## SUBCHAPTER G. DISCRETIONARY CONDITIONS OF PAROLE OR MANDATORY SUPERVISION



## SUBCHAPTER H. WARRANTS



## SUBCHAPTER I. HEARINGS AND SANCTIONS

## SUBCHAPTER J. MISCELLANEOUS





## SUBCHAPTER A. GENERAL PROVISIONS

### §508.001. Definitions.

In this chapter:

(1) "Board" means the Board of Pardons and Paroles.

(2) "Community supervision and corrections department" means a department established under Chapter 76.

(3) "Director" means the director of the pardons and paroles division.

(4) "Division" means the pardons and paroles division.

(5) "Mandatory supervision" means the release of an eligible inmate sentenced to the institutional division so that the inmate may serve the remainder of the inmate's sentence not on parole but under the supervision of the pardons and paroles division.

(6) "Parole" means the discretionary and conditional release of an eligible inmate sentenced to the institutional division so that the inmate may serve the remainder of the inmate's sentence under the supervision of the pardons and paroles division.

(7) "Parole officer" means a person appointed by the director and assigned the duties of assessment of risks and needs, investigation, case management, and supervision of releasees to ensure that releasees are complying with the conditions of parole or mandatory supervision.

(8) "Policy board" means the Board of Pardons and Paroles Policy Board.

(9) "Releasee" means a person released on parole or to mandatory supervision.
*(Added by L.1997, chap. 165(12.01); chgd. by L.1999, chap. 62(10.01), eff. 9/1/99.)*

### §508.002. Clemency, commutation distinguished.

Neither parole nor mandatory supervision is a commutation of sentence or any other form of clemency. *(Added by L.1997, chap. 165(12.01), eff. 9/1/97.)*

### §508.003. Inapplicable to juveniles and certain inmates.

(a) This chapter does not apply to an emergency absence under escort granted to an inmate by the institutional division under Section 501.006.

(b) Except as provided by Subsection (c), this chapter does not apply to release on parole from an institution for juveniles.

(c) The provisions of this chapter not in conflict with Section 508.156 apply to parole of a person from the Texas Youth Commission under that section.
*(Added by L.1997, chap. 165(12.01), eff. 9/1/97.)*

### §§508.004 to 508.030. *(Reserved.)*

## SUBCHAPTER B. BOARD OF PARDONS AND PAROLES

### §508.031. Composition of board.

(a) The board consists of 18 members appointed by the governor with the advice and consent of the senate.

(b) Appointments to the board must be made without regard to the race, color, disability, sex, religion, age, or national origin of the appointed members.
*(Added by L.1997, chap. 165(12.01); chgd. by L.1999, chap. 554(1), eff. 9/1/99.)*

## §508.032. Requirements for membership.

(a) Board members must be representative of the general public.

(b) A member must have resided in this state for the two years before appointment.

*(Added by L.1997, chap. 165(12.01), eff. 9/1/97.)*

## §508.033. Disqualifications.

(a) A person is not eligible for appointment as a member of the board if the person or the person's spouse:

(1) is employed by or participates in the management of a business entity or other organization receiving funds from the department or the board;

(2) owns or controls, directly or indirectly, more than a 10-percent interest in a business entity or other organization:

(A) regulated by the department; or

(B) receiving funds from the department or the board; or

(3) uses or receives a substantial amount of tangible goods, services, or funds from the department or the board, other than compensation or reimbursement authorized by law for board membership, attendance, or expenses.

(b) In determining eligibility under Subsection (a)(3), the compensation or reimbursement that a board member's spouse receives as an employee of the board or the department may not be considered. This subsection does not affect any restriction on employment or board membership imposed by any other law.

(c) A person may not be a member of the board and may not be an employee of the division or the board employed in a "bona fide executive, administrative, or professional capacity," as that phrase is used for purposes of establishing an exemption to the overtime provisions of the federal Fair Labor Standards Act of 1938 (29 U.S.C. Section 201 et seq.) and its subsequent amendments, if:

(1) the person is an officer, employee, or paid consultant of a Texas trade association in the field of criminal justice; or

(2) the person's spouse is an officer, manager, or paid consultant of a Texas trade association in the field of criminal justice.

(d) A person who is required to register as a lobbyist under Chapter 305 because of the person's activities for compensation in or on behalf of a profession related to the operation of the board may not:

(1) serve as a member of the board; or

(2) act as the general counsel to the board or division.

(e) In this section, "Texas trade association" means a cooperative and voluntarily joined association of business or professional competitors in this state designed to assist its members and its industry or profession in:

(1) dealing with mutual business or professional problems; and

(2) promoting their common interests.

*(Added by L.1997, chap. 165(12.01); chgd. by L.1999, chaps. 62(10.02), (10.03), (10.04), 554(2), eff. 9/1/99.)*

## §508.034. Grounds for removal.

(a) It is a ground for removal from the board that a member:

(1) does not have at the time of taking office the qualification required by Section 508.032(b) for appointment to the board;

(2) is ineligible for membership under Section 508.033;

(3) is unable to discharge the member's duties for a substantial part of the term for which the member is appointed because of illness or disability; or

(4) is absent from more than half of the regularly scheduled board or panel meetings that the member is eligible to attend during each calendar year, except when the absence is excused by majority vote of the board.

(b) It is a ground for removal from the board and the policy board if a member of the policy board is absent from more than half of the regularly scheduled policy board meetings that the member is eligible to attend during each calendar year.

(c) The board administrator or the board administrator's designee shall provide to members of the board, to members of the policy board, and to employees, as often as necessary, information regarding their qualification for office or employment under this chapter and their responsibilities under applicable laws relating to standards of conduct for state officers or employees.

(d) The validity of an action of:

(1) the board or panel is not affected by the fact that the action is taken when a ground for removal of a board member exists; and

(2) the policy board is not affected by the fact that the action is taken when a ground for removal of a member of the policy board exists.

(e) If the general counsel to the board has knowledge that a potential ground for removal exists, the general counsel shall notify the presiding officer of the board of the potential ground. The presiding officer shall notify the governor and the attorney general that a potential ground for removal exists. If the potential ground for removal involves the presiding officer, the general counsel to the board shall notify the governor and the attorney general that a potential ground for removal exists.

*(Added by L.1997, chap. 165(12.01); chgd. by L.1999, chaps. 62(10.05), 554(3), eff. 9/1/99.)*

### §508.035. Presiding officer.

(a) The governor shall designate one member to serve as presiding officer of the board.

(b) The presiding officer serves in that capacity at the pleasure of the governor.

*(Added by L.1997, chap. 165(12.01), eff. 9/1/97.)*



### §508.036. Policy board: composition; general duties.

(a) The governor shall designate six members of the board to serve as the Board of Pardons and Paroles Policy Board. The governor shall designate the presiding officer of the board as one of the six members of the policy board, and the presiding officer of the board shall serve as presiding officer of the policy board. Service on the policy board is an additional duty of office for members appointed to the policy board.

(b) Members of the board designated as members of the policy board serve on the policy board for six-year terms that are concurrent with their six-year terms on the board, with the service of two members expiring February 1 of each odd-numbered year.

(c) The policy board shall:

(1) adopt rules relating to the decision-making processes used by the board and parole panels;

(2) establish caseloads for members of the board and assign duties to members of the policy board that are in addition to the duties those members have in handling a caseload;

(3) update parole guidelines, assign precedential value to previous decisions of the board relating to the granting of parole and the revocation of parole or mandatory supervision, and develop policies to ensure that members of the board use guidelines and previous decisions of the board in making decisions under this chapter;

(4) require members of the board to file activity reports, on forms provided by the policy board, that provide information on release decisions made by members of the board, the workload of the members of the board, and the use of parole guidelines by members of the board; and

(5) report at least annually to the governor and the legislature on board activities, parole release decisions, and the use of parole guidelines by the board.

*(Added by L.1997, chap. 165(12.01); repealed and added by L.1999, chap. 62(10.06), eff. 9/1/99.)*

### §508.0361. Policy board: general administrative provisions.

(a) The policy board shall:

(1) develop and implement policies that clearly separate the policy-making responsibilities of the policy board and the management responsibilities of the board administrator and the staff of the board;

(2) prepare information of public interest describing the functions of the board and make the information available to the public and appropriate state agencies;

(3) comply with federal and state laws related to program and facility accessibility; and

(4) prepare annually a complete and detailed written report that meets the reporting requirements applicable to financial reporting provided in the General Appropriations Act and accounts for all funds received and disbursed by the board during the preceding fiscal year.

(b) The board administrator shall prepare and maintain a written plan that describes how a person who does not speak English can be provided reasonable access to the board's programs and services.

(c) The policy board is subject to the open meetings law, Chapter 551, and the administrative procedure law, Chapter 2001, as if it were, respectively, a governmental body or a state agency under those laws. This subsection does not affect the provisions of Section 2001.223 exempting hearings and interviews conducted by the board or the division from Section 2001.038 and Subchapters C-H, Chapter 2001.

(d) Members of the board who are not members of the policy board may participate in policy board meetings but may not vote.
*(Added by L.1999, chap. 62(10.07), eff. 9/1/99.)*

### §508.0362. Training required.

(a) A person who is appointed to and qualifies for office as a member of the board or the policy board may not vote, deliberate, or be counted as a member in attendance at a meeting of the board or policy board until the person completes at least one course of a training program that complies with this section.

(b) A training program must provide information to the person regarding:

(1) the enabling legislation that created the board and the policy board;

(2) the programs operated by the board;

(3) the role and functions of the board;

(4) the rules of the board;

(5) the current budget for the board;

(6) the results of the most recent formal audit of the board;

(7) the requirements of the:

(A) open meetings law, Chapter 551;

(B) open records law, Chapter 552; and

(C) administrative procedure law, Chapter 2001;

(8) the requirements of the conflict of interest laws and other laws relating to public officials; and

(9) any applicable ethics policies adopted by the policy board or the Texas Ethics Commission.

(c) A person appointed to the board or policy board is entitled to reimbursement, as provided by the General Appropriations Act, for the travel expenses incurred in attending the training program regardless of whether the attendance at the program occurs before or after the person qualifies for office.
*(Added by L.1999, chap. 62(10.08), eff. 9/1/99; chgd. by L.1999, chap. 554(4), eff. 9/1/99.)*

### §508.037. Terms; removal.

(a) A board member holds office for a term of six years.

(b) The terms of one-third of the members expire February 1 of each odd-numbered year.

(c) The governor may remove a board member, other than a member appointed by another governor, at any time and for any reason.
*(Added by L.1997, chap. 165(12.01), eff. 9/1/97.)*

### §508.038. Vacancies.

If a vacancy occurs, the governor shall appoint in the same manner as other appointments are made a person to serve the remainder of the unexpired term. *(Added by L.1997, chap. 165(12.01), eff. 9/1/97.)*

### §508.039. Compensation.

A board member is paid the salary the legislature determines in the General Appropriations Act. *(Added by L.1997, chap. 165(12.01), eff. 9/1/97.)*

### §508.040. Personnel.

(a) The policy board shall employ and supervise:

(1) a general counsel to the board;

(2) a board administrator to manage the day-to-day activities of the board;

(3) hearing officers;

(4) personnel to assist in clemency matters; and

(5) secretarial or clerical personnel.

(b) The board administrator or the board administrator's designee shall prepare and maintain a written policy statement that implements a program of equal employment opportunity under which all personnel decisions of the board are made without regard to race, color, disability, sex, religion, age, or national origin. The policy statement must include:

(1) personnel policies, including policies relating to recruitment, evaluation, selection, training, and promotion of personnel, that show the intent of the board to avoid the unlawful employment practices described by Chapter 21, Labor Code; and

(2) an analysis of the extent to which the composition of the board's personnel is in accordance with state and federal law and a description of reasonable methods to achieve compliance with state and federal law.

(c) The policy statement must be updated annually, be reviewed by the Commission on Human Rights for compliance with Subsection (b)(1), and be filed with the governor's office.

(d) The board administrator or the board administrator's designee shall develop an intra-agency career ladder program that addresses opportunities for mobility and advancement for employees within the board. The program shall require intra-agency posting of all positions concurrently with any public posting.

(e) The board administrator or the board administrator's designee shall develop a system of annual performance evaluations that are based on documented employee performance. All merit pay for board employees must be based on the system established under this subsection.
*(Added by L.1997, chap. 165(12.01); chgd. by L.1999, chaps. 62(10.09), 554(5), eff. 9/1/99.)*

## §508.041. Designee training; handbook.

(a) The policy board shall develop and implement:

(1) a training program that each newly hired employee of the board designated to conduct hearings under Section 508.281 must complete before conducting a hearing without the assistance of a board member or experienced designee; and

(2) a training program to provide an annual update to designees of the board on issues and procedures relating to the revocation process.

(b) The policy board shall prepare and biennially update a procedural manual to be used by designees of the board. The policy board shall include in the manual:

(1) descriptions of decisions in previous hearings determined by the policy board to have value as precedents for decisions in subsequent hearings;

(2) laws and court decisions relevant to decision making in hearings; and

(3) case studies useful in decision making in hearings.

(c) The policy board shall prepare and update as necessary a handbook to be made available to participants in hearings under Section 508.281, such as defense attorneys, persons released on parole or mandatory supervision, and witnesses. The handbook must describe in plain language the procedures used in a hearing under Section 508.281.
*(Added by L.1997, chap. 165(12.01); repealed and added by L.1999, chap. 62(10.10), eff. 9/1/99.)*

## §508.042. Training program for members.

(a) The policy board shall develop for board members a comprehensive training and education program on the criminal justice system, with special emphasis on the parole process.

(b) A new member may not participate in a vote of the board or a panel, deliberate, or be counted as a member in attendance at a meeting of the board or policy board until the member completes the program.
*(Added by L.1997, chap. 165(12.01); chgd. by L.1999, chaps. 62(10.11), 554(6), eff. 9/1/99.)*

## §508.043. Gifts and grants.

The board may apply for and accept gifts or grants from any public or private source for use in any lawful purpose of the board. *(Added by L.1997, chap. 165(12.01), eff. 9/1/97.)*

## §508.044. Powers and duties of board.

(a) A board member shall give full time to the duties of the member's office.

(b) In addition to performing the duties imposed on the board by the Texas Constitution, board members shall determine:

(1) which inmates are to be released on parole;

(2) conditions of parole or mandatory supervision;

(3) which releasees may be released from supervision and reporting; and

(4) the revocation of parole or mandatory supervision.

(c) The policy board shall develop and implement a policy that clearly defines circumstances under which a board member should disqualify himself or herself from voting on:

(1) a parole decision; or

(2) a decision to revoke parole or mandatory supervision.

(d) The policy board may adopt reasonable rules as the policy board considers proper or necessary relating to:

(1) the eligibility of an inmate for release on parole or release to mandatory supervision;

(2) the conduct of a parole or mandatory supervision hearing; or

(3) conditions to be imposed on a releasee.

(e) The policy board may provide a written plan for the administrative review of actions taken by a parole panel by the entire membership or by a subset of the entire membership of the board. *(Added by L.1997, chap. 165(12.01); chgd. by L.1999, chap. 62(10.12), (10.13), (10.14), eff. 9/1/99.)*

**§508.045. Parole panels.**

(a) Except as provided by Section 508.046, board members shall act in panels composed of three persons each in matters of:

(1) release on parole;

(2) release to mandatory supervision; and

(3) revocation of parole or mandatory supervision.

(b) The presiding officer of the board shall designate the composition of each panel.

(c) A parole panel may:

(1) grant, deny, or revoke parole;

(2) revoke mandatory supervision; and

(3) conduct parole revocation hearings and mandatory supervision revocation hearings.

*(Added by L.1997, chap. 165(12.01), eff. 9/1/97.)*



**§508.046. Extraordinary vote required.**

To release on parole an inmate who was convicted of a capital felony or an offense under Section 21.11(a)(1) or 22.021, Penal Code, or who is required under Section 508.145(c) to serve 35 calendar years before becoming eligible for release on parole, all members of the board must vote on the release on parole of the inmate, and at least two-thirds of the members must vote in favor of the release on parole. A member of the board may not vote on the release unless the member first receives a copy of a written report from the department on the probability that the inmate would commit an offense after being released on parole. *(Added by L.1997, chap. 165(12.01), eff. 9/1/97.)*

**§508.047. Meetings.**

(a) The members of the policy board shall meet at least once in each quarter of the calendar year at a site determined by the presiding officer.

(b) The members of the board are not required to meet as a body to perform the members' duties in clemency matters.

(c) A majority of each parole panel constitutes a quorum for the transaction of the panel's business. A panel's decision must be by majority vote.

(d) The members of a parole panel are not required to meet as a body to perform the members' duties, except to conduct a hearing under Section 508.281.

*(Added by L.1997, chap. 165(12.01); chgd. by L.1999, chap. 62(10.15), eff. 9/1/99.)*

**§508.048. Subpoenas.**

(a) A parole panel may issue a subpoena requiring the attendance of a witness or the production of any record, book, paper, or document the panel considers necessary for investigation of the case of a person before the panel.

(b) A member of the board may sign a subpoena and administer an oath.

(c) A peace officer, parole officer, or community supervision and corrections department officer may serve the subpoena in the same manner as similar process in a court of record having original jurisdiction of criminal actions is served.

(d) A person who testifies falsely, fails to appear when subpoenaed, or fails or refuses to produce material under the subpoena is subject to the same orders and penalties to which a person taking those actions before a court is subject.

(e) On application of the board, a court of record having original jurisdiction of criminal actions may compel the attendance of a witness, the production of material, or the giving of testimony before the board, by an attachment for contempt or in the same manner as the court may otherwise compel the production of evidence.

*(Added by L.1997, chap. 165(12.01), eff. 9/1/97.)*

**§508.049. Mission statement.**

(a) The policy board, after consultation with the governor and the Texas Board of Criminal Justice, shall adopt a mission statement that reflects the responsibilities for the operation of the parole process that are assigned to the policy board, the board, the division, the department, or the Texas Board of Criminal Justice.

(b) The policy board shall include in the mission statement a description of specific locations at which the board intends to conduct business related to the operation of the parole process. *(Added by L.1997, chap. 165(12.01); chgd. by L.1999, chap. 62(10.16), eff. 9/1/99.)*

### §508.050. Report to governor.

(a) On request of the governor, the board shall investigate a person being considered by the governor for:

(1) pardon;
(2) commutation of sentence;
(3) reprieve;
(4) remission of fine; or
(5) forfeiture.

(b) The board shall report to the governor on its investigation and make recommendations about the person to the governor.
*(Added by L.1997, chap. 165(12.01), eff. 9/1/97.)*

### §508.051. Sunset provision.

The Board of Pardons and Paroles is subject to review under Chapter 325 (Texas Sunset Act), but is not abolished under that chapter. The board shall be reviewed during the period in which the Texas Department of Criminal Justice is reviewed. *(Added by L.1997, chap. 165(12.01); chgd. by L.1999, chap. 62(10.17), eff. 9/1/99.)*



### §508.052. Computers; office space; other equipment.

(a) The department by interagency contract may provide to the board necessary computer equipment and computer access to all computerized records and physical access to all printed records in the custody of the department that are related to the duties and functions of the board.

(b) The department by interagency contract may provide to the board necessary and appropriate:

(1) office space at locations designated by the presiding officer of the board; and
(2) utilities and communications equipment.

*(Added by L.1997, chap. 165(12.01), eff. 9/1/97.)*

### §§508.053 to 508.080. *(Reserved.)*

## SUBCHAPTER C. REPRESENTATION OF INMATES

### §508.081. Definitions.

In this subchapter:

(1) "Compensation" has the meaning assigned by Section 305.002.
(2) "Inmate" includes:
(A) an administrative releasee;
(B) an inmate imprisoned in the institutional division; and
(C) a person confined in a transfer facility or county jail awaiting:
(i) transfer to the institutional division; or
(ii) a revocation hearing.
(3) "Represent" means to directly or indirectly contact in person or by telephone, facsimile transmission, or correspondence a member or employee of the board or an employee of the department on behalf of an inmate.

*(Added by L.1997, chap. 165(12.01), eff. 9/1/97.)*

### §508.082. Rules.

The policy board shall adopt rules relating to:

(1) the submission and presentation of information and arguments to the board, a parole panel, and the department for and in behalf of an inmate; and
(2) the time, place, and manner of contact between a person representing an inmate and:
(A) a member of the board;
(B) an employee of the board; or
(C) an employee of the department.

*(Added by L.1997, chap. 165(12.01); chgd. by L.1999, chap. 62(10.18), eff. 9/1/99.)*

### §508.083. Eligibility to represent inmates.

(a) A person who represents an inmate for compensation must:

(1) be an attorney licensed in this state; and

(2) register with the division.

(b) A person serving as a member or employee of the board or the Texas Board of Criminal Justice may not, before the 10th anniversary of the date the person ceases to be a board member or employee:

(1) represent any person in a matter before the board or a parole panel; or

(2) receive compensation for services rendered on behalf of any person regarding a matter pending before the board or a parole panel.

(c) A person, other than a person subject to Subsection (b), who is employed by the department may not, before the 10th anniversary of the date the person terminates service with the department:

(1) represent an inmate in a matter before the board or a parole panel; or

(2) receive compensation for services rendered on behalf of any person regarding a matter pending before the board or a parole panel.

(d) A former member or employee of the board or the Texas Board of Criminal Justice or a former employee of the department may not represent any person or receive compensation for services rendered on behalf of any person regarding a matter pending before the board or a parole panel with which the former member or employee, during the period of service on or with either board or employment with the department or board, was directly concerned either:

(1) through personal involvement; or

(2) because the matter was within the member's or employee's official responsibility while associated with the board or the department.

*(Added by L.1997, chap. 165(12.01), eff. 9/1/97.)*



### §508.084. Fee affidavit.

(a) A person required to register under Section 508.083, before the person first contacts a member of the board, an employee of the board, or an employee of the department on behalf of an inmate, shall file a fee affidavit with the department in a form prescribed by the department for each inmate the person represents for compensation.

(b) The fee affidavit must be written and verified and contain a statement of:

(1) the registrant's full name and address;

(2) the registrant's normal business, business phone number, and business address;

(3) the full name of any former member or employee of the board or the Texas Board of Criminal Justice or any former employee of the department with whom the registrant:

(A) is associated;

(B) has a relationship as an employer or employee; or

(C) maintains a contractual relationship to provide services;

(4) the full name and institutional identification number of the inmate the registrant represents;

(5) the amount of compensation the registrant has received or expects to receive in exchange for the representation; and

(6) the name of the person providing the compensation.

(c) If a registrant receives compensation in excess of the amount reported on the fee affidavit, the registrant shall file with the department, not later than the fifth day after the date the registrant receives compensation in excess of the reported amount, a supplemental fee affidavit in a form prescribed by the department indicating the total amount of compensation received for representing the inmate.

(d) For each fee affidavit and supplemental fee affidavit received, the department shall:

(1) keep a copy of the affidavit in a central location; and

(2) not later than the third day after the date the affidavit is filed, place a copy of the affidavit in the inmate's file that is reviewed by a parole panel or the board.

*(Added by L.1997, chap. 165(12.01), eff. 9/1/97.)*

### §508.085. Representation summary form.

(a) A person required to register under Section 508.083 shall, for each calendar year in which the person represents an inmate, file a representation summary form with the division on a form prescribed by the division.

(b) The form must be filed not later than January 31 of the year succeeding the year for which the report is filed and must include a statement of:

(1) the registrant's full name and address;

(2) the registrant's normal business, business phone number, and business address;

(3) the full name of any former member or employee of the board or the Texas Board of Criminal Justice or any former employee of the department with whom the registrant:

(A) is associated;

(B) has a relationship as an employer or employee; or

(C) maintains a contractual relationship to provide services;

(4) the full name and institutional identification number of each inmate the registrant represented in the previous calendar year; and

(5) the amount of compensation the registrant has received for representing each inmate in the previous calendar year.

(c) A person who files a form under this section and for whom the information required for the form has changed shall, not later than the 10th day after the date the information changes, file a supplemental statement with the division indicating the change.
*(Added by L.1997, chap. 165(12.01), eff. 9/1/97.)*

### §508.086. Criminal penalties.

(a) A former member or employee of the board or the Texas Board of Criminal Justice or a former employee of the department commits an offense if the former member or employee violates Section 508.083(b), (c), or (d).

(b) A person who represents an inmate for compensation commits an offense if the person is not an attorney licensed in this state.

(c) A person who is required to file an affidavit under Section 508.084(a) or (c) or a form or statement under Section 508.085 commits an offense if the person fails to file the affidavit, form, or statement.

(d) An offense under Subsection (a) is a Class A misdemeanor. An offense under Subsection (b) or (c) is a Class C misdemeanor.
*(Added by L.1997, chap. 165(12.01), eff. 9/1/97.)*

### §§508.087 to 508.110. *(Reserved.)*

## SUBCHAPTER D. PARDONS AND PAROLES DIVISION

### §508.111. Director.

(a) The executive director shall hire the director of the division.

(b) The director is responsible for the administration of the division.
*(Added by L.1997, chap. 165(12.01), eff. 9/1/97.)*

### §508.112. Duty of division.

The division is responsible for the investigation and supervision of all releasees. *(Added by L.1997, chap. 165(12.01), eff. 9/1/97.)*

### §508.113. Parole officers, supervisors: qualifications.

(a) This subsection and Subsection (b) apply only to a person employed as a parole officer or supervisor on or before September 1, 1990. A person may not be employed as a parole officer or supervisor, or be responsible for investigating or supervising a releasee, unless the person has:

(1) four years of successfully completed education in an accredited college or university;

(2) two years of full-time paid employment in responsible correctional work with adults or juveniles or in a related field; and

(3) any other qualifications that may be specified by the director.

(b) Additional experience in a category described by Subsection (a)(2) may be substituted year for year for the required college education, with a maximum substitution of two years.

(c) The director shall establish qualifications for parole officers and supervisors that are the same as qualifications for community supervision and corrections department officers imposed by Section 76.005. A person may not begin employment as a parole officer or supervisor after September 1, 1990, unless the person meets the qualifications established by the director.

(d) A person who is serving as a peace officer or as a prosecuting attorney may not act as a parole officer or be responsible for supervising a releasee.
*(Added by L.1997, chap. 165(12.01), eff. 9/1/97.)*

### §508.114. Parole officers, supervisors: additional duties.

(a) The judge of a court having original jurisdiction of criminal actions may, with the approval of the director, designate a parole officer or supervisor as a community supervision and corrections department officer. The director must give prior written approval for the payment of a proportional part of the salary paid to the parole officer or supervisor in compensation for service as a community supervision and corrections department officer. The director shall periodically report to the governor and the legislature the proportional salary payments.

(b) A parole officer or supervisor, on request of the governor or on order of the director, shall be responsible for supervising an inmate placed on conditional pardon or granted an emergency absence under escort.

*(Added by L.1997, chap. 165(12.01), eff. 9/1/97.)*

### §508.1141. Specialized training: gang members.

The department shall develop and provide specialized training for parole officers supervising releasees previously identified by the department as being members of prison gangs, criminal street gangs, or security threat groups. *(Added by L.1999, chap. 490(1), eff. 9/1/99.)*



### §508.115. Notification of release of inmate.

(a) Not later than the 11th day before the date the board orders the release on parole of an inmate or not later than the 11th day after the date the board recommends that the governor grant executive clemency, the division shall notify the sheriffs, each chief of police, the prosecuting attorneys, and the district judges in the county in which the inmate was convicted and the county to which the inmate is released that the board is considering release on parole or the governor is considering clemency.

(b) In a case in which there was a change of venue, the division shall notify the sheriff, the prosecuting attorney, and the district judge in the county in which the prosecution was originated if, not later than the 30th day after the date the inmate was sentenced, those officials request in writing that the division give the officials notice under this section of a release of the inmate.

(c) Not later than the 10th day after the date a parole panel orders the transfer of an inmate to a halfway house under this chapter, the division shall give notice in accordance with Subsection (d) to:

(1) the sheriff of the county in which the inmate was convicted;

(2) the sheriff of the county in which the halfway house is located and each chief of police in the county; and

(3) the attorney who represents the state in the prosecution of felonies in the county in which the halfway house is located.

(d) The notice must state:

(1) the inmate's name;

(2) the county in which the inmate was convicted; and

(3) the offense for which the inmate was convicted.

*(Added by L.1997, chap. 165(12.01); chgd. by L.1999, chap. 62(10.19), eff. 9/1/99.)*

### §508.116. Parole information program.

(a) The division shall develop and implement a comprehensive program to inform inmates, the inmates' families, and other interested parties about the parole process.

(b) The division shall update the program annually.

*(Added by L.1997, chap. 165(12.01), eff. 9/1/97.)*

### §508.117. Victim notification.

(a) Before a parole panel considers for release on parole an inmate who is serving a sentence for an offense in which a person was a victim, the division, using the name and address provided on the victim impact statement, shall make a reasonable effort to notify:

(1) the victim;

(2) if the victim has a guardian, the guardian; or

(3) if the victim is deceased, a close relative of the deceased victim.

(b) A victim, guardian of a victim, or close relative of a deceased victim who would have been entitled to notification of parole consideration by the division but failed to provide a victim impact statement containing the person's name and address may file with the division a written request for notification. After receiving the written request, the division shall grant to the person all privileges, including notification under this section, to which the person would have been entitled had the person submitted a completed victim impact statement.

(c) If the notice is sent to a guardian or close relative of a deceased victim, the notice must contain a request by the division that the guardian or relative inform other persons having an interest in the matter that the inmate is being considered for release on parole.

(d) The failure of the division to comply with notice requirements of this section is not a ground for revocation of parole.

(e) Before an inmate is released from the institutional division on parole or to mandatory supervision, the pardons and paroles division shall give notice of the release to a person entitled to notification of parole consideration for the inmate under Subsection (a) or (b).

(f) Except as necessary to comply with this section, the board or the department may not disclose to any person the name or address of a person entitled to notice under this section unless:

(1) the person approves the disclosure; or

(2) a court determines that there is good cause for disclosure and orders the board or the department to disclose the information.

(g) In this section:

(1) "Close relative of a deceased victim" means a person who was:

(A) the spouse of the victim at the time of the victim's death;

(B) a parent of the deceased victim; or

(C) an adult brother, sister, or child of the deceased victim.

(2) "Guardian of a victim" means a person who is the legal guardian of a victim, whether or not the legal relationship between the guardian and the victim exists because of the age of the victim or the physical or mental incompetency of the victim.

(3) "Victim" means a person who:

(A) is a victim of sexual assault, kidnapping, aggravated robbery, or felony stalking; or

(B) has suffered bodily injury or death as the result of the criminal conduct of another.

*(Added by L.1997, chap. 165(12.01), eff. 9/1/97.)*



## §508.118. Halfway houses.

(a) The division, in conjunction with the institutional division, shall use halfway houses to divert from housing in regular units of the institutional division suitable low-risk inmates and other inmates who would benefit from a smoother transition from incarceration to supervised release.

(b) Before transferring an inmate to a halfway house, the division shall send to the director of the halfway house all information relating to the inmate that the division determines will aid the halfway house in helping the inmate make a transition from the institutional division to supervised release.

(c) The division is responsible for supervising an inmate:

(1) for whom a presumptive parole date has been established; and

(2) who is transferred into a preparole residence in a halfway house under Subchapter A, Chapter 499.

*(Added by L.1997, chap. 165(12.01), eff. 9/1/97.)*

## §508.119. Community residential facilities.

(a) The purpose of a community residential facility is to provide housing, supervision, counseling, personal, social, and work adjustment training, and other programs to:

(1) releasees who are required by a parole panel as a condition of release on parole or to mandatory supervision to serve a period in a community residential facility; and

(2) releasees whose parole or mandatory supervision has been continued or modified under Section 508.283 and on whom sanctions have been imposed under that section.

(b) The division may establish and operate, or contract for the operation of, community residential facilities.

(c) The division may contract with a public or private vendor for the financing, construction, operation, or management of a community residential facility using a lease-purchase or installment sale contract to provide or supplement housing, board, or supervision for releasees placed in a community residential facility. A releasee housed or supervised in a facility operated by a vendor under a contract is subject to the same laws as if the housing or supervision were provided directly by the division.

(d) Unless the division or a vendor proposing to operate a community residential facility provides notice of a following proposed action and a hearing on the issues in the same manner as required under Section 509.010, the division may not:

(1) establish or contract for a community residential facility;

(2) change the use of a community residential facility;

(3) significantly increase the capacity of a community residential facility; or

(4) increase the capacity of a community residential facility to more than 500 residents, regardless of whether the increase is significant.

(e) Subsection (d) applies to any residential facility that the division establishes or contracts for under:

(1) this chapter;

(2) Subchapter C, Chapter 497; or

(3) Subchapter A, Chapter 499.

(f) The Texas Board of Criminal Justice shall adopt rules necessary for the management of a community residential facility.

(g) The division may charge to a releasee housed in a community residential facility a reasonable fee for the cost of housing, board, and the part of the administrative costs of the facility that is properly allocable to the releasee. The fee may not exceed the actual costs to the division for services to that releasee. The division may not deny placement in a community residential facility to a releasee because the releasee is unable to pay the fee.

(h) A parole panel or a designated agent of the division may grant a limited release to a releasee placed in a community residential facility to maintain or seek employment or participation in an education or training course or to seek housing after release from the facility.

(i) The notice required by Subsection (d) must clearly state that the proposed action concerns a facility in which persons who have been released from prison on parole or to mandatory supervision are to be housed.

*(Added by L.1997, chap. 165(12.01); chgd. by L.1999, chap. 62(10.20), eff. 9/1/99.)*



### §§508.120 to 508.140. *(Reserved.)*

## SUBCHAPTER E. PAROLE AND MANDATORY SUPERVISION; RELEASE PROCEDURES

### §508.141. Authority to consider and order release on parole.

(a) A parole panel may consider for release and release on parole an inmate who:

(1) has been sentenced to a term of imprisonment in the institutional division;

(2) is confined in a penal or correctional institution, including a jail in this state, a federal correctional institution, or a jail or a correctional institution in another state; and

(3) is eligible for release on parole.

(b) A parole is issued only on the order of a parole panel.

(c) Before releasing an inmate on parole, a parole panel may have the inmate appear before the panel and interview the inmate.

(d) A parole panel may release an inmate on parole during the parole month established for the inmate if the panel determines that the inmate's release will not increase the likelihood of harm to the public.

(e) A parole panel may release an inmate on parole only when:

(1) arrangements have been made for the inmate's employment or for the inmate's maintenance and care; and

(2) the parole panel believes that the inmate is able and willing to fulfill the obligations of a law-abiding citizen.

(f) A parole panel may order a parole only for the best interest of society and not as an award of clemency.

*(Added by L.1997, chap. 165(12.01), eff. 9/1/97.)*

### §508.142. Period of parole.

(a) The institutional division shall provide the board with sentence time credit information for each inmate who is eligible for release on parole.

(b) Good conduct time credit is computed for an inmate as if the inmate were confined in the institutional division during the entire time the inmate was actually confined.

(c) The period of parole is computed by subtracting from the term for which the inmate was sentenced the calendar time served on the sentence.

*(Added by L.1997, chap. 165(12.01), eff. 9/1/97.)*

### §508.143. Legal custody of releasee.

(a) A releasee while on parole is in the legal custody of the division.

(b) A releasee while on mandatory supervision is in the legal custody of the state.

*(Added by L.1997, chap. 165(12.01), eff. 9/1/97.)*

### §508.144. Parole guidelines.

(a) The board shall:

(1) develop according to an acceptable research method the parole guidelines that are the basic criteria on which a parole decision is made;

(2) base the guidelines on the seriousness of the offense and the likelihood of a favorable parole outcome;

(3) implement the guidelines; and

(4) review the guidelines periodically.

(b) If a board member deviates from the parole guidelines in voting on a parole decision, the member shall:

(1) produce a brief written statement describing the circumstances regarding the departure from the guidelines; and

(2) place a copy of the statement in the file of the inmate for whom the parole decision was made.

(c) The board shall keep a copy of a statement made under Subsection (b) in a central location.

*(Added by L.1997, chap. 165(12.01), eff. 9/1/97.)*

### §508.145. Eligibility for release on parole; computation of parole eligibility date.

(a) An inmate under sentence of death is not eligible for release on parole.

(b) An inmate serving a life sentence for a capital felony is not eligible for release on parole until the actual calendar time the inmate has served, without consideration of good conduct time, equals 40 calendar years.

(c) An inmate serving a life sentence under Section 12.42(c)(2), Penal Code, is not eligible for release on parole until the actual calendar time the inmate has served, without consideration of good conduct time, equals 35 calendar years.

(d) An inmate serving a sentence for an offense described by Section 3g(a)(1)(A), (C), (D), (E), (F), (G), or (H), Article 42.12, Code of Criminal Procedure, or for an offense for which the judgment contains an affirmative finding under Section 3g(a)(2) of that article, is not eligible for release on parole until the inmate's actual calendar time served, without consideration of good conduct time, equals one-half of the sentence or 30 calendar years, whichever is less, but in no event is the inmate eligible for release on parole in less than two calendar years.

(e) An inmate serving a sentence for which the punishment is increased under Section 481.134, Health and Safety Code, is not eligible for release on parole until the inmate's actual calendar time served, without consideration of good conduct time, equals five years or the term to which the inmate was sentenced, whichever is less.

(f) Except as provided by Section 508.146, any other inmate is eligible for release on parole when the inmate's actual calendar time served plus good conduct time equals one-fourth of the sentence imposed or 15 years, whichever is less.

*(Added by L.1997, chap. 165(12.01); chgd. by L.1999, chap. 62(10.21), eff. 9/1/99.)*

### §508.146. Special needs parole.

(a) An inmate serving a sentence for which parole eligibility is otherwise determined under Section 508.145(f) may become eligible for release on special needs parole on a date designated by a parole panel that is earlier than the date computed under that section if:

(1) the institutional division identifies the inmate as being elderly, physically handicapped, mentally ill, terminally ill, or mentally retarded;

(2) the parole panel determines that, based on the inmate's condition and a medical evaluation, the inmate does not constitute a threat to public safety or a threat to commit an offense; and

(3) the pardons and paroles division has prepared for the inmate a special needs parole plan that ensures appropriate supervision, service provision, and placement.

(b) An inmate diagnosed as mentally ill or mentally retarded may be released on special needs parole only if the inmate's special needs parole plan under Subsection (a)(3) is approved by the Texas Council on Offenders with Mental Impairments.

*(Added by L.1997, chap. 165(12.01), eff. 9/1/97.)*

### §508.147. Release to mandatory supervision.

(a) Except as provided by Section 508.149, a parole panel shall order the release of an inmate who is not on parole to mandatory supervision when the actual calendar time the inmate has served plus any accrued good conduct time equals the term to which the inmate was sentenced.

(b) An inmate released to mandatory supervision is considered to be released on parole.

(c) To the extent practicable, arrangements for the inmate's proper employment, maintenance, and care must be made before the inmate's release to mandatory supervision.
*(Added by L.1997, chap. 165(12.01), eff. 9/1/97.)*

**§508.148. Period of mandatory supervision.**

(a) The period of mandatory supervision is computed by subtracting from the term for which the inmate was sentenced the calendar time served on the sentence.

(b) The time served on mandatory supervision is computed as calendar time.
*(Added by L.1997, chap. 165(12.01), eff. 9/1/97.)*

**§508.149. Inmates ineligible for mandatory supervision.**

(a) An inmate may not be released to mandatory supervision if the inmate is serving a sentence for or has been previously convicted of:

(1) an offense for which the judgment contains an affirmative finding under Section 3g(a)(2), Article 42.12, Code of Criminal Procedure;

(2) a first degree felony or a second degree felony under Section 19.02, Penal Code;

(3) a capital felony under Section 19.03, Penal Code;

(4) a first degree felony or a second degree felony under Section 20.04, Penal Code;

(5) a second degree felony or a third degree felony under Section 21.11, Penal Code;

(6) a second degree felony under Section 22.011, Penal Code;

(7) a first degree felony or a second degree felony under Section 22.02, Penal Code;

(8) a first degree felony under Section 22.021, Penal Code;

(9) a first degree felony under Section 22.04, Penal Code;

(10) a first degree felony under Section 28.02, Penal Code;

(11) a second degree felony under Section 29.02, Penal Code;

(12) a first degree felony under Section 29.03, Penal Code;

(13) a first degree felony under Section 30.02, Penal Code; or

(14) a felony for which the punishment is increased under Section 481.134, Health and Safety Code.

(b) An inmate may not be released to mandatory supervision if a parole panel determines that:

(1) the inmate's accrued good conduct time is not an accurate reflection of the inmate's potential for rehabilitation; and

(2) the inmate's release would endanger the public.

(c) A parole panel that makes a determination under Subsection (b) shall specify in writing the reasons for the determination.

(d) A determination under Subsection (b) is not subject to administrative or judicial review, except that the parole panel making the determination shall reconsider the inmate for release to mandatory supervision at least twice during the two years after the date of the determination.
*(Added by L.1997, chap. 165(12.01); chgd. by L.1999, chap. 62(10.22), eff. 9/1/99.)*

**§508.150. Consecutive felony sentences.**

(a) If an inmate is sentenced to consecutive felony sentences under Article 42.08, Code of Criminal Procedure, a parole panel shall designate during each sentence the date, if any, the inmate would have been eligible for release on parole if the inmate had been sentenced to serve a single sentence.

(b) For the purposes of Article 42.08, Code of Criminal Procedure, the judgment and sentence of an inmate sentenced for a felony, other than the last sentence in a series of consecutive sentences, cease to operate:

(1) when the actual calendar time served by the inmate equals the sentence imposed by the court; or

(2) on the date a parole panel designates as the date the inmate would have been eligible for release on parole if the inmate had been sentenced to serve a single sentence.

(c) A parole panel may not:

(1) consider consecutive sentences as a single sentence for purposes of parole; or

(2) release on parole an inmate sentenced to serve consecutive felony sentences before the date the inmate becomes eligible for release on parole from the last sentence imposed on the inmate.

(d) A parole panel may not use calendar time served and good conduct time accrued by an inmate that are used by the panel in determining when a judgment and sentence cease to operate:

(1) for the same purpose in determining that date in a subsequent sentence in the same series of consecutive sentences; or

(2) for determining the date an inmate becomes eligible for release on parole from the last sentence in a series of consecutive sentences.
*(Added by L.1997, chap. 165(12.01), eff. 9/1/97.)*

**§508.151. Presumptive parole date.**

(a) For the purpose of diverting inmates to halfway houses under Section 508.118, a parole panel, after reviewing all available pertinent information, may designate a presumptive parole date for an inmate who:

(1) has never been convicted of an offense listed under Section 3g(a)(1), Article 42.12, Code of Criminal Procedure; and

(2) has never had a conviction with a judgment that contains an affirmative finding under Section 3g(a)(2), Article 42.12, Code of Criminal Procedure.

(b) The presumptive parole date may not be a date that is earlier than the inmate's initial parole eligibility date computed under Section 508.145.

(c) A parole panel may rescind or postpone a previously established presumptive parole date on the basis of a report from an agent of the division responsible for supervision or an agent of the institutional division acting in the case.

(d) If an inmate transferred to preparole status has satisfactorily served the inmate's sentence in the halfway house to which the inmate is assigned from the date of transfer to the presumptive parole date, without rescission or postponement of the date, the parole panel shall order the inmate's release on parole and issue an appropriate certificate of release. The releasee is subject to the provisions of this chapter governing release on parole.
*(Added by L.1997, chap. 165(12.01), eff. 9/1/97.)*



**§508.152. Proposed program of institutional progress.**

(a) Not later than the 120th day after the date an inmate is admitted to the institutional division, the department shall obtain all pertinent information relating to the inmate, including:

(1) the court judgment;

(2) any sentencing report;

(3) the circumstances of the inmate's offense;

(4) the inmate's previous social history and criminal record;

(5) the inmate's physical and mental health record;

(6) a record of the inmate's conduct, employment history, and attitude in the institutional division; and

(7) any written comments or information provided by local trial officials or victims of the offense.

(b) The department shall:

(1) establish for the inmate a proposed program of measurable institutional progress; and

(2) submit the proposed program to the board at the time of the board's consideration of the inmate's case for release.

(c) The board shall conduct an initial review of an eligible inmate not later than the 180th day after the date of the inmate's admission to the institutional division.

(d) Before the inmate is approved for release on parole, the inmate must agree to participate in the programs and activities described by the proposed program of measurable institutional progress.

(e) The institutional division shall:

(1) work closely with the board to monitor the progress of the inmate in the institutional division; and

(2) report the progress to the board before the inmate's release.
*(Added by L.1997, chap. 165(12.01), eff. 9/1/97.)*

**§508.153. Statements of victim.**

(a) A parole panel considering for release on parole an inmate who is serving a sentence for an offense in which a person was a victim shall allow:

(1) the victim, a guardian of the victim, a close relative of the deceased victim, or a representative of the victim, the victim's guardian, or the victim's close relative to provide a written statement to the panel; and

(2) the victim, guardian of the victim, or close relative of the deceased victim to appear in person before the board members to present a statement of the person's views about:

(A) the offense;

(B) the inmate; and

(C) the effect of the offense on the victim.

(b) If more than one person is entitled to appear in person before the board members, only the person chosen by all persons entitled to appear as the persons' sole representative may appear before the board members.

(c) The panel shall consider the statements and the information provided in a victim impact statement in determining whether to recommend an inmate for release on parole.

(d) This section does not limit the number of persons who may provide written statements for or against the release of the inmate on parole.

(e) In this section, "close relative of a deceased victim," "guardian of a victim," and "victim" have the meanings assigned by Section 508.117.

*(Added by L.1997, chap. 165(12.01), eff. 9/1/97.)*

## §508.154. Contract on release.

(a) An inmate to be released on parole shall be furnished a contract stating in clear and intelligible language the conditions and rules of parole.

(b) Acceptance, signing, and execution of the contract by the inmate to be paroled is a precondition to release on parole.

(c) An inmate released to mandatory supervision shall be furnished a written statement stating in clear and intelligible language the conditions and rules of mandatory supervision.

(d) A releasee while on parole or mandatory supervision must be amenable to the conditions of supervision ordered by a parole panel.

*(Added by L.1997, chap. 165(12.01), eff. 9/1/97.)*



## §508.155. Completion of parole period.

(a) To complete a parole period, a releasee must serve the entire period of parole.

(b) The time on parole is computed as calendar time.

(c) The division may allow a releasee to serve the remainder of the releasee's sentence without supervision and without being required to report if:

(1) the releasee has been under supervision for at least one-half of the time that remained on the releasee's sentence when the releasee was released from imprisonment;

(2) during the period of supervision the releasee's parole or release to mandatory supervision has not been revoked; and

(3) the division determines:

(A) that the releasee has made a good faith effort to comply with any restitution order imposed on the releasee by a court; and

(B) that allowing the releasee to serve the remainder of the releasee's sentence without supervision and reporting is in the best interest of society.

(d) The division may require a person released from supervision and reporting under Subsection (c) to resubmit to supervision and resume reporting at any time and for any reason.

*(Added by L.1997, chap. 165(12.01), eff. 9/1/97.)*

## §508.156. Determinate sentence parole.

(a) Before the release of a person who is transferred under Section 61.081(f) or 61.084(f) or (g), Human Resources Code, to the division for release on parole, a parole panel shall review the person's records and may interview the person or any other person the panel considers necessary to determine the conditions of parole. The panel may impose any reasonable condition of parole on the person that the panel may impose on an adult inmate under this chapter.

(b) The panel shall furnish the person with a written statement clearly describing the conditions and rules of parole. The person must accept and sign the statement as a precondition to release on parole.

(c) While on parole, the person remains in the legal custody of the state and shall comply with the conditions of parole ordered by a panel under this section.

(d) The period of parole for a person released on parole under this section is the term for which the person was sentenced less calendar time served at the Texas Youth Commission and in a juvenile detention facility in connection with the conduct for which the person was adjudicated.

(e) If a parole panel revokes the person's parole, the panel may require the person to serve the remaining portion of the person's sentence in the institutional division. The remaining portion of the person's sentence is computed without credit for the time from the date of the person's release to the date of revocation. The panel may not recommit the person to the Texas Youth Commission.

(f) For purposes of this chapter, a person released from the Texas Youth Commission on parole under this section is considered to have been convicted of the offense for which the person has been adjudicated.

*(Added by L.1997, chap. 165(12.01), eff. 9/1/97.)*

**§§508.157 to 508.180.** *(Reserved.)*

## SUBCHAPTER F. MANDATORY CONDITIONS OF PAROLE OR MANDATORY SUPERVISION

### §508.181. Residence during release.

(a) Except as provided by Subsections (b) and (c), a parole panel shall require as a condition of parole or mandatory supervision that the releasee reside in the county in which:

(1) the releasee resided at the time of committing the offense for which the releasee was sentenced to the institutional division; or

(2) the releasee committed the offense for which the releasee was sentenced to the institutional division, if the releasee was not a resident of this state at the time of committing the offense.

(b) A parole panel may require a releasee to reside in a county other than the county required under Subsection (a) to:

(1) protect the life or safety of:

(A) a victim of the releasee's offense;

(B) the releasee;

(C) a witness in the case; or

(D) any other person; or

(2) increase the likelihood of the releasee's successful completion of parole or mandatory supervision, because of:

(A) written expressions of significant public concern in the county in which the releasee would otherwise be required to reside;

(B) the presence of family members or friends in the other county who have expressed a willingness to assist the releasee in successfully completing the conditions of the releasee's parole or mandatory supervision;

(C) the verified existence of a job offer in the other county; or

(D) the availability of a treatment program, educational program, or other social service program in the other county that is not available in the county in which the releasee is otherwise required to reside under Subsection (a).

(c) At any time after a releasee is released on parole or to mandatory supervision, a parole panel may modify the conditions of parole or mandatory supervision to require the releasee to reside in a county other than the county required by the original conditions. In making a decision under this subsection, a parole panel must consider the factors listed under Subsection (b).

(d) If a parole panel initially requires the releasee to reside in a county other than the county required under Subsection (a), the parole panel shall subsequently require the releasee to reside in the county described under Subsection (a) if the requirement that the releasee reside in the other county was based on:

(1) the verified existence of a job offer under Subsection (b)(2)(C) and the releasee is no longer employed or actively seeking employment; or

(2) the availability of a treatment program, educational program, or other social service program under Subsection (b)(2)(D) and the releasee:

(A) no longer regularly participates in the program as required by a condition of parole or mandatory supervision; or

(B) has successfully completed the program but has violated another condition of the releasee's parole or mandatory supervision.

(e) If a parole panel requires the releasee to reside in a county other than the county required under Subsection (a), the panel shall:

(1) state in writing the reason for the panel's decision; and

(2) place the statement in the releasee's permanent record.

(f) This section does not apply to a decision by a parole panel to require a releasee to serve the period of parole or mandatory supervision in another state.

(g) The division shall, on the first working day of each month, notify the sheriff of any county in which the total number of sex offenders under the supervision and control of the division residing in the county exceeds 10 percent of the total number of sex offenders in the state under the supervision and control of the division. If the total number of sex offenders under the supervision and control of the division residing in a county exceeds 22 percent of the total number of sex offenders in the state under the supervision and control of the division, a parole panel may require a sex offender to reside in that county only as required by Subsection (a) or for the reason stated in Subsection (b)(2)(B). In this subsection, "sex offender" means a person who is released on parole or to mandatory supervision after serving a sentence for an offense described by Section 508.187(a).

(h) If a parole panel requires a releasee to reside in a county other than the county required under Subsection (a), the division shall include the reason for residency exemption in the required notification to the sheriff of the county in which the defendant is to reside, the chief of police of the municipality in which the halfway house is located, and the attorney who represents the state in the prosecution of felonies in that county.
*(Added by L.1997, chap. 165(12.01); chgd. by L.1999, chap. 62(10.23), (10.24), eff. 9/1/99.)*

## §508.182. Parole supervision fee; administrative fee.

(a) A parole panel shall require as a condition of parole or mandatory supervision that a releasee pay to the division for each month during which the releasee is under parole supervision:

(1) a parole supervision fee of $10; and

(2) an administrative fee of $8.

(b) A fee under this section applies to an inmate released in another state who is required as a condition of the inmate's release to report to a parole officer or supervisor in this state for parole supervision.

(c) On the request of the releasee, a parole panel may allow the releasee to defer one or more payments under this section. The releasee remains responsible for payment of the fee and shall pay the amount of the deferred payment not later than the second anniversary of the date the payment becomes due.

(d) The Texas Board of Criminal Justice shall adopt rules relating to the method of payment required of the releasee.

(e) The division shall remit fees collected under this section to the comptroller. The comptroller shall deposit the fees collected under:

(1) Subsection (a)(1) in the general revenue fund; and

(2) Subsection (a)(2) in the compensation to victims of crime fund.

(f) In a parole or mandatory supervision revocation hearing under Section 508.281 at which it is alleged only that the releasee failed to make a payment under this section, it is an affirmative defense to revocation that the releasee is unable to pay the amount as ordered by a parole panel. The releasee must prove the affirmative defense by a preponderance of the evidence.
*(Added by L.1997, chap. 165(12.01), eff. 9/1/97.)*

## §508.183. Educational skill level.

(a) A parole panel shall require as a condition of release on parole or release to mandatory supervision that an inmate demonstrate to the parole panel whether the inmate has an educational skill level that is equal to or greater than the average skill level of students who have completed the sixth grade in a public school in this state.

(b) If the parole panel determines that the inmate has not attained that skill level, the parole panel shall require as a condition of parole or mandatory supervision that the inmate as a releasee attain that level of educational skill, unless the parole panel determines that the inmate lacks the intellectual capacity or the learning ability to ever achieve that level of skill.
*(Added by L.1997, chap. 165(12.01), eff. 9/1/97.)*

## §508.184. Controlled substance testing.

(a) A parole panel shall require as a condition of parole or mandatory supervision that a releasee submit to testing for controlled substances on evidence that:

(1) a controlled substance is present in the releasee's body;

(2) the releasee has used a controlled substance; or

(3) the use of a controlled substance is related to the offense for which the releasee was convicted.

(b) The Texas Board of Criminal Justice by rule shall adopt procedures for the administration of a test required under this section.
*(Added by L.1997, chap. 165(12.01), eff. 9/1/97.)*

## §508.185. Substance abuse treatment.

(a) A parole panel shall require as a condition of release on parole or release to mandatory supervision that an inmate who immediately before release is a participant in the program established under Section 501.0931 participate as a releasee in a drug or alcohol abuse continuum of care treatment program.

(b) The Texas Commission on Alcohol and Drug Abuse shall develop the continuum of care treatment program.
*(Added by L.1997, chap. 165(12.01), eff. 9/1/97.)*

**§508.186. Sex offender registration.**

(a) A parole panel shall require as a condition of parole or mandatory supervision that a releasee required to register as a sex offender under Chapter 62, Code of Criminal Procedure:

(1) register under that chapter; and

(2) pay to the releasee's supervising officer an amount equal to the cost, as evidenced by written receipt, incurred by the applicable local law enforcement authority for providing notice for publication to a newspaper as required by that chapter.

(b) The division shall remit an amount collected under this section to the applicable local law enforcement authority.

(c) In a parole or mandatory supervision revocation hearing under Section 508.281 at which it is alleged only that the releasee failed to make a payment under this section, it is an affirmative defense to revocation that the releasee is unable to pay the amount as ordered by a parole panel. The releasee must prove the affirmative defense by a preponderance of the evidence.

*(Added by L.1997, chap. 165(12.01); chgd. by L.1999, chap. 62(10.25), eff. 9/1/99.)*

**§508.187. Child safety zone.**

(a) This section applies only to a releasee serving a sentence for an offense under:

(1) Section 43.25 or 43.26, Penal Code;

(2) Section 21.11, 22.011, 22.021, or 25.02, Penal Code;

(3) Section 20.04(a)(4), Penal Code, if the releasee committed the offense with the intent to violate or abuse the victim sexually; or

(4) Section 30.02, Penal Code, punishable under Subsection (d) of that section, if the releasee committed the offense with the intent to commit a felony listed in Subdivision (2) or (3).

(b) A parole panel shall establish a child safety zone applicable to a releasee if the panel determines that a child as defined by Section 22.011(c), Penal Code, was the victim of the offense, by requiring as a condition of parole or mandatory supervision that the releasee:

(1) not:

(A) supervise or participate in any program that includes as participants or recipients persons who are 17 years of age or younger and that regularly provides athletic, civic, or cultural activities; or

(B) go in, on, or within a distance specified by the panel of premises where children commonly gather, including a school, day-care facility, playground, public or private youth center, public swimming pool, or video arcade facility; and

(2) attend psychological counseling sessions for sex offenders with an individual or organization that provides sex offender treatment or counseling as specified by the parole officer supervising the releasee after release.

(c) A parole officer who under Subsection (b)(2) specifies a sex offender treatment provider to provide counseling to a releasee shall:

(1) contact the provider before the releasee is released;

(2) establish the date, time, and place of the first session between the releasee and the provider; and

(3) request the provider to immediately notify the officer if the releasee fails to attend the first session or any subsequent scheduled session.

(d) At any time after the imposition of a condition under Subsection (b)(1), the releasee may request the parole panel to modify the child safety zone applicable to the releasee because the zone as created by the panel:

(1) interferes with the releasee's ability to attend school or hold a job and consequently constitutes an undue hardship for the releasee; or

(2) is broader than necessary to protect the public, given the nature and circumstances of the offense.

(e) A parole officer supervising a releasee may permit the releasee to enter on an event-by-event basis into the child safety zone that the releasee is otherwise prohibited from entering if:

(1) the releasee has served at least two years of the period of supervision imposed on release;

(2) the releasee enters the zone as part of a program to reunite with the releasee's family;

(3) the releasee presents to the parole officer a written proposal specifying:

(A) where the releasee intends to go within the zone;

(B) why and with whom the releasee is going; and

(C) how the releasee intends to cope with any stressful situations that occur;

(4) the sex offender treatment provider treating the releasee agrees with the officer that the releasee should be allowed to attend the event; and

(5) the officer and the treatment provider agree on a chaperon to accompany the releasee, and the chaperon agrees to perform that duty.

(f) In this section, "playground," "premises," "school," "video arcade facility," and "youth center" have the meanings assigned by Section 481.134, Health and Safety Code.
*(Added by L.1997, chap. 165(12.01), eff. 9/1/97.)*

### §508.188. Community service for certain releasees.

A parole panel shall require as a condition of parole or mandatory supervision that a releasee for whom the court has made an affirmative finding under Article 42.014, Code of Criminal Procedure, perform not less than 300 hours of community service at a project designated by the parole panel that primarily serves the person or group that was the target of the releasee. *(Added by L.1997, chap. 165(12.01), eff. 9/1/97.)*

### §508.189. Parole fee for certain releasees.

(a) A parole panel shall require as a condition of parole or mandatory supervision that a releasee convicted of an offense under Section 21.08, 21.11, 22.011, 22.021, 25.02, 43.25, or 43.26, Penal Code, pay to the division a parole supervision fee of $5 each month during the period of parole supervision.

(b) The division shall send fees collected under this section to the comptroller. The comptroller shall deposit the fees in the general revenue fund to the credit of the sexual assault program fund established under Section 44.0061, Health and Safety Code.
*(Added by L.1997, chap. 165(12.01), eff. 9/1/97.)*



### §508.190. Avoiding victim of stalking offense.

(a) A parole panel shall require as a condition of parole or mandatory supervision that a releasee serving a sentence for an offense under Section 42.072, Penal Code, not:

(1) communicate directly or indirectly with the victim;

(2) go to or near the residence, place of employment, or business of the victim; or

(3) go to or near a school, day-care facility, or similar facility where a dependent child of the victim is in attendance.

(b) If a parole panel requires the prohibition contained in Subsection (a)(2) or (3) as a condition of parole or mandatory supervision, the parole panel shall specifically describe the prohibited locations and the minimum distances, if any, that the releasee must maintain from the locations.
*(Added by L.1999, chap. 62(10.26), eff. 9/1/99.)*

### §508.191. No contact with victim.

(a) If a parole panel releases a defendant on parole or to mandatory supervision, the panel shall require as a condition of parole or mandatory supervision that the defendant not intentionally or knowingly communicate directly or indirectly with a victim of the offense or intentionally or knowingly go near a residence, school, place of employment, or business of a victim. At any time after the defendant is released on parole or to mandatory supervision, a victim of the offense may petition the panel for a modification of the conditions of the defendant's parole or mandatory supervision allowing the defendant contact with the victim subject to reasonable restrictions.

(b) Notwithstanding Subsection (a), a defendant may participate in victim-offender mediation authorized by Section 508.324 on the request of the victim or a guardian of the victim or a close relative of a deceased victim.

(c) In this section, "victim" has the meaning assigned by Article 56.01(3), Code of Criminal Procedure.
*(Added by L.1999, chap. 62(10.27), eff. 9/1/99.)*

### §§508.192 to 508.220. *(Reserved.)*

## SUBCHAPTER G. DISCRETIONARY CONDITIONS OF PAROLE OR MANDATORY SUPERVISION

### §508.221. Conditions permitted generally.

A parole panel may impose as a condition of parole or mandatory supervision any condition that a court may impose on a defendant placed on community supervision under Article 42.12, Code of Criminal Procedure, including the condition that a releasee submit to testing for controlled substances or submit to electronic monitoring if the parole panel determines that without testing for controlled substances or participation in an electronic monitoring program the inmate would not be released on parole. *(Added by L.1997, chap. 165(12.01), eff. 9/1/97.)*

**§508.222. Payment of certain damages.**

A parole panel may require as a condition of parole or mandatory supervision that a releasee make payments in satisfaction of damages for which the releasee is liable under Section 500.002. *(Added by L.1997, chap. 165(12.01), eff. 9/1/97.)*

**§508.223. Psychological counseling.**

A parole panel may require as a condition of parole or mandatory supervision that a releasee serving a sentence for an offense under Section 42.072, Penal Code, attend psychological counseling sessions of a type and for a duration as specified by the parole panel, if the parole panel determines in consultation with a local mental health services provider that appropriate mental health services are available through the Texas Department of Mental Health and Mental Retardation in accordance with Section 534.053, Health and Safety Code, or through another mental health services provider. *(Added by L.1997, chap. 165(12.01); chgd. by L.1999, chap. 62(10.28), eff. 9/1/99.)*

**§508.224. Substance abuse counseling.**

A parole panel may require as a condition of parole or mandatory supervision that the releasee attend counseling sessions for substance abusers or participate in substance abuse treatment services in a program or facility approved or licensed by the Texas Commission on Alcohol and Drug Abuse if:

(1) the releasee was sentenced for an offense involving a controlled substance; or

(2) the panel determines that the releasee's substance abuse was related to the commission of the offense.

*(Added by L.1997, chap. 165(12.01), eff. 9/1/97.)*

**§508.225. Child safety zone.**

(a) If the nature of the offense for which an inmate is serving a sentence warrants the establishment of a child safety zone, a parole panel may establish a child safety zone applicable to an inmate serving a sentence for an offense listed in Section 3g(a)(1), Article 42.12, Code of Criminal Procedure, or for which the judgment contains an affirmative finding under Section 3g(a)(2), Article 42.12, Code of Criminal Procedure, by requiring as a condition of parole or release to mandatory supervision that the inmate not:

(1) supervise or participate in any program that includes as participants or recipients persons who are 17 years of age or younger and that regularly provides athletic, civic, or cultural activities; or

(2) go in or on, or within a distance specified by the panel of, a premises where children commonly gather, including a school, day-care facility, playground, public or private youth center, public swimming pool, or video arcade facility.

(b) At any time after the imposition of a condition under Subsection (a), the inmate may request the parole panel to modify the child safety zone applicable to the inmate because the zone as created by the panel:

(1) interferes with the ability of the inmate to attend school or hold a job and consequently constitutes an undue hardship for the inmate; or

(2) is broader than is necessary to protect the public, given the nature and circumstances of the offense.

(c) This section does not apply to an inmate described by Section 508.187.

(d) In this section, "playground," "premises," "school," "video arcade facility," and "youth center" have the meanings assigned by Section 481.134, Health and Safety Code.

*(Added by L.1999, chap. 56(2), eff. 9/1/99. See other section 508.225 below.)*

**§508.225. Orchiectomy as condition prohibited.**

A parole panel may not require an inmate to undergo an orchiectomy as a condition of release on parole or to mandatory supervision. *(Added by L.1999, chap. 62(10.29), eff. 9/1/99. See other section 508.225 above.)*

**§§508.226 to 508.250.** *(Reserved.)*

## SUBCHAPTER H. WARRANTS

### §508.251. Issuance of warrant or summons.

(a) In a case of parole or mandatory supervision, the director or a designated agent of the director or, in another case, the board on order by the governor, may issue a warrant as provided by Section 508.252 for the return of:

(1) a releasee;

(2) an inmate released although not eligible for release;

(3) a resident released to a preparole or work program;

(4) an inmate released on emergency reprieve or on emergency absence under escort; or

(5) a person released on a conditional pardon.

(b) A warrant issued under Subsection (a) must require the return of the person to the institution from which the person was paroled or released.

(c) Instead of the issuance of a warrant under this section, the division may issue to the person a summons requiring the person to appear for a hearing under Section 508.281. The summons must state the time, date, place, and purpose of the hearing.

(d) A designated agent of the director acts independently from a parole officer and must receive specialized training as determined by the director.

*(Added by L.1997, chap. 165(12.01), eff. 9/1/97.)*



### §508.252. Grounds for issuance of warrant.

A warrant may be issued under Section 508.251 if:

(1) there is reason to believe that the person has been released although not eligible for release;

(2) the person has been arrested for an offense;

(3) there is a document that is self-authenticating as provided by Rule 902, Texas Rules of Evidence, stating that the person violated a rule or condition of release; or

(4) there is reliable evidence that the person has exhibited behavior during the person's release that indicates to a reasonable person that the person poses a danger to society that warrants the person's immediate return to custody.

*(Added by L.1997, chap. 165(12.01); chgd. by L.1999, chap. 62(10.30), eff. 9/1/99.)*

### §508.253. Effect on sentence after issuance of warrant.

If it appears a releasee has violated a condition or provision of the releasee's parole or mandatory supervision, the date of the issuance of the warrant to the date of the releasee's arrest is not counted as a part of the time served under the releasee's sentence. *(Added by L.1997, chap. 165(12.01), eff. 9/1/97.)*

### §508.254. Detention under warrant.

(a) A person who is the subject of a warrant may be held in custody pending a determination of all facts surrounding the alleged offense, violation of a rule or condition of release, or dangerous behavior.

(b) A warrant authorizes any officer named by the warrant to take custody of the person and detain the person until a parole panel orders the return of the person to the institution from which the person was released.

(c) Pending a hearing on a charge of parole violation, ineligible release, or violation of a condition of mandatory supervision, a person returned to custody shall remain confined.

*(Added by L.1997, chap. 165(12.01), eff. 9/1/97.)*

### §508.255. Status as fugitive from justice.

(a) After the issuance of a warrant, a person for whose return a warrant was issued is a fugitive from justice.

(b) The law relating to the right of the state to extradite a person and return a fugitive from justice and Article 42.11, Code of Criminal Procedure, relating to the waiver of all legal requirements to obtain extradition of a fugitive from justice from another state to this state, are not impaired by this chapter and remain in full force and effect.

*(Added by L.1997, chap. 165(12.01), eff. 9/1/97.)*

### §508.256. Withdrawal of warrant.

At any time before setting a revocation hearing date under Section 508.282, the division may withdraw a warrant and continue supervision of a releasee. *(Added by L.1997, chap. 165(12.01), eff. 9/1/97.)*

**§§508.257 to 508.280.** *(Reserved.)*

## SUBCHAPTER I. HEARINGS AND SANCTIONS

### §508.281. Hearing.

(a) A releasee, a person released although ineligible for release, or a person granted a conditional pardon is entitled to a hearing before a parole panel or a designated agent of the board under the rules adopted by the policy board and within a period that permits a parole panel, a designee of the board, or the department to dispose of the charges within the periods established by Sections 508.282(a) and (b) if the releasee or person:

(1) is accused of a violation of the releasee's parole or mandatory supervision or the person's conditional pardon, on information and complaint by a peace officer or parole officer; or

(2) is arrested after an ineligible release.

(b) If a parole panel or designated agent of the board determines that a releasee or person granted a conditional pardon has been convicted of a felony offense committed while an administrative releasee and has been sentenced to a term of confinement in a penal institution, the determination is considered to be a sufficient hearing to revoke the parole or mandatory supervision or recommend to the governor revocation of a conditional pardon without further hearing, except that the parole panel or designated agent shall conduct a hearing to consider mitigating circumstances if requested by the releasee or person granted a conditional pardon.

*(Added by L.1997, chap. 165(12.01); chgd. by L.1999, chap. 62(10.31), eff. 9/1/99.)*



### §508.2811. Preliminary hearing.

A parole panel or a designee of the board shall provide within a reasonable time to an inmate or person described by Section 508.281(a) a preliminary hearing to determine whether probable cause or reasonable grounds exist to believe that the inmate or person has committed an act that would constitute a violation of a condition of release, unless the inmate or person:

(1) waives the preliminary hearing; or

(2) after release:

(A) has been charged only with an administrative violation of a condition of release; or

(B) has been adjudicated guilty of or has pleaded guilty or nolo contendere to an offense committed after release, other than an offense punishable by fine only involving the operation of a motor vehicle, regardless of whether the court has deferred disposition of the case, imposed a sentence in the case, or placed the inmate or person on community supervision.

*(Added by L.1999, chap. 62(10.32), eff. 9/1/99.)*

### §508.282. Deadlines.

(a) Except as provided by Subsection (b), a parole panel, a designee of the board, or the department shall dispose of the charges against an inmate or person described by Section 508.281(a):

(1) before the 61st day after the date on which:

(A) a warrant issued as provided by Section 508.251 is executed, if the inmate or person is arrested only on a charge that the inmate or person has committed an administrative violation of a condition of release, and the inmate or person is not charged before the 61st day with the commission of an offense described by Section 508.2811(2)(B); or

(B) the sheriff having custody of an inmate or person alleged to have committed an offense after release notifies the department that:

(i) the inmate or person has discharged the sentence for the offense; or

(ii) the prosecution of the alleged offense has been dismissed by the attorney representing the state in the manner provided by Article 32.02, Code of Criminal Procedure; or

(2) within a reasonable time after the date on which the inmate or person is returned to the custody of the department, if:

(A) immediately before the return the inmate or person was in custody in another state or in a federal correctional system; or

(B) the inmate or person is transferred to the custody of the department under Section 508.284.

(b) A parole panel, a designee of the board, or the department is not required to dispose of the charges against an inmate or person within the period required by Subsection (a) if:

(1) the inmate or person is in custody in another state or a federal correctional institution;

(2) the parole panel or a designee of the board is not provided a place by the sheriff to hold the hearing, in which event the department, parole panel, or designee is not required to dispose of the

charges against the inmate or person until the 60th day after the date on which the sheriff provides a place to hold the hearing; or

(3) the inmate or person is granted a continuance by a parole panel or a designee of the board in the inmate's or person's hearing under Section 508.281(a), but in no event may a parole panel, a designee of the board, or the department dispose of the charges against the person later than the 30th day after the date on which the parole panel, designee, or department would otherwise be required to dispose of the charges under this section, unless the inmate or person is released from custody and a summons is issued under Section 508.251 requiring the inmate or person to appear for a hearing under Section 508.281.

(c) In Subsections (a) and (b), charges against an inmate or person are disposed of when:

(1) the inmate's or person's conditional pardon, parole, or release to mandatory supervision is:

(A) revoked; or

(B) continued or modified and the inmate or person is released from the county jail;

(2) the warrant for the inmate or person issued under Section 508.251 is withdrawn; or

(3) the inmate or person is transferred to a facility described by Section 508.284 for further proceedings.

(d) A sheriff, not later than the 10th day before the date on which the sheriff intends to release from custody an inmate or person described by Section 508.281(a) or transfer the inmate or person to the custody of an entity other than the department, shall notify the department of the intended release or transfer.

(e) If a warrant for an inmate or person issued under Section 508.251 is withdrawn, a summons may be issued requiring the inmate or person to appear for a hearing under Section 508.281.
*(Added by L.1997, chap. 165(12.01); repealed and added by L.1999, chap. 62(10.33), eff. 9/1/99.)*



### §508.283. Sanctions.

(a) After a parole panel or designated agent of the board has held a hearing under Section 508.281, the board may, in any manner warranted by the evidence:

(1) recommend to the governor to continue, revoke, or modify the conditional pardon; or

(2) continue, revoke, or modify the parole or mandatory supervision.

(b) If a person's parole, mandatory supervision, or conditional pardon is revoked, the person may be required to serve the remaining portion of the sentence on which the person was released. The remaining portion is computed without credit for the time from the date of the person's release to the date of revocation.

(c) If a warrant is issued charging a violation of a release condition or a summons is issued for a hearing under Section 508.281, the sentence time credit may be suspended until a determination is made in the case. The suspended time credit may be reinstated if the parole, mandatory supervision, or conditional pardon is continued.
*(Added by L.1997, chap. 165(12.01); chgd. by L.1999, chap. 62(10.34), eff. 9/1/99.)*

### §508.284. Transfer pending revocation hearing.

The department, as provided by Section 508.282(c), may authorize a facility that is otherwise required to detain and house an inmate or person to transfer the inmate or person to a correctional facility operated by the department or under contract with the department if:

(1) the department determines that adequate space is available in the facility to which the inmate or person is to be transferred; and

(2) the facility to which the inmate or person is to be transferred is located not more than 150 miles from the facility from which the inmate or person is to be transferred.
*(Added by L.1999, chap. 62(10.35), eff. 9/1/99.)*

### §§508.285 to 508.310. *(Reserved.)*

## SUBCHAPTER J. MISCELLANEOUS

### §508.311. Duty to provide information.

On request of a member of the board or employee of the board or department, a public official of the state, including a judge, district attorney, county attorney, or police officer, who has information relating to an inmate eligible for parole shall send to the department in writing the information in the official's possession or under the official's control. *(Added by L.1997, chap. 165(12.01), eff. 9/1/97.)*

### §508.312. Information on recidivism of releasees.

The Texas Board of Criminal Justice shall collect information on recidivism of releasees under the supervision of the division and shall use the information to evaluate operations. *(Added by L.1997, chap. 165(12.01), eff. 9/1/97.)*

### §508.313. Confidential information.

(a) All information obtained and maintained, including a victim protest letter or other correspondence, a victim impact statement, a list of inmates eligible for release on parole, and an arrest record of an inmate, is confidential and privileged if the information relates to:

(1) an inmate of the institutional division subject to release on parole, release to mandatory supervision, or executive clemency;

(2) a releasee; or

(3) a person directly identified in any proposed plan of release for an inmate.

(b) Statistical and general information relating to the parole and mandatory supervision system, including the names of releasees and data recorded relating to parole and mandatory supervision services, is not confidential or privileged and must be made available for public inspection at any reasonable time.

(c) The department may provide information that is confidential and privileged under Subsection (a) to:

(1) the governor;

(2) a member of the board;

(3) the Criminal Justice Policy Council in performing duties of the council under Section 413.021; or

(4) an eligible entity requesting information for a law enforcement, prosecutorial, correctional, clemency, or treatment purpose.

(d) In this section, "eligible entity" means:

(1) a government agency, including the office of a prosecuting attorney;

(2) an organization with which the department contracts or an organization to which the department provides a grant; or

(3) an organization to which inmates are referred for services by the department.

(e) This section does not apply to information relating to a sex offender that is authorized for release under Chapter 62, Code of Criminal Procedure.

(f) This section does not apply to information that is subject to required public disclosure under Section 552.029.

*(Added by L.1997, chap. 165(12.01); chgd. by L.1999, chaps. 62(10.36), 783(3), eff. 9/1/99, 6/18/99, respectively.)*

### §508.314. Access to inmates.

The department shall:

(1) grant to a member or employee of the board access at all reasonable times to any inmate;

(2) provide for the member or employee or a representative of the member or employee facilities for communicating with or observing an inmate; and

(3) furnish to the member or employee:

(A) any report the member or employee requires relating to the conduct or character of an inmate; or

(B) other facts a parole panel considers pertinent in determining whether an inmate will be released on parole.

*(Added by L.1997, chap. 165(12.01), eff. 9/1/97.)*

### §508.315. Electronic monitoring programs.

(a) To establish and maintain an electronic monitoring program under this chapter, the department may:

(1) fund an electronic monitoring program in a parole office;

(2) develop standards for the operation of an electronic monitoring program in a parole office; and

(3) fund the purchase, lease, or maintenance of electronic monitoring equipment.

(b) In determining whether electronic monitoring equipment should be leased or purchased, the department shall consider the rate at which technological change makes electronic monitoring equipment obsolete.

*(Added by L.1997, chap. 165(12.01), eff. 9/1/97.)*

**§508.316. Special programs.**

(a) The department may contract for services for releasees if funds are appropriated to the department for the services, including services for releasees who have a history of:

(1) mental impairment or mental retardation;

(2) substance abuse; or

(3) sexual offenses.

(b) The department shall seek funding for a contract under this section as a priority item.

*(Added by L.1997, chap. 165(12.01), eff. 9/1/97.)*

**§508.317. Intensive supervision program; super-intensive supervision program.**

(a) The department shall establish a program to provide intensive supervision to inmates released under Subchapter B, Chapter 499, and other inmates determined by a parole panel or the department to require intensive supervision.

(b) The Texas Board of Criminal Justice shall adopt rules that establish standards for determining which inmates require intensive supervision.

(c) The program must provide the level of supervision the department provides that is higher than any level of supervision other than the level of supervision described by Subsection (d).

(d) The department shall establish a program to provide super- intensive supervision to inmates released on parole or mandatory supervision and determined by parole panels to require super-intensive supervision. The program must provide the highest level of supervision provided by the department.

*(Added by L.1997, chap. 165(12.01); chgd. by L.1999, chap. 62(10.37), eff. 9/1/99.)*



**§508.318. Continuing education program.**

(a) The Texas Board of Criminal Justice and the Texas Education Agency shall adopt a memorandum of understanding that establishes the respective responsibilities of the board and the agency in implementing a continuing education program to increase the literacy of releasees.

(b) The Texas Board of Criminal Justice and the agency shall coordinate the development of the memorandum of understanding and each by rule shall adopt the memorandum.

*(Added by L.1997, chap. 165(12.01), eff. 9/1/97.)*

**§508.319. Program to assess and enhance educational and vocational skills.**

(a) The department, with the assistance of public school districts, community and public junior colleges, public and private institutions of higher education, and other appropriate public and private entities, may establish a developmental program based on information obtained under Section 508.183 for an inmate to be released to the supervision of the division.

(b) The developmental program may provide the inmate with the educational and vocational training necessary to:

(1) meet the average skill level required under Section 508.183; and

(2) acquire employment while in the custody of the division to lessen the likelihood that the inmate will return to the institutional division.

(c) To decrease state expense for a program established under this section, the Texas Workforce Commission shall provide to the department and the other entities described by Subsection (a) information relating to obtaining financial assistance under applicable programs of public or private entities.

(d) The department may establish a developmental program similar to the program described by Subsection (a) for inmates released from the institutional division who will not be supervised by the department.

*(Added by L.1997, chap. 165(12.01), eff. 9/1/97.)*

**§508.320. Contracts for lease of federal facilities.**

(a) The department may contract with the federal government for the lease of a military base or other federal facility that is not being used by the federal government.

(b) The department may use a facility leased under this section to house releasees in the custody of the division.

(c) The department may not enter into a contract under this section unless funds have been appropriated specifically to make payments on a contract under this section.

(d) The department shall attempt to enter into contracts that will provide the department with facilities located in various parts of the state.

*(Added by L.1997, chap. 165(12.01), eff. 9/1/97.)*

**§508.321. Reporting, management, and collection services.**

The department, with the approval of the Texas Board of Criminal Justice, may contract with a public or private vendor to provide telephone reporting, automated caseload management, or collection services for:

(1) fines, fees, restitution, or other costs ordered to be paid by a court; or

(2) fees collected by the division.

*(Added by L.1997, chap. 165(12.01), eff. 9/1/97.)*

**§508.322. Releasee restitution fund.**

(a) The releasee restitution fund is a fund outside the treasury and consists of restitution payments made by releasees. Money in the fund may be used only to pay restitution as required by a condition of parole or mandatory supervision to victims of criminal offenses.

(b) The comptroller is the trustee of the releasee restitution fund as provided by Section 404.073.

(c) When the board orders the payment of restitution from a releasee as provided by Article 42.037(h), Code of Criminal Procedure, the department shall:

(1) collect the payment for disbursement to the victim;

(2) deposit the payment in the releasee restitution fund; and

(3) transmit the payment to the victim as soon as practicable.

(d) If a victim who is entitled to restitution cannot be located, immediately after receiving a final payment in satisfaction of an order of restitution for the victim, the department shall attempt to notify the victim of that fact by certified mail, mailed to the last known address of the victim. If a victim then makes a claim for payment, the department promptly shall remit the payment to the victim.

(e) Money that remains unclaimed shall be transferred to the compensation to victims of crime auxiliary fund on the fifth anniversary of the date the money was deposited to the credit of the releasee restitution fund.

*(Added by L.1997, chap. 165(12.01), eff. 9/1/97.)*

**§508.323. Audit.**

The financial transactions of the division and the board are subject to audit by the state auditor in accordance with Chapter 321. *(Added by L.1997, chap. 165(12.01), eff. 9/1/97.)*

**§508.324. Victim-offender mediation.**

If the pardons and paroles division receives notice from the victim services office of the department that a victim of the defendant, or the victim's guardian or close relative, wishes to participate in victim-offender mediation with a person released on parole or to mandatory supervision, the division shall cooperate and assist the person if the person chooses to participate in the mediation program provided by the office. The pardons and paroles division may not require the defendant to participate and may not reward the person for participation by modifying conditions of release or the person's level of supervision or by granting any other benefit to the person. *(Added by L.1999, chap. 62(10.38), eff. 9/1/99.)*

# TITLE 5. OPEN GOVERNMENT; ETHICS

*(Added by L.1993, chap. 268(1), eff. 9/1/93.)*

## SUBTITLE A. OPEN GOVERNMENT

## CHAPTER 552. PUBLIC INFORMATION

*(Added by L.1993, chap. 268(1); heading chgd. by L.1995, chap. 1035(1), eff. 9/1/95.)*
*(Selected Subchapter)*

## SUBCHAPTER I. CRIMINAL VIOLATIONS



Section



## SUBCHAPTER I. CRIMINAL VIOLATIONS

### §552.351. Destruction, removal, or alteration of public information.

(a) A person commits an offense if the person wilfully destroys, mutilates, removes without permission as provided by this chapter, or alters public information.

(b) An offense under this section is a misdemeanor punishable by:

(1) a fine of not less than $25 or more than $4,000;

(2) confinement in the county jail for not less than three days or more than three months; or

(3) both the fine and confinement.

*(Added by L.1993, chap. 268(1); chgd. by L.1995, chap. 1035(25), eff. 9/1/95.)*

### §552.352. Distribution of confidential information.

(a) A person commits an offense if the person distributes information considered confidential under the terms of this chapter.

(b) An offense under this section is a misdemeanor punishable by:

(1) a fine of not more than $1,000;

(2) confinement in the county jail for not more than six months; or

(3) both the fine and confinement.

(c) A violation under this section constitutes official misconduct.

*(Added by L.1993, chap. 268(1), eff. 9/1/93.)*

### §552.353. Failure or refusal of officer for public information to provide access to or copying of public information.

(a) An officer for public information, or the officer's agent, commits an offense if, with criminal negligence, the officer or the officer's agent fails or refuses to give access to, or to permit or provide copying of, public information to a requestor as provided by this chapter.

(b) It is an affirmative defense to prosecution under Subsection (a) that the officer for public information reasonably believed that public access to the requested information was not required and that the officer:

(1) acted in reasonable reliance on a court order or a written interpretation of this chapter contained in an opinion of a court of record or of the attorney general issued under Subchapter G;

(2) requested a decision from the attorney general in accordance with Subchapter G, and the decision is pending; or

(3) not later than the 10th calendar day after the date of receipt of a decision by the attorney general that the information is public, filed a petition for a declaratory judgment, a writ of mandamus, or both, against the attorney general in a Travis County district court seeking relief from compliance with the decision of the attorney general, and a petition is pending.

(c) It is an affirmative defense to prosecution under Subsection (a) that a person or entity has, not later than the 10th calendar day after the date of receipt by a governmental body of a decision by the attorney general that the information is public, filed a cause of action seeking relief from compliance with the decision of the attorney general, and the cause is pending.

(d) It is an affirmative defense to prosecution under Subsection (a) that the defendant is the agent of an officer for public information and that the agent reasonably relied on the written instruction of the officer for public information not to disclose the public information requested.

(e) An offense under this section is a misdemeanor punishable by:

(1) a fine of not more than $1,000;

(2) confinement in the county jail for not more than six months; or

(3) both the fine and confinement.

(f) A violation under this section constitutes official misconduct.

*(Added by L.1993, chap. 268(1); chgd. by L.1995, chap 1035(25), eff. 9/1/95.)*

## CHAPTER 557. SEDITION, SABOTAGE, AND COMMUNISM

*(Added by L.1993, chap. 268(1), eff. 9/1/93.)*



### SUBCHAPTER A. SEDITION

Section



### SUBCHAPTER B. SABOTAGE



### SUBCHAPTER C. COMMUNISM



### SUBCHAPTER A. SEDITION

**§557.001. Sedition.**

(a) A person commits an offense if the person knowingly:

(1) commits, attempts to commit, or conspires with one or more persons to commit an act to overthrow, destroy, or alter the constitutional form of government of this state or of any political subdivision of this state by force or violence;

(2) under circumstances that constitute a clear and present danger to the security of this state or a political subdivision of this state, advocates, advises, or teaches or conspires with one or more persons to advocate, advise, or teach a person to commit or attempt to commit an act described in Subdivision (1); or

(3) participates, with knowledge of the nature of the organization, in the management of an organization that engages in or attempts to engage in an act intended to overthrow, destroy, or alter the constitutional form of government of this state or of any political subdivision of this state by force or violence.

(b) An offense under this section is a felony punishable by:

(1) a fine not to exceed $20,000;

(2) confinement in the institutional division of the Texas Department of Criminal Justice for a term of not less than one year or more than 20 years; or

(3) both fine and imprisonment.

(c) A person convicted of an offense under this section may not receive probation under Article 42.12, Code of Criminal Procedure.

*(Added by L.1993, chap. 268(1), eff. 9/1/93.)*

### §557.002. Disqualification.

A person who is finally convicted of an offense under Section 557.001 may not hold office or a position of profit, trust, or employment with the state or any political subdivision of the state. *(Added by L.1993, chap. 268(1), eff. 9/1/93.)*

### §557.003. Seditious organizations.

(a) An organization, either incorporated or unincorporated, may not engage in or have as a purpose activities intended to overthrow, destroy, or alter the constitutional form of government of this state or a political subdivision of this state by force or violence.

(b) An organization that violates Subsection (a):

(1) may not lawfully exist, function, or operate in this state; and

(2) is not entitled to the rights, privileges, and immunities granted to organizations under the law of this state.

(c) A district attorney, criminal district attorney, or county attorney may bring an action against an organization in a court of competent jurisdiction. If the court finds that the organization has violated Subsection (a), the court shall order:

(1) the organization dissolved;

(2) if the organization is incorporated in the state or has a permit to do business in the state, the organization's charter or permit revoked;

(3) all funds, records, and property of the organization forfeited to the state; and

(4) all books, records, and files of the organization turned over to the attorney general.

(d) It is prima facie evidence that an organization engages in or has as a purpose engaging in activities intended to overthrow, destroy, or alter the constitutional form of the government of this state or a political subdivision of this state by force or violence if it is shown that the organization has a parent or superior organization that engages in or has as a purpose engaging in activities intended to overthrow, destroy, or alter the constitutional form of the government of this state or a political subdivision of this state by force or violence.
*(Added by L.1993, chap. 268(1), eff. 9/1/93.)*

### §557.004. Enforcement.

(a) A district court may, on application by a district attorney, criminal district attorney, or county attorney, order injunctive or other equitable relief appropriate to enforce this subchapter.

(b) The procedure for relief sought under Subsection (a) of this section is the same as that for other similar relief in the district court except that the proceeding may not be instituted unless the director of the Department of Public Safety of the State of Texas or the director's assistant in charge is notified by telephone, telegraph, or in person that injunctive or other equitable relief will be sought.

(c) An affidavit that states that the notice described in Subsection (b) was given and that accompanies the application for relief is sufficient to permit filing of the application.

(d) Injunctive or other equitable relief sought to enforce this subchapter may not be granted in a labor dispute.

(e) The internal security section of the Department of Public Safety of the State of Texas shall assist in the enforcement of this subchapter.
*(Added by L.1993, chap. 268(1), eff. 9/1/93.)*

### §557.005. Judicial powers in labor disputes.

This subchapter does not affect the powers of the courts of this state or of the United States under the law of this state in a labor dispute. *(Added by L.1993, chap. 268(1), eff. 9/1/93.)*

## SUBCHAPTER B. SABOTAGE

### §557.011. Sabotage.

(a) A person commits an offense if the person, with the intent to injure the United States, this state, or any facility or property used for national defense sabotages or attempts to sabotage any property or facility used or to be used for national defense.

(b) An offense under this section is a felony punishable by confinement in the institutional division of the Texas Department of Criminal Justice for a term of not less than two years or more than 20 years.

(c) If conduct constituting an offense under this section also constitutes an offense under another provision of law, the actor may be prosecuted under both sections.

(d) In this section, "sabotage" means to wilfully and maliciously damage or destroy property.
*(Added by L.1993, chap. 268(1), eff. 9/1/93.)*

### §557.012. Capital sabotage.

(a) A person commits an offense if the person commits an offense under Section 557.011(a) and the sabotage or attempted sabotage causes the death of an individual.

(b) An offense under this section is punishable by:

(1) death; or

(2) confinement in the institutional division of the Texas Department of Criminal Justice for:

(A) life; or

(B) a term of not less than two years.

(c) If conduct constituting an offense under this section also constitutes an offense under other law, the actor may be prosecuted under both sections.
*(Added by L.1993, chap. 268(1), eff. 9/1/93.)*

### §557.013. Enforcement.

The attorney general, a district or county attorney, the department, and any law enforcement officer of this state shall enforce this subchapter. *(Added by L.1993, chap. 268(1), eff. 9/1/93.)*

## SUBCHAPTER C. COMMUNISM

### §557.021. Definitions.

In this subchapter:

(1) "Communist" means a person who commits an act reasonably calculated to further the overthrow of the government:

(A) by force or violence; or

(B) by unlawful or unconstitutional means and replace it with a communist government.

(2) "Department" means the Department of Public Safety of the State of Texas.

(3) "Government" means the government of this state or any of its political subdivisions.
*(Added by L.1993, chap. 268(1), eff. 9/1/93.)*

### §557.022. Restrictions.

(a) The name of a communist may not be printed on the ballot for any primary or general election in this state or a political subdivision of this state.

(b) A person may not hold a nonelected office or position with the state or any political subdivision of the state if:

(1) any of the compensation for the office or position comes from public funds of this state or a political subdivision of this state; and

(2) the employer or superior of the person has reasonable grounds to believe that the person is a communist.
*(Added by L.1993, chap. 268(1), eff. 9/1/93.)*

### §557.023. Enforcement.

The attorney general, a district or county attorney, the department, and any law enforcement officer of this state shall enforce this subchapter. *(Added by L.1993, chap. 268(1), eff. 9/1/93.)*

Printed in the U.S.A. 2t

# HEALTH AND SAFETY CODE

*(Added by L.1989, chap. 678(1), eff. 9/1/89.)*

## TITLE 2. HEALTH

## CHAPTER 12. POWERS AND DUTIES OF TEXAS DEPARTMENT OF HEALTH

*(Selected Subchapter)*

## SUBCHAPTER H. MEDICAL ADVISORY BOARD

*(Added by L.1995, chap. 165(9), eff. 9/1/95.)*

Section


### §12.091. Definitions.

In this subchapter:

(1) "Medical standards division" means the Medical Standards on Motor Vehicle Operations Division of the department.

(2) "Panel" means a panel of the medical advisory board.

*(Added by L.1995, chap. 165(9), eff. 9/1/95.)*

### §12.092. Medical advisory board; board members.

(a) The commissioner shall appoint the medical advisory board members from:

(1) persons licensed to practice medicine in this state, including physicians who are board certified in internal medicine, psychiatry, neurology, physical medicine, or ophthalmology and who are jointly recommended by the Texas Department of Health and the Texas Medical Association; and

(2) persons licensed to practice optometry in this state who are jointly recommended by the department and the Texas Optometric Association.

(b) The medical advisory board shall assist the Department of Public Safety of the State of Texas in determining whether:

(1) an applicant for a driver's license or a license holder is capable of safely operating a motor vehicle; or

(2) an applicant for or holder of a license to carry a concealed handgun under the authority of Subchapter H, Chapter 411, Government Code, is capable of exercising sound judgment with respect to the proper use and storage of a handgun.

*(Added by L.1995, chap. 165(9); chgd. by L.1997, chap. 1261(21); L.1999, chap. 62(9.23), eff. 9/1/99.)*

### §12.093. Administration; rules.

(a) The medical advisory board is administratively attached to the medical standards division.

(b) The medical standards division:

(1) shall provide administrative support for the medical advisory board and panels of the medical advisory board; and

(2) may collect and maintain the individual medical records necessary for use by the medical advisory board and the panels under this section from a physician, hospital, or other health care provider.

*(Added by L.1995, chap. 165(9), eff. 9/1/95.)*

### §12.094. Rules relating to medical advisory board members.

(a) The board:

(1) may adopt rules to govern the activities of the medical advisory board;

(2) by rule may establish a reasonable fee to pay a member of the medical advisory board for the member's professional consultation services; and

(3) if appropriate, may authorize per diem and travel allowances for each meeting a member attends, not to exceed the amounts authorized for state employees by the General Appropriations Act.

(b) The fee under Subsection (a)(2) may not be less than $75 or more than $150 for each meeting that the member attends.

*(Added by L.1995, chap. 165(9), eff. 9/1/95.)*

## §12.095. Board panels; powers and duties.

(a) If the Department of Public Safety of the State of Texas requests an opinion or recommendation from the medical advisory board as to the ability of an applicant or license holder to operate a motor vehicle safely or to exercise sound judgment with respect to the proper use and storage of a handgun, the commissioner or a person designated by the commissioner shall convene a panel to consider the case or question submitted by that department.

(b) To take action as a panel, at least three members of the medical advisory board must be present.

(c) Each panel member shall prepare an individual independent written report for the Department of Public Safety of the State of Texas that states the member's opinion as to the ability of the applicant or license holder to operate a motor vehicle safely or to exercise sound judgment with respect to the proper use and storage of a handgun, as appropriate. In the report the panel member may also make recommendations relating to that department's subsequent action.

(d) In its deliberations, a panel may examine any medical record or report that contains material that may be relevant to the ability of the applicant or license holder.

(e) The panel may require the applicant or license holder to undergo a medical or other examination at the applicant's or holder's expense. A person who conducts an examination under this subsection may be compelled to testify before the panel and in any subsequent proceedings under Subchapter N, Chapter 521, Transportation Code, concerning the person's observations and findings.

*(Added by L.1995, chap. 165(9); chgd. by L.1997, chap. 1261(22), eff. 9/1/97.)*

## §12.096. Physician report.

(a) A physician licensed to practice medicine in this state may inform the Department of Public Safety of the State of Texas or the medical advisory board, orally or in writing, of the name, date of birth, and address of a patient older than 15 years of age whom the physician has diagnosed as having a disorder or disability specified in a rule of the Department of Public Safety of the State of Texas.

(b) The release of information under this section is an exception to the patient-physician privilege requirements imposed under Section 5.08, Medical Practice Act (Article 4495b, Texas Civil Statutes).

*(Added by L.1995, chap. 165(9), eff. 9/1/95.)*

## §12.097. Confidentiality requirements.

(a) All records, reports, and testimony relating to the medical condition of an applicant or license holder:

(1) are for the confidential use of the medical advisory board, a panel, or the Department of Public Safety of the State of Texas;

(2) are privileged information; and

(3) may not be disclosed to any person or used as evidence in a trial except as provided by Subsection (b).

(b) In a subsequent proceeding under Subchapter N, Chapter 521, Transportation Code, the medical standards division may provide a copy of the report of the medical advisory board or panel and a medical record or report relating to an applicant or license holder to:

(1) the Department of Public Safety of the State of Texas;

(2) the applicant or license holder; and

(3) the officer who presides at the hearing.

*(Added by L.1995, chap. 165(9), eff. 9/1/95.)*

## §12.098. Liability.

A member of the medical advisory board, a member of a panel, a person who makes an examination for or on the recommendation of the medical advisory board, or a physician who reports to the medical advisory board or a panel under Section 12.096 is not liable for a professional opinion, recommendation, or report made under this subchapter. *(Added by L.1995, chap. 165(9), eff. 9/1/95.)*

# CHAPTER 161. PUBLIC HEALTH PROVISIONS
*(Selected Subchapters)*

## SUBCHAPTER H
## DISTRIBUTION OF CIGARETTES OR TOBACCO PRODUCTS
*(Selected Sections)*
*(Heading chgd. by L.1997, chap. 671(1.01), eff. 9/1/97.)*

Section




### §161.081. Definitions.

In this subchapter:

(1) "Cigarette" has the meaning assigned by Section 154.001, Tax Code.

(2) "Permit holder" has the meaning assigned by Section 154.001 or 155.001, Tax Code, as applicable.

(3) "Retail sale" means a transfer of possession from a retailer to a consumer in connection with a purchase, sale, or exchange for value of cigarettes or tobacco products.

(4) "Retailer" has the meaning assigned by Section 154.001 or 155.001, Tax Code, as applicable.

(5) "Tobacco product" has the meaning assigned by Section 155.001, Tax Code.

(6) "Wholesaler" has the meaning assigned by Section 154.001 or 155.001, Tax Code, as applicable.

*(Added by L.1997, chap. 671(1.01), eff. 9/1/97. Former section 161.081 renumbered to 161.082 by L.1997, chap. 671(1.01), eff. 9/1/97.)*

### §161.082. Sale of cigarettes or tobacco products to persons younger than 18 years of age prohibited; proof of age required.

(a) A person commits an offense if the person, with criminal negligence:

(1) sells, gives, or causes to be sold or given a cigarette or tobacco product to someone who is younger than 18 years of age; or

(2) sells, gives, or causes to be sold or given a cigarette or tobacco product to another person who intends to deliver it to someone who is younger than 18 years of age.

(b) If an offense under this section occurs in connection with a sale by an employee of the owner of a store in which cigarettes or tobacco products are sold at retail, the employee is criminally responsible for the offense and is subject to prosecution.

(c) An offense under this section is a Class C misdemeanor.

(d) It is a defense to prosecution under Subsection (a)(1) that the person to whom the cigarette or tobacco product was sold or given presented to the defendant apparently valid proof of identification.

(e) A proof of identification satisfies the requirements of Subsection (d) if it contains a physical description and photograph consistent with the person's appearance, purports to establish that the person is 18 years of age or older, and was issued by a governmental agency. The proof of identification may include a driver's license issued by this state or another state, a passport, or an identification card issued by a state or the federal government.

*(Added by L.1989, chap. 678(1); chgd. by L.1991, chap. 14(50); renumbered from 161.081 and chgd. by L.1997, chap. 671(1.01), eff. 9/1/97.)*

### §161.083. Sale of cigarettes or tobacco products to persons younger than 27 years of age.

(a) Pursuant to federal regulation under 21 C.F.R. Section 897.14(b), a person may not sell, give, or cause to be sold or given a cigarette or tobacco product to someone who is younger than 27 years of age unless the person to whom the cigarette or tobacco product was sold or given presents an apparently valid proof of identification.

(b) A retailer shall adequately supervise and train the retailer's agents and employees to prevent a violation of Subsection (a).

(c) A proof of identification described by Section 161.082(e) satisfies the requirements of Subsection (a).

(d) Notwithstanding any other provision of law, a violation of this section is not a violation of this subchapter for purposes of Section 154.1142 or 155.0592, Tax Code.

*(Added by L.1997, chap. 671(1.01), eff. 1/1/98.)*

## §161.084. Warning notice.

(a) Each person who sells cigarettes or tobacco products at retail or by vending machine shall post a sign in a location that is conspicuous to all employees and customers and that is close to the place at which the cigarettes or tobacco products may be purchased.

(b) The sign must include the statement:

PURCHASING OR ATTEMPTING TO PURCHASE TOBACCO PRODUCTS BY A MINOR UNDER 18 YEARS OF AGE IS PROHIBITED BY LAW. SALE OR PROVISION OF TOBACCO PRODUCTS TO A MINOR UNDER 18 YEARS OF AGE IS PROHIBITED BY LAW. UPON CONVICTION, A CLASS C MISDEMEANOR, INCLUDING A FINE OF UP TO $500, MAY BE IMPOSED. VIOLATIONS MAY BE REPORTED TO THE TEXAS COMPTROLLER'S OFFICE BY CALLING (insert toll-free telephone number).

(c) The comptroller by rule shall determine the design and size of the sign.

(d) The comptroller on request shall provide the sign without charge to any person who sells cigarettes or tobacco products. The comptroller may provide the sign without charge to distributors of cigarettes or tobacco products or wholesale dealers of cigarettes or tobacco products in this state for distribution to persons who sell cigarettes or tobacco products. A distributor or wholesale dealer may not charge for distributing a sign under this subsection.

(e) A person commits an offense if the person intentionally fails to display a sign as prescribed by this section. An offense under this subsection is a Class C misdemeanor.

*(Added by L.1991, chap. 14(50); renumbered from 161.082 and chgd. by L.1997, chap. 671(1.01), eff. 9/1/97.)*

## §161.086. Vendor assisted sales required; vending machines.

(a) Except as provided by Subsection (b), a retailer or other person may not:

(1) offer cigarettes or tobacco products for sale in a manner that permits a customer direct access to the cigarettes or tobacco products; or

(2) install or maintain a vending machine containing cigarettes or tobacco products.

(b) Subsection (a) does not apply to:

(1) a facility or business that is not open to persons younger than 18 years of age at any time;

(2) that part of a facility or business that is a humidor or other enclosure designed to store cigars in a climate-controlled environment; or

(3) a premises for which a person holds a package store permit issued under the Alcoholic Beverage Code.

(c) The comptroller or a peace officer may, with or without a warrant, seize, seal, or disable a vending machine installed or maintained in violation of this section. Property seized under this subsection must be seized in accordance with, and is subject to forfeiture to the state in accordance with, Subchapter H, Chapter 154, Tax Code, and Subchapter E, Chapter 155, Tax Code.

(d) A person commits an offense if the person violates Subsection (a). An offense under this subsection is a Class C misdemeanor.

*(Added by L.1997, chap. 671(1.01); chgd. by L.1999, chap. 567(1), eff. 9/1/99.)*

## §161.087. Distribution of cigarettes or tobacco products.

(a) A person may not distribute to persons younger than 18 years of age:

(1) a free sample of a cigarette or tobacco product; or

(2) a coupon or other item that the recipient may use to receive a free or discounted cigarette or tobacco product or a sample cigarette or tobacco product.

(b) Except as provided by Subsection (c), a permit holder may not accept or redeem, offer to accept or redeem, or hire a person to accept or redeem a coupon or other item that the recipient may use to receive a free or discounted cigarette or tobacco product or a sample cigarette or tobacco product if the recipient is younger than 18 years of age. A coupon or other item that such a recipient may use to receive a free or discounted cigarette or tobacco product or a sample cigarette or tobacco product may not be redeemable through mail or courier delivery.

Printed in the U.S.A. 17

(c) Subsections (a)(2) and (b) do not apply to a transaction between permit holders unless the transaction is a retail sale.

(d) A person commits an offense if the person violates this section. An offense under this subsection is a Class C misdemeanor.
*(Added by L.1997, chap. 671(1.01), eff. 9/1/97.)*

### §161.088. Enforcement; unannounced inspections.

(a) The comptroller shall enforce this subchapter in partnership with local law enforcement agencies and with their cooperation and shall ensure the state's compliance with Section 1926 of the federal Public Health Service Act (42 U.S.C. Section 300x-26) and any implementing regulations adopted by the United States Department of Health and Human Services. Except as expressly authorized by law, the comptroller may not adopt any rules governing the subject matter of this subchapter or Subchapter K, N, or O.

(b) The comptroller may make block grants to counties and municipalities to be used by local law enforcement agencies to enforce this subchapter in a manner that can reasonably be expected to reduce the extent to which cigarettes and tobacco products are sold or distributed to persons who are younger than 18 years of age. At least annually, random unannounced inspections shall be conducted at various locations where cigarettes and tobacco products are sold or distributed to ensure compliance with this subchapter. The comptroller shall rely, to the fullest extent possible, on local law enforcement agencies to enforce this subchapter.

(c) To facilitate the effective administration and enforcement of this subchapter, the comptroller may enter into interagency contracts with other state agencies, and those agencies may assist the comptroller in the administration and enforcement of this subchapter.

(d) The use of a person younger than 18 years of age to act as a minor decoy to test compliance with this subchapter shall be conducted in a fashion that promotes fairness. A person may be enlisted by the comptroller or a local law enforcement agency to act as a minor decoy only if the following requirements are met:

(1) written parental consent is obtained for the use of a person younger than 18 years of age to act as a minor decoy to test compliance with this subchapter;

(2) at the time of the inspection, the minor decoy is younger than 17 years of age;

(3) the minor decoy has an appearance that would cause a reasonably prudent seller of cigarettes or tobacco products to request identification and proof of age;

(4) the minor decoy carries either the minor's own identification showing the minor's correct date of birth or carries no identification, and a minor decoy who carries identification presents it on request to any seller of cigarettes or tobacco products; and

(5) the minor decoy answers truthfully any questions about the minor's age.

(e) The comptroller shall annually prepare for submission by the governor to the secretary of the United States Department of Health and Human Services the report required by Section 1926 of the federal Public Health Service Act (42 U.S.C. Section 300x-26).
*(Added by L.1997, chap. 671(1.01); chgd. by L.1999, 1156(1), eff. 9/1/99.)*

### §161.090. Reports of violation.

A local or state law enforcement agency or other governmental unit shall notify the comptroller, on the 10th day of each month, or the first working day after that date, of any violation of this subchapter that occurred in the preceding month that the agency or unit detects, investigates, or prosecutes. *(Added by L.1997, chap. 671(1.01), eff. 9/1/97.)*

## SUBCHAPTER N. TOBACCO USE BY MINORS

*(Added by L.1997, chap. 671(3.01), eff. 1/1/98.)*

Section

## §161.251. Definitions.

In this subchapter:

(1) "Cigarette" has the meaning assigned by Section 154.001, Tax Code.

(2) "Tobacco product" has the meaning assigned by Section 155.001, Tax Code.

*(Added by L.1997, chap. 671(3.01), eff. 1/1/98.)*

## §161.252. Possession, purchase, consumption, or receipt of cigarettes or tobacco products by minors prohibited.

(a) An individual who is younger than 18 years of age commits an offense if the individual:

(1) possesses, purchases, consumes, or accepts a cigarette or tobacco product; or

(2) falsely represents himself or herself to be 18 years of age or older by displaying proof of age that is false, fraudulent, or not actually proof of the individual's own age in order to obtain possession of, purchase, or receive a cigarette or tobacco product.

(b) It is an exception to the application of this section that the individual younger than 18 years of age possessed the cigarette or tobacco product in the presence of:

(1) an adult parent, a guardian, or a spouse of the individual; or

(2) an employer of the individual, if possession or receipt of the tobacco product is required in the performance of the employee's duties as an employee.

(c) It is an exception to the application of this section that the individual younger than 18 years of age is participating in an inspection or test of compliance in accordance with Section 161.088.

(d) An offense under this section is punishable by a fine not to exceed $250.

*(Added by L.1997, chap. 671(3.01), eff. 1/1/98.)*

## §161.253. Tobacco awareness program; community service.

(a) On conviction of an individual for an offense under Section 161.252, the court shall suspend execution of sentence and shall require the defendant to attend a tobacco awareness program approved by the commissioner. The court may require the parent or guardian of the defendant to attend the tobacco awareness program with the defendant.

(b) On request, a tobacco awareness program may be taught in languages other than English.

(c) If the defendant resides in a rural area of this state or another area of this state in which access to a tobacco awareness program is not readily available, the court shall require the defendant to perform eight to 12 hours of tobacco-related community service instead of attending the tobacco awareness program.

(d) The tobacco awareness program and the tobacco-related community service are remedial and are not punishment.

(e) Not later than the 90th day after the date of a conviction under Section 161.252, the defendant shall present to the court, in the manner required by the court, evidence of satisfactory completion of the tobacco awareness program or the tobacco-related community service.

(f) On receipt of the evidence required under Subsection (e), the court shall:

(1) if the defendant has been previously convicted of an offense under Section 161.252, execute the sentence, and at the discretion of the court, reduce the fine imposed to not less than half the fine previously imposed by the court; or

(2) if the defendant has not been previously convicted of an offense under Section 161.252, discharge the defendant and dismiss the complaint or information against the defendant.

(g) If the court discharges the defendant under Subsection (f)(2), the defendant is released from all penalties and disabilities resulting from the offense except that the defendant is considered to have been convicted of the offense if the defendant is subsequently convicted of an offense under Section 161.252 committed after the dismissal under Subsection (f)(2).

*(Added by L.1997, chap. 671(3.01), eff. 1/1/98.)*

## §161.254. Driver's license suspension or denial.

(a) If the defendant does not provide the evidence required under Section 161.253(e) within the period specified by that subsection, the court shall order the Department of Public Safety to suspend or deny issuance of any driver's license or permit to the defendant. The order must specify the period of the suspension or denial, which may not exceed 180 days after the date of the order.

(b) The Department of Public Safety shall send to the defendant notice of court action under Subsection (a) by first class mail. The notice must include the date of the order and the reason for the order and must specify the period of the suspension or denial.

*(Added by L.1997, chap. 671(3.01); chgd. by L.1999, chap. 1409(8), eff. 9/1/99.)*

### §161.255. Expungement of conviction.

An individual convicted of an offense under Section 161.252 may apply to the court to have the conviction expunged. If the court finds that the individual satisfactorily completed the tobacco awareness program or tobacco-related community service ordered by the court, the court shall order the conviction and any complaint, verdict, sentence, or other document relating to the offense to be expunged from the individual's record and the conviction may not be shown or made known for any purpose. *(Added by L.1997, chap. 671(3.01), eff. 1/1/98.)*

### §161.256. Jurisdiction of courts.

A justice court or municipal court may exercise jurisdiction over any matter in which a court under this subchapter may:

(1) impose a requirement that a defendant attend a tobacco awareness program or perform tobacco-related community service; or

(2) order the suspension or denial of a driver's license or permit.

*(Added by L.1997, chap. 671(3.01), eff. 1/1/98.)*

### §161.257. Application of other law.

Title 3, Family Code, does not apply to a proceeding under this subchapter. *(Added by L.1997, chap. 671(3.01), eff. 1/1/98.)*

### §§161.258 to 161.300. *(Reserved.)*

# SUBTITLE H. PUBLIC HEALTH PROVISIONS

## CHAPTER 166. FEMALE GENITAL MUTILATION*

*(Complete Chapter)*

*(Heading added by L.1999, chap. 642(1), eff. 6/18/99.)*

*(*Two versions of Chapter 166 were enacted. See other Chapter 166 below.*)



### §166.001. Female genital mutilation prohibited.

(a) A person commits an offense if the person knowingly circumcises, excises, or infibulates any part of the labia majora or labia minora or clitoris of another person who is younger than 18 years of age.

(b) An offense under this section is a state jail felony.

(c) It is a defense to prosecution under Subsection (a) that:

(1) the person performing the act is a physician or other licensed health care professional and the act is within the scope of the person's license; and

(2) the act is performed for medical purposes.

*(Added by L.1999, chap. 642(1), eff. 6/18/99.)*

## CHAPTER 166. ADVANCE DIRECTIVES*

*(Selected Subchapter)*

*(Heading added by L.1999, chap. 450(1.01), eff. 9/1/99.)*

*(Two versions of Chapter 166 were enacted. See other Chapter 166 above.)*

## SUBCHAPTER B. DIRECTIVE TO PHYSICIANS

*(Selected Section)*

*(Redesignated from Chapter 672, Health and Safety Code by L.1999, chap. 450(1.03), eff. 9/1/99.)*



## SUBCHAPTER B. DIRECTIVE TO PHYSICIANS

### §166.048. Criminal penalty; prosecution.

(a) A person commits an offense if the person intentionally conceals, cancels, defaces, obliterates, or damages another person's directive without that person's consent. An offense under this subsection is a Class A misdemeanor.

(b) A person is subject to prosecution for criminal homicide under Chapter 19, Penal Code, if the person, with the intent to cause life-sustaining treatment to be withheld or withdrawn from another person contrary to the other person's desires, falsifies or forges a directive or intentionally conceals or withholds personal knowledge of a revocation and thereby directly causes life-sustaining treatment to be withheld or withdrawn from the other person with the result that the other person's death is hastened.

*(Renumbered from 672.018 and chgd. by L.1999, chap. 450(1.03), eff. 9/1/99.)*

# TITLE 3. VITAL STATISTICS

## CHAPTER 192. BIRTH RECORDS

*(Selected Section)*



### §192.0021. Heirloom birth certificate.

(a) The department may design the form of an heirloom birth certificate and may promote and sell copies of the certificate. An heirloom birth certificate must contain the same information as, and have the same effect of, a certified copy of another birth record. The department shall prescribe a fee for the issuance of an heirloom birth certificate in an amount that does not exceed $30.

(b) Proceeds from the sale of heirloom birth certificates shall be deposited to the credit of the general revenue fund. An amount not to exceed the costs of administering this section as determined by the comptroller shall be appropriated to the department for administering this section.

Printed in the U.S.A.

# TITLE 5. SANITATION AND ENVIRONMENTAL QUALITY

## SUBTITLE B. SOLID WASTE, TOXIC CHEMICALS, SEWAGE, LITTER, AND WATER

*(Heading chgd. by L.1991, chap. 14(130); L.1991, 1st C.S., chap. 3(1.046), eff. 8/12/91.)*

## CHAPTER 365. LITTER

### SUBCHAPTER A. GENERAL PROVISIONS



### SUBCHAPTER B. CERTAIN ACTIONS PROHIBITED



### SUBCHAPTER C. SPECIAL PROVISIONS



### SUBCHAPTER A. GENERAL PROVISIONS

#### §365.001. Short title.

This chapter may be cited as the Texas Litter Abatement Act. *(Added by L.1989, chap. 678(1), eff. 9/1/89.)*

#### §365.002. Water pollution controlled by Water Code.

The pollution of water in the state is controlled by Chapter 26, Water Code, and other applicable law. *(Added by L.1989, chap. 678(1), eff. 9/1/89.)*

#### §365.003. Litter on beaches controlled by Natural Resources Code.

The regulation of litter on public beaches is controlled by Subchapters C and D, Chapter 61, Natural Resources Code. *(Added by L.1989, chap. 678(1), eff. 9/1/89.)*

**§365.004. Disposal of garbage, refuse, and sewage in certain areas under control of Parks and Wildlife Department.**

The Parks and Wildlife Commission may adopt rules to govern the disposal of garbage, refuse, and sewage in state parks, public water in state parks, historic sites, scientific areas, and forts under the control of the Parks and Wildlife Department. *(Added by L.1989, chap. 678(1), eff. 9/1/89.)*

**§365.005. Venue and recovery of costs.**

(a) Venue for the prosecution of a criminal offense under Subchapter B or Section 365.032 or 365.033 or for a suit for injunctive relief under any of those provisions is in the county in which the defendant resides, in the county in which the offense or the violation occurs, or in Travis County.

(b) If the attorney general or a local government brings a suit for injunctive relief under Subchapter B or Section 365.032 or 365.033, a prevailing party may recover its reasonable attorney fees, court costs, and reasonable investigative costs incurred in relation to the proceeding. *(Added by L.1991, chap. 14(125), eff. 9/1/91.)*

**§§365.006 to 365.010.** *(Reserved.)*

## SUBCHAPTER B. CERTAIN ACTIONS PROHIBITED

*(Chgd. by L.1991, 1st C.S., chap. 3(8.161), eff. 9/1/91.)*

**§365.011. Definitions.**

In this subchapter:

(1) "Approved solid waste site" means:

(A) a solid waste site permitted or registered by the Texas Natural Resource Conservation Commission;

(B) a solid waste site licensed by a county under Chapter 361; or

(C) a designated collection area for ultimate disposal at a permitted or licensed municipal solid waste site.

(2) "Boat" means a vehicle, including a barge, airboat, motorboat, or sailboat, used for transportation on water.

(3) "Commercial purpose" means the purpose of economic gain.

(4) "Commercial vehicle" means a vehicle that is operated by a person for a commercial purpose or that is owned by a business or commercial enterprise.

(5) "Dispose" and "dump" mean to discharge, deposit, inject, spill, leak, or place litter on or into land or water.

(6) "Litter" means:

(A) decayable waste from a public or private establishment, residence, or restaurant, including animal and vegetable waste material from a market or storage facility handling or storing produce or other food products, or the handling, preparation, cooking, or consumption of food, but not including sewage, body wastes, or industrial by-products; or

(B) nondecayable solid waste, except ashes, that consists of:

(i) combustible waste material, including paper, rags, cartons, wood, excelsior, furniture, rubber, plastics, yard trimmings, leaves, or similar materials;

(ii) noncombustible waste material, including glass, crockery, tin or aluminum cans, metal furniture, and similar materials that do not burn at ordinary incinerator temperatures of 1800 degrees Fahrenheit or less; and

(iii) discarded or worn-out manufactured materials and machinery, including motor vehicles and parts of motor vehicles, tires, aircraft, farm implements, building or construction materials, appliances, and scrap metal.

(7) "Motor vehicle" has the meaning assigned by Section 541.201, Transportation Code.

(8) "Public highway" means the entire width between property lines of a road, street, way, thoroughfare, bridge, public beach, or park in this state, not privately owned or controlled, if any part of the road, street, way, thoroughfare, bridge, public beach, or park:

(A) is opened to the public for vehicular traffic;

(B) is used as a public recreational area; or

(C) is under the state's legislative jurisdiction through its police power.

(9) "Solid waste" has the meaning assigned by Section 361.003.

*(Added by L.1989, chap. 678(1); chgd. by L.1991, 1st C.S., chap. 3(8.161); L.1993, chap. 740(1); L.1995, chap. 76(11.111); L.1997, chaps. 165(30.206), 286(1), eff. 9/1/97, 5/26/97, respectively.)*

 Zt

## §365.012. Illegal dumping; criminal penalties.

(a) A person commits an offense if the person disposes or allows or permits the disposal of litter or other solid waste at a place that is not an approved solid waste site, including a place on or within 300 feet of a public highway, on a right-of-way, on other public or private property, or into inland or coastal water of the state.

(b) A person commits an offense if the person receives litter or other solid waste for disposal at a place that is not an approved solid waste site, regardless of whether the litter or other solid waste or the land on which the litter or other solid waste is disposed is owned or controlled by the person.

(c) A person commits an offense if the person transports litter or other solid waste to a place that is not an approved solid waste site for disposal at the site.

(d) An offense under this section is a Class C misdemeanor if the litter or other solid waste to which the offense applies weighs 15 pounds or less or has a volume of 13 gallons or less.

(e) An offense under this section is a Class B misdemeanor if the litter or other solid waste to which the offense applies weighs more than 15 pounds but less than 500 pounds or has a volume of more than 13 gallons but less than 100 cubic feet.

(f) An offense under this section is a Class A misdemeanor if:

(1) the litter or other solid waste to which the offense applies weighs 500 pounds or more or has a volume of 100 cubic feet or more; or

(2) the litter or other solid waste is disposed for a commercial purpose and weighs more than five pounds or has a volume of more than 13 gallons.

(g) If it is shown on the trial of the defendant for an offense under this section that the defendant has previously been convicted of an offense under this section, the punishment for the offense is increased to the punishment for the next highest category.

(h) On conviction for an offense under this section, the court shall provide to the defendant written notice that a subsequent conviction for an offense under this section may result in the forfeiture under Chapter 59, Code of Criminal Procedure, of the vehicle used by the defendant in committing the offense.

(i) The offenses prescribed by this section include the unauthorized disposal of litter or other solid waste in a dumpster or similar receptacle.

(j) This section does not apply to the temporary storage for future disposal of litter or other solid waste by a person on land owned by that person, or by that person's agent. The commission by rule shall regulate temporary storage for future disposal of litter or other solid waste by a person on land owned by the person or the person's agent.

(k) This section does not apply to an individual's disposal of litter or other solid waste if:

(1) the litter or waste is generated on land the individual owns;

(2) the litter or waste is not generated as a result of an activity related to a commercial purpose;

(3) the disposal occurs on land the individual owns; and

(4) the disposal is not for a commercial purpose.

(*l*) A municipality or county may offer a reward of $50 for reporting a violation of this section that results in a prosecution under this section.

*(Added by L.1989, chap. 678(1); chgd. by L.1991, 1st C.S., chap. 3(1.036); repealed and added by L.1991, 1st C.S., chap. 3(8.161); chgd. by L.1993, chaps. 740(2), 828(3); L.1995, chap. 76(17.01)(28); L.1997, chap. 286(2), eff. 5/26/97.)*

## §365.013. Rules and standards; criminal penalty.

(a) The Texas Natural Resource Conservation Commission shall adopt rules and standards regarding processing and treating litter disposed in violation of this subchapter.

(b) A person commits an offense if the person violates a rule adopted under this section.

(c) An offense under this section is a Class A misdemeanor.

*(Added by L.1989, chap. 678(1); chgd. by L.1991, 1st C.S., chap. 3(1.037); repealed and added by L.1991, 1st C.S., chap. 3(8.161); chgd. by L.1995, chap. 76(11.112), eff. 9/1/95.)*

## §365.014. Application of subchapter; defenses; presumptions.

(a) This subchapter does not apply to farmers:

(1) in handling anything necessary to grow, handle, and care for livestock; or

(2) in erecting, operating, and maintaining improvements necessary to handle, thresh, and prepare agricultural products or for conservation projects.

(b) A person who dumps more than five pounds or 13 gallons of litter or other solid waste from a commercial vehicle in violation of this subchapter is presumed to be dumping the litter or other solid waste for a commercial purpose.

(c) It is an affirmative defense to prosecution under Section 365.012 that:

(1) the storage, processing, or disposal took place on land owned or leased by the defendant;

(2) the defendant received the litter or other solid waste from another person;

(3) the defendant, after exercising due diligence, did not know and reasonably could not have known that litter or other solid waste was involved; and

(4) the defendant did not receive, directly or indirectly, compensation for the receipt, storage, processing, or treatment.

*(Added by L.1989, chap. 678(1); repealed and added by L.1991, 1st C.S., chap. 3(8.161); chgd. by L.1993, chap. 740(3), eff. 9/1/93.)*

### §365.015. Injunction; venue; recovery of costs.

(a) A district attorney, a county attorney, or the attorney general may bring a civil suit for an injunction to prevent or restrain a violation of this subchapter. A person affected or to be affected by a violation is entitled to seek injunctive relief to enjoin the violation.

(b) Venue for prosecution of a criminal offense under this subchapter or for a civil suit for injunctive relief under this subchapter is in the county in which the defendant resides, the county in which the offense or violation occurred, or in Travis County.

(c) In a suit for relief under this section, the prevailing party may recover its reasonable attorney fees, court costs, and reasonable investigative costs incurred in relation to the proceeding.

*(Added by L.1989, chap. 678(1); repealed and added by L.1991, 1st C.S., chap. 3(8.161), eff. 9/1/91.)*



### §365.016. Disposal of litter in a cave; criminal penalty.

(a) A person commits an offense if the person disposes litter, a dead animal, sewage, or any chemical in a cave.

(b) An offense under this section is a Class C misdemeanor unless:

(1) it is shown on the trial of the defendant that the defendant previously has been convicted once of an offense under this section, in which event the offense is a Class A misdemeanor; or

(2) it is shown on the trial of the defendant that the defendant previously has been convicted two or more times of an offense under this section, in which event the offense is a felony of the third degree.

*(Added by L.1989, chap. 678(1); repealed and added by L.1991, 1st C.S., chap. 3(8.161), eff. 9/1/91.)*

### §365.017. Regulation of litter in certain counties.

(a) The commissioners court of a county may adopt regulations to control the disposal of litter and the removal of illegally dumped litter from private property in unincorporated areas of that county. The commissioners court may not adopt regulations under this section concerning the disposal of recyclable materials as defined in Chapter 361 of the Health and Safety Code.

(b) Prior to the adoption of regulations the commissioners court of a county must find that the proposed regulations are necessary to promote the public health, safety, and welfare of the residents of that county.

(c) The definitions of Section 365.011 apply in this Act. "Illegally dumped litter" means litter dumped anywhere other than in an approved solid waste site. "Litter" has the meaning assigned by Section 365.011, except that the term does not include equipment used for agricultural purposes.

(d) The regulations adopted by the commissioners court may require the record property owners to pay for the cost of removal after the commissioners court has given the record property owner 30 days written notice to remove the illegally dumped litter.

(e) Regulations adopted under this section are in addition to any other law regarding this issue and the stricter law shall apply.

(f) In addition to any other remedy provided by law, a district attorney, a county attorney, or the attorney general may bring a civil suit to enjoin violation of regulations adopted under this section and to recover the costs of removal of illegally dumped litter. In such a suit the prevailing party may recover its reasonable attorney fees, court fees, and reasonable investigative costs incurred in relation to that proceeding.

*(Added by L.1993, chap. 828(4); chgd. by L.1995, chap. 439(1), eff. 8/28/95.)*

### §§365.018 to 365.030. *(Reserved.)*

## SUBCHAPTER C. SPECIAL PROVISIONS

### §365.031. Litter, garbage, refuse, and rubbish in Lake Sabine.

The governing body of Port Arthur by ordinance may prohibit the depositing or placing of litter, garbage, refuse, or rubbish into or on the waters of Lake Sabine within the municipal limits. *(Added by L.1989, chap. 678(1), eff. 9/1/89.)*

### §365.032. Throwing certain substances in or near Lake Lavon; criminal penalty.

(a) The definitions provided by Section 365.011 apply to this section.

(b) A person commits an offense if the person throws, leaves, or causes to be thrown or left wastepaper, glass, metal, a tin can, refuse, garbage, waste, discarded or soiled personal property, or any other noxious or poisonous substance in the water of or near Lake Lavon in Collin County if the substance is detrimental to fish or to a person fishing in Lake Lavon.

(c) An offense under this section is a Class C misdemeanor unless it is shown on the trial of the defendant that the defendant has previously been convicted of an offense under this section, in which event the offense is a Class A misdemeanor.

*(Added by L.1989, chap. 678(1), eff. 9/1/89.)*

### §365.033. Discarding refuse in certain county parks; criminal penalty.

(a) The definitions provided by Section 365.011 apply to this section.

(b) In this section, "beach" means an area in which the public has acquired the right of use or an easement and that borders on the seaward shore of the Gulf of Mexico or extends from the line of mean low tide to the line of vegetation bordering on the Gulf of Mexico.

(c) This section applies only to a county park located in a county that has the Gulf of Mexico as one boundary, but does not apply to a beach located in that park.

(d) A person commits an offense if the person discards in a county park any junk, garbage, rubbish, or other refuse in a place that is not an officially designated refuse container or disposal unit.

(e) An offense under this section is a Class C misdemeanor unless it is shown on the trial of the defendant that the defendant has previously been convicted of an offense under this section, in which event the offense is a Class A misdemeanor.

*(Added by L.1989, chap. 678(1), eff. 9/1/89.)*

### §365.034. County regulation of litter near public highway; criminal penalty.

(a) The commissioners court of a county may:

(1) by order prohibit the accumulation of litter for more than 30 days on a person's property within 50 feet of a public highway in the county;

(2) provide for the removal and disposition of litter accumulated near a public highway in violation of an order adopted under this section; and

(3) provide for the assessment against a person who owns the property from which litter is removed under Subdivision (2) of the costs incurred by the county in removing and disposing of the litter.

(b) Before the commissioners court takes any action to remove or dispose of litter under this section, the court shall send a notice by certified mail to the record owners of the property on which the litter is accumulated in violation of an order adopted under this section. The court may not remove or dispose of the litter or assess the costs of the removal or disposition against a property owner before the 30th day after the date the notice is sent under this subsection.

(c) If a person assessed costs under this section does not pay the costs within 60 days after the date of assessment:

(1) a lien in favor of the county attaches to the property from which the litter was removed to secure the payment of the costs and interest accruing at an annual rate of 10 percent on any unpaid part of the costs; and

(2) the commissioners court shall file a record of the lien in the office of the county clerk.

(d) The violation of an order adopted under this section is a Class C misdemeanor.

(e) In this section:

(1) "Litter" has the meaning assigned by Section 365.011 except that the term does not include equipment used for agricultural purposes.

(2) "Public highway" has the meaning assigned by Section 365.011.

*(Added by L.1991, chap. 14(126); chgd. by L.1991, 1st C.S., chap. 3(8.162), eff. 9/1/91.)*

Printed in the U.S.A. Zt

# SUBTITLE C. AIR QUALITY

## CHAPTER 382. CLEAN AIR ACT

## SUBCHAPTER B. POWERS AND DUTIES OF COMMISSION
*(Selected Sections)*

Section




### §382.037. Vehicle emissions inspection and maintenance program.

(a) The commission by resolution may request the Public Safety Commission to establish a vehicle emissions inspection and maintenance program under Subchapter F, Chapter 548, Transportation Code, in accordance with this section and rules adopted under this section. The commission by rule may establish, implement, and administer a program requiring emissions-related inspections of motor vehicles to be performed at inspection facilities consistent with the requirements of the federal Clean Air Act (42 U.S.C. Section 7401 et seq.).

(a-1) *(Repealed by L.1997, chap. 1069(19)(1), eff. 6/1/97)*

(b) The commission by rule may require emissions-related inspection and maintenance of land vehicles, including testing exhaust emissions, examining emission control devices and systems, verifying compliance with applicable standards, and other requirements as provided by federal law or regulation.

(c) If the program is established under this section, the commission :

(1) shall adopt vehicle emissions inspection and maintenance requirements for certain areas as required by federal law or regulation; and

(2) may adopt vehicle emissions inspection and maintenance requirements for counties not subject to a specific federal requirement in response to a formal request by resolutions adopted by the county and the most populous municipality within the county according to the most recent federal decennial census.

(d) On adoption of a resolution by the commission and after proper notice, the Department of Public Safety of the State of Texas shall implement a system that requires, as a condition of obtaining a safety inspection certificate issued under Subchapter C, Chapter 548, Transportation Code , in a county that is included in a vehicle emissions inspection and maintenance program under Subchapter F of that chapter, that the vehicle, unless the vehicle is not covered by the system, be annually or biennially inspected under the vehicle emissions inspection and maintenance program as required by the state's air quality state implementation plan. The Department of Public Safety shall implement such a system when it is required by any provision of federal or state law, including any provision of the state's air quality state implementation plan.

(e) The commission may assess fees for vehicle emissions- related inspections performed at inspection or reinspection facilities authorized and licensed by the commission in amounts reasonably necessary to recover the costs of developing, administering, evaluating, and enforcing the vehicle emissions inspection and maintenance program. If the program relies on privately operated or contractor-operated inspection or reinspection stations, an appropriate portion of the fee as determined by commission rule may be retained by the station owner or operator to recover the cost of performing the inspections and provide a reasonable margin of profit. Any portion of the fee collected by the commission is a Clean Air Act fee under Section 382.0622.

(f) The commission shall examine the efficacy of annually inspecting diesel vehicles for compliance with applicable federal emission standards, compliance with an opacity or other emissions- related standard established by commission rule, or both and shall implement that inspection program if the commission determines the program would minimize emissions. For purposes of this subsection, a diesel engine not used in a vehicle registered for use on public highways is not a diesel vehicle.

(g) The commission may not establish vehicle fuel content standards to provide for vehicle fuel content for clean motor vehicle fuels other than those standards promulgated by the United States Environmental Protection Agency unless specifically authorized by the legislature or unless it is demonstrated to be necessary for the attainment of federal ozone ambient air quality standards or, following appropriate health studies and in consultation with the Texas Department of Health, it is determined to be necessary for the protection of public health.

(h) to (j) *(Repealed by L.1995, chap. 34(9)(3), eff. 5/2/97.)*

(k) The commission by rule may establish classes of vehicles that are exempt from vehicle emissions inspections and by rule may establish procedures to allow and review petitions for the exemption of individual vehicles, according to criteria established by commission rule. Rules adopted by the commission under this subsection must be consistent with federal law. The commission by rule may establish fees to recover the costs of administering this subsection. Fees collected under this subsection shall be deposited to the credit of the clean air account, an account in the general revenue fund, and may be used only for the purposes of this section.

(*l*) *(Repealed.)*

(m) Except as provided by this subsection, a person who sells or transfers ownership of a motor vehicle for which a vehicle emissions inspection certificate has been issued is not liable for the cost of emission control system repairs that are required for the vehicle subsequently to receive an emissions inspection certificate. This subsection does not apply to repairs that are required because emission control equipment or devices on the vehicle were removed or tampered with before the sale or transfer of the vehicle.

(n) The commission may conduct audits to determine compliance with this section.

(*o*), (p) *(Repealed.)*

*(Chgd. by L.1997, chaps. 165(30.207), 333(73), eff. 9/1/97; chap. 1069(1), eff. 6/19/97.)*



## §382.0372. Vehicles subject to program; exemptions.

(a) The inspection and maintenance program applies to any gasoline-powered vehicle that is:

(1) required to be registered in and is primarily operated in Dallas, Tarrant, El Paso, or Harris County; and

(2) at least two and less than 25 years old.

(b) In addition to a vehicle described by Subsection (a), the program applies to:

(1) a vehicle with United States governmental plates primarily operated in Dallas, Tarrant, El Paso, or Harris County;

(2) a vehicle operated on a federal facility in Dallas, Tarrant, El Paso, or Harris County; and

(3) a vehicle primarily operated in Dallas, Tarrant, El Paso, or Harris County that is exempt from motor vehicle registration requirements or eligible under Chapter 502, Transportation Code, to display an "exempt" license plate.

(c) The Department of Public Safety of the State of Texas may waive program requirements, in accordance with standards adopted by the commission, for certain vehicles and vehicle owners, including:

(1) the registered owner of a vehicle who:

(A) cannot afford to comply with the program, based on reasonable income standards; or

(B) has spent a reasonable amount of money, set by the commission, to repair the vehicle, without bringing the vehicle into compliance with emissions standards; and

(2) a vehicle that cannot be brought into compliance with emissions standards by performing repairs.

(d) The program does not apply to a:

(1) motorcycle;

(2) slow-moving vehicle as defined by Section 547.001, Transportation Code; or

(3) circus vehicle.

*(Added by L.1997, chap. 1069(2), eff. 6/19/97.)*

## §382.0373. Remote sensing program component.

(a) The commission and the Department of Public Safety of the State of Texas jointly shall develop a program component for enforcing emissions standards by use of remote or automatic emissions detection and analysis equipment.

(b) The program component may be employed in any county designated as a nonattainment area within the meaning of Section 107(d) of the Clean Air Act (42 U.S.C. Section 7407).

*(Added by L.1997, chap. 1069(2), eff. 6/19/97.)*

## §382.0374. Inspection equipment and procedures.

(a) The commission by rule may adopt:

(1) standards and specifications for motor vehicle emissions testing equipment;

(2) recordkeeping and reporting procedures; and

(3) measurable emissions standards a vehicle must meet to pass the inspection.

(b) The Department of Public Safety of the State of Texas by rule shall adopt:

(1) testing procedures in accordance with motor vehicle emissions testing equipment specifications; and

(2) procedures for issuing or denying an emissions inspection certificate.

(c) Subject to Subsection (d), the commission and the Department of Public Safety of the State of Texas by rule may allow alternative vehicle emissions testing, including onboard diagnostic testing, if:

(1) the technology provides accurate and reliable results;

(2) the technology is widely and readily available to persons interested in performing alternative vehicle emissions testing; and

(3) the use of alternative testing is not likely to substantially affect federal approval of the state's air quality state implementation plan.

(d) A rule adopted under Subsection (c) may not be more restrictive than federal regulations governing vehicle emissions testing.

*(Added by L.1997, chap. 1069(2); chgd. by L.1999, chap. 1189(42), eff. 9/1/99.)*

## §382.0375. Collection of data; report.

(a) The commission and the Department of Public Safety of the State of Texas may collect inspection and maintenance information derived from the emissions inspection and maintenance program, including:

(1) inspection results;

(2) inspection station information;

(3) information regarding vehicles operated on federal facilities;

(4) vehicle registration information; and

(5) other data the United States Environmental Protection Agency requires.

(b) The commission shall:

(1) report the information to the United States Environmental Protection Agency; and

(2) compare the information on inspection results with registration information for enforcement purposes.

*(Added by L.1997, chap. 1069(2), eff. 6/19/97.)*

## §382.038. Inspection stations; quality control audits.

(a) The Department of Public Safety of the State of Texas by rule shall adopt standards and procedures for establishing vehicle emissions inspection stations authorized and licensed by the state.

(b) A vehicle emissions inspection may be performed at a decentralized independent inspection station or at a centralized inspection facility operated or licensed by the state. In developing the program for vehicle emissions inspections, the Department of Public Safety shall make all reasonable efforts to preserve the present decentralized system.

(c) After consultation with the Texas Department of Transportation, the commission shall require state and local transportation planning entities designated by the commission to prepare long-term projections of the combined impact of significant planned transportation system changes on emissions and air quality. The projections shall be prepared using air pollution estimation methodologies established jointly by the commission and the Texas Department of Transportation. This subsection does not restrict the Texas Department of Transportation's function as the transportation planning body for the state or its role in identifying and initiating specific transportation-related projects in the state.

(d) The Department of Public Safety may authorize enforcement personnel or other individuals to remove, disconnect, adjust, or make inoperable vehicle emissions control equipment, devices, or systems and to operate a vehicle in the tampered condition in order to perform a quality control audit of an inspection station or other quality control activities as necessary to assess and ensure the effectiveness of the vehicle emissions inspection and maintenance program.

(e) The Department of Public Safety shall develop a challenge station program to provide for the reinspection of a motor vehicle at the option of the owner of the vehicle to ensure quality control of a vehicle emissions inspection and maintenance system.

(f) The commission may contract with one or more private entities to operate a program established under this section.

(g) In addition to other procedures established by the commission, the commission shall establish procedures by which a private entity with whom the commission has entered into a contract to operate a program established under this section may agree to perform:

(1) testing at a fleet facility or dealership using mobile test equipment;

(2) testing at a fleet facility or dealership using test equipment owned by the fleet or dealership but calibrated and operated by the private entity's personnel; or

(3) testing at a fleet facility or dealership using test equipment owned and operated by the private entity and installed at the fleet or dealership facility.

(h) The fee for a test conducted as provided by Subsection (g) shall be set by the commission in an amount not to exceed twice the fee otherwise provided by law or by rule of the commission. An appropriate portion of the fee, as determined by the commission, may be remitted by the private entity to the fleet facility or dealership.

**§382.039. Attainment program.**

(a) The commission shall coordinate with federal, state, and local transportation planning agencies to develop and implement transportation programs and other measures necessary to demonstrate and maintain attainment of national ambient air quality standards and to protect the public from exposure to hazardous air contaminants from motor vehicles.

(b) Participating agencies include the Texas Department of Transportation and metropolitan planning organizations designated by the governor.

# TITLE 6. FOOD, DRUGS, ALCOHOL, AND HAZARDOUS SUBSTANCES

## SUBTITLE A. FOOD AND DRUG HEALTH REGULATIONS

## CHAPTER 431 TEXAS FOOD, DRUG, AND COSMETIC ACT

*(Selected Subchapters)*

### SUBCHAPTER A. SHORT TITLE; DEFINITIONS

Section



### SUBCHAPTER B. PROHIBITED ACTS



### SUBCHAPTER C. ENFORCEMENT

## SUBCHAPTER E. DRUGS AND DEVICES



## SUBCHAPTER H. FAIR PACKAGING AND LABELING; FALSE ADVERTISING



## SUBCHAPTER I. WHOLESALE DRUG DISTRIBUTORS



## SUBCHAPTER K. GENERAL ADMINISTRATIVE PROVISIONS AND RULEMAKING AUTHORITY

## SUBCHAPTER A. SHORT TITLE; DEFINITIONS

### §431.001. Short title.

This chapter may be cited as the Texas Food, Drug, and Cosmetic Act. *(Added by L.1989, chap. 678(1), eff. 9/1/89.)*

### §431.002. Definitions.

In this chapter:

(1) "Advertising" means all representations disseminated in any manner or by any means, other than by labeling, for the purpose of inducing, or that are likely to induce, directly or indirectly, the purchase of food, drugs, devices, or cosmetics.

(2) "Animal feed," as used in Subdivision (23), in Section 512 of the federal Act, and in provisions of this chapter referring to those paragraphs or sections, means an article intended for use as food for animals other than man as a substantial source of nutrients in the diet of the animals. The term is not limited to a mixture intended to be the sole ration of the animals.

(3) "Authorized agent" means an employee of the department who is designated by the commissioner to enforce the provisions of this chapter.

(4) "Board" means the Texas Board of Health.

(5) "Butter" means the food product usually known as butter that is made exclusively from milk or cream, or both, with or without common salt or additional coloring matter, and containing not less than 80 percent by weight of milk fat, after allowing for all tolerances.

(6)(A) "Color additive" means a material that:

(i) is a dye, pigment, or other substance made by a process of synthesis or similar artifice, or extracted, isolated, or otherwise derived, with or without intermediate or final change of identity from a vegetable, animal, mineral, or other source; and

(ii) when added or applied to a food, drug, or cosmetic, or to the human body or any part of the human body, is capable, alone or through reaction with other substance, of imparting color. The term does not include any material exempted under the federal Act.

(B) "Color" includes black, white, and intermediate grays.

(C) Paragraph (A) does not apply to any pesticide chemical, soil or plant nutrient, or other agricultural chemical solely because of its effect in aiding, retarding, or otherwise affecting, directly or indirectly, the growth or other natural physiological processes of produce of the soil and thereby affecting its color, whether before or after harvest.

(7) "Commissioner" means the commissioner of health.

(8) "Consumer commodity," except as otherwise provided by this subdivision, means any food, drug, device, or cosmetic, as those terms are defined by this chapter or by the federal Act, and any other article, product, or commodity of any kind or class that is customarily produced or distributed for sale through retail sales agencies or instrumentalities for consumption by individuals, or for use by individuals for purposes of personal care or in the performance of services ordinarily rendered within the household, and that usually is consumed or expended in the course of the consumption or use. The term does not include:

(A) a meat or meat product, poultry or poultry product, or tobacco or tobacco product;

(B) a commodity subject to packaging or labeling requirements imposed under the Federal Insecticide, Fungicide, and Rodenticide Act (7 U.S.C. 136), or Section 8, Virus-Serum-Toxin Act (21 U.S.C. 158);

(C) a drug subject to the provisions of Section 431.113(c)(1) or 431.112(k), or Section 503(b)(1) or 506 of the federal Act;

(D) a beverage subject to or complying with packaging or labeling requirements imposed under the Federal Alcohol Administration Act (27 U.S.C. 205(e)); or

(E) a commodity subject to the provisions of Chapter 61, Agriculture Code, relating to the inspection, labeling, and sale of agricultural and vegetable seed.

(9) "Contaminated with filth" applies to any food, drug, device, or cosmetic not securely protected from dust, dirt, and as far as may be necessary by all reasonable means, from all foreign or injurious contaminations.

(10) "Cosmetic" means articles intended to be rubbed, poured, sprinkled, or sprayed on, introduced into, or otherwise applied to the human body or any part of the human body for cleaning, beautifying, promoting attractiveness, or altering the appearance, and articles intended for use as a component of those articles. The term does not include soap.

(11) "Counterfeit drug" means a drug, or the container or labeling of a drug, that, without authorization, bears the trademark, trade name, or other identifying mark, imprint, or device of a drug manufacturer, processor, packer, or distributor other than the person who in fact manufactured, processed, packed, or distributed the drug, and that falsely purports or is represented to be

the product of, or to have been packed or distributed by, the other drug manufacturer, processor, packer, or distributor.

(12) "Department" means the Texas Department of Health.

(13) "Device," except when used in Sections 431.003, 431.021(1), 432.082(g), 431.112(c) and 431.142(c), means an instrument, apparatus, implement, machine, contrivance, implant, in vitro reagent, or other similar or related article, including any component, part, or accessory, that is:

(A) recognized in the official United States Pharmacopoeia National Formulary or any supplement to it;

(B) intended for use in the diagnosis of disease or other conditions, or in the cure, mitigation, treatment, or prevention of disease in man or other animals; or

(C) intended to affect the structure or any function of the body of man or other animals and that does not achieve any of its principal intended purposes through chemical action within or on the body of man or other animals and is not dependent on metabolization for the achievement of any of its principal intended purposes.

(14) "Drug" means articles recognized in the official United States Pharmacopoeia National Formulary, or any supplement to it, articles designed or intended for use in the diagnosis, cure, mitigation, treatment, or prevention of disease in man or other animals, articles, other than food, intended to affect the structure or any function of the body of man or other animals, and articles intended for use as a component of any article specified in this subdivision. The term does not include devices or their components, parts, or accessories. A food for which a claim is made in accordance with Section 403(r) of the federal Act, and for which the claim is approved by the secretary, is not a drug solely because the label or labeling contains such a claim.

(15) "Federal Act" means the Federal Food, Drug and Cosmetic Act (21 U.S.C. 301 et seq.).

(16) "Food" means:

(A) articles used for food or drink for man;

(B) chewing gum; and

(C) articles used for components of any such article.

(17) "Food additive" means any substance the intended use of which results or may reasonably be expected to result, directly or indirectly, in its becoming a component or otherwise affecting the characteristics of any food (including any substance intended for use in producing, manufacturing, packing, processing, preparing, treating, packaging, transporting, or holding food; and including any source of radiation intended for any use), if such substance is not generally recognized, among experts qualified by scientific training and experience to evaluate its safety, as having been adequately shown through scientific procedures (or, in the case of a substance used in food prior to January 1, 1958, through either scientific procedures or experience based on common use in food) to be safe under the conditions of its intended use; except that such term does not include:

(A) a pesticide chemical in or on a raw agricultural commodity;

(B) a pesticide chemical to the extent that it is intended for use or is used in the production, storage, or transportation of any raw agricultural commodity;

(C) a color additive;

(D) any substance used in accordance with a sanction or approval granted prior to the enactment of the Food Additives Amendment of 1958, Pub. L. No. 85-929, 52 Stat. 1041 (codified as amended in various sections of 21 U.S.C.), pursuant to the federal Act, the Poultry Products Inspection Act (21 U.S.C. 451 et seq.) or the Meat Inspection Act of 1907 (21 U.S.C. 603); or

(E) a new animal drug.

(18) "Health authority" means a physician designated to administer state and local laws relating to public health.

(19) "Immediate container" does not include package liners.

(20) "Infant formula" means a food that is represented for special dietary use solely as a food for infants by reason of its simulation of human milk or is suitability as a complete or partial substitute for human milk.

(21) "Label" means a display of written, printed, or graphic matter upon the immediate container of any article; and a requirement made by or under authority of this chapter that any word, statement, or other information that appears on the label shall not be considered to be complied with unless the word, statement, or other information also appears on the outside container or wrapper, if any, of the retail package of the article, or is easily legible through the outside container or wrapper.

(22) "Labeling" means all labels and other written, printed, or graphic matter (1) upon any article or any of its containers or wrappers, or (2) accompanying such article.

(23) "Manufacture" means:

(A) the process of combining or purifying food or packaging food for sale to a person at wholesale or retail, and includes repackaging or labeling of any food;

(B) the process of preparing, propagating, compounding, processing, packaging, repackaging, labeling, testing, or quality control of a drug or drug product, but does not include compounding that is done within the practice of pharmacy and pursuant to a prescription from a practitioner for a patient;

(C) the process of preparing, fabricating, assembling, processing, packing, repacking, labeling, or relabeling a device; or

(D) the making of any cosmetic product by chemical, physical, biological, or other procedures, including manipulation, sampling, testing, or control procedures applied to the product.

(24) "New animal drug" means any drug intended for use for animals other than man, including any drug intended for use in animal feed:

(A) the composition of which is such that the drug is not generally recognized among experts qualified by scientific training and experience to evaluate the safety and effectiveness of animal drugs as safe and effective for use under the conditions prescribed, recommended, or suggested in the labeling of the drug (except that such an unrecognized drug is not deemed to be a "new animal drug" if at any time before June 25, 1938, it was subject to the Food and Drug Act of June 30, 1906, and if at that time its labeling contained the same representations concerning the conditions of its use);

(B) the composition of which is such that the drug, as a result of investigations to determine its safety and effectiveness for use under those conditions, has become recognized but that has not, otherwise than in the investigation, been used to a material extent or for a material time under those conditions; or

(C) is composed wholly or partly of penicillin, streptomycin, chlortetracycline, chloramphenicol, or bacitracin, or any derivative of those substances, unless:

(i) a published order of the secretary is in effect that declares the drug not to be a new animal drug on the grounds that the requirement of certification of batches of the drug, as provided by Section 512(n) of the federal Act, is not necessary to ensure that the objectives specified in Section 512(n)(3) of that Act are achieved; and

(ii) Paragraph (A) or (B) of this subdivision does not apply to the drug.

(25) "New drug" means:

(A) any drug, except a new animal drug, the composition of which is such that such drug is not generally recognized among experts qualified by scientific training and experience to evaluate the safety and effectiveness of drugs, as safe and effective for use under the conditions prescribed, recommended, or suggested in the labeling thereof (except that such an unrecognized drug is not a "new drug" if at any time before May 26, 1985, it was subject to the Food and Drug Act of June 30, 1906, and if at that time its labeling contained the same representations concerning the conditions of its use); or

(B) any drug, except a new animal drug, the composition of which is such that such drug, as a result of investigations to determine its safety and effectiveness for use under such conditions, has become so recognized, but which has not, otherwise than in such investigations, been used to a material extent or for a material time under such conditions.

(26) "Official compendium" means the official United States Pharmacopoeia National Formulary, or any supplement to it.

(27) "Package" means any container or wrapping in which a consumer commodity is enclosed for use in the delivery or display of that consumer commodity to retail purchasers. The term includes wrapped meats enclosed in papers or other materials as prepared by the manufacturers thereof for sale. The term does not include:

(A) shipping containers or wrappings used solely for the transportation of a consumer commodity in bulk or in quantity to manufacturers, packers, or processors, or to wholesale or retail distributors;

(B) shipping containers or outer wrappings used by retailers to ship or deliver a commodity to retail customers if the containers and wrappings do not bear printed matter relating to any particular commodity; or

(C) containers subject to the provisions of the Standard Barrel Act (Apple Barrels) (15 U.S.C. 231, 21 U.S.C. 20) or the Standard Barrel Act (Fruits and Vegetables) (15 U.S.C. 234-236).

(28) "Person" includes individual, partnership, corporation, and association.

(29) "Pesticide chemical" means any substance which, alone, in chemical combination or in formulation with one or more other substances, is a "pesticide" within the meaning of the Federal Insecticide, Fungicide, and Rodenticide Act (7 U.S.C. 136(u)), as now in force or as amended, and that is used in the production, storage, or transportation of raw agricultural commodities.

(30) "Principal display panel" means the part of a label that is most likely to be displayed, presented, shown, or examined under normal and customary conditions of display for retail sale.

(31) "Raw agricultural commodity" means any food in its raw or natural state, including all fruits that are washed, colored, or otherwise treated in their unpeeled natural form prior to marketing.

(32) "Saccharin" includes calcium saccharin, sodium saccharin, and ammonium saccharin.

(33) "Safe" refers to the health of humans or animals.

(34) "Secretary" means the secretary of the United States Department of Health and Human Services.

*(Added by L.1989, chap. 678(1); chgd. by L.1991, chaps. 14(149), 539(1); L.1993, chap. 459(1); L.1997, chap. 629(1), eff. 9/1/97.)*

## §431.003. Article misbranded because of misleading labeling or advertising.

If an article is alleged to be misbranded because the labeling or advertising is misleading, then in determining whether the labeling or advertising is misleading, there shall be taken into account, among other things, not only representations made or suggested by statement, word, design, device, sound, or any combination of these, but also the extent to which the labeling or advertising fails to reveal facts material in the light of such representations or material with respect to consequences which may result from the use of the article to which the labeling or advertising relates under the conditions of use prescribed in the labeling or advertising thereof, or under such conditions of use as are customary or usual. *(Added by L.1989, chap. 678(1); chgd. by L.1991, chap. 14(150), eff. 9/1/91.)*

## §431.004. Representation of drug as antiseptic.

The representation of a drug, in its labeling, as an antiseptic shall be considered to be a representation that the drug is a germicide, except in the case of a drug purporting to be, or represented as, an antiseptic for inhibitory use as a wet dressing, ointment, dusting powder, or such other use as involves prolonged contact with the body. *(Added by L.1989, chap. 678(1), eff. 9/1/89.)*

## §431.005. Provisions regarding sale of food, drugs, devices, or cosmetics.

The provisions of this chapter regarding the selling of food, drugs, devices, or cosmetics, shall be considered to include the manufacture, production, processing, packaging, exposure, offer, possession, and holding of any such article for sale; and the sale, dispensing, and giving of any such articles in the conduct of any food, drug, or cosmetic establishment. *(Added by L.1989, chap. 678(1), eff. 9/1/89.)*

## §431.006. Certain combination products.

*(As added by L.1999, chap. 132(1). See other Section 431.006 below.)*

If the United States Food and Drug Administration determines, with respect to a product that is a combination of a drug and a device, that:

(1) the primary mode of action of the product is as a drug, a person who engages in wholesale distribution of the product is subject to licensure under Subchapter I; and

(2) the primary mode of action of the product is as a device, a distributor or manufacturer of the product is subject to licensure under Subchapter L.

*(Added by L.1999, chap. 132(1), eff. 5/20/99.)*

## §431.006. Compliance with other law; molluscan shellfish.

*(As added by L.1999, chap. 1298(1). See other Section 431.006 above.)*

A person who is subject to this chapter and who handles molluscan shellfish, as that term is defined by Section 436.002, shall comply with Section 436.105.

*(Added by L.1999, chap. 1298(1), eff. 6/18/99.)*

## §§431.007 to 431.020. *(Reserved.)*

# SUBCHAPTER B. PROHIBITED ACTS

## §431.021. Prohibited acts.

The following acts and the causing of the following acts within this state are unlawful and prohibited:

(a) the introduction or delivery for introduction into commerce of any food, drug, device, or cosmetic that is adulterated or misbranded;

(b) the adulteration or misbranding of any food, drug, device, or cosmetic in commerce;

(c) the receipt in commerce of any food, drug, device, or cosmetic that is adulterated or misbranded, and the delivery or proffered delivery thereof for pay or otherwise;

(d) the distribution in commerce of a consumer commodity, if such commodity is contained in a package, or if there is affixed to that commodity a label that does not conform to the provisions of this chapter and of rules adopted under the authority of this chapter; provided, however, that this prohibition shall not apply to persons engaged in business as wholesale or retail distributors of consumer commodities except to the extent that such persons:

(1) are engaged in the packaging or labeling of such commodities; or

(2) prescribe or specify by any means the manner in which such commodities are packaged or labeled;

(e) the introduction or delivery for introduction into commerce of any article in violation of Section 431.084, 431.114, or 431.115;

(f) the dissemination of any false advertisement;

(g) the refusal to permit entry or inspection, or to permit the taking of a sample or to permit access to or copying of any record as authorized by Sections 431.042-431.044; or the failure to establish or maintain any record or make any report required under Section 512(j), (*l*), or (m) of the federal Act, or the refusal to permit access to or verification or copying of any such required record;

(h) the manufacture within this state of any food, drug, device, or cosmetic that is adulterated or misbranded;

(i) the giving of a guaranty or undertaking referred to in Section 431.059, which guaranty or undertaking is false, except by a person who relied on a guaranty or undertaking to the same effect signed by, and containing the name and address of the person residing in this state from whom the person received in good faith the food, drug, device, or cosmetic; or the giving of a guaranty or undertaking referred to in Section 431.059, which guaranty or undertaking is false;

(j) the use, removal, or disposal of a detained or embargoed article in violation of Section 431.048;

(k) the alteration, mutilation, destruction, obliteration, or removal of the whole or any part of the labeling of, or the doing of any other act with respect to a food, drug, device, or cosmetic, if such act is done while such article is held for sale after shipment in commerce and results in such article being adulterated or misbranded;

(*l*)(1) forging, counterfeiting, simulating, or falsely representing, or without proper authority using any mark, stamp, tag, label, or other identification device authorized or required by rules adopted under this chapter or the regulations promulgated under the provisions of the federal Act;

(2) making, selling, disposing of, or keeping in possession, control, or custody, or concealing any punch, die, plate, stone, or other thing designed to print, imprint, or reproduce the trademark, trade name, or other identifying mark, imprint, or device of another or any likeness of any of the foregoing on any drug or container or labeling thereof so as to render such drug a counterfeit drug;

(3) the doing of any act that causes a drug to be a counterfeit drug, or the sale or dispensing, or the holding for sale or dispensing, of a counterfeit drug;

(m) the using by any person to the person's own advantage, or revealing, other than to the commissioner, an authorized agent, a health authority or to the courts when relevant in any judicial proceeding under this chapter, of any information acquired under the authority of this chapter concerning any method or process that as a trade secret is entitled to protection;

(n) the using, on the labeling of any drug or device or in any advertising relating to such drug or device, of any representation or suggestion that approval of an application with respect to such drug or device is in effect under Section 431.114 or Section 505, 515, or 520(g) of the federal Act, as the case may be, or that such drug or device complies with the provisions of such sections;

(*o*) the using, in labeling, advertising or other sales promotion of any reference to any report or analysis furnished in compliance with Sections 431.042-431.044 or Section 704 of the federal Act;

(p) in the case of a prescription drug distributed or offered for sale in this state, the failure of the manufacturer, packer, or distributor of the drug to maintain for transmittal, or to transmit, to any practitioner licensed by applicable law to administer such drug who makes written request for information as to such drug, true and correct copies of all printed matter that is required to be included in any package in which that drug is distributed or sold, or such other printed matter as is approved under the federal Act. Nothing in this subsection shall be construed to exempt any person from any labeling requirement imposed by or under other provisions of this chapter;

(q)(1) placing or causing to be placed on any drug or device or container of any drug or device, with intent to defraud, the trade name or other identifying mark, or imprint of another or any likeness of any of the foregoing;

(2) selling, dispensing, disposing of or causing to be sold, dispensed, or disposed of, or concealing or keeping in possession, control, or custody, with intent to sell, dispense, or dispose of, any drug, device, or any container of any drug or device, with knowledge that the trade name or other identifying mark or imprint of another or any likeness of any of the foregoing has been placed thereon in a manner prohibited by Subdivision (1) of this subsection; or

(3) making, selling, disposing of, causing to be made, sold, or disposed of, keeping in possession, control, or custody, or concealing with intent to defraud any punch, die, plate, stone, or other thing designed to print, imprint, or reproduce the trademark, trade name, or other identifying mark, imprint, or device of another or any likeness of any of the foregoing on any drug or container or labeling of any drug or container so as to render such drug a counterfeit drug;

(r) dispensing or causing to be dispensed a different drug in place of the drug ordered or prescribed without the express permission in each case of the person ordering or prescribing;

(s) the failure to register in accordance with Section 510 of the federal Act, the failure to provide any information required by Section 510(j) or (k) of the federal Act, or the failure to provide a notice required by Section 510(j)(2) of the federal Act;

(t)(1) the failure or refusal to:

(A) comply with any requirement prescribed under Section 518 or 520(g) of the federal Act; or

(B) furnish any notification or other material or information required by or under Section 519 or 520(g) of the federal Act;

(2) with respect to any device, the submission of any report that is required by or under this chapter that is false or misleading in any material respect;

(u) the movement of a device in violation of an order under Section 304(g) of the federal Act or the removal or alteration of any mark or label required by the order to identify the device as detained;

(v) the failure to provide the notice required by Section 412(b) or 412(c), the failure to make the reports required by Section 412(d)(1)(B), or the failure to meet the requirements prescribed under Section 412(d)(2) of the federal Act;

(w) the acceptance by a person of an unused prescription or drug, in whole or in part, for the purpose of resale, after the prescription or drug has been originally dispensed, or sold;

(x) engaging in the wholesale distribution of drugs or operating as a distributor or manufacturer of devices in this state without filing a licensing statement with the commissioner as required by Section 431.202 or having a license as required by Section 431.272, as applicable;

(y) engaging in the manufacture of food in this state without first registering with the department as required by Section 431.222; or

(z) unless approved by the United States Food and Drug Administration pursuant to the federal Act, the sale, delivery, holding, or offering for sale of a self-testing kit designed to indicate whether a person has a human immunodeficiency virus infection, acquired immune deficiency syndrome, or a related disorder or condition.

*(Added by L.1989, chap. 678(1); chgd. by L.1991, chaps. 14(151), 539(2); L.1993, chap. 440(1); L.1995, chap. 1047(6); L.1997, chap. 282(1), eff. 5/26/97.)*

### § 431.022. Offense: transfer of product containing ephedrine.

(a) A person commits an offense if the person knowingly sells, transfers, or otherwise furnishes a product containing ephedrine to a person 17 years of age or younger, unless:

(1) the actor is:

(A) a practitioner or other health care provider licensed by this state who has obtained, as required by law, consent to the treatment of the person to whom the product is furnished; or

(B) the parent, guardian, or managing conservator of the person to whom the product is furnished;

(2) the person to whom the product is furnished has had the disabilities of minority removed for general purposes under Chapter 31, Family Code; or

(3) the product is a drug.

(b) An offense under this section is a Class C misdemeanor unless it is shown on the trial of the offense that the defendant has been previously convicted of an offense under this section, in which event the offense is a Class B misdemeanor.

(c) A product containing ephedrine that is not described in Subsection (a)(3) must be labeled in accordance with rules adopted by the Texas Department of Health to indicate that sale to persons 17 years of age or younger is prohibited.

*(Added by L.1999, chap. 151(1), eff. 9/1/99.)*

## SUBCHAPTER C. ENFORCEMENT

### §431.041. Definition.

In this subchapter,"detained or embargoed article" means a food, drug, device, cosmetic, or consumer commodity that has been detained or embargoed under Section 431.048. *(Added by L.1989, chap. 678(1), eff. 9/1/89.)*

### §431.042. Inspection.

(a) To enforce this chapter, the commissioner, an authorized agent, or a health authority may, on presenting appropriate credentials to the owner, operator, or agent in charge:

(1) enter at reasonable times an establishment, including a factory or warehouse, in which a food, drug, device, or cosmetic is manufactured, processed, packed, or held for introduction into commerce or held after the introduction;

(2) enter a vehicle being used to transport or hold the food, drug device, or cosmetic in commerce; or

(3) inspect at reasonable times, within reasonable limits, and in a reasonable manner, the establishment or vehicle and all equipment, finished and unfinished materials, containers, and labeling of any item and obtain samples necessary for the enforcement of this chapter.

(b) The inspection of an establishment, including a factory, warehouse, or consulting laboratory, in which a prescription drug or restricted device is manufactured, processed, packed, or held for introduction into commerce extends to any place or thing, including a record, file, paper, process, control, or facility, in order to determine whether the drug or device:

(1) is adulterated or misbranded;

(2) may not be manufactured, introduced into commerce, sold, or offered for sale under this chapter; or

(3) is otherwise in violation of this chapter.

(c) An inspection under Subsection (b) may not extend to:

(1) financial data;

(2) sales data other than shipment data;

(3) pricing data;

(4) personnel data other than data relating to the qualifications of technical and professional personnel performing functions under this chapter;

(5) research data other than data:

(A) relating to new drugs, antibiotic drugs, and devices; and

(B) subject to reporting and inspection under regulations issued under Section 505(i) or (j), 507(d) or (g), 519, or 520(g) of the federal Act; or

(6) data relating to other drugs or devices that, in the case of a new drug, would be subject to reporting or inspection under regulations issued under Section 505(j) of the federal Act.

(d) An inspection under Subsection (b) shall be started and completed with reasonable promptness.

(e) This section does not apply to:

(1) a pharmacy that:

(A) complies with the Texas Pharmacy Act (Article 4542a-1, Texas Civil Statutes);

(B) regularly engages in dispensing prescription drugs or devices on prescriptions of practitioners licensed to administer the drugs or devices to their patients in the course of their professional practice; and

(C) does not, through a subsidiary or otherwise, manufacture, prepare, propagate, compound, or process a drug or device for sale other than in the regular course of its business of dispensing or selling drugs or devices at retail;

(2) a practitioner licensed to prescribe or administer a drug who manufactures, prepares, propagates, compounds, or processes the drug solely for use in the course of the practitioner's professional practice;

(3) a practitioner licensed to prescribe or use a device who manufactures or processes the device solely for use in the course of the practitioner's professional practice; or

(4) a person who manufactures, prepares, propagates, compounds, or processes a drug or manufactures or processes a device solely for use in research, teaching, or chemical analysis and not for sale.

(f) The board may exempt a class of persons from inspection under this section if the board finds that inspection as applied to the class is not necessary for the protection of the public health.

(g) An authorized agent or health authority who makes an inspection under this section to enforce the provisions of this chapter applicable to infant formula shall be permitted, at all reasonable times, to have access to and to copy and verify records:

(1) in order to determine whether the infant formula manufactured or held in the inspected facility meets the requirements of this chapter; or

(2) that are required by this chapter.

(h) An authorized agent or health authority who makes an inspection of an establishment, including a factory or warehouse, and obtains a sample during or on completion of the inspection and before leaving the establishment, shall give to the owner, operator, or the owner's or operator's agent a receipt describing the sample.
*(Added by L.1989, chap. 678(1), eff. 9/1/89.)*

### §431.043. Access to records.

A person who is required to maintain records under this chapter or Section 519 or 520(g) of the federal Act or a person who is in charge or custody of those records shall, at the request of an authorized agent or health authority, permit the authorized agent or health authority at all reasonable times access to and to copy and verify the records. *(Added by L.1989, chap. 678(1), eff. 9/1/89.)*

### §431.044. Access to records showing movement in commerce.

(a) To enforce this chapter, a carrier engaged in commerce or other person receiving a food, drug, device, or cosmetic in commerce or holding a food, drug, device, or cosmetic received in commerce shall, at the request of an authorized agent or health authority, permit the authorized agent or health authority at all reasonable times to have access to and to copy all records showing:

(1) the movement in commerce of the food, drug, device, or cosmetic;

(2) the holding of the food, drug, device, or cosmetic after movement in commerce; and

(3) the quantity, shipper, and consignee of the food, drug, device, or cosmetic.

(b) The carrier or other person may not refuse access to and copying of the requested record if the request is accompanied by a written statement that specifies the nature or kind of food, drug, device, or cosmetic to which the request relates.

(c) Evidence obtained under this section or evidence that is directly or indirectly derived from the evidence obtained under this section may not be used in a criminal prosecution of the person from whom the evidence is obtained.

(d) A carrier is not subject to other provisions of this chapter because of the carrier's receipt, carriage, holding, or delivery of a food, drug, device, or cosmetic in the usual course of business as a carrier.
*(Added by L.1989, chap. 678(1), eff. 9/1/89.)*

### §431.045. Emergency order.

(a) The commissioner or a person designated by the commissioner may issue an emergency order, either mandatory or prohibitory in nature, in relation to the manufacture of a food, drug, device, or cosmetic in the department's jurisdiction if the commissioner or the person designated by the commissioner determines that:

(1) the manufacture of the food, drug, device, or cosmetic creates or poses an immediate and serious threat to human life or health; and

(2) other procedures available to the department to remedy or prevent the occurrence of the situation will result in unreasonable delay.

(b) The commission or a person designated by the commissioner may issue the emergency order without notice and hearing if the commissioner or a person designated by the commissioner determines this is practicable under the circumstances.

(c) If an emergency order is issued without a hearing, the department shall determine a time and place for a hearing at which the emergency order is affirmed, modified, or set aside. The hearing shall be held under the contested case provisions of Chapter 2001, Government Code, and the board's formal hearing rules.

(d) This section prevails over Sections 11.013 and 12.001.
*(Added by L.1989, chap. 678(1); chgd. by L.1997, chap. 629(4), eff. 9/1/97.)*

### §431.046. Violation of rules.

A violation of a rule adopted under this chapter is a violation of this chapter. *(Added by L.1989, chap. 678(1), eff. 9/1/89.)*

### §431.047. Violation; injunction.

(a) The commissioner, an authorized agent, or a health authority may petition the district court for a temporary restraining order to restrain a continuing violation of Subchapter B or a threat of a continuing violation of Subchapter B if the commissioner, authorized agent, or health authority finds that:

Printed in the U.S.A. 47

(1) a person has violated, is violating, or is threatening to violate Subchapter B; and

(2) the violation or threatened violation creates an immediate threat to the health and safety of the public.

(b) A district court, on petition of the commissioner, an authorized agent, or a health authority, and on a finding by the court that a person is violating or threatening to violate Subchapter B shall grant any injunctive relief warranted by the facts.

(c) Venue for a suit brought under this section is in the county in which the violation or threat of violation is alleged to have occurred or in Travis County.

(d) The commissioner and the attorney general may each recover reasonable expenses incurred in obtaining injunctive relief under this section, including investigative cost, court costs, reasonable attorney fees, witness fees, and deposition expenses. The expenses recovered by the commissioner are hereby appropriated to the department for the administration and enforcement of this chapter. The expenses recovered by the attorney general are hereby appropriated to the attorney general.

*(Added by L.1989, chap. 678(1); chgd. by L.1991, chap. 539(3), eff. 9/1/91.)*

## §431.048. Detained or embargoed article.

(a) The commissioner or an authorized agent shall affix to an article that is a food, drug, device, cosmetic, or consumer commodity a tag or other appropriate marking that gives notice that the article is, or is suspected of being, adulterated or misbranded and that the article has been detained or embargoed if the commissioner or the authorized agent finds or has probable cause to believe that the article:

(1) is adulterated;

(2) is misbranded so that the article is dangerous or fraudulent under this chapter; or

(3) violates Section 431.084, 431.114, or 431.115.

(b) The tag or marking on a detained or embargoed article must warn all persons not to use the article, remove the article from the premises, or dispose of the article by sale or otherwise until permission for use, removal, or disposal is given by the commissioner, the authorized agent, or a court.

(c) A person may not use a detained or embargoed article, remove a detained or embargoed article from the premises, or dispose of a detained or embargoed article by sale or otherwise without permission of the commissioner, the authorized agent, or a court. The commissioner or the authorized agent may permit perishable goods to be moved to a place suitable for proper storage.

(d) The commissioner or an authorized agent shall remove the tag or other marking from an embargoed or detained article if the commissioner or an authorized agent finds that the article is not adulterated or misbranded.

*(Added by L.1989, chap. 678(1); chgd. by L.1997, chap. 282(2), eff. 5/26/97.)*

## §431.049. Removal order for detained or embargoed article.

(a) If the claimant of the detained or embargoed articles or the claimant's agent fails or refuses to transfer the articles to a secure place after the tag or other appropriate marking has been affixed as provided by Section 431.048, the commissioner or an authorized agent may order the transfer of the articles to one or more secure storage areas to prevent their unauthorized use, removal, or disposal.

(b) The commissioner or an authorized agent may provide for the transfer of the article if the claimant of the article or the claimant's agent does not carry out the transfer order in a timely manner. The costs of the transfer shall be assessed against the claimant of the article or the claimant's agent.

(c) The claimant of the article or the claimant's agent shall pay the costs of the transfer.

(d) The commissioner may request the attorney general to bring an action in the district court in Travis County to recover the costs of the transfer. In a judgment in favor of the state, the court may award costs, attorney fees, court costs, and interest from the time the expense was incurred through the date the department is reimbursed.

*(Added by L.1989, chap. 678(1); chgd. by L.1991, chap. 14(152); L.1997, chap. 282(3), eff. 5/26/97.)*

## §431.0495. Recall orders.

(a) In conjunction with the issuance of an emergency order under Section 431.045 or the detention or embargo of an article under Section 431.048, the commissioner may order a food, drug, device, cosmetic, or consumer commodity to be recalled from commerce.

(b) The commissioner's recall order may require the articles to be removed to one or more secure areas approved by the commissioner or an authorized agent.

(c) The recall order must be in writing and signed by the commissioner.

(d) The recall order may be issued before or in conjunction with the affixing of the tag or other appropriate marking as provided by Section 431.048(a) or in conjunction with the commissioner's issuance of an emergency order under Section 431.045.

(e) The recall order is effective until the order:

(1) expires on its own terms;

(2) is withdrawn by the commissioner;

(3) is reversed by a court in an order denying condemnation under Section 431.050; or

(4) is set aside at the hearing provided to affirm, modify, or set aside an emergency order under Section 431.045.

(f) The claimant of the articles or the claimant's agent shall pay the costs of the removal and storage of the articles removed.

(g) If the claimant or the claimant's agent fails or refuses to carry out the recall order in a timely manner, the commissioner may provide for the recall of the articles. The cost of the recall shall be assessed against the claimant of the articles or the claimant's agent.

(h) The commissioner may request the attorney general to bring an action in the district court of Travis County to recover the costs of the recall. In a judgment in favor of the state, the court may award costs, attorney fees, court costs, and interest from the time the expense was incurred through the date the department is reimbursed.

*(Added by L.1991, chap. 14(153), eff. 9/1/91.)*

### §431.050. Condemnation.

An action for the condemnation of an article may be brought before a court in whose jurisdiction the article is located, detained, or embargoed if the article is adulterated, misbranded, or in violation of Section 431.084, 431.114, or 431.115. *(Added by L.1989, chap. 678(1), eff. 9/1/89.)*

### §431.051. Destruction of article.

(a) A court shall order the destruction of a sampled article or a detained or embargoed article if the court finds that the article is adulterated or misbranded.

(b) After entry of the court's order, an authorized agent shall supervise the destruction of the article.

(c) The claimant of the article shall pay the cost of the destruction of the article.

(d) The court shall tax against the claimant of the article or the claimant's agent all court costs and fees, and storage and other proper expenses.

*(Added by L.1989, chap. 678(1), eff. 9/1/89.)*

### §431.052. Correction by proper labeling or processing.

(a) A court may order the delivery of a sampled article or a detained or embargoed article that is adulterated or misbranded to the claimant of the article for labeling or processing under the supervision of an agent of the commissioner or an authorized agent if:

(1) the decree has been entered in the suit;

(2) the costs, fees, and expenses of the suit have been paid;

(3) the adulteration or misbranding can be corrected by proper labeling or processing; and

(4) a good and sufficient bond, conditioned on the correction of the adulteration or misbranding by proper labeling or processing, has been executed.

(b) The claimant shall pay the costs of the supervision.

(c) The court shall order that the article be returned to the claimant and the bond discharged on the representation to the court by the commissioner or an authorized agent that the article no longer violates this chapter and that the expenses of the supervision are paid.

*(Added by L.1989, chap. 678(1), eff. 9/1/89.)*

### §431.053. Condemnation of perishable articles.

(a) The commissioner or an authorized agent shall immediately condemn or render by any means unsalable as human food an article that is a nuisance under Subsection (b) and that the commissioner or authorized agent finds in any room, building, or other structure or in a vehicle.

(b) Any meat, seafood, poultry, vegetable, fruit, or other perishable article is a nuisance if it:

(1) is unsound;

(2) contains a filthy, decomposed, or putrid substance; or

(3) may be poisonous or deleterious to health or otherwise unsafe.

*(Added by L.1989, chap. 678(1), eff. 9/1/89.)*

## §431.054. Administrative penalty.

(a) The commissioner may assess an administrative penalty against a person who violates Subchapter B or an order adopted or registration issued under this chapter.

(b) In determining the amount of the penalty, the commissioner shall consider:

(1) the person's previous violations;

(2) the seriousness of the violation;

(3) any hazard to the health and safety of the public;

(4) the person's demonstrated good faith; and

(5) Such other matters as justice may require.

(c) The penalty may not exceed $25,000 a day for each violation.

(d) Each day a violation continues may be considered a separate violation.

*(Added by L.1989, chap. 678(1); chgd. by L.1991, chap. 539(4), eff. 9/1/91.)*

## §431.055. Administrative penalty assessment procedure.

(a) An administrative penalty may be assessed only after a person charged with a violation is given an opportunity for a hearing.

(b) If a hearing is held, the commissioner shall make findings of fact and shall issue a written decision regarding the occurrence of the violation and the amount of the penalty that may be warranted.

(c) If the person charged with the violation does not request a hearing, the commissioner may assess a penalty after determining that a violation has occurred and the amount of the penalty that may be warranted.

(d) After making a determination under this section that a penalty is to be assessed against a person, the commissioner shall issue an order requiring that the person pay the penalty.

(e) The commissioner may consolidate a hearing held under this section with another proceeding.

*(Added by L.1989, chap. 678(1), eff. 9/1/89.)*

## §431.056. Payment of administrative penalty.

(a) Not later than the 30th day after the date an order finding that a violation has occurred is issued, the commissioner shall inform the person against whom the order is issued of the amount of the penalty for the violation.

(b) Not later than the 30th day after the date on which a decision or order charging a person with a penalty is final, the person shall:

(1) pay the penalty in full; or

(2) if the person seeks judicial review of the amount of the penalty, the fact of the violation, or both:

(A) send the amount of the penalty to the commissioner for placement in an escrow account; or

(B) post with the commissioner a bond for the amount of the penalty.

(c) A bond posted under this section must be in a form approved by the commissioner and be effective until all judicial review of the order or decision is final.

(d) A person who does not send money to the commissioner or post the bond within the period prescribed by Subsection (b) waives all rights to contest the violation or the amount of the penalty.

*(Added by L.1989, chap. 678(1), eff. 9/1/89.)*

## §431.057. Refund of administrative penalty.

Not later than the 30th day after the date of a judicial determination that an administrative penalty against a person should be reduced or not assessed, the commissioner shall:

(1) remit to the person the appropriate amount of any penalty payment plus accrued interest; or

(2) execute a release of the bond if the person has posted a bond.

*(Added by L.1989, chap. 678(1), eff. 9/1/89.)*

## §431.058. Recovery of administrative penalty by attorney general.

The attorney general at the request of the commissioner may bring a civil action to recover an administrative penalty under this subchapter. *(Added by L.1989, chap. 678(1), eff. 9/1/89.)*

## §431.0585. Civil penalty.

(a) At the request of the commissioner, the attorney general or a district, county, or city attorney shall institute an action in district court to collect a civil penalty from a person who has violated Section 431.021.

(b) The civil penalty may not exceed $25,000 a day for each violation. Each day of violation constitutes a separate violation for purposes of the penalty assessment.

(c) The court shall consider the following in determining the amount of the penalty:

(1) the person's history of any previous violations of Section 431.021;

(2) the seriousness of the violation;

(3) any hazard posed to the public health and safety by the violation; and

(4) demonstrations of good faith by the person charged.

(d) Venue for a suit brought under this section is in the city or county in which the violation occurred or in Travis County.

(e) A civil penalty recovered in a suit instituted by a local government under this section shall be paid to that local government.

*(Added by L.1991, chap. 14(154), eff. 9/1/91.)*

## §431.059. Criminal penalty; defenses.

(a) A person commits an offense if the person violates any of the provisions of Section 431.021 relating to unlawful or prohibited acts. An offense under this subsection is a Class A misdemeanor. In a criminal proceeding under this section, it is not necessary to prove intent, knowledge, recklessness, or criminal negligence of the defendant beyond the degree of culpability, if any, stated in Section 431.021 to establish criminal responsibility for the violation.

(b) A person is not subject to the penalties of Subsection (a):

(1) for having received an article in commerce and having delivered or offered delivery of the article, if the delivery or offer was made in good faith, unless the person refuses to furnish on request to the commissioner, an authorized agent, or a health authority, the name and address of the person from whom the article was received and copies of any documents relating to the receipt of the article;

(2) for having violated Section 431.021(a) or (e) if the person establishes a guaranty or undertaking signed by, and containing the name and address of, the person residing in this state from whom the person received in good faith the article, to the effect that;

(A) in the case of an alleged violation of Section 431.021(a), the article is not adulterated or misbranded within the meaning of this chapter; and

(B) in the case of an alleged violation of Section 431.021(e), the article is not an article that may not, under the provisions of Section 404 or 405 of the federal Act or Section 431.084 or 431.114, be introduced into commerce;

(3) for having violated Section 431.021, if the violation exists because the article is adulterated by reason of containing a color additive not from a batch certified in accordance with regulations promulgated under the federal Act, if the person establishes a guaranty or undertaking signed by, and containing the name and address of, the manufacturer of the color additive, to the effect that the color additive was from a batch certified in accordance with the applicable regulations promulgated under the federal Act;

(4) for having violated Section 431.021(b), (c), or (k) by failure to comply with Section 431.112(j) with respect to an article received in commerce to which neither Section 503(a) nor Section 503(b)(1) of the federal Act applies if the delivery or offered delivery was made in good faith and the labeling at the time of the delivery or offer contained in the same directions for use and warning statements as were contained in the labeling at the same time of the receipt of the article; or

(5) for having violated Section 431.021(*l*)(2) if the person acted in good faith and had no reason to believe that use of the punch, die, plate, stone, or other thing would result in a drug being a counterfeit drug, or for having violated Section 431.021(*l*)(3) if the person doing the act or causing it to be done acted in good faith and had no reason to believe that the drug was a counterfeit drug.

(c) A publisher, radio-broadcast licensee, or agency or medium for the dissemination of an advertisement, except the manufacturer, packer, distributor, or seller of the article to which a false advertisement relates, is not liable under this section for the dissemination of the false advertisement, unless the person has refused, on the request of the commissioner to furnish the commissioner the name and post-office address of the manufacturer, packer, distributor, seller, or advertising agency, residing in this state who caused the person to disseminate the advertisement.

(d) A person is not subject to the penalties of Subsection (a) for a violation of Section 431.021 involving misbranded food if the violation exists solely because the food is misbranded under Section 431.082 because of its advertising, and a person is not subject to the penalties of Subsection (a) for such a violation unless the violation is committed with the intent to defraud or mislead.

*(Added by L.1989, chap. 678(1), eff. 9/1/89; chgd. by L.1991, chap. 14(155), eff. 9/1/91.)*

### §431.060. Initiation of proceedings.

(a) The attorney general, or a district, county, or municipal attorney to whom the commissioner, an authorized agent, or a health authority reports a violation of this chapter, shall initiate and prosecute appropriate proceedings without delay.

(b) The commissioner, the commissioner's authorized agent, or the attorney general may, as authorized by Section 307 of the federal Act, bring in the name of this state a suit for civil penalties or to restrain a violation of Section 401 or Section 403(b) through (i), (k), (q), or (r) of the federal Act if the food that is the subject of the proceedings is located in this state.

(c) The commissioner, the commissioner's authorized agent, or the attorney general may not bring a proceeding under Subsection (b):

(1) before the 31st day after the date on which the state has given notice to the secretary of its intent to bring a suit;

(2) before the 91st day after the date on which the state has given notice to the secretary of its intent to bring a suit if the secretary has, not later than the 30th day after receiving notice from the state, commenced an informal or formal enforcement action pertaining to the food that would be the subject of the suit brought by the state; or

(3) if the secretary is diligently prosecuting a suit in court pertaining to that food, has settled a suit pertaining to that food, or has settled the informal or formal enforcement action pertaining to that food.

*(Added by L.1989, chap. 678(1); chgd. by L.1993, chap. 459(2), eff. 9/1/93.)*



### §431.061. Minor violation.

This chapter does not require the commissioner, an authorized agent, or a health authority to report for prosecution or the institution of proceedings under this chapter a minor violation of this chapter if the commissioner, authorized agent, or health authority believes that the public interest is adequately served by a suitable written notice or warning. *(Added by L.1989, chap. 678(1), eff. 9/1/89.)*

### §§431.062 to 431.080. *(Reserved.)*

## SUBCHAPTER E. DRUGS AND DEVICES

### §431.111. Adulterated drug or device.

A drug or device shall be deemed to be adulterated:

(a)(1) if it consists in whole or in part of any filthy, putrid, or decomposed substance; or

(2)(A) if it has been prepared, packed, or held under insanitary conditions whereby it may have been contaminated with filth, or whereby it may have been rendered injurious to health; or

(B) if it is a drug and the methods used in, or the facilities or controls used for, its manufacture, processing, packing, or holding do not conform to or are not operated or administered in conformity with current good manufacturing practice to assure that such drug meets the requirements of this chapter as to safety and has the identity and strength, and meets the quality and purity characteristics, which it purports or is represented to possess; or

(3) if its container is composed, in whole or in part, of any poisonous or deleterious substance which may render the contents injurious to health; or

(4) if it:

(A) bears or contains, for purposes of coloring only, a color additive that is unsafe under Section 431.161(a); or

(B) is a color additive, the intended use of which in or on drugs or devices is for purposes of coloring only, and is unsafe under Section 431.161(a); or

(5) if it is a new animal drug that is unsafe under Section 512 of the federal Act.

(b) if it purports to be or is represented as a drug, the name of which is recognized in an official compendium, and its strength differs from, or its quality or purity falls below, the standards set forth in such compendium. Such determination as to strength, quality or purity shall be made in accordance with the tests or methods of assay set forth in such compendium, or in the absence of or inadequacy of such tests or methods of assay, those prescribed under the authority of the federal Act. No drug defined in an official compendium shall be deemed to be adulterated under this paragraph because it differs from the standards of strength, quality, or purity therefor set forth in such compendium, if its difference in strength, quality, or purity from such standards is plainly stated on its label. Whenever a drug is recognized in the United States Pharmacopoeia National Formulary, it shall be subject to the requirements of the United States Pharmacopoeia National Formulary;

(c) if it is not subject to the provision of Paragraph (b) and its strength differs from, or its purity or quality falls below, that which it purports or is represented to possess;

(d) if it is a drug and any substance has been:

(1) mixed or packed therewith so as to reduce its quality or strength; or

(2) substituted wholly or in part therefor;

(e) if it is, or purports to be or is represented as, a device that is subject to a performance standard established under Section 514 of the federal Act, unless the device is in all respects in conformity with the standard;

(f)(1) if it is a class III device:

(A)(i) that is required by a regulation adopted under Section 515(b) of the federal Act to have an approval under that section of an application for premarket approval and that is not exempt from Section 515 as provided by Section 520(g) of the federal Act; and

(ii)(I) for which an application for premarket approval or a notice of completion of a product development protocol was not filed with the United States Food and Drug Administration by the 90th day after the date of adoption of the regulation; or

(II) for which that application was filed and approval was denied or withdrawn, for which that notice was filed and was declared incomplete, or for which approval of the device under the protocol was withdrawn;

(B) that was classified under Section 513(f) of the federal Act into class III, which under Section 515(a) of the federal Act is required to have in effect an approved application for premarket approval, that is not exempt from Section 515 as provided by Section 520(g) of the federal Act, and that does not have the application in effect; or

(C) that was classified under Section 520(*l*) of the federal Act into class III, which under that section is required to have in effect an approved application under Section 515 of the federal Act, and that does not have the application in effect, except that:

(2)(A) in the case of a device classified under Section 513(f) of the federal Act into class III and intended solely for investigational use, Subdivision (1)(B) does not apply to the device during the period ending on the 90th day after the date of adoption of the regulations prescribing the procedures and conditions required by Section 520(g)(2) of the federal Act; and

(B) in the case of a device subject to a regulation adopted under Section 515(b) of the federal Act, Subdivision (1) does not apply to the device during the period ending on whichever of the following dates occurs later:

(i) the last day of the 30-day calendar month beginning after the month in which the classification of the device into class III became effective under Section 513 of the federal Act; or

(ii) the 90th day after the date of adoption of the regulation;

(g) if it is a banned device;

(h) if it is a device and the methods used in, or the facilities or controls used for its manufacture, packing, storage, or installation are not in conformity with applicable requirements under Section 520(f)(1) of the federal Act or an applicable condition as prescribed by an order under Section 520(f)(2) of the federal Act; or

(i) if it is a device for which an exemption has been granted under Section 520(g) of the federal Act for investigational use and the person who was granted the exemption or any investigator who uses the device under the exemption fails to comply with a requirement prescribed by or under that section.

*(Added by L.1989, chap. 678(1); chgd. by L.1993, chap. 440(2), eff. 9/1/93.)*

### §431.112. Misbranded drug or device.

A drug or device shall be deemed to be misbranded:

(a)(1) if its labeling is false or misleading in any particular; or

(2) if its labeling or packaging fails to conform with the requirements of Section 431.181.

(b) if in a package form unless it bears a label containing (1) the name and place of business of the manufacturer, packer, or distributor; and (2) an accurate statement of the quantity of the contents in terms of weight, measure, or numerical count; provided, that under Subdivision (2) reasonable variations shall be permitted, and exemptions as to small packages shall be allowed in accordance with regulations prescribed by the secretary under the federal Act;

(c) if any word, statement, or other information required by or under authority of this chapter to appear on the label or labeling is not prominently placed thereon with such conspicuousness (as compared with other words, statements, designs, or devices, in the labeling) and in such terms as to render it likely to be read and understood by the ordinary individual under customary conditions of purchase and use;

(d) if it is for use by man and contains any quantity of the narcotic or hypnotic substance alpha-eucaine, barbituric acid, betaeucaine, bromal, cannabis, carbromal, chloral, coca, cocaine, codeine, heroin, marihuana, morphine, opium, paraldehyde, peyote, or sulphonmethane, or any chemical derivative of such substance, which derivative, after investigation, has been found to be designated as habit forming, by regulations issued by the secretary under Section 502(d) of the federal Act, unless its label bears the name and quantity or proportion of such substance or derivative and in juxtaposition therewith the statement, "Warning: May be habit forming";

(e)(1) if it is a drug, unless:

(A) its label bears, to the exclusion of any other nonproprietary name (except the applicable systematic chemical name or the chemical formula):

(i) the established name (as defined in Subdivision (3)) of the drug, if any; and

(ii) in case it is fabricated from two or more ingredients, the established name and quantity of each active ingredient, including the quantity, kind, and proportion of any alcohol, and also including, whether active or not, the established name and quantity or proportion of any bromides, ether, chloroform, acetanilid, acetphenetidin, amidopyrine, antipyrine, atropine, hyoscine, hyoscyamine, arsenic, digitalis, digitalis glucosides, mercury, ouabain, strophanthin, strychnine, thyroid, or any derivative or preparation of any such substances, contained therein; provided, that the requirement for stating the quantity of the active ingredients, other than the quantity of those specifically named in this subparagraph shall apply only to prescription drugs; and

(B) for any prescription drug the established name of the drug or ingredient, as the case may be, on the label (and on any labeling on which a name for such drug or ingredient is used) is printed prominently and in type at least half as large as that used thereon for any proprietary name or designation for such drug or ingredient; and provided, that to the extent that compliance with the requirements of Paragraph (A)(ii) or this paragraph is impracticable, exemptions shall be allowed under regulations promulgated by the secretary under the federal Act;

(2) if it is a device and it has an established name, unless its label bears, to the exclusion of any other nonproprietary name, its established name (as defined in Subdivision (4)) prominently printed in type at least half as large as that used thereon for any proprietary name or designation for such device, except that to the extent compliance with this subdivision is impracticable, exemptions shall be allowed under regulations promulgated by the secretary under the federal Act;

(3) as used in Subdivision (1), the term "established name," with respect to a drug or ingredient thereof, means:

(A) the applicable official name designated pursuant to Section 508 of the federal Act; or

(B) if there is no such name and such drug, or such ingredient, is an article recognized in an official compendium, then the official title thereof in such compendium; or

(C) if neither Paragraph (A) nor Paragraph (B) applies, then the common or usual name, if any, of such drug or of such ingredient; provided further, that where Paragraph (B) applies to an article recognized in the United States Pharmacopoeia National Formulary, the official title used in the United States Pharmacopoeia National Formulary shall apply;

(4) as used in Subdivision (2), the term "established name" with respect to a device means:

(A) the applicable official name of the device designated pursuant to Section 508 of the federal Act;

(B) if there is no such name and such device is an article recognized in an official compendium, then the official title thereof in such compendium; or

(C) if neither Paragraph (A) nor Paragraph (B) applies, then any common or usual name of such device;

(f) unless its labeling bears:

(1) adequate directions for use; and

(2) such adequate warnings against use in those pathological conditions or by children where its use may be dangerous to health, or against unsafe dosage or methods or durations of administration or application, in such manner and form, as are necessary for the protection of users unless the drug or device has been exempted from those requirements by the regulations adopted by the secretary;

(g) if it purports to be a drug the name of which is recognized in an official compendium, unless it is packaged and labeled as prescribed therein unless the method of packing has been modified with the consent of the secretary. Whenever a drug is recognized in the United States Pharmacopoeia National Formulary, it shall be subject to the requirements of the United States Pharmacopoeia National Formulary with respect to packaging and labeling. If there is an inconsistency between the requirements of this subsection and those of Subsection (e) as to the name by which the drug or its ingredients shall be designated, the requirements of Subsection (e) prevail;

(h) if it has been found by the secretary to be a drug liable to deterioration, unless it is packaged in such form and manner, and its label bears a statement of such precautions, as the secretary shall by regulations require as necessary for the protection of public health;

(i) if:

(1) it is a drug and its container is so made, formed, or filled as to be misleading; or

(2) it is an imitation of another drug; or

(3) it is offered for sale under the name of another drug;

(j) if it is dangerous to health when used in the dosage, or manner or with the frequency or duration prescribed, recommended, or suggested in the labeling thereof;

(k) if it is, or purports to be, or is represented as a drug composed wholly or partly of insulin, unless:

(1) it is from a batch with respect to which a certificate or release has been issued pursuant to Section 506 of the federal Act; and

(2) such certificate or release is in effect with respect to such drug;

(*l*) if it is, or purports to be, or is represented as a drug (except a drug for use in animals other than man) composed wholly or partly of any kind of penicillin, streptomycin, chlortetracycline, chloramphenicol, bacitracin, or any other antibiotic drug, or any derivative thereof, unless:

(1) it is from a batch with respect to which a certificate or release has been issued pursuant to Section 507 of the federal Act; and

(2) the certificate or release is in effect with respect to the drug; provided, that this subdivision shall not apply to any drug or class of drugs exempted by regulations promulgated under Section 507(c) or (d) of the federal Act;

(m) if it is a color additive, the intended use of which is for the purpose of coloring only, unless its packaging and labeling are in conformity with such packaging and labeling requirements applicable to such color additive, as may be contained in rules issued under Section 431.161(b);

(n) in the case of any prescription drug distributed or offered for sale in this state, unless the manufacturer, packer, or distributor thereof includes in all advertisements and other descriptive printed matter issued or caused to be issued by the manufacturer, packer, or distributor with respect to that drug a true statement of:

(1) the established name as defined in Subsection (e), printed prominently and in type at least half as large as that used for any trade or brand name;

(2) the formula showing quantitatively each ingredient of the drug to the extent required for labels under Subsection (e); and

(3) other information in brief summary relating to side effects, contraindications, and effectiveness as required in regulations issued under Section 701(e) of the federal Act;

(*o*) if it was manufactured, prepared, propagated, compounded, or processed in an establishment in this state not registered under Section 510 of the federal Act, if it was not included in a list required by Section 510(j) of the federal Act, if a notice or other information respecting it was not provided as required by that section or Section 510(k) of the federal Act, or if it does not bear symbols from the uniform system for identification of devices prescribed under Section 510(e) of the federal Act as required by regulation;

(p) if it is a drug and its packaging or labeling is in violation of an applicable regulation issued under Section 3 or 4 of the Federal Poison Prevention Packaging Act of 1970 (21 U.S.C. 1472 or 1473);

(q) if a trademark, trade name, or other identifying mark, imprint or device of another, or any likeness of the foregoing has been placed thereon or on its container with intent to defraud;

(r) in the case of any restricted device distributed or offered for sale in this state, if:

(1) its advertising is false or misleading in any particular; or

(2) it is sold, distributed, or used in violation of regulations prescribed under Section 520(e) of the federal Act ;

(s) in the case of any restricted device distributed or offered for sale in this state, unless the manufacturer, packer, or distributor thereof includes in all advertisements and other descriptive printed matter issued by the manufacturer, packer, or distributor with respect to that device:

(1) a true statement of the device's established name as defined in Section 502(e) of the federal Act, printed prominently and in type at least half as large as that used for any trade or brand name thereof; and

(2) a brief statement of the intended uses of the device and relevant warnings, precautions, side effects, and contraindications and in the case of specific devices made subject to regulations issued under the federal Act, a full description of the components of such device or the formula showing quantitatively each ingredient of such device to the extent required in regulations under the federal Act;

(t) if it is a device subject to a performance standard established under Section 514 of the federal Act, unless it bears such labeling as may be prescribed in such performance standard; or

(u) if it is a device and there was a failure or refusal:

(1) to comply with any requirement prescribed under Section 518 of the federal Act respecting the device; or

(2) to furnish material required by or under Section 519 of the federal Act respecting the device.

*(Added by L.1989, chap. 678(1); chgd. by L.1997, chap. 282(4), eff. 5/26/97.)*

## §431.113. Exemption for certain drugs and devices.

(a) The board is directed to adopt rules exempting from any labeling or packaging requirement of this chapter drugs and devices that are, in accordance with the practice of the trade, to be processed, labeled, or repacked in substantial quantities at establishments other than those where originally processed or packaged on condition that such drugs and devices are not adulterated or misbranded under the provisions of this chapter on removal from such processing, labeling, or repacking establishment.

(b) Drugs and device labeling or packaging exemptions adopted under the federal Act shall apply to drugs and devices in this state except insofar as modified or rejected by rules of the board.



(c)(1) A drug intended for use by man that:

(A) is a habit-forming drug to which Section 431.112(d) applies; or

(B) because of its toxicity or other potentiality for harmful effect, or the method of its use, or the collateral measures necessary to its use, is not safe for use except under the supervision of a practitioner licensed by law to administer such drug; or

(C) is limited by an approved application under Section 505 of the federal Act to use under the professional supervision of a practitioner licensed by law to administer such drug shall be dispensed only:

(i) on a written prescription of a practitioner licensed by law to administer such drug; or

(ii) on an oral prescription of such practitioner that is reduced promptly to writing and filed by the pharmacist; or

(iii) by refilling any such written or oral prescription if such refilling is authorized by the prescriber either in the original prescription or by oral order that is reduced promptly to writing and filed by the pharmacist. The act of dispensing a drug contrary to the provisions of this paragraph shall be deemed to be an act that results in a drug being misbranded while held for sale.

(2) Any drug dispensed by filling or refilling a written or oral prescription of a practitioner licensed by law to administer such drug shall be exempt from the requirements of Section 431.112, except Sections 431.112(a)(1), (i)(2), (i)(3), (k), and (*l*), and the packaging requirements of Sections 431.112(g), (h), and (p), if the drug bears a label containing the name and address of the dispenser, the serial number and date of the prescription or of its filling, the name of the prescriber, and, if stated in the prescription, the name of the patient, and the directions for use and cautionary statements, if any, contained in such prescription. This exemption shall not apply to any drugs dispensed in the course of the conduct of business of dispensing drugs pursuant to diagnosis by mail, or to a drug dispensed in violation of Subdivision (1).

(3) The board may, by rule, remove drugs subject to Section 431.112(d) and Section 505 of the federal Act from the requirements of Subdivision (1) when such requirements are not necessary for the protection of the public health.

(4) A drug that is subject to Subdivision (1) shall be deemed to be misbranded if at any time prior to dispensing its label fails to bear the statement "Caution: Federal Law Prohibits Dispensing Without Prescription," or "Caution: State Law Prohibits Dispensing Without Prescription." A drug to which Subdivision (1) does not apply shall be deemed to be misbranded if at any time prior to dispensing its label bears the caution statement quoted in the preceding sentence.

*(Added by L.1989, chap. 678(1), eff. 9/1/89.)*

## §431.114. New drugs.

(a) A person shall not sell, deliver, offer for sale, hold for sale or give away any new drug unless:

(1) an application with respect thereto has been approved and the approval has not been withdrawn under Section 505 of the federal Act; and

(2) a copy of the letter of approval or approvability issued by the Federal Food and Drug Administration is on file with the commissioner if the product is manufactured in this state.

(b) A person shall not use in or on human beings or animals a new drug or new animal drug limited to investigational use unless the person has filed with the Federal Food and Drug Administration a completed and signed "Notice of claimed investigational exemption for a new drug" form in accordance with 21 C.F.R. 312.1 (1980) and the exemption has not been terminated. The drug shall be plainly labeled in compliance with Section 505(i) or 507(d) of the federal Act.

(c) This section shall not apply:

(1) to any drug that is not a new drug as defined in the federal Act;

(2) to any drug that is licensed under the Public Health Services Act of July 1, 1944 (42 U.S.C. 201 et seq.); or

(3) to any drug approved by the commissioner by the authority of any prior law.

*(Added by L.1989, chap. 678(1); chgd. by L.1991, chap. 14(157), eff. 9/1/91.)*

### §431.115. New animal drugs.

(a) A new animal drug shall, with respect to any particular use or intended use of the drug, be deemed unsafe for the purposes of this chapter unless:

(1) there is in effect an approval of an application filed pursuant to Section 512(b) of the federal Act with respect to the use or intended use of the drug; and

(2) the drug, its labeling, and the use conforms to the approved application.

(b) A new animal drug shall not be deemed unsafe for the purposes of this chapter if the article is for investigational use and conforms to the terms of an exemption in effect with respect thereto under Section 512(j) of the federal Act.

(c) This section does not apply to any drug:

(1) licensed under the virus-serum-toxin law of March 4, 1913 (21 U.S.C. 151-159);

(2) approved by the United States Department of Agriculture; or

(3) approved by the commissioner by the authority of any prior law.

*(Added by L.1989, chap. 678(1); chgd. by L.1991, chap. 14(158), eff. 9/1/91.)*

### §§431.116 to 431.140. *(Reserved.)*

## SUBCHAPTER H. FAIR PACKAGING AND LABELING; FALSE ADVERTISING

### §431.181. Fair packaging and labeling.

(a) All labels of consumer commodities, as defined by this chapter, shall conform with the requirements for the declaration of net quantity of contents of Section 4 of the Fair Packaging and Labeling Act (15 U.S.C. 1451 et seq.) and the regulations promulgated pursuant thereto; provided, that consumer commodities exempted from the requirements of Section 4 of the Fair Packaging and Labeling Act also be exempt from this subsection.

(b) The label of any package of a consumer commodity that bears a representation as to the number of servings of the commodity contained in the package shall bear a statement of the net quantity (in terms of weight, measure, or numerical count) of each serving.

(c) No person shall distribute or cause to be distributed in commerce any packaged consumer commodity of any qualifying words or phrases appear in conjunction with the separate statement of the net quantity of contents required by Subsection (a), but nothing in this subsection shall prohibit supplemental statements at other places on the package describing in nondeceptive terms the net quantity of contents; provided, that the supplemental statements of net quantity of contents shall not include any term qualifying a unit of weight, measure, or count that tends to exaggerate the amount of the commodity contained in the package.

(d) Whenever the board determines that rules containing prohibitions or requirements other than those prescribed by Subsection (a) are necessary to prevent the deception of consumers or to facilitate value comparisons as to any consumer commodity, the board shall adopt with respect to that commodity rules effective to:

(1) establish and define standards for the characterization of the size of a package enclosing any consumer commodity, which may be used to supplement the label statement of net quantity of contents of packages containing such commodity, but this paragraph shall not be construed as authorizing any limitation on the size, shape, weight, dimensions, or number of packages that may be used to enclose any commodity;

(2) regulate the placement on any package containing any commodity, or on any label affixed to the commodity, of any printed matter stating or representing by implication that such commodity is offered for retail sale at a price lower than the ordinary and customary retail sale price or that a retail sale price advantage is accorded to purchasers thereof by reason of the size of that package or the quantity of its contents;

(3) require that the label on each package of a consumer commodity (other than one which is a food within the meaning of Section 431.002(15)) bear:

(A) the common or usual name of the consumer commodity, if any; and

(B) in case the consumer commodity consists of two or more ingredients, the common or usual name of each ingredient listed in order of decreasing predominance, but nothing in this paragraph shall be deemed to require that any trade secret be divulged; or

(4) prevent the nonfunctional slack-fill of packages containing consumer commodities. For the purpose of this subdivision, a package shall be deemed to be nonfunctionally slack-filled if it is filled of substantially less than its capacity for reasons other than:

(A) protection of the contents of the package; or

(B) the requirements of the machine used for enclosing the contents in the package.

*(Added by L.1989, chap. 678(1), eff. 9/1/89.)*

### §431.182. False advertisement.

(a) An advertisement of a food, drug, device, or cosmetic shall be deemed to be false if it is false or misleading in any particular.

(b) The advertising of a food that incorporates a health claim not in conformance with or defined by Section 403(r) of the federal Act is deemed to be false or misleading for the purposes of this chapter.

*(Added by L.1989, chap. 678(1); chgd. by L.1993, chap. 459(5), eff. 9/1/93.)*



### §431.183. False advertisement of drug or device.

(a) An advertisement of a drug or device is false if the advertisement represents that the drug or device affects:

(1) infectious and parasitic diseases;

(2) neoplasms;

(3) endocrine, nutritional, and metabolic diseases and immunity disorders;

(4) diseases of blood and blood-forming organs;

(5) mental disorders;

(6) diseases of the nervous system and sense organs;

(7) diseases of the circulatory system;

(8) diseases of the respiratory system;

(9) diseases of the digestive system;

(10) diseases of the genitourinary system;

(11) complications of pregnancy, childbirth, and the puerperium;

(12) diseases of the skin and subcutaneous tissue;

(13) diseases of the musculoskeletal system and connective tissue;

(14) congenital anomalies;

(15) certain conditions originating in the perinatal period;

(16) symptoms, signs, and ill-defined conditions; or

(17) injury and poisoning.

(b) Subsection (a) does not apply to an advertisement of a drug or device if the advertisement does not violate Section 431.182 and is disseminated:

(1) to the public for self-medication and is consistent with the labeling claims permitted by the federal Food and Drug Administration;

(2) only to members of the medical, dental, and veterinary professions and appears only in the scientific periodicals of those professions; or

(3) only for the purpose of public health education by a person not commercially interested, directly or indirectly, in the sale of the drug or device.

(c) The board by rule shall authorize the advertisement of a drug having a curative or therapeutic effect for a disease listed under Subsection (a) if the board determines that an advance in medical science has made any type of self-medication safe for the disease. The board may impose conditions and restrictions on the advertisement of the drug necessary in the interest of public health.

(d) This section does not indicate that self-medication for a disease other than a disease listed under Subsection (a) is safe or effective.

*(Added by L.1989, chap. 678(1); chgd. by L.1991, chap. 14(160), eff. 9/1/91.)*

### §§431.184 to 431.200. *(Reserved.)*

## SUBCHAPTER I. WHOLESALE DRUG DISTRIBUTORS

### §431.201. Definitions.

In this subchapter:

(1) "Wholesale distribution" means distribution to a person other than a consumer or patient, and includes distribution by a manufacturer, repacker, own label distributor, jobber, or wholesaler.

(2) "Place of business" means each location at which a drug for wholesale distribution is located.

*(Added by L.1989, chap. 678(1), eff. 9/1/89.)*

### §431.202. License statement required.

(a) A person may not engage in wholesale distribution of drugs in this state unless the person has filed with the commissioner a signed and verified license statement on a form furnished by the commissioner.

(b) The license statement must be filed annually.

*(Added by L.1989, chap. 678(1); chgd. by L.1991, chaps. 14(161), 539(5), eff. 9/1/91.)*



### §431.2021. Exemption from licensing.

(a) A person who engages in wholesale distribution of prescription drugs in this state for use in humans is exempt from this subchapter if the person is exempt under:

(1) the Prescription Drug Marketing Act of 1987, as amended (21 U.S.C. Section 353(c)(3)(B));

(2) the regulations adopted by the secretary to administer and enforce that Act; or

(3) the interpretations of that Act set out in the compliance policy manual of the United States Food and Drug Administration.

(b) An exemption from the licensing requirements under this section does not constitute an exemption from the other provisions of this Act or the rules adopted by the board to administer and enforce this Act.

*(Added by L.1991, chap. 539(6); chgd. by L.1993, chap. 375(1), eff. 6/2/93.)*

### §431.203. Contents of license statement.

The license statement must contain:

(1) the name under which the business is conducted;

(2) the address of each business that is licensed;

(3) the name and residence address of:

(A) the proprietor, if the business is a proprietorship;

(B) all partners, if the business is a partnership; or

(C) all principals, if the business is an association;

(4) the date and place of incorporation, if the business is a corporation;

(5) the names and residence addresses of the individuals in an administrative capacity showing:

(A) the managing proprietor, if the business is a proprietorship;

(B) the managing partner, if the business is a partnership;

(C) the officers and directors, if the business is a corporation; or

(D) the persons in a managerial capacity, if the business is an association; and

(6) the residence address of an individual in charge of each place of business.

*(Added by L.1989, chap. 678(1); chgd. by L.1991, chap. 539(7), eff. 9/1/91.)*

### §431.2031. Effect of operation in other jurisdictions; reports.

(a) A person who engages in the wholesale distribution of drugs outside this state may engage in the wholesale distribution of drugs in this state if the person holds a license issued by the department.

(b) The department may accept reports from authorities in other jurisdictions to determine the extent of compliance with this chapter and the minimum standards adopted under this chapter.

(c) The department may issue a license to a person who engages in the wholesale distribution of drugs outside this state to engage in the wholesale distribution of drugs in this state, if after an examination of the reports of the person's compliance history and current compliance record, the department determines that the person is in compliance with this subchapter and the board's rules.

(d) The department shall consider each licensing statement filed by a person who wishes to engage in wholesale distribution of drugs in this state on an individual basis.

*(Added by L.1991, chap. 539(8), eff. 9/1/91.)*

### §431.204. Fees.

(a) The board shall collect fees for:

(1) a license that is filed or renewed;

(2) a license that is amended, including a notification of a change in the location of a licensed place of business required under Section 431.206; and

(3) an inspection performed in enforcing this subchapter and rules adopted under this subchapter.

(b) The board may charge annual fees.

(c) The board by rule shall set the fees in amounts that allow the department to recover at least 50 percent of the annual expenditures of state funds by the department in:

(1) reviewing and acting on a license;

(2) amending and renewing a license;

(3) inspecting a licensed facility; and

(4) implementing and enforcing this subchapter, including a rule or order adopted or a license issued under this subchapter.

(d) Fees collected under this section shall be deposited to the credit of the food and drug registration fee account of the general revenue fund and may be appropriated to the department only to carry out this chapter.

*(Added by L.1989, chap. 678(1); chgd. by L.1991, chap. 539(9), eff. 9/1/91.)*



### §431.205. Expiration date.

(a) The board by rule may provide that licenses expire on different dates during the year.

(b) If the board changes a license expiration date, the board shall prorate the license fee payable on or before September 1 so that the licensee is required to pay only that portion of the fee that is allocable to the number of months during which the license is valid.

(c) The total renewal license fee is payable when the license is renewed on the new expiration date.

*(Added by L.1989, chap. 678(1); chgd. by L.1991, chap. 539(9), eff. 9/1/91.)*

### §431.206. Change of location of place of business.

Not fewer than 30 days in advance of the change, the licensee shall notify the commissioner or the commissioner's designee in writing of the licensee's intent to change the location of a licensed place of business. The notice shall include the address of the new location, and the name and residence address of the individual in charge of the business at the new location. Not more than 10 days after the completion of the change of location, the licensee shall notify the commissioner or the commissioner's designee in writing to verify the change of location, the address of the new location, and the name and residence address of the individual in charge of the business at the new address. Notice will be deemed adequate if the licensee provides the intent and verification notices to the commissioner or the commissioner's designee by certified mail, return receipt requested, mailed to the central office of the department. *(Added by L.1989, chap. 678(1); chgd. by L.1991, chap. 539(9), eff. 9/1/91.)*

### §431.207. Refusal to license; suspension or revocation of license.

(a) The commissioner may refuse an application for a license or may suspend or revoke a license if the applicant or licensee:

(1) has been convicted of a felony or misdemeanor that involves moral turpitude;

(2) is an association, partnership, or corporation and the managing officer has been convicted of a felony or misdemeanor that involves moral turpitude;

(3) has been convicted in a state or federal court of the illegal use, sale, or transportation of intoxicating liquors, narcotic drugs, barbiturates, amphetamines, desoxyephedrine, their compounds or derivatives, or any other dangerous or habit-forming drugs;

(4) is an association, partnership, or corporation and the managing officer has been convicted in a state or federal court of the illegal use, sale, or transportation of intoxicating liquors, narcotic drugs, barbiturates, amphetamines, desoxyephedrine, their compounds or derivatives, or any other dangerous or habit-forming drugs; or

(5) has not complied with this chapter or the board's rules implementing this chapter.

(b) The commissioner may refuse an application for a license or may suspend or revoke a license if the commissioner determines from evidence presented during a hearing that the applicant or licensee:

(1) has violated Section 431.021(*l*) (3), relating to the counterfeiting of a drug or the sale or holding for sale of a counterfeit drug;

(2) has violated Chapter 481 (Texas Controlled Substances Act) or 483 (Dangerous Drugs); or

(3) has violated the rules of the director of the Department of Public Safety, including being responsible for a significant discrepancy in the records that state law requires the applicant or licensee to maintain.

(c) The refusal to license an applicant or the suspension or revocation of a license by the commissioner and the appeal from that action are governed by the board's formal hearing procedures and the procedures for a contested case hearing under Chapter 2001, Government Code.
*(Added by L.1989, chap. 678(1); chgd. by L.1991, chap. 539(9); L.1995, chap. 76(5.95)(49), eff. 9/1/95.)*

## SUBCHAPTER K. GENERAL ADMINISTRATIVE PROVISIONS AND RULEMAKING AUTHORITY

### §431.241. Rulemaking authority.

(a) The board may adopt rules for the efficient enforcement of this chapter.

(b) The board may conform its rules, if practicable, with regulations adopted under the federal Act.

(c) The enumeration of specific federal laws and regulations in Sections 431.244 and 431.245 does not limit the general authority granted to the board in Subsection (b) to conform its rules to those adopted under the federal Act.

(d) The board may adopt the federal regulations issued by the secretary pursuant to the Prescription Drug Marketing Act of 1987 (21 U.S.C. Sections 331, 333, 353, and 381), as necessary or desirable so that the state wholesale drug distributor licensing program in Subchapter I of this chapter may achieve compliance with that Act.

(e) The board and the Texas Department of Human Services shall not establish a drug formulary that restricts by any prior or retroactive approval process a physician's ability to treat a patient with a prescription drug that has been approved and designated as safe and effective by the United States Food and Drug Administration, in compliance with federal law and subject to review by the Texas Department of Human Services, Vendor Drug Advisory Subcommittee.

(f) Nothing in this section shall effect a prior approval program in operation on the effective date of this section nor shall any portion of this chapter prohibit a prior approval process on any federally exempted products.

(g) The department may assess a fee for the issuance of a certificate of free sale and another certification issued under this chapter. The board by rule shall set each fee in an amount sufficient to recover the cost to the department of issuing the particular certificate.
*(Added by L.1989, chap. 678(1); chgd. by L.1991, chap. 539(11); L.1993, chap. 675(7), eff. 9/1/93.)*

### §431.242. Contested case hearings and appeals.

A hearing under this chapter or an appeal from a final administrative decision shall be conducted under Chapter 2001, Government Code. *(Added by L.1989, chap. 678(1); chgd. by L.1995, chap. 76(5.95)(49), eff. 9/1/95.)*

### §431.243. Persons to conduct hearings.

The commissioner or an officer, agent, or employee designated by the commissioner shall conduct a hearing authorized or required under this chapter. *(Added by L.1989, chap. 678(1), eff. 9/1/89.)*

### §431.244. Federal regulations adopted as state rules.

(a) A regulation adopted by the secretary under the federal Act concerning pesticide chemicals, food additives, color additives, special dietary use, processed low acid food, acidified food, infant formula, bottled water, or vended bottled water is a rule for the purposes of this chapter, unless the board modifies or rejects the rule.

(b) A regulation adopted under the Fair Packaging and Labeling Act (15 U.S.C. 1451 et seq.) is a rule for the purposes of this chapter, unless the board modifies or rejects the rule. The board may not adopt a rule that conflicts with the labeling requirements for the net quantity of contents required under Section 4 of the Fair Packaging and Labeling Act (15 U.S.C. 1453) and the regulations adopted under that Act.

(c) A regulation adopted by the secretary under Sections 403(b) through (i) of the federal Act is a rule for the purposes of this chapter unless the board modifies or rejects the rule. The board may not adopt a rule that conflicts with the limitations provided by Sections 403(q) and (r) of the federal Act.

(d) A federal regulation that this section provides as a rule for the purposes of this chapter is effective:

(1) on the date that the regulation becomes effective as a federal regulation; and

(2) whether or not the department has fulfilled the rulemaking provisions of Chapter 2001, Government Code.

(e) If the board modifies or rejects a federal regulation, the board shall comply with the rulemaking provisions of Chapter 2001, Government Code.
*(Added by L.1989, chap. 678(1); chgd. by L.1991, chap. 539(12); L.1993, chap. 459(6); L.1995, chap. 76(5.95)(49), eff. 9/1/95.)*

## §431.245. Definition or standard of identity, quality, or fill of container.

(a) A definition or standard of identity, quality, or fill of container of the federal Act is a definition or standard of identity, quality, or fill of container in this chapter, except as modified by board rules.

(b) The board by rule may establish definitions and standards of identity, quality, and fill of container for a food if:

(1) a federal regulation does not apply to the food; and

(2) the board determines that adopting the rules will promote honest and fair dealing in the interest of consumers.

(c) A temporary permit granted for interstate shipment of an experimental pack of food that varies from the requirements of federal definitions and standards of identity is automatically effective in this state under the conditions of the permit.

(d) The commissioner may issue additional permits if the commissioner determines that:

(1) it is necessary for the completion of an otherwise adequate investigation; and

(2) the interests of consumers are safeguarded.

(e) A permit issued under Subsection (d) is subject to the terms and conditions of board rules.
*(Added by L.1989, chap. 678(1), eff. 9/1/89.)*

## §431.246. Removal of adulterated item from stores.

The board shall adopt rules that provide a system for removing adulterated items from the shelves of a grocery store or other retail establishment selling those items. *(Added by L.1989, chap. 678(1), eff. 9/1/89.)*

## §431.247. Delegation of powers or duties.

(a) The board by rule may delegate a power or duty imposed on the commissioner by this chapter to a designee of the board, including the power or duty to issue an emergency rule, an emergency manufacturing permit, or an order or to render a final administrative decision.

(b) A health authority may, unless otherwise restricted by law, delegate a power or duty imposed on the health authority by this chapter to an employee of the local health department, the local health unit, or the public health district in which the health authority serves.
*(Added by L.1989, chap. 678(1), eff. 9/1/89.)*

## §431.2471. Texas Department of Health peace officers.

(a) The department may employ a peace officer to administer and enforce this chapter.

(b) The department may not employ a peace officer under this section unless:

(1) the employee will enforce the food and drug portions of this chapter;

(2) the Commission on Law Enforcement Officer Standards and Education certifies the employee as qualified to be a peace officer;

(3) the commissioner recommends the employee to the department as being qualified to enforce the food and drug laws within the jurisdiction of the department; and

(4) the employee also serves simultaneously as the director of the food and drugs division of the department.

(c) A person employed as a peace officer under this section has the powers, privileges, and immunities of a peace officer while carrying out the employee's duties under this chapter.
*(Added by L.1993, chap. 339(1), eff. 9/1/93.)*

## §431.248. Memorandum of understanding with Department of Agriculture.

(a) The department and the Department of Agriculture shall execute a memorandum of understanding that:

(1) requires each agency to disclose to the other agency any positive results of testing conducted by the agency for pesticides in food; and

(2) specifies how each agency will assist the other in performing its duties regarding pesticides in food.

(b) The department and the Department of Agriculture shall adopt the memorandum of understanding as a rule.

(c) The department and the Department of Agriculture shall request the federal Food and Drug Administration to join in execution of the memorandum of understanding.
*(Added by L.1989, chap. 678(1), eff. 9/1/89.)*

### §431.249. Dissemination of information.

(a) The commissioner may publish reports summarizing the judgments, decrees, and court orders rendered under this chapter, including the nature and disposition of the charge.

(b) The commissioner may disseminate information regarding a food, drug, device, or cosmetic in a situation that the commissioner determines to involve imminent danger to health or gross deception of consumers.

(c) This section does not prohibit the commissioner from collecting, reporting, and illustrating the results of an investigation by the commissioner.
*(Added by L.1989, chap. 678(1), eff. 9/1/89.)*



## SUBTITLE B. ALCOHOL AND SUBSTANCE ABUSE PROGRAMS

## CHAPTER 462. TREATMENT OF CHEMICALLY DEPENDENT PERSONS
*(Selected Section)*



### §462.041. Apprehension by peace officer without warrant.

(a) A peace officer, without a warrant, may take a person into custody if the officer:

(1) has reason to believe and does believe that:

(A) the person is chemically dependent; and

(B) because of that chemical dependency there is a substantial risk of harm to the person or to others unless the person is immediately restrained; and

(2) believes that there is not sufficient time to obtain a warrant before taking the person into custody.

(b) A substantial risk of serious harm to the person or others under Subsection (a)(1)(B) may be demonstrated by:

(1) the person's behavior; or

(2) evidence of severe emotional distress and deterioration in the person's mental or physical condition to the extent that the person cannot remain at liberty.

(c) The peace officer may form the belief that the person meets the criteria for apprehension:

(1) from a representation of a credible person; or

(2) on the basis of the conduct of the apprehended person or the circumstances under which the apprehended person is found.

(d) A peace officer who takes a person into custody under Subsection (a) shall immediately transport the apprehended person to:

(1) the nearest appropriate inpatient treatment facility; or

(2) if an appropriate inpatient treatment facility is not available, a facility considered suitable by the county's health authority.

(e) A person may not be detained in a jail or similar detention facility except in an extreme emergency. A person detained in a jail or a nonmedical facility shall be kept separate from any person who is charged with or convicted of a crime.

(f) A peace officer shall immediately file an application for detention after transporting a person to a facility under this section. The application for detention must contain:

(1) a statement that the officer has reason to believe and does believe that the person evidences chemical dependency;

(2) a statement that the officer has reason to believe and does believe that the person evidences a substantial risk of serious harm to himself or others;

(3) a specific description of the risk of harm;

(4) a statement that the officer has reason to believe and does believe that the risk of harm is imminent unless the person is immediately restrained;

(5) a statement that the officer's beliefs are derived from specific recent behavior, overt acts, attempts, or threats that were observed by or reliably reported to the officer;

(6) a detailed description of the specific behavior, acts, attempts, or threats; and

(7) the name and relationship to the apprehended person of any person who reported or observed the behavior, acts, attempts, or threats.

(g) The person shall be released on completion of a preliminary examination conducted under Section 462.044 unless the examining physician determines that emergency detention is necessary and provides the statement prescribed by Section 462.044(b). If a person is not admitted to a facility, is not arrested and does not object, arrangements shall be made to immediately return the person to:

(1) the location of the person's apprehension;

(2) the person's residence in this state; or

(3) another suitable location.

(h) The county in which the person was apprehended shall pay the costs of the person's return.

(i) A treatment facility may provide to a person medical assistance regardless of whether the facility admits the person or refers the person to another facility.

*(Added by L.1991, chap. 14(175), eff. 9/1/91.)*



## CHAPTER 463. CONTRIBUTING TO DELINQUNECY OF HABITUAL DRUNKARD OR NARCOTIC ADDICT
*(Selected Subchapters)*

## SUBCHAPTER A. CONTRIBUTING TO DELINQUENCY OF HABITUAL DRUNKARD



## SUBCHAPTER B. CONTRIBUTING TO NARCOTIC ADDICTION



## SUBCHAPTER A. CONTRIBUTING TO DELINQUENCY OF HABITUAL DRUNKARD

### §463.001. Contributing to delinquency of habitual drunkard; criminal penalty.

(a) In this section, "delinquency" means any act that tends to debase or injure the morals, health, or welfare of a habitual drunkard and includes:

(1) drinking intoxicating liquor;

(2) entering or remaining in any bawdy house, assignation house, disorderly house, roadhouse, hotel, or public dance hall where prostitutes, gamblers, or thieves are permitted to enter and ply their trade;

(3) entering a place where intoxicating liquors are kept, drunk, used, or sold;

(4) associating with thieves and immoral persons;

(5) causing a habitual drunkard to leave home or to leave the custody of the drunkard's parents, guardian, or person acting for the drunkard's parents or guardian without first receiving their consent or against their will; or

(6) causing the habitual drunkard, by undue influence, to unlawfully cohabit with a person known by the actor to be a habitual drunkard.

(b) A person commits an offense if the person by any act or in any manner encourages, causes, acts in conjunction with, or contributes to the delinquency, dependency, or neglect of a habitual drunkard, regardless of the drunkard's previous convictions.

(c) An offense under this section is punishable by a fine of not more than $500, confinement in jail for not more than one year, or both.

### §463.002. Conflicting offenses.

To the extent of any conflict, the offenses prescribed by the Penal Code or other law enacted after June 9, 1949, prevail over the offense prescribed by Section 463.001.

## SUBCHAPTER B. CONTRIBUTING TO NARCOTIC ADDICTION

### §463.011. Contributing to delinquency of narcotic addict; criminal penalty.

(a) In this section, "delinquency" means any act that tends to debase or injure the morals, health, or welfare of a narcotic addict, and includes:

(1) drinking intoxicating liquor;

(2) going into or remaining in any bawdy house, assignation house, disorderly house, roadhouse, hotel, or public dance hall where prostitutes, gamblers, or thieves are permitted to enter and ply their trade;

(3) going into a place where intoxicating liquors are kept, drunk, used, or sold;

(4) associating with thieves and immoral persons;

(5) causing a narcotic addict to leave home or to leave the custody of the addict's parents, guardian, or person acting for the addict's parent or guardian without first receiving that person's consent or against that person's will; or

(6) causing the addict, by undue influence, to unlawfully cohabit with a person known by the actor to be a narcotic addict.

(b) A person commits an offense if the person, by any act or in any manner, encourages, causes, acts in conjunction with, or contributes to the delinquency, dependency, or neglect of a narcotic addict, regardless of the addict's previous convictions.

(c) An offense under this section is punishable by a fine of not more than $500, confinement in jail for not more than one year, or both.

### §463.012. Conflicting offenses.

To the extent of any conflict, the offenses defined by the Penal Code or other law enacted after June 9, 1949, prevail over the offense defined by Section 463.011.

# CHAPTER 466. REGULATION OF NARCOTIC DRUG TREATMENT PROGRAMS

*(Chgd. by L.1991, chap. 14(193), eff. 9/1/91.)*

## SUBCHAPTER A. GENERAL PROVISIONS

Section



## SUBCHAPTER B. PERMIT

## SUBCHAPTER C. ENFORCEMENT



## SUBCHAPTER A. GENERAL PROVISIONS

### §466.001. Legislative intent.

(a) It is the intent of the legislature that the department exercise its administrative powers and regulatory authority to ensure the proper use of approved narcotic drugs in the treatment of narcotic dependent persons.

(b) Treatment of narcotic addiction by permitted treatment programs is recognized as a specialty chemical dependency treatment area using the medical model.

(c) Short-term goals should have an emphasis of personal and public health, crime prevention, reintegration of narcotic addicted persons into the public work force, and social and medical stabilization. Narcotic treatment programs are an important component of the state's effort to prevent the further proliferation of the AIDS virus. Total drug abstinence is recognized as a long-term goal of treatment, subject to medical determination of the medical appropriateness and prognosis of the narcotic addicted person.
*(Added by L.1991. chap. 14(193); chgd. by L.1999, chap. 1411(1.12), eff. 9/1/99.)*



### §466.002. Definitions.

In this chapter:

(1) "Approved narcotic drug" means a drug approved by the United States Food and Drug Administration for maintenance or detoxification of a person physiologically addicted to the opiate class of drugs.

(2) "Authorized agent" means an employee of the department who is designated by the commissioner to enforce this chapter.

(3) "Board" means the Texas Board of Health.

(4) "Commissioner" means the commissioner of public health.

(5) "Department" means the Texas Department of Health.

(6) "Facility" includes a medical office, an outpatient clinic, a general or special hospital, a community mental health center, and any other location in which a structured narcotic dependency program is conducted.

(7) "Narcotic drug" has the meaning assigned by Chapter 481 (Texas Controlled Substances Act).
*(Redesignated and chgd. by L.1991, chap. 14(193); chgd. by L.1999, chap. 1411(1.13), eff. 9/1/99.)*

### §466.003. Exclusion of cocaine.

Cocaine is excluded for the purpose of this chapter. *(Added by L.1991, chap. 14(193), eff. 9/1/91.)*

### §466.004. Powers and duties of board and department.

(a) The board shall adopt and the department shall administer and enforce rules to ensure the proper use of approved narcotic drugs in the treatment of narcotic drug-dependent persons, including rules that:

(1) require an applicant or a permit holder to make annual, periodic, and special reports that the department determines are necessary;

(2) require an applicant or permit holder to keep records that the department determines are necessary;

(3) provide for investigations that the department determines are necessary; and

(4) provide for the coordination of the approval of narcotic drug treatment programs by the United States Food and Drug Administration and the United States Drug Enforcement Administration.

(b) The board shall adopt rules for the issuance of permits to operate narcotic drug treatment programs including rules:

(1) governing the submission and review of applications;

(2) establishing the criteria for the issuance and renewal of permits; and
(3) establishing the criteria for the suspension and revocation of permits.
*(Redesignated and chgd. by L.1991, chap. 14(193); chgd. by L.1999, chap. 1411(1.14), eff. 9/1/99.)*

**§466.005.** *(Repealed by L.1999, chap. 1411(1.18), eff. 9/1/99.)*

**§§466.006 to 466.020.** *(Reserved.)*

## SUBCHAPTER B. PERMIT

**§466.021. Permit required.**
A person may not operate a narcotic drug treatment program unless the person has a permit issued under this chapter. *(Redesignated and chgd. by L.1991, chap. 14(193), eff. 9/1/91.)*

**§466.022. Limitation on prescription, order, or administration of narcotic drug.**
A physician may not prescribe, order, or administer a narcotic drug for the purpose of treating drug dependency unless the physician prescribes, orders, or administers an approved narcotic drug for the maintenance or detoxification of drug-dependent persons as part of a program permitted by the department. *(Added by L.1991, chap. 14(193); chgd. by L.1999, chap. 1411(1.15), eff. 9/1/99.)*

**§466.023. Application for permit; fees.**
(a) The department shall issue a permit to an applicant who qualifies under rules and standards adopted by the board.
(b) A permit issued under this section is valid until suspended or revoked by the department or surrendered by the permit holder in accordance with board rules.
(c) A person must obtain a permit for each facility that the person operates.
(d) A permit issued by the department is not transferable from one facility to another facility and must be returned to the department if the permit holder sells or otherwise conveys the facility to another person.
(e) The board by rule shall establish and collect a nonrefundable application fee to defray the cost to the department of processing each application for a permit. The application fee must be submitted with the application. An application may not be considered unless the application is accompanied by the application fee.
(f) The board shall adopt rules that set permit fees in amounts sufficient for the department to recover not less than half of the actual annual expenditures of state funds by the department to:
(1) amend permits;
(2) inspect facilities operated by permit holders; and
(3) implement and enforce this chapter.
(g) Fees collected by the department shall be deposited in the state treasury to the credit of the narcotic treatment permitting fee fund.
*(Redesignated and chgd. by L.1991, chap. 14(193), eff. 9/1/91.)*

**§466.024. Permit limitations.**
(a) The department may issue a permit to:
(1) a person constituting a legal entity organized and operating under the laws of this state; or
(2) a physician.
(b) The department may issue a permit to a person other than a physician only if the person provides health care services under the supervision of one or more physicians licensed by the Texas State Board of Medical Examiners.
*(Added by L.1991, chap. 14(193), eff. 9/1/91.)*

**§466.025. Inspection.**
(a) An authorized agent may enter the facility of a person who is an applicant for a permit or who is a permit holder during any hours in which the facility is in operation for the purpose of inspecting the facility to determine:
(1) if the person meets the standards set in the rules of the board for the issuance of a permit; or
(2) if a person who holds a permit is in compliance with this chapter, the standards set in the rules of the board for the operation of a facility, any special provisions contained in the permit, or an order of the commissioner or the department.

(b) The inspection may be conducted without prior notice to the applicant or the permit holder.

(c) The authorized agent shall provide the applicant or permit holder with a copy of the inspection report. An inspection report shall be made a part of the applicant's submission file or the permit holder's compliance record.
*(Added by L.1991, chap. 14(193), eff. 9/1/91.)*

### §466.026. Multiple enrollment prevention.

The department shall work with representatives from permitted narcotic treatment programs in this state to develop recommendations for a plan to prevent the simultaneous multiple enrollment of persons in narcotic treatment programs. The board may adopt rules to implement these recommendations. *(Added by L.1991, chap. 14(193), eff. 9/1/91.)*

### §466.027. Denial, suspension, or revocation of permit.

(a) After notice to an applicant or a permit holder and after the opportunity for a hearing, the department may:

(1) deny an application of the person if the person fails to comply with this chapter or the rules establishing minimum standards for the issuance of a permit adopted under this chapter; or

(2) suspend or revoke the permit of a person who has violated this chapter, an order issued under this chapter, or a minimum standard required for the issuance of a permit.

(b) The board may adopt rules that establish the criteria for the denial, suspension, or revocation of a permit.

(c) Hearings, appeals from, and judicial review of final administrative decisions under this section shall be conducted according to the contested case provisions of Chapter 2001, Government Code and the board's formal hearing rules.

(d) This section does not prevent the informal reconsideration of a case before the setting of a hearing or before the issuance of the final administrative decision under this section. The program rules must contain provisions establishing the procedures for the initiation and conduct of the informal reconsideration by the department.
*(Redesignated and chgd. by L.1991, chap. 14(193); chgd. by L.1995, chap. 76(5.95)(49), eff. 9/1/95.)*

### §§466.028 to 466.040. *(Reserved.)*

## SUBCHAPTER C. ENFORCEMENT

### §466.041. Emergency orders.

(a) The commissioner or the commissioner's designee may issue an emergency order, either mandatory or prohibitory in nature, in relation to the operation of a permitted facility or the treatment of patients by the facility staff, in the department's jurisdiction. The order may be issued if the commissioner or the commissioner's designee determines that the treatment of patients by the staff of the permit holder creates or poses an immediate and serious threat to human life or health and other procedures available to the department to remedy or prevent the occurrence of the situation will result in an unreasonable delay.

(b) The commissioner or the commissioner's designee may issue the emergency order, including an emergency order suspending or revoking a permit issued by the department, without notice and hearing, if the commissioner or the commissioner's designee determines that action to be practicable under the circumstances.

(c) If an emergency order is issued without a hearing, the department shall determine a time and place for a hearing at which the emergency order is affirmed, modified, or set aside. The hearing shall be held under the contested case provisions of Chapter 2001, Government Code and the board's formal hearing rules.

(d) If the emergency order is issued to suspend or revoke the permit, the department shall ensure that treatment services for the patients are maintained at the same location until appropriate referrals to an alternate treatment program are made.
*(Redesignated and chgd. by L.1991, chap. 14(193); chgd. by L.1995, chap. 76(5.95)(49), eff. 9/1/95.)*

### §466.042. Injunction.

(a) The commissioner, the commissioner's designee, or an authorized agent may request the attorney general or a district, county, or municipal attorney to petition the district court for a temporary restraining order to restrain:

(1) a continuing violation of this chapter, a rule adopted under this chapter, or an order or permit issued under this chapter; or

(2) a threat of a continuing violation of this chapter, a rule, or an order or permit.

(b) To request a temporary restraining order, the commissioner, commissioner's designee, or an authorized agent must find that a person has violated, is violating, or is threatening to violate this chapter, a rule adopted under this chapter, or an order or permit issued under this chapter and:

(1) the violation or threatened violation creates an immediate threat to the health and safety of the public; or

(2) there is reasonable cause to believe that the permit holder or the staff of the permit holder is party to the diversion of a narcotic drug or drugs in violation of Chapter 481 (Texas Controlled Substances Act).

(c) On finding by the court that a person is violating or threatening to violate this chapter, a rule adopted under this chapter, or an order or permit issued under this chapter, the court shall grant the injunctive relief warranted by the facts.

(d) Venue for a suit brought under this section is in the county in which the violation or threat of violation is alleged to have occurred or in Travis County.
*(Redesignated and chgd. by L.1991, chap. 14(193), eff. 9/1/91.)*

### §466.043. Administrative penalty.

If a person violates this chapter, a rule adopted under this chapter, or an order or permit issued under this chapter, the commissioner may assess an administrative penalty against the person as provided by Chapter 431 (Texas Food, Drug, and Cosmetic Act). *(Redesignated and chgd. by L.1991, chap. 14(193), eff. 9/1/91.)*

### §466.044. Criminal penalty.

(a) A person commits an offense if the person operates a narcotic drug treatment program without a permit issued by the department.

(b) An offense under this section is a Class A misdemeanor.
*(Redesignated and chgd. by L.1991, chap. 14(193), eff. 9/1/91.)*

### §466.045. Civil penalty.

(a) If it appears that a person has violated this chapter, a rule adopted under this chapter, or an order or permit issued under this chapter, the commissioner may request the attorney general or the district, county, or municipal attorney of the municipality or county in which the violation occurred to institute a civil suit for the assessment and recovery of a civil penalty.

(b) The penalty may be in an amount not to exceed $10,000 for each violation.

(c) In determining the amount of the penalty, the court shall consider:

(1) the person's history of previous violations;

(2) the seriousness of the violation;

(3) any hazard to the health and safety of the public; and

(4) the demonstrated good faith of the person charged.

(d) A civil penalty recovered in a suit instituted by the attorney general under this chapter shall be deposited in the state treasury to the credit of the General Revenue Fund. A civil penalty recovered in a suit instituted by a local government under this chapter shall be paid to the local government.
*(Redesignated and chgd. by L.1991, chap. 14(193), eff. 9/1/91.)*

# SUBTITLE C. SUBSTANCE ABUSE REGULATION AND CRIMES

# CHAPTER 481. TEXAS CONTROLLED SUBSTANCES ACT

## SUBCHAPTER A. GENERAL PROVISIONS

## SUBCHAPTER B. SCHEDULES



## SUBCHAPTER C. REGULATION OF MANUFACTURE, DISTRIBUTION, AND DISPENSATION OF CONTROLLED SUBSTANCES, CHEMICAL PRECURSORS, AND CHEMICAL LABORATORY APPARATUS





**So in original. Probably should be "481.062.".*

## SUBCHAPTER D. OFFENSES AND PENALTIES

## SUBCHAPTER E. FORFEITURE



## SUBCHAPTER F. INSPECTIONS, EVIDENCE, AND MISCELLANEOUS LAW ENFORCEMENT PROVISIONS

## SUBCHAPTER G. THERAPEUTIC RESEARCH PROGRAM



## SUBCHAPTER A. GENERAL PROVISIONS

### §481.001. Short title.

This chapter may be cited as the Texas Controlled Substances Act. *(Added by L.1989, chap. 678(1), eff. 9/1/89.)*



### §481.002. Definitions.

In this chapter:

(1) "Administer" means to directly apply a controlled substance by injection, inhalation, ingestion, or other means to the body of a patient or research subject by:

(A) a practitioner or an agent of the practitioner in the presence of the practitioner; or

(B) the patient or research subject at the direction and in the presence of a practitioner.

(2) "Agent" means an authorized person who acts on behalf of or at the direction of a manufacturer, distributor, or dispenser. The term does not include a common or contract carrier, public warehouseman, or employee of a carrier or warehouseman acting in the usual and lawful course of employment.

(3) "Commissioner" means the commissioner of public health or the commissioner's designee.

(4) "Controlled premises" means:

(A) a place where original or other records or documents required under this chapter are kept or are required to be kept; or

(B) a place, including a factory, warehouse, other establishment, or conveyance, where a person registered under this chapter may lawfully hold, manufacture, distribute, dispense, administer, possess, or otherwise dispose of a controlled substance or other item governed by this chapter, including a chemical precursor and a chemical laboratory apparatus.

(5) "Controlled substance" means a substance, including a drug, an adulterant, a dilutant, and an immediate precursor, listed in Schedules I through V or Penalty Groups 1, 1-A, or 2 through 4. The term includes the aggregate weight of any mixture, solution, or other substance containing a controlled substance.

(6) "Controlled substance analogue" means:

(A) a substance with a chemical structure substantially similar to the chemical structure of a controlled substance in Schedule I or II or Penalty Group 1, 1-A, or 2; or

(B) a substance specifically designed to produce an effect substantially similar to, or greater than, the effect of a controlled substance in Schedule I or II or Penalty Group 1, 1-A, or 2.

(7) "Counterfeit substance" means a controlled substance that, without authorization, bears or is in a container or has a label that bears an actual or simulated trademark, trade name, or other identifying mark, imprint, number, or device of a manufacturer, distributor, or dispenser other than the person who in fact manufactured, distributed, or dispensed the substance.

(8) "Deliver" means to transfer, actually or constructively, to another a controlled substance, counterfeit substance, or drug paraphernalia, regardless of whether there is an agency relationship. The term includes offering to sell a controlled substance, counterfeit substance, or drug paraphernalia.

(9) "Delivery" or "drug transaction" means the act of delivering.

(10) "Designated agent" means an individual designated under Section 481.073 to communicate a practitioner's instructions to a pharmacist.

(11) "Director" means the director of the Department of Public Safety or an employee of the department designated by the director.

(12) "Dispense" means the delivery of a controlled substance in the course of professional practice or research, by a practitioner or person acting under the lawful order of a practitioner, to an ultimate user or research subject. The term includes the prescribing, administering, packaging, labeling, or compounding necessary to prepare the substance for delivery.

(13) "Dispenser" means a practitioner, institutional practitioner, pharmacist, or pharmacy that dispenses a controlled substance.

(14) "Distribute" means to deliver a controlled substance other than by administering or dispensing the substance.

(15) "Distributor" means a person who distributes.

(16) "Drug" means a substance, other than a device or a component, part, or accessory of a device, that is:

(A) recognized as a drug in the official United States Pharmacopoeia, official Homeopathic Pharmacopoeia of the United States, official National Formulary, or a supplement to either pharmacopoeia or the formulary;

(B) intended for use in the diagnosis, cure, mitigation, treatment, or prevention of disease in man or animals;

(C) intended to affect the structure or function of the body of man or animals but is not food; or

(D) intended for use as a component of a substance described by Paragraph (A), (B), or (C).

(17) "Drug paraphernalia" means equipment, a product, or material that is used or intended for use in planting, propagating, cultivating, growing, harvesting, manufacturing, compounding, converting, producing, processing, preparing, testing, analyzing, packaging, repackaging, storing, containing, or concealing a controlled substance in violation of this chapter or in injecting, ingesting, inhaling, or otherwise introducing into the human body a controlled substance in violation of this chapter. The term includes:

(A) a kit used or intended for use in planting, propagating, cultivating, growing, or harvesting a species of plant that is a controlled substance or from which a controlled substance may be derived;

(B) a material, compound, mixture, preparation, or kit used or intended for use in manufacturing, compounding, converting, producing, processing, or preparing a controlled substance;

(C) an isomerization device used or intended for use in increasing the potency of a species of plant that is a controlled substance;

(D) testing equipment used or intended for use in identifying or in analyzing the strength, effectiveness, or purity of a controlled substance;

(E) a scale or balance used or intended for use in weighing or measuring a controlled substance;

(F) a dilutant or adulterant, such as quinine hydrochloride, mannitol, inositol, nicotinamide, dextrose, lactose, or absorbent, blotter-type material, that is used or intended to be used to increase the amount or weight of or to transfer a controlled substance regardless of whether the dilutant or adulterant diminishes the efficacy of the controlled substance;

(G) a separation gin or sifter used or intended for use in removing twigs and seeds from or in otherwise cleaning or refining marihuana;

(H) a blender, bowl, container, spoon, or mixing device used or intended for use in compounding a controlled substance;

(I) a capsule, balloon, envelope, or other container used or intended for use in packaging small quantities of a controlled substance;

(J) a container or other object used or intended for use in storing or concealing a controlled substance;

(K) a hypodermic syringe, needle, or other object used or intended for use in parenterally injecting a controlled substance into the human body; and

(L) an object used or intended for use in ingesting, inhaling, or otherwise introducing marihuana, cocaine, hashish, or hashish oil into the human body, including:

(i) a metal, wooden, acrylic, glass, stone, plastic, or ceramic pipe with or without a screen, permanent screen, hashish head, or punctured metal bowl;

(ii) a water pipe;

(iii) a carburetion tube or device;

(iv) a smoking or carburetion mask;

(v) a chamber pipe;

(vi) a carburetor pipe;

(vii) an electric pipe;

(viii) an air-driven pipe;

(ix) a chillum;

(x) a bong; or

(xi) an ice pipe or chiller.

(18) "Federal Controlled Substances Act" means the Federal Comprehensive Drug Abuse Prevention and Control Act of 1970 (21 U.S.C. Section 801 et seq.) or its successor statute.

(19) "Federal Drug Enforcement Administration" means the Drug Enforcement Administration of the United States Department of Justice or its successor agency.

(20) "Hospital" means:

(A) a general or special hospital as defined by Section 241.003 (Texas Hospital Licensing Law); or

(B) an ambulatory surgical center licensed by the Texas Department of Health and approved by the federal government to perform surgery paid by Medicaid on patients admitted for a period of not more than 24 hours.

(21) "Human consumption" means the injection, inhalation, ingestion, or application of a substance to or into a human body.

(22) "Immediate precursor" means a substance the commissioner finds to be and by rule designates as being:

(A) a principal compound commonly used or produced primarily for use in the manufacture of a controlled substance;

(B) a substance that is an immediate chemical intermediary used or likely to be used in the manufacture of a controlled substance; and

(C) a substance the control of which is necessary to prevent, curtail, or limit the manufacture of a controlled substance.

(23) "Institutional practitioner" means an intern, resident physician, fellow, or person in an equivalent professional position who:

(A) is not licensed by the appropriate state professional licensing board;

(B) is enrolled in a bona fide professional training program in a base hospital or institutional training facility registered by the Federal Drug Enforcement Administration; and

(C) is authorized by the base hospital or institutional training facility to administer, dispense, or prescribe controlled substances.

(24) "Lawful possession" means the possession of a controlled substance that has been obtained in accordance with state or federal law.

(25) "Manufacture" means the production, preparation, propagation, compounding, conversion, or processing of a controlled substance other than marihuana, directly or indirectly by extraction from substances of natural origin, independently by means of chemical synthesis, or by a combination of extraction and chemical synthesis, and includes the packaging or repackaging of the substance or labeling or relabeling of its container. However, the term does not include the preparation, compounding, packaging, or labeling of a controlled substance:

(A) by a practitioner as an incident to the practitioner's administering or dispensing a controlled substance in the course of professional practice; or

(B) by a practitioner, or by an authorized agent under the supervision of the practitioner, for or as an incident to research, teaching, or chemical analysis and not for delivery.

(26) "Marihuana" means the plant Cannabis sativa L., whether growing or not, the seeds of that plant, and every compound, manufacture, salt, derivative, mixture, or preparation of that plant or its seeds. The term does not include:

(A) the resin extracted from a part of the plant or a compound, manufacture, salt, derivative, mixture, or preparation of the resin;

(B) the mature stalks of the plant or fiber produced from the stalks;

(C) oil or cake made from the seeds of the plant;

(D) a compound, manufacture, salt, derivative, mixture, or preparation of the mature stalks, fiber, oil, or cake; or

(E) the sterilized seeds of the plant that are incapable of germination.

(27) "Medical purpose" means the use of a controlled substance for relieving or curing a mental or physical disease or infirmity.

(28) "Medication order" means an order from a practitioner to dispense a drug to a patient in a hospital for immediate administration while the patient is in the hospital or for emergency use on the patient's release from the hospital.

(29) "Narcotic drug" means any of the following, produced directly or indirectly by extraction from substances of vegetable origin, independently by means of chemical synthesis, or by a combination of extraction and chemical synthesis:

(A) opium and opiates, and a salt, compound, derivative, or preparation of opium or opiates;

(B) a salt, compound, isomer, derivative, or preparation of a salt, compound, isomer, or derivative that is chemically equivalent or identical to a substance listed in Paragraph (A) other than the isoquinoline alkaloids of opium;

(C) opium poppy and poppy straw; or

(D) cocaine, including:

(i) its salts, its optical, position, or geometric isomers, and the salts of those isomers;

(ii) coca leaves and a salt, compound, derivative, or preparation of coca leaves; and

(iii) a salt, compound, derivative, or preparation of a salt, compound, or derivative that is chemically equivalent or identical to a substance described by Subparagraph (i) or (ii), other than decocainized coca leaves or extractions of coca leaves that do not contain cocaine or ecgonine.

(30) "Opiate" means a substance that has an addiction-forming or addiction-sustaining liability similar to morphine or is capable of conversion into a drug having addiction-forming or addiction-sustaining liability. The term includes its racemic and levorotatory forms. The term does not include, unless specifically designated as controlled under Subchapter B, the dextrorotatory isomer of 3-methoxy-n-methylmorphinan and its salts (dextromethorphan).

(31) "Opium poppy" means the plant of the species Papaver somniferum L., other than its seeds.

(32) "Patient" means a human for whom or an animal for which a drug is administered, dispensed, delivered, or prescribed by a practitioner.

(33) "Person" means an individual, corporation, government, business trust, estate, trust, partnership, association, or any other legal entity.

(34) "Pharmacist" means a person licensed by the Texas State Board of Pharmacy to practice pharmacy and who acts as an agent for a pharmacy.

(35) "Pharmacist-in-charge" means the pharmacist designated on a pharmacy license as the pharmacist who has the authority or responsibility for the pharmacy's compliance with this chapter and other laws relating to pharmacy.

(36) "Pharmacy" means a facility licensed by the Texas State Board of Pharmacy where a prescription for a controlled substance is received or processed in accordance with state or federal law.

(37) "Poppy straw" means all parts, other than the seeds, of the opium poppy, after mowing.

(38) "Possession" means actual care, custody, control, or management.

(39) "Practitioner" means:

(A) a physician, dentist, veterinarian, podiatrist, scientific investigator, or other person licensed, registered, or otherwise permitted to distribute, dispense, analyze, conduct research with respect to, or administer a controlled substance in the course of professional practice or research in this state;

(B) a pharmacy, hospital, or other institution licensed, registered, or otherwise permitted to distribute, dispense, conduct research with respect to, or administer a controlled substance in the course of professional practice or research in this state; or

(C) a person practicing in and licensed by another state as a physician, dentist, veterinarian, or podiatrist, having a current Federal Drug Enforcement Administration registration number, who may legally prescribe Schedule II, III, IV, or V controlled substances in that state.

(40) "Prescribe" means the act of a practitioner to authorize a controlled substance to be dispensed to an ultimate user.

(41) "Prescription" means an order by a practitioner to a pharmacist for a controlled substance for a particular patient that specifies:

(A) the date of issue;

(B) the name and address of the patient or, if the controlled substance is prescribed for an animal, the species of the animal and the name and address of its owner;

(C) the name and quantity of the controlled substance prescribed with the quantity shown numerically followed by the number written as a word if the order is written or, if the order is communicated orally or telephonically, with the quantity given by the practitioner and transcribed by the pharmacist numerically;

(D) directions for the use of the drug;

(E) the intended use of the drug unless the practitioner determines the furnishing of this information is not in the best interest of the patient; and

(F) the legibly printed or stamped name, address, Federal Drug Enforcement Administration registration number, and telephone number of the practitioner at the practitioner's usual place of business.

(42) "Principal place of business" means a location where a person manufactures, distributes, dispenses, analyzes, or possesses a controlled substance. The term does not include a location where a practitioner dispenses a controlled substance on an outpatient basis unless the controlled substance is stored at that location.

(43) "Production" includes the manufacturing, planting, cultivating, growing, or harvesting of a controlled substance.

(44) "Raw material" means a compound, material, substance, or equipment used or intended for use, alone or in any combination, in manufacturing a controlled substance.

(45) "Registrant" means a person who is registered under Section 481.063.

(46) "Substitution" means the dispensing of a drug or a brand of drug other than that which is ordered or prescribed.

(47) "Official prescription form" means a prescription form that contains the prescription information required by Section 481.075.

(48) "Ultimate user" means a person who has lawfully obtained and possesses a controlled substance for the person's own use, for the use of a member of the person's household, or for administering to an animal owned by the person or by a member of the person's household.

(49) "Adulterant or dilutant" means any material that increases the bulk or quantity of a controlled substance, regardless of its effect on the chemical activity of the controlled substance.

(50) "Abuse unit" means:

(A) except as provided by Paragraph (B):

(i) a single unit on or in any adulterant, dilutant, or similar carrier medium, including marked or perforated blotter paper, a tablet, gelatin wafer, sugar cube, or stamp, or other medium that contains any amount of a controlled substance listed in Penalty Group 1-A, if the unit is commonly used in abuse of that substance; or

(ii) each quarter-inch square section of paper, if the adulterant, dilutant, or carrier medium is paper not marked or perforated into individual abuse units; or

(B) if the controlled substance is in liquid form, 40 micrograms of the controlled substance including any adulterant or dilutant.

(51) *(Repealed by L.1999, chap. 145(5)(1), eff. 9/1/99.)*

(52) "Department" means the Department of Public Safety.

(53) *(Repealed by L.1999, chap. 145(5)(1), eff. 9/1/99.)*

(54) *(Repealed by L.1999, chap. 145(5)(1), eff. 9/1/99.)*

(55) *(Repealed by L.1999, chap. 145(5)(1), eff. 9/1/99.)*

*(Added by L.1989, chap. 678(1); chgd. by L.1989, chap. 1100(5.02(b)); L.1993, chaps. 351(27), 789(15), 900(2.01); L.1997, chap. 745(1), (2); L.1999, chap. 145(1), 145(5)(1), eff. 9/1/99.)*



### §481.003. Rules.

(a) The director may adopt rules to administer and enforce this chapter.

(b) The director by rule shall prohibit a person in this state, including a person regulated by the Texas Department of Insurance under the Insurance Code or the other insurance laws of this state, from using a practitioner's Federal Drug Enforcement Administration number for a purpose other than a purpose described by federal law or by this chapter. A person who violates a rule adopted under this subsection commits a Class C misdemeanor.

*(Added by L.1997, chap. 745(3); chgd. by L.1999, chap. 1266(1), eff. 9/1/99.)*

### §§481.004 to 481.030. *(Reserved.)*

## SUBCHAPTER B. SCHEDULES

### §481.031. Nomenclature.

Controlled substances listed in Schedules I through V and Penalty Groups 1 through 4 are included by whatever official, common, usual, chemical, or trade name they may be designated.

*(Added by L.1989, chap. 678(1); reenacted by L.1997, chap. 745(4), eff. 1/1/98.)*

### §481.032. Schedules.

(a) The commissioner shall establish and modify the following schedules of controlled substances under this subchapter: Schedule I, Schedule I-A, Schedule II, Schedule III, Schedule IV, and Schedule V.

(b) A reference to a schedule in this chapter means the most current version of the schedule established or altered by the commissioner under this subchapter and published in the Texas Register on or after January 1, 1998.

*(Added by L.1997, chap. 745(4), eff. 1/1/98.)*

### §481.033. Exclusion from schedules and application of act.

(a) A nonnarcotic substance is excluded from Schedules I through V if the substance may lawfully be sold over the counter without a prescription, under the Federal Food, Drug, and Cosmetic Act (21 U.S.C. Section 301 et seq.).

(b) The commissioner may not include in the schedules:

(1) a substance described by Subsection (a); or

(2) distilled spirits, wine, malt beverages, or tobacco.

(c) A compound, mixture, or preparation containing a stimulant substance listed in Schedule II and having a potential for abuse associated with a stimulant effect on the central nervous system is excepted from the application of this chapter if the compound, mixture, or preparation contains one or more active medicinal ingredients not having a stimulant effect on the central nervous system and if the admixtures are included in combinations, quantity, proportions, or concentrations that vitiate the potential for abuse of the substance having a stimulant effect on the central nervous system.

(d) A compound, mixture, or preparation containing a depressant substance listed in Schedule III or IV and having a potential for abuse associated with a depressant effect on the central nervous system is excepted from the application of this chapter if the compound, mixture, or preparation contains one or more active medicinal ingredients not having a depressant effect on the central nervous system and if the admixtures are included in combinations, quantity, proportions, or concentrations that vitiate the potential for abuse of the substance having a depressant effect on the central nervous system.

(e) A nonnarcotic prescription substance is exempted from Schedules I through V and the application of this chapter to the same extent that the substance has been exempted from the application of the Federal Controlled Substances Act, if the substance is listed as an exempt prescription product under 21 C.F.R. Section 1308.32 and its subsequent amendments.

(f) A chemical substance that is intended for laboratory, industrial, educational, or special research purposes and not for general administration to a human being or other animal is exempted from Schedules I through V and the application of this chapter to the same extent that the substance has been exempted from the application of the Federal Controlled Substances Act, if the substance is listed as an exempt chemical preparation under 21 C.F.R. Section 1308.24 and its subsequent amendments.

(g) An anabolic steroid product, which has no significant potential for abuse due to concentration, preparation, mixture, or delivery system, is exempted from Schedules I through V and the application of this chapter to the same extent that the substance has been exempted from the application of the Federal Controlled Substances Act, if the substance is listed as an exempt anabolic steroid product under 21 C.F.R. Section 1308.34 and its subsequent amendments.

*(Added by L.1989, chap. 678(1); chgd. by L.1993, chap. 532(1); renumbered from section 481.037 and chgd. by L.1997, chap. 745(4), eff. 1/1/98.)*

**§481.034. Establishment and modification of schedules by commissioner.**

(a) The commissioner shall annually establish the schedules of controlled substances. These annual schedules shall include the complete list of all controlled substances from the previous schedules and modifications in the federal schedules of controlled substances as required by Subsection (g). Any further additions to and deletions from these schedules, any rescheduling of substances and any other modifications made by the commissioner to these schedules of controlled substances shall be made:

(1) in accordance with Section 481.035;

(2) in a manner consistent with this subchapter; and

(3) with approval of the Texas Board of Health.

(b) Except for alterations in schedules required by Subsection (g), the commissioner may not make an alteration in a schedule unless the commissioner holds a public hearing on the matter in Austin and obtains approval from the Texas Board of Health.

(c) The commissioner may not:

(1) add a substance to the schedules if the substance has been deleted from the schedules by the legislature;

(2) delete a substance from the schedules if the substance has been added to the schedules by the legislature; or

(3) reschedule a substance if the substance has been placed in a schedule by the legislature.

(d) In making a determination regarding a substance, the commissioner shall consider:

(1) the actual or relative potential for its abuse;

(2) the scientific evidence of its pharmacological effect, if known;

(3) the state of current scientific knowledge regarding the substance;

(4) the history and current pattern of its abuse;

(5) the scope, duration, and significance of its abuse;

(6) the risk to the public health;

(7) the potential of the substance to produce psychological or physiological dependence liability; and

(8) whether the substance is an immediate precursor of a substance already controlled under this chapter.

 Zt

(e) After considering the factors listed in Subsection (d), the commissioner shall make findings with respect to those factors and adopt a rule controlling the substance if the commissioner finds the substance has a potential for abuse.

(f) If the commissioner designates a substance as an immediate precursor, a substance that is a precursor of the controlled precursor is not subject to control solely because it is a precursor of the controlled precursor.

(g) Except as otherwise provided by this subsection, if a substance is designated, rescheduled, or deleted as a controlled substance under federal law and notice of that fact is given to the commissioner, the commissioner similarly shall control the substance under this chapter. After the expiration of a 30-day period beginning on the day after the date of publication in the Federal Register of a final order designating a substance as a controlled substance or rescheduling or deleting a substance, the commissioner similarly shall designate, reschedule, or delete the substance, unless the commissioner objects during the period. If the commissioner objects, the commissioner shall publish the reasons for the objection and give all interested parties an opportunity to be heard. At the conclusion of the hearing, the commissioner shall publish a decision, which is final unless altered by statute. On publication of an objection by the commissioner, control as to that particular substance under this chapter is stayed until the commissioner publishes the commissioner's decision.

(h) Not later than the 10th day after the date on which the commissioner designates, deletes, or reschedules a substance under Subsection (a), the commissioner shall give written notice of that action to the director and to each state licensing agency having jurisdiction over practitioners.
*(Added by L.1989, chap. 678(1); renumbered from section 481.038 and chgd. by L.1997, chap. 745(4), eff. 1/1/98.)*



### §481.035. Findings.

(a) The commissioner shall place a substance in Schedule I if the commissioner finds that the substance:

(1) has a high potential for abuse; and

(2) has no accepted medical use in treatment in the United States or lacks accepted safety for use in treatment under medical supervision.

(b) The commissioner shall place a substance in Schedule II if the commissioner finds that:

(1) the substance has a high potential for abuse;

(2) the substance has currently accepted medical use in treatment in the United States; and

(3) abuse of the substance may lead to severe psychological or physical dependence.

(c) The commissioner shall place a substance in Schedule III if the commissioner finds that:

(1) the substance has a potential for abuse less than that of the substances listed in Schedules I and II;

(2) the substance has currently accepted medical use in treatment in the United States; and

(3) abuse of the substance may lead to moderate or low physical dependence or high psychological dependence.

(d) The commissioner shall place a substance in Schedule IV if the commissioner finds that:

(1) the substance has a lower potential for abuse than that of the substances listed in Schedule III;

(2) the substance has currently accepted medical use in treatment in the United States; and

(3) abuse of the substance may lead to a more limited physical or psychological dependence than that of the substances listed in Schedule III.

(e) The commissioner shall place a substance in Schedule V if the commissioner finds that the substance:

(1) has a lower potential for abuse than that of the substances listed in Schedule IV;

(2) has currently accepted medical use in treatment in the United States; and

(3) may lead to a more limited physical or psychological dependence liability than that of the substances listed in Schedule IV.
*(Added by L.1989, chap. 678(1); renumbered from section 481.039 by L.1997, chap. 745(4), eff. 1/1/98.)*

### §481.036. Publication of schedules.

(a) The commissioner shall publish the schedules by filing a certified copy of the schedules with the secretary of state for publication in the Texas Register not later than the fifth working day after the date the commissioner takes action under this subchapter.

(b) Each published schedule must show changes, if any, made in the schedule since its latest publication.

(c) An action by the commissioner that establishes or modifies a schedule under this subchapter may take effect not earlier than the 21st day after the date on which the schedule or modification is published in the Texas Register unless an emergency exists that necessitates earlier action to avoid an imminent hazard to the public safety.
*(Added by L.1989, chap. 678(1); renumbered from section 481.040 and chgd. by L.1997, chap. 745(4), eff. 1/1/98.)*

**§§481.037 to 481.060.** *(Reserved.)*

## SUBCHAPTER C. REGULATION OF MANUFACTURE, DISTRIBUTION, AND DISPENSATION OF CONTROLLED SUBSTANCES, CHEMICAL PRECURSORS, AND CHEMICAL LABORATORY APPARATUS

### §481.061. Registration required.

(a) Except as otherwise provided by this chapter, a person who is not a registrant may not manufacture, distribute, prescribe, possess, analyze, or dispense a controlled substance in this state.

(b) A person who is registered by the director to manufacture, distribute, analyze, dispense, or conduct research with a controlled substance may possess, manufacture, distribute, analyze, dispense, or conduct research with that substance to the extent authorized by the person's registration and in conformity with this chapter.

(c) A separate registration is required at each principal place of business or professional practice where the applicant manufactures, distributes, analyzes, dispenses, or possesses a controlled substance. However, the director may not require separate registration for a practitioner engaged in research with a nonnarcotic controlled substance listed in Schedules II through V if the registrant is already registered under this subchapter in another capacity.
*(Chgd. by L.1989, chap. 678(1); L.1997, chap. 745(5), eff. 1/1/98.)*

### *§461.062. Exemptions.

(a) The following persons are not required to register and may possess a controlled substance under this chapter:

(1) an agent or employee of a registered manufacturer, distributor, analyzer, or dispenser of the controlled substance acting in the usual course of business or employment;

(2) a common or contract carrier, a warehouseman, or an employee of a carrier or warehouseman whose possession of the controlled substance is in the usual course of business or employment;

(3) an ultimate user or a person in possession of the controlled substance under a lawful order of a practitioner or in lawful possession of the controlled substance if it is listed in Schedule V;

(4) an officer or employee of this state, another state, or the United States who is lawfully engaged in the enforcement of a law relating to a controlled substance or drug or to a customs law and authorized to possess the controlled substance in the discharge of the person's official duties; or

(5) if the substance is tetrahydrocannabinol or one of its derivatives:

(A) a Texas Department of Health official, a medical school researcher, or a research program participant possessing the substance as authorized under Subchapter G; or

(B) a practitioner or an ultimate user possessing the substance as a participant in a federally approved therapeutic research program that the commissioner has reviewed and found, in writing, to contain a medically responsible research protocol.

(b) The director by rule may waive the requirement for registration of certain manufacturers, distributors, or dispensers if the director finds it consistent with the public health and safety and if the attorney general of the United States has issued a similar waiver under the Federal Controlled Substances Act.
*(Added by L.1989, chap. 678(1); chgd. by L.1997, chap. 745(6), eff. 1/1/98.)*
**So in original. Probably should be "§481.062".*

### §481.0621. Exceptions.

(a) This subchapter does not apply to an educational or research program of a school district or a public or private institution of higher education. This subchapter does not apply to a manufacturer, wholesaler, retailer, or other person who sells, transfers, or furnishes materials covered by this subchapter to those educational or research programs.

(b) The department and the Texas Higher Education Coordinating Board shall adopt a memorandum of understanding that establishes the responsibilities of the board, the department, and the public or private institutions of higher education in implementing and maintaining a program for reporting information concerning controlled substances, controlled substance analogues, chemical precursors, and chemical laboratory apparatus used in educational or research activities of institutions of higher education.

(c) The department and the Texas Education Agency shall adopt a memorandum of understanding that establishes the responsibilities of the agency, the department, and school districts in implementing and maintaining a program for reporting information concerning controlled substances, controlled substance analogues, chemical precursors, and chemical laboratory apparatus used in educational or research activities of those schools and school districts.

*(Added by L.1989, chap. 1100(5.02(e)); chgd. by L.1997, chaps. 165(6.45), 745(7), eff. 9/1/97, 1/1/98, respectively.)*



### §481.063. Registration application; issuance or denial.

(a) The director may refuse to issue a registration to a person to manufacture, distribute, analyze, or conduct research with a controlled substance if the person fails or refuses to provide to the director a consent form signed by the person granting the director the right to inspect the person's controlled premises and any record, controlled substance, or other item covered by this chapter.

(b) The director may not issue a registration to a person to dispense a controlled substance unless the director receives a consent form signed by the person granting the director the right to inspect records as required by this chapter.

(c) The director shall register a person to manufacture, distribute, or analyze a controlled substance listed in Schedules II through V if:

(1) the person furnishes the director evidence that the person is registered for that purpose under the Federal Controlled Substances Act;

(2) the person has made proper application and paid the applicable fee; and

(3) the person has not been found by the director to have violated a provision of Subsection (e).

(d) The director shall register a person to dispense or conduct research with a controlled substance listed in Schedules II through V if the person:

(1) is a practitioner licensed under the laws of this state;

(2) has made proper application and paid the applicable fee; and

(3) has not been found by the director to have violated a provision of Subsection (e).

(e) An application for registration to manufacture, distribute, analyze, dispense, or conduct research with a controlled substance may be denied on a finding that the applicant:

(1) has furnished material information in an application filed under this chapter that the applicant knows is false or fraudulent;

(2) has been convicted of or placed on community supervision or other probation for:

(A) a felony;

(B) a violation of this chapter or of Chapters 482-485; or

(C) an offense reasonably related to the registration sought;

(3) has voluntarily surrendered or has had suspended, denied, or revoked a registration or application for registration to manufacture, distribute, analyze, or dispense controlled substances under the Federal Controlled Substances Act;

(4) has had suspended, probated, or revoked a registration or a practitioner's license under the laws of this state or another state;

(5) has intentionally or knowingly failed to establish and maintain effective security controls against diversion of controlled substances into other than legitimate medical, scientific, or industrial channels as provided by federal regulations or laws, this chapter, or a rule adopted under this chapter;

(6) has intentionally or knowingly failed to maintain records required to be kept by this chapter or a rule adopted under this chapter;

(7) has refused to allow an inspection authorized by this chapter or a rule adopted under this chapter;

(8) has intentionally or knowingly violated this chapter or a rule adopted under this chapter; or

(9) has voluntarily surrendered a registration that has not been reinstated.

(f) The director may inspect the premises or establishment of an applicant for registration in accordance with this chapter.

(g) A registration is valid until the first anniversary of the date of issuance and may be renewed annually under rules adopted by the director, unless a rule provides for a longer period of validity or renewal.

(h) Chapter 2001, Government Code does not apply to a denial, suspension, or revocation of a registration under Subsection (e)(3).

(i) For good cause shown, the director may probate the denial of an application for registration. If a denial of an application is probated, the director may require the person to report regularly to the department on matters that are the basis of the probation or may limit activities of the person to those prescribed by the director, or both.

*(Added by L.1989, chap. 678(1); chgd. by L.1989, chap. 1100(5.02)(f); L.1993, chap. 790(19); L.1995, chap. 76(5.95)(49); L.1997, chap. 745(8), eff. 1/1/98.)*

### §481.064. Registration fees.

(a) The director may charge an annual registration fee of not more than $25. The director by rule shall set the amount of the fee at the amount that is necessary to cover the cost of administering and enforcing this subchapter. Except as provided by Subsection (b), registrants shall pay the fees to the director.

(b) The director may authorize a contract between the department and an appropriate state agency for the collection and remittance of the fees. The director by rule may provide for remittance of the fees collected by state agencies for the department.

(c) The director shall deposit the collected fees to the credit of the operator's and chauffeur's license account in the general revenue fund. The fees may be used only by the department in the administration or enforcement of this subchapter.

*(Added by L.1989, chap. 678(1); chgd. by L.1997, chap. 745(9), eff. 1/1/98.)*



### §481.065. Authorization for certain activities.

(a) The director may authorize the possession, distribution, planting, and cultivation of controlled substances by a person engaged in research, training animals to detect controlled substances, or designing or calibrating devices to detect controlled substances. A person who obtains an authorization under this subsection does not commit an offense involving the possession or distribution of controlled substances to the extent that the possession or distribution is authorized.

(b) A person may conduct research with or analyze substances listed in Schedule I in this state only if the person is a practitioner registered under federal law to conduct research with or analyze those substances and the person provides the director with evidence of federal registration.

*(Added by L.1989, chap. 678(1), eff. 9/1/89.)*

### §481.066. Voluntary surrender, cancellation, suspension, probation, or revocation of registration.

(a) The director may accept a voluntary surrender of a registration.

(b) The director may cancel, suspend, or revoke a registration, place on probation a person whose license has been suspended, or reprimand a registrant for a cause described by Section 481.063(e).

(c) The director may cancel a registration that was issued in error.

(d) The director may limit the cancellation, suspension, probation, or revocation to the particular schedule or controlled substance within a schedule for which grounds for cancellation, suspension, probation, or revocation exist.

(e) After accepting the voluntary surrender of a registration or ordering the cancellation, suspension, probation, or revocation of a registration, the director may seize or place under seal all controlled substances owned or possessed by the registrant under the authority of that registration. If the director orders the cancellation, suspension, probation, or revocation of a registration, a disposition may not be made of the seized or sealed substances until the time for administrative appeal of the order has elapsed or until all appeals have been concluded, except that the director may order the sale of perishable substances and deposit of the proceeds of the sale in a special interest-bearing account in the general revenue fund. When a surrender or cancellation, suspension, probation, or revocation order becomes final, all controlled substances may be forfeited to the state as provided under Subchapter E.

(f) The operation of a registrant in violation of this section is a public nuisance, and the director may apply to any court of competent jurisdiction for an injunction suspending the registration of the registrant.

(g) Chapter 2001, Government Code, applies to a proceeding under this section to the extent that that chapter does not conflict with this subchapter.

(h) The director shall promptly notify appropriate state agencies of an order accepting a voluntary surrender or canceling, suspending, probating, or revoking a registration and the forfeiture of controlled substances.

(i) The director shall give written notice to the applicant or registrant of the acceptance of a voluntary surrender of a registration, or of the cancellation, suspension, probation, revocation, or denial of a registration. The notice shall be sent by registered mail, return receipt requested, to the most current address of the applicant or registrant contained in the files of the Department of Public Safety.

(j) After a voluntary surrender, cancellation, suspension, probation, revocation, or denial of a registration, on petition of the applicant or former registrant, the director may issue or reinstate the registration for good cause shown by the petitioner.
*(Added by L.1989, chap. 678(1); chgd. by L.1997, chap. 745(10), eff. 1/1/98.)*



### §481.067. Records.

(a) A person who is registered to manufacture, distribute, analyze, or dispense a controlled substance shall keep records and maintain inventories in compliance with recordkeeping and inventory requirements of federal law and with additional rules the director adopts. Records and inventories must be retained for at least two years after the date they are made.

(b) The pharmacist-in-charge of a pharmacy shall maintain the records and inventories required by this section.
*(Added by L.1989, chap. 678(1), eff. 9/1/89.)*

### §481.068. Confidentiality.

(a) The director may authorize a person engaged in research on the use and effects of a controlled substance to withhold the names and other identifying characteristics of individuals who are the subjects of the research. A person who obtains the authorization may not be compelled in a civil, criminal, administrative, legislative, or other proceeding to identify the individuals who are the subjects of the research for which the authorization is obtained.

(b) Except as provided by Section 481.074(b) and 481.075(d), a practitioner engaged in authorized medical practice or research may not be required to furnish the name or identity of a patient or research subject to the Department of Public Safety, the director of the Texas Commission on Alcohol and Drug Abuse, or any other agency, public official, or law enforcement officer. A practitioner may not be compelled in a state or local civil, criminal, administrative, legislative, or other proceeding to furnish the name or identity of an individual that the practitioner is obligated to keep confidential.

(c) The director may not provide to a federal, state, or local law enforcement agency the name or identity of a patient or research subject whose identity could not be obtained under Subsection (b).
*(Added by L.1989, chap. 678(1), eff. 9/1/89.)*

### §481.069. Order forms.

A registrant may not distribute or order a controlled substance listed in Schedule I or II to or from another registrant except under an order form. A registrant complying with the federal law concerning order forms is in compliance with this section. *(Added by L.1989, chap. 678(1); chgd. by L.1989, chap. 1100(5.02)(g), eff. 9/1/89.)*

### §481.070. Administering or dispensing Schedule I controlled substance.

Except as permitted by this chapter, a person may not administer or dispense a controlled substance listed in Schedule I. *(Added by L.1989, chap. 678(1), eff. 9/1/89.)*

### §481.071. Medical purpose required before prescribing, dispensing, delivering, or administering controlled substance.

(a) A practitioner defined by Section 481.002(39)(A) may not prescribe, dispense, deliver, or administer a controlled substance or cause a controlled substance to be administered under the practitioner's direction and supervision except for a valid medical purpose and in the course of medical practice.

(b) An anabolic steroid or human growth hormone listed in Schedule III may only be:

(1) dispensed, prescribed, delivered, or administered by a practitioner, as defined by Section 481.002(39)(A), for a valid medical purpose and in the course of professional practice; or

(2) dispensed or delivered by a pharmacist according to a prescription issued by a practitioner, as defined by Section 481.002(39)(A) or (C), for a valid medical purpose and in the course of professional practice.

(c) For the purposes of Subsection (b), bodybuilding, muscle enhancement, or increasing muscle bulk or strength through the use of an anabolic steroid or human growth hormone listed in Schedule III by a person who is in good health is not a valid medical purpose.
*(Added by L.1989, chap. 678(1); chgd. by L.1989, chap. 1100(5.03)(b); L.1997, chap. 745(11), eff. 1/1/98.)*

**§481.072. Medical purpose required before distributing or dispensing Schedule V controlled substance.**

A person may not distribute or dispense a controlled substance listed in Schedule V except for a valid medical purpose. *(Added by L.1989, chap. 678(1), eff. 9/1/89.)*

**§481.073. Communication of prescriptions by agent.**

(a) Only a practitioner defined by Section 481.002(39)(A) and an agent designated in writing by the practitioner in accordance with rules adopted by the Department of Public Safety may communicate a prescription by telephone. A pharmacy that receives a telephonically communicated prescription shall promptly write the prescription and file and retain the prescription in the manner required by this subchapter. A practitioner who designates an agent to communicate prescriptions shall maintain the written designation of the agent in the practitioner's usual place of business and shall make the designation available for inspection by investigators for the Texas State Board of Medical Examiners, the State Board of Dental Examiners, the State Board of Veterinary Medical Examiners, and the Department of Public Safety. A practitioner who designates a different agent shall designate that agent in writing and maintain the designation in the same manner in which the practitioner initially designated an agent under this section.

(b) On the request of a pharmacist, a practitioner shall furnish a copy of the written designation authorized under Subsection (a).

(c) This section does not relieve a practitioner or the practitioner's designated agent from the requirement of Section 40, Texas Pharmacy Act (Article 4542a-1, Texas Civil Statutes). A practitioner is personally responsible for the actions of the designated agent in communicating a prescription to a pharmacist.
*(Added by L.1989, chap. 678(1), eff. 9/1/89.)*

**§481.074. Prescriptions.**

(a) A pharmacist may not:

(1) dispense or deliver a controlled substance or cause a controlled substance to be dispensed or delivered under the pharmacist's direction or supervision except under a valid prescription and in the course of professional practice;

(2) fill a prescription that is not prepared or issued as prescribed by this chapter;

(3) permit or allow a person who is not a licensed pharmacist or pharmacist intern to dispense, distribute, or in any other manner deliver a controlled substance even if under the supervision of a pharmacist, except that after the pharmacist or pharmacist intern has fulfilled his professional and legal responsibilities, a nonpharmacist may complete the actual cash or credit transaction and delivery; or

(4) permit the delivery of a controlled substance to any person not known to the pharmacist, the pharmacist intern, or the person authorized by the pharmacist to deliver the controlled substance without first requiring identification of the person taking possession of the controlled substance, except as provided by Subsection (n).

(b) Except in an emergency as defined by rule of the director or as provided by Section 481.075(j), a person may not dispense or administer a controlled substance listed in Schedule II without the written prescription of a practitioner on an official prescription form that meets the requirements of and is completed by the practitioner in accordance with Section 481.075, and if the controlled substance is to be dispensed, the practitioner must be registered under Section 481.063. In an emergency, a person may dispense or administer a controlled substance listed in Schedule II on the oral or telephonically communicated prescription of a practitioner. The person who administers or dispenses the substance shall:

(1) if the person is a prescribing practitioner or a pharmacist, promptly comply with Subsection (c); or

(2) if the person is not a prescribing practitioner or a pharmacist, promptly write the oral or telephonically communicated prescription and include in the written record of the prescription the name, address, and Federal Drug Enforcement Administration number of the prescribing practitioner, all information required to be provided by a practitioner under Section 481.075(e)(1), and all information required to be provided by a dispensing pharmacist under Section 481.075(e)(2).

(c) Not later than 72 hours after authorizing an emergency oral or telephonically communicated prescription, the prescribing practitioner shall cause a written prescription, completed in the manner required by Section 481.075, to be delivered in person or mailed to the dispensing pharmacist at the pharmacy where the prescription was dispensed. The envelope of a prescription delivered by mail must be postmarked not later than 72 hours after the prescription was authorized. On receipt of the prescription, the dispensing pharmacy shall file the transcription of the telephonically communicated prescription and the pharmacy copy. The pharmacist or the pharmacy that employs the pharmacist shall send all information required by the director, including any information required to complete an official prescription form, to the director by electronic transfer, a universal claim form customarily used by pharmaceutical service providers, or other form approved by the director not later than the 30th day after the date the prescription was dispensed.

(d) Except as specified in Subsections (e) and (f) of this section, a person may not fill a prescription for a controlled substance listed in Schedule II after the end of the seventh day after the date on which the prescription is issued. A person may not refill a prescription for a substance listed in Schedule II.

(e) The partial filling of a prescription for a controlled substance listed in Schedule II is permissible, if the pharmacist is unable to supply the full quantity called for in a written or emergency oral prescription and the pharmacist makes a notation of the quantity supplied on the face of the written prescription or written record of the emergency oral prescription. The remaining portion of the prescription may be filled within 72 hours of the first partial filling; however, if the remaining portion is not or cannot be filled within the 72-hour period, the pharmacist shall so notify the prescribing individual practitioner. No further quantity may be supplied beyond 72 hours without a new prescription.

(f) A prescription for a Schedule II controlled substance written for a patient in a long-term care facility (LTCF) or for a patient with a medical diagnosis documenting a terminal illness may be filled in partial quantities to include individual dosage units. If there is any question about whether a patient may be classified as having a terminal illness, the pharmacist must contact the practitioner prior to partially filling the prescription. Both the pharmacist and the practitioner have a corresponding responsibility to assure that the controlled substance is for a terminally ill patient. The pharmacist must record the prescription on an official prescription form and must indicate on the form whether the patient is "terminally ill" or an "LTCF patient." A prescription that is partially filled and does not contain the notation "terminally ill" or "LTCF patient" shall be deemed to have been filled in violation of this Act. For each partial filling, the dispensing pharmacist shall record on the back of the official prescription form the date of the partial filling, the quantity dispensed, the remaining quantity authorized to be dispensed, and the identification of the dispensing pharmacist. Prior to any subsequent partial filling, the pharmacist is to determine that the additional partial filling is necessary. The total quantity of Schedule II controlled substances dispensed in all partial fillings must not exceed the total quantity prescribed. Schedule II prescriptions for patients in a long-term care facility or patients with a medical diagnosis documenting a terminal illness shall be valid for a period not to exceed 30 days from the issue date unless sooner terminated by discontinuance of the medication.

(g) A person may not dispense a controlled substance in Schedule III or IV that is a prescription drug under the Federal Food, Drug, and Cosmetic Act (21 U.S.C. Section 301 et seq.) without a written, oral, or telephonically communicated prescription of a practitioner defined by Section 481.002(39)(A), except that the practitioner may dispense the substance directly to an ultimate user. A prescription for a controlled substance listed in Schedule III or IV may not be filled or refilled later than six months after the date on which the prescription is issued and may not be refilled more than five times, unless the prescription is renewed by the practitioner.

(h) A pharmacist may dispense a controlled substance listed in Schedule III, IV, or V under an original written prescription issued by a practitioner defined by Section 481.002(39)(C) and only if the pharmacist determines that the prescription was issued for a valid medical purpose and in the course of professional practice. A prescription issued under this subsection may not be filled or refilled later than six months after the date the prescription is issued, and a prescription authorized to be refilled on the original prescription may not be refilled more than five times.

(i) A person may not dispense a controlled substance listed in Schedule V and containing 200 milligrams or less of codeine, or any of its salts, per 100 milliliters or per 100 grams, or containing 100 milligrams or less of dihydrocodeine, or any of its salts, per 100 milliliters or per 100 grams, without the prescription of a practitioner defined by Section 481.002(39)(A), except that a practitioner may dispense the substance directly to an ultimate user. A prescription issued under this subsection may not be filled or refilled later than six months after the date the prescription is issued and may not be refilled more than five times, unless the prescription is renewed by the practitioner.

(j) A practitioner or institutional practitioner may not allow a patient, on the patient's release from the hospital, to possess a controlled substance prescribed by the practitioner unless:

(1) the substance was dispensed under a medication order while the patient was admitted to the hospital;

(2) the substance is in a properly labeled container; and

(3) the patient possesses not more than a seven-day supply of the substance.

(k) A prescription for a controlled substance must show:

(1) the quantity of the substance prescribed:

(A) numerically, followed by the number written as a word, if the prescription is written; or

(B) if the prescription is communicated orally or telephonically, as transcribed by the receiving pharmacist;

(2) the date of issue;

(3) the name and address of the patient or, if the controlled substance is prescribed for an animal, the species of the animal and the name and address of its owner;

(4) the name and strength of the controlled substance prescribed;

(5) the directions for use of the controlled substance;

(6) the intended use of the substance prescribed unless the practitioner determines the furnishing of this information is not in the best interest of the patient; and

(7) the legibly printed or stamped name, address, Federal Drug Enforcement Administration registration number, and telephone number of the practitioner at the practitioner's usual place of business.

(*l*) A pharmacist may exercise his professional judgment in refilling a prescription for a controlled substance in Schedule III, IV, or V without the authorization of the prescribing practitioner provided:

(1) failure to refill the prescription might result in an interruption of a therapeutic regimen or create patient suffering;

(2) either:

(A) a natural or manmade disaster has occurred which prohibits the pharmacist from being able to contact the practitioner; or

(B) the pharmacist is unable to contact the practitioner after reasonable effort;

(3) the quantity of prescription drug dispensed does not exceed a 72-hour supply;

(4) the pharmacist informs the patient or the patient's agent at the time of dispensing that the refill is being provided without such authorization and that authorization of the practitioner is required for future refills; and

(5) the pharmacist informs the practitioner of the emergency refill at the earliest reasonable time.

(m) A pharmacist may permit the delivery of a controlled substance by an authorized delivery person, by a person known to the pharmacist, a pharmacist intern, or the authorized delivery person, or by mail to the person or address of the person authorized by the prescription to receive the controlled substance. If a pharmacist permits delivery of a controlled substance under this subsection, the pharmacist shall retain in the records of the pharmacy for a period of not less than two years:

(1) the name of the authorized delivery person, if delivery is made by that person;

(2) the name of the person known to the pharmacist, a pharmacist intern, or the authorized delivery person if delivery is made by that person; or

(3) the mailing address to which delivery is made, if delivery is made by mail.

(n) A pharmacist may permit the delivery of a controlled substance to a person not known to the pharmacist, a pharmacist intern, or the authorized delivery person without first requiring the identification of the person to whom the controlled substance is delivered if the pharmacist determines that an emergency exists and that the controlled substance is needed for the immediate well-being of the patient for whom the controlled substance is prescribed. If a pharmacist permits delivery of a controlled substance under this subsection, the pharmacist shall retain in the records of the pharmacy for a period of not less than two years all information relevant to the delivery known to the pharmacist, including the name, address, and date of birth or age of the person to whom the controlled substance is delivered.

*(Added by L.1989, chap. 678(1); chgd. by L.1989, chap. 1100(5.02)(h); L.1991, chaps. 615(10), 761(6); L.1993, chaps. 351(28), 789(16); L.1997, chap. 745(12), (13); L.1999, chap. 145(2), eff. 9/1/99.)*

**§481.075. Official prescription program.**

(a) A practitioner who prescribes a controlled substance listed in Schedule II shall, except as provided by rule adopted under Section 481.0761, record the prescription on an official prescription form that includes the information required by this section.

(b) Each official prescription form must be sequentially numbered.

(c) The director shall issue official prescription forms to practitioners for a fee covering the actual cost of printing, processing, and mailing the forms at 100 a package. Before mailing or otherwise delivering prescription forms to a practitioner, the director shall print on each form the number of the form and any other information the director determines is necessary.

(d) A person may not obtain an official prescription form unless the person is a practitioner as defined by Section 481.002(39)(A) or an institutional practitioner.

(e) Each official prescription form used to prescribe a Schedule II controlled substance must contain:

(1) information provided by the prescribing practitioner, including:

(A) the date the prescription is written;

(B) the controlled substance prescribed;

(C) the quantity of controlled substance prescribed, shown numerically followed by the number written as a word;

(D) the intended use of the controlled substance or the diagnosis for which it is prescribed and the instructions for use of the substance;

(E) the practitioner's name, address, and Federal Drug Enforcement Administration number; and

(F) the name, address, and date of birth or age of the person for whom the controlled substance is prescribed;

(2) information provided by the dispensing pharmacist, including the date the prescription is filled; and

(3) the signatures of the prescribing practitioner and the dispensing pharmacist.

(f) Not more than one prescription may be recorded on an official prescription form, except as provided by rule adopted under Section 481.0761.

(g) Except for oral prescriptions prescribed under Section 481.074(b), the prescribing practitioner shall:

(1) legibly fill in, or direct a designated agent to legibly fill in, on the official prescription form, each item of information required to be provided by the prescribing practitioner under Subsection (e)(1), unless the practioner* determines that:

**So in original. Probably should be "practitioner".*

(A) under rule adopted by the director for this purpose, it is unnecessary for the practitioner or the practitioner's agent to provide the patient identification number; or

(B) it is not in the best interest of the patient for the practitioner or practitioner's agent to provide information regarding the intended use of the controlled substance or the diagnosis for which it is prescribed; and

(2) sign the official prescription form and give the form to the person authorized to receive the prescription.

(h) In the case of an oral prescription prescribed under Section 481.074(b), the prescribing practitioner shall give the dispensing pharmacy the information needed to complete the form.

(i) Each dispensing pharmacist shall:

(1) fill in on the official prescription form each item of information given orally to the dispensing pharmacy under Subsection (h), the date the prescription is filled, and the dispensing pharmacist's signature;

(2) retain with the records of the pharmacy for at least two years:

(A) the official prescription form; and

(B) the name or other patient identification required by Section 481.074(m) or (n); and

(3) send all information required by the director, including any information required to complete an official prescription form, to the director by electronic transfer or another form approved by the director, including a universal claim form customarily used by pharmaceutical services providers, not later than the 30th day after the date the prescription is filled or not later than the 30th day after the completion of a prescription dispensed under Section 481.074(f).

(j) A medication order written for a patient who is admitted to a hospital at the time the medication order is written and filled is not required to be on a form that meets the requirements of this section.

(k) Not later than the 30th day after the date a practitioner's department registration number, Federal Drug Enforcement Administration number, or license to practice has been denied, suspended, canceled, surrendered, or revoked, the practitioner shall return to the department all official prescription forms in the practitioner's possession that have not been used for prescriptions.

(*l*) Each prescribing practitioner:

(1) may use an official prescription form only to prescribe a controlled substance;

(2) shall date or sign an official prescription form only on the date the prescription is issued; and

(3) shall take reasonable precautionary measures to ensure that an official prescription form issued to the practitioner is not used by another person to violate this subchapter or a rule adopted under this subchapter.

(m) A pharmacy in this state may fill a prescription for a controlled substance listed in Schedule II issued by a practitioner in another state if:

(1) a share of the pharmacy's business involves the dispensing and delivery or mailing of controlled substances;

(2) the prescription is issued by a prescribing practitioner in the other state in the ordinary course of practice; and

(3) the prescription is filled in compliance with a written plan providing the manner in which the pharmacy may fill a Schedule II prescription issued by a practitioner in another state that:

(A) is submitted by the pharmacy to the director; and

(B) is approved by the director in consultation with the Texas State Board of Pharmacy.

(n) *(Repealed by L.1999, chap. 145(5)(2), eff. 9/1/99.)*

*(Added by L.1989, chap. 678(1); chgd. by L.1989, chap. 1100(5.02)(i); L.1993, chap. 789(17); L.1997, chap. 745(14); L.1999, chap. 145(3), 145(5)(2), eff. 9/1/99.)*

## §481.076. Official prescription information.

(a) The director may not permit any person to have access to information submitted to the director under Section 481.075 except:

(1) an investigator for the Texas State Board of Medical Examiners, the Texas State Board of Podiatric Medical Examiners, the State Board of Dental Examiners, the State Board of Veterinary Medical Examiners, or the Texas State Board of Pharmacy;

(2) an authorized officer or member of the department engaged in the administration, investigation, or enforcement of this chapter or another law governing illicit drugs in this state or another state; or

(3) if the director finds that proper need has been shown to the director:

(A) a law enforcement or prosecutorial official engaged in the administration, investigation, or enforcement of this chapter or another law governing illicit drugs in this state or another state;

(B) a pharmacist or practitioner who is a physician, dentist, veterinarian, or podiatrist and is inquiring about the recent Schedule II prescription history of a particular patient of the practitioner; or

(C) a pharmacist or practitioner who is inquiring about the person's own dispensing or prescribing activity.

(b) This section does not prohibit the director from creating, using, or disclosing statistical data about information received by the director under this section if the director removes any information reasonably likely to reveal the identity of each patient, practitioner, or other person who is a subject of the information.

(c) The director by rule shall design and implement a system for submission of information to the director by electronic or other means and for retrieval of information submitted to the director under this section and Section 481.075. The director shall use automated information security techniques and devices to preclude improper access to the information. The director shall submit the system design to the Texas State Board of Pharmacy and the Texas State Board of Medical Examiners for review and approval or comment a reasonable time before implementation of the system and shall comply with the comments of those agencies unless it is unreasonable to do so.

(d) Information submitted to the director under this section may be used only for:

(1) the administration, investigation, or enforcement of this chapter or another law governing illicit drugs in this state or another state;

(2) investigatory or evidentiary purposes in connection with the functions of an agency listed in Subsection (a)(1); or

(3) dissemination by the director to the public in the form of a statistical tabulation or report if all information reasonably likely to reveal the identity of each patient, practitioner, or other person who is a subject of the information has been removed.

(e) The director shall remove from the information retrieval system, destroy, and make irretrievable the record of the identity of a patient submitted under this section to the director not later than the end of the 12th calendar month after the month in which the identity is entered into the system. However, the director may retain a patient identity that is necessary for use in a specific ongoing investigation conducted in accordance with this section until the 30th day after the end of the month in which the necessity for retention of the identity ends.

(f) If the director permits access to information under Subsection (a)(2) relating to a person licensed or regulated by an agency listed in Subsection (a)(1), the director shall notify and cooperate with that agency regarding the disposition of the matter before taking action against the person, unless the director determines that notification is reasonably likely to interfere with an administrative or criminal investigation or prosecution.

(g) If the director permits access to information under Subsection (a)(3)(A) relating to a person licensed or regulated by an agency listed in Subsection (a)(1), the director shall notify that agency of the disclosure of the information not later than the 10th working day after the date the information is disclosed.

(h) If the director withholds notification to an agency under Subsection (f), the director shall notify the agency of the disclosure of the information and the reason for withholding notification when the director determines that notification is no longer likely to interfere with an administrative or criminal investigation or prosecution.

(i) Information submitted to the director under Section 481.075 is confidential and remains confidential regardless of whether the director permits access to the information under this section.

(j) *(Repealed by L.1999, chap. 145(5)(3), eff. 9/1/99.)*

*(Added by L.1989, chap. 678(1); chgd. by L.1995, chap. 965(81); L.1997, chap. 745(15); L.1999, chap. 145(4), 145(5)(3), eff. 9/1/99.)*



### §481.0761. Rules; authority to contract.

(a) The director shall consult with the Texas State Board of Pharmacy and by rule establish and revise as necessary a standardized database format that may be used by a pharmacy to transmit the information required by Section 481.075(i) to the director electronically or to deliver the information on storage media, including disks, tapes, and cassettes.

(b) The director shall consult with the Texas Department of Health, the Texas State Board of Pharmacy, and the Texas State Board of Medical Examiners and by rule may:

(1) remove a controlled substance listed in Schedule II from the official prescription program, if the director determines that the burden imposed by the program substantially outweighs the risk of diversion of the particular controlled substance; or

(2) return a substance previously removed from Schedule II to the official prescription program, if the director determines that the risk of diversion substantially outweighs the burden imposed by the program on the particular controlled substance.

(c) The director by rule may:

(1) permit more than one prescription to be administered or dispensed and recorded on one official prescription form;

(2) remove from or return to the official prescription program any aspect of a practitioner's or pharmacist's hospital practice, including administering or dispensing;

(3) waive or delay any requirement relating to the time or manner of reporting;

(4) establish compatibility protocols for electronic data transfer hardware, software, or format;

(5) establish a procedure to control the release of information under Sections 481.075 and 481.076; and

(6) establish a minimum level of prescription activity below which a reporting activity may be modified or deleted.

(d) The director by rule shall authorize a practitioner to determine whether it is necessary to obtain a particular patient identification number and to provide that number on the official prescription form.

(e) In adopting a rule relating to the electronic transfer of information under this subchapter, the director shall consider the economic impact of the rule on practitioners and pharmacists and, to the extent permitted by law, act to minimize any negative economic impact, including the imposition of costs related to computer hardware or software or to the transfer of information. The director may not adopt a rule relating to the electronic transfer of information under this subchapter that imposes a fee in addition to the fee authorized by Section 481.064.

(f) The director may authorize a contract between the department and another agency of this state or a private vendor as necessary to ensure the effective operation of the official prescription program.

(g) *(Repealed by L.1999, chap. 145(5)(4), eff. 9/1/99.)*

*(Added by L.1997, chap. 745(16); chgd. by L.1999, chap. 145(5)(4), eff. 9/1/99.)*

## §481.077. Chemical precursor records and reports.

(a) Except as provided by Subsection (*l*), a person who sells, transfers, or otherwise furnishes any of the following precursor substances to a person shall make an accurate and legible record of the transaction and maintain the record for at least two years after the date of the transaction:

(1) Methylamine;
(2) Ethylamine;
(3) D-lysergic acid;
(4) Ergotamine tartrate;
(5) Diethyl malonate;
(6) Malonic acid;
(7) Ethyl malonate;
(8) Barbituric acid;
(9) Piperidine;
(10) N-acetylanthranilic acid;
(11) Pyrrolidine;
(12) Phenylacetic acid;
(13) Anthranilic acid;
(14) Ephedrine;
(15) Pseudoephedrine;
(16) Norpseudoephedrine; or
(17) Phenylpropanolamine.

(b) The director by rule may:

(1) name an additional chemical substance as a precursor for purposes of Subsection (a) if the director determines that public health and welfare are jeopardized by evidenced proliferation or use of the substance in the illicit manufacture of a controlled substance or controlled substance analogue; or

(2) delete a substance listed in Subsection (a) if the director determines that the substance does not jeopardize public health and welfare or is not used in the illicit manufacture of a controlled substance or a controlled substance analogue.

(c) This section and Section 481.078 do not apply to a person to whom a registration has been issued under Section 481.063.

(d) Before selling, transferring, or otherwise furnishing to a person in this state a precursor substance subject to Subsection (a), a manufacturer, wholesaler, retailer, or other person shall:

(1) if the recipient does not represent a business, obtain from the recipient:

(A) the recipient's driver's license number or other personal identification certificate number, date of birth, and residential or mailing address, other than a post office box number, from a driver's license or personal identification card issued by the Department of Public Safety that contains a photograph of the recipient;

(B) the year, state, and number of the motor vehicle license of the motor vehicle owned or operated by the recipient;

(C) a complete description of how the substance is to be used; and

(D) the recipient's signature; or

(2) if the recipient represents a business, obtain from the recipient:

(A) a letter of authorization from the business that includes the business license or comptroller tax identification number, address, area code, and telephone number and a complete description of how the substance is to be used; and

(B) the recipient's signature; and

(3) for any recipient, sign as a witness to the signature and identification of the recipient.

(e) If the recipient does not represent a business, the recipient shall present to the manufacturer, wholesaler, retailer, or other person a permit issued in the name of the recipient by the Department of Public Safety under Section 481.078.

(f) Except as provided by Subsection (h), a manufacturer, wholesaler, retailer, or other person who sells, transfers, or otherwise furnishes to a person in this state a precursor substance subject to Subsection (a) shall submit, at least 21 days before the delivery of the substance, a report of the transaction on a form obtained from the director that includes the information required by Subsection (d).

(g) The director shall supply to a manufacturer, wholesaler, retailer, or other person who sells, transfers, or otherwise furnishes a precursor substance subject to Subsection (a) a form for the submission of:

(1) the report required by Subsection (f);
(2) the name and measured amount of the precursor substance delivered; and
(3) any other information required by the director.

Printed in the U.S.A. 17

(h) The director may authorize a manufacturer, wholesaler, retailer, or other person to submit a comprehensive monthly report instead of the report required by Subsection (f) if the director determines that:

(1) there is a pattern of regular supply and purchase of the substance between the furnisher and the recipient; or

(2) the recipient has established a record of use of the substance solely for a lawful purpose.

(i) A manufacturer, wholesaler, retailer, or other person who receives from a source outside this state a substance subject to Subsection (a) or who discovers a loss or theft of a substance subject to Subsection (a) shall:

(1) submit a report of the transaction to the director in accordance with department rule; and

(2) include in the report:

(A) any difference between the amount of the substance actually received and the amount of the substance shipped according to the shipping statement or invoice; or

(B) the amount of the loss or theft.

(j) A report under Subsection (i) must:

(1) be made not later than the third day after the date that the manufacturer, wholesaler, retailer, or other person learns of the discrepancy, loss, or theft; and

(2) if the discrepancy, loss, or theft occurred during a shipment of the substance, include the name of the common carrier or person who transported the substance and the date that the substance was shipped.

(k) Unless the person is the holder of only a permit issued under Section 481.078(b)(1), a manufacturer, wholesaler, retailer, or other person who sells, transfers, or otherwise furnishes any substance subject to Subsection (a) or a permit holder, commercial purchaser, or other person who receives a substance governed by Subsection (a):

(1) shall maintain records and inventories in accordance with rules established by the director;

(2) shall allow a member of the Department of Public Safety or a peace officer to conduct audits and inspect records of purchases and sales and all other records made in accordance with this section at any reasonable time; and

(3) may not interfere with the audit or with the full and complete inspection or copying of those records.

(*l*) This section does not apply to the sale or transfer of a nonnarcotic product that includes a precursor substance subject to Subsection (a) if the sale or transfer complies with federal law and involves a product that may be sold lawfully with a prescription or over the counter without a prescription under the Federal Food, Drug, and Cosmetic Act (21 U.S.C. Section 301 et seq.) or a rule adopted under that Act.

*(Added by L.1989, chap. 678(1); chgd. by L.1989, chap. 1100(5.02)(k); L.1997, chap. 745(17), eff. 1/1/98.)*

**§481.078. Chemical precursor transfer permit.**

(a) A person must obtain a chemical precursor transfer permit from the Department of Public Safety to the eligible:

(1) to sell, transfer, or otherwise furnish a precursor substance subject to Section 481.077(a) to a person in this state;

(2) to receive a precursor substance subject to Section 481.077(a) from a source outside this state; or

(3) to receive a precursor substance subject to Section 481.077(a) if the person, in receiving the substance, does not represent a business.

(b) The director by rule shall adopt procedures and standards for the issuance and renewal or the voluntary surrender, cancellation, suspension, probation, or revocation of:

(1) a permit for one sale, transfer, receipt, or otherwise furnishing of a controlled substance precursor; or

(2) a permit for more than one sale, transfer, receipt, or otherwise furnishing of a controlled substance precursor.

(c) A permit issued or renewed under Subsection (b)(1) is valid only for the transaction indicated on the permit. A permit issued or renewed under Subsection (b)(2) is valid for one year after the date of issuance or renewal.

(d) A permit holder must report in writing or by telephone to the director a change in the holder's business name, address, area code, and telephone number not later than the seventh day after the date of the change.

(e) The director may not issue a permit under this section unless the person applying for the permit delivers to the director a written consent to inspect signed by the person that grants to the director the right to inspect any controlled premises, record, chemical precursor, or other item governed by this chapter in the care, custody, or control of the person. After the director receives the consent, the director may inspect any controlled premises, record, chemical precursor, or other item to which the consent applies.

(f) The director may adopt rules to establish security controls and provide for the inspection of a place, entity, or item to which a chemical precursor transfer permit applies.
*(Added by L.1989, chap. 1100(5.02)(l); chgd. by L.1997, chap. 745(18), eff. 1/1/98.)*

**§481.079.** *(Repealed by L.1997, chap. 745(37), eff. 1/1/98.)*

**§481.080. Chemical laboratory apparatus record-keeping requirements and penalties.**

(a) In this section, "chemical laboratory apparatus" means any item of equipment designed, made, or adapted to manufacture a controlled substance or a controlled substance analogue, including:

(1) a condenser;
(2) a distilling apparatus;
(3) a vacuum drier;
(4) a three-neck or distilling flask;
(5) a tableting machine;
(6) an encapsulating machine;
(7) a filter, Buchner, or separatory funnel;
(8) an Erlenmeyer, two-neck, or single-neck flask;
(9) a round-bottom, Florence, thermometer, or filtering flask;
(10) a Soxhlet extractor;
(11) a transformer;
(12) a flask heater;
(13) a heating mantel; or
(14) an adaptor tube.

(b) A manufacturer, wholesaler, retailer, or other person who sells, transfers, or otherwise furnishes chemical laboratory apparatus shall make an accurate and legible record of the transaction and maintain the record for at least two years after the date of the transaction.

(c) The director may adopt rules to implement this section.

(d) The director by rule may:

(1) name additional chemical laboratory apparatus for purposes of Subsection (a) if the director determines that public health and welfare are jeopardized by evidenced proliferation or use of a chemical laboratory apparatus in the illicit manufacture of a controlled substance or controlled substance analogue; or

(2) delete an apparatus listed in Subsection (a) if the director determines that the apparatus does not jeopardize public health and welfare or is not used in the illicit manufacture of a controlled substance or a controlled substance analogue.

(e) This section and Section 481.081 do not apply to a person to whom a registration has been issued under Section 481.063.

(f) Before selling, transferring, or otherwise furnishing to a person in this state an apparatus subject to Subsection (a), a manufacturer, wholesaler, retailer, or other person shall:

(1) if the recipient does not represent a business, obtain from the recipient:

(A) the recipient's driver's license number or other personal identification certificate number, date of birth, and residential or mailing address, other than a post office box number, from a driver's license or personal identification card issued by the Department of Public Safety that contains a photograph of the recipient;

(B) the year, state, and number of the motor vehicle license of the motor vehicle owned or operated by the recipient;

(C) a complete description of how the apparatus is to be used; and

(D) the recipient's signature; or

(2) if the recipient represents a business, obtain from the recipient:

(A) a letter of authorization from the business that includes the business license or comptroller tax identification number, address, area code, and telephone number and a complete description of how the apparatus is to be used; and

(B) the recipient's signature; and

(3) for any recipient, sign as a witness to the signature and identification of the recipient.

Printed in the U.S.A. Zt

(g) If the recipient does not represent a business, the recipient shall present to the manufacturer, wholesaler, retailer, or other person a permit issued in the name of the recipient by the Department of Public Safety under Section 481.081.

(h) Except as provided by Subsection (j), a manufacturer, wholesaler, retailer, or other person who sells, transfers, or otherwise furnishes to a person in this state an apparatus subject to Subsection (a) shall, at least 21 days before the delivery of the apparatus, submit a report of the transaction on a form obtained from the director that includes the information required by Subsection (f).

(i) The director shall supply to a manufacturer, wholesaler, retailer, or other person who sells, transfers, or otherwise furnishes an apparatus subject to Subsection (a) a form for the submission of:

(1) the report required by Subsection (h);

(2) the name and number of apparatus delivered; and

(3) any other information required by the director.

(j) The director may authorize a manufacturer, wholesaler, retailer, or other person to submit a comprehensive monthly report instead of the report required by Subsection (h) if the director determines that:

(1) there is a pattern of regular supply and purchase of the apparatus between the furnisher and the recipient; or

(2) the recipient has established a record of use of the apparatus solely for a lawful purpose.

(k) A manufacturer, wholesaler, retailer, or other person who receives from a source outside this state an apparatus subject to Subsection (a) or who discovers a loss or theft of an apparatus subject to Subsection (a) shall:

(1) submit a report of the transaction to the director in accordance with department rule; and

(2) include in the report:

(A) any difference between the number of the apparatus actually received and the number of the apparatus shipped according to the shipping statement or invoice; or

(B) the number of the loss or theft.

(*l*) A report under Subsection (k) must:

(1) be made not later than the third day after the date that the manufacturer, wholesaler, retailer, or other person learns of the discrepancy, loss, or theft; and

(2) if the discrepancy, loss, or theft occurred during a shipment of the apparatus, include the name of the common carrier or person who transported the apparatus and the date that the apparatus was shipped.

(m) This subsection applies to a manufacturer, wholesaler, retailer, or other person who sells, transfers, or otherwise furnishes any apparatus subject to Subsection (a) and to a permit holder, commercial purchaser, or other person who receives an apparatus governed by Subsection (a) unless the person is the holder of only a permit issued under Section 481.081(b)(1). A person covered by this subsection:

(1) shall maintain records and inventories in accordance with rules established by the director;

(2) shall allow a member of the Department of Public Safety or a peace officer to conduct audits and inspect records of purchases and sales and all other records made in accordance with this section at any reasonable time; and

(3) may not interfere with the audit or with the full and complete inspection or copying of those records.

*(Added by L.1989, chap. 1100(5.02)(l); chgd. by L.1997, chap. 745(19), eff. 1/1/98.)*

## §481.081. Chemical laboratory apparatus transfer permit.

(a) A person must obtain a chemical laboratory apparatus transfer permit from the Department of Public Safety to be eligible:

(1) to sell, transfer, or otherwise furnish an apparatus subject to Section 481.080(a) to a person in this state;

(2) to receive an apparatus subject to Section 481.080(a) from a source outside this state; or

(3) to receive an apparatus subject to Section 481.080(a) if the person, in receiving the apparatus, does not represent a business.

(b) The director by rule shall adopt procedures and standards for the issuance and renewal or the voluntary surrender, cancellation, suspension, probation, or revocation of:

(1) a permit for one sale, transfer, receipt, or otherwise furnishing of a chemical laboratory apparatus; or

(2) a permit for more than one sale, transfer, receipt, or otherwise furnishing of a chemical laboratory apparatus.

(c) A permit issued or renewed under Subsection (b)(1) is valid only for the transaction indicated on the permit. A permit issued or renewed under Subsection (b)(2) is valid for one year after the date of issuance or renewal.

(d) A permit holder must report in writing or by telephone to the director a change in the holder's business name, address, area code, and telephone number not later than the seventh day after the date of the change.

(e) The director may not issue a permit under this section unless the person applying for the permit delivers to the director a written consent to inspect signed by the person that grants to the director the right to inspect any controlled premises, record, chemical laboratory apparatus, or other item governed by this chapter in the care, custody, or control of the person. After the director receives the consent, the director may inspect any controlled premises, record, chemical laboratory apparatus, or other item to which the consent applies.

(f) The director may by rule establish security controls and provide for the inspection of a place, entity, or item to which a chemical laboratory apparatus transfer permit applies. *(Added by L.1989, chap. 1100(5.02)(l); chgd. by L.1997, chap. 745(20), eff. 1/1/98.)*

**§481.082.** *(Repealed by L.1997, chap. 745(37), eff. 1/1/98.)*

**§§481.083 to 481.100.** *(Reserved.)*

## SUBCHAPTER D. OFFENSES AND PENALTIES

### §481.101. Criminal classification.

For the purpose of establishing criminal penalties for violations of this chapter, controlled substances, including a material, compound, mixture, or preparation containing the controlled substance, are divided into Penalty Groups 1 through 4. *(Added by L.1989, chap. 678(1); chgd. by L.1989, chap. 1100(5.02)(n), eff. 9/1/89.)*

### §481.102. Penalty group 1.

Penalty Group 1 consists of:

(1) the following opiates, including their isomers, esters, ethers, salts, and salts of isomers, esters, and ethers, unless specifically excepted, if the existence of these isomers, esters, ethers, and salts is possible within the specific chemical designation:

Alfentanil;
Allylprodine;
Alphacetylmethadol;
Benzethidine;
Betaprodine;
Clonitazene;
Diampromide;
Diethylthiambutene;
Difenoxin not listed in Penalty Group 3 or 4;
Dimenoxadol;
Dimethylthiambutene;
Dioxaphetyl butyrate;
Dipipanone;
Ethylmethylthiambutene;
Etonitazene;
Etoxeridine;
Furethidine;
Hydroxypethidine;
Ketobemidone;
Levophenacylmorphan;
Meprodine;
Methadol;
Moramide;
Morpheridine;
Noracymethadol;
Norlevorphanol;
Normethadone;
Norpipanone;

Phenadoxone;
Phenampromide;
Phenomorphan;
Phenoperidine;
Piritramide;
Proheptazine;
Properidine;
Propiram;
Sufentanil;
Tilidine; and
Trimeperidine;

(2) the following opium derivatives, their salts, isomers, and salts of isomers, unless specifically excepted, if the existence of these salts, isomers, and salts of isomers is possible within the specific chemical designation:

Acetorphine;
Acetyldihydrocodeine;
Benzylmorphine;
Codeine methylbromide;
Codeine-N-Oxide;
Cyprenorphine;
Desomorphine;
Dihydromorphine;
Drotebanol;
Etorphine, except hydrochloride salt;
Heroin;
Hydromorphinol;
Methyldesorphine;
Methyldihydromorphine;
Monoacetylmorphine;
Morphine methylbromide;
Morphine methylsulfonate;
Morphine-N-Oxide;
Myrophine;
Nicocodeine;
Nicomorphine;
Normorphine;
Pholcodine; and
Thebacon;

(3) the following substances, however produced, except those narcotic drugs listed in another group:

(A) Opium and opiate not listed in Penalty Group 3 or 4, and a salt, compound, derivative, or preparation of opium or opiate, other than thebaine derived butorphanol, nalmefene and its salts, naloxone and its salts, and naltrexone and its salts, but including:

Codeine not listed in Penalty Group 3 or 4;
Ethylmorphine not listed in Penalty Group 3 or 4;
Granulated opium;
Hydrocodone not listed in Penalty Group 3;
Hydromorphone;
Metopon;
Morphine not listed in Penalty Group 3;
Opium extracts;
Opium fluid extracts;
Oxycodone;
Oxymorphone;
Powdered opium;
Raw opium;
Thebaine; and
Tincture of opium;

(B) a salt, compound, isomer, derivative, or preparation of a substance that is chemically equivalent or identical to a substance described by Paragraph (A), other than the isoquinoline alkaloids of opium;

(C) Opium poppy and poppy straw;

(D) Cocaine, including:

(i) its salts, its optical, position, and geometric isomers, and the salts of those isomers;

(ii) coca leaves and a salt, compound, derivative, or preparation of coca leaves;

(iii) a salt, compound, derivative, or preparation of a salt, compound, or derivative that is chemically equivalent or identical to a substance described by Subparagraph (i) or (ii), other than decocainized coca leaves or extractions of coca leaves that do not contain cocaine or ecgonine; and

(E) concentrate of poppy straw, meaning the crude extract of poppy straw in liquid, solid, or powder form that contains the phenanthrine alkaloids of the opium poppy;

(4) the following opiates, including their isomers, esters, ethers, salts, and salts of isomers, if the existence of these isomers, esters, ethers, and salts is possible within the specific chemical designation:

Acetyl-alpha-methylfentanyl (N-(1-(1-methyl-2-phenethyl)-4-piperidinyl)-N-phenylacetamide);

Alpha-methylthiofentanyl (N-(1-methyl-2-(2-thienyl)ethyl-4-piperidinyl)-N-phenylpropanamide);

Alphaprodine;

Anileridine;

Beta-hydroxyfentanyl (N-(1-(2-hydroxy-2-phenethyl)-4-piperidinyl)-N-phenyl-propanamide);

Beta-hydroxy-3-methylfentanyl;

Bezitramide;

Carfentanil;

Dihydrocodeine not listed in Penalty Group 3 or 4;

Diphenoxylate not listed in Penalty Group 3 or 4;

Fentanyl or alpha-methylfentanyl, or any other derivative of Fentanyl;

Isomethadone;

Levomethorphan;

Levorphanol;

Metazocine;

Methadone;

Methadone-Intermediate, 4-cyano-2-dimethylamino-4, 4-diphenyl butane;

3-methylfentanyl(N-(3-methyl-1-(2-phenylethyl)-4-piperidyl)-N-phenylpropanamide);

3-methylthiofentanyl(N-(3-methyl-1-(2-thienyl) ethyl-4-piperidinyl)-N-phenyl-propanamide);

Moramide-Intermediate, 2-methyl-3-morpholino-1, 1-diphenyl-propane-carboxylic acid;

Para-fluorofentanyl(N-(4-fluorophenyl)-N-(1-(2-phenylethyl)-4-piperidinyl)propanamide);

PEPAP (1-(2-phenethyl)-4-phenyl-4-acetoxypiperidine);

Pethidine (Meperidine);

Pethidine-Intermediate-A, 4-cyano-1-methyl-4-phenylpiperidine;

Pethidine-Intermediate-B, ethyl-4-phenylpiperidine-4 carboxylate;

Pethidine-Intermediate-C, 1-methyl-4-phenylpiperidine-4-carboxylic acid;

Phenazocine;

Piminodine;

Racemethorphan;

Racemorphan; and

Thiofentanyl(N-phenyl-N-(1-(2-thienyl)ethyl-4-piperidinyl)-propanamide);

(5) Flunitrazepam (some trade or other names: Rohypnol);

(6) Methamphetamine, including its salts, optical isomers, and salts of optical isomers;

(7) Phenylacetone and methylamine, if possessed together with intent to manufacture methamphetamine;

(8) Phencyclidine, including its salts*; and*

(9) Gamma hydroxybutyrate, including its salts.

*(Added by L.1989, chap. 678(1); chgd. by L.1989, chap. 1100(5.02)(n); L.1991, chap. 761(1); L.1997, chap. 745(21), eff. 1/1/98.)*

## §481.1021. Penalty group 1-A.

Penalty Group 1-A consists of lysergic acid diethylamide (LSD), including its salts, isomers, and salts of isomers. *(Added by L.1997, chap. 745(22), eff. 1/1/98.)*

**§481.103. Penalty group 2.**

(a) Penalty Group 2 consists of:

(1) any quantity of the following hallucinogenic substances, their salts, isomers, and salts of isomers, unless specifically excepted, if the existence of these salts, isomers, and salts of isomers is possible within the specific chemical designation:

alpha-ethyltryptamine;

4-bromo-2, 5-dimethoxyamphetamine (some trade or other names: 4-bromo-2, 5-dimethoxy-alpha-methylphenethylamine; 4-bromo-2, 5-DMA);

4-bromo-2, 5-dimethoxyphenethylamine;

Bufotenine (some trade and other names: 3-(beta-Dimethylaminoethyl)-5-hydroxyindole; 3-(2-dimethylaminoethyl)-5-indolol; N, N-dimethylserotonin; 5-hydroxy-N, N-dimethyltryptamine; mappine);

Diethyltryptamine (some trade and other names: N, N-Diethyltryptamine, DET);

2, 5-dimethoxyamphetamine (some trade or other names: 2, 5-dimethoxy-alpha-methylphenethylamine; 2, 5-DMA);

2, 5-dimethoxy-4-ethylamphetamine (some trade or other names: DOET);

Dimethyltryptamine (some trade and other names: DMT);

Dronabinol (synthetic) in sesame oil and encapsulated in a soft gelatin capsule in a U.S. Food and Drug Administration approved drug product (some trade or other names for Dronabinol: (a6aR-trans)-6a,7,8,10a-tetrahydro-6,6,9-trimethyl-3-pentyl-6H-dibenzo (b,d)pyran-1-ol or (-)-delta-9-(trans)-tetrahydrocannabinol);

Ethylamine Analog of Phencyclidine (some trade or other names: N-ethyl-1-phenylcyclohexylamine, (1-phenylcyclohexyl) ethylamine, N-(1-phenylcyclohexyl) ethylamine, cyclohexamine, PCE);

Ibogaine (some trade or other names: 7-Ethyl-6, 6, beta 7, 8, 9, 10, 12, 13-octahydro-2-methoxy-6, 9-methano-5H-pyrido (1', 2':1, 2) azepino (5, 4-b) indole; tabernanthe iboga.);

Mescaline;

5-methoxy-3, 4-methylenedioxy amphetamine;

4-methoxyamphetamine (some trade or other names: 4-methoxy-alpha-methylphenethylamine; paramethoxyamphetamine; PMA);

1-methyl-4-phenyl-4-propionoxypiperidine (MPPP, PPMP);

4-methyl-2, 5-dimethoxyamphetamine (some trade and other names: 4-methyl-2, 5-dimethoxy-alpha-methylphenethylamine; "DOM"; "STP");

3,4-methylenedioxy methamphetamine (MDMA, MDM);

3,4-methylenedioxy amphetamine;

3,4-methylenedioxy N-ethylamphetamine (Also known as N-ethyl MDA);

Nabilone (Another name for nabilone: (+)-trans-3-(1,1-dimethylheptyl)-6,6a,7,8,10,10a-hexahydro-1-hydroxy-6,6-dimethyl-9H-dibenzo(b,d)pyran-9-one;

N-ethyl-3-piperidyl benzilate;

N-hydroxy-3,4-methylenedioxyamphetamine (Also known as N-hydroxy MDA);

4-methylaminorex;

N-methyl-3-piperidyl benzilate;

Parahexyl (some trade or other names: 3-Hexyl-1-hydroxy-7, 8, 9, 10-tetrahydro-6, 6, 9-trimethyl-6H-dibenzo (b, d) pyran; Synhexyl);

1-Phenylcyclohexylamine;

1-Piperidinocyclohexanecarbonitrile (PCC);

Psilocin;

Psilocybin;

Pyrrolidine Analog of Phencyclidine (some trade or other names: 1-(1-phenylcyclohexyl)-pyrrolidine, PCPy, PHP);

Tetrahydrocannabinols, other than marihuana, and synthetic equivalents of the substances contained in the plant, or in the resinous extractives of Cannabis, or synthetic substances, derivatives, and their isomers with similar chemical structure and pharmacological activity such as:

delta-1 cis or trans tetrahydrocannabinol, and their optical isomers;

delta-6 cis or trans tetrahydrocannabinol, and their optical isomers;

delta-3, 4 cis or trans tetrahydrocannabinol, and its optical isomers;

compounds of these structures, regardless of numerical designation of atomic positions, since nomenclature of these substances is not internationally standardized;

Thiophene Analog of Phencyclidine (some trade or other names: 1-(1-(2-thienyl) cyclohexyl) piperidine; 2-Thienyl Analog of Phencyclidine; TPCP, TCP);

1-(1-(2-thienyl)cyclohexyl)pyrrolidine (some trade or other names: TCPy); and

3,4,5-trimethoxy amphetamine;

(2) Phenylacetone (some trade or other names: Phenyl-2-propanone; P2P, Benzymethyl ketone, methyl benzyl ketone); and

(3) unless specifically excepted or unless listed in another Penalty Group, a material, compound, mixture, or preparation that contains any quantity of the following substances having a potential for abuse associated with a depressant or stimulant effect on the central nervous system:

Aminorex (some trade or other names: aminoxaphen; 2-amino-5-phenyl-2-oxazoline; 4,5-dihydro-5-phenyl-2-oxazolamine);

Amphetamine, its salts, optical isomers, and salts of optical isomers;

Cathinone (some trade or other names: 2-amino-1-phenyl-1-propanone, alpha-aminopropiophenone, 2-aminopropiophenone);

Etorphine Hydrochloride;

Fenethylline and its salts;

Mecloqualone and its salts;

Methaqualone and its salts;

Methcathinone (some trade or other names: 2-methylamino-propiophenone; alpha-(methylamino)propriophenone; 2-(methylamino)-1-phenylpropan-1-one; alpha-N-methylaminopropriophenone; monomethylpropion; ephedrone, N-methylcathinone; methylcathinone; AL-464; AL-422; AL-463; and UR 1431);

N-Ethylamphetamine, its salts, optical isomers, and salts of optical isomers; and

N,N-dimethylamphetamine (some trade or other names: N,N,alpha-trimethylbenzeneethaneamine; N,N,alpha-trimethylphenethylamine), its salts, optical isomers, and salts of optical isomers.

(b) For the purposes of Subsection (a)(1) only, the term "isomer" includes an optical, position, or geometric isomer.

*(Added by L.1989, chap. 678(1); chgd. by L.1989, chap. 1100(5.02)(n); L.1991, chap. 761(2); L.1997, chap. 745(23), eff. 1/1/98.)*

## §481.104. Penalty group 3.

(a) Penalty Group 3 consists of:

(1) a material, compound, mixture, or preparation that contains any quantity of the following substances having a potential for abuse associated with a stimulant effect on the central nervous system:

Methylphenidate and its salts; and

Phenmetrazine and its salts;

(2) a material, compound, mixture, or preparation that contains any quantity of the following substances having a potential for abuse associated with a depressant effect on the central nervous system:

a substance that contains any quantity of a derivative of barbituric acid, or any salt of a derivative of barbituric acid not otherwise covered by this subsection;

a compound, mixture, or preparation containing amobarbital, secobarbital, pentobarbital, or any salt of any of these, and one or more active medicinal ingredients that are not listed in any penalty group;

a suppository dosage form containing amobarbital, secobarbital, pentobarbital, or any salt of any of these drugs, and approved by the United States Food and Drug Administration for marketing only as a suppository;

Alprazolam;

Amobarbital;

Bromazepam;

Camazepam;

Chlordiazepoxide;

Chlorhexadol;

Clobazam;

Clonazepam;

Clorazepate;

Clotiazepam;

Cloxazolam;

Delorazepam;

Diazepam;

Estazolam;

Ethyl loflazepate;

Fludiazepam;

Flurazepam;

Glutethimide;
Halazepam;
Haloxzolam;
Ketazolam;
Loprazolam;
Lorazepam;
Lormetazepam;
Lysergic acid, including its salts, isomers, and salts of isomers;
Lysergic acid amide, including its salts, isomers, and salts of isomers;
Mebutamate;
Medazepam;
Methyprylon;
Midazolam;
Nimetazepam;
Nitrazepam;
Nordiazepam;
Oxazepam;
Oxazolam;
Pentazocine, its salts, derivatives, or compounds or mixtures thereof;
Pentobarbital;
Pinazepam;
Prazepam;
Quazepam;
Secobarbital;
Sulfondiethylmethane;
Sulfonethylmethane;
Sulfonmethane;
Temazepam;
Tetrazepam;
Tiletamine and zolazepam in combination, and its salts. (some trade or other names for a tiletamine-zolazepam combination product: Telazol, for tiletamine: 2-(ethylamino)-2-(2-thienyl)-cyclohexanone, and for zolazepam: 4-(2-fluorophenyl)-6, 8-dihydro-1,3,8,-trimethylpyrazolo-(3,4-e)(1,4)-d diazepin-7(1H)-one, flupyrazapon);
Triazolam; and
Zolpidem;

(3) Nalorphine;

(4) a material, compound, mixture, or preparation containing limited quantities of the following narcotic drugs, or any of their salts:

not more than 1.8 grams of codeine, or any of its salts, per 100 milliliters or not more than 90 milligrams per dosage unit, with an equal or greater quantity of an isoquinoline alkaloid of opium;

not more than 1.8 grams of codeine, or any of its salts, per 100 milliliters or not more than 90 milligrams per dosage unit, with one or more active, nonnarcotic ingredients in recognized therapeutic amounts;

not more than 300 milligrams of dihydrocodeinone (hydrocodone), or any of its salts, per 100 milliliters or not more than 15 milligrams per dosage unit, with a fourfold or greater quantity of an isoquinoline alkaloid of opium;

not more than 300 milligrams of dihydrocodeinone (hydrocodone), or any of its salts, per 100 milliliters or not more than 15 milligrams per dosage unit, with one or more active, nonnarcotic ingredients in recognized therapeutic amounts;

not more than 1.8 grams of dihydrocodeine, or any of its salts, per 100 milliliters or not more than 90 milligrams per dosage unit, with one or more active, nonnarcotic ingredients in recognized therapeutic amounts;

not more than 300 milligrams of ethylmorphine, or any of its salts, per 100 milliliters or not more than 15 milligrams per dosage unit, with one or more active, nonnarcotic ingredients in recognized therapeutic amounts;

not more than 500 milligrams of opium per 100 milliliters or per 100 grams, or not more than 25 milligrams per dosage unit, with one or more active, nonnarcotic ingredients in recognized therapeutic amounts;

not more than 50 milligrams of morphine, or any of its salts, per 100 milliliters or per 100 grams with one or more active, nonnarcotic ingredients in recognized therapeutic amounts; and

not more than 1 milligram of difenoxin and not less than 25 micrograms of atropine sulfate per dosage unit;

(5) a material, compound, mixture, or preparation that contains any quantity of the following substances:

Barbital;
Chloral betaine;
Chloral hydrate;
Ethchlorvynol;
Ethinamate;
Meprobamate;
Methohexital;
Methylphenobarbital (Mephobarbital);
Paraldehyde;
Petrichloral; and
Phenobarbital;

(6) Peyote, unless unharvested and growing in its natural state, meaning all parts of the plant classified botanically as Lophophora, whether growing or not, the seeds of the plant, an extract from a part of the plant, and every compound, manufacture, salt, derivative, mixture, or preparation of the plant, its seeds, or extracts;

(7) unless listed in another penalty group, a material, compound, mixture, or preparation that contains any quantity of the following substances having a stimulant effect on the central nervous system, including the substance's salts, optical, position, or geometric isomers, and salts of the substance's isomers, if the existence of the salts, isomers, and salts of isomers is possible within the specific chemical designation:

Benzphetamine;
Cathine ((+)-norpseudoephedrine);
Chlorphentermine;
Clortermine;
Diethylpropion;
Fencamfamin;
Fenfluramine;
Fenproporex;
Mazindol;
Mefenorex;
Pemoline (including organometallic complexes and their chelates);
Phendimetrazine;
Phentermine;
Pipradrol; and
SPA ((-)-1-dimethylamino-1,2-diphenylethane);

(8) unless specifically excepted or unless listed in another penalty group, a material, compound, mixture, or preparation that contains any quantity of the following substance, including its salts:

Dextropropoxyphene (Alpha-(+)-4-dimethylamino-1,2-diphenyl-3-methyl-2-propionoxybutane); and

(9) an anabolic steroid or any substance that is chemically or pharmacologically related to testosterone, other than an estrogen, progestin, or corticosteroid, and promotes muscle growth, including:

Boldenone;
Chlorotestosterone (4-chlortestosterone);
Clostebol;
Dehydrochlormethyltestosterone;
Dihydrotestosterone (4-dihydrotestosterone);
Drostanolone;
Ethylestrenol;
Fluoxymesterone;
Formebulone;
Mesterolone;
Methandienone;
Methandranone;
Methandriol;
Methandrostenolone;
Methenolone;
Methyltestosterone;
Mibolerone;

Nandrolone;
Norethandrolone;
Oxandrolone;
Oxymesterone;
Oxymetholone;
Stanolone;
Stanozolol;
Testolactone;
Testosterone; and
Trenbolone.

(b) Penalty Group 3 does not include a compound, mixture, or preparation containing a stimulant substance listed in Subsection (a)(1) if the compound, mixture, or preparation contains one or more active medicinal ingredients not having a stimulant effect on the central nervous system and if the admixtures are included in combinations, quantity, proportion, or concentration that vitiate the potential for abuse of the substances that have a stimulant effect on the central nervous system.

(c) Penalty Group 3 does not include a compound, mixture, or preparation containing a depressant substance listed in Subsection (a)(2) or (a)(5) if the compound, mixture, or preparation contains one or more active medicinal ingredients not having a depressant effect on the central nervous system and if the admixtures are included in combinations, quantity, proportion, or concentration that vitiate the potential for abuse of the substances that have a depressant effect on the central nervous system.

*(Added by L.1989, chap. 678(1); chgd. by L.1989, chap. 1100(5.02)(n); L.1991, chap. 761(3); L.1997, chap. 745(24), eff. 1/1/98.)*

## §481.105. Penalty Group 4.

Penalty Group 4 consists of:

(1) a compound, mixture, or preparation containing limited quantities of any of the following narcotic drugs that includes one or more nonnarcotic active medicinal ingredients in sufficient proportion to confer on the compound, mixture, or preparation valuable medicinal qualities other than those possessed by the narcotic drug alone:

not more than 200 milligrams of codeine per 100 milliliters or per 100 grams;

not more than 100 milligrams of dihydrocodeine per 100 milliliters or per 100 grams;

not more than 100 milligrams of ethylmorphine per 100 milliliters or per 100 grams;

not more than 2.5 milligrams of diphenoxylate and not less than 25 micrograms of atropine sulfate per dosage unit;

not more than 15 milligrams of opium per 29.5729 milliliters or per 28.35 grams; and

not more than 0.5 milligrams of difenoxin and not less than 25 micrograms of atropine sulfate per dosage unit;

(2) unless specifically excepted or unless listed in another penalty group, a material, compound, mixture, or preparation containing the narcotic drug Buprenorphine or its salts; and

(3) unless specifically exempted or excluded or unless listed in another penalty group, any material, compound, mixture, or preparation that contains any quantity of pyrovalerone, a substance having a stimulant effect on the central nervous system, including its salts, isomers, and salts of isomers.

*(Added by L.1989, chap. 678(1); chgd. by L.1989, chap. 1100(5.04)(a); L.1991, chap. 761(4); L.1997, chap. 745(25), eff. 1/1/98.)*

**§§481.106. 481.107.** *(Added by L.1989, chap. 678(1); repealed by L.1993, chap. 900(2.07), eff. 9/1/94.)*

## §481.108. Preparatory offenses.

Title 4, Penal Code, applies to an offense under this chapter. *(Added by L.1989, chap. 678(1); chgd. by L.1993, chap. 900(2.02); L.1995, chap. 318(36), eff. 9/1/95.)*

**§§481.109, 481.110.** *(Added by L.1989, chap. 678(1); repealed by L.1991, chap. 141(6)(a), eff. 9/1/91.)*

## §481.111. Exemptions.

(a) The provisions of this chapter relating to the possession and distribution of peyote do not apply to the use of peyote by a member of the Native American Church in bona fide religious ceremonies of the church. However, a person who supplies the substance to the church must register and maintain appropriate records of receipts and disbursements in accordance with rules adopted by the director. An exemption granted to a member of the Native American Church under this section does not apply to a member with less than 25 percent Indian blood.

(b) The provisions of this chapter relating to the possession of denatured sodium pentobarbital do not apply to possession by personnel of a humane society or an animal control agency for the purpose of destroying injured, sick, homeless, or unwanted animals if the humane society or animal control agency is registered with the Federal Drug Enforcement Administration. The provisions of this chapter relating to the distribution of denatured sodium pentobarbital do not apply to a person registered as required by Subchapter C, who is distributing the substance for that purpose to a humane society or an animal control agency registered with the Federal Drug Enforcement Administration.

(c) A person does not violate Section 481.113, 481.116, 481.121, or 481.125 if the person possesses or delivers tetrahydrocannabinols or their derivatives, or drug paraphernalia to be used to introduce tetrahydrocannabinols or their derivatives into the human body, for use in a federally approved therapeutic research program.

(d) The provisions of this chapter relating to the possession and distribution of anabolic steroids do not apply to the use of anabolic steroids that are administered to livestock or poultry.
*(Added by L.1989, chap. 678(1); chgd. by L.1989, chap. 1100(5.03)(d), eff. 9/1/89.)*

### §481.112. Offense: Manufacture or delivery of substance in Penalty Group 1.

(a) Except as authorized by this chapter, a person commits an offense if the person knowingly or intentionally manufactures, delivers, or possesses with intent to manufacture or deliver a controlled substance listed in Penalty Group 1.

(b) An offense under Subsection (a) is a state jail felony if the amount of the controlled substance to which the offense applies is, by aggregate weight, including adulterants or dilutants, less than one gram.

(c) An offense under Subsection (a) is a felony of the second degree if the amount of the controlled substance to which the offense applies is, by aggregate weight, including adulterants or dilutants, one gram or more but less than four grams.

(d) An offense under Subsection (a) is a felony of the first degree if the amount of the controlled substance to which the offense applies is, by aggregate weight, including adulterants or dilutants, four grams or more but less than 200 grams.

(e) An offense under Subsection (a) is punishable by imprisonment in the institutional division of the Texas Department of Criminal Justice for life or for a term of not more than 99 years or less than 10 years, and a fine not to exceed $100,000, if the amount of the controlled substance to which the offense applies is, by aggregate weight, including adulterants or dilutants, 200 grams or more but less than 400 grams.

(f) An offense under Subsection (a) is punishable by imprisonment in the institutional division of the Texas Department of Criminal Justice for life or for a term of not more than 99 years or less than 15 years, and a fine not to exceed $250,000, if the amount of the controlled substance to which the offense applies is, by aggregate weight, including adulterants or dilutants, 400 grams or more.
*(Added by L.1989, chap. 678(1); chgd. by L.1993, chap. 900(2.02), eff. 9/1/94.)*

### §481.1121. Offense: Manufacture or delivery of substance in penalty group 1-A.

(a) Except as provided by this chapter, a person commits an offense if the person knowingly manufactures, delivers, or possesses with intent to manufacture or deliver a controlled substance listed in Penalty Group 1-A.

(b) An offense under this section is:

(1) a state jail felony if the number of abuse units of the controlled substance is fewer than 20;

(2) a felony of the second degree if the number of abuse units of the controlled substance is 20 or more but fewer than 80;

(3) a felony of the first degree if the number of abuse units of the controlled substance is 80 or more but fewer than 4,000; and

(4) punishable by imprisonment in the institutional division of the Texas Department of Criminal Justice for life or for a term of not more than 99 years or less than 15 years and a fine not to exceed $250,000, if the number of abuse units of the controlled substance is 4,000 or more.
*(Added by L.1997, chap. 745(26), eff. 1/1/98.)*

## §481.113. Offense: Manufacture or delivery of substance in Penalty Group 2.

(a) Except as authorized by this chapter, a person commits an offense if the person knowingly or intentionally manufactures, delivers, or possesses with intent to manufacture or deliver a controlled substance listed in Penalty Group 2.

(b) An offense under Subsection (a) is a state jail felony if the amount of the controlled substance to which the offense applies is, by aggregate weight, including adulterants or dilutants, less than one gram.

(c) An offense under Subsection (a) is a felony of the second degree if the amount of the controlled substance to which the offense applies is, by aggregate weight, including adulterants or dilutants, one gram or more but less than four grams

(d) An offense under Subsection (a) is a felony of the first degree if the amount of the controlled substance to which the offense applies is, by aggregate weight, including adulterants or dilutants, four grams or more but less than 400 grams.

(e) An offense under Subsection (a) is punishable by imprisonment in the institutional division of the Texas Department of Criminal Justice for life or for a term of not more than 99 years or less than 10 years, and a fine not to exceed $100,000, if the amount of the controlled substance to which the offense applies is, by aggregate weight, including adulterants or dilutants, 400 grams or more.

*(Added by L.1989, chap. 678(1); chgd. by L.1993, chap. 900(2.02), eff. 9/1/94.)*

## §481.114. Offense: Manufacture or delivery of substance in Penalty Group 3 or 4.

(a) Except as authorized by this chapter, a person commits an offense if the person knowingly or intentionally manufactures, delivers, or possesses with intent to manufacture or deliver a controlled substance listed in Penalty Group 3 or 4.

(b) An offense under Subsection (a) is a state jail felony if the amount of the controlled substance to which the offense applies is, by aggregate weight, including adulterants or dilutants, less than 28 grams.

(c) An offense under Subsection (a) is a felony of the second degree if the amount of the controlled substance to which the offense applies is, by aggregate weight, including adulterants or dilutants, 28 grams or more but less than 200 grams.

(d) An offense under Subsection (a) is a felony of the first degree if the amount of the controlled substance to which the offense applies is, by aggregate weight, including adulterants or dilutants, 200 grams or more but less than 400 grams.

(e) An offense under Subsection (a) is punishable by imprisonment in the institutional division of the Texas Department of Criminal Justice for life or for a term of not more than 99 years or less than 10 years, and a fine not to exceed $100,000, if the amount of the controlled substance to which the offense applies is, by aggregate weight, including any adulterants or dilutants, 400 grams or more.

*(Added by L.1989, chap. 678(1); chgd. by L.1993, chap. 900(2.02), eff. 9/1/94.)*

## §481.115. Offense: Possession of substance in Penalty Group 1.

(a) Except as authorized by this chapter, a person commits an offense if the person knowingly or intentionally possesses a controlled substance listed in Penalty Group 1, unless the person obtained the substance directly from or under a valid prescription or order of a practitioner acting in the course of professional practice.

(b) An offense under Subsection (a) is a state jail felony if the amount of the controlled substance possessed is, by aggregate weight, including adulterants or dilutants, less than one gram.

(c) An offense under Subsection (a) is a felony of the third degree if the amount of the controlled substance possessed is, by aggregate weight, including adulterants or dilutants, one gram or more but less than four grams.

(d) An offense under Subsection (a) is a felony of the second degree if the amount of the controlled substance possessed is, by aggregate weight, including adulterants or dilutants, four grams or more but less than 200 grams.

(e) An offense under Subsection (a) is a felony of the first degree if the amount of the controlled substance possessed is, by aggregate weight, including adulterants or dilutants, 200 grams or more but less than 400 grams.

(f) An offense under Subsection (a) is punishable by imprisonment in the institutional division of the Texas Department of Criminal Justice for life or for a term of not more than 99 years or less than 10 years, and a fine not to exceed $100,000, if the amount of the controlled substance possessed is, by aggregate weight, including adulterants or dilutants, 400 grams or more.

*(Added by L.1989, chap. 678(1); chgd. by L.1993, chap. 900(2.02), eff. 9/1/94.)*

**§481.1151. Offense: Possession of substance in Penalty Group 1-A.**

(a) Except as provided by this chapter, a person commits an offense if the person knowingly possesses a controlled substance listed in Penalty Group 1-A.

(b) An offense under this section is:

(1) a state jail felony if the number of abuse units of the controlled substance is fewer than 20;

(2) a felony of the third degree if the number of abuse units of the controlled substance is 20 or more but fewer than 80;

(3) a felony of the second degree if the number of abuse units of the controlled substance is 80 or more but fewer than 4,000;

(4) a felony of the first degree if the number of abuse units of the controlled substance is 4,000 or more but fewer than 8,000; and

(5) punishable by imprisonment in the institutional division of the Texas Department of Criminal Justice for life or for a term of not more than 99 years or less than 15 years and a fine not to exceed $250,000, if the number of abuse units of the controlled substance is 8,000 or more.
*(Added by L.1997, chap. 745(26), eff. 1/1/98.)*

**§481.116. Offense: Possession of substance in Penalty Group 2.**

(a) Except as authorized by this chapter, a person commits an offense if the person knowingly or intentionally possesses a controlled substance listed in Penalty Group 2, unless the person obtained the substance directly from or under a valid prescription or order of a practitioner acting in the course of professional practice.

(b) An offense under Subsection (a) is a state jail felony if the amount of the controlled substance possessed is, by aggregate weight, including adulterants or dilutants, less than one gram.

(c) An offense under Subsection (a) is a felony of the third degree if the amount of the controlled substance possessed is, by aggregate weight, including adulterants or dilutants, one gram or more but less than four grams.

(d) An offense under Subsection (a) is a felony of the second degree if the amount of the controlled substance possessed is, by aggregate weight, including adulterants or dilutants, four grams or more but less than 400 grams.

(e) An offense under Subsection (a) is punishable by imprisonment in the institutional division of the Texas Department of Criminal Justice for life or for a term of not more than 99 years or less than five years, and a fine not to exceed $50,000, if the amount of the controlled substance possessed is, by aggregate weight, including adulterants or dilutants, 400 grams or more.
*(Added by L.1989, chap. 678(1); chgd. by L.1993, chap. 900(2.02), eff. 9/1/94.)*

**§481.117. Offense: Possession of substance in Penalty Group 3.**

(a) Except as authorized by this chapter, a person commits an offense if the person knowingly or intentionally possesses a controlled substance listed in Penalty Group 3, unless the person obtains the substance directly from or under a valid prescription or order of a practitioner acting in the course of professional practice.

(b) An offense under Subsection (a) is a Class A misdemeanor if the amount of the controlled substance possessed is, by aggregate weight, including adulterants or dilutants, less than 28 grams.

(c) An offense under Subsection (a) is a felony of the third degree if the amount of the controlled substance possessed is, by aggregate weight, including adulterants or dilutants, 28 grams or more but less than 200 grams.

(d) An offense under Subsection (a) is a felony of the second degree, if the amount of the controlled substance possessed is, by aggregate weight, including adulterants or dilutants, 200 grams or more but less than 400 grams.

(e) An offense under Subsection (a) is punishable by imprisonment in the institutional division of the Texas Department of Criminal Justice for life or for a term of not more than 99 years or less than five years, and a fine not to exceed $50,000, if the amount of the controlled substance possessed is, by aggregate weight, including adulterants or dilutants, 400 grams or more.
*(Added by L.1989, chap. 678(1); chgd. by L.1993, chap. 900(2.02), eff. 9/1/94.)*

**§481.118. Offense: Possession of substance in Penalty Group 4.**

(a) Except as authorized by this chapter, a person commits an offense if the person knowingly or intentionally possesses a controlled substance listed in Penalty Group 4, unless the person obtained the substance directly from or under a valid prescription or order of a practitioner acting in the course of practice.

(b) An offense under Subsection (a) is a Class B misdemeanor if the amount of the controlled substance possessed is, by aggregate weight, including adulterants or dilutants, less than 28 grams.

(c) An offense under Subsection (a) is a felony of the third degree if the amount of the controlled substance possessed is, by aggregate weight, including adulterants or dilutants, 28 grams or more but less than 200 grams.

(d) An offense under Subsection (a) is a felony of the second degree, if the amount of the controlled substance possessed is, by aggregate weight, including adulterants or dilutants, 200 grams or more but less than 400 grams.

(e) An offense under Subsection (a) is punishable by imprisonment in the institutional division of the Texas Department of Criminal Justice for life or for a term of not more than 99 years or less than five years, and a fine not to exceed $50,000, if the amount of the controlled substance possessed is, by aggregate weight, including adulterants or dilutants, 400 grams or more.
*(Added by L.1989, chap. 678(1); chgd. by L.1993, chap. 900(2.02), eff. 9/1/94.)*

## §481.119. Offense: Manufacture, delivery, or possession of miscellaneous substances.

(a) A person commits an offense if the person knowingly or intentionally manufactures, delivers, or possesses with intent to manufacture or deliver a controlled substance listed in a schedule by an action of the commissioner under this chapter but not listed in a penalty group. An offense under this subsection is a Class A misdemeanor.

(b) A person commits an offense if the person knowingly or intentionally possesses a controlled substance listed in a schedule by an action of the commissioner under this chapter but not listed in a penalty group. An offense under this subsection is a Class B misdemeanor.
*(Added by L.1989, chap. 678(1), eff. 9/1/89.)*

## §481.120. Offense: Delivery of marihuana.

(a) Except as authorized by this chapter, a person commits an offense if the person knowingly or intentionally delivers marihuana.

(b) An offense under Subsection (a) is:

(1) a Class B misdemeanor if the amount of marihuana delivered is one-fourth ounce or less and the person committing the offense does not receive remuneration for the marihuana;

(2) a Class A misdemeanor if the amount of marihuana delivered is one-fourth ounce or less and the person committing the offense receives remuneration for the marihuana;

(3) a state jail felony if the amount of marihuana delivered is five pounds or less but more than one-fourth ounce;

(4) a felony of the second degree if the amount of marihuana delivered is 50 pounds or less but more than five pounds;

(5) a felony of the first degree if the amount of marihuana delivered is 2,000 pounds or less but more than 50 pounds; and

(6) punishable by imprisonment in the institutional division of the Texas Department of Criminal Justice for life or for a term of not more than 99 years or less than 10 years, and a fine not to exceed $100,000, if the amount of marihuana delivered is more than 2,000 pounds.
*(Added by L.1989, chap. 678(1); chgd. by L.1993, chap. 900(2.02), eff. 9/1/94.)*

## §481.121. Offense: Possession of marihuana.

(a) Except as authorized by this chapter, a person commits an offense if the person knowingly or intentionally possesses a usable quantity of marihuana.

(b) An offense under Subsection (a) is:

(1) a Class B misdemeanor if the amount of marihuana possessed is two ounces or less;

(2) a Class A misdemeanor if the amount of marihuana possessed is four ounces or less but more than two ounces;

(3) a state jail felony if the amount of marihuana possessed is five pounds or less but more than four ounces;

(4) a felony of the third degree if the amount of marihuana possessed is 50 pounds or less but more than 5 pounds;

(5) a felony of the second degree if the amount of marihuana possessed is 2,000 pounds or less but more than 50 pounds; and

(6) punishable by imprisonment in the institutional division of the Texas Department of Criminal Justice for life or for a term of not more than 99 years or less than 5 years, and a fine not to exceed $50,000, if the amount of marihuana possessed is more than 2,000 pounds.
*(Added by L.1989, chap. 678(1); chgd. by L.1993, chap. 900(2.02), eff. 9/1/94.)*

**§481.122. Offense: Delivery of controlled substance or marihuana to minor.**

(a) Except as provided by this chapter, a person commits an offense if the person knowingly delivers a controlled substance listed in Penalty Group 1, 1-A, 2, or 3 or knowingly delivers marihuana and the person delivers the controlled substance or marihuana to a person:

(1) who is 17 years of age or younger;

(2) who the actor knows or believes intends to deliver the controlled substance or marihuana to a person 17 years of age or younger;

(3) who is enrolled in an elementary or secondary school; or

(4) who the actor knows or believes intends to deliver the controlled substances or marihuana to a person who is enrolled in an elementary or secondary school.

(b) It is an affirmative defense to prosecution under this section that:

(1) the actor was younger than 18 years of age when the offense was committed; or

(2) the actor was younger than 21 years of age when the offense was committed and delivered only marihuana in an amount less than one-fourth ounce for which the actor did not receive remuneration.

(c) An offense under this section is a felony of the second degree.

*(Added by L.1989, chap. 678(1); chgd. by L.1993, chap. 900(2.02); L.1997, chap. 745(27), eff. 1/1/98.)*

**§481.123. Offense: Delivery, manufacture, or possession of controlled substance analogue.**

(a) For the purposes of this chapter, a controlled substance analogue is considered to be a controlled substance listed in Penalty Group 1 or 1-A if the analogue in whole or in part is intended for human consumption and:

(1) the chemical structure of the analogue is substantially similar to the chemical structure of a controlled substance listed in Schedule I or Penalty Group 1 or 1-A; or

(2) the analogue is specifically designed to produce an effect substantially similar to or greater than the effect of a controlled substance listed in Schedule I or Penalty Group 1 or 1-A.

(b) For the purposes of this chapter, a controlled substance analogue is considered to be a controlled substance listed in Penalty Group 2 if the analogue in whole or in part is intended for human consumption and:

(1) the chemical structure of the analogue is substantially similar to the chemical structure of a controlled substance listed in Schedule II or Penalty Group 2; or

(2) the analogue is specifically designed to produce an effect substantially similar to or greater than the effect of a controlled substance listed in Schedule II or Penalty Group 2.

(c) Except as authorized by this chapter, a person commits an offense if the person knowingly or intentionally manufactures, delivers, or possesses with intent to manufacture or deliver a controlled substance analogue described by Subsection (a).

(d) Except as authorized by this chapter, a person commits an offense if the person knowingly or intentionally possesses a controlled substance analogue described by Subsection (a).

(e) Except as authorized by this chapter, a person commits an offense if the person knowingly or intentionally manufactures, delivers, or possesses with intent to manufacture or deliver a controlled substance analogue described by Subsection (b).

(f) Except as authorized by this chapter, a person commits an offense if the person knowingly or intentionally possesses a controlled substance analogue described by subsection (b).

(g) This section does not apply to:

(1) a controlled substance;

(2) a substance for which there is an approved new drug application under Section 505 of the Federal Food, Drug, and Cosmetic Act (21 U.S.C. Section 355);

(3) a substance for which an exemption for investigational use has been granted under Section 505 of the Federal Food, Drug, and Cosmetic Act (21 U.S.C. Section 355), to the extent that the substance is possessed, manufactured, or delivered by a particular person under the exemption and the person's conduct with respect to the substance is in accord with the exemption; or

(4) a substance, to the extent the substance is not intended for human consumption, before an exemption under Section 505 of the Federal Food, Drug, and Cosmetic Act (21 U.S.C. Section 355), takes effect with regard to the substance.

(h) For the purposes of this section, Section 505 of the Federal Food, Drug, and Cosmetic Act (21 U.S.C. Section 355) applies to the introduction or delivery for introduction of any new drug into intrastate, interstate, or foreign commerce.

(i) An offense under Subsection (c) is punishable in the same manner as if the controlled substance analogue were a controlled substance manufactured, delivered, or possessed with intent to manufacture or deliver under Section 481.112.

(j) An offense under Subsection (d) is punishable in the same manner as if the controlled substance analogue were a controlled substance possessed under Section 481.115.

(k) An offense under Subsection (e) is punishable in the same manner as if the controlled substance analogue were a controlled substance manufactured, delivered, or possessed with intent to manufacture or deliver under Section 481.113.

(*l*) An offense under Subsection (f) is punishable in the same manner as if the controlled substance analogue were a controlled substance possessed under Section 481.116.
*(Added by L.1989, chap. 678(1); chgd. by L.1997, chap. 745(28), eff. 1/1/98.)*

**§481.124.** *(Repealed by L.1989, chap. 1100(5.02)(j); added by L.1991, chap. 14(197), but failed to take effect under L.1991, chap. 141(6)(b), eff. 9/1/91.)*

### §481.125. Offense: Possession or delivery of drug paraphernalia.

(a) A person commits an offense if the person knowingly or intentionally uses or possesses with intent to use drug paraphernalia to plant, propagate, cultivate, grow, harvest, manufacture, compound, convert, produce, process, prepare, test, analyze, pack, repack, store, contain, or conceal a controlled substance in violation of this chapter or to inject, ingest, inhale, or otherwise introduce into the human body a controlled substance in violation of this chapter.

(b) A person commits an offense if the person knowingly or intentionally delivers, possesses with intent to deliver, or manufactures with intent to deliver drug paraphernalia knowing that the person who receives or who is intended to receive the drug paraphernalia intends that it be used to plant, propagate, cultivate, grow, harvest, manufacture, compound, convert, produce, process, prepare, test, analyze, pack, repack, store, contain, or conceal a controlled substance in violation of this chapter or to inject, ingest, inhale, or otherwise introduce into the human body a controlled substance in violation of this chapter.

(c) A person commits an offense if the person commits an offense under Subsection (b), is 18 years of age or older, and the person who receives or who is intended to receive the drug paraphernalia is younger than 18 years of age and at least three years younger than the actor.

(d) An offense under Subsection (a) is a Class C misdemeanor.

(e) An offense under Subsection (b) is a Class A misdemeanor, unless it is shown on the trial of a defendant that the defendant has previously been convicted under Subsection (b) or (c), in which event the offense is punishable by confinement in jail for a term of not more than one year or less than 90 days.

(f) An offense under Subsection (c) is a state jail felony.
*(Added by L.1989, chap. 678(1); chgd. by L.1993, chap. 900(2.02), eff. 9/1/94.)*

### §481.126. Offense: Illegal expenditure or investment.

(a) A person commits an offense if the person knowingly or intentionally:

(1) expends funds the person knows are derived from the commission of an offense punishable under Section 481.112(e) or (f), 481.113(e), 481.114(e), 481.115(f), 481.116(e), 481.117(e), 481.118(e), 481.120(b)(6), or 481.121(b)(6); or

(2) finances or invests funds the person knows or believes are intended to further the commission of an offense for which the punishment is listed under Subdivision (1).

(b) An offense under this section is a felony of the first degree.
*(Added by L.1989, chap. 678(1); chgd. by L.1993, chap. 900(2.02); L.1995, chap. 318(37), eff. 9/1/95.)*

### §481.127. Offense: Unauthorized disclosure of information.

(a) A person commits an offense if the person knowingly gives, permits, or obtains unauthorized access to information submitted to the director under Section 481.075.

(b) An offense under this section is a state jail felony.
*(Added by L.1989, chap. 678(1); chgd. by L.1993, chap. 900(2.02); L.1997, chap. 745(29), eff. 1/1/98.)*

### §481.128. Offense and civil penalty: Commercial matters.

(a) A registrant or dispenser commits an offense if the registrant or dispenser knowingly:

(1) distributes, delivers, administers, or dispenses a controlled substance in violation of Sections 481.070-481.075;

(2) manufactures a controlled substance not authorized by the person's registration or distributes or dispenses a controlled substance not authorized by the person's registration to another registrant or other person;

Zt Printed in the U.S.A.

(3) refuses or fails to make, keep, or furnish a record, report, notification, order form, statement, invoice, or information required by this chapter;

(4) prints, manufactures, possesses, or produces a prescription sticker or official prescription form without the approval of the director;

(5) delivers or possesses a counterfeit prescription sticker or official prescription form;

(6) refuses an entry into a premise for an inspection authorized by this chapter;

(7) refuses or fails to return a prescription sticker as required by Section 481.075(k);

(8) refuses or fails to make, keep, or furnish a record, report, notification, order form, statement, invoice, or information required by a rule adopted by the director; or

(9) refuses or fails to maintain security required by this chapter or a rule adopted under this chapter.

(b) If the registrant or dispenser knowingly refuses or fails to make, keep, or furnish a record, report, notification, order form, statement, invoice, or information or maintain security required by a rule adopted by the director, the registrant or dispenser is liable to the state for a civil penalty of not more than $5,000 for each act.

(c) An offense under Subsection (a) is a state jail felony.

(d) If a person commits an act that would otherwise be an offense under Subsection (a) except that it was committed without the requisite culpable mental state, the person is liable to the state for a civil penalty of not more than $1,000 for each act.

(e) A district attorney of the county where the act occurred may file suit in district court in that county to collect a civil penalty under this section, or the district attorney of Travis County or the attorney general may file suit in district court in Travis County to collect the penalty.

*(Added by L.1989, chap. 678(1); chgd. by L.1991, chap. 761(5); L.1993, chap. 900(2.02); L.1997, chap. 745(30), eff. 1/1/98.)*

### §481.129. Offense: Fraud.

(a) A person commits an offense if the person knowingly:

(1) distributes as a registrant or dispenser a controlled substance listed in Schedule I or II, unless the person distributes the controlled substance under an order form as required by Section 481.069;

(2) uses in the course of manufacturing, prescribing, or distributing a controlled substance a registration number that is fictitious, revoked, suspended, or issued to another person;

(3) uses a prescription sticker issued to another person to prescribe a Schedule II controlled substance;

(4) possesses or attempts to possess a controlled substance:

(A) by misrepresentation, fraud, forgery, deception, or subterfuge;

(B) through use of a fraudulent prescription form; or

(C) through use of a fraudulent oral or telephonically communicated prescription; or

(5) furnishes false or fraudulent material information in or omits material information from an application, report, record, or other document required to be kept or filed under this chapter.

(b) A person commits an offense if the person knowingly or intentionally:

(1) makes, distributes, or possesses a punch, die, plate, stone, or other thing designed to print, imprint, or reproduce an actual or simulated trademark, trade name, or other identifying mark, imprint, or device of another on a controlled substance or the container or label of a container for a controlled substance, so as to make the controlled substance a counterfeit substance; or

(2) manufactures, delivers, or possesses with intent to deliver a counterfeit substance.

(c) A person commits an offense if the person knowingly or intentionally:

(1) delivers a prescription or a prescription form for other than a valid medical purpose in the course of professional practice; or

(2) possesses a prescription for a controlled substance or a prescription form unless the prescription or prescription form is possessed:

(A) during the manufacturing or distribution process;

(B) by a practitioner, practitioner's agent, or an institutional practitioner for a valid medical purpose during the course of professional practice;

(C) by a pharmacist or agent of a pharmacy during the professional practice of pharmacy;

(D) under a practitioner's order made by the practitioner for a valid medical purpose in the course of professional practice; or

(E) by an officer or investigator authorized to enforce this chapter within the scope of the officer's or investigator's official duties.

(d) An offense under Subsection (a) is:

(1) a felony of the second degree if the controlled substance that is the subject of the offense is listed in Schedule I or II;

(2) a felony of the third degree if the controlled substance that is the subject of the offense is listed in Schedule III or IV; and

(3) a Class A misdemeanor if the controlled substance that is the subject of the offense is listed in Schedule V.

(e) An offense under Subsection (b) is a Class A misdemeanor.

(f) An offense under Subsection (c)(1) is:

(1) a felony of the second degree if the defendant delivers:

(A) a prescription form; or

(B) a prescription for a controlled substance listed in Schedule II; and

(2) a felony of the third degree if the defendant delivers a prescription for a controlled substance listed in Schedule III, IV, or V.

(g) An offense under Subsection (c)(2) is:

(1) a state jail felony if the defendant possesses:

(A) a prescription form; or

(B) a prescription for a controlled substance listed in Schedule II or III; and

(2) a Class B misdemeanor if the defendant possesses a prescription for a controlled substance listed in Schedule IV or V.

*(Added by L.1989, chap. 678(1); chgd. by L.1989, chap. 1100(5.02)(p); chgd. by L.1993, chap. 900(2.02); L.1997, chap. 745(31), eff. 1/1/98.)*



## §481.130. Penalties under other law.

A penalty imposed for an offense under this chapter is in addition to any civil or administrative penalty or other sanction imposed by law. *(Added by L.1989, chap. 678(1), eff. 9/1/89.)*

## §481.131. Offense: Diversion of controlled substance property or plant.

(a) A person commits an offense if the person intentionally or knowingly:

(1) converts to the person's own use or benefit a controlled substance property or plant seized under Section 481.152 or 481.153; or

(2) diverts to the unlawful use or benefit of another person a controlled substance property or plant seized under Section 481.152 or 481.153.

(b) An offense under this section is a state jail felony.

*(Added by L.1991, chap. 141(2); chgd. by L.1993, chap. 900(2.02), eff. 9/1/94.)*

## §481.132. Multiple prosecutions.

(a) In this section, "criminal episode" means the commission of two or more offenses under this chapter under the following circumstances:

(1) the offenses are committed pursuant to the same transaction or pursuant to two or more transactions that are connected or constitute a common scheme, plan, or continuing course of conduct; or

(2) the offenses are the repeated commission of the same or similar offenses.

(b) A defendant may be prosecuted in a single criminal action for all offenses arising out of the same criminal episode. If a single criminal action is based on more than one charging instrument within the jurisdiction of the trial court, not later than the 30th day before the date of the trial, the state shall file written notice of the action.

(c) If a judgment of guilt is reversed, set aside, or vacated and a new trial is ordered, the state may not prosecute in a single criminal action in the new trial any offense not joined in the former prosecution unless evidence to establish probable guilt for that offense was not known to the appropriate prosecution official at the time the first prosecution began.

(d) If the accused is found guilty of more than one offense arising out of the same criminal episode prosecuted in a single criminal action, sentence for each offense for which the accused has been found guilty shall be pronounced, and those sentences run concurrently.

(e) If it appears that a defendant or the state is prejudiced by a joinder of offenses, the court may order separate trials of the offenses or provide other relief as justice requires.

(f) This section provides the exclusive method for consolidation and joinder of prosecutions for offenses under this chapter. This section is not a limitation of Article 36.09 or 36.10, Code of Criminal Procedure.

*(Added by L.1991, chap. 193(1); renumbered by L.1991, 1st C.S., chap. 14(8.01)(17a), eff. 11/12/91.)*

## §481.133. Offense: Falsification of drug test results.

(a) A person commits an offense if the person knowingly or intentionally uses or possesses with intent to use any substance or device designed to falsify drug test results.

(b) A person commits an offense if the person knowingly or intentionally delivers, possesses with intent to deliver, or manufactures with intent to deliver a substance or device designed to falsify drug test results.

(c) In this section, "drug test" means a lawfully administered test designed to detect the presence of a controlled substance or marihuana.

(d) An offense under Subsection (a) is a Class B misdemeanor.

(e) An offense under Subsection (b) is a Class A misdemeanor.

*(Added by L.1991, chap. 274(1); renumbered by L.1991, 1st C.S., chap. 14(8.01)(17b), eff. 11/12/91.)*

## §481.134. Drug-free zones.

(a) In this section:

(1) "Minor" means a person who is younger than 18 years of age.

(2) "Institution of higher education" means any public or private technical institute, junior college, senior college or university, medical or dental unit, or other agency of higher education as defined by Section 61.003, Education Code.

(3) "Playground" means any outdoor facility that is not on the premises of a school and that:

(A) is intended for recreation;

(B) is open to the public; and

(C) contains three or more separate apparatus intended for the recreation of children, such as slides, swing sets, and teeterboards.

(4) "Premises" means real property and all buildings and appurtenances pertaining to the real property.

(5) "School" means a private or public elementary or secondary school or a day-care center, as defined by Section 42.002, Human Resources Code.

(6) "Video arcade facility" means any facility that:

(A) is open to the public, including persons who are 17 years of age or younger;

(B) is intended primarily for the use of pinball or video machines; and

(C) contains at least three pinball or video machines.

(7) "Youth center" means any recreational facility or gymnasium that:

(A) is intended primarily for use by persons who are 17 years of age or younger; and

(B) regularly provides athletic, civic, or cultural activities.

(b) An offense otherwise punishable as a state jail felony under Section 481.112, 481.113, 481.114, or 481.120 is punishable as a felony of the third degree, and an offense otherwise punishable as a felony of the second degree under any of those sections is punishable as a felony of the first degree, if it is shown at the punishment phase of the trial of the offense that the offense was committed:

(1) in, on, or within 1,000 feet of premises owned, rented, or leased by an institution of higher learning or a playground; or

(2) in, on, or within 300 feet of the premises of a public or private youth center, public swimming pool, or video arcade facility.

(c) The minimum term of confinement or imprisonment for an offense otherwise punishable under Section 481.112(c), (d), (e), or (f), 481.113(c), (d), or (e), 481.114(c), (d), or (e), 481.115(c)-(f), 481.116(c), (d), or (e), 481.117(c), (d), or (e), 481.118(c), (d), or (e), 481.120(b)(4), (5), or (6), or 481.121(b)(4), (5), or (6) is increased by five years and the maximum fine for the offense is doubled if it is shown on the trial of the offense that the offense was committed:

(1) in, on, or within 1,000 feet of premises of a school; or

(2) on a school bus.

(d) An offense otherwise punishable under Section 481.112(b), 481.113(b), 481.114(b), 481.115(b), 481.116(b), 481.120(b)(3), or 481.121(b)(3) is a felony of the third degree if it is shown on the trial of the offense that the offense was committed:

(1) in, on, or within 1,000 feet of any real property that is owned, rented, or leased to a school or school board; or

(2) on a school bus.

(e) An offense otherwise punishable under Section 481.117(b), 481.119(a), 481.120(b)(2), or 481.121(b)(2) is a state jail felony if it is shown on the trial of the offense that the offense was committed:

(1) in, on, or within 1,000 feet of any real property that is owned, rented, or leased to a school or school board; or

(2) on a school bus.

(f) An offense otherwise punishable under Section 481.118(b), 481.119(b), 481.120(b)(1), or 481.121(b)(1) is a Class A misdemeanor if it is shown on the trial of the offense that the offense was committed:

(1) in, on, or within 1,000 feet of any real property that is owned, rented, or leased to a school or school board; or

(2) on a school bus.

(g) Subsection (f) does not apply to an offense if:

(1) the offense was committed inside a private residence; and

(2) no minor was present in the private residence at the time the offense was committed.

(h) Punishment that is increased for a conviction for an offense listed under this section may not run concurrently with punishment for a conviction under any other criminal statute.

*(Added by L.1993, chap. 888(1); chgd. by L.1995, chaps. 260(39), 318(38); L.1997, chap. 1063(9), eff. 9/1/97.)*

### §481.135. Maps as evidence of location or area.

(a) In a prosecution under Section 481.134, a map produced or reproduced by a municipal or county engineer for the purpose of showing the location and boundaries of drug-free zones is admissible in evidence and is prima facie evidence of the location or boundaries of those areas if the governing body of the municipality or county adopts a resolution or ordinance approving the map as an official finding and record of the location or boundaries of those areas.

(b) A municipal or county engineer may, on request of the governing body of the municipality or county, revise a map that has been approved by the governing body of the municipality or county as provided by Subsection (a).

(c) A municipal or county engineer shall file the original or a copy of every approved or revised map approved as provided by Subsection (a) with the county clerk of each county in which the area is located.

(d) This section does not prevent the prosecution from:

(1) introducing or relying on any other evidence or testimony to establish any element of an offense for which punishment is increased under Section 481.134; or

(2) using or introducing any other map or diagram otherwise admissible under the Texas Rules of Criminal Evidence.

*(Added by L.1993, chap. 888(3), eff. 9/1/93.)*

### §481.136. Offense: Unlawful transfer or receipt of chemical precursor.

(a) A person commits an offense if the person sells, transfers, furnishes, or receives a precursor substance listed in Section 481.077(a) and the person:

(1) does not hold a precursor transfer permit as required by Section 481.078 at the time of the transaction;

(2) does not comply with Section 481.077;

(3) knowingly makes a false statement in a report or record required by Section 481.077 or 481.078; or

(4) knowingly violates a rule adopted under Section 481.077 or 481.078.

(b) An offense under this section is a state jail felony, unless it is shown on the trial of the offense that the defendant has been previously convicted of an offense under this section or Section 481.137, in which event the offense is a felony of the third degree.

*(Added by L.1997, chap. 745(32), eff. 1/1/98.)*

### §481.137. Offense: Transfer of precursor substance for unlawful manufacture.

(a) A person commits an offense if the person sells, transfers, or otherwise furnishes a precursor substance listed in Section 481.077(a) with the knowledge or intent that the recipient will use the substance to unlawfully manufacture a controlled substance or controlled substance analogue.

(b) An offense under this section is a felony of the third degree.

*(Added by L.1997, chap. 745(32), eff. 1/1/98.)*

### §481.138. Offense: Unlawful transfer or receipt of chemical laboratory apparatus.

(a) A person commits an offense if the person sells, transfers, furnishes, or receives an apparatus described by Section 481.080(a) and the person:

(1) does not have an apparatus transfer permit as required by Section 481.081 at the time of the transaction;

(2) does not comply with Section 481.080;

(3) knowingly makes a false statement in a report or record required by Section 481.080 or 481.081; or

(4) knowingly violates a rule adopted under Section 481.080 or 481.081.

(b) An offense under this section is a state jail felony, unless it is shown on the trial of the offense that the defendant has been previously convicted of an offense under this section, in which event the offense is a felony of the third degree.

*(Added by L.1997, chap. 745(32), eff. 1/1/98.)*

### §481.139. Offense: Transfer of chemical laboratory apparatus for unlawful manufacture.

(a) A person commits an offense if the person sells, transfers, or otherwise furnishes an apparatus described by Section 481.080(a) with the knowledge or intent that the recipient will use the apparatus to unlawfully manufacture a controlled substance or controlled substance analogue.

(b) An offense under Subsection (a) is a felony of the third degree.

*(Added by L.1997, chap. 745(32), eff. 1/1/98.)*

### §§481.140 to 481.150. *(Reserved.)*

## SUBCHAPTER E. FORFEITURE

*(Chgd. by L.1991, chap. 141(1), eff. 9/1/91.)*

### §481.151. Definitions.

In this subchapter:

(1) "Department" means the Department of Public Safety.

(2) "Controlled substance property" means a controlled substance, mixture containing a controlled substance, controlled substance analogue, counterfeit controlled substance, drug paraphernalia, chemical precursor, or raw material.

(3) "Controlled substance plant" means a species of plant from which a controlled substance listed in Schedule I or II may be delivered.

*(Repealed by L.1989, 1st C.S., chap. 12(6); added by L.1991, chap. 141(1), eff. 9/1/91.)*

### §481.152. Seizure and summary forfeiture and destruction of controlled substance plants.

(a) Controlled substance plants are subject to seizure and summary forfeiture to the state if:

(1) the plants have been planted, or cultivated, or harvested in violation of this chapter;

(2) the plants are wild growths; or

(3) the owners or cultivators of the plants are unknown.

(b) Subsection (a) does not apply to unharvested peyote growing in its natural state.

(c) If a person who occupies or controls land or premises on which the plants are growing fails on the demand of a peace officer to produce an appropriate registration or proof that the person is the holder of the registration, the officer may seize and forfeit the plants.

(d) If a controlled substance plant is seized and forfeited under this section, a court may order the disposition of the plant under Section 481.159, or the department or a peace officer may summarily destroy the property under the rules of the department.

*(Added by L.1989, chap. 678(1); chgd. by L.1991, chap. 141(1), eff. 9/1/91.)*

### §481.153. Seizure and summary forfeiture and destruction of controlled substance property.

(a) Controlled substance property that is manufactured, delivered, or possessed in violation of this chapter is subject to seizure and summary forfeiture to the state.

(b) If an item of controlled substance property is seized and forfeited under this section, a court may order the disposition of the property under Section 481.159, or the department or a peace officer may destroy the property under the rules of the department.

*(Repealed by L.1989, 1st C.S., chap. 12(6); added by L.1991, chap. 141(1), eff. 9/1/91.)*

### §481.154. Rules.

(a) The director may adopt reasonable rules and procedures, not inconsistent with the provisions of this chapter, concerning:

(1) summary forfeiture and destruction of controlled substance property or plants;

(2) establishment and operation of a secure storage area;

(3) delegation by a law enforcement agency head of the authority to access a secure storage area; and

(4) minimum tolerance for and the circumstances of loss or destruction during an investigation.

(b) The rules for the destruction of controlled substance property or plants must require:

(1) more than one person to witness the destruction of the property or plants;

(2) the preparation of an inventory of the property or plants destroyed; and

(3) the preparation of a statement that contains the names of the persons who witness the destruction and the details of the destruction.

(c) A document prepared under a rule adopted under this section must be completed, retained, and made available for inspection by the director.

*(Repealed by L.1989, 1st C.S., chap. 12(6); added by L.1991, chap. 141(1), eff. 9/1/91.)*

**§§481.155, 481.156.** *(Repealed by L.1989, 1st C.S., chap. 12(6), eff. 10/18/89.)*

**§481.157.** *(Added by L.1989, chap. 678(1); chgd. by L.1989, chap. 1100(5.02)(q); repealed by L.1989, 1st C.S., chap. 12(6); repealed by L.1991, chap. 14(198), eff. 9/1/91.)*

**§481.158.** *(Repealed by L.1989, 1st C.S., chap. 12(6), eff. 10/18/89.)*

**§481.159. Disposition of controlled substance property or plant.**

(a) If a district court orders the forfeiture of a controlled substance property or plant under Chapter 59, Code of Criminal Procedure, or under this code, the court shall also order a law enforcement agency to:

(1) retain the property or plant for its official purposes, including use in the investigation of offenses under this code;

(2) deliver the property or plant to a government agency for official purposes;

(3) deliver the property or plant to a person authorized by the court to receive it;

(4) deliver the property or plant to a person authorized by the director to receive it for a purpose described by Section 481.065(a); or

(5) destroy the property or plant that is not otherwise disposed of in the manner prescribed by this subchapter.

(b) The district court may not require the department to receive, analyze, or retain a controlled substance property or plant forfeited to a law enforcement agency other than the department.

(c) In order to ensure that a controlled substance property or plant is not diluted, substituted, diverted, or tampered with while being used in the investigation of offenses under this code, law enforcement agencies using the property or plant for this purpose shall:

(1) employ a qualified individual to conduct qualitative and quantitative analyses of the property or plant before and after their use in an investigation;

(2) maintain the property or plant in a secure storage area accessible only to the law enforcement agency head and the individual responsible for analyzing, preserving, and maintaining security over the property or plant; and

(3) maintain a log documenting:

(A) the date of issue, date of return, type, amount, and concentration of property or plant used in an investigation; and

(B) the signature and the printed or typed name of the peace officer to whom the property or plant was issued and the signature and the printed or typed name of the individual issuing the property or plant.

(d) A law enforcement agency may contract with another law enforcement agency to provide security that complies with Subsection (c) for controlled substance property or plants.

(e) A law enforcement agency may adopt a written policy with more stringent requirements than those required by Subsection (c). The director may enter and inspect, in accordance with Section 481.181, a location at which an agency maintains records or controlled substance property or plants as required by this section.

(f) If a law enforcement agency uses a controlled substance property or plant in the investigation of an offense under this code and the property or plant has been transported across state lines before the forfeiture, the agency shall cooperate with a federal agency in the investigation if requested to do so by the federal agency.

(g) Under the rules of the department, a law enforcement agency head may grant to another person access to a secure storage facility under Subsection (c)(2).

(h) A county, justice, or municipal court may order forfeiture of a controlled substance property or plant, unless the lawful possession of and title to the property or plant can be ascertained. If the court determines that a person had lawful possession of and title to the controlled substance property or plant before it was seized, the court shall order the controlled substance property or plant returned to the person, if the person so desires. The court may only order the destruction of a controlled substance property or plant that is not otherwise disposed of in the manner prescribed by Section 481.160.

(i) If a controlled substance property or plant seized under this chapter was forfeited to an agency for the purpose of destruction or for any purpose other than investigation, the property or plant may not be used in an investigation unless a district court orders disposition under this section and permits the use of the property or plant in the investigation.

*(Added by L.1989, chap 678(1); chgd. by L.1989, 1st C.S., chap. 12(5)(a); L.1991, chap. 141(1), eff. 9/1/91.)*

### §481.160. Destruction of items for health, environmental, or safety reasons.

(a) All hazardous waste, raw materials, residuals, contaminated glassware, associated equipment, and by-products from illicit chemical laboratories or similar operations that create health or environmental hazards or prohibit safe storage may be immediately destroyed by a law enforcement agency without court order if current environmental protection standards are followed.

(b) A law enforcement agency seizing materials described in Subsection (a) shall ensure that photographs are taken that reasonably demonstrate the total amount of the materials seized and the manner in which the materials were physically arranged or positioned before seizure and disposal.

*(Added by L.1989, chap. 678(1); chgd. by L.1989, chap. 1100(5.02)(r), L.1991, chap. 14(199), eff. 9/1/91. See other sec. 481.160 below.)*

### §481.160. Destruction of excess quantities.

(a) If a controlled substance property or plant is forfeited under this code or under Chapter 59, Code of Criminal Procedure, the law enforcement agency that seized the property or plant or to which the property or plant is forfeited may summarily destroy the property or plant without a court order before the disposition of a case arising out of the forfeiture if the agency ensures that:

(1) at least five random and representative samples are taken from the total amount of the property or plant and a sufficient quantity is preserved to provide for discovery by parties entitled to discovery;

(2) photographs are taken that reasonably demonstrate the total amount of the property or plant; and

(3) the gross weight or liquid measure of the property or plant is determined, either by actually weighing or measuring the property or plant or by estimating its weight or measurement after making dimensional measurements of the total amount seized.

(b) If the property consists of a single container of liquid, taking and preserving one representative sample complies with Subsection (a)(1).

(c) A representative sample, photograph, or record made under this section is admissible in civil or criminal proceedings in the same manner and to the same extent as if the total quantity of the suspected controlled substance property or plant was offered in evidence, regardless of whether the remainder of the property or plant has been destroyed. An inference or presumption of spoliation does not apply to a property or plant destroyed under this section.

(d) All controlled substance property, hazardous waste, residuals, contaminated glassware, associated equipment, and by-products from illicit chemical laboratories or similar operations that create health or environmental hazards or prohibit safe storage may be disposed of under Subsection (a) or may be seized and immediately destroyed by a law enforcement agency without court order if current environmental protection standards are followed.

(e) A law enforcement agency seizing and destroying or disposing of materials described in Subsection (d) shall ensure that photographs are taken that reasonably demonstrate the total amount of the materials seized and the manner in which the materials were physically arranged or positioned before seizure.

(f) A law enforcement agency may petition a court to require, as a condition of community supervision under Article 42.12, Code of Criminal Procedures, a person to reimburse the agency for the cost of the confiscation, analysis, storage, or disposal of raw materials, controlled substances, chemical precursors, drug paraphernalia, or other materials seized in connection with an offense committed by the person under this chapter.

*(Added by L.1989, chap. 678(1); chgd. by L.1989, chap. 1100(5.02)(r); L.1991, chaps. 141(1), 285(2); L.1997, chap. 745(33), eff. 1/1/98. See other sec. 481.160 above.)*

### §§481.161 to 481.180. *(Reserved.)*

## SUBCHAPTER F. INSPECTIONS, EVIDENCE, AND MISCELLANEOUS LAW ENFORCEMENT PROVISIONS

### §481.181. Inspections.

(a) The director may enter controlled premises at any reasonable time and inspect the premises and items described by Subsection (b) in order to inspect, copy, and verify the corrections of a record, report, or other document required to be made or kept under this chapter and to perform other functions under this chapter. The director shall state the purpose of the entry and present to the owner, operator, or agent in charge of the premises appropriate credentials and a written notice of inspection authority.

(b) The director may:

(1) inspect and copy a record, report, or other document required to be made or kept under this chapter;

(2) inspect, within reasonable limits and in a reasonable manner, the controlled premises and all pertinent equipment, finished and unfinished drugs, other substances, and materials, containers, labels, records, files, papers, processes, controls, and facilities as appropriate to verify a record, report, or document required to be kept under this chapter or to administer this chapter;

(3) examine and inventory stock of a controlled substance and obtain samples of the controlled substance;

(4) examine a hypodermic syringe, needle, pipe, or other instrument, device, contrivance, equipment, control, container, label, or facility relating to a possible violation of this chapter; and

(5) examine a material used, to be used, or capable of being used to dilute or adulterate a controlled substance.

(c) Unless the owner, operator, or agent in charge of the controlled premises consents in writing, the director may inspect:

(1) financial data;

(2) sales data other than shipment data; or

(3) pricing data.

*(Added by L.1989, chap. 678(1), eff. 9/1/89.)*

### §481.182. Search warrants.

A search warrant may be issued to search for and seize a controlled substance possessed or manufactured in violation of this chapter. The application for the issuance of and the execution of a search warrant under this section must conform to applicable provisions of the Code of Criminal Procedure. *(Added by L.1989, chap. 678(1), eff. 9/1/89.)*

### §481.183. Evidentiary rules relating to delivery or drug paraphernalia.

(a) For the purpose of establishing the delivery of a controlled substance, counterfeit substance, or drug paraphernalia, proof of an offer to sell must be corroborated by a person other than the offeree or by evidence other than a statement of the offeree.

(b) In considering whether an item is drug paraphernalia under this chapter, a court or other authority shall consider, in addition to all other logically relevant factors, and subject to rules of evidence:

(1) statements by an owner or person in control of the object concerning its use;

(2) the existence of any residue of a controlled substance on the object;

(3) direct or circumstantial evidence of the intent of an owner or other person in control of the object to deliver it to a person whom the person knows or should reasonably know intends to use the object to facilitate a violation of this chapter;

(4) oral or written instructions provided with the object concerning its use;

(5) descriptive material accompanying the object that explains or depicts its use;

(6) the manner in which the object is displayed for sale;

(7) whether the owner or person in control of the object is a supplier of similar or related items to the community, such as a licensed distributor or dealer of tobacco products;

(8) direct or circumstantial evidence of the ratio of sales of the object to the total sales of the business enterprise;

(9) the existence and scope of uses for the object in the community;

(10) the physical design characteristics of the item; and

(11) expert testimony concerning the item's use.

(c) The innocence of an owner or other person in charge of an object as to a direct violation of this chapter does not prevent a finding that the object is intended or designed for use as drug paraphernalia.

*(Added by L.1989, chap. 678(1), eff. 9/1/89.)*

### §481.184. Burden of proof; liabilities

(a) The state is not required to negate an exemption or exception provided by this chapter in a complaint, information, indictment, or other pleading or in any trial, hearing, or other proceeding under this chapter. A person claiming the benefit of an exemption or exception has the burden of going forward with the evidence with respect to the exemption or exception.

(b) In the absence of proof that a person is the duly authorized holder of an appropriate registration or order form issued under this chapter, the person is presumed not to be the holder of the registration or form. The presumption is subject to rebuttal by a person charged with an offense under this chapter.

(c) This chapter does not impose a liability on an authorized state, county, or municipal officer engaged in the lawful performance of the officer's duties.

*(Added by L.1989, chap. 678(1), eff. 9/1/89.)*

### §481.185. Arrest reports.

(a) Each law enforcement agency in this state shall file monthly with the director a report of all arrests made for drug offenses and quantities of controlled substances seized during the preceding month. The agency shall make the report on a form provided by the director and shall provide the information required by the form.

(b) The director shall publish an annual summary of all drug arrests and controlled substances seized in the state.

*(Added by L.1989, chap. 678(1), eff. 9/1/89.)*

### §481.186. Cooperative arrangements.

(a) The director shall cooperate with federal and state agencies in discharging the director's responsibilities concerning traffic in controlled substances and in suppressing the abuse of controlled substances. The director may:

(1) arrange for the exchange of information among government officials concerning the use and abuse of controlled substances;

(2) cooperate in and coordinate training programs concerning controlled substances law enforcement at local and state levels;

(3) cooperate with the Federal Drug Enforcement Administration and state agencies by establishing a centralized unit to accept, catalog, file, and collect statistics, including records on drug-dependent persons and other controlled substance law offenders in this state and, except as provided by Section 481.068, make the information available for federal, state, and local law enforcement purposes; and

(4) conduct programs of eradication aimed at destroying wild or illegal growth of plant species from which controlled substances may be extracted.

(b) In the exercise of regulatory functions under this chapter, the director may rely on results, information, and evidence relating to the regulatory functions of this chapter received from the Federal Drug Enforcement Administration and state agencies.

*(Added by L.1989, chap. 678(1), eff. 9/1/89.)*

### §§481.187 to 481.200. *(Reserved.)*

## SUBCHAPTER G. THERAPEUTIC RESEARCH PROGRAM

### §481.201. Research program; review board.

(a) The Texas Board of Health may establish a controlled substance therapeutic research program for the supervised use of tetrahydrocannabinols for medical and research purposes to be conducted in accordance with this chapter.

(b) If the Texas Board of Health establishes the program, the board shall create a research program review board. The review board members are appointed by the Texas Board of Health and serve at the will of the board.

(c) The review board shall be composed of:

(1) a licensed physician certified by the American Board of Ophthalmology;

(2) a licensed physician certified by the American Board of Internal Medicine and certified in the subspecialty of medical oncology;

(3) a licensed physician certified by the American Board of Psychiatry;

(4) a licensed physician certified by the American Board of Surgery;

(5) a licensed physician certified by the American Board of Radiology; and

(6) a licensed attorney with experience in law pertaining to the practice of medicine.

(d) Members serve without compensation but are entitled to reimbursement for actual and necessary expenses incurred in performing official duties.
*(Added by L.1989, chap. 678(1), eff. 9/1/89.)*

### §481.202. Review board powers and duties.

(a) The review board shall review research proposals submitted and medical case histories of persons recommended for participation in a research program and determine which research programs and persons are most suitable for the therapy and research purposes of the program. The review board shall approve the research programs, certify program participants, and conduct periodic reviews of the research and participants.

(b) The review board, after approval of the Texas Board of Health, may seek authorization to expand the research program to include diseases not covered by this subchapter.

(c) The review board shall maintain a record of all persons in charge of approved research programs and of all persons who participate in the program as researchers or as patients.

(d) The Texas Board of Health may terminate the distribution of tetrahydrocannabinols and their derivatives to a research program as it determines necessary.
*(Added by L.1989, chap. 678(1), eff. 9/1/89.)*



### §481.203. Patient participation.

(a) A person may not be considered for participation as a recipient of tetrahydrocannabinols and their derivatives through a research program unless the person is recommended to a person in charge of an approved research program and the review board by a physician who is licensed by the Texas State Board of Medical Examiners and is attending the person.

(b) A physician may not recommend a person for the research program unless the person:

(1) has glaucoma or cancer;

(2) is not responding to conventional treatment for glaucoma or cancer or is experiencing severe side effects from treatment; and

(3) has symptoms or side effects from treatment that may be alleviated by medical use of tetrahydrocannabinols or their derivatives.
*(Added by L.1989, chap. 678(1), eff. 9/1/89.)*

### §481.204. Acquisition and distribution of controlled substances.

(a) The Texas Board of Health shall acquire the tetrahydrocannabinols and their derivatives for use in the research program by contracting with the National Institute on Drug Abuse to receive tetrahydrocannabinols and their derivatives that are safe for human consumption according to the regulations adopted by the institute, the Food and Drug Administration, and the Federal Drug Enforcement Administration.

(b) The Texas Board of Health shall supervise the distribution of the tetrahydrocannabinols and their derivatives to program participants. The tetrahydrocannabinols and derivatives of tetrahydrocannabinols may be distributed only by the person in charge of the research program to physicians caring for program participant patients, under rules adopted by the Texas Board of Health in such a manner as to prevent unauthorized diversion of the substances and in compliance with all requirements of the Federal Drug Enforcement Administration. The physician is responsible for dispensing the substances to patients.
*(Added by L.1989, chap. 678(1), eff. 9/1/89.)*

### §481.205. Rules; reports.

(a) The Texas Board of Health shall adopt rules necessary for implementing the research program.

(b) If the Texas Board of Health establishes a program under this subchapter, the commissioner shall publish a report not later than January 1 of each odd-numbered year on the medical effectiveness of the use of tetrahydrocannabinols and their derivatives and any other medical findings of the research program.
*(Added by L.1989, chap. 678(1), eff. 9/1/89.)*

## CHAPTER 482. SIMULATED CONTROLLED SUBSTANCES

Section

### §482.001. Definitions.

In this chapter:

(1) "Controlled substance" has the meaning assigned by Section 481.002 (Texas Controlled Substances Act).

(2) "Deliver" means to transfer, actually or constructively, from one person to another a simulated controlled substance, regardless of whether there is an agency relationship. The term includes offering to sell a simulated controlled substance.

(3) "Manufacture" means to make a simulated controlled substance and includes the preparation of the substance in dosage form by mixing, compounding, encapsulating, tableting, or any other process.

(4) "Simulated controlled substance" means a substance that is purported to be a controlled substance, but is chemically different from the controlled substance it is purported to be.
*(Added by L.1989, chap. 678(1), eff. 9/1/89.)*

### §482.002. Unlawful delivery or manufacture with intent to deliver; criminal penalty.

(a) A person commits an offense if the person knowingly or intentionally manufactures with the intent to deliver or delivers a simulated controlled substance and the person:

(1) expressly represents the substance to be a controlled substance;

(2) represents the substance to be a controlled substance in a manner that would lead a reasonable person to believe that the substance is a controlled substance; or

(3) states to the person receiving or intended to receive the simulated controlled substance that the person may successfully represent the substance to be a controlled substance to a third party.

(b) It is a defense to prosecution under this section that the person manufacturing with the intent to deliver or delivering the simulated controlled substance was:

(1) acting in the discharge of the person's official duties as a peace officer;

(2) manufacturing the substance for or delivering the substance to a licensed medical practitioner for use as a placebo in the course of the practitioner's research or practice; or

(3) a licensed medical practitioner, pharmacist, or other person authorized to dispense or administer a controlled substance, and the person was acting in the legitimate performance of the person's professional duties.

(c) It is not a defense to prosecution under this section that the person manufacturing with the intent to deliver or delivering the simulated controlled substance believed the substance to be a controlled substance.

(d) An offense under this section is a state jail felony.
*(Added by L.1989, chap. 678(1); chgd. by L.1993, chap. 900(2.03), eff. 9/1/94.)*

### §482.003. Evidentiary rules.

(a) In determining whether a person has represented a simulated controlled substance to be a controlled substance in a manner that would lead a reasonable person to believe the substance was a controlled substance, a court may consider, in addition to all other logically relevant factors, whether:

(1) the simulated controlled substance was packaged in a manner normally used for the delivery of a controlled substance;

(2) the delivery or intended delivery included an exchange of or demand for property as consideration for delivery of the substance and the amount of the consideration was substantially in excess of the reasonable value of the simulated controlled substance; and

(3) the physical appearance of the finished product containing the substance was substantially identical to a controlled substance.

(b) Proof of an offer to sell a simulated controlled substance must be corroborated by a person other than the offeree or by evidence other than a statement of the offeree.
*(Added by L.1989, chap. 678(1), eff. 9/1/89.)*

### §482.004. Forfeiture.

A simulated controlled substance seized as a result of an offense under this chapter is subject to summary forfeiture and to destruction or disposition in the same manner as is a controlled substance property under Subchapter E, Chapter 481. *(Added by L.1989, chap. 678(1); chgd. by L.1991, chap. 141(3), eff. 9/1/91.)*

**§482.005. Preparatory offenses.**

Title 4, Penal Code, applies to an offense under this chapter. *(Added by L.1995, chap. 318(39), eff. 9/1/95.)*

# CHAPTER 483. DANGEROUS DRUGS

## SUBCHAPTER A. GENERAL PROVISIONS



## SUBCHAPTER B. DUTIES OF PHARMACISTS, PRACTITIONERS, AND OTHER PERSONS



## SUBCHAPTER C. CRIMINAL PENALTIES



## SUBCHAPTER D. CRIMINAL AND CIVIL PROCEDURE

## SUBCHAPTER A. GENERAL PROVISIONS

### §483.0001. Short title.

This Act may be cited as the Texas Dangerous Drug Act. *(Added by L.1993, chap. 789(18), eff. 9/1/93.)*

### §483.001. Definitions.

In this chapter:

(1) "Board" means the Texas State Board of Pharmacy.

(2) "Dangerous drug" means a device or a drug that is unsafe for self-medication and that is not included in Schedules I through V or Penalty Groups 1 through 4 of Chapter 481 (Texas Controlled Substances Act). The term includes a device or a drug that bears or is required to bear the legend:

(A) Caution: federal law prohibits dispensing without prescription; or

(B) Caution: federal law restricts this drug to use by or on the order of a licensed veterinarian.

(3) "Deliver" means to sell, dispense, give away, or supply in any other manner.

(4) "Designated agent" means:

(A) a licensed nurse, physician assistant, pharmacist, or other individual designated by a practitioner to communicate prescription drug orders to a pharmacist;

(B) a licensed nurse, physician assistant, or pharmacist employed in a health care facility to whom the practitioner communicates a prescription drug order; or

(C) a registered nurse or physician assistant authorized by a practitioner to carry out a prescription drug order for dangerous drugs under Section 3.06(d)(5) or (6), Medical Practice Act (Article 4495b, Texas Civil Statutes).

(5) "Dispense" means to prepare, package, compound, or label a dangerous drug in the course of professional practice for delivery under the lawful order of a practitioner to an ultimate user or the user's agent.

(6) "Manufacturer" means a person, other than a pharmacist, who manufactures dangerous drugs. The term includes a person who prepares dangerous drugs in dosage form by mixing, compounding, encapsulating, entableting, or any other process.

(7) "Patient" means:

(A) an individual for whom a dangerous drug is prescribed or to whom a dangerous drug is administered; or

(B) an owner or the agent of an owner of an animal for which a dangerous drug is prescribed or to which a dangerous drug is administered.

(8) "Person" includes an individual, corporation, partnership, and association.

(9) "Pharmacist" means a person licensed by the Texas State Board of Pharmacy to practice pharmacy.

(10) "Pharmacy" means a facility where prescription drug or medication orders are received, processed, dispensed, or distributed under this chapter, Chapter 481, and the Texas Pharmacy Act (Article 4542a-1, Texas Civil Statutes). The term does not include a narcotic drug treatment program that is regulated by Chapter 466, Health and Safety Code.

(11) "Practice of pharmacy" means:

(A) provision of those acts or services necessary to provide pharmaceutical care;

(B) interpretation and evaluation of prescription drug orders or medication orders;

(C) participation in drug and device selection as authorized by law, drug administration, drug regimen review, or drug or drug-related research;

(D) provision of patient counseling;

(E) responsibility for:

(i) dispensing of prescription drug orders or distribution of medication orders in the patient's best interest;

(ii) compounding and labeling of drugs and devices, except labeling by a manufacturer, repackager, or distributor of nonprescription drugs and commercially packaged prescription drugs and devices;

(iii) proper and safe storage of drugs and devices; or

(iv) maintenance of proper records for drugs and devices. In this subdivision, "device" has the meaning assigned by the Texas Pharmacy Act (Article 4542a-1, Texas Civil Statutes); or

(F) performance of a specific act of drug therapy management for a patient delegated to a pharmacist by a written protocol from a physician licensed by the state under the Medical Practice Act (Article 4495b, Texas Civil Statutes).

(12) "Practitioner" means a person licensed:

(A) by the Texas State Board of Medical Examiners, State Board of Dental Examiners, Texas State Board of Podiatric Medical Examiners, Texas Optometry Board, or State Board of Veterinary Medical Examiners to prescribe and administer dangerous drugs;

(B) by another state in a health field in which, under the laws of this state, a licensee may legally prescribe dangerous drugs; or

(C) in Canada or Mexico in a health field in which, under the laws of this state, a licensee may legally prescribe dangerous drugs.

(13) "Prescription" means an order from a practitioner, or an agent of the practitioner designated in writing as authorized to communicate prescriptions, or an order made in accordance with Section 3.06(d)(5) or (6), Medical Practice Act (Article 4495b, Texas Civil Statutes), or Section 16A, Texas Midwifery Act (Article 4512i, Texas Civil Statutes), to a pharmacist for a dangerous drug to be dispensed that states:

(A) the date of the order's issue;

(B) the name and address of the patient;

(C) if the drug is prescribed for an animal, the species of the animal;

(D) the name and quantity of the drug prescribed;

(E) the directions for the use of the drug;

(F) the intended use of the drug unless the practitioner determines the furnishing of this information is not in the best interest of the patient;

(G) the name, address, and telephone number of the practitioner at the practitioner's usual place of business, legibly printed or stamped; and

(H) the name, address, and telephone number of the documented midwife, registered nurse, or physician assistant, legibly printed or stamped, if signed by a documented midwife, registered nurse, or physician assistant.

(14) "Warehouseman" means a person who stores dangerous drugs for others and who has no control over the disposition of the drugs except for the purpose of storage.

(15) "Wholesaler" means a person engaged in the business of distributing dangerous drugs to a person listed in Sections 483.041(c)(1)-(6).

*(Added by L.1989, chap. 678(1); chgd. by L.1989, chap. 1100(5.04)(b); L.1991, chaps. 14(200), 237(10), 588(26); L.1993, chaps. 351(29), 789(18); L.1995, chaps. 965(6), 965(82); L.1997, chaps. 1095(18), 1180(22), eff. 9/1/97.)*



### §483.002. Rules.

The board may adopt rules for the proper administration and enforcement of this chapter. *(Added by L.1989, chap. 678(1), eff. 9/1/89.)*

### §483.003. Board of Health hearings regarding certain dangerous drugs.

(a) The Texas Board of Health may hold public hearings in accordance with Chapter 2001, Government Code to determine whether there is compelling evidence that a dangerous drug has been abused, either by being prescribed for nontherapeutic purposes or by the ultimate user.

(b) On making that finding, the Texas Board of Health may limit the availability of the abused drug by permitting its dispensing only on the prescription of a practitioner described by Section 483.001(12)(A) or (B).

*(Added by L.1989, chap. 678(1); chgd. by L.1995, chap. 76(5.95)(49); L.1997, chap. 1180(23), eff. 9/1/97.)*

### §483.004. Commissioner of Health emergency authority relating to dangerous drugs.

If the commissioner of health has compelling evidence that an immediate danger to the public health exists as a result of the prescription of a dangerous drug by practitioners described by Section 483.001(12)(C), the commissioner may use the commissioner's existing emergency authority to limit the availability of the drug by permitting its prescription only by practitioners described by Section 483.001(12)(A) or (B). *(Added by L.1989, chap. 678(1), eff. 9/1/89.)*

### §§483.005 to 483.020. *(Reserved.)*

## SUBCHAPTER B. DUTIES OF PHARMACISTS, PRACTITIONERS, AND OTHER PERSONS

### §483.021. Determination by pharmacist on request to dispense drug.

(a) A pharmacist who is requested to dispense a dangerous drug under a prescription issued by a practitioner described by Section 483.001(12)(C) shall determine, in the exercise of the pharmacist's professional judgment, that:

(1) the prescription is authentic;

(2) the prescription was issued under a valid patient-physician relationship; and

(3) the prescribed drug is considered necessary for the treatment of illness.

(b) A pharmacist who is requested to dispense a dangerous drug under a prescription issued by a therapeutic optometrist shall determine, in the exercise of the pharmacists's professional judgment, whether the prescription is for a dangerous drug that a therapeutic optometrist is authorized to prescribe under Section 1.03, Texas Optometry Act (Article 4552-1.01 et seq., Texas Civil Statutes).

*(Added by L.1989, chap. 678(1); chgd. by L.1991, chap. 588(27), eff. 9/1/91.)*



### §483.022. Practitioner's designated agent; practitioner's responsibilities.

(a) A practitioner shall provide in writing the name of each designated agent as defined by Section 483.001(4)(A) and (C), and the name of each healthcare facility which employs persons defined by Section 483.001(4)(B).

(b) The practitioner shall maintain at the practitioner's usual place of business a list of the designated agents or healthcare facilities as defined by Section 483.001(4).

(c) The practitioner shall provide a pharmacist with a copy of the practitioner's written authorization for a designated agent as defined by Section 483.001(4) on the pharmacist's request.

(d) This section does not relieve a practitioner or the practitioner's designated agent from the requirements of Section 40, Texas Pharmacy Act (Article 4542a-1, Texas Civil Statutes).

(e) A practitioner remains personally responsible for the actions of a designated agent who communicates a prescription to a pharmacist.

(f) A practitioner may designate a person who is a licensed vocational nurse or has an education equivalent to or greater than that required for a licensed vocational nurse to communicate prescriptions of an advanced practice nurse or physician assistant authorized by the practitioner to sign prescription drug orders under Section 3.06(d)(5) or (6), Medical Practice Act (Article 4495b, Vernon's Texas Civil Statutes).

*(Added by L.1989, chap. 678(1); chgd. by L.1991, chaps. 14(201), 237(11); L.1993, chap. 789(19); L.1999, chap. 428(4), eff. 9/1/99.)*

### §483.023. Retention of prescriptions.

A pharmacy shall retain a prescription for a dangerous drug dispensed by the pharmacy for two years after the date of the initial dispensing or the last refilling of the prescription, whichever date is later. *(Added by L.1989, chap. 678(1), eff. 9/1/89.)*

### §483.024. Records of acquisition or disposal.

The following persons shall maintain a record of each acquisition and each disposal of a dangerous drug for two years after the date of the acquisition or disposal:

(1) a pharmacy;

(2) a practitioner;

(3) a person who obtains a dangerous drug for lawful research, teaching, or testing purposes, but not for resale;

(4) a hospital that obtains a dangerous drug for lawful administration by a practitioner; and

(5) a manufacturer or wholesaler registered with the commissioner of health under Chapter 431 (Texas Food, Drug, and Cosmetic Act).

*(Added by L.1989, chap. 678(1), eff. 9/1/89.)*

### §483.025. Inspections; inventories.

A person required to keep records relating to dangerous drugs shall:

(1) make the records available for inspection and copying at all reasonable hours by any public official or employee engaged in enforcing this chapter; and

(2) allow the official or employee to inventory all stocks of dangerous drugs on hand.

*(Added by L.1989, chap. 678(1), eff. 9/1/89.)*

**§483.026.** *(Repealed by L.1989, chap. 1100(5.03)(h), eff. 9/1/89.)*

**§§483.027 to 483.040.** *(Reserved.)*

## SUBCHAPTER C. CRIMINAL PENALTIES

### §483.041. Possession of dangerous drug.

(a) A person commits an offense if the person possesses a dangerous drug unless the person obtains the drug from a pharmacist acting in the manner described by Section 483.042(a)(1) or a practitioner acting in the manner described by Section 483.042(a)(2).

(b) Except as permitted by this chapter, a person commits an offense if the person possesses a dangerous drug for the purpose of selling the drug.

(c) Subsection (a) does not apply to the possession of a dangerous drug in the usual course of business or practice or in the performance of official duties by the following persons or an agent or employee of the person:

(1) a pharmacy licensed by the board;

(2) a practitioner;

(3) a person who obtains a dangerous drug for lawful research, teaching, or testing, but not for resale;

(4) a hospital that obtains a dangerous drug for lawful administration by a practitioner;

(5) an officer or employee of the federal, state, or local government;

(6) a manufacturer or wholesaler licensed by the commissioner of health under Chapter 431 (Texas Food, Drug, and Cosmetic Act);

(7) a carrier or warehouseman;

(8) a home and community support services agency licensed under and acting in accordance with Chapter 142; or

(9) a documented midwife who obtains oxygen for administration to a mother or newborn or who obtains a dangerous drug for the administration of prophylaxis to a newborn for the prevention of ophthalmia neonatorum in accordance with Section 16A, Texas Midwifery Act (Article 4512i, Texas Civil Statutes).

(d) An offense under this section is a Class A misdemeanor.

*(Added by L.1989, chap. 678(1); chgd. by L.1989, chap. 1100(5.03)(f); L.1993, chaps. 16(2), 789(20); L.1995, chaps. 307(2), 318(41); L.1997, chaps. 1095(19), 1129(2), eff. 9/1/97.)*



### §483.042. Delivery or offer of delivery of dangerous drug.

(a) A person commits an offense if the person delivers or offers to deliver a dangerous drug:

(1) unless:

(A) the dangerous drug is delivered or offered for delivery by a pharmacist under:

(i) a prescription issued by a practitioner described by Section 483.001(12)(A) or (B);

(ii) a prescription signed by a registered nurse or physician assistant in accordance with Section 3.06(d)(5) or (6), Medical Practice Act (Article 4495b, Texas Civil Statutes); or

(iii) an original written prescription issued by a practitioner described by Section 483.001(12)(C); and

(B) a label is attached to the immediate container in which the drug is delivered or offered to be delivered and the label contains the following information:

(i) the name and address of the pharmacy from which the drug is delivered or offered for delivery;

(ii) the date the prescription for the drug is dispensed;

(iii) the number of the prescription as filed in the prescription files of the pharmacy from which the prescription is dispensed;

(iv) the name of the practitioner who prescribed the drug and, if applicable, the name of the registered nurse or physician assistant who signed the prescription;

(v) the name of the patient and, if the drug is prescribed for an animal, a statement of the species of the animal; and

(vi) directions for the use of the drug as contained in the prescription; or

(2) unless:

(A) the dangerous drug is delivered or offered for delivery by:

(i) a practitioner in the course of practice; or

(ii) a registered nurse or physician assistant in the course of practice in accordance with Section 3.06(d)(5) or (6), Medical Practice Act (Article 4495b, Texas Civil Statutes); and

(B) a label is attached to the immediate container in which the drug is delivered or offered to be delivered and the label contains the following information:

(i) the name and address of the practitioner who prescribed the drug, and if applicable, the name and address of the registered nurse or physician assistant;

(ii) the date the drug is delivered;

(iii) the name of the patient and, if the drug is prescribed for an animal, a statement of the species of the animal; and

(iv) the name of the drug, the strength of the drug, and directions for the use of the drug.

(b) Subsection (a) does not apply to the delivery or offer for delivery of a dangerous drug to a person listed in Section 483.041(c) for use in the usual course of business or practice or in the performance of official duties by the person.

(c) The labeling provisions of Subsection (a) do not apply when the dangerous drug is prescribed for administration to an ultimate user who is institutionalized. The board shall adopt rules for the labeling of such drugs.

(d) Proof of an offer to sell a dangerous drug must be corroborated by a person other than the offeree or by evidence other than a statement by the offeree.

(e) An offense under this section is a state jail felony. *(See other subsection (e) below.)*

(e) The labeling provisions of Subsection (a) do not apply to a dangerous drug prescribed or dispensed for administration to a patient who is institutionalized. The board shall adopt rules for the labeling of such a drug. *(See other subsection (e) above.)*

(f) Provided all federal requirements are met, the labeling provisions of Subsection (a) do not apply to a dangerous drug prescribed or dispensed for administration to food production animals in an agricultural operation under a written medical directive or treatment guideline from a veterinarian licensed under The Veterinary Licensing Act (Article 8890, Revised Statutes) and its subsequent amendments.

*(Added by L.1989, chap. 678(1); chgd. by L.1989, chap. 1100(5.03)(g); L.1993, chaps. 789(21), 900(2.04); L.1995, chap. 965(7); L.1997, chap. 1180(24); L.1999, chap. 1404(1), eff. 9/1/99.)*



## §483.043. Manufacture of dangerous drug.

(a) A person commits an offense if the person manufactures a dangerous drug and the person is not authorized by law to manufacture the drug.

(b) An offense under this section is a state jail felony.

*(Added by L.1989, chap. 678(1); chgd. by L.1993, chap. 900(2.05), eff. 9/1/94.)*

## §483.044. *(Repealed by L.1989, chap. 1100(5.03)(h), eff. 9/1/89.)*

## §483.045. Forging or altering prescription.

(a) A person commits an offense if the person:

(1) forges a prescription or increases the prescribed quantity of a dangerous drug in a prescription;

(2) issues a prescription bearing a forged or fictitious signature;

(3) obtains or attempts to obtain a dangerous drug by using a forged, fictitious, or altered prescription;

(4) obtains or attempts to obtain a dangerous drug by means of a fictitious or fraudulent telephone call; or

(5) possesses a dangerous drug obtained by a forged, fictitious, or altered prescription or by means of a fictitious or fraudulent telephone call.

(b) An offense under this section is a Class B misdemeanor unless it is shown on the trial of the defendant that the defendant has previously been convicted of an offense under this chapter, in which event the offense is a Class A misdemeanor.

*(Added by L.1989, chap. 678(1), eff. 9/1/89.)*

## §483.046. Failure to retain prescription.

(a) A pharmacist commits an offense if the pharmacist:

(1) delivers a dangerous drug under a prescription; and

(2) fails to retain the prescription as required by Section 483.023.

(b) An offense under this section is a Class B misdemeanor unless it is shown on the trial of the defendant that the defendant has previously been convicted of an offense under this chapter, in which event the offense is a Class A misdemeanor.

*(Added by L.1989, chap. 678(1), eff. 9/1/89.)*

### §483.047. Refilling prescription without authorization.

(a) Except as authorized by Subsection (b), a pharmacist commits an offense if the pharmacist refills a prescription unless:

(1) the prescription contains an authorization by the practitioner for the refilling of the prescription, and the pharmacist refills the prescription in the manner provided by the authorization; or

(2) at the time of refilling the prescription, the pharmacist is authorized to do so by the practitioner who issued the prescription.

(b) A pharmacist may exercise his professional judgment in refilling a prescription for a dangerous drug without the authorization of the prescribing practitioner provided:

(1) failure to refill the prescription might result in an interruption of a therapeutic regimen or create patient suffering;

(2) either:

(A) a natural or manmade disaster has occurred which prohibits the pharmacist from being able to contact the practitioner; or

(B) the pharmacist is unable to contact the practitioner after reasonable effort;

(3) the quantity of drug dispensed does not exceed a 72-hour supply;

(4) the pharmacist informs the patient or the patient's agent at the time of dispensing that the refill is being provided without such authorization and that authorization of the practitioner is required for future refills; and

(5) the pharmacist informs the practitioner of the emergency refill at the earliest reasonable time.

(c) An offense under this section is a Class B misdemeanor unless it is shown on the trial of the defendant that the defendant has previously been convicted under this chapter, in which event the offense is a Class A misdemeanor.

*(Added by L.1989, chap. 678(1); chgd. by L.1993, chap. 789(22), eff. 9/1/93.)*



### §483.048. Unauthorized communication of prescription.

(a) An agent of a practitioner commits an offense if the agent communicates by telephone a prescription unless the agent is designated in writing under Section 483.022 as authorized by the practitioner to communicate prescriptions by telephone.

(b) An offense under this section is a Class B misdemeanor unless it is shown on the trial of the defendant that the defendant has previously been convicted of an offense under this chapter, in which event the offense is a Class A misdemeanor.

*(Added by L.1989, chap. 678(1), eff. 9/1/89.)*

### §483.049. Failure to maintain records.

(a) A person commits an offense if the person is required to maintain a record under Section 483.023 or 483.024 and the person fails to maintain the record in the manner required by those sections.

(b) An offense under this section is a Class B misdemeanor unless it is shown on the trial of the defendant that the defendant has previously been convicted of an offense under this chapter, in which event the offense is a Class A misdemeanor.

*(Added by L.1989, chap. 678(1), eff. 9/1/89.)*

### §483.050. Refusal to permit inspection.

(a) A person commits an offense if the person is required to permit an inspection authorized by Section 483.025 and fails to permit the inspection in the manner required by that section.

(b) An offense under this section is a Class B misdemeanor unless it is shown on the trial of the defendant that the defendant has previously been convicted of an offense under this chapter, in which event the offense is a Class A misdemeanor.

*(Added by L.1989, chap. 678(1), eff. 9/1/89.)*

### §483.051. Using or revealing trade secret.

(a) A person commits an offense if the person uses for the person's advantage or reveals to another person, other than to an officer or employee of the board or to a court in a judicial proceeding relevant to this chapter, information relating to dangerous drugs required to be kept under this chapter, if that information concerns a method or process subject to protection as a trade secret.

(b) An offense under this section is a Class B misdemeanor unless it is shown on the trial of the defendant that the defendant has previously been convicted of an offense under this chapter, in which event the offense is a Class A misdemeanor.

*(Added by L.1989, chap. 678(1), eff. 9/1/89.)*

### §483.052. Violation of other provision.

(a) A person commits an offense if the person violates a provision of this chapter other than a provision for which a specific offense is otherwise described by this chapter.

(b) An offense under this section is a Class B misdemeanor, unless it is shown on the trial of the defendant that the defendant has previously been convicted of an offense under this chapter, in which event the offense is a Class A misdemeanor.

*(Added by L.1989, chap. 678(1), eff. 9/1/89.)*

### §483.053. Preparatory offenses.

Title 4, Penal Code, applies to an offense under this subchapter. *(Added by L.1995, chap. 318(40), eff. 9/1/95.)*

### §§483.054 to 483.070. *(Reserved.)*

## SUBCHAPTER D. CRIMINAL AND CIVIL PROCEDURE

### §483.071. Exceptions; burden of proof.

(a) In a complaint, information, indictment, or other action or proceeding brought for the enforcement of this chapter, the state is not required to negate an exception, excuse, proviso, or exemption contained in this chapter.

(b) The defendant has the burden of proving the exception, excuse, proviso, or exemption.

*(Added by L.1989, chap. 678(1), eff. 9/1/89.)*

### §483.072. Uncorroborated testimony.

A conviction under this chapter may be obtained on the uncorroborated testimony of a party to the offense. *(Added by L.1989, chap. 678(1), eff. 9/1/89.)*

### §483.073. Search warrant.

A peace officer may apply for a search warrant to search for dangerous drugs possessed in violation of this chapter. The peace officer must apply for and execute the search warrant in the manner prescribed by the Code of Criminal Procedure. (A.C.S. Art. 4476-14, Sec. 15A.)

### §483.074. Seizure and destruction.

(a) A dangerous drug that is manufactured, sold, or possessed in violation of this chapter is contraband and may be seized by an employee of the board or by a peace officer authorized to enforce this chapter and charged with that duty.

(b) If a dangerous drug is seized under Subsection (a), the board may direct an employee of the board or an authorized peace officer to destroy the drug. The employee or authorized peace officer directed to destroy the drug must act in the presence of another employee of the board or authorized peace officer and shall destroy the drug in any manner designated appropriate by the board.

(c) Before the dangerous drug is destroyed, an inventory of the drug must be prepared. The inventory must be accompanied by a statement that the dangerous drug is being destroyed at the direction of the board, by an employee of the board or authorized peace officer, and in the presence of another employee of the board or authorized peace officer. The statement must also contain the names of the persons in attendance at the time of destruction, state the capacity in which each of those persons acts, be signed by those persons, and be sworn by those persons that the statement is correct. The statement shall be filed with the board.

*(Added by L.1989, chap. 678(1); chgd. by L.1991, chap. 237(12), eff. 9/1/91.)*

### §483.075. Injunction.

The board may institute an action in its own name to enjoin a violation of this chapter. *(Added by L.1989, chap. 678(1), eff. 9/1/89.)*

### §483.076. Legal representation of board.

(a) If the board institutes a legal proceeding under this chapter, the board may be represented only by a county attorney, a district attorney, or the attorney general.

(b) The board may not employ private counsel in any legal proceeding instituted by or against the board under this chapter.

*(Added by L.1989, chap. 678(1), eff. 9/1/89.)*

# CHAPTER 484. VOLATILE CHEMICALS





## §484.001. Definitions.

In this chapter:

(1) "Deliver" means to actually transfer from one person to another.

(2) "Delivery" means the act of delivering.

(3) "Inhalant paraphernalia" means equipment, products, or materials of any kind that are used or intended for use in inhaling, ingesting, or otherwise introducing into the human body a substance containing a volatile chemical, and the term includes:

(A) a can, tube, or other container that was used as the original receptacle for a volatile chemical by the manufacturer or packager of the substance; or

(B) a can, tube, balloon, bag, fabric, bottle, or other container used to contain, concentrate, or hold in suspension a substance containing a volatile chemical.

(4) "Person" means an individual, corporation, or association.

(5) "Sell" means to offer for sale, convey, exchange, barter, or trade to a consumer or user.

*(Added by L.1989, chap. 678(1), eff. 9/1/89.)*

## §484.002. Volatile chemicals.

In this chapter, the following chemicals or their isomers are volatile chemicals:

(1) toluene;
(2) hexane;
(3) trichloroethylene;
(4) acetone;
(5) ethyl acetate;
(6) methyl ethyl ketone;
(7) trichloroethane;
(8) carbon tetrachloride;
(9) methanol;
(10) methyl isobutyl ketone;
(11) methyl cellosolve acetate;
(12) cyclohexanone;
(13) amyl nitrite;
(14) butyl nitrite;
(15) chloroform;
(16) diethyl ether;
(17) petroleum distillate;
(18) aliphatic hydrocarbons;
(19) chlorinated hydrocarbons;
(20) ketone solvent;
(21) glycol ether solvent;
(22) glycol ether inter solvent;
(23) xylol or xylene; and
(24) chlorofluorocarbons.

*(Added by L.1989, chap. 678(1), eff. 9/1/89.)*

## §484.003. Possession and use; criminal penalty

(a) A person commits an offense if the person inhales, ingests, applies, uses, or possesses a substance containing a volatile chemical with the intent to inhale, ingest, apply, or use the substance in a manner:

(1) contrary to directions for use, cautions, or warnings appearing on a label of a container of the substance; and

(2) designed to:

(A) affect the person's central nervous system;

(B) create or induce a condition of intoxication, hallucination, or elation; or

(C) change, distort, or disturb the person's eyesight, thinking process, balance, or coordination.

(b) An offense under this section is a Class B misdemeanor.

*(Added by L.1989, chap. 678(1), eff. 9/1/89.)*

## §484.004. Inhalant paraphernalia; criminal penalty.

(a) A person commits an offense if the person knowingly or intentionally uses or possesses with intent to use inhalant paraphernalia to inhale, ingest, apply, use, or otherwise introduce into the human body a substance containing a volatile chemical in violation of section 484.003.

(b) A person commits an offense if the person:

(1) knowingly or intentionally:

(A) delivers or sells inhalant paraphernalia;

(B) possesses, with intent to deliver or sell, inhalant paraphernalia; or

(C) manufactures, with intent to deliver or sell, inhalant paraphernalia; and

(2) at the time of the act described by Subdivision (1), knows that the person who receives or is intended to receive the paraphernalia intends that it be used to inhale, ingest, apply, use, or otherwise introduce into the human body a substance containing a volatile chemical in violation of Section 484.003.

(c) An offense under Subsection (a) is a Class B misdemeanor, and an offense under Subsection (b) is a Class A misdemeanor.

*(Added by L.1989, chap. 678(1); chgd. by L.1991, chap. 14(202), eff. 9/1/91.)*



## §484.005. Delivery to a minor; criminal penalty.

(a) A person commits an offense if:

(1) the person intentionally, knowingly, or recklessly sells or delivers a substance containing a volatile chemical to a person younger than 18 years of age; and

(2) the substance is subject to special labeling requirements concerning precautions against inhalation established under the Federal Hazardous Substances Act (15 U.S.C. Section 1261 et seq.) as that law existed on January 1, 1985, and the federal regulations adopted under that Act (16 C.F.R. 1500.14) and in effect on that date.

(b) It is an affirmative defense to prosecution under this section that the person to whom the substance was sold or delivered exhibited to the defendant an apparently valid Texas driver's license or an identification card issued by the Department of Public Safety, containing a physical description consistent with the person's appearance, that purported to establish that the person was 17 years of age or older.

(c) It is a defense to prosecution under this section that the person delivering the substance containing the volatile chemical was:

(1) a physician, dentist, veterinarian, scientific investigator, or other person licensed, registered or otherwise permitted to distribute, dispense, analyze, administer, or conduct research with respect to a volatile chemical in the course of professional practice or research, and the sale or delivery was within the limits of that person's official authority; or

(2) a pharmacy, hospital, or other institution licensed, registered, or otherwise permitted to distribute, dispense, administer, or conduct research with respect to a volatile chemical in the course of professional practice or research, and the sale or delivery was within the limits of that institution's official authority.

(d) It is an exception to the application of Subsection (a) that the substance sold or delivered was gasoline, aerosol paint, glue, or adhesive cement.

(e) Except as provided by Subsection (f), an offense under this section is:

(1) a Class B misdemeanor if the actor is the owner of or is an employee of a business establishment covered for the location of the sale by a sales tax permit issued under Chapter 151, Tax Code, and the offense was committed at the business establishment; or

(2) a state jail felony if the actor is any person other than a person described by Subdivision (1) who committed the offense at a business establishment described by that subdivision.

(f) An offense under this section is a felony of the third degree if it is shown at the punishment phase of the trial of the offense that the offense was committed:

(1) in, on, or within 1,000 feet of:

(A) the premises of a school or any premises owned, rented, or leased by an institution of higher education;

(B) a playground; or

(C) any real property owned, rented, or leased to a school or school board;

(2) on a school bus; or

(3) in, on, or within 300 feet of the premises of a public or private youth center, public swimming pool, or video arcade facility.

(g) Subsection (f) does not apply to an offense if:

(1) the offense was committed inside a private residence and no person younger than 18 years of age was present in the private residence at the time the offense was committed; or

(2) the actor was at the time of the offense an owner or employee described by Subsection (e)(1) and the offense was committed at a business location described by that subsection.

(h) In this section, "institution of higher education," "playground," "premises," "school," "video arcade facility," and "youth center" have the meanings assigned by Section 481.134. *(Added by L.1989, chap. 678(1); chgd. by L.1999, chap. 684(1), eff. 9/1/99.)*

### §484.006. Proof of offer to sell or deliver.

Proof of an offer to sell or deliver a substance containing a volatile chemical must be corroborated by a person other than the offeree or by evidence other than a statement of the offeree. *(Added by L.1989, chap. 678(1), eff. 9/1/89.)*



### §484.007. Summary forfeiture.

A volatile chemical or inhalant paraphernalia seized as a result of an offense under this chapter is subject to summary forfeiture and to destruction or disposition in the same manner as controlled substance property under Subchapter E, Chapter 481. *(Added by L.1991, chap. 141(4), eff. 9/1/91.)*

### §484.008. Preparatory offenses.

Title 4, Penal Code, applies to an offense under this chapter. *(Added by L.1995, chap. 318(42), eff. 9/1/95.)*

## CHAPTER 485. ABUSABLE GLUES AND AEROSOL PAINTS

## SUBCHAPTER A. GENERAL PROVISIONS

Section



## SUBCHAPTER B. ADDITIVES, SALES PERMITS, AND SIGNS



## SUBCHAPTER C. CRIMINAL PENALTIES

## SUBCHAPTER D. ADMINISTRATIVE PENALTY





## SUBCHAPTER A. GENERAL PROVISIONS

### §485.001. Definitions.

In this chapter:

(1) "Abusable glue or aerosol paint" means glue or aerosol paint that is:

(A) packaged in a container holding a pint or less by volume or less than two pounds by weight; and

(B) labeled in accordance with the labeling requirements concerning precautions against inhalation established under the Federal Hazardous Substances Act (15 U.S.C. Section 1261 et seq.), and under regulations adopted under that Act.

(2) "Aerosol paint" means an aerosolized paint product, including a clear or pigmented lacquer or finish.

(3) "Commissioner" means the commissioner of health.

(4) "Deliver" means to make the actual or constructive transfer from one person to another of an abusable glue or aerosol paint, regardless of whether there is an agency relationship. The term includes an offering to sell an abusable glue or aerosol paint.

(5) "Delivery" means the act of delivering.

(6) "Department" means the Texas Department of Health.

(7) "Glue" means an adhesive substance intended to be used to join two surfaces.

(8) "Inhalant paraphernalia" means equipment, products, or materials of any kind that are used or intended for use in inhaling, ingesting, or otherwise introducing into the human body an abusable glue or aerosol paint in violation of Section 485.031. The term includes:

(A) a can, tube, or other container used as the original receptacle for an abusable glue or aerosol paint; or

(B) a can, tube, balloon, bag, fabric, bottle, or other container used to contain, concentrate, or hold in suspension an abusable glue or aerosol paint, or vapors of the glue or paint.

*(Added by L.1989, chap. 678(1), eff. 9/1/89.)*

### §§485.002 to 485.010. *(Reserved.)*

## SUBCHAPTER B. ADDITIVES, SALES PERMITS, AND SIGNS

### §485.011. Additives.

(a) The commissioner by rule shall:

(1) approve and designate additive materials to be included in abusable glue or aerosol paint; and

(2) prescribe the proportions of additive materials to be placed in abusable glue or aerosol paint.

(b) The rules must be designed to safely and effectively discourage intentional abuse by inhalation of abusable glue or aerosol paint at the lowest practicable cost to the manufacturers and distributors of the glue or paint.

*(Added by L.1989, chap. 678(1), eff. 9/1/89.)*

## §485.012. Permit required.

A person may not sell abusable glue or aerosol paint at retail unless the person or the person's employer has, at the time of the sale, a glue and paint sales permit for the location of the sale. *(Added by L.1989, chap. 678(1), eff. 9/1/89.)*

## §485.013. Issuance and renewal of permit.

(a) To be eligible for the issuance or renewal of a glue and paint sales permit, a person must:

(1) have a sales tax permit that has been issued to the person;

(2) complete and return to the department an application as required by the department; and

(3) pay to the department a $25 application fee for each location at which abusable glue and aerosol paint may be sold by the person on obtaining a glue and paint sales permit.

(b) The department shall adopt rules as necessary to administer this chapter, including application procedures and procedures by which the department shall give each permittee reasonable notice of permit expiration and renewal requirements.

(c) The department shall issue or deny a permit and notify the applicant of the department's action not later than the 60th day after the date on which the department receives the application and appropriate fee. If the department denies an application, the department shall include in the notice the reasons for the denial.

(d) A permit issued or renewed under this chapter is valid for one year from the date of issuance or renewal.

(e) A permit is not valid if the permit holder has been convicted more than once in the preceding year of an offense that is committed:

(1) at the location for which the permit is issued; and

(2) under Section 484.005(a), 485.031, 485.032, 485.033, or 485.034.

(f) A permit issued by the department is the property of the department and must be surrendered on demand by the department.

(g) The department shall prepare an annual roster of permit holders.

(h) The department shall monitor and enforce compliance with this chapter.

*(Added by L.1989, chap. 678(1); chgd. by L.1991, chap. 14(203), eff. 9/1/91.)*

## §485.014. Permit available for inspection.

A permit holder must have the glue and paint sales permit or a copy of the permit available for inspection by the public at the place where the permit holder sells abusable glue and aerosol paint. *(Added by L.1989, chap. 678(1), eff. 9/1/89.)*

## §485.015. Refusal to issue or renew permit.

A proceeding for the failure to issue or renew a glue and paint sales permit under Section 485.013 or for an appeal from that proceeding is governed by the contested case provisions of Chapter 2001, Government Code. *(Added by L.1989, chap. 678(1); chgd. by L.1995, chap. 76(5.95)(49), eff. 9/1/95.)*

## §485.016. Disposition of funds; education and prevention programs.

(a) The department shall receive and account for all funds received under Section 485.013 and send the funds as they are received to the comptroller.

(b) The comptroller shall deposit those funds to the credit of the general revenue fund to be used to:

(1) administer, monitor, and enforce this chapter; and

(2) finance education projects concerning the hazards of abusable glue or aerosol paint and the prevention of inhalant abuse.

(c) The department shall enter into a memorandum of understanding with the Texas Commission on Alcohol and Drug Abuse to implement the education and prevention programs.

*(Added by L.1989, chap. 678(1); chgd. by L.1991, chap. 14(204), eff. 9/1/91.)*

## §485.017. Signs.

A business establishment that sells abusable glue or aerosol paint at retail shall display a conspicuous sign, in English and Spanish, that states the following:

It is unlawful for a person to sell or deliver abusable glue or aerosol paint to a person under 18 years of age. Except in limited situations, such an offense is a 3rd degree felony.

It is also unlawful for a person to abuse glue or aerosol paint by inhaling, ingesting, applying, using, or possessing with intent to inhale, ingest, apply, or use glue or aerosol paint in a manner designed to affect the central nervous system. Such an offense is a Class B misdemeanor.

*(Added by L.1989, chap. 678(1), eff. 9/1/89.)*

### §485.018. Prohibited ordinance and rule.

(a) A political subdivision or an agency of the state may not enact an ordinance or rule that requires a business establishment to display abusable glue or aerosol paint in a manner that makes the glue or aerosol paint accessible to patrons of the business only with the assistance of personnel of the business.

(b) This section does not apply to an ordinance or rule that was enacted before September 1, 1989.

*(Added by L.1991, chap. 14(205), eff. 9/1/91.)*

### §485.019. Restriction of access to aerosol paint.

(a) A business establishment that holds a permit under Section 485.012 and that displays aerosol paint shall display the paint:

(1) in a place that is in the line of sight of a cashier or in the line of sight from a workstation normally continuously occupied during business hours;

(2) in a manner that makes the paint accessible to a patron of the business establishment only with the assistance of an employee of the establishment; or

(3) in an area electronically protected, or viewed by surveillance equipment that is monitored, during business hours.

(b) This section does not apply to a business establishment that has in place a computerized checkout system at the point of sale for merchandise that alerts the cashier that a person purchasing aerosol paint must be over 18 years of age.

(c) A court may issue a warning to a business establishment or impose a civil penalty of $50 on the business establishment for a first violation of this section. After receiving a warning or penalty for the first violation, the business establishment is liable to the state for a civil penalty of $100 for each subsequent violation.

(d) For the third violation of this section in a calendar year, a court may issue an injunction prohibiting the business establishment from selling aerosol paint for a period of not more than two years. A business establishment that violates the injunction is liable to the state for a civil penalty of $100, in addition to any other penalty authorized by law, for each day the violation continues.

(e) If a business establishment fails to pay a civil penalty under this section, the court may issue an injunction prohibiting the establishment from selling aerosol paint until the establishment pays the penalty, attorney's fees, and court costs.

(f) The district or county attorney for the county in which a violation of this section is alleged to have occurred, or the attorney general, if requested by the district or county attorney for that county, may file suit for the issuance of a warning, the collection of a penalty, or the issuance of an injunction.

(g) A penalty collected under this section shall be sent to the comptroller for deposit in the state treasury to the credit of the general revenue fund.

(h) This section applies only to a business establishment that is located in a county with a population of 75,000 or more.

*(Added by L.1997, chap. 593(4), eff. 9/1/97.)*

### §§485.020 to 485.030. *(Reserved.)*

## SUBCHAPTER C. CRIMINAL PENALTIES

### §485.031. Possession and use.

(a) A person commits an offense if the person inhales, ingests, applies, uses, or possesses an abusable glue or aerosol paint with intent to inhale, ingest, apply, or use abusable glue or aerosol paint in a manner:

(1) contrary to directions for use, cautions, or warnings, appearing on a label of a container of the glue or paint; and

(2) designed to:

(A) affect the person's central nervous system;

(B) create or induce a condition of intoxication, hallucination, or elation; or

(C) change, distort, or disturb the person's eyesight, thinking process, balance, or coordination.

(b) An offense under this section is a Class B misdemeanor.

*(Added by L.1989, chap. 678(1), eff. 9/1/89.)*

## §485.032. Manufacture and delivery.

(a) A person commits an offense if the person intentionally manufactures, delivers, or possesses with intent to manufacture or deliver abusable glue or aerosol paint that does not contain additive material in accordance with rules adopted by the commissioner.

(b) It is an affirmative defense to prosecution under this section that the abusable glue or aerosol paint is packaged in bulk quantity containers, each of which holds at least two gallons, and is intended for ultimate use only by industrial or commercial enterprises.

(c) An offense under this section is a Class A misdemeanor.

*(Added by L.1989, chap. 678(1), eff. 9/1/89.)*

## §485.033. Delivery to a minor.

(a) A person commits an offense if the person intentionally, knowingly, or recklessly delivers abusable glue or aerosol paint to a person who is younger than 18 years of age.

(b) It is a defense to prosecution under this section that the abusable glue or aerosol paint that was delivered contains additive material that effectively discourages intentional abuse by inhalation or is in compliance with rules adopted by the commissioner under Section 485.011.

(c) It is an affirmative defense to prosecution under this section that:

(1) the person making the delivery is an adult having supervisory responsibility over the person younger than 18 years of age and:

(A) the adult permits the use of the abusable glue or aerosol paint only under the adult's direct supervision and in the adult's presence and only for its intended purpose; and

(B) the adult removes the substance from the person younger than 18 years of age on completion of that use; or

(2) the person to whom the abusable glue or aerosol paint was delivered presented to the defendant an apparently valid Texas driver's license or an identification card, issued by the Department of Public Safety of the State of Texas and containing a physical description consistent with the person's appearance, that purported to establish that the person was 18 years of age or older.

(d) Except as provided by Subsections (e) and (f), an offense under this section is a state jail felony.

(e) An offense under this section is a Class B misdemeanor if it is shown on the trial of the defendant that at the time of the delivery the defendant or the defendant's employer had a glue and paint sales permit for the location of the sale.

(f) An offense under this section is a Class A misdemeanor if it is shown on the trial of the defendant that at the time of the delivery the defendant or the defendant's employer:

(1) did not have a glue and paint sales permit but did have a sales tax permit for the location of the sale; and

(2) had not been convicted previously under this section for an offense committed after January 1, 1988.

*(Added by L.1989, chap. 678(1); chgd. by L.1993, chap. 900(2.06), eff. 9/1/94.)*



## §485.034. Inhalant paraphernalia.

(a) A person commits an offense if the person intentionally or knowingly uses or possesses with intent to use inhalant paraphernalia to inhale, ingest, or otherwise introduce into the human body an abusable glue or aerosol paint in violation of Section 485.031.

(b) A person commits an offense if the person:

(1) knowingly or intentionally:

(A) delivers or sells inhalant paraphernalia;

(B) possesses, with intent to deliver or sell, inhalant paraphernalia; or

(C) manufactures, with intent to deliver or sell, inhalant paraphernalia; and

(2) at the time of the act described by Subdivision (1), knows that the person who receives or is intended to receive the paraphernalia intends that it be used to inhale, ingest, apply, use, or otherwise introduce into the human body a substance containing a volatile chemical in violation of Section 485.031.

(c) An offense under Subsection (a) is a Class B misdemeanor, and an offense under Subsection (b) is a Class A misdemeanor.

*(Added by L.1989, chap. 678(1); chgd. by L.1991, chap. 14(206), eff. 9/1/91.)*

## §485.035. Failure to post sign.

(a) A person commits an offense if the person sells abusable glue or aerosol paint in a business establishment and the person does not display a sign as required by Section 485.017.

(b) An offense under this section is a Class C misdemeanor.

*(Added by L.1989, chap. 678(1), eff. 9/1/89.)*

**§485.036. Sale without permit.**

(a) A person commits an offense if the person sells abusable glue or aerosol paint in violation of Section 485.012 and the purchaser is 18 years of age or older.

(b) An offense under this section is a Class B misdemeanor.

*(Added by L.1989, chap. 678(1), eff. 9/1/89.)*

**§485.037. Proof of offer to sell.**

Proof of an offer to sell an abusable glue or aerosol paint must be corroborated by a person other than the offeree or by evidence other than a statement of the offeree. *(Added by L.1989, chap. 678(1), eff. 9/1/89.)*

**§485.038. Summary forfeiture.**

An abusable glue, aerosol paint, or inhalant paraphernalia seized as a result of an offense under this chapter is subject to summary forfeiture and to destruction or disposition in the same manner as controlled substance property under Subchapter E, Chapter 481. *(Added by L.1991, chap. 141(5), eff. 9/1/91.)*

**§485.039. Preparatory offenses.**

Title 4, Penal Code, applies to an offense under this subchapter. *(Added by L.1995, chap. 318(43), eff. 9/1/95.)*

## SUBCHAPTER D. ADMINISTRATIVE PENALTY

**§485.101. Imposition of penalty.**

(a) The department may impose an administrative penalty on a person who sells abusable glue or aerosol paint at retail who violates this chapter or a rule or order adopted under this chapter.

(b) A penalty collected under this subchapter shall be deposited in the state treasury in the general revenue fund.

*(Added by L.1999, chap. 1411(6.01), eff. 9/1/99.)*

**§485.102. Amount of penalty.**

(a) The amount of the penalty may not exceed $1,000 for each violation, and each day a violation continues or occurs is a separate violation for purposes of imposing a penalty. The total amount of the penalty assessed for a violation continuing or occurring on separate days under this subsection may not exceed $5,000.

(b) The amount shall be based on:

(1) the seriousness of the violation, including the nature, circumstances, extent, and gravity of the violation;

(2) the threat to health or safety caused by the violation;

(3) the history of previous violations;

(4) the amount necessary to deter a future violation;

(5) whether the violator demonstrated good faith, including when applicable whether the violator made good faith efforts to correct the violation; and

(6) any other matter that justice may require.

*(Added by L.1999, chap. 1411(6.01), eff. 9/1/99.)*

**§485.103. Report and notice of violation and penalty.**

(a) If the department initially determines that a violation occurred, the department shall give written notice of the report by certified mail to the person.

(b) The notice must:

(1) include a brief summary of the alleged violation;

(2) state the amount of the recommended penalty; and

(3) inform the person of the person's right to a hearing on the occurrence of the violation, the amount of the penalty, or both.

*(Added by L.1999, chap. 1411(6.01), eff. 9/1/99.)*

**§485.104. Penalty to be paid or hearing requested.**

(a) Within 20 days after the date the person receives the notice sent under Section 485.103, the person in writing may:

(1) accept the determination and recommended penalty of the department; or

(2) make a request for a hearing on the occurrence of the violation, the amount of the penalty, or both.

(b) If the person accepts the determination and recommended penalty or if the person fails to respond to the notice, the commissioner by order shall approve the determination and impose the recommended penalty.

*(Added by L.1999, chap. 1411(6.01), eff. 9/1/99.)*

### §485.105. Hearing.

(a) If the person requests a hearing, the commissioner shall refer the matter to the State Office of Administrative Hearings, which shall promptly set a hearing date and give written notice of the time and place of the hearing to the person. An administrative law judge of the State Office of Administrative Hearings shall conduct the hearing.

(b) The administrative law judge shall make findings of fact and conclusions of law and promptly issue to the commissioner a proposal for a decision about the occurrence of the violation and the amount of a proposed penalty.

*(Added by L.1999, chap. 1411(6.01), eff. 9/1/99.)*



### §485.106. Decision by commissioner.

(a) Based on the findings of fact, conclusions of law, and proposal for a decision, the commissioner by order may:

(1) find that a violation occurred and impose a penalty; or

(2) find that a violation did not occur.

(b) The notice of the commissioner's order under Subsection (a) that is sent to the person in accordance with Chapter 2001, Government Code, must include a statement of the right of the person to judicial review of the order.

*(Added by L.1999, chap. 1411(6.01), eff. 9/1/99.)*

### §485.107. Options following decision: Pay or appeal.

Within 30 days after the date the order of the commissioner under Section 485.106 that imposes an administrative penalty becomes final, the person shall:

(1) pay the penalty; or

(2) file a petition for judicial review of the commissioner's order contesting the occurrence of the violation, the amount of the penalty, or both.

*(Added by L.1999, chap. 1411(6.01), eff. 9/1/99.)*

### §485.108. Stay of enforcement of penalty.

(a) Within the 30- day period prescribed by Section 485.107, a person who files a petition for judicial review may:

(1) stay enforcement of the penalty by:

(A) paying the penalty to the court for placement in an escrow account; or

(B) giving the court a supersedeas bond approved by the court that:

(i) is for the amount of the penalty; and

(ii) is effective until all judicial review of the commissioner's order is final; or

(2) request the court to stay enforcement of the penalty by:

(A) filing with the court a sworn affidavit of the person stating that the person is financially unable to pay the penalty and is financially unable to give the supersedeas bond; and

(B) sending a copy of the affidavit to the commissioner by certified mail.

(b) If the commissioner receives a copy of an affidavit under Subsection (a)(2), the commissioner may file with the court, within five days after the date the copy is received, a contest to the affidavit. The court shall hold a hearing on the facts alleged in the affidavit as soon as practicable and shall stay the enforcement of the penalty on finding that the alleged facts are true. The person who files an affidavit has the burden of proving that the person is financially unable to pay the penalty or to give a supersedeas bond.

*(Added by L.1999, chap. 1411(6.01), eff. 9/1/99.)*

### §485.109. Collection of penalty.

(a) If the person does not pay the penalty and the enforcement of the penalty is not stayed, the penalty may be collected.

(b) The attorney general may sue to collect the penalty.

*(Added by L.1999, chap. 1411(6.01), eff. 9/1/99.)*

### §485.110. Decision by court.

(a) If the court sustains the finding that a violation occurred, the court may uphold or reduce the amount of the penalty and order the person to pay the full or reduced amount of the penalty.

(b) If the court does not sustain the finding that a violation occurred, the court shall order that a penalty is not owed.

*(Added by L.1999, chap. 1411(6.01), eff. 9/1/99.)*

### §485.111. Remittance of penalty and interest.

(a) If the person paid the penalty and if the amount of the penalty is reduced or the penalty is not upheld by the court, the court shall order, when the court's judgment becomes final, that the appropriate amount plus accrued interest be remitted to the person within 30 days after the date that the judgment of the court becomes final.

(b) The interest accrues at the rate charged on loans to depository institutions by the New York Federal Reserve Bank.

(c) The interest shall be paid for the period beginning on the date the penalty is paid and ending on the date the penalty is remitted.

*(Added by L.1999, chap. 1411(6.01), eff. 9/1/99.)*



### §485.112. Release of bond.

(a) If the person gave a supersedeas bond and the penalty is not upheld by the court, the court shall order, when the court's judgment becomes final, the release of the bond.

(b) If the person gave a supersedeas bond and the amount of the penalty is reduced, the court shall order the release of the bond after the person pays the reduced amount.

*(Added by L.1999, chap. 1411(6.01), eff. 9/1/99.)*

### §485.113. Administrative procedure.

A proceeding to impose the penalty is considered to be a contested case under Chapter 2001, Government Code.

*(Added by L.1999, chap. 1411(6.01), eff. 9/1/99.)*

# TITLE 8. DEATH AND DISPOSITION OF THE BODY

## SUBTITLE A. DEATH

## CHAPTER 672. NATURAL DEATH ACT
*(Selected Section)*



**§672.018.** *(Renumbered to 166.048 by L.1999, chap. 450(1.03), eff. 9/1/99.)*

## CHAPTER 714. MISCELLANEOUS PROVISIONS RELATING TO CEMETERIES
*(Selected Section)*



### §714.001. Depth of graves; criminal penalty.

(a) The body of a decedent may not be buried in a manner so that the outside top surface of the container of the body is:

(1) less than two feet below the surface of the ground if the container is not made of an impermeable material; or

(2) not less than 1½ feet below the surface of the ground if the container is made of an impermeable material.

(b) The governing body of a political subdivision of this state may, because of subsurface soil conditions or other relevant considerations, permit, by ordinance or rule, burials in that political subdivision at a shallower depth than that required by Subsection (a).

(c) This section does not apply to burials in a sealed surface reinforced concrete burial vault.

(d) A person commits an offense if the person buries the body of a decedent in violation of this section or in violation of an ordinance or rule adopted under this section.

(e) An offense under this section is a misdemeanor punishable by a fine of not less than $100 or more than $200.

*(Added by L.1989, chap. 678(1), eff. 9/1/89.)*

# TITLE 9. SAFETY

## SUBTITLE A. PUBLIC SAFETY

## CHAPTER 751. MASS GATHERINGS



Section



### §751.001. Short title.

This chapter may by cited as the Texas Mass Gatherings Act. *(Added by L.1989, chap. 678(1), eff. 9/1/89.)*

### §751.002. Definitions.

In this chapter:

(1) "Mass gathering" means a gathering that is held outside the limits of a municipality and that attracts or is expected to attract more than 5,000 persons who will remain at the meeting location for more than five continuous hours.

(2) "Person" means an individual, group of individuals, firm, corporation, partnership, or association.

(3) "Promote" includes organize, manage, finance, or hold.

(4) "Promoter" means a person who promotes a mass gathering.

*(Added by L.1989, chap. 678(1); chgd. by L.1999, chap. 553(1), eff. 6/18/99.)*

### §751.003. Permit requirement.

A person may not promote a mass gathering without a permit issued under this chapter. *(Added by L.1989, chap. 678(1), eff. 9/1/89.)*

### §751.004. Application procedure.

(a) At least 45 days before the date on which a mass gathering will be held, the promoter shall file a permit application with the county judge of the county in which the mass gathering will be held.

(b) The application must include:

(1) the promoter's name and address;

(2) a financial statement that reflects the funds being supplied to finance the mass gathering and each person supplying the funds;

(3) the name and address of the owner of the property on which the mass gathering will be held;

(4) a certified copy of the agreement between the promoter and the property owner;

(5) the location and a description of the property on which the mass gathering will be held;

(6) the dates and times that the mass gathering will be held;

(7) the maximum number of persons the promoter will allow to attend the mass gathering and the plan the promoter intends to use to limit attendance to that number;

(8) the name and address of each performer who has agreed to appear at the mass gathering and the name and address of each performer's agent;

(9) a description of each agreement between the promoter and a performer;

(10) a description of each step the promoter has taken to ensure that minimum standards of sanitation and health will be maintained during the mass gathering;

(11) a description of all preparations being made to provide traffic control, to ensure that the mass gathering will be conducted in an orderly manner, and to protect the physical safety of the persons who attend the mass gathering;

(12) a description of the preparations made to provide adequate medical and nursing care; and

(13) a description of the preparations made to supervise minors who may attend the mass gathering.

*(Added by L.1989, chap. 678(1), eff. 9/1/89.)*

## §751.005. Investigation.

(a) After a permit application is filed with the county judge, the county judge shall send a copy of the application to the county health authority, the county fire marshal or the person designated under Subsection (c), and the sheriff.

(b) The county health authority shall inquire into preparations for the mass gathering. At least five days before the date on which the hearing prescribed by Section 751.006 is held, the county health authority shall submit to the county judge a report stating whether the health authority believes that the minimum standards of health and sanitation prescribed by state and local laws, rules, and orders will be maintained.

(c) The county fire marshal shall investigate preparations for the mass gathering. If there is no county fire marshal in that county, the commissioners court shall designate a person to act under this section. At least five days before the date on which the hearing prescribed by Section 751.006 is held, the county fire marshal or the commissioners court designee shall submit to the county judge a report stating whether the fire marshal or designee believes that the minimum standards for ensuring public fire safety and order as prescribed by state and local laws, rules, and orders will be maintained.

(d) The sheriff shall investigate preparations for the mass gathering. At least five days before the date on which the hearing prescribed by Section 751.006 is held, the sheriff shall submit to the county judge a report stating whether the sheriff believes that the minimum standards for ensuring public safety and order that are prescribed by state and local laws, rules, and orders will be maintained.

(e) The county judge may conduct any additional investigation that the judge considers necessary.

(f) The county health authority, county fire marshal or commissioners court designee, and sheriff shall be available at the hearing prescribed by Section 751.006 to give testimony relating to their reports.

*(Added by L.1989, chap. 678(1); chgd. by L.1999, chap. 553(2), eff. 6/18/99.)*

## §751.006. Hearing.

(a) Not later than the 10th day before the date on which a mass gathering will begin, the county judge shall hold a hearing on the application. The county judge shall set the date and time of the hearing.

(b) Notice of the time and place of the hearing shall be given to the promoter and to each person who has an interest in whether the permit is granted or denied.

(c) At the hearing, any person may appear and testify for or against granting the permit.

*(Added by L.1989, chap. 678(1), eff. 9/1/89.)*

## §751.007. Findings and decision of county judge.

(a) After the completion of the hearing prescribed by Section 751.006, the county judge shall enter his findings in the record and shall either grant or deny the permit.

(b) The county judge may deny the permit if he finds that:

(1) the application contains false or misleading information or omits required information;

(2) the promoter's financial backing is insufficient to ensure that the mass gathering will be conducted in the manner stated in the application;

(3) the location selected for the mass gathering is inadequate for the purpose for which it will be used;

(4) the promoter has not made adequate preparations to limit the number of persons attending the mass gathering or to provide adequate supervision for minors attending the mass gathering;

(5) the promoter does not have assurance that scheduled performers will appear;

(6) the preparations for the mass gathering do not ensure that minimum standards of sanitation and health will be maintained;

(7) the preparations for the mass gathering do not ensure that the mass gathering will be conducted in an orderly manner and that the physical safety of persons attending will be protected;

(8) adequate arrangements for traffic control have not been provided; or

(9) adequate medical and nursing care will not be available.

*(Added by L.1989, chap. 678(1), eff. 9/1/89.)*

### §751.008. Permit revocation.

(a) The county judge may revoke a permit issued under this chapter if the county judge finds that preparations for the mass gathering will not be completed by the time the mass gathering will begin or that the permit was obtained by fraud or misrepresentation.

(b) The county judge must give notice to the promoter that the permit will be revoked at least 24 hours before the revocation. If requested by the promoter, the county judge shall hold a hearing on the revocation.

*(Added by L.1989, chap. 678(1), eff. 9/1/89.)*



### §751.009. Appeal.

A promoter or person affected by the action of a county judge in granting, denying, or revoking a permit may appeal that action to a district court having jurisdiction in the county in which the mass gathering will be held. *(Added by L.1989, chap. 678(1), eff. 9/1/89.)*

### §751.010. Rules.

(a) After notice and a public hearing, the Texas Board of Health shall adopt rules relating to minimum standards of health and sanitation to be maintained at mass gatherings.

(b) After notice and a public hearing, the Department of Public Safety shall adopt rules relating to minimum standards that must be maintained at a mass gathering to protect public safety and maintain order.

*(Added by L.1989, chap. 678(1), eff. 9/1/89.)*

### §751.011. Criminal penalty.

(a) A person commits an offense if the person violates Section 751.003.

(b) An offense under this Section is a misdemeanor punishable by a fine of not more than $1,000, confinement in the county jail for not more than 90 days, or both.

*(Added by L.1989, chap. 678(1), eff. 9/1/89.)*

### §751.012. Inspections.

(a) The county health authority may inspect a mass gathering during the mass gathering to ensure that the minimum standards of health and sanitation prescribed by state and local laws, rules, and orders are being maintained. If the county health authority determines a violation of the minimum standards is occurring, the health authority may order the promoter of the mass gathering to correct the violation.

(b) The county fire marshal or the person designated under Section 751.005(c) may inspect a mass gathering during the mass gathering to ensure that the minimum standards for ensuring public fire safety and order as prescribed by state and local laws, rules, and orders are being maintained. If the marshal or commissioners court designee determines a violation of the minimum standards is occurring, the marshal or designee may order the promoter of the mass gathering to correct the violation.

(c) The sheriff may inspect a mass gathering during the mass gathering to ensure that the minimum standards for ensuring public safety and order prescribed by state and local laws, rules, and orders are being maintained. If the sheriff determines a violation of the minimum standards is occurring, the sheriff may order the promoter of the mass gathering to correct the violation.

(d) A promoter who fails to comply with an order issued under this section commits an offense. An offense under this section is a Class C misdemeanor.

*(Added by L.1999, chap. 553(3), eff. 6/18/99.)*

**§751.013. Inspection fees.**

(a) A commissioners court may establish and collect a fee for an inspection performed under Section 751.012. The fee may not exceed the amount necessary to defray the costs of performing the inspections. The fee shall be deposited into the general fund of the county.

(b) A commissioners court may use money collected under this section to reimburse the county department or, if a state agency performs the inspection on behalf of the county, the state agency, the cost of performing the inspection.

*(Added by L.1999, chap. 553(3), eff. 6/18/99.)*

# TITLE 10. HEALTH AND SAFETY OF ANIMALS
*(Selected Chapters)*

## CHAPTER 821. TREATMENT AND DISPOSITION OF ANIMALS
*(Selected Sections)*

### SUBCHAPTER B. DISPOSITION OF CRUELLY TREATED ANIMALS





### SUBCHAPTER B. DISPOSITION OF CRUELLY TREATED ANIMALS

**§821.022. Seizure of cruelly treated animal.**

(a) If a county sheriff, constable, or deputy constable or an officer who has responsibility for animal control in a municipality has reason to believe that an animal has been or is being cruelly treated, he may apply to a justice court in the county or to a municipal court in the municipality in which the animal is located for a warrant to seize the animal.

(b) On a showing of probable cause to believe that the animal has been or is being cruelly treated, the court shall issue the warrant and set a time within 10 days of the date of issuance for a hearing in the court to determine whether the animal has been cruelly treated.

(c) The officer executing the warrant shall cause the animal to be impounded and shall give written notice to the owner of the animal of the time and place of the hearing.

## CHAPTER 822. REGULATION OF ANIMALS
*(Selected Sections)*

### SUBCHAPTER A. DOGS THAT ARE A DANGER TO PERSONS



### SUBCHAPTER C. COUNTY REGISTRATION AND REGULATION OF DOGS



### SUBCHAPTER D. DANGEROUS DOGS

## SUBCHAPTER A. DOGS THAT ARE A DANGER TO PERSONS

### §822.001. Definitions.

In this Subchapter:

(1) "Animal control authority" means a municipal or county animal control office with authority over the area in which the dog is kept or the county sheriff in an area that does not have an animal control office.

(2) "Serious bodily injury" means an injury characterized by severe bite wounds or severe ripping and tearing of muscle that would cause a reasonably prudent person to seek treatment from a medical professional and would require hospitalization without regard to whether the person actually sought medical treatment.

*(Chgd. by L.1997, chap. 99(1), eff. 9/1/97.)*



### §822.003. Hearing.

(a) The court shall set a time for a hearing to determine whether the dog caused the death of or serious bodily injury to a person by attacking, biting, or mauling the person. The hearing must be held not later than the 10th day after the date on which the warrant is issued.

(b) The court shall give written notice of the time and place of the hearing to:

(1) the owner of the dog or the person from whom the dog was seized; and

(2) the person who made the complaint.

(c) Any interested party, including the county attorney or city attorney, is entitled to present evidence at the hearing.

(d) The court shall order the dog destroyed if the court finds that the dog caused the death of a person by attacking, biting, or mauling the person. If that finding is not made, the court shall order the dog released to:

(1) its owner;

(2) the person from whom the dog was seized; or

(3) any other person authorized to take possession of the dog.

(e) The court may order the dog destroyed if the court finds that the dog caused serious bodily injury to a person by attacking, biting, or mauling the person. If that finding is not made, the court shall order the dog released to:

(1) its owner;

(2) the person from whom the dog was seized; or

(3) any other person authorized to take possession of the dog.

(f) The court may not order the dog destroyed if the court finds that the dog caused the serious bodily injury to a person by attacking, biting, or mauling the person and:

(1) the dog was being used for the protection of a person or person's property, the attack, bite, or mauling occurred in an enclosure in which the dog was being kept, and:

(A) the enclosure was reasonably certain to prevent the dog from leaving the enclosure on its own and provided notice of the presence of a dog; and

(B) the injured person was at least eight years of age, and was trespassing in the enclosure when the attack, bite, or mauling occurred;

(2) the dog was not being used for the protection of a person or person's property, the attack, bite, or mauling occurred in an enclosure in which the dog was being kept, and the injured person was at least eight years of age and was trespassing in the enclosure when the attack, bite, or mauling occurred;

(3) the attack, bite, or mauling occurred during an arrest or other action of a peace officer while the peace officer was using the dog for law enforcement purposes;

(4) the dog was defending a person from an assault or person's property from damage or theft by the injured person; or

(5) the injured person was younger than eight years of age, the attack, bite, or mauling occurred in an enclosure in which the dog was being kept, and the enclosure was reasonably certain to keep a person younger than eight years of age from entering.

*(Chgd. by L.1997, chap. 99(1), eff. 9/1/97.)*

## SUBCHAPTER C. COUNTY REGISTRATION AND REGULATION OF DOGS

### §822.031. Unregistered dogs prohibited from running at large.

The owner or person having control of a dog at least six months of age in a county adopting this subchapter may not allow the dog to run at large unless the dog:

(1) is registered under this subchapter with the county in which the dog runs at large; and
(2) has fastened about its neck a dog identification tag issued by the county.

### §822.032. Unmuzzled dogs prohibited from running at large.

The owner of a dog in a county adopting this subchapter may not allow the dog to run at large between sunset of one day and sunrise of the following day unless the dog has a leather or metallic muzzle securely fastened about its mouth that will effectively prevent the dog from killing or injuring sheep, goats, calves, or other domestic animals or fowls.

### §822.033. Dogs that attack domestic animals.

(a) A dog that is attacking, is about to attack, or has recently attacked sheep, goats, calves, or other domestic animals or fowls may be killed by any person witnessing or having knowledge of the attack.

(b) A person who kills a dog as provided by this section is not liable for damages to the owner of the dog.

(c) A dog known or suspected of having killed sheep, goats, calves, or other domestic animals or fowls is a public nuisance. Any person may detain or impound the dog until the dog's owner is notified and all damage done by the dog has been determined and paid to the proper persons.

(d) The owner of a dog that is known to have attacked sheep, goats, calves, or other domestic animals or fowls shall kill the dog. A sheriff, deputy sheriff, cons able, police officer, magistrate, or county commissioner may enter the premises of the owner of the dog and kill the dog if the owner fails to do so.

### §822.035. Criminal penalty.

(a) A person commits an offense if the person intentionally:
(1) fails or refuses to register a dog required to be registered under this subchapter;
(2) fails or refuses to allow a dog to be killed when ordered by the proper authorities to do so; or
(3) violates this subchapter.

(b) An offense under this section is a misdemeanor punishable by a fine of not more than $100, confinement in the county jail for not more than 30 days, or both.

## SUBCHAPTER D. DANGEROUS DOGS

### §822.044. Attack by dangerous dog.

(a) A person commits an offense if the person is the owner of a dangerous dog and the dog makes an unprovoked attack on another person outside the dog's enclosure and causes bodily injury to the other person.

(b) An offense under this section is a Class C misdemeanor, unless the attack causes serious bodily injury or death, in which event the offense is a Class A misdemeanor.

(c) If a person is found guilty of an offense under this section, the court may order the dangerous dog destroyed by a person listed in Section 822.003.

(d) In addition to criminal prosecution, a person who commits an offense under this section is liable for a civil penalty not to exceed $10,000. An attorney having civil jurisdiction in the county or an attorney for a municipality where the offense occurred may file suit in a court of competent jurisdiction to collect the penalty. Penalties collected under this subsection shall be retained by the county or municipality.

### §822.045. Violations.

(a) A person who owns or keeps custody or control of a dangerous dog commits an offense if the person fails to comply with Section 822.042 or Section 822.0422(b) or an applicable municipal or county regulation relating to dangerous dogs.

(b) Except as provided by Subsection (c), an offense under this section is a Class C misdemeanor.

(c) An offense under this section is a Class B misdemeanor if it is shown on the trial of the offense that the defendant has previously been convicted under this section.
*(Chgd. by L.1997, chap. 99(2), eff. 9/1/97.)*

# CHAPTER 823. ANIMAL SHELTERS
*(Selected Sections)*



## §823.003. Standards for animal shelters; criminal penalty.

(a) Each animal shelter operated in this state shall comply with the standards for housing and sanitation existing on September 1, 1982, and adopted under Chapter 826 (Rabies Control Act of 1981).

(b) An animal shelter shall separate animals in its custody at all times by species, by sex (if known), and if the animals are not related to one another, by size.

(c) An animal shelter may not confine healthy animals with sick, injured, or diseased animals.

(d) Each person who operates an animal shelter shall employ a veterinarian at least once a year to inspect the shelter to determine whether it complies with the requirements of this chapter. The veterinarian shall file copies of his report with the person operating the shelter and with the department on forms prescribed by the department.

(e) The board may require each person operating an animal shelter to keep records of the date and disposition of animals in its custody, to maintain the records on the business premises of the animal shelter, and to make the records available for inspection at reasonable times.

(f) A person commits an offense if the person substantially violates this section. An offense under this subsection is a Class C misdemeanor.



## §823.006. Prohibited methods of death.

(a) A person commits an offense if the person kills a dog, cat, or other small animal in the custody of an animal shelter by shooting, except in emergency field conditions, by clubbing, by using a decompression chamber, or by administering any of the following:

(1) unfiltered or uncooled carbon monoxide;

(2) curariform drugs, used alone, including curare, succinylcholine, pancuronium, and glyceryl fenesin;

(3) magnesium salts, used alone;

(4) chloral hydrate;

(5) nicotine; or

(6) strychnine.

(b) An offense under this section is a Class C misdemeanor.

# CHAPTER 825. PREDATORY ANIMALS AND ANIMAL PESTS
*(Selected Sections)*

## SUBCHAPTER A. COOPERATION BETWEEN STATE AND FEDERAL AGENCIES IN CONTROLLING PREDATORY ANIMALS AND RODENTS



## SUBCHAPTER A. COOPERATION BETWEEN STATE AND FEDERAL AGENCIES IN CONTROLLING PREDATORY ANIMALS AND RODENTS

## §825.008. Tampering with traps; criminal penalty.

(a) A person commits an offense if the person maliciously or wilfully tampers with all or any part of a trap set under this subchapter or removes a trap from the position in which it is placed by a hunter or trapper acting under this subchapter.

(b) An offense under this section is punishable by a fine of not less than $50 or more than $200.

### §825.009. Stealing traps; criminal penalty.

(a) A person commits an offense if the person steals or fraudulently takes a trap belonging to the state or the United States Department of the Interior.

(b) An offense under this section is a misdemeanor punishable by a fine of not less than $100 or more than $200.

### §825.010. Stealing animals from traps; criminal penalty.

(a) A person commits an offense if the person steals an animal listed in Section 825.001 from a trap set under this subchapter or takes the animal from the trap without authority.

(b) An offense under this section is a misdemeanor punishable by a fine of not less than $100 or more than $200.

(c) An animal stolen or taken in violation of this section is the property of the state. A complaint alleging a violation of this section must allege that the animal is owned by the state, and the only proof necessary to establish ownership shall consist of proving that the animal was taken from a trap that had been set by a hunter or trapper acting under this subchapter.



## CHAPTER 826. RABIES
*(Selected Sections)*

## SUBCHAPTER C. RABIES VACCINATIONS



## SUBCHAPTER D. REGISTRATION AND RESTRAINT OF DOGS AND CATS



## SUBCHAPTER E. REPORTS AND QUARANTINE



## SUBCHAPTER F. QUARANTINE AND IMPOUNDMENT FACILITIES



## SUBCHAPTER C. RABIES VACCINATIONS

### §826.021. Vaccination of dogs and cats required.

(a) Except as otherwise provided by board rule, the owner of a dog or cat shall have the animal vaccinated against rabies by the time the animal is four months of age and at regular intervals thereafter as prescribed by board rule.

(b) A veterinarian who vaccinates a dog or cat against rabies shall issue to the animal's owner a vaccination certificate in a form that meets the minimum standards approved by the board.

(c) A county or municipality may not register or license an animal that has not been vaccinated in accordance with this section.

### §826.022. Vaccination; criminal penalty.

(a) A person commits an offense if the person fails or refuses to have each dog or cat owned by the person vaccinated against rabies and the animal is required to be vaccinated under:

(1) Section 826.021 and board rules; or

(2) ordinances or rules adopted under this chapter by a county or municipality within whose jurisdiction the act occurs.

(b) An offense under this section is a Class C misdemeanor.

(c) If on the trial of an offense under this section the court finds that the person has been previously convicted of an offense under this section, the offense is a Class B misdemeanor.

## SUBCHAPTER D. REGISTRATION AND RESTRAINT OF DOGS AND CATS

### §826.034. Restraint; criminal penalty.

(a) A person commits an offense if:

(1) the person fails or refuses to restrain a dog or cat owned by the person; and

(2) the animal is required to be restrained under the ordinances or rules adopted under this chapter by a county or municipality within whose jurisdiction the act occurs.

(b) An offense under this section is a Class C misdemeanor.



## SUBCHAPTER E. REPORTS AND QUARANTINE

### §826.042. Quarantine of animals.

(a) The board shall adopt rules governing the testing of quarantined animals and the procedure for and method of quarantine.

(b) The local rabies control authority or a veterinarian shall quarantine or test in accordance with board rules any animal that the local rabies control authority or veterinarian has probable cause to believe is rabid, may have been exposed to rabies, or may have exposed a person to rabies.

(c) An owner shall submit for quarantine an animal that:

(1) is reported to be rabid or to have exposed an individual to rabies; or

(2) the owner knows or suspects is rabid or has exposed an individual to rabies.

(d) The owner shall submit the animal to the local rabies control authority of the county or municipality in which the exposure occurs.

(e) A veterinarian shall quarantine an animal that:

(1) is in the possession of the veterinarian; and

(2) the veterinarian knows or suspects is rabid or has exposed an individual to rabies.

### §826.044. Quarantine; criminal penalty.

(a) A person commits an offense if the person fails or refuses to quarantine or present for quarantine or testing an animal that:

(1) is required to be placed in quarantine or presented for testing under Section 826.042 and board rules; or

(2) is required to be placed in quarantine under ordinances or rules adopted under this chapter by a county or municipality within whose jurisdiction the act occurs.

(b) An offense under this section is a Class C misdemeanor.

## SUBCHAPTER F. QUARANTINE AND IMPOUNDMENT FACILITIES

### §826.055. Quarantine or impoundment facility; criminal penalty.

(a) A person commits an offense if the person operates a facility for quarantined or impounded animals that fails to meet standards for approval established by:

(1) board rules; or

(2) ordinances or rules adopted under this chapter by a county or municipality.

(b) An offense under this section is a Class C misdemeanor.

# TITLE 11. CIVIL COMMITMENT OF SEXUALLY VIOLENT PREDATORS
*(Selected Chapter)*

## CHAPTER 841. CIVIL COMMITMENT OF SEXUALLY VIOLENT PREDATORS

### SUBCHAPTER A. GENERAL PROVISIONS



### SUBCHAPTER B. NOTICE OF POTENTIAL PREDATOR; INITIAL DETERMINATIONS



### SUBCHAPTER C. PETITION ALLEGING PREDATOR STATUS



### SUBCHAPTER D. TRIAL



### SUBCHAPTER E. CIVIL COMMITMENT



### SUBCHAPTER F. COMMITMENT REVIEW



### SUBCHAPTER G. PETITION FOR RELEASE

## SUBCHAPTER H. MISCELLANEOUS PROVISIONS



## SUBCHAPTER A. GENERAL PROVISIONS

### §841.001. Legislative findings.

The legislature finds that a small but extremely dangerous group of sexually violent predators exists and that those predators have a behavioral abnormality that is not amenable to traditional mental illness treatment modalities and that makes the predators likely to engage in repeated predatory acts of sexual violence. The legislature finds that the existing involuntary commitment provisions of Subtitle C, Title 7, are inadequate to address the risk of repeated predatory behavior that sexually violent predators pose to society. The legislature further finds that treatment modalities for sexually violent predators are different from the traditional treatment modalities for persons appropriate for involuntary commitment under Subtitle C, Title 7. Thus, the legislature finds that a civil commitment procedure for the long- term supervision and treatment of sexually violent predators is necessary and in the interest of the state.
*(Added by L.1999, chap. 1188(4.01), eff. 9/1/99.)*



### §841.002. Definitions.

In this chapter:

(1) "Attorney representing the state" means an attorney employed by the prison prosecution unit to initiate and pursue a civil commitment proceeding under this chapter.

(2) "Behavioral abnormality" means a congenital or acquired condition that, by affecting a person's emotional or volitional capacity, predisposes the person to commit a sexually violent offense, to the extent that the person becomes a menace to the health and safety of another person.

(3) "Case manager" means a person employed by or under contract with the council to perform duties related to outpatient treatment and supervision of a person committed under this chapter.

(4) "Council" means the Interagency Council on Sex Offender Treatment.

(5) "Predatory act" means an act that is committed for the purpose of victimization and that is directed toward:

(A) a stranger;

(B) a person of casual acquaintance with whom no substantial relationship exists; or

(C) a person with whom a relationship has been established or promoted for the purpose of victimization.

(6) "Repeat sexually violent offender" has the meaning assigned by Section 841.003.

(7) "Secure correctional facility" means a county jail or a confinement facility operated by or under contract with any division of the Texas Department of Criminal Justice.

(8) "Sexually violent offense" means:

(A) an offense under Section 21.11(a)(1), 22.011, or 22.021, Penal Code;

(B) an offense under Section 20.04(a)(4), Penal Code, if the defendant committed the offense with the intent to violate or abuse the victim sexually;

(C) an offense under Section 30.02, Penal Code, if the offense is punishable under Subsection (d) of that section and the defendant committed the offense with the intent to commit an offense listed in Paragraph (A) or (B);

(D) an attempt, conspiracy, or solicitation, as defined by Chapter 15, Penal Code, to commit an offense listed in Paragraph (A), (B), or (C);

(E) an offense under prior state law that contains elements substantially similar to the elements of an offense listed in Paragraph (A), (B), (C), or (D); or

(F) an offense under the law of another state, federal law, or the Uniform Code of Military Justice that contains elements substantially similar to the elements of an offense listed in Paragraph (A), (B), (C), or (D).

(9) "Sexually violent predator" has the meaning assigned by Section 841.003.

(10) "Tracking service" means an electronic monitoring service, global positioning satellite service, or other appropriate technological service that is designed to track a person's location.
*(Added by L.1999, chap. 1188(4.01), eff. 9/1/99.)*

### §841.003. Sexually violent predator.

(a) A person is a sexually violent predator for the purposes of this chapter if the person:

(1) is a repeat sexually violent offender; and

(2) suffers from a behavioral abnormality that makes the person likely to engage in a predatory act of sexual violence.

(b) A person is a repeat sexually violent offender for the purposes of this chapter if the person is convicted of more than one sexually violent offense and a sentence is imposed for at least one of the offenses or if:

(1) the person:

(A) is convicted of a sexually violent offense, regardless of whether the sentence for the offense was ever imposed or whether the sentence was probated and the person was subsequently discharged from community supervision;

(B) enters a plea of guilty or nolo contendere for a sexually violent offense in return for a grant of deferred adjudication;

(C) is adjudged not guilty by reason of insanity of a sexually violent offense; or

(D) is adjudicated by a juvenile court as having engaged in delinquent conduct constituting a sexually violent offense and is committed to the Texas Youth Commission under Section 54.04(d)(3) or (m), Family Code; and

(2) after the date on which under Subdivision (1) the person is convicted, receives a grant of deferred adjudication, is adjudged not guilty by reason of insanity, or is adjudicated by a juvenile court as having engaged in delinquent conduct, the person commits a sexually violent offense for which the person:

(A) is convicted, but only if the sentence for the offense is imposed; or

(B) is adjudged not guilty by reason of insanity.

*(Added by L.1999, chap. 1188(4.01), eff. 9/1/99.)*

### §841.004. Prison prosecution unit.

A special division of the prison prosecution unit, separate from that part of the unit responsible for prosecuting criminal cases, is responsible for initiating and pursuing a civil commitment proceeding under this chapter.

*(Added by L.1999, chap. 1188(4.01), eff. 9/1/99.)*

### §841.005. Office of state counsel for offenders.

The Office of State Counsel for Offenders shall represent a person subject to a civil commitment proceeding under this chapter.

*(Added by L.1999, chap. 1188(4.01), eff. 9/1/99.)*

### §841.006. Application of chapter.

This chapter does not:

(1) prohibit a person committed under this chapter from filing at any time a petition for release under this chapter; or

(2) create for the committed person a cause of action against another person for failure to give notice within a period required by Subchapter B.

*(Added by L.1999, chap. 1188(4.01), eff. 9/1/99.)*

### §841.007. Duties of interagency council on sex offender treatment.

The Interagency Council on Sex Offender Treatment is responsible for providing appropriate and necessary treatment and supervision through the case management system.

*(Added by L.1999, chap. 1188(4.01), eff. 9/1/99.)*

## SUBCHAPTER B. NOTICE OF POTENTIAL PREDATOR; INITIAL DETERMINATIONS

### §841.021. Notice of potential predator.

(a) Before the person's anticipated release date, the Texas Department of Criminal Justice shall give to the multidisciplinary team established under Section 841.022 written notice of the anticipated release of a person who:

(1) is serving a sentence for a sexually violent offense; and

(2) may be a repeat sexually violent offender.

(b) Before the person's anticipated discharge date, the Texas Department of Mental Health and Mental Retardation shall give to the multidisciplinary team established under Section 841.022 written notice of the anticipated discharge of a person who:

(1) is committed to the department after having been adjudged not guilty by reason of insanity of a sexually violent offense; and

(2) may be a repeat sexually violent offender.

(c) The Texas Department of Criminal Justice or the Texas Department of Mental Health and Mental Retardation, as appropriate, shall give the notice described by Subsection (a) or (b) not later than the first day of the 16th month before the person's anticipated release or discharge date, but under exigent circumstances may give the notice at any time before the anticipated release or discharge date. The notice must contain the following information:

(1) the person's name, identifying factors, anticipated residence after release or discharge, and criminal history;

(2) documentation of the person's institutional adjustment and actual treatment; and

(3) an assessment of the likelihood that the person will commit a sexually violent offense after release or discharge.

*(Added by L.1999, chap. 1188(4.01), eff. 9/1/99.)*



### §841.022. Multidisciplinary team.

(a) The executive director of the Texas Department of Criminal Justice and the commissioner of the Texas Department of Mental Health and Mental Retardation jointly shall establish a multidisciplinary team to review available records of a person referred to the team under Section 841.021. The team must include:

(1) two persons from the Texas Department of Mental Health and Mental Retardation;

(2) three persons from the Texas Department of Criminal Justice, one of whom must be from the victim services office of that department;

(3) one person from the Texas Department of Public Safety; and

(4) one person from the council.

(b) The multidisciplinary team may request the assistance of other persons in making a determination under this section.

(c) Not later than the 30th day after the date the multidisciplinary team receives notice under Section 841.021(a) or (b), the team shall:

(1) determine whether the person is a repeat sexually violent offender and whether the person is likely to commit a sexually violent offense after release or discharge;

(2) give notice of that determination to the Texas Department of Criminal Justice or the Texas Department of Mental Health and Mental Retardation, as appropriate; and

(3) recommend the assessment of the person for a behavioral abnormality, as appropriate.

*(Added by L.1999, chap. 1188(4.01), eff. 9/1/99.)*

### §841.023. Assessment for behavioral abnormality.

(a) Not later than the 30th day after the date of a recommendation under Section 841.022(c), the Texas Department of Criminal Justice or the Texas Department of Mental Health and Mental Retardation, as appropriate, shall determine whether the person suffers from a behavioral abnormality that makes the person likely to engage in a predatory act of sexual violence. To aid in the determination, the department required to make the determination shall use an expert to examine the person. That department may contract for the expert services required by this subsection. The expert shall make a clinical assessment based on testing for psychopathy, a clinical interview, and other appropriate assessments and techniques to aid in the determination.

(b) If the Texas Department of Criminal Justice or the Texas Department of Mental Health and Mental Retardation determines that the person suffers from a behavioral abnormality, the department making the determination shall give notice of that determination and provide corresponding documentation to the attorney representing the state not later than the 30th day after the date of a recommendation under Section 841.022(c).

*(Added by L.1999, chap. 1188(4.01), eff. 9/1/99.)*

## SUBCHAPTER C. PETITION ALLEGING PREDATOR STATUS

### §841.041. Petition alleging predator status.

(a) If a person is referred to the attorney representing the state under Section 841.023, the attorney may file, in a Montgomery County district court other than a family district court, a petition alleging that the person is a sexually violent predator and stating facts sufficient to support the allegation.

(b) A petition described by Subsection (a) must be filed not later than the 60th day after the date the person is referred to the attorney representing the state.
*(Added by L.1999, chap. 1188(4.01), eff. 9/1/99.)*

## SUBCHAPTER D. TRIAL

### §841.061. Trial.

(a) Not later than the 60th day after the date a petition is filed under Section 841.041, the judge shall conduct a trial to determine whether the person is a sexually violent predator.

(b) The person or the state is entitled to a jury trial on demand. A demand for a jury trial must be filed in writing not later than the 10th day before the date the trial is scheduled to begin.

(c) The person and the state are entitled to an immediate examination of the person by an expert.

(d) Additional rights of the person at the trial include the following:

(1) the right to appear at the trial;

(2) the right to present evidence on the person's behalf;

(3) the right to cross-examine a witness who testifies against the person; and

(4) the right to view and copy all petitions and reports in the court file.

(e) The attorney representing the state may rely on the petition filed under Section 841.041 and supplement the petition with documentary evidence or live testimony.
*(Added by L.1999, chap. 1188(4.01), eff. 9/1/99.)*

### §841.062. Determination of predator status.

(a) The judge or jury shall determine whether, beyond a reasonable doubt, the person is a sexually violent predator. Either the state or the person is entitled to appeal the determination.

(b) A jury determination that the person is a sexually violent predator must be by unanimous verdict.
*(Added by L.1999, chap. 1188(4.01), eff. 9/1/99.)*

### §841.063. Continuance.

The judge may continue a trial conducted under Section 841.061 if the person is not substantially prejudiced by the continuance and:

(1) on the request of either party and a showing of good cause; or

(2) on the judge's own motion in the due administration of justice.
*(Added by L.1999, chap. 1188(4.01), eff. 9/1/99.)*

### §841.064. Mistrial.

A trial following a mistrial must begin not later than the 90th day after the date a mistrial was declared in the previous trial, unless the later trial is continued as provided by Section 841.063.
*(Added by L.1999, chap. 1188(4.01), eff. 9/1/99.)*

## SUBCHAPTER E. CIVIL COMMITMENT

### §841.081. Civil commitment of predator.

If at a trial conducted under Subchapter D the judge or jury determines that the person is a sexually violent predator, the judge shall commit the person for outpatient treatment and supervision to be coordinated by the case manager. The outpatient treatment and supervision must begin on the person's release from a secure correctional facility or discharge from a state hospital and must continue until the person's behavioral abnormality has changed to the extent that the person is no longer likely to engage in a predatory act of sexual violence.
*(Added by L.1999, chap. 1188(4.01), eff. 9/1/99.)*

### §841.082. Commitment requirements.

(a) Before entering an order directing a person's outpatient civil commitment, the judge shall impose on the person requirements necessary to ensure the person's compliance with treatment and supervision and to protect the community. The requirements shall include:

(1) requiring the person to reside in a particular location;

(2) prohibiting the person's contact with a victim or potential victim of the person;

(3) prohibiting the person's use of alcohol or a controlled substance;

(4) requiring the person's participation in a specific course of treatment;

(5) requiring the person to submit to tracking under a particular type of tracking service and to any other appropriate supervision;

(6) prohibiting the person from changing the person's residence without prior authorization from the judge and from leaving the state without that authorization;

(7) if determined appropriate by the judge, establishing a child safety zone in the same manner as a child safety zone is established by a judge under Section 13B, Article 42.12, Code of Criminal Procedure, and requiring the person to comply with requirements related to the safety zone;

(8) requiring the person to notify the case manager within 48 hours of any change in the person's status that affects proper treatment and supervision, including a change in the person's physical health or job status and including any incarceration of the person; and

(9) any other requirements determined necessary by the judge.

(b) The judge shall provide a copy of the requirements imposed under Subsection (a) to the person and to the council. The council shall provide a copy of those requirements to the case manager and to the service providers.

(c) Immediately after the person's commitment, the judge shall transfer jurisdiction of the case to a district court, other than a family district court, having jurisdiction in the county in which the defendant is residing.

*(Added by L.1999, chap. 1188(4.01), eff. 9/1/99.)*

## §841.083. Treatment; supervision.

(a) The council shall approve and contract for the provision of a treatment plan for the committed person to be developed by the treatment provider. A treatment plan may include the monitoring of the person with a polygraph or plethysmograph. The treatment provider may receive annual compensation in an amount not to exceed $6,000 for providing the required treatment.

(b) The case manager shall provide supervision to the person. The provision of supervision shall include tracking services and, if required by court order, supervised housing.

(c) The council shall enter into an interagency agreement with the Texas Department of Public Safety for the provision of tracking services. The Department of Public Safety shall contract with the General Services Commission for the equipment necessary to implement those services.

(d) The council shall contract for any necessary supervised housing. The committed person may not be housed for any period of time in a mental health facility, state school, or community center. In this subsection:

(1) "Community center" means a center established under Subchapter A, Chapter 534.

(2) "Mental health facility" has the meaning assigned by Section 571.003.

(3) "State school" has the meaning assigned by Section 531.002.

(e) The case manager shall:

(1) coordinate the outpatient treatment and supervision required by this chapter, including performing a periodic assessment of the success of that treatment and supervision;

(2) make timely recommendations to the judge on whether to allow the committed person to change residence or to leave the state and on any other appropriate matters; and

(3) provide a report to the council, semiannually or more frequently as necessary, which must include:

(A) any known change in the person's status that affects proper treatment and supervision; and

(B) any recommendations made to the judge.

*(Added by L.1999, chap. 1188(4.01), eff. 9/1/99.)*

## §841.084. Provider status reports.

A treatment provider or a supervision provider other than the case manager shall submit, monthly or more frequently if required by the case manager, a report to the case manager stating whether the person is complying with treatment or supervision requirements, as applicable.

*(Added by L.1999, chap. 1188(4.01), eff. 9/1/99.)*

## §841.085. Criminal penalty.

A person commits an offense if the person violates a requirement imposed under Section 841.082. An offense under this section is a felony of the third degree. *(Added by L.1999, chap. 1188(4.01), eff. 9/1/99.)*

## SUBCHAPTER F. COMMITMENT REVIEW

### §841.101. Biennial examination.

(a) A person committed under Section 841.081 shall receive a biennial examination. The council shall contract for an expert to perform the examination.

(b) In preparation for a judicial review conducted under Section 841.102, the case manager shall provide a report of the biennial examination to the judge. The report must include consideration of whether to modify a requirement imposed on the person under this chapter and whether to release the person from all requirements imposed on the person under this chapter. The case manager shall provide a copy of the report to the council.
*(Added by L.1999, chap. 1188(4.01), eff. 9/1/99.)*

### §841.102. Biennial review.

(a) The judge shall conduct a biennial review of the status of the committed person.

(b) The person is entitled to be represented by counsel at the biennial review, but the person is not entitled to be present at that review.

(c) The judge shall set a hearing if the judge determines at the biennial review that:

(1) a requirement imposed on the person under this chapter should be modified; or

(2) probable cause exists to believe that the person's behavioral abnormality has changed to the extent that the person is no longer likely to engage in a predatory act of sexual violence.
*(Added by L.1999, chap. 1188(4.01), eff. 9/1/99.)*

### §841.103. Hearing.

(a) At a hearing set by the judge under Section 841.102, the person and the state are entitled to an immediate examination of the person by an expert.

(b) If the hearing is set under Section 841.102(c)(1), hearsay evidence is admissible if it is considered otherwise reliable by the judge.

(c) If the hearing is set under Section 841.102(c)(2), the committed person is entitled to be present and to have the benefit of all constitutional protections provided to the person at the initial civil commitment proceeding. On the request of the person or the attorney representing the state, the court shall conduct the hearing before a jury. The burden of proof at that hearing is on the state to prove beyond a reasonable doubt that the person's behavioral abnormality has not changed to the extent that the person is no longer likely to engage in a predatory act of sexual violence.
*(Added by L.1999, chap. 1188(4.01), eff. 9/1/99.)*

## SUBCHAPTER G. PETITION FOR RELEASE

### §841.121. Authorized petition for release.

(a) If the case manager determines that the committed person's behavioral abnormality has changed to the extent that the person is no longer likely to engage in a predatory act of sexual violence, the case manager shall authorize the person to petition the court for release.

(b) The petitioner shall serve a petition under this section on the court and the attorney representing the state.

(c) The judge shall set a hearing on a petition under this section not later than the 30th day after the date the judge receives the petition. The petitioner and the state are entitled to an immediate examination of the petitioner by an expert.

(d) On request of the petitioner or the attorney representing the state, the court shall conduct the hearing before a jury.

(e) The burden of proof at the hearing is on the state to prove beyond a reasonable doubt that the petitioner's behavioral abnormality has not changed to the extent that the petitioner is no longer likely to engage in a predatory act of sexual violence.
*(Added by L.1999, chap. 1188(4.01), eff. 9/1/99.)*

### §841.122. Right to file unauthorized petition for release.

On a person's commitment and annually after that commitment, the case manager shall provide the person with written notice of the person's right to file with the court and without the case manager's authorization a petition for release. *(Added by L.1999, chap. 1188(4.01), eff. 9/1/99.)*

### §841.123. Review of unauthorized petition for release.

(a) If the committed person files a petition for release without the case manager's authorization, the person shall serve the petition on the court and the attorney representing the state.

(b) On receipt of a petition for release filed by the committed person without the case manager's authorization, the judge shall attempt as soon as practicable to review the petition.

(c) Except as provided by Subsection (d), the judge shall deny without a hearing a petition for release filed without the case manager's authorization if the petition is frivolous or if:

(1) the petitioner previously filed without the case manager's authorization another petition for release; and

(2) the judge determined on review of the previous petition or following a hearing that:

(A) the petition was frivolous; or

(B) the petitioner's behavioral abnormality had not changed to the extent that the petitioner was no longer likely to engage in a predatory act of sexual violence.

(d) The judge is not required to deny a petition under Subsection (c) if probable cause exists to believe that the petitioner's behavioral abnormality has changed to the extent that the petitioner is no longer likely to engage in a predatory act of sexual violence.

*(Added by L.1999, chap. 1188(4.01), eff. 9/1/99.)*



### §841.124. Hearing on unauthorized petition for release.

(a) If as authorized by Section 841.123 the judge does not deny a petition for release filed by the committed person without the case manager's authorization, the judge shall conduct as soon as practicable a hearing on the petition.

(b) The petitioner and the state are entitled to an immediate examination of the person by an expert.

(c) On request of the petitioner or the attorney representing the state, the court shall conduct the hearing before a jury.

(d) The burden of proof at the hearing is on the state to prove beyond a reasonable doubt that the petitioner's behavioral abnormality has not changed to the extent that the petitioner is no longer likely to engage in a predatory act of sexual violence.

*(Added by L.1999, chap. 1188(4.01), eff. 9/1/99.)*

## SUBCHAPTER H. MISCELLANEOUS PROVISIONS

### §841.141. Rulemaking authority.

(a) The council by rule shall administer this chapter. Rules adopted by the council under this section must be consistent with the purposes of this chapter.

(b) The council by rule shall develop standards of care and case management for persons committed under this chapter.

*(Added by L.1999, chap. 1188(4.01), eff. 9/1/99.)*

### §841.142. Release or exchange of information.

(a) To protect the public and to enable a determination relating to whether a person is a sexually violent predator, any entity that possesses relevant information relating to the person shall release the information to an entity charged with making a determination under this chapter.

(b) To protect the public and to enable the provision of supervision and treatment to a person who is a sexually violent predator, any entity that possesses relevant information relating to the person shall release the information to the case manager.

(c) On the written request of any attorney for another state or a political subdivision in another state, the Texas Department of Criminal Justice, the council, a service provider contracting with one of those agencies, the multidisciplinary team, and the attorney representing the state shall release to the attorney any available information relating to a person that is sought in connection with an attempt to civilly commit the person as a sexually violent predator in another state.

(d) To protect the public and to enable a determination relating to whether a person is a sexually violent predator or to enable the provision of supervision and treatment to a person who is a sexually violent predator, the Texas Department of Criminal Justice, the council, a service provider contracting with one of those agencies, the multidisciplinary team, and the attorney representing the state may exchange any available information relating to the person.

(e) Information subject to release or exchange under this section includes information relating to the supervision, treatment, criminal history, or physical or mental health of the person, as appropriate, regardless of whether the information is otherwise confidential and regardless of

when the information was created or collected. The person's consent is not required for release or exchange of information under this section.
*(Added by L.1999, chap. 1188(4.01), eff. 9/1/99.)*

### §841.143. Report, record, or statement submitted to court.

(a) A psychological report, drug and alcohol report, treatment record, diagnostic report, medical record, or victim impact statement submitted to the court under this chapter is part of the record of the court.

(b) Notwithstanding Subsection (a), the report, record, or statement must be sealed and may be opened only:

(1) on order of the judge;

(2) as provided by this chapter; or

(3) in connection with a criminal proceeding as otherwise provided by law.

*(Added by L.1999, chap. 1188(4.01), eff. 9/1/99.)*

### §841.144. Counsel.

(a) At all stages of the civil commitment proceedings under this chapter, a person subject to a proceeding is entitled to the assistance of counsel.

(b) If the person is indigent, the court shall appoint counsel through the Office of State Counsel for Offenders to assist the person.

*(Added by L.1999, chap. 1188(4.01), eff. 9/1/99.)*

### §841.145. Expert.

(a) A person who is examined under this chapter may retain an expert to perform an examination or participate in a civil commitment proceeding on the person's behalf.

(b) On the request of an indigent person examined under this chapter, the judge shall determine whether expert services for the person are necessary. If the judge determines that the services are necessary, the judge shall appoint an expert to perform an examination or participate in a civil commitment proceeding on the person's behalf.

(c) The court shall approve reasonable compensation for expert services rendered on behalf of an indigent person on the filing of a certified compensation claim supported by a written statement specifying:

(1) time expended on behalf of the person;

(2) services rendered on behalf of the person;

(3) expenses incurred on behalf of the person; and

(4) compensation received in the same case or for the same services from any other source.

(d) The court shall ensure that an expert retained or appointed under this section has for purposes of examination reasonable access to a person examined under this chapter, as well as to all relevant medical and psychological records and reports.

*(Added by L.1999, chap. 1188(4.01), eff. 9/1/99.)*

### §841.146. Civil commitment proceeding; procedure and costs.

(a) On request, a person subject to a civil commitment proceeding under this chapter and the attorney representing the state are entitled to a jury trial or a hearing before a jury for that proceeding, except for a proceeding set by the judge under Section 841.102(c)(1). The number and selection of jurors are governed by Chapter 33, Code of Criminal Procedure.

(b) A civil commitment proceeding is subject to the rules of procedure and appeal for civil cases.

(c) In an amount not to exceed $1,600, the state shall pay the costs of a civil commitment proceeding conducted under Subchapter D. For any civil commitment proceeding conducted under this chapter, the state shall pay the costs of state or appointed counsel or experts and the costs of the person's outpatient treatment and supervision.

*(Added by L.1999, chap. 1188(4.01), eff. 9/1/99.)*

### §841.147. Immunity.

The following persons are immune from liability for good faith conduct under this chapter:

(1) an employee or officer of the Texas Department of Criminal Justice, the Texas Department of Mental Health and Mental Retardation, or the council;

(2) a member of the multidisciplinary team established under Section 841.022;

(3) the attorney representing the state; and

(4) a person contracting, appointed, or volunteering to perform a service under this chapter.

*(Added by L.1999, chap. 1188(4.01), eff. 9/1/99.)*

# HUMAN RESOURCES CODE

## TITLE 2. DEPARTMENT OF HUMAN SERVICES AND DEPARTMENT OF PROTECTIVE AND REGULATORY SERVICES

*(Heading chgd. by L.1995, chap. 920(2), eff. 9/1/95.)*
*(Selected Chapters)*

## CHAPTER 33. NUTRITIONAL ASSISTANCE PROGRAMS

*(Selected Section)*

Section




**§33.011. Prohibited activities; penalties.† [*Food stamp benefit permits; offenses; penalties.*]**

(a) A person commits an offense if the person knowingly uses, alters, or transfers food stamp benefit permits in any manner not authorized by law. An offense under this subsection is a Class A misdemeanor if the value of the food stamp benefit permits is less than $200 and a felony of the third degree if the value of the food stamp benefit permits is $200 or more.

(b) A person commits an offense if the person knowingly possesses food stamp benefit permits when not authorized by law to possess them, knowingly redeems food stamp benefit permits when not authorized by law to redeem them, or knowingly redeems food stamp benefit permits for purposes not authorized by law. An offense under this subsection is a Class A misdemeanor if the value of the food stamp benefit permits is less than $200 and a felony of the third degree if the value of the food stamp benefit permits is $200 or more.

(c) A person commits an offense if the person knowingly possesses blank authorizations to participate in the food stamp program when not authorized by law to possess them. An offense under this subsection is a felony of the third degree.

(d) When cash, exchange value, or food stamp benefit permits of various values are obtained in violation of this section pursuant to one scheme or continuing course of conduct, whether from the same or several sources, the conduct may be considered as one offense and the values aggregated in determining the grade of the offense.

(e) The department may contract with county commissioners courts to provide funds to pay for professional and support services necessary for the enforcement of any criminal offense that involves illegally obtaining, possessing, or misusing food stamps.

(f) For the purposes of Subsections (a) and (b), the value of food stamp benefit permits is the cash or exchange value obtained in violation of this section.

(g) In this section, "food stamp benefit permits" includes:

(1) food stamp coupons;

(2) electronic benefit transfer (EBT) cards; and

(3) authorizations to participate in the food stamp program.

*(Chgd. by L.1993, chap. 249(1), (2); L.1997, chap. 788(1), eff. 9/1/97.)*

## CHAPTER 42. REGULATION OF CERTAIN FACILITIES, HOMES, AND AGENCIES THAT PROVIDE CHILD-CARE SERVICES

*(Heading chgd. by L.1997, chap. 1063(1), eff. 9/1/97.)*
*(Selected Section)*

Section


**§42.055. Sign posting.**

(a) Each child-care facility shall post in a location that is conspicuous to all employees and customers a sign that includes:

(1) a description of the provisions of Chapter 261, Family Code relating to the duty to report child abuse or neglect; and

(2) a description of the penalties for violating the reporting provisions of Chapter 261, Family Code.

(b) The department by rule shall determine the design, size, and wording of the sign.

(c) The department shall provide the sign to each child-care facility without charge.

(d) A person who operates a child-care facility commits an offense if the department provides a sign to the facility as provided by this section and the person intentionally fails to display the sign in the facility as prescribed by this section. An offense under this subsection is a Class C misdemeanor.

*(Added by L.1989, 1st C.S., chap. 20(1); renumbered from section 42.056 and chgd. by L.1997, chap. 1063(7); chgd. by chap. 165(7.47), eff. 9/1/97.)*

# TITLE 3. FACILITIES AND SERVICES FOR CHILDREN

## CHAPTER 61. TEXAS YOUTH COUNCIL

### SUBCHAPTER F. RELEASE

*(Selected Section)*



**§61.0841. Determinate sentence parole.**

(a) Not later than the 90th day before the date the commission transfers a person to the custody of the pardons and paroles division of the Texas Department of Criminal Justice for release on parole under Section 61.081(f) or 61.084(f) or (g), the commission shall submit to the department all pertinent information relating to the person, including:

(1) the juvenile court judgment;

(2) the circumstances of the person's offense;

(3) the person's previous social history and juvenile court records;

(4) the person's physical and mental health record;

(5) a record of the person's conduct, employment history, and attitude while committed to the commission;

(6) a record of the sentence time served by the person at the commission and in a juvenile detention facility in connection with the conduct for which the person was adjudicated; and

(7) any written comments or information provided by the commission, local officials, or victims of the offense.

(b) The commission shall provide instruction for parole officers of the pardons and paroles division relating to juvenile programs at the commission. The commission and the pardons and paroles division shall enter into a memorandum of understanding relating to the administration of this subsection.

*(Added by L.1997, chap. 165(12.20), eff. 9/1/97.)*

# TITLE 8. RIGHTS AND RESPONSIBILITIES OF PERSONS WITH DISABILITIES

*(Heading chgd. by L.1997, chap. 649(1), eff. 9/1/97.)*
*(Selected Chapter)*

## CHAPTER 121. PARTICIPATION IN SOCIAL AND ECONOMIC ACTIVITIES

*(Selected Section)*





### §121.007. Blind and disabled pedestrians.

(a) No person may carry a white cane on a public street or highway unless the person is totally or partially blind.

(b) The driver of a vehicle approaching an intersection or crosswalk where a pedestrian guided by an assistance animal or carrying a white cane is crossing or attempting to cross shall take necessary precautions to avoid injuring or endangering the pedestrian. The driver shall bring the vehicle to a full stop if injury or danger can be avoided only by that action.

(c) The failure of a totally or partially blind or otherwise disabled person to carry a white cane or be guided or aided by an assistance animal does not deprive the person of the rights and privileges conferred by law on pedestrians crossing streets or highways and does not constitute evidence of contributory negligence.

(d) A person who violates this section commits a Class C misdemeanor.

*(Chgd. by L.1997, chap. 649(8), eff. 9/1/97.)*

This page intentionally left blank.

# INSURANCE CODE

## TITLE 1. THE INSURANCE CODE OF 1951

*(Heading added by L.1999, chap. 101(2), eff. 9/1/99.)*

## CHAPTER 5. RATING AND POLICY FORMS

*(Selected Articles)*



### Art. 5.06. Policy forms and endorsements.

(1) The Board shall adopt a policy form and endorsements for each type of motor vehicle insurance subject to this subchapter. The coverage provided by a policy form adopted under this subsection is the minimum coverage that may be provided under an insurance policy for that type of insurance in this State. Each policy form must provide the coverages mandated under Articles 5.06-1 and 5.06-3 of this code, except that the coverages may be rejected by the named insured as provided by those articles.

(2) Except as provided by Subsections (3) and (4) of this article, an insurer may only use a form adopted by the Board under this section in writing motor vehicle insurance delivered, issued for delivery, or renewed in this State. A contract or agreement not written into the application and policy is void and of no effect and in violation of the provisions of this subchapter, and is sufficient cause for revocation of license of such insurer to write automobile insurance within this State.

(3) The Board may approve the use of a policy form adopted by a national organization of insurance companies, or similar organization, if the form, with any endorsement to the form required and approved by the Board, provides coverage equivalent to the coverage provided by the form adopted by the Board under Subsection (1) of this section.

(4) An insurer may use an endorsement to the policy form adopted or approved by the Board under this article if the endorsement is approved by the Board.

(5) An insurer, if in compliance with applicable requirements and conditions, may issue and deliver a certificate of insurance as a substitute for the entire policy of insurance. The certificate of insurance shall make reference to and identify the policy form adopted or approved by the Board for which the substitution of certificate is made. The certificate shall be in such form as is prescribed by the Board. The certificate will represent the policy of insurance, and when issued, shall be evidence that the certificate holder is insured under the identified policy form. The certificate is subject to the same limitations, conditions, coverages, selection of options, and other provisions of the policy as are provided in the policy, and that insurance policy information is to be shown on and adequately referenced by the certificate of insurance issued by the insurer to the insured. Reference shall be made in the certificate, or in subsequent attachments, to all endorsements to the policy of insurance. The certificate shall be executed in the same manner as though a policy were issued. When the certificate is substituted for the policy of insurance by an insurer, the insurer shall simultaneously furnish to the insured receiving the certificate an "outline of coverages", the form and content of which has been approved by the Board. At the request of an insured at any time, an insurer which has substituted a certificate for a policy of insurance shall provide a copy of the policy.

(6) The Board may promulgate such rules as are necessary to implement the certificate in lieu of policy provision herein, including a rule limiting the application thereof to private passenger automobile policies.

(7) The Board may not adopt or approve a policy form for private passenger automobile insurance or any endorsement to the policy if the policy or endorsement is not in plain language. For the purposes of this subsection, a policy or endorsement is written in plain language if it achieves the minimum score established by the commissioner on the Flesch reading ease test or an equivalent test selected by the commissioner, or, at the option of the commissioner, if it conforms to the language requirements in a National Association of Insurance Commissioners model act relating to plain language. This subsection does not apply to policy language that is mandated by state or federal law.

(8) The Board may withdraw its approval of a policy or endorsement form at any time, after notice and hearing.

(9) An insurance policy or other document evidencing proof of purchase of a personal automobile insurance policy written for a term of less than 30 days may not be used to obtain an

original or renewal driver's license, an automobile registration or license plates, or a motor vehicle inspection certificate and must contain a statement as follows:

"TEXAS LAW PROHIBITS USE OF THIS DOCUMENT TO OBTAIN A MOTOR VEHICLE INSPECTION CERTIFICATE, AN ORIGINAL OR RENEWAL DRIVER'S LICENSE, OR AN AUTOMOBILE REGISTRATION OR LICENSE PLATES."

(10) Before accepting any premium or fee for a personal automobile insurance policy or binder for a term of less than 30 days, an agent or insurer must make the following written disclosure to the applicant or insured:

"TEXAS LAW PROHIBITS USE OF THIS POLICY OR BINDER TO OBTAIN A MOTOR VEHICLE INSPECTION CERTIFICATE, AN ORIGINAL OR RENEWAL DRIVER'S LICENSE, OR AN AUTOMOBILE REGISTRATION OR LICENSE PLATES."

### Art. 5.06-5. Recovery prohibited for vehicles impounded for drug violations.

(a) A motor vehicle insurance policy delivered or issued for delivery in this state may not provide payment on final conviction of the named insured for loss for a covered motor vehicle that is seized by federal or state law enforcement officers as evidence in a case against the named insured under Chapter 481, Health and Safety Code or the federal Controlled Substances Act, 21 U.S.C. Section 801 et seq. For the purpose of this section a named insured shall be the person named on the declaration page of an automobile insurance policy and his or her spouse if the policy is written on an individual. If a policy is other than an individual policy, a named insured shall be the company or corporation named on the declaration page of an automobile insurance policy and any officer, director, or stockholder of that company or corporation.

(b) An insurer may not deliver or issue for delivery in this state a motor vehicle insurance policy that provides payment on final conviction of the named insured for loss for a covered motor vehicle that is seized by federal or state law enforcement officers as evidence in a case against the named insured under Chapter 481, Health and Safety Code or the federal Controlled Substances Act, 21 U.S.C. Section 801 et seq.

*(Added by L.1989, chap. 568(1); chgd. by L.1991, chap. 14(284)(42), eff. 9/1/91.)*

### Art. 5.46. Report of information on fire losses.

(A) The State Fire Marshal, any fire marshal of a political subdivision in Texas, or the chief of any established fire department in Texas, or any peace officer in Texas, may request any insurance company investigating a fire loss of real or personal property in which damages or losses exceed $1,000 to release information in its possession relative to that loss. The company shall release the information and cooperate with any official authorized to request such information pursuant to this section. The information may include but not exceed:

(1) any insurance policy relevant to a fire loss under investigation and any application for such a policy;

(2) policy premium payment records;

(3) history of previous claims made by the insured for fire loss;

(4) material relating to the investigation of the loss, including statements of any person, proof of loss, or other relevant evidence.

(5) The provisions of this section shall not be construed to authorize a public official or agency to promulgate or require any type or form of periodic report by an insurer.

(B) If an insurance company has reason to suspect that a fire loss to its insured's real or personal property was caused by incendiary means and if it receives a request for information pursuant to Section (A) of this article, the company shall notify the requesting official and furnish him with all relevant material acquired during its investigation of the fire loss, cooperate with and take such action as may be requested of it by any law enforcement agency, and permit any person ordered by a court to inspect any of its records pertaining to the policy and the loss.

(C) In the absence of fraud or malice no insurance company or person who furnished information on its behalf is liable for damages in a civil action or subject to criminal prosecution for oral or written statement made or any other action taken that is necessary to supply information required pursuant to this section.

(D) The officials and departmental and agency personnel receiving any information furnished pursuant to this section shall hold the information in confidence until such time as its release is required pursuant to a criminal or civil proceeding.

(E) Any official referred to in Section (A) of this article may be required to testify as to any information in his possession regarding the fire loss of real or personal property in any civil action in which any person seeks recovery under a policy against an insurance company for the fire loss.

(F)(1) No person shall purposely refuse to release any information requested pursuant to Section (A) of this article.

Printed in the U.S.A. Zt

(2) No person shall purposely refuse to notify the fire marshal of a fire loss required to be reported pursuant to Section (B) of this article.

(3) No person shall purposely refuse to supply the fire marshal with pertinent information required to be furnished pursuant to Section (B) of this article.

(4) No person shall purposely fail to hold in confidence information required to be held in confidence by Section (D) of this article.

This page intentionally left blank.

# LOCAL GOVERNMENT CODE

## CHAPTER 130. MISCELLANEOUS FINANCIAL PROVISIONS AFFECTING COUNTIES

*(Selected Sections)*

## SUBCHAPTER A. PAYMENT OF FEES AND TAXES BY CHECK, CREDIT CARD, OR ELECTRONIC MEANS

Section





## SUBCHAPTER A. PAYMENT OF FEES AND TAXES BY CHECK, CREDIT CARD, OR ELECTRONIC MEANS

*(Heading chgd. by L.1997, chap. 148(1), eff. 9/1/97.)*

### §130.001. Definitions.

In this subchapter:

(1) "Check" means an instrument signed by the maker, containing an unconditional promise or order to pay a sum certain in money, containing no other promise, order, obligation, or power given by the maker, payable on demand, and drawn on a bank.

(2) "Credit card invoice" means the document authorized by the holder of a credit card to be used to provide payment of an amount from the holder's credit card account.

(3) "Maker" means the drawer of a check or the holder of a credit card who authorizes a credit card invoice.

(4) "Payment by electronic means" means payment by telephone or computer but does not include payment in person or by mail.

*(Added by L.1989, chap. 1(23)(a)(3); chgd. by L.1989, chap. 737(3); L.1997, chap. 148(2), eff. 9/1/97.)*

### §130.002. Acceptance of check or credit card payment of certain fees and taxes.

A county tax assessor-collector may accept a check or credit card invoice for the payment of:

(1) motor vehicle registration fees under Chapter 502, Transportation Code;

(2) motor vehicle sales taxes imposed by Chapter 152, Tax Code;

(3) occupation taxes paid to the assessor-collector under Chapter 191, Tax Code;

(4) motor vehicle title transfer fees under Chapter 501, Transportation Code;

(5) license or permit fees under the Alcoholic Beverage Code; and

(6) property taxes.

*(Added by L.1989, chap. 1(23)(a)(3); chgd. by L.1989, chap. 737(3); L.1997, chap. 165(30.215), eff. 9/1/97.)*

### §130.003. Payment conditional.

(a) The acceptance of a check or credit card invoice for the payment of a fee or tax does not constitute payment of the fee or tax. The fee or tax is not considered paid until the check is honored by the bank on which the check is drawn or the credit card invoice is honored by the issuer.

(b) This section does not prohibit a county tax assessor- collector from issuing receipts, license plates, certificates, or other instruments on the receipt of a check or credit card invoice, but the issuance is conditional on the payment of the check by the drawee bank or the honoring of the credit card invoice by the credit card issuer.

*(Added by L.1989, chap. 1(23)(a)(3); chgd. by L.1989, chap. 737(3), eff. 8/28/89.)*

## §130.004. Identification required.

When a county tax assessor-collector receives a check or credit card invoice as conditional payment of a fee or tax, the assessor- collector shall require adequate identification of the maker and note on the check or invoice or otherwise record the type of identification of the maker and information from the identification to assist in locating the maker in the event the check or invoice is not honored. *(Added by L.1989, chap. 1(23)(a)(3); chgd. by L.1989, chap. 737(3), eff. 8/28/89.)*

## §130.0045. Credit card payment processing fee.

If a county tax assessor-collector accepts a credit card invoice as conditional payment of a fee or tax, the assessor-collector shall collect a fee for processing the invoice. The collector shall set the fee in an amount that is reasonably related to the expense incurred in processing the credit card invoice, not to exceed five percent of the amount of the fee or tax. The processing fee is in addition to the amount of the fee or tax, and may be paid conditionally by including the amount of the processing fee on the credit card invoice. *(Added by L.1989, chap. 737(3), eff. 8/28/89.)*

## §130.0046. Fee for payment by electronic means.

A county tax assessor-collector that accepts payment by electronic means as conditional payment of a county or state fee or tax may collect a handling fee for processing the payment. The handling fee is in addition to the amount of the fee or tax and may be paid conditionally by electronic means at the same time the tax or fee is paid. *(Added by L.1997, chap. 148(3), eff. 9/1/97.)*

Printed in the U.S.A.

## §130.005. Liability of assessor-collector and bondsman.

Except as provided by Section 130.008, a county tax assessor- collector and the assessor-collector's bondsman are not liable for the amount of any fee or tax for which the assessor-collector has accepted a check that is not honored by the drawee bank or credit card invoice that is not honored by the credit card issuer if the assessor- collector complied with the requirements of Section 130.004 and if the assessor-collector did not know or should not reasonably have known that the check was not properly drawn, that the credit card payment was not properly made, or that the check or credit card invoice would not be honored. *(Added by L.1989, chap. 1(23)(a)(3); chgd. by L.1989, chap. 737(3), eff. 8/28/89.)*

## §130.006. Procedures for collection of dishonored checks and invoices.

A county tax assessor-collector may establish procedures for the collection of dishonored checks and credit card invoices. The procedures may include:

(1) official notification to the maker that the check or invoice has not been honored and that the receipt, registration, certificate, or other instrument issued on the receipt of the check or invoice is not valid until payment of the fee or tax is made;

(2) notification of the sheriff or other law enforcement officers that a check or credit card invoice has not been honored and that the receipt, registration, certificate, or other instrument held by the maker is not valid; and

(3) notification to the Texas Department of Transportation, the comptroller of public accounts, or the Department of Public Safety that the receipt, registration, certificate, or other instrument held by the maker is not valid.

*(Added by L.1989, chap. 1(23)(a)(3); chgd. by L.1989, chap. 737(3); L.1995, chap. 165(22)(46), eff. 9/1/95.)*

## §130.007. Remission to state not required; state assistance in collection.

(a) If a fee or tax is required to be remitted to the comptroller or the Texas Department of Transportation and if payment was made to the county tax assessor-collector by a check that was not honored by the drawee bank or by a credit card invoice that was not honored by the credit card issuer, the amount of the fee or tax is not required to be remitted, but the assessor-collector shall notify the appropriate department of:

(1) the amount of the fee or tax;

(2) the type of fee or tax involved; and

(3) the name and address of the maker.

(b) The Texas Department of Transportation and the comptroller shall assist the county tax assessor-collector in collecting the fee or tax and may cancel or revoke any receipt, registration, certificate, or other instrument issued in the name of the state conditioned on the payment of the fee or tax.

*(Added by L.1989, chap. 1(23)(a)(3); chgd. by L.1989, chap. 737(3); L.1995, chap. 165(22)(46), eff. 9/1/95.)*

### §130.008. Liability of tax collector for violations of subchapter.

If the comptroller or the Texas Department of Transportation determines that the county tax assessor-collector has accepted payment for fees and taxes to be remitted to that department in violation of Section 130.004 or that more than two percent of the fees and taxes to be received from the assessor-collector are not remitted because of the acceptance of checks that are not honored by the drawee bank or of credit card invoices that are not honored by the credit card issuer, the department may notify the assessor-collector that the assessor- collector may not accept a check or credit card invoice for the payment of any fee or tax to be remitted to that department. A county tax assessor-collector who accepts a check or credit card invoice for the payment of a fee or tax, after notice that the assessor-collector may not receive a check or credit card invoice for the payment of fees or taxes to be remitted to a department, is liable to the state for the amount of the check or credit card invoice accepted. *(Added by L.1989, chap. 1(23)(a)(3); chgd. by L.1989, chap. 737(3); L.1995, chap. 165(22)(46), eff. 9/1/95.)*

### §130.009. State rules.

The comptroller and the Texas Department of Transportation may make rules concerning the acceptance of checks or credit card invoices by a county tax assessor-collector and for the collection of dishonored checks or credit card invoices. *(Added by L.1989, chap. 1(23)(a)(3); chgd. by L.1989, chap. 737(3); L.1995, chap. 165(22)(46), eff. 9/1/95.)*



## CHAPTER 341. MUNICIPAL LAW ENFORCEMENT
*(Selected Sections)*

Section


### §341.904. Possession or use of law enforcement identification, insignia, or vehicle in populous municipality.

(a) In this section, "police identification item" means a badge, identification card, insignia, shoulder emblem, or uniform of a municipal police department.

(b) In a municipality with a population of one million or more, a person commits an offense if he intentionally or knowingly:

(1) uses, possesses, or wears:

(A) a police identification item of the municipal police department;

(B) an item bearing the insignia or design prescribed by the police chief of the municipality for officers and employees of the municipal police department to use while engaged in official activities; or

(C) within the municipal police department's jurisdiction, an item that is deceptively similar to a police identification item of the department;

(2) uses, within the municipal police department's jurisdiction, the name of the department in connection with an object to create the appearance that the object belongs to or is being used by the department; or

(3) uses, possesses, or operates, within the municipal police department's jurisdiction, a marked patrol vehicle that is deceptively similar to a department patrol vehicle.

(c) An item or vehicle is deceptively similar to a police identification item or patrol vehicle of a municipal police department if the circumstances under which the object is used could mislead a reasonable person as to the object's identity.

(d) An offense under this section is a Class B misdemeanor.

(e) It is an affirmative defense to prosecution under this section that:

(1) the object was used or intended to be used exclusively for decorative purposes and:

(A) the actor was not engaged in an activity involving police work or security work; or

(B) the object was used only in an artistic or dramatic presentation;

(2) the actor was engaged in the commercial manufacturing or commercial sales of the items described by Subsection (b);

(3) the actor was a licensed peace officer who:

(A) was on active duty discharging an official duty for an agency listed under Article 2.12, Code of Criminal Procedure, and acting under the agency's direct supervision; and

(B) was not privately employed as or hired on an individual or independent contractor basis as a patrolman, guard, watchman, flagman, or traffic conductor;

(4) the police chief consented, after determining that consent would serve law enforcement interests in the municipality, to the actor's:

(A) using or possessing a police identification item or other insignia of the municipal police department;

(B) using, possessing, or wearing an item or insignia similar to a police identification item or insignia of the municipal police department; or

(C) operating a vehicle similar to a patrol vehicle of the municipal police department; or

(5) the actor prosecuted under this section for wearing a uniform wore a light blue uniform shirt in a municipality that uses a light blue uniform shirt with navy blue pocket flaps and epaulets for its police officers, if the actor's shirt did not have:

(A) the contrasting navy blue pocket flaps or epaulets found on the municipal police officer's uniform shirts; and

(B) a shoulder emblem similar in shape, color, or design to an emblem found on the municipal police officers' uniform shirts.

(f) The attorney general or a municipal attorney, district attorney, or prosecuting attorney performing the duties of district attorney for the district in which a court is located may apply to the district court to enjoin a violation of this section. A district court shall grant an injunction if evidence demonstrates that a violation has occurred or will likely occur.

*(Added by L.1995, chap. 76(10.05)(a), eff. 9/1/95.)*



### §341.905. Juvenile curfew in general-law municipality.

(a) To provide for the public safety, the governing body of a general-law municipality has the same authority to adopt a juvenile curfew ordinance that a county has under Section 351.903.

(b) The governing body of a general-law municipality may adopt by ordinance a juvenile curfew order adopted by the commissioners court of the county in which any part of the municipality is located and may adapt the order to fit the needs of the municipality.

(c) If the governing body of a general-law municipality adopts an ordinance under this section, a person commits an offense if the person violates a restriction or prohibition imposed by the ordinance.

(d) An offense under this section is a Class C misdemeanor.

*(Added by L.1995, chap. 262(93); renumbered from section 341.904 by L.1997, chap. 165(31.01(67)), eff. 9/1/97.)*

## CHAPTER 351. COUNTY JAILS AND LAW ENFORCEMENT

*(Selected Section)*

Section



### §351.903. County juvenile curfew.

(a) To provide for the public safety, the commissioners court of a county by order may adopt a curfew to regulate the movements or actions of persons under 17 years of age during the period beginning one-half hour after sunset and extending until one-half hour before sunrise or during school hours, or both. The order applies only to the unincorporated area of the county.

(b) This authority includes the authority to:

(1) establish the hours of the curfew, including different hours for different days of the week;

(2) apply different curfew hours to different age groups of juveniles;

(3) describe the kinds of conduct subject to the curfew;

(4) determine the locations to which the curfew applies;

(5) determine which persons incur liability if a violation of the curfew occurs;

(6) prescribe procedures, in compliance with Section 52.028, Family Code, a police officer must follow in enforcing the curfew; and

(7) establish exemptions to the curfew, including but not limited to exemptions for times when there are no classes being conducted, for holidays, and for persons going to or from work.

(c) If the commissioners court adopts an order under this section, a person commits an offense if the person violates a restriction or prohibition imposed by the order.

(d) an order under this section is a Class C misdemeanor.

*(Added by L.1995, chap. 262(94), eff. 5/31/95.)*

# NATURAL RESOURCES CODE

## TITLE 3. OIL AND GAS

## SUBTITLE B. CONSERVATION AND REGULATION OF OIL AND GAS
*(Selected Chapter)*

## CHAPTER 85. CONSERVATION OF OIL AND GAS
*(Selected Section)*



**§85.389. Criminal penalty.**

(a) A person who is not the owner or operator of an oil well, gas well, or oil and gas well, a purchaser under contract of oil, gas, or oil and gas from a well, a gatherer with written authorization from the owner, operator, or purchaser, or an authorized representative of the commission who knowingly destroys, breaks, removes, or otherwise tampers with or attempts to destroy, break, remove, or otherwise tamper with any cap, seal, or other device placed on an oil well, gas well, oil and gas well, or associated oil or gas gathering equipment by the owner or operator for the purpose of controlling or limiting the operation of the well or associated equipment commits an offense.

(b) An offense under this section is a felony of the third degree.

## SUBTITLE D. REGULATION OF SPECIFIC BUSINESSES AND OCCUPATIONS
*(Selected Chapters)*

## CHAPTER 112. USED OIL FIELD EQUIPMENT DEALERS

### SUBCHAPTER A. GENERAL PROVISIONS



### SUBCHAPTER B. SALE OF USED EQUIPMENT



### SUBCHAPTER C. ENFORCEMENT; PENALTY



### SUBCHAPTER A. GENERAL PROVISIONS

**§112.001. Definitions.**

In this chapter:

(1) "Pipeline equipment" means all pipe, fittings, pumps, telephone and telegraph lines, and all other material and equipment used as part of or incident to the construction, maintenance, and operation of a pipeline for the transportation of oil, gas, water, or other liquid or gaseous substance.

(2) "Oil and gas equipment" means equipment and materials that are part of or incident to the exploration, development, maintenance, and operation of oil and gas properties and includes

equipment and materials that are part of or incident to the construction, maintenance, and operation of oil and gas wells, oil and gas leases, gasoline plants, and refineries.

(3) "Used materials" means pipeline equipment or oil and gas equipment after the equipment has once been placed in the use for which it first was manufactured and intended.

(4) "Dealer" means every person whose primary business is buying, selling, or otherwise dealing in used materials and who has a fixed, designated place or places of business within the state.

(5) "Broker" means every person whose primary business is buying, selling, or otherwise dealing in used materials as agent for the seller of the used materials, or as agent for the buyer of the used materials, or as agent for both.

(6) "Peddler" means every person who is not a dealer or broker and whose primary business is buying, selling, or otherwise dealing in used materials.

### §112.002. Applicability.

The provisions of this chapter shall not apply if the reasonable market value of the purchase made is less than $25.



## SUBCHAPTER B. SALE OF USED EQUIPMENT

### §112.011. Bill of sale.

Before purchasing or acquiring by exchange used materials, a dealer, broker, or peddler shall require that a bill of sale for the used materials be executed by the seller or the person who exchanges the materials. The dealer, broker, or peddler shall keep a copy of each bill of sale at his place of business.

### §112.012. Required information.† [*Information on bill of sale.*]

(a) The bill of sale shall include:

(1) the name and address of the dealer, broker, or peddler;

(2) the serial number, if any;

(3) the kind, make, size, weight, length, and quantity of the used materials purchased or acquired by exchange;

(4) the date of the purchase or acquisition by exchange, if different from the date of the bill of sale;

(5) the name and address of the seller or person who exchanged the materials;

(6) the place of location of the property at the time purchased or acquired by exchange;

(7) the license number of each motor vehicle used in transporting a purchased or exchanged item to the dealer's, broker's or peddler's place of business; and

(8) the driver's license number of the seller or person who exchanged the materials.

(b) A dealer, broker, or peddler under this chapter shall keep at his regular place of business all records required to be kept by this chapter for two years after the date of the purchase or acquisition by exchange of the materials.

## SUBCHAPTER C. ENFORCEMENT; PENALTY

### §112.031. Injunctive relief.

In the name and on behalf of the State of Texas, the attorney general or any district attorney or county attorney in this state may enjoin a dealer, peddler, or broker from continuing in business in this state as a dealer, peddler, or broker on violation of any of the provisions of this chapter.

### §112.032. Criminal penalty.

A person, dealer, peddler, or broker who violates any of the provisions of this chapter is guilty of a misdemeanor and on conviction is subject to a fine of not less than $500 for each violation.

### §112.033. Inspection.

(a) Any Texas Ranger or other officer commissioned by the Department of Public Safety, any sheriff or deputy sheriff, or any municipal police officer may enter the business premises of a dealer, broker, or peddler under this chapter during normal business hours to inspect the premises and the records of the dealer, broker, or peddler to determine whether the dealer, broker, or peddler is in compliance with this chapter.

(b) A dealer, broker, or peddler under this chapter must allow and shall not interfere with inspections conducted pursuant to this chapter.

(c) Each inspection conducted under this chapter shall be commenced and completed with reasonable promptness and shall be conducted in a reasonable manner.

# CHAPTER 115. REGULATION OF CERTAIN TRANSPORTERS OF OIL OR PETROLEUM PRODUCTS

*(Selected Sections)*

## SUBCHAPTER A. GENERAL PROVISIONS

Section





## SUBCHAPTER B. TENDERS AND MANIFESTS



## SUBCHAPTER D. ENFORCEMENT AND PENALTIES



## SUBCHAPTER A. GENERAL PROVISIONS

### §115.001. Definitions.

In this chapter:

(1) "Commission" means the Railroad Commission of Texas.

(2) "Commission order" includes a rule or order adopted by the commission under the oil and gas conservation statutes of this state, including this title and Subtitle B, Title 3, Utilities Code.

(3) "Gas" includes natural gas, bradenhead gas, casinghead gas, or gas produced from an oil or gas well.

(4) "Manifest" includes a document issued by a shipper that covers oil or a petroleum product transported by motor vehicle.

(5) "Oil" includes crude petroleum oil:

(A) in its natural state as produced; or

(B) from which only the basic sediment and water have been removed.

(6) "Person" includes an individual, corporation, association, partnership, receiver, trustee, guardian, executor, administrator, or representative.

(7) "Petroleum product" includes:

(A) refined crude oil;

(B) crude tops;

(C) topped crude;

(D) processed crude petroleum;

(E) residue from crude petroleum;

(F) cracking stock;
(G) uncracked fuel oil;
(H) fuel oil;
(I) treated crude oil;
(J) residuum;
(K) gas oil;
(L) casinghead gasoline;
(M) natural gas gasoline;
(N) naphtha;
(O) distillate;
(P) gasoline;
(Q) kerosene;
(R) benzine;
(S) wash oil;
(T) waste oil;
(U) blended gasoline;
(V) lubricating oil;
(W) blends or mixtures of petroleum; or
(X) any other liquid petroleum product or byproduct derived from crude petroleum oil or gas.

(8) "Shipping papers" includes:
(A) a bill of lading that covers oil or a petroleum product transported by railway;
(B) a manifest; or
(C) a document that covers oil or a petroleum product transported by pipeline, boat, or barge.

(9) "Tender" means a permit or certificate of clearance for the transportation of oil or a petroleum product that is approved and issued or registered under the authority of the commission.

(10) "Unlawful gas" includes gas produced or transported in violation of a law of this state or commission order.

(11) "Unlawful petroleum product" includes a petroleum product:
(A) any part of which was processed or derived in whole or in part from:
(i) unlawful oil;
(ii) a product of unlawful oil; or
(iii) unlawful gas; or
(B) transported in violation of a law of this state or commission order.

*(Added by L.1997, chap. 166(7), eff. 9/1/97.)*

## §115.002. Exception.

This chapter does not apply to the retail purchase of a petroleum product if that product is:
(1) contained in the ordinary equipment of a motor vehicle; and
(2) used only to operate the motor vehicle in which it is contained.

*(Added by L.1997, chap. 166(7), eff. 9/1/97.)*

## §115.003. Definition of unlawful oil; presumption.

(a) For purposes of this chapter, oil is unlawful if the oil is:
(1) produced in this state from a well in excess of the amount allowed by a commission order or otherwise in violation of a law of this state or commission order; or
(2) transported in violation of a law of this state or commission order.

(b) It is presumed that oil is "unlawful oil" for purposes of this chapter if the oil is retained in storage for more than six years without being used, consumed, or moved into regular commercial channels.

(c) The presumption under Subsection (b) may be rebutted by proof that the oil:
(1) was produced from a well within the production allowable then applying to that well;
(2) was not produced in violation of a law of this state or commission order; and
(3) if transported from the lease from which it was produced, was not transported in violation of a law of this state or commission order.

*(Added by L.1997, chap. 166(7), eff. 9/1/97.)*

## SUBCHAPTER B. TENDERS AND MANIFESTS

### §115.011. Tender requirements.

The commission by order may require that a tender be obtained before oil or a petroleum product may be transported or received for transportation by pipeline, railway, boat, or barge. *(Added by L.1997, chap. 166(7), eff. 9/1/97.)*

### §115.012. Tender; application requirements.

(a) The commission by order shall prescribe the form of a tender and a tender application.

(b) The form must show:

(1) the name and address of the shipper or other person who tenders oil or a petroleum product for transportation;

(2) the name and address of the transporter if the commission order requires the transporter to be designated;

(3) the quantity and classification of each commodity authorized to be transported;

(4) each location at which delivery is to be made to the transporter; and

(5) other related information as prescribed by commission order.

(c) Each tender must:

(1) bear a date and serial number;

(2) state the expiration date of the tender; and

(3) be executed by an agent authorized by the commission to deny, approve, or register tenders.

(d) An agent may not approve or register a tender for the transportation of unlawful oil or an unlawful petroleum product.

*(Added by L.1997, chap. 166(7), eff. 9/1/97.)*

### §115.013. Action on tender application.

(a) If an agent of the commission rejects an application for a tender, the agent shall return a copy of the application to the applicant with the reasons for the rejection indicated on the copy.

(b) A person whose tender application is not acted on before the 21st day after the date on which the application is filed is entitled to judicial review in the manner provided by Section 115.014 for the appeal of a rejection of a tender application.

*(Added by L.1997, chap. 166(7), eff. 9/1/97.)*

### §115.014. Judicial review.

(a) A person whose tender application is rejected may appeal that action by filing a petition against the commission in a district court of Travis County for review of the agent's decision.

(b) The clerk of the court shall issue to the commission a notice setting forth briefly the cause of action stated in the petition. The court may not enter an order on the petition until the court conducts a hearing. The court must conduct the hearing not later than the fifth day after the date of issuance of the notice.

(c) The court may sustain, modify, or overrule the agent's decision and may issue a restraining order or injunction as warranted by the facts.

(d) A person dissatisfied with the decision of the district court may appeal to the court of appeals.

*(Added by L.1997, chap. 166(7), eff. 9/1/97.)*

### §115.015. Transfer under tender.

(a) A person who obtains a tender may not transport or deliver, or cause or permit to be transported or delivered, any more or any different commodity than that authorized by the tender.

(b) A connecting carrier or consignee who receives oil or a petroleum product from another transporter by pipeline, railway, boat, or barge under authority of shipping papers executed by the initial transporter that bear the date and serial number of a tender issued to that initial transporter is considered to receive the oil or petroleum product by authority of that tender if the commission order provides that a connecting carrier or consignee may rely on the shipping papers.

*(Added by L.1997, chap. 166(7), eff. 9/1/97.)*

### §115.016. Issuance of manifest.

(a) A person who obtains a tender required under this subchapter shall sign and issue a manifest to the operator of each motor vehicle used to transport the oil or petroleum product that is covered by the tender.

(b) The person shall issue a separate manifest for each load carried by the motor vehicle.

*(Added by L.1997, chap. 166(7), eff. 9/1/97.)*

### §115.017. Form of manifest.

(a) The commission by order may prescribe the form of a manifest.

(b) A manifest must:

(1) bear a certificate signed by the shipper that states the amount of oil or petroleum products to be transported and specifies each petroleum product to be transported; and

(2) include, if required by commission order:

(A) the date and serial number of the tender that authorizes the transportation or a seal, number, or other evidence of the tender, if a tender is required;

(B) the amount and classification of each petroleum product to be transported;

(C) the name and address of the transporter, the name and address of the shipper, and the name and address of the consignee, if known;

(D) the name and address of the operator of the motor vehicle;

(E) the license plate number of the motor vehicle;

(F) the date, time, and place at which the motor vehicle was loaded and the destination, if known, of the load; and

(G) other related information as required by commission order.

(c) If the form of the manifest is not prescribed by commission order, each shipper required to issue a manifest to a transporter shall use a form of manifest that is:

(1) commonly used in commercial transactions; or

(2) required by another state agency to accompany the movement of gasoline.

*(Added by L.1997, chap. 166(7), eff. 9/1/97.)*

### §115.018. Transfer under manifest; restrictions.

(a) A person authorized to transport oil or a petroleum product on a manifest issued by a shipper may not receive:

(1) a commodity for transportation that is different from the commodity described in the manifest; or

(2) oil or a petroleum product in an amount exceeding the amount authorized by the manifest.

(b) A person authorized to transport oil or a petroleum product by a shipper-issued manifest that bears on its face the date and serial number of the tender may rely on the manifest delivered to that person and each consignee or person to whom the transporter delivers oil or a petroleum product covered by that manifest may rely on the manifest as authority to receive the commodity delivered if the manifest:

(1) appears to be valid on its face;

(2) is signed by the shipper; and

(3) bears the certificate of the shipper that the transportation of the oil or petroleum product is authorized by the tender.

(c) If the commission by order prohibits the transportation of oil or a petroleum product by motor vehicle without a manifest that shows the date and serial number of a tender authorizing the transportation, a person may not ship or transport or cause to be shipped or transported by motor vehicle oil or a petroleum product unless the person furnishes the manifest to the operator of the motor vehicle. The person transporting the oil or petroleum product shall maintain the manifest in the vehicle at all times during the shipment. If the person to whom the tender is issued is the operator of the motor vehicle and the tender identifies the motor vehicle by license number and covers one load, the person may carry the tender in the vehicle in lieu of a manifest.

*(Added by L.1997, chap. 166(7), eff. 9/1/97.)*

### §115.019. Receipt required.

A person who transports oil or a petroleum product by motor vehicle under conditions that require a tender or manifest shall obtain a receipt from each person to whom any part of the oil or petroleum product is delivered. The receipt must be on the reverse side of the tender or manifest and must indicate:

(1) the number of gallons of oil or of each petroleum product delivered;

(2) the date of delivery; and

(3) the signature and address of the purchaser or consignee of the oil or petroleum product.

*(Added by L.1997, chap. 166(7), eff. 9/1/97.)*

### §115.020. Records; inspection.

(a) A person who transports by motor vehicle and delivers oil or a petroleum product shall keep in this state for two years each tender or manifest issued to the person, together with the receipts and endorsements on the tender or manifest.

(b) A tender or manifest is at all times subject to inspection by the commission or an agent or inspector of the commission.
*(Added by L.1997, chap. 166(7), eff. 9/1/97.)*

## SUBCHAPTER D. ENFORCEMENT AND PENALTIES

### §115.041. Enforcement; arrests.

(a) To enforce this chapter, an agent of the commission or a peace officer of this state who has probable cause and reasonable grounds to believe that a motor vehicle is transporting unlawful oil or an unlawful petroleum product may stop the vehicle to take samples of the cargo and to inspect the shipping papers.

(b) If, on examination of the motor vehicle, the agent or officer finds that the vehicle is transporting unlawful oil or an unlawful petroleum product or is transporting oil or a petroleum product without a required tender, the agent or officer, with or without a warrant, shall arrest the operator of the vehicle and file a complaint against the operator under this chapter.

(c) In a criminal action under this chapter, the agent or officer is not entitled to a fee for executing a warrant of arrest or capias or for making an arrest with or without a warrant.
*(Added by L.1997, chap. 166(7), eff. 9/1/97.)*



### §115.042. Publication of commission order prior to enforcement.

A criminal action may not be maintained against a person involving the violation of a rule or order that the commission adopts, modifies, or amends until the commission publishes a complete copy of the rule or order. *(Added by L.1997, chap. 166(7), eff. 9/1/97.)*

### §115.043. Certificate as evidence.

(a) A certificate that sets forth the terms of a commission order and states that the order has been adopted and published and was in effect on a specified date or during a specified period is prima facie evidence of those facts if the certificate is:

(1) made under the seal of the commission; and

(2) executed by a member or the secretary of the commission.

(b) The certificate is admissible in evidence in any civil or criminal action that involves the order without further proof of the adoption, publication, or contents of the order.
*(Added by L.1997, chap. 166(7), eff. 9/1/97.)*

### §115.044. Service of process.

(a) In an action or proceeding that involves the enforcement of this chapter or a commission order, a Texas Ranger or agent of the commission may serve any judicial process, warrant, subpoena, or writ as directed by the court issuing the process and shall serve the process in the same manner as a peace officer.

(b) The ranger or agent may serve the process, warrant, or subpoena anywhere in this state although it may be directed to the sheriff or a constable of a particular county.

(c) The ranger or agent shall make the same return as any other officer, sign the return, and add under the name the title "State Ranger" or "Agent, Railroad Commission of Texas," as appropriate, which is sufficient to make the writ valid if the writ is otherwise properly prepared.

(d) A Texas Ranger or agent of the commission is not entitled to a fee in addition to that person's regular compensation for a service provided under this section.
*(Added by L.1997, chap. 166(7), eff. 9/1/97.)*

### §115.047. Penalties.

(a) A person commits an offense if the person is the operator of a motor vehicle that transports oil or a petroleum product and the person:

(1) intentionally fails to stop the vehicle on the command of an agent of the commission or peace officer; or

(2) intentionally fails to permit inspection by the agent or officer of the contents of or the shipping papers accompanying the vehicle.

(b) A person commits an offense if the person:

(1) knowingly violates Section 115.011, 115.015(a), 115.016, 115.018, 115.019, or 115.020;

(2) knowingly ships or transports or causes to be shipped or transported unlawful oil or an unlawful petroleum product by motor vehicle over a public highway in this state;

(3) knowingly ships or transports or causes to be shipped or transported by motor vehicle oil or a petroleum product without the authority of a tender if a tender is required by a commission order; or

(4) if a tender is required by a commission order, knowingly receives from a motor vehicle or knowingly delivers to a motor vehicle oil or a petroleum product that is not covered by a tender authorizing the transportation of the oil or petroleum product.

(c) A person commits an offense if the person:

(1) knowingly ships or transports or causes or permits to be shipped or transported by pipeline, railway, boat, or barge unlawful oil or an unlawful petroleum product;

(2) knowingly receives or delivers for transportation by pipeline, railway, boat, or barge unlawful oil or an unlawful petroleum product;

(3) knowingly ships or transports or causes or permits to be shipped or transported by pipeline, railway, boat, or barge oil or a petroleum product without authority of a tender if a tender is required by a commission order; or

(4) knowingly receives or delivers by pipeline, railway, boat, or barge oil or a petroleum product without authority of a tender if a tender is required by a commission order.

(d) An offense under this section is punishable by a fine of not less than $50 or more than $200.

*(Added by L.1997, chap. 166(7), eff. 9/1/97.)*

Printed in the U.S.A.

# OCCUPATIONS CODE

*(Added by L.1999, chap. 388(1), eff. 9/1/99.)*

# TITLE 3. HEALTH PROFESSIONS

## SUBTITLE B. PHYSICIANS

## CHAPTER 158. AUTHORITY OF PHYSICIAN TO PROVIDE CERTAIN DRUGS AND SUPPLIES

Section


### §158.001. Provision of drugs and other supplies.

(a) A physician licensed under this subtitle may supply a patient with any drug, remedy, or clinical supply necessary to meet the patient's immediate needs.

(b) This section does not permit a physician to operate a retail pharmacy without complying with Chapter 558. (V.A.C.S. Art. 4495b, Sec. 5.09(a).)
*(Added by L.1999, chap. 388(1), eff. 9/1/99.)*

### §158.002. Provision of free samples.

(a) This chapter does not prohibit a physician from supplying a pharmaceutical sample to a patient free of charge if, in the physician's opinion, it is advantageous to the patient, in adhering to a course of treatment prescribed by the physician, to receive the sample.

(b) A pharmaceutical sample provided under this section must be:

(1) provided to the physician from the manufacturer free of charge and delivered to a patient free of any direct or indirect charge;

(2) prepackaged by the original manufacturer and not repackaged; and

(3) marked on the immediate container to indicate that it is a sample or recorded in records that indicate it is a sample.

(c) Each state and federal labeling and recordkeeping requirement must be followed and documented. A record maintained under Subsection (b)(3) must be accessible as provided under state and federal law. (V.A.C.S. Art. 4495b, Sec. 5.09(b) (part).)
*(Added by L.1999, chap. 388(1), eff. 9/1/99.)*

### §158.003. Dispensing of dangerous drugs in certain rural areas.

(a) In this section, "reimbursement for cost" means an additional charge, separate from that imposed for the physician's professional services, that includes the cost of the drug product and all other actual costs to the physician incidental to providing the dispensing service. The term does not include a separate fee imposed for the act of dispensing the drug itself.

(b) This section applies to an area located in a county with a population of 5,000 or less, or in a municipality or an unincorporated town with a population of less than 2,500, that is within a 15-mile radius of the physician's office and in which a pharmacy is not located. This section does not apply to a municipality or an unincorporated town that is adjacent to a municipality with a population of 2,500 or more.

(c) A physician who practices medicine in an area described by Subsection (b) may:

(1) maintain a supply of dangerous drugs in the physician's office to be dispensed in the course of treating the physician's patients; and

(2) be reimbursed for the cost of supplying those drugs without obtaining a license under Chapter 558.

(d) A physician who dispenses dangerous drugs under Subsection (c) shall:

(1) comply with each labeling provision under Subtitle J applicable to that class of drugs; and

(2) oversee compliance with packaging and recordkeeping provisions applicable to that class of drugs.

(e) A physician who desires to dispense dangerous drugs under this section shall notify both the Texas State Board of Pharmacy and the board that the physician practices in an area described by Subsection (b). The physician may continue to dispense dangerous drugs in the area until the Texas State Board of Pharmacy determines, after notice and hearing, that the physician no longer practices in an area described by Subsection (b). (V.A.C.S. Art. 4495b, Sec. 5.09(c).)
*(Added by L.1999, chap. 388(1), eff. 9/1/99.)*

# SUBTITLE J. PHARMACY AND PHARMACISTS

## CHAPTER 563. PRESCRIPTION REQUIREMENTS; DELEGATION OF ADMINISTRATION AND PROVISION OF DANGEROUS DRUGS

### SUBCHAPTER A. PRESCRIPTION REQUIREMENTS FOR PRACTITIONERS

Section


### SUBCHAPTER B. DELEGATION OF ADMINISTRATION AND PROVISION OF DANGEROUS DRUGS



### SUBCHAPTER A. PRESCRIPTION REQUIREMENTS FOR PRACTITIONERS

#### §563.001. Prescription issued by practitioner.

A practitioner may not issue a prescription to be dispensed unless the prescription contains the following typed, printed, or stamped information:

(1) the practitioner's name, address, and telephone number; and

(2) the practitioner's required identification number. (V.A.C.S. Art. 4542a-1, Sec. 33(e).)
*(Added by L.1999, chap. 388(1), eff. 9/1/99.)*

#### §563.002. Requirements related to prescription forms.

(a) A written prescription issued by a practitioner must be on a form that:

(1) contains two signature lines of equal prominence, side by side, at the bottom of the form;

(2) has printed clearly, under one signature line, the words "product selection permitted"; and

(3) has printed clearly, under the other signature line, the words "dispense as written."

(b) The practitioner shall communicate dispensing instructions to the pharmacist by signing on the appropriate line.

(c) A prescription form furnished a practitioner may not contain a preprinted order for a drug product by brand name, generic name, or manufacturer. (V.A.C.S. Art. 4542a-1, Sec. 40(h) (part).)
*(Added by L.1999, chap. 388(1), eff. 9/1/99.)*

### SUBCHAPTER B. DELEGATION OF ADMINISTRATION AND PROVISION OF DANGEROUS DRUGS

#### §563.051. General delegation of administration and provision of dangerous drugs.

(a) A physician may delegate to any qualified and properly trained person acting under the physician's supervision the act of administering or providing dangerous drugs in the physician's office, as ordered by the physician, that are used or required to meet the immediate needs of the physician's patients. The administration or provision of the dangerous drugs must be performed in compliance with laws relating to the practice of medicine and state and federal laws relating to those dangerous drugs.

(b) A physician may also delegate to any qualified and properly trained person acting under the physician's supervision the act of administering or providing dangerous drugs through a facility licensed by the board, as ordered by the physician, that are used or required to meet the needs of the physician's patients. The administration of those dangerous drugs must be in compliance with laws relating to the practice of medicine, professional nursing, and pharmacy and state and federal drug laws. The provision of those dangerous drugs must be in compliance with:

(1) laws relating to the practice of medicine, professional nursing, and pharmacy;

(2) state and federal drug laws; and

(3) rules adopted by the board.

(c) The administration or provision of the drugs may be delegated through a physician's order, a standing medical order, a standing delegation order, or another order defined by the Texas State Board of Medical Examiners.

(d) This section does not authorize a physician or a person acting under the supervision of a physician to keep a pharmacy, advertised or otherwise, for the retail sale of dangerous drugs, other than as authorized under Section 158.003, without complying with the applicable laws relating to the dangerous drugs. (V.A.C.S. Art. 4542a-1, Secs. 33(a), (b) (part).)
*(Added by L.1999, chap. 388(1), eff. 9/1/99.)*

### §563.052. Suitable container required.

A drug or medicine provided under this subchapter must be supplied in a suitable container labeled in compliance with applicable drug laws. A qualified and trained person, acting under the supervision of a physician, may specify at the time of the provision of the drug the inclusion on the container of the date of the provision and the patient's name and address. (V.A.C.S. Art. 4542a-1, Sec. 33(b) (part).) *(Added by L.1999, chap. 388(1), eff. 9/1/99.)*

### §563.053. Dispensing of dangerous drugs in certain rural areas.

(a) In this section, "reimbursement for cost" means an additional charge, separate from that imposed for the physician's professional services, that includes the cost of the drug product and all other actual costs to the physician incidental to providing the dispensing service. The term does not include a separate fee imposed for the act of dispensing the drug itself.

(b) This section applies to an area located in a county with a population of 5,000 or less, or in a municipality or an unincorporated town with a population of less than 2,500, that is within a 15-mile radius of the physician's office and in which a pharmacy is not located. This section does not apply to a municipality or an unincorporated town that is adjacent to a municipality with a population of 2,500 or more.

(c) A physician who practices medicine in an area described by Subsection (b) may:

(1) maintain a supply of dangerous drugs in the physician's office to be dispensed in the course of treating the physician's patients; and

(2) be reimbursed for the cost of supplying those drugs without obtaining a license under Chapter 558.

(d) A physician who dispenses dangerous drugs under Subsection (c) shall:

(1) comply with each labeling provision under this subtitle applicable to that class of drugs; and

(2) oversee compliance with packaging and recordkeeping provisions applicable to that class of drugs.

(e) A physician who desires to dispense dangerous drugs under this section shall notify both the board and the Texas State Board of Medical Examiners that the physician practices in an area described by Subsection (b). The physician may continue to dispense dangerous drugs in the area until the board determines, after notice and hearing, that the physician no longer practices in an area described by Subsection (b). (V.A.C.S. Art. 4542a-1, Sec. 33(c).)
*(Added by L.1999, chap. 388(1), eff. 9/1/99.)*

### §563.054. Administration of dangerous drugs.

(a) A veterinarian may:

(1) administer or provide dangerous drugs to a patient in the veterinarian's office, or on the patient's premises, if the drugs are used or required to meet the needs of the veterinarian's patients;

(2) delegate the administration or provision of dangerous drugs to a person who:

(A) is qualified and properly trained; and

(B) acts under the veterinarian's supervision; and

(3) itemize and receive compensation for the administration or provision of the dangerous drugs under Subdivision (1).

(b) This section does not permit a veterinarian to maintain a pharmacy for the retailing of drugs without complying with applicable laws.

(c) The administration or provision of dangerous drugs must comply with:

(1) laws relating to the practice of veterinary medicine; and

(2) state and federal laws relating to dangerous drugs. (V.A.C.S. Art. 4542a-1, Sec. 33(d).)
*(Added by L.1999, chap. 388(1), eff. 9/1/99.)*

# TITLE 10. OCCUPATIONS RELATED TO LAW ENFORCEMENT AND SECURITY

## CHAPTER 1701. LAW ENFORCEMENT OFFICERS
*(Selected Sections)*

## SUBCHAPTER F. TRAINING PROGRAMS AND SCHOOLS

Section


## SUBCHAPTER H. CONTINUING EDUCATION AND YEARLY WEAPONS PROFICIENCY



## SUBCHAPTER F. TRAINING PROGRAMS AND SCHOOLS
*(Selected Section)*

### §1701.253. School curriculum.

(a) The commission shall establish minimum curriculum requirements for preparatory and advanced courses and programs for schools subject to approval under Section 1701.251(c)(1).

(b) In establishing requirements under this section, the commission shall require courses and programs to provide training in:

(1) the investigation and documentation of cases that involve:

(A) child abuse or neglect;

(B) family violence; and

(C) sexual assault; and

(2) issues concerning sex offender characteristics.

(c) As part of the minimum curriculum requirements, the commission shall establish a statewide comprehensive education and training program on civil rights, racial sensitivity, and cultural diversity for persons licensed under this chapter.

(d) Training in documentation of cases required by Subsection (b) shall include instruction in:

(1) making a written account of the extent of injuries sustained by the victim of an alleged offense;

(2) recording by photograph or videotape the area in which an alleged offense occurred and the victim's injuries; and

(3) recognizing and recording a victim's statement that may be admissible as evidence in a proceeding concerning the matter about which the statement was made. (Government Code, Sec. 415.032.)

*(Added by L.1999, chap. 388(1), eff. 9/1/99.)*

## SUBCHAPTER H. CONTINUING EDUCATION AND YEARLY WEAPONS PROFICIENCY
*(Selected Sections)*

### §1701.351. Continuing education required for peace officers.

(a) Each peace officer shall complete a continuing education program at least once every 24 months. The commission may suspend the license of a peace officer who fails to comply with this requirement.

(b) The commission by rule shall provide for waiver of the requirements of this section when mitigating circumstances exist. (Government Code, Sec. 415.034(g).)

*(Added by L.1999, chap. 388(1), eff. 9/1/99.)*

### §1701.352. Continuing education programs.

(a) The commission shall recognize, prepare, or administer continuing education programs for officers and county jailers.

(b) The commission shall require a state, county, special district, or municipal agency that appoints or employs peace officers to provide each peace officer with a training program at least once every 24 months. At least 20 hours of the instruction must be on topics selected by the agency. The course must:

(1) be approved by the commission;

(2) contain curricula that incorporate the learning objectives developed by the commission; and

(3) include education and training in:

(A) civil rights, racial sensitivity, and cultural diversity; and

(B) unless determined by the agency head to be inconsistent with the officer's assigned duties:

(i) the recognition and documentation of cases that involve child abuse or neglect, family violence, and sexual assault; and

(ii) issues concerning sex offender characteristics; and

(4) include other education and training only if determined by the agency head to be consistent with the officer's assigned duties.

(c) A course provided under Subsection (b):

(1) may not exceed 40 hours; and

(2) may use instructional materials developed by the agency or its trainers or by entities having training agreements with the commission in addition to materials included in curricula developed by the commission.

(d) A peace officer appointed to the officer's first supervisory position must receive in-service training on supervision as part of the course provided for the officer under Subsection (b) during the 24-month period after the date of that appointment.

(e) The commission may require a state, county, special district, or municipal agency that appoints or employs a reserve law enforcement officer, county jailer, or public security officer to provide each of those persons with education and training in civil rights, racial sensitivity, and cultural diversity at least once every 24 months.

(f) Training in documentation of cases required by Subsection (b) shall include instruction in:

(1) making a written account of the extent of injuries sustained by the victim of an alleged offense;

(2) recording by photograph or videotape the area in which an alleged offense occurred and the victim's injuries; and

(3) recognizing and recording a victim's statement that may be admissible as evidence in a proceeding concerning the matter about which the statement was made. (Government Code, Secs. 415.034(a); (b), as amended Acts 74th Leg., R.S., Chs. 254, 538, 562, 585; (c), as amended Acts 74th Leg., R.S., Chs. 254, 538, 585; (d); (f); (i).)

*(Added by L.1999, chap. 388(1), eff. 9/1/99.)*

### §1701.353. Continuing education procedures.

(a) The commission by rule shall adopt procedures to:

(1) ensure the timely and accurate reporting by agencies and peace officers of information related to training programs offered under this subchapter, including procedures for creating training records for individual peace officers; and

(2) provide adequate notice to agencies and peace officers of impending noncompliance with the training requirements of this subchapter so that the agencies and peace officers may comply within the 24-month period.

(b) The commission shall require agencies to report in a timely manner the reasons that a peace officer is in noncompliance after receiving notice by the commission of the peace officer's noncompliance. The commission shall, following receipt of an agency's report or on a determination that the agency has failed to report in a timely manner, conduct a hearing consistent with Section 1701.504 if the peace officer claims that:

(1) mitigating circumstances exist; or

(2) the peace officer failed to complete the required training because the officer's employing agency did not provide an adequate opportunity for the officer to attend the required training course. (Government Code, Sec. 415.034(h).)

*(Added by L.1999, chap. 388(1), eff. 9/1/99.)*

**§1701.355. Continuing demonstration of weapons proficiency.**

(a) An agency that employs at least two peace officers shall designate a firearms proficiency officer and require each peace officer the agency employs to demonstrate weapons proficiency to the firearms proficiency officer at least annually. The agency shall maintain records of the weapons proficiency of the agency's peace officers.

(b) On request, the commission may waive the requirement that a peace officer demonstrate weapons proficiency on a determination by the commission that the requirement causes a hardship.

(c) The commission by rule shall define weapons proficiency for purposes of this section. (Government Code, Sec. 415.0345.)

*(Added by L.1999, chap. 388(1), eff. 9/1/99.)*

# TITLE 11. REGULATION OF SALES AND SOLICITATION

## CHAPTER 1803. SOLICITATION FOR PUBLIC SAFETY ORGANIZATIONS

### SUBCHAPTER A. GENERAL PROVISIONS



### SUBCHAPTER B. REGISTRATION AND BOND REQUIREMENTS



### SUBCHAPTER C. SOLICITATION RESTRICTIONS



### SUBCHAPTER D. ENFORCEMENT AND PENALTIES



### SUBCHAPTER A. GENERAL PROVISIONS

**§1803.001. Definitions.**

In this chapter:

(1) "Law enforcement personnel" means commissioned peace officers who are employees of government law enforcement agencies.

(2) "Public safety entity" means a public safety promoter or public safety organization.

(3) "Public safety organization" means a nongovernmental organization that, in a manner that reasonably implies that the organization is composed of law enforcement or public safety personnel or that a contribution, purchase, or membership will benefit public safety personnel, uses the term "officer," "peace officer," "police officer," "police," "law enforcement," "reserve officer,"

"deputy," "deputy sheriff," "constable," "deputy constable," "fireman," "firefighter," "volunteer fireman," "emergency medical service provider," "civilian employee," or any other term:

(A) in its name;

(B) in a publication of the organization; or

(C) in a solicitation for:

(i) contributions to the organization;

(ii) membership in the organization;

(iii) the purchase of advertising in a publication of the organization; or

(iv) the purchase of products or tickets to an event sponsored by or for the benefit of the organization by a solicitor.

(4) "Public safety personnel" means employees or volunteers of a public safety organization, including:

(A) firefighters;

(B) emergency medical service providers; or

(C) civilian employees of a public safety organization.

(5) "Public safety promoter" means a person who:

(A) is not affiliated with a public safety organization; and

(B) in the name of public safety or in a name associated with public safety makes a request for a donation or the sale of tickets or advertising.

(6) "Public safety publication" means a nongovernmental publication with a name that includes the term "officer," "peace officer," "police officer," "police," "law enforcement," "reserve officer," "deputy," "deputy sheriff," "constable," "deputy constable," "fireman," "firefighter," "volunteer fireman," "emergency medical service provider," "civilian employee," or any other term in a manner that reasonably implies that the publication is published by a public safety organization or benefits public safety.

(7) "Public safety solicitor" means a person who:

(A) contracts for or receives money for providing solicitation services for a public safety entity or public safety publication; and

(B) solicits:

(i) contributions in person, by telephone, by electronic media, or by mail;

(ii) membership in a public safety organization from an individual not employed by a public safety agency of the United States, this state, or a political subdivision of this state; or

(iii) the purchase of:

(a) advertising; or

(b) goods, services, or tickets to an event sponsored by or for the benefit of a public safety organization or for the cause of public safety. (V.A.C.S. Art. 9023c, Sec. 1 (part); New.) *(Added by L.1999, chap. 388(1), eff. 9/1/99.)*

### §1803.002. Effect on municipal ordinance.

This chapter preempts any municipal ordinance applicable to public safety entities, public safety publications, public safety solicitors, or solicitations related to a person registered under this chapter. (V.A.C.S. Art. 9023c, Sec. 16.) *(Added by L.1999, chap. 388(1), eff. 9/1/99.)*

## SUBCHAPTER B. REGISTRATION AND BOND REQUIREMENTS

### §1803.051. Registration.

(a) A public safety entity or public safety publication may not solicit unless the entity or publication:

(1) files a registration statement under Section 1803.053; and

(2) pays a registration fee under Section 1803.054.

(b) A public safety entity or public safety publication may not use a public safety solicitor, and a person may not act as a public safety solicitor unless the solicitor:

(1) files a registration statement and pays the registration fee under Section 1803.055; and

(2) files and maintains a bond under Section 1803.056. (V.A.C.S. Art. 9023c, Sec. 2.) *(Added by L.1999, chap. 388(1), eff. 9/1/99.)*

### §1803.052. Eligibility to use solicitor.

(a) A public safety organization may register under Section 1803.053 and use a public safety solicitor only if the organization is a bona fide membership organization consisting of individual members:

(1) of whom at least five percent or 500 members, whichever is less, are employed as law enforcement personnel or public safety personnel by a public safety agency of the United States, this state, or a political subdivision of this state; and

(2) who have signed membership agreements with the organization and paid an annual membership fee of at least $10.

(b) A public safety promoter may register under Section 1803.053 and use a public safety solicitor if the disclosure required by Section 1803.101 is made. (V.A.C.S. Art. 9023c, Sec. 3.)
*(Added by L.1999, chap. 388(1), eff. 9/1/99.)*

## §1803.053. Registration statement by public safety entity or publication.

(a) Before beginning solicitations, a public safety entity or public safety publication shall file with the secretary of state:

(1) a registration statement signed by two of its officers or directors; and

(2) if the public safety entity or publisher of the publication, as applicable, is a nonresident, an irrevocable written consent appointing the secretary of state as agent for service of process on the entity or publisher for any action relating to a violation of this chapter.

(b) The registration statement must disclose:

(1) the name, street address, and telephone number of any public safety solicitor for the registering entity;

(2) the name, street address, and telephone number of each public safety organization, public safety publication, or fund for which any part of the contributions will be used, or if there is no organization, publication, or fund, a statement describing how the contributions will be used;

(3) whether the registering entity or fund that the contributions are being solicited for has a federal and state charitable tax exemption;

(4) the name and public safety agency or former agency of each active and retired public safety officer serving on the board of directors or governing body of the registering entity;

(5) the number of members and the percentage of members who are active and retired public safety officers of the United States, this state, or a political subdivision of this state, as determined on December 31 of the year preceding the year in which the registration is made and the contributions are solicited, if the registering entity is a public safety organization;

(6) the name of the local chapter, lodge, association, or group of licensed public safety officers of the public safety organization for which contributions are being solicited, if the registering entity is a public safety organization;

(7) a copy of the most recent tax or informational return filed with the Internal Revenue Service by the registering entity;

(8) the amount of money collected during the previous year by the registering entity by solicitations of nonmembers of the public safety organization for which the funds were collected and the amount of funds paid as expenses to maintain the solicitation operation;

(9) the amount of money, if known or projected, expected to be collected during the year of filing by the registering entity by nonmember solicitations described by Subdivision (8);

(10) a copy of any contract or agreement between the registering entity and a solicitor; and

(11) if the registering entity is a public safety publication, information on:

(A) the total number of copies of each issue of the publication printed during the previous year;

(B) the frequency of the publication; and

(C) the date and circulation of the most recent issue of the publication.

(c) A registration statement takes effect on the date the secretary of state issues a certificate and is valid for one year. The statement may be renewed annually by filing a renewal registration statement and paying the registration fee required by Section 1803.054.

(d) A public safety entity or public safety publication shall file an updated statement with the secretary of state not later than the 30th day after the date of a change of street address, phone number, or name. (V.A.C.S. Art. 9023c, Sec. 4.)
*(Added by L.1999, chap. 388(1), eff. 9/1/99.)*

## §1803.054. Public safety entity registration fee.

(a) Except as provided by Subsection (b), a public safety entity registering under Section 1803.053 shall pay to the secretary of state an annual registration fee of $250.

(b) A public safety organization consisting of members who are volunteer firefighters for a local political subdivision and that solicits only in the area of the firefighters' jurisdiction is not required to pay a registration fee.

(c) Subsection (b) does not apply to a statewide association of volunteer firefighters. (V.A.C.S. Art. 9023c, Sec. 5.)
*(Added by L.1999, chap. 388(1), eff. 9/1/99.)*

### §1803.055. Solicitor registration statement and fee.

(a) Before beginning solicitations for a public safety entity or public safety publication, a public safety solicitor shall file with the secretary of state a registration statement containing:

(1) the name, street and mailing address, and telephone number of the solicitor;

(2) the name, street and mailing address, and telephone number of each public safety entity or public safety publication for whom the solicitor solicits or will solicit in this state; and

(3) if the solicitor is a nonresident, an irrevocable written consent appointing the secretary of state as agent for service of process on the solicitor for any action pertaining to a violation of this chapter.

(b) The registration statement required by Subsection (a) must be accompanied by:

(1) a $500 registration fee; and

(2) a bond as required by Section 1803.056.

(c) A registration statement takes effect on the date the secretary of state issues a certificate and is valid for one year. The statement may be renewed annually by filing a renewal registration statement and paying the registration fee required by Subsection (b).

(d) A solicitor shall file an updated statement with the secretary of state not later than the 30th day after the date of a change of street address, mailing address, phone number, or name. (V.A.C.S. Art. 9023c, Sec. 6.)

*(Added by L.1999, chap. 388(1), eff. 9/1/99.)*

### §1803.056. Solicitor bond.

(a) A public safety solicitor shall post with the secretary of state a $10,000 surety bond issued by a surety company authorized to do business in this state.

(b) The bond must be payable to the state and conditioned on compliance with this chapter. (V.A.C.S. Art. 9023c, Sec. 7.)

*(Added by L.1999, chap. 388(1), eff. 9/1/99.)*

## SUBCHAPTER C. SOLICITATION RESTRICTIONS

### §1803.101. Solicitation disclosure.

(a) An oral or a written disclosure shall be given to each person before the person delivers any consideration to a public safety entity, public safety publication, or public safety solicitor.

(b) A written disclosure must be in contrasting eight-point type or larger.

(c) A disclosure must include:

(1) the name of the public safety organization registered under Section 1803.053, if an organization is involved;

(2) a statement that the promotion is independent of affiliation with any public safety organization, if a public safety promoter is involved;

(3) the name of any public safety solicitor employed;

(4) a general statement of the use of net funds received; and

(5) the name, street address, and statewide telephone number established under Section 1803.102 that a person may use to obtain from the secretary of state additional information on the public safety entity, public safety publication, or public safety solicitor. (V.A.C.S. Art. 9023c, Sec. 8.)

*(Added by L.1999, chap. 388(1), eff. 9/1/99.)*

### §1803.102. Solicitation information hotline.

The secretary of state shall establish and operate a toll-free telephone line known as the Solicitation Information Hotline that enables a person to call the hotline number to:

(1) obtain information concerning a public safety entity, public safety publication, or public safety solicitor that has filed a registration statement with the secretary of state under this chapter; or

(2) report an alleged violation of this chapter by a public safety entity, public safety publication, or public safety solicitor. (V.A.C.S. Art. 9023c, Sec. 9.)

*(Added by L.1999, chap. 388(1), eff. 9/1/99.)*

### §1803.103. Prohibited practices.

In soliciting for a Public safety entity or public safety publication, a person may not:

(1) use, unless authorized in writing by a public safety Agency or public safety organization:

(A) any representation that implies that the contribution is For or on behalf of the agency or organization; or

(B) any emblem, device, or printed matter belonging to or Associated with the agency or organization;

(2) use a name, symbol, or statement similar to a name, Symbol, or statement used by a public safety agency or organization in A manner intended to confuse or mislead a person being solicited;

(3) knowingly represent or imply that the solicitation Proceeds are being used for a purpose other than the purpose for which The funds are actually used;

(4) represent or imply that the solicitor is a peace officer Or member of a public safety agency or public safety organization if The solicitor is not an officer or a member;

(5) use or exploit the fact of filing with the secretary of State in a manner leading a person to believe that filing, in any way, Constitutes an endorsement by or approval of the state;

(6) knowingly file incomplete, false, or misleading Information in a document required to be filed with the secretary of State under this chapter;

(7) solicit for a public safety entity or public safety Publication, or represent that those responding affirmatively to the Solicitation will receive favored treatment by public safety Personnel;

(8) collect a contribution or membership fee solicited at a Person's residence by an in-person or telephone solicitation by means Other than payment through the united states mail or parcel post Courier;

(9) solicit for a public safety organization in a county in Which members of the organization do not have jurisdiction; or

(10) commit another unfair or deceptive act or practice. (V.A.C.S. Art. 9023c, Sec. 10.) *(Added by L.1999, chap. 388(1), eff. 9/1/99.)*



### §1803.104. Failure to file timely report.

A public safety entity or public safety publication that fails to timely file the information required by this chapter or that files information required by this chapter that is found to contain material misrepresentation may not use a public safety solicitor until it provides or corrects the information. (V.A.C.S. Art. 9023c, Sec. 14(b).) *(Added by L.1999, chap. 388(1), eff. 9/1/99.)*

## SUBCHAPTER D. ENFORCEMENT AND PENALTIES

### §1803.151. Audit by attorney general.

(a) The attorney general may make a written request for information from a public safety entity, public safety publication, or public safety solicitor to audit or verify a representation contained in a registration statement.

(b) A public safety entity, public safety publication, or public safety solicitor shall provide information requested by the attorney general under Subsection (a) not later than the 10th working day after the date of the attorney general's request.

(c) Wilful failure to provide timely information under this section is a ground for bond forfeiture or suspension of registration. (V.A.C.S. Art. 9023c, Sec. 11.)
*(Added by L.1999, chap. 388(1), eff. 9/1/99.)*

### §1803.152. Criminal penalties.

(a) A person commits an offense if the person knowingly violates this chapter.

(b) An offense under this chapter is a Class A misdemeanor.

(c) A corporation or association may be held criminally responsible for conduct by a person acting on its behalf if the person's conduct:

(1) constitutes an offense under this chapter; and

(2) is done with the knowledge and approval of the corporation or association. (V.A.C.S. Art. 9023c, Sec. 12.)
*(Added by L.1999, chap. 388(1), eff. 9/1/99.)*

### §1803.153. Civil penalty and injunction.

(a) The attorney general may bring an action in a Travis County district court:

(1) for a civil penalty for a violation of this chapter; and

(2) to enjoin a person from violating this chapter.

(b) The attorney general shall notify the defendant of the alleged prohibited conduct not later than the seventh day before the date the action is commenced.

(c) Notice is not required if the attorney general intends to request that the court issue a temporary restraining order. (V.A.C.S. Art. 9023c, Sec. 13.)
*(Added by L.1999, chap. 388(1), eff. 9/1/99.)*

**§1803.154. Civil penalties.**

(a) A person who violates this chapter or an injunction issued under Section 1803.153 is liable to the state for a civil penalty of not more than:

(1) $2,500 for a single violation; or

(2) $10,000 for all of the violations.

(b) If a person found to have violated this chapter or an injunction has filed a bond under this chapter, the suit may be brought against the bond. (V.A.C.S. Art. 9023c, Sec. 14(a).) *(Added by L.1999, chap. 388(1), eff. 9/1/99.)*

**§1803.155. Service on secretary of state.**

(a) A service of process or pleading served on the secretary of state as the agent for a nonresident public safety solicitor, public safety entity, or public safety publication must be served in triplicate.

(b) The secretary of state shall file one copy in the secretary of state's office and immediately forward the other copies by certified mail, return receipt requested, to the address of the nonresident, as shown on the nonresident's registration statement.

(c) Service on the secretary of state shall be returned not later than the 30th day after the date of service. (V.A.C.S. Art. 9023c, Sec. 15.) *(Added by L.1999, chap. 388(1), eff. 9/1/99.)*



# TITLE 13. SPORTS, AMUSEMENTS, AND ENTERTAINMENT

## SUBTITLE A. GAMING

## CHAPTER 2003. INSPECTION AND REGULATION OF GAMBLING VESSELS

### SUBCHAPTER A. GENERAL PROVISIONS

Section



### SUBCHAPTER B. STATE INSPECTION AND REGULATION



### SUBCHAPTER C. MUNICIPAL INSPECTION AND REGULATION



### SUBCHAPTER A. GENERAL PROVISIONS

**§2003.001. Definition.**

In this chapter, "department" means the Department of Public Safety of the State of Texas. (V.A.C.S. Art. 179f, Sec. 1, as added Acts 71st Leg., R.S., Ch. 1030.) *(Added by L.1999, chap. 388(1), eff. 9/1/99.)*

**§2003.002. Application of chapter.**

This chapter applies only to a vessel on which activity described by Section 47.02(a), Penal Code, is regularly conducted, whether or not the activity occurs in this state. (V.A.C.S. Art. 179f, Sec. 2, as added Acts 71st Leg., R.S., Ch. 1030.) *(Added by L.1999, chap. 388(1), eff. 9/1/99.)*

## SUBCHAPTER B. STATE INSPECTION AND REGULATION

### §2003.051. Criminal history record information.

(a) The department may request criminal history record information from the Federal Bureau of Investigation or any other law enforcement agency relating to a person who owns, has a financial interest in, operates, or is employed by a person who operates a vessel in this state, including the territorial waters of this state, whether or not the operation of the vessel is in violation of law.

(b) The department may maintain records of information obtained under Subsection (a). (V.A.C.S. Art. 179f, Sec. 3, as added Acts 71st Leg., R.S., Ch. 1030.)
*(Added by L.1999, chap. 388(1), eff. 9/1/99.)*

### §2003.052. Inspection.

The department may inspect a vessel located in this state, including the territorial waters of this state, to ensure that the vessel is operated in compliance with state or other law. (V.A.C.S. Art. 179f, Sec. 4, as added Acts 71st Leg., R.S., Ch. 1030.) *(Added by L.1999, chap. 388(1), eff. 9/1/99.)*



## SUBCHAPTER C. MUNICIPAL INSPECTION AND REGULATION

### §2003.101. Regulation.

(a) A municipality, by ordinance, may impose regulations for the protection of the health and safety of the passengers or crew of a vessel that:

(1) regularly boards passengers in the municipality; or

(2) is regularly loaded, fueled, repaired, stored, or docked in the municipality.

(b) A municipal ordinance may not prohibit an activity relating to a vessel that is expressly permitted under Chapter 47, Penal Code, or other state law. (V.A.C.S. Art. 179f, Secs. 5(a), (c), as added Acts 71st Leg., R.S., Ch. 1030.)
*(Added by L.1999, chap. 388(1), eff. 9/1/99.)*

### §2003.102. Inspection.

A municipality may inspect a vessel docked in the municipality to determine if the vessel is operated in compliance with Chapter 47, Penal Code, a municipal ordinance, or other law. (V.A.C.S. Art. 179f, Sec. 5(b), as added Acts 71st Leg., R.S., Ch. 1030.) *(Added by L.1999, chap. 388(1), eff. 9/1/99.)*

# SUBTITLE B. SPORTS

## CHAPTER 2053. RIDING STABLES
*(Selected Sections)*

## SUBCHAPTER C. REGISTRATION



## SUBCHAPTER D. ENFORCEMENT AND DISCIPLINARY PROCEDURES



## SUBCHAPTER C. REGISTRATION

### §2053.021. Registration required.

A person may not operate a riding stable unless the person holds a certificate of registration issued by the department for each location at which the person operates a stable. (Health and Safety Code, Sec. 827.003(a).)*(Added by L.1999, chap. 388(1), eff. 9/1/99.)*

## SUBCHAPTER D. ENFORCEMENT AND DISCIPLINARY PROCEDURES

**§2053.038. Criminal offense.**

(a) A person commits an offense if the person knowingly operates a riding stable in violation of Section 2053.021.

(b) An offense under this section is a Class B misdemeanor.

(c) A person commits a separate offense for each day the person engages in conduct prohibited by Subsection (a). (Health and Safety Code, Sec. 827.011.)
*(Added by L.1999, chap. 388(1), eff. 9/1/99.)*

# SUBTITLE C. ARTS AND MUSIC



# CHAPTER 2104. REGULATION OF OUTDOOR MUSIC FESTIVALS

## SUBCHAPTER A. GENERAL PROVISIONS



## SUBCHAPTER B. PROMOTER REGISTRATION



## SUBCHAPTER C. OUTDOOR MUSIC FESTIVAL PERMIT



## SUBCHAPTER D. PENALTIES



## SUBCHAPTER A. GENERAL PROVISIONS

**§2104.001. Definitions.**

In this chapter:

(1) "Outdoor music festival" means any form of musical entertainment provided by live performances that occurs on two or more consecutive days or on any two days during a three-day period if:

(A) more than 5,000 persons attend any performance;

(B) any performer or audience member is not within a permanent structure; and

(C) the performance occurs outside the boundaries of a municipality.

(2) "Promoter" means a person who attempts to organize or promote an outdoor music festival, or to solicit funds for the organization or promotion of an outdoor music festival. (V.A.C.S. Art. 9003, Sec. 1.)
*(Added by L.1999, chap. 388(1), eff. 9/1/99.)*

## SUBCHAPTER B. PROMOTER REGISTRATION

### §2104.051. Promoter registration.

(a) A promoter shall register with the county clerk of the county in which the outdoor music festival is to be held.

(b) The registration must include:

(1) the name and address of:

(A) the promoter; and

(B) each of the promoter's associates or employees assisting in the promotion of the festival; and

(2) a statement indicating whether the promoter, or an associate or employee of the promoter, has been convicted of a crime involving the misappropriation of funds, theft, burglary, or robbery.

(c) The promoter must submit a $5 registration fee with the registration.

(d) The registration must be verified by the promoter and be based on the promoter's best information and belief. (V.A.C.S. Art. 9003, Sec. 3.)

*(Added by L.1999, chap. 388(1), eff. 9/1/99.)*



## SUBCHAPTER C. OUTDOOR MUSIC FESTIVAL PERMIT

### §2104.101. Festival permit application.

(a) A promoter shall, before the 60th day before the date the promoter holds an outdoor music festival, file a permit application with the county clerk of the county in which the festival is to be held.

(b) The application must include:

(1) the name and address of:

(A) the promoter; and

(B) each of the promoter's associates or employees assisting in the promotion of the festival;

(2) a financial statement of the promoter and a statement specifying the sources and amounts of capital being supplied for the festival;

(3) a description of the festival location;

(4) the name and address of the owner of the festival location;

(5) a statement describing the terms and conditions of the agreement allowing the promoter to use the festival location;

(6) the dates and times of the festival;

(7) the maximum number of persons the promoter will allow to attend the festival;

(8) a statement describing the promoter's plan to control the number of persons attending the festival;

(9) a description of the agreement between the promoter and each performer who is scheduled to appear at the festival; and

(10) a complete statement describing the promoter's festival preparations to comply with the minimum standards of sanitation and health prescribed by Chapter 341, Health and Safety Code.

(c) The promoter shall submit a $5 filing fee with the permit application.

(d) The permit application must be verified by the promoter and be based on the promoter's best information and belief. (V.A.C.S. Art. 9003, Sec. 4.)

*(Added by L.1999, chap. 388(1), eff. 9/1/99.)*

### §2104.102. Health report.

(a) On the filing of a permit application under Section 2104.101, the county clerk shall forward a copy of the application to the county health officer.

(b) The county health officer shall make a written report to the commissioners court. A report made under this subsection must:

(1) state whether the county health officer believes that the preparations described in the application would, if carried out, be sufficient to:

(A) protect the community and the persons attending the outdoor music festival from health dangers; and

(B) avoid a violation of Chapter 341, Health and Safety Code; and

(2) be filed with the county clerk before the second day before the date of the hearing on the permit application.

(c) The county health officer shall be present at the hearing on the permit application and may be called to testify by a person having an interest in the permit. (V.A.C.S. Art. 9003, Sec. 5.)

*(Added by L.1999, chap. 388(1), eff. 9/1/99.)*

### §2104.103. Hearing.

(a) The commissioners court shall set a date and time for a hearing on the permit application.

(b) The hearing must be held:

(1) after the 15th day after the date the permit application is filed; and

(2) before the 30th day before the date set for the first performance of the outdoor music festival.

(c) A promoter is entitled to at least 10 days notice before the hearing date.

(d) Any person may appear at the hearing and testify for or against the grant of the permit. (V.A.C.S. Art. 9003, Sec. 6.)

*(Added by L.1999, chap. 388(1), eff. 9/1/99.)*

### §2104.104. Decision on permit application.

The commissioners court shall grant a permit application filed under Section 2104.101 unless, by a majority vote, the court finds, from a preponderance of the evidence presented at the hearing, that:

(1) the permit application contains false or misleading information;

(2) required information is omitted from the application;

(3) the promoter does not have sufficient financial backing or stability to:

(A) carry out the preparations described in the application; or

(B) ensure the faithful performance of the promoter's agreements;

(4) the preparations described in the application are insufficient to:

(A) protect the community or the persons attending the outdoor music festival from health dangers; or

(B) avoid a violation of Chapter 341, Health and Safety Code;

(5) the times of the festival and the festival location create a substantial danger of congestion and disruption of other lawful activities in the immediate vicinity of the festival;

(6) the preparations described in the application are insufficient to limit the number of persons attending the festival to the maximum number stated in the application; or

(7) the promoter does not have adequate agreements with performers to ensure with reasonable certainty that persons advertised to perform at the festival will appear. (V.A.C.S. Art. 9003, Sec. 7.)

*(Added by L.1999, chap. 388(1), eff. 9/1/99.)*

### §2104.105. Effect of permit.

A permit issued under this chapter authorizes the promoter to hold an outdoor music festival at a specified location at specified times. (V.A.C.S. Art. 9003, Sec. 8.) *(Added by L.1999, chap. 388(1), eff. 9/1/99.)*

### §2104.106. Permit revocation.

(a) At any time before the fifth day before the date of the first performance of the outdoor music festival, the commissioners court may, after reasonable notice to the promoter and a hearing, revoke the permit on a finding, by a majority of the court, that:

(1) the preparations for the event will not be completed in time for the first performance; and

(2) the failure to carry out the preparations will result in a serious threat to the health of the community or persons attending the festival.

(b) A permit may not be revoked during the period beginning with the fifth day before the date of the first performance of the festival and ending with the final day of the festival. (V.A.C.S. Art. 9003, Sec. 9.)

*(Added by L.1999, chap. 388(1), eff. 9/1/99.)*

### §2104.107. Appeal.

(a) A person affected by an action of the commissioners court in granting, denying, or revoking a permit issued under this chapter may appeal the action by filing a petition in a district court in the county in which the commissioners court presides.

(b) The district court shall review the action of the commissioners court under the substantial evidence rule.

(c) An appeal under this section does not suspend an action of the commissioners court unless the district court orders a suspension. (V.A.C.S. Art. 9003, Sec. 10.)

*(Added by L.1999, chap. 388(1), eff. 9/1/99.)*

## SUBCHAPTER D. PENALTIES

### §2104.151. Prohibited acts; criminal offense.

(a) A person may not act as a promoter of an outdoor music festival unless the person registers with the county clerk of the county in which the festival is to be held.

(b) A person may not direct, control, or participate in the direction or control of an outdoor music festival unless the festival is authorized by a permit issued under this chapter.

(c) A person commits an offense if the person violates this section.

(d) An offense under this section is a misdemeanor punishable by:

(1) confinement in a county jail for a term not to exceed 30 days;

(2) a fine not to exceed $1,000; or

(3) both the fine and confinement. (V.A.C.S. Art. 9003, Secs. 2, 11.)

*(Added by L.1999, chap. 388(1), eff. 9/1/99.)*

# SUBTITLE D. OTHER AMUSEMENTS AND ENTERTAINMENT

# CHAPTER 2152. REGULATION OF CIRCUSES, CARNIVALS, AND ZOOS

*(Selected Sections)*

## SUBCHAPTER C. LICENSE REQUIREMENTS



## SUBCHAPTER E. ENFORCEMENT



## SUBCHAPTER C. LICENSE REQUIREMENTS

### §2152.101. License required.

A person may not operate a circus, carnival, or zoo unless the person holds a license issued under this chapter for the circus, carnival, or zoo. (Health and Safety Code Sec. 824.003.) *(Added by L.1999, chap. 388(1), eff. 9/1/99.)*

## SUBCHAPTER E. ENFORCEMENT

### §2152.202. Criminal penalty.

(a) A person commits an offense if the person knowingly violates Section 2152.101.

(b) An offense under this section is a Class C misdemeanor. (Health and Safety Code Sec. 824.016.)

*(Added by L.1999, chap. 388(1), eff. 9/1/99.)*

# PARKS AND WILDLIFE CODE

## CHAPTER 12. POWERS AND DUTIES CONCERNING WILDLIFE
*(Selected Sections)*



### §12.101. Definitions.

In this subchapter:

(1) "Aircraft" means a device, including an airplane, ultralight airplane, or helicopter, that can be used for flight in the air.

(2) "Contraband" means:

(A) an aircraft, vehicle, firearm, or other device used to commit a violation of Subchapter G, Chapter 43, of this code or a regulation of the commission adopted under that subchapter;

(B) a vessel that is not documented by the United States Coast Guard or registered as provided by Chapter 31 and that is used to commit an offense under Section 66.006 of this code;

(C) equipment, including a vessel, seized as provided by Section 66.2011 of this code; or

(D) any aircraft or vessel used to commit a second or subsequent offense under Section 61.022, 62.003, 62.004, or 62.005.

*(Added by L.1995, chap. 966(1); chgd. by L. 1999, chap. 959(1), eff. 9/1/99.)*

### §12.104. Right to search and inspect.

(a) A game warden or other peace officer commissioned by the department may search a game bag, vehicle, vessel, or other receptacle if the game warden or peace officer has a reasonable, articulable suspicion that the game bag, vehicle, vessel, or receptacle contains a wildlife resource that has been unlawfully killed or taken.

(b) A game warden or other peace officer commissioned by the department may inspect a wildlife resource or a part or product of a wildlife resource that is discovered during a search under Subsection (a) of this section.

(c) In this section "wildlife resource" means an animal, bird, reptile, amphibian, fish, or other aquatic life the taking or possession of which is regulated in any manner by this code.

*(Chgd. by L.1991, chap. 261(1), eff. 8/26/91.)*

### §12.1105. Seizure and disposition of unlawful fishing devices.

(a) When a game warden or other peace officer finds in or on the public water of the state a seine, net, trawl, trap, or other device that is in or on the water in violation of a provision of this code or in violation of a lawful regulation of the commission or is aboard a vessel in violation of a provision of this code or a lawful regulation of the commission, the warden or other peace officer shall seize without a warrant the seine, net, trawl, trap, or device.

(b) When an alleged violator is charged with an offense in connection with the unlawful use or possession of the seine, net, trawl, trap, or device seized by the warden or other peace officer, the warden or other peace officer shall hold the seine, net, trawl, trap, or device as evidence. Except as provided in Subsection (e) of this section, on a final conviction for the offense of the alleged violator, including a final judgment arising from a plea of nolo contendere, the warden or other peace officer shall destroy the seine, net, trawl, trap, or device. If the alleged violator is not guilty of the offense or if the charge is not prosecuted and dismissed, the seine, net, trawl, trap, or device shall be returned to the owner.

(c) If no person is charged with an offense in connection with the seizure of a seine, net, trawl, trap, or other device under this section, and no person is found in possession of the seine, net, trawl, trap, or device, the warden or other peace officer shall give notice of the seizure to the county judge or a judge of a county court at law or justice court of the county where the seizure occurred. The notice must include a description of the items seized and the location of the seizure. The court shall then direct the sheriff or a constable to post a copy of the notice in the county courthouse for not less than 10 days. At the expiration of 10 days, the court shall hold a hearing to determine if the seine, net, trawl, trap, or device was used or possessed in violation of a provision of this code or of a lawful regulation of the commission. Except as provided in Subsection (e) of this section, if the use or possession was unlawful, the warden or other peace officer shall destroy the seine, net, trawl, trap, or device.

(d) A game warden or other peace officer who seizes items under this section is immune from liability and from suit for a seizure or destruction of a net as authorized by this section.

(e) The Parks and Wildlife Department, when requested by authorized representatives of units of The University of Texas System, The Texas A&M University System, and the Texas State University System engaged in teaching and research related to marine science and oceanography, may transfer to such units of said universities and university systems nets, seines, and other marine equipment, which have been seized under this section, to be used in carrying out the teaching and research programs within said institutions.

*(Chgd. by L.1991, chap. 781(1); L.1995, chap. 1061(10); L.1997, chap. 227(7); L.1999, chap. 851(1), eff. 9/1/99.)*

## §12.1106. Seizure and disposition of contraband; immunity.

(a) A game warden or other peace officer who has probable cause to believe property is contraband may seize the property without a warrant.

(b) The warden or officer shall give notice of the seizure, including a description of the seized property and the location and date of seizure, to the county judge or a judge of a county court at law, justice court, or district court of the county where the seizure occurred:

(1) when a person pleads guilty or nolo contendere to, is convicted of, or is placed on deferred adjudication for:

(A) an offense under Section 66.006, Section 66.2011, or Subchapter G, Chapter 43, of this code; or

(B) a second or subsequent offense under Section 61.022, 62.003, 62.004, or 62.005 of this code; or

(2) if no person is arrested for an offense immediately after the warden or officer seizes the property.

(c) The court shall direct the sheriff or a constable to post a copy of the notice in the county courthouse for not less than 10 days. At the expiration of 10 days, the court shall hold a hearing to determine if the seized property is contraband.

(d) The court shall order the seized property:

(1) forfeited to the department if the court determines by a preponderance of the evidence that:

(A) the seized property is contraband and a person pleaded guilty or nolo contendere to, was convicted of, or was placed on deferred adjudication for:

(i) an offense under Section 66.006, Section 66.2011, or Subchapter G, Chapter 43, of this code; or

(ii) a second or subsequent offense under Section 61.022, 62.003, 62.004, or 62.005 of this code; or

(B) the seized property is contraband and no person was arrested for an offense immediately after the warden or officer seized the property; or

(2) released to the owner if:

(A) the person charged with an offense under Section 66.006, Section 66.2011, or Subchapter G, Chapter 43, of this code or a second or subsequent offense under Section 61.022, 62.003, 62.004, or 62.005 of this code is acquitted or the charge is dismissed; or

(B) the court determines that the seized property is not contraband.

(e) If the department receives a forfeiture order from a court as authorized by this section, the department may:

(1) use the seized property in its normal operations;

(2) sell or transfer the property; or

(3) destroy the property.

(f) A warden or officer who seizes property under this section is immune from liability and from suit for a seizure and disposition of property as authorized by this section.

(g) The commission may adopt rules to implement this section.

(h) The department shall deposit money received under this section in the state treasury to the credit of the game, fish, and water safety account.

*(Added by L.1991, chap. 808(1); chgd. by L.1993, chap. 679(12); L.1995, chap. 966(2); L.1999, chaps. 851(2), 959(2), eff. 9/1/99.)*

# CHAPTER 31. WATER SAFETY

*(Selected Section)*

**§31.097.** *(Repealed by L.1993, chap. 900(1.12), eff. 9/1/94.)*

# CHAPTER 66. FISH
*(Selected Section)*



## §66.006. Possession of illegal fishing devices.

(a) No person may possess a device designed to catch fish or other aquatic wildlife in or on the public water of this state where the use of the device is not permitted by this code or by a proclamation of the commission under this code unless the device is on board a vessel that is in public coastal water and is:

(1) in port; or

(2) in a marked channel and the vessel is going directly to or from public water in this state where the use of the device is permitted.

(b) No person may possess or use for the purpose of catching finfish a seine, strike net, gill net, or trammel net in or on the public water of this state unless the seine, strike net, gill net, or trammel net is equipped with floats at intervals of six feet or less and of sufficient buoyancy to maintain the seine, strike net, gill net, or trammel net in an upright position in the water so that the floats are visible on the surface of the water thereby avoiding a hazard to motorboat traffic.

(c)(1) No person may possess a seine, strike net, gill net, or trammel net on or within 500 yards of any public coastal water of this state where the use of the seine or net for the catching of fish is not permitted by this code or by a proclamation of the commission under this code.

(2) It is a defense to prosecution under this subsection that the seine, strike net, gill net, or trammel net was possessed within 500 yards of a public coastal water of this state for a lawful fishing activity.

*(Added by L.1989, chap. 27(1), eff. 9/1/89.)*

This page intentionally left blank.

# PROPERTY CODE

## CHAPTER 24. FORCIBLE ENTRY AND DETAINER
*(Selected Sections)*



### §24.004. Jurisdiction.

A justice court in the precinct in which the real property is located has jurisdiction in eviction suits. Eviction suits include forcible entry and detainer and forcible detainer suits. *(Chgd. by L.1997, chap. 1205(1), eff. 9/1/97.)*

### §24.0061. Writ of possession.

(a) A landlord who prevails in an eviction suit is entitled to a judgment for possession of the premises and a writ of possession. In this chapter, "premises" means the unit that is occupied or rented and any outside area or facility that the tenant is entitled to use under a written lease or oral rental agreement, or that is held out for the use of tenants generally.

(b) A writ of possession may not be issued before the sixth day after the date on which the judgment for possession is rendered unless a possession bond has been filed and approved under the Texas Rules of Civil Procedure and judgment for possession is thereafter granted by default.

(c) The court shall notify a tenant in writing of a default judgment for possession by sending a copy of the judgment to the premises by first class mail not later than 48 hours after the entry of the judgment.

(d) The writ of possession shall order the officer executing the writ to:

(1) post a written warning of at least 8-1/2 by 11 inches on the exterior of the front door of the rental unit notifying the tenant that the writ has been issued and that the writ will be executed on or after a specific date and time stated in the warning not sooner than 24 hours after the warning is posted; and

(2) when the writ is executed:

(A) deliver possession of the premises to the landlord;

(B) instruct the tenant and all persons claiming under the tenant to leave the premises immediately, and, if the persons fail to comply, physically remove them;

(C) instruct the tenant to remove or to allow the landlord, the landlord's representatives, or other persons acting under the officer's supervision to remove all personal property from the rental unit other than personal property claimed to be owned by the landlord; and

(D) place, or have an authorized person place, the removed personal property outside the rental unit at a nearby location, but not blocking a public sidewalk, passageway, or street and not while it is raining, sleeting, or snowing.

(e) The writ of possession shall authorize the officer, at the officer's discretion, to engage the services of a bonded or insured warehouseman to remove and store, subject to applicable law, part or all of the property at no cost to the landlord or the officer executing the writ.

(f) The officer may not require the landlord to store the property.

(g) The writ of possession shall contain notice to the officer that under Section 7.003, Civil Practice and Remedies Code, the officer is not liable for damages resulting from the execution of the writ if the officer executes the writ in good faith and with reasonable diligence.

(h) A sheriff or constable may use reasonable force in executing a writ under this section. *(Chgd. by L.1989, chaps. 2(13.01), 688(5); L.1997, chap. 1205(4), eff. 9/1/97.)*

## CHAPTER 70. MISCELLANEOUS LIENS
*(Selected Sections)*

**§70.001. Worker's lien.**

(a) A worker in this state who by labor repairs an article, including a vehicle, motorboat, vessel, or outboard motor, may retain possession of the article until:

(1) the amount due under the contract for the repairs is paid; or

(2) if no amount is specified by contract, the reasonable and usual compensation is paid.

(b) If a worker relinquishes possession of a motor vehicle, motorboat, vessel, or outboard motor in return for a check, money order, or a credit card transaction on which payment is stopped, has been dishonored because of insufficient funds, no funds or because the drawer or maker of the order or the credit card holder has no account or the account upon which it was drawn or the credit card account has been closed, the lien provided by this section continues to exist and the worker is entitled to possession of the vehicle, motorboat, vessel, or outboard motor until the amount due is paid, unless the vehicle, motorboat, vessel, or outboard motor is possessed by a person who became a bona fide purchaser of the vehicle after a stop payment order was made. A person entitled to possession of property under this subsection is entitled to take possession thereof in accordance with the provisions of Section [9.503] *9.603*, Business & Commerce Code.

(c) A worker may take possession of an article under Subsection (b) only if the person obligated under the repair contract has signed a notice stating that the article may be subject to repossession under this section. A notice under this subsection must be:

(1) separate from the written repair contract; or

(2) printed on the written repair contract, credit agreement, or other document in type that is boldfaced, capitalized, underlined, or otherwise set out from surrounding written material so as to be conspicuous with a separate signature line.

(d) A worker who takes possession of an article under Subsection (b) may require a person obligated under the repair contract to pay the costs of repossession as a condition of reclaiming the article only to the extent of the reasonable fair market value of the services required to take possession of the article. For the purpose of this subsection, charges represent the fair market value of the services required to take possession of an article if the charges represent the actual cost incurred by the worker in taking possession of the article.

(e) A worker may not transfer to a third party, and a person who performs repossession services may not accept, a check, money order, or credit card transaction that is received as payment for repair of an article and that is returned to the worker because of insufficient funds or no funds, because the drawer or maker of the check or money order or the credit card holder has no account, or because the account on which the check or money order is drawn or the credit card account has been closed.

(f) A person commits an offense if the person transfers or accepts a check, money order, or credit card transaction in violation of Subsection (e). An offense under this subsection is a Class B misdemeanor.

(g) A motor vehicle that is repossessed under this section shall be promptly delivered to the location where the repair was performed or a vehicle storage facility licensed under the Vehicle Storage Facility Act (Article 6687-9a, Revised Statutes). The motor vehicle must remain at the repair location or a licensed vehicle storage facility at all times until the motor vehicle is lawfully returned to the motor vehicle's owner or a lienholder or is disposed of as provided by this subchapter.

*(Chgd. by L.1993, chap. 754(1), (2); L.1995, chap. 375(1); L.1999, chaps. 414(2.38), 978(1), eff. 7/1/2001, 9/1/99, respectively. Matter in brackets eff. only until 7/1/2001. Matter in italics eff. 7/1/2001.)*



**§70.003. Stable keeper's, garageman's, pasturer's, and cotton ginner's liens.**

(a) A stable keeper with whom an animal is left for care has a lien on the animal for the amount of the charges for the care.

(b) An owner or lessee of a pasture with whom an animal is left for grazing has a lien on the animal for the amount of the charges for the grazing.

(c) A garageman with whom a motor vehicle, motorboat, vessel, or outboard motor is left for care has a lien on the motor vehicle, motorboat, vessel, or outboard motor for the amount of the charges for the care, including reasonable charges for towing the motor vehicle, motorboat, vessel, or outboard motor to the garageman's place of business.

(d)(1) A cotton ginner to whom a cotton crop has been delivered for processing or who, under an agreement, is to be paid for harvesting a cotton crop has a lien on the cotton processed or harvested for the amount of the charges for the processing or harvesting. The lienholder is entitled to retain possession of the cotton until the amount of the charge due under an agreement is paid or, if an amount is not specified by agreement, the reasonable and usual compensation is paid. If the cotton owner's address is known and the amount of the charge is not paid before the 31st day after the date the cotton ginner's work is completed or the date payment is due under a written agreement, whichever is later, the lienholder shall request the owner to pay the unpaid charge due and shall notify the owner and any other person having a lien on the cotton which is properly recorded under applicable law with the secretary of state of the fact that unless payment is made not later than the 15th day after the date the notice is received, the lienholder is entitled to sell the cotton under any procedure authorized by Section [9.504] *9.610*, Business & Commerce Code. If the cotton owner's address is not known and the amount of the charge is not paid before the 61st day after the date the cotton ginner's work is completed or the date payment is due under a written agreement, whichever is later, the lienholder is entitled to sell the cotton without notice at a commercially reasonable sale. The proceeds of a sale under this subsection shall be applied first to charges due under this subsection, and any remainder shall be paid in appropriate proportion to:

(A) any other person having a lien on the cotton which is properly recorded under applicable law with the secretary of state; and

(B) the cotton owner.

(2) Nothing in this subsection shall be construed to place an affirmative burden on the cotton ginner to perform any lien searches except as may be appropriate to provide notices required by this section.

*(Chgd. by L.1989, chap. 629(1); L.1997, chap. 462(1), (2); L.1999, chap. 414(2.39), eff. 7/1/2001. Matter in brackets eff. only until 7/1/2001. Matter in italics eff. 7/1/2001.)*



### §70.004. Possession of motor vehicle, motorboat, vessel, or outboard motor.

(a) A holder of a lien under Section 70.003 on a motor vehicle, motorboat, vessel, or outboard motor who obtains possession of the motor vehicle, motorboat, vessel, or outboard motor under a state law or city ordinance shall give notice for a motor vehicle, motorboat, vessel, or outboard motor registered in this state to the last known registered owner and each lienholder of record not later than the fifth day after the day possession is obtained. If the motor vehicle, motorboat, vessel, or outboard motor is registered outside this state, the notice shall be given to the last known registered owner and each lienholder of record not later than the 14th day after the day possession is obtained.

(b) Except as provided by Subsection (c), the notice must be sent by certified mail with return receipt requested and must contain:

(1) a request to remove the motor vehicle, motorboat, vessel, or outboard motor;

(2) a request for payment;

(3) the location of the motor vehicle, motorboat, vessel, or outboard motor; and

(4) the amount of accrued charges.

(c) The notice may be given by publishing the notice once in a newspaper of general circulation in the county in which the motor vehicle, motorboat, vessel, or outboard motor is stored if:

(1) the motor vehicle, motorboat, vessel, or outboard motor is registered in another state;

(2) the holder of the lien submits a written request by certified mail, return receipt requested, to the governmental entity with which the motor vehicle, motorboat, vessel, or outboard motor is registered requesting information relating to the identity of the last known registered owner and any lienholder of record;

(3) the holder of the lien:

(A) is advised in writing by the governmental entity with which the motor vehicle, motorboat, vessel, or outboard motor is registered that the entity is unwilling or unable to provide information on the last known registered owner or any lienholder of record; or

(B) does not receive a response from the governmental entity with which the motor vehicle, motorboat, vessel, or outboard motor is registered on or before the 21st day after the date the holder of the lien submits a request under Subdivision (2);

(4) the identity of the last known registered owner cannot be determined;

(5) the registration does not contain an address for the last known registered owner; and

(6) the holder of the lien cannot determine the identities and addresses of the lienholders of record.

(d) The holder of the lien is not required to publish notice under Subsection (c) if a correctly addressed notice is sent with sufficient postage under Subsection (b) and is returned as unclaimed or refused or with a notation that the addressee is unknown or has moved without leaving a forwarding address.

(e) A person is entitled to fees for towing, impoundment, preservation, and notification and to reasonable storage fees for up to five days before the day that the notice is mailed or published, as applicable. After the day that the notice is mailed or published, the person is entitled to reasonable storage, impoundment, and preservation fees until the motor vehicle, motorboat, vessel, or outboard motor is removed and accrued charges are paid.

(f) A person charging fees under Subsection (e) commits an offense if the person charges a storage fee for a period of time not authorized by that subsection. An offense under this subsection is punishable by a fine of not less than $200 nor more than $1,000.
*(Chgd. by L.1999, chap. 70(2), eff. 9/1/99.)*

## §70.006. Sale of motor vehicle, motorboat, vessel, or outboard motor.

(a) A holder of a lien under this subchapter or Chapter 59 on a motor vehicle subject to Chapter 501, Transportation Code, or on a motorboat, vessel, or outboard motor for which a certificate of title is required under Subchapter B, Chapter 31, Parks and Wildlife Code, as amended, who retains possession of the motor vehicle, motorboat, vessel, or outboard motor for 30 days after the day that the charges accrue shall give written notice to the owner and each holder of a lien recorded on the certificate of title. If the motor vehicle, motorboat, vessel, or outboard motor is registered outside this state, the holder of a lien under this subchapter who retains possession during that period shall give notice to the last known registered owner and each lienholder of record.

(b) Except as provided by Subsection (c), the notice must be sent by certified mail with return receipt requested and must include the amount of the charges and a request for payment.

(c) The notice may be given by publishing the notice once in a newspaper of general circulation in the county in which the motor vehicle, motorboat, vessel, or outboard motor is stored if:

(1) the holder of the lien submits a written request by certified mail, return receipt requested, to the governmental entity with which the motor vehicle, nmotorboat, vessel, or outboard motor is registered requesting information relating to the identity of the last known registered owner and any lienholder of record;

(2) the holder of the lien:

(A) is advised in writing by the governmental entity with which the motor vehicle, motorboat, vessel, or outboard motor is registered that the entity is unwilling or unable to provide information on the last known registered owner or any lienholder of record; or

(B) does not receive a response from the governmental entity with which the motor vehicle, motorboat, vessel, or outboard motor is registered on or before the 21st day after the date of the lien submits a request under Subdivision (1);

(3) the identity of the last known registered owner cannot be determined;

(4) the registration does not contain an address for the last known registered owner; and

(5) the holder of the lien cannot determine the identities and addresses of the lienholders of record.

(d) The holder of the lien is not required to publish notice under Subsection (c) if a correctly addressed notice is sent with sufficient postage under Subsection (b) and is returned as unclaimed or refused or with a notation that the addressee is unknown or has moved without leaving a forwarding address.

(e) After notice is given under this section to the owner of or the holder of a lien on the motor vehicle, motorboat, vessel, or outboard motor, the owner or holder of the lien may obtain possession of the motor vehicle, motorboat, vessel, or outboard motor by paying all charges due to the holder of a lien under this subchapter and Chapter 59 before the 31st day after the date the notice is mailed or published as provided by this section.

(f) If the charges are not paid before the 31st day after the day that the notice is mailed or published, as applicable, the lienholder may sell the motor vehicle, motorboat, vessel, or outboard motor at a public sale and apply the proceeds to the charges. The lienholder shall pay excess proceeds to the person entitled to them.
*(Chgd. by L.1997, chap. 165(30.248); L.1999, chap. 70(3), eff. 9/1/99.)*

## §70.007. Unclaimed excess.

(a) If a person entitled to excess proceeds under this subchapter is not known or has moved from this state or the county in which the lien accrued, the person holding the excess shall pay it to the county treasurer of the county in which the lien accrued. The treasurer shall issue the person a receipt for the payment.

(b) If the person entitled to the excess does not claim it before two years after the day it is paid to the treasurer, the excess becomes a part of the county's general fund.

### §70.008. Attorney's fees.

The court in a suit concerning possession of a motor vehicle, motorboat, vessel, or outboard motor and a debt due on it may award reasonable attorney's fees to the prevailing party.

### §70.301. Lien.

(a) A person who stores, repairs, or performs maintenance work on an aircraft has a lien on the aircraft for:

(1) the amount due under a contract for the storage, repairs, or maintenance work; or

(2) if no amount is specified by contract, the reasonable and usual compensation for the storage, repairs, or maintenance work.

(b) This subchapter applies to a contract for storage only if it is:

(1) written; or

(2) oral and provides for a storage period of at least 30 days.

*(Added by L.1989, chap. 250(1); chgd. by L.1995, chap. 946(1), eff. 8/28/95.)*



### §70.302. Possession.

(a) A holder of a lien under this subchapter may retain possession of the aircraft subject to the lien until the amount due is paid.

(b) Except as provided by Subsection (c), if the holder of a lien under this subchapter relinquishes possession of the aircraft before the amount due is paid, the person may retake possession of the aircraft as provided by Section [9.503] *9.609*, Business & Commerce Code.

(c) The holder of a lien under this subchapter may not retake possession of the aircraft from a bona fide purchaser for value who purchases the aircraft without knowledge of the lien before the date the lien is recorded under Section 70.303.

*(Added by L.1989, chap. 250(1); chgd. by L.1999, chap. 414(2.41), eff. 7/1/2000. Matter in brackets eff. only until 7/1/2000. Matter in italics eff. 7/1/2000.)*

### §70.303. Recording of lien.

A holder of a lien under this subchapter may record the lien on the aircraft by filing with the Federal Aviation Administration Aircraft Registry not later than the 120th day after the date of the completion of the contractual storage period or the performance of the last repair or maintenance a verified document in the form and manner required by applicable federal laws and regulations that states:

(1) the name, address, and telephone number of the holder of the lien under this subchapter;

(2) the amount due for storage, repairs, or maintenance;

(3) a complete description of the aircraft; and

(4) the name and address of the owner of the aircraft and the number assigned the aircraft by the Federal Aviation Administration, if known.

*(Added by L.1989, chap. 250(1); chgd. by L.1995, chap. 946(1), eff. 8/28/95.)*

### §70.304. Notice to owner and lienholders.

(a) Not later than the 30th day after the date of the completion of the contractual storage period or the performance of the last repair or maintenance, a holder of a lien under this subchapter who retains possession of the aircraft shall notify the owner shown on the certificate of registration and each holder of a lien on the aircraft as shown by the records maintained for that purpose by the Federal Aviation Administration Aircraft Registry. The notice must state:

(1) the name, address, and telephone number of the holder of the lien under this subchapter;

(2) the amount due for storage, repairs, or maintenance;

(3) a complete description of the aircraft; and

(4) the legal right of the holder of the lien under this subchapter to sell the aircraft at public auction and apply the proceeds to the amount due.

(b) The notice must be delivered by certified or registered mail, return receipt requested.

*(Added by L.1989, chap. 250(1); chgd. by L.1991, chap. 538(1); L.1995, chap. 946(1), eff. 8/28/95.)*

### §70.305. Sale of aircraft.

If the holder of a lien under this subchapter provides the notice required by Section 70.304 and the amount due remains unpaid after the 60th day after the date of the completion of the contractual storage period or the performance of the last repair or maintenance, the holder of the lien may sell the aircraft at a public sale and apply the proceeds to the amount due. The lienholder shall pay any excess proceeds to the person entitled to them. *(Added by L.1989, chap. 250(1); chgd. by L.1995, chap. 946(1), eff. 8/28/95.)*

### §70.306. Attorney's fees.

The court in a suit brought under this subchapter may award reasonable attorney's fees to the prevailing party.

## CHAPTER 301. TEXAS FAIR HOUSING ACT

*(Added by L.1993, chap. 268(40), eff. 9/1/93.)*

*(Selected Section)*

## SUBCHAPTER I. CRIMINAL PENALTY



## SUBCHAPTER I. CRIMINAL PENALTY

### §301.171. Intimidation or interference.

(a) A person commits an offense if the person, without regard to whether the person is acting under color of law, by force or threat of force intentionally intimidates or interferes with a person:

(1) because of the person's race, color, religion, sex, disability, familial status, or national origin and because the person is or has been selling, purchasing, renting, financing, occupying, or contracting or negotiating for the sale, purchase, rental, financing, or occupation of any dwelling or applying for or participating in a service, organization, or facility relating to the business of selling or renting dwellings; or

(2) because the person is or has been or to intimidate the person from:

(A) participating, without discrimination because of race, color, religion, sex, disability, familial status, or national origin, in an activity, service, organization, or facility described by Subdivision (1); or

(B) affording another person opportunity or protection to so participate; or

(C) lawfully aiding or encouraging other persons to participate, without discrimination because of race, color, religion, sex, disability, familial status, or national origin, in an activity, service, organization, or facility described by Subdivision (1).

(b) An offense under this section is a Class A misdemeanor.

*(Added by L.1993, chap. 268(40), eff. 9/1/93.)*

# TAX CODE

## CHAPTER 152. TAXES ON SALE, RENTAL, AND USE OF MOTOR VEHICLES
*(Selected Sections)*



**§152.027. Tax on metal dealer plates.**

(a) A use tax is imposed on each person to whom is issued a metal dealer's plate authorized by Chapter 503, Transportation Code.

(b) The tax is $25 for each plate issued.

(c) The tax imposed by this section is in lieu of any other tax imposed by this chapter. *(Chgd. by L.1997, chap. 165(30.252), eff. 9/1/97.)*



**§152.042. Collection of tax on metal dealer plates.**

A person required to pay the tax imposed by Section 152.027 shall pay the tax to the Texas Department of Transportation, and the department may not issue the metal dealer's plates until the tax is paid. *(Chgd. by L.1995, chap. 165(22)(70), eff. 9/1/95.)*

## CHAPTER 159. CONTROLLED SUBSTANCES TAX
*(Added by L.1989, chap. 1152(1), eff. 9/1/89.)*

### SUBCHAPTER A. GENERAL PROVISIONS



### SUBCHAPTER B. IMPOSITION, RATE, AND PAYMENT OF TAX



### SUBCHAPTER C. CRIMINAL PROVISIONS



### SUBCHAPTER D. DISPOSITION OF PROCEEDS



### SUBCHAPTER A. GENERAL PROVISIONS

**§159.001. Definitions.**

In this chapter:

(1) "Controlled substance" has the meaning assigned by Section 481.002, Health and Safety Code.

(2) "Counterfeit substance" has the meaning assigned by Section 481.002, Health and Safety Code.

(3) "Dealer" means a person who in violation of the law of this state imports into this state or manufactures, produces, acquires, or possesses in this state:

(A) seven grams or more of a taxable substance consisting of or containing a controlled substance, counterfeit substance, or simulated controlled substance;

(B) fifty dosage units or more of a taxable substance not commonly sold by weight, consisting of or containing a controlled substance, counterfeit substance, or simulated controlled substance; or

(C) more than four ounces of a taxable substance consisting of or containing marihuana.

(4) "Marihuana" has the meaning assigned by Section 481.002, Health and Safety Code.

(5) "Simulated controlled substance" has the meaning assigned by Section 482.001, Health and Safety Code.

(6) "Tax payment certificate" means a stamp or other device provided by the comptroller under Section 159.003 of this code for use under this chapter.

(7) "Taxable substance" means a controlled substance, a counterfeit substance, a simulated controlled substance, or marihuana, or a mixture of any materials that contains a controlled substance, counterfeit substance, simulated controlled substance, or marihuana.

(8) "Dosage unit" means a tablet, pill, capsule, vial, ampule, or other identifiable or separated unit designed or packaged to be used, taken, or ingested at one time.

*(Added by L.1989, chap. 1152(1); chgd. by L.1991, chaps. 14(284)(45), (65), 705(20); L.1993, chap. 1031(23), eff. 9/1/93.)*



### §159.002. Measurements.

For purposes of this chapter, the weight of a taxable substance is its weight in the possession of the dealer. *(Added by L.1989, chap. 1152(1), eff. 9/1/89.)*

### §159.003. Tax payment certificates.

(a) The comptroller shall adopt a uniform system for providing, affixing, and displaying official tax payment certificates to be attached to a taxable substance as evidence that the tax imposed by this chapter has been paid.

(b) A tax payment certificate may not be used more than once.

*(Added by L.1989, chap. 1152(1), eff. 9/1/89.)*

### §159.004. No defense or immunity.

Nothing in this chapter provides a defense or affirmative defense to, exception to, or immunity from prosecution under the penal laws of this state relating to controlled substances, counterfeit substances, simulated controlled substances, or marihuana. *(Added by L.1989, chap. 1152(1), eff. 9/1/89.)*

### §159.005. Confidential information.

(a) Information provided by a person in a report or return made for purposes of paying a tax imposed by this chapter is confidential.

(b) The comptroller or any other public official or employee commits an offense if he reveals information made confidential by this section to any person other than:

(1) to the comptroller or a public official or employee whose duties involve the administration or collection of the taxes imposed by this chapter; or

(2) in a judicial proceeding involving a tax imposed by this chapter.

(c) An offense under Subsection (b) of this section is a Class A misdemeanor.

(d) Except in a prosecution directly related to a tax imposed by this chapter, information made confidential by this section may not be used in any way in a prosecution of the dealer for whom the report or return is made unless the information is obtained independently of the report or return.

*(Added by L.1989, chap. 1152(1), eff. 9/1/89.)*

## SUBCHAPTER B. IMPOSITION, RATE, AND PAYMENT OF TAX

### §159.101. Tax imposed; rate of tax.

(a) A tax is imposed on the possession, purchase, acquisition, importation, manufacture, or production by a dealer of a taxable substance on which a tax has not previously been paid under this chapter.

(b) The rate of the tax is:

(1) $200 for each gram of a taxable substance consisting of or containing a controlled substance, counterfeit substance, or simulated controlled substance;

(2) $3.50 for each gram of a taxable substance consisting of or containing marihuana; and

(3) $2,000 on each 50 dosage units, or portion of 50 dosage units, if the total amount is less than 50 dosage units, of a controlled substance that is not sold by weight.

(c) The tax becomes due immediately when a dealer possesses, purchases, acquires, manufactures, or produces in this state or imports into this state the taxable substance on which the tax has not previously been paid.

(d) In determining the total weight of taxable substance, a part of a gram remaining after the measurement of whole grams is considered as one gram.

(e) For purposes of this section, if a taxable substance consists of a mixture containing both marihuana and another substance listed in the definition of taxable substance provided by Section 159.001 of this code, the taxable substance is taxable under Subsection (b)(1) of this section and not under Subsection (b)(2) of this section.

(f) If a determination made under this chapter becomes final without payment of the amount of the determination being made, the comptroller shall add to the amount a penalty of 10 percent of the amount of the tax and interest.

(g) In a redetermination proceeding held or a judicial proceeding brought under this chapter, a certificate from the comptroller that shows the issued determination is prima facie evidence of:

(1) the determination of the stated tax or amount of the tax;

(2) the stated amount of the penalties and interest; and

(3) the compliance of the comptroller with this chapter in computing and determining the amount due.

(h) The suppression of evidence on any ground in a criminal case that arises out of facts on which a determination is made under this chapter or the dismissal of criminal charges in such a case does not affect a determination made under this chapter.

*(Added by L.1989, chap. 1152(1); chgd. by L.1991, chaps. 484(1), 705(21); L.1995, chap. 1000(57), eff. 10/1/95.)*

### §159.102. Tax payment certificate required.

(a) A dealer who pays a tax imposed by this chapter shall securely affix in the manner required by the comptroller to the taxable substance the appropriate tax payment certificate to show payment of the tax.

(b) A dealer shall obtain the necessary tax payment certificates before the tax becomes due as provided by Section 159.101 of this code. The possession of a taxable substance without the possession of the requisite amount or number of certificates is prima facie evidence that and is notice that the tax has not been paid as required by this chapter.

(c) The comptroller's rules shall provide for the return of unused certificates and for the refund of money for returned certificates.

*(Added by L.1989, chap. 1152(1), eff. 9/1/89.)*

### §159.103. Exemption.

The possession, purchase, acquisition, importation, manufacture, or production of a taxable substance is exempt from the tax imposed by this chapter if the activity is authorized by law.

*(Added by L.1989, chap. 1152(1); chgd. by L.1995, chap. 1000(58), eff. 10/1/95.)*

## SUBCHAPTER C. CRIMINAL PROVISIONS

*(Heading chgd. by L.1995, chap. 1000(59), eff. 10/1/95.)*

### §159.201. Possession of item if tax unpaid.

(a) A dealer commits an offense if the dealer possesses a taxable substance on which the tax imposed by this chapter has not been paid.

(b) An offense under this section is a felony of the third degree. In addition to the fine provided by law for a felony of the third degree, a person convicted of an offense under this section shall be fined an amount equal to the amount of tax due and unpaid on the taxable substance that is the subject of the offense.

(c) An indictment for an offense under this section may be presented within six years from the date of the offense and not afterward.

*(Added by L.1989, chap. 1152(1), eff. 9/1/89.)*

### §159.202. Counterfeit tax payment certificates.

(a) A person commits an offense if the person:

(1) prints, engraves, makes, issues, sells, or circulates a counterfeit tax payment certificate;

(2) possesses with intent to use, sell, circulate, or pass a counterfeit tax payment certificate; or

(3) places or causes to be placed a counterfeit tax payment certificate on a taxable substance.

(b) An offense under this section is a felony of the third degree.

(c) Venue of a prosecution under this section is in Travis County.

*(Added by L.1989, chap. 1152(1), eff. 9/1/89.)*

### §159.203. Previously used certificates.

(a) A person commits an offense if the person:

(1) uses, sells, offers for sale, or possesses for use or sale previously used tax payment certificates; or

(2) attaches or causes to be attached a previously used tax payment certificate to a taxable substance.

(b) An offense under this section is a felony of the third degree.

(c) Venue of a prosecution under this section is in Travis County.

*(Added by L.1989, chap. 1152(1); chgd. by L.1995, chap. 1000(60), eff. 10/1/95.)*

### §159.204. *(Added by L.1989, chap. 1152(1); repealed by L.1995, chap. 1000(73), eff. 10/1/95.)*

### §159.205. Right to collect subordinate to other laws.

(a) The right of the comptroller to collect the tax imposed by this chapter, including applicable penalty and interest, is subordinate to the right of a federal, state, or local law enforcement authority to seize, forfeit, and retain property under Chapter 481, Health and Safety Code; Chapter 59, Code of Criminal Procedure; or any other criminal forfeiture law of this state or of the United States. A lien filed by the comptroller as a result of the failure of a dealer to pay the tax, penalty, or interest due under this chapter is also subordinate to those rights.

(b) This section does not affect the validity of a lien or a collection action relating to the tax imposed by this chapter under any other circumstance.

*(Added by L.1989, chap. 1152(1); chgd. by L.1991, chaps. 14(284)(54), 705(22); L.1995, chap. 1000(61), eff. 10/1/95.)*

### §159.206. Settlement or compromise of tax.

The comptroller may settle or compromise a tax, penalty, or interest imposed under this chapter only if:

(1) the prosecutor of a criminal offense under this chapter or of another offense arising out of the same incident or transaction requests in writing that the comptroller settle or compromise and specifies the reasons for the request; and

(2) the comptroller determines that the settlement or compromise is in the best interest of the state.

*(Added by L.1991, chap. 705(23); chgd. by L.1995, chap. 1000(62), eff. 10/1/95.)*

## SUBCHAPTER D. DISPOSITION OF PROCEEDS

### §159.301. Disposition of proceeds.

All proceeds from the collection of the tax, penalty, and interest imposed by this chapter shall be deposited to the credit of the general revenue fund. The fine imposed by Section 159.201(b) of this code and the fine provided by law for a felony shall be deposited to the credit of the county treasury of the county in which the offense occurred. *(Added by L.1989, chap. 1152(1); chgd. by L.1991, chap. 705(24), eff. 9/1/91.)*

# UTILITIES CODE

*(Added by L.1997, chap. 166(1), eff. 9/1/97.)*

## TITLE 4. DELIVERY OF UTILITY SERVICES

## SUBTITLE B. PROVISIONS REGULATING DELIVERY OF SERVICES

## CHAPTER 186. PROVISIONS TO ENSURE THE RELIABILITY AND INTEGRITY OF UTILITY SERVICE

*(Selected Sections)*



### SUBCHAPTER A. CONTINUITY OF UTILITY SERVICE



### SUBCHAPTER B. MANIPULATION OF SERVICE FOR CERTAIN LAW ENFORCEMENT PURPOSES



### SUBCHAPTER C. FRAUDULENT OBTAINING OF SERVICE



### SUBCHAPTER D. AVAILABILITY OF EMERGENCY TELEPHONE SERVICE



### SUBCHAPTER A. CONTINUITY OF UTILITY SERVICE

#### §186.004. Unlawful picketing, threats, or intimidation.

(a) A person may not:

(1) picket the plant, premises, or other property of a public utility with intent to disrupt the service of that utility or to prevent the maintenance of that service; or

(2) engage in picketing that has the effect of disrupting the service of a public utility or preventing the maintenance of that service.

(b) A person may not:

(1) intimidate, threaten, or harass an employee of a public utility with intent to disrupt the service of the utility or prevent the maintenance of that service; or

(2) intimidate, threaten, or harass an employee of a public utility if that conduct has the effect of disrupting the service of the utility or preventing the maintenance of that service.
*(Added by L.1997, chap. 166(1), eff. 9/1/97.)*

#### §186.005. Restraining order.

(a) A district court shall immediately inquire into the matter if a public utility presents a verified petition to the court:

(1) alleging that in the judicial district of the court a person is violating or threatening to violate Section 186.004 and that the violation or threatened violation will interfere with the maintenance of adequate water, electric, or gas service; and

(2) describing the acts committed in violation of Section 186.004, or the threatened acts that, if committed, will violate Section 186.004.

(b) If it appears that there is a violation or threatened violation of Section 186.004, the court shall immediately issue an order restraining the person, the person's agent, and any other person acting with them from committing an act prohibited by that section.

(c) A restraining order issued under this section is effective when the petitioner files with the clerk of the court a good and sufficient bond in an amount set by the court to cover court costs that may reasonably accrue in connection with the case. A judgment rendered in the case may not be superseded pending appeal.

(d) Venue for a suit under this section is in any judicial district in which the violation or threat to violate occurs.
*(Added by L.1997, chap. 166(1), eff. 9/1/97.)*



## SUBCHAPTER B. MANIPULATION OF SERVICE FOR CERTAIN LAW ENFORCEMENT PURPOSES

*(Selected Section)*

### §186.021. Emergency involving hostage or armed suspect.

(a) In an emergency in which the supervising law enforcement official having jurisdiction in the geographical area has probable cause to believe that an armed and barricaded suspect or a person holding a hostage is committing a crime, the supervising law enforcement official may order a designated telephone company security official to cut or otherwise control telephone lines to prevent telephone communication by the armed suspect or the hostage holder with a person other than a peace officer or person authorized by a peace officer.

(b) The serving telephone company in the geographical area of a law enforcement unit shall designate a telephone company security official and an alternate to provide all required assistance to law enforcement officials to carry out this section.

(c) Good faith reliance on an order given by a supervising law enforcement official under this section is a complete defense to a civil or criminal action brought against a telephone company or the company's director, officer, agent, or employee as a result of compliance with the order.
*(Added by L.1997, chap. 166(1), eff. 9/1/97.)*

## SUBCHAPTER C. FRAUDULENT OBTAINING OF SERVICE

### §186.031. Definitions.

In this subchapter:

(1) "Publish" means to communicate information to another by any means.

(2) "Telecommunications service" means the transmission of a message or other information by a public utility, including a telephone or telegraph company.
*(Added by L.1997, chap. 166(1), eff. 9/1/97.)*

### §186.032. Fraudulently obtaining telecommunications services.

(a) A person commits an offense if:

(1) knowing that another will use the published information to avoid payment of a charge for telecommunications service, the person publishes:

(A) an existing, cancelled, revoked, or nonexistent telephone number;

(B) a credit number or other credit device; or

(C) a method of numbering or coding that is used in issuing telephone numbers or credit devices, including credit numbers; or

(2) the person makes or possesses equipment specifically designed to be used fraudulently to avoid charges for telecommunications service.

(b) An offense under this section is a misdemeanor punishable by a fine of not more than $500, by confinement in jail for not more than 60 days, or by both, unless the person has been previously convicted of an offense under this section. A second or subsequent offense is a felony punishable by a fine of not more than $5,000, by imprisonment in the penitentiary for not less than two years and not more than five years, or by both.

(c) This section does not apply to an employee of a public utility who provides telecommunications service while acting in the course of employment.
*(Added by L.1997, chap. 166(1), eff. 9/1/97.)*

### §186.033. Disposition of certain equipment.

(a) A peace officer may seize equipment described by Section 186.032(a)(2) under a warrant or incident to a lawful arrest.

(b) If the person who possessed equipment seized under Subsection (a) is convicted under Section 186.032, the court entering the judgment of conviction shall order the sheriff to destroy the equipment.
*(Added by L.1997, chap. 166(1), eff. 9/1/97.)*

## SUBCHAPTER D. AVAILABILITY OF EMERGENCY TELEPHONE SERVICE



### §186.041. Definitions.

In this subchapter:

(1) "Emergency" means a situation in which property or human life is in jeopardy and the prompt summoning of aid is essential.

(2) "Party line" means a subscriber's telephone circuit, consisting of two or more main telephone stations connected with the circuit, each station with a distinctive ring or telephone number.
*(Added by L.1997, chap. 166(1), eff. 9/1/97.)*

### §186.042. Obstruction of emergency telephone call; penalty.

(a) A person commits an offense if:

(1) the person wilfully refuses to relinquish a party line immediately on being informed that the line is needed for an emergency call described by Subdivision (2); and

(2) the party line is needed for an emergency call:

(A) to a fire or police department; or

(B) for medical aid or an ambulance service.

(b) An offense under this section is a misdemeanor punishable by:

(1) a fine of not less than $25 and not more than $500;

(2) confinement in the county jail for not more than one month; or

(3) both fine and confinement.
*(Added by L.1997, chap. 166(1), eff. 9/1/97.)*

### §186.043. Falsification of emergency telephone call; penalty.

(a) A person commits an offense if the person secures the use of a party line by falsely stating that the line is needed for an emergency call:

(1) to a fire or police department; or

(2) for medical aid or an ambulance service.

(b) An offense under this section is a misdemeanor punishable by:

(1) a fine of not less than $25 and not more than $500;

(2) confinement in the county jail for not more than one month; or

(3) both fine and confinement.
*(Added by L.1997, chap. 166(1), eff. 9/1/97.)*

### §186.044. Notice of certain offenses required.

(a) A telephone directory distributed to the public in this state that lists the telephone numbers of an exchange located in this state must contain a notice explaining the offenses under Sections 186.042 and 186.043. The notice must be:

(1) printed in type not smaller than the smallest type on the same page; and

(2) preceded by the word "warning" printed in type at least as large as the largest type on the same page.

(b) At least once each year, a person providing telephone service shall enclose in the telephone bill mailed to each person who uses a party line telephone a notice of Sections 186.042 and 186.043.

(c) This section does not apply to a directory, commonly known as a classified directory, that is distributed solely for business advertising purposes.
*(Added by L.1997, chap. 166(1), eff. 9/1/97.)*

**§186.045. Failure to provide notice; penalty.**

(a) A person providing telephone service commits an offense if the person:

(1) distributes copies of a telephone directory subject to Section 186.044(a) from which the notice required by that section is wilfully omitted; or

(2) wilfully fails to enclose in telephone bills the notice required by Section 186.044(b).

(b) An offense under this section is a misdemeanor punishable by a fine of not less than $25 and not more than $500.

*(Added by L.1997, chap. 166(1), eff. 9/1/97.)*

# WATER CODE

## TITLE 2. WATER ADMINISTRATION

*(Title heading chgd. by L.1995, chap. 933(1), eff. 9/1/95.)*
*(Selected Chapter)*

## CHAPTER 26. WATER QUALITY CONTROL

*(Selected Section)*

Section
26.3574. Fee on delivery of certain petroleum products.

**§26.3574. Fee on delivery of certain petroleum products.** *(Selected Subsections)*

(r) A person forfeits to the state a civil penalty of not less than $25 nor more than $200 if the person:

(1) refuses to stop and permit the inspection and examination of a motor vehicle transporting petroleum products on demand of a peace officer or the comptroller;

* * *

(s) A person commits an offense if the person:

(1) refuses to stop and permit the inspection and examination of a motor vehicle transporting petroleum products on the demand of a peace officer or the comptroller;

* * *

(8) refuses, while transporting petroleum products, to stop the motor vehicle he is operating when called on to do so by a person authorized to stop the motor vehicle;

(9) transports petroleum products for which a cargo manifest is required to be carried without possessing or exhibiting on demand by an officer authorized to make the demand a cargo manifest containing the information required to be shown on the manifest;

* * *

(t) The following criminal penalties apply to the offenses enumerated in Subsection (s) of this section:

(1) an offense under Subdivision (1) is a Class C misdemeanor;

* * *

(3) an offense under Subdivisions (8) and (9) is a Class A misdemeanor;

* * *

(u) The court may not fine a corporation or association under Section 12.51(c), Penal Code, unless the amount of the fine under that subsection is greater than the amount that could be fixed by the court under Section 12.51(b), Penal Code.

(v) In addition to a sentence imposed on a corporation, the court shall give notice of the conviction to the attorney general as required by Article 17A.09, Code of Criminal Procedure.
*(Added by L.1989, chap. 228(17), eff. 5/31/89.)*

* * *

## TITLE 4. GENERAL LAW DISTRICTS

*(Selected Chapters)*

## CHAPTER 49. PROVISIONS APPLICABLE TO ALL DISTRICTS

*(Added by L.1995, chap. 715(2), eff. 9/1/95.)*
*(Selected Section)*

Section
49.217. Operation of certain motor vehicles on or near public facilities.

**§49.217. Operation of certain motor vehicles on or near public facilities.**

(a) In this section, "motor vehicle" means a self-propelled device in, upon, or by which a person or property is or may be transported or drawn on a road or highway.

(b) Except as provided in Subsections (c) and (d), a person may not operate a motor vehicle on a levee, in a drainage ditch, or on land adjacent to a levee, canal, ditch, exposed conduit, pipeline, pumping plant, storm water facility, or other facility for the transmission, storage, treatment, or distribution of water, sewage, or storm water owned or controlled by a district.

(c) A district may authorize the use of motor vehicles on land that it owns or controls by posting signs on the property.

(d) This section does not prohibit a person from:

(1) driving on a public road or highway; or

(2) operating a motor vehicle used for repair or maintenance of public water, sewer, or storm water facilities.

(e) A person who operates a motor vehicle in violation of Subsection (b) commits an offense. An offense under this section is a Class C misdemeanor, except that if a person has been convicted of an offense under this section, a subsequent offense is a Class B misdemeanor.
*(Added by L.1995, chap. 715(2), eff. 9/1/95.)*

## CHAPTER 50. PROVISIONS GENERALLY APPLICABLE TO DISTRICTS

*(Repealed by L.1995, chap. 715(39), eff. 9/1/95.)*
*(Selected Section)*

**§50.058.** *(Repealed by L.1995, chap. 715(39), eff. 9/1/95.)*

# CONSTITUTIONS/UNITED STATES CODE

## UNITED STATES CONSTITUTION

### ARTICLE I

*(Selected Sections)*

**Section 6, Clause 1. Compensation of Members; Privilege from Arrest.**

The Senators and Representatives shall receive a Compensation for their services, to be ascertained by Law, and paid out of the Treasury of the United States. They shall in all Cases, except Treason, Felony and Breach of Peace, be privileged from Arrest during their Attendance at the Session of their respective Houses, and in going to and returning from the same; and for any Speech or Debate in either House, they shall not be questioned in any other Place.

**Section 9, Clause 2. Suspension of Habeas Corpus.**

The Privilege of the Writ of Habeas Corpus shall not be suspended, unless when in Cases of Rebellion or Invasion the public Safety may require it.



### THE BILL OF RIGHTS

*(The first fourteen amendments to the U.S. Constitution.)*

**1st Amendment.**

Congress shall make no law respecting an establishment of religion, or prohibiting the free exercise thereof; of abridging the freedom of speech, or of the press; or the right of the people peaceably to assemble, and to petition the Government for a redress of grievances.

**2nd Amendment.**

A well regulated Militia, being necessary to the security of a free State, the right of the people to keep and bear Arms, shall not be infringed.

**3rd Amendment.**

No Soldier shall, in time of peace be quartered in any house, without the consent of the Owner, nor in time of war, but in a manner to be prescribed by law.

**4th Amendment.**

The right of the people to be secure in their persons, houses, papers, and effects, against unreasonable searches and seizures, shall not be violated, and no Warrants shall issue, but upon probable cause, supported by Oath or affirmation, and particularly describing the place to be searched, and the persons or things to be seized.

**5th Amendment.**

No person shall be held to answer for a capital, or otherwise infamous crime, unless on a presentment or indictment of a Grand Jury, except in cases arising in the land or naval forces, or in the Militia, when in actual service in time of War or public danger; nor shall any person be subject for the same offense to be twice put in jeopardy of life or limb; nor shall be compelled in any criminal case to be a witness against himself, nor be deprived of life, liberty, or property, without due process of law; nor shall private property be taken for public use, without just compensation.

**6th Amendment.**

In all criminal prosecutions, the accused shall enjoy the right to a speedy and public trial, by an impartial jury of the State and district wherein the crime shall have been committed, which district shall have been previously ascertained by law, and to be informed of the nature and cause of the accusation; to be confronted with the witnesses against him, to have compulsory process for obtaining Witnesses in his favor, and to have the Assistance of Counsel for this defense.

**7th Amendment.**

In Suits at common law, where the value in controversy shall exceed twenty dollars, the right of trial by jury shall be preserved, and no fact tried by a jury, shall be otherwise reexamined in any Court of the United States, then according to the rules of the common law.

**8th Amendment.**

Excessive bail shall not be required, nor excessive fines imposed, nor cruel and unusual punishments inflicted.

**9th Amendment.**

The enumeration in the Constitution, of certain rights, shall not be construed to deny or disparage others retained by the people.

**10th Amendment.**

The powers not delegated to the United States by the Constitution, nor prohibited by it to the States, are reserved to the States respectively, or to the people.

**11th Amendment.**

The Judicial power of the United States shall not be construed to extend to any suit in law or equity, commenced or prosecuted against one of the United States by Citizens of another State, or by Citizens or Subjects of any Foreign State.

**12th Amendment.**

The Electors shall meet in their respective states, and vote by ballot for President and Vice-President, one of whom, at least, shall not be an inhabitant of the same state with themselves; they shall name in their ballots the person voted for as President, and in distinct ballots the person voted for as Vice-President, and they shall make distinct lists of all persons voted for as President, and of all persons voted for as Vice-President, and of the number of votes for each, which lists they shall sign and certify, and transmit sealed to the seat of the government of the United States, directed to the President of the Senate; The President of the Senate shall, in the presence of the Senate and House of Representatives, open all the certificates and the votes shall then be counted; The person having the greatest number of votes for President, shall be the President, if such number be a majority of the whole number of Electors appointed; and if no person have such majority, then from the persons having the highest numbers not exceeding three on the list of those voted for as President, the House of Representatives shall choose immediately, by ballot, the President. But in choosing the President, the votes shall be taken by states, the representation from each state having one vote; a quorum for this purpose shall consist of a member or members from two-thirds of the states, and a majority of all the states shall be necessary to a choice. And if the House of Representatives shall not choose a President whenever the right of choice shall devolve upon them, before the fourth day of March next following, then the Vice-President shall act as President, as in the case of the death or other constitutional disability of the President.ùThe person having the greatest number of votes as Vice-President, shall be the Vice-President, if such number be a majority of the whole number of Electors appointed, and if no person have a majority, then from the two highest numbers on the list, the Senate shall choose the Vice-President; a quorum for the purpose shall consist of two-thirds of the whole number of Senators, and a majority of the whole number shall be necessary to a choice. But no person constitutionally ineligible to the office of President shall be eligible to that of Vice-President of the United States.

**13th Amendment.**

**Section 1.** Neither slavery nor involuntary servitude, except as a punishment for crime whereof the party shall have been duly convicted, shall exist within the United States, or any place subject to their jurisdiction.

**Section 2.** Congress shall have power to enforce this article by appropriate legislation.

**14th Amendment.**

**Section 1.** All persons born or naturalized in the United States, and subject to the jurisdiction thereof, are citizens of the United States and of the State wherein they reside. No State shall make or enforce any law which shall abridge the privileges or immunities of citizens of the United States; nor shall any State deprive any person of life, liberty, or property, without due process of law; nor deny to any person within its jurisdiction the equal protection of the laws.

**Section 2.** Representatives shall be apportioned among the several States according to their respective numbers, counting the whole number of persons in each State, excluding Indians not taxed. But when the right to vote at any election for the choice of electors for President and Vice President of the United States, Representatives in Congress, the Executive and Judicial officers of a State, or the members of the Legislature thereof, is denied to any of the male inhabitants of such State, being twenty-one years of age, and citizens of the United States, or in any way abridged, except for participation in rebellion, or other crime, the basis of representation therein shall be reduced in the proportion which the number of such male citizens shall bear to the whole number of male citizens twenty-one years of age in such State.

**Section 3.** No person shall be a Senator or Representative in Congress, or elector of President and Vice President, or hold any office, civil or military, under the United States, or under any State, who, having previously taken an oath, as a member of Congress, or as an officer of the United States, or as a member of any State legislature, or as an executive or judicial officer of any State, to support the Constitution of the United States, shall have engaged in insurrection or rebellion against the same, or given aid or comfort to the enemies thereof. But Congress may by a vote of two-thirds of each House, remove such disability.

**Section 4.** The validity of the public debt of the United States, authorized by law, including debts incurred for payment of pensions and bounties for services in suppressing insurrection or rebellion, shall not be questioned. But neither the United States nor any State shall assume or pay any debt or obligation incurred in aid of insurrection or rebellion against the United States, or any claim for the loss or emancipation of any slave; but all such debts, obligations and claims shall be held illegal and void.

**Section 5.** The Congress shall have power to enforce, by appropriate legislation, the provisions of this article.



# TEXAS CONSTITUTION
*(Selected Sections)*

## ARTICLE I. BILL OF RIGHTS

### Section 9. Searches and Seizures.

The people shall be secure in their persons, houses, papers and possessions, from all unreasonable seizures or searches, and no warrant to search any place, or to seize any person or thing, shall issue without describing them as as near as may be, nor without probable cause, supported by oath or affirmation.

### Section 10. Rights of Accused in Criminal Prosecutions.

In all criminal prosecutions the accused shall have a speedy public trial by an impartial jury. He shall have the right to demand the nature and cause of the accusation against him, and to have a copy thereof. He shall not be compelled to give evidence against himself, and shall have the right of being heard by himself or counsel, or both, shall be confronted by the witnesses against him and shall have compulsory process for obtaining witnesses in his favor, except that when the witness resides out of the State, and the offense charged is a violation of any of the anti-trust laws of this State, the defendant and the State shall have the right to produce and have the evidence admitted by deposition, under such rules and laws as the Legislature may hereafter provide; and no person shall be held to answer for a criminal offense, unless on an indictment of a grand jury, except in cases in which the punishment is by fine or imprisonment, otherwise than in the penitentiary, in cases of impeachment, and in cases arising in the army or navy, or in the militia, when in actual service in time of war or public danger.

### Section 11. Bail.

All prisoners shall be bailable by sufficient sureties, unless for capital offenses, when the proof is evident; but this provision shall not be so construed as to prevent bail after indictment found upon examination of the evidence, in such manner as may be prescribed by law.

### Section 11a. Multiple Convictions; Denial of Bail.

(a) Any person (1) accused of a felony less than capital in this State, who has been theretofore twice convicted of a felony, the second conviction being subsequent to the first, both in point of time of commission of the offense and conviction therefor, (2) accused of a felony less than capital in this State, committed while on bail for a prior felony for which he has been indicted, (3) accused of a felony less than capital in this State involving the use of a deadly weapon after being convicted of a prior felony, or (4) accused of a violent or sexual offense committed while under the supervision of a criminal justice agency of the State or a political subdivision of the State for a prior felony, after a hearing, and upon evidence substantially showing the guilt of the accused of the offense in (1) or (3) above, of the offense committed while on bail in (2) above, or of the offense in (4) above committed while under the supervision of a criminal justice agency of the State or a political subdivision of the State for a prior felony, may be denied bail pending trial, by a district judge in this State, if said order denying bail pending trial is issued within seven calendar days subsequent to the time of incarceration of the accused; provided, however, that if the accused is not accorded a trial upon the accusation under (1) or (3) above, the accusation and indictment used under (2) above, or the accusation or indictment used under (4) above within sixty (60) days from the time of his incarceration upon the accusation, the order denying bail shall be automatically set aside, unless a continuance is obtained upon the motion or request of the accused; provided, further, that the right of appeal to the Court of Criminal Appeals of this State is expressly accorded the accused for a review of any judgment or order made hereunder, and said appeal shall be given preference by the Court of Criminal Appeals.

(b) In this section:

(1) "Violent offense" means:

(A) murder;

(B) aggravated assault, if the accused used or exhibited a deadly weapon during the commission of the assault;

(C) aggravated kidnapping; or

(D) aggravated robbery.

(2) "Sexual offense" means:

(A) aggravated sexual assault;

(B) sexual assault; or

(C) indecency with a child.

*(Amended November 2, 1993.)*



## ARTICLE III. LEGISLATIVE DEPARTMENT

### Section 14. Privileged From Arrest.

Senators and Representatives shall, except in cases of treason, felony, or breach of the peace, be privileged from arrest during the session of the Legislature, and in going to and returning from the same[, allowing one day for every twenty miles such member may reside from the place at which the Legislature is convened].

*(Matter in brackets removed upon voter approval on 11/2/99; chgd. by L.1999, H.J.R. 62(7); eff. upon voter approval on 11/2/99.)*

## ARTICLE VI. SUFFRAGE

### Section 5. Privilege of voters from arrest.

Voters shall, in all cases, except treason, felony or breach of the peace, be privileged from arrest during their attendance at elections, and in going to and returning therefrom.

## ARTICLE XVII. MODE OF AMENDING THE CONSTITUTION OF THIS STATE

### Section 1. Proposed Amendments; Publication; Submission to Voters; Adoption.

[(a)] The Legislature, at any regular session, or at any special session when the matter is included within the purposes for which the session is convened, may propose amendments revising the Constitution, to be voted upon by the qualified [voters ]*electors* for statewide offices and propositions, as defined in the Constitution and statutes of this State. The date of the elections shall be specified by the Legislature. The proposal for submission must be approved by a vote of two-thirds of all the members elected to each House, entered by yeas and nays on the journals.

[(b)] A brief explanatory statement of the nature of a proposed amendment, together with the date of the election and the wording of the proposition as it is to appear on the ballot, shall be published twice in each newspaper in the State which meets requirements set by the Legislature for the publication of official notices of offices and departments of the state government. The explanatory statement shall be prepared by the Secretary of State and shall be approved by the Attorney General. The Secretary of State shall send a full and complete copy of the proposed amendment or amendments to each county clerk who shall post the same in a public place in the courthouse at least 30 days prior to the election on said amendment. The first notice shall be published not more tha 60 days nor less than 50 days before the date of the election, and the second notice shall be published on the same day in the succeeding week. The Legislature shall fix the standards for the rate of charge for the publication, which may not be higher than the newspaper's published national rate for advertising per column inch.

[(c)] The election shall be held in accordance with procedures prescribed by the Legislature, and the returning officer in each county shall make returns to the Secretary of State of the number of legal votes cast at the election for and against each amendment. If it appears from the returns that a majority of the votes cast have been cast in favor of an amendment, it shall become a part of this Constitution, and proclamation thereof shall be made by the Governor. (Amended Nov. 7, 1972.) *(Matter in brackets removed and matter in italics added upon voter approval on 11/2/99; chgd. by L.1999, H.J.R. 62(54); eff. upon voter approval on 11/2/99.)*

# UNITED STATES CODE
*(Selected Title)*

# TITLE 22. FOREIGN RELATIONS AND INTERCOURSE
*(Selected Chapter)*

## CHAPTER 6. FOREIGN DIPLOMATIC AND CONSULAR OFFICERS
*(Selected Sections)*



Section


### §§251 to 254. *(Repealed.)*

### §254a. Definitions.

As used in this Act [22 USCU 254a et seq.] -

(1) the term "members of a mission" means -

(A) the head of a mission and those members of a mission who are members of the diplomatic staff or who, pursuant to law, are granted equivalent privileges and immunities,

(B) members of the administrative and technical staff of a mission, and

(C) members of the service staff of a mission,

as such terms are defined in Article 1 of the Vienna Convention;

(2) the term "family" means -

(A) the members of the family of a member of a mission described in paragraph (1)(A) who form part of his or her household if they are not nationals of the United States, and

(B) the members of the family of a member of a mission described in paragraph (1)(B) who form part of his or her household if they are not nationals or permanent residents of the United States,

within the meaning of Article 37 of the Vienna Convention;

(3) the term "mission" includes missions within the meaning of the Vienna Convention and any missions representing foreign governments, individually or collectively, which are extended the same privileges and immunities, pursuant to law, as are enjoyed by missions under the Vienna Convention; and

(4) the term "Vienna Convention" means the Vienna Convention on Diplomatic Relations of April 18, 1961 (T.I.A.S. numbered 7502; 23 U.S.T. 3227), entered into force with respect to the United States on December 13, 1972.

### §254b. Privileges and immunities of mission of nonparty to Vienna Convention.

With respect to a nonparty to the Vienna Convention, the mission, the members of the mission, their families, and diplomatic couriers shall enjoy the privileges and immunities specified in the Vienna Convention.

### §254c. Extension of more favorable or less favorable treatment than provided under Vienna Convention; authority of President.

The President may, on the basis of reciprocity and under such terms and conditions as he may determine, specify privileges and immunities for the mission, the members of the mission, their families, and the diplomatic couriers which result in more favorable treatment or less favorable treatment than is provided under the Vienna Convention.

This page intentionally left blank.

# TEXAS CRIMINAL LAW AND MOTOR VEHICLE HANDBOOK INDEX

*All references are to sections or rules of the following:*

*Alcoholic Beverage Code (ABC)*
*Agriculture Code (AG)*
*Business and Commerce Code (BCC)*
*Civil Practice and Remedies Code (CPR)*
*Civil Statutes (CS)*
*Code of Criminal Procedure (CCP)*
*Constitution of State of Texas (CON)*
*Education Code (ED)*
*Election Code (EL)*
*Family Code (FAM)*
*Finance Code (FC)*
*Government Code (GC)*
*Health and Safety Code (HSC)*
*Human Resources Code (HRC)*
*Insurance Code (IC)*
*Local Government Code (LGC)*
*Natural Resources Code (NRC)*
*Occupations Code (OC)*
*Parks and Wildlife Code (PWC)*
*Penal Code (PC)*
*Property Code (PRC)*
*Rules of Evidence (RE)*
*Tax Code (TC)*
*Transportation Code (TRC)*
*U.S. Code (USC)*
*U.S. Constitution (USCON)*
*Utilities Code (UC)*
*Vehicle Laws (V)*
*Water Code (W)*

*(Index entries in brackets eff. only until 9/1/2000. Entries in italics eff. 9/1/2000.)*

Printed in the U.S.A. Zt

Zt

 Zt

Zt

Zt

Printed in the U.S.A.

Printed in the U.S.A. Zt

Printed in the U.S.A. Zt

Printed in the U.S.A. Zt

Printed in the U.S.A. Zt

Printed in the U.S.A. Zt

Printed in the U.S.A. 27

Printed in the U.S.A. 21

Zt

Printed in the U.S.A. Zt

Printed in the U.S.A.

Printed in the U.S.A. Zt

Printed in the U.S.A. 17

Printed in the U.S.A. Zt

Zt

This page intentionally left blank.

# GOULD'S QUICK FIND LOCATOR™



**HOW TO USE**

**To find individual titles, bend the edge and follow the arrow to the corresponding black mark.**

***For titles in the left hand column, use the mark nearest the front cover.***
***For titles in the right hand column, use the mark nearest the back cover.***